The Almanac of American Politics
★ 2002 ★

THE **Senators**, THE **Representatives**

AND THE **Governors**:

THEIR **Records** AND **Election Results**,

THEIR **States** AND **Districts**

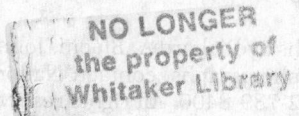
Michael Barone
Richard E. Cohen
with Charles E. Cook Jr.

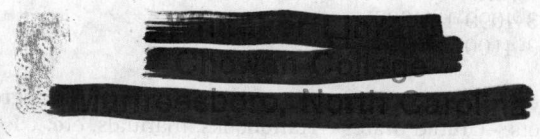

National
Journal

Washington, D.C.

NATIONAL JOURNAL GROUP INC.

Printed in the United States of America by United Book Press. Database design by CDIS, Inc.; composition by Impressions Book and Journal Services Inc. Distributed to the trade by LPC Group.

Photographs by Richard A. Bloom, John Eisele, Liz Lynch and Bruce Reedy. For information regarding photographs, contact: National Journal, 1501 M Street, N.W., Washington, D.C. 20005. 202-739-8400. All rights reserved.

The Almanac of American politics. — 1972 –

v. : ill. ; 24 cm.

Biennial
Published by Gambit 1972– ; by National Journal 1988–

ISSN: 0362-076X
ISBN 0-8923-4099-1 (2002)
ISBN 0-8923-4100 (Gambit 2002)

1. United States. Congress—Biography. 2. United States. Congress—Committees. 3. Election districts—United States—Handbooks, manuals, etc. I. Barone, Michael. II. Ujifusa, Grant. III. Matthews, Douglas.

JK1012 .A44
328.73/005

70-160417

THE ALMANAC OF AMERICAN POLITICS 2002

Author
Michael Barone

Co-Author
Richard E. Cohen

Founding Editor
Grant Ujifusa

Editor
Eleanor Evans

Associate Editor & Research Director
Gideon Berger

Assistant Editor
Cherie Galyean

Research Associates
Chris M. Cillizza, Jennifer Lucas,
Bryan S. Murphy

Research Assistants
Jason Ellenburg, Mark Murray

Contributing Editor
Charlie Cook

Contributing Writers
Jennifer E. Duffy, Amy Walter

Editorial Assistant
Claire Mathy

Photography Editor
Liz Lynch

Presidential Election Results
NCEC Services Inc.

State Maps
Election Data Services Inc.

CONTENTS

8   Contents

10   **Contents**

GUIDE TO USAGE

The *Almanac of American Politics* is designed to be self-explanatory. The following guide provides a brief description of each section and a list of sources from which information was derived, both of which serve as a road map to understanding the meaning behind the figures. In addition some of the data, such as interest group ratings and key votes of the 107th Congress, will be updated regularly on the Almanac website. This website is for the exclusive use of purchasers of the 2002 edition of The Almanac. For information on how to subscribe to this free service, please see the insert card towards the middle of the book.

The People

POPULATION. All population figures, excluding unemployment rates and voter registration, are from the Bureau of the Census, U.S. Department of Commerce, Washington D.C. 20230, 301-457-4608, www.census.gov. Official April 1, 2000 Census figures are used for each state.

RACE AND ETHNIC ORIGIN. For the 2000 Census, the Census Bureau asked people what their race or ethnic origin was. Race, as defined by the Bureau of the Census, reflects the individual respondents' perception of his or her racial identity and does not reflect any biological or anthropological definition. The basic racial categories are: American Indian or Alaska Native; Asian; Native Hawaiian or other Pacific Islander; Black or African American; White; and two or more races. The race statistics used in the Almanac are drawn from respondents reporting only one race category. Hispanic origin is defined as an ethnicity, and includes those who classified themselves in one of three specific Hispanic categories on the census form (Cuban, Mexican, Puerto Rican) or as of "other Spanish/Hispanic origin"; *persons of Hispanic origin may be of any race.*

AGE. The Bureau of the Census defines age as based on the number of years a person completed as of April 1, 2000. This definition was used to determine the voting age population. Many people, however, provided their age as of the date they completed the census form rather than the definition provided by the Bureau of the Census.

UNEMPLOYMENT. All unemployment figures are from the Bureau of Labor Statistics, U.S. Department of Labor, Washington, D.C. 20210, 202-691-5200, www.bls.gov. These figures represent the average rate of unemployment for each state for 2000.

REGISTERED VOTERS. Registered voter numbers are from the individual states' election bureaus or political parties, and represent the number of voters officially registered as close as possible to the November 2000 election. Some states have no voter registration.

POLITICAL LINEUP. This block includes the names of top state officials as well as a breakdown by party of the state legislative bodies. The names of U.S. senators and a party breakdown of the state's congressional delegation are also provided.

PRESIDENTIAL VOTE. The 1996 and 2000 presidential vote is included for each state and congressional district. Presidential vote by congressional district was derived from state, county and precinct results as compiled by the staff of the National Committee for an Effective Congress (NCEC), 122 C Street, NW, Washington, DC 20001, 202-638-8300, www.ncec.org. The 1996 presidential vote by congressional district was recalculated in eight states to reflect redistricting (remapping) changes. The eight states are: Florida, Georgia, Kentucky, Louisiana, New York, North Carolina, Texas and Virginia. Results of the presidential primaries were provided by the states and the FEC; caucus results are not provided. The general election returns for the states were compiled from official state election results. The total of the congressional district votes may not add up to the total state vote, because some votes (overseas, military) cannot be assigned to a congressional district. By June 2000, the third party vote for Texas was unavailable at the congressional district level. While the vote totals for Bush and Gore are correct, the percentages could vary slightly with the addition of the third party data; the additional data will be posted on our website when it becomes available.

BIOGRAPHY. This section lists when each governor, senator and representative was elected or appointed, date and place of birth, home, college education and degrees obtained (if any), religion, marital status and, if applicable, spouse's name. The number of terms listed reflects full, elected terms. Also listed is a brief outline of the politician's past elected offices, professional career and military service and his or her office addresses and telephone numbers. Committee and subcommittee assignments, as of June 15, 2000, are provided as well. (Note: On many committees, the chairman and ranking minority member are ex officio members of each subcommittee on which they do not hold a regular assignment.)

Ratings

GROUP RATINGS. The congressional rating statistics of 11 interest groups provide an idea of a legislator's general ideology and the degree to which the legislator represents different groups' interests. Not just a record of liberal/conservative voting behavior, these ratings come from a range of groups concerned with everything from single issues (environmental concerns) to the political interests of a particular sector (e.g., businesses). The order of the groups is such that the more "liberal" groups are on the left and the more "conservative" are on the right. Four groups, ACLU, ITIC, NTLC and CHC provide one rating for the two-year congressional session. Following is a general description of each organization, its address and telephone number.

ADA   Americans for Democratic Action
1625 K St., N.W., #210, Washington, D.C. 20006, 202-785-5980, www.adaction.org.
Liberal: Since its founding in 1947, ADA members have pushed for legislation designed to reduce inequality, curtail rising defense spending, prevent encroachments on civil liberties and promote international human rights. The ADA uses a broad spectrum of issues for its vote analysis.

ACLU   American Civil Liberties Union
122 Maryland Ave., N.E., Washington, D.C. 20002, 202-544-1681, www.aclu.org.
Pro-individual liberties: ACLU seeks to protect individuals from legal, executive and congressional infringement on basic rights guaranteed by the Bill of Rights. The ACLU ratings are published for every Congress; the 2000 ratings include the years 1999 and 2000.

AFS   American Federation of State, County and Municipal Employees (AFSCME)
1625 L St., N.W., Washington, D.C. 20036, 202-429-1000, www.afscme.org.
Liberal Labor: As the nation's largest public employee and health care workers union, representing more than 1.3 million members, AFSCME is committed to achieving dignity and improving working conditions through collective bargaining. The AFSCME voting records are based on a representative sample of roll call votes from the First and Second Sessions of the 106th Congress.

LCV   League of Conservation Voters
1920 L St., N.W., #800, Washington, D.C. 20036, 202-785-8683, www.lcv.org.
Environmental: Formed in 1970, LCV is the national, non-partisan arm of the environmental movement. LCV works to elect pro-environmental candidates to Congress.

LCV ratings are based on key votes concerning energy, environment and natural resource issues, selected by leaders from major national environmental organizations.

CON Concord Coalition
1819 19th St., N.W., #800, Washington, D.C. 20006, 202-467-6222,
www.concordcoalition.org.

Pro-Balanced Budget: The Concord Coalition is a nonpartisan, grassroots organization dedicated to eliminating the federal budget deficit and reforming entitlement programs. The Coalition, with members and active chapters in all 50 states, is determined to educate the American public about the dangers of the federal deficit.

ITIC Information Technology Industry Council
1250 I Street, N.W., #200, Washington, DC 20005, 202-737-8888, www.itic.org.

High Technology Industry: ITI represents the leading U.S. providers of information technology products and services. ITI's mission is to help shape policies that advance electronic commerce, open new markets, rely on market-based solutions, and foster innovation. ITI's *High Tech Voting Guide* ratings are based on key votes that encourage productivity and innovation and sustain U.S. economic growth and leadership in the Information Age.

NTU National Taxpayers Union
108 N. Alfred St., Alexandria, VA 22314, 703-683-5700, www.ntu.org.

Pro-Taxpayer Rights: NTU is the nation's largest and oldest taxpayers' rights group, representing 300,000 members in all 50 states. NTU analyzes every roll call vote taken during both sessions of Congress that significantly affects federal taxes, spending, debt, or regulatory impact.

COC Chamber of Commerce of the United States
1615 H Street, N.W., Washington, D.C. 20062, 202-659-6000, www.uschamber.org.

Pro-business: Founded in 1912 as a voice for organized business, COC represents local, regional and state chambers of commerce in addition to trade and professional organizations.

ACU American Conservative Union
1007 Cameron St., Alexandria, VA 22314, 703-836-8602, www.conservative.org.

Conservative: Since 1971, ACU ratings have provided a means of gauging the conservatism of members of Congress. Foreign policy, social and budget issues are their primary concerns.

NTLC National Tax-Limitation Committee
151 North Sunrise Ave., #901, Roseville, CA 95661, 916-786-9400,
www.limittaxes.org.

Pro-tax limitation: NTLC was organized in 1975 to seek constitutional and other limits on taxes, spending and deficits at the state and federal levels. NTLC actively pursues a balanced budget/tax limitation amendment to the U.S. Constitution. These ratings are based on budget issue votes and bills which would have a major impact on long-term government taxing and spending programs.

CHC Christian Coalition
499 South Capitol Street, S.W., #615, Washington, D.C. 20003, 202-479-6900,
www.cc.org.

Conservative: Pro-family citizen organization and national lobby founded in 1989 working for family-friendly public policy on a local, state and national level with over 1.5 million members and activists.

NATIONAL JOURNAL RATINGS. *National Journal*'s rating system establishes an objective method of analyzing congressional voting. A panel of *National Journal* editors and staff initially compiled a list of congressional roll call votes and classified them as either economic, social or foreign policy-related. The interrelationship of these votes was shown by a statistical procedure called "principal components analysis," which revealed which "yea" votes and which "nay" votes fit a liberal or a conservative pattern. The votes in each of the three subject areas were computer-weighted to reflect the degree they fit the common pattern. All members of Congress who participated in at least half of the votes in each area received ratings; those who missed more that half the votes were not scored (shown as *). Absences and abstentions were not counted.

Members of Congress were then ranked according to relative liberalism and conservatism. Finally, they were assigned percentiles showing their rank relative to others in their chamber. Percentile scores range from a minimum of 0 to a maximum of 99. Because some members voted liberal or conservative on every roll call, however, there are ties at the liberal and conservative ends of each scale. For that reason, the maximum percentiles often turn out to be less than 99.

Election Results

Listed for each member of the House are results of the 2000 general, runoff and primary elections, as well as the 1998 general elections (results of any special elections are also listed). Gubernatorial and senatorial results are presented in a like manner. Votes and percentages are included, indicating the margin of victory (due to the process of rounding up and rounding down, some totals may equal more or less than 100%). Candidates receiving less than 4% of the total vote are grouped together and listed as "Other." Dollar amounts listed to the right of the vote totals are campaign expenditures as reported by the candidate to the Federal Election Commission. Election returns were collected from the individual states.

Campaign Finance

All data are derived from candidates' campaign finance reports and party reports available from the Federal Election Commission (FEC), 999 E St., NW, Washington, D.C. 20463, 202-694-1000 (toll free, 1-800-424-9530). The dollar figure, in parentheses to the right of the election results, represent the candidates net disbursements (expenditures) for the period beginning January 1, 1997, and ending December 31, 1998. *These figures may not include candidate loans which have been repaid, nor does it include any corrections or amendments filed with the FEC after May 1, 1999.*

Abbreviations

ABC	Americans for Better Childcare Act	**AS**	American Samoa
ACLU	American Civil Liberties Union	**ASI**	American Systems Independent Party (PA)
ACP	A Connecticut Party	**BGH**	Bovine Growth Hormone
ACU	American Conservative Union	**BVP**	Brooklyn Voters Party (NY)
ADA	Americans for Democratic Action, Americans with Disabilities Act	**C**	Conservative Party (NY)
		CAB	Civil Aeronautics Board
AFDC	Aid to Families with Dependent Children	**CAFE**	Corporate Average Fuel Economy
AFS	American Federation of State, County & Municipal Employees (AFSCME)	**CFA**	Consumer Federation of America
		CFC	Conscience for Congress
		CCP	Change Congress Party
AI	Alaska Independent Party	**CHC**	Christian Coalition
ANWR	Alaska National Wildlife Refuge	**CHOB**	Cannon House Office Building

CIA	Central Intelligence Agency
CNP	Constitution Party
COC	Chamber of Commerce of the United States
COLA	Cost of Living Adjustment
CON	Concord Coalition
DCCC	Democratic Congressional Campaign Committee
DFL	Democratic-Farmer-Labor Party (MN)
DLC	Democratic Leadership Council
DNC	Democratic National Committee
DSCC	Democratic Senatorial Campaign Committee
DSOB	Dirksen Senate Office Building
EMILY	EMILY's List (Early Money is Like Yeast)
ERISA	Employee Retirement Income Security Act
FEC	Federal Election Commission
FR	Freedom Party (NY)
GATT	General Agreement on Tariffs Trade
GREEN	Green Party
H	Capitol Building Room–House side
HMO	Stop HMO Abuses Party
HSOB	Hart Senate Office Building
I	Independent
IC	Independent Conservative
Ind	Independence Party
INF	Independent Fusion Party
INN	Independent Neighbors Party (NY)
IR	Independent-Republican Party (MN)
ISTEA	Intermodal Surface Transportation Efficiency Act
IVP	Independent Voters Party
JBS	Jobs Party (NY)
L	Liberal Party
LCV	League of Conservation Voters
LHOB	Longworth House Office Building
LIB	Libertarian Party
LIF	Long Island First Party (NY)
LU	Liberty Union
MFN	Most Favored Nation
NAFTA	North American Free Trade Agreement
NAP	New Alliance Party (MA)
NARAL	National Abortion Rights Action League
NEA	National Endowment for the Arts
NFIB	National Federation of Independent Business
NL	Natural Law
NRCC	National Republican Congressional Committee
NRSC	National Republican Senatorial Committee
NTLC	National Tax-Limitation Committee
NTU	National Taxpayers Union
P&F	Peace & Freedom Party (CA)
PAC	Pacific Green Party (OR)
PDP	Popular Democratic Party (PR)
POP	Populist Party
PR	Puerto Rico
PRG	Progressive Party
PS	Protect Seniors Party (NY)
Ref	Reform Party
RHOB	Rayburn House Office Building
RLDS	Reorganized Church of the Latter Day Saints
RMM	Ranking Minority Member
RNC	Republican National Committee
RP	Republican Moderate Party (AK)
RSOB	Russell Senate Office Building
RTL	Right-to-Life Party
S	Capitol Building Room, Senate side
SCH	School Choice Party
SDI	Strategic Defense Initiative
SIS	Staten Island Secession Party (NY)
SM	Save Medicare Party (NY)
SOC	Socialist Party
SOL	Solidarity Party (IL)
SWP	Socialist Workers Party (MN)
TFC	Twenty-First Century Party (NY)
TXB	Tax Break Party (NY)
UAW	United Auto Workers
VNS	Voter News Service
VRP	Voters Rights Party (NY)
WIC	Women and Infant Children
WF	Working Families

KEY VOTES OF THE 107TH CONGRESS

KEY VOTES. The Key Votes section attempts to illustrate a legislator's stance on important votes where he or she must vote *for* or *against* a national issue. The process grossly oversimplifies the legislative system where months of debate, amendment, pressure, persuasion, and compromise go into a final floor vote. However, the voting record remains the best indication of a member's general ideologies and position on specific issues. Following is a list of key votes used. A member who was absent, voted present, or who was not in office at the time of a particular vote receives an "*". Roll-call data were drawn from Congressional Observer Publications at *www.proaxis.com/cop*, a private legislative tracking company.

HOUSE VOTES, 107TH CONGRESS:

1. **Patient Bill of Rights** (HR 2723) Establish a patients' "bill of rights" in dealing with health maintenance organizations. Oct. 7, 1999. (275-151) (D: 206-2; R: 68-149; I: 1-0)
2. **Accelerate Min. Wage** (HR 3846) Increase the minimum wage by $1.00 in two years, rather than three years as reported by the House committee. March 9, 2000. (246-179) (D: 203-5; R: 42-173; I: 1-1)
3. **Strike Ban on Ergo. Stnd.** (HR 4577) Strike ban on federal standard for ergonomic protection. June 8, 2000. (203-220) (D: 188-16; R: 14-203; I: 1-1)
4. **Ovrd. Estate Tax Veto** (HR 8) Override President Clinton's veto of phase-out of estate and gift taxes. Sept. 7, 2000. (274-157; failed to receive the required two-thirds) (D: 53-155; R: 220-1; I: 1-1)
5. **Bar RU-486 $ for FDA** (HR 1906) Bar funding for Food and Drug Administration review of the RU-486 drug for the chemical inducement of abortion. June 8, 1999. (217-214) (D: 36-173; R: 181-40; I: 0-1)
6. **Display 10 Commandments** (HR 1501) Permit state and local governments to display the Ten Commandments on public property. June 17, 1999. (248-180) (D: 45-164; R: 203-15; I: 0-1)
7. **Gun Show Bkgrnd. Checks** (HR 2122) Require certain gun show dealers to perform background checks within three days. June 17, 1999. (193-235) (D: 159-49; R: 33-186; I: 1-0)
8. **Ban Part.-Birth Abortion** (HR 3660) Ban partial-birth abortions. April 5, 2000. (287-141) (D: 77-132; R: 209-8; I: 1-1)
9. **NATO War in Serbia** (HConRes 42) Authorize deployment of U.S. military forces in the NATO peacekeeping operation planned for Kosovo. March 11, 1999. (219-191) (D: 174-18; R: 44-173; I: 1-0)
10. **Perm. Trade with China** (HR 4444) Authorize permanent trade relations with China. May 24, 2000. (237-197) (D: 73-138; R: 164-57; I: 0-2)
11. **Debt Relief for 3rd World** (HR 4811) Provide debt relief for heavily-indebted nations. July 13, 2000. (216-211) (D: 189-16; R: 26-194; I: 1-1)
12. **Drop Cuba Econ. Embargo** (HR 4871) Drop enforcement of U.S. economic embargo of Cuba. July 20, 2000. (174-241) (D: 149-52; R: 24-188; I: 1-1)

SENATE VOTES, 107TH CONGRESS:

1. **Educ. Savings Accts.** (S 1134) Establish tax-free education savings accounts for children in public or private schools. March 2, 2000. (61-37) (D: 9-35; R: 52-2)
2. **Prescrip. Drug Benefit** (SConRes 101) Procedural vote to establish a prescription-drug benefit for Medicare beneficiaries. April 5, 2000. (51-49; failed to receive the required 60 votes) (D: 45-0; R: 6-49)
3. **Delay Ergo. Standards** (HR 4577) Delay federal standards for ergonomic protection for one year. June 22, 2000. (57-41) (D: 3-40; R: 54-1)

4. **Phase Out Estate Tax** (HR 8) Phase out estate and gift taxes from the income tax code. July 14, 2000. (59-39) (D: 9-35; R: 50-4)
5. **Review Movie Violence** (S 254) Require federal review of violence in movies or television shows produced on federal property. May 19, 1999. (66-34) (D: 16-29; R: 50-5)
6. **Gun Show Bckgrnd. Checks** (S 254) Require background checks on persons who buy guns at gun shows. May 20, 1999. (51-50; Vice President Gore broke tie) (D: 44-1; R: 6-49)
7. **Ban Part.-Birth Abortion** (S 1692) Approve ban on late-term procedure known as partial-birth abortion. Oct. 21, 1999. (63-34) (D: 14-31; R: 48-3)
8. **Broaden Hate Crimes List** (S 2549) Broaden coverage of federal hate crimes. June 20, 2000. (57-42) (D: 44-1; R: 13-41)
9. **NATO War in Serbia** (SConRes 21) Authorize Clinton to wage aircraft and missile operations as part of the NATO campaign against Yugoslavia. March 23, 1999. (58-41) (D: 42-3; R: 16-38)
10. **Table Cuba Travel Ban** (S 1234) Table proposal to bar presidential regulation of U.S. citizens traveling to Cuba. June 30, 1999. (55-43) (D: 12-33; R: 43-10)
11. **Nuclear Test Ban Treaty** Ratify the Comprehensive Nuclear Test Ban Treaty. Oct. 13, 1999. (48-51) (D: 44-0; R: 4-51) (Bob Smith (NH) technically voted as an Independent.)
12. **Perm. Trade with China** (HR 4444) Authorize permanent trade relations with China. Sept. 19, 2000. (83-15) (D: 37-7; R: 46-8)

THE 49% NATION

By Michael Barone

The United States at the end of the 20th Century was a nation divided down the middle. In 1996 Bill Clinton was re-elected with 49.2% of the vote. That same year Republicans held the House when their candidates led Democrats by a 48.9% to 48.5% margin. In 1998 Republicans held onto the House when their candidates led in popular vote by 48.9% to 47.8%. On November 7, 2000—although the final result was not known until five weeks later—George W. Bush won 47.9% of the vote and Al Gore 48.4%. The same day House Republican candidates led Democrats by a 49.2% to 47.9% margin. Round off these numbers and you have 49%, 49%, 49%, 49%, 48%, 48%, 48%, 49%, 48%—essentially the same number over and over. We haven't had such stasis in successive election results since the 1880s, which was also the last decade when a president was elected despite trailing in the popular vote and when the Senate was equally divided between the two major parties.

Halfway through the 1990s no one foresaw this result. Both parties had reason to believe they could forge majority coalitions by 2000. Republicans believed that their 1980s presidential majorities (which averaged 54%–43%) and their 1994 congressional majority (52%–45%) represented a fundamental Republican majority, which could sweep the presidential and congressional races. Conservative strategist Grover Norquist argued that there was a majority "leave-us-alone" coalition of economic and cultural conservatives which Republicans, if they framed the issues skillfully, could summon into being. Newt Gingrich looked past his disappointment at Bob Dole's defeat, confidently predicted that a Republican president and Congress would be elected in 2000, and said he looked forward to serving his last term as Speaker in 2001–02 working with a Republican president.

At the same time Democrats believed that Bill Clinton's high job approval ratings (in the 60% level from 1995 through 1998, and even higher that year) and his 50%-plus showings in most polls against Bob Dole represented a fundamental Democratic majority which could sweep the presidential and congressional races. Liberal columnist E. J. Dionne, Jr., argued in his book *They Only Look Dead* that there was a natural majority for moderate but activist government which Democrats, if they framed the issues skillfully, could summon into being. Democrats looked past their disappointment at not recapturing the House in 1996 and confidently predicted that a Democratic president and Congress would be elected in 2000, and looked forward to eight years of Al Gore following eight years of Bill Clinton.

But neither majority materialized. Bill Clinton survived impeachment and continued to receive 55%–60% job approval ratings. But Democrats failed to win back the House in 1998. Republicans held onto majorities of both houses of Congress that year, but their failure to gain seats in the House led to the ouster of Newt Gingrich as Speaker. Then, in 2000, neither side won a majority for president or in races for the House. We have now had three straight presidential elections and three straight House elections in which neither party has won 50% of the vote. The last time there were three straight presidential races without a majority was in 1884–1892. The last time there were three straight House races without a majority, aside from 1910–16 and 1890–98, when there were many third-party Progressive and Populist candidates, was apparently (data are not easy to come by) in the 1880s.

Both parties have strong incentives to amass a popular majority, and have striven mightily to do so. But in 2000 both failed. The Republicans failed to reproduce the Reagan-Bush majority and the Democrats failed to produce a Clinton-Gore majority. At the beginning of the 1990s it was conventional wisdom that the Republicans had a lock on the presidency and the Democrats had a lock on Congress. In 1995 some thought the Democrats had a lock on the presidency and the Republicans had a lock on Congress. Now no one has a lock on either.

That is evidence of strongly-held partisan attachments, on both sides. One of the unsung features of the politics of the 1990s and 2000 has been the reemergence of straight-ticket voting, which is more pronounced than in any decade since the 1940s. From 1968 to 1992, Democrats ran stronger and Republicans weaker in congressional than in presidential elections. Now, with ticket-splitting in decline and straight-ticket voting the rule, both have been winning 48% or 49% in both presidential and congressional elections.

To see how the political changes of the 1990s have left us a closely divided nation, compare the results of the 1988 and 2000 presidential elections. In 1988 the older George Bush defeated Michael Dukakis 53%–46%; in 2000 George W. Bush tied Al Gore 48%–48%. Nationally, the Republican percentage was down 5.5%, the Democratic percentage up 2.7%. This might be taken as a show of the weakness of George W. Bush and the strength of Al Gore and the record of the Clinton-Gore administration. But it should be kept in mind that the factors of peace and prosperity worked for the Republican ticket in 1988 and worked for the Democratic ticket in 2000. In past decades when the peace and prosperity advantage swung from one party to another in a few years, the swing in party votes was much higher. Peace and prosperity favored the Democrats in 1964 and the Republicans in 1972. Between those two elections the Republican percentage was up 22.2% and the Democratic percentage down 23.6%. The fact that the party percentages changed much less between 1988 and 2000 is evidence of the strength of party allegiance and the stubbornness of political attachments.

But, that said, the changes in party preference that did take place between 1988 and 2000 were far from evenly distributed. There were stark differences between the largest metropolitan areas—those with more than 2 million people—and the rest of the country. The figures below show the percentage for the two major party candidates in 1988 and 2000 for the major metro and non-major metro parts of the country. They are roughly equal in size: The major metro areas cast 46% of the nation's votes in 1988 and 45% in 2000.

	1988		**2000**		**Diff.**	
	R	– D	R	– D	R	– D
U.S.	53.5	– 45.7	48.1	– 48.3	–5.4	+2.6
Major metro	50.6	– 48.5	40.8	– 55.3	–9.8	+6.8
Non-major metro	55.9	– 43.2	54.0	– 42.5	–1.9	–0.7

The contrast is stark. Democrats made significant gains in major metro areas, but actually lost ground outside them; Republicans suffered serious losses in the major metro areas but only small losses outside them. The vote was about evenly split, but George W. Bush carried 30 states, 2,480 counties and 228 congressional districts to Gore's 20 states, 674 counties and 207 congressional districts.

The picture may be clearer if we subdivide each of these categories. Among the major metro areas, let us distinguish between the seven largest major metro areas[1] and

---

1. New York, Los Angeles, Chicago, San Francisco, Philadelphia, Detroit, and Washington. Boston, which

the 16 other, smaller major metro areas.[2] Outside the major metro areas, let us distinguish between those in the North and those in the South. These four groups are roughly similar in size. In 1988, the top 7 major metro areas cast 24% of the votes, the next 15 major metro areas 22%, the non-major metro North 32%, and the non-major metro South 22%. In 2000 the percentages of the votes were slightly different: 22% for the top 7 major metro areas, 23% for the next 16 major metro areas, 31% for the non-major metro North, and 24% for the non-major metro South.

	1988		**2000**		**Diff.**	
	R – **D**		**R** – **D**		**R** – **D**	
U.S.	53.5 –	45.7	48.1 –	48.3	− 5.4	+ 2.6
Top 7 major metro	49.5 –	49.8	36.7 –	59.6	− 12.8	+ 9.8
Next 16 major metro	51.9 –	47.1	44.8 –	51.0	− 7.1	+ 3.9
Non-major metro North	54.7 –	44.5	52.8 –	42.8	− 1.9	− 1.7
Non-major metro South	57.7 –	41.6	55.7 –	42.1	− 2.0	+ 0.5

Let us look at each of these areas in turn.

THE TOP 7 MAJOR METRO AREAS. In these vast, sprawling major metro areas, places where people have almost no personal contact with major elected officials, with their sophisticated, cynical, secular voters, Clinton-Gore Democrats made major gains in the 1990s; indeed, these areas account for most of the Democrats' percentage gains in the entire country. Here Clinton's performance got high approval and his personal peccadilloes raised few hackles. These are not places where Al Gore's "people versus the powerful" theme had much appeal. They are the most affluent parts of the country, where voters in the 1990s saw gains not only in income, but in wealth: Housing values are high and stock ownership widespread. Opposition to tax increases helped Bush here in 1988; but in 2000, with increased wealth, tax cuts had relatively little appeal. At the same time, they are also metro areas, which for decades were plagued by high crime and welfare dependency, factors which increased the appeal of Republicans here in the 1980s. But with the sharp drops in crime and welfare dependency in the 1990s, these issues faded and the Democrats were no longer vulnerable on them. These 7 major metro areas were even in the 1988 election but gave Al Gore a 23% margin in 2000.

THE NEXT 16 MAJOR METRO AREAS. In many respects these metro areas are similar to the larger ones. But they are not as large, people are closer to elected officials; they tend to be somewhat less affluent, and less secular and cynical. Some (Minneapolis, St. Louis) have major right-to-life movements; some (Denver, Dallas) have had an influx of culturally conservative young families. In some of them the Democratic gain in 1988–2000 was as great as in the top 7 major metro areas—Miami, Tampa-Orlando, Phoenix, San Diego, Boston, Baltimore, Atlanta. In others Democrats gained only 1% to 4% in that period—Seattle, St. Louis, Cleveland. And in six of these major metro areas, Gore actually had lower percentages than Dukakis—Pittsburgh, Minneapolis, Denver, Hous-

---

ranks about the same, is not included because the VNS election figures do not aggregate New England results by county. Arbitrarily, all of Massachusetts, Connecticut, Rhode Island, and New Hampshire were counted as major metro; all of Maine and Vermont as non-major metro. These adjustments make for only a minor difference in the totals.

2. Atlanta, Baltimore, Boston, Cleveland, Dallas-Fort Worth, Denver, Houston, Miami-Fort Lauderdale-West Palm Beach, Minneapolis-St. Paul, Phoenix, Pittsburgh, Portland, St. Louis, San Diego, Seattle, Tampa-Orlando. Careful readers will notice minor departures from official definitons.

ton, Dallas, Portland. Note that all but one of these last five are centered in states where Bush in 2000 ran ahead of his father.

NON-MAJOR METRO NORTH. This is the most populous of these areas, and one generally ignored in political coverage. Here voters are more anti-corruption, tradition-minded, and religious than the national average. They reacted negatively to Bill Clinton's personal immorality and to his cultural liberalism on issues like abortion, gay rights, and gun control. Clinton-Gore positions of the environment were unpopular in many parts of the West, the Farm belt and in the eastern coal country. In places where the Democratic Party has been traditionally strong for historical reasons—because of Civil War loyalties, the union organizing drives of the 1930s, agrarian radicalism—there were major Republican gains. Lumberjack Democrats, mine-worker Democrats, country music Democrats—all surged toward Bush.

NON-MAJOR METRO SOUTH. The non-metropolitan South has been voting for Republican presidential candidates since 1972 and, in some cases, 1964. What is interesting here is that the non-major metro area South is now voting for Republican congressional candidates as well. The Tennessee-born Gore made only the most minor of gains here over Massachusetts-born Michael Dukakis, and those gains did not matter much in the electoral college: No southern state except Florida was close.

These countervailing shifts in partisan preference have created a new political map in 2000, a map which puzzled many of the election experts. Florida, which voted 61% for Bush in 1988, was the number one target state of both candidates in 2000 and the result, as the world knows, was excruciatingly close. The reason is simple: 53% of Florida's votes were cast in major metro areas—the Gold Coast running from Miami to Palm Beach County and the I-4 corridor from Tampa-St. Petersburg to Orlando. These metro areas showed some of the sharpest shifts to the Democrats in the 1990s, 14% in the Gold Coast and 10% in the I-4 corridor. New Jersey, one of George H. W. Bush's best megastates in 1988, is almost totally included in two of the top 7 major metro areas; it was so heavily Democratic in 2000 that it was not a target for either campaign. Illinois, which Bush narrowly won in 1988, has 63% of its votes in metro Chicago and another 5% in metro St. Louis; it was Al Gore's strongest Midwestern state all along. California, which went comfortably for Bush in 1988, has 68% of its votes in metro Los Angeles and San Francisco, plus 8% in metro San Diego; in 2000 Bush spent $20 million there and Gore zero, but Gore carried it 54%–41%.

But changes in partisan preference in non-major metro areas favored Bush. He carried West Virginia with its 5 precious electoral votes, a state which since 1928 has voted Republican only for incumbent presidents winning landslide victories. He carried Al Gore's Tennessee and Bill Clinton's Arkansas. He came within 1% of carrying Iowa, Wisconsin, and Oregon—which together had as many electoral votes as Florida—all of which went for Michael Dukakis and against the older George Bush in 1988.

It was almost as if two different Americas were voting. In one America, in the major metro areas, the choice between Gore and Bush looked almost as stark as the choice in 1964 between Lyndon Johnson and Barry Goldwater. Gore carried Manhattan 80%–14% and Los Angeles County 64%–32%; Johnson carried Manhattan 81%–19% and Los Angeles County 57%–43%. In another America, in the rural areas and some of the fast-growing metropolitan fringe, the choice between Bush and Gore looked like the choice in 1972 between Richard Nixon and George McGovern. Bush carried 30 counties in Kentucky with bigger percentages than Nixon, including four ancestrally Democratic counties carried by McGovern; he carried Idaho 69%–28% and Montana 58%–33%, compared to Nixon's 64%–26% in Idaho and 58%–38% in Montana.

There will be some who will say that the closeness of the 2000 election, and the fact that both major parties have been consistently winning 49% and 48% of the voter is happenstance, that different results were possible in 2000, that the final tie vote was the result of contingencies which could have turned out differently. And of course it is always possible to imagine how things might have turned out differently—how often did partisans of both parties roll those possibilities over in their minds during the five-week struggle over Florida!

Al Gore, it is often said, and at least as often by Democrats as by Republicans, did not run an optimum campaign. For seven years he had known he would run for president in 2000, yet he had three campaign managers and four or five different campaign strategies—clear signs that he might have done better. The campaign theme he finally adopted at the Los Angeles convention—"the people versus the powerful"—was arguably weaker than the New Democratic argument that he had the formula for showing how a limited but helpful government could lay the groundwork for technological innovation and bounteous prosperity. Certainly "the people versus the powerful" did not staunch the loss of Democratic votes in economically ailing West Virginia. But the Gore campaign did some things right. With a few exceptions, it targeted states well: It spent more money than anywhere else in Florida and spent nothing in California, outspending Bush in the former and saving money in the latter. Political scientists argued, based on formulas developed from the results of several past elections, that Gore should have won as much as 60% of the two-party vote. But those formulas were based on economic indicators, and elections are also about other things; Gore consistently trailed in polls up to the August convention, when voters were well aware of the nation's low-inflation economic growth, and his judgment that harping on it would not change their minds was almost surely sound. It is said that he should have used Bill Clinton more; but Clinton's personal deficiencies stood to lose him as many votes as his professional accomplishments would gain, and in any case to have relied heavily on his boss would have made him seem less than presidential in stature. It is true that if you add Ralph Nader's vote to Gore's that would take him over 50%; but there was no way to get Nader out of the race and polling suggests that if he were not running less than half his supporters would have voted for Gore; some would have voted for Bush and others wouldn't have voted at all. A Naderless race might have produced a victory for Gore, but it probably would not have gotten him to 50% of the vote.

Anyway, it could also be argued that George W. Bush ran less than an optimum campaign. He coasted after the second debate and made some obvious targeting mistakes—spending two days in California in the last two weeks, for example. He failed to anticipate the last-weekend surge toward Gore, which seems to have been the result of doubts that Bush was up to the job. But he also put together a platform without which he would not have come as close as he did. He effectively framed the campaign as being about something other than a generally satisfactory status quo. He consolidated the Republican base early, targeted some seemingly unlikely states (West Virginia, Tennessee), and got just enough votes to win.

Would we still have had a 48%–48% election if the parties had chosen other nominees? An imponderable: but it's not clear that we wouldn't. It might be argued that John McCain would have been a stronger Republican nominee. But McCain's famous temper may have flared and cost him some votes, and in any case many of the Independents and Democrats who found him so attractive when he was challenging Bush would have decided that he was not so attractive once he became the nominee of a basically conservative Republican Party, and when his mostly conservative voting record and positions on issues had been publicized by the liberal-leaning press. One might argue as well that Bill Bradley, or one of the other possible Democratic candidates scared out of the race by the Clinton-Gore White House might have done better than Gore.

Maybe. But a strong case can be made that Bush and Gore were probably their parties' strongest candidates. They consolidated their parties' base vote, Bush early and Gore at his convention, and those party bases were just about equal in size. Both campaigns, with just a few exceptions, did a good job of targeting states, often against the conventional political wisdom. In a competitive political marketplace, two parties with generally competent candidates will come up with campaign strategies that tend to maximize their support. These candidates did that, and ended up with 48% each. That, and the results of the 1996 and 1998 elections, suggests very strongly that when we are looking at repeated 49% and 48% results, we are looking at something pretty fundamental. The nation is divided right down the middle, not deeply perhaps, but at least very evenly.

Politics, said the political scientist Paul Lazarsfeld, is about who gets how much when. In other words, politics is about economics. Lazarsfeld came from Europe, where intellectuals spun Marxist theories and where large socialist parties had become major competitors for power in the first half of the 20th century; and he was writing in 1948, when American politics seemed to be a struggle between New Deal Democrats and reactionary Republicans, between those who wanted to use government to redistribute wealth and income and those who wanted it to leave well enough alone, between a party backed by rapidly growing labor unions and a party with almost unanimous backing from corporate and financial leaders. But American politics even then was about more than economics. The polling evidence is pretty clear that Franklin Roosevelt would not have won a third term in 1940 except for the fact that war had broken out in Europe and Hitler was overruning the continent. Otherwise most Americans' strong feeling that no president should serve more than two terms would have determined the result. Over the long course of American history, cultural factors have been more important than economic factors in determining how people vote—not all important, for economics counts for something, but more important. The election of 2000 provides a good example.

Look at the VNS exit poll and see how those with incomes over $100,000 voted: 54%–43% for Bush. Voters in the $75,000-$100,000 range voted for Bush by 52%–45%. Republican margins, to be sure, but not very big ones: The senior Bush in 1988 had carried over $100,000 income voters by 65%–32% and $50,000-$100,000 voters (perhaps a better proxy) by 62%–37%. And the highest-income voters had a lot to gain economically from a Bush victory in 2000: He promised to cut their marginal income tax rate from 39.6% to 33%, while Al Gore made it clear he would never do so. Or look at voters with incomes under $15,000. They voted for Gore by 57%–37%, as did voters with $15,000-$30,000 incomes by 54%–41%—the only significant Gore margins among income groups. Under $15,000 voters in 1988, in contrast, were 62%–37% for Dukakis.

In other words, neither Al Gore's championship of "the people versus the powerful" nor George W. Bush's promise of a big tax cut did much of a job of rallying his party's New Deal economic constituencies. One reason is that the economic factor that is important in American politics today is not so much income as it is wealth. Voters are not much concerned about temporary drops in income in a country that has suffered only six months of recession in the last 17 years: Low-inflation economic growth has prevailed for 97% of the time, and has come to seem the norm. What voters are concerned about is how well they are doing in the lifetime project of accumulating wealth, in residential real estate and, increasingly, in the stock market. The older George Bush's greatest loss of votes in 1992 came in New Hampshire and southern California—which were also the parts of the nation where housing values dropped most in the 1990–91 recession. Then, as the stock market boomed after the Republicans won control of Congress in 1994—personal household assets, a good measure of voters' wealth, increased by 8.5% a year from 1994 to 1999—the electorate entered a period of great contentment. Lower-income voters did not feel in much need of the economic benefits that Democrats might promise. Higher-income voters did not care much about tax rates when they were making vast gains in the stock market. The increase in wealth helps explain why affluent suburban voters in the major metro areas have shifted away from Republicans: Taxes were the one issue that inclined them to Republicans in 1988, and the issue was much weaker in 2000. But the bottom line is that in 2000 economic status explained very little about voting behavior. Other factors were more important.

One such factor was race. Whites voted 54%–42% for Bush; blacks voted 90%–9% for Gore. Other "people of color" voted for Gore as well, but the picture is more complicated than national figures suggest. Hispanics voted 62%–35% for Gore, despite Bush's strong appeals for their votes and greater fluency in Spanish. But Hispanics, unlike blacks, are not a bloc of voters homogeneous across the nation. Bush got only 18% of the Hispanic vote in New York and 29% in California; but he got 43% of the Hispanic vote in Texas and won the Hispanic vote 49%–48% in Florida. If no Hispanics had been voting nationally, Gore would not have won his popular vote plurality. But if no Hispanics had voted in Florida, Gore would have carried the state and would have been elected president. Nationally, Asians voted 55%–41% for Gore. But most of this margin came in Hawaii, where Gore won 62% of the Asian majority in the state. In California, the vote was 49%–48% for Gore, and Asian voters appear to have been equally divided in the other 48 states as well. Far from behaving like "people of color," Asians voted much more like whites than blacks.

Other factors have little explanatory value. The by now familiar gender gap appeared once again, as it has in every election since 1980: men voted 53%–42% for Bush, women 54%–43% for Gore. But the gap is the work almost entirely of unmarried women; married women split 49%–48% for Bush. This was not a generational battle. There was no statistically significant difference between the responses of any age group. Education made some difference, but not in a straight-line way. Voters who graduated from high school, went to college and graduated from college all cast small pluralities for Bush. Those who never graduated from high school and those with graduate degrees cast somewhat larger pluralities for Gore. Sense can be made of this. Clients of the state (non-high school graduates) and employees of the state (the teachers, social workers, health care workers and lawyers who make up most of those with graduate degrees) tend to prefer the party that favors a larger state, while those who depend less on the state (the large majority with middling levels of education) do not.

So what is it that divides the two nations? What demographic factor separates voters more than any other? The answer is: religion. White voters who identified as members of the religious right—14% of the electorate—voted for Bush by an 80%–18% margin. Jews—4%—voted for Gore by 79%–18% percent, and those with other non-Christian religions or no religion—15% of the electorate—voted for Gore by 61%–29%. The difference in voting behavior between the religious right and non-Christians is bigger than the difference between blacks and whites. These are the groups on the outer edges; look now at the larger masses. White Protestants—56% of the electorate—voted for Bush by 63%–34%. White Catholics—25% of the electorate—voted for Bush by 52%–45%, despite the historic preference of Catholics for the Democratic Party. One of the untold stories of the campaign is how the Bush forces worked subtly through little-publicized channels to win over strong, tradition-minded Catholics, obviously with some success. Those who attended religious services weekly or more often—42% of the electorate—voted 59%–39% for Bush. Those who attend religious services seldom or never—another 42% of the electorate—voted 56%–39% for Gore. The middle group, the 14% who said they attended religious services monthly, voted 51%–46% for Gore.

The same picture emerges from the post-election survey conducted by the University of Akron and sponsored by the Ethics and Public Policy Center and the Pew Charitable Trusts. The survey separated Americans into 14 different groups based on religious belief and practice. Distinctions were made between different kinds of Protestant denominations (Evangelical and Mainline) and, in some cases, between more and less observant members of a group; more observent were those who reported church attendance once a week or more often. The results are arrayed in the following table according to the percentage of the two-party vote cast for George W. Bush:

	Bush	Gore
Mormons	88%	12%
White Evangelical Protestants, more observant	84%	16%
White Mainline Protestants, more observant	66%	34%
White Mainline Protestants, less observant	57%	43%
Roman Catholics, more observant	57%	43%
White Evangelical Protestants, less observant	55%	45%
Roman Catholics, less observant	41%	59%
Seculars	35%	65%
Hispanic Protestants	33%	67%
Other Christians	28%	72%
Hispanic Catholics	24%	76%
Jews	23%	77%
Other non-Christians	20%	80%
Black Protestants	4%	96%

More than half, 54%, of Bush's voters were more observant Protestants or Catholics; only 15% were blacks, Hispanics or non-Christians. More than half of Gore's voters, 51%, were blacks, Hispanics or non-Christians; only 20% were more observant Protestants or Catholics. Although they may be uncomfortable with the fact, Americans increasingly vote as they pray—or don't pray.

To put it another way, the two Americas apparent in the 48%–48% 2000 election are two nations of different faiths. One is observant, tradition-minded, moralistic. The other is unobservant, liberation-minded, relativist. One nation was repelled by Bill Clinton—his frequent lies, his fundraising scandals, his affair with a White House intern, his lies under oath in a United States District Court proceeding. The other nation was pleased with Bill Clinton—his charm and fluency, his support of feminism and gay rights, his closeness to Hollywood figures—or was ready to subordinate any personal distaste to satisfaction with the peace and prosperity, the steep declines in crime and welfare dependency, that occurred during his presidency. The first nation saw in Al Gore many of Clinton's deficiencies; the second nation saw in him many of his strengths. So it makes sense that the major metro areas, less observant, more relativist, trended toward Gore, and the non-major metro majority, observant, moralistic, trended toward Bush.

Interestingly, the specific issues on which these groups are most deeply divided are issues that were seldom mentioned by either candidate in the campaign or in debate, issues on which they addressed with obvious reluctance in the debates. They are abortion, gun control, the environment. In the mid–1990s Democrats were slavering at the prospect of making these major issues. They were convinced that abortion, gun control, and the environment would sweep many voters their way. And indeed they did—or, rather, had. But by 2000 the gains Democrats hoped for on these issues had already been made. The places where their positions on abortion, gun control, and the environment were popular were by 2000 safely Democratic—California, New Jersey, the major metro areas. But they were also unpopular in significant portions of target states—among the large right-to-life movements in Minnesota and Missouri, among hunters in Pennsylvania and Michigan, among voters who believed Clinton environmental policies were threatening their livelihood and way of life. Voters in eastern Washington and Oregon felt threatened by the proposal to breach dams on the Snake River to protect salmon, voters in West Virginia and Kentucky felt threatened by restrictions on the use of coal, voters in the Rocky Mountain West felt threatened by land use policy that fenced off grazing land and protected the grizzly bear, voters in the Farm Belt felt threatened by EPA's proposal to regulate non-point source pollution—which, put in plain English, meant that farmers would have to get an EPA permit every time they used a new fertilizer.

They were aggrieved, in other words, by what they saw as a busybody Democratic government which was trying to impose the values of the major metro areas on their local communities, to impose the values of one nation on another. On these issues— abortion, gun control, the environment—the Clinton-Gore government was practicing, or was seen to be practicing, a kind of cultural imperialism. The Gore nation wants abortions honored, guns regulated or outlawed, and the environment protected by intrusive regulators. The Bush nation believes that abortions are immoral, guns part of a healthy way of life, and the land and water best protected by those who use it every day. The two nations on these issues have diametrically opposite views of what is decent and moral, just as they have diametrically opposite views on Bill Clinton's personal morality and Al Gore's assertion that he was under "no controlling authority."

The brings to mind the famous passage from Benjamin Disraeli's novel *Sybil*, published in 1845, just after the Chartist movement led great marches against the government. "Our Queen," says Disraeli's character Egremont, "reigns over the greatest nation that has ever existed." "Which nation?" Morley, the Chartist agitator asks, "for she reigns over two." Egremont seemed puzzled. "Yes," Morley went on. "Two nations between whom there is no intercourse and no sympathy; who are as ignorant of each other's habits, thoughts, and feelings, as if they were dwellers in different zones or inhabitants of different planets; who are formed by a different breeding, are fed by a different food, are ordered by different manners, and are not governed by the same laws." "You speak of?" Egremont asks. The answer, in bold capital letters, "THE RICH AND THE POOR." In early 21st Century America the divide is not economic but cultural. But there are two nations, of almost equal size, between which there is little intercourse and sympathy, which are ignorant of each other's habits, thoughts and feelings, which "are fed by a different food, are ordered by different manners, and are not governed by the same laws." They are as different as Bill Clinton's preferred vacation spot, Martha's Vineyard, and George W. Bush's ranch in Crawford, Texas.

Can these two nations live together? The historian Robert Wiebe once wrote that Americans could live together because Americans lived separately. In Florida, during impeachment, when gun control and abortion are raised as issues, the two Americas have found themselves no longer separate, but living together, uncomfortably. On each of these very different issues, the arguments have raged along similar lines. One nation has called for obeying old rules. The other nation has called for creating new rules. The Florida imbroglio generated great discord not just because so much was at stake, but also because the arguments reprised old themes. The Republicans insisted that the rules for counting the votes should stay the same as they were when the votes were cast. The Democrats argued that the rules were unfairly leaving some people out and so should be changed. The circumstances of Florida forced an argument: Neither side was going to back down. But most Americans prefer to avoid such arguments if they can. In the peace and prosperity of the late 1990s, they have been mostly content with things as they are, and reelected incumbents of both parties at record rates. But when they were forced by the political calendar to choose, between George W. Bush and Al Gore, between a Republican government and a Democratic government, the two nations, almost precisely equal in size, had to face each other, to confront their differences—as much as both candidates and both parties wished to avoid the confrontation.

George W. Bush now has the opportunity to govern in a way that will extend his party's base as Clinton extended his party's base in the 1990s. He starts off with no reliable national majority, but neither did Clinton. There may be an analogy here with the last time the American political balance was so even, in the 1880s. Then Americans were divided by a central non-economic issue, the Civil War. But in the 1890s other issues came along—free silver and hard money, protectionism and imperialism—which shifted the balance. The key figure was a president seldom remembered today, but often cited by Bush's chief political strategist, Karl Rove. William McKinley was elected and re-elected with a bare majority of 51%. But he used the new issues to break across the old cultural barriers and establish the working Republican majority that prevailed for the long generation from 1896 to 1930. Rove believes that Bush can do the same.

The cultural divisions will remain. Abortions and guns will never be outlawed; the demands of neither nation will never be fully satisfied. But the saliency of those issues may decline, and other issues may take their place. There is a common theme to all of the major Bush domestic proposals, on education, Social Security, Medicare, and taxes, which is to provide citizens with more choice and to rely less on centralized authority. When Bush was trailing in the polls in early September, he put up ads which explicitly presented the election as a contest between more choice and more government, and his standing rose. This is in line with the increasingly decentralized character of American society and responsive to the fact that we are, in important ways, two separate nations who live uncomfortably together. Postindustrial America in many ways more closely resembles the decentralized, culturally divided preindustrial America that Alexis de Tocqueville described in *Democracy in America* than it does the industrial America in which the generation of Bush, Gore and Clinton grew up—an America that seemed culturally homogeneous and economically and governmentally centralizing. In this view, George W. Bush, though he won fewer votes than Al Gore, is more in line with the grain of American history.

That means, among other things, that the Bush administration is less likely to practice the kind of cultural imperialism practiced by the Clinton administration. The Bush nation is less inclined to want to change the Gore nation—indeed, it despairs that it cannot change the Gore nation—than it is to simply want to be left alone. The passage of restrictions on abortion, and even the repeal of *Roe v. Wade* by a new Supreme Court majority would leave the current American abortion regime largely intact: Abortions will still be widely available, though there may be a further decline in their number. We will continue to have the current gun control regime, in which about 50% of the people live in the 33 states which allow law-abiding citizens to carry concealed handguns and about 50% live in the 17 states that don't (not surprisingly, most of the former voted for Bush and most of the latter for Gore). Crime, incidentally, has declined more in states with carry-concealed-weapons laws; it appears that criminals are deterred if there is a serious possibility that a potential victim may have a handgun. As for the environment, urban-based environmental activists will be unhappy, and will prosper from direct mail campaigns seeking contributions. But Bush policies will reduce the discontent with attempts to change local ways of life.

Bush's proposals for education seem unlikely to invade local autonomy or to impose one nation's values on the other. He seeks greater accountability and testing, and in fact American education has been moving, rapidly in some states, fitfully in others, in the same direction. We will get less of centralized bureaucracy trying to impose values from Washington. The Democratic policy followed for the last 30 years—pump more money into schools and prevent them from being held accountable for results—is increasingly regarded as bankrupt, and would have been at least modified even if Gore had won.

Bush's major economic initiatives—on taxes, Social Security, and Medicare—have some potential for increasing support for Republicans in the major metro areas where they lost ground in the 1990s. Affluent suburban voters may not be particularly eager for tax cuts today. But once they get them, they may be wary that the Democrats will raise rates if they get back in—the posture of the tax issue that favored the older George Bush in 1988. As for providing individual investment accounts as part of Social Security, this should appeal most to younger voters who have become accustomed to accumulating wealth by investing in the market. Here is a reform which goes very much with the grain of life in major metro America, and not against the grain in the rest of the country. Similarly, on Medicare the Bush reform would provide the elderly with more choices of medical insurance, and replace a system that is centrally directed and therefore inefficient and inherently unable to keep up with technological and scientific advance. And since the incredibly complex and rigid Medicare regulations currently tend to govern the dispensing of medical care to all patients, a more supple, adaptable Medicare would produce better results for everyone in ways that may become visible over time. The Clinton health care finance plan failed in 1994 in large part because it attempted to impose a single system on a nation that has, in effect, many health care finance systems. A health care finance plan that allows more choices is more likely to be found acceptable in such a nation.

Demography is moving, slowly, toward the Bush nation. Some Republicans look with foreboding at the major metro areas where they have fallen behind the opposition. Who cares if you make gains in West Virginia when you lose ground in California? But the major metro areas are not growing as fast as the rest of the country; they cast a smaller share of the nation's votes in 2000 than in 1988. The 2000 Census showed the trend. If the electoral vote had been based on the reapportionment mandated by the 2000 Census and announced in early 2001, George W. Bush would have won not 271 electoral votes, but 278. He carried all of the states that gained House seats except California—Arizona, Colorado, Florida, Georgia, Nevada, North Carolina, and Texas—while most of those that lost seats were carried by Gore. The Americans of the Bush nation tend to have more children than the Americans of the Gore nation, and the communities of the Bush nation tend to welcome growth while the communities of the Gore nation tend to limit it: California's culturally conservative Central Valley is growing faster than the culturally liberal San Francisco Bay area. The fastest-growing parts of the United States are formerly rural counties on the metropolitan fringe, beyond the edge city office centers, now filling up with family-sized subdivisions, outlet shopping malls and booming mega-churches. Though many of these are within the boundaries of major metro areas, these counties tend to vote strongly Republican, and with their growth have produced Republican majorities almost large enough to offset the Democratic margins in heavily black or culturally liberal central cities. These are places like Collin County, Texas, which grew by 86% in the 1990s and voted 73%–24% for Bush; Forsyth County, Georgia, which grew by 123% and voted 78%–19% percent for Bush; and Douglas County, Colorado, which grew by 191% and voted 65%–31% for Bush. These edge counties are usually ignored by reporters and political scientists, who can't imagine living in such places, but they are in many ways the cutting edge of America, the wave of the future.

The two Americas face no revolution, like the one Disraeli feared; for the most part Americans leave plenty of space for their fellow citizens to live as they want. But our politics, in these mostly placid times, will continue to register the angers and the passions that are aroused when one of the nations seems to be threatening to use government to impinge on the other. The prospect ahead is for close elections, closely divided

Congresses, bitterly fought battles over issues and nominations—and for the two nations with two different faiths to continue to live together, mostly peaceably, economically productive, militarily powerful, culturally creative, often seeming to be spinning out of control, but ultimately stable, two nations united by the politics that seems to divide us.

The Political Government

The Founding Fathers did not intend to make American government easy. They set up three branches of government, with powers intertwined with each other. The president would be Commander-in-Chief, but Congress would declare war; the state's electors would choose the president, but the House could do so when no one got an electoral majority; the president would administer, but the Congress would appropriate, and only the House could initiate taxation; the president would conduct foreign policy, but the Senate must approve treaties. All voters would choose members of the House, but state legislatures, originally, chose members of the Senate, and the method of electing the president was left to the state legislatures. Where exactly the Supreme Court would fit into all this the Founders left ambiguous; and it remains ambiguous still, even as the Supreme Court effectively determined who would become president in January 2001.

The political branches of the United States government on the inauguration of George W. Bush were, technically, in the hands of the Republican Party, for the first time since 1953–55. But it would be a mistake to say that the Republican Party, was in control of a government which in any circumstances is difficult to control and when the Republican control was so tenuous—as was made clear when James Jeffords's party switch gave Democrats control of the Senate in May 2001. George W. Bush was elected president with 271 electoral votes, one more than the required 270. The Senate, Republican by virtue of the tie-breaking vote of Vice President Richard Cheney from January 20 to May 29, and was technically controlled by Democrats from January 3 to January 20, 2001, when Al Gore was still vice president and was controlled by them again after the Jeffords party switch. The balance could be altered again any time by another party switch or by the death or resignation of one of the 29 Democratic or 18 Republican senators whose states have governors of a different party; Washington has focused on the possibility of a vacancy in the seat of Strom Thurmond, who turned 98 in December 2000, but in the last Congress it was the death not of Thurmond, but of 61-year-old Paul Coverdell which changed the party balance in the Senate. Following the election, the House of Representatives had a Republican majority of 222–213, counting the two Independents with the party with which they ordinarily vote, and not counting as a Republican Democrat Jim Traficant, who voted for Dennis Hastert for speaker and lost his Democratic committee assignments.

This is not control. But it is incumbency, and incumbents ordinarily have one great power in government and politics, the power to set the agenda. That power can move from one branch of the government to another, as it did from Bill Clinton's White House to Newt Gingrich's House of Representatives in November 1994; and it can move back again. It can move outside government altogether: in the spring of 1992 Ross Perot and his cries for cutting deficits and reforming government eclipsed the incumbent president and the man who would be elected his successor. In early 2001, despite the narrowness of his margin and the bitterness of the Florida contest, the power to set the agenda for government was solidly in the hands of George W. Bush. A divided Democratic Party, disheartened by the last-minute pardons issued by Bill Clinton, and a Republican congressional leadership, suddenly relieved of the exhausting tasks of endless negotiations with Clinton—neither was in any condition to set an agenda. So it is with the presidency that we begin.

The Presidency

"An institution is the lengthened shadow of one man," wrote Ralph Waldo Emerson, and the presidency has been the lengthened shadows of the 42 men who have held the office. This presidency will be the lengthened shadow of George W. Bush, a man Washington had difficulty understanding during the 2000 campaign but who, when observed over his not overlong political career, is a comprehensible and coherent figure. Washington has always been fascinated by the supposed aristocratic pedigree of the Bush family and of its supposed roots in the Northeast. But the pedigree is not ancient and the Northeastern roots never deep. To be sure, George W. Bush's grandfather Prescott Bush was a partner at Brown Brothers Harriman and Senator from Connecticut. But his father had owned a steel factory in Columbus, Ohio—he was neither a Northeasterner nor an aristocrat. George H. W. Bush left the Northeast in 1948, at age 24, to make his fortune in west Texas and has lived in Texas, except when he has held government office, for the rest of his life (though he does summer in Maine). George W. Bush grew up in Midland, Texas and speaks with a west Texas accent (much more so than his younger brother, Florida Governor Jeb Bush, who did most of his growing up in Houston). At Andover and Yale, his father's schools, George W. Bush flaunted his Texas background and was never entirely at ease with Northeasterners, whether the traditional preppies who dominated the schools in the early 1960s, or the campus radicals who dominated them when he graduated from Yale in 1968 and while he was at Harvard Business School in 1973–75.

The years in between he lived in Texas; he returned to Midland after business school and ran for Congress in 1978. It was not a winning campaign. Midland was a white-collar Republican town, but the rest of west Texas was still ancestrally Democratic, and the district, which stretched from Midland to Lubbock, elected instead an ambitious young Democrat named Kent Hance. Hance co-sponsored the Reagan tax cuts in 1981 and later turned Republican, and ran losing races for senator and governor. Bush stuck to business, with little success in the "awl bidness" and more success as managing partner of the Texas Rangers. He worked on his father's 1988 presidential campaign and had some exposure to the workings of the Bush White House. His father's defeat in 1992 left him with the option of a political career of his own in a Texas that was increasingly Republican. In 1993 he set out to run for governor, against the popular Democratic incumbent Ann Richards, who in 1988 memorably described his father as "born with a silver foot in his mouth."

Bush's 1993–94 campaign for governor was methodical, dogged, clearly focused on issues, underestimated by the opposition—a campaign that was very much the model for his 1999–2000 campaign for president. With the help of his chief strategist Karl Rove, who had worked for most successful Texas Republicans, he set out to learn about state government issues and how government worked on the ground. He assembled a team of smart issues experts and drew up a four-point program for reform. Then for more than a year he delivered again and again his same four-point message. The fame he enjoyed as a president's son enabled him to avoid primary competition and to gain voters' attention. His four-point message slowly helped him win their votes. Invariably he was respectful of his opponent; Richards referred to him derisively as "Shrub," but he always called her "Governor." When in debate she paid tribute to volunteers who gave aid in a disaster, he began, "Well spoken, Governor." Bush trailed in polls until mid-October; in Texas and Washington he was widely expected to lose. Instead he won by a 53%–46% margin.

In his first year in office he worked with legislators of both parties and put his four-point program into law. He spoke frankly and negotiated openly with Democrats as well as Republicans and worked especially closely with Lieutenant Governor Bob Bullock, a grizzled Democrat who endorsed him for reelection in 1998. He was not entirely successful with the 1997 legislature, but was re-elected by a 68%–31% margin in 1998. With discipline, he worked to pass his program through the legislature and did not begin any outward presidential campaigning until after it adjourned in May 1999.

The presidential campaign was in many ways a copy of his first campaign for governor. Quietly, with Rove and aides Karen Hughes and Joe Albaugh by his side, he assembled teams of experts, most of them people he had not known before, and studied government—how the federal government worked in theory and on the ground. Shrewd political consultants advise their clients that the best way to campaign is to come up with a limited set of priority issues, on which the candidate's stand is in line with the voters', a set of issues which will work in the primary, work in the general election and work in governing. It is not easy to do: there is always a tension between what the party's hard core wants and what middle-of-the-road voters will accept, and between what sounds good on the campaign trail and in ads and what will work in legislative sessions and in an administration. But Bush managed to do it. He took certain risks. He called for individual investment accounts as part of Social Security—a stand which went against all conventional wisdom. He called for vouchers as a part of his education program—a stand that does not do well in polls. He called for reform of Medicare—an issue on which Democrats thought they had an inordinate advantage. He called for changes in defense—although the men who turned out to be his strongest opponents, John McCain and Al Gore, had much experience on defense issues and he had none. And he called for large tax cuts—an issue that did not poll especially well and was sure to be denounced by Democrats and leading editorial pages as a giveaway to the rich.

Bush also worked skillfully at minimizing primary competition and maximizing Republican support. His initial high ratings in polls came not just because he had a familiar name; they also came because Republicans, and Americans generally, were seeking in the next president what they found lacking in the current one. And they found it easy to believe that the honesty and good character so plainly lacking in Bill Clinton could be found in George and Barbara Bush's son. Bush corralled the support of all of his fellow Republican governors and most senators; he won an outpouring of support from Republican contributors. His chief primary opponent turned out to be John McCain, whose story of courage and defiance under torture inspired many voters eager for a president with character and whose call for campaign finance reform attracted many Independents, Democrats and journalists. But McCain could not expand his appeal to committed Republicans. His emphasized issues—campaign finance, taxes—on which his message resembled the Democrats' and downplayed issues—abortion, defense—on which his message had great appeal to Republicans. He picked a fight with prominent Christian conservatives, although religious conservatives are a large Republican constituency.

Meanwhile, Bush showed he could respond in crisis. After McCain surged to victory in New Hampshire as a reformer, Bush started calling himself a "reformer with results," citing his issue successes in Texas. In early September, when he fell behind Al Gore in the polls and suffered through 10 days of adverse coverage, he started running ads and giving speeches arguing that his reforms—the same five issues he emphasized all along—would give people choices while the Democrats' programs would give them more government. He rose to the occasion in his acceptance speech in August and in the three debates in October. While Al Gore, who had known for seven years that he would be running, had three campaign managers, four or five campaign themes and several changes of clothes, Bush stuck closely to the same course he had set long before, much as he had in Texas.

But not with quite the same result. The first exit polls took Bush aback: he expected to win by several points. But the polling evidence makes it clear that in the weekend before the campaign there was a movement away from Bush and toward Gore. The chief reason was not the last-week revelation that Bush had had a DUI conviction in 1976; it was that a fair number of voters in the middle still were worried that he was not up to the job—a theme the Gore campaign shrewdly hammered on for the last five days. The result was that Bush trailed in the popular vote, and hung on to only the narrowest of leads in Florida during the 36-day battle for the state's crucial 25 electoral votes. Though he seemed unsure of himself in some public appearances, Bush performed steadily through the crisis, making crisp decisions and forging ahead, mostly behind the scenes, in selecting appointees for what he could not be completely sure was going to be his administration. His penchant for preparation became clear in the 38-day transition between the Supreme Court decision and the inauguration, when he crisply announced appointments and set out once again his policy goals.

What is striking is how different George W. Bush's campaign was from the campaigns his father waged in 1992. The older Bush emphasized foreign policy and seemed disconnected from the domestic concerns of the voters. He seemed to regard campaigning as a dirty business beneath his dignity. The younger Bush emphasized domestic issues and imposed a coherent framework of reform around his separate proposals. He seemed to enjoy campaigning and to relish the opportunity to state his five-point message once again. It was Bush's opponents who were more preoccupied with their fathers. John McCain entitled his book *Faith of My Fathers* and described his supposed failing to live up to his father's example. Al Gore in the peroration to his convention speech invoked his father's demand that he never forget the victims of the Great Depression. Gore's "people versus the powerful" message and his use of expressions like "I know where the rats in the barn are" made his campaign resemble more closely those of his father, who had been defeated for office 30 years before, than Bush's campaign resembled those of his father, who had been beaten eight years before.

Bush did something else in his campaign that Gore failed to do: he connected with the mood of the American people. In the early 1990s Americans preferred confrontation to consensus. They were in an angry, in-your-face mood, punishing incumbents and rewarding challengers whose stands on issues were "crunchy," in the terminology of a famous 1988 editorial in *The Economist*. In 1990 and 1992, for the first times in half a century, incumbent congressmen of both parties saw their percentages fall; in 1992, an incumbent president was defeated and got only 37% of the vote; in 1994, the Democratic Party which had controlled the House of Representatives for 40 years and the Senate for 34 of that 40 lost its majorities in both houses of Congress. Then the mood changed, quite suddenly; perhaps the critical event was the bombing of the Oklahoma City federal building in April 1995. After that Americans have preferred consensus to confrontation. They have been in a happy, contented mood, as crime and welfare rolls fell sharply and incomes and household wealth grew. In this mood they punished politicians who were angry and argumentative and rewarded incumbents and politicians whose stands on issues were, in the terminology of the same *Economist* editorial, "soggy." In this atmosphere the consensus-minded Bill Clinton won reelection by 1996 by campaigning against a confrontation-minded alternative named Dole Gingrich. In 1996 and 1998 House Republicans and incumbent governors held on to their jobs by downplaying the crunchiness they'd displayed in 1994 and adapting to the appetite for sogginess.

In 2000 the balance was different from 1996. Al Gore, as the candidate of the party in power at a time of peace and prosperity, was well-positioned to campaign as the candidate of consensus. But that was simply not his bent. Gore, though he has a moderate record on some issues, is one of the most fiercely partisan politicians in recent times, one who seems to burn with a hatred for the opposition that many close observers think dates back to his father's defeat for reelection after a bitterly fought campaign in

1970. "I'm going to fight for you!" Gore loved to proclaim, as he framed the election as a choice of "the people versus the powerful." Bush, in contrast, seems deeply consensus-minded. In Texas running for governor and across the nation running for president, he promised to work with members of both parties. In Texas he was able to build on a tradition of bipartisanship in Austin. Operating on the national stage, he called for a new era of civility and mutual respect between those with different views. After the war room operations of the Clinton era, all too visible to most Americans in the 1998–99 impeachment struggle, voters were ready for Bush's appeal. Voters in 2000 clearly yearned for a bipartisan approach to issues. They could believe they would get it with Bush. It was hard to see how they could get it with Gore. Polls suggest that, for all the rancor when Bush finally won in Florida, there would have been more if the state had been awarded to Gore.

In his first weeks as president, Bush performed much as promised. He continued to advance his issues agenda, moving first on education and taxes, instructing Defense Secretary Donald Rumsfeld to prepare recommendations for a new role for defense, and setting aside Medicare and Social Security for later. Senate Democrats voiced loud opposition to the nomination of John Ashcroft as Attorney General and House Democrats voiced loud opposition to how Republican leaders quickly pushed through tax cuts. There were few visible Democrats among major Bush appointees. But the potential remained for Bush to win Democratic votes on many of his proposals, even while keeping all or almost all Republicans on board. Bush seemed to be moving to do the things he'd said he'd do.

To Washington, which always looks for hidden motives, secret agendas, clever strategies, Bush seemed a puzzle. Bill Clinton, for all his surface ariculateness, was always opaque. There was always room to ask which Clinton was in charge, and what he was aiming to do. George W. Bush, in contrast, seems amazingly transparent. He gets up early in the morning, keeps to his schedule, makes judgments about personnel and decisions about issues quickly and crisply, and sticks mostly to his long-set-out plans. Deadlines are set and met, speech texts reviewed and speeches given, meetings proceed as scheduled, public appearances go off as planned. George W. Bush is the first business school graduate to become president. His operating style resembles most closely, among former presidents, that of Dwight Eisenhower, who had been more of a manager than a warrior as a general. Like Eisenhower, he has appointed people of great accomplishment outside politics, including some with views which seem different from his own; like Eisenhower, he seems confident he can manage them to produce the results he wants. And like Eisenhower, he is not banking on getting his programs through Congress on Republican votes only.

Also like Eisenhower, he is often underestimated. His lack of fluency, especially in comparison to Bill Clinton, is striking and, to the press, suggests that he is dumb: the chattering class likes people who are good at chattering. But his crisp four- and five-point programs are based on more than polls and focus groups. His convention speech showed a sense of history; it spun out a narrative in which Republican presidents have rescued the nation from the consequences of weakness abroad and have reformed its institutions at home, a narrative which places him in a line with Eisenhower, Nixon, Ford, Reagan and his father. His inaugural speech was suffused with a sense of the importance of religion in helping the nation set its course: "Compassion is the work of a nation, not just a government. And some needs and hurts are so deep they will only respond to a mentor's touch or a pastor's prayer. Church and charity, synagogue and mosque, lend our communities their humanity, and the will have an honored place in our plans and in our laws." It is said by his critics that Bush has no understanding of the complexity of issues, that he cannot match Bill Clinton in the exegesis of detail. Perhaps not. But he seems to be operating with the confidence that Ronald Reagan showed when he said that issues are not complex, they're simple; they're just not easy. Adherence to principle, the upholding of simple and understandable rules, a firm insistence on moral precept: these are what hold together the half of the nation that voted for George W. Bush, and they may prove to have some appeal to the other half. For perhaps it was their proclivity to the opposite—adjustment to circumstance, the assertion that complexity trumps common sense, the sense that moral rules are always adjustable—which prevented the Clinton-Gore Democrats from winning more than half the vote even as the nation enjoyed peace and prosperity.

The House of Representatives

John Dingell, the senior member of the House of Representatives, was first elected in December 1955, 11 months after the expiration of the last Republican House that served during the administration of a Republican president. No House member has any memory of what it is like to serve in a Republican House with a Republican president, though Senator Robert Byrd served in the last such House as a Democrat. That House was Republican by a 221–213 margin, with one Independent. This House began with a Republican majority of 222–213, counting the two Independents with the parties with which they ordinarily vote, and not counting as a Republican Democrat Jim Traficant, who voted for Dennis Hastert for speaker and lost his Democratic committee assignments.

Republicans would surely prefer a larger majority. Yet there are some advantages to having a small majority in the House. When one party controls both the executive and legislative branch, large majorities encourage the passage of legislation which proves harmful to the party in the long run—indeed, at the next election. The last time the Republicans had large majorities, in 1929–30, they passed the Smoot-Hawley tariff, one of the great causes of the Depression; they lost 49 seats in the 1930 election and another 101 in 1932. The Democratic Congress of 1965–66 obediently passed Lyndon Johnson's Great Society programs with hardly any changes; Democrats lost 47 seats and effective control of the House in 1966. In 1993–94, the Democratic Congress passed Bill Clinton's tax increases and spent much of its time and energy on Hillary Rodham Clinton's health care program; Democrats lost 52 seats and, for the first time in 40 years, control of the House in 1994.

And control matters, very much, in the House as it has operated for the last quarter century. In this regard, the House today is still very much the House that Tip O'Neill made. For the four decades before O'Neill became Speaker in 1977, the House was a much more bipartisan place than it has been since. The two parties were more heterogeneous. As many as half the House Democrats were from the South, and most were conservatives who voted with Republicans on most issues. Two or three dozen Republicans were liberals, from constituencies heavy with labor union members or urban ethnics, who voted with liberal Democrats on most issues. For most of the years from 1937, when Franklin Roosevelt's court-packing plan was defeated, until 1977, the House was controlled on most issues by an informal but effective coalition of conservative Southern Democrats and conservative Midwestern and Northeastern Republicans—by the county courthouses of the South and of Illinois and Ohio and Upstate New York. A bipartisan conservative coalition controlled the crucial House Rules Committee, which sets the terms for debate and the number of amendments allowed, under the chairmanships of Howard Smith and William Colmer from 1955 to 1973. The effective lobbying force for the Kennedy-Johnson legislative programs of the 1960s came not from the Democratic leadership but from the AFL-CIO. On the January 1961 vote to expand the Rules Committee, Kennedy prevailed by only 217–212 in a 262–175

Democratic House, and won only because the AFL-CIO brought in the votes of 22 Republicans. Even after that liberals often lost in Rules, and hence on the floor. Only when the Democratic majority was overwhelming, as in the Great Society Congress, did liberal Democrats effectively control the House.

Tip O'Neill saw an opportunity to change that. He was a strong partisan who grew up in a politics in which almost all Catholics were Democrats and almost all Protestants were Republicans, and where political battles were fought with a bitterness reminiscent of the religious wars of the 17th century. When Democrats to everyone's surprise got a majority in the state House in 1948 and O'Neill became Speaker, he found that the outgoing Republicans had stripped every piece of furniture and telephone from his office. When he became Speaker in the U.S. House in 1977, he saw no reason to continue the bipartisan pattern of the past. By then there were fewer liberal Republicans than in the 1960s, and the AFL-CIO lobbying operation had grown weaker. Conservative Democrats on the Rules Committee had retired or been defeated, and its 9–4 Democratic majority meant that the speaker could have solid control over procedure. O'Neill surely understood that Democrats would not always have the 292–143 margin they enjoyed in January 1977. As time went on, to a degree generally unappreciated, he fashioned legislative programs with an eye to maintaining support from moderate Democrats and those with conservative-leaning districts.

O'Neill made little or no effort to seek Republican votes. He made it clear that the House leadership expected that all party members, regardless of their views on the substantive issue at stake, will support Rules on procedural votes, and they almost always have. This makes for confrontational, crunchy debate and much bitter partisanship. The minority party will always have an incentive to argue that the rules are unfair, that the majority is framing the issue in a way that guarantees or at least enhances its chances for success on the floor. Of course often those charges will be true; plausible arguments can usually be made on both sides of a procedural issue. This course has been followed under his successors as Speaker, Democrats Jim Wright and Thomas Foley and Republicans Newt Gingrich and Dennis Hastert.

The speaker's power over committee chairmen has also been increased. Speaker Sam Rayburn was so respectful of committee chairmen that he literally disappeared in the days before the Rules Committee fight of 1961; he did not want to antagonize Howard Smith and other Southern committee chairmen. O'Neill was the beneficiary of a reform effected by Phillip Burton in December 1974, under which all committee chairmen were elected by secret vote of the Democratic Caucus. Since the Caucus was overwhelmingly liberal, that gave conservatives who were or wished to become chairmen an incentive to allow more liberal legislation through and to compile more liberal voting records themselves—which they promptly did. After the Republicans won their majority in 1994, Newt Gingrich went one or two steps further than Burton. Confident that he had the votes of the conservative freshmen just elected, he passed over senior members and simply appointed chairmen who he thought would advance his program. And he instituted a three-term limit on chairmen of committees and subcommittees, a measure designed to prevent even his new chairmen from being dominated by the culture of committees like Appropriations and making chairmen and those hopeful of becoming chairmen responsive to the conservative majority of the Republican Conference. Under Speaker Dennis Hastert, chairmen are effectively chosen in behind-closed-doors meetings of the House Republican Steering Committee, on which Hastert casts five votes and usually prevails.

These changes have made the House a more rational, comprehensible and accountable institution. But it also made it one which is more partisan and confrontational—whichever party is in control. Democrats' complaints about the majority's control of the December 1998 impeachment debate, familiar to television viewers and persuasive to many, echo almost eerily Republicans' complaints, few seen by such large audiences, against hundreds of Democratic rules during their long ascendancy. The partisan atmosphere has been increased by the increasing homogeneity of the parties in the House. The House Republican Conference has become more uniformly conservative and the House Democratic Caucus has become more uniformly liberal. There are exceptions, enough to make a difference on some issues in a closely-divided House. But Gingrich and Hastert, like the Democratic speakers before them, spent much time holding together their party, and succeeded far more often in doing so than not. Managing the House is not an easy thing: Its rules are the most complex parliamentary rules in the world, not written down in any one source; its members represent a complex and variegated nation, and have geographical, economic, cultural and committee interests that are often in tension; holding together majorities large as well as small is not an easy thing to do. That Hastert, Gingrich, Foley, Wright and O'Neill—all highly able, dedicated, politically sophisticated leaders—have been able to do so as often as they have is what is remarkable, not that they sometimes failed.

Now that may change. The Republican House in its first years put forward an agenda of its own, and it was more successful than is generally realized. Its standstill, no-spending-increase budget of 1996, passed after the showdown with Bill Clinton that was labelled the government shutdown, was one of three essential steps to erasing the budget deficits that seemed chronic in the early 1990s. (The other two were the increased tax rates on high-income taxpayers, the product of the Democratic Congress, and the end of the savings and loan crisis, which was inevitable as the government finished paying off depositors and started selling off S&L assets.) It passed welfare reform and, 14 weeks before the 1996 election, got Bill Clinton to sign it. It passed a major budget bill in May 1997, which included halts in Medicare spending, and financial services deregulation in 1999. It passed, after laborious negotiations with the Clinton administration, budgets that allowed federal spending increases to creep up toward levels one would expect from a Democratic Congress. It handled the crunchy issue of impeachment in a dignified way. Republicans seemed to lose their nerve after they nearly lost control in the 1996 election; there was a failed coup against Newt Gingrich in July 1997, and he was forced to resign after the November 1998 elections when Republicans lost seats rather than making gains as they expected. But the new Speaker, Dennis Hastert, after a sometimes shaky start, kept the trains running, though not always on time: But the hard thing in any legislature is to get anything passed at all. On some issues party lines were breached. Many Republicans backed Democrats' positions on the minimum wage, campaign finance and HMO regulation; they forced the leadership to allow open votes which they lost. Many Democrats backed Republicans' positions on the marriage penalty, the estate tax and the partial-birth abortion ban; the leadership was happy to move those forward, even toward Bill Clinton vetoes.

Now the initiative has passed from the House Republican leadership to the Republican president. And the legislative strategy he seems likely to pursue is quite different from the strategy of the House leadership of both parties over the last quarter century. Bush's strategy seems based on his experience in the very much more bipartisan atmosphere of Texas. When he became governor in 1995, Democrats still held majorities in both the state House and Senate, as they had since Reconstruction. But the two houses were not organized on partisan lines. Committee chairmen were chosen by the speaker in the House and the lieutenant governor (elected separately from the governor) in the Senate, not on partisan lines, but on the basis of support for the speaker's or lieutenant governor's program. Some chairmanships went to Republicans; members of the minority party often carried legislation. This was no doubt easier because many Democratic legislators were conservative, with views similar to those of most Republicans. But Bush made no move to obtain a coherent, partisan Republican majority. He worked closely with Democratic Speaker Pete Laney and the late Lieuten-ant Governor Bob Bullock, who endorsed him for re-election in 1998 and predicted he would be a great president. He made little effort to win Democratic seats in elections. The rule was that any Democrat who supported him on any of his top priority issues would not get serious opposition. If Republicans gained open seats or beat uniformly hostile Democrats, that was fine. Republicans did in fact win a majority of the state Senate in 1996, but Democrats kept several chairmanships.

The strategy was mostly successful. Bush's one loss on a major issue, his 1997 tax plan, came from opposition by conservative Republicans. For the most part, Bush could regard Republican legislators as a solid bloc of support and Democratic legislators as a reservoir from which he can find enough votes, from some members on one issue and other members on others, to pass his bills with significant bipartisan majorities. His proposals on the five issues he emphasized in the 2000 campaign—education, taxes, defense, Medicare, Social Security—were clearly fashioned with a view to amassing bipartisan majorities. On each he incorporated measures that have drawn significant Democratic support on Capitol Hill or have been endorsed by prominent Democrats. His education bill was very similar to one sponsored by New Democrats Joseph Lieber-man and Evan Bayh. Many Democrats voted in 2000 to end the marriage penalty and repeal the estate tax. Defense spending was increased in 2000, for the first time since the 1980s, with significant Democratic support. Bush's Medicare plan is modeled on the one recommended in March 1999 by Democratic Senator John Breaux when he chaired the Medicare Commission. A number of prominent Democrats have endorsed individual retirement accounts as part of Social Security.

This is not to say that Bush's program will inevitably succeed. On the first major measure to reach the floor of the House, income tax cuts, only 10 Democrats voted with Bush, as did every Republican. But there is no reason why Bush's plan must fail either. It will require, however, party leaders in the House to behave differently. The Republican leadership must be more open to compromise with Democrats, and holding Republicans together in support of compromises many may not like.

House Democratic leaders have a harder task. Their first instinct is surely for con-frontation, for both institutional and ideological reasons. Institutionally, because they are used to fighting partisan battles in a partisan House, and given how the House is run they will have reason to object: House Minority Leader Dick Gephardt protested loudly when the Rules Committee refused to allow a vote on a Democratic version of the income tax cut. Ideologically, because Gephardt, Minority Whip David Bonior and most other members of the Democratic leadership oppose the Bush proposals on the merits, for principled reasons. Many other House Democrats are eager for confronta-tion. Nearly one-fifth of them are members of the Congressional Black Caucus, most of them far to the left on both issues and unreconciled to the result in Florida. So are many of the party's other liberals. Yet there are also some moderates in Democratic ranks—and different kinds of moderates. The Blue Dog Democrats tend to be conser-vative on cultural issues and liberal on economics; the New Democrat Coalition tends to be conservative on economics and liberal on cultural issues. Both include many members that are inclined toward the Bush position on one or more of his priority positions.

Constituency politics could move many Democrats in the same direction. Alto-gether 46 of the 213 House Democrats represent districts carried by George W. Bush in 2000. Of these districts 23 are in the South and 23 elsewhere, mainly in the Midwest. Few have ever had to grapple with the problem of how to stay popular at home while serving with a popular Republican president: 27 of the 46 were elected in 1992 or later. In contrast, there are 40 Republicans elected from districts carried by Al Gore; 21 of these are in the East and 19 elsewhere. All but the five freshmen have had plenty of practice maintaining their local popularity while voting at least at times against the position of a locally popular Bill Clinton.

Democrats have one additional problem. They entered the 107th Congress far less confident than they entered the 106th Congress that they would be in the majority in the next Congress. In 1999 they seemed supremely confident they would gain a majority in the 2000 elections, and that helped them maintain a degree of unity and good fellowship that they had by no means always showed when they were in fact the majority. Gephardt did a splendid job of persuading veteran members not to retire or run for other office, on the grounds that they would be chairmen again soon. He put Patrick Kennedy, no keen strategist but a great draw at fundraisers, in as campaign committee chairmen and raised enough money to actually give them a fundraising advantage over Republicans. Gephardt worked his heart out, recruiting candidates, speaking at fundraisers, rallying lobbyist-moneygivers to the cause. But on election day 2000 Democrats fell short. Immediately afterwards many were not in a mood for another all-out effort. Kennedy declined to be campaign committee chairman again. Veteran members started to think about retirement or other office; in early 2001 Bonior was setting about running for governor of Michigan.

In this setting, it is going to be hard for even as talented and indefatigable a leader as Gephardt to hold the Democratic Caucus together and to persuade members again and again that they should not consider voting for even one of the Bush proposals. Gephardt would obviously like to force the Bush White House to negotiate directly with him, and to extract major concessions for any Democratic support. But it does not seem that all Democratic votes are theirs to withhold. Indeed, Democrats who wish to avoid serious competition in 2002 could do that by supporting Bush on one of his major issues if he follows his practice in Texas of making sure that such Democrats are not seriously opposed. Democratic leaders can still hope for some success on measures where significant numbers of Republican members have come their way—the minimum wage, HMO regulation, campaign finance. But they no longer have the presidential veto to back them up; it tends to undercut them instead. And Bush certainly remembers the 1990 budget negotiations in which his father gave up his "Read my lips, no new taxes" promise for rather minor concessions from the Democratic leaders. Direct negotiations with Democratic leaders are seen by him as a forum for surrender, not a necessary ingredient of bipartisan government.

But can't the Democrats look forward to controlling the House since out-of-presidential parties inevitably gain seats in non-presidential years? The answer is not necessarily yes. For out parties don't inevitably gain in offyears: They didn't in 1934 or, more familiarly to today's politicians, in 1998. The offyear out-party dynamic exists because the in-party tends to be saddled with a single national program, some parts of which will almost always be unpopular in some kinds of constituencies, while the out-party's offyear candidates are not saddled with a single platform and can adapt their appeals to the local terrain. Thus Democrats lost many districts in 1994 where their support of gun control, though popular nationally, was unpopular locally. But George W. Bush carried more districts than Al Gore in 2000, and it is not clear that Democrats will have a lot of ready targets; Republicans in Gore districts, as mentioned, have already learned how to survive. At the same time, Republicans will have obvious targets in Democrats elected from Bush districts who support none of the Bush program.

Finally, redistricting means that there may be more Bush seats in the House elected in 2002 than in the House elected in 2000. The 2000–02 redistricting cycle is the first redistricting cycle in 40 years in which redistricting will cut in favor of the party in control of the White House heading into offyear elections. The results of the 1962 elections show what can happen when the party in power is possible: John Kennedy's Democrats lost 4 seats in the House and Republicans gained 2. (The difference came because the newly admitted states of Alaska and Hawaii raised the number of House members elected in 1960 temporarily to 437.) This is the third best result ever for a party in presidential power, after 1934 and 1998. Redistricting accounted for a net gain of 6 seats for Democrats, thanks almost entirely to California, which gained 8 seats and whose Democratic redistricting plan gave the Democrats 11 more seats and Republicans 3 less. In contrast, redistricting in the 1981–82 cycle gained the Democrats a net of 15 seats. Many observers made much of the fact that Democrats gained 25 seats in the 1982 elections. But most of the gains were due to redistricting; apart from redistricting, the incumbent Reagan Republicans did about as well as the incumbent Kennedy Democrats did apart from redistricting in 1962.

Redistricting for 2002 will likely give the Republicans a net gain of between 5 and 10 seats. This is despite California, where Democrats control the process and will draw the lines of 53 districts, 1 more than at present. They can probably extend the Democrats' current lead from 32–20 in the delegation to 35–18. But offsetting these Democratic gains will be Republican gains in Texas, where Republicans will dominate the drawing of lines in Texas, the state that currently has the most partisan Democratic districting plan. Republicans are likely (absent unpredictable court decisions) to have total control in Michigan, Ohio, Pennsylvania, and Florida, which could net them half a dozen seats altogether. Democrats will have control in fast-growing Georgia and North Carolina, but will be hard put to gain more than a seat each because the fastest-growing areas of those states are heavily Republican. Split control over the process will mean neither party will monopolize the seats gained in Arizona, Colorado and Nevada. In other states losing one seat—Connecticut, Illinois, Indiana, Mississippi, Oklahoma and Wisconsin—losses will be split between the two parties. Control over redistricting is split in New York, which loses 2 seats, most likely 1 from each party.

The Senate

On March 14, 1881, the United States Senate met to elect officers and consider committee assignments. Of the 76 senators, 37 were Democrats, 37 were Republicans, one was an Independent committed to voting with Democrats, and one, William Mahone of Virginia, was—well, no one was sure. "All eyes came to rest on Mahone when the clerk reached his name," writes Senator Robert Byrd in his graceful and authoritative *The Senate, 1789–1989*. "When the dramatic moment arose, Mahone, from his seat on the Democratic side, cast his vote with the Republicans. Having thereby clinched control of the Senate, the Republicans rocked the chamber with cheers and shouts." Only it wasn't quite control: After further votes and the resignation of two Republicans over a patronage dispute, the Senate edged into a sort of compromise. "Leadership of the Senate committees remained in Republican hands"—Mahone got Agriculture—"while the Democrats continued to control the offices of secretary and sergeant at arms."

So it went the last time the Senate was equally divided between the two parties, an event so long ago that is beyond the living memory of even Strom Thurmond. As in 1881, so in 2000 it was not immediately apparent that the Senate would be equally divided after the election. Six months before the new Congress would assemble, Republicans held a 55–45 majority in the Senate. Then in July Senator Paul Coverdell of Georgia died, and was replaced by Democrat Zell Miller. In the November election, Republicans defeated Senator Charles Robb of Virginia and won the Nevada open seat as expected, while Republicans lost in Delaware, Minnesota and Florida by significant margins. Republicans Senators John Ashcroft of Missouri and Spencer Abraham of Michigan, ahead in polls in October, lost by 2% and 1%, respectively, in November. The result in Washington was in doubt. Republican Senator Slade Gorton led during most of the count (about one-quarter of Washington's ballots are cast by mail). But in mid-December the victory went to Democrat Maria Cantwell. That meant that the Senate would have 50 Democrats and 50 Republicans. Ties would be broken by Republican Vice President Richard Cheney.

But that did not settle the issue of control. Democratic leader Tom Daschle demanded that Democrats be given equal numbers of members on each committee and equal staffs and budgets. Some Republican committee chairmen let it be known that would accept equal numbers; others bridled. For Daschle's demand there was a strong institutional argument. Committees are supposed to reflect the balance of opinion on the floor, so that they will tend to produce legislation the majority of members will tend to support. Republican Leader Trent Lott, after four-and-a-half years as Majority Leader, was loath to accept Daschle's demand. But Democrats started talking about holding up Senate business for days unless equal membership was granted. It was feared that a senator might make an objection at the joint session on January 6 to the casting of Florida's 25 electoral votes for George W. Bush; that would trigger a long and acrimonious debate on the Florida count. So on January 5 Lott capitulated and accepted equal membership. He added the proviso that legislation on which a committee was equally divided could be brought to the floor by the chairman or ranking minority member or by either party's floor leader.

This was a solution suited to the Senate's institutional character. The Framers created the Senate as a balance wheel, a cooling saucer for hot coffee, a place where superior wisdom and experience could prevent unwise and rash mistakes. With only one-third of its members elected every two years, with a fair number of its members freed from political pressures because of their personal relationship with voters in small or one-party states, with its rules allowing even the politically weakest and personally least regarded of its members to stop the forward motion of legislation for some precious period of time, with its allowance of unlimited discussion and non-germane amendments and its rules that require a 60% supermajority for passage of strongly-opposed legislation, the Senate supplies some caution to the enthusiasms of the House. The Senate majority leader, many in Washington seem to assume, runs the Senate. What he does in fact is schedule business, and his schedule is usually subject to unanimous consent: He can stop things from happening, but he can't get things going if some significant body of opinion wants them stopped. The majority leader title goes back only to 1911, and many of its holders have been obscure party wheelhorses; the idea that it is a powerful position is rooted in the extraordinary use of it made by Lyndon Johnson in four years in the 1950s when the Senate was nearly evenly divided between the parties; as Johnson's successor Mike Mansfield, in a speech intended to be given on November 22, 1963, and not delivered until 1997 at the first Leader's Lecture, put it, the majority leader is the Senate's servant, not its master.

The Lott-Daschle agreement went with the grain of the basic character of the Senate. It allows the Senate to do its work in committees which represent the balance of opinion on the floor, while it puts a sensible limitation on the power of deadlock to stop all action. It pushes senators toward working together, and toward using their power with forebearance to others. It was not lost on either Daschle or Lott that control of a 50–50 Senate can shift at any time. From January 3 to January 20, 2001, while Al Gore was still vice president, Democrats were technically in control; Democrats presided at committee hearings on the cabinet nominations of President-elect George W. Bush. In early 2001 there was much focus on whether Strom Thurmond, who turned 98 in December 2000, would serve out the remaining two years of his term (he has promised not to seek another). But death does not always single out the old; in the preceding Congress it was the unexpected death of the 61-year-old Coverdell that put

Democrats in the way of winning their 50 seats. Thurmond was only one of 47 senators, nearly half the body—18 Republicans and 29 Democrats—who were from states with governors of a different party.

And then there was the possibility of a party switch, a possibility that became a reality when James Jeffords left the Republican Party in May and announced he would vote to organize the Senate with the Democrats. This was not the first time the partisan balance in the Senate has shifted markedly and unexepctedly in just a few months. If the Republicans lost six seats between July 2000 and May 2001, the Democrats lost 10 between November 1994, when they lost eight seats in the offyear election, and March 1995, by which point both Richard Shelby of Alabama and Ben Nighthorse Campbell of Colorado switched parties. Over the last 10 years the Senate has had as many as 57 Democrats and as many as 55 Republicans. In these circumstances, and given its rules, it is unwise to say that any party controls, or could control, the Senate.

Despite their achievement in gaining a 51–49 majority before November 2002, Democrats are not necessarily well positioned to stop Bush priorities from being approved in the Senate. Fully 20 of the 50 Democratic senators are from states carried by George W. Bush, and 13 of those 20 are from states which Bush carried by margins ranging from 8% upward to 29%. It could be a political liability for them to be seen as obdurate Bush opponents; indeed, Democratic Leader Tom Daschle's standing, after he vocally opposed the Bush tax program, fell in polls in South Dakota, which Bush carried 60%–38%. Moreover, four of those Democrats from states Bush carried by wide margins are up for reelection in 2002: Max Cleland of Georgia, Mary Landrieu of Louisiana, Max Baucus of Montana and Tim Johnson of South Dakota. In contrast, only 10 of the 50 Republican senators are from states carried by Al Gore, and only three from states that Gore carried by 8% or more; none of the latter is up for reelection in 2002.

But Democrats do have the advantage of greater cohesiveness and fellow feeling. Since his selection as minority leader in 1994, Tom Daschle has done a superb job of welding Democrats together, keeping in touch with each Democratic senator and getting them to work together and to avoid embarrassing their colleagues. Democratic senators have also contributed generously to each other's campaigns. That cohesion was on display during the impeachment trial, in which Democrats hung together unanimously. It was apparent also in early 2001 after Democrat Zell Miller, a senator only since July 2000, came out in full-throated support of the Bush tax cut. Daschle complained that Miller gave him no notice, and made it clear that he expected any other dissenters to do so; obviously, in such conversations he would try to talk them out of it—or ask them to delay. In the next two months, no other Democrats joined Miller, though some surely doubted the wisdom of Daschle's aggressive opposition to the Bush tax cuts. With committee majorities, Democrats will be able to keep Bush nominees—especially judicial nominees—from being confirmed. And Daschle's ability to schedule business will undoubtedly be deftly used to frustrate Bush on matters large and small. But there is a limit to the majority leader's power to schedule. Senators can threaten to obstruct all floor business unless some issue they are deeply concerned about comes to the floor. This is how John McCain forced a reluctant Trent Lott to schedule two weeks' debate on campaign finance in March 2001, and it is how supporters of the Bush agenda, Democrats as well as Republicans, may persuade Daschle to schedule issues of great importance which he would prefer to block.

In contrast, Senate Republicans have little cohesion. Majority Leader Trent Lott and Majority Whip Don Nickles are not close; Nickles appeared to disagree with Lott's granting Democrats equal committee membership in January 2001. John McCain, the Republican senator most popular nationally, has insisted on advancing his own agenda, not only demanding an early debate on the campaign finance measure he had long supported but also joining with Edward Kennedy on healthcare regulation. But Republican senators appear to have a clear sense that their fate is tied to that of the Bush administration, and it may supply the cohesion Senate Republicans have conspicuously lacked.

What will happen to the Senate in the 2002 elections? Almost anything. In spring 2001 Democrats seemed very confident of winning a majority of seats then, as House Democrats seemed very confident of winning a majority of seats in 2002; as in that case, there are good reasons for optimism, but victory is by no means assured. The fact is that the statistical margin of error for predicting Senate elections is very high, because there are only a few races and a party that wins most of the close races can do much better than the oddsmakers thought. This is what happened when Republicans won a majority of the Senate in 1980 and when they lost it again in 1986. In 2002, 34 Senate seats will be up, 20 held by Republicans and 14 by Democrats. But 13 of the Republican seats and only 7 of the Democratic seats seem absolutely solid: which leaves the number of seats that could conceivably change hands at 7 Republican and 7 Democratic. In early 2001 the most vulnerable Republicans appeared to be Tim Hutchinson of Arkansas, Susan Collins of Maine, Bob Smith of New Hampshire and Jesse Helms of North Carolina. In 2000 Bush carried three of those four states, and lost Maine by only 49%–44%. The most vulnerable Democrats appeared to be Max Cleland of Georgia, Tom Harkin of Iowa, Mary Landrieu of Louisiana and Jean Carnahan of Missouri. In 2000 Bush carried three of those four states, and lost Iowa by only 49%–48%. The prospect is for a closely divided Senate up through the 2004 election, with control perhaps switching in unpredictable ways.

EIGHT SIGHS, FOUR EXAGGERATIONS AND ONE HELL OF AN ELECTION

By Charlie Cook

This is truly a fascinating time in American politics. The entire political landscape has changed over the last decade and a half. We've gone from virtually a Republican hegemony over the presidency and Democratic domination of the Congress to a partisan equilibrium on almost every governmental level, save governorships. National elections are supposed to produce definitive winners and losers, but this election resulted in a tie. As Michael Barone so ably stated it in his introduction to this book, "The 49% Nation," America is split right down the middle. Fifteen years ago, the "Republican lock on the Electoral College" theory popularized by the late Horace Busby, a former aide to Lyndon Johnson, seemed firmly in place, as was a Democratic stranglehold on the House and, to a lesser extent, the Senate. Today both notions are a distant memory.

Partisan Voting

Equally divided as this election was, it was also the most partisan election we have seen in many years. Of the 39% of the electorate who called themselves Democrats in 2000, Gore pulled 86% of the vote, which was not only higher than Bill Clinton in 1992 or 1996 but also the highest percentage for any Democratic nominee in at least the last seven presidential elections. Of the 35% who considered themselves Republicans, Bush won 91%, second only to Ronald Reagan's 92% performance in his 1984 landslide victory over former Vice President Walter Mondale, and tying Bush's father's party support against former Massachusetts Governor Michael Dukakis in 1988. The partisans almost canceled each other out in 2000. The larger base of Democrats gave Gore a narrow advantage over the even more solidified, but smaller, group of Republicans for Bush. As Barone points out, we have seen a substantial increase in straight-ticket voting in recent years, a reversal from a previous pattern of more ticket splitting.

While partisans largely stayed loyal to their parties, independents split straight down the middle, with Bush edging out Gore by just 47%–45%—not quite enough to overcome Gore's small edge among partisans. This was the closest split among independents in modern history; the second closest was in 1992 when Bill Clinton beat President Bush among independents 38%–32%.

Forces at Work

While some have characterized the 2000 election as a freakish election, the political equivalent of a hundred-year flood, it actually may be the confluence of a number of dynamics that will keep this equilibrium in place until some dramatic event gives one party a majority.

The Great and Growing Cultural Divide

The divisions among the electorate went far beyond the simple equation of Democrats backing a Democrat, Republicans supporting a Republican, and independents splitting down the middle. From 1968 through 1988, Republicans won four out of five presidential elections, losing only in 1976 after the Watergate scandal. During that period a clear pattern emerged. Democrats routinely carried the big cities by huge margins and won moderately sized cities and towns by somewhat smaller margins. At the same time, Republicans won small towns and rural areas by wide margins, and carried the suburbs by comfortable 10–22 point margins. The Republican recipe of winning big in rural, small-town and suburban America was almost always sufficient to overwhelm the Democratic vote in the cities.

That pattern changed in 1992, however, when the political divide between urban and rural voters began to increase rather dramatically. Clinton's 58% in 1992 in the big cities (population over 500,000) grew to 68% in 1996. Gore took a whopping 71% in these areas in 2000. Although Gore improved only a half-dozen points over Clinton's 1992 number in the overall vote, he doubled that margin in the big cities. While Gore received one percentage point less than Clinton did in 1996, he ran three points ahead of Clinton in those big cities and seven points better among voters in cities with populations between 50,000 and 500,000. Much, but not all, of that increase came in increased Democratic performance among African-American voters. Gore beat Bush among black voters by 90%–8%, the worst performance by a Republican in modern history. Though Bush did better among Hispanic voters than any Republican has since Ronald Reagan in 1984, it did not offset the impact of that strongly Democratic, African-American vote, resulting in Bush getting buried in the cities.

At the same time, Bush easily bested recent Republican performances among voters in rural America, winning 59%. By comparison, Dole pulled only 46% of the rural vote in 1996. The elder Bush only took 40% and 44% in 1992 and 1988, respectively. Bush's performance was second in recent times only to Reagan's 1984 landslide. While Bush outperformed Dole by seven percentage points this year in the national vote, he bettered Dole by 13 points among these rural voters and surpassed him by 18 points among those in communities with populations between 10,000 and 50,000.

In short, there is a huge and growing divide between the voting patterns of the 29% of Americans who live in big and medium-sized cities and the 28% living in small-town and rural America. Urban America is getting more Democratic, while rural and small town America is getting more Republican. This was very true on the presidential level and fairly accurate on the congressional level. For Democrats, as veteran Democratic media consultant David Dixon said, "If you didn't have a Starbucks in your district, you were hurtin'."

What remains, of course, are the suburbs, which in 2000 made up a whopping 43% of the total vote. The Republican recipe of running up the score in suburban, rural and small-town America fell apart this year due to their drop in performance in the suburbs. In 1980, 1984 and 1988, Republican presidential nominees pulled between 55% and 61% of the suburban vote, running between four and 10 points better in the suburbs than in the nation as a whole. But in 1992, 1996 and 2000, the GOP nominees ran between one and three points worse in the suburbs than nationally, with Clinton actually carrying the suburbs by two points in 1992 and five points in 1996. Bush edged out Gore in 2000 by 49%–47%. Importantly, Bush's scant two-point victory in suburbs this year was driven by carrying Southern suburbs by 20 points, while losing non-Southern suburbs by about 15 points.

Why has this happened? A good guess is that social and cultural issues have contributed to these divisions. As Republicans increasingly become identified with conservative and/ or moralistic positions on social and cultural issues, such as abortion and gun control, their fortunes have improved in the heartland of America—small towns and farms and in the South. But those same issues are hurting them badly among urban and previously Republican leaning, non-Southern, suburban voters, turning the suburbs into a battleground. The environment and education were additional factors motivating many of these relatively affluent suburban voters to begin voting Democratic—particularly after Republicans sought to abolish the Department of Education during the Contract with America days, which was seen by voters as the federal government trying to divest itself of any responsibility for education. After their 1994 electoral debacle, Democrats generally moved to the middle on economics, emphasizing federal debt retirement—not withstanding Gore's turn to the left in his convention acceptance speech—and so became more acceptable to middle-class and upscale suburban voters outside the South. But Bush so successfully emphasized the education issue that for the first time in memory, Republicans are now seen as better on education than Democrats. But while Republicans captured the education issue in the 2000 election, abortion, gun control and the environment remained problem spots for them with swing suburban voters.

Another factor in the new competitiveness of the suburbs is that the nature of them has changed. The image of suburbs used to be lily-white communities as seen in *Ozzie and Harriet*, *Father Knows Best* and *Leave it to Beaver*. In more recent years, however, closer-in, older suburban communities have become much more racially and ethnically diverse as more city-dwellers have crossed the line, bringing with them their urban-Democratic voting patterns. But as suburbs reach farther out into places that were once rural countryside, these new areas are remaining very conservative.

In short, these profound changes in the suburbs and in suburban voting patterns, though seen far more in areas outside the South, has had a dramatic impact on the political balance of power in this country. Old patterns are gone. The size of the suburban vote is increasingly dramatically, while simultaneously becoming more of a swing, rather than Republican, vote. These changes are profoundly impacting the nation's political landscape. The population shift from the Democratic urban and Republican rural areas to the suburbs has only accelerated this trend.

Continuity versus ChangeHistorians and political scientists are fond of saying that our presidential elections usually amount to a contest between the desire for continuity and the competing desire for change. Normally, one sentiment easily outweighs the other. In this election, though, Americans were deeply divided on this idea as well.

When Americans went to the polls in November 2000, the economy seemed solid and was in its 73rd consecutive month of economic growth since April 1991. Americans seemed to think that the economy and maybe the country were on cruise control, needing a minimum of attention. As a result, they gave political leaders very little credit for this extraordinary period of economic expansion, awarding some to Federal Reserve Board Chairman Alan Greenspan, with Presidents Bush and Clinton and congressional Republicans and Democrats alike sharing a little. To the extent that Americans attributed a cause to this prosperity, they pointed to technology, a more productive workforce and streamlined management. While not giving Vice President Gore much credit for the strong economy, they certainly were not looking for change or showing concern about their jobs.

On matters relating to policy, Americans were also very content. After Clinton and congressional Democrats veered too far to the left in 1993 and 1994—and as a result suffered devastating electoral losses in 1994—they moved toward the center and, generally speaking, have occupied a center-left position ever since. After their huge 1994 victory, Republicans veered off to the right, losing seats and another presidential election in 1996, and then started to move back toward the center, though they took a detour to the right in 1998 for impeachment. Since then, however, both in policy and style, Republicans have toned down and moved to a center-right position.

With a center-left Democratic president being kept in check by a center-right Republican Congress, and vice versa, neither party strayed too far from the middle. To the extent that Democrats and Republicans, Clinton and Congress, agreed on very little, little happened. They couldn't agree on much on spending, so big budget-busting spending packages did not pass. They couldn't agree much on taxes—which ones to cut, for whom and by how much—so taxes did not get significantly cut. The end result: Big spending increases and deep tax cuts alike were kept to a minimum. The economy was expanding at an explosive pace and federal budget deficits evaporated; surpluses soared and the national debt stopped growing for the first time since the beginning of the Vietnam War. Voters looked and said, "This is good." While individual voters and constituencies fretted over a lack of action on many specific issues, on balance, Americans were on a policy level as contented as we have seen in many years.

On another level, though, there was a desire for change. Americans had grown weary of eight years of scandals, embarrassment and controversies. While many of these ended up being petty or inconsequential—the president, first lady and their staffs and supporters were less culpable than critics suggested—they still took a toll. It all culminated with the Monica Lewinsky affair in 1998. That scandal and the ensuing impeachment trial rank among the most unsavory periods of American political history. While polls showed that a majority of Americans opposed removing President Clinton from office, opinion of him as a person plummeted. National polls typically gave Clinton 60% positive job approval ratings, but also usually gave him a 60% negative personal rating. Generally speaking, about 40% approved of Clinton's job performance and of him as a person. This group, not surprisingly, was made up almost entirely of Democrats. Another 40% disapproved of him in both categories, these being almost exclusively Republicans. The remaining 20%, including very few Democrats or Republicans but a lot of independents, approved of the job Clinton was doing but disapproved of him as a person. Indeed, in only two of eight polls conducted last cycle with a hypothetical matchup between Bush and Clinton did Clinton lead the Texas governor. Interestingly, earlier in the year, Bush typically beat Clinton by high single digits in similar matchups, while as the election drew nearer Clinton took a four-to-five point lead.

While it can be argued that the marginal difference between how Clinton and Gore would have performed might have made the difference between victory and defeat for Democrats, this data says a lot more about just how conflicted the American electorate was by November of 2000. Voters wanted the scandals and controversies to end and wanted some of the luster that once surrounded the presidency to be restored. So instead of making a choice between either continuity or change, voters wanted both: continuity in policy—a middle-of-the-road approach to governing—and an end to scandals and controversies.

Voters then were confronted with questions about the presidential nominees. Did Al Gore represent enough change from what they had not liked about the Clinton presidency over the last eight years and did George Bush represent too much? While it is easy for Gore supporters to say that he represented all that was good in the Clinton years, Gore's role in campaign fundraising controversies and his unflinching support of Clinton during the Monica Lewinsky affair, reinforced by his exaggerations, likely created questions in voters' minds. Undoubtedly, some wondered whether a Gore win might not end the era of half-truths and parsed statements that defined the Clinton years.

The Perceptions of Bush and Gore

In many ways, voters knew whom they were voting for before the identities of the two nominees became known. Most Democrats were going to vote for the Democrat no matter what. Even before the GOP convention in Philadelphia, Bush had already coalesced most of the Republican base. For Gore, many of the possible defectors came back into the fold after his pick of Senator Joe Lieberman to be his running mate. After the Democratic convention, Gore's support within his own party was nearly comparable to

Bush's already high support among Republicans. It was the weakest of Democratic and Republican voters, and independents, who determined this election.

One key factor in determining how these voters would break was to look at how they perceived the two candidates. Neither candidate came into the contest with the political equivalent of a full set of tools. Gore entered the race with voters seeing him as very intelligent, knowledgeable and experienced, and better prepared for the job than Bush. Bush was appealing to voters on a different level. People liked and trusted him, felt more comfortable with him, and saw him as an antidote to the partisanship and finger pointing that has wracked Washington for so long. But in many cases, Gore's advantages of expertise and experience were offset by a feeling that he was aloof and untrustworthy. Gore effectively addressed many of his problems with the Lieberman selection and the Democratic convention, pulling ahead with a lead that would continue until the first debate. The warmth and trust that many felt for Bush, on the other hand, was undercut by reservations about whether he was smart and knowledgeable enough and whether he had the right kind of experience to be an effective president. Whether it was due to Gore's repeated, sarcastic sighs during the debate or the heightened scrutiny of every thing he said, attacks on Gore's honesty effectively reminded swing voters of the truthfulness problem that had surrounded the White House for eight years. This perception caused Gore to drop behind for most of the next month, only to come back during the final 72 hours before the election.

The Late Shift

In a superb post-election analysis, Bill McInturff, Glen Bolger and Neil Newhouse of the highly regarded Republican polling firm Public Opinion Strategies (POS) argue that while Bush was ahead for much of October, the race tightened up considerably in the final weekend before the election. In the end, late deci---- ---ers who made up their mind during the last week to the d-- ------- ---- heavily in favor of Gore, which helped Gore win the ----------- ---- ors that allowed Gore to surge ahead at the end wer- ---- ---- ------ a toward Social Security and the movement toward ---- --------- s who believed that the country was headed in the r--- --------- ---

In a pre-election survey, conduc--- ------ ------ Health Insurance Association of America, Bush le-- ---- ----- ------ lose numbers were consistent with what most other ------ --- ---- ----- ime. But the post-election POS analysis cites Voter ------ ------ --- ---- that had Bush leading by four points among the vote- ---- ---- --- made up their minds prior to September—50% of the eventual electo--- -- Among the 13% who made their minds up during the month of September, Bush also led by four points. But among those who said they made their minds up during the first two weeks of October—about 8% of the electorate—Gore led by two points. Among the 10% who made their minds up during the last two weeks of October, Gore led by one point. Then the real movement occurred: Among the 9% of the electorate who said they made their minds up "during the last few days before the election," Gore led by 18 points, and among the 8% who said they decided on Election Day, Gore prevailed by 16 points. While these numbers don't precisely track with what polls were saying at those specific points, the difference could be that some voters were fluctuating between the two candidates.

In their last pre-election track, the weekend before the election, POS found that Bush's six-point lead had narrowed to three points, 45%–42%. As such, POS concluded "among the 17% of late deciders, Bush dropped 2.5 to three points in the last few days before the election." When asked in an open-ended question why they voted as they did, POS found that "early deciders for both Bush and Gore were more likely to cite the fact that their choice was based on the party affiliation of their candidate." POS went on to point out that "on most topics and issues there are no vast differences between the responses of late deciders and those who made up their minds early in the candidate consideration process." But they did find that Gore late deciders based their choice on experience, abortion, protecting the surplus, and that Gore would do a better job taking care of the elderly. Among the far fewer late deciders who ended up in the Bush camp, including quite a few independent and Democratic voters who crossed party lines, the reasons most cited to explain their support of Bush were "abortion and moral issues." POS also cited data showing that among those voters who believed the country was headed in the right direction, Gore ended up pulling a substantially larger share than he earlier had enjoyed.

Clinton Fatigue

Many say that given the strong economy, the election was Gore's to lose, that the status quo was the default preference for voters, that if he and his campaign had not been so inept, he would have won. In my view, however, this argument ignores the important factor of Clinton fatigue. Though happy with the economy and satisfied with most of the substantive positions of the Clinton administration, they were tired of lying and embarrassed by the personal behavior of their president. Gore's exaggerations, prior to and during the first debate, reattached the umbilical cord between Gore and Clinton.

Some have argued that Gore's refusal to use Clinton more and better during the campaign cost him the election. But this argument ignores the fact that Gore campaign polls and focus groups made clear that while Clinton was hugely popular among the Democratic base (which ultimately turned out in high numbers), he was radioactive among swing voters. Given the economy and moderate positions of the administration, the only reason many of these voters weren't automatically for Gore was Clinton. While many may have approved of the job that Clinton had done as president, they were sick of him in many other respects and wanted him and all reminders of him gone, quickly. In an era of television, it simply isn't possible to have a high-profile personality such as the president of the United States campaign incognito, even if just in Arkansas.

Taken with Gore's performance during that first debate, it can legitimately be argued that the vice president was eight sighs and four exaggerations away from being elected president. Gore was ahead or tied in almost every reliable poll taken between the end of the Democratic convention and the first debate. Obviously it is impossible to determine whether Gore would have won the election had he performed well in that (and subsequent) debates or whether some other factor would have pushed Bush ahead.

On a technical level, both campaigns seemed to be very well planned and executed. Though the Bush campaign leadership lacked senior-level, presidential campaign experience, they were exceedingly effective in reverse engineering past campaigns: analyzing who won, who lost and why. They exploited Clinton and Gore weaknesses well and pulled off, given the economy, what might be called an inside straight. As for Gore, he beat the point spread, winning the popular vote and coming within a few hundred votes of winning Florida and the presidency, when most expected he would lose the election by two to four percentage points in the popular vote and by dozens of electoral votes.

In the end, this was a hell of an election and was the closest presidential contest that any of us will ever likely see. Still, it will be months, even a year or two before we know whether any of the major factors that affected this election will develop into lasting trends that will affect the mid-term elections in 2002 and the next presidential election. If two years is a lifetime in American politics, four years is an eternity.

President George W. Bush (R)

Elected 2000, term expires Jan. 2005; 1st term; born, July 6, 1946, New Haven, CT; home, Austin; Yale U., B.A. 1968, Harvard U., M.B.A. 1975; Methodist; married (Laura).

Military Career: TX Air Natl. Guard, 1968–73

Elected Office: TX Gov., 1994–2000

Professional Career: Founder & CEO, Bush Exploration Oil & Gas Co., 1975–87; Sr. Advisor, Bush Presidential Camp., 1988; Managing Gen. Partner, Texas Rangers baseball org., 1989–98

Office: The White House, 1600 Pennsylvania Ave., NW, Washington, DC 20500, 202-456-1414.

Vice President Richard (Dick) B. Cheney (R)

Elected 2000, term expires Jan. 2005; 1st term; born, Jan. 30, 1941, Lincoln, NE; home, Casper, WY; U. of WY, B.A. 1965, M.A. 1966; United Methodist; married (Lynne).

Elected Office: U.S. House of Reps., 1978–89

Professional Career: Spec. Asst. to the Dir. of OEO, 1969–70; White House Staff Asst., 1971; Asst. Dir., Cost of Living Cncl., 1971–73; V.P., Bradley, Woods & Co., 1973–74; Dep. Asst. to Pres. Gerald Ford, 1974–75; White House Chief of Staff, 1975–77; U.S. Secy. of Defense, 1989–93; Sr. Fellow, American Enterprise Inst., 1993–95; Chmn. & CEO, Halliburton Co., 1993–2000

Office: The White House, 1600 Pennsylvania Ave., NW, Washington, DC 20500, 202-456-1414.

2000 Presidential Vote			**1996 Presidential Vote**		
George W. Bush (R)	50,456,169	(47.8%)	Clinton (D)	47,401,185	(49%)
Al Gore (D)	50,996,116	(48.4%)	Dole (R)	39,1197,469	(41%)
Ralph Nader (Green)	2,831,066	(2.7%)	Perot (I)	8,085,294	(8%)

THE PEOPLE: Est. Pop. 2000: 281,421,906; Pop. 1990: 248,765,170, up 13.1% 1990–2000. 100% of U.S. total; 75.1% White, 12.3% Black, 3.6% Asian, 0.9% Amer. Indian, 0.1% Hawaiian, 2.4% Two+ races, 5.5% Other; 12.5% Hispanic Origin. 4% Unemployment. 2000 Voting age pop.: 209,128,094. 2000 Turnout: 106,913,005; 51% of VAP. Registered voters (2000): 159,076,685.

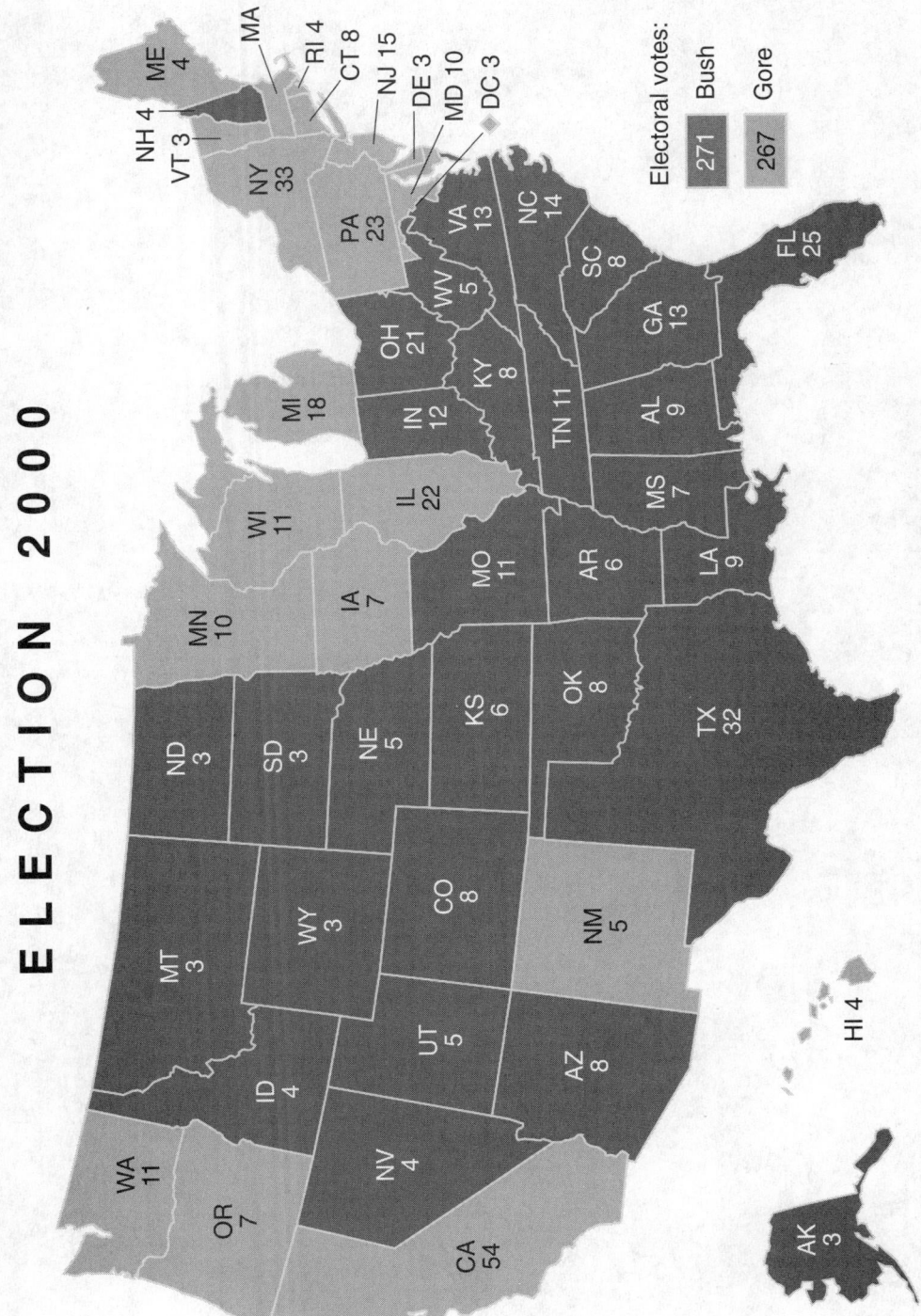

ELECTION 2000

Electoral votes:

271	Bush
267	Gore

ME 4

NH 4
VT 3

MA 12
RI 4
CT 8
NJ 15
DE 3
MD 10
DC 3

NY 33

PA 23

WV 5
VA 13
NC 14
SC 8
FL 25

OH 21

MI 18

KY 8
TN 11
GA 13
AL 9

IN 12

WI 11

IL 22

MS 7

MN 10

IA 7

MO 11

AR 6

LA 9

ND 3

SD 3

NE 5

KS 6

OK 8

TX 32

MT 3

WY 3

CO 8

NM 5

ID 4

UT 5

AZ 8

WA 11

OR 7

NV 4

CA 54

HI 4

AK 3

★ ALABAMA ★

On a hill in downtown Montgomery, Dexter Avenue connects two buildings that capture much of southern history. Atop the hill is the restored Greek Revival Alabama Capitol, where the first Confederate Congress convened and Jefferson Davis took the oath of office as president of the Confederacy in February 1861. A few blocks down the hill is the Dexter Avenue Baptist Church, where in December 1956 the 27-year-old Martin Luther King Jr. led the boycott that began when Rosa Parks refused to move to the back of the bus. One building symbolizes the breakout of fiery defiance that led to the tragedy of the Civil War, the other the dignified resistance that produced the success of the civil rights revolution. Today both the Confederacy and the civil rights movement are celebrated, though as time goes on with less emphasis on the first and more on the latter: Maya Lin's circular Civil Rights Memorial in Montgomery, the Civil Rights Institute across the street from the 16th Street Baptist Church in Birmingham's Civil Rights District, the Pettus Bridge in Selma and the Dexter Avenue Baptist Church are among the many sites of civil rights and black history preserved and promoted by the state.

Yet for all the classic symmetry of the Capitol and the calm simplicity of the black churches, nature still seems untamed in Alabama, and the raw passions of the first settlers that gave life to these serene buildings often seem ready to break into anger and even violence. There has been a raucous tone to Alabama's history since the first Jacksonian farmers pushed the Indians west and plowed the steeply inclined red clay hills of northern Alabama, and the first plantation owners shipped in hundreds of slaves to grow cotton in the dark Black Belt soil. It was the violent reactions of white Alabamans that led to the greatest triumphs of civil rights: The police dogs and fire hoses of Birmingham in 1963 motivated President Kennedy to endorse what would become the Civil Rights Act of 1964, and the beatings on the bridge to Selma spurred President Johnson to propose the Voting Rights Act of 1965. Even in Alabama's peaceful economic development is evidence of the clang of metal on rock: miners hacking away in the 1880s at the solid-iron Red Mountain to feed newly cast steel mills glaring in the valley of Birmingham below; motorists today speeding past exposed red earth of gouged-out hillsides towards the factories and Wal-Mart shopping centers that have sprouted up.

There is a similar rawness to Alabama's politics, as it has shifted from one of the nation's most Democratic to one of its more Republican states. In the 1930s and 1940s Alabama elected populist Democrats, crusaders against Wall Street and against the local economic potentates they called the "Big Mules": Hugo Black, a senator until he became a Supreme Court justice in 1937; Lister Hill and John Sparkman, who as senators sponsored landmark health and housing legislation; a House delegation that passed housing, health and public works bills. The dominant governor was Kissin' Jim Folsom, elected in 1946 and 1954, outsized in build and eloquence, whose career ended in 1962 when he appeared drunk in a late campaign appearance on the new medium of television; he lost the governor's race to his onetime protege, a young lawyer named George Wallace.

While Wallace was politicking, Martin Luther King was leading what turned out to be a civil rights revolution whose moral force he was among the first to comprehend. In the South of that day what King demanded seemed impossible, and in the short run it helped the politicians who most strongly proclaimed their opposition to desegregation. But in the long run it changed public life in America and in Alabama. But not before George Wallace made himself a national figure. Believing he had lost the 1958 governor's primary because he was "out-segged," he vowed that he never would be again. Elected governor in 1962, he pledged to stand in the schoolhouse door to prevent desegregation—a charade, but a dangerous one, for it encouraged violent resistance. It was the acts of Alabama officials—Birmingham Police Commissioner Bull Connor's police dogs and fire hoses in 1963, Sheriff Jim Clark's cordons in Selma in 1965—which, transmitted on evening newscasts, made civil rights a national issue. The North was no longer able to turn its eyes away from the South's legally imposed segregation, and most Americans decided it must end.

Despite his defeat, Wallace went national. With a shrewd sense of ordinary voters' resentment at elites' cultural liberalism, Wallace ran well in the 1964 and 1972 northern Democratic

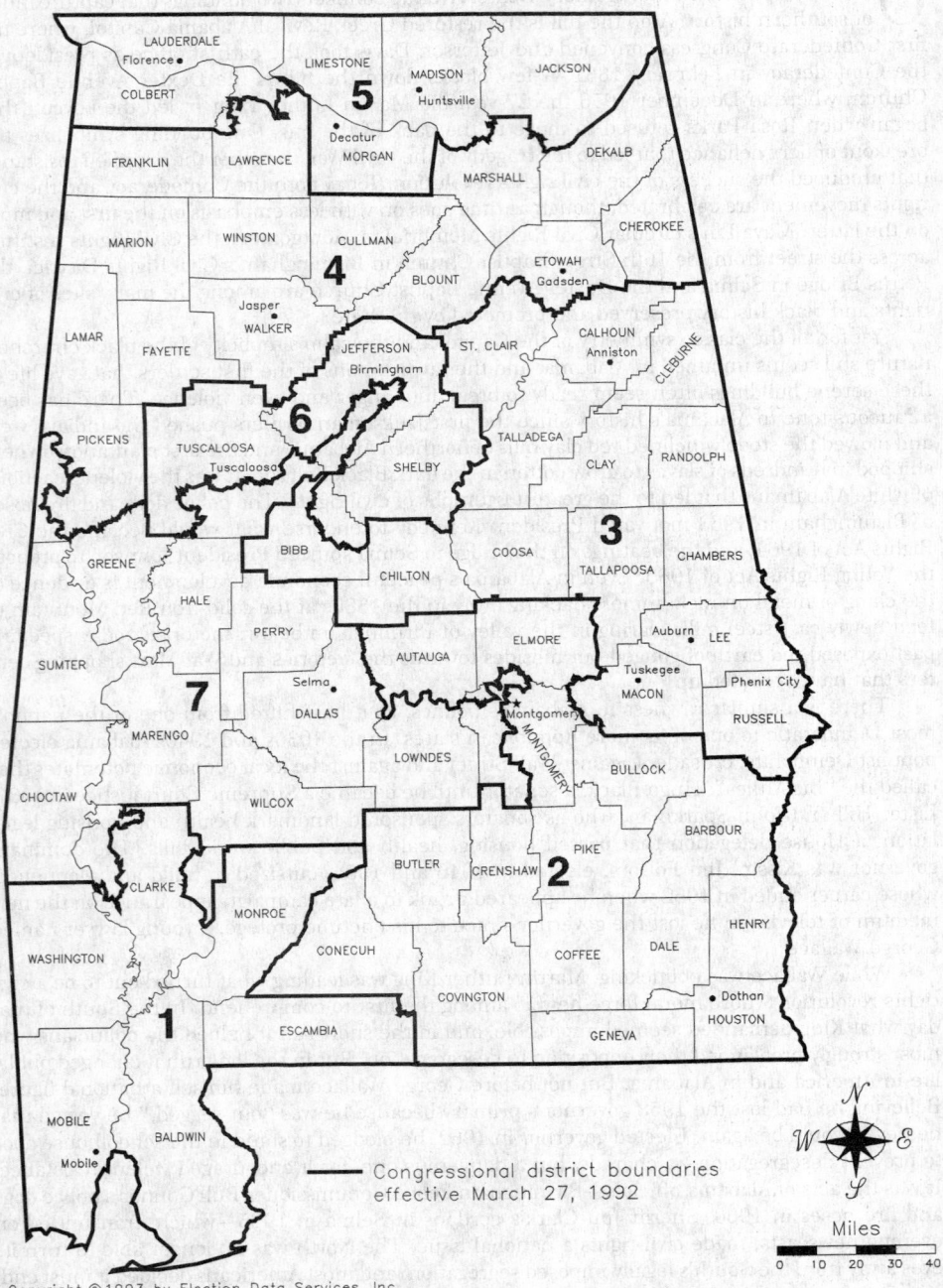

LAUDERDALE
Florence
COLBERT
LIMESTONE
MADISON
Huntsville
JACKSON
5
FRANKLIN
LAWRENCE
Decatur
MORGAN
MARSHALL
DEKALB
MARION
WINSTON
CULLMAN
BLOUNT
CHEROKEE
ETOWAH
Gadsden
4
Jasper
WALKER
JEFFERSON
Birmingham
ST. CLAIR
CALHOUN
Anniston
CLEBURNE
LAMAR
FAYETTE
PICKENS
TUSCALOOSA
Tuscaloosa
6
SHELBY
TALLADEGA
CLAY
RANDOLPH
GREENE
BIBB
CHILTON
COOSA
TALLAPOOSA
3
CHAMBERS
HALE
PERRY
AUTAUGA
ELMORE
Auburn
LEE
SUMTER
Selma
DALLAS
7
Montgomery
Tuskegee
MACON
Phenix City
RUSSELL
MARENGO
LOWNDES
MONTGOMERY
BULLOCK
CHOCTAW
WILCOX
BARBOUR
CLARKE
MONROE
BUTLER
CRENSHAW
2
PIKE
HENRY
WASHINGTON
CONECUH
COFFEE
DALE
1
ESCAMBIA
COVINGTON
GENEVA
Dothan
HOUSTON
MOBILE
BALDWIN
Mobile

—— Congressional district boundaries
effective March 27, 1992

N
W   E
S

Miles
0   10   20   30   40

presidential primaries, and as a third-party candidate in the 1968 presidential race won 13.5% of the vote. He was partially paralyzed by a gunshot wound while campaigning in May 1972, and lost all force as a national politician when he lost to Jimmy Carter in the March 1976 Florida primary. But he remained the key figure in Alabama for a decade, retiring as governor in 1978 but returning to office in 1982 until his final retirement in 1986. He spent his last sad years apologizing for his acts, meeting with the student he tried to block in the schoolhouse door, and proclaiming, "The South has changed, and for the better," until his death in September 1998.

Unfortunately, in the Wallace years Alabama lost important ground. While Atlanta was peacefully desegregating and beginning three decades of vibrant white-collar growth, Birmingham was violently resisting the civil rights movement, only to see the shrinkage of its once substantial blue-collar base—the steel industry—and an outflow of talented people of all races. The state's economy, regarded as progressive when manufacturing was the leading edge of growth, seemed backward at the end of the Wallace era.

Wallace delayed for a generation the rise of the Republicans in Alabama and the non-metropolitan South, but since his retirement Alabama has moved toward Republicans. It is now solidly Republican in presidential elections. It has elected Republican governors in three of the last four contests, though one was forced from office and the other defeated for re-election. It has been electing Republicans to downballot state offices and they now control the state Supreme Court—a battleground between trial lawyers and their business adversaries—by 8–1. The state's House delegation has been 5–2 Republican since 1996.

The opposing political forces partly resemble those of 50 years ago. "Big Mules," angry at Alabama's ultraliberal tort law, are pro-Republican, but small business and tradition-minded Protestants are a bigger source of support; Republican enclaves are no longer confined to affluent urban precincts, but have spread out along the interstates to sprawling new subdivisions. The Democrats' institutional base is among teachers' unions and trial lawyers. The Republicans' base is larger, but more volatile: business conservatives on the one hand and religious conservatives on the other, determined to assert their beliefs in the public square. In 1998 they clashed when Governor Fob James was opposed for renomination by businessman Winton Blount Jr., who argued that James had looked foolish promoting prayer in schools and allowed trial lawyers too much influence. For the first time ever, more Alabamians voted in the Republican than the Democratic primary, 359,000 to 358,000—a sign of vitality perhaps for Republicans. But the Democrats were united in their support for Lieutenant Governor Don Siegelman, and when James eventually won a fractious runoff, Siegelman easily defeated him in November.

Siegelman has not been entirely successful. His key campaign pledge—a lottery to finance education—was defeated in a referendum. His attempt to strip incoming Republican Lieutenant Governor Steve Windom of power to appoint state Senate committees and direct the flow of legislation was only partly successful. The 11th Circuit federal court of appeals upheld a 1993 law approving voluntary, student-led prayer in schools, over the public address system and at graduations, and in 2000 Judge Roy Moore, who posted the Ten Commandments in his courtroom, was elected Chief Justice. Alabama voters in 2000 did approve a referendum, backed by Siegelman and leading Republicans as well, to repeal the state's long since ineffective ban on interracial marriages. But it passed by only 59%–41%, losing in heavily white rural counties, and it was apparent that most whites voted against it. Alabama is proud that Mercedes Benz decided to build its North American plant in Tuscaloosa County in 1993, moved partly by promises of tax forebearance, and that Daimler Benz announced in 2000 it would double its size and create 2,000 more jobs, at the same time that Honda was building a big new plant in Talladega County, off I-20 east of Birmingham. But Alabama's job growth still lags behind that of other southern states and, though its larger cities and counties along the interstates are growing, its rural counties seemed to be falling behind, bemoaning drought and pine beetle infestation in 2000. Even Alabama's water supply was threatened by a dispute with Georgia, which wants to use the headwaters of the Chattahoochee River for an ever-growing Atlanta; Alabama, ever feisty, may fight the case up to the Supreme Court.

Governor   Don Siegelman, elected governor on his second try in 1998, grew up in Mobile, went to the University of Alabama and was elected student body president in 1968. While at

Georgetown Law he worked as a Capitol policeman. He studied at Oxford and practiced law in Birmingham with Robert Vance, a federal judge who was later murdered. Siegelman became executive director of the state Democratic Party while Vance was chairman. He has been elected to statewide office five times now, as secretary of State in 1978 and 1982, attorney general in 1986 and lieutenant governor in 1994; he ran second in the Democratic primary for governor in 1990. As lieutenant governor, he ran the state Senate, and came out on the side of trial lawyers' in tort reform controversies. By 1998 he had no serious opposition in the primary for governor.

But the Republicans did have a fierce fight, between incumbent Governor Fob James and businessman Winton Blount. James had made headlines urging schools to defy a federal court order banning a state law allowing voluntary school prayer; when Judge Roy Moore, a county judge, was ordered to remove a copy of the Ten Commandments posted in his courtroom, James threatened to call out the National Guard to protect him. Blount charged that James had done little for economic development and had embarrassed the state. (Ironically, the state law was upheld on appeal in 1999 and Moore was elected Chief Justice in 2000.) James led in the first primary 48%–41% and won the runoff 56%–44%. But damage was done; as Siegelman put it, "Fob has done for me what I could never do for myself: divide the Republican Party and at the same time unite the Democratic Party." Siegelman campaigned for a lottery with the $150 million proceeds to go to merit-based college scholarship, pre-kindergarten programs and computers for schools, a plan modeled on the highly popular lottery and HOPE scholarships of Georgia Governor (now Senator) Zell Miller. Siegelman won by an impressive 58%–42% margin, carrying all but 11 counties. He carried the big urban counties, usually Republican, by large margins. James's percentage fell by only 4% among under-$30,000 voters, but by 18% among $30,000–75,000 voters; Siegelman carried college graduates 59%–40%.

Siegelman has been a consensus-minded governor: On inauguration day he laid a wreath on the Confederate memorial outside the Capitol and visited Martin Luther King, Jr.'s Dexter Avenue Baptist Church. His lottery proposal passed in June, but was immediately opposed by many ministers and signatures were obtained for an October referendum. As one reporter put it, "There was barely a pastor in the state, of any denomination, who did not issue fiery instructions to defeat gambling as moral corruption and an injustice to the poor." Siegelman' side outspent lottery opponents by 3–1, but with a big turnout (only 4% lower than in November 1998) Alabamans rejected the lottery 54%–46%. It carried in Birmingham and the Black Belt but lost in the rest of the state. "I have no Plan B," said Siegelman glumly, and refused to back a tax increase for education (he had lost the 1990 governor primary after calling for one).

Siegelman was more successful in 2000. Per his request, the legislature voted to raise teacher salaries gradually to the national average and to make it easier to fire bad principals and teachers. "When the schools fail, principals will be fired." Also passing were tougher penalties for drunk driving and domestic violence. Siegelman approved some restrictions on abortion. On the November 2000 ballot Siegelman placed Amendment One, to allow the state to use $35 million in royalties from offshore natural gas to finance $425 million in bonds for roads, bridges, laboratories, the State Docks in Mobile, and industrial projects. Siegelman was shown campaigning for the measure on rotting old bridges and marshaled support from the Alabama Farmers Federation by promising support for animal diagnostic labs and a textile technology center. It was supported by Republican Attorney General Bill Pryor and the Alabama Business Council, but opposed by Republican Lieutenant Governor Steve Windom. It passed by the resounding margin of 63%–37%.

In search of more money for education, Siegelman has called for performance measurement in state agencies, starting with Mental Health, Youth Services, and Human Resources—which among others had been operating under federal court supervision. He worked with state House Speaker Seth Hammett for performance-based budgeting and to eliminate pass-through pork barrel spending long favored by the state Senate. He established bonuses up to $5,000 for state employees whose suggestions save the state money. He worked hard to attract businesses to Alabama, spending most of his time at the Los Angeles Democratic convention calling on them. But a March 1999 U.S. Supreme Court decision overturning Alabama's higher tax on out-of-state businesses seems likely to cost the state hundreds of millions in refunds. Then in early 2001 tax collections dropped, and the state mandated cuts to compensate for the $266 million deficit.

Siegelman called a special session, but lawmakers refused to support any of his proposals, including creating a "rainy day fund"for education and shifting cuts from elementary to higher education. This forced him to support 6% budget cuts in education, prompting outrage from one of his core constituencies, teachers' unions.

In early 2001 Siegelman seemed to be in reasonably strong shape for re-election in 2002, though he has been embarrassed by minor scandals involving some of his appointees.

Cook's Call   *Potentially Competitive.* Unlike Democratic governors in neighboring Southern states, Siegelman seems to lose more battles than he wins. But Republicans will need to recruit a very credible challenger if they are to defeat him. Congressman Bob Riley, Lieutenant Governor Steve Windom and wealthy developer Stan Pate have expressed interest in the race, but have not yet committed to running.

Senior Senator   Richard Shelby grew up in Birmingham, the son of a steelworker. After earning two degrees from the University of Alabama, he stayed in Tuscaloosa and went into law practice with Walter Flowers, later a conservative Democratic congressman; Shelby was well enough politically connected to be elected state senator in 1970, at 36. When Flowers ran for the Senate in 1978, and lost the Democratic primary to Howell Heflin, Shelby ran for his House seat. The critical contest was the Democratic runoff against Chris McNair, a black legislator whose daughter had been killed in the 1963 Birmingham church bombing; the district had the highest black percentage in Alabama at the time. Once in office Shelby had a conservative voting record, opposing the Voting Rights Act extension and the Martin Luther King Holiday. In the 1986 Senate race, he won the primary with 51% after getting a liberal to withdraw, then ran TV ads attacking incumbent Jeremiah Denton, a retired admiral who had been a prisoner of war in Vietnam, for voting to cut Social Security and owning two Mercedes (not a likely negative now, with the Mercedes plant in Tuscaloosa County). Shelby won by 7,000 votes.

As one of half a dozen or so conservative southern Democrats in the Senate, Shelby at first attracted little notice. He voted for the confirmation of Clarence Thomas and for the Gulf war resolution. He voted against the campaign finance bill supported by almost all Democrats and he voted for the Strategic Defense Initiative. He was a major sponsor of a law to enforce court orders on fathers who default on child support payments. In 1992 he was re-elected 65%–33%; this broke the jinx on this seat which, before Shelby's election in 1986, had four occupants in 10 years.

Shelby's break with the Democratic Party came soon after Bill Clinton took office. In February 1993, angered by Shelby's criticism of the president's just-released economic plan—"the taxman cometh"—Clinton strategists ostentatiously decided to make an example of him and Shelby ostentatiously decided to make a display of his independence. At a meeting in which Vice President Al Gore tried to persuade Shelby to support the plan, Shelby turned to 19 Alabama TV cameras and, embarrassing Gore, further denounced the Clinton program as "high on taxes, low on spending cuts." As punishment, it was announced that a multi-million dollar space facility would be built not in Alabama but in Texas (it eventually went up in Alabama). But, as Clinton's ratings slid downward, this only raised Shelby's popularity ratings to the highest level in the state, making a politician previously known more for his suppleness of maneuver now appear an embattled defender of principle. Relentlessly, Shelby voted against the administration again and again and lined up with Republicans on almost every partisan issue, criticizing the Democrats' health care plan as "ill-conceived, unworkable and unwanted by the American people."

So it was not much of a surprise when, the day after Republicans regained control of the Senate in 1994, Shelby announced he was switching parties and increased the Republican majority to 53–47. Republicans happily allowed him to keep his seniority on the Banking Committee, ahead of those elected as Republicans in the same year, and gave him seats on Appropriations and its Defense Subcommittee and on Intelligence as well; he chaired the Treasury-Postal Appropriations Subcommittee, and in 1997 moved over to chair the Transportation Subcommittee. He became chairman of Intelligence in 1997.

As a Republican, Shelby has maintained his conservative record and has sponsored many conservative measures, but he is not a doctrinaire market conservative. Despite his party switch he has remained friendly with trial lawyers, who usually support Democrats in Alabama. He opposed his colleague Jeff Sessions' amendment to cap lawyers' fees in tobacco cases, and insists tort reform should be only a state issue. He was the only Senate Republican to vote against financial services deregulation in November 1999, and moved to block Orrin Hatch's patent reform from getting to the floor. One of his great causes is privacy, and from his seat on Banking he has sought to prevent financial institutions from disclosing Social Security numbers and other information unless consumers agree in writing. His measure, supported by nine Democrats, failed to get out of committee on a 10–10 vote in July 2000. After a hearing on Firestone tires in September 2000, he thundered, "Ford and Firestone had at a minimum a moral obligation to make sure that the products they sell to the American public and other people in other countries are safe. And yet they both failed to bring this issue to consumers' attention and the federal government's attention, at the cost of dozens of lives, I'm afraid."

He has not been shy about using his seat on Appropriations to channel money to Alabama. Projects totaling more than $80 million have gone to Huntsville (a missile and space intelligence center, advanced research center, battle integration center, software engineering complex) and to a tornado preparedness center in the town of Arab. The latter was attacked as pork by John McCain in July 1997 and line-item vetoed by Bill Clinton. But Shelby got it into an emergency spending bill—and had the satisfaction of seeing Clinton visit Alabama in May 1998 the week after a tornado. Alabama was the number three state receiving special appropriations for universities between 1996 and 2000. He worked to delay the creation of peanut-free zones on airplanes to 2001 (Alabama grows peanuts) and he got $2 million to repair the statue of Vulcan in Birmingham. He co-sponsored with Democrat Frank Lautenberg the bill to reduce drunk driving blood alcohol levels to 0.8% and blocked a regulation that would reduce the number of hours truckers could drive per week. His move to cut $278 million in mass transit funds for New York and California was defeated by the Senate.

As chairman of Intelligence he kept a close and often hostile eye on the Clinton administration. He criticized and helped kill Anthony Lake's nomination as CIA director in 1997. He called the Wye River Memorandum's use of CIA officers to monitor compliance "troubling," and promised to investigate the use of American-made satellites by the Chinese to gather military intelligence. In 1999, charging that the Clinton administration had done little to address Chinese spying at the Los Alamos National Laboratory, he introduced a measure that would curb visits to nuclear labs by foreign scientists. He criticized the handling of the Wen Ho Lee spy case in September 2000. "I believe the FBI's counterintelligence investigation was a gravely flawed exercise characterized by inadequate resources, lack of management attention and missed opportunities . . . I am concerned about the apparent imbalance between the serious charges against Dr. Lee and the leniency of the sentence agreed to in the plea bargain." He told Energy Secretary Bill Richardson that he had "lost all credibility" after promising improvements in security. In the November 2000 intelligence reauthorization he included a provision making it a crime for a government official to disclose "properly" classified information. This was supported by the Justice Department and the CIA and by House Intelligence Chairman Porter Goss. But it was opposed by news organizations, many liberals, and by conservatives like Henry Hyde and Bob Barr, and the bill was vetoed by Bill Clinton. He spoke out strongly against China early in the Bush administration when a standoff occurred over a fallen spy plane: "We need to realize that China is not our strategic partner. China is our competitor, economically and militarily."

Shelby was re-elected easily in 1998. He raised over $5 million, and no serious Democrat ran. The state AFL-CIO even discouraged Democrats from running, fearing Shelby would turn out Republican voters. The Democratic nominee, Clayton Suddith, a retired ironworker and former Franklin County commissioner, mortgaged his pickup truck to pay the $2,672 filing fee and was arrested for public intoxication at 11 a.m. one August morning. Shelby won 63%–37%, with most of the $5 million unspent. There has been little speculation yet about who will run for this seat in 2004.

Junior Senator   Jeff Sessions had the satisfaction of being elected in 1996 to replace the Democrat who had blocked his nomination to a federal judgeship in 1986, Howell Heflin. Sessions grew up in Alabama's Black Belt, practiced law in a small town near the Tennessee Valley, became a federal prosecutor and then practiced law in Mobile. He was appointed U.S. Attorney in 1981, at 36, where he became known as a tough, aggressive prosecutor. In 1985 he was nominated for federal judge, but was attacked by some liberals for "gross insensitivity" in racial matters, and defended by conservatives; Heflin voted against him in the Judiciary Committee and his nomination never went to the floor. In 1994 Sessions ran against state Attorney General Jimmy Evans, who had successfully prosecuted Governor Guy Hunt the year before. Sessions won that race 57%–43% and, when Heflin announced his retirement in March 1995, Sessions started running and became the favorite among the seven Republicans and four Democrats who ran.

Sessions started early, avoiding debates and controversy, and relying on his base in southern Alabama, territory that not long ago cast almost no Republican primary votes. Long-distance carrier executive Sid McDonald, who spent more than $1 million, attacked Sessions for office-hopping, accepting a lenient plea bargain for a murderer, and improperly favoring tobacco and insurance companies. From Birmingham north, it was a close race: McDonald led in the June 4 primary by 30%–29%. But in the rest of the state, Sessions led 48%–12%, for a 38%–22% statewide margin. In the runoff McDonald continued his attacks and Sessions ducked debates. McDonald extended his lead north from Birmingham, 54%–46%, but almost half the votes were cast to the south, and there Sessions led 73%–27%, for a 59%–41% win.

The Democratic nominee was trial lawyer Roger Bedford was financed by trial lawyers and endorsed by key public employee unions and black organizations—the heart of today's Alabama Democratic Party. In the past Democratic primaries had turnouts of nearly 1 million, with the advantage going to moderate or conservative candidates, like Glen Browder, the 3d District Congressman who had a moderate record in the House. But only 315,000 voted in the Democratic primary in 1996, about half of them black—a much more liberal electorate. Bedford won 45% in the June 4 primary, to only 29% for Browder and 23% for Natalie Davis, a liberal political scientist and pollster. In the June 25 runoff, Browder attacked Bedford for supporting NAFTA and gambling, and for being backed by trial lawyers, but Bedford had more money and won 62%–38%.

Bedford also proved the better campaigner in the general, was competitive in fundraising, and ran close in the polls. "The old liberal days of tax and spend are over," he insisted, and opposed abortion, gun control, and gays in the military. Sessions avoided debates, at which Bedford excelled, and attacked the Democrat as a Ted Kennedy backer and for leading the battle against tort reform in the Alabama Senate in January 1996. He called government "a ball and chain on private enterprise" and signed the Americans for Tax Reform anti-tax pledge, while Bedford didn't. Sessions won 52%–45%, running best in the suburbanizing counties around Alabama's cities; Bedford carried the Black Belt and many rural counties in the north.

In the Senate, Sessions has had a very conservative voting record and has proved himself a stickler for details that many senators ignore; he has been known to read GAO reports during the congressional recess. He serves on the Judiciary Committee, where he has held up more than a few judicial nominations; for example he led the campaign against Judge Richard Paez, who had approved the Justice Department plea bargain with mum Clinton fundraiser John Huang, but Paez was confirmed in March 2000. He passed an amendment limiting attorneys' fees in tobacco cases only to see it effectively overruled, 50–48. But he did successfully sponsor laws to punish civilians who commit crimes while overseas with military personnel, to provide $768 million over six years to upgrade state crime laboratories and to protect church employee benefit plans from state regulation. He favors bankruptcy reform, but has not always taken the side of big business. Many businesses like to require aggrieved consumers to submit to arbitration; Sessions sponsored a bill to require arbitrators to be neutral, to waive costs in hardship cases and to require clear disclosure in contracts that contain a mandatory arbitration clause. In October 2000, by proposing 17 amendments he killed a noncontroversial bill ending the requirement that franchised auto dealers must submit to binding arbitration in disputes with auto companies; presumably he wants to revisit arbitration issues in the 107th Congress.

Sessions has put forth proposals on a wide variety of issues. In November 1999 he tried to prevent HHS Secretay Donna Shalala from making decisions on organ donations until Congress completed the reauthorization, in a battle over organ allocation policies. He seeks lower capital gains on timber producers and an extension of tax breaks on prepaid college tuition programs like Alabama's. He wants to amend the special education statute to allow uniform disciplinary standards for all students. He sought a one-year moratorium on Interior Secretary Bruce Babbitt's authority to license Indian casinos; the Poarch Creek Indians want to build a casino near Wetumpka, which Sessions and Governor Don Siegelman oppose. He helped persuade major retailers not to sell mature-rated video games to minors. He is willing to take on colleagues: He disagreed with colleague Richard Shelby and supported a bill to provide $75 million yearly for purchase and conservation of land in Alabama. He attacked Trent Lott for designating Madison County, Mississippi, a "renewal community," which would give it tax immunity helpful in competing for a Nissan plant also sought by Opelika, Alabama. He sought a GAO report on the cost of Bill Clinton's overseas travel and called the $292 million total "exorbitant." Sessions' seat comes up in 2002. When 5th District Representative Bud Cramer announced in May 2001 that he would not challenge Sessions, a number of Democrats were expected to consider the race.

Cook's Call   *Potentially Competitive.* As conservative and Republican as Alabama has become, Sessions will not get a free ride in his first bid for re-election. Democrats appear headed toward a primary between attorney Julian McPhillips and state Auditor Susan Parker. This could work to Sessions' advantage, but the Democratic gubernatorial victory in 1998 keeps this race worth watching.

Presidential politics   Alabama is one of the most Republican states in presidential elections. In 2000 Alabama whites voted 73%–25% for George W. Bush and Alabama blacks voted 91%–8% for Al Gore; Gore's best county in the nation was heavily black Macon County, where he won 86% of the vote. As head of the Alabama Democratic Conference Joe Reed has said, "Blacks are the base of the Democratic Party"; blacks often cast most of the votes in Democratic primaries. But overall the state went 56%–42% for Bush.

Alabama's presidential primary is in June—too late to count for much. An attempt to change the date failed in 1999.

Congressional districting   Democrats control the legislature and the governorship, but will be hard pressed to redraw Alabama's congressional district lines to help their party. The Voting Rights Act, as revised in 1982, is generally interpreted as requiring the creation of majority-minority districts where possible; a November 2000 U.S. Supreme Court ruling, unanimously dismissing six white voters' claims that the districts were biased, strengthens that interpretation. For 2002, that probably means retention of the Birmingham-Black Belt 7th District seat, which is safely Democratic but drains Democratic votes away from adjacent districts. Presumably the 5th District in the TVA country in the north, which Democrat Bud Cramer held against some tough challenges in the 1990s, will remain intact. But it will be hard to draw lines that endanger the Republicans who hold the other five districts.

THE PEOPLE: Pop. 2000: 4,447,100; Pop. 1990: 4,040,587, up 10.1% 1990–2000. 1.6% of U.S. total, 23d largest; 71.1% White, 26% Black, 0.7% Asian, 0.5% Amer. Indian, 1% Two+ races, 0.7% Other; 1.7% Hispanic Origin. 4.6% Unemployment. 2000 Voting age pop.: 3,323,678. 2000 Turnout: 1,665,573; 50% of VAP. Registered voters (2000): 2,882,348; no party registration.

POLITICAL LINEUP: Governor, Don Siegelman (D); Lt. Gov., Steve Windom (R); Secy. of State, Jim Bennett (R); Atty. Gen., Bill Pryor (R); Treasurer, Lucy Baxley (D); Auditor, Susan D. Parker (D); State Senate, 35 (24 D, 11 R); Senate Pres. Pro Tempore, Lowell Ray Barron (D); Majority Leader, Tom Butler (D); State Assembly, 105 (68 D, 37 R); House Speaker, Seth Hammett (D). Senators, Richard C. Shelby (R) and Jeff Sessions (R). Representatives, 7 (2 D, 5 R).

ELECTIONS DIVISION: 334-242-7205; **FILING DEADLINE FOR U.S. CONGRESS:** April 5, 2002.

2000 Presidential Vote

Bush (R)	941,173	(56%)
Gore (D)	692,611	(42%)
Nader (Green)	18,323	(1%)
Others	14,165	(1%)

1996 Presidential Vote

Dole (R)	768,826	(50%)
Clinton (D)	662,066	(43%)
Perot (I)	92,628	(6%)

2000 Republican Presidential Primary

Bush (R)	171,077	(84%)
Keyes (R)	23,394	(12%)
Uncommitted	8,608	(4%)

2000 Democratic Presidential Primary

Gore (D)	214,541	(77%)
Uncommitted	48,521	(17%)
LaRouche (D)	15,465	(6%)

Gov. Don Siegelman (D)

Elected 1998, term expires Jan. 2003, 1st term; b. Feb. 24, 1946, Mobile; home, Montgomery; U. of AL, B.A. 1968, Georgetown U., J.D. 1972, Oxford U. 1972–73; Catholic; married (Lori).

Military Career: Air Natl. Guard, 1968–69.

Elected Office: AL Secy. of State, 1978–86; AL Atty. Gen., 1986–90; AL Lt. Gov., 1994–98.

Professional Career: Practicing atty.; Capitol Hill Policeman, 1971; Law Clerk, U.S. Dept of Justice; Vestavia City Prosecutor; Exec. Dir, AL Dem. Party, 1973–78.

Office: Alabama State Capitol, 11 S. Union St., Montgomery, 36130, 334-242-7150; Fax: 334-242-4407; Web site: www.state.al.us.

Election Results

1998 general	Don Siegelman (D)	760,155	(58%)
	Fob James (R)	554,746	(42%)
1998 primary	Don Siegelman (D)	280,181	(78%)
	Lenora Pate (D)	59,300	(17%)
	Others	18,698	(5%)
1994 general	Fob James (R)	604,926	(50%)
	James Folsom Jr. (D)	594,169	(49%)

Sen. Richard C. Shelby (R)

Elected 1986, seat up 2004, 3d term; b. May 6, 1934, Birmingham; home, Tuscaloosa; U. of AL, B.A. 1957, LL.B. 1963; Presbyterian; married (Annette).

Elected Office: AL Senate, 1970–78; U.S. House of Reps., 1978–86.

Professional Career: Practicing atty., 1963–78.

DC Office: 110 HSOB, 20510, 202-224-5744; Fax: 202-224-3416; Web site: www.senate.gov/~shelby.

State Offices: Birmingham, 205-731-1384; Huntsville, 256-772-0460; Mobile, 334-694-4164; Montgomery, 334-223-7303; Tuscaloosa, 205-759-5047.

Committees: *Aging (Special). Appropriations:* Defense; Foreign Operations; Transportation (RMM); Treasury & General Government; VA, HUD & Independent Agencies. *Banking, Housing & Urban Affairs:* Financial Institutions; Housing & Transportation; Securities & Investment. *Energy & Natural Resources:* Energy Research, Development, Production & Regulation; Forests & Public Land Management; Water & Power. *Intelligence (Select)* (Vice Chmn.).

Group Ratings

	ADA	ACLU	AFS	LCV	CON	ITIC	NTU	COC	ACU	NTLC	CHC
2000	0	29	0	0	11	70	73	93	100	97	85
1999	10	—	0	0	40	—	77	71	84	—	—

National Journal Ratings

	1999 LIB	—	1999 CONS		2000 LIB	—	2000 CONS
Economic	40%	—	57%		14%	—	75%
Social	7%	—	92%		27%	—	70%
Foreign	40%	—	56%		5%	—	86%

Key Votes of the 106th Congress

1. Educ. Savings Accts.	Y	5. Review Movie Violence	Y	9. NATO War in Serbia	Y
2. Prescrip. Drug Benefit	N	6. Gun Show Bckgrnd. Checks	N	10. Table Cuba Travel Ban	Y
3. Delay Ergonomic Standards	Y	7. Ban Part.-Birth Abortion	Y	11. Nuclear Test-Ban Treaty	N
4. Phase Out Estate Tax	Y	8. Broaden Hate Crimes List	N	12. Perm. Trade with China	Y

Election Results

1998 general	Richard C. Shelby (R)	817,973	(63%)	($1,890,484)
	Clayton Suddith (D)	474,568	(37%)	($15,723)
1998 primary	Richard C. Shelby (R)	unopposed		
1992 general	Richard C. Shelby (D)	1,022,698	(65%)	($2,807,764)
	Richard Sellers (R)	522,015	(33%)	($149,578)
	Others	31,811	(2%)	

Sen. Jeff Sessions (R)

Elected 1996, seat up 2002, 1st term; b. Dec. 24, 1946, Hybert; home, Mobile; Huntingdon Col., B.A. 1969, U. of AL, J.D. 1973; Methodist; married (Mary).

Military Career: Army Reserves, 1973–86.

Elected Office: AL Atty. Gen., 1994–96.

Professional Career: Practicing atty., 1973–75, 1977–81, 1993–94; Asst. U.S. Atty., 1975–77; U.S. Atty., 1981–93.

DC Office: 493 RSOB, 20510, 202-224-4124; Fax: 202-224-3149; Web site: www.senate.gov/~sessions.

State Offices: Birmingham, 205-731-1500; Huntsville, 256-533-0979; Mobile, 334-414-3083; Montgomery, 334-265-9507.

Committees: *Armed Services*: Airland Forces; Seapower (RMM); Strategic Forces. *Health, Education, Labor & Pensions*: Employment, Safety & Training; Public Health. *Judiciary*: Administrative Oversight & the Courts (RMM); Technology, Terrorism & Government Information; Youth Violence. *Joint Economic Committee* (8th of 10 Sens.).

Group Ratings

	ADA	ACLU	AFS	LCV	CON	ITIC	NTU	COC	ACU	NTLC	CHC
2000	0	14	0	0	59	85	77	86	100	100	100
1999	0	—	0	0	87	—	80	88	100	—	—

National Journal Ratings

	1999 LIB	—	1999 CONS		2000 LIB	—	2000 CONS
Economic	26%	—	71%		14%	—	75%
Social	13%	—	84%		0%	—	90%
Foreign	10%	—	84%		0%	—	95%

Key Votes of the 106th Congress

1. Educ. Savings Accts.	Y	5. Review Movie Violence	Y	9. NATO War in Serbia	N
2. Prescrip. Drug Benefit	N	6. Gun Show Bckgrnd. Checks	N	10. Table Cuba Travel Ban	Y
3. Delay Ergonomic Standards	Y	7. Ban Part.-Birth Abortion	Y	11. Nuclear Test-Ban Treaty	N
4. Phase Out Estate Tax	Y	8. Broaden Hate Crimes List	N	12. Perm. Trade with China	Y

Election Results

1996 general	Jeff Sessions (R)	786,436	(52%)	($3,862,359)
	Roger Bedford (D)	681,651	(45%)	($2,284,801)
	Others	31,306	(2%)	
1996 runoff	Jeff Sessions (R)	81,681	(59%)	
	Sid McDonald (R)	56,156	(41%)	
1996 primary	Jeff Sessions (R)	80,694	(38%)	
	Sid McDonald (R)	47,320	(22%)	
	Charles Woods (R)	23,796	(11%)	
	Frank McRight (R)	21,818	(10%)	
	Walter Clark (R)	18,513	(9%)	
	Jimmy Blake (R)	15,305	(7%)	
	Others	7,600	(4%)	
1990 general	Howell Heflin (D)	717,814	(61%)	($3,437,073)
	Bill Cabaniss (R)	467,190	(39%)	($1,853,869)

FIRST DISTRICT

Mobile, the port where the Tombigbee and Alabama rivers flow into the Gulf of Mexico, was long a key point on the American frontier. Spanish until after the Revolutionary War, it was wrested away by threats of war from Secretary of State John Quincy Adams. During the Civil War it was one of the major Confederate ports; here in 1864 Admiral David Farragut, while steaming into the harbor lashed to his mast, cried, "Damn the torpedoes! Full speed ahead." Today Mobile is full of graceful signs of its slightly exotic past: Behind the docks and rail lines are downtown buildings and old houses with Spanish motifs, French accents, or tropical Art Deco lines. Further inland are neighborhoods with spacious houses, often with double porches, overhung by huge live oaks, graced with Spanish moss. Mobile is a Gulf Coast version of Charleston or a smaller, more comfortable New Orleans, with a taste for shellfish and spicy food and an even older Mardi Gras, which the locals have been celebrating since 1703. (Unlike the Big Easy, Mobile imposes a $500 fine on people caught openly consuming alcohol.) As befits a frontier city with a martial past, Mobile is bristling with arms: One of the city's proudest possessions is the battleship *U.S.S. Alabama*, moored at the head of Mobile Bay, with its guns aimed out toward the Gulf. Mobile's economy was based originally on docks and shipyards, factories and terminals, but with a determination to impose touches of beauty on its hot, flat landscape. For years this southern seaboard of the Confederacy and the Union has been one of the most hawkish parts of America, and today it is solidly Republican in national elections. Its economy is thriving again; the shipyards and chemical plants have been busy and upriver new timber and paper mills are running. The capital-improvements Amendment One approved by voters in 2000 includes $100 million for improvement of Mobile's State Docks, through which it is hoped the Mercedes plant in Tuscaloosa County will ship in parts and ship out cars.

Mobile is the focus of Alabama's 1st Congressional District, which extends north along the lazily flowing Tombigbee and Alabama Rivers, near the old forts and mansions. This was the home of great writers—Truman Capote and his childhood playmate, Harper Lee, whose *To Kill a Mockingbird* is set here; and Winston Groom, author of *Forrest Gump*. Also here are surviving back-country settlements of blacks and Cajans (who may or may not be descended from Louisiana Cajuns) and Creek Indians. To the south, along the shores of the Gulf of Mexico, are fast-growing condominium communities; the glorious Gulf beaches are one of the South's best-kept secrets and this is one of the fastest-growing—and most Republican—parts of Alabama.

The congressman from the 1st District is Sonny Callahan, a gregarious Republican with a rags-to-riches biography, a party-switcher who has influence as one of the House's "cardinals." The oldest boy in a family of nine children whose father died young, Callahan went to work at the age of 12, during World War II; fortunately, the boss was his uncle, a warehouse company owner. He served in the Navy during Korea, then rose to become president of the company at 32 and expanded into real estate and insurance. Like so many go-getters, he ran for the state legislature and was elected at 38. As a Democrat, he lost the 1982 primary for lieutenant governor to liberal Bill Baxley. Then 1st District Republican Congressman Jack Edwards decided to retire in 1984 after 20 years and asked Callahan to run as a Republican; he did and won. For years he had a very conservative voting record; with the Republican majority pushing the House toward the right, he winds up as a bit moderate on economic and foreign policy.

From his modest beginnings and provincial political base, Callahan for six years occupied a key position in American foreign policy as chairman of the Appropriations Foreign Operations Subcommittee. During the previous decade, he voted against all foreign aid bills; in 1995, as chairman, he started writing them and exerted influence just by talking. Bill Clinton sought his advice; it was Callahan with whom Clinton was talking on the phone while he was busy with Monica Lewinsky in November 1995. When the story came out in August 1998 Callahan said, "I can say unequivocally and without hesitation that I had no knowledge I was sharing the president's time or attention with anyone else." Throughout his chairmanship, he remained a foreign-aid skeptic. Even when Clinton raised the prospect at the end of his presidency of a Middle East peace deal, Callahan doubted that a peace agreement "can be secured simply by promising even more money than has been promised before." But he did sign on to the debt-relief initiative pushed by international leaders from Pope John Paul II to Bono, the Irish rock star. On occasion, Callahan supported Clinton when leading Democrats did not—as with funds to fight drugs in Colombia. "Your lack of confidence in your president is stunning to me," he told senior Appropriations Democrat David Obey. He also voted "present" when Republicans tried to prohibit deployment in Serbia, saying that Clinton should be allowed time to work out an agreement first. When the Republicans' term limits rule for chairmen forced him to take a new subcommittee in 2001, he shifted to Energy and Water where he will be able to bring home more local projects.

Callahan has insisted that voters are "sick of being asked to pay more, only to make government bigger, but not necessarily better," but he has protected the interests of south Alabama. He sought parity with Mississippi and Louisiana when the National Marine Fisheries Service said red snapper was overfished by commercial shrimp trawlers—an attempt to keep Mobile fishermen working. And he has remained true to his start as a trucker by opposing Transportation Department rules to limit drivers' hours at the wheel.

He has been re-elected easily, without major-party opposition in the past two elections. His Libertarian challenger Dick Coffee in 2000 said that he had no major qualms with Callahan but that it was "un-American" to run unopposed. Redistricting will remove some precincts from his growing district, but Callahan should be able to set his timetable to take his houseboat back to the 1st District when he retires.

Cook's Call *Safe*. Since first winning this seat in 1984 with 51%, Callahan has not had to work up much of a sweat to hold onto this Mobile-based district. Moderate population growth here means that the district is likely to be altered, but it should not be significant enough to have any real impact on Callahan's stability in this district.

THE PEOPLE: Pop. 2000: 646,181; Pop. 1990: 577,375, up 11.9% 1990–2000. 68% White, 28.6% Black, 1% Asian, 1% Amer. Indian, 1% Two+ races, 0.4% Other; 1.3% Hispanic Origin.

2000 Presidential Vote

Bush (R)	140,489	(60%)
Gore (D)	88,358	(38%)
Nader (Green)	2,776	(1%)
Others	2,164	(1%)

1996 Presidential Vote

Dole (R)	112,999	(53%)
Clinton (D)	83,920	(39%)
Perot (I)	14,660	(7%)

Rep. Sonny Callahan (R)

Elected 1984, 9th term; b. Sept. 11, 1932, Mobile; home, Mobile; U. of AL, 1959–60; Catholic; married (Karen).

Military Career: Navy, 1952–54.

Elected Office: AL House of Reps., 1970–78; AL Senate, 1978–82.

Professional Career: Finch Cos. 1955–85, Pres., 1964–85.

DC Office: 2372 RHOB 20515, 202-225-4931; Fax: 202-225-0562; Web site: www.house.gov/callahan.

District Office: Mobile, 334-690-2811.

Committees: *Appropriations* (9th of 35 R): Energy & Water Development (Chmn.); Foreign Operations & Export Financing; Transportation.

Group Ratings

	ADA	ACLU	AFS	LCV	CON	ITIC	NTU	COC	ACU	NTLC	CHC
2000	0	21	0	7	3	100	56	85	69	65	100
1999	10	—	0	0	37	—	53	84	91	—	—

National Journal Ratings

	1999 LIB	—	1999 CONS		2000 LIB	—	2000 CONS
Economic	30%	—	64%		36%	—	63%
Social	10%	—	85%		0%	—	79%
Foreign	50%	—	50%		33%	—	62%

Key Votes of the 106th Congress

1. Patient Bill of Rights	Y	5. Bar RU-486 $ for FDA	Y	9. NATO War in Serbia		*
2. Accelerate Min. Wage	N	6. Display 10 Commandments	Y	10. Perm. Trade with China		Y
3. Strike Ban on Ergo. Stnd.	N	7. Gun Show Bkgrnd. Checks	N	11. Debt Relief for 3rd World		N
4. Ovrd. Estate Tax Veto	Y	8. Ban Part.-Birth Abortion	Y	12. Drop Cuba Econ. Embargo		N

Election Results

2000 general	Sonny Callahan (R)	151,188	(91%)	($344,493)
	Dick Coffee (LIB)	14,031	(8%)	
2000 primary	Sonny Callahan (R)	unopposed		
1998 general	Sonny Callahan (R)	unopposed		($263,347)

SECOND DISTRICT

The thick green countryside is everywhere in southern Alabama. Even in Montgomery the stone and brick buildings that rise in the irregular downtown grid do not mask the contours of the hills or hide the lush foliage. You can look downhill from the restored Greek Revival Capitol toward Dexter Avenue Baptist Church where Martin Luther King Jr. was pastor, or out past the impressive theater where the Alabama Shakespeare Festival is held, toward new subdivisions and shopping malls, and easily imagine when this land was covered with pine trees and cotton fields. The atmosphere is even more rural in southeast Alabama's Wiregrass region, named for the stiff native grass, around the town of Dothan, past Daleville and the Army's Fort Rucker to Enterprise, site of the Boll Weevil Monument that commemorates the insect that destroyed two-thirds of the cotton crop here in 1915 and then spread throughout the South; in 1998 the statue was removed after someone hacked off the goddess's arms and stole the insect. Peanuts are now the main crop, with 25% of U.S. production within 75 miles of Dothan.

The 2d Congressional District covers most of the southeast corner of the state. The district includes all of Montgomery County except for an 80% black segment that is part of the black-majority 7th District, plus 78% white Elmore and Autauga Counties across the Alabama River. Without these adjustments, prompted by the Voting Rights Act, the 2d District would be closely split between the parties. But as now drawn, it is heavily Republican, for politics in southern Alabama remains racially polarized: blacks vote almost unanimously Democratic, whites vote very heavily (but not quite unanimously) Republican in national and statewide contests. It would be a mistake to see these preferences as purely racial, however. The civil rights laws of the 1960s have long since been accepted. Blacks here tend to support a larger and more generous government, and hence vote Democratic. Alabama whites tend to take a hard line on defense and crime, want government to promote traditional cultural values, and hence vote Republican.

The congressman from the 2d District is Terry Everett, a businessman from the Wiregrass first elected in 1992. He served in Air Force Intelligence in Germany in the 1950s, learned Russian, worked as a sports and police beat reporter and circulation manager for southern Alabama newspapers. He bought some newspapers himself and sold them for far more, and ended up heading a S&L and owning a large farm and real estate development firm. In 1992, when he decided to run for the seat being vacated by 28-year incumbent Republican Bill Dickinson, he was far from the favorite. But he beat two career politicians, a Montgomery legislator in the Republican primary and in the general state Treasurer George Wallace III, son of the former governor. Everett spent $600,000 of his own money and, echoing an old George Wallace slogan, called on voters to "Send them a message, not a politician." Everett carried the Montgomery area and the Wiregrass and lost the Black Belt and rural areas.

Everett's voting record is conservative on most issues, though he shows a practical-minded concern about local issues. One example is peanuts: In 1995 Everett formed a Peanut Caucus and on the Agriculture Committee held out against the Freedom to Farm Act until he got the peanut program continued, though with a 10% cut in the support price and a lower national quota. Since then Everett and the Peanut Caucus have been nibbling back; the quotas have been increased and Everett has advocated a higher price for Segregation 3 peanuts (damaged peanuts). "Vigilance and hard work will continue to be necessary if we are to ensure the current and future profitability of the peanut program," he said. In January 2001, Everett was chosen to chair the new Specialty Crops and Foreign Agricultural Programs Subcommittee, where he will be in a strong position to save the peanut quota system.

As Oversight and Investigations Subcommittee chairman for the Veterans Affairs Committee, he took credit for a $1.7 billion increase for veterans' health care spending in 1999 plus the opening of four new national cemeteries for the nation's aging vets. But he clashed with Clinton Administration officials over a General Accounting Office report showing that serious mistakes in patient-care remain a major problem at veterans' hospitals. The report also criticized the failure to downsize those facilities—a problem for which Congress shares responsibility because many members view them as budget pork. Following his subcommittee's report on Clinton waivers allowing burials of non-veterans in Arlington National Cemetery, which he called "one of Washington's dirty little secrets," he won House passage of a bill to tighten the waiver process.

Everett has been re-elected easily. Although his 2000 Democratic opponent Charles Woods won only 30% of the vote, his maverick history is noteworthy: After his face and hands were badly burned in a World War Two airplane crash in which his doctors gave him up for dead, Woods became a wealthy developer of a nationwide media empire. In 1992, he won 39% against Harry Reid in the Senate Democratic primary in Nevada; then, he was third out of seven in Alabama's Republican primary for an open Senate seat in 1996. Unlike those races, this time he spent little money on his campaign.

Cook's Call　*Safe.* The district is very conservative, highly dependent on both the military and agriculture, with Everett focusing his congressional energies on both. Everett hasn't had a tough race in years, and will likely continue that streak through 2002.

THE PEOPLE: Pop. 2000: 650,321; Pop. 1990: 577,203, up 12.7% 1990–2000. 69.3% White, 28% Black, 0.7% Asian, 0.4% Amer. Indian, 1.1% Two+ races, 0.5% Other; 1.5% Hispanic Origin.

2000 Presidential Vote
(Data not available as of June 1, 2001)

1996 Presidential Vote
Dole (R)	121,306	(56%)
Clinton (D)	81,148	(37%)
Perot (I)	12,691	(6%)

Rep. Terry Everett (R)

Elected 1992, 5th term; b. Feb. 15, 1937, Dothan; home, Enterprise; Baptist; married (Barbara).

Military Career: Air Force, 1955–59.

Professional Career: Newspaper reporter, 1959–61, 1966–68; Businessman, 1961–64; Editor & Publisher, 1968–88; Real estate developer, 1988–92; Owner & Pres., *Union Springs Herald*, 1988–present.

DC Office: 2312 RHOB 20515, 202-225-2901; Fax: 202-225-8913; Web site: www.house.gov/everett.

District Offices: Dothan, 334-794-9680; Montgomery, 334-277-9113; Opp, 334-493-9253.

Committees: *Agriculture* (6th of 27 R): General Farm Commodities & Risk Management; Specialty Crops & Foreign Agriculture Programs (Chmn.). *Armed Services* (9th of 32 R): Military Installations & Facilities; Military Procurement. *Veterans' Affairs* (5th of 17 R): Oversight & Investigations.

Group Ratings
	ADA	ACLU	AFS	LCV	CON	ITIC	NTU	COC	ACU	NTLC	CHC
2000	0	21	0	7	10	87	61	78	90	72	100
1999	5	—	0	6	56	—	58	80	91	—	—

National Journal Ratings
	1999 LIB	—	1999 CONS		2000 LIB	—	2000 CONS
Economic	16%	—	78%		17%	—	82%
Social	0%	—	96%		0%	—	79%
Foreign	10%	—	86%		24%	—	75%

Key Votes of the 106th Congress

1. Patient Bill of Rights	N	5. Bar RU-486 $ for FDA	Y	9. NATO War in Serbia	N
2. Accelerate Min. Wage	N	6. Display 10 Commandments	Y	10. Perm. Trade with China	Y
3. Strike Ban on Ergo. Stnd.	N	7. Gun Show Bkgrnd. Checks	N	11. Debt Relief for 3rd World	N
4. Ovrd. Estate Tax Veto	Y	8. Ban Part.-Birth Abortion	Y	12. Drop Cuba Econ. Embargo	N

Election Results

2000 general	Terry Everett (R)	151,830	(68%)	($304,981)
	Charles Woods (D)	64,958	(29%)	
	Other	5,848	(3%)	
2000 primary	Terry Everett (R)	unopposed		
1998 general	Terry Everett (R)	131,428	(69%)	($567,408)
	Joe Fondren (D)	58,136	(31%)	($22,134)

THIRD DISTRICT

Forty years ago, Lineville, Alabama, in the red hills of Clay County, was Ku Klux Klan country, with whites determined to resist race-mixing and blacks intimidated by threats of violence. Recently in Lineville, reported *The Washington Post*'s Eugene Robinson, integrated crowds regularly cheer integrated high school teams, people of all races work amicably together, though they tend to pray separately on Sundays. Interracial dating is getting more common—though a high school principal in Wedowee made national headlines when he canceled the 1994 prom because of it—and Alabamans of both races are wondering how they will adjust to their new Hispanic neighbors. Lineville's progress perhaps echoes that of America's most integrated institution, the military; for the small town produced more men and women per capita for Operation Desert Storm than any other community in the nation.

The 3d Congressional District is centered geographically and perhaps spiritually in Lineville. There are other places of distinction: Horseshoe Bend, where Andrew Jackson won a climactic battle against the Indians; Tuskegee, home of Booker T. Washington's Tuskegee Institute; Auburn, home of Auburn University and its renowned sports teams and veterinary school; Talladega, home of the Alabama Institute for the Deaf and Blind, which is perhaps America's most user-friendly city for the disabled. This looks and feels like rural country, though few people here make a living off their farms; instead they ride in to work at Tysons Food or Wal-Mart or in dozens of textile mills and small- or medium-sized factories. Politically, this was long one of the heartlands of the Democratic Party, the home of populist white Democrats—patriotic supporters of the military, cautious supporters of some domestic programs—who won power so often in the House and Senate. But the interstates have brought in new businesses and new families and the towns have been trending Republican, and the 3d is now a Republican-held district. Still, the Black Belt's Macon County is notable not only as the home of Tuskegee Institute but also as the county which gave 86% of its vote to Al Gore in November 2000, his highest percentage in any county nationwide. But the rest of the district was solidly for George W. Bush.

The congressman from the 3d is Bob Riley, who grew up as a seventh-generation Clay County resident. Riley was a University of Alabama student, watching when George Wallace stood in the schoolhouse door in 1963. Two years later he returned home with a business degree, and at 20 he and his brother started selling eggs door-to-door. That became a large egg-and-poultry company; he also ran a grocery store, airport, pharmacy, and sold real estate. He ended up with a car dealership (Midway Ford and Chrysler), a trucking company (Midway Transit), half a shopping center, and a cattle farm, and served on the city council in Ashland. In 1996, when Glen Browder, the 3d District's moderate Democratic congressman, ran for the Senate and lost to trial lawyer Roger Bedford in the primary, Riley ran for the House.

He was not the best-known candidate. But Riley proved a strong and energetic campaigner, a supporter of school prayer, term limits, tax cuts, and a balanced budget amendment, and an opponent of abortion, gun control, and racial quotas. His Democratic opponent was state Senator Ted Little, who opposed NAFTA, promised to "stand up to Newt Gingrich," and opposed cuts in Medicare and education. Riley pounded home his conservative views and assailed Little as a trial lawyer. Little had more political experience but the tide was running Riley's way: The Alabama

Farmers Federation withdrew its endorsement of Little and endorsed Riley at the end of October. As Republicans Bob Dole and Jeff Sessions carried the 3d, so did Riley, 50%–47%.

In the House, Riley has a dependable conservative voting record. He said he came to Washington meaning to be bipartisan, but his first three months made him "become the most partisan person on the Hill," in his own words. Like many Southern conservatives he is not averse to federal spending in his district, especially for local military bases. Sometimes these local issues have national implications. After Fort McClellan was shut down in the 1995 base closings, Riley fought to save the 3,600 jobs at the Anniston Army Depot, which refurbishes tanks with tracks. As a member of the Depot Caucus, Riley moved to stop the Clinton Administration's "privatization in place" of depots designed to save McClellan and Kelly Air Force bases in Sacramento and San Antonio. He was a prime mover in defeating an amendment brought forward by 2d District Congressman Terry Everett, which would have essentially upheld the Clinton plan. He added that the Clinton plan for two more base closings "is dead on arrival," as indeed it proved to be. And the depot was revived in 2000 by a $4 billion project to hire 140 additional workers to handle final work on armored vehicles. Riley also bolstered the depot with an $800 million incinerator for destruction of military gases.

Democrats targeted the 3d District in 1998, and recruited Joe Turnham, son of a longtime legislator and state party chairman for three years, to run. But Riley raised money furiously and contributed $845,000 of his own. Turnham carried only two Black Belt counties, losing his home county, and Riley won 58%–42%. Apparently chastened, Democrats failed to nominate a candidate in 2000. Riley says that he will "go home soon," but to return to private life, not to run statewide, although his name has been mentioned as a possible gubernatorial candidate against Don Siegelman.

Cook's Call   *Probably Safe.* After running serious races against Riley in 1996 and 1998 and coming up woefully short, Democrats gave Riley a pass in 2000. In its present form, the district has a substantial black population and as recently as 1994 voters here were comfortably voting for moderate Democrats. Still, Riley has proven to be a solid fit for this district. But, with rumors that Riley may run for governor in 2002, Democrats may have a shot at putting this once solidly Democratic district back into their fold. Plus, with Democrats in control of redistricting in the state, they are going to try to make some of the more marginal districts in the state competitive.

THE PEOPLE: Pop. 2000: 643,525; Pop. 1990: 577,116, up 11.5% 1990–2000. 72.6% White, 25.3% Black, 0.5% Asian, 0.3% Amer. Indian, 0.8% Two + races, 0.5% Other; 1.3% Hispanic Origin.

2000 Presidential Vote			1996 Presidential Vote		
Bush (R)	126,421	(57%)	Dole (R)	97,798	(49%)
Gore (D)	91,872	(41%)	Clinton (D)	88,156	(44%)
Nader (Green)	2,488	(1%)	Perot (I)	13,112	(7%)
Others	1,930	(1%)			

Rep. Bob Riley (R)

Elected 1996, 3d term; b. Oct. 3, 1944, Ashland; home, Ashland; U. of AL, B.A. 1965; Baptist; married (Patsy).

Elected Office: Ashland City Cncl., 1972–76.

Professional Career: Owner, egg & poultry co.; Rancher; Owner, Midway Transit, 1965–present.

DC Office: 322 CHOB 20515, 202-225-3261; Fax: 202-225-5827; Web site: www.house.gov/riley.

District Offices: Anniston, 256-236-5655; Clanton, 205-755-1522; Opelika, 334-745-6222.

Committees: *Agriculture* (15th of 27 R): General Farm Commodities & Risk Management; Livestock & Horticulture. *Armed Services* (21st of 32 R): Military Readiness (Vice Chmn.); Military Research & Development.

Financial Services (19th of 37 R): Capital Markets, Insurance & Government Sponsored Enterprises; Financial Institutions & Consumer Credit; Housing & Community Opportunity.

Group Ratings

	ADA	ACLU	AFS	LCV	CON	ITIC	NTU	COC	ACU	NTLC	CHC
2000	5	21	14	7	50	71	64	75	91	85	100
1999	5	—	0	0	56	—	60	79	91	—	—

National Journal Ratings

	1999 LIB —	1999 CONS	2000 LIB —	2000 CONS
Economic	22%	77%	6%	85%
Social	0%	96%	0%	79%
Foreign	31%	66%	0%	88%

Key Votes of the 106th Congress

1. Patient Bill of Rights	N	5. Bar RU-486 $ for FDA	Y	9. NATO War in Serbia	N
2. Accelerate Min. Wage	N	6. Display 10 Commandments	Y	10. Perm. Trade with China	N
3. Strike Ban on Ergo. Stnd.	N	7. Gun Show Bkgrnd. Checks	N	11. Debt Relief for 3rd World	N
4. Ovrd. Estate Tax Veto	Y	8. Ban Part.-Birth Abortion	Y	12. Drop Cuba Econ. Embargo	N

Election Results

2000 general	Bob Riley (R)	147,317	(87%)	($527,222)
	John Sophocleus (LIB)	21,119	(12%)	
2000 primary	Bob Riley (R)	unopposed		
1998 general	Bob Riley (R)	101,731	(58%)	($1,985,984)
	Joe Turnham (D)	73,357	(42%)	($447,051)

FOURTH DISTRICT

The Appalachians' corduroy ridges, dividing the Atlantic coast from the interior, are America's coal-and-steel industrial spine, from the black coal country of western Pennsylvania to the red hill country of northern Alabama. Here rose America's two premier steel cities, Pittsburgh and Birmingham; around both, and for many miles in between them, is the country settled by feisty Scots-Irish farmers in the years between the Revolution and the Civil War. In valley land accessible to railroads are the great steel factories built in the 80 years after the Civil War and smaller factories that produce underwear and tires, glass and chemicals, socks and chickens. Politically, the two regions were separated by the Civil War: Western Pennsylvania was overwhelmingly Republican until the 1930s, while northern Alabama was solidly Democratic through the 1950s. But they shared the same political impulses—populist on economics, conservative on culture—which made them both Democratic heartlands during the New Deal and in congressional politics for years afterwards. Now they seem to have traded partisan allegiances: Western Pennsylvania is Democratic, though less solidly so when the Democrats emphasize cultural liberalism; northern Alabama has moved toward the Republicans, even though it has benefited from massive federal public works programs, and the movement is most pronounced in counties close to Birmingham and along the interstates.

Alabama's 4th District crosses the state and the Appalachian ridges, from the Georgia line near the gritty factory town of Gadsden to the Mississippi line near lightly populated rural counties. It has the lowest black percentage of Alabama's congressional districts and, next to the black-majority 7th District, the 4th and the 5th just to the north are the most Democratic districts in the state. But neither gave a plurality to Bill Clinton in 1992 or 1996, and both cast solid majorities for George W. Bush in 2000.

The congressman is Robert Aderholt, a Republican first elected in 1996 to replace 30-year Democrat Tom Bevill, a senior Appropriations member and benefactor of great federal projects, including the Tennessee-Tombigbee Waterway project. Aderholt is from Winston County, the one ancestrally Republican county in north Alabama, which opposed secession in the Civil War and declared itself the Free State of Winston. His father was a circuit judge for over 30 years; his wife's father was a state senator and state commissioner of Agriculture and Industry. In 1992 he was appointed Haleyville municipal judge; in 1995 he became a top aide to Governor Fob James.

With that pedigree he decided to run for Congress when Bevill retired. After he won 49% in the primary, the runner-up decided not to seek a runoff. Democrats nominated state Senator Bob Wilson Jr., whose father was a state senator who nominated George Wallace for president at the 1972 Democratic convention. Wilson called himself a Democrat "in the Tom Bevill tradition" and said he supported family values. Aderholt recognized that Bevill did a lot for the district: To his proposed five-year moratorium on federal highway construction he made an exception for Corridor X, Bevill's idea for an interstate-quality road from Birmingham to Memphis. But in this culturally conservative district, Aderholt didn't hedge on cultural issues. Against abortion, gun control and same-sex marriage, and for school prayer, he said, "We want to go to Washington to deliver a message, and that is, don't mess with our traditional family values." He attacked Wilson for his support from unions and trial lawyers, and invited Newt Gingrich to the district. This was a nationally targeted race, seriously contested, and Aderholt won 50%–48%.

Recognizing Aderholt's electoral vulnerability, Republican leaders put Aderholt on Appropriations and saw to it that he got more highway money than most Republicans, including an additional $100 million for Corridor X. And he didn't forget the social issues. When local judge Roy Moore was ordered to remove a copy of the Ten Commandments from his courtroom, Aderholt protested (in 2000 Moore was elected Alabama's Chief Justice). Aderholt sponsored legislation commending public display of the Ten Commandments in government buildings, including courthouses. He sponsored a Religious Freedom constitutional amendment, which got a majority but not the required two-thirds. But perhaps Aderholt's most clever legislative moves in an otherwise conservative voting record was working with national steel companies and unions to earmark federal subsidies. Plus, those steel interests received some satisfaction with his co-sponsoring a bill passed by the House but not the Senate setting stricter standards for review of illegal dumping of steel by foreign countries; Aderholt, reaching out further to industrial unions, voted against permanent trade relations for China.

In his two re-election campaigns, he fared surprisingly well against familiar names in Alabama politics. In 1998, Democrats prevailed on Don Bevill, son of the former congressman. But unlike his father he had no seniority and no assurance of being in the majority party. Aderholt increased his percentage to 56%. Two years later, Democrats enthused about Martha Folsom, the state's former First Lady when her husband was Acting Governor in 1993–94. She had more than $1 million to fund an aggressive advertising campaign, including inaccurate accusations that Aderholt supported Internet gambling. This time, Aderholt increased his vote to 61%, an impressive performance. National Rifle Association president Charlton Heston made a late appearance for him. Folsom may have been damaged for failing to appear at an anti-abortion forum in Walker County typically frequented by candidates. And Aderholt injected witchcraft into the campaign when he linked the practice to one of 50 members in an interfaith alliance friendly to Folsom.

This cannot be counted as an utterly safe seat, especially with some other strong Democrats in these hills and Democrats controlling redistricting. But Aderholt appears to have quickly entrenched himself.

Cook's Call   *Probably Safe.* Aderholt's impressive win in 2000 should give even the most ambitious Democrat pause about challenging the third term Republican. Though legendary Democratic Rep. Tom Bevill easily held onto this district for years and the registration here still favors Democrats, this district, like so many former southern Democratic strongholds, continues to trend toward Republicans. Growth in the Huntsville-based 5th District and Birmingham-based 6th could have an impact on the lines here.

THE PEOPLE: Pop. 2000: 643,275; Pop. 1990: 577,058, up 11.5% 1990–2000. 90.3% White, 6.3% Black, 0.2% Asian, 0.7% Amer. Indian, 1.1% Two+ races, 1.4% Other; 3% Hispanic Origin.

2000 Presidential Vote

Bush (R)	137,593	(59%)
Gore (D)	91,566	(39%)
Nader (Green)	2,134	(1%)
Others	2,472	(1%)

1996 Presidential Vote

Dole (R)	101,636	(48%)
Clinton (D)	91,625	(43%)
Perot (I)	17,687	(8%)

Rep. Robert Aderholt (R)

Elected 1996, 3d term; b. July 22, 1965, Haleyville; home, Haleyville; Birmingham Southern U., B.A. 1987, Samford U., J.D. 1990; Congregationalist; married (Caroline).

Professional Career: Haleyville Municipal Judge, 1992–96; Asst. Legal Advisor, Gov. Fob James, 1995–96.

DC Office: 1433 LHOB 20515, 202-225-4876; Fax: 202-225-5587; Web site: www.house.gov/aderholt.

District Offices: Cullman, 256-734-6043; Gadsden, 256-546-0201; Jasper, 205-221-2310.

Committees: *Appropriations* (26th of 35 R): Military Construction; Transportation; VA, HUD & Independent Agencies.

Group Ratings

	ADA	ACLU	AFS	LCV	CON	ITIC	NTU	COC	ACU	NTLC	CHC
2000	15	21	14	7	61	72	64	71	88	76	100
1999	5	—	0	0	79	—	62	80	84	—	—

National Journal Ratings

	1999 LIB —	1999 CONS		2000 LIB —	2000 CONS
Economic	16%	78%		25%	72%
Social	0%	96%		0%	79%
Foreign	15%	85%		45%	53%

Key Votes of the 106th Congress

1. Patient Bill of Rights	N	5. Bar RU-486 $ for FDA	Y	9. NATO War in Serbia	N
2. Accelerate Min. Wage	Y	6. Display 10 Commandments	Y	10. Perm. Trade with China	N
3. Strike Ban on Ergo. Stnd.	N	7. Gun Show Bkgrnd. Checks	N	11. Debt Relief for 3rd World	Y
4. Ovrd. Estate Tax Veto	Y	8. Ban Part.-Birth Abortion	Y	12. Drop Cuba Econ. Embargo	N

Election Results

2000 general	Robert Aderholt (R)	140,009	(61%)	($1,583,278)
	Marsha Folsom (D)	86,400	(37%)	($1,134,694)
	Other	4,697	(2%)	
2000 primary	Robert Aderholt (R)	unopposed		
1998 general	Robert Aderholt (R)	106,297	(56%)	($1,605,092)
	Donald Bevill (D)	82,065	(44%)	($662,224)

FIFTH DISTRICT

Twice this century, the federal government has transformed the northern Alabama counties along the Tennessee River. The first time was when it created the Tennessee Valley Authority in 1933. Proposed by Nebraska Senator George Norris, a favorite of President Franklin Roosevelt, TVA took the World War I federal munitions plant at Muscle Shoals on the unnavigable Tennessee River, and built a series of dams to control flooding and produce cheap hydroelectric power. This was backwards country then: Poor white farmers scratched a living out of hardscrabble land, were housed in shacks without electricity or running water, and lived off a diet that produced pellagra and rickets; and TVA was intended to showcase what an enlightened, generous federal government could do. The second major federal project here was the space program. After the Soviets put up Sputnik in 1957, the Redstone Arsenal in Huntsville became the nation's major missile development center. NASA built its Marshall Space Flight Center nearby in the 1960s and the Huntsville-Decatur area achieved high-tech critical mass. In recent years, the Boeing research center here has been a prime contractor for the space station which—after surviving a legislative funding battle by one vote in 1993—has remained a major project of NASA. Recently, Boeing rolled its first Delta IV booster out of the local factory.

The 5th District of Alabama takes in most of the state's TVA and space counties. TVA and the space program were primarily Democratic projects, and for years most voters here were staunch New Deal Democrats, liberal on economics and not much interested in race, like the longtime Senator John Sparkman, the party's vice presidential nominee in 1952. But professional and technical people in the space business tend to combine high-tech and traditional values, and this has made much of northern Alabama marginal-to-Republican country in the 1990s. The 5th District has voted Republican for president since the departure of Jimmy Carter, and in the 1990s it had seriously contested congressional elections.

The congressman from the 5th District is Bud Cramer Jr., a Democrat first elected in 1990. He was born in Huntsville, served as an Army tank officer after law school, beat the incumbent district attorney in 1980, at 33. In 1985 he set up the Child Advocacy Center, a child-friendly environment for abused children; as congressman, he set up a $5 million federal program to encourage such centers across the country. "We are the Mayo Clinic there in Huntsville of child abuse," he boasted. When Congressman Ronnie Flippo ran for governor in 1990, Cramer ran for Congress. He won the general election 2–1.

In the House, Cramer became a tireless booster of the beleaguered Space Station. He won funding for an Atlanta-Memphis highway through Huntsville, which he said would boost economic development. In the TVA tradition he supported the Democratic leadership on key issues. But his votes for the Clinton budget and tax package in 1993 and for the Clinton crime bill with its gun control provisions were unpopular locally, and were seized upon by Republican Wayne Parker, Huntsville native and son-in-law of Ways and Means senior Republican Bill Archer of Texas. With $288,000 from PACs, Cramer outspent Parker, and he had massive support from local media. But the issues worked against him, and he barely won, 50%–49%.

After that, Cramer has avoided liberal votes on visible issues and worked to get federal dollars and contracts. No project was too small. He fought a National Weather Service decision to close its Huntsville office, ultimately unsuccessfully, and broke ground for a Next Generation radar station in northeast Alabama to track the area's frequent tornadoes. Prior to the 2000 election, he announced that he had secured in an agriculture spending bill $725,000 for red snapper research, $600,000 for catfish disease research, and $500,000 for peanut allergy research.

With his seat on Appropriations, he became the first Blue Dog Democrat there. Cramer's overall voting record was in the middle of the House, but he voted conservative on key issues: He was one of 31 Democrats to vote for the Republicans' impeachment inquiry and one of 27 Democrats to vote for the Religious Freedom constitutional amendment, which would allow prayer in schools; he voted to ban partial-birth abortions and needle exchanges. The League of Conservation Voters put Cramer on its "dirty dozen" list in June 1998, saying that his environmental record "has taken a nose dive." But he also voted to allow abortions in military hospitals and against eliminating the National Endowment for the Arts. In 2001, he was one of only four Democrats to vote for both repealing the Clinton ergonomic standards and President Bush's income tax cuts.

With this dextrous balancing, Cramer has entrenched himself in the district. Against Republican Gil Aust, a Huntsville physician, he romped home 70%–30% in 1998. And Republicans did not run anyone against him two years later. After the 2000 election, Cramer was said to be under consideration for a job in the Bush administration. He also was touted as a possible challenger to Jeff Sessions in the 2002 Senate campaign but in May 2001 decided not to run. Cramer is among moderates of both parties and well positioned to exercise influence and seek bipartisanship in the 107th Congress. Since Democrats control redistricting in Alabama, they could tweak the lines to make the 5th District a bit more Democratic.

Cook's Call   *Probably Safe.* Though Cramer represents an increasingly conservative and suburban district, he continues to elude defeat. Redistricting will also be interesting to watch here: This district experienced some of most significant population growth in the state over the last 10 years.

THE PEOPLE: Pop. 2000: 654,886; Pop. 1990: 577,235, up 13.5% 1990–2000. 79.9% White, 16.2% Black, 1% Asian, 0.7% Amer. Indian, 1.5% Two+ races, 0.7% Other; 2% Hispanic Origin.

2000 Presidential Vote

Bush (R)	139,337	(55%)
Gore (D)	107,553	(43%)
Nader (Green)	3,282	(1%)
Others	2,619	(1%)

1996 Presidential Vote

Dole (R)	111,652	(49%)
Clinton (D)	98,401	(43%)
Perot (I)	18,403	(8%)

Rep. Bud Cramer, Jr. (D)

Elected 1990, 6th term; b. Aug. 22, 1947, Huntsville; home, Huntsville; U. of AL, B.S. 1969, J.D. 1972; Methodist; widowed.

Military Career: Army, 1972; Army Reserves, 1976–78.

Professional Career: Instructor, U. of AL Law Schl., Dir., Clinical Studies Program, 1972–73; Madison Cnty. Asst. Dist. Atty., 1973–75; Practicing atty., 1975–80; Madison Cnty. Dist. Atty., 1981–90; Founder, Natl. Children's Advocacy Ctr., 1985.

DC Office: 2367 RHOB 20515, 202-225-4801; Fax: 202-225-4392; Web site: www.house.gov/cramer.

District Offices: Decatur, 256-355-9400; Huntsville, 205-551-0190; Muscle Shoals, 205-381-3450.

Committees: *Appropriations* (19th of 29 D): Commerce, Justice & State; VA, HUD & Independent Agencies.

Group Ratings

	ADA	ACLU	AFS	LCV	CON	ITIC	NTU	COC	ACU	NTLC	CHC
2000	35	21	57	36	2	94	38	80	40	41	60
1999	55	—	83	25	71	—	24	72	41	—	—

National Journal Ratings

	1999 LIB	—	1999 CONS		2000 LIB	—	2000 CONS
Economic	52%	—	48%		50%	—	49%
Social	48%	—	52%		49%	—	50%
Foreign	54%	—	45%		56%	—	42%

Key Votes of the 106th Congress

1. Patient Bill of Rights	Y	5. Bar RU-486 $ for FDA	N	9. NATO War in Serbia	Y
2. Accelerate Min. Wage	Y	6. Display 10 Commandments	Y	10. Perm. Trade with China	Y
3. Strike Ban on Ergo. Stnd.	Y	7. Gun Show Bkgrnd. Checks	N	11. Debt Relief for 3rd World	N
4. Ovrd. Estate Tax Veto	Y	8. Ban Part.-Birth Abortion	Y	12. Drop Cuba Econ. Embargo	Y

Election Results

2000 general	Bud Cramer Jr. (D)	186,059	(89%)	($512,728)
	Alan Barksdale (LIB)	22,110	(11%)	
2000 primary	Bud Cramer Jr. (D)	unopposed		
1998 general	Bud Cramer Jr. (D)	134,819	(70%)	($1,122,250)
	Gil Aust (R)	58,536	(30%)	($819,992)

SIXTH DISTRICT

Birmingham, once one of America's booming industrial cities, then the site of violence in the civil rights revolution, now has future prospects far more hopeful than seemed possible even a decade ago. This is a new city by southern standards: Before the Civil War there was nothing here but a few creeks running below Red Mountain. But Red Mountain is almost pure iron ore, and by 1890 Birmingham had the South's largest steel mills. In the early 20th Century, as the statue of Vulcan, Roman god of fire and metalworking, looked out over the smokestack-rich valley, Birmingham seemed the most up-to-date and progressive city in the South. But the worldwide overcapacity in steel and technological obsolescence at home sent the American steel industry into long-term decline starting in the 1950s. Industrial Birmingham's political leaders plotted to avoid desegregation, and the city's violent reaction to civil rights—Police Commissioner Bull Connor set dogs and fire hoses against peaceful demonstrators, and Ku Klux Klansmen bombed the 16th Street

Baptist Church, killing four young girls in 1963, for which Thomas Blanton, 62, was convicted in May 2001, the second conviction of the four original suspects—made a vivid impression over the new medium of television news, spurring the Civil Rights Act of 1964, and created a reputation from which Birmingham still suffered a generation later.

But over the years, Birmingham developed a new economic base to generate growth and worked to improve race relations. Health care is one major industry: Birmingham has some of the largest and most advanced medical care centers in the South, and is especially renowned for its sports medicine facilities and specialists who have treated such greats as Michael Jordan. Banking is the other: While Atlanta's banks foundered and were acquired by outsiders, Birmingham became the largest southern banking center after Charlotte, North Carolina, with headquarters of SouthTrust, AmSouth Bancorp, Regions Financial, Compass Bancshares and Colonial Bancgroup. There is still racial polarization here. Most blacks live in Birmingham itself and the series of factory towns north of Red Mountain, an area that is about two-thirds black. A new Birmingham has grown up along the freeways south of Red Mountain, starting with the old high-income suburb of Mountain Brook and spreading south into Shelby County, whose booming suburbs grew 69% in the 1990s; the county is 90% white. Leaders of both races have promoted the Birmingham Pledge, a six-sentence promise to eliminate racism, and a week of pledge events in September 2000 featured a teen forum and town hall meeting on race relations. Signers have included President Clinton and South African Desmond Tutu.

The 6th Congressional District, which once included all of Birmingham and most of its suburbs, is now, thanks to prevailing interpretations of the 1982 Voting Rights Act amendments, the white Birmingham-area district. It includes only a small part of the city, plus the high-income suburbs south of Red Mountain and in Shelby County and the middle-income suburbs north of Birmingham. It runs south to the white areas of the university town of Tuscaloosa. This is one of the most Republican districts in the nation, voting 57% for George W. Bush in 2000.

The congressman from the 6th District is Republican Spencer Bachus. A Birmingham native, he owned a sawmill company and practiced law, and boasted that he was a good enough trial lawyer to have produced four straight acquittals in murder trials. Elected to the state legislature in 1982, he was an activist though one of very few Republicans. After running unsuccessfully for attorney general in 1990, he became Republican state chairman. When the new 6th District seat was drawn in 1992, he won a Republican runoff and defeated incumbent Ben Erdreich, moderate Democrat. Erdreich outspent Bachus nearly 2–1 and led in polls, but Bachus won 52%–45%.

Bachus has a mostly, though not quite totally, conservative voting record and has been an aggressive lawmaker and investigator. He enacted a resolution recognizing the contribution of the Birmingham Pledge. He won House passage of Senator Evan Bayh's bill to require the Justice Department to tabulate crimes against senior citizens. And, serving on the Transportation Committee, he was proud that Alabama highway spending grew by 61% in the 1998 highway bill.

As chairman of the House Banking General Oversight and Investigation Subcommittee, he discovered that the Community Development Financial Institute, which President Clinton established in the Treasury Department in 1994, directed $11 million in loans (one-third of its funds) to four banks with ties to Hillary Rodham Clinton without proper documentation; the two top CDFI officials resigned as a consequence. Earlier, he demanded Controller of the Currency Eugene Ludwig turn over papers of his meeting with leading bankers and Democratic fundraisers at a May 1996 White House "coffee." Bacchus also took on an unlikely cause: He became an unlikely crusader for international debt relief for poor Third World nations. After sending $1.20 of his own money to each House member—to demonstrate the cost to each American per year—he joined a broad coalition of domestic and international activists. His efforts, which included joining Ohio Democrat Tony Hall in a one-day fast to demand action, ultimately proved successful. He voted for permanent trade relations with China after winning concessions on imported coke, which is used in steel processing.

Bachus has not faced a competitive challenge for re-election. He has considered a statewide bid in 2002, which led Republican Secretary of State Jim Bennett to express interest in the House seat if there's an opening.

Cook's Call   *Safe*. Redistricting in 1991 helped to turn this once competitive district into the Republican stronghold that it is today. In 2000, Bush won by his largest margin in the state (41 %) here. It is not possible to alter the 6th much without upsetting the black majority of the 7th District. This seat should remain safe.

THE PEOPLE: Pop. 2000: 664,795; Pop. 1990: 577,170, up 15.2% 1990–2000. 82.1% White, 14.9% Black, 1.2% Asian, 0.3% Amer. Indian, 0.8% Two+ races, 0.7% Other; 1.8% Hispanic Origin.

2000 Presidential Vote
(Data not available as of June 1, 2001)

1996 Presidential Vote

Dole (R)	169,870	(68%)
Clinton (D)	68,545	(27%)
Perot (I)	10,995	(4%)

Rep. Spencer Bachus (R)

Elected 1992, 5th term; b. Dec. 28, 1947, Birmingham; home, Birmingham; Auburn U., B.A. 1969, U. of AL, J.D. 1972; Baptist; married (Linda).

Military Career: Natl. Guard, 1969–71.

Elected Office: AL Senate, 1983–84; AL House of Reps., 1984–87.

Professional Career: Owner, Lumber Co.; Practicing atty., 1972–92; AL Repub. Party Chmn., 1991–92.

DC Office: 442 CHOB 20515, 202-225-4921; Fax: 202-225-2082; Web site: www.house.gov/bachus.

District Offices: Birmingham, 205-969-2296; Northport, 205-333-9894.

Committees: *Financial Services* (6th of 37 R): Capital Markets, Insurance & Government Sponsored Enterprises; Financial Institutions & Consumer Credit (Chmn.); Housing & Community Opportunity. *Judiciary* (14th of 21 R): Courts, the Internet & Intellectual Property; The Constitution. *Transportation & Infrastructure* (11th of 42 R): Aviation; Railroads.

Group Ratings

	ADA	ACLU	AFS	LCV	CON	ITIC	NTU	COC	ACU	NTLC	CHC
2000	5	0	0	14	2	94	55	85	88	67	93
1999	20	—	16	0	10	—	54	76	84	—	—

National Journal Ratings

	1999 LIB	—	1999 CONS		2000 LIB	—	2000 CONS
Economic	41%	—	59%		29%	—	67%
Social	16%	—	82%		0%	—	79%
Foreign	15%	—	81%		33%	—	62%

Key Votes of the 106th Congress

1. Patient Bill of Rights	Y	5. Bar RU-486 $ for FDA	Y	9. NATO War in Serbia	N
2. Accelerate Min. Wage	N	6. Display 10 Commandments	Y	10. Perm. Trade with China	Y
3. Strike Ban on Ergo. Stnd.	N	7. Gun Show Bkgrnd. Checks	N	11. Debt Relief for 3rd World	Y
4. Ovrd. Estate Tax Veto	Y	8. Ban Part.-Birth Abortion	Y	12. Drop Cuba Econ. Embargo	N

Election Results

2000 general	Spencer Bachus (R)	212,751	(88%)	($577,565)
	Terry Reagin (LIB)	28,189	(12%)	
2000 primary	Spencer Bachus (R)	unopposed		
1998 general	Spencer Bachus (R)	154,761	(72%)	($603,504)
	Donna Wesson Smalley (D)	60,657	(28%)	($27,860)

SEVENTH DISTRICT

Alabama celebrates its black heritage more than any other state, building striking memorials to the civil rights movement in Montgomery and Birmingham, commemorating with dignified restraint a history that was full of raucous hatred and moving sacrifice. Blacks first came here as slaves; the last slave ship to the United States, the *Clotilde*, docked in Mobile in 1859, where its cargo was then set free. Blacks were part of the great migration into the cottonlands after the Jacksonians swept the Indians out of the Southeast and sent them on their Trail of Tears to what is now Oklahoma. Today, Alabama's rural blacks are still clustered in the Black Belt of fertile dark soil across the center of the state: Around Montgomery, where Rosa Parks refused to move to the back of a city bus in 1955 and a young minister named Martin Luther King Jr. led a bus boycott; and around Selma, founded by Alabama's one vice president, William Rufus King, and where Sheriff Jim Clark's troops beat up peaceful marchers on the Edmund Pettus Bridge in demonstrations that led to the march on Montgomery and the 1965 Voting Rights Act. The city's troubled past was recalled when federal prosecutors in May 2001 convicted Thomas Blanton, 62, of the murder of four black girls in the 1963 explosion of Birmingham's 16th Street Baptist Church; that incident became the topic of *Four Little Girls*, a film documentary by Spike Lee. All 10 of Alabama's majority-black counties are in the rich farm country of the Black Belt. But most Alabama blacks now live in urban areas, one-quarter in metropolitan Birmingham, the childhood home of Alma Powell, wife of Secretary of State Colin Powell, and of Bush National Security Advisor Condoleezza Rice.

The 7th Congressional District, with its convoluted boundaries, was created in 1992 as a black-majority district. Some 45% of its people live in the narrow valley of Birmingham and Jefferson County where the population is 75% black; another 13% are in an 80% black portion of Montgomery County. The rest of the district includes Black Belt counties where the Alabama and Tombigbee Rivers flow past old plantations, plus part of Tuscaloosa, home of the University of Alabama, and nearby Vance, site of the much sought-after new Mercedes factory. The district thus combines the remnants of Alabama's old cotton economy with neighborhoods built in the shadows of Birmingham's once booming steel mills. A 1997 lawsuit challenged the boundaries as racially motivated, but it was rejected by the U.S. Supreme Court in November 2000, when in any case it was too late to draw lines based on the 1990 Census.

The congressman from the 7th District is Earl Hilliard, the first black representative from Alabama since Republican Jeremiah Haralson retired in 1877, who later went west and, according to the Biographical Directory of the U.S. Congress, was "killed by wild beasts near Denver, Colorado, in 1916." Hilliard grew up in segregated Birmingham and was educated in historically black schools—Morehouse, Howard, Atlanta University. In 1974, at 32, he was elected to the Alabama legislature, one of the first blacks there since Reconstruction; 10 years later he became a committee chairman. He pushed for horse racing in Birmingham and sponsored tax abatement bills. In 1992 he outmaneuvered others and became the main Birmingham-based candidate for the new 7th District seat. The decisive Democratic primary was a "friends and neighbors" contest reminiscent of the old days of Southern white politics. Hilliard led in the primary with 31%, winning Jefferson County but running far behind elsewhere. The runoff was a contest with state Senator Hank Sanders, who won in his base, the Black Belt, and narrowly in Montgomery; but Hilliard's 71% in Jefferson County was enough for a 50.5%–49.5% victory.

In the House Hilliard has a largely liberal voting record. He voted for school prayer and flag amendments, but he has filed legislation to restore voting rights to former prisoners and eliminate mandatory minimum sentences for crack cocaine offenses. In August 1997 Hilliard visited Libya, despite its designation as a terrorist state, and was soon sharply criticized by the 6th District's Spencer Bachus. But the Treasury ruled that he didn't engage in financial transactions and the House ethics committee noted that he did not stamp his passport, with both declaring that he did not violate U.S. sanctions. He has called for a national commission to apologize for slavery and to decide on reparations: "It's often said that you can't fault the offspring of slaveholders. I would say that's incorrect because [some of] the offspring are still living off the wealth created by the labor of my ancestors. They are still benefiting from the work of my forefathers." He chaired the Congressional Black Caucus task force that helped to organize in October 2000 the Million Family March, sponsored by Nation of Islam leader Louis Farrakhan. On the House Agriculture Committee, he is the ranking Democrat on Rural Development and Research Subcommittee.

Although Hilliard has won re-election easily, he faced a competitive primary in 2000. Harvard-educated attorney Artur Davis of Birmingham cited Hilliard's trip to Libya and said he failed to aid his financially pressed district and that he had "deep vulnerabilities." Davis was enthusiastically endorsed by Birmingham Mayor Bernard Kincaid, who had replaced Richard Arrington, a longtime Hilliard ally. Davis also criticized Hilliard's support from the National Rifle Association and his votes against gun control. Hilliard, who largely ignored the challenge, won 58%–34%, though his margin in Jefferson County was only 51%–47%. In November Hilliard won 75%–23%, though the contest was closer in the rural areas. After being forced to defend himself against various campaign finance irregularities, Hilliard's campaign account was depleted after the election. Although the district seems certain to remain Democratic, redistricting and another primary challenge could pose risks for Hilliard.

Cook's Call   *Safe.* This district has grown the slowest of any in the state, with Birmingham losing more than 23,000 people over the last 10 years. But, the Voting Rights Act virtually precludes any changes in the overall make-up of this district. One of the top Democratic districts in the country, Gore beat Bush here by 46 % in 2000.

THE PEOPLE: Pop. 2000: 544,117; Pop. 1990: 577,430, down 5.8% 1990–2000. 28.7% White, 70% Black, 0.2% Asian, 0.2% Amer. Indian, 0.6% Two+ races, 0.3% Other; 1% Hispanic Origin.

2000 Presidential Vote
(Data not available as of June 1, 2001)

1996 Presidential Vote

Clinton (D)	150,271	(72%)
Dole (R)	53,565	(26%)
Perot (I)	5,080	(2%)

Rep. Earl Hilliard (D)

Elected 1992, 5th term; b. Apr. 9, 1942, Birmingham; home, Birmingham; Morehouse Col., B.A. 1964, Howard U., J.D. 1967, Atlanta U., M.B.A. 1970; Baptist; married (Mary).

Elected Office: AL House of Reps., 1974–80; AL Senate, 1980–92.

Professional Career: Practicing atty., 1972–92.

DC Office: 1314 LHOB 20515, 202-225-2665; Fax: 202-226-0772; Web site: www.house.gov/hilliard.

District Offices: Birmingham, 205-328-2841; Montgomery, 334-281-0531; Selma, 334-872-2684; Tuscaloosa, 205-752-3578.

Committees: *Agriculture* (6th of 24 D): Conservation, Credit, Rural Development & Research (RMM); Department Operations, Oversight, Nutrition & Forestry. *International Relations* (10th of 23 D): Africa.

Group Ratings

	ADA	ACLU	AFS	LCV	CON	ITIC	NTU	COC	ACU	NTLC	CHC
2000	90	71	100	57	24	60	19	52	12	12	7
1999	80	—	100	69	12	—	12	24	4	—	—

National Journal Ratings

	1999 LIB —	1999 CONS	2000 LIB —	2000 CONS
Economic	88% —	0%	74% —	26%
Social	67% —	32%	70% —	29%
Foreign	95% —	0%	77% —	21%

Key Votes of the 106th Congress

1. Patient Bill of Rights	Y	5. Bar RU-486 $ for FDA	N	9. NATO War in Serbia	Y
2. Accelerate Min. Wage	Y	6. Display 10 Commandments	N	10. Perm. Trade with China	N
3. Strike Ban on Ergo. Stnd.	Y	7. Gun Show Bkgrnd. Checks	N	11. Debt Relief for 3rd World	Y
4. Ovrd. Estate Tax Veto	N	8. Ban Part.-Birth Abortion	N	12. Drop Cuba Econ. Embargo	Y

Election Results

2000 general	Earl Hilliard (D)	148,243	(75%)	($432,730)
	Ed Martin (R)	46,134	(23%)	($18,431)
	Other	4,256	(2%)	
2000 primary	Earl Hilliard (D)	36,249	(58%)	
	Artur Davis (D)	20,973	(34%)	
	Wayne Sowell (D)	5,155	(8%)	
1998 general	Earl Hilliard (D)	unopposed		($212,829)

★ ALASKA ★

A laska is America in the Arctic, in the far northwest extension of North America, a state that was the creation of a federal government that it now often resents and an individualistic society that has responded to its unique situation in creative ways that commend themselves to the attention of what Alaskans call the Lower 48 or, more simply, Outside. Alaska would not be American at all but for the expansive dream of Secretary of State William Seward, who took advantage of a fleeting opportunity to create an American Pacific empire by purchasing it from Russia in 1867 for $7.2 million. The Alaska Territory owed most of its early growth to decisions made by the federal government. It started growing feverishly with the Klondike gold rush in 1897, just as William McKinley reaffirmed the gold standard. Anchorage, the major city here, had its beginnings in 1913 as the chief worksite of the federal government's Alaska Railroad. The Alcan Highway, connecting Alaska to the Lower 48, was built by the Army in the grim war days of 1942, when the Aleutian island of Attu was held by the Japanese, the only part of the United States occupied by a foreign enemy since the War of 1812. During the Cold War, Alaska was the only state abutting the Soviet Union, across the Bering Strait and over the North Pole. Even today Alaska remains militarily strategic, and the military remains a major presence, in Elmendorf Air Force Base near Anchorage and Fort Wainwright near Fairbanks. Alaska's giant size remains hard for Americans to comprehend: If superimposed on the Lower 48, it would stretch from Florida to southern California to Lake Superior. One-third of Alaskans have no access to the state's roads and are reachable only by boat or airplane; Alaska has per capita six times the number of pilots and 14 times the number of airplanes as the rest of the nation, 325 airports and another 1,100 designated landing areas. Yet only 626,000 of 281 million Americans live here, more than 40% in the Anchorage area, the rest in Fairbanks in the interior and Juneau in the Panhandle and scattered in small towns and Native settlements over millions of acres of stunning scenery.

Statehood was won in 1959, after a valiant campaign. But statehood did not end federal decision-making power over Alaska—or the widespread resentment of it. Alaska's economy at statehood depended on fishing, oil production in Cook Inlet around Anchorage and the military—all federally regulated or controlled. But less than a decade later Alaska's economy and public life were reshaped by the discovery of North Slope oil. It began suddenly, accidentally: On the day after Christmas 1967, at Prudhoe Bay on the Arctic coast, an undulating roar as loud as four jumbo jets directly overhead drew a crowd of 40 men, heavily clothed against the 30-below weather, to an oil rig. Suddenly a natural gas flare shot 30 feet straight up: This was the great 12 billion barrel North Slope oil field. Earlier oil companies had drilled seven dry wells on Prudhoe Bay, and ARCO chief executive Robert Anderson wouldn't have ordered this last try, except that he had a drilling rig nearby. This was the greatest oil strike ever in the United States and the beginning of much of today's Alaska.

Finding oil in Prudhoe Bay was something like finding it on the moon. It was not clear in 1967 who owned the oil or how it could be taken out. The Statehood Act of 1959 provided for the state to choose its own public lands, but only after settling Native land claims. Congress, not Alaska, settled such claims in the 1971 Alaska Native Claims Act which set up 12 regional and 220 village Native corporations, gave them $962 million and time to select their own 44 million acres, and ended the Interior Department's freeze that enabled the state to stake claims to mineral-rich acreage. The only feasible way to get the oil out—the Arctic Ocean ice only breaks up

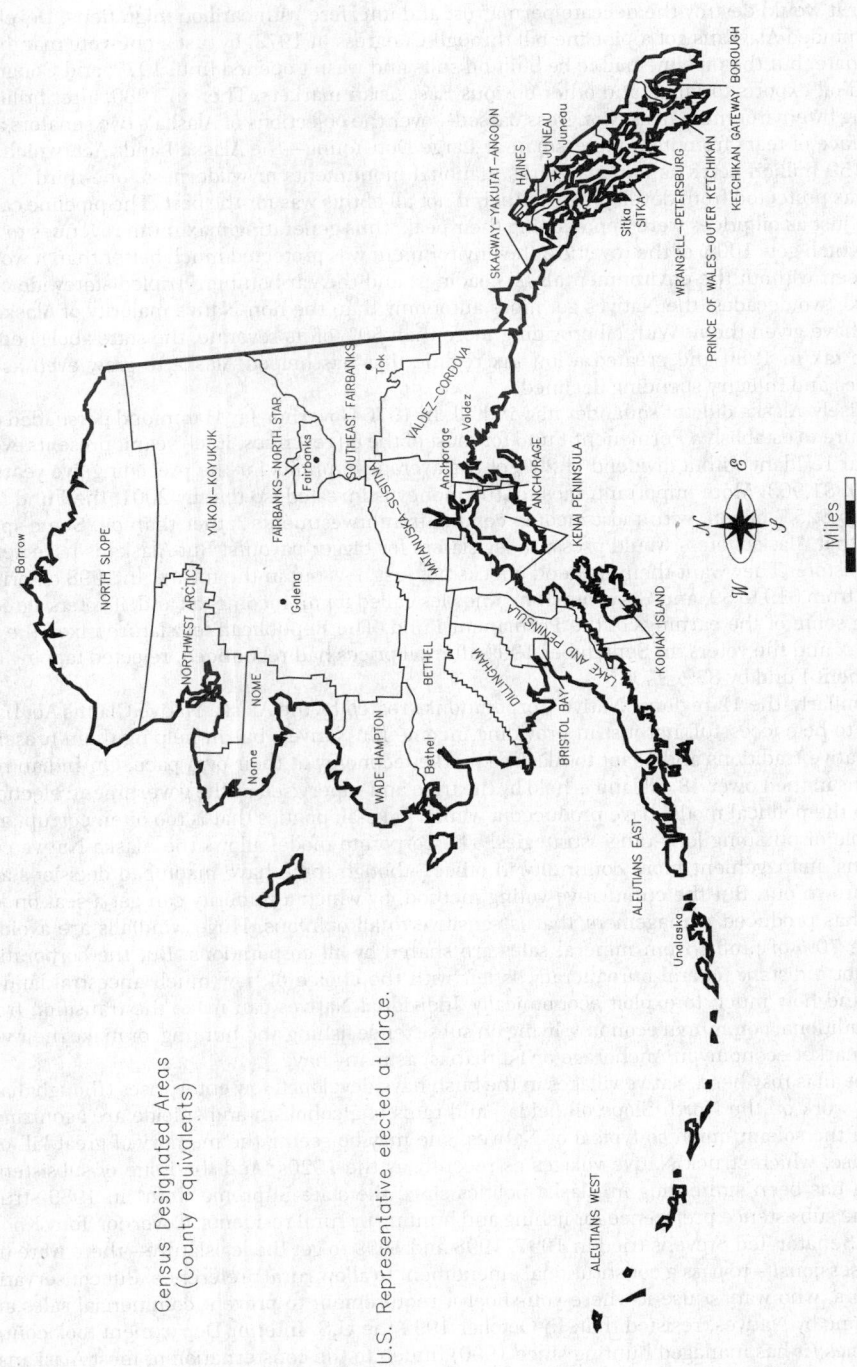

Census Designated Areas
(County equivalents)

U.S. Representative elected at large.

Miles

0 20 40 60 80

Copyright © 1993 by Election Data Services, Inc.

in late July for six weeks of the year—was a pipeline. But that was opposed by environmentalists for fear it would destroy the delicate permafrost and interfere with caribou migrations. Development-minded Alaskans got a pipeline bill through Congress in 1973, by just a one-vote margin in the Senate, but the pipeline had to be built on stilts and wasn't opened until 1977, and Congress banned oil exports to Japan and other obvious East Asian markets. Then in 1980, after brilliant lobbying by environmentalists, Congress passed—over the objections of Alaska's two senators and in the face of tears from its Congressman-at-Large Don Young—the Alaska Lands Act, which set aside 159 million acres as national parks, national monuments or wilderness: one-third of the state was protected from development. Much if not all of this was for the best. The pipeline came on line just as oil prices were approaching their peak, thus generating maximum revenues to the state, which gets 100% of the royalties; the environment was protected much better than it would have been without the environmentalists' goadings, and the caribou herd tripled statewide over the next two decades; the Natives got more autonomy than the non-Native majority of Alaskans would have given them. With oil providing more than 80% of its revenue, the state abolished its income tax in 1980 and created a low-tax regime that has helped Alaska to grow even as oil revenues and military spending declined.

Wisely, Alaska did not squander its windfall. In 1976 Governor Jay Hammond persuaded the legislature to establish a Permanent Fund for most of the oil revenues. Each year it presents every one-year resident with a dividend of 20% of the average of profits for the preceding five years—in 2000, $1,963. More important, most of the money is invested, so that by 2001, the Fund had grown to $25.7 billion, with most income coming from investments rather than oil. Some speculated that Alaska voters would pressure legislators for bigger payouts. But Alaskans have acted like investors: They want their dividend checks not just now but in the future. In 1998 oil prices dipped from $19 to $9, and Governor Tony Knowles called for an income tax and, if voters agreed, tapping some of the earnings of the Permanent Fund. The Republican legislature nixed the income tax and the voters, in September 1999 after oil prices had rebounded, rejected tapping the Permanent Fund by 83%–17%.

Similarly, the 12 regional Native Corporations created by the Alaska Native Claims Act have proved to be successful, not just in providing income for Natives, but in helping them preserve their Native traditions and adapt to Alaska's market economy at their own pace. On Indian reservations in the Lower 48, all land is held by the tribe and supervised by the government; elections held on the political model have produced a winner-take-all politics that is too often corrupt and incapable of pursuing long-range strategies. The corporate model allows the Alaska Native corporations' management more continuity in office—though some have made bad decisions and been thrown out. But the cumulative voting method, by which a minority can get a seat on the board, has produced management that is sensitive to all opinions. Huge windfalls are avoided because 70% of profits from mineral sales are shared by all corporations. But the corporation itself, not a distant federal bureaucracy, is left with the choice of how much ancestral land to retain and how much to exploit economically. Individual Natives can make the transition from their traditional communal economy, living on subsistence fishing and hunting, or make their way in the market economy in Anchorage or Fairbanks, as many have.

Not all is rosy here. Native villages in the bush have developed few enterprises (though many Natives work on the North Slope oil fields), and rates of alcoholism and suicide are agonizingly high. In the solemn mien so typical of Natives, one may be seeing the memory of great kill-offs by disease, which struck Native villages as recently as the 1920s. And the issue of subsistence hunting has been simmering in Alaska politics since the state Supreme Court in 1989 struck down the subsistence preference for fishing and hunting by rural residents. Governor Tony Knowles and Senator Ted Stevens tried in 1997, 1998 and 1999 to get the legislature—there were five special sessions!—to pass a constitutional amendment to allow rural preference. But conservative legislators, who want a use-it-where-you-shoot-it requirement to prevent commercial sales and overfishing by Natives, resisted that. In October 1999 the U.S. Interior Department took control of fisheries (it has managed hunting since 1990), much to the consternation of most Alaskans.

Alaska's three-member congressional delegation, with key committee positions and 80 years of seniority going into the 107th Congress, has fought hard but, up through early 2001, with little success to preserve logging in the Tongass National Forest and to allow oil drilling in the Arctic National Wildlife Refuge, which some claim contains 12 million barrels of oil. Oil drilling in ANWR, just east of Prudhoe Bay, seemed about to be approved by Congress when the Exxon *Valdez* ran aground in Prince William Sound in March 1989. That disaster killed the proposal, and the delegation spent most of its efforts on oil-spill legislation. In the 1990s, environmentalists made ANWR one of their top issues. Stevens got ANWR drilling into the reconciliation bill in 1995, but Bill Clinton vetoed it; George W. Bush backed it in the 2000 campaign and made it one of his major energy proposals, but in early 2001 it seemed possible that enough Republicans would oppose it to defeat it in Congress. The issue on the Tongass is whether logging should be allowed at all in his dense primeval forest, since it is already banned in 94% of its area; its great champion is Senator Frank Murkowski, who grew up in the area. The Forest Service under Clinton canceled an old contract to harvest timber and squelched attempts to revive it. In late September 1996, by holding up the national parks bill, Murkowski got a promise of two more years of logging and he went along with a May 1997 Forest Service logging plan. In January 2001 Clinton approved a Forest Service order banning new roads and commercial logging in 9.3 million acres in Alaska, a ban that threatened to cut the Tongass timber harvest 95% and eliminate 400 jobs. In May 2001 the Bush administration said it would carry out the rules with major amendments, but shortly afterward a federal judge rejected the order for its "irreparable long-term harm."

For all this controversy, on many issues there seems to be a convergence of opinion in Alaska, and considerable progress, as the classic battles between Alaska's boomers and Washington's environmentalists have become less important and Alaska's successes—for some of which all sides can claim some credit—have become more apparent. In August 1998 Interior Secretary Bruce Babbitt approved oil drilling in most of the 23-million acre National Petroleum Reserve-Alaska, just west of Prudhoe Bay, except for the bird-breeding swamps along Lake Teshekpuk. Oil companies wanted more drilling and some environmentalists wanted less; but Alaska environmentalists concede that today's drilling practices on the North Slope—with small "footprints" for wellheads and horizontal drilling to leave the surface mostly undisturbed—are much less objectionable than the techniques of 30 years ago. Similarly, environmentalists have endorsed, indeed helped prepare, the Yukon Pacific proposal to build a parallel pipeline to ship out the North Slope's currently unused natural gas, and environmental concerns helped convince Stevens and Murkowski to support a natural gas pipeline route from the North Slope to Fairbanks and then southeast along the Alaska Highway to the Midwest, over a plan to build it along the Arctic Sea and then southeast along the Mackenzie River—a project that seems more attractive now that natural gas prices are high. The Alaska Railroad, sold to the state by the federal government, is being run like a business and making a profit. The congressional delegation, with support from the Clinton administration, repealed the economically mindless prohibition on exporting Alaskan oil to its obvious and lucrative markets in Japan and East Asia. And they revised the Magnuson Act to protect seafood stocks from being overfished.

Alaska remains heavily dependent on oil and on the federal government, so there is some reason for unease about its economy. At the end of 1999 and 2000 oil prices shot up, and Alaska, despite a $44 million cut in military spending, got an additional $536 million in non-defense spending, on construction, highways, sewers and harbors—"the Stevens effect," some call it, since he is chairman of the Senate Appropriations Committee. But there are no guarantees that oil prices will stay high and Stevens will not remain in the Senate forever. Yet even when oil prices were low and before Stevens chaired Appropriations, population and jobs in Alaska were growing. One reason is tourism, with more than 1.3 million visitors a year, many on cruise ships and others headed to Denali National Park and Mount McKinley; Alaska is now trying to build winter tourism, with a ski resort in Girdwood near Anchorage, where winter temperatures are milder than in the Rockies. There are complaints about cruise ship waste dumping and Juneau slapped a $5 per passenger tax on them, but cruise ship passengers spend $160 million a year in Alaska. Another spur is the air freight business. Anchorage airport, near the top of the world, is seven hours from New York, Tokyo and London, and is a major transfer point for UPS and FedEx. More all-cargo, wide-bodied aircraft move through Anchorage International than any other U.S. airport. A third reason is that this is a low-tax, low-regulation state, which has been attracting independent-spirited, entrepreneurial-minded young families. Big institutions don't run things here: Unions, politically pivotal 25 years ago, aren't any more, and the oil companies, while not unpopular, weren't able to stop higher state oil taxes. The biggest private employers now are not the oil companies but Safeway and Providence Alaska Medical Center: This is an economy that buzzes with small business success.

Politically, Alaska is heavily Republican, with a libertarian streak. As one Matanuska-Susitna Republican says, "We are very individualistic people and we don't want dictatorship by government." In national politics it has been solidly Republican since the 1970s because national Democrats have favored locking up natural resources. In 2000 George W. Bush carried Alaska 59%–28%, carrying even the traditionally Democratic Panhandle and the Native-majority bush country beyond Anchorage and Fairbanks. But there were some quirky results: Girdwood, home of Alaska's one ski resort, cast a plurality of its votes for Ralph Nader. No Democrat has been elected to Congress since 1974, though some contests have been close. Democrat Tony Knowles was elected governor in 1994 and 1998, but the first time by only 536 votes and the second with 51% after the Republican Party repudiated its nominee and launched a write-in candidacy against him. The legislature is not only solidly Republican, but conservative, pushing constantly for spending cuts and bucking Knowles and Stevens on subsistence. Referendums show Alaskans to be increasingly conservative, though with a libertarian tinge: In 1998 they voted for medical marijuana, English-only and a ban on same-sex marriage, but a ban on wolf snaring was defeated. In 2000 they rejected an initiative that would not only have legalized marijuana but would have paid restitution to those convicted of marijuana offenses.

Some regional differences persist. Anchorage is much like a prosperous Rocky Mountains' metropolis with longer summer days and winter nights; it is affluent and booming, with perhaps the highest percentage of working women in the country. Politically, it is solidly Republican. So are the smaller settlements in a 200-mile arc around Anchorage, which have been growing even more rapidly: the Matanuska Valley (one of the few places in Alaska where farming is possible), Seward, the Kenai peninsula and the little port of Valdez at the southern terminus of the pipeline. Fairbanks, Alaska's second-largest city, is a pipeline and mineral service center deep in the interior, unprotected from Arctic winds in winter and crowds of mosquitoes in the brief but hot summer. It tends to vote Republican too.

The old Alaska, first settled by Russians, can be seen in the fishing towns of the Panhandle and in the capital of Juneau, located on an inlet of the Pacific up against a steep mountain; Alaskans voted to move the capital to a site near Anchorage in 1974 but defeated referendums to pay for it in 1978 and 1982, and Juneau prevailed in a 1994 referendum by 55%–45%. The Panhandle, historically Democratic, is now more evenly split. Mostly Democratic is the bush, the villages where Natives—Athabaskans, Aleuts, Yupiks, Inupiats—are the large majority. Natives make up 16% of Alaska's population and nearly 50% in the vast lands north and west of Anchorage and Fairbanks. They are greatly outnumbered and outvoted on many issues, and yet are the object of awed respect for their achievement in building civilizations in such a forbidding environment.

Governor   Tony Knowles, a Democrat who was elected governor in 1994 and 1998, was born in Oklahoma, served in the 82d Airborne in Vietnam, graduated from Yale (where he was a fraternity brother of George W. Bush), and came to Alaska in 1968 and worked as a roughneck. In 1969 he started a hamburger chain called the Grizzly Burger, then later started the Downtown Deli; in the mode of local businessmen, he served on the council (the Anchorage Assembly) and as mayor from 1982–87. He built the Alaska Center for Performing Arts, the Egan Convention Center, and the 11-mile Tony Knowles Coastal Trail, used for cyclists and joggers, plus the most extensive cross-country ski trails of any city in the nation. In 1990 he ran for governor and lost to Walter Hickel, 39%–31%. In 1994 Knowles ran again, against Republican Jim Campbell and Lieutenant Governor Jack Coghill, who ran on Hickel's Alaska Independence ticket. Campbell started out favored but was hurt by his attacks on Knowles, who won by 536 votes, 41.1%–40.8%, with 13% for Coghill. Knowles had huge leads in the bush and Juneau, but ran behind in urban areas.

In office, Knowles clashed repeatedly with the conservative Republican legislature. In 2000 legislative leaders boasted that they had cut $250 million in spending from Knowles' budgets over five years. But they reached some agreement on welfare reform and teacher tenure. Knowles has stressed "jobs and families" issues, spotlighting child abuse and providing health care insurance for low-income families with children. He worked closely with the oil and tourism industries, urging the Clinton administration to approve oil drilling in the National Petroleum Reserve-Alaska, as it did in August 1998. He angered some Native leaders by appealing the 9th Circuit *Venetie* decision declaring a Native village "Indian territory"; this was unanimously reversed by the U.S. Supreme Court. He did not support the congressional delegation on logging in the Tongass National Forest, but advanced his own initiatives to keep the Ketchikan pulp mill running. He unsuccessfully tried to get the legislature to put a constitutional amendment on subsistence fishing and hunting before the voters, and was unable to prevent the Interior Department from taking over regulation. He proposed the nation's highest taxes on tobacco and alcohol, and eventually got a $1 cigarette tax—America's second highest.

In 1998, when Knowles ran for re-election, no governor had won a consecutive second term in 20 years. But conservative Republicans were split between state Senator Robin Taylor and Anchorage lawyer Wayne Ross, who both were heavily outspent by former University of Alaska Anchorage Chancellor and newspaper owner John Lindauer. Lindauer left the chancellor's office under criticism and his newspaper chain folded in 1992. But he had married a rich Chicago woman in 1995 and proceeded to spend $857,000 on his primary campaign. In Alaska's all-party primary, Knowles won just 36%; Lindauer's 23% was ahead of Taylor and Ross, who won 16% each. But Lindauer's residency and financing proved to be fishy. Alaska requires seven years of residency for a governor, but for two years in the 1990s Lindauer had not applied for his Permanent Fund dividend. On October 20, the state Republican party withdrew its support for Lindauer and backed Robin Taylor as a write-in candidate. Knowles, generally popular and flush with contributions from state and oil company employees, cruised to a 51% victory. Lindauer won only 18% of the vote, while Taylor took 20%.

In his second term Knowles continued to spar with the legislature. With oil prices plummeting to $9 in December 1998, he proposed an income tax and tapping into the earnings of the Permanent Fund. The legislature rejected the income tax and voters in September 1999, after oil prices had started rising, opposed tapping the Permanent Fund by an 83%–17% margin. Knowles kept pressing, without success, for a long-term budget plan, to accommodate wildly oscillating oil prices; the budget was balanced by drawing on the state's reserve, but at rates that threatened to deplete it in several years. Knowles proposed a major school building program and called for a "children's budget": more money for Head Start, child care and foster care, background checks for foster parents, a Quality Schools Initiative to help students prepare for the new high school exit exams. He beat back the legislature's attempts to stop the southward extension of the Tony Knowles Coastal Trail. In 2000 he declined to order a kill-off of wolves threatening moose near McGrath on the Iditarod Trail (where the 1,160-mile Iditarod sled dog race is held every winter) and tried to stop overfishing of salmon in the Yukon and Kuskokwin Rivers. In September 2000 he lambasted the cruise ship industry for discharging waste in the coastal waters of Southeast Alaksa.

The energy industry has consumed much of Knowles' attention. When BP Amoco announced its proposed takeover of Arco in summer 1999, Knowles was alarmed that one company would own about 70% of the North Slope oil fields and the pipeline. He negotiated and in December 1999 got BP Amoco to agree to sell some oil leases and part of its production and pipeline ownership. In February 2000 he defended the merger against the FTC's 3–2 decision to oppose it. Like most Alaskans, Knowles has consistently and strongly supported oil drilling in the Arctic National Wildlife Reserve. When former President Jimmy Carter came to Anchorage in August 2000 to celebrate the 20th anniversary of the Alaska Lands Act, Knowles was absent at the celebrations. When Carter called on Bill Clinton to declare ANWR a national monument, Knowles responded in a blistering letter. "I feel you abused this welcome by your actions yesterday. Without any meaningful dialogue with the people of Alaska, you used our state as a media prop and platform to project your message to President Clinton. . . . You are wrong in calling for executive action at the midnight hour instead of an open, public democratic process." Little wonder that during the Florida recount there was speculation that Knowles might serve in a Bush, but not in a Gore, cabinet.

Knowles is term-limited and cannot run again in 2002. The new governor will evidently not face Alaska's old all-party primary, which in a California case was outlawed by the U.S. Supreme Court in 2000. For 2000 the state had a makeshift system, a Republican primary for registered Republicans only and a simultaneous all-other-party primary for all the other parties. For 2002 the legislature may make modifications: The Republicans want to keep other voters out of their primary while the Democrats, who have benefited from the all-party primary in gubernatorial elections, want the their ballot open to independent voters. In spring 2001, the only Democrat mentioned as a serious candidate was Lieutenant Governor Fran Ulmer. Potential Republicans include state Senators Loren Leman, Robin Taylor and Drue Pearce, former Anchorage Mayor Rick Mystrom, 1998 candidate Wayne Ross, state Representative Gail Phillips and Alaska Railroad Board Chairman Johne Binkley. There is the possibility, widely mooted every four years, that Senator Frank Murkowski might run.

Cook's Call   *Probable Republican Pick Up.* Democrats will be hard-pressed to hold on to the governorship after Knowles' eight-year run. The state party does not have much of a bench and enthusiasm seems limited, particularly given Bush's 31-point win last November. The Republican field, however, has yet to emerge as potential candidates are waiting to see whether Senator Frank Murkowski will run.

Senior Senator   No other senator fills so central a place in his state's public and economic life as Ted Stevens of Alaska. "They sent me here," Stevens said in one impassioned debate, "to stand up for the state of Alaska." Stevens is now the second most senior Republican senator, and ranking member of the Appropriations Committee and of its Defense subcommittee; he has also been for two decades the leading public policymaker for and about Alaska. "We ask for special consideration," Stevens is not too shy to say, "because no one else is that far away, no one else has the problems that we have or the potential that we have, and no one else deals with the federal government day in and day out the way we do." Probably more than any other senator, Stevens has shaped the public institutions and private economy of his state.

He has had plenty of training. Stevens grew up in Indiana and California in very modest surroundings, served in World War II flying C-46s and C-47s, graduated from UCLA and Harvard Law, then moved to Alaska in 1950, driving up the Alaska Highway with his new bride. He was U.S. attorney in Fairbanks and worked in the Interior Department in Washington, served in the legislature in Juneau and was appointed to the Senate by Governor Walter Hickel in December 1968, at 45. He quickly gained a seat on Appropriations and worked on Alaska issues of all description. He has not been entirely successful. He could not stop the Alaska Lands Act in 1980 and could not get approval of Arctic National Wildlife Refuge oil drilling in 1991 or 1995. But he played a major role on the Native Claims Act in 1971 and got the oil pipeline through by one vote in 1973. In 1995 he finally secured the repeal of the 1977 law forbidding exports of Alaskan oil, thus opening up the obvious East Asian markets. He managed the oil spill bill of 1989 in response to the *Valdez* accident, requiring double hulls and compensating Alaska.

When he succeeded Mark Hatfield as chairman of the Appropriations Committee in 1997, Stevens told colleagues, "Senator Hatfield had the patience of Job and the disposition of a saint. I don't. The watch has changed. I'm a mean, miserable SOB." But if he is terrible-tempered (or wants others to think so), he is also hard-working. On the Defense subcommittee, he has generally supported robust defense spending and has been an advocate of missile defense. He works hard to fund the National Guard, to raise military salaries and to keep troops in readiness. When House Defense Appropriations Subcommittee Chairman Jerry Lewis moved to cut off the F-22 jet fighter, Stevens was its great champion and produced a compromise that allowed development to proceed if the jet could pass flight tests. He worked to stop Clinton administration changes in the Army Corps of Engineers.

Since he became Appropriations chairman, Alaskans have started referring matter-of-factly to "Stevens money" for projects he has been able to fund. Stevens sees his work in a broader context: "Congress has not awakened to the fact that we've got a state with one-fifth the land in this country. My mission is to try to make Congress understand that the promise of statehood is that we should have the ability to establish a workable private-enterprise economy in the areas of Alaska that want it. And that's basically 90% of the state." His prowess is legendary. In 1998 Stevens sought a land trade for a seven-mile road through the Izembeck National Wildlife Refuge—which the Clinton Interior Department wanted to declare off-limits—so that the tiny Aleutian village of King Cove would have access to medical facilities. The administration offered three alternatives, and Stevens took all three: $37.7 million for an airport road, medical clinic and doctor and nurse. In 1999 Stevens got, often through earmarks on appropriations, $22 million to compensate loggers for restrictions on the Tongass National Forest, $26 million to relieve southeastern Alaska fishermen, research on fetal alcohol syndrome, research into weather in the Bering Sea, and the Anchorage Museum of History and Art. In 2000 Stevens got $55 million for rural water and sewers, $80 million for highways and transportation, $20 million for the Alaska Railroad in Fairbanks, $45 million for the Ship Creek train and bus station in Anchorage, and $10 million in disaster aid because of the Bering Sea snow crab harvest collapse. He funded a $30 million Arctic Region Supercomputing Center in Fairbanks, which helped to triple in 2000 federal funding of the University of Alaska. He has boosted funding for Boys and Girls Clubs, for the National Guard's Challenge boot camps for troubled teens. Defense spending in Alaska dipped in 2000, but total federal spending increased by $512 million. As the *Anchorage Daily News* wrote, "It's a good bet that Stevens is the second-largest engine of the Alaska economy."

In 2000 federal spending per capita in Alaska was $8,521, the highest in the nation, and Citizens Against Government Waste put Stevens at the top of their list in their "pig book." Stevens is unapologetic. And even his critics must concede that he does not shovel money into projects willy-nilly; his knowledge of detail is astonishing, and he is prepared to defend every single project on the merits. Issues involving tiny villages or a few fishermen get his attention: He intervened to exempt Alaska from Endangered Species limits on chinook salmon, to provide $30 million for research on the decline of the Stellar sea lion (holding up passage of the whole federal budget on the latter in December 2000), and to ban Native subsistence hunting of Cook Inlet beluga whales absent an agreement with the National Marine Fisheries Service. Stevens has worked tirelessly with Alaska Native leaders, skillfully eliciting consensus when opinion is divided, getting more health and sanitation aid to bush villages and funding for health research on fetal alcohol syndrome and cancers common among Natives, and allowing the CIRI Native corporation to raise capital by reselling its wireless licenses earlier than allowed under FCC small business rules. He tends to set the consensus on larger Alaska issues, hailing the concessions Governor Tony Knowles exacted in return for approval of BP Amoco's takeover of Arco and favoring the Fairbanks-Alaska Highway route for a natural gas pipeline. He generally works in tandem with colleagues Frank Murkowski and Don Young, though at one point he disagreed with Murkowski's push to continue allowing commercial fishing in Glacier Bay National Park.

After surgery for prostate cancer in 1991, Stevens pushed for more funding for breast, cervical and prostate cancer research, plus telemedicine projects to connect rural Alaskans to hospitals and specialists. He is a big booster of exercise and physical education programs. He supports the Corporation for Public Broadcasting: Alaska's public TV and radio stations have the nation's largest audience shares. He helped to pass the 1999 law allowing satellite broadcasters to beam local network stations into local markets. And, with the large government work force in high-cost Alaska, he supports increased salaries and benefits for federal workers and argues volubly for higher salaries for senators and Senate staffers.

Stevens's work has not gone unappreciated. In January 2000 he was named Alaskan of the Century; he responded, "I can think of at least two dozen people who deserve it more than I." In May 2000 a Ted Stevens Foundation was established, to dispose of his papers. In July 2000 Anchorage Airport was named the Ted Stevens International Airport and the Challenger Center in Kenai became the Ted and Catherine Stevens Center for Space Science Technology. Stevens has been re-elected easily. His toughest competition recently came in the August 1996 primary when a banker and former legislator spent $1.3 million of his own money and charged that Stevens was insufficiently conservative. Stevens won 59%–27%. The Democratic nominee that fall, former Anchorage school board member Theresa Obermeyer, blamed Stevens for her husband's failure to pass the Alaska bar on 22 separate tries; she sometimes wore black-and-white prisoner stripes and a ball-and-chain to his public events. Democratic Governor Tony Knowles announced he was voting for Stevens, who won 77%, followed by Green Party candidate Jed Whittaker with 13%, and Obermeyer with 10%. No one doubts Stevens will win re-election in 2002. In 2003 the Republicans' six-year term-limit on chairmanships will force him to relinquish the Appropriations chair, but he has said he will claim the chairmanship (or ranking minority position) on Commerce.

Cook's Call   *Safe.* On the Senate Appropriations Committee, Stevens delivers for Alaska and voters there seem to know who butters their bread. Stevens won 77% in his 1996 re-election bid and should almost match that in 2002, with only nominal opposition.

Junior Senator   Frank Murkowski, first elected to the Senate in 1980, is ranking member of the Energy and Natural Resources Committee. Murkowski grew up in Seattle and Ketchikan, served in the Coast Guard in Alaska, and became a banker in Fairbanks. A department head under Governor Walter Hickel in the 1960s, he ran for Congress and lost in 1970. He was elected to the Senate in 1980 by winning 54% against liberal Democrat Clark Gruening.

Murkowski has played a major role on environmental and energy issues. In 1996 he produced a parks bill giving legal status to the Presidio Trust in San Francisco, Sterling Forest in New York and New Jersey, the Tallgrass Prairie Natural Preserve in Kansas, the New Bedford Whaling National Park, and the Selma-to-Montgomery National Historic Trail. He tried to hold it up in October 1996 to get concessions on the Tongass, then allowed it to go through. He has been an advocate of storing all high-level nuclear waste at a site in Yucca Mountain in Nevada, a proposal resisted fiercely by Nevada senators, backed up for eight years by the veto of Bill Clinton, who carried the state twice on this issue. In 1997 he passed a bill for interim storage at Nevada through the Senate, and a version passed the House; but the Senate vote, 65–34, was two short of a veto override. In February 2000 he was trying to provide for temporary storage, but dropped a provision requiring the Energy Department to pay for storing spent nuclear fuel at reactors across the country after seven governors objected. Again the bill passed by a wide margin, but two votes short of a veto override. In 1999 Murkowski worked for a law creating a new agency in the Energy Department to handle nuclear weapons research and production. He supported the Conservation and Reinvestment Act in 2000, despite opposition from many Republicans, but it passed only after dropping provisions making federal payments for state land purchases an entitlement, with less annual funding. In 2000 he sponsored a bill to provide $2 billion over 10 years to help businesses develop anti-pollution technologies. He has sponsored a bill to separate Alaska and five other western states from the 9th Circuit Court of Appeals, whose often liberal decisions on resource issues have been overturned in 77% of cases heard by the U.S. Supreme Court.

Murkowski has worked on East Asia issues, from Taiwan to North Korea, which he visited; in late 1994 he criticized the Clinton administration's accord with North Korea, but declined to try to overturn it, and has said he is anxious to facilitate "meaningful dialogue" between North and South Korea. Somewhat closer to home, he has criticized working conditions and human rights abuses in the Commonwealth of the Northern Mariana Islands, and in 2000 got the Senate to pass unanimously a bill to change those conditions. But on this issue he had solid opposition from his Alaska colleague Don Young, then chairman of the corresponding House committee, who refused to allow a bill to come up. They differ also on territorial issues: Young sponsored a bill for a referendum on statehood in Puerto Rico, which passed the House 209–208 in March 1998 but Murkowski saw that it went nowhere in the Senate.

Naturally, Murkowski has been a major force on Alaska issues. He helped secure a ban on drift net fishing in international waters; the Native Languages Preservation Act, initiating contacts between Alaska and Siberia; lifting of the ban on Alaskan oil exports, a 1977 policy that stayed on the books until November 1995. He has been frustrated in attempts to allow oil drilling in the Arctic National Wildlife Reserve. He opposed making ANWR a national monument, and in February 2001 introduced another bill to allow ANWR drilling, which is strongly supported by President Bush. Murkowski has opposed Clinton administration attempts to stamp out logging in the Tongass National Forest, but the amount of timber taken there declined 75% in the 1990s. He did obtain commitments for a dependable timber supply plan for the pulp mill in Ketchikan, where he grew up, and worked successfully for large amounts in compensation; he also supported the 2000 law requiring steady federal payments for counties and cities which lost tax revenue from federal bans on logging. He worked for an October 2000 tax bill amendment worth $40 million in Medicaid payments to Alaska. In October 2000, working with Don Young, he got authorization for a $384 million electric power grid for southeast Alaska; this was a classic example of log rolling, in which the two got critical support from colleagues by supporting a $75 million Navajo electrification project, $291 million to compensate South Dakota for payments owed to the Sioux, and extension of a Civil War battlefield in Richmond, Virginia. In 2000 he sponsored a law that banned waste dumping by cruise ships inside the three-mile limit. He got a commission to study the extension of the Alaska Railroad to Canada. He questioned Interior's requiring of cumulative environmental impact statements to secure approval of the oil companies' pipeline lease, which expires in December 2003. He was the first member of the Alaska delegation to support BP Amoco's takeover of Arco after BP Amoco agreed with Governor Tony Knowles to sell off some assets. On many of these matters, Murkowski worked harmoniously with Ted Stevens, sometimes with one taking the lead, sometimes the other, though they have differed on a few issues, notably on subsistence hunting and fishing, and on commercial fishing in Glacier Bay National Park.

Murkowski has been re-elected three times in contests that attracted little attention outside Alaska. In 1986 and 1992 Murkowski won by 54%–44% and 53%–38%. In 1998 he was pressed to, but decided not to, run against Governor Knowles. Murkowski's Democratic opponent had run unsuccessfully for mayor of Juneau, state House and the U.S. Senate. Murkowski won 74%–20%. In February 2001 Murkowski said he would consider running for governor and would announce a decision by September. He was considered a heavy favorite to win if he ran, just as he would be for re-election in 2004.

Representative-At-Large   Don Young has been Alaska's congressman-at-large since 1973. He is a one-time tugboat captain on the Yukon and the only licensed mariner in Congress—in his words, "not one of these smooth, namby-pamby politicians." He is a hot-tempered, salty-tongued true believer, given to malapropisms ("Pribilof's dog" and "bladderdash") and provocative insults (Republicans soft on the environment are "squishies"). Young grew up in rural California, served in the Army, then moved to Alaska, captained his tugboat and was elected mayor of Fort Yukon. He was elected to the legislature in 1966 and ran for Congress in 1972; his opponent, incumbent Nick Begich, was killed in a plane crash, and Young won the March 1973 special election to succeed him. Young is not a free-market conservative, and casts many liberal economic votes; but he is a cultural and foreign policy conservative, and an unceasing advocate of what he considers Alaska's interests.

Young has done much of his legislating on the Resources Committee, where from 1985–1995 he was ranking minority member and from 1995–2001 chairman. Resources handles many Alaska issues, and in the 1970s and 1980s it was packed with members, including some Republicans, who opposed Young's positions and followed the lead of national environmental organizations. Their numbers were trimmed after the Republican victory of 1994, but environmental groups still have great sway on the floor of the House, where many Republicans from the Northeast, Florida and Arizona are eager to score high on the groups' scoresheets; that often comes at Alaska's, or Young's, expense. Alaska's two senators can use the Senate's dilatory rules to get their way; in the tightly controlled House, Young can be efficiently steamrollered, as he was often when in the minority—most notably when the Alaska Lands Act passed in 1980. He was stymied as well by Bill Clinton's vetoes, particularly after the House finally approved oil drilling in Arctic National Wildlife Refuge in 1995 and when Congress rallied to maintain logging in the Tongass National Forest. He was stymied in the House in his efforts to rewrite the Endangered Species Act, on which his aggressive efforts in 1995 antagonized some other Republicans. But he did succeed in allowing gambling on Alaska cruise ships inside the three-mile limit. He is not afraid to make enemies and name names: in 1998 he inquired whether Forest Service employees were members of environmental groups that made deals with the office without notifying affected landowners; in 1999 he charged that an Interior appointee was turning over negative information on Republican congressmen to the Democrats' campaign committee (he was, and he resigned); in 2000 he sought a contempt resolution against an environmental group which brought a lawsuit and paid Interior and Energy officials who provided information with whistleblower fees of $383,000.

But Young has also shown a talent for consensus. In 1997 he passed, by 419–1, the National

Wildlife Improvement Act, which sets new guidelines for the nation's 500-plus wildlife refuges. The bill, endorsed by Clinton and environmental groups, allows for recreational activities that are compatible with the refuges' conservation mission. He steered a reform of the 30-year-old ANWR Act to passage, with the help of its original sponsor John Dingell, by 388–37 in October 1995; but the Senate failed to act on it. With memories of Alaska's struggle for statehood, Young has been sympathetic to advocates of statehood for Puerto Rico and in 1998 spent much time drawing up a bill setting terms for a plebiscite there with alternatives intended to be acceptable to Congress. This was a special project of then-Speaker Newt Gingrich, who thought it would make Republicans more attractive to Hispanic voters. Young labored hard and in March 1998 his bill passed by a 209–208 margin, with most yes votes coming from Democrats. But it went nowhere in the Senate. The pro-statehood party in Puerto Rico sponsored a referendum in December 1998, in which statehood finished second to "none of the above" by a 50%–46% margin. Another major issue for Young is missile defense. He vigorously and persistently opposed the 1995 Clinton National Intelligence Estimate that asked whether the U.S. would be safe from a hostile missile force for the next 15 years; Alaska and Hawaii, Young argued persuasively, are not excluded from the constitutional requirement that the federal government provide for the common defense. In fact, Alaska is now vulnerable to North Korean missiles, and Young will surely keep pushing for missile defense.

Young has had his disagreements, some of them stormy, with Alaska's two senators, though mostly the delegation works closely together. He saved Ted Stevens's Denali Commission by making a timely point of order when it was zeroed out in an appropriation bill in October 1999. He attacked Frank Murkowski's cruise ship bill in September 2000 as unnecessary and perhaps impinging on fishing fleets. Yet in October he was working with Murkowski to authorize a $384 million electric power grid for southeast Alaska. Young's principal focus in 2000 was on the Conservation and Reinvestment Act, to provide federal dollars for state purchases of land. His original version would require that $3 billion be spent every year, independent of the appropriations process, for 15 years; Alaska would be guaranteed $163 million a year in compensation for the environmental costs of oil drilling, more than all but two other states. This was opposed by many conservative Republicans as a federal power grab, but Young pushed it through the House by a wide margin in May 2000—"the crowning achievement of his career," said the *Anchorage Daily News*. But it was not a popular cause in the Senate, where Rocky Mountain Republicans carry greater weight and others thought the money should be subject to the appropriations process, and the Clinton administration moved toward opposing it. Finally, in October 2000 a scaled-down version—CARA lite, Murkowski called it—was passed as part of the Interior appropriation; it authorized $12 billion over six years, subject to appropriators, with about $50 million a year authorized for Alaska.

But Young was already looking ahead to getting around appropriators. House Republican rules limited him to six years as chairman of Resources but didn't prevent him from chairing another committee. And Young was second in seniority to Chairman Bud Shuster on Transportation and Infrastructure. Under Shuster's chairmanship, the committee passed huge transportation bills, with local projects earmarked for every cooperative member, and funding guaranteed through the gas and other dedicated taxes without having to go through the appropriators. In consequence, it became the largest committee in the House; members got even more generous slices of pork. In March 2000 Young criticized Murkowski for supporting a suspension of the gas tax as "absolutely the dumbest thing ever thought of"—a remark that makes sense if you are about to become chairman of Transportation. Young got the chairmanship in December 2000, while some speculated that Shuster might retain power by chairing a huge Surface Transportation Subcommittee, which would get first cut at reauthorizing the transportation bill in 2003. But as the 107th Congress assembled, Shuster abruptly announced that he was resigning, and Young could look forward to a placid time chairing a committee much less partisan than Resources, on which no one would object to his helping Alaska. As he said, "It will be great for the state. Our state is in the embryo stage as far as infrastructure is concerned."

Young has had his ups and downs with Alaska voters over the years, with significant opposition in 1978, 1984, 1986, 1990 and 1992. For years the *Anchorage Daily News'* criticisms hurt him in that usually Republican city, but his work for Native causes (he has pushed constantly for more federal jobs for Natives, as promised in the Alaska Native Claims Act) helped him run well ahead of party lines in the bush. As chairman, he has won by wide margins: 63%–35% in 1998; 70%–17% over Democrat Clifford Greene, with 8% for Green Party nominee Anna Young, in 2000.

Cook's Call   *Safe*. Don Young's controversial and colorful style caused Democrats to consistently place this district on their target lists through the 70s and 80s. Now that he chairs the Transportation Committee, any hopes of Democrat's knocking Young off have evaporated. When Young eventually steps aside, the voting patterns of the state are so Republican that only a Democrat with some extraordinary personal appeal would have a reasonable chance of picking up this seat.

Presidential politics   In presidential elections, Alaska votes Alaska issues, but this was not always so: In 1960 and 1968 its votes came eerily close to the national average. Since then it has voted against the national Democrats: In the year of the Alaska Lands Act, it gave only 26% of its votes to Jimmy Carter, who in some places ran behind Libertarian Ed Clark. In 1992 Ross Perot won 28% here, his second-best showing in the country. In 2000 George W. Bush won 59%–28%, but Ralph Nader got 10% of the vote—his best showing in the country. There was a big gender gap: men voted 65%–24% for Bush, which recalls the plaint of Alaskan women who are outnumbered by men: "the odds are good but the goods are odd."

Alaska has no presidential primary. Party true believers tend to dominate the caucuses. In the January 1996 straw poll or "beauty contest," Alaska Republicans voted 33% for Pat Buchanan, 31% for Steve Forbes, and 17% for Bob Dole. This gave Buchanan the confidence and verve he showed weeks later in Louisiana, where he beat Phil Gramm, and in other early contests climaxed by his win in New Hampshire on February 20. But Buchanan got only 2% here in November 2000. In November 1999 the Republican Party committee voted 39–36 to hold precinct caucuses and a straw poll on January 24, 2000. About 4,000 Alaskans voted, and George W. Bush led Forbes by 5 votes. Alaska, unlike Florida, didn't have a recount.

THE PEOPLE: Pop. 2000: 626,932; Pop. 1990: 550,043, up 14% 1990–2000. 0.2% of U.S. total, 48th largest; 69.3% White, 3.5% Black, 4% Asian, 15.6% Amer. Indian, 0.5% Hawaiian, 5.4% Two + races, 1.6% Other; 4.1% Hispanic Origin. 6.6% Unemployment. 2000 Voting age pop.: 436,215. 2000 Turnout: 281,812; 65% of VAP. Registered voters (2000): 469,866; 76,248 D (16%), 115,966 R (25%), 277,652 unaffiliated and minor parties (59%).

POLITICAL LINEUP: Governor, Tony Knowles (D); Lt. Gov., Fran Ulmer (D); Atty. Gen., Bruce M. Botelho (D); Commissioner of Revenue, Wilson Condon (D); State Senate, 20 (6 D, 14 R); Senate President, Rick Halford (R); Majority Leader, Loren Leman (R); State House, 40 (13 D, 27 R); House Speaker, Brian Porter (R). Senators, Ted Stevens (R) and Frank Murkowski (R). Representative, 1 R at large.

ELECTIONS DIVISION: 907-465-4611; **FILING DEADLINE FOR U.S. CONGRESS:** June 1, 2002.

2000 Presidential Vote			1996 Presidential Vote		
Bush (R)	167,398	(59%)	Dole (R)	122,746	(51%)
Gore (D)	79,004	(28%)	Clinton (D)	80,380	(33%)
Nader (Green)	28,747	(10%)	Perot (I)	26,333	(11%)
Others	10,411	(4%)	Others	12,161	(5%)

Gov. Tony Knowles (D)

Elected 1994, term expires Jan. 2003, 2d term; b. Jan. 1, 1943, Tulsa, OK; home, Juneau; Yale U., B.A. 1968; nondenominational; married (Susan).

Military Career: Army, 1962–65 (Vietnam).

Elected Office: Anchorage Assembly, 1975–79; Anchorage Mayor, 1982–87.

Professional Career: Restaurant owner, 1969–present.

Office: P.O. Box 110001, Juneau, 99811, 907-465-3500; Fax: 907-465-3532; Web site: www.state.ak.us.

Election Results

1998 general	Tony Knowles (D)	112,879	(51%)
	Robin Taylor (write-in)	43,571	(20%)
	John Lindauer (R)	39,331	(18%)
	Ray Metcalfe (RP)	13,540	(6%)
	Others	10,856	(5%)
1998 primary	Tony Knowles (D)	38,798	(36%)
	John Lindauer (R)	25,048	(23%)
	Robin Taylor (R)	17,671	(16%)
	Wayne Ross (R)	17,447	(16%)
	Others	10,062	(9%)
1994 general	Tony Knowles (D)	87,693	(41%)
	James O. (Jim) Campbell (R)	87,157	(41%)
	John B. (Jack) Coghill (I)	27,838	(13%)
	Jim Sykes (Green)	8,727	(4%)

Sen. Ted Stevens (R)

Appointed Dec. 1968, seat up 2002, 5th term; b. Nov. 18, 1923, Indianapolis, IN; home, Girdwood; U.C.L.A., B.A. 1947, Harvard, LL.B. 1950; Episcopalian; married (Catherine).

Military Career: Army Air Corps, 1943–46 (WWII).

Elected Office: AK House of Reps., 1964–68.

Professional Career: Practicing atty., 1950–53, 1961–68; U.S. Atty., 1953–56; U.S. Dept. of Interior, Legis. Cnsl., 1956–58, Asst. to Secy., 1958–60, Solicitor, 1960–61.

DC Office: 522 HSOB, 20510, 202-224-3004; Fax: 202-224-2354; Web site: www.senate.gov/~stevens.

State Offices: Anchorage, 907-271-5915; Fairbanks, 907-456-0261; Juneau, 907-586-7400; Kenai, 907-283-5808; Ketchikan, 907-225-6880; Wasilla, 907-376-7665.

Committees: *Appropriations* (RMM): Commerce, Justice, State & Judiciary; Defense (RMM); Interior; Labor, HHS & Education; Legislative Branch. *Commerce, Science & Transportation*: Aviation; Communications; Oceans & Fisheries; Science, Technology & Space; Surface Transportation & Merchant Marine. *Governmental Affairs*: Government Management, Restructuring and the District of Columbia; International Security, Proliferation & Federal Services; Investigations (Permanent). *Rules & Administration.*

Group Ratings

	ADA	ACLU	AFS	LCV	CON	ITIC	NTU	COC	ACU	NTLC	CHC
2000	5	29	0	0	11	100	73	100	92	91	69
1999	10	—	16	0	8	—	72	88	84	—	—

National Journal Ratings

	1999 LIB	—	1999 CONS		2000 LIB	—	2000 CONS
Economic	32%	—	65%		14%	—	75%
Social	46%	—	52%		46%	—	53%
Foreign	23%	—	67%		36%	—	58%

Key Votes of the 106th Congress

1. Educ. Savings Accts.	Y	5. Review Movie Violence	N	9. NATO War in Serbia	N
2. Prescrip. Drug Benefit	N	6. Gun Show Bckgrnd. Checks	N	10. Table Cuba Travel Ban	Y
3. Delay Ergonomic Standards	Y	7. Ban Part.-Birth Abortion	Y	11. Nuclear Test-Ban Treaty	N
4. Phase Out Estate Tax	Y	8. Broaden Hate Crimes List	Y	12. Perm. Trade with China	Y

Election Results

1996 general	Ted Stevens (R)	177,893	(77%)	($2,711,710)
	Jed Whittaker (Green)	29,037	(13%)	
	Theresa Obermeyer (D)	23,977	(10%)	
1996 primary	Ted Stevens (R)	71,042	(59%)	
	Dave W. Cuddy (R)	32,994	(27%)	
	Others	16,640	(14%)	
1990 general	Ted Stevens (R)	125,806	(66%)	($1,618,098)
	Michael Beasley (D)	61,115	(32%)	($445)
	Others	2,999	(2%)	

Sen. Frank Murkowski (R)

Elected 1980, seat up 2004, 4th term; b. Mar. 28, 1933, Seattle, WA; home, Fairbanks; U. of Santa Clara, Seattle U., B.A. 1955; Catholic; married (Nancy).

Military Career: Coast Guard, 1955–56.

Professional Career: Pacific Natl. Bank of Seattle, 1957–58; Natl. Bank of AK, 1959–67; Commissioner, AK Dept. of Econ. Devel., 1966–70; Pres., AK Natl. Bank of the North, 1971–80.

DC Office: 322 HSOB, 20510, 202-224-6665; Fax: 202-224-5301; Web site: www.senate.gov/~murkowski.

State Offices: Anchorage, 907-271-3735; Fairbanks, 907-456-0233; Juneau, 907-586-7400; Kenai, 907-283-5808; Ketchikan, 907-225-6880; Wasilla, 907-376-7665.

Committees: *Energy & Natural Resources* (RMM). *Finance*: International Trade; Long-Term Growth & Debt Reduction (RMM); Taxation & IRS Oversight. *Indian Affairs. Veterans' Affairs. Joint Committee on Taxation* (5th of 5 Sens.).

Group Ratings

	ADA	ACLU	AFS	LCV	CON	ITIC	NTU	COC	ACU	NTLC	CHC
2000	0	14	0	0	11	100	75	100	100	94	92
1999	5	—	0	0	36	—	76	88	92	—	—

National Journal Ratings

	1999 LIB	—	1999 CONS		2000 LIB	—	2000 CONS
Economic	17%	—	82%		14%	—	75%
Social	28%	—	71%		10%	—	81%
Foreign	23%	—	67%		25%	—	74%

Key Votes of the 106th Congress

1. Educ. Savings Accts.	Y	5. Review Movie Violence	Y	9. NATO War in Serbia	N
2. Prescrip. Drug Benefit	N	6. Gun Show Bckgrnd. Checks	N	10. Table Cuba Travel Ban	Y
3. Delay Ergonomic Standards	Y	7. Ban Part.-Birth Abortion	Y	11. Nuclear Test-Ban Treaty	N
4. Phase Out Estate Tax	Y	8. Broaden Hate Crimes List	N	12. Perm. Trade with China	Y

Election Results

1998 general	Frank Murkowski (R)	165,227	(74%)	($911,926)
	Joseph Sonneman (D)	43,743	(20%)	($26,091)
	Others	12,837	(6%)	
1998 primary	Frank Murkowski (R)	76,635	(72%)	
	Joseph Sonneman (D)	10,716	(10%)	
	Frank Vondersaar (D)	6,343	(6%)	
	William L. Hale (R)	6,312	(6%)	
	Jeffrey Gottlieb (Green)	4,793	(4%)	
	Others	1,986	(2%)	
1992 general	Frank Murkowski (R)	127,163	(53%)	($1,910,759)
	Tony Smith (D)	92,065	(38%)	($910,138)
	Mary Jordan (Green)	20,019	(8%)	($4,091)

Rep. Don Young (R)

Elected Mar. 1973, 14th term; b. June 9, 1933, Meridian, CA; home, Fort Yukon; Yuba Jr. Col., A.A. 1952, Chico St. Col., B.A. 1958; Episcopalian; married (Lu).

Military Career: Army, 1955–57.

Elected Office: Fort Yukon City Cncl., 1960–64; Fort Yukon Mayor, 1964–68; AK House of Reps., 1966–70; AK Senate, 1970–73.

Professional Career: School teacher, Fort Yukon, 1960–68; Riverboat captain, 1960–68.

DC Office: 2111 RHOB, 20515, 202-225-5765; Fax: 202-225-0425; Web site: www.house.gov/donyoung.

District Offices: Anchorage, 907-271-5978; Fairbanks, 907-456-0210; Juneau, 907-586-7400; Kenai, 907-283-5808; Ketchikan, 907-225-6880; Mat-Su, 907-376-7665.

Committees: *Resources* (Vice Chmn. of 28 R): Fisheries Conservation, Wildlife & Oceans. *Transportation & Infrastructure* (Chmn. of 42 R).

Group Ratings

	ADA	ACLU	AFS	LCV	CON	ITIC	NTU	COC	ACU	NTLC	CHC
2000	10	29	14	7	3	73	57	78	73	80	80
1999	10	—	0	6	4	—	54	88	86	—	—

National Journal Ratings

	1999 LIB	—	1999 CONS		2000 LIB	—	2000 CONS
Economic	16%	—	78%		33%	—	67%
Social	24%	—	75%		29%	—	70%
Foreign	23%	—	73%		33%	—	67%

Key Votes of the 106th Congress

1. Patient Bill of Rights	N	5. Bar RU-486 $ for FDA	Y	9. NATO War in Serbia	N
2. Accelerate Min. Wage	Y	6. Display 10 Commandments	Y	10. Perm. Trade with China	N
3. Strike Ban on Ergo. Stnd.	N	7. Gun Show Bkgrnd. Checks	N	11. Debt Relief for 3rd World	N
4. Ovrd. Estate Tax Veto	*	8. Ban Part.-Birth Abortion	Y	12. Drop Cuba Econ. Embargo	N

Election Results

2000 general	Don Young (R)	190,862	(70%)	($1,030,168)
	Clifford Greene (D)	45,372	(17%)	($412)
	Anna C. Young (Green)	22,440	(8%)	
	Jim Dore (AI)	10,085	(4%)	
	Others	5,634	(2%)	
2000 primary	Don Young (R)	unopposed		
1998 general	Don Young (R)	139,676	(63%)	($1,385,073)
	Jim Duncan (D)	77,232	(35%)	($570,894)
	Others	6,392	(3%)	

★ ARIZONA ★

Youth and age, new and old: Arizona is home to America's oldest continuous community and is one of America's fastest-growing and most rapidly changing states. The Hopi Indians, living as shepherds on plateaus east of the Grand Canyon, have not changed much in perhaps 500 years. In 1680 they killed the local Franciscan priests and burned their churches and have spurned Christianity since; more recently they have been involved in land disputes with the far more numerous Navajo. The Hopi are the oldest Arizonans; the newest are moving in every day, into subdivisions rising up out of the empty desert east, north, and west of Phoenix, hemmed in only by dry river beds, upcrops of mountains, and Indian reservation boundaries.

For Arizona was one of the boom states of the 1990s, when its population rose by 40%, the highest except for next-door Nevada, a state with an economy now sophisticated and decentralized enough that there is no easy explanation, as there once was, of how and why Arizona grows. The first explanation was copper: the dome of the state Capitol dome is encased in copper; one of Arizona's leading public figures was Lewis Douglas, copper heir and congressman, Franklin Roosevelt's first budget director and Harry Truman's ambassador to Britain. In those years Arizona depended heavily on the federal government, and on politicians like Carl Hayden, Democratic congressman from statehood in 1912 and senator from 1927–69, whose public works projects watered Arizona's cotton, citrus and cattle farms.

Then in the decades after World War II, businessmen, lawyers, developers and water companies, notably the Salt River Project, built an Arizona based on something like the opposite of New Deal principles: with minimal government and precious little regulation of business, a welcoming of new technological ideas and shunning of new cultural liberalism; like Disneyland, a more gleaming and spotless embodiment of old values than America had ever been. Their political champion was Barry Goldwater, city council member and senator and the nation's Mr. Conservative for much of the 1950s and 1960s. He helped to make Arizona Republican, the only state to vote Republican for president in every election from 1952–92.

This Arizona has grown phenomenally, from 700,000 people at the end of World War II to 3.6 million in 1990 and then to 5.1 million in 2000—an increase in 10 years larger than twice its whole population in 1945. It is growth based on high-tech and low taxes. It is not growth based on an influx of elderly retirees—Arizona may have Sun City, but its proportion of people over 65 is near the national average; nor is it based on farming subsidized by cheap water, since thirsty cotton farms are being phased out for urban users who can easily outbid them, and the Valley around Phoenix lost nearly half its farmland between 1975 and 2000. Nor is it based on, though it is helped by, immigration; Arizona has attracted immigrants from Mexico and Latin America eager for entry-level jobs, so eager that many cross the lightly guarded border in the desert—more than 800 were rescued and 100 found dead by the Border Patrol and other officers during a 12-month period in 1999–2000. More than anything else, the engine of Arizona's growth has been technology: Phoenix has been attracting high-tech industries since Motorola built a research center for military electronics there in 1948, and big employers now include Motorola's semiconductor operation, Allied Signal, Honeywell flight systems, Intel and Raytheon's missile systems division. Landlocked Arizona is a major exporter—nearly $4.6 billion to Mexico and $1.5 billion to Canada in 2000.

Arizona is a place where the private sector is expanding apace and the public sector, if not shriveling away, is yielding ground. Arizona cut state taxes sharply in the 1990s, though voters did approve a sales tax increase for education and a hotel and rental car increase for stadiums and tourism promotion in 2000. It has pioneered in providing choice in education, with America's largest proportion of charter schools (some 20% of the total) and the for-profit University of Phoenix, based here but with branches in many states, which leases space and hires working-age adults to teach job-related skills to working-age adults. Local choice prevails: the inaptly named Youngtown, near Phoenix, bars children from living there; so does Superstition Heights. Where government once used to allocate precious water, now "shadow governments" (Joel Garreau's term) like the Salt River District do so, heeding the market signals that say urban users will pay

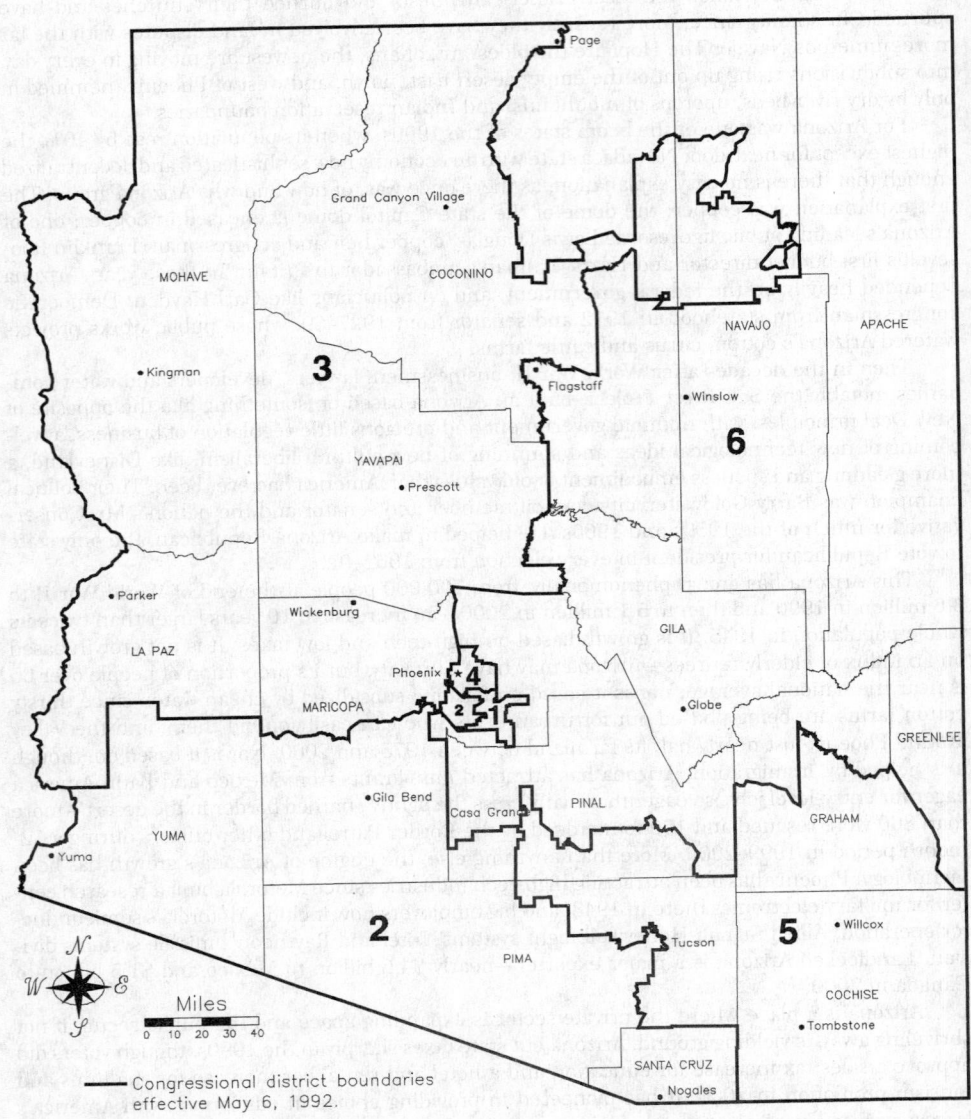

Congressional district boundaries
effective May 6, 1992.

more than farmers. It is a place wide open for entrepreneurs, some of them perhaps a bit shady, others at times wildly overoptimistic, many crossing traditional barriers. Phoenix is the number three metro area for women business owners per capita, and there are a burgeoning number of Latino-owned businesses.

This wide-openness can be reflected in politics. Former Governor Fife Symington was ousted from office when a jury convicted him of fraudulent dealings as a developer (his conviction was reversed on appeal and, though a Republican, he was pardoned by Bill Clinton in January 2001), and in 1998 Arizona became the first state to elect women to all of its top five statewide executive offices: Governor Jane Hull, Secretary of State Betsey Bayless, Attorney General Janet Napolitano, Treasurer Carol Springer, Superintendent of Public Instruction Lisa Graham Keegan; all but Napolitano are Republicans. Although Bill Clinton carried Arizona in 1996 and came close in 1992, the state remains heavily Republican in other elections and the Democratic party—which has had talented leaders like the late Congressman Morris Udall and former Governor and Clinton Interior Secretary Bruce Babbitt—has been since 1994 uncompetitive at most levels.

In the exuberance of growth mistakes are made. An April 2000 bill giving state subsidy for alternative-fuel vehicles was worded so that any car that installed a one-gallon alternative-fuel tank qualified for subsidies that averaged $22,000; the program, expected to cost $5 million, zoomed up toward $500 million—one-tenth of the state budget—before Hull could call a special session of the legislature and have it repealed. That mistake was touted as an anti-pollution measure, and Phoenix's air quality is not good. Yet Arizona has been spared some of the worst effects of growth. The expansion of subdivisions has not led to abandonment of old downtowns or deterioration of central city neighborhoods as it has in eastern cities; and the imperatives of growth in parched desert areas mean that lot sizes are smaller and land use more parsimonious than in a heavily-watered boom area like Atlanta. In 2000 voters rejected by 2–1 a ballot initiative, similar to one also rejected in Colorado, which would have put tough Oregon-like limits on growth and new development. And Arizonans preserve common sense; in November 2000 they voted 63%–37% to require that Spanish-speaking pupils be transferred into English-language instruction rather than be kept in "bilingual" classes for years, despite the opposition of most politicians.

Governor   Arizona's governor is Jane Hull, who came to office when Fife Symington was convicted of financial fraud in September 1997 (the conviction was later reversed on appeal). She was the fourth junior state official to succeed to the office in 20 years: Secretary of State Wesley Bolin became governor when Raul Castro resigned to become ambassador to Argentina in October 1977, Attorney General Bruce Babbitt became governor when Bolin died in March 1978, and Rose Mofford became governor when Evan Mecham was impeached and removed in April 1988. Hull grew up in Mission, Kansas, a suburb of Kansas City. She graduated from the University of Kansas, became a teacher, married and moved to the Navajo Reservation where her husband was a doctor with the U.S. Public Health Service. They moved to Phoenix, where he practiced medicine, she raised four children and—a Goldwater conservative since she saw him speak in Kansas—started volunteering in political campaigns. In 1978 Hull was elected to the state House and in time became majority whip (1987–89) and speaker (1989–92). In that post she presided over the House during the AzScam scandal in which numerous legislators were charged with bribery. In 1993 she resigned to run for secretary of state and was elected in 1994.

In her early days in the legislature, Hull was known as a strong conservative; her later stands on education, juvenile justice and abortion gained her the label of a moderate. But she supported Symington's relentless tax cutting. In her first year in office she kept most of Symington's staff and got through cuts in vehicle license income and business taxes of $140 million. But the state budget rose 13%, to $5.9 billion, mostly because of two Hull programs. One was a $150 million KidsCare program, to finance health care for low-income children, mostly with money from the tobacco tax and the federal government. Hull worked months and had to call a special session to get passage of a school funding law that would pass court muster; under her Students FIRST bill the state would spend $372 million to equalize funding, but still allow local districts to raise money by issuing bonds.

Hull started off her 1998 campaign well ahead in polls. In October 1997 Eddie Basha, the "chubby grocer" who was the Democratic nominee in 1994, decided not to run. In May 1998 conservative Republican Congressman Matt Salmon bowed out of the race, while suggesting he might run in 2002. Hull's major opponent turned out to be Paul Johnson, successful entrepreneur and mayor of Phoenix from 1990–94. Johnson criticized Hull's conservative record as a legislator and her position on abortion. She had voted for abortion restrictions as a legislator, but as speaker kept them from coming to the floor; more recently she has supported the partial-birth abortion ban, but says "there are times . . . when abortion is very definitely a decision between a woman, her physician and her spouse." In a pro-incumbent year the result was no surprise: Hull won 61%–36%. She carried not only Republican Maricopa County but also Democratic Pima County (Tucson).

Hull's next two years in office were more controversial. She pushed for a 0.6% sales tax increase for education, including accountability provisions, and a tax on rental cars and hotels to pay for a football stadium for the Arizona Cardinals; both were approved by voters in November 2000. She proposed to use tobacco money for health programs, including an $80 million mental hospital. She took conservative stands on some issues, signing a parental consent for abortion law, repeal of Smog Dogs (roadside vans reading the exhaust fumes of passing vehicles) and a ban on local gun control laws, and she vetoed $54 million from spending bills. She criticized Bill Clinton for designating new national monuments in Arizona without seeking local input. She proposed a Growing Smarter measure to allow the legislature to preserve the extensive state trust lands sold or leased to fund public schools. Hull and business interests had backed a proposition approved by voters in 1998 authorizing $220 million to preserve open land from development and barring the legislature from requiring local governments to maintain open space, and she opposed the Sierra Club's 2000 initiative, rejected by voters, which would have imposed severe Oregon-style limits on growth. She has sought a guest worker program for immigrants, without success, and urged the federal government to do a better job of patrolling the border with Mexico.

Her biggest mistake was signing the alternative fuels program pushed by House Speaker Jeff Groscost. This provided huge subsidies, averaging over $20,000, to cars equipped to run on alternative fuels—propane, natural gas, electricity. The law did not require motorists to use the alternative fuels, and soon car owners were installing small propane tanks in their SUVs and demanding huge rebates. The program was billed as costing $5 million, but over the fall the cost zoomed up toward $500 million—one-tenth of the state budget. Hull called a special session of the state legislature in November 2000 and suggested the state would pay the rebates over five years; Attorney General Janet Napolitano argued that the rebates could be voided if the law was repealed in the same tax year it was passed. Eventually the law was repealed in December 2000, but the cost to the state has been huge.

Hull also aroused some controversy in presidential politics. In October 1999 she endorsed George W. Bush, not Arizona's John McCain, for president. Her relations with McCain were "not particularly warm" she said. This went back a ways: McCain remembered that Hull endorsed one of his opponents in his 1982 House primary. McCain won the Arizona primary and when Hull said she wanted to head the delegation to the convention, she was rebuffed; it was the candidate's wife who announced the state's votes in Philadelphia. Hull is ineligible to run in 2002.

Cook's Call   *Competitive.* As long as state Attorney General Janet Napolitano gets into the race, Democrats have a shot at the governorship for the first time since 1982. On the Republican side, former Congressman Matt Salmon appears to be the standard bearer but will probably get a minor primary challenge. Arizona is not as Republican as it once was, but the party still enjoys an advantage and Salmon will be a formidable candidate.

Senior Senator   John McCain is the closest thing American politics has to a national hero, a presidential candidate in 2000 who was admired by voters of both parties. His personal story is a dramatic one, told beautifully by Robert Timberg in *The Nightingale's Song* and by McCain himself and Mark Salter in the 1999 bestseller *Faith of My Fathers*. McCain is the son and grandson of Navy admirals, a decorated Navy pilot himself who was shot down over Vietnam and who spent five years, most of it in pain and torture, in Communist prisoner of war camps; he refused to be let out ahead of those who had been in longer when he was offered release because of his father's rank. McCain returned to the United States in March 1973. His final assignment in the Navy was as Senate liaison. In 1980 he retired and moved to Arizona, his wife's home state; in 1982 he ran for an open House seat. Attacked as an outsider, he responded, "The longest place I ever lived in was Hanoi." He led 32%–26% in a four-way primary, and won the 1982 and 1984 general elections and then the 1986 Senate contest easily.

McCain is Ranking Member of the Commerce Committee and a member of Armed Services, but he is anything but a member of the Senate club; his crusades for campaign finance regulation and against pork-barrel spending have provided plenty of material for his self-deprecating jokes about how unpopular he is with many colleagues. On several highly visible issues, he has taken stands opposed by almost all Republicans and backed by almost all Democrats—on campaign finance for several years, on tobacco legislation in 1999, on HMO regulation in 2000. He brings to his work a sense of righteousness and a conviction that what have become the normal workings of the political process—campaign contributions, backing local projects—are deeply corrupt. He has worked on difficult and complex legislation but has had, as he concedes, less than complete success in his efforts.

In his first years in the Senate he had a low profile. His first major issue was one on which he had great expertise: Vietnam. In the early 1990s McCain worked hard with Massachusetts' John Kerry, also a decorated Vietnam veteran, on the special committee investigating charges that American POWs or MIAs remained in Vietnam; they found no evidence of any. With Kerry he supported ending the trade embargo on and pressed for establishing diplomatic relations with Vietnam. But his support for reconciliation with our former enemies has not dimmed his memories of how his captors treated his fellow prisoners of war. On other defense issues, McCain has called for more defense spending but has shown a professional military officer's caution about committing American troops without a clear end in sight, most notably in Bosnia, where he opposed the use of air power alone. He called the Clinton administration's 1994 agreement with North Korea "appeasement" and said sanctions against North Korean nuclear proliferation should be backed by explicit threats of air strikes. He was extremely vocal on Kosovo, pushing Clinton to either press for victory or get out; in May 1999 the Senate shelved McCain's proposal to authorize "all necessary force" including ground forces.

McCain served as chairman of the Indian Affairs Committee in 1995–96. Arizona has one of the nation's largest percentages of Indians, and McCain, like Barry Goldwater and Morris Udall, obviously feels sympathy for them. "Never deceive them," he says. "They have been deceived too many times in the last 200 years." Generally, McCain has supported the tribal agenda. He cooperated with the vast expansion in the 1990s of Indian gambling. He has worked for Indian self-governance and sovereignty, but has also pushed laws on child abuse on reservations. He backed limited changes in the law that allows tribes to control the adoptions even of children born off the reservation with low percentages of Indian blood.

McCain was a pilot in the Navy, and on the Commerce Committee he has worked on aviation issues. He authored the law banning small airplanes from flying over the Grand Canyon. He has long pushed for nonstop flights from Washington Reagan National Airport to Phoenix's Sky Harbor, and sponsored the law opening up slots at Reagan National, Chicago's O'Hare and New York's Kennedy and LaGuardia airports. In 1999 he held hearings on complaints against the airlines, and proposed an Airline Passenger Fairness Act, which would require disclosure of overbooked planes and flight delays. But when the airlines announced new policies, he switched to a bill emphasizing voluntary compliance. He took little part in shaping the compromise Telecommunications Act of 1996, and voted against it, arguing that it did not effectively ensure competition; he called for an auction, not a giveaway, of the digital TV spectrum to networks. When he became chairman of Commerce in 1997, McCain led key senators and congressmen to agree not to legislate for three years if the networks would come up with code letters for violence, sexual content and foul language in their programs; in September 2000 he held hearings on the marketing of violent movies, music and video games to children, which studio heads ducked but at which Joseph Lieberman and Lynne Cheney testified. McCain sponsored the Internet Tax Freedom Act and has sought its renewal. He sponsored an Internet privacy act, to require websites to disclose their privacy policies and limit disclosure of data to third parties unless it is related to products or services on the site. He was the chief sponsor of the Muhammad Ali Act, to protect boxers, and wants to ban gambling on amateur sports in Nevada—which he believes would prevent newspapers from reporting the point spread on college football and basketball games.

The tobacco issue was thrust on McCain as Commerce chairman: Majority Leader Trent Lott told him to put together a bill with bipartisan support, and McCain's bill passed 19–1 in April 1998. It provided for closer regulation of tobacco advertising and marketing and stiffer penalties if the teenage smoking rate did not decline, plus a $1.10 cigarette tax; the cost was estimated at $516 billion—opponents said it was higher. At first the bill had little articulate opposition, but John Ashcroft, a non-smoker thinking of running for president, forthrightly opposed the tax. And the big tobacco companies, noting that the cost was well above the $368 billion in the settlement agreed to with state attorneys general in 1997, argued that the McCain bill did not protect them against lawsuits as that settlement did; when the Finance Committee raised the tax to $1.50, the companies decided to oppose it. They ran a huge ad campaign against the tobacco tax—naming McCain in, as he noted, Arizona, Iowa and New Hampshire. Although just about everyone in Washington seemed to favor McCain's bill, an NBC- *Wall Street Journal* poll showed that voter opinion was about evenly divided. McCain was obviously angered by the opposition, but the bill was dropped in June 1998 after only 57 senators voted to stop the filibuster. In November 1998 the attorneys general of 46 states reached a $206 billion settlement with the tobacco companies, which would restrict advertising and marketing but provide no protection against other lawsuits.

McCain's interest in campaign finance may have come from when he was one of the "Keating five" senators investigated for meeting in 1987 with regulators on behalf of Charles Keating's Arizona savings and loan. McCain was kept in the case by Democrats, though he had done nothing for Keating, because he was the one Republican involved and thus made the scandal bipartisan; he was cited for nothing more than bad judgment. Vindicated by re-election in 1992, in the majority after the election of 1994, he sought out Democrat Russ Feingold, whose campaign finance bill had gotten nowhere that year. The McCain-Feingold bills have gone through several transformations. The 1998 bill purported to ban soft money contributions to political parties and to limit "issue ads" run by independent organizations within 60 days of an election. It was fiercely opposed as an infringement of free speech and as a threat to the Republican Party by Mitch McConnell of Kentucky. Majority Leader Trent Lott yanked the bill from the Senate floor in February 1998; it returned in September, after the House passed a similar bill, but could summon up no more than 52 votes and was killed. In September 1999, after the House passed a similar bill again, McCain and Feingold introduced a new version that attacked soft money but did not address issue ads. The obvious intent was to get a bill to conference and generate enough public support that McConnell and other Republican opponents would have to back down. But in October McConnell, noting that McCain had charged that the current campaign finance system produces corruption, challenged McCain to name senators who had been corrupted. Robert Bennett of Utah chimed in and demanded to know what soft money had been responsible for his own amendment, criticized by McCain as pork, to build sewers for the 2002 Winter Olympics in Salt Lake City. McCain refused to name names and said the system was corrupt in general. Against McConnell's filibuster a few days later McCain and Feingold were able to summon up only 55 votes for cloture, five short of the 60 needed, and the bill was taken off the floor.

By that time McCain was already embarked on his presidential campaign. He wisely decided to avoid the Iowa caucuses (McCain had long campaigned against ethanol subsidies as pork) and concentrated on New Hampshire, where he traveled around the state in his "Straight Talk Express" bus. At first only a few reporters traveled with him and crowds were sparse. But it soon became clear McCain was striking a chord. To increasingly large and fervent crowds he told his personal story in self-deprecating terms, and pledged, "I will never tell you a lie." He talked about defense and foreign policy issues—the only candidate to do so much—and invariably called for campaign finance reform. On the bus McCain was always available to answer reporters' questions and banter with the press, while making fun of his aides and consultant Mike Murphy (who later called the press "our constituency"). McCain did not have much support from politicians. Only four fellow senators endorsed him (Jon Kyl, Chuck Hagel, Fred Thompson and Mike DeWine) and Arizona Governor Jane Hull, apparently because of abrasive treatment by McCain, endorsed George W. Bush; the *Arizona Republic* wrote editorials warning of McCain's "volcanic" temper.

But the strength of feeling among his ever-larger crowds was palpable. George W. Bush predicted victory in New Hampshire, but on February 1 McCain beat him by an impressive 49%–31% margin, and suddenly became, if not the frontrunner, at least the most admired of either party's presidential candidates.

From there the "Straight Talk Express" had mixed success. It went down to South Carolina, whose early primary had been invented by the late Lee Atwater for the older George Bush in 1988, and where both the Republican establishment and Christian conservatives supported George W. Bush in 2000. There the campaigning got negative. McCain ran an ad saying Bush "twists the truth like Clinton"; a Bush ad said that McCain "will say one thing and then do another." After a tearful woman at one McCain appearance told how her son was crushed by a negative phone message about McCain, McCain promised to cut all negative ads. That may have hurt him, but what hurt even more was his failure to win over self-identified Republicans. His emphasis on campaign finance reform and his criticisms of Bush's tax plan for giving too much to the rich helped with independents, but sounded like enemy talk to Republicans. On February 18 Bush won 53%–42% in South Carolina, in what turned out to be as decisive a victory as his father's there had been 12 years before. The New Hampshire and South Carolina results were templates for what happened elsewhere; in New Hampshire and other Northeastern states McCain ran about even with Bush among self-identified Republicans and way ahead among self-identified independents and self-identified Democrats; in South Carolina and other states outside the Northeast, Bush ran way ahead among Republicans and behind among independents and Democrats. On February 22 McCain won in Arizona and, in a big 50%–43% upset, in Michigan; but Michigan has no party registration, and 20% of Republican primary voters there were Democrats (most of them as hostile toward Governor John Engler (who backed Bush) as most Republicans are to Bill Clinton) and 30% were independents—much higher figures than in any other state.

McCain might have done better if he had emphasized other issues on which he had consistently taken stands in line with most Republicans' thinking—defense, tax cuts (he had an interesting tax cut plan himself, but he spent less time on it than on attacking Bush's), abortion, Social Security individual investment accounts. Instead, after South Carolina, he gave a speech in Virginia Beach attacking the religious right and in an offhand comment on the bus called Pat Robertson and Jerry Falwell "forces of evil." As he explained the next day, this was sarcastic "Luke Skywalker talk," which reporters often heard on the bus but which rarely appeared in their reports. But to many Christian conservatives, a large segment of the Republican primary vote, it sounded like angry hostility, and McCain lost in Virginia and Washington on February 29. On Super Tuesday, March 7, McCain won in Massachusetts, Connecticut, Rhode Island and Vermont. But he lost decisively in New York, Ohio and California and "suspended" his campaign on March 9. Much attention was focused on the fact that he did not "endorse" Bush, and when they finally met in Pittsburgh in May reporters practically had to extract the word from his mouth. He made it clear he did not want to be nominated for vice president and said he wanted no cabinet post, making the plausible argument that he operated better as his own man than as someone else's appointee. He insisted on having his wife Cindy McCain, not Jane Hull, head the Arizona delegation to the convention, and he gave a moving, elegiac speech that ended as if in a minor key. Reporters speculated that he might run again in 2004 or 2008. But the campaign was clearly a moving and unique experience for him: "I would never do this again. I think it's fun once. I don't see how it's fun twice."

Some defeated presidential candidates sulk in their tents; McCain became more legislatively active than ever. In May he sponsored the law putting Section 527 organizations under the campaign finance acts. With Bill Frist he sponsored a bill to discourage teen smoking. He voted with the Democrats in July on HMO regulation and worked with Democrat John Edwards to craft a bipartisan bill, unsuccessfully. With Charles Schumer, he sponsored a bill to make it easier to produce generic drugs. He tried in October, after the Firestone tire revelations, to impose criminal penalties on manufacturers who knowingly market defective products. He was the only Republican to vote against the water projects bill in October, charging that it contained $1.2 billion of special projects earmarked for districts. He campaigned tirelessly for Republican House candidates, and tried, with some success, to get them to support his campaign finance bill. He appeared in ads in Colorado and Oregon for ballot propositions requiring background checks for sales at gun shows.

In March 2001, the Senate again took up campaign finance reform. After two weeks of remarkably civilized but spirited debate, during which McCain and Feingold fended off several poison-pill amendments, the legislation passed April 2 by a 59–41 vote. An amendment by Fred Thompson and Dianne Feinstein was passed to raise limits on individual contributions from $1,000 to $2,000, but the bill retained the soft-money ban and limit on issue ads prior to the election, which some senators fear will be struck down by the courts as an unconstitutional ban of free speech. Just prior to the final vote, McCain saluted his nemesis on the issue, Mitch McConnell, who afterward acknowledged that the outcome was "a tribute to [McCain's] tenacity." McCain also appeared to make amends with Chuck Hagel, a fellow Vietnam veteran and his closest friend in the Senate, who had offered a losing amendment during debate to limit, instead of ban, soft money.

McCain may have irritated some Arizona Republican politicians, but his standing with the state's voters is very strong. He won the Senate seat in 1986 by 60%–40%. In 1992 he was re-elected 56%–32%, with 11% for conservative former Governor Evan Mecham. In 1998 he was opposed by Ed Ranger, an environmental lawyer in Arizona and Mexico who put 70,000 miles on a Harley Davidson and converted 1970s school bus traveling through the state. McCain won by an impressive 69%–27%, carrying the heavily Navajo and Democratic Apache County 54%–42% and winning the Hispanic vote 52%–42%. He attributed this not to his one $12,000 ad on Spanish-language radio, but to his longstanding positions on issues: "I favor bilingual education that works, I'm opposed to 'English only,' I favor legal immigration."

Junior Senator   Jon Kyl is a Republican first elected in 1994. His father John Kyl was a Republican congressman from Iowa (1959–65, 1967–73), who eventually lost his seat in redistricting; Jon Kyl moved to a state that, in effect, was gaining the Republican seats Great Plains states like Iowa were losing. Kyl went to college and law school in Arizona, practiced law in Phoenix, worked on Republican campaigns and headed the Phoenix Chamber of Commerce; he won the heavily Republican 4th District seat in 1986 by beating former (1973–77) Congressman John Conlan, who had support from the religious right, 60%–28%.

In the House, Kyl was a leader among Republicans on the Strategic Defense Initiative, the balanced budget amendment, and for disclosing the names of House members with overdrafts on the House bank—one of the causes that destabilized Democrats' control of the House in 1993 and 1994. But by that time Kyl was running for the Senate seat held for three terms by Democrat Dennis DeConcini, whose reputation was stained by his involvement in the Keating Five scandal. Kyl had no primary opposition and the further good fortune that one-term Congressman Sam Coppersmith won the September 13 primary by only 59 votes of 255,000 cast and after a two-week recount. Kyl, with far more money, ran ads with home movie texture showing him traveling through the desert countryside, dressed in jeans and working on ranches, while talking about how he and his wife first fell in love with the state (he has climbed Mount Camelback "more than 1,000 times"). Coppersmith stressed his pro-choice stand on abortion and said he would welcome a campaign visit from President Clinton. Kyl won solidly, 54%–40%.

Kyl has a solidly conservative record. Quietly, he has become a major force on defense policy. He is perhaps the Senate's biggest champion of a missile defense system. A 1996 speech he made in Europe on the future of NATO impressed Margaret Thatcher and Henry Kissinger, who accepted his invitation to a conference at the Arizona Biltmore. In 1997 he led with Jesse Helms the losing fight against the Chemical Weapons Convention. Learning from that experience, he organized the winning fight to reject the Comprehensive Test Ban Treaty, submitted by Bill Clinton to the Senate in September 1997. Starting in 1998, Kyl studied the details and worked to persuade Republican colleagues to oppose the treaty. In May 1999 he told Majority Leader Trent Lott that he had 34 solid votes against, enough to prevent ratification, but Foreign Relations Chairman Jesse Helms insisted that he get more before he would let the treaty come to the floor. All 45 Democrats, unaware in the increasingly partisan Senate of Kyl's efforts, wrote Helms in July demanding the treaty be brought forward by September. Helms replied dismissively that he would not do so until he got action on the Kyoto treaty and amendments to the ABM treaty. In September North Dakota Democrat Byron Dorgan promised to "plant myself on the floor like a potted plant" until the CTBT was considered. The ranking Foreign Relations Democrat still thought that 25 Republicans could be persuaded to vote for the treaty, and concurred when Lott promised to bring it up in October. Only then did Senate Democrats and the Clinton White House begin to discover that they had conspired to defeat their own treaty. Kyl had done his work well: the CTBT did not even get a majority, much less the required two-thirds, as it was defeated 48–51. "Our success," Kyl said, "depended on being quiet about what we did."

Kyl serves on Judiciary and is sponsor, with Dianne Feinstein, of a constitutional amendment on victims' rights. It would give victims of crime a right to be informed, to be present and to be heard at critical stages in the judicial process, a right to speedy trial and final conclusion free from unreasonable delay, full restitution from the criminal, and protection from violence or intimidation. It had 40 co-sponsors but was shelved in April 2000 because it lacked the necessary two-thirds. Kyl has also co-sponsored with Feinstein a bill to prepare defenses for attacks by terrorists with chemical and biological weapons. He has introduced bills outlawing identity theft, Internet gambling and on-line casinos. He was a lead Senate sponsor of the bill to ban racial quotas and preferences. He has worked to beef up the Border Patrol and to track legal immigrants who overstay their visas. He supports cuts in legal immigration and new rules for family-based immigration—the kind of measures that have cost Republicans Hispanic votes. He worked with Congressman Ed Pastor, the only Democrat in the Arizona delegation, to create three new federal judgeships and to confirm the Democratic appointees in October 2000 after Democrats put a hold on them. Alarmed by increasing numbers of illegal border crossings in Arizona, and by occasional violence by local farmers against illegal immigrants, he has worked to increase the number of Border Patrol agents in Arizona, nearly doubling the Tucson office and getting $3 million for new facilities in Douglas, Tucson, Yuma and Florence.

On other issues, Kyl is prime sponsor of the bill, vetoed by Bill Clinton, to phase out the estate tax. He was the Senate leader on the move to change the Clinton administration's barring of doctors who take Medicare patients from contracting with patients for more services or higher fees. He has worked patiently to settle the water rights claims of Arizona Indian tribes. He was the prime sponsor of a 1999 law setting up a semiautonomous division of the Energy Department to oversee nuclear weapons research and production. In June 2000, after security lapses were discovered at the Los Alamos labs, Kyl called for Energy Secretary Bill Richardson's resignation.

Kyl is not an active seeker of publicity, and is far less well known in Arizona and Washington than his colleague John McCain. But in June 2000 he was interviewed by Richard Cheney, whom he had chosen as a kind of model when he came to the House, as a possible vice-presidential candidate; he was interviewed a second time in July but recommended against his own selection. Kyl came up for re-election in 2000, and in July 1999 the Democratic Senatorial Campaign Committee called him "the most vulnerable Republican incumbent." But Democrats were not able to get anyone to run, and Kyl became the only senator without major party opposition that year. He won 79% of the vote against an independent, a Green Party candidate and a Libertarian.

Presidential politics   Far from the media centers of the East Coast, Arizona has tried to make itself another Iowa or New Hampshire in presidential primary politics, with little success. In 1972 it had an early Democratic primary, the improbable winner of which was Republican-turned-Democrat New York Mayor John Lindsay. But he went nowhere anywhere else. Twenty-four years later Arizona tried again, attempting to set its primary for the same date as New Hampshire; when that failed it set it one week later. The intended beneficiary was Republican Phil Gramm, running with the support of Arizona's John McCain. But Gramm pulled out of the race a week before New Hampshire, and Arizona became a battleground between Bob Dole, who now had McCain's support; Pat Buchanan, who urged his followers to "mount up and ride" after his narrow victory in New Hampshire; and Steve Forbes, who peppered the state with ads boosting his flat tax and attacking Washington politicians. Buchanan's campaigning in gunslinger costume wearing a black hat was a bit too much, and he finished third, with 27%, ending any serious chance he had to win the nomination. Dole finished second with 30%; Forbes won 33% and all the delegates, after which his campaign, like that of his fellow easterner Lindsay a quarter-century before, went nowhere.

In 2000 Arizona tried other innovations. McCain had irritated local Republicans enough that Governor Jane Hull and other party leaders endorsed George W. Bush. McCain, however, won a solid victory in his home state in the February primary, but it was overshadowed by his misleading triumph in Michigan the same day—misleading since he won that open-primary state because 20% of Republican primary voters were self-identified Democrats, double the percentage in any other contest that year. As for the Democrats, they ran and paid for their own primary in March, because Arizona's February date was outside the "window" allowed by national Democratic Party rules. They allowed voting by Internet, and about 35,000 Arizonans typed in their choices; another 20,000 voted by mail; still others voted by computer or paper ballot at the polls. But the Internet voting was not flawless and the primary was trivial since Al Gore had already clinched the nomination.

Between the 1940s and the 1990s, Arizona had not been competitive in presidential elections: Republicans won every contest between 1952 and 1992, and only once, when native son Barry Goldwater beat Lyndon Johnson here, was the margin close. But in the 1990s Arizona suddenly became competitive. In 1992 George Bush carried the state by only 38%–37%, as Ross Perot won 24%. In 1996 Clinton actually won by a 47%–44% margin—the first Democrat to carry the state since Harry Truman in 1948. The winning issue was not so much Medicare—Arizona does not have an especially large elderly population, and the air seemed to go out of the Medicare issue in mid-October—as it was the environment. Arizona has a much lower percentage of rural and small town voters than other Rocky Mountain states: nearly 80% of Arizonans live in metro Phoenix and Tucson, and they want to preserve the environment that is so visibly being transformed by their own success. Clinton's staging of the announcement of a Utah land preserve at the Grand Canyon may have carried Arizona single-handedly (it may also have defeated the only Democratic congressman in Utah). Indeed, Clinton went on to create new National Monuments in Arizona—four in 2000 alone—over the opposition of local elected officials, and perhaps in the hope of aiding Al Gore. If so, it was in vain. Gore won 45% here, a good showing for a national Democrat, but George W. Bush won 51%, carrying not only Phoenix and Maricopa County, as Republican nominees had in 1992 and 1996, but also the smaller counties outside the Phoenix and Tucson metro areas, which they had not: The non-metropolitan backlash against Clinton-Gore environmental policies worked for Bush in Arizona as it did in Colorado and other Rocky Mountain states.

Congressional districting   Arizona gained two House seats in the 2000 Census, after gaining one each in the Censuses of 1960, 1970, 1980 and 1990. This time, thanks to Proposition 106, passed in November 2000, redistricting will be done not by the legislature but by a five-member commission. Two Republican and two Democratic legislators will appoint four members, and the fifth, to be neither a Democrat nor a Republican, will be picked by the other four. The results are unpredictable: The current map, like those in the past, has all but one district based in metro Phoenix, with the other based in Tucson; a majority-Hispanic district, the only one currently represented by a Democrat, stretches from south Phoenix to west Tucson.

The commission could continue this pattern, or it could do something quite different. The northern counties of the state have about the right population for one district. No incumbent lives there, and the area has only a slight Republican edge; this would be a classic marginal seat. The southern counties including Tucson's Pima County have the about the right population for two districts, both of which would have to be based in the Tucson area. These counties are closely balanced politically; presumably the result would be one heavily Hispanic Democratic district and one safe Republican district; presumably one for Tucson-area Republican Jim Kolbe and another for a Democratic newcomer. Phoenix's Maricopa County plus the much smaller Pinal County next door have about the right population for five districts. Here one could expect a heavily Hispanic and Democratic district in south Phoenix plus four more or less heavily Republican districts. Such a plan would change Arizona's current 5–1 Republican delegation to 6–2 or perhaps even 5–3 Republican, with reasonably safe seats for four current incumbents plus one Republican newcomer.

THE PEOPLE: Pop. 2000: 5,130,632; Pop. 1990: 3,665,228, up 40% 1990–2000. 1.8% of U.S. total, 20th largest; 75.5% White, 3.1% Black, 1.8% Asian, 5% Amer. Indian, 0.1% Hawaiian, 2.9% Two+ races, 11.6% Other; 25.3% Hispanic Origin. 3.9% Unemployment. 2000 Voting age pop.: 3,763,685. 2000 Turnout: 1,559,520; 41% of VAP. Registered voters (2000): 2,173,122; 830,904 D (38%), 942,078 R (43%), 400,140 unaffiliated and minor parties (18%).

POLITICAL LINEUP: Governor, Jane Dee Hull (R); Secy. of State, Betsey Bayless (R); Atty. Gen., Janet Napolitano (D); Treasurer, Carol Springer (R); Super. of Public Instruction, Lisa Graham Keegan (R); State Senate, 30 (15 D, 15 R); Senate President, Randall Gnant (R); Senate Floor Leader, Jack Brown (D); State House, 60 (24 D, 36 R); House Speaker, Jim Weiers (R). Senators, John McCain (R) and Jon Kyl (R). Representatives, 6 (1 D, 5 R).

ELECTIONS DIVISION: 602-542-8683; **FILING DEADLINE FOR U.S. CONGRESS:** June 12, 2002.

2000 Presidential Vote
Bush (R)	781,652	(51%)
Gore (D)	685,341	(45%)
Nader (Green)	45,645	(3%)
Others	19,268	(1%)

1996 Presidential Vote
Clinton (D)	653,288	(47%)
Dole (R)	622,073	(44%)
Perot (I)	112,074	(8%)

2000 Republican Presidential Primary
McCain (R)	193,708	(60%)
Bush (R)	115,115	(36%)
Keyes (R)	11,500	(4%)

2000 Democratic Presidential Primary
Gore (D)	67,582	(78%)
Bradley (D)	16,383	(19%)
Other	2,797	(3%)

Gov. Jane Dee Hull (R)

Assumed office Sept.1997, term expires Jan. 2003, 1st term; b. Aug. 8, 1935, Kansas City, MO; home, Phoenix; U. of KS, B.S. 1957; AZ St. U., 1974–79; Josephson Ethics Inst., 1993; Catholic; married (Terry).

Elected Office: AZ House of Reps., 1978–93, Maj. Whip, 1987–89, Speaker, 1989–92; AZ Secy. of State., 1994–97.

Professional Career: Jr. High Teacher, 1957–63.

Office: 1700 W. Washington, Phoenix, 85007, 602-542-4331; Fax: 602-542-7601; Web site: www.state.az.us.

Election Results
1998 general	Jane Dee Hull (R)	620,188	(61%)
	Paul Johnson (D)	361,552	(36%)
	Others	35,876	(4%)
1998 primary	Jane Dee Hull (R)	177,324	(77%)
	Jim Howl (R)	30,699	(13%)
	Charles Brown (R)	23,710	(10%)
1994 general	Fife Symington (R)	593,492	(53%)
	Eddie Basha (D)	500,702	(44%)
	Others	35,413	(3%)

Sen. John McCain (R)

Elected 1986, seat up 2004, 3d term; b. Aug. 29, 1936, Panama Canal Zone; home, Phoenix; U.S. Naval Acad., B.S. 1958, Natl. War Col., 1973–74; Episcopalian; married (Cindy).

Military Career: Navy, 1958–80 (Vietnam).

Elected Office: U.S. House of Reps., 1982–1986.

Professional Career: Dir., Navy Senate Liaison Ofc., 1977–81.

DC Office: 241 RSOB, 20510, 202-224-2235; Fax: 202-228-2862; Web site: www.senate.gov/~mccain.

State Offices: Mesa, 480-897-6289; Phoenix, 602-952-2410; Tucson, 520-670-6334.

Committees: *Armed Services*: Personnel; Readiness & Management Support; Seapower. *Commerce, Science & Transportation* (RMM). *Indian Affairs*.

Group Ratings

	ADA	ACLU	AFS	LCV	CON	ITIC	NTU	COC	ACU	NTLC	CHC
2000	5	0	16	0	98	90	82	75	81	94	91
1999	5	—	0	11	97	—	87	75	77	—	—

National Journal Ratings

	1999 LIB	—	1999 CONS		2000 LIB	—	2000 CONS
Economic	18%	—	81%		47%	—	52%
Social	33%	—	66%		32%	—	67%
Foreign	44%	—	54%		34%	—	64%

Key Votes of the 106th Congress

1. Educ. Savings Accts.	*	5. Review Movie Violence	Y	9. NATO War in Serbia	Y
2. Prescrip. Drug Benefit	N	6. Gun Show Bckgrnd. Checks	N	10. Table Cuba Travel Ban	Y
3. Delay Ergonomic Standards	Y	7. Ban Part.-Birth Abortion	Y	11. Nuclear Test-Ban Treaty	N
4. Phase Out Estate Tax	Y	8. Broaden Hate Crimes List	N	12. Perm. Trade with China	Y

Election Results

1998 general	John McCain (R)	696,577	(69%)	($2,461,900)
	Ed Ranger (D)	275,224	(27%)	($371,439)
	Others	41,479	(4%)	
1998 primary	John McCain (R)	unopposed		
1992 general	John McCain (R)	771,395	(56%)	($3,766,588)
	Claire Sargent (D)	436,321	(32%)	($287,682)
	Evan Mecham (I)	145,361	(11%)	($86,433)
	Others	28,974	(2%)	

Sen. Jon Kyl (R)

Elected 1994, seat up 2006, 2d term; b. Apr. 25, 1942, Oakland, NE; home, Phoenix; U. of AZ, B.A. 1964, L.L.B. 1966; Presbyterian; married (Caryll).

Elected Office: U.S. House of Reps., 1986–94.

Professional Career: Practicing atty., 1966–86; Chmn., Phoenix Chamber of Commerce, 1984–85.

DC Office: 730 HSOB, 20510, 202-224-4521; Fax: 202-224-2207; Web site: www.senate.gov/~kyl.

State Offices: Phoenix, 602-840-1891; Tucson, 520-575-8633.

Committees: *Energy & Natural Resources*: Energy Research, Development, Production & Regulation; Forests & Public Land Management; Water & Power. *Finance*: Health Care; Long-Term Growth & Debt Reduction; Social

Security & Family Policy (RMM). *Intelligence (Select)*. *Judiciary*: Constitution, Federalism & Property Rights; Immigration; Technology, Terrorism & Government Information (RMM).

Group Ratings

	ADA	ACLU	AFS	LCV	CON	ITIC	NTU	COC	ACU	NTLC	CHC
2000	0	14	0	0	67	85	83	85	100	100	100
1999	0	—	0	0	58	—	83	82	100	—	—

National Journal Ratings

	1999 LIB	—	1999 CONS		2000 LIB	—	2000 CONS
Economic	0%	—	83%		32%	—	64%
Social	29%	—	69%		22%	—	73%
Foreign	37%	—	60%		0%	—	95%

Key Votes of the 106th Congress

1. Educ. Savings Accts.	Y	5. Review Movie Violence	Y	9. NATO War in Serbia	N
2. Prescrip. Drug Benefit	N	6. Gun Show Bckgrnd. Checks	N	10. Table Cuba Travel Ban	Y
3. Delay Ergonomic Standards	Y	7. Ban Part.-Birth Abortion	Y	11. Nuclear Test-Ban Treaty	N
4. Phase Out Estate Tax	Y	8. Broaden Hate Crimes List	N	12. Perm. Trade with China	Y

Election Results

2000 general	Jon Kyl (R)	1,108,196	(79%)	($2,503,674)
	William Toel (I)	109,230	(8%)	($21,491)
	Vance Hansen (Green)	108,926	(8%)	
	Barry J. Hess, II (Lib)	70,724	(5%)	
2000 primary	Jon Kyl (R)	unopposed		
1994 general	Jon Kyl (R)	600,999	(54%)	($4,138,203)
	Sam Coppersmith (D)	442,510	(40%)	($1,577,556)
	Scott Grainger (Lib)	75,493	(7%)	

FIRST DISTRICT

The metropolis of Phoenix is exceedingly young—yet bears traces of a lost Indian civilization a millennium old. Barry Goldwater, born in 1909 and living on into 1998, grew up knowing men and women who remembered when the Valley of the Sun—or the Valley, as most people say—was virtually empty, with a few parched settlements set above the dry river bed; eerily, this empty land was crisscrossed by more than 200 miles of irrigation channels built some 500 years ago by the Hohokam, who then mysteriously disappeared. Phoenix was founded in the years after the Civil War, near the Pueblo Grande Indian ruins and still functioning canals, as a haymarket for cavalry horses at Fort McDowell 40 miles away. On the usually dry Salt River, Tempe was founded in 1871 as Hayden's Ferry, by the father of future Senator (1927–69) Carl Hayden; it was renamed in 1879 for an ancient Greek vale, and is now home of Arizona State University, founded in 1885, and the Fiesta Bowl. Further east is Mesa, founded by Mormons in 1878 on a square mile, laid out with broad streets with huge blocks holding just four homesites, using Indian canals built 1,100 years before; a gleaming white Mormon Temple was built there in 1927, one of the few in the United States. North of the Salt River, directly east of Phoenix and in the shadows of Camelback Mountain, is Scottsdale, founded much more recently, with its trendy shops carefully decked out in Old West style.

For half a century this remained mostly empty land: As late as 1950 only 106,000 people lived in Phoenix and only 331,000 in all of Maricopa County. But in the years after World War II the air conditioner and military technology—in 1948 Motorola built an electronics research center here—transformed Phoenix, from a sleepy whistle-stop, where the small tufa stone turn-of-the-century Capitol was the most prominent building, to today's high-rise studded metropolis, with 1.3 million people in Phoenix and 3 million in Maricopa County. This is not, as some think, a giant retirement village; nor is it totally overrun with crooked land salesmen or fast-buck artists, though freewheeling Phoenix has attracted more than its share of both. The typical cactus-decorated, desert-brown adobe tract house here is occupied by a growing family, living a more traditional life than many occupants of more traditional-looking houses back east. Mesa, with almost

400,000 people, is larger than Minneapolis or Pittsburgh; but it struggles to overcome its past image as a trailer-park haven and to emerge from Phoenix's shadow as a bedroom community. Its voters rejected a project to construct a convention center and a football stadium for the Arizona Cardinals.

The 1st District of Arizona includes much of the historic heart of Phoenix: Pueblo Grande and the old Indian School in Phoenix, Arizona State in Tempe and the Mormon Temple in Mesa and Old Town Scottsdale; it also goes south to include most of Chandler. Its boundaries are convoluted, designed to maximize the number of Hispanics in the 2d District and Indians (in the Salt River and Gilva River Reservations) in the 6th; geographically, it sits south of Camelback Mountain, west of the Superstition Mountains, east of South Mountain. It includes some high-income neighborhoods, but its cultural tone is resolutely middle class, hard working, church going; traditionally, it has been heavily Republican.

The congressman from the 1st District is Jeff Flake, a Republican elected in 2000. A fifth-generation Arizonian, he is a practicing Mormon who was born and raised on a ranch in Snow-flake; the town was named, in part, after his great-great grandfather. The fifth of 11 children, Flake served a Mormon mission in South Africa and Zimbabwe before he attended Brigham Young University. In 1987 he moved to Washington, D.C. and worked in a lobbying firm. He returned to southern Africa to serve as executive director of the Foundation for Democracy, which monitored democratic progress in Namibia. Following Namibian independence in 1990 and two more years in Washington representing Namibian companies, he returned to Arizona and became executive director of the Goldwater Institute, where he led the fight for Arizona's charter school law, the most successful in the nation.

In 2000, then-Congressman Matt Salmon kept his pledge to serve only three terms (and left the door open to run for governor in 2002), he handpicked Flake to succeed him. Flake faced four opponents in a hard-fought September primary, in which he was the most conservative candidate. Flake had the support of several prominent Republican state leaders and was bolstered by the endorsement and more than $200,000 from the Club for Growth, a political action committee of Wall Street financiers that promotes conservative economic ideology. When he resigned as a consultant for the Arizona School Choice Trust to launch his campaign, his opponents criticized him for taking a $50,000 donation from his campaign chairman, developer Ira Fulton; Flake agreed to repay his consulting fee to the trust. In its closing days, the primary was marred by a bitter clash when two of the other candidates—Phoenix attorney Tom Liddy (son of G. Gordon Liddy) and Susan Bitter Smith—accused each other of dirty campaigning; both agreed to take polygraph tests, and both passed. Flake won with 32%, an unexpectedly large margin over the runner-up, Phoenix Councilman Sal DiCiccio, who had 24%. Smith, who was runner-up to Salmon in the 1994 primary, won the same 22% of the vote. Liddy, who was backed by Senator John McCain, had 21%. In the general, Flake won 54%–42% over Democrat David Mendoza, a longtime lobbyist for public employees, who also ran for the seat in 1998—when he lost 65%–35%. Probably the most difficult part of the fall campaign came in early October when Flake was thrown from a horse at his ranch and suffered a punctured lung, broken shoulder and three broken ribs.

His campaign was based on his political philosophy—"Government which governs least, governs best." Flake promised to serve no more than three terms and "continue to rock the boat," much as his predecessor did for six years (it was Salmon's refusal to vote for Newt Gingrich for speaker which led to Gingrich's decision to quit in 1998). He plans to work for charter schools, and he has said that his term-limit pledge gives him the freedom to stand up against corporate interests. He favors replacing the income tax with a national sales tax. He also is an ardent foe of abortion. Redistricting probably will shrink this district, perhaps to one based largely in Mesa.

Cook's Call *Potentially Competitive.* Almost no other city in America has experienced the rampant growth over the last 10 years as Phoenix, which is the major reason the state will be getting two new seats in Congress. But, this growth could also have a major impact on the outlines of the three Phoenix based seats like this on. Already the least Republican of the three, the 1st District could see a very competitive contest in 2002.

THE PEOPLE: Pop. 2000: 829,492; Pop. 1990: 610,817, up 35.8% 1990–2000. 76.7% White, 3.9% Black, 3.1% Asian, 2% Amer. Indian, 0.2% Hawaiian, 3.1% Two+ races, 11% Other; 22.7% Hispanic Origin.

2000 Presidential Vote		
Bush (R)	127,057	(51%)
Gore (D)	108,920	(44%)
Nader (Green)	7,939	(3%)
Others	3,018	(1%)

1996 Presidential Vote		
Dole (R)	109,137	(46%)
Clinton (D)	107,698	(45%)
Perot (I)	17,048	(7%)

Rep. Jeff Flake (R)

Elected 2000, 1st term; b. Dec. 31, 1962, Snowflake; home, Mesa; Brigham Young U., B.A. 1986, M.A. 1987; Mormon; married (Cheryl).

Professional Career: Pub. Plcy. Exec., Shipley, Smoak & Henry, 1987–89; Exec. Dir., Fndt. for Democracy (Namibia), 1989–90; Owner, Interface Pub. Affairs, 1990–92; Exec. Dir., The Goldwater Inst., 1992–99.

DC Office: 512 CHOB 20515, 202-225-2635; Fax: 202-226-4386; Web site: www.house.gov/flake.

District Office: Mesa, 480-833-0092.

Committees: *International Relations* (24th of 26 R): Africa; East Asia & the Pacific. *Judiciary* (21st of 21 R): Commercial & Administrative Law; Immigration & Claims. *Resources* (26th of 28 R): Energy & Mineral Resources; Water & Power.

Group Ratings and Key Votes: Newly Elected

Election Results

2000 general	Jeff Flake (R)	123,289	(54%)	($505,210)
	David Mendoza (D)	97,455	(42%)	($74,451)
	Jon Burroughs (Lib)	9,227	(4%)	
2000 primary	Jeff Flake (R)	16,745	(32%)	
	Sal DiCiccio (R)	12,490	(24%)	
	Susan Bitter Smith (R)	11,763	(22%)	
	Tom Liddy (R)	10,898	(21%)	
	Others	764	(1%)	
1998 general	Matt Salmon (R)	98,840	(65%)	($362,374)
	David Mendoza (D)	54,108	(35%)	($4,058)

SECOND DISTRICT

Southern Arizona, though technically part of Mexico for hundreds of years, was never a home to Hispanic civilization like northern New Mexico. Here the hot desert land was inhabited mainly by Indians who kept their native ways and language until English-speaking whites came in on cavalry horses, miners' wagons and railroad cars in the late 19th Century. Today's Hispanic Arizonans are mostly descendants of later immigrants from Mexico, some who came over the border in the sleepier days before World War II, when it was scarcely patrolled, and many more who came in the 1980s and 1990s to partake in the dazzling economic growth which has served as both an attraction and an example to so many *norteno* Mexicans.

The 2d District of Arizona was designed to be the state's Hispanic district; its population in 2000 was 63% Hispanic. On a map, it looks regularly shaped, but in fact it is a collection of three distant communities connected by many acres of uninhabited desert. One center is central Phoenix, including the old downtown, the state Capitol to the west and the skyscraper districts on North Central Avenue out toward Camelback Road. The stereotypical Hispanic neighborhood here is a collection of 1940s and 1950s bungalows, spaced out by empty lots, not far from the railroad or Sky Harbor Airport or nestling within view of South Mountain. The west side of Tucson, with about one-third of the people in the 2d, is similar. The 2d also includes Yuma, on a Colorado River crossing, in an irrigated agricultural valley, often the hottest place in the country, with a desalination plant to protect the farmlands and extensive recreational facilities. Across the desert, past the Luke Air Force Base shooting range, the Organ Pipe Cactus National Monument, and the Tohono O'odham Indian Reservation, is the Mexican border town of Nogales, 94% Hispanic and near many maquiladora plants, the scene of many illegal crossings until the Border Patrol was beefed up, as well as an entry point for illegal drugs, and recently the locale for a bullfighting revival at the old stadium across the border. In a sign of their growing cooperation plus the booming industrial growth on both sides of the border, the sister cities of Nogales, Arizona and Nogales, Mexico have signed an agreement to jointly prevent and respond to emergencies involving fire or hazardous materials. The 2d is the one solidly Democratic district in Arizona.

The congressman from the 2d is Ed Pastor, a Democrat who won a special election in September 1991 to replace Morris Udall, longtime chairman of the House Interior Committee. Pastor grew up in Claypool, a mining town in Gila County, where his parents "taught me the value of education, the need of tolerance and the responsibility of community service. But especially they taught me the reward of a hard day's work." Pastor has been a career politician: after teaching high school he got a law degree at Arizona State, worked as an assistant to Governor Raul Castro in 1975, then was elected in 1976 to the Maricopa County Board of Supervisors, where he served until elected to Congress. In the 1991 special he beat Republican Pat Connor 56%–44%.

Since 1994 Pastor has been the only Arizona Democrat in Congress; all along he has been a faithful follower of the Democratic leadership and has a mostly liberal voting record. He supported NAFTA, despite strong labor opposition, but he opposed permanent trade relations with China. He vigorously opposed Arizona's English Only law and supports bilingual ballots, but says that "everyone acknowledges that English is the common language of our country." He strongly opposed the 1996 Immigration Act's limits on welfare for legal migrants and family unification preference for low-income households. He was proud of sponsoring the U.S.'s only current Hispanic U.S. Attorney and the first Hispanic woman federal judge in Arizona; he worked with Jon Kyl to get three new federal judges for the state and Kyl helped get them confirmed in October 2000.

Much of Pastor's work has been on the Appropriations Committee, on which he got a seat in his first full term (though he lost it for a while after Democrats lost control of the House). Now he sits on the Energy and Water Development and the Transportation Subcommittees, and brings home the bacon to southern Arizona—$16.5 million for transit projects in the Phoenix area, $11 million for the city airport, $5 million for Tucson transit projects, and $4.2 million for 62 new housing units for the elderly at Tucson's Barrio Historico Neighborhood Association. He has worked on a proposed $52 million project to transform the barren Salt River bottom into a wetland wildlife habitat. With John McCain and Jim Kolbe, Pastor worked on creating the Institute for Environmental Conflict Resolution in the Morris K. Udall Foundation; the idea is to settle environmental arguments by arbitration rather than lawsuits. In 2000, he won enactment of his proposal to authorize a new international port of entry at the border in Yuma, with conveyance of 330 acres to the Greater Yuma Port Authority; the project was designed to relieve congestion that often causes delays of several hours for commercial vehicles at San Luis five miles to the west. As an appropriator, he has had the thankless task of ranking Democrat on the Legislative Branch subcommittee that funds Capitol Hill.

Pastor has been re-elected easily, but with Arizona's gain of two seats, the 2d is likely to be significantly changed. One possibility is the creation of a heavily Hispanic district entirely in the Phoenix area and the creation of a new, Democratic-leaning district including much of Tucson. In that case Pastor would presumably run from Phoenix, but there is likely to be a heavily Hispanic and solidly Democratic district for him in 2002.

Cook's Call   *Safe*. The 2nd District was designed to be Democratic and has been reliably so for Ed Pastor. Though the state will undergo tremendous change in redistricting, the Voting Rights Act ensures that this majority Hispanic district will not be altered very much. The only question now is if one of the states two new districts will also be majority Hispanic.

THE PEOPLE: Pop. 2000: 773,824; Pop. 1990: 610,266, up 26.8% 1990–2000. 55.8% White, 5.1% Black, 1% Asian, 4.4% Amer. Indian, 0.1% Hawaiian, 3.7% Two+ races, 29.9% Other; 62.5% Hispanic Origin.

2000 Presidential Vote		
Gore (D)	78,169	(62%)
Bush (R)	43,017	(34%)
Nader (Green)	4,091	(3%)
Others	1,680	(1%)

1996 Presidential Vote		
Clinton (D)	81,678	(63%)
Dole (R)	36,584	(28%)
Perot (I)	9,292	(7%)

Rep. Ed Pastor (D)

Elected Sept. 1991, 5th term; b. June 28, 1943, Claypool; home, Phoenix; AZ St. U., B.A. 1966, J.D. 1974; Catholic; married (Verma).

Elected Office: Maricopa Cnty. Bd. of Supervisors, 1976–91.

Professional Career: High schl. teacher, 1966–69; Asst., AZ Gov. Castro, 1975.

DC Office: 2465 RHOB 20515, 202-225-4065; Fax: 202-225-1655; Web site: www.house.gov/pastor.

District Offices: Phoenix, 602-256-0551; Tucson, 520-624-9986; Yuma, 520-726-2234.

Committees: *Chief Deputy Minority Whip. Appropriations* (15th of 29 D): Energy & Water Development; Transportation. *Standards of Official Conduct* (3d of 5 D).

Group Ratings

	ADA	ACLU	AFS	LCV	CON	ITIC	NTU	COC	ACU	NTLC	CHC
2000	90	86	100	71	69	72	18	52	8	12	0
1999	100	—	100	81	90	—	22	24	0	—	—

National Journal Ratings

	1999 LIB —	1999 CONS		2000 LIB —	2000 CONS
Economic	67% —	32%		75% —	24%
Social	87% —	0%		77% —	22%
Foreign	93% —	5%		80% —	16%

Key Votes of the 106th Congress

1. Patient Bill of Rights	Y	5. Bar RU-486 $ for FDA	N	9. NATO War in Serbia	Y
2. Accelerate Min. Wage	Y	6. Display 10 Commandments	N	10. Perm. Trade with China	N
3. Strike Ban on Ergo. Stnd.	Y	7. Gun Show Bkgrnd. Checks	Y	11. Debt Relief for 3rd World	Y
4. Ovrd. Estate Tax Veto	N	8. Ban Part.-Birth Abortion	N	12. Drop Cuba Econ. Embargo	Y

Election Results

2000 general	Ed Pastor (D)	84,034	(69%)	($569,648)
	Bill Barenholtz (R)	32,990	(27%)	($80,566)
	Others	5,581	(5%)	
2000 primary	Ed Pastor (D)	unopposed		
1998 general	Ed Pastor (D)	57,178	(68%)	($418,113)
	Ed Barron (R)	23,628	(28%)	
	Others	3,557	(4%)	

THIRD DISTRICT

Most of Arizona's physical landscape, for all the vibrant metropolitan growth of Phoenix and Tucson, remains much as it was when white men first settled here. Beneath mountains and along mostly dry creek beds, they built towns that still have an Old West look, like Prescott, originally a gold mining camp, home since 1888 of America's oldest annual rodeo and now decorated with statutes of everyone from early settlers to Vietnam veterans, and Wickenburg, the oldest Arizona town north of Tucson, still very Western in style. The landscape retains a beauty that can overpower mere buildings and parking lots: think of the red rocks of Sedona, an esoteric resort between Prescott and Flagstaff, with its own film festival. Some landscape is intentionally preserved, like the sere uplands of the Hopi Indian Reservation. There are some abrupt juxtapositions of settlement and nature: the real London Bridge transplanted to Lake Havasu City, a retirement community on the Colorado River; or Bullhead City, one-third of whose people work in "family gambler" casinos in Laughlin, Nevada, just across the bridge over the rock-lined, piping-hot river. And there is the Grand Canyon, impossible to take in all at once.

All these areas are part of the 3d Congressional District of Arizona, which stretches from the west side of Phoenix to cover most of the northwest quadrant of the state. Most of its people are clustered in its southeast corner, in metro Phoenix. Here, west of the Black Canyon Freeway, is the mushrooming suburb of Glendale, not so long ago just a crossroads but with 219,000 people in 2000; just west are Peoria, as Middle American as its namesake in Illinois, and the huge retirement community of Sun City. The 3d also includes the fast-growing corridor along the westbound I-10 Papago Freeway, past Litchfield Park and its Wigwam resort to the once open spaces of Goodyear and Buckeye. This is heavily Republican territory: The retirees here remember— and the upwardly-striving, family-oriented young migrants who have populated these new towns in the desert still try to live—the culturally conservative, Ozzie-and-Harriet lifestyle of the 1950s. Culture, more than affluence, which by national standards is not all that striking here, accounts for their political conservatism. Similarly Republican are the Colorado River new cities and Prescott, where Barry Goldwater used to end all his campaigns.

The 3d District's congressman is Bob Stump, who was first elected as a Democrat in 1976 and who is now the Republican chairman of the Armed Services Committee. He grew up in Arizona, enlisted at 16 in the Navy during World War II, and took part in the bloody invasions of Luzon, Iwo Jima and Okinawa. After the war he grew cotton and grain, and was elected to the legislature in 1958: he has been a legislator for more than 40 years. Like many older Arizonans, he was a "pinto" (conservative) Democrat, elected to Congress as a Democrat in 1976. In 1981, after voting for the Reagan budget and tax cuts, he switched parties, to reflect both his constituency and his convictions. It was a smooth switch: He won 64% as a Democrat in 1980 and 63% as a Republican in 1982. When Stump switched, Republicans gave him seats on the Armed Services and Veterans' Affairs Committees, whose conservatism was compatible with his own. He is tight-lipped; the *Arizona Republic* called him "the most low-key committee chairman in Congress" and Mississippi Democrat Sonny Montgomery once said of Stump: "His longest speech has been two minutes." He has no press secretary and has only four employees in his Washington office; he sometimes answers the office phone.

Stump became chairman of the Veterans Affairs Committee after the Republicans won control in 1994, but he kept to the policies he supported when Montgomery was chairman, including the innovative Montgomery G.I. veterans' benefits package of the 1980s. Stump made some headlines after it was found that ambassador and big Democratic contributor Larry Lawrence had been buried in Arlington National Cemetery under false pretenses. With ranking Democrat Lane Evans, he sponsored a bill limiting burial in Arlington to veterans who were killed on active duty or who won major medals; it passed the House unanimously in March 1998 but went nowhere in the Senate. For the most part he ran Veterans Affairs on a bipartisan basis, though there was some partisan warfare in early 1999. His bill to expand Arlington National Cemetery to accommodate 30,000 more gravesites became law in October 1999. In 2000 he noted that the Clinton budget failed to include benefits he and Evans sought, and then the administration came out for them a day before the committee markup.

House Republicans' six-year term limits on committee chairmen put Stump in line for the chairmanship of the Armed Services Committee. He did have spirited competition from Curt Weldon, a strong proponent of missile defense who was three seats behind in seniority. Stump did not put on a visible campaign, but he did give $150,000 to the Republicans' Battleground 2000 program and approached members on the floor; he prevailed in the Republican Steering Committee. He can be expected to support significant defense spending increases, and is likely to have a good relationship with ranking Democrat Ike Skelton; they were fellow Democratic freshmen in the class of 1976. Stump is a strong supporter of missile defense. He also believes that homosexuality is incompatible with military service.

On other issues, Stump backed repeal of the Social Security earnings tax (a popular stand in Sun City). He opposed then-Interior Secretary Bruce Babbitt's plan to designate the Shivwits Plateau northwest of the Grand Canyon as a national monument; Stump wanted continued mining, road construction and air tours. He opposes individual investment accounts for Social Security and wants to limit immigration to 300,000 a year. He was displeased when Citizens Against Government Waste, an anti-pork barrel group admiring of John McCain, labeled as pork Stump's provision for a $10 million land purchase at the Barry Goldwater Range. He was the one member of the Arizona Republican delegation who did not endorse McCain for president, instead staying neutral.

Except for the anti-incumbent year of 1990, when his percentage dipped to 57%, Stump has been re-elected easily in this strongly Republican district. In 1996 and 1998 he was won 67%–33%; in 2000, 66%–31%. After the 2000 election, he strongly criticized the Gore-Lieberman campaign for its systematic effort to disqualify absentee military ballots in Florida.

Cook's Call   *Probably Safe.* While Phoenix will likely undergo serious restructuring in redistricting, Bob Stump is no stranger to running and winning in newly created districts. Stump has survived two previous map changes with flying colors. For the first time, however, a nonpartisan commission instead of the legislature will draw district lines. That will makes the process (and the outlines for his seat) more unpredictable.

THE PEOPLE: Pop. 2000: 997,565; Pop. 1990: 610,424, up 63.4% 1990–2000. 82.6% White, 2.5% Black, 1.3% Asian, 2.6% Amer. Indian, 0.1% Hawaiian, 2.5% Two + races, 8.3% Other; 18.1% Hispanic Origin.

2000 Presidential Vote
Bush (R)	177,572	(56%)
Gore (D)	126,950	(40%)
Nader (Green)	8,571	(3%)
Others	4,511	(1%)

1996 Presidential Vote
Dole (R)	130,887	(48%)
Clinton (D)	113,635	(41%)
Perot (I)	26,993	(10%)

Rep. Bob Stump (R)

Elected 1976, 13th term; b. Apr. 4, 1927, Phoenix; home, Tolleson; AZ St. U., B.S. 1951; Seventh Day Adventist; divorced.

Military Career: Navy, 1943–46 (WWII).

Elected Office: AZ House of Reps., 1958–66; AZ Senate, 1966–76, Senate Pres., 1975–76.

Professional Career: Cotton & grain farmer.

DC Office: 211 CHOB 20515, 202-225-4576; Fax: 202-225-6328.

District Office: Phoenix, 602-379-6923.

Committees: *Armed Services* (Chmn. of 32 R). *Veterans' Affairs* (3d of 17 R): Oversight & Investigations (Vice Chmn.).

Group Ratings
	ADA	ACLU	AFS	LCV	CON	ITIC	NTU	COC	ACU	NTLC	CHC
2000	0	21	0	0	31	94	67	76	92	88	100
1999	0	—	0	6	44	—	61	84	92	—	—

National Journal Ratings
	1999 LIB	—	1999 CONS		2000 LIB	—	2000 CONS
Economic	0%	—	84%		25%	—	72%
Social	10%	—	85%		0%	—	79%
Foreign	20%	—	78%		25%	—	69%

Key Votes of the 106th Congress

1. Patient Bill of Rights	N	5. Bar RU-486 $ for FDA	Y	9. NATO War in Serbia	N
2. Accelerate Min. Wage	N	6. Display 10 Commandments	Y	10. Perm. Trade with China	Y
3. Strike Ban on Ergo. Stnd.	N	7. Gun Show Bkgrnd. Checks	N	11. Debt Relief for 3rd World	N
4. Ovrd. Estate Tax Veto	Y	8. Ban Part.-Birth Abortion	Y	12. Drop Cuba Econ. Embargo	N

Election Results

2000 general	Bob Stump (R)	198,367	(66%)	($377,426)
	Gene Scharer (D)	94,676	(31%)	($6,993)
	Others	8,927	(3%)	
2000 primary	Bob Stump (R)	60,143	(83%)	
	Dick Hensley (R)	12,427	(17%)	
1998 general	Bob Stump (R)	137,618	(67%)	($246,233)
	Stuart Marc Starky (D)	66,979	(33%)	($29,211)

FOURTH DISTRICT

In May 1998 Barry Goldwater died at his home in the Phoenix suburb of Paradise Valley. His life had spanned almost the whole history of Arizona. He was born on New Year's Day 1909, when Arizona was still a territory, and could remember when it was the "baby state," the fourth-least populous in the nation, ahead of only Delaware, Wyoming and Nevada. When he returned from World War II, Paradise Valley was still empty land and Phoenix not much more than a small town, an outpost of American civilization in a sizzling desert. Today Arizona has 5.1 million people, with 3.2 million in metropolitan Phoenix; the city has been transformed from a frontier outpost to a diversified high-tech center, an example of how creativity and ingenuity can build a sophisticated city with relatively minimalist government and low taxes.

From Camelback Mountain, 1800 feet above Phoenix and Paradise Valley, or from Frank Lloyd Wright's Taliesin West home and studio, you can with equal awe get a sense of what this land was originally like and an understanding of how impressively Phoenix has grown. South of Camelback, subdivisions were often built with grass and greenery; in the affluent areas north of Camelback and spreading out Scottsdale Road and the Black Canyon Freeway, the natural desert look is more common. In 1998, a master-planned community of Anthem was created 35 miles north of downtown and it is expected to grow to 50,000 within a decade. Grass is discouraged, and often banned by subdivision covenant; planting anything but desert flora is frowned upon. The architecture of the houses tends toward unadorned stucco with picture windows facing away from the sun; the idea is to suggest that there is a horse corral over in the next lot and sometimes, especially in the northern edges of Phoenix, there is.

The 4th Congressional District of Arizona consists of this northern part of Phoenix, northern Scottsdale, Paradise Valley and part of Glendale, bounded approximately by Camelback Road on the south, Pima Road and the Salt River Indian Reservation on the east, Pinnacle Peak Road on the north and 47th and Grand Avenues on the west. For all its rustic and unplanned air, this is a highly affluent district, and usually a heavily Republican one.

The congressman from the 4th is John Shadegg, elected in 1994, with a fine Arizona Republican pedigree. His father, Stephen Shadegg, managed Barry Goldwater's first campaign for the Senate in 1952, when he upset Senate Majority Leader Ernest McFarland; the older Shadegg helped deliver campaign press releases in those pre-fax days. The younger Shadegg is a lawyer who served as special assistant to the state attorney general and a special counsel to the Arizona House Republican Caucus. When 4th District Congressman Jon Kyl ran for the Senate in 1994, Shadegg ran for the House seat and won 43% in the Republican primary, to 30% for a former aide to controversial Governor Evan Mecham, and 21% for a county supervisor. He won the general election easily, 60%–36%.

In the House, Shadegg was one of the firebrand 1994 Republican freshmen, a rebel against Democratic policies and often against his own party's leadership. He refused to back the balanced budget amendment without a three-fifths supermajority for tax increases, in defiance of Speaker Newt Gingrich and Majority Leader Dick Armey. He pushed to defund the National Endowment for the Arts, even when the leadership compromised. He was one of 15 freshman to vote against a keep-the-government-open compromise in January 1996 and he voted against the Clinton-Gingrich budget deal in May 1997, saying its claims of budget balance and tax relief were "over-blown and exaggerated." On the Budget Committee, he proposed in April 1998 a budget with more domestic spending cuts, more defense increases and more tax cuts than then-Chairman John Kasich's. As chairman of the House's Conservative Action Team in 2000, Shadegg wanted to allow states to "opt out" of minimum wage increases; but party leaders pleaded and he backed off. His CATs group agreed to support the budget resolution that year only on the condition that Kasich agreed to enhanced enforcement of budget limits; Shadegg won that battle but by the end of the year, Congress had approved spending more than $30 billion above the original ceiling. "Our base doesn't expect us to win, but they want to make sure we're fighting for them," he told *The New York Times,* in a mellowing of the earlier radical rhetoric. He filed a bill requiring the federal government to turn over 22,000 acres of land to Arizona, which Shadegg and other Arizonans contend was part of the 1910 statehood agreement. The Bureau of Land Management hasn't denied the claim but it reportedly has "moved slowly"—for more than 90 years so far.

On the Commerce Committee, Shadegg worked with Tom Coburn on an alternative managed-care reform plan, which permitted some lawsuits against HMOs, though limited in amount and with losing litigants paying costs—a position arguably to the left of the House leadership but prepared at the request of Speaker Dennis Hastert. When House Republicans were pressured to support the more sweeping Norwood-Dingell alternative, Shadegg's version gave them some cover, though it exposed him to attack from both insurance companies and trial lawyers. The plan was defeated by the House 238–193, with only two Democrats in favor but 29 mostly moderate Republicans opposed.

Shadegg's anti-leadership stands cost him a seat on Ways and Means in 1997 (it went to the 6th District's J.D. Hayworth instead). But he has been entrusted with several leadership assignments. When Gingrich relinquished the GOPAC chairmanship in May 1995, Shadegg replaced him. He was asked to help head recruitment by the National Republican Congressional Committee in September 1997 and was named one of six vice chairmen by Tom Davis in November 1998. He was named as one of five Republicans on the Census 2000 subcommittee—to handle an issue Republican leaders regarded as vital to their party. He skillfully grilled Attorney General Janet Reno in hearings on the Waco massacre and campaign finance charges against Al Gore. When Bill Clinton decided to create the Ironwood National Forest Monument outside Tucson, an unhappy Shadegg objected to the abuse of presidential authority and said, "I would draw a parallel to Hitler. He resisted the will of the German people to resist evil;" Shadegg later voiced regret about the Hitler analogy, though not about his general point.

Shadegg has won re-election with at least 64% of the vote three times against weak opposition. Redistricting will shrink Shadegg's geographic base but it should not significantly change its political make-up. He has voiced interest in seeking a Senate seat if and when John McCain steps down.

Cook's Call *Probably safe.* Rep. John Shadegg represents the most conservative district in the state. How redistricting will impact his district is unknown, but it is likely that Phoenix will retain at least one heavily Republican seat.

THE PEOPLE: Pop. 2000: 735,344; Pop. 1990: 610,708, up 20.4% 1990–2000. 81.6% White, 3.1% Black, 2.4% Asian, 1.8% Amer. Indian, 0.1% Hawaiian, 2.9% Two + races, 8.2% Other; 18.8% Hispanic Origin.

2000 Presidential Vote

Bush (R)	121,685	(52%)
Gore (D)	101,960	(44%)
Nader (Green)	6,216	(3%)
Others	3,024	(1%)

1996 Presidential Vote

Dole (R)	115,094	(48%)
Clinton (D)	103,878	(44%)
Perot (I)	16,547	(7%)

Rep. John Shadegg (R)

Elected 1994, 4th term; b. Oct. 22, 1949, Phoenix; home, Phoenix; U. of AZ, B.A. 1972, J.D. 1975; Episcopalian; married (Shirley).

Military Career: Air Natl. Guard, 1969–75.

Professional Career: Practicing atty., 1975–94; US Spec. Asst. Atty. Gen., 1983–90; Spec. Cnsl., AZ House Republican Caucus, 1991–92; Cnsl., AZ Wildlife Conservation, 1992.

DC Office: 432 CHOB 20515, 202-225-3361; Fax: 202-225-3462; Web site: www.house.gov/shadegg.

District Office: Phoenix, 602-263-5300.

Committees: *Energy & Commerce* (18th of 31 R): Commerce, Trade & Consumer Protection; Energy & Air Quality; Health. *Financial Services* (28th of 37 R): Capital Markets, Insurance & Government Sponsored Enterprises; Domestic Monetary Policy, Technology & Economic Growth; Oversight & Investigations.

Group Ratings

	ADA	ACLU	AFS	LCV	CON	ITIC	NTU	COC	ACU	NTLC	CHC
2000	5	21	0	7	93	100	79	80	96	100	100
1999	0	—	0	6	88	—	70	79	96	—	—

National Journal Ratings

	1999 LIB	—	1999 CONS		2000 LIB	—	2000 CONS
Economic	0%	—	84%		25%	—	72%
Social	10%	—	85%		0%	—	79%
Foreign	0%	—	97%		0%	—	88%

Key Votes of the 106th Congress

1. Patient Bill of Rights	N	5. Bar RU-486 $ for FDA	Y	9. NATO War in Serbia	N
2. Accelerate Min. Wage	N	6. Display 10 Commandments	Y	10. Perm. Trade with China	Y
3. Strike Ban on Ergo. Stnd.	N	7. Gun Show Bkgrnd. Checks	N	11. Debt Relief for 3rd World	N
4. Ovrd. Estate Tax Veto	Y	8. Ban Part.-Birth Abortion	Y	12. Drop Cuba Econ. Embargo	N

Election Results

2000 general	John Shadegg (R)	140,396	(64%)	($572,248)
	Ben Jankowski (D)	71,803	(33%)	($1,250)
	Others	7,298	(3%)	
2000 primary	John Shadegg (R)	unopposed		
1998 general	John Shadegg (R)	102,722	(65%)	($525,849)
	Eric Ehst (D)	49,538	(31%)	($14,206)
	Others	6,562	(4%)	

FIFTH DISTRICT

Arizona's first frontier was just south of today's Tucson, where Franciscan friars built San Xavier del Bac mission in the 18th Century. To the east the late 19th Century mining towns of Tombstone and Bisbee sprang up on desert mountainsides, where miners dug up gold and silver and, for many years, much of America's copper; Cochise County, including those two towns, was the most populous county when Arizona became the 48th state in 1912. Here the white man last subdued the Indians, when the Apache leader Geronimo faced the U.S. Army in 1900. In the late 1990s Cochise County became an active frontier again. After the Border Patrol reduced illegal crossings in California and Texas, Mexicans wishing to enter the United States came to Agua Prieta, just across the border from the town of Douglas. Every night they fan out east and west and then, often with guides, cross the barbed wire and enter the United States. In the dozens they tramp across ranches and rural homelots; some ranchers have taken to tracking them down and turning them over to the Border Patrol. In eight months in 1999 and 2000, some 40 of these immigrants were found dead; in the month of May 2000, 43,000 were sent back to Mexico by the Border Patrol.

One of their destinations is Tucson, Arizona's second metropolis, much smaller, more rough-hewn and politically less conservative than Phoenix. Tucson is a high-tech city and home of the University of Arizona. It is sometimes at odds with the rest of the state; the city government wants to require contractors to pay employees more than the minimum wage, while the state legislature says no. Tucson is also tourist country, with famed resorts. Nearby is the site of Biosphere II, the greenhouse-like structure in the desert in which eight men and women lived more or less self-sufficiently from September 1991 until September 1993; it is now a research site run by Columbia University. For nearly 40 years, Tucson was the political base of the brothers Udall: Stewart, congressman in the 1950s, Interior secretary in the 1960s, now an Arizona lawyer again; Morris, congressman for 30 years and Interior Committee chairman, who retired in 1991 because of Parkinson's disease and died in 1998.

The 5th Congressional District of Arizona includes most, but not all, of Tucson and Pima County—the Latino west side of town is in the 2d District. The 5th also includes much south-eastern Arizona desert real estate: all of Cochise County, including Tombstone, Bisbee, Douglas and Sierra Vista near Fort Huachuca; and some small farming and mining towns in Pinal and Graham Counties. Politically, it is fairly evenly divided, voting Republican in state politics and twice for Bill Clinton but voting for George W. Bush in 2000, 49%–46%.

The congressman from the 5th is Jim Kolbe, a Republican first elected in 1984. He comes originally from Illinois, served in the Navy in Vietnam, became an assistant to Illinois' Republican Governor Richard Ogilvie in 1972, and moved to Arizona shortly thereafter and went into real estate. In 1976 he was elected to the Arizona Senate. In 1982 he ran in the new 5th District and lost to Democrat Jim McNulty 50%–48%. In 1984 he ran again and beat him 51%–48%.

Kolbe's voting record on economics has been mostly conservative; he ranks near the middle of the House on cultural and foreign issues. He is a strong booster of free trade and of the maquiladora program, in which U.S.-made components shipped to Mexico for assembly can reenter the U.S. without paying full duty. He was one of the Republican leaders in the successful fight to pass NAFTA in the House in November 1993. He supported GATT, fast track and the WTO and has called for a free-trade zone covering Central America. He attended the Seattle WTO meeting and chairs the Inter-Parliamentary Group for Mexico. He was one of the leading House spokesmen for PNTR for China in 2000. In response to the surge in illegal immigration in the 5th District, he worked for more Border Patrol officers and got $2 million to address border problems in June 2000. Looking farther ahead, he has called for a guest worker program, to provide a legal way for Mexicans and others to work in tight-labor markets like Arizona. Another Kolbe cause is Social Security reform; he believes that America should move toward an individual account system. He served on the Center for Strategic and International Studies reform commission with Democrat Charles Stenholm and Senators John Breaux and Judd Gregg, and has sponsored their proposal which would raise the retirement age gradually, put 2% of the payroll tax into individual retirement accounts and guarantee a baseline pension.

From 1997–2000 Kolbe was chairman of the Appropriations subcommittee with jurisdiction over the Treasury, the White House and Congress itself. He demanded an accounting in May 1997 of the cost of Bill Clinton's 938 overnight guests in the Lincoln bedroom. In 2000 he held hearings on the cost to the government of transporting Senate candidate Hillary Rodham Clinton to New York campaign events; as of July 2000 he found that her trips cost the Air Force $698,000 but her campaign had reimbursed the government only $112,000. Clinton apologists argued that she was obliged to use government aircraft because of her position as First Lady; Kolbe noted that she had traveled on a chartered plane on a book tour, for which she or her publisher would have to pick up the tab. In 1997 and 1999 he pushed for passage of appropriations without the usual language barring cost-of-living pay increases for members of Congress. In 1999 he sponsored an increase in the president's salary from $200,000, the level set in 1969, to $400,000, to take effect in January 2001. He has also used his Appropriations seat for Arizona causes—a $14 million Navajo-Hopi hospital, $4 million for land acquisition in the Saguaro National Park (East) just outside Tucson, $4 million for the Fort Apache Reservation. With John McCain and Ed Pastor, he got $5.5 million to establish an Institute for Environmental Conflict Resolution at the Morris K. Udall Foundation in Tucson. He has been working to create a wildlife and recreation corridor linking mountain ranges and national forests from the Mexican border, which would encourage land conservation but allow grazing and other uses of private property there; the first step was the December 2000 law establishing the Las Cienagas National Conservation Area. For the 107th Congress, Kolbe moved over to chair the Foreign Operations Subcommittee.

On cultural issues Kolbe is often liberal. He angered many Republicans by supporting funding for the National Endowment for the Arts and was one of the few Republicans to vote against the partial-birth abortion ban. He voted for the 1994 crime bill with its gun control provisions but in 1999 voted against Carolyn McCarthy's amendment to toughen a Republican bill to require background checks at gun shows—Kolbe voted for the final bill, which failed. He voted for the Defense of Marriage Act and in July 1996, pressured by an impending article in *The Advocate*, announced that he is gay. This had little apparent impact on the 1996 election, in which he beat Morris Udall's chiropractor 69%–26%. He supported hate crimes legislation before the Matthew Shepard slaying and said afterward, "Thank God Wyoming has the death penalty." In July 1998 he opposed Joel Hefley's amendment to overturn Bill Clinton's order banning discrimination against homosexuals in federal employment, saying, "It's a bad signal for Republicans to be sending, that we want to alienate this substantial group." Republican leaders got Hefley to agree not to offer his amendment to Kolbe's appropriation; when it came up later, Kolbe helped persuade 63 Republicans to vote against it.

In 1998 Kolbe had an unexpectedly close race for re-election. His opponent was Tom Volgy, University of Arizona political scientist, Tucson councilman for 10 years and mayor from 1987–91. His biggest issue was campaign finance: He limited his campaign to $250,000 and championed the plan he instituted in Tucson, which limits total contributions and bans PAC money. Although Kolbe spent nearly three times as much money, he won by only 52%–45%, and many wondered whether his sexual orientation was a hidden liability. In August 2000 Kolbe was the first openly gay speaker at a Republican National Convention. As he spoke about the importance of free trade, his assigned topic and one on which he had a strong record, several members of the Texas delegation in the front took off their cowboy hats and bowed their heads in prayer; Kolbe said he didn't notice. In September he easily dispatched a primary opponent by 79%–21%. In November he had what some considered his strongest opponent, George Cunningham, a former state Senator and chief of staff to Governor Rose Mofford. He ran ads showing schoolchildren attacking Kolbe for his votes on education; Kolbe responded with ads showing Senator John McCain and Governor Jane Hull attacking Cunningham's tactics. Kolbe spent much more money and won by a solid 60%–35%.

Kolbe had some hopes of a Bush appointment, perhaps as Special Trade Representative; but it was unlikely that, with such a closely divided House, Republicans would want a special election in this district. Redistricting could pose some difficulties for Kolbe. A district like the present one would probably be most favorable to him; a district that lumped together the heavily Republican precincts of east Tucson with the heavily Democratic precincts of west Tucson would be problematic, though not unwinnable, since Kolbe ran well ahead of George W. Bush in 2000.

Cook's Call   *Competitive.* But for one tighter than expected race in 1998, Jim Kolbe has easily carried this district, originally drawn to be a swing seat, for 16 years. There is some talk that the Tucson area will pick up a new seat in 2002 with one seat located in the inner Tucson region and one seat taking the outer Tucson suburbs and rural parts of southern Arizona.

THE PEOPLE: Pop. 2000: 793,256; Pop. 1990: 611,128, up 29.8% 1990–2000. 82.1% White, 3.1% Black, 2.1% Asian, 1.2% Amer. Indian, 0.1% Hawaiian, 3% Two + races, 8.4% Other; 20.5% Hispanic Origin.

2000 Presidential Vote

Bush (R)	143,179	(49%)
Gore (D)	135,963	(46%)
Nader (Green)	11,330	(4%)
Others	3,245	(1%)

1996 Presidential Vote

Clinton (D)	126,223	(47%)
Dole (R)	116,965	(44%)
Perot (I)	20,732	(8%)

Rep. Jim Kolbe (R)

Elected 1984, 9th term; b. June 28, 1942, Evanston, IL; home, Tucson; Northwestern U., B.A. 1965, Stanford U., M.B.A. 1967; United Methodist; divorced.

Military Career: Navy, 1968–69 (Vietnam), Naval Reserves, 1970–77.

Elected Office: AZ Senate, 1976–82.

Professional Career: Asst., IL Bldg. Authority Architect, 1970–72; Asst., IL Gov. Ogilvie, 1972–73; Vice Pres., land planning firm; Real estate consultant.

DC Office: 2266 RHOB 20515, 202-225-2542; Fax: 202-225-0378; Web site: www.house.gov/kolbe.

District Offices: Sierra Vista, 520-459-3115; Tucson, 520-881-3588.

Committees: *Appropriations* (8th of 35 R): Commerce, Justice & State; Foreign Operations & Export Financing (Chmn.); Interior.

Group Ratings

	ADA	ACLU	AFS	LCV	CON	ITIC	NTU	COC	ACU	NTLC	CHC
2000	20	57	0	29	41	94	63	80	68	64	50
1999	20	—	0	19	37	—	58	91	70	—	—

National Journal Ratings

	1999 LIB	—	1999 CONS		2000 LIB	—	2000 CONS
Economic	0%	—	84%		25%	—	72%
Social	55%	—	45%		54%	—	45%
Foreign	50%	—	48%		33%	—	62%

Key Votes of the 106th Congress

1. Patient Bill of Rights	N	5. Bar RU-486 $ for FDA	N	9. NATO War in Serbia	N
2. Accelerate Min. Wage	N	6. Display 10 Commandments	Y	10. Perm. Trade with China	Y
3. Strike Ban on Ergo. Stnd.	N	7. Gun Show Bkgrnd. Checks	N	11. Debt Relief for 3rd World	N
4. Ovrd. Estate Tax Veto	Y	8. Ban Part.-Birth Abortion	N	12. Drop Cuba Econ. Embargo	N

Election Results

2000 general	Jim Kolbe (R)	172,986	(60%)	($1,541,478)
	George Cunningham (D)	101,564	(35%)	($552,735)
	Others	13,059	(5%)	
2000 primary	Jim Kolbe (R)	35,263	(79%)	
	Joseph Sweeney (R)	9,477	(21%)	
1998 general	Jim Kolbe (R)	103,952	(52%)	($707,776)
	Tom Volgy (D)	91,030	(45%)	($257,651)
	Others	6,491	(3%)	

SIXTH DISTRICT

Arizona has one of the nation's largest and fastest-growing Indian populations. There are small, sparsely populated reservations across the state, but by far the largest Indian tribe is the Navajo, in the northeast corner of the state who form the majority in (oddly) Apache County and a large minority in Navajo County to the west. The Navajo have their own tribal politics, complete with fiercely contested elections for tribal chief; and, alas, considerable corruption. The political form of governance, with winner-take-all elections, seems not to have served the Navajo well: unemployment runs around 30% and nearly 30% live without running water and electricity. An alternative might be the corporate form that has worked much better for Alaska Natives.

The 6th Congressional District covers nearly half of Arizona, including the Navajo country and some of northern Phoenix and Scottsdale. The 6th also takes in the old mining towns of Globe and Clifton; Flagstaff, south of the Grand Canyon, in the midst of ponderosa pine forests which the fire department thins by cutting trees and controlled burns; Page, to the north, where townspeople making money off the recreational Lake Powell oppose the Sierra Club's proposal to get rid of the Glen Canyon Dam and the lake. Much of this is wild country: Mexican wolves were released in 1998 in the mountains of the Apache National Forest, and environmentalists rejoiced when the federal government in 2000 paid $1 million to stop pumice-mining operations on the San Francisco Peaks. Here also is the sparsely populated, wind-swept desert with seven Indian reservations in all (the erose boundaries exclude the Hopis, who have a long and angry boundary dispute with the Navajo). Closer to Phoenix, the 6th takes in the suburbs of Carefree and Cave Creek, rustic areas where the mile-square grids are far from filled in and the local stores are more likely to feature horse feed than designer clothes, and the Salt River and Gila Valley reservations, their edges now sprouting Wal-marts and Kmarts. Politically, this is a sharply divided district. The Maricopa County portions, which cast 60% of the vote in 2000, are usually heavily Republican. Navajo County is recently, and the copper mining country has been historically, heavily Democratic; Flagstaff is moving that way. The Navajo vote heavily Democratic. The result is that the 6th District was fiercely contested in the first four elections after it was created in 1992.

The congressman from the 6th District is J.D. Hayworth, a conservative Republican who grew up in North Carolina and made his way upward in the hierarchy of local TV stations as a sportscaster, from Raleigh to Greenville to Cincinnati and then, in 1987, to Phoenix. Hayworth is 6'5", weighs 290, speaks with a booming voice and has a certain resemblance—a help in some quarters, a hindrance in others—to Rush Limbaugh. Certainly he was well known when he ran for Congress in 1994 and won the five-way Republican primary with 45%. In the general he faced incumbent Democrat Karan English, who won the newly created seat in 1992 by 53%–41%. Hayworth attacked English for voting for the Clinton tax increase and framed the race as "between a citizen who pays taxes and a career politician who raises them." He carried Maricopa County 65%–32%, enough to easily overcome deficits on the Indian reservations and around Flagstaff, and won 55%–41%.

Hayworth became a strong voice and a solid vote in the new Republican majority. He seemed to irritate Democrats more than just about any other freshman. Veteran Democrat David Obey told him, "You are one of the most impolite members I have ever seen in my service in this House." Hayworth voted solidly with Gingrich and the Republican leadership, even as his 1994 Arizona colleagues Matt Salmon and John Shadegg were leading rebellion. He worked on some local issues, meeting with Indian leaders though that was not likely to win him much support, and traveled around the district in a Subaru Outback specially designed for his large frame.

Early on Democrats targeted him. Steve Owens, an aide to then-Senator Al Gore in the 1980s and later Arizona Democratic chairman, returned to the district to run against Hayworth in 1996. Through most of the fall the race was even in the polls. Hayworth called Owens a carpetbagger—a strange charge in a state where most people are from somewhere else—and ran ads pointing out that Owens had taken $5,000 from the Laborers' Union whose "bosses have admitted their connection to organized crime." Hayworth spent more than $1 million, Owens some $750,000; labor's money was balanced by Republican National Committee ads. Hayworth won 48%–47%, one of the closest results in the country.

In the House Hayworth continued his conservative rhetoric but also became an inside player. He reaped his reward for loyalty when Gingrich gave him a seat on Ways and Means, and bypassed Shadegg. On that committee Hayworth organized a bipartisan coalition to defeat by 22–16 a $1.9 billion proposed tax on Indian gambling. He was also a lead sponsor of the successful $500 per child tax credit. When Bill Clinton line-item vetoed funds for the experimental Case Grande copper mine, Hayworth got commitments for funds from Budget Director Jacob Lew and Interior Secretary Bruce Babbitt. The *Arizona Republic* still referred to his "infamous bluster," Matt Salmon called him "Foghorn Leghorn" and a *Washingtonian* survey named him number one in Congress in the "no rocket scientist" category and number two in "biggest windbag." In 1998 Steve Owens ran again. This time he asked the AFL-CIO to stay out of the race and campaigned for a patient's bill of rights against "insurance company bureaucrats" and for the McCain-Feingold campaign finance reform bill. Hayworth won by the fairly comfortable margin of 53%–44%. He carried Maricopa County 61%–36% and lost the rest of the district 53%–44%.

In the 106th Congress Hayworth continued to make noise. He attacked the "controlled burns" that got out of control at Los Alamos and the North Rim of the Grand Canyon as "misguided management," calling instead of thinning and timber harvesting, and said the seizure of

Elian Gonzalez was "the lowest point of the Clinton presidency." He called for the resignations of National Security Advisor Sandy Berger because of Chinese theft of nuclear secrets and of White House Press Secretary Joe Lockhart for saying that Southern Baptists "perpetuate ancient religious hatred." But he also worked on local issues. A Hayworth bill passed the House in June 1999 allowing local school districts to buy up to 80 acres of Forest Service lands at $10 an acre for educational purposes, and he delayed a change in Medicare for Maricopa County, where many more recipients have HMO contracts and pay less than the national average for insurance. He got the House to pass a bill giving the DEA control over the GBL dietary supplemental that nearly killed Phoenix Suns basketball player Tom Gugliotta.

In 2000 the Democrats had a hard time coming up with a candidate and ended up running a copper miner from San Manuel. Hayworth won 61%–36%; he carried Maricopa 67%–30% and won in the rest of district as well, 53%–44%. Redistricting will certainly change the shape of this fast-growing district, as Arizona gains two new seats. But there will surely be a district anchored in northeast Maricopa County for Hayworth to win.

Cook's Call   *Potentially Competitive.* 1991 redistricting helped to create this sprawling district, but it is not yet clear how 2001 redistricting will impact it. Early in the decade this seat was a top target thanks in large part to Hayworth's blustery and flamboyant image that polarized the electorate here. But, after a close call in 1996, Hayworth has won comfortably.

THE PEOPLE: Pop. 2000: 1,001,151; Pop. 1990: 611,885, up 63.6% 1990–2000. 73% White, 1.5% Black, 1.2% Asian, 15.6% Amer. Indian, 0.1% Hawaiian, 2.2% Two+ races, 6.5% Other; 14.2% Hispanic Origin.

2000 Presidential Vote		
Bush (R)	169,142	(54%)
Gore (D)	133,379	(43%)
Nader (Green)	7,498	(2%)
Others	3,790	(1%)

1996 Presidential Vote		
Clinton (D)	120,176	(47%)
Dole (R)	113,406	(44%)
Perot (I)	21,462	(8%)

Rep. J.D. Hayworth (R)

Elected 1994, 4th term; b. July 12, 1958, High Point, NC; home, Scottsdale; NC St. U., B.A. 1980; Baptist; married (Mary).

Professional Career: Sports Reporter/Anchor: WPTF-TV Raleigh, NC, 1980–81; WTFF-TV Greenville, SC, 1981–86; WLWT-TV, Cincinnati, OH, 1986–87; KTSP-TV Phoenix, AZ, 1987–94; Insurance agent & PR consultant, 1994.

DC Office: 2434 RHOB 20515, 202-225-2190; Fax: 202-225-3263; Web site: www.house.gov/hayworth.

District Offices: Casa Grande, 520-876-4095; Flagstaff, 520-556-8760; Mesa, 480-926-4151.

Committees: *Veterans' Affairs* (10th of 17 R): Benefits (Chmn.). *Ways & Means* (17th of 24 R): Select Revenue Measures; Social Security.

Group Ratings

	ADA	ACLU	AFS	LCV	CON	ITIC	NTU	COC	ACU	NTLC	CHC
2000	5	29	16	0	91	72	70	84	100	100	93
1999	10	—	0	13	63	—	63	80	100	—	—

National Journal Ratings

	1999 LIB —	1999 CONS		2000 LIB —	2000 CONS
Economic	0% —	84%		0% —	94%
Social	10% —	85%		0% —	79%
Foreign	20% —	78%		0% —	88%

Key Votes of the 106th Congress

1. Patient Bill of Rights	N	5. Bar RU-486 $ for FDA	Y	9. NATO War in Serbia	N
2. Accelerate Min. Wage	N	6. Display 10 Commandments	Y	10. Perm. Trade with China	N
3. Strike Ban on Ergo. Stnd.	N	7. Gun Show Bkgrnd. Checks	N	11. Debt Relief for 3rd World	N
4. Ovrd. Estate Tax Veto	Y	8. Ban Part.-Birth Abortion	Y	12. Drop Cuba Econ. Embargo	*

Election Results

2000 general	J.D. Hayworth (R)	186,687	(61%)	($1,183,832)
	Larry Nelson (D)	108,317	(36%)	($39,522)
	Others	9,000	(3%)	
2000 primary	J.D. Hayworth (R)	unopposed		
1998 general	J.D. Hayworth (R)	106,891	(53%)	($1,839,460)
	Steve Owens (D)	88,001	(44%)	($836,074)
	Others	6,645	(3%)	

★ ARKANSAS ★

Arkansas, like America, has entered the post-Clinton era, but perhaps more poignantly than anywhere else. For Clinton is likely to be the ninth former president (the others were Grant, Cleveland, Taft, Wilson, Hoover, Eisenhower, Nixon and Ford) to spend little time back in his home state, and Arkansas' feelings about him are full of ambivalence. Arkansans interviewed by national reporters evoked varied responses. "He didn't start with much. He wasn't born rich. Look where he got. He did us proud," said carpenter Robert Keeling, "Proud enough." Retired Little Rock banker Edward Penick sounded another note: "In Arkansas he's remembered as a great embarrassment." An anonymous Arkansan said that when Clinton left Little Rock for Washington in January 1993, "I distinctly remember thinking that this was finally going to wipe away the stain left by Faubus," implying that some of the stain is still left. Arkansas is justly proud of Clinton's great talents, but is abashed that he seldom returned here on vacation, and that the scandals associated with him, if they did not bring him down, tarnished the reputations of many other Arkansans. Independent counsel Kenneth Starr, much reviled here, shut down his Arkansas office in August 1999, having secured 14 convictions, including that of Governor Jim Guy Tucker, who was forced to resign in July 1996. Six blocks of Little Rock's Markham Street have been renamed President Clinton Avenue—but not the 30 blocks originally proposed—and the President Clinton Library and Museum is scheduled to rise near the Old State House along the Arkansas River. But in his final full day in office, Clinton publicly admitted to giving misleading (but not false) testimony about his affair with Monica Lewinsky and agreed to a five-year suspension of his Arkansas law license in a settlement with Independent Counsel Robert Ray that ended the Whitewater criminal probe. And as details about Clinton's controversial last-minute pardons emerged, a piqued Justice Department and Congress began a new series of investigations.

Arkansas, like Clinton, began life without many advantages. In area, it's the smallest state between the Mississippi and the Pacific; in population, it's the smallest state in the South; it has not been blessed with any great natural resource—unless you count flame-retarding bromine, of which it produces half the world supply—or any growing major industry. Arkansas is the land left over when Louisiana and Missouri were carved out of the Louisiana Purchase and what is now Oklahoma was fenced off as Indian Territory. Settled by poor farmers with large families, few slaves, and little cash, it has had no Atlanta or Dallas or even Memphis to be a focus of growth. As Arkansas political scientist Diane Blair noted, Arkansas never had a power elite of great plantation owners or economic robber barons. That has left it a heritage without honored traditions or tight standards, but has also made Arkansas a land of great opportunities, where talented people can move up fast—like Blair and her husband Jim, the former house counsel at Tyson Foods, who guided Hillary Rodham Clinton's commodities trading that netted her a quick $100,000.

This Arkansas produced old style politicians like John McClellan and William Fulbright, who represented Arkansas in the Senate for a total of 65 years from the 1940s to the 1970s while chairing the Appropriations and Foreign Relations committees; Wilbur Mills, chairman of the

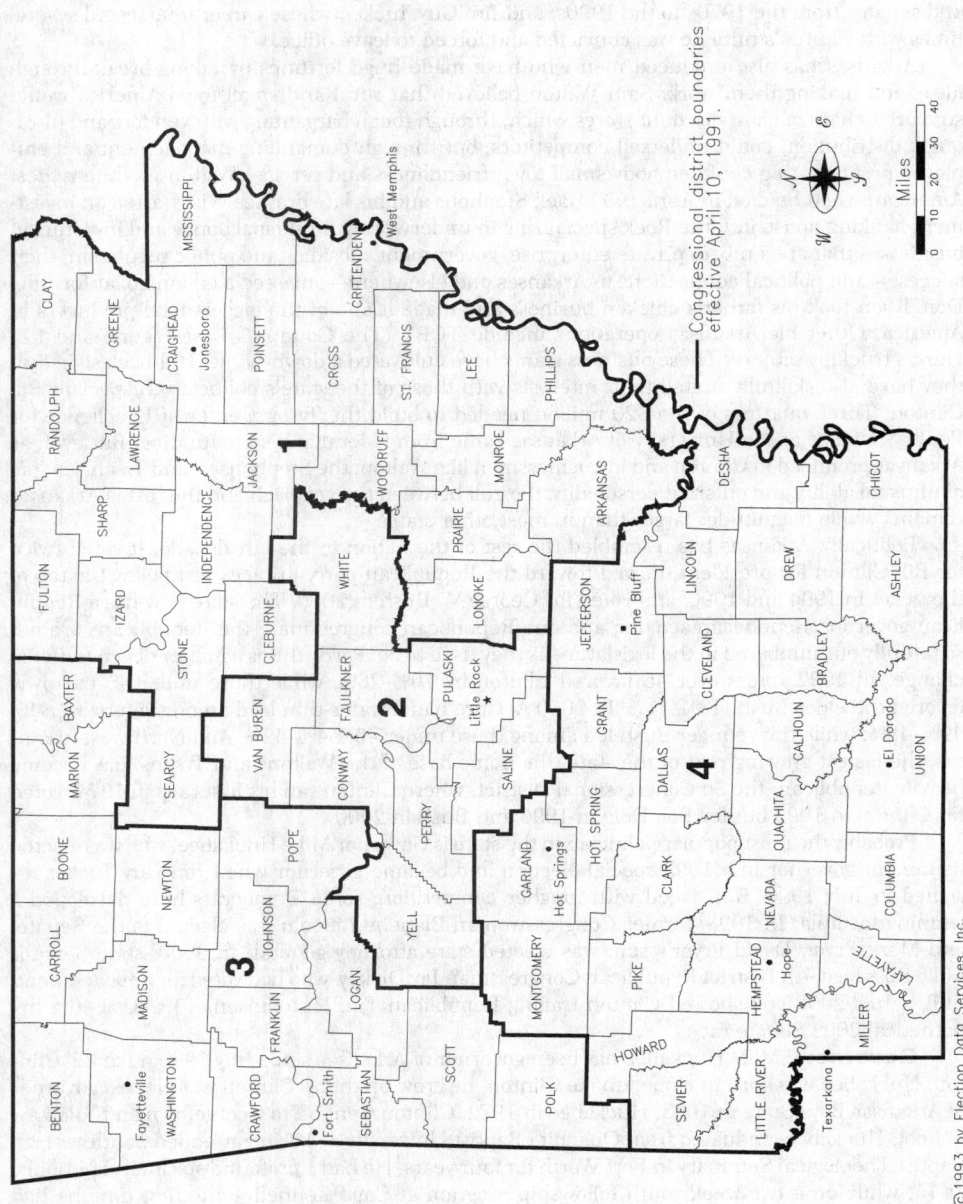

Congressional district boundaries effective April 10, 1991.

House Ways and Means Committee from 1958–74; Governor Orval Faubus, who shamed Little Rock and Arkansas around the world by resisting integration at Central High School in 1957; and Governor Winthrop Rockefeller, who steered the state toward integration a decade later. Arkansas produced moderate Democrats like Dale Bumpers and David Pryor, who each served as governor and senator from the 1970s to the 1990s, and Jim Guy Tucker, whose career intersected several times with Clinton's until he was convicted and forced to leave office.

Arkansas has also produced men who have made huge fortunes by taking break-through ideas and making them work. Sam Walton believed that rural and small town America would support a chain of giant discount stores which, through tough bargaining with vendors and ultra-quick distribution, could undersell competitors, but through demanding management and employee profit-sharing could embody small town friendliness and service; Walton was the richest American when he died in April 1992. Jack Stephens and his late brother Witt started an investment banking house in Little Rock specializing in underwriting municipal bonds and investing in businesses that are a mix of private enterprise, government subsidies and public regulation; their success—and political connections in Arkansas and elsewhere—amassed a billion dollar fortune. Don Tyson took his father's chicken business and made it one of the biggest food producers in America. Other big Arkansas operations include TCBY (The Country's Best Yogurt) and J.B. Hunt's trucking empire. These business giants have cultivated a down-home, laid-back style. But they have also skillfully united their interests with those of the state's politicians, especially Bill Clinton. Three-quarters of the $20 million needed to build the Tyson Center of Excellence for Poultry Science at the University of Arkansas came from federal and state funding. But even as Arkansas produced in Clinton and in businessmen like Walton, the Stephenses, and Tyson, leaders of unusual ability and outsized personality, the gulf between the very rich and the rest of Arkansas remains whole magnitudes larger than in most other states.

Politically, Arkansas has resembled the rest of the nation in the last decade. It voted twice for Bill Clinton for president, moved toward the Republican party in races just below the top of the ticket in 1994 and 1996, and voted for George W. Bush in 2000. The state now has a Republican governor, Republican senator, and one Republican congressman; the Republicans are not so pitifully outnumbered in the legislature as they used to be. Partly this is a matter of generational change. In 1992 voters over 45 favored Clinton by 70%–26%, while those under 45 narrowly favored the elder Bush, 43%–41%. In 2000 Al Gore had a wafer-thin lead among voters over 45, 49%–48%, while the younger Bush led among those under 45, 54%–42%. And Northwest Arkansas, the fastest-growing part of the state, the home base of the Waltons and Tysons, has become heavily Republican: the 3d Congressional District, where Clinton ran his first race in 1974, voted for Clinton in 1992 but for Bob Dole in 1996 and Bush in 2000.

Probably the most popular politician in the state is Governor Mike Huckabee, who was elected lieutenant governor in a 1993 special election and became governor when Jim Guy Tucker resigned in July 1996. But, faced with tougher competition, some Democrats have developed a winning formula. In 1998, former Congresswoman Blanche Lincoln was elected to the Senate, and Mark Pryor, David Pryor's son, was elected state attorney general. In 2000, state Senator Mike Ross beat 4th District Republican Congressman Jay Dickey, who had voted for impeachment. Still, a July 2000 poll showed Clinton trailing Republican Tim Hutchinson, 49%–41%, in a hypothetical 2002 Senate race.

Governor　Mike Huckabee has been governor of Arkansas since July 1996. Like Bill Clinton, Huckabee was born in Hope; unlike Clinton, he grew up there. Clinton was elected governor of Arkansas Boys State in 1963, Huckabee in 1972. Clinton went off to Georgetown and Yale Law School; Huckabee graduated from Ouachita Baptist University at 19 and attended Southwestern Baptist Theological Seminary in Fort Worth for four years. He had a profound spiritual experience at 15, while on a two-week youth fellowship program at Cape Kennedy—the first time he had been outside Arkansas. In the 1980s Huckabee was a Baptist minister in Pine Bluff and then Texarkana; in both towns he started a 24-hour television station, where he produced documentaries and hosted a program called *Positive Alternatives*. In 1989 he became president of the Arkansas Baptist Convention, with a membership of 490,000.

Huckabee's first stab at politics was running against Senator Dale Bumpers in 1992; he lost

60%–40%. Then, after Jim Guy Tucker replaced Bill Clinton as governor, Huckabee ran for lieutenant governor. It was July 1993, the Clinton tax plan and gays in the military had been in the headlines, and Huckabee beat pro-Clinton Democrat Nate Coulter 51%–49%; he was re-elected 59%–41% in November 1994. In October 1995, after David Pryor said he was retiring from the Senate, Huckabee announced for the seat and was ahead in the polls. But in May 1996 Tucker was convicted on one count of arranging nearly $3 million in fraudulent loans. Tucker promised to resign July 15; on that day, claiming he had a good case on appeal, he hesitated, then finally in the early evening he resigned. Huckabee, who had already bowed out of the Senate race, had insisted Tucker resign and handled the transition gracefully but firmly.

As governor, Huckabee promoted a tiny (0.125%) tax increase to promote tourism as an alternative to casino gambling, which was defeated on the 1996 ballot. In the 1997 session he tussled with Democratic legislators who overrode many of his vetoes. But he also had some successes: $90 million in income tax cuts, a partial-birth abortion ban, and his ARKids plan providing health insurance for parents of disabled children above the Medicaid income limits—some 30,000 qualified. Another Huckabee favorite was a $7.6 million Smart Start program for the first five grades, to teach "the basic skills of reading, math, and character." In November 1998 he faced Democrat Bill Bristow, an attorney representing state trooper Danny Ferguson in the case Paula Jones brought against Bill Clinton. Bristow charged that Huckabee spent Governor's Mansion funds on personal items and called for a bond issue for road repairs similar to a Tucker bond issue that lost on the ballot 87%–13% in 1996. He criticized Huckabee for capitalizing on tragedy when he wrote a book called *Kids Who Kill*, and began it with an account of the two Jonesboro youths who turned guns on their schoolmates in March 1998. Both opposed an initiative that would have abolished the property tax; it was removed from the ballot in mid-October. Huckabee outspent Bristow and won 60%–39%, carrying all but eight lightly populated counties in eastern Arkansas.

In 1999 Huckabee worked more cooperatively with the legislature; one reason may have been that term limits had kicked in and 57 of the 100 House members were freshmen. Together they passed property tax reform, putting on the November 2000 ballot a measure to increase the sales tax by 0.5% to fund a $300 homestead property tax credit; it passed 62%–38%. Taxes were cut by another $84 million, but the gas and diesel tax was increased for highway construction and repair. Legislation was passed to encourage charter schools and to require an annual report on every school, including test scores. In response to the Jonesboro school shootings they passed a law allowing children to be given life sentences for such crimes. Another new law prohibits cities and counties from suing gun manufacturers.

Huckabee did have disagreements with Democrats, on the tobacco settlement, on whether parents should be given a choice between ARKids First and Medicaid (Democrats wanted them all on Medicaid), on whether lawyers for a tiny school district should be given a $32 million fee for bringing a case challenging the state aid formula. Major scandal erupted when longtime state Senator Nick Wilson and nine colleagues were accused of plundering more than $1 million from a fund for providing legal representation to children and parents in domestic cases; Wilson was convicted for tax evasion in November 1999 and racketeering the following year. Huckabee made other headlines, in July 2000 when he and his family moved into a triple-wide trailer—"manufactured housing" as the industry calls it—while the Governor's Mansion was renovated, and a day before the November election when on Don Imus' radio program Huckabee said Arkansas was a "banana republic" because Democratic local elections officials were allowing early voting on Sunday; Huckabee said the issue was "serious; the manner in which I talked about it was clearly done with a sense of humor." In 2000 he published his third book, *Living Beyond Your Lifetime*, about baby boomers facing mortality and "turning away from material prosperity to spiritual fullness."

Huckabee campaigned heavily for George W. Bush and was pleased when he carried the state and Republicans gained seats in the legislature; he was unhappy about the defeats of Congressman Jay Dickey and the Republican state Supreme Court nominee. After the election, he proposed a tight budget and $3,000 in teacher-pay increases and installed his choice, 78-year-old former Congressman John Paul Hammerschmidt, as Republican state chairman. Huckabee has said he will run for re-election in 2002 and does not regret missing the chance to run for the

Senate seat he sought in 1996. "The Senate would be very difficult and very frustrating." Potential opponents include two former Clinton cabinet members: FEMA Director Jamie Lee Witt and Transportation Secretary Rodney Slater. Arkansas Secretary of State Sharon Priest and a number of state senators may throw their hats in as well.

Cook's Call   *Safe*. Arkansas is not particularly conservative or Republican, but Huckabee appears to have a very firm hold on the governorship. He has managed to govern competently and—in contrast with his two immediate predecessors—with minimal controversy. Since most first-tier potential Democratic challengers see more opportunity in next year's Senate race, it is likely that Huckabee will have only nominal opposition.

Senior Senator   Tim Hutchinson, elected in 1996, is the first Republican senator from Arkansas since 1879. Hutchinson grew up on a farm in Northwest Arkansas, attended Bob Jones University and became a Baptist minister; he also owned and managed a radio station and was founder and administrator of a Christian school in Rogers. In 1984 he was elected to the Arkansas House, where Bill Clinton called him "No-Tax Tim." His brother Asa Hutchinson was the Republican nominee against Senator Dale Bumpers in 1986, later served as Republican state chairman, and ultimately succeeded Tim in the House. In 1992 Tim Hutchinson ran for Congress and won the three-candidate Republican primary impressively, 53%–32%, over a fellow state legislator. In the general, he backed term limits, the balanced budget amendment, the line-item veto—essentially the Contract with America two years early—and called for a base-closings-type commission to curb government spending. He called attacks on him as a religious extremist scare tactics reflecting a kind of intolerance. But Democrat John Van Winkle raised more money, Clinton carried the district, and Hutchinson won by just 50%–47%.

In the House, Hutchinson had a conservative record, supporting NAFTA after watching U.S. exports sell in a Wal-Mart in Mexico City. He was re-elected easily in 1992 and seemed headed for a third term when Governor Jim Guy Tucker was convicted of fraud in May 1996 and announced he would resign in July. That elevated Republican Lieutenant Governor Mike Huckabee, who was the Republican nominee for the Senate seat being vacated by Democrat David Pryor. Huckabee opted out of the Senate race on May 30, and on June 3, Hutchinson said he would not run. But no other candidate seemed strong enough to win a seat Republicans had counted on as a sure gain, and on June 15, a Republican convention nominated Hutchinson. The winner of the Democratic primary was Attorney General Winston Bryant, a seasoned politician who had won seven statewide races for various offices, but he won the June 11 runoff over liberal state Senator Lu Hardin by only 54%–46%.

Hutchinson started his general campaign with an ad showing John Kennedy and saying that his father had voted for Kennedy while teaching Tim to have an open mind and open heart. Democrats squawked, and Bryant ran ads tying Hutchinson to Newt Gingrich and accusing him of government shut downs in 1995. But Hutchinson, one of only four House Republicans to vote to release the outside counsel's report on Gingrich, brushed the attacks aside, responding, "For 15 years Winston Bryant's been very liberal with your money." On Election Day, Hutchinson won 53%–47%. He carried all of Arkansas west and north of Little Rock and ran just about even in the capital. His brother Asa was elected to his old 3d District House seat, and the two became the second pair of congressional brothers (the others are Democrats Sander and Carl Levin of Michigan). The political impulse seems to be hereditary: Tim's son Jeremy Hutchinson was elected to the Arkansas House from a Little Rock district in March 2000.

Hutchinson's Senate voting record has been pretty solidly conservative. He passed an amendment denying U.S. visas to foreign officials involved in abortion, sterilization, genital mutilation, or religious persecution—originally aimed at China but broadened to include all countries. Hutchinson opposed Permanent Normal Trade Relations with China because of its human rights abuses, though big Arkansas businesses like Wal-Mart and Tyson Foods backed it and his brother Asa voted for it: a rare instance of fraternal disagreement. He opposed the nomination of David Satcher as surgeon general because Satcher opposed the partial-birth abortion ban; he called for tighter restrictions on the abortifacient RU-486 than required by the FDA; he sponsored a bill for extra penalties for those who kill a fetus while committing a federal crime. Hutchinson led a move to scrap the entire Internal Revenue Code by the end of 2002 and saw it defeated by a 49–49 tie in July 1998, after it passed the House. In 2000 he helped form a Bio-Technology Caucus to defend bio-engineered corn and other genetically altered crops against attacks from Europeans and others. He has argued that EPA has no authority to regulate "non-point source" water pollution—runoff from farms—and has tried, sometimes in opposition to his Arkansas colleague Blanche Lincoln, to bar EPA from doing so; his edgy relations with her were said to have been changed to a "detente" in summer 2000.

Hutchinson serves on the Armed Services Committee and is the top Republican on the Personnel Subcommittee. He was one of three Republican senators to insist in October 1999 on a vote on the Comprehensive Test Ban Treaty, which was defeated. With John Warner, he wants to allow over-65 military retirees to stay in the Tricare military health plan rather than be moved to Medicare—a $41 billion item over 10 years. He has a bill to deny federal aid to high schools which bar military recruiters. He has been critical of the military's troubled anthrax vaccine program. Hutchinson has defended Little Rock Air Force Base's position as the chief C-130 training base, putting a hold on Air Force officer nominations in October 1999 to get a commitment to deliver more C-130s there—this pitted him against Trent Lott, who wanted them transferred to Mississippi. When the Air Force confirmed Little Rock as the chief C-130 base Hutchinson sought to further its missions.

On other local issues, Hutchinson sought low-interest loans for chicken producers after 10.5 million Arkansas chickens died in a blizzard in January 2000 and in October 2000 got a $2 million community center for Arkansas State University in Mountain Home. Some 554 methamphetamine labs were seized in Arkansas in 1999, the most per capita in the nation; Hutchinson sought $2.3 million from drug czar Barry McCaffrey to combat methamphetamines. Working with Trent Lott, he got $8 million in initial funding for the proposed Great River Bridge over the Mississippi.

Hutchinson comes up for re-election in 2002. Some observers wondered whether he would have problems with his base constituency when he divorced his wife in 1999 and, a year later, married a former staffer. In 2001 Christian conservative state Representative Jim Bob Duggar announced he would challenge him in the primary. But in an October 2000 poll, matched against Bill Clinton, Hutchinson led 49%–41%. "I would relish the race," said Hutchinson in 1999 when rumors circulated that Clinton might run. But with the Clintons' purchase of new houses in New York and Washington, that seems unlikely. Democratic state Attorney General Mark Pryor, son of the popular Arkansas U.S. Senator David Pryor (1979–97), announced in April 2001 he would challenge Hutchinson, which prompted 1st District Representative Marion Berry to drop out of the race. But as a Republican incumbent in a pro-incumbent time in a now pro-Republican state, Hutchinson would have to be regarded as the favorite.

Cook's Call *Highly Competitive.* A conservative voting record and a well-publicized divorce and remarriage have made Hutchinson a prime Democratic target in 2002. Democrats had wanted either former FEMA Director James Lee Witt or former Transportation Secretary Rodney Slater to run, but state Attorney General Mark Pryor has emerged as the party's candidate. Given Hutchinson's problems, and the fact that Arkansas is arguably the least conservative and Republican state in the Deep South, this is definitely a race to watch.

Junior Senator Blanche Lincoln was elected to the Senate in 1998 after showing something close to perfect political pitch in her 1990s electoral career. She grew up in Helena, on the flat rice lands of eastern Arkansas, where her father and brother are the sixth and seventh generations running a farm raising rice, wheat, soybeans, and cotton, and where she stayed in public schools after they were integrated. Cheerful, active, endowed with good political sense, she lists her hobbies as duck hunting, fishing and yard sales. After college, in 1982, she worked as a staffer for 1st District Congressman Bill Alexander, then after two years worked as a lobbyist for, among others, Billy Broadhurst, Gary Hart's host on the *Monkey Business* cruise. In 1992 she moved back to Arkansas and, as Blanche Lambert (she was married in 1993) ran against Alexander, sensing he was in trouble. He had lost a leadership race in 1986, was named in a lawsuit for a $308,000 debt, and had 487 overdrafts totaling $208,000 on the House bank. "I'll promise you one thing," the 31-year-old challenger said, "I can sure enough balance my checkbook." She won the primary 61%–39%, carrying 23 of 25 counties.

In the House, Lincoln compiled a moderate voting record and got a seat on the Commerce

Committee. She saw Japan open its market to Arkansas rice and denounced the Supplemental Security Income program that provided disability checks to kids who act up in school. She supported much of the Contract with America in 1995. But when the moratorium on regulations threatened duck hunting season and national wildlife refuges were closed, she got laws changed to ensure it wouldn't happen again. Her re-election margin in 1994 was only 53%–47%, but she seemed well positioned to hold the seat when, in January 1996, she announced that she was pregnant with twin boys and would not run for reelection because of the strain of campaigning in an Arkansas summer during a difficult pregnancy.

When Senator Dale Bumpers announced he would not run for reelection in 1998, Lincoln got into the race. She flashed snapshots of her twins and ran ads showing her overseeing mealtime, balancing one twin on her lap, bouncing the other on her knee, laying her head on her husband's shoulder. "Daughter, wife, mother, congresswoman . . . Living our rock-solid Arkansas values." On the issues Lincoln was not terribly specific: she promised to work on children's and women's health issues; she wanted to improve education; she wanted to keep the budget balanced, and to use the surplus to replenish the Social Security trust fund and cut taxes. Though she has spent most of her adult life in Washington, she boasted to rice farmers, "I was one of the few members of the Agriculture Committee that ever walked a rice levee." In the primary she faced Attorney General Winston Bryant, the Democratic nominee in the 1996 Senate race. She led by an impressive 45%–27% in the May primary, with 64% in her old 1st District, which cast nearly one-third of the votes. She won the June runoff 62%–38%.

In the general election, Lincoln staunched the Republican tide that had been running since Bill Clinton left the state, and then some. The Republican nominee was Fay Boozman (pronounced in the Dutch manner, like Bozeman, Montana), an ophthalmologist from Rogers who attends the same church as Senator Tim Hutchinson. Boozman had a profound religious experience in 1992, sold his medical practice, and ran for the state Senate; there he was the champion of the partial-birth abortion ban. Boozman called on Bill Clinton to resign and ran tough comparative ads on Lincoln. He said the Bible dictated his anti-tax philosophy and made a serious gaffe when he said it is rare for women to get pregnant by rape because fear triggers a hormonal change that blocks conception. Lincoln won 55%–42%, a more solid win than Tim Hutchinson's in 1996; Boozman carried the northwest corner of the state and little else.

Lincoln's voting record has been a bit to the left of the midpoint of the Senate; she was one of nine Democrats to form a moderate caucus, similar to the House's Blue Dogs, in February 2000. Working with her 1st District successor, Marion Berry, she promoted farm exports, joining the WTO caucus in October 1999 and in May 2000 visiting Cuba, which before Fidel Castro had purchased much of Arkansas's rice. She described Castro as "very cordial" and "still very much in command and in control," and accepted two boxes of cigars, worth $1,250. She strongly supported ending the embargo on trade in Cuba; the Cuban American National Foundation ran TV ads against her position in the Little Rock market after her trip. She has opposed the Freedom to Farm Act and introduced her own bill to expand crop insurance and expand the Conservation Reserve Program.

On other issues, Lincoln got passed bills exempting scrap metal recyclers from a waste liability law and (co-sponsored with Peter Fitzgerald, who also has young children) requiring the National Highway Transportation Safety Administration to test car seats in cars rather than simulators. She supported the bipartisan Chafee-Graham prescription drug benefit and worked for a bipartisan middle path on HMO regulation. She voted for the partial-birth abortion ban: "always a difficult vote." With Spencer Abraham, she called for research on the slaves who built the Capitol and the White House (the Abraham-Lincoln resolution, someone said).

On local issues, Lincoln sponsored a bill providing $90 million to rebuild watershed dams, of which Arkansas has more than 100, and promised to seek more funding; she seeks $1 million to promote tourism at 20 dam-created lakes, including Lake Ouachita in Arkansas. With Berry she sought $30 million for the Delta Regional Authority, and got the Senate to pass $12 million to decontaminate the Southwest Experimental Fast Oxide Reactor near Fayetteville. In 2000 she got $1.1 million for a pedestrian and bicycle bridge over the Arkansas River at Murray Lock and Dam in Little Rock.

For the 107th Congress Lincoln became the third woman to win a seat on the Finance Committee. She comes up for re-election in 2004. In the meantime, her Senate Internet site includes "the BBQ bandwagon" with 42 "hot spot" barbecue restaurants, from Kibb's in Pine Bluff to Bubba's in Eureka Springs and Penguin Ed's in Fayetteville.

Presidential politics   Arkansas voted 53% for Bill Clinton in 1992 and 54% in 1996; these were his best and eighth-best percentages those years. In 2000 it voted only 46% for Al Gore, his 29th-best state. George W. Bush, who targeted the state and appeared in Northwest Arkansas on election eve, won 51% here, his lowest percentage in the South except of course for Florida. But with Clinton out of office and out of state, Arkansas does not seem likely to vote Democratic for president any time soon.

The Arkansas presidential primary, held in May, attracts little attention; nor did it in 1992 when it was held on Super Tuesday. There is no party registration requirement and Republican turnout has typically been very low; 85% of those voting in the May primary voted Democratic.

Congressional districting   The boundaries of Arkansas's four congressional districts will need adjustment to meet the equal-population standard. The legislature, with enough Democratic votes to override a veto by Republican Governor Mike Huckabee, will probably want to safeguard the state's three Democratic congressmen, especially freshman Mike Ross. But the heavily Republican 3d District will have to be reduced in size, and any counties pared off will make adjacent districts more Republican. Most likely there will be minimal changes.

THE PEOPLE: Pop. 2000: 2,673,400; Pop. 1990: 2,350,725, up 13.7% 1990–2000. 0.9% of U.S. total, 33d largest; 80% White, 15.7% Black, 0.8% Asian, 0.7% Amer. Indian, 0.1% Hawaiian, 1.3% Two+ races, 1.5% Other; 3.2% Hispanic Origin. 4.4% Unemployment. 2000 Voting age pop.: 1,993,031. 2000 Turnout: 921,781; 46% of VAP. Registered voters (2000): 1,553,356; no party registration.

POLITICAL LINEUP: Governor, Mike Huckabee (R); Lt. Gov., Winthrop P. Rockefeller (R); Secy. of State, Sharon Priest (D); Atty. Gen., Mark Pryor (D); Treasurer, Jimmie Lou Fisher (D); Auditor, Gus Wingfield (D); Commissioner of State Lands, Charlie Daniels (D); State Senate, 35 (27 D, 8 R); Senate Pres. Pro Tempore, Mike Beebe (D); Majority Leader, John A. Riggs (D); State House, 100 (70 D, 30 R); House Speaker, Shane Broadway (R). Senators, Tim Hutchinson (R) and Blanche Lincoln (D). Representatives, 4 (3 D, 1 R).

ELECTIONS DIVISION: 501-682-5070; **FILING DEADLINE FOR U.S. CONGRESS:** April 2, 2002.

2000 Presidential Vote

Bush (R)	472,940	(51%)
Gore (D)	422,768	(46%)
Nader (Green)	13,421	(1%)
Others	12,652	(1%)

1996 Presidential Vote

Clinton (D)	475,171	(54%)
Dole (R)	325,416	(37%)
Perot (I)	69,884	(8%)
Others	13,791	(2%)

2000 Republican Presidential Primary

Bush (R)	35,759	(80%)
Keyes (R)	8,814	(20%)

2000 Democratic Presidential Primary

Gore (D)	193,750	(78%)
LaRouche (D)	53,150	(22%)

Gov. Mike Huckabee (R)

Assumed office, July 1996, term expires Jan. 2003, 1st term; b. Aug. 24, 1955, Hope; home, Little Rock; Ouachita Baptist U., B.A. 1975, Southwestern Baptist Theological Seminary, 1976–80; Baptist; married (Janet).

Elected Office: AR Lt. Gov., 1993–96.

Professional Career: Advertising Dir., Focus, 1976–80; Baptist Minister, 1980–92; Pres., ACTS-TV, 1983–86; Pres., KBSC-TV, 1987–92; Pres., Cambridge Comm., 1992–96.

Office: State Capitol, Little Rock, 72201, 501-682-2345; Fax: 501-682-3597; Web site: www.state.ar.us.

Election Results

1998 general	Mike Huckabee (R)	421,989	(60%)
	Bill Bristow (D)	272,923	(39%)
	Others	11,099	(2%)
1998 primary	Mike Huckabee (R)	51,627	(90%)
	Gene McVay (R)	5,581	(10%)
1994 general	Jim Guy Tucker (D)	428,936	(60%)
	Sheffield Nelson (R)	287,904	(40%)

Sen. Tim Hutchinson (R)

Elected 1996, seat up 2002, 1st term; b. Aug. 11, 1949, Gravette; home, Bentonville; Bob Jones U., B.A. 1979, U. of AR, M.A. 1990; Baptist; married (Randi Fredholm).

Elected Office: AR House of Reps., 1984–92; US House of Reps., 1992–96.

Professional Career: Baptist Minister; Founder & Admin., Benton Cnty. Christian Schl., 1975–85; Co-owner & Mgr., KBCV Radio, 1982–89; Prof., John Brown U., 1989–92.

DC Office: 239 DSOB, 20510, 202-224-2353; Fax: 202-228-3973; Web site: www.senate.gov/~hutchinson.

State Offices: El Dorado, 870-863-6406; Fayetteville, 501-582-1935; Jonesboro, 870-935-5022; Little Rock, 501-324-6336.

Committees: *Aging (Special). Agriculture, Nutrition & Forestry*: Forestry, Conservation & Rural Revitalization; Research, Nutrition & General Legislation. *Armed Services*: Airland Forces; Emerging Threats & Capabilities; Personnel (RMM). *Health, Education, Labor & Pensions*: Aging (RMM); Public Health. *Veterans' Affairs*.

Group Ratings

	ADA	ACLU	AFS	LCV	CON	ITIC	NTU	COC	ACU	NTLC	CHC
2000	5	29	20	0	0	70	70	85	91	97	100
1999	5	—	0	0	26	—	77	94	100	—	—

National Journal Ratings

	1999 LIB —	1999 CONS		2000 LIB —	2000 CONS
Economic	26% —	71%		0% —	86%
Social	23% —	72%		0% —	90%
Foreign	0% —	94%		0% —	95%

Key Votes of the 106th Congress

1. Educ. Savings Accts.	Y	5. Review Movie Violence	Y	9. NATO War in Serbia	N
2. Prescrip. Drug Benefit	N	6. Gun Show Bckgrnd. Checks	N	10. Table Cuba Travel Ban	Y
3. Delay Ergonomic Standards	Y	7. Ban Part.-Birth Abortion	Y	11. Nuclear Test-Ban Treaty	N
4. Phase Out Estate Tax	*	8. Broaden Hate Crimes List	N	12. Perm. Trade with China	N

Election Results

1996 general	Tim Hutchinson (R)	445,942	(53%)	($1,604,014)
	Winston Bryant (D)	400,241	(47%)	($1,577,838)
1996 primary	Tim Hutchinson (R)	nominated by convention		
1990 general	David Pryor (D)	unopposed		($622,479)

Sen. Blanche Lincoln (D)

Elected 1998, seat up 2004, 1st term; b. Sept. 30, 1960, Helena; home, Horseshoe Lake; U. of AR, 1979–80, Randolph Macon Col., B.S. 1982; Episcopalian; married (Steve).

Elected Office: US House of Reps., 1992–96.

Professional Career: Staff Asst., U.S. Rep. Bill Alexander, 1982–84; Lobbyist & govt. affairs rep., 1985–91.

DC Office: 355 DSOB, 20510, 202-224-4843; Fax: 202-228-1371; Web site: www.senate.gov/~lincoln.

State Offices: Fort Smith, 501-782-9215; Jonesboro, 870-910-6896; Little Rock, 501-375-2993.

Committees: *Aging (Special)*. *Agriculture, Nutrition & Forestry*: Forestry, Conservation & Rural Revitalization (Chmn.); Production & Price Competitiveness. *Ethics (Select)*. *Finance*: Health Care; International Trade; Taxation & IRS Oversight.

Group Ratings

	ADA	ACLU	AFS	LCV	CON	ITIC	NTU	COC	ACU	NTLC	CHC
2000	70	43	57	57	46	100	10	86	20	3	23
1999	95	—	100	11	32	—	7	65	12	—	—

National Journal Ratings

	1999 LIB	—	1999 CONS		2000 LIB	—	2000 CONS
Economic	56%	—	42%		57%	—	41%
Social	62%	—	36%		61%	—	36%
Foreign	62%	—	29%		86%	—	12%

Key Votes of the 106th Congress

1. Educ. Savings Accts.	N	5. Review Movie Violence	Y	9. NATO War in Serbia	Y
2. Prescrip. Drug Benefit	Y	6. Gun Show Bckgrnd. Checks	Y	10. Table Cuba Travel Ban	N
3. Delay Ergonomic Standards	Y	7. Ban Part.-Birth Abortion	Y	11. Nuclear Test-Ban Treaty	Y
4. Phase Out Estate Tax	Y	8. Broaden Hate Crimes List	Y	12. Perm. Trade with China	Y

Election Results

1998 general	Blanche Lincoln (D)	385,878	(55%)	($3,122,776)
	Fay Boozman (R)	292,906	(42%)	($1,093,007)
	Others	21,860	(3%)	
1998 runoff	Blanche Lincoln (D)	134,203	(62%)	
	Winston Bryant (D)	80,889	(38%)	
1998 primary	Blanche Lincoln (D)	145,009	(45%)	
	Winston Bryant (D)	87,183	(27%)	
	Scott Ferguson (D)	44,761	(14%)	
	Nate Coulter (D)	41,848	(13%)	
1992 general	Dale Bumpers (D)	553,635	(60%)	($2,016,112)
	Mike Huckabee (R)	366,373	(40%)	($910,212)

FIRST DISTRICT

The Mississippi Delta, the flat, mushy, river-crossed lowland on both sides of the great river, was some of the country's first industrial farmland. This land was uncultivated in most of the 19th Century, when plows were still pulled by mules and muddy flatlands were impassable. Then, about a century ago, big landowners used machines to drain the marshlands and persuaded poor blacks to move here to tend fields of cotton, rice, and later, soybeans. The results were bountiful agriculture and impoverished people. Around 1940, the Delta began to change slowly: the first minimum wage and war industry jobs up North drew young people out of the Delta and the mechanical cotton picker forced many off the farms. But this land—stretching flat as far as the eye can see, past rows of telephone poles and ribbons of asphalt that shimmer in the heat—remains poor by national standards and the people are undereducated and underemployed.

The 1st Congressional District includes most of Arkansas's Delta lands and stretches west to the cool green Ozarks. The Delta started off heavily Democratic, while some of the hill counties are ancestrally Republican. That changed as partisan preferences oscillated wildly just after the civil rights revolution, but the district returned to its historical norm by the late 1980s, and the Delta provided critical support for, perhaps saving the career of, Bill Clinton in 1990; in 1992 Delta counties voted up to 69% for Clinton, among his best county percentages in the country. Unsurprisingly, Clinton supported creating the $30 million Delta Regional Authority, to promote economic development in the counties with the lowest average income.

The congressman from the 1st District is Marion Berry, a Democrat and Clinton supporter who was first elected in 1996. Berry grew up in Bayou Meto in Arkansas County in the Delta. He earned a pharmacy degree in Little Rock, then ran a pharmacy for two years, and has been a family farmer since 1968, with a net worth of more than $1 million. Berry first met Clinton when he was running for attorney general in 1976, and was impressed with his fluency and knowledge: "You thought to yourself right then—even though you didn't know him—that this guy could be governor, even president, one day." Governor Clinton appointed him to the Arkansas Soil & Water Conservation Commission in 1986, and President Clinton appointed him White House liaison to the Agriculture Department in 1993.

Berry returned to Arkansas in 1996, after Congresswoman Blanche Lincoln announced she would not run for re-election because she was pregnant with twins. Berry had tough opposition for the seat. In the Democratic primary, Tom Donaldson, a 28-year-old deputy prosecutor in Crittenden County, spent little money but ran rural radio ads criticizing Berry for accepting farm subsidies. He held Berry to a 48%–30% lead in the primary. Lincoln endorsed Berry and he brought in Agriculture Secretary Dan Glickman to campaign for him. Yet he won the runoff by only 52%–48%. In the general, Berry faced Republican Warren DuPwe, a former Jonesboro city attorney who won 47% against Lincoln in 1994. They sparred over Medicare; both candidates opposed abortion rights and gun control and favored a balanced budget. Berry's Washington contacts proved more generous than DuPwe's; Berry outspent him nearly 2–1. In a district that has never elected a Republican, Berry won 53%–44%.

Berry got seats on the Agriculture and Transportation committees—good spots for a constituency-oriented member. His voting record is moderate to liberal; a Blue Dog Democrat, he supported the balanced budget amendment and said he wanted to pay off the national debt and save Social Security and Medicare. With his background, Berry was a natural as co-founder of the Prescription Drug Task Force. He complained when Republicans agreed to a loophole-filled version of his proposal to allow the re-importation of prescription from other nations. He sponsored bills on rural health and fought a USDA and FDA investigation of dioxin spills that he said unwarrantedly threatened the local catfish and chicken industries. He opposed EPA rules to set pollution limits on waterways, which led the Sierra Club to run radio ads against him. Berry voted for Permanent Normal Trade Relations with China; he visited Cuba with Lincoln to promote an end to the trade embargo, hoping that Arkansas farmers could sell rice and feed products there. But not all of his local Democratic base was happy. At a meeting with the Black Farmers and Agriculturalists Association, Berry was confronted by farmers complaining that the Agriculture Department had reneged on its settlement of a lawsuit on discrimination in lending practices. They claimed that the department had stopped making $50,000 payments to 18,000 black farmers. He walked out of the meeting.

Berry was unopposed in 1998. In 2000 he faced Susan Myshka, a Jonesboro chiropractor who criticized him as a liberal on abortion and gun votes. He won 60%–40%, but lost three counties in the Ozarks, while Al Gore was carrying the district by only 50%–47%.

Cook's Call   *Probably safe.* Although this sprawling rural district should be considered very competitive, Republicans have not given Berry any serious opposition since his first race in 1996. Berry's conservative voting record and strong agricultural background help to solidify his hold here. Though the 1st District is slightly under the ideal congressional district population, redistricting is unlikely to make much of a dent in the make-up here. If Berry decides to run for the Senate, Republicans could make this a competitive race.

THE PEOPLE: Pop. 2000: 629,974; Pop. 1990: 588,588, up 7% 1990–2000. 80% White, 17.7% Black, 0.3% Asian, 0.4% Amer. Indian, 1% Two+ races, 0.5% Other; 1.6% Hispanic Origin.

2000 Presidential Vote			1996 Presidential Vote		
Gore (D)	102,664	(50%)	Clinton (D)	116,634	(58%)
Bush (R)	96,009	(47%)	Dole (R)	65,707	(33%)
Nader (Green)	2,558	(1%)	Perot (I)	16,269	(8%)
Others	2,270	(1%)			

Rep. Marion Berry (D)

Elected 1996, 3d term; b. Aug. 27, 1942, Bayou Meto; home, Gillett; U. of AR, B.S. 1965; Methodist; married (Carolyn).

Professional Career: Pharmacist, 1965–67; farmer, 1968–present; AR Soil & Water Conservation Comm., 1986–94, Chmn. 1992; Special Asst. to the Pres., Domestic Policy Cncl., White House, 1993–96.

DC Office: 1113 LHOB 20515, 202-225-4076; Fax: 202-225-5602; Web site: www.house.gov/berry.

District Office: Jonesboro, 870-972-4600.

Committees: *Agriculture* (11th of 24 D): Department Operations, Oversight, Nutrition & Forestry; General Farm Commodities & Risk Management. *Transportation & Infrastructure* (28th of 34 D): Economic Development, Public Buildings & Emergency Management; Water Resources & Environment.

Group Ratings

	ADA	ACLU	AFS	LCV	CON	ITIC	NTU	COC	ACU	NTLC	CHC
2000	35	21	42	21	78	78	36	76	48	24	53
1999	60	—	83	31	60	—	28	58	29	—	—

National Journal Ratings

	1999 LIB —	1999 CONS		2000 LIB —	2000 CONS
Economic	54% —	46%		58% —	41%
Social	48% —	51%		42% —	57%
Foreign	74% —	23%		77% —	21%

Key Votes of the 106th Congress

1. Patient Bill of Rights	Y	5. Bar RU-486 $ for FDA	Y	9. NATO War in Serbia	Y
2. Accelerate Min. Wage	Y	6. Display 10 Commandments	Y	10. Perm. Trade with China	Y
3. Strike Ban on Ergo. Stnd.	N	7. Gun Show Bkgrnd. Checks	Y	11. Debt Relief for 3rd World	Y
4. Ovrd. Estate Tax Veto	Y	8. Ban Part.-Birth Abortion	Y	12. Drop Cuba Econ. Embargo	Y

Election Results

2000 general	Marion Berry (D)	120,266	(60%)	($1,169,274)
	Susan Myshka (R)	79,437	(40%)	($298,491)
2000 primary	Marion Berry (D)	unopposed		
1998 general	Marion Berry (D)	unopposed		($303,952)

SECOND DISTRICT

Little Rock has been the capital, largest city and central focus of Arkansas for more than a century. It is one of those capitals located at its state's geographical center, and in a state that has no other metropolis, it stands out. For a long moment, Little Rock became internationally famous. That was in September 1957, when Governor Orval Faubus, eager for a third term, sent in the National Guard to block a desegregation order at Central High School. President Eisenhower sent in U.S. troops and federalized the Guard to enforce the order, and Little Rock became a synonym for bigotry around the world. Forty years later, the Little Rock nine who had integrated the high school returned for an anniversary commemoration, and heard a speech by none other than Bill Clinton. "It was Little Rock that made racial equality a driving obsession in my life," he said, and added that American life still was in too many ways segregated. Also speaking was Republican Governor Mike Huckabee, who said, "Today we come to say once and for all that what happened here 40 years ago was simply wrong." Most impressive were the Little Rock nine themselves and what these graying and now 50-something adults had achieved, as suggested by their occupations: writer, managing director of an investment bank, real estate broker, chairman of a university psychology department, magazine publisher, financial specialist for the Department of Defense, teacher, public relations specialist and journalist. And Central High School today, about 60% black, gets academic prizes and Ivy League admissions: Little Rock has reasons to be proud.

Little Rock is also the political center of Arkansas. It sets the tone of the public life of its state as do only a few other state capitals—Boston, Providence, Atlanta, Denver, Honolulu. Little Rock is home to the *Arkansas Democrat-Gazette*, the feisty, conservative paper whose editor Paul Greenberg christened Clinton "Slick Willie." It is home to the state government, to Jack Stephens' investment banking firm, Worthen Bank, Dillards department stores, the TCBY yogurt chain, Excelsior Hotel, and the now-defunct Madison Guaranty Savings & Loan. Little Rock may not be upscale by national standards, but it is in Arkansas.

The 2d Congressional District of Arkansas includes Little Rock, with its large black and affluent white neighborhoods, and North Little Rock, a kind of industrial suburb across the Arkansas River known informally for years as Dog Town. (At the turn of the century, Little Rock officials, peeved that North Little Rock was allowed to incorporate separately, dumped all their stray dogs there.) It also includes surrounding counties that have grown rapidly as people move farther out on the freeways, and a couple of small hill counties. On the banks of the Arkansas River is the site of the William J. Clinton Presidential Library Complex, which will include an apartment for Clinton and is scheduled to open in 2003. Politically, Little Rock was long a progressive force in a state with widely divergent political tendencies; it provided key support to Clinton when he was in political trouble in the 1990 primary and general, and again in 1992. Yet like much of Arkansas, it has been trending Republican, and fast-growing Saline County to the southwest has been heavily Republican. In 2000 Little Rock's Pulaski County voted for Al Gore, but the other counties voted for George W. Bush, who won Bill Clinton's home district 49%–48%.

The congressman from the 2d District is Vic Snyder, a Democrat elected in 1996. He is an unusual politician, "an inveterately private man in a public profession, quite content to be all alone," wrote the *Arkansas Democrat-Gazette*'s Michael Leahy. He grew up fatherless in Medford, Oregon, dropped out of Willamette University, and at 20 signed up in the Marine Corps and served in Vietnam. Then he returned to Oregon for college and medical school and became a practicing physician, and went on medical missions in Thailand, Honduras, Sierra Leone and Sudan. He got a law degree but never practiced law. In 1990 he was elected to the state Senate and made news when he called for repeal of Arkansas's anti-sodomy law and when he refused to accept a pension.

When the incumbent retired in 1996, Snyder, consulting no one, decided to run for Congress. He campaigned as a reformer, promising not to accept a congressional pension until the establishment of an equitable system for federal employees. His main Democratic opponents had more political backgrounds. The most formidable was Mark Stodola, the county prosecutor in Little Rock, a strong Clinton backer who said he would work to solve the root causes of crime. Snyder cited his experience as a doctor and legislator and pressed the attack. Stodola led in the May primary 48%–32%. Snyder won the June runoff in an upset, 51%–49%. The Republican nominee, lawyer Bud Cummins, ran an aggressive campaign; Snyder continued to sound reform themes while outspending him. With the Little Rock area was moving toward Republicans, Snyder won narrowly, 52%–48%.

Snyder's voting record is close to the center of the House Democrats, which is liberal for this district. He voted against the partial-birth abortion ban and for needle exchanges; he was the single Democrat to vote against a resolution to urge an international tribunal to try Saddam Hussein for "crimes against humanity." But Snyder has bragged of supporting more moderate measures—the balanced budget, tax cuts, a strong education system—and has stressed his military record and service on the Armed Services Committee. He has filed legislation to protect Vietnam veterans suffering from Hepatitis C. On his first trip back to Vietnam, when he accompanied Clinton, he said that the local population doesn't remember the war but they are interested in America. At home, he pushed to passage a law naming Central High School a National Historic Site.

Snyder has been twice re-elected by 58%–42% margins, in 1998 against Phil Wyrick, who was elected as a Republican in January 1997 to replace Snyder in the state Senate, and in 2000 against Bob Thomas, an orthopedic-supply company manager who called for more tax cuts and said that Snyder's record showed that "he's no leader." Thomas defeated the Republican party favorite in the primary, but received little national assistance. With several Republican-leaning counties across the district's borders, redistricting could make it more competitive.

Cook's Call *Potentially Competitive.* This Little Rock-based district is the most marginal seat in the state. Though Clinton won here by 18 % in 1996, Bush won it by 1 % in 2000. Snyder's impressive wins here in 1998 and 2000 are proof that he is well liked by voters and that his own personal appeal has proven strong enough to overcome the competitive nature of the district. But, as this state and district continue to trend away from its Democratic roots, Snyder could face a serious challenge down the road. This seat will have to pick up some population, but it is not likely to alter the district significantly.

THE PEOPLE: Pop. 2000: 666,058; Pop. 1990: 587,412, up 13.4% 1990–2000. 76.6% White, 19.5% Black, 0.9% Asian, 0.5% Amer. Indian, 1.3% Two+ races, 1.1% Other; 2.4% Hispanic Origin.

2000 Presidential Vote			**1996 Presidential Vote**		
Bush (R)	116,075	(49%)	Clinton (D)	124,545	(55%)
Gore (D)	112,720	(48%)	Dole (R)	83,218	(37%)
Nader (Green)	3,421	(1%)	Perot (I)	14,667	(6%)
Others	3,396	(1%)			

Rep. Victor F. Snyder (D)

Elected 1996, 3d term; b. Sept. 27, 1947, Medford, OR; home, Little Rock; Willamette U., B.A. 1975, U. of OR, M.D. 1979, U. of AR, J.D. 1988; Presbyterian; single.

Military Career: Marine Corps, 1967–69 (Vietnam).

Elected Office: AR Senate, 1990–96.

Professional Career: Practicing physician, 1982–present.

DC Office: 1319 LHOB 20515, 202-225-2506; Fax: 202-225-5903; Web site: www.house.gov/snyder.

District Office: Little Rock, 501-324-5941.

Committees: *Armed Services* (12th of 28 D): Military Installations & Facilities; Military Personnel (RMM). *Veterans' Affairs* (7th of 14 D): Oversight & Investigations (RMM).

Group Ratings

	ADA	ACLU	AFS	LCV	CON	ITIC	NTU	COC	ACU	NTLC	CHC
2000	70	79	85	79	55	78	21	55	4	15	13
1999	85	—	100	88	73	—	15	29	4	—	—

National Journal Ratings

	1999 LIB	—	1999 CONS		2000 LIB	—	2000 CONS
Economic	62%	—	38%		77%	—	22%
Social	74%	—	25%		70%	—	29%
Foreign	77%	—	22%		85%	—	10%

Key Votes of the 106th Congress

1. Patient Bill of Rights	Y	5. Bar RU-486 $ for FDA	N	9. NATO War in Serbia	Y
2. Accelerate Min. Wage	Y	6. Display 10 Commandments	N	10. Perm. Trade with China	Y
3. Strike Ban on Ergo. Stnd.	Y	7. Gun Show Bkgrnd. Checks	Y	11. Debt Relief for 3rd World	Y
4. Ovrd. Estate Tax Veto	N	8. Ban Part.-Birth Abortion	N	12. Drop Cuba Econ. Embargo	Y

Election Results

2000 general	Victor F. Snyder (D)	126,957	(58%)	($623,489)
	Bob Thomas (R)	93,692	(42%)	($261,200)
2000 primary	Victor F. Snyder (D)	unopposed		
1998 general	Victor F. Snyder (D)	100,334	(58%)	($963,053)
	Phil Wyrick (R)	72,737	(42%)	($607,999)

THIRD DISTRICT

The northwest corner of Arkansas has become one of America's boom areas, with major corporate headquarters and dozens of small factories, tourist attractions and retirement developments, some of America's richest families and growing numbers of hard-working Hispanic immigrants. It is home to the handsome University of Arkansas in Fayetteville, the mountain-bound resort town of Eureka Springs and the sparkling Northwest Arkansas Regional Airport, opened in 1998, the second major new airport in the country since 1972. This would have seemed most unlikely for most of the 20th Century, when these rounded green mountains and pleasant wide valleys, farm-houses and small towns seemed left behind. But the friendly atmosphere and strong religious faith of these communities have proved to be assets, not liabilities, conducive to economic crea-tivity and personal serenity. There have also been touches of genius. Sam Walton, who opened his first Wal-Mart on the town square of Bentonville (it's now a small museum), had the inspiration of building a retail chain in tradition-minded small towns and rural areas using sophisticated computerized management; it made him the richest man in America, though he still drove a pickup truck and some of the metal panels have fallen off the Wal-Mart headquarters building outside Bentonville. Don Tyson took his family chicken business and made Tyson Foods, in its sparkling headquarters outside Springdale, the nation's leading chicken producer and processor.

The 3d Congressional District covers Northwest Arkansas, including Bentonville, Fayetteville and Springdale, plus Fort Smith on the Oklahoma line and several mountain and upcountry counties to the east and south. Some of these mountain counties have been Republican since the Civil War, for there were few slaves here and much suspicion of planters; others started leaning Republican in the 1950s, and a Republican congressman, John Paul Hammerschmidt, was elected here in 1966. He was strong enough even in Democratic 1974 to beat Bill Clinton, then 28, in his first election, though Clinton did get an impressive 48%. Lately this area has become even more Republican, as Christian conservatives have entered politics and new migrants and million-aires have voted heavily Republican. The 3d voted for Clinton 43%–42% in 1992, but in 1996 it went 45%–44% for Bob Dole and George W. Bush won 59%–37% in 2000. The big companies may work with Democrats—Wal-Mart had Hillary Rodham Clinton on its board and Don Tyson's house counsel put her in the way of making unbelievable profits in commodities trades—but most voters here are staunchly Republican.

The congressman from the 3d District is Asa Hutchinson, a Republican elected in 1996 to replace his older brother Tim Hutchinson, who was elected to the Senate. The Hutchinsons grew up on a farm in Gravette, the fifth and sixth children of a couple who started a Christian radio station and the Benton County Christian School. Both went to Bob Jones University (Asa defended George W. Bush when he was criticized for speaking there during the South Carolina primary), and then came back to Arkansas—graduate school for Tim, law school for Asa. Asa entered the University of Arkansas Law School the year Bill Clinton started teaching there; this would not be the final time their careers intertwined. Hutchinson was Bentonville coordinator for Frank White, the Republican who beat one-term Governor Clinton in 1980. Recommended by Hammersch-midt, Hutchinson became U.S. attorney in western Arkansas in 1981, the youngest U.S. attorney in the country. There he prosecuted a Republican sheriff for marijuana possession and Roger Clinton for cocaine possession; his signal achievement was the prosecution of a paramilitary group called the Covenant, the Sword, and the Arm of the Lord. In 1986 he ran for the Senate and lost to Dale Bumpers 62%–38%; in 1990 he ran for attorney general and lost to Democrat Winston Bryant. He practiced law in Fort Smith—taking a lot of civil rights and sex discrimination cases, "things you wouldn't think of a Republican lawyer doing"—and was state Republican chairman from 1990–95.

In early 1996, Asa Hutchinson wasn't running for Congress. But after Governor Jim Guy Tucker was convicted of fraud and announced he would resign, Lieutenant Governor Mike Huckabee withdrew from the Senate race; Tim Hutchinson, after some hesitation, became the Republican candidate for Senate. That left the 3d District nomination open. Asa Hutchinson seemed the clear favorite to win. The Democrats tapped Ann Henry, a University of Arkansas business law professor and former Fayetteville councilwoman. She was a close friend of Bill and Hillary Rodham Clinton—they held their wedding reception at her house—and put $130,000 into her campaign and spent more than Hutchinson. She campaigned as an opponent of "the Gingrich agenda." But Hutchinson's personal strength and party affiliation gave him a 56%–42% victory—better than brother Tim's 50%–47% four years before.

In the House, Hutchinson has combined a conservative voting record with an open and pleasant manner to become an important member in a short time. In addition to seats on Government Reform and Transportation, he got a committee assignment on Judiciary. He sought to have the tranquilizer Rohypnol, used by rapists to quiet victims, made a Schedule 1 drug. With his brother, he protested China's human rights violations and "adopted" a Chinese "prisoner of conscience" and pledged to work for his release. He played a mediating role on impeachment. Early on, as Democrats angrily turned the hearings partisan, he, Lindsey Graham and Ed Pease began meeting with Democrats William Delahunt and Howard Berman to see if they could reach some common ground. Not much was found. But Hutchinson in his statements on the committee and on television struck a positive, open-minded, even friendly tone that was sharply in contrast with much of the discourse on the issue.

Hutchinson sought bipartisan agreement on incremental measures on health care finance and, most notably, campaign finance reform. With Democrat Tom Allen of Maine, he co-sponsored a so-called "freshman bill," to ban soft money but not issue advocacy—though it did rouse some protest from Arkansas Right to Life. But most Democrats wanted to pass the Shays-Meehan bill, which did ban issue advocacy ads within 60 days of an election, and the Hutchinson-Allen bill lost 147–226, with most Republicans voting for it. Subsequently, Hutchinson endorsed a simplified version of the McCain-Feingold reform bill. He also became a proponent of privacy protection, with authorship of the bipartisan Privacy Commission Act; he served on Speaker Hastert's Task Force for a Drug-Free America; he called for junking the current tax code to force Congress to debate a simpler, fairer system. For the 107th Congress, Hutchinson won a seat on the Intelligence Committee.

In the 1998 election, Hutchinson's only opponent was Ralph Forbes, former member of the American Nazi Party and the National Socialist White People's Party, who sued Arkansas Public Broadcasting for excluding him from a 1992 debate and, in a well-argued case, lost in the Supreme Court. There was speculation that Democrats would retaliate against Hutchinson for supporting impeachment, but in 2000 they could find no one to run and Hutchinson was re-elected without opposition. He has said that he would be interested in a leadership bid if the right opportunity came along, but in May 2001 he was nominated to lead the Drug Enforcement Administration. Several state legislators expressed interest in the seat. Should the seat become available state parties have ten days to decide if they want to hold a special primary election. (If one party does, they all hold primaries.) The governor sets a date for candidate filings at least ten days afterwards and the special primary is at least 30 but no more than 45 days after the deadline. The election must be at least ten days after the primary.

Cook's Call   *Safe.* The most Republican district in the state (Bush won the district by 22%) is also the state's fastest growing. With about 100,000 more people than the ideal congressional district, this Fort Smith-based district will contract a bit in redistricting, but it will retain its heavily Republican base.

THE PEOPLE: Pop. 2000: 764,853; Pop. 1990: 589,523, up 29.7% 1990–2000. 90.8% White, 1.8% Black, 1.3% Asian, 1.3% Amer. Indian, 0.1% Hawaiian, 1.8% Two+ races, 2.8% Other; 5.8% Hispanic Origin.

2000 Presidential Vote
Bush (R)	160,001	(59%)
Gore (D)	100,297	(37%)
Nader (Green)	5,005	(2%)
Others	4,082	(2%)

1996 Presidential Vote
Dole (R)	110,457	(45%)
Clinton (D)	107,096	(44%)
Perot (I)	22,976	(9%)
Others	4,419	(2%)

Rep. Asa Hutchinson (R)

Elected 1996, 3d term; b. Dec. 3, 1950, Gravette; home, Fort Smith; Bob Jones U., B.S. 1972, U. of AR, J.D. 1975; Baptist; married (Susan).

Professional Career: U.S. Atty., AR Western Dist., 1982–85; Practicing atty., 1986–96; AR Repub. Party Chmn., 1990–95.

DC Office: 1421 LHOB 20515, 202-225-4301; Fax: 202-225-5713; Web site: www.house.gov/hutchinson.

District Offices: Fayetteville, 501-442-5258; Fort Smith, 501-782-7787; Harrison, 870-741-6900.

Committees: *Judiciary* (11th of 21 R): Courts, the Internet & Intellectual Property; Crime; The Constitution. *Permanent Select Committee on Intelligence* (10th of 11 R): Human Intelligence, Analysis & Counterintelligence; Intelligence Policy & National Security. *Standards of Official Conduct* (4th of 5 R). *Transportation & Infrastructure* (16th of 42 R): Aviation; Water Resources & Environment.

Group Ratings
	ADA	ACLU	AFS	LCV	CON	ITIC	NTU	COC	ACU	NTLC	CHC
2000	0	21	0	0	39	100	63	85	83	67	93
1999	10	—	16	6	12	—	60	91	72	—	—

National Journal Ratings
	1999 LIB	—	1999 CONS		2000 LIB	—	2000 CONS
Economic	28%	—	71%		6%	—	85%
Social	35%	—	64%		37%	—	62%
Foreign	23%	—	73%		24%	—	76%

Key Votes of the 106th Congress
1. Patient Bill of Rights	N	5. Bar RU-486 $ for FDA	Y	9. NATO War in Serbia	N
2. Accelerate Min. Wage	N	6. Display 10 Commandments	Y	10. Perm. Trade with China	Y
3. Strike Ban on Ergo. Stnd.	N	7. Gun Show Bkgrnd. Checks	N	11. Debt Relief for 3rd World	N
4. Ovrd. Estate Tax Veto	Y	8. Ban Part.-Birth Abortion	Y	12. Drop Cuba Econ. Embargo	N

Election Results
2000 general	Asa Hutchinson (R)	unopposed		($949,743)
2000 primary	Asa Hutchinson (R)	unopposed		
1998 general	Asa Hutchinson (R)	154,780	(81%)	($296,736)
	Ralph Forbes (Ref)	36,917	(19%)	

FOURTH DISTRICT

West from the Delta flatlands along the Mississippi River, where the water-soaked fields produce America's largest rice crop, across small cities with antique pasts like Pine Bluff and El Dorado, southern Arkansas runs west to the Ouachita Mountains and the border town of Texarkana, where the main street divides two states and Texan Ross Perot grew up five blocks west of Arkansas. This is the northwestern corner of the Deep South. There is still a large black population here, a reminder that parts of southern Arkansas were once plantation country; there is also oil production, a reminder that this is the beginning of the Southwest. The broiler chicken industry looms large in these parts, and the accent is clearly Arkansan: El Dorado, Nevada and Lafayette are all pronounced with long As and penultimate syllable accents, and Ouachita is, with a bow to the original French, *waSHEEta*. The district also includes the little railroad-crossing, county seat town of Hope, where President Bill Clinton and his first White House Chief of Staff Mack McLarty were classmates at Miss Mary's kindergarten, and where Arkansas's Governor Mike Huckabee grew up a decade later; and Hot Springs, the spa resort and gambling haven where Clinton's stepfather sold Buicks, his mother bet on the horses, and he excelled in high school as he began his climb from southern Arkansas to world eminence.

The 4th Congressional District occupies almost all of the southern geographical half of Arkansas, from the Mississippi River to the Ouachita Mountains, the Delta to Texarkana. It is historically a Democratic district, and one that for most of this century has elected young men to the House and kept them there for years, to cut deals with the Democratic leadership and bring home the bacon. During the 1990s it had a very different congressional politics: bipartisan, with rancorous debates on national issues followed by narrow election victories.

The congressman from the 4th District is Mike Ross, a Democrat who defeated four-term Representative Jay Dickey, the only House Republican outside California who was defeated in 2000. A fifth generation Arkansan, Ross was born in Texarkana. He graduated from Hope High School and received his bachelor's degree in political science from the University of Arkansas at Little Rock in 1987. He got his start in local politics in 1982 as a travel aide for Bill Clinton's successful bid to regain the governor's office. Then, while working on his degree, he served on the staff of Lieutenant Governor Winston Bryant, including five years as his chief of staff; he also was executive director of the Arkansas Youth Suicide Prevention Commission. Then Ross sold insurance and worked as a sales manager for a pharmaceutical company. He owns Holly's Health Mart in rural Prescott, where he lives with his wife Holly, who is the store's pharmacist. Ross was elected to the state senate in 1990 and served there until he ran for Congress. In 1998, he led hearings into allegations of abuse and neglect within the state Youth Services Division.

This was perhaps the only district in the nation where impeachment played a pivotal role in 2000. For Jay Dickey, representing Bill Clinton's boyhood homes, had voted for impeachment, and Clinton vowed to get back at him and took a close interest in the campaign. Dickey prided himself for working his Appropriations Committee seat to bring home federal largesse—most recently $94 million to complete I-49 from Texarkana to the Louisiana border—and to aid local black farmers. But Democrats rallied blacks and limited Dickey's inroads into this constituency. Both candidates raised more than $1 million; Republicans criticized Ross for raising nearly half of his money from political action committees. There were plenty of independent expenditures as well, by pharmaceutical groups against Ross, by labor unions against Dickey. Ross encountered unexpected trouble winning the party nomination. In the primary, he received 45% of the vote and was forced into a runoff against former television reporter Dewayne Graham, who barely finished second with 22%; trailing by 234 votes in third place was Judy Smith, a former state representative who ran against Dickey in 1998 and had support from black and women's groups. Graham, a political neophyte and party maverick who borrowed $75,000 from his credit card to finance his campaign and later supported Dickey (as did Judy Smith), said that Ross was selling voters "a bill of goods" and that Dickey better understood local people; Ross won the runoff, 58%–42%.

In the rough-and-tumble general, Ross portrayed himself as a small-town guy who found himself pitted against his own pharmaceutical industry in his fight to lower prescription drug prices and stop telemarketing harassment. He also focused on lowering class sizes and making schools safer. Although Dickey often was a thorn in the Republican leadership's side, Ross reprised Democratic challenges from previous years, claiming that "the real Jay Dickey" voted to cut Medicare and Social Security to fund tax cuts for the wealthy. Dickey responded that Ross was getting his script from "his liberal masters in Washington." Clinton had an impact: He helped raise $300,000 for Ross at fundraisers, orchestrated endorsements from other administration officials with Arkansas roots, and campaigned for Ross in Pine Bluff on the Sunday before the election. Ross won, 51%–49%, taking 18 of 26 counties—with an especially big 58%–42% margin in Pine Bluff and Jefferson County. Dickey ran best in El Dorado and Hot Springs.

In the House, Ross joined the Blue Dogs. Although the district already leaned strongly Democratic, he will look for more help on redistricting from former colleagues in the legislature. A tough primary fight in 2002 is possible.

Cook's Call   *Potentially Competitive.* As the only Democrat outside of California to defeat an incumbent and as one of the few Democrats to win in a primarily rural district, it would seem likely that Ross would be a top target in 2002. Though Republican Jay Dickey (whom Ross defeated) held onto this seat for eight years, this district has a serious Democratic lean to it. And, this sprawling district, which takes in five media markets, is a tough (and expensive) district in which to get known. It looks likely that this 26 county district will get even bigger after redistricting as it the slowest growing in the state. A down year for Democrats (or a misstep by Ross), could give Republicans an opening here.

THE PEOPLE: Pop. 2000: 612,515; Pop. 1990: 585,202, up 4.7% 1990–2000. 70.1% White, 26.6% Black, 0.4% Asian, 0.5% Amer. Indian, 1.1% Two+ races, 1.3% Other; 2.7% Hispanic Origin.

2000 Presidential Vote		
Gore (D)	107,107	(50%)
Bush (R)	100,855	(47%)
Nader (Green)	2,437	(1%)
Others	2,904	(1%)

1996 Presidential Vote		
Clinton (D)	126,896	(60%)
Dole (R)	66,034	(31%)
Perot (I)	15,972	(8%)

Rep. Mike Ross (D)

Elected 2000, 1st term; b. Aug. 2, 1961, Texarkana; home, Prescott; U. of AR, B.A. 1987; Methodist; married (Holly).

Elected Office: AR Senate, 1990–2000.

Professional Career: Chief of Staff, AR Lt. Gov. Winston Bryant, 1984–89; Owner, Holly's Health Mart, 1993-present.

DC Office: 514 CHOB 20515, 202-225-3772; Fax: 202-225-1314; Web site: www.house.gov/ross.

District Offices: El Dorado, 870-881-0681; Hot Springs, 501-520-5892; Pine Bluff, 870-536-3376; Prescott, 870-887-6787.

Committees: *Agriculture* (21st of 24 D): General Farm Commodities & Risk Management; Livestock & Horticulture. *Financial Services* (32d of 32 D): Capital Markets, Insurance & Government Sponsored Enterprises; Domestic Monetary Policy, Technology & Economic Growth. *Small Business* (15th of 17 D): Tax, Finance & Exports; Workforce, Empowerment & Government Programs.

Group Ratings and Key Votes: Newly Elected

Election Results

2000 general	Mike Ross (D)	108,143	(51%)	($1,626,164)
	Jay W. Dickey (R)	104,017	(49%)	($1,786,307)
2000 runoff	Mike Ross (D)	28,286	(58%)	
	Dewayne Graham (D)	20,392	(42%)	
2000 primary	Mike Ross (D)	41,668	(45%)	
	Dewayne Graham (D)	20,575	(22%)	
	Judy Smith (D)	20,341	(22%)	
	Bruce Carleton Harris (D)	10,539	(11%)	
1998 general	Jay W. Dickey (R)	92,346	(58%)	($842,243)
	Judy Smith (D)	68,194	(42%)	($316,927)

★ CALIFORNIA ★

California is America's largest state, a nation-state really, with an economy larger than all but 5 nations; it is the site of the world's most advanced cutting-edge technology, and a state that at the dawn of the 21st Century was subject, like some Third World country, to rolling blackouts of electricity. Its growth has been awesome: The 2000 Census counted 33.9 million Californians, far ahead of second-place Texas's 20.8 million; metro Los Angeles had 16.4 million people, second only to metro New York's 21.2 million, and the San Francisco Bay area had 7.0 million, not so far behind Chicagoland's 9.2 million. California, moreover, owes its current preeminence not to natural advantage but to human ingenuity. Los Angeles, with no natural resources and no natural harbor, is the nation's leading manufacturer and port, as well as the world's entertainment center. The Bay area, which once lived by exporting food, is now the world's leader in computers and high tech. California has grown not because it had to but because people wanted it to. But it has not grown without contradictions. California loves its physical environment, but also has the largest urban sprawl in the United States; it likes to think of itself as the America of the future, even as it watches the electricity flicker out; it likes to see itself as the political leader of the nation, but lives now with a president who did not come close to winning here and has a public sector that in important ways has been dysfunctional over the past decade. California today is solidly Democratic, well off to the left on cultural issues, secular more than religious. If it could imagine itself leading the nation when Bill Clinton was president, it is all too conscious that the nation is not following its lead now that Clinton has been succeeded by George W. Bush.

Most of all California has been a state that is always transforming itself, whose economy has been transformed several times over, whose population has been transformed by one group of newcomers after another and whose politics is periodically transformed with the suddennesss of an earthquake. If other states have changed gradually on an analog scale over the years, California has changed sharply on a digital scale: this is quantum physics, not wave mechanics. So it has been from its American beginning. In 1848, when California passed from Mexico to the United States by the Treaty of Guadalupe Hidalgo, this was an almost entirely empty land, inhabited by a few thousand Indians and Mexicans and by a few hundred American soldiers and men on the make. Then in 1849 gold was found in Sutter's Mill and thousands arrived in the Gold Rush; within months San Francisco became one of America's 25 largest cities. The big money was made not by the miners but by the grocers and dry goods merchants who provisioned them, like the Big Four—Crocker, Hopkins, Huntington, Stanford—who built the Central and Southern Pacific Railroads. The railroads sold off vast chunks of the Central Valley to large farming operations and enticed settlers with low fares to newly-platted suburbs in the Los Angeles Basin. Engineers built great aqueducts that stretched hundreds of miles, from the Hetch Hetchy Valley in Yosemite to San Francisco and from the Owens River to Los Angeles, without which these cities could not exist. Early 20th Century California was affluent and cultured, with great universities already, Berkeley and Stanford, and fine museums and libraries; it was America's window on the Pacific, alert to developments in China and Japan, eager to extend America's economic reach and military strength, but still, as Carey McWilliams wrote, an "island" separated from the rest of the country. Then in World War II California became one of the great defense industry states, building ships and airplanes by the thousands. Millions of Americans came here and millions stayed: The population rose from 7 million in 1940 to 17 million in 1963, when California passed New York and became the nation's most populous state.

California's future was planned by the heads of the big units of government and business—Franklin Roosevelt and Henry J. Kaiser, who built vast shipyards and steel and aluminum factories; Governor Earl Warren, who husbanded tax monies to build schools and freeways in the years after the war; Robert Sproul and Clark Kerr, who built the University of California into what Kerr called "the multiversity," Governor Pat Brown, who completed the vast system of canals and aqueducts that brought water from the wet north to the thirsty south. But the real engine of growth was the little people who took advantage of this infrastructure and built a humming economy on it. When California's defense plants closed down after World War II, leaders imagined

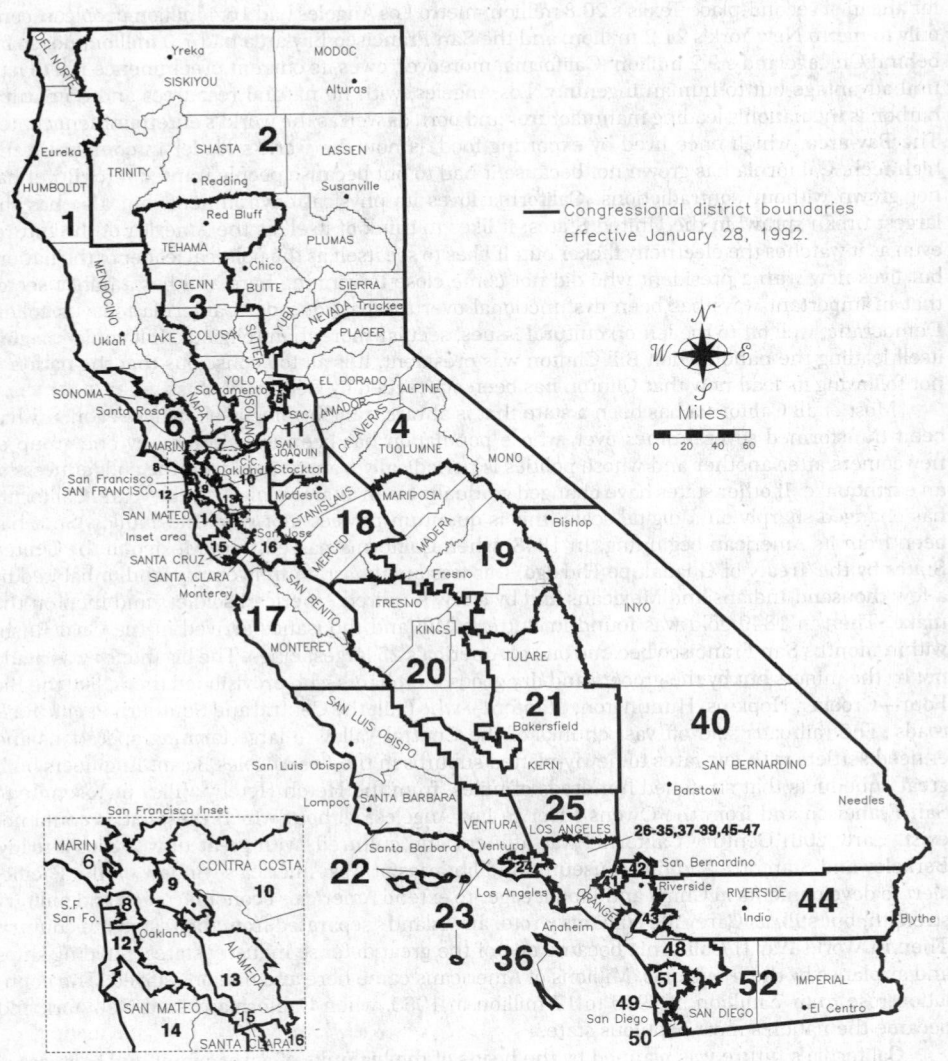

Congressional district boundaries
effective January 28, 1992.

that hundreds of thousands would have to head back east. Instead, as urbanologist Jane Jacobs points out, one-eighth of all the new jobs in the nation in the late 1940s were created in metro Los Angeles. This small scale growth, multiplied thousands of times over, made California the nation's largest state. This infusion of new people transformed California politically. Before World War II this was a Republican state, with progressive leanings; political struggles took place inside the Republican Party. The in-rush of the G.I. generation, with its love of the New Deal, the building for the first time here of auto and steel factories with unionized work forces, made California a two-party state. Earl Warren's progressive Republicans still were dominant through the mid-1950s, but with the election of Democratic Governor Pat Brown in 1958 a group of talented liberal Democrats took over. Things turned sour in the mid-1960s, when student rebellions starting in Berkeley in 1964 and the Watts riot of 1965 upset the New Deal order. Californians responded by calling in a disillusioned New Dealer espousing the conformist cultural conservatism of the G.I. generation, Ronald Reagan, who presaged the course the nation would follow in the 1980s.

California veered off on a different path in the 1970s, electing Jerry Brown as governor, entranced for a time by his idiosyncratic version of Baby Boomer liberalism (though he was too old to be a Boomer himself), as the World War II generation started to die out and California received a new infusion of migrants, well-educated whites attracted to the state's groovy lifestyle and, little noticed at first, Mexicans and other Latin Americans looking for work. Voters soon soured on Brown's liberalism: They passed Proposition 13 in 1978, banning property tax increases in a state where rapidly rising housing values were the chief source of people's wealth; they decried his spraying of Medfly-infested crops with an overly-effective insecticide that peeled paint on houses; they ousted, after he left office, three of his Supreme Court nominees who had overturned death penalty verdicts and struck down tough-on-crime laws. Brown lost a Senate race in 1982 and was succeeded by 16 years of Republican governors; he ran a quixotic campaign for president in 1992 (pointing presciently to the corruption of Bill and Hillary Rodham Clinton) and is now the tough-on-crime mayor of Oakland.

With Brown gone, politics and government more or less disappeared from TV stations' newscasts and voters' minds. In the 1980s, with Reagan as president and quiet Republican George Deukmejian as governor, California's defense industry boomed and Silicon Valley flowered off I-280 south of San Francisco. Public policy was mostly set by Willie Brown, speaker of the California Assembly from 1980–95 and now mayor of San Francisco, and the Democratic legislature surreptitiously furthered the causes of their clients—teachers' unions, trial lawyers and the criminal defense bar. The response was government by referendum, usually a clumsy matter but sometimes effective, on criminal justice, aid to immigrants, racial quotas and preferences. California schools in the post-World War II years taught the basics and inculcated students in mainstream American culture, readying them for the rapidly growing network of universities and community colleges and for an expanding and increasingly high-skill private sector. But now they changed course. "Multicultural" policies slotted newcomers into quota-fed monocultural enclaves in schools, universities, and big corporations. Public schools, with the pace set by teachers' unions, held students in "bilingual" Spanish-speaking programs long past the age when it is easiest to learn English—a policy not ended until voters approved Proposition 227 in June 1998. The Los Angeles Unified school district, the nation's second largest, became "an experiment in social dysfunction" in one reporter's words. The state Education Department pushed the education school nostrum "whole language," which left a generation unable to read or write standard English at levels acceptable in advanced workplaces—a mistake, the then-state superintendent later admitted, which shortchanged five million students. Civil liberties-minded legislators hobbled the criminal justice system, leaving teenage gangs to rule large swathes of central cities. The affluent hired private security systems, moved to gated communities and sent their children to elite school districts or private schools. The less well-off and the new immigrants from Latin America and Asia were left behind.

In the 1990s California went through another transformation, as a series of natural disasters and a massive economic downturn drained the state of confidence and set it off in a new political direction. Defense industry cutbacks hit metropolitan Los Angeles hard, costing hundreds of thousands of jobs and sending housing values that had skyrocketed in the 1980s plummeting downward in the early 1990s. Television screens were absorbed by disasters natural and manmade—the Loma Prieta earthquake in the San Francisco Bay area in October 1989, the Central Valley floods in early 1991, the Los Angeles riot following the acquittal of policemen accused of beating Rodney King in May 1992, the Malibu fires of September 1992, the Northridge earthquake of January 1994, the O.J. Simpson case, from the murder in June 1994 to the acquittal in October 1995. Long proud of its efficient and incorruptible government, California has seen it grow larger and increasingly dysfunctional, as documented by California's greatest reporter, Lou Cannon, in his book *Official Negligence*, the definitive story of the Rodney King beating, the Los Angeles riot and the trials that followed. In the 1990s California lost its trademark big businesses to mergers—Security Pacific and First Interstate Banks and the Bank of America, Carter Hawley Hale stores, Unocal and Getty Oil and Arco, even Times Mirror—so that today downtown Los Angeles has not a single Fortune 500 company headquarters. In the first half of the 1990s, about two million Californians, mostly white and affluent, abandoned California for other western states or went even further back east. In the meantime, and in increasing numbers in the late 1990s, immigrants kept arriving. The 2000 Census showed that 32% of California's population was Hispanic, up from 26% in 1990; the Asian population was 11%, up from 10%; in the meantime the number classifying themselves as white fell to 60% from 69%, while those classifiying themselves as black remained steady at 7%.

The defense downturn of the 1990s produced a huge fiscal crisis for incoming Governor Pete Wilson in 1991. His plans for preventive government to address social breakdown had to be put aside, and budgets whacked down. In the process Wilson discovered the state was spending billions on illegal immigrants and their children—for welfare (though Latinos in poverty apply for welfare much less than anyone else), for schools, for prison spaces. In 1994, uncertain of reelection against state Treasurer Kathleen Brown, Jerry Brown's sister, he supported Proposition 187, which denied non-emergency state government spending on illegal aliens and their children. In speeches Wilson was careful to differentiate between legal and illegal immigrants, and voters did too; at least one-third of Latino voters voted for 187, which passed by a wide margin. But campaign ads make a much greater impression than politicians' careful statements in a state where TV news coverage of politics and government is miniscule. Wilson's ad showing Mexicans running across the border, with the announcer proclaiming ominously, "They just keep coming," was taken by many as a slur, suggesting that all Latinos were more interested in welfare than work, which stung all the more because it is simply not true—Hispanic males have the highest work force participation rate of any measured group. And Republican firebrand Robert Dornan's challenge in 1997 of Loretta Sanchez's 984-vote victory over him in an Orange County congressional district, heavily publicized on Spanish-language television, was taken as a sign that Republicans did not want Latinos to vote, though Dornan insisted he was just challenging non-citizens' votes. The result was that Latino turnout increased and Latinos increasingly turned to the Democratic Party. The Latino vote increased from 10% of the vote in 1994 to 14% in 1998, and Gray Davis beat Republican Dan Lungren among Hispanics by 78%–16%—a huge drop for Republicans, since Wilson got almost 40% of the Latino vote in 1990. This was ominous news for Republicans, and not just in the short run. In 2000, 44% of Californians under 18 were Hispanic; they are going to be a lot more than 14% of the electorate, and unless Republicans can become competitive among them, it is hard to see how they can win many statewide races again.

This was one of the factors moving California from its status as a marginal state in 1990, one in which Republicans had won, with the exception of a close victory by Alan Cranston in 1986, seven consecutive contests for president, governor and senator, to its status in 2000 as a solidly Democratic state. In 1998 California voted 58%–38% for Democrat Gray Davis for governor and 53%–43% for Democratic Senator Barbara Boxer. In 2000 it voted 54%–42% for Al Gore over George W. Bush, although Bush spent $20 million on California media and Gore not a penny, and 56%–37% for Democratic Senator Dianne Feinstein over Republican Congressman Tom Campbell, in a contest that was never visible or close; Feinstein now has twice won more votes, by far, than any other senator in American history. Another factor was Bill Clinton. In 1992 Clinton carried California with 46% of the vote, as Californians, dismayed over plunging housing values and the senior George Bush's seeming indifference to their economy, moved from voting 51% for

Bush in 1988 to 33% four years later. Clinton understood that if he could lock up California's 54 electoral votes he would be a long way toward being assured of re-election. He courted the state with dozens of appearances, with special attention to California issues and projects, with assiduous cultivation of Hollywood celebrities and Silicon Valley cybermillionaires. Clinton's combination of moderation on economic issues and liberalism on cultural issues was a perfect fit for a critical block of California voters, the affluent professionals and techies who support abortion rights and gun control without question and who were increasingly fearful of the prominence of Christian conservatives in the national and to some extent the state Republican Party. Affluent Americans increasingly are not moored to any one locality, but can choose where they live, from an array of places with widely different cultural atmospheres. Those who espouse traditional values and have traditional religious views tend to pick metropolises like Denver, Atlanta, Dallas and Houston; those with liberation-minded values and secular or non-Christian religious attitudes tend to pick Los Angeles and the San Francisco Bay area. The quantum of all these personal decisions over the last decade made Colorado, Georgia and Texas more Republican and made California more Democratic. Liberation-minded voters happily rallied to Clinton during the Monica Lewinsky scandal and the impeachment crisis; polling evidence suggests that even after the furor of Clinton's last-minute pardons of Marc Rich and others, he remained a widely admired, even beloved figure here, assumed to be a Californian at heart even if, because of his wife's election to the Senate, he must live in New York.

The anatomy of Democrats' strength in California can be seen in the 2000 VNS exit poll. Gore carried every income group but those over $100,000, which went 51%–45% for Bush; the college-educated voted for Gore, and by greater margins than high school grads: cultural liberalism trumped promised tax cuts. Gore's best age group was those 30–44: many of them are people who have chosen to move to California over the past 15 years. White men voted 53%–41% for Bush, but white women were 53%–42% for Gore: the feminist left is strong here. Blacks, only 7% of the electorate, voted 86%–11% for Gore, a little lower than his national percentage among blacks. Hispanics, 14% of the electorate, despite Bush's efforts went 68%–29% for Gore: the campaign for Proposition 187 still rankles. Asians, 6% of the electorate, are reported as 48%–47% for Gore, a result statistically indistinguishable from that among whites. In the early 1990s Asians cast Republican margins; some groups, notably Chinese and Vietnamese, seemed to be moving away from Republicans in the late 1990s, perhaps disturbed by Republican campaigning against Al Gore's Buddhist temple fundraiser and John Huang's illegal fundraising or the prosecution of Wen Ho Lee. Koreans still seem solidly Republican, Filipinos more Democratic: this is not a single voting bloc, nor is it part of a single bloc of "people of color." Bush did not win as large a margin here as in most states among those who attend church at least once a week, and there are fewer of them in California than in almost any other state; those who never attend church voted 61%–30% for Gore, while Jews, more numerous here than in any other state but New York, voted 82%–15% for Gore.

Los Angeles County, which from the 1950s through the early 1990s was politically marginal, is now heavily Democratic. It gave Al Gore a 64%–32% margin, far better than the 57%–43% margin Lyndon Johnson won in his landslide victory of 1964. The reason for this shift is obvious to any traveler who gets beyond the mostly white precincts of Beverly Hills: Los Angeles County is now the greatest immigrant entry point in the United States—what New York was a century ago. The 2000 Census recorded Los Angeles County's population of 9.5 million as 45% Hispanic, 12% Black and 10% Asian. Here you can find the world's largest numbers of Mexicans, Iranians, Samoans, Filipinos, Salvadorans, Armenians, Guatemalans, Koreans and Thais outside their native countries. Mexicans and other Latinos are concentrated most heavily east and south of downtown Los Angeles; the old factory suburbs east of Alameda Street, filled with southern-born whites 40 years ago, are now 90% Hispanic. Latinos are moving into once heavily black neighborhoods in Watts and South Central as well as east from East Los Angeles to Pico Rivera, Baldwin Park and Santa Fe Springs. Asians are most heavily concentrated north of the I-10 east of downtown, and are a majority in Monterey Park, 49% in San Gabriel, Rosemead and high-income San Marino, 47% in Alhambra and 45% in Arcadia. But for the most part in L.A. County you find not ghettoes, but mixtures, in varying proportions, in the most polyglot constituency in America.

The battle for this constituency was played out in the 2001 Los Angeles mayoral election. The April primary featured 15 candidates, of which the top two finishers were both Democrats: former state House Speaker Antonio Villaraigosa, who had 30%; and city attorney James Hahn, who had 25% (Republican businessman Steve Sobroff finished third with 21%, Republican-turned independent city Councilman Joel Wachs was fourth with 11%, and Democratic Congressman Xavier Becerra was a distant fifth with 6%). "There's virtually no difference between the surviving candidates' prescriptions for meeting Los Angeles' needs in transportation, education, public safety and economic development," wrote David Broder of the *Washington Post*. "So the election turns on the contrast in their personalities—and their ethnic support." Seeking to become the city's first Latino mayor since 1872, the colorful and controversial Villaraigosa energized the East Side Latino community and made alliances with West Side Jewish leaders; he also won the endorsement of term-limited Republican Mayor Richard Riordan. A 20-year City Hall veteran, the phlegmatic Hahn courted older African-American leaders, such as Congresswoman Maxine Waters, who had been helped by his father, a former Los Angeles County supervisor; he drew support from an older Los Angeles, where non-Hispanic whites were still the majority of typical voters. In a late TV ad, Hahn cited a 1996 letter by Villaraigosa urging clemency for a convicted drug dealer whose sentence was commuted by President Clinton in his final hours in office, concluding, "Los Angeles can't trust Antonio Villaraigosa." Despite an unusually large Latino turnout, Hahn won the June runoff, 54%–46%. The old Los Angeles had one more, but perhaps final, victory.

Southern California beyond Los Angeles County was once the political bulwark of Ronald Reagan, heavily Republican; he made his last campaign appearances in 1980, 1984 and 1988 in San Diego, his "lucky city," and held his 1984 campaign kickoff in Mile Square Park in Orange County. But Orange County's image as an all-white enclave is two decades out of date. Santa Ana is one of the entry points for migrants from Mexico and Central America, and 76% Hispanic; Latinos are at least one-third of the populations of Anaheim, Garden Grove and Fullerton. Only when you get to Newport Beach on the coast or Mission Viejo inland are you in affluent, heavily Republican territory. George W. Bush carried Orange County 56%–40%; in 1988 his father carried it 68%–31%. The fastest-growing part of metro L.A. is the Inland Empire, San Bernardino and Riverside Counties, where the temperature is hotter, the air dirtier and the housing cheaper than in coastal L.A. Bush narrowly carried both in 2000. In 1988, the senior George Bush carried southern California 63%–36%, with a big enough margin to offset Democratic margins in Los Angeles County and the San Francisco Bay area put together. In 2000, George W. Bush carried this area by 52%–44%, not enough to offset L.A. County, much less the Bay area. This is a prime example of the Democratic trend in the nation's largest metro areas in the Clinton-Gore 1990s.

Economically affluent, culturally liberal, complaining about high housing prices and congested freeways, the San Francisco Bay area has been one of America's greatest success stories— and a place which is profoundly and proudly out of line with what used to be called Middle America. It has been Democratic since Earl Warren, who first won office as city attorney in Oakland, left the state, and in the 1990s has become overwhelmingly Democratic, more so than any other major metro area. All of its congressmen are Democrats, as are 8 of 9 state senators and 18 of its 19 members of the California Assembly. The Bay area voted 64%–30% for Al Gore. Republicans tried to court Silicon Valley by arguing that Democrats were overregulating high tech and favoring trial lawyers over entrepreneurs; they pointed out that the one bill on which Congress overrode Bill Clinton's veto was a 1995 measure, which would protect high-tech companies from frivolous suits by trial lawyers. George W. Bush's campaign did manage to be competitive with Al Gore's in fundraising in the Valley, but not in votes.

The rest of California is usually forgotten, yet it amounts to one-quarter of the state—and is large enough that if it were a state by itself it would rank 12th in population; the media markets of Sacramento and Fresno in the Central Valley taken together would be the nation's tenth largest. It is forgotten also because it has been trending in the opposite direction from the rest of the state. From the New Deal era through the 1960s the Central Valley was strongly Democratic, while the more affluent coast was Republican; now that cultural issues are at the center of politics in California, those positions are reversed. Here also are the counties with the biggest percentage population increase in California, foothill counties filling up with cultural conservatives who left the cosmopolitan major metro areas, Central Valley counties with commuters to the Bay area who can't afford houses there. George W. Bush carried the Central Valley and the rest of California by a 51%–43%, a margin similar to the 54%–44% his father won there in 1988 when he carried the state. This is a prime example of the 1990s trend against the Democrats and toward the Republicans outside America's major metro areas.

Presiding over this California—or these Californias—is Governor Gray Davis, who as 2000 turned into 2001 seemed in political command of all he surveyed. He won his first term in 1998 by a 58%–38% margin, one that exceeded the impressive first-term margins of Ronald Reagan (58%–42%) and Pat Brown (60%–40%). His fellow Democrats had a 26–14 margin in the state Senate and a 50–30 margin in the Assembly. Only one Republican held lower statewide office, Secretary of State Bill Jones; Insurance Commissioner Chuck Quackenbush had resigned amid scandal in 2000. Davis presided over, and did much to create, a moderate consensus replacing the clash and conflict between a liberal-left Democratic legislature and a Republican governor or angry voters speaking through referenda that had prevailed from 1978 to 1998. From his long experience in state government—seven years as chief of staff to Jerry Brown, four years in the Assembly, eight years as controller and four years as lieutenant governor—he had learned many lessons, foremost among them being not to defy the voters and seek by judicial decree or administrative legerdemain to overturn their verdicts in referenda. From his long cultivation of liberal Westside money-givers and of Sacramento lobbyists, he had raised $26 million for his re-election campaign by January 2001. The state's economy was humming. As Joel Kotkin, the greatest chronicler of California business, put it, "We have an economy something like the Internet, with a bunch of random connections and poles that are always recreating themselves."

There was only one problem: In early 2001 the lights kept going out. Here, as with the public schools and the LAPD, the problem is the public sector. In 1996 California passed electricity deregulation, in a bill backed unanimously in the legislature, signed by Governor Pete Wilson, embraced by the utilities and praised by just about every civic voice. But, as put into effect by regulators, the bill was not actually deregulation: Consumers were guaranteed no rate increase until 2002, and the electric utilities were required to buy all their electricity in a state-run spot market and could not, as businesses usually do, hedge against higher prices by entering into long-term contracts. In summer 2000 energy prices spiked up, for not totally unpredictable reasons—natural gas prices rose, low rainfall held hydroelectric power production down, no new power plant has been built in California with its tight environmental laws and nitpicking regulators for more than 10 years. The San Diego utility was faced with high spot market prices, escaping from the regulatory scheme by paying off previous debt, but regulators capped prices in August 2000 when prices spiked and California got through a cool summer without much problem. Pacific Gas and Electric Company and Southern California Edison sought and received permission to enter into long-term contracts to buy power at $50 per megawatt-hour, less than a third the average for August 2000, but no long-term contracts were signed and the utility companies and the public utilities commission continued to blame each other for the inaction. Supplies grew much worse in the winter and the two leading utilities, PG&E and Southern California Edison quickly accumulated debts of $12 billion buying electricity at spot prices ranging from $250 to $1,500 per megawatt hour; power suppliers were reluctant to sell to PG&E and Southern California Edison because there was no assurance they would be paid. Rolling blackouts started in January: night school classes were taught by flashlight, citizens directed traffic below defunct traffic signals, dairy farmers were unable to process milk, Orange County factories ran only on nights and weekends, dentists postponed surgery. California, with the most advanced economy anywhere, was suddenly living in the Third World.

Davis's initial response was to allow higher rates briefly and promise to avoid them hereafter, and once said that he could solve the problem in 20 minutes if he raised rates; he evidently feared that so-called consumer advocates would resort to ballot initiatives that would wreck the system. California voters evidently believed that they were possessed of certain virtues which entitled them not to pay more for electricity, even though it costs more to produce and everyone in the other 49 states had to pay higher rates. In January, Davis asked George W. Bush to continue a Clinton administration order requiring suppliers to sell power to California utilities; Bush said he would extend it for two weeks, but that California would have to fix its own deregulation law. In February Davis persuaded the legislature to approve a bill to let the state buy power through long-term contracts with revenue bonds and to pass it along to the utilities; the measure also included higher rates for consumers who exceeded baseline usage, a measure that could have much greater impact in Republican-leaning inland California, where air conditioning is a must for comfortable living, than in mostly Democratic coastal California, where air conditioning is usually optional. And Davis ordered 20% rebates to consumers who cut their usage 20% from the previous year. Later that month Davis agreed to buy Edison's transmission grid and to guarantee its bonds to pay off its debts. But Davis had difficulty obtaining electricity at rates that would prevent increases to consumers. In March the Public Utility Commission ordered a $5 billion a year rate increase; Davis, who had often said that he expected his appointees, even judges, to follow his policies, said he had no part in the decision. In April PG&E announced it was going into bankruptcy. Three days later, Davis and Edison announced its deal to sell the transmission lines. Davis then attempted to purchase PG&E's portion of the grid in bankruptcy court, although he still needed legislative approval for all his proposals. He called a special session in May 2001, and presented a 98 page bill to authorize the state to pay $2.76 billion to buy Edison's transmission lines, selling bonds to finance the purchase, and earmarking part of ratepayers' monthly utility bills to pay off the utilities' debt. In Washington Senators Dianne Feinstein and Barbara Boxer introduced bills to impose price controls on wholesale power prices in the Western states. But they went nowhere, and the Bush-appointed FERC chairman, Curt Hebert, refused to consider temporary price controls; temporary controls, he argued, would never be suspended, and controls would reduce supply.

As the electricity crisis went on, Davis's job rating started to sag somewhat, though it still remained positive. Other politicians spotted weakness: Secretary of State Bill Jones announced he would run against Davis, and state Treasurer Phil Angelides, Controller Kathleen Connell and state Senator Don Perata criticized his handling of the electricity crisis. It seemed very likely that there would be rolling blackouts in summer 2001, and that the state's economy would be slowed down. As of May 2001 it is impossible to say how the crisis would play out, and what effect it would have on Davis and other Democrats in 2002; but it raises the possibility that the governor's race could be competitive. But, even apart from the fact that so many smart people missed what in retrospect seems an obvious flaw in the 1996 bill, the electricity crisis raises serious questions about the governance of California. California's economically productive, culturally non-judgmental electorate seems to feel itself entitled to all good things at minimal cost. Internet servers consume huge amounts of electricity, and the unanticipated increases in demand from Silicon Valley's servers are one reason the state got caught short of electricity. Yet Internet giant Cisco lobbied successfully the San Jose City Council to block a power plant near its headquarters. Californians are so religiously intent on protecting their environment that no new power plants are built—and then are affronted when they are asked to pay more for electricity. For example, a February 2001 poll found 64% of Californians "adamantly" opposed easing environmental standards to increase electricity supplies, but 50% disapproved of paying higher prices for electricity purchased through state-issued bonds. The public appetite for news of crimes and freeway crashes means that elected officials operate in a cocoon in the company town of Sacramento, insulated from scrutiny, immune from accountability, determined to maintain high poll ratings by offending no one at the risk of neglecting problems that may loom ahead.

California in 2001 is much like New York in 1901: the nation's largest state, its greatest immigrant magnet, with its most productive and creative economy. But it seems to lack two things which enabled New York over the first half of the 20th Century to develop its full potential and become a national leader, to create an image of itself as an "empire state" in which every citizen could take pride. One is a coherent and competent civic and political elite. The other is a pattern to interweave the newcomers into the American fabric. California's loss of corporate headquarters has deprived it of many business leaders, although others—real estate billionaire Eli Broad, entrepreneur and former Los Angeles Mayor Richard Riordan—have sometimes stepped in. But Hollywood leaders are transfixed by their own narcissism and by their preoccupation with the censure of the tradition-minded right, and Silicon Valley leaders have been too busy building their own businesses or protecting them from downturns to take much part in civic affairs; a rare exception is that of a small player in the Valley, Ron Unz, whose Proposition 227 put an end to California's dysfunctional bilingual education—a problem the political elite, left and right, neglected for 20 years. The political elite includes many competent and dedicated people, Governors Pete Wilson and Gray Davis among them. But too often they have been unable or unwilling to break deadlocks, and they are hampered by media that leave the public woefully underinformed.

The other thing California lacks is an idea of how to interweave immigrants into the American fabric. Culturally the dominant style in California is laissez faire: let people do pretty much anything they want (except smoke). But tolerance can segue into indifference. And it does not necessarily translate into a sense of common identity and purpose. The California of Earl Warren, Pat Brown and Ronald Reagan had a kind of nationalism, a shared vision of itself, like the New York of Theodore Roosevelt, Al Smith, Franklin Roosevelt, Fiorello LaGuardia and Thomas Dewey. That seems to be missing in California today. Instead articulate elites, focusing on changing demography, paint a vision of California as a "multicultural" polity, with a Third World majority (or approaching it) of "people of color." But the immigrants of today's California are no more a single united mass striving to overthrow the system than were the immigrants of New York 100 years ago; they came to the United States not to change this country but to become part of it. California businesses and political elites, like those in the United States generally, have responded to these newcomers with racial quotas and preferences, which cast doubt on their achievements, and with bilingual education, which consigns them to low-wage jobs. Fortunately, California voters have chosen another course, and Gray Davis has risked the wrath of Democratic legislators by vetoing their bills to overturn the voters' verdicts. In 1996 voters adopted Proposition 209, which banned state racial quotas and preferences. University administrators howled in agony, and demonstrators claimed that this was a return to Jim Crow. Far from it. The number of "minority" freshmen at the University of California was actually higher in 2000 than it was in 1997, the last quota year; there were smaller numbers at the highly selective Berkeley and Los Angeles campus, where many low-scoring Hispanics and blacks admitted under quotas had dropped out, but more at other campuses, where administrators worked with local high schools to prepare Hispanic and black students for college work. In 1998 voters adopted Proposition 227 that limited so-called bilingual education. Again elites fretted and demonstrators howled. But test scores immediately shot up among Hispanic elementary school children. Policies designed to address the problems faced by blacks in the 1960s and 1970s are ill-suited to the needs of immigrants in the 1990s and 2000s. California elites in the name of "multiculturalism" have denied Latino students the chance to master English and have blocked high-scoring Asian students from places in selective universities. They need to learn the lessons taught by the New York elites of a century ago: to help immigrants move forward to become Americans. Immigrants are striving not to create a "people of color" California, with separate compartments for separate races, where the heritage of "white Europeans" will be set aside, but an American California, with a rich mix of talented and enterprising people capable of making their own way, proud of their talents and achievements, willing to meet common obligations and respectful of worthy traditions.

Governor Gray Davis, the Governor of California, was elected in 1998—only the fourth Democratic governor of California in the 20th century (and only the second not named Brown). Davis grew up in Connecticut and, after age 11, in Los Angeles; he graduated from Stanford and Columbia Law School, then served in the Army in Vietnam, where he earned a Bronze Star. In 1969 he returned to California and almost immediately plunged into politics. In 1973 he worked on Tom Bradley's first successful campaign for mayor; in 1974, at 31, he ran for state treasurer, and lost the primary to former Speaker Jess Unruh. Later that year, he worked on Jerry Brown's successful campaign for governor, and in 1975 he became Brown's chief of staff. To the always improvisatory and provocative Brown, Davis was a balance wheel: well-organized, unflappable, propitiating conventional politicians and bureaucrats, learning the ways of the powers-that-be not only in Sacramento but across the state. When Brown launched into the 1982 Senate campaign which he lost to Pete Wilson, Davis moved to Westside Los Angeles and, pre-empting serious primary opposition, won a safe Democratic seat in the Assembly. There he served two terms as a conventional California liberal, during which he had surgery for removal of a benign brain tumor.

No other state legislative seat in the country has as many big Democratic contributors, and Davis cultivated them tirelessly.

That enabled him to move from top-level staffer and Assembly insider to statewide office. In 1986 he ran for controller, the one statewide position with significant patronage, and won; in 1990, when Attorney General John Van de Kamp and former San Francisco Mayor Dianne Feinstein slugged it out for the gubernatorial nomination, Davis was cruising to re-election. In 1992 he made his one false step, running against Feinstein for the nomination for the last two years of Wilson's Senate term; he ran ads comparing Feinstein to convicted tax evader Leona Helmsley and enraged her and many feminists in the "year of the woman." He lost the primary 57%–33%. But in 1994 he recovered and ran for lieutenant governor. As in 1986, he chose his spot well. His fundraising capacity deterred other potentially strong candidates; his base in the liberal Westside was strong enough to allow him to take moderate positions on some issues, like supporting the death penalty; his braininess and knowledge of state government made him an eminently respectable choice for editorial writers and endorsement groups. He won the primary easily and, while Pete Wilson was beating Democrat Kathleen Brown by 55%–40%, Davis was elected by 52%–40% over little-known and poorly-financed Simi Valley state Senator Cathie Wright.

It was no secret that Davis was aiming to run to succeed the term-limited Wilson, with whom he had almost no relationship. Politics and government are everything to Davis: he and his wife live in a tiny West Hollywood apartment; he has never made large amounts of money and his taste for California social life is undetectable. It was widely thought also that he was unelectable—too boring and uncharismatic, many said, too gray. Two seemingly dazzling and self-financed candidates entered the Democratic primary. Former Northwest Airlines Co-Chairman Al Checchi, with a net worth around $550 million, conducted a serious study of California government and called for striking education reforms; he was articulate, attractive (with a Spanish-speaking wife) and he spent more than $38 million on his campaign. And Congresswoman Jane Harman, after three terms representing the Los Angeles beachfront, decided to enter the race in March 1998. Harman also spent freely of her own money and raised more to spend $20 million. She argued that as a woman she was better able to listen to Californians and understand their needs: a seemingly strong platform in a state where Democrats had not nominated a man for governor or senator in 10 years.

But Davis was able to take advantage of mistakes made by the big money candidates. In March Harman surged momentarily into a lead in the polls, and Checchi ran negative ads against her. The result was that both sank in the polls. But their candidacies had deeper flaws. Checchi called for change in a year in which voters were mostly content; Harman, despite her competence at dealing with issues in the House, was not well schooled in state government. Davis's slogan was "Experience money can't buy," which established his incumbent status and his knowledge of state government. And if he was heavily outspent by his rivals, he was able to use his Westside contacts to raise $10 million, an impressive amount in any context except this one. Davis had the forethought to save most of his money to run ads in the last weeks before the June primary, during which he was able to match his opponents' ad buys. The result was a blowout victory for Davis: of the votes cast for Democrats, he won 58%, to 21% for Checchi and 20% for Harman.

In the general election Davis positioned himself shrewdly. Sensing the mood of the voters, he called for an end to the confrontations promoted by Republicans over issues like capital punishment, welfare for immigrants and racial quotas and preferences, and for an era of cooperation and amity. He took some controversial issues off the table: although he had opposed Propositions 187, 209 and 227, he promised to respect the voters' choice and enforce them. Others he embraced: for years he had supported capital punishment, backed by some 80% of voters and the key issue in Pete Wilson's defeat of Kathleen Brown. Despite the fact that he had voted in the Assembly in lockstep with the teachers' unions, he proposed education reforms which, while crafted carefully to minimally annoy union leaders, still diverged from the liberal policies which had destroyed California's public schools. He joked about his lack of charisma, especially when welcoming Vice President Al Gore to the state, and emphasized at every turn his status as a Vietnam veteran. And he pounced on his opponent's mistakes. The Republican nominee was Attorney General Dan Lungren. Lungren has an outgoing personality, the aggressive friendliness of the California of the 1950s he grew up in, in the then-Middle American city of Long Beach, the son of Richard Nixon's doctor. In polls until midyear he ran roughly even with Davis and the other Democrats. Until well into October he emphasized the crime issue, and tried to argue that Davis was a closet liberal. But Davis's long record against capital punishment gave him no opening. He tried to portray Davis as a clone of Jerry Brown, who after three quixotic presidential campaigns was attracting attention as a candidate for mayor of Oakland. But Davis's positions on issues made this unpersuasive. Lungren ran few ads and talked little about education, which polls showed to be far and away the number one issue; Davis, whose party had mostly run the public schools, was able to establish himself as the candidate who would reform them. When Davis battered him for his opposition to abortion, Lungren could only say that as a believing Catholic he opposed abortion—not a good excuse for many voters in this increasingly secular state—and that the only relevant issues were parental consent and partial-birth abortions.

Davis won by the landslide margin of 58%–38%—a margin of the magnitude of George Deukmejian's 61%–37% in 1986, Jerry Brown's 56%–36% in 1978, Ronald Reagan's 58%–42% in 1966 and Pat Brown's 60%–40% in 1958. Davis carried the Bay Area 69%–28% and Los Angeles County by nearly as much, 66%–31%; he even carried the rest of southern California 49%–47% and the rest of the state 50%–45%. Davis carried blacks with 83% of the vote, Hispanics with 78%, Asians with 67%, white women with 60% and even white men with 54%. California became only the second state (Hawaii was the other) with a Democratic governor, two Democratic senators, a Democratic House delegation and a Democratic legislature. It was a victory as sweeping as that of Tony Blair's New Labour party in Britain in May 1997 and left Davis, like Blair, with a mandate to pursue conciliatory moderate policies not so far out of line as one might think with the confrontational policies of his increasingly inept conservative predecessors. He also came into office at a time when California's surging economy was producing budget surpluses—very different from the early 1990s, when Pete Wilson announced a $14 billion deficit.

Davis pledged to "govern neither from the left nor the right, but from the center," and in his first two years kept his word. Education he proclaimed as his "first, second and third" priorities. Davis called a special session of the legislature and presented four bills—for peer review for teachers, enhanced reading instruction, a school-rating system and a standardized test for high schools. Democratic legislators watered them down and delayed some reforms until 2003 and 2004, but in March 1999 versions of all four were passed, and Davis claimed victory. He vetoed laws which would have undone Proposition 227 by restoring bilingual education and Proposition 209 by reimposing racial quotas and preferences; but he declined to appeal a federal judge's ruling against Proposition 187. He vetoed liberals' bills which would have banned racial profiling (though he signed a study of whether it was occurring a year later), limited big box discount stores, provided stiffer regulation of nursing homes, imposed taxes on Internet transactions, revised the "three strikes and you're out" law and granted journalists more access to prison inmates. He resisted unions' pressure to liberalize workmen's comp. He negotiated an HMO regulation bill that stopped short of what liberals wanted. He opposed the trial lawyers' proposal to raise the cap on medical malpractice awards. He signed several gun control bills in 1999, but said he would veto any others until he saw how those worked. He negotiated an agreement that allowed Indian casinos, but barred other casinos from the state. He opposed gay marriage and a bill to give rights to live-in partners, but signed a bill banning harassment of gays in schools and one setting up a domestic partners registry. Working with the legislature, he produced on-time budgets with big spending increases and some tax cuts, as revenues came gushing in. He increased spending on transportation.

"I've been underestimated my whole life, and I don't want it to change. It's my greatest strength. You know, this whole business is exceeding expectations," Davis once said. But by the end of 2000 Davis was the colossus of California government. Of Democratic legislators he said, "Their job is to implement my vision," and he added that he expected his appointees, including judges, to resign if they could not in conscience act in accord with his policies. He clearly had sway with voters on 2000 referenda. They rejected 71%–29% the school voucher proposal advanced by Silicon Valley venture capitalist Tim Draper; Davis appeared in ads against it. They followed him in backing a proposal to reduce the required majority for approving school bond issues from two-thirds to 55%. They followed his early endorsement of Al Gore by giving him a big margin over Bill Bradley in the March 2000 primary and by giving him a solid majority over George W. Bush in November (though in October Davis consultant Garry South criticized Gore for not spending money in California and for distancing himself from Bill Clinton). As the California economy blossomed, voters seemed to share his philosophy. "There's nothing government can do to substitute for a growing economy. Twenty-five, 30 years ago I might have thought differently, but now I'm convinced that government has to do a few things and do them well."

Then in early 2001 came the electricity crisis (see California, above). At first Davis's ratings seemed to hold up well, as he came forward with plans to keep electricity flowing. But by early April 2001 there were signs that his support from voters was flagging, and other politicians started to circle in for the kill. Davis has spent most of his adult lifetime in California government, and has learned from the mistakes of others. From Jerry Brown's opposition to the death penalty and his penchant for appointing administrators and judges who used insider skills to produce results opposite from what the public wanted, he learned that he must always respect the will of the people when solemnly expressed in referendum or in sustained responses to polls over the years. He learned from Pete Wilson's crunchy opposition to aid for illegal immigrants that he must not disrespect any substantial segment of the electorate. He learned from the failure of liberal schemes across the country that he must not allow legislation to add too great a burden to a bountiful and creative private sector. But nothing prepared him for the electricity crisis. He worked to deny utilities' pleas to allow them to make long-term contracts for power in summer 2000 because he feared that voters would resent the somewhat higher utility rates they would cause and that so-called consumer advocates would put up ballot initiatives promising low-cost power which would "pass in a heartbeat." The result was that the utilities were bankrupted by much higher spot market rates six months later, and the higher costs would have to be passed on to consumers and/or taxpayers, or both.

At this writing, nothing definitive can be said of Davis's chances for reelection in 2002. Straight-line extrapolation from early 2001 poll results suggested that he would win easily, and escape serious opposition. But Davis's middle-of-the-road stance has left him without last-ditch allies. Liberal Democrats in the legislature see him as more an adversary than an advocate; Republicans admire his skills, but have no investment in his success; his institutional base of Westside fundraisers helped him to amass a campaign treasury of $26 million by January 2001, but he himself has seen how popularity engendered by campaign spending of that magnitude can evaporate overnight. Davis's popularity depends on the success of the California economy, which as summer 2001 approached and rolling blackouts seemed certain, seemed likely to diminish, and on his stance as a calm, soothing arbiter in the culture wars, which as the 1990s segued into the 2000s seemed increasingly distant. In March 2001 no serious opposition to Davis's reelection was visible. In April 2001 he began to be criticized by fellow Democrats—state Treasurer Philip Angelides, who as Democratic state chairman was critical of his campaign against Feinstein in 1992; State Controller Kathleen Connell, who ran unsuccessfully for L.A. Mayor in 2001; Attorney General Bill Lockyer, a Bay area liberal; State senator Don Perata, an advocate of the view that Californians should never have to pay for increases in the price of electricity. In late March 2001 Secretary of State Bill Jones announced he was running for governor, charging that Davis had not shown leadership on the electricity crisis. In April 2001 Republican William Simon Jr., investor and son of former Treasury Secretary William Simon, was mulling his candidacy; actor Arnold Schwarzenegger, after a publicity binge, decided not to run. California's hapless Republican party has no institutional base for a serious challenge, and events may prove favorable to Davis—if rolling blackouts do not occur in summer 2001, if electricity supplies increase and rates are tamped down by the market, if Davis's initiatives produce a reliable supply of electricity and Californians feel free once again to enter an elevator without visiting the bathroom first. In the meantime, talk is vanishing of Davis running for president in 2004; he has always insisted that he was not interested in being a national candidate, and in fact his whole career has been devoted to California politics and government, and he has shown less interest in national and international issues than George W. Bush showed as a baseball team owner. He has always wanted to be governor of California and, against great odds, achieved his ambition and became for a time the most dominant governor since Pat Brown in the late 1950s and early 1960s. Whether he can sustain that position depends on how he is perceived as handling an issue which neither he nor anyone else expected would be the defining event of his administration.

Cook's Call *Probably Safe.* Davis has a campaign war chest in excess of $26 million and the state Republican party is on life support. But he is vulnerable to charges that he allowed the state's energy crisis to get completely out of control, relying on politics over policy to address the problem. The two announced Republican candidates are Secretary of State Bill Jones and businessman William Simon Jr., whose father was Treasury secretary in the Reagan cabinet. But the White House is trying to persuade former Los Angeles Mayor Richard Riordan to run, and venture capitalist Tim Draper is also interested. While Davis' war chest—which could reach $40 million—may keep him in office, incumbent state legislators could bear the brunt of voter fury over the availability and cost of energy.

Senior Senator Dianne Feinstein, California's senior senator, has twice won far more popular votes than any other senator in American history. Feinstein grew up in San Francisco, in lush Presidio Heights, went to Stanford and later studied criminology. She was appointed by Governor Pat Brown to the women's parole board in 1960, at 27. In 1969 she was elected to the San Francisco County Board of Supervisors—the city's council—and twice ran for mayor and lost. As president of the board, she became mayor in 1978 when Mayor George Moscone and Supervisor Harvey Milk were murdered by former Supervisor Dan White; she discovered Moscone's body and showed steadiness and a sense of command that calmed the city. In 1984, Walter Mondale seriously considered her for vice president, but passed over her for Geraldine Ferraro because of qualms about the business dealings of her husband, Richard Blum. Feinstein presided gracefully that year over the Democratic National Convention in San Francisco—while Ferraro juggled questions about *her* family's business. In fact, Feinstein and Blum's investments have thrived; the Capitol Hill newspaper *Roll Call* estimated their net worth in 2001 at $50 million, the eighth highest in Congress. Some of Blum's investments were in businesses in China, which sparked attacks on Feinstein, a strong supporter of trade ties with China; in the 2000 campaign Blum said that he had divested all his China investments, though questions were raised about just when.

Feinstein left the mayor's office in 1987, ineligible for a third full term, and ran for governor in 1990. She won the Democratic primary impressively, then lost 49%–46% to Pete Wilson. When Wilson appointed Orange County state Senator John Seymour—an unknown and bland choice—to replace him in the Senate, Feinstein quickly announced for the seat, even though the 1992 race was for only the last two years of Wilson's term, and she could have run for the seat being vacated by Alan Cranston the same year. She had primary competition from Gray Davis, then state controller, who ran a spot against her campaign finance practices comparing her to Leona Helmsley; Feinstein won 58%–33% and one can assume that relations between her and Davis, now governor, are not entirely warm. In the general election nothing worked for the hapless Seymour—not his switches to pro-choice on abortion and anti-offshore oil drilling, not his attacks on Feinstein's arguably tricky financing of her 1990 gubernatorial campaign (which resulted in a $190,000 fine), not fears of immigration, not Seymour's tending to agricultural interests. Feinstein won 54%–38%, coming close even in Seymour's southern California base.

California has a long tradition of having one senator who expresses ideological views and another who works hard to represent the state's economic interests. Feinstein chose the latter workhorse role, as did her predecessors Wilson, Cranston and Thomas Kuchel. She got a seat on Appropriations, where she could funnel money to California, and on Judiciary, where she was one of the women chosen by then-chairman Joseph Biden, who sought to spare himself the flak he got for allowing cross-examination of Anita Hill. Feinstein has a generally but not uniformly liberal voting record; she also has a tough, prosecutorial demeanor, and on the podium she can be one of the best speakers in American politics today. She kept a certain distance from the Clinton administration, negotiating for changes before voting for the 1993 budget, voting against NAFTA, withdrawing her support of the Clinton health care plan in May 1994, condemning Bill Clinton's "I did not have sexual relations with that woman, Miss Lewinsky" comment which she had heard in person.

In her first two years she had two major legislative achievements. One was the attachment of the assault weapons ban to the 1994 crime bill—good politics for her and many Democrats in metropolitan states, but a liability to Democrats in much of the West and South. When Idaho's Larry Craig argued that her definition of assault weapons was not rigorous enough and challenged her knowledge of firearms, she responded by saying: "I know something about what firearms can do; I came to be mayor of San Francisco as a product of assassination." Her other major achievement was a California Desert Protection Act. Similar measures had been stymied by the state's Republican senators as too restrictive, but now that there was no Republican senator, Feinstein managed it through enactment.

Feinstein surely hoped that she would face weak competition in 1994 and that her early and hard work raising money would enable her to win essentially unopposed. But then came Michael Huffington, with the determination and the cash to be the biggest spending Senate candidate, as of then. Huffington moved to Santa Barbara in 1991 and in 1992 beat an 18-year Republican congressman in the primary by spending over $3 million. His Senate campaign was lavishly financed—with nearly $30 million of his own money—and shrewd. When Feinstein ran an ad accusing him of refusing to act as an advocate for Raytheon, a company located in his district, he ran one arguing that her constituency service made her a "career politician." Huffington pulled even in polls in September, and Feinstein was clearly flustered and angry that she could not count on heavily outspending him. Huffington slipped when it was revealed that he and his wife employed an illegal alien as a nanny. On the Thursday before the election, it was revealed that Feinstein, despite her earlier denials, had employed a woman whose work permit had expired; but the news media ran stories saying that federal officials cast doubt on whether the woman was an illegal. That probably made the difference. Feinstein won 47%–45%, carrying the Bay Area 63%–30% and Los Angeles County 52%–40%, while losing the rest of southern California 56%–35% and the north outside the Bay Area 51%–40%.

Feinstein has a moderate to liberal voting record, and has differed on quite a few issues from her colleague and Bay area neighbor Barbara Boxer; she sponsored the Y2K liability act opposed by trial lawyers, for example, and voted to repeal the marriage penalty and the estate tax. With Jon Kyl she has sponsored a victim's right constitutional amendment which has failed to get the needed two-thirds support and a bill to promote counterterrorism measures. She has continued to push for gun control measures, like a ban on the import of high-capacity ammunition clips, with less success than in 1994; in 2000 she introduced a bill to require licensing of all guns—something gun control opponents argue would lead to confiscation. She has co-sponsored bills to criminalize false identification on the Internet and identity theft. In October 2000 she amended the H1-B visa bill to require the INS to process H-1B and other non-immigrant visas within 30 days and naturalization and immigration visas within six months. Her bill, co-sponsored by Orrin Hatch, to allow disabled people to qualify for citizenship even if they can't take the oath became law in 2000. She amended the 2000 intelligence reauthorization to require declassification of records on Japanese atrocities committed between 1931 and 1945.

Feinstein has sponsored bills to ban denial of hospitalization for mastectomies, and with Kay Bailey Hutchison has co-sponsored the breast cancer stamp, with proceeds directed to cancer research. Like others on the feminist left, she opposed impeachment of Bill Clinton, but wrote a proposal to censure Clinton for "immoral and reckless behavior." That did not come to the floor, and she dropped it after the Senate voted for acquittal. She has supported various versions of the McCain-Feingold campaign finance legislation, with reservations. She opposed anti-bundling provisions because they would hamper ideological PACs like EMILY's List. And, remembering her race against a self-financer in 1994, she has pushed for increasing the $1,000 limit on individual contributions which has not been adjusted for inflation since 1974. In March 2001 she and Fred Thompson passed an amendment raising it to $2,000.

When San Francisco and Shanghai became sister cities in 1979, Feinstein got to know Mayor Jiang Zemin, now President of China. She has been one of the most vocal supporters of renewing normal trade relations with China every year and of Permanent Normal Trade Relations in 2000. She argues that trade is driving political change in China and that if trade ties are cut China will just withdraw and remain dictatorial. "No matter how you look at it, this benefits the United

States." With Russ Feingold, she has sought to remove patent protection from AIDS drugs in Africa. They threatened to filibuster the Africa free trade agreement in May 2000, and desisted only when the Clinton administration promised to issue an executive order waiving patent rights; in March 2001, after several pharmaceutical companies promised to make such drugs available in Africa at cost, she and Feingold called for writing the executive order into law.

In late 1997 Feinstein gave thought to running for governor, and delivered a speech stingingly criticizing California's public school system. Polls showed her the strongest Democratic candidate. But memories of past campaigns evidently deterred her: investor Al Checchi was spending much of his own fortune on the race, as Huffington had, and also running was Gray Davis, who had run those negative ads against her in 1992. She has continued to work on California issues, successfully brokering a deal for Pacific Lumber to sell redwood groves in the Headwaters Forest on the north coast, passing a Lake Tahoe cleanup bill, seeking $240 million to deal with buildup of forest fuels on federal lands and securing $4.2 million to refurbish the visitors' center at the Manzanar Internment Camp where Japanese Americans were held during World War II.

In 2000 Feinstein came up for reelection—her fourth statewide race in 10 years. The first Republicans to announce were Ron Unz, the Silicon Valley entrepreneur whose 1998 Proposition 227 ended the state's bilingual education program, state Senator Ray Haynes and San Diego County Supervisor Bill Horn—none of them a well-known figure. Then in October 1999 Congressman Tom Campbell got into the race, at which point Unz dropped out. Campbell is an unusual figure, a Stanford Law professor often called the brainiest member of Congress, with an unusual set of issue positions. He was elected to the House in 1988 and 1990, when Silicon Valley was much more hospitable country for Republicans; he ran for the Senate in 1992 and lost the Republican primary 38%–36% to conservative Bruce Herschensohn (many observers believe Campbell would have beaten Barbara Boxer in the fall); he then got elected to the state Senate in 1993 and to the House again in 1995. There Campbell voted against Newt Gingrich for speaker in January 1997; forced a vote on the Kosovo bombing in 1999 and then sued to stop it, unsuccessfully; took a conservative line on economics; and supported abortion rights. In 1999 and 2000 his big issue was drugs: he favored more treatment and less imprisonment, and called for use of heroin in drug treatments. This was scarcely Republican holy writ, but Campbell's name was more familiar and in the March 2000 all-party primary he won 56% of the votes cast for Republicans, to 22% for Haynes and 15% for Horn.

Ominously for Campbell, Feinstein, with only nominal Democratic opposition, won 51% of all votes cast to 41% for all the Republicans put together. From there on out Campbell did not get a break—except perhaps when Feinstein broke her leg in Aspen in September. Campbell spent only $4.8 million to Feinstein's $10.3 million, and his emphasis on the drug issue failed to make him inroads among Democrats. In October 1999 a poll showed Feinstein leading Campbell 55%–30%; in November 2000 she won 56%–37%. As in 1992, Feinstein led in all regions of the state and among practically every demographic group except white males. Campbell is back at Stanford. But House Republicans are miffed because the seat, which Campbell would surely have held on to, was lost to a Democrat.

Feinstein began her second full term by opposing John Ashcroft for attorney general—an early sign of solidarity among Senate Democrats—and by criticizing Bill Clinton's pardon of Marc Rich and others. She dropped her bid for a Finance Committee seat because there was no assurance that the Appropriations seat she would have to relinquish would go to Boxer; evidently Appropriations ranking Democrat did not believe that California should be regarded as entitled to a seat. As California faced rolling blackouts of electricity, she and Boxer called for controls on wholesale electricity prices; this seemed unlikely to pass, and Feinstein and Oregon Republican Gordon Smith sponsored a bill giving FERC the choice between imposing price controls or setting cost-based rates to be passed along to consumers.

Junior Senator Barbara Boxer was first elected in 1992. She grew up in Brooklyn, where she was a victim of sexual harassment by a college professor and was refused work as a stockbroker; she moved to California in 1965 and worked on civic affairs and political campaigns and ultimately for Democratic Congressman (and now state Senate President pro tem) John Burton. In 1972 she ran for the Marin County Board of Supervisors, in the ultra-trendy suburbs nestled between Mount Tamalpais and the Bay, north of the Golden Gate Bridge. She lost, but in 1976, when women candidates were more accepted, she won a seat on the board. Boxer is energetic, usually good-humored, unafraid to challenge authority, voluble in support of her issue positions but not always candid about her goals. When Burton retired unexpectedly in 1982, she ran for the House and was easily elected. She made many splashes in the House, unearthing the Air Force's $7,622 coffee pot in 1984, denouncing the Persian Gulf war with more ardor than anyone, and leading a march of angry women on the Senate when Anita Hill was testifying against Clarence Thomas. She also compiled the highest-dollar voting record in the House on spending in 1992.

In the 1980s it seemed improbable that anyone as liberal as Boxer could be elected senator from California, which had after all voted Republican for president in all but one election from 1952 to 1988. But in the 1990s Boxer was elected twice, by decisive and rising margins. In 1992 she started off as neither the best-known nor the best-financed candidate, but this turned out to be the year of the woman, in which the enthusiasm of the feminist left produced important victories for Democratic women. Boxer won the June 1992 Democratic primary with 44% of the vote, to 31% for Lieutenant Governor Leo McCarthy, a familiar name after four statewide races, and 22% for Congressman Mel Levine, who emphasized his support of the Gulf war resolution. Her general election opponent was Bruce Herschensohn, a Los Angeles TV and radio commentator, Nixon speechwriter and Reagan enthusiast, backer of a flat tax and offshore oil drilling and opponent of abortion. Herschensohn had edged Silicon Valley moderate Congressman Tom Campbell 38%–36% in the primary, with the help of then-Palm Springs Mayor Sonny Bono, who won 17% of the vote. The Boxer-Herschensohn race was a battle of opposites, the far left versus the far right of the American electoral spectrum. Boxer was helped by the collapse of the Bush candidacy in California, by hearty support from Feinstein and by the revelation by state Democratic political director Bob Mulholland during the last week of the campaign that Herschensohn attended nude dancer night clubs. Boxer won 48%–43%, carrying the Bay Area 61%–30% and Los Angeles County 53%–40%, while losing southern California 52%–38% and the rest of the state 49%–42%.

Boxer's voting record has been strongly liberal, the most liberal in the Senate in 1999 and 2000 according to *National Journal's* ratings. She is perhaps the personification of the feminist left, and is one of the strongest proponents of abortion rights in the Senate; she vehemently opposed the partial-birth abortion ban and tried to overturn George W. Bush's ban on funding international family planning organizations that provide abortions. But she was also a staunch defender of Bill Clinton. In 1998, the senator who had marched across the Capitol to protest the cross-examination of Anita Hill, found little to believe in the charges against Clinton until he admitted their truth, and even then limited her condemnation to a perfunctory statement combined with a total commitment to defeat impeachment. And in 1999 the crusader against the Gulf war resolution solidly backed the bombing campaign against Serbia.

Gun control is also one of Boxer's causes. She was one of the first to sponsor a bill to require child-proof safety locks on all handguns, and has come forward with provocative proposals embarrassing gun control opponents, like her amendment to ban sales of guns to people who are intoxicated. She has been a critic of the oil industry. In 1999 she fought to keep Congress from blocking Clinton administration plans to increase oil and gas royalties on federal lands; the companies were engaged, she said, in "out and out thievery." She held up the Strategic Petroleum Reserve reauthorization in 2000 by successfully insisting that oil companies not be allowed to pay federal royalties in kind. As California was hit by rolling blackouts of electricity in early 2001, she proposed a windfall profits tax on energy producers and, with colleague Dianne Feinstein, sponsored a bill to impose temporary price controls on wholesale electric power suppliers. But she split with Feinstein by backing the two Oregon senators' unsuccessful amendment to the bankruptcy reform bill that would have barred PG&E and Southern California Edison from discharging their debts in bankruptcy; a few weeks later PG&E sought bankruptcy protection. Since 1997 she has sought to phase out the polluting gasoline additive MTBE; in September 2000, with support from Chairman Bob Smith, the Environment Committee voted for her bill for a phaseout by 2004, and allowing governors to phase it out earlier (as Gray Davis has been trying to do since 1999). In response to complaints by Los Angeles area constituents, she introduced a bill calling for tough water quality standards for Chromium-6 and for a review of the cleanup at Rocketdyne's Santa Susana Field Lab. She scored a great success in pushing the public-private trust for the Presidio in the 1996 parks bill, and helped broker a last-minute compromise between the White House and Alaska Senator Frank Murkowski on the Tongass National Forest, which enabled the bill to pass. After the 2000 election, ranking Appropriations Democrat Robert Byrd reportedly frowned on Boxer replacing Feinstein on that committee. So Feinstein gave up her plan to switch to Finance and stayed on Appropriations, while Boxer got a seat on Commerce.

For all her partisanship, on some issues Boxer has worked with Republicans. With Smith she has co-sponsored a brownfields bill which would exempt some old industrial sites from Superfund standards. With Phil Gramm she proposed in March 2001 to exempt Mexico from annual drug certification. She took the lead for California citrus growers, normally a conservative group, in trying to keep apparently diseased Argentina citrus out of the United States. But she can be the toughest of partisans. For nearly four years Republicans held up the confirmation of Judge Richard Paez to the liberal 9th Circuit Court of Appeals. In fall 1999 Boxer put a hold on the nomination of a friend of Majority Leader Trent Lott to the TVA board; Lott agreed to hold a floor vote on Paez and he was confirmed. In January 2001 she was the first senator to oppose the nomination for attorney general of her former colleague John Ashcroft. "This nomination is driving a stake into the heart of large numbers of Americans." She has raised money for many Democratic candidates for Senate and House; in December 2000 Democrats created a new leadership position, and she became Chief Deputy Whip for Strategic Outreach.

During her first three years in the Senate Boxer's job ratings were among the Senate's lowest. But California with its large metro areas trended sharply toward the Democrats in the 1990s, and by early 1997 Boxer's job rating was up to 50%, and prominent Republicans—Congressman Tom Campbell, San Diego Mayor Susan Golding, 1994 Senate nominee Michael Huffington—decided not to run. In the all-party primary, state Treasurer Matt Fong edged businessman (and now Congressman) Darrell Issa. On paper Fong was a strong candidate, with an Asian heritage, a moderate record on issues and a Democratic heritage; his mother March Fong Eu, a Democrat, was California's Secretary of State from 1974 to 1994. But Boxer raised $15 million and campaigned long and hard. She launched an ad campaign attacking Fong for his ambiguous stances on issues like abortion. She guarded herself from contact with reporters so she would not have to answer questions about Bill Clinton; the president's brother-in-law Tony Rodham was then married to her daughter Nicole, though she filed for divorce in 2000. At one point her staff told reporters she had a bad back though she danced at a Democratic gathering soon after. Fong attacked her for the hypocrisy of her stand on the Clinton scandals. But Fong spoke hesitantly and unconvincingly in the sound bites which are the staple of California politics and never succeeded in raising much money. For much of September and October he was off the air, while Boxer was pounding the airwaves mercilessly.

Boxer won 53%–43%. She won 61%–36% in Los Angeles County, a big improvement over 1992; she won 64%–33% in the Bay Area, by the same margin as in 1992, in the part of the state with the largest Asian population. She lost by 51%–44% in the South, not a bad margin for a Democrat, and by 50%–45% in the rest of the state. In the one part of California that has been moving to Republicans in the 1990s, the Central Valley, she ran poorly. But she made up for that with good showings in coastal counties, even carrying historically Republican Santa Barbara. This was a gender gap race, an even 48%–48% among men and 57%–39% for Boxer among women. Boxer is up for reelection in 2004, and her prospects look good so long as California continues its current heavy preference for the Democratic party; a January 2001 Field Poll showed her with a 51% positive job rating.

Presidential politics California, which in the 1970s and 1980s was said to have established a lock on the presidency for the Republicans, now seems heavily Democratic in presidential politics. Actually, California was not that heavily Republican: Republicans won handily when they nominated Californians—Richard Nixon in 1972 and Ronald Reagan in 1980 and 1984—but they won only narrowly in 1976 and 1988 when they didn't. Then, in the 1990s it was the Democrats who seemed to have a lock on California and the presidency. Now, after the 2000 election, it is apparent that you can win the presidency without California—indeed, if George W. Bush's percentages rise uniformly in every state in 2004, he could win the presidency with 373 electoral votes without carrying California. California's solid Democratic status owes something to its increasing number of Latino voters and their distaste, rooted in California politics, for Republicans; it owes much to Californians' affection for and assiduous cultivation by Bill Clinton; it owes much as well to the liberal attitude on cultural issues here—abortion and gun control and the environment—which has trumped any desire for lower taxes. In the 1990s Americans in the nation's largest metropolitan areas trended toward Clinton-Gore Democrats, and three-quarters of California voters live in the large metropolitan areas centered on Los Angeles, San Francisco and San Diego.

Still, California seems just too big to ignore. In 2000 it cast 54 electoral votes; in 2004 it will cast 55, 20% of those necessary to win. Despite the Democrats' sweep here in 1998, despite Bill Clinton's and Al Gore's cultivation of the state, despite daunting polls, George W. Bush made a serious attempt to carry California. California Republicans had been tired of raising money only to see it spent elsewhere. So Bush enlisted fundraiser Gerald Parsky to raise $20 million and kept his promise to spend it all in California. On top of that, Bush spent two days in the last two weeks in California, precious time which, if spent in Wisconsin, Iowa and Oregon might have made the controversy over Florida's electoral votes irrelevant. It mattered not. The Gore campaign coolly assessed its prospects here, and spent nothing; and Gore carried the state by the unambiguous margin of 54%–42%, with another 4% for Ralph Nader.

Some can still recall when California's June primary was the national tie-breaker. This state was the center of national attention when Nelson Rockefeller lost here to Barry Goldwater in 1964, when Robert Kennedy and Eugene McCarthy slugged it out in 1968—Kennedy won and was murdered on primary night—and when George McGovern edged Hubert Humphrey in 1972. California was all the more important because it was winner-take-all: Voters chose between slates pledged to each candidate, and whoever won a plurality won every vote in the largest delegation in each party's convention. But since the 1980s nominations have been sewed up a lot earlier than June, and California for some time was an irrelevancy.

For 1996 California moved its presidential primary from the first week in June to March 26; that was still too late to make any difference. So in 2000 it moved it back to March 7. That was still a problem. California's all-party primary, adopted by referendum, allowed anyone, not just registered Democrats or Republicans, to vote for a Democrat or a Republican: not kosher under Democratic Party rules. But Secretary of State Bill Jones, a Republican, came up with a computer-assisted double counting procedure, which would allow a total of just registered Democrats' votes to be counted for Democratic delegates. Under those rules Al Gore won 34% of all votes and 80% of those cast for a Democrat; George W. Bush won 29% and John McCain 23% of all votes. Among those voting for Republicans, Bush led McCain 52%–43%. This is not a result that mattered, as it turned out, and it was conducted under a system that is now extinct: The Supreme Court, in response to a challenge from four of California's political parties, outlawed the all-party primary (a longstanding institution in Washington and Alaska) in June 2000. But California is still stuck with holding its primary for all offices in early March, when few voters will have focused on the election.

Congressional districting   California has gained House seats in every Census going back to 1850, when it became a state; over that century and a half it has grown from 2 seats to 53, the most of any state in history. But California grew less rapidly in the early 1990s, and so it gained only 1 seat from the 2000 Census, the first time in a century it has not gained 2 or more. The tradition of partisan redistricting goes way back: Republicans drew the lines to their advantage in the 1940s and 1950s, Democrats in the 1960s, 1970s and 1980s, as the California House delegation grew from 23 in the 1940s to 30, 38, 43, 45 and 52. The great genius of redistricting here was Democratic Congressman Phillip Burton, who dominated the line-drawing for House seats and for the state Senate and Assembly as well (and intervened behind the scenes in other states too); his 1982 plan, slightly revised for 1984–90, left Democrats in secure control of the delegation even though he died in 1983. In the 1990s neither party had full control. Governor Pete Wilson, after hard-nosed bargaining with the Democratic legislature, persuaded the state

Supreme Court to adopt a plan drawn up by his appointed commission in 1992. This was a relatively evenhanded plan, with generally regular boundaries; the fact that Democrats had a 32–20 margin in the delegation after the 2000 election reflected the party's strength in most parts of the state, not any acuity in drawing district lines.

Now Democrats control the redistricting process once again, and can draw what lines they please. But it is not clear that they will make big gains as in the past. Given the political demography of the state, it is hard to see how even the most ingenious Democratic districter can avoid creating 17 or 18 Republican seats. That would leave Democrats with a 36–17 or 35–18 margin. In effect the party has already made most of its redistricting gains in the 1998 and 2000 elections. Moreover, districters will face a couple of new problems. The first is that the rules have changed. Ten years ago the prevailing interpretation of the Voting Rights Act amendments of 1982 required maximizing the number of majority-minority district—that is, districts with black or Hispanic majorities or near-majorities. But a series of Supreme Court cases since have suggested that districts that have weirdly shaped boundaries drawn along racial lines are invalid. As it happens, California has four black representatives (all are women), but no current district is more than 35% black. Creating districts with higher black percentages would be difficult, and might actually reduce the number of black members. Hispanics are much more numerous here—32% of the population in the 2000 Census, compared to 7% for blacks—but Hispanics are not as geographically concentrated as blacks, are often not citizens and even when citizens have low voter turnout: 14% of California voters in 2000 were Hispanic. Of the current districts, 11 have Hispanic majorities, but three of them have white and two have black representatives. Central city districts did not gain population in the 1990s as they did in the 1980s; there may be one more Hispanic-majority district after redistricting.

The other problem redistricters will face is that political power is less centralized than it used to be. In the old days before term limits, legislative leaders like Willie Brown could guarantee passage of redistricting plans, the Senate did not mess with the Assembly plan and vice versa, and both deferred to the congressional delegation for the House plan. The story was that Phil Burton insisted that legislators vote for his plans before he would let them see the lines. But California's term limits, approved in 1990, have kicked in, and members of the Assembly, limited to six years, spend much of that time frantically looking for other offices to run for. Redistricting software is widely available, and anyone can draw his own plan. With Assembly members looking for Senate and House seats, it may be hard to assemble majorities for a plan which has purely partisan aims. In addition, Governor Gray Davis has said that he does not want plans that maximize Democratic representation and that he wants to create a plan that will survive a court challenge. There are several incumbent Republican congressmen who could be significantly weakened by only minor redrawings of the lines. But the exigencies of putting together plans which can get majority support may prevent that from happening.

THE PEOPLE: Pop. 2000: 33,871,648; Pop. 1990: 29,760,021, up 13.8% 1990–2000. 12% of U.S. total, 1st largest; 59.5% White, 6.7% Black, 10.9% Asian, 1% Amer. Indian, 0.3% Hawaiian, 4.7% Two+ races, 16.8% Other; 32.4% Hispanic Origin. 4.9% Unemployment. 2000 Voting age pop.: 24,621,819. 2000 Turnout: 11,142,843; 45% of VAP. Registered voters (2000): 15,707,307; 7,134,601 D (45%), 5,485,492 R (35%), 3,087,214 unaffiliated and minor parties (20%).

POLITICAL LINEUP: Governor, Gray Davis (D); Lt. Gov., Cruz Bustamante (D); Secy. of State, Bill Jones (R); Atty. Gen., Bill Lockyer (D); Treasurer, Philip Angelides (D); Commissioner of Insurance, Harry W. Low (D); Controller, Kathleen Connell (D); Super. of Public Instruction, Delaine Eastin; State Senate, 40 (26 D, 14 R); Senate Pres. Pro Tempore, John Burton (D); Majority Leader, Richard Polanco (D); State Assembly, 80 (50 D, 29 R, 1 vacancy); Assembly Speaker, Robert M. Hertzberg (D). Senators, Dianne Feinstein (D) and Barbara Boxer (D). Representatives, 52 (31 D, 20 R, 1 vacancy).

ELECTIONS DIVISION: 916-657-2166; **FILING DEADLINE FOR U.S. CONGRESS:** December 7, 2001.

2000 Presidential Vote

Gore (D)	5,861,203	(53%)
Bush (R)	4,567,429	(42%)
Nader (Green)	418,707	(4%)
Others	118,517	(1%)

1996 Presidential Vote

Clinton (D)	5,119,815	(51%)
Dole (R)	3,828,368	(38%)
Perot (I)	697,845	(7%)
Others	372,553	(4%)

2000 Republican Presidential Primary

Bush (R)	2,168,466	(52%)
McCain (R)	1,780,570	(43%)
Keyes (R)	170,442	(4%)

2000 Democratic Presidential Primary

Gore (D)	2,609,950	(80%)
Bradley (D)	642,654	(20%)

Gov. Gray Davis (D)

Elected 1998, term expires Jan. 2003, 1st term; b. Dec. 26, 1942, New York, NY; home, Los Angeles; Stanford U., B.A. 1964, Columbia U., J.D. 1967; Catholic; married (Sharon).

Military Career: Army, 1967–69 (Vietnam).

Elected Office: CA Assembly, 1982–86; CA Controller, 1986–94; CA Lt. Gov., 1995–98.

Professional Career: Finance Dir., Tom Bradley mayoral campaign, 1972–74; Chief of Staff, Gov. Jerry Brown Jr., 1974–82.

Office: State Capitol Bldg., Sacramento, 95814, 916-445-2841; Fax: 916-445-4633; Web site: www.state.ca.gov.

Election Results

1998 general	Gray Davis (D)	4,858,817	(58%)
	Dan Lungren (R)	3,216,749	(38%)
	Others	306,305	(4%)
1998 primary	Gray Davis (D)	2,083,396	(35%)
	Dan Lungren (R)	2,023,618	(34%)
	Al Checchi (D)	748,828	(12%)
	Jane Harman (D)	741,251	(12%)
	Others	399,697	(7%)
1994 general	Pete Wilson (R)	4,777,674	(55%)
	Kathleen Brown (D)	3,517,777	(41%)
	Others	363,430	(4%)

Sen. Dianne Feinstein (D)

Elected 1992, seat up 2006, 2d term; b. June 22, 1933, San Francisco; home, San Francisco; Stanford U., B.A. 1955; Jewish; married (Richard C. Blum).

Elected Office: San Francisco Bd. of Supervisors, 1970–78, Pres., 1970–71, 1974–75, 1978; San Francisco Mayor, 1978–88.

Professional Career: CA Women's Parole Bd., 1960–66.

DC Office: 331 HSOB, 20510, 202-224-3841; Fax: 202-228-3954; Web site: www.senate.gov/~feinstein.

State Offices: Fresno, 559-485-7430; Los Angeles, 310-914-7300; San Diego, 619-231-9712; San Francisco, 415-393-0707.

Committees: *Appropriations*: Agriculture & Rural Development; Defense; Energy & Water Development; Interior; Military Construction (Chmn.). *Energy & Natural Resources*: Energy Research, Development, Production

& Regulation; Forests & Public Land Management; Water & Power. *Intelligence (Select)*. *Judiciary*: Immigration; Technology, Terrorism & Government Information (Chmn.); Youth Violence. *Rules & Administration*. *Joint Committee on Printing* (4th of 5 Sens.).

Group Ratings

	ADA	ACLU	AFS	LCV	CON	ITIC	NTU	COC	ACU	NTLC	CHC
2000	70	57	57	86	2	100	20	54	28	20	15
1999	100	—	100	100	51	—	3	53	4	—	—

National Journal Ratings

	1999 LIB —	1999 CONS		2000 LIB —	2000 CONS
Economic	68%	29%		60%	39%
Social	88%	0%		66%	21%
Foreign	87%	0%		72%	15%

Key Votes of the 106th Congress

1. Educ. Savings Accts.	Y	5. Review Movie Violence	N	9. NATO War in Serbia	Y
2. Prescrip. Drug Benefit	Y	6. Gun Show Bckgrnd. Checks	Y	10. Table Cuba Travel Ban	N
3. Delay Ergonomic Standards	N	7. Ban Part.-Birth Abortion	N	11. Nuclear Test-Ban Treaty	Y
4. Phase Out Estate Tax	Y	8. Broaden Hate Crimes List	Y	12. Perm. Trade with China	Y

Election Results

2000 general	Dianne Feinstein (D)	5,932,522	(56%)	($10,346,170)
	Tom Campbell (R)	3,886,853	(37%)	($4,378,283)
	Others	804,233	(8%)	
2000 primary	Dianne Feinstein (D)	3,759,560	(52%)	
	Tom Campbell (R)	1,697,208	(23%)	
	Ray Haynes (R)	679,034	(9%)	
	Bill Horn (R)	453,630	(6%)	
	Others	759,405	(10%)	
1994 general	Dianne Feinstein (D)	3,977,063	(47%)	($14,407,179)
	Michael Huffington (R)	3,811,501	(45%)	($29,969,695)
	Others	714,500	(8%)	

Sen. Barbara Boxer (D)

Elected 1992, seat up 2004, 2d term; b. Nov. 11, 1940, Brooklyn, NY; home, Greenbrae; Brooklyn Col., B.A. 1962; Jewish; married (Stewart).

Elected Office: Marin Cnty. Bd. of Supervisors, 1976–82; U.S. House of Reps., 1982–92.

Professional Career: Stockbroker & researcher, 1962–65; Journalist, *Pacific Sun*, 1972–74; Dist. aide, U.S. Rep. John Burton, 1974–76.

DC Office: 112 HSOB, 20510, 202-224-3553; Fax: 202-228-4056; Web site: www.senate.gov/~boxer.

State Offices: Fresno, 559-497-5109; Los Angeles, 213-894-5000; Sacramento, 916-448-2787; San Bernardino, 909-888-8525; San Diego, 619-239-3884; San Francisco, 415-403-0100.

Committees: *Commerce, Science & Transportation*: Communications; Consumer Affairs, Foreign Commerce & Tourism; Oceans & Fisheries; Surface Transportation & Merchant Marine. *Environment & Public Works*: Superfund, Waste Control & Risk Assessment (Chmn.); Transportation & Infrastructure. *Foreign Relations*: African Affairs; International Operations & Terrorism (Chmn.); Near Eastern & South Asian Affairs.

Group Ratings

	ADA	ACLU	AFS	LCV	CON	ITIC	NTU	COC	ACU	NTLC	CHC
2000	85	71	80	86	73	93	14	41	4	3	15
1999	100	—	100	89	95	—	10	47	4	—	—

National Journal Ratings

	1999 LIB	—	1999 CONS		2000 LIB	—	2000 CONS
Economic	90%	—	0%		93%	—	6%
Social	88%	—	0%		79%	—	0%
Foreign	87%	—	0%		95%	—	0%

Key Votes of the 106th Congress

1. Educ. Savings Accts.	N	5. Review Movie Violence	N	9. NATO War in Serbia	Y
2. Prescrip. Drug Benefit	Y	6. Gun Show Bckgrnd. Checks	Y	10. Table Cuba Travel Ban	N
3. Delay Ergonomic Standards	*	7. Ban Part.-Birth Abortion	N	11. Nuclear Test-Ban Treaty	Y
4. Phase Out Estate Tax	N	8. Broaden Hate Crimes List	Y	12. Perm. Trade with China	Y

Election Results

1998 general	Barbara Boxer (D)	4,410,056	(53%)	($13,737,548)
	Matt Fong (R)	3,575,078	(43%)	($10,764,892)
	Others	326,771	(4%)	
1998 primary	Barbara Boxer (D)	2,574,264	(41%)	
	Matt Fong (R)	1,292,662	(21%)	
	Darrell Issa (R)	1,142,567	(18%)	
	John M. Brown (R)	489,741	(8%)	
	Frank D. Riggs (R)	295,886	(5%)	
	Others	507,257	(8%)	
1992 general	Barbara Boxer (D)	5,173,443	(48%)	($10,415,811)
	Bruce Herschensohn (R)	4,644,139	(43%)	($7,649,072)
	Others	981,781	(9%)	

FIRST DISTRICT

The North Coast of California is unlike any other place in America. It is the only part of the Lower 48 states first settled by Russians, who built Fort Ross in 1812; they sold it in 1841 to a Swiss named John Augustus Sutter, whose discovery of gold near Sacramento started the Gold Rush eight years later. It is the only part of the world with large numbers of redwood trees, shooting up in the moist and drizzly air hundreds of feet toward the sky. It is wet country, and for years it has been one of America's prime lumbering areas: Eureka and smaller lumber towns are filled with filigreed Victorian houses and old lumber mills, saloons and waterfront hotels. It has moved on to other crops: in sunny valleys sealed off the from Coast Range ridges grow some of the nation's premium wine grapes, and Mendocino County has been known since the late 1960s for its premier marijuana fields. Thirty years ago, there were only 20 wineries in Napa Valley. Today, there are more than 300, with more just west of the ridges in Sonoma County; most are highly profitable. Napa is building a $50 million cultural center to celebrate achievements in winemaking and the arts. These valleys were some of California's earliest literary haunts: Robert Louis Stevenson took his honeymoon near Calistoga in Napa, and Jack London owned a giant house in Sonoma which mysteriously burned down in 1913.

The 1st Congressional District consists of most of the North Coast (though just missing Fort Ross), plus much of the wine-growing area inland and just a bit of the vast Central Valley interior. The North Coast lumbering area from Mendocino on north, once filled with rough-hewn working men, was historically Democratic country; but their business became hostage to concern about the northern spotted owl, and the area backlashed toward the Republicans on cultural issues. In the 1990s, as veterans of the counterculture settled in Mendocino County and along the coast, it moved toward the cultural left. Inland, the wine-growing country around Healdsburg and in Napa County was once Republican, but now pretty much concurs in the San Francisco Bay area's liberal consensus. The district's inland portion is around Fairfield, home of Travis Air Force Base. The mix of different economies and cultures, of generations with sharply different experiences and outlooks, made this for much of the 1990s one of California's politically most unstable districts, and it changed partisan hands four times during the decade. But the district voted solidly for Bill Clinton twice and for Al Gore in 2000, with 8% for Ralph Nader.

The congressman from the 1st District is Mike Thompson, a Democrat elected in 1998. Thompson grew up in the Napa Valley town of St. Helena, served in the Army in Vietnam and earned a Purple Heart, and later owned a vineyard and worked as a maintenance supervisor for Beringer, a big winery in the valley. He taught at San Francisco State University and California State University-Chico. In 1982 he was chosen an Assembly Fellow, and from 1984–90 was chief of staff to two veteran Bay Area Assembly members. In 1990 he ran for the state Senate, survived redistricting, and was re-elected in 1994. He chaired the Senate Budget Committee and helped broker the controversial Headwaters Forest deal, an on-again, off-again plan, finally approved in 1999, to buy out and preserve the last privately held stand of redwoods owned by the corporate raider Charles Hurwitz.

In 1998, facing California's legislative term limits, Thompson decided to run for the House seat held, precariously, by Republican Frank Riggs. Riggs, whose background was in law enforcement, was first elected in 1990, lost the seat in 1992, then was elected again in 1994 and 1996. In his three victories, Riggs defeated a Democratic career politician, a counter-culture figure who taught Chinese to foreigners in China, and the 28-year-old granddaughter of former San Francisco Mayor Joseph Alioto. By the 1998 election the political terrain had changed. Loggers who had lost their jobs had moved away; the Headwaters Forest deal seemed on the way to completion. Possibly fearing a challenge from Thompson, who had had been eyeing the seat, Riggs announced in January 1998 he would run for Barbara Boxer's Senate seat; with no name identification beyond the district and little money, he left that race in April. Thompson faced weak opposition and won support from almost every interest group: unions, medical providers, vintners, oil and timber interests, law enforcement groups, fishermen. His issue stands—opposition to oil drilling off the California coast, support of abortion rights and the death penalty—were broadly popular. He won the June primary easily, 78%–22%, and won the general by 62%–33%: this is a district Republicans conceded. He easily won a second term in 2000.

In the House, Thompson joined both the New Democrats and the Blue Dogs, and he pledged bipartisanship. With Republican George Radanovich, he started the House Wine Caucus. Mindful of local businesses, he voted to override Bill Clinton's veto of the estate tax repeal. He lost a battle with conservative senators and beer and alcohol wholesalers over the wine industry's opposition to a bill giving states new power to restrict sales over the Internet; Thompson said that the wholesalers were seeking to preserve their monopolistic distribution system. Before deciding to vote for Permanent Normal Trade Relations with China, he got the White House's agreement to resolve a nine-year battle over a new local ZIP code. He won $19 million for improvements at Travis.

Thompson's strong electoral performances and his success at bridging over the differences that shaped politics in this district for a decade, suggest that he will have a longer and more serene tenure than his immediate predecessors. Democratic redistricters may shift some Republicans into his district and some Democrats elsewhere to cause problems for adjacent Republicans—especially Doug Ose in the 3rd.

Cook's Call   *Probably Safe.* Although sophomore Mike Thompson has never had a tough race here, this sprawling northern California district was one of the most volatile in California during the early 1990's. Democrats control the redistricting process in the state and may try to help ensure Thompson's political safety by playing around with the margins here.

THE PEOPLE: Pop. 2000: 644,525; Pop. 1990: 572,870, up 12.5% 1990–2000. 76.6% White, 4.6% Black, 3.6% Asian, 2.8% Amer. Indian, 0.3% Hawaiian, 4.6% Two+ races, 7.4% Other; 16.5% Hispanic Origin.

2000 Presidential Vote			1996 Presidential Vote		
Gore (D)	124,039	(50%)	Clinton (D)	113,861	(48%)
Bush (R)	101,630	(41%)	Dole (R)	83,669	(35%)
Nader (Green)	19,500	(8%)	Perot (I)	23,024	(10%)
Others	2,891	(1%)	Others	15,695	(7%)

Rep. Mike Thompson (D)

Elected 1998, 2d term; b. Jan. 24, 1951, St. Helena; home, St. Helena; CA St. U., B. A. 1982, M. A. 1996.; Catholic; married (Janet).

Military Career: Army, 1969–73 (Vietnam).

Elected Office: CA Senate, 1990–98.

Professional Career: Owner, Beringer Winery; CA Assembly fellow, 1982–83; Chief of Staff, CA Assemblyman Lou Papan, 1984–87; Chief of Staff, CA Assemblywoman Jacqueline Speier, 1987–90.

DC Office: 119 CHOB 20515, 202-225-3311; Fax: 202-225-4335; Web site: www.house.gov/mthompson.

District Offices: Eureka, 707-269-9595; Fort Bragg, 707-962-0933; Napa, 707-226-9898.

Committees: *Agriculture* (17th of 24 D): Conservation, Credit, Rural Development & Research; General Farm Commodities & Risk Management; Specialty Crops & Foreign Agriculture Programs. *Armed Services* (24th of 28 D): Military Installations & Facilities; Military Research & Development.

Group Ratings

	ADA	ACLU	AFS	LCV	CON	ITIC	NTU	COC	ACU	NTLC	CHC
2000	75	71	71	86	50	89	25	66	8	9	7
1999	95	—	83	69	75	—	15	44	4	—	—

National Journal Ratings

	1999 LIB	—	1999 CONS		2000 LIB	—	2000 CONS
Economic	62%	—	37%		65%	—	34%
Social	76%	—	23%		68%	—	31%
Foreign	78%	—	17%		69%	—	28%

Key Votes of the 106th Congress

1. Patient Bill of Rights	Y	5. Bar RU-486 $ for FDA	N	9. NATO War in Serbia	Y
2. Accelerate Min. Wage	Y	6. Display 10 Commandments	N	10. Perm. Trade with China	Y
3. Strike Ban on Ergo. Stnd.	Y	7. Gun Show Bkgrnd. Checks	Y	11. Debt Relief for 3rd World	Y
4. Ovrd. Estate Tax Veto	Y	8. Ban Part.-Birth Abortion	N	12. Drop Cuba Econ. Embargo	Y

Election Results

2000 general	Mike Thompson (D)	155,638	(65%)	($851,612)
	Russel J. Chase (R)	66,987	(28%)	($11,730)
	Other	16,710	(7%)	
2000 primary	Mike Thompson (D)	112,185	(65%)	
	Russel J. Chase (R)	21,456	(12%)	
	Kenneth A. Hitt (R)	14,489	(8%)	
	Lawrence R. Wiesner (R)	14,351	(8%)	
	Other	11,096	(6%)	
1998 general	Mike Thompson (D)	121,710	(62%)	($941,795)
	Mark Luce (R)	64,622	(33%)	($123,061)
	Others	10,437	(5%)	

SECOND DISTRICT

Rising 14,000 feet over low foothills and the Central Valley, visible for 100 miles, is the snow-capped volcanic cone of Mount Shasta, one of a string of (supposedly) burnt-out volcanoes that march up and down the Pacific Coast states. This is the far northern end of California, where truck traffic on Interstate 5 is the only reminder of the choked metropolitan areas where most of the state's people live. This is lumber country mostly, where the mountains that rise on all sides—the Coast Range to the east, the Sierra Nevada to the west, the scattered mountains sealing off the Central Valley north of Redding—are carpeted with trees: rough flannel-shirt, two-lane-road country that was left behind economically when Los Angeles and San Francisco boomed after World War II. In the last dozen years, however, the northern end of California has been attracting people, mostly young families who come here to raise their children in a small town atmosphere, but also retirees looking for a calm atmosphere and low cost of living. There are few minorities here; the population is 86% white, one of the highest in California.

The 2d Congressional District of California covers most of this area. The district has two major population areas: one around Redding, just below Mount Shasta, and the other farther south, at the edge of the Sierra foothills, around the Butte County communities of Paradise and Chico. Chico is a liberal oasis amid sprawling orchards—home to a state university campus and Sierra Nevada Pale Ale. But the rest of the district is culturally conservative and angry at the diktats of urban environmentalists. The region has a Democratic heritage. Until 1980, it elected rough-and-ready Democrats who pulled strings in Sacramento and Washington to build roads and dams. Now it elects abstemious Republicans who have solidly conservative voting records and tend to local needs. George W. Bush carried the 2nd with 59% of the vote, his third best California district.

The congressman from the 2d District is Republican Wally Herger, an ardent conservative, businessman and rancher first elected to the Assembly in 1980. In 1986 he was elected to Congress after winning solid margins over the mayor of Redding in the primary and a Shasta County supervisor in the general. He has served rather quietly on the Ways and Means Committee, favoring balanced budgets and lower taxes. He passed as part of welfare reform a provision to prevent prisoners in local and state jails from collecting Supplemental Security Income benefits. Sheriffs and prison departments were given a bonus for identifying prisoners who receive illegal benefits, and in 1998 the program was estimated to save the taxpayers $3.46 billion over seven years. Herger has been a leader of the rhetorical battle to create so-called "lock boxes" to set aside the surpluses in the Social Security and Medicare trust funds. In 2001, he took over as chairman of the Human Resources Subcommittee, which faced a statutory deadline to review the 1996 welfare reform.

On local issues, Herger tends to local water projects, lamenting in the 1997 floods the failure to shore up levees, and opposing the Central Valley Project water bill for legislating "a permanent drought." He sponsored an exemption of flood control activities from the Endangered Species Act. One of his most significant efforts was providing clout for the Quincy Library Group, a collection of loggers and (some) local environmentalists in Plumas County in the Sierras who decided to meet at the library in Quincy—the only place where they couldn't shout at each other. They hammered out a plan that permitted the logging of smaller, more crowded trees in national forests as a way to reduce wildfires and provide a steady supply of timber for local mills. (After decades of resource extraction, there are few old-growth forests still left here.) Initially, even the Clinton Administration backed the proposal, believing it melded with a Clinton-Gore effort to promote collaboration, rather than litigation, to solve environmental problems. In 1997 the House passed the Quincy plan 429–1. But then national environmental groups came out full-bore against it, fearing it would set a precedent for greater local control of federal lands. Senator Barbara Boxer stalled Herger's bill for months, but legislators did an end-run around her by inserting language into the omnibus spending package that passed in October 1998. By summer 2000, loggers complained that the deal was not working because of bureaucratic delays by the Forest Service; Herger tried to cut through the delays by securing $25 million in additional funding. Meanwhile, the unusual coalitions continued as local businesses fought a Clinton plan for more aggressive logging in the Sierras because of concern that it would harm tourism. When the Bush Administration took over, Herger backed efforts to postpone Clinton's road-building ban in national forests, including nearly 2 million acres in the Sierras.

Herger has been consistently reelected with more than 60% of the vote against weak opponents. If anything, Democratic redistricters are likely to make his district even safer by packing in more Republicans.

Cook's Call *Safe.* Since he was elected in 1986, Wally Herger has had little trouble winning in this heavily conservative district. Rumors that Democrats will try to alter the nearby 3rd District to their liking would have an impact on Herger's district. But, it is unlikely that those alterations could dramatically change a district that Bush won by 25% in 2000.

THE PEOPLE: Pop. 2000: 633,808; Pop. 1990: 573,226, up 10.6% 1990–2000. 86.3% White, 1.6% Black, 2.5% Asian, 2.4% Amer. Indian, 0.1% Hawaiian, 3.7% Two+ races, 3.4% Other; 8.5% Hispanic Origin.

2000 Presidential Vote
Bush (R)	155,841	(59%)
Gore (D)	89,859	(34%)
Nader (Green)	13,855	(5%)
Others	3,807	(1%)

1996 Presidential Vote
Dole (R)	126,430	(51%)
Clinton (D)	89,736	(36%)
Perot (I)	22,161	(9%)
Others	10,058	(4%)

Rep. Wally Herger (R)

Elected 1986, 8th term; b. May 20, 1945, Yuba City; home, Marysville; American River Comm. Col., A.A. 1967, CA St. U., 1968–69; Mormon; married (Pamela).

Elected Office: CA Assembly, 1980–86.

Professional Career: Rancher; Owner, Herger Gas Inc., 1969–80.

DC Office: 2268 RHOB 20515, 202-225-3076; Web site: www.house.gov/herger.

District Offices: Chico, 530-893-8363; Redding, 530-223-5898.

Committees: *Ways & Means* (6th of 24 R): Human Resources (Chmn.); Trade.

Group Ratings
	ADA	ACLU	AFS	LCV	CON	ITIC	NTU	COC	ACU	NTLC	CHC
2000	0	21	0	0	87	100	72	85	95	88	100
1999	5	—	0	6	65	—	68	88	92	—	—

National Journal Ratings
	1999 LIB —	1999 CONS		2000 LIB —	2000 CONS
Economic	0% —	84%		0% —	94%
Social	0% —	96%		0% —	79%
Foreign	0% —	97%		38% —	61%

Key Votes of the 106th Congress
1. Patient Bill of Rights	N	5. Bar RU-486 $ for FDA	Y	9. NATO War in Serbia	N
2. Accelerate Min. Wage	N	6. Display 10 Commandments	Y	10. Perm. Trade with China	Y
3. Strike Ban on Ergo. Stnd.	N	7. Gun Show Bkgrnd. Checks	N	11. Debt Relief for 3rd World	N
4. Ovrd. Estate Tax Veto	Y	8. Ban Part.-Birth Abortion	Y	12. Drop Cuba Econ. Embargo	Y

Election Results
2000 general	Wally Herger (R)	168,172	(66%)	($664,374)
	Stan Morgan (D)	72,075	(28%)	
	Other	15,609	(6%)	
2000 primary	Wally Herger (R)	120,375	(65%)	
	Stan Morgan (D)	48,858	(26%)	
	John McDermott (NL)	11,647	(6%)	
	Other	4,634	(2%)	
1998 general	Wally Herger (R)	128,372	(63%)	($608,996)
	Roberts Braden (D)	70,837	(34%)	($35,424)
	Others	6,158	(3%)	

THIRD DISTRICT

California's Sacramento Valley is one of nature's, and man's, miracles. Nature has sculpted a floor of almost perfectly flat land, surrounded on three sides by mountains, alternately purple and brown in the light. To this fertile lush black loam, man has added roads and fences—as straight as the lines in a geometry text—and, most importantly, water. Pacific clouds pour rain into the mountains, but the water used to run off quickly before it was penned in reservoirs and distributed through a system of canals and aqueducts, levees and pumping plants. The Sacramento and Central valleys now produce a marvelous variety of crops: rice, plums, almonds, olives, asparagus, pears, hops, beans, celery, onions, potatoes, plus caviar-yielding sturgeon in pools of filtered water. The Sacramento Valley has always guarded its water jealously, and in the days before one-person-one-vote, it had enough seats in the California Senate to veto water decisions it didn't like; today it must fight to keep enough for its farms against the demands of the cities to the south and to maintain the levees which broke during the 1997 floods. The metropolis of this valley is Sacramento. Its historic foundation is apparent to those coming into town on the West Sacramento Freeway, elevated above utterly flat rice lands on the dense, hard clay that is painstakingly drained by a network of canals. As you hurtle over the Sacramento River on the M Street Bridge you see, framed perfectly in its arch, California's glorious golden-domed Capitol. On this landing Sacramento was born, and the state government, plus the agriculture symbolized by those rice fields, were for years its lifeblood. Now Sacramento spreads far to the south, east and north, with 1.8 million people—one of the nation's fastest-growing big metropolitan areas.

The Third Congressional District includes part of metropolitan Sacramento and much of the Sacramento Valley to the north. It takes in many of the suburbs just north of Sacramento and the American River—all or part of Carmichael, Citrus Heights, North Highlands and Foothills Farms. Sacramento, filled with government employees, is historically Democratic, but these suburbs are increasingly Republican. The 3rd also includes heavily Democratic Yolo County, with industrial West Sacramento just across the Sacramento River from the Capitol and, on the flat farmlands, the tree-shaded, bicycle-pathed town of Davis, with its University of California campus. In the Sacramento Valley it extends north along I-5 to Red Bluff.

The congressman from the 3rd District is Doug Ose, a Republican elected in 1998 to a seat which, in its various versions, had elected only Democrats since it was created in 1962. Ose grew up in Sacramento and went into the family real estate development business after graduating from Berkeley in 1977. In 1985, he struck out on his own, mainly to build mini-storage units. This is a booming business in a fast-growing metropolitan area filling up with subdivision houses on narrow lots and garden apartments with little room to store a lifetime's paraphernalia. Ose had accumulated enough of a fortune to self-finance a House campaign. The occasion came when Vic Fazio, congressman and chairman of the Democratic Caucus, announced he would not seek re-election after 20 years in the House. Despite his prominence in Washington and connections in Sacramento, redistricting in 1992 gave Fazio this Republican-leaning district, which he fought hard to hold. His retirement made Republicans the clear favorite for the district. Their two leading candidates were Ose, who had not run for office before, and Assemblywoman Barbara Alby, a strong conservative. Spending freely of his own money, Ose ran a stream of attacks against Alby; one ad asserted that Alby had missed two of every 10 legislative votes in 1997 (some of them due to a "junket to Hawaii," a charge that was accompanied in the ad by dancing hula dolls). The attacks worked. In the nine-candidate all-party June primary, Ose finished first, with 30%, to Alby's 19%. Sandie Dunn, a water and land-use attorney endorsed by Fazio, won the Democratic nomination with 23%.

In the general, both candidates showed strengths. Dunn campaigned as a moderate, with special expertise in water law and experience in the Sacramento Valley on this issue; she opposed the moribund Auburn Dam. Ose campaigned for tax cuts and giving local governments control over environmental protection. The two candidates raised similar sums from individuals and PACs. But Ose spent another $1.43 million of his own money. With turnout low, the district's Republican lean prevailed, and Ose won 53%–45%. Yolo County, which cast one-quarter of the district's votes, went 57%–41% for Dunn. But Sacramento County and the Sacramento Valley counties, each with three-eighths of the district's votes, went for Ose by 52%–45% and 60%–37% respectively.

In Washington, Ose was more conservative on economic than on cultural and foreign issues. He tended to the needs of rice farmers, whose prices had been battered by oversupply and the Asian financial crisis. He passed a bill allowing the port of Sacramento to deliver dirt dredged from its man-made waterway to other government agencies for restoring wetlands and reinforcing levees. And he got $14 million for a microelectronics program to assist conversion of McClellan Air Force Base to a civilian facility. But he ran into some problems in the complex world of California politics. John Doolittle helped to scuttle Ose's plan for improvement of Sacramento River levees in the Natomas area. And when he agreed to eastern environmentalists' demands to drop his proposed bar on a wildlife refuge in the Yolo Bypass in exchange for the Fish and Wildlife Service slowing work on the project, some Yolo County officials objected that he had caved in to bureaucrats.

In January 2001, Ose became chairman of the Energy Policy, Natural Resources and Regulatory Affairs Subcommittee of Government Reform, from which he oversaw California's electricity crisis plus water problems that Republicans contend the Clinton Administration exacerbated. Although he handily won reelection—though again losing Yolo, this time by 53%–44%—he faces a serious threat to a third term. Democrats control redistricting, and seem set on removing rural areas from the 3rd District; that would require sacrifices by safe Democrats in adjacent areas, though the Census showed that the district already needed to shed 36,000 persons. With Ose's base in Sacramento plus his personal resources, he will probably put up a strong fight.

Cook's Call   *Competitive.* This once reliably Democratic seat has been trending away from Democrats since it was reshaped in the 1991 redistricting. But, Democrats, who control the redistricting process in the state this year, are very enthusiastic about putting this seat back into their fold. To do so, there is talk of forcing the sophomore Ose to run against another Republican incumbent (like 4th District Representative John Doolittle) or creating a district that has a much more Democratic lean to it. But Ose should not be underestimated: His personal wealth and moderate voting record will give him some advantages in a competitive general election contest.

THE PEOPLE: Pop. 2000: 675,618; Pop. 1990: 571,545, up 18.2% 1990–2000. 73.2% White, 3.8% Black, 6.4% Asian, 1.3% Amer. Indian, 0.3% Hawaiian, 5.1% Two+ races, 9.9% Other; 19.5% Hispanic Origin.

2000 Presidential Vote		
Bush (R)	122,587	(51%)
Gore (D)	104,639	(44%)
Nader (Green)	9,842	(4%)
Others	2,778	(1%)

1996 Presidential Vote		
Clinton (D)	103,507	(45%)
Dole (R)	101,651	(44%)
Perot (I)	15,921	(7%)
Others	7,858	(3%)

Rep. Doug Ose (R)

Elected 1998, 2d term; b. June 27, 1955, Sacramento; home, Sacramento; U. of CA at Berkeley, B.S. 1977; Lutheran; married (Lynnda).

Professional Career: Project mgr., Ose Properties, 1977–85; Real estate developer, 1985-present.

DC Office: 215 CHOB 20515, 202-225-5716; Fax: 202-226-1298; Web site: www.house.gov/ose.

District Office: Woodland, 530-669-3540.

Committees: *Agriculture* (17th of 27 R): Conservation, Credit, Rural Development & Research; General Farm Commodities & Risk Management. *Financial Services* (23d of 37 R): Capital Markets, Insurance & Government Sponsored Enterprises; Domestic Monetary Policy, Technology & Economic Growth; International Monetary Policy & Trade (Vice Chmn.). *Government Reform* (15th of 24 R): Criminal Justice, Drug Policy & Human Resources; Energy Policy, Natural Resources and Regulatory Affairs (RMM); Government Efficiency, Financial Management & Intergovernmental Relations; Technology & Procurement Policy.

Group Ratings

	ADA	ACLU	AFS	LCV	CON	ITIC	NTU	COC	ACU	NTLC	CHC
2000	15	36	0	7	8	100	59	85	76	61	53
1999	30	—	0	6	51	—	54	92	68	—	—

National Journal Ratings

	1999 LIB —	1999 CONS		2000 LIB —	2000 CONS
Economic	0% —	84%		6% —	85%
Social	54% —	46%		49% —	50%
Foreign	52% —	48%		25% —	69%

Key Votes of the 106th Congress

1. Patient Bill of Rights	N	5. Bar RU-486 $ for FDA	N	9. NATO War in Serbia	Y
2. Accelerate Min. Wage	N	6. Display 10 Commandments	Y	10. Perm. Trade with China	Y
3. Strike Ban on Ergo. Stnd.	N	7. Gun Show Bkgrnd. Checks	Y	11. Debt Relief for 3rd World	N
4. Ovrd. Estate Tax Veto	Y	8. Ban Part.-Birth Abortion	Y	12. Drop Cuba Econ. Embargo	N

Election Results

2000 general	Doug Ose (R)	129,254	(56%)	($593,164)
	Bob Kent (D)	93,067	(40%)	($258,524)
	Other	7,861	(3%)	
2000 primary	Dous Ose (R)	101,571	(61%)	
	Bob Kent (D)	58,250	(35%)	
	Other	6,270	(4%)	
1998 general	Doug Ose (R)	100,621	(52%)	($2,373,133)
	Sandie Dunn (D)	86,471	(45%)	($622,964)
	Others	4,914	(3%)	

FOURTH DISTRICT

California sprang suddenly into existence: The Gold Rush of 1849 was followed by statehood and the creation of the first 27 counties in 1850. The new state's first boom area was the Mother Lode country in the foothills of the Sierras above Sacramento. Mining camps the size of eastern cities grew up in vacant valleys locked amid steep hills, with thousands of would-be millionaires gathered to find gold—though most of those who actually got rich did so by catering to miners' needs. In Placerville, John Studebaker had a buggy shop, Phillip Armour ran a butcher shop and Mark Hopkins had a dry goods store. The biggest mine in California was sunk in Grass Valley in 1857 and worked for half a century. But long before that, most of the Mother Lode country emptied out, leaving ghost towns and villages with hundreds of deserted houses: an antique vacation country left behind in time.

As they celebrated the sesquicentennial, local residents sought to resurrect their area into a booming ex-urban and tourist mecca. "The American River near Coloma becomes a virtual free-way of whooping rafters on summer weekends," reported *USA Today*. "The Mother Lode also offers modern-day prospectors an intriguing pastiche of bed-and-breakfast inns, musty antique stores and such blink-and-you'll-miss-'em outposts as Volcano, Fiddletown, Rough and Ready"–named after President Zachary Taylor. Thousands of Californians—many of them families from smog-filled, middle-class suburbs of the Los Angeles Basin and the San Francisco Bay area—looking for a more pleasant, small-town, orderly environment, have found it here along fast-flowing creeks where the '49ers camped. For the first time since the 1860 Census, county populations rose sharply in the past three decades. Politically, this migration has changed the Mother Lode country from Democrat to Republican. The new migrants are tired of the cultures of therapy of the big metro areas and ready for more discipline. In 1976, nine Mother Lode counties from Sierra to Mariposa cast 118,000 votes, and voted 50%–47% for Jimmy Carter over Gerald Ford: close to the California average. In 2000 they cast 286,000 votes, and voted 57%–37% for George W. Bush over Al Gore: results closer to Idaho's than California's.

The 4th Congressional District consists of most of the Mother Lode country plus the north-eastern suburbs of Sacramento—Fair Oaks, Citrus Heights, Orangevale—and the old town of Folsom. The district runs northeast along I-80 into Auburn and Roseville in Placer County where the Mother Lode hills start, then up to the crest of the Sierra Nevada and over to the California shore of Lake Tahoe and the arid salt flats around Mono Lake. This heavily Republican district was also the fastest-growing California district north of Los Angeles in the 1990s, when its population increased 27%.

The congressman from the 4th District is John Doolittle, a Republican with one of the most conservative voting records in the House. Doolittle grew up in the Los Angeles area and went to high school in Cupertino, in what now is Silicon Valley. His conservatism was annealed in the fires of adversity: He graduated from the University of California at Santa Cruz in 1972, when the campus was 97% for George McGovern. After law school he moved to the edge of the Sacramento metro area where the foothills begin, and in 1980 was elected at 30 to the state Senate from a district that stretched up to the Oregon border. As a senator he opposed gun control and abortion, and favored a crime victims' bill of rights and widespread AIDS testing. When the incumbent retired in 1990 in a district that then stretched from the Mother Lode country to Stockton, Doolittle ran for the seat. He had tougher competition than expected from Democrat Patricia Malberg, who was pro-choice on abortion, against nuclear power and for defense spending cuts; Doolittle won by just 50%–46%.

As a freshman, Doolittle was one of the Republicans' Gang of Seven, who were the advance guard for Newt Gingrich's 1994 revolution. Perhaps to curry favor with the 25% of the district who voted for Ross Perot in 1992, Doolittle joined "United We Stand America." In the Republican House, Doolittle was given a subcommittee chair the old Democrats who represented this area would have relished: Water and Power. But his agenda resembled theirs only in his support for the Auburn Dam, which he and other Sacramento area congressmen for decades have wanted to build on the American River, 35 miles east of Sacramento. Doolittle insisted on a design that could supply water to the Mother Lode. But in 1996 the dam was rejected in committee, 35–28, by a combination of environmentalists and spending opponents. When he continued the fight, the Senate Environment and Public Works Committee, led by the Bay Area's Barbara Boxer, blocked his efforts in 1998. Doolittle then blocked Robert Matsui's proposal for higher levees and more outlets in the Folsom Dam. The deadlock left unresolved attempts to address Sacramento's flood-control needs. Doolittle's other subcommittee plans were also unrealized. He wanted to sell the government's Power Marketing Administrations, which subsidize electric power in some areas because they needed power lines built in the 1930s. He sought to change the environmental provisions imposed on the Central Valley Project in 1992. Some of those changes may be more likely with George W. Bush as president, but Doolittle gave up the subcommittee in 2001 to take a long-desired slot on the Appropriations Committee. Doolittle did play a constructive role in assisting the rehabilitation of Yosemite National Park—the district line runs through the Yosemite Valley—after its devastating 1997 flood led Congress to spend $178 million to restore the site, while also decongesting it. By eliminating most parking and launching a park-and-ride transit system, Doolittle and the environmentalists cooperated on more efficient use of the park. However, after George W. Bush became President, Doolittle and neighboring Representative George Radanovich wanted the plan reconsidered.

He has worked closely with Tom DeLay on several issues, including opposing the Shays-Meehan campaign-finance reform as "an abomination" and offering their own alternative—defeated by the House, 117–306—to remove restrictions on fundraising but provide daily disclosure of contributions: free expression and transparency. (This has been the position of former Senator Eugene McCarthy.) In a political odd couple, he and Maxine Waters revived an old proposal: In lieu of a pay raise, agree to per-diem allowances to cover expenses, of the kind they received as California Assemblymen; others said this would be attacked as a $20,000-plus tax-free pay increase, and the proposal went nowhere. Back home, he got a firm hold on the district in 1994, and he has stayed above 60% since then. Redistricting will remove some parts, but there is sure to be another heavily Republican seat in the foothills.

Cook's Call   *Probably Safe.* With talk of significant changes to the neighboring 3rd District, there is a chance that Doolittle's district could feel the fall-out. Doolittle's past electoral experience suggests that when faced with a high quality challenger, he can be pushed into a competitive race but perhaps not beaten, and against weak opposition he will win comfortably every time. Still, it is hard to see Democrats putting much effort into ousting Doolittle in 2002. After all, this is a district that Bush won by 21 % in 2000.

THE PEOPLE: Pop. 2000: 725,180; Pop. 1990: 571,027, up 27% 1990–2000. 87.7% White, 1.6% Black, 2.7% Asian, 1.1% Amer. Indian, 0.2% Hawaiian, 3.3% Two+ races, 3.5% Other; 9.2% Hispanic Origin.

2000 Presidential Vote		
Bush (R)	189,521	(58%)
Gore (D)	120,519	(37%)
Nader (Green)	12,605	(4%)
Others	3,579	(1%)

1996 Presidential Vote		
Dole (R)	145,223	(51%)
Clinton (D)	107,076	(38%)
Perot (I)	21,233	(7%)
Others	9,775	(3%)

Rep. John Doolittle (R)

Elected 1990, 4th term; b. Oct. 30, 1950, Glendale; home, Rocklin; U. of CA at Santa Cruz, B.A. 1972, U. of the Pacific, J.D. 1978; Mormon; married (Julia).

Elected Office: CA Senate, 1980–90, Repub. Caucus Chmn., 1987–90.

Professional Career: Practicing atty., 1978–80.

DC Office: 2410 RHOB 20515, 202-225-2511; Fax: 202-225-5444; Web site: www.house.gov/doolittle.

District Office: Roseville, 916-786-5560.

Committees: *Appropriations* (31st of 35 R): District of Columbia; Energy & Water Development. *Budget* (15th of 24 R). *House Administration* (5th of 6 R).

Group Ratings

	ADA	ACLU	AFS	LCV	CON	ITIC	NTU	COC	ACU	NTLC	CHC
2000	5	36	0	0	9	83	63	76	88	88	100
1999	5	—	0	6	47	—	70	80	91	—	—

National Journal Ratings

	1999 LIB	—	1999 CONS		2000 LIB	—	2000 CONS
Economic	41%	—	57%		29%	—	67%
Social	35%	—	64%		0%	—	79%
Foreign	14%	—	85%		0%	—	88%

Key Votes of the 106th Congress

1. Patient Bill of Rights	N	5. Bar RU-486 $ for FDA	Y	9. NATO War in Serbia	N
2. Accelerate Min. Wage	N	6. Display 10 Commandments	Y	10. Perm. Trade with China	Y
3. Strike Ban on Ergo. Stnd.	N	7. Gun Show Bkgrnd. Checks	N	11. Debt Relief for 3rd World	N
4. Ovrd. Estate Tax Veto	Y	8. Ban Part.-Birth Abortion	Y	12. Drop Cuba Econ. Embargo	N

Election Results

2000 general	John Doolittle (R)	197,503	(63%)	($587,722)
	Mark A. Norberg (D)	97,974	(31%)	($14,540)
	Other	15,946	(5%)	
2000 primary	John Doolittle (R)	149,735	(66%)	
	Mark A. Norberg (D)	63,130	(28%)	
	Other	13,413	(6%)	
1998 general	John Doolittle (R)	155,306	(63%)	($489,083)
	David Shapiro (D)	85,394	(34%)	
	Others	7,524	(3%)	

FIFTH DISTRICT

Sacramento, capital of the nation's largest state, focus of California's third-largest media market (19th in the nation), home of a national sports franchise (the NBA's Sacramento Kings) and an 18-mile light rail system, is no longer just a small city with a lot of civil servants and a vegetable-packing economy. It is a vibrant American metropolis, with some of the nation's highest job growth and is 13th in the number of homes with on-line access. Sacramento started as a river port on the sluggish waters of the Sacramento and American rivers. It was the destination of many overland migrants, the site of Sutter's Fort, where John Augustus Sutter found the gold that set off the Gold Rush of 1849, and the western terminus of the Pony Express in 1860. This was the natural choice to be California's capital, halfway between the San Francisco Bay and the Mother Lode country in the foothills of the Sierras, and in the middle of California's vast valley. Agriculture continues to be important today in Sacra-tomato (as some call it): it has the world's largest almond processing plant.

In the old days, government was not a big business. Just a few lobbyists hung out in saloons on K or J streets, the governor's mansion was a musty antique, and the 100-plus degree summers emptied out what there was of the city. But air conditioning has replaced awnings, freeways and shopping malls have followed the city's growth east and north toward the Sierra foothills, and affluence has made this one of America's higher income metropolitan areas. In the 1980s metropolitan Sacramento grew 35% and in the 1990s by 22%, so that it now has 1.8 million people, about the same as metro Cincinnati or Kansas City. The high-tech growth has moved east from Silicon Valley, with Intel and Hewlett-Packard housing large campuses. Government expanded, too, and the platoons of lobbyists, lawyers and consultants have grown anew since Democrat Gray Davis claimed the governor's office. As Sacramento has grown, this once Democratic, pro-government, working-class bastion has become closer to an upscale Sun Belt boom town. A long generation ago, in 1966, Sacramento was just about the only part of California beyond the Bay Area that stuck with Pat Brown over challenger Ronald Reagan. In 1998, the Sacramento area favored Democrat Gray Davis, but with 55%, 3% below his statewide average; Al Gore carried Sacramento County by only 49%–45%, and George W. Bush carried the four-county metro area by 48%–46%.

The 5th District of California consists of the center of metropolitan Sacramento. The 5th contains affluent neighborhoods on older grid streets and scattered low-income black, Mexican-American and Hmong neighborhoods, plus new condominiums north of the American River and middle-class subdivisions south of downtown. This is the solidly Democratic part of metro Sacramento, and the 5th is the most Democratic district in the great valley from Bakersfield north to Oregon.

The congressman from the 5th is Robert Matsui, a Democrat first elected in 1978, third-ranking Democrat on the Ways and Means Committee. Born in 1941, the infant Matsui and his family were among the West Coast Japanese Americans forced into internment camps in 1942, and although he has no memory of the experience himself, he does remember the silence his family and others maintained about it. It was Asian shame, when none of the victims had anything to be ashamed about. He was one of the lead sponsors of the 1988 Japanese American redress law which apologized for the internment policy and provided monetary compensation for every survivor of the camps and for so-called "voluntary evacuees." He also sponsored the creation of the Manzanar National Historic Site, near Bishop, California, to preserve the memory of this episode.

Matsui has been dependably liberal, but at the risk of offending current Democratic dogma by pressing for expanded international trade. In 1993 he took the lead among House Democrats in seeking approval of the North American Free Trade Agreement, at a time when the Clinton Administration was lukewarm, then-Majority Leader Dick Gephardt was opposed and then-Minority Whip Newt Gingrich was not engaged in the issue. Working with Republican Jim Kolbe of Arizona, he rallied support and let the White House know that NAFTA was foundering and would not pass without a major push. Both the White House and Gingrich went all out, and NAFTA passed by a comfortable majority. Matsui hoped for a similar outcome on fast-track negotiating authority in 1997. But he found himself isolated as one of very few Democrats strongly supporting fast track; when he and the White House were unable to produce the number of Democratic votes they had promised, Speaker Gingrich pulled the measure at the last minute. The Republicans brought it back up for a vote in September 1998, even though it was apparent it had lost rather than gained votes. Matsui bitterly termed the vote "an attempt to embarrass members of my party," though the question might be asked whether the Democrats, only 29 of whom voted for fast track, embarrassed themselves. When the ranking Democratic seat on the Social Security Subcommittee opened up in 1999, Matsui was eager to switch, and he was more comfortable advocating traditional Democratic policy on an issue where he was not nearly so far out of line with his party. But he remained a key figure on trade issues, especially in support of Permanent Normal Trade Relations with China; Bill Clinton took his advice not to deliver a nationally televised address on the issue for fear of alienating many Democrats. At Ways and Means, he has become a party leader on tax issues, objecting to excessive Republican cuts. But he has sponsored more narrow tax benefits, including repeal of the 3% telephone excise tax and a new tax credit for the deployment of broadband services.

Matsui has been active in Democratic fundraising, as treasurer of the Democratic National Committee from 1991–95 and deputy chairman in 1995 and 1996; his wife Doris Matsui was deputy director of public liaison in the Clinton White House until 1998. The retirement of Vic Fazio in the 3rd District increased the burden on Matsui to work on local projects. The Sacramento delegation worked together for years to build the Auburn Dam to provide greater flood protection for Sacramento, but they split after losing to a coalition of environmentalists and fiscal conservatives. Matsui conceded that the Auburn Dam would not be built and introduced a plan, endorsed by the Clinton administration, to raise the height of downstream American River levees. As 2000 ended, neither plan had been approved, and the deadlock over Sacramento's flood control system continued.

In the past, Matsui has flirted with running for statewide office—against then-Senator Pete Wilson in 1988, for attorney general in 1990, for the vacant Senate seat in 1992—but decided each time not to. He once contemplated a challenge to Charles Rangel for the ranking minority position on Ways and Means, but the two of them lately have gotten along well. The district's boundaries will have to be pared back in redistricting, and Democratic redistricters might put some Democratic precincts in the 3rd or 11th districts to weaken Republican incumbents there. But Matsui likely will continue to win re-election easily every two years.

Cook's Call   *Safe.* This Sacramento-based district is strongly Democratic and has re-elected Matsui rather easily for over 22 years. With Democrats in control of the redistricting process in 2001, it is possible that they will move some of the surplus Democrats from the 5th into adjacent districts (like the 3rd) to boost their chances in those seats.

THE PEOPLE: Pop. 2000: 669,412; Pop. 1990: 573,659, up 16.7% 1990–2000. 52.6% White, 13.6% Black, 15.5% Asian, 1.2% Amer. Indian, 0.8% Hawaiian, 6.5% Two + races, 9.8% Other; 19.9% Hispanic Origin.

2000 Presidential Vote			1996 Presidential Vote		
Gore (D)	126,007	(57%)	Clinton (D)	119,678	(57%)
Bush (R)	81,592	(37%)	Dole (R)	70,925	(34%)
Nader (Green)	10,309	(5%)	Perot (I)	10,863	(5%)
Others	2,833	(1%)	Others	8,159	(4%)

Rep. Robert T. Matsui (D)

Elected 1978, 12th term; b. Sept. 17, 1941, Sacramento; home, Sacramento; U. of CA at Berkeley, A.B. 1963, J.D. 1966; United Methodist; married (Doris).

Elected Office: Sacramento City Cncl., 1971–78.

Professional Career: Practicing atty., 1967–78.

DC Office: 2308 RHOB 20515, 202-225-7163; Fax: 202-225-0566; Web site: www.house.gov/matsui.

District Office: Sacramento, 916-498-5600.

Committees: *Ways & Means* (3d of 17 D): Social Security (RMM).

Group Ratings

	ADA	ACLU	AFS	LCV	CON	ITIC	NTU	COC	ACU	NTLC	CHC
2000	85	86	85	93	53	76	16	47	4	15	7
1999	100	—	100	94	28	—	12	29	0	—	—

National Journal Ratings

	1999 LIB	—	1999 CONS		2000 LIB	—	2000 CONS
Economic	75%	—	23%		85%	—	11%
Social	83%	—	13%		84%	—	15%
Foreign	85%	—	12%		85%	—	10%

Key Votes of the 106th Congress

1. Patient Bill of Rights	Y	5. Bar RU-486 $ for FDA	N
2. Accelerate Min. Wage	Y	6. Display 10 Commandments	N
3. Strike Ban on Ergo. Stnd.	Y	7. Gun Show Bkgrnd. Checks	Y
4. Ovrd. Estate Tax Veto	N	8. Ban Part.-Birth Abortion	N

9. NATO War in Serbia	Y
10. Perm. Trade with China	Y
11. Debt Relief for 3rd World	Y
12. Drop Cuba Econ. Embargo	Y

Election Results

2000 general	Robert T. Matsui (D)	147,025	(69%)	($769,342)
	Ken Payne (R)	55,945	(26%)	($44,395)
	Other	11,089	(5%)	
2000 primary	Robert T. Matsui (D)	112,132	(71%)	
	Ken Payne (R)	38,158	(24%)	
	Other	8,081	(5%)	
1998 general	Robert T. Matsui (D)	130,715	(72%)	($586,491)
	Robert S. Dinsmore (R)	47,307	(26%)	($17,530)
	Others	3,816	(2%)	

SIXTH DISTRICT

When the Golden Gate bridge was opened in 1937, San Francisco was one of the nation's best-known cities, but few knew much about the land beyond the bridge's north pierhead. There were fewer than 50,000 people in Marin County then and another 65,000 just to the north in Sonoma County. For San Franciscans, Marin was known for the ferry terminus in Sausalito, a fishing village and art colony, and as the beginning of the Redwood Empire, with its giant trees in Muir Woods, which has a dense concentration of spotted owls; near the Bay was the state prison at San Quentin, with its infamous gas chamber. Farther north, in a sunny valley protected from the fog by the Coast Range, was Santa Rosa, site of agronomist Luther Burbank's laboratory, a town that looked Middle American enough to be the set for dozens of movies. Politically, the area was then typical of the nation: traditionally Republican, but favoring Franklin Roosevelt in the 1930s.

Today this part of California is far more populous, with 247,000 people in Marin and 458,000 in Sonoma, solidly a part of the San Francisco Bay Area, affluent beyond the dreams of Americans of 50 years ago and extreme in its cultural attitudes. Trendy Marin, with its hot tubs and its fashionable people getting in touch with themselves, became a national caricature in the late 1970s: economically affluent, culturally liberationist. Until it was surpassed by the Silicon Valley in the late 1990s, it was the nation's most expensive housing market. After a while such an image feeds on itself; a place like Marin attracts affluent people who share its values, while those who don't, go elsewhere—in the Bay Area to the more conservative San Ramon Valley, beyond the mountains east of Oakland. Indeed the Bay Area as a whole seems to attract liberals and repel conservatives, just as Dallas does the opposite. And Marin and Sonoma are attracting the most liberal of the liberal—averse to traditional religion, derisive of traditional sexual and marriage mores, viscerally anti-military. In Sonoma's vineyard town of Sebastopol, Greens hold three of five elected positions.

The 6th Congressional District includes all of Marin County and Sonoma except for its most rural corner. Marin County has been transformed politically over the last generation. In 1980 it voted for Ronald Reagan over Jimmy Carter by a 46%–36% margin. In the Reagan years it moved left and in 1988 voted for Michael Dukakis over George Bush by a 59%–41% margin. Now Republicans seem almost an endangered species here: in 2000 Marin voted for Al Gore over George

W. Bush by a 64%–28% margin. The public dialogue here is increasingly monopartisan, and, in this community priding itself on its tolerance, nary a dissenting word is heard.

The congresswoman from the 6th District is Lynn Woolsey, a Democrat elected in 1992 when 10-year incumbent Barbara Boxer was elected to the Senate. Woolsey grew up in the Pacific Northwest, moved to Marin and was a housewife with three children under 6 when her marriage ended in 1968. She went on welfare, got a low-paying job and left her children with 13 different babysitters in a year. Deliverance appeared in the form of a job with a high-tech startup firm where she rose to become a top executive. She remarried and moved to a house in Petaluma where her mother could live and look after the kids. As she wrote in her campaign literature, "Finally I could concentrate on work. The children had good care at last!" She put herself through business school at night, earned a degree in human resources and started her own personnel service. In 1984 Woolsey won a seat on the Petaluma Council and was proud of its record in limiting growth, setting up affirmative action programs and a Women of Color Task Force, requiring that 15% of new housing be reserved for low-income buyers and establishing a voucher system for low-income families' child care. In 1992 she won the House seat in a nine-candidate primary with 26%, well ahead of the next candidate's 19%. In the general she faced liberal Republican Assemblyman Bill Filante. But he had surgery for a brain tumor and stopped campaigning, and she won 65%–34%.

Woolsey has one of the most liberal voting records in the House. As the only known former welfare recipient in Congress, she co-chaired the Democrats' task force on welfare reform. She opposed the 1996 Welfare Reform Act and calls for easing work requirements and providing more child care; she wants mothers to be able to stay at home until their children are 11. She lobbied against banning gays in the military, accompanied by her son who is gay. She wants to let school districts use federal aid to provide health services. When the child-nutrition program was re-newed, she took credit for a pilot program to expand school breakfast to all children regardless of income and for opening eligibility to teenagers in after-school snack programs. She led a delegation of ten House women to the Senate Foreign Relations Committee in October 1999, where they protested chairman Jesse Helms's blocking action on a treaty against the discrimination of women; when they failed to heed his attempt to gavel them to silence, he scolded Woolsey—"Please be a lady!"—and ordered Capitol police to remove them. Republicans sought to embarrass Democrats by calling for a vote in September 2000 on Woolsey's bill to revoke the federal charter for the Boy Scouts because the group excludes gays; "We are not saying that the Boy Scouts are bad. We are saying that intolerance is bad," she explained; her bill was defeated 12–362. On occasion, Woolsey has teamed with Republicans: with Henry Hyde on a proposal to have the IRS enforce child-support collection, and with Wally Herger on moving Social Security revenues out of federal budget calculations. For the 107th Congress, she set improved teacher quality as a top priority, and will seek welfare-reform changes to reward states that address barriers such as domestic violence, lack of child care and deficient job training. She wants to finance parental-leave pro-grams in state governments.

Her big local project has been to expand the protected area around the Point Reyes National Seashore by purchasing easements from nearby farmers and barring them from selling their land to nonagricultural users. Many farmers complained about a federal "land grab" and the proposal languished; Woolsey in 1999 warned the landowners that they could expect a stricter bill if Dem-ocrats regain the House. She got $3 million in the 1999 budget to tow the battleship *Iowa* from Newport, Rhode Island to the San Francisco waterfront. Another local favorite is her call for export subsidies for winemakers.

Woolsey has been easily re-elected and that will likely continue.

Cook's Call *Safe.* This Marin and Sonoma based district has consistently supported liberal women representatives for the past 18 years and there is no sign today that redistricting will do much to change that fact in 2002. While not as overwhelmingly Democratic as other Bay Area districts, the 6th retains a strong Democratic core and Woolsey should be considered safe for 2002.

THE PEOPLE: Pop. 2000: 644,600; Pop. 1990: 571,360, up 12.8% 1990–2000. 82.6% White, 2.1% Black, 3.8% Asian, 0.9% Amer. Indian, 0.2% Hawaiian, 3.9% Two+ races, 6.6% Other; 14.4% Hispanic Origin.

2000 Presidential Vote

Gore (D)	181,497	(62%)
Bush (R)	88,144	(30%)
Nader (Green)	20,944	(7%)
Others	2,440	(1%)

1996 Presidential Vote

Clinton (D)	155,513	(57%)
Dole (R)	78,166	(29%)
Perot (I)	18,431	(7%)
Others	21,199	(8%)

Rep. Lynn Woolsey (D)

Elected 1992, 5th term; b. Nov. 3, 1937, Seattle, WA; home, Petaluma; U. of San Francisco, B.A. 1980; Presbyterian; divorced.

Elected Office: Petaluma City Cncl., 1985–92, Vice Mayor, 1986, 1991.

Professional Career: Human Resources Mgr., Harris Digital Telephone, 1969–80; Owner, Woolsey Personnel Svc., 1980–92.

DC Office: 2263 RHOB 20515, 202-225-5161; Fax: 202-225-5163; Web site: www.house.gov/woolsey.

District Offices: San Rafael, 415-507-9554; Santa Rosa, 707-542-7182.

Committees: *Education & the Workforce* (9th of 22 D): Education Reform; Workforce Protections. *Science* (6th of 22 D): Energy (RMM).

Group Ratings

	ADA	ACLU	AFS	LCV	CON	ITIC	NTU	COC	ACU	NTLC	CHC
2000	100	93	100	93	54	44	21	40	8	16	0
1999	95	—	100	100	44	—	21	12	4	—	—

National Journal Ratings

	1999 LIB —	1999 CONS	2000 LIB —	2000 CONS
Economic	88% —	0%	95% —	0%
Social	87% —	0%	94% —	0%
Foreign	83% —	16%	77% —	21%

Key Votes of the 106th Congress

1. Patient Bill of Rights	Y	5. Bar RU-486 $ for FDA	N	9. NATO War in Serbia	Y
2. Accelerate Min. Wage	Y	6. Display 10 Commandments	N	10. Perm. Trade with China	N
3. Strike Ban on Ergo. Stnd.	Y	7. Gun Show Bkgrnd. Checks	Y	11. Debt Relief for 3rd World	Y
4. Ovrd. Estate Tax Veto	N	8. Ban Part.-Birth Abortion	N	12. Drop Cuba Econ. Embargo	Y

Election Results

2000 general	Lynn Woolsey (D)	182,116	(64%)	($576,539)
	Ken McAuliffe (R)	80,169	(28%)	($17,979)
	Justin Moscoso (Green)	13,248	(5%)	
	Other	7,585	(3%)	
2000 primary	Lynn Woolsey (D)	135,941	(66%)	
	Ken McAuliffe (R)	57,478	(28%)	
	Other	11,415	(6%)	
1998 general	Lynn Woolsey (D)	158,446	(68%)	($634,563)
	Ken McAuliffe (R)	69,295	(30%)	($97,352)
	Others	5,240	(2%)	

SEVENTH DISTRICT

The journey inward from the Pacific Ocean to the vast flatness of California's Central Valley passes through wondrous terrain. The traveler starts at the Golden Gate, with the lush green Presidio on one side and the bluff of the Marin mountains on the other; through the waters of San Francisco Bay, looked down upon by ridges above the East Bay on one side and the cone of Mount Tamalpais on the other; through the narrow Carquinez Strait to Suisun Bay, with its sloughs and marshes, fed by the sluggish waters of the Sacramento and San Joaquin Delta; and finally past the mountains and waters, to the flat, fertile expanse of California's great interior. This is not a journey most tourists make, but it was a familiar route to the first Californians and it passes by much of the industrial base of the Bay Area. On the east side of the bay is Richmond, developed almost instantaneously during World War II when Henry J. Kaiser built a shipyard in its deep-water port and 91,000 people from all over the country were put to work building ships for the Pacific theater; what became known as Rosie the Riveter Memorial Park is now a national park, and the city now has a 36% black population and is attracting high-tech spinoffs. Across Carquinez Strait is Vallejo, named for a Mexican general and member of the first California Senate, the site from 1853 to 1996 of the giant Mare Island Naval Shipyard, now being redeveloped. Across the strait are tank farms and factories in Rodeo and Pittsburg and Martinez, the seat of Contra Costa County (literally, the coast opposite San Francisco).

The 7th Congressional District of California includes most of this passage, from Richmond and El Cerrito along both sides of Carquinez Strait and Suisun Bay to Vallejo, Rodeo, Martinez and Pittsburg. It also proceeds inland through the intermountain interstices of Contra Costa County to include most of middle-income Concord, but excludes the heavily Republican and higher-income interior Contra Costa communities around Walnut Hill and the San Ramon Valley. Politically, this industrial area was blue-collar, labor-union Democratic back in the days when San Francisco, with its larger white-collar population, often voted Republican. It has experienced a surge in housing values as home buyers look to the East Bay for better values. But it remains heavily Democratic, liberal on most issues; it voted 69%–27% for Al Gore in 2000.

The congressman from the 7th District is George Miller, one of four remaining Democrats of the Watergate class of 1974 (the others are John LaFalce, James Oberstar, and Henry Waxman), the first baby-boom liberal to chair a House committee. He is heir to a tradition of Bay Area working-class politics. His father was chairman of the state Senate Finance Committee; when he died in 1969, Miller lost the race to succeed him, but became a staffer for Senate Leader (and later San Francisco Mayor) George Moscone. Miller was also a protege of San Francisco Congressman Phillip Burton, who did so much to establish liberal hegemony in the House in the 1970s. To his work Miller brings an aggressiveness and zest for political combat reminiscent of Burton. He is a strong backer of protecting the environment against what he sees as greedy private sector operators and of furthering the causes of labor unions. Like Burton, Miller has grasped for top party leadership posts but hasn't made it. But he has learned a legislator's virtues of patience, timing and creativity.

Miller began the 1990s in a position of power, able to advance his causes forward; in the mid-1990s he found himself defending yesterday's gains and trying to prevent losses. In 1991 he became chairman of Interior (he renamed it Natural Resources in 1993 and Republicans renamed it Resources in 1995) and proceeded, in his words, "to kick ass and take names." He had long crusaded against water reclamation projects that provided cheap water to farmers. In 1992, amid a California drought, he passed a Central Valley Project law that raised farmers' prices closer to those of urban users and imposed environmental restrictions, over the fierce opposition of Central Valley politicians and Governor Pete Wilson. The victory was sealed when Bill Clinton in 1993 appointed a top Miller aide as head of the Bureau of Reclamation. But the Clinton Administration was not always helpful on other Miller priorities. He strongly backed higher mining, grazing and timber fees for companies operating on federal lands, and he was dismayed when Clinton deep-sixed Interior Secretary Bruce Babbitt's proposal for these. He passed the California desert bill, with Senator Dianne Feinstein, in October 1994; it was the last major legislation of the Democratic Congress.

In the minority, he has worked more to prevent change than to make change. He helped to stymie John Doolittle's attempt to revise the Central Valley Project and was part of the coalition opposing the Auburn Dam sought by Doolittle and others from the Sacramento area. He harshly criticized Republicans for trying to change the Endangered Species Act, EPA regulations, Arctic National Wildlife Refuge oil drilling, Tongass Forest logging and commercial sponsorship of national parks; for the most part, he was successful, with help from the Clinton Administration. He worked for the Presidio private-public trust fund and Bay-Delta funding in the successful 1996 parks bill, for the Manzanar National Historic Site commemorating one of the Japanese American detention camps in World War II; although the Senate scuttled a more sweeping version, he won with Republican Don Young in 2000 a major expansion of the Land and Water Conservation Fund to protect national assets. He successfully moved to award Congressional Medals of Honor to black World War II veterans who were unfairly overlooked, and sought to reopen the mutiny verdicts of black sailors who refused to report for duty after munitions explosions at Port Chicago in 1944. He showed open-mindedness by working with Republican Senator Mike DeWine to change the focus of the Family Reunification Act, which Miller sponsored in 1980, to the best interests of children. And he ventured far afield, criticizing the Park Service's proposals for a visitors' center at Gettysburg and attacking Republican Whip Tom DeLay for supporting what Miller considers sweatshops in the Commonwealth of the Northern Mariana Islands.

From time to time Miller's short fuse is on display. In 1997 he and DeLay had a red-faced confrontation over Miller's charge that DeLay let lobbyists write legislation in his office. Later, he obstructed the House by objecting to routine procedures in order to force a vote on the campaign finance bill. Miller mocked what he considered Republicans' obsession with Monica Lewinsky, speculating they would take her blue dress "through their districts like the Olympic torch or something and see if that helps." But he was the one member who did not vote on impeachment in December 1998, for a good reason: he had just had hip-replacement surgery and his California doctor advised against air travel. In January 2000, he took on the unlikely cause of his old friend Bill Bradley's campaign for President, spending five days campaigning in Iowa before the caucuses. "This is an opportunity to change the course from incrementalism," he told *The San Francisco Chronicle*. "I'm not for another four, eight years of business as usual—that's not why I went to Washington."

The election of George W. Bush unexpectedly returned Miller to the center ring. He replaced the retired Bill Clay as ranking Democrat on the Education and the Workforce Committee and, with the help of matchmaking by new committee chairman John Boehner, Miller struck up a cordial relationship with the new President—who called him "Big George"—and sought bipartisanship on Bush's education program. Miller said he agreed with the Bush's plans to improve teacher compensation and training, on early reading programs, and for school accountability; they disagreed on vouchers, but Miller and most Democrats assumed that would not be a sticking point. "I'm going to help him on education," Miller said in February 2001. Bush exulted when the bill—aside from vouchers—gained approval from the Boehner-Miller axis.

Miller has no cause for concern at home, although Democratic redistricters want him to give up some of his liberal base in hopes of making the adjacent 3rd District more Democratic.

Cook's Call   *Safe*. A fixture of Bay Area and California politics for over 25 years, George Miller (nicknamed Big George by President Bush with whom he has a congenial working relationship) has not had to worry about a race in years. The lines of the district will likely change a bit in redistricting, but Miller should have no problem running and winning in 2002.

THE PEOPLE: Pop. 2000: 636,367; Pop. 1990: 572,857, up 11.1% 1990–2000. 50.5% White, 16.5% Black, 15.1% Asian, 0.7% Amer. Indian, 0.6% Hawaiian, 6.1% Two + races, 10.5% Other; 21.6% Hispanic Origin.

2000 Presidential Vote			**1996 Presidential Vote**		
Gore (D)	148,302	(69%)	Clinton (D)	131,707	(65%)
Bush (R)	57,930	(27%)	Dole (R)	50,140	(25%)
Nader (Green)	7,964	(4%)	Perot (I)	12,178	(6%)
Others	1,694	(1%)	Others	7,321	(4%)

Rep. George Miller (D)

Elected 1974, 14th term; b. May 17, 1945, Richmond; home, Martinez; San Francisco St. U., B.A. 1968, U. of CA at Davis, J.D. 1972; Catholic; married (Cynthia).

Professional Career: Legis. aide, CA Senate Majority Ldr., 1969–74; Practicing atty., 1972–74.

DC Office: 2205 RHOB 20515, 202-225-2095; Fax: 202-225-5609; Web site: www.house.gov/georgemiller.

District Offices: Concord, 925-602-1880; Richmond, 510-262-6500; Vallejo, 707-645-1888.

Committees: *Education & the Workforce* (RMM of 22 D). *Resources* (2d of 25 D): Water & Power.

Group Ratings

	ADA	ACLU	AFS	LCV	CON	ITIC	NTU	COC	ACU	NTLC	CHC
2000	95	93	100	93	95	41	31	38	12	19	7
1999	100	—	83	94	98	—	37	4	8	—	—

National Journal Ratings

	1999 LIB —	1999 CONS	2000 LIB —	2000 CONS
Economic	68%	31%	90%	8%
Social	80%	19%	91%	6%
Foreign	78%	17%	85%	10%

Key Votes of the 106th Congress

1. Patient Bill of Rights	Y	5. Bar RU-486 $ for FDA	N	9. NATO War in Serbia	Y
2. Accelerate Min. Wage	Y	6. Display 10 Commandments	N	10. Perm. Trade with China	N
3. Strike Ban on Ergo. Stnd.	Y	7. Gun Show Bkgrnd. Checks	Y	11. Debt Relief for 3rd World	Y
4. Ovrd. Estate Tax Veto	N	8. Ban Part.-Birth Abortion	N	12. Drop Cuba Econ. Embargo	Y

Election Results

2000 general	George Miller (D)	159,692	(76%)	($443,578)
	Christopher A. Hoffman (R)	44,154	(21%)	($5,188)
	Other	4,943	(2%)	
2000 primary	George Miller (D)	98,451	(75%)	
	Christopher A. Hoffman (R)	18,926	(14%)	
	Nicholas Mraovich (R)	10,503	(8%)	
	Other	2,792	(2%)	
1998 general	George Miller (D)	125,842	(77%)	($343,658)
	Norman H. Reece (R)	38,290	(23%)	($28,183)

EIGHTH DISTRICT

On February 20, 1915, Governor Hiram Johnson and Mayor James Rolph led 150,000 people onto the grounds of the Panama-Pacific International Exposition to see the Spanish-Italian baroque style building built on reclaimed land in what became San Francisco's Marina district. The Exposition ostensibly celebrated the completion of the Panama Canal, but it was clearly intended to show off San Francisco's recovery from the 1906 earthquake. It also spotlighted San Francisco as the central focus of an America that was becoming, with its acquisition of Hawaii and the Philippines and its interest in an open-door policy with China and trade with Japan, a power in the Pacific. The Exposition set the physical style of San Francisco: It encouraged the use of Mediterranean color, accent and detail that characterizes most post-Victorian houses and commercial structures in The City (as the *San Francisco Examiner* called it for years). It created the picturesque Marina district, whose old buildings were among those damaged in the 1989 earthquake, and today's tourist waterfront around Fisherman's Wharf and Ghirardelli Square. This San Francisco has many facets: On a sunny day it looks almost tropical, with brown mountains baking in the sun and light shining off the pastel stucco buildings; when the clouds scud in from the Pacific, it can look sinister, full of dark corners where a private detective's partner might be ambushed by a pretty girl. The buildings can be majestic, like the monumental Beaux Arts City Hall, or tawdry, like the hotels of the Tenderloin; it is a city that looks exotic at first but, when you look closely, can only be American.

San Francisco has been a dynamic city, capable of great growth, carrying the American tradition of tolerance of diversity to new lengths; it grew from nothing to a major city in the single year of 1850; its American origins are obvious from the regular grids of streets named after politicians and local developers. The San Francisco of 1915 was proud of the writers who had flourished there—Jack London, Ambrose Bierce, Frank Norris—and of the home-town traditions of the arts and crafts movement, just as San Francisco later would have a Herb Caen-ish pride in the beats of the 1950s North Beach, the hippies who thronged Haight-Ashbury in 1967, and the gays of Castro in the 1970s and since. Over the years, the city's booming economy, based initially on food processing, but now on finance, high-tech and clothing (Levi Strauss, The Gap) attracted talented newcomers, weighted increasingly toward those who find its liberation-minded cultural attitudes congenial.

Politically, San Francisco was a progressive Republican town, like the two men who led the way into the Exposition. The sour-tempered Hiram Johnson made his name as a reformer throwing out crooked city politicians; his administration gave California primary elections, referenda and recall, and strong civil service laws. "Sunny Jim" Rolph, mayor from 1911–30 and then governor, built the civic center, parks, schools, streetcars and the Hetch Hetchy aqueduct—the antique infrastructure of San Francisco today. Sympathetic to the conservation movement, willing to deal with organized labor in a union town that had America's only general strike in 1934, tolerant of the diversity of California, these progressive Republicans were the recognizable ancestors of, though certainly not identical to, the San Franciscans who in the 1970s and 1980s became increasingly liberal and even radical.

But San Francisco's hipness can be overstated. For if its distinctive style attracted liberal singles and gays in increasing numbers, its economic dynamism on the Pacific Rim has attracted Asians—as indeed San Francisco did from 1850 until immigration was shut off by the Chinese Exclusion Act in 1882. The city has elected strong liberal politicians—notably, Mayor George Moscone and openly gay Supervisor Harvey Milk, who were shot to death in 1978 by a political opponent who was acquitted of murder by a liberal jury on the bizarre theory that he had been crazed by junk food. Over the next decade, the city's cultural liberalism was tempered by Mayor Dianne Feinstein, who vetoed a gay marriage ordinance and opposed commercial rent control. In 1995, Willie Brown, ousted after 15 years as speaker of the Assembly, returned home and was elected mayor. After the first two years, in which he reaped admiring publicity, Brown's record suddenly seemed dismal. While the affluent neighborhoods were enriched with new Silicon Valley millionaires, the Chinese, Filipino and other Asian immigrants in the southern and western parts of the city were beleaguered by high taxes that supported the pampered public employee unions. But he was re-elected in 1999 and continues to preside with aplomb over a prosperous city complaining about high housing prices and clogged freeways.

The 8th Congressional District takes in four-fifths of San Francisco, all but the southwest corner. It has all of San Francisco's high-rise downtown, the crowded and bustling Chinatown, Telegraph, Nob and Russian Hills, North Beach (which was once really a beach), Pacific Heights (which is still on heights) and the Marina District (which does not have a very big marina). In the valleys are the mostly black Fillmore and Western Addition areas, but only 9% of the district's residents in 2000 were black (a drop from 13% in 1990), 16% were Hispanic and 28% Asian— the third highest Asian percentage of any district outside Hawaii. The 8th also has the gay Castro district and Noe Valley, Haight-Ashbury, once the bedraggled center of hippiedom and now another yup-and-coming San Francisco neighborhood, and Portrero Hill with its restored houses overlooking downtown. Farther south are the old residential areas overlooking I-280, with pastel houses strewn along grid streets that hug the steep hills. The district is overwhelmingly Democratic: 77%–15% for Al Gore in 2000, with 8% for Ralph Nader.

The 8th District is represented by Nancy Pelosi, a Democrat with deep political roots, who was elected in June 1987. She has the energy and shrewdness of one who has handled the most delicate political chores and the charm and unflappability of one who is the mother of five children. Pelosi grew up in Maryland; her father, Thomas D'Alessandro, served in the House from 1939–47 and was mayor of Baltimore for 12 years after that, and her brother, Thomas D'Alessandro Jr., was mayor from 1967–71. Married to a successful San Francisco businessman, she was California Democratic Party chairman in the early 1980s, chaired the national party's Compliance Review Commission on delegate rules for 1984, and served as the Democratic Senatorial Campaign Committee's finance chairman in 1985. Since the 1960s, San Francisco's congressional politics were dominated by Phillip Burton, an old-fashioned labor-liberal Democrat. But Burton died in 1983 and his widow Sala, elected to succeed him, died in 1987. Pelosi ran and won 35%–31% in the special against gay supervisor Harry Britt.

Pelosi has taken the lead on important issues of local sensitivity. One is human rights, especially in China. After the Tiananmen Square massacre, she sponsored an amendment to give Chinese students the right to remain in the United States; George Bush vetoed it. In 1991 she became the lead sponsor of the bill to condition China's Most Favored Nation status on human rights reforms; the House overrode Bush's veto but it was upheld in the Senate. After that, Pelosi led the annual fight against permanent normal trade relations, PNTR, as it is now called, and sharply criticized China. "I don't believe in the concept of trickle-down liberty. Economic reform does not necessarily lead to political reform," she said, arguing that the Chinese make concessions not when the U.S. bows to their wishes but when it threatens to walk away. She said that Bill Clinton was either in denial or ill-informed about what's going on in China. When President Jiang Zemin visited Washington in 1997, she termed the White House state dinner shameful and attended a stateless dinner hosted by actor and pro-Tibet activist Richard Gere. When Clinton two years later agreed to terms for China's entry into the World Trade Organization, Pelosi led even more furious opposition to PNTR. When the American spy plane was downed in China in April 2001, she said, "It's constructive for others to be disabused of any idealist notions they might have about China." Although bitter about the setbacks, she vowed to maintain her human rights vigil. She has done all this at some political risk: Pelosi's position is by no means universally popular with Asian Americans in her district; many think the U.S. should trade and negotiate quietly with China. One of her chief adversaries on the issue is her San Francisco neighbor, Senator Dianne Feinstein; their houses are just a few blocks apart.

On AIDS funding, Pelosi has used her Appropriations seat to get money for victims and wants access to new therapies and drugs without regard to ability to pay; she got AIDS spending increased even in the Republican Congress. Another cause is the Presidio, which was transferred from the military to the National Park Service in 1995. There is no more stunning piece of urban property in America, but it is extremely expensive to maintain. Pelosi spent four years trying to devise a private-public trust fund for the Presidio. She succeeded by getting Republican support for a trust that would lease the buildings to provide enough revenue to pay the Park Service to maintain the open spaces and renovate the old buildings, with the proviso, insisted on by Republicans, that it be self-supporting in 15 years.

On other issues Pelosi has a perfectly liberal voting record. She has worked to restore welfare for legal immigrants, and has supported needle exchanges. She has been a leader in encouraging family planning and environmental protection overseas. Although she worked well with Republicans on China and the Presidio, she is a strong partisan. She turned down Dick Gephardt's entreaties to lead the Democratic Congressional Campaign Committee, but she ran a vigorous campaign against Steny Hoyer to become majority whip in 2000—raising more than $3 million for her party's candidates and agreeing to head a major fundraising push among non-members. Unfortunately for Democrats and Pelosi, who stood a good chance to win, Republicans kept control and Tom DeLay remained majority whip. After the election, she said that Democrats needed to do a better job at grass-roots organizing. As the Californian perhaps best-positioned for a House Democratic leadership position, her career continues to flourish. She took over in 2001 as the senior Democrat on the Intelligence Committee. With David Bonior planning to leave the House to run for governor of Michigan in 2002, she and Hoyer revved up their leadership bids again—this time, perhaps, in a contest to succeed him as minority whip during the 107th Congress. At home, Pelosi has been re-elected by huge margins.

Cook's Call *Safe.* It's almost impossible to imagine how Democrats could lose the 8th District, which is among the two-dozen most Democratic and liberal in the nation. Without a competitive race to worry about, Pelosi is much more focused on a campaign for majority whip, should Democrats take control of the House in 2002, than a general election.

THE PEOPLE: Pop. 2000: 617,094; Pop. 1990: 573,192, up 7.7% 1990–2000. 49.5% White, 9.1% Black, 28.4% Asian, 0.5% Amer. Indian, 0.6% Hawaiian, 4.4% Two+ races, 7.6% Other; 16.1% Hispanic Origin.

2000 Presidential Vote

Gore (D)	190,636	(77%)
Bush (R)	36,224	(15%)
Nader (Green)	20,143	(8%)
Others	1,466	(1%)

1996 Presidential Vote

Clinton (D)	114,906	(66%)
Dole (R)	31,282	(18%)
Perot (I)	7,104	(4%)
Others	20,853	(12%)

Rep. Nancy Pelosi (D)

Elected June 1987, 7th term; b. Mar. 26, 1940, Baltimore, MD; home, San Francisco; Trinity Col., B.A. 1962; Catholic; married (Paul).

Professional Career: CA Dem. Party, Northern Chmn., 1977–81, St. Chmn., 1981–83; DSCC Finance Chmn., 1985–87; PR exec., Ogilvy & Mather, 1986–87.

DC Office: 2457 RHOB 20515, 202-225-4965; Fax: 202-225-8259; Web site: www.house.gov/pelosi.

District Office: San Francisco, 415-556-4862.

Committees: *Appropriations* (8th of 29 D): Foreign Operations & Export Financing; Labor, HHS & Education. *Permanent Select Committee on Intelligence* (RMM of 9 D).

Group Ratings

	ADA	ACLU	AFS	LCV	CON	ITIC	NTU	COC	ACU	NTLC	CHC
2000	100	92	100	93	89	67	25	42	8	16	0
1999	95	—	100	94	88	—	21	12	0	—	—

National Journal Ratings

	1999 LIB —	1999 CONS		2000 LIB —	2000 CONS
Economic	88%	0%		92%	5%
Social	87%	0%		94%	0%
Foreign	89%	8%		85%	10%

Key Votes of the 106th Congress

1. Patient Bill of Rights	Y	5. Bar RU-486 $ for FDA	N	9. NATO War in Serbia	Y
2. Accelerate Min. Wage	Y	6. Display 10 Commandments	N	10. Perm. Trade with China	N
3. Strike Ban on Ergo. Stnd.	Y	7. Gun Show Bkgrnd. Checks	Y	11. Debt Relief for 3rd World	Y
4. Ovrd. Estate Tax Veto	N	8. Ban Part.-Birth Abortion	N	12. Drop Cuba Econ. Embargo	Y

Election Results

2000 general	Nancy Pelosi (D)	181,847	(85%)	($608,318)
	Adam Sparks (R)	25,298	(12%)	
	Other	8,283	(4%)	
2000 primary	Nancy Pelosi (D)	109,246	(86%)	
	Adam Sparks (R)	13,501	(11%)	
	Other	4,964	(4%)	
1998 general	Nancy Pelosi (D)	148,027	(86%)	($523,136)
	David J. Martz (R)	20,781	(12%)	
	Others	3,654	(2%)	

NINTH DISTRICT

Oakland and Berkeley, on the East Bay opposite San Francisco, stand today on one of the lushest sites in America, overlooking the Bay Bridge and the Golden Gate, basking in the sunshine that is more common here than across the Bay. Both cities are the homes of great institutions, but in different ways they are also museum pieces, antiques from a moment in the 1960s when both, especially Berkeley, gained identities that became hard to shake. Berkeley was founded as a university town, named after the 18th Century Irish philosopher Bishop George Berkeley, for his proclamation, "Westward the course of empire takes its way." Famous for years as the home of first-rate scholarship at the University of California, Berkeley became famous politically in 1964 as the home of student rebellion when the Free Speech Movement, protesting an administrator's refusal to let students set up a card table to sign up volunteers for Lyndon Johnson's campaign, led to months of riots, student strikes and classroom confrontation. In 1969, students led protests at "People's Park," a lot owned by the university, and Governor Ronald Reagan sent in the National Guard to protect state property from conversion to a playground: an episode in which both sides relished confrontation more than success. Berkeley in the 1960s gave birth to a street culture that still exists. Its denizens made common cause with the Black Panthers, a violent quasi-political gang from nearby Oakland, and smoked marijuana with the Hell's Angels motorcycle gang, also once based in Oakland. Berkeley's city council features bizarre political wars in which Democrats very liberal by national standards are the right wing. The Berkeley campus, with its view of the Bay, remains beautiful, and old buildings like the shingled Claremont Hotel are grand. But Berkeley has had little commercial development, and its public facilities have a low-maintenance, almost Third World look.

Oakland has a different history, centered around commerce and building its own civic institutions (Gertrude Stein was wrong: there is a there there). It became the western terminus of the transcontinental railroad in 1870 and was connected by ferry to San Francisco; it has always had heavy industry, and its port today is the busiest on the bay. The docks attracted young roustabouts like the writer Jack London, after whom a downtown square is named; civic affairs were run by the local elite, like the Knowland family who owned the *Oakland Tribune*. With the Bay Area's largest black community, Oakland spawned the Black Panthers in the 1960s; blacks took control of city government in the 1970s and, through the late editor-owner Bob Maynard, the *Tribune* in the 1980s. But Oakland was anything but thriving, with high crime rates, poor public schools and little economic development. Onto the scene came Jerry Brown, governor of California 20 years before, unsuccessful presidential candidate in 1976, 1980 and 1992; in 1998, he ran an unorthodox campaign for mayor, and won. Brown irritated local politicos by firing department heads and ignoring political alliances, but he seemed to take seriously his mission of propelling Oakland to the prominence its geographic position suggests it can occupy. He sounded like a conservative, with his tough talk on crime and advocate of big commercial development projects that drove up rents. The local economy thrived, partly with the growth of dot-com businesses. If Brown's victory was a rejection of the Oakland political establishment, so even more was the Assembly victory in a 1999 special election of Green Party nominee Audie Bock; but she lost the seat to a Democrat in 2000.

The 9th Congressional District consists of Oakland and Berkeley, plus adjacent towns like Alameda, site of an old Navy base. It has the largest black percentage of any northern California district (26% in 2000, down from 32% in 1990); in 2000 its population was 17% Asian and 17% Hispanic. Politically, it is way off to the left: 79% for Al Gore, with George W. Bush's 12% only barely keeping him in second place ahead of Ralph Nader's 9%.

The congresswoman from the 9th District is Barbara Lee, a Democrat chosen in a 1998 special election. She grew up in Texas and the San Fernando Valley, graduated from Mills College in Oakland and got a social work degree at Berkeley. She started a community mental health center in Berkeley and then worked as a staffer for 12 years for Congressman Ronald Dellums, elected in 1970 as a left Democrat and, in time, chairman of the Armed Services Committee. In 1990 Lee was elected to the California Assembly; in 1996, she was elected to the California Senate. She chaired the Housing and Land Use Committee, and worked to promote the Sonoma Baylands project, which broke the logjam on bay dredging. She passed laws on many subjects and worked for closer ties between California and Africa. After Dellums announced he was resigning—later remaining active as chair of Bill Clinton's advisory council on HIV/AIDS—he endorsed Lee as his successor, and she won the special election with 67% of the vote.

In the House Lee stands at the far left of the ideological spectrum. She wants to reduce the nation's weapons stockpiles and cut Pentagon spending sharply. She continued Dellums' efforts to convert closed military bases in Oakland to civilian use. She sponsored a ban on insurance company redlining in the financial services deregulation bill, a provision removed by Republicans. In May 2001, the International Relations Committee passed her bill to reverse President Bush's policy on denying funding to international groups who offer abortion counseling of services, but later that month the House voted to strike the language from the State Department authorization bill, 218–210, a slightly better showing than a similar vote the year before. She became vice-chair of the Progressive Caucus. After a visit to Cuba, she called for steps to end the 40-year embargo of Castro's island. She criticized Bill Clinton's renewed bombing of Iraq in late 1998. As most Democrats voted to authorize bombing of Serbia in March 1999, Lee was the only House member to oppose a resolution supporting U.S. troops; she argued that it wrongfully "embraces the notion that the president can authorize the commitment of U.S. troops to war without congressional approval."

She was twice reelected with more than 80%. Redistricting must add 42,000 people to the district, but is unlikely to shift the ideological balance.

Cook's Call   *Safe.* This Oakland-based district is one of the safest Democratic seats in the nation. But, census data show it to be one of the slower growing in the Bay Area and will need to pick up some population. Lee will hold this seat as long as she wants it.

THE PEOPLE: Pop. 2000: 597,285; Pop. 1990: 573,669, up 4.1% 1990–2000. 41.3% White, 26.2% Black, 17.4% Asian, 0.6% Amer. Indian, 0.4% Hawaiian, 5.2% Two+ races, 8.9% Other; 17.3% Hispanic Origin.

2000 Presidential Vote			**1996 Presidential Vote**		
Gore (D)	177,840	(79%)	Clinton (D)	156,998	(75%)
Bush (R)	27,154	(12%)	Dole (R)	26,321	(13%)
Nader (Green)	19,243	(9%)	Perot (I)	6,277	(3%)
Others	1,980	(1%)	Others	19,498	(9%)

Rep. Barbara Lee (D)

Elected April 1998, 2d term; b. July 16, 1946, El Paso, TX; home, Oakland; Mills Col., B.A. 1973, U. of CA at Berkeley, M.A. 1975; no religious affiliation; divorced.

Elected Office: CA Assembly, 1990–96; CA Senate, 1996–98.

Professional Career: Chief of Staff, U.S. Rep. Ron Dellums, 1975–87.

DC Office: 426 CHOB 20515, 202-225-2661; Fax: 202-225-9817; Web site: www.house.gov/lee.

District Office: Oakland, 510-763-0370.

Committees: *Financial Services* (17th of 32 D): Domestic Monetary Policy, Technology & Economic Growth; Financial Institutions & Consumer Credit; Housing & Community Opportunity; International Monetary Policy & Trade. *International Relations* (17th of 23 D): Africa; Europe.

Group Ratings

	ADA	ACLU	AFS	LCV	CON	ITIC	NTU	COC	ACU	NTLC	CHC
2000	90	86	100	100	60	35	26	33	4	12	0
1999	100	—	100	94	54	—	34	16	8	—	—

National Journal Ratings

	1999 LIB —	1999 CONS	2000 LIB —	2000 CONS
Economic	73%	26%	81%	16%
Social	87%	0%	94%	0%
Foreign	53%	47%	80%	16%

Key Votes of the 106th Congress

1. Patient Bill of Rights	Y	5. Bar RU-486 $ for FDA	N	9. NATO War in Serbia	Y
2. Accelerate Min. Wage	Y	6. Display 10 Commandments	N	10. Perm. Trade with China	N
3. Strike Ban on Ergo. Stnd.	Y	7. Gun Show Bkgrnd. Checks	Y	11. Debt Relief for 3rd World	Y
4. Ovrd. Estate Tax Veto	N	8. Ban Part.-Birth Abortion	N	12. Drop Cuba Econ. Embargo	Y

Election Results

2000 general	Barbara Lee (D)	182,352	(85%)	($452,812)
	Arneze Washington (R)	21,033	(10%)	
	Other	11,265	(5%)	
2000 primary	Barbara Lee (D)	117,173	(85%)	
	Arneze Washington (R)	13,563	(10%)	
	Other	6,898	(5%)	
1998 general	Barbara Lee (D)	140,722	(83%)	($504,240)
	Claiborne (Clay) Sanders (R)	22,431	(13%)	($9,555)
	Others	6,742	(4%)	

TENTH DISTRICT

In the 1950s, when the streets of San Francisco and Oakland were already crowded, the rolling grasslands on the east of the mountain ridges, over the hill and through the tunnel from Oakland, were still mostly empty. In the years since, they have filled up. Freeways took the first commuters through the Caldecott Tunnel to the woodsy trail-like roads of Orinda and Lafayette; I-580 brought people east from the southern East Bay towns to the Amador Valley and Livermore, site of one of the nation's nuclear laboratories; I-680 running north-south provided a spine for businesses and shopping centers up and down the San Ramon Valley, from burgeoning Concord through Walnut Creek, Danville and Dublin; BART stations in Walnut Creek and Orinda took commuters to downtown San Francisco. Not all this area is filled in yet, and there is resistance to overdevelopment. But what has evolved in this sunny land, shielded by the mountains from the ocean fogs and rains, is an advanced civilization of highly skilled and educated people. Affluent and generally tolerant of—if a little put off by—what happens in San Francisco, they are respectful of economic markets and wary of government, but concerned about preserving a physical environment that is one of America's most pleasant: Livermore voters in 2000 passed a growth control initiative. As Bruce Cain of Berkeley's Institute of Governmental Studies put it, "These are basically secular professionals."

This is the land of the 10th Congressional District of California, a seat created by the redistricting of 1992. It consists almost entirely of the interior portion of the Bay Area, with just a few towns beyond—the suburb of Castro Valley on the East Bay, where population grew 18% in the 1990s, plus the town of Antioch on the San Joaquin River Delta, which had 46% growth over the previous decade and now requires developers to provide two jobs for every home they want to build. This area had been voting Republican for years but had been split up between four Democratic districts. It is now easily the most Republican Bay Area district, but not very Republican by national standards: the senior George Bush won here 58%–42% in 1988, but in 2000 George W. Bush was beaten by Al Gore 51%–45%.

The congresswoman from the 10th District is Ellen Tauscher, a Democrat elected in 1996. Tauscher grew up in New Jersey, where her father ran a grocery store; she won a seat on the New York Stock Exchange at 25, where she was a stock trader and investment banker. In 1989, she and her then-husband, owner of Vanstar (formerly ComputerLand), moved to California. After a difficult childbirth, Tauscher started the ChildCare Registry, the first company to offer (for $140) background information on child-care providers. "Here we are, on the front porch of the 21st Century, and we don't have standards for caring for the most precious things in the world," she said. In 1995 she decided to run against two-term Republican Congressman Bill Baker, a fiscal conservative who was also a tart-tongued conservative on cultural issues. She ran as a moderate Democrat and spent liberally of her own money, some $1.7 million in all. Baker ran ads comparing her to a lottery winner buying a congressional seat. Tauscher's ads called Baker an "extremist" on gun control, abortion and the environment. She claimed not to have special interests supporting her, but union operatives were out working precincts. All of this proved a winning combination, though only barely. Tauscher won 49%–47%.

In the House, Tauscher has a more moderate voting record than other Bay Area Democrats—"Tauscherism," as *Time* called it. She joined the moderate Blue Dog Democrats and the New Democrat Coalition and chaired its entitlement reform task force. As the region's only Transportation and Infrastructure Committee member, she took the lead on behalf of both highway projects in her district and Bay Area transit plans. She claimed credit for $14 million to study a BART extension to Antioch and Livermore, and criticized delay in the approval of highway improvements. She voted for the Republicans' impeachment inquiry resolution and called on Bill Clinton to stop "legal hairsplitting and speak plain English to the American people." She sponsored model child care and school infrastructure bills. Though a junior member of the minority party, she said she had the ability to make bipartisan deals: "I feel like I'm back on Wall Street. If you have a sensory touch that can tell there's a deal in the room—and I have a great one—you can get things done." Alone among Bay Area Democrats, she voted to override Clinton vetoes of the marriage-penalty and estate tax repeals, and she favored Permanent Normal Trade Relations with China. In 2001, she became vice-chair of the Democratic Leadership Council. She showed her centrism and local independence by endorsing Steny Hoyer—against San Franciscan Nancy Pelosi—in the 2000 contest for majority whip, a contest that proved to be academic since Democrats did not win a majority.

Tauscher has had competitive re-election contests. In 1998, Charles Ball, a national-security analyst at the Lawrence Livermore National Laboratory, put together a serious platform and raised $1 million to Tauscher's $1.3 million. The national Republican Party spent another $500,000 on ads attacking Tauscher on taxes. Ball argued that Tauscher's record in Washington was more liberal than she advertised. She won 53%–43%. In 2000 she won 53%–44% against community banker Claude Hutchison, who favored abortion rights and argued that Tauscher neglected local transportation. The Chamber of Commerce endorsed Tauscher. Those were not overwhelming margins, and might suggest trouble ahead.

Cook's Call   *Potentially Competitive.* The most marginal of the Bay Area districts, the 10th is also projected to be the fastest growing in this region. But, with Democrats in complete control of the line drawing process in the state this year, there is an effort underway to help make this seat friendlier for the New Democrat Tauscher. Tauscher has never won big here, but in a district where Gore took just 51% in 2000, her showing was just about as good as any Democrat could do here. Still, Tauscher could remain an attractive target for Republicans.

THE PEOPLE: Pop. 2000: 713,341; Pop. 1990: 571,979, up 24.7% 1990–2000. 77.2% White, 3.7% Black, 9.3% Asian, 0.5% Amer. Indian, 0.3% Hawaiian, 4.4% Two+ races, 4.6% Other; 12.1% Hispanic Origin.

2000 Presidential Vote

Gore (D)	161,773	(51%)
Bush (R)	141,285	(45%)
Nader (Green)	9,719	(3%)
Others	2,368	(1%)

1996 Presidential Vote

Clinton (D)	138,386	(48%)
Dole (R)	122,296	(43%)
Perot (I)	17,930	(6%)
Others	8,375	(3%)

Rep. Ellen Tauscher (D)

Elected 1996, 3d term; b. Nov. 15, 1951, Newark, NJ; home, Alamo; Seton Hall U., B.A. 1973; Catholic; divorced.

Professional Career: Wall Street Invest. Banker, 1974–88, NYSE member, 1977–79; Founder & CEO, Registry Cos., 1992–96.

DC Office: 1122 LHOB 20515, 202-225-1880; Fax: 202-225-5914; Web site: www.house.gov/tauscher.

District Offices: Antioch, 925-757-7187; Dublin, 925-829-0813; Walnut Creek, 925-932-8899.

Committees: *Armed Services* (20th of 28 D): Military Personnel; Military Procurement. *Transportation & Infrastructure* (21st of 34 D): Aviation; Highways & Transit.

Group Ratings

	ADA	ACLU	AFS	LCV	CON	ITIC	NTU	COC	ACU	NTLC	CHC
2000	70	79	57	100	24	94	33	71	20	24	7
1999	100	—	83	81	51	—	13	68	8	—	—

National Journal Ratings

	1999 LIB	—	1999 CONS		2000 LIB	—	2000 CONS
Economic	57%	—	42%		60%	—	40%
Social	73%	—	26%		74%	—	24%
Foreign	68%	—	30%		80%	—	16%

Key Votes of the 106th Congress

1. Patient Bill of Rights	Y	5. Bar RU-486 $ for FDA	N	9. NATO War in Serbia	Y
2. Accelerate Min. Wage	Y	6. Display 10 Commandments	N	10. Perm. Trade with China	Y
3. Strike Ban on Ergo. Stnd.	Y	7. Gun Show Bkgrnd. Checks	Y	11. Debt Relief for 3rd World	Y
4. Ovrd. Estate Tax Veto	Y	8. Ban Part.-Birth Abortion	N	12. Drop Cuba Econ. Embargo	Y

Election Results

2000 general	Ellen Tauscher (D)	160,429	(53%)	($1,540,830)
	Claude B. Hutchison Jr. (R)	134,863	(44%)	($1,127,901)
	Other	9,527	(3%)	
2000 primary	Ellen Tauscher (D)	110,702	(54%)	
	Claude B. Hutchison Jr. (R)	36,257	(18%)	
	Gordon Blake (R)	30,532	(15%)	
	Dennis M. Kilian (R)	21,039	(10%)	
	Other	5,324	(3%)	
1998 general	Ellen Tauscher (D)	127,134	(53%)	($1,355,053)
	Charles Ball (R)	103,299	(43%)	($1,066,829)
	Others	7,376	(3%)	

ELEVENTH DISTRICT

People from back East looking for clues about California might consider avoiding Beverly Hills and Nob Hill and taking a look at Stockton. For Stockton, just 50 miles south of Sacramento, is in the middle of the Central Valley, which saw much of California's most rapid growth during the past two decades. This is not a new part of the state: Stockton was a Gold Rush trading town founded in 1847, named after Robert Stockton, the second U.S. military governor of California, who captured Santa Barbara and Los Angeles from Mexico and proclaimed California United States territory. The Central Valley, criss-crossed with railroads and canals, became one of the world's greatest agriculture areas; the San Joaquin River channel was deepened to 37 feet and Stockton today is the Central Valley's ocean port. The rich farming attracted immigrants from all over: Mexicans coming up Route 99 joined North Dakotans flocking to the town of Lodi; Italian and Yugoslav immigrants bringing their Old World crops; Yankees and Okies bringing their distinct churches and systems of belief; and now Southeast Asian refugees crowd into the older streets of Stockton. In the 1990s, Stockton positioned itself to take advantage of the region's economic strength by turning into a warehouse and distribution center for northern California. This growth came as farms were squeezed by inexorable factors: the move toward reducing water subsidies, the difficulty of attracting migrant workers for harvests, declines in crop prices. And it has brought sky-high housing prices to the San Francisco Bay area; Bay area workers with modest incomes are increasingly buying cheaper houses around Tracy and Stockton and commuting to work on I-580. In 2001, building permits in the county were up 80% from two years earlier.

The 11th Congressional District includes Stockton and most of surrounding San Joaquin County, plus the southern part of Sacramento County, an area of farms and a few subdivisions, dredge tailings and marshy, rich-soiled islands in the delta of the Sacramento and San Joaquin Rivers. This was once a solidly Democratic area; towns near Stockton were the home base of two House Democratic whips, John McFall, who was defeated for re-election in 1980, and Tony Coelho, who resigned in 1989. But the Valley has increasingly moved to the right, angry at the intrusiveness of federal environmental regulators, puzzled by the cultural liberalism of Bay Area and Los Angeles Democrats. George W. Bush carried seven of the nine congressional districts partially or wholly in the Valley; his margin in the 11th was 50%–47%.

The congressman from the 11th District is Richard Pombo, a Republican elected when the district was created in 1992 and one of the leaders of the property rights movement in Congress. Pombo grew up in Tracy, attended Cal Poly Pomona, worked on the family cattle ranch; he often wears a cowboy hat and boots, some of which are eel and ostrich skin. "I'm not going to fit in too well, because I'm anything but politically correct," Pombo described himself. With a nearly perfectly conservative voting record, he has tilted with environmentalists on the Resources Committee and with subsidy advocates on Agriculture (most Valley crops are not subsidized). In the majority, Resources Chairman Don Young put him in charge of rewriting the Endangered Species Act; he held hearings with stories of absurd regulations (one Fish and Wildlife Service official wanted to reduce the speed limit on a section of I-10 to 15 miles an hour to avoid bothering a rare fly) and produced a bill to compensate landowners whose property values declined greatly. In 1996, he and liberal Republican Sherwood Boehlert co-chaired a Speaker's Task Force on the Environment, and in fact the Republican 104th produced more environmental legislation than the Democratic 103d—the Safe Drinking Water, Coastal Zone Management, Food Quality Protection and Water Resources Development Acts, plus Freedom to Farm conservation sections and Everglades protection amendments. He opposed Robert Matsui's proposal for higher levees on the American River, and his suit to have the American Heritage Rivers program declared unconstitutional was rejected by the Supreme Court. He opposed Don Young's annual $3 billion conservation fund proposal, viewing government as "not a welcome neighbor." As chairman of the Livestock and Horticulture Subcommittee, Pombo remained unhappy with his lack of success in revising other laws affecting farmers, including pesticide regulation and guest-worker limits, though he conceded that one benefit of gridlock is it "forces you to go slow and deliberately." Environmentalists complained that his pesticide bill was written by a chemical industry lobbyist, but Pombo denied any ethical impropriety. Pombo eventually found common ground with Barney Frank on one issue: winning $24 million for a military base in Portugal's Azores. Pombo's grandparents came from the islands, as have many of Frank's constituents.

Pombo first won the seat by defeating a moderate in the 1992 Republican primary and then beating the wife of state Senator John Garamendi 48%–46%. He has not had serious competition since. But Democrats control redistricting, and some tweaking of the district lines could perhaps prompt a serious challenge.

Cook's Call   *Probably Safe.* Considered a swing district after it was redistricted in 1991, this Central Valley seat has been trending more Republican over the decade (as has most of the Central Valley). Clinton won the here by 2 % in 1992, but Bush won here by 3 % in 2000. Pombo looks well positioned for 2002.

THE PEOPLE: Pop. 2000: 684,178; Pop. 1990: 571,650, up 19.7% 1990–2000. 60.4% White, 6.6% Black, 11% Asian, 1.1% Amer. Indian, 0.4% Hawaiian, 6% Two+ races, 14.5% Other; 27.8% Hispanic Origin.

2000 Presidential Vote
Bush (R) 106,466 (50%)
Gore (D) 99,899 (47%)
Nader (Green) 5,792 (3%)
Others 2,142 (1%)

1996 Presidential Vote
Clinton (D) 85,117 (46%)
Dole (R) 84,303 (45%)
Perot (I) 12,373 (7%)
Others 4,187 (2%)

Rep. Richard Pombo (R)

Elected 1992, 5th term; b. Jan. 8, 1961, Tracy; home, Tracy; CA Polytechnic Inst., 1979–82; Catholic; married (Annette).

Elected Office: Tracy City Cncl., 1990–92.

Professional Career: Cattle rancher; Co-founder, Citizens Land Alliance, 1986.

DC Office: 2411 RHOB 20515, 202-225-1947; Fax: 202-226-0861; Web site: www.house.gov/pombo.

District Office: Stockton, 209-951-3091.

Committees: *Agriculture* (4th of 27 R): Department Operations, Oversight, Nutrition & Forestry; Livestock & Horticulture (Chmn.). *Resources* (11th of 28 R): Fisheries Conservation, Wildlife & Oceans; Water & Power. *Transportation & Infrastructure* (22d of 42 R): Highways & Transit; Water Resources & Environment.

Group Ratings

	ADA	ACLU	AFS	LCV	CON	ITIC	NTU	COC	ACU	NTLC	CHC
2000	5	36	14	0	43	78	66	76	100	88	87
1999	5	—	0	6	15	—	59	88	100	—	—

National Journal Ratings

	1999 LIB	—	1999 CONS		2000 LIB	—	2000 CONS
Economic	16%	—	78%		0%	—	94%
Social	25%	—	72%		0%	—	79%
Foreign	10%	—	86%		0%	—	88%

Key Votes of the 106th Congress

1. Patient Bill of Rights	N	5. Bar RU-486 $ for FDA	Y	9. NATO War in Serbia	N
2. Accelerate Min. Wage	N	6. Display 10 Commandments	Y	10. Perm. Trade with China	N
3. Strike Ban on Ergo. Stnd.	N	7. Gun Show Bkgrnd. Checks	N	11. Debt Relief for 3rd World	N
4. Ovrd. Estate Tax Veto	Y	8. Ban Part.-Birth Abortion	Y	12. Drop Cuba Econ. Embargo	N

Election Results

2000 general	Richard Pombo (R)	120,635	(58%)	($451,956)
	Tom Y. Santos (D)	79,539	(38%)	($12,510)
	Other	8,433	(4%)	
2000 primary	Richard Pombo (R)	87,160	(61%)	
	Tom Y. Santos (D)	30,817	(22%)	
	Robert L. Figueroa (D)	19,152	(13%)	
	Other	5,661	(4%)	
1998 general	Richard Pombo (R)	95,496	(61%)	($517,830)
	Robert L. Figueroa (D)	56,345	(36%)	($12,625)
	Others	3,608	(2%)	

TWELFTH DISTRICT

Running south from San Francisco is the Peninsula, which connects the city with the mainland of the United States. This is geologically interesting, and active, country: The San Andreas Fault runs just east of the Coast Range, underneath the reservoirs that store San Francisco's water supply. To the west are green mountains running down into the foggy ocean. To the east is a zone of flat land between mountain and bay, an unbroken chain of suburbs and urban settlement, with light industry and salt flats along the bay front, and residential neighborhoods and some commercial strips from the Bayshore Freeway up through the Junipero Serra Freeway atop the mountain ridge. Historically, the Peninsula has seemed separate from San Francisco. Lately, the action has been on the Peninsula, which separates the Silicon Valley workplaces of some of the Bay Area's most productive people from the San Francisco neighborhoods where some of them like to cocoon.

The 12th Congressional District consists of the northern Peninsula suburbs plus the southwest quadrant of San Francisco—the city's middle-income Sunset district, with older houses amid unburied telephone and electric wires, lying on curving hills that were once sand dunes, and affluent St. Francis's Wood. Just to the south, across the San Mateo County line at the southern extension of the BART lines, is Daly City, with substantial numbers of Mexican-Americans and Asians; nearby, South San Francisco proclaims itself "the industrial city" in big letters on San Bruno Mountain near the Bayshore Freeway; the streets lined with boxy houses in San Bruno and Pacifica wind over sweeping hillsides facing cemeteries where many San Franciscans and veterans of Pacific wars are buried. That is the view from one side of the Junipero Serra Freeway; from the other, the vista is of San Francisco Bay, broader than one might expect, and the airport next door, connecting this metropolis with others on the Pacific Rim; to the south is the neat suburban city of San Mateo and, on twisting streets in the hills above the Burlingame Country Club, the rich suburb of Hillsborough, home to much of the city's WASP elite.

This is an ethnically diverse and economically prosperous constituency. Fully 31% of its residents are Asian—the highest of any district outside Hawaii—and another 16% are Hispanic. The economic orientation here was historically toward San Francisco but now is increasingly south toward Silicon Valley. Income levels are, if not among the highest in the country, very far above average. Housing values spiked up in 1999 with the high-tech bubble, to $327,000 in blue collar Daly City and $990,000 in middle-income Burlingame, and office rents were higher than in Manhattan. The political heritage is mostly Democratic, from historic ethnic and labor union ties, and from liberal cultural attitudes. Al Gore carried the 12th 67%–27% in 2000.

The congressman from the 12th District, Tom Lantos, has several distinctions, but none more important than the fact that he is the only Holocaust survivor ever to serve in Congress. Lantos was born in Hungary and as a teenager fought in the underground against the Nazis; he was imprisoned and was one of the Jews saved by Swedish diplomat Raoul Wallenberg. So was his wife Annette, his childhood sweetheart and now his unpaid assistant; these two Holocaust survivors have two daughters and 17 grandchildren. Lantos has shown energy and competence throughout his career. He taught economics at San Francisco State, made money as an investor, appeared on television as a foreign policy expert. He had the political insight to challenge a Republican incumbent in the Peninsula in 1980, a Republican year nationally though not so much here, and he has shown great capacity for publicizing his crusades in congressional hearings and on television. In early 1999, he was featured in the release of a documentary by Steven Spielberg, *The Last Days*, which recounts the Nazis' 1944 destruction of Hungary's Jewish community. "It's been very difficult to watch it," Lantos said of the Oscar-winning film, which he promoted in four cities across the country.

Lantos has spent much of his time in the House on foreign policy and is now ranking minority member on the International Relations Committee. Unlike other Bay Area Democrats, he has not brought to his work an instinctive mistrust of American policy or doubts of American good intentions. He founded the Congressional Human Rights Caucus, focusing on Communist regimes as well as the right-wing dictatorships other liberal Democrats denounced. He is among the most enthusiastic supporters of Israel and called for economic sanctions against Iraq back in 1988 for its gassing of the Kurds; he continued to support sanctions against Iraq in 2000 when other Bay area members tried to end them. During the collapse of Communism, Lantos stayed in close touch with Eastern Europe, especially Hungary, as new democracies rose up; in 1990 he was the first American official to visit Albania since 1946. He sponsored the first U.S. aid to the newly free countries of Eastern Europe and strongly backed NATO expansion. He advocated a more active American role in Bosnia and other parts of the former Yugoslavia. He has attacked human rights violations in China, opposes normalizing of Chinese trade status and in September

2000 sponsored a resolution urging that Beijing not be selected as the site of the 2008 Olympics. Lantos has been part of the U.S. delegations to the European Parliament and the United Nations; he became friends with Secretary General Kofi Annan, whose wife Nane Annan is Raoul Wallenberg's niece. He sponsored the bust of Wallenberg, which was unveiled in the Capitol in 1995, and the conferring of honorary U.S. citizenship on him—the only person besides Winston Churchill ever so honored. And he has worked with the Swedish-Russian Working Group and others to discover the truth about Wallenberg, which the Soviets concealed for decades. He and Republican Chris Smith have sponsored a Torture Victims Relief Act and, with other colleagues, a Human Rights Information Act. In May 2001, he and Republican Henry Hyde passed an amendment in the House to withhold $244 million in U.N. arrears after the United States lost its seat on the U.N. Human Rights Commission.

Lantos showed a flair for showmanship as chairman of a Government Operations subcommittee. Unlike almost all other congressional Democrats, he initially pursued Clinton Administration scandals, including the Waco massacre and the handling of FBI files in the White House. But he became a harsh critic when chairman Dan Burton began investigating Bill Clinton's 1996 campaign finance abuses, terming the inquiry authoritarian and dictatorial. Lantos's defense of the Clinton administration grew more heated at a committee hearing when he compared Independent Counsel Donald Smaltz's investigation of former Agriculture Secretary Mike Espy to the conduct of ex-United Nations Secretary General and Nazi war criminal Kurt Waldheim. Republicans, aghast at the comparison, said that Lantos had lost his credibility.

Other Lantos causes include regulation of the owning of wild animals as pets; he invited actresses Tippi Hedren and her daughter Melanie Griffith to a hearing on the subject. Locally, Lantos helped add 1,000 acres to the Golden Gate National Recreation Area and obtained $3.75 million for soundproofing homes in San Bruno and schools in South San Francisco near San Francisco Airport. In 2000 he worked to find a compromise to preserve daytime access to the levees around Redwood Shores for joggers and strollers while protecting the habitat of the California clapper rail and the salt marsh harvest mouse.

Lantos spent $1.7 million on his 1980 and 1982 campaigns and has won easily ever since. Later his fundraising was targeted to his son-in-law Dick Swett, who was elected congressman from New Hampshire in 1990 and 1992, but was defeated in 1994 and lost for the Senate in 1996; Swett served as Bill Clinton's last Ambassador to Denmark.

Cook's Call   *Safe.* Tom Lantos has won effortlessly in this Bay Area district ever since he was first elected in 1980 with just 46%. There have been rumors that the 71-year old Lantos may retire but even then the seat will remain in Democratic hands.

THE PEOPLE: Pop. 2000: 615,370; Pop. 1990: 571,667, up 7.6% 1990–2000. 52.9% White, 2.7% Black, 30.9% Asian, 0.4% Amer. Indian, 1% Hawaiian, 5.2% Two+ races, 6.8% Other; 15.9% Hispanic Origin.

2000 Presidential Vote

Gore (D)	156,791	(67%)
Bush (R)	63,561	(27%)
Nader (Green)	10,914	(5%)
Others	1,482	(1%)

1996 Presidential Vote

Clinton (D)	191,973	(70%)
Dole (R)	58,260	(21%)
Perot (I)	11,994	(4%)
Others	10,291	(4%)

Rep. Tom Lantos (D)

Elected 1980, 11th term; b. Feb. 1, 1928, Budapest, Hungary; home, San Mateo; U. of WA, B.A. 1949, M.A. 1950, U. of CA, Ph.D. 1953; Jewish; married (Annette).

Professional Career: Economist, Bank of America, 1952–53; TV Commentator, San Francisco, 1955–63; Dir. of Intl. Programs, CA St. U., 1962–71; Advisor, U.S. Sen. Joseph R. Biden Jr., 1978–79; Mbr., Pres. Task Force on Defense & Foreign Policy, 1976; Prof., San Francisco St. U., 1950–80.

DC Office: 2217 RHOB 20515, 202-225-3531; Web site: www.house.gov/lantos.

District Office: San Mateo, 650-342-0300.

Committees: *Government Reform* (2d of 19 D): Energy Policy, Natural Resources and Regulatory Affairs; National Security, Veterans' Affairs & Intl. Relations. *International Relations* (RMM of 23 D).

Group Ratings

	ADA	ACLU	AFS	LCV	CON	ITIC	NTU	COC	ACU	NTLC	CHC
2000	85	79	85	93	41	47	23	47	4	6	0
1999	85	—	100	69	25	—	18	14	0	—	—

National Journal Ratings

	1999 LIB	—	1999 CONS		2000 LIB	—	2000 CONS
Economic	83%	—	17%		78%	—	20%
Social	77%	—	23%		79%	—	17%
Foreign	88%	—	11%		85%	—	10%

Key Votes of the 106th Congress

1. Patient Bill of Rights	Y	5. Bar RU-486 $ for FDA	N	9. NATO War in Serbia	Y
2. Accelerate Min. Wage	Y	6. Display 10 Commandments	N	10. Perm. Trade with China	N
3. Strike Ban on Ergo. Stnd.	Y	7. Gun Show Bkgrnd. Checks	Y	11. Debt Relief for 3rd World	Y
4. Ovrd. Estate Tax Veto	N	8. Ban Part.-Birth Abortion	N	12. Drop Cuba Econ. Embargo	Y

Election Results

2000 general	Tom Lantos (D)	158,404	(75%)	($310,957)
	Mike Garza (R)	44,162	(21%)	
	Other	9,990	(5%)	
2000 primary	Tom Lantos (D)	103,807	(74%)	
	Mike Garza (R)	14,165	(10%)	
	Bob Evans (R)	8,274	(6%)	
	James D. Williams Jr. (R)	7,694	(6%)	
	Other	5,886	(4%)	
1998 general	Tom Lantos (D)	128,135	(74%)	($254,400)
	Robert H. Evans Jr. (R)	36,562	(21%)	
	Michael J. Moloney (Lib)	8,515	(5%)	

THIRTEENTH DISTRICT

The East Bay is the workaday, unglamorous side of metropolitan San Francisco—the margin of land perhaps five miles wide between San Francisco Bay and the surprisingly high mountains that rise just to the east. The shoreline is not picturesque, with its closed-down Navy bases, docks, airports and salt evaporators; the Bay Bridge, bisected by Yerba Buena Island, cuts an inspiring figure, but the San Mateo Bridge to the south is at best utilitarian. Sixty years ago, when the shipyards of Richmond and the Navy yard in Oakland were buzzing, the East Bay south of Oakland was still largely uninhabited farm fields. In the postwar years, it filled up, south along Route 17: San Leandro, originally settled by Portuguese, Castro Valley with its Japanese Gardens, Hayward with its Cal State University campus, Union City with its rail yards, and Fremont, home of the famous NUMMI auto plant where Chevrolets and Toyotas are produced together, and of the California School for the Deaf. Underneath is the Hayward Fault, not as famous as the San Andreas, but equally—if not more—hazardous.

The 13th Congressional District is made up of this string of East Bay towns, somewhat lower income than the Peninsula towns across the Bay. The district is racially and ethnically mixed in the California manner. Koreans and other Asians have moved in large numbers to Fremont and other East Bay towns; in 2000 the district was 30% Asian—the second highest Asian percentage in any district outside Hawaii, just behind the 12th district across the Bay—22% Hispanic and 7% black. This has long been a Democratic area, and in the 1990s it became more Democratic than ever: the 13th voted 66%–30% for Al Gore in 2000.

The congressman from the 13th District is Pete Stark, a liberal Democrat and product of the peace movement of the 1960s who in the first half of the 1990s was one of four senior Democratic House committee and subcommittee chairmen elected from four East Bay districts. Since then, two of them retired and Stark has been a senior member of the minority. Stark grew up in Wisconsin, served in the Air Force, got an engineering degree at MIT and an M.B.A. at Berkeley and in 1961 started a bank in Walnut Creek. He attracted attention, and accounts, all over the Bay Area when he put a giant peace symbol atop the bank headquarters and peace symbols on all checks. In 1972 he ran for Congress, spending his own money freely; he beat an 81-year-old incumbent in the primary 56%–22% and held on in the McGovern undertow to win the general with 53%. By his third term he had a safe seat back home and was on Ways and Means, on which he now is the second ranking Democrat; he chaired its Health Subcommittee from 1985–95.

Stark brought to that post a desire to use government powers to make health care more available. He has not always been successful on policy. He did expand Medicare benefits and provided COBRA benefit continuation to younger workers. But his major achievement was the Catastrophic Health Care Act of 1988, which created a new benefit for Medicare recipients but was repealed by an overwhelming vote in 1989 after an outpouring of public protest: the problem was that its tax on the high-income elderly was very unpopular while benefits seemed puny. He has supported universal health insurance in various forms. That was overtaken by the Clinton health care plan, from whose formulation Stark and other members complained that they were shut out. In 1994, he worked his subcommittee hard, eventually producing a majority for a bill that modified the Clinton plan with some Stark features; that narrowly passed Ways and Means. But, with moderate Democrats fearful of its big-government features, it lacked majority support in the House and did not reach the floor.

In the minority since then, he has mostly criticized and found few areas of agreement with Republicans. He was one of two votes against the 1996 Kennedy-Kassebaum bill, on the grounds it did not include mental health coverage and extended patent protection for a drug. But he worked more amicably with fellow Californian Bill Thomas and called his 1997 Medicare bill "not bad," except for its provisions encouraging medical savings accounts. He argues that Medicare would save money if it could buy drugs at the prices the Veterans Administration pays, saying, "Drug industry charges to Medicare are a scandal." He won enactment in November 2000 of needle safety legislation that requires medical facilities to use safer syringes and blood-drawing devices. When George W. Bush backed prescription-drug coverage for seniors, Stark said in January 2001 Congress should discard his proposal for a stopgap program run by states and advance one with more control by Washington. On other issues in 2000, he was one of two House members to vote against repeal of the 3% telephone excise tax, and—citing church-state conflict—he was the only one to oppose a resolution condemning the Vatican's reduced influence at the United Nations.

Stark has been re-elected by wide margins, and his insouciance continues. When he missed the 1999 swearing-in because he stayed in Hawaii with his three-year-old who had an ear infection, he told a reporter, "I didn't think it made a difference if I was there." He supported Bill Bradley in the 2000 presidential primary; referring to the 44 million Americans without health care, Stark called him "the only candidate who's been willing to say this is a problem we must address." The continuing rapid population growth plus redistricting may shrink some of his lines, but should not cause problems. A bigger question may be whether, at age 70, he runs again.

Cook's Call   *Safe.* Since winning this seat in 1972 with 53%, Pete Stark has not had a truly competitive race. Like so many other Bay area districts, the 13th is congenitally Democratic, and when the 68-year old Stark decides to retire, this seat should remain safely in Democratic hands.

THE PEOPLE: Pop. 2000: 678,177; Pop. 1990: 572,333, up 18.5% 1990–2000. 44.5% White, 7.4% Black, 30.1% Asian, 0.6% Amer. Indian, 0.9% Hawaiian, 6.2% Two+ races, 10.3% Other; 22.1% Hispanic Origin.

2000 Presidential Vote

Gore (D)	127,994	(66%)
Bush (R)	57,042	(30%)
Nader (Green)	5,815	(3%)
Others	2,056	(1%)

1996 Presidential Vote

Clinton (D)	115,633	(62%)
Dole (R)	51,084	(28%)
Perot (I)	13,085	(7%)
Others	5,843	(3%)

Rep. Fortney H. (Pete) Stark (D)

Elected 1972, 15th term; b. Nov. 11, 1931, Milwaukee, WI; home, Fremont; MIT, B.S. 1953, U. of CA at Berkeley, M.B.A. 1960; Unitarian; married (Deborah).

Military Career: Air Force, 1955–57.

Professional Career: Founder, Beacon Savings & Loan Assn., 1961; Founder & Pres., Security Natl. Bank, Walnut Creek, 1963–72.

DC Office: 239 CHOB 20515, 202-225-5065; Fax: 202-226-3805; Web site: www.house.gov/stark.

District Office: Fremont, 510-494-1388.

Committees: *Ways & Means* (2d of 17 D): Health (RMM); Human Resources. *Joint Committee on Taxation* (5th of 5 Reps.). *Joint Economic Committee* (7th of 10 Reps.).

Group Ratings

	ADA	ACLU	AFS	LCV	CON	ITIC	NTU	COC	ACU	NTLC	CHC
2000	95	86	100	79	97	21	32	25	4	13	0
1999	95	—	100	88	91	—	39	8	8	—	—

National Journal Ratings

	1999 LIB —	1999 CONS		2000 LIB —	2000 CONS
Economic	79% —	20%		80% —	20%
Social	87% —	0%		94% —	0%
Foreign	54% —	46%		80% —	16%

Key Votes of the 106th Congress

1. Patient Bill of Rights	Y	5. Bar RU-486 $ for FDA	N	9. NATO War in Serbia	Y
2. Accelerate Min. Wage	Y	6. Display 10 Commandments	N	10. Perm. Trade with China	N
3. Strike Ban on Ergo. Stnd.	Y	7. Gun Show Bkgrnd. Checks	Y	11. Debt Relief for 3rd World	Y
4. Ovrd. Estate Tax Veto	N	8. Ban Part.-Birth Abortion	N	12. Drop Cuba Econ. Embargo	Y

Election Results

2000 general	Fortney H. (Pete) Stark (D)	129,012	(70%)	($414,879)
	James R. Goetz (R)	44,499	(24%)	
	Other	9,635	(5%)	
2000 primary	Fortney H. (Pete) Stark (D)	77,905	(69%)	
	James R. Goetz (R)	22,488	(20%)	
	Saundra Duffy (R)	7,736	(7%)	
	Other	5,194	(5%)	
1998 general	Fortney H. (Pete) Stark (D)	101,671	(71%)	($313,711)
	James R. Goetz (R)	38,050	(27%)	
	Others	3,066	(2%)	

FOURTEENTH DISTRICT

Silicon Valley is a place and a state of mind, an area that had no distinctive identity two decades ago but which people all over the world now recognize, admire and try to imitate. For Silicon

Valley has been the center of America's computer industry, a place where creative minds have developed products that large corporations never thought would sell. Its beginnings can be traced back to 1939, when William Hewlett and David Packard started their electronics firm in a Palo Alto garage, or perhaps to 1891, when Stanford University was founded on the estate of a California governor and senator.

But Silicon Valley did not achieve critical mass until the late 1970s and early 1980s, when Steve Jobs started Apple in a garage in Cupertino with the idea of making a computer ordinary people could use, and Gordon Moore, Robert Noyce and Andrew Grove started Intel in nearby Santa Clara to make the microchips that let computers process data much faster than almost anyone thought possible. What follows was suggested by Moore's law: that computer capacity tends to double every 18 months. One revolution has followed another, and not every aspect of the computer business is centered here. Microsoft, routinely disparaged in every Palo Alto espresso shop and bar, is up in Redmond, Washington, and IBM is off in Armonk, New York. But Silicon Valley is where most of the giants, and very much of the creativity, of the high-tech business—as well as the ghosts of dot.coms whose stock has melted down to zero—is based.

Rapidly growing businesses are inherently unstable, but the Valley's enduring advantages have made it amazingly adaptable. One advantage is Stanford, the students it attracts and produces, and fact that it has always encouraged profit-making activity by faculty. Another is venture capital, widely available from innovation-minded old San Francisco money, dispensed mostly from nondescript office buildings on Sand Hill Road off I-280. A third, perhaps the greatest, is that Silicon Valley is the kind of place where smart young innovators like to live. Elite law and medical school graduates head to the prestigious, high-salary jobs of central cities; but techies are free to live in this pleasant, healthy environment. Sheltered by hills from coastal fogs and rains, Silicon Valley boasts a sunny climate with perceptible but gentle seasons, perfect for year-round outdoor sports; there may well be more jogging trails and bicycle paths here than anywhere else in the country. There is a sort of pure Americana here: these communities were rustic but never poor, rural but never bigoted, country-like but still easily accessible to the luxuries of civilization. People here were ahead of the rest of the nation in fighting for the environment, in favoring natural over processed foods, and in indulging in regular exercise. Innovation extends even to government. The city of Sunnyvale, with its results-oriented management and flexible job definitions in the semi-conductor, aerospace and biotechnology firms, is the hero of David Osborne's *Reinventing Government*. Physically, Silicon Valley's office parks are unremarkable. Yet this is where computer hackers have turned tinkerers' dreams into multi-billion dollar companies and innovators have produced business after business that out-think public planners and out-compete subsidized foreign consortiums.

The 14th Congressional District coincides almost exactly with Silicon Valley. Though it reaches to the Pacific and homey Half Moon Bay with its pumpkin farms, the 14th's population lies mostly on the Bay side of the mountains, in the strip of flat land from Belmont, not far south of San Francisco Airport, through Redwood City, Menlo Park, Palo Alto (home of Stanford), Mountain View, Sunnyvale and Cupertino (home of Apple). There are a few ultra-wealthy enclaves, with real estate prices pushed skyward into the multiple millions by entrepreneurs' paper profits: Atherton, with its stone-walled lots; Woodside, with its 1850s country store and mansions dotting the hills; Portola Valley and Los Altos Hills, with stark contemporary homes overlooking the Bay. The 14th's political heritage is progressive: a sort of environmentalist, dovish, healthy-lifestyle, but entrepreneurial Republicanism, typified by former Congressmen Pete McCloskey (1967–83), Ed Zschau (1983–87) and Tom Campbell (1989–93), each of whom ran unsuccessfully for the Senate. But this kind of Republican has become an endangered species (Campbell lost his second Senate bid in 2000 and is now a Stanford law professor again), and in the 1990s Silicon Valley has become very Democratic. It is liberal on cultural issues and was enchanted by the attentions it received from Bill Clinton and Al Gore, and even forgiving when Clinton vetoed the securities litigation bill high-tech entrepreneurs wanted at the behest of trial lawyer William Lerach; perhaps it helped that this was the one Clinton veto Congress overrode. Despite its Republican heritage, the 14th voted 55%–45% for Michael Dukakis over the older George Bush in 1988. In 2000 it was no contest: Al Gore carried the district 62%–32%.

The congresswoman from the 14th District is Anna Eshoo, a Democrat elected in 1992. Born back East, she is the only member of Congress of Assyrian descent. She was a full time homemaker, then chaired the San Mateo County Democratic Party and was elected to the San Mateo Board of Supervisors in 1982. In 1988, she ran for the House, facing Tom Campbell, already a Stanford Law professor and economics Ph.D. The two spent a total of $2.5 million, and Eshoo was the first congressional candidate to distribute videotapes to voters—a slick video with hip music, showing her in a postmodern office, telling voters that the Silicon Valley, unlike Orange County or Iowa, should be represented by someone special. Campbell won 52%–46%. But in 1992 he ran for the Senate and Eshoo ran for the House. In the primary she beat an assemblyman redistricted out of his seat at age 30, by 40%–36%. In the general, she distributed a 58-page booklet of her issue positions and boasted of her work on setting up a managed-competition health plan for county government; she outspent her Republican opponent and while George Bush had only 26% of the vote here, Eshoo won 57%–39%.

In the House Eshoo's voting record is solidly liberal. She was a bit nervous in 1993 about supporting the Clinton budget and tax package, which hit this high-income area hard, and hesitated long before supporting NAFTA and fast track. In the Republican Congress she has crossed the aisle—sometimes to the dismay of liberal Democrats and consumerists—to work successfully for several bills: securities litigation reform (including the 1996 bill passed over Bill Clinton's veto and the 1998 bill taking cases out of state courts), liability relief for Y2K computer problems, FDA reform, in which she focused on gaining quicker regulatory approval for new medical devices from the biotechnology industry, and Permanent Normal Trade Relations with China. In 2000, she co-sponsored a law to extend Medicaid coverage to low-income women with breast or cervical cancer. She initially supported estate-tax repeal, but switched and voted against overriding Clinton's veto. In telecommunications reform she passed an amendment barring the FCC from setting a standard for cable compatibility and from establishing gatekeeper technology for home automation systems. She sought looser controls on high-tech exports, and opposed the FASB accounting board proposal to charge stock options against earnings. She sponsored a bill to improve the safety of imported fruits and vegetables and got $10 million to purchase Bair Island for the Don Edwards San Francisco Bay National Wildlife Refuge. Responding to the state's electricity crisis in January 2001, she co-sponsored with Republican Duncan Hunter a bill to give the Secretary of Energy authority to cap "unreasonable" prices on the wholesale market.

Eshoo has not been seriously challenged for reelection. Ironically, her most visible appearance in a campaign "attack" ad may have come in 2000, when the National Republican Congressional Committee mistakenly included her photo in a spot that was attacking Shelley Berkeley of Nevada. Democrats control redistricting, and with slow-growth zoning policies keeping population growth in the Bay area steady, district lines will not have to be changed much.

Cook's Call   *Safe.* This affluent Silicon Valley district had routinely elected culturally liberal but pro-business Republicans for almost three decades; since 1992, however, voters here have taken to electing Anna Eshoo easily. Without Eshoo on the ballot, it's easy to see how a moderate to liberal Republican could win this seat but it's highly unlikely that she will ever be unseated.

THE PEOPLE: Pop. 2000: 615,917; Pop. 1990: 571,058, up 7.9% 1990–2000. 64.9% White, 3.2% Black, 18.9% Asian, 0.4% Amer. Indian, 0.8% Hawaiian, 3.8% Two+ races, 8.1% Other; 17.2% Hispanic Origin.

2000 Presidential Vote

Gore (D)	150,035	(62%)
Bush (R)	77,773	(32%)
Nader (Green)	10,645	(4%)
Others	2,886	(1%)

1996 Presidential Vote

Clinton (D)	137,561	(58%)
Dole (R)	73,302	(31%)
Perot (I)	13,939	(6%)
Others	13,193	(6%)

Rep. Anna G. Eshoo (D)

Elected 1992, 5th term; b. Dec. 13, 1942, New Britain, CT; home, Atherton; Canada Col., A.A. 1975; Catholic; divorced.

Elected Office: San Mateo Cnty. Bd. of Supervisors, 1982–92, Pres., 1986.

Professional Career: Chmn., San Mateo Cnty Dem. Party, 1980; Chief of Staff, CA Assembly Speaker McCarthy, 1981.

DC Office: 205 CHOB 20515, 202-225-8104; Fax: 202-225-8890; Web site: www-eshoo.house.gov.

District Office: Palo Alto, 650-323-2984.

Committees: *Energy & Commerce* (12th of 26 D): Commerce, Trade & Consumer Protection; Health; Tele-communications & The Internet.

Group Ratings

	ADA	ACLU	AFS	LCV	CON	ITIC	NTU	COC	ACU	NTLC	CHC
2000	75	86	57	100	88	94	33	55	8	12	0
1999	95	—	83	94	87	—	26	28	4	—	—

National Journal Ratings

	1999 LIB	—	1999 CONS		2000 LIB	—	2000 CONS
Economic	73%	—	26%		78%	—	22%
Social	82%	—	17%		78%	—	21%
Foreign	78%	—	17%		85%	—	10%

Key Votes of the 106th Congress

1. Patient Bill of Rights	Y	5. Bar RU-486 $ for FDA	N	9. NATO War in Serbia	Y
2. Accelerate Min. Wage	Y	6. Display 10 Commandments	N	10. Perm. Trade with China	Y
3. Strike Ban on Ergo. Stnd.	Y	7. Gun Show Bkgrnd. Checks	Y	11. Debt Relief for 3rd World	Y
4. Ovrd. Estate Tax Veto	N	8. Ban Part.-Birth Abortion	N	12. Drop Cuba Econ. Embargo	Y

Election Results

2000 general	Anna G. Eshoo (D)	161,720	(70%)	($642,146)
	Bill Quraishi (R)	59,338	(26%)	
	Other	9,204	(4%)	
2000 primary	Anna G. Eshoo (D)	111,136	(71%)	
	Bill Quraishi (R)	17,817	(11%)	
	Craig L. DeLue (R)	11,662	(7%)	
	Henry E. (Bud) Manzler (R)	11,453	(7%)	
	Other	5,314	(3%)	
1998 general	Anna G. Eshoo (D)	129,663	(69%)	($450,368)
	John C. (Chris) Haugen (R)	53,719	(28%)	($35,529)
	Others	5,528	(3%)	

FIFTEENTH DISTRICT

The broad valley of Santa Clara County around San Jose a few decades ago was mostly orchards and vineyards. Sheltered by mountains from the chilly ocean fogs, with soil incredibly fertile once it was irrigated, this valley produced peaches, plums, prunes, apricots and grapes and made San Jose half a century ago the nation's biggest fruit-packing center. Today, almost all the orchards have been replaced by subdivisions and shopping centers and office buildings, for Santa Clara County has become a metropolitan area of 1.7 million people. San Jose, with a growing downtown, an arena for its National Hockey League team (the San Jose Sharks), and a population of 895,000 (30% Hispanic and 27% Asian), has become a major American city. Santa Clara County is also the center of Silicon Valley, site of many creative firms that have made the United States the world's computer and microchip industry center, a phenomenon predicted by few if any national policymakers or corporate leaders a quarter-century ago.

The 15th Congressional District of California is made up of the central slice of Santa Clara County, plus, over the mountains to the south, a small portion of Santa Cruz County. Downtown San Jose is in the 16th District to the east, and Silicon Valley towns like Cupertino and Mountain View are in the 14th District to the northwest; the 15th District lies in between. At its northern end, near the salt evaporators and wetlands around San Francisco Bay, is the Great America theme park, not far from where a huge Lockheed plant was once the nation's largest defense contractor. Just to the south is Santa Clara, with its old mission and Santa Clara University. The 15th includes much of the upscale and middle-income neighborhoods of western San Jose, with more than 300,000 people. It also has high-income suburbs nestled in what used to be vineyards beneath the encroaching mountains: Saratoga, Los Gatos, Monte Sereno. After all this settlement, the mountains remain surprisingly wild, a haunt of Ken Kesey's Merry Pranksters in the 1960s, now inhabited with rustic cabins and high-income houses in narrow valleys. Prosperous and pleased with its environment, confident in free-market economics and uneasy about the performance of the public sector, people here have been somewhat more conservative than in other quadrants of the Bay Area. There are fewer singles and gays here than farther north, fewer Mexican-Americans than farther east; Asian Americans are far likelier to be high-income producers than low-income wage earners. But the 1990s trend here, as elsewhere in the Bay Area and in contrast to much of the country, was toward the Democrats. This is a place where any trace of cultural conservatism hurts the Republicans.

The congressman from the 15th District is Democrat Mike Honda, elected in 2000. A Japanese-American, Honda was born in Walnut Creek, and he spent his early childhood in a World War Two internment camp in Colorado. He received undergraduate and master's degrees from San Jose State University. From 1978 to 1986, Honda was a principal at two area elementary schools, and served on the San Jose Unified School Board and the Santa Clara County Board of Supervisors. In 1996, he was elected to the first of two terms in the California Assembly. He worked to secure an apology from Japan for its wartime atrocities against other Asian nations. In 2000 iconoclastic Republican 15th district Congressman Tom Campbell decided to run against Senator Dianne Feinstein; the authorities at Stanford Law School had told him he would lose tenure if he stayed in Congress, so instead of winning another term in the House as he could easily have done, he decided to gamble and win either the Senate or Stanford. Predictably, Stanford won.

At first Honda was reluctant to run for the House, even though California's term limits meant that if he won another term in the Assembly it would be his last. Days before the filing deadline, he told supporters that he would not run for the open seat. But persuasive telephone calls from several leading House Democrats and, finally, from Bill Clinton changed his mind. "All the pieces were not in place, but they are coming together now," he said in explaining his decision to run. One reason for his initial reluctance was the prospect of running against former Carter Administration Pentagon official Bill Peacock, a venture capitalist who was ready to spend $1 million of his own money and had secured significant endorsements, including that of the mayor of San Jose. But this was no contest: Honda won the March primary with 67% of the votes cast for Democrats, to 24% for Peacock. Moreover, 60% of all votes cast went to Democrats and only 40% to Republicans.

His Republican opponent was Jim Cunneen, a well-regarded Republican assemblyman whose state assembly district was from the heart of the congressional seat, while much of Honda's assembly district was in the neighboring 16th district. Cunneen was a protege of Campbell and was strongly supported by national Republican leaders, and the contest seemed to be one of the year's most competitive. Cunneen favored abortion rights, gun control, environmental groups' priorities—the liberal positions on cultural issues so popular in metropolitan California—and as a former global corporate affairs manager for Applied Materials was able to get support from many Silicon Valley capitalists. He tried to depict the contest as a referendum on the old economy versus the new economy. After the primary, despite his close ties to organized labor, Honda supported Permanent Normal Trade Relations with China—a politically shrewd move to connect with the high-tech industry. Bill Clinton honored his pledge to campaign for him. Honda reached out to the Democratic base by talking about the fight for social justice and calling for more federal aid to education. In the closing days, the contest turned ugly as Honda blasted Republican mailers that depicted him in a jail cell background, and Cunneen attacked Democratic ads that misled voters on his views on abortion. In November the 15th district voted 57%–38% for Al Gore—this was actually the second best Republican showing in the Bay area—and 54%–42% for Honda.

In the House, Honda won seats on the Budget and Transportation Committee. Democrats control redistricting, and can adjust the district boundaries to help Honda in 2002.

Cook's Call   *Probably safe.* Mike Honda's impressive 12 point victory over a well-funded moderate Republican should make even the most ambitious Republican candidates rethink a challenge to Honda in 2002. Not as Democratic as the nearby 14th or 16th Districts, the 15th still has a serious Democratic core and gave Gore a 19-point margin of victory in 2002. Should Honda stray too far from the moderate values of this district, the right Republican could give him a real race. For now, however, Republicans may want to put their efforts in more hospitable districts than this one.

THE PEOPLE: Pop. 2000: 612,416; Pop. 1990: 572,360, up 7% 1990–2000. 69.5% White, 2.1% Black, 17.6% Asian, 0.5% Amer. Indian, 0.3% Hawaiian, 4.6% Two+ races, 5.4% Other; 13.3% Hispanic Origin.

2000 Presidential Vote			1996 Presidential Vote		
Gore (D)	138,407	(57%)	Clinton (D)	125,438	(53%)
Bush (R)	92,230	(38%)	Dole (R)	83,846	(35%)
Nader (Green)	10,117	(4%)	Perot (I)	17,506	(7%)
Others	3,477	(1%)	Others	11,155	(5%)

Rep. Mike Honda (D)

Elected 2000, 1st term; b. June 27, 1941, Walnut Creek; home, San Jose; San Jose St. U., B.S. 1969, B.A. 1970, M.A. 1973; Protestant; married (Jeanne).

Elected Office: San Jose Unified Schl. Bd., 1981–90; Santa Clara Cnty. Bd. of Supervisors, 1990–96; CA Assembly, 1996–2000.

Professional Career: Peace Corps, 1965–67; Elem. schl. principal, 1978–90.

DC Office: 503 CHOB 20515, 202-225-2631; Fax: 202-225-2699; Web site: www.house.gov/honda.

District Office: San Jose, 408-244-8085.

Committees: *Budget* (16th of 20 D). *Science* (22d of 22 D): Research. *Transportation & Infrastructure* (33d of 34 D): Aviation; Highways & Transit; Water Resources & Environment.

Group Ratings and Key Votes: Newly Elected

Election Results

2000 general	Mike Honda (D)	128,545	(54%)	($2,125,541)	
	Jim Cunneen (R)	99,866	(42%)	($1,429,904)	
	Other	8,493	(4%)		
2000 primary	Mike Honda (D)	62,876	(39%)		
	Jim Cunneen (R)	53,282	(33%)		
	Bill Peacock (D)	22,499	(14%)		
	Dale C. Mead (R)	8,638	(5%)		
	Other	12,979	(8%)		
1998 general	Tom Campbell (R)	111,876	(61%)	($791,634)	
	Dick Lane (D)	70,059	(38%)	($15,484)	
	Others	2,851	(2%)		

SIXTEENTH DISTRICT

With more people than San Francisco, higher per capita income than San Diego, a tradition of high-tech innovation that rivals any on earth, and a major league sports team, San Jose has great claims on national attention and respect. Yet San Jose does not bulk as large in the national consciousness as it should. At the southern end of the Bay, it remains in the shadow. San Francisco is every tourist's idea of a city: geographically compact, with picturesque public transportation, old-time and new immigrant groups, an economy historically based on heavy industry and sea trade, a large city bureaucracy symbolized by a monumental city hall. San Jose is quite different. It got its start as a farm-market town, with canneries and fruit-packing operations for the produce from the surrounding fertile plains. It sits not on the Bay, but on the Southern Pacific line above the marshes and salt evaporators; its major transportation arteries are the freeways—U.S. 101, Interstates 280 and 680, California 17—which encircle its revitalized downtown. For many years there were Mexican-Americans here, originally farm workers; now there is a major immigrant presence, with large numbers from Latin America and East and South Asia. Starting in the 1950s, San Jose has grown out in every direction, developers hip-hopping across the farmland, putting up subdivisions faster sometimes than the few city employees could update the street map. Economically, San Jose has been sustained by everything from its traditional agriculture to manufacturing to the high-tech businesses that are centered in Silicon Valley towns just to the west but are omnipresent here: an American city, 21st Century style.

The 16th Congressional District of California consists of the larger part of San Jose, plus its urban fringe to the east and the still agricultural Santa Clara Valley to the south, including Gilroy, the garlic capital of the United States. It includes the old and new downtowns and the heavily Mexican-American areas to the east. This is the most heavily Hispanic district in the Bay Area (40%) and is also heavily Asian (27%), with the largest concentration of Vietnamese in the U.S. Politically, it is solidly Democratic. Its future leanings depend on the trends among Latinos and Asians, who are family-oriented and not necessarily as favorable to big government as blacks.

The congresswoman from the 16th District is Zoe Lofgren, a Democrat elected in 1994. Lofgren grew up in the Bay Area, where her father was a Teamster truck driver and her mother worked for the Machinists Union, went to Stanford and Santa Clara Law School, worked for eight years as a staffer to Congressman Don Edwards; while still a law student, she worked for him while he served on the Judiciary Committee that voted to impeach Richard Nixon. In 1980 she was elected to the Santa Clara County Board of Supervisors, where she spearheaded a 1984 ballot proposition to give local governments control of freeway building and moved the jails from the sheriff's office to the local corrections department. In 1994, when Edwards retired after 32 years in the House, Lofgren ran for the seat. Her chief Democratic opponent, former San Jose Mayor Tom McEnery, started off better known. But Lofgren raised almost twice as much money with the support of the National Women's Political Caucus, the National Organization for Women, EMILY's List, Senator Barbara Boxer and Congresswomen Anna Eshoo and Lynn Woolsey. She won the primary 45%–42%. She easily won the general election and looked forward to putting into effect her ideas for early intervention to fight gun violence and drug abuse and to help underprivileged children.

To her surprise she found herself in the minority. "It has been frustrating because so much of what the Gingrich agenda has been is stuff I don't agree with," she said. Nonetheless she has had some impact, and her voting record, while mostly liberal, includes some free-market positions responsive to local businesses. Despite some conflicts on Latino immigration fairness issues with her chief ally David Dreier, she won an expanded allotment from 115,000 to 195,000 in the H-1B visa program for high-tech workers. She passed an amendment to exempt AIDS drugs from some FDA procedures. A major cause has been to get schools wired to the Internet; she strongly supports the "e-rate" tax on telephones, dedicated to wiring schools to the Internet. She pushed for looser controls on encryption exports, securities litigation reform, and relaxation of trade restraints on supercomputers—all big Silicon Valley causes. She opposed the Communications Decency Act and sponsored a bill to require Internet service providers to offer filtering software. She sponsored a bill (the "Zzzzz's to A's Act") to encourage local school districts to start the school day later, after her own adolescent children became whiny about early starts. In 2000, she backed Bill Clinton on Permanent Normal Trade Relations with China. She voted to repeal the estate tax but, after a presidential phone call, voted against overriding Clinton's veto.

The Clinton impeachment inquiry suddenly put Lofgren in the national spotlight. As the only

Judiciary member to have served as a staffer during the Nixon proceedings, she attempted to put her experience to use. She brought forward the 1974 committee staff report that had set forth grounds for impeachment, and insisted the committee members vote on what is an impeachable offense –though, of course, Judiciary did not have such a vote 24 years before. This argument suited Democrats' partisan purposes, and they included it in their impeachment resolution, which is presumably why it was not acceptable to Chairman Henry Hyde and the Republicans. Impeachment was a "national embarrassment," Lofgren said, and laughed loudly at arguments made by the other side. She argued that a Senate trial would paralyze the nation for six months and prevent the Supreme Court from doing business—which did not turn out to be true. And she said that Clinton's acts did not impair the operations of government. Her stand was popular with her constituents and with the local press.

Lofgren has had no trouble winning reelection. In early 2001, there were reports, denied by Lofgren, of a possible challenge to San Jose Mayor Ron Gonzales—fueled, perhaps, by unhappiness with life in the House minority, or from long-standing clashes with Gonzales. Democrats control redistricting, and the lines will be changed somewhat; some Democratic areas may be shifted to the less heavily Democratic next-door 15th district.

Cook's Call   *Safe.* Another California Democrat with not a re-election woe in the world is Zoe Lofgren. This San Jose-based seat, which gave Gore 64% in 2000, is about as safe as they come.

THE PEOPLE: Pop. 2000: 689,817; Pop. 1990: 571,460, up 20.7% 1990–2000. 41.3% White, 3.6% Black, 26.9% Asian, 1% Amer. Indian, 0.4% Hawaiian, 5.1% Two+ races, 21.7% Other; 39.8% Hispanic Origin.

2000 Presidential Vote		
Gore (D)	108,515	(64%)
Bush (R)	53,502	(32%)
Nader (Green)	4,498	(3%)
Others	2,488	(1%)

1996 Presidential Vote		
Clinton (D)	91,786	(61%)
Dole (R)	43,257	(29%)
Perot (I)	9,659	(6%)
Others	5,195	(3%)

Rep. Zoe Lofgren (D)

Elected 1994, 4th term; b. Dec. 21, 1947, San Mateo; home, San Jose; Stanford U., B.A. 1970, U. of Santa Clara Law Schl., J.D. 1975; Protestant; married (John Collins).

Elected Office: Santa Clara Bd. of Supervisors, 1980–94.

Professional Career: Staff Asst., U.S. Rep. Don Edwards, 1970–78; Practicing atty., 1978–80; Prof., U. of Santa Clara Law Schl., 1981–94.

DC Office: 227 CHOB 20515, 202-225-3072; Fax: 202-225-3336; Web site: zoelofgren.house.gov.

District Office: San Jose, 408-271-8700.

Committees: *Judiciary* (8th of 17 D): Courts, the Internet & Intellectual Property; Immigration & Claims. *Science* (8th of 22 D): Environment, Technology and Standards; Space & Aeronautics. *Standards of Official Conduct* (4th of 5 D).

Group Ratings

	ADA	ACLU	AFS	LCV	CON	ITIC	NTU	COC	ACU	NTLC	CHC
2000	85	86	71	71	88	80	36	52	4	7	7
1999	95	—	100	63	87	—	26	29	4	—	—

National Journal Ratings

	1999 LIB —	1999 CONS		2000 LIB —	2000 CONS
Economic	72% —	28%		76% —	23%
Social	78% —	22%		85% —	14%
Foreign	64% —	35%		92% —	6%

Key Votes of the 106th Congress

1. Patient Bill of Rights	Y	5. Bar RU-486 $ for FDA	N	9. NATO War in Serbia		*
2. Accelerate Min. Wage	Y	6. Display 10 Commandments	N	10. Perm. Trade with China	Y	
3. Strike Ban on Ergo. Stnd.	Y	7. Gun Show Bkgrnd. Checks	Y	11. Debt Relief for 3rd World	Y	
4. Ovrd. Estate Tax Veto	N	8. Ban Part.-Birth Abortion	N	12. Drop Cuba Econ. Embargo	Y	

Election Results

2000 general	Zoe Lofgren (D)	115,118	(72%)	($486,365)
	Horace (Gene) Thayn (R)	37,213	(23%)	
	Other	7,415	(5%)	
2000 primary	Zoe Lofgren (D)	72,515	(72%)	
	Horace (Gene) Thayn (R)	23,652	(23%)	
	Other	4,678	(5%)	
1998 general	Zoe Lofgren (D)	85,503	(73%)	($221,568)
	Horace (Gene) Thayn (R)	27,494	(23%)	
	Others	4,417	(4%)	

SEVENTEENTH DISTRICT

The California coast around Monterey Bay is for many a working definition of paradise. This kernel of California, where Spanish and then Mexicans governed a virtually empty land and Californians set up their first state capital, still makes a fine living off the land and sea, as it has for nearly 150 years. The fields around Salinas supply much of the nation's lettuce and cauliflower, the fields around Castroville supply almost all of its artichokes, and the vast greenhouses around Watsonville supply a goodly portion of its roses. The fishing fleet and 18 canneries of Monterey are no longer a major industry (the last cannery closed 30 years ago) but they have generated a new industry: Cannery Row is refurbished with upscale shops and hotels, and the magnificent Monterey Bay Aquarium is one of California's top tourist destinations. Monterey Bay has become the nation's language learning capital, with the Defense Language Institute, the AT&T Language Line and Cal State's Monterey Bay Center for Intensive Language and Culture on the site of Fort Ord, the Army's old language school, which was closed in the early 1990s. There are other attractions on the Monterey peninsula as well, like the Pebble Beach golf courses and the Del Monte Lodge, and Carmel, whose restrictive laws—no house numbers, no door-to-door mail delivery, no live entertainment, no stop lights, no cutting trees without city council permission—reflect an effort to maintain the atmosphere of 80 years ago, when it really was an artists' colony.

The 17th Congressional District includes all the coast of Monterey Bay and then follows the Big Sur coastline south almost to William Randolph Hearst's castle, San Simeon, past some of the most beautiful scenery in America. The district extends inland, into sunny valleys sheltered from ocean mists, and covers some of the nation's richest farmland. Most of the farm workers are Latino, and in the 1990s the district's Latino population rose from 31% to 43%—the largest rise in any northern California district. This area is a prime example of how the California coast has trended Democratic. Thirty years ago this was a solidly Republican area, dominated politically by the landowners in Salinas and the townspeople who sympathize with them, retirees in Santa Cruz and the Monterey Peninsula. But an influx of liberation-minded young people now in their prime years, attracted less by the economy than by the atmosphere, moved the coast to the left. Also, the University of California branch at Santa Cruz is so liberal (97% for McGovern in 1972) that it has changed the political balance of the whole county. As late as 1980, Monterey and Santa Cruz counties were voting less Democratic than the nation. But since 1984 they have been 6% to 10% more Democratic than the nation. In 2000 Al Gore won by 60%–33% a district that was carried four times by Ronald Reagan.

The congressman from the 17th is Sam Farr, a Democrat elected in June 1993. A fifth-generation Californian, he grew up in the area, where his father Fred Farr was a state senator for many years. Sam Farr after college signed up for the Peace Corps, learned Spanish at the Monterey Institute of International Studies and served two years in Colombia. He was a staffer in the California Assembly for a decade, became a Monterey County supervisor in 1975, and was elected to the Assembly in 1980. There he wrote one of the nation's strictest oil spill liability laws and expanded the state park system. When Leon Panetta, congressman since 1977, resigned to become Office of Management and Budget director, Farr ran for the House. He entered the race as the overwhelming favorite, and in the all-party primary won 26% to beat two other Democrats who had 19% and 14%. But in the runoff, after the Clinton budget and tax increase had been introduced, he had trouble against Republican Bill McCampbell, who had been beaten 72%–24% by Panetta seven months before. Farr won, but by just 52%–43%.

The 1991 base-closing had shut Fort Ord, one of the biggest closures in the country. Once elected, Farr worked to start the California State University campus there and to install a Defense Department finance center. In November 1994 Farr again faced McCampbell and lost Monterey County, winning by enough in Santa Cruz for a 52%–44% victory. After the election there was terrible flooding. A local official "asked me whether, being in the minority, I was able to handle disasters. I said becoming the minority was a disaster. I am disaster equipped." But Farr had some successes, as well as some failures, in the Republican Congress. He got more funding for Cal State and a new veterans' clinic. He saved 300 jobs at Social Security's Salinas Data Operations Center. Working with environmental groups, he urged more recycling on Capitol Hill. He opposed Richard Pombo's bill to allow in 250,000 foreign farm workers, arguing that growers who pay good wages don't need to import workers; this was a contrast to Panetta's sponsorship in the 1980s of guest worker programs. He got Clinton to give federal protection to all of California's off-shore islands. In voting against the fast-track trade bill, Farr cited the administration's failure to restrict imports of cut flowers from Colombia, which have harmed a major local industry; the flowers are allowed across the border with no tariff as an incentive for Colombia to grow crops other than narcotics. He criticized Republican unwillingness to negotiate a compromise on estate-tax repeal. He proposed a ban on elephants in traveling circuses. He fought a proposed bombing range for Navy fighter pilots off Big Sur.

With a seat on the Appropriations Committee, Farr has focused on two major local issues: farming and military bases. Farr is also chairman of the California Democratic delegation in the House. Starting in 1996, he has been reelected easily.

Cook's Call *Probably safe.* Since his close call in 1994 when he took just 52%, Sam Farr has never dipped below 59%. Like most of northern coastal California, this district has been very supportive of Democrats at the presidential level giving both Clinton and Gore big winning margins. Republicans have talked in the past about the possibility of a strong state legislator making a run against Farr, but at this point, he looks well positioned for 2002.

THE PEOPLE: Pop. 2000: 653,209; Pop. 1990: 571,077, up 14.4% 1990–2000. 61.2% White, 2.7% Black, 5% Asian, 1.1% Amer. Indian, 0.3% Hawaiian, 4.9% Two + races, 24.8% Other; 42.6% Hispanic Origin.

2000 Presidential Vote			1996 Presidential Vote		
Gore (D)	127,791	(60%)	Clinton (D)	109,941	(55%)
Bush (R)	70,750	(33%)	Dole (R)	64,178	(32%)
Nader (Green)	13,918	(6%)	Perot (I)	12,795	(6%)
Others	2,050	(1%)	Others	12,020	(6%)

Rep. Sam Farr (D)

Elected June 1993, 4th term; b. July 4, 1941, San Francisco; home, Carmel; Willamette U., B.S. 1963; Episcopalian; married (Shary).

Elected Office: Monterey Cnty. Bd. of Supervisors, 1975–80, Chmn., 1979; CA Assembly, 1980–93.

Professional Career: Peace Corps, Colombia, 1963–65; Staff, CA Assembly, 1965–75.

DC Office: 1221 LHOB 20515, 202-225-2861; Fax: 202-225-6791; Web site: www.house.gov/farr.

District Offices: Salinas, 831-424-2229; Santa Cruz, 831-429-1976.

Committees: *Appropriations* (24th of 29 D): Agriculture, Rural Development, & FDA; Military Construction.

Group Ratings

	ADA	ACLU	AFS	LCV	CON	ITIC	NTU	COC	ACU	NTLC	CHC
2000	95	86	85	93	62	72	22	45	8	6	0
1999	100	—	100	88	73	—	13	17	0	—	—

National Journal Ratings

	1999 LIB	—	1999 CONS	2000 LIB	—	2000 CONS
Economic	83%	—	16%	81%	—	16%
Social	87%	—	0%	91%	—	6%
Foreign	95%	—	0%	92%	—	6%

Key Votes of the 106th Congress

1. Patient Bill of Rights	Y	5. Bar RU-486 $ for FDA	N	9. NATO War in Serbia	Y
2. Accelerate Min. Wage	Y	6. Display 10 Commandments	N	10. Perm. Trade with China	N
3. Strike Ban on Ergo. Stnd.	Y	7. Gun Show Bkgrnd. Checks	Y	11. Debt Relief for 3rd World	Y
4. Ovrd. Estate Tax Veto	N	8. Ban Part.-Birth Abortion	N	12. Drop Cuba Econ. Embargo	Y

Election Results

2000 general	Sam Farr (D)	143,219	(69%)	($692,932)
	Clint Engler (R)	51,557	(25%)	($29,951)
	E. Craig Coffin (Green)	8,215	(4%)	
	Other	5,769	(3%)	
2000 primary	Sam Farr (D)	83,275	(57%)	
	Clint Engler (R)	21,258	(14%)	
	Rob Roberts (R)	11,467	(8%)	
	Joe Grossman (D)	8,104	(6%)	
	Debra Whitmore (D)	7,661	(5%)	
	Carole Dooley (R)	6,495	(4%)	
	Other	8,571	(6%)	
1998 general	Sam Farr (D)	103,719	(65%)	($413,023)
	Bill McCampbell (R)	52,470	(33%)	($108,905)
	Others	4,501	(3%)	

EIGHTEENTH DISTRICT

The Central Valley of California is a miraculous man-made landscape, an outdoor factory stretching as far as the eye can see. Nature created the vast flatlands, rimmed by mountains rising surreally in the distant haze. But man in the last century has disciplined the land with a remorseless mile-square grid of roads, and the sluggish-flowing California Aqueduct and dozens of arrow-straight canals; pipes fitted with valves and gauges to pump water and fertilizer and pesticides to the fields in measured quantities give an air of industrial precision. The crops grow in carefully spaced rows, filling the fields, for the rich soil and the irrigated water are too precious to waste on decoration or flower gardens. Farming here has never been a way of life, but a business; in the 19th Century the land was not given to 160-acre homesteaders but sold to thousands-of-acres capitalist enterprises.

The Central Valley has become one of California's surprise boom areas, growing not just crops but people. Middle-wage employees in the San Francisco Bay area drive east at the end of the day on I-580, past surreal windmills whirling on the bare hills of the Altamont pass, across the Westlands fields to modestly priced homes in Modesto, the town immortalized (when it was much smaller) in *American Graffiti*. Warehouses and factories have sprung up on land that, for all its farming value, is cheaper than industrial land in the Bay Area, and some croplands have been given over to pasture, as subsidized water was cut off from cultivators of cotton, and water prices are moving slowly toward market levels far above those of government subsidy. The result is not stagnation but growth, and a more well-rounded economy. But there are costs. Traffic is a problem, air pollution on bad days approaches coastal metropolitan levels, and the pace of life is getting more hectic.

The 18th Congressional District includes a large chunk of the Central Valley from Modesto and Stanislaus County south through Merced almost to Fresno. The political tradition here is Democratic: Democrats in Washington and Democratic Governor Pat Brown built the irrigation canals and authorized the water subsidies; Democrats own the McClatchy newspapers, the predominant Valley chain; Democrats staffed the Bank of America, long the dominant financial force here; on the walls of insider law firms are signed pictures of Franklin Roosevelt and Pat Brown, not Ronald Reagan and Pete Wilson. Today the voters of the 18th District are more selectively Democratic. There are many Latinos here, 36% of the population in 2000; there are some voters of white Southern ancestry, used to voting for local Democrats though happy to vote Republican for president. The Central Valley is the part of California with the highest proportion of families and children, and there is a natural cultural conservatism here, shared by successful local Democratic politicians. The Valley, from Modesto south to Bakersfield, is one part of California where George W. Bush ran as strong as his father had in his winning race 12 years before and where Al Gore ran behind Michael Dukakis. Bush carried the 18th district 53%–44%.

The congressman from the 18th District is Gary Condit, a Democrat chosen in a September 1989 election to replace the Democratic Whip Tony Coelho after he resigned, and now one of the key moderate Democrats in a closely divided House. Condit grew up in Oklahoma, the son of a Baptist minister. At 19 he married and, with his young family and father, moved to Ceres in the Central Valley; he worked his way through college and in 1972, the year he graduated, he was elected to the Ceres Council. In 1982, at 34, he was elected to the Assembly; there he made a moderate to conservative record on crime and taxes and was one of the "Gang of Five" Democrats who nearly toppled Speaker Willie Brown in 1988—and were fiercely retaliated against. When Coelho surprised everyone by resigning, Condit seized the chance to run for Congress. He raised money efficiently and ran an absentee voter drive that essentially won the election before the polls opened, and won 57%–35%.

Condit has the most conservative voting record of any California Democrat: for the balanced budget amendment and line-item veto, against publicly funded abortions, for relaxed environmental restrictions. He gained influence after the 1994 election when Republicans won control. He was the prime Democratic co-sponsor of the unfunded mandates act, which disclosed the costs bills would impose on state and local governments. When Dick Gephardt refused to appoint him to the conference committee, Newt Gingrich did instead. Condit backed regulatory reform, including risk assessment and cost-benefit analysis. He supported tort reform, product liability reform, and sunset of the Internal Revenue Code. But he opposed school vouchers, NAFTA and privatizing Social Security.

Condit was a founding member of the Blue Dog Democrats; they were not yellow dog Democrats, they said, always faithful to the party, but dogs who were choked til they were blue by liberal Democrats. "We are not a hostile group and we are not mad at anyone. We just want to do what's right for the country and vote our conscience," he insists. The Blue Dogs produced their own budget in 1995, which went nowhere as Gingrich's Republicans and the Clinton White House slugged it out. But the 1997 balanced budget deal partook of the Blue Dog approach, and as the federal deficit became history, Condit could take satisfaction in achieving one of his goals. And he joined the top negotiations, in which he became friends with John Kasich. They attended Pearl Jam and Rolling Stones concerts together, and Kasich pledged to contribute to Condit's campaign, which later led angry California Republicans to block his participation at a February 1999 Republican presidential candidates "cattle show." Condit also worked with Republicans for a compromise minimum-wage increase.

Condit's friendliness and apparent lack of guile has enabled him to make friends across all lines. In 1997 he assembled a coalition of Blue Dogs, New Democrats and Congressional Black Caucus members to support reform of Superfund, most of whose money goes to lawyers, not environmental cleanup. He was one of 31 House Democrats to vote for the Clinton impeachment inquiry, though he later voted against impeachment. Republicans often urged Condit to switch parties, but after 1995 he said switching was "over with." And in the closely divided House he has more leverage than ever. Gephardt, who once snubbed him, invited him to serve on the party's leadership council. One of George W. Bush's early targets for bipartisanship, he was among 10

House Democrats in March 2001 to break ranks in support of the cut in income tax rates and 1 of 6 House Democrats in May to vote for the final agreement on the fiscal 2002 budget.

He does not neglect local politics. He endorsed Gray Davis for governor in January 1998, when Davis seemed mired in third place in the primary, and accompanied him to Valley events. After the election, Davis named Condit one of three co-chairmen of a commission on farm and water policy—a clear sign Davis would not pursue the anti-Valley policies of Jerry Brown. "No elected official has a closer political union with [Davis] than Condit," the *Sacramento Bee* wrote in December 2000. The results included unprecedented state funds and appointments for the Valley; Condit's son Chad was the governor's point man on Valley issues. Condit organized Team California, a bipartisan group of California federal, state and local officials, to get the ideologically divided California delegation moving in the same direction on at least some state issues. But his efforts to enact a foreign guest-worker plan for 400,000 illegal immigrants were stymied in December 2000 by Senate Republicans. Following the bankruptcy of a local peach canning co-op, he urged 100% duties on European canned peaches.

Condit's close connections have generated talk of possible high-level jobs in Washington and Sacramento. Condit, who rides a Harley when he is back home, says he is happy with his current job; he is confident enough of re-election that he gives campaign funds to charities. He has not been seriously challenged. The district lines in the fast-growing Central Valley will be shifted at least somewhat by redistricting. Democrats control the redistricting process, and could try to make the 18th more Democratic, although Condit will likely be safe whatever the boundaries.

Cook's Call   *Safe.* Though many Democrats begrudge Gary Condit for his conservative voting record, it is this profile that has helped him to get re-elected in this conservative, agriculturally dependent, Central Valley district. Condit and Lois Capps of the 22nd District are the only Democrats in the delegation who represent a district that Bush won in 2000. As one of the founders of the "Blue Dog" faction of House Democrats, the conservative Condit appears to have found the right recipe for this district but in an open seat situation, there could be a real fight here.

THE PEOPLE: Pop. 2000: 683,642; Pop. 1990: 571,358, up 19.7% 1990–2000. 65% White, 3.1% Black, 4.9% Asian, 1.2% Amer. Indian, 0.3% Hawaiian, 5.4% Two+ races, 20.1% Other; 36.4% Hispanic Origin.

2000 Presidential Vote		
Bush (R)	97,175	(53%)
Gore (D)	81,179	(44%)
Nader (Green)	4,663	(3%)
Others	1,700	(1%)

1996 Presidential Vote		
Clinton (D)	77,560	(46%)
Dole (R)	76,217	(45%)
Perot (I)	12,161	(7%)
Others	3,470	(2%)

Rep. Gary Condit (D)

Elected Sept. 1989, 6th term; b. Apr. 21, 1948, Salina, OK; home, Ceres; Modesto Jr. Col., A.A. 1970, CA St. U., B.A. 1972; Protestant; married (Carolyn).

Elected Office: Ceres City Cncl., 1972–76; Ceres Mayor, 1974–76; Stanislaus Cnty. Bd. of Supervisors, 1976–82; CA Assembly, 1982–89.

DC Office: 2234 RHOB 20515, 202-225-6131; Fax: 202-225-0819; Web site: www.house.gov/gcondit.

District Offices: Merced, 209-383-4455; Modesto, 209-527-1914.

Committees: *Agriculture* (2d of 24 D): Livestock & Horticulture; Specialty Crops & Foreign Agriculture Programs (RMM). *Permanent Select Committee on Intelligence* (4th of 9 D): Human Intelligence, Analysis & Counterintelligence; Intelligence Policy & National Security (RMM).

Group Ratings

	ADA	ACLU	AFS	LCV	CON	ITIC	NTU	COC	ACU	NTLC	CHC
2000	50	36	71	64	38	61	43	57	44	55	53
1999	70	—	50	44	81	—	42	64	44	—	—

National Journal Ratings

	1999 LIB —	1999 CONS		2000 LIB —	2000 CONS
Economic	51% —	49%		52% —	48%
Social	60% —	39%		62% —	37%
Foreign	48% —	51%		53% —	45%

Key Votes of the 106th Congress

1. Patient Bill of Rights	Y	5. Bar RU-486 $ for FDA	N	9. NATO War in Serbia	N
2. Accelerate Min. Wage	Y	6. Display 10 Commandments	Y	10. Perm. Trade with China	N
3. Strike Ban on Ergo. Stnd.	Y	7. Gun Show Bkgrnd. Checks	Y	11. Debt Relief for 3rd World	N
4. Ovrd. Estate Tax Veto	Y	8. Ban Part.-Birth Abortion	Y	12. Drop Cuba Econ. Embargo	Y

Election Results

2000 general	Gary Condit (D)	121,003	(67%)	($686,683)
	Steve R. Wilson (R)	56,465	(31%)	($31,087)
	Other	2,860	(2%)	
2000 primary	Gary Condit (D)	80,543	(65%)	
	Steve R. Wilson (R)	35,335	(29%)	
	Rodger McAfee (D)	6,142	(5%)	
	Other	1,262	(1%)	
1998 general	Gary Condit (D)	118,842	(87%)	($439,331)
	Linda M. Degroat (Lib)	18,089	(13%)	

NINETEENTH DISTRICT

Fresno, in California's Central Valley, between the flat Westlands and the Sierras, is a city agricultural and industrial, middle American and ethnically diverse. It is a creation of the industrial age, founded by the Central Pacific Railroad; its city fathers bred the local wine grape, developed the raisin industry and introduced the Smyrna fig. But these are not all of Fresno's crops, which include cotton, lima beans, tomatoes, cantaloupes, plums, peaches and alfalfa: Fresno produces more farm products in dollar value than any other county in the United States. Central Valley agriculture is industrial in its precision, its thoroughness and its ownership by large corporations: the vineyards outside Fresno radiate in mechanical precision, with vines just 10 feet apart and exposed to the relentless summer sun: nothing romantic or quaint here. The city of Fresno started as a farm-marketing center—one high-income neighborhood is called Fig Garden because that's what it used to be—and as a tourists' stop-off point on the way to Yosemite National Park. But it has long since grown out north, east and west from its old downtown, and its economy has diversified.

Like all the Central Valley, Fresno has always been ethnically diverse, with a telephone book that reads like the United Nations; it has America's second largest Armenian community, after Los Angeles. Its already large Latino population has more than doubled in the last 20 years, and Fresno County was 44% Hispanic in 2000; Asians, including Chinese, Filipinos, Vietnamese and Hmong, were 8% of the county's population. Fresno grew lustily in the 1990s, despite high unemployment rates; there were violent teenage gangs and air pollution that made the Sierra Nevada invisible on many days. Historically, Fresno was a Democratic town, the prime Democratic bastion in the Valley south of Sacramento. But in the 1990s it elected a Republican mayor, religious broadcaster Jim Patterson, who cut crime and tried to reduce burdens on business. It voted for Bob Dole in 1996, Republican governor candidate Dan Lungren in 1998 and George W. Bush in 2000, all of whom lost statewide by solid margins. This is one part of California that trended toward Republicans in the 1990s, when most of the state was moving the other way.

The 19th Congressional District of California includes most of Fresno, all but the old downtown and a Latino area in the Hispanic-majority 20th District. The 19th spreads with an erose boundary over the farm country below the Sierra foothills from Visalia, south of Fresno, to mountainous Mariposa County. Most of its land mass is part of the Sierra Nevada, and it contains most of three major national parks: Yosemite, Kings Canyon and Sequoia.

The congressman from the 19th District is George Radanovich, a Republican elected in 1994. Radanovich is the son of Croatian immigrants, with relatives all over the Valley. He worked on the family farm, served on the Mariposa County Planning Commission in the 1980s and won a seat on the Board of Supervisors in 1989. In 1986, after studying local microclimates, he opened the first winery in Mariposa County and made it work; the Radanovich Winery ships 4,000 cases of sauvignon blanc, zinfandel and cabernet sauvignon. In 1992 he ran for Congress, losing the primary 33%–30% to 28-year-old Tal Cloud, who lost to incumbent Democrat Richard Lehman 47%–46%. Lehman was an adept professional politician, but all his fundraising and skills could not avail him in 1994 as Radanovich, an easy winner in this primary, attacked him for supporting the Clinton Administration and California Democrat George Miller's efforts to raise the price of Valley water. Radanovich won 57%–40% in the widest defeat of a non-freshman incumbent in 1994. Radanovich became the first full-time professional winemaker to serve in the House.

In the House, Radanovich was elected president of the 74-member freshmen Republican class. Sometimes moderate on economics, he has mostly had a conservative voting record. He defended the government shutdown, even when it closed Yosemite during the holiday season, and said he would prefer government default before voting to increase the debt limit. In 1996 he passed with David Bonior an amendment to require Turkey to acknowledge the Armenian genocide of 1915; Turkey spurned aid under such conditions. In 2000, Radanovich secured $90 million in aid for Armenia—one of the largest recipients of U.S. aid; but Speaker Dennis Hastert acceded to Clinton's personal appeal to abandon another resolution on Armenian genocide. He held out on fast track trade negotiating authority, agreeing to support it only after the Clinton administration agreed to address Mexican wine tariffs. As co-chairman with Mike Thompson of the Congressional Wine Caucus, he sought to educate members on the industry's issues. Radanovich worked on local issues, calling for light rail in Yosemite even if other parks had to be closed to fund it, and getting 67 families continued access to isolated cabins in Sequoia National Park. Angry with eastern environmentalists, he sought to delay approval of the new Wilson Bridge over the Potomac River and demanded a tit-for-tat strict compliance with endangered-species rules. In 2001, he joined the wide-ranging Energy and Commerce Committee, and pledged to deal with hydroelectric problems in the Sierra Nevadas. He urged the Bush Administration to postpone Clinton's road-building ban in national forests; Agriculture Secretary Ann Veneman is a Modesto native.

Two days after the 1998 election, he challenged House Republican Conference chairman John Boehner, but switched to support J.C. Watts when he entered the race. Back home, Radanovich has won re-election easily. The 19th district has grown rapidly and must be pared back in redistricting, which is controlled by Democrats. But this area is so heavily Republican that there will surely be a safe district for Radanovich in 2002.

Cook's Call   *Safe*. Though Democrat Richard Lehman held this district for 10 years, redistricting in 1991 slashed Democratic registration by 12 % and added more rural sections to the district, making it a safe Republican seat. And, as the Central Valley continues to trend away from Democrats (Bush won this district with 58%), there is little hope of Democrats mounting a competitive effort unless the lines are moved substantially.

THE PEOPLE: Pop. 2000: 709,622; Pop. 1990: 573,077, up 23.8% 1990–2000. 63.7% White, 4.5% Black, 7.2% Asian, 1.8% Amer. Indian, 0.1% Hawaiian, 4.8% Two + races, 18% Other; 32.9% Hispanic Origin.

2000 Presidential Vote		
Bush (R)	132,193	(58%)
Gore (D)	87,661	(38%)
Nader (Green)	7,519	(3%)
Others	2,141	(1%)

1996 Presidential Vote		
Dole (R)	111,666	(52%)
Clinton (D)	85,744	(40%)
Perot (I)	12,495	(6%)
Others	4,816	(2%)

Rep. George Radanovich (R)

Elected 1994, 4th term; b. June 20, 1955, Mariposa; home, Mariposa; CA Polytechnic U., B.S. 1978; Catholic; married (Ethie).

Elected Office: Mariposa Cnty. Planning Comm., 1982–86, Chmn., 1985–86; Mariposa Cnty. Bd. of Supervisors, 1989–92.

Professional Career: Farmer; Founder & Owner, Radanovich Winery, 1986–present.

DC Office: 123 CHOB 20515, 202-225-4540; Fax: 202-225-3402; Web site: www.house.gov/radanovich.

District Office: Fresno, 559-248-0800.

Committees: *Energy & Commerce* (26th of 31 R): Commerce, Trade & Consumer Protection; Energy & Air Quality; Environment & Hazardous Materials. *Resources* (13th of 28 R): National Parks, Recreation & Public Lands; Water & Power (Vice Chmn.).

Group Ratings

	ADA	ACLU	AFS	LCV	CON	ITIC	NTU	COC	ACU	NTLC	CHC
2000	5	21	0	14	67	100	66	90	100	85	93
1999	5	—	0	6	8	—	59	96	88	—	—

National Journal Ratings

	1999 LIB	—	1999 CONS		2000 LIB	—	2000 CONS
Economic	0%	—	84%		18%	—	76%
Social	0%	—	96%		0%	—	79%
Foreign	28%	—	70%		0%	—	88%

Key Votes of the 106th Congress

1. Patient Bill of Rights	N	5. Bar RU-486 $ for FDA	Y	9. NATO War in Serbia	Y
2. Accelerate Min. Wage	N	6. Display 10 Commandments	Y	10. Perm. Trade with China	Y
3. Strike Ban on Ergo. Stnd.	N	7. Gun Show Bkgrnd. Checks	N	11. Debt Relief for 3rd World	N
4. Ovrd. Estate Tax Veto	Y	8. Ban Part.-Birth Abortion	Y	12. Drop Cuba Econ. Embargo	N

Election Results

2000 general	George Radanovich (R)	144,517	(65%)	($659,104)
	Dan Rosenberg (D)	70,578	(32%)	($179,555)
	Other	7,520	(3%)	
2000 primary	George Radanovich (R)	109,723	(67%)	
	Dan Rosenberg (D)	33,921	(21%)	
	John S. Hernandez (D)	15,647	(9%)	
	Other	5,623	(3%)	
1998 general	George Radanovich (R)	131,105	(79%)	($452,642)
	Jonathan Richter (Lib)	34,044	(21%)	

TWENTIETH DISTRICT

California's Central Valley by car seems a monotonous landscape: mile after mile of farmland with mile-square grid roads, cut across by diagonal railroads and canals, with an occasional cluster town. The land is hilly and gets more water near the Sierra Nevada, and this is where the larger cities cluster. On the other side is the Westlands, where the land is flatter and the water scarcer. Here the land was always developed and sold in large plots, and it has some of the world's largest farming operations today. And it produces plenty: alfalfa, cantaloupes, cotton, grapes, lima beans, olives, peaches, plums, raisins, sugar beets, tomatoes, walnuts, wheat. The owners are a hardy lot, but like most entrepreneurs they have been happy to have government help: crop price supports, agricultural research, exceptions to the immigration laws, irrigation systems and (most important) subsidized water. They have fought hard against liberals' efforts at change, from Governor Jerry Brown's attempts to encourage Cesar Chavez's United Farm Workers in the 1970s to former House Natural Resources Committee Chairman George Miller's 1992 law to draw off more water to the Sacramento delta and charge higher prices for it in the Valley. But the greatest threats may come from conservatives: In a free market for water, Los Angeles users may outbid the farmers, and tighter restrictions on illegal immigrants have cut into the supply of farm workers; Congress has so far declined to approve guest worker programs pushed by Valley members.

The 20th Congressional District includes most of the Westlands of the Central Valley, from north of Bakersfield to south of Fresno. Its irregular boundaries were drawn to maximize the Hispanic population and possibly elect a Hispanic congressman, so the 20th includes the old downtown neighborhoods of both Bakersfield and Fresno, but none of their newer suburbs; it includes heavily Latino towns like Delano, long Chavez's headquarters, but not more Anglo places like Tulare. The 20th's Hispanic population increased to 64% in 2000, about double that in other Central Valley districts, but the share of voters who are Latino is lower, 34% in 1990 and around 40% in 2000. Still, this is the most Democratic Valley seat between Sacramento and Los Angeles; the Valley has been trending Republican, but the 20th district voted for Al Gore, albeit by only a 50%–48% margin.

The congressman from the 20th is Calvin Dooley, a Democrat elected in 1990. He is a farmer, growing cotton, alfalfa and walnuts, as his great-grandfather did before him. In 1987 he became a staffer for Tulare state Senator Rose Ann Vuich. In 1990, he ran for Congress in a more Republican-leaning district. Luck was with him: The incumbent had accepted contributions from S&L operator Charles Keating and interceded on his behalf with regulators. Dooley won with a solid 55%. When new district lines were announced in 1992, Dooley and 10-year incumbent Democrat Richard Lehman both eyed the 20th, but Dooley staked it out quickly and Lehman ran in the more Republican 19th, where he lost in 1994.

Dooley's endurance has been partly a testimonial to his moderate voting record, which is the most conservative of California Democrats except for Gary Condit's. He tottered before voting for the Clinton budget and tax package, and he supported the balanced budget amendment and the line-item veto. Dooley voted for much of the Contract with America and supported most of welfare reform. On the Agriculture and Resources Committees, he tended to district interests. He was one of three committee Democrats to vote for Richard Pombo's guest worker bill and supported lifting the ban on food sales to Cuba. He has co-chaired the Congressional Beef Caucus, the Western Water Caucus and the Biotechnology Caucus. He opposed Clinton Interior Secretary Bruce Babbitt's plan to restore the original flow of the Trinity River—which was opposed by Valley farmers dependent on its water and power. He strongly backed Permanent Normal Trade Relations with China and voted to override Bill Clinton's veto of estate tax repeal. He is a founder and co-chairman of the New Democrat Coalition, formerly the Mainstream Forum, a group of 72 moderate House Democrats who bill themselves as seeking bipartisan solutions to the nation's problems. After the 1998 election, he ran for vice-chairman of the House Democratic Caucus, seeking to assemble a coalition of conservatives and Californians. But he failed to lock up either camp, and lost 124–81 on the second ballot to Robert Menendez of New Jersey. Afterward, Minority Leader Dick Gephardt asked Dooley to be one of five members of a new Democratic Leadership Council designed to encourage dialogue among Democratic factions.

Dooley is active on local issues, including flood control projects, increased dam capacity, and additional funds for farm workers. He helped obtain a $3.8 million grant to assist Southeast Asian refugees in Fresno County learn English and get jobs; he supported the bill to waive the English language requirement for citizenship for Hmong and Lao veterans who were recruited by the U.S. military in the 1960s and 1970s. He organized in Fresno a bipartisan summit, including the state's two Senators, to seek solutions to the methamphetamine crisis.

Despite the seat's Democratic leaning, Dooley has had well-financed and competitive re-election challenges. The most serious came in 2000 from Rich Rodriguez, a former Fresno TV news anchorman, who was wooed and supported by national Republicans especially keen that he is Latino—although he does not speak Spanish. Rodriguez made mistakes common for political newcomers and was not always familiar with the issues: When the Mexican-American Political Association endorsed Dooley, Rodriguez's campaign manager called the group "liberal Cesar Chavez types." But Rodriguez had high name recognition and won the endorsement from the California Farm Bureau Federation, whose members griped that Dooley appeared to give as much attention to Silicon Valley as to the Central Valley and had failed to establish a guest-worker program. George W. Bush joined Rodriguez at a rally in Fresno the week before the election. Dooley countered with Dianne Feinstein, Gray Davis and Bill Clinton, and he raised nearly twice as much money as the challenger—much of it from leaders of agricultural organizations like Sunkist and Blue Diamond. Dooley won 52%–45%, running just 2% ahead of Al Gore. Rodriguez won in Kings and Tulare Counties 53%–42% but they cast only 35% of the total vote. Dooley prevailed with strong showings in the Hispanic sections of Fresno and Bakersfield; the Republican strategy had a flawed messenger. Following the election, despite continuing hard feelings, Dooley sought to make peace with the farm groups.

Redistricting will prove vital for Dooley. "The 20th Congressional district was made for a Hispanic—a Hispanic Democrat," *The Fresno Bee* concluded. The 2000 Census showed that the district grew 24% in the 1990s, and most of that growth came from Latinos. Democrats control redistricting, and the obvious way to boost the Democratic percentage is to draw a district with as many Latinos as possible. But that may give a strong Latino challenger in the Democratic primary some time in the coming decade.

Cook's Call *Competitive.* Dooley's tough race against TV broadcaster Rich Rodriguez may be a preview of difficult races down the road for the six-term Democrat. By the numbers this seat is supposed to be the most Democratic in the Central Valley (thanks in part to the fact it has a 64% Latino population), but like the rest of the agriculturally dependent Central Valley, this seat has begun to behave more conservatively. In 1992 Clinton won the district by 10 %, but Gore won the seat by just 2 % in 2000. Rodriguez has said he won't run again, but a good Republican candidate in the right political environment could give Dooley another tight race.

THE PEOPLE: Pop. 2000: 711,574; Pop. 1990: 573,555, up 24.1% 1990–2000. 43% White, 5.9% Black, 4.7% Asian, 1.6% Amer. Indian, 0.1% Hawaiian, 4.5% Two + races, 40.3% Other; 63.7% Hispanic Origin.

2000 Presidential Vote			1996 Presidential Vote		
Gore (D)	63,592	(50%)	Clinton (D)	62,164	(52%)
Bush (R)	60,989	(48%)	Dole (R)	48,446	(41%)
Nader (Green)	2,148	(2%)	Perot (I)	6,617	(6%)
Others	1,355	(1%)			

Rep. Calvin Dooley (D)

Elected 1990, 6th term; b. Jan. 11, 1954, Visalia; home, Visalia; U. of CA at Davis, B.S. 1977, Stanford U., M.A. 1987; Methodist; married (Linda).

Professional Career: Farmer, 1978–91; A.A., CA Sen. Rose Ann Vuich, 1987–89.

DC Office: 1201 LHOB 20515, 202-225-3341; Fax: 202-225-9308; Web site: www.house.gov/dooley.

District Office: Fresno, 559-441-7496.

Committees: *Agriculture* (4th of 24 D): General Farm Commodities & Risk Management (RMM); Livestock & Horticulture. *Resources* (10th of 25 D): Energy & Mineral Resources; Water & Power.

Group Ratings

	ADA	ACLU	AFS	LCV	CON	ITIC	NTU	COC	ACU	NTLC	CHC
2000	70	71	42	57	15	100	27	90	20	21	13
1999	80	—	66	50	79	—	16	80	8	—	—

National Journal Ratings

	1999 LIB	—	1999 CONS		2000 LIB	—	2000 CONS
Economic	54%	—	46%		54%	—	46%
Social	68%	—	31%		79%	—	17%
Foreign	74%	—	23%		85%	—	10%

Key Votes of the 106th Congress

1. Patient Bill of Rights	Y	5. Bar RU-486 $ for FDA	N	9. NATO War in Serbia	Y
2. Accelerate Min. Wage	Y	6. Display 10 Commandments	Y	10. Perm. Trade with China	Y
3. Strike Ban on Ergo. Stnd.	N	7. Gun Show Bkgrnd. Checks	Y	11. Debt Relief for 3rd World	Y
4. Ovrd. Estate Tax Veto	Y	8. Ban Part.-Birth Abortion	N	12. Drop Cuba Econ. Embargo	Y

Election Results

2000 general	Calvin Dooley (D)	66,235	(52%)	($1,775,089)
	Rich Rodriguez (R)	57,563	(45%)	($1,257,145)
	Other	2,736	(2%)	
2000 primary	Calvin Dooley (D)	43,608	(52%)	
	Rich Rodriguez (R)	38,661	(46%)	
	Other	2,143	(3%)	
1998 general	Calvin Dooley (D)	60,599	(61%)	($634,240)
	Cliff Unruh (R)	39,183	(39%)	($222,368)

TWENTY-FIRST DISTRICT

Bakersfield, at the apex of the southern end of California's Central Valley, has been the focus of great migrations four times—in a gold rush in 1885, when oil was discovered here in 1899, during the 1930s when the Okies drove their jalopies from the Dust Bowl of Oklahoma and Kansas and Texas across the Southwest on U.S. 66, and again in the 1980s and 1990s, when Bakersfield and Kern County grew more rapidly than California's biggest metro areas. Bakersfield's oil rigs pump more oil than is produced annually in Oklahoma, but the migration that made the deepest imprint was in the 1930s. The Okies drove over one thousand miles of brown landscape, then through the Tehachapi Pass, and found this vast green valley, with its irrigated fields and its eucalyptus-shaded towns, the richest farming country in the world. The story is told vividly in John Steinbeck's *The Grapes of Wrath*, though his vision of the Okies as workers eager to join together with their fellow proletarians and rise up against their bosses did not get the picture quite right. More accurate is Dan Morgan's *Rising in the West*, which shows the strong Pentecostal beliefs that drove many migrants and, unlike Steinbeck, explains how they prospered in California.

The area around Bakersfield has become the one Southern-accented part of California, the home of country singers Buck Owens and Merle Haggard and a thriving contemporary country music scene, culturally conservative with a strong drive toward discipline and little empathy for the therapy that is so common in Los Angeles, 110 miles south. "I hope you all agree with me that Bakersfield is boring," LA Mayor Richard Riordan once said on radio—and then came up for a tour in 106-degree heat and heard the Kern County DA tell him that motorists are not fired at on Bakersfield's freeways, its citizens don't riot when they don't like a jury verdict and its celebrities are not on trial for murder.

The 21st Congressional District, the southernmost district in the Central Valley, is centered on Bakersfield and takes in most of Kern and Tulare counties; it also includes Edwards Air Force Base where Chuck Yeager flew the X-1 and where the space shuttle frequently lands. The district's boundaries are irregular to maximize the Hispanic percentage of the next-door 20th District, but the 21st was still 31% Hispanic in 2000, up from 20% in 1990. The 21st includes most of Bakersfield and its surroundings, oil fields and high-income subdivisions, and Kern County desert and mountain communities. The rich farm land produces a majority of the olives grown in the United States and is the nation's largest dairy-producing region. Politically, this was Democratic territory in the early 1960s—when, for that matter, so was Oklahoma; by the late 1960s, both had become solidly Republican in national politics, and today both seem Republican up and down the ticket. In 1996 the 21st District voted 56%–34% for Bob Dole, a showing he matched in only one other California district, the 48th in Orange and San Diego Counties. In 2000 the 21st voted 64%–33% for George W. Bush, his best performance in any California district.

The congressman from the 21st, Bill Thomas, was first elected in 1978 and is now Chairman of the House Ways and Means Committee. Thomas grew up in Orange County; his father was a union plumber and his parents never graduated from high school; he lived for a time in public housing. He graduated from San Francisco State and taught political science from 1965–74 in the community college in Bakersfield. In 1974 he was elected to the Assembly, a conservative in a liberal-run legislature; when Congressman Bill Ketchum died after the 1978 primary, he ran as the relative moderate at the party convention and won the seat. He is bright and testy; he has, wrote Faye Fiore in the *Los Angeles Times*, "an intellect so sharp he is considered one of the brightest members of the House and a temper so mercurial some say he may be one of the meanest." Some of that may have come from being beaten again and again by Democrats on elections issues. On the House Administration Committee he was the Republicans' point man on the challenge to Indiana's 8th District result in 1985, in which the Democrats voted in their man though the state authorities said the Republican had won—"rape," said Thomas, who added that if Republicans ever got a majority, "We will not be civilized. We will not assume it's business as usual. We will not go back to playing the lackey." He was also attacked by conservatives for being too moderate, and in December 1992 Newt Gingrich and others ran Paul Gillmor of Ohio against him for ranking-member on House Administration; Thomas won by only 12 votes. "That particular event changed his life. It taught him, in a very serious way, that leadership in the House is a team sport," said Gingrich later. Thomas was unsuccessful in fighting George Miller's 1992 Central Valley Water Project Act and the 1994 Desert Protection Act.

Now things are different. After Republicans won the majority in 1994, Thomas was given two tough assignments by Gingrich. As chairman of House Administration, Thomas managed the Republicans' bills reducing the House budget by $50 million, reducing committee staffs by one-third, providing an independent audit of the House and applying to Congress the laws it applies to others. He opposed Democratic campaign finance measures and proposed his own reforms. Following the July 1998 murder of two Capitol policemen, Thomas took control of efforts to impose additional security restrictions, including the long-planned construction of a visitors center under the Capitol's east plaza.

On Ways and Means, and as chairman of its Health Subcommittee, Thomas has been the majority Republicans' lead man on Medicare. He studied the issue intensively, rising at 4:00 a.m. to crack the books, and reflected on the situation of his parents (his mother was killed and his father gravely injured in a Kern County car crash). He managed to passage in the House the 1995 Medicare reform reducing the rate of spending increases and giving seniors more choices. Though Democratic candidates hammered Republicans hard on Medicare, polling after the Republican counteroffensive in October 1996 showed that it was not a net minus for Republican House candidates, who ran even with Democrats among the elderly. Thomas played a lead role in the Medicare reforms and spending cuts—including steps to give senior citizens additional private-insurance options—that were enacted as part of the Clinton-Republican Congress budget agreement of May 1997. In November 1999 he worked with the Clinton White House to put additional funds into Medicare. Thomas was co-chairman, with Senator John Breaux, of the National Bipartisan Commission on the Future of Medicare set up under the 1997 law. Breaux and Thomas produced a "premium support" package, modeled on the Federal Employees Health Benefits Plan, which would give seniors enough money to pay for a certain minimum amount of coverage, plus the option of entering into other plans; in March 1999 it got the votes of 10 members of the 17-member commission, but not the 11-vote supermajority required to be its official recommendation. It was spurned by Bill Clinton, but it became the basis for George W. Bush's plan for Medicare in the 2000 campaign. In early 2001 it seemed likely that Bush would like to see Medicare addressed later in the year; Thomas will be the key man on the issue in the House.

On other health issues, Thomas took the lead in establishing deductibility of health care insurance for the self-employed. He helped work out the plan for HMO regulation that the Republican leadership offered as an alternative to the Dingell-Norwood bill. Starting in spring 2000, he devised the Republican plan for prescription drugs for seniors, which passed the House in June 2000. It consisted mainly of subsidies to insurers for providing prescription drug coverage for less affluent seniors; in response to criticism, Thomas agreed in June to make the government the insurer of last resort. In early 2001 Thomas seemed likely to tackle the prescription drug issue in tandem with Medicare. Up through 2000, Thomas did not work so much on taxes and trade, although he consistently supported tax cuts and free trade.

Throughout 2000 Thomas was running, quietly, for Ways and Means chairman. Chairman

Bill Archer, limited to six years by Republicans' term limits, was retiring from Congress. The next committee Republican in seniority was Philip Crane, who had not been nearly as productive legislatively; in March 2000 Crane admitted he had a problem with alcohol, and spent some weeks in treatment. But in June Thomas was hit with a *Bakersfield Californian* story charging that he had an "intensely personal relationship" with health care lobbyist Deborah Steelman; Thomas denied any professional impropriety, and the story had relatively little impact. His greater problem was his temper. He takes pride in his knowledge, and has shown contempt for those with less. Even his hobbies are unsociable: he likes to disassemble and reassemble old cars and take apart computers. Thomas recognized the problem and assured Republican leaders that he would contain his temper: "I realize that to be chairman of the committee I can't be the Bill Thomas you're used to seeing on the committee." In 1999 and 2000 Crane raised some $2.5 million for other Republicans; Thomas pointed out that he had raised $1.6 million for other Republicans since 1995, starting long before the chairmanship contest. Crane had backing from some economic and religious conservatives, but Thomas got the backing of Speaker Dennis Hastert, even though both he and Crane are from Illinois. Evidently Hastert decided that he needed Thomas's knowledge and skills since the committee would have to address three of George W. Bush's five top issues, tax cuts, Medicare and Social Security. Thomas was the choice of the Republican Steering Committee, a choice ratified by the Republican Conference.

As chairman, Thomas moved first on taxes. Noting the signs that the economy was weakening and taking note of Federal Reserve Chairman Alan Greenspan's testimony favoring a tax cut, he decided in late January 2001 to advance the income-tax cut in George W. Bush's $1.6 trillion package. It passed in committee in February and was passed by the House, with a few Democratic votes, in early March. In the next month, Thomas gained bipartisan support, although Bush did not get the whole $1.6 trillion in the spring, Thomas said that additional tax cuts were likely later in the year; he is likely to be a key player throughout. As he said in March 2001, "To get into the room you have to knock on the door. If you're on the inside, you don't have to do any of that. I don't need to knock on the door. I'm inside."

Thomas has been reelected easily every two years in his heavily Republican district. He has also been the California House Republicans' point man on redistricting issues: a difficult position, because it was clear from November 1998 that Democrats would control redistricting. To forestall that, Thomas concocted a ballot proposition in 1999 that would turn redistricting over to the California Supreme Court (most of whose justices were appointed by Republicans) and also cut legislators' salaries. The House Republicans' campaign committee, fearful that it could lose eight seats in redistricting, put up $1.3 million to get it on the ballot. But in December 1999 the state Supreme Court ruled it was invalid because it included two subjects. Thomas then split the proposal into two separate initiatives, but in March 2000 the campaign committee declined to put up any more money to get it on the ballot. That may have been wise. Previous redistricting ballot propositions have been voted down in California, and Republicans lost four California seats in November 2000. They are down to a 32–20 disadvantage on the delegation, and redistricting will probably not make that worse than 36–17. But Thomas is not likely to be eliminated. Although the Democrats who control redistricting were said in early 2001 to be contemplating putting him in the same district with another incumbent, his strength in the heavily Republican Bakersfield area and his status as Ways and Means Chairman suggest that he can be assured of reelection in 2002.

Cook's Call   *Safe.* The fact that Bush, who lost the state by 11 %, won the 21st with 64% gives a good indication of how solidly Republican this district is. There were some rumors that Thomas' district would fall victim to the redistricting pen (Thomas' relationship with both Republican and Democratic legislators got rather rocky after his support for a redistricting initiative that would have slashed legislators' salaries). But it will be very difficult to draw a tough district for Thomas without impacting marginal Democratic incumbents. Thomas should be safe in 2002.

THE PEOPLE: Pop. 2000: 666,684; Pop. 1990: 571,143, up 16.7% 1990–2000. 68.1% White, 4.5% Black, 3% Asian, 1.6% Amer. Indian, 0.2% Hawaiian, 4.3% Two+ races, 18.3% Other; 31.4% Hispanic Origin.

2000 Presidential Vote

Bush (R)	129,401	(64%)
Gore (D)	67,577	(33%)
Nader (Green)	4,184	(2%)
Others	2,345	(1%)

1996 Presidential Vote

Dole (R)	109,344	(56%)
Clinton (D)	66,492	(34%)
Perot (I)	15,000	(8%)
Others	3,513	(2%)

Rep. Bill Thomas (R)

Elected 1978, 12th term; b. Dec. 6, 1941, Wallace, ID; home, Bakersfield; San Francisco St. U., B.A. 1963, M.A. 1965; Baptist; married (Sharon).

Elected Office: CA Assembly, 1974–78.

Professional Career: Prof., Bakersfield Comm. Col., 1965–74.

DC Office: 2208 RHOB 20515, 202-225-2915; Fax: 202-225-8798; Web site: www.house.gov/billthomas.

District Offices: Bakersfield, 661-327-3611; Visalia, 559-627-6549.

Committees: *Ways & Means* (Chmn. of 24 R). *Joint Committee on Printing* (1st of 5 Reps.). *Joint Committee on Taxation* (Chmn. of 5 Reps.). *Joint Committee on the Library of Congress* (Vice Chmn. of 6 Reps.).

Group Ratings

	ADA	ACLU	AFS	LCV	CON	ITIC	NTU	COC	ACU	NTLC	CHC
2000	10	27	0	7	24	95	61	90	80	67	77
1999	10	—	0	6	33	—	51	96	66	—	—

National Journal Ratings

	1999 LIB —	1999 CONS		2000 LIB —	2000 CONS
Economic	30% —	64%		6% —	85%
Social	42% —	58%		51% —	48%
Foreign	28% —	70%		12% —	78%

Key Votes of the 106th Congress

1. Patient Bill of Rights	N	5. Bar RU-486 $ for FDA	N	9. NATO War in Serbia	N
2. Accelerate Min. Wage	N	6. Display 10 Commandments	*	10. Perm. Trade with China	Y
3. Strike Ban on Ergo. Stnd.	N	7. Gun Show Bkgrnd. Checks	*	11. Debt Relief for 3rd World	N
4. Ovrd. Estate Tax Veto	Y	8. Ban Part.-Birth Abortion	Y	12. Drop Cuba Econ. Embargo	N

Election Results

2000 general	Bill Thomas (R)	142,539	(72%)	($1,529,664)
	Pedro Martinez Jr. (D)	49,318	(25%)	
	James Manion (LIB)	7,243	(4%)	
2000 primary	Bill Thomas (R)	98,088	(74%)	
	Pedro Martinez Jr. (D)	29,511	(22%)	
	James Manion (LIB)	5,430	(4%)	
1998 general	Bill Thomas (R)	115,989	(79%)	($1,172,167)
	John Evans (RP)	30,994	(21%)	($6,464)

TWENTY-SECOND DISTRICT

Santa Barbara is one of California's most paradisical places, a collection of red tile roofs and leafy live oaks, sheltered by towering mountains just above the sea. The impression is a bit misleading, for Santa Barbara has its problems, and its Spanish style is a creation not of 18th-Century Mission culture, but of the 20th Century. Most of its white stucco buildings were put up after a 1925 earthquake leveled much of the town and the most distinguished of the Spanish Revival buildings were designed by an architect with the marvelously un-Latin name of George Washington Smith. Santa Barbara, like Disneyland, does not reproduce the past but presents a bigger, more attractive, cleaner version of it, maintained not by a company but by an architectural review board. But Santa Barbara's affluence isn't ersatz. This has long been one of the nation's richest retirement communities, and one increasingly devoted to preserving its environment and serenity. Both features came under threat spectacularly in 1969, when an underwater oil well ruptured, coating the beach with oil; pictures of the oil slick in the channel and of volunteers trying to wash oil off grounded birds, helped to launch the environmental movement. Almost all the wells are closed now (though some old 19th Century wells still send globs of oil to the beach at nearby Summerland), but the oil spill did leave a residue in Santa Barbara's politics—and helped attract high-tech businesses to replace the defense jobs lost in the early 1990s. This has been a mostly Republican community, uninterested in redistribution of wealth, but very concerned about the environment (it has built the nation's largest desalination plant) and moderate to liberal on cultural issues.

The 22d Congressional District consists of all of Santa Barbara County except the town of Carpinteria at its southeast corner, plus San Luis Obispo County to the north. Not all of this area resembles Santa Barbara. The most notable feature in northern Santa Barbara County, across the Santa Ynez Mountains from Ronald Reagan's former ranch, is Vandenberg Air Force Base, and the nearby town of Santa Maria is pro-military and conservative. San Luis Obispo County is pleasant and as untrendy a place as you could find on this coast, culturally more Middle American than is Santa Barbara; it voted 52%–41% for George W. Bush and the 22nd was, by a narrow margin, a Bush district.

The congresswoman from the 22d District is Lois Capps, a Democrat chosen in a March 1998 special election, and its fourth Representative since 1992. Capps grew up in Wyoming and Montana, the daughter of a Lutheran minister; she graduated from college with a nursing degree and was head nurse at Yale New Haven Hospital where she met her husband, Walter Capps, a student at Yale Divinity School. In 1964 he became a professor at the University of California at Santa Barbara. Lois Capps became the head elementary school nurse for the Santa Barbara school system, director of the county's teenage pregnancy and parenting project, and a part-time instructor at Santa Barbara City Community College. In 1994, when Michael Huffington gave up the seat after one term to run for the Senate, Walter Capps ran and lost 49.3%–48.5% to Andrea Seastrand, a conservative Republican assemblywoman from San Luis Obispo County. Capps, who said he wanted to promote conciliation in the House, ran again in 1996 and won 48%–44%. He died suddenly in October 1997.

National Republicans had great hopes of picking up the seat. Speaker Newt Gingrich encouraged the candidacy of Assemblyman Brooks Firestone—an heir to the Firestone tire fortune and successful winemaker, and a centrist in favor of abortion rights and gun control. But also running was Assemblyman Tom Bordonaro, the favorite of Christian conservatives. Bordonaro, a paraplegic since a car accident in college, emphasized his "blue-collar roots and common values" and attacked Firestone's wealthy status; after a Firestone fundraiser with former President Gerald Ford, Bordonaro said caustically, "I don't have the luxury of hob-nobbing with celebrities from Palm Springs." House conservatives were angered by Gingrich's support of Firestone; Majority Whip Tom DeLay steered about $30,000 to Bordonaro during the primary. Meanwhile, Lois Capps announced her candidacy, with support from many of Walter Capps's admirers as well as from labor and environmental groups. Both Capps and Firestone spent about $450,000 in the primary, while Bordonaro spent only $130,000. In the January 1998 all-party primary, Capps finished first with 45%, Bordonaro was second with 29% and Firestone had 25%. The turning point for Bordonaro may have been a $100,000 independent ad campaign sponsored by the Campaign for Working Families, featuring Bordonaro's opposition to partial-birth abortions. In the fiercely-contested runoff, Capps ran a better-organized campaign, including a superior absentee-ballot effort, and Bordonaro suffered from lingering animosity of Firestone supporters plus voter backlash against the outside groups' advertising. Also, term limits advocates ran ads against the younger Bordonaro, who refused to limit his terms; Capps said that at her age she was happy to limit herself to three terms. She won by a surprisingly large 53%–45%. That did not end their competition; both were on the ballot again in November. But national Republicans had few hopes of winning this time, and it was not a priority race. She won 55%–43%, carrying San Luis Obispo narrowly and winning Santa Barbara 58%–40%.

With her seat on Energy and Commerce and background as a health-care professional, Capps focused on HMO regulation and protecting the privacy of medical records, including genetic tests. After four seriously contested Capps' campaigns in four years, she was an advocate of changes in campaign finance laws. She backed legislation to bar offshore oil drilling off the Santa Barbara and San Luis Obispo coasts. But she was less of a down-the-line liberal than her husband. She was one of only three California Democrats who voted to override Bill Clinton's vetoes of the marriage penalty and estate-tax repeal. Following her vote to support Permanent Normal Trade Relations with China, the Teamsters claimed that Capps betrayed them and withdrew their endorsement. On local issues, Capps got $2.1 million for a Central Coast research park.

Capps had serious competition in 2000 from moderate Republican Mike Stoker, a former Santa Barbara County Supervisor and California Agricultural Labor Relations Board Chairman. Stoker hoped for the local Farm Bureau's endorsement but the group deadlocked. He supported Roe v. Wade, but favored parental notification for minors and the partial birth abortion ban. Capps had a big fundraising edge and she won 53%–44%, a slight downtick from 1998, but 8% ahead of Al Gore. Redistricting could strengthen her bid for a third and, if she keeps her promise, last term in 2002. Democrats control redistricting, and by removing some or all of San Luis Obispo County and substituting Oxnard in Ventura County, they could make this a significantly more Democratic district.

Cook's Call *Competitive.* As one of the most Republican districts in the state held by a Democrat (Bush won here by 4 %), it is no wonder that Lois Capps has never won this seat by particularly large margins. But, Republicans have also fallen short in finding top-notch candidates to run against her. A moderate and well-known Republican could give Capps a very tight race. With Democrats in control of redistricting in the state, there has been talk of finding a way to make this district friendlier for Capps.

THE PEOPLE: Pop. 2000: 631,659; Pop. 1990: 572,956, up 10.2% 1990–2000. 77.3% White, 2.2% Black, 3.6% Asian, 1.1% Amer. Indian, 0.2% Hawaiian, 4% Two + races, 11.6% Other; 27% Hispanic Origin.

2000 Presidential Vote
Bush (R) 126,180 (49%)
Gore (D) 115,221 (45%)
Nader (Green) 14,872 (6%)
Others 2,334 (1%)

1996 Presidential Vote
Dole (R) 108,722 (44%)
Clinton (D) 108,208 (44%)
Perot (I) 17,311 (7%)
Others 11,656 (5%)

Rep. Lois Capps (D)

Elected March 1998, 2d term; b. Jan. 10, 1938, Ladysmith, WI; home, Santa Barbara; Pacific Lutheran U., B.S. 1959, Yale U., M.A. 1964, U. of CA at Santa Barbara, M.A. 1990; Lutheran; widowed.

Professional Career: Staff nurse, Visiting Nurses Assn., 1963–64; Head nurse, Yale New Haven Hospital, 1960–63; Instructor, Santa Barbara City Col., 1983–95; Nurse, Santa Barbara Schl. Dist., 1979–96.

DC Office: 1118 LHOB 20515, 202-225-3601; Fax: 202-225-5632; Web site: www.house.gov/capps.

District Offices: San Luis Obispo, 805-546-8348; Santa Barbara, 805-730-1710; Santa Maria, 805-349-9313.

Committees: *Energy & Commerce* (23d of 26 D): Commerce, Trade & Consumer Protection; Environment & Hazardous Materials; Health.

Group Ratings

	ADA	ACLU	AFS	LCV	CON	ITIC	NTU	COC	ACU	NTLC	CHC
2000	70	71	71	93	11	88	34	75	16	20	13
1999	100	—	100	81	59	—	13	44	8	—	—

National Journal Ratings

	1999 LIB	—	1999 CONS		2000 LIB	—	2000 CONS
Economic	62%	—	38%		61%	—	39%
Social	73%	—	26%		68%	—	31%
Foreign	77%	—	22%		69%	—	28%

Key Votes of the 106th Congress

1. Patient Bill of Rights	Y	5. Bar RU-486 $ for FDA	N	9. NATO War in Serbia		*
2. Accelerate Min. Wage	Y	6. Display 10 Commandments	N	10. Perm. Trade with China	Y	
3. Strike Ban on Ergo. Stnd.	Y	7. Gun Show Bkgrnd. Checks	Y	11. Debt Relief for 3rd World	Y	
4. Ovrd. Estate Tax Veto	Y	8. Ban Part.-Birth Abortion	N	12. Drop Cuba Econ. Embargo	Y	

Election Results

2000 general	Lois Capps (D)	135,538	(53%)	($1,498,955)
	Mike Stoker (R)	113,094	(44%)	($770,000)
	Other	6,438	(3%)	
2000 primary	Lois Capps (D)	105,850	(55%)	
	Mike Stoker (R)	73,256	(38%)	
	Allen Rowe (R)	8,385	(4%)	
	Other	4,036	(2%)	
1998 general	Lois Capps (D)	109,517	(55%)	($990,611)
	Tom J. Bordonaro Jr. (R)	85,927	(43%)	($392,149)
	Others	3,820	(2%)	

TWENTY-THIRD DISTRICT

On a golden mountainside, looking westward over a valley hemmed in by mountains north and south, five United States presidents gathered in November 1991 to dedicate the Ronald Reagan Library. This was the first time in 202 years that five presidents stood together in one place—one which the Founding Fathers surely did not imagine would ever be American and yet today seems quintessentially so. Simi Valley, famous a few months later as the site of the trial of police officers accused of assaulting Rodney King, is a product of the 1960s, the expansive and still optimistic postwar years when the vast stream of migrants who had come from all over the United States to Los Angeles spread beyond city and county limits to fill up barren valleys between golden mountains. They brought a willingness to work hard, high competence and high tech, an appreciation of the local environment and a distaste for crime and rioting that seemed all too common in the Los Angeles basin they left behind.

Simi Valley is just one of several communities in the valleys and narrow coastal margins of Ventura County, west of Los Angeles, that have been filling up with people leaving Los Angeles and the San Fernando Valley and building new communities in what had been an agricultural county with a gritty port and Navy base; Simi Valley claims more cars per capita than anywhere else in the United States and the county's population rose 12% in the 1990s. After the King trial, Simi Valley was criticized for being all-white and racist. In fact it is ethnically diverse: Ventura County was 33% Hispanic and 5% Asian in 2000. It also has some of the nation's lowest crime rates and some of the highest percentages of intact families in California, vivid contrasts with L.A. It also has a reminder, where the five presidents met in 1991, that traditional American values are not just material but are also moral: Pieces of the Berlin Wall, which President Reagan called on Mikhail Gorbachev to tear down, stand at the edge of the hill as you look toward the west.

The 23d Congressional District includes almost all of Ventura County except Thousand Oaks—places such as Simi Valley, Moorpark, Camarillo, Ventura, Oxnard, and the Point Mugu Navy base—plus a corner of Santa Barbara County and the town of Carpinteria. Politically, this was strong Reagan country when he was elected governor and president, though it lost some of its cheerful optimism when the California economy crashed in the early 1990s. As the district's Hispanic population has grown, from 30% in 1990 to 38% in 2000, it has become more Democratic. This district was carried 61%–39% by the senior George Bush in 1988; in 2000 it voted 48%–47% for Al Gore.

The congressman from the 23d District is Elton Gallegly. He grew up in the working class suburb of Huntington Park (now 96% Hispanic), dropped out of college and became a real estate broker. He was elected at 35 to the Simi Valley city council, became mayor in 1980, then was elected to Congress in 1986. In 1992, when redistricting moved much of Republican Robert Lagomarsino's district into the new Ventura County-based seat, Gallegly moved fast to push Lagomarsino into running in the 22d District to the north, where he lost the primary to Michael Huffington's $3 million campaign. Gallegly had minimal primary opposition but a spirited challenge from Democrat Anita Perez Ferguson, who raised large sums from the feminist left in "the year of the woman" and held Gallegly to 54%–41%.

Gallegly has a moderate-to-conservative voting record and has played a part on major issues. Foremost among them is illegal immigration. He called for a constitutional amendment to deny citizenship to babies of illegal immigrants, a tougher Border Patrol, an end to welfare for illegal immigrants and a tamperproof identification card for legal aliens. He criticized the INS IDs as easily forgeable, carrying one around himself as evidence. "One of the reasons that I am such a strong opponent of illegal immigration, other than the fact that it's illegal, is because it poses the greatest threat to legal immigration," he said. In 1996, he got the full House to pass his amendment allowing states to deny education to children who are illegal immigrants. This was heartily supported by Bob Dole, campaigning in California, and opposed by Bill Clinton. After a filibuster threat in the Senate, Republicans agreed to drop it.

On other issues, he sought to minimize labeling requirements on vitamins and dietary supplements issued by the Food and Drug Administration in response to a 1990 law sponsored by Henry Waxman. He passed a law to identify criminal aliens in U.S. prison, with a view toward deportation, and another to allow government agencies to give away their dogs—superannuated drug-sniffers and guard dogs—to their handlers. In 2000, Clinton signed his bill to add to the Vietnam Veterans Memorial on the Washington Mall a plaque honoring unnamed vets who died of causes not directly related to combat wounds. After pressure from local growers, he decided in the final hours to support Permanent Normal Trade Relations with China. The first measure passed by the House in 2001 was Gallegly's bill to raise the retirement age for federal firefighters from 55 to 57. Locally, he worked hard to save the Point Mugu Navy base, threatened with closure and with 18,000 related jobs, Ventura County's largest employer; he worked to get a wing of 16 E-2 radar planes assigned there, plus two new C-130s to fight forest fires. He secured funding to help widen the Santa Clara River Bridge to 12 lanes, and he gained an additional 8,500 acres for Santa Cruz Island, the largest in Channel Islands National Park.

Gallegly, a non-lawyer, has passed up several opportunities to chair a Judiciary subcommittee and declined to serve as a House manager during the Senate impeachment trial of Clinton. In the 107th Congress, he became chairman of the new Europe Subcommittee of International Relations. His strongest recent reelection challenge came in 2000 from corporate attorney and political newcomer Michael Case, who attacked his views on abortion and guns; Gallegly won 54%–41%. Redistricting could be a huge problem for him. Gallegly appears to be one of the chief targets of the Democrats who control redistricting. In early 2001 they seemed to be contemplating a major reconfiguration of the district lines in this part of the state, with a view toward forcing Gallegly and 25th district Republican Buck McKeon into the same district. Democratic portions of the district would be added to make adjacent districts—the 22nd and 24th—more Democratic. It is not clear whether the demographics will permit this; Gallegly survived redistricting against the odds in 1992 and perhaps will do so again in 2002.

Cook's Call   *Competitive.* The fact that Elton Gallegly took just 54% in 2000 highlights how marginal this Ventura County district has become over the last few years. Democrats have talked about tinkering with the lines here to make this seat even more attractive to a Democrat. But with the Pacific Ocean to the west, Lois Capps' 22nd District to the north, and the Republican-leaning 25th to the east, there is not that much room to work with. Still, even with its present lines, a well-funded challenger could give Gallegly a real race.

THE PEOPLE: Pop. 2000: 642,427; Pop. 1990: 571,562, up 12.4% 1990–2000. 66.9% White, 2.1% Black, 5.3% Asian, 1% Amer. Indian, 0.2% Hawaiian, 4.2% Two + races, 20.3% Other; 37.7% Hispanic Origin.

2000 Presidential Vote

Gore (D)	110,746	(48%)
Bush (R)	107,859	(47%)
Nader (Green)	8,810	(4%)
Others	2,493	(1%)

1996 Presidential Vote

Clinton (D)	93,046	(45%)
Dole (R)	85,508	(42%)
Perot (I)	19,237	(9%)
Others	6,745	(3%)

Rep. Elton Gallegly (R)

Elected 1986, 8th term; b. Mar. 7, 1944, Huntington Park; home, Simi Valley; Los Angeles St. Col., 1962–63; Protestant; married (Janice).

Elected Office: Simi Valley City Cncl., 1979–80; Simi Valley Mayor, 1980–86.

Professional Career: Owner, real estate firm.

DC Office: 2427 RHOB 20515, 202-225-5811; Fax: 202-225-1100; Web site: www.house.gov/gallegly.

District Office: Oxnard, 805-485-2300.

Committees: *International Relations* (7th of 26 R): Europe (Chmn.); Western Hemisphere. *Judiciary* (6th of 21 R): Courts, the Internet & Intellectual Property; Immigration & Claims. *Resources* (5th of 28 R): National Parks, Recreation & Public Lands.

Group Ratings

	ADA	ACLU	AFS	LCV	CON	ITIC	NTU	COC	ACU	NTLC	CHC
2000	5	14	0	36	14	90	56	85	72	67	73
1999	25	—	0	13	6	—	52	84	79	—	—

National Journal Ratings

	1999 LIB —	1999 CONS		2000 LIB —	2000 CONS
Economic	30% —	64%		29% —	67%
Social	35% —	64%		43% —	55%
Foreign	23% —	73%		33% —	62%

Key Votes of the 106th Congress

1. Patient Bill of Rights	Y	5. Bar RU-486 $ for FDA	Y	9. NATO War in Serbia	N
2. Accelerate Min. Wage	N	6. Display 10 Commandments	Y	10. Perm. Trade with China	Y
3. Strike Ban on Ergo. Stnd.	N	7. Gun Show Bkgrnd. Checks	N	11. Debt Relief for 3rd World	N
4. Ovrd. Estate Tax Veto	Y	8. Ban Part.-Birth Abortion	Y	12. Drop Cuba Econ. Embargo	N

Election Results

2000 general	Elton Gallegly (R)	119,479	(54%)	($1,022,565)
	Michael Case (D)	89,918	(41%)	($726,953)
	Other	11,637	(5%)	
2000 primary	Elton Gallegly (R)	92,010	(63%)	
	Michael Case (D)	36,221	(25%)	
	Albert Maxwell Goldberg (D)	8,786	(6%)	
	Other	8,547	(6%)	
1998 general	Elton Gallegly (R)	96,322	(60%)	($282,187)
	Daniel Gonzalez (D)	64,032	(40%)	($33,777)

TWENTY-FOURTH DISTRICT

The San Fernando Valley, in the early 20th Century when the movie business was young, was a vast expanse of empty land, annexed to Los Angeles in 1915; moviemakers, looking for filming sites for a western, drove past the vacant lots of Westwood, up narrow roads through the Santa Monica Mountains and over into the vast Valley, sheltered from ocean breezes and rain-bearing clouds by the mountains. Since then this vast bowl of land has been transformed, first into 1950s suburbia, then into a postmodern city of its own, economically vital and yeastily ethnic. Even in its suburban years, the San Fernando Valley was not entirely residential: big factories—the General Motors Van Nuys assembly plant, the Anheuser Busch brewery, Rockwell and Litton defense plants—provided jobs. In those years this was fast-growing, family-friendly territory; politically, it was turf fought over hard by Republicans and Democrats. By the 1970s young white Anglo families were fleeing, as the Los Angeles Unified School District was hit by a busing order. There is plenty of upscale territory left in the uplands in the rims of the Valley, in heavily Jewish Sherman Oaks and Encino and to the west in Woodland Hills and Chatsworth; the office blocks and mini-malls along Ventura and Woodland Hills Boulevard show unmistakable signs of affluence. In the inner lowlands of the Valley, new immigrants have moved in. Some old neighborhoods have become rough enclaves, with youth gangs and boarded-up houses and apartments weakened by the Northridge earthquake; Iranians and Chinese, Mexicans and Koreans, Israelis and Filipinos are keeping other neighborhoods solidly middle-class.

The 24th Congressional District of California includes most of the southern and western San Fernando Valley, from the hillside mansions of Encino to the gang territory around the Van Nuys plant. Two-thirds of the 24th's people live in the Valley; others live directly west, in new communities nestled amid mountains along U.S. 101—ranch-like Agoura, jewel-like Westlake Village and Ventura County's sprawling Thousand Oaks, home of the biotechnology giant Amgen. The 24th also takes in Malibu, with $1 million beach houses five feet from each other and Pepperdine University's campus in the hills. Politically, this is a mixed area. The Jewish precincts are solidly Democratic, and have become more so in the 1990s; Thousand Oaks is heavily Republican; the immigrant areas fluctuate and have been going Democratic; Malibu is trendy showbiz liberal.

The congressman from the 24th is Brad Sherman, a Democrat elected in 1996. Sherman grew up in Monterey Park, in the San Gabriel Valley east of Los Angeles; he started working on Democratic campaigns at age 6, licking stamps and stuffing envelopes, and set up his own stamp wholesaling firm at 14. He graduated with high honors from UCLA, worked as an accountant, then went to Harvard Law and practiced tax law in L.A. He always had the political bug, and in 1990 was elected to the state Board of Equalization. This five-member body is a sort of tax court; Sherman's district was most of Los Angeles County. He was known as a stickler for detail, a "tax nerd," as one former staffer said, who used the office with a keen scent for political advantage. He led the fight against Pete Wilson's snack tax in 1991, and got Bill Clinton to side with his opinion on taxing foreign-owned businesses, which he says saved California $2 billion. But he irritated cartoonists with a ruling that exempted them from the state tax on artwork but not on illustrations; they set up a Website, the Sherman Gallery, in which they vied in caricaturing the balding and bespectacled Sherman.

Sherman decided to run for Congress, and moved his residence from Santa Monica to Sherman Oaks, when Anthony Beilenson announced he would retire in 1996 after 20 years in the House. Sherman had an active Republican opponent, businessman Rich Sybert, who had lost to Beilenson by 49%–48% in 1994. Both of these self-financers (Sherman spent $578,000 of his own money) stressed their moderation. Sherman ran against Newt Gingrich and the Republican Congress; but he also supported the death penalty, wanted racial quotas and preferences phased out and favored tough measures on illegal immigration. Sybert stressed his independence of Gingrich, favoring abortion rights and environmental protections. Sybert was intense, Sherman a bit humorous (he handed out combs to voters, saying "You'll be able to use it more than I can"). Sherman won 49%–44%.

In the House, Sherman's voting record has been notably more moderate than those of other Los Angeles County Democrats. One of the few CPAs in Congress, he serves on Financial Services. He passed an amendment appropriating an extra $599 million for parkland acquisition and claimed credit for $5 million for the Santa Monica Mountains National Recreation Area; he also announced money for the Backbone Trail for hikers. He sponsored a national hotline for parents to check if teachers and coaches were convicted sexual predators. He urged a mandatory curfew at Burbank Airport and opposed takeoffs over the Valley. He opposed the proposed huge Ahmanson Ranch development in Ventura because of concerns over traffic and endangered species. He pushed to study the San Diego-Ventura Freeway interchange in the Valley, the fourth busiest in

California, but a $1.5 million earmark was rejected in 2000. He got House passage of $10 million in international funding to combat AIDS.

Sherman has won reelection by increasing margins. In 1998, against Magellan Systems founder Randy Hoffman who spent $426,000 of his own money, Sherman won 57%–38%; he carried the Los Angeles County portion of the district 61%–35% while losing the Ventura County portion by 51%–45%. This was evidence of the leftward trend in metro Los Angeles. In 2000 former Doobie Brothers guitarist and missile defense enthusiast Jeff "Skunk" Baxter decided not to run, and Sherman beat former "Babylon 5" TV actor Jerry Doyle, although he was criticized for taking some contributions to pay himself back for earlier campaign loans. During the presidential election recount, Sherman called for abolishing the Electoral College, describing it as a "relic." In redistricting, he would like to shed Thousand Oaks. But Democratic redistricters may put the needs of other Democrats in this area ahead of his, and he has in any case demonstrated he can carry the district as it is.

Cook's Call   *Safe*. In the mid-1990s this district was considered one of the most competitive in southern California. In 1994 Democratic incumbent Tony Beilenson won by just 3,500 votes and Sherman won his first race in 1996 with just 49%. Since 1998, this district has been behaving like a Democratic stronghold. Sherman won with 57% in 1998 against a well-funded challenger, took 66% in 2000, and Gore beat Bush in the district with 58%. Sherman looks well positioned for 2002.

THE PEOPLE: Pop. 2000: 629,832; Pop. 1990: 572,287, up 10.1% 1990–2000. 75.5% White, 2.9% Black, 7.8% Asian, 0.5% Amer. Indian, 0.1% Hawaiian, 4.4% Two+ races, 8.9% Other; 19.8% Hispanic Origin.

2000 Presidential Vote

Gore (D)	144,778	(58%)
Bush (R)	94,235	(38%)
Nader (Green)	8,154	(3%)
Others	2,666	(1%)

1996 Presidential Vote

Clinton (D)	117,724	(52%)
Dole (R)	83,412	(37%)
Perot (I)	16,165	(7%)
Others	8,054	(4%)

Rep. Brad Sherman (D)

Elected 1996, 3d term; b. Oct. 24, 1954, Los Angeles; home, Sherman Oaks; U.C.L.A., B.A. 1974, Harvard U., J.D. 1979; Jewish; single.

Elected Office: CA St. Board of Equalization, 1990–95, Chmn., 1991–95.

Professional Career: Accountant, 1980–90.

DC Office: 1524 LHOB 20515, 202-225-5911; Fax: 202-225-5879; Web site: www.house.gov/sherman.

District Offices: Thousand Oaks, 805-449-2372; Woodland Hills, 818-999-1990.

Committees: *Financial Services* (14th of 32 D): Capital Markets, Insurance & Government Sponsored Enterprises; Financial Institutions & Consumer Credit; International Monetary Policy & Trade. *International Relations* (11th of 23 D): Europe; Middle East & South Asia.

Group Ratings

	ADA	ACLU	AFS	LCV	CON	ITIC	NTU	COC	ACU	NTLC	CHC
2000	90	79	100	93	54	75	25	47	20	30	13
1999	95	—	100	100	28	—	18	32	8	—	—

National Journal Ratings

	1999 LIB	—	1999 CONS		2000 LIB	—	2000 CONS
Economic	67%	—	32%		75%	—	24%
Social	73%	—	26%		79%	—	17%
Foreign	61%	—	37%		69%	—	28%

Key Votes of the 106th Congress

1. Patient Bill of Rights	Y	5. Bar RU-486 $ for FDA	N	9. NATO War in Serbia	Y
2. Accelerate Min. Wage	Y	6. Display 10 Commandments	N	10. Perm. Trade with China	N
3. Strike Ban on Ergo. Stnd.	Y	7. Gun Show Bkgrnd. Checks	Y	11. Debt Relief for 3rd World	Y
4. Ovrd. Estate Tax Veto	N	8. Ban Part.-Birth Abortion	N	12. Drop Cuba Econ. Embargo	N

Election Results

2000 general	Brad Sherman (D)	155,398	(66%)	($539,122)
	Jerry Doyle (R)	70,169	(30%)	($126,148)
	Other	9,877	(4%)	
2000 primary	Brad Sherman (D)	99,236	(66%)	
	Jerry Doyle (R)	43,762	(29%)	
	Other	6,865	(5%)	
1998 general	Brad Sherman (D)	103,491	(57%)	($1,185,937)
	Randy Hoffman (R)	69,501	(38%)	($1,040,934)
	Others	7,588	(4%)	

TWENTY-FIFTH DISTRICT

One tragedy of the 1994 Northridge earthquake was at the intersection of the I-5 and Route 14 freeways at the north edge of the San Fernando Valley, where an overpass collapsed and a motorcycle patrolman hurtled to his death. Destruction of the interchange had an economic and personal impact for months afterwards, for the settled area of Los Angeles County no longer ends at the mountains at the northern rim of the San Fernando Valley. It continues along Route 14 past the mountain-surrounded city of Santa Clarita, with 151,000 people in 2000, and 25 miles beyond, where the mountains stop at the San Andreas Fault and the desert stretches out low and flat, divided into mile-square grids. This is the Antelope Valley, with huge aerospace plants and military bases around the fast-growing towns of Palmdale and Lancaster, where more than 235,000 people live. Because of mountain terrain, when the chokepoint intersection was crushed, thousands of commuters lined up for hours to get to work.

The 25th Congressional District covers all three of these areas. It includes the northwest quadrant of the San Fernando Valley, Granada Hills and Chatsworth, with 180,000 mostly affluent Anglos inside the LA city limits; it takes in Santa Clarita, with its Old West air and its industrial park, spreading subdivisions and Six Flags Magic Mountain theme park, home of a boosterish Republicanism; it includes the aerospace country of the Antelope Valley, with somewhat lower-income. All three parts of the district are heavily Republican, especially the desert area; this safe Republican district was created after the 1990 Census.

The congressman from the 25th since 1992 is Howard "Buck" McKeon, who grew up in Southern California, graduated from Brigham Young University and was a co-owner of Howard and Phil's Western wear, a family business that expanded to 52 stores in California, Arizona, Nevada and Utah in the early 1990s, but closed in 2000. McKeon was the first mayor of Santa Clarita, when it was incorporated by joining several unincorporated county areas, and served five years on the council. He won the 1992 primary 40%–38% over Assemblyman Phil Wyman, who once proposed to ban the allegedly satanic practice of recording certain words into songs backwards.

McKeon, became Republican freshman class president and helped abolish four select committees in 1993. With a seat on the Armed Services Committee, he worked to save local defense jobs—this was the production base for the B-1 and B-2 bombers, and SR-71 fighter planes. He helped get new contracts for the X-33, the next generation Space Shuttle and the Joint Strike Fighter; in 2000, he enacted a requirement that the Pentagon study building the fighter in the Antelope Valley, instead of the chief competing sites in St. Louis or Fort Worth. He tried to authorize more B-2s and got NASA to perform Space Shuttle modifications to Air Force Base Plant 42 in Palmdale, and criticized the Clinton Administration for failing to meet military readiness needs.

He has been a leader at the Education and the Workforce Committee. He put together in 1995 a bill restructuring job training, literacy and youth employment programs, but it was not reconciled with the Senate version. In 1998, his subcommittee reauthorized the Higher Education act, brokering a truce with the Clinton administration over student loan programs; bank-based and government-run programs would continue to coexist. He fought an Equal Employment Opportunity Commission religious harassment guideline that, he felt, would bar people from keeping a Bible on their desk or wearing religious symbols like the Star of David at work. After the 1998 election, he briefly considered a challenge to Majority Leader Dick Armey, but correctly concluded that Armey would prevail. Instead, he moved into the inner circle of Speaker-designate Bob Livingston, who named McKeon one of his top lieutenants. But that assignment disappeared with Livingston's surprise announcement that he was resigning. In the 107th Congress, McKeon lost out to John Doolittle for an Appropriations seat; instead, he became chairman of the 21st Century Competitiveness Subcommittee, which deals mostly with higher education issues.

On local issues, he has pressed for transportation improvements for his rapidly-growing district, including development of a Palmdale regional airport. He opposed Los Angeles's request for $100 million for the Red Line subway and got funding for interchange improvements in Santa Clarita and the Antelope Valley. He won language to enforce a 190 million ton trash dump in Elsmere Canyon. In 2000, he got $3.4 million to repair the gym and pool at the Veterans Administration medical center in Sepulveda, which were damaged in the earthquake, plus $3.4 million to relocate a stretch of the Pacific Crest Trail in the Agua Dulce area. He demanded to know why the Housing and Urban Development Department sold years later condominiums in North Hills that had been damaged by the earthquake.

McKeon has been re-elected without serious opposition. Even though his district—and its Republicans—grew by 22% in the 1990s, redistricting could be a problem. Redistricting is controlled by Democrats, and in early 2001 they seemed bent on placing McKeon and 23rd district Republican Elton Gallegly in the same district; this would presumably be done as part of a ripple effect resulting from the creation of new Latino seats in central L.A., pushing other Democratic districts outward.

Cook's Call   *Safe.* Though not the most Republican district in the state, it is nonetheless safe territory for McKeon.

THE PEOPLE: Pop. 2000: 699,526; Pop. 1990: 573,189, up 22% 1990–2000. 67.4% White, 7.9% Black, 7.6% Asian, 0.8% Amer. Indian, 0.2% Hawaiian, 4.6% Two+ races, 11.6% Other; 25% Hispanic Origin.

2000 Presidential Vote			1996 Presidential Vote		
Bush (R)	120,463	(51%)	Dole (R)	97,002	(47%)
Gore (D)	104,593	(45%)	Clinton (D)	84,212	(41%)
Nader (Green)	6,294	(3%)	Perot (I)	18,320	(9%)
Others	2,826	(1%)	Others	5,775	(3%)

Rep. Howard P. (Buck) McKeon (R)

Elected 1992, 5th term; b. Sept. 9, 1938, Los Angeles; home, Santa Clarita; Brigham Young U., B.S. 1985; Mormon; married (Patricia).

Elected Office: William S. Hart School District Bd., 1979–87; Santa Clarita Mayor, 1987–88; Santa Clarita City Cncl., 1988–92.

Professional Career: Small businessman; Owner, Howard & Phil's Western Wear, 1973–2000; Chmn., Valencia Natl. Bank, 1987–88.

DC Office: 2242 RHOB 20515, 202-225-1956; Fax: 202-226-0683; Web site: www.house.gov/mckeon.

District Offices: Palmdale, 661-274-9688; Santa Clarita, 661-254-2111.

Committees: *Armed Services* (11th of 32 R): Military Procurement; Military Readiness. *Education & the Workforce* (6th of 27 R): 21st Century Competitiveness (Chmn.); Employer-Employee Relations. *Veterans' Affairs* (11th of 17 R): Health.

Group Ratings

	ADA	ACLU	AFS	LCV	CON	ITIC	NTU	COC	ACU	NTLC	CHC
2000	5	23	0	7	22	100	63	85	92	66	79
1999	5	—	0	6	21	—	55	96	79	—	—

National Journal Ratings

	1999 LIB	—	1999 CONS		2000 LIB	—	2000 CONS
Economic	0%	—	84%		18%	—	76%
Social	34%	—	65%		33%	—	66%
Foreign	23%	—	77%		12%	—	78%

Key Votes of the 106th Congress

1. Patient Bill of Rights	N	5. Bar RU-486 $ for FDA	Y	9. NATO War in Serbia	N
2. Accelerate Min. Wage	N	6. Display 10 Commandments	*	10. Perm. Trade with China	Y
3. Strike Ban on Ergo. Stnd.	N	7. Gun Show Bkgrnd. Checks	N	11. Debt Relief for 3rd World	N
4. Ovrd. Estate Tax Veto	Y	8. Ban Part.-Birth Abortion	Y	12. Drop Cuba Econ. Embargo	N

Election Results

2000 general	Howard P. (Buck) McKeon (R)	138,628	(62%)	($674,238)
	Sid Gold (D)	73,921	(33%)	($34,112)
	Other	10,229	(5%)	
2000 primary	Howard P. (Buck) McKeon (R)	92,342	(63%)	
	Sid Gold (D)	39,748	(27%)	
	Hal Brent Meyers (R)	7,842	(5%)	
	Other	5,999	(4%)	
1998 general	Howard P. (Buck) McKeon (R)	114,013	(75%)	($405,024)
	Bruce R. Acker (Lib)	38,669	(25%)	

TWENTY-SIXTH DISTRICT

A hiker looking north from the crest of the Santa Monica Mountains in 1910 would have seen spread out, almost totally empty and barren, 20 miles wide and 12 miles deep, the San Fernando Valley. Separated by the Cahuenga Pass from rapidly growing Los Angeles and Hollywood, the Valley was bought up in massive tracts by civic leaders even as they were urging city engineer William Mulholland to build a huge 250-mile aqueduct from the Owens Valley to give Los Angeles water and persuading the city in 1915 to annex 200 square miles of the Valley. In the years after World War II, this was modern suburbia, filled with *Leave It to Beaver* families. Today the San Fernando Valley is postmodern urban, with a look you can see in exaggerated form in Disney headquarters buildings in Burbank or Universal City's CityWalk shopping mall: The driver topping the crest today sees office towers looming out over slightly hazy air, shopping centers, occasional palm trees, lines of grid streets stretching out into the distance beyond stucco subdivisions and the squat factory and warehouse buildings that make Los Angeles County the nation's number-one manufacturer.

The people in the Valley have also changed. The white Anglo families with stay-at-home moms in the 1950s have been replaced by hard-working Latino families, with children waiting at the bus stops for schools and parents juggling two jobs. But there is continuity: These remain places where people work hard and try to raise children who will have better chances and make better livings than they have. Pacoima, at the northern end of the Valley, where Rodney King was pulled over and beaten and arrested, is mostly black and Latino. Farther south, in Canoga Park, Van Nuys and Burbank, are the big aerospace plants; the GM assembly plants have been shut down since 1989, with thousands of jobs lost. Less visible are the hundreds of small factories and multimedia plants where thousands of jobs have been created. The lower income areas here are farther from the central city; the southern rim of the Valley, around Studio City and North Hollywood, is still heavily Jewish and is attracting new families who often send their kids to religious schools. In 1988 this district voted 56%–44% for Michael Dukakis; in 2000 it had moved left and voted 70%–25% for Al Gore.

The 26th Congressional District of California consists of the Golden State and Hollywood Freeway corridors of the Valley—roughly its eastern half—proceeding as far west as Van Nuys and the San Diego Freeway. Overall, the district was 52% Hispanic in 1990 and 65% in 2000. But Latinos are still not the majority voting bloc here; many are not citizens, many are children or young people not yet in the voting stream; and the tradition among Latinos today, as among Italians 100 years ago, is to trust family and hard work, not politics and government, to get ahead. The rising Democratic percentages here are due as much to Jewish as to Latino voters, who have both trended Democratic in the late 1990s, one group in response to the emergence of the Christian right, the other in response to the campaign for cutting off aid to illegal aliens which suggested, wrongly, that Latinos are interested more in welfare than hard work.

The congressman from the 26th is Howard Berman, one of the most aggressive and creative members of the House—and one of the most clear-sighted operators in American politics. He grew up in Los Angeles in modest circumstances, got involved in politics, and was elected to the Assembly from a formerly Republican Hollywood Hills district in 1972, at 31. This was the beginning of the so-called Berman-Waxman political machine—not so much a precinct organization as a group of consultants who raised money, redrew district lines and endorsed candidates through direct mail. Their core constituency was liberal Westside Jews. Berman became Assembly majority leader in his first term. In 1980 he tried to unseat Speaker Leo McCarthy; ultimately both lost to Willie Brown, who served 15 years. Berman's consolation prize was a Valley-based congressional seat in 1982. The machine fell on hard times in the 1990s, as Republicans wrested away control of redistricting, the feminist left became the Democratic Party's driving force and Berman-Waxman ally Mel Levine lost the 1992 Senate primary to Barbara Boxer. Since then, Berman has been a political force on his own, with a record that is mostly but not always liberal.

Berman has been an active legislator even more than a political operator, and on all manner of issues. On foreign policy, he started off less as a Vietnam war dove than as a backer of Israel, and he is not one of those Democrats who think America has habitually been on the wrong side in the world. For a decade he floor-managed foreign aid authorization bills, defending aid to many countries as well as Israel. With Henry Hyde he wrote the law authorizing embargoes on nations that condone terrorism; in April 1990 he called for sanctions on Iraq, four months before Saddam Hussein invaded Kuwait. Berman voted for the Gulf war resolution, but was understandably critical of the Bush administration—if it had followed his advice there might well have been no need for war. Berman has worked to stop the export of missile and nuclear weapons technology—an uphill battle in the Clinton years. He also was among the few Democrats to buck organized labor and back President Clinton's request for fast-track trade authority. "We can't afford to sit on the sidelines while the rest of the world hammers out new trade agreements," he said.

Berman passed a law banning the double-issuing of U.S. passports to coddle Arab countries that refuse to honor passports with Israeli marks. He pushed through the International Broadcasting Act, consolidating and downsizing agencies but maintaining Radio Free Europe and establishing Radio Free Asia. He worked hard to save the National Endowment for Democracy. He has worked on reorganizing the State Department and other foreign policy agencies. He sponsored a law in 2000 to take action against any country that proliferates weapons of mass destruction to Iran. He offered an amendment to revoke Permanent Normal Trade Relations with China if it attacks, invades or blockades Taiwan and, when that was rejected, voted against PNTR. He protested Canadian government policies that he said led unfairly to "runaway" film-making in Canada.

Immigration is another issue on which Berman has been a major legislator. In 1988 he sponsored the provision allowing 20,000 immigrant visas for migrants without close relatives here, to be selected randomly by computer—"Berman visa applications," they are called. He secured in 1990 more family reunification slots, expediting the immigration of Soviet Jews (a vivid presence in L.A), and gaining amnesty provisions for more family members to remain in this country. He worked to pass an amendment taking federal responsibility for the cost of jailing illegal aliens, and in 2000 got $565 million spent on it; much of course goes to California. On the 1996 immigration bill he co-sponsored the amendment separating legal and illegal immigration. Berman also helped to kill Republican Richard Pombo's amendment to let in 250,000 guest farm workers. In May 2000, as support grew for guest worker legislation, Berman entered negotiations with their sponsors to get provisions to protect incoming farm workers. "Let's make a coalition of farmers and farm workers, and all the folks affiliated with these groups. The question is, how can we accomplish what the growers need to accomplish, in a way that's good for farm workers." He pushed especially for legal status for farm workers who have worked in this country for 150 days. The measure was killed in the Senate in December 2000 by Phil Gramm and Trent Lott, but will undoubtedly be revisited. In early 2001, Berman and Hilda Solis introduced a bill to grant a year of amnesty to Salvadorans illegally in this country after that country suffered a devastating earthquake, on the theory that those workers would send home remittances that would help rebuild that country.

In the 106th Congress, Berman gave up his ranking position on the Asia and Pacific Subcommittee of International Affairs, and took the ranking position on the Courts and Intellectual Property Subcommittee of Judiciary, one of vital importance to Hollywood interests. There he passed an anti-cybersquatting law, to discourage pouncing on website names. He questioned whether methods of business patents, like Amazon.com's one-click, should be granted for computer uses of techniques obvious elsewhere, and sought to open a dialogue on the issue. He worked to modify a bill to ensure adequate incentives to create databases. He tried unsuccessfully to stop compulsory licensing for satellite broadcasts because of damage to copyright holders. He decried websites like Napster and Gnutella that systematically deprive copyright holders a return on their intellectual property.

In January 1997 Minority Leader Dick Gephardt prevailed on Berman to become ranking minority member of the ethics committee, which had become badly scarred by partisanship during the investigation of Newt Gingrich. With his tacit encouragement, few ethics complaints have been filed for partisan reasons. On local issues, he worked with other area congressmen to rebuild the VA gym at the Sepulveda campus, to fund the California Institute of the Arts in Santa Clarita and to stock the Hansen Dam Recreation Lake with catfish. He fought to enforce the voluntary 11:00 p.m. to 7:00 a.m. curfew on flights into and out of Burbank Airport.

The rising percentage of Latinos in the 26th district has been seen by some as a political threat to Berman. Although many Latinos do not vote, the Latino percentage of the electorate rose to above one-third by 2000. In December 1997 Berman sent a letter to constituents warning about "vandals, burglars, rapists and murderers that roam our streets," and arguing that though improvements have been made, "the crime rate in our area remains appallingly high!" Raul Gordinez, Mayor of San Fernando (an enclave inside Los Angeles), took umbrage, noting that crime in San Fernando was down 20% in three years. Berman responded, "The crime rate is still too high." In March 1998 Godinez started running for the 26th District seat, portraying himself as a David challenging a Goliath, criticizing Berman's efforts to create a recreation area at Hansen Lake in the northern Valley. Berman campaigned hard in district neighborhoods, and in the June primary Berman prevailed 67%–33%. At the same time, there was a much more vitriolic primary in the overlapping 20th state Senate district between former Assemblyman Richard Katz and L.A. Councilman Richard Alarcon, which Alarcon won by just 29 votes.

Redistricting poses some problems for Berman. The 26th district could be kept in much its current form; it is only about 20,000 too large, and the high Latino percentage would answer demands by Latino politicians to maximize the number of heavily Latino districts. But Democratic redistricters, with whom Berman is in close touch, reportedly have plans to alter nearby districts. So the 26th district might move east, to take over some Republican and Anglo areas in the 27th district that Democrat Adam Schiff captured in 2000, or it could move south to include Jewish neighborhoods in Studio City. In all likelihood Berman will end up with a favorable constituency.

Cook's Call   *Safe.* As one of the most Democratic districts in the state (and the country), there is no chance that 20-year incumbent Howard Berman will ever have to worry about a competitive general election contest here. But, there has been talk that Berman could face a serious challenge from a Latino in the 2002 primary (this district is already heavily minority). But Berman, one of the most plugged in members in the L.A. area, has a leg up on redistricting: His brother Michael is the chief Democratic consultant on the map drawing.

THE PEOPLE: Pop. 2000: 660,224; Pop. 1990: 571,538, up 15.5% 1990–2000. 46.4% White, 5.1% Black, 6.6% Asian, 1% Amer. Indian, 0.1% Hawaiian, 5.7% Two+ races, 35.1% Other; 65.4% Hispanic Origin.

2000 Presidential Vote

Gore (D)	88,710	(70%)
Bush (R)	32,004	(25%)
Nader (Green)	3,761	(3%)
Others	1,633	(1%)

1996 Presidential Vote

Clinton (D)	71,416	(65%)
Dole (R)	27,129	(25%)
Perot (I)	7,930	(7%)
Others	3,150	(3%)

Rep. Howard L. Berman (D)

Elected 1982, 10th term; b. Apr. 15, 1941, Los Angeles; home, N. Hollywood; U.C.L.A., B.A. 1962, LL.B. 1965; Jewish; married (Janis).

Elected Office: CA Assembly, 1973–82, Majority Ldr., 1974–79.

Professional Career: Practicing atty., 1967–72.

DC Office: 2330 RHOB 20515, 202-225-4695; Fax: 202-225-3196; Web site: www.house.gov/berman.

District Office: Mission Hills, 818-891-0543.

Committees: *International Relations* (2d of 23 D): Middle East & South Asia. *Judiciary* (3d of 17 D): Courts, the Internet & Intellectual Property (RMM); Immigration & Claims. *Standards of Official Conduct* (RMM of 5 D).

Group Ratings

	ADA	ACLU	AFS	LCV	CON	ITIC	NTU	COC	ACU	NTLC	CHC
2000	100	85	100	86	64	68	22	50	4	12	7
1999	95	—	100	94	51	—	15	26	0	—	—

National Journal Ratings

	1999 LIB —	1999 CONS		2000 LIB —	2000 CONS
Economic	88%	12%		92%	8%
Social	87%	0%		83%	17%
Foreign	84%	15%		94%	5%

Key Votes of the 106th Congress

1. Patient Bill of Rights	Y	5. Bar RU-486 $ for FDA	N	9. NATO War in Serbia	Y
2. Accelerate Min. Wage	Y	6. Display 10 Commandments	N	10. Perm. Trade with China	N
3. Strike Ban on Ergo. Stnd.	Y	7. Gun Show Bkgrnd. Checks	Y	11. Debt Relief for 3rd World	Y
4. Ovrd. Estate Tax Veto	N	8. Ban Part.-Birth Abortion	N	12. Drop Cuba Econ. Embargo	*

Election Results

2000 general	Howard L. Berman (D)	96,500	(84%)	($521,478)
	Bill Farley (LIB)	13,052	(11%)	($38)
	David L. Cossak (NL)	5,229	(5%)	
2000 primary	Howard L. Berman (D)	60,896	(85%)	
	Bill Farley (LIB)	8,190	(11%)	
	David L. Cossak (NL)	2,887	(4%)	
1998 general	Howard L. Berman (D)	69,000	(82%)	($690,408)
	Juan Carlos Ros (Lib)	6,556	(8%)	($672)
	Maria Armoudian	4,858	(6%)	
	Others	3,248	(4%)	

TWENTY-SEVENTH DISTRICT

In the early years of the 20th Century, when Los Angeles was growing to become one of America's major cities, its richest citizens settled not on the beach (too clammy and cold) or on the west side (too dusty and remote), but in communities they built at the base of the San Gabriel Mountains that rise 10,000 feet above the city, their snow-capped peaks visible most of the year. The premier such community was Pasadena, with its institutions of national stature—the Rose Bowl,

Cal Tech—and the premier structures were Pasadena's baroque-domed City Hall and railroader Henry Huntington's house in next-door San Marino, now the Huntington Library, one of the world's great scholarly institutions. Pasadena and South Pasadena have proudly preserved their bungalow neighborhoods, and Pasadena preserved and rebuilt the 80-year old curving Colorado Boulevard Bridge over Arroyo Seco. More middle class is Glendale, north of downtown Los Angeles, site of Forest Lawn Cemetery; just west, beneath the Verdugo Mountains, is Burbank (named not for botanist Luther Burbank but for a local dentist-developer), famous now for the NBC Studios and Disney headquarters and home to many small entertainment multimedia companies as well. With their lower taxes and business-friendly attitude, and despite earlier loss of aerospace jobs, Glendale and Burbank are booming while inside the city limits of high-tax and high-regulation Los Angeles, Hollywood has become seedy and commercial buildings have huge vacancy rates.

The 27th Congressional District takes in all these affluent foothill communities plus—sandwiched between the Verdugo and San Gabriel Mountains—La Canada, La Crescenta, Sunland and Tujunga. For years these places were traditionally, indeed stereotypically, Republican, but in the 1990s they moved sharply toward the Democrats. There are black communities in Pasadena and Altadena, the boyhood home of Jackie Robinson. Style-conscious young couples are moving into Arts and Crafts houses in Pasadena and South Pasadena. Immigrants have moved in: Latinos in Glendale and other towns, Asians into San Marino (now 49% Asian). In 2000 the 27th district was 23% Hispanic, 13% Asian and 7% black. Glendale is now the center of the nation's largest Armenian community and has many Iranians, Koreans, Filipinos—nearly half its residents are foreign-born. There are also immigrants as well as upscale singles in showbizzy Burbank. This district, with a very different electorate, voted 57%–43% for the senior George Bush in 1988. In 2000 it voted 53%–41% for Al Gore. The change has been registered down the ballot too. In 1996, the two Assembly districts that cover the area—safe Republican seats since the 1940s—both elected Democrats. And it 2000 the 27th district rejected a Republican congressman and elected a Democrat.

The congressman from the 27th is Adam Schiff, a Democrat elected in 2000 over Republican James Rogan in the nation's most expensive House race. Schiff grew up throughout the country, graduating from high school in northern California, and went on to Stanford and Harvard Law School. From 1987 to 1993, he was a criminal prosecutor with the U.S. Attorney in Los Angeles. He ran for the Assembly and lost three times—twice to Rogan. But in 1996 he was elected to the state Senate, where he became its youngest member. In his first two years, he authored 40 measures that Pete Wilson signed into law. Schiff also has taught political science at Glendale Community College.

Rogan had been elected to the House in 1996 after a 24-year Republican veteran retired, but he won by only 50%–43%; he was reelected 51%–46% in 1998. But it was Rogan's role in the impeachment of Bill Clinton that made him the Democrats' most visible target in 2000. Rogan was a leading player in the Judiciary Committee's deliberations and an eloquent voice for the case against Clinton. He was among the most articulate and persuasive of the House managers in the Senate's impeachment trial. He obviously knew that supporting impeachment carried political risks; while most impeachment managers had safe seats, Rogan's was anything but. Hollywood Democrats were almost hysterical in attacking Rogan. Entertainment mogul—and Clinton pal—David Geffen promised to raise millions to oppose him. "Jim Rogan is done," state Democratic Chairman Art Torres said in February 1999. "Now he has been exposed as the far-right zealot he is." After exploring the possibility of running against Dianne Feinstein, Rogan decided not to, despite the support of many state Republicans and the obvious difficulty of his reelection race. The Schiff-Rogan race became a fundraising contest; both candidates, buoyed by responses to direct mail, raised more than $10 million, and more was spent by Clinton lovers and Clinton haters. James Bennet in *The New York Times Magazine* called the contest "the politico ad absurdum of our times.Thanks to the bandwagon effect of political finance, the more money you raise, the more money you raise [and] thanks to the scare tactics of political finance, the more money your opponent raises, the more money you raise, provided you are competitive to begin with." The candidates disagreed on health care, abortion, gun control and taxes. Rogan branded his opponent as a traditional tax-and-spend liberal, who would "run naked through the Treasury, spending everything he can." Schiff attacked Rogan for calling abortion a "Holocaust" for the African-American community and saying that the Ku Klux Klan "couldn't do a better job on committing genocide on African Americans." They also battled for more than 60,000 local Armenians. Rogan was a lead sponsor of a House resolution commemorating their "genocide" from 1915 to 1923 by the Ottoman Turks; he was promised a floor vote in October by Speaker Dennis Hastert, but Hastert reneged after phone calls from Bill Clinton and his foreign policy appointees. Schiff cosponsored a state senate resolution declaring "a day of remembrance of Armenian genocide," and got $400,000 from state taxpayers to produce a documentary about Armenian issues. On local issues, Schiff said that Rogan's focus on partisan Washington had led him to ignore problems, such as expansion of the Burbank airport and a controversial proposed housing development in the Glendale hillsides. Rogan had no apologies for his work on impeachment: "It was history, important history, and it was for a principle."

Republicans were not optimistic about the result. But Schiff's 53%–44% margin was surprisingly large; he had a solid lead among Armenians. Schiff said that he was ready to work across party lines, though few of his issue positions offered early opportunity to cooperate with the new Bush administration. In his post mortem, Rogan called impeachment "the right thing to do," even though he knew that his career was in jeopardy. In the House, Schiff won seats on International Relations and Judiciary—both useful local platforms. Based on their mutual experiences in high-cost contests, he teamed up with Republican freshman Mark Kirk to form a "Freshmen for Reform" coalition for campaign finance overhaul. But Schiff also needed to tend to redistricting. Democrats control the redistricting process, but it was not clear how they would accommodate demands for a Latino district in the San Fernando Valley with the needs of the 26th district's Howard Berman, who has long been the Democratic delegation's point man on redistricting. Berman may want some of Schiff's current territory, while Schiff may want some of Berman's heavily Democratic precincts. In such a contest Berman is likely to prevail, but there is unlikely to be another Republican district here in what was for so long solid Republican territory.

Cook's Call   *Potentially Competitive.* Once considered a Republican stronghold, this district has been steadily trending Democratic over the last 10 years and has a seven point Democratic edge in registration today. As such, Schiff's 53% win over embattled incumbent and House impeachment manager Jim Rogan in 2000 was not that big of a shock. It remains to be seen if Republicans are going to want to put in the effort (and money) needed to make this seat competitive in 2002. But, even minor redistricting could change the flavor of the district enough to give Schiff some problems in his race in 2002. It is a race to watch.

THE PEOPLE: Pop. 2000: 600,986; Pop. 1990: 572,629, up 5% 1990–2000. 62.5% White, 6.6% Black, 13.2% Asian, 0.5% Amer. Indian, 0.1% Hawaiian, 6.9% Two+ races, 10.2% Other; 23.1% Hispanic Origin.

2000 Presidential Vote		
Gore (D)	118,944	(53%)
Bush (R)	92,278	(41%)
Nader (Green)	9,031	(4%)
Others	2,509	(1%)

1996 Presidential Vote		
Clinton (D)	98,348	(49%)
Dole (R)	81,282	(41%)
Perot (I)	13,324	(7%)
Others	7,540	(4%)

Rep. Adam Schiff (D)

Elected 2000, 1st term; b. June 22, 1960, Framingham, MA; home, Burbank; Stanford U., B.A. 1982; Harvard U., J.D. 1985; Jewish; married (Eve).

Elected Office: CA Senate, 1996–2000.

Professional Career: Prosecutor, U.S. Atty. Gen. Ofc., L.A., CA 1987–93; Practicing atty. 1986–87, 1995–96.

DC Office: 437 CHOB 20515, 202-225-4176; Fax: 202-225-5828; Web site: www.house.gov/schiff.

District Office: Pasadena, 626-304-2727.

Committees: *International Relations* (23d of 23 D): International Operations and Human Rights; Middle East & South Asia. *Judiciary* (16th of 17 D).

Group Ratings and Key Votes: Newly Elected

Election Results

2000 general	Adam Schiff (D)	113,708	(53%)	($4,351,025)
	James E. Rogan (R)	94,518	(44%)	($6,889,947)
	Other	7,548	(3%)	
2000 primary	Adam Schiff (D)	70,449	(49%)	
	James E. Rogan (R)	68,179	(47%)	
	Other	5,737	(4%)	
1998 general	James E. Rogan (R)	80,702	(51%)	($1,259,523)
	Barry A. Gordon (D)	73,875	(46%)	($516,259)
	Others	4,489	(3%)	

TWENTY-EIGHTH DISTRICT

It is the great route west to California: Passengers on the Santa Fe railroad's *Super Chief* or motorists on U.S. 66, after hours and days in barren desert, descended through the El Cajon Pass into the Los Angeles Basin, moving in a stately procession beneath the 10,000-foot snow-capped San Gabriel Mountains, marveling at orange groves and exotic plants. The railroad and highway ran through a line of towns, built by Midwestern Protestants as independent communities and now mostly high-income suburbs with their own civic institutions: Claremont, home of the academically strong Claremont Colleges; La Verne and Glendora; Azusa, named by a Chicago manufacturer for his wife; Duarte, with the City of Hope Medical Center; Monrovia and Arcadia, site of the Santa Anita race track and the Los Angeles County Arboretum. Today, the traveler arriving in Los Angeles can see the same sights—if the air is clear—as the jet glides down the flightpath to LAX.

The 28th Congressional District covers much of this territory in the San Gabriel Valley, with the exception of Azusa, which is part of the Hispanic-majority 31st District. Its eastern end reaches south from Claremont and Glendora to include Covina and West Covina, classic 1950s suburbs now with many Mexican-Americans, where city ordinances require that lawns be kept watered: 1950s homeowner values continue to govern here. The District's western end reaches south from Monrovia and Arcadia to include Temple City, where many towns are trying to revive their old downtowns. It is far from monocultural: 32% Hispanic and 19% Asian in 2000. Latinos have been moving in large numbers into the towns on the plain, while affluent communities near the mountains have become home to large numbers of Chinese, Koreans and other Asians. This has changed the political complexion of the area, though not as much as one might think. Latinos do vote heavily Democratic, but many of the whites who used to vote in the lower towns did as well. And Asians in California were evenly split in the 2000 presidential election, not heavily Democratic as many people assume. However, they are replacing whites who were heavily Republican. The result is that this historically Republican area has been getting more Democratic. In 1988 the 28th district voted 63%–37% for the senior George Bush. In 2000 it voted 49%–47% for Al Gore.

The congressman from the 28th district is David Dreier, first elected in 1980 and now chairman of the House Rules Committee. Dreier grew up in Kansas City, Missouri, then spent a decade mostly on the Claremont McKenna campus, as a student and administrator, before he was elected to Congress in 1980. Dreier first ran in 1978, at 25, and lost to Democratic incumbent Jim Lloyd. He beat Lloyd in 1980 and in 1982 beat fellow Republican Wayne Grisham after they were redistricted together. At that point, Dreier evidently decided never to be pressed for funds again; he raised plenty and spent little, which takes more self-discipline than one might think. After the 2000 campaign, in which he spent $1.1 million, he had $2.3 million cash on hand, among the highest in the House.

Dreier personifies the intellectually rigorous conservatism and free market economics that has thrived at Claremont and maintains a California cheerfulness and good humor characteristic of California—even after serving for 14 years in the minority, chiefly on the Rules Committee, where Republicans were outnumbered 9–4 and lost almost every vote. Now Dreier is on the long end of the 9–4 split, and the complaints are coming from the Democrats. He had already exerted influence in his first months in the majority when he worked to realign the House's committee structure: Three committees were abolished, almost half of the other panels were renamed and saw some shifting of jurisdictional lines, committee staff was cut by one-third, and six-year term limits were established for committee and subcommittee chairmen. Dreier encouraged committees to establish websites on the Internet, and held the first interactive subcommittee hearing in May 1996; his reforms adopted in 1997 include Internet access, allowing members to ask questions for more than five minutes and allowing committees to sit while the House is considering amendments.

The Rules chairman, once upon a time an independent operator, has become an operating member of the House leadership since Democrats instituted election of committee chairmen in 1974. Rules sets the terms for debate and limits the amendments that can be offered—an essential procedural function in a legislature with 435 members, and one which can be and often is used to shape substantive outcome. The 9–4 ratio and the careful selection of members guarantee the chairman control over committee votes, but over time it must be tempered by a sense of fairness: An outraged minority party can store up grievances and wait for a chance to overturn a rule on the floor. In 1999 and 2000, Dreier's Rules Committee produced 229 rules, and not one was defeated on the floor. "I see my job as moving our agenda, number one, and doing it in the fairest way possible. Some might say those conflict, but the priority is moving our agenda," Dreier said. He also led a bipartisan process that reduced the number of standing House rules from 51 to 27, and expanded the Subcommittee on Technology and the House. But he was less successful in persuading the House to adopt a biennial budget process, a move he led with Jim Nussle and Ben Cardin; it was rejected 217–201. In January 2001 Dreier showed Rules's clout again when, at the leadership's urging, he produced a bill restructuring committee jurisdictions and renaming the Banking Committee to Financial Services; this was done to give Michael Oxley, who lost out on the Energy and Commerce chairmanship, a chairmanship of his own, and was done over the angry protests of Energy and Commerce's John Dingell.

Dreier also has a policy agenda: free trade, high-tech, San Gabriel Valley water. He was one of the leading advocates of Permanent Normal Trade Relations with China, and led the fight for many months when it seemed short of votes. Days before the vote, to counter complaints about China's suppression of religious freedom, he circulated a carefully worded letter from Billy Graham seeming to favor open trade ties. PNTR passed 237–197 in May 2000; Dreier argues, "The most effective way to change the Chinese is to expose them to American products, ideas and values." His next goals are giving the new president Trade Promotion Authority (this used to be called fast track) and seeking a Free Trade Area of the Americas. On high-tech he was a lead sponsor of legislation to limit liability in law suits stemming from the Y2K computer problem, and he was one of the chief sponsors, with the Silicon Valley's Zoe Lofgren, of increasing the number of H1-B visas. He urges what he calls modernization of export controls, arguing that current controls cover many products which are not secret, and has spoken out against Internet taxes.

The San Gabriel Valley's water supply is threatened by perchlorates that have contaminated the groundwater; apparently they came from emissions from defense plants in the 1950s and

1960s. This is obviously a major problem which Dreier has addressed by, among other things, hosting a hearing with local officials testifying live with an Internet video hookup. In March 2000 the House authorized an $85 million, multi-year cleanup, plus $25 million more for research on perchlorates; in September 2000 the House appropriated $25 million for the project. Dreier has also supported cancer research at the City of Hope Medical Center in Duarte, the advanced space programs at Jet Propulsion Laboratory in Pasadena and funding for roads in communities near the Angeles National Forest.

Dreier is a regular spokesman for Republicans on cable TV talk shows; he even appeared with sparring partner Charles Rangel in a made-for-TV movie: show business imitating politics imitating show business. He serves on the Republican Steering Committee in the House, became Chairman of GOPAC, one of the vehicles Newt Gingrich used to produce the Republican majority, and served as Parliamentarian at the Republican National Convention. Those last duties were light; he produced the rationale of the Republicans' three-day "rolling roll call." He supported George W. Bush early in the 2000 race for president; they have been acquainted since Dreier sat next to Bush at a training school for Republican congressional candidates in 1978. That year neither won; 22 years later they were elected and became Rules Committee Chairman and President.

With his youthful, photogenic demeanor, Dreier's skill and stubbornness can be underestimated. "His ambition is masked by an easygoing style, an infectious grin, a charming spontaneity," wrote Nina Easton and Gebe Martinez in the *Los Angeles Times*. He has considered running for statewide office in California, though now the state looks forbiddingly Democratic, and he has expressed hopes that some day he may be speaker. But first he must contend with redistricting. He was reelected in 2000 by 57%–40%, a solid margin but his closest contest since 1980. The 28th district is inexorably becoming more Democratic within its current boundaries. His district is 30,000 short of the population average, and redistricting is controlled by the Democrats. They could easily make his seat more Democratic by adding Latino neighborhoods to the south or west and by removing Republican areas. Whether this is done depends probably less on Dreier than on whether Democrats feel a need to create a new Latino- or Asian-influence district in eastern Los Angeles County. If they do, they may take Democratic territory away from the 28th. That would strengthen Dreier, though it also might put him in the same district with another Republican incumbent.

Cook's Call *Probably Safe.* There is little question that this suburban Los Angeles district, once a Republican stronghold, has become much more competitive over the last 10 years. George H.W. Bush won the seat in 1992 by 3 % but Clinton won it by 1 point in 1996 and Gore won here by 2 % in 2000. In fact, this was one of only three districts in the state that voted for a Republican congressman and Gore. Even Dreier's margins have been slipping over the years. After regularly winning with margins in the 60s and low 70s, Dreier has not been able to break out of the high 50s since 1996, even against lackluster Democratic opponents. Whether Democrats can knock off the affable Rules chairman still remains a big question mark: Dreier is one of the most prolific fundraisers in the House and had over $2 million in the bank at the end of 2000.

THE PEOPLE: Pop. 2000: 609,233; Pop. 1990: 572,189, up 6.5% 1990–2000. 56.9% White, 4.8% Black, 19.4% Asian, 0.7% Amer. Indian, 0.2% Hawaiian, 4.4% Two + races, 13.7% Other; 31.6% Hispanic Origin.

2000 Presidential Vote

Gore (D)	106,203	(49%)
Bush (R)	101,698	(47%)
Nader (Green)	6,440	(3%)
Others	2,434	(1%)

1996 Presidential Vote

Clinton (D)	88,709	(45%)
Dole (R)	86,358	(44%)
Perot (I)	15,215	(8%)
Others	5,441	(3%)

Rep. David Dreier (R)

Elected 1980, 11th term; b. July 5, 1952, Kansas City, MO; home, San Dimas; Claremont McKenna Col., B.A. 1975, Claremont Grad. Schl., M.A. 1976; Christian Scientist; single.

Professional Career: Corp. Relations Dir., Claremont McKenna Col., 1975–78; Mktg. Dir., Industrial Hydrocarbons, 1979–80; Vice Pres., Dreier Development Co., 1985–present.

DC Office: 237 CHOB 20515, 202-225-2305; Fax: 202-225-7018; Web site: dreier.house.gov.

District Office: Covina, 626-339-9078.

Committees: *Chairman, Committee on Rules. Rules* (Chmn. of 9 R): Rules & Organization of the House; The Legislative & Budget Process.

Group Ratings

	ADA	ACLU	AFS	LCV	CON	ITIC	NTU	COC	ACU	NTLC	CHC
2000	5	29	0	7	41	100	58	90	92	64	87
1999	10	—	0	6	33	—	51	96	80	—	—

National Journal Ratings

	1999 LIB —	1999 CONS		2000 LIB —	2000 CONS
Economic	30%	64%		29%	67%
Social	35%	64%		0%	79%
Foreign	49%	50%		12%	78%

Key Votes of the 106th Congress

1. Patient Bill of Rights	N	5. Bar RU-486 $ for FDA	Y	9. NATO War in Serbia	Y
2. Accelerate Min. Wage	N	6. Display 10 Commandments	Y	10. Perm. Trade with China	Y
3. Strike Ban on Ergo. Stnd.	N	7. Gun Show Bkgrnd. Checks	N	11. Debt Relief for 3rd World	N
4. Ovrd. Estate Tax Veto	Y	8. Ban Part.-Birth Abortion	Y	12. Drop Cuba Econ. Embargo	N

Election Results

2000 general	David Dreier (R)	116,557	(57%)	($1,130,755)
	Janice M. Nelson (D)	81,804	(40%)	($188,122)
	Other	6,838	(3%)	
2000 primary	David Dreier (R)	88,837	(62%)	
	Janice M. Nelson (D)	47,971	(34%)	
	Other	5,444	(4%)	
1998 general	David Dreier (R)	90,607	(58%)	($893,029)
	Janice M. Nelson (D)	61,721	(39%)	($122,994)
	Others	4,872	(3%)	

TWENTY-NINTH DISTRICT

The Westside: The term was not much used 20 years ago, but is now shorthand for what might be the biggest and flashiest concentration of affluence in the world. It is the heartland of one of America's most productive and creative industries and one of the nation's major exports, show business. The first moviemakers came here earlier in the century, looking for a place to shoot silent films where the sunlight was more dependable than in Astoria, Queens, or Englewood, New Jersey. They found it in Hollywood, a suburb just annexed by burgeoning Los Angeles when the first movie studio was built in 1911. In 1923 came the Hollywood sign, overlooking the soon-famous intersection of Hollywood and Vine. By the 1930s, big studio lots were scattered around town, over the mountains in Burbank or out toward the ocean in Westwood and Culver City. Miraculously, the studio bosses of that era—most of them Jewish immigrants with little ancestral experience of America—created a popular culture that was universally accessible and embodied the American spirit in a way that still captures the imagination. This was the universal American culture of the 1940s movies that Ronald Reagan understood and transferred into politics. Today's showbiz moguls, by contrast, sometimes seem absorbed in the solipsistic enterprise of putting their own personal idiosyncrasies on the screen or the tube or tapes or CDs.

Showbiz still sets the tone for the Westside. It remains tremendously profitable, in large part because it's not run by big business units but by thousands of craftsmen and entrepreneurs who keep it anchored in Los Angeles because so many of them remain here. People on the Westside like to portray themselves as artists in a garret, willing to risk starving to make art and speak truth to bourgeois society. But their yen for fashionable new moral standards make them disdainful of the ordinary people who are the market of any mass entertainment. The Westside loves to congratulate itself on its moral daring when it makes a movie or TV show revealing businessmen or priests as criminals. And yet the marketplace may be teaching showbiz some lessons. As Michael Medved, movie critic and author of *Hollywood vs. America*, has pointed out, Hollywood's most obscene, anti-business and anti-religious products don't sell nearly as well as its family fare; and television shows and movies started reflecting a wider range of subjects and values. Showbiz rejoiced in the election of Bill Clinton and in his frequent forays into California and obvious fascination with entertainers, and it rejected with fury the notion that there was something wrong about his affair with a White House intern from the Westside or with lying under oath in a sexual harassment case in a United States District Court.

Not everyone on the Westside is in show business, of course. This is also the home of thousands of small entrepreneurs, manufacturers, and inventors and marketers of everything imaginable, who sparked the huge growth of the Los Angeles Basin, and there are even traces of pre-show business Los Angeles money, which is also plentiful. There are large numbers of singles and gays here: apartment-renters provided majorities for Santa Monica's city government, which thrived when it imposed rent control but foundered when it invited in more homeless. The core of Hollywood itself has gone seedy and is the home now of many Central American immigrants, a high-crime and riot zone, but the Fairfax neighborhood remains solidly middle-class Jewish—though many of its Jews today are recent Russian immigrants. Hancock Park looks as aristocratic as it did when it was built, when Beverly Hills was vacant land. The Westside has been the home of a former president who does not at all exemplify its politics, Ronald Reagan; before his Alzheimer's Disease worsened, he kept his office on the former Fox lot that is now Century City. It is the center of the second largest Jewish community in the United States, as well as the focus of the 1980s immigration of Iranians to the United States. It is also the locus of some of America's most expensive residential real estate, where people buy houses for multiples of $1 million, knock down the structure and build something new for a few more millions, and of one of the world's premier high-priced shopping areas—Rodeo Drive, once a quite ordinary shopping street.

The 29th Congressional District of California contains almost all the major elements of Westside Los Angeles, from old, high-income Los Feliz and the gay neighborhood around Silver Lake through Hollywood and Hancock Park, west through Beverly Hills and Westwood, Bel Air and Brentwood, Santa Monica and Pacific Palisades. It is solidly Democratic and not just in votes: It probably contributes more money to Democratic candidates and liberal causes than any other district with the exception of Manhattan's New York 14th. Its boundaries are carefully sculpted to put blacks in the 32nd District to the south and Hispanics and Asians in the 30th to the east; far from being racially diverse, it has the highest percentage of non-Hispanic whites of any Los Angeles Basin district.

The congressman from the 29th is Henry Waxman, a Democrat elected in 1974, one of the ablest members of the House, a shrewd political operator who is a skilled and idealistic policy entrepreneur. There is no Westside glitz about him: He grew up over his family's store in Watts, his personal demeanor is quiet, he has never attended the Oscars ceremony. He moved up rapidly in politics by spying openings before others did and taking advantage of them. He ran against Assemblyman Lester McMillan in the mostly Jewish Fairfax area in 1968, at 28, and won 64% in the primary. From 1971–72 he chaired the redistricting committee, a good place to make friends, but he went to Congress in 1974 in a district designed, he points out, not by his committee but by a court. Waxman's biggest break came after the 1978 election, when he was elected chairman of the Commerce Committee's Health and Environment Subcommittee. This was one of the first times House Democrats decided to ignore seniority in handing out subcommittee chairs. Nevertheless, Waxman argued his case on the issues and—in a move quite unprecedented at the time, though common in Sacramento and now also in Washington—made campaign contributions to other Democrats on the full committee, and won the post, 15–12, over the widely respected Richardson Preyer of North Carolina.

The campaign contributions were no accident. Waxman and his friend Howard Berman built their own political machine in Los Angeles. Its power came not from patronage but from fundraising and savvy. Their specialty was targeted direct mail, with hundreds of customized letters and endorsement slates sent out to different lists of people. In the apolitical commonwealth of California, where television advertising is exceedingly expensive and people seem to avoid politics, this made them critical though not always successful players. But in 1992 their machine foundered: Westsider Mel Levine lost the Senate nomination to Barbara Boxer in "the year of the woman," and Tom Hayden beat a Waxman-Berman ally for state senator. Since then, Waxman has rarely taken an active role in Los Angeles area politics; an exception came in the April 2001 primary for the vacant 32nd District, when he backed the unsuccessful Kevin Murray.

Waxman has been a major national policymaker for two decades—arguably, the most important lawmaker on environmental issues. In 1981 and 1982 he prevented the Reagan Administration and Commerce Committee Chairman John Dingell from revising the Clean Air Act; biding his time, he worked to strengthen the law in its 1990 revision. He and Dingell—frequent shouting-match partners who nevertheless maintained a working relationship—hammered out a compromise, delaying stricter California-type auto standards until 1994 and moving more aggressively on non-auto issues. Another great Waxman project has been expanding Medicaid for the poor. His strategy was to threaten to hold up budget reconciliation bills unless they required states to expand Medicaid eligibility. Between 1984 and 1990, he got coverage for all poor children up to 18, all children under seven and pregnant women in families under 133% of poverty income. This helped raise Medicaid from 9% to 14% of state spending in the 1980s, and helps to explain why Waxman was so disliked by many governors.

Waxman had less success on reforming national health care. He wanted to move to something like a single-payer program and supported the Clinton plan but to no avail. He has secured more funding for AIDS research, important in the 29th District with its large gay population. He passed a law providing damages to children injured by required immunizations, sponsored measures to require testing of mammography devices, expanded the availability of generic drugs, extended patent protection for drugs for time spent during the approval process, and tried unsuccessfully to legalize the use of heroin to reduce the pain of terminal cancer patients. In early 1994, in widely publicized hearings, he lined up the chief executive officers of leading tobacco companies and accused them of adding nicotine and other substances to cigarettes and of lying in their testimony. All this had no immediate legislative result, and when Thomas Bliley of Virginia, became Commerce Committee chair, the hearings stopped. But Waxman brought the tobacco issue into public view, and he helped to inspire the lawsuits against tobacco companies which have resulted in the biggest redistribution of corporate assets—from the tobacco companies to state governments and trial lawyers—in history.

Waxman reacted with dismay to the Republican takeover of Congress, but with no slackening of effort. On some issues, he worked to negotiate compromises with Republicans, notably the Safe Drinking Water Act and the pesticide standards in the Food Quality Provision Act of 1996; part of his strategy was "right-to-know" amendments listing contaminants. He led the fight against Republicans' regulatory reform and Medicare and Medicaid changes. He had staff investigate nursing homes in Los Angeles in 1999 and found "appalling" conditions and sought to impose sanctions for nursing homes that violate federal health standards. He and Lincoln Diaz-Balart sought to establish nationally the California practice of not barring immigrants from Medicaid. In 2000 he co-sponsored the bill to let families with disabled children receive Medicaid even if family income rises above the limit; after opposition from the Senate leadership, he reintroduced it with a lower limit in 2001 with Republican Pete Sessions and Senators Charles Grassley and Edward Kennedy.

In 1997 Waxman gave up the ranking position on Health to be ranking Democrat on the Government Reform Committee. There he sharply attacked Chairman Dan Burton's investigation of Clinton campaign misdeeds, arguing that Burton had given himself unprecedented subpoena power and was misusing it, and he emerged as perhaps the House's most articulate defender of Clinton against scandal charges. Waxman did stop short of defending Clinton in some cases. In September 1999 he said he "probably" wouldn't have granted clemency to Puerto Rican FALN terrorists as Clinton had in August, evidently to help his wife's Senate campaign in New York. And in February 2001 he said that Clinton showed "incredibly poor judgment" in pardoning Marc Rich. But overall he has peppered Burton with criticism and, in the opinion of some observers, run circles around him. In 1999 he ridiculed Burton for not noticing that evidence of the use of tear gas cannisters at Waco had been provided to the committee back in 1995; Burton said that the committee had been buried by an avalanche of 100,000 documents. Waxman has criticized Burton for offenses that are not strictly political. In January 2000 he questioned the scheduling of a closed-session hearing on Russian threats to the United States in Los Angeles; Burton was attending a golf tournament in Palm Springs. In April 2000 he said that a Burton hearing was stacked to show a connection between autism and vaccination; Burton has an autistic granddaughter. And he goes after other Republicans: he served on the 1999 committee to choose a new House chaplain, and charged that anti-Catholic bias prevented the selection of the priest who was the informal choice of the committee.

Waxman has always won re-election easily, and has contributed generously to other Democrats' campaigns. The 29th district had little population growth in the 1990s, and must be expanded by nearly 60,000 people, but Democrats close to Waxman control the redistricting process and there is likely to be another Westside district that will be happy to reelect him.

Cook's Call   *Safe.* Another incumbent with no re-election concerns is Henry Waxman. Since winning the seat in 1974 his closest electoral call was a 61% win in 1992. This seat will stay firmly planted in the Democratic column.

THE PEOPLE: Pop. 2000: 584,823; Pop. 1990: 571,386, up 2.4% 1990–2000. 76.5% White, 3.3% Black, 9.8% Asian, 0.3% Amer. Indian, 0.1% Hawaiian, 4.6% Two+ races, 5.4% Other; 12.1% Hispanic Origin.

2000 Presidential Vote			1996 Presidential Vote		
Gore (D)	183,361	(72%)	Clinton (D)	150,771	(66%)
Bush (R)	56,705	(22%)	Dole (R)	53,354	(24%)
Nader (Green)	11,936	(5%)	Perot (I)	10,639	(5%)
Others	2,346	(1%)	Others	12,002	(5%)

Rep. Henry A. Waxman (D)

Elected 1974, 14th term; b. Sept. 12, 1939, Los Angeles; home, Los Angeles; U.C.L.A., B.A. 1961, J.D. 1964; Jewish; married (Janet).

Elected Office: CA Assembly, 1968–74.

Professional Career: Practicing atty., 1965–68.

DC Office: 2204 RHOB 20515, 202-225-3976; Fax: 202-225-4099; Web site: www.house.gov/waxman.

District Office: Los Angeles, 323-651-1040.

Committees: *Energy & Commerce* (2d of 26 D): Commerce, Trade & Consumer Protection; Energy & Air Quality; Environment & Hazardous Materials; Health. *Government Reform* (RMM of 19 D).

Group Ratings

	ADA	ACLU	AFS	LCV	CON	ITIC	NTU	COC	ACU	NTLC	CHC
2000	90	86	85	93	80	56	28	45	4	9	0
1999	95	—	100	100	76	—	24	17	0	—	—

National Journal Ratings

	1999 LIB	—	1999 CONS		2000 LIB	—	2000 CONS
Economic	88%	—	0%		95%	—	0%
Social	87%	—	0%		89%	—	10%
Foreign	95%	—	0%		94%	—	6%

Key Votes of the 106th Congress

1. Patient Bill of Rights	Y	5. Bar RU-486 $ for FDA	N	9. NATO War in Serbia	Y
2. Accelerate Min. Wage	Y	6. Display 10 Commandments	N	10. Perm. Trade with China	Y
3. Strike Ban on Ergo. Stnd.	Y	7. Gun Show Bkgrnd. Checks	Y	11. Debt Relief for 3rd World	Y
4. Ovrd. Estate Tax Veto	N	8. Ban Part.-Birth Abortion	N	12. Drop Cuba Econ. Embargo	Y

Election Results

2000 general	Henry A. Waxman (D)	180,295	(76%)	($389,766)
	Jim Scileppi (R)	45,784	(19%)	
	Other	12,122	(5%)	
2000 primary	Henry A. Waxman (D)	114,147	(76%)	
	Jim Scileppi (R)	27,870	(19%)	
	Jack Anderson (LIB)	5,419	(4%)	
	Other	2,135	(1%)	
1998 general	Henry A. Waxman (D)	131,561	(74%)	($276,306)
	Mike Gottlieb (R)	40,282	(23%)	($47,641)
	Others	6,251	(4%)	

THIRTIETH DISTRICT

Surrounding downtown Los Angeles are neighborhoods just now becoming antique, as the early 20th Century buildings stop looking familiar and start taking on the patina of the historic. Downtown LA, with its 1980s marble slabs and pink cylinders jutting up to 70 stories from what was once a low-rise business district, seems soulless and detached from its neighborhoods, which change character with every new immigration flow. Not far east, over the Los Angeles River, is Boyle Heights, once an entry neighborhood for Irish and Jewish immigrants and for the last 30 years predominantly Mexican-American, low in income but with enough community cohesion not to riot in April 1992. In between downtown and Boyle Heights is Toytown, the center of toy manufacturing and importing in the United States. South of downtown is the garment district, with factories in nondescript buildings, an economically vibrant area and one of the reasons Los Angeles is the number one manufacturing city in America today. To the north is Lincoln Heights, a heavily Hispanic area centering on the busy shopping street of North Broadway, plus the neighborhoods of Highland Park and Eagle Rock, white middle-class 30 years ago, now mostly Latino but with Asians as well. West of downtown are Pico Union, an entry point for new immigrants, lower Sunset Boulevard, the Koreatown strip along Western Avenue, site of the worst damage during the 1992 riot, Thai Town along Hollywood Boulevard between Normandie and Western, much of Hollywood and some of South Central. Hollywood has a seedy look: it has not sprouted the office buildings you can see in Burbank or Glendale, because of Los Angeles's high taxes and daffy regulations. Central Americans rioted in Hollywood in 1992, and the Hollywood Boulevard subway line caved in during the 1994 earthquake: not auspicious signs.

In Los Angeles's booming 1980s these neighborhoods were suddenly thronged with immigrants, more thickly populated than a quarter-century before, with small houses and garden apartments full of large families and many children; new migrants stayed with those who have been here a few years, with beds assigned to family members working different shifts so they're slept in 24 hours a day. To most American eyes, they looked like poverty neighborhoods, but this is the snapshot view; in the video version they are the first frames on the way to prosperity, the first way-station on freeways out to middle-income American comfort. Indeed, in the 1990s the population surge stopped, as the newcomers of the decade before moved out to more middle class neighborhoods and as incoming immigrants spread more evenly around the Los Angeles Basin.

Almost all of these areas, centering geographically on Dodger Stadium, are part of California's 30th Congressional District. The population here in 2000 was recorded as 64% Hispanic and 20%

Asian. The 2000 Census showed 583,000 people living here, the smallest of any of California's 52 districts. And of course very many of them are not registered voters, or even citizens. In 2000 only 64,000 voted in the open primary and only 100,000 in the general election, compared to 150,000 in the primary and 238,000 in the general in the adjacent Westside 29th District. This is a heavily Democratic district, 75%–19% for Al Gore in 2000.

The congressman from the 30th District is Xavier Becerra, a Democrat elected in 1992. He grew up in California, went to college and law school at Stanford, worked for legal services, then worked for state Senator (now state Democratic chairman) Art Torres and Attorney General John Van de Kamp, and married a Harvard Medical School graduate who teaches at George Washington University. In 1990 he was elected to the Assembly, and had a liberal record on the environment and called for making AIDS drugs available; he backed campaign finance reform and tougher penalties for gang activities near schools. In 1992, the redrawn 30th District was expected to re-elect Edward Roybal, California's first Latino congressman, elected 30 years before; his daughter, Assemblywoman Lucille Roybal-Allard, was running in the neighboring 33d District. But Roybal announced late in the game that he was retiring, and Becerra jumped into the race, although his residence was in Monterey Park outside the district. Becerra's main Latino competitor, Leticia Quezada, was a member of the Los Angeles school board, a powerful engine for publicity. But Becerra had the endorsements of Roybal, Congressman Esteban Torres and County Supervisor Gloria Molina. In a primary in which only 33,000 voters turned out, Becerra won with 32% to 22% for Quezada. His 10,417 votes effectively made him the representative of more than half a million people; he won the general in this heavily Democratic district 58%–24%.

In the House, he was among the most liberal members. When Republicans took control, the fast-moving Becerra was legislatively active, if not always successful. On the Judiciary Committee he moved for refunds of the $80 fee paid by the one million visa applicants who would be ineligible under the proposed immigration rules and called for an appeals process for workers denied jobs by errors in the proposed new identification program. He said declaring English as the official language "sends a message of intolerance for those trying to learn English." He opposed a law to allow local law enforcement agents to enter pacts with the Department of Justice to enforce immigration laws. He opposed restrictions on bilingual education and Republican efforts to stop census sampling techniques.

When Becerra visited Cuba and met with Fidel Castro in 1996, he did not denounce his regime or demand free elections as other members have done on such visits. In January 1997 he was elected chairman of the Hispanic Caucus by 12–7 and immediately found himself on the defensive, when Republicans Ileana Ros-Lehtinen and Lincoln Diaz-Balart announced their resignation. That year, he also became a member of the Ways and Means Committee, where he advocated tax-code changes to prevent the overseas exodus of jobs in the entertainment industry, including a tax credit for labor costs of independent film producers. He supported Permanent Normal Trade Relations with China, in hopes of encouraging democracy there and benefiting Los Angeles's economy. He filed a bill to require gun manufacturers to test-fire guns before their sale, thus leaving "fingerprints" that make it easier to track down the gun that fired a bullet. When President Clinton's last-minute pardons included convicted Los Angeles cocaine dealer Carlos Vignali, Becerra was at the center of contacts made on his behalf. Although Vignali's father had been a major campaign contributor, Becerra denied any connection nor did he investigate the accuracy of claims for the pardon. "I told Horacio Vignali I thought it was a longshot to do this," he told *The Los Angeles Times* in February 2001.

Becerra's pleasant and businesslike manner combined with his obvious ambition could make him a force in the House, but his views left him not very effective in a Republican majority. That helps to explain why he ran for mayor of Los Angeles in 2001. But he started off with low name recognition and did not raise much money. He was overshadowed by the candidacy of former Assembly Speaker Antonio Villaraigosa, who started off better known and with more fundraising contacts. Other Latino leaders held private meetings in late 2000 to urge one or the other to withdraw. Villaraigosa reportedly said he would drop out if Becerra agreed not to run again for the House even if he lost the Mayor's race; that presumably would have given Villaraigosa an opportunity for a seat in Congress. Becerra was evidently uninterested in such a deal. Villaraigosa won the endorsements of several labor unions and, to the surprise of many, Governor Gray Davis, and spent nearly $3 million on ads; Becerra was scarcely a presence in the ad wars. In the April 10 primary vote, Becerra finished fifth, with 6% of the vote, far behind Villaraigosa's 30% and James Hahn's 25%. Some 21% of city voters were Hispanic, a big rise from the 8% in 1993; Villaraigosa won 62% of their votes and Becerra 17%. Interestingly, the combined Villaraigosa-Becerra vote was 36%, nearly double the Latino total; half of their votes were cast by non-Latinos. There was ethnic preference in the Los Angeles voting, but also a widespread willingness to vote across ethnic lines.

Becerra is certain to survive redistricting, but pressure for additional Latino districts in Los Angeles could reduce the Hispanic percentage in his district, which also needs to expand by 56,000.

Cook's Call   *Safe*. Xavier Becerra has won easily here since 1992 and should have no problems in 2002. This district is a lock for Democrats.

THE PEOPLE: Pop. 2000: 582,745; Pop. 1990: 572,604, up 1.8% 1990–2000. 34.7% White, 3% Black, 19.6% Asian, 1% Amer. Indian, 0.1% Hawaiian, 5.5% Two + races, 36% Other; 64.3% Hispanic Origin.

2000 Presidential Vote			1996 Presidential Vote		
Gore (D)	80,011	(75%)	Clinton (D)	61,114	(71%)
Bush (R)	20,626	(19%)	Dole (R)	17,053	(20%)
Nader (Green)	4,818	(5%)	Perot (I)	4,165	(5%)
Others	1,228	(1%)	Others	3,713	(4%)

Rep. Xavier Becerra (D)

Elected 1992, 5th term; b. Jan. 26, 1958, Sacramento; home, Los Angeles; Stanford U., B.A. 1980, J.D. 1984; Catholic; married (Carolina Reyes).

Elected Office: CA Assembly, 1990–92.

Professional Career: Staff Atty., Legal Assistance Corp. of Central MA; Dist. Dir., CA Sen. Art Torres, 1986; CA Dep. Atty. Gen., 1987–90.

DC Office: 1119 LHOB 20515, 202-225-6235; Fax: 202-225-2202; Web site: www.house.gov/becerra.

District Office: Los Angeles, 213-483-1425.

Committees: *Ways & Means* (14th of 17 D): Social Security; Trade.

Group Ratings

	ADA	ACLU	AFS	LCV	CON	ITIC	NTU	COC	ACU	NTLC	CHC
2000	90	86	85	86	64	84	17	45	8	16	0
1999	100	—	100	100	82	—	24	22	0	—	—

National Journal Ratings

	1999 LIB —	1999 CONS		2000 LIB —	2000 CONS
Economic	88% —	0%		90% —	8%
Social	87% —	0%		88% —	12%
Foreign	95% —	0%		91% —	8%

Key Votes of the 106th Congress

1. Patient Bill of Rights	Y	5. Bar RU-486 $ for FDA	N	9. NATO War in Serbia			*
2. Accelerate Min. Wage	Y	6. Display 10 Commandments	N	10. Perm. Trade with China	Y
3. Strike Ban on Ergo. Stnd.	Y	7. Gun Show Bkgrnd. Checks	Y	11. Debt Relief for 3rd World	Y
4. Ovrd. Estate Tax Veto	N	8. Ban Part.-Birth Abortion	N	12. Drop Cuba Econ. Embargo	Y

Election Results

2000 general	Xavier Becerra (D)	83,223	(83%)	($1,046,470)
	Tony Goss (R)	11,788	(12%)	
	Other	4,909	(5%)	
2000 primary	Xavier Becerra (D)	53,145	(84%)	
	Tony Goss (R)	6,919	(11%)	
	Other	3,640	(6%)	
1998 general	Xavier Becerra (D)	58,230	(81%)	($361,813)
	Patricia Parker (R)	13,441	(19%)	

THIRTY-FIRST DISTRICT

Anyone interested in the future of America and today's immigrants should drive straight east from downtown Los Angeles on the San Bernardino Freeway, through the string of suburbs that grew up in the 1940s and 1950s. These were once white middle-class communities, with grids of stucco houses above the dry riverbeds; they were filled with Midwest and East Coast migrants who discovered California during World War II and decided to stay, or who learned of its golden reputation from the new medium of television in the days before smog became part of the language. The atmosphere then was Midwestern, cheerful, busy, with children always underfoot. Over the next generation or so, there has been almost a complete population turnover here, but some things remain the same. Mexican-Americans have spread out from their original East Los Angeles base to become majorities in blue-collar suburbs like El Monte, Baldwin Park and Azusa, all with many more residents than in their Anglo days. The 2000 Census showed that Chinese and other Asians have become the majority in Monterey Park and are just under 50% of the population in Alhambra, San Gabriel and, Rosemead. But these are not ghettoes in any sense of the word. Almost every neighborhood is mixed, with people whose origins are in different continents and cultures, and the new people here have not downgraded but upgraded the neighborhoods, bringing in energy and money, the enthusiasm of the young and the community-spiritedness of the homeowner. There are no empty storefronts, but busy shops with new signs; no housing riddled with vandalism and neglect, but newly painted homes with carefully tended gardens; these are neighborhoods still filled with children whose parents believe in traditional values. When blacks and Latinos were rioting in South Central and Hollywood, East Los Angeles and the San Gabriel Valley were quiet and orderly. Some time later in this century, novels will be written describing the by-then vanished atmosphere of these immigrant suburbs, that will surely tell more about the human condition than TV series and movies about the clueless youth of Beverly Hills.

In the 1950s, these were Democratic areas—New Dealers bringing their voting habits west—but the new Latinos and Asians seem up for grabs. They voted strongly for Ronald Reagan in 1984 and were only 5% to 8% more Democratic than average in the 1988 and 1990 elections. In the early 1990s Asians, dismayed by the civic elite's response to the Los Angeles riot, which seemed more interested in ministering to the complaints of the rioters than compensating the store owners whose property was ruined and lives threatened, moved toward the Republicans. Then in the middle 1990s Latinos, less because of Proposition 209's prohibition of racial quotas than because of Republican immigration and welfare laws removing aid to legal immigrants and because Republican campaign ads suggested Latinos were more interested in welfare than work, moved heavily toward the Democrats; Asians moved a bit in the same direction. Now this area is very heavily Democratic.

The 31st Congressional District covers much of the territory from the LA city limit east through East Los Angeles, Alhambra, San Gabriel, Rosemead, El Monte, Baldwin Park and Azusa; it brushes, but excludes, higher-income suburbs up against the San Gabriel Mountains. The 2000 Census reported that it was 59% Hispanic and 28% Asian—the highest Asian percentage and one of the lowest percentages of non-Hispanic whites in southern California. In 1988 the 31st District voted for Michael Dukakis by a narrow 54%–46% margin. In 2000 it voted overwhelmingly, 69%–27%, for Al Gore.

The congresswoman from the 31st District is Hilda Solis, a Democrat elected in 2000. The daughter of a union shop steward, Solis grew up in southern California, graduated from California

State Polytechnic University in 1979, and got a master's degree in public administration from the University of Southern California. She worked in the Carter White House's Office of Hispanic Affairs. Solis began her career as an elected official in 1984 when she won a seat on the Rio Hondo Community College Board of Trustees. She was elected to the Assembly in 1992, and in 1994 became the first Latino woman elected to the state Senate. Her work for environmental justice led the John F. Kennedy Library Foundation to give her a Profiles in Courage Award.

Solis was term-limited in 2002, and her state Senate district overlapped the 31st Congressional District (in California state Senate districts are larger than congressional districts), and so it is not surprising that in 2000 she ran against Congressman Matthew Martinez. Martinez was originally elected in 1982 with the support of the Berman-Waxman machine; he lost support among feminist and labor activists by voting for a ban on late-term abortions and fast-track trade authority and helping to stall gun control. Solis was endorsed by organized labor, EMILY's List, Sierra Club, Senator Barbara Boxer and Congresswoman Loretta Sanchez. Martinez was supported by colleagues Lucille Roybal-Allard and Grace Napolitano; Berman and Waxman were neutral. Solis raised four times as much money as Martinez and had hundreds of volunteers from reinvigorated unions in the Los Angeles area. She won 62%–29%. The contest was caustic. Before he conceded defeat in the March 2000 primary, Martinez called Solis "obnoxious" and accused her of putting out "a lot of things in her fliers that are absolute untruths." Solis proclaimed, "The community is ready for a change." With no Republican opposition, she effectively won election 10 months before taking office. After the primary, a bitter Martinez voted mostly with Republicans, and he switched parties in July. But his efforts to urge Latinos to vote Republican fell flat and the party switch had no perceptible effect in the 31st District.

In the House, Solis got seats on Resources, and Education and the Workforce. With Howard Berman, she filed a bill to grant undocumented Salvadoran immigrants a one-year amnesty because of their country's devastating January 2001 earthquake. Redistricting is her next political problem. The process is controlled by Democrats, and they will certainly be listening to Latino demands to protect the seats of Latino House members. But there may also be demands to create a district with a maximized Asian percentage—even though Asians are of many different national origins. The focus of such a district would be towns now in the 31st District, but its boundaries would be somewhat different. Most likely this poses no threat to Solis.

Cook's Call *Safe.* Hilda Solis' victory over Matthew Martinez in the 2000 Democratic primary was the first major example of the influence of state term limits on the national political environment. With Solis termed out of the state Senate, she set her sights on Congress and Martinez. Martinez never took this race seriously enough, and it showed in the final vote, 62%–29%. Solis will never have to worry about a tough general election in this overwhelmingly Democratic seat.

THE PEOPLE: Pop. 2000: 600,376; Pop. 1990: 572,758, up 4.8% 1990–2000. 34.9% White, 1.3% Black, 28.2% Asian, 1.1% Amer. Indian, 0.1% Hawaiian, 4.2% Two+ races, 30.2% Other; 59.4% Hispanic Origin.

2000 Presidential Vote		
Gore (D)	86,956	(69%)
Bush (R)	34,389	(27%)
Nader (Green)	2,859	(2%)
Others	1,317	(1%)

1996 Presidential Vote		
Clinton (D)	70,288	(65%)
Dole (R)	27,736	(26%)
Perot (I)	7,043	(7%)
Others	2,468	(2%)

Rep. Hilda Solis (D)

Elected 2000, 1st term; b. Oct. 20, 1957, Los Angeles; home, El Monte; CA St. Polytechnic U., B.A. 1979; U. of Southern CA, M.A. 1981; Catholic; married (Sam Sayyad).

Elected Office: CA Assembly, 1992–94; CA Senate 1994–2000.

Professional Career: Editor, White House Ofc. of Hispanic Affairs, 1980–81; Management Analyst, Ofc. of Management & Budget, 1981.

DC Office: 1641 LHOB 20515, 202-225-5464; Fax: 202-225-5467; Web site: www.house.gov/solis.

District Office: El Monte, 626-448-1271.

Committees: *Education & the Workforce* (20th of 22 D): Education Reform; Workforce Protections. *Resources* (22d of 25 D): National Parks, Recreation & Public Lands; Water & Power.

Group Ratings and Key Votes: Newly Elected

Election Results

2000 general	Hilda Solis (D)	89,600	(79%)	($978,263)
	Krista Lieberg-Wong (Green)	10,294	(9%)	
	Michael McGuire (LIB)	7,138	(6%)	
	Richard D. Griffin (NL)	5,882	(5%)	
2000 primary	Hilda Solis (D)	48,531	(62%)	
	Matthew G. Martinez (D)	22,241	(29%)	
	Krista Lieberg-Wong (Green)	3,296	(4%)	
	Other	3,995	(5%)	
1998 general	Matthew G. Martinez (D)	61,173	(70%)	($124,583)
	Frank Moreno (R)	19,786	(23%)	
	Krista Lieberg-Wong	4,377	(5%)	
	Others	2,024	(2%)	

THIRTY-SECOND DISTRICT

One of the myths of the Los Angeles riots of 1992 and 1965 is that black Angelenos live in conditions of isolation and poverty. Some do, but in levels of income and in degree of residential integration with non-blacks, Los Angeles blacks rank among the top in the United States. Its black-owned businesses have the highest revenues of any city in the nation. Californians have historically shown less prejudice against blacks than most Americans, and job opportunities in Los Angeles—up to and including the office of mayor for 20 years—have been plenteous for blacks. This is apparent in the hills just west of Crenshaw, an Art Deco neighborhood built in the 1920s and 1930s in vacant flat land southwest of downtown LA and the birthplace of West Coast hip-hop music. Here, in Baldwin Hills, where on clear days you can see the towers of downtown and the snow-capped San Gabriel Mountains beyond, is a high-income black neighborhood, one of the strongest in the country, and where Magic Johnson built his successful multiplex theaters. To the north and west are other comfortable black-majority neighborhoods; on the flatlands south of Beverly Hills and the Fairfax district not far away, many affluent blacks are buying houses.

This part of Los Angeles is the heart of the 32d Congressional District, which runs approximately from the Harbor Freeway west past Baldwin Hills to Culver City almost to the ocean, and south from Olympic Boulevard past the Santa Monica Freeway down almost to Inglewood and the LAX airport. The 32d vies with the Maryland 4th, New York 6th and the Georgia 4th for the largest numbers of affluent blacks in any district. Politically there has been no serious trend toward Republicans. Indeed, affluent, well-educated blacks seem if anything to be culturally more liberal than low-income black voters who may have closer ties to church and tradition. Many have profited on the way up from some form of government intervention—a student loan, a public sector job, an affirmative action program—and many still hold public sector jobs. Yet, though blacks set the political tone here, they are not the majority. In 2000, only 33% of the district's residents were black, down from 40% in 1990. The Hispanic percentage rose from 30% to 37%, although of course many are not eligible to vote. What seems to be happening is that non-affluent blacks are leaving the Los Angeles area, often moving to the South, while Latinos are moving in and are spreading out into South Central and other formerly black neighborhoods. Many are not eligible or registered to vote, and the electorate in this area will probably remain black-plurality for most of the decade.

The congresswoman from the 32nd district is Diane Watson, elected officially in the June 2001 runoff but effectively chosen in an April 2001 special primary election. She replaces Julian Dixon, the incumbent since 1978, who died in December 2000. Dixon was chairman of the ethics committee when it filed charges that led to the resignation of Speaker Jim Wright and at the time of his death was ranking Democrat on the Intelligence Committee; he handled difficult assignments with tact and skill. Watson grew up in Los Angeles, and received both her bachelors and masters degrees from UCLA. She worked in a variety of education-related fields as an elementary school teacher, school psychologist and lecturer at Cal State Los Angeles. Watson began her political career in 1975 as the first black woman elected to the Los Angeles Board of Education, where she worked on school desegregation issues. Three years later, she ran for the state Senate, again becoming the first black woman in that body. She served as chairman of the Health and Human Services Committee for 17 years before term limits forced her to retire in 1998. During her tenure, Watson was a spokeswoman for women's rights. She stirred controversy in 1989 when she defended the practice of granting legislative perks, which have since been outlawed; she argued that legislators deserved special treatment because they were not "ordinary people." In October 1999, Watson was confirmed as U.S. Ambassador to Micronesia, where she replaced former (and, perhaps, future) California Secretary of State March Fong Eu; she returned to the U.S. in January 2001 to run in the special election to replace Dixon. Her chief opponents were state Senator Kevin Murray, whose father once served in the Assembly, and Councilman Nate Holden, who lost a 1978 primary to Dixon. Maxine Waters of the neighboring 35th District sought to avoid a primary contest, but such an opening may come only once in a generation, and California legislators and Los Angeles council members are term-limited. Watson's theme was familiarity: "People have trusted me, and I have not let them down. People have read my name on the ballot for 25 years. They have been born, grown up and gotten married in that time. That means a great deal. When you work your base, you win." Murray argued that, at 41 and 26 years younger than Watson—and 30 years younger than Holden—he could build seniority; Watson countered by campaigning with her 91-year-old mother. The race was, among other things, a battle of endorsements. Watson was endorsed and funded by EMILY's List; in the waning days of the race, she garnered the endorsement of former L.A. Laker Magic Johnson. Murray was endorsed by Waters, Dixon's widow Bettye, and Henry Waxman and Howard Berman; Holden was endorsed by outgoing Mayor Richard Riordan.

Turnout was high, with 83,000 voting in the April open primary; it was doubtless spurred by the simultaneous primary for mayor of Los Angeles, since most of the district is in the city. Watson won 33% of the vote, to 26% for Murray and 17% for Holden. The all female slate that moved on to the June runoff included Watson; 1998 unsuccessful lieutenant governor candidate and Republican Noel Hentschel, who took 5% in the primary; Reform Party candidate and 2000 Patrick Buchanan running mate Ezola Foster, who took less than 1% in April; and Green Party candidate Donna Warren who garnered just over 1% in the primary. The June 5 runoff, which again coincided with the L.A. mayoral election where just two Democrats were running, propelled Watson to her stunning 75% victory. Hentschel, who took 20%, ran a game campaign and was able to lend herself $400,000, but she never had a chance.

Even before Dixon's death, local black Democrats were worried that the declining number of blacks in the 32nd and neighboring areas and the rapid growth among Latinos would make it hard to maintain three black-represented districts in the Los Angeles area. Population must be added to each of the three, which will reduce black percentages further. Most likely a similarly-shaped district will emerge, though perhaps with changes that could undermine Watson in some future contest; Kevin Murray serves on the state Senate's redistricting committee.

Cook's Call *Safe.* There was never any doubt that a Democrat would win the special election here, but it is not yet clear what the district will look like after the redraw. Heavy Latino growth in this district and the surrounding Los Angeles area means that this district may no longer be majority black.

THE PEOPLE: Pop. 2000: 586,031; Pop. 1990: 572,630, up 2.3% 1990–2000. 31.8% White, 32.9% Black, 7.8% Asian, 0.7% Amer. Indian, 0.2% Hawaiian, 5% Two+ races, 21.6% Other; 37.1% Hispanic Origin.

2000 Presidential Vote			
Gore (D)	146,706	(83%)
Bush (R)	22,852	(13%)
Nader (Green)	4,904	(3%)
Others	1,485	(1%)

1996 Presidential Vote			
Clinton (D)	130,394	(81%)
Dole (R)	19,348	(12%)
Perot (I)	5,764	(4%)
Others	4,854	(3%)

Rep. Diane Watson (D)

Elected 2000, 1st term; b. Nov. 12, 1933, Los Angeles; home, Los Angeles; LA City College; U.C.L.A., B.A. 1954; CA State U., M.S. 1968; Claremont Graduate U., Ph.D. 1987; Catholic; single.

Elected Office: L.A. Bd. of Education, 1975–78; CA Senate, 1978–98.

Professional Career: Teacher & school psychologist, 1954–75; lecturer, CA State L.A. & CA State Long Beach; U.S. Ambassador, Micronesia 1999–2001.

DC Office: 2413 RHOB , 202-225-7084; Fax: 202-226-4571.

District Office: Los Angeles, 323-678-5424.

Committees: *International Relations* (23d of 23 D).

Group Ratings and Key Votes: Newly Elected

Election Results

2001 special	Diane Watson (D)	72,955	(75%)	($103,832)
	Noel I. Hentschel (R)	19,403	(20%)	($709,138)
	Donna Warren (Green)	3,661	(4%)	
	Other	1,512	(2%)	
2001 spec. prim.	Diane Watson (D)	27,600	(33%)	
	Kevin Murray (D)	22,273	(26%)	
	Nate Holden (D)	14,038	(17%)	
	Noel I. Hentschel (R)	4,479	(5%)	
	Leo James Terrell (D)	4,127	(5%)	
	Other	11,561	(14%)	
2000 general	Julian C. Dixon (D)	137,447	(85%)	($161,211)
	Kathy Williamson (R)	19,924	(12%)	($3,077)
	Other	7,156	(4%)	
2000 primary	Julian C. Dixon (D)	84,307	(79%)	
	Kathy Williamson (R)	13,040	(12%)	
	Elisha Smith (D)	6,351	(6%)	
	Other	3,682	(3%)	

THIRTY-THIRD DISTRICT

A block from the 452-foot white tower of Los Angeles's "modern architecture" City Hall—long the symbol of the city, but now dwarfed by 60- and 70-story postmodern marble slabs and pink cylinders a few blocks away—is the huge retail shopping street of Broadway. The sidewalks are thronged, the signs are mostly in Spanish, the merchandise is often strewn on tables: this could be Mexico City or Lima. It is Latin America transplanted a block from a gleaming symbol of Yankee propriety and gaudy emblems of North American prosperity. Broadway, now somewhat in decline from its retail heyday, is neither the geographical nor spiritual center of Los Angeles's Latino communities and it is just one of many shopping areas. But it is an emblem of the entry-level Latino neighborhoods of the nation's second largest city, the places where many immigrants, not only from Mexico but from Central and South America, come to find a cheap place to live— doubling and tripling up with other families and single newcomers, close enough to drive an old car to work in factories and warehouses that fill so much of the acreage south and east of downtown.

Broadway and many of these entry-level neighborhoods make up much of the 33d Congressional District. It includes downtown and MacArthur Park—once beautiful, then a drug dealers' hangout, now cleaned up—plus Pico Union, where many Central and South American immigrants make their first homes. It also includes the giant factories south of downtown along the Southern Pacific Railroad and Santa Ana Freeway and it takes in part of East Los Angeles. To the south it includes the garment factories of Vernon and the 1940s working-class suburbs: Huntington Park—with its vibrant shopping strip on the wide Pacific Boulevard and with a youthful population that has more than doubled since 1980—South Gate, Bell and Bell Gardens, Commerce, Maywood and Cudahy, all of which are now heavily Latino. In 2000, the 33d District was 86% Hispanic, by far the highest figure of any California district, and the only one that can be called monocultural. Politically, these neighborhoods are overwhelmingly Democratic. The lag in voter participation is growing smaller. In 1990, the registered voters were 48% Latino; by 1997, 62% were—the highest share in California. Still, this is mostly a non-voting constituency, with only 132,354 registered voters in October 2000: Newcomers may not be citizens, many residents are children, workers at two jobs may be too busy to register, and Latinos tend to see private sector work, not public sector protections, as their way up in the world. As a result, in 2000 only 37,000 people voted in the 33d District's House Democratic primary and only 71,000 in the general election, compared to 238,000 in November in the Westside 29th District and between 100,000 and 149,000 in the Hispanic-majority 26th, 30th, 31st and 34th Districts. The 33d District looks like a version of a rotten borough, Old-Sarum-on-the-Pacific-Rim, but it is a district where people work hard and play by the American rules, with high rates of family stability and low levels of people who count on welfare—the home of people rising into the middle class.

The 33d District's congresswoman is Lucille Roybal-Allard, first elected in 1992, the daughter of 30-year Congressman Edward Roybal; his roots were in New Mexico, not Mexico, and in 1949 he was the first Latino elected to the Los Angeles city council. Lucille Roybal-Allard dreamed of a show-business career as a teenager and later worked as a department-store clerk and for non-profit organizations. After raising a family—her two children are both lawyers—she entered politics at age 45, at the encouragement of local activists. She was elected to the Assembly in 1986 and sponsored bills on sexual assault, domestic violence and requiring more environmental impact reports for toxic waste incinerators (a move prompted by protests against a proposed incinerator in Vernon.) She entered the 1992 House race before her father announced his retirement in the adjacent 30th District, and she won 75% in the Democratic primary and 63% in the general election.

As the first Mexican-American woman elected to Congress, Roybal-Allard says she is "dedicated to community empowerment at all levels," and she has compiled an almost perfectly liberal voting record. In 1999, she won two key assignments. On the Appropriations Committee, where her father had been a subcommittee chairman, she has dealt heavily with immigration issues. As chairman of the Hispanic Caucus, she challenged the "East coast mentality in Washington" and sought to move beyond internal divisions over Cuba and Fidel Castro. She sought fairness in immigration policy, with proposals to give immigrants from all of Central America and the Caribbean the same right to permanent resident status as those from Cuba and Nicaragua, and to make amnesty available to all persons who have lived in the United States since 1986. She criticized the lack of support from congressional Republicans and urged George W. Bush to "help us bring fairness to Latinos." On other issues, she won House passage of an amendment to allow breast-feeding in national parks and museums. She won $34 million in 2000 for a new federal court house in downtown Los Angeles, which is swamped by the needs of immigrants. She sought inclusion of anti-drinking messages to youths in the government's campaign against illegal drugs, but the effort died at the hands of the alcohol and beer lobbies.

Back home, in her office at the Edward R. Roybal Federal Building, Roybal-Allard sponsors health fairs and workshops on home-buying and U.S. citizenship. She has been re-elected without difficulty, and has promised to work on redistricting to increase the number of Latinos elected in the Los Angeles area.

Cook's Call *Safe.* It is not yet clear how redistricting will alter the district, but it is unlikely that Roybal-Allard will have much to worry about.

THE PEOPLE: Pop. 2000: 600,695; Pop. 1990: 570,893, up 5.2% 1990–2000. 37.6% White, 3.9% Black, 4.5% Asian, 1.2% Amer. Indian, 0.1% Hawaiian, 4.9% Two+ races, 47.8% Other; 86% Hispanic Origin.

2000 Presidential Vote		
Gore (D)	63,370	(83%)
Bush (R)	11,402	(15%)
Nader (Green)	1,333	(2%)
Others	657	(1%)

1996 Presidential Vote		
Clinton (D)	48,636	(80%)
Dole (R)	8,538	(14%)
Perot (I)	2,691	(4%)
Others	1,146	(2%)

Rep. Lucille Roybal-Allard (D)

Elected 1992, 5th term; b. June 12, 1941, Los Angeles; home, Los Angeles; CA St. U. at Los Angeles, B.A. 1965; Catholic; married (Edward Allard).

Elected Office: CA Assembly, 1986–92.

DC Office: 2435 RHOB 20515, 202-225-1766; Fax: 202-226-0350; Web site: www.house.gov/roybal-allard.

District Office: Los Angeles, 213-628-9230.

Committees: *Appropriations* (23d of 29 D): Commerce, Justice & State; Energy & Water Development.

Group Ratings

	ADA	ACLU	AFS	LCV	CON	ITIC	NTU	COC	ACU	NTLC	CHC
2000	90	86	100	79	68	53	15	35	8	12	0
1999	95	—	100	94	56	—	16	16	0	—	—

National Journal Ratings

	1999 LIB —	1999 CONS		2000 LIB —	2000 CONS
Economic	88% —	0%		95% —	0%
Social	87% —	0%		88% —	12%
Foreign	95% —	0%		77% —	21%

Key Votes of the 106th Congress

1. Patient Bill of Rights	Y	5. Bar RU-486 $ for FDA	N	9. NATO War in Serbia	Y
2. Accelerate Min. Wage	Y	6. Display 10 Commandments	N	10. Perm. Trade with China	N
3. Strike Ban on Ergo. Stnd.	Y	7. Gun Show Bkgrnd. Checks	Y	11. Debt Relief for 3rd World	Y
4. Ovrd. Estate Tax Veto	N	8. Ban Part.-Birth Abortion	N	12. Drop Cuba Econ. Embargo	Y

Election Results

2000 general	Lucille Roybal-Allard (D)	60,510	(85%)	($292,932)
	Wayne Miller (R)	8,260	(12%)	
	Other	2,801	(4%)	
2000 primary	Lucille Roybal-Allard (D)	37,618	(85%)	
	Wayne Miller (R)	5,364	(12%)	
	Other	1,465	(3%)	
1998 general	Lucille Roybal-Allard (D)	43,310	(87%)	($143,600)
	Wayne Miller (R)	6,364	(13%)	

THIRTY-FOURTH DISTRICT

One of the great population surges in the United States is the upward social movement of the hundreds of thousands of immigrants to the Los Angeles Basin, from crowded entry-level neighborhoods out on freeways to the suburbs. It is visible east and southeast of Los Angeles, in suburbs that over a generation have changed from solidly white Anglo to largely Latino. Many have made their way up working in small smokeless factories along railroad tracks and near river beds, beneath roaring freeways and on grid streets near stucco garden apartment blocks and in small business offices and stores; these have made Los Angeles the nation's number-one manufacturing metro area. These people came to the United States not to re-create their Third World environment but to rise above it, and they see this country not as a land of oppression but of opportunity. Their values resemble those of working-class Americans of the 1960s: pro-family and respectful of traditional personal morals (LA-area Latinos have lower than average divorce rates), patriotic and pro-military (they are more likely than average to volunteer for military service), working for economic advancement (Latino males have the highest work force participation of any measured group and the incomes of U.S.-born Los Angeles County Latino incomes are at the county average).

Vast numbers of these new residents—whose rise through hard work has gone largely unnoticed in the mainstream press—live in the 34th Congressional District. The percentage of Hispanic voters rose from 43% in 1990 to 51% in 1997, the second highest of any California district. This is a swath of suburban Los Angeles County anchored by three suburbs. On the northwest is Montebello, a working-class suburb just beyond East Los Angeles, now 75% Hispanic. To the east is La Puente, 83% Hispanic, a center of the light-manufacturing economy that created hundreds of thousands of jobs in the Los Angeles Basin in the 1980s, and in which increasing numbers of small businesses are owned by Asians, Latinos and blacks. To the south are Whittier—a town founded by Midwestern Quakers, where Richard Nixon grew up and went to Whittier College—and Norwalk, the district's largest city, farther south astride the Santa Ana Freeway; they are 56% and 63% Hispanic. Overall, the 34th District's population in 2000 was 72% Hispanic, up from 62% in 1990.

The congresswoman from the 34th District is Grace Flores Napolitano, a Democrat elected in 1998. Napolitano grew up in the Lower Rio Grande Valley of Texas, married at 18, and had five children and moved to California by the time she was 23. She worked as a secretary at Ford Motor Company for 22 years. After her first husband died, she married Frank Napolitano and in 1980 they started a pizzeria business. She served on the city council in Norwalk from 1986–92, and served one term as mayor, becoming the first Latina to hold either position. In 1992 she was elected to the California Assembly from a district that covered 60% of this congressional district. She chaired the International Trade and Development Committee and got a 100% rating from the AFL-CIO.

Term-limited in 1998, she got the opportunity to run for Congress when 16-year incumbent Esteban Torres announced three days before the filing deadline that he was retiring. Torres's surprise move seemed designed to promote the election of Jamie Casso, his son-in-law and chief of staff, who immediately announced his candidacy. But Napolitano was not deterred. She convinced the state AFL-CIO to vote an "open endorsement," although the executive board had backed Casso and Torres had been a senior United Auto Workers official under Walter Reuther in the 1960s. Napolitano and Casso waged a fierce campaign. She criticized his failure to live in the district; he criticized her $180,000 loan to her campaign at an unusual 18% interest rate, which he said left her little reason to repay the principal. Torres was featured prominently in Casso's campaign literature and appearances. Napolitano had the financial backing of national women's organizations, including EMILY's List, plus the benefit of higher name-identification. The two candidates had few differences on major issues, except that Napolitano signed a pledge to serve only four terms. Napolitano won the primary by 618 votes, 51%–49% among Democratic voters. Her victory in November was routine.

In 2000, she won enactment of a $300 million authorization to remove a leaking 10-million ton pile of radioactive uranium tailings from the defunct Pentagon-contracting mill of Atlas Corporation at Moab, Utah—600 feet from the Colorado River, a prime source of Southern California's drinking water. The House approved for 1999 and 2000 $4 million that she requested to clean up the vacated site in Pico Rivera where Northrop Grumman produced B-2 bombers. She filed bills aimed at reducing the high rate of school drop-outs and suicides among Latino teens. Despite initial concern, she had no Democratic opposition in 2000, and has not faced competitive Republican challenges. Redistricting will change the boundaries of the district in some way, but there is likely to be another heavily Hispanic district in this area.

Cook's Call   *Safe.* Grace Napolitano seamlessly took over this suburban Los Angeles County seat from eight-term Representataive Esteban Torres in 1998 and should be able to hold it for as long as she wants.

THE PEOPLE: Pop. 2000: 617,343; Pop. 1990: 573,456, up 7.7% 1990–2000. 46.9% White, 1.9% Black, 8.9% Asian, 1.2% Amer. Indian, 0.2% Hawaiian, 4.9% Two+ races, 36% Other; 72.4% Hispanic Origin.

2000 Presidential Vote

Gore (D)	107,003	(67%)
Bush (R)	46,974	(30%)
Nader (Green)	3,461	(2%)
Others	1,552	(1%)

1996 Presidential Vote

Clinton (D)	91,603	(64%)
Dole (R)	39,277	(27%)
Perot (I)	10,396	(7%)
Others	2,930	(2%)

Rep. Grace Napolitano (D)

Elected 1998, 2d term; b. Dec. 4, 1936, Brownsville, TX; home, Norwalk; Catholic; married (Frank).

Elected Office: Norwalk City Cncl., 1986–92; Norwalk Mayor, 1989–92; CA Assembly, 1992–98.

Professional Career: Employee, Ford Motor Co., 1970–1992.

DC Office: 1609 LHOB 20515, 202-225-5256; Fax: 202-225-0027; Web site: www.house.gov/napolitano.

District Office: Pico Rivera, 562-801-2134.

Committees: *International Relations* (22d of 23 D): International Operations and Human Rights; Western Hemisphere. *Resources* (16th of 25 D): Energy & Mineral Resources; Water & Power. *Small Business* (11th of 17 D): Tax, Finance & Exports.

Group Ratings

	ADA	ACLU	AFS	LCV	CON	ITIC	NTU	COC	ACU	NTLC	CHC
2000	95	79	100	93	71	82	21	47	4	12	7
1999	90	—	100	81	31	—	16	45	0	—	—

National Journal Ratings

	1999 LIB	—	1999 CONS		2000 LIB	—	2000 CONS
Economic	66%	—	33%		92%	—	5%
Social	83%	—	13%		72%	—	26%
Foreign	93%	—	7%		84%	—	15%

Key Votes of the 106th Congress

1. Patient Bill of Rights	Y	5. Bar RU-486 $ for FDA	N	9. NATO War in Serbia	Y
2. Accelerate Min. Wage	Y	6. Display 10 Commandments	N	10. Perm. Trade with China	N
3. Strike Ban on Ergo. Stnd.	Y	7. Gun Show Bkgrnd. Checks	Y	11. Debt Relief for 3rd World	Y
4. Ovrd. Estate Tax Veto	N	8. Ban Part.-Birth Abortion	N	12. Drop Cuba Econ. Embargo	Y

Election Results

2000 general	Grace Napolitano (D) 105,980	(71%)	($298,484)
	Robert Arthur Canales (R) 33,445	(22%)	($1,689)
	Julia F. Simon (NL) 9,262	(6%)	
2000 primary	Grace Napolitano (D) 68,631	(70%)	
	Robert Arthur Canales (R) 24,140	(24%)	
	Other 6,053	(6%)	
1998 general	Grace Napolitano (D) 76,471	(68%)	($618,421)
	Ed Perez (R) 32,321	(29%)	($15,819)
	Others 4,283	(4%)	

THIRTY-FIFTH DISTRICT

In April 1992, the corner of Florence and Normandie in South Central Los Angeles became for a moment the most famous intersection in America: the epicenter of the Los Angeles riot. This was not, as was commonly said, simply an outpouring of anger at the Rodney King verdict; if it were, there would have been rioting everywhere in the Los Angeles Basin, since few citizens agreed with the Simi Valley jury. It was rather, like the urban riots of the 1960s, a collection of criminal acts suddenly committed by people in the expectation that so many others would be doing the same thing that all would have impunity; and even so, the rioting this time clearly would have been stopped but for the dereliction of Los Angeles Police Department Chief Daryl Gates, who had prepared no contingency plan and spent hours on his way to and from a political fundraiser as the rioting broke out. The definitive story is told by the brilliant reporter Lou Cannon in his book *Official Negligence*. The rioting stopped after some 36 hours once Governor Pete Wilson and President George Bush announced that 25,000 troops were being ordered to Los Angeles, eliminating potential rioters' expectation that they would not be punished. But great damage was done. Most visible was the harm to individuals: Black and Latino onlookers were killed and injured by rioters and law enforcement personnel; a white truck driver was viciously beaten at Florence and Normandie; Asian and Latino storeowners were singled out by black and Central American rioters and treated as oppressors, when in fact they were providing goods and services which no one else—for reasons later painfully apparent—was willing to provide. More than 9,000 businesses were destroyed and at least 6,000 jobs lost.

Among those commenting most vociferously on the riot was Congresswoman Maxine Waters, whose 35th Congressional District includes Florence and Normandie as well as much of the South Central and Watts corridors which formed California's first black-majority district 30 years ago. The 35th also includes the suburb of Inglewood, home of the Inglewood Forum; Hawthorne, birthplace of the Beach Boys; and Gardena, with California's first licensed poker clubs at which some of the most cutthroat games in the country are played. Over the last two decades the ethnic composition of this area has changed. Twenty years ago Inglewood and the Los Angeles parts of the district were heavily black, Hawthorne and Gardena mostly white. But in the 1980s and 1990s many Latinos have moved into all these areas. The 35th District was 42% black and 43% Hispanic in 1990. In 2000 it was 35% black and 54% Hispanic. Blacks are still the voting majority, since many Latinos are not citizens or are not registered to vote.

Maxine Waters grew up in St. Louis and came to California in 1961; she worked in a garment factory and raised two children, got a sociology degree at California State University in Los Angeles and became an assistant Head Start teacher after the Watts riot of 1965. In 1976 she won a seat in the California Assembly. There she supported Willie Brown and passed minority, women's and tenants' rights laws, limits on police strip searches and a provision mandating divestiture of state pension funds from South Africa. She became a Democratic national committeewoman in 1980 and Phil Burton consulted her on 1982 redistricting. When Augustus Hawkins retired in 1990 after 28 years in the House and 28 years in the California Assembly, Waters was the obvious choice for the seat and won it easily.

Waters comes from a background of poverty and believes with fervor in federal aid for the poor and for racial preferences to help blacks overcome years of slavery, segregation and discrimination; she favors drastic reductions in defense spending and was one of six members who voted against supporting the Gulf war once it started, asking how urban gang members could be expected to stop fighting when America's own leaders were waging battles. She brings to her work a fury that is almost palpable, and an insistence that she will assert herself regardless of protocol, partly perhaps a result of anger but also a weapon she uses shrewdly and cynically to get both publicity and results. "I don't have time to be polite," she says, beginning her career by getting herself included in a post-riot White House meeting with George Bush. The Los Angeles riot was occasion for both Waters' best and worst moments. She flew home immediately and roused the Department of Water and Power to restore water to the riot area, and was effective in gaining provisions to the post-riot emergency act that eventually made it through Congress and was signed into law. But she also over-emotionally claimed, "Los Angeles is under siege . . . the violence could spill over to many other cities in this country."

She has produced specific legislation, including the Community Reinvestment Act racial quotas, a "Youth Fair Chance Act" with job training and counseling for unemployed young men 17 to 30, and a Center for Women Veterans within the Department of Veterans Affairs. She has worked for many set-asides for women and minorities. Her husband, a former professional football player and Mercedes Benz salesman, became Bill Clinton's ambassador to the Bahamas. Even so, she voted against the crime bill rule in August 1994 when the administration desperately needed votes, because she said she "could not vote for a crime bill that sweepingly expands the death penalty to include sixty new crimes." In 1994 she protested Clinton's cutoff of Haitian refugees and was arrested at the gates of the White House. In 1996, again opposing Clinton, she denounced his signing of the welfare bill and called for a vast expansion of government spending and powers. And in January 2001 she complained that Bill Clinton's choice for Democratic national chairman, Terry McAuliffe, was "anointed without our participation," and backed Maynard Jackson instead.

Waters often makes news. In 1996 and 1997, she pushed the theory, supported in a story in the *San Jose Mercury News* (later repudiated by the paper), that the CIA had worked with Nicaraguan Contras to import crack cocaine into South Central Los Angeles. Waters gained her greatest national publicity during the Judiciary Committee's Clinton impeachment inquiry, where she assailed "trumped-up charges," and termed Kenneth Starr "guilty" of "raw, unmasked, unbridled hatred and meanness that drives this impeachment coup d'etat." She said Senators John Ashcroft and Christopher Bond committed an "evil, racist act" when they blocked the confirmation of Ronnie White for federal judge. She called the partial birth abortion bill a "ritualistic attack on women." She waded into the Elian Gonzalez case, meeting with Elian's father in Cuba and with the boy's grandmothers in Washington, arguing that he should be returned to his father in Cuba. In a rare legislative success in the Republican House, Waters sponsored an amendment to triple spending for the erasure of the debts of poor nations, mostly in Africa; many Republicans crossed over, and it passed 216–211. At the Los Angeles Democratic Convention she announced she was not prepared to endorse the Gore-Lieberman ticket until Lieberman appeared before the convention's Black Caucus and explained his stands on education, criminal justice and racial quotas and preferences. Lieberman appeared and began by leading a chorus of "Happy Birthday" for Waters (it was her 62nd) and explained that he had never supported Proposition 209 and that he had voted in 1995 and 1998 for racial set-asides in transportation contracts; this brought loud applause, and Waters endorsed him. (But 15,000 of Waters's "official sample ballots" mailed out before Election Day had a red circle around Ralph Nader; a printing mistake, she said.) Waters protested loudly during the session at which the electoral votes were counted, and appeared at a "mourning of the inauguration" rally in Pershing Square on inauguration day. Waters's penchant for confrontation does not always help her in the House; in February 2001 she was passed over for a seat on Appropriations. After Minority Leader Dick Gephardt named her the head of a special Democratic committee on election reform, it was taken by Republicans as a signal that Gephardt was not interested in bipartisan action.

Waters has been re-elected without difficulty. With her political skills and capacity for shrewdly directed outrage, she is likely to emerge from redistricting, which is controlled by Democrats, with a favorable district. But however that is done, Latinos are likely to cast an increasing percentage of the vote, and it is possible that Waters could be challenged in the primary by a Latino candidate by the end of the decade.

Cook's Call   *Safe*. Maxine Waters will never have to worry about a general election in a district that gave Gore 86% in 2000. But, redistricting could cause her some headaches. With the heavy growth of Latinos in the Los Angeles area, there has been talk of creating a new majority-Latino district that could have an impact on Waters' seat.

THE PEOPLE: Pop. 2000: 607,944; Pop. 1990: 570,697, up 6.5% 1990–2000. 22.9% White, 34.6% Black, 4.3% Asian, 0.8% Amer. Indian, 0.4% Hawaiian, 4.5% Two+ races, 32.6% Other; 54.2% Hispanic Origin.

2000 Presidential Vote		
Gore (D)	104,812	(86%)
Bush (R)	14,605	(12%)
Nader (Green)	1,695	(1%)
Others	968	(1%)

1996 Presidential Vote		
Clinton (D)	92,773	(84%)
Dole (R)	12,063	(11%)
Perot (I)	4,129	(4%)
Others	1,727	(2%)

Rep. Maxine Waters (D)

Elected 1990, 6th term; b. Aug. 15, 1938, St. Louis, MO; home, Los Angeles; CA St. U. at Los Angeles, B.A. 1970; Christian; married (Sidney Williams).

Elected Office: CA Assembly, 1976–90.

Professional Career: Head Start teacher, 1966; Dpty., City Councilman David Cunningham, 1973–76.

DC Office: 2344 RHOB 20515, 202-225-2201; Fax: 202-225-7854; Web site: www.house.gov/waters.

District Office: Los Angeles, 323-757-8900.

Committees: *Chief Deputy Minority Whip. Financial Services* (4th of 32 D): Financial Institutions & Consumer Credit (RMM); Housing & Community Opportunity; International Monetary Policy & Trade. *Judiciary* (10th of 17 D): Commercial & Administrative Law; Courts, the Internet & Intellectual Property.

Group Ratings

	ADA	ACLU	AFS	LCV	CON	ITIC	NTU	COC	ACU	NTLC	CHC
2000	85	85	100	86	82	37	31	26	0	3	0
1999	100	—	100	94	82	—	30	12	0	—	—

National Journal Ratings

	1999 LIB —	1999 CONS		2000 LIB —	2000 CONS
Economic	88% —	0%		95% —	0%
Social	87% —	0%		79% —	21%
Foreign	95% —	0%		91% —	9%

Key Votes of the 106th Congress

1. Patient Bill of Rights	Y	5. Bar RU-486 $ for FDA	*	9. NATO War in Serbia	Y
2. Accelerate Min. Wage	Y	6. Display 10 Commandments	N	10. Perm. Trade with China	N
3. Strike Ban on Ergo. Stnd.	Y	7. Gun Show Bkgrnd. Checks	Y	11. Debt Relief for 3rd World	Y
4. Ovrd. Estate Tax Veto	N	8. Ban Part.-Birth Abortion	N	12. Drop Cuba Econ. Embargo	Y

Election Results

2000 general	Maxine Waters (D)	100,569	(87%)	($266,309)
	Carl McGill (R)	12,582	(11%)	($7,671)
	Other	3,064	(3%)	
2000 primary	Maxine Waters (D)	64,176	(85%)	
	Carl McGill (R)	8,898	(12%)	
	Other	2,108	(3%)	
1998 general	Maxine Waters (D)	78,732	(89%)	($177,584)
	Gordon Michael Mego (AI)	9,413	(11%)	

THIRTY-SIXTH DISTRICT

For many southern Californians, there is no better place to be than the beach. It is not a perfect environment: In the morning there may be mists, the winter air is damp and clammy, even in summer the weather can be chilly, the water is never very warm and is sometimes polluted. But for many this is echt-California, and in this democratic polity, there is a beach to suit the taste of just about everyone. The funkiest of all is Venice, with its beach houses jammed together and the long-stagnant canals dug by a developer in 1904, with the boardwalk where skateboarding got its start and roller blading is *de rigueur*. Right behind is Marina Del Rey, with sleek modern apartment complexes and expensive yacht moorings. Just south, across an inlet, is LAX; the swooping arches of its theme building, intended in 1961 to symbolize the jet era, are now an historic landmark, like Disneyland's Tomorrowland or the *Jetsons*, an antique version of a surpassed future. To the south is El Segundo, named for Chevron's second oil refinery. Next are Manhattan Beach, one of the favorites four decades ago of the Beach Boys who grew up a couple of miles inland in Hawthorne, and tiny Hermosa Beach, with tightly packed frame houses originally the homes of elderly retirees, now filled with the young and would-be young. To the south are the flower-planted rises of Redondo Beach and the larger city of Torrance, whose vast inland expanse is filled with the American headquarters of Japanese companies. The South Bay beaches end where the Palos Verdes Peninsula looms high over the ocean, seismically active and socioeconomically upscale. Just to the east is the harbor town of San Pedro, once working-class, but moving up as well, overlooking LA's eerily modern containerport.

All this beach territory, from Venice south to San Pedro (both of which are within the Los Angeles city limits, though the area in between is not), makes up the 36th Congressional District. California today is mostly multiethnic, but the beach communities are still, as if in the 1950s, filled mostly with white Anglos: In 2000 the district was 19% Hispanic, the second lowest percentage of any Los Angeles area district, 15% Asian and 4% black. Historically Republican, this area is still leery of taxes, but culturally it is libertarian—against restrictions or even aspersions on its various lifestyles. When those issues are paramount, the Beach area trends Democratic, as in the mid-1970s and mid-1990s; when economics and defense are more important, it is solidly Republican, as in the 1960s and early-1980s. For this has been one of America's leading defense and aerospace areas, where Howard Hughes built planes half a century ago and where so much of the 1980s defense buildup took place. The most recent trends are apparent in the presidential results here. In the defense-buildup 1980s, the senior George Bush carried the district 60%–40%. In the cultural-war year of 2000, Al Gore carried the 36th 51%–44%.

The congresswoman from the 36th District is Democrat Jane Harman, who regained the seat in 2000 that she held for six years before running for governor in 1998. Born in New York City, she grew up in Los Angeles as the daughter of a Westside physician and was in the gallery as a volunteer usher when John F. Kennedy was nominated at the 1960 Democratic National Convention in Los Angeles. She graduated from Smith College and Harvard Law School, when women were still rare there. In the 1970s, she worked for California Senator John Tunney and the Senate Judiciary Committee. She later served in the Carter White House and as a special counsel in the Defense Department. After her stints in government, Harman practiced law and worked as a lobbyist in Washington. When she saw the new 1992 district lines, she returned to California and ran for Congress. Harman is one of the richest members of Congress, with a net worth of $200 million, according to *Roll Call*; her husband Sidney Harman is founder of Harman International Industries, and she has spent large amounts of her own money on her campaigns. In 1992, the "year of the woman," she campaigned as "pro-choice and pro-change," defeating a pro-life Republican woman 48%–42%; she was narrowly re-elected in 1994 and 1996 against Susan Brooks, a Rancho Palos Verdes council member. She decided late to run for governor, getting into the race only after Senator Dianne Feinstein announced in January 1998 that she would not run. Harmon spent more than $20 million, but finished a disappointing third among Democrats. In 1999, she was appointed as a Regents' professor at UCLA. Congressional and state Democrats lobbied her hard to seek her former House seat, which Republican Steven Kuykendall narrowly won over Democrat Janice Hahn in 1998. With Kuykendall's pro-choice and pro-environment views plus efforts on behalf of local businesses, many Democrats believed that only Harman could defeat him.

In the March 2000 all-party primary, Kuykendall narrowly edged Harman 43%–41% among all voters, with Republicans winning another 8% and other Democrats another 6%. Harman attacked Kuykendall for failing to support the Democrats' proposal for a prescription drug benefit in Medicare and for voting to repeal the estate tax, and tried to tie him to Republican leaders Dick Armey and Tom DeLay. She stressed her earlier House record, economically somewhat conservative and culturally liberal. Her assiduous work on defense issues in the 1990s was perhaps less relevant now that the area has become much less dependent on defense industries. Dick Gephardt promised to restore her seniority. Kuykendall may have been hurt by the deadlock between the Republican leadership and the Clinton White House that kept Congress in session through October, and he was certainly hurt by the lack of appeal of George W. Bush in coastal California. This was a race targeted by both parties, requiring expensive purchases of Los Angeles TV time; each candidate spent just a shade under $2 million; the AFL-CIO and Natural Resources Defense Council ran ads as well. Harman won 48%–47%; it took more a week of absentee-ballot counting after election day before Kuykendall conceded.

On her return to the House, Harman gave up her Armed Services Committee seat and joined Energy and Commerce, where she can deal with a range of issues—including locally relevant communications and environmental problems—and develop additional campaign fundraising sources. She regained her seat on the Intelligence Committee, though she was disappointed that she did not get the ranking Democratic post, which instead went to Nancy Pelosi. The district must add 48,000 people; most likely they will come from Democratic precincts in neighboring districts, of which there are plenty.

Cook's Call   *Potentially Competitive.* With a good political wind at her back (Gore won the district by 7 %), Democrat Jane Harman defeated Steve Kuykendall to win back her former congressional seat. In its current form, this is a moderate, swing district that could still give Harman some troubles, especially in a down year for the party (Harman has never won here by more than 52%). But, it is hard to see how Republicans could put up a better candidate than Kuykendall. Democrats, who control the redistricting process in the state, are expected to help Harman considerably in redistricting.

THE PEOPLE: Pop. 2000: 591,448; Pop. 1990: 573,665, up 3.1% 1990–2000. 67.5% White, 3.9% Black, 15.3% Asian, 0.5% Amer. Indian, 0.4% Hawaiian, 4.7% Two+ races, 7.7% Other; 18.8% Hispanic Origin.

2000 Presidential Vote			1996 Presidential Vote		
Gore (D)	126,440	(51%)	Clinton (D)	109,244	(47%)
Bush (R)	110,507	(44%)	Dole (R)	96,872	(41%)
Nader (Green)	9,504	(4%)	Perot (I)	18,510	(8%)
Others	3,058	(1%)	Others	9,375	(4%)

Rep. Jane Harman (D)

Elected 2000, 1st term; b. June 28, 1945, New York, NY; home, Rolling Hills; Smith Col., B.A. 1966, Harvard, J.D. 1969; Jewish; married (Sidney).

Elected Office: U.S. House of Reps., 1992–98.

Professional Career: Legis. Dir., U.S. Sen. John Tunney, 1972–73; Chief Cnsl. & Staff Dir., Senate Judiciary Subcmtee., 1973–77; Dep. Cabinet Secy., White House, 1977; Defense Dept. Special Cnsl., 1979; Harman Intl. Industries, Corp. Secy., 1985–92, Dir., 1990–92; Practicing atty., 1987–92; Regents Prof., U.C.L.A., 1999.

DC Office: 229 CHOB 20515, 202-225-8220; Fax: 202-226-7290; Web site: www.house.gov/harman.

District Office: Redondo Beach, 310-372-1600.

Committees: *Energy & Commerce* (26th of 26 D): Commerce, Trade & Consumer Protection; Environment & Hazardous Materials; Telecommunications & The Internet. *Permanent Select Committee on Intelligence* (3d of 9 D): Technical & Tactical Intelligence.

Group Ratings and Key Votes: Newly Elected

Election Results

2000 general	Jane Harman (D)	115,651	(48%)	($1,998,739)
	Steven T. Kuykendall (R)	111,199	(47%)	($1,988,938)
	Other	12,281	(5%)	
2000 primary	Steven T. Kuykendall (R)	66,520	(43%)	
	Jane Harman (D)	63,013	(41%)	
	Robert T. Pegram (R)	12,653	(8%)	
	James C. Cavuoto (D)	6,423	(4%)	
	Other	7,055	(4%)	
1998 general	Steven T. Kuykendall (R)	88,843	(49%)	($785,085)
	Janice Hahn (D)	84,624	(47%)	($692,076)
	Others	8,239	(5%)	

THIRTY-SEVENTH DISTRICT

Los Angeles is the creation not of nature but of man: there is little natural water supply here and no natural port, little in the way of natural resources except for oil which turned out not to be enough for California; it is a place for people who plan big. Nearly a century ago, Los Angeles's city fathers decided to build a port where the usually-dry Los Angeles River debouches into the ocean; in 1906 they annexed an eight-mile-long, four-block-wide corridor of land (christened Harbor Gateway in 1984) and the harbor areas of Wilmington and San Pedro, and converted a shallow bay with a few marshy inlets into what has become the biggest port on the West Coast, ahead of the splendid natural harbors of San Francisco and San Diego. Inland, along the rail lines that hug the river bed, heavy and light industry developed: oil tank farms and big factories, small job shops and warehouses. Interspersed were subdivisions. To the north was Watts, the epicenter of the 1965 riot and also the site of one of the strangest made-by-man structures in this made-by-man city, the 107-foot-high Watts Tower, built from 1921–54 by Simon Rodia out of all manner of salvaged material.

The 37th Congressional District of California takes in a swath of low-income industrial suburbs from Watts and the new Century Freeway, the most expensive road in history, south to Wilmington and the port. Here are Compton and Lynwood, which switched from all-white to all-black in the 1960s and in the 1980s became heavily Latino. Here also are Carson, with recent subdivisions amid freeway interchanges and tank farms, and Wilmington, facing a spankingly modern port. The district's population in 2000 was 26% black and 57% Hispanic, but a near-majority of registered voters are black.

The congresswoman from the 37th District is Juanita Millender-McDonald, chosen in a March 1996 special election. She was born in Alabama, raised a family in Carson, and earned a bachelor's degree in 1979, at 40. She worked as a teacher and editor/writer for the Los Angeles Unified School District and was manuscript editor for *IMAGES*, a state textbook designed for young women to enhance self-esteem and explore non-traditional careers. She later became director of gender equity programs for the district and was appointed to the National Commission on Teaching and America's Future, chaired by North Carolina Governor Jim Hunt. In 1990 she was elected to the Carson City Council. In 1992 she ran for the Assembly and beat an incumbent in the primary. She chaired the Insurance and the Revenue and Taxation Committees for a year each and sponsored the bill qualifying for designation as a National Transportation Artery the Alameda Corridor—a $1.8 billion combination of underground rail and freeway lanes connecting the port to major east-west rail lines and freeways.

Her opening to run for Congress came in December 1995, when two-term Congressman Walter Tucker was convicted of extortion and tax fraud as mayor of Compton and sentenced to 27 months in federal prison. A special election was set for the following March, the same day as the regular primary; since no Republicans ran, it determined the winner. Already running was

Assemblyman Willard Murray, who had been chief of staff to former (1981–93) Congressman Mervyn Dymally and is the father of state Senator Kevin Murray, who lost the April 2001 special primary in the 32nd district. Murray started off better-known, but with help from EMILY's List, Millender-McDonald raised much more money. Murray had other problems. He favored building a prison for Compton, which voters there turned down 87%–13%, and he favored the state take-over of Compton's public schools. Millender-McDonald won the nine-candidate special with 27% to 20% for Murray. The regular primary on the same ballot was a bit closer because of the presence of another candidate, Susan Carrillo, who got 15%. Millender-McDonald won this contest by just 24%–21%.

In the House, Millender-McDonald got a seat on the Transportation and Infrastructure Committee, where she made the Alameda Corridor her first priority. She also made national news in 1996. The *San Jose Mercury News* (in a story it later repudiated) charged that the CIA aided Nicaraguan Contras in smuggling crack cocaine to Los Angeles; and Millender-McDonald invited CIA Director John Deutsch to a public meeting in her district. Astonishingly, he accepted, and was denounced by dozens of speakers and booed and interrupted with obscenities by many others despite Millender-McDonald's pleas for order. Other causes included a cervical cancer awareness resolution, the Faces of AIDS stamp, expanding the bone marrow registry for minorities and people of mixed ancestry, asthma awareness, and the Digital Divide. She chairs the Democratic Women's Caucus, and was a prime organizer during impeachment of a delegation of House Democratic women to visit Hillary Rodham Clinton to "refocus the political dialogue on issues that really matter." She backed the Chinese-government-owned China Ocean Shipping Company's bid to build a container terminal at the former Long Beach Naval Air Station. But despite its likely benefits for the port, she voted against Permanent Normal Trade Relations with China because of its human rights abuses.

She has easily won re-election. Vernon Van, a part-time actor and her challenger in 2000, became a Republican two years earlier after he dabbled in witchcraft during a trip to New York City. "Demons attacked me when I was asleep. They had me by the throat," he told *The Los Angeles Times*. Millender-McDonald won 82%–11%. Redistricting likely will change some lines throughout this area—the district must add 23,000 people, and Millender-McDonald may face a Latino challenger before the decade is out.

Cook's Call *Safe*. This district is pretty barren territory for any Republican. But, Millender-McDonald, like many of her Los Angeles area Democratic colleagues, needs to be wary about the impact of redistricting on her district. Solid Latino growth in the area means that once majority black districts may have to give way to districts that are more heavily Hispanic. This could mean that the third-term incumbent could have a competitive primary election.

THE PEOPLE: Pop. 2000: 616,103; Pop. 1990: 572,191, up 7.7% 1990–2000. 24.6% White, 25.9% Black, 8.3% Asian, 0.9% Amer. Indian, 1.3% Hawaiian, 4.6% Two+ races, 34.6% Other; 57.2% Hispanic Origin.

2000 Presidential Vote			**1996 Presidential Vote**		
Gore (D)	99,748	(83%)	Clinton (D)	88,877	(81%)
Bush (R)	17,777	(15%)	Dole (R)	13,874	(13%)
Nader (Green)	1,706	(1%)	Perot (I)	4,798	(4%)
Others	1,165	(1%)			

Rep. Juanita Millender-McDonald (D)

Elected March 1996, 3d term; b. Sept. 7, 1938, Birmingham, AL; home, Carson; U. of Redlands, B.S. 1979, CA St. U., M.Ed. 1981; Baptist; married (James).

Elected Office: Carson City Cncl., 1990–92; Carson Mayor Pro-Tem, 1991–92; CA Assembly, 1993–96.

Professional Career: Teacher & Schl. Admin., 1981–90.

DC Office: 125 CHOB 20515, 202-225-7924; Fax: 202-225-7926; Web site: www.house.gov/millender-mcdonald.

District Office: Torrance, 310-538-1190.

Committees: *Small Business* (2d of 17 D): Workforce, Empowerment & Government Programs (RMM). *Transportation & Infrastructure* (17th of 34 D): Aviation; Highways & Transit; Water Resources & Environment.

Group Ratings

	ADA	ACLU	AFS	LCV	CON	ITIC	NTU	COC	ACU	NTLC	CHC
2000	90	85	100	86	58	72	18	50	8	13	7
1999	100	—	100	100	12	—	15	30	0	—	—

National Journal Ratings

	1999 LIB	—	1999 CONS		2000 LIB	—	2000 CONS
Economic	88%	—	0%		92%	—	5%
Social	87%	—	0%		94%	—	0%
Foreign	85%	—	12%		85%	—	10%

Key Votes of the 106th Congress

1. Patient Bill of Rights	Y	5. Bar RU-486 $ for FDA	N	9. NATO War in Serbia	Y
2. Accelerate Min. Wage	Y	6. Display 10 Commandments	N	10. Perm. Trade with China	N
3. Strike Ban on Ergo. Stnd.	Y	7. Gun Show Bkgrnd. Checks	Y	11. Debt Relief for 3rd World	Y
4. Ovrd. Estate Tax Veto	N	8. Ban Part.-Birth Abortion	N	12. Drop Cuba Econ. Embargo	Y

Election Results

2000 general	Juanita Millender-McDonald (D)	93,269	(82%)	($169,214)
	Vernon Van (R)	12,762	(11%)	
	Margaret Glazer (NL)	4,094	(4%)	
	Other	3,150	(3%)	
2000 primary	Juanita Millender-McDonald (D)	58,646	(82%)	
	Vernon Van (R)	8,048	(11%)	
	Other	4,999	(7%)	
1998 general	Juanita Millender-McDonald (D)	70,026	(85%)	($205,223)
	Saul E. Lamkster (R)	12,301	(15%)	

THIRTY-EIGHTH DISTRICT

Long Beach, founded in 1888, with 461,000 people in 2000, would be a major metropolis almost anywhere but in Los Angeles County, where it seems just the largest of many suburbs. But it has an identity of its own. Started as a beach resort, it soon became a port when Los Angeles civic leaders decided that if their town were to be a world-class city it must have a world-class harbor; nature not having provided one, they built it where the Los Angeles River merges into the ocean at Long Beach. By 1909, Los Angeles had annexed the harbor towns of San Pedro and Wilmington next to Long Beach; over the next decades the two cities persuaded federal government to dredge channels and build a breakwater and turning basins. Long Beach was developing other businesses as well: It sprouted oil derricks in the 1920s and briefly became one of the nation's big oil producers; it was the site of major aircraft plants in the 1940s and after. By the 1980s, the Los Angeles-Long Beach port was the nation's largest, the fastest-growing major cargo center in the world, with huge steel-gray container ships pulling quietly up to enormous automated loading facilities— a 21st Century contrast to the rotting docks of New York and San Francisco. Long Beach even acquired the *Queen Mary*, which became its biggest tourist attraction, plus, until it was sawed apart and taken to a museum in Oregon, Howard Hughes's *Spruce Goose*, the huge cargo seaplane that was piloted just once across the harbor in 1946. Long Beach's downtown, once full of run-down 1920s buildings and pawn shops, now has an array of glittering high-rises and the area has become a favorite for Japanese and Asian companies' American headquarters. Long Beach was hurt by closure of its naval shipyard and cutbacks at the huge McDonnell Douglas plant before the company was purchased by Boeing, but small businesses have grown. In August 2000, as the Democratic National Convention was about to open in Los Angeles, Long Beach again played second-fiddle: this time, hosting the comic-opera Reform Party Convention that nominated Patrick Buchanan for president and Los Angeles County resident Ezola Foster for vice president.

The 38th Congressional District includes most of Long Beach—the beachfront, harbor and airport. It extends north and inland to include the post-World War II suburbs of Lakewood, Paramount, Bellflower and Downey. This is middle-class country, but not monochromatic; the 38th excludes some black areas of Long Beach but in 2000 was 40% Hispanic, up from 25% in 1990, and 9% Asian. It has a large Cambodian community, a core of union members, and a large gay population. Defense contracts and bases remain important in Long Beach, and Downey has the Boeing (formerly Rockwell) plant that built the space shuttle. Politically, the 38th was long politically marginal. But like so much of metro Los Angeles it trended sharply Democratic in the 1990s, as ethnic change and liberal cultural attitudes both pushed it leftward. In 1988 the 38th voted 56%–44% for the senior George Bush; in 2000 it voted 58%–37% for Al Gore.

The congressman from the 38th District is Steve Horn, a Republican first elected in 1992. Horn grew up on a farm near San Juan Bautista, California, and worked his way through Stanford and Harvard. He was an aide to President Eisenhower's labor secretary in the 1950s and to California Senator Thomas Kuchel in the 1960s. He was in Everett Dirksen's office helping draft the Voting Rights Act in those stirring days of 1965, and he served on the U.S. Commission on Civil Rights from 1969–82. As a political scientist, Horn has written books on parliamentary procedures, the Senate Appropriations Committee and campaign finance. He worked at the Brookings Institution, was a dean at American University in Washington, and then from 1970–88 was president of Cal State at Long Beach, leaving the job when he first ran for an open seat in Congress. That race was in a district that stretched from Long Beach far into Orange County; he ran third in the primary, with 20%, behind the more conservative and flamboyant Dana Rohrabacher. In 1992 he ran in the newly drawn 38th. In the primary, the pro-choice Horn beat anti-abortion former Assemblyman Dennis Brown by 105 votes out of 45,000 cast. In the general, he faced Long Beach Councilman Evan Anderson Braude, stepson of 22-year incumbent and Public Works Chairman Glenn Anderson. Horn accepted no PAC money and ran his campaign out of his son's apartment, sending out 50,000 15-minute videos to voters. He won 49%–43%.

Horn has a mostly moderate voting record, but has been downright liberal on cultural issues (for abortion rights, gun control, gays in the military). He played a key role in obtaining funds for the Alameda Corridor, the underground rail and freeway connection from the port to the main east-west links, and secured $25 million in 2000 to clean up contamination of the underground water supply that extends to South Bay. He supported the Democrats' HMO regulation bill, plus additional mental health initiatives, and enacted an expansion in overseas adoption opportunities for U.S. citizens.

As chairman of the renamed Subcommittee on Government Efficiency, Financial Management, and Intergovernmental Relations, Horn often worked in bipartisan fashion: He produced a Debt Collection Act, aimed at getting back some $60 billion the government is owed in non-tax debts but has not collected. He took the lead in raising concerns about the capacity of government agencies to meet the Y2K problem. Like an old-time professor, he took to grading government agencies on how they handled it: Horn noted the agencies' progress every three months, and when the New Year's deadline arrived, Horn gave the overall grade of "B +." But the end of the Y2K crisis did not end Horn's reviews of federal performance. In September 2000, he gave failing grades to seven of 24 agencies for their computer security, and he urged appointment of a government-wide chief information officer to handle technology policy.

Horn's moderate record and taste for bipartisanship have sparked opposition from several quarters. The leftward trend in southern California steadily narrowed Horn's margin from his 58%–37% in 1994. His contest in 2000 against Democrat Gerrie Schipske, an openly gay woman, was so close that it took three weeks of absentee ballot counting to determine the winner. Schipske, a nurse practitioner and health-care attorney who served on Janet Reno's Advisory Council on Violence Against Women, campaigned on gun control, health care reform and education. After Horn finally won 48.5%–47.5%, House Democrats second-guessed their leaders' failure to give more support to Schipske. Horn probably faces more trouble in 2002. Democrats control redistricting and regard him as one of the most vulnerable remaining California Republican incumbents. He was the first House Republican to visit the Bush White House in early 2001 as part of its incumbent-protection program. It would be easy to draw a Long Beach area district that would be significantly more Democratic. He turns 71 in 2002, and might choose to retire after a career that spans five decades in public life.

Cook's Call   *Highly Competitive.* As a Republican sitting in an overwhelmingly Democratic district (Gore won here by 21%), Steve Horn is the equivalent of a political miracle. His moderate, sometimes liberal voting record has helped him survive here, and Democrats have been unable to round up a top-tier nominee to challenge him. Horn's latest squeaker of a victory has given Democrats renewed vigor for winning this seat. With control of the redistricting process in the state, Democrats are determined to make sure that Horn is extremely vulnerable in 2002.

THE PEOPLE: Pop. 2000: 634,392; Pop. 1990: 572,676, up 10.8% 1990–2000. 52.1% White, 10.7% Black, 8.9% Asian, 0.9% Amer. Indian, 0.7% Hawaiian, 5.1% Two+ races, 21.5% Other; 40.1% Hispanic Origin.

2000 Presidential Vote			1996 Presidential Vote		
Gore (D)	109,436	(58%)	Clinton (D)	91,673	(53%)
Bush (R)	70,439	(37%)	Dole (R)	62,053	(36%)
Nader (Green)	6,753	(4%)	Perot (I)	14,310	(8%)
Others	2,360	(1%)	Others	5,472	(3%)

Rep. Steve Horn (R)

Elected 1992, 5th term; b. May 31, 1931, San Juan Bautista; home, Long Beach; Stanford U., A.B. 1953, Harvard U., M.P.A. 1955, Stanford U., Ph.D. 1958; Protestant; married (Nini).

Military Career: Army Reserves, Strategic Intelligence, 1954–62.

Professional Career: A.A., U.S. Labor Secy. James Mitchell, 1959–60; Legis. Asst., U.S. Sen. Thomas Kuchel, 1960–66; Sr. Fellow, Brookings Inst., 1966–69; Dean, Grad. Studies, American U., 1969–70; Vice Chmn./Mbr., U.S. Commission on Civil Rights, 1969–82; Pres., CA St. U. at Long Beach, 1970–88; Chmn., Amer. Assn. of State Cols. & Universities, 1985–86; Prof., CA St. U. at Long Beach 1988–92.

DC Office: 2331 RHOB 20515, 202-225-6676; Fax: 202-226-1012; Web site: www.house.gov/horn.

District Office: Lakewood, 562-425-1336.

Committees: *Government Reform* (7th of 24 R): Government Efficiency, Financial Management & Intergovernmental Relations (Chmn.); Technology & Procurement Policy. *Transportation & Infrastructure* (7th of 42 R): Aviation; Water Resources & Environment.

Group Ratings

	ADA	ACLU	AFS	LCV	CON	ITIC	NTU	COC	ACU	NTLC	CHC
2000	35	50	42	71	16	78	53	66	56	62	47
1999	55	—	50	56	23	—	47	72	44	—	—

National Journal Ratings

	1999 LIB —	1999 CONS		2000 LIB —	2000 CONS
Economic	48%	— 50%		51%	— 49%
Social	62%	— 37%		68%	— 31%
Foreign	43%	— 55%		49%	— 49%

Key Votes of the 106th Congress

1. Patient Bill of Rights	Y	5. Bar RU-486 $ for FDA	N	9. NATO War in Serbia	N
2. Accelerate Min. Wage	Y	6. Display 10 Commandments	N	10. Perm. Trade with China	N
3. Strike Ban on Ergo. Stnd.	Y	7. Gun Show Bkgrnd. Checks	Y	11. Debt Relief for 3rd World	Y
4. Ovrd. Estate Tax Veto	Y	8. Ban Part.-Birth Abortion	N	12. Drop Cuba Econ. Embargo	N

Election Results

2000 general	Steve Horn (R)	87,266	(48%)	($580,445)
	Gerrie Schipske (D)	85,498	(47%)	($738,427)
	Other	7,358	(4%)	
2000 primary	Steve Horn (R)	59,209	(51%)	
	Gerrie Schipske (D)	17,676	(15%)	
	Erin Gruwell (D)	16,062	(14%)	
	Peter Matthews (D)	13,937	(12%)	
	Ken Graham (D)	7,248	(6%)	
	Other	3,161	(3%)	
1998 general	Steve Horn (R)	71,386	(53%)	($238,560)
	Peter Mathews (D)	59,767	(44%)	($165,594)
	Others	3,722	(3%)	

THIRTY-NINTH DISTRICT

When Walt Disney began planning Disneyland in the late 1940s, he did not have to drive far from downtown Los Angeles before arriving at agricultural land. Dairy farms and orange groves covered most of southeast Los Angeles County and Orange County, which had only 216,000 people in 1950. As Disneyland opened there in 1955 and became a vast success, the area around it—a mass of flat land surrounded by mountains and sea—found itself directly in the path of the most explosively growing metropolitan area in the United States. Orange County's population rose to 703,000 in 1960, 1.4 million in 1970, 1.9 million in 1980, 2.4 million in 1990, 2.8 million in 2000. It is now the nation's fourth largest county, just a tad ahead of San Diego County.

Always Republican, Orange County became a symbol of conservatism first in California and then nationally: In 1988, its 317,000-vote plurality for George Bush was the largest of any county. Orange County's conservatism reflected a belief in technological progress and traditional values as unyielding as the mile-square grid the county's founders imposed on most of its land, a belief in the market economics that had produced such wonders as Disneyland and the area's advanced military technologies. In 1994, the county government declared bankruptcy because of the county treasurer's sloppy investment and bookkeeping practices; shortly afterwards, the Disney company shelved plans for a $2 billion resort development that would have doubled the size of Disneyland. But Orange County has rebounded, and so has Disney, which in February 2001 opened its California Adventure amusement park here. In the 1990s Orange County, like all of the nation's second largest metropolitan area, trended toward the Democrats. In 2000 it still voted Republican, but gave George W. Bush only a 149,000-vote margin.

The 39th Congressional District of California consists of an area that was mostly farmland when Disneyland was being laid out. In Los Angeles County, its largest community is Cerritos, once all dairy farms, now a suburb with an unusual Angeleno mix: 59% Asian, 27% white Anglos, 10% Hispanic. La Mirada to the north is more upscale, as are the La Habra communities that span the LA-Orange County line. The biggest Orange County city here is Fullerton, with its own branch of Cal State University; to the southwest are Buena Park, home of Knott's Berry Farm, the earliest theme park (c. 1940), plus Cypress, Los Alamitos and Rossmoor. The 39th also pushes east of Fullerton to include, by just a few blocks, the Richard Nixon Library and birthplace in Yorba Linda. Overall the 39th district is 30% Hispanic, 18% Asian and 3% black—hardly the all-white Orange County stereotype.

The life of the 39th District's congressman, Ed Royce, almost precisely covers the area's growth. Like Orange County, he has long been conservative: He was in the Young Americans for Freedom at Cal State Fullerton; he worked several years as a tax and capital projects manager for a cement company. In 1982, a bunch of conservative legislators known as "the Cave Men" took him to a Black Angus restaurant—no avocado and sprout sandwiches for them—and after a few beers persuaded him to run for the state Senate. He won at age 31. When the legislature refused to pass his legislation allowing crime victims to object to trial delays, giving grand juries more power and ending shopping for juries, he put it on the ballot as an initiative and it passed by a wide margin. With many Vietnamese in Orange County, Royce passed a law making it easier for University of Saigon medical graduates to practice in California.

In 1992 Royce ran for the House. With the blessing of Orange County Republican leaders, he was unopposed in the decisive primary and easily won the general. In the House, Royce has a conservative voting record, though a bit less so on foreign issues. He worked to pass anti-stalking legislation, first in the 1994 crime bill, then as part of a defense appropriation in 1996. He pushes a victim's rights constitutional amendment, plus another to ban retroactive taxation. He co-chairs the House "porkbusters," risking others' wrath by opposing appropriations bills with dubious projects. He worked with appropriator Frank Wolf to stop highway "demonstration projects," but the 1998 transportation bill had a record number of "earmarks." He advocated a breakup of the Energy Department and the abolition of the Overseas Private Investment Corporation, which guarantees foreign investments, as a form of corporate welfare. He got a rules change requiring unauthorized spending to be listed separately in appropriations bills. His proposal in 2000 to ensure that nonprofit religious organizations have access to all necessary financial resources was a forerunner of George W. Bush's faith-based initiative.

As chairman of the International Relations Subcommittee on Africa and an ardent free-trader, Royce backed an Africa free trade bill with ranking Ways and Means Democrat Charles Rangel; it came at a time when, after three decades of economic stagnation and dictatorship, several African countries were moving toward market economics and democracy. Despite Rangel's sponsorship, the issue divided the Black Caucus; Jesse Jackson Jr. called for forgiving of African nations' foreign debts instead. But Royce helped steer the bill to enactment in 2000. Although he had never set foot in Africa before he became chairman, he was widely praised for learning about the continent and was the only Republican on Bill Clinton's 1998 visit to Africa. Royce also has a strong interest in Asia; he co-chairs the Congressional Caucus on India and Indian Americans and urges a stronger trade relationship between the two nations.

Back home Royce has been re-elected easily.

Cook's Call *Safe*. Ed Royce has had little problem holding onto this Republican-leaning Orange and Los Angeles County-based seat since winning it in 1992. He should be safe in 2002.

THE PEOPLE: Pop. 2000: 622,921; Pop. 1990: 573,941, up 8.5% 1990–2000. 59.3% White, 3.1% Black, 18.4% Asian, 0.7% Amer. Indian, 0.3% Hawaiian, 4.3% Two+ races, 13.8% Other; 30.4% Hispanic Origin.

2000 Presidential Vote			1996 Presidential Vote		
Bush (R)	114,680	(53%)	Dole (R)	97,247	(48%)
Gore (D)	93,977	(43%)	Clinton (D)	83,246	(41%)
Nader (Green)	5,752	(3%)	Perot (I)	15,909	(8%)
Others	2,515	(1%)	Others	4,841	(2%)

Rep. Ed Royce (R)

Elected 1992, 5th term; b. Oct. 12, 1951, Los Angeles; home, Fullerton; CA St. U., Fullerton, B.A. 1977; Catholic; married (Marie).

Elected Office: CA Senate, 1982–92.

Professional Career: Tax Mgr., 1979–82.

DC Office: 2202 RHOB 20515, 202-225-4111; Fax: 202-226-0335; Web site: www.house.gov/royce.

District Office: Fullerton, 714-992-8081.

Committees: *Financial Services* (9th of 37 R): Capital Markets, Insurance & Government Sponsored Enterprises; Domestic Monetary Policy, Technology & Economic Growth; Financial Institutions & Consumer Credit. *International Relations* (11th of 26 R): Africa (Chmn.); East Asia & the Pacific.

Group Ratings

	ADA	ACLU	AFS	LCV	CON	ITIC	NTU	COC	ACU	NTLC	CHC
2000	0	29	0	14	99	89	79	80	100	94	100
1999	5	—	0	13	93	—	77	76	96	—	—

National Journal Ratings

	1999 LIB	—	1999 CONS		2000 LIB	—	2000 CONS
Economic	0%	—	84%		0%	—	94%
Social	28%	—	71%		23%	—	74%
Foreign	10%	—	86%		0%	—	88%

Key Votes of the 106th Congress

1. Patient Bill of Rights	N	5. Bar RU-486 $ for FDA	Y	9. NATO War in Serbia	N
2. Accelerate Min. Wage	N	6. Display 10 Commandments	Y	10. Perm. Trade with China	Y
3. Strike Ban on Ergo. Stnd.	N	7. Gun Show Bkgrnd. Checks	N	11. Debt Relief for 3rd World	N
4. Ovrd. Estate Tax Veto	Y	8. Ban Part.-Birth Abortion	Y	12. Drop Cuba Econ. Embargo	N

Election Results

2000 general	Ed Royce (R)	129,294	(63%)	($327,284)
	Gill G. Kanel (D)	64,938	(32%)	($24,805)
	Other	11,872	(6%)	
2000 primary	Ed Royce (R)	91,626	(68%)	
	Gill G. Kanel (D)	35,816	(27%)	
	Other	7,441	(5%)	
1998 general	Ed Royce (R)	97,366	(63%)	($487,001)
	Cecy R. Groom (D)	52,815	(34%)	($120,134)
	Others	5,284	(3%)	

FORTIETH DISTRICT

Over the last two decades the great American movement west has turned back east, at least in California. As settlement reached the Pacific Coast, young families looking for affordable houses, neighborhoods and schools, where traditional values are respected, moved away from the liberation-minded and high-crime coast and toward the sunny, often hot, valleys inland. This impulse has resulted in rapid growth in the Central Valley, the repopulation of the Mother Lode country in the foothills of the Sierras and the startling growth in the eastern end of the Los Angeles Basin, around San Bernardino and Riverside, and east and north past the mountain rims into the desert. This Inland Empire grew from 1.6 million in 1980 to 3.2 million in 2000.

The 40th Congressional District, which covers most of the land area of San Bernardino County, is larger physically than nine states and has more people than 12 states. Much of this population is concentrated in the southwest corner of the county, within the Los Angeles Basin, including the eastern edge of San Bernardino itself, Loma Linda, Redlands and Yucaipa—small towns formed by pious Midwesterners at the base of 10,000-foot mountains, now part of the expanding Los Angeles suburban strip. North of the mountains, out beyond the wind-torn El Cajon Pass in the scorching desert, with its Joshua trees and California poppies, are Victorville and Apple Valley, once tiny gas station stops on the road to Las Vegas; Roy Rogers and Dale Evans lived for years on a ranch here, with their stuffed Trigger, Buttermilk and Bullet in a nearby museum. Now vast subdivisions and the new city of Hesperia have grown up here, housing more than 180,000 people. The rest of the people of the 40th are scattered across the desert, in ghost towns and weapons testing sites, in Twentynine Palms and its Marine base. The 40th has some of the nation's hottest temperatures and some of its lowest rainfall, the lower 48 states' highest point at Mount Whitney and lowest point in Death Valley.

The congressman from the 40th District is Jerry Lewis, a House member since 1978 and chairman of the Defense Appropriations Subcommittee. Lewis grew up in San Bernardino, worked as a lifeguard and graduated from UCLA. (He maintains his swimming skills, and once saved former Speaker Jim Wright off the shore of Hawaii.) He was an insurance agent in Redlands, a joiner in civic causes, and was elected to the California Assembly in 1968, at 34. In 1978, when the incumbent retired, he was elected to the House. In 1980, he got a seat on the Appropriations Committee, where bipartisan cooperation was the norm, enabling even minority members to confer favors on their districts. With a small city background and an accommodationist attitude toward Democrats, he steadily won leadership positions—chairman of the Republican Research Committee in 1984, chairman of the Policy Committee in 1986, Conference chairman in 1988, and seemed headed towards the minority leader post. But a small group of young conservatives around Newt Gingrich resented Lewis's cooperation with Democrats, and believed that Republicans could break out of the minority if they confronted Democrats more. In March 1989 the minority whip position came open when Dick Cheney was appointed secretary of Defense. Lewis considered running, but declined and Gingrich won by an 87–85 vote. In December 1992, Dick Armey, with support from Gingrich, challenged Lewis for the Conference chair Lewis and won 88–84. Those two votes put in place the two top leaders of the Republican majority that emerged after November 1994.

Lewis recovered from that setback, and when Republicans won their majority in 1994, he became chairman of the VA-HUD Appropriations Subcommittee—a member of the "college of cardinals," as appropriations subcommittee chairmen are known. Here he got his agencies' attention by reporting a bill making deep cuts in NASA, including closing the Goddard space center in Greenbelt, Maryland. Goddard was saved, but Lewis forced other cuts at NASA. He focused on eliminating waste and fraud in federal housing programs to assure, he said, that federal dollars actually get to people they are intended to help. Lewis also has worked for relief appropriations after the Northridge earthquake of 1994 and has promoted the Alameda Corridor rail connection to the Los Angeles-Long Beach port. He supported Gingrich against the July 1997 coup.

In 1999 Lewis became chairman of the Defense Subcommittee, with the largest share of federal spending of any of the 13 subcommittees. He attracted attention when the subcommittee voted unanimously to cut the $1.8 billion for building the first six of the Air Force's F-22s. This was a bolt out of the blue, and something that would not have happened had Gingrich still been speaker—the F-22 is produced in a Lockheed Martin plant in Gingrich's former district. Lewis was disturbed by a report that the Air Force had been spending money on programs Congress never authorized, including an $800 million military communications satellite and updates to the C-5. He argued that the F-22 was a Cold War super weapon, whose high cost left the Air Force as "very close to a broken branch" of the military, and he pointed out that the old F-15 did just fine in the spring 1999 bombing of Kosovo, while the Air Force was short of tankers and radar-jamming aircraft there. Funds were restored by the Senate; but the program was cut by $500 million, and the Pentagon's attention was gained. In May 2000 the subcommittee cut $150 million from money requested for the Joint Strike Fighter.

As an appropriator, Lewis has been able to channel funds into his district. In 2000 he got $10 million for seismic refitting (including using a laser to strengthen buildings at Loma Linda University Medical Center), $26 million for medical research, $100,000 to maintain Hillside Cemetery in Redlands and $500,000 to tear down shacks built years before by people taking advantage of a 1938 homestead act but long since abandoned. Lewis even got $1 million to rebuild the Perris Hill Plunge, a WPA-built pool where he was a lifeguard and taught dozens of children to swim. In 2000 Loma Linda University got more non-competitive federal grants than any other university, some $36 million, more than half the amount for all universities in California.

One issue that Lewis has fought fiercely is the Desert Protection Act sponsored by Dianne Feinstein and George Miller and passed over Lewis's opposition, but with some of his limiting amendments, in 1994. Later Lewis tried to condition money for purchase of old Southern Pacific lands for the Mojave Desert established by the act on agreement to expand Fort Irwin, a move opposed by environmentalists who said it would endanger the desert tortoise. In 2000 the private Wildlands Conservancy donated $15 million for the land purchase, so no more federal money was needed, but in October the Army, the Interior Department, Feinstein and Lewis agreed to expand Fort Irwin.

Lewis has been re-elected easily in this heavily Republican and fast-growing district. Redistricting should not cause him too much of a problem, and even politically hostile redistricters usually accommodate senior appropriators. But Lewis has noticed that the Hispanic percentage here has been rising, from 16% in 1990 to 24% in 2000, and he has been taking Spanish lessons, including time spent with a family in Mexico City.

Cook's Call *Safe.* Growth in San Bernadino and Riverside Counties means that this district will have to contract. Early estimates indicate that the 40th District is about 51,000 people over the ideal congressional population.

THE PEOPLE: Pop. 2000: 674,431; Pop. 1990: 573,939, up 17.5% 1990–2000. 71.9% White, 6.6% Black, 3.5% Asian, 1.6% Amer. Indian, 0.3% Hawaiian, 4.8% Two+ races, 11.4% Other; 23.8% Hispanic Origin.

2000 Presidential Vote
Bush (R)	116,349	(56%)
Gore (D)	81,703	(39%)
Nader (Green)	6,277	(3%)
Others	3,389	(2%)

1996 Presidential Vote
Dole (R)	94,916	(49%)
Clinton (D)	73,316	(38%)
Perot (I)	20,719	(11%)
Others	5,467	(3%)

Rep. Jerry Lewis (R)

Elected 1978, 12th term; b. Oct. 21, 1934, Seattle, WA; home, Redlands; U.C.L.A., B.A. 1956; Presbyterian; married (Arlene).

Elected Office: CA Assembly, 1968–78.

Professional Career: Insurance exec., 1959–78; Field rep., U.S. Rep. Jerry Pettis, 1968.

DC Office: 2112 RHOB 20515, 202-225-5861; Fax: 202-225-6498; Web site: www.house.gov/jerrylewis.

District Office: Redlands, 909-862-6030.

Committees: *Appropriations* (3d of 35 R): Defense (Chmn.); Foreign Operations & Export Financing; The Legislative Branch.

Group Ratings
	ADA	ACLU	AFS	LCV	CON	ITIC	NTU	COC	ACU	NTLC	CHC
2000	0	46	0	14	13	94	61	80	64	59	57
1999	20	—	16	6	33	—	48	92	73	—	—

National Journal Ratings
	1999 LIB —	1999 CONS	2000 LIB —	2000 CONS
Economic	39%	59%	37%	62%
Social	41%	59%	29%	71%
Foreign	52%	48%	45%	53%

Key Votes of the 106th Congress
1. Patient Bill of Rights	N	5. Bar RU-486 $ for FDA	Y	9. NATO War in Serbia	Y
2. Accelerate Min. Wage	N	6. Display 10 Commandments	Y	10. Perm. Trade with China	Y
3. Strike Ban on Ergo. Stnd.	N	7. Gun Show Bkgrnd. Checks	N	11. Debt Relief for 3rd World	N
4. Ovrd. Estate Tax Veto	Y	8. Ban Part.-Birth Abortion	Y	12. Drop Cuba Econ. Embargo	N

Election Results
2000 general	Jerry Lewis (R)	151,069	(80%)	($805,526)
	Frank N. Schmit (NL)	19,029	(10%)	
	Jay Lindberg (LIB)	18,924	(10%)	
2000 primary	Jerry Lewis (R)	86,315	(84%)	
	Frank N. Schmit (NL)	8,687	(8%)	
	Marion J. Lindberg (LIB)	8,155	(8%)	
1998 general	Jerry Lewis (R)	97,406	(65%)	($465,377)
	Robert Conaway (D)	47,897	(32%)	($7,017)
	Others	4,822	(3%)	

FORTY-FIRST DISTRICT

The fastest growth in the Los Angeles metropolitan area over the last 20 years has been in the eastern end of the Los Angeles Basin—the Inland Empire, as it is now called. Mostly orange groves and dairy farms a couple of decades ago, this territory now is the site of a booming economy, personal upward mobility and ethnic and cultural harmony. The economic-growth secret is small entrepreneurial businesses, usually started by people with no particular connections or advantages—often, of Asian or Latino immigrant background. California has never been a land of leisure, as stereotype would have it, but rather a place for hard work, where the amazing fertility of the soil and the amazing productivity of the people have happened with a lot of effort and a tolerant attitude toward newcomers. California hasn't always welcomed people from strange places—anti-Asian feeling expressed itself in the Chinese Exclusion Act of 1882 and the Japanese American internment camps of 1942–44—but certainly since World War II this has been one of the least prejudiced and most welcoming places on earth, which helps to explain why it has been receiving more immigrants than any other state.

The 41st Congressional District is one place where such trends are visible. It is centered in the Inland Empire on the point where Los Angeles, San Bernardino and Orange Counties come together. In San Bernardino County it includes most of Ontario and its airport and industrial zone, plus the higher income towns of Montclair and Upland, plus Chino, site of a low-security prison, and the Chino Dairy Area, which is now becoming transformed into subdivisions. In Los Angeles County it includes the old town of Pomona, now much expanded, site of the Los Angeles County Fair, and fast-growing Diamond Bar. Over the hills in Orange County it includes Yorba Linda, site (just beyond the district line) of the birthplace of Richard Nixon in 1913 (when Orange County had only 40,000 residents). Ethnically diverse, in 2000 its residents were 41% Hispanic and 15% Asian, believers still in traditional values, working their way up through the private sector—and leaning toward Republicans. Like other parts of metro Los Angeles, this area moved toward the Democrats in the 1990s, but not all the way: in 2000 it voted 50%–47% for George W. Bush.

The congressman from the 41st District is Gary Miller, a Republican elected in 1998. He was born in Arkansas but grew up in Whittier, and in his early 20s became a homebuilder, and developed planned communities. His public service began in 1988 when Los Angeles County Supervisor Pete Schabarum appointed him to the Diamond Bar Municipal Advisory Council. A year later, after Diamond Bar was incorporated, Miller was elected to the city council and served as mayor. In 1995, he was elected to the state Assembly in a special election to replace Republican Paul Horcher, who was recalled after he supported Democrat Willie Brown for Assembly speaker. In Sacramento, Miller became chairman of the Budget Committee in his freshman year. He helped pass many law-enforcement bills in addition to his work on budget and tax issues.

In November 1997 he decided to run for the House against scandal-tarred incumbent Jay Kim, who lived just two blocks away in Diamond Bar. Kim, the first Korean-American in Congress, was elected in 1992. In August 1997 Kim and his wife pleaded guilty to accepting and concealing $230,000 in illegal campaign contributions between 1992 and 1996. In March 1998 he was sentenced to house arrest, confined to the House and his apartment in suburban Virginia, and was required to wear an electronic bracelet around his ankle for two months. As a result, he could not campaign back home for the June primary. Local leaders appealed to Miller to run, and he was endorsed by Governor Pete Wilson; the National Republican Congressional Committee, which normally endorses incumbents, remained neutral. Miller emphasized standard Republican themes—lower taxes, tougher penalties for crime, improved local education—and largely financed his own campaign. The result was unambiguous. Two-thirds of the votes in the all-party primary were cast for Republican candidates, and Miller won 48% of Republican votes, to 26% for Kim and 22% for Orange County-based Pete Pierce. This was not a seriously contested race in November; Miller won 53%–41%.

Miller has had a very conservative voting record in the House and advanced some original proposals. In the California Assembly he had written an anti-spam law, inspired by a constituent whose business e-mail address was used as a false return address on a spam, as a result of which he went out of business for several days. In the House Miller sponsored an anti-spam bill, to allow Internet Service Providers to decide whether they want to allow spamming and, if not, to give them a cause of action against spammers, with $500 per message damages. This measure was combined with other anti-spam bills plus a provision that would let the FCC go after spammers. It passed 427–1 in July 2000. Miller also succeeded in getting $2 million authorized for the second generation of a spectrometer being developed by the Army which provides through a single instrument early detection of chemical and biological weapons; the device is produced by a firm in Pomona. Other successful district projects included $51 million for improvements to the Prado Dam and purchase of right-of-way and flood control infrastructure in Ontario and Chino. His first bill in the 107th Congress would authorize $50 million for a desalinization and reclamation project in the Chino Dairy area, $20 million for an Inland Empire regional water recycling project and $50 million for a study of northern California brine lines to reduce the salinity of Colorado River water.

Miller's 2000 Democratic opponent was a former Ontario councilman who was demoted while working for the California Youth Authority for trading inmate labor to a contractor in return for a gazebo. Miller won 59%–37%.

Cook's Call *Safe.* Miller shook off any doubt that he would have problems holding onto this Republican-leaning district with his solid showing in his 2000 race. This district has not grown as much as some of the other San Bernadino County districts.

THE PEOPLE: Pop. 2000: 666,225; Pop. 1990: 572,529, up 16.4% 1990–2000. 52.8% White, 5.9% Black, 14.7% Asian, 0.8% Amer. Indian, 0.2% Hawaiian, 4.5% Two+ races, 21% Other; 40.9% Hispanic Origin.

2000 Presidential Vote		
Bush (R)	95,093	(50%)
Gore (D)	88,174	(47%)
Nader (Green)	4,230	(2%)
Others	1,997	(1%)

1996 Presidential Vote		
Dole (R)	76,867	(47%)
Clinton (D)	71,393	(43%)
Perot (I)	13,007	(8%)
Others	3,732	(2%)

Rep. Gary Miller (R)

Elected 1998, 2d term; b. Oct. 16, 1948, Huntsville, AR; home, Diamond Bar; Mt. San Antonio Col. 1971, 1988–89; Christian; married (Cathy).

Military Career: Army, 1967.

Elected Office: Diamond Bar City Cncl., 1989–95; Diamond Bar Mayor, 1992; CA Assembly, 1995–98.

Professional Career: Businessman, real estate developer, G. Miller Development Co., 1971–98.

DC Office: 1037 LHOB 20515, 202-225-3201; Fax: 202-226-6962; Web site: www.house.gov/garymiller.

District Office: Diamond Bar, 909-612-4677.

Committees: *Budget* (11th of 24 R). *Financial Services* (30th of 37 R): Capital Markets, Insurance & Government Sponsored Enterprises; Housing & Community Opportunity; International Monetary Policy & Trade. *Science* (17th of 25 R): Research; Space & Aeronautics.

Group Ratings

	ADA	ACLU	AFS	LCV	CON	ITIC	NTU	COC	ACU	NTLC	CHC
2000	0	21	0	0	74	100	68	95	100	82	93
1999	5	—	0	0	8	—	56	96	88	—	—

National Journal Ratings

	1999 LIB	—	1999 CONS		2000 LIB	—	2000 CONS
Economic	0%	—	84%		0%	—	94%
Social	10%	—	85%		0%	—	79%
Foreign	31%	—	66%		12%	—	78%

Key Votes of the 106th Congress

1. Patient Bill of Rights	N	5. Bar RU-486 $ for FDA	Y	9. NATO War in Serbia	N
2. Accelerate Min. Wage	N	6. Display 10 Commandments	Y	10. Perm. Trade with China	Y
3. Strike Ban on Ergo. Stnd.	N	7. Gun Show Bkgrnd. Checks	N	11. Debt Relief for 3rd World	N
4. Ovrd. Estate Tax Veto	Y	8. Ban Part.-Birth Abortion	Y	12. Drop Cuba Econ. Embargo	N

Election Results

2000 general	Gary Miller (R)	104,695	(59%)	($482,491)
	Rodolfo Favila (D)	66,361	(37%)	($81,937)
	David Kramer (NL)	6,560	(4%)	
2000 primary	Gary Miller (R)	60,953	(59%)	
	Rodolfo Favila (D)	32,528	(31%)	
	Tony Ma (R)	7,140	(7%)	
	Other	3,519	(3%)	
1998 general	Gary Miller (R)	68,310	(53%)	($569,494)
	Eileen R. Ansari (D)	52,264	(41%)	($100,802)
	Others	7,840	(6%)	

FORTY-SECOND DISTRICT

The gateway to the Los Angeles Basin for decades was San Bernardino, situated on flat land where the route through the twisting, windy El Cajon Pass took passengers on the Santa Fe Railroad and motorists on U.S. 66 from the hot and dusty desert to the greener, tree-lined Los Angeles basin. There were orange groves around the little railroad towns and vineyards to the west; this was an agricultural zone until World War II, when Henry J. Kaiser built the West Coast's first major steel mill between the Santa Fe and Southern Pacific lines in Fontana, just west of San Bernardino. Today, these lands have largely filled up. This Inland Empire, as it is called, may be where the smog piles up against the mountains, but it also has some of the lowest real estate prices in the Los Angeles Basin and an energetic small business economy.

The 42d Congressional District consists of most of San Bernardino and the towns running west—Rialto, Fontana, where many businesses replaced the closed steel mill (the blast furnaces were dismantled in 1994 and reassembled in China), and fast-growing Rancho Cucamonga. Politically this area trended Republican in the 1980s, as the cultural liberalism of California Democrats repelled family-oriented residents. But when the economy slowed in the early 1990s it trended to the Democrats, and in the late 1990s California Latinos' aversion to Republicans shifted it still farther to the left. The Hispanic percentage in the 42nd District grew from 34% in 1990 to 51% in 2000; in addition, in 2000 12% were black, the highest percentage in any district outside central Los Angeles, the San Francisco Bay area and Sacramento. In 1988 the 42nd District voted 54%–46% for the senior George Bush. In 2000 it voted 57%–39% for Al Gore.

The congressman from the 42d District is Joe Baca, a Democrat who won a special election in November 1999. Baca was born in Belen, New Mexico, the youngest of 15 children. His family moved to Barstow, California, when he was four years old. His father worked as a laborer for the Santa Fe Railroad; Baca followed his example even as a child, shining shoes at age 10 and later selling newspapers and working as a janitor. He served in the Army as a paratrooper during the Vietnam war, but did not see combat. After graduating from California State University at Los Angeles, Baca moved to the San Bernardino area, where he spent 15 years as a community affairs representative for General Telephone and Electric, and was elected four times to the San Bernardino Community College board. After two unsuccessful bids, he won a seat in the Assembly in 1992. Baca was quickly elected speaker pro tempore of the Assembly, becoming the first Latino to serve in this capacity in California. He earned a reputation as a hard worker, introducing more bills than any other member in his first year, but his aggressiveness rubbed some colleagues the wrong way. A moderate to conservative Democrat, he worked to reduce welfare rolls, lower taxes on middle-income earners, and increase penalties for drug dealers. Facing term limits in 1998, he threatened a primary against veteran Congressman George Brown. Instead, Baca ran for the state Senate, spending $2 million to raise his local profile for an expected future congressional run.

Baca's opportunity came soon enough, when Brown died in July 1999 at age 79 and in his 18th term; he had a very liberal voting record and served as chairman of the Science Committee. The contest to replace Brown took on an unusual tone when Baca ran a vigorous campaign against Marta Macias Brown, George Brown's widow. Before this election, widows of sitting members had won 35 of 36 congressional races, according to the Congressional Research Service. But Minority Leader Dick Gephardt refused to honor Marta Brown's request to clear the Democratic field. Gun control emerged as the major issue in the primary. Brown highlighted Baca's support by the National Rifle Association and his opposition to a gun control measure that overwhelmingly passed the state legislature that summer. But Baca benefited from the support of organized labor and the growing Hispanic population in the district. Baca won the September all-party primary with 32% of the vote; Brown finished second with 30%, losing by 518 votes.

The Republican nominee was real estate developer Elia Pirozzi, who in 1998 lost to Brown 55%–40%; state Senator Jim Brulte, probably the strongest Republican locally, declined to run. During the two-month campaign Republicans filed two campaign finance complaints against Baca, one for failing to file a financial disclosure statement and one charging that he used a taxpayer-funded brochure to promote his candidacy. Baca had filed his financial report late and said his staff simply forgot to print on the brochure that it was paid for by his campaign committee. Pirozzi highlighted his opposition to abortion and support for school vouchers, aiding local businesses and the death penalty. Baca emphasized his centrist voting record and his support for targeted tax cuts, a minimum wage increase and abortion rights. Brown, apparently harboring bitter feelings from the primary, did not endorse Baca. In a light turnout, Baca won 51%–45%.

In the House, Baca took George Brown's former seats on the Agriculture and Science Committees; his efforts to change committee assignments in 2001 were unsuccessful. He joined the Blue Dog Coalition, where he said that he wanted to push bipartisanship; he co-chairs its education task force. In the Hispanic Caucus, he focused on empowerment for Hispanics, was elected whip, and sought to increase the number of Latinos elected to Congress.

Republicans had a short time to find an opponent for Baca; the 2000 primary was in March. They had a scare when former 41st District Congressman Jay Kim said he was interested in running: Kim had pleaded guilty to three misdemeanor charges of accepting illegal campaign contributions in 1997, and was beaten in the 1998 primary by Gary Miller. Their fallback was to urge a reluctant Pirozzi to run a third time. Pirozzi beat Kim 80%–20% in March, and Baca beat Pirozzi 60%–35% in November. This seat, marginal in much of the 1990s, is now safely Democratic. The district must lose about 60,000 people in redistricting, which is controlled by Democrats; its basic shape and character will not likely change.

Cook's Call   *Probably Safe.* Through much of the early 1990's, when the late Democrat George Brown represented this district, this seat was considered one of the most competitive in the state. But, since Joe Baca won the special election in 1999, he has had little trouble winning here. Growth in and around the Inland Empire means that this seat will be altered a bit.

THE PEOPLE: Pop. 2000: 700,491; Pop. 1990: 571,595, up 22.6% 1990–2000. 48.8% White, 12.4% Black, 3.7% Asian, 1.2% Amer. Indian, 0.3% Hawaiian, 5.3% Two+ races, 28.3% Other; 50.8% Hispanic Origin.

2000 Presidential Vote		
Gore (D)	89,955	(57%)
Bush (R)	62,058	(39%)
Nader (Green)	3,712	(2%)
Others	2,228	(1%)

1996 Presidential Vote		
Clinton (D)	76,745	(53%)
Dole (R)	51,106	(36%)
Perot (I)	12,342	(9%)
Others	3,329	(2%)

Rep. Joe Baca (D)

Elected Nov. 16, 1999, 1st term; b. Jan. 23, 1947, Belen, NM; home, Rialto; Cal State U.-Los Angeles, B.A., 1971; Roman Catholic; married (Barbara).

Military Career: Army, 1966–68.

Elected Office: CA House, 1992–98; CA Senate, 1998–99.

Professional Career: Community affairs rep., General Telephone and Electric, 1974–89; Co-owner, Interstate World Travel, 1989-present.

DC Office: 1133 LHOB 20515, 202-225-6161; Fax: 202-225-8671; Web site: www.house.gov/baca.

District Office: San Bernardino, 909-885-2222.

Committees: *Agriculture* (19th of 24 D): Conservation, Credit, Rural Development & Research; General Farm Commodities & Risk Management. *Science* (18th of 22 D): Environment, Technology and Standards; Research.

Group Ratings (Only Served Partial Term)

	ADA	ACLU	AFS	LCV	CON	ITIC	NTU	COC	ACU	NTLC	CHC
2000	80	0	83	57	34	60	23	44	16	0	
1999	*	—	*	*	*	*	—	*	*	—	—

National Journal Ratings (Only Served Partial Term)

	1999 LIB —	1999 CONS	2000 LIB —	2000 CONS
Economic	*	—	67%	33%
Social	*	*	57%	43%
Foreign	*	*	58%	40%

Key Votes of the 106th Congress (Only Served Partial Term)

1. Patient Bill of Rights	*	5. Bar RU-486 $ for FDA	*	9. NATO War in Serbia	*
2. Accelerate Min. Wage	Y	6. Display 10 Commandments	*	10. Perm. Trade with China	N
3. Strike Ban on Ergo. Stnd.	Y	7. Gun Show Bkgrnd. Checks	*	11. Debt Relief for 3rd World	Y
4. Ovrd. Estate Tax Veto	N	8. Ban Part.-Birth Abortion	Y	12. Drop Cuba Econ. Embargo	*

Election Results

2000 general	Joe Baca (D)	90,585	(60%)	($1,347,431)
	Elia Pirozzi (R)	53,239	(35%)	($831,552)
	Other	7,753	(5%)	
2000 primary	Joe Baca (D)	49,234	(56%)	
	Elia Pirozzi (R)	27,947	(32%)	
	Jay Kim (R)	7,119	(8%)	
	Other	3,921	(4%)	
1999 special	Joe Baca (D)	23,690	(51%)	($901,965)
	Elia Pirozzi (R)	21,018	(45%)	($647,795)
	Rick Simon (Ref)	1,198	(3%)	
	John (Scott) Ballard (L)	956	(2%)	
1999 spec. prim.	Joe Baca (D)	12,089	(32%)	
	Marta Macias Brown (D)	11,571	(30%)	
	Elia Pirozzi (R)	10,526	(28%)	
	David R. Eshelman (D)	1,676	(4%)	
	Others	2,400	(6%)	
1998 general	George Brown (D)	62,007	(55%)	($676,044)
	Elia Pirozzi (R)	45,328	(40%)	($585,522)
	Others	4,985	(4%)	

FORTY-THIRD DISTRICT

Riverside was a sleepy town of 34,000, a couple hours' drive from Los Angeles, when Richard and Pat Nixon were married in 1940 in the gaudy Mission Inn, with its bell towers, altars, fountains, rotunda, stained-glass windows and wrought-iron grilles. Riverside was not much larger, with 46,000 people, when Ronald and Nancy Reagan spent their honeymoon at the Mission Inn a dozen years later, in 1952. Riverside then was a citrus center, a market town amid orange groves, where the local agricultural college developed among other things the navel orange. Today the Mission Inn is still doing business, but Riverside has changed completely. The city has expanded to some 255,000 people, and Riverside County, which had 105,000 people in 1940, now has 1.5 million people, more than doubling since 1980. Riverside County stretches east to Arizona, so some of this increase was in the desert, but much was in the Inland Empire around Riverside, where the flat Los Angeles Basin plains are interrupted by odd-shaped hills and ridges, and the vegetation has an other-worldly air. This has been a boom part of California since the 1980s, where modest-income families found new houses in inexpensive developments and small businesses expanded mightily; it was hit hard by the recession of the early 1990s but rebounded and is growing strongly again.

The 43rd Congressional District is one of two that were formed in 1992 from the one district that had covered most of Riverside County, which was the fastest-growing congressional district in the nation in the 1980s. In the 1990s, these new districts were two of the three fastest-growing in California (the fastest growth was in the 48th District in Orange and San Diego Counties). The change in the past decade included a near-doubling of the county's Hispanic population to 560,000. The 43rd District includes all of Riverside and the towns immediately nearby; another population node just to the west, around Corona; and new subdivisions scattered around I-215 and I-15, which run south from Riverside and Corona until they join at Murietta Hot Springs, just north of the new town of Temecula.

The congressman from the 43d is Ken Calvert, a Republican elected in 1992. Calvert grew up in Corona; during college, he was a congressional intern at the Senate Watergate hearings of 1973. Later, he ran the family restaurant back home and in 1980 entered the commercial real estate business. In 1982, at 29, he ran for Congress in the old Riverside County district and lost a nine-candidate primary to Al McCandless by a 25%–24% margin: 868 votes kept him out of Congress for 10 years. He remained active in civic affairs and chaired the local Republican Party. In 1992 he ran for Congress in the new 43d and won the primary with 28%. His Democratic opponent was Mark Takano, an eighth grade teacher and Riverside Community College trustee with institutional support from teachers' unions and financial support from Japanese Americans. In a district where George Bush beat Bill Clinton by 797 votes, Calvert beat Takano by 519 votes.

In the House, Calvert compiled a conservative voting record. But he ran into trouble back home, when the Riverside *Press-Enterprise* reported that he had been stopped by police with a convicted prostitute in his car; Calvert apologized for the "embarrassing and inappropriate" incident, and said that he was upset because his wife had divorced him the month before and his father had recently committed suicide. It was, as he said, "an extremely embarrassing situation," of which his opponents rushed to take advantage. Calvert won the 1994 primary 51%–49%, with only an 884-vote margin, against business professor Joseph Khoury. Takano, running again in the general, ran an ad with the song "The Liar" and accused him of "flagrant womanizing." But the Republican tide of the year showed up in the election results, with Calvert winning by a thumping 55%–38%.

Since his near political-death experiences, Calvert has settled down. As chairman of the Energy and Mineral Resources Subcommittee in 1995, he produced a bill to reform the Mining Law of 1872, which allows mining companies to stake claims on federal lands for absurdly low fees; he would have required them to pay fair market value and a royalty of 3%. But Democrats and some Republicans called that "anemic," and no legislation passed. In 1997, as chairman of the Energy and Environment Subcommittee of Science, he challenged the Clinton administration's support of the global warming pact then being negotiated in Kyoto, Japan. He criticized the Fish and Wildlife Service's heavy-handed enforcement of endangered species laws, which he says is strangling development in southern California. On other issues, he enacted a pro-privacy bill in 2000 to prevent the Treasury Department from displaying Social Security numbers on checks. With Democrat Alan Mollohan, he co-chaired the Generic Drug Equity Caucus to improve consumer access to lower-cost medications. In 2001, he joined the Armed Services Committee, and he took over as chairman of the Water and Power Subcommittee at Resources—a prime distributor of pork.

In the 1998 primary, Calvert again faced Khoury, who argued that both Calvert and Bill Clinton "have shown they lack the common decency, sense of right and wrong, concern for the truth and respect for women that the rest of us learned as children." After five years, voters apparently had moved beyond Calvert's first-term misdeed. He won the primary 56%–35%. In 2000, Democrats ran no challenger against him. But redistricting, controlled by Democrats, holds risks for him and Mary Bono of the 44th District. The growth in both districts means that lines must be redrawn; the 43d is almost 100,000 people larger than the required average. Redistricters could try to increase the Hispanic percentages in one of the districts, which would make it more Democratic.

Cook's Call   *Potentially Competitive.* Due to the tremendous growth in Riverside County, this district will need to be altered in 2001. One scenario has the Riverside-San Bernadino area gaining a new Latino-majority district. Another has Calvert and Mary Bono's 44th District combined into one seat. Either way, this part of the state will undergo some serious transformation in 2002.

THE PEOPLE: Pop. 2000: 736,634; Pop. 1990: 571,090, up 29% 1990–2000. 64.7% White, 6.2% Black, 4.6% Asian, 1% Amer. Indian, 0.3% Hawaiian, 4.8% Two + races, 18.4% Other; 35.5% Hispanic Origin.

2000 Presidential Vote
Bush (R)	111,212	(52%)
Gore (D)	94,293	(44%)
Nader (Green)	5,666	(3%)
Others	2,333	(1%)

1996 Presidential Vote
Dole (R)	82,940	(45%)
Clinton (D)	78,384	(43%)
Perot (I)	16,406	(9%)
Others	4,687	(3%)

Rep. Ken Calvert (R)

Elected 1992, 5th term; b. June 8, 1953, Corona; home, Corona; San Diego St. U., B.A. 1975; Protestant; divorced.

Professional Career: Restaurant owner, 1975–80; Real estate broker, 1980–92; Chmn., Riverside Cnty. Repub. Party, 1984–88.

DC Office: 2201 RHOB 20515, 202-225-1986; Fax: 202-225-2004; Web site: www.house.gov/calvert.

District Office: Riverside, 909-784-4300.

Committees: *Armed Services* (25th of 32 R): Military Installations & Facilities; Military Research & Development. *Resources* (9th of 28 R): Water & Power (Chmn.). *Science* (8th of 25 R): Energy; Space & Aeronautics.

Group Ratings
	ADA	ACLU	AFS	LCV	CON	ITIC	NTU	COC	ACU	NTLC	CHC
2000	0	14	0	7	10	100	60	80	84	61	87
1999	5	—	0	0	22	—	56	96	80	—	—

National Journal Ratings
	1999 LIB —	1999 CONS		2000 LIB —	2000 CONS
Economic	0% —	84%		25% —	72%
Social	10% —	85%		23% —	74%
Foreign	46% —	53%		39% —	57%

Key Votes of the 106th Congress
1. Patient Bill of Rights	N	5. Bar RU-486 $ for FDA	Y	9. NATO War in Serbia	Y
2. Accelerate Min. Wage	N	6. Display 10 Commandments	Y	10. Perm. Trade with China	Y
3. Strike Ban on Ergo. Stnd.	N	7. Gun Show Bkgrnd. Checks	N	11. Debt Relief for 3rd World	N
4. Ovrd. Estate Tax Veto	Y	8. Ban Part.-Birth Abortion	Y	12. Drop Cuba Econ. Embargo	N

Election Results

2000 general	Ken Calvert (R)	140,201	(74%)	($421,029)
	Bill Reed (LIB)	29,755	(16%)	
	Nat Adam (NL)	20,376	(11%)	
2000 primary	Ken Calvert (R)	73,660	(58%)	
	Martin Collen (R)	31,907	(25%)	
	Bill Reed (LIB)	9,627	(8%)	
	Nat Adam (NL)	6,956	(5%)	
	Khalid Jafri (R)	4,448	(4%)	
1998 general	Ken Calvert (R)	83,012	(56%)	($790,556)
	Mike Rayburn (D)	56,373	(38%)	
	Others	9,686	(6%)	

FORTY-FOURTH DISTRICT

From the air two decades ago, a night flight east from Los Angeles showed the lights of 10 million persons' streets and houses and then almost perfect darkness: a vast metropolis surrounded by almost uninhabited territory. Today the sprinkled pattern of white lights has spread into the Inland Empire around Riverside and San Bernardino and is multiplying outward into the desert. The Inland Empire has filled up with instant towns like Moreno Valley, which did not exist in 1980 and had 142,000 people in 2000. The surreal landscape to the south and east, around the old towns of Perris and Hemet, is filling up with new places like Sun City and Valle Vista. Over the 10,000-foot San Jacinto Mountains, desert communities have boomed: Palm Springs, once the lone winter resort for the stars, is now one of a string of communities along Highway 111 and Frank Sinatra and Bob Hope Drives. Among rich retirees, the vogue for the coast lessened as beach cities filled up with enviro-activists and rent control crusaders; the clean, dry, roomy desert, where the days are almost always crystal clear and the sky usually blue and cloudless, became more attractive, and, with everything air-conditioned, a comfortable year-round home for more than 170,000 in 2000. That's 220,000 if you count Indio, the heavily Latino center of the fast-growing Coachella Valley, which has 75% of the country's date palms and features camel races at its annual date festival. Two presidents retired to the desert, Dwight Eisenhower in Palm Desert for the winters and Gerald Ford in nearby Rancho Mirage.

The 44th Congressional District covers all the desert in Riverside County and proceeds west to Moreno Valley, including most of the region around Perris and Hemet. It was heavily Republican in most elections, but trended Democratic in the 1990s. The result is a district very marginal in presidential contests. It voted 40%–36% for Bill Clinton in 1992, 45%–44% for Bob Dole in 1996 and 49%–47% for George W. Bush in 2000. During the Florida dispute, Riverside gained attention as the nation's most populous county that has converted entirely to touch-screen voting.

The congresswoman from the 44th District is Mary Bono, who won the seat held until his death in January 1998 by her husband Sonny Bono, onetime showbiz celebrity, restauranteur and mayor of Palm Springs. He was on a family vacation when he died in a skiing accident in South Lake Tahoe, California. His funeral—televised by CNN—was attended by Hollywood stars, former President Ford, Governor Pete Wilson and dozens of congressmen, including Speaker Newt Gingrich. Mary Bono was strongly encouraged to run for the seat by House Republican leaders who believed that only she could avert a Republican primary bloodbath and a possible loss of the seat, and she agreed to run. "Sonny would have encouraged me to continue his work," she said. She grew up as Mary Whitaker in South Pasadena, where she was an accomplished gymnast; she remains a fitness buff, a certified personal fitness instructor who has studied karate and Tae Kwan Do. They met when she was celebrating her college graduation at his Los Angeles restaurant in 1984 and were married two years later. Before her campaign, she had no political experience and was little known in Washington. She calls herself a "mainstream conservative," and has more centrist views on the environment and on labor protections than did her husband.

Her chief opponent in the special election was actor Ralph Waite, best known as "Pa" Walton in *The Waltons*. But Waite was hurt during the brief campaign because he kept a commitment to play Willy Loman in *Death of a Salesman* six times a week in a New Jersey theater. The campaign's biggest controversy came when Sonny's 83-year-old mother said that her son would have opposed Mary's candidacy, preferring that she care for their children (did that win Mary Bono the anti-mother-in-law vote?). But it was no contest: Bono won 64%–29%, a bigger margin than Sonny's two victories.

That was only the start of Mary Bono's unusual year. Bono won her husband's former seat on the Armed Services Committee to tend to the district's military installations. Her chief legislative priority was passage of Sonny's bill to restore the Salton Sea, an artificial body of water in the desert created when a canal burst early in the century; it has been shrinking in recent decades, increasing the salinity of the water and the pollution from agricultural runoff. Although some Democrats objected to taking funds from other California projects, Mary Bono secured $13.4 million for what became the Sonny Bono Salton Sea National Wildlife Refuge. In November, as the only female Republican on the Judiciary Committee and the panel's most junior member, this non-lawyer played a visible role in the impeachment inquiry. *Newsweek* said, "Bono was citizen Jane—the everywoman in a room of blowhards." She voted for impeachment. On local issues, she got $4 million for a radar system at the Palm Springs Airport and $14 million for a settlement with an Indian tribe whose reservation was flooded in 1905 when the Salton Sea was created. Although she said she favored abortion rights, Bono was criticized by abortion advocates when she backed a bill for counseling pregnant women against abortion. In January 2001, she won a seat on the Energy and Commerce Committee.

Bono was re-elected by wide margins in 1998 and 2000, but she may face some perils in redistricting for 2002. Democrats control the redistricting process, and the 44th, which is the second largest district in the state, must shed 103,000 people to reach the statewide average. If redistricters add heavily Hispanic and Democratic Imperial County to the district and remove 200,000 people at its western end, the result would be a district carried by Al Gore, not George W. Bush, in 2000—and, possibly, more serious competition for Bono. Even so, she would be the favorite; indeed, California Republicans, desperate for strong candidates, have even mentioned her as an opponent for Senator Barbara Boxer in 2004. There would be a certain piquancy to that: Sonny Bono ran for the seat in 1992, and finished third in the Republican primary.

Cook's Call *Potentially Competitive.* Bono's sprawling Riverside County district is estimated to be the fastest growing district in the state and it is likely to undergo a lot of changes. Democrats, who are interested in gaining a toehold in this part of the state, may try to play around with the lines here to give themselves a seat.

THE PEOPLE: Pop. 2000: 742,718; Pop. 1990: 571,843, up 29.9% 1990–2000. 65.3% White, 6.5% Black, 2.7% Asian, 1.3% Amer. Indian, 0.2% Hawaiian, 4% Two+ races, 20.1% Other; 38.5% Hispanic Origin.

2000 Presidential Vote			1996 Presidential Vote		
Bush (R)	106,011	(49%)	Dole (R)	86,414	(45%)
Gore (D)	100,754	(47%)	Clinton (D)	85,397	(44%)
Nader (Green)	5,535	(3%)	Perot (I)	17,830	(9%)
Others	2,394	(1%)	Others	3,914	(2%)

Rep. Mary Bono (R)

Elected April 1998, 2d term; b. Oct. 24, 1961, Cleveland, OH; home, Palm Springs; U. of S. CA, B.F.A. 1984; Protestant; widowed.

Professional Career: Gen. Mgr., Bono restaurant, 1986–90.

DC Office: 404 CHOB 20515, 202-225-5330; Fax: 202-225-2961; Web site: www.house.gov/bono.

District Offices: Hemet, 909-658-2312; Moreno Valley, 909-485-4827; Palm Springs, 760-320-1076.

Committees: *Energy & Commerce* (29th of 31 R): Commerce, Trade & Consumer Protection; Energy & Air Quality; Environment & Hazardous Materials.

Group Ratings

	ADA	ACLU	AFS	LCV	CON	ITIC	NTU	COC	ACU	NTLC	CHC
2000	5	36	0	14	15	90	56	100	68	66	80
1999	15	—	0	0	2	—	54	79	76	—	

National Journal Ratings

	1999 LIB	—	1999 CONS		2000 LIB	—	2000 CONS
Economic	24%	—	72%		18%	—	76%
Social	46%	—	53%		43%	—	55%
Foreign	45%	—	55%		39%	—	57%

Key Votes of the 106th Congress

1. Patient Bill of Rights	Y	5. Bar RU-486 $ for FDA	Y	9. NATO War in Serbia	Y
2. Accelerate Min. Wage	N	6. Display 10 Commandments	Y	10. Perm. Trade with China	Y
3. Strike Ban on Ergo. Stnd.	N	7. Gun Show Bkgrnd. Checks	N	11. Debt Relief for 3rd World	N
4. Ovrd. Estate Tax Veto	Y	8. Ban Part.-Birth Abortion	Y	12. Drop Cuba Econ. Embargo	Y

Election Results

2000 general	Mary Bono (R)	123,738	(59%)	($582,684)
	Ron Oden (D)	79,302	(38%)	($124,866)
	Other	6,147	(3%)	
2000 primary	Mary Bono (R)	79,365	(56%)	
	Ron Oden (D)	20,079	(14%)	
	Tom Harney (D)	13,170	(9%)	
	Bud Mathewson (R)	9,800	(7%)	
	Jon Gordon (D)	9,765	(7%)	
	Doug Wofford (D)	6,124	(4%)	
	Other	2,392	(2%)	
1998 general	Mary Bono (R)	97,013	(60%)	($364,834)
	Ralph Waite (D)	57,697	(36%)	($34,184)
	Jim J. Meuer (NL)	6,818	(4%)	

FORTY-FIFTH DISTRICT

In the 1950s, when the Beach Boys were at Hawthorne High School, surfers would drive far down the coast to the vast expanse of Huntington Beach in Orange County to catch a wave. This was empty country then, vegetable fields and orange groves, with nary a freeway or shopping center in sight. Today the beach itself is eerily empty, with swampland across the highway where surfers' pickups are parked, and it was shut for two months in 1999 because of contamination; but the rest of Orange County is pretty much filled in. Huntington Beach is a city of 190,000, a mixture of family subdivisions and garden apartments and home of the International Surfing Museum. To the north are Stanton and Westminster, the latter the center of the nation's biggest Vietnamese-American community. South along San Diego Freeway is Fountain Valley, the central focus of many Asian-owned high-tech businesses, an engine of Southern California growth. Near the coast is Costa Mesa, site of South Coast Plaza's luxury stores, and Newport Beach, with its large harbor and expensive mansions a block or two from the ocean.

The 45th Congressional District includes all this territory. Politically, it is heavily Republican, though Democrats have sometimes been competitive in Stanton and Westminster. The Vietnamese here are conservative, angry with America—not for going into Vietnam but for leaving it. There is confidence here in free enterprise despite the Orange County bankruptcy of 1994 (spawned by the speculative excess of the county's one Democratic office-holder, Treasurer Robert Citron, but accepted by local government Republicans greedy for revenue). There is also a desire, despite the wildness of the beach and the seeming anarchy of the freeway, for discipline to supplant therapy and reassert the order that seemed so solid when Orange County was starting to grow in the 1950s. But this is not the monoracial Orange County of the 1960s: the district's population in 2000 was 21% Hispanic and 15% Asian.

The congressman from the 45th is Dana Rohrabacher, a Republican elected in 1988. Rohrabacher calls himself a surfer Republican and sports an American flag surfboard. He grew up in southern California, went to college and experimented with drugs, and once had a folk band called the Goldwaters. He worked on the 1976 and 1980 Reagan presidential campaigns, wrote editorials for *The Orange County Register* and was a Reagan White House speechwriter. He returned to Southern California in 1988 when Long Beach-based Congressman Dan Lungren decided not to run again (Lungren was elected attorney general in 1990 but lost for governor in 1998). Rohrabacher, with fundraising help from Oliver North, won the primary with 35%, compared to 22% for an Orange County supervisor who had padded her resume, and 20% for Steve Horn, now congressman from the 38th District. After redistricting, Rohrabacher tussled with Robert Dornan and won, running in this heavily Republican district while Dornan ran in the marginal 46th, where he lost in 1996. Rohrabacher persuaded the mayor of Huntington Beach not to run and won the 1992 primary with 48% of the vote against three Costa Mesa and Huntington Beach councilmen.

Rohrabacher has made waves in the House. As chairman of the Space and Aeronautics Subcommittee on Science, he worked for the single-stage-to-orbit vehicle. In 1997, he cut a deal with House Democrats to give them their weather-observing satellite project—which he had publicly derided as trendy science aimed at ozone depletion and other "liberal clap-trap"—in exchange for his reusable rockets. Later, as the reusable vehicle program met problems, he said that the concept was "Al Gore's baby" and that Congress should not be blamed. He strongly opposes illegal immigration, which he says is "going to bankrupt America," and he sharply criticized as "a betrayal of American workers" the generally-popular policy to give 600,000 skilled foreign workers temporary visas in the United States. After having asked the Clinton administration in 1993 to lift the ban on the launching from China of satellites manufactured by Los Angeles-based Hughes Electronics, he switched course in 1998, making an impassioned House speech criticizing Clinton's decision to relax export controls on satellites to China. "In retrospect, I shouldn't have believed the administration's assurances," he said. He has been a long-time critic of China's rulers, strongly opposed Permanent Normal Trade Relations, and has been a friend of Taiwan. In 2000, the House soundly defeated his attempt to block expanded trade with Vietnam. But, reversing earlier opposition, he had kind words for Cambodian prime minister Hun Sen following a January 2001 visit to Phnom Penh.

In 1998 Rohrabacher had an atypically serious re-election challenge from Patricia Neal, a real-estate agent and former president of the California Association of Realtors. For the first time in his career, organized labor actively opposed Rohrabacher, believing he might be defeated. "Dana does not have any other verbiage except 'pinko, communist, liberal, tax-and-spend left'," Neal said. She criticized him for avoiding the draft during the Vietnam war. Rohrabacher conceded, "I respect those guys who went a lot more than I respect myself for showing that X-ray" of a high school hip injury to win his deferment. With more than $200,000 of her own money, Neal outspent him. But in a pro-incumbent year, he won 59%–37%. In 2000, he won his customary easy re-election; he had a bit of a scare when Robert Dornan, ruing that he had stepped aside in 1992, threatened to run in the primary. But Dornan decided to stay on the talk-show circuit. In redistricting, Democrats have talked of returning to Rohrabacher some Republican precincts from the 38th district.

Cook's Call *Safe.* In a district that went for Bush by 16% in 2000, it is hard to see how Rohrabacher will have a tough general election in 2002. Orange County has not grown as quickly as neighboring Riverside and San Bernadino Counties to the east, but redistricting could certainly have an impact.

THE PEOPLE: Pop. 2000: 619,092; Pop. 1990: 570,991, up 8.4% 1990–2000. 68.2% White, 1.4% Black, 15.4% Asian, 0.6% Amer. Indian, 0.5% Hawaiian, 4% Two+ races, 9.9% Other; 21.2% Hispanic Origin.

2000 Presidential Vote

Bush (R)	128,175	(56%)
Gore (D)	91,915	(40%)
Nader (Green)	7,571	(3%)
Others	2,980	(1%)

1996 Presidential Vote

Dole (R)	108,240	(50%)
Clinton (D)	81,299	(38%)
Perot (I)	17,831	(8%)
Others	6,972	(3%)

Rep. Dana Rohrabacher (R)

Elected 1988, 7th term; b. June 21, 1947, Coronado; home, Huntington Beach; Long Beach St. Col. B.A. 1969, U. of S. CA, M.A. 1975; Baptist; married (Rhonda).

Professional Career: Radio & print journalist, 1970–80; Sr. Speechwriter, Special Asst. to Pres. Reagan, 1981–88.

DC Office: 2338 RHOB 20515, 202-225-2415; Fax: 202-225-0145; Web site: www.house.gov/rohrabacher.

District Office: Huntington Beach, 714-960-6483.

Committees: *International Relations* (10th of 26 R): East Asia & the Pacific; Middle East & South Asia. *Science* (6th of 25 R): Energy; Space & Aeronautics (Chmn.).

Group Ratings

	ADA	ACLU	AFS	LCV	CON	ITIC	NTU	COC	ACU	NTLC	CHC
2000	10	29	14	7	97	75	75	61	96	97	93
1999	5	—	0	13	88	—	76	76	96	—	—

National Journal Ratings

	1999 LIB	—	1999 CONS		2000 LIB	—	2000 CONS
Economic	0%	—	84%		0%	—	94%
Social	32%	—	66%		23%	—	74%
Foreign	3%	—	92%		45%	—	53%

Key Votes of the 106th Congress

1. Patient Bill of Rights	N	5. Bar RU-486 $ for FDA	Y	9. NATO War in Serbia	N
2. Accelerate Min. Wage	N	6. Display 10 Commandments	Y	10. Perm. Trade with China	N
3. Strike Ban on Ergo. Stnd.	N	7. Gun Show Bkgrnd. Checks	N	11. Debt Relief for 3rd World	N
4. Ovrd. Estate Tax Veto	Y	8. Ban Part.-Birth Abortion	Y	12. Drop Cuba Econ. Embargo	N

Election Results

2000 general	Dana Rohrabacher (R)	136,275	(62%)	($300,724)
	Ted Crisell (D)	71,066	(32%)	($52,674)
	Don Hull (LIB)	8,409	(4%)	
	Other	3,635	(2%)	
2000 primary	Dana Rohrabacher (R)	89,174	(62%)	
	Ted Crisell (D)	37,755	(26%)	
	Long K. Pham (R)	10,942	(8%)	
	Other	7,109	(5%)	
1998 general	Dana Rohrabacher (R)	94,296	(59%)	($275,748)
	Patricia W. Neal (D)	60,022	(37%)	($587,903)
	Others	6,452	(4%)	

FORTY-SIXTH DISTRICT

Orange County is the fourth most populous county in the United States, having grown steadily from 130,000 in 1940 to 703,000 in 1960, 1.9 million in 1980, and 2.8 million in 2000. It is now a community with the patina of maturity—in some places an aging community, fraying around the edges. The county can no longer double its population, as it did in the 1950s and 1960s, when Disneyland sprung up on empty land and mile-square grids of orange groves and bean fields were transformed into one suburban subdivision, shopping center or office tower after another. A distinctive civilization was implanted here: mostly white and middle-class, confident of its traditional values and its market capitalism, proud of American principles and American military might. Orange County has been transformed in the years since by its openness to economic and ethnic change. Its economy was constantly reshaped by the inevitable upheavals of capitalism: There is no single industry here—not even defense—that is totally responsible for the prosperity of Orange County, and people here must be ready to adapt almost as deftly as the Taiwanese on the other side of the Pacific Rim. It was hit hard by the defense cutbacks and recession of the early 1990s but it bounced back, pitched forward by new startups and small entrepreneurial successes not anticipated by government or corporate planners. And it was not much phased by the bankruptcy of the county government in 1994, caused by the improvident investments of (the aptly named) County Treasurer Robert Citron.

Just as Orange County was once transformed by newcomers from Los Angeles County and the Midwest, so Orange County is again being transformed by immigrants from the Pacific Rim, from Mexico and other parts of Latin America, and from Vietnam, Taiwan, Korea and other parts of East Asia. By 1990 the county's population was 23% Hispanic and 10% Asian; now the figures are higher: 31% Hispanic and 14% Asian. Some of these new Orange County residents are direct migrants: Santa Ana, the county seat, is one of two major arrival points for immigrants from Mexico, and its population more than 76% Hispanic. Others have moved out along the freeways, like so many southern Californians before them, working hard at jobs, commuting on freeways and living in stucco subdivisions like anyone else. There are concentrations in various places—Latinos in Santa Ana and much of Anaheim, Vietnamese in Westminster and Garden Grove—but many of these new Californians are just speckled through the county. These changes have made for some political wobble, but until the mid-1990s not very much: Asians tend to vote Republican and Latinos were registered in very small numbers. Since then, the number of Latino voters has increased sharply, even as they have switched toward the Democrats.

The 46th Congressional District is the geographic heart of Orange County. About half its people live in Santa Ana in neighborhoods full of large families and many workers. The district also includes most of Garden Grove, with many Latinos and Vietnamese—though the main Vietnamese shopping area is across the line in Westminster—and most of Anaheim, including Disneyland and territory just across the street from Orange County landmarks: Anaheim Stadium, Knott's Berry Farm and John Wayne Airport. In February 2001, Disney opened its California Adventure amusement park that took five years to complete and created 8,500 jobs—making Disney the county's largest employer. Overall, the district's population in 2000 was 62% Hispanic and 15% Asian; registered voters, only 18% Latino in 1990, were an estimated 30% Latino in 2000. Even before these population influxes, this was the least Republican part of Orange County, and in the 1960s, 1970s and 1980s Democratic redistricters carefully sculpted districts willing to elect locally popular Democrats. The 1990s trend toward Democrats is apparent from the presidential results: The 46th District voted for the senior George Bush by 62%–38% in 1988 and 40%–37% in 1992; it voted for Bill Clinton by 49%–41% in 1996 and Al Gore by 54%–42% in 2000. In 12 years a 24% Republican margin was transformed into a 12% Democratic margin.

The congresswoman from the 46th District is Loretta Sanchez, a Democrat elected in 1996. Sanchez grew up in Anaheim and graduated from Chapman University in Orange. She worked as a financial analyst, providing advice to public agencies and private businesses; she established her own firm in the early 1990s. For a time she and her husband lived in Palos Verdes Estates, far from Orange County, but in 1994 she ran for the city council in Anaheim under her married name, Loretta Sanchez-Brixey, and lost. In 1996, she ran for the House against one of the loudest voices of American conservatism, Robert Dornan. In the primary against three Anglo male Democrats (she had registered as a Democrat in February 1992), she won with 35% of the vote; she carried the Latino vote heavily, winning 72 of 85 precincts in Santa Ana.

Her primary victory attracted little attention, not even from Dornan. But she shrewdly counted on increasing Latino turnout ("Latinos will vote for Latinos," she said). Sanchez calculated that she could attract contributions from the many enemies that Dornan had made over a political career that went back to 1976 and included a quixotic presidential campaign that took him far from Orange County during 1995 and 1996 (he won only 1,029 votes for president in the 46th District). Sanchez outspent Dornan by $811,000 to $742,000. The campaign was acrimonious: Dornan would not debate Sanchez; Sanchez's husband tore down two Dornan signs and was prosecuted and fined $640. Bill Clinton came to Santa Ana late in the campaign to stump for Sanchez, and this may have made the difference. She won by 984 votes, 47%–46%.

There was great cheering in the White House and in many liberal precincts at Dornan's defeat. From Dornan there were bellows of rage and charges of vote fraud; if he had put as much effort into his congressional campaign earlier as he did in fighting his loss later, he probably would have won. Dornan brought his case to the House Contested Elections Task Force, which issued many subpoenas. Dornan argued that there were 1,789 illegal voters some of which had been registered to vote by a group called Hermandad Mexicana Nacional; this fell short of proving the result was wrong, but raised questions about the netherworld of voter registration in Orange County. Dornan, using the privileges afforded to former members, regularly appeared on the House floor trying to convince his ex-colleagues to call for a special election in the 46th District; Democrats charged that he was abusing his privileges by promoting a personal agenda and the House voted to bar him from the floor after a heated discussion between Dornan and New Jersey Democrat Bob Menendez. Finally, in February 1998 the House Oversight Committee (which later regained its name as House Administration) upheld Sanchez's victory. The panel later reimbursed the two candidates for nearly $600,000 in legal expenses, which angered Sanchez: She feared—correctly—that it would finance Dornan's next campaign.

When Dornan sought vindication in the 1998 election, many dubious Republican leaders sought a less controversial candidate and backed lawyer Lisa Hughes. But Dornan won the primary by 49%–27%—a less than a stunning victory for a long-time incumbent. By the fall it was obvious to everyone that Sanchez would win: Latino registration was up, and Sanchez had become a Latino-magazine celebrity and was the third-biggest fundraiser in the House in 1998. She won by 56%–39%, and Dornan retired to a daily show on Talk Radio Network that he aired from his suburban Virginia home.

After the election, Sanchez was named general co-chairwoman of the Democratic National Committee to lead a Hispanic voter-registration drive, and Vice President Gore tapped her as honorary chair of his political action committee. But that proved a mixed blessing for both Sanchez and her party. She scheduled a fundraiser during the week of the 2000 Democratic National Convention at Hugh Hefner's Playboy Mansion. Gore and many House Democrats—including other Latinos, from whom she has kept her distance—were not amused and said that she was mocking the party's claim of family values. At first quietly, then more bluntly, they urged her to choose a new site and warned that she was jeopardizing her rise up the party ladder. Finally, after National Chairman Joe Andrew removed her from the scheduled list of convention speakers, she relented and moved the event to Universal Studio's City Walk. A month later, Sanchez cancelled a local fundraising event with Bill Clinton after the White House changed it from a sit-down dinner to a reception. "In her self-absorption and her unpredictable and at times even loopy behavior," the *Orange County Register* noted, Sanchez had become "eerily akin" to Dornan.

In the House, her voting record leaned to the middle and she occasionally bolted her party, as when she voted to override Clinton's veto of the estate and gift tax repeal. Accompanying Clinton on his visit to Vietnam, she met with dissidents to discuss human rights. She fought unsuccessfully to remove the ban on abortions in overseas military hospitals. Sanchez's independence seemed to play well at home. In the 2000 election, she was challenged by Gloria Matta Tuchman, a teacher in Santa Ana public schools who in 1998 was co-author of Proposition 227, which ended the system of bilingual education that kept children many years in Spanish language instruction. But Sanchez had vastly superior fundraising, and won 60%–35%. Democrats control redistricting, and will probably massage the district lines to give Sanchez an even safer district.

Cook's Call   *Probably Safe.* With three big wins under her belt, Sanchez looks to have locked up this one time Republican stronghold. The most Democratic of the Orange County districts (Gore won here by 12 %), it is unlikely that Republicans will be able to bring this district back into their fold. Sanchez looks well positioned for 2002.

THE PEOPLE: Pop. 2000: 663,548; Pop. 1990: 570,963, up 16.2% 1990–2000. 43.9% White, 1.8% Black, 15.2% Asian, 1.1% Amer. Indian, 0.4% Hawaiian, 4.7% Two+ races, 32.9% Other; 62.3% Hispanic Origin.

2000 Presidential Vote			1996 Presidential Vote		
Gore (D)	64,569	(54%)	Clinton (D)	51,330	(49%)
Bush (R)	50,505	(42%)	Dole (R)	42,780	(41%)
Nader (Green)	2,749	(2%)	Perot (I)	8,229	(8%)
Others	1,518	(1%)	Others	2,609	(2%)

Rep. Loretta Sanchez (D)

Elected 1996, 3d term; b. Jan. 7, 1960, Lynwood; home, Santa Ana; Chapman U., B.A. 1982, American U., M.B.A. 1984; Catholic; married (Stephen Brixey).

Professional Career: Mgr. & Financial Analyst, Orange Cnty. Transp. Auth., 1984–87; Asst. Vice Pres., Fieldman, Rolapp & Assoc., 1987–90; Assoc., Booz, Allen & Hamilton, 1990–93; Principal, Amiga Advisors.

DC Office: 1230 LHOB 20515, 202-225-2965; Fax: 202-225-5859; Web site: www.house.gov/sanchez.

District Office: Garden Grove, 714-621-0102.

Committees: *Armed Services* (15th of 28 D): Military Personnel; Military Research & Development. *Education & the Workforce* (15th of 22 D): Education Reform; Select Education; Workforce Protections.

Group Ratings

	ADA	ACLU	AFS	LCV	CON	ITIC	NTU	COC	ACU	NTLC	CHC
2000	65	71	83	93	6	65	32	63	17	28	20
1999	95	—	100	75	51	—	21	36	4	—	—

National Journal Ratings

	1999 LIB —	1999 CONS		2000 LIB —	2000 CONS
Economic	62%	37%		62%	38%
Social	73%	26%		89%	10%
Foreign	78%	17%		74%	26%

Key Votes of the 106th Congress

1. Patient Bill of Rights	Y	5. Bar RU-486 $ for FDA	N	9. NATO War in Serbia	Y
2. Accelerate Min. Wage	Y	6. Display 10 Commandments	N	10. Perm. Trade with China	N
3. Strike Ban on Ergo. Stnd.	Y	7. Gun Show Bkgrnd. Checks	Y	11. Debt Relief for 3rd World	Y
4. Ovrd. Estate Tax Veto	Y	8. Ban Part.-Birth Abortion	N	12. Drop Cuba Econ. Embargo	*

Election Results

2000 general	Loretta Sanchez (D)	70,381	(60%)	($1,640,175)
	Gloria Matta Tuchman (R)	40,928	(35%)	($296,060)
	Other	5,599	(5%)	
2000 primary	Loretta Sanchez (D)	40,031	(58%)	
	Gloria Matta Tuchman (R)	16,606	(24%)	
	Howard Garber (R)	9,518	(14%)	
	Other	3,200	(5%)	
1998 general	Loretta Sanchez (D)	47,964	(56%)	($2,535,243)
	Bob Dornan (R)	33,388	(39%)	($3,864,920)
	Others	3,650	(4%)	

FORTY-SEVENTH DISTRICT

As one drives southeast in Orange County, there are still some patches of vacant land, places where one can see what this metropolis must have looked like before the vast growth starting in the 1950s. The Irvine Ranch, originally stretching 10 miles along the Pacific Coast and 22 miles inland to the mountains, was sold to developers by the Irvine family in the late 1970s but is still not entirely developed. Arrayed at the edges of the Irvine Ranch are Orange County landmarks. One is John Wayne Airport, named after the movie star who lived in Newport Beach and who symbolized patriotism though he never served in the military himself. Another is South Coast Plaza, the highest-volume upscale shopping center in southern California, standing in what not so long ago was a lima bean field. Another is University of California-Irvine, with 1,000 acres donated by the Irvine Ranch developers. On all sides are comfortable settlements—Orange, an orderly community, within sight of the hills, where even the street signs are orange; Newport Beach around its harbor; Irvine, with its planned communities, handsome clusters of office towers, landscaped shopping plazas and groups of houses and condominiums (but no cemeteries); artsy-craftsy Laguna Beach between mountains and the sea. Orange County is assailed by some as monotonous and sterile and boring, but for most of its residents it is a promised land, economically creative and ethnically diverse, orderly without being authoritarian, crowded perhaps but with privacy, sunny without being too hot.

The 47th Congressional District is centered geographically on the Irvine Ranch lands. On the coast it includes about half of Newport Beach as well as most of Irvine and runs south to Laguna Beach. It includes the growing subdivisions near the now closed El Toro Marine Corps Air Station in Lake Forest (the name was changed from El Toro, but some locals object that there is little forest or lake here and the new name is bull) and Laguna Hills. About half its residents live to the north, in and around Orange; the other half is split between the ocean communities and those inland. Politically, this is a conservative area, long one of the most Republican districts in the United States. Its people like the sense of order conveyed by its grid street patterns and the feeling of protection imparted by subdivision walls. They have felt comfortable as well with the military nearby. Although there are some distinctively rich communities here, the people do not feel that they are some kind of elite; they tend to see themselves as ordinary Americans with classic values who have worked hard and are entitled to enjoy their comfort. The Democratic trend in metro Los Angeles has, however, been operating here. The senior George Bush carried this area, when it had less population, by 71%–29% in 1988. George W. Bush carried it in 2000, but by only 57%–39%.

The congressman from the 47th District is Christopher Cox, a Republican first elected in 1988. Cox grew up in St. Paul, Minnesota, graduated from the University of Southern California in three years, went to Harvard Law and Business Schools jointly, practiced law at Latham & Watkins in Orange County, then was part of the Reagan White House counsel's staff. In 1988, when the local incumbent retired, Cox ran for the House—one of 14 Republican candidates. With the support of Oliver North, Robert Bork and members of the Irvine family, he won the primary with 31%. He has since won primary and general elections without difficulty. Cox's intellect and range of interests are impressive: from the former Soviet Union (he and his father published an English translation of *Pravda* from 1984–88) to lobbying for more local control of highway funds and a proposed monorail system in Orange County. Cox did more than lament Orange County Treasurer Robert Citron's reckless investments, which bankrupted the county government; he backed local Republican John Moorlach's criticism of Citron's practices and afterwards proposed that public sector investors be required to make the same disclosures as private.

With the Republican victory in 1994, Cox came into his own, becoming chairman of the Republican Policy Committee and a leading legislator on many fronts. On the first day of the new Congress, he led the move to end baseline budgeting, which typically had given each agency and department either an inflation increase or the previous year's increase, whichever was higher, and an opportunity to argue for even more: This practically insured that government grew faster than the private economy. His radical idea was to state budget totals in dollar terms, so that an increase is an increase and a cut is a cut. Another specialty is tort reform. Cox passed through the House bills limiting "injured feelings" recovery to $250,000 and repealing joint and several liability. He wrote the securities litigation reform to prevent predatory suits against high-tech and other companies, which got two-thirds support in both houses and was the only bill passed over Bill Clinton's veto in his first term. His bill to limit appeals of death penalties became law in April 1995. Cox oversaw House passage in 1997 of the "Policy for Freedom" package of 11 bills dealing with a range of human rights and free market issues in China. An Internet surfer, Cox won enactment in 1998 of an important proposal for the emerging marketplace. With Democratic Senator Ron Wyden of Oregon, he passed the Internet Tax Freedom Act, which placed a three-year moratorium on state and local governments from imposing special taxes on electronic commerce.

He also chaired the special committee investigating technology transfers from U.S. companies to China. Thanks to Cox and ranking Democrat Norman Dicks, this investigation was conducted on a bipartisan basis, without leaks, and produced a unanimous report documenting an extensive operation by China to acquire military technology, including nuclear weapons design, by groups with links to the Chinese military or state intelligence service. It faulted the policies of the Reagan, Bush and Clinton administrations. The report was finally made public in May 1999, after more than four months of negotiations with the White House over what material could be declassified. Cox won much bipartisan praise over his handling of the report. "Chris Cox has been a man of his word," said Dicks.

Amid all these big issues, Cox also worked on small ones. He passed a Corrections Day bill easing requirements for metric conversion in federal projects to what is practical. He passed a law allowing FedEx, UPS and other private delivery services to meet the IRS "timely-mailing-as-timely-filing" requirement. He sponsored a law to allow deputizing state and local law enforcement officers to enforce immigration law. And he pushed through a land exchange between the Orange County Boy Scouts Council and the U.S. Forest Service.

In early 2001, Cox was actively promoted by George W. Bush to be a judge on the Ninth Circuit Court of Appeals; but Cox withdrew his name from consideration in the Spring when Democrats took over the Senate majority, noting that he wouldn't be confirmed without a long and contentious battle. Cox has been re-elected easily in the 47th District. He considered running for the Senate in 1994 against Dianne Feinstein, but decided not to enter the primary against Michael Huffington, who spent freely of his own money. Cox also was mentioned as a candidate against Senator Barbara Boxer in 1998 and against Feinstein again in 2000, but declined to run. George Will suggested he would be a good choice for vice president. During the House Republican turmoil in late 1998, Cox twice showed interest in running for speaker but he backed off each time—first in November, when Bob Livingston wrapped up support a few days after Newt Gingrich decided to quit; then, for a few hours December 19, until Republicans decided to quickly rally behind Denny Hastert after Bob Livingston's sudden resignation. The sobering lesson for Cox was that to win he needed to work harder at the House's inside game. (Winning the endorsement of the *Wall Street Journal* editorial page, as Cox did, doesn't count for much in a contest for speaker, even among House Republicans.) On the other hand, he has already shown the capacity for handling national and international issues of the highest importance.

Cook's Call *Safe.* Cox's district is projected to be one of the fastest growing in Orange County. But, in a district that gave Bush 57%, this heavy population surge has certainly not hurt the underlying Republican performance.

THE PEOPLE: Pop. 2000: 715,625; Pop. 1990: 571,605, up 25.2% 1990–2000. 71.6% White, 1.6% Black, 13.6% Asian, 0.5% Amer. Indian, 0.2% Hawaiian, 4% Two+ races, 8.5% Other; 19.7% Hispanic Origin.

2000 Presidential Vote

Bush (R)	165,909	(57%)
Gore (D)	112,136	(39%)
Nader (Green)	7,657	(3%)
Others	2,993	(1%)

1996 Presidential Vote

Dole (R)	137,024	(54%)
Clinton (D)	91,916	(36%)
Perot (I)	17,680	(7%)
Others	7,206	(3%)

Rep. Christopher Cox (R)

Elected 1988, 7th term; b. Oct. 16, 1952, St. Paul, MN; home, Newport Beach; U. of S. CA, B.A. 1973, Harvard U., M.B.A., J.D., 1977; Catholic; married (Rebecca).

Professional Career: Clerk, U.S. Court of Appeals, Judge Hebert Choy, 1977; Practicing atty., 1978–86; Lecturer, Harvard Bus. Schl., 1982–83; Sr. Assoc. Cnsl., White House, 1986–88.

DC Office: 2402 RHOB 20515, 202-225-5611; Fax: 202-225-9177; Web site: www.house.gov/chriscox.

District Office: Newport Beach, 949-756-2244.

Committees: *Republican Policy Committee Chairman. Energy & Commerce* (8th of 31 R): Energy & Air Quality; Telecommunications & The Internet. *Financial Services* (16th of 37 R): Capital Markets, Insurance & Government Sponsored Enterprises; Oversight & Investigations.

Group Ratings

	ADA	ACLU	AFS	LCV	CON	ITIC	NTU	COC	ACU	NTLC	CHC
2000	0	21	0	14	96	88	74	80	100	94	100
1999	0	—	0	6	79	—	71	75	95	—	—

National Journal Ratings

	1999 LIB	—	1999 CONS		2000 LIB	—	2000 CONS
Economic	0%	—	84%		0%	—	94%
Social	29%	—	71%		0%	—	79%
Foreign	38%	—	62%		0%	—	88%

Key Votes of the 106th Congress

1. Patient Bill of Rights	N	5. Bar RU-486 $ for FDA	Y	9. NATO War in Serbia	N
2. Accelerate Min. Wage	N	6. Display 10 Commandments	Y	10. Perm. Trade with China	Y
3. Strike Ban on Ergo. Stnd.	N	7. Gun Show Bkgrnd. Checks	N	11. Debt Relief for 3rd World	N
4. Ovrd. Estate Tax Veto	Y	8. Ban Part.-Birth Abortion	Y	12. Drop Cuba Econ. Embargo	N

Election Results

2000 general	Christopher Cox (R)	181,365	(66%)	($1,171,803)
	John Graham (D)	83,186	(30%)	($17,922)
	Other	11,850	(4%)	
2000 primary	Christopher Cox (R)	134,959	(69%)	
	John Graham (D)	18,913	(10%)	
	Don Irvine (D)	16,510	(8%)	
	Jim Keysor (D)	10,010	(5%)	
	Maziar Mafi (D)	8,953	(5%)	
	Other	7,511	(4%)	
1998 general	Christopher Cox (R)	132,711	(68%)	($1,417,508)
	Christina Avalos (D)	57,938	(30%)	($9,781)
	Others	5,667	(3%)	

FORTY-EIGHTH DISTRICT

The California coast between Los Angeles and San Diego has never entirely filled up with development and never will as long as the Marine Corps retains custody of Camp Pendleton, the giant training base just south of the Orange-San Diego County line. But on both sides of Pendleton up and down the coast and for miles inland on the pleasant hills and in sunny valleys, there has been tremendous growth. Little wonder: This area has perhaps the most agreeable climate in the continental United States, beautiful scenery, the physical infrastructure typical of California and much lower crime rates than Los Angeles or even San Diego. A quarter century ago, this was largely empty territory—never fertile enough to produce a large farm community, never endowed with much manufacturing, never actively promoted as a retirement community. By 1990 there were half a million people just north and south of Pendleton, and the Interior Department was struggling to come up with a district plan that would protect the ecosystem of the four-inch gnat-catcher bird and other endangered species in the area.

The 48th Congressional District occupies the southwestern corner of Orange County, the northern part of San Diego County (referred to as North County in these parts) and a small slice of Riverside County, the instant town of Temecula. It was the fastest-growing California district in the 1990s, with a population increase of 35%.It includes the seaside communities of San Clemente, where Richard Nixon resided after leaving the White House, and San Juan Capistrano, to which the swallows famously return every year. Inland, there are the newer condominium communities of Mission Viejo and Laguna Niguel; just south of Pendleton in San Diego County are Oceanside and Vista. Farther inland amid the hills are Fallbrook and, in Riverside County, Temecula, in the mid-1980s a corner-grocery town serving a vineyard district, now the center of an area with more than 100,000 people, mostly commuters to Orange County and other distant areas attracted by low-priced homes and traditional values. People in all these areas tend to be Republican; they are affluent enough to identify with the party of property, conventional enough in their personal lives to identify with what describes itself as the party of traditional values, undivided enough by ethnic differences to identify with the party that fancies it is made up of an unethnic majority.

The congressman from the 48th is Darrell Issa, a Republican first elected in 2000. He grew up in Cleveland and graduated from Siena Heights University in Adrian, Michigan. After a 10-year career in the Army, Issa started a car alarm company in Cleveland, but he moved the business to North County and renamed it Directed Electronics, where it became the world's largest man-ufacturer of vehicle security systems, with the industry's largest R&D budget. The firm, the first with a programmable personal computer system, made him a fortune estimated at $200 million as he found a way to capitalize legally on America's high crime rates. He became active in the high-tech industry, serving as chairman of the Consumer Electronics Association. In the early 1990s he turned to politics, contributing to Republicans and chairing the 1996 campaign to pass Proposition 209, which banned state use of racial quotas and preferences. In 1998 he ran for the Senate and spent $12 million of his own money. Despite that, he lost the Republican primary 45%–40% to Matt Fong—perhaps a lucky thing, since he probably would not have beaten Barbara Boxer either, and he saved the millions he would have spent between June and November.

In November 1999, nine-term incumbent and Appropriations Subcommittee chairman Ron Packard announced he would retire in 2000. It was obvious that his successor would be chosen in the March 2000 Republican primary, which attracted 10 candidates. First to enter was Bill Morrow, a conservative state senator. Former 46th district Congressman Robert Dornan expressed interest in a comeback attempt, but he ended up deferring to his son, Mark Dornan, who ended up trailing behind. The race turned into a bruising two-man contest. Morrow questioned Issa's business practices. Issa raised questions about his opponent's honesty. When Issa sent a last-minute mailer linking Morrow to former state senator Frank Hill, who went to federal prison for extortion, Morrow responded by suing Issa. On most issues, the candidates took similar positions; they supported streamlining government, opposed abortion and favored rebuilding the military. Issa spent $1.5 million of his own money on the primary, and beat Morrow 46%–30%. Issa won 41%–32% in Orange County and 50%–29% in San Diego County. In the fall the Democratic nominee disconnected his phone and abandoned his campaign because his party, predictably, gave him little support. Issa talked up Social Security reform. He won 61%–28%.

In the House, Issa hoped for a seat on Energy and Commerce, but no freshmen were assigned there. Instead, he was placed on International Relations, Judiciary and Small Business. Demo-crats complained that Issa and other Republicans, during George W. Bush's first speech to Con-gress, filled up the seats Democrats left vacant on their side of the aisle to protest Republican opposition to Census sampling. Issa now holds what must be regarded as a safe seat. Democratic redistricters must remove 134,000 people, but whatever way the district lines are drawn, there will be a heavily Republican seat based in North County that Issa should be able to win.

Cook's Call   *Safe.* This district grew a great deal over the last decade and could undergo some changes in 2001 redistricting. Still, the increase in population has not hurt the Republican performance of the district. Issa won with 61% and Bush took 60% in 2000.

THE PEOPLE: Pop. 2000: 773,292; Pop. 1990: 573,211, up 34.9% 1990–2000. 76% White, 3.3% Black, 4.8% Asian, 1.1% Amer. Indian, 0.5% Hawaiian, 4.1% Two+ races, 10.3% Other; 22.5% Hispanic Origin.

2000 Presidential Vote		
Bush (R)	169,514	(60%)
Gore (D)	100,148	(36%)
Nader (Green)	7,976	(3%)
Others	3,167	(1%)

1996 Presidential Vote		
Dole (R)	132,545	(56%)
Clinton (D)	80,646	(34%)
Perot (I)	18,731	(8%)
Others	6,462	(3%)

Rep. Darrell Issa (R)

Elected 2000, 1st term; b. Nov. 1, 1953, Cleveland, OH; home, Vista; Siena Heights U., B.A. 1976; Protestant; married (Kathy).

Military Career: Army, 1970–80.

Professional Career: Founder & Pres., Directed Electronics, 1982–99.

DC Office: 1725 LHOB 20515, 202-225-3906; Fax: 202-225-3303; Web site: www.house.gov/issa.

District Offices: San Clemente, 949-496-2343; Temecula, 909-693-2447; Vista, 760-940-4380.

Committees: *International Relations* (22d of 26 R): East Asia & the Pacific; Middle East & South Asia. *Judiciary* (19th of 21 R): Commercial & Administrative Law; Immigration & Claims. *Small Business* (13th of 19 R): Tax, Finance & Exports; Workforce, Empowerment & Government Programs.

Group Ratings and Key Votes: Newly Elected

Election Results

2000 general	Darrell Issa (R)	160,627	(61%)	($2,300,907)
	Peter Kouvelis (D)	74,073	(28%)	($17,069)
	Eddie Rose (Ref)	11,240	(4%)	
	Other	15,538	(6%)	
2000 primary	Darrell Issa (R)	67,732	(35%)	
	Bill Morrow (R)	45,223	(24%)	
	Peter Kouvelis (D)	20,789	(11%)	
	Richard K. Maguire (D)	13,704	(7%)	
	Mark Dornan (R)	9,534	(5%)	
	Joe Snyder (R)	8,480	(4%)	
	Other	26,565	(14%)	
1998 general	Ronald C. Packard (R)	138,948	(77%)	($288,822)
	Sharon K. Miles (NL)	23,262	(13%)	
	Daniel L. Muhe (Lib)	18,509	(10%)	

FORTY-NINTH DISTRICT

When the United States was dictating the terms of the Treaty of Guadalupe Hidalgo in 1848, after its successful war with Mexico, it made sure the southern boundary of its new California territory was just south of the port of San Diego. This is one of three splendid natural harbors on the Pacific Coast and the major West Coast U.S. Navy base for more than 50 years. The port and Navy base in the sheltered harbor remain the central focus of a metropolis that has grown tenfold over that time and now stretches far inland and to the north. On one side is downtown, booming with post-modern buildings like the Horton Plaza amid a few well-preserved early 20th Century relics like the Spreckels Theatre. Across the harbor, on the sand spit that guards it against the ocean, is the white frame castle of the Hotel Del Coronado, with its surprisingly dark wooden interior—the U.S.'s largest wooden structure and a favored resort of past American presidents; the town of Coronado has long been a favorite retirement place for Navy admirals and captains.

But San Diego is not all harbor and Navy. To the north, the Pacific waves pound against the beach beneath erose cliffs of unique rock formations that stride up and down the coast on which stand some of San Diego's great cultural institutions: the Scripps Institute of Oceanography, the University of California San Diego campus, the Salk Institute and the Torrey Pines reserve, home of this unique, wide-spreading pine tree. They look out over the ocean through clear and gentle air south to La Jolla, the city's highest-income neighborhood, and north toward Del Mar and the race track that made San Diego a tourist mecca 50 years ago when the track was owned by Bing Crosby and friends. The weather—a sunny 70 degrees most of the time—has lured people to San Diego; the informal resort atmosphere of La Jolla and Mission Beach appeal to tourists. But this is a working town as well, a sophisticated high-tech center with around 200,000 full and part-time students at its colleges and universities and growing biotech, electronics, software and telecommunications industries; someone who looks like a professional surfer may turn out to be a high-tech engineer. It is a manufacturing center as well, with maquiladora factories clustering near the Mexican border. Facing the state's electricity crisis, the county's leading home builder announced in February 2001 construction of the nation's largest subdivision equipped with solar-powered fuel cells.

The 49th Congressional District, which includes about half the city of San Diego plus Coronado and Imperial Beach, takes in most of the harbor and Navy bases and much of its high-tech businesses and workers. It reaches as far south as the Mexican border and includes most of downtown San Diego and Balboa Park, with its justly famous zoo. It reaches inland where the city's freeway network, denser and more practical than San Francisco's or even Los Angeles's, efficiently shuttles commuters from scattered employment centers to their homes on hilltop subdivisions. San Diego under Mayor (1971–83) Pete Wilson wouldn't let developers build on the sides of the hills, so it lacks the picturesque but precarious hillside streets of the Hollywood Hills or Pacific Heights—but rather has the natural landscape that the Portuguese explorer Cabrillo saw in the 1500s and the American adventurer Richard Henry Dana saw three centuries later. The district includes Ocean Beach, Mission Bay and La Jolla and reaches north to Torrey Pines and inland to the outer boundary of Miramar Naval Air Station. Voters here tend to be Republican and free market on economics but liberal on cultural issues like abortion and the environment— much like Mayors Wilson and, later, Susan Golding. Limits on growth help to explain why this was the fourth slowest-growing district in California during the 1990s, trailing only three inner-city Los Angeles districts. Historically, this was a Republican district, but it has trended Democratic in the 1990s: cultural liberalism trumping market economics. In 1988 it voted 57%–43% for the senior George Bush; in 2000 it voted 53%–41% for Al Gore.

The congresswoman from the 49th district is Susan Davis, a Democrat elected in 2000. She grew up in Richmond, California, graduated from the University of California at Berkeley and took a social work degree at the University of North Carolina. Her father and husband have both been doctors. She moved to San Diego in 1973, and became president of the local League of Women Voters and a community producer for the local public television station. Davis got her first taste of politics in 1983, when she won a seat on the San Diego school board. In 1990, she became the executive director of the Aaron Price Fellows Program, which helps teach leadership and citizen skills to multi-ethnic high school students. She returned to politics in 1994, winning the first of three terms in the California Assembly. She advocated guaranteeing patients the right to a second medical opinion. To combat San Diego's many boating accidents, she wrote a bill in 1999 requiring mandatory licensing of all boaters, stricter life-jacket rules, and increased education; but Governor Gray Davis vetoed it because he opposed written tests and the added bureaucracy.

In 2000, the term-limited Davis challenged Republican Congressman Brian Bilbray, who had won three close elections in this competitive district. She tried to portray him as a conservative, even though he held pro-choice and pro-environment views and made a point of not attending the Republican convention in Philadelphia. "He talks moderate in San Diego but votes conservative in Washington," Davis said. She attacked Bilbray for supporting bills that would deny citizenship to children of illegal immigrants and that would allow private insurers to provide prescription drug benefits to seniors; she called for coverage under Medicare. Davis also said that Bilbray had failed to deliver more federal dollars to the district. She had campaign visits from Dick Gephardt, Donna Shalala, and Gloria Steinem; when Bill Clinton came to San Diego in June to raise money for her, she stayed in Sacramento. The AFL-CIO ran so much advertising on her behalf that Davis requested that they stop. Bilbray had help from Citizens for Better Medicare. He criticized Davis for her handling of utility deregulation. He cited his support for John McCain's campaign finance bill, and said that he was comfortable with his pro-impeachment votes for a president he called "a perpetual liar." Davis won 50%–46%, running 3% behind Gore. In the House, she got plum assignments to Armed Services and Education and the Workforce.

Democrats control redistricting and will seek to strengthen Davis' seat while adding 52,000 people but three of the four adjoining districts are heavily Republican; the only source of Democratic precincts is the 50th District. There, incumbent Bob Filner might not mind losing Latino precincts to the 49th and picking up some Republican precincts from it; this would help protect him from a Latino primary challenge. But Latino legislators may block such a strategy.

Cook's Call *Competitive.* Since 1992, when redistricting significantly altered it, this seat has been one of the most heavily contested races in the country and over that time has ousted two incumbents. Democrats, wary of the district's marginal nature, will work to shore up freshman Susan Davis in redistricting.

THE PEOPLE: Pop. 2000: 586,882; Pop. 1990: 573,437, up 2.3% 1990–2000. 74.1% White, 5.2% Black, 8.1% Asian, 0.7% Amer. Indian, 0.4% Hawaiian, 4.4% Two + races, 7.1% Other; 16.7% Hispanic Origin.

2000 Presidential Vote			1996 Presidential Vote		
Gore (D)	123,997	(53%)	Clinton (D)	110,920	(49%)
Bush (R)	97,785	(41%)	Dole (R)	91,478	(40%)
Nader (Green)	11,204	(5%)	Perot (I)	15,084	(7%)
Others	2,674	(1%)	Others	9,514	(4%)

Rep. Susan Davis (D)

Elected 2000, 1st term; b. Apr. 13, 1944, Cambridge; home, San Diego; U.of CA (Berkeley), B.A. 1965; U. of NC, M.A. 1968; Jewish; married (Steve).

Elected Office: San Diego School Bd., 1983–1992; CA Assembly, 1994–2000.

Professional Career: Exec. Dir., Aaron Price Fellows, 1990–93; Devel. Assoc., KPBS Radio, 1980–83.

DC Office: 1517 LHOB 20515, 202-225-2040; Fax: 202-225-2948; Web site: www.house.gov/susandavis.

District Office: San Diego, 619-291-1430.

Committees: *Armed Services* (26th of 28 D): Military Personnel; Military Readiness. *Education & the Workforce* (21st of 22 D): Education Reform; Select Education.

Group Ratings and Key Votes: Newly Elected

Election Results

2000 general	Susan Davis (D)	113,400	(50%)	($1,926,497)
	Brian P. Bilbray (R)	105,515	(46%)	($1,846,574)
	Other	9,574	(4%)	
2000 primary	Brian P. Bilbray (R)	79,473	(51%)	
	Susan Davis (D)	71,443	(46%)	
	Other	5,243	(3%)	
1998 general	Brian P. Bilbray (R)	90,516	(49%)	($1,278,210)
	Christine Kehoe (D)	86,400	(47%)	($1,263,299)
	Others	8,603	(5%)	

FIFTIETH DISTRICT

San Diego, at one corner of the continental United States, not so long ago a small Navy town known for its good harbor and splendid weather, is now a major metropolis, a city of 1.2 million people and the center of a metro area of 2.8 million. It is also, to its sometime discomfort, one of the largest cities anywhere directly on an international border and between countries with strikingly different economic conditions, political systems and cultural traditions. Not many other Americans think about it, but Mexican presidential candidate Luis Donaldo Colosio was murdered in March 1994 just a few blocks from the border in Tijuana.

This is, in fact, the busiest border crossing in the world, but most of San Diego seems to look away, toward the ocean. Tijuana looks to the United States, to the lower-income part of San Diego—the industrial zone on brown hills in Otay Mesa and San Ysidro, the industrial suburbs of Chula Vista and National City and the grid streets south of downtown and behind the harbor in San Diego itself. Latinos are scattered in various parts of the city, in the southern corridor and in Encanto and Chollas Park in the east. Oddly, there is not much evidence of Mexican style in San Diego—less even than in Los Angeles, as if the border city was insisting on its Yanqui origins, just as San Diego's civic leaders bridled at the idea of a bi-national airport on the border. Even the city's favorite symbol, the red Tijuana Trolley that takes tourists from downtown to the San Ysidro-Tijuana border station, is as resolutely Yanqui as Main Street in Disneyland. Although real estate remained in strong demand, some of the beauty has faded. "When you're stalled on a jammed freeway, look around at what used to be beautiful canyons. Developers have lopped off the tops, filled in the valleys, and plunked pinkish purple tract homes on top of them," lamented the *San Diego Union-Tribune's* Don Bauder.

The 50th Congressional District—the first 50th district in the history of the House of Representatives—covers the southern and eastern ends of San Diego, and includes National City and Chula Vista toward the border. The district was 51% Hispanic in 2000, up from 40% in 1990; the percentage of Latino voters is over 30%, up from 22% 10 years before. This is by far the most Democratic district in the San Diego area, carried by Al Gore in 2000 by a 59%–37% margin.

The congressman from the 50th District is Bob Filner, a Democrat elected in 1992, when the district was newly created. Filner grew up in New York and was a Freedom Rider in 1961, imprisoned for two months in Mississippi. He earned a Ph.D. at Cornell, taught history at San Diego State and directed the Lipinsky Institute for Judaic Studies; he took time off to work on Senator Hubert Humphrey's staff in the 1970s, was elected to the San Diego school board in 1979 and to the city council in 1987, where he made a name for himself favoring graffiti removal and expansion of Jack Murphy Stadium. In the 1992 primary for the open seat, he had strong backing from blacks and Latinos although he had two better-known rivals. Filner won with 26%, to 23% for Waddie Deddeh, state senator and assemblyman since 1966, but 71 and recovering from heart surgery; and 20% for Jim Bates, four-term congressman beaten in 1990 after being disciplined for sexual harassment; and 19% for Juan Carlos Vargas, returned to San Diego after training to be a Jesuit priest and then switching to Harvard Law School.

Filner is politically savvy, with some original ideas about policy, aggressive to the point of abrasiveness, and a consistent House liberal. He told the 1993 Democratic freshmen they should vote as a bloc for internal reform; they did not, and many lost, as Filner foresaw. In 1995, he worked with Republican Brian Bilbray to get funding for the international sewage treatment center and supported the permanent waiver from sewage treatment standards; in 2000, they teamed to enact a plan for the Bajagua private sewage treatment plant in Tijuana. "No other members of Congress have raw sewage flowing into their districts from another country," Filner said. He proposed with Bilbray a "Jobs Train" to reopen the now-defunct San Diego and Arizona Eastern Railroad, providing a connection between the port of San Diego and the east; he lost 238–162, as the other three San Diego County Republicans opposed the plan to trigger a $7.9 million loan guarantee. When San Diego suffered its huge electricity-rate increases in summer 2000, he called it a "poster child" and warned against national electricity deregulation. In early 2001, he demanded that President Bush order federal energy regulators to fix local rates and urged House

Democrats to focus more intensively on California's problem, which he warned could threaten incumbents in both parties.

As the number-two Democrat on the Veterans' Affairs Committee, Filner has become an eager advocate of veterans' rights, a popular cause in his district of many military retirees. He has paid particular attention to restoring benefits denied to Filipino veterans who fought for the U.S. in World War II; he and 15 of the veterans were arrested in 1997 after they chained themselves to a White House fence. In 1999, he was one of only two members to vote against further restrictions on burials at Arlington Cemetery. On other issues, he was one of only five House members to vote against both parties' impeachment inquiries, and one of two who opposed the Medicare "lockbox" proposal in February 2001. In 2000, he relived his Freedom Riders experience—including his arrest with House colleague John Lewis—by touring the Civil Rights Institute in Birmingham.

In the March 1996 primary, Filner was challenged by Vargas, who had been elected to succeed him on the council in 1993. Filner, whose ads said Vargas was "anti-choice," bragged of fighting Newt Gingrich on Medicare and saving taxpayers $3 billion on sewage treatment. Vargas ran as a moderate and responded with an ad showing his wife praising his positive, door-to-door campaign ("a candidate who doesn't throw mud to win elections"), and with him saying, "It's wrong to cut Medicare and veterans' benefits, and it's wrong to burn the American flag"—a reference to Filner's vote against the flag amendment. Filner won, but by just 55%–45%. In the next two cycles, Filner was not seriously challenged in the primary or general election. In 1999, he decided against a bid for mayor, saying that he could accomplish more for the city by working to create a Democratic-controlled House in which he might chair a committee.

Filner has two obvious worries about re-election. One is that he may be challenged by Vargas or another strong Latino as the district's Latino percentage grows. The other worry is redistricting. It is controlled by Democrats, but Vargas, now an assemblyman, and therefore term-limited, could try to draw a district more favorable to a future challenge. That would mean adding nearby precincts that are heavily Latino, or seem likely to become so. Filner's interests might actually be served by making the district somewhat less Democratic. That would also serve the interests of 49th district Democrat Susan Davis. Transferring Latino precincts from the 50th to the 49th might help both—but that would be fought by Latinos in Sacramento, without whose votes Democrats lack majorities in both houses of the legislature.

Cook's Call   *Safe*. This San Diego based seat is very Democratic and rather barren territory for Republicans, but shoring up Susan Davis in the more marginal 49th district may require Filner to give up some of his more Democratic territory.

THE PEOPLE: Pop. 2000: 641,790; Pop. 1990: 573,244, up 12% 1990–2000. 41.2% White, 11.4% Black, 14.3% Asian, 0.8% Amer. Indian, 0.7% Hawaiian, 5.7% Two + races, 26% Other; 50.8% Hispanic Origin.

2000 Presidential Vote

Gore (D)	85,408	(59%)
Bush (R)	53,898	(37%)
Nader (Green)	3.992	(3%)
Others	1,533	(1%)

1996 Presidential Vote

Clinton (D)	78,881	(60%)
Dole (R)	42,730	(32%)
Perot (I)	7,764	(6%)
Others	2,765	(2%)

Rep. Bob Filner (D)

Elected 1992, 5th term; b. Sept. 4, 1942, Pittsburgh, PA; home, San Diego; Cornell U., B.A. 1963, Ph.D. 1973, U. of DE, M.A. 1969; Jewish; married (Jane).

Elected Office: San Diego Schl. Bd., 1979–83, Pres., 1982–83; San Diego City Cncl., 1987–92, Dpty. Mayor, 1991.

Professional Career: Prof., San Diego St. U., 1970–92; Legis. Asst., U.S. Sen. Hubert Humphrey, 1974; Legis. Asst., U.S. Rep. Don Fraser, 1975.

DC Office: 2463 RHOB 20515, 202-225-8045; Fax: 202-225-9073; Web site: www.house.gov/filner.

District Office: Chula Vista, 619-422-5963.

Committees: *Transportation & Infrastructure* (13th of 34 D): Highways & Transit; Railroads; Water Resources & Environment. *Veterans' Affairs* (2d of 14 D): Health (RMM).

Group Ratings

	ADA	ACLU	AFS	LCV	CON	ITIC	NTU	COC	ACU	NTLC	CHC
2000	95	86	100	93	76	47	23	27	0	12	0
1999	100	—	100	100	44	—	25	20	0	—	—

National Journal Ratings

	1999 LIB —	1999 CONS		2000 LIB —	2000 CONS
Economic	88%	—	0%	95%	— 0%
Social	83%	—	13%	94%	— 0%
Foreign	93%	—	5%	97%	— 0%

Key Votes of the 106th Congress

1. Patient Bill of Rights	Y	5. Bar RU-486 $ for FDA	N	9. NATO War in Serbia	Y
2. Accelerate Min. Wage	Y	6. Display 10 Commandments	N	10. Perm. Trade with China	N
3. Strike Ban on Ergo. Stnd.	Y	7. Gun Show Bkgrnd. Checks	Y	11. Debt Relief for 3rd World	Y
4. Ovrd. Estate Tax Veto	N	8. Ban Part.-Birth Abortion	N	12. Drop Cuba Econ. Embargo	Y

Election Results

2000 general	Bob Filner (D)	95,191	(68%)	($357,015)
	Bob Divine (R)	38,526	(28%)	($11,002)
	Other	5,755	(4%)	
2000 primary	Bob Filner (D)	61,742	(67%)	
	Bob Divine (R)	18,339	(20%)	
	Alexander Sorongon (R)	5,420	(6%)	
	Other	6,165	(7%)	
1998 general	Bob Filner (D)	77,354	(99%)	($433,671)
	Others	596	(1%)	

FIFTY-FIRST DISTRICT

When longtime (1924–72) FBI Director J. Edgar Hoover came to the races at Del Mar for two weeks every summer in the 1940s and 1950s, the rest of north San Diego County, from the track north to the Marine Corps's Camp Pendleton, was mostly uninhabited: There were a few thousand people in the beach towns of Oceanside and Carlsbad and a few thousand more scattered over the dry, brownish hills that rolled inland. Today about 650,000 people live in North County, and who can blame them? For this is one of America's most beautiful and comfortable environments, with ocean and mountain scenery, sunny and warm weather, no rural poverty and low crime. Here, amid dry but not desert landscape, you can see miles of rolling hills, with occasional sur-realistic trees and sagebrush-like bushes; mountains clump up not in ridges, but here and there, seemingly at random. This land has attracted thousands of new migrants—many, but by no means all, retirees. Outside the Los Angeles media market, not frequented by many entertainment ce-lebrities, North County does not have a high media profile. Although the local convention and visitors bureau complained that the area "doesn't have a distinct image," that probably suits just fine the quietly successful people who have moved here.

The 51st Congressional District covers much of North County and grew by 25% in the 1990s. It includes more than 200,000 people in San Diego itself—not in its urbanized core, but in land it annexed during Pete Wilson's long tenure as mayor, including the Rancho Bernardo planned community, San Diego's Wild Animal Park and Miramar Naval Air Station. It also includes the gorgeous suburb of Rancho Sante Fe, with its multi-million dollar mansions set amid rolling hills and lush greenery. The 51st district takes in the beach communities from Del Mar north to Carlsbad and the nearby La Costa resort. Inland, with its red-tile roofs filling a sunny valley and its splendid arts center, is fast-growing Escondido, with 134,000 people in 2000. Politically, this is overwhelmingly Republican territory, though with a taste for Ross Perot in 1992: rather conservative on cultural issues, against bigger government, nationalistic on foreign policy.

The congressman from the 51st is Randy (Duke) Cunningham, a Republican elected in 1990. Born the day after Pearl Harbor, he taught and coached swimming in Hinsdale, Illinois, and San Diego; in 1966, at 25, he joined the Navy and became one of the most decorated pilots in the Vietnam war. He then trained pilots at Miramar in the Top Gun program; he retired from the Navy in 1987 and started a business in San Diego. In 1990 he ran in a Democratic district against Congressman Jim Bates, who had been charged with sexual harassment; Cunningham beat a former ambassador to Qatar in the Republican primary 46%–30%, and in the general beat Bates 46%–45%. In 1992, faced with a choice of districts to run in, he passed up the marginal and culturally more liberal 49th on the coast and ran in the 51st. Incumbent Bill Lowery, a Republican who had 300 overdrafts at the House bank, withdrew from the race in April 1992, and Cunningham comfortably won the primary and general.

Cunningham arrived just in time for the Gulf war debate and in his first years worked to make Filipino Gulf war veterans eligible to apply for U.S. citizenship and to prevent base closings in the San Diego area. He was one of four congressmen who in October 1992 met with George Bush and prompted him to ask questions about Bill Clinton's student trip to Moscow and Eastern Europe, an issue that hurt the Republican ticket. With Republican control, he switched to the Appropriations Committee and has assignments on its two subcommittees with the largest budgets: Defense; and Labor, Health and Human Services, and Education. He has emerged as a forceful advocate of more Pentagon spending. Cunningham was the lead sponsor of the English-as-official-language bill passed by the House in 1996. "We must take this defining step to avoid our nation becoming divided into many ethnic enclaves." He has pressed for stricter enforcement of immigration laws and sponsored a "no frills prison act." He successfully opposed efforts to terminate the mothballed Selective Service draft, is a leading advocate of the constitutional amendment to bar flag desecration, and co-authored legislation to ensure that military overseas ballots are counted. On local issues, he sought to direct $200 million to Navy ship-repair in San Diego, and he won in 2000 a change in the allocation formula to give California an additional $13.5 million for education. He also enacted his bill to ban the harvesting of shark fins by Hawaiian fishing boats.

Cunningham has a gift for pungent comments. At one hearing, he said, "I do not believe they [troops] can be well led when they have a commander-in-chief who has turned his back on them." He said that Clinton's anti-war past would result in being "tried as a traitor and even shot" if he had lived in another country. After he said Jim Moran "switched his vote and turned his back on Desert Storm," Moran pushed him in the hall, then apologized. In 1995, he triggered a firestorm by calling gays "homos" on the House floor. In 1998 he dressed down an Army official at a subcommittee hearing about "B.S." efforts to combat sexual harassment and discrimination in the military. "Our kids don't like that. They don't like the political correctness," Cunningham lectured. And in 2000, his critique of "our liberal and socialist friends" in the House drew a complaint from Progressive Caucus head Peter DeFazio about the "bizarre and inaccurate accusations."

In recent years, he has had several personal setbacks. When he ran for the Republican Conference secretary position in 1997, he was winnowed out on the second ballot. Also that year, his 27-year-old son was arrested and charged with flying a plane to Boston with 400 pounds of marijuana. He said, "As a parent this is the most anguishing thing that can happen to you. We love him. If the charges are true, we are disappointed, and he must face his responsibilities."

When his son later was sentenced to two years in federal prison, Cunningham appeared in court for the sentencing and admitted in a tear-choked voice that he had not spent enough time with the boy when he was growing up. Also in 1998, he underwent surgery for prostate cancer, crediting early detection with saving his life. That led him to advocate a federal office of men's health to promote early detection.

Cunningham was re-elected routinely in 2000. Redistricting could change the district's boundaries some; exactly how depends on how Democrats resolve the boundaries of the 49th and 50th districts. But there is so much heavily Republican territory in this part of San Diego County that Cunningham should have no problems.

Cook's Call   *Safe.* Former "Top Gun" instructor Duke Cunningham is also a high flier in this district. Heavy growth in this district means that it will have to contract some in redistricting, but there is no indication that this will give him problems in 2002.

THE PEOPLE: Pop. 2000: 713,746; Pop. 1990: 572,850, up 24.6% 1990–2000. 73.9% White, 2.1% Black, 11.1% Asian, 0.6% Amer. Indian, 0.3% Hawaiian, 4% Two+ races, 8% Other; 17.6% Hispanic Origin.

2000 Presidential Vote

Bush (R)	156,855	(55%)
Gore (D)	115,219	(41%)
Nader (Green)	9,137	(3%)
Others	3,008	(1%)

1996 Presidential Vote

Dole (R)	130,459	(52%)
Clinton (D)	97,128	(38%)
Perot (I)	16,963	(7%)
Others	7,918	(3%)

Rep. Randy (Duke) Cunningham (R)

Elected 1990, 6th term; b. Dec. 8, 1941, Los Angeles; home, San Diego; U. of MO, B.A. 1964, M.S. 1965, National U., M.B.A. 1985; Christian; married (Nancy).

Military Career: Navy, 1966–87 (Vietnam).

Professional Career: Businessman, 1987–90.

DC Office: 2350 RHOB 20515, 202-225-5452; Fax: 202-225-2558; Web site: www.house.gov/cunningham.

District Office: Escondido, 760-737-8438.

Committees: *Appropriations* (21st of 35 R): Defense; District of Columbia; Labor, HHS & Education. *Permanent Select Committee on Intelligence* (7th of 11 R): Human Intelligence, Analysis & Counterintelligence; Technical & Tactical Intelligence.

Group Ratings

	ADA	ACLU	AFS	LCV	CON	ITIC	NTU	COC	ACU	NTLC	CHC
2000	5	14	0	14	20	100	62	95	92	76	93
1999	10	—	0	6	40	—	59	92	88	—	—

National Journal Ratings

	1999 LIB	—	1999 CONS		2000 LIB	—	2000 CONS
Economic	0%	—	84%		15%	—	83%
Social	15%	—	85%		26%	—	71%
Foreign	15%	—	81%		33%	—	62%

Key Votes of the 106th Congress

1. Patient Bill of Rights	N	5. Bar RU-486 $ for FDA	Y	9. NATO War in Serbia	N
2. Accelerate Min. Wage	N	6. Display 10 Commandments	Y	10. Perm. Trade with China	Y
3. Strike Ban on Ergo. Stnd.	N	7. Gun Show Bkgrnd. Checks	N	11. Debt Relief for 3rd World	N
4. Ovrd. Estate Tax Veto	Y	8. Ban Part.-Birth Abortion	Y	12. Drop Cuba Econ. Embargo	N

Election Results

2000 general	Randy (Duke) Cunningham (R)	172,291	(64%)	($572,440)
	George Barraza (D)	81,408	(30%)	
	Other	14,100	(5%)	
2000 primary	Randy (Duke) Cunningham (R)	126,038	(68%)	
	George Barraza (D)	50,245	(27%)	
	Other	9,961	(5%)	
1998 general	Randy (Duke) Cunningham (R)	126,229	(61%)	($436,528)
	Dan Kripke (D)	71,706	(35%)	($92,708)
	Others	8,943	(4%)	

FIFTY-SECOND DISTRICT

San Diego began as a port, but today most metropolitan area residents live out of sight of the sea, in hilltop neighborhoods inland that look out over distant ridges and freeways or in warm, sunny valleys amid the mountains which become denser and higher as one travels east from the Pacific. There is a discernible difference in attitudes and values between those who have settled inland and those nearer the ocean, part of the split that became critical in California's political struggles and culture wars since the 1980s. In San Diego, both groups tend to identify as Republicans, and coastal people may be more affluent. But those who settle inland are more likely to be conventionally religious and to have traditional moral values; they tend to be more supportive of the military and assertive foreign policy; they are more dubious about the ability of government to shape poor citizens' lives. They are more conservative on most of the cultural and foreign issues of recent times, and therefore more reliably Republican: When oceanfront voters in San Diego shifted sharply toward Democrats in the 1990s, the movement was much less among voters inland.

The 52d Congressional District takes in many of the inland San Diego suburbs and proceeds eastward across mountains and desert and the man-made Salton Sea to the drained-dry Colorado River on the Arizona border. More than half its people are clustered in suburbs directly east of San Diego, off I-8 and Routes 94 and 67: Lemon Grove, La Mesa, Spring Valley, El Cajon, Santee. These are places little noticed by the media—or were little noticed, until March 2001 when a teenager at Santana High School in Santee went on a shooting spree and killed two and injured 13; two weeks later, in nearby El Cajon, another high school student opened fire and wounded three classmates and two teacher. El Cajon, quite unnoticed, includes America's second largest (after Detroit) community of Chaldeans, Christian Arabs from Iraq, who own 80% of San Diego's liquor stores and are known for their toughness—it's not easy being a Christian in Iraq—and penchant for doing business in cash. The rest of the people in the 52nd District are scattered in pockets around rural San Diego County and in the Imperial Valley, irrigated desert land where low-paid farm workers harvest some of America's most bounteous crops. Along the southern edge of the district, from the Pacific Ocean to Otay Mountain, is being built the 14-mile, 15-foot-high fence, 150 feet north of an existing steel barrier to vehicles, along the border with Mexico mandated by a 1996 law, and scheduled to be completed in 2002, at a cost of $25 million, twice the original estimate, and despite the risk to the endangered California gnat catcher and Least Bell's vireo.

The congressman from the 52d district is Duncan Hunter, first elected in 1980, an upset winner in the Reagan landslide who now leads a strain of America-first Republicanism, which is not represented in large numbers in the House (Hunter was one of the few Pat Buchanan supporters in the House in 1996), but which Hunter thinks has greater support among ordinary voters. Hunter grew up in Riverside and served in the Army in Vietnam in helicopter combat assaults, and was an antipoverty lawyer afterwards. In 1980, at 32, he beat an incumbent Democrat and came to the House brash and confident he had the right answers. In the 1980s he was part of the group of young conservative Republicans around Newt Gingrich. On the Armed Services Committee, he was an ardent backer of the Strategic Defense Initiative and of the buildup of the Navy. He worked to block relaxation of export controls on high-tech products. He has continued to work for higher defense expenditures on particular programs. But he has strongly opposed free trade measures, once taking a sledgehammer to a Japanese car. And, representing a district with hundreds of miles along the Mexican border, he was the chief sponsor of the 1996 law requiring the border fence.

On Armed Services he continues to argue for increases in defense spending, even against the Republican leadership. In March 2000 he and six other ranking members of Armed Services threatened to withhold their votes for the budget resolution unless Speaker Dennis Hastert added $4 billion in defense spending to the supplemental spending bill; the threat worked. Included were funds for repairing ships in San Diego. For six years he was chairman of the Military Procurement Subcommittee, calling for accelerated F-22 development because of its stealth capabilities, even though the F-15 has a long shelf life, and for building more B-2s. He has tried to push the Pentagon to build more nuclear submarines and match apparent Russian gains in quiet technology. He objected to San Diego area colleague Duke Cunningham's request for different flight paths for noisy helicopters over Cunningham's North County district; politics should be ignored on military decisions, Hunter wrote the commander of Miramar Marine Corps Air Station. When Armed Services Chairman Floyd Spence was rotated off as chairman because of House Republicans' six-year term limit, Hunter supported the next most senior member, Bob Stump, over Curt Weldon, who ranked behind Hunter in seniority, but said he would run if Stump lost. "I respect seniority and I support Bob Stump. But if he doesn't wind up in the chairmanship, then I'm running." Stump won.

Hunter ardently opposed NAFTA and claimed in 1996 that it cost the United States 250,000 jobs. He also vociferously opposed GATT in 1994, the Mexico bailout in 1995, and fast track in 1997. He became a vociferous opponent of expanding trade with China. In 1998, he led the successful effort to deny Bill Clinton the authority to issue a waiver allowing the China Ocean Shipping Company to lease a terminal at the former Long Beach naval station. In 2000 he voted against Permanent Normal Trade Relations with China. "Whichever side of this debate one is on, everyone here has to concede American dollars are arming Communist China today." In 2000 he sponsored an amendment to detail how lie detector tests should be administered in Department of Energy laboratories; this was defeated in committee 25–23.

Representing the southwest corner of the continental United States, Hunter takes a San Diegocentric view of issues. He opposes Bob Filner's proposal to fund the San Diego & Arizona Eastern Railroad line which dips into Mexico on its way from San Diego to Imperial County; this "jobs train" (Filner's phrase) would give too many opportunities for illegal immigrants and drug traffickers to evade border guards in Hunter's view. In 1999 he urged huge tax breaks—tax credits for shipbuilders, exemption from corporate income tax, halving the depreciation period, additional tax credits for U.S.-made engines—for builders and operators of cruise ships, a growing industry in San Diego. When electric rates spiked upward in San Diego in summer 2000, he was as scornful of market economics as liberal Democrat Filner, arguing that FERC must roll back rates that are not "just and reasonable," and sponsoring a bill to order refunds from power companies if the regulators refused to control prices. He put together a proposal to get the city and county to buy or lease electricity generating units and build a power plant at Miramar; incoming San Diego Mayor Dick Murphy was reluctant because "the city has a $400 million ballpark to finish"—one form of municipal socialism trumping another in this conservative metropolis. He opposes the Clinton ban on vehicles from 49,000 acres of Imperial Valley desert and, with Filner and Cunningham, moved to stop the Cuyapaipe Indians from building a casino on a health clinic site on I-8 east of San Diego.

In 2000 Hunter had more active Democratic opposition than usual from a University of San Diego business professor who said, "Duncan's attitude about Mexico is counterproductive. His isolationist view is bad for San Diego's economy, because it is an impediment to trade." Hunter won 65%–31%. His district will likely be changed somewhat by redistricting, which is controlled by Democrats, but the changes will be incidental to what they hope to accomplish elsewhere. He could lose Imperial County to Mary Bono's 44th District, which would be made more marginal, and he could find the borders changed to the west, depending on how Democrats redraw the boundaries between the Democratic-held 49th and 50th Districts. He is next in line in seniority for the Armed Services chair after Stump, who turns 75 in 2002.

Cook's Call　*Safe.* Hunter's district has not grown as much as the nearby 51st, but it will undergo some minor changes. Still, it is hard to see how Hunter gets a tough race in 2002.

THE PEOPLE: Pop. 2000: 640,630; Pop. 1990: 573,355, up 11.7% 1990–2000. 71.8% White, 4.7% Black, 3% Asian, 1.2% Amer. Indian, 0.3% Hawaiian, 4.5% Two+ races, 14.4% Other; 29.7% Hispanic Origin.

2000 Presidential Vote

Bush (R)	115,402	(54%)
Gore (D)	87,365	(41%)
Nader (Green)	6,581	(3%)
Others	2,790	(1%)

1996 Presidential Vote

Dole (R)	94,035	(48%)
Clinton (D)	81,401	(41%)
Perot (I)	16,657	(8%)
Others	5,531	(3%)

Rep. Duncan Hunter (R)

Elected 1980, 11th term; b. May 31, 1948, Riverside; home, Alpine; U. of MT, U. of CA, Western St. U., B.S.L & J.D. 1976; Baptist; married (Lynne).

Military Career: Army, 1969–71 (Vietnam).

Professional Career: Practicing atty., 1976–80.

DC Office: 2265 RHOB 20515, 202-225-5672; Fax: 202-225-0235; Web site: www.house.gov/hunter.

District Offices: El Cajon, 619-579-3001; Imperial, 760-353-5420.

Committees: *Armed Services* (3d of 32 R): Military Readiness; Military Research & Development (Chmn.).

Group Ratings

	ADA	ACLU	AFS	LCV	CON	ITIC	NTU	COC	ACU	NTLC	CHC
2000	10	21	14	0	34	56	62	71	76	73	87
1999	15	—	0	0	21	—	55	70	84	—	—

National Journal Ratings

	1999 LIB	—	1999 CONS		2000 LIB	—	2000 CONS
Economic	36%	—	64%		29%	—	67%
Social	0%	—	96%		0%	—	79%
Foreign	45%	—	54%		25%	—	69%

Key Votes of the 106th Congress

1. Patient Bill of Rights	Y	5. Bar RU-486 $ for FDA	Y	9. NATO War in Serbia	Y
2. Accelerate Min. Wage	N	6. Display 10 Commandments	Y	10. Perm. Trade with China	N
3. Strike Ban on Ergo. Stnd.	N	7. Gun Show Bkgrnd. Checks	N	11. Debt Relief for 3rd World	N
4. Ovrd. Estate Tax Veto	Y	8. Ban Part.-Birth Abortion	Y	12. Drop Cuba Econ. Embargo	N

Election Results

2000 general	Duncan Hunter (R)	131,345	(65%)	($856,691)
	Craig Barkacs (D)	63,537	(31%)	($270,663)
	Other	8,112	(4%)	
2000 primary	Duncan Hunter (R)	103,667	(71%)	
	Craig Barkacs (D)	36,715	(25%)	
	Other	5,863	(4%)	
1998 general	Duncan Hunter (R)	116,251	(76%)	($605,857)
	Lynn Badler (Lib)	21,933	(14%)	
	Adrienne Pelton (NL)	15,380	(10%)	

★ COLORADO ★

At the Front Range of the Rocky Mountains, Colorado is also at the front edge of economic, cultural and political change. Colorado is an island of 4.3 million people surrounded by the sea of the Great Plains and the ramparts of the Rockies. With vistas of vast emptiness, it is mostly an urban state: More than half its people live in metropolitan Denver and four-fifths in the urban strip paralleling the Front Range, where the Rockies rise suddenly from the mile-high plateau. And its very ruggedness is inviting more settlement: As the eastern plains continue to lose population, the valley-crevices between the mountains are being filled with second-home condominiums and ranchettes. While much of Colorado's positive change has gone unnoticed in the rest of the country, the state came glaringly into the national spotlight in April 1999 when Columbine High School, in the affluent Denver suburb of Littleton, became the site of the deadliest school massacre in the nation's history.

Colorado started off with a boom, with the discovery of gold and silver in the crevasses of the Rockies. Evidence of this mining boom can be seen still in the opera houses and storefronts of Cripple Creek and Central City, Aspen and Telluride, built when Denver was just a village on the creek that is the South Platte River. Then Denver grew, as a meatpacking, banking and manufacturing center, and also as the state capital and regional headquarters of the federal government. Then came the booms of the high-energy-price 1970s, when the Denver skyline sprouted new buildings overlooking the Capitol's golden dome and entrepreneurs built ever more ski resorts and year-round mountain condominiums. Colorado's economy sagged during the long-energy-price 1980s but, based more on telecommunications than energy, boomed again in the 1990s.

The visible signs of this boom are all around—in the skyscrapers of downtown Denver, bearing at various times, the names of Qwest and TCI and other telecommunications and high-tech companies; in the retro Coors Field baseball park set amid Denver's LoDo, where warehouses have been renovated into restaurants and clubs; in the startling architecture of the new Denver International Airport far out in the plains; in the sprawling Denver Tech Center south of the city; in the fast-growing tracts of subdivisions and office parks in Douglas County south of Denver, the second fastest-growing American county in the 1990s. Colorado has attracted well-educated newcomers from around the country, with many from California; by 1998 it had the highest number of high-tech workers per capita of any state and ranked third in venture capital financing per capita. Its economy grew in 1992–98 at 6.6% per year, the fifth highest in the nation; unemployment fell toward the vanishing point. The physical environment—the mountains, the nearby wilderness—has done much to attract people here, but even more important has been the presence of critical mass of entrepreneurial spirit and technological competence. These newcomers tend to be high-tech, family-oriented cultural conservatives: In the 1990s public school enrollment rose 14%, while private school enrollment was up 33% and the number of home-schooled children tripled.

Colorado's waves of growth have changed its politics. The pre-1970s Colorado was politically just a bit more Republican than the nation as a whole, with cautious Democrats alternating in office with conventionally conservative Republicans. But in the 1970s, a wave of liberal newcomers swept the state's politics by calling for slow growth and reached the national stage—slow-growth Governor Dick Lamm, Senator Gary Hart, Congresswoman Patricia Schroeder, Congressman Tim Wirth. Now all of them, though in the prime of life, are out of politics. Democrats held the governorship for years—Lamm until 1986, then Roy Romer until 1998—but Republicans captured the legislature. Romer pushed for higher taxes for education and for regional planning and a light rail system, but was limited by the legislature and by an increasingly conservative electorate. For the new migrants of the 1980s and 1990s have not been liberals looking for an environment to preserve but conservatives looking for an environment in which to prosper. If the spirit of the 1970s newcomers was embodied in Boulder, with its pedestrian mall, outdoor sports shops and vegetarian restaurants, dominated politically by environmentalist liberals, the spirit of the 1990s newcomers is embodied in Colorado Springs, the home of the Air Force Academy and Fort Carson, and dominated politically by religious and family-oriented conservatives—a contrast to environ-

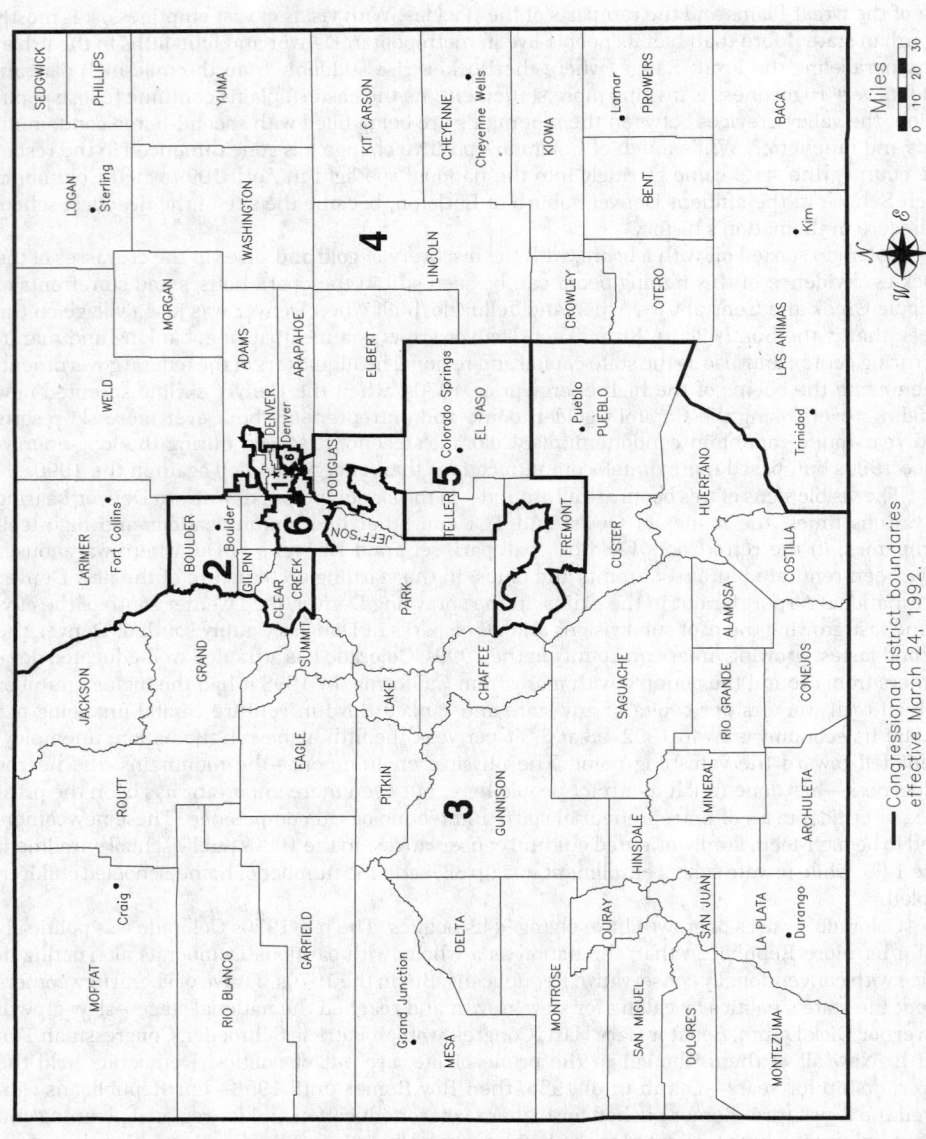

—Congressional district boundaries
effective March 24, 1992.

Copyright © 1993 by Election Data Services, Inc.

ment-conscious and secular Boulder. Just as Boulder's spirit seemed to migrate down the old U.S. 36 to Denver in the 1970s, so Colorado Springs's spirit seemed to surge up the wide Interstate 25, through Douglas County.

The conservatives started to move ahead politically in the early 1990s. They won two big victories by referendum. In 1990 Colorado became one of the first states to pass term limits; in 1992 it passed a measure requiring a popular vote to raise taxes—much to Romer's frustration— and another, later struck down by the U.S. Supreme Court, barring localities from passing gay rights laws. In 1992 Democrats were still competitive in Colorado: Congressman Ben Nighthorse Campbell from the Western Slope was elected to the U.S. Senate and Bill Clinton carried the state, even as Ross Perot won 23%, one of his highest percentages. But after that Republicans surged. They won Campbell's House seat in 1992. In 1995 Campbell switched parties, giving Colorado two Republican senators for the first time since 1972. In 1996 Colorado was one of three states (the others were Montana and Georgia) to switch from Bill Clinton to Bob Dole, and Republican Wayne Allard was elected to the Senate. In 1998 Bill Owens became the first Republican elected governor since 1970, and Republicans controlled both houses of the legislature. In 2000, Colorado seemed conservative enough that it was not targeted by either presidential campaign. It voted 51%–42% for George W. Bush; the central city of Denver (62%–31% for Al Gore) and Boulder County (50%–36% Gore) were outvoted by Colorado Spring's El Paso County (64%–31% Bush) and Douglas County (65%–31% Gore).

Colorado's ebullience and perhaps its conservatism have been tempered by the Columbine massacre. The immediate political response was a demand for gun control, which killed a proposed carry-concealed-weapons law and embarrassed the National Rifle Association which had scheduled its convention in Denver. In 2000 voters did pass a referendum, supported by Owens, requiring background checks for gun sales at gun shows. But they also rejected an initiative which would have required counties to set aside no growth zones subject to approval by voters and only narrowly, 53%–47%, approved an initiative requiring K-12 education spending to rise at inflation plus 1% for 10 years.

Governor Bill Owens grew up in Texas and was appointed a page by Congressman Jim Wright, whom Owens's father had supported in his first victory in 1954. He went to Austin State University, where he demonstrated with a red-white-and-blue armband against anti-Vietnam war demonstrators, and to the University of Texas's Lyndon B. Johnson School, where he was one of the few Republicans during the Watergate scandal. He moved to Colorado and went to work for an oil producers' association. In 1982 he was elected to the state House and in 1988 to the state Senate. There he sponsored a successful charter schools law in 1993 and public school choice in 1994. He opposed Governor Roy Romer's 1% tax for education. He worked for deregulation of taxis, limousines, messengers and off-road charters, and for the three-strikes law. In 1994 he was elected state treasurer.

In the 1998 race to succeed Romer, who was term-limited, Owens was one of two Republicans running. Owens won the party nomination in convention, and went on to win the primary against Senate President Tom Norton, 59%–41%. On the Democratic side Lieutenant Governor Gail Schoettler was opposed by state Senate Minority Leader Mike Feeley, who was endorsed by the AFL-CIO and the Colorado Education Association; she won 53%–45%.

In the general the issues were squarely raised. Owens favored cutting the state income tax and eliminating the property tax on business property like computers and machines; he called for tort reform; he called for holding teachers and students accountable for results, while reducing education regulation; he wanted more emphasis on buses rather than light rail. Schoettler, riding across the state on a Tennessee walking horse named Sam to promote her views, represented continuity with past policies; she had worked for Governor Dick Lamm and then was elected treasurer and lieutenant governor. Schoettler cut into the usual Republican vote among high-earning and high-education voters; Owens depended heavily on the support of the elderly. Romer argued that it would be dangerous to turn over control to "an increasingly conservative legislature and a very conservative governor." It was a close election, but Owens won 49%–48%. Schoettler had a 52%–46% margin in metro Denver, but Owens carried the rest of the state by 51%–46%, including 61%–36% in Colorado Springs and El Paso County.

In his first two years Owens delivered on many of his promises, though not always as some Republicans liked. He backed two big transportation bond referenda, with $1.6 billion to add lanes and widen roads, especially I-25 which could be called the state's main street, and $457 million to quadruple the light rail system in Denver and five suburban counties. Voters rejected transportation initiatives in 1997 and 1998, but in 1999 Owens raised $1.8 million and campaigned with Romer and Denver Mayor Wellington Webb, and the bond proposal passed. To spotlight Colorado's strengths as a high-tech center, Owens created a state Office of Innovation and Technology, headed by investor and onetime Pennsylvania congressional candidate Mark Holtzman, and made trips to Silicon Valley, Austin, Texas, and to meet Bill Gates in Redmond, Washington, to encourage entrepreneurs to locate businesses in Colorado. Owens's greatest crisis in 1999 was, of course, Columbine, to which he responded with much attention and state aid. Later, reflecting on the tragedy, he called for changes in police tactics and longer school hours for teenagers, and said, "Some people are quick to blame it on guns . . . In fact, those two killers broke scores of laws, and one more law—or even a dozen laws—wouldn't have changed the hate that resided so deeply in their hearts. Others might want to blame the parents. After all, how could they not know that their sons were building an arsenal of bombs within their homes? Many of us have wanted to blame violent movies and video games and even Internet sites. However, what all these contributing factors boil down to is the fact that our culture is badly in need of repair and healing."

Owens's major effort in 2000 was education reform. His proposal to expand the use of state assessment tests and to issue letter grades to each school based on performance was loudly opposed by Democrats and the Colorado Education Association, but was passed by the Republican legislature. Owens also secured a large increase in state spending on education, much more than Romer had gotten, and settled a lawsuit over construction in poor districts; he pushed an initiative to spend $50 million a year on math and science. Owens opposed a November ballot proposition to require inflation plus 1% increases in state education spending for schools, but it passed anyway. In 2001 he sought more money for school construction and more Read to Achieve literacy program grants. Owens failed to get the legislature to pass a law requiring background checks for sales at gun shows, but it passed in initiative form in November.

Owens has achieved notice in other ways. Lieutenant Governor Joe Rogers feuded with him when Owens sought background checks of office employees; they patched things up in a meeting in October 1999. In October 1999 Owens said the parents of murdered Jon Benet Ramsey should stop hiding behind their lawyers and return to Colorado; in March 2000 he said, "The focus in this case is really on Patsy Ramsey." He criticized Clinton administration federal lands policies and called off negotiations on a federal land swap after Clinton without local input created the Canyons of the Ancients National Monument in June 2000. He endorsed and campaigned for George W. Bush. Owens comes up for re-election in 2002.

Cook's Call   *Safe.* Owens has been forced to deal with more than his share of crises in his first term—the school shootings in Columbine, in particular—but has handled them well and has not suffered politically. He is not likely to get a top-tier challenger (there is more interest in taking on Senator Wayne Allard) and the only Democrat said to be seriously looking at the race is businessman Rollie Heath, whose wife was the party's 1990 Senate nominee.

Senior Senator   Ben Nighthorse Campbell is the only Native American Indian in the Senate—only the eighth to serve in Congress, and a former Democrat who switched to the Republican Party in March 1995. He is a distinctive figure, with his neck scarves and his pony tail, Western-cut sport coats and Levi's Sta Prest pants, riding a motorcycle (he owns eight of them) as he did in a parade at the 1996 Republican National Convention, or riding a horse wearing full Indian headdress as he did at the 1993 Presidential Inaugural Parade. He worked his way through college driving trucks, and renewed his trucker's license in time to truck in the 2000 Capitol Christmas tree. Campbell had a rough early life; he was placed in an orphanage, dropped out of high school, joined the Air Force and served in Korea. He studied judo for four years in Japan and was captain of the 1964 U.S. Olympic judo team and carried the American flag in the opening ceremonies. He settled not in a trendy ski resort but in the small town of Ignacio, on the plain below Durango, near the New Mexico border, where he bred horses and built a successful jewelry-making business. He is a member of the Northern Cheyenne tribe and attends tribal ceremonies in Montana.

Campbell got into politics serendipitously. One day in 1982 his plane was grounded and he attended a Democratic Party meeting for a friend being nominated for sheriff; Campbell spoke briefly and was soon drafted to run for the legislature. He spent $13,000 of his own money and won. In 1986 he ran for Congress and beat a Republican incumbent who had personal financial problems. In the House he had a moderate record, showing more interest in economic growth than in preserving the environment. In 1992, when Tim Wirth retired from the Senate, Campbell plunged into the race. In the primary he faced former Governor Dick Lamm, environmentalist and opponent of immigration, who once said the terminally ill have a "duty to die." Campbell, with backing from the Western Slope and other non-upscale areas, beat the Denver-based Lamm 46%–36%. In the general election Campbell faced former state Senator Terry Considine, who started the national term limits movement in Colorado. In the weeks before his election, Campbell kept with him a ceremonial eagle feather tuft and Northern Cheyennes held a series of ritual ceremonies and prayer meetings on his behalf. As Bill Clinton was carrying Colorado, and with support from the active Colorado Perot organization, and with the help of his moderate record, Campbell won 52%–43%.

In the Senate, Campbell criticized Clinton's stands on grazing fees and Mining Act revision. Then, in March 1995, the day after the balanced budget amendment failed in the Senate by one vote, he switched parties. He acted partly out of irritation with Denver area liberals, for their environmental stands and also maybe their penchant for reform: He was upset when he was denied an exemption from congressional income limits on his jewelry making, even though book royalties and investment income is exempted. As a Republican, he switched on some issues—the partial-birth abortion ban, oil-drilling in the Arctic National Wildlife Reserve, the assault weapons ban. But he continued to support labor unions' positions on many issues, and his voting record on economic and cultural issues has been near the middle of the Senate.

From his seat on the Indian Affairs Committee, Campbell co-sponsored the 1989 law authorizing the National Museum of the American Indian on the Mall in Washington, and in 1999 broke ground for the building. But he insists that "I'm Colorado's senator, not the Indian senator-at-large," and opposes changing the name of Columbus Day. He has loudly denounced the Interior and Treasury Departments' handling of trust accounts for 200 tribes and 300,000 Indians and charges that the government is unable to account for $2.5 billion due Indians over the years. "The record of the United States is shameful and the destruction of [162 boxes of documents by the Treasury] is just the latest shameless development." He opposed attempts to waive tribes' sovereign immunity from civil litigation and to means-test assistance to tribes, and he wants tribes to be able to consolidate land which has been fractionalized by inheritances. He wants to have Indian nickels minted again, in Denver, and has called for a memorial at the site of the 1864 Sand Creek massacre in Colorado.

Campbell has been criticized for his work to create an Animas-LaPlata water project in his home area. This, the last major western dam under consideration, has been scaled back and has been repackaged as an attempt to settle the water rights claims for the Southern Ute tribe. Environmentalists charged him with ethics violations because, the Pine River Irrigation District, in which as a rancher he owns shares, would receive water under a bill he sponsored. In 1999 the Senate Ethics Committee found "no technical violation . . . which would require disciplinary action," but added "the committee strongly agrees with Senator Campbell's decision not to reintroduce this legislation." He was criticized again in October 2000 when he amended the Utes bill to require that three-quarters of the tribe's cash settlement be spent in partnership with neighboring non-Indian communities on water projects, even though the tribe had no objection.

On other issues Campbell voted in February 2000 against temporary storage of nuclear waste in Nevada because it would have to be transported, dangerously he thought, through Colorado. That same month he called on the Capitol Police to buy more American-made motorcycles. "These little foreign bikes, they break down and look like junk." He cast a critical vote in July 2000 against a bill to spend $3 billion in offshore oil revenues to buy public land. He voted against Permanent Normal Trade Relations with China in September 2000. "I think it is wrong to reward a country that steals our nuclear secrets and sells them to our enemies, that puts priests in prison and puts children to work in factories making sneakers." He was enraged when a *Denver Post* columnist attacked him in October 1999 for accepting a $5,000 PAC contribution from a forest products company and supporting clear-cutting in two Colorado national forests, and concluded in an article that "A pimp's a pimp, after all, even if he looks good in a headdress." The paper later apologized.

Campbell was re-elected in 1998, the first Colorado senator to seek re-election since 1984 and the first to have been elected in two different parties since Henry Teller in 1903. It was a little bumpy along the way. Western Slope Congressman Scott McInnis, who believed Campbell would run for governor, had raised $850,000 for a Senate race, and vowed to run anyway; national Republican leaders, eager to protect a party-switcher, persuaded him to withdraw in October 1999. A conservative got 43% against Campbell in the Republican state convention, but national Republicans backed him and he won the primary 71%–29%. Democratic Governor Roy Romer and Congressman David Skaggs both decided not to run, and to retire from office, but Campbell got spirited opposition in the general from Dottie Lamm, wife of his 1992 primary opponent and for 17 years a *Denver Post* columnist. She was opposed by unions and Hispanics put off by her husband's opposition to immigration, and beat lightly-financed state Senator Gil Romero in the Democratic primary by only 58%–42%.

In the general Lamm ran an ingenious ad campaign hitting Campbell for his flip-flops on issues from gay rights to campaign finance reform. She noted his switch on ANWR and his opposition to the tobacco settlement—and the contributions he received from oil and tobacco PACs. Campbell countered with radio ads of a clock repairman discussing Lamm's columns—17 years of potentially controversial material!—with his wife. As he read words questioning organ transplants to seniors and life support for the smallest premature babies, the listener suddenly heard, "Cuckoo, cuckoo." But Lamm carried little more than the liberal base in a state mostly trending conservative—Denver, Boulder, Aspen, Telluride—and not by wide margins. Campbell swamped her in rural areas and in the Denver suburbs, and won 62%–35%. He has pledged to serve no more than three terms.

Junior Senator   Wayne Allard is a Republican senator elected in 1996. He grew up in the northern end of the Front Range, attended veterinary school, and built a veterinary practice in Loveland—a lively business in an area with vast feedlots. In 1982 he was elected to the state Senate, where he succeeded in limiting the length of legislative sessions—so legislators would be more in touch with their constituents, he said. In 1990, when Congressman Hank Brown ran for the Senate, the solidly conservative Allard ran for the House in the 4th District, which covered much of the High Plains and the northern end of the Front Range. Against a former local university president and legislator, Allard barely carried the Front Range, but he won 61% on the conservative High Plains, for a solid 54% victory. He was easily re-elected in 1992 and 1994 and, when Brown retired from the Senate after just one term, Allard ran for the seat.

Allard's voting record was one of the most conservative in the House. He returned more than $1 million in unspent office funds, and sponsored a Citizens Congress Act, to abolish the congressional pension system, require votes on pay raises, ban personal use of frequent flier miles, and ban unsolicited mailings. He moved to de-fund the National Biological Survey in 1994, charging that it leads to misuse of the Endangered Species Act. He sponsored a bill for regulatory relief for the farm credit system and a bill to improve the process of approving drugs for animals, both of which passed.

Allard was scarcely the most prominent candidate going into 1996, but others better known declined to run—former Senator Gary Hart, Governor Roy Romer, former Governor Dick Lamm. His primary opponent, Attorney General Gale Norton—now Bush's Interior secretary, lost in the Supreme Court defending Colorado's anti-gay rights Amendment 2 a month before the June 1996 nominating convention, and her support of abortion rights rankled many Republican activists and voters. With strong support from religious conservatives, Allard led 40%–31% at the convention. With more money, he ran a blitz of ads before the primary, stressing his background as a veterinarian: "Four candidates for the U.S. Senate. Three more lawyers and Wayne Allard." In the

August 13 primary, Norton ran close to even in metro Denver, but Allard took 62% in the rest of the state, and won 57%–43%.

The Democratic nominee was Tom Strickland, law partner of Phil Brownstein, one of the key fundraisers and political insiders in Colorado. Strickland had more money and sophistication, but Allard ended up with more votes. Strickland held fundraisers with Robert Redford and Gloria Steinem and Strickland attacked Allard's "Neanderthal" positions on the environment; Allard said he was interested in "sound science" rather than emotional appeals, more local decision-making and less bureaucracy. Allard went on to run ads attacking Strickland for defending clients with environmental problems, including one company trying to build a medical waste incinerator in a poor Denver neighborhood. Allard won 51%–46%, trailing only narrowly in metro Denver (47%–51%) and winning solidly in the rest of the state (56%–41%).

Allard has had a very conservative voting record in the Senate and has often been part of small minorities taking conservative stands—on the Chemical Weapons convention and the May 1997 budget deal, for instance. He has tried to attach to appropriations his proposal to pay down the national debt at $12 billion a year, with varying success. In May 1999, in the wake of Columbine, an Allard amendment allowing display of crosses and other religious symbols on public property after school shootings was passed 85–13. In October 1999 he blocked a federal judge nominee chosen by a selection committee headed by Denver Congresswoman Diana DeGette; he pointed out that the Democratic state attorney general supported another candidate. On the Strategic Subcommittee of Armed Services, Allard has worked to develop low-yield nuclear weapons that can burrow into the ground and destroy hardened target and to create a space-based radar capability—defense in inner space and outer space. In September 2000 he criticized George W. Bush's call for reducing U.S. nuclear arsenals. Allard was appointed to the Agriculture Committee in 2000, where he spent six years as a House member.

Allard gets low ratings from national environmental grounds, but has done much work on his own environmental causes. He pushed successfully to ban aircraft flights over Rocky Mountain National Park. He supported the 3d District's Scott McInnis' proposal to make the Great Sand Dunes in the San Luis Valley into a national park and to authorize the government to purchase the adjacent Baca Ranch, whose owners threatened to sell water to Front Range users. With 2d District Democrat Mark Udall, he has called for the Rocky Mountain Flats, site of a much-polluted nuclear plant closed in 1989 and scheduled to be cleaned up by 2006, to become a national wildlife refuge; this was modeled on his action as a House member, when he joined with Democrat Patricia Schroeder to make the Rocky Mountain Arsenal site a wildlife refuge. He successfully obtained designation of the Spanish Peaks as a wilderness area and succeeded in getting the Fort Lyon Veterans' Medical Center transferred to the state government for use as a prison. When EPA's ombudsman was barred access to EPA employees while investigating the Shattuck Superfund site in Denver in 1999, he called for making the ombudsman entirely independent. He voted in February 2000 for shipping nuclear waste to Nevada, arguing that too much waste was remaining on-site in Colorado.

One of Allard's most interesting proposals is a ban on the interstate shipment of birds for cockfighting. He explains: "I'm a veterinarian. I've never supported the idea of animal fighting. My training is not to encourage that kind of treatment of animals with no purpose other than fighting." By summer 2000 Allard had rounded up 56 senators and 188 congressmen as cosponsors; cockfighting is illegal in every state but Louisiana, Oklahoma, and New Mexico. But he has had trouble getting the measure to the floor of the Senate and former Senators Bennett Johnston and Steven Symms have been lobbying against it in the House.

Allard promised in 1996 to hold town meetings in all 63 counties every year, and in his first four years he kept that promise. In 2000 he even added a town meeting in Broomfield, near Boulder, which was scheduled to become a separate county in November 2001. Allard comes up for re-election in 2002, and as a Republican in an increasingly Republican state seems likely to start as the favorite to win.

Cook's Call   *Potentially Competitive.* Despite holding more than 500 town meetings since winning the seat, Allard enters his first re-election campaign unusually undefined in the minds of those outside his old 4th Congressional District of the Front Range. Congressman Mark

Udall and former U.S. Attorney and 1996 Senate nominee Tom Strickland are looking at the race. Either could give Allard a credible contest, but the uncontroversial incumbent starts as the favorite.

Presidential politics   Colorado was a three-way battleground in the 1992 presidential race, a two-way battleground in 1996, and not much of a battleground at all in 2000.

Colorado has had an early March presidential primary since 1992, when it was won by Jerry Brown; now mayor of Oakland, California. The 2000 primary came just after Super Tuesday, which ended the campaigns of Bill Bradley and John McCain.

Congressional districting   Colorado gained a House seat from the 2000 Census, as it did from the Censuses of 1970 and 1980. Republicans would have had total control had they not lost, by one seat, their margin in the state Senate in 2000. Demographically, however, the likelihood is that the new seat will be created in the fast-growing Denver suburbs, which are heavily Republican; one possible and oft-mentioned candidate is former Denver Broncos quarterback and now car dealer John Elway. In return Senate Democrats may seek to make Mark Udall's 2d District seat more safely Democratic.

THE PEOPLE: Pop. 2000: 4,301,261; Pop. 1990: 3,294,394, up 30.6% 1990–2000. 1.5% of U.S. total, 24th largest; 82.8% White, 3.8% Black, 2.2% Asian, 1% Amer. Indian, 0.1% Hawaiian, 2.8% Two+ races, 7.2% Other; 17.1% Hispanic Origin. 2.7% Unemployment. 2000 Voting age pop.: 3,200,466. 2000 Turnout: 1,741,368; 54% of VAP. Registered voters (2000): 2,883,948; 863,749 D (30%), 1,022,019 R (35%), 998,189 unaffiliated and minor parties (35%).

POLITICAL LINEUP: Governor, Bill Owens (R); Lt. Gov., Joe Rogers (R); Secy. of State, Donetta Davidson (D); Atty. Gen., Ken Salazar (D); Treasurer, Mike Coffman (R); State Senate, 35 (18 D, 17 R); Senate Pres. Pro Tempore, Ed Perlmutter (D); Senate President, Stan Matsunaki (D); Majority Leader, Bill Thiebaut (D); State House, 65 (27 D, 38 R); House Speaker, Doug Dean (R). Senators, Ben Nighthorse Campbell (R) and Wayne Allard (R). Representatives, 6 (2 D, 4 R).

ELECTIONS DIVISION: 303-894-2680; **FILING DEADLINE FOR U.S. CONGRESS:** TBA.

2000 Presidential Vote

Bush (R)	883,748	(51%)
Gore (D)	738,227	(42%)
Nader (Green)	91,434	(5%)
Others	27,959	(2%)

1996 Presidential Vote

Dole (R)	691,846	(46%)
Clinton (D)	671,150	(44%)
Perot (I)	99,628	(7%)
Others	45,646	(3%)

2000 Republican Presidential Primary

Bush (R)	116,897	(65%)
McCain (R)	48,996	(27%)
Keyes (R)	11,871	(7%)

2000 Democratic Presidential Primary

Gore (D)	63,384	(75%)
Bradley (D)	20,663	(24%)
Other	821	(1%)

Gov. Bill Owens (R)

Elected 1998, term expires Jan. 2003, 1st term; b. Oct. 22, 1950, Ft. Worth, TX; home, Aurora; Austin St. U., B.S. 1973; U. of TX, M.P.A. 1975; Catholic; married (Frances).

Elected Office: CO House of Reps., 1982–88; CO Senate, 1988–94; CO Treasurer, 1994–98.

Professional Career: Consultant, Touche Ross & Co., 1975–77; Project Mgr., Gates Corp., 1977–80, Assoc. Dir., 1980–82; Exec. Dir., CO trade assn., 1982–95.

Office: 136 State Capitol, Denver, 80203, 303-866-2471; Fax: 303-866-2003; Web site: www.state.co.us.

Election Results

1998 general	Bill Owens (R)	648,202	(49%)
	Gail Schoettler (D)	639,905	(48%)
	Others	33,200	(3%)
1998 primary	Bill Owens (R)	126,613	(59%)
	Tom Norton (R)	87,269	(41%)
1994 general	Roy Romer (D)	619,205	(55%)
	Bruce Benson (R)	432,042	(39%)
	Others	65,060	(6%)

Sen. Ben Nighthorse Campbell (R)

Elected 1992, seat up 2004, 2d term; b. Apr. 13, 1933, Auburn, CA; home, Ignacio; San Jose St. U., B.A. 1957, Meiji U., Japan, 1960–64; no religious affiliation; married (Linda).

Military Career: Air Force, 1951–53 (Korea).

Elected Office: CO House of Reps., 1982–86; U.S. House of Reps, 1986–92.

Professional Career: Rancher; Horse trainer; Jewelry designer.

DC Office: 380 RSOB, 20510, 202-224-5852; Fax: 202-224-1933; Web site: www.senate.gov/~campbell.

State Offices: Colorado Springs, 719-636-9092; Ft. Collins, 970-224-1909; Grand Junction, 970-241-6631; Greenwood Village, 303-843-4100; Pueblo, 719-542-6987.

Committees: *Appropriations*: Commerce, Justice, State & Judiciary; Foreign Operations; Interior; Transportation; Treasury & General Government (RMM). *Energy & Natural Resources*: Energy Research, Development, Production & Regulation; National Parks, Historic Preservation & Recreation; Water & Power. *Environment & Public Works*: Clean Air, Wetlands, Private Property & Nuclear Safety; Fisheries, Wildlife & Water. *Indian Affairs* (Vice Chmn.). *Veterans' Affairs*.

Group Ratings

	ADA	ACLU	AFS	LCV	CON	ITIC	NTU	COC	ACU	NTLC	CHC
2000	5	43	16	14	11	78	74	84	96	94	77
1999	15	—	0	0	8	—	72	94	88	—	—

National Journal Ratings

	1999 LIB —	1999 CONS		2000 LIB —	2000 CONS
Economic	43%	—	56%	41% —	57%
Social	34%	—	64%	33% —	66%
Foreign	23%	—	67%	17% —	75%

Key Votes of the 106th Congress

1. Educ. Savings Accts.	Y	5. Review Movie Violence	Y	9. NATO War in Serbia	N
2. Prescrip. Drug Benefit	N	6. Gun Show Bckgrnd. Checks	N	10. Table Cuba Travel Ban	Y
3. Delay Ergonomic Standards	Y	7. Ban Part.-Birth Abortion	Y	11. Nuclear Test-Ban Treaty	N
4. Phase Out Estate Tax	Y	8. Broaden Hate Crimes List	N	12. Perm. Trade with China	N

Election Results

1998 general	Ben Nighthorse Campbell (R)	829,370	(62%)	($3,045,982)
	Dottie Lamm (D)	464,754	(35%)	($1,818,801)
	Others	33,111	(3%)	
1998 primary	Ben Nighthorse Campbell (R)	154,702	(71%)	
	Bill Eggert (R)	64,347	(29%)	
1992 general	Ben Nighthorse Campbell (D)	803,725	(52%)	($1,561,347)
	Terry Considine (R)	662,893	(43%)	($2,215,791)
	Others	85,671	(6%)	

Sen. Wayne Allard (R)

Elected 1996, seat up 2002, 1st term; b. Dec. 2, 1943, Fort Collins; home, Loveland; CO St. U., D.V.M. 1968; Protestant; married (Joan).

Elected Office: CO Senate, 1982–90; US House of Reps., 1990–96.

Professional Career: Veterinarian, 1968–present; Loveland City Health Officer, 1970–78; Owner, Allard Animal Hosp., 1970–90.

DC Office: 525 DSOB, 20510, 202-224-5941; Fax: 202-224-6471; Web site: www.senate.gov/~allard.

State Offices: Colorado Springs, 719-634-6071; Englewood, 303-220-7414; Grand Junction, 970-245-9553; Greeley, 970-351-7582; Pueblo, 719-545-9751.

Committees: *Agriculture, Nutrition & Forestry*: Forestry, Conservation & Rural Revitalization; Research, Nutrition & General Legislation. *Armed Services*: Emerging Threats & Capabilities; Personnel; Strategic Forces (RMM). *Banking, Housing & Urban Affairs*: Financial Institutions; Housing & Transportation (RMM); Securities & Investment. *Budget.*

Group Ratings

	ADA	ACLU	AFS	LCV	CON	ITIC	NTU	COC	ACU	NTLC	CHC
2000	0	14	0	0	11	100	84	93	100	100	100
1999	0	—	0	0	87	—	84	100	95	—	—

National Journal Ratings

	1999 LIB —	1999 CONS	2000 LIB —	2000 CONS
Economic	0%	83%	14%	75%
Social	6%	93%	0%	90%
Foreign	10%	84%	5%	86%

Key Votes of the 106th Congress

1. Educ. Savings Accts.	Y	5. Review Movie Violence	Y	9. NATO War in Serbia	N
2. Prescrip. Drug Benefit	N	6. Gun Show Bckgrnd. Checks	N	10. Table Cuba Travel Ban	Y
3. Delay Ergonomic Standards	Y	7. Ban Part.-Birth Abortion	Y	11. Nuclear Test-Ban Treaty	N
4. Phase Out Estate Tax	Y	8. Broaden Hate Crimes List	N	12. Perm. Trade with China	Y

Election Results

1996 general	Wayne Allard (R)	750,325	(51%)	($2,233,429)
	Tom Strickland (D)	677,600	(46%)	($2,894,916)
	Others	41,686	(3%)	
1996 primary	Wayne Allard (R)	115,064	(57%)	
	Gale Norton (R)	87,394	(43%)	
1990 general	Hank Brown (R)	569,048	(56%)	($3,684,020)
	Josie Heath (D)	425,746	(42%)	($1,943,422)

FIRST DISTRICT

The mile high city: one mile above sea level (as the plaque on the 14th step of the gold-domed Capitol reads), a few miles from where the High Plains yield to the sharp peaks of the Front Range of the Rockies, on no historic trade route and with a fresh water supply adequate for a town one-tenth of its size, stands the great metropolitan center of Denver. With 2.4 million people, it has been the economic and cultural capital for 100 years of the whole Rocky Mountain region. On top of its Old West heritage and early 20th Century elegance, Denver has developed an exuberant postmodern style. The National Western Stock Show held here every year and the LoDo entertainment district redeveloped near the railyards along the South Platte evoke the Old West; the Capitol, the spacious parks, the aspens which line so many streets, give the city a lush, burnished air, in contrast to the dry high plains and the stark Rocky peaks. Amid its downtown grid, slanted on a 45-degree angle to align with the South Platte and the railroads, are the skyscrapers of the 1970s energy and 1990s high-tech booms, plus the new-old Coors Stadium and Elitch Gardens amusement park. Denver has not lost population as many central cities have, and most of its neighborhoods have vitality, including the black neighborhoods of northeastern Denver, filled with well-maintained 1950s bungalows, and the Hispanic quarter northwest of downtown. But three-quarters of the metro area's people now live in the suburbs, and Denver has disproportionate numbers of singles and cultural liberals who value an urban lifestyle, in the gentrified areas south of the Capitol and the rich neighborhood where the Tattered Cover, among the nation's premier independent book stores, sits opposite posh Cherry Creek Shopping Center.

Denver increasingly is the liberal heart of Colorado, heavily Democratic as the state mostly votes Republican, strongly liberation-minded on cultural issues, cautiously liberal on economic issues. Though it remains majority white Anglo, it has elected Hispanic and black mayors since 1983—Federico Pena, who became Bill Clinton's Transportation and then Energy secretary, and the current incumbent Wellington Webb. In the early 1970s Denver liberals were hostile to growth and boosterism; today's Denver has shown that growth can improve a city. Twenty years ago Denver's winters were palled by "brown cloud" air pollution. But the city has cut down on wood fires and used non-polluting de-icing agents and oxygenated gasoline, and now boasts of brown-cloudless winters. From Cherry Creek to LoDo, Denver has shown that growth can produce more of the distinctiveness that people here like. The civic pride is rampant: At the start of the 21st Century, boosters noted that Denver was ranked among the nation's top 10 cities in its business climate, livability, libraries, and bikeways. The down side can be seen if you are stalled in traffic on I-25 and its horrendous interchange with I-70.

The 1st Congressional District of Colorado includes all of Denver and extends northeast toward Denver International Airport, taking in Commerce City and the northern part of Aurora, places with warehouses and trucking terminals on main streets and curved-street subdivisions behind. This is a heavily Democratic district, including most of metro Denver's blacks and Hispanics, singles and gays: The percentage of households with married couples and children is among the lowest in America. In an era when cultural attitudes are a better clue to voting behavior than economic status, this once politically marginal area has become a solidly Democratic constituency.

The congresswoman from the 1st District is Diana DeGette, a Democrat elected in 1996. DeGette is a fourth-generation Denverite who went away to law school and returned to practice employment law and became involved in politics. In 1992, at 35, she was elected to the Colorado House, where she was surprisingly productive for a member of the minority. She sponsored a "bubble" bill placing a zone of protection around abortion clinics and their clients, which the Supreme Court upheld in 2000; she developed a Voluntary Cleanup and Redevelopment Act to encourage businesses and citizens to clean up the environment; she passed a bill protecting families of accident victims from being contacted by lawyers within 30 days.

In 1995, Denver Congresswoman Patricia Schroeder announced she was retiring after 24 years in the House; she was a pioneer of the feminist left, who gave serious consideration in 1987 to running for president and whose persistence on the Armed Services Committee helped change the military culture. Today, in a place like Denver, the feminist left is the heart of the Democratic Party (as the religious right is the heart of the Republican Party in Colorado Springs) and DeGette—feminist, organizationally adept and legislatively creative—has become a worthy successor to Schroeder. DeGette has a very liberal voting record; she was disinvited from a Catholic rewards dinner by an archbishop because of her stand on abortion. And she has shown on the Commerce Committee, as she did in Denver, some legislative successes even though in the minority. She has focused especially on health-care issues. One victory was an amendment creating "presumptive eligibility" for Medicaid for poor families with children. The idea is to let hospitals and care-givers initiate the application for government aid, so that they get paid rather than provide their services for free. She won House passage of an amendment to ensure that organ-transplant legislation recognizes the needs of children; the House passed the controversial measure with bipartisan support. She has worked with Republican John Mica and Democrat Henry Waxman to promote new controls over all human research programs. She also filed legislation to permit Medicare and Medicaid coverage of the cost of smoking-cessation treatments. Separate from her committee work, she angered her labor supporters—but pleased local business groups—by supporting Permanent Normal Trade Relations with China.

DeGette also showed independence in presidential politics. Her endorsement of Bill Bradley early in the 2000 campaign caused unhappiness in what remains of Colorado's Democratic establishment. In November she won 69%–27% over Jesse Thomas, a government affairs worker for the Colorado Access health care plan. DeGette said that her third-term focus will be on health care for children, plus stronger gun controls. Republican redistricters will likely expand the district to include more Democrats from adjacent suburbs.

Cook's Call　*Safe.* Though DeGette will never have trouble holding onto this heavily Democratic Denver-based district in a general election, she may face a competitive 2002 Democratic primary. Already Denver City Council President Ramona Martinez, hoping to take advantage of the growing Hispanic presence in the district (now at about 33%), has indicated that she will challenge DeGette. But, DeGette is pretty well entrenched here and will not be easy to beat.

THE PEOPLE: Pop. 2000: 662,711; Pop. 1990: 549,053, up 20.7% 1990–2000. 64.6% White, 11.3% Black, 2.8% Asian, 1.3% Amer. Indian, 0.1% Hawaiian, 3.9% Two+ races, 16% Other; 33.4% Hispanic Origin.

2000 Presidential Vote			1996 Presidential Vote		
Gore (D)	135,666	(61%)	Clinton (D)	133,032	(61%)
Bush (R)	69,758	(32%)	Dole (R)	66,427	(31%)
Nader (Green)	12,504	(6%)	Perot (I)	10,367	(5%)
Others	3,287	(1%)	Others	7,676	(4%)

Rep. Diana DeGette (D)

Elected 1996, 3d term; b. July 29, 1957, Tachikawa, Japan; home, Denver; CO Col., B.A. 1979, N.Y.U., J.D. 1982; Presbyterian; married (Lino Lipinsky).

Elected Office: CO House of Reps., 1992–96, Asst. Minority Ldr., 1994–95.

Professional Career: Practicing atty., 1982–96.

DC Office: 1530 LHOB 20515, 202-225-4431; Fax: 202-225-5657; Web site: www.house.gov/degette.

District Office: Denver, 303-844-4988.

Committees: *Energy & Commerce* (20th of 26 D): Commerce, Trade & Consumer Protection; Oversight & Investigations; Telecommunications & The Internet.

Group Ratings

	ADA	ACLU	AFS	LCV	CON	ITIC	NTU	COC	ACU	NTLC	CHC
2000	75	86	85	93	58	83	29	47	8	12	0
1999	100	—	100	100	73	—	26	24	0	—	—

National Journal Ratings

	1999 LIB —	1999 CONS		2000 LIB —	2000 CONS
Economic	84%	—	12%	90%	—	10%
Social	83%	—	13%	74%	—	26%
Foreign	74%	—	23%	85%	—	10%

Key Votes of the 106th Congress

1. Patient Bill of Rights	Y	5. Bar RU-486 $ for FDA	N	9. NATO War in Serbia	Y
2. Accelerate Min. Wage	Y	6. Display 10 Commandments	N	10. Perm. Trade with China	Y
3. Strike Ban on Ergo. Stnd.	Y	7. Gun Show Bkgrnd. Checks	Y	11. Debt Relief for 3rd World	Y
4. Ovrd. Estate Tax Veto	N	8. Ban Part.-Birth Abortion	N	12. Drop Cuba Econ. Embargo	Y

Election Results

2000 general	Diana DeGette (D)	141,831	(69%)	($542,495)
	Jesse L. Thomas (R)	56,291	(27%)	($63,514)
	Other	8,312	(4%)	
2000 primary	Diana DeGette (D)	unopposed		
1998 general	Diana DeGette (D)	116,628	(67%)	($775,271)
	Nancy McClanahan (R)	52,452	(30%)	($42,440)
	Others	5,225	(3%)	

SECOND DISTRICT

Nestled right up against the Front Range of the Rockies, Boulder the home of the University of Colorado, is billed by its convention bureau as "a combination of lycra-clad athletes, New Age artists, and thoughtful intellectuals sipping cappuccinos." It was called the nation's number one town for outdoor sports by *Outdoor* magazine, and an "international mecca for people who thrive on physical challenge and risk" by Colorado journalist Clifford May. Boulder, dubbed the "adventure capital of the U.S." is one of the nation's leading centers for bungee jumping, mountain biking, snowshoe running, rock and ice climbing, downhill skiing, land surfing and hot-air ballooning, plus the home of the Buddhist Naropa Institute and the Boulder School of Massage Therapy. All of which is suggested by the terrain: Boulder literally looks up at erose rows of peaks rising to 14,000 feet from a mile-high plain laid out in mile-square grids much farther than the eye can see. Its pedestrian mall lined by kicky restaurants and shops is full of friendly fit people. But not all is happy in this paradise: Boulder is where JonBenet Ramsey was murdered in 1996, and where a police detective charged in 1998 that District Attorney Alex Hunter "effectively crippled" the investigation of the killing.

The 2d Congressional District of Colorado is centered on Boulder. It extends west to some lightly-populated but picturesque Rocky Mountains acreage, including Central City with its new gambling casino, and south to north and northwest of Denver—Arvada, Wheat Ridge, Westminster, Thornton, Northglenn, Broomfield (which will secede from Boulder County in November 2001 to form its own county). Here families of comfortable affluence and struggling finances, of fundamentalist religion and environment-loving liberalism, live in subdivisions with views of the mountains. Greater Boulder has grappled with the effects of commercial and residential "growth management," as development is restricted to just 1% annually and open space is protected by a "blue line" barrier, causing housing prices to soar. The Metro North area is politically marginal while Boulder is heavily Democratic. Overall, this is one of just a few Democratic-leaning districts in the Rocky Mountain states.

The congressman from the 2d District is Mark Udall, a Democrat elected in a close race in 1998. Udall is the son of longtime (1961–91) Arizona Congressman Morris Udall, who ran for president in 1976 and died in December 1998 after a long battle with Parkinson's disease, and the nephew of Stewart Udall, who served in the House before his brother and was Interior secretary from 1961–68. "I can remember the excitement I felt sitting in a corner of Stewart's kitchen listening to my father, Stewart, Bob McNamara, Bobby Kennedy and Justice Douglas talk about the issues of the day and there was a sense of optimism and sense of involvement and sense of meaning," Mark said. He is also a cousin of Oregon Senator Gordon Smith, a Republican, and of New Mexico Congressman Tom Udall, a Democrat also elected in 1998. "Vote for the Udall nearest you," as Mark put it.

Soon after college, Udall moved to Boulder to work for the Colorado Outward Bound School and headed it for 10 years; he is an accomplished mountaineer (though he didn't quite make it to the top of Mount Everest), rock climber and kayaker. In 1996 he ran for the state House, and with his family and ideological connections raised 40% of his money out of state and won. In October 1997, Udall was one of several candidates spurred to run when incumbent Democrat David Skaggs retired. Republicans nominated Bob Greenlee, mayor of Boulder, who put more than $1 million of his own money into his campaign; Udall stressed environmental protection, growth management and education. Greenlee ran well in the suburbs, but even with all his involvement in local government and charities in Boulder, he still lost Boulder County, where nearly half the votes were cast, 56%–41%. That gave Udall a 50%–47% victory; local difficulties in vote-counting—not paid as much national heed in 1998 as in 2000—made it one of the last results announced.

With seats on the Resources and Science Committees and his co-chairmanship of the Renewable Energy Caucus, Udall focused on the West and environmental issues, and was elected Western regional whip by his colleagues. When House Republicans moved legislation in June 2000 to remove as a potential federal wilderness area Utah's San Rafael Swell, Udall sought to restrict the change. In a largely party-line showdown on the House floor, he lost by 1 vote. But its Utah sponsors ultimately agreed to pull their bill from the House floor. The Sierra Club—where his wife works—praised Udall's efforts. His other lands-based efforts have included a proposal to thin forests that are vulnerable to summer fires, and support of a state initiative (defeated in November 2000) to require Colorado municipalities and counties to present growth plans to local voters for their approval.

Udall had a relatively easy re-election in 2000, despite the district's demographic trends. Republican challenger Carolyn Cox, a retired businesswoman, spent $450,000 of her own money and focused on her earlier work for Social Security reform. But national Republicans did not target the district, and Udall won 55%–39%—a significant increase over his 1998 margin. Perhaps his biggest scare was the threat from Green Party candidate Ron Forthofer, a retired professor who echoed Ralph Nader's themes in criticizing Udall for blurring partisan lines; but he ran behind Nader's 12% in Boulder County and got only 4% of the vote. Udall's political future is promising, if uncertain. With Colorado gaining a seat from reapportionment, there was speculation that Republican redistricters might make the seat less Democratic. But Democrats won a one-vote majority in the state Senate, and Republicans might hesitate to strip Democratic areas from this district lest they make adjacent Republican districts more marginal. There has been speculation that Udall might run against Senator Wayne Allard in 2002, but that would be a risky race in much less favorable terrain, and Udall co-sponsored with Allard a proposal to make the Rocky Flats former nuclear plant, now under cleanup, a national wildlife refuge.

Cook's Call   *Competitive.* There is some speculation that Udall will run for the Senate in 2002 and thereby leave open a very competitive district. Heavy growth in the suburbs surrounding Denver and Boulder also mean that redistricting will impact this district. But Democrats are heartened that they won control of the state Senate in 2000, which will help them block what could have been a drastic redraw of the 2nd to the benefit of Republicans. Regardless of what decision Udall ultimately makes, this district, one of the most marginal in the state, could be a competitive one in 2002.

THE PEOPLE: Pop. 2000: 702,336; Pop. 1990: 548,953, up 27.9% 1990–2000. 87.1% White, 1% Black, 3.3% Asian, 0.8% Amer. Indian, 0.1% Hawaiian, 2.5% Two+ races, 5.4% Other; 13.7% Hispanic Origin.

2000 Presidential Vote			1996 Presidential Vote		
Gore (D)	143,142	(48%)	Clinton (D)	127,702	(49%)
Bush (R)	125,221	(42%)	Dole (R)	102,107	(40%)
Nader (Green)	23,349	(8%)	Perot (I)	16,605	(6%)
Others	5,221	(2%)	Others	12,074	(5%)

Rep. Mark Udall (D)

Elected 1998, 2d term; b. July 18, 1950, Tucson, AZ; home, Boulder; Williams Col., B.A. 1972; no religious affiliation; married (Maggie L. Fox).

Elected Office: CO House of Reps., 1996–98.

Professional Career: CO Outward Bound Course Dir., 1975–85, Exec. Dir., 1985–95.

DC Office: 115 CHOB 20515, 202-225-2161; Fax: 202-226-7840; Web site: www.house.gov/markudall.

District Office: Westminster, 305-457-4500.

Committees: *Resources* (18th of 25 D): Forests & Forest Health; National Parks, Recreation & Public Lands. *Science* (13th of 22 D): Environment, Technology and Standards; Space & Aeronautics. *Small Business* (13th of 17 D).

Group Ratings

	ADA	ACLU	AFS	LCV	CON	ITIC	NTU	COC	ACU	NTLC	CHC
2000	85	86	71	100	21	61	30	47	12	9	0
1999	100	—	100	100	82	—	22	28	4	—	—

National Journal Ratings

	1999 LIB	—	1999 CONS		2000 LIB	—	2000 CONS
Economic	75%	—	23%		70%	—	29%
Social	80%	—	19%		74%	—	24%
Foreign	83%	—	16%		80%	—	16%

Key Votes of the 106th Congress

1. Patient Bill of Rights	Y	5. Bar RU-486 $ for FDA	N	9. NATO War in Serbia	Y
2. Accelerate Min. Wage	Y	6. Display 10 Commandments	N	10. Perm. Trade with China	N
3. Strike Ban on Ergo. Stnd.	Y	7. Gun Show Bkgrnd. Checks	Y	11. Debt Relief for 3rd World	Y
4. Ovrd. Estate Tax Veto	N	8. Ban Part.-Birth Abortion	N	12. Drop Cuba Econ. Embargo	Y

Election Results

2000 general	Mark Udall (D)	155,725	(55%)	($1,330,529)
	Carolyn Cox (R)	109,338	(39%)	($512,085)
	Ronald N. Forthofer (Green)	12,398	(4%)	($37,912)
	Other	5,655	(2%)	
2000 primary	Mark Udall (D)	unopposed		
1998 general	Mark Udall (D)	113,946	(50%)	($1,226,580)
	Bob Greenlee (R)	108,385	(47%)	($1,879,887)
	Others	6,111	(3%)	

THIRD DISTRICT

On a clear night from the air they look like tiny mottled veins with small clots here and there, thicker near Denver but never very bright: the lights of the civilization Americans have built on the Western Slope of the Rockies in Colorado. The lights follow the trails of valley roads and mountainside switchbacks; the nodes mark the dozens of little towns built during mining boom years: the gold rush of the 1870s, the uranium boom of the 1950s, the oil shale boomlet of the 1970s. The Western Slope—everything west of the Front Range, with dozens of peaks over 14,000 feet—has always blocked east-west movement; except for mining and now skiing, no one would have followed the Ute Indians and settled here. The miners who tracked gold and silver and lead ores also built Victorian towns with opera houses and gingerbread storefronts in Leadville and Salida in valleys and defiles scarcely accessible to the outside world. Now many of these towns have been restored by ski resort operators and joined by dozens of new condominiums and shopping malls. Cries of overdevelopment have followed, and stimulated different responses. One is extreme: the "Earth Liberation Front" has announced it burned $12 million of Vail's resort expansion facilities "on behalf of the lynx," whose reintroduction to the area began in February 1999. But there is also consensus between former adversaries: Cattlemen and environmentalists are using land trusts to preserve open land in pastures around Steamboat Springs.

The political map of the Western Slope is as diverse as its history. Aspen and Telluride, with Victorian houses and counter-cultural substrata, are liberal and Democratic. Vail and Crested Butte, with contemporary condominiums, formerly Republican, are trending left. (Recent signs of problems in paradise: Aspen has had difficulty finding service-industry workers, and Vail's continuing development plans have raised local objections.) The rough-handed mining area around Grand Junction, where piles of tailings still crackle with radioactivity, and the northwest corner of the state, where people remember the oil shale boom with nostalgia, is hostile to environmentalists and heavily Republican.

The 3d Congressional District of Colorado includes all the Western Slope plus the small industrial city of Pueblo. There, on the banks of the Arkansas River, the Rockefellers built large steel factories before World War I to make barbed wire and rails; now this blue-collar town has attracted new plants from Unisys and B.F. Goodrich. Pueblo is heavily Democratic and so are Hispanic Conejos and Costilla counties just to the south. Hispanic, not Mexican-American: Spanish-speaking people have been living here, as in northern New Mexico, for 350 years. Politically, the 3d District has been moving to the right, voting for Bill Clinton in 1992 but for Bob Dole in 1996 and George W. Bush in 2000—though Al Gore won Pueblo County.

The congressman from the 3d District is Scott McInnis, a Republican elected in 1992, when then-Democratic Congressman Ben Nighthorse Campbell was elected to the Senate. McInnis grew up in Glenwood Springs, in a crevassed valley west of Aspen and Vail, site of a 100-year-old hot springs resort. He worked as a local policeman and went to law school, practiced law and was elected to the legislature in 1982, at 29. Colorado was one of the few states in the 1980s with a Republican legislature, and McInnis became House majority leader in 1990. In 1992 he won the 3d District Republican nomination unopposed; he outworked and outcampaigned Lieutenant Governor Mike Callihan to win 55%–44%.

McInnis has a moderate-to-conservative voting record, with some maverick tendencies; he supports funding for the National Endowment for the Arts and for Denver's light rail, for example. When House managers learned that he and other junior members were sleeping overnight in the House gym to save rental fees, they cracked down—forcing McInnis to bed down in his office during mid-week. He also has followed in the footsteps of members from Henry Gonzalez to Newt Gingrich with frequent late-night "special orders" on the House floor, during which he often speaks for an hour about his party's or his own latest ideas. He has criticized such local sacred cows as the Air Force Academy (for allowing its graduates to cut short their active duty so they can play professional football) and United Airlines (for its poor service in Denver, where it's the dominant carrier). But McInnis has been enough of a party regular to win a coveted Ways and Means Committee seat, where he has advocated repealing the estate tax. He won passage of a significant package of federal lands bills for Colorado, which sought to strike a balance between environmentalists and developers. One dealt with the desert lands of Colorado Canyons and Black Ridge Canyons near Grand Junction. Another was the Great Sand Dunes project near Alamosa, an area whose beauty McInnis describes in poetic terms. The bill also included authorization of the purchase of the adjacent Baca Ranch, whose owners to the dismay of locals wanted to sell water to Front Range users. Colorado colleague Joel Hefley described the area as simply a "pile of sand" and blocked referral of McInnis's bill from the National Parks Subcommittee, where Hefley served; but the resourceful McInnis won Speaker Denny Hastert's support to circumvent the committee, and the House overwhelmingly passed and President Clinton signed the measure. "We've cheapened the title of national park," Hefley stridently objected.

McInnis remains upwardly mobile. His earlier plan to run for the Senate in 1998 was foiled when Campbell dropped plans to run for governor following his 1995 party switch and ran for reelection to the Senate. McInnis grudgingly dropped out under pressure from national Republicans who were eager not to penalize a party-switcher. But his campaign war chest exceeds $1 million in case another statewide opportunity beckons. His focus on lands issues could help him: The *Denver Post* called McInnis "a surprisingly strong conservationist."

McInnis's switch on his 1992 pledge to limit himself to four terms didn't bother his constituents much. He has a zest for getting around the district and for political combat: "I love campaigning. I don't feel good unless I wake up in the morning and know I'm going to have a good fight." In 2000, he was re-elected with 66%–29% against a part-time actor best known for winning an annual donkey race to the top of a local mountain peak.

Cook's Call   *Probably Safe.* McInnis' big wins over the past four cycles are due to a combination of his own strengths and the fact that he has had relatively weak opponents. But the district itself is not as Republican as McInnis' big wins would have you think (Bush took just 53% here in 2000). The state's new seat is expected to be located in the fast growing Denver suburbs, but heavy growth in the Western Slope will have an impact on how this district is shaped after redistricting.

THE PEOPLE: Pop. 2000: 723,533; Pop. 1990: 549,120, up 31.8% 1990–2000. 87.4% White, 0.7% Black, 0.5% Asian, 1.7% Amer. Indian, 0.1% Hawaiian, 2.3% Two+ races, 7.2% Other; 18.9% Hispanic Origin.

2000 Presidential Vote

Bush (R)	165,723	(53%)
Gore (D)	120,779	(39%)
Nader (Green)	19,222	(6%)
Others	4,947	(2%)

1996 Presidential Vote

Dole (R)	122,826	(45%)
Clinton (D)	116,628	(43%)
Perot (I)	23,571	(9%)
Others	8,711	(3%)

Rep. Scott McInnis (R)

Elected 1992, 5th term; b. May 9, 1953, Glenwood Springs; home, Grand Junction; Ft. Lewis Col., B.A. 1975, St. Mary's U., J.D. 1980; Catholic; married (Lori).

Elected Office: CO House of Reps., 1982–92, Majority Ldr., 1990–92.

Professional Career: Glenwood Springs Police Officer, 1976; Practicing atty., 1980–92.

DC Office: 320 CHOB 20515, 202-225-4761; Fax: 202-226-0622; Web site: www.house.gov/mcinnis.

District Offices: Durango, 970-259-2754; Glenwood Springs, 970-928-0637; Grand Junction, 970-245-7107; Pueblo, 719-543-8200.

Committees: *Resources* (10th of 28 R): Forests & Forest Health (Chmn.). *Ways & Means* (20th of 24 R): Human Resources; Oversight.

Group Ratings

	ADA	ACLU	AFS	LCV	CON	ITIC	NTU	COC	ACU	NTLC	CHC
2000	10	23	0	29	79	100	71	84	95	90	100
1999	20	—	0	13	74	—	67	88	92	—	—

National Journal Ratings

	1999 LIB	—	1999 CONS		2000 LIB	—	2000 CONS
Economic	16%	—	78%		40%	—	60%
Social	19%	—	79%		36%	—	64%
Foreign	10%	—	86%		0%	—	88%

Key Votes of the 106th Congress

1. Patient Bill of Rights	N	5. Bar RU-486 $ for FDA	Y	9. NATO War in Serbia	N
2. Accelerate Min. Wage	N	6. Display 10 Commandments	Y	10. Perm. Trade with China	Y
3. Strike Ban on Ergo. Stnd.	N	7. Gun Show Bkgrnd. Checks	N	11. Debt Relief for 3rd World	N
4. Ovrd. Estate Tax Veto	Y	8. Ban Part.-Birth Abortion	Y	12. Drop Cuba Econ. Embargo	*

Election Results

2000 general	Scott McInnis (R)	....	199,204	(66%)	($545,836)
	Curtis Imrie (D)	....	87,921	(29%)	
	Other	....	15,415	(5%)	
2000 primary	Scott McInnis (R)	....	unopposed		
1998 general	Scott McInnis (R)	....	156,501	(66%)	($410,491)
	Robert Reed Kelley (D)	....	74,479	(31%)	($47,101)
	Others	....	5,673	(2%)	

FOURTH DISTRICT

The High Plains of eastern Colorado are dusty brown, gently rolling grasslands that seem flat but actually slope imperceptibly downward toward the Mississippi River. The land is fertile but dry: Rainfall is rare, the rivers are just a trickle most of the year, and in many places groundwater is equally scarce. It is fine wheat country when irrigated and one of the foremost beef cattle regions. But it has been squeezed in recent decades between declining prices for wheat and declining demand for beef on the one hand, and increased prices for water because of high demand in Denver and along the Front Range on the other. Local farmers are now finding that the value of their water rights to greedy metro Denver far exceeds what they hope to gain by farming, and their neighbors condemn them for selling out and betraying a way of life that seems destined to decline. The prairie lands and small towns of the High Plains have small reminders of their past: the Pawnee National Grasslands, where antelope, coyotes and prairie dogs still roam, and Burlington's 1905 carousel, one of the few with the original paint. But the free market that once peopled the High Plains with farmers and ranchers and made it the scene of farm protests and revolts is now causing it to empty out and revert to untamed land, ready again for now increasingly numerous buffalo.

The 4th Congressional District of Colorado contains almost all of the High Plains plus the medium-sized towns of Greeley, Fort Collins and Loveland—the northern end of the densely populated Front Range. By heritage and usually by inclination, this is Republican territory: It was evenly split in 1992 but later gave solid margins to Bob Dole and George W. Bush. The only Democratic parts are working-class Adams County suburbs north of Denver and Las Animas County on the New Mexico border.

The congressman from the 4th District is Bob Schaffer, a Republican elected in 1996. Schaffer grew up in Cincinnati; after college in Ohio, he moved to Fort Collins and bought and managed rental property. In 1986, at 24, he was elected to the state Senate, where he favored tax cuts, education reform, tougher sentences and welfare reform. A solid conservative, he seized AIDS pamphlets on display at the Capitol in 1993 as unsuitable for children and supported a bill to enable parents to take children out of sex education classes more easily. He sponsored a law to end judicial review of initiatives passed by the voters. In 1994 he ran unsuccessfully for lieutenant governor.

In 1996, when Congressman Wayne Allard ran for the Senate, Schaffer was one of three Republican legislators running for the House. Schaffer portrayed himself as a "true conservative," a gun control opponent whose first priority was balancing the budget. His two opponents both supported limited abortion rights. Schaffer, with support from all over the district, won with 40%. In the general, running against University of Colorado Regent Guy Kelley, Schaffer called for lower taxes on farmers, opening up foreign markets to agricultural exports, and revision of the Endangered Species Act. Kelley accused Schaffer of running on a right-wing agenda undermining public education, abortion rights and gun control. Schaffer won 56%–38%, carrying the Adams County suburbs and losing only two southern counties to Kelley.

In the House, Schaffer was elected president of his freshman class and has made a mostly conservative voting record. "It's far, far more partisan here than in the state legislature," he said. But, he noted, "I didn't come to Washington to make friends with the alligators. I want to help drain the swamp." On taxes, he proposed to eliminate the marriage penalty, exempt small amounts of interest income, institute 100% deductibility for health insurance for the self-employed, expand prepaid tuition programs and exempt family farms and ranches from the estate tax. He sued Bill Clinton in 1997 to stop the American Heritage Rivers Initiative, and lost. Following the House's impeachment vote, he and the 6th District's Tom Tancredo chose not to attend the 1999 State of the Union. Schaffer has taken the lead on behalf of the home school movement and wants to permit parents to move their children from schools that they believe are unsafe. In July 2000, despite liberal objections in floor debate, he won the House's voice-vote approval of his proposal to display the motto "In God We Trust" in public buildings. "Too many American children grow up without adequate knowledge of the impetus that drove our founding fathers to search for freedom."

Schaffer had a vigorous opponent in 1998, a college professor who served as mayor of Fort Collins. Schaffer focused on tax cuts, and won easily 59%–41%, carrying their common home county by 54%–46%. In 2000, he had no major-party opposition. He unexpectedly became the center of controversy following the election, when he publicly second-guessed his earlier pledge to limit himself to six years. Although he said that he had no plans to seek a fourth term in 2002, he said that he was angry for making the pledge when he first sought office. "It was probably the biggest political mistake I ever made," he said. Fellow Coloradoan Scott McInnis suffered no ill effects when he abandoned a similar pledge, and Schaffer may be popular enough to survive if he changes his mind. But several Republicans quickly voiced interest in succeeding him, and former Senator Bill Armstrong, who quit after two terms though he could easily have won, warned that "integrity trumps seniority" if Schaffer wants to continue his political career.

Cook's Call   *Safe.* Over the last ten years, this sprawling eastern Colorado district has been growing rapidly and will need to be altered significantly in redistricting. Since being elected in 1996, Schaffer has had little trouble holding onto this district and Bush won here with 56% in 2000.

THE PEOPLE: Pop. 2000: 748,228; Pop. 1990: 549,216, up 36.2% 1990–2000. 85.9% White, 1.1% Black, 1.4% Asian, 0.9% Amer. Indian, 0.1% Hawaiian, 2.5% Two+ races, 8.2% Other; 18.4% Hispanic Origin.

2000 Presidential Vote

Bush (R)	169,552	(56%)
Gore (D)	112,086	(37%)
Nader (Green)	13,692	(5%)
Others	5,083	(2%)

1996 Presidential Vote

Dole (R)	122,840	(49%)
Clinton (D)	102,355	(41%)
Perot (I)	18,644	(7%)
Others	6,683	(3%)

Rep. Bob Schaffer (R)

Elected 1996, 3d term; b. July 24, 1962, Cincinnati, OH; home, Fort Collins; U. of Dayton, B.A. 1984; Catholic; married (Maureen).

Elected Office: CO Senate, 1986–96.

Professional Career: Legis. Research, OH Senate, 1984–85; Press Secy., CO Senate, 1985–87; Owner, Northern Front Range Mktg. Co., 1989–94.

DC Office: 212 CHOB 20515, 202-225-4676; Fax: 202-225-5870; Web site: www.house.gov/schaffer.

District Offices: Fort Collins, 970-493-9132; Greeley, 970-353-3507; LaJunta, 719-384-7370; Sterling, 970-522-1788.

Committees: *Agriculture* (10th of 27 R): Specialty Crops & Foreign Agriculture Programs. *Education & the Workforce* (13th of 27 R): Education Reform (Vice Chmn.); Select Education. *Resources* (18th of 28 R): National Parks, Recreation & Public Lands.

Group Ratings

	ADA	ACLU	AFS	LCV	CON	ITIC	NTU	COC	ACU	NTLC	CHC
2000	15	29	14	7	88	89	81	84	100	88	93
1999	15	—	0	6	92	—	77	80	100	—	—

National Journal Ratings

	1999 LIB	—	1999 CONS		2000 LIB	—	2000 CONS
Economic	0%	—	84%		28%	—	71%
Social	15%	—	84%		23%	—	74%
Foreign	10%	—	86%		47%	—	51%

Key Votes of the 106th Congress

1. Patient Bill of Rights	N	5. Bar RU-486 $ for FDA	Y	9. NATO War in Serbia	N
2. Accelerate Min. Wage	*	6. Display 10 Commandments	Y	10. Perm. Trade with China	Y
3. Strike Ban on Ergo. Stnd.	N	7. Gun Show Bkgrnd. Checks	N	11. Debt Relief for 3rd World	Y
4. Ovrd. Estate Tax Veto	Y	8. Ban Part.-Birth Abortion	Y	12. Drop Cuba Econ. Embargo	N

Election Results

2000 general	Bob Schaffer (R)	209,078	(79%)	($248,736)
	Dan Sewell Ward (NL)	19,721	(7%)	($4,444)
	Kordon L. Baker (LIB)	19,713	(7%)	
	Leslie J. Hanks (AC)	9,955	(4%)	
	Other	4,539	(2%)	
2000 primary	Bob Schaffer (R)	unopposed		
1998 general	Bob Schaffer (R)	131,318	(59%)	($514,662)
	Susan Kirkpatrick (D)	89,973	(41%)	($291,909)

FIFTH DISTRICT

In 1893 Katherine Lee Bates took the cog railway up from Colorado Springs to the top of 14,110-foot Pikes Peak and, looking out at the purple mountain's majesty above amber waves of grain, wrote the lines of "America the Beautiful." Pike's Peak, espied by Zebulon Pike in 1806, and Colorado Springs, with the Garden of the Gods and the Broadmoor Hotel, have been tourist attractions for more than 100 years. In the second half of the 20th Century, Colorado Springs, safe in the fastness of North America, has also become a great American military fortress, the home of Fort Carson, the site of the Air Force Academy, and, most recently, at Falcon Air Force Base, site of space-based defense research.

Around them Colorado Springs has built a high-tech, innovative economy—"silicon mountain." And with the arrival of Dr. James Dobson's Focus on the Family in 1994 and other Christian organizations, it has been a center of conservative Christianity, the home of Colorado's young conservatism, the counterpoint to Denver's aging liberalism. This was the birthplace of Colorado's anti-tax initiatives and of Amendment 2, which in 1992 repealed city gay rights ordinances but was overturned by the U.S. Supreme Court. More recently, Colorado Springs's conservative activists have had some local opposition; the city even passed a tax increase to fund purchases of open land. But overall, this is one of America's most Republican metropolitan areas: Colorado Spring's El Paso County in 2000 cast more votes than Denver County, and its 64%–31% margin for George W. Bush gave him a bigger popular vote margin than Denver's 62%–31% margin for Al Gore.

Between Colorado Springs and Denver is Douglas County, which until the 1970s was a sparsely-populated patch of the High Plains just east of the Front Range. In the 1990s it has the second fastest-growing county in the United States, as young families move into huge subdivisions around Castle Rock and Parker just south of the Denver Tech Center. This is a high-tech, highly educated, culturally traditional population, even more conservative by most measures than Colorado Springs's El Paso County. Douglas County offered home buyers "the chance to have a semi-rural lifestyle, views of the mountains—and yet be close to work," the *Denver Post* wrote. In 2000 it voted 65 %–31% for George W. Bush. El Paso County and most of Douglas County make up almost all of Colorado's 5th Congressional District, which spreads into a couple of mountain counties as well. This is by any measure Colorado's most Republican district, and one of the nation's.

The congressman from the 5th District is Joel Hefley, a Republican first elected in 1986. Hefley grew up in Oklahoma, and originally came to Colorado seeking work as a cowboy. He moved to Colorado Springs in 1965, became a professional civic leader, and was elected to the legislature in 1976. In the House he has a very conservative voting record. Long before the Contract with America, he called for zeroing out the National Endowment for Democracy, the EDA and the then-Interstate Commerce Commission, issued a Porker of the Week award for greedy colleagues, sought to end unfunded mandates and called for a three-fifths supermajority for tax increases.

Hefley came to Congress just as defense cutbacks were beginning; he now supports increased military spending, and has long been a staunch supporter of missile defense. As chairman of the Armed Services Subcommittee on Military Installations and Facilities, which has jurisdiction over base closings, he opposed the Clinton administration's request for new rounds of closings. Hefley is concerned that the high cost of environmental cleanup of closed bases will impinge on military needs. "To go through another round of base closures, when we are still spending billions of dollars trying to close bases because of the cleanup makes no sense at all," he said. Instead of closing facilities, Hefley has led efforts to privatize housing construction at the bases, with a pilot program at Fort Carson in Colorado Springs.

On other issues, Hefley favors abolishing the IRS and moving to a flat or sales tax. He was one of three Republicans who voted against Bush's budget resolution on May 9, 2001. He has backed a number of other so-far lost causes—blocking the Clinton Administration ban on discrimination against gay federal workers, passing a federal law like Colorado's grant of immunity to polluters who voluntarily disclose their violations, setting a 10-year term for federal judges. But he also has had some successes. In 2000 he enacted his plan encouraging the Park Service to assess filmmakers fees to use the parks. He also won approval of a new Historic Preservation Fund to preserve historic sites and resources. Following the 2000 election, Hefley took up the dubious honor of chairing the Standards of Official Conduct (ethics) Committee.

Hefley essentially won this seat in the 1986 primary and has held it easily ever since. Colorado's gain of a House seat in reapportionment may change the boundaries, but Hefley will surely end up with a safe Colorado Springs-based district.

Cook's Call   *Safe*. This Colorado Springs-based district is the most Republican in the state giving Bush 63% in 2000 and Hefley 83%. It is estimated that this district has grown the fastest of any in the state (it is about 200,000 people over the ideal congressional population). It is conceivable the fast-growing Douglas and Jefferson County portions of this district are peeled off to help create the state's new 7th district.

THE PEOPLE: Pop. 2000: 810,423; Pop. 1990: 549,264, up 47.5% 1990–2000. 85.2% White, 4.8% Black, 2.5% Asian, 0.8% Amer. Indian, 0.2% Hawaiian, 3.1% Two+ races, 3.5% Other; 9.3% Hispanic Origin.

2000 Presidential Vote			1996 Presidential Vote		
Bush (R)	214,261	(63%)	Dole (R)	158,790	(59%)
Gore (D)	107,084	(32%)	Clinton (D)	88,057	(33%)
Nader (Green)	11,209	(3%)	Perot (I)	16,583	(6%)
Others	5,172	(2%)	Others	5,928	(2%)

Rep. Joel Hefley (R)

Elected 1986, 8th term; b. Apr. 18, 1935, Ardmore, OK; home, Colorado Springs; OK Baptist U., B.A. 1957; OK St. U., M.S. 1962; Baptist; married (Lynn).

Elected Office: CO House of Reps., 1976–78; CO Senate, 1978–86.

Professional Career: Exec. Dir., Community Planning & Research Cncl., 1966–86.

DC Office: 2230 RHOB 20515, 202-225-4422; Fax: 202-225-1942.

District Offices: Colorado Springs, 719-520-0055; Englewood, 303-843-0401.

Committees: *Armed Services* (6th of 32 R): Military Installations & Facilities; Military Procurement. *Resources* (7th of 28 R): National Parks, Recreation & Public Lands (Chmn.). *Small Business* (3d of 19 R). *Standards of Official Conduct* (Chmn. of 5 R).

Group Ratings

	ADA	ACLU	AFS	LCV	CON	ITIC	NTU	COC	ACU	NTLC	CHC
2000	10	21	14	21	92	78	74	84	100	100	100
1999	20	—	0	13	91	—	76	79	100	—	—

National Journal Ratings

	1999 LIB —	1999 CONS	2000 LIB —	2000 CONS
Economic	30%	64%	6%	85%
Social	16%	82%	0%	79%
Foreign	3%	92%	12%	78%

Key Votes of the 106th Congress

1. Patient Bill of Rights	Y	5. Bar RU-486 $ for FDA	Y	9. NATO War in Serbia	N
2. Accelerate Min. Wage	N	6. Display 10 Commandments	Y	10. Perm. Trade with China	N
3. Strike Ban on Ergo. Stnd.	N	7. Gun Show Bkgrnd. Checks	N	11. Debt Relief for 3rd World	N
4. Ovrd. Estate Tax Veto	Y	8. Ban Part.-Birth Abortion	Y	12. Drop Cuba Econ. Embargo	N

Election Results

2000 general	Joel Hefley (R)	253,330	(83%)	($127,282)
	Kerry Kantor (LIB)	37,719	(12%)	
	Randy MacKenzie (NL)	15,260	(5%)	
2000 primary	Joel Hefley (R)	unopposed		
1998 general	Joel Hefley (R)	155,790	(73%)	($151,194)
	Ken Alford (D)	55,609	(26%)	($5,422)
	Others	2,871	(1%)	

SIXTH DISTRICT

A generation ago, most people in metro Denver lived in the city itself; at the city limits the tree-shaded sidewalks gave way to the empty High Plains. Today, three-quarters of metro Denver residents live outside the city. Just south of Denver, in Arapahoe County, are the comfortable and affluent suburbs, pioneered in the 1940s and 1950s, of Englewood, Cherry Hills and Littleton; the latter, which has restored its century-old buildings, reveled in its small-town way of life before it became famous as the site in April 1999 of children killing children in the nation's deadliest school massacre. Aurora, to the east, benefited at first from the growth around now-closed Stapleton Airport, but has grown big enough—from 50,000 in 1965 to 258,000 in 2000—to support its own regional mall. West in Jefferson County, which casts more votes than Denver, are Lakewood and Wheat Ridge, creations of the 1960s and 1970s, affluent but not elite suburbs with winding streets and office complexes, including Lakewood's gigantic Denver Federal Center. Up against the Front Range is Golden, the headquarters of Coors beer and the Coors family which funds so many conservative causes, and of the National Renewable Energy Laboratory, which develops solar energy exports.

The 6th Congressional District of Colorado covers most of this suburban territory. This is mostly Republican terrain. The dominant tone is technical and managerial, and many people here yearn for the certainty of traditional limits. They value the environment, but they also see the need for economic growth and scientific innovation—both of which they think liberals tend to underrate.

The congressman from the 6th District is Tom Tancredo, a self-described religious right Republican, who was elected after a turbulent campaign in 1998. Tancredo grew up on the northside of Denver, taught junior high school civics, and in 1976, at 30, was elected to the state House. He was part of a group called "the Crazies," who zeroed out the sales tax on food and utilities, the inheritance tax and the auto safety inspection tax. In 1981 he became head of the regional office of the Education Department; he cut its staff by two-thirds. A lapsed Catholic who began attending an evangelical Presbyterian church in 1990, he became in 1993 head of the Independence Institute, a libertarian think tank in Golden.

After Dan Schaefer, previously the 6th's only congressman, retired in 1998, Tancredo, an energetic and active speaker, jumped into the race. But he was not the only candidate in the primary; four other well-known Republicans ran from across the ideological spectrum. Tancredo campaigned by walking the district and running radio ads the last 10 days; his big break was an endorsement by former Senator (1979–91) Bill Armstrong, a religious conservative who has stayed active in the Denver area. Armstrong's endorsement was worth 5% of the vote, Tancredo said, and he needed it: He led with 25% to 22% for Bill Schroeder, a moderate endorsed by road contractors and home builders. When Democrats nominated 70-year-old businessman Henry Strauss, Tancredo's victory and Strauss's money—he gave his campaign $230,000— gave them hope they might win. Strauss, a refugee from Nazi Germany as a child, attacked Tancredo for opposing minimum wage increases, light rail funding and federal aid to education. Then he ran a TV ad based on a speech Tancredo had given: "Gathering at night to lash out at our government—a militia group with featured speaker, Tom Tancredo. A militia linked to white supremacists and the racist Aryan Nation . . . and called 'dangerous' by the FBI." Then, "Tom Tancredo admits he's met with groups even more extreme than this militia." But Tancredo had spoken to many groups and the "more extreme" groups he mentioned were forums with liberal Denver Congresswoman Patricia Schroeder. The *Rocky Mountain News* called this ad a smear and wrote, "If Strauss really believes this, then he is one of the silliest men in America." Tancredo won comfortably, 56%–42%.

Tancredo got attention from the start. Invited to the White House for a reception for new members, he declined: "I'm not going. I've been to the White House when we had a real president." He also did not attend the 1999 State of the Union address. He introduced legislation during his early weeks to emphasize his conservative roots. Then, the Columbine High School incident reshaped the career of Tancredo, whose home in Littleton is six bocks from Columbine. Gun ownership was prevalent in that working class neighborhood, and he supported the Second Amendment, pointing out that Colorado has stronger gun-control laws than the federal government. "If I had my way, I would take away the evil in man's heart that makes it destructive," he said. But after more than a year in which his hometown had become the symbol for a large national debate led by President Clinton, Tancredo said that he had enough. When District of Columbia delegate Eleanor Holmes Norton said, "The shadow of Columbine [is] hanging over the Congress," he exploded. "I don't know why I think I can ever get near a microphone" without hearing about Columbine, he told the House. "I need no one to remind me how it happened or what happened." He responded legislatively by winning House voice-vote passage to establish school violence hotlines across the nation. He was the only Coloradoan in the House to vote with the National Rifle Association for its gun control package, saying that he wanted something to pass. Later, he made a point of refusing campaign donations from any group in the gun-control debate. Tancredo's other work included leading the fight to require school districts to obtain parents' written permission before admitting students to bilingual education classes. He was the only Coloradoan to oppose opening trade with Cuba.

Tancredo's views and high profile gave national Democrats hopes of winning his seat. Their candidate was Ken Toltz, an Englewood dry-cleaning owner who had been Gary Hart's national finance director in 1984. Toltz said Tancredo's views were out of the mainstream, and he had plenty of money. But Toltz proved to be a weak challenger, and the district decided to move on from its Columbine tragedy. With endorsements from Denver-area newspapers, Tancredo outpolled George W. Bush in the district and won 54%–42%—a slight downtick from his 1998 margin, but an unambiguous victory. Redistricting could reshape this district. Colorado's new 7th seat will likely be created in the Denver suburbs, and while a Republican legislature and governor would certainly protect Tancredo, Democrats gained a one-seat margin in the state Senate in 2000 and so will have a veto on the plan. The speculation is that there will be a new suburban, heavily Republican district ready to elect former Denver Broncos quarterback and prominent car dealer John Elway, a conservative Republican. But Tancredo is likely to find a hospitable district in which to seek the third term, to which he promised in 1998 he would limit himself.

Cook's Call *Potentially Competitive.* Although this suburban Denver district has a Republican edge, it is not overly conservative; Bush only won the district with 51%. Tancredo has toned down his controversial demeanor and looks more settled in this district going into 2002 than he was going into 2000. With a new seat likely to be centered in and on this district, the 6th CD will certainly feel some impact.

THE PEOPLE: Pop. 2000: 654,030; Pop. 1990: 548,788, up 19.2% 1990–2000. 85% White, 4.8% Black, 3% Asian, 0.8% Amer. Indian, 0.1% Hawaiian, 2.7% Two+ races, 3.7% Other; 10.5% Hispanic Origin.

2000 Presidential Vote		
Bush (R)	139,208	(51%)
Gore (D)	119,474	(44%)
Nader (Green)	11,459	(4%)
Others	4,275	(2%)

1996 Presidential Vote		
Dole (R)	118,856	(49%)
Clinton (D)	103,376	(43%)
Perot (I)	13,858	(6%)
Others	4,574	(2%)

Rep. Tom Tancredo (R)

Elected 1998, 2d term; b. Dec. 20, 1945, Denver; home, Littleton; U. of N. CO, B.A. 1968; Presbyterian; married (Jackie).

Elected Office: CO House of Reps., 1976–81.

Professional Career: Jr. high teacher, 1968–81; Regional rep., U.S. Dept. of Education, 1981–93; Pres., Independence Inst., 1993–98.

DC Office: 418 CHOB 20515, 202-225-7882; Fax: 202-226-4623; Web site: www.house.gov/tancredo.

District Office: Littleton, 720-283-9773.

Committees: *Education & the Workforce* (17th of 27 R): Education Reform; Employer-Employee Relations. *International Relations* (18th of 26 R): Africa; International Operations and Human Rights. *Resources* (23d of 28 R): Energy & Mineral Resources; Forests & Forest Health.

Group Ratings

	ADA	ACLU	AFS	LCV	CON	ITIC	NTU	COC	ACU	NTLC	CHC
2000	5	21	14	21	96	75	76	71	96	100	93
1999	10	—	0	13	73	—	73	88	100	—	—

National Journal Ratings

	1999 LIB —	1999 CONS		2000 LIB —	2000 CONS
Economic	0% —	84%		6% —	85%
Social	10% —	85%		30% —	68%
Foreign	10% —	86%		0% —	88%

Key Votes of the 106th Congress

1. Patient Bill of Rights	N	5. Bar RU-486 $ for FDA	Y	9. NATO War in Serbia	N
2. Accelerate Min. Wage	N	6. Display 10 Commandments	Y	10. Perm. Trade with China	N
3. Strike Ban on Ergo. Stnd.	N	7. Gun Show Bkgrnd. Checks	N	11. Debt Relief for 3rd World	N
4. Ovrd. Estate Tax Veto	Y	8. Ban Part.-Birth Abortion	Y	12. Drop Cuba Econ. Embargo	N

Election Results

2000 general	Tom Tancredo (R)	141,410	(54%)	($1,123,854)
	Kenneth A. Toltz (D)	110,568	(42%)	($994,094)
	Other	10,499	(4%)	
2000 primary	Tom Tancredo (R)	unopposed		
1998 general	Tom Tancredo (R)	111,374	(56%)	($527,796)
	Henry L. Strauss (D)	82,662	(42%)	($393,280)
	Others	5,152	(3%)	

★ CONNECTICUT ★

C onnecticut is the nation's highest-income state and quite likely the wealthiest, not through any natural advantage but by virtue of its own pluck. Through most of its history this small chunk of rocky terrain has been isolated and insular, while politically Connecticut has been an odd duck of a state: one of the last to renounce an established church (in 1818) and one of the last to impose an income tax (in 1991), one of the last to back the Federalist Party (1816) and one of the few to vote to re-elect Herbert Hoover (1932). Life here still bears the imprint of the original 17th Century settlers, even though most Connecticut residents today are descendants of Catholic immigrants who arrived here between 1840 and 1924. Connecticut was founded by Puritans who found Massachusetts too lenient and backsliding, and Connecticut Yankees for years have been flintier and more unyielding, more tight-fisted and set in their ways, than their Bay State brethren.

These characteristics have yielded economic advantage. For Connecticut's affluence has come not from any windfall but from a knack for tinkering. In 1831, Alexis de Tocqueville was struck by how this spot on the map gave America "the clock-peddler, the schoolmaster, and the senator. The first gives you time, the second tells you what to do with it, and the third makes your law and civilization." Connecticut made clocks of wood and metal and hats of felt and invented vulcanized rubber; it produced combs, cigars, clocks, silk thread, pins, matches, furniture; it invented and still manufactures Pez candy in Orange, Pepperidge Farm bread and Nivea cream in Norwalk, the Stanley Powerlock tape measure in New Britain and the Wiffle Ball in Shelton. Connecticut—one of the least violent parts of America—has always specialized in arms. The quintessential Connecticut Yankee, Eli Whitney, was the inventor not only of the cotton gin— which may have been the proximate cause of the Civil War—but also of the rifles with inter-changeable parts. Connecticut has been an arms maker ever since Samuel Colt won a War Department contract to manufacture guns for the Mexican-American War; during the Reagan defense buildup of the 1980s it produced Air Force jets and Army helicopters and, in the Electric Boat Shipyard in New London, most of the Navy's nuclear submarines. But it is hostile to guns: The attorney general subpoenaed records from gun companies when Smith & Wesson charged its competitors with harassment after it agreed to voluntary restrictions on selling its guns.

These arms industries, like Connecticut's civilian manufacturers, depend heavily on metic-ulous work. For years, the state was the center of the brass industry, the nation's main producer of precision instruments. Over the last quarter century, manufacturing productivity has risen as output went up 33% while manufacturing jobs declined by 33%. Through decades of immigration Connecticut workers never lost the Yankee knack: Connecticut ranks second in new patents per capita, and a Millken Institute study ranked Connecticut number three among states in its ability to excel in the information economy. Over the years Connecticut has accumulated capital and invested shrewdly, with great skill at assessing risk; it is the home of several of the nation's great insurance companies, and its laws are uniquely friendly to creditors and harsh on bankrupts.

For all its skills Connecticut fell on hard times in the early 1990s. The insurance companies were hit by huge casualty losses and have been downsizing and merging ever since. The end of the Cold War and cuts in defense spending cost Connecticut nearly 150,000 manufacturing jobs, down from a peak of 420,000 in 1982. Connecticut's small central cities—New Haven, Hartford, Bridgeport, Waterbury—have been plagued by crime and have lost manufacturing jobs and people (to the point that Hartford now casts far fewer votes than high-income Stamford). The 1990–91 recession struck hard at wealth by slashing housing values, and growth was retarded by passage in 1991 of a state income tax. Now Connecticut is on the rebound, but its trajectory is a bit different. The state's biggest employer and taxpayer is the Foxwoods Casino, opened in 1992, run by a battery of lawyers and lobbyists and developers working for the 650-member Mashantucket Pequot tribe; Foxwoods says it has generated 41,000 new jobs and $1.2 billion a year to the state economy. Connecticut has the nation's highest per capita income and in December 2000 un-employment fell to 1.5%, the lowest ever. Highways such as I-95, I-91 and I-84 are choked with traffic. Housing values are booming, most spectacularly in wealthy Greenwich, in the state's south-

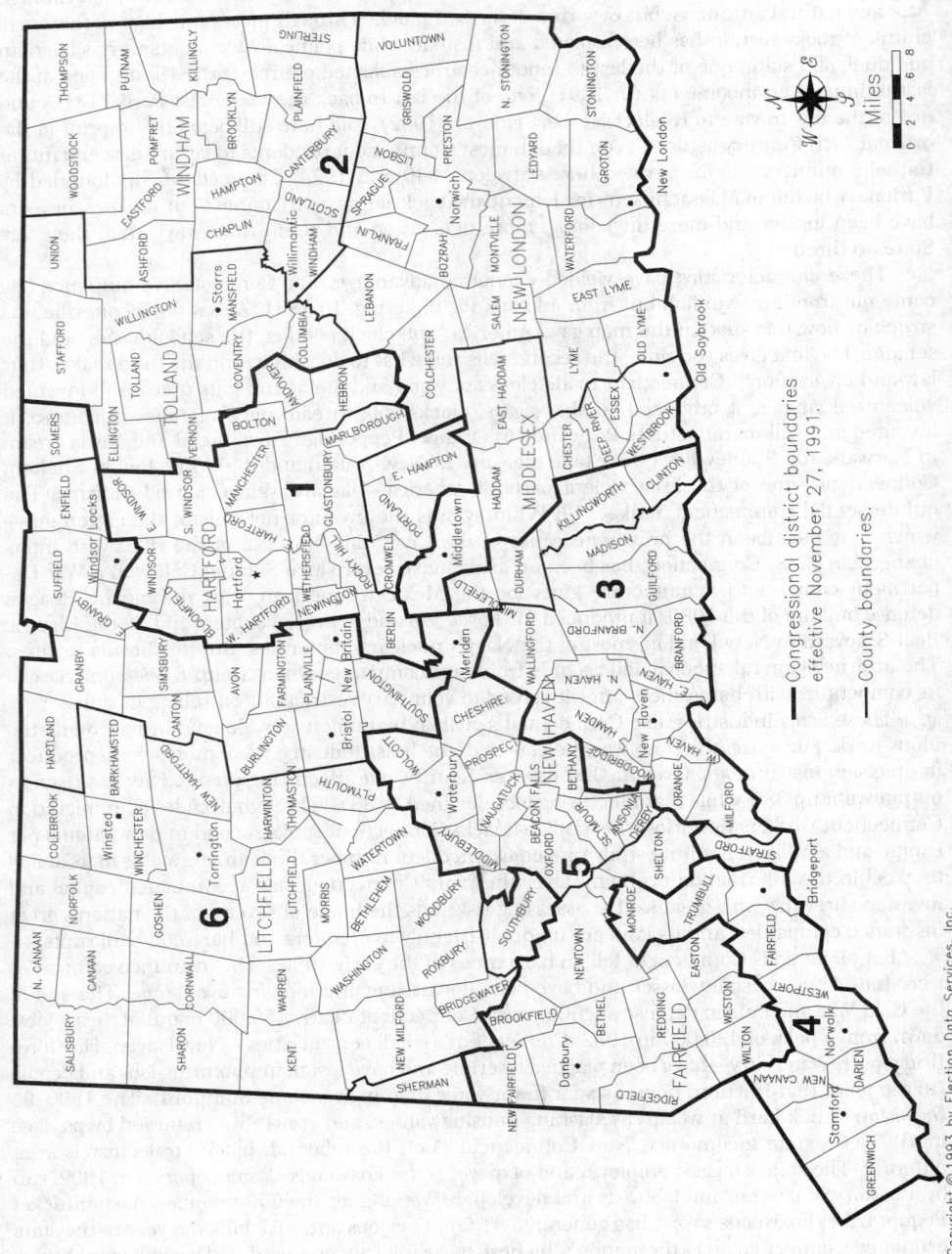

Copyright © 1993 by Election Data Services, Inc.

west corner, and the state income tax has been reduced. There has been an influx of immigrants from Mexico, Peru, the Dominican Republic and other parts of Latin America, who fill jobs others let go begging; Hispanics are now the state's largest minority group. Even wildlife has thrived in an ever-woodsier Connecticut: Deer have become a major pest in southern Connecticut, spreading Lyme disease and eating garden flowers; fishers, small animals that eat cats, rodents and even porcupines, have been returning to the growing-back forests in the north; 50 to 100 bears roam the high-priced terrain of Litchfield County.

For most of the 20th Century, Connecticut politics has been an ethnic struggle between Yankee Republicans and Catholic Democrats. Slowly, as Catholic birthrates exceeded Protestant, Democrats gained ground; their great leader was John Bailey, state Democratic chairman from 1946–75, a master legislative strategist and ticket-balancer, who was one of the first to endorse John Kennedy for president. Traces of the old Protestant-Catholic divide are apparent today in geographic voting patterns, but not much in political rhetoric; splitting tickets is now common in a state where the straight-party lever dominated politics a generation ago. Connecticut voters with their high incomes endure high taxes—the nation's highest, by some measures, including a 32-cent gas tax—but bristle at what they consider the imposition of old moral codes. The rigorous Congregationalism of the Federalists and the censoriousness of mid-20th Century Catholicism are just memories now, and the whiff of political correctness is in the air: In March 2000 *The Hartford Courant*, founded in 1764 and the oldest continuously published newspaper in the United States, apologized for having run ads for sales of slaves from 1765 to 1823.

These days Connecticut is a mostly Democratic state, and in 2000 voters here backed native son Joseph Lieberman twice, voting 63%–34% to re-elect him as U.S. senator and 56%–38% to elect him vice president and, incidentally, Al Gore as president. Democrats ran well ahead among all age groups except the elderly—good news for them in the long term. Senator Christopher Dodd has been re-elected by wide margins. But Republicans sometimes prevail. After independent Governor Lowell Weicker forced through an income tax in the early 1990s, he was replaced by Republican John Rowland, who promises to hold taxes down; Republicans also scored a surprise win against 20-year incumbent Congressman Sam Gejdenson in the 2nd District in 2000.

Governor   John Rowland, in his second term as governor, is a grizzled veteran of Connecticut's political wars, with some scar tissue and muscular strength he didn't have when he started. Rowland grew up in Waterbury, the high-skill factory town with its own tough politics. His family has owned an insurance agency for four generations and his father and grandfather were city comptrollers. He was elected to the state House from a Democratic district, in 1980, at 23, and ran for Congress in 1984, upsetting a Democratic incumbent and becoming the youngest member of the House. He has run for governor in the last three elections, losing with 37% in 1990 (to former Republican Senator Lowell Weicker's 40%) and winning with 36% in 1994 (to Democrat Bill Curry's 33%). Dominating state politics then were issues of spending and taxes. State government spending went up by double-digit percentages yearly in the 1980s, as defense-driven revenues surged in; then the recession hit hard and resulted in huge deficits. Weicker's solution was a 4.5% income tax, enacted in 1991; it was unpopular, and he retired in 1994. Rowland campaigned against the income tax in 1990 and promised to repeal it in 1994.

In his first year as governor, even with a divided legislature, Rowland had surprising success—but he didn't get rid of the income tax. Connecticut passed a "tough love" welfare bill limiting payments to 21 months and encouraging recipients to get a job and work their way up. The income tax was cut marginally. Business taxes were lowered and unemployment and workmen's comp were made more business-friendly. Parents delinquent with child support were denied all state licenses. A new death penalty law and Megan's law to inform communities of released sex offenders were passed. The state workforce was cut by 2,500 and the lottery was privatized. State spending increases were minimal. Although Democrats captured the state Senate in 1996 and held the House throughout, Rowland was able to push through tax cuts every year, as the state's economy revived and revenues rose.

In 1998 Democrats Bill Curry and Bridgeport Mayor Joseph Ganim thought about opposing him, until the field was preempted in September 1997 by 1st District Congresswoman Barbara Kennelly. But her insider political skills didn't translate into campaigning, and voters believed

Rowland when he talked of the Connecticut comeback, and many credited his tax cuts—which now total more than $2 billion—and welfare reform. In fall 1997 and spring 1998 Rowland unveiled proposals for redevelopment of ailing central cities, school construction, state purchase of open space, and a cut of 5,000 state employees. He got reluctant Democrats to approve an income tax rebate, over Kennelly's opposition. He even got a limited school choice program. Borrowing from Bill Clinton's 1995–96 playbook, Rowland in January 1998 started running ads touting his accomplishments. The income tax rebates were sent out in July 1998 with the message, "It's your money. We're giving it back." Rowland surged to big leads in the polls. He was hit for changing positions on issues (abortion in 1990, school vouchers in 1997, the minimum wage and patients suing health insurers in 1998), but that had little impact; neither did ethics charges that he accepted discounted tickets to a Jimmy Buffett concert or that state troopers gave his children state surplus sleeping bags and canteens (he paid a $2,000 fine for the Buffett tickets—ticket scalping). Rowland won by 63%–35%, carrying all but eight of Connecticut's cities and towns.

The first Connecticut governor to win with an absolute majority in 12 years, Rowland faced some setbacks in his second term. He had unveiled a grandiose plan for a riverfront development in Hartford with a convention center, restaurants, hotels and shopping centers, capped by a stadium for the New England Patriots to be financed with $375 million in state bonds; Patriots owner Robert Kraft signed an agreement to move to Hartford. But in April 1999 Kraft, offered a $70 million subsidy to stay in Massachusetts, reneged on the deal. Rowland eventually got a $2.4 million check from the National Football League for Connecticut's out-of-pocket expenses, and the next day announced a scaled-back riverfront project; but city business leaders acknowledged that the loss of the Patriots squashed any hopes for a downtown redevelopment. Another setback came in September 1999, when former state Treasurer Paul Silvester, a Republican appointed by Rowland but defeated in 1998, pleaded guilty to federal charges arising out of a scheme to steer state pension funds to conspiring investment firms in return for campaign contributions. Rowland had attended some of the fundraisers, but an October 2000 indictment of Silvester aides and investment firm executives did not implicate Rowland.

On the defensive, Rowland called in October 1999 for an examination of state election and ethics laws. In May 2000 he vetoed the Democratic legislature's campaign finance bill, which would have provided public financing to state candidates who accepted voluntary limits on spending. But he also had some successes. In 1999 the legislature passed his sales tax rebate. He got a 7-cent cut in the state's 32-cent gas tax. He tried but failed to abolish the office of high sheriff, the last vestige of county government in Connecticut. In January 2001 he called for overhauling the state transportation system, with more cargo flights to Hartford's Bradley International Airport and more river shipping (Hartford for many years was a seaport), for expanding mental health care services and increasing education spending. He nonplussed leaders of both parties by proposing that anyone who got the signatures of 2% of a party's registered members (a small number, since Connecticut has a plurality of independents) can automatically get on the primary ballot; Connecticut pols are used to a system where candidates have to get a certain percentage of the votes at party conventions before getting on the ballot.

In November 2000 Rowland said he would decide within a year whether to run again. The most prominent possible Democratic opponent is Attorney General Richard Blumenthal, but he would have to give up power to serve as governor; he has played a major role in the national tobacco and Microsoft cases. Other possible Democratic candidates include 1995 nominee Bill Curry, who served a stint in the Clinton White House, Bridgeport Mayor Joseph Ganim, state Senator Majority Leader George Jepsen, Secretary of State Susan Bysiewicz and state Controller Nancy Wyman.

Cook's Call   *Potentially Competitive.* Rowland—or any Republican for that matter—can never feel completely safe in a state that appears to be becoming increasingly Democratic. Nevertheless, he seems to be in very good shape for a third term.

Senior Senator   Christopher Dodd was almost born into politics, one of three senators who are sons of senators (Evan Bayh and Bob Bennett are the others). His father Thomas Dodd, a prosecutor at the Nuremberg trials, was elected to the House in 1952, when Chris was eight; he lost a Senate race to Prescott Bush, George Bush's father, in 1956, then won in 1958. Chris

Dodd served in the Peace Corps in the Dominican Republic from 1966–68. In 1967 the older Dodd was censured by the Senate for misuse of funds; he ran as an independent in 1970 and Chris Dodd managed his campaign, in which he finished behind Republican Lowell Weicker and Democrat Joseph Duffey, for whom Yale Law School student Bill Clinton was working as a volunteer. Almost immediately after law school, Christopher Dodd ran for the House in the open-seat eastern Connecticut 2d District and, in the Watergate year of 1974, won comfortably. He was re-elected easily and in 1980 outmaneuvered fellow Watergate Democrat Toby Moffett to get the Democratic nomination to succeed Senator Abraham Ribicoff, and won that race by a wide margin.

Dodd, who speaks fluent Spanish, has often played a role on Latin American issues. On the Western Hemisphere Subcommittee in the 1980s he took the lead in opposing U.S. military aid to El Salvador's government and aid to the Nicaraguan contras. He opposed the process of certifying anti-drug efforts of foreign countries each year, arguing that this causes needless friction with Latin countries, especially Mexico, without helping the anti-drug effort; it was ended in 1997. He has long backed freer travel to and trade with Castro's Cuba. He strongly supported sending 6-year-old Elian Gonzalez back to Cuba, and said that Elian's case would spotlight what he considers the wrongheadedness of isolating Cuba. But he opposed the language in the House Republicans' June 2000 bill on lifting the embargo on food and medicine, which he said would restrict the president's ability to open up travel to Cuba. Dodd threatened a filibuster on the issue, and prevented it from being passed in June 2000 with the aid package that included the Clinton administration's $1 billion-plus Plan Colombia. In October, with some grumbling, he voted for the bill lifting the embargo, which passed by a wide margin. In contrast to his wariness of U.S. military aid in Central America in the 1980s, he supported Plan Colombia, to provide equipment and military training to Colombians fighting the FARC guerrillas. "Whether we like it or not, we are engaged . . . in Colombia," he said. "This is not some distant conflict without any ramifications here at home." He sponsored an amendment to allow the Pentagon and Colombia to decide which helicopters to use; they were expected to favor Connecticut-made Black Hawks, while Congress preferred the less expensive Texas-made Hueys. The amendment failed by a 51–47 vote, and Dodd voted for the full measure.

Dodd worked on the 1990 ABC child care bill, which established Child Care and Development Block Grants, funding for which was sharply increased in 2000. He was the lead sponsor of the Family and Medical Leave Act vetoed by George Bush and signed by Bill Clinton in early 1993—and cited often by Clinton as one of his greatest achievements. With Ohio Republican Mike DeWine, Dodd has worked to promote testing of psychiatric drugs prescribed for young children. They also co-sponsored the Firefighter Investment and Response Enhancement Act of 2000 and got $100 million funding for it; this was the first federal aid program for firefighters, a vivid contrast with the $11 billion of federal aid to police and state and local law enforcement. With Joseph Lieberman Dodd sponsored the bill passed to curtail the use of restraint and seclusion in mental health facilities.

Connecticut, with its big insurance companies, has long been a creditor state, and one leery of trial lawyers. Dodd was the chief Democratic sponsor of the securities litigation bill sought by high-tech companies and fought by trial lawyers. "People shouldn't make a business out of ambulance chasing when a stock simply fluctuates on the market," he said. When Clinton vetoed it, Dodd immediately started lobbying Senate and House Democrats, and both houses in December 1995 voted to override. In 1996 and 1998 he worked with Phil Gramm and Alfonse D'Amato to successfully pass a law barring class-action securities litigation suits from state courts, requiring them to be heard in federal court where the rules are stricter. He was a lead sponsor of the product liability bill vetoed by Clinton in May 1996. He sponsored the Y2K litigation law of 1999, which created a 90-day waiting period before Y2K lawsuits could be brought; the aim was to encourage mitigation of those problems and alternative dispute resolution and to discourage predatory class action suits.

Dodd has a pleasant, friendly manner and seems unfazed by opposition and approaches debates with an affable air, deflating opponents' indignation and suggesting that they are all in this game together. That has served him well when he took the national stage in 1996, though not in the role he first sought or with the encore he might have wished. In November 1994 he launched a quick and nearly successful campaign for Senate Democratic leader after his original choice, Jim Sasser, had been defeated for re-election. After a month-long campaign, Dodd lost to Tom Daschle by just 24–23. Dodd was promptly asked by Bill Clinton to be Democratic National Committee chairman. Dodd performed ably in public debates and set-tos with Republican Chairman Haley Barbour, but was embarrassed in October 1996 when he followed White House orders to stonewall on charges that DNC top-level fundraiser John Huang raised millions in illegal foreign contributions. Dodd plausibly denied that he knew much about Huang, who was placed at the committee personally by Clinton; he was less plausible when he said he never thought the White House coffees, some of which he attended, were fundraisers. Dodd dropped the chairmanship in January 1997, and mostly avoided investigations of the DNC thereafter. In 1998 he seemed genuinely angry with Clinton for carrying on the Lewinsky affair and then lying about it for seven months: "On issues, I've stood up and fought for things and all of a sudden, the idiot throws [the Lewinsky scandal] in the midst of all this." In 2000 he lobbied hard to get his junior colleague Joseph Lieberman nominated for vice president, assuring Jesse Jackson, NEA head Bob Chase, and AFL-CIO President John Sweeney that Lieberman was a good Democrat. Never did he show a sign of jealousy or envy; on the contrary, when Lieberman reached him with the news, while Dodd was at a rest stop on the New Jersey Turnpike, Dodd quipped, "Here I am at this rest stop eating a hamburger and you've got all this Secret Service protection."

Dodd was easily re-elected in 1998. His Republican opponent was Gary Franks, elected congressman in 1990 and defeated in 1996 in the often marginal 5th District, and one of the few black Republicans to serve in Congress. Franks' attacks on Dodd's closeness to Clinton and his attendance record struck no sparks, especially since Franks was outspent by $3 million. In October the *New Haven Register* reported that a lien had been placed on Franks' home in Waterbury; he had several unconvincing explanations, and Dodd actually scolded a reporter for raising the issue. "Why should I vote for you?" a student at Guilford High School asked. "Because I'm a hell of a guy," Dodd replied, with a big smile. He won 65%–32%, carrying all but six of the state's cities and towns. In February 2001 Dodd said he would run for re-election in 2004.

Junior Senator Joseph Lieberman is now a national figure of some eminence after his candidacy for vice president in 2000. He has been admired for some time for his independence of mind, civility of spirit and fidelity to causes in which he believes; and if this reputation was not enhanced by the 2000 campaign, which after all was an inevitably partisan enterprise, it was not badly damaged. Lieberman has always been an intensely political person, balancing a solid allegiance to the Democratic Party with a commitment to intellectual rigor and honesty—a balancing act that is never easy and occasionally impossible. Lieberman grew up in Stamford, the son of a liquor store owner, and was interested in politics early on; he remembers coming home from school at age nine eager to watch the televised Kefauver hearings. He went to Yale College and Yale Law School, became chairman of the *Yale Daily News* and worked summers for Senator Abraham Ribicoff and the Democratic National Committee. His political ambitions were no secret; other students called him "the Senator." In college he wrote an admiring yet revealing biography of that quintessential political boss John Bailey, Connecticut Democratic chairman from 1946–1975. Writing a book that was intellectually honest enough to pass academic scrutiny but tactful enough not to displease a man who could make or break his political career was a challenge, and Lieberman met it. At the same time, he was not afraid to challenge the political establishment. He helped found a reform and antiwar Caucus of Connecticut Democrats; in 1970 he ran for state Senate in New Haven against state Senate Majority Leader Edward Marcus, and won with help from, among others, a Yale Law student volunteer named Bill Clinton. In 1980 he ran for an open House seat and lost 52%–46%; in 1982 he was elected attorney general, where he took action against fake charities, crooked car dealers and gouging merchants.

In 1988 Lieberman challenged Senator Lowell Weicker, another maverick, but of a different sort. Weicker was well to the left of most Republicans on economic and cultural issues, Lieberman more conservative than most Democrats on cultural issues and foreign policy. Lieberman is an Orthodox Jew—he didn't attend the convention that nominated him because it was held on Saturday, and sent in a videotape instead—and a believer that "we in government should look to religion as a partner, as I think the Founders of our country did." He favored the death penalty and a moment of silence in schools, and opposed Weicker's proposed 30-cent gas tax increase. He ran witty ads, one showing a bear sleeping through work—a nice take-off on the growling but erratic Weicker. Lieberman won 50%–49%; the contest cut across party lines, with Lieberman running well in industrial towns and Weicker in Hartford, college towns and tony towns in Litchfield County.

Lieberman has made a distinctive mark in foreign policy. He was one of the leaders in the fight for the Gulf war resolution in January 1991, and without his earnest but vehement support it might not have passed. Presciently, he called for "final victory" over Saddam Hussein. He is a strong supporter of Israel but favored F-15 sales to Saudi Arabia in 1992; in spring 1998 he spoke against an American ultimatum to Israel. He favored U.S. ground troops in Bosnia and action against Bosnian Serb war criminals. He backed NATO expansion in Eastern Europe. In 1998 he successfully led a fight for sanctions to stop Russia from exporting missile technology to Iran. In 1999 hearings, he said there was "a shocking lack of thoroughness, competence and urgency" in government investigations of the leaking of nuclear secrets to China. In 2000 he cast a vote in a closed-door markup in the Armed Services Committee to authorize five new nuclear submarines, a $10 billion commitment of great benefit to Connecticut's Electric Boat.

On economic issues, Lieberman has backed capital gains tax cuts for small business ("you can't be pro-jobs and anti-business") and urged Bill Clinton to sign the 1996 welfare reform bill—both stands opposed by many Democrats. He is a sponsor of Auto Choice reform, which would allow car owners to opt out of pain and suffering damages and get much cheaper insurance premiums. He and the late John Chafee sponsored a bill to give credit to companies that voluntarily reduce emissions of greenhouse gases. He has supported gun-control measures, but worked to get a gun produced by Connecticut-based Colt removed from the 1994 assault weapon ban and voted against making lawsuits against gunmakers non-dischargeable in bankruptcy. With John McCain, he sponsored the 2000 law required tax-exempt Section 527 groups to disclose their contributors. With Rick Santorum, he sponsored a package of incentives for economic development in poor areas that was double the cost of the Clinton-Hastert plan; the Lieberman bill emphasized individual development accounts, on which tax credits would be given banks that match deposits to special savings accounts.

Lieberman has spoken out eloquently on moral issues. In 1995 he joined with *Book of Virtues* author William Bennett and criticized gangsta rap records, and shamed Time Warner into selling their Interscope label; in 1998 they said the purchaser, Seagram, failed to keep its promises to clean up the words, and gave it a Silver Sewer award. In highly publicized Commerce Committee hearings in September 2000 he denounced the marketing of violent movies, music and video games with children. But during that fall campaign, after he attended a Hollywood fundraiser and spoke of being a "noodge" to the industry, Bennett criticized him for abandoning their fight against obscenity and violence. One thing that made Lieberman an attractive running mate for Al Gore was the fact that he was one of the few Democrats who was not a lockstep defender of Bill Clinton. He was dismayed by Clinton's August 17, 1998, speech in which he grudgingly admitted lying about the Lewinsky affair for seven months. When the Senate resumed in September, Lieberman took the floor and said, "Such behavior is . . . wrong and unacceptable and should be followed by some measure of public rebuke and accountablity." But he was persuaded by Senate Minority Leader Tom Daschle not to call for censure, and he stopped well short of backing impeachment or resignation.

Gore's selection of Lieberman as his vice presidential nominee was history-making: He was the first Jew on a major party ticket in American history. Gore knew Lieberman from the Senate, where they were friends—Gore did not have many close personal relationships with colleagues. But two things probably pushed Gore toward his choice: Lieberman's reputation for probity and denunciation of Clinton, which gave the ticket some insulation from the Clinton scandals, and Lieberman's moderate record on many issues and undoubted ability. Another asset proved to be Lieberman's fervent avowals of religious faith and that it has a rightful place in politics; what might have been resented from a Christian conservative seemed attractive coming from an Orthodox Jew. Lieberman was criticized for his faith talk by the Anti-Defamation League; he replied,

"This is really less a matter of programs or legislation than it is of giving respect to the constructive role that faith can play in the lives of individuals and in the lives of the community." Some Democrats criticized him for running for vice president and for re-election as senator at the same time; if he won both, Connecticut's Republican Governor John Rowland could have appointed a Republican replacement.

Overall, Lieberman was clearly an asset to the ticket. His poll ratings were high, and if there was general agreement that Dick Cheney excelled at the October 6 vice presidential debate, Lieberman also performed well; some observers wondered whether the order of the tickets should be reversed. Lieberman's Judaism seems not to have hurt the ticket anywhere, and it probably helped in crucial Florida; he made memorable campaign appearances in heavily Jewish Broward and Palm Beach Counties, which voted nearly 2–1 for Gore (the exact margin, of course, turned out to be in some dispute). But there was some tension between positions Lieberman had taken before August 2000 and what he said during the campaign. He had questioned racial quotas and preferences, and refused to oppose Proposition 209 in California in 1996, which banned racial quotas and preferences by paraphrasing the Civil Rights Act of 1964. Lieberman told the Black Caucus at the Democratic convention, to great applause, that he had voted against abolishing racial setasides in transportation contracts. Lieberman had supported vouchers for students in the failing District of Columbia schools; he told teachers' union leaders that he was for demonstration vouchers, but overall wanted to put money into public schools. He had said that Social Security was headed on a disastrous course and needed an injection of funds from private markets; but in the campaign he said that the transition costs for George W. Bush's plan were too high. Vice presidential candidates always have to defer to presidential nominees, and turn their backs on some positions they have taken; but did Lieberman have to go quite as far as he did? In the Florida controversy, Lieberman took what to some was a surprisingly partisan role—of course this was a quintessentially partisan issue. On Sunday interview shows he said that he and Al Gore would never challenge legitimately cast military absentee ballots. But on the preceding Friday night lawyers working for the Gore-Lieberman ticket did precisely that, and raised their fists in the air in triumph when the military votes were disqualified.

On Election Day, the Gore-Lieberman ticket carried Connecticut 56%–38% and Lieberman was re-elected to the Senate by a 63%–34% margin over Waterbury Mayor Phil Giordano. Governor Rowland tried to keep Giordano from running, on the theory that a contest would only bring out Democratic votes; the result of the race was never in doubt, and Lieberman did not bother to show up at one debate. The margin was a slight downtick from Lieberman's 67%–31% victory in 1994, but his position in Connecticut seems rock-solid. He returned to the Senate as a major national figure. He had been chairman for several years of the moderate Democratic Leadership Council, and in February 2000 helped form a group of moderate Senate Democrats, whose membership swelled to 19 in early 2001. He has the potential to be a major force on bipartisan legislation. The Bush education program was largely modeled on the education bill Lieberman and Evan Bayh introduced in February 2000, which would provide more funding, more local control and more accountability; it was voted down 84–13 in May 2000, but seemed to be the consensus position in 2001. On defense he is a likely partner for new Bush policies. On Social Security, there is some question; will changes in the economic picture persuade him that we can afford to move to individual investment accounts? Lieberman is certainly a strong potential candidate for the presidency in 2004, although he has said he would not run against Al Gore. But he will have to contend, as he has contended throughout his career, mostly successfully, with the challenge of remaining true to his independent beliefs while remaining an effective partisan politician.

Presidential politics   Why does the nation's highest income state vote Democratic for president? Because liberal stands on cultural issues trump the hunger for tax cuts among most of these often cynical voters; because most people here regard themselves as members of ethnic groups with a historic Democratic heritage; because, in 2000, Connecticut's own Joe Lieberman was on the Democratic ticket: The Gore-Lieberman ticket ran well ahead of Clinton-Gore. Over the years Connecticut has oscillated between the parties, moving toward Republicans in the 1970s and 1980s as cultural conflicts split the old Democratic majority, moving toward Democrats in the 1990s in response to the 1990–91 recession and also out of increasing distaste for Southern-accented Republican conservatism. Connecticut had little appetite for either Jimmy Carter or George W. Bush.

Connecticut's presidential primary, though held fairly early in the process, has not been quite early enough and has made little difference. Gary Hart won here in 1984, Jerry Brown in 1992; but they fared no better than the Federalists Connecticut favored in 1816. In 2000 John McCain won here, as elsewhere in New England, and Al Gore beat Bill Bradley by a comparatively close 56%–41%.

Congressional districting   Connecticut has devised a bipartisan process for redistricting. Two Republicans and two Democrats from each house of the legislature meet and try to draw lines; if they are approved by a two-thirds vote in both chambers, they become law. Otherwise, a ninth member is chosen by the other eight, and they try to reach consensus. It worked 10 years ago, when a plan that made minimal changes in the congressional district lines was approved. It will be harder this time, for in the 2000 Census, Connecticut lost one of the six House seats it has had since the 1930 Census. But the potential for a fair fight solution is in sight. The four counties in the east have just about the exact population for a district; districts could be drawn centered on Hartford, New Haven and Bridgeport, all similar to current districts, and a final district would include most of the current 5th and 6th Districts, held by Democrat James Maloney and Republican Nancy Johnson. The narrow and elongated 5th has often been targeted as the logical district to eliminate—Maloney's hold on it is tenuous—and it is hard to see a way to improve his position that doesn't endanger Democrats in the neighboring districts.

THE PEOPLE: Pop. 2000: 3,405,565; Pop. 1990: 3,287,116, up 3.6% 1990–2000. 1.2% of U.S. total, 29th largest; 81.6% White, 9.1% Black, 2.4% Asian, 0.3% Amer. Indian, 2.2% Two+ races, 4.3% Other; 9.4% Hispanic Origin. 2.3% Unemployment. 2000 Voting age pop.: 2,563,877. 2000 Turnout: 1,459,525; 57% of VAP. Registered voters (2000): 2,031,626; 701,017 D (35%), 485,593 R (24%), 845,016 unaffiliated and minor parties (42%).

POLITICAL LINEUP: Governor, John G. Rowland (R); Lt. Gov., M. Jodi Rell (R); Secy. of State, Susan Bysiewicz (D); Atty. Gen., Richard Blumenthal (D); Treasurer, Denise Nappier (D); Comptroller, Nancy Wyman (D); State Senate, 36 (21 D and 15 R); Senate Pres. Pro Tempore, Kevin B. Sullivan (D); Majority Leader, George Jepson (D); State House, 151 (100 D, 51 R); House Speaker, Moira Lyons (D). Senators, Christopher J. Dodd (D) and Joseph I. Lieberman (D). Representatives, 6 (3 D, 3 R).

ELECTIONS DIVISION: 860-509-6100; **FILING DEADLINE FOR U.S. CONGRESS:** August 5, 2002.

2000 Presidential Vote

Gore (D)	816,015	(56%)
Bush (R)	561,094	(38%)
Nader (Green)	64,452	(4%)
Others	17,920	(1%)

1996 Presidential Vote

Clinton (D)	735,740	(53%)
Dole (R)	483,109	(35%)
Perot (I)	139,523	(10%)
Others	34,237	(2%)

2000 Republican Presidential Primary

McCain (R)	87,270	(49%)
Bush (R)	82,871	(46%)
Other	8,920	(5%)

2000 Democratic Presidential Primary

Gore (D)	99,563	(56%)
Bradley (D)	74,075	(41%)
Other	5,418	(3%)

Gov. John G. Rowland (R)

Elected 1994, term expires Jan. 2003, 2d term; b. May 24, 1957, Waterbury; home, Hartford; Villanova U., B.S. 1979; Catholic; married (Patricia).

Elected Office: CT House of Reps., 1980–84; U.S. House of Reps., 1984–90.

Professional Career: Insurance Agent, 1979–84.

Office: Executive Chamber, State Capitol, Hartford, 06106, 860-566-4840; Fax: 860-566-4677; Web site: www.state.ct.us.

Election Results

1998 general	John G. Rowland (R)	628,707	(63%)
	Barbara Kennelly (D)	354,187	(35%)
	Others	16,641	(2%)
1998 primary	John G. Rowland (R)	nominated	
1994 general	John G. Rowland (R)	415,201	(36%)
	Bill Curry (D)	375,133	(33%)
	Eunice Strong Groark (ACP)	216,585	(19%)
	Tom Scott (I)	130,128	(11%)

Sen. Christopher J. Dodd (D)

Elected 1980, seat up 2004, 4th term; b. May 27, 1944, Willimantic; home, East Haddam; Providence Col., B.A. 1966, U. of Louisville, J.D. 1972; Catholic; married (Jackie Clegg).

Military Career: Army Reserves, 1969–75.

Elected Office: U.S. House of Reps., 1974–80.

Professional Career: Peace Corps, Dominican Republic, 1966–68; Practicing atty., 1972–74.

DC Office: 448 RSOB, 20510, 202-224-2823; Fax: 202-224-1083; Web site: www.senate.gov/~dodd.

State Office: Wethersfield, 860-258-6940.

Committees: *Banking, Housing & Urban Affairs:* Financial Institutions; Housing & Transportation; Securities & Investment (Chmn.). *Foreign Relations:* African Affairs; European Affairs; Western Hemisphere, Peace Corps, Narcotics Affairs (Chmn.). *Health, Education, Labor & Pensions:* Aging; Children & Families (Chmn.); Employment, Safety & Training. *Rules & Administration* (Chmn.).

Group Ratings

	ADA	ACLU	AFS	LCV	CON	ITIC	NTU	COC	ACU	NTLC	CHC
2000	95	71	85	86	82	100	12	53	13	3	15
1999	95	—	100	89	72	—	4	53	0	—	—

National Journal Ratings

	1999 LIB	—	1999 CONS		2000 LIB	—	2000 CONS
Economic	71%	—	28%		89%	—	10%
Social	81%	—	12%		79%	—	0%
Foreign	78%	—	13%		72%	—	15%

Key Votes of the 106th Congress

1. Educ. Savings Accts.	N	5. Review Movie Violence	Y	9. NATO War in Serbia	Y
2. Prescrip. Drug Benefit	Y	6. Gun Show Bckgrnd. Checks	Y	10. Table Cuba Travel Ban	N
3. Delay Ergonomic Standards	N	7. Ban Part.-Birth Abortion	N	11. Nuclear Test-Ban Treaty	Y
4. Phase Out Estate Tax	N	8. Broaden Hate Crimes List	Y	12. Perm. Trade with China	Y

Election Results

1998 general	Christopher J. Dodd (D)	628,306	(65%)	($4,442,567)
	Gary A. Franks (R)	312,177	(32%)	($1,478,307)
	Others	23,974	(2%)	
1998 primary	Christopher J. Dodd (D) ...... nominated by convention			
1992 general	Christopher J. Dodd (D-ACP)	882,569	(59%)	($4,553,792)
	Brook Johnson (R)	572,036	(38%)	($2,395,262)
	Others	46,104	(3%)	

Sen. Joseph I. Lieberman (D)

Elected 1988, seat up 2006, 3d term; b. Feb. 24, 1942, Stamford; home, New Haven; Yale U., B.A. 1964, LL.B. 1967; Jewish; married (Hadassah).

Elected Office: CT Senate, 1970–80, Majority Ldr., 1974–80; CT Atty. Gen., 1983–88.

Professional Career: Practicing atty., 1964–80.

DC Office: 706 HSOB, 20510, 202-224-4041; Fax: 202-224-9750; Web site: www.senate.gov/~lieberman.

State Office: Hartford, 860-549-8463.

Committees: *Armed Services:* Airland Forces (Chmn.); Emerging Threats & Capabilities; Seapower. *Environment & Public Works:* Clean Air, Wetlands, Private Property & Nuclear Safety (Chmn.); Transportation & Infrastructure. *Governmental Affairs* (Chmn.). *Small Business.*

Group Ratings

	ADA	ACLU	AFS	LCV	CON	ITIC	NTU	COC	ACU	NTLC	CHC
2000	75	57	83	86	87	100	16	33	20	9	15
1999	95	—	100	100	68	—	8	47	0	—	—

National Journal Ratings

	1999 LIB	—	1999 CONS		2000 LIB	—	2000 CONS
Economic	59%	—	37%		63%	—	36%
Social	64%	—	31%		66%	—	21%
Foreign	62%	—	29%		57%	—	42%

Key Votes of the 106th Congress

1. Educ. Savings Accts.	Y	5. Review Movie Violence	Y	9. NATO War in Serbia	Y
2. Prescrip. Drug Benefit	Y	6. Gun Show Bckgrnd. Checks	Y	10. Table Cuba Travel Ban	Y
3. Delay Ergonomic Standards	N	7. Ban Part.-Birth Abortion	N	11. Nuclear Test-Ban Treaty	Y
4. Phase Out Estate Tax	N	8. Broaden Hate Crimes List	Y	12. Perm. Trade with China	*

Election Results

2000 general	Joseph I. Lieberman (D)	828,902	(63%)	($3,786,665)
	Phil Giordano (R)	448,077	(34%)	($1,080,020)
	Other	34,282	(3%)	
2000 primary	Joseph I. Lieberman (D) .... unopposed			
1994 general	Joseph I. Lieberman (D)	723,842	(67%)	($4,017,520)
	Jerry Labriola (R)	334,833	(31%)	($166,064)
	Others	20,989	(2%)	

FIRST DISTRICT

In 1871, Mark Twain moved to Hartford to become director of an insurance company, and in time became the Connecticut capital's most famous citizen. Hartford, already more than two centuries old, home of the nation's longest circulating newspaper (since 1764), *The Hartford Courant*, was becoming the nation's best-known insurance center. This was not what the harsh Puritans who founded Hartford had in mind, but Connecticut's Yankees turned out to be shrewd businessmen. Thanks to the broad Connecticut River, Hartford also became a seaport; its merchants, prevented from trading and writing marine insurance by Thomas Jefferson's Embargo Act of 1807, turned to writing fire insurance and using the capital they had accumulated in the Napoleonic Wars to finance their ventures. One was Samuel Colt's gun factory just south of downtown Hartford, which became one of the nation's great arms plants—and whose company became a symbol of Connecticut's recession when it went into Chapter XI in 1992.

Insurance and arms are still economic mainstays of Hartford, Connecticut's capital and the center of its largest metropolitan concentration. Though affected by downsizing and mergers, Aetna and Travelers are still big employers; across the river is the Pratt and Whitney jet engine plant in East Hartford, cornerstone of Connecticut-based United Technologies—even though its local work force is barely one-third its size in 1980, it still builds engines for more than 8,000 airlines around the world. The small central city of Hartford is otherwise in bad shape, its high-crime neighborhoods abandoned and bedraggled, its school system taken over by the state after a private firm was fired. But metropolitan Hartford has long since spread miles into pleasant hills, and most Hartford suburbs are in good economic shape from the surging economic growth of the late 1990s.

The 1st Congressional District is centered on Hartford, but the city lost 15% of its residents in the 1990s, dropping from Connecticut's second-largest to its third-largest city; in 2000 it was 41% Hispanic, 38% black. When Hartford's unemployment was 5% in January 2001, the statewide rate was 2.3%. Politically, the area has long been more Democratic than the rest of Connecticut: Hartford in Connecticut is something like Boston in Massachusetts, a commercial metropolis more statist than its surroundings. It owes some of its Democratic character to longtime state (1946–75) and national (1961–68) Democratic chairman, John Bailey, an old-fashioned political boss with a scandal-free career who promoted a raft of first-class candidates.

The congressman from the 1st District is John Larson, a Democrat elected in 1998 to replace Barbara Kennelly, Bailey's daughter, who ran for governor after 16 years in the House and lost by a wide margin. Larson grew up in the Mayberry Village public housing project in East Hartford, one of eight children; his father was a fireman at Pratt & Whitney, and his mother worked at the state Capitol. He graduated from Central Connecticut State, taught high school and coached athletics; he then became an insurance agent. He comes from a political family—his brother Timothy became mayor of East Hartford—and in 1982, at 34, John Larson was elected to the state Senate. Four years later he was Senate president. There Larson sponsored one of the nation's first family medical leave laws, a prototype for the law sponsored by Senator Christopher Dodd and signed by Bill Clinton in 1993. He created neighborhood resource centers for preschoolers, where parents could receive a variety of services. He seemed headed for the governorship, and in 1994 he won the party designation at the state convention. But Comptroller Bill Curry built an organization of unionists and liberal activists, and beat him 55%–45% in the primary. Larson then returned to private life and promoted a volunteer Connect '96 project to hook up libraries and schoolrooms to the information superhighway.

When Kennelly announced her retirement in September 1997, Larson was an obvious candidate; another was Secretary of State Miles Rapoport, from more affluent West Hartford, who had the support of unions, the Sierra Club, and the Connecticut Citizens Action group. They had clashed in the legislature, where Rapoport helped lead the push for a state income tax in 1991 and Larson was one of the few Democrats who opposed it. Rapoport led in polls and fundraising. But Larson raised impressive sums as well, built a local organization, did lots of door-to-door campaigning, and benefited from the support of Hartford Mayor Mike Peters. Larson ended up with a surprise 46%–43% win. Rapoport won in the northwest part of the district, including Hartford, West Hartford, and heavily Jewish Bloomfield; Larson carried most of the rest, with a big vote in East Hartford. The general election was vigorously contested by Kevin O'Connor, a 31-year-old former law clerk and SEC lawyer, who returned to the Hartford area and enlisted the help of his large extended family; he held fundraisers in sports bars, bought signs on buses, had his young nephews blow kisses to motorists as volunteers held signs. He generated enough enthusiasm to get the endorsement of *The Hartford Courant* and the dispatch of $70,000 for ads from the House Republican campaign committee. Larson supported gun control and gay rights, opposed late-term abortions, and boasted of his experience on family medical leave and neighborhood resources center. Of O'Connor he said, "He says all the time, 'a fresh face.' I think that's just another way of saying, 'I have no record.'" Larson won with 58%, just one point shy of Bill Clinton's percentage here in 1996.

In the House, Larson pulled together several Democratic caucuses to prepare a package of bills to close the digital divide between technology haves and have-nots; he called for a Technology Corps of volunteers to train students how to use the Internet. He worked to reverse the Appropriations Committee's decision in 1999 to stop funding for F-22 fighter jets. He voted against permanent normal trade relations with China, he said, because of a promise he had made to labor unions. For a freshman, the former history teacher took an unusual interest in the institution—pushing successfully for the Library of Congress to write an illustrated, narrative history of the House, to match the fine history of the Senate written by Senator Robert Byrd.

In 2000 Larson faced a celebrity challenger in former World Wrestling Federation champion Bob Backlund, but this was to be no repeat of the Jesse Ventura phenomenon. Backlund had little experience in public life, raised little money, and lost every town as he was defeated 72%–28%. Redistricting will probably enlarge the district, but it will likely remain centered on Hartford and safe for Larson.

Cook's Call   *Safe.* The loss of one of the state's six districts will be felt in just about every district in the state. Still, there is little chance that this Hartford-based district will be altered enough to give Larson any trouble in 2002.

THE PEOPLE: Pop. 2000: 552,127; Pop. 1990: 547,979, up 0.8% 1990–2000. 71.1% White, 15.6% Black, 2.7% Asian, 0.2% Amer. Indian, 0.1% Hawaiian, 2.6% Two+ races, 7.7% Other; 13.1% Hispanic Origin.

2000 Presidential Vote		
Gore (D)	148,858	(62%)
Bush (R)	77,423	(32%)
Nader (Green)	9,296	(4%)
Others	3,350	(1%)

1996 Presidential Vote		
Clinton (D)	136,775	(59%)
Dole (R)	68,483	(30%)
Perot (I)	20,862	(9%)
Others	5,204	(2%)

Rep. John Larson (D)

Elected 1998, 2d term; b. July 22, 1948, Hartford; home, E. Hartford; Central CT St. U., B.S. 1971; Catholic; married (Leslie).

Elected Office: E. Hartford Bd. of Ed., 1977–79; E. Hartford Town Cncl., 1979–83; CT Senate, 1983–95, Pres. Pro-Tem 1986–95.

Professional Career: High schl. teacher, 1972–77; Insurance broker, 1977–98; Sr. Fellow, Yale Bush Ctr., 1995–present.

DC Office: 1419 LHOB 20515, 202-225-2265; Fax: 202-225-1031; Web site: www.house.gov/larson.

District Office: Hartford, 860-278-8888.

Committees: *Armed Services* (25th of 28 D): Military Research & Development. *Science* (12th of 22 D): Research; Space & Aeronautics.

Group Ratings

	ADA	ACLU	AFS	LCV	CON	ITIC	NTU	COC	ACU	NTLC	CHC
2000	95	79	85	93	31	83	19	57	12	13	13
1999	100	—	100	94	63	—	17	38	4	—	—

National Journal Ratings

	1999 LIB	—	1999 CONS		2000 LIB	—	2000 CONS
Economic	78%	—	21%		78%	—	20%
Social	76%	—	24%		79%	—	17%
Foreign	74%	—	23%		79%	—	21%

Key Votes of the 106th Congress

1. Patient Bill of Rights	Y	5. Bar RU-486 $ for FDA	N	9. NATO War in Serbia	Y
2. Accelerate Min. Wage	Y	6. Display 10 Commandments	N	10. Perm. Trade with China	N
3. Strike Ban on Ergo. Stnd.	Y	7. Gun Show Bkgrnd. Checks	Y	11. Debt Relief for 3rd World	Y
4. Ovrd. Estate Tax Veto	N	8. Ban Part.-Birth Abortion	N	12. Drop Cuba Econ. Embargo	Y

Election Results

2000 general	John Larson (D)	151,932	(72%)	($715,753)
	Bob Backlund (R)	59,331	(28%)	($69,042)
2000 primary	John Larson (D)	unopposed		
1998 general	John Larson (D)	97,681	(58%)	($1,181,517)
	Kevin O'Connor (R)	69,668	(41%)	($389,948)
	Others	915	(1%)	

SECOND DISTRICT

Eastern Connecticut, one of the longest-settled parts of the United States, had great, and some-times painful, change in the 1990s—a change comparable to those of the 1640s or 1810s or 1950s. When the Puritan settlers from Massachusetts and England arrived, these flinty hills were the home of small Indian tribes, whose numbers were slashed by warfare and even more by disease. This was never fertile farming country, but New London and Norwich were among the 13 colonies' leading workshops and ports. Not long after, factories developed around mills in little villages on the fast-flowing Quinebaug and Shetucket Rivers. Sandbars kept oceangoing ships out of the rivers, but they docked at New London. In the mid-20th Century new technology shaped the area. Four nuclear power plants were built here, more than in any similarly populated part of the United States. In Groton, the "Submarine Capital of the World" across the Thames River from New London and downriver from the Coast Guard Academy, is General Dynamics' Electric Boat Com-pany, which built the nuclear submarines that may very well have deterred nuclear war.

By the 1990s this latest high-tech economy was in trouble. Nuclear plants were wearing out and being shut down across the country. And with the end of the Cold War, much of the Electric Boat force was laid off, though some remained to work on the next-generation Virginia-class submarine; the base is home port to more than 20 subs, still the nation's most active submarine port, and about 10,000 employees. Suddenly the area's economic base shifted to entertainment. Some of that was tourism—Mystic Seaport and the Coast Guard Academy. Much more important was the Foxwoods Casino, built by the 650-member Mashantucket Pequot tribe and the legions of managers and lawyers and lobbyists it has hired. Foxwoods is now the largest casino in the East, and with hotels and golf courses and a convention center, it is the largest employer in Connecticut. A university study commissioned by Foxwoods claims that it attracts 50,000 visitors a day, has created 41,000 jobs and sends to state government 25% of its gross slot machine rev-enues—$174 million in 1999, 1.5% of the revenue for Connecticut state government. The tribe has reaped enormous profits, donating $10 million to the National Museum of the American Indian and is becoming one of the nation's biggest political contributors.

The 2d Congressional District includes most of eastern Connecticut, centering on New Lon-don and Norwich, including mill towns and the University of Connecticut town of Storrs nestled in the rocky hills to the north. The 2d also stretches west to Middletown, once ethnic and now a college town that has a riverfront development project, and affluent antique-filled small towns like Essex and Old Lyme on Long Island Sound. For many years this was a politically marginal district, with close battles between Yankee Republicans and Catholic Democrats. In the early 1990s it was the scene of political rebellions. It voted 27% for Ross Perot in 1992—his best showing in New England after the two Maine districts—and in 1994 it came within 21 votes of defeating its Democratic Congressman Sam Gejdenson. Then, with the economy revived, it gave Bill Clinton a wide margin in 1996 and in 1998 voted solidly for incumbents—a Democratic senator, a Republican governor, and a Democratic congressman. But the latter changed in 2000.

The congressman from the 2nd District is Rob Simmons, a Republican elected in 2000. Simmons grew up in New York City and enlisted in the Army after graduating from Haverford College in 1965; he spent 19 months in Vietnam, where he earned two Bronze Star medals. In 1969 he joined the CIA, working as an operations officer for a decade, including five years on assignment in East Asia. Simmons joined the staff of Senator John Chafee in 1979 and was staff director for the Senate Intelligence Committee from 1981–85. When he left Washington, he said that he never expected to return. He earned a master's in public policy administration from the Kennedy School of Government and was a doctoral candidate in political science at the University of Connecticut from 1988–92. He has been an associate fellow of Yale's Berkeley College, where he taught courses on military intelligence; he also chaired the Stonington police commission. In 1990 Simmons was elected to the Connecticut General Assembly, serving five terms in a Democratic leaning district and voting against the state's new income tax. He remained in the Army Reserve, with the rank of colonel.

Then Simmons decided to run against 20-year incumbent Democratic Congressman Sam Gejdenson in 2000. He began the race with little recognition outside his New London-area district and seemed a long shot. Gejdenson tried to portray him as too conservative for the district and criticized his support for individual investment accounts for Social Security. Simmons said Gejdenson was too entrenched in Washington, where he was ranking minority member of the House International Relations Committee, and was out of touch with the district—living in his wife's home in a gated community in Branford, in the 3d District. Simmons also made an issue of the Mashantucket Pequot Indian tribe land claims. In 1983, Gejdenson voted to give the tribe—whose lineage to the original Pequots was in question—federal recognition and settlement land for a reservation within the state, all of which was essential to the development of Foxwoods. But by 2000 officials in neighboring towns were complaining of traffic problems, and others were resisting the Pequots' claims to more lands. There were other issues. Human rights groups criticized Gejdenson's support for military aid to Colombia to fight drug trafficking—a package that included 18 Black Hawk helicopters built by Stratford-based Sikorsky Aircraft. Simmons argued that the $1.7 billion in military aid would be better spent for border protection and drug education treatment in this country. In the campaign's closing days, Gejdenson fired two aides who admitted planting with reporters a story critical of Simmons's service in Vietnam. For some time House Democratic strategists figured Gejdenson was home free because of the popularity of Connecticut's Joe Lieberman and that he was able to outspend Simmons by $1.6 million to $1 million. When they realized in October that Gejdenson was in trouble, they sent money in, but it was too late. Simmons won by 2,860 votes—51%–49%. He ran strongly in his home base in the district's southeast corner and won 34 of 54 towns, while Gejdenson's ran best in the college towns of Middletown, Storrs and Willimantic.

In the House, Simmons won his first objective of a seat on the Armed Services Committee, where he pledged to protect workers at Electric Boat who he said have felt betrayed by Gejdenson, plus seats on Transportation and Veterans Affairs. His biggest challenge in 2002 may be to survive redistricting. Possible Democratic opponents for 2002 include Norwich businessman James Sullivan, state Senator Donald Williams and former state Representative Joseph Courtney, who was the Democratic candidate for lieutenant governor in 1998.

Cook's Call   *Highly Competitive.* Simmons' surprise defeat of 20-year incumbent Democrat Sam Gejdenson means that he will be put very high on the target list for Democrats in 2002. This district, which gave Gore 55% in 2000, has a good Democratic lean to it. Redistricting will also have an impact. Simmons' moderate profile could help insulate him from defeat, but he should expect a serious challenge in 2002.

THE PEOPLE: Pop. 2000: 568,007; Pop. 1990: 548,018, up 3.6% 1990–2000. 89.1% White, 4.2% Black, 1.9% Asian, 0.6% Amer. Indian, 2.1% Two+ races, 2% Other; 4.7% Hispanic Origin.

2000 Presidential Vote

Gore (D)	137,128	(55%)
Bush (R)	92,844	(38%)
Nader (Green)	14,284	(6%)
Others	3,035	(1%)

1996 Presidential Vote

Clinton (D)	123,595	(53%)
Dole (R)	73,863	(32%)
Perot (I)	29,790	(13%)
Others	6,991	(3%)

Rep. Robert Simmons (R)

Elected 2000, 1st term; b. Feb. 11, 1943, New York, NY; home, Stonington; Haverford Col., B.A. 1965; Harvard U., M.A. 1979; Episcopalian; married (Heidi Paffard).

Military Career: Army, 1965–69 (Vietnam); Army Reserves, 1969–2000.

Elected Office: CT House of Reps., 1990–2000.

Professional Career: Operations Ofcr., CIA, 1969–79; Staff, Sen. John Chafee, 1979–81; Staff Dir., Sel. Cmte. on Intelligence, 1981–85; Visiting Lecturer, Yale U., 1985–95; Teaching asst., U. of CT, 1988–91.

DC Office: 511 CHOB 20515, 202-225-2076; Fax: 202-225-4977; Web site: www.house.gov/simmons.

District Offices: Middletown, 860-346-1123; Norwich, 860-886-0139.

Committees: *Armed Services* (26th of 32 R): Military Personnel; Military Procurement. *Transportation & Infrastructure* (27th of 42 R): Coast Guard & Maritime Transportation; Highways & Transit; Railroads. *Veterans' Affairs* (15th of 17 R): Health.

Group Ratings and Key Votes: Newly Elected

Election Results

2000 general	Robert Simmons (R)	114,380	(51%)	($1,060,197)
	Sam Gejdenson (D)	111,520	(49%)	($1,616,863)
2000 primary	Robert Simmons (R)	unopposed		
1998 general	Sam Gejdenson (D)	99,567	(61%)	($1,041,564)
	Gary M. Koval (R)	57,860	(35%)	($126,650)
	Others	5,774	(4%)	

THIRD DISTRICT

The beginnings of Connecticut's defense industry came two centuries ago, in 1798, when Eli Whitney, a young Yale graduate, won an order from the federal government to produce 10,000 muskets at $13.40 each. Six years before, Whitney had invented the cotton gin, which revolutionized the South but for years only embroiled him in a patent suit. On the musket contract, he was determined to make a profit right off, so he set up a system of interchangeable parts and invented a milling machine and gauges: the beginning of standardized American manufacturing. It was also the beginning of New Haven as a manufacturing center, for Whitney set up his factory along a small, rapidly flowing river just north of this town established more than 150 years before as a religious haven for strict Puritans. For the next 150 years or so, the town mass-produced rifles, clocks, locks, hardware and toys—anything its tinkerers and entrepreneurs could fashion. Today there are few factories left in New Haven, and Connecticut's defense contracts have been cut way back. Southern Connecticut around New Haven is mostly prosperous, but the city itself, with significant crime rates and many neighborhoods scarred by abandoned homes, has only two-thirds of its peak population. Yale, with its Gothic spires, redbrick halls and modernist skating rink, has always been the visual focus of the city; now Yale is left as New Haven's largest employer. In the late 1990s, the city had a bit of an economic revival—sparked, in part, by Yale's homebuyers' program of incentives to faculty and staff and by $1 billion in campus-area investments by biotech firms. A $500 million plan for a shopping mall along Long Wharf has sparked controversy.

The 3d Congressional District of Connecticut covers the New Haven metropolitan area, which has long since spread beyond the narrow city limits over the hills of what were once Yankee villages and countryside; New Haven cast only 14% of its votes in 2000. Politics in the New Haven area for years was a three-cornered battle, between Yankee Republicans, Irish Democrats, and Italians who became its largest ethnic group and usually voted Republican. Though often regarded as a Democratic seat, the 3d has sometimes been marginal, changing partisan hands in the 1980s as well as the 1940s and 1950s.

Rosa DeLauro, congresswoman from the 3d District, is well connected in New Haven and Washington. She grew up in New Haven's Wooster Square, where her father Ted was alderman; her mother, Luisa DeLauro, retired in 1999 after 35 years as New Haven's longest-serving alderman. Rosa's husband Stanley Greenberg was Bill Clinton's chief pollster from 1991–94 and worked for Tony Blair's New Labour Party in Britain, for Ehud Barak in Israel's 1999 and 2001 elections and for Al Gore in 2000. Rosa DeLauro has been in politics for years: She was a development administrator in New Haven in the 1970s, chief of staff to Senator Christopher Dodd from 1980–87, then spent a year working to stop U.S. military aid to Nicaraguan contras before going on to become director of EMILY's List, the spectacularly successful liberal women's fundraising group. In 1990, when 3d District incumbent Bruce Morrison ran for governor, DeLauro ran for Congress and won 52%–48% over anti-tax and anti-abortion legislator Tom Scott, after spending an impressive $957,000.

DeLauro is now one of the Democratic leadership's loudest champions on the floor. In November 1998 she ran for caucus chairman, and lost narrowly, 108–97, to Martin Frost of Texas. But Dick Gephardt, responsive to demands by Democratic women for a leadership post, named her an assistant to the leader to work on the party message. She has a consistently liberal record and supported the Clinton administration faithfully; she backed the idea of 100,000 more teachers and called for no tax cut in order to save Social Security. Like most House Democratic leaders, she voted against NAFTA and permanent normal trade relations with China. She has been an active and enthusiastic supporter of women's issues. A cancer survivor herself, she sponsored the law to require 48-hour hospital stays for mastectomies and argues for coverage of early-detection tests of cervical cancer. She introduced the Paycheck Fairness Act which would allow women to collect punitive damages for pay discrimination. She has sought unsuccessfully to remove abortion restrictions on federal employees' health benefits.

DeLauro remains an active and intense political strategist, "a live wire whose words rush out like sparks," wrote Frank Bruni of *The New York Times*. As a House Democratic leader, she sought political focus on gun control and sponsored the "Columbine Clock" as a symbol of congressional inaction. In 2000, she helped to crystallize House Democrats' attacks on George W. Bush and organized pre-election bus tours for women members in battleground states. On local matters, she has sought defense contracts for locally built Black Hawk helicopters. With her seat on Appropriations, she secured $7.3 million to support lobstermen victimized by dying lobsters in Long Island Sound.

DeLauro's last serious competition came in 1992, when she beat Scott 66%–34%. She has been reelected easily since then. When Joe Lieberman's vice presidential candidacy raised the possibility that his Senate seat would become open, she expressed interest in running for it. For now, though, she has to focus on protecting her district. Redistricting could expand it in various directions, but the likelihood is that she will get a New Haven-centered district from which she can easily be re-elected.

Cook's Call *Safe.* After her initial narrow victory in 1990, DeLauro has won easily in this solidly Democratic district. But, redistricting could have an impact here. There has been some talk about parceling out the 5th District between the 4th, 6th and this New Haven-based district.

THE PEOPLE: Pop. 2000: 561,576; Pop. 1990: 547,904, up 2.5% 1990–2000. 78.8% White, 12.8% Black, 2.7% Asian, 0.2% Amer. Indian, 2% Two+ races, 3.5% Other; 8% Hispanic Origin.

2000 Presidential Vote
Gore (D)	146,540	(60%)
Bush (R)	82,344	(34%)
Nader (Green)	11,847	(5%)
Others	3,120	(1%)

1996 Presidential Vote
Clinton (D)	129,756	(57%)
Dole (R)	71,009	(31%)
Perot (I)	22,916	(10%)
Others	5,531	(2%)

Rep. Rosa DeLauro (D)

Elected 1990, 6th term; b. Mar. 2, 1943, New Haven; home, New Haven; Marymount Col., B.A. 1964, London Sch. of Econ., 1962–63, Columbia U., M.A. 1966; Catholic; married (Stanley Greenberg).

Professional Career: Exec. Asst., New Haven Mayor Frank Logue, 1976–77; Exec. Asst. & Develop. Admin., City of New Haven, 1977–79; Chief of Staff, U.S. Sen. Christopher Dodd, 1980–87; Exec. Dir., Countdown '87, 1987–88; Exec. Dir., EMILY's List, 1989.

DC Office: 2262 RHOB 20515, 202-225-3661; Fax: 202-225-4890; Web site: www.house.gov/delauro.

District Office: New Haven, 203-562-3718.

Committees: *Appropriations* (12th of 29 D): Agriculture, Rural Development, & FDA; Labor, HHS & Education.

Group Ratings
	ADA	ACLU	AFS	LCV	CON	ITIC	NTU	COC	ACU	NTLC	CHC
2000	90	86	100	93	50	56	20	42	8	12	0
1999	100	—	100	100	40	—	14	16	0	—	—

National Journal Ratings
	1999 LIB —	1999 CONS		2000 LIB —	2000 CONS
Economic	84%	12%		85%	11%
Social	87%	0%		79%	17%
Foreign	85%	12%		80%	16%

Key Votes of the 106th Congress
1. Patient Bill of Rights	Y	5. Bar RU-486 $ for FDA	N	9. NATO War in Serbia	Y
2. Accelerate Min. Wage	Y	6. Display 10 Commandments	N	10. Perm. Trade with China	N
3. Strike Ban on Ergo. Stnd.	Y	7. Gun Show Bkgrnd. Checks	Y	11. Debt Relief for 3rd World	Y
4. Ovrd. Estate Tax Veto	N	8. Ban Part.-Birth Abortion	N	12. Drop Cuba Econ. Embargo	Y

Election Results
2000 general	Rosa DeLauro (D)	156,910	(72%)	($680,778)
	June M. Gold (R)	60,037	(28%)	($73,864)
	Other	1,258	(1%)	
2000 primary	Rosa DeLauro (D)	unopposed		
1998 general	Rosa DeLauro (D)	109,726	(71%)	($463,460)
	Martin T. Reust (R)	42,090	(27%)	($22,274)
	Others	2,035	(1%)	

FOURTH DISTRICT

It was a fitting place, perhaps, for one of the most spectacular financial failures in history: the collapse in September 1998 of Long Term Capital Management, in Greenwich, Connecticut. In the far southwestern corner of New England, Greenwich never seemed destined for wealth, and yet it is arguably the wealthiest community of its size in the world. The Connecticut towns along Long Island Sound were lightly populated Yankee farm country in the 17th and 18th Centuries. In the 19th Century, Bridgeport, several towns east of Greenwich, became a factory town, famous as the home of P. T. Barnum. By the early 20th Century Greenwich and other Yankee villages clustered around commuter railroad stations became the home of some of New York's elite. Greenwich has beautifully manicured hills, elaborately simple boat docks, carefully casual roads, good manners and dull haircuts, 16 private clubs and nine private schools—and houses which are routinely sold for more than $1 million and then torn down to make way for grander mansions. Starting in the 1950s, New York-based CEOs, eager to minimize their own commutes and avoid New York income taxes, moved their headquarters out to Greenwich and Stamford and Fairfield and points inland: General Electric, American Brands, Union Carbide, Champion International, Pitney Bowes, and Olin. Many other firms, including LTCM, followed, so that Stamford, just east of Greenwich, is now the focus of an edge city that is the biggest office center between Manhattan and Boston.

The 4th Congressional District covers all of Connecticut along Long Island Sound from industrial Bridgeport to Greenwich, plus several inland towns. It includes Joe Lieberman's hometown of Stamford, chock full of office complexes; woodsy Darien and New Canaan; Norwalk, with its industrial zone, new office buildings, and modest neighborhoods down by the tracks; artsy-craftsy Westport; Fairfield, home of GE, arguably the world's most valuable corporation; and Bridgeport, an odd duck, industrial and low-income town, though spruced up when the state-financed Ballpark at Harbor Yard opened up for minor league baseball in 1998. The Stamford-Norwalk 1% unemployment rate was the lowest in the nation in December 2000. The basic political balance has been the same since the 1940s, when the heavily affluent suburbs attracted enough people to outvote Bridgeport and elect Republican Claire Boothe Luce to the House in 1942 and 1944. More than the rest of Connecticut, the 4th is oriented to New York rather than Hartford or Boston. People here watch New York TV stations: they are Yankee, not Red Sox, fans; their political attitudes are shaped by what is happening in the City as much as in Hartford. Hatred of the state income tax enabled Republican Governor John Rowland to win by big margins here three times in the 1990s. But the specter of the religious right eroded the Episcopalian Republican vote and helped Bill Clinton make a dead heat of the race here against Greenwich native George Bush in 1992, and beat Bob Dole 51%–40% in 1996. With 4th District native Lieberman on the ticket, Al Gore carried this district 55%–41% in 2000.

The 4th District's congressman, Christopher Shays, is a product of the upscale towns and one of the most pivotal Republicans in the House. Shays grew up in Darien. After college he and his wife volunteered for the Peace Corps and served in Fiji; after graduate school he was elected to the Connecticut House at 29 and served for 12 years, working with Common Cause on rules reform. He won the U.S. House seat in a 1987 special election by beating a culturally conservative Democrat from Bridgeport. Shays is a pleasant man with a stubborn streak and considerable legislative savvy; his voting record is near the middle of the House on most issues, a bit left on cultural issues. When he feels strongly, he will risk everything: He registered for conscientious objector status during the Vietnam war, and says he would not have served if drafted; as a legislator, he went to jail for seven days in 1986 to protest judicial system corruption.

Despite his dissent from many Republicans' views—on campaign finance reform, abortion, gun control, subsidies to the arts, gay rights, the minimum wage, defense spending, Census sampling—he was a partisan Republican from the time he was ignored by the House's Democratic leaders and impressed by a speech in Connecticut by a backbencher named Newt Gingrich. In August 1994 Shays withdrew his vote for the Clinton crime bill in protest over Democratic tactics, and with Gingrich's support negotiated a new version—an episode that helped break up the Democratic majority. The first major bill passed the first day of the Republican Congress was managed by Shays, the Congressional Accountability Act, imposing on Congress the laws it imposes on others; it passed unanimously. Shays was also chief sponsor of the gift ban law and the Lobby Disclosure Act. "I am very much a part of the Republican revolution—and I do think it is a revolution—but I am still an independent person," Shays said in January 1996, amid the budget fight; he supported Gingrich on ethics charges and warned him of the other leaders' coup in 1997. Yet he soured on other Republicans in 1998 as Gingrich went to great lengths to sink his campaign finance reform bill; his tune was different: "I am a Republican who can't be proud of how my Republicans are conducting themselves."

Shays's great cause remains campaign finance reform. His Shays-Meehan bill in its latest version—it has been rewritten several times—would ban soft money in federal elections and bar issue advocacy ads within 60 days of an election. Most Republicans initially opposed it as harmful to their party, and added that some of its provisions would be unconstitutional under current Supreme Court precedents. After Shays filed a discharge petition in May 1999 to force a vote that year, which Representative John Doolittle called "treason," the House passed Shays-Meehan in September 1999, 252–177, with 54 Republicans voting for. As Democrats in 2000—in both the presidential and congressional campaigns—came close to matching Republicans' soft money fundraising, Shays gained more Republican supporters with his argument that his proposal also made sense in partisan terms. In April 2001, the Senate passed its version, McCain-Feingold, but House Republican leaders did not embrace Shays-Meehan.

As chairman of a Government Reform subcommittee, Shays zeroed in on Gulf war illnesses. A large number of veterans have reported various symptoms, some of which may be related to exposure to chemical weapons, and the Pentagon failed to reveal for years the use of some gas by Iraq or contact with it by American troops. Shays became convinced that the Pentagon and the Veterans' Administration were "plagued by arrogant incuriosity and a pervasive myopia that sees lack of evidence as proof." After a 20-month investigation, the subcommittee voted to take jurisdiction away from the Pentagon and VA altogether.

Shays's cooperation with the Republican revolution may have cost him some votes at home. His 1996 opponent attacked him for supporting Gingrich, and his percentage dropped from 74% in 1994 to 60% in 1996. In 1998 he won easily. In 2000, Shays was faced with a primary challenge from Jim Campbell, who said Shays was too independent and too liberal, and complained that, after agonizing (and telecast on C-SPAN) district hearings he had voted against the impeachment of Bill Clinton. But Campbell withdrew in May 2000; though he won 37% of the vote in delegate primaries, Shays won all the delegates. Shays won the general 58%–41%. In 1999 Shays moved his residence to a not very affluent neighborhood in Bridgeport, and there was talk that he would run for governor in 2002, if John Rowland steps down.

Cook's Call   *Safe.* This district was one of only 40 in the country that split their ticket for Gore and a Republican House candidate and, like the rest of New England's former Republican strongholds, continues to trend Democratic. As a moderate, reform-oriented Republican, Shays is a good fit for this swing district. The loss of a seat in the state will have an impact on the lines and Republicans are hoping to get Republican leaning Danbury, now in the 5th District, put into the 4th to help shore up Shays.

THE PEOPLE: Pop. 2000: 574,101; Pop. 1990: 547,561, up 4.8% 1990–2000. 74.2% White, 13.4% Black, 3.5% Asian, 0.2% Amer. Indian, 2.8% Two+ races, 5.9% Other; 14.8% Hispanic Origin.

2000 Presidential Vote			1996 Presidential Vote		
Gore (D)	125,843	(55%)	Clinton (D)	113,411	(51%)
Bush (R)	94,079	(41%)	Dole (R)	88,181	(40%)
Nader (Green)	6,938	(3%)	Perot (I)	14,825	(7%)
Others	2,791	(1%)	Others	5,355	(2%)

Rep. Christopher Shays (R)

Elected Aug. 1987, 7th term; b. Oct. 18, 1945, Darien; home, Bridgeport; Principia Col., B.A. 1968, NYU, M.B.A. 1974, M.P.A. 1978; Christian Scientist; married (Betsi).

Elected Office: CT House of Reps., 1974–87.

Professional Career: Peace Corps, Fiji, 1968–70; Aide, Trumbull Mayor, 1971–72.

DC Office: 1126 LHOB 20515, 202-225-5541; Fax: 202-225-9629; Web site: www.house.gov/shays.

District Offices: Bridgeport, 203-579-5870; Norwalk, 203-866-6469; Stamford, 203-357-8277.

Committees: *Financial Services* (27th of 37 R): Capital Markets, Insurance & Government Sponsored Enterprises; Domestic Monetary Policy, Technology & Economic Growth; International Monetary Policy & Trade. *Government Reform* (4th of 24 R): Energy Policy, Natural Resources and Regulatory Affairs; National Security, Veterans' Affairs & Intl. Relations (Chmn.). *Science* (4th of 25 R): Environment, Technology and Standards.

Group Ratings

	ADA	ACLU	AFS	LCV	CON	ITIC	NTU	COC	ACU	NTLC	CHC
2000	40	43	14	93	91	100	73	76	60	76	40
1999	55	—	0	100	97	—	72	60	44	—	—

National Journal Ratings

	1999 LIB	—	1999 CONS	2000 LIB	—	2000 CONS
Economic	46%	—	53%	48%	—	52%
Social	66%	—	34%	62%	—	37%
Foreign	40%	—	59%	53%	—	45%

Key Votes of the 106th Congress

1. Patient Bill of Rights	Y	5. Bar RU-486 $ for FDA	N	9. NATO War in Serbia	N
2. Accelerate Min. Wage	Y	6. Display 10 Commandments	Y	10. Perm. Trade with China	Y
3. Strike Ban on Ergo. Stnd.	N	7. Gun Show Bkgrnd. Checks	Y	11. Debt Relief for 3rd World	Y
4. Ovrd. Estate Tax Veto	Y	8. Ban Part.-Birth Abortion	Y	12. Drop Cuba Econ. Embargo	Y

Election Results

2000 general	Christopher Shays (R)	119,155	(58%)	($1,039,573)
	Stephanie Sanchez (D)	84,472	(41%)	($172,155)
	Other	3,131	(2%)	
2000 primary	Christopher Shays (R)	unopposed		
1998 general	Christopher Shays (R)	94,767	(69%)	($604,689)
	Jonathan Kantrowitz (D)	40,988	(30%)	
	Others	1,449	(1%)	

FIFTH DISTRICT

Central Connecticut's stony hills are physically isolated, the climate is forbidding, local manners are frosty, there is nothing to suggest lavishness: this might be the Switzerland of America. Yet in the last 200 years, the mountains of Switzerland and the hills of Connecticut have been transformed from subsistence farmland to some of the most productive and affluent places on earth. Their secrets have been thrift, hard work, inventiveness and an intolerance for imprecision. But Switzerland has prospered by closing others out, while Connecticut, like the rest of America, is an open society, welcoming newcomers and imbuing immigrants with the Yankee knack for tinkering and precision work. It has also been quick to adapt to market changes. Danbury was once the nation's leading producer of hats; now it cuts almost no felt but is a major corporate headquarters and has reinvented itself as a commercial mecca with the 200-store Danbury Fair Mall plus a $9 million ice skating complex. Meriden once made ivory combs, clocks, cutlery, and silver; now it produces electrical signaling equipment, jewelry, biotech filters, and nuclear instruments. Waterbury, once the nation's largest producer of brass, saw the last of its big three brass fabricators shut down in 1985, but has replaced that with health care and two local hospitals are the city's biggest employers; the old Scovill brass factory is now a shopping mall. And it is one of America's political cockpits: as a former Democratic state chairman said, "Waterbury is one of the toughest political places that you can find. It's got a lot of Southie in it and a lot of Charlestown, too. If you can make it in Waterbury, you can make it anywhere."

The 5th Congressional District is an irregularly shaped slice of central Connecticut, entirely inland, from Meriden west through Waterbury to Danbury and the high-income havens of Ridgefield and Wilton. This was the Federalist heartland in the early 19th Century. It voted Republican for nearly a century, then became Democratic as Catholics started outnumbering Protestants. Now cultural conservatism and economic growth have tilted it toward Republicans again; it produced the lowest margins of any Connecticut district for Bill Clinton in 1996 and the Gore-Lieberman ticket in 2000. But it is closely balanced enough to be marginal often, and has voted out incumbent congressmen of both parties in 1972, 1978, 1984, 1996, and came close to doing so in 1998. In recent years the 5th was represented by Republicans John Rowland, reelected governor by a wide margin in 1998, and Gary Franks, who lost to Senator Christopher Dodd by a wide margin the same year.

The congressman from the 5th District is now James Maloney, a Democrat who defeated Franks in 1996 and withstood tough challenges in 1998 and 2000. Maloney grew up in Danbury, and after college and law school spent a year as a Vista volunteer. From 1974–78 he headed Danbury's antipoverty agency. In 1986 he was elected to the state Senate, where he worked on a family leave act, voted against the state income tax, and supported business tax cuts. In 1994 he decided to run against Franks, then the only black Republican in the House. Maloney held him to a 52%–46% margin in 1994, the second lowest margin for a Republican incumbent that year, and in early 1996 decided to run again. Helped when a primary opponent dropped out, Maloney ran on a somewhat conservative platform: for the balanced budget amendment, favoring job opportunities and no cash payments for welfare recipients. Maloney criticized Franks for receiving a $100,000 advance from HarperCollins for a book; unperturbed, Franks spent much of summer 1996 on a 17-city book tour. Franks lost 52%–46% in 1996.

Maloney proceeded to compile a moderate voting record. He supported a tax cut and the partial-birth abortion ban. He sponsored a bill, which passed the House in 1998, to spend $20 million on hiring police officers who would be stationed in schools. With Christopher Shays, he sponsored a brownfields bill to help finance new construction on old factory sites in Danbury, Meriden, Derby, Seymour, and Waterbury. He submitted a $122 million proposal to restore electric power along a 23-mile Metro-North rail line from Danbury to South Norwalk.

Not surprisingly Maloney had serious opposition in 1998, from 34-year-old Danbury state Senator Mark Nielsen. Republican leaders called the 5th "one of our top targets in the nation," and Nielsen, whose opponent for the nomination dropped out before the primary, had nearly as much money as the incumbent. Scandal issues played some role. On August 18, the day after Bill Clinton's grand jury appearance, Nielsen called on him to resign; Maloney voted for the Republican motion to hold impeachment hearings. Maloney also was dogged by campaign finance charges. In January 1998 his brother was convicted of reimbursing contributors to his 1996 campaign, and fined $256,000, though James Maloney was not implicated. Then in October the Maloney campaign returned $5,000 and redesignated $29,000 of contributions classified as pre-primary, but which were contributed between the July convention and the September primary where Maloney had no opposition; Nielsen ran ads attacking these irregularities. More positively, he called for welfare reform and tax cuts and called himself a "John Rowland Republican." This was not quite enough, and Maloney won 50%–48%. He carried Meriden in the east and Danbury in the west, plus the Naugatuck valley factory towns narrowly, but he scarcely carried Waterbury and lost most of the smaller towns.

Nielsen tried again in 2000, with the charges at least as nasty as in 1998: Nielson depicted Maloney as a corrupt puppet on strings pulled by union bosses, while Maloney attacked his opponent for vicious ads. Although he was one of only five Democrats voting for the Republican's prescription-drug measure and he split from Democrats on ending the marriage penalty on taxpayers plus estate and gift taxation, Maloney decided in the final hour to oppose permanent normal trade relations with China. But the contest in this swing district wasn't as close, with Maloney winning 54%–44%, easily taking the industrial centers plus 17 of 27 towns overall; Nielson fared best in the western towns.

Now Maloney's problem is redistricting. Connecticut lost one House district in the 2000 Census, and a bipartisan commission is tasked with drawing up the redistricting plan. One obvious solution is to divide the elongated 5th District among its neighbors. This would not be entirely to Maloney's detriment: the current 5th is the least Democratic of Connecticut's current six districts in presidential elections, and he would surely not mind losing heavily Republican towns at its southern edge. But he could then be forced into a contest against 6th District Republican Nancy Johnson. For 2002 Maloney could find himself, as he did in 1998, in one of the most seriously contested House races in the cycle.

Cook's Call   *Highly Competitive.* The 5th District, already the most marginal district in the state, stands out as the biggest target for line drawers in the state to eliminate. Tucked into the middle of the state, the 5th has no major city to anchor it, and could be parceled into the three surrounding districts. It is also conceivable that the 5th and the 6th are combined into one seat. But Maloney, who has beat back two very serious challenges in 1998 and 2000, is no stranger to tough races and is likely to run regardless of how this district looks in 2002.

THE PEOPLE: Pop. 2000: 581,903; Pop. 1990: 547,907, up 6.2% 1990–2000. 85.3% White, 5.7% Black, 2.2% Asian, 0.2% Amer. Indian, 2.1% Two+ races, 4.4% Other; 10% Hispanic Origin.

2000 Presidential Vote		
Gore (D)	123,207	(51%)
Bush (R)	107,360	(44%)
Nader (Green)	9,857	(4%)
Others	3,017	(1%)

1996 Presidential Vote		
Clinton (D)	110,596	(48%)
Dole (R)	92,570	(40%)
Perot (I)	24,265	(10%)
Others	4,694	(2%)

Rep. James H. Maloney (D)

Elected 1996, 3d term; b. Sept. 17, 1948, Quincy, MA; home, Danbury; Harvard U., B.A. 1972, Boston U., J.D. 1980; Catholic; married (Mary Draper).

Elected Office: CT Senate, 1986–95.

Professional Career: Exec. Dir., Danbury Anti-Poverty Agency, 1974–78; Practicing atty., 1980–96.

DC Office: 1427 LHOB 20515, 202-225-3822; Fax: 202-225-5746; Web site: www.house.gov/jimmaloney.

District Offices: Danbury, 203-790-6856; Derby, 203-735-5005; Meriden, 203-630-1903; Waterbury, 203-573-1418.

Committees: *Armed Services* (16th of 28 D): Military Procurement; Military Readiness. *Financial Services* (11th of 32 D): Capital Markets, Insurance & Government Sponsored Enterprises; Domestic Monetary Policy, Technology & Economic Growth; Financial Institutions & Consumer Credit.

Group Ratings

	ADA	ACLU	AFS	LCV	CON	ITIC	NTU	COC	ACU	NTLC	CHC
2000	55	50	71	93	0	61	39	52	36	19	27
1999	85	—	100	81	23	—	24	44	28	—	—

National Journal Ratings

	1999 LIB —	1999 CONS	2000 LIB —	2000 CONS
Economic	61%	39%	55%	45%
Social	65%	35%	68%	32%
Foreign	58%	41%	64%	34%

Key Votes of the 106th Congress

1. Patient Bill of Rights	Y	5. Bar RU-486 $ for FDA	N	9. NATO War in Serbia	Y
2. Accelerate Min. Wage	Y	6. Display 10 Commandments	N	10. Perm. Trade with China	N
3. Strike Ban on Ergo. Stnd.	Y	7. Gun Show Bkgrnd. Checks	Y	11. Debt Relief for 3rd World	N
4. Ovrd. Estate Tax Veto	Y	8. Ban Part.-Birth Abortion	Y	12. Drop Cuba Econ. Embargo	N

Election Results

2000 general	James H. Maloney (D)	118,932	(54%)	($2,065,122)
	Mark Nielsen (R)	98,229	(44%)	($1,393,319)
	Other	4,660	(2%)	
2000 primary	James H. Maloney (D)	unopposed		
1998 general	James H. Maloney (D)	78,394	(50%)	($1,377,977)
	Mark Nielsen (R)	76,051	(48%)	($939,775)
	Others	2,712	(2%)	

SIXTH DISTRICT

From its Yankee past to its Ellis Islander present and ahead to its third wave of immigrants future, Connecticut has been a land of tinkerers specializing in precision work, of inventors able to transform vagrant ideas into profitable products. Over the years this stony soil has become the home of some of the most affluent people in the nation and the world. This is true even in the hills of northwest Connecticut, off the interstates and far from Connecticut's small urban capital of Hartford and its sometime booming edge city of Stamford. Here are exquisite Yankee towns like Washington and Kent, prosperous once in the post-Revolutionary era when Connecticut's ship owners accumulated capital and invested it in factories and mills, and now the "anti-Hamptons," a country-home mecca for ultra-rich New Yorkers seeking to avoid the glitz of Southampton and Easthampton. Not far away are small industrial cities like New Britain, America's ball bearing capital for years, and Bristol, where sports announcer Bill Rasmussen dreamed up the idea of transmitting satellite feeds of UConn games to his neighbors by cable TV, an idea which became ESPN, now headquartered on its 43-acre Bristol campus. Nearby is the American Clock and Watch Museum (northwest Connecticut is where Americans started manufacturing clocks) and the New England Carousel Museum (not far from America's oldest amusement park, Lake Compounce).

The 6th Congressional District of Connecticut covers approximately the northwest corner of the state, stretching from Enfield and Windsor Locks, north of Hartford on the Connecticut River, across the affluent Farmington valley suburbs of Hartford to industrial New Britain and Bristol, and includes all of Litchfield County. Here is Winsted, the hometown of Ralph Nader, where he has kept his voting residence. Historically, this was rock-ribbed Federalist and Republican territory; in the 20th Century, with Italian immigrants heading to Enfield and Windsor Locks and Poles to New Britain, it moved toward being politically marginal.

The congresswoman from the 6th District is Nancy Johnson, a Republican first elected in 1982. She grew up in Chicago, daughter of a Republican state legislator, came east to school, then lived in New Britain as a doctor's wife and a teacher, raising three children while active in charitable and community affairs. She was elected to the Connecticut Senate in 1976 from a heavily Democratic district. When 6th District Congressman Toby Moffett ran against Senator Lowell Weicker in 1982, Johnson won the House seat, beating Bill Curry, then a 30-year-old nuclear freeze organizer and later the 1994 Democratic candidate for governor and a Clinton White House aide.

Johnson is now a high-ranking member of Ways and Means and chair of its Health Subcommittee. Her record has been mostly market-oriented on economics, fairly liberal on cultural issues. For some years she has been one of the most active and productive legislators in the House. She opposed the Clinton health care plan, enduring gratuitous and sexist insults from then-Chairman Pete Stark in hearings, and her efforts contributed to its demise. She was the lead sponsor of the 1997 CHIP program for health insurance for uninsured children, which passed in July 1997. After many health insurers started paying for Viagra, she and Nita Lowey sponsored a bill to provide contraceptives to federal employees with health insurance covering prescriptions. She has worked on reshaping Medicare, sponsoring the first preventive health care benefits for seniors, measures to strengthen community hospitals, nursing homes and Medicare Choice plans. She helped to make premiums for long-term health insurance deductible from income taxes and seeks a $3,000 tax credit for families' spending on long-term care. She got funding for children's hospitals to conduct training for children's health care and more mammograms to detect breast cancer. On Medicare, she stands to play a key role. The Bush administration has said its model for reform is the bill developed on the Medicare Commission by Senator John Breaux and Bill Thomas, now Ways and Means chairman; that may very well go through Johnson's subcommittee. She says her first priorities are a prescription drug benefit for seniors and making long-term care more affordable.

Also on Ways and Means she took the lead on eliminating the old child care tax credit, which tended to help high-income parents, and replaced it with $300 million in vouchers to low-income working mothers. She worked to increase the Independent Living program for older foster care children and to help fathers on welfare get jobs and develop parental skills. In 1999 and 2000 she worked with ranking Democrat Charles Rangel to develop a $25 billion tax credit for school construction bonds, but this foundered as other committee Republicans concentrated on education savings accounts and the Clinton administration demanded school construction be covered by the pro-union Davis-Bacon Act. As chair of the Oversight Subcommittee, she was a chief sponsor of the IRS reform bill, which moved the presumption of correctness away from the agency and otherwise changed rules of many years standing.

Johnson has often bucked the House Republican leadership on issues. She voted against the Contract with America crime package, has supported abortion rights (Johnson harshly criticized George W. Bush's executive order reimposing a ban on federal aid to international organizations that promote abortion), was one of the first Republicans to sign a discharge petition for the Shays-Meehan campaign finance bill, and in February 2001 introduced legislation to prevent oil drilling in the Arctic National Wildlife Refuge's coastal plain. But she also worked cooperatively with Speaker Newt Gingrich on many issues, and her connection with Gingrich ended up causing her electoral trouble.

In 1996 Johnson chaired the House ethics committee, which was considering the charges brought by Democrats against Gingrich, an issue committee Democrats were determined not to drop. At home, Johnson faced a sudden electoral challenge. Charlotte Koskoff, a Democrat Johnson had beaten 64%–32% in 1994, now had the endorsement of the National Organization for Women, which had long endorsed Johnson, and greater funding. Bill Clinton carried the 6th District 50%–36%, and Johnson was hard pressed. The networks reported on election night that she lost; in fact she ended up winning 50%–49%. Johnson readily admitted that her role on the ethics committee "absolutely hurt me." On January 21 the House voted 395–28 to reprimand and fine Gingrich an unprecedented $300,000; Johnson, her term up, immediately left the committee. Koskoff was off and running again, and Johnson went into legislative high gear, sponsoring funding of the National Endowment for the Arts, an American Heritage Rivers bill and a law barring convicted sex offenders from federally financed public housing—as well as health and tax legislation. Koskoff called her "an enabler and participant in the right-wing Republican agenda," and national liberal groups targeted the district. The hottest argument came over a bill Johnson sponsored to prevent the Customs Bureau from changing the rule allowing companies to market tools including overseas-made components as "Made in the U.S.A." Among the companies interested was Stanley Works of New Britain, and in October 1997 it was revealed that Johnson owns over $100,000 of Stanley stock (her husband inherited it from his father, who was a Stanley foreman). Koskoff ran ads accusing Johnson of helping Stanley Works export jobs, and accusing her of trying to benefit herself and responding to $6,000 in contributions from Stanley Works executives. Johnson replied tartly that the bill would increase jobs in Connecticut and added, "I've busted my butt for local industry." Outspending Koskoff more than 3–1, Johnson rebounded, winning 58%–40%, carrying practically all small towns but one and losing only in New Britain, Bristol, and (Koskoff's home town) Plainville. In 2000, against weaker opposition, Johnson was re-elected 63%–33%, carrying every city and town except New Britain.

Just before the November 2000 election Governor John Rowland said he would appoint Johnson to the Senate if Joseph Lieberman were elected vice president. But that became moot December 13. Now comes the question of redistricting. Connecticut lost one of its six House seats in the 2000 Census, and under state law the new lines will be drawn by a bipartisan commission appointed by the legislature. It has long been thought that the district most likely to be eliminated would be the elongated 5th District, just south of the 6th, and that Johnson and Democrat James Maloney would be put in the same district. The advantage would seem to lie with Johnson. Amid all her national legislating she has kept working on local projects—redevelopment in New Britain, funding to protect the Great Mountain Forest and the Black Revolutionary War Patriots Memorial, Army contracts for Tru-Hitch Inc. in Torrington. But this could be a seriously contested district.

Cook's Call *Highly Competitive.* As a moderate Republican who isn't afraid to buck the Republican leadership, Johnson has built a profile that is well suited for this district. However, it is likely to be impacted greatly by redistricting: There is serious talk that her New Britain-based district will be combined with Democrat Jim Maloney's 5th District which would create a showdown between two very skilled, moderate politicians.

THE PEOPLE: Pop. 2000: 567,851; Pop. 1990: 547,747, up 3.7% 1990–2000. 91% White, 3.2% Black, 1.5% Asian, 0.2% Amer. Indian, 1.5% Two+ races, 2.5% Other; 5.8% Hispanic Origin.

2000 Presidential Vote
Gore (D)	134,439	(52%)
Bush (R)	107,044	(42%)
Nader (Green)	12,230	(5%)
Others	2,651	(1%)

1996 Presidential Vote
Clinton (D)	121,607	(50%)
Dole (R)	89,003	(36%)
Perot (I)	26,865	(11%)
Others	6,462	(3%)

Rep. Nancy L. Johnson (R)

Elected 1982, 10th term; b. Jan. 5, 1935, Chicago, IL; home, New Britain; U. of Chicago, 1951–53, Radcliffe Col., B.A. 1957, U. of London, 1957–58; Unitarian; married (Theodore).

Elected Office: CT Senate, 1976–82.

Professional Career: Pres., Sheldon Community Guidance Clinic; Adjunct Prof., Central CT St. Col., 1968–71.

DC Office: 2113 RHOB 20515, 202-225-4476; Fax: 202-225-4488; Web site: www.house.gov/nancyjohnson.

District Office: New Britain, 860-223-8412.

Committees: *Ways & Means* (4th of 24 R): Health (Chmn.); Human Resources.

Group Ratings
	ADA	ACLU	AFS	LCV	CON	ITIC	NTU	COC	ACU	NTLC	CHC
2000	35	50	14	64	14	100	49	90	56	53	27
1999	55	—	33	69	49	—	50	83	36	—	—

National Journal Ratings
	1999 LIB —	1999 CONS	2000 LIB —	2000 CONS
Economic	48% —	50%	49% —	51%
Social	61% —	38%	66% —	34%
Foreign	50% —	48%	49% —	49%

Key Votes of the 106th Congress
1. Patient Bill of Rights	N	5. Bar RU-486 $ for FDA	N	9. NATO War in Serbia	Y
2. Accelerate Min. Wage	Y	6. Display 10 Commandments	Y	10. Perm. Trade with China	Y
3. Strike Ban on Ergo. Stnd.	N	7. Gun Show Bkgrnd. Checks	Y	11. Debt Relief for 3rd World	N
4. Ovrd. Estate Tax Veto	Y	8. Ban Part.-Birth Abortion	N	12. Drop Cuba Econ. Embargo	Y

Election Results
2000 general	Nancy L. Johnson (R)	143,698	(63%)	($1,163,610)
	Paul Valenti (D)	75,471	(33%)	($11,142)
	Other	10,374	(5%)	
2000 primary	Nancy L. Johnson (R)	unopposed		
1998 general	Nancy L. Johnson (R)	101,630	(58%)	($1,768,957)
	Charlotte Koskoff (D)	69,201	(40%)	($551,881)
	Others	3,950	(2%)	

★ DELAWARE ★

Delaware, the first state to ratify the Constitution, the second smallest state in area, sixth smallest in population, is a small corner of America, with some considerable claims on the national attention. The mouth of the Delaware River was explored by Henry Hudson, and the Dutch and Swedes built settlements on the west bank in the 1630s. But the three counties of Delaware owe their separate existence to the politics of the proprietors of William Penn's colony of Pennsylvania, and to Delawareans' own speed in ratifying the Constitution which made it literally the "First State."

Through most of its history Delaware has been unusually affluent. It had the nation's highest income levels during the early 20th Century and high incomes in the prosperous 1990s. It houses, in beautiful cobblestone mansions in its chateau country, many members of the most numerous wealthy family in America, the du Ponts. Delaware's ethnic and racial mixture is much like that along the rest of the East Coast and not that much different than the nation's, though with fewer than average Hispanics and Asians; there is a mixture here of suburbs, old immigrant neighborhoods, urban black neighborhoods, attractive beach towns and farmlands. Sussex County in southern Delaware is a world of its own, one of the centers of the nation's chicken industry, where 10,000 workers produce 60 million pounds of chicken a week. If not all parts of the nation can follow Delaware's exact path to continued prosperity, perhaps they can get an idea of the direction to travel.

The central focus of Delaware's economy for two centuries was the business started when Eleuthere Irenee du Pont, the practical, business-minded son of a dreamy, idealistic French immigrant, built a gunpowder mill on the banks of Brandywine Creek in 1802. This was the first enterprise of the family du Pont, and it expanded to become one of America's great munitions and chemical companies. It grew especially rapidly during World War I, generating so much capital that the Du Pont Company bought a huge block of stock in General Motors in the 1920s and controlled GM for thirty years while it was America's largest corporation. That capital also financed what was arguably the world's finest research and development program. In the years during and after World War II, Du Pont prospered by bringing to the consumer and industrial market new synthetics and plastics like rayon, nylon, cellophane, polyethylene, lucite and teflon: "Better Living Through Chemistry." Delaware continues to be a high-tech state today; it boasts that it ranks number one in scientists and engineers with Ph.D.s per capita and highest in patents per capita.

Delaware has also thrived in finance. In the late 19th Century, it pioneered liberal laws of incorporation, giving more flexibility and power to managers and owners. A large share of the nation's big companies are incorporated in Delaware—their legal births take place in a federal-style building near the Capitol in Dover—which means that much of the nation's corporate law, especially on mergers and acquisitions and unfriendly takeovers, is made in Delaware courts. Banking prospered here starting in the 1980s when Governor Pete du Pont's succeeded in liberalizing Delaware's banking laws to encourage out-of-state banks to locate operations here. Today banking accounts for more than 30,000 jobs in Delaware, more than any other business, and several of the nation's leading credit card companies are headquartered here. Charles Cawley, head of MBNA, the largest credit card issuer, has emerged as Delaware's leading civic and business leader, overshadowing every du Pont. Pete du Pont's systematic lowering of the income tax rate, continued by his successors, Republican Mike Castle and Democrat Thomas Carper, has also contributed mightily to Delaware's prosperity. Its economy grew robustly in the 1980s, paused only a little in the recession of 1990–91, and surged again as its population grew more in the 1990s than than any other Northeastern or Midwestern state—indeed, it was the only one that grew faster than the national average.

On both sides of the Mason and Dixon line, with immigrants in Wilmington and southern-accented farmers in Kent and Sussex Counties (plus Latino migrants working in chicken plants), with suburbs ranging from very affluent to not-so-affluent in New Castle County, Delaware has long had a robust two-party politics. But in the 1990s Delaware, like so many of America's largest

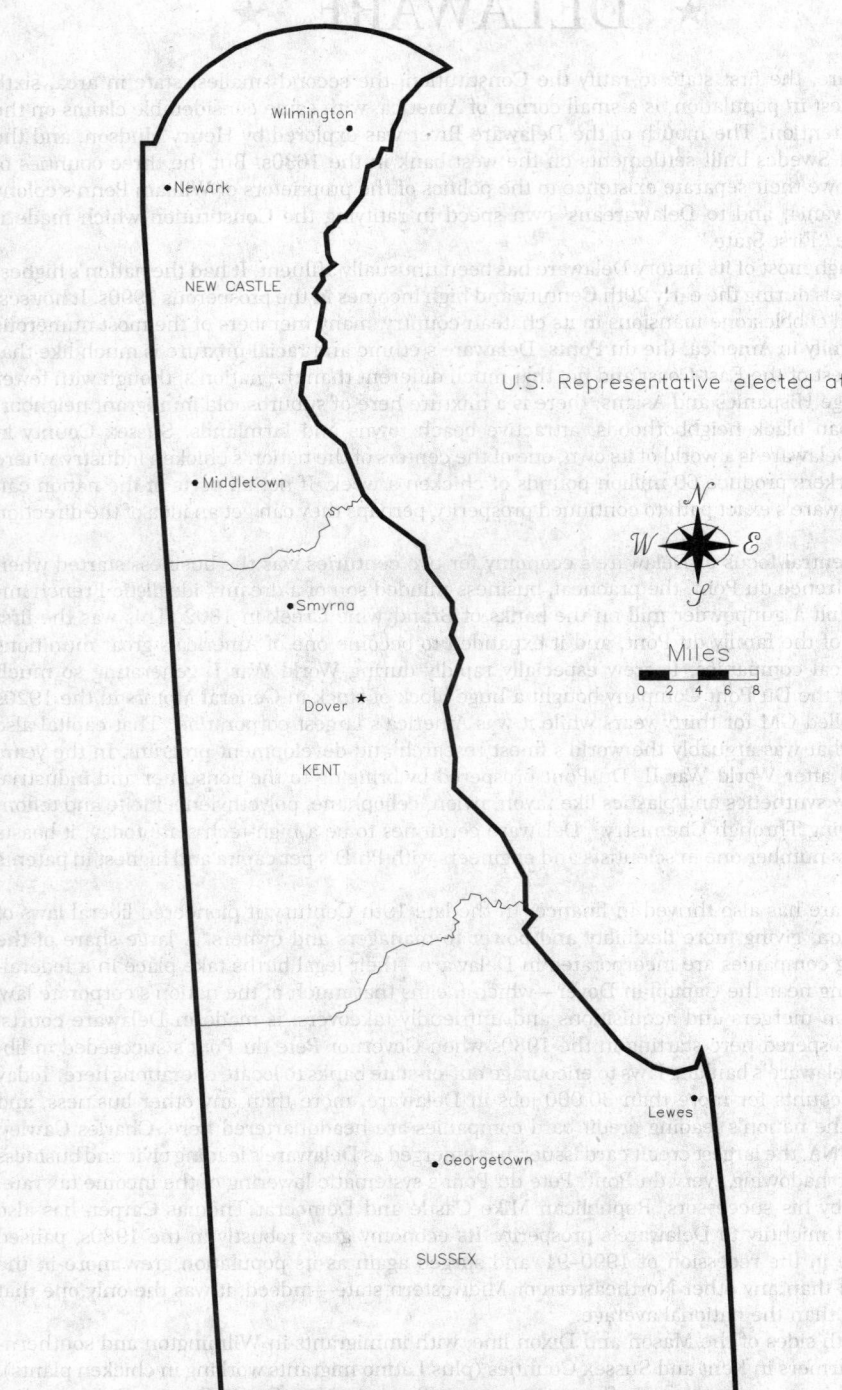

Wilmington

Newark

NEW CASTLE

U.S. Representative elected at large.

Middletown

N
W • E
S

Smyrna

Miles
0 2 4 6 8

Dover ★

KENT

Lewes

Georgetown

SUSSEX

metro areas, trended toward the Democrats, and now Democrats hold both the governorship and both Senate seats, while a popular former Republican governor has held onto the state's single seat in the U.S. House. For a half century, from 1952–96, Delaware voted for every winning presidential candidate. But in the pre-election 100% Recycled Paperboard Presidential Poll in Sussex County, in which backers of both candidates heaved pumpkins as far as they could, the Gore pumpkins were propelled 13% farther than the Bush pumpkins, and, perhaps coincidentally, Al Gore carried Delaware 55%–42%. At the same time five-term Republican Senator William Roth was defeated by Democratic Governor Tom Carper by a wider than expected 56%–44%, and Democrat Ruth Ann Minner was elected governor by 59%–40%.

But these were not bitter contests. Thanks to Delaware's small size there is still an intimacy to politics here. Senator Joseph Biden has returned home to suburban Wilmington every night for nearly 30 years, and runs into constituents at the drug store or cleaners. Most of Delaware is reached (though politically ignored) by Philadelphia TV, so personal campaigning is still important. The candidates for governor made the rounds of 33 scheduled joint appearances, starting at the Jewish Community Center in Talleyville. Roth campaigned, as always, with his trademark St. Bernards; he may have been hurt politically when he fell during one parade. The day after the election is "Return Day," when winning and losing candidates—opponents ride in the same car—come back to the Sussex County seat of Georgetown to receive the bipartisan cheers of the voters and, literally, bury a hatchet.

Governor Ruth Ann Minner, a Democrat, was elected governor in 2000. She grew up in southern Delaware, the daughter of a sharecropper; she dropped out of high school to work on the farm, and got married at 17. In 1967, her husband died; at 32, she was left with three sons and no high school diploma. She worked as an agricultural worker and a librarian, got her GED, and in 1972 landed a job as a receptionist in the office of Governor Sherman Tribbitt. "I never had any intention of getting deeply involved in politics," she says, but she had done political volunteer work as a teen and she obviously found politics congenial. In 1974 she ran for the state House and, in one of Delaware's small districts (they average 19,000 residents today), won. In 1982 she was elected to the state Senate. In the legislature she helped build the state's open space protection program, worked on education and public safety and chaired a commission that reorganized state agencies. She also married again, and she and her husband started a car-towing business; he died in 1991, but her sons still run the business. In 1992 she ran for lieutenant governor as Democratic Congressman-at-Large Tom Carper's running mate, but the offices are elected separately. So when Minner ran for governor in 2000, she had already won two statewide elections.

Minner, the favorite in the election, was unopposed in the Democratic primary. The Republicans had a close primary between former state Senate Majority Leader John Burris and former Judge Bill Lee. Burris owns a chain of tire stores, a tire recapping factory and a frozen food distribution company; he was backed by MBNA Chairman Charles Cawley, and company executives contributed $147,000 to his campaign. Lee attacked Burris for being too close to MBNA, and that apparently had some resonance. Some 27,000 voters voted in the Republican primary; Burris won by exactly 46 votes.

Both candidates were from southern Delaware, and both were generally counted as moderates. Minner ran as a successor to Carper, who had continued former Governor Pete du Pont's policy of cutting income taxes even as, helped by the state's surging economy, he increased state spending by 40%. Burris called for addressing the state's high rates of cancer and drug abuse, and for addressing environmental problems by smart planning. Burris attacked the state's education testing program, which produced high fail rates among students; Minner said it was an improvement over the past, but called for extra classes for failing students on afternoons and Saturdays, rather than summer school.

Minner was ahead in polls all along. She won 59%–40%, leading among men by only 50%–48% but among women by 68%–32%; she carried working women 70%–29% and ran particularly well among younger voters. In January 2001 she proposed a patient's bill of rights, providing review of decisions by an independent panel or arbitration, and guaranteeing emergency room care without physician preapproval, access to prescription drugs not on HMO lists and the right to see specialists without getting referrals from primary care physicians each time.

Senior Senator   Joseph Biden, Delaware's senior senator on the Senate Foreign Relations Committee, was first elected in 1972, at age 29 (he reached the constitutional age of 30 by the time he took office); in January 2003 he will have spent most of his life as a senator. Biden grew up in the suburbs of Wilmington in a middle class home; his father was a car salesman and one grandfather was a state senator in Pennsylvania. As a teenager he had a stutter, but taught himself to deliver a speech to his whole school; he is now one of the Senate's most fluent orators. He married and started a family while still in law school. After school he moved back to the Wilmington suburbs, practiced law, and in 1970, at 27, was elected to the New Castle County Council. In 1972 he ran for the Senate, against a popular incumbent who seemed ready to retire, while this young challenger had energy, an attractive extended family and an ability to connect with voters' emotions. He won 51%–49%. A month later his wife and daughter were killed in an auto accident; his two young sons were injured. He thought about resigning, but was persuaded to serve, and began his practice, kept to this day, of commuting from his home near Wilmington on Amtrak, 80 minutes to and from Washington every day. He remains a familiar figure in, and one familiar with, his constituency.

In the Senate, Biden has a moderate-to-liberal voting record. For many years he did much of his most visible work on the Judiciary Committee, which he chaired from 1987–95 and served as ranking Democrat on from 1981–87 and 1995–97. The issues that arise here—abortion, flag-burning, capital punishment, crime control—cut deeply, and for years the cultural liberals in the Democratic Party differed sharply on most of them from the constituents Biden saw in Delaware every day. As chairman, Biden presided over the most contentious Supreme Court confirmation hearings in history. In his 1987 hearings, nominee Robert Bork set a high standard for intellectual seriousness, but some of his opponents used his candor to vote against him for disgracefully dishonest reasons, from which Biden's attempts to construct an honestly based, anti-Bork rationale proved politically indistinguishable; no other nominee since has testified so frankly. The 1991 hearings on Clarence Thomas exploded when someone leaked charges of sexual harassment by Anita Hill against the nominee. Biden was bitterly criticized for covering up this information, but he had shared it with committee members, who agreed that Hill's initial unwillingness to testify publicly meant that any reference to it would be unfair to Thomas. Once the story was out though, Hill and then Thomas testified to fascinated television audiences. Despite the strong pro-Hill bias of the press, Thomas was confirmed, over Biden's opposition.

In the middle of the Bork hearings came a climactic moment for Biden, who in 1987 started running for president. He hoped to inspire a new generation as John Kennedy had inspired his. But Biden decided to leave the race when a Michael Dukakis staffer leaked an "attack video" showing similarities between Biden's stump speech about his background and a speech by British Labour Party leader Neil Kinnock. Paraphrasing someone else's words is not a political crime—most political discourse is conducted in familiar shorthand terms—but Biden in dramatizing his background actually distorted it, for unlike Kinnock he did not rise from working class roots, and unlike in Britain, upward social mobility is a common experience in the United States. In 1988, Biden nearly died of an aneurysm, but recovered fully.

After the Thomas hearings, Biden seemed defensive about attacks from the feminist left, the greatest source of activism in the Democratic Party, as the religious right is in the Republican Party; he sought out women to serve on Judiciary and worked hard on the 1994 Violence Against Women Act; he helped renew it in 2000, although part of it was declared unconstitutional by the Supreme Court. He worked hard on the 1994 crime bill, which came very close to being whip-sawed between liberals who prefer therapy to harsh punishment and conservatives who oppose gun control and favor tough sentences. In later years, Biden helped pass a methamphetamine control law, a nationwide tracking system for sex offenders, a bill to crack down on Rohypnol, the "date rape" drug, and death penalties for many offenses (though in June 2000 he called for a moratorium on executions). In 2000 Biden, addressing "the digital divide," successfully sponsored a public-private partnership to provide 27,000 computers with Internet access to Boys and Girls Club. He was the sponsor in Judiciary of the bankruptcy reform legislation, backed strongly by

Delaware's MBNA and other credit card issuers, which was vetoed by Bill Clinton in 2000 but due to be signed by George W. Bush in 2001.

Biden became ranking Democrat on the Foreign Relations Committee in 1997 and, to the surprise of many, entered into a constructive working relationship with Chairman Jesse Helms. Once part of a Democratic majority wary of another Vietnam and of the extension of American power, Biden was now part of a Democratic minority who, after the U.S. victory in the Cold War, has sought to maintain American involvement in the world. He worked hard to preserve Radio Free Europe and Radio Liberty and to establish Radio Free Asia, and he is the author of the law setting up a separate international broadcasting agency, apart from the State Department or USIA. He favored NATO expansion, while remaining concerned about whether Europeans would share burdens equally, and with Helms led the move to approve expansion. When democracy in the former Yugoslavia was thwarted by state-led terrorism and when multilateral instrumentalities proved ineffective, Biden was among the strongest voices—and the best positioned, with his high-ranking seat on Foreign Relations—to call for lifting the arms embargo on Bosnia and training Bosnian Muslims, demanding that the United States and NATO investigate war crimes there, and arguing for NATO air strikes. He once called Slobodan Milosevic a "war criminal" to his face, and in 1999 pushed the Senate to approve the use of U.S. air power in Kosovo. With John McCain and Chuck Hagel, he co-authored the resolution authorizing the ground war in Kosovo.

Of course Biden and Helms have not always agreed. He opposed Helms' Taiwan legislation in 1999—"the equivalent of waving a red cape at the Chinese and inviting them to charge." He fought hard for the ratification of the Chemical Weapons Treaty in 1998. He supported the Comprehensive Test Ban Treaty in 1999, and was one of the Democrats who called for it to be reported to the floor. When it was in September 1999, it turned out that Jon Kyl had already lined up almost every Republican in opposition, and Biden and others demanded that it be pulled back. It was defeated in October despite Biden's warning. "When we reject this treaty, we are rejecting American leadership in the world, and embracing Fortress America. We're embracing a return to nuclear testing around the world." He said in early 2000 that Bill Clinton should leave the decision on deploying missile defense to the next president, but left no doubt that he thought that "the shield of dreams" would fail to protect the United States, would provoke Russia and China, and if it were needed we should get Russia to agree to modify the ABM treaty and convince China that it doesn't threaten its deterrent. "This system is not ready for prime time. No president—this one or the next one, unless things change drastically—should in fact deploy this system." But Biden and Helms together achieved some goals that most thought unreachable. They won a long-delayed reorganization of foreign policy agencies, plus an increase in the State Department budget. Biden backed Helms' effort to have the U.S. share of UN dues reduced in return for U.S. repayment of most back UN dues and reform of the swollen UN bureaucracy. This was of course stoutly resisted. But Ambassador to the UN Richard Holbrooke took Helms' charge seriously, and achieved a near total acceptance of his demands; Helms agreed on repaying the back dues, and Biden paid handsome tribute to them both.

Biden remains a familiar everyday figure in Delaware and has tended to its most local needs. He is proud of having achieved the designation of White Clay Creek as Delaware's only National Wild Wild and Scenic River in 2000, and of gaining $1.5 million to restore Pea Patch Island at Fort Delaware, blocking the Army Corps of Engineers from removing the St. George Bridge, getting $6.7 million of Army research projects at the University of Delaware, $7 million for the 148-person Army National Guard Readiness Center in Smyrna and $3.5 million for replenishment of Delaware's beaches. And naturally he has supported Amtrak funding. On his daily commutes, he has come to know the Amtrak crew members personally and hosts an annual Christmas dinner for the crews; crew members in turn keep track of his seniority—he was 7th in seniority among senators in early 2001, but only about 65th among the Amtrak crew.

Biden's most visible gift is an articulateness that can verge on the mellifluous; he can inspire, but can also drone on at great length (being elected a senator at 29 does not curb a tendency to verbosity). But this has not reduced the appreciation most Delawareans have for his admirable personal qualities. He was re-elected by wide margins in 1984 (60%–40%), 1990 (63%–36%) and 1996 (60%–38%). His 1996 opponent was a Naval Academy graduate and businessman who walked, rode a bicycle and rollerbladed through the state, raised $1 million and questioned the sale of Biden's house to an executive of MBNA, the big credit card company whose top executives gave generously to Biden's campaign. But Biden won by his accustomed majority.

Will he run for president again? In 1997 he said, "The honest-to-God truth is that I have no desire to run for president, no plans to run for president and I've taken no action to run for president. But who knows what will happen in four years or eight years if I'm still around?" In August 2000, when he was asked if he would run if Al Gore lost, he said, "Would I consider running for president again? Yes. Am I going to run for president again? I don't know." In early 2001 he was taking a tough line on the incoming Bush administration, taking the lead in opposing the nomination of John Ashcroft for attorney general and charging that the Bush tax cut "will eat our seed corn." Asked about running for president in January 2001, he said, "Assuming I'm re-elected, I'll take a look at it then."

Cook's Call   *Safe.* There are no indications that Biden is in any trouble and Republicans are regrouping after losing gubernatorial and Senate races in 2000. With a likely third-tier opponent, Biden can focus his efforts on a potential White House bid in 2004.

Junior Senator   Democrat Thomas Carper was elected Delaware's junior senator in 2000, after already serving 24 years in statewide elective office. His election meant that Delaware has two Democratic senators for the first time since January 1943. He grew up in southside Virginia and Ohio and went to college in Ohio. He first came to Delaware as an ensign in the Navy, then returned to get his M.B.A after service in Southeast Asia, where he piloted submarine-hunting planes. In 1976, he was elected state treasurer, at 29; he ran for Congress in 1982 and beat a scandal-tarred incumbent. In the House, Carper had a moderate voting record and worked to let banks into the securities business and to prevent ocean sludge dumping, both causes supported by Delaware constituencies. In 1992, when Republican Governor Mike Castle had served his two allotted terms and ran for Congress, Carper ran for governor and won the general with 65%.

As governor, Carper pursued an agenda in many ways more conservative than liberal. He continued du Pont's policy of cutting taxes, reducing income tax rates about 10% and also cutting small business and utility taxes. Revenues kept gushing in from Delaware's strong economy, and he increased the "rainy day" fund and boosted the state's credit rating to an historic high even as state spending rose 40% in eight years. He inherited Mike Castle's standard-based education reform, raised standards, started testing students in 1998 and provided public school choice, utilized by 8% of students, tried to raise teacher salaries, instituted charter schools and passed a teacher accountability bill in 2000. His June 1995 "A Better Chance" welfare reform imposed four-year limits on welfare payments, required recipients to work, and discouraged teen pregnancy by denying additional welfare aid to families that increase in size; it cut welfare rolls 23% in two years. He has tried to take action against chicken waste, a major problem in southern Delaware and called for a business-friendly "new environmentalism." His major defeats came when the legislature voted to allow slot machines at harness racing tracks over his opposition. He was re-elected by 70%–31% over then-Treasurer Janet Rzewnicki. Barred from a third term, he was an obvious candidate for the Senate seat held by Republican William Roth since 1970.

This was a battle of positives. Both candidates had very high approval ratings, and both were familiar figures to many voters; they brought a combined total of 58 years in statewide office to the race. Roth had a record of achievements that paid direct benefits to people in this generally affluent state: the Kemp-Roth tax cut of 1981, the Roth IRAs enacted in 1997, the reform of the Internal Revenue Service passed in 1998, $2.3 billion for capital improvements in Amtrak in 1998 and $10 billion in bonds in 2000. As chairman of the Finance Committee, he held a position of power, though Republicans' six-year term limit meant that he would have to relinquish the post after the 2002 election. Roth's main problem was that he was 79 in 2000. After serving as head of the National Governors Association, Carper announced that he was running for the Senate in September 1999. A poll that month showed him ahead 48%–38%. Carper was careful not to campaign negatively against Roth or to attack him for his age, but his slogan "A Senator for Our Future" spotlighted the contrast between their ages and his 16-hour days of campaigning at factories, bowling alleys and parades was a contrast with Roth, who stayed in Washington legislating much of the time and made many fewer campaign appearances with his trademark St. Bernards. "People can be too old, or senior, at 59. The question is whether people are effective. I think that his effectivenes has waned," Carper said. As Roth unveiled initiatives—Amtrak funding, a program to aid states to pay for prescription drugs for low-income seniors—Carper suggested that Roth's tax cuts were too large and his prescription drug plan too stingy. Roth, able to raise large sums as Finance chairman, outspent Carper by $4.3 million to $2.5 million, but the Democratic Party spent some $4 million of soft money in Delaware, more than evening the score. In October, Roth fainted twice on the campaign trail, once in full view of cameras. Polls showed the race close to even in September and October, but on November 7 Carper won by a solid 56%–44% margin. This was nearly a carbon copy of Al Gore's 55%–42% margin in the state; Carper ran especially well with younger voters, and with those who were married with children.

In Washington Carper enlisted in the ranks of moderate Senate Democrats, and got seats on the Banking, Environment and Governmental Affairs Committees.

Representative-At-Large Michael Castle, a Republican first elected in 1992, has been in public life his entire career. A direct descendant of Benjamin Franklin, he grew up in Delaware and, after college and law school, returned to be a deputy attorney general. In 1966, at 27, he was elected to the Delaware House from a Democratic district. Two years later he was elected to the Senate, and in time became minority leader; in 1980 he was elected lieutenant governor; he was elected governor in 1984 and 1988. In that office he cut tax rates, started a program to make health care services available to all children, built lots of roads, developed an "Environmental Legacy" program to address issues in the coming decade, and increased teacher salaries. In 1992, barred from running for re-election by term limits, he traded jobs with Democratic Congressman-at-Large Thomas Carper. Castle won the Republican primary for Congress by 56%–30% over state Treasurer Janet Rzewnicki, and won the general 55%–43% over former Senate candidate and Lieutenant Governor S. B. Woo, who raised more in individual contributions (mostly from Chinese-Americans) than any other non-incumbent in 1992.

At that point it seemed unlikely that Castle, as a moderate member of a conservative minority party, could be influential; yet he was. He was a leader of the bipartisan freshmen who offered their own budget cuts. In August 1994 he withdrew his support from the crime bill when he thought Democrats overreached, then at Newt Gingrich's suggestion led a group of moderate Republicans to negotiate with the Clinton administration. This delivered a stinging rebuke to Democrats—it broke their majority apart, in fact—and yet ultimately produced a crime bill with less spending on prevention but with the gun control provisions which Castle, unlike most Republicans, supported.

Castle has a voting record at the middle of the House; he was one of the 10 Republicans to support Clinton administration positions on most issues and has been a leader of the informal Tuesday Group of moderate Republicans; he was one of the conveners of a bipartisan group of moderates that met in December 2000. "We're here to make laws, not to make politics," he said. In August 1996, when Republicans revived their twice-vetoed welfare reform, Castle and Tennessee Democrat John Tanner proposed an alternative. It was rejected, but several of its provisions were included in the final bill, for which Castle voted and which Bill Clinton, after vetoing two earlier welfare reform bills, signed. In March 1997 he came forward with his own budget plan, with no tax cuts until the budget was balanced; Castle and future Speaker Dennis Hastert called for considering tax cuts separately from the budget; in 1998 he attacked John Kasich's budget for cutting spending too much. In July 1999 he opposed the Republican leadership's tax cut as overlarge, and was one of a group of moderates who got the leadership to agree to make the income tax cut contingent on progress in reducing the national debt; then he was one of four Republicans who voted against the tax cut anyway. He voted for Bush's across-the-board income tax reduction with some skepticism, but voted against repeal of the "death tax." But he is not an enthusiast for every spending program. He rejected $15 million in local highway projects offered by Transportation Chairman Bud Shuster in 1999, and in 1999 authored his own list of the most wasteful programs, including research on cleaner-burning coal, roadbuilding in national forests and, closer to Delaware, the National Flood Insurance Program.

Castle is on the Financial Services Committee, which is of great importance to Delaware.

He held hearings on the new $100 and $20 bills, and pushed for a new dollar coin, more distinctive than the failed Susan B. Anthony dollar; he wanted the Statue of Liberty on one side, but Treasury Secretary Robert Rubin's panel chose the Indian guide Sacajawea instead. Castle sponsored the bill for the commemorative quarter, with different designs for each state. He was present when the first such coin was issued, which shows Delaware Revolutionary leader Caesar Rodney, atop a galloping horse, rushing to Philadelphia in 1776 to sign the Declaration of Independence. On Delaware issues, he has pushed successfully for beach replenishment and a study of *Pfiesteria piscicida*, when it was ravaging rivers in the Delmarva peninsula.

Castle now chairs the Education Reform Subcommittee, and while he may support higher spending than some other Republicans, he also questions the worth of programs mostly fashioned by Democrats. "Eliminating the Department of Education is not the answer. But neither is simply spending more for programs that fail to give our children the education they deserve." In May 1999 he called for consolidation of the 27 federal programs for technology education, administered by five agencies. In March 2000 he challenged the notion that putting computers in classrooms was the key to improving education. In July 2000 he called for an overhaul of education research, pointing out that only rarely does education research use control groups. "Research needs to be conducted on a more scientific basis." Castle has strongly supported the Shays-Meehan campaign finance legislation. He was one of the first four Republicans to sign a discharge petition on it in May 1999, and worked on the successful July 2000 bill to require disclosure of Section 527 committees. In early 2001 he was optimistic that Shays-Meehan could be passed.

Castle played a role in the elevation of Speaker Dennis Hastert. In November 1998, after Newt Gingrich announced his resignation, he and Thomas Ewing of Illinois moved to draft Hastert to run for majority leader; Hastert demurred, because he had committed to Dick Armey. But when Bob Livingston renounced the speakership December 19, Hastert was quickly selected to be speaker. Castle has been re-elected by wide margins in Delaware, 66%–32% in 1998 and 68%–31% in 2000. He has often been mentioned as a candidate for the Senate in this small state, and said that he would have run if Republican Senator William Roth had retired in 1994. But Roth chose to run again then and, at 79, in 2000, when he lost. But even if Roth had not run, Castle might not have; he said in 1998, "as time has evolved, I have grown to like my role in the House." Still, it is interesting that both of Delaware's Democratic senators won their seats by beating 70-something incumbents who chose to run despite the fact that younger popular Republicans (Pete du Pont in 1972, Castle in 2000) were waiting in the wings.

Cook's Call   *Safe.* As politically competitive as Delaware is, it has a weak spot for incumbents. Indeed, Senator Bill Roth was the first incumbent House or Senate member to lose re-election since 1972. Castle, a moderate Republican, is a good profile for a state that gave Gore 55% in 2000. Should Castle leave the seat it would be highly competitive. For now, Castle looks in great shape for 2002.

Presidential politics   Delaware has been competitive in presidential elections since the Federalists were battling the Jeffersonians. Until 2000, it could claim to be the nation's presidential bellwether: It had voted for every winner since 1952, the longest winning streak of any state. Wilmington is heavily Democratic but casts relatively few votes, the two lower counties lean Republican and the balance is struck by the New Castle County suburbs. But in 2000 suburban New Castle County, like the suburban Philadelphia counties to the north, trended heavily to the Democrats, and Al Gore, though losing the two southern counties, carried the state by a wide margin. There was a big gender gap; working women voted 65%–33% for Gore, while people married with children, a Bush group in most other states, voted 56%–42% for Gore. Blacks voted 89%–9% for Gore, white Protestants 56%–42% for Bush and white Catholics 50%–46% for Gore. Delaware's days as a bellwether are at least temporarily over.

In 1996 Delaware vied for attention by holding its presidential primary February 24, just four days after New Hampshire. But New Hampshire Republicans put pressure on candidates to ignore Delaware, and only Steve Forbes and Alan Keyes showed up here. Forbes advertised heavily on Philadelphia TV and won the contest with 33% of the vote, to 27% for Bob Dole, 19% for Pat Buchanan, and 13% for Lamar Alexander. For 2000 Republicans decided not to hold a primary on February 4, four days after New Hampshire, and voted February 9 instead. George W. Bush, who spent two full days in Delaware, led with 51%, well ahead of John McCain (25%) and the still-remembered Steve Forbes (20%). Democrats held a primary February 4, but its result was not recognized under party rules, and neither candidate campaigned. Only 5% of registered voters turned out; Al Gore led Bill Bradley 57%–40%.

THE PEOPLE: Pop. 2000: 783,600; Pop. 1990: 666,168, up 17.6% 1990–2000. 0.3% of U.S. total, 45th largest; 74.6% White, 19.2% Black, 2.1% Asian, 0.3% Amer. Indian, 1.7% Two + races, 2% Other; 4.8% Hispanic Origin. 4% Unemployment. 2000 Voting age pop.: 589,013. 2000 Turnout: 335,053; 57% of VAP. Registered voters (2000): 503,614; 214,456 D (43%), 171,446 R (34%), 117,712 unaffiliated and minor parties (23%).

POLITICAL LINEUP: Governor, Ruth Ann Minner (D); Lt. Gov., John C. Carney Jr. (D); Secy. of State, Harriet Smith Windsor (D); Atty. Gen., M. Jane Brady (R); Treasurer, Jack Markell (D); Commissioner of Insurance, Donna Lee Williams (R); Auditor, R. Thomas Wagner Jr. (R); State Senate, 21 (13 D, 8 R); Senate Pres. Pro Tempore, Thomas B. Sharp (D); Majority Leader, Thurman G. Adams Jr. (D); State House, 41 (15 D, 26 R); House Speaker, Terry Spence (R). Senators, Joseph R. Biden Jr. (D) and Thomas R. Carper (D). Representative, 1 R at large.

ELECTIONS DIVISION: 302-577-3464; **FILING DEADLINE FOR U.S. CONGRESS:** July 26, 2002.

2000 Presidential Vote
Gore (D)	180,638	(55%)
Bush (R)	137,081	(42%)
Nader (Green)	8,288	(3%)
Others	1,863	(1%)

1996 Presidential Vote
Clinton (D)	140,355	(52%)
Dole (R)	99,062	(37%)
Perot (I)	28,719	(11%)

2000 Republican Presidential Primary
Bush (R)	15,250	(51%)
McCain (R)	7,638	(25%)
Forbes (R)	5,883	(20%)
Keyes (R)	1,148	(4%)

2000 Democratic Presidential Primary
Gore (D)	6,377	(57%)
Bradley (D)	4,476	(40%)
LaRouche (D)	288	(3%)

Gov. Ruth Ann Minner (D)

Elected 2000, term expires Jan. 2005, 1st term; b. Jan. 17, 1935, Milford; home, Dover; G.E.D. 1968; Methodist; widowed.

Elected Office: DE House of Reps., 1974–82; DE Senate, 1982–1992; DE Lt. Gov. 1992–2000.

Professional Career: Owner, Roger Minner Towing, 1969-present; Receptionist, Gov. Sherman Tribbitt, 1973.

Office: Legislative Hall, Dover, 19901, 302-739-4101; Fax: 302-739-2775; Web site: www.state.de.us.

Election Results
2000 general	Ruth Ann Minner (D)	191,484	(59%)
	John M. Burris (R)	128,436	(40%)
	Others	3,263	(1%)
2000 primary	Ruth Ann Minner (D)	unopposed	
1996 general	Thomas R. Carper (D)	188,300	(70%)
	Janet C. Rzewnicki (R)	82,654	(30%)

Sen. Joseph R. Biden, Jr. (D)

Elected 1972, seat up 2002, 5th term; b. Nov. 20, 1942, Scranton, PA; home, Wilmington; U. of DE, B.A. 1965, Syracuse U., J.D. 1968; Catholic; married (Jill).

Elected Office: New Castle Cnty. Cncl., 1970–72.

Professional Career: Practicing atty., 1968–72.

DC Office: 221 RSOB, 20510, 202-224-5042; Fax: 202-224-0139; Web site: www.senate.gov/~biden.

State Offices: Dover, 302-678-9483; Georgetown, 302-856-9275; Wilmington, 302-573-6345.

Committees: *Foreign Relations* (Chmn.): East Asian & Pacific Affairs; European Affairs (Chmn.); International Operations & Terrorism. *Judiciary*: Technology, Terrorism & Government Information; Youth Violence (Chmn.).

Group Ratings

	ADA	ACLU	AFS	LCV	CON	ITIC	NTU	COC	ACU	NTLC	CHC
2000	80	57	71	100	63	85	22	60	16	14	31
1999	95	—	100	78	32	—	9	47	4	—	—

National Journal Ratings

	1999 LIB	—	1999 CONS		2000 LIB	—	2000 CONS
Economic	80%	—	17%		69%	—	30%
Social	60%	—	38%		79%	—	0%
Foreign	87%	—	0%		70%	—	28%

Key Votes of the 106th Congress

1. Educ. Savings Accts.	Y	5. Review Movie Violence	Y	9. NATO War in Serbia	Y
2. Prescrip. Drug Benefit	Y	6. Gun Show Bckgrnd. Checks	Y	10. Table Cuba Travel Ban	N
3. Delay Ergonomic Standards	N	7. Ban Part.-Birth Abortion	Y	11. Nuclear Test-Ban Treaty	Y
4. Phase Out Estate Tax	N	8. Broaden Hate Crimes List	Y	12. Perm. Trade with China	Y

Election Results

1996 general	Joseph R. Biden Jr. (D)	165,465	(60%)	($2,466,499)
	Raymond J. Clatworthy (R)	105,088	(38%)	($1,126,427)
	Others	5,038	(2%)	
1996 primary	Joseph R. Biden Jr. (D)	unopposed		
1990 general	Joseph R. Biden Jr. (D)	112,918	(63%)	($2,550,061)
	M. Jane Brady (R)	64,554	(36%)	($240,669)

Sen. Thomas R. Carper (D)

Elected 2000, seat up 2006, 1st term; b. Jan. 23, 1947, Beckley, WV; home, Wilmington; OH St. U., B.A. 1968, U. of DE, M.B.A. 1975; Presbyterian; married (Martha).

Military Career: Navy, 1968–73 (Vietnam); Naval Reserves, 1973–91.

Elected Office: DE Treas., 1976–82; U.S. House of Reps., 1982–92; DE Gov. 1992–2000.

Professional Career: Industrial Devel. Specialist, DE Div. of Econ. Devel., 1975–76.

DC Office: 513 HSOB, 20510, 202-224-2441; Fax: 202-228-2190; Web site: carper.senate.gov.

State Office: Dover, 302-674-3308; Georgetown, 302-856-7690; Wilmington, 302-573-6291.

Committees: *Aging* (Special). *Banking, Housing & Urban Affairs*: Financial Institutions; Housing & Transportation; Securities & Investment. *Environment & Public Works*: Clean Air, Wetlands, Private Property & Nuclear

Safety; Superfund, Waste Control & Risk Assessment. *Governmental Affairs*: Government Management, Restructuring and the District of Columbia; International Security, Proliferation & Federal Services; Investigations (Permanent).

Group Ratings and Key Votes: Newly Elected

Election Results

2000 general	Thomas R. Carper (D)	181,387	(56%)	($2,608,942)
	William V. Roth Jr. (R)	142,683	(44%)	($4,366,884)
	Others	2,144	(1%)	
2000 primary	Thomas R. Carper (D)	unopposed		
1994 general	William V. Roth Jr. (R)	111,088	(56%)	($2,310,474)
	Charles M. Oberly III (D)	84,554	(42%)	($1,561,440)
	Others	3,387	(2%)	

Rep. Michael N. Castle (R)

Elected 1992, 5th term; b. July 2, 1939, Wilmington; home, Wilmington; Hamilton Col., B.A. 1961, Georgetown U., LL.B. 1964; Catholic; married (Jane).

Elected Office: DE House of Reps., 1966–68; DE Senate, 1968–76, Minority Ldr., 1975–76; DE Lt. Gov., 1980–84; DE Gov., 1984–92.

Professional Career: DE Dep. Atty. Gen., 1965–66.

DC Office: 1233 LHOB, 20515, 202-225-4165; Fax: 202-225-2291; Web site: www.house.gov/castle.

District Office: Dover, 302-736-1666; Georgetown, 302-856-3334; Wilmington, 302-428-1902.

Committees: *Education & the Workforce* (7th of 27 R): 21st Century Competitiveness; Education Reform (Chmn.). *Financial Services* (7th of 37 R): Capital Markets, Insurance & Government Sponsored Enterprises; Financial Institutions & Consumer Credit; International Monetary Policy & Trade. *Permanent Select Committee on Intelligence* (3d of 11 R): Intelligence Policy & National Security; Technical & Tactical Intelligence (Chmn.).

Group Ratings

	ADA	ACLU	AFS	LCV	CON	ITIC	NTU	COC	ACU	NTLC	CHC
2000	30	50	0	71	88	94	60	80	68	70	47
1999	55	—	33	75	95	—	50	72	44	—	—

National Journal Ratings

	1999 LIB —	1999 CONS		2000 LIB —	2000 CONS
Economic	45% —	54%		46% —	52%
Social	65% —	35%		61% —	38%
Foreign	48% —	51%		45% —	53%

Key Votes of the 106th Congress

1. Patient Bill of Rights	Y	5. Bar RU-486 $ for FDA	N	9. NATO War in Serbia	Y
2. Accelerate Min. Wage	Y	6. Display 10 Commandments	N	10. Perm. Trade with China	Y
3. Strike Ban on Ergo. Stnd.	N	7. Gun Show Bkgrnd. Checks	Y	11. Debt Relief for 3rd World	Y
4. Ovrd. Estate Tax Veto	Y	8. Ban Part.-Birth Abortion	Y	12. Drop Cuba Econ. Embargo	N

Election Results

2000 general	Michael N. Castle (D)	211,546	(68%)	($588,911)
	Michael C. Miller (R)	96,538	(31%)	($28,831)
	Others	4,832	(2%)	
2000 primary	Michael N. Castle (D)	unopposed		
1998 general	Michael N. Castle (R)	119,811	(66%)	($331,621)
	Dennis E. Williams (D)	57,446	(32%)	($1,297)
	Others	3,270	(2%)	

★ DISTRICT OF COLUMBIA ★

The District of Columbia is on the way up. For most of the last 25 years, Washington, D.C., the capital of the most successful democracy in the history of the world, was a dysfunctional polity, a city with above-average incomes and a vibrant commercial property base, but with a local government so bloated with employees yet so indifferent to its duties that it destroyed one marginal neighborhood after another. Now Marion Barry, mayor for 16 of the 20 years from 1978–98, is out of office, and the new mayor, Anthony Williams, and the city Council are bent on reform; the culture of the District government is in the process of being transformed and the city's neighborhoods are becoming more peaceful and prosperous.

The problem of how to govern the nation's capital is not new. In 1787 the framers of the Constitution, familiar with contemporary London and Paris mobs and remembering how crowds had threatened Congress in Philadelphia, purposely gave the new federal government control of the 10-mile-square enclave that came to be called the District of Columbia. Over the years Congress kept control, for its own advantage and, later, out of distrust of the city's large black population. Blacks had consistently made up one-quarter of the population of Washington and surrounding counties since the 1790s, and the city was a center for free blacks even before the Civil War and Emancipation. Radical Republicans gave the District self-government in the era of Reconstruction in 1871, but Governor Alexander "Boss" Shepherd in building great public works spent the District into bankruptcy, and the experiment ended in 1874. Later Washington's vast growth, starting with the New Deal and World War II, resulted in the growth of large, mostly white suburbs, and blacks became a larger percentage of the city's population—a majority in the 1960 Census. During the 1960s civil rights revolution, it began to seem absurd to deny the vote to Washington. So in 1964 District residents began to cast three electoral votes for president, in 1968 they were allowed to vote for school board, in 1971 they finally got to elect a non-voting delegate to Congress, and in 1974 they got home rule and could vote for a mayor and city Council.

The results were tragic. Barry, a man of great ability and charm, a leader of protest organizations with few connections to Washington's established black middle class, was elected narrowly in 1978. He inherited a government that was already overlarge and undermanaged, and over the years made it more so. He raised money from public employee unions and real estate developers and increasingly won votes from poor blacks by attacking any critic as racist. Crime rates were among the nation's highest, while the police department was in shambles. Nor was the delivery of social services much better. Poor neighborhoods in the District had levels of infant mortality worse than in Sri Lanka or Jamaica. The public schools were in dreadful shape. Then, in January 1990 Barry was arrested in a D.C. hotel using crack cocaine, a crime for which he was eventually convicted and imprisoned. A reform-minded mayor, Sharon Pratt Kelly, was elected, but flinched when it came time to cut the payroll. She asked for a larger federal payment in lieu of taxes and begged for statehood (voted down by the Democratic House 277–153 in 1992). Barry, out of prison and elected to the Council in 1992, ran for mayor in 1994 and won the Democratic primary with 47% to 37% for Councilman John Ray and only 13% for Kelly. In the general, Republican Carol Schwartz, a longtime Council member, ran a gallant campaign, but Barry won 56%–42%.

In the meantime the District had changed. Even as the District payroll was peaking—at 51,300 in 1992—the District's population was falling, and becoming more white. Washington's population fell from 802,000 in 1950 to 572,000 in 2000. In the 1950s and 1960s, the District saw white flight; in the Barry years it saw black flight. The District lost 6% of its population in the 1990s, as blacks headed to majority-black Prince Georges County, Maryland, and other suburbs, where three-quarters of Washington-area blacks live. At the same time, Ward 3 and gentrifying neighborhoods near downtown have been growing in population, so that the black percentage of the population has declined from a peak of 71% in 1970 to 60% in 2000, and in some elections whites account for nearly half the vote. But the region's 16% growth rate for the 1990s topped that of all metro areas outside the Sun Belt.

After Barry returned to office in 1995 the District faced a fiscal crisis and Congress took most of the government out from under Barry's control. This was not a hostile takeover: House Speaker

Newt Gingrich appointed as chairman of the D.C. subcommittee Tom Davis, a Republican Congressman from Northern Virginia long sympathetic to the District, and he worked closely with the District's elected delegate, Eleanor Holmes Norton. They got Congress to establish a five-member financial control board in April 1995, which demanded cuts in spending and payroll. The control board took over the public schools in November 1996 and in August 1997 Congress stripped Barry of power over nine city departments, including Police, Public Works, Human Services, and Consumer and Regulatory Affairs; Barry kept the libraries and parks. The federal government assumed the District's $4.8 billion in unfunded pension liabilities in return for a two-thirds cut in the federal payment, and ordered closure of the scandal-tarred Lorton prison in northern Virginia. The control board's chief financial officer, Anthony Williams, a former city official in St. Louis and Boston, hacked away at the payroll, reformed management practices and literally cleaned up messes in District offices.

The electorate changed as well. It remains overwhelmingly Democratic: in 2000 Al Gore carried the District over George W. Bush 85%–9%, with 5% for Ralph Nader; whites voted for Gore 67%–20%, a higher percentage than in any state. But in a December 1997 citywide special election to the Council, Republican David Catania defeated Democrat and former Council Chairman Arrington Dixon. Turnout was relatively high in Ward 3 and other affluent areas but plummeted in Barry's strongholds in Anacostia, and Catania, who is gay, carried the heavily gay DuPont Circle area with over 80%. Catania turned out to be a stickler for holding city officials responsible for the performance of his department, and his election—the fact that a Republican beat a Democrat in a city which has voted 9% Republican for president—was a harbinger of the future. In May 1998 Barry announced he would not run again. Four Council members were in the race, Schwartz and three Democrats. Then there was a move, encouraged by *The Washington Post*, to draft Anthony Williams.

Williams was an unlikely candidate. He was not from Washington at all: He grew up in Los Angeles, a foster child adopted when he was 3 and did not talk; he was once an alderman in New Haven, Connecticut; when he took the CFO job in 1995 he moved first to Virginia and only later to Washington's Foggy Bottom. Williams had a history of changing course: he participated in anti-Vietnam war demonstrations, enlisted in the Air Force and served, then applied for conscientious objector status and got an honorable discharge. After seven years he graduated with honors from Yale, started an antique map business, then got degrees from Harvard Law and the Kennedy School and worked in Connecticut, Boston and St. Louis. Always dressed in a bow tie, diffident at first with crowds, he did not seem to have a political touch. But that may have been an asset. As CFO Williams had moved the District from huge deficits to a $185 million surplus in February 1998; he had cut payrolls deeply, provoking many squawks; he had changed the way many departments were managed. His leading primary opponent, Kevin Chavous, emphasized the need for a compassionate government and called Williams a bean counter. But Williams quickly surged and some key Barry supporters jumped on his bandwagon. He won the September Democratic primary by 50% to 35%, carrying five of the eight wards; in Ward 3 he beat Chavous 77%–9%. In the general Schwartz attacked Williams as an interloper and a heartless bureaucrat who fired too many people. But Williams, endorsed by the conservative *Washington Times* as well as *The Washington Post*, won 66%–30%.

The control board immediately delegated power to the new mayor. In fall 2000 judges returned control of most District departments to the city. The number of foster child adoptions tripled, and by 2000 the city had 27 charter schools—one of the highest rates in the nation. In 1999 Davis passed through Congress a law, first suggested by *Post* publisher Don Graham, allowing District students to attend public colleges in Maryland and Virginia at in-state rates. In June 2000 voters narrowly approved a new, partly appointed school board, with Ward 3 again leading the way. There were still problems. Williams did not get along well with the Council, and Catania and other members pushed successfully for reforms and for big tax cuts over Williams's opposition. Some city departments still performed abysmally. Many were shocked when 23-month-old Brianna Blackmond, often returned by city workers to her mother, was killed by her mother and godmother. The Police Department's homicide division was a mess, with dozens of unsolved and uninvestigated cases, and the child welfare agency seemed to do little to help neglected children.

But on balance progress was being made. The District budget was in surplus and was approved by Congress. Payrolls were reduced to 32,000 city employees. Lorton is being converted to a park. The culture of the city bureaucracy seemed to be changing, though many complaints were directed at Williams and the Council. As veteran city official Dwight Cropp said, "What we're seeing is a movement away from a lot of government programs addressing the needs of certain sectors of the community to an emphasis on economic development and an overall strategy for reviving the city." Some complaints still rankled and some disaffected Democrats in March 2001 began a campaign to draft former Clinton Transportation Secretary Rodney Slater to run against Williams in 2002. Courts turned down the District's suit claiming a constitutional right to voting representation in Congress; and Congress is not likely to grant it any time soon. District license plates, at the suggestion of radio commentator Mark Plotkin, carry the legend, "Taxation without representation." But it now seems possible the world's greatest democracy will have, for the first time in its history, a capital city with competent self-government.

D.C. Delegate   Eleanor Holmes Norton, first elected delegate from the District of Columbia in 1990, is a Washington native. She graduated from Antioch and Yale Law School, worked for the ACLU and the New York City Commission on Human Rights, and was head of the Equal Employment Opportunity Commission in the Carter administration. Afterward, she taught law at Georgetown. When the delegate seat came open in 1990, she ran and was criticized because her husband hadn't filed their income taxes for several years. But in the primary she edged past city Councilwoman Betty Anne Kane, 39%–33%. Norton has been re-elected easily since.

In the House she had the difficult and sometimes vexing task of responding to the fiscal collapse of the District government just as Republicans took over Congress. She has been hard-working, competent, intellectually honest, able to get along with opponents as well as fellow partisans and willing to take personal and political risks. She established good relations with Republicans active on District matters before 1994, even though she led the drive, much resented by Republicans in 1993 and repealed by them in 1995, to give her and the four territorial delegates to the House—all of whom were then Democrats—votes on most legislation in the House. In March 2001, she and Joseph Lieberman introduced legislation to exempt D.C. residents from federal income taxes until they are represented in Congress. In 1995 she worked with Tom Davis and Newt Gingrich to create the fiscal control board to superintend District finances; in 1997 she and Davis came up with the package that rescued District finances and removed control over most of the District government from Marion Barry. She initially hailed it as "a great day for the District," and with some cause. It also included tax breaks for downtown and some other areas. In return, the District gave up the $660 million federal payment for a $198 million "contribution," which, Norton argues, should in the long run remove the District from the close superintendency of Congress. Norton changed her tone momentarily after Barry criticized the measure for stripping the mayor of effective power over most of the District government. But the powers were restored after Anthony Williams was elected mayor in 1998.

Norton has spoken out effectively for District interests even though she doesn't have a vote on the floor. She obtained $1 billion for much needed street repairs and $75 million for the water system. She also got District borrowing authority for a new convention center. In 1999 she co-sponsored the bill to provide in-state tuition rates for District students at state colleges in Maryland and Virginia and, she argues, other states. She worked effectively for the District to take control of its renovated City Hall, most of which it ceded to the federal government in 1996. She argued in 1999 that the Blue Plains Sewage Treatment plant should be cleaned up by customers of the D.C. Water and Sewer Authority, not by the District. She criticized Attorney General Janet Reno for seeking the death penalty for the Starbucks killer, because the District repealed its death penalty in 1981 and voted against it in referendum in 1992. She bristled when the House Appropriations subcommittee moved to nullify a Council requirement for health insurance for contraception, even though Williams had said he would veto it. She protested when the House passed an amendment repealing the District's ban on handguns; it was quickly reversed. She got the District of Columbia included in the state quarter program. When delay in passing the District budget threatened D.C. General Hospital in November 2000, she worked effectively with Speaker Dennis Hastert to pass it and expressed concern about Williams' plan to privatize it.

Norton has plenty of future goals for the District. She has backed the reopening of Pennsylvania Avenue in front of the White House. She has worked for a new land agency to build a new Metrorail station at New York and Florida Avenues, N.E., and to redevelop the 55 acre federal Navy Yard property on the Anacostia River. She backs a private proposal to build a memorial for Frederick Douglass on federal land. She was reelected in 2000 by a 90%–6% margin.

THE PEOPLE: Pop. 2000: 572,059; Pop. 1990: 606,900, down 5.7% 1990–2000. 0.2% of U.S. total, 50th largest; 30.8% White, 60% Black, 2.7% Asian, 0.3% Amer. Indian, 0.1% Hawaiian, 2.4% Two+ races, 3.8% Other; 7.9% Hispanic Origin. 5.8% Unemployment. 2000 Voting age pop.: 457,067. 2000 Turnout: 205,748; 45% of VAP. Registered voters (2000): 354,410; 271,380 D (77%), 26,485 R (7%), 56,545 unaffiliated and minor parties (16%).

POLITICAL LINEUP: Delegate, 1 D at large.

2000 Presidential Vote		
Gore (D)	171,923	(85%)
Bush (R)	18,073	(9%)
Nader (Green)	10,576	(5%)
Others	1,322	(1%)

1996 Presidential Vote		
Clinton (D)	158,220	(85%)
Dole (R)	17,339	(9%)
Perot (I)	3,611	(2%)
Others	6,566	(4%)

2000 Republican Presidential Primary		
Bush (R)	1,771	(73%)
McCain (R)	593	(24%)
Other	69	(3%)

2000 Democratic Presidential Primary		
Gore (D)	18,621	(96%)
LaRouche (D)	796	(4%)

Del. Eleanor Holmes Norton (D)

Elected 1990; 6th term; b. June 13, 1937, Washington, D.C.; home, Washington, D.C.; Antioch Col., B.A. 1960, Yale, M.A. 1963, LL.B. 1964; Episcopalian; divorced.

Professional Career: Asst. Legal Dir., ACLU, 1965–70; New York City Human Rights Comm., 1970–77; Equal Empl. Oppor. Comm., 1977–81; Sr. Fellow, The Urban Inst., 1981–82; Prof., Georgetown U. Law Ctr., 1982–present.

DC Office: 2136 RHOB, 20515, 202-225-8050; Fax: 202-225-3002; Web site: www.house.gov/norton.

District Offices: Washington, D.C., 202-678-8900; Washington, D.C., 202-783-5065.

Committees: *Government Reform* (8th of 19 D): Civil Service & Agency Organization; District of Columbia (RMM). *Transportation & Infrastructure* (8th of 34 D): Aviation; Economic Development, Public Buildings & Emergency Management.

Election Results

2000 general	Eleanor Holmes Norton (D)	158,824	(90%)	($162,346)
	Edward H. Wolterbeek (R)	10,258	(6%)	
	Other	6,549	(4%)	
2000 primary	Eleanor Holmes Norton (D)	19,372	(97%)	
	Other	570	(3%)	
1998 general	Eleanor Holmes Norton (D)	118,520	(90%)	($143,495)
	Edward H. Wolterbeek (R)	8,288	(6%)	
	Others	4,910	(4%)	

★ FLORIDA ★

F lorida: For 36 days it was the cynosure of all eyes, the state that would determine who would become president of the United States, the most evenly balanced political state in the nation. To many this seemed astonishing. Sixty years before, Florida was the smallest Southern state, with just 5 congressional districts and 7 electoral votes, overwhelmingly Democratic. In 2000 it was the fourth-largest state in the nation, with 23 congressional districts and 25 electoral votes—and about to get 2 more from the 2000 Census. Only 12 years earlier, Florida had voted 61% for then-Vice President George Bush; he carried 66 of its 67 counties. Military-minded Southerners in the northern part of the state, affluent retirees on the Gulf Coast, middle-class conservatives in Tampa Bay and Orlando and around Disney World, Cubans in Miami and Dade County—all voted Republican, easily outnumbering the state's scattered black communities and its Jewish voters concentrated in Broward and Palm Beach County on the Gold Coast. But by 2000 Florida had become a state with political divisions as deep and political preferences as starkly different as any in the nation. Broward and Palm Beach on the Gold Coast voted 65%–33% for Al Gore; Escambia, Santa Rosa and Okaloosa Counties, on the western end of the Panhandle around what is called, perhaps unkindly, the Redneck Riviera, voted 68%–30% for George W. Bush. How Florida came to be the pivot of American politics is a story of growth and change, and over the past 60 years Florida has grown more rapidly and changed more vividly than just about any other part of the United States.

Florida has an exotic past. It is the only Atlantic Coast state that was not part of the colonial United States; through the exertions of John Quincy Adams and Andrew Jackson it was acquired from Spain in 1819. Starting off as a forgotten swamp and semitropical resort, Florida has emerged as almost an empire of its own, a prototype in many ways of America's future, with an international flavor and sometimes almost with its own foreign policy. For many years, Florida was the place which millions of retirees looked forward to: the sunny, year-round warmth after eternal gray skies over winter factories and dark offices. But in the 1980s and 1990s Florida's population of children grew rapidly as young couples, from the South, from various points north and from Latin America, chose to raise their families and make their livings in a booming economy, with jobs and opportunities in communities that did not exist a generation ago. For refugees from Cuba and Haiti and immigrants from all over the Caribbean and Latin America, Florida has been a land of freedom and security from authoritarian regimes and totalitarian police states. For Americans and foreigners of all kinds—some 74 million of them in 2000—Florida is the place to visit, with attractions, year-round swimming, restaurants and rooms to suit every taste and pocketbook. Yet all is not sunny: crime is down, but still a threat; the economic future is, as always, uncertain; the melting pot seems to work slowly, and Florida's Hispanic population seems often to live in a world apart.

Florida is a creation not of America's elite—though a few millionaires like Henry Flagler and Marcus Plant pioneered tourism here—but a place for which ordinary people have voted with their feet. Before World War II it was the least populous state in the South, with 1.4 million people, isolated, disease-ridden, bigoted, with no mineral resources but phosphate mines, not much agriculture outside its citrus groves, and hardly any manufacturing at all; today it has 16 million people. Florida is on the leading edge of where the nation is going: This is a state one-fifth of whose economy is based on tourism in a country where tourism is one of the great growth industries; a state with an economy based on services in a country increasingly service-oriented; the state with the largest proportion of elderly and retired citizens in a country where an increasing percentage will live many years in retirement; a state also with a growing number of school children in a country which, replenished by immigration, is growing faster and more robustly than any other advanced nation. And Florida is becoming a show business center, with actual movie production on the lots at the Universal and Disney World theme parks near Orlando: tourist attractions becoming workplaces, life imitating art imitating life.

Florida today has one of America's most buoyant economies, though its economic base may seem a mystery to outsiders. This is an economy is based on small business—98% of businesses

— Congressional district boundaries
  effective May 2, 1996.

South Florida Inset

have fewer than 100 employees—with a significant high-tech sector (sixth in the country); international merchandise trade, which increased from $24 billion in 1987 to $73 billion in 2000; while foreign investment increased from $9.5 billion to $29.6 billion. Miami for two decades has been the economic and commercial capital of Latin America, as well as its mecca for political exiles. A sign in Miami, "Gateway to Latin America," was updated to "Bridge to Latin America" and then "Capital of the Americas." You can fly nonstop from Miami to just about any place in Latin America, both English and Spanish are commonly understood, and it has been the one place where Latins could be sure their money and their persons were safe from government takeover. But Miami's position is not secure: As democracy, property rights and the rule of law become more secure in Latin America, Miami loses much of its uniqueness, and perhaps much of its business. Florida's economic future is tied up with trade, but since NAFTA was approved in 1993—over the objections of Florida's congressmen who wanted to protect its politically adept, but economically not that important, agricultural interests—opportunities to open trade further with Latin America have been missed, at an unknown cost to Florida.

What may be fragile in Florida is civil society; Florida can be disorderly and chaotic. Most people here do not have deep roots in the state, most communities sprang into existence within living memory and, if Florida gives people more freedom and options than they may ever have imagined, it has also given them more disruption and crime than they surely anticipated. Many of Florida's great fortunes were made elsewhere, and brought here partly because the state has no income or inheritance taxes. Government is weak here, and even in fighting crime Florida has let citizens take the lead. This was the first major state with a law allowing law-abiding citizens to routinely be licensed to carry guns. The result has been lower crime rates because, backers say, criminals hesitate to attack people who may be armed.

This new Florida, like today's America, has no real center. Its largest urban focus, Miami, is geographically off to one corner and culturally uniquely Cuban, with its eyes increasingly on Latin America. Even before the 2000 imbroglio, Miami's politics held it up to ridicule, as in March 1998 when the Miami city elections were voided because of absentee ballot fraud. But Miami holds only 362,000 of the 2.25 million people in the renamed Miami-Dade County, which has among other accomplishments developed one of the largest and best community college systems in the country. The rest of the Gold Coast, north past West Palm Beach, while containing almost one-third of Floridians, is also atypical, with a population drawn heavily from New York (the largest migration between any two states is from New York to Florida) and other Northeastern metro areas, plus non-Latino migrants from Miami-Dade, with large numbers of Jews, and huge retiree condos lining the ocean front. Then there is Central Florida, the I-4 corridor from Tampa-St. Petersburg through citrus and tourist country and Orlando, then finally to the Space Coast. This is mostly family, not retiree, country, living off high-tech industries as much as tourism. A year-round rather than seasonal civilization, this area has seen so much growth in the 1990s that it is becoming its own megalopolis—a "Tamplando" or "Orlampa," as the *Orlando Sentinel* called it. There is also the Gulf Coast, the affluent and burgeoning communities south of Tampa Bay and the more modest retirement counties to the north. Growing even more rapidly is the area along the hard-sand-beach Atlantic Coast around Jacksonville and Daytona Beach. Very Southern culturally is the western Panhandle, the Redneck Riviera around Pensacola and Panama City, which has Florida's most luxuriant white sand beaches.

Politically, this all adds up to a Florida that is uniquely balanced between the parties: in the 1990s the Republicans slowly captured control of state offices, winning the state House in 1994, the state Senate in 1996, and the governorship in 1998, even as the Democratic Party increased its strength in national elections so that in 2000 Florida came achingly close to electing Al Gore and elected its second Democratic U.S. senator. These contests were often close: Republican Jeb Bush lost to Democratic Governor Lawton Chiles by 51%–49% in 1994, then beat acting Governor Buddy McKay 55%–45% in 1998; Democrat Bill Nelson was elected to the Senate by 51%–46% in 2000, and of course the presidential election was decided by a 48.85%–48.84% margin. Republicans have won solid majorities in the legislature—25–15 in the Senate, 77–43 in the House—by organizing intensively and patiently capturing one marginal district after another; they have been helped by term limits, which keeps politically adept Democrats from holding onto Republican-leaning districts forever. Republicans have maintained a 15–8 margin in the U.S. House delegation in the same way, and by adapting shrewdly to local terrain; those with agricultural constituencies opposed NAFTA, the two Cuban-Americans opposed welfare reform because of the ban on aid to legal immigrants, those from affluent areas have voted pro-environment.

But Republicans have been able to prevent Democrats from changing the political balance of the state. In 1988 George Bush carried the Gold Coast 53%–46%, just as he carried narrowly most of the big metropolitan areas like New York, Philadelphia, Chicago and Detroit, capitalizing on voters' opposition to higher taxes and aggravation with high crime and welfare rolls. He carried the I-4 corridor 61%–38%, capitalizing on family values and the prosperity of the Reagan years. And he won the rest of the state, the culturally Southern counties of the center and north and the affluent retiree counties of the Gulf Coast, by 65%–34%. The Bush vote fell 17% to 21% in each of these areas in 1992—almost all a direct loss to Ross Perot. In the next eight years, the record of the Clinton administration and changing attitudes on cultural attitudes enabled Bill Clinton in 1996 and Al Gore in 2000 to, in effect, win over almost all of the Perot percentages. In 1996 Clinton carried the Gold Coast 60%–33%; Gore carried it 60%–38% in 2000. As crime and welfare rolls fell, those issues lost saliency, and cultural issues like the environment, abortion and gun control took their place; as in metro New York, Philadelphia, Chicago and Detroit, this greatly helped Democrats. Also, the increasing Jewish population in Broward and Palm Beach Counties moved them toward Democrats; Joe Lieberman campaigned extensively, and before enthusiastic crowds, in the Gold Coast in 2000. In 1996 Clinton carried the I-4 corridor 47%–43%; in 2000 Gore lost it 49%–48%. The biggest loss of Republican margin in any county in Florida between 1988 and 2000 was in Osceola County, which contains part of Disney World and the Disney-sponsored "new town" of Celebration. In the 1980s Disney World was still an epitome of traditional values; by 2000 Disney was hosting Gay Day—a shift in attitudes that is mirrored in the I-4 corridor's election returns. There was less change in the other half of Florida, which voted for Bob Dole 47%–42% in 1996 and for George W. Bush 55%–42% in 2000. As compared with 1988, the Bush margin fell significantly in counties with large in-migration from the North or from immigrants from abroad, and fell much less—in some cases rose a bit—in counties with a Southern cultural tone or large military installations. This mild change was similar to that in other Southern states, all of which Bush carried easily. But in Florida it was just enough to—barely—win.

Whither Florida in 2004, and 2002? The divisions appear pretty deeply etched. A comparison of George W. Bush's narrow victory in 2000 and Jeb Bush's narrow loss in 1994 show very similar patterns, with both Bushes losing big in the Gold Coast and narrowly carrying the I-4 corridor. The difference is that Jeb Bush's opponent, Lawton Chiles, with his roots in culturally southern Polk County, was able to hold his losses in the rest of the state to a lower margin than Al Gore did in 2000. During the Florida controversy in November and December 2000, many Democrats and their sympathizers in the press predicted that Jeb Bush would have a hard time winning reelection in 2002, and that angry Democrats would retaliate against him. But his job approval ratings remained well above 50% in late 2000 and early 2001, and it was not apparent that Democrats had a candidate with the stature and the claims to moderate status that recent winners like Senators Bob Graham and Bill Nelson brought to statewide races. As for 2004, Florida will surely be a target state again unless, as seems unlikely, the contest is heavily one-sided; and there will be new voters, and a different administration's record to be assessed. Florida, always ready for a hurricane, should be ready for another battle.

Two more things are worth noting about Florida politics. The first is that politics here is not driven by an elderly population terrified of losing government benefits. To be sure, the elderly are a larger percentage of the electorate here than in any other state, but the difference is not overwhelming; most new residents come here to work, not to retire. When Democrats ran against Medicare "cuts" in 1996, the damage to Republicans was minimal. Bob Dole actually ran better than George Bush had four years before in Gulf Coast counties heavily peopled by retirees, while he ran worse in the Gold Coast, especially in Miami-Dade County, and in the Orlando area, which has relatively few retirees. And Republican congressmen who had supported the Republican leadership on Social Security and Medicare were re-elected in districts with the largest elderly percentages in the nation. In 2000 George W. Bush called for individual investment accounts as a part of Social Security. Even so, he carried the over 65 vote in Florida by a 52%–46% margin—a margin essential to his carrying the state. The elderly tend to vote in line with long-established partisan preferences, not in rapid response to the latest proposal on Social Security.

The second point is that the environment is an increasingly important issue in Florida, but one which may not cut in a partisan way. People come to Florida partly because of the kind of place it is; migrants from New York or Illinois may not have cared much about environmental issues when they lived there, but they came to Florida in large part because of the climate and setting, and don't want to see oil drilled on the Gulf coast or the Everglades paved over. This is a change from history. The Everglades were seen as a nuisance for years: In 1845, when Florida was admitted to the Union, the legislature called for "reclaiming" the Everglades, and in 1850 Congress passed the Swamp and Overflowed Lands Act. The Army Corps of Engineers started building a dike across Lake Okeechobee in 1930 and for nearly 50 years worked to straighten the Kissimmee River and build dikes and channels to reclaim land for farming. But with the publication in 1947 of *The Everglades: River of Grass* by Marjory Stoneman Douglas, who died in 1998 at 108, Floridians began to appreciate the Everglades, which is essentially a flow of water south, from the Kissimmee River near Disney World, through Lake Okeechobee down to Florida Bay and the Gulf of Mexico. In the 1990s Congress ordered the Corps to restore the original flow of the Kissimmee River and in 1996 voters approved an amendment for cleaning up the Everglades (though disapproving a one-cent sugar tax to pay for it). Then both parties came together to call for restoring the Everglades. The Clinton administration package was announced in October 1998 by Al Gore (White House strategists were targeting Florida even then): a $7.8 billion Central and Southern Florida Project to build huge reservoirs above and under ground, a vast plant to recycle Miami waste water and a system of 70 massive pumps in the Everglades and to make the Tamiami Trail a causeway, like Alligator Alley 25 miles to the north. It was promptly supported by Governor Jeb Bush, who persuaded the Republican legislature to set aside $2 billion over 10 years for the project. Both houses of Congress, with leadership from the Florida delegation and from New Hampshire Republican Senator Bob Smith, approved the Everglades project before the 2000 election. It is not clear that it will work—it requires storing water in 1,000-foot wells, which has never been done and south Florida in early 2001 was enduring the worst drought in state history, with record low water levels in Lake Okeechobee—and it may well turn out to be more expensive than predicted. But it does appear that the Florida of the mid-21st Century will, for all its development, be closer in one important way to the natural Florida of the Seminoles than the Florida of today.

Governor Jeb Bush was elected governor of Florida in 1998, the second son of former President George Bush to be elected a big state governor in the 1990s. Jeb grew up in Midland and Houston, Texas. He majored in Latin American studies at the University of Texas and there met his wife, Columba, who is originally from Mexico. He speaks Spanish fluently—but with more a Mexican than Cuban accent, he notes. In 1981 he moved to Miami and started a real estate development company. For a year or so he was Commerce secretary under Republican Governor Bob Martinez. With a well-known name and strong convictions on issues, he decided to run for governor in 1994, vanquishing competition in the Republican primary and leading in polls during most of the fall. He called for fewer appeals for death row inmates and speedier executions, said Florida should withdraw from Aid to Families with Dependent Children and replace it with limited temporary assistance, and called for school choice and demanded voter approval of all state and local tax increases. There was a rigid tone to Bush's campaign; when one black man asked him what he would do to help him, Bush replied, "Probably nothing." Incumbent Governor Lawton Chiles responded with negative ads on Bush's business dealings; a Bush ad on crime backfired. Chiles started emphasizing his "cracker" roots and called himself "the he-coon [who] always walks before the light of day." The result was a 51%–49% Chiles victory. It was a polarized election: Blacks were 94% and Jews 75% for Chiles, Cubans 74% and Christian conservatives 91% for Bush.

Bush immediately started running again. He set up a foundation which produced intellectually serious government reform proposals and visited shelters for abused women and children in foster care. Challenged by the teachers' union head to spend more time in classrooms, he visited more than 200 schools and, with the Urban League of Miami, founded and taught at a charter school in Miami's Liberty City neighborhood. Bush lobbied the legislature to cut unemployment taxes in 1997 and to better handle abused children in foster care in 1998. "I started listening more," he said later and, while his positions on issues did not change much, his approach and his tone did. Republican rule "does not mean that we don't need to create consensus and build some common ground." The consensus in Florida had been moving for some time toward Bush—Chiles had produced welfare and reinventing government reforms—and now Bush came some distance toward the consensus.

Bush entered 1998 as the heavy favorite for governor while Democrats inflicted damage on themselves. In January state House Democrats ousted party leader-designate Willie Logan, an African American from Opa-Locka; Bush called Logan and held informal sessions with him and other black legislators, and got endorsements from a black legislator in Broward County and the mayor of Fort Lauderdale. Black legislators joined Republicans in overturning Chiles' vetoes of the partial-birth abortion ban, school vouchers and parental notification of abortions. After Senator Bob Graham and Insurance Commissioner (and now Senator) Bill Nelson said they would not run, Democrats noisily looked for alternatives to the likely nominee, Lieutenant Governor Buddy MacKay, though MacKay had received good press for his work in office and nearly beat Connie Mack for senator in 1988. In time MacKay found his voice, bragging about the Healthy Kids insurance program and calling for higher education standards and a patients' bill of rights; he attacked Bush on vouchers, abortion and gun control, and criticized "questionable deals" and "mismanagement" in his business. Bush won 55%–45%. The electorate was a bit less polarized this time: Bush's percentage rose among blacks (to 14%) but was down among Christian conservatives (to 83%). Bush still lost the Gold Coast by a 56%–44% margin despite all his attentions. He won a solid 57%–43% in the I-4 corridor and 61%–39% in the rest of the state. In mid-December Chiles unexpectedly died; his greatest legacy was the tobacco lawsuit which he initiated by pushing through a law changing the standard of proof. Buddy MacKay was governor for the last weeks of the term.

With a Republican legislature, Bush got off to a fast start. He killed a high speed Miami-Orlando "Bullet Train," and pushed through a $1 billion tax cut. He passed an education reform plan, which provided school vouchers for students in schools that persisted in being rated failing; teachers' unions hated this and got a Leon County Circuit Court judge to rule it unconstitutional, but that decision was overturned on appeal. A February 2001 study showed that the threat of vouchers spurred low-performing schools to improve their students' academic performance. Bush got civil justice reform, longer prison terms for gun-toting criminals, and a speedier process for death-penalty appeals, though the latter was overturned by the Florida Supreme Court. He vetoed a record $313 million of legislators' pet projects. In mid-1999 Bush was alarmed when Ward Connerly, sponsor of California's 1996 Proposition 209 which outlawed state government racial quotas and preferences, moved to put a similar proposition on the Florida ballot. Bush said Connerly would start a "war" and in November 1999 put forward his own One Florida proposal, to curtail quotas and setasides in state contracts, get rid of quotas and preferences in state colleges and universities and replace them by guaranteeing places in the state's 10 public colleges to the top 20% of every high school graduating class. There was loud protest: Two African-American legislators staged a 25-hour sit-in in the governor's office, and 10,000 protesters chanted while Bush delivered his 2000 State of the State address. But by 2001 minority contracting was up a whopping 90%; meanwhile, Bush had quietly taken a Confederate flag out of the Capitol and sent it to the Florida Museum of History. In 2000 Bush continued to be successful with the legislature, cutting taxes by $500 million, spending $6 billion on roads and getting a $2 billion, 10-year commitment to the bipartisan program to restore the Everglades. The legislature passed a prescription drug program for seniors and Medicaid recipients, expanded KidCare and passed a patient protection plan. Bush supported a new law school for historically black Florida A&M University.

Jeb Bush did not take a highly visible role in the 2000 presidential campaign. He seldom traveled outside Florida and spoke only every week or so with his brother George W. Bush. A more visible role was played by Jeb Bush's 24-year-old son, George P. Bush, who made appearances before Hispanic audiences, cut a TV spot in Spanish and English and spoke at the podium of the Republican National Convention. In the controversy over Florida's vote, Jeb Bush recused himself from the three-member board of elections, substituting Agriculture Commissioner Bob Crawford, a Democrat who endorsed George W. Bush; charges that he orchestrated Secretary of State Katherine Harris' decisions to certify George W. Bush as the winner have foundered for lack of evidence. He did say that he would sign a proclamation by the Florida legislature that the Republican electors had won, but there was nothing to back the charges that somehow the governor of Florida had stolen the election for his brother. The day after the election was decided, he appeared with officials of both parties and announced the formation of a bipartisan commission to study Florida's election procedures. In March 2001 it came forward with its recommendations, including getting rid of punch card ballots, leasing optical scanning equipment for all counties for the 2002 election and setting a uniform standard for recounts; an election reform bill was signed by Governor Bush in May 2001.

There was much speculation during the Florida controversy and after that Bush would have difficulty winning reelection in 2002. Angry Democrats threatened retaliation and black leaders angrily charged that he had stolen the election for his brother. But his standing in public polls remained high, and the best-known state Democrat, Attorney General Bob Butterworth, said that he would not run. In early 2001 Senators Bob Graham and Bill Nelson were trying to recruit Ambassador to Vietnam and former 2nd District Congressman Pete Peterson, who would start off relatively unknown but seemed to have the potential to be a serious statewide competitor. Others mentioned as possible candidates included former Clinton Attorney General and Miami-Dade Attorney Janet Reno, Congressmen Bob Wexler and Jim Davis, state House Democratic leader Lois Frankel, state Senator Daryl Jones, Tallahassee Mayor Scott Maddox and Tampa attorney Bill McBride. In the meantime, Bush was wrestling with budget problems: the amount of unallocated funds in early 2001 was one-third what it had been a year earlier, and Democrats were attacking him for proposing cuts in the intangibles tax. Bush proposed setting aside $3.8 billion in reserves and cutting spending from projected levels by $1.9 billion. He signed a bill in May 2001 eliminating the state Board of Regents, replacing it with a seven-member board appointed by the governor—a move attacked by Graham—and called for more spending to recruit teachers and improve nursing homes. In January 2001 he attracted national attention when he called on the Interior Department to cancel planned oil leases in the Gulf of Mexico off the Alabama coast. Florida politicians of both parties have long opposed oil drilling in the Gulf off the Florida coast, and Bush claimed that drilling nearby would endanger Florida beaches and threaten the tourism industry, but Vice President Dick Cheney in May said the administration favored drilling.

Cook's Call   *Competitive.* This race is where Democrats would like to exact some retribution for the outcome of the presidential contest. Before November 2000, Bush did not seem particularly vulnerable, but Democrats now appear incredibly energized—especially minorities. There is a long list of Democratic possibilities, including Congressmen Jim Davis and Bob Wexler, former Congressman and Ambassador to Vietnam Pete Peterson, and former U.S. Attorney General Janet Reno. Although running a statewide campaign here is difficult and very expensive, the Democratic nominee is likely to be very well funded and the race will be under the national media spotlight.

Senior Senator   Bob Graham was first elected in 1986. He is careful, methodical, thorough, hard-working, reliable—always wearing his Florida ties, recording every meeting and meal in notebooks, scheduling meetings with every member of the Florida House delegation and with lobbyists on both sides of important issues. He comes from a prominent Florida family. His father started out with a Miami-area dairy farm and developed the planned mini-city of Miami Lakes; his half-brother Philip Graham was publisher of *The Washington Post.* He has been in politics almost all his adult life; he was elected to the state House in 1966, at 30, and to the state Senate in 1970. In 1978 he ran for governor. After a come-from-behind win in the Democratic runoff, he won the general with a solid 56%. He was highly popular and easily won reelection in 1982. In 1986 he ran against Republican Senator Paula Hawkins, and after a spirited campaign won 55%–45%. His trademark campaign device since 1978 has been work days (invented by Senator Tom Harkin for his 1974 House race): Graham worked one day a week at some local job, from bagging groceries to construction. He keeps it up still, once a month, and in January 2001 logged his 365th work day—a full year of work days—as an airline gate attendant and flight attendant in Tallahassee, Tampa and Miami.

Graham's voting record in the Senate has been moderate and he is part of the New Democrat Coalition. He has been a hardliner on crime legislation, supporting capital punishment, seeking federal reimbursement to states which jail criminal aliens. A staunch opponent of Fidel Castro, Graham has strongly backed the embargo on Cuba. He wanted to stem the flow of Haitian refugees to Florida, and backed the dispatch of U.S. troops to Haiti. In late 2000 and early 2001 he argued that the Elian Gonzalez case should be settled in state court: "Elian and every child like him should have access to the same values of justice and due process that have sustained our democracy for more than two centuries." He co-sponsored the bill to make the boy a U.S. citizen. He got a commitment from Bill Clinton not to seize Elian at night, arguing that otherwise his Miami relatives would be deprived of sleep and might be more difficult to deal with. When Clinton reneged, and the boy was seized at gunpoint in the middle of the night, Graham was outraged: "There was an insensitivity and crudeness to this. To do this at one of the most deeply religious periods of the year, to do it at a time when families are reflecting on spiritual values, to do it in the middle of the night, . . . to do it under all of those circumstances was absolutely intolerable, unnecessary, outrageous and has left a scar on this community." Later, he introduced a bill to bar the INS from sending immigrant children who arrive in the U.S. without their parents to juvenile detention centers and giving the attorney general discretion to grant permanent residency status to 500 such children a year. He also sponsored a bill curtailing indefinite detention for immigrants whose countries won't take them back and tried to negotiate a compromise on guest workers, to allow 1 million temporary visas for farm workers and grant amnesty to 570,000 currently illegal workers.

On national issues, Graham often supports Democratic policy but is sometimes willing to buck both party and constituency. He voted unhesitatingly for the Gulf war resolution. He supports the balanced budget amendment and the McCain-Feingold campaign finance legislation. He has called for means-testing Medicare and reducing cost-of-living increases in Social Security—not Democratic orthodoxy and risky in Florida. In 1998 he sponsored with Republican John Chafee an HMO regulation bill requiring an internal appeal process, but without the right-to-sue favored by many Democrats or the medical savings accounts favored by many Republicans. In 1999 he helped pass a law prohibiting nursing homes from evicting Medicaid patients. He called for Medicare to use managed care techniques, like negotiating contracts with competitive bidding, to hold down costs. In 2000 he proposed a tax credit for long-term care expenses and for deductibility of premiums for long-term care insurance. He pushed for Medicare coverage of hypertension and glaucoma screenings and preventive medications. He sponsored the Senate Democrats' prescription drug bill in June 2000, with premiums of $40 a month and a deductible of $250 and full payment of costs over $4,000 for those below a certain income level; it was rejected on party lines. Graham sits on the Finance Committee, which he sees as a "laboratory for bipartisanship," and says, "I don't think being a centrist is necessarily a cautious position. It's a position that tries to get something accomplished." In the closely divided Senate he may be a key maker of bipartisan compromise. On tobacco he backed Florida's law, passed under Governor Lawton Chiles, to eliminate the defense of contributory negligence—a law that made the national tobacco cases possible.

As a former governor, Graham has kept a close eye on Florida issues. In 1997 he and John McCain succeeded in getting changes in the veterans' health funding formula, to recognize the needs in rapidly growing states like Florida and Arizona. In 1998 he worked for a highway funding formula more favorable to Florida. He has sponsored bills to exempt pre-paid college tuition programs, like Florida's, from taxation and to allow schools to be built by private corporations with tax-exempt private activity bonds. He passed a bill in March 2000 to reduce the cost of crop insurance to citrus growers. He hailed the signing of the bill reducing tariffs on textiles, apparels and other exports from the Caribbean, Central America and sub-Saharan Africa. He has worked hard on restoring the Everglades, starting with returning to its natural state the Kissimmee River and culminating in the November 2000 Everglades Act, which authorized $1.4 billion toward an eventual $7.8 billion for the dozens of projects to restore the natural flow of water through the Everglades.

Graham was re-elected by wide margins in 1992 and 1998. He was clearly disturbed by the Lewinsky affair and was one of the Senate Democrats who seemed to be wavering for a while on the impeachment of Bill Clinton. In 2000 Graham was on the short list of vice presidential nominees. Polls showed that he would have improved Al Gore's showing in Florida: Joe Lieberman surely had a positive effect on the ticket in Broward and Palm Beach Counties on the Gold Coast, but Graham has run far ahead of party lines not only there but in the I-4 corridor and in the rest of the state—he carried 63 of 67 counties in 1998. After the 2000 election, Graham headed for a vacation in the Galapagos, but returned to defend local Democratic election officials from charges of partisanship. He has worked with, but has also been sharply critical of, Governor Jeb Bush. In early 2001 he was angered when Governor Bush signed legislation to replace the state Board of Regents with a new board appointed by the governor. In February 2001 state Republican Chairman Al Cardenas challenged Graham to run for governor, and Democrats hoped he would do so; but within a week he said he would not run, and later was pushing for Ambassador to Vietnam and former Congressman Pete Peterson to be the candidate.

Junior Senator   Bill Nelson, elected in 2000, is a freshman now after nearly 30 years in politics. He grew up in Melbourne, on what is now the Space Coast, the son of a developer and real estate investor who died when he was 14; Nelson likes to recall that his great-grandfather arrived in Florida on boat as a stowaway. From his family home, Rock Point, he could see rockets blast off from what is now the Kennedy Space Center in the 1950s and 1960s. Nelson was active in student government and has always been something of a straight arrow; he doesn't drink, smoke or swear. He went to the University of Florida for two years, then graduated from Yale and the University of Virginia Law School. Then he served two years in the Army, returned to Melbourne and briefly practiced law. He worked on the staff of Governor Reubin Askew. In 1972, at 30, he was elected to the state House of Representatives. There he sponsored a local land planning law that passed in 1975, wrote a computer crime law and pushed through a lobbyist disclosure law.

In 1978, when Republican Congressmen Louis Frey retired, Nelson ran for Congress, from a seat that then included the Space Coast's Brevard County and most of Orlando's Orange County. His religious faith and traditional values, his indefatigable campaigning and folksy manner helped make him popular in an area that was trending heavily Republican. He won the seat 61%–39% and in five succeeding elections won between 61% and 73% of the vote, in a district that voted 29% for Michael Dukakis. In Congress he was not entirely sure-footed. He got a seat on the Budget Committee in his freshman year, where he wobbled on the Reagan budget and tax cuts. On the Science Committee he got his fellow Democrats to vote him rather than the more liberal George Brown chairman of the Space Subcommittee—obviously of prime importance to the district. Nelson not only boosted the space program in every possible way, he also rode the space shuttle himself, in early January 1986. Less than two weeks later the *Challenger* exploded. Nelson pressed successfully for funding of the space shuttle and space station, institutionalizing, he said, the manned space program for some time to come.

In 1989, with the support of leading Florida Democrats, Nelson set out to run against Republican Governor Bob Martinez, who was not faring well in polls. But in early 1990, some Democrats became antsy about Nelson's prospects, and got Lawton Chiles, who had retired from the Senate in 1988 after three terms, to run. Nelson stayed in the race and attacked Chiles for land deals and said that his use of Prozac meant that health was an issue. Chiles charged that Nelson's votes on the Banking Committee may have worsened the savings and loan crisis. But Chiles was always far ahead, and won the September primary 69%–31%. Nelson returned to his 77-acre oceanfront home in Melbourne, his political career seemingly over. But in 1994 he found an opening when state Insurance Commissioner Tom Gallagher, a Republican, ran for governor (he finished third in the primary, with 13% to Jeb Bush's 46%). Nelson was elected in November to an office whose full title is Treasurer, Insurance Commissioner and State Fire Marshal, and proceeded to make a highly publicized activist record. He helped to rebuild the homeowners insurance market, devastated since Hurricane Andrew in 1992; in time, 34 new insurers entered the field and the Joint Underwriters Association's number of policies dropped from 937,000 to 65,000. He ordered auto insurers to decrease rates for good drivers, fined big insurers for "churning" life insurance policies on the elderly, investigated insurers who targeted blacks with "junk burial" policies, cracked down on insurance fraud (staged auto accidents, padded medical bills) enough to allow rates to be lowered, and helped get European insurers to honor unpaid Holocaust-related claims. He supported mandatory hospital stays for mastectomies and put two decades of malpractice complaints on the Internet. As a member of Florida's Cabinet, he ranged far afield, opposing offshore oil drilling (as almost all Florida politicians do), worked for the Healthy Kids program and organized voluntary food giveaways. As Fire Marshal, he fought a power company's plan to use the untested fuel Orimulsion in Tampa Bay, set up a Church Arson Task Force in 1996 and gave away 50,000 smoke detectors to the poor.

Nelson was obviously setting himself up to run for higher statewide office, and his opening came in March 1999, when Senator Connie Mack said he would not run for reelection in 2000. Mack, a Republican, had worked closely with Democratic Senator Bob Graham on state issues and was the key Republican in seeking a doubling of research spending at the National Institutes of Health over five years. He was highly popular and would easily have won reelection; his retirement left a seat up for grabs in a state which, as election night viewers learned in November 2000, was very closely divided between the parties. And Republicans appeared to have a rough primary contest—always a problem in a state with a late September primary and an even later October runoff if no candidate got a majority. The contestants were 20-year, Orlando-based Congressman Bill McCollum, one of the House's impeachment managers, and Tom Gallagher, the Florida Education Commissioner. Not until June 2000, after a meeting with Governor Jeb Bush and state Republican Chairman Al Cardenas, did Gallagher take himself out of the race, to run for Insurance Commissioner, the office he had relinquished to Nelson in 1994. A possible problem for Nelson was the independent candidacy of Willie Logan, a veteran African-American legislator whom Democrats had ousted as Speaker-designate in January 1998 on the grounds that he wasn't raising enough money. But Logan, who was getting 5% in many polls, ended up winning just 1.4% in November.

Washington observers considered the race a contest over the wisdom of impeachment, and Nelson played on that occasionally, saying in May 2000, "We've seen what happened to politics in America in the last few years, the politics of personal attacks, the politics of excessive partisanship and ideological intolerance." But mostly it was a battle of competing styles. Nelson, running his fourth statewide race in 10 years, always led in polls. His easygoing, folksy manner contrasted favorably with McCollum's stiff, often aggressive manner. McCollum, with a long conservative record on abortion and gun control, attempted to modulate his positions, but only succeeded in antagonizing his base. His longstanding support of harsh restrictions on immigration probably worked against him in a state with an increasing number of voters of recent immigrant origin. Nelson may have been embarrassed momentarily, when Democrats, reading from White House talking points, were attacking vice presidential nominee Dick Cheney for having voted against a resolution calling for freedom for Nelson Mandela in 1986; it turned out that Nelson, who appeared with Bill Clinton that day, had voted against the resolution too. But McCollum's charge that Nelson was a "liberal" and a proponent of "class warfare" proved unconvincing. There was demagoguery on both sides: McCollum hit Nelson for voting in 1983 to raise the Social Security retirement age, while Nelson attacked McCollum for voting in 1995 and 1996 for Medicare "cuts" which were actually increases in spending.

This was the most expensive Senate race in Florida history, with each candidate spending over $8.5 million. But none of it seemed to move votes. In the September primaries, 52% of the two-party vote was cast on the Democratic side; in the November general election, 52% of the two-party vote was cast for the Democrat, as Nelson won 51%–46%. Nelson won 60%–37% in the Gold Coast, almost exactly the same margin as in the presidential race. In the I-4 corridor, which included McCollum's district and most of the district Nelson had represented in the House, Nelson won 51%–46%; superior name identification was not Nelson's only advantage. In the rest of the state Nelson lost by only 52%–46%, compared to the 55%–42% margin by which Al Gore lost there. Folksiness and Florida roots counted.

In Washington, Nelson joined the New Democrat Coalition, but sounded quite partisan notes on issues in early 2001. He vowed to use his Budget Committee seat to defeat the Bush tax cut and voted against the confirmation of John Ashcroft. He said he would use his seat on Foreign Relations to fight terrorism and his seat on Armed Services to allow Internet voting for military personnel overseas—a response, perhaps, to the concerted Democratic attempt in Florida to disqualify the legitimate votes of overseas military personnel whose ballots arrived without a postmark. In a show of respect for his political acumen, he was named vice chairman of the Democratic Senatorial Campaign Committee.

Presidential politics   Political pundits may not have predicted that Florida would be the most closely contested state in the 2000 presidential campaign, but the candidates foresaw it. Al Gore targeted it early and visited it often, even conducting his debate prep sessions in Sarasota County; this was the one close state where Joe Lieberman's Jewish faith paid political dividends. George W. Bush for a time seemed to believe that the state where his brother was governor would fall into his column without too much prodding, and his campaign was outspent here by Gore's. But Bush ended up devoting lots of time and money to Florida as well. Gore's position on Elian Gonzalez—that his custody should be determined by a state court—was widely taken as a turnabout and a bid for Miami-Dade County's Cuban-American vote; in fact it was consistent with Gore's longstanding views on Cuban policy, and availed him little since the violent seizure of the 6-year-old boy by armed agents of the Clinton administration put the Cuban vote solidly in favor of Bush.

Indeed, the Cuban vote was so heavily for Bush that he carried Hispanics overall by a 50%–48% margin: this Spanish-speaking president owes his election to Latinos. Blacks voted heavily for Gore, 93%–7%, and the VNS exit poll showed black turnout up sharply from 1996, to 16%. What is clear is that there was no organized effort to bar black voters from the polls, nor any significant incidents where they were barred, contrary to the charges of Jesse Jackson and the lame duck Civil Rights Commission. Florida was not another Selma. There were other differences between groups of voters which are worth noting. Jewish voters voted overwhelmingly for the Clinton-Gore ticket, and those with no religion voted 68%–24% for Gore; white Protestants voted 65%–33% and white Catholics 54%–42% for Bush. Voters with incomes under $30,000 voted more heavily for Gore and voters with incomes over $100,000 voted more heavily for Bush than in the nation generally: there was more economic polarization in Florida. Voters over 65 voted 52%–46% for Bush, a sign that Social Security individual investment accounts are not abhorrent to the elderly. But voters under 30 voted 56%–38% for Gore, a good omen for Democrats in future Florida elections.

The story of the Florida recount will not be fully told here. The Gore campaign was again first off the mark, at first claiming that the butterfly ballot in Palm Beach County (designed by a Democratic official and approved by both parties) had been so unfair that it required a county-wide revote, then settling on a two-pronged strategy of disqualifying legitimately cast military absentee ballots sent in without a postmark, and qualifying as votes dimpled chads and bumps on punch card ballots in four carefully selected heavily Democratic counties. The Bush strategy was to oppose hand counts of punch card ballots, on the grounds that counting was inevitably subjective and subject to political manipulation. Of course that was factually correct, as the hand count in Broward County showed, where Democratic officials gave Gore about 500 net votes from dimpled chads and bumps. The Democratic hand counters in Palm Beach County, however, employed a tougher standard, counting dimpled chads only where ballots had dimpled chads for several offices. In Miami-Dade County (the name was changed from Dade County in 1997) the canvassers started hand counting in heavily Democratic precincts and counted dimpled chads. But when Republicans protested when they attempted to segregate ballots with no presidential vote in a room from which outside observers would be barred, in violation of Florida's sunshine law, the canvassers stopped the hand count; as it happened, the un-hand-counted part of the county had voted for Bush, and press examination of the ballots later suggested that Bush, rather than Gore, would have benefited from a continuation of the hand count.

At no point did Gore ever take the lead away from Bush. Gore had great help from the Florida Supreme Court, all seven of whose members had been chosen by Democratic governors (one was co-chosen by then-Governor-elect Bush), a court known for its liberal judicial interventionism. But to the surprise of many, rulings of the Florida court rewriting (in the guise of interpreting) state election law were overturned twice by the U.S. Supreme Court. The Gore campaign, accustomed to a press inclined to accept its arguments, was evidently unaware of how unfair its strategy of hand-counting only four heavily Democratic counties would seem to the U.S. Supreme Court justices, seven out of nine of whom ruled that it was so unfair as to be unconstitutional. The Bush campaign's hard-line opposition to hand counts, even in counties where they might help Bush, proved the better strategy. The official 537-vote margin, by the way, still includes the Broward and Palm Beach hand counts, which gained Gore votes by counting dimpled chads. The best guess, fortified by post-election press examinations, is that Bush actually won Florida by a little more than 1,000 votes—a paper thin margin, out of 5,963,100 recorded. To charges that the Palm Beach ballot changed the outcome of the election, perhaps the final word should go to Palm Beach County Democratic Chairman Monte Friedkin, speaking in March 2001: "Frankly the system is bad, the machines are not user-friendly, but at the end of the day it's as much the fault of the voters as the process. We can make all the excuses we want, but the facts are the facts and George Bush is president."

Florida has had a presidential primary in March for many years; since 1988 it has been part of Southern Super Tuesday. It was once a pivotal contest: Jimmy Carter's victory here in 1976 tossed George Wallace out of national politics and helped put Carter in the White House. Now, as one of many states voting on a single day—albeit the second largest—it attracts less attention, though certainly no serious candidate, knowing what it could mean in November, will avoid it.

Congressional districting   Florida has gained congressional districts from every Census since 1930, when it was still the smallest state in the South: in 1930 it elected four House members; in 2002 it will elect 25, two more than in 2000. Ten years ago, when the state gained four seats, Democrats controlled the redistricting process, but they were so conflicted they could not produce a plan, and the current lines were drawn by a federal court in May 1992. The plan included three black-majority districts and two Hispanic-majority districts, some with very peculiar shapes; boundaries of the other 18 districts were not so driven by politics, but sometimes ended up grotesque because of next-door minority districts. The result was the election of three black Democrats, two Cuban-American Republicans and a Republican edge that increased from 10–9 in 1990 to 15–8 after November 1994; Florida now has the second largest Republican delegation in the House. In April 1996, the 3d District, which meandered through half the swamps of north Florida, was ruled unconstitutional, and redrawn amicably by a split-party legislature; its black percentage fell from 51% to 40%, but incumbent Democrat Corinne Brown has been re-elected since.

With the governorship and big margins in the state legislature, Republicans control the process in 2001. State House Speaker Tom Feeney, a national figure momentarily when he led the Florida House in voting to cast the state's electoral votes for Bush as the candidate certified by the secretary of State, has said that the three heavily black and two heavily Hispanic seats will not be seriously disturbed. Geography will control some lines, in the Panhandle particularly, and demographics will limit the degree to which Republicans can help their cause. Shaky Republican incumbents—Clay Shaw in the Gold Coast 22d District and Ric Keller in the Orlando-area 8th District—will probably be shored up. Incumbent Democrats will probably fare pretty well: They either come from heavily Democratic areas or from places where paring off Democratic areas will endanger Republicans in adjacent seats. Central Florida, the state's fastest-growing region, will probably gain at least one new seat; where the other will come from probably depends on Tallahassee politics.

THE PEOPLE: Pop. 2000: 15,982,378; Pop. 1990: 12,937,926, up 23.5% 1990–2000. 5.7% of U.S. total, 4th largest; 78% White, 14.6% Black, 1.7% Asian, 0.3% Amer. Indian, 0.1% Hawaiian, 2.4% Two + races, 3% Other; 16.8% Hispanic Origin. 3.6% Unemployment. 2000 Voting age pop.: 12,336,038. 2000 Turnout: 6,138,765; 50% of VAP. Registered voters (2000): 8,752,717; 3,803,081 D (43%), 3,430,238 R (39%), 1,519,398 unaffiliated and minor parties (17%).

POLITICAL LINEUP: Governor, Jeb Bush (R); Lt. Gov., Frank Brogan (R); Secy. of State, Katherine Harris (R); Atty. Gen., Robert A. Butterworth (D); Treasurer and Insurance Commissioner, Tom Gallagher (R); Comptroller, Robert Milligan (R); Commissioner of Education, Charlie Crist (R); Commissioner of Agriculture, Charles Bronson (R); State Senate, 40 (15 D, 25 R); Senate Pres. Pro Tempore, Ginny Brown-Waite (R); Senate President, John M. McKay (R); Majority Leader, James E. King (R); State House, 120 (43 D, 77 R); House Speaker, Tom Feeney (R). Senators, Bob Graham (D) and Bill Nelson (D). Representatives, 23 (8 D,15 R).

ELECTIONS DIVISION: 850-488-7697; **FILING DEADLINE FOR U.S. CONGRESS:** July 12, 2002.

2000 Presidential Vote

Bush (R)	2,912,790	(49%)
Gore (D)	2,912,253	(49%)
Nader (Green)	97,488	(2%)
Others	40,579	(1%)

1996 Presidential Vote

Clinton (D)	2,545,690	(48%)
Dole (R)	2,242,951	(43%)
Perot (I)	483,761	(9%)

2000 Republican Presidential Primary

Bush (R)	516,161	(74%)
McCain (R)	139,397	(20%)
Keyes (R)	32,343	(5%)

2000 Democratic Presidential Primary

Gore (D)	451,657	(82%)
Bradley (D)	100,259	(18%)

Gov. Jeb Bush (R)

Elected 1998, term expires Jan. 2003, 1st term; b. Feb. 11, 1953, Midland, TX; home, Miami; U. of TX, B.A. 1974; Catholic; married (Columba).

Elected Office: FL Commerce Secy., 1987–88; Candidate for FL Gov., 1994.

Professional Career: Pres. & COO, Codina Group, 1981–94; Founder & Chmn., Foundation for Florida's Future, 1995–98.

Office: The Capitol, Tallahassee, 32399, 904-488-7146; Fax: 904-487-0801; Web site: www.state.fl.us.

Election Results

1998 general	Jeb Bush (R)	2,192,105	(55%)
	Buddy MacKay (D)	1,773,054	(45%)
1998 primary	Jeb Bush (R)	unopposed	
1994 general	Lawton Chiles (D)	2,135,008	(51%)
	Jeb Bush (R)	2,071,068	(49%)

Sen. Bob Graham (D)

Elected 1986, seat up 2004, 3d term; b. Nov. 9, 1936, Coral Gables; home, Miami Lakes; U. of FL, B.A. 1959, Harvard, J.D. 1962; United Church of Christ; married (Adele).

Elected Office: FL House of Reps., 1966–70; FL Senate, 1970–78; FL Gov., 1978–1986.

Professional Career: The Graham Cos., Sengra Development Corp., 1962–66.

DC Office: 524 HSOB, 20510, 202-224-3041; Fax: 202-224-2237; Web site: www.senate.gov/~graham.

State Offices: Miami, 305-536-7293; Tallahassee, 850-907-1100; Tampa, 813-228-2476.

Committees: *Energy & Natural Resources*: Energy Research, Development, Production & Regulation (Chmn.); National Parks, Historic Preservation & Recreation; Water & Power. *Environment & Public Works*: Fisheries, Wildlife & Water (Chmn.); Transportation & Infrastructure. *Finance*: Health Care; International Trade; Long-Term Growth & Debt Reduction (Chmn.). *Intelligence (Select)* (Chmn.). *Veterans' Affairs*.

Group Ratings

	ADA	ACLU	AFS	LCV	CON	ITIC	NTU	COC	ACU	NTLC	CHC
2000	80	57	85	86	95	93	20	60	16	3	15
1999	100	—	100	78	98	—	16	35	4	—	—

National Journal Ratings

	1999 LIB	—	1999 CONS		2000 LIB	—	2000 CONS
Economic	87%	—	10%		76%	—	22%
Social	75%	—	20%		66%	—	21%
Foreign	56%	—	40%		58%	—	38%

Key Votes of the 106th Congress

1. Educ. Savings Accts.	N	5. Review Movie Violence	N	9. NATO War in Serbia	Y
2. Prescrip. Drug Benefit	Y	6. Gun Show Bckgrnd. Checks	Y	10. Table Cuba Travel Ban	Y
3. Delay Ergonomic Standards	N	7. Ban Part.-Birth Abortion	N	11. Nuclear Test-Ban Treaty	Y
4. Phase Out Estate Tax	N	8. Broaden Hate Crimes List	Y	12. Perm. Trade with China	Y

Election Results

1998 general	Bob Graham (D)	2,436,402	(62%)	($5,094,581)
	Charlie Crist (R)	1,463,749	(38%)	($1,487,498)
1998 primary	Bob Graham (D)	unopposed		
1992 general	Bob Graham (D)	3,245,565	(65%)	($3,318,473)
	Bill Grant (R)	1,716,505	(35%)	($242,251)

Sen. Bill Nelson (D)

Elected 2000, seat up 2006, 1st term; b. Sept. 29, 1942, Miami; home, Tallahassee; Yale U., B.A. 1965; U. of VA, J.D. 1968; Episcopalian; married (Grace Cavert).

Military Career: U.S. Army, 1968–70; U.S. Army Reserves, 1965–71.

Elected Office: FL House of Reps., 1972–78; U.S. House of Reps., 1978–90; FL Treasurer, Insurance Comm. & Fire Marshal, 1994–2000.

Professional Career: Practicing atty., 1970–79, 1991–94; Legis. asst., FL Gov. Reubin Askew, 1971; Astronaut crew member, 1986.

DC Office: 716 HSOB, 20510, 202-224-5274; Fax: 202-228-2183; Web site: billnelson.senate.gov.

State Offices: Orlando, 407-872-7161; Tallahassee, 850-942-8415.

Committees: *DSCC Vice Chairman. Armed Services*: Airland Forces; Emerging Threats & Capabilities; Strategic Forces. *Budget. Foreign Relations*: International Economic Policy, Export & Trade Promotion; International Operations & Terrorism; Western Hemisphere, Peace Corps, Narcotics Affairs.

Group Ratings and Key Votes: Newly Elected

Election Results

2000 general	Bill Nelson (D)	2,989,487	(51%)	($6,535,832)
	Bill McCollum (R)	2,705,348	(46%)	($8,664,112)
	Others	161,896	(3%)	
2000 primary	Bill Nelson (D)	692,147	(78%)	
	Newall J. Daughtrey (D)	105,650	(12%)	
	David B. Higginbottom (D)	95,492	(11%)	
1994 general	Connie Mack (R)	2,894,726	(71%)	($5,729,359)
	Hugh E. Rodham (D)	1,210,412	(29%)	($617,190)

FIRST DISTRICT

The "Redneck Riviera" is the affectionate local name for the Gulf Coast beaches of Florida's Panhandle, from Pensacola east to Destin. This has been military country ever since John Quincy Adams persuaded Spain to sell Florida to the U.S. in 1819 to get the port of Pensacola. It was the site of the nation's first naval aviation training base and the birthplace of carrier aviation. The Air Force also has a massive presence in Eglin Air Force Base, which spreads over the lion's share of three counties. Culturally part of Dixie, this was economically backward land for years, dependent in the 1940s and 1950s on the military bases for growth. More recently, as the South has become more prosperous, this American Riviera has become a major vacation and retirement spot for Southerners who enjoy its vast, fine-grained white sand beaches, perhaps the finest in the country, and its pleasant inlet-filled bays; it also has become a leading destination of college students for their spring break. Its cultural conservatism has remained ingrained from that earlier era, and it has become economically more conservative as well, while militarily it is supportive of assertive American policies around the world.

The 1st Congressional District includes the end of the Panhandle, so far west it's in the Central time zone—which became a sore point in the 2000 Election when some TV networks declared Al Gore the winner of Florida's electoral votes ten minutes before the polls in the Panhandle closed. The 1st District stretches from Pensacola and the Alabama border east to include part of Panama City. Politically, this is Republican territory. It voted solidly against Bill Clinton in 1992 and 1996 and voted overwhelmingly for George W. Bush in 2000: the Panhandle and Cuban-American parts of Miami-Dade County, separated by 800 miles, are the two most Republican parts of Florida.

The congressman from the 1st District is Joe Scarborough, a Republican first elected in 1994. Scarborough grew up in Pensacola and taught high school and coached the football team, then practiced law and was active in community affairs. In October 1993 he helped collect 3,000 signatures to protest the city government's 65% property tax increase. He had never run for office, but had long been interested in politics: his family remembers him at 5, in 1968, coloring in states red and blue depending on whether they went Democrat or Republican. When Democratic Congressman Earl Hutto, who won with only 52% in 1990 and 1992, decided to retire, Scarborough ran for the seat. He was one of five Republicans in the race, and far from the best known. In the September primary, Scarborough, conservative and anti-abortion, built on petition contacts and finished second with 30.6%, just behind Lois Benson, a pro-choice legislator and Pensacola council member, with 31.4%. Scarborough won the October runoff 54%–46%. In the general Scarborough advocated a five-year federal spending freeze, school vouchers and tax credits for home schoolers and a ban on offshore oil drilling. Riding the national Republican wave, Scarborough won by the whopping margin of 62%–38%.

Temperamentally, Scarborough is a cheerful rebel. His fellow freshmen elected him their political director and then-Speaker Newt Gingrich named him to head a Republican task force on education. "Our goal is to get as much money, power and authority out of Washington and get as much money, power and authority into the classroom as possible," Scarborough said. He urged intransigence in the 1995–96 government shutdown. One of the youngest freshmen, he kept a coonskin cap in his office and liked to wear jeans on Fridays. He called for ending corporate welfare, including royalty relief for offshore oil drillers and aid to large tobacco and sugar companies. He led opposition to oil drilling in the Gulf of Mexico.

In contrast to some 1994 freshmen who entered the political mainstream, Scarborough continued his rebel ways. He supported the coup against Gingrich in July 1997, and voted against the transportation bill and omnibus budget in 1998. He joined an effort to name the Justice Department headquarters for Robert Kennedy, his political hero. He worked to shut down the School of the Americas at Fort Benning and to fund D.C. advisory neighborhood commissions. He was one of the few congressmen to speak at the Tibet Freedom Rally on the steps of the Capitol, and—though he was the only member to miss the vote—he said he opposed permanent normal trade relations with China because of its human rights violations. When Clinton's antitrust chief Joel Klein testified at the Judiciary Committee, Scarborough took issue with his prosecution of Microsoft, contending that most consumers believe that "Microsoft is in the right here." While appearing often on TV political programs, he played a role in expanding in 2000 TRICARE, the military's health insurance system, to a permanent entitlement for military retirees. As chairman of the Civil Service Subcommittee he also helped to enact that year a bill to make long-term care insurance available to federal employees, retirees and their families. He has played guitar in his rock band, Regular Joe, with lyrics ranging from transvestites to taking bribes; when he sang at the Republican convention in Philadelphia he had a more uplifting focus on immigration and opportunity. His friends in Congress are mostly Democrats, he said, because although most members are clueless on music and pop culture, "Democratic members are less clueless than Republicans."

Scarborough considered running for the open Senate seat in 2000, but decided in June 1999 that the time wasn't right and "my heart was in Pensacola." A few months later, he ruptured two discs in his back and had surgery after he fell from a plank leading to his sons' tree house. He was re-elected in 1996 with 73%, and then twice without opposition in the general; in 2000, he got 77% in the primary. After spending time at home recuperating from the back surgery, he said "I'd be very surprised if I ran in 2002." In early 2001, he tried and failed to win an Appropriations Committee seat. On May 25, he announced his plan to resign, effective September 6, to devote more attention to his two sons. This free spirit's future is not predictable, but his seat is almost certain to remain in Republican hands, and a number of Republicans expressed immediate interest in the seat.

Cook's Call   *Safe.* Scarborough's decision to resign on September 6th forces a special election to be held on October 16, 2001. Republicans will have no trouble holding onto this conservative and increasingly Republican seat. Bush took 68% here in 2000. Heavy growth in the district means that the lines will be altered, but it's hard to see how Democrats can capture this seat in the special or in 2002.

THE PEOPLE: Pop. 2000: 683,987; Pop. 1990: 562,575, up 21.6% 1990–2000. 81% White, 12.9% Black, 1.9% Asian, 0.9% Amer. Indian, 0.1% Hawaiian, 2.3% Two+ races, 0.9% Other; 3% Hispanic Origin.

2000 Presidential Vote

Bush (R)	187,720	(68%)
Gore (D)	82,817	(30%)
Nader (Green)	4,048	(1%)
Others	2,629	(1%)

1996 Presidential Vote

Dole (R)	146,794	(59%)
Clinton (D)	77,070	(31%)
Perot (I)	24,322	(10%)

Rep. Joe Scarborough (R)

Elected 1994, 4th term; b. Apr. 9, 1963, Atlanta, GA; home, Pensacola; U. of AL, B.A. 1985, U. of FL, J.D. 1990; Baptist; divorced.

Professional Career: Teacher, 1985–87; Practicing atty., 1990–94.

DC Office: 127 CHOB 20515, 202-225-4136; Fax: 202-225-3414; Web site: www.house.gov/scarborough.

District Offices: Ft. Walton Beach, 850-664-1266; Pensacola, 850-479-1183.

Committees: *Armed Services* (17th of 32 R): Military Installations & Facilities; Military Research & Development. *Government Reform* (11th of 24 R): Civil Service & Agency Organization (Chmn.); District of Columbia. *Judiciary* (15th of 21 R): Courts, the Internet & Intellectual Property.

Group Ratings

	ADA	ACLU	AFS	LCV	CON	ITIC	NTU	COC	ACU	NTLC	CHC
2000	5	42	0	43	93	85	64	66	95	93	85
1999	15	—	0	31	94	—	69	74	85	—	—

National Journal Ratings

	1999 LIB	—	1999 CONS		2000 LIB	—	2000 CONS
Economic	37%	—	63%		38%	—	61%
Social	37%	—	63%		26%	—	71%
Foreign	27%	—	73%		0%	—	88%

Key Votes of the 106th Congress

1. Patient Bill of Rights	*	5. Bar RU-486 $ for FDA	Y	9. NATO War in Serbia	N
2. Accelerate Min. Wage	*	6. Display 10 Commandments	Y	10. Perm. Trade with China	*
3. Strike Ban on Ergo. Stnd.	N	7. Gun Show Bkgrnd. Checks	N	11. Debt Relief for 3rd World	N
4. Ovrd. Estate Tax Veto	Y	8. Ban Part.-Birth Abortion	Y	12. Drop Cuba Econ. Embargo	N

Election Results

2000 general	Joe Scarborough (R) .... unopposed			($772,995)
2000 primary	Joe Scarborough (R)	54,032	(77%)	
	Bob Condon (R)	15,808	(23%)	
1998 general	Joe Scarborough (R) .... unopposed			($395,976)

SECOND DISTRICT

For most of the 36 days from November 7 to December 13, 2000, Tallahassee was the epicenter of the political universe during the controversy over who carried Florida and who would be the next president. Reporters complained—especially when they were evicted from their motels in the weekend of the Florida State-University of Florida game—and must have wondered why this small city, not much more than a small town, located far from Florida's booming metropolises and amid swampy lowlands, far from a decent beach, should be the capital of the nation's fourth-largest state. The answer lies in history. The site was chosen in the days when almost all Floridians—and there weren't many of them—lived along the state's northern edge and Tallahassee was, more or less, the center of population. Ralph Waldo Emerson, visiting Tallahassee in the 19th Century, said it was a "grotesque place, rapidly settled by public officers, land speculators and desperadoes." Today the countryside around is distinctly Dixie: cotton fields, soft pine stands, catfish farms, large families, small towns with big churches, both black and white. And until recently Tallahassee was not much more than a Spanish-mossed county seat with a handsome Creole capitol, built in 1845 and preserved opposite its 1977 skyscraper replacement, and two state universities. But in the past 20 years Tallahassee has spread out and become a middling-sized city, with a tight-knit and sometimes fractious political and legal elite, bringing to the state's north end some of the new urbanized Florida, with an additional pro-government tilt: some 37% of Tallahassee area jobs are now in city and state government, compared to 12% statewide. Tallahassee has not attained the critical mass of the capitals of the three more populous states (Sacramento, Austin, and Albany), but it is on its way.

The 2d Congressional District of Florida is centered on Tallahassee, but extends westward to Panama City and eastward almost to Jacksonville. Historically, this was Democratic country, Jeffersonian and segregationist. Today, it is still mostly Democratic, though for different reasons; there is a large black percentage (25% in 2000, the fourth largest in Florida) and a strong Democratic preference among state employees and those dependent on them. Tallahassee's Leon County gave solid margins twice to Bill Clinton and, with two adjacent counties with high black percentages, voted heavily for Al Gore: the Florida law that establishes Leon County as the venue for election cases clearly favors the Democrats. But the rest of the district's counties gave majorities to George W. Bush. The result is a district that was close-to-evenly divided in the very close-to-evenly divided presidential election of 2000.

The congressman from the 2d District is Allen Boyd, a Democrat first elected in 1996. A lifelong farmer, Boyd grew up in Monticello in Jefferson County just east of Tallahassee. He served in Vietnam and graduated from Florida State. His political career began when he won a special election to the state House in January 1989. There he was majority whip and chairman of two committees and helped form the Conservative Democratic Caucus.

Boyd decided to run for the House when incumbent Pete Peterson, a moderate Democrat and Vietnam prisoner-of-war, retired after three terms, saying he believed in term limits; in March

1996 he was named our first ambassador to Vietnam, but in May 2001 he said he would resign to run to challenge Governor Jeb Bush. In a high-turnout Democratic primary Boyd won 48% of the vote to 26% for Leon County Commissioner Anita Davis and 25% for retired Gulf County Judge David Taunton. Boyd easily won the runoff 64%–36%. In the general Boyd campaigned with Blue Dog conservative Democrats and, more important, outspent the Republican by 2–1. He won a solid 59%–40% victory.

In the House Boyd became Blue Dog whip. He sought to be a behind-the-scenes consensus builder and worked for the 1997 balanced budget agreement and for a campaign finance bill; he called himself a "moderate Democrat with a social conscience." In 1998 he was head of the Blue Dogs' PAC and worked with the Democratic Congressional Campaign Committee to elect several more Blue Dogs; later he became the group's communications co-chair. He worked to keep open Tyndall Air Force Base near Panama City. At home he spearheaded a Coalition for a Drug-Free North Florida. He backed a bill to allow private timber harvesters to enter national forests and remove trees damaged in fires or floods, and later backed a bill for increased payments for schools and roads in counties with national forests. He was unperturbed when animal rights advocates picketed the Annual Boyd Family Dove Hunt in 1998, and was the only Florida Democrat to vote for an amendment that helped kill the 1999 gun control bill. He criticized the Environmental Protection Agency for "unrealistic" enforcement of pesticide rules for products long used by farmers, and sought a statutory change requiring more detailed justification by EPA. He voted to sustain Bill Clinton's vetoes of the marriage-penalty and estate-tax repeals, and favored permanent normal trade relations with China. In 1999 he got a seat on Appropriations. After the 2000 election, he spoke positively about prospects for a centrist coalition in the House.

Boyd was easily re-elected twice against late-filing Republican challengers. With big population gains in the 1st and 2nd Districts, redistricting likely will shift each slightly toward the west. That may increase their Republican percentage, but probably not enough to threaten Boyd or change Tallahassee's position as the center of his district.

Cook's Call   *Safe*. Based on presidential voting patterns, Florida's 2d district looks like it should be a classic swing district (in fact it was the only district in the state that went for Bush and a Democratic House candidate). But Boyd, a conservative Democrat, has a good profile for this district and has had little difficulty winning here. Boyd can probably hold this seat as long as he wants, but don't be surprised to see a strong Republican someday making a very credible challenge in an open seat situation.

THE PEOPLE: Pop. 2000: 678,025; Pop. 1990: 562,359, up 20.6% 1990–2000. 70.7% White, 25.2% Black, 1.1% Asian, 0.5% Amer. Indian, 1.5% Two+ races, 0.9% Other; 3.4% Hispanic Origin.

2000 Presidential Vote			1996 Presidential Vote		
Bush (R)	130,631	(49%)	Clinton (D)	114,601	(48%)
Gore (D)	127,328	(48%)	Dole (R)	99,487	(42%)
Nader (Green)	3,885	(1%)	Perot (I)	25,455	(11%)
Others	2,478	(1%)			

Rep. Allen Boyd, Jr. (D)

Elected 1996, 3d term; b. June 6, 1945, Valdosta, GA; home, Monticello; N. FL Jr. Col., A.A. 1966, FL St. U., B.S. 1969; Methodist; married (Cissy).

Military Career: Army 1969–71 (Vietnam).

Elected Office: FL House of Reps., 1989–96.

Professional Career: Farmer.

DC Office: 107 CHOB 20515, 202-225-5235; Fax: 202-225-5615; Web site: www.house.gov/boyd.

District Offices: Panama City, 850-785-0812; Tallahassee, 850-561-3979.

Committees: *Appropriations* (27th of 29 D): Agriculture, Rural Development, & FDA; Military Construction.

Group Ratings

	ADA	ACLU	AFS	LCV	CON	ITIC	NTU	COC	ACU	NTLC	CHC
2000	50	36	28	36	75	89	27	80	40	9	27
1999	70	—	66	44	87	—	17	68	20	—	—

National Journal Ratings

	1999 LIB	—	1999 CONS		2000 LIB	—	2000 CONS
Economic	52%	—	48%		56%	—	44%
Social	58%	—	42%		52%	—	48%
Foreign	68%	—	30%		47%	—	51%

Key Votes of the 106th Congress

1. Patient Bill of Rights	Y	5. Bar RU-486 $ for FDA	N	9. NATO War in Serbia	Y
2. Accelerate Min. Wage	N	6. Display 10 Commandments	Y	10. Perm. Trade with China	Y
3. Strike Ban on Ergo. Stnd.	N	7. Gun Show Bkgrnd. Checks	N	11. Debt Relief for 3rd World	N
4. Ovrd. Estate Tax Veto	N	8. Ban Part.-Birth Abortion	Y	12. Drop Cuba Econ. Embargo	N

Election Results

2000 general	Allen Boyd Jr. (D)	185,579	(72%)	($378,202)
	Doug Dodd (R)	71,754	(28%)	($16,227)
2000 primary	Allen Boyd Jr. (D)	unopposed		
1998 general	Allen Boyd Jr. (D)	unopposed		($281,015)

THIRD DISTRICT

Before the Civil War, most of Florida was still an unchartered watery wilderness, festooned with exotic greenery, inhabited by unusual animals: a part of the United States so far out of the experience of most Americans as to seem foreign. As late as 1940, Florida had the smallest population of any Southern state, and most of the people here lived in classic Dixie rural counties with small courthouse towns, where civic affairs were run by the richest white men; blacks lived in poorly constructed, unpainted shotgun houses propped up on blocks, with little money and no vote. This was a land of swamps and lakes and orange groves, of Marjorie Kinnan Rawlings's Cross Creek, where she wrote the great children's classic *The Yearling*, and the Florida of the broad St. Johns River, one of the few North American rivers that flows (if only sluggishly) north, through the orange grove country to the port of Jacksonville, for many years Florida's largest city.

The 3d Congressional District occupies much of this old Florida terrain. The district was created in 1992 to be north Florida's black majority seat, and its boundaries were modified in 1996, by an almost unanimous vote of the legislature, after it was overturned by a court order; it was 50% black in 2000. The boundaries are less convoluted: it no longer has a tentacle reaching out to Gainesville and Ocala, but extends more or less straight south, along the St. Johns River from Jacksonville to Orlando. Almost half of the district's population lives in Jacksonville, almost one quarter in and near Orlando (including all-black Eatontown, home of author Zora Neale Hurston). Much of it follows Florida watercourses: it touches on Cross Creek as well as the St. Johns River and numerous swamps.

The congresswoman from the 3d District is Corrine Brown, a Democrat elected in 1992. She grew up in Jacksonville, taught at the community college, was a guidance counselor and in 1982 was elected to the Florida House. With her Jacksonville base, she was the obvious favorite in 1992. In the Democratic primary she faced white talk radio host Andy Johnson, who called himself "the blackest candidate in the race." Brown led 43%–31% in the primary and won 64%–36% in the runoff; she won the general 59%–41%. Johnson brought the case challenging the district boundaries, but was not pleased with the results.

Brown has compiled a liberal record on most issues, though she supports her district in backing more defense spending than many on the left; she stresses that the military can be a source of opportunity, a lesson many black Americans have learned from personal experience. She has used her seats on Transportation and Veterans' Affairs to bring economic development to her district, working to secure an $86 million federal courthouse for Jacksonville and to promote

LYNX in Orlando and a cross-Florida high-speed rail. On the Transportation Committee she was a strong backer of the Step-21 formula which guaranteed all states at least 95% of their gas tax revenues (Florida used to get 74%). On the Veterans' Committee she spearheaded a law to provide better health care for women in veterans' hospitals and clinics; she helped pass the VERA (Veterans Equitable Resource Allocation) formula that gives Florida reimbursement for veterans who move there or use health facilities while visiting. She also sought additional veterans cemeteries for Florida, which is the home to more veterans than any other state except California. She fought to preserve the Medicaid payments for disproportionate share hospitals (those with lots of low-income patients). When Jesse Helms delayed in scheduling a Senate Foreign Relations hearing to confirm former Senator Carol Moseley-Braun as ambassador to New Zealand, Brown joined several House colleagues protesting at his office. She called Helms a "rude, mean man" after he directed Capitol police to remove Brown and the other congresswomen; Moseley-Braun was confirmed.

Brown has had spirited campaign opposition, which is unusual for Florida incumbents. Although she opposed the redistricting lawsuit, she embraced the legislature's new lines with enthusiasm and won 61%–39% in 1996. She faced her most difficult contest in 1998, with her problems largely of her own making. That April the *St. Petersburg Times* reported that she received $10,000 from Baptist minister Henry Lyons, who had since been indicted on theft charges; she said the money was for his help in a rally protesting the redistricting case. In June the same paper reported that her daughter, attorney and EPA employee Shantrel Brown, was given a $50,000 Lexus by agents of African millionaire Foutanga Sissoko; he had been imprisoned in Miami on federal charges of paying an illegal gratuity to a Customs Service officer, and Brown worked furiously to get him released, lobbying Attorney General Janet Reno to have him deported to Africa to continue his humanitarian work. A third charge was that she kept a jazz singer on her payroll as a "congressional outreach specialist," who occasionally visited the district from her New York City home. Brown reacted with fury: she filed a criminal contempt charge against the *Times* reporters with the Capitol Police, claiming they "accosted" her and their questions made her cry. A federal prosecutor said there was not enough to indict them for impeding a member of Congress.

These charges attracted national Republican attention. They had a presentable candidate: Bill Randall, also black, a former General Motors management employee who had become a minister and worked as a sales manager for a cable company; he opposed abortion, favored local control of schools and school vouchers. As Randall admitted, "I think this race has gotten on the radar screen based on what this candidate has done to herself. It's not so much that I'm all that great a candidate or anything." There were further wrinkles. On October 18, the *Daytona News-Journal* reported two allegations against Randall. One was that he bounced a check for $1,300 in 1988 when the IRS froze his bank account because of failure to pay $30,000 in taxes. Randall said he was paying off the arrears and that one reason he was running was his mistreatment by the IRS. The paper also charged that Randall fathered a child with an unmarried woman in 1980. "An absolute lie," he said immediately. But two days later, surrounded by his wife, daughter and grandchildren, he acknowledged the charge, and said it was the catalyst that got him to attend the seminary. This undercut the ad the Republicans were running: "We need public officials to be honest and preserve the rule of law. But look at Corinne Brown's record." All the charges did cost Brown something: she won by 55%–45%. Randall made inroads among white Democrats and got 77% in heavily Republican Clay County.

But the ramifications were not finished. The Congressional Accountability Project requested that the House ethics committee investigate the $10,000 contribution and the Lexus gift, which her daughter later sold and gave the proceeds to charity. In September 2000 the committee concluded that Brown "demonstrated, at the least, poor judgment and created substantial concerns regarding both the appearance of impropriety and the reputation of the House," but dropped the case because it was unable to question key witnesses, including Sissoko. Brown responded, "This is a great day." She faced a vigorous re-election challenge from Republican Jennifer Carroll, a retired Navy officer with 20 years of service, who criticized Brown's lack of vision and her inability to work with people. Brown, who called Carroll "a zero" and "a Republican puppet," was outspent during the campaign by Carroll, who is also black. But she had help from an October campaign rally with Bill Clinton and a strong local grass-roots organization. Brown won 58%–42%. Carroll won the five counties between Jacksonville and Orlando, but Brown ran strongly in the two urban anchors and most heavily populated counties: 61%–39% in Duval, and 72%–28% in Orange. During the subsequent presidential recount, Brown was outspoken in her insistence that voting irregularities discriminated against black voters.

In the 107th Congress, Brown became ranking Democrat on the Coast Guard and Maritime Transportation Subcommittee, a useful post for her local constituents. Republicans control redistricting, but have indicated that they will continue to draw three heavily black districts, including the 3d, though it will need to add 53,000 persons.

Cook's Call *Safe.* In 1998 and 2000 Republicans put a lot of effort (and money) to try and knock the scandal-tainted Brown from this overwhelmingly Democratic, majority-black district. While Brown was forced to take these races seriously, she never came too close to losing and it is unlikely that Republicans will target this seat in 2002. The Voting Rights Act prevents linedrawers from altering this district all that much.

THE PEOPLE: Pop. 2000: 586,694; Pop. 1990: 562,080, up 4.4% 1990–2000. 44.4% White, 49.7% Black, 1.3% Asian, 0.3% Amer. Indian, 2.1% Two+ races, 2.1% Other; 5.8% Hispanic Origin.

2000 Presidential Vote		
Gore (D)	103,808	(59%)
Bush (R)	68,883	(39%)
Nader (Green)	1,587	(1%)
Others	1,518	(1%)

1996 Presidential Vote		
Clinton (D)	110,701	(58%)
Dole (R)	66,057	(35%)
Perot (I)	12,633	(7%)

Rep. Corrine Brown (D)

Elected 1992, 5th term; b. Nov. 11, 1946, Jacksonville; home, Jacksonville; FL A&M, B.S. 1969, M.S., 1971; Baptist; single.

Elected Office: FL House of Reps., 1982–92.

Professional Career: Prof., FL Commun. Col., 1977–82, Guidance Counselor, 1982–92.

DC Office: 2444 RHOB 20515, 202-225-0123; Fax: 202-225-2256; Web site: www.house.gov/corrinebrown.

District Offices: Jacksonville, 904-354-1652; Orlando, 407-872-0656.

Committees: *Transportation & Infrastructure* (11th of 34 D): Aviation; Coast Guard & Maritime Transportation (RMM); Highways & Transit. *Veterans' Affairs* (4th of 14 D): Benefits.

Group Ratings

	ADA	ACLU	AFS	LCV	CON	ITIC	NTU	COC	ACU	NTLC	CHC
2000	80	79	100	71	63	56	17	50	9	12	13
1999	100	—	100	88	12	—	14	28	0	—	—

National Journal Ratings

	1999 LIB —	1999 CONS	2000 LIB —	2000 CONS
Economic	88% —	0%	85% —	11%
Social	83% —	13%	90% —	9%
Foreign	74% —	23%	72% —	27%

Key Votes of the 106th Congress

1. Patient Bill of Rights	Y	5. Bar RU-486 $ for FDA	N	9. NATO War in Serbia	Y
2. Accelerate Min. Wage	Y	6. Display 10 Commandments	N	10. Perm. Trade with China	N
3. Strike Ban on Ergo. Stnd.	Y	7. Gun Show Bkgrnd. Checks	Y	11. Debt Relief for 3rd World	Y
4. Ovrd. Estate Tax Veto	N	8. Ban Part.-Birth Abortion	N	12. Drop Cuba Econ. Embargo	Y

Election Results

2000 general	Corrine Brown (D)	102,143	(58%)	($479,828)
	Jennifer S. Carroll (R)	75,228	(42%)	($1,035,709)
2000 primary	Corrine Brown (D)	unopposed		
1998 general	Corrine Brown (D)	66,621	(55%)	($488,690)
	Bill Randall (R)	53,530	(45%)	($465,865)

FOURTH DISTRICT

With more than 1 million people in the surrounding area, Jacksonville is twice as large as any other Florida city, with a National Football League franchise (the Jaguars), an agreement to host the 2005 Super Bowl, and bold new skyscrapers looming above a wide river and a shopping mall overshadowing grid streets of tiny shotgun houses. The wide freeways leading to huge beachfront subdivisions are not far from primeval wetlands. Mayport, one of the Navy's biggest bases, and other military installations are nearby. But Floridians tend to overlook Jacksonville. While its gleaming downtown is just one of a dozen in a state that had little commercial office development a generation ago, Jacksonville was known not long ago as a smelly, slow-growing insurance and paper mill town. Attracting big installations from AT&T, Brockway International, Prudential, Sears, UPS, American Express and the Mayo Clinic, Jacksonville has grown, while still maintaining its big military bases and insurance headquarters. With bipartisan support, Duval County voters agreed in 2000 to a half-penny sales tax increase to finance their growth management, especially traffic congestion and environmental protection. In the past decade, St. Johns and Flagler counties just to the south of Jacksonville were among the fastest growing in Florida, with a more than 50% increase. Vast condominiums have been built along the Atlantic coastline from Amelia Island south through Ponte Vedra; farther south the new city of Palm Coast has grown up not far from St. Augustine, the oldest European settlement in the United States. Growth has continued around Ormond Beach, where John D. Rockefeller used to spend his winters, and nearby Daytona Beach with its hard sand and stock car races, where Dale Earnhart met his death in February 2001.

The 4th Congressional District of Florida includes most of Jacksonville (minus the mostly black areas in the 3d District) and the beach areas to the north and south as far as Daytona Beach. The area is heavily Republican and voted solidly for George W. Bush in 2000.

The congressman from the 4th District is Ander Crenshaw, a Republican first elected in 2000. He grew up in Jacksonville and attended the University of Georgia on a basketball scholarship, then graduated from the University of Florida Law School. His wife's father, Claude Kirk, was elected governor, the first Republican since Reconstruction, in 1966, then defeated in 1970. Crenshaw was elected to the state House in 1972 and served for six years until he left to become an investment banker. In 1980 he ran for the Senate and finished third of six in the 1980 Republican primary won by Paula Hawkins. From 1986 until 1993 he served in the state Senate, and in 1992 became its first Republican president in 118 years; in that post he helped to kill a big tax increase proposed by Governor Lawton Chiles. He ran for governor in 1994 but was fourth in the primary, far behind Jeb Bush, who narrowly lost to Chiles in November.

Crenshaw's opportunity to run for the House came when Tillie Fowler, vice chairman of the House Republican Conference and an influential member of the Armed Services Committee, announced in January 2000 that she would honor her promise to serve only four terms and not seek reelection in 2000. Crenshaw announced his candidacy a week later and was promptly endorsed by local Republican leaders. That discouraged several other possible candidates, including state Senator Jim Horne and outgoing House Speaker John Thrasher. Crenshaw's campaign focused on lowering taxes and a "government that does more for less." He was opposed in the primary by a 31-year-old newcomer who moved to the district only four months before he declared his candidacy and had served as an intern in Ronald Reagan's post-presidential office in California and built a vending machine business in Washington, D.C. Crenshaw's only misstep in the September primary was a rebuke from a Reagan staffer for using in an ad a photo of himself with the former president. Crenshaw won 70%–30%, and easily won the general 67%–31%.

After the election, Crenshaw displayed his political savvy, becoming freshman class liaison to the Republican leadership, and winning seats on Armed Services, Budget and Veterans' Affairs. He pledged that his top priority was the district's large military facilities. His toughest political decision may be whether to run again statewide. Redistricting will shrink this district and could leave an additional Republican area for Horne, a legislative powerhouse who said he wants to carve out a seat for himself.

Cook's Call   *Safe.* This Jacksonville-based district has grown substantially over the last ten years and as such it will have to contract for 2002 elections. But it is likely that this heavily Republican district will remain safe for Crenshaw.

THE PEOPLE: Pop. 2000: 734,246; Pop. 1990: 562,459, up 30.5% 1990–2000. 85.5% White, 9% Black, 2.4% Asian, 0.3% Amer. Indian, 0.1% Hawaiian, 1.7% Two+ races, 1% Other; 4% Hispanic Origin.

2000 Presidential Vote			1996 Presidential Vote		
Bush (R)	191,012	(63%)	Dole (R)	145,760	(56%)
Gore (D)	106,658	(35%)	Clinton (D)	94,843	(37%)
Nader (Green)	4,400	(1%)	Perot (I)	19,071	(7%)
Others	2,636	(1%)			

Rep. Ander Crenshaw (R)

Elected 2000, 1st term; b. Sept. 1, 1944, Jacksonville; home, Jacksonville; U. of GA, B.A. 1966; U. of FL, J.D. 1969; Episcopalian; married (Kitty).

Elected Office: FL House of Reps., 1972–78; FL Senate 1986–93.

Professional Career: Investment banker, 1980–2000.

DC Office: 510 CHOB 20515, 202-225-2501; Fax: 202-225-2504; Web site: www.house.gov/crenshaw.

District Offices: Jacksonville, 904-598-0481; Ormand Beach, 386-672-0754.

Committees: *Armed Services* (27th of 32 R): Military Installations & Facilities; Military Research & Development. *Budget* (22d of 24 R). *Veterans' Affairs* (16th of 17 R): Benefits; Health.

Group Ratings and Key Votes: Newly Elected

Election Results

2000 general	Ander Crenshaw (R)	203,090	(67%)	($863,422)
	Tom Sullivan (D)	94,587	(31%)	($143,241)
	Others	5,609	(2%)	
2000 primary	Ander Crenshaw (R)	47,588	(70%)	
	Dan Quiggle (R)	20,816	(30%)	
1998 general	Tillie K. Fowler (R)	unopposed		($162,361)

FIFTH DISTRICT

Over the past quarter century, Florida's urban areas have grown in every unlikely direction, occupying the high ground between the swamps and wetlands that still take up much of the state's peninsula. The pattern of development is clear in the North Sun Coast, the Gulf Coast counties north of St. Petersburg and Tampa, where subdivisions, trailer parks and shopping centers with Eckerd drug stores and Publix and Winn Dixie supermarkets sprang up in what were sleepy little towns with low brick buildings baking in the Florida sun, and residents are proud of their fresh water springs that are a haven for manatees. More than a half million people live in the towns starting with Clearwater and Tampa's northern suburbs that run up the spines of U.S. 19, just off the Gulf Coast, or U.S. 41 and I-75 inland near the orange groves. Though there are plenty of working people here, this is retirement country. People are comfortable though not usually affluent here, and if the existence of such communities is taken for granted by most Americans, their construction—the creation of an infrastructure of water and sewer lines, underground electricity, and phone and TV cables—is an example of the miracles of modern technology.

The 5th Congressional District, created after the 1990 Census, occupies much of the fast-growing area, including the New Port Richey area on the Pasco County coast and Citrus and Hernando counties to the north. The 5th travels northward to include Gainesville, home of the University of Florida, where students from the more wealthy urban corridors of central and south Florida study in a town with many flimsy houses from the impoverished South of 50 years ago; here they can become part of a Florida elite bonded by shared memories of the Gator Growl festivities. The population of this area quadrupled from 1960–90, and increased by close to one-fourth in the 1990s. Politically, the Gulf Coast counties are marginal territory—very closely divided in the 2000 presidential election—while Gainesville is solidly liberal and Democratic.

The congresswoman from the 5th District is Karen Thurman, a Democrat who has shown something like perfect political pitch while spending most of her adult life in public office. An Air Force brat, she grew up in Florida and elsewhere, worked as a middle school math teacher for eight years before being elected to the Dunnellon Council, then became mayor. Elected to the Florida Senate in 1982, at 31, she was re-elected in 1986 with more votes than any other senator. As chairman in 1992 of the reapportionment committee she carefully included her hometown in the new 5th District. She easily won the primary and in the general faced a former prosecutor who called her a "professional, big money politician." She outraised him 2–1 and won 49%–43%.

In the House Thurman has compiled a moderate-to-liberal voting record and has been responsive to constituent interests. She casts conservative votes on many issues but has supported at some risk the Democratic position on some key votes, like the 1993 tax increase. One of her chief causes is regulatory relief: She was a lead Democrat for requiring EPA to conduct risk-assessment studies before issuing regulations. In the 104th Congress she was one of four Democrats to vote in committee to freeze new federal regulations until Congress could review the underlying statutes. On the 1999 gun bill, she opposed additional checks on gun show sales because "this matter has been addressed already in Florida."

Thurman sits on the Ways and Means Committee, where she is an avid advocate of protecting Social Security. Noting that 37% of her district's seniors have no prescription-drug coverage, she has been a leading proponent of adding that benefit to Medicare. She also wants Medicare to cover annual Pap smears to detect cervical cancer. She won enactment in 2000 of her proposal to permit Medicare-eligible military retirees to participate in the Pentagon's mail-order prescription drug program. She secured two new V.A. primary care clinics for her district.

Thurman has performed well against unconventional opponents. She was targeted by Republicans in 1994 and her opponent, former drag racing champion Don "Big Daddy" Garlits, attracted attention, calling for "medieval-style prisons" and public paddling of juveniles in town squares. Thurman carried all but one county and won 57%–43%. She was helped by a 1996 redistricting case that added black and white liberal precincts in Gainesville and Alachua County from the 3d District. In 1998 her opponent was Jack Gargan, running on the Reform Party ticket and later its national leader. He promised to poll constituents and vote accordingly. To get enough ballot signatures, he promised to raffle off $50,000 of his salary to petition signers and campaign volunteers. He got the signatures, but Thurman won 66%–34%. In 2000, against the Gainesville Chamber of Commerce's lawyer, she easily carried all counties and won 64%–36%. Republicans control redistricting for 2002, but they will be hard put to jeopardize Thurman.

Cook's Call   *Potentially Competitive.* Having carefully drawn this seat for herself while serving in the state Senate in 1991, Thurman has had a fairly easy time holding onto this Gainesville-based district. But in this round of redistricting, it is Republicans in control of the process and they have their sites on this district. Already, at least one Republican, Senate President Pro Tempore Ginny Brown-Waite, has indicated an interest in running for what is likely to be a newly redrawn 5th District. This could be a race to watch in 2002.

THE PEOPLE: Pop. 2000: 689,672; Pop. 1990: 562,926, up 22.5% 1990–2000. 86.9% White, 8.6% Black, 1.6% Asian, 0.3% Amer. Indian, 1.5% Two+ races, 1% Other; 4.5% Hispanic Origin.

2000 Presidential Vote
Gore (D) 148,870   (50%)
Bush (R) 138,382   (46%)
Nader (Green) 8,230   (3%)
Others 3,009   (1%)

1996 Presidential Vote
Clinton (D) 135,496   (50%)
Dole (R) 100,603   (37%)
Perot (I) 34,973   (13%)

Rep. Karen L. Thurman (D)

Elected 1992, 5th term; b. Jan. 12, 1951, Rapid City, SD; home, Dunnellon; U. of FL, B.A. 1973; Episcopalian; married (John).

Elected Office: Dunnellon City Cncl., 1974–82; Dunnellon Mayor, 1979–81; FL Senate, 1982–92.

Professional Career: Middle schl. teacher, 1974–82.

DC Office: 201 CHOB 20515, 202-225-1002; Fax: 202-226-0329; Web site: www.house.gov/thurman.

District Offices: Gainesville, 352-336-6614; Inverness, 352-344-3044; New Port Richey, 727-849-4496.

Committees: *Ways & Means* (15th of 17 D): Health; Oversight.

Group Ratings

	ADA	ACLU	AFS	LCV	CON	ITIC	NTU	COC	ACU	NTLC	CHC
2000	80	77	85	71	97	84	21	57	20	23	8
1999	85	—	100	56	92	—	16	29	4	—	—

National Journal Ratings

	1999 LIB —	1999 CONS	2000 LIB —	2000 CONS
Economic	73%	26%	81%	16%
Social	69%	31%	70%	29%
Foreign	71%	27%	64%	34%

Key Votes of the 106th Congress

1. Patient Bill of Rights	Y	5. Bar RU-486 $ for FDA	N	9. NATO War in Serbia	Y
2. Accelerate Min. Wage	Y	6. Display 10 Commandments	N	10. Perm. Trade with China	Y
3. Strike Ban on Ergo. Stnd.	Y	7. Gun Show Bkgrnd. Checks	N	11. Debt Relief for 3rd World	Y
4. Ovrd. Estate Tax Veto	N	8. Ban Part.-Birth Abortion	N	12. Drop Cuba Econ. Embargo	Y

Election Results

2000 general	Karen L. Thurman (D)	180,338	(64%)	($643,355)
	Pete Enwall (R)	100,244	(36%)	($274,771)
2000 primary	Karen L. Thurman (D)	unopposed		
1998 general	Karen L. Thurman (D)	132,005	(66%)	($472,959)
	Jack Gargan (Ref)	67,147	(34%)	($28,485)

SIXTH DISTRICT

The flat grasslands of central Florida, once bypassed by southbound tourists heading for the coast, in the last two decades have become one of the prime growth areas in this high-growth state. Central Florida's economy once depended on farming, on state institutions (the University of Florida in Gainesville, the big state prison in Raiford) and on passing tourists getting off the interstate to see attractions like Silver Springs, the world's largest formation of clear artesian springs. Then retirees began settling in places like the bluegrass country around Ocala (one of America's prime horse breeding grounds) and the plenteous lakes in Lake County to the south; the area was studded with trailer parks and mobile home developments. In the 1990s growth accelerated, pitched a bit more upscale; voter turnout around Ocala and Leesburg grew faster than almost anywhere else in Florida.

The 6th Congressional District of Florida takes up much of this territory. It includes almost all of Ocala and Marion County and most of Lake and Sumter Counties just to the south. These counties, once marginal, are now solidly Republican. About half of its people live around Ocala or in Lake County; about one-third live on the west side of Jacksonville or in Clay County.

The congressman from the 6th District is Cliff Stearns, a Republican first elected in 1988. Stearns grew up and attended public schools in Washington, D.C. and served in the Air Force. In 1972 he went into Florida real estate and ended up owning five motels, three restaurants and other property—"someone who works in the community, goes to church with his neighbors, and doesn't live in Tallahassee," as he put it in his 1988 campaign, when he beat the favorite, state House Speaker Jon Mills, 54%–46%.

"I was elected to put the federal government on a diet," Stearns said, and he has compiled a solidly conservative voting record. He was first noticed on Capitol Hill for cutting staff pay raises. He pushed for funding cuts in the National Endowment for the Arts, and backed the move to post the Ten Commandments in public buildings. In 1994 he penned the letter signed by 87 Republicans calling for the resignation of then-Surgeon General Joycelyn Elders. He was able to convince HUD to issue rules protecting seniors-only housing developments from discrimination suits. Since losing a low-level leadership contest in 1994, he has shown independence of the leadership. He opposed IMF funding, fast-track trade authority and permanent normal trade relations with China. He voted against the 1997 budget agreement and the 1998 omnibus budget. As chairman of the Veterans' Health Subcommittee, he sponsored a research center on Gulf war syndrome and won new medical facilities and benefits for disabled vets. On the Energy and Commerce Committee he has worked for privacy for health care and genetic records. In 2000 he helped pass the Cardiac Arrest Survival Act, which encourages the use of defibrillators and installs them in all federal buildings. He has been a leader in letting the states take the lead in utility deregulation and wants to drop the requirement that utilities purchase power from renewable and non-traditional energy sources.

Following the 2000 election, Stearns criticized the television networks' coverage of the Florida results and helped to launch the Energy and Commerce Committee investigation. Although he wanted to chair the Telecommunications Subcommittee, he became the new chairman of the revamped Commerce, Trade and Consumer Protection Subcommittee, whose jurisdiction includes Internet privacy. Stearns is also interested in funds that mean jobs for north Florida. He took credit for situating a new 3,000-bed federal prison in Sumter County and then expanding it, and for a Marion County veterans' outpatient clinic. He got $6 million for an interchange on Florida's Turnpike at County Road 470 in Lake County.

Stearns ran unopposed in 1998 and 2000, and in the latter year broke a 1988 promise to serve only six terms. Redistricting will change the lines in central Florida considerably and remove more than 116,000 persons, but Stearns should be safe wherever the lines are drawn.

Cook's Call   *Safe*. Central Florida has grown substantially over the last ten years and it is expected to gain at least one of the state's two new seats. It is not likely that redistricting will have a detrimental impact on Stearns' hold of this now solidly Republican district.

THE PEOPLE: Pop. 2000: 755,939; Pop. 1990: 562,219, up 34.5% 1990–2000. 84.1% White, 11.1% Black, 1.1% Asian, 0.4% Amer. Indian, 1.5% Two+ races, 1.6% Other; 5.3% Hispanic Origin.

2000 Presidential Vote			**1996 Presidential Vote**		
Bush (R)	176,004	(59%)	Dole (R)	124,489	(50%)
Gore (D)	113,776	(38%)	Clinton (D)	96,135	(39%)
Nader (Green)	4,211	(1%)	Perot (I)	27,762	(11%)
Others	3,668	(1%)			

Rep. Cliff Stearns (R)

Elected 1988, 7th term; b. Apr. 16, 1941, Washington, DC; home, Ocala; George Washington U., B.S. 1963; Presbyterian; married (Joan).

Military Career: Air Force, 1963–67.

Professional Career: Data Control Systems Inc., 1967–68; Negotiator, CBS, 1969–70; Pres., Stearns House Inc., 1972–present.

DC Office: 2227 RHOB 20515, 202-225-5744; Fax: 202-225-3973; Web site: www.house.gov/stearns.

District Offices: Leesburg, 352-326-8285; Ocala, 352-351-8777; Orange Park, 904-269-3203.

Committees: *Energy & Commerce* (5th of 31 R): Commerce, Trade & Consumer Protection (Chmn.); Oversight & Investigations; Telecommunications & The Internet (Vice Chmn.). *Veterans' Affairs* (8th of 17 R): Health (Vice Chmn.).

Group Ratings

	ADA	ACLU	AFS	LCV	CON	ITIC	NTU	COC	ACU	NTLC	CHC
2000	5	21	14	7	90	78	74	80	100	88	100
1999	10	—	0	13	81	—	66	72	92	—	—

National Journal Ratings

	1999 LIB	—	1999 CONS		2000 LIB	—	2000 CONS
Economic	16%	—	78%		0%	—	94%
Social	10%	—	85%		0%	—	79%
Foreign	3%	—	92%		0%	—	88%

Key Votes of the 106th Congress

1. Patient Bill of Rights	N	5. Bar RU-486 $ for FDA	Y	9. NATO War in Serbia	N
2. Accelerate Min. Wage	N	6. Display 10 Commandments	Y	10. Perm. Trade with China	N
3. Strike Ban on Ergo. Stnd.	N	7. Gun Show Bkgrnd. Checks	N	11. Debt Relief for 3rd World	N
4. Ovrd. Estate Tax Veto	Y	8. Ban Part.-Birth Abortion	Y	12. Drop Cuba Econ. Embargo	N

Election Results

2000 general	Cliff Stearns (R)	.... unopposed	($213,747)
2000 primary	Cliff Stearns (R)	.... unopposed	
1998 general	Cliff Stearns (R)	.... unopposed	($189,345)

SEVENTH DISTRICT

In ever-changing Florida, new communities and towns continue to spring up on the landscape, replacing older town centers with which tourists have been familiar. Just down the road from Daytona Beach, where 600,000 motorcyclists gather at the Speedway each March for Bike Week, is New Smyrna Beach, a new town established on the site of an old settlement. Fifteen miles inland, close to Sanford, where Amtrak's Auto-Train unloads its Florida-bound travelers, is Deltona, a vast five-mile square development that drained part of a Florida swamp and designed curving streets meandering around small lakes and golf courses, set aside land for shopping centers and office space and then marketed the place nationwide. It became an instant city: in 2000, 70,000 people lived in Deltona—where there were 15,000 in 1980 and 4,800 in 1970.

The 7th Congressional District of Florida includes Deltona, New Smyrna Beach and part of Daytona Beach, as well as most of Sanford. Stretching from Daytona across the marshy St. Johns River basin to Seminole County, it includes large Orlando suburbs like Altamonte Springs and small old towns like Oviedo, and goes south to include part of Orlando itself. In most elections this is a solidly Republican district, although the area around Daytona has a conservative Democratic heritage and voted for Al Gore in 2000.

The congressman from the 7th is John Mica, a spirited Republican and a political veteran who came to office as an opponent of the status quo. He grew up in south Florida, in a bipartisan political family: His younger brother Dan Mica was a Democratic congressman from Palm Beach County from 1978–88, when he lost a primary for U.S. Senate, another brother worked for Democratic Governor Lawton Chiles and a third is a lobbyist for the Florida oil and gas industry—John Mica is the only Florida congressman who supports drilling in the Gulf of Mexico. He made a small fortune by turning 360 feet of New Smyrna beachfront into a real estate business, served as a staffer to Senator Paula Hawkins from 1981–85, then became a lobbyist. When attacked in the 1992 Republican primary as an insider representing special interests, Mica lobbied pro bono for the Daytona airport and got a runway extension, and won 53%–34%. In the general he outraised his opponent, attacked him as a liberal backed by trial lawyers and labor unions and won 56%–44%. He has since been re-elected by wide margins.

Mica has been a consistent conservative and brash reformer, leading the charge to abolish House select committees and to make public the names of those signing petitions to discharge legislation. He also pushed a plan to require the EPA to subject new regulations to a cost-benefit analysis, versions of which ultimately passed. When Republicans took control of the House, Mica became chairman of the Government Reform's Civil Service Subcommittee. There he helped pass the White House Accountability Act of 1996, imposing on the White House, as a Republican-pushed law imposed on Congress, the laws the legislative and executive branches impose on others. He sought to expand federal employees' health insurance to include long-term coverage at group rates. When support for a Capitol Visitors Center below the East Front of the Capitol increased after two Capitol Police officers were killed by a gunman in 1998, he managed to put $100 million into the budget with the remainder then planned to come from private funds. With Lucille Roybal-Allard, he proposed a media campaign to prevent underage drinking. In 2001 he took over as chairman of the Aviation Subcommittee at Transportation and Infrastructure, which should assist continued development of Sanford's rapidly growing Orlando Sanford airport; he pledged faster building of runways across the nation.

Mica has said that his biggest issue is fighting drugs. With Senator Bob Graham, he announced in 1998 a new Central Florida High Intensity Drug Trafficking Area, headquartered in the Orlando area; he told local police, "We want you to kick butt." Mica and Clay Shaw introduced a bill to revoke the Clinton administration's certification of Mexico's drug-fighting efforts. He held a hearing in 1999 to criticize Mexico as a continuing safe haven for drug traffickers, and later said that the White House had "sabotaged" the war on drugs by sharply reducing Pentagon interdiction. He held a hearing in June 2000 in Sioux City, Iowa, to examine the spread of methamphetamines in the Midwest and the "mind-boggling" foothold by Mexican traffickers. Barry McCaffrey, Clinton's drug policy adviser, criticized Mica for "unprecedented oversight and interference."

On local issues, Mica has supported the light-rail system in Orlando, proposed a bus, train and light-rail station in Sanford to connect with the Auto Train, Amtrak and LYNX, and backed the plan by Governor Jeb Bush to replace the clogged St. John River Bridge on I-4. He worked to keep the Army simulation training command in Orlando, where it has spawned many local businesses.

Cook's Call *Safe.* Since first capturing this seat in 1992, Mica has had little trouble winning reelection in this very Republican district. Growth along the central part of the state means that the district will have to shed at least 70,000 voters.

THE PEOPLE: Pop. 2000: 722,139; Pop. 1990: 563,552, up 28.1% 1990–2000. 85% White, 7.9% Black, 1.9% Asian, 0.3% Amer. Indian, 2% Two + races, 2.8% Other; 10% Hispanic Origin.

2000 Presidential Vote			1996 Presidential Vote		
Bush (R)	140,802	(50%)	Dole (R)	108,636	(47%)
Gore (D)	131,792	(47%)	Clinton (D)	100,603	(43%)
Nader (Green)	4,235	(2%)	Perot (I)	22,863	(10%)
Others	2,541	(1%)			

Rep. John L. Mica (R)

Elected 1992, 5th term; b. Jan. 27, 1943, Binghamton, NY; home, Winter Park; Miami-Dade Commun.' Col., A.A. 1965, U. of FL, B.A. 1967; Episcopalian; married (Patricia).

Elected Office: FL House of Reps., 1976–80.

Professional Career: Exec. Dir., Palm Beach & Orange Cnty. Govt. Charter Study Commissions, 1970–74; Pres., MK Development, 1975–92; A.A., U.S. Sen. Paula Hawkins, 1981–85; Partner, Mica, Dudinsky & Assoc., 1985–92.

DC Office: 2445 RHOB 20515, 202-225-4035; Fax: 202-226-0821; Web site: www.house.gov/mica.

District Offices: Casselberry, 407-657-8080; Deltona, 407-860-1499; Port Orange, 904-756-9798.

Committees: *Government Reform* (8th of 24 R): Civil Service & Agency Organization; Criminal Justice, Drug Policy & Human Resources. *House Administration* (3d of 6 R). *Transportation & Infrastructure* (8th of 42 R): Aviation (Chmn.); Highways & Transit; Railroads.

Group Ratings

	ADA	ACLU	AFS	LCV	CON	ITIC	NTU	COC	ACU	NTLC	CHC
2000	5	7	14	14	44	89	62	80	88	78	93
1999	10	—	0	0	36	—	59	88	80	—	—

National Journal Ratings

	1999 LIB	—	1999 CONS		2000 LIB	—	2000 CONS
Economic	16%	—	78%		18%	—	76%
Social	19%	—	79%		23%	—	74%
Foreign	30%	—	70%		12%	—	78%

Key Votes of the 106th Congress

1. Patient Bill of Rights	N	5. Bar RU-486 $ for FDA	Y	9. NATO War in Serbia	N
2. Accelerate Min. Wage	N	6. Display 10 Commandments	Y	10. Perm. Trade with China	N
3. Strike Ban on Ergo. Stnd.	N	7. Gun Show Bkgrnd. Checks	N	11. Debt Relief for 3rd World	N
4. Ovrd. Estate Tax Veto	Y	8. Ban Part.-Birth Abortion	Y	12. Drop Cuba Econ. Embargo	N

Election Results

2000 general	John L. Mica (R)	171,018	(63%)	($206,125)
	Dan Vaughen (D)	99,531	(37%)	($40,088)
2000 primary	John L. Mica (R)	unopposed		
1998 general	John L. Mica (R)	unopposed		($117,344)

EIGHTH DISTRICT

Who would have supposed 40 years ago that the most popular tourist destination in the world would rise amid the swamps and orange groves of central Florida? The answer: Walt Disney, and just about no one else. In the middle 1960s he looked at the map and decided that the intersection of I-4 and Florida's Turnpike, the "crossroads of Florida," just a few miles southwest of Orlando, was the perfect place for the vast theme park he was planning. The spirit of this place was set by a man who never lived here but created something now taken for granted. Disney conceived the first theme park in the flatlands of Orange County, California, but he perfected it in the 17,000 acres of swamp and lakes in Florida's Orange County. With the invention of the theme park, Disney also pioneered sophisticated communications, utility, and waste-disposal methods—all out of sight and underground. Yet Disney World is not just an engineering marvel; it requires some 54,000 people with know-how and unfailing cheerfulness. Disney's vision of a future that was labor-intensive as well as high-tech—in which the critical ingredient is the provision of services—accurately forecast the service-driven economy that has grown so lustily.

In 1960 metro Orlando had fewer people—88,000—than the Orlando area has hotel rooms today; Walt Disney World's Magic Kingdom opened in 1971, followed by EPCOT Center, Disney/

MGM Studios, Sea World, Universal Studios, Disney's Animal Kingdom, Universal's Islands of Adventure and dozens of other attractions bring in millions of visitors from around the world each year. Metro Orlando grew by 54% in the 1970s, 52% in the 1980s and 34% in the 1990s, more than tripling in three decades from 522,000 to 1,645,000. In 1999 metro Orlando built 13,153 apartment units, more than any other area in the nation. And the economy has diversified beyond tourism: Martin Marietta has a big defense plant here, and greater Orlando has a high-tech economy and a population weighted toward young families with children rather than retirees. The recent completion of new expressways and water lines opened the way to more growth. The University of Central Florida, which opened in 1968 and has more than 34,000 students, is one of the fastest growing in the nation.

The 8th Congressional District includes most of Orlando and surrounding Orange County. It excludes most heavily black neighborhoods and towns placed in the 3d District. It includes central and eastern Orlando and all its suburbs directly to the east, plus most to the south and west. It also takes in most of the Kissimmee area in Osceola County just to the south and Disney World's Magic Kingdom. Politically, this Orange County is less Republican than the Orange County where the original Disneyland was built; it was historically Democratic, like all of central Florida, then swung toward Republicans in the 1970s and 1980s. In the 1990s, like most other major metro areas in the country, it trended toward Bill Clinton's Democrats. In 1996 and 2000, the 8th District cast only narrow margins for Bob Dole and George W. Bush, though Orange County—including the black Orlando precincts in the 3d District—in 2000 went narrowly Democratic.

The congressman from the 8th District is Ric Keller, a Republican first elected in 2000 in one of the closest races in the country. A political newcomer, he was born in Tennessee but grew up mostly in Orlando, in a one-bedroom house with his brother, sister, mother and grandmother. With financial help from Pell grants, he graduated first in his class at East Tennessee State University, and graduated from Vanderbilt Law School. In 1992 he moved to Orlando and practiced law, and quickly earned conservative credentials. His firm served as general counsel to a business coalition that won passage of tort reform in the Florida legislature. He chaired a successful mentoring program for local students at risk of dropping out of high school in Orange County, which has one of the nation's lowest graduation rates.

When Republican Congressman Bill McCollum, who had held the seat for 20 years, decided to run for the Senate seat being vacated by Connie Mack, Keller ran for Congress. He had tough primary competition from state Representative Bill Sublette, who boasted of delivering state funds to the area and was supported by most of the local Republican establishment. With his greater name recognition, Sublette led in most polls. Keller focused on conservative hot-button issues like abortion and gun-owners' rights. Sublette led Keller in the September primary 43%–31%; since neither had a majority, the nomination would be decided in the October 3 runoff. Democrats had a strong candidate in Linda Chapin, a former Orange County chairman, who was recruited and highly touted by national party leaders. Fearful that there would be little time after the runoff, the National Republican Congressional Committee began running ads against her even as Keller and Sublette increased their attacks on each other. Two factors helped Keller win the nomination. One was an endorsement from the third-place finisher, who disagreed with Sublette's support of abortion rights. The other was contributions of more than $200,000 from the Club for Growth, a group of Wall Street financiers who wanted to elect economically conservative Republicans and were willing to antagonize party leaders, who suspected that a moderate would be stronger in the general election. Keller won the runoff 52%–48%, with a margin of 1,215 votes; he had prepared a concession speech and admitted that he was surprised.

In the general Keller again was considered the underdog. Chapin argued that her moderate views plus her experience as a long-time county official put her more in line with district voters. To combat Keller's anti-tax message, Chapin sought the votes of "swing" moderate Republican women by stressing her work for the community and her support for gun control. Keller played up his outsider status, while Republican ads lampooned Chapin for providing frills for the county jail and other local facilities, including $150,000 for palm trees. Chapin objected that the ads were inaccurate and many were pulled; for example, cable TV was only provided to prisoners on work release, not to inmates, as the ads alleged. Keller generated additional controversy when he called Palestinians "lower than pond scum" because of the intifada in Israel. This was an exceedingly close race—Keller won 50.8%–49.2%—and a great disappointment to House Democratic leaders, who had long expected to win it. But it may have been decided by the personal touch: Keller's folksy, self-deprecating style made him "an easy man to like," wrote Tamara Lytle of the *Orlando Sentinel*.

In the House Keller got seats on the Education and the Workforce and Judiciary Committees. Although he supported George W. Bush's plan for private-school vouchers, he also favored the Democrats' priority for school-construction plus a higher support level for Pell grants. With a 39% increase, this was the fastest-growing district in the northern half of Florida during the 1990s and it will need to shrink by more than 143,000 persons. With Republicans in control of redistricting, Keller likely will benefit from more favorable lines in 2002. He has pledged to serve only four terms.

Cook's Call   *Potentially Competitive.* Keller's narrow 51% win here in 2000 and the fact that Bush only won here by 2 % would normally make the freshman Republican a big target in 2002. But it is unlikely that Democrats could find a better candidate than their 2000 nominee. Heavy growth in the Orlando area also means that this district will look different in 2002.

THE PEOPLE: Pop. 2000: 782,397; Pop. 1990: 562,244, up 39.2% 1990–2000. 76.4% White, 8.8% Black, 3.6% Asian, 0.4% Amer. Indian, 0.1% Hawaiian, 3.4% Two+ races, 7.3% Other; 23% Hispanic Origin.

2000 Presidential Vote			1996 Presidential Vote		
Bush (R)	127,400	(50%)	Dole (R)	95,300	(47%)
Gore (D)	123,028	(48%)	Clinton (D)	88,306	(44%)
Nader (Green)	3,742	(1%)	Perot (I)	17,231	(9%)
Others	1,763	(1%)			

Rep. Ric Keller (R)

Elected 2000, 1st term; b. Sept. 5, 1964, Johnson City, TN; home, Orlando; E. TN St. U., B.S. 1986; Vanderbilt U., J.D. 1992; Methodist; married (Cathy).

Professional Career: Practicing atty., 1992–2000.

DC Office: 419 CHOB 20515, 202-225-2176; Fax: 202-225-0999; Web site: www.house.gov/keller.

District Office: Orlando, 407-872-1962.

Committees: *Education & the Workforce* (25th of 27 R): Education Reform; Workforce Protections. *Judiciary* (18th of 21 R): Courts, the Internet & Intellectual Property; Crime.

Group Ratings and Key Votes: Newly Elected

Election Results

2000 general	Ric Keller (R)	125,253	(51%)	($1,318,044)
	Linda W. Chapin (D)	121,295	(49%)	($1,669,191)
2000 runoff	Ric Keller (R)	16,292	(52%)	
	Bill Sublette (R)	15,077	(48%)	
2000 primary	Bill Sublette (R)	18,196	(43%)	
	Ric Keller (R)	12,981	(31%)	
	Bob Hering (R)	10,736	(26%)	
1998 general	Bill McCollum (R)	104,298	(66%)	($648,553)
	Al Krulick (D)	54,245	(34%)	($38,882)

NINTH DISTRICT

Half a century ago, the land north of St. Petersburg and Tampa was scarcely inhabited. The Gulf is lined with swamps and inland the terrain is spotted with lakes and was covered with dense semitropical forests. Over the years, development has moved up the coast and up the major highways inland. Much of this area originally was designed for retirees—condominiums, garden apartments, trailer parks. But this is working country as well. Businesses grew up around Clearwater in northern Pinellas County and inland in Pasco County off I-75. And people brought their ancestral political beliefs with them. In the 1950s and 1960s, only white-collar retirees could afford to buy new places in Florida, and they were heavily Republican. As blue-collar workers and union members became more affluent in the 1970s and 1980s, they came with their traditional Democratic party identification and cultural conservatism. In the 1990s there were retirees and young in-migrants of all political stripes, and these crosscurrents have made this area prime marginal territory in Florida politics.

The 9th Congressional District of Florida covers much of this area north of St. Petersburg and Tampa. About half its population is in northern Pinellas County around Clearwater and Tarpon Springs, an old resort first settled by Greek sponge divers early in the 20th Century. Another quarter is in northern Hillsborough County, on the suburban fringe of Tampa. The final quarter is the inland portion of Pasco County, north of Tampa, where former crossroads like Zephyrhills have become significant population centers.

The congressman from the 9th District is Michael Bilirakis, a Republican who grew up near Pittsburgh; he served in the Air Force, and then worked his way through college, toiling in a steel mill. He also worked for the government in Washington and an aerospace contractor in Florida, then practiced law. He believes strongly that Americans can work their way up, with occasional government assistance (like the G.I. Bill that helped him through school). Originally a Democrat, he switched to the Republican Party in 1980, and in 1982, when this district was created, he won though it had been designed for a Democrat.

Bilirakis has a moderate record on economics and is more conservative on other issues. He has made something of an environmental record, opposing Western water subsidies and offshore oil drilling on the Gulf Coast. Early in his career, Bilirakis won a seat on the Commerce Committee, and starting in 1995 he held one of the most potentially powerful chairmanships in Congress, that of the Health and Environment Subcommittee; he managed to retain it in 2001, despite House Republicans' six-year term limit, by arguing that it had been reconfigured to merely the Health Subcommittee and thus wasn't the same subcommittee any more.

In 1993 and 1995, Bilirakis sponsored a bill which tried to make health insurance portable and to stop insurers from denying coverage for pre-existing conditions; it was put aside in 1994 in the debate over the Clinton health care plan, but something very like it was passed in 1996, known from its Senate sponsors as Kennedy-Kassebaum. Bilirakis also sponsored the Food Quality Protection Act, which eliminated the Delaney clause and substituted a provision allowing pesticides only when there is a reasonable certainty of no harm to the consumer. Bilirakis helped to pass the 1997 FDA overhaul intended to speed up approval of lifesaving drugs. After a Tampa nursing home evicted residents because they were on Medicaid in April 1998, Bilirakis, Jim Davis of Tampa and Senator Bob Graham sponsored a bill to prevent that practice; a version became law in March 1999. Bilirakis served on the Medicare Commission and was part of the majority that supported the Breaux-Thomas premium support plan; a version of that has been supported by George W. Bush and Bilirakis may play a role in Medicare legislation. Bilirakis also sponsored a bill to provide a state-based prescription drug benefit for the poorest and sickest Medicare beneficiaries. "An overly broad approach will simply spread limited resources too thin, without helping those most in need of assistance," he argued. This became the Republican party's plan, and again Bush has supported something quite similar. Bilirakis supported the Dingell-Norwood HMO regulation bill, and was its only supporter placed on the conference committee by Speaker Dennis Hastert. Bilirakis sponsored the November 1999 law to establish a pediatric research institute at NIH. He was chief sponsor of the bill to take control of the organ transplant program away from HHS and grant it to the government contractor UNOS; this was supported by smaller transplant centers that did not want organs to be shared over wider geographic areas and was passed by the House in 2000.

Bilirakis is also vice-chairman of the Veterans Committee. He sponsored a 1997 law to provide "forgotten widows" of veterans with a minimum annuity of $165 a month, and a 1999 law to enable severely disabled military retirees to collect retirement as well as disability benefits. He has proposed giving survivor benefits to spouses of prisoners of war. For most of his congressional career, Bilirakis has backed a center to treat veterans with spinal cord injuries; ground was broken in Tampa in March 2000 for the $17 million facility.

On local issues, Bilirakis in October 1999 questioned EPA's mound-and-cap solution for the Stauffer Chemical Superfund site on the Pinellas-Pasco county line. At a June 2000 hearing in Tarpon Springs, EPA ombudsman Bob Martin and chief investigator Hugh Kaufman sharply questioned EPA officials, who abruptly walked out after 10 minutes. Bilirakis praised Martin and Kaufman and objected later when Kaufman was removed from his duties. But weeks later EPA agreed to halt its plan.

Bilirakis had no Democratic opponent in 1998 or 2000. In 2000 he was opposed by the Reform Party's Jon Duffey, who took Bilirakis aside and offered to withdraw if he would contribute $600,000 to a health care trust fund for residents near the Stauffer site, refuse to accept PAC money, and hire Duffey as an unpaid "ethical adviser." Bilirakis responded, "Silly boy." Bilirakis in October 1999 talked of retiring: "I have said that I'm very engrossed in what's happening on health care, and I'd hate to leave that undone. I'm tired, but there's an obligation here. . . . I don't intend to stay there much longer. I think one more term." That suggests he may not run again in 2002. Because Hillsborough and Pasco Counties have grown faster than Pinellas, redistricting will change the lines of the districts in central Florida. This is a marginal area; without Bilirakis, Republicans could lose the newly drawn seat in 2002.

Cook's Call   *Safe.* While the 9th is certainly a Republican-leaning district, since winning this open seat in 1982, Bilirakis has consistently won victories far larger than might be expected. This part of the state has grown, though it is not estimated to have grown as quickly as the eastern part of the state.

THE PEOPLE: Pop. 2000: 722,068; Pop. 1990: 562,814, up 28.3% 1990–2000. 90.3% White, 4.2% Black, 1.9% Asian, 0.3% Amer. Indian, 1.6% Two+ races, 1.6% Other; 7.4% Hispanic Origin.

2000 Presidential Vote			1996 Presidential Vote		
Bush (R)	166,000	(52%)	Dole (R)	119,658	(45%)
Gore (D)	142,138	(45%)	Clinton (D)	118,996	(45%)
Nader (Green)	6,812	(2%)	Perot (I)	27,335	(10%)
Others	2,278	(1%)			

Rep. Michael Bilirakis (R)

Elected 1982, 10th term; b. July 16, 1930, Tarpon Springs; home, Palm Harbor; U. of Pittsburgh, B.S. 1959, U. of FL, J.D. 1963; Greek Orthodox; married (Evelyn).

Military Career: Air Force, 1951–55.

Professional Career: Steelworker, 1955–59; Govt. contract negotiator, 1959–60; Petroleum engineer, 1960–63; Practicing atty., 1969–83.

DC Office: 2269 RHOB 20515, 202-225-5755; Fax: 202-225-4085; Web site: www.house.gov/bilirakis.

District Offices: Clearwater, 727-441-3721; Land O'Lakes, 813-996-7441.

Committees: *Energy & Commerce* (2d of 31 R): Health (Chmn.); Oversight & Investigations; Telecommunications & The Internet. *Veterans' Affairs* (Vice Chmn. of 17 R): Oversight & Investigations.

Group Ratings

	ADA	ACLU	AFS	LCV	CON	ITIC	NTU	COC	ACU	NTLC	CHC
2000	5	21	14	29	29	78	55	71	80	64	93
1999	20	—	16	0	33	—	52	88	84	—	—

National Journal Ratings

	1999 LIB	—	1999 CONS		2000 LIB	—	2000 CONS
Economic	41%	—	59%		29%	—	67%
Social	19%	—	79%		23%	—	74%
Foreign	3%	—	92%		12%	—	78%

Key Votes of the 106th Congress

1. Patient Bill of Rights	Y	5. Bar RU-486 $ for FDA	Y	9. NATO War in Serbia	N
2. Accelerate Min. Wage	N	6. Display 10 Commandments	Y	10. Perm. Trade with China	N
3. Strike Ban on Ergo. Stnd.	N	7. Gun Show Bkgrnd. Checks	N	11. Debt Relief for 3rd World	N
4. Ovrd. Estate Tax Veto	Y	8. Ban Part.-Birth Abortion	Y	12. Drop Cuba Econ. Embargo	N

Election Results

2000 general	Michael Bilirakis (R)	210,318	(82%)	($518,118)
	Jon Duffey (Ref)	46,474	(18%)	($12,775)
2000 primary	Michael Bilirakis (R)	unopposed		
1998 general	Michael Bilirakis (R)	unopposed		($323,890)

TENTH DISTRICT

St. Petersburg, established in 1888 and named for the then-Russian capital, known for decades as the American city with the largest percentage of elderly residents, in the 1990s finally reached a certain balance. It started off promoting itself as a retirement center, and in the early 1900s *St. Petersburg Times* editor W. L. Straub tried to stop the industrialization of the waterfront, setting the city's character by establishing parks and park benches. By the 1950s St. Petersburg had become a national cliche, bringing to mind old folks trying to drum up a game of shuffleboard. Starting off on the grid streets facing Tampa Bay, spreading later toward the beaches on the Gulf Coast, St. Petersburg filled up to a greater extent than any other American city with retirees, mostly from the North and modestly affluent. They adapted easily to a city whose civic tone was set by the *St. Petersburg Times* and its longtime owners Nelson and Henrietta Poynter: sober, good-humored, supportive of clean government and civil rights. In recent decades retirees have sought homes in less urban settings, and St. Petersburg has become a more conventional central city, with a larger working population, more families and blacks and Hispanics, office buildings and civic attractions. They include the Salvador Dali Museum, a major collection of the Spanish artist's works purchased from a Beachwood, Ohio, collector, and Sunken Gardens, now being restored with grants from the federal and state governments and proceeds from the Penny for Pinellas county sales tax.

St. Petersburg and southern Pinellas County, including Largo and the string of barrier island beach towns from Mullet Key to Belleair Beach, make up Florida's 10th Congressional District. Like any retirement center, St. Petersburg has had rapid population turnover, reflected in its political trends. White-collar Yankee retirees in the 1940s and 1950s made St. Petersburg the first Republican center in ancestrally Democratic Florida; it voted for Thomas Dewey in 1948 and elected a Republican congressman in 1954. Then, as more blue-collar workers could afford Florida retirement and the affluent moved farther down the Gulf Coast, St. Petersburg trended Democratic in the 1970s and 1980s. St. Petersburg and Pinellas County gave Al Gore a small plurality in 2000, even as Tampa and Hillsborough County across the bay, once more Democratic, gave a small majority to George W. Bush.

The congressman from the 10th District is Bill Young, a Republican first elected in 1970, tied for second in seniority among House Republicans and chairman of the Appropriations Committee. Young grew up in a dirt-poor Pennsylvania coal town. His first home was a shotgun shack that was swept down a river when he was 6; at 16 he was shot in a hunting accident. The family moved to Florida, and Young dropped out of high school to support his ill mother by hauling concrete blocks and mixing mortar; at 25 he applied for a job as an insurance salesman, and ultimately ran a successful insurance agency. In the 1950s he worked for St. Petersburg's first Republican congressman, William Cramer. Young was elected to the state Senate in 1960, at 29; when Cramer ran for the Senate in 1970, Young ran for his House seat and won. In the early 1970s Social Security was vastly increased and indexed to inflation and St. Petersburg basked in prosperity; Young delivered constituency services and had a moderate to conservative voting record.

Early on, Young got a seat on Appropriations, where he, like many Republicans, worked closely with the Democratic chairmen. Young's special project has been the bone marrow donor program, originated by Dr. Robert Good of All Children's Hospital in St. Petersburg. Working from his seat on the Defense Subcommittee, he originally placed the program in the Pentagon; in 1987 it started off with $2.1 million; by 1998 it had $34 million, with 3.5 million volunteers. He has backed child health research centers, juvenile diabetes centers, more money for pediatric AIDS, and the University of Florida's Brain Institute.

Despite his seniority, Young did not become full committee chairman after Republicans won their majority in 1994. Speaker-designate Newt Gingrich passed over him and two more senior Republicans for being too accommodating to Democrats. Young says that Gingrich offered him the job, but that he preferred to chair the Defense Subcommittee, on which he had done much of his work. In that post he worked to produce bipartisan appropriations out of the spotlight; he has said he knew every dime that goes into secret "black" military and intelligence operations. Young sharply criticized the Clinton administration for stretching the military too thin. His philosophy, he says, goes back to his memories of hearing about Pearl Harbor as a child. In his office he has kept a "horseshoe nail" list ("for want of the nail, the shoe was lost") of small items the military needs; on a scroll, it stretched across the room and included items like more training hours for pilots, barracks repair and more bullets, compasses, tents and flashlights.

In 1998 Young considered retiring, but at the end of the year he was suddenly catapulted into the Appropriations chairmanship. It happened three days after the November election, when Gingrich decided to resign; Appropriations Chairman Bob Livingston quickly became the Speaker-designate, and Young became chairman. He was something of an unknown quantity: "When I came to this job, a lot of members didn't know me. The reason is that my whole life since I came to Congress has been national defense and intelligence. Most of that work is done behind closed doors." Speaker Dennis Hastert and Majority Whip Tom DeLay promised to have the 13 appropriation bills considered in a timely manner. But Young had a tough time as conservative Republican Tom Coburn filed dozens of cost-cutting amendments. Young also got into disputes with Senate Majority Leader Trent Lott. He called "excessive" Lott's funding of ships not sought by the Pentagon in a shipyard in his hometown. But in the appropriations crunch in fall 2000, he was upbraided by DeLay for his concessions to Clinton administration negotiators on education spending, the ergonomics rule and a rule that prevented dispensing of the morning-after pill in schools.

With his expertise on defense, Young occasionally spoke out on foreign policy. He charged that Bill Clinton gave Slobodan Milosevic an advantage by ruling out ground troops in March 1999. In September 1999 he restored funding for the F-22, which had been axed by his successor as Defense Appropriations Subcommittee chairman and the full House two months earlier. In October 2000 he moved to withhold foreign aid to Yemen until the U.S. was sure it was cooperating with the investigation of the attack on the *U.S.S. Cole*.

Locally, Young pushed hard for the Everglades bill in November 2000, and reluctantly accepted the price—not fighting the addition of nearly $400 million elsewhere in new pork-barrel spending. In 1999 he got $116 million for Florida projects—a reservoir in Hillsborough County, an instrument landing system at St. Petersburg-Clearwater airport, bioterrorism research grants for the University of South Florida. In 2000 he did better: $286 million—an Army Reserve unit and a $17.8 million hangar for the St. Petersburg-Clearwater airport, $26 million for a ballistics project for the ATF at the Star Center converted defense plant, $58 million to compensate citrus farmers for citrus canker, $6.6 million for dredging St. Petersburg Harbor, $60 million for military construction in Jacksonville, the Panhandle and Homestead Air Force Base, $10 million for an Army training center in Pinellas County, four new Coast Guard cutters in St. Petersburg, $50 million for safety improvements on U.S. 19.

The 10th District voted for Al Gore in 2000 but Young has not had serious competition in many years. In 1995 he said that he would abide by Florida's "eight is enough" term limit and not run again in 2000. After becoming chairman he said it was up to his constituents, who were happy to re-elect him. Its 4% increase made this the slowest-growing white-majority district in Florida during the 1990s, but Republican redistricters will surely accommodate Young with a St. Petersburg-based seat that he can easily win. Should Young retire, Democrats could seriously contest it.

Cook's Call   *Safe.* Based on presidential voting patterns alone, the 10th District should be at least a competitive district, if not in Democratic hands. It is one of only three districts in the state to split their tickets between Gore and a Republican congressional candidate in 2000. But Democrats have had little luck in even coming close to knocking off Young. With Young now at the helm of the Appropriations Committee, it's unlikely that he'll be unseated.

THE PEOPLE: Pop. 2000: 583,809; Pop. 1990: 562,301, up 3.8% 1990–2000. 83.3% White, 11.3% Black, 2.3% Asian, 0.3% Amer. Indian, 0.1% Hawaiian, 1.7% Two+ races, 1% Other; 4.1% Hispanic Origin.

2000 Presidential Vote		
Gore (D)	129,568	(53%)
Bush (R)	107,582	(44%)
Nader (Green)	6,602	(3%)
Others	1,879	(1%)

1996 Presidential Vote		
Clinton (D)	120,716	(52%)
Dole (R)	89,928	(38%)
Perot (I)	23,579	(10%)

Rep. C. W. (Bill) Young (R)

Elected 1970, 16th term; b. Dec. 16, 1930, Harmarville, PA; home, Indian Rocks Beach; United Methodist; married (Beverly).

Military Career: Army Natl. Guard, 1948–57.

Elected Office: FL Senate, 1960–70, Minority Ldr., 1966–70.

Professional Career: Aide, U.S. Rep. William Cramer, 1957–60.

DC Office: 2407 RHOB 20515, 202-225-5961; Fax: 202-225-9764; Web site: www.house.gov/young.

District Offices: Largo, 727-581-0980; St. Petersburg, 727-893-3191.

Committees: *Appropriations* (Chmn. of 35 R): Defense; Labor, HHS & Education.

Group Ratings

	ADA	ACLU	AFS	LCV	CON	ITIC	NTU	COC	ACU	NTLC	CHC
2000	5	21	0	0	55	100	58	84	72	53	93
1999	20	—	16	0	24	—	54	86	73	—	—

National Journal Ratings

	1999 LIB —	1999 CONS		2000 LIB —	2000 CONS
Economic	41% —	59%		33% —	66%
Social	32% —	66%		26% —	74%
Foreign	36% —	64%		39% —	61%

Key Votes of the 106th Congress

1. Patient Bill of Rights	Y	5. Bar RU-486 $ for FDA	Y	9. NATO War in Serbia	N
2. Accelerate Min. Wage	Y	6. Display 10 Commandments	Y	10. Perm. Trade with China	Y
3. Strike Ban on Ergo. Stnd.	N	7. Gun Show Bkgrnd. Checks	N	11. Debt Relief for 3rd World	N
4. Ovrd. Estate Tax Veto	Y	8. Ban Part.-Birth Abortion	Y	12. Drop Cuba Econ. Embargo	N

Election Results

2000 general	C. W. (Bill) Young (R)	146,799	(76%)	($336,372)
	Josette Green (NL)	26,908	(14%)	($11,938)
	Randy Heine (I)	20,296	(11%)	
2000 primary	C. W. (Bill) Young (R)	unopposed		
1998 general	C.W. (Bill) Young (R)	unopposed		($178,796)

ELEVENTH DISTRICT

Tampa is one of America's boomtowns whose history goes back just a little more than a century. Its industrial past can be traced to 1886, when Cuban cigarmakers left Key West for what became the Ybor City neighborhood of Tampa. Soon after, it was the major takeoff spot for U.S. troops in the Spanish-American War of 1898. It also became a major citrus distribution center. The old industrial city developed along the waterfront, where today you can find the world's longest sidewalk (6.5 miles along Bayshore Boulevard) and still see the 13 minarets of Tampa pioneer Henry B. Plant's 1890s Arabian-style Tampa Bay Hotel (long since taken over by the University of Tampa). For a time, Tampa was Florida's one industrial city. Now, with a diversified economy, a fast-growing service sector, tourist attractions led by Busch Gardens, and a famously pleasant and convenient airport, it has moved ahead, with subdivisions and condominiums, office towers and low-rise commercial buildings spreading inland across swamps and lowlands.

Through all this, and in contrast to St. Petersburg with its many retirees, Tampa has remained a city of families and young people, a place with a blue-collar past that is quickly moving upscale as it expands—with a major league baseball franchise since 1995 and the Super Bowl in 2001. The Bureau of Labor Statistics called it the number-one area nationwide in job growth in 1999. Tampa is an important military command center: Central Command, which ran the Gulf war, is headquartered at the still-thriving MacDill Air Force Base, and General Norman Schwarzkopf, a strong supporter of George W. Bush in 2000, remains a Tampa-area resident.

The 11th Congressional District of Florida consists of Tampa and two-thirds of surrounding Hillsborough County. Tampa was historically Democratic as St. Petersburg was Republican, though the two sides of Tampa Bay have more or less converged politically; in 2000 Hillsborough cast a majority for George W. Bush while Pinellas went for Al Gore. But the 11th District voted twice for Bill Clinton and then for Gore.

The congressman from the 11th District is Jim Davis, a Democrat first elected in 1996. Davis grew up in Tampa, returned after law school, was elected in 1988, at 31, to the state House. There he showed insider skills and interests, favoring a requirement that criminals serve 85% of their sentences and rewriting the education formula to help Hillsborough County. After the 1994 election he was elected state House Majority Leader—the last Democrat to hold that job, since Republicans won a majority in 1996. That year, Congressman Sam Gibbons decided to retire after 34 years, including seven months as Ways and Means chairman and a frustrating final two years in the minority. Davis was far from the best-known candidate, but he showed great skill at raising money and was the only one running TV ads for the September primary. Sandy Freedman, Tampa's mayor from 1986–95, led that contest with 35%, to 25% for Davis. Both supported the balanced budget amendment, the 1996 welfare reform and called for more managed care. Davis won the runoff 56%–44% and in the general faced Republican Mark Sharpe, who had given Gibbons two close contests. He attacked Davis as a fan of higher taxes and a career politician. Davis insisted he was a New Democrat, supporting the Defense of Marriage Act and opposing the penny-per-pound sugar tax on the Florida ballot; he also called for more education spending. Davis won by a solid 58%–42%.

Davis was elected the Democratic freshman class president and got a seat on the Budget Committee. He favored a number of New Democrat causes: fast-track on trade, federal funding of charter schools, the partial-birth abortion ban. He helped enact a Medicare anti-fraud bill. Prompted by eviction of Medicaid beneficiaries from a Tampa nursing home, he joined Republican Michael Bilirakis and Senator Bob Graham in sponsoring a bill to stop such evictions, which Clinton signed in 1999. On impeachment, he started off saying, "I'm not in the camp of 'I believe the president.' I'm in the camp of 'Let's have a thorough investigation and learn the facts.'" But he voted against the Republicans' impeachment inquiry resolution and against impeachment. In 1999 he voted with Republicans on their education bill after they accepted his Transition to Teaching proposal for recruiting teachers at mid-career from other jobs; Hillsborough County has been plagued by teacher vacancies. "It's not the first time, and it won't be the last," Davis said about voting against his party. When that bill deadlocked, he won $34 million for a version of his proposal in the 2000 budget. He opposed Governor Jeb Bush's voucher program as harmful to public schools. After securing a deal to liberalize trade in manufactured fertilizers, whose chief U.S. shipping port is Tampa, Davis voted for permanent normal trade relations with China.

Davis has entrenched himself in the seat, with no major-party opposition in 2000. In the House, however, he was "deeply, deeply disappointed" over his failure to win a seat on the Energy and Commerce Committee in January 2001. He has expressed interest in running for governor in 2002. Republican redistricters could create a Tampa-centered seat which leans more their way, though that would be at the cost of making neighboring districts more vulnerable, all of which have Republican incumbents.

Cook's Call *Potentially Competitive.* Though this is hardly a safe Democratic district, Davis has not had any trouble racking up big margins since his first win in 1996. But Republicans, who control the redistricting process, are interested in marginalizing this seat in 2002. Talk that Davis is interested in running for governor could give them more flexibility. But too much tickering with this district could tilt it either way. This is a seat to keep an eye on during the battle over redistricting.

THE PEOPLE: Pop. 2000: 628,167; Pop. 1990: 562,293, up 11.7% 1990–2000. 69.3% White, 20.4% Black, 2.2% Asian, 0.4% Amer. Indian, 0.1% Hawaiian, 2.9% Two + races, 4.6% Other; 20% Hispanic Origin.

2000 Presidential Vote		
Gore (D)	110,026	(53%)
Bush (R)	92,309	(44%)
Nader (Green)	4,794	(2%)
Others	1,553	(1%)

1996 Presidential Vote		
Clinton (D)	98,028	(52%)
Dole (R)	75,004	(40%)
Perot (I)	14,849	(8%)

Rep. Jim Davis (D)

Elected 1996, 3d term; b. Oct. 11, 1957, Tampa; home, Tampa; Wash. & Lee U., B.A. 1979, U. of FL, J.D. 1982; Episcopalian; married (Peggy).

Elected Office: FL House of Reps., 1988–96, Majority Ldr. 1994–96.

Professional Career: Practicing atty., 1982–96.

DC Office: 424 CHOB 20515, 202-225-3376; Fax: 202-225-5652; Web site: www.house.gov/jimdavis.

District Office: Tampa, 813-354-9217.

Committees: *Budget* (5th of 20 D). *House Administration* (3d of 3 D). *International Relations* (12th of 23 D): East Asia & the Pacific; Europe.

Group Ratings

	ADA	ACLU	AFS	LCV	CON	ITIC	NTU	COC	ACU	NTLC	CHC
2000	75	50	71	86	81	90	19	57	16	16	20
1999	80	—	83	63	92	—	16	44	12	—	—

National Journal Ratings

	1999 LIB —	1999 CONS		2000 LIB —	2000 CONS
Economic	60% —	39%		77% —	22%
Social	65% —	34%		66% —	34%
Foreign	74% —	23%		61% —	38%

Key Votes of the 106th Congress

1. Patient Bill of Rights	Y	5. Bar RU-486 $ for FDA	N	9. NATO War in Serbia	Y
2. Accelerate Min. Wage	Y	6. Display 10 Commandments	N	10. Perm. Trade with China	Y
3. Strike Ban on Ergo. Stnd.	Y	7. Gun Show Bkgrnd. Checks	Y	11. Debt Relief for 3rd World	Y
4. Ovrd. Estate Tax Veto	N	8. Ban Part.-Birth Abortion	Y	12. Drop Cuba Econ. Embargo	N

Election Results

2000 general	Jim Davis (D) 149,465	(85%)	($447,707)
	Charlie Westlake (LIB) 27,197	(15%)	($14,604)
2000 primary	Jim Davis (D) .... unopposed		
1998 general	Jim Davis (D) 85,262	(65%)	($756,141)
	Joe Chillura (R) 46,176	(35%)	($48,041)

TWELFTH DISTRICT

With their skyscrapers rising over bays and rivers, the great gleaming cities of Florida are found near the Atlantic or Gulf coasts. Inland are parts of the state that were most heavily settled half a century ago. One is Polk County, the biggest inland county in Florida, with its small lakes and small cities of Lakeland, Bartow, Lake Wales and Winter Haven scattered about. The citrus business remains a mainstay of the local economy and orange groves abound, although periodic freezes have convinced some growers to move south or to produce tomatoes instead. Turpentine distilleries, dependent on the big stands of pine, and phosphate mining businesses can be found also; there are more manufacturing jobs here proportionately (though not that many) than almost anywhere else in Florida. Retired *Ladies Home Journal* editor Edward Bok built the most prominent landmarks here: the gothic Bok Tower and the surrounding Mountain Lake Sanctuary and gardens. But little of Bok's prestige remains and the area has not become a major retiree haven.

Polk County historically was Democratic, the home of Spessard Holland and Lawton Chiles; Holland was senator 1946–71, after serving as governor, and Chiles was senator 1970–88 and then was elected governor in 1990 and 1994. But as in most of the Deep South, Republicans have picked up strength in Polk County. Chiles kept it in the Democratic column in 1990 but it voted against him and for Jeb Bush in 1994. It has been consistently Republican since then and gave George W. Bush a 54%–45% majority in 2000.

The 12th District of Florida includes all but the northeast edge of Polk County, plus the western, rapidly suburbanizing edge of Tampa's Hillsborough County. It extends into old-fashioned Florida agricultural country north of Polk County, around Dade City in Pasco County, and to the south, in Hardee, DeSoto and a slice of Highlands Counties. Historically Democratic, this has been a Republican seat since Congressman Andy Ireland switched parties in 1984.

The congressman from the 12th is Adam Putnam, a Republican elected in 2000 who entered the House as its youngest member, at 26. A fifth-generation member of a Bartow family, he graduated from the University of Florida and worked in his family's citrus and cattle business. In 1996 he was elected to the state House, where as Agriculture Committee chairman he supported several pieces of controversial legislation, including a "sovereign lands" bill that would have given shoreline property on inland waters to adjacent property owners and was strongly opposed by environmentalists. He also sponsored a bill that set mandatory maximum sentences on prisoners who had been released early and then committed another crime. When Congressman Charles Canady retired at age 46, keeping his pledge to serve only four terms and taking a job as the chief lawyer to Jeb Bush, Putnam was unopposed in his own party. He became the clear frontrunner when former Democratic state Senator Rick Dantzler, the party's nominee for lieutenant governor in 1998, decided against running. Putnam supported most parts of the Republican agenda: He is against abortion and gun control, opposes the marriage and estate taxes, wants to lower the capital gains tax and allow workers to invest part of their Social Security tax in private investments, and favors a missile defense system.

Putnam had a tougher than expected challenge from auto-dealer and first-time candidate Michael Stedem, who described himself as pro-business and centrist, and said that Putnam did not have enough life experience for the job. Stedem's message gained some traction. "Putnam is 26 and looks as if he's going on 13," wrote Daniel Ruth of *The Tampa Tribune* in October 2000, in a story headlined, "Opie runs for Congress." Stedem was bolstered by substantial fundraising and attention from House Democrats. But Putnam won the seat 57%–43%, winning comfortably in all six counties; in Polk, which cast 69% of the district vote, he led 55%–45%.

Putnam got seats on Agriculture, Government Reform, and Budget—where he planned to focus on Social Security inter-generational problems. Redistricting will shrink the 12th District, but Republicans control the process and will probably create a district dominated by Polk County where he can win easily.

Cook's Call *Probably Safe.* Though Putnam struggled early in the 2000 race to replace Charles Canady, he seemed to catch his stride in the late stretches of the campaign and ended up winning big. It is hard to see Democrats targeting this seat in 2002: They were unable to convince a top-tier candidate to run here even when this was an open seat. This district has grown a bit since 1990, but it is not apparent that will make this district any more competitive in 2002.

THE PEOPLE: Pop. 2000: 671,347; Pop. 1990: 562,381, up 19.4% 1990–2000. 79.1% White, 12.6% Black, 1% Asian, 0.4% Amer. Indian, 1.7% Two+ races, 5.2% Other; 12.3% Hispanic Origin.

2000 Presidential Vote			1996 Presidential Vote		
Bush (R)	127,263	(55%)	Dole (R)	96,140	(47%)
Gore (D)	98,472	(43%)	Clinton (D)	89,296	(43%)
Nader (Green)	3,076	(1%)	Perot (I)	20,770	(10%)
Others	2,395	(1%)			

Rep. Adam Putnam (R)

Elected 2000, 1st term; b. June 30, 1974, Bartow; home, Bartow; U. of FL, B.S. 1995; Episcopalian; married (Melissa).

Elected Office: FL House of Reps., 1996–2000.

Professional Career: Rancher, Putnam Groves, Inc.

DC Office: 506 CHOB 20515, 202-225-1252; Fax: 202-226-0585; Web site: www.house.gov/putnam.

District Office: Bartow, 863-534-3530.

Committees: *Agriculture* (26th of 27 R): Conservation, Credit, Rural Development & Research; Department Operations, Oversight, Nutrition & Forestry; Livestock & Horticulture; Specialty Crops & Foreign Agriculture Programs. *Budget* (23d of 24 R). *Government Reform* (21st of 24 R): Government Efficiency, Financial Management & Intergovernmental Relations; National Security, Veterans' Affairs & Intl. Relations. *Joint Economic Committee* (6th of 10 Reps.).

Group Ratings and Key Votes: Newly Elected

Election Results

2000 general	Adam Putnam (R)	125,224	(57%)	($1,047,257)
	Mike Stedem (D)	94,395	(43%)	($650,578)
2000 primary	Adam Putnam (R)	unopposed		
1998 general	Charles Canady (R)	unopposed		($116,254)

THIRTEENTH DISTRICT

Everyone else followed the circus to Sarasota. When the Ringling Brothers made a success of the circus they founded in the 1880s, they needed a place for performers and animals to rest during the winter months. They settled on the bayfront village of Sarasota behind a barrier island along the Gulf of Mexico. It was just far enough north to be reachable by railroad, just far enough south to be semitropical so the elephants would not get sick and die. Here, John Ringling established the Ringling Museum of Art, with its huge sculpture garden and built his own Venetian palace, the Ca'd'Zan. After World War II, when people began spending their retirement years in warmer climates, the Gulf Coast started attracting new settlers—affluent, WASPy Republicans from upper crust suburbs of northern cities. The population exploded, with Manatee and Sarasota counties growing from 63,000 in 1950 to 589,959 in 2000.

The 13th Congressional District of Florida includes Sarasota and Manatee counties and slivers of Tampa's Hillsborough County on the north and Charlotte County on the south. It is mostly a collection of Gulf Coast towns, from Tampa Bay south past Venice (where the circus now has its winter quarters). It is retiree and tourist country. It also includes huge tomato and strawberry fields in Ruskin. But some high-tech firms recently have diversified the economy. *Money* magazine in 2000 called Sarasota the best small city in the nation. The 13th for many years was heavily Republican, though it became somewhat less so in the 1990s.

The congressman from the 13th District is Dan Miller, a Republican first elected in 1992. Miller is a native of Michigan, with an M.B.A. and a Ph.D., who taught economics at Georgia State and then moved to Bradenton in the 1970s and started small businesses—the Memorial Pier Restaurant, the Suncoast Manor Nursing Center, the Barnett Bank Building and Riverview Center. He served on local commissions, the hospital board of directors and the judicial nominating commission. After 1992, Andy Ireland, who had represented most of the new 12th and 13th Districts, retired. Miller was one of five Republican and two Democratic candidates. Calling for less government, fewer regulations, and lower taxes, he ran second in the primary, 143 votes behind former Bush administration appointee Brad Baker; in the runoff, with Ireland's endorsement, Miller won 53%–47%. Against Democrat Rand Snell, former aide to Senator Lawton Chiles, Miller won 58%–42%.

His voting record has been conservative on economics and moderate on cultural issues. Miller voted for the assault weapons ban and has supported abortion rights. He has taken some political risks. He spearheaded opposition to the Clinton health care plan in 1993 and helped put together the Republican Medicare proposal in 1995. One area of spending he looks favorably on is medical research: As an appropriator, he worked to increase Clinton's requests for the National Institutes of Health and the Centers for Disease Control and Prevention. Every year he conducts a Congressional Classroom program, bringing one junior from every high school in the district to meet Washington leaders and stage a mock Congress.

Miller has embarked on several crusades in Congress. The first was against the sugar program, which places quotas on imports from other nations and subsidizes U.S. producers because the domestic price is double the world price—"corporate welfare," in Miller's view. It has stimulated overproduction in Florida and the phosphorus runoff has killed plants and wildlife in the Everglades. Miller and Democrat Charles Schumer led an effort to kill the program; in February 1996 their amendment lost on the floor by only 217–208. Miller has persisted, but has not come as close since. Another Miller cause is renegotiating the extradition treaty with Mexico. He was outraged when Mexico refused to extradite a man who murdered a Sarasota mother of six, even after the district attorney waived (as the treaty allows Mexico to demand) capital punishment. He voted against the transportation bill in 1998 (though it contained a Sarasota project) as having "more pork than a Memphis barbecue." But he sought to shift to Florida more operations of the National Oceanic and Atmospheric Administration.

Then there is the Census. In a September 1997 floor debate he attacked the Clinton administration proposal for Census sampling, pointing out that his Ph.D. is in marketing and statistics. "I used to make the statement, 'Tell me the point you want to make, and I will prove it with statistics,' because it can be done," he said. In November he was made chairman of a new and politically vital Census Subcommittee. The Census became a major struggle between Bill Clinton and Congress. Miller argued that the Clinton plan to headcount just 90% of the population and to use a 750,000-person sample to adjust the count left open the possibility of fraud (the sample would be conducted by local people, perhaps chosen by political operatives) and required a far larger and faster survey than the Census Bureau ever conducted. His position was strengthened in January 1999 when the Supreme Court upheld two appeals court decisions and said the sampling plan could not be used for apportionment of House seats among the states. The administration then said it would conduct two counts, and that sample-produced numbers could be used for redistricting within states. Miller, who supported Democrats' proposals for outreach efforts to improve the head count, opposed funding for two counts. But Congress agreed to leave the final decision on sampling for the new president. As it turned out, outreach efforts made the 2000 Census head count considerably more accurate than the 1990 Census. In March 2001, Census

Bureau professionals ruled that they could not say that the 750,000-person sample was more accurate than the head count, and recommended against sampling. Commerce Secretary Donald Evans, who had assumed final authority, ruled against sampling and for the head count. This was a complete and overwhelming victory for Miller. Democrats and big city mayors said they would sue, but it is highly unlikely that a court would overturn a decision concurred with Census officials and the Commerce secretary.

Miller has won reelection easily. Following the 2000 election, he said that he would keep his term-limit pledge to retire in 2002. Secretary of State Katherine Harris, who was primed to certify George W. Bush as the winner in Florida until she was barred from doing so by the state Supreme Court, and who later certified him as winner in accordance with state law, has indicated an interest in running for this seat; she is from Sarasota and has been active in civic affairs. Redistricting could change the lines, but Harris or another Republican nominee would be heavily favored in any seat in this area.

Cook's Call *Safe.* Miller has made it clear that he intends to retire this term. Republicans should have little difficulty holding onto the Republican leaning 13th District in 2002.

THE PEOPLE: Pop. 2000: 677,666; Pop. 1990: 562,501, up 20.5% 1990–2000. 89.5% White, 5.7% Black, 0.8% Asian, 0.3% Amer. Indian, 1.2% Two+ races, 2.4% Other; 7.5% Hispanic Origin.

2000 Presidential Vote			1996 Presidential Vote		
Bush (R)	160,230	(52%)	Dole (R)	133,005	(47%)
Gore (D)	137,596	(45%)	Clinton (D)	122,884	(43%)
Nader (Green)	7,304	(2%)	Perot (I)	29,634	(10%)
Others	1,740	(1%)			

Rep. Dan Miller (R)

Elected 1992, 5th term; b. May 30, 1942, Highland Park, MI; home, Bradenton; U. of FL, B.S./B.A. 1964, Emory U., M.B.A. 1965, Louisiana St. U., Ph.D. 1970; Episcopalian; married (Glenda).

Professional Career: Businessman, Miller Enterprises, 1973–present; Asst. Prof., Georgia St. U., 1969–73; Adjunct Prof., U. of S. FL, 1975–83.

DC Office: 102 CHOB 20515, 202-225-5015; Fax: 202-226-0828; Web site: www.house.gov/danmiller.

District Offices: Bradenton, 941-747-9081; Sarasota, 941-951-6643.

Committees: *Appropriations* (16th of 35 R): Commerce, Justice & State; Labor, HHS & Education; Military Construction. *Government Reform* (14th of 24 R): Census (Chmn.); Criminal Justice, Drug Policy & Human Resources; Government Efficiency, Financial Management & Intergovernmental Relations.

Group Ratings

	ADA	ACLU	AFS	LCV	CON	ITIC	NTU	COC	ACU	NTLC	CHC
2000	10	36	0	29	72	94	67	75	88	75	73
1999	15	—	16	31	44	—	63	83	68	—	—

National Journal Ratings

	1999 LIB	—	1999 CONS		2000 LIB	—	2000 CONS
Economic	28%	—	71%		29%	—	67%
Social	52%	—	48%		47%	—	53%
Foreign	23%	—	73%		0%	—	88%

Key Votes of the 106th Congress

1. Patient Bill of Rights	N	5. Bar RU-486 $ for FDA	N	9. NATO War in Serbia	N
2. Accelerate Min. Wage	N	6. Display 10 Commandments	Y	10. Perm. Trade with China	Y
3. Strike Ban on Ergo. Stnd.	N	7. Gun Show Bkgrnd. Checks	N	11. Debt Relief for 3rd World	N
4. Ovrd. Estate Tax Veto	Y	8. Ban Part.-Birth Abortion	Y	12. Drop Cuba Econ. Embargo	N

2000 general	Dan Miller (R)	175,918	(64%)	($369,407)
	Daniel E. Dunn (D)	99,568	(36%)	($40,948)
2000 primary	Dan Miller (R)	unopposed		
1998 general	Dan Miller (R)	unopposed		($191,313)

FOURTEENTH DISTRICT

On the edge of the Tropics, in a physical environment once teeming with diseases and inhospitable to advanced civilization only two generations ago, Florida's Gulf Coast has sprung up as a model of what America will be for many when they retire. This was once Seminole country, from which the last Seminoles were sent on boats to the West in 1858; there were only a few white settlements, like Fort Myers, built in 1850 as an Army base to get rid of the Seminoles. For another century, few people lived here. But in time the wide white sand beaches with gentle breakers, the inlets and broad estuaries that abound for boating, the wetlands filled with exotic birds, made this prime resort country: Thomas Edison had his winter home in Fort Myers, Henry Ford used to visit here, Walter Reuther, after his gunshot wound, recuperated by building a modest house near the Caloosahatchee River. But the local economy could not support many permanent residents, and at the beginning of World War II, there were only 68,000 people living on the Gulf Coast from Bradenton south to Naples.

By 2000 there were 1.4 million: the climate and environment attracted affluent suburbanites from the Midwest and Northeast, with the added lure of no state income or inheritance taxes. Developers like Barron Collier, who built the Tamiami Trail across the Everglades and designed Naples with the wealthy in mind (and gave his name to Collier County, the richest in Florida), were determined to avoid the high-rise canyons that line the Atlantic from Miami to Palm Beach. The alternative has been low-rise, city-sized developments like fast-growing Cape Coral and Port Charlotte, with canals in most backyards, and thinly paved roads along the sand spits next to the sultry, lapping waves of the Gulf, or the luxurious boutique town of Naples set amid preserved coastal islands and St. Augustine grass and banyan trees. This is very much retirement country.

The 14th Congressional District of Florida occupies the southern half of this Gulf Coast, from Charlotte County past Cape Coral and Fort Myers south to Naples. This district has the highest Republican registration of any in Florida, and votes heavily Republican, though recently Democrats have picked up some strength, and in 2000 it gave George W. Bush a smaller majority than in the much less affluent Panhandle.

The congressman from the 14th District is Porter Goss, a Republican first elected in 1988. After graduating from Yale, he worked 10 years in the CIA's Clandestine Services in Latin America, the Caribbean and Europe. He then retired and moved to Sanibel Island (whose famous shells are now scarce). There he founded a prize-winning newspaper, served on the city council and passed growth management laws and was appointed to the Lee County Commission by then-Governor Bob Graham. When incumbent Connie Mack ran for the Senate in 1988, Goss ran for this seat and effectively won it in the Republican primary, leading 38%–29%–19% over former Congressman Skip Bafalis and retired General Jim Dozier.

Goss has been chairman of the Intelligence Committee since 1997. There he led efforts to increase intelligence spending in the October 1998 omnibus budget bill. "There is no question in my view that we have hollowed out our defense unnecessarily, including our intelligence, and we have to rebuild," he said. He intended the increased spending to enable intelligence agencies to recapitalize technological intelligence collection, rebuild espionage capabilities, develop the ability to respond with covert action to transnational threats and hostile states and to increase analytic depth and breadth. He also called on intelligence agencies to do more to learn about the drug trade in Latin America. In 1999 he criticized the Clinton administration harshly for allowing Chinese spying: "We allowed ourselves to be victimized. The inept handling of counterintelligence matters at the Department of Energy, the insufficient attention paid to security at our national laboratories and elsewhere, and the predominance of trade considerations over those of national security were all the driving forces behind the disaster at hand." In April 2000 he said the CIA had acted properly in firing the intelligence officer responsible for the bombing of the Chinese

Embassy in Belgrade. When a computer hard drive was discovered missing at Los Alamos in June 2000, he said, "Throughout this White House's tenure, there has existed a culture of disdain towards security that continually rises to the surface."

Goss's concern for security is balanced by a realization that there can be too much secrecy. In October 1999 he and Senator Daniel Patrick Moynihan sponsored a bill to create a Public Interest Declassification Board to declassify old documents, especially those relating to historical controversies; Goss compared it to a bathtub and said this would be "a slightly larger drain." In October 2000 he supported the anti-leak criminal measure sponsored by Senate Intelligence Chairman Richard Shelby; to those, liberal and conservative, who said this would be onerous, he argued that the government would have to prove that leaked material was "properly" classified. But the measure was vetoed by Bill Clinton. Goss has opposed loosening export controls on encryption. He was mentioned as a possible director of Central Intelligence in December 2000, but showed no interest. In his final two years as chairman he promises to make cybersecurity a major issue.

On foreign policy, Goss was concerned that the United States was becoming "overengaged" in Kosovo in spring 1999. He supported removal of U.S. troops from Haiti in 2000 and supported the Taiwan legislation, with some reservations. He supported the Clinton administration's $1.7 billion Plan Colombia, and in September 2000 traveled to Colombia with Clinton to show bipartisan support.

Goss is the second-ranking Republican on the Rules Committee and has reliably supported the Republican leadership. He was called in by Speaker Dennis Hastert in October 1999 to manage the Republican version of managed care reform, which was defeated. He has called for changing the budget process so that Congress and the president would early on agree on a budget resolution. On most issues he has taken conservative stands. In line with Gulf Coast opinion, he has supported and worked to extend the 1982 moratorium on oil drilling in the Gulf of Mexico off the Florida shore. He worked for the Everglades restoration bill that was passed in November 2000. He was the chief sponsor of the Ricky Ray Hemophilia Relief Fund Act, which compensates hemophiliacs who contracted AIDS through tainted transfusions. Ricky Ray was one of three south Florida brothers so infected; Goss introduced the bill in 1995, it became law in October 1998 and was funded in December 2000. It sets up a $750 million fund to provide $100,000 to each recipient. "If there is ever any reason to serve in public this is it," Goss said. On local matters, he has pushed for a new VA outpatient clinic and a new federal courthouse in Fort Myers and expansion of the Southwest Florida International Airport.

Goss has been re-elected without difficulty. When Connie Mack announced his retirement from the Senate, Goss was mentioned as a possible candidate, but took himself out of the running in September 1999. In May 2000 he said he would serve one more term in the House. The district grew by 41% in the 1990s, but Republicans control redistricting and are expected to create another heavily Republican district in this area; some have discussed extending a new district across the state. The next congressman will presumably be decided in a multi-candidate Republican primary, with perhaps a runoff in October 2002. Possible contenders included Lee County Commissioners John Albion and Andy Coy, and former Cape Coral Mayor John Mazurkiewicz.

Cook's Call   *Safe.* Goss hasn't had a real race since he first won the seat in 1982. This district is one of the fastest growing in the state (it is expected to need to shed over 120,000 people). But this was also one of Bush's best districts in the state, giving him a 21-point margin of victory.

THE PEOPLE: Pop. 2000: 790,852; Pop. 1990: 562,489, up 40.6% 1990–2000. 88% White, 5.5% Black, 0.7% Asian, 0.3% Amer. Indian, 1.7% Two+ races, 3.7% Other; 11.9% Hispanic Origin.

2000 Presidential Vote			1996 Presidential Vote		
Bush (R)	194,780	(59%)	Dole (R)	140,921	(51%)
Gore (D)	125,036	(38%)	Clinton (D)	105,027	(38%)
Nader (Green)	6,097	(2%)	Perot (I)	29,735	(11%)
Others	1,745	(1%)			

Rep. Porter J. Goss (R)

Elected 1988, 7th term; b. Nov. 26, 1938, Waterbury, CT; home, Sanibel; Yale U., B.A. 1960; Presbyterian; married (Mariel).

Military Career: Army Intelligence, 1960–62.

Elected Office: Sanibel City Cncl., 1974–82; Sanibel Mayor, 1974–77, 1980; Lee Cnty. Commissioner 1983–88.

Professional Career: CIA Clandestine Svcs. 1960–71; Businessman & newspaper publ., 1973–78.

DC Office: 108 CHOB 20515, 202-225-2536; Fax: 202-225-6820; Web site: www.house.gov/goss.

District Offices: Ft. Myers, 941-332-4677; Naples, 941-774-8060; Punta Gorda, 941-639-0051.

Committees: *Permanent Select Committee on Intelligence* (Chmn. of 11 R). *Rules* (2d of 9 R): The Legislative & Budget Process (Vice Chmn.).

Group Ratings

	ADA	ACLU	AFS	LCV	CON	ITIC	NTU	COC	ACU	NTLC	CHC
2000	0	29	0	43	59	100	63	80	96	76	73
1999	10	—	0	25	37	—	62	92	80	—	—

National Journal Ratings

	1999 LIB	—	1999 CONS		2000 LIB	—	2000 CONS
Economic	0%	—	84%		34%	—	64%
Social	35%	—	64%		0%	—	79%
Foreign	43%	—	55%		0%	—	88%

Key Votes of the 106th Congress

1. Patient Bill of Rights	N	5. Bar RU-486 $ for FDA	Y	9. NATO War in Serbia	Y
2. Accelerate Min. Wage	N	6. Display 10 Commandments	Y	10. Perm. Trade with China	Y
3. Strike Ban on Ergo. Stnd.	N	7. Gun Show Bkgrnd. Checks	N	11. Debt Relief for 3rd World	N
4. Ovrd. Estate Tax Veto	Y	8. Ban Part.-Birth Abortion	Y	12. Drop Cuba Econ. Embargo	N

Election Results

2000 general	Porter J. Goss (R)	242,614	(85%)	($259,684)
	Sam Farling (NL)	41,988	(15%)	($7,215)
2000 primary	Porter J. Goss (R)	unopposed		
1998 general	Porter J. Goss (R)	unopposed		($158,856)

FIFTEENTH DISTRICT

When Cape Canaveral was chosen as the nation's rocket testing site in the 1940s, there were only 20,000 people in all of Brevard County, which stretches along 63 miles of the coast north and south of the Cape. It was a backward place with no industry, picked because it was on the sunny Atlantic coast: rockets here have to be launched eastward so spent parts fall into the ocean. Today, Brevard County north and south of the Cape has 476,000 people. It is a prototype of America's future, with no city center but plenty of shopping centers along strip highways, with a white-collar, service economy, knit together by interest in the space program. With proximity to Disney World also has come growth in the local cruise business, including Disney mega-ships.

The 15th Congressional District of Florida includes all of the Space Coast and Brevard County and extends south into Indian River County and the fast-growing retirement areas around Vero Beach. It continues west past the vast new town of Palm Bay, now the district's largest city, to what is left of primeval Florida. More may come: the Army Corps of Engineers, which straightened out the Kissimmee River in the early 1970s, is now restoring it to its natural snake-like course—a process that will be followed farther south by restoration of the Everglades, under a law passed in November 2000. Nearby in the Three Lakes Wildlife Management Area, whooping cranes were released to propagate in the wild. The Space Coast is Republican, distrustful of many national Democrats' disdain for the space program, though Brevard County was represented in the House by Democratic Senator Bill Nelson from 1978 to 1990.

The congressman from the 15th District is Dave Weldon, a Republican first elected in 1994. Weldon grew up on Long Island, went to medical school in Buffalo, served in the Army in Fort Stewart, Georgia, then in 1987 joined Melbourne Internal Medicine Associates in Florida. In 1989 he founded the Space Coast Family Forum "to promote family-friendly issues and positions." Weldon ran for the House in 1994, when moderate Democrat Jim Bacchus retired, and was considered a weak candidate because of his strong conservative views on cultural issues. He led the seven-candidate Republican primary, but with only 24% of the vote, and in the runoff won 54%–46% over Carole Jordan, who campaigned as a pro-choice moderate. Democrats ran Sue Munsey, a pro-choice former Republican and Space Coast Chamber of Commerce head. Weldon called for phasing out welfare and banning abortion. He won 54%–46%, and Speaker Newt Gingrich, whom Weldon called an "idol," gave him a seat on Science and made him vice chairman of the Space and Aeronautics Subcommittee.

Weldon started off defending the Kennedy Space Center and promoting the Space Shuttle, protecting their funding even when NASA funding was going down. But in time he moved from defending an existing program to transforming it. With Senator Bob Graham, he passed a bill in 1998 to move toward commercialization of space. The idea was to increase U.S. commercial launching capacity, by using antiquated (and disposable) ballistic missiles. The U.S. currently produces most commercial satellites, but has launching capacity for only about 40% of them; the French launch roughly one-half, with the remainder largely split between Russia and China. Increased capacity would mean less reliance on countries like China, and less incentive for U.S. satellite companies to betray American technology to China, as some evidently did. The bill would also ease licensing requirements for commercial re-entry vehicles, to provide competition for NASA's Space Shuttle. And it orders NASA to improve its tracking machinery at launching sites. Weldon supported the space station the U.S. operated jointly with Russia, but questioned whether Russia could provide the needed financing. With commercial competition may come long-term challenges to the Cape Canaveral area. With NASA's funding problems, Weldon backed cancellation of an oceanography satellite project—of which Al Gore was an enthusiast. In 1999 Weldon raised concern that shrinking budgets were indirectly responsible for the failure of two Mars missions.

Weldon has a very conservative voting record; he favors increased defense spending, a 17% flat tax, school vouchers and education IRAs. In 1999 he got $16 million for Port Canaveral dredging and Brevard County beach renourishment. He demanded that Energy Secretary Bill Richardson resign for the loss of nuclear weapon secrets from the Los Alamos lab. Citing labor and human rights abuses plus undercutting of the U.S. space launch industry, he voted against permanent normal trade relations with China. By 2000, Weldon conceded that Republican revolutionary fervor from the Contract with America had faded but he had no regrets about their work or Gingrich's leadership. "Newt was the right man to take us from minority to the majority," Weldon said. "He had trouble transitioning to the governing mode." In January 2001 he sponsored a change in House rules to prohibit a member from having a spouse on payroll; the rule was intended to discourage the practice of a lawmaker divorcing a spouse and then marrying an aide, he said.

Weldon's reputation for outspoken conservatism—he home-schools his children—has inspired strong opposition. But he has survived with comfortable margins. In 2000 he had a well-financed opponent, Patsy Kurth, a state Senator and cousin of Dick Gephardt; she criticized Weldon's failure to prevent NASA cutbacks. Kurth supported abortion rights and wanted to use the budget surplus to strengthen Social Security and pay down the debt. Weldon won 59%–39%. Redistricting will reduce the size of the district, but probably will not jeopardize Weldon. Since the eve of the 2000 election, he said he was reconsidering his initial pledge to limit himself to four terms.

Cook's Call *Probably Safe.* Though not the most Republican-leaning district in the state, this Space Coast-area seat does have a Republican core that makes it tough for Democrats to oust three-term Representative Dave Weldon.

THE PEOPLE: Pop. 2000: 718,294; Pop. 1990: 562,542, up 27.7% 1990–2000. 86.5% White, 7.9% Black, 1.3% Asian, 0.4% Amer. Indian, 0.1% Hawaiian, 1.8% Two+ races, 1.9% Other; 7.2% Hispanic Origin.

2000 Presidential Vote		
Bush (R)	167,426	(53%)
Gore (D)	137,949	(44%)
Nader (Green)	6,016	(2%)
Others	2,457	(1%)

1996 Presidential Vote		
Dole (R)	125,430	(46%)
Clinton (D)	111,263	(41%)
Perot (I)	34,594	(13%)

Rep. Dave Weldon (R)

Elected 1994, 4th term; b. Aug. 31, 1953, Amityville, NY; home, Palm Bay; S.U.N.Y. Stony Brook, B.A. 1978, S.U.N.Y. Buffalo, M.D. 1981; Christian; married (Nancy).

Military Career: Army Medical Corps, 1981–87, Army Reserves, 1987–92.

Professional Career: Practicing physician, 1987–94.

DC Office: 332 CHOB 20515, 202-225-3671; Fax: 202-225-3516; Web site: www.house.gov/weldon.

District Office: Melbourne, 407-632-1776.

Committees: *Financial Services* (17th of 37 R): Capital Markets, Insurance & Government Sponsored Enterprises; Financial Institutions & Consumer Credit (Vice Chmn.); Oversight & Investigations. *Government Reform* (19th of 24 R): Civil Service & Agency Organization (Vice Chmn.); Criminal Justice, Drug Policy & Human Resources; National Security, Veterans' Affairs & Intl. Relations. *Science* (12th of 25 R): Space & Aeronautics (Vice Chmn.).

Group Ratings

	ADA	ACLU	AFS	LCV	CON	ITIC	NTU	COC	ACU	NTLC	CHC
2000	5	14	14	7	43	78	68	76	92	85	100
1999	10	—	0	6	28	—	61	88	92	—	—

National Journal Ratings

	1999 LIB —	1999 CONS		2000 LIB —	2000 CONS
Economic	24%	72%		6%	85%
Social	10%	85%		0%	79%
Foreign	31%	66%		0%	88%

Key Votes of the 106th Congress

1. Patient Bill of Rights	Y	5. Bar RU-486 $ for FDA	Y	9. NATO War in Serbia	N
2. Accelerate Min. Wage	N	6. Display 10 Commandments	Y	10. Perm. Trade with China	N
3. Strike Ban on Ergo. Stnd.	N	7. Gun Show Bkgrnd. Checks	N	11. Debt Relief for 3rd World	N
4. Ovrd. Estate Tax Veto	Y	8. Ban Part.-Birth Abortion	Y	12. Drop Cuba Econ. Embargo	N

Election Results

2000 general	Dave Weldon (R)	176,189	(59%)	($910,906)
	Patsy Ann Kurth (D)	117,511	(39%)	($698,292)
	Others	5,745	(2%)	
2000 primary	Dave Weldon (R)	unopposed		
1998 general	Dave Weldon (R)	129,278	(63%)	($508,032)
	David Golding (D)	75,654	(37%)	($26,640)

SIXTEENTH DISTRICT

Urban Florida has fanned far across the swamplands from its original nuclei in beachfront resort communities. Thus Palm Beach has spread out from its original locus around the plush Breakers Hotel and the Addison Mizner villas, across Lake Worth and well beyond the refurbished city of West Palm Beach: these are now just neighborhoods in a vast metropolitan area. Old beach towns, such as Hobe Sound, located northward along the ocean, have become the hub of extremely affluent developments that stretch all the way to Stuart in Martin County. Farther north, near the old town of Fort Pierce, are larger but more modest developments like Port St. Lucie. These spring training sites compete for baseball franchises that direct millions of dollars to local economies. Entire square miles west and northwest of West Palm Beach have been reclaimed from swampland and made into condo communities such as Century Village, surrounded by golf courses or tracts of factories and warehouses. Once, metro Palm Beach was a narrow stretch along Lake Worth; now it runs inland almost halfway to Lake Okeechobee.

The 16th Congressional District of Florida includes much of greater West Palm. Its boundaries include the beach towns from Jupiter north to Port St. Lucie, but they are convoluted to avoid the black-majority 23d District. The district also takes in many recently and soon-to-be developed parcels in inland Palm Beach County. A small chunk of the district's residents live in citrus and vegetable growing areas around Lake Okeechobee, and as far away as Sebring, site of an auto racing track: here is the source of the Everglades, the 50-mile-wide and six-inch-deep "river of grass" that flows slowly to the Gulf of Mexico—and which is to be restored to its natural state under the Everglades Restoration Act of 2000. This is a Republican-leaning district, though much of Palm Beach County has been trending Democratic, as became evident during the presidential recount.

The congressman from the 16th District is Mark Foley, a Republican first elected in 1994. Foley was born in Massachusetts, moved to Florida at age 3, dropped out of Palm Beach Community College and opened The Lettuce Patch restaurant in Lake Worth at 20. He was active in politics, working for Democratic Congressman Paul Rogers; he was a real estate broker and served on civic boards. Foley was elected to the Lake Worth City Commission at 23, to the state House as a Republican in 1990, and the state Senate from a Democratic district in 1992. When Republican Congressman Tom Lewis decided to retire after 12 years, he and the local Republican organization supported Foley, who won a three-way primary with 61%. In the general, he outraised the Democrat and outpolled him 58%–42%, though by only 52%–48% in Palm Beach County.

In the House, Foley's political skills caught the leadership's eye, and he was named a deputy whip and a member of task forces to abolish government departments. But Foley also displayed an independent streak and concentrated on issues with local ramifications: immigration and agriculture. He proved capable of shifting on issues, voting in 1995 to cut EPA monies and in 1996 against such cuts; his vote to repeal the assault weapons ban contrasted with his support of some gun control measures in Florida. His moderate record on cultural issues includes support for funding of AIDS research, family planning and public broadcasting. He pushed for the deportation of imprisoned illegal immigrants, and to amend the Constitution so that children born here are not automatically citizens. But he also worked to increase the number of immigrants admitted as farmworkers, although many overstay their visas and never return home. He was part of the Green Scissors Coalition seeking to eliminate expensive programs like the Gas Turbine Modular Helium Reactor. He sponsored an amendment to force insurance companies to open up records of policies of Holocaust victims. In 1998 his Volunteers for Children Act was passed; it allows volunteer groups like the Boy Scouts to check records in the FBI database. On the Ways and Means Committee since 1999, he worked with Sander Levin to give additional preventive screening tests to Medicare beneficiaries. Speaker Dennis Hastert tapped Foley to lead an entertainment task force for House Republicans to sell themselves to Hollywood; his work extended from escorting actors across Capitol Hill to shepherding a treaty that protects creative work from Internet pirates and opposing legislative limits on "violent" material. "It's easy to blame crime on a movie," he told the *Los Angeles Times*. "But I saw 'Bonnie and Clyde' five times and it didn't make me rob banks."

Much of his work focused on the Everglades. In 1996 he got Newt Gingrich and Bob Dole to earmark $200 million for Everglades restoration—land acquisition and water filtration—into the farm bill. And he supported the Everglades Restoration Act in 2000. But he also took the side of the sugar industry, opposing the Florida referendum for a one-cent tax on sugar and opposing Dan Miller's effort to repeal the sugar program.

Foley appears to have entrenched himself in the district. He was unopposed in 1998. In 2000 his Democratic opponent was a public relations consultant who borrowed money from her IRA because she believed that the impeachment of Bill Clinton would make voters anger at Foley. Although was well-financed, her campaign had organizational problems; it faded during the months before the election and gained little national attention. Foley was held to 55% in Palm Beach County, which cast 44% of the vote. During the presidential recount, he was a prominent talk-show fixture delivering lively sound bites against Democratic protests.

Redistricting could be a problem for Foley. Palm Beach County has been growing rapidly and has become more Democratic, with many Jewish and other new residents from the Northeast; the 16th District has the second most registered voters in Florida. But Foley is likely to end up with a favorable district, though its lines may change considerably.

Cook's Call　*Probably Safe*. Though this is more of a swing district than a Republican one (Gore won here by 3 % in 2000 and Clinton by 5% in 1996), Foley has never dropped below 58% since his first race in 1994. His affable personality, socially moderate voting record, and history of standing up for the district's sugar cane growers make him a good fit for this district.

THE PEOPLE: Pop. 2000: 758,365; Pop. 1990: 561,856, up 35% 1990–2000. 86.2% White, 7.2% Black, 1.2% Asian, 0.3% Amer. Indian, 0.1% Hawaiian, 1.8% Two+ races, 3.2% Other; 11.8% Hispanic Origin.

2000 Presidential Vote

Gore (D)	155,033	(50%)
Bush (R)	146,308	(47%)
Nader (Green)	4,872	(2%)
Others	2,775	(1%)

1996 Presidential Vote

Clinton (D)	131,252	(47%)
Dole (R)	116,630	(42%)
Perot (I)	29,321	(11%)

Rep. Mark Foley (R)

Elected 1994, 4th term; b. Sept. 8, 1954, Newton, MA; home, West Palm Beach; Palm Beach Commun. Col., 1974; Catholic; single.

Elected Office: Lake Worth City Comm., 1977–83; Vice Mayor, 1983–84; FL House of Reps., 1990–92; FL Senate, 1992–94.

Professional Career: Restaurateur, 1974–84; Real estate broker, 1984–90.

DC Office: 104 CHOB 20515, 202-225-5792; Fax: 202-225-3132; Web site: www.house.gov/foley.

District Offices: Palm Beach Gardens, 561-627-6192; Port St. Lucie, 561-878-3181.

Committees: *Ways & Means* (22d of 24 R): Oversight; Select Revenue Measures.

Group Ratings

	ADA	ACLU	AFS	LCV	CON	ITIC	NTU	COC	ACU	NTLC	CHC
2000	20	43	0	43	50	94	56	80	68	79	47
1999	35	—	16	38	44	—	56	72	64	—	—

National Journal Ratings

	1999 LIB	—	1999 CONS		2000 LIB	—	2000 CONS
Economic	39%	—	59%		34%	—	64%
Social	56%	—	43%		60%	—	39%
Foreign	31%	—	66%		0%	—	88%

Key Votes of the 106th Congress

1. Patient Bill of Rights	Y	5. Bar RU-486 $ for FDA	N	9. NATO War in Serbia	N
2. Accelerate Min. Wage	N	6. Display 10 Commandments	Y	10. Perm. Trade with China	Y
3. Strike Ban on Ergo. Stnd.	N	7. Gun Show Bkgrnd. Checks	N	11. Debt Relief for 3rd World	N
4. Ovrd. Estate Tax Veto	Y	8. Ban Part.-Birth Abortion	Y	12. Drop Cuba Econ. Embargo	N

Election Results

2000 general	Mark Foley (R)	176,153	(60%)	($1,544,903)
	Jean Elliott Brown (D)	108,782	(37%)	($559,210)
	Others	7,565	(3%)	
2000 primary	Mark Foley (R)	unopposed		
1998 general	Mark Foley (R)	unopposed		($399,472)

SEVENTEENTH DISTRICT

North from downtown Miami, alongside the railroad tracks that Henry Flagler built shortly after Miami was founded in 1896 and alongside I-95, Miami's main north-south artery, is the city's largest black community, stretching from the Orange Bowl near downtown Miami north through Allapattah and Liberty City toward the suburb of Opalocka. This has been a kind of frontierland in Miami, the scene where hostilities between Miami's blacks and its Cuban-American majority have been played out. In 1980, 18 people died in a riot after the acquittal of a police officer charged with killing a black insurance salesman; this was the first public crisis for Janet Reno, then the Dade County District Attorney. Many Miami blacks have resented the economic upward mobility and political strength of the Cubans, the first generation of which rose while still speaking mostly Spanish, and of other Latins—including the Haitians in Little Haiti—who have been moving upward as well. The Elian Gonzalez affair left many local blacks resentful of the national preoccupation with his plight while many Haitians were deported without notice. This animosity is reflected in partisan politics: blacks here vote more than 90% Democratic, while Cuban Americans vote 70% to 80% Republican.

The 17th Congressional District of Florida covers most of northeast Miami-Dade County (the name was changed in 1997) except for the coast. It runs along the I-95 and 27th Avenue corridors from the Miami River north to the Broward County line. The mostly white high-rise gated condominiums on the shore of Biscayne Bay and heavily Cuban Hialeah were carefully excluded from the district. It extends south along a narrow corridor on either side of Dixie Highway, expanding here and there to bring in heavily black areas all the way to Homestead, site of Hurricane Andrew's worst damage in 1992. In one of his final acts as president, Bill Clinton cited environmental concerns and rejected a plan to convert the former Homestead Air Force Base to a commercial airport; instead, 700 acres were transferred to the county for likely use by developers. But local officials continued to fight for a new airport and the Bush administration is reviewing the decision.

The congresswoman from the 17th is Carrie Meek, a Democrat first elected in 1992, when the district was created. The granddaughter of a slave, Meek was born in Tallahassee and grew up near the old Capitol in a neighborhood called the Bottom. She was a gifted athlete when she attended Florida A&M's lab school; she went to Florida A&M and the University of Michigan (Florida government paid the tuition because its graduate schools were segregated). When she returned to Miami, she taught physical education at Miami-Dade Community College. Here she became active in politics and, when pioneer black legislator Gwen Cherry died in an auto accident, Meek was elected to the state House in 1978. Particularly effective in the legislature, Meek passed a bill to criminalize stalking, a Minority Business Enterprise law, and promoted literacy and drop-out prevention programs. In the state Senate, she helped to draw the new 17th District after the 1990 Census. Clearly the best-known and most-liked politician here, she was nominated with 83% of the vote in the primary and elected with no Republican opposition.

Meek has a very liberal voting record, except on some foreign policy issues—she is a strong critic of Fidel Castro. In her first term, she demonstrated her determination and savvy by being the only freshman Democrat to win a seat on the Appropriations Committee. She said her first priority was creating jobs through federal programs and private initiatives to help blacks develop their own businesses and banks as, she notes, Cuban-Americans have. She worked successfully to change the Social Security rules for household employees and sought to extend Supplemental Security Income to the aged, blind and handicapped legal aliens. She worked hard to protect Haitian immigrants and refugees allowed to remain temporarily in the country but not included in the November 1997 Nicaraguan Adjustment and Central America Relief Act, and she protested their unfair treatment by the INS and Justice Department under Janet Reno.

Meek was an outspoken advocate of Census sampling, and said her district had a large undercount in 1990: "My people died for the right to vote. And if you are going to skew the figures because you don't want to count them correctly, that removes the humor from this situation for me." After the Supreme Court ruled against sampling in 1999, she persuaded Census Subcommittee Chairman Dan Miller to support her bill to allow recipients of welfare to hold temporary census jobs without fear of losing benefits; the aim was to get a more accurate count of poor neighborhoods by using members of those communities to assist in the counting. Miller's support of Meek's outreach measures helped make the Census head count in 2000 much more accurate than in 1990, which prompted Census officials to reject sampling—the opposite of the result Meek wanted.

Meek has had no serious re-election challenges, and was unopposed in the past two campaigns. She protested that her voters had been "cheated" and their rights "trampled" in 2000. When President Bush invited the Congressional Black Caucus to the White House in February 2001, Meek refused to attend because she remained angry with the Florida ballot count. "The president wants to placate us, but you can't just spin the kind of hurt we felt in Florida," she said. With a growth of only 2% in the 1990s, this was the state's slowest-growing district. But redistricting should not be problem: state House Speaker Tom Feeney has said the legislature will preserve Florida's three heavily black congressional districts.

Cook's Call   *Safe.* There are few members of Congress with safer seats than Meek. This majority-minority seat will not be altered all that much in 2002 redistricting. She'll hold this seat as long as she wants it.

THE PEOPLE: Pop. 2000: 577,167; Pop. 1990: 563,284, up 2.5% 1990–2000. 29.3% White, 60.3% Black, 1.1% Asian, 0.3% Amer. Indian, 4.8% Two+ races, 4.1% Other; 27.4% Hispanic Origin.

2000 Presidential Vote			**1996 Presidential Vote**		
Gore (D)	122,462	(84%)	Clinton (D)	115,732	(85%)
Bush (R)	21,890	(15%)	Dole (R)	16,802	(12%)
Nader (Green)	731	(1%)	Perot (I)	3,944	(3%)

Rep. Carrie P. Meek (D)

Elected 1992, 5th term; b. Apr. 29, 1926, Tallahassee; home, Miami; FL A&M U., B.A. 1946, U. of MI, M.S. 1948; Primitive Baptist; divorced.

Elected Office: FL House of Reps, 1978–82; FL Senate 1982–92.

Professional Career: Admin., Miami-Dade Commun. Col., 1949–92.

DC Office: 2433 RHOB 20515, 202-225-4506; Fax: 202-226-0777; Web site: www.house.gov/meek.

District Office: Miami, 305-576-9303.

Committees: *Appropriations* (16th of 29 D): Treasury, Postal Service & General Government; VA, HUD & Independent Agencies.

Group Ratings

	ADA	ACLU	AFS	LCV	CON	ITIC	NTU	COC	ACU	NTLC	CHC
2000	80	86	100	64	55	50	15	52	8	10	7
1999	90	—	100	81	28	—	12	25	0	—	—

National Journal Ratings

	1999 LIB —	1999 CONS		2000 LIB —	2000 CONS
Economic	88% —	0%		85% —	15%
Social	87% —	0%		91% —	6%
Foreign	95% —	0%		74% —	24%

Key Votes of the 106th Congress

1. Patient Bill of Rights	Y	5. Bar RU-486 $ for FDA	N	9. NATO War in Serbia	Y
2. Accelerate Min. Wage	Y	6. Display 10 Commandments	N	10. Perm. Trade with China	N
3. Strike Ban on Ergo. Stnd.	Y	7. Gun Show Bkgrnd. Checks	Y	11. Debt Relief for 3rd World	Y
4. Ovrd. Estate Tax Veto	N	8. Ban Part.-Birth Abortion	N	12. Drop Cuba Econ. Embargo	Y

Election Results

2000 general	Carrie P. Meek (D)	unopposed	($298,389)
2000 primary	Carrie P. Meek (D)	unopposed	
1998 general	Carrie P. Meek (D)	unopposed	($267,089)

EIGHTEENTH DISTRICT

A century ago it was a tiny tropical village where the Miami River empties into Biscayne Bay. Today it is a world-city, not just America's "Gateway to Latin America" but the "Capital of the Americas," as welcoming signs have proclaimed. The surrealistic high-rises of Brickell Boulevard, the re-minders of the 1920s in the pseudo-Spanish Villa Vizcaya and the winding lanes of Coral Gables, the shimmer of orange and pink neon signs in the hot night air: the lights of the grid streets stretching for miles and then abruptly turning to darkness at the bayfront or the Everglades: this is Miami today. It lives on the cusp of two civilizations, North American and Latin American, with different traditions, styles and sensibilities converging in this one place, despite some friction, toward an amalgam with the strengths of both. Miami has become commercially and economically the capital of Latin America, the one place from which it is easiest to fly directly to any other part of Latin America, where top business and banking services are available to a sophisticated Span-ish-speaking (and usually also English-speaking) clientele.

The 1980s TV program "Miami Vice" showed the underside of Miami, the air of menace in streets where many are armed and vast quantities of drugs and cash regularly change hands and killings are not at all unusual. The news columns have focused on violence, the riots by blacks in 1980 and 1989, and on the shenanigans of the city's politicians in 1997 and 1998, when corrup-tion charges were lodged at several officeholders and the mayor thrown out after the courts ruled that vote fraud produced his winning margin, and on the controversy over six-year-old Elian Gonzalez in 1999 and 2000. But such episodes are common enough in the history of high-im-migration American cities, and the negatives are often exaggerated: crime is down from the 1980s, the drug trade not as menacing, the city of Miami is just one small governmental unit in a giant county, renamed in 1997 Miami-Dade, which provides services about as competently and honestly as most large American local governments. What is striking about Miami is not its vices but its virtues—the vitality and creativity of entrepreneurs and artists, the cosmopolitan sophistication of people living and making their way ahead in two (or more) cultures, the successful American-ization of Cubans and other Latinos who make up more than half of Miami-Dade's population, together with the retention of a cultural flavor that is linked to the past but headed fast into the future.

John Quincy Adams believed that Cuba must inevitably become a part of the United States. That never happened, but a large part of the Cuban people have become Americans. And the epicenter of Cuban America has been Miami, since the days the first refugees fled Fidel Castro's regime in 1959. That has caused a certain amount of resentment among those who were previ-ously the majority. In the 1960s, as the Cuban population grew, the tone of Miami civic life was set by the large Jewish community and the liberal voice of the *Miami Herald*: Dade County was the one liberal bastion in a state dominated by George Wallace Democrats and rising conservative Republicans. But the Cubans, implacably opposed to the totalitarian Castro and estranged by John Kennedy's betrayal of their cause at the Bay of Pigs, entered the voting stream heavily Republican. Liberals bristled at the late Cuban activist Jorge Mas Canosa's charges that the *Miami Herald* "manipulates information just like *Granma*," the Castro paper in Havana. On its face, the com-ment was absurd; but many goodhearted liberals have failed to appreciate the totalitarianism of Castro's regime and glossed over the brutality—the imprisonment of political dissenters, the per-secution of homosexuals—that has been its steady conduct. Anglo-Americans, after years of poli-tics in which the shades of difference between candidates are often subtle and in which basic liberties and property are not threatened, have a hard time understanding the enthusiasm of Americans with backgrounds in Latin America, where the differences between political creeds can be enormous and where liberties have frequently been in danger. The result has been seen in *The New York Times* coverage of the Elian Gonzalez controversy, in which Cuban Americans were lampooned as crazed and violent enthusiasts, and the people who wanted to send a child back to become the icon of totalitarian Cuba were portrayed as caring and compassionate.

In the early 1960s Cubans were a noisy minority in the Miami area; now they are the dominant part of a Latino majority in Miami-Dade County. The Hispanic population in 2000 was 57%, and blacks 19%, leaving whites the fading minority. South Florida's Jewish community has mostly moved north, to Broward and Palm Beach counties. Little Havana around Calle Ocho (Southwest 8th Street in English) now has many Nicaraguans, Hondurans and Peruvians; its annual spring carnival has featured the world's largest paella (serving 300,000 people) and the longest conga line (four miles). Miami-Dade's Latinos tend to stay in the area, go to school at Miami-Dade Community College (one of the nation's largest) and Florida International University; they start businesses and practice professions in Miami's booming economy. Politically, Miami-Dade is now trending Republican. It voted 57%–38% for Bill Clinton in 1996, after he signed the Helms-Burton Act and responded angrily to the shooting down of two Brothers to the Rescue planes. But it then soured on him, as he suspended Helms-Burton and clashed with the community in the Elian Gonzalez affair, which culminated in April 2000 when immigration agents seized the 6-year-old from his relatives' home in an armed pre-dawn raid and returned him to his father and ultimately to totalitarian Cuba. Among the consequences was that Miami Mayor Joe Carollo fired City Manager Donald Warshaw—who had refused to fire the police chief following the incident—and replaced him with fire chief Carlos Gimenez. Some blacks and Anglos referred to City Hall as a "banana republic;" even after he was jailed overnight in February 2001 on a domestic violence charge, Carollo said that he would seek reelection. Vice President Al Gore, in line with his longtime antipathy to Castro, called for settling Elian's status in state courts—a stand that was, inaccurately, called a change of positions by liberal Democrats. But the Elian case soured Cuban Americans on anything connected with the Clinton administration, and Gore, despite overwhelming support from Miami-Dade's blacks and Jews, carried the county by only 53%–46%.

The 18th Congressional District of Florida is the slower-growing of two Hispanic-majority districts in Miami-Dade County, more than half Cuban-American, and usually heavily Republican. It includes the corridor along Calle Ocho and spreads south and west toward Miami Airport and the suburb of Kendall. It stretches all the way down to Homestead, site of Hurricane Andrew's worst damage, and then extends back north, around the black-majority 17th, to include the neighborhoods of Coconut Grove and Miami Beach's trendy South Beach, with old art deco hotels that used to house elderly retirees and has become a home to the glitziest celebrities of North America, Latin America and Europe.

The representative from the 18th District is Ileana Ros-Lehtinen, the first Cuban-American elected to Congress. She was born in Cuba, came to Miami at 7, graduated from Miami-Dade Community College and Florida International University. She became a teacher, then was the owner of a private school. She was elected to the Florida House in 1982, at 30, and to the state Senate in 1986; her husband Dexter Lehtinen also served in both houses of the legislature and served as U.S. attorney in Miami during the first Bush administration. Ros-Lehtinen ran for the House in the special election after the death in 1989 of Claude Pepper, one of the most enduring liberals in American politics and a great champion of Social Security, who was a staunch opponent of Castro. In this acrimonious contest, voting ran almost entirely on ethnic lines: exit polls showed that 96% of blacks and 88% of non-Hispanic whites voted for Democratic nominee Gerald Richman, while 90% of Hispanics voted for Ros-Lehtinen. Hispanic turnout was 58%, compared to 42% for non-Hispanic whites, and Ros-Lehtinen won with 53%. With a much more heavily Latino district since 1992, she has won without serious opposition.

Ros-Lehtinen has a mixed voting record: moderate on economics policy, more conservative on cultural and foreign issues. Despite the long-term local economic benefit, she opposed NAFTA (which extends only to Mexico), and spoke out against it. She refused to sign the Contract with America, and was a harsh critic of Republican attempts to pass English-only legislation, to cut off welfare for legal immigrants, and to reduce the immigration quota for relatives of U.S. citizens. "I wish our party would be more aggressive in courting this Hispanic vote but because of welfare and immigration reform and English-only issues we are afraid to try and solicit their support," she said. Noting that Miami-Dade has the highest percentage of immigrants in the United States—about half its residents were born in other countries—she says, "I think Miami is just a microcosm of all that's good in immigration. You take people in and give them an opportunity and look at what they've done with that opportunity." In 1999 she was chief sponsor of the Child Custody Protection Act, to bar the transport of minors across state lines for abortions; the House voted for it 270–159, but it died in the Senate.

Ros-Lehtinen serves on the International Relations Committee, where much of her energy has been devoted to Cuban and Latin issues. She strongly backed the Cuban Democracy Act and Helms-Burton. With Lincoln Diaz-Balart of Miami-Dade and Robert Menendez of New Jersey, she opposed Senator John Warner's proposal for a commission to review Cuban policy. In 2000 she opposed an amendment by farm-state Republicans to relax the trade embargo on Cuba, which passed in a diluted version. In 2001 she gained added leverage over many of these issues when she became chairwoman of the International Operations and Human Rights Subcommittee. She sought to scuttle the House Republicans' term limits on committee chairmen because she said it was causing a "brain drain," but was resoundingly defeated.

Ros-Lehtinen has been re-elected without opposition since 1994. Redistricting could change her district lines to accommodate a third Cuban-American district in Miami-Dade, though that is by no means a sure thing.

Cook's Call   *Safe*. Ros-Lehtinen is firmly ensconced in this heavily Republican district.

THE PEOPLE: Pop. 2000: 597,947; Pop. 1990: 562,394, up 6.3% 1990–2000. 85.4% White, 5.1% Black, 1.3% Asian, 0.2% Amer. Indian, 3.3% Two+ races, 4.7% Other; 70.5% Hispanic Origin.

2000 Presidential Vote		
Bush (R)	110,833	(61%)
Gore (D)	68,151	(38%)
Nader (Green)	1,897	(1%)

1996 Presidential Vote		
Dole (R)	86,005	(52%)
Clinton (D)	71,673	(43%)
Perot (I)	7,788	(5%)

Rep. Ileana Ros-Lehtinen (R)

Elected Aug. 1989, 6th term; b. July 12, 1952, Havana, Cuba; home, Miami; Miami-Dade Commun. Col., A.A. 1972, FL Intl. U., B.S. 1975, M.S. 1986; Catholic; married (Dexter).

Elected Office: FL House of Reps., 1982–86; FL Senate, 1986–89.

Professional Career: Teacher, Principal & Owner, Eastern Academy Elem. Schl., 1978–85.

DC Office: 2160 RHOB 20515, 202-225-3931; Fax: 202-225-5620; Web site: www.house.gov/ros-lehtinen.

District Office: Miami, 305-275-1800.

Committees: *Government Reform* (5th of 24 R): Criminal Justice, Drug Policy & Human Resources; National Security, Veterans' Affairs & Intl. Relations. *International Relations* (8th of 26 R): International Operations and Human Rights (Chmn.); Western Hemisphere.

Group Ratings

	ADA	ACLU	AFS	LCV	CON	ITIC	NTU	COC	ACU	NTLC	CHC
2000	15	15	28	21	13	71	57	71	64	66	91
1999	25	—	0	31	3	—	51	71	73	—	—

National Journal Ratings

	1999 LIB	—	1999 CONS		2000 LIB	—	2000 CONS
Economic	48%	—	52%		34%	—	64%
Social	44%	—	55%		40%	—	59%
Foreign	23%	—	73%		25%	—	69%

Key Votes of the 106th Congress

1. Patient Bill of Rights	Y	5. Bar RU-486 $ for FDA		9. NATO War in Serbia	N
2. Accelerate Min. Wage	Y	6. Display 10 Commandments	Y	10. Perm. Trade with China	N
3. Strike Ban on Ergo. Stnd.	N	7. Gun Show Bkgrnd. Checks	Y	11. Debt Relief for 3rd World	N
4. Ovrd. Estate Tax Veto	Y	8. Ban Part.-Birth Abortion	Y	12. Drop Cuba Econ. Embargo	N

Election Results

2000 general	Ileana Ros-Lehtinen (R)	unopposed	($192,368)
2000 primary	Ileana Ros-Lehtinen (R)	unopposed	
1998 general	Ileana Ros-Lehtinen (R)	unopposed	($152,709)

NINETEENTH DISTRICT

When the first millionaires came to Palm Beach in the 1920s to winter in their new Addison Mizner pseudo-Mediterranean mansions, and as the first real estate speculators arrived in Miami, there was virtually nothing man-made between these two cites. In 1920, Dade, Broward and Palm Beach counties had some 66,000 residents. Now, 5 million people live in the 5- to 15-mile strip between the Atlantic Ocean and the protected Everglades—an increase of 1 million during the 1990s. The contrast between the 1920s and today is especially glaring in Boca Raton, where Mizner built in 1926 what is now the Boca Raton Hotel and Club. Its azure-tiled fountains and red-tiled roofs, its pseudo-Moorish columns and pink stucco walls bespeak a vision of a holiday Florida, a bit mannered and antique to today's eye, but still exuberant. Boca Raton has grown inland and is still solidly affluent, but has become more functional and workaday. Affluent retirees from the Northeast and Canada ("snowbirds") live in unadorned high-rise towers, enjoying the weather and the lack of a state income tax. But there are also major corporate headquarters here—W.R. Grace and an IBM-Intel joint venture: high-tech and big money at work in what used to be just paradise.

The 19th Congressional District of Florida includes former swampland and citrus groves in Palm Beach and Broward counties. It does not touch the ocean at all, kept from it by the majority-black 23d District, which collects the black neighborhoods just inland from the Intracoastal Waterway. It stretches south from the edge of West Palm Beach, travels through Lantana, Boynton Beach, Boca Raton, Deerfield Beach and Sunrise. With the growth in northern Broward and southern Palm Beach counties, the district's largest communities are not beach towns, but new inland communities: Coral Springs, Margate, Tamarac. Liberal condominium associations, mobilized by "condo commandos," are political powers. The 19th has a large Jewish population in both counties, is heavily Democratic and grew by 42% in the 1990s.

The congressman from the 19th is Robert Wexler, a Democrat first elected in 1996. Wexler grew up in Florida from age 10, and after law school went into practice in Boca Raton. In 1990, at 29, he was elected to the state Senate, where he sponsored tough prison sentencing guidelines, called for chemical castration of sex offenders, put a cap on money taxpayers contributed to Everglades cleanup and more funds for education. When four-term Democrat Harry Johnston retired in 1996, Wexler was one of three Democratic legislators who jumped into the race. It was close in Broward, but Wexler won in Palm Beach County, which cast over half the votes. He led with 47% to 29% for state Senator Peter Weinstein. The October 1 runoff was bitter. Wexler won 65%–35%, carrying Palm Beach County 83%–17% and losing Broward County 59%–41%; afterwards Weinstein filed a $10 million defamation suit against him, citing an unflattering picture of Weinstein in a Wexler TV ad (the suit was dropped in early 1997). In this heavily Democratic district, Wexler won the general 66%–34%.

Wexler has a fairly liberal voting record in the House and a flare for gaining attention. In 1997 he and Republican Mark Foley proposed a constitutional amendment to allow states to change "gain time" rules for prisoners retroactively. On the International Relations Committee, he traveled to the Middle East with Madeleine Albright; he was the only member of the House in attendance at the Wye River accords. Later, he said Yasir Arafat needed to do more to prepare Palestinians for peace. At the Judiciary Committee, he was the only Democrat to favor a three-year pilot program giving temporary visas to an unlimited number of foreign workers for seasonal farm work. He criticized George W. Bush's initiative to assist "faith-based" groups as blurring church-state lines.

But Wexler made his greatest mark as an ardent defender of Bill Clinton. Producers of cable shows are always looking for someone who can be relied on to take one side of an issue and to bring energy to the broadcast: one look at Wexler convinced bookers that he would fill the bill, and he seemed to turn down few invitations. He denounced Clinton's personal conduct to be sure, but then bellowed with rage over the acts of Independent Counsel Kenneth Starr, House Judiciary Committee Republicans and everyone who was preventing him from working on issues like health care, education and Social Security. One typical plaint: "The president betrayed his wife; he did not betray his country. God help this nation if we fail to recognize the difference." Wexler—sometimes, with Foley—gained another opportunity to hit the cable circuit during the Florida vote controversy. "Confusion is confusion, and the presidency shouldn't hinge on it," Wexler told Larry King the day after the election. As the deadlock continued, he received death threats; but that didn't keep him from appearing on *Rivera Live*.

Some have speculated that Wexler was trying to strengthen himself in his district or to set himself up as a statewide candidate. But his standing in the 19th is solid—he has had no trouble winning reelection—and he quickly abandoned a possible run for the Senate in 2000; he left the door open to a run for governor in 2002, depending in part on redistricting. Republicans control the redistricting process, but this district grew more than any other in Florida and the Democratic constituency is large enough here that it seems unlikely he could not find a district in which to run and easily win.

Cook's Call *Safe.* There are rumors that Wexler's burgeoning southeastern district will be heavily altered in 2001, perhaps putting him and 20th District Democratic Representative Peter Deutsch in the same seat. But it is not clear why Republicans would or should do this. In its present form this seat is one of the most Democratic in the state.

THE PEOPLE: Pop. 2000: 800,902; Pop. 1990: 562,978, up 42.3% 1990–2000. 84.9% White, 7.7% Black, 2.3% Asian, 0.2% Amer. Indian, 2.3% Two+ races, 2.7% Other; 12.2% Hispanic Origin.

2000 Presidential Vote		
Gore (D)	225,286	(68%)
Bush (R)	97,231	(30%)
Nader (Green)	3,648	(1%)
Others	2,800	(1%)

1996 Presidential Vote		
Clinton (D)	189,336	(65%)
Dole (R)	81,020	(28%)
Perot (I)	20,094	(7%)

Rep. Robert Wexler (D)

Elected 1996, 3d term; b. Jan. 2, 1961, Queens, NY; home, Boca Raton; U. of FL, B.A. 1982, George Washington U., J.D. 1985; Jewish; married (Laurie).

Elected Office: FL Senate, 1990–96.

Professional Career: Practicing atty., 1985–96.

DC Office: 213 CHOB 20515, 202-225-3001; Fax: 202-225-5974; Web site: www.house.gov/wexler.

District Offices: Boca Raton, 561-988-6302; Margate, 954-972-6454.

Committees: *International Relations* (11th of 23 D): Europe; Middle East & South Asia. *Judiciary* (13th of 17 D): Courts, the Internet & Intellectual Property.

Group Ratings

	ADA	ACLU	AFS	LCV	CON	ITIC	NTU	COC	ACU	NTLC	CHC
2000	85	79	100	93	14	50	22	52	17	22	13
1999	100	—	100	100	53	—	12	20	8	—	—

National Journal Ratings

	1999 LIB	—	1999 CONS		2000 LIB	—	2000 CONS
Economic	84%	—	12%		71%	—	28%
Social	79%	—	20%		85%	—	14%
Foreign	78%	—	17%		64%	—	34%

Key Votes of the 106th Congress

1. Patient Bill of Rights	Y	5. Bar RU-486 $ for FDA	N	9. NATO War in Serbia	Y
2. Accelerate Min. Wage	Y	6. Display 10 Commandments	N	10. Perm. Trade with China	N
3. Strike Ban on Ergo. Stnd.	Y	7. Gun Show Bkgrnd. Checks	Y	11. Debt Relief for 3rd World	Y
4. Ovrd. Estate Tax Veto	N	8. Ban Part.-Birth Abortion	N	12. Drop Cuba Econ. Embargo	N

Election Results

2000 general	Robert Wexler (D)	171,080	(72%)	($447,274)
	Morris Kent Thompson (R)	67,789	(28%)	($10,620)
2000 primary	Robert Wexler (D)	unopposed		
1998 general	Robert Wexler (D)	unopposed		($280,724)

TWENTIETH DISTRICT

Fort Lauderdale, back when Connie Francis made it famous in the 1960 spring break movie *Where the Boys Are*, was just a small town with a strip of motels along the beach and some nice houses fronting canals. Now it is the center of a vast metropolitan area with its own major airport. Fort Lauderdale and Broward County had fewer than 100,000 people in 1950; now it has more than 1.6 million. The land from the strip of beach along the Atlantic Ocean west to the Sawgrass Expressway and the Everglades Wildlife Management Area has filled up with subdivisions, shopping centers, office complexes, warehouses and trucking terminals. Broward County is no longer just vacation country; it is also a major port and business center with high-tech companies and startups that have become national giants, including Blockbuster Video.

As it has grown, the ethnic composition of Broward County has changed. In the 1950s, it was understood that Jews couldn't buy houses or rent hotel rooms this far north of Miami. Today, after four decades of Cubans moving into the Miami area and many Jews moving out, Broward County is the most heavily Jewish part of Florida, indeed one of the most heavily Jewish parts of the United States. Nearer the coast, especially in the huge high-rises of Hollywood and Hallandale, most of Broward's Jews are retirees from New York and other Northeastern metro areas. But inland, in towns like booming Pembroke Pines, Davie, Plantation and Sunrise that didn't exist a few decades ago, there are many young Jewish parents raising families in communities that pride themselves on fine schools and high property values. This is one reason that in the 1990s the number of children in Florida rose more rapidly than the number of seniors, with school enrollment rising more than 35% in Broward alone.

The 20th Congressional District of Florida includes most of southern Broward County, though not the precincts nearest the beach. The district also takes in the mostly unpopulated Everglades west of the Sawgrass in Broward and Miami-Dade Counties, plus the Florida Keys. At the end of the Overseas Highway is Key West, now a bustling tropical outpost that echoes its historic seafaring roots. This southern-most city in the continental United States was long accessible only by sea, and treasures from shipwrecks along the miles of coral reefs once gave its residents the highest per capita income in the nation. Key West has attracted famous residents—Ernest Hemingway, Tennessee Williams, Jimmy Buffett—and a large gay population, many living in restored "conch houses," quaint clapboard bungalows. Politically, this is a heavily Democratic district.

The congressman from the 20th District is Peter Deutsch, a Democrat first elected in 1992. Deutsch grew up in New York, graduated from Yale Law School in 1982, moved to Florida and five months later was elected to the legislature. Two years later, he was reelected with the largest vote in Florida and was unopposed in the next three elections. A *Miami Herald* reporter said Deutsch was "viewed by colleagues as bright but abrasive, and an expert at using procedural rules to advance or torpedo legislation." The newly drawn 20th District looked as if it were drawn for Deutsch. Dante Fascell, chairman of the Foreign Affairs Committee, confronted with the prospect of a district dominated by unfamiliar Broward County, decided to retire after 38 years in the House. Deutsch won the primary nearly 2–1 and the general election 55%–39%.

Deutsch has a mostly liberal voting record and is a member of the New Democrat Coalition. His early achievements were passage of a law to protect the health care benefits of police officers and fire fighters injured in the line of duty, named after two Plantation fire fighters injured in a 1995 explosion, and a $1.5 million law enforcement training program on missing children. He opposed raising the Medicare age in tandem with Social Security, a $5 fee for home health visits and means-testing to determine Medicare premiums. He went with Bill Clinton to the Middle East. In 1998 he charged that a United Nations agency was funding anti-semitic textbooks in Palestinian schools, and got language in the State Department appropriation to end it. He supports the Helms-Burton Act and Radio and TV Marti, and criticized Fidel Castro for the burdens he has placed on his people.

Deutsch has spent much time on Everglades restoration and water quality in the Keys, with considerable progress. He was active in helping to enact on the eve of the 2000 election the Everglades Restoration Plan, which he calls the "largest ecosystem restoration project in the world." The Florida Keys have different interests: Deutsch has faced protests from a Conch Coalition of fishermen, real estate agents and treasure hunters opposed to government bureaucrats declaring, despite previous assurances, no-fishing zones in the Florida Keys National Marine Sanctuary. He won House passage in May 2000 of a bill to improve water quality in the Keys, and the Senate finally agreed to $100 million for improvements as part of the omnibus budget.

Deutsch has won reelection easily, but not without raising plenty of money. He has handled it well, too: he invested $700,000 of campaign funds in January 1997 and it grew to $1.1 million 15 months later. He was unopposed in 1998 and 2000, and had $2.4 million cash on hand at the end of the year, even after giving $250,000 to the Gore campaign—which he called "the largest hard-dollar contribution in U.S. history." During the Florida recount, Deutsch served as an official observer in Broward and an ever-ready voice for the Democratic party line on cable TV. He was the first member to protest on the House floor during the formal certification of the Electoral College vote. All of which raises the question of whether he wants to run for statewide office. So far, he has opted out, waiting for the right opportunity. Republicans, who control redistricting, have said that Deutsch will lose pieces of his district in Miami-Dade and the Keys. But Broward has enough Democrats that his House seat probably will remain safe.

Cook's Call   *Safe.* Like the rest of south Florida, this Dade/Broward County-based district has grown tremendously over the last 10 years. It is not yet clear how this district will be affected in redistricting, but state House Speaker Tom Feeney has indicated that Republicans are not likely to tinker with it.

THE PEOPLE: Pop. 2000: 783,412; Pop. 1990: 562,673, up 39.2% 1990–2000. 80.2% White, 10.8% Black, 2.7% Asian, 0.3% Amer. Indian, 0.1% Hawaiian, 2.8% Two+ races, 3.1% Other; 23.1% Hispanic Origin.

2000 Presidential Vote			1996 Presidential Vote		
Gore (D)	184,311	(63%)	Clinton (D)	148,289	(59%)
Bush (R)	105,037	(36%)	Dole (R)	78,699	(31%)
Nader (Green)	4,274	(1%)	Perot (I)	23,296	(9%)

Rep. Peter R. Deutsch (D)

Elected 1992, 5th term; b. Apr. 1, 1957, New York, NY; home, Lauderhill; Swarthmore Col., B.A. 1979, Yale Law Schl., J.D. 1982; Jewish; married (Lori).

Elected Office: FL House of Reps., 1982–92.

Professional Career: Practicing atty., 1983–92.

DC Office: 2421 RHOB 20515, 202-225-7931; Fax: 202-225-8456; Web site: www.house.gov/deutsch.

District Office: Pembroke Pines, 954-437-3936.

Committees: *Energy & Commerce* (10th of 26 D): Commerce, Trade & Consumer Protection; Environment & Hazardous Materials; Health; Oversight & Investigations (RMM).

Group Ratings

	ADA	ACLU	AFS	LCV	CON	ITIC	NTU	COC	ACU	NTLC	CHC
2000	65	64	85	93	24	67	28	57	28	21	7
1999	95	—	100	94	49	—	13	40	8	—	—

National Journal Ratings

	1999 LIB —	1999 CONS	2000 LIB —	2000 CONS
Economic	67%	32%	67%	33%
Social	71%	28%	72%	26%
Foreign	63%	36%	58%	40%

Key Votes of the 106th Congress

1. Patient Bill of Rights	Y	5. Bar RU-486 $ for FDA	N	9. NATO War in Serbia	Y
2. Accelerate Min. Wage	Y	6. Display 10 Commandments	N	10. Perm. Trade with China	N
3. Strike Ban on Ergo. Stnd.	Y	7. Gun Show Bkgrnd. Checks	Y	11. Debt Relief for 3rd World	Y
4. Ovrd. Estate Tax Veto	N	8. Ban Part.-Birth Abortion	N	12. Drop Cuba Econ. Embargo	N

Election Results

2000 general	Peter R. Deutsch (D)	unopposed	($558,259)
2000 primary	Peter R. Deutsch (D)	unopposed	
1998 general	Peter R. Deutsch (D)	unopposed	($259,016)

TWENTY-FIRST DISTRICT

Miami's Cuban-American community has been one of America's most dynamic over the last 40 years (see 18th District), growing from 50,000 in 1960, the year after Fidel Castro took over Cuba, to well over 1 million today. Over those years, the Cuban-American neighborhoods centered along 8th Street—Calle Ocho—expanded to the southwest, west and northwest. Development first filled the land all the way to the Palmetto Expressway; in the 1980s, development reached outward to the Homestead Extension of Florida's Turnpike. The Cuban-Americans moved out and beyond Hialeah, whose now-closed racetrack was constructed in the 1920s beyond the edge of urban development; its 90% Hispanic population is the highest in the Miami area. To the south, West-wood and Kendale Lakes—southwest suburbs of Miami with large Cuban-American populations—have been growing outward into what once was swampland. Here, planned communities and subdivisions often have just one guarded entrance, with streets fanning out around lakes and golf courses.

The 21st Congressional District of Florida includes most of these new Cuban-American communities, taking in Hialeah and, just to the north, the planned community of Miami Lakes developed in 1962 by Senator Bob Graham and his father. To the south, it is centered on Kendall Lakes, and its boundaries go out to the Everglades Wildlife Management Area. The district is 78% Hispanic—mostly but not all Cuban-American—and usually heavily Republican. Knowing first hand the evils of Communism, Cuban-Americans appreciate the blessings of free enterprise, cherish traditional moral values, and for years preferred Republicans to Democrats on all these counts. In 1996 Bill Clinton cut into the Cuban vote by condemning the Cubans who shot down the Brothers to the Rescue pilots, supporting the Helms-Burton Act, and opposing cutoffs of welfare to legal aliens; by the end of his presidency, after seeking accommodation with Castro and his handling of the Elian Gonzalez affair, Clinton was far more unpopular here.

The congressman from the 21st District is Lincoln Diaz-Balart, a Republican first elected when the district was created in 1992. Diaz-Balart was born in Cuba where his grandfather and father served in the Cuban Congress; the family left Cuba in 1959, shortly after Castro took over and their house was looted and burned. His aunt was the former wife of Fidel Castro and the mother of Castro's only recognized child. Diaz-Balart started off as a poverty lawyer and a Democrat, but switched parties. He was elected to the state House as a Republican in 1986 with 78% of the vote and to the state Senate in 1989 with 82%, a year after his younger brother Mario was elected to the state House. In the legislature Diaz-Balart was tough on crime, but he also backed home construction and substance abuse programs. In 1989 Jorge Mas Canosa's Cuban American National Foundation convinced Diaz-Balart not to run against Ileana Ros-Lehtinen in the then-18th District special election to replace Claude Pepper. In 1992 the organization endorsed Diaz-Balart to run in the new 21st. But fellow state Senator Javier Souto, also Cuban-born, opposed him in the primary, charging that Diaz-Balart was backed by wealthy contributors and was not a lifelong Republican. Diaz-Balart won 69%–31%.

Diaz-Balart has a voting record that is rather liberal on economics, veering far from market principles on issues from the minimum wage to NAFTA, though he has said he believes a hemispheric common market is inevitable. When Republicans took over the House, Speaker Newt Gingrich named Diaz-Balart to the Rules Committee. But he was one of three Republican incumbents who refused to sign the Contract with America in 1994, and he voted against the Republican welfare bills because of their provisions denying welfare to legal immigrants. Many older Cubans who have not taken U.S. citizenship because they hoped some day to return to Cuba are dependent on Supplemental Security Income and other aid. He persevered, and his bill to restore SSI benefits to legal immigrants passed in 1997. In 2000 he led a bipartisan group that sought to reduce from five years to two the ban on legal immigrants from receiving federal or state health care insurance.

Naturally he has favored sanctions against Cuba, and when the Clinton administration announced in 1995 that it would no longer give automatic safe haven to Cuban refugees and instead would return them to Cuba, Diaz-Balart was arrested while protesting this switch. When Colorado Democrat David Skaggs tried to cut funding for Radio Marti and TV Marti broadcasts to Cuba, Diaz-Balart successfully cut $23 million in funding for the National Institute of Standards and Technology in Skaggs's district. Diaz-Balart wrote the section of Helms-Burton codifying the embargo against Cuba. He sponsored the Central American Relief Act of 1997 that prevented deportation of Nicaraguans, Salvadorans and Guatemalans—several hundred thousand—who qualified for legal resident or immigrant status temporarily, and had become law-abiding residents for many years. He objected to Cuba's building a Chernobyl-style nuclear reactor, called Canadian policy "racist" for boycotting Nigeria but not Cuba, and objected when the Clinton administration declared almost all of Florida's coast a "security zone" requiring small vessels to get permits to enter Cuban waters. He protested the Clinton administration's 1999 decision to permit charter flights to Cuba. He worked with Tom DeLay in 2000 to defeat farm-state Republicans who wanted to relax the trade embargo; they prevailed in denying a significant opening of hard-currency dollars.

During the Elian Gonzalez affair, Diaz-Balart closely advised the Miami family—he gave the six-year-old a black Labrador puppy—and he was a prominent spokesman for the local community. Some have said that the party's split on the issue showed that the Cuban-American leadership's hard line on Elian weakened its national political clout. But Diaz-Balart, who advised George W. Bush during the presidential campaign, told *National Journal* that Bush embraced the core of his recommendations and that the candidate's position was "very firm and consistent in private."

The Federal Election Commission announced in November 2000 that an audit of the Diaz-Balart campaign for 1997–98 showed $114,000 in missing cash and a failure to cooperate with auditors. His campaign manager acknowledged some mistakes but said that they had been corrected; in 2001 she was forced to make refunds. Diaz-Balart has had no re-election problems. His brother Mario, now a state Senator and chairman of the redistricting committee, has been mentioned as a possible candidate for a new Miami-based district that might result from redistricting. The current 21st—78% Hispanic and needing to drop 150,000 persons—would offer a good start.

Cook's Call   *Safe.* Diaz-Balart is safely settled in this solidly Republican, overwhelmingly Cuban district. But a new seat in southern Florida will have an impact on the lines of this district.

THE PEOPLE: Pop. 2000: 789,742; Pop. 1990: 562,402, up 40.4% 1990–2000. 84.5% White, 4.8% Black, 1.6% Asian, 0.1% Amer. Indian, 3.6% Two+ races, 5.3% Other; 77.5% Hispanic Origin.

2000 Presidential Vote		
Bush (R)	126,991	(62%)
Gore (D)	74,304	(37%)
Nader (Green)	1,569	(1%)

1996 Presidential Vote		
Dole (R)	82,384	(51%)
Clinton (D)	72,844	(45%)
Perot (I)	7,901	(5%)

Rep. Lincoln Diaz-Balart (R)

Elected 1992, 5th term; b. Aug. 13, 1954, Havana, Cuba; home, Miami; U. of S. FL, B.S. 1977, Case Western Reserve U., J.D. 1979; Catholic; married (Cristina).

Elected Office: FL House of Reps., 1986–89; FL Senate 1989–92.

Professional Career: Practicing atty., 1979–92; Asst. FL Atty., 1983–84.

DC Office: 2244 RHOB 20515, 202-225-4211; Fax: 202-225-8576; Web site: www.house.gov/diaz-balart.

District Office: Miami, 305-470-8555.

Committees: *Rules* (5th of 9 R): Rules & Organization of the House (Vice Chmn.).

Group Ratings

	ADA	ACLU	AFS	LCV	CON	ITIC	NTU	COC	ACU	NTLC	CHC
2000	20	21	42	14	7	61	57	65	56	62	87
1999	25	—	0	25	2	—	50	60	64	—	—

National Journal Ratings

	1999 LIB	—	1999 CONS		2000 LIB	—	2000 CONS
Economic	48%	—	50%		44%	—	55%
Social	44%	—	55%		41%	—	58%
Foreign	45%	—	55%		39%	—	57%

Key Votes of the 106th Congress

1. Patient Bill of Rights	Y	5. Bar RU-486 $ for FDA	Y	9. NATO War in Serbia	Y
2. Accelerate Min. Wage	Y	6. Display 10 Commandments	Y	10. Perm. Trade with China	N
3. Strike Ban on Ergo. Stnd.	N	7. Gun Show Bkgrnd. Checks	Y	11. Debt Relief for 3rd World	N
4. Ovrd. Estate Tax Veto	Y	8. Ban Part.-Birth Abortion	Y	12. Drop Cuba Econ. Embargo	N

Election Results

2000 general	Lincoln Diaz-Balart (R)	unopposed		($294,122)
2000 primary	Lincoln Diaz-Balart (R)	unopposed		
1998 general	Lincoln Diaz-Balart (R)	84,018	(75%)	($482,166)
	Patrick Cusack (D)	28,378	(25%)	($28,635)

TWENTY-SECOND DISTRICT

The barrier islands of Florida's Gold Coast have been developed in spasms of speculative frenzy, not just as vacation places and retirement homes but as embodiments of dreams and fantasies.

Consider Palm Beach, the great beach resort of the 1920s, where rich WASPs would leave their snow-covered Tudor or Georgian mansions and live in Addison Mizner's pseudo-Mediterranean confections. Consider also Miami Beach: the great resort of the 1950s, where Jews who had grown up amid prejudice and made their fortunes in ebullient postwar America vacationed in surrealistically curved and embellished skyscraper hotels—like Morris Lapidus's Fontainebleau and Eden Roc—giant variations on the themes set out in the much smaller Art Deco hotels at the beach's south end. Or think of the 1970s and 1980s, as the coastline of Miami-Dade, Broward and Palm Beach counties were lined with one high-rise condo after another, a promised land for retirees, free from winter frost and state and city income taxes.

Almost all of this beach area is now gathered together into Florida's 22d Congressional District, a thin strip of land 91 miles long and never more than three miles wide, along the barrier islands from Juno Beach in the north through Palm Beach south through Fort Lauderdale to the Lincoln Road mall in Miami Beach. Palm Beach has been maintained as if under glass by great wealth; the Fort Lauderdale beach went downhill and has now been refurbished; Miami's South Beach, its Art Deco buildings restored, has become a kind of amalgam of North American, Latin American and European cultures. The 22d District has had the highest percentage of over-65 residents and quite possibly the highest percentage of high-rise dwellers, of any district in America, and one of the highest Jewish percentages of any district. For many years this affluent territory usually voted Republican, but in the 1990s, like many areas in the nation's very largest metropolitan areas, it trended toward Democrats, and it delivered solid margins for Bill Clinton in 1992 and 1996 and Al Gore in 2000.

The congressman from the 22d District is Clay Shaw, first elected in 1980. Shaw grew up in Fort Lauderdale, practiced law and served as a judge and councilman; in 1975, at 36, he became the city's mayor. In 1980 he ran for the House in a very differently shaped district, and had the good fortune of seeing the Democratic incumbent lose his primary to a Miami lawyer. Shaw won the seat handily and held it despite the Fort Lauderdale area's increasing Democratic tilt. For eight years he served on Judiciary, working on drug and crime bills. In July 1988 he switched to Ways and Means. There he drafted an alternative to the statist ABC child care bill, first supported and then in 1989 opposed the Catastrophic Health Care Act, worked on the nanny tax bill in 1993–94 and opposed taxes on Social Security earnings.

In the Republican Congress Shaw has taken on the really big issues—first welfare reform, then Social Security. After Republicans won control in 1994, Shaw became chairman of the Way and Means subcommittee handling welfare. His little-noticed 1993 bill, to end the federal entitlement to welfare and take most recipients off the rolls and require them to work after two years, was part of the Contract with America and became one of House Republicans' major priorities. Shaw's bills were passed twice in 1995, in somewhat different form, and vetoed twice by Bill Clinton. They generally turned over control of welfare to the states, but not without some strings: cash benefits were barred for mothers under 18 and the two-years-and-work rule could not be dropped. In early 1996 House Republicans hoped that Bob Dole could use the welfare issue against Clinton. By July 1996 they decided that Dole was likely to lose anyway, and so decided to pass welfare reform a third time, giving Dole an issue if Clinton vetoed it again and giving House Republicans an accomplishment if Clinton signed it. They had no idea what he would do, but in the end he signed, and a major change in American public policy was made. Shaw continued to be involved in welfare issues in 1997 and 1998. He tried but failed to keep workfare participants exempt from the various requirements and conditions that unions have exacted for others on local public payrolls; he retreated in October 1997 when it was plain that the Senate wouldn't act. But around the country workfare continued.

After the 1998 election, Shaw, representing the House district with the nation's highest percentage of those 65 and over, became chairman of the Social Security Subcommittee. He said he wanted to reform the system and preserve it for baby boomers' retirements. In April 1999, Shaw and Ways and Means Chairman Bill Archer introduced a bill to give workers income tax credits to fund personal retirement accounts. But the Republican leadership did not want to go forward, and the effort foundered in summer 1999. In the next year Shaw focused on the earnings tax on Social Security recipients; he managed to pass a bill repealing it for Social Security recipients age 65 to 69. Shaw had other accomplishments in the 106th Congress. With Karen Thurman he introduced a bill requiring Medicare to pay for annual pap smears; into the final budget bill he got a measure for pap smears every two years, plus increased fees for digital mammography. Shaw had worked for many years on restoring the Everglades, and was lauded as the $7.8 billion Everglades Restoration Act was passed just before the November 2000 election.

This could not have hurt politically, for in 2000 Shaw had the strongest opposition since he first won the seat. It came from state Representative Elaine Bloom, who had a base in the condominiums and raised large sums from national liberal and feminist groups. Bloom ran an ad saying that Shaw had "voted" for privatization of Social Security, but he never had (there were no votes on the issue), and she had to pull the spot. With both candidates buying Miami and West Palm Beach television, this was one of the most expensive House races in the country: Bloom spent $2.4 million and Shaw $3 million. Bloom campaigned on her support for abortion and gun control, and on her support of Al Gore and Joe Lieberman, who were running far ahead in the district. Bloom called for lower prescription drug prices for seniors. In mid-October Shaw attacked Bloom for keeping seniors from buying drugs at lower prices; she owned $5 million of stock in and served on the board of generic drugmaker Andrx, which in June 2000 had been found guilty in federal court of violating the antitrust laws by taking $89 million from the maker of Cardizem CD in return for keeping its cheaper generic drug, CartiaXT, off the market. Bloom attacked him for "vicious personal attacks." But she was embarrassed when it was revealed that her personal physician wrote a prescription to her campaign manager for Cardizem CD and CartiaXT so the candidate could use them as props in a debate—a prescription that could under Florida law trigger disciplinary action. This turned out to be one of the closest races in the country. The initial count showed Shaw ahead by 599 votes; the mechanical recount required by Florida law didn't change the margin. Bloom sought a hand count, but the three county boards of canvassers, willing to order hand counts for Al Gore, declined to do so in this race (Miami-Dade did hand count six precincts, three chosen by each candidate). Shaw ran far ahead, 58%–42%, in Palm Beach County and carried his home base in Broward County by 55%–45%. He lost in the Miami-Dade County portion 67%–33%.

After the election, Shaw offered himself as a dark horse candidate for Ways and Means chairman. But the Republican Steering Committee, passing over the senior member, Philip Crane, picked the next most senior, Bill Thomas. Shaw remains chairman of the Social Security Subcommittee. The closeness of the 2000 election may stimulate opposition; as early as February 2001, Boca Raton Councilman Bill Glass said he was seriously considering running. But Republicans control redistricting, and they have an obvious way to protect Shaw: remove the Miami-Dade County section and move the district further north.

Cook's Call   *Competitive.* Shaw's close call in 2000 highlights just how marginal this southeastern district really is. Currently, this seat is the most Democratic district in the state held by a Republican (Gore won the district with 58%). It is likely that Republican redistricters will try to find a way to help make this district more amenable to Shaw for 2002.

THE PEOPLE: Pop. 2000: 630,775; Pop. 1990: 560,959, up 12.4% 1990–2000. 86.3% White, 6.7% Black, 1.4% Asian, 0.2% Amer. Indian, 0.1% Hawaiian, 2.7% Two+ races, 2.7% Other; 20.6% Hispanic Origin.

2000 Presidential Vote

Gore (D)	140,133	(58%)
Bush (R)	94,358	(39%)
Nader (Green)	3,951	(2%)
Others	1,447	(1%)

1996 Presidential Vote

Clinton (D)	124,715	(55%)
Dole (R)	86,668	(38%)
Perot (I)	17,418	(8%)

Rep. E. Clay Shaw, Jr. (R)

Elected 1980, 11th term; b. Apr. 19, 1939, Miami; home, Ft. Lauderdale; Stetson U., B.S. 1961, U. of AL, M.B.A. 1963, Stetson U., J.D. 1966; Catholic; married (Emilie).

Elected Office: Ft. Lauderdale City Comm., 1971–73; Ft. Lauderdale Vice Mayor, 1973–75, Mayor, 1975–80.

Professional Career: Practicing atty., 1966–68; Ft. Lauderdale Chief Prosecutor, 1968–69; Assoc. Municipal Judge, 1969–71.

DC Office: 2408 RHOB 20515, 202-225-3026; Fax: 202-225-8398; Web site: www.house.gov/shaw.

District Offices: Ft. Lauderdale, 954-522-1800; West Palm Beach, 561-832-3007.

Committees: *Ways & Means* (3d of 24 R): Social Security (Chmn.); Trade. *Joint Committee on Taxation* (3d of 5 Reps.).

Group Ratings

	ADA	ACLU	AFS	LCV	CON	ITIC	NTU	COC	ACU	NTLC	CHC
2000	10	15	0	21	61	95	54	80	68	61	77
1999	20	—	0	13	40	—	52	88	60	—	—

National Journal Ratings

	1999 LIB	—	1999 CONS		2000 LIB	—	2000 CONS
Economic	39%	—	59%		40%	—	59%
Social	49%	—	51%		48%	—	52%
Foreign	43%	—	55%		12%	—	78%

Key Votes of the 106th Congress

1. Patient Bill of Rights	Y	5. Bar RU-486 $ for FDA	Y	9. NATO War in Serbia	Y
2. Accelerate Min. Wage	N	6. Display 10 Commandments	Y	10. Perm. Trade with China	Y
3. Strike Ban on Ergo. Stnd.	N	7. Gun Show Bkgrnd. Checks	Y	11. Debt Relief for 3rd World	N
4. Ovrd. Estate Tax Veto	Y	8. Ban Part.-Birth Abortion	Y	12. Drop Cuba Econ. Embargo	N

Election Results

2000 general	E. Clay Shaw Jr. (R)	105,855	(50%)	($3,086,708)
	Elaine Bloom (D)	105,256	(50%)	($2,378,327)
2000 primary	E. Clay Shaw Jr. (R)	unopposed		
1998 general	E. Clay Shaw Jr. (R)	unopposed		($353,968)

TWENTY-THIRD DISTRICT

In the morning shadow of the high-rise condominiums that line the Atlantic Ocean from Palm Beach to Miami Beach, behind the waterways that separate the barrier islands from the mainland, usually a few blocks off of old U.S. 1 and behind the railroad lines, are the black neighborhoods of South Florida's Gold Coast. They are gatherings of older stucco homes and commercial storefronts, ranging from enclaves of upper-middle-class residents to rundown slums. These are neighborhoods overlooked by most tourists and feared by many local residents.

Florida's 23d Congressional District, created by the May 1992 court redistricting, gathers together many of these black neighborhoods in a constituency that is ethnically defined and geographically grotesque. A little more than half its residents live in Broward County, a little more than one-third live in Palm Beach County, and the rest are scattered: a few in north Miami-Dade County, more in a geographically expansive but lightly populated segment that includes migrant worker camps around Lake Okeechobee and the old black neighborhood of Fort Pierce, a small city 120 miles north of Miami. Slightly more than half of the population is black.

The congressman from the 23d District is Alcee Hastings, a Democrat elected in 1992, the only member of Congress ever to have been impeached and removed from office as a federal judge. Hastings is articulate and charming, the son of a hotel maid from Orlando; he practiced law, ran for the U.S. Senate in 1970 and was appointed a federal judge in 1979. He was impeached by the House of Representatives by a vote of 413–3 in 1988 and convicted by the Senate by a vote of 69–26. Hastings was charged with conspiring with a friend to take a $150,000 bribe and give two convicted swindlers light sentences. Hastings was acquitted by a Miami jury in 1983, but the friend was convicted. The 11th Circuit Court of Appeals called for impeachment in 1987 and referred the case to Congress. In the House the case for impeachment was made by John Conyers, senior member of the Congressional Black Caucus; the case was heard by a panel of 12 senators, and Hastings was removed in 1989. Footnote: in 1997 the Department of Justice in investigating the FBI crime lab found that an agent falsely testified against Hastings, and he and Conyers moved to reopen the case. Nothing came of that: can a removed federal judge be restored to office?

After his removal Hastings was unapologetic. In 1990 he ran an abortive campaign for governor, then lost the primary for secretary of State. When the 23d District was created, he sprang into that race. In the primary Hastings edged out another black candidate for second place, 28%–27%. In the October runoff he faced Palm Beach County legislator Lois Frankel, a national celebrity as state House Democratic leader during the November-December 2000 Florida controversy. He was helped by a ruling by federal Judge Stanley Sporkin that his removal from office was invalid since the full Senate did not hear the charges; the Supreme Court ruled to the contrary in a case involving another federal judge in January 1993, but by that time Hastings was in Congress. Frankel blasted Hastings for his record, and Hastings responded, "The bitch is a racist," and won the runoff 58%–42%, with voting closely following racial lines. He won the general election 59%–31%.

"I sort of came back like gangbusters, didn't I?" he said later, but in the House he treated colleagues pleasantly and respectfully. "I'm not a vengeful person," he said. His voting record has been close to the most liberal in the Florida delegation. He focused on international issues, strongly supporting the U.S. intervention in Kosovo. As a member of the International Relations Committee, he serves on the Organization for Security and Cooperation in Europe and has been Rapporteur of the OSCE Committee on Political Affairs and Security. In the 107th Congress he became the senior Democrat on the Europe Subcommittee. He has worked with Fort Lauderdale neighbor Clay Shaw for funds for Port Everglades and its customs officers.

Naturally, Hastings's opinion was sought when the subject of impeachment arose, and it was exuberantly given. He saw Clinton's impeachment as being driven by prosecutors as his own was, in his view, by judges—in both cases abusing their powers: "In my case, they nullified a jury. In this case, they are nullifying an election." In September 1998 he moved to impeach Independent Counsel Kenneth Starr; his motion was voted down 340–71. When one senator estimated that a trial would take just three weeks, Hastings replied, "Hello? I don't think so. Over on Ego Mountain they don't have a clue."

But even as he opposed Republicans in Congress, he was opposing Democrats back home. In January 1998 Florida House Democrats ousted Willie Logan, a black from Opa-Locke, as Speaker-designate, claiming that he wasn't a good fundraiser. Hastings responded with more outrage than Logan, who declared himself a "free agent." In a March special election for a state Senate vacancy in Broward, he backed the Republican over a Democrat who had voted against Logan. The Democrat still won, but in black precincts where Jeb Bush had won 4% for governor in 1994 the Republican state Senate candidate won 54% in 1998. In April 2000 Hastings criticized Governor Jeb Bush's One Florida plan to end race and gender preferences in state colleges and universities, contending that white men have developed a "good old boy system . . . and a whole bunch of other things that are preferences." And he called the presidential-election recount in Florida "a stain on democracy."

Cook's Call   *Safe.* Being the only member of the House to have been impeached by the House and convicted by the Senate as a then-Federal judge, certainly hasn't hurt Hastings politically in this overwhelmingly minority and Democrat-dominated district. Republicans have said they do not expect to alter any of the state's majority-black districts in redistricting.

THE PEOPLE: Pop. 2000: 618,766; Pop. 1990: 563,645, up 9.8% 1990–2000. 34.7% White, 55.3% Black, 0.9% Asian, 0.3% Amer. Indian, 0.1% Hawaiian, 4.7% Two+ races, 4% Other; 13.1% Hispanic Origin.

2000 Presidential Vote

Gore (D) 119,806 (78%)
Bush (R) 30,431 (20%)
Nader (Green) 1,409 (1%)
Others 1,173 (1%)

1996 Presidential Vote

Clinton (D) 107,884 (75%)
Dole (R) 27,531 (19%)
Perot (I) 9,193 (6%)

Rep. Alcee L. Hastings (D)

Elected 1992, 5th term; b. Sept. 5, 1936, Altamonte Springs; home, Miramar; Fisk U., B.A. 1958, Howard U., 1958–60, FL A&M, J.D. 1963; Methodist; single.

Elected Office: Broward Cnty. Circuit Court Judge, 1977–79.

Professional Career: Practicing atty., 1964–77; Federal Judge, U.S. District Court, 1979–89.

DC Office: 2235 RHOB 20515, 202-225-1313; Web site: www.house.gov/alceehastings.

District Offices: Ft. Lauderdale, 954-733-2800; West Palm Beach, 561-684-0565.

Committees: *Permanent Select Committee on Intelligence* (6th of 9 D): Human Intelligence, Analysis & Counterintelligence; Technical & Tactical Intelligence. *Rules* (4th of 4 D).

Group Ratings

	ADA	ACLU	AFS	LCV	CON	ITIC	NTU	COC	ACU	NTLC	CHC
2000	80	92	100	86	82	53	17	55	4	16	8
1999	80	—	100	88	19	—	11	22	0	—	—

National Journal Ratings

	1999 LIB	—	1999 CONS		2000 LIB	—	2000 CONS
Economic	39%	—	59%		85%	—	15%
Social	87%	—	0%		94%	—	0%
Foreign	83%	—	16%		85%	—	10%

Key Votes of the 106th Congress

1. Patient Bill of Rights	Y	5. Bar RU-486 $ for FDA	N	9. NATO War in Serbia	Y
2. Accelerate Min. Wage	Y	6. Display 10 Commandments	N	10. Perm. Trade with China	N
3. Strike Ban on Ergo. Stnd.	Y	7. Gun Show Bkgrnd. Checks	Y	11. Debt Relief for 3rd World	Y
4. Ovrd. Estate Tax Veto	N	8. Ban Part.-Birth Abortion	N	12. Drop Cuba Econ. Embargo	Y

Election Results

2000 general	Alcee L. Hastings (D)	89,179	(76%)	($375,037)
	Bill Lambert (R)	27,630	(24%)	
2000 primary	Alcee L. Hastings (D) .... unopposed			
1998 general	Alcee L. Hastings (D) .... unopposed			($263,794)

★ GEORGIA ★

G eorgia and Atlanta—the megacity whose metropolitan area spreads out over the red clay hills of 20 of Georgia's 159 counties—were one of the great American success stories of the last decade. Between 1990 and 2000, Georgia's population grew by 26%, the sixth highest rate of population growth among states, the highest east of Colorado, and the highest rate of growth for Georgia since the 1870s, when Atlanta rose literally from the ashes of the Civil War and Henry Grady's New South sprang into being. Atlanta and Georgia have been in many ways for many years the center of the South, at least since William Tecumseh Sherman marched here in 1864. This is where John Stith Pemberton invented Coca-Cola, where Margaret Mitchell wrote *Gone With the Wind*, where Martin Luther King Jr. grew up, and where most of the civil rights organizations that changed America were headquartered. But in growth and flamboyance, Georgia for decades was outdazzled by other parts of the South—by Texas with its oil wells and high-tech industries, by Florida with Miami Beach and Disney World, even by North Carolina with its Research Triangle and college basketball champions.

In the 1990s, however, Georgia grew faster than any of them, and by 2000 was the tenth-largest state—the first time it has been in the top 10 since the Census of 1850. Almost all this growth has come in the booming Atlanta metropolitan area, not in the core city, but amid the hills of suburban counties for almost 100 miles around. Atlanta, long a regional capital, has become a world city, a status suitably memorialized when it hosted the 1996 Summer Olympics, and re-emphasized every day as travelers all over the world watch the news from the CNN Broadcast Center. Just to the north is Georgia Tech and a few miles to the east are the Jimmy Carter Presidential Center, Emory University and the Centers for Disease Control and Prevention. Atlanta in the 1990s was part of literature as well: It was the central focus of Tom Wolfe's *A Man in Full*. If leading Atlantans were not entirely pleased with his portrait of a football player-turned-real estate developer with a mansion in Buckhead and a 29,000-acre hunting estate in south Georgia who manufactures a Ku Klux Klan rally to deflate the price of property he wants to buy, or of conniving local black politicians and the tension between light-skinned and dark-skinned blacks, they could console themselves that Wolfe's Atlanta was not as cynical as Balzac's Paris or as lugubrious as Dickens's London, and that Wolfe, on his book tour here in 1998, continually lauded the city's ambition and optimism, good manners and unfailing generosity.

Neither Atlanta's rise to world eminence nor its role as the capital of the South was inevitable. This was only a small, though well located, railroad crossroads when it was burned by General William Tecumseh Sherman's troops as they conducted their "march to the sea." Richmond, Charleston and New Orleans all had stronger claims to being the central focus of the South a century ago. But in the 20th Century two figures imprinted Atlanta on the national imagination. One was Margaret Mitchell, whose 1936 novel *Gone with the Wind* inspired the 1939 movie. The other was Martin Luther King Jr., reared in Atlanta and based there during most of his career, as a leader and ultimately the national symbol of the civil rights revolution that changed the South and the nation. Linking the two was Atlanta's business community, notably Robert Woodruff, who headed Coca-Cola from 1932–60 and made Coke a worldwide enterprise. Perhaps aware that a world company could not indefinitely be associated with racial segregation, Woodruff and William Hartsfield, mayor from 1937–61, cooperated with blacks and promoted Atlanta as "the city too busy to hate." Hartsfield's successor, Ivan Allen, elected in 1961 and 1965, supported the Civil Rights Act of 1964, as Peachtree Center and the first atriumed Hyatt Regency were going up in downtown Atlanta.

This new Atlanta was growing up amid a mostly rural, deeply segregationist Georgia that as late as 1960 cast the second-highest Democratic percentage of any state for president: hatred of Sherman was still strong. Political contests typically matched Atlanta-supported moderates against rural-supported segregationists, and the latter invariably won: Georgia's electoral votes were cast for Barry Goldwater in 1964 and George Wallace in 1968. Then came change in the person of Jimmy Carter, a former nuclear submarine officer and one-term state senator who was elected governor in 1970 with a rural base as well as conspicuous black support. On taking office he

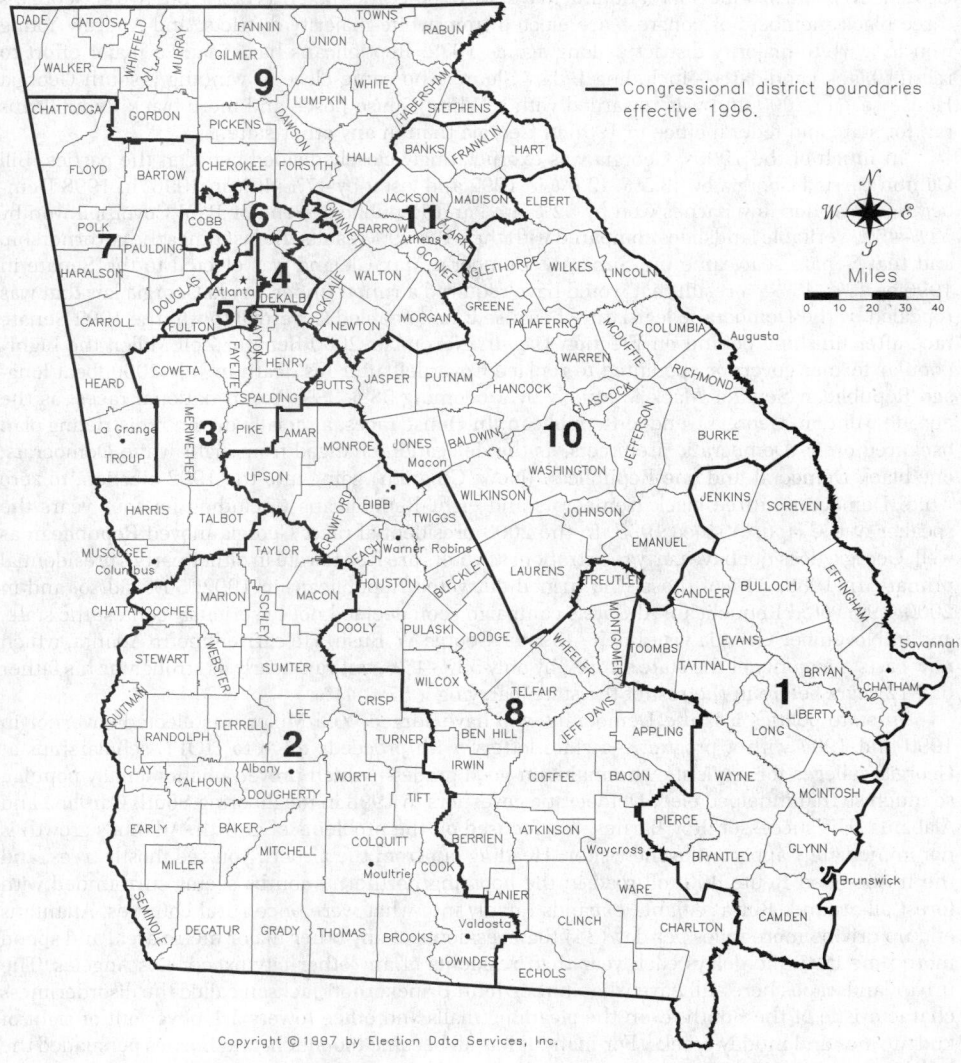

Congressional district boundaries effective 1996.

proclaimed a reconciliation of the races and installed a portrait of Martin Luther King Jr. in the Capitol. Carter thus became one of the first politicians from the rural South to celebrate and honor the civil rights revolution and in the process set himself on the road to being elected president in 1976. Without exactly saying so, Georgia has developed what Charles Moskos and John Sibley Butler in their book on races in the Army, *All We Can Be*, call an Anglo-African culture, a merger of traditions that were long associated intimately in private life but rigidly and even violently separated in public. This is the dominant culture of the Army, Moskos and Butler argue, and could turn out to be—though Tom Wolfe doesn't seem to think so—the dominant culture of Georgia. In politics, criticisms of Atlanta mayors are sometimes taken as racist, but two of Georgia's three black members of congress are elected from white-majority districts, and Andrew Young won in a white-majority district as long ago as 1972. Republicans have made a major effort to recruit black candidates—including Dylan Glenn, who came close to winning a south Georgia House seat in 2000 and was rewarded with a White House post—and more black Republicans ran for state and federal office in 1998 in Georgia than in any other state.

In much of the 1990s, Georgia was excruciatingly closely divided between the parties. Bill Clinton carried Georgia by 43.5%–42.9% in 1992 and lost it by 47%–46% in 1996. In 1998 Democratic Governor Roy Barnes won by 52%–44% and Republican Senator Paul Coverdell won by 52%–45%, veritable landslides compared with the 51%–49% results the last times the governorship and that Senate seat came up. Similarly, Democrat Max Cleland was elected to the Senate in 1996 by 49%–48%—a result that would have required a runoff under an old Georgia law that was repealed by the Democratic legislature because it had enabled Coverdell to win the 1992 Senate race after finishing behind on Election Day. In November 2000 Senator Zell Miller, the highly popular former governor appointed to replace Coverdell after his death in July 2000, beat long-ago Republican Senator Mack Mattingly by a booming 58%–38%. Yet in national races, as the decade went on, Georgia trended Republican. In House races, a racially-driven redistricting plan backfired on its Democratic architects, as the delegation changed from eight white Democrats, one black Democrat and one Republican (Newt Gingrich) going into the 1992 election, to zero white Democrats, three black Democrats and eight Republicans (including for four years the speaker of the House) since 1995. In the 2000 presidential race, Georgia moved Republican as well. Georgia does not have party registration, so voters are free to vote in either party's presidential primary. In 1988, 39% of those who turned out voted Republican; in 1992, 50% did so, and in 2000, 69% voted Republican. Al Gore's campaign soon decided not to seriously contest the state, and in November Georgia voted 55%–43% for George W. Bush. He carried metro Atlanta, which now casts a majority of the state's votes, by only 53%–45%, but ran nearly as strongly as his father had 12 years before in the rest of the state, carrying it 57%–41%.

In state politics it is the Democrats who have surged. Zell Miller was elected governor in 1990 and 1994 with a program—a state lottery, with proceeds to go to HOPE scholarships at Georgia colleges for students who maintain good grades—which proved phenomenally popular, so much so that it helped elect Democratic governors in 1998 in neighboring South Carolina and Alabama. His successor, Roy Barnes, has focused on the problems of growth. Atlanta's growth is not immediately apparent to the visitor: Heading out from the airport, you see mostly trees, and the traffic-filled Route 400 toll road in the booming northern suburbs seems surrounded with forest all around. But as Atlanta expands rapidly into what were once rural counties, Atlantans end up driving more miles per day (34) than residents of any other major metro area, and spend more time in traffic delays each year than residents of any other city except Los Angeles. The urban landscapes here still have what author John Brinckerhoff Jackson called the disorderliness characteristic of the South; even the gleaming malls and office towers are never out of sight of kudzu vines and muddy creeks. For many, it has all become too much, and Barnes persuaded the legislature in March 1999 to create a transportation superagency with broad powers to impose transit systems and highways on local governments. Barnes also got $300 million for rapidly growing counties to buy up to 20% of their land and set it aside as open space. Atlanta's growth has even threatened to make water as precious a resource as it is in the parched megacities of the West: Georgia is in a legal battle with Florida and Alabama over increasing its use of water from the Chattahoochee River.

Barnes's education program, with new higher standards, and his HMO regulation also appealed to residents of suburban counties. Once overwhelmingly Republican, they are now getting more black residents and Latino and Asian immigrants as well, and enough are voting Democratic to enable Democrats like Barnes and Miller to win. Barnes has supported racial preferences at the University of Georgia, and in February 2001 signed legislation to take the Confederate stars and bars out of its prominent place on the state flag and instead place it as one of five historic flags below a large rendition of the state seal—a bill that passed the state legislature with most of its support from black Democrats and suburban Republicans. Barnes also proposed spending $200,000 to improve Georgia's voting systems; seven African-American voters filed a lawsuit in January 2001 alleging political disenfranchisement—an assertion reflected by a Southern Regional Council study that found ballots cast by black voters were twice as likely to not be counted than those cast by whites due to voting irregularities.

Governor   Roy Barnes, elected governor in 1998, is a lawyer and professional politician who has spent almost all his adult life in public office. Barnes grew up in Cobb County when it was mostly rural and Marietta was a courthouse town dependent on the Lockheed aircraft factory—not the booming edge city burgeoning with small businesses it is today. He returned from college and law school, became a prosecutor in the Cobb district attorney's office, was elected to the state Senate in 1974, at 26, and served 16 years in the then-large Democratic majority. He ran for governor in 1990, finishing third in the Democratic primary with 21% against tough competition from Zell Miller (41%) and Andrew Young (29%). In 1992 he was elected to the state House from an increasingly Republican county.

Approaching the 1998 election Barnes was anything but a favorite. Much speculation focused on Republicans—first on Attorney General Mike Bowers, whose candidacy collapsed in June 1997 when he admitted a 10-year affair with a former state employee, then on Guy Millner, who started the Norrell temporary employee firm and spent freely of his $160-million-plus fortune to lose narrowly to Governor Zell Miller in 1994 and Senator Max Cleland in 1996. Barnes entered the race in August 1997, when Lieutenant Governor Pierre Howard announced he would not run. His chief primary opponent, Secretary of State Lewis Massey, was 36 and looked younger; two other intellectually serious candidates were poorly funded. Barnes raised $4 million by the primary and stressed the issue of the hour: providing more choice of doctors in managed care health insurance plans. With his folksy manner and in some respects conservative record—he was endorsed by the National Rifle Association and apologized for a 1980s vote against the Martin Luther King Jr. holiday—he ran well in rural counties. Barnes led Massey in the July 1998 primary by 49%–28%; two days later Massey withdrew from the runoff. Meanwhile, Guy Millner had beaten Bowers by only 50.4%–39.9%, avoiding a runoff by only 1,574 votes. Millner started by running ads accusing Barnes of being soft on crime; Barnes promised to cut residential property taxes. But Millner's previous races apparently did not leave all voters with a favorable impression and the overall mood worked for Barnes. "I don't see all those negative things that Guy Millner sees. I see a Georgia that prospers," Barnes said. He won by a solid 52%–44% margin. He was helped by black turnout, which according to the VNS exit poll was 29% of the total, slightly higher than the black share of population; he also did especially well among the youngest voters—a good omen for Democrats. Barnes carried most rural counties and cut into the Republican base in the suburbs.

Barnes has had spectacular success with the legislature in his first two years. All 27 of his bills passed in 1999, including creation of the Georgia Regional Transportation Authority which gave him control over transportation and development in the 20-county metro Atlanta area—more power than any other governor (some said the acronym stood for Give Roy Total Authority). The legislature also provided $300 million to allow metro Atlanta and other fast-growing counties to purchase up to 20% of their land area to maintain open space. Barnes got a $640 million annual property tax cut; an HMO regulation, including the rights to choose a doctor and to sue HMOs; an open meetings law; and a corporate child care tax credit. Then there was the Yamacraw Mission, named after the bluff where James Oglethorpe first settled Georgia, to foster high-tech with 85 professorships and 2,000 semiconductor designers to concentrate on high-capacity communications channels. In 2000 the legislature passed an automatic five-year sentence for felons who try to buy guns, higher campaign contribution limits (up to $16,000 for candidates who face runoffs) and—thanks to Tom Murphy, the nation's longest serving House speaker (since 1975)—a new department of motor vehicles.

Barnes' centerpiece in 2000 was education reform. Dismayed at Georgia's low test scores, he pushed through a bill requiring annual testing from first grade to 12th, with increased class time for low-scoring students and an end to tenure for newly hired teachers: "Tenure is an outdated concept, born of a time when we treasured process over performance." Barnes' plan had bonuses for teachers in high-performing schools and consequences for those in low-performing ones. Teacher-pupil ratios were required to be cut sharply. Critics said the plan would be too expensive and would squeeze out non-academic programs. It was opposed by some teachers' unions, the Christian Coalition and Republican state School Superintendent Linda Schrenko. But it passed, and despite Schrenko's success in beating a couple of legislative supporters in Republican primaries, there was no perceptible backlash in November. Barnes backtracked only a bit, apologizing to teachers for blaming them for student failure. Barnes campaigned heavily for Democratic legislators, and his party lost only two state Senate seats and picked up two in the state House, leaving solid Democratic majorities to deal with redistricting.

Looming in 2001 were long-term projects like creating a state water management authority (Georgia has been sued by Alabama and Florida for taking too much water from the Chattahoochee River for Atlanta) and creating a cancer treatment center in Atlanta. But in early 2001 all eyes were on Georgia's flag. In 1956, when Georgia politicians were vowing to defy school desegregation, the state adopted the Confederate stars and bars as the state flag. Fearing embarrassment when Georgia hosted the 1996 Olympics and out of strong conviction, Governor Zell Miller in 1993 called for redesigning the flag. But a poll showed that 64% of voters were opposed, and he dropped the issue after the legislature resisted. In 2000, pressure was building up again for redesign, and all sides agreed on "no flag talk till after the election." In January 2001 Barnes unveiled a new design, in which the state seal would occupy most of the flag and it would include at the bottom small depictions of five flags that have flown over the state, including the Confederate flag. A poll showed opinion now closer: 49% against redesign, 33% in favor. Barnes's bill passed the state House 94–82 in January, with support from black Democrats, suburban Republicans and a few Democrats outside metro Atlanta; the state Senate passed it by a 43–22 vote later that month, with six metro-area Republicans voting in favor.

Barnes appears to be in strong shape for re-election in 2002. Republicans may run on issues they failed to get through the legislature—an income tax cut, ethics reform, biennial auto emissions testing, school vouchers.

Cook's Call   *Probably Safe.* Barnes has adeptly handled a number of controversial issues and has enjoyed a lengthy honeymoon with the state legislature. He is in the strongest political shape of any of the Southern Democratic Governors up for re-election in 2002. The two leading Republican candidates are state School Superintendent Linda Schrenko, who has long been at odds with Barnes, and Cobb County Commission Chairman Bill Byrne. In either case, Barnes is a clear favorite.

Senior Senator   Max Cleland was elected senator in 1996, after a long career in public life and having overcome grievous injuries sustained during the Vietnam war. Cleland grew up in Lithonia, now an Atlanta suburb in DeKalb County, but then a country town that could have been hundreds of miles from the city. After college and a master's degree in American history at Emory, he volunteered for the Army and went to Vietnam in 1967, at 25; he lost both legs and one arm when a loose grenade he thought to be his own accidentally exploded, but in March 1999 the marine who saved Cleland's life told him the grenade had belonged to another soldier, lifting Cleland's emotional burden from the accident. He has chronicled his life in his 2000 book *Going for the Max*. In 1970 Cleland was elected to the Georgia Senate, where he wrote a law to make public facilities accessible to the handicapped. In 1977 Jimmy Carter appointed him head of the Veterans Administration, the youngest ever. In 1982 he was elected Georgia secretary of State, and was re-elected by wide margins three times. In October 1995, after Sam Nunn said he would retire from the Senate in 1996, Cleland promptly announced he would run and had no primary opposition.

The leader in the Republican primary was Guy Millner, the 1994 (and later 1998) gubernatorial nominee who founded the Norrell temporary employee firm and made a fortune, and who ran on a staunch conservative platform. Also running were Johnny Isakson, Republican gubernatorial nominee in 1990 and Newt Gingrich's successor in the House since 1999; and Clint Day, scion of the Days Inn family, who ran as a Christian conservative. In the July 9 primary, Millner led Isakson, 42%–35%. The Atlanta Olympics began 10 days later, overshadowing the campaign. Millner won the August 6 runoff 53%–47%.

Cleland's campaign was mostly positive, making folksy, self-deprecating speeches, running soft-focus positive ads showing him shaving, putting on a tie, and driving, saying, "I was raised to believe you can't expect help if you don't help yourself." His issue stands were mostly conservative: for a balanced budget amendment, term limits, the 1996 welfare reform bill, the death penalty for drug dealers, victims' rights, and a constitutional amendment allowing limits on campaign spending. Millner spent more than $9 million and ran tough ads charging that Cleland sought parole for a killer with a politically connected father who, when released, committed another murder; he criticized Cleland for a $300,000 settlement paid to a worker in his office when she blew the whistle on his use of state computers for political purposes. The result was exceedingly close. Cleland won 49%–48%; Millner had a microscopic edge in metro Atlanta and ran well in north Georgia, but he carried few counties south of Atlanta. These percentages were identical to those four years earlier, when Democrat Wyche Fowler led Republican Paul Coverdell, triggering a runoff three weeks later that Coverdell won. But in the meantime the Democratic legislature, led by Speaker Tom Murphy, had repealed the runoff law, and Millner did not have another chance.

Cleland has compiled a mixed voting record, quite liberal on economic issues, more moderate on cultural and foreign issues. He has split sometimes from his fellow Democrats, on the minimum wage bill in 1999, on repeal of the estate tax and marriage penalty in 2000, and on the Bush budget in 2001. In May 1999 he opposed Democrats' measures to require background checks on sales at gun shows and then, two days later, voted for the bill, which he said had been changed and which passed with Al Gore's tie-breaking vote 51–50: "I don't want my high schools, in my state, in this country, to turn into a miniature Vietnam, where you've got to come through a barricade and have an inner perimeter and an outer perimeter."

Cleland got Sam Nunn's place on Armed Services, and also on the Personnel Subcommittee, which he now chairs. In 2000 he passed a bill to give access to long-term health insurance at reduced group rates to federal employees and active duty, reserve and retired military personnel. But he was not able to get his proposal to allow military personnel to transfer their education benefits to family members into the October 2000 defense appropriation. He and John McCain sponsored the law to build a monument to honor disabled military veterans, and Cleland got a 770-acre site in Cherokee County for a veterans cemetery. He met frequently and worked with the other five Vietnam veterans in the Senate in 1999 and 2000, co-sponsoring a bill to create an education center near the Vietnam Veterans Memorial and another to use $5 million of Vietnam's annual payment to the United States to fund student exchange programs.

On local issues, Cleland worked for funds for transportation projects, including $25 million for MARTA expansion, and he made sure that Governor Roy Barnes's new Georgia Regional Transportation Authority was eligible for federal funds. He has lobbied for faster completion of the fifth runway at Hartsfield Airport—scheduled to be completed in 2005. He worked with others in the Georgia delegation to get the Pentagon to commit to building four new C-130s at Lockheed Martin's Marietta plant where otherwise, the company said, the plant would be shut down. Cleland concentrated on lobbying Vice President Al Gore, pressing him on an Air Force Two flight in fall 1999 and in rides to Hartsfield; at the January 2000 State of the Union message, Gore caught Cleland's eye and gave him a thumbs-up. Cleland in turn spoke out for Gore during the 2000 campaign. Gore, he said at one stop, "never said he was a combat hero. He went to the war of his generation. Bush didn't and Cheney never served. I find it ironic that these men who avoided the wars of their generation are now big defense experts." After Democrats in Florida successfully challenged absentee military ballots without postmarks, Cleland asked for Armed Services hearings on military postmarks and their relationship to state absentee ballot laws. Striking a bipartisan note, after the election he called for regular lunches for the Georgia delegation, which has been sharply split on partisan lines.

Cleland comes up for re-election in 2002, and there has been some speculation that he will retire for health reasons. "I find life a constant series of being broken and then recovering and then moving on and overcoming," he once said, but when pressed about running again, he said in late 2000, "The only retirement I'll take is if the Georgia voters send me home." All of the state's Republican congressmen except Johnny Isakson have been reported to be considering the race. Another possible candidate is businessman Lewis Jordan, who got into and then bowed out of the special Senate election in 2000 against Zell Miller.

Cook's Call   *Potentially Competitive.* Polls show that while voters very much like and appreciate who and what Cleland is—a highly decorated Vietnam veteran with a compelling personal history—they know very little about what he has done since entering public office. As of spring 2001, seven of Georgia's Republican House members were looking at this race; who ultimately runs may hinge on the outcome of the redistricting process. But the odd-man-out method of selecting a nominee may not be the most effective way to pick a winning challenger.

Junior Senator   Zell Miller, a Democrat, was appointed to the Senate to replace Paul Coverdell after his death in July 2000 and was elected to fill out the remainder of his term in November. Miller grew up in the mountains of north Georgia in the town of Young Harris (of which his mother was mayor), and joined the Marines after high school; his 1997 book is entitled *Corps Values: Everything You Need to Know, I Learned in the Marines.* He returned home, went back to school, and was elected to the Georgia Senate in 1960, at 28; he worked for Lester Maddox in his last two years as governor, and ran the state Democratic Party when Jimmy Carter was governor. Miller was elected lieutenant governor in 1974 and held the office, whose occupant tends to run the state Senate, for 16 years. In 1990 he finally ran for governor. In the Democratic primary he led with 41% of the vote to 29% for Andrew Young, longtime Atlanta mayor, congressman and ambassador to the United Nations, and 21% for Roy Barnes, then a state senator and now Miller's successor as governor. In the runoff he beat Young 62%–38%. In the general he beat Johnny Isakson, now 6th District congressman, 53%–45%.

Miller's main issue in his 1990 campaign was a lottery, with revenues to go to education. The lottery passed, and the money went to fund pre-kindergarten for four-year-olds and to fund HOPE scholarships—free tuition at any Georgia college, public or private, for freshmen who maintain B averages in high school. In a few years Georgia led the nation in percentage of four-year-olds in pre-kindergarten and 97% of instate freshmen at the University of Georgia and Georgia Tech had HOPE scholarships. Miller had occasional defeats: In 1993 he tried to get the Confederate stars and bars removed from the Georgia flag (it was placed there in 1956, when politicians were opposing school desegregation) but the legislature resisted.

Miller was an early supporter of Bill Clinton for president (Miller was a client of James Carville in 1990) and in 1992 got the Georgia primary rescheduled a week earlier, on March 3. Clinton's victory there was a key step in his nomination, and Miller's support helped him carry Georgia in November by 13,000 votes (43.5%–42.9%). But his association with Clinton hurt in 1994 when Miller was opposed by Guy Millner, founder of the Norrell temporary employee firm. Miller won by only 51%–49% in this heavily Republican year, and took tougher stands on welfare and taxes in his second term. His job approval rating rose to as high as 85%. Term-limited, he decided to retire and teach at Young Harris College and Emory University, declaring, "I will never be a candidate ever again, and we might as well go further and say that I will not take a job or an appointment in Washington."

Coverdell had been re-elected in 1998 by 52%–45% and became an important part of the Republican leadership, handling numerous issues for Majority Leader Trent Lott with a minimum amount of self-publicity; he was also a policy innovator, co-sponsoring education savings accounts with Bob Torricelli and anti-drug laundering measures with Dianne Feinstein. Then, entirely unexpectedly, in three days in July 2000 Coverdell was hospitalized, underwent surgery and died of a stroke. The appointment to fill his seat was in the hands of Governor Roy Barnes. He asked Miller, who refused. Barnes tried again, and Miller finally agreed: He had, after all, tried to keep his promise by turning down this Senate seat twice. The appointment lasted only until November, when under Georgia law voters would choose among candidates listed without party affiliation for the remaining four years of Coverdell's term; if no candidate received 50%, there would be a runoff. Miller, with his high job ratings, was the immediate favorite, and Georgia's eight Republican congressmen, most interested in the race, quickly dropped out. Two Republicans remained. One was Lewis Jordan, founder of ValuJet, who promised to put $3 million of his own into the race; this earned the endorsement of Republican Senate campaign committee head Mitch McConnell. The other was Mack Mattingly, who won the seat against troubled veteran Herman Talmadge in 1980 by 51%–49% and lost it to Democrat Wyche Fowler in 1986 by 51%–49%. (In 1992 Coverdell beat Fowler by, you guessed it, 51%–49%.) Concerned that having two Republicans in the race would cost the party any chance of winning, Jordan bowed out in early August 2000.

Miller was far ahead in the polls; his appointment, *National Journal*'s Charlie Cook wrote at the time, "effectively puts control of the Senate into play for the first time in this election cycle"—and indeed if Democrats had not held the seat, Republicans would have emerged from the election with a 51–49 majority. But Miller insisted that he would not be a partisan senator, and recalled his work with Coverdell in the state Senate and promised to continue his work on at least some issues. "I will support the Democrats when I think they are right and I will oppose them whenever I think they are wrong, and the same way with the president and his programs," he said, and started off his career by joining Republicans and voting for repeal of estate tax and marriage penalty, a measure Clinton vowed to veto. Mattingly based much of his campaign on the Republican label. "Paul and I have identical beliefs and values, and I'm the only one who can become a subcommittee chairman. Zell Miller can't." In debates and ads Miller reached back to Mattingly's Senate record and accused him of voting to increase the retirement age and limit Social Security inflation increases (he would "destroy Social Security as we know it") and of "voting no" on education 14 times. He admitted that he supported Al Gore for president, but only, he said, because Gore helped with the Atlanta Olympics and with recovery from natural disasters. Mattingly attacked the HOPE scholarship program for not doing enough to raise students' basic knowledge; Miller said Mattingly was "dissing" teachers. Mattingly ran a spot showing Coverdell's widow saying, "If Paul were here, he'd wish Zell well, but he'd work day and night to elect Mack to follow in his true conservative footsteps." A Miller ad—there were more of them, for he had more funding—signed off, "Zell Miller—the man who brought HOPE to Georgia." George W. Bush cut a spot for Mattingly, but even as Bush carried the state 55%–43%, Miller whipped Mattingly 58%–38%. Bush carried 125 of Georgia's 159 counties; Mattingly carried only 10.

Miller carried out his promise to be bipartisan early in the 107th Congress. Soon after former Senator John Ashcroft was nominated to be attorney general, Miller said he would support him—the first Democrat to do so. And in George W. Bush's first week in office, Miller joined Texas Republican Phil Gramm, a Georgia native, in co-sponsoring Bush's tax program. Some Senate Democrats were miffed that Miller did not consult with them first, or hold back, as they certainly would have urged. But in May 2001, amid rumors of defection, he stated, "I am not going to switch to the Republican Party. I am saying it as plainly as I know how." But one of Miller's "Corps values" is to speak out loudly for what he believes and—fearless and evidently not caring much about re-election to a seat he accepted only under the most unusual circumstances—he is likely to do so until his term expires in 2005.

Presidential politics   Georgia used to be an outlier in presidential politics—the second-most Democratic state in 1960, for Barry Goldwater in 1964 and George Wallace in 1968, heavily Republican in 1972, strongly for native son Jimmy Carter in 1976 and 1980. In the 1990s it was a prime marginal state—for Bill Clinton by 13,000 votes in 1992, for Bob Dole by 27,000 votes in 1996. In 2000 its 13 electoral votes went solidly for George W. Bush. But with all its new voters, and the Democratic strength in state races, it is possible that its augmented 15 electoral votes will be seriously contested in 2004 or 2008.

Georgia's 1992 presidential primary was scheduled one week before Super Tuesday at the insistence of Governor Zell Miller, who wanted to help Bill Clinton, and did: Clinton won smartly to balance losses in Maryland and Colorado the same day. George Bush's 64%–36% victory here over Pat Buchanan showed the Buchanan brigades were not about to overrun the South. Since then, Georgia's primary has been of little consequence, except as a measure of its Republican presidential trend since voters are free to mark the ballot for either party. In 1988, when both parties had contests, 622,000 voted Democratic and 400,000 voted Republican; in 1992, 454,631 voted Democratic and 453,990 voted Republican; in 2000, 284,000 voted Democratic and 643,000 Republican.

Congressional districting   With a burgeoning population spreading rapidly across the hills of north Georgia within a nearly 100-mile radius of downtown Atlanta, Georgia is a redistricter's dream—or nightmare. For the 1990s, Democratic Speaker Tom Murphy drew up a plan that was intended to end the career of Newt Gingrich, safeguard Democratic incumbents and create three black-majority seats. But each of those goals was frustrated. Gingrich moved to a heavily Republican suburban Atlanta seat; Democratic incumbents retired, were beaten or switched parties, to the point that a 9–1 Democratic delegation in October 1992 was 8–3 Republican by April 1995. In June 1995 the Supreme Court struck down the convoluted black-majority 11th District, extending from Atlanta to Savannah, as a "racial gerrymander," and a new plan, with just one black-majority district, was drawn up by a federal court in December 1995 and approved by the Supreme Court in June 1997. In fact, all the black incumbents were re-elected; the idea that white Georgians are unwilling to vote for black candidates was refuted as long ago as 1972, when Andrew Young was elected in a majority-white district.

The 2000 Census gave Georgia two new House seats, and Democrats control both chambers and the governorship. The four south Georgia seats—the 1st, 2d, 8th and 10th—come close to the new population standard and could pretty much be left alone. But look for the legislature to shuffle counties between them, to strengthen the Democrat Sanford Bishop in the 2d by moving the district toward Democratic Macon, and to weaken the three Republicans by giving them new territory. State Senator Charles Walker might try to increase the black percentage in the 10th District and then challenge Charlie Norwood, while other Democrats may want to weaken Saxby Chambliss in the 8th. In the northern suburbs of Atlanta, rapid growth will probably force the legislature to create one new heavily Republican suburban seat. But the legislature might try to create a new district anchored in southern Cobb County, Roy Barnes's home base, where Republican incumbent Bob Barr trailed in 2000, which will be within reach of a Democrat; many Democrats want to target Barr, as they targeted Gingrich 10 years ago, but Barr like Gingrich might elude them by shifting to a more heavily Republican district. The heavily black 4th and 5th Districts will probably not be much disturbed. But Democrats will have to make tough choices: If they create too many close seats, they may lose them, as they did in the 1990s. And Republicans may try to make a deal with black legislators, as they did in other Southern states after the 1990 Census, to put most black voters in three heavily Democratic districts, leaving the others more Republican.

THE PEOPLE: Pop. 2000: 8,186,453; Pop. 1990: 6,478,216, up 26.4% 1990–2000. 2.9% of U.S. total, 10th largest; 65.1% White, 28.7% Black, 2.1% Asian, 0.3% Amer. Indian, 0.1% Hawaiian, 1.4% Two+ races, 2.4% Other; 5.3% Hispanic Origin. 3.7% Unemployment. 2000 Voting age pop.: 6,017,219. 2000 Turnout: 2,655,325; 44% of VAP. Registered voters (2000): 4,648,210; no party registration.

POLITICAL LINEUP: Governor, Roy Barnes (D); Lt. Gov., Mark Taylor (D); Secy. of State, Cathy Cox (D); Atty. Gen., Thurbert Baker (D); Commissioner of Insurance, John Oxendine (R); Superintendent of Education, Linda C. Schrenko (R); Commissioner of Agriculture, Tommy Irvin (D); Commissioner of Labor, Michael L. Thurmond (D); State Senate, 56 (32 D, 24 R); Senate Pres. Pro Tempore, Terrell Starr (D); Majority Leader, Charles Walker (D); State House, 180 (105 D, 75 R); House Speaker, Thomas B. Murphy (D). Senators, Max Cleland (D) and Zell Miller (D). Representatives, 11 (3 D, 8 R).

ELECTIONS DIVISION: 404-656-2871; **FILING DEADLINE FOR U.S. CONGRESS:** April 26, 2002.

2000 Presidential Vote

Bush (R)	1,419,720	(55%)
Gore (D)	1,116,230	(43%)
Others	47,258	(2%)

1996 Presidential Vote

Dole (R)	1,080,840	(47%)
Clinton (D)	1,053,848	(46%)
Perot (I)	146,337	(6%)

2000 Republican Presidential Primary

Bush (R)	430,480	(67%)
McCain (R)	179,046	(28%)
Keyes (R)	29,640	(5%)

2000 Democratic Presidential Primary

Gore (D)	238,396	(84%)
Bradley (D)	46,035	(16%)

Gov. Roy Barnes (D)

Elected 1998, term expires Jan. 2003, 1st term; b. Mar. 11, 1948, Atlanta; home, Marietta; U. of GA, A.B. 1969, J.D. 1972; Methodist; married (Marie).

Elected Office: Cobb County Asst. D.A., 1972–74; GA Senate, 1974–90; GA House of Reps., 1993–98.

Professional Career: Practicing atty., 1975–98.

Office: 203 State Capitol, Atlanta, 30334, 404-656-1776; Fax: 404-657-7332; Web site: www.state.ga.us.

Election Results

1998 general	Roy Barnes (D)	941,076	(52%)
	Guy Millner (R)	790,201	(44%)
	Others	61,531	(3%)
1998 runoff	Roy Barnes (D)	221,651	(83%)
	Lewis A. Massey (D)	45,735	(17%)
1998 primary	Roy Barnes (D)	239,517	(49%)
	Lewis A. Massey (D)	135,920	(28%)
	David Poythress (D)	65,860	(14%)
	Steve Langford (D)	31,543	(6%)
	Others	14,001	(3%)
1994 general	Zell Miller (D)	788,926	(51%)
	Guy Millner (R)	756,371	(49%)

Sen. Max Cleland (D)

Elected 1996, seat up 2002, 1st term; b. Aug. 24, 1942, Atlanta; home, Lithonia; Stetson U., B.A. 1964, Emory U., M.A. 1968; Methodist; single.

Military Career: Army, 1965–68 (Vietnam).

Elected Office: GA Senate, 1970–75; GA Secy. of State, 1982–96.

Professional Career: Staff Mbr., Senate Veterans' Affairs Cmte., 1975–77; Administrator, U.S. Veterans' Admin., 1977–81.

DC Office: 461 DSOB, 20510, 202-224-3521; Fax: 202-224-0072; Web site: www.senate.gov/~cleland.

State Offices: Albany, 229-430-7796; Atlanta, 404-331-4811; Augusta, 706-722-4040; Columbus, 706-649-7705; Dalton, 706-275-8905; Macon, 478-755-1779; Savannah, 912-352-8283.

Committees: *Armed Services*: Airland Forces; Personnel (Chmn.); Readiness & Management Support. *Commerce, Science & Transportation*: Aviation; Communications; Science, Technology & Space; Surface Transportation & Merchant Marine. *Governmental Affairs*: International Security, Proliferation & Federal Services; Investigations (Permanent). *Small Business*.

Group Ratings

	ADA	ACLU	AFS	LCV	CON	ITIC	NTU	COC	ACU	NTLC	CHC
2000	70	57	57	86	46	85	20	73	24	17	15
1999	100	—	100	89	65	—	8	47	0	—	—

National Journal Ratings

	1999 LIB —	1999 CONS	2000 LIB —	2000 CONS
Economic	84%	13%	57%	41%
Social	69%	28%	61%	36%
Foreign	56%	40%	62%	34%

Key Votes of the 106th Congress

1. Educ. Savings Accts.	Y	5. Review Movie Violence	N	9. NATO War in Serbia	Y
2. Prescrip. Drug Benefit	Y	6. Gun Show Bckgrnd. Checks	Y	10. Table Cuba Travel Ban	N
3. Delay Ergonomic Standards	N	7. Ban Part.-Birth Abortion	N	11. Nuclear Test-Ban Treaty	Y
4. Phase Out Estate Tax	Y	8. Broaden Hate Crimes List	Y	12. Perm. Trade with China	Y

Election Results

1996 general	Max Cleland (D)	1,103,993	(49%)	($2,926,391)
	Guy Millner (R)	1,073,969	(48%)	($9,858,955)
	Others	81,270	(4%)	
1996 primary	Max Cleland (D)	unopposed		
1990 general	Sam Nunn (D)	unopposed		($1,214,695)

Sen. Zell Miller (D)

Appointed July 2000, seat up 2004, 1st term; b. Feb. 24, 1932, Young Harris; home, Young Harris; U. of GA, A.B. 1957, M.A. 1958; Methodist; married (Shirley).

Military Career: Marine Corps, 1953–56.

Elected Office: Mayor, Young Harris, 1958–60; GA Senate, 1960–64; GA Lt. Gov., 1974–90; GA Gov. 1990–98.

Professional Career: Dir., St. Board of Probation, Personnel Officer, GA Dept. of Corrections, 1965–66; Exec. Secy., Gov. Lester Maddox, 1969–71; Exec. Dir., GA Dem. Party, 1971–73; Professor, Young Harris College, Emory U. & U. of GA, 1999–2000.

DC Office: 257 DSOB, 20510, 202-224-3643; Fax: 202-228-2090; Web site: miller.senate.gov.

State Offices: Atlanta, 404-347-2202; Macon, 478-745-5949; Moultrie, 912-985-8113; Savannah, 912-238-3244; Young Harris, 706-379-9950.

Committees: *Agriculture, Nutrition & Forestry*: Production & Price Competitiveness; Research, Nutrition & General Legislation. *Banking, Housing & Urban Affairs*: Economic Policy; Financial Institutions; International Trade & Finance. *Veterans' Affairs*.

Group Ratings and Key Votes: Newly Elected

Election Results

2000 special	Zell Miller (D)	1,413,224	(58%)	($2,533,746)
	Mack Mattingly (R)	920,478	(38%)	($1,093,408)
	Other	94,540	(4%)	
1998 general	Paul Coverdell (R)	918,540	(52%)	($6,936,745)
	Michael Coles (D)	791,904	(45%)	($5,275,419)
	Others	43,467	(2%)	
1998 primary	Paul Coverdell (R)	unopposed		

FIRST DISTRICT

Georgia's South Atlantic coast, long one of the poorest parts of the country, has been booming in recent years. The area was settled in the 1730s by James Oglethorpe as Britain's 13th coastal colony as a refuge and reformatory for convicts. It did not take long for the sea islands and lowlands along the wide rivers and inlets to become plantation country. Savannah, the state's first capital, was by the 1830s one of America's booming cotton ports; it languished after the Civil War, living off paper mills and chemical plants in the 20th Century, while impoverished blacks on the islands a few miles away still spoke Gullah dialects. Then, a few decades ago, preservationists started restoring houses and churches on the grid punctuated by 24 squares that Oglethorpe had laid out more than 200 years before. Today Savannah is one of the most graciously preserved cities in the country, and a major tourism mecca and convention center thanks to the popularity of John Berendt's *Midnight in the Garden of Good and Evil*, a somewhat-based-on-facts story of eccentricity and murder that was on the bestseller lists from 1994 to 1998. The city competes actively with neighboring Charleston, South Carolina, not only for tourists but also for shipping.

The 1st Congressional District of Georgia includes the state's entire Atlantic coast and goes 50 or so miles inland, through cotton and tobacco fields and softwood forests. There are more exotic products here as well: Toombs County is the home of the fragrant Vidalia onions that folks say are so sweet you can eat 'em like an apple, while Claxton in tiny Evans County has for nearly a century been home to two of the nation's prime fruitcake makers. The boundaries were changed a bit in the 1995 court-mandated redistricting, in which the 1st lost some rural counties and gained black neighborhoods in Savannah; the black percentage rose from 23% to 31%. Though the counties in the 1st District are ancestrally Democratic, most voters here are conservative on cultural and military issues. That, plus coastal prosperity, has made this area Republican at the top of the ticket and even in some statewide contests.

The congressman from the 1st District is Jack Kingston, a Republican first elected in 1992. Kingston grew up in Texas, Ethiopia, and Athens, Georgia, the son of a professor; after college he moved to Savannah and became a commercial insurance agent. In 1984 he was elected to the Georgia House, at 29, and served eight years. In 1992, when incumbent Democrat Lindsay Thomas retired to work on the Summer Olympics, Kingston ran for Congress. Against Democrat Barbara Christmas, a school principal, he won decisively—58%–42%, with a 2–1 margin in his home base of Savannah and Chatham County.

In the House Kingston has a mostly conservative voting record and has tended to district interests as well as Democratic congressmen of yore. Opposing the House's five-day work week, he said, "I'm just enough of a populist to believe that the real action is on the streets of America and not in Washington." He has led the Republicans' "theme team," which coordinates the party's national message on the House floor and at home. He parted company with the Republican leadership on trade issues, notably NAFTA, GATT and PNTR for China, and he decries the World Trade Organization. He serves on the Agriculture Subcommittee of Appropriations, where he has used his vote and lobbied his colleagues for district interests. One is sugar. The nation's largest sugar refinery, Savannah Foods, is in the 1st District, and in May 1996 he tried to get a cap of 21 cents a pound on the price of raw sugar, but succumbed to spirited opposition from lawmakers from cane- and sugar beet-producing states. More successful was a Kingston amendment to a spending bill barring requests for FBI files except for those of presidential appointees or regarding clear threats to national security, as attested by the attorney general or White House counsel; this was prompted by the fact that the files of Kingston's top aide were among those found in the Clinton White House.

On other local issues, Kingston has fought for historic preservation and looked after Fort Stewart, with its 25,900 military and civilian employees. As an appropriator, he has brought millions of dollars to improve the water flow of the Savannah River and complete the Sidney Lanier drawbridge in Brunswick, plus $250,000 for dredging the Brunswick harbor; he has pushed for $230 million to dredge the Savannah harbor, despite criticism from environmentalists and from South Carolina port interests. He defended the construction of F-22 fighters, which Lockheed builds in Marietta, when they came under attack from Pentagon critics.

Kingston has been consistently re-elected by better than 2–1 margins. His percentage has dipped slightly in Chatham County, as whites move to subdivisions farther out, but was over 80% in the two adjacent counties. When Senator Paul Coverdell died in July 2000, Kingston gave serious thought to running in the special election; but, like other Georgia House Republicans, he backed out when Democrat Zell Miller agreed to take the seat. His interest in running statewide has remained strong, and in early 2001 Kingston was considered a possible candidate against Senator Max Cleland in 2002.

Cook's Call   *Probably Safe.* Although Kingston has continued to win here by impressive margins, this district is theoretically competitive. With Kingston taking a serious look at running for the Senate, this district could become competitive in 2002, especially if Democrats (who control redistricting in the state) are able to tweak the lines here. Still, this conservative district will not be an easy one for Democrats to win.

THE PEOPLE: Pop. 2000: 692,199; Pop. 1990: 588,541, up 17.6% 1990–2000. 64.4% White, 31.1% Black, 1.1% Asian, 0.3% Amer. Indian, 0.1% Hawaiian, 1.3% Two+ races, 1.7% Other; 3.6% Hispanic Origin.

2000 Presidential Vote			1996 Presidential Vote		
Bush (R)	113,818	(57%)	Dole (R)	87,895	(49%)
Gore (D)	83,837	(42%)	Clinton (D)	81,804	(45%)
Others	1,425	(1%)	Perot (I)	11,491	(6%)

Rep. Jack Kingston (R)

Elected 1992, 5th term; b. Apr. 24, 1955, Bryan, TX; home, Savannah; U. of GA, B.S. 1978; Episcopalian; married (Libby).

Elected Office: GA House of Reps., 1984–92.

Professional Career: Insurance agent, 1979–92.

DC Office: 1034 LHOB 20515, 202-225-5831; Fax: 202-226-2269; Web site: www.house.gov/kingston.

District Offices: Brunswick, 912-265-9010; Savannah, 912-352-0101; Statesboro, 912-489-8797.

Committees: *Appropriations* (17th of 35 R): Agriculture, Rural Development, & FDA; Foreign Operations & Export Financing; Interior.

Group Ratings

	ADA	ACLU	AFS	LCV	CON	ITIC	NTU	COC	ACU	NTLC	CHC
2000	5	15	14	7	69	72	67	80	100	87	100
1999	0	—	0	6	77	—	68	75	95	—	—

National Journal Ratings

	1999 LIB —	1999 CONS		2000 LIB —	2000 CONS
Economic	0% —	84%		0% —	94%
Social	10% —	85%		0% —	79%
Foreign	15% —	81%		12% —	78%

Key Votes of the 106th Congress

1. Patient Bill of Rights	N	5. Bar RU-486 $ for FDA	Y	9. NATO War in Serbia	N
2. Accelerate Min. Wage	N	6. Display 10 Commandments	Y	10. Perm. Trade with China	N
3. Strike Ban on Ergo. Stnd.	N	7. Gun Show Bkgrnd. Checks	N	11. Debt Relief for 3rd World	N
4. Ovrd. Estate Tax Veto	Y	8. Ban Part.-Birth Abortion	Y	12. Drop Cuba Econ. Embargo	N

Election Results

2000 general	Jack Kingston (R)	131,684	(69%)	($652,186)
	Joyce Marie Griggs (D)	58,776	(31%)	($70,119)
2000 primary	Jack Kingston (R)	unopposed		
1998 general	Jack Kingston (R)	unopposed		($232,812)

SECOND DISTRICT

The southwest corner of Georgia, plantation country before the Civil War, still is mostly farmland today: cotton fields, peanut acreage, pecan groves, pine lands. In the south, near the Florida border, is the Plantation Trace area around Thomasville, where rich Northerners have come to shoot quail and ducks in winters since the 1880s—a part of Georgia memorialized in Tom Wolfe's *A Man in Full*. A bit to the north is Albany, the largest city in these parts, with several factories and a civil rights museum and the site of Martin Luther King Jr.'s least successful civil rights protests in the 1960s. Two counties north is the village of Plains, the home since childhood of Jimmy Carter. This is hardscrabble country: As recently as World War II most rural residents lived in clapboard cabins without power or running water, eking a living out of over-tilled soil. Today this remains one of the low-income quarters of America. But rural electrification and then air-conditioning made homes and workplaces comfortable; automobiles and good roads have given people options they never had before (such as outlet malls); racial desegregation has given dignity to all in a way few dreamed possible thirty-some years ago.

This is the land of Georgia's 2d Congressional District. For the 1992 and 1994 elections this was a seat with ragged boundaries designed to make it black-majority; it included black neighborhoods in Columbus, Macon, and Valdosta, as well as Albany and the heavily black counties along the Alabama border. But the Supreme Court overturned the Georgia districting, and the 1995 court-drawn plan had new boundaries along county lines that excluded Columbus and Macon, and reduced the black percentage from 57% to 39%—which increased to 41% in 2000.

The congressman from the 2d District is Sanford Bishop, a Democrat first elected in 1992. Bishop grew up in Mobile, Alabama, where his father was a state college president. He went to Morehouse College in Atlanta, where he was student body president in 1968 and sang at Martin Luther King Jr.'s funeral. He was an award-winning student at Emory Law School, then served in the Army. After a year in New York he settled in Columbus, practiced law, joined the church choir and many civic organizations, and was elected to the state legislature in 1976, at 29. He served there until 1990, when he was elected to the Georgia Senate. There Bishop helped push through an ethics law, a training program for welfare recipients, and established the Commission on Equal Opportunity and the Office of Child Support Receiver. In 1992 he ran for the House against incumbent Charles Hatcher, who gained his greatest public notice when it was revealed he had 819 overdrafts on the House bank. Bishop defeated Hatcher in the runoff 53%–47%, and won the general election 64%–36%.

Bishop describes himself as "a moderate conservative on fiscal issues and a 'traditionalist' on so-called family issues." His style is not confrontational, and his voting record is far more moderate than that of most other black Democrats, including Georgia's John Lewis and Cynthia McKinney. He supported the balanced budget, school prayer, the partial-birth abortion ban, and anti-flag burning amendments. He voted for welfare reform in 1996 and was one of ten Democrats to support Bush's income tax cut in 2001. In his first term he voted for the assault weapons ban, but switched, joined the NRA and started hunting doves. He joined the conservative Blue Dog Democrats. He works to protect local military bases, like the School of the Americas that trains Latin American soldiers at Fort Benning, which was reopened in January and renamed the Western Hemisphere Institute for Security Cooperation.

Bishop serves on the Agriculture Committee and on its Specialty Crops Subcommittee, which has jurisdiction over peanuts and tobacco. In the 1996 farm bill debate, Bishop realized he could not save the old peanut program and fashioned what he calls a "market-oriented, no-net cost" program. Working with 8th District Republican Saxby Chambliss, Bishop lobbied hard to pass it, and it prevailed in the House by three votes; he points out that 23 members of the Congressional Black Caucus voted for it and suggests his work was crucial in getting these votes. He delivered more help to peanut farmers in 2000 when Congress passed a $35 million bailout for their previous year's losses resulting from a surplus harvest. He also visited Cuba to promote new markets for U.S. farm products.

The 1995 redistricting made the seat more difficult to hold: Clinton's 1992 percentage fell from 60% to 49% after the changes. Bishop moved to Albany in 1996 and regularly attends the Big Pig Jig in Vienna and Rattlesnake Roundup in Whigham. In 1998 he attracted two serious Republican challengers: Dylan Glenn, a 29-year-old former Bush White House and Republican National Committee staffer; and Joe McCormick, a white 35-year-old Albany businessman. A native of Columbus who left for the Washington area while in high school, Glenn was urged into the race by Speaker Newt Gingrich, who believed that a black Republican could dip into Bishop's black support, and got primary support from the National Republican Congressional Committee. Turnout in the Republican primary was low, though not so low as what it was in many of these counties 20 years ago (zero). McCormick won 53%–47%, in what seems to have been a friends-and-neighbors rather than racial pattern. But in the pro-incumbent climate Bishop increased his margin in the general and won 57%–43%. He carried 27 of 31 counties and won almost 40% of the white vote.

Glenn ran again in 2000 and was unopposed for the Republican nomination. The unprecedented contest between two African-Americans in a rural, majority-white district was strikingly lacking in racial notes. Instead, Bishop largely ignored the challenger and ran on his record, while Glenn offered the perspective of a new generation focusing on economic growth; at the Republican convention in Philadelphia, MTV followed him around for a "young candidates" special. Interestingly, as a law student, Bishop was friendly with Glenn's mother, when young Dylan was a toddler. But in the election Bishop's help for peanut farmers proved more important than the personal tales. Bishop won 54%–47%, carrying heavily black rural counties by wide margins. But Glenn won the counties containing the fair-sized towns of Valdosta, Thomasville, Moultrie and Tifton, and Lee County just outside Albany, which has a fast-growing white population.

Democratic redistricters will have a chance to make the district safer for Bishop. One way would be to add Columbus's Muscogee County, which voted for Al Gore over George W. Bush, and to subtract several of the counties that Glenn carried—but that could strengthen Republican Saxby Chambliss in the next-door 8th District.

Cook's Call   *Potentially Competitive.* Bishop's 54% showing in 2000 indicates just how competitive (and conservative) this rural southwestern Georgia district really is. Bush won here by 9 %. Bishop has worked hard to make a distinction between himself and the more predictably liberal record of most other members of the Congressional Black Caucus. It is likely that Democrats will shore up this seat for Bishop in redistricting.

THE PEOPLE: Pop. 2000: 650,392; Pop. 1990: 587,583, up 10.7% 1990–2000. 55.9% White, 40.5% Black, 0.6% Asian, 0.3% Amer. Indian, 0.9% Two+ races, 1.8% Other; 3.3% Hispanic Origin.

2000 Presidential Vote			**1996 Presidential Vote**		
Bush (R)	97,749	(54%)	Clinton (D)	82,429	(49%)
Gore (D)	82,086	(45%)	Dole (R)	72,934	(44%)
Others	1,258	(1%)	Perot (I)	11,494	(7%)

Rep. Sanford D. Bishop, Jr. (D)

Elected 1992, 5th term; b. Feb. 4, 1947, Mobile, AL; home, Albany; Morehouse Col., B.A. 1968, Emory U., J.D. 1971; Baptist; divorced.

Military Career: Army, 1970–71.

Elected Office: GA House of Reps., 1976–90; GA Senate, 1990–92.

Professional Career: Practicing atty., 1971–92.

DC Office: 2429 RHOB 20515, 202-225-3631; Fax: 202-225-2203; Web site: www.house.gov/bishop.

District Offices: Albany, 912-439-8067; Dawson, 912-995-3991; Valdosta, 912-247-9705.

Committees: *Agriculture* (8th of 24 D): General Farm Commodities & Risk Management; Specialty Crops & Foreign Agriculture Programs. *Permanent Select Committee on Intelligence* (2d of 9 D): Intelligence Policy & National Security (RMM); Technical & Tactical Intelligence (RMM).

Group Ratings

	ADA	ACLU	AFS	LCV	CON	ITIC	NTU	COC	ACU	NTLC	CHC
2000	50	43	71	36	6	76	36	78	43	33	47
1999	65	—	83	50	18	—	21	56	28	—	—

National Journal Ratings

	1999 LIB	—	1999 CONS		2000 LIB	—	2000 CONS
Economic	59%	—	41%		55%	—	45%
Social	58%	—	40%		58%	—	42%
Foreign	68%	—	30%		53%	—	45%

Key Votes of the 106th Congress

1. Patient Bill of Rights	Y	5. Bar RU-486 $ for FDA	N	9. NATO War in Serbia	Y
2. Accelerate Min. Wage	Y	6. Display 10 Commandments	Y	10. Perm. Trade with China	Y
3. Strike Ban on Ergo. Stnd.	Y	7. Gun Show Bkgrnd. Checks	N	11. Debt Relief for 3rd World	Y
4. Ovrd. Estate Tax Veto	Y	8. Ban Part.-Birth Abortion	Y	12. Drop Cuba Econ. Embargo	Y

Election Results

2000 general	Sanford D. Bishop Jr. (D)	96,430	(54%)	($1,069,838)
	Dylan Glenn (R)	83,870	(47%)	($953,867)
2000 primary	Sanford D. Bishop Jr. (D)	unopposed		
1998 general	Sanford D. Bishop Jr. (D)	77,953	(57%)	($626,373)
	Joe McCormick (R)	59,305	(43%)	($419,229)

THIRD DISTRICT

Running south from Atlanta, within an hour or so by car, you can see the most modern parts of Georgia and some of the most traditional. The modern is Atlanta's Hartsfield International Airport, built by Mayor William Hartsfield on the site of Candler Racetrack eight miles south of Atlanta's Five Points. Hartsfield was the mayor whose moderation on racial issues made Atlanta known as "the city too busy to hate," and whose airport, completely rebuilt in the 1980s, is now the world's busiest, surpassing Chicago O'Hare in 1996. Not far south are the old courthouse towns of Jonesboro and Fayetteville, now surrounded by new suburbs, but both with claims to be the spiritual homes of *Gone With the Wind*; near Jonesboro, where high-school football games have been preceded by prayers in defiance of the Supreme Court ban, is the mansion long owned by Senator (1957–81) Herman Talmadge, which looks a lot like Tara.

Eventually—farther south each year, it seems—the suburbs thin out, and you are in rural Georgia; a county past Sprayberry's Barbecue in booming Newnan is the village of Warm Springs and the faded hotel and pool where Franklin Roosevelt recuperated from polio in the 1920s, and where he died in 1945. Roosevelt liked to look over the wooded hills of Meriwether County, where few dwellings had central heat or indoor plumbing and almost everyone voted Democratic, just as they had since General Sherman marched his troops not too many miles away from Atlanta to the sea. Farther south is another Georgia, the small industrial city of Columbus and next-door Fort Benning, long the home of the Army's Infantry School; it's the place where George Marshall's brilliant talents were first noticed and where he kept his little book on the gifted officers whom he would make generals in World War II, and which now includes the George C. Marshall European Center for Security Studies in Germany, which fosters democratic militaries in former Communist nations.

The 3d Congressional District of Georgia takes in all this territory, starting just south of the airport, passing through suburbs and fields to Columbus. About seven in ten votes here are cast in the Atlanta communities. The Clayton County neighborhoods around Hartsfield are now mostly black and heavily Democratic. Farther out, the new communities are affluent but not dominated by any establishment, liberation-minded in much of their lifestyles but often tradition-minded in their yearnings. Politically, this is conservative country, full of young families moving up who prefer the relatively bucolic culture of the smaller counties. Mostly white, their ancestral politics may be Democratic but their current preferences lean heavily Republican, including for George W. Bush in 2000. The 1995 federal court redistricting removed some rural counties and added Warm Springs and black neighborhoods in Columbus; this increased the black percentage from 18% to 25%—which increased to 31% in 2000—and made the 3d somewhat more Democratic.

The congressman from the 3d is Mac Collins, a switcher to the Republican Party in the 1980s. Collins grew up in Jackson and started his trucking company at age 18, hauling logs for Georgia-Pacific; he is known, a local paper said, for "his lumbering stature and signature boots." He served as a Democrat on the Butts County Commission in the late 1970s, lost in 1980, then convinced the Butts County Republicans to elect him chairman. In 1988, he was elected to the state Senate, where he worked on welfare and ethics reforms and bills to fight drug dealing. In 1992, he ran for Congress in a newly fashioned district. Collins capitalized on a fierce Democratic primary battle between incumbent Congressman Richard Ray and David Worley, who had come close to beating Gingrich in the old 6th District in 1990. Ray won 51%–32%. Collins, like Worley, attacked Ray as an insider; Ray spent $1.1 million, but Collins won 55%–45%.

Collins has a mostly conservative voting record. Hartsfield International Airport was his chief early focus; he pushed for a repeal of the airline fuel tax slated for fall 1995, arguing the levy would cripple the industry, including Georgia-based Delta. He voted to pare spending at almost every opportunity, except for defense and 3d District projects. He made a point of opting out of the congressional pension plan. On Ways and Means since his second term, Collins backed welfare reform, a lower tax on earnings by Social Security recipients, and temporary repeal of the federal gasoline tax. He voted for the Freedom to Farm Act. On trade issues he voted against NAFTA, GATT and PNTR with China. He came out for impeachment and removal of Bill Clinton in September 1998 and suggested the new president should nominate Sam Nunn for vice president. He won House approval in June 2000 to delay EPA enforcement of strict air quality standards until a new President took office (although Bush later upheld the standards). Clinton signed his bill to give families of American victims of friendly fire in Iraq the same compensation that foreign victims received.

Collins has not faced a serious re-election challenge since he was first elected. He has voiced an interest in running against Senator Max Cleland in 2002. Whatever his plans, the 3rd District could be significantly changed in redistricting, which is controlled by Democrats. But there is enough fast-growing conservative territory here to be the basis of a Republican-leaning district.

Cook's Call   *Safe.* Since winning the seat in 1992, Mac Collins has had few re-election concerns, even after the Federal Courts boosted the black percentage in his district from 18% to 25%. Collins, like most of the state's Republican delegation, is taking a look at running for the Senate in 2002. But, as presently configured, this is a solidly Republican district.

THE PEOPLE: Pop. 2000: 781,694; Pop. 1990: 589,718, up 32.6% 1990–2000. 63.8% White, 30.6% Black, 2% Asian, 0.3% Amer. Indian, 0.1% Hawaiian, 1.5% Two + races, 1.7% Other; 4.1% Hispanic Origin.

2000 Presidential Vote

Bush (R) 137,086 (57%)
Gore (D) 100,188 (41%)
Others 4,398 (2%)

1996 Presidential Vote

Dole (R) 104,286 (51%)
Clinton (D) 87,911 (43%)
Perot (I) 13,550 (7%)

Rep. Mac Collins (R)

Elected 1992, 5th term; b. Oct. 15, 1944, Jackson; home, Hampton; Methodist; married (Julie).

Military Career: Army Natl. Guard, 1964–70.

Elected Office: Chmn., Butts Cnty. Commission, 1977–80; GA Senate, 1988–92.

Professional Career: Founder & Pres., Collins Trucking Co., 1962–92; Chmn., Butts Cnty. Repub. Party, 1981–82.

DC Office: 1131 LHOB 20515, 202-225-5901; Fax: 202-225-2515; Web site: www.house.gov/maccollins.

District Offices: Columbus, 706-327-7228; Jonesboro, 770-603-3395; Newnan, 770-304-8812.

Committees: *Budget* (9th of 24 R). *Ways & Means* (13th of 24 R): Social Security.

Group Ratings

	ADA	ACLU	AFS	LCV	CON	ITIC	NTU	COC	ACU	NTLC	CHC
2000	5	7	14	14	82	74	68	76	96	97	87
1999	15	—	0	19	21	—	62	80	92	—	—

National Journal Ratings

	1999 LIB	—	1999 CONS		2000 LIB	—	2000 CONS
Economic	16%	—	78%		6%	—	85%
Social	4%	—	91%		0%	—	79%
Foreign	10%	—	86%		25%	—	69%

Key Votes of the 106th Congress

1. Patient Bill of Rights	N	5. Bar RU-486 $ for FDA	Y	9. NATO War in Serbia	N
2. Accelerate Min. Wage	N	6. Display 10 Commandments	Y	10. Perm. Trade with China	N
3. Strike Ban on Ergo. Stnd.	N	7. Gun Show Bkgrnd. Checks	N	11. Debt Relief for 3rd World	N
4. Ovrd. Estate Tax Veto	Y	8. Ban Part.-Birth Abortion	Y	12. Drop Cuba Econ. Embargo	N

Election Results

2000 general	Mac Collins (R)	150,200	(64%)	($697,766)
	Gail Notti (D)	86,309	(37%)	($131,447)
2000 primary	Mac Collins (R)	39,153	(89%)	
	Herb Galloway (R)	4,744	(11%)	
1998 general	Mac Collins (R) .... unopposed			($335,801)

FOURTH DISTRICT

In 1920, when Gutzom Borglum began sculpting Jefferson Davis, Robert E. Lee and Stonewall Jackson into the side of Stone Mountain, the huge outcropping of granite was a day's drive into the country from central Atlanta. Even when the memorial (the largest single piece of sculpture in the world) was completed in 1972, suburban development barely reached this far. But today, after two decades of some of the most explosive metropolitan growth in the country, DeKalb County, which Stone Mountain overlooks, is part of the core of the Atlanta metropolitan area, and this monument to the Confederacy sits in one of the most cosmopolitan and liberal constituencies in the South. Not far from Stone Mountain is Emory University, just beyond the old mansions of Druid Hills. A few miles away are the Centers for Disease Control and Prevention, one of the federal government's superb research institutions. All around in north DeKalb County are affluent suburbs, including much of Atlanta's Jewish community, with voting habits somewhat more liberal than other suburbs. Also, southern DeKalb is being transformed from mostly rural territory 25 years ago to one of the nation's largest collections of affluent black neighborhoods, rivaled only by Prince George's County, Maryland. This has pushed DeKalb County's politics well to the left: It was a Republican county when rural Georgia was almost all Democratic in the 1960s, now it is the most heavily Democratic major county in Georgia, considerably more so than next-door Fulton County which includes central Atlanta; in 2000 Dekalb voted 71%–27% for Al Gore, his best percentage except for one tiny rural county in all the 159 counties of Georgia.

The 4th Congressional District of Georgia consists of almost all of DeKalb County plus a small slice of the more Republican Gwinnett County to the northeast. It is the product of the 1995 redistricting, in which a federal court, enforcing a Supreme Court decision, reduced the number of black-majority districts in Georgia from three to one. This also produced some nimble district-hopping. Cynthia McKinney, elected in 1992 and 1994 from the old black-majority 11th District, which stretched from DeKalb County all the way to Savannah, decided to run here: South DeKalb is her political base. And Republican John Linder, who represented much of DeKalb in the old 4th District, moved to Gwinnett County to run in the new 11th District that stretches to the South Carolina border.

Cynthia McKinney grew up in Atlanta, just long enough ago to remember many great events of the civil rights revolution; she recalls riding on her father's shoulders as a child in civil rights marches. Her father, Billy McKinney, was one of the first blacks on the Atlanta police force and was elected to the legislature in 1973. Cynthia McKinney went to college in California, taught at Spelman College, Clark Atlanta University, and Agnes Scott College, and is a doctoral candidate in international relations at the Fletcher School at Tufts University. In 1988 she was elected to the Georgia House and became part of the country's only father-daughter legislative team. She got a seat on the legislature's 1991 redistricting committee and worked long and hard to craft the new black-majority districts. In 1992 she ran in the 11th, one of those districts. With her south DeKalb base, she led the Democratic primary with 31%, then won the runoff with 56%.

McKinney has a very liberal voting record and a confrontation-prone temperament not afraid to ruffle feathers. "I'm attracted to fights," she said as she insisted on wearing pants on the floor of the House. She complained loudly when White House guards in 1996 and again in 1998 did not recognize her or treat her like other members of Congress: "I am absolutely sick and tired of having to have my appearance at the White House validated by white people." In 1998, she defended Jane Fonda after Fonda apologized to Governor Zell Miller for comparing parts of Georgia to starving Third World nations. Later that year, McKinney harshly criticized Bill Clinton: "His reckless behavior with Monica Lewinsky has brought us to the brink of a constitutional crisis. His lost credibility means he is no help to me raising my son, his leadership is missing in action on Capitol Hill, he has shattered the confidence of too many people in my district." During the 2000 campaign, following a complaint by black Secret Service agents, her office issued a statement attacking Al Gore's low "Negro tolerance level" and accused him of rarely having more than one black agent with him. Not until a week later, with Gore in Atlanta, did she state that the release was not intended for public distribution.

McKinney has spent much time and effort on Africa, which she has called "the forgotten and ignored continent." She has called for respect for human rights and has hailed new African leaders who are willing to allow the private sector to get involved in economic development. She supported Laurent Kabila's attempts to overthrow the Mobutu dictatorship in what is now Congo, but later called for investigation of the Kabila government's human rights abuses. She described IMF agreements as a "cruel hoax," because they require countries to spend money on repayment of loans they can never pay off rather than on health care and education. On some of these issues, she has cooperated with conservative House Republicans, with the unpredictability adding credibility. With Dana Rohrabacher, she has sponsored legislation to cancel IMF debts of the poorest nations owed to the United States. With Chris Smith, she has written a State Department authorization bill, including her code of conduct for permissible U.S. arms sales to other nations.

As late as 1998 McKinney was still expressing resentment for the 1995 Supreme Court decision calling her old 11th District a "racial gerrymander," and the court-drawn plan which constructed her current district. The new 4th District was only 33% black (compared to 60% in the old 11th) in 1990, but since then many middle-income blacks moved into DeKalb from Atlanta and the district was 50% black in 2000, while whites in the area have proved entirely open to voting for a black candidate. In the 1996 election, Republican John Mitnick attacked McKinney for opposing school vouchers while sending her son to the elite Paideia school, for attending a 1995 panel discussion at Howard University with Louis Farrakhan, and then for voting against a resolution to condemn him. When Billy McKinney called Mitnick "a racist Jew," she asked him to apologize publicly—"he's my dad and I love him, but I am with him when he's right and I tell him when he's wrong"—and he withdrew from her campaign. McKinney won 58%–42%, carrying south DeKalb overwhelmingly and running well in north DeKalb. McKinney argued that her victory was the result of incumbency, that she could not have won an initial election in such a district. Not, perhaps, if she had run the identical campaign she had in 1992, when she pitched her appeal entirely to black voters; but if she had taken the more moderate tone of her 1996 ads she might well have won then within the lines of the current district.

In 1998 and 2000, McKinney was opposed by black Republican businesswoman Sunny Warren. Years earlier, McKinney had told *USA Today*, "My impression of modern-day black Republicans is they have to pass a litmus test in which all black blood is extracted." Warren campaigned in red power suits and showed an attitude different from McKinney's: "I've broken all the barriers, and I'm still a black female doing it. The barriers have come down because I haven't made that an issue." Interestingly, the two candidates never shared the same stage, nor even met during their campaigns. Each time, McKinney lost some white precincts in north DeKalb, but won the district 61%–39%, a solid margin but not as large as Gore's. Since McKinney has shown she can win this district handily, its lines may not be much changed for 2002.

Cook's Call   *Safe.* Though 1996 redistricting slashed the black population almost in half, this district is still pretty safe for Democrats and McKinney. McKinney is nowhere near the ideological 50-yard line for this district but Republicans have not yet been successful in taking advantage of that fact. McKinney seems pretty well solidified here.

THE PEOPLE: Pop. 2000: 744,717; Pop. 1990: 589,431, up 26.3% 1990–2000. 37.7% White, 49.5% Black, 5.3% Asian, 0.3% Amer. Indian, 0.1% Hawaiian, 2.3% Two+ races, 4.8% Other; 11% Hispanic Origin.

2000 Presidential Vote			1996 Presidential Vote		
Gore (D)	148,795	(70%)	Clinton (D)	141,078	(64%)
Bush (R)	60,063	(28%)	Dole (R)	69,912	(32%)
Others	5,005	(2%)	Perot (I)	8,014	(4%)

Rep. Cynthia McKinney (D)

Elected 1992, 5th term; b. Mar. 17, 1955, Atlanta; home, Lithonia; U. of S. CA, B.A. 1978; Catholic; divorced.

Elected Office: GA House of Reps., 1988–92.

Professional Career: Diplomatic Fellow, Spelman Col., 1984; Atlanta Bd. of Health Svcs. Plng. Cncl., 1990–92; Adjunct Prof., Agnes Scott Women's Col., 1991–92.

DC Office: 124 CHOB 20515, 202-225-1605; Fax: 202-226-0691; Web site: www.house.gov/mckinney.

District Office: Decatur, 404-377-6900.

Committees: *Armed Services* (19th of 28 D): Military Personnel; Military Procurement. *International Relations* (8th of 23 D): International Operations and Human Rights (RMM).

Group Ratings

	ADA	ACLU	AFS	LCV	CON	ITIC	NTU	COC	ACU	NTLC	CHC
2000	95	86	100	100	65	42	40	23	12	37	7
1999	95	—	100	94	44	—	28	8	8	—	—

National Journal Ratings

	1999 LIB	—	1999 CONS		2000 LIB	—	2000 CONS
Economic	88%	—	0%		73%	—	26%
Social	83%	—	13%		79%	—	17%
Foreign	53%	—	47%		85%	—	15%

Key Votes of the 106th Congress

1. Patient Bill of Rights	Y	5. Bar RU-486 $ for FDA	N	9. NATO War in Serbia	N
2. Accelerate Min. Wage	Y	6. Display 10 Commandments	N	10. Perm. Trade with China	N
3. Strike Ban on Ergo. Stnd.	Y	7. Gun Show Bkgrnd. Checks	Y	11. Debt Relief for 3rd World	Y
4. Ovrd. Estate Tax Veto	N	8. Ban Part.-Birth Abortion	N	12. Drop Cuba Econ. Embargo	Y

Election Results

2000 general	Cynthia McKinney (D)	139,579	(61%)	($410,270)
	Sunny Warren (R)	90,277	(39%)	($302,012)
2000 primary	Cynthia McKinney (D)	unopposed		
1998 general	Cynthia McKinney (D)	100,622	(61%)	($414,368)
	Sunny Warren (R)	64,146	(39%)	($160,593)

FIFTH DISTRICT

Venture out of the quiet of the Ebenezer Baptist Church or the shade of Martin Luther King Jr.'s boyhood home two blocks away and into the steamy heat of the sun on Auburn Avenue—Sweet Auburn—and you can see, a mile away, downtown Atlanta's atrium-skyscrapers towering in their glory. They are evidence of the wealth and vibrant growth of the commercial capital of the South, the metropolis that has grown up where there was little more than a railroad junction at the time of the War Between the States. But the awesome achievement that is downtown Atlanta is over-shadowed by the revolution made in very large part by a man who grew up on Auburn Avenue, where people who never felt air-conditioning moved slowly in the sweltering heat, and around Morehouse and Spelman colleges, where proud professionals struggled and worked hard and raised their families. Atlanta's white establishment, led by Mayors William Hartsfield and Ivan Allen and Coca-Cola's Robert Woodruff, deserve credit for abandoning segregation, but it was King and other civil rights leaders who took the risks that led them to do so. Atlanta's city fathers acted out of good will, but also with an eye for the economic growth of their city, which they knew would be hurt by violent resistance.

Yet, sadly, not all is entirely well in Atlanta. Downtown Atlanta's primacy in office buildings is being eclipsed by north-side edge cities in Buckhead and along I-285. Many of Atlanta's black neighborhoods today have been abandoned by families who have headed to subdivisions in DeKalb County, leaving the central city with vacant housing and street crime. Mayor Bill Campbell raised eyebrows in September 2000 when he compared the FBI to "the KGB in Communist Russia" for investigating alleged corruption at City Hall, and the city and county government have been sued for their generous racial-setaside programs which allot 34% of contracts to minority-controlled firms, even as Coca-Cola agreed to a $192 million settlement in a lawsuit claiming racial segre-gation. But Atlanta also has its glories: the headquarters of world-girdling Coca-Cola and CNN, the gigantic Hartsfield International Airport, the modern Martin Luther King Jr. Center that depicts the triumphs of the civil rights movement, the Jimmy Carter Presidential Center, the antique Cyclorama that shows Atlanta burning during the Civil War, and the stadiums and sports facilities built for the 1996 Summer Olympics.

The 5th Congressional District of Georgia includes most of Atlanta and a few suburbs, from posh Buckhead and Sandy Springs in the north to middle-class and increasingly black East Point in the south, plus rural southwest Fulton County and a black neighborhood around the airport in Clayton County. The district was 62% black in 1990 and 63% so in 2000 despite the migration of middle-class blacks outward to DeKalb County and growth in heavily white Buckhead.

The congressman from the 5th District is John Lewis, who made history a generation ago as a hero of the civil rights movement, as he recounts in his 1998 autobiography, *Walking With the Wind*. A sharecropper's son from Troy, Alabama, he was seized by religious fervor as a child, preaching in the barnyard, determined to be a minister. Lewis was the first in his family to finish high school; he wrote to Ralph Abernathy for help in suing for the right to enter Troy State College; he met Martin Luther King Jr. when he was 18. In 1959, at 19, he helped organize the first lunch-counter sit-in, which was received with open hostility hard to imagine today. In 1960, the day after John Kennedy was elected, Lewis sat in the Krystal Diner in Nashville while a waitress poured cleansing powder down his back and water over his food; he went to talk to the manager, who turned a fumigating machine on him. In May 1961, he was on the first of the Freedom Rides, riding buses as they were attacked and burned; he was viciously beaten in Rock Hill, South Carolina and Montgomery, Alabama. He spoke at the 1963 March on Washington, criticizing Kennedy liberals for inaction on civil rights and calling for massive help for the poor. In 1964, he helped coordinate the Mississippi Freedom Project. In 1965, he led the Selma-to-Montgomery march to petition for voting rights and was beaten by policemen who fractured his skull. Modestly, quietly, maintaining his poise and good judgment under harsh circumstances, Lewis was one of the people who risked their lives many times to make the civil rights revolution happen. He worked for Robert Kennedy for president in 1968, and was with him in Indianapolis when they heard King was killed, and in Los Angeles just before Kennedy himself was shot.

Lewis's first foray into electoral politics was unsuccessful: He ran in 1977 to replace Andrew Young in the House and was soundly beaten by Wyche Fowler (but ran ahead of Republican Paul Coverdell, who beat Fowler in the 1992 Senate election). After winning a seat on the Atlanta Council in 1981, Lewis ran for Congress in 1986, and trailed Julian Bond 47%–35% in the primary. But even though Bond won more than 60% of the black vote, Lewis won the runoff by assembling a coalition of poor blacks and affluent whites: "Vote for the tugboat, not the showboat" was his slogan, stressing his hard work on local issues. He has been re-elected easily since.

Lewis has been a strong partisan, with one of the most liberal voting records in the House, and an impassioned supporter of Bill Clinton on issues and amid scandal. Usually quiet, he can speak in the cadences of black preachers, as he did on the Gulf war resolution in January 1991 and impeachment in November 1998. He is one of the Democrats' four chief deputy whips, an integral part of the leadership, and has a seat on Ways and Means. Only occasionally does he defect from his party, as when he opposed the 1994 crime bill because of his disapproval of capital punishment. He furiously voiced his disappointment when Republicans captured the House in 1994. Lewis argued passionately against the Republican welfare bills: "They're coming for the children. They're coming for the poor. They're coming for the sick, the elderly and the disabled"— implicitly comparing the Republicans to Nazis by paraphrasing an anti-Nazi German theologian against them.

Lewis has worked to commemorate the civil rights revolution in which he played such a large part. He got a federal building in Atlanta named for Martin Luther King Jr. and got the route from Selma to Montgomery designated a National Historic Trail. His vision remains clear: "You can have an integrated society without losing diversity. But you can also have a society that transcends race, where you can lay down the burden of race . . . and treat people as human beings, regardless of the color of their skin." He has said affirmative action should move from race to class as a criterion, but he has stoutly defended racial quotas and preferences and opposed school vouchers for low-income children in Washington, D.C. With Republican J. C. Watts, he sponsored a bill to honor the slaves who helped construct the Capitol and the White House. He passed a Minority Health and Health Disparities Research and Education Act, setting up a research center at the National Institutes of Health. He spotlighted what he thought was racial profiling in Customs searches. He sponsored a bill to exempt from tax an employer's gift of computers or Internet access (Delta had such a program) and he helped secure $52 million for the MARTA extension to North Springs.

In August 1999, Lewis declared that he was running for majority whip should Democrats win a House majority; Nancy Pelosi and Steny Hoyer had already started lining up support. But not all Congressional Black Caucus members supported him (Cynthia McKinney, of the next-door 4th district, backed Pelosi), and Lewis left the race (which turned out to be academic) in July 2000. At the same time he said he would "gladly" accept appointment to the Senate seat vacated by the death of Republican Paul Coverdell, but Governor Roy Barnes appointed former Governor Zell Miller instead. Lewis supported Al Gore for president in 1999, and noted that the Georgia primary would be held on the 35th anniversary of the Selma march. At the Los Angeles Democratic National Convention, Lewis took to the podium to give testimony for vice presidential nominee Joseph Lieberman, who was suspect by some blacks for having voiced doubts about racial quotas and preferences: "From my lips to God's ears. That is a Yiddish expression of hope that came to my mind when I heard that Al Gore chose Joe Lieberman as his running mate. From our lips to God's ears, I believe and I know that America is ready for Joe Lieberman and Joe Lieberman is ready for America. This man, our next vice president, has dedicated his life toward the building of a truly interracial democracy."

Lewis was re-elected by a wide margin in 2000, and it is unlikely that the Democratic redistricters will fail to create an Atlanta-based district from which he can be re-elected for another decade.

Cook's Call   *Safe*. To say that John Lewis is safe is an understatement. Since first winning this seat in 1986 with 75%, Lewis has consistently won with 70% or more, only once dipping to 69%.

THE PEOPLE: Pop. 2000: 646,184; Pop. 1990: 589,380, up 9.6% 1990–2000. 31.1% White, 62.9% Black, 2.1% Asian, 0.2% Amer. Indian, 1.4% Two+ races, 2.3% Other; 5.2% Hispanic Origin.

2000 Presidential Vote

Gore (D)	147,164	(74%)
Bush (R)	48,546	(24%)
Others	3,334	(2%)

1996 Presidential Vote

Clinton (D)	134,597	(74%)
Dole (R)	41,346	(23%)
Perot (I)	4,980	(3%)

Rep. John Lewis (D)

Elected 1986, 8th term; b. Feb. 21, 1940, Troy, AL; home, Atlanta; Amer. Baptist Theol. Seminary, B.A. 1961, Fisk U., B.A. 1963; Baptist; married (Lillian).

Elected Office: Atlanta City Cncl., 1981–86.

Professional Career: Chmn., Student Nonviolent Coord. Cmte., 1963–66; Field Foundation, 1966–67; Community Organization Dir., Southern Regional Cncl., 1967–70; Exec. Dir., Voter Educ. Project, 1970–76; Assoc. Dir., ACTION, 1977–80; Community Affairs Dir., Natl. Coop. Bank, 1980–82.

DC Office: 343 CHOB 20515, 202-225-3801; Fax: 202-225-0351; Web site: www.house.gov/johnlewis.

District Office: Atlanta, 404-659-0116.

Committees: *Chief Deputy Minority Whip. Ways & Means* (9th of 17 D): Health; Oversight.

Group Ratings

	ADA	ACLU	AFS	LCV	CON	ITIC	NTU	COC	ACU	NTLC	CHC
2000	95	86	100	93	66	53	24	42	4	15	0
1999	95	—	100	94	84	—	21	9	0	—	—

National Journal Ratings

	1999 LIB —	1999 CONS		2000 LIB —	2000 CONS
Economic	88% —	0%		95% —	0%
Social	87% —	0%		90% —	10%
Foreign	95% —	0%		91% —	9%

Key Votes of the 106th Congress

1. Patient Bill of Rights	Y	5. Bar RU-486 $ for FDA	N	9. NATO War in Serbia	Y
2. Accelerate Min. Wage	Y	6. Display 10 Commandments	N	10. Perm. Trade with China	N
3. Strike Ban on Ergo. Stnd.	Y	7. Gun Show Bkgrnd. Checks	Y	11. Debt Relief for 3rd World	Y
4. Ovrd. Estate Tax Veto	N	8. Ban Part.-Birth Abortion	N	12. Drop Cuba Econ. Embargo	Y

Election Results

2000 general	John Lewis (D)	137,333	(77%)	($811,850)
	Hank Schwab (R)	40,606	(23%)	($25,836)
2000 primary	John Lewis (D)	unopposed		
1998 general	John Lewis (D)	109,177	(79%)	($307,440)
	John H. Lewis Sr. (R)	29,877	(21%)	($11,938)

SIXTH DISTRICT

In the red clay hills north of Atlanta, over the last three decades an almost wholly new metropolitan quarter has grown up as affluent Atlanta has spread out from Ansley Park, just north of downtown, and the rolling hills of Buckhead, within the city limit, past the I-285 Perimeter into territory that was once just farms, small towns and little factory cities. Where there were perhaps 100,000 people in the 1950s, there are more than 1 million today. No longer is downtown Atlanta the only focus: The edge cities of Buckhead, Perimeter Center and the area near Cumberland Mall are now not just shopping but major office centers, rivaling downtown Atlanta in square footage. Cobb County around Marietta is the headquarters of Home Depot and the Weather Channel; Dunwoody in northern DeKalb County is the home of Holiday Inn. Yet physically this Golden Crescent north of the Perimeter and between I-75 in Cobb County and I-85 in Gwinnett County seems not to have changed greatly: The buildings are tree-shaded and lush foliage and large-lot requirements have given most of the communities a woodsy look.

The 6th Congressional District of Georgia occupies a large portion of this Golden Crescent north of Atlanta, including most of Cobb County, Fulton County north of the Perimeter, and to the east a chunk of Gwinnett County. This was a newly created seat in 1992, the seat Georgia gained in the 1990 Census, in recognition of how much the affluent suburban ring around Atlanta has contributed to the state's growth. It would surely surprise Georgians a generation or two ago to learn that one of their congressional districts would rank among the nation's richest and most educated. It is easily the most Republican district in Georgia, and by some measures one of the most heavily Republican districts in the country. But another change recently has taken place. What not so long ago was a local Republican majority dominated by religious conservatives has lately become more socially moderate and focused on conventional suburban concerns such as managing sprawl and improving education.

The congressman from the 6th District is Republican Johnny Isakson, who won a 1999 special election to replace Newt Gingrich, who had resigned as the 50th speaker of the House. A real estate agent, Isakson became president of Sandy Springs-based Northside Realty in 1979. He was elected to the Georgia House in 1976, serving as Republican leader from 1983 until 1990, when he lost the gubernatorial election to Zell Miller, 53%–45%. In the state House, Isakson authored and passed legislation on growth policy and regional planning, major issues in the sprawling Atlanta metro region. He was elected to the state Senate in 1993, serving until 1996, when he sought to challenge Democratic Senator Max Cleland. But Isakson had tough competition from Guy Millner, the millionaire founder of the Norrell temporary employee firm and Clint Day of the Days Inn family, and the race was overshadowed by the Summer Olympics. Millner won the primary with 42%, compared to 35% for Isakson and 19% for Day, and carried the runoff against Isakson 53%–47%. That December, Governor Miller appointed Isakson chairman of the state Board of Education.

Gingrich's story, now well known, shows how in our politics one can come from obscurity and, with insight and effort and not a little luck, make an enormous difference. But he also aroused furious opposition. In November 1998, after Republicans lost five House seats rather than—as everyone expected—gained a few, backbencher Matt Salmon said that he and five other Republicans would not vote for Gingrich for speaker. On Friday, November 6, Gingrich announced he would stand down and resign from the House. The only suspense in the six-candidate, nonpartisan special election was whether Gingrich's handpicked successor—the moderate, pro-choice Isakson—would win with a majority and thus avoid a runoff. Isakson was by far the best-known, most experienced and best-financed candidate in the February 23 special election. The one Democrat was attorney Gary "Bats" Pelphrey, who had lost to Gingrich in November 1998, 71%–29%. The only other candidate with significant name recognition was Kennesaw State University professor Christina Jeffrey, whom Gingrich hired and then dismissed as House historian in 1995 after Democrats attacked her criticism of a high school Holocaust course for not describing the views of the Nazis. Jeffrey ran as a conservative, pro-life alternative to Isakson, who embraced much of the Republican leadership's economic agenda while playing down his moderate stands on social issues. But no one could compete with the $1 million Isakson had raised and the additional $500,000 he contributed of his own money, which allowed him to maintain a steady advertising presence for weeks. Isakson avoided a runoff, winning 65% of the vote and carrying all four counties; Jeffrey finished second with 25%, Pelphrey third with 5%.

Isakson won a seat on the Transportation Committee, where he helped push for a rapid-transit line for the overburdened Georgia 400 corridor on the north side. He complained to Cobb County businessmen when state legislators passed a bill requiring only biennial automobile emissions testing, rather than the annual testing to be required under a federal agreement with Atlanta area officials. Isakson also gained a seat on the Education Committee, where chairman Bill Goodling named him to the Web-Based Education Commission to examine education technology issues. When Bill Clinton pushed Congress to fund 100,000 new teachers, Isakson objected on the ground that there wasn't a large enough supply of available teachers even with the money, and he got Republican leaders to change the initiative to a block grant allowing the states discretion in how they hire instructors. Unlike his more-conservative Georgia Republican House colleagues, he has called for safety locks on handguns and supported the federal ban on assault weapons. Serving as a link between speakers, he became friendly with Gingrich's successor Denny Hastert, getting an invitation to the speaker's delegation visiting the Pacific Rim.

Isakson was easily re-elected in 2000. He was mentioned as a possible candidate for senator or governor in 2002, but in March 2001 said it would be "irresponsible" of him to consider a statewide race while trying to pass the President's education proposal. Democratic redistricters will probably change the district lines in the fast-growing northern suburbs, but there will still be a heavily Republican district here, or rather two, for the 2000 Census showed that the 6th now has more than 940,000 people, nearly enough for two districts.

Cook's Call   *Safe.* Since being elected in a 1999, Isakson has never had to break a sweat to hold onto this quintessentially Republican district. Heavy growth in Republican leaning Cobb and Gwinnett Counties means that one of the state's two new seats will likely be located in this area. Isakson is a sure bet for 2002.

THE PEOPLE: Pop. 2000: 943,373; Pop. 1990: 589,018, up 60.2% 1990–2000. 79.6% White, 10.9% Black, 4.7% Asian, 0.2% Amer. Indian, 1.8% Two+ races, 2.8% Other; 6.6% Hispanic Origin.

2000 Presidential Vote			1996 Presidential Vote		
Bush (R)	221,268	(65%)	Dole (R)	186,084	(62%)
Gore (D)	110,329	(32%)	Clinton (D)	100,714	(33%)
Others	9,072	(3%)	Perot (I)	15,416	(5%)

Rep. Johnny Isakson (R)

Elected Feb. 1999, 1st term; b. Dec. 28, 1944, Atlanta; home, Marietta; U. of GA, B.B.A. 1966; Methodist; married (Dianne).

Military Career: GA Air Natl. Guard, 1966–72.

Elected Office: GA House of Reps., 1976–90, Repub. Ldr., 1983–90; GA gubernatorial candidate, 1990; GA Senate, 1993–96; U.S. Senate candidate, 1996.

Professional Career: Northside Realty, 1967–99, Pres., 1979–99; Co-chair, Dole GA presidential campaign, 1988, 1996; Chmn., GA Board of Ed., 1997.

DC Office: 132 CHOB 20515, 202-225-4501; Fax: 202-225-4656; Web site: www.house.gov/isakson.

District Office: Atlanta, 404-252-5239.

Committees: *Education & the Workforce* (20th of 27 R): 21st Century Competitiveness (Vice Chmn.); Workforce Protections. *Transportation & Infrastructure* (25th of 42 R): Aviation; Highways & Transit.

Group Ratings

	ADA	ACLU	AFS	LCV	CON	ITIC	NTU	COC	ACU	NTLC	CHC
2000	5	15	0	14	27	100	57	85	72	76	80
1999	10	—	0	18	6	—	56	91	66	—	—

National Journal Ratings

	1999 LIB	—	1999 CONS		2000 LIB	—	2000 CONS
Economic	0%	—	84%		18%	—	76%
Social	47%	—	53%		46%	—	53%
Foreign	35%	—	64%		12%	—	78%

Key Votes of the 106th Congress

1. Patient Bill of Rights	N	5. Bar RU-486 $ for FDA	N	9. NATO War in Serbia	N
2. Accelerate Min. Wage	N	6. Display 10 Commandments	Y	10. Perm. Trade with China	Y
3. Strike Ban on Ergo. Stnd.	N	7. Gun Show Bkgrnd. Checks	N	11. Debt Relief for 3rd World	N
4. Ovrd. Estate Tax Veto	Y	8. Ban Part.-Birth Abortion	Y	12. Drop Cuba Econ. Embargo	N

Election Results

2000 general	Johnny Isakson (R)	256,595	(75%)	($1,601,856)
	Brett DeHart (D)	86,666	(25%)	($35,168)
2000 primary	Johnny Isakson (R)	unopposed		
1999 special	Johnny Isakson (R)	51,548	(65%)	($912,413)
	Christina Jeffrey (R)	20,115	(25%)	($215,736)
	Gary (Bats) Pelphrey (D)	4,014	(5%)	
	Others	3,536	(4%)	
1998 general	Newt Gingrich (R)	164,966	(71%)	($7,578,716)
	Gary (Bats) Pelphrey (D)	68,366	(29%)	($11,232)

SEVENTH DISTRICT

North Georgia, home of the Cherokee Nation before they were sent west in the 1830s on the Trail of Tears, has been manufacturing country for the last century. There are hundreds of textile mills and dozens of carpet mills located near the supply of natural cotton and along the railroad lines heading southwest at the base of the southern Appalachian chain. Factories were hailed as the vanguard of technological progress by the late 19th Century propagandists of the New South, and in fact the factories produced a higher standard of living than farms on this stubborn land. But mill work put scant premium on education or the cultivation of civic virtues and did little to bring in higher-skill white-collar work. All-white hiring practices maintained racial segregation in mostly white north Georgia. Today, north Georgia is developing a different kind of economy, as the example of Atlanta spreads out over highways north into what used to be mill towns. Cobb County, once centered on the Lockheed aircraft factory in Marietta, has been transformed into an upscale suburb and office center; places like the textile mill town of LaGrange or the carpet mill town of Rome are seeing change as well, as Latino immigrants have become a major part of the mill work force.

The 7th Congressional District includes much of this part of north Georgia. It extends along the state's western boundary from LaGrange to Rome, east to Cartersville, where U.S. 41 starts its four-lane roll toward Atlanta, and takes in a somewhat downscale part of western Cobb County, including the old center of Marietta. This was Democratic territory from the time of General Jackson and General Sherman until the civil rights revolution of the 1960s. In the 1970s, Carrollton, in the western part of the 7th, was the home of a West Georgia College professor who, in his third try, became a Republican congressman: Newt Gingrich.

The congressman from the 7th is Bob Barr, a Republican elected in 1994 who almost immediately became prominent on national issues. Like most members of the Georgia delegation, Barr grew up elsewhere; his father was in the Army and he went to high school in Tehran and college at the University of Southern California. In the 1970s he worked as a CIA analyst while he went to Georgetown law school. In 1978 he left the agency and moved to Georgia to practice law; in 1986 he became U.S. attorney in Atlanta, a high-profile job. Yet for all his successes he remains humorless, pessimistic, sarcastic, to the point that his wife beeps him when he is on TV, "Smile, honey." He says he has no close friends on Capitol Hill and usually sleeps in his office.

In 1992 Barr ran for the Senate and lost the Republican runoff to Paul Coverdell by 1,548 votes, 50.5%–49.5%. Undaunted, he ran for the House in 1994. In the general election he faced incumbent Buddy Darden, a Democrat with a mixed voting record in a Republican-leaning district. Barr's campaign gave out t-shirts showing Darden jogging with Bill Clinton, and he attacked Darden's votes for the Clinton tax hike and crime bill. Darden replied that he opposed the Clinton health care plan and favored the balanced budget amendment, but he could not deny he was a Clinton supporter. Barr won 52%–48%.

Barr has a strongly conservative voting record. He is a stern opponent of gun control and proponent of family values, though he is not a gun enthusiast and has been divorced twice. In his first term, while ranking 20th of 20 Republicans on Judiciary, he played a lead role on three national issues. On the anti-terrorism bill sought after the Oklahoma City bombing, he led a House fight to amend the committee bill and stitched together a coalition of conservative Republicans angry at government misconduct at Waco and Ruby Ridge and liberal Democrats long opposed to government infringements of civil liberties. The amendment passed 246–171, with support from most Republicans and about one-third of Democrats. Two months later he introduced the Defense of Marriage Act, allowing states to refuse to recognize same-sex marriages and to define marriage for federal benefit purposes as the legal union of one man and one woman. This was a response to the Hawaii court case that threatened to legalize same-sex marriages there, which ordinarily would cause them to be honored in every state by the Constitution's full faith and credit clause. The bill passed overwhelmingly and a reluctant but reelection-minded Bill Clinton signed it in the dark of night in September 1996. Barr's third accomplishment was sponsoring repeal of the assault weapons ban, which passed the House 239–173, but never came to a Senate vote.

Barr's ardent conservatism occasionally produces alliance with the ACLU. "It's really come to the point of no return with government taking so much power," he said. "I really have a tremendous fear of government taking away our freedoms." He opposes a national identification card and unique health identifiers and won a one-year delay of a federal rule encouraging states to use Social Security numbers on drivers' licenses. He sees great dangers in giving the government access to burgeoning databases and would force private employers to tell their employees if their computer use or phone calls are monitored or their email is scanned. He opposed a bill to provide every welfare recipient with a debit card so the government can track expenditures. He objected to a legislative deal—signed by Clinton—that criminalized all "properly classified" government information, predicting that it would have a chilling effect on speech and would create an "official secrets act." On local issues, he criticized Atlanta Mayor Bill Campbell for not obeying a decree to stop illegal discharges in the Chattahoochee River, which runs through the 7th District. He also has tried to stop barge traffic on the Chattahoochee because of the huge amount of lake water needed to keep them afloat.

But what Barr is best known for is, of course, impeachment. Back in May 1997 he asked Independent Counsel Kenneth Starr to give the House Judiciary Committee any evidence that might be grounds to impeach Clinton. In November 1997, before Monica Lewinsky had been summoned as a witness in the Paula Jones case, he and 17 other members filed an inquiry of impeachment. "I care about the rule of law," he said, a theme he would repeat many times. In December 1998 Barr made his presentation to the House. "Anyone not possessing an infinite capacity for self-delusion knows," he said, "that the president perjured himself on multiple occasions and committed other acts of obstruction of justice." That month, it was revealed he had spoken six months before to the Council of Conservative Citizens, a group with racist material on its Web site. Barr replied, "If I were aware white supremacists' views occupied any place in the Council's philosophy, I would never have agreed to speak." In January 1999 he made his presentation to the Senate—and seemed dour and understandably pessimistic about the result. Two years later he would request an investigation of reports that Clinton staffers vandalized the White House on their way out, although it found no evidence of destruction.

Not surprisingly, impeachment placed Barr high on the Democrats target list. As he said, "I suspect that there are a lot of Democrats who hate me, and I don't think it's just a mild dislike." And his 55%–45% victory against a poorly funded challenger in 1998 gave them hope. They recruited Roger Kahn, the former vice chairman of the Georgia state elections board and a millionaire businessman in liquor wholesaling and radio broadcasting. Kahn had retired to Florida but, Barr said, returned to run against him, even though he no longer had local ties. Kahn, who said that impeachment was not an issue because he agreed with Barr on Clinton, spent at least $2.9 million of his own money on the race, highlighting Barr's personal failings and his inattention to local jobs. Barr responded by softening his image—reading with local school children and using humor in his campaign ads. Kahn proved to be not so skillful as Democrats had hoped in identifying with local voters and he probably suffered some from Al Gore's weak showing in the district. Barr trailed consistently behind George W. Bush, but he won every county except his portion of Cobb County, which is also the base of Democratic Governor Roy Barnes and to which many black Atlantans have been moving. Overall he won by the same 55%–45% margin by which he beat his 1998 challenger, who spent 0.5% as much money.

Barr will likely be one of the prime targets of the Democrats who control redistricting. They may create a district based on Democratic-trending Cobb County, perhaps with enough black Atlanta precincts to tilt it heavily toward Democrats. But their strategy could boomerang, as did their targeting on Newt Gingrich 10 years ago. Then, as now, population increases will force the creation of a new, heavily Republican district in the northern suburbs, like the 6th to which Gingrich moved in 1992. Barr may move to such a district, or he may move outward to counties that he carried in the 2000 election. There is also the possibility that he may run against Senator Max Cleland.

Cook's Call   *Potentially Competitive.* Barr has never won this suburban Atlanta district by big margins, despite the fact that the district has a reliable Republican edge (Bush won here with 60%). Barr's polarizing nature and his less than impressive wins make him a tempting target for Democrats. Expecting a major redraw of his burgeoning district, Barr has put his home up for sale. Whether Democrats can make Barr or this district more vulnerable remains to be seen. It is a seat to watch.

THE PEOPLE: Pop. 2000: 752,161; Pop. 1990: 589,915, up 27.5% 1990–2000. 76.8% White, 18.2% Black, 0.9% Asian, 0.3% Amer. Indian, 1.3% Two+ races, 2.5% Other; 5% Hispanic Origin.

2000 Presidential Vote			1996 Presidential Vote		
Bush (R)	152,723	(60%)	Dole (R)	99,320	(51%)
Gore (D)	96,570	(38%)	Clinton (D)	77,741	(40%)
Others	5,011	(2%)	Perot (I)	16,603	(9%)

Rep. Bob Barr (R)

Elected 1994, 4th term; b. Nov. 5, 1948, Iowa City, IA; home, Smyrna; U. of S. CA, B.A. 1970, George Washington U., M.A. 1972, Georgetown U., J.D. 1977; Methodist; married (Jeri).

Professional Career: CIA Analyst, 1971–78; Practicing atty., 1978–86, 1990–94; U.S. Atty., N. GA District, 1986–90; Dir., SE Legal Foundation, 1990–92.

DC Office: 1207 LHOB 20515, 202-225-2931; Fax: 202-225-2944; Web site: www.house.gov/barr.

District Offices: Carrollton, 770-836-1776; LaGrange, 706-812-1776; Marietta, 770-429-1776; Rome, 706-290-1776.

Committees: *Financial Services* (12th of 37 R): Capital Markets, Insurance & Government Sponsored Enterprises; Financial Institutions & Consumer Credit; Housing & Community Opportunity. *Government Reform* (13th of 24 R): Census; Criminal Justice, Drug Policy & Human Resources. *Judiciary* (9th of 21 R): Commercial & Administrative Law (Chmn.); Crime.

Group Ratings

	ADA	ACLU	AFS	LCV	CON	ITIC	NTU	COC	ACU	NTLC	CHC
2000	10	29	14	14	90	68	72	71	100	100	93
1999	15	—	16	19	65	—	72	76	100	—	—

National Journal Ratings

	1999 LIB —	1999 CONS		2000 LIB —	2000 CONS
Economic	36%	64%		6%	85%
Social	10%	85%		0%	79%
Foreign	0%	97%		0%	88%

Key Votes of the 106th Congress

1. Patient Bill of Rights	Y	5. Bar RU-486 $ for FDA	Y	9. NATO War in Serbia	N
2. Accelerate Min. Wage	N	6. Display 10 Commandments	Y	10. Perm. Trade with China	N
3. Strike Ban on Ergo. Stnd.	N	7. Gun Show Bkgrnd. Checks	N	11. Debt Relief for 3rd World	N
4. Ovrd. Estate Tax Veto	Y	8. Ban Part.-Birth Abortion	Y	12. Drop Cuba Econ. Embargo	N

Election Results

2000 general	Bob Barr (R)	126,312	(55%)	($3,495,641)
	Roger Kahn (D)	102,272	(45%)	($3,859,860)
2000 primary	Bob Barr (R)	unopposed		
1998 general	Bob Barr (R)	85,982	(55%)	($1,424,519)
	James F. Williams (D)	69,293	(45%)	($13,633)

EIGHTH DISTRICT

South Georgia has been under attack and enemy occupation more than almost any other part of America. Most famously, of course, when General William Tecumseh Sherman's troops set out from Atlanta, without supplies or lines of communication, to march through Georgia to the sea, burning its antebellum mansions, destroying its crops, capturing its leader (the Jefferson Davis Memorial in Ocilla marks the spot where Union troops took him in May 1865), leaving memories of slaves freed, handed down as family lore for more than a century. But the land bears, if only on its road signs, the memory of another invasion, when poor white farmers aided by Andrew Jackson's troops drove the Cherokees and other Indians off this land, where Indians had lived for perhaps thousands of years, west over the Trail of Tears to what is now Oklahoma. And there was the oppression of blacks by whites under the old systems of slavery and legal segregation, the latter not long dead—a past recalled by Macon's Harriet Tubman Historical and Cultural Museum.

The 8th Congressional District runs down the center of Georgia, roughly along these lines of occupation, past immense stands of soft lumber pines, in forests with wild hogs and bears, through counties where 80% of the nation's and more than half the world supply of kaolin (clay used for china and ceramics) is mined, all the way from Macon to the Okefenokee Swamp, where local opposition halted a proposed DuPont titanium mine, and activists are now lobbying for a research and education center. The district lines were more regular for 1996 than for 1992 and 1994, thanks to a federally court-ordered plan handed down in 1995 after the Supreme Court overturned the former lines as a "racial gerrymander." The 8th now includes all of Macon, home of music legends Otis Redding, Little Richard and the Allman Brothers, a city proud of its restored houses and Japanese cherry trees (it has 20 times as many as Washington, D.C.). This has been Democratic country since Sherman's troops came through, and the 1995 redistricting made the 8th more Democratic, primarily by increasing the black percentage from 21% to 31%. Bill Clinton carried this 8th district twice, and it voted solidly for Senator Max Cleland in 1996 and Governor Roy Barnes in 1998. But in 2000 it switched; Macon and four small counties narrowly voted for Al Gore, but the other 25 counties voted, by as much as 68%, for George W. Bush.

The congressman from the 8th District is Saxby Chambliss, a Republican elected in 1994 to replace a retiring conservative Democrat. Chambliss grew up in Shreveport, Louisiana, the son of an Episcopalian minister, went to college in Georgia, and practiced business and agriculture law in Moultrie starting in 1968. In 1992 he ran for the House and lost the Republican primary; in 1994 he was the sole Republican candidate, while Democrats, as in days of yore, had a multi-candidate contest. The winner was Craig Mathis, the 32-year-old son of Congressman (1971–81)

Dawson Mathis and a former House staffer. Chambliss called for targeting repeat offenders and reducing the deficit; he opposed Dick Armey's proposal to zero out peanut subsidies. Chambliss won 63%–37%.

In the House, Newt Gingrich saw that Chambliss had the committee assignments he needed most—Armed Services to look after Robins Air Force Base near Macon, and Agriculture to protect subsidies for peanut farmers in the counties to the south. In his first term Chambliss toured every military base in Georgia (80-plus years of Carl Vinson, Richard Russell and Sam Nunn is a tough legacy to follow) and worked with locals to remove Robins, an air logistics center, from the final Base Closing Commission list in 1995. He formed and co-chaired an Air Power Caucus and sought support for the F-22 Raptor.

To protect peanut farmers, Chambliss voted in committee against the Freedom to Farm Act in 1995 with four other Republicans, which defeated it temporarily; he opposed a provision to end the cotton-marketing program as well. When the leadership folded the farm bill into the budget, Chambliss threatened not to support it but backed down under pressure. With Sanford Bishop of the 2d District, he devised a new "no-net-cost, market-oriented" peanut program, with a quota set at the projected domestic demand for edible peanuts; this was put into the final Freedom to Farm Act. When the Department of Transportation tried to force airlines to offer peanut-free zones around passengers who claimed allergies, Chambliss retaliated with a ban on such action that made its way into the October 1998 omnibus budget bill. In June 2000 he placed a $35 million peanut farmer bailout in the military appropriation and backed Governor Roy Barnes's plan to pay some tobacco settlement money to tobacco farmers.

Chambliss usually votes with the Republican leadership, but he was one of the 1994 freshman class members who wanted a lower income cap on the $500 per child tax credit. He opposes gun control and became vice chairman of the Sportsmen's Caucus, which sponsored the first Congressional Shoot-out; he has proposed a Sportsmen's Bill of Rights, to allow hunting and fishing on federal land unless specifically forbidden by Congress. An avid outdoorsman, Chambliss said, "On one of those rare outdoor occasions when my mind turns to a pending issue in Congress, I have found no better place to be alone with my thoughts than my favorite fishing hole." He has worked for funding to purchase the DuPont Okefenokee titanium mine, for the Tubman museum, to get the Army to donate a Civil War cannon to Macon's Cannonball House, to build a $14 million Reserve Command headquarters and a $3.3 million KC-135 flight simulator at Warner Robins. He challenged EPA's plan to require farmers to get discharge permits and sponsored a bill to allow military dependents abroad to be prosecuted under military law.

Democrats have targeted Chambliss since the 1995 redistricting, which removed his own home from the district; he moved to an apartment in Macon. But he vastly outspent the 1996 nominee, Jim Wiggins—a Vietnam veteran and prosecutor—and Chambliss ran as the savior of the peanut program. He won 53%–47%. In 1998 Democrats' first choice candidate did not run, and Chambliss spent time raising money for his PAC, the Common Sense Leadership Fund, which donated to other Republicans. He won 62%–38%. In 2000 he was opposed by former Macon Mayor and Vietnam combat veteran Jim Marshall, who campaigned almost exclusively on prescription drugs for seniors. But independent ads praised Chambliss' prescription drug plan and he won 59%–41%, running about even with George W. Bush in Macon and ahead in rural counties.

Chambliss also talked about the likelihood that he would become chairman of the Budget Committee. In November 1998, Bob Livingston, then speaker-designate, put Chambliss on the Budget Committee and named him vice chairman; in July 1999, Chairman John Kasich announced his retirement and Chambliss started a campaign for the post. In July 2000, after Senator Paul Coverdell's sudden death, Chambliss considered running in the November special election; he had also pondered running for governor in 1998. But Speaker Dennis Hastert persuaded him to stay in the House, and Chambliss came away feeling he would get the Budget chair. But he had competition from Jim Nussle, who was supported by Majority Leader Dick Armey, who had clashed with Chambliss over the peanut program and the base closing process. The Republican Steering Committee interviewed both candidates, and in December 2000 picked Nussle. But in January 2001 Chambliss was chosen to chair the Agriculture subcommittee on General Farm Commodities and Risk Management.

Chambliss is said to be one of the chief targets of Democratic redistricters. They may shuffle counties in south Georgia to strengthen Democrat Sanford Bishop and force Republicans to run in unfamiliar territory. Shifting Macon into Bishop's 2d District would force Chambliss to move back to Moultrie—and perhaps to run against another Republican. It is also possible that Chambliss will run against Senator Max Cleland in 2002.

Cook's Call *Potentially Competitive.* Although this district was made more competitive during 1996 redistricting, Chambliss has continued to win by solid margins. And, while Democrats are interested in making this seat even more competitive in redistricting this year, Chambliss, now in his fourth term, is popular and well situated here. But, with Chambliss taking a serious look at running for the Senate, Democrats could certainly make an open seat race very competitive.

THE PEOPLE: Pop. 2000: 662,811; Pop. 1990: 587,912, up 12.7% 1990–2000. 64.4% White, 32.3% Black, 0.7% Asian, 0.2% Amer. Indian, 0.9% Two+ races, 1.3% Other; 2.8% Hispanic Origin.

2000 Presidential Vote			1996 Presidential Vote		
Bush (R)	115,875	(57%)	Clinton (D)	90,662	(47%)
Gore (D)	85,989	(42%)	Dole (R)	85,224	(45%)
Others	2,167	(1%)	Perot (I)	14,643	(8%)

Rep. Saxby Chambliss (R)

Elected 1994, 4th term; b. Nov. 10, 1943, Warrenton, NC; home, Macon; U. of GA, B.A. 1966, U. of TN, J.D. 1968; Episcopalian; married (Julianne).

Professional Career: Practicing atty., 1968–94.

DC Office: 1019 LHOB 20515, 202-225-6531; Fax: 202-225-3013; Web site: www.house.gov/chambliss.

District Offices: Macon, 912-752-0800; Waycross, 912-287-1180.

Committees: *Agriculture* (8th of 27 R): General Farm Commodities & Risk Management (Chmn.); Specialty Crops & Foreign Agriculture Programs. *Armed Services* (15th of 32 R): Military Readiness; Military Research & Development. *Permanent Select Committee on Intelligence* (11th of 11 R): Intelligence Policy & National Security; Technical & Tactical Intelligence.

Group Ratings

	ADA	ACLU	AFS	LCV	CON	ITIC	NTU	COC	ACU	NTLC	CHC
2000	0	7	0	14	56	83	63	90	91	76	100
1999	10	—	0	6	28	—	58	80	80	—	—

National Journal Ratings

	1999 LIB —	1999 CONS	2000 LIB —	2000 CONS
Economic	37% —	61%	18% —	76%
Social	16% —	82%	0% —	79%
Foreign	23% —	73%	22% —	76%

Key Votes of the 106th Congress

1. Patient Bill of Rights	Y	5. Bar RU-486 $ for FDA	Y	9. NATO War in Serbia	N
2. Accelerate Min. Wage	N	6. Display 10 Commandments	Y	10. Perm. Trade with China	Y
3. Strike Ban on Ergo. Stnd.	N	7. Gun Show Bkgrnd. Checks	N	11. Debt Relief for 3rd World	N
4. Ovrd. Estate Tax Veto	Y	8. Ban Part.-Birth Abortion	Y	12. Drop Cuba Econ. Embargo	N

Election Results

2000 general	Saxby Chambliss (R)	113,380	(59%)	($1,841,653)
	Jim Marshall (D)	79,051	(41%)	($846,565)
2000 primary	Saxby Chambliss (R)	unopposed		
1998 general	Saxby Chambliss (R)	87,993	(62%)	($708,556)
	Ronald L. Cain (D)	53,079	(38%)	($10,459)

NINTH DISTRICT

In the last years of the 20th Century, the hills and mountains of north Georgia have suddenly become one of the boom areas of the South. This is a sharp turn in their history: Since the Cherokee were driven out early in the 19th Century this has been poor country, where small farmers scratched a living off rocky land. It was devastated by the Civil War, by General Sherman's troops and because so many young men who left to fight for the Confederacy (and a few who left from mountain counties to fight for the Union) never returned. After the war not much changed for a while. Most communities lived in isolation; roads with hairpin curves led to remote hills where until very recently moonshine stills were more common than summer cabins. In time, textile mills began springing up along the railroads, around Gainesville poultry production became a big business, and in Dalton the craft tradition of tufted bedspread handiwork was transformed into the world's largest carpet industry, producing 60% of the world's tufted carpet. But these were low-wage industries and all white; there had never been many slaves here, and in 1912 Forsyth County made headlines when it drove out its few black residents.

In the 1980s and especially the 1990s there has been a rush of change. Interstate highways have brought north Georgia in easy range of the world-city of Atlanta; the carpet industry has become more high-tech; small manufacturing is booming, with higher-skill work replacing low-tech mills; vacation and retirement communities have been built in mountains and around lakes. Forsyth and Cherokee counties are now part of the booming ring around Atlanta, even 50-plus miles from Peachtree Street. So tight are the labor markets that tens of thousands of Latinos from Texas and Latin countries have come to Dalton, Gainesville and the area around to snap up the jobs the boom is creating.

The 9th Congressional District covers the whole northern end of the state, from the Georgia suburbs of Chattanooga and Dalton in the west to the old Republican and new resort counties in the east. It extends south to include Forsyth County and part of Cherokee. A few counties here have always been Republican, many started switching in the 1970s and 1980s, and Cherokee and Forsyth now are among the most heavily Republican counties in the South—73% and 78% for George W. Bush in 2000. Economic prosperity and cultural traditionalism have sent politics here in one direction, even against national tides: Despite north Georgia native Senator Zell Miller's wide victory in the Senate race, most north Georgia counties voted at least 2–1 for Bush.

The congressman from the 9th District is Nathan Deal, first elected in 1992, who switched parties and became a Republican in April 1995. Deal grew up in Gainesville, went to Mercer University, then served in the Army from 1966–68; he returned home to practice "street level law," with offices always on the ground floor, and public offices a young lawyer takes as civic duty: assistant district attorney, juvenile court judge, county attorney. In 1980, at 38, he was elected to the state Senate as a Democrat. Jimmy Carter was still president, the legislature was overwhelmingly Democratic, and it would have been quixotic to run as a Republican. He proved a capable legislator and was elected Senate president pro tem in 1989 and 1991. In 1992, 16-year incumbent Ed Jenkins, a power on the Ways and Means Committee, retired. Deal ran, defeating a Republican abortion opponent with 59% of the vote.

In the House, Deal opposed the new Clinton administration's economic policies, voting against the 1993 budget, for the line-item veto and balanced budget amendment. He helped found a 26-Democrat Fiscal Caucus. Many saw Deal as a potential party-switcher, but while campaigning in 1994 he said, "If I choose to switch during the term, I think the honest thing to do is resign and have a special election." He beat an underfunded Republican, but with only 58%—a sign of increasing Republican sentiment. In early 1995 he soldiered on as a Democrat and worked with other Democrats to offer an alternative to the Republicans' welfare reform package. On Monday, April 3, Deal said how pleased he was by Democrats' support for that plan. Two days later, he was unhappy with Democrats' opposition to tax cuts and with senior Democrats' criticisms of Clean Water Act revisions he and Louisiana's Jimmy Hayes (later a party-switcher himself) had won on a bipartisan committee vote. On April 10, back home in Gainesville, Deal announced he was a Republican. He said the national Democratic Party was unwilling to admit it was "out of touch with mainstream America," and "I think that it is important that at some point you get away from the schizophrenia I have had to deal with." Democrats were stunned, and Newt Gingrich was clearly delighted; Deal was rewarded with a seat on the Commerce Committee.

Deal has not proved to be a totally party-line Republican. In 1996 he backed the minimum wage increase and in August 1998 he supported the Shays-Meehan campaign finance bill. But his voting record is mostly conservative, and constituents did not protest vehemently at the Tailgate Talk public meetings where he drives his pickup truck to town squares every summer. Deal worked to get a community veterans' clinic opened in Gainesville, sponsored a Web site for disabled people to become aware of assistive technology, and was a co-sponsor of Megan's Law. He sponsored higher penalties for illegal aliens and smugglers of aliens. Deal said he was aware that this may hurt politically in a district with a rapidly growing Hispanic population, but said, "We're a nation of laws. It's our responsibility to forge support for the concept of law." On the Commerce Committee, he has worked to improve local TV coverage for home-satellite users, an important issue in rural areas.

Since 1995, Deal had no Republican primary opposition and his two Democratic challengers have not come close enough to be taken seriously. It's hard to see how redistricting will leave Democrats any opportunity across northern Georgia.

Cook's Call   *Safe.* Sometimes party-switching "takes," sometimes it "doesn't take." Clearly, Nathan Deal's 1995 switch "took," as he has won by large margins since then. Presently configured, this is the most Republican seat in the state (Bush won here with 70% in 2000). As one of the fastest growing districts in the state, it will be altered in the redistricting process.

THE PEOPLE: Pop. 2000: 814,305; Pop. 1990: 589,355, up 38.2% 1990–2000. 90.5% White, 3.2% Black, 0.7% Asian, 0.3% Amer. Indian, 0.1% Hawaiian, 1.1% Two+ races, 4.1% Other; 8.4% Hispanic Origin.

2000 Presidential Vote			1996 Presidential Vote		
Bush (R)	180,533	(70%)	Dole (R)	115,306	(55%)
Gore (D)	73,195	(28%)	Clinton (D)	73,861	(35%)
Others	5,421	(2%)	Perot (I)	20,809	(10%)

Rep. Nathan Deal (R)

Elected 1992, 5th term; b. Aug. 25, 1942, Millen; home, Lula; Mercer U., B.A. 1964, J.D. 1966; Baptist; married (Sandra).

Military Career: Army, 1966–68.

Elected Office: Hall Cnty. Juvenile Court Judge, 1971–72; GA Senate, 1980–92, Pres. Pro-Tem, 1989–90, 1991–92.

Professional Career: Hall Cnty. Atty., 1966–70; Asst. Dist. Atty., NE Judicial Circuit, 1970–71; Practicing atty., 1971–92.

DC Office: 2437 RHOB 20515, 202-225-5211; Fax: 202-225-8272; Web site: www.house.gov/deal.

District Offices: Dalton, 706-226-5320; Gainesville, 770-535-2592; Lafayette, 706-638-7042.

Committees: *Energy & Commerce* (9th of 31 R): Commerce, Trade & Consumer Protection (Vice Chmn.); Health; Telecommunications & The Internet.

Group Ratings

	ADA	ACLU	AFS	LCV	CON	ITIC	NTU	COC	ACU	NTLC	CHC
2000	5	14	14	14	85	67	67	71	96	82	73
1999	10	—	0	13	33	—	63	84	80	—	—

National Journal Ratings

	1999 LIB	—	1999 CONS		2000 LIB	—	2000 CONS
Economic	0%	—	84%		6%	—	85%
Social	19%	—	79%		26%	—	71%
Foreign	3%	—	92%		25%	—	69%

Key Votes of the 106th Congress

1. Patient Bill of Rights	N	5. Bar RU-486 $ for FDA	Y	9. NATO War in Serbia	N
2. Accelerate Min. Wage	N	6. Display 10 Commandments	Y	10. Perm. Trade with China	N
3. Strike Ban on Ergo. Stnd.	N	7. Gun Show Bkgrnd. Checks	N	11. Debt Relief for 3rd World	N
4. Ovrd. Estate Tax Veto	Y	8. Ban Part.-Birth Abortion	Y	12. Drop Cuba Econ. Embargo	N

Election Results

2000 general	Nathan Deal (R)	183,171	(75%)	($429,979)
	James Harrington (D)	60,360	(25%)	($69,884)
2000 primary	Nathan Deal (R)	unopposed		
1998 general	Nathan Deal (R)	unopposed		($224,137)

TENTH DISTRICT

Augusta, Georgia, is one of those small American cities that pops up now and again in our history. Founded in 1735 on the site of a fur-trading post, it is far older than Atlanta and just about as old as coastal Savannah. It was missed, fortunately, on General Sherman's march through Georgia; in those same years it was the boyhood home of Woodrow Wilson. Its antique Medical College of Georgia dates back to 1835. It is best known for its Augusta National Golf Course, where President Eisenhower used to tee off, and where the Masters Tournament is held every year. Augusta was once a cotton port on the Savannah River, with its own Cotton Exchange; now it has a Riverwalk on the site of the old levee. The paper industry, stoked by the pines that grow in profusion on the flat Piedmont land, is important here; so are nuclear weapons, produced until 1989 and now under disarmament downriver in South Carolina at the Savannah River site.

The 10th Congressional District of Georgia includes Augusta and its fast-growing suburbs—they account for more than half the population and votes—plus 22 mostly rural counties in every direction. This district was very much changed by the 1995 redistricting, which followed a Supreme Court decision overturning the previous boundaries as a "racial gerrymander." The old 10th District did not include the black neighborhoods of Augusta, and most of its other counties were toward the Gwinnett County suburbs of Atlanta. The new 10th includes all of Augusta, plus several black-majority counties to the south—once big plantation country and now an area with far slower growth than the Atlanta region. Previously 18% black, it's now 38% black.

The congressman from the 10th District is Charlie Norwood, a Republican elected by a smashing margin in 1994. Norwood grew up in Valdosta, went to college and dental school, served in the Army in Vietnam and at Fort Gordon, then practiced dentistry in Augusta. He was president of the Georgia Dental Association and also started small businesses—Northwood Tree Nursery and Park Avenue Fabrics. In 1993 he decided to sell his dental practice and run against Congressman Don Johnson, a freshman elected in 1992 "I calculated one time that if my grandson was a dentist and we kept going the way we were going, he'd have to do 900 crowns just to pay his part of the interest on the national debt," said Norwood. Johnson came under scathing criticism when he broke a campaign promise to vote against any tax increase and supported the Clinton budget and tax package in 1993. Norwood's toughest race in 1994 turned out to be the primary; he came from behind to beat Ralph Hudgens in the runoff 51%–49%. When Johnson said he wanted Bill Clinton or Al Gore to visit the 10th District only if "they are coming down to endorse my opponent," Norwood invited Clinton and offered to pay his plane fare. Norwood won 65%–35%, as Johnson took one of the worst lickings of a non-scandal-tarred incumbent in recent history.

In his first term Norwood had a conservative voting record. His one major dissent from the leadership was his successful opposition in 1995 to the sale of the Southeastern Power Administration for the purpose of deficit reduction; he was afraid private utilities would charge higher rates. Redistricting put him in obvious political danger. The Democratic nominee, state legislator David Bell, campaigned as a conservative and said he would support the Blue Dog Democrats in the House, but criticized Norwood on education, the environment, Medicare and the minimum wage. But Norwood excelled in fundraising, and collected $664,000 in PAC contributions for the 1996 election. Norwood challenged the accuracy of AFL-CIO ads and persuaded all but one Augusta station not to run them; he purchased his own ads, to be run right after those spots, calling them lies and urging viewers to switch channels. And when Bell ran an ad in which a cartoon fish said, "Sorry, Charlie," Norwood's campaign alerted StarKist Tuna, which called it a trademark infringement on its Charlie the Tuna ads and demanded it be yanked. This was the closest House election in Georgia in 1996. Norwood carried the Augusta area 55%–45% and Bell won narrowly the rest of the district; overall Norwood won 52%–48%.

In his third term Norwood suddenly became one of the House's most influential members. The reason was PARCA, the Patient Access to Responsible Care Act, regulating health maintenance organizations, which Norwood sponsored and pushed with great vehemence: "This is something that has been festering in my soul for a long time. People are trying to deny our patients treatment." In his dental practice, Norwood was in an HMO for three years and decided, "This was no way to go." To some critics, PARCA looked like "provider protection." But Norwood insisted, "This is not about money for physicians. It is about them losing control of their ability to practice medicine." To push his bill, Norwood pestered Speaker Newt Gingrich on flights to Atlanta and, more importantly, assembled at one point 230 co-sponsors, including 90 Republicans. PARCA provided that patients could sue HMOs when they overrule doctors and refuse to pay for treatments that turn out to have been needed; that patients can visit emergency rooms without the permission of the insurer; that doctors couldn't be prohibited from discussing alternative treatments (the gag rule); that patients have free selection of doctors, hospitals and treatments; and that patients can see specialists on a doctor's recommendation. Ironically, it would be enforced mainly by the Labor Department; it was heavy-handed OSHA regulation that inspired Norwood to get into politics.

PARCA produced new political alliances and results. Large businesses and the Chamber of Commerce were appalled, and predicted it would raise insurance costs by 35%. HMOs and the Blues opposed it as well. The American Medical Association, American Dental Association and the American College of Emergency Physicians came out in favor. Most Democrats favored the idea, as did Republican Greg Ganske, an Iowa plastic surgeon who sat with Norwood on the Commerce Committee. In January 1998, as momentum was growing, Gingrich appointed a Republican working group headed by Chief Deputy Whip Dennis Hastert. Norwood judged that he couldn't pass his full bill, and so was ready to compromise; Ganske, in contrast, joined with Democrats to back their bill. When the working group came up with a bill, it did not include the right to sue, but did include a ban on the gag rule, emergency room visits without previous approval, and allowing patients to appeal decisions to an outside arbitrator. Some of Hastert's initiatives were added: "HealthMarts," cooperative purchasing agreements to give small businesses access to lower-cost insurance, and malpractice reforms. The working group's proposal, the Patient Protection Act, passed 216–210; a Democratic "Patient Bill of Rights" failed 212–217; but the Senate did not act.

When the issue returned in the 106th Congress, Hastert had become speaker but he could no longer stop the tide once Norwood signed on with senior Democrat John Dingell. With the Senate having passed a more-limited version, 68 House Republicans signed up with Norwood to have the differences resolved by a conference committee; in October 1999 Norwood-Dingell passed 275–151. Norwood was now many Democrats' favorite Republican, and Bill Clinton embraced the bill as "a major victory for every family." Then something unexpected happened. For the next year, all sorts of negotiations took place: Republican-Democratic, House-Senate, Congress-White House. But the bill remained logjammed. Unwilling to add further burdens to the courts, Republicans gambled that momentum for HMO regulation had waned. And many Democrats moved on to their new health-care issue *du jour*: prescription-drug coverage for seniors. Norwood did not lend his name to the patients' rights bill introduced in January 2001 after meeting with White House aides.

To some surprise, Norwood's standing remained strong among top Republicans; Hastert appeared at a Norwood fundraiser in Augusta and he was named chairman of the Workforce Protections panel on the Education and the Workforce Committee for the 107th Congress. With his new bipartisan persona, Norwood's problems in the once-competitive district faded. His big funding advantage scared away potential challengers. Against an ordained Baptist woman minister with sparse funding, Norwood won 60% in 1998 and 63% in 2000. Still, some Democrats see

Norwood as a redistricting target. State senate Majority Leader Charles Walker, who is black and a potential challenger, is said to want to increase the black percentage in the district. But that can be done only at the cost of frustrating Democrats' attempts to weaken Saxby Chambliss in the adjacent 8th District. Norwood has also been mentioned as a possible candidate against Senator Max Cleland in 2002.

Cook's Call   *Potentially Competitive.* Like Saxby Chambliss in the 8th District, after the 1995 redrawing of lines, Charlie Norwood was drawn into a more competitive district. But, Democrats have not had much luck recruiting a serious candidate over the last two cycles, and Norwood has yet to drop below 60% since 1996. This is another area where Democrats may want to tinker with the lines to create a more favorable district, but Norwood, who is well established here, will not be so easy to knock off. Democratic state Senate Majority Leader Charles Walker is said to be interested in running in a newly configured 10th District.

THE PEOPLE: Pop. 2000: 662,201; Pop. 1990: 588,046, up 12.6% 1990–2000. 58.2% White, 38.5% Black, 1.1% Asian, 0.2% Amer. Indian, 0.1% Hawaiian, 1.1% Two+ races, 0.8% Other; 2% Hispanic Origin.

2000 Presidential Vote			**1996 Presidential Vote**		
Bush (R)	115,661	(55%)	Clinton (D)	94,968	(48%)
Gore (D)	93,892	(44%)	Dole (R)	90,213	(46%)
Others	2,100	(1%)	Perot (I)	11,669	(6%)

Rep. Charlie Norwood (R)

Elected 1994, 4th term; b. July 27, 1941, Valdosta; home, Evans; GA S. U., B.S. 1964, Georgetown U., D.D.S. 1967; Methodist; married (Gloria).

Military Career: Army, 1967–69 (Vietnam).

Professional Career: Small businessman, 1969–present; Practicing dentist, 1969–93; Pres., GA Dental Assn., 1983.

DC Office: 1707 LHOB 20515, 202-225-4101; Fax: 202-226-5995; Web site: www.house.gov/norwood.

District Offices: Augusta, 706-733-7066; Dublin, 912-275-2814; Milledgeville, 912-453-0373.

Committees: *Education & the Workforce* (12th of 27 R): Select Education; Workforce Protections (Chmn.). *Energy & Commerce* (14th of 31 R): Energy & Air Quality; Health (Vice Chmn.).

Group Ratings

	ADA	ACLU	AFS	LCV	CON	ITIC	NTU	COC	ACU	NTLC	CHC
2000	5	21	14	14	80	72	65	71	100	77	100
1999	10	—	16	6	25	—	59	71	88	—	—

National Journal Ratings

	1999 LIB —	1999 CONS		2000 LIB —	2000 CONS
Economic	41% —	57%		29% —	67%
Social	4% —	91%		0% —	79%
Foreign	3% —	92%		22% —	76%

Key Votes of the 106th Congress

1. Patient Bill of Rights	Y	5. Bar RU-486 $ for FDA	Y	9. NATO War in Serbia	N
2. Accelerate Min. Wage	N	6. Display 10 Commandments	Y	10. Perm. Trade with China	N
3. Strike Ban on Ergo. Stnd.	N	7. Gun Show Bkgrnd. Checks	N	11. Debt Relief for 3rd World	N
4. Ovrd. Estate Tax Veto	Y	8. Ban Part.-Birth Abortion	Y	12. Drop Cuba Econ. Embargo	N

Election Results

2000 general	Charlie Norwood (R)	122,590	(63%)	($787,855)
	Marion Spencer Freeman (D)	71,309	(37%)	($26,713)
2000 primary	Charlie Norwood (R)	unopposed		
1998 general	Charlie Norwood (R)	88,527	(60%)	($1,104,431)
	Marion Spencer Freeman (D)	60,004	(40%)	($48,136)

ELEVENTH DISTRICT

Greater Atlanta has grown out in every direction, south past the airport, west over the Chatta-hoochee, north past Buckhead and the Perimeter Mall, and east and northeast past Stone Mountain. Gwinnett County, on I-85, has become an urban community of its own: It cast 21,000 votes in 1972 and nearly 190,000 in 2000, a level approaching Fulton County, which includes central Atlanta, or DeKalb just to the east. Now similar growth is heading east to Walton and Barrow Counties, the then-rural home of Senator (1933–71) Richard Russell, and south to Rockdale County, where spiritualist Nancy Fowler channeled messages said to be from the Virgin Mary. Politically, these new growth areas favor market forces over government regulation on economic issues and traditional values over liberal ones on cultural issues; they vote overwhelmingly Republican.

But there is another Georgia in the counties beyond, a state of still rural communities, and Athens, home of the University of Georgia, the country's oldest chartered state university. Athens is the site of one of America's finest collections of Greek Revival buildings—gleaming white columns, perfectly proportioned little Parthenons and flat-roofed square houses surrounded by fluted columns with Corinthian capitals, all dating from the 1830s-50s. Politically, Athens remains liberal and Democratic, though neighboring Oconee County has been—Gwinnett-like—growing and trending Republican.

The 11th Congressional District of Georgia consists of much of this territory, from Gwinnett County east to Athens, then northeast to the Savannah River. Gwinnett and the other counties in metro Atlanta cast about 70% of the votes, with the rest split nearly equally between Athens and Oconee County and the rural counties. The current 11th District was created when the Supreme Court in 1995 declared Georgia's district lines a "racial gerrymander." The former 11th was a black-majority district that snaked from heavily black south DeKalb County across the state to black precincts in Savannah and Augusta; none of the new 11th is contained within these lines. Athens and most of the rural counties were formerly part of the 10th District.

The congressman from the 11th District is John Linder, a Republican first elected in 1992 in the old 4th District, which combined north DeKalb County and half of Gwinnett. Like most of the Georgia delegation, Linder grew up elsewhere, in his case Minnesota, where he went to college and dental school. After two years in the Air Force he moved to greater Atlanta and practiced dentistry for 13 years. In 1977 he started Linder Financial Corporation, a lending institution for entrepreneurial ventures in the South. In 1974, at 32, he was elected to the Georgia House, where he served all but two of the next 16 years. In 1990 he challenged Democratic Congressman Ben Jones and lost 52%–48%. Following the 1992 redistricting, Linder ran again in the new 4th, where he was first in a six-candidate primary and won the runoff with 62%. In the general, he faced Democratic state Senator Cathey Steinberg and, in a race that ran along national party lines, won by just 51%–49%.

From this tenuous beginning Linder quickly became an important congressman. One reason was electoral security: In heavily Republican 1994 he won 58%–42%, and since 1996 he has had a safe seat in the 11th. Another benefit for a time was that he was a close ally to Newt Gingrich. They went back a ways: In 1975 Linder, Gingrich and Paul Coverdell began meeting to try to build a strong Georgia Republican Party, surely not imagining that within 20 years they would be congressman, speaker and senator. In 1984 they developed Operation Breakthrough for electing Republicans in conservative-leaning legislative districts which had never been seriously contested before. A decade later, they were setting political strategy for congressional Republicans. But they could not have imagined in mid-1998 that two years later, Gingrich would be out as speaker, Linder would have lost his leadership position, and Coverdell would be dead.

Linder has a calm, usually humorous demeanor; his views are solidly conservative—though a bit more Wall Street than Main Street. He says his "over-arching ideology [is] that individuals will make better decisions for their families than the government." After Republicans won control, Gingrich gave Linder a seat on the House Rules Committee and called on him often to preside over contentious debates; he floor-managed rules on complex bills like the 1996 Telecommunications Act. Linder also became the informal head of a group of Republicans determined to defend Gingrich on ethics charges.

After the 1996 election, Gingrich chose Linder to replace Bill Paxon as chairman of the National Republican Congressional Committee. He excelled at fundraising, amassing some $40 million for the committee and relentlessly prevailing on incumbents to contribute to Republican challengers. He did a good job at recruiting candidates. He shared the assumption of most observers that Republicans would gain seats as the out party in a presidential off-year election. His targeting was good but one of his ads misfired: at the behest of Gingrich, it raised the trust and impeachment issues against Bill Clinton. While run in only a few districts, the ad was publicized nationally; it yielded a minimum of gain and a maximum of pain. When the Republicans actually lost five seats Linder was obviously in deep trouble. Linder said the problem was the lack of a "strong message," which "was not my responsibility"—an obvious reference to Gingrich, who paid a far bigger price for the election outcome. Gingrich, before resigning and already under attack, said that the next NRCC head would be elected by the conference rather than appointed by him. Tom Davis, a highly competent election buff, started running for the job, with the support of Whip Tom DeLay. Linder reacted bitterly: "I remember when Newt Gingrich's wife left a press conference in tears when he blamed her. So I don't think he has any compunction about blaming me." That was Thursday, two days after the election. Gingrich announced his retirement late on Friday; 12 days later Linder lost to Davis 130–77.

Taking a far lower profile, Linder resumed his legislative work and got on well with the new Republican leadership; Rules is not a good committee for a party rebel. He turned his long-term attention toward leading the fight for fundamental tax reform. Working with the Americans for Fair Taxation, he joined Democrat Collin Peterson in calling for abolition of individual and corporate income taxes and their replacement with a 23% national sales tax on new goods and services at the retail level. He was prepared for a lengthy fight, but one that seems unlikely to become a centerpiece before a second Bush term—when Linder, not coincidentally, might have additional clout as Rules Committee chairman.

Back home, he built support to make Highway 316 into an Interstate between Atlanta and Athens. His upheaval in Washington seemed to have no impact in the district. Curiously, Linder had the same opponent in the past two elections but in different sequences. In 1998 Vincent Littman ran as a Democrat and lost 69%–31%; in 2000 he ran in the Republican primary and lost 87%–13%. Redistricting might change the boundaries of the 11th, but there will likely be a heavily Republican Gwinnett County-based district in which Linder can continue to win.

Cook's Call   *Safe.* Like the rest of the suburban Atlanta delegation, Linder has seen his district grow tremendously over the last ten years (it is estimated that the district will need to shed at least 200,000 people). And, like many of his colleagues, Linder is also taking a look at the race for the U.S. Senate. It is too early to tell what impact redistricting will have on this seat, but for now Linder looks safe in a seat that gave Bush 64%.

THE PEOPLE: Pop. 2000: 836,416; Pop. 1990: 589,317, up 41.9% 1990–2000. 78.9% White, 14.6% Black, 2.9% Asian, 0.2% Amer. Indian, 1.4% Two + races, 2% Other; 5% Hispanic Origin.

2000 Presidential Vote			1996 Presidential Vote		
Bush (R)	175,570	(64%)	Dole (R)	128,320	(55%)
Gore (D)	92,672	(34%)	Clinton (D)	88,083	(38%)
Others	8,163	(3%)	Perot (I)	17,668	(8%)

Rep. John Linder (R)

Elected 1992, 5th term; b. Sept. 9, 1942, Deer River, MN; home, Tucker; U. of MN, B.S. 1964, D.D.S., 1967; Presbyterian; married (Lynne).

Military Career: Air Force, 1967–69.

Elected Office: GA House of Reps., 1974–80, 1982–90.

Professional Career: Practicing dentist, 1969–82; Founder & Pres., Linder Financial Corp., 1977–92.

DC Office: 1727 LHOB 20515, 202-225-4272; Fax: 202-225-4696; Web site: linder.house.gov.

District Offices: Athens, 706-355-9909; Duluth, 770-931-9550.

Committees: *House Administration* (4th of 6 R). *Rules* (3d of 9 R): Rules & Organization of the House (Chmn.).

Group Ratings

	ADA	ACLU	AFS	LCV	CON	ITIC	NTU	COC	ACU	NTLC	CHC
2000	0	29	0	7	46	94	63	90	87	82	93
1999	10	—	0	13	61	—	57	92	87	—	—

National Journal Ratings

	1999 LIB —	1999 CONS	2000 LIB —	2000 CONS
Economic	41%	57%	6%	85%
Social	25%	75%	0%	79%
Foreign	15%	81%	33%	62%

Key Votes of the 106th Congress

1. Patient Bill of Rights	N	5. Bar RU-486 $ for FDA	Y	9. NATO War in Serbia	Y
2. Accelerate Min. Wage	N	6. Display 10 Commandments	Y	10. Perm. Trade with China	Y
3. Strike Ban on Ergo. Stnd.	N	7. Gun Show Bkgrnd. Checks	N	11. Debt Relief for 3rd World	N
4. Ovrd. Estate Tax Veto	Y	8. Ban Part.-Birth Abortion	Y	12. Drop Cuba Econ. Embargo	Y

Election Results

2000 general	John Linder (R)	.... unopposed		($418,105)
2000 primary	John Linder (R)	 43,563	(87%)	
	Vincent Littman (R)	 6,717	(13%)	
1998 general	John Linder (R)	 120,909	(69%)	($717,543)
	Vincent Littman (D)	 53,510	(31%)	($11,541)

★ HAWAII ★

Trouble in paradise. That was the story of Hawaii for most of the 1990s. While the rest of the nation has surged to prosperity, Hawaii has fallen behind. From 1992 to 1998 the gross state product declined an average of 0.5% a year, the worst in the nation. The number of jobs peaked in 1991, then fell 4% by 1997, and only began to rise again in 1999. Foreign investment plummeted from $3.6 billion in 1990 to half a billion four years later. Bankruptcies increased fivefold between 1990 and 1997. Home sales dropped 55% from 1990 to 1997. While the 49 other states have cut welfare rolls since 1993, Hawaii had a 36% increase in caseloads in a half dozen years; the caseload peaked at 25,000 in 1997 and fell to 20,000 in 2000. Child poverty rose 20% from 1992 to 1997. One reason for Hawaii's economic trouble was tourism, the mainstay of Hawaii's economy, which declined from a peak of 7 million in 1990 to 6.1 million in 1993, and did not reach 7 million again until 2000: the early 1990s recession in California and the decade-long recession in Japan. Tourism picked up in 1999 and 2000, unemployment declined, the construction industry revived. But in 2000 the Corporation for Enterprise Development still gave Hawaii a grade of D for economic performance and an F for business vitality. Hawaii's economy may be starting to grow, but the problems in paradise are not just economic. There are threats as well that some of the defining characteristics that have made Hawaii strong and tolerant in the nearly six decades after Pearl Harbor might turn sour.

Hawaii was settled only about a thousand years ago by Polynesians who paddled across vast Pacific expanses in small outrigger canoes; when Captain Cook came here in 1776, he found his Maori interpreter from New Zealand could understand Hawaiian. On these geologically young islands, teeming with food and seldom inconvenienced by bad weather, Hawaiians built a fierce civilization, with harsh taboos and cannibalism as well as alluring music and dance. The islands were united politically in 1779 by King Kamehameha I, who ate one of his rivals and maintained the old culture. In 1819, within a year of his death, his consort Kaahumanu outlawed the Hawaiian religious taboos and welcomed the American missionary Hiram Bingham. New England missionaries and their trader cousins came—while British and Russian ships occasionally put into port— and established the predominant culture. By the 1850s, laborers from China, Japan, Portugal and the Philippines streamed in to work the sugar and pineapple plantations. American planters and businessmen bridled at the caprices of the royal line and, in January 1893, with the help of U.S. Marines, ousted Queen Liliuokalani from the Iolani Palace and called on the United States to annex Hawaii. President Grover Cleveland demurred, and Hawaii for five years was a republic; it was annexed by President William McKinley in July 1898.

This history is a source of regret for some; an *Onipa'a* ceremony remembering Liliuokalani's overthrow was staged by John Waihee, the first governor of native Hawaiian descent, in January 1993, with the American flag conspicuously absent; in 1998, native Hawaiians staged a protest demonstration on the Mall in Washington. Yet Hawaii is a civilization both American and Pacific, which has created a better life for its citizens than almost any island or native commonwealth of 100 years ago. Its ethnic mixing began a century ago when disease reduced the native Hawaiians to 45,000; they shared Liliuokalani's Hawaii with 3,000 Americans, 20,000 Chinese and 25,000 Japanese. Hawaii was well on it way to being "the gathering place of peoples," as Walter McDougall called it in his history of the North Pacific, *Let the Sea Make a Noise*.

To that Americana, each group has made a positive contribution. The Asian migrant laborers brought traditions of hard work, family loyalty and group solidarity that found expression most vividly in the performance of the 442d "Go for Broke" Regimental Combat Team, made up mostly of sons of Japanese immigrants, which became the most decorated unit in U.S. military history. The Yankee spirit has been evident in Hawaii's commercial success and in its attachment to the rule of Anglo-American law. The Hawaiian spirit is alive in the vitality of the *aloha* ambience, the welcoming of others despite their differences, and a willingness to absorb the teachings of others while maintaining a certain Polynesian attitude toward life. When Pearl Harbor was attacked by the Japanese in December 1941, no one in Hawaii or on the Mainland doubted that this was part of America. Ironically, it was Hawaii's super-American tolerance that inspired segregationist

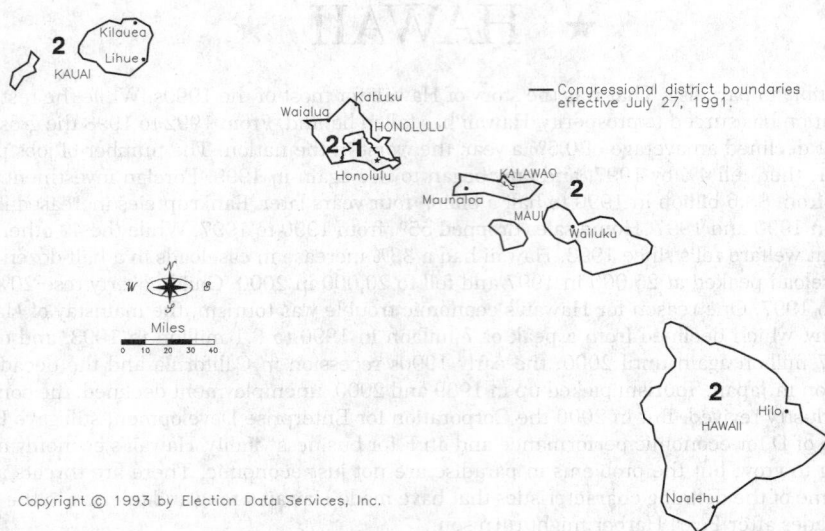

Southern Democrats to block its admission to the Union for years. Today, Hawaiians retain pride in their ethnic heritage—or heritages: about half of non-military weddings are "out" marriages and most babies are of mixed ethnicity. The 2000 Census reported that 24% of Hawaiians called themselves white, 2% black, 42% Asian, 9% Native Hawaiian or Pacific Islander, 7% Hispanic—and 21% said they were of two or more races.

Hawaii's economy was built first on agriculture, by the Big Five trading companies that shipped out sugar and pineapple and shipped in almost anything else; then on the military, important for nearly 100 years in this strategic site in the middle of the world's largest ocean. But the sugar and pineapple plantations have become uneconomic; there were just 7,650 farming jobs by 2000 compared to 11,300 in 1982. The total number of military and civilian federal employees has also fallen from 97,800 in 1988 to 64,700 in 2000. The engine of Hawaii's economy for the last quarter-century has been tourism, which accounts for one-quarter of Hawaii's economy and one-third of its jobs. But tourism dropped dramatically in the 1990s.

In this downturn Hawaii was no longer able to afford the expensive and intrusive governmental apparatus constructed by the Democrats who have controlled state government since 1962 and, despite a near-loss of the governorship in 1998, still control it today. This machine had its beginning in the 1950s, when returning World War II veterans like Daniel Inouye, Spark Matsunaga and George Ariyoshi joined forces with former Mainlander John Burns, who as a policeman during the war helped prevent persecution of Japanese Americans. They allied themselves with the then-powerful International Longshoremen's and Warehousemen's Union, and cemented the allegiance of Japanese American voters. The Burns-Inouye machine built on the grievances against the *haole* (white) owners of the big companies and triumphed. Inouye was elected as a Democrat to the House in 1959 and to the Senate in 1962; Burns was elected governor in 1962, and the office has been passed down in lineal succession to George Ariyoshi, John Waihee and now Benjamin Cayetano—a balanced ticket, of Japanese, native Hawaiian and Filipino descent. As agriculture and the docks became less important, the ILWU's power waned; it has been replaced by the public employee unions which are strongly Democratic. Voting has long tended to run along ethnic lines. Japanese Americans, used to working in organizations in unions and government, have tended to be the heart of the Democratic Party; whites, with relatively high incomes, tend toward Republicans; Filipinos, often in menial jobs, are heavily Democratic; Chinese, somewhat less so; native Hawaiians, heavily Democratic but not as likely to be active in politics.

Over the years this machine has built a large government. Despite some 1990s tax cuts, Hawaii in 2000 had the third highest per capita tax burden in the nation and the highest number of state and local employees per capita. This is centralized government: Hawaii has five counties (with one, Honolulu, covering 72% of the population), one school district, one statewide health care plan. And it is thick with regulations. It can be ridiculously generous: Until recently, Hawaii paid workmen's comp to workers who were traumatized by being laid off. The culture created by one-party control and a large state apparatus seems to be characterized in a phrase of Cayetano's, "You've got to support your friends and you have to punish your enemies." Law professor Randall Roth, a backer of Republican governor candidate Linda Lingle in 1998, explains her failure to win support among business groups by saying, "There is a fear of retribution. With regulation and centralized government, you just can't afford to be seen as an enemy of the administration."

Eight public and private entities own 69% of Hawaii's land: the federal government 16%, the state 29%, and six private landowners 24%. The Bishop Estate (Mrs. Bishop was the last surviving descendant of Kamehameha I) owns 9%. A 1984 U.S. Supreme Court decision upheld a Hawaii law forcing the estate to sell land held in 99-year leaseholds when they expire, and with the resulting cash the estate has made vast investments. It's total net worth is some $10 billion, and its purpose is to fund the Kamehameha Schools for native Hawaiians. Until 1999 its five trustees were appointed by the state Supreme Court, which is to say the Democratic machine, and paid more than $900,000 a year. But in 1998 the five trustees were embroiled in lawsuits: a criminal charge of breach of fiduciary duty was brought against one; an ouster suit was brought against four; one trustee sought the ouster of two others. Meanwhile, students at the schools charged that one trustee undermined the headmaster's authority and created an oppressive atmosphere on campus with her arbitrary and intimidating actions. All five ultimately had to settle a lawsuit, brought by the state attorney general's office, for $20.1 million for excessive compensation and mismanagement of the estate. For 2000 a probate judge picked the five trustees from seven nominees found by a court appointed committee. Salaries were slashed to $97,000, terms are limited, and the 116 year old Bishop Estate is now called the Kamehameha Schools Estate.

All these problems came to a head in the 1998 governor's race. Republican Linda Lingle, then mayor of Maui, ran a vigorous campaign calling for reform of Hawaii's swollen government, and led for a while in polls. Incumbent Governor Ben Cayetano, who had already cut taxes and government payrolls somewhat, responded with ads appealing to Hawaiian ethnic groups, recalling among other things the difficulties Japanese Americans experienced in the 1940s and 1950s. It worked, barely: Cayetano won 50%–49%. Two years later, many of Lingle's volunteers ran for the legislature, and 19 Republicans were elected to the state House—still far behind the 32 Democrats, but a big jump from before. After the election, Cayetano conceded that Democrats were seen as too close to the Bishop Estate and public employee unions and must make painful changes. "The big problem we've got is that for Democrats, the changes that this state needs are changes that are going to affect members of our family. It's going to affect organized labor; and civil service reform will affect state workers, and those are all part of our Democratic base. But we have to do these things for the good of the overall community." Hawaii still has great potential. It is still the favorite tourist destination of the Japanese, who throng to the King Kamehameha Hula Competition every June. It still has great potential as a central Pacific emporium—the stability of the American flag and dollar, the wondrous climate and physical beauty of these islands. The last is almost too good: Hawaii's island ecology means there are few species here and the islands can be easily overrun by intruders; Hawaiians are desperate to keep out the tree snake that has infested Guam and the Miconia calvescens plant that has overrun Tahiti. It has a heritage of tolerance and openness to diversity second to none.

But there may be problems here too, from the native Hawaiian sovereignty movement. Consciousness of native ancestry grew in the 1990s: in the 2000 Census, 9% of the state's residents described themselves simply as Native Hawaiian or Pacific Islander and another 8% described themselves as Native Hawaiian or Pacific Islander and another race or races (it is generally thought that less than 1% of Hawaii residents are of entirely native ancestry). More people are learning the Hawaiian language. The centennials of the overthrow of Queen Liliuokolani (1993) and of U.S. annexation of Hawaii (1998) inspired demonstrations and expressions of bitterness over the end of the Hawaiian kingdom; a Hawaiian who claims he is still living under the pre-1893 constitution has brought a case in the World Court. A state sovereignty commission met for two years and in 1996 sponsored a referendum of native Hawaiians; 73% of those eligible (with some native blood) voted yes on the question, "Shall the Hawaiian people elect delegates to propose a native Hawaiian government?" The problem is that no one is quite sure what sovereignty means. A few activists have called for independence; others seek a commonwealth status something like Puerto Rico's (though in Puerto Rico support for statehood is rising); some want native Hawaiians to be a "nation within a nation," like various North American Indian tribes. But native Hawaiians live scattered all over the Islands, and few if any native Hawaiians live in aboriginal communities; and who would say that the condition of life on Indian reservations is appealing? Nor is Indian gambling likely to be approved in Hawaii, which is one of the three states (Utah and Tennessee are the others) with no legalized gambling.

Hawaii's officeholders take a typically tolerant view. Cayetano says sovereignty will be fine if it is "acceptable to the non-Hawaiians, as well as the United States government"; the four-member Hawaiian congressional delegation promised to abide by the results of the referendum, and in the 106th Congress introduced a bill which would give native Hawaiians the same status as most Mainland Indian tribes and a "government-to-government" relation with the federal government. The U.S. Supreme Court took another view. In a case argued by Theodore Olson, George W. Bush's Solicitor General, the Court in February 2000 declared unconstitutional the 1978 Hawaii constitutional amendment setting up native-Hawaiian-only elections for the Office of Hawaiian Affairs, which administers a $400 million trust fund. "It demeans the dignity and worth of a person to be judged by ancestry instead of by his or her own merit," the Court wrote. That decision casts doubt on other provisions of the 1978 amendment, including the Hawaiian Homes Commission and the recognition of native gathering rights on private property. The bill granting native Hawaiians Indian status was passed in the U.S. House in September 2000, but was not acted on by the Senate when it adjourned in December 2000; its advocates considered it effectively killed by the election of George W. Bush. Matters may not end there. One Hawaiian nationalist (and University of Hawaii professor) predicted civil disobedience by a native Hawaiian underclass and said, "We need a land base to improve our conditions." But nurturing ethnic grievances and confining people to a racial reservation seems a far less attractive future than living in the tolerant society and First World economy that is Hawaii. Surely the sensible future for Hawaii is not to create ethnic enclaves or racial preference, but to nurture the special strengths of all the peoples who have made Hawaii tolerant and affluent—just as Hawaii, to protect its 10,000 unique biological and botanical species, needs not to put them under glass but to maintain the environment in which they have flourished. Western ideology has made Hawaii a free, tolerant, and prosperous state, and the stability of being an unquestioned part of the United States is one of the assets Hawaii can deploy to diversify its economy beyond tourism.

Governor   Ben Cayetano has twice been elected governor of Hawaii by narrow margins, and is the first American governor of Filipino descent. He grew up in Honolulu, went to college and law school in Los Angeles, then went into private practice in Hawaii; he was elected to the legislature in 1974, at 34, and served 12 years, working on low-income housing loans, auto insurance premium rollbacks and Agent Orange compensation. He was elected lieutenant governor in 1986 and was former Governor John Waihee's choice for succession. But Cayetano had serious competition in 1994. In the September primary he beat state health care program director Jack Lewin by 55%–38%. In the general he faced former Congresswoman Pat Saiki, a strong though losing candidate against Senator Daniel Akaka in 1990, and of Japanese descent; and Frank Fasi, who formed his own The Best Party using as his symbol the Hawaiian good luck gesture of a raised thumb and little finger. Fasi is the termagent of Hawaii politics, mayor of Honolulu for all but four years from 1968–94, a candidate for governor five times on the Democratic, Republican and Best Party tickets, accusing Democratic machine politicians of corruption and accused by them of it in turn. Cayetano said he was concerned about education and ran a half-hour ad telling his personal story; Saiki ran an unfocused campaign; Fasi rallied his supporters in Honolulu and came near to winning. Cayetano won with 37%, to 31% for Fasi and 29% for Saiki.

In office, Cayetano, facing big deficits, moved to hold down spending and cut the state work force. He reformed workmen's compensation, cutting business costs, and gave more authority to local schools. Telecom was deregulated. He doubled to $60 million the state's marketing budget for tourism, built a $350 million convention center on the Honolulu waterfront and started a $5 million venture capital operation, the Hawaii Technology Fund. But he insisted that he wanted to maintain state government's safety net, and the economy still sputtered. Only parts of the fall 1997 commission stimulus package were passed by the heavily Democratic legislature, and the expensive welfare system was little touched by reform.

Linda Lingle, Republican mayor of Maui since 1990, mounted a challenge. Maui had been gaining jobs during the recession: "the Maui miracle," she called it: "It's time for a change, and change is about joining the other 49 states with economic revitalization that is taking place across the country." Lingle led in polls throughout the campaign. But Cayetano appealed to Hawaii's Democratic tradition. "We Democrats have built the state." In a June 1998 poll, voters by a 49%–23% margin said Republicans were better for the economy, but by a 68%–19% said Democrats were closer to Hawaii's mainstream.In August, Lingle accused the Cayetano campaign of spreading the false rumor that she is gay. But Senator Daniel Inouye did say later, "I would prefer to have a governor who's had a family. Ben's my man." The outcome may have been determined by Lingle's decision to take state matching funds and abide by a $2.7 million spending limit; she was heavily outspent by Cayetano in the last two weeks. Voting tended to fall on ethnic lines, with Cayetano carrying heavily Filipino and Japanese American areas, and Lingle carrying 21 of the 29 state House districts where whites are the largest ethnic group.

In his second term Cayetano had more difficulty getting along with the legislature, especially the heavily Democratic Senate, which refused to reappoint Attorney General Margery Bronster (active in the Bishop Estate case) and Budget Director Earl Anzai. In 1999 it rebuffed his education and civil service proposals. In 2000 it passed his proposals to spend more for education, but again rejected most of his civil service changes—he wanted to get rid of binding arbitration for public employee contacts and wanted to fire state employees when they had a second positive drug test. Environmentalists were pleased when Cayetano, by mistake, signed new land use regulations that make it easier for the bureaucracy to impose conditions on developers. In June 2000 Cayetano signed a medical marijuana law, the first in the nation passed by a legislature and not by referendum. He was criticized by Lieutenant Governor Mazie Hirono and the state's two congressmen for joining other states in challenging the application of the Americans with Disabilities Act to state government; he said it was a states' rights issue and that Congress had exempted the federal government. Of Hawaiian sovereignty he said, "This issue could tear us apart." After the U.S. Supreme Court ruled unconstitutional the native-Hawaiians-only elections to the board of the Office of Hawaiian Affairs, he appointed non-natives to fill vacancies. Native Hawaiian activists charged that he was trying to get a settlement favorable to the state on the issue of ceded lands—native Hawaiian lands taken by the federal government after annexation and given to the state to hold in trust for the betterment of native Hawaiians. When he said he felt Hawaiian himself, which native activist Haunani-Kay Trask said was ridiculous, because only people with Hawaiian blood can feel Hawaiian. Cayetano's response to such criticism: "And if you look at, listen to comments by those who are in OHA right now, it's the same game that I used to see being played on white people on the Mainland—the guilt game, you know what I mean? If you disagree with me, you're anti-Hawaiian. That kind of dialogue never helps anybody."

After Republicans, led by Lingle, now state party chairman, made gains in legislative elections, Cayetano announced that the budget was headed toward red ink. He called for more spending on classrooms and computers, and more concentration on engineering, medicine and business at the University of Hawaii. He criticized a bill passed by Senator Daniel Inouye—still the most powerful figure in Hawaii politics—that would bar gambling on cruise ships beginning and ending voyages in Hawaii. In late 2000 and early 2001 the labor negotiation rules Cayetano had sought to change seemed to be forcing huge increases in state spending. A strike by teacher's unions and University of Hawaii faculty basically shut down the public school system for three weeks in April 2001, until agreement was reached on a 10% payraise over two and a half years for teachers and a 12% raise over two years for the university faculty.

In early 2001 it appeared that three candidates would run for governor in 2002. One was

Republican Linda Lingle, who had promised to run again soon after losing in 1998. Another was Democratic Lieutenant Governor Mazie Hirono, who tended to take more liberal positions than Cayetano. The third was Democratic Honolulu Mayor Jeremy Harris. Cayetano's prediction: "If it's Lingle against Harris—no contest. If it's Hirono and Lingle, it will be a slightly tougher race, but in the end Hirono is going to win. You know, even though the Democrats keep on shooting ourselves in the foot, the Republicans do it more often."

Cook's Call   *Competitive.* After 36 years of Democratic governors, the signs are growing that Hawaiians are in the mood for change: Republicans picked up 19 seats in the state legislature in 2000. Republicans start as the underdog, but this could be a very competitive race.

Senior Senator   The largest figure in Hawaii's public life remains Senator Daniel K. Inouye, who has held elective office here since Hawaii attained statehood in 1959, and before. Inouye grew up in Honolulu, the son of Japanese immigrants; his ambition was to become a surgeon. He served in the 442d Regimental Combat Team in World War II, in which capacity he earned 15 medals and citations and, in the last days of the war, lost his right arm. Unsure of what to do, recovering in a Michigan veterans' hospital, he asked a Kansas veteran whose right arm had been shattered what his plans were; the man said he was going to law school, would run for the legislature and "when the opportunity presents itself, I am going to Congress": it was Bob Dole. They served together two years in the House and 28 in the Senate. Inouye graduated from the University of Hawaii and George Washington University Law School, then became a leader of a group of young veterans who took over Hawaii's creaking Democratic party. He was elected to the territorial legislature in 1954, the House in 1959, and the Senate in 1962. He was keynoter at the turbulent 1968 Democratic National Convention, a tenacious member of the Senate Watergate Committee in 1973–74 and the first chairman of the Senate Intelligence Committee, in 1976. Inouye believes in the Senate, the Democratic Party, Hawaii, the armed services, and Native Americans—among other things. He is the fourth most senior member of the Senate, after Strom Thurmond, Robert Byrd and Edward Kennedy. In June 2000 he was awarded the Congressional Medal of Honor.

Inouye is chairman of the Appropriations Defense Subcommittee and the second ranking Democrat on Appropriations; the committee's ranking Republican is Ted Stevens of Alaska, which gives enormous clout to two senators in office since the 1960s from the two states most recently admitted to the Union, both with their own special claims on the federal government. Inouye's voting record has generally been very liberal, but not always. On foreign and defense issues he is close to the center of the Senate. He and Hawaii colleague Daniel Akaka were two of the four Democrats who joined all Republicans in 1998 in seeking to deploy a ballistic missile defense system; the Clinton administration's opposition to deployment was based in part on an intelligence estimate that there will be no missile threat within the next 10 years to the continental 48 states—which seems to exclude Hawaii and Alaska from the "common defense" the Constitution promises.

Inouye has long used his seat on Appropriations to fund projects he finds worthy, from his alma mater of George Washington University to native Hawaiian education. Over the years the federal government spent $445 million to clean up the Kahoolawe bombing range, and Inouye obtained $1.2 billion in emergency aid after Hurrican Iniki in 1992. He persisted 25 years to build the "interstate" highway H-3 from the Windward Coast to Pearl Harbor, finally opened in 1997. In 1999 Hawaii received $800 million in federal spending, in 2000 $1.25 billion, most of it from the military budget, which is to say it passes through Inouye's subcommittee. "Considering the situation, I think we've done pretty well," Inouye said in 2000. "I'm here to see that it continues." In 1997 he saw that the American Classic cruise line received a 25-year virtual monopoly on interisland cruises in return for the company's promise to spend $1.4 billion on new ships to be built in Ingalls Shipyard in Pascagoula, Mississippi, the home town of Senator Trent Lott; construction began in 1999. He helped to persuade the Navy that the *U.S.S. Missouri's* final berth would be at Pearl Harbor.

He has proudly earmarked projects for Hawaii in the defense appropriations bill; the December 2000 bill included $41 million for ocean resources and marine research—$1 million to the Pacific Coastal Services Cooperative Center, $8 million to convert the Adventurous, a mothballed

Navy vessel, to a high-endurance fisheries and oceanographic research vessel, $13.5 million for the East-West Center at University of Hawaii. Like his colleague and friend Ted Stevens, Inouye takes a kind of proprietary interest in the public policy of his home area, with a sense of responsibility for its long-term development and character. In 2000 he moved quickly to pass a law banning gambling on cruise ships beginning and ending their voyages in Hawaii. "I have made it clear that I do not want gambling in Hawaii many times . . . I have been unwavering in my position that gambling on voyages beginning and ending in Hawaii will not be accepted practice." In 1999 he introduced a bill to spend $100 million to preserve coral reefs in the waters off northwestern Hawaii; but he and others opposed giving the area national monument status which would ban all fishing. In December 2000 Bill Clinton declared 84 million acres of the ocean—an area larger than Florida and Georgia combined—a nature preserve, banning oil and gas exploration and any dumping or alterations of seabed or coral, but allowing fishing at recent or current levels.

Inouye chaired the Indian Affairs Committee from 1989–94, and was moved by their tragic history. He described his reaction: "By God, did we do all these things? We should be embarrassed and ashamed of ourselves." He was an early backer of Indian gaming, which has transformed the life of many tribes, and worked to authorize a new building on Washington's Mall to house part of the American Indian Museum collection. He and Jeff Bingaman of New Mexico sponsored the bill to award the Congressional Gold Medal to the 29 Navajo code talkers who served during World War II. He evidently sees many analogies between the condition of Mainland Indians and native Hawaiians. He was a co-sponsor of the 1993 law in which the United States apologized for overthrowing the Hawaiian monarchy. He supported the Hawaiian Homes Commission Act and in 2000 finally secured funding for native Hawaiians purchasing property in the Home Lands, the 200,000 acres set aside in 1920 for a permanent homeland for native Hawaiians. He secured reauthorization of native Hawaiian health care programs in 2000, but did not succeed in giving it entitlement status. On the heated issue of native Hawaiian sovereignty, some native Hawaiian activists consider him lukewarm. In October 1999 Office of Hawaiian Affairs Trustee Mililani Trask attacked him with vile insults; Inouye said he was saddened. In December 2000 he and colleague Daniel Akaka did not succeed in getting through the Senate the House-passed bill granting Indian tribe status to native Hawaiians and a "government-to-government" relation with the federal government. Some Republican senators objected, and its prospects seem dim while George W. Bush is president.

On the Commerce Committee, Inouye was long involved in communications issues and tended to favor government regulation over markets. He backed cable reregulation and was pleased that the Telecommunications Act of 1996 imposed a competition checklist for local services on the Regional Bells before they could enter the long-distance market. Inouye wanted to set aside up to 20% of the information superhighway for libraries, schools, state and local governments and nonprofits, but the provision was not included in the final bill.

Honolulu is a long two flights from Washington, and Inouye's local influence has varied, but is generally great. Despite some disagreements with Governor Ben Cayetano, he has supported every governor since 1962. His apparent choice for 2002 is Lieutenant Governor Mazie Hirono. Inouye has always been re-elected by wide margins. His greatest trouble came in 1992, when Republican Rick Reed ran an ad with tapes of a woman who was long Inouye's barber making charges about events many years before. On election day, Inouye won with a much reduced percentage, 57%, to 27% for Reed and 14% for the Green Party's Linda Martin. In 1998 he faced less controversy. In October, Republican Crystal Young alleged that actress Shirley MacLaine implanted electromagnetic needles in her. MacLaine said she had not been in Hawaii in "years and years and years," and added, "I don't know anything about this and she certainly won't get my vote." She didn't get many others, either. Inouye won 79%–18%. He seems likely to win re-election again, if he runs, in 2004.

Junior Senator   Daniel Akaka is the first senator of (partial) native Hawaiian descent. Born four days after Daniel Inouye, he served in the Army Corps of Engineers in the 1940s, went to college, taught school and became a principal. As he tells it, "People have asked me, 'When did you plan to run for the Senate?' I say, 'I never did.' As an educator, my goal was to be superintendent. That's it." In 1971, at 47, he became director of the Hawaii antipoverty program; in

1975, he became an assistant to Governor George Ariyoshi. The next year, when both of Hawaii's congressmen ran for the Senate, he was elected to the House, where he served quietly on the Appropriations Committee. In May 1990, after the death of Senator Spark Matsunaga, Governor John Waihee appointed Akaka to the Senate. He has thus been an integral part of the dominant Democratic organization and a quiet but diligent worker on Hawaii issues for nearly 30 years. As he says, "My priorities have been first for Hawaii, unless it affects our country."

Akaka, though a member of Congress since 1976, is not well known in Washington. "I do much of my work with members in committees," he said. "I do it that way because it works, it's where you find out whether you have heavy opposition, which could cause you to change tactics or not even bring [the issue] up." In 1997, as a member of the Governmental Affairs Committee investigating Clinton-Gore campaign finances, Akaka charged that Clinton had dropped Asian-Americans from consideration for Cabinet posts because of the controversy and criticized the Democratic National Committee for having auditors ask Asian-Americans about "whether they were citizens, how they earn their money, if they would provide their tax returns, and other intrusive questions." In July 1997 he said, "I am seriously concerned with the negative impact that the allegations of fundraising abuse have had on the Asian-Pacific-American community."

Akaka has a mostly liberal voting record, somewhat less so on foreign and defense issues; he and Inouye were two of the four Democrats supporting deployment of a ballistic missile defense system in 1998. Hawaii, out in the Pacific, is much more vulnerable to North Korean missiles than the U.S. Mainland. Akaka also worked for a 1991 ban on German chemical weapons dumping on Johnston Island, 700 miles southwest of Hawaii, and in 1996 he opposed a proposed nuclear waste dump on Palmyra Island, 1,000 miles southwest. He vehemently opposed French nuclear testing in the South Pacific. He sponsored the Hawaiian Home Lands Recovery Act of 1995, to reclaim Native lands in Lualualei unlawfully withdrawn from the home lands when Hawaii was a territory; it was partly implemented in 1998. He sponsored a 1998 law to allow Hawaii energy companies during an emergency to buy oil at the average price of successful bids for Strategic Petroleum Reserve oil.

Much of Akaka's time has been spent on the issue of native Hawaiian sovereignty. He was the sponsor of the 1993 Apology Resolution, signed by Bill Clinton, in which the United States acknowledged as illegal the overthrow of the Kingdom of Hawaii in 1893 and the denial of native Hawaiians' right to self-determination. In 1998 and 1999 he pushed the Clinton administration to recognize native Hawaiians as an aboriginal people with whom the U.S. has a special relationship, as it does with Indian tribes. But in February 2000 the U.S. Supreme Court ruled that the Hawaii Constitution provision limiting voting for the Office of Hawaiian Affairs to those of native Hawaiian descent was unconstitutional racial discrimination; the Clinton administration assertion of a special relationship was rejected. Other lawsuits were brought against OHA activities. In response, in July 2000 Akaka introduced a native recognition bill, which would recognize native Hawaiians as an indigenous people with a right to self-determination and set up a process for formation of a native Hawaiian governing body to have, as many Indian tribes do, a government-to-government relationship with the United States. Thanks to the energetic efforts of Congressman Neil Abercrombie, this passed the House in September 2000. But in the Senate some Republicans objected to unanimous consent, and it died there in December. Akaka promises to bring the issue up again, but with George W. Bush as president it seems unlikely to become law.

Other Akaka causes include the 1995 law for a review of service records in World War II with a view to awarding higher medals to deserving Asian Americans (under this, Senator Daniel Inouye was awarded the Congressional Medal of Honor in 2000), a law making permanent the waiver of visa requirements from certain countries including Japan (2 million Japanese visit Hawaii every year), laws expanding (and renaming) the Hawaii Volcanoes National Park and requiring the FAA and the National Park Service to negotiate limits on air tours over Haleakala and a five-year study of the energy potential of methane hydrates.

Akaka had one tough election in 1990—indeed the only Senate election in Hawaii that has generated any suspense since 1976. His opponent, Republican Congresswoman Pat Saiki, conceded that Akaka was congenial, but suggested he was ineffective and not too bright. Akaka struck back with ads attacking drugs and his work to end the use of the island of Kahoolawe as a target range. The Democratic organization worked hard and Akaka won 54%–45%, carrying not just the Democratic Neighbor Islands and poorer areas of Honolulu, but most of Oahu as well. In 1994 Akaka was easily re-elected, 72%–24%. In 2000, his Republican opponent campaigned against the native recognition bill, and lost 73%–25%. Akaka has not said whether he will run again in 2006, when he turns 82.

Presidential politics Hawaii's presidential voting over the years has been the product of two, sometimes countervailing, forces. One is the Islands' strong Democratic partisan preference, since voters tend to favor big government and value racial tolerance and diversity. This helps explain why Hawaii voted Democratic when most states didn't in 1980 and 1988. The other is an inclination to support incumbents in a state that takes patriotism very seriously, in part because the patriotism of so many of its citizens was once unjustly questioned and in part because, in these heavily fortified Pacific islands, foreign threats seem more menacing. This helps explain why Hawaii supported Ronald Reagan solidly in 1984 and came close to voting for Gerald Ford in 1976, though it wasn't nearly enough to help George Bush in 1992: Ross Perot's military background, and the presence of Hawaiian Orson Swindle among his top leaders, gave him 14% and helped Bill Clinton carry Hawaii 48%–37%. In 1996 and 2000, as in 1968 and 1980, both those forces were moving in the same direction, and Hawaii voted 57%–32% for Bill Clinton and a nearly identical 56%–37% for Al Gore.

Hawaii chooses presidential delegates by caucus. Sometimes insurgents have been able to swamp thinly-attended meetings and win, as Jesse Jackson and Pat Robertson did in 1988. Since then Hawaii's caucus-goers have gone for the frontrunners.

Congressional districting Hawaii has two congressional districts: the 1st includes urban Honolulu (city elections now cover all of Oahu) and extends westward to Pearl Harbor and the rural area beyond; the 2d includes the rest of Oahu and the Neighbor Islands. Both districts are represented by liberal Democrats who had served in the past, then lost elections, ran again and won in 1990 and have been re-elected since. The boundaries will probably be adjusted slightly by the heavily Democratic legislature.

THE PEOPLE: Pop. 2000: 1,211,537; Pop. 1990: 1,108,229, up 9.3% 1990–2000. 0.4% of U.S. total, 42d largest; 24.3% White, 1.8% Black, 41.6% Asian, 0.3% Amer. Indian, 9.4% Hawaiian, 21.4% Two+ races, 1.3% Other; 7.2% Hispanic Origin. 4.3% Unemployment. 2000 Voting age pop.: 915,770. 2000 Turnout: 371,033; 41% of VAP. Registered voters (2000): 637,349; no party registration.

POLITICAL LINEUP: Governor, Benjamin J. Cayetano (D); Lt. Gov. & Secy. of State, Mazie Hirono (D); Atty. Gen., Earl I. Anzai (D); Comptroller, Raymond Sato (D); State Senate, 25 (22 D, 3 R); Senate President, Robert Bunda (D); Co-Majority Leader, Jonathon Chun (D); Co-Majority Leader, Cal Kawamoto (D); State House, 51 (32 D, 19 R); House Speaker, Calvin Say (D). Senators, Daniel K. Inouye (D) and Daniel K. Akaka (D). Representatives, 2 (2 D).

ELECTIONS DIVISION: 808-453-8683; **FILING DEADLINE FOR U.S. CONGRESS:** July 20, 2002.

2000 Presidential Vote

Gore (D)	205,286	(56%)
Bush (R)	137,845	(37%)
Nader (Green)	21,623	(6%)
Others	3,197	(1%)

1996 Presidential Vote

Clinton (D)	205,012	(57%)
Dole (R)	113,943	(32%)
Perot (I)	27,362	(8%)
Others	13,807	(4%)

Gov. Benjamin J. Cayetano (D)

Elected 1994, term expires Jan. 2003, 2d term; b. Nov. 14, 1939, Honolulu; home, Honolulu; U. of CA, B.A. 1968, Loyola Law Schl., J.D. 1971; Christian; married (Vicki).

Elected Office: HI House of Reps., 1974–78; HI Senate 1978–86; HI Lt. Gov., 1986–90.

Professional Career: Practicing atty., 1971–86.

Office: State Capitol, Executive Chambers, Honolulu, 96813, 808-586-0034; Fax: 808-586-0006; Web site: www.state.hi.us.

Election Results

1998 general	Benjamin J. Cayetano (D)	204,206	(50%)
	Linda Lingle (R)	198,952	(49%)
	Others	4,398	(1%)
1998 primary	Benjamin J. Cayetano (D)	95,797	(86%)
	Jim Brewer (D)	6,169	(6%)
	Others	8,914	(8%)
1994 general	Benjamin J. Cayetano (D)	134,978	(37%)
	Frank F. Fasi (Best)	113,158	(31%)
	Patricia F. Saiki (R)	107,908	(29%)
	Others	12,969	(4%)

Sen. Daniel K. Inouye (D)

Elected 1962, seat up 2004, 7th term; b. Sept. 7, 1924, Honolulu; home, Honolulu; U. of HI, B.A. 1950, George Washington U., J.D. 1952; United Methodist; married (Margaret).

Military Career: Army, 1943–47 (WWII).

Elected Office: HI House of Reps., 1954–58; HI Senate, 1958–59; U.S. House of Reps., 1959–62.

Professional Career: Honolulu Dpty. Public Prosecutor, 1953–54.

DC Office: 722 HSOB, 20510, 202-224-3934; Fax: 202-224-6747; Web site: www.senate.gov/~inouye.

State Offices: Hilo, 808-935-0844; Honolulu, 808-541-2542; Kauai, 808-245-4610; Kona, 808-935-0844; Maui, 808-242-9702; Molokai, 808-642-0203.

Committees: *Appropriations*: Commerce, Justice, State & Judiciary; Defense (Chmn.); Foreign Operations; Labor, HHS & Education; Military Construction. *Commerce, Science & Transportation*: Aviation; Communications; Oceans & Fisheries; Surface Transportation & Merchant Marine (Chmn.). *Indian Affairs* (Chmn.). *Rules & Administration*.

Group Ratings

	ADA	ACLU	AFS	LCV	CON	ITIC	NTU	COC	ACU	NTLC	CHC
2000	60	71	75	57	73	85	10	69	23	0	15
1999	95	—	100	33	51	—	4	50	0	—	—

National Journal Ratings

	1999 LIB	—	1999 CONS		2000 LIB	—	2000 CONS
Economic	66%	—	32%		73%	—	25%
Social	88%	—	0%		79%	—	0%
Foreign	78%	—	13%		62%	—	34%

Key Votes of the 106th Congress

1. Educ. Savings Accts.	*	5. Review Movie Violence	N	9. NATO War in Serbia	Y
2. Prescrip. Drug Benefit	Y	6. Gun Show Bckgrnd. Checks	Y	10. Table Cuba Travel Ban	N
3. Delay Ergonomic Standards	*	7. Ban Part.-Birth Abortion	N	11. Nuclear Test-Ban Treaty	Y
4. Phase Out Estate Tax	N	8. Broaden Hate Crimes List	Y	12. Perm. Trade with China	Y

Election Results

1998 general	Daniel K. Inouye (D)	315,252	(79%)	($1,375,601)
	Crystal Young (R)	70,964	(18%)	
	Others	11,908	(3%)	
1998 primary	Daniel K. Inouye (D)	108,891	(93%)	
	Richard Thompson (D)	8,468	(7%)	
1992 general	Daniel K. Inouye (D)	208,266	(57%)	($3,515,722)
	Rick Reed (R)	97,928	(27%)	($438,851)
	Linda B. Martin (Green)	49,921	(14%)	($6,687)
	Others	7,547	(2%)	

Sen. Daniel K. Akaka (D)

Appointed May 1990, seat up 2006, 2d term; b. Sept. 11, 1924, Honolulu; home, Honolulu; U. of HI, B.Ed. 1952, M.A. 1966; Congregationalist; married (Mary Mildred).

Military Career: Army Corps of Engineers, 1945–47 (WWII).

Elected Office: U.S. House of Reps., 1976–90.

Professional Career: Public schl. teacher, principal & admin., 1953–71; Dir., HI Office of Econ. Oppor., 1971–74; Asst., HI Gov. Ariyoshi, 1975–76; Dir., Progressive Neighborhoods Program, 1975–76.

DC Office: 141 HSOB, 20510, 202-224-6361; Fax: 202-224-2126; Web site: www.senate.gov/~akaka.

State Offices: Hilo, 808-935-1114; Honolulu, 808-522-8970.

Committees: *Armed Services:* Personnel; Readiness & Management Support (Chmn.); Strategic Forces. *Energy & Natural Resources:* Energy Research, Development, Production & Regulation; Forests & Public Land Management; National Parks, Historic Preservation & Recreation (Chmn.). *Ethics (Select). Governmental Affairs:* Government Management, Restructuring and the District of Columbia; International Security, Proliferation & Federal Services (Chmn.); Investigations (Permanent). *Indian Affairs. Veterans' Affairs.*

Group Ratings

	ADA	ACLU	AFS	LCV	CON	ITIC	NTU	COC	ACU	NTLC	CHC
2000	85	71	100	71	73	86	10	46	12	0	15
1999	100	—	100	89	51	—	3	41	4	—	—

National Journal Ratings

	1999 LIB —	1999 CONS		2000 LIB —	2000 CONS
Economic	90% —	0%		94% —	4%
Social	75% —	20%		79% —	0%
Foreign	78% —	13%		69% —	30%

Key Votes of the 106th Congress

1. Educ. Savings Accts.	N	5. Review Movie Violence	N	9. NATO War in Serbia	Y
2. Prescrip. Drug Benefit	Y	6. Gun Show Bckgrnd. Checks	Y	10. Table Cuba Travel Ban	N
3. Delay Ergonomic Standards	N	7. Ban Part.-Birth Abortion	N	11. Nuclear Test-Ban Treaty	Y
4. Phase Out Estate Tax	N	8. Broaden Hate Crimes List	Y	12. Perm. Trade with China	*

Election Results

2000 general	Daniel K. Akaka (D)	251,215	(73%)	($428,516)
	John Carroll (R)	84,701	(25%)	($97,407)
	Others	9,707	(3%)	
2000 primary	Daniel K. Akaka (D)	13,857	(91%)	
	Art P. Reyes (D)	1,317	(9%)	
1994 general	Daniel K. Akaka (D)	256,189	(72%)	($1,017,872)
	Maria M. Hustace (R)	86,320	(24%)	($29,293)
	Richard O. Rowland (Lib)	14,393	(4%)	

FIRST DISTRICT

Tourists in Honolulu see the airport and adjacent Hickam Air Force Base, the *Arizona* monument in Pearl Harbor, perhaps the downtown with its wondrously Victorian Iolani Palace, and of course Waikiki, with its 40-story hotels rising within a few feet of one another. This is tight-packed Hawaii, between the 3,000-foot Koolau Range and the beaches and harbor, where tropical bungalows and garden apartments house Hawaiians of all incomes. Here are Hawaii's largest shopping centers and its state university; here are neighborhoods where the rich overlook the ocean and neighborhoods where the relatively poor are packed into people-clogged streets. Hawaii's topography also jams cars into just a few freeways and avenues, where traffic slows during rush hour and the *aloha* spirit is sorely tested.

Politically, the neighborhoods around Honolulu's downtown and the university campus are lower income and usually Democratic. To the west, around the harbor, are many military families in modest neighborhoods who may vote for Democrats but can be attracted to Republicans. To the east, past Waikiki, around Diamond Head and out to the Kahala and Koko Head beach areas, is higher-income territory, voting for Republicans when they seriously contest a race.

The congressman from the 1st District is Neil Abercrombie, a Democrat with a graying beard who used to sport a pony tail (he cut it off because "it was getting in the way of getting things done"). He has been called an aging hippie but celebrated his 60th birthday by bench-pressing 260 pounds in the House gym; he debates with an aggressiveness and bombast tempered by enthusiasm and good humor. After college in Upstate New York, he taught school, moved to Hawaii, earned a Ph.D. in sociology; he was elected to the Hawaii legislature in 1974 and served 12 years. Abercrombie first came to the House in 1986, when he won a special election, and served only three months; he lost a primary for the full term to a Democrat who then lost to Republican Pat Saiki. When she ran for the Senate, Abercrombie won a three-way primary in 1990 for the House seat and won the general election easily.

Abercrombie is one of the distinctive and often delightful figures in the House. His voting record is mostly, but not entirely, liberal. He serves on the Armed Services Committee and sees no contradiction between his protests of the Vietnam war and votes for military spending in Hawaii and elsewhere. "I see my work on Armed Services as a fulfillment of my principles and the motivating force of my life. I never opposed the military. . . . It's not about pro-war or anti-war, but how do you keep the peace." He did vote against military intervention in Bosnia and Kosovo, because he believed diplomatic options had not been exhausted. But he still gets things done on Armed Services. He helped to get $277 million in military construction for Hawaii in 2000, for example, and added a $275 reimbursement to transferred-in military personnel for pet quarantines (Hawaii, with its fragile ecology, charges $655 and $1,080 for quarantines). In April 2000 he got a Navy admiral to commit to keeping nuclear submarine jobs in Hawaii, but endorsed a later plan to move some subs to Guam. "By building up Guam, we build up Hawaii. The logistical tail that runs from Guam runs right through Hawaii."

On other issues Abercrombie is not always predictable. In July 2000 he joined Resources Committee Republicans in voting for a contempt citation opposed by other Democrats. He cosponsored repeal of the inheritance tax—there are a lot of small businesses in Hawaii, he said. Despite Hawaii's trade interests, he voted against Permanent Normal Trade Relations with China. He defended the Hawaiian Education Act money against John Boehner's charge that it was just subsidizing the Bishop Estate. He won a signal and surprising victory in September 2000 as House sponsor of the native recognition act, which would recognize native Hawaiians as an indigenous people with a right to self-determination and set up a process for formation of a native Hawaiian governing body to have, as many Indian tribes do, a government-to-government relationship with the United States. He won the support of Resources Chairman Don Young, who has always been sympathetic to the Natives in his home state of Alaska, and the bill was passed unanimously by the committee. It was brought to the floor as a noncontroversial matter and passed there. The lead Senate sponsor Daniel Akaka did not have such luck. He got the Indian Affairs Committee to let the House version come to the floor, but only under a rule of unanimous consent; when some conservative Republicans voiced objection, the bill was dead.

Despite the Democratic nature of the 1st District, Abercrombie had serious competition in 1994 and 1996 from Orson Swindle, Marine Corps pilot and Vietnam POW, a national leader of Ross Perot's United We Stand America in 1992 and later member of the Federal Communications Commission. In 1994 Swindle charged that Abercrombie was too dovish, but Abercrombie outraised him and won 54%–43%. In 1996 Swindle labeled Abercrombie a far left hippie and called for big spending cuts. Abercrombie only narrowly outspent him, and won by only 50%–46%, even as Bill Clinton was smashing Bob Dole locally. In 1997 it looked like he would be opposed by Quentin Kawananakoa, a descendant of King Kalakaua and Queen Kapiolanoi and minority leader—of the then 12 Republicans—in the state House. But in August Kawananakoa left the race for health reasons, and Abercrombie won 62%–36%. In 2000, against Phil Meyers, the son of former Kansas Republican Congresswoman Jan Meyers, Abercrombie again won 69%–29%.

Cook's Call *Safe.* Abercrombie's close calls in1994 and 1996 gave Republicans every reason to be enthusiastic about reclaiming a seat they held from 1986–90. But, convincing wins in 1998 and 2000 and Gore's 55% showing here in 2000 should temper Republican enthusiasm for targeting Abercrombie in 2002.

THE PEOPLE: Pop. 2000: 568,524; Pop. 1990: 554,174, up 2.6% 1990–2000. 19.5% White, 2.1% Black, 53.5% Asian, 0.2% Amer. Indian, 6.8% Hawaiian, 16.9% Two+ races, 1% Other; 5.4% Hispanic Origin.

2000 Presidential Vote		
Gore (D)	95,628	(55%)
Bush (R)	67,356	(39%)
Nader (Green)	8,568	(5%)
Others	1,282	(1%)

1996 Presidential Vote		
Clinton (D)	99,351	(57%)
Dole (R)	58,906	(34%)
Perot (I)	10,741	(6%)
Others	5,521	(3%)

Rep. Neil Abercrombie (D)

Elected 1990, 6th term; b. June 26, 1938, Buffalo, NY; home, Honolulu; Union Col., B.A. 1959, U. of HI, M.A.1964, Ph.D. 1974; no religious affiliation; married (Nancie Caraway).

Elected Office: HI House of Reps., 1974–78; HI Senate, 1978–86; U.S. House of Reps., 1986–87; Honolulu City Cncl., 1988–90.

Professional Career: College teacher, 1959–63; Probation Officer, Marin Cnty., CA, 1964–67; Sociologist, 1967–74; Asst. prof., HI Loa Col., 1979–80; Consultant, 1983–87, 1989–90; Asst., HI Superintendent of Educ., 1987–88.

DC Office: 1502 LHOB 20515, 202-225-2726; Fax: 202-225-4580; Web site: www.house.gov/abercrombie.

District Office: Honolulu, 808-541-2570.

Committees: *Armed Services* (6th of 28 D): Military Installations & Facilities (RMM); Military Research & Development. *Resources* (7th of 25 D): Fisheries Conservation, Wildlife & Oceans.

Group Ratings

	ADA	ACLU	AFS	LCV	CON	ITIC	NTU	COC	ACU	NTLC	CHC
2000	80	86	85	86	11	39	24	42	12	21	7
1999	100	—	100	94	37	—	9	17	4	—	—

National Journal Ratings

	1999 LIB	—	1999 CONS		2000 LIB	—	2000 CONS
Economic	88%	—	0%		66%	—	33%
Social	87%	—	0%		86%	—	12%
Foreign	55%	—	45%		77%	—	21%

Key Votes of the 106th Congress

1. Patient Bill of Rights	Y	5. Bar RU-486 $ for FDA		N	9. NATO War in Serbia	*
2. Accelerate Min. Wage	Y	6. Display 10 Commandments		N	10. Perm. Trade with China	N
3. Strike Ban on Ergo. Stnd.	Y	7. Gun Show Bkgrnd. Checks		Y	11. Debt Relief for 3rd World	Y
4. Ovrd. Estate Tax Veto	Y	8. Ban Part.-Birth Abortion		N	12. Drop Cuba Econ. Embargo	Y

Election Results

2000 general	Neil Abercrombie (D)	108,517	(69%)	($722,133)
	Phil Meyers (R)	44,989	(29%)	($22,042)
	Others	3,688	(2%)	
2000 primary	Neil Abercrombie (D)	unopposed		
1998 general	Neil Abercrombie (D)	116,693	(62%)	($1,082,330)
	Gene Ward (R)	68,905	(36%)	($701,480)
	Others	3,973	(2%)	

SECOND DISTRICT

The 2d District of Hawaii includes not only the Neighbor Islands but most of Oahu's acreage beyond the city of Honolulu. It has Wheeler Air Force Base, still looking much as it did in December 1941, and the farmlands north of Pearl Harbor, between two jagged chains of mountains that lift the island out of the sea. Over the mountains to the west is the Leeward Coast—calm, sultry and lightly populated; over the mountains to the northeast is the Windward Coast with many prosperous and Republican subdivisions in and around Kaneohe and Kailua. The Neighbor Islands have distinct personalities. Hawaii, the Big Island, is large enough to boast huge cattle ranches, the active volcano of Kilauea, and Mauna Kea, the highest mountain in the world if you count from its base far under the ocean to the peak; tourists are told that it is bad luck to take pieces of lava home, and many send them back. On the north shore, with heavy rainfall and tropical foliage, is the old port of Hilo and Hawaii's macadamia nut industry; this is a blue-collar Democratic area. On the Kona Coast, where there is little rainfall and the landscape is dominated by lava flows, there are retirement condominiums and a higher-income, more Republican population. Maui, favored more by North American than Asian tourists, has dozens of luxury condominiums and vast upscale resorts. But there is risk in paradise: Many of Hawaii's native plants are facing extinction due to the pigs, goats and diseases introduced to the islands since Captain Cook arrived in 1776. Kauai, much of which was devastated by Hurricane Iniki in 1992, is the least-developed and most agricultural of the main islands; parts of it have the nation's highest rainfall, while others seldom get wet. Its large farm work force makes it the most Democratic of the islands.

The 2d District is represented by Patsy Mink, still exuberant and enthusiastically liberal after a long political career. She grew up in Hawaii, went to law school in Chicago, then practiced law in Honolulu starting in 1953 and became involved in politics as part of the liberal Democratic group that won a majority in the territorial legislature in 1954. She was first elected to the House in 1964, gave up the seat to run unsuccessfully for the Senate in 1976, then, after losing races for governor in 1986 and mayor of Honolulu in 1988, won the House seat again in 1990 after incumbent Daniel Akaka was appointed to the Senate. She is thus one of only three House members—the others are Michigan Democrats John Dingell and John Conyers—who served in the Great Society Congress of 1965–66. (Four senators also served in the Senate in that Congress: Strom Thurmond, Robert Byrd, Edward Kennedy and Daniel Inouye.) Mink helped feminism grow from a fringe cause to one of the main rallying cries for Democrats, and sponsored a gender equity act, which passed the House and then the Senate—though in a more diluted form—and women's health care measures. She spoke with special vehemence in March 1995 against product liability reform. (She sued a drug company and hospital 44 years ago after she was prescribed the anti-miscarriage drug DES; it was later thought to expose children to a greater risk of cancer, and Mink collected a $250,000 settlement.)

After spending most of her legislative career in the majority—often a large one—the minority seems not to suit Mink. She has served for many years on the committee now called Education and the Work Force. With great vehemence Mink has criticized the Republicans. She opposed a $1.4 million review of labor laws. As ranking member on Peter Hoekstra's Oversight Subcommittee, she called his hearings on the Teamsters a "sham," sought delays at many turns and opposed issuance of subpoenas. Mink has taken the Democratic line on education, calling for smaller class sizes and more money for special education, computers and school construction. But she split with the party by supporting repeal of the estate tax and with the Clinton administration by opposing Permanent Normal Trade Relations with China. She has called for research on medical marijuana.

On Hawaii legislation Mink has steered her own course. She sponsored the law for financing home purchases by native Hawaiians in or near the Hawaiian homelands, and sponsored a change from "Unknown" to "Dec. 7, 1941, U.S.S. Arizona" on 74 graves in the Punchbowl cemetery. She sought money for observers required by a court decision on longline fishing boats, and got money for a study on restoring the wetlands in Kealia Pond National Wildlife Refuge, home of the endangered Hawaiian stilt and Hawaiian coot. On the native recognition bill sought by her House colleague Neil Abercrombie and Senator Daniel Akaka, she showed skepticism. This legislation would recognize native Hawaiians as an indigenous people with a right to self-determination and set up a process for formation of a native Hawaiian governing body to have, as many Indian tribes do, a government-to-government relationship with the United States. In the spring of 2000 she said the bill needed more work, and declined in the summer to become a co-sponsor. In September 2000 she said it "should merely state that the federal government is ready to recognize the native Hawaiian people as aboriginal and indigenous and enable them to assemble as such to petition the United States for such recognition as they deem appropriate." The Supreme Court in February 2000 had overturned as unconstitutional racial discrimination the Hawaii Constitution provision that limited voting for the Office of Hawaiian Affairs trustees to native Hawaiians, and Mink evidently felt uncomfortable with federal legislation based on specifying that members of a certain race had certain rights; she said also that native Hawaiians need more time to think about what sovereignty means. She did vote for the bill when, surprisingly, it passed the House in September 2000 under a procedure for uncontroversial legislation; it died, however, in the Senate and seems unlikely to become law while George W. Bush is president.

Mink won the seat in 1990 by narrowly edging former 1st District nominee Mufi Hannemann in the primary; she won easily in 1992 and 1994. In 1996 she had primary opposition from four Democrats, including state Senator Robert Bunda who ran as a "moderate alternative." Mink won the primary by 60%–32%, a wide margin. In 1998 and 2000 she was easily re-elected. Redistricting should pose no problems for her.

Cook's Call   *Safe.* Early in the 2000 cycle, Republicans were enthusiastic about their chances against 11-term incumbent Patsy Mink. Though Mink's winning percentage for the last ten years has not dropped below 60%, Republicans argued that she was vulnerable to a challenge from former New England Patriot football star Russ Francis. But, Francis never turned out to be much of a threat and Mink coasted to another easy win. This year, state Representative Bob McDermott has announced that he intends to challenge Mink in 2002, but Mink looks pretty safe.

THE PEOPLE: Pop. 2000: 643,013; Pop. 1990: 554,055, up 16.1% 1990–2000. 28.5% White, 1.6% Black, 31.1% Asian, 0.4% Amer. Indian, 11.7% Hawaiian, 25.4% Two+ races, 1.5% Other; 8.9% Hispanic Origin.

2000 Presidential Vote		
Gore (D)	109,658	(56%)
Bush (R)	70,488	(36%)
Nader (Green)	13,055	(7%)
Others	1,915	(1%)

1996 Presidential Vote		
Clinton (D)	105,661	(57%)
Dole (R)	55,037	(30%)
Perot (I)	16,621	(9%)
Others	8,286	(4%)

Rep. Patsy Mink (D)

Elected Sept. 1990, 6th term; b. Dec. 6, 1927, Paia, Maui; home, Hilo; U. of HI, B.A. 1948, U. of Chicago, J.D. 1951; Protestant; married (John Francis).

Elected Office: HI House of Reps., 1956–58; HI Senate, 1959, 1963–64; U.S. House of Reps., 1964–76; Honolulu City Cncl., 1983–87.

Professional Career: Practicing atty., 1953–64, 1987–90; U.S. Asst. Secy. of State for Oceans, Intl. Environment & Scientific Affairs, 1977–78; Pres., Americans for Democratic Action, 1978–81.

DC Office: 2210 RHOB 20515, 202-225-4906; Fax: 202-225-4987; Web site: www.house.gov/mink.

District Offices: Hilo, 808-935-3756; Honolulu, 808-541-1986; Kauai, 808-245-1951; Maui, 808-242-1818.

Committees: *Education & the Workforce* (5th of 22 D): 21st Century Competitiveness (RMM); Workforce Protections. *Government Reform* (6th of 19 D): Energy Policy, Natural Resources and Regulatory Affairs; Technology & Procurement Policy.

Group Ratings

	ADA	ACLU	AFS	LCV	CON	ITIC	NTU	COC	ACU	NTLC	CHC
2000	85	100	85	93	29	39	28	52	16	24	7
1999	95	—	100	94	56	—	22	28	8	—	—

National Journal Ratings

	1999 LIB	—	1999 CONS		2000 LIB	—	2000 CONS
Economic	80%	—	18%		67%	—	33%
Social	87%	—	0%		86%	—	12%
Foreign	60%	—	40%		77%	—	23%

Key Votes of the 106th Congress

1. Patient Bill of Rights	Y	5. Bar RU-486 $ for FDA	N	9. NATO War in Serbia	*
2. Accelerate Min. Wage	Y	6. Display 10 Commandments	N	10. Perm. Trade with China	N
3. Strike Ban on Ergo. Stnd.	Y	7. Gun Show Bkgrnd. Checks	Y	11. Debt Relief for 3rd World	Y
4. Ovrd. Estate Tax Veto	Y	8. Ban Part.-Birth Abortion	N	12. Drop Cuba Econ. Embargo	Y

Election Results

2000 general	Patsy Mink (D)	112,856	(62%)	($337,420)
	Russ Francis (R)	65,906	(36%)	($195,390)
	Others	4,468	(2%)	
2000 primary	Patsy Mink (D)	13,204	(88%)	
	Charles (Lucky) Collins (D)	1,877	(12%)	
1998 general	Patsy Mink (D)	144,254	(69%)	($221,165)
	Carol J. Douglas (R)	50,423	(24%)	($9,495)
	Noreen Leilehua Chun (Lib)	13,194	(6%)	

★ IDAHO ★

I daho, with just 1.3 million people, tucked off near the northwest edge of the country, has been one of America's leading growth states over the last decade. Since the early 1990s it has been one of the nation's leading states in population growth, technological progress and economic creativity; it also led at least part of the nation in cultural attitudes and politics, in a direction that many, especially the national media, resented and resisted. Idaho's growth has tapered off a bit, but it still has a robust and growing economy. Its biggest businesses are big: J.R. Simplot is the nation's largest potato processer; Micron Technology, the state's number one employer, is a leader in semiconductors; Albertson's is the nation's second largest supermarket chain. And dozens of smaller high-tech and service businesses have sprung up. From California a few highly publicized liberal entertainment personalities and a much larger number of conservative engineers and entrepreneurs have come to Idaho for a fresh environment and fresh start, clean air and few crowds, and no cumbersome or expensive regulations, where family lifestyles are still prevalent, traditional values respected, and traditional rules enforced.

The wilderness is never far away in Idaho, nor is the experience of the first settlers. Towering over the state Capitol in Boise is the vast peak of Shafer Butte, and not far away are impassable mountains of the Frank Church River of No Return Wilderness: Idaho ranks third in National Wilderness lands, behind California and Alaska. This was the last North American area European pioneers—fur traders—set eyes on. In the 1840s, New England Yankees led by ministers made their way west on the Oregon Trail through southern Idaho. Idaho's northern panhandle, an extension of Washington's Columbia Valley, was first settled by miners seeking gold and silver, then by loggers seeking timber. Mormons moved north from Utah and settled eastern Idaho. But federal water reclamation projects first authorized in 1894 brought the most settlers, and they transformed the barren Snake River Valley into some of the nation's best volcanic soil-enriched farmland. Fresh in family lore are the people who pioneered this state, built the first towns and farms, established the first churches and schools and became its community leaders. Yet Idaho is also cosmopolitan. It exports potatoes—mostly frozen french fries—across the Pacific Rim, and its high-tech companies have competitors all over the world. If Idaho politicians used to concentrate on water and maintaining irrigation, now they also work to curb Canadian potato imports and South Korean semiconductor subsidies.

Idaho politics for years was run by two bosses—Democrat Tom Boise from the panhandle and Republican Lloyd Adams from the Mormon east—who could patch together statewide alliances from the regional divisions still apparent today. Although its first settlers had a Republican heritage, silver-mining Idaho went for William Jennings Bryan and free silver in 1896, and then supported Woodrow Wilson and Franklin D. Roosevelt; as late as 1960, John F. Kennedy won 46% of the vote here. Idaho produced prominent national politicians of both parties—notably, Senate Foreign Relations Committee Chairmen William Borah, a Republican, and Frank Church, a Democrat. Democrats—Cecil Andrus, John Evans, then Andrus again—held the governorship from 1970–94.

But that is in the past. Logging and unions have declined in the panhandle, while the Mormon east is growing and Boise has become heavily Republican. The result is that Idaho is arguably the nation's most one-sidedly Republican state. George W. Bush won here in 2000 by a 67%–28% margin, his third best in the country; he lost only Blaine County, with Sun Valley and its trendy newcomers, and by only 220 votes. Today most Idahoans think of themselves not as downtrodden employees of absentee corporations needing a protective federal government, but as pioneering entrepreneurs who need to get a bloated, bossy federal government off their backs. The federal government owns 62.5% of Idaho's land, and most Idahoans have been furious at how Clinton appointees managed it. Idaho would have been the state most affected by Clinton plans to stop roadbuilding in national forests. "The scum in Washington, D.C, are taking our freedom away from us once again," one logger said, and Idaho officials said the proposal could cost the state $163 million in revenue for roads and schools. The *Idaho Statesman* and local environmentalists have called for breaching of the dams on the Snake River to protect salmon whose numbers have

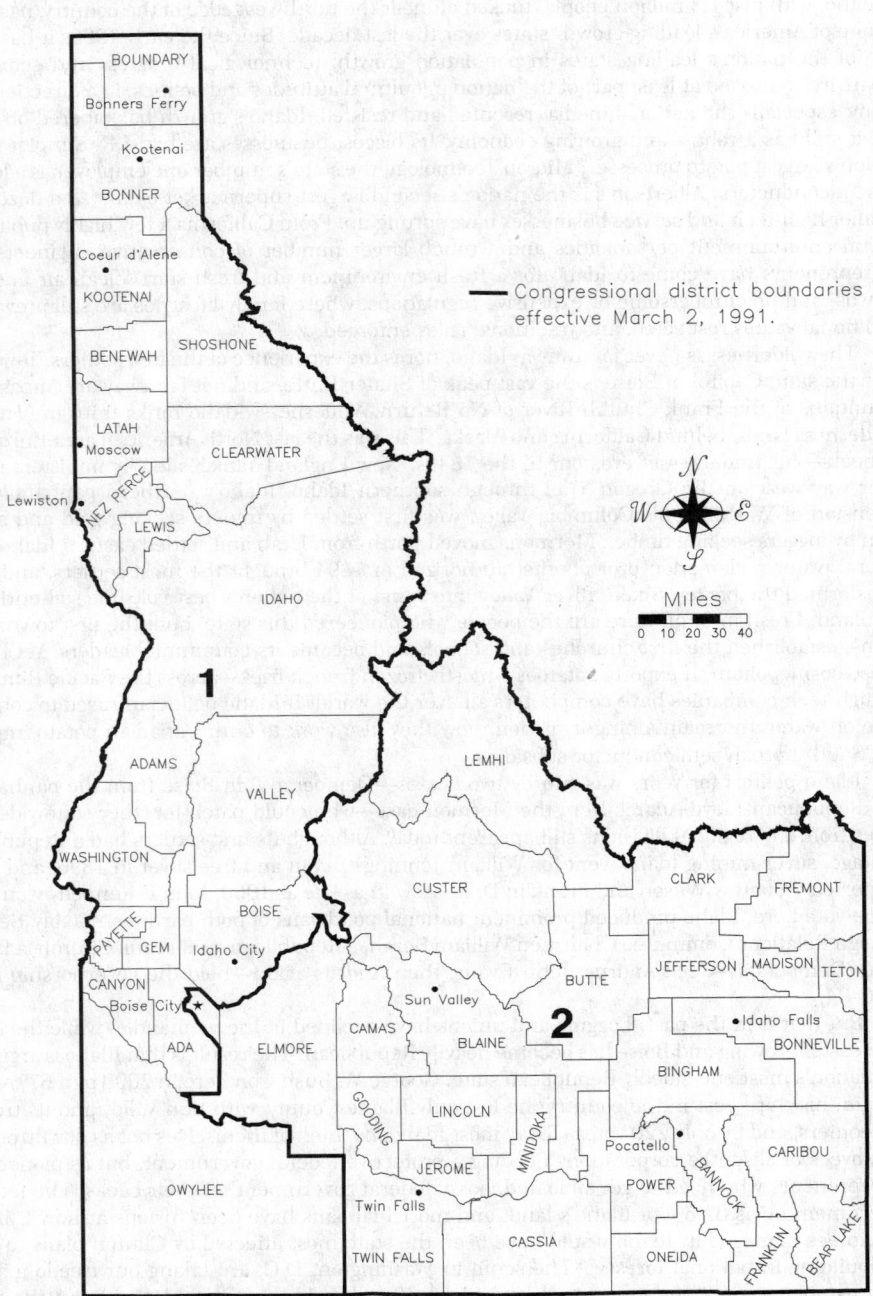

Congressional district boundaries
effective March 2, 1991.

BOUNDARY
Bonners Ferry
Kootenai
BONNER
Coeur d'Alene
KOOTENAI
BENEWAH
SHOSHONE
LATAH
Moscow
CLEARWATER
Lewiston
NEZ PERCE
LEWIS
IDAHO

1

ADAMS
VALLEY
WASHINGTON
BOISE
PAYETTE
GEM
Idaho City
CANYON
Boise City ★
ADA
ELMORE
OWYHEE

LEMHI
CUSTER
CLARK
FREMONT
BUTTE
JEFFERSON   MADISON   TETON
Sun Valley
CAMAS
BLAINE
Idaho Falls
BONNEVILLE
BINGHAM

2

GOODING
LINCOLN
MINIDOKA
Pocatello
CARIBOU
JEROME
POWER   BANNOCK
Twin Falls
CASSIA
ONEIDA   FRANKLIN   BEAR LAKE
TWIN FALLS

N
W   E
S

Miles
0 10 20 30 40

been depleted (half the salmon are trucked down the river to get to the ocean). Idaho Republican politicians strongly opposed breaching the dams, and so did George W. Bush in the 2000 campaign; Al Gore refused to take a position. Just after the election, the Fish and Wildlife Service announced it would reintroduce grizzly bears into the Bitterroot Range in 2002; whether that will take place in the Bush administration is unclear. There have been protests about failure to clean up toxic waste at the Idaho National Engineering and Environmental Laboratory (INEEL) near Idaho Falls; in March 2000 INEEL scrapped plans for an incinerator after a lawsuit was brought by celebrities with houses downwind in Jackson Hole, Wyoming. Idaho has received bad publicity from a group called the Aryan Nations living in a compound near Coeur d'Alene; in September 2000 a Coeur d'Alene jury brought in a verdict of $6.3 million against Aryan Nations leader Richard Butler for the beating and shooting of two people by his security guards; Butler was forced to give up the compound, but continued to receive financing from Silicon Valley millionaire and recent Idaho resident, Vincent Bertollini. To those who portray Idaho as a den of intolerance, Idahoans have an answer: In 2000 they raised nearly $1 million in response to a challenge by former Prodigy Chairman Greg Carr to build an Idaho Anne Frank Human Rights education and conference center on the site of the Aryan Nations compound.

Today Republicans hold almost all of Idaho's elective offices, and have won most by wide margins. In 1998, Senator Dirk Kempthorne won 68% of the votes for governor and Congressman Mike Crapo won 70% for the Senate. In 2000 House races, the two Republican candidates carried every county and won with 65% and 71% of the vote. Senator Larry Craig won in 1990 and 1996 by comfortable margins. In the legislature, Republicans' overall lead is 93–12. Republicans hold all but two of the seven statewide elected offices. Republican successes cannot be ascribed to just a matter of tradition: The VNS exit poll showed the highest percentages for Republicans under 30 (76%–22% for Bush). But Republican majorities are not monolithic, or everlasting: Term limits will help give Democrats a chance to fasten on local grievances and raise new issues which will surely some day yield them more than they have now.

Governor   Dirk Kempthorne was elected governor of Idaho in 1998 after six years in the U.S. Senate. He was born in San Diego, grew up in Spokane, Washington, and graduated from the University of Idaho. He has spent most of his adult life in the political arena, starting in state government, then working for the Idaho Home Builders Association and FMC Corporation. He managed Phil Batt's unsuccessful gubernatorial campaign in 1982 (Batt finally won in 1994) and was mayor of Boise for seven boom years from 1986–93. Kempthorne was elected to the Senate seat vacated in 1992 by two-term incumbent Republican Steve Symms and over tough competition from Democratic Congressman Richard Stallings, a Mormon and a conservative on abortion and gun control and three-time congressman from the eastern Idaho 2d District. Kempthorne won with 57%, barely carrying the northern panhandle, but running far ahead in the Boise market and carrying the Mormon areas in the east.

Kempthorne started off 100th in seniority in a Democratic Senate, concentrating on the nonstarter issue of unfunded mandates. But after the Republicans's 1994 victory, Bob Dole made Kempthorne's unfunded mandates bill S.1, the first order of legislative business. Kempthorne impressed colleagues with his knowledge of detail and his willingness to face off with Robert Byrd, who fought mightily against the bill as an infringement of congressional prerogatives; it passed the Senate easily with bipartisan support. Kempthorne also worked hard on the Safe Drinking Water Act, which passed with bipartisan support in 1996, and worked on a bipartisan Endangered Species Act revision which never passed the House.

But Idaho beckoned. Phil Batt, elected at 67, decided to retire after a long career in state politics and one successful four-year term as governor. Welfare rolls were cut more than 75%, crime was sharply down, taxes and state payrolls were cut, and in 1996, voters had endorsed by 63%–37% the 40-year compact with the federal government Batt negotiated on nuclear waste disposal. In September 1997 Batt announced his decision to retire; in October 1997 Kempthorne announced he was running. He was willing to give up what easily could have been a lifetime Senate seat for, at most, two term-limited terms as governor. "I truly do believe power now is irreversibly returning to the states, and that is where the important action will be," he said. Once Kempthorne was in, the race was essentially over. Former state Supreme Court Justice Robert

Huntley ran, he said, to maintain two-party competition. Kempthorne won 68%–29%, carrying every county but the one including Sun Valley.

Kempthorne lives modestly in a two-bedroom condominium; he travels around the state to sign bills. In 1999 he got the legislature to pass a $5.5 million reading initiative; he passed a $2.5 million immunization bill and signed a phase-out of the state marriage tax. Criticized for aloofness, he held an open house in his office for legislators in 2000. Then he passed an $873 million education budget, an increase in hunting and fishing license fees and consolidation of endangered species issues in the governor's office. He signed a controverisal Free Exercise of Religion Act, but only with a one-year delay in effectiveness, hoping that competing views could come together. He lobbied for and got $5 million in federal funds to crackdown on and clean up illicit metham-phetamine labs that have flourished across the state; the meth habit contributed to Idaho's bur-geoning prison population that grew faster than any other state in 1999. After the summer 2000 wildfires, he predicted there would be more unless timber and underbrush are removed from national forests. "This summer, any justification for continuing the status quo forest policy just went up in flames—across the state of Idaho and throughout the West." In September 2000 he called for ending the exemption of farm workers from the $5.15 minimum wage. He opposed the November 2000 decision of the Fish and Wildlife Service to reintroduce grizzly bears into the Bitterroot Range.

Kempthorne has gubernatorial good looks and a certain charm; veteran Secretary of State Pete Cenarrusa, who has known 13 Idaho governors, says, "I see instances of Ronald Reagan in Governor Kempthorne. He conveys his feelings, makes a good impression, and he's convincing." And a Coeur d'Alene resort owner hands out "Kempthorne for governor in 2008" stickers. In early 2001 there was no visible opposition, and he seemed likely to be easily re-elected in 2002.

Cook's Call   *Safe.* Bush won this state by 39 points, making it unlikely that Democrats have much hope of recruiting the caliber of candidate who can unseat Kempthorne. He should cruise to a second term.

Senior Senator   Larry Craig was first elected to the Senate in 1990. Born on a ranch homesteaded by his grandfather in 1899, he was elected to the state Senate in 1974, at 29, and to the U.S. House in 1980, at 35. In 1990, when Senator James McClure retired, he was elected to the Senate. Throughout his career he has had a very conservative voting record and has been a well-informed and persistent critic of Western lands policies favored by environmentalists or, as he says, "environmental extremism." In the Senate he became chairman of the informal con-servative Steering Committee, whose members seemed to win most of the leadership positions. After Bob Dole's resignation in June 1996, Craig became chairman of the Republican Policy Committee, the number four leadership position. He was, Idaho reporter Dan Popkey wrote, "poised to become the fourth face on Idaho's Mount Rushmore, joining Senators William Borah, Frank Church, and Jim McClure."

Craig has used his seats on the Appropriations, Agriculture and Energy committees to fight for what he considers sensible environmental policies. He opposed Clinton efforts to revise the Mining Act of 1872 and increase grazing fees. He opposes the introduction of grizzly bears into Idaho's Bitterroot Range and the moratorium on logging roads in the national forests. He is against breaching the Snake River dams to allow salmon to swim more easily upstream and sponsored a bill to require the Fish and Wildlife Service to consider many factors, including the effect on farming, when it makes decisions on salmon protection programs; in October 2000 the Senate passed unanimously a bill sponored by Craig and Idaho colleague Mike Crapo that would cut FWS administrative expenses in half and direct more gun and fishing tackle tax revenues into hunter safety and range development. In 2000 Craig highlighted a study showing that the government spends directly and indirectly $935 million a year on salmon protection programs: "The bureau-cracy of salmon rolls on."

Craig seems engaged in a continual battle to change the policies and institutional culture of the Forest Service. In the wake of the summer 2000 wildfires that raged in Idaho, he strongly criticized the Clinton administration for failing to fund fire prevention and, with Pete Domenici, called for $240 million for federal agencies to remove timber and brush. He has a reorganization bill to streamline planning procedures, limit court challenges to local people who commented during the planning process, and forbid deviations from the plan once adopted. It would allow states and private organizations, with congressional approval, to take over management of National Forest and Bureau of Land Management lands. He would also let state management practices be determinative in enforcing the Clean Water Act. He opposed expansion of the Craters of the Moon National Monument, and sponsored a bill to create certain requirements for presidents to declare national monuments, as Bill Clinton frequently did. In 2000, after considerable negotiations and holdups because of Wyden's defense of Oregon's assisted suicide law, both houses passed the bill sponsored by Craig and Oregon Democrat Ron Wyden to increase payments to counties with national forests. Since the Clinton administration cut way back on timber harvesting, these payments in Idaho had fallen from $23 million to $7.5 million; the bill would raise them back to $22.5 million.

Another Craig cause is nuclear waste. He has been pushing relentlessly for the government to meet its commitment to establish a permanent nuclear waste repository at Yucca Mountain in Nevada. Opposition came from Nevada's two senators and from Bill Clinton, who carried Nevada twice by narrow margins after promising to veto bills to establish a temporary waste facility there. In August 1997 Craig got the Senate to pass his nuclear waste policy act by 65–34—just two votes short of what is needed to override a veto. In April 2000 the Senate again passed a bill requiring storage of nuclear waste in Yucca Mountain beginning in 2007, but it was again vetoed by Clinton, and there were not enough votes to override.

Craig has taken on a variety of national issues. He was a lead sponsor of the constitutional amendment to require a balanced budget in the House in 1982 and in the Senate in 1995. The high-water mark for this measure came in early 1995, when it passed the House with 300 votes and came within one vote of the required two-thirds margin in the Senate. Now the issue seems mooted by large federal surpluses. He has supported free trade measures and went to China in 1999 to promote an open trade agreement with the city of Xiamen. And he has was one of the leaders in the gun control debate in the Senate in 1999, sponsoring a measure to allow (but not force) unlicensed sellers at gun shows to conduct background checks. He has been a major promoter of adoption. He was a lead sponsor of the Adoption and Safe Families Act of 1997, which promotes the adoption of foster children; he was proud that Idaho more than doubled the number of adoptions of foster children in 1999. He has sought a $2,000 benefit for federal employees who adopt and pushed succesfully for approval of The Hague Convention on Intercountry Adoption in 2000. A strong critic of the Kyoto Treaty, he was convinced at the November 2000 conference at The Hague that global warming exists and is partly human-caused; he called for credits for farmers whose crops reduce carbon dioxide in the air.

Craig became chairman of the Republican Policy Committee in 1996, after the Bob Dole resigned as majority leader. He is often a conduit between Trent Lott and Republican conservatives, and is not close to Whip Don Nickles, who held up the Craig-Wyden bill for reimbursing counties with national forests because of his opposition to Wyden's defense of Oregon's assisted suicide law. In December 2000 Craig was challenged for the Policy Committee leadership by the more senior and more conciliation-minded Pete Domenici. It was one of two serious leadership challenges after Senate Republicans had seen their 54–46 majority converted by the 2000 elections to a 50–50 tie, and some saw Domenici's challenge as a vote of no confidence in Lott. Craig just barely prevailed, by a 26–24 margin.

On Idaho issues, Craig has used his Appropriations seat to get $13.5 million for roads in southern Idaho, which may get heavy traffic from the 2002 Winter Olympics in Salt Lake City, $1 million for the Sacajawea interpretive center in Salmon and $500,000 for other projects for the 2005 Lewis and Clark bicentennial.

Craig won the seat relatively easily in 1990, with 59% in the primary against Attorney General Jim Jones and with 61% in the general. In 1996 he was opposed by building materials millionaire Walt Minnick, who spent $945,000 of his own money. He attacked Craig sharply for backing Governor Phil Batt's nuclear waste compact and ran "Lying Larry" ads associating him with nuclear pollution, clear-cutting, gill-netting and national parks destruction. Craig responded by rafting down the river with his family and running ads predicting toxic desolation if the nuclear waste compact was not carried out. Craig won 57%–40%, losing only three counties. His seat comes up again in 2002, and he is likely to be a heavy favorite if he runs. There was some speculation in 2000 that he might retire while still in the prime of life, as James McClure did in 1990.

Cook's Call   *Safe.* Federal offices in Idaho have become a wasteland for Democrats: Even when they field unusually strong candidates, they get massacred. It's unlikely that Craig will draw any more than token opposition.

Junior Senator   Mike Crapo is a Republican elected to the House in 1992 and the Senate in 1998. He grew up in Idaho Falls, went to Brigham Young University and Harvard Law School, is a faithful Mormon who was named a bishop in the church at 31. He was elected to the state Senate in 1984, at 33, and became state Senate leader in 1988. Crapo ran for the House in 1992 and campaigned against all tax increases, for spending cuts, a balanced budget amendment and the line-item veto—the Contract with America two years early. He won the primary 68%–32%. "Cowboy Democrat" J. D. Williams, the state controller, ran on a "put America first" stand on industrial policy and trade. Crapo won 61%–35%.

With a self-professed "passion for reform," Crapo became Republican freshman class leader and championed institutional reforms—on discharge petitions, select committees, closed rules, closed committee meetings, open voting—many of which were adopted after Republicans won control in 1994. Like many Republicans, he favored simple, hard-and-fast rules—a balanced budget, term limits, across-the-board discretionary spending cuts (excluding Social Security)—to force tough decisions. He sponsored the deficit reduction lock box bill which passed the House in 1995; he served on Agriculture as it passed the Freedom To Farm Act. He was a founding member of the Congressional Water Caucus and a member of the fabled Congressional Boot Caucus, an informal group of Western lawmakers who wear boots. His overall voting record has been very conservative, with some exceptions on economics. He opposed NAFTA in 1993 but supported PNTR for China in 2000; he said that opening markets would help China's citizens "realize that there are other ways of governing." At the WTO meeting in Seattle he worked to get China to agree to imports of 1.5 million metric tons of wheat from the Pacific Northwest.

In 1997 Crapo, who prides himself on returning to Idaho Falls every weekend, faced a career choice that many House members would like to face. In September Governor Phil Batt announced his retirement and in October Senator Dirk Kempthorne said he would run for governor. Within days Crapo announced he would run for the Senate. His opponent was former Democratic chairman and Boise trial lawyer Bill Mauk. He attacked Crapo for accepting tobacco PAC money; Crapo replied he had stopped taking it some time ago. Idaho, one-quarter Mormon, had never elected a Mormon senator. This time it did. Crapo led in polls by a wide margin and Mauk, vastly outspent, made little headway. Crapo won 70%–28%, carrying every county.

In his first years in the Senate Crapo became chairman of the subcommittee with jurisdiction over the troubled Superfund program and many EPA programs. Hoping to force overall Superfund reform, which had gone nowhere in previous Congresses, he got Trent Lott to pledge in writing that he would not let piecemeal Superfund bills come to the floor. But in September 2000 broad-based Superfund reform was brought up in the House on suspension calendar and failed to get the two-thirds vote required under that procedure. And in October Lott seemed willing to bring forward a brownfields bill, supported by Democrats who were against the broader reform, which would change Superfund rules in cities. Superfund reform would have to wait for another Congress. In 1999 Crapo sponsored, with Pete Domenici and the late John Chafee, a reform of the Endangered Species Act which would require scientific information and economic impacts to be determined before the designation of critical habitat; this was designed to prevent restrictions on large areas with little scientific evidence. In 2000 Crapo worked to delay EPA's proposed rules on runoff pollution, which threatened to require that farmers and loggers get agency permission before making even minor changes in their operations.

On Idaho issues, Crapo supported former Governor Phil Batt's nuclear waste compact with the federal government, allowing waste to be transported now to INEEL in return for a promise of later shipment to waste sites in New Mexico and Nevada. He strongly opposes breaching the Snake dams and he opposes spring drawdowns on lower Snake River dams; he wants to maintain the flow of Snake River water to Idaho farms. He opposes reintroduction of grizzly bears to the

Bitterroot Mountains. He wants decisions on issues like grazing, water quality and grizzly bear management to be made at local forums. In 1999 he developed Project SEARCH, a $1.3 million program to help cities with less than 2,500 people to apply for federal grants and comply with federal mandates; it was inspired by difficulties encountered by the town of Stanley in Custer County.

Presidential politics   Idaho is one of the most Republican states in national politics. George W. Bush and Bob Dole carried it easily; in 1992 Bill Clinton only narrowly beat out Ross Perot for second place, 28%–27%. From 1988–96, Idaho's presidential primary was held in late May, but was not binding for Democrats, who select their presidential nominee in the early March caucus. Idaho considered joining other Rocky Mountain states voting in an early March 2000 primary, but the state House voted it down in March 1999.

Congressional districting   Idaho has two congressional districts, which split Boise between them. After the 2000 Census, a bipartisan commission is scheduled to draw new boundaries; given Idaho's geography, it will most likely push the boundary west a couple of miles to somewhere between Maple Grove and Eagle Roads.

THE PEOPLE: Pop. 2000: 1,293,953; Pop. 1990: 1,006,749, up 28.5% 1990–2000. 0.5% of U.S. total, 39th largest; 91% White, 0.4% Black, 0.9% Asian, 1.4% Amer. Indian, 0.1% Hawaiian, 2% Two+ races, 4.2% Other; 7.9% Hispanic Origin. 4.9% Unemployment. 2000 Voting age pop.: 924,923. 2000 Turnout: 516,647; 56% of VAP. Registered voters (2000): 728,085; no party registration.

POLITICAL LINEUP: Governor, Dirk Kempthorne (R); Lt. Gov., Jack Riggs (R); Secy. of State, Pete T. Cenarrusa (R); Atty. Gen., Alan G. Lance (R); Treasurer, Ron Crane (R); Controller, J.D. Williams (D); Super. of Public Instruction, Marilyn Howard (D); State Senate, 35 (3 D, 32 R); Senate Pres. Pro Tempore, Robert L. Geddes (R); Majority Leader, Jim Risch (R); State House, 70 (9 D, 61 R); House Speaker, Bruce Newcomb (R). Senators, Larry Craig (R) and Mike Crapo (R). Representatives, 2 (2 R).

ELECTIONS DIVISION: 208-334-2852; **FILING DEADLINE FOR U.S. CONGRESS:** April 5, 2002.

2000 Presidential Vote

Bush (R)	336,937	(67%)
Gore (D)	138,637	(28%)
Nader (Green)	12,292	(2%)
Others	13,749	(3%)

1996 Presidential Vote

Dole (R)	256,595	(52%)
Clinton (D)	165,443	(34%)
Perot (I)	62,518	(13%)

2000 Republican Presidential Primary

Bush (R)	116,385	(73%)
Keyes (R)	30,263	(19%)
None Shown	11,798	(7%)

2000 Democratic Presidential Primary

Gore (D)	27,025	(76%)
None Shown	5,722	(16%)
LaRouche (D)	2,941	(8%)

Gov. Dirk Kempthorne (R)

Elected 1998, term expires Jan. 2003, 1st term; b. Oct. 29, 1951, San Diego, CA; home, Boise; U. of ID, B.A. 1975; Methodist; married (Patricia).

Elected Office: Boise Mayor, 1986–93; U.S. Senate, 1992–98.

Professional Career: Exec. Asst. to Dir., ID Dept. of Public Lands, 1976–78; Exec. V.P., ID Home Builders Assn., 1978–81; Campaign Mgr., Phil Batt for Gov., 1982; ID Public Affairs Mgr., FMC Corp, 1983–86.

Office: State House, Boise, 83720, 208-334-2100; Fax: 208-334-2175; Web site: www.state.id.us.

Election Results

1998 general	Dirk Kempthorne (R)	258,095	(68%)
	Robert C. Huntley (D)	110,815	(29%)
	Others	12,338	(3%)
1998 primary	Dirk Kempthorne (R)	111,658	(87%)
	David Shepherd (R)	16,332	(13%)
1994 general	Phil Batt (R)	216,123	(52%)
	Larry EchoHawk (D)	181,363	(44%)
	Ronald D. Rankin (I)	15,793	(4%)

Sen. Larry Craig (R)

Elected 1990, seat up 2002, 2d term; b. July 20, 1945, Midvale; home, Payette; U. of ID, B.A. 1969; United Methodist; married (Suzanne).

Military Career: Army Natl. Guard, 1970–74.

Elected Office: ID Senate, 1974–80; U.S. House of Reps., 1980–90.

Professional Career: Rancher, farmer.

DC Office: 520 HSOB, 20510, 202-224-2752; Fax: 202-228-1067; Web site: www.senate.gov/~craig.

State Offices: Boise, 208-342-7985; Coeur d'Alene, 208-667-6130; Idaho Falls, 208-523-5541; Lewiston, 208-743-0792; Pocatello, 208-236-6817; Twin Falls, 208-734-6780.

Committees: *Republican Policy Committee Chairman. Aging (Special)* (RMM). *Appropriations*: Agriculture & Rural Development; Energy & Water Development; Labor, HHS & Education; Military Construction; VA, HUD & Independent Agencies. *Energy & Natural Resources*: Energy Research, Development, Production & Regulation; Forests & Public Land Management (RMM); Water & Power. *Veterans' Affairs*.

Group Ratings

	ADA	ACLU	AFS	LCV	CON	ITIC	NTU	COC	ACU	NTLC	CHC
2000	0	43	0	0	59	100	75	93	100	97	92
1999	0	—	0	0	62	—	78	88	96	—	—

National Journal Ratings

	1999 LIB	—	1999 CONS		2000 LIB	—	2000 CONS
Economic	0%	—	83%		14%	—	75%
Social	18%	—	79%		10%	—	81%
Foreign	0%	—	94%		17%	—	75%

Key Votes of the 106th Congress

1. Educ. Savings Accts.	Y	5. Review Movie Violence	Y	9. NATO War in Serbia	N
2. Prescrip. Drug Benefit	N	6. Gun Show Bckgrnd. Checks	N	10. Table Cuba Travel Ban	Y
3. Delay Ergonomic Standards	Y	7. Ban Part.-Birth Abortion	Y	11. Nuclear Test-Ban Treaty	N
4. Phase Out Estate Tax	Y	8. Broaden Hate Crimes List	N	12. Perm. Trade with China	Y

Election Results

1996 general	Larry Craig (R)	283,532	(57%)	($2,992,451)
	Walt Minnick (D)	198,422	(40%)	($2,140,878)
	Others	15,279	(3%)	
1996 primary	Larry Craig (R)	unopposed		
1990 general	Larry Craig (R)	193,641	(61%)	($1,620,304)
	Ron J. Twilegar (D)	122,295	(39%)	($544,419)

Sen. Mike Crapo (R)

Elected 1998, seat up 2004, 1st term; b. May 20, 1951, Idaho Falls; home, Idaho Falls; Brigham Young U., B.A. 1973, Harvard U., J.D. 1977; Mormon; married (Susan).

Elected Office: ID Senate, 1984–92, Senate Ldr., 1988–92; U.S. House of Reps., 1992–98.

Professional Career: Practicing atty., 1977–92.

DC Office: 111 RSOB, 20510, 202-224-6142; Web site: www.senate.gov/~crapo.

State Offices: Boise, 208-334-1776; Caldwell, 208-455-0360; Coeur D'Alene, 208-664-5490; Idaho Falls, 208-522-9779; Pocatello, 208-236-6775; Twin Falls, 208-734-2515.

Committees: *Agriculture, Nutrition & Forestry*: Forestry, Conservation & Rural Revitalization (RMM); Research, Nutrition & General Legislation. *Banking, Housing & Urban Affairs*: Financial Institutions; International Trade & Finance; Securities & Investment. *Environment & Public Works*: Clean Air, Wetlands, Private Property & Nuclear Safety; Fisheries, Wildlife & Water (RMM); Superfund, Waste Control & Risk Assessment. *Small Business. Joint Economic Committee* (9th of 10 Sens.).

Group Ratings

	ADA	ACLU	AFS	LCV	CON	ITIC	NTU	COC	ACU	NTLC	CHC
2000	0	43	0	0	59	100	75	93	100	100	100
1999	0	—	0	0	79	—	83	88	100	—	—

National Journal Ratings

	1999 LIB	—	1999 CONS		2000 LIB	—	2000 CONS
Economic	0%	—	83%		14%	—	75%
Social	16%	—	83%		10%	—	81%
Foreign	0%	—	94%		26%	—	73%

Key Votes of the 106th Congress

1. Educ. Savings Accts.	Y	5. Review Movie Violence	Y	9. NATO War in Serbia	N
2. Prescrip. Drug Benefit	N	6. Gun Show Bckgrnd. Checks	N	10. Table Cuba Travel Ban	Y
3. Delay Ergonomic Standards	Y	7. Ban Part.-Birth Abortion	Y	11. Nuclear Test-Ban Treaty	N
4. Phase Out Estate Tax	Y	8. Broaden Hate Crimes List	N	12. Perm. Trade with China	Y

Election Results

1998 general	Mike Crapo (R)	262,966	(70%)	($1,563,811)
	Bill Mauk (D)	107,375	(28%)	($241,443)
	Others	7,833	(2%)	
1998 primary	Mike Crapo (R)	unopposed		
1992 general	Dirk Kempthorne (R)	270,468	(57%)	($1,305,338)
	Richard Stallings (D)	208,036	(43%)	($1,222,222)

FIRST DISTRICT

The 1st District of Idaho stretches from the Nevada border to Canada, including most of usually Republican Boise and all of the panhandle, historically Democratic but more recently known as the home of militias, an image that local leaders have worked to dispel. It includes two of Idaho's big growth areas, the west side of Boise and the Coeur d'Alene area; high-tech and tourism increasingly are important to the economy. Politically, it is marginally less Republican than the 2d, but not very Democratic: Bill Clinton and Al Gore did not win more than 35% here in three tries. Northern mining counties were once the district's Democratic base; that base is now the university town of Moscow.

The congressman from the 1st District is C.L. "Butch" Otter, a Republican first elected in 2000. His father was a journeyman electrician and life-long Democrat. He entered an abbey to pursue the priesthood but quickly decided that was not his calling; in 1967, he graduated from the College of Idaho. He went to work for his then father-in-law, billionaire J.R. Simplot, at the

J.R. Simplot Company, the largest potato processor in the world. In 1972 he was elected to the state House. Otter ran for governor in 1978, finishing third in the Republican primary. In 1986, he was elected lieutenant governor, and served under three governors until he was elected to Congress. Otter, who is also a wealthy independent ranch owner, believes strongly in gun ownership and property rights. But he is not the social conservative that his predecessor Helen Chenoweth-Hage was. While he opposes abortion, he believes that the government should stay out of people's lives. He also declined to take a term-limits pledge. He wants to check the power of the Environmental Protection Agency. This isn't a surprise: As a ranch owner, Otter has been charged three times by the EPA for violating the Clean Water Act; the last time he was fined $80,000 for dredging and filling wetlands without a permit. But violating federal environmental regulations is not necessarily the worst offense in Idaho. Otter, who said that his pond-digging was designed to improve the wetlands, responded that he showed he's willing to "stand up for folks in Idaho against a government that is arrogant, intransigent."

In 2000, when Helen Chenoweth-Hage kept her pledge to limit herself to three terms, a venomous Republican primary between Otter and Dennis Mansfield, who founded the religious right group Idaho Family Forum, ensued. Mansfield's supporters highlighted Otter's drunk-driving conviction in 1993, following which he agreed to perform 72 hours of community service and attend 16 hours of an alcohol treatment program; he apologized and went on a speaking tour to youngsters across Idaho. One of Mansfield's ads stated: "Just what we need in Washington—another bad example for our children." It was later discovered that Mansfield's teenage son had recently pleaded guilty to drug charges. But Otter had the support of most Republican insiders, including Governor Dirk Kempthorne and 29 of 31 state senators. He argued that Washington had usurped the power of local governments, and that states can better make decisions that affect peoples' lives. He also supports individual investment accounts in Social Security. Mansfield, running as a political outsider, backed term limits and was endorsed by the Wall Street-based Club for Growth. In the May primary, Otter won all 19 counties and defeated Mansfield 48%–27%, with former state Republican chairman Ron McMurray taking 17%. Otter benefited from a late get-out-the-vote campaign by the National Rifle Association and local farming and ranching interests, plus a more than 3–1 fundraising advantage. Democrats had some hopes of defeating Otter, but their candidate raised little PAC or party money. Otter won 65%–31%.

While running for the House, Otter confessed that he would rather be governor. But that may not be open soon; Kempthorne seems likely to win re-election easily in 2002. Redistricting will slice off some of the Boise and Ada County precincts from the 1st district, with no effect on the political balance.

Cook's Call   *Safe.* This district, like the rest of the state, has been trending Republican for the last ten years. Democrats' inability in 1996 or 1998 to knock off Helen Chenoweth, one of the most controversial Republicans in the country, illustrated just how difficult it is for a Democrat to make any headway in this district. Don't look for them to spend much time or energy here in 2002.

THE PEOPLE: Pop. 2000: 702,521; Pop. 1990: 503,141, up 39.6% 1990–2000. 91.6% White, 0.3% Black, 1% Asian, 1.3% Amer. Indian, 0.1% Hawaiian, 2% Two+ races, 3.6% Other; 6.8% Hispanic Origin.

2000 Presidential Vote			1996 Presidential Vote		
Bush (R)	182,498	(66%)	Dole (R)	134,783	(51%)
Gore (D)	77,926	(28%)	Clinton (D)	91,297	(35%)
Nader (Green)	6,986	(3%)	Perot (I)	33,130	(13%)
Others	7,456	(3%)	Others	4,142	(2%)

Rep. C. L. (Butch) Otter (R)

Elected 2000, 1st term; b. May 3, 1942, Caldwell; home, Star; Col. of ID, B.A. 1967; Catholic; divorced.

Military Career: ID Natl. Guard, 1967–73.

Elected Office: ID House of Reps., 1972–76; ID Lt. Gov., 1986–2000.

Professional Career: Rancher; Dir., Food Products Div., Pres., Simplot Livestock, Pres., Simplot Intl., 1963–1993.

DC Office: 1711 LHOB 20515, 202-225-6611; Fax: 202-225-3029; Web site: www.house.gov/otter.

Committees: *Government Reform* (22d of 24 R): Civil Service & Agency Organization; Energy Policy, Natural Resources and Regulatory Affairs (Vice Chmn.); National Security, Veterans' Affairs & Intl. Relations. *Resources* (24th of 28 R): Energy & Mineral Resources; Forests & Forest Health; Water & Power. *Transportation & Infrastructure* (38th of 42 R): Highways & Transit; Water Resources & Environment.

Group Ratings and Key Votes: Newly Elected

Election Results

2000 general	C.L. (Butch) Otter (R)	173,743	(65%)	($1,005,580)
	Linda Pall (D)	84,080	(31%)	($72,061)
	Others	10,293	(4%)	
2000 primary	C.L. (Butch) Otter (R)	41,516	(48%)	
	Dennis Mansfield (R)	23,559	(27%)	
	Ron McMurray (R)	14,434	(17%)	
	Others	7,651	(9%)	
1998 general	Helen Chenoweth (R)	113,231	(55%)	($1,331,487)
	Dan Williams (D)	91,653	(45%)	($876,308)

SECOND DISTRICT

The 2d District of Idaho, from central Boise east to the Utah border, is one of America's most Republican districts in presidential elections. It's also one of the most picturesque. In the year-round resort community of Sun Valley, celebrities from Bill Gates to Arnold Schwarzenegger have spurred rapid development with soaring costs, which has led to calls for restrictions on growth. Southeast Idaho is part of the Mormon heartland, and the district is almost half Mormon. Most of the farm counties and towns here are heavily Republican. The old frontier and railroad town of Pocatello sometimes votes for Democrats; Sun Valley is in the one Idaho county that voted for Al Gore, by 220 votes; and the 2d's portion of Boise includes the city's few Denverish-liberal neighborhoods. The other whole counties in the 2nd District gave between 69% and 89% of their votes to George W. Bush.

The congressman from the 2d District is Mike Simpson, a Republican elected in 1998 when incumbent Mike Crapo was elected to the Senate. He grew up in Blackfoot, became a dentist and joined his father's practice there and was elected to the city council in 1982 and the state House in 1984; he didn't declare himself as a Republican until then and was opposed by the local party organization. In 1993 he became speaker, but kept up his dental practice as well. In the legislature he was known as a moderate in a conservative House, affable and able to get differing sides together. He pushed the Martin Luther King Jr. holiday, workmen's compensation for farm workers and property tax relief. When Governor Phil Batt announced he would retire in 1998, Simpson wanted to run for his office. But Senator Dirk Kempthorne's decision to run for governor closed that option. Then 2d District Congressman Mike Crapo ran for Kempthorne's Senate seat, and Simpson entered the 2d District race.

But his elevation to the House required some work. In the Republican primary Simpson was opposed by state Representative Mark Stubbs and two former state senators. Simpson called for tax reform, Stubbs for lower payroll taxes; Stubbs had opposed nuclear programs at the Idaho

Nation Engineering and Environmental Laboratory in the 1980s, while Simpson wanted more work at the facility. But the big issue was term limits. Simpson refused to take US Term Limits's pledge to serve only three terms; the other three did. Americans for Term Limits spent large sums to run TV ads against Simpson. Enraged by these ads, Governor Phil Batt endorsed Simpson five days before the election; Simpson ran ads against "outsiders" and "out-of-state folk;" Batt recorded a message for him which was delivered to 47,000 households by telemarketing. Simpson beat Stubbs, 47%–41%. The Democratic nominee was Richard Stallings, a former history professor elected to the House in 1984 and re-elected three times; in 1992 he ran against Kempthorne for the Senate and lost 57%–43%. Stallings talked about his conservative voting record in the House, called for more education spending and pointed with anxiety at falling farm commodity prices. Simpson wanted a smaller federal role in education; he favored tax cuts and Republican Social Security reform. As farm prices plummeted, Simpson called for trade talks to open markets, with possible tariffs if others didn't go along, and renegotiating NAFTA. Simpson won 53%–45%, losing the most visible parts of the district—Pocatello, Sun Valley, Boise—but carrying just about everything else, and in the Mormon southeast and ultraconservative northeast by considerable margins.

In the House, Simpson dedicated much of his first two years to building relationships with his 434 colleagues—preferably, he said, in one-on-one informal conversations. But he did not get to know all of them—the House is a big place—and that reinforced his opposition to term limits. More than most western Republicans, he has reached out to Democrats on economic and social issues. "Sometimes we get a little too partisan," he told the *Idaho Statesman* at the end of his first term, complaining that greater willingness to compromise would have permitted enactment of tax cuts. Although he was the only Idahoan to vote for the emergency appropriations in May 1999 to pay for the military operation in Kosovo, he urged President Clinton to accelerate efforts to remove United States troops. Despite his call for a middle ground on resource issues, he endorsed a prohibition on breaching dams along the Columbia and Snake Rivers. He criticized Bill Clinton for acting unilaterally to expand the Craters of the Moon National Monument and he filed a bill to prevent similar actions.

Simpson had an easier time winning in 2000 than in 1998. His Democratic opponent, a retired Air Force fighter pilot trainer, refused campaign contributions and relied on the Internet to get his message out. It evidently didn't get far: Simpson won 71%–26%. Redistricting should add more of Boise and Ada County to the 2d District, but will not change the political balance materially.

Cook's Call   *Safe.* In 1998, when Democrats ran their best possible candidate, former Rep. Richard Stallings, it became clear just how Republican Idaho is: In what elsewhere was a good year for Democrats, they still came up short. Simpson should be able to hold onto this seat for as long as he wants it.

THE PEOPLE: Pop. 2000: 591,432; Pop. 1990: 503,608, up 17.4% 1990–2000. 90.3% White, 0.5% Black, 0.8% Asian, 1.4% Amer. Indian, 0.1% Hawaiian, 1.9% Two+ races, 4.9% Other; 9.1% Hispanic Origin.

2000 Presidential Vote		
Bush (R)	154,439	(68%)
Gore (D)	60,711	(27%)
Nader (Green)	5,306	(2%)
Others	6,293	(3%)

1996 Presidential Vote		
Dole (R)	121,812	(53%)
Clinton (D)	74,146	(32%)
Perot (I)	29,388	(13%)

Rep. Mike Simpson (R)

Elected 1998, 2d term; b. Sept. 8, 1950, Burley; home, Blackfoot; UT St. U., 1968–72; WA U. Dental Schl., D.D.S. 1977; Mormon; married (Kathy).

Elected Office: Blackfoot City Cncl., 1982–86; ID House of Reps., 1984–98, Speaker, 1993–98.

Professional Career: Practicing dentist, 1977-present.

DC Office: 1440 LHOB 20515, 202-225-5531; Fax: 202-225-8216; Web site: www.house.gov/simpson.

District Offices: Boise, 208-334-1953; Idaho Falls, 208-523-6701; Pocatello, 208-478-4160; Twin Falls, 208-734-7219.

Committees: *Agriculture* (16th of 27 R): Department Operations, Oversight, Nutrition & Forestry; Specialty Crops & Foreign Agriculture Programs. *Resources* (22d of 28 R): Forests & Forest Health; National Parks, Recreation & Public Lands; Water & Power. *Transportation & Infrastructure* (24th of 42 R): Aviation; Water Resources & Environment. *Veterans' Affairs* (13th of 17 R): Health.

Group Ratings

	ADA	ACLU	AFS	LCV	CON	ITIC	NTU	COC	ACU	NTLC	CHC
2000	0	21	0	0	38	100	63	90	88	73	87
1999	10	—	16	0	15	—	57	100	84	—	—

National Journal Ratings

	1999 LIB —	1999 CONS	2000 LIB —	2000 CONS
Economic	30%	70%	29%	67%
Social	29%	69%	30%	68%
Foreign	28%	70%	25%	69%

Key Votes of the 106th Congress

1. Patient Bill of Rights	N	5. Bar RU-486 $ for FDA	Y	9. NATO War in Serbia	N
2. Accelerate Min. Wage	N	6. Display 10 Commandments	Y	10. Perm. Trade with China	Y
3. Strike Ban on Ergo. Stnd.	N	7. Gun Show Bkgrnd. Checks	N	11. Debt Relief for 3rd World	N
4. Ovrd. Estate Tax Veto	Y	8. Ban Part.-Birth Abortion	Y	12. Drop Cuba Econ. Embargo	N

Election Results

2000 general	Mike Simpson (R)	158,912	(71%)	($532,746)
	Craig Williams (D)	58,265	(26%)	
	Others	7,542	(3%)	
2000 primary	Mike Simpson (R)	unopposed		
1998 general	Mike Simpson (R)	91,337	(53%)	($888,208)
	Richard H. Stallings (D)	77,736	(45%)	($648,952)
	Others	4,872	(3%)	

★ ILLINOIS ★

A century ago America seemed destined to center on Chicago. This brash new city on the lake had grown from 112,000 residents in 1860, when it was host to the Republican Convention that nominated Illinois' Abraham Lincoln, to 1.4 million when it hosted the Columbian Exposition in 1893. "Make no little plans," Chicago architect Daniel Burnham exhorted. And Chicago was making vast plans: building grand parks on the lakefront, erecting America's first downtown of skyscrapers, building expansive retail palaces, becoming the headquarters of the new American Medical and American Bar Associations, creating a great university from scratch on the Exposition's Midway Plaisance, housing the union agitators and their liberal advocate Clarence Darrow as well as the corporate leaders and attorneys who bested them, hosting the Democratic Convention of 1896 that nominated 36-year-old William Jennings Bryan after his "cross of gold" speech, and becoming the headquarters of the brilliant campaign Marcus Hanna waged for William McKinley that beat Bryan in the fall. Chicago started with the advantage of a great location, where the Great Lakes meet the prairies of the vast Mississippi Valley, and Chicago's entrepreneurs made it the hub of the nation's railroad network and the center of the nation's trade in lumber, grain and meat, as William Cronon describes in *Nature's Metropolis*.

A century later, Chicago is the nation's third-largest metropolis, sometimes overshadowed by and often ignored by the media of coastal New York and Los Angeles; but it is still a productive and creative world-city. Illinois, after near-zero population growth in the 1970s and 1980s, saw its population rise 9% in the 1990s, more than any decade since the 1960s. In commerce, Chicago remains a prime producer and processor of food products, a great manufacturing center with the strongest white-collar and service economy between the coasts, the home of the world's greatest commodities exchanges and futures markets. O'Hare Airport, promoted and nurtured by longtime (1955–76) Mayor Richard J. Daley and long the world's busiest airport, has been edged into second place by Atlanta's Hartsfield, but is still a great hub of commerce. Chicago and Illinois remain a focus of national attention. In May 2001 Chicago beat out Dallas and Denver as Boeing's choice for its new corporate headquarters. The state and city offered about $60 million in tax breaks over 20 years to lure the aerospace company from Seattle. Boeing will surpass McDonald's, Sears and Motorola as Illinois' biggest company in terms of sales in September 2001, when the move is expected to be complete. In the great home run duel of 1998, Illinois was split, between Cubs fans on the North Side of Chicago and suburbs rooting for Sammy Sosa and St. Louis Cardinals fans in much of Downstate rooting for Mark McGwire. All the nation joined Chicago in celebrating the career and lamenting the retirement of Michael Jordan in January 1999.

Politically, Chicago and Illinois did not produce any presidents in the 20th Century, but they have produced crucial votes and pivotal politicians. The list starts with Charles Dawes, a 30-year-old lawyer sent to Chicago by Hanna to manage McKinley's campaign—later he was a World War I general, the first Budget Bureau (now Office of Management and Budget) director, and vice president under Calvin Coolidge. Next comes Chicago lawyer Harold Ickes, who was Franklin Roosevelt's great Interior secretary. Prominent Illinois Republicans have included House Speaker Joseph Cannon, Senate Republican Leader Everett Dirksen, Senator Charles Percy and House Republican Leader Robert Michel; prominent Democrats have included Governor Adlai Stevenson, Mayor Richard J. Daley and Ways and Means Chairman Dan Rostenkowski. For much of the 20th Century, Illinois was a key political battleground, closely divided between (usually) Democratic Chicago and (mostly) Republican Downstate, with the growing ring of suburbs around Chicago becoming increasingly pivotal. Its mixture of blacks and whites and Hispanics, immigrants and pioneers, city-dwellers and suburbanites and farmers, the affluent and the impoverished, heavy industry and high-tech, make it a rough proxy for the nation. For a century Illinois was a political bellwether, voting only twice for losing presidential candidates between 1896 and 1996—in 1916 and 1976. Now it has seemed to move a bit to the left of the nation—primarily because of Democratic inroads in the suburbs, which cast about 40% of the state's votes—leaning pro-market on economics and *laissez faire* on cultural issues. These views sent Illinois toward Gerald Ford when Jimmy Carter was winning, but tilted the state heavily toward Bill Clinton in

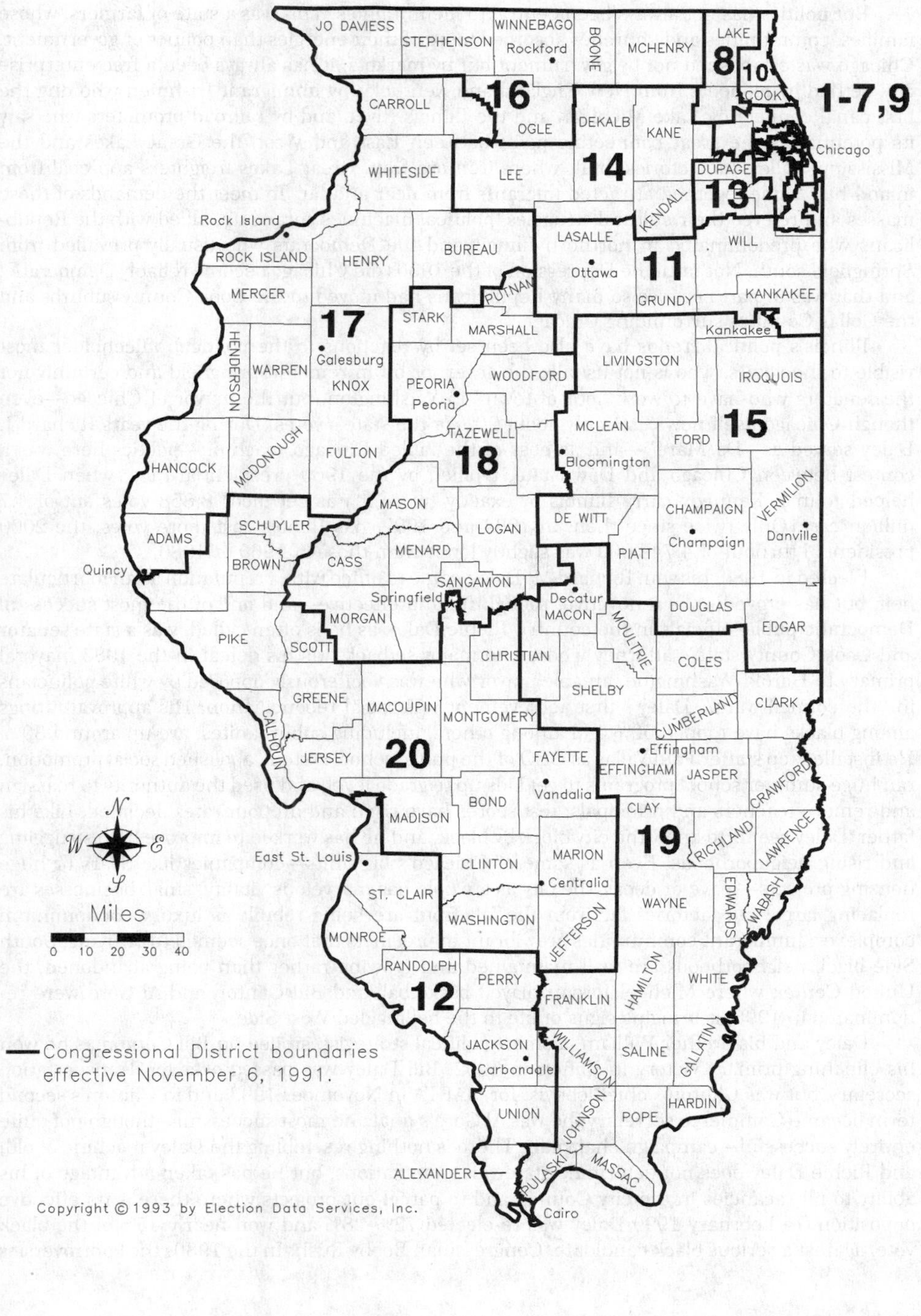

JO DAVIESS
STEPHENSON
WINNEBAGO
Rockford
BOONE
MCHENRY
LAKE
8
10
16
CARROLL
OGLE
DEKALB
KANE
COOK
1-7,9
Chicago
WHITESIDE
LEE
14
DUPAGE
13
KENDALL
Rock Island
ROCK ISLAND
HENRY
BUREAU
LASALLE
Ottawa
11
WILL
MERCER
PUTNAM
GRUNDY
KANKAKEE
17
STARK
MARSHALL
Kankakee
HENDERSON
Galesburg
WARREN
KNOX
LIVINGSTON
PEORIA
Peoria
WOODFORD
IROQUOIS
MCDONOUGH
FULTON
TAZEWELL
MCLEAN
FORD
15
HANCOCK
18
Bloomington
VERMILION
MASON
DE WITT
CHAMPAIGN
SCHUYLER
LOGAN
Champaign
Danville
ADAMS
BROWN
CASS
MENARD
PIATT
Quincy
SANGAMON
Springfield
Decatur
MACON
DOUGLAS
MORGAN
MOULTRIE
EDGAR
PIKE
SCOTT
CHRISTIAN
COLES
SHELBY
GREENE
MACOUPIN
MONTGOMERY
CUMBERLAND
CLARK
CALHOUN
JERSEY
20
FAYETTE
Effingham
EFFINGHAM
JASPER
CRAWFORD
Vandalia
BOND
MADISON
CLAY
19
RICHLAND
LAWRENCE
East St. Louis
CLINTON
MARION
Centralia
ST. CLAIR
WAYNE
EDWARDS
WABASH
MONROE
WASHINGTON
JEFFERSON
RANDOLPH
HAMILTON
PERRY
12
FRANKLIN
WHITE
JACKSON
Carbondale
WILLIAMSON
SALINE
GALLATIN
UNION
POPE
HARDIN
JOHNSON
ALEXANDER
PULASKI
MASSAC
Cairo
N
W
E
S
Miles
0 10 20 30 40
Congressional District boundaries
effective November 6, 1991.
Copyright © 1993 by Election Data Services, Inc.

the 1990s and Al Gore in 2000, when Illinois—for the first time in a century—was not seriously contested in a close presidential race. And suburban Republican strongholds like DuPage County, which George W. Bush's father carried by 39 percentage points in 1988, were much closer in 2000, when Bush only won by 13 points.

But politics has not always been central to life in Illinois. This was a state of farmers, whose families, communities and churches absorbed more of their energies than politics or government. Chicago was established not by government but by markets; it has always been a free enterprise city, settled by pioneers from New England and Kentucky, by immigrant Irishmen who dug the first canal connecting Lake Michigan and the Illinois River, and by railroad promoters who saw its potential as the great connecting point between East and West, the Great Lakes and the Mississippi Valley. Its factories, built where iron ore from Great Lakes freighters and coal from inland hills came together, attracted migrants from near and far. To meet the demands of these masses and referee their cultural struggles, political machines sprang up, allied with the Republicans who predominated in northern Illinois and the Democrats who usually prevailed from Springfield south. Not until the Depression of the 1930s did Chicago become reliably Democratic, and that was in part because so many Republicans had moved to the Cook County suburbs and the Collar Counties surrounding Chicago.

Illinois's political trends have also been set by reactions to the political officeholder most visible to the voters, who is not usually the governor off in remote Springfield and certainly not the senators who have to work "out of town" in Washington, but the mayor of Chicago—even though Chicago itself now casts only about 20% of the state's votes. During the years Richard J. Daley served as "Da Mare"—and as boss of the fabled Chicago machine—politics here was a contest between Chicago and Downstate, typified by the 1960 presidential race, when Daley helped John F. Kennedy carry Illinois by exactly (or so it was certified) 8,858 votes out of 4.7 million cast. Only twice since then, in 1984 and 1992, has Illinois cast more votes; the 2000 presidential turnout of 4,742,000 was slightly lower than those of 1960 or 1980.

Elected in 1989, his son, Richard M. Daley, came to office with a reputation as an inarticulate heir, but has proved to be innovative, thoughtful and effective—and one of the most successful Democratic public officials in the country. Richie Daley, as he is often called, was a state senator and Cook County state's attorney whose one major setback was his defeat in the 1983 mayoral primary to Harold Washington, an able mayor who was vociferously opposed by white politicians in "the council wars." Daley's first achievement was racial reconciliation: His approval ratings among blacks have topped 50% and among others, including suburbanites, are up around 80%. He installed top staffer Paul Vallas as CEO of the public school system, abolished social promotion, ran huge summer school programs to get kids up to grade level, and used the authority to reassign and remove teachers and principals; test scores have risen and dropout rates declined. Like his father, Daley seems to know the city block by block, and he has worked to improve both struggling and rising neighborhoods. Even as some of Chicago's big units—companies like Sears or huge housing projects—leave or decay, the city as a whole has marvelous vitality: small businesses are replacing large; old factories far from the lakefront are being rebuilt as luxury condominium complexes; immigrant communities are vibrant in precincts that once seemed to be dying; South Side black neighborhoods are well maintained and growing rather than being abandoned; the United Center, where Michael Jordan played basketball and Bill Clinton and Al Gore were renominated in 1996, is bringing signs of life to the bedraggled West Side.

Daley and his brother William, a smart political strategist, smiled on Bill Clinton as he won his clinching primary victory in Illinois in 1992. Bill Daley was passed over for Transportation secretary, but was Clinton's chief lobbyist for NAFTA in November 1993 and in Clinton's second term became Commerce secretary; he was Al Gore's final and most successful—though not quite entirely successful—campaign chairman. There is nothing resembling the Daley machine of old, and Richie Daley does not determine statewide nominations, but he has taken advantage of his ability to fill vacancies in the city Council and to parcel out projects where there is no effective opposition. In February 1999 Daley was re-elected 72%–28% and won nearly 45% of the black vote, against a serious black candidate, Congressman Bobby Rush. In the 1980s the controversies of Mayor Washington helped move Illinois toward the Republicans; in the 1990s the success of Mayor Daley helped move Illinois toward the Democrats.

Republicans control the Illinois Senate, Democrats the Illinois House; both parties elect downballot statewide officials. The U.S. House delegation has been split 10–10 since 1994, though it will not be after 2002, since the state lost one House seat in the 2000 Census. The most notable members of the delegation today are Speaker Dennis Hastert and Henry Hyde, who led the efforts to impeach Bill Clinton when he was Judiciary Committee chairman. Clinton twice carried Illinois by large margins—49%–34% over George Bush in 1992 and 54%–37% over Bob Dole in 1996, when Clinton carried the suburbs 48%–43% as well as the city 79%–16%; in 2000 Al Gore carried the state 55%–43%, barely winning the suburbs and sweeping all 50 of Chicago's wards (a feat that eluded Democrats even at the zenith of Richard J. Daley's power) for an 80%–17% victory in the Windy City. The suburbs—anti-tax, secular, if not liberal, on cultural issues—were mostly satisfied with Clinton and Gore; but they were also satisfied with the moderate Republican governors who succeeded James Thompson—Jim Edgar in 1990 and George Ryan in 1998. In the latter year, the suburbs, with much bigger turnout than eight years before, reacted negatively to Democratic nominee Glenn Poshard, a Downstater who opposed abortion and gun control. Yet they also gave a solid margin in the Senate race to conservative Republican Peter Fitzgerald over scandal-scarred Democratic incumbent Carol Moseley-Braun. Illinois' primary election, held in March, is one of the nation's first for statewide and congressional races, and has sometimes been a bellwether. The defeat of Senator Alan Dixon and four congressmen in the 1992 primary was a harbinger of the anti-incumbent trend that year. The fizzling of anti-incumbent challenges in 1996, 1998 and 2000 has foreshadowed the pro-incumbent sentiments in those years.

Governor George Ryan was elected governor in 1998 after a long career in politics. He grew up in Kankakee, served in Korea, got a degree in pharmacology and ran a family pharmacy in Kankakee, a town on the border of Chicagoland and Downstate Illinois. In 1966, prodded by a friend after complaining about local government, he ran for the county board and served six years. In 1972 he was elected to the state House, becoming minority leader in 1976 and speaker in 1980; that was the last term before Illinois's 177-member "Big House," with each district electing two from one party and one from the other, was slimmed down to 118 elected from single-member districts. The Big House was an environment that encouraged accommodation and deal-making (good and bad words for the same thing), in which Ryan continued to excel. In 1982 he was elected lieutenant governor and served eight years; in 1990 he was edged out of the race for governor by Jim Edgar, and was elected secretary of State instead. Ryan used the office, which issues driver's licenses and other documents, to political advantage. He opened offices on Saturdays and placed his name everywhere, on drunken driving pamphlets, ads for organ donations, refrigerator magnets for a seniors' hotline and promotions for family reading night.

When Edgar stunned everyone by announcing in August 1997 his retirement from elective politics, Ryan jumped into the race. So did several Democrats, hungry for an office their party has not occupied since 1976. Former Attorney General Roland Burris, with strong backing from black voters, started off leading in polls, but never raised enough money for a big ad campaign. Former Justice Department official John Schmidt seemed to have the backing of Mayor Richard M. Daley, more important for his popularity than his organization, and raised plenty of money. Then there was Congressman Glenn Poshard, from far Downstate Illinois—closer to Jackson, Mississippi, than Jackson Boulevard in Chicago, noted George Will—who had reached his self-imposed limit of five terms. In the March primary, Poshard won with 38%; he carried all but two Downstate counties, with a total of 70%. Burris, with backing from blacks—who formed almost one-quarter of the primary electorate—won 31%; Schmidt won 25%.

Ryan entered the general election campaign with a big fundraising advantage (he eventually raised $15 million to Poshard's $5.9 million). Poshard, meanwhile, was battered by Chicago-area liberals who disliked his opposition to abortion (which was even greater than that of Ryan, who made exceptions for rape and incest), his votes against some gay rights positions, and his opposition to some gun-control measures. The Independent Voters of Illinois refused to endorse him, and gay rights leaders, after meeting with Poshard, announced they were sticking with Ryan. Mayor Daley did support Poshard, but admitted he had always gotten on well with Ryan. Ryan, meanwhile, had backed gun control since 1989, supported gay rights, opposed more riverboat gambling but favored changes to make Illinois boats more competitive with those in Indiana, Iowa and Missouri. He set out his own priorities: putting 51% of new state revenues into schools, life sentences for criminals who use guns and injure or kill people, disentangling the "Hillside Strangler" intersection of the Eisenhower Expressway and two tollways. When he went on TV in July, an ad showed him striding down the center of the legislature and quoted him as saying he could always work with people on both sides of the aisle, while another hit Poshard as too conservative and "extreme, extreme, extreme." But there was a shadow over Ryan's campaign: Employees at a Secretary of State's office in Melrose Park were accused of bribery for issuing more than 250 truck driver's licenses to unqualified applicants, and Ryan was criticized for getting campaign contributions from employees in his office. Ryan won by just 51%–47% after leading by much wider margins in the polls. He made some inroads into the Democratic base—18% among blacks, 62% among Jews, 26% of self-identified Democrats—but Poshard also was strong in his home base, winning his old district convincingly, and holding Ryan to a 50%–49% margin Downstate. The difference was the suburbs, which went about 2–1 for Ryan.

As governor Ryan worked closely with the legislature and Mayor Daley—indeed, closer on many issues with Democrats than Republicans. He passed a bill requiring 51% of new revenues to go to education, but did not get the $1,000 vocational school scholarships he had promised for high school graduates. In 1999 he secured a five-year, $12 billion Illinois FIRST program to build roads, bridges, schools and sewers, funded by increases in vehicle registration fees and liquor taxes (which included $75 million to buy land for a Peotone airport south of Chicago). He allowed riverboat gambling in Cook County. Bills were passed to require longer sentences for crimes committed with guns and to limit children's access to guns. He vetoed a bill that would have limited Medicaid abortions. Ryan traveled to Cuba in fall 1999, attending Catholic Mass and meeting with Fidel Castro. In response to a *Chicago Tribune* series charging that 12 Illinois death row inmates had been wrongly convicted, he declared a moratorium in January 2000 on all executions and suggested later that he would probably adhere to it as long as he was governor. He backed a compromise bill making the unlawful carrying of weapons a first-time felony—even though many Republicans and Downstaters charged that this would result in the harassment of hunters. In the 2000 legislative session he got a property tax rebate of up to $300. In June 2000 he and the legislature suspended the 5% gas tax for six months.

Meanwhile, the shadow that fell on Ryan's 1998 campaign grew darker. In early 2000 a former top aide in the secretary of State's office was indicted for covering up information about the sale of commercial truck licenses (he pleaded guilty in January 2001); one particular sale was to an unqualified driver who caused an accident that killed six children. In January 2000 Ryan apologized for the corruption that existed in that department and said he had not been aware of it. But evidence came out that whistleblowers in the department had been fired and had tried to get information to Ryan and others close to him. In March 2001 he unveiled an ethics reform package. But in May 2001 another former high-ranking official in the Secretary of State's office admitted to trading coveted low-number license plates for campaign contributions. A February 2001 poll found that 45% of Illinois residents thought he should resign.

Heading into the 2002 election, some Illinois Republicans were hoping Ryan would not run for re-election. Besides his image problems from the ongoing license scandal, conservatives in the party were dissatisfied with his record of increasing spending, strengthening gun-control laws and his veto of a bill to ban public funding of abortions. Most Republicans considered state Attorney General Jim Ryan (no relation) to be the best candidate should Ryan not run. On the Democratic side, former Attorney General Roland Burris was the early favorite in spring 2001. Democrats in any case seem overdue for a victory in this increasingly Democratic state where they have not elected a governor since 1972 (Illinois changed its governor elections to off-years in 1978).

Cook's Call   *Highly Competitive.* If Ryan—who has been drowning in controversy and scandal since the day he was elected—runs for re-election and manages to hold his nomination, he would almost certainly lose the general. Attorney General Jim Ryan tops the list of likely alternate Republican nominees and might have the best chance to keep this contest competitive, although other Republicans have already thrown their hats into the primary contest. There is a long line of potential Democratic challengers, including Congressman Rod Blagojevich, former Treasurer Patrick Quinn, Secretary of State Jesse White, Cook County Assessor James Houlihan, Cook County Attorney Richard Devine and former Congressman and 1998 gubernatorial nominee Glenn Poshard. In the race already are 1998 Democratic nomination hopeful John Schmidt, former state attorney general and 1998 candidate Roland Burris and state Representative Louis Lang.

Senior Senator   Richard Durbin is a Democrat elected in 1996. Durbin grew up in East St. Louis, and for almost all his adult life has been in politics: Right out of law school he joined Paul Simon's staff when he was lieutenant governor (1969–73), then was a state Senate staffer in the 1970s. He lost two races for office in the 1970s, but in 1982 won the nomination to oppose Republican Congressman Paul Findley, who had characterized himself as Yasir Arafat's best friend in Congress; that helped Durbin raise large sums from Israel supporters. Durbin won that race, got a seat on the Agriculture Committee and then moved to Appropriations, where in 1993 he became chairman of the Agriculture Subcommittee. There Durbin worked on Illinois projects—not just Downstate projects like the research center at the Lincoln home, but the $750 million Chicago Circulator trolley project as well. He worked to promote ethanol and soybean-based ink in government documents—big causes in the homeland of Dwayne Andreas's Archer-Daniels-Midland. Durbin's father died of lung cancer when he was 14, and Durbin's most prominent achievement was the 1988 ban on smoking on domestic airline flights; he followed that up by trying to limit tobacco subsidies and in 1994 moved unsuccessfully to direct the FDA to regulate tobacco as a health hazard.

Senator Paul Simon announced his retirement in November 1994, and in June 1995, Durbin decided to run for the seat. He had lost his subcommittee chair after Republicans won the House in 1994. His recent House races had been uncomfortably close; he won against a serious opponent with 57% in 1992, then won with just 55% in 1994 against a construction worker and John Birch Society member who spent only $55,000. Simon immediately endorsed him, which surely helped him Downstate. Durbin's chief problem—an almost total lack of name identification in Chicago, which cast nearly half the primary votes—was solved with money: He raised more than $1 million for the March 19 primary, vastly outspending his only serious opponent, former state Treasurer Pat Quinn; he won the primary 65%–30%. Meanwhile, the Republican primary was won in an upset. Governor Jim Edgar and other insiders had worked to persuade a reluctant Lieutenant Governor Bob Kustra to run. But Kustra, who at one point in 1994 announced he was retiring from politics to be a talk radio host, seemed to have little fire in his belly. His opponent, trial lawyer and abortion opponent Al Salvi, did, and spent more than $1 million of his own money in the primary. Despite a meek demeanor and total lack of name identification, Salvi came from behind to edge Kustra 48%–43%.

The general election was a battle of broad-brush charges in a state where few voters knew much about either candidate. Salvi called Durbin a tax-raiser, and hit him for opposing the balanced budget amendment; a bartender in one of his ads called Durbin "a big-taxin', big-spendin', pay-grabbin' liberal congressman." Perhaps the leading issue was gun control. Salvi's opposition to the assault weapons ban was undoubtedly unpopular, especially in the suburbs, and an October endorsement from gun control activists Jim and Sarah Brady surely helped Durbin. But more important was an astonishing mistake by Salvi: In late October, someone he met at a rally told him that Jim Brady used to sell machine guns and, without checking out the story, Salvi repeated it in a radio interview. It was totally untrue and Salvi had to apologize, but any chance of his overtaking Durbin was gone. Durbin won 56%–41%, with a huge margin in Chicago and narrow edges in the suburbs and Downstate. Durbin's 56% was almost exactly identical to Bill Clinton's 54% and Democratic House candidates' 55%.

In the Senate Durbin has compiled a liberal voting record, though he has supported welfare reform and the death penalty, and has been a dependable Democratic partisan on the floor and on cable news networks. He got a seat on Appropriations in 1998. He defended the Clinton-Gore campaign resolutely in Fred Thompson's 1997 investigation of campaign finance irregularities and staunchly opposed impeachment in 1999, but did criticize Clinton in February 2001 for pardoning Marc Rich. Durbin has long been a critic of the Electoral College system, and in November 2000 he and Downstate Republican Ray LaHood revived their constitutional amendment to do away with it and elect the president by popular vote.

On tobacco, Durbin took a lead role at several stages. He moved to repeal the tax credit for tobacco companies; he lost 78–22 in July 1997, then won 95–3 in September 1997. He opposed provisions to limit FDA regulation of tobacco or "any additive ingredient of a tobacco product." In July 1998 he moved to ban smoking on international flights, and he pushed to increase the size of the tobacco settlement. On other health issues, Durbin wants patients to be able to sue HMOs. "The insurance companies hate the idea of being sued in court like the devil hates holy water," he said. In the House Durbin favored restrictions on abortion, including the Hyde amendment and the Human Life Amendment; in the Senate, and with perhaps an eye on national office, he has backed abortion rights and introduced a bill to ban abortions once the fetus can survive outside the womb, except where two physicians certify that a woman's life is at risk or she faces "grievous injury" to physical health. He supported his anti-abortion Downstate colleague Glenn Poshard in the 1998 primary for governor.

Durbin has tried to move his goal of gun control incrementally forward, calling for a ban on gun possession by foreigners on non-immigrant visas, a ban on certain cheap handguns, criminal penalties for parents whose children get hold of guns, and a permanent extension of the Brady bill's five-day waiting requirement (the original bill had it lapse to be replaced by an instant criminal background check). Durbin has a very strong pro-union voting record, but split with them on trade, supporting NAFTA in the House and PNTR for China in the Senate: Illinois is a big exporter. He sponsored a bill to give the FDA power to approve genetically modified foods but would not require labeling. In March 1999 he was one of three senators to oppose a national missile defense system, and in July 2000 he sponsored a bill to require more testing and an independent review of missile testing systems, which was defeated 52–48. He unsuccessfully fought against Senate passage of a Republican bankruptcy reform bill in March 2001. On the D.C. Appropriations Committee, he abandoned his usual deference to District officials' policies and in July 1999 tried to stop the District from cutting taxes, using a college scholarship bill as hostage.

As *Chicago Sun-Times* columnist Steve Neal points out, Durbin has followed the career path of Everett Dirksen, who also was an appropriator in both House and Senate and who as a practical politician worked with Illinois colleagues of both parties. Durbin and Republican Senator Peter Fitzgerald hold weekly breakfasts for Illinois constituents. At one such gathering in March 2000, Fitzgerald announced that Durbin was under serious consideration for the Democratic nomination for vice president, and Durbin-Gore buttons were handed out that month in Chicago's St. Patrick's Day parade. Durbin's name appeared on unofficial short lists for VP. But in August Durbin explained that he had been contacted by Warren Christopher in June and asked for information for the vetting process, but Durbin had called back four days later to say they he did not want to be considered. Neal speculated that Durbin's nomination became impossible in June when William Daley, who had looked for candidates to oppose Durbin in the 1996 Senate primary, became Gore's campaign chairman.

Like most statewide elected officials in this megastate, Durbin is not well known by most voters; an October 2000 poll showed Durbin with 47%–17% favorable ratings, with more than one-third unable to respond. He nevertheless remains perhaps the best-known Democrat in Illinois except for Mayor Richard M. Daley. He chaired the Democrats' 2000 platform committee and aroused some criticism when he insisted on being one of three white males to announce the Illinois vote on the roll call at the Democratic Convention in Los Angeles. There was speculation starting in summer 2000 that he would run for governor, as incumbent Republican George Ryan continued to rate poorly in the polls, but in December 2000 Durbin said he would not seek the governorship.

Cook's Call   *Probably Safe.* While Illinois voters have developed a reputation for tossing incumbents, there is little evidence that Durbin is vulnerable, and Illinois Republicans have their hands full holding onto the governorship. To compete in this race, Republicans would need to recruit a moderate candidate who can finance some or all of the campaign. They believe Jack Ryan, a Goldman Sachs executive turned public school teacher, might fit that bill, but Ryan might not be the best last name to have on an Illinois ballot in 2002 given Republican Governor George Ryan's substantial problems.

Junior Senator   Peter Fitzgerald, a Republican born in 1960 and elected to the Senate in 1998, is the youngest member of the Senate. He grew up in the affluent northwest suburb of Inverness—as Republican as Chicago is Democratic. His father started a suburban bank chain and sold it to the Bank of Montreal in 1991, netting his son some $40 million in stock. Fitzgerald went to Catholic schools and majored in Latin and Greek at Dartmouth; after a year in Greece he went to Michigan Law School. In his college years he was an intern for Congressman Philip Crane—now the senior Republican in the House—and organized a New Hampshire rally for Crane's 1980 presidential campaign. In 1988 Fitzgerald lost a close primary for the state House; in 1992 he was elected to the state Senate. There he opposed tax increases and was known as one of the "Fab Five" conservatives. He voted to allow law-abiding citizens to carry concealed weapons and favored competitive bidding for casino licenses. In 1994 he spent more than $700,000 of his own money challenging Crane in a primary, and lost by only 40%–33%.

Fitzgerald won his Senate seat by beating incumbent Democrat Carol Moseley-Braun, who had become the first black woman senator in 1992. She had a mostly liberal record but tended closely to Chicago and Downstate business interests; she was articulate, with a winning manner. But she also had terrible problems, including a report that she had split among herself and siblings a $28,750 inheritance owed to her mother, a nursing home resident who was supposed to have reimbursed Medicaid with the money; a month-long trip to Africa after her election with her South African campaign manager and ex-fiance Kgosie Matthews, where they allegedly spent some $281,000 in campaign funds; and a "private" visit to Nigeria with Matthews, a former registered agent of the Nigerian government, where they met with now-deceased dictator General Sani Abacha without the normal checking-in with the State Department. As a result, Moseley-Braun's poll numbers dropped to near-record lows. But Democrats shied away from challenging the only black senator, and the best-known Republicans declined to run: Governor Jim Edgar announced his retirement from public office, Secretary of State George Ryan announced for governor, and Attorney General Jim Ryan, recovering from cancer, declined to run.

Fitzgerald had announced in April 1997, but Edgar and other Republican leaders, fresh from watching abortion opponent Al Salvi lose the 1996 Senate race, did not want an abortion opponent as the nominee. They encouraged Comptroller Loleta Didrickson, though she was reluctant to run. Fitzgerald spent some $7 million in the primary, starting off with warm ads showing him as a basic suburban father, then calling for lower taxes. When Moseley-Braun said, "Loleta Didrickson and I voted very much alike when we were in the state legislature together," Fitzgerald seized on the theme and attacked Didrickson as a tax-raiser. Didrickson called him "the trust fund kid" and argued that he would lose the general election. She was heavily outspent, but Fitzgerald won by only 52%–48%, losing the suburbs narrowly but carrying Downstate 59%–41%.

In the general, Fitzgerald attacked "six years of scandal and controversy" and said that Moseley-Braun had "been to Nigeria more than she's been to Rockford." Moseley-Braun fought back. In ads she conceded, "I know I've made some mistakes and disappointed some people. But I want you to know that I've always tried to do what's best for Illinois." Bill Clinton, Al Gore and Illinois native Hillary Rodham Clinton came in to raise money and campaign for her. Moseley-Braun accused Fitzgerald of running a stealth campaign and relying on ads, and she performed creditably in debate. But Fitzgerald, with more than $14 million of his own money, outspent her 2–1. Fitzgerald won by just 50%–47%, losing Cook and four small Downstate counties and carrying the other 97. Moseley-Braun carried Cook County heavily, but Fitzgerald was ahead in the suburbs and he carried the rest of the state 60%–36%, even though it went for George Ryan over Downstater Glenn Poshard in the gubernatorial race by only 50%–49%. She carried blacks 93%–7%; he carried white Protestants 65%–32% and white Catholics 69%–30%.

In the Senate Fitzgerald has set his own course, opposing fellow Republicans on key issues and building a cooperative relationship with Democratic Senator Richard Durbin, while compiling a mostly conservative record. One pet cause was his Truth in Budgeting Act, to require that government use generally accepted accounting practices and provide separate audits for trust funds; he claims the government is shortchanging Social Security. With his conservative reputation, Fitzgerald surprised colleagues when he voted for patients' rights to sue HMOs and background checks at gun shows in 1999, for the Democrats' prescription drug and HMO regulation bills in 2000, and with only two other Republicans in favor of a Democratic lockbox proposal for Medicare in March 2001. He bucked Western Republican senators on logging regulations in national forests, disposal of toxic mining wastes on federal lands, and mountaintop mining; Fitzgerald even received a 57% rating from the League of Conservation Voters, the fourth-highest among Senate Republicans. But he was one of two votes against confirming Moseley-Braun as ambassador to New Zealand in November 1999 (the other was Jesse Helms). He has an eye for the popular measure: in June 2000, when Chicago area gas prices zoomed above $2, he called for suspending the 18.3-cent federal gas tax for 90 days. Fitzgerald's net worth, between $26 and $51 million, is one of the highest in the Senate. In March 2001 with just 11 other Republicans he voted to kill Chuck Hagel's amendment to the McCain-Feingold bill to limit, instead of ban, soft money. He has not put his holdings into a blind trust, but has refrained from voting on bills with impact on banking, like the financial services deregulation bill.

Durbin and Moseley-Braun had held weekly breakfasts for Illinois constituents; despite their political differences, Fitzgerald persuaded Durbin to continue the practice, and they ended up working together on funding ethanol-manufacturing plants and ethanol studies at Southern Illinois University, expanding commuter rail lines, rebuilding the Lake Michigan shoreline in Chicago, maintaining the Army weapons factory in Rock Island. Fitzgerald supports a third Chicago-area airport. He has opposed increasing the number of slots at O'Hare, and against John McCain's bill to do so in October 1999 he filed 304 amendments. McCain accused him of jeopardizing the safety of airline passengers and Fitzgerald withdrew the amendments and agreed to 30 more slots at O'Hare—far fewer than in New York's LaGuardia. But his fight was in vain: the AIR-21 bill that passed in March 2000 will abolish O'Hare's slots by 2002 and ultimately increase its air traffic.

Fitzgerald's most acerbic fight was to impose federal competitive bidding standards on the $115 million Abraham Lincoln Library project in Springfield. In October 2000 Fitzgerald conducted a two-day filibuster, insisting on federal standards. He charged that the state's competitive bidding process would result in a sweetheart contract for Springfield developer William Cellini. This was a head-on attack on a bipartisan compromise reached by Governor George Ryan and the Illinois delegation. Speaker Dennis Hastert, who supported the Illinois competitive-bidding system in the House, responded in language rare for one co-partisan to another: "I find Senator Fitzgerald's political grandstanding on the Abraham Lincoln Library outrageous." Fitzgerald's filibuster ultimately did not prevail.

There was talk that Fitzgerald might challenge Ryan in the 2002 governor primary; Ryan's poll numbers were low amid charges that secretary of State employees had sold commercial truck licenses when he held the office. An October 2000 poll showed Fitzgerald leading Ryan in a primary by 62%–26%, and Fitzgerald could run without giving up his Senate seat, which is not up until 2004; in February 2001 he said Ryan should not run for a second term and began recruiting other Republicans to challenge the incumbent governor, without ruling himself out as a candidate. But in early 2001 it seemed likely that Fitzgerald would wait and run for re-election in 2004; he pledged in 1998 to serve only two terms. In the meantime, this self-financing senator has been unafraid to provide plenty of headaches for Illinois' more pragmatic politicians and many of his Senate colleagues.

Presidential politics   Illinois's presidential primary, for years held fittingly on or around St. Patrick's Day, clinched the nominations for Republican victors Gerald Ford in 1976, Ronald Reagan in 1980 and George Bush in 1988, and Democratic victors Jimmy Carter in 1980, Walter Mondale in 1984 and Bill Clinton in 1992. In 1988 the Democratic nomination would probably have been clinched here for Michael Dukakis, except for the dominance of two Illinois candidates, Paul Simon and Jesse Jackson. But as more states vote earlier, Illinois was too late to decide any nomination in 1996 or 2000. Illinois' Republican primary voters are about evenly split between the suburbs, with their affluent free-market dislike for taxes, and Downstate, with their old-fashioned, practical-minded Midwestern politics. More than 60% of Illinois' Democratic primary votes are cast in Cook County, most of them in Chicago.

In the close presidential elections of 1976 and 1988, Illinois went Republican, on the strength of big majorities in Chicago's suburbs. But in 2000 Illinois went solidly for Al Gore, 55%–43%, as the suburban Collar Counties voted only narrowly, 53%–44% for George W. Bush while the Cook County suburbs went for Gore, with an even greater than usual Democratic landslide in the city of Chicago. This gave Gore a huge 59%–38% in metro Chicago over George W. Bush, whose father carried the metro area 50%–49% in 1988. But the younger Bush carried Downstate Illinois 51%–47%, the same margin as his father's 52%–48%.

Congressional districting   Illinois's congressional district lines for the last 20 years have been drawn by courts. The 1980s plan favored Democrats, the 1990s plan Republicans. New lines can cause political upsets: four incumbents lost in the 1992 primary. Illinois lost one seat in the 2000 Census, and control of redistricting is split between a Republican governor and state Senate and a Democratic state House. The 5th District, created 10 years ago for Dan Rosten-kowski, was expected to be eliminated because its current incumbent, Democrat Rod Blagojevich, expressed interest in running for governor. But the dramatic decline in the population of southern Illinois during the 1990s made such a plan unworkable. In a bipartisan agreement reached by House Speaker Dennis Hastert and Democrat William Lipinski, the 5th District will be preserved while most of the Downstate 19th District of Democrat David Phelps will be combined with the 15th District of freshman Republican Tim Johnson, setting up a contest between the two incumbents in 2002 favoring Johnson.

THE PEOPLE: Pop. 2000: 12,419,293; Pop. 1990: 11,430,602, up 8.6% 1990–2000. 4.4% of U.S. total, 5th largest; 73.5% White, 15.1% Black, 3.4% Asian, 0.2% Amer. Indian, 1.9% Two+ races, 5.8% Other; 12.3% Hispanic Origin. 4.4% Unemployment. 2000 Voting age pop.: 9,173,842. 2000 Turnout: 4,932,192; 54% of VAP. Registered voters (2000): 7,129,026; no party registration.

POLITICAL LINEUP: Governor, George H. Ryan (R); Lt. Gov., Corinne Wood (R); Secy. of State, Jesse White (D); Atty. Gen., James E. Ryan (R); Treasurer, Judy Baar Topinka (R); Comptroller, Daniel W. Hynes (D); State Senate, 59 (27 D, 32 R); Senate President, James (Pate) Philip (R); Majority Leader, Stanley B. Weaver (R); State Assembly, 118 (62 D, 56 R); Assembly Speaker, Mike Madigan (D). Senators, Richard J. Durbin (D) and Peter G. Fitzgerald (R). Representatives, 20 (10 D, 10 R).

ELECTIONS DIVISION: 217-782-4141; **FILING DEADLINE FOR U.S. CONGRESS:** December 17, 2001.

2000 Presidential Vote
Gore (D)	2,589,026	(55%)
Bush (R)	2,019,421	(43%)
Nader (Green)	103,759	(2%)
Others	29,902	(1%)

1996 Presidential Vote
Clinton (D)	2,341,744	(54%)
Dole (R)	1,587,021	(37%)
Perot (I)	346,408	(8%)

2000 Republican Presidential Primary
Bush (R)	496,646	(67%)
McCain (R)	158,752	(22%)
Keyes (R)	66,057	(9%)
Other	15,402	(2%)

2000 Democratic Presidential Primary
Gore (D)	682,916	(84%)
Bradley (D)	115,317	(14%)

Gov. George H. Ryan (R)

Elected 1998, term expires Jan. 2003, 1st term; b. Feb. 24, 1934, Maquoketa, IA; home, Kankakee; Butler U. 1952, Ferris State Col., B.S., 1961; Methodist; married (Lura Lynn).

Military Career: Army, 1954–56 (Korea).

Elected Office: Kankakee Cnty. Bd., 1966–72; IL House of Reps., 1972–82, Minority Ldr., 1977–81, Speaker, 1981–82; IL Lt. Gov., 1982–90; IL Secy. of State, 1990–98.

Professional Career: Pharmacist & co-owner, family pharmacy, 1962–90.

Office: 207 State House, Springfield, 62706, 217-782-6830; Fax: 217-524-1676; Web site: www.state.il.us.

Election Results

1998 general	George H. Ryan (R)	1,714,094	(51%)
	Glenn Poshard (D)	1,594,191	(47%)
	Others	50,420	(2%)
1998 primary	George H. Ryan (R)	608,940	(86%)
	Chad Koppie (R)	98,466	(14%)
1994 general	Jim Edgar (R)	1,984,318	(64%)
	Dawn Clark Netsch (D)	1,069,850	(34%)
	Others	52,398	(2%)

Sen. Richard J. Durbin (D)

Elected 1996, seat up 2002, 1st term; b. Nov. 21, 1944, E. St. Louis; home, Springfield; Georgetown U., B.S. 1966, J.D. 1969; Catholic; married (Loretta).

Elected Office: U.S. House of Reps., 1982–96.

Professional Career: Staff, Lt. Gov. Paul Simon, 1969–72; Legal Cnsl., IL Sen. Judiciary Cmte., 1972–82; Prof., S. IL Schl. of Medicine, 1978–82.

DC Office: 332 DSOB, 20510, 202-224-2152; Fax: 202-228-0400; Web site: www.senate.gov/~durbin.

State Offices: Chicago, 312-353-4952; Marion, 618-998-8812; Springfield, 217-492-4062.

Committees: *Appropriations*: Agriculture & Rural Development; Defense; District of Columbia; Foreign Operations; Legislative Branch (Chmn.); Transportation. *Governmental Affairs*: Government Management, Restructuring and the District of Columbia (Chmn.); Investigations (Permanent). *Intelligence (Select)*. *Judiciary*: Administrative Oversight & the Courts; Constitution, Federalism & Property Rights; Immigration; Youth Violence.

Group Ratings

	ADA	ACLU	AFS	LCV	CON	ITIC	NTU	COC	ACU	NTLC	CHC
2000	95	71	85	100	54	90	10	50	4	6	8
1999	100	—	100	100	68	—	3	35	4	—	—

National Journal Ratings

	1999 LIB —	1999 CONS		2000 LIB —	2000 CONS
Economic	90%	— 0%		90%	— 7%
Social	88%	— 0%		79%	— 0%
Foreign	71%	— 24%		86%	— 12%

Key Votes of the 106th Congress

1. Educ. Savings Accts.	N	5. Review Movie Violence	N	9. NATO War in Serbia	Y
2. Prescrip. Drug Benefit	Y	6. Gun Show Bckgrnd. Checks	Y	10. Table Cuba Travel Ban	N
3. Delay Ergonomic Standards	N	7. Ban Part.-Birth Abortion	N	11. Nuclear Test-Ban Treaty	Y
4. Phase Out Estate Tax	N	8. Broaden Hate Crimes List	Y	12. Perm. Trade with China	Y

Election Results

1996 general	Richard J. Durbin (D)	2,384,028	(56%)	($4,966,804)
	Al Salvi (R)	1,728,824	(41%)	($4,696,065)
	Others	137,870	(3%)	
1996 primary	Richard J. Durbin (D)	512,520	(65%)	
	Pat Quinn (D)	233,138	(30%)	
	Others	44,397	(6%)	
1990 general	Paul Simon (D)	2,115,377	(65%)	($8,665,789)
	Lynn Martin (R)	1,135,628	(35%)	($4,921,613)

Sen. Peter G. Fitzgerald (R)

Elected 1998, seat up 2004, 1st term; b. Oct. 20, 1960, Elgin; home, Inverness; Dartmouth Col., A.B. 1982, U. of MI Law Schl., J.D. 1986; Catholic; married (Nina).

Elected Office: IL Senate, 1992–98.

Professional Career: Practicing atty., 1986–96.

DC Office: 555 DSOB, 20510, 202-224-2854; Fax: 202-228-1372; Web site: www.senate.gov/~fitzgerald.

State Offices: Chicago, 312-886-3506; Dixon, 815-288-3140; Glen Carbon, 618-692-0364; Springfield, 217-492-5089.

Committees: *Aging (Special)*. *Agriculture, Nutrition & Forestry*: Marketing, Inspection & Product Promotion (RMM); Production & Price Competitiveness. *Commerce, Science & Transportation*: Aviation; Communications; Consumer Affairs, Foreign Commerce & Tourism (RMM); Manufacturing & Competitiveness; Oceans & Fisheries; Science, Technology & Space; Surface Transportation & Merchant Marine. *Small Business*.

Group Ratings

	ADA	ACLU	AFS	LCV	CON	ITIC	NTU	COC	ACU	NTLC	CHC
2000	25	17	14	57	67	100	71	71	95	94	100
1999	15	—	33	44	96	—	79	88	92	—	—

National Journal Ratings

	1999 LIB	—	1999 CONS		2000 LIB	—	2000 CONS
Economic	32%	—	65%		50%	—	49%
Social	48%	—	51%		45%	—	54%
Foreign	10%	—	84%		47%	—	52%

Key Votes of the 106th Congress

1. Educ. Savings Accts.	Y	5. Review Movie Violence	Y	9. NATO War in Serbia	N
2. Prescrip. Drug Benefit	Y	6. Gun Show Bckgrnd. Checks	Y	10. Table Cuba Travel Ban	Y
3. Delay Ergonomic Standards	Y	7. Ban Part.-Birth Abortion	Y	11. Nuclear Test-Ban Treaty	N
4. Phase Out Estate Tax	Y	8. Broaden Hate Crimes List	N	12. Perm. Trade with China	Y

Election Results

1998 general	Peter G. Fitzgerald (R)	1,709,041	(50%)	($17,678,198)
	Carol Moseley-Braun (D)	1,610,496	(47%)	($7,200,895)
	Others	74,984	(2%)	
1998 primary	Peter G. Fitzgerald (R)	372,916	(52%)	
	Loleta Didrickson (R)	346,606	(48%)	
1992 general	Carol Moseley-Braun (D)	2,631,229	(53%)	($6,699,942)
	Richard S. Williamson (R)	2,126,833	(43%)	($2,300,924)
	Others	181,496	(4%)	

FIRST DISTRICT

The South Side of Chicago has been the nation's largest urban black community for nearly a century now. At first there were just a few blocks where black families from the South would settle; this ghetto grew rapidly with the first influx of blacks from the Mississippi Delta in the 1910s. By the 1920s the South Side was well established, a center of blues music in America and of black-owned businesses. Politically, the South Side was a heavily Republican constituency throughout those years; the comfortable white Protestants who settled in solid brick houses here believed in the party of Yankee propriety, and the blacks had faith in the party of Lincoln. This was one of the heartlands of the Republican party, represented in Congress by Minority Leader James R. Mann and then Appropriations Chairman Martin Madden. After Madden died in the Appropriations Committee room in 1928, the 1st District elected Oscar DePriest, the first black elected to the House in the 20th Century. Blacks remained faithful to the party of Lincoln even during the Depression, voting for Herbert Hoover and DePriest in 1932.

The New Deal and the racial liberalism of New Dealers like Eleanor Roosevelt and Interior Secretary Harold Ickes (a former Chicago Republican himself) attracted blacks to the Democratic Party, and DePriest was beaten by a black Democrat in 1934. The South Side has been Democratic ever since. For 40 years it was a cooperative part of Chicago's Democratic machine; then, after the death of longtime Congressman William Dawson, it rebelled against Mayor Richard J. Daley. The South Side seemed to take over the city when Congressman Harold Washington was elected mayor in 1983 and 1987. But control of political office does not mean what it once did. Patronage jobs became fewer as a result of court decisions. After Washington died in November 1987, other black South Side politicians flailed at each other, even though Chicago's electorate is only 40% black and a black candidate needs non-black voters to win.

The 1st Congressional District of Illinois includes about half of Chicago's black South Side community within its oddly shaped boundaries. It also extends out into the suburbs and is no longer even the city's highest-percentage black district, but is by most measures Illinois' most Democratic. It includes the Gothic spires of the University of Chicago and the mansions of Kenwood, once the home of Chicago's Jewish aristocracy and more recently the headquarters of the Nation of Islam and home to its leader, Louis Farrakhan. Miles and miles of the district are made up of bungalow neighborhoods, with single-family houses lining arrow-straight streets. Many of these neighborhoods have shown signs of vitality and growth in recent years: Citizens have banded together to fight crime using high-sodium streetlights and roadblocks; the South Shore Development Bank has provided loans to minority business owners. The 1st District's odd shape follows historic patterns: The eastern half of the district roughly approximates the boundaries of 1st Districts going back to the 1960s; the western half, to which it is connected by a strip a mile wide, has some all-black neighborhoods, but also includes the higher-income Irish-American neighborhoods of Morgan Park and Beverly, where the annual South Side Irish St. Patrick's Day Parade is held. It goes as far south as the industrial suburbs of Alsip and Blue Island.

The congressman from the 1st District is a man who has gone through several transformations. Bobby Rush grew up on the North Side, a Boy Scout whose mother was a Republican precinct captain. In the Army he became involved in the Student Non-Violent Coordinating Committee in the South, then went AWOL and founded the Illinois Black Panthers, where he recruited Fred Hampton, later killed in a raid by police in 1969. Rush served six months in prison for illegal possession of firearms, but also during his time with the Black Panthers he had run a medical clinic that developed the nation's first mass sickle cell anemia testing program. "I don't repudiate any of my involvement in the Panther party—it was part of my maturing," Rush has since said. In 1983 he was elected 2d Ward alderman and became a strong Harold Washington supporter. In 1992, with the district expanded, he challenged incumbent Congressman Charles Hayes, an older generation politician with a union background. Just before the March 1992 primary it was revealed that Hayes had 716 overdrafts on the House bank. Rush beat Hayes 42%–39%, carrying eight of 12 black wards plus Morgan Park and Beverly, where many white police veterans live and where Rush was helped by state House Speaker and 13th Ward Committeeman Michael Madigan.

In the House, Rush has a liberal voting record and a seat on the Commerce Committee. He voted for the securities litigation reform bill that was passed over President Clinton's veto. But he has also been willing to protest what he considers injustice. He was so angry that Clinton signed the 1996 welfare bill that he would have thrown away his delegate credential for the 1996 Democratic National Convention but for his wife's urging. He called the requirement of community service for public housing tenants "involuntary servitude." He attacked Chicago's anti-gang loitering law as "police state tactics [that] make scapegoats and criminals of innocent people."

Rush's rhetoric has toned down over the years. "Most African-Americans just want a comfortable, middle-class lifestyle," he said in 1992. "Twenty-five years ago, I didn't know that." On crime, he said, "Blacks are killing blacks. Young blacks are killing other young blacks. We don't need to make excuses for our young people. We need to challenge them." That reality was brought painfully home to Rush in October 1999, when his son Huey Rich—who was born three weeks before the 1969 police raid, and although raised by an aunt had recently grown close with his father—was murdered by a man wielding a handgun as he returned to his South Side home with his fiance. "My son's death was a senseless death," Rush told supporters a day later at Jesse

Jackson's PUSH headquarters. "We've got to rid our communities of guns. Violence and guns don't belong in a civilized society."

After his re-election in 1998 Rush launched a quixotic mayoral challenge to Daley, of whom he has sometimes been a harsh critic. During the campaign, he attacked the mayor for tolerating police brutality, inadequate mass-transit service and "cronyism." House colleagues Jesse Jackson Jr. and Danny Davis were at his side, but only three of the 50 aldermen endorsed him—many had been appointed by Daley to fill vacancies and he worked with almost all of them on local projects. Rush insisted that he wanted to build a multiracial coalition, but for practical purposes his only chance was with black voters, and not all of them supported him. Daley's record was too popular and his financial advantage overwhelming. Even prominent black ministers endorsed the mayor and Jackson said that Rush should have focused more on economic issues. Daley won the February election by 72%–28%, with nearly 45% of the black vote, an achievement that reflects more on his record than on Rush.

After that pounding, Rush found himself challenged in the primary for his own re-election in 2000 by two state senators—Donne Trotter and Barack Obama. Obama, a civil rights lawyer who was the first black president of the Harvard Law Review, made the more spirited challenge. But he badly slipped by missing a gun-control vote in the state Senate two months before the election, when he remained late on a visit to Hawaii because, he said, his infant daughter was ill. With an additional boost from a primary-eve endorsement from Bill Clinton, Rush ran well in both the city and suburbs, and won an unexpectedly strong 61%, with Obama and Trotter receiving 30% and 7%, respectively.

Rush needs to remain on guard against future Democratic challenges, including redistricting mischief. The 1st District needs to find 93,000 additional people, and the lines on the South Side could be redrawn to benefit local challengers.

Cook's Call   *Safe*. Bobby Rush is sitting in what must be among the half dozen or so most Democratic districts in the nation (Gore won here with 87%) and as such will never have to sweat a general election. After handily beating back a field of three other Democrats in the 2000 primary, it remains to be seen if he gets another serious challenge in the 2002.

THE PEOPLE: Pop. 2000: 560,239; Pop. 1990: 571,908, down 2% 1990–2000. 23% White, 70.3% Black, 1.4% Asian, 0.2% Amer. Indian, 1.5% Two+ races, 3.6% Other; 7.5% Hispanic Origin.

2000 Presidential Vote			1996 Presidential Vote		
Gore (D)	194,432	(87%)	Clinton (D)	179,767	(85%)
Bush (R)	24,276	(11%)	Dole (R)	22,914	(11%)
Nader (Green)	2,867	(1%)	Perot (I)	6,378	(3%)

Rep. Bobby Rush (D)

Elected 1992, 5th term; b. Nov. 23, 1946, Albany, GA; home, Chicago; Roosevelt U., B.A. 1973, U. of IL, M.A. 1994, McCormick Seminary, M.A. 1998; Baptist; married (Carolyn).

Military Career: Army, 1963–68.

Elected Office: Chicago City Alderman, 1983–92; 2nd Ward Committeeman, 1984–present.

Professional Career: Member, Student Non-Violent Coord. Cmte., 1966–68; Co-founder, IL Black Panther Party, 1968; Med. Clinic Dir., 1970–1973; insurance agent, 1978–83.

DC Office: 2416 RHOB 20515, 202-225-4372; Fax: 202-226-0333; Web site: www.house.gov/rush.

District Offices: Chicago, 773-224-6500; Evergreen Park, 708-422-4055.

Committees: *Energy & Commerce* (11th of 26 D): Commerce, Trade & Consumer Protection; Energy & Air Quality; Oversight & Investigations; Telecommunications & The Internet.

Group Ratings

	ADA	ACLU	AFS	LCV	CON	ITIC	NTU	COC	ACU	NTLC	CHC
2000	90	86	100	79	41	61	21	36	0	10	0
1999	100	—	100	69	47	—	23	23	0	—	—

National Journal Ratings

	1999 LIB —	1999 CONS	2000 LIB —	2000 CONS
Economic	88%	0%	95%	0%
Social	87%	0%	83%	17%
Foreign	95%	0%	97%	0%

Key Votes of the 106th Congress

1. Patient Bill of Rights	Y	5. Bar RU-486 $ for FDA	N	9. NATO War in Serbia	Y
2. Accelerate Min. Wage	Y	6. Display 10 Commandments	N	10. Perm. Trade with China	N
3. Strike Ban on Ergo. Stnd.	Y	7. Gun Show Bkgrnd. Checks	Y	11. Debt Relief for 3rd World	Y
4. Ovrd. Estate Tax Veto	N	8. Ban Part.-Birth Abortion	N	12. Drop Cuba Econ. Embargo	Y

Election Results

2000 general	Bobby Rush (D)	172,271	(88%)	($656,599)
	Raymond G. Wardingly (R)	23,915	(12%)	
2000 primary	Bobby Rush (D)	59,599	(61%)	
	Barack Obama (D)	29,649	(30%)	
	Donne E. Trotter (D)	6,915	(7%)	
	Other	1,501	(2%)	
1998 general	Bobby Rush (D)	151,890	(87%)	($243,587)
	Marlene White Ahimaz (R)	18,429	(11%)	
	Others	4,046	(2%)	

SECOND DISTRICT

Chicago is a great center of both commerce and industry, and if its white-collar offices are heavily concentrated in the Loop, its blue-collar heavy industries are most visible on the far South Side. This Chicago, diminished in importance economically today, is historically significant and, with the remnants of its great hulking factories around Lake Calumet and the nearby rail yards, has a certain undeniable majesty. Thomas Geoghegan, who writes more poetically than a lawyer ought to be able to, has told in his book, *Which Side Are You On?*, of the fights to wrest severance benefits and pension rights for the workers whose steel mills shut down, of the decline in the labor movement in a place where it got much of its inspiration. This is where the Pullman strike of 1894 was broken by federal troops and where policemen killed 10 union supporters in the Little Steel strike of 1937. Over the years, Chicago grew around the tight ethnic neighborhoods where workers went home at shift break each afternoon or midnight; today they are mostly empty buildings that suburbanites speed by on the Calumet and Dan Ryan Expressways.

The 2d Congressional District of Illinois includes much of Chicago's old South Side industrial area plus many suburbs to the south. About two-thirds of its people live in Chicago, in widely separated neighborhoods. Some are in the old factory towns around Lake Calumet, some in the once heavily Jewish South Shore neighborhood, some in black wards west of Halsted Street. The Chicago portion of the 2d is overwhelmingly black; many blacks, especially young parents fleeing Chicago public schools, are moving into suburbs directly to the south—Harvey, Dolton, Posen (a reminder of its Polish origin), Markham. Farther south are Homewood and Flossmoor, with significant Jewish populations, high-income Olympia Fields, the planned town of Park Forest, and Chicago Heights, home town of America's premier political reporter for four decades now, David Broder. Three-fourths of the district's voters are black—the most in the state—and most are middle class.

The congressman from the 2d District is Jesse Jackson Jr., a Democrat first elected in December 1995, and son of civil rights activist and 1984 and 1988 presidential candidate Jesse Jackson. Jesse Jackson Jr. was born in Greenville, South Carolina, while his father was marching to Selma; he went to the St. Albans School in Washington (as did former Vice President Al Gore and Congressman Harold Ford Jr.), then to North Carolina A&T (as did his father), and got a masters degree at Chicago Theological Seminary and a law degree at the University of Illinois. He worked for his father's Rainbow Coalition and did not run for office until the spectacular rise and fall of 2d District Congressman Mel Reynolds, who was hailed nationally when he defeated the anti-Semitic Gus Savage in the 1992 primary and then disgraced when he was convicted and sentenced to five years in prison for having sexual relations with a teenage campaign worker. When Reynolds announced he would resign Jackson promptly decided to run. He faced serious opposition in Emil Jones, a 23-year legislator and state Senate minority leader who had the support of Mayor Richard M. Daley. Jones boasted of his clout and political experience; Jackson said being his father's son was a lifetime of political experience. He talked of bringing dollars to the South Side and, echoing the argument Dan Rostenkowski made to Mayor Richard J. Daley in 1957, said, "The only way one grows into leadership in Congress is to get elected young enough that you become speaker of the House or chairman of the Ways and Means Committee." In a close primary, Jackson won with 46% to Jones' 37%; a state legislator endorsed by Louis Farrakhan and Gus Savage won only 2%. Jackson easily won the special general election with 76%.

In office, Jackson has combined liberal advocacy with careful attention to the interests of his district and a steady advancement of his own influence. He called for a law to create full employment through job training and a single-payer universal health care system—both would be nonstarters even in a Democratic Congress. He called for a federal moratorium on the death penalty. He opposed requiring eight hours per month community service by public housing tenants; "Will picking cotton qualify?" he caustically asked. He waged unexpectedly fierce opposition to the Crane-Rangel bill to relax trade restrictions on Africa, saying that he feared exploitation of African workers. With support from labor unions and other foes of free trade agreements, Jackson faulted the lack of labor and environmental protection and said that a better alternative was debt reduction, more U.S. aid to Africa, and preferential access for African goods to the American market. Charles Rangel, a long-time ally of the senior Jackson, was furious—calling the attack on his bill "unprofessional." The bill was enacted, but the dispute badly split the Congressional Black Caucus.

Jackson has worked on local projects, notably on flooding and the unpotable water supply in Ford Heights. His great cause is the building of a third Chicago area airport in Peotone, 45 miles south of the Loop and just south of the 2d District along Interstate 57. He sees it as an economic development project: "The point is, the third airport will provide 236,000 jobs . . . on the South Side and in the south suburbs. . . . It means a livable wage and union jobs. It means school funding." This fight has pitted him against fellow Democrats, including Congressman William Lipinski, the great protector of Midway Airport in his 3d District, and Daley, the great protector of O'Hare; his allies have included Republicans like former Governor Jim Edgar, who first suggested Peotone, Congressman Henry Hyde, who is worried about O'Hare noise over his suburban 6th District, and Governor George Ryan. In the 1998 gubernatorial race, Jackson refused to endorse Democrat Glenn Poshard, who opposed Peotone, and made friendly noises about Ryan. He was ambivalent about Al Gore—telling a forum during the 2000 Democratic Convention, "If there was another campaign that was speaking to our issues that had the possibility and plausibility of winning, we should support that campaign."

Jackson has been mentioned as a candidate for higher office—including mayor, the only office that matters for Chicago pols. But with a seat on the Appropriations Committee, he seems bent on remaining in the House. "His ultimate goal is to become the first black speaker of the House," reported the *Chicago Daily Herald*. Jackson has been careful not to exploit his huge name recognition or to be seen as exclusively the "black issues" congressman. In his first five years in the House he held only five press conferences, according to his press secretary. Still, his name and voice guarantee an audience. During the 2000 fall campaign he warned that narrow Democratic control of Congress would leave conservatives in charge. "Democrats shouldn't be talking about a few seats here, a few seats there," he told *The Nation*. "We should be talking about how do we get to a supermajority," to pass universal health care, plus quality education and housing benefits for everyone. That's not a conventional stand for a prospective party leader, but Jackson—like his father—does not play by the usual rules.

In the 1999 mayor's race, Jackson endorsed his House colleague Bobby Rush with considerable enthusiasm, but also made a point of saying nice things about Daley, who was re-elected easily in March: "As you know, this Mayor Daley has issued no 'shoot to kill' orders. This Mayor Daley has positioned African-Americans on the School Board, in the Police Department . . . and has done a fairly decent job of fighting to include more African-Americans at every level of his administration." Middle-class blacks, the heart of Jackson's constituency, are moving in large numbers from Chicago to the suburbs, which reduces his core constituency for some future race for mayor; redistricting after the 2000 Census may make this a more suburban district, like the black-majority Maryland 4th and Georgia 4th Districts. Jackson's advocacy of the Peotone airport suggests he has anticipated this and is set on representing a mostly suburban, mostly black district for some time.

Cook's Call   *Safe.* Like Bobby Rush's 1st District, Jesse Jackson Jr. enjoys a commandingly Democratic district. Redistricting may change the outlines here, as this South Side district needs to pick up about 90,000 people.

THE PEOPLE: Pop. 2000: 556,482; Pop. 1990: 572,188, down 2.7% 1990–2000. 18.1% White, 75.8% Black, 0.5% Asian, 0.2% Amer. Indian, 1.4% Two+ races, 4% Other; 7.8% Hispanic Origin.

2000 Presidential Vote			1996 Presidential Vote		
Gore (D)	188,289	(89%)	Clinton (D)	170,819	(85%)
Bush (R)	21,838	(10%)	Dole (R)	22,204	(11%)
Nader (Green)	1,626	(1%)	Perot (I)	6,395	(3%)

Rep. Jesse Jackson, Jr. (D)

Elected Dec. 1995, 3d term; b. Mar. 11, 1965, Greenville, SC; home, Chicago; NC A&T, B.S. 1987, Chicago Theological Seminary, M.A. 1990, U. of IL, J.D. 1993; Baptist; married (Sandra).

Professional Career: Civil rights activist; Pres., Keep Hope Alive PAC, 1989–90; V.P., Operation PUSH 1991–95; Field Dir., Natl. Rainbow Coalition 1993–95.

DC Office: 313 CHOB 20515, 202-225-0773; Fax: 202-225-0899; Web site: www.jessejacksonjr.org.

District Office: Homewood, 708-798-6000.

Committees: *Appropriations* (25th of 29 D): Foreign Operations & Export Financing; Labor, HHS & Education.

Group Ratings

	ADA	ACLU	AFS	LCV	CON	ITIC	NTU	COC	ACU	NTLC	CHC
2000	100	86	100	100	75	39	25	23	4	12	0
1999	100	—	100	100	96	—	31	8	8	—	—

National Journal Ratings

	1999 LIB —	1999 CONS		2000 LIB —	2000 CONS
Economic	88%	0%		95%	0%
Social	87%	0%		94%	0%
Foreign	61%	37%		92%	6%

Key Votes of the 106th Congress

1. Patient Bill of Rights	Y	5. Bar RU-486 $ for FDA	N	9. NATO War in Serbia	Y
2. Accelerate Min. Wage	Y	6. Display 10 Commandments	N	10. Perm. Trade with China	N
3. Strike Ban on Ergo. Stnd.	Y	7. Gun Show Bkgrnd. Checks	Y	11. Debt Relief for 3rd World	Y
4. Ovrd. Estate Tax Veto	N	8. Ban Part.-Birth Abortion	N	12. Drop Cuba Econ. Embargo	Y

Election Results

2000 general	Jesse Jackson Jr. (D)	175,995	(90%)	($304,619)
	Robert Gordon III (R)	19,906	(10%)	
2000 primary	Jesse Jackson Jr. (D)	unopposed		
1998 general	Jesse L. Jackson Jr. (D)	148,985	(89%)	($245,478)
	Robert Gordon III (R)	16,075	(10%)	
	Others	1,608	(1%)	

THIRD DISTRICT

A century ago, Finley Peter Dunne's fictional Mr. Dooley pontificated on matters political in a saloon on Archer Avenue. This was, and is, Archer Avenue on the South Side of Chicago, one of the radial streets that cuts across what was once open prairie near the Loop and out the Chicago River and the Chicago and Sanitary Ship Canal. Archer Avenue was one of the paths of outward migration and upward mobility for the children and grandchildren of Chicago's ethnic and cultural groups, and still is. Italians from the river wards along the Canal moved west; the South Side Irish moved west and south along Cicero Avenue toward Oak Lawn; the Bohemians (as they were called then, now Czechs) were heavily concentrated in the neat bungalows of the industrial suburbs of Berwyn and Cicero, famous as a haven for Al Capone's mobsters in the 1920s. Today, Latinos are driving these same avenues, up before dawn to arrive at large factories and small, or heading to the Loop on the CTA or to "edge city" jobs out the expressways or the Tollway, then home past storefronts with Spanish signs to carefully refurbished old bungalows.

The 3d Congressional District of Illinois consists of much of this territory, crisscrossed by the Canal, the radial streets and the railroad lines and switching yards so common in this, the center of the nation's rail network. It includes the far west edge of Chicago and most of Cicero and Berwyn; Riverside, with its early 20th Century prairie-style houses; a few older affluent suburbs like Western Springs and the more recent and middle-income expanses of Oak Lawn and Palos Heights. Politically, this is marginal territory. Ancestral political preferences are mostly Democratic, but this is a culturally conservative area, with a sense of patriotism. Cicero, hostile to blacks in the 1960s, has grown with an influx of Hispanics, who now make up about 77% of the town. But its tradition of extortion and corruption lives on: nearly a dozen former Cicero officials and employees have been indicted by federal grand juries in recent years and the Justice Department sent 25 federal observers to monitor a February 2001 primary for town board president.

The congressman from the 3d District, Democrat William Lipinski, grew up in southwest Chicago, started off as a patronage employee with the Parks District, was elected 23d Ward alderman and ward committeeman in 1975—he still holds the latter position in the ward that includes Midway Airport and Chicago's westernmost stretch of Archer Avenue. He ran for Congress and beat an aging incumbent in the 1982 primary 61%–36%. His credo: "I know the people of the 3d District—what they believe in, what they want for their future and their children's future. . . . I have never been so involved in what was happening in Washington that I lost sight of my constituents and their needs."

Lipinski is by far the most conservative Democrat in the Chicago delegation, but his views seem to mirror those of his constituents. He is anti-abortion, was strongly against gays in the military and for the Defense of Marriage Act. He favors the death penalty and opposed NAFTA, GATT and PNTR with China. He was one of the few Democrats to favor education vouchers for poor children in Washington, D.C., and tax-free education savings accounts. He was one of 30 Democrats to vote for the Republican welfare reform bill. He was proud of the passage of his amendment, co-sponsored by two Republicans, denying welfare benefits to fugitive criminals (previously, it barred benefits only to those in jail; those who escaped were entitled). He supported restrictions on welfare for legal immigrants, but also got an amendment to help 832 refugees who had left Poland and Hungary before fall 1989 gain permanent resident status.

Lipinski is on the Transportation and Infrastructure Committee and is the ranking Democrat on its Aviation Subcommittee. He is a staunch advocate of Midway Airport, which generates more jobs than any other site in the 3d District. He supported Mayor Richard M. Daley's $3 per passenger charge but insisted that the money be used to upgrade Midway and O'Hare, and not to start a third airport in Peotone, 45 miles south of Chicago—part of that money has been used for rehabilitating Midway and rebuilding its terminal. He is frequently at odds with Jesse Jackson Jr., a strong backer of Peotone, for that reason. On other aviation issues, he opposed the naming of Washington National Airport for Ronald Reagan (but said he'd vote to put him on Mount Rushmore), called for requiring FAA and Justice Department approval of airline alliances and congressional approval of international aviation agreements, and helped to lift flight caps at O'Hare by 2002. On local projects, Lipinski is proud of his work to complete the CTA's Orange Line and reconstruction of its Blue Line Douglas branch, to rebuild the Stevenson Expressway and Lower Wacker Drive. He has pushed a provision allowing local communities to regulate train whistles; it may not sound like much, but when your district has (probably) the largest number of freight yards and surface crossings in the nation and whistle-blowing is mandatory, you will hear about it.

Lipinski is often out of line with the Democratic Party and sometimes with Mayor Richard M. Daley, but is a close ally of Michael Madigan, who is speaker of the Illinois House, but, perhaps more important, 13th Ward committeeman, just south of the 23d. "Unless the ethnic position is listened to and we're not looked upon as outsiders," Lipinski once warned, "I think that there will be an even greater exodus from the Democratic Party among ethnic voters." In 1998 he supported the gubernatorial candidacy of Glenn Poshard, his Downstate conservative colleague, and helped him win the Democratic nomination. Lipinski took a stern attitude toward Bill Clinton. He was one of 31 Democrats to vote for the Republican impeachment inquiry; on the day before the vote, Lipinski said Clinton should resign but that he "unfortunately" would not vote for impeachment. He has become a close friend of Speaker Denny Hastert, whose district starts about 15 miles to the west and who helped Lipinski win $832 million for the CTA. And he was sufficiently nonpartisan to be mentioned as a possible Transportation secretary for President George W. Bush.

Lipinski has coped well with the major threat to his tenure: redistricting. When Cook County lost a district in the 1990 Census, he was placed in the same district with fellow Democratic incumbent Marty Russo. Russo, with a seat on Ways and Means, had much more money, but Lipinski had support from Mayor Daley and the *Chicago Tribune* called him "more important to the future of Illinois"; he won 58%–37%. Now, after the 2000 Census, Illinois has lost another seat, but Lipinski is well positioned with Illinois' two speakers. In late 2000 he started negotiating new lines with U.S. House Speaker Dennis Hastert, and his interests were kept in mind by Madigan, who worked on lines with Republican Governor George Ryan and Republican Senate President Pate Philip. In redistricting, Lipinski may lose some Hispanic precincts and gain the southwest townships in Cook County that are now in the 13th, and possibly some Will County townships.

Cook's Call   *Safe*. Lipinski's past wins belie the fact that the 3rd District is not reliably Democratic. Gore took just 55% here while he racked up margins in the 70s and 80s in the other Chicago-based districts. Lipinski, along with House Speaker Dennis Hastert, created the bipartisan congressional redistricting map, which protects most incumbents, that was passed by the state legislature.

THE PEOPLE: Pop. 2000: 629,597; Pop. 1990: 570,902, up 10.3% 1990–2000. 78.5% White, 4.5% Black, 1.7% Asian, 0.3% Amer. Indian, 2.9% Two+ races, 12.1% Other; 24.3% Hispanic Origin.

2000 Presidential Vote

Gore (D)	118,342	(55%)
Bush (R)	88,458	(41%)
Nader (Green)	5,537	(3%)
Others	1,271	(1%)

1996 Presidential Vote

Clinton (D)	114,089	(53%)
Dole (R)	78,853	(37%)
Perot (I)	19,441	(9%)

Rep. William Lipinski (D)

Elected 1982, 10th term; b. Dec. 22, 1937, Chicago; home, Chicago; Loras Col., 1956–57; Catholic; married (Rose Marie).

Military Career: Army Reserves, 1961–67.

Elected Office: Chicago City Alderman, 1975–83; Committeeman, 23d Ward, 1975–present.

Professional Career: Chicago Parks & Recreation Dept., 1958–75.

DC Office: 2470 RHOB 20515, 202-225-5701; Fax: 202-225-1012; Web site: www.house.gov/lipinski.

District Offices: Chicago, 312-886-0481; LaGrange, 708-352-0524; Oak Lawn, 708-952-0860.

Committees: *Transportation & Infrastructure* (4th of 34 D): Aviation (RMM); Highways & Transit; Railroads.

Group Ratings

	ADA	ACLU	AFS	LCV	CON	ITIC	NTU	COC	ACU	NTLC	CHC
2000	45	23	85	50	27	38	36	40	37	22	71
1999	55	—	66	75	37		26	28	45	—	—

National Journal Ratings

	1999 LIB	—	1999 CONS		2000 LIB	—	2000 CONS
Economic	54%	—	45%		60%	—	40%
Social	46%	—	53%		43%	—	57%
Foreign	52%	—	48%		55%	—	44%

Key Votes of the 106th Congress

1. Patient Bill of Rights	Y	5. Bar RU-486 $ for FDA	Y	9. NATO War in Serbia	*
2. Accelerate Min. Wage	Y	6. Display 10 Commandments	Y	10. Perm. Trade with China	N
3. Strike Ban on Ergo. Stnd.	Y	7. Gun Show Bkgrnd. Checks	Y	11. Debt Relief for 3rd World	Y
4. Ovrd. Estate Tax Veto	Y	8. Ban Part.-Birth Abortion	Y	12. Drop Cuba Econ. Embargo	N

Election Results

2000 general	William Lipinski (D)	145,498	(76%)	($387,674)
	Karl Groth (R)	47,005	(24%)	($18,073)
2000 primary	William Lipinski (D)	46,459	(90%)	
	R. Benedict Mayers (D)	5,009	(10%)	
1998 general	William Lipinski (D)	115,887	(72%)	($326,204)
	Robert Marshall (R)	44,012	(28%)	($100,518)

FOURTH DISTRICT

Just west of the Loop, the Chicago River splits into North and South branches, both penetrating the heart of old neighborhoods where immigrants fresh off the boat first got their start in Chicago. The South Branch is the guts of Chicago, the site of one of Western civilization's astonishing engineering feats: here in 1900 the course of the river was reversed so that sewage flowed Downstate through a canal rather than out into Lake Michigan. Just blocks away was Maxwell Street, then thronged with market stalls, long the arrival neighborhood for Chicago's Jews; not far away, in an Italian-American neighborhood on Halsted Street, was Jane Addams's Hull House, the original settlement house, where social workers told new immigrants not how to rebel against middle-class American mores but how to live up to them. To the south were Bridgeport, home of the Irish and of the mayors of Chicago from 1933–79 and again from 1989 until Richard M. Daley moved to the South Loop—and Pilsen, arrival neighborhood for the Bohemians (Czechs). Off the North Branch of the River was Milwaukee Avenue, the main street of Polish-Americans and Ukrainian-Americans for a century now.

Today, many of these places are arrival neighborhoods again, mostly for Chicago's wide variety of Hispanic immigrants. On the South Side, in the old river wards, is Chicago's Mexican-American community, extending west into the once Bohemian suburb of Cicero; on the North Side are many Puerto Ricans and other Hispanics. In the 1990s Chicago's Hispanic population increased from 545,000 to 754,000, by far the largest Latino concentration north of Texas and Florida and between the two coasts; that number also is approaching the total of 1.1 million blacks in Chicago. They have been attracted, as immigrants were 100 years ago, by a vibrant economy that provides opportunity to those who work hard.

The 4th Congressional District of Illinois is the Hispanic-majority district that was deemed mandatory under the Voting Rights Act amendments of 1982. The problem was that the South Side Mexican-American and the North Side Puerto Rican communities were separated by the West Side black ghetto. The solution was today's 4th, with arguably the most convoluted shape of any congressional district in the country. Essentially these two Latino communities, defined by erose boundaries to maximize the Hispanic percentage, are connected by a thin line of territory stretching around the West Side black-majority 7th District to meet at the Cook-DuPage County line. Most of this salient consists of parkland, railroad yards and cemeteries; more than 95% of the votes are in Chicago or Cicero. The Hispanic share of the district's population rose to 70% in 2000. Even so, because many have not become citizens and some who have do not vote, Latinos may be only a bare majority of the electorate. Not surprisingly, the lines were challenged in court. In 1996 the Supreme Court sent the case back to a three-judge federal district court, which then ruled the lines in order; in 1998 three Supreme Court justices, but not the required four, voted to hear the appeal.

The congressman from the 4th District since it was created has been Democrat Luis Gutierrez. He is of Puerto Rican descent, grew up in Chicago and returned for two years to Puerto Rico as a teacher after college. Back in Chicago he worked as a cab driver and social worker. In 1983 he ran for 32d Ward committeeman against Dan Rostenkowski (who with his father held the post for more than 50 years), and lost decisively. Then he became a staffer for Mayor Harold Washington, ran for alderman in 1984 and lost; two years later he ran again on the North Side in one of two new Hispanic-majority aldermanic seats. He and Juan Solis won—crucial victories that gave Washington a majority on the city Council for the first time. Then Washington died in 1987 and, in the 1989 election to succeed him, Gutierrez backed (and Solis opposed) Richard M. Daley. For that, Gutierrez was richly rewarded: He became chairman of the Housing Committee and pushed through his "New Homes for Chicago" affordable housing plan. He also authored a bill prohibiting discrimination against gays and the disabled. In both cases he helped Daley cement support with crucial groups in the middle 20% of the electorate: Latinos and gays.

Another "payback," as Gutierrez called it, came in the 1992 race for the new 4th Congressional District. Gutierrez and Solis were again rivals. Gutierrez called crime the number one problem and bragged of his council record; Solis talked about trade and health care and called Gutierrez a machine candidate. Certainly Gutierrez seemed a multi-ethnic candidate: "There is a Hispanic agenda . . . it's the same as the Polish, Irish and Lithuanian agenda. If you work hard, sweat and toil and play by the rules, you will be rewarded . . . with clean streets, safer and better schools, the opportunity to send your kids to college. Tell me who in America and in the 4th Congressional District doesn't want these things?" Gutierrez won 60%–40%. The 1994 primary was a rematch and Gutierrez won again, 64%–36%; he has not had serious competition since. Gutierrez has a high profile in the district, running recycling drives, a Gutierrez Community Corps to remove graffiti and citizenship enrollment meetings.

In the House, Gutierrez's in-your-face style has produced mixed results. His outspoken opposition to congressional pay raises and his appearance on a February 1994 *60 Minutes* broadcast, in which he called the House "the belly of the beast" and charged that the Democratic leadership stifled reform and that some freshmen Democrats "sold out," was not well received. "I've gotten my rear end kicked around here," Gutierrez told *The Washington Post*; a leadership staffer said Gutierrez "will never get a choice committee" and "will always end up on the Banking Committee." He's still there, though it's been renamed the Financial Services Committee. In a 1999 return visit to *60 Minutes*, he was not repentant but he did say, "I'm more careful" in speaking out. Gutierrez has staked out liberal positions and has been more a commentator than a legislative craftsman. He called for setting aside $1.5 billion for AIDS research; former North Shore Congressman John Porter, the generous appropriator for NIH, said no. Gutierrez called for raising mass transit aid from $4.8 billion to $7 billion while Bud Shuster and others crafted the transportation bill. In a deft maneuver, he criticized the Clinton administration's national education testing standards, while praising those set by Daley and Chicago public schools CEO Paul Vallas.

Gutierrez, as a leader of the Hispanic Caucus, has cheered on efforts to restore food stamp eligibility and other benefits to legal immigrants. He opposed the INS's increase from $95 to $200 or more the fee for processing applications as "a glaring example of the government imposing a higher price on its customers while continuing to offer inadequate and inefficient service." When Clinton in the 2000 lame-duck session agreed to Republican demands to drop clarifications of the status of immigrants facing the threat of deportation, Gutierrez accused the White House of "capitulating" to reach a budget deal. In the 107th Congress he introduced a sweeping immigration amnesty bill that would grant legal status by 2007 to illegal immigrants who entered the country by February 6, 2001. At the 2000 Democratic national convention he complained that "three white males" were delivering the Illinois votes.

In the debate on Don Young's bill authorizing a status referendum in Puerto Rico, Gutierrez took the lead for the opposition. He has long backed independence ("Puerto Rico is not just a territory, it is a nation"), a position favored in referenda by fewer than 3% of Puerto Ricans, and argued that Young's bill was tilted toward statehood. It passed 209–208 in March 1998, despite Gutierrez's attempt to switch votes at the last minute; but there was never any chance the Senate would take it up. To the Clinton White House's dismay, he has vehemently opposed the Navy's bombing on the island of Vieques off Puerto Rico's coast. Even with tentative agreement in 1999 to limit out the bombing to 90 days a year and phase out the practice by 2004, Gutierrez—with much of his family still in Puerto Rico—remained dissatisfied. He was arrested with others in May 2000 for protesting at a makeshift chapel on Vieques inside the bombing range and again a year later when the Navy resumed its exercises, after which he complained of "inhumane" treatment.

One preoccupation now must be redistricting. The courts may not approve a similar-shaped district after the 2000 Census and Gutierrez has already been thinking of alternatives. The geographical problem is that the 7th District is almost totally surrounded by the 4th, and it must gain population. One solution would be to make the two parts of the 4th connect through a single point. Territory from the 5th District, just to the north of the current 4th, could be added, but new groups beyond his Puerto Rican base could endanger Gutierrez. He could also be challenged in the 2002 primary—by Solis, who is still an alderman, or some other candidate supported by Mayor Richard M. Daley. The mayor was displeased when Gutierrez endorsed Bill Bradley over Al Gore.

Cook's Call   *Safe.* Since reconfigured to be a Hispanic seat in 1992, Gutierrez has easily won and held this seat. This seat is protected by the Voting Rights Act and is not likely to be altered significantly even though it needs to pick up about 25,000 new people. There are rumblings that Gutierrez may have a serious opponent in the Democratic primary, however.

THE PEOPLE: Pop. 2000: 625,941; Pop. 1990: 571,162, up 9.6% 1990–2000. 44.7% White, 8.1% Black, 2.6% Asian, 0.7% Amer. Indian, 0.1% Hawaiian, 4.2% Two+ races, 39.6% Other; 70.1% Hispanic Origin.

2000 Presidential Vote		
Gore (D)	93,735	(78%)
Bush (R)	21,276	(18%)
Nader (Green)	4,384	(4%)
Others	633	(1%)

1996 Presidential Vote		
Clinton (D)	82,225	(80%)
Dole (R)	14,661	(14%)
Perot (I)	5,160	(5%)

Rep. Luis Gutierrez (D)

Elected 1992, 5th term; b. Dec. 10, 1953, Chicago; home, Chicago; NE IL U., B.A. 1975; Catholic; married (Soraida).

Elected Office: Chicago City Alderman, 1986–92, Pres. Pro Tem, 1989–92.

Professional Career: Teacher, Puerto Rico, 1977–78; Social Wkr., Chicago Dept. of Children & Family Svcs., 1979–83; Advisor, Chicago Mayor Harold Washington, 1984–86.

DC Office: 2452 RHOB 20515, 202-225-8203; Fax: 202-225-7810; Web site: www.house.gov/gutierrez.

District Offices: Chicago, 773-579-0902; Chicago, 773-509-0999.

Committees: *Financial Services* (6th of 32 D): Financial Institutions & Consumer Credit; International Monetary Policy & Trade; Oversight & Investigations (Chmn.). *Veterans' Affairs* (3d of 14 D): Health (RMM).

Group Ratings

	ADA	ACLU	AFS	LCV	CON	ITIC	NTU	COC	ACU	NTLC	CHC
2000	90	79	100	93	71	50	26	38	9	15	0
1999	95	—	100	94	24	—	26	16	0	—	—

National Journal Ratings

	1999 LIB —	1999 CONS	2000 LIB —	2000 CONS
Economic	84%	12%	95%	0%
Social	83%	13%	88%	11%
Foreign	89%	8%	73%	26%

Key Votes of the 106th Congress

1. Patient Bill of Rights	Y	5. Bar RU-486 $ for FDA	N	9. NATO War in Serbia	Y
2. Accelerate Min. Wage	Y	6. Display 10 Commandments	N	10. Perm. Trade with China	N
3. Strike Ban on Ergo. Stnd.	Y	7. Gun Show Bkgrnd. Checks	Y	11. Debt Relief for 3rd World	Y
4. Ovrd. Estate Tax Veto	N	8. Ban Part.-Birth Abortion	N	12. Drop Cuba Econ. Embargo	N

Election Results

2000 general	Luis Gutierrez (D)	89,487	(89%)	($454,558)
	Stephanie Sailor (LIB)	11,476	(11%)	
2000 primary	Luis Gutierrez (D)	35,593	(82%)	
	Joseph L. Pagan (D)	7,663	(18%)	
1998 general	Luis Gutierrez (D)	54,244	(82%)	($349,887)
	John Birch (R)	10,529	(16%)	
	Others	1,583	(2%)	

FIFTH DISTRICT

No place in America today has more variety—ethnic and cultural—than the North Side of Chicago. From the air, the geometric grid streets lit by high-sodium lamps seem monotonous; on the ground, on a winter's day with snow swirling, its brick buildings look stolid and forbidding. This has been the homeland of one immigrant group after another and the chosen neighborhoods of all manner of successful middle-class people. Wooden workingman's cottages from the late 19th Century give way to sturdy huge brick houses of the early 1900s and then to the prairie bungalows of the 1920s and white-shuttered, orange-brick colonials of the 1950s. Chicago was America's number one immigrant destination for Poles, Lithuanians, Czechs, Slovaks, Ukrainians and Romanians; something about the heavy dull clouds of the long winters, the short hot summers, a climate suited to potatoes and cabbage and other hardy vegetables, may have reminded them of central and eastern Europe. By the late 1980s new upwardly mobile immigrants from Mexico and Guatemala, Korea and the Philippines, have moved in; the 1990s have seen immigrants from Poland and Ukraine, Pakistan and India. Family ties, webs of acquaintance that reach back to ancestral villages, have made the North Side of Chicago a natural port of entry for Eastern bloc migrants, even as newcomers establish new family ties and webs of relationships extending to Latin America and Southeast Asia.

The 5th Congressional District of Illinois covers an oddly shaped slice of Chicago's North Side, running from the lakefront to the suburbs directly south of O'Hare Airport. Its boundaries were carefully drawn to put most Hispanics in the 4th District just to the south, but otherwise it reflects the full variety of the North Side. It includes Chicago's most glamorous lakefront apartments facing the Oak Street beach and the gentrified neighborhoods of Old Town, where old houses and factories are being converted into upscale condominiums. It takes in the Polish-American and Ukrainian-American neighborhoods around Milwaukee Avenue, and the old Italian neighborhoods running west on Grand Avenue. It includes, a couple of blocks from the Chicago River, the grand old church of St. Stanislaus Kostka—a traditional center of the Polish community since the 19th Century but now with Masses in Spanish—and the residence across Pulaski Park of Dan Rostenkowski, chairman of the House Ways and Means Committee from 1981 to 1994, for whom the district was originally designed.

The congressman from the 5th District is Rod Blagojevich, a Democrat elected in 1996 over incumbent Republican Michael Flanagan, who upset Rostenkowski in 1994 following his indictment for mismanaging his official finances. Blagojevich is of Serbian descent; he was a Golden Gloves boxer who graduated from Northwestern and Pepperdine Law School. He practiced law and worked two years in state's Attorney Richard M. Daley's office in the 1980s. In 1992 he was elected state representative. Politics in Chicago is often a matter of genealogy, and it did not hurt that Blagojevich is the son-in-law of 33d Ward Alderman Dick Mell, long one of the major powers in Chicago politics.

Blagojevich was surely as surprised as anyone when Flanagan beat Rostenkowski 54%–46% and he immediately began eyeing this Democratic seat. Although he voted against Speaker Newt Gingrich's budget, Flanagan's record was mostly conservative and he seemed to have few political skills and little party backing. Not surprisingly, Blagojevich had primary opposition, chiefly from state Representative Nancy Kaszak. Blagojevich had Mell's ward organization and the backing of Mayor Daley; Kaszak had fundraising help from EMILY's List and roughly matched his money. Blagojevich won 50%–38%. In the general, Blagojevich focused on guns and tobacco, saying that Flanagan might as well be a lobbyist for the National Rifle Association and the American Tobacco Institute. It was no contest: Bill Clinton had run far ahead in this district; Blagojevich outspent Flanagan and won 64%–36%.

In the House, Blagojevich has pushed for gun control legislation. He sponsored bills to require child-proof locks on handguns, to abolish the Civilian Marksmanship program and to ban police departments from commercially trading officers' old guns for discounts on new ones. He wants to outlaw semi-automatic and easily concealable handguns, known as "pocket rockets," said to be popular with Chicago criminals. He was a leading supporter of background checks to close the gun-show loophole, but none of this passed the Republican Congress.

Blagojevich also opposed fast track, PNTR with China and the B-2 stealth bomber. He remains a fine athlete, recruited for the Democratic team in the congressional baseball game. He continued to run marathons, even training during a congressional visit to 8,500-foot-high, heavily polluted, terrorist-threatened Bogota; a Coast Guard lieutenant detailed to accompany him on his run couldn't keep up. Blagojevich said he is frustrated by having low seniority, but understands where he is in the Chicago political firmament: "I'm just a congressman. In Chicago, I'm not even [as high up] as an alderman yet." But he raised his political rank and profile in May 1999, when he traveled to Serbia with Jesse Jackson to successfully secure the release of three American POWs after he tired of the White House's non-response to his offers of help. Blagojevich, who used his Serbian-American contacts to set up the historic meeting with president Slobodan Milosevic, is fluent in Serbian and served as chief negotiator. Clinton administration officials remained cool even as Blagojevich urged Clinton to get more involved in the Kosovo conflict.

Facing serious problems in redistricting, Blagojevich in 2000 began talking about running for governor. His candidacy is no sure thing and he would surely have competition in the Democratic primary. Republican Governor George Ryan, with low approval ratings, may not run for a second term, and other possible Republican nominees, notably Attorney General Jim Ryan, might be strong in the general election.

Cook's Call   *Probably Safe*. With the state slated to lose one seat in redistricting, all eyes were on Cook County. Blagojevich's public flirting with running for governor certainly would make it easier for mapmakers to eliminate this seat. But the final bipartisan congressional map has the state losing a seat Downstate, leaving the Chicago districts, including this one, intact.

THE PEOPLE: Pop. 2000: 635,824; Pop. 1990: 571,053, up 11.3% 1990–2000. 76.8% White, 2% Black, 6.1% Asian, 0.3% Amer. Indian, 0.1% Hawaiian, 3.6% Two+ races, 11.1% Other; 25% Hispanic Origin.

2000 Presidential Vote

Gore (D)	130,064	(63%)
Bush (R)	68,942	(33%)
Nader (Green)	6,630	(3%)
Others	1,147	(1%)

1996 Presidential Vote

Clinton (D)	120,132	(63%)
Dole (R)	56,532	(30%)
Perot (I)	12,915	(7%)

Rep. Rod R. Blagojevich (D)

Elected 1996, 3d term; b. Dec. 10, 1956, Chicago; home, Chicago; Northwestern U., B.A. 1979, Pepperdine U., J.D. 1983; Eastern Orthodox; married (Patti).

Elected Office: IL House of Reps., 1992–96.

Professional Career: Practicing atty., 1984–96; Asst. Cook County Atty., 1986–88.

DC Office: 331 CHOB 20515, 202-225-4061; Fax: 202-225-5603; Web site: www.house.gov/blagojevich.

District Offices: Chicago, 773-868-3240; Elmwood Park, 708-583-1948.

Committees: *Armed Services* (9th of 28 D): Military Procurement; Military Research & Development. *Government Reform* (11th of 19 D): Criminal Justice, Drug Policy & Human Resources; Energy Policy, Natural Resources and Regulatory Affairs.

Group Ratings

	ADA	ACLU	AFS	LCV	CON	ITIC	NTU	COC	ACU	NTLC	CHC
2000	80	71	85	93	3	56	30	52	25	21	7
1999	100	—	100	94	26	—	17	30	8	—	—

National Journal Ratings

	1999 LIB	—	1999 CONS		2000 LIB	—	2000 CONS
Economic	77%	—	22%		63%	—	37%
Social	74%	—	25%		71%	—	28%
Foreign	61%	—	39%		66%	—	33%

Key Votes of the 106th Congress

1. Patient Bill of Rights	Y	5. Bar RU-486 $ for FDA	N	9. NATO War in Serbia	N
2. Accelerate Min. Wage	Y	6. Display 10 Commandments	Y	10. Perm. Trade with China	N
3. Strike Ban on Ergo. Stnd.	Y	7. Gun Show Bkgrnd. Checks	Y	11. Debt Relief for 3rd World	Y
4. Ovrd. Estate Tax Veto	Y	8. Ban Part.-Birth Abortion	N	12. Drop Cuba Econ. Embargo	N

Election Results

2000 general	Rod R. Blagojevich (D)	142,161	(87%)	($277,035)
	Matt Beauchamp (LIB)	20,728	(13%)	($28,231)
2000 primary	Rod R. Blagojevich (D)	unopposed		
1998 general	Rod R. Blagojevich (D)	95,738	(74%)	($384,964)
	Alan Spitz (R)	33,687	(26%)	($20,509)

SIXTH DISTRICT

In World War II, what is now the nation's second-busiest airport was an apple orchard on which a defense plant was built (hence its current three-letter code: ORD); to the east was the Forest

Preserve along the Des Plaines River, to the west little suburban villages strung along rail lines, separated by cornfields. But in the 1940s, Chicago politicians, in search of a new airport site, annexed the orchard and named it after a World War II airman awarded the Medal of Honor, who got a military appointment from the feds after his father gave state's evidence against Al Capone and was gunned down. Mayor Richard J. Daley opened O'Hare in 1955 and promoted its development, convinced that a great airport could maintain in the 20th Century the economic strength Chicago gained from railroad stations and rail yards in the 19th Century—as it has. Today, O'Hare is surrounded on all sides by suburbs as densely settled as the bungalow wards of the city, with hotels and office buildings clustered near the interchanges in Rosemont, and characteristic Chicago yellow-orange brick houses in orderly rows in suburbs like Park Ridge, where Hillary Rodham Clinton grew up at 235 Wisner. Politically, these suburbs have long been solidly Republican, as were the Rodhams, convinced that civic virtues could best be realized by opposing the party of City Hall in Chicago and that economic growth could best be assured by opposing the party that backed stifling government regulation.

The 6th Congressional District of Illinois includes much of this suburban area. It includes Park Ridge and Des Plaines just north of O'Hare, and to the west the newer suburb of Elk Grove Village, headquarters of United Airlines. The larger part of the district is over the line in DuPage County, including the string of long-settled suburbs directly west of the Loop: Elmhurst, Villa Park, Lombard, Glen Ellyn, Wheaton. It also takes in the newer suburbs along I-290 and Lake Street: Bensenville, Addison, Wood Dale, Bloomingdale. Economically, this is high-income territory; culturally, it is cautiously moderate; politically, it is one of the most Republican districts in Illinois.

The congressman from the 6th is Henry Hyde, former chairman of the House Judiciary Committee, chief manager of the impeachment of Bill Clinton and one of the most respected and intellectually honest members of the House. Hyde springs from Chicago earth, was raised a Catholic and a Democrat; he was an all-city basketball center and played against basketball great George Mikan; he went off to college at Georgetown and enlisted in the Navy and served at Lingayen Gulf. After the war he finished college and law school, practiced law in Chicago, and in 1958 switched parties, convinced that Republicans were more in line with his anti-Communist beliefs. He ran for the House in 1962 in northwest Chicago and lost 53%–47% to incumbent Roman Pucinski. He was elected to the Illinois House in 1966 and in the Democratic year of 1974 was elected, as one of only 144 Republicans, to the U.S. House.

There he first made his name as an opponent of abortion, attaching to Appropriations subcommittee bills his Hyde amendments prohibiting the use of federal funds to pay for abortions in various circumstances. He had been appalled by abortion since a colleague in Springfield asked him to support a liberalized abortion law in 1968. "I look for the common thread in slavery, the Holocaust and abortion," he said in 1998. "To me, the common thread is dehumanizing people." In 1976 he was asked by conservative Robert Bauman to sponsor an amendment to an appropriation bill cutting spending on abortion; that year the first Hyde amendment was passed, banning Medicaid abortions. It has remained in force ever since, though states can spend their own money on abortions, and some do; exceptions for saving the life of the mother, and victims of rape and incest were added in 1993. Hyde is concerned about born as well as unborn children. He was one of the few Republicans who supported the family leave bill, and has sponsored bills to expand the number of women eligible for pregnancy benefits under the children's health insurance program. Hyde also joined the bipartisan effort on the 1996 welfare bill to add tough measures against "deadbeat dads" who fail to support their family. He opposes assisted suicide as part of a "culture of death" and sponsored the bill passed by the House in October 1999 (but not by the Senate) to criminalize the prescription of lethal drugs to terminally ill patients contemplating ending their lives—an attempt to nullify Oregon's assisted suicide law.

On many occasions, including several times during the impeachment process, Hyde has proven himself one of the most eloquent members of the House. His speeches against term limits and in favor of the flag-burning amendment are classics; his evisceration of the nuclear freeze resolution helped turn the tide on foreign policy in the House in the 1980s. He defended the Reagan administration on Iran-Contra and in the process said, somewhat to his embarrassment in the impeachment debate, that to condemn all lying "seems to me too simplistic. In the murkier grayness of the real world, choices must often be made." He irked many junior Republicans by opposing term limits, and he supported reauthorization of the independent counsel bill in 1994 when it was passed by the Democratic Congress and signed, presumably to his later regret, by Bill Clinton. He voted for the Brady bill waiting period for gun purchases and sponsored a compromise proposal with a 24-hour background check for gun sales at gun shows after the Columbine murders of May 1999. Three major Hyde measures passed both houses but were vetoed by Clinton: the partial-birth abortion ban, product liability and tort reform.

None of these challenges he had faced before was as great or as public as the challenge of impeachment. From the first Hyde had little taste for the subject, yet realized he had the responsibility to handle it. Early on he said that any impeachment resolution must be bipartisan if it were to be credible, but it became clear by September that almost every Democrat was determined to defend Bill Clinton at every turn. He noted that "bipartisanship is defined by Democrats as Republican surrender." Hyde assembled a staff headed by David Schippers, a longtime Chicago lawyer and a Democrat, and modeled his procedures on those used by Chairman Peter Rodino in the impeachment of Richard Nixon 24 years before. Democrats resisted his resolution for an impeachment inquiry but felt obliged to advance one of their own, with time limits and with Zoe Lofgren's requirement that members vote first on the definition of an impeachable offense. All Republicans and 31 Democrats voted for the Republican resolution.

The hearings were fractious, and Clinton backers tried to put Hyde on the defensive. In September, cyber-magazine *Salon*, often a White House mouthpiece, reported that Hyde had had an affair 30 years before; "youthful indiscretions," Hyde said in response. As the facts of Clinton's conduct became known, Hyde obviously decided that the president had lied under oath in a United States District Court proceeding, and that that could not be forgiven. He ran the hearings with scrupulous fairness, despite the diatribes of some Democrats, and even with occasional humor. In his summation to the House he was genuinely eloquent, and impeachment was voted on two of four counts.

Then came the historic march of Hyde and the 12 other House managers to the Senate presided over by Chief Justice William Rehnquist. The managers were pitted against Clinton's professional litigators, and the discomfort of almost all senators was obvious. (In 1996, Hyde rebuffed requests that he run for the Senate, adding "I'd be a great senator—God, I'd be so arrogant.") Remembering his own experience in combat, he summoned up memories of Americans who had fallen in battle and urged the senators to uphold the rule of law. But Democrats did not waver, and the articles of impeachment were rejected, the first by 55–45, the second by 50–50.

In 1999 and 2000 Hyde continued to work on other issues. Much of his district lies under O'Hare flight paths, and he has been a champion of building a third Chicago-area airport in Peotone in Will County; in this his chief ally has been the 2d District's Jesse Jackson Jr. In June 2000 he held hearings on the proposed United-USAirways merger and criticized the airlines for suppressing competition. He supported bankruptcy reform, passed by the House in May 1999 and in December 2000 by the Senate, but sought unsuccessfully to give judges discretion to determine reasonable living allowances for debtors. In October 2000 he opposed the Intelligence Committee bill that would criminalize disclosure of all classified government papers marked secret, and with ranking Democrat John Conyers argued that the subject required hearings in Judiciary—it was eventually vetoed by Bill Clinton. That same month he sought to cut taxes on Nobel Prizes and forced the House to include uranium miners in the bill to compensate workers at uranium enrichment plants.

After the impeachment trial, Hyde considered not running for re-election in 2000, but decided to do so after hearing Democrats' threats to target the House impeachment managers. In 1998, before the impeachment vote, he was re-elected 67%–30%. In 2000, against a more moderate Democrat, he won 59%–41%; evidently he paid some political price for his stand. After the election he tried to get the House Republican leadership to waive the six-year term limited on chairmanships, arguing that he had lost one year of chairing Judiciary to impeachment. But they declined, and instead gave Hyde the chairmanship of the International Relations Committee.

Redistricting may change the boundaries of the 6th District somewhat, but it is likely that there will continue to be a district anchored in northern DuPage County, where Hyde—if he wants to run again—can be re-elected.

Cook's Call   *Safe.* This suburban Chicago district has been steadily trending away from the Republican stronghold it once was. In 1992, Bush won the district by 14%, but in 2000 George W. Bush won here by just 7%. Hyde's 59% showing in 2000 was his lowest winning margin since being elected here in 1974. Still, he continues to have a good hold on this district, but when he retires, this seat could be in play.

THE PEOPLE: Pop. 2000: 615,419; Pop. 1990: 572,268, up 7.5% 1990–2000. 83.8% White, 2.4% Black, 7.7% Asian, 0.2% Amer. Indian, 1.9% Two+ races, 4% Other; 10.9% Hispanic Origin.

2000 Presidential Vote

Bush (R)	121,014	(52%)
Gore (D)	104,192	(45%)
Nader (Green)	5,822	(3%)
Others	1,355	(1%)

1996 Presidential Vote

Dole (R)	105,797	(48%)
Clinton (D)	93,358	(42%)
Perot (I)	18,796	(9%)

Rep. Henry J. Hyde (R)

Elected 1974, 14th term; b. Apr. 18, 1924, Chicago; home, Wood Dale; Georgetown U., B.S. 1947, Loyola U., J.D. 1949; Catholic; widowed.

Military Career: Navy, 1944–46 (WWII); Naval Reserves, 1946–68.

Elected Office: IL House of Reps., 1966–74, Majority Ldr., 1971–72.

Professional Career: Practicing atty., 1950–75.

DC Office: 2110 RHOB 20515, 202-225-4561; Fax: 202-225-1166; Web site: www.house.gov/hyde.

District Office: Addison, 630-832-5950.

Committees: *International Relations* (Chmn. of 26 R). *Judiciary* (2d of 21 R): Courts, the Internet & Intellectual Property.

Group Ratings

	ADA	ACLU	AFS	LCV	CON	ITIC	NTU	COC	ACU	NTLC	CHC
2000	10	21	14	14	30	85	53	71	76	58	93
1999	15	—	0	0	60	—	55	75	72	—	—

National Journal Ratings

	1999 LIB	—	1999 CONS		2000 LIB	—	2000 CONS
Economic	44%	—	55%		42%	—	58%
Social	32%	—	66%		39%	—	60%
Foreign	47%	—	52%		12%	—	78%

Key Votes of the 106th Congress

1. Patient Bill of Rights	Y	5. Bar RU-486 $ for FDA	Y	9. NATO War in Serbia	Y
2. Accelerate Min. Wage	Y	6. Display 10 Commandments	Y	10. Perm. Trade with China	Y
3. Strike Ban on Ergo. Stnd.	N	7. Gun Show Bkgrnd. Checks	N	11. Debt Relief for 3rd World	N
4. Ovrd. Estate Tax Veto	Y	8. Ban Part.-Birth Abortion	Y	12. Drop Cuba Econ. Embargo	N

Election Results

2000 general	Henry J. Hyde (R)	133,327	(59%)	($2,436,839)
	Brent Christensen (D)	92,880	(41%)	($234,608)
2000 primary	Henry J. Hyde (R)	unopposed		
1998 general	Henry J. Hyde (R)	111,603	(67%)	($514,349)
	Thomas A. Cramer (D)	49,906	(30%)	
	Others	4,199	(3%)	

SEVENTH DISTRICT

The cross-country flyer on a lucky day can get a clear view of the biggest man-made cityscape between the Atlantic and Pacific Oceans: Chicago's Loop. High-rise buildings were pioneered a century ago in the Loop—named in 1897 for the circle the elevated train forms around the city's center—by architects like Louis Sullivan and Daniel Burnham. International School modernists built their most impressive collection of buildings here and along Lake Shore Drive in the years after World War II; in the last dozen years, postmodernists have decorated the Chicago River and reinvented the skyscraper. The Loop now spreads beyond the El, up the wondrous shopping street of North Michigan Avenue with a peak at the John Hancock Tower, and west beyond the commodities exchanges to the Sears Tower on the Chicago River. This is the face Chicago likes to present to the world: giant structures rising where the prairies meet the inland sea, a vast concentration of brains and muscle, the nerve center of the markets of the nation and the world.

Behind the lakefront, where the air traveler sees the grid spread out below with occasional radials, is the muscle and sinew, gristle and fat of the city. It also has parts that do not work so well: houses and apartment buildings are abandoned; commercial space stands empty and vandalized; giant, crime-racked housing projects, like the Robert Taylor Homes off the Dan Ryan Expressway, built by one Mayor Richard Daley in the 1960s (he preferred low-rise projects, but the feds wouldn't finance them) and now being torn down by another. The West Side of Chicago, the vast acres directly west of the Loop, for years was a dreadful slum, with some areas almost emptied out; the decay spread west to the Austin neighborhood, just before the border of upper-income—and for decades racially integrated—Oak Park. In the 1990s there was some revival. The United Center, the erstwhile home court of Michael Jordan and site of the 1996 Democratic National Convention, sparked commercial development of the West Side, and lower crime rates have raised the value of land once again.

The 7th Congressional District of Illinois contains the Loop and most of the North Michigan corridor and the Near North Side, where the infamous Cabrini-Green housing project is being replaced by new, mixed-market housing. It also goes south, past 19th Century Prairie Avenue mansions to take in a few heavily black South Side neighborhoods. Its heart, demographically and spiritually, is the black ghetto of the West Side, more depopulated and socially disorganized than the South Side. To the west are Oak Park, the boyhood home of Ernest Hemingway and location of the Frank Lloyd Wright home and museum and many of his prairie-style houses; River Forest; and the much more modest Maywood, which is black-majority; and Broadview and Hillside, site of a one-lane bottleneck on the Chicago freeway system known as the Hillside Strangler. A bit less than two-thirds of the people here are black; there remain few Hispanics since they were confined by careful drawing to the 4th District, which practically encircles the 7th on three sides.

The congressman from the 7th District is Danny Davis, a Democrat first elected in 1996 after two unsuccessful tries in the 1980s. Davis grew up on a cotton farm in Arkansas, graduated from college there, then moved to Chicago and worked as a teacher, assistant principal and guidance counselor in Chicago public schools. For 10 years he ran a community health project on the West Side. He was elected alderman in the 29th Ward on the boundary of Oak Park in 1979 and supported Mayor Harold Washington in the council wars of the 1980s, but lost his 29th Ward committeeman post to a Daley-backed challenger in March 2000. In 1990 he was elected a Cook County commissioner; in 1991 he made a quixotic run against Mayor Richard M. Daley.

In 1996, when Cardiss Collins retired after nearly 24 years in the House, Davis decided to run. His major opponents were 3d Ward Alderman Dorothy Tillman, an ally of Mayor Daley, and 37th Ward Alderman Ed Smith. The fiery Tillman told one crowd she had a "contract" on Newt Gingrich; Smith was for welfare reform and had once called for martial law on the West Side. Davis campaigned as a big-government liberal, calling for a $7.60 minimum wage, affirmative action, and a national health care plan; he said his goal was "the development of an urban strategy, and urban agenda, that reclaims the inner cities of America." Davis won with 33%, followed by Tillman with 20% and Smith with 12%. He won the general with ease and has not faced a serious challenge.

In the House, Davis has a very liberal voting record. He was one of three Illinois Democrats to vote against the 1997 tax cuts: "We cannot have a great, civilized and humane nation without paying the cost; if all we can do is cut, cut, cut, all that we will get is blood, blood, blood." He said that many of his friends found Ralph Nader's presidential candidacy "intriguing" but that the "practical" ones voted for Gore. He opposed the sugar program as corporate welfare and called charter schools a "sinister move to dismantle public education." He protested the low percentage of minority law clerks on the Supreme Court, a protest brusquely rejected by Chief Justice William Rehnquist. Still, Davis has worked with Republicans, co-sponsoring with Jim Talent and J. C. Watts the American Community Renewal Act, to provide tax cuts and credits for businesses locating in troubled central city neighborhoods. Aspects of that proposal were embraced by Bill Clinton and Speaker Dennis Hastert as the "new markets" tax incentive and enacted into law.

Davis speaks in impressive sepulchral tone, and his self-evident sincerity and concern for the poor has helped him achieve additional success in a mostly conservative House. In 1998 he was the only member to get Transportation Chairman Bud Shuster not to oppose an amendment to the big transportation bill: an increase from $42 million to $150 million in a pilot program to provide transportation for low-income central city residents to get to work sites in the suburbs; this was supported by UPS and United Airlines. The bill also contained $250 million for the reconstruction of Wacker Drive.

Davis's hold on the district seems secure, but redistricting could pose problems. The 7th needs to gain population but is nearly encircled by the 4th District. While there will surely be another black-majority district based in the West Side, its boundaries could include black politicians eager for Davis's seat.

Cook's Call   *Safe.* This Chicago district is currently ranked as one of the 15 most Democratic in the country. Redistricting could have an impact here, but Davis should have no problem holding onto this majority black district in 2002.

THE PEOPLE: Pop. 2000: 569,470; Pop. 1990: 572,039, down 0.4% 1990–2000. 28% White, 63.3% Black, 4.8% Asian, 0.2% Amer. Indian, 0.1% Hawaiian, 1.5% Two+ races, 2.2% Other; 5.2% Hispanic Origin.

2000 Presidential Vote

Gore (D)	176,635	(83%)
Bush (R)	31,150	(15%)
Nader (Green)	3,499	(2%)

1996 Presidential Vote

Clinton (D)	152,606	(82%)
Dole (R)	25,757	(14%)
Perot (I)	5,037	(3%)

Rep. Danny K. Davis (D)

Elected 1996, 3d term; b. Sept. 6, 1941, Parkdale, AR; home, Chicago; AR AM&N Col., B.A. 1961, Chicago St. U., M.S. 1968, Union Inst., Ph.D. 1977; Baptist; married (Vera).

Elected Office: Chicago City Alderman, 1979–90; Cook Cnty. Commissioner, 1990–96.

Professional Career: Teacher, Chicago Public Schls., 1962–69; Health Care Planner, 1969–79.

DC Office: 1222 LHOB 20515, 202-225-5006; Fax: 202-225-5641; Web site: www.house.gov/davis.

District Office: Chicago, 773-533-7520.

Committees: *Government Reform* (12th of 19 D): Census; Civil Service & Agency Organization (RMM); Criminal Justice, Drug Policy & Human Resources. *Small Business* (3d of 17 D): Tax, Finance & Exports; Workforce, Empowerment & Government Programs.

Group Ratings

	ADA	ACLU	AFS	LCV	CON	ITIC	NTU	COC	ACU	NTLC	CHC
2000	100	83	100	93	77	39	27	33	4	9	0
1999	100	—	100	100	56	—	27	17	0	—	—

National Journal Ratings

	1999 LIB	—	1999 CONS		2000 LIB	—	2000 CONS
Economic	88%	—	0%		95%	—	0%
Social	87%	—	0%		94%	—	0%
Foreign	93%	—	5%		96%	—	3%

Key Votes of the 106th Congress

1. Patient Bill of Rights	Y	5. Bar RU-486 $ for FDA	N	9. NATO War in Serbia	Y
2. Accelerate Min. Wage	Y	6. Display 10 Commandments	N	10. Perm. Trade with China	N
3. Strike Ban on Ergo. Stnd.	Y	7. Gun Show Bkgrnd. Checks	Y	11. Debt Relief for 3rd World	Y
4. Ovrd. Estate Tax Veto	N	8. Ban Part.-Birth Abortion	N	12. Drop Cuba Econ. Embargo	Y

Election Results

2000 general	Danny K. Davis (D)	164,155	(86%)	($196,566)
	Robert Dallas (R)	26,872	(14%)	
2000 primary	Danny K. Davis (D)	unopposed		
1998 general	Danny K. Davis (D)	130,984	(93%)	($160,147)
	Dorn E. Van Cleave III (Lib)	9,984	(7%)	

EIGHTH DISTRICT

Schaumburg may not be nationally known, but it is one of America's major corporate headquarters cities and one of several edge cities northwest of Chicago. Sixty years ago this was farmland, half a dozen miles beyond the orchard that is now O'Hare Airport. Today, Schaumburg—near the intersection of the Northwest Tollway and I-290, with lots of office space and Woodfield Mall and miles of subdivisions, with moderately priced apartments and with some black residents—is the site of the headquarters of Motorola and Zurich American Life Insurance; nearby are the head-quarters of Sears and Kemper Insurance. Yet Schaumburg yearns for traditions. It has built a performing arts center, formed an orchestra for young people, and has built from scratch a tra-ditional downtown.

The 8th Congressional District of Illinois is made up of Schaumburg and dozens of similar communities, on the prairies and hilly lakelands northwest of Chicago. Near Schaumburg are Streamwood, Hoffman Estates, Arlington Heights, Rolling Meadows, Palatine: Over half the dis-trict's population is in the far northwest extremity of Cook County. The 8th also includes the filling-up western half of Lake County, with little lake communities being surrounded by new suburbs. The tone of life here is not elite, but it is highly affluent; culturally, this is part of the great rural Midwest as much as—perhaps more than—it is of yeasty, lusty Chicago. Economically, it is suspicious of government spending, which it associates with the corrupt big city of yore. By most measures this is the most Republican district in Illinois and one of the most Republican in the nation.

The congressman from the 8th District is Philip Crane, now the most senior Republican in the House. Crane grew up in Indiana, one of several sons of a doctor who had his own radio program; he went to Hillsdale College, got a Ph.D. at Indiana University, and was a conservative intellectual when that seemed an oxymoron. He moved to the Chicago area in 1967 and, at 39, won a November 1969 special election to the House, replacing Donald Rumsfeld, who was then Richard Nixon's poverty program director, and was later Defense secretary for both Gerald Ford and George W. Bush. Crane supported a set of ideas which then seemed backward-looking but which have been on the ascendant in the nation and the world since: free market economics, a strong national defense, traditional values.

In his first years in the House Crane sat largely unnoticed on the back benches and had meager influence. In 1980 he ran for president, hoping, as the truer libertarian, to cut in on the elderly Ronald Reagan's support and then take it over when the Reagan candidacy faded. But his strategy totally failed and through the 1980s he seemed embittered and unfocused; he was never a part of the young conservative movement led by Jack Kemp, Newt Gingrich and Trent Lott. By the early 1990s Crane was in trouble back home. In the anti-incumbent year of 1992, in a redis-tricted seat with unfamiliar territory, he beat Gary Skoien, a former aide to Governor James Thompson, by only 55%–45% in the Republican primary and won the general by only 56%–40%.

In the 1994 primary he faced Skoien and then-state Senator Peter Fitzgerald, who spent $700,000 of his own money; Crane won with 40% of the vote to Fitzgerald's 33% and Skoien's 21%.

After those close scrapes Crane suddenly found himself part of a Republican majority. He was not a committee chairman—Bill Archer had seniority over him on Ways and Means—but he did become chairman of its Trade subcommittee. Crane is as much of a pure free trader as anyone who has ever served in Congress: He supported NAFTA, GATT, fast track, and often chided the Clinton administration for not lobbying for bipartisan support of free trade measures it nominally supported. He got assurances from top Clinton aides that the administration would not support labor and environmental clauses sought by anti-free trade demonstrators in Seattle; then, as he led the congressional delegation there, he saw Bill Clinton do just that. Crane shepherded through Most Favored Nation status for Bulgaria, Romania and Cambodia. Then in 1999 and 2000 he had quite spectacular success. He worked hard to pass the Africa trade bill originated in the Black Caucus and co-sponsored by Ways and Means ranking Democrat Charles Rangel. This was a thankless task: There is not much constituency for it in the 8th District or in Republican circles, and it was fiercely opposed by textile interests, unions, Jesse Jackson Jr. and several other Black Caucus members. But Crane and Rangel managed to strike a House-Senate deal in May 2000 and it became law. That agreement also lowered trade barriers with nations in the Caribbean Basin. Starting in early 1999 he pushed for action on permanent normal trade relations with China. The House passed PNTR in May 2000 and the Senate did likewise in September.

At the same time, Crane was campaigning for the Ways and Means chairmanship; Republican rules limit chairmen to six-year terms and Bill Archer had announced long ago that he would retire in 2000. But Newt Gingrich had established in November 1994 the precedent that Republicans would not always honor seniority, and Crane had serious competition from the next most senior member, Bill Thomas. While Crane had long been a supporter of the flat tax, he had played little part in tax legislation; in the July 1999 sessions considering the tax cut, Archer and Thomas had taken lead roles while Crane was mostly silent. Nor was he a factor on health care issues, on which Thomas as chairman of the Health Subcommittee took the lead. In the 105th Congress, Crane had scorned Gingrich's demand that members seeking chairmanships raise money to elect other Republicans; in October 1998, in a response to requests for funds, he sent in a desultory $25,000 with a tart note: "I understand, however, that a career of service to our party and our candidates means little today, and the only question that now apparently matters, at least when it comes to 'properly securing' a chairmanship, is 'what have you done for me lately?' "

Gingrich's downfall in November 1998 and his replacement by Crane's fellow Illinoisan Dennis Hastert in January 1999 gave heart to Crane's campaign for the chairmanship. His attitude toward fundraising changed, but there was a widespread feeling that Thomas would be a more competent and active leader; one member in early March 2000 said, "There aren't five votes in the Conference" for Crane. Then in mid-March 2000, eight friends and family members confronted Crane in an intervention and demanded that he seek treatment for alcoholism; he had fallen into the habit, exacerbated by his daughter's death from cancer around Christmas 1997, of drinking 10 Heinekens a night. Crane asked for a 30-day leave of absence for treatment and issued a statement: "Over a period of time I have sensed an increased dependence on alcohol. This dependence has taken a toll on my health and other aspects of my life." He returned to the House a month later, the object of many warm remarks, and stepped up his legislative work—and his fundraising. With help from friends—one of whom, Silicon Valley executive Tom Siebel, gave $500,000—Crane raised some $2.5 million for the National Republican Congressional Committee and Republican candidates, plus $251,000 from his campaign committee and $816,000 for Battleground 2000. But Thomas was raising money in similar magnitudes and Hastert, despite his friendliness, would not commit to observing seniority. In January 2001 the Republican Steering Committee voted overwhelmingly to give the chairmanship to Thomas and the decision was ratified by the Republican Conference.

This surely was a great disappointment to Crane, and raises the question of whether he will seek re-election in 2002. He does have the consolation of continuing as chairman of the Trade subcommittee, and redistricting is likely to create another heavily Republican district in this area.

But the Ways and Means chairmanship—or ranking minority member post—looks out of reach until after the 2006 election, when Crane will turn 76.

Cook's Call   *Safe.* There are rumors that 32-year incumbent Phil Crane may retire, but insiders say that is unlikely. Regardless of his decision, this northwestern suburban Chicago seat is one of the most Republican in the state and will be held easily by Republicans.

THE PEOPLE: Pop. 2000: 699,513; Pop. 1990: 571,464, up 22.4% 1990–2000. 83.4% White, 2.7% Black, 7.4% Asian, 0.2% Amer. Indian, 1.9% Two+ races, 4.4% Other; 11.3% Hispanic Origin.

2000 Presidential Vote			1996 Presidential Vote		
Bush (R)	138,554	(55%)	Dole (R)	105,742	(49%)
Gore (D)	104,351	(42%)	Clinton (D)	86,907	(41%)
Nader (Green)	5,551	(2%)	Perot (I)	19,482	(9%)
Others	1,383	(1%)			

Rep. Philip M. Crane (R)

Elected Nov. 1969, 16th term; b. Nov. 3, 1930, Chicago; home, Wauconda; Hillsdale Col., B.A. 1952, IN U., M.A. 1961, Ph.D. 1963; Protestant; married (Arlene).

Military Career: Army, 1954–56.

Professional Career: Instructor, IN U., 1960–63; Asst. Prof., Bradley U., 1963–67; Dir., Westminster Academy, 1967–68.

DC Office: 233 CHOB 20515, 202-225-3711; Fax: 202-225-7830; Web site: www.house.gov/crane.

District Offices: Lake Villa, 847-265-9000; Palatine, 847-358-9160.

Committees: *Ways & Means* (2d of 24 R): Health; Trade (Chmn.). *Joint Committee on Taxation* (2d of 5 Reps.).

Group Ratings

	ADA	ACLU	AFS	LCV	CON	ITIC	NTU	COC	ACU	NTLC	CHC
2000	0	31	0	14	98	100	70	85	100	93	93
1999	5	—	0	13	75	—	73	91	100	—	—

National Journal Ratings

	1999 LIB —	1999 CONS		2000 LIB —	2000 CONS
Economic	0% —	84%		18% —	82%
Social	10% —	85%		0% —	79%
Foreign	3% —	92%		24% —	75%

Key Votes of the 106th Congress

1. Patient Bill of Rights	N	5. Bar RU-486 $ for FDA	Y	9. NATO War in Serbia	N
2. Accelerate Min. Wage	N	6. Display 10 Commandments	Y	10. Perm. Trade with China	Y
3. Strike Ban on Ergo. Stnd.	N	7. Gun Show Bkgrnd. Checks	N	11. Debt Relief for 3rd World	N
4. Ovrd. Estate Tax Veto	Y	8. Ban Part.-Birth Abortion	*	12. Drop Cuba Econ. Embargo	N

Election Results

2000 general	Philip M. Crane (R)	141,918	(61%)	($970,024)
	Lance Pressl (D)	90,777	(39%)	($280,791)
2000 primary	Philip M. Crane (R)	unopposed		
1998 general	Philip M. Crane (R)	104,242	(69%)	($833,853)
	Mike Rothman (D)	47,614	(31%)	

NINTH DISTRICT

"Make no little plans," commanded architect Daniel Burnham, who made no little plans for the Chicago lakefront. The glorious parks he designed are among America's urban jewels, and the row of high-rise apartment buildings—some austere works of masters of the International style, some in traditional styles evocative of some other place and time, some sleek Art Deco works of the 1920s and 1930s—are a splendid accompaniment. Behind the lakefront is all the diversity of Chicago. In sturdy brick houses, with scarcely a shoehorn's space between them, or in stubby apartment buildings, are ethnic and racial groups of all sorts, from Argentineans to Slavs, Plains Indians to Indian plainsmen. In the 1970s the neighborhoods behind the lakefront seemed to be getting grimier and heading downhill. Since the late 1980s, they have been busy gentrifying, as young couples and gays, professionals and entrepreneurs renovate old houses and open new businesses. Today this part of Chicago has as much urban energy and lively diversity as any place in America.

The lakefront has long been the most heavily Jewish part of Chicago. Chicago's Jewish community, prominent for more than a century, has never been as much a force for big government as in New York, nor is it connected as much to a glamorous industry as in Los Angeles. Yet these Jewish voters' liberal impulses have been strong: the 19th Century impulse to resist state authority and imposition of cultural uniformity and the 20th Century impulse to increase state responsibility for individuals' lives. Chicago's North Side Jews, on the lakefront or in neighborhoods like Rogers Park and nearby suburbs like Skokie and Niles, have been a solidly Democratic voting bloc, involved with—but skeptical of—the old Democratic machine. In the racial city politics of the 1980s, as in state politics, Jewish voters and lakefront liberals of all backgrounds were a key swing group.

The 9th Congressional District of Illinois covers most of Chicago's lakefront, from Diversey Harbor north to Evanston, the home of Northwestern University and a city that has moved gracefully from historic Yankee Republican-ness to trendy post-graduate Democratic-ness. The 9th presses inland from the Rogers Park neighborhood at the north end of Chicago west into Polish-American areas at the northwest edge of the city; from Evanston it reaches west through heavily Jewish Skokie to Morton Grove and Niles.

The representative from the 9th District is Jan Schakowsky, a Democrat elected in 1998. She grew up in Rogers Park, worked two years as a teacher; in 1969 she formed National Consumers Unite and worked for date-of-freshness labels on food. Later she joined Illinois Public Action, a consumer group that worked to stop utilities from shutting off heat for delinquent bills in winter; in 1985 she became executive director of the Illinois State Council of Senior Citizens. In 1990 she was elected to the state House from Evanston and Skokie. There she worked for day care centers and hate crime laws and chaired the Labor and Commerce Committee.

Schakowsky was selected in the Democratic primary to replace Sidney Yates, who had represented the Lakefront in Congress for all but two of the preceding 50 years, chiefly as chairman of the Interior Appropriations Subcommittee. Her strategy was to run from the left—"I don't think I can be defined as too far left in a district like this"—and to build a volunteer organization. With ads in college papers, she got 400 young people to apply for 20 field organizer jobs; they set about identifying Schakowsky voters. She also raised plenty of money, $1.4 million, with help from EMILY's List; she survived attacks based on the fact that her husband Robert Creamer had resigned as head of Citizens Action of Illinois because of a federal investigation. Schakowsky's two opponents had a different strategy. Longtime state Senator Howard Carroll, with roots in the heavily Jewish 50th Ward, had the support of most Democratic ward committeemen. He attacked Schakowsky for her opposition to the death penalty. J. B. Pritzker, a member of the billionaire family that started Hyatt hotels, put $1.5 million into his own campaign. On primary day, Schakowsky's campaign fielded 1,500 workers, 250 from unions; she won 31,443 votes, enough for a 45%–34% win over Carroll. Of course, she easily won the general election; the Republican nominee was once her physician.

In the House, Schakowsky quickly began to work with party leaders, gaining their support to expand her training program for political organizers. She wants to expand Medicare to cover everybody—single payer government health insurance, in effect—and has advanced a proposal to have a government-run investment fund that taxpayers could use to supplement Social Security, similar to the USA Accounts Bill Clinton proposed in 1999. She called for child safety locks to be sold with all handguns. When gasoline prices soared in the Chicago area, she attacked the oil companies' big profit increases. Schakowsky quickly made her mark as a fundraiser in the

Democrats' effort to win back the House and in March 2001 was tapped to head the Democratic Congressional Campaign Committee's Women LEAD fundraising program. She was re-elected with 76% in 2000.

Although redistricting could significantly change her district—which is 60,000 shy of the population requirement for the new decade—it is not likely to cause Schakowsky any problems, especially given her organizational skills.

Cook's Call   *Safe*. Jan Schakowsky should have little trouble retaining this liberal Democratic district.

THE PEOPLE: Pop. 2000: 593,205; Pop. 1990: 571,611, up 3.8% 1990–2000. 66.8% White, 12.2% Black, 12.1% Asian, 0.3% Amer. Indian, 0.1% Hawaiian, 3.6% Two+ races, 4.9% Other; 12.3% Hispanic Origin.

2000 Presidential Vote		
Gore (D)	156,524	(70%)
Bush (R)	59,206	(26%)
Nader (Green)	7,860	(3%)
Others	1,185	(1%)

1996 Presidential Vote		
Clinton (D)	139,166	(69%)
Dole (R)	52,263	(26%)
Perot (I)	9,732	(5%)

Rep. Jan Schakowsky (D)

Elected 1998, 2d term; b. May 26, 1944, Chicago; home, Evanston; U. of IL, B.S. 1965; Jewish; married (Robert Creamer).

Elected Office: IL House of Reps., 1990–98.

Professional Career: Fdr., Natl. Consumers Unite, 1969–73; Prog. Dir., IL Public Action, 1976–85; Exec. Dir., IL State Cncl. of Sr. Citizens, 1985–90.

DC Office: 515 CHOB 20515, 202-225-2111; Fax: 202-226-6890; Web site: www.house.gov/schakowsky.

District Offices: Chicago, 773-506-7100; Evanston, 847-328-3409.

Committees: *Financial Services* (20th of 32 D): Housing & Community Opportunity; International Monetary Policy & Trade; Oversight & Investigations. *Government Reform* (16th of 19 D): Government Efficiency, Financial Management & Intergovernmental Relations (RMM); National Security, Veterans' Affairs & Intl. Relations.

Group Ratings

	ADA	ACLU	AFS	LCV	CON	ITIC	NTU	COC	ACU	NTLC	CHC
2000	85	86	100	86	52	28	28	40	4	12	0
1999	100	—	100	94	66	—	30	20	4	—	—

National Journal Ratings

	1999 LIB —	1999 CONS		2000 LIB —	2000 CONS
Economic	80% —	18%		80% —	20%
Social	83% —	13%		94% —	0%
Foreign	78% —	17%		97% —	0%

Key Votes of the 106th Congress

1. Patient Bill of Rights	Y	5. Bar RU-486 $ for FDA	N	9. NATO War in Serbia	Y
2. Accelerate Min. Wage	Y	6. Display 10 Commandments	N	10. Perm. Trade with China	N
3. Strike Ban on Ergo. Stnd.	Y	7. Gun Show Bkgrnd. Checks	Y	11. Debt Relief for 3rd World	Y
4. Ovrd. Estate Tax Veto	N	8. Ban Part.-Birth Abortion	N	12. Drop Cuba Econ. Embargo	Y

Election Results

2000 general	Jan Schakowsky (D)	147,002	(76%)	($694,724)
	Dennis J. Driscoll (R)	45,344	(24%)	($98,852)
2000 primary	Jan Schakowsky (D)	unopposed		
1998 general	Jan Schakowsky (D)	107,878	(75%)	($1,440,606)
	Herbert Sohn (R)	33,448	(23%)	($24,631)
	Others	3,284	(2%)	

TENTH DISTRICT

Since 1855, when the first Chicago & Northwestern opened the railroad line from downtown Chicago north along the lakeshore, the North Shore suburbs along Lake Michigan have been the favorite residence for Chicago's elite. The North Shore starts in Evanston, founded by Methodists to promote temperance (a cause that has never prospered in Chicago), and goes on to Wilmette, Winnetka, Glencoe, Highland Park, Lake Forest—each with a slightly different personality and character, each long established, mightily prosperous and with a patina of age. Not far from the gritty, monosyllabic city, these are communities of pleasant, affluent, well-educated people living in an environment whose natural beauty—the long water vista and blue light off the lake, the gentle hills and fine trees—is kept carefully disciplined.

The 10th Congressional District of Illinois is the North Shore district, starting at the Baha'i Temple on the Wilmette lakefront, just north of Evanston, reaching up past Fort Sheridan (which was closed in 1993) to the city of Waukegan (once famous as the home of comedian Jack Benny) and the Wisconsin border beyond. The district also goes inland to what for many years was just cornfields to Northbrook and Deerfield, just west of Glencoe and Highland Park. Farther inland are suburbs like Arlington Heights, developed in the 1950s and 1960s on the Northwestern railroad line, and Wheeling, developed in the 1960s and 1970s near I-294. To the north are Long Grove and Libertyville, near where the Adlai Stevensons, the late presidential candidate and his son the former senator, have owned what is now one of the last farms only a few miles from Lake Michigan.

The congressman from the 10th District is Mark Kirk, a Republican first elected in 2000 and the successor to his former boss John Porter. Porter retired after serving 20 years, the final six as chairman of the Appropriations Labor-HHS-Education Subcommittee, where he was one of the prime movers in doubling the National Institutes of Health budget over five years. Kirk was born downstate in Champaign but spent the better part of his childhood in the affluent Chicago suburb of Kenilworth. As a 16-year-old, he nearly died of hypothermia after a boating accident, an incident that he said helped influence him to go into public service. Kirk graduated from Cornell in 1981 and the London School of Economics in 1982, and worked as a staffer in Porter's Washington office and became the chief of staff after just three years. Kirk left Porter's office in 1990 and moved on to a number of Washington jobs, first at the World Bank, then as a State Department aide working on the Central American peace process. After two years of international law practice, he served four years as counsel to the House International Relations Committee; he was also a lieutenant commander in the Naval Reserves, with tours of duty in Turkey, Serbia, Bosnia. Haiti, Panama and the Persian Gulf.

In 1999, when Porter announced his retirement, Kirk returned home to the 10th District, where he was one of no fewer than 11 competitors in the Republican primary. This contest included six millionaires who spent nearly $4 million of their own money. Kirk did not spend nearly as much, but he had two great advantages: the endorsement of the immensely popular Porter and the fact that he was the only candidate with moderate views on cultural issues. Also, Kirk had much more experience than his rivals. He won just 31% in the March primary, but this was enough to put him well ahead of the 15% for R.R. Donnelley & Sons printing company heiress Shawn Margaret Donnelley, who ran an astonishing number of radio ads, and the 14% for Northbrook Mayor Mark Damisch.

This seat in ancestral Republican territory was seriously contested in the general election. Democratic state Representative Lauren Beth Gash won the nomination without opposition after Chris Kennedy, son of Robert F. Kennedy and an executive of Chicago's Merchandise Mart, decided not to run. Both Kirk and Gash campaigned as candidates in the Porter mold, promising to carry on his fiscally conservative, culturally moderate record. Gash, an attorney, tried to downplay Kirk's years in Washington, touting her own legislative experience while focusing on protecting Social Security and making prescription drugs more affordable for seniors. Kirk wooed voters with his policy-making experience and promised to deliver on local issues, such as cleaning up Waukegan Harbor, removing nuclear waste from the Zion nuclear power plant and maintaining the Veterans Administration hospital in North Chicago. Both candidates were moderate and polite—

befitting the district. But there were negative TV ads paid for by the parties: Democrats depicted Kirk as unable to make up his mind about Social Security, while Republicans accused Gash of trying to mislead voters. Kirk won the Cook County suburbs 54%–46% and lost in Lake County 51%–49%, leaving him a 51%–49% victory. He called his election a mandate to continue "the thoughtful, independent leadership of our district" and promised to retain a positive focus. After taking office, Kirk continued Porter's tradition of regularly holding town meetings and in February 2001 he and Democratic freshman Adam Schiff of California formed a bipartisan Freshmen for Reform coalition to promote campaign finance reform.

Like his predecessor, Kirk faces the threat of primaries from the right and general election challenges from the left. Redistricting may change the lines somewhat, but the district is in a corner of the state and is only 25,000 short of the required population.

Cook's Call   *Competitive*. This North Shore district, once considered a safe Republican area, has become much more competitive in recent years. In fact, this district was one of only two in the state that voted for Gore and for a Republican House candidate. These demographics may encourage Democrats to target the freshman Kirk, who won with just 51% in 2000. But Kirk is a good fit for this district and won't be easy to oust from this seat.

THE PEOPLE: Pop. 2000: 627,793; Pop. 1990: 571,501, up 9.8% 1990–2000. 79.1% White, 6.7% Black, 5.7% Asian, 0.2% Amer. Indian, 1.9% Two + races, 6.3% Other; 13.9% Hispanic Origin.

2000 Presidential Vote				**1996 Presidential Vote**		
Gore (D)	130,972	(53%)		Clinton (D)	112,105	(50%)
Bush (R)	110,427	(45%)		Dole (R)	97,434	(43%)
Nader (Green)	4,540	(2%)		Perot (I)	13,418	(6%)

Rep. Mark Kirk (R)

Elected 2000, 1st term; b. Sept. 15, 1959, Champaign; home, Kenilworth; Universidad Nacional Autonoma de Mexico, 1977–78; Cornell U., B.A. 1981; London Sch. of Econ., M.Sc. 1982; Georgetown U., J.D. 1992; Congregationalist; married (Kimberly Vertolli).

Military Career: U.S. Naval Reserve, 1989-present.

Professional Career: Parliamentary aide, British House of Commons, 1981–83; A.A., U.S. Rep. John E. Porter, 1984–89; Staffer, World Bank, 1990–91; Spec. Asst., U.S. Dept. of State, 1991–93; Practicing atty., 1993–95; Counsel, U.S. House Cmte. on Intl. Relations, 1995–2000.

DC Office: 1531 LHOB 20515, 202-225-4835; Web site: www.house.gov/kirk.

District Offices: Deerfield, 847-940-0202; Waukegan, 847-662-0101.

Committees: *Armed Services* (28th of 32 R): Military Personnel; Military Procurement. *Budget* (24th of 24 R). *Transportation & Infrastructure* (31st of 42 R): Aviation; Highways & Transit.

Group Ratings and Key Votes: Newly Elected

Election Results

2000 general	Mark Kirk (R)	121,582	(51%)	($2,015,292)
	Lauren Beth Gash (D)	115,924	(49%)	($1,967,426)
2000 primary	Mark Kirk (R)	19,717	(31%)	
	Shawn Margaret Donnelley (R)	9,585	(15%)	
	Mark William Damisch (R)	9,016	(14%)	
	Andrew Hochberg (R)	7,480	(12%)	
	John H. Cox (R)	6,339	(10%)	
	Scott Phelps (R)	3,712	(6%)	
	Tom Lachner (R)	2,555	(4%)	
	Other	4,401	(7%)	
1998 general	John Edward Porter (R)	unopposed		($489,275)

ELEVENTH DISTRICT

The low-lying land west and south of Chicago, where sluggishly flowing rivers run circles around industrial sites, is a great divide over which French explorers portaged the easiest path from the inland oceans of the Great Lakes to the Mississippi River valley. Today there is still a kind of borderland here, as the factories and shopping centers and subdivisions stop somewhere past the Cook County line and downstate prairies begin, cornfields bisected by highways and railroads radiating out from the Loop and the rail yards of the nation's transportation hub. Politically, this is a borderland as well, between the traditionally Democratic Chicago metropolitan area, with its hard-bitten machine politics, and heavily Republican Downstate Illinois, with its tradition of governance by local civic leaders that stretches back to the days of Abraham Lincoln.

The 11th Congressional District of Illinois covers much of this borderland. It includes the old 10th Ward of Chicago plus the suburbs of South Holland, Calumet City and Lansing near the Indiana line. This is heavy industry country; many of the factories around Lake Calumet are empty now—if not torn down—but the rows of workers' houses on the grid streets remain. This is the home of the struggling white working class, ancestrally Democratic. To the west is Joliet in Will County, whose 40% growth in the 1990s was the second fastest in Illinois. Once a canal boat town, and later the producer of one-third of America's wallpaper, Joliet now has two big prisons; with the federal Joliet Arsenal closed, Joliet owes its current prosperity to two riverboat casinos built since 1992. To the south is Kankakee, a county seat amid rich prairie earth on the Illinois Central main line and the hometown of Governor George Ryan; this is Republican territory. Farther west, on bluffs above the Illinois River heading down to the Mississippi, are the factory towns of Ottawa and LaSalle and, to the south, Streator; this is LaSalle County, the politically marginal area in the district.

The congressman from the 11th District is Jerry Weller, a hard-working, politically savvy Republican who won the seat in 1994. Weller grew up on a Grundy County farm, where his family still raises hogs; out of college, he was a staffer to Congressman Tom Corcoran and Agriculture Secretary John Block; in the mid-1980s he returned to Illinois and was elected to the state House in 1988. In 1994, when Democratic Congressman George Sangmeister retired, Weller was one of six Republicans and seven Democrats to run for the seat. He boasted of reforming health care via market-based principles, holding criminals accountable and promoting markets for ethanol fuels and soybean inks; he was proud of replacing the "granny tax" on nursing home residents with a cigarette tax as a way to pay for health care. Against Democrat Frank Giglio, a state legislator for 20 years, who said of Congress, "Wouldn't this be a nice way to finish my career?" Weller won 61%–39%.

In the House, Weller has shown impressive insider skills. With the help of then-Chief Deputy Whip Dennis Hastert, he was named one of three freshmen on the Republican Steering Committee. On the Veterans Affairs' Committee he steered to passage a law allowing the Veterans' Administration to contract outpatient care with private clinics and hospitals. After a close re-election in 1996 Weller ran hard for a seat on the Ways and Means Committee, arguing that no one there represented Chicago. With help again from Hastert he won one of the four open seats. He became a prime sponsor of ending the marriage penalty, giving couples the option of the current system or his new provision. And he backed several other tax cuts, including the end of the Social Security earnings limit on seniors, which Bill Clinton signed, and elimination of the estate tax, which the president opposed. On behalf of Republicans, Weller reached out to the motion picture and casino industries with favorable tax policy. He also worked up a proposal, with the help of Chicago Mayor Richard M. Daley, for tax incentives to clean up brownfields, contaminated former industrial sites. And he led the fight for elimination of the 3% telephone excise tax, first passed to pay for the Spanish-American War. After a Joliet nine-year-old was targeted by sexual predators on the Internet, he proposed higher penalties for Internet sex crimes; this passed the House in June 1998 after Weller brought in the girl's parents to testify and the language was modified to satisfy Judiciary Committee Republicans.

Weller did not neglect local concerns. On Transportation, he promoted the third Chicago-area airport proposed for Peotone, 45 miles south of Chicago and a few miles north of Kankakee.

He has pushed for a feasibility study of a Calumet Ecological Park in the old industrial zone of the south suburbs; he placed veterans' medical clinics in the south suburbs and LaSalle County; he fought to save impact aid for schools near the closed Joliet Arsenal and won enactment of his provision to bar the deposit of garbage from outside Will County at a landfill there; he got $17 million for the Deep Tunnel and Reservoir Project in the often flood-sodden south suburbs. But his attempt to name a new Joliet veterans' cemetery after Abraham Lincoln was foiled by Ray LaHood, who feared confusion with the cemetery in Springfield where Lincoln is buried.

Weller has been active in internal House Republican politics. He lost a race for Republican Conference secretary in July 1997, after some bad publicity when he held a breakfast and promised $1,500 contributions to each member who attended; he withdrew from a race for chairman of the Policy Committee in November 1998. But in December 1998, when Speaker-designate Bob Livingston stunned everyone by announcing his retirement, Weller worked the phones for Dennis Hastert, along with Tom DeLay and Tom Davis, and helped Hastert win the speakership within hours. In early 2001, Weller was named finance chairman of the National Republican Congressional Committee.

Weller won re-election easily in 1998 and 2000, spending about $1 million against lightly funded opponents, but was held below 60% each time. Redistricting may push Jesse Jackson Jr.'s 2d and Bill Lipinski's 3d Districts farther south into Weller's Democratic-leaning Cook County precincts, which should suit him fine.

Cook's Call *Potentially Competitive.* Weller has taken what should be a very competitive seat (Gore won here by 8%) and, with a combination of strong political skills and solid fundraising, has made it relatively safe. Still, this unwieldy district is not totally safe Republican territory and can feel the impact of a national tide and redistricting. It was also one of the fastest growing districts in the state.

THE PEOPLE: Pop. 2000: 635,653; Pop. 1990: 571,050, up 11.3% 1990–2000. 79.4% White, 13.2% Black, 0.7% Asian, 0.2% Amer. Indian, 1.6% Two+ races, 4.8% Other; 10.5% Hispanic Origin.

2000 Presidential Vote

Gore (D)	129,905	(53%)
Bush (R)	110,313	(45%)
Nader (Green)	4,806	(2%)
Others	1,642	(1%)

1996 Presidential Vote

Clinton (D)	112,110	(51%)
Dole (R)	83,648	(38%)
Perot (I)	23,162	(11%)

Rep. Gerald C. (Jerry) Weller (R)

Elected 1994, 4th term; b. July 7, 1957, Streator; home, Morris; U. of IL, B.S. 1979; Christian; divorced.

Elected Office: IL House of Reps., 1988–94.

Professional Career: Farmer; Aide, U.S. Rep. Tom Corcoran, 1980–81; Aide, U.S. Agriculture Secy. John Block, 1981–85.

DC Office: 1210 LHOB 20515, 202-225-3635; Fax: 202-225-3521; Web site: www.house.gov/weller.

District Office: Joliet, 815-740-2028.

Committees: *Ways & Means* (18th of 24 R): Oversight; Select Revenue Measures.

Group Ratings

	ADA	ACLU	AFS	LCV	CON	ITIC	NTU	COC	ACU	NTLC	CHC
2000	15	29	33	29	24	100	57	68	66	73	93
1999	15	—	16	13	73	—	61	88	80	—	—

National Journal Ratings

	1999 LIB	—	1999 CONS		2000 LIB	—	2000 CONS
Economic	37%	—	61%		46%	—	52%
Social	25%	—	72%		45%	—	55%
Foreign	36%	—	63%		24%	—	76%

Key Votes of the 106th Congress

1. Patient Bill of Rights	N	5. Bar RU-486 $ for FDA	Y	9. NATO War in Serbia	N
2. Accelerate Min. Wage	Y	6. Display 10 Commandments	Y	10. Perm. Trade with China	Y
3. Strike Ban on Ergo. Stnd.	Y	7. Gun Show Bkgrnd. Checks	N	11. Debt Relief for 3rd World	N
4. Ovrd. Estate Tax Veto	Y	8. Ban Part.-Birth Abortion	Y	12. Drop Cuba Econ. Embargo	*

Election Results

2000 general	Gerald C. (Jerry) Weller (R)	132,384	(56%)	($976,795)
	James P. Stevenson (D)	102,485	(44%)	($144,916)
2000 primary	Gerald C. (Jerry) Weller (R)	unopposed		
1998 general	Gerald C. (Jerry) Weller (R)	100,597	(59%)	($1,514,474)
	Gary S. Mueller (D)	70,458	(41%)	($195,774)

TWELFTH DISTRICT

The nation's two mightiest rivers, the Mississippi and Missouri, their waters roiling together, join just a few miles above St. Louis and just a few miles below Alton, Illinois. Most views of this center of the Mississippi Valley focus on the Gateway Arch and the buildings of downtown St. Louis. But the Mississippi shoreline of Illinois is worthy of attention as well. Alton's 19th Century buildings recall its turbulent history, when it was the home of the anti-slavery agitator Elijah Lovejoy, who was murdered by a mob; more recently it was the longtime home of conservative crusader and columnist Phyllis Schlafly. Just across from the Gateway Arch is East St. Louis, where dozens of rail lines and highways funnel into bridges over the river. Once a rail and stockyards center second only to Chicago, East St. Louis is now almost entirely black and one of America's poorest and most troubled cities, a half-abandoned slum with one of the nation's highest crime rates and a rapidly declining tax base, almost entirely dependent on a riverboat casino and an adjacent waterfront hotel for its tax revenue.

South of East St. Louis and the industrial area around Belleville, the river counties are lightly inhabited, but they were not always unimportant: This was the site of the French Kaskaskia settlement that became Illinois's first capital in 1818. Farther south, the river abuts coal country and the town of Carbondale, once a coal center but now, as the home of Southern Illinois University, bustling with students from Downstate Illinois and Chicago and the retirement base of former Senator Paul Simon. The land here is sometimes known as Egypt, the southern end of Illinois where the Ohio River meets the Mississippi: flat, fertile farmland, protected by giant man-made levees because it is susceptible to yearly floods. There is more than a touch of Dixie here: The unofficial capital of Egypt, Cairo (pronounced *KAYroh*), is a declining town closer to Mississippi than to Chicago with its own occasional racial violence.

The 12th District of Illinois covers all of this riverfront from Alton south to Cairo, with some inland territory as well. Most of its population is in St. Clair (East St. Louis and Belleville) and Madison (Alton) Counties, but one-third of the votes are cast in counties running south to Cairo. The population of the district and of St. Clair County each declined by several thousand during the 1990s.

The congressman from the 12th District is Jerry Costello, a Democrat first elected in 1988. He grew up in a St. Clair political family, worked for the courts after college, then became chairman of the St. Clair County Board of Supervisors. He waited with some impatience for the retirement of Congressman Mel Price, first elected in 1944, who was re-elected by only 943 votes in 1986 and announced his retirement not long after and died in office in April 1988. Experienced, well connected, supported by organized labor, Costello was the obvious successor. Yet he received only 51% of the votes in the special election and 53% for a full term.

Costello is a practical-minded politician with a seat on the Transportation and Infrastructure Committee and a voting record more liberal on economics than on cultural and foreign issues.

He opposed George Bush's Clean Air Act and Bill Clinton's NAFTA, bucked Clinton on the balanced budget amendment and House Republicans on public works votes. He trumpets his accomplishments without subtlety. Bridges are important in a river district: Costello has worked to replace the Clark Bridge in Alton and, with the late Congressman Bill Emerson of Missouri, to build a new bridge to Cape Girardeau that is named after Emerson. His biggest ongoing project has been creating the Mid-America Airport at Scott Air Force Base near Belleville; it opened in 1997 but, alas, has no scheduled airline service. He has pushed for $60 million for an 8.9-mile rail link to the airport. In the 1998 transportation bill he got funding for a $4.8 million I-64 interchange in O'Fallon, $5.6 million for an industrial park in Alton and $4.5 million for a two-mile road through the new Sauget Business Park.

But a cloud has hung over Costello. In September 1996 federal prosecutors indicted Amiel Cueto, Costello's longtime friend and business partner, for trying to stop an investigation of a gambling operation run by a client and for conspiring to get himself installed as St. Clair County state's attorney. In May 1997 a federal judge ruled that Costello was an "unindicted co-conspirator;" prosecutors said he was a silent partner in a plan to build an Indian casino and that he worked in Congress to get recognition of an Indian tribe to sponsor it. Costello denied all in June 1997, arguing that he had no interest in the casino, his role in the Indian designation was minimal, and he had tried to get a rival to vacate the state's attorney job only to avoid the political fuss of a primary.

Cueto was convicted and Costello was never indicted. But he put aside plans to run for secretary of State and found himself opposed in 1998 by Bill Price, an orthopedic surgeon and son of Mel Price, who switched parties and ran as a Republican. Price said Costello was taking credit for projects that were his father's, that he was undercutting Mid-America Airport by backing a new runway for Lambert Airport in St. Louis County, Missouri, and that he allowed southern Illinois highway money to be shifted to Chicago projects. Price came close to equaling Costello's $1 million in spending. But Costello won by a solid 60%–40%. Interestingly, Costello ran weakest in his home territory, where knowledge of the Cueto case was presumably greatest, with just 55% in St. Clair County, and lost fast-growing Monroe County just to the south.

The overall result, though, suggests that Costello is safe in this basically Democratic district, and in 2000 he had no Republican challenger. If only because the 20th needs an additional 93,000 persons, redistricting will change the boundaries.

Cook's Call   *Safe.* This southwestern Illinois district was one of the slowest growing in the state; St. Clair County, which currently makes up about 45% of the district, has lost 6,700 people since 1990. To pick up population, a bipartisan redistricting plan devised by Speaker Hastert and Bill Lipinski pushed the 12th District eastward into parts of the current 19th District. Costello is well entrenched here and has proven that he can run and win tough races. If Republicans couldn't knock him off when he was in the midst of a political scandal, it's hard to see how they'd get him now.

THE PEOPLE: Pop. 2000: 560,912; Pop. 1990: 571,441, down 1.8% 1990–2000. 78.3% White, 18.5% Black, 0.9% Asian, 0.3% Amer. Indian, 1.2% Two+ races, 0.8% Other; 2% Hispanic Origin.

2000 Presidential Vote

Gore (D)	123,566	(55%)
Bush (R)	96,096	(42%)
Nader (Green)	4,777	(2%)
Others	1,813	(1%)

1996 Presidential Vote

Clinton (D)	120,389	(56%)
Dole (R)	72,652	(34%)
Perot (I)	19,777	(9%)

Rep. Jerry F. Costello (D)

Elected Aug. 1988, 7th term; b. Sept. 25, 1949, E. St. Louis; home, Belleville; Belleville Area Col. A.A. 1970, Maryville Col. B.A. 1972; Catholic; married (Georgia).

Elected Office: Chmn., St. Clair Cnty. Bd. of Supervisors, 1980–88.

Professional Career: Dir., IL Court Svcs. & Probation, 1973–80; Chmn., Region's Cncl. of Govts., 1980–84.

DC Office: 2454 RHOB 20515, 202-225-5661; Fax: 202-225-0285; Web site: www.house.gov/costello.

District Offices: Belleville, 618-233-8026; Carbondale, 618-529-3791; Chester, 618-826-3043; E. St. Louis, 618-397-8833; Granite City, 618-451-7065.

Committees: *Science* (3d of 22 D): Energy. *Transportation & Infrastructure* (7th of 34 D): Aviation; Economic Development, Public Buildings & Emergency Management (RMM); Highways & Transit.

Group Ratings

	ADA	ACLU	AFS	LCV	CON	ITIC	NTU	COC	ACU	NTLC	CHC
2000	55	23	85	64	34	44	33	47	33	16	53
1999	65	—	100	69	73	—	25	24	24	—	—

National Journal Ratings

	1999 LIB —	1999 CONS		2000 LIB —	2000 CONS
Economic	63%	36%		61%	38%
Social	45%	54%		43%	57%
Foreign	57%	43%		61%	38%

Key Votes of the 106th Congress

1. Patient Bill of Rights	Y	5. Bar RU-486 $ for FDA	Y	9. NATO War in Serbia	N
2. Accelerate Min. Wage	Y	6. Display 10 Commandments	Y	10. Perm. Trade with China	N
3. Strike Ban on Ergo. Stnd.	Y	7. Gun Show Bkgrnd. Checks	N	11. Debt Relief for 3rd World	Y
4. Ovrd. Estate Tax Veto	Y	8. Ban Part.-Birth Abortion	Y	12. Drop Cuba Econ. Embargo	Y

Election Results

2000 general	Jerry F. Costello (D)	unopposed		($373,057)
2000 primary	Jerry F. Costello (D)	37,234	(90%)	
	Kenneth Wiezer (D)	4,189	(10%)	
1998 general	Jerry F. Costello (D)	99,605	(60%)	($1,097,159)
	Bill Price (R)	65,409	(40%)	($846,057)

THIRTEENTH DISTRICT

Most residents of Chicagoland now live not in the city but in the suburbs, and increasingly not even in Cook County but in the Collar Counties all around. DuPage County, straight west of Chicago, had 103,000 residents in 1940; in 2000, there were 904,000—a 16% increase from the previous decade—with new subdivisions still springing up. Nor are these just bedroom communities. Here in Oak Brook are the headquarters of Ace Hardware, Federal Signal, the Spiegel catalogue, and most prominently, McDonald's and its Hamburger University. One out of eight young Americans has worked at McDonald's, and millions have learned from this corporation the basics of arithmetic and literacy, good work habits and cheerful service, lessons not always taught in today's public schools. Nearby are gracefully older railroad commuter towns like Hinsdale and Downers Grove, but also Naperville, once a country village, now an edge city, with a school district ranked number one in the world in science in an international exam. And vast government laboratories have sprung up, sparking private research firms, the Argonne National Laboratory along the Sanitary and Ship Canal and the Des Plaines River.

The 13th Congressional District of Illinois includes the southern slice of DuPage County, including Oak Brook, Downers Grove and Naperville, the southwest corner of Cook County around Palos Hills, and the northern slice of Will County north of Joliet. Politically, this has been a heavily Republican area, suspicious of the motives and operations of Chicago's Democrats, devoted to free enterprise and hostile to higher taxes. DuPage County has indeed become Illinois' Republican powerhouse, the home base of state Senate President Pate Philip and House Minority Leader (and former Speaker) Lee Daniels.

The congresswoman from the 13th is Judy Biggert, a Republican elected in 1998. She grew up in Kenilworth, on the affluent North Shore, graduated from New Trier Township High School, Stanford and Northwestern Law School and clerked for a federal appeals judge. She raised four children in Hinsdale, practicing estate and real estate law out of her home, served on the Hinsdale Township Board of Education, was chairman of the Visiting Nurses Association of Chicago—a "former car pool mom and assistant soccer coach," as her campaign put it. In 1992 she was elected to the state House, and was soon part of the leadership. There she supported tort reform, property tax caps, repeal of the Structural Work Act, tougher sentencing for child pornographers and education reform.

In August 1997, incumbent Republican Harris Fawell announced his retirement and three months later endorsed Biggert, who ran as a supporter of abortion rights. She said she opposed most gun control measures for constitutional reasons, though she had campaigned for gun control in 1992. She pledged to limit herself to three terms. She had primary opposition from state Representative Peter Roskam, who moved into the district to run. He attacked her on abortion and criticized her for voting for a $485 million school funding bill that included tax increases on cigarettes, casino gambling and telephones. Gary Bauer's Campaign for Working Families ran ads against Biggert, but Biggert raised far more money, including $402,000 of her own funds and contributions from Planned Parenthood and the Human Rights Campaign (she has voted for gay rights bills). Biggert won the March 1998 primary by 45%–40%, carrying DuPage 50%–38% while trailing in Will and Cook counties. Biggert won the general election 61%–39%.

Even before being sworn in, Biggert was the only freshman to take part in a White House conference on Social Security; she favors individual investment accounts. She supported the Violence Against Women Act and a 24-hour, but not 72-hour, background check for gun sales at gun shows in June 1999. Her amendment passed the House in October 1999 to eliminate the waiting period for homeless children to enroll in schools and give them a choice between the nearest or their current school. She sponsored a bill for $20 billion to pay interest costs on school construction loans. In October 1999 Biggert abandoned her pledge to serve only three terms. "If I knew what I know now, I wouldn't have signed," she said. "I didn't realize how important seniority was." A supporter of free trade, she attended the Seattle WTO conference in 1999 but could not leave her hotel due to the protests; she criticized Clinton: "Labor isn't a trade issue. He was only trying to placate the unions, and it undercut our negotiations."

Biggert's abandonment of her term-limits pledge did not inspire strong opposition; she was re-elected 66%–34%. She launched a late candidacy for secretary of the House Republican Conference, but on November 14 lost to Barbara Cubin of Wyoming, 122–73, who argued that she would bring more regional diversity to the conference. Because Biggert's district grew by 33% in the 1990s, it will need to shrink by 105,000 residents—possibly its Cook County suburbs.

Cook's Call   *Safe.* This western Chicagoland district is one of the most reliably Republican in the state. DuPage and Will Counties, which currently make up 80% of the district, are two of the fastest growing counties in the state. This district will need to contract in redistricting, but it is likely to remain safe Republican territory.

THE PEOPLE: Pop. 2000: 759,124; Pop. 1990: 571,344, up 32.9% 1990–2000. 85.8% White, 4.5% Black, 6.2% Asian, 0.1% Amer. Indian, 1.6% Two+ races, 1.8% Other; 5.4% Hispanic Origin.

2000 Presidential Vote			1996 Presidential Vote		
Bush (R)	171,335	(55%)	Dole (R)	126,594	(50%)
Gore (D)	132,472	(42%)	Clinton (D)	104,713	(41%)
Nader (Green)	6,769	(2%)	Perot (I)	21,701	(9%)
Others	1,611	(1%)			

Rep. Judy Biggert (R)

Elected 1998, 2d term; b. Aug. 15, 1937, Chicago; home, Hinsdale; Stanford U., B.A. 1959, Northwestern U., J.D. 1963; Episcopalian; married (Rody).

Elected Office: IL House of Reps., 1992–98.

Professional Career: Clerk, U.S. Ct. of Appeals, 1963–64; Practicing atty., 1975–98.

DC Office: 1213 LHOB 20515, 202-225-3515; Fax: 202-225-9420; Web site: www.house.gov/biggert.

District Office: Clarendon Hills, 630-655-1061.

Committees: *Education & the Workforce* (22d of 27 R): Education Reform; Workforce Protections (Vice Chmn.). *Financial Services* (24th of 37 R): Capital Markets, Insurance & Government Sponsored Enterprises; Financial Institutions & Consumer Credit; International Monetary Policy & Trade. *Science* (18th of 25 R): Energy; Research. *Standards of Official Conduct* (5th of 5 R).

Group Ratings

	ADA	ACLU	AFS	LCV	CON	ITIC	NTU	COC	ACU	NTLC	CHC
2000	20	50	0	36	5	94	56	100	68	70	60
1999	30	—	16	31	21	—	59	96	60	—	—

National Journal Ratings

	1999 LIB —	1999 CONS		2000 LIB —	2000 CONS
Economic	24%	72%		36%	64%
Social	58%	42%		53%	46%
Foreign	41%	58%		39%	57%

Key Votes of the 106th Congress

1. Patient Bill of Rights	N	5. Bar RU-486 $ for FDA	N	9. NATO War in Serbia	Y
2. Accelerate Min. Wage	N	6. Display 10 Commandments	Y	10. Perm. Trade with China	Y
3. Strike Ban on Ergo. Stnd.	N	7. Gun Show Bkgrnd. Checks	N	11. Debt Relief for 3rd World	N
4. Ovrd. Estate Tax Veto	Y	8. Ban Part.-Birth Abortion	Y	12. Drop Cuba Econ. Embargo	Y

Election Results

2000 general	Judy Biggert (R)	193,250	(66%)	($381,623)
	Thomas Mason (D)	98,768	(34%)	
2000 primary	Judy Biggert (R)	unopposed		
1998 general	Judy Biggert (R)	121,889	(61%)	($1,294,853)
	Susan W. Hynes (D)	77,878	(39%)	($222,656)

FOURTEENTH DISTRICT

A few dozen miles beyond the Loop there is an invisible line marking two different Chicagos. One is the Chicago dominated by blacks and descendants of the vast immigrations of 1840–1924 and 1970–90, a Chicago where certain loyalties are taken for granted: loyalty to ethnic group, to church (usually the Catholic Church, often with an ethnic prefix), and to party (almost always the Democrats). This Chicago is a gritty city, where personal cheerfulness and courtesy lighten up days otherwise as cold and impersonal as the gray winter sky. The other Chicago is the beginning of the Great Plains, originally a white Anglo-Saxon Protestant Chicago, a place whose residents are products of the first great wave of immigration to America. The tone of this Chicago is lighter, its streets and highways cleaner and neater, its daily life generally free from evidence of unpleasantness and deprivation. Ronald Reagan grew up in Downstate Illinois within the orbit of this Chicago (though he did live in the city briefly), and its spirit helped to characterize his presidency. His migration to southern California, incidentally, is not atypical: You can see in the geometric grids and Republican voting patterns of Orange County or Phoenix almost exact replicas of the grids and patterns in Chicago's suburban Collar Counties, transported to the once-empty Southwest on the Atchison, Topeka & Santa Fe or out the old U.S. 66 from their beginnings in Chicago's Loop.

The 14th Congressional District straddles this line between metropolitan Chicago and Downstate Illinois. It gets as close as 30 miles to Chicago's Loop, in western DuPage County, with two great Chicagoland landmarks—Cantigny, the estate of Colonel Robert McCormick, longtime publisher of the *Chicago Tribune*, and FermiLab, the world's fastest energy particle accelerator and employer of some 2,000 people—icons of political conservatism and high technology within two miles of each other. The 14th also contains the Fox River Valley and its industrial cities of Elgin and resurgent Aurora—which grew to the third-largest city in Illinois in 2000—plus antique St. Charles in the heart of the Collar Counties. Farther west, amid what may be the world's richest cornfields, the 14th passes through DeKalb, long the world's leading manufacturer of barbed wire, and goes on to Kendall and Lee Counties, including Reagan's boyhood home in Dixon. This is some of the most heavily Republican territory in the country. Northern Illinois was settled when Chicago was just a frontier village by Yankees from Ohio, Indiana, Upstate New York and New England, and by Germans emigrating after the failed revolutions of 1848: people who formed the heart of the Republican Party from its founding in 1854 and who would form the core of the Grand Army of the Republic a few years later. Their descendants, in this extension of Chicagoland, remain solidly Republican today.

The congressman from the 14th is Dennis Hastert, a Republican first elected in 1986, and today the 51st speaker of the House. Like many congressmen from high-income districts he comes from a modest background. He grew up on a farm; his father had a feed supply business, and Denny and his brothers hoisted 100-pound bags and delivered milk in the early morning and he worked as a fry cook in his parents' restaurant. At high school in Oswego—then a rural town, now exploding with subdivisions—he wrestled and played football; after graduating from Wheaton College he became a high school teacher at Yorkville High School, a rural town a few miles farther from Chicago. There he taught history and coached wrestling for 16 years. But his experience was not as limited as that description may suggest. In summers he traveled as a teacher for the YMCA or other groups to Japan, Colombia, Venezuela, Europe and the Soviet Union. And as a wrestling coach he excelled: His team won the state championship and he was named the national coach of the year in 1976.

After a trip to Washington in 1978, when Democrats had a 2–1 majority in the House, Hastert got involved in politics, interning with state Senator John Grotberg. In 1980 he finished third in an Illinois House primary, then the incumbent became fatally ill and Hastert was chosen to take his place on the November ballot. After the March 1986 primary, Grotberg, now a member of Congress, was fatally stricken with cancer and Hastert again was chosen by the party as a replacement. The election was unusually close, but Hastert won 52%–48%.

In the House, Hastert had a conservative voting record and made few waves. But he gained valuable experience. He got a seat on the Commerce Committee and on the subcommittees handling health, energy and telecommunications issues. He built a relationship with Minority Leader Robert Michel, from Illinois 18th District. He worked together with Tom DeLay of Texas for Ed Madigan in the race for minority whip in March 1989; Madigan lost by just two votes to an upstart from Georgia named Newt Gingrich. In the 1992 campaign he and Bill Emerson of Missouri worked hard for the National Republican Congressional Committee. In 1994 he was chief organizer for Tom DeLay's campaign for whip, the one leadership post won by a non-Gingrichite after the big Republican gains that fall. Afterwards Hastert was named chief deputy whip and shared an office and staff with DeLay.

To his work Hastert brought the habits of a coach, listening long to colleagues' goals and complaints, sizing up their character and capacity, then insisting firmly on a course of action when he reached a judgment. He operated with minimal ego and a bear-like friendliness, putting his arm around a colleague when asking advice or seeking intelligence; increasingly he was looked to by other leaders to help Republicans reach consensus and to negotiate difficult issues with Democrats, particularly health care. In 1993 he was on a Republican task force responding to Hillary Rodham Clinton's health care plan. In 1996 he worked on the health-care portability bill passed by both houses of Congress; it included removal of preexisting conditions, allowed small businesses to use pools to buy insurance, created medical savings accounts, increased on a sliding scale tax deductibility of health insurance for the self-employed and reformed malpractice laws. In 1997 he helped put together the Republicans' Medicare bill. Gingrich made him head of a task force that hammered out a patients' rights bill, which was passed by the House in August 1998. Hastert was active in negotiations on the 1996 telecommunications bill and on repealing the Social Security "earnings tax"—the deduction of benefits among senior citizens who earn over a certain figure—in the 1995 Contract With America. Over the years, Hastert has continued his trips abroad, including to Japan, and has been supportive of free trade; central Illinois, where the largest company is Caterpillar, produces more exports than just about anywhere else in the country. He has helped get funding for FermiLab and Argonne National Laboratory, and in 1998 got $250,000 in the defense budget for "pharmacokinetics research," which turned out to be a study of caffeinated chewing gum by Amurol Confections Company of Yorkville.

Until December 1998, Hastert, well known in the House, was almost unknown to the general public. Then, three days after Republicans lost five seats in the November elections, Speaker Newt Gingrich announced his retirement. Challenges loomed against everyone in the leadership, with the conspicuous exception of DeLay. Many members urged Hastert to run against Majority Leader Dick Armey. But Hastert had pledged to support him; when he asked to be released from the pledge, Armey said no; and so he stuck to it and didn't run for a position he probably could have won. This behavior, unusual among Republican leaders who had been targeting each other for more than a year, was recalled on December 19, when just before the impeachment vote Speaker-designate Bob Livingston announced his retirement too. Gingrich told Hastert, "You are the only one in this conference who could pull this body together. You are going to have to be the next speaker of the House." At 1 p.m. he announced; by the end of the day he had more than 100 votes, and the speakership.

In his opening speech on January 6, Hastert made a point of walking down from the podium and speaking from the well of the House. "My legislative home is here on the floor with you, and so is my heart," he said. He invoked his authority as a coach: "Everyone on the squad has something to offer. You never get to the finals without a well-rounded team. Above all, a coach worth his salt will instill in his team a sense of fair play, camaraderie, respect for the game and for the opposition. . . . It is work, not talk, that wins championships." He readily conceded that he did not have Gingrich's articulateness and zest for abstract ideas; but he treated members more respectfully and deferred more to committee chairmen and said that he would concentrate on getting appropriations passed on time. But, even as Democrats exuded confidence that they would win control of the House in 2000, Hastert went about setting legislative priorities. Early on the House and then the Senate passed "EdFlex" bills, block grants for the states, a proposal supported by all 50 governors. He got Republicans to back what he called a "lockbox" on Social Security, so that they could say they had not tapped the trust fund. In April 1999 he stayed neutral while the House considered a resolution "authorizing" the five-week-old bombing campaign in Kosovo; he finally voted for it but Majority Whip Tom DeLay and most Republicans voted against it, and it failed on a tie vote 213–213. Minority Leader Dick Gephardt took umbrage at Hastert's actions, and relations between them were chilly to nonexistent until after the November 2000 election.

Other frustrations followed. Before the Memorial Day recess in 1999, the House rejected appropriations bills, as Republicans rebelled. In June Hastert gave Republicans a pep talk: "I need you to stand together. To not just cry out for leadership, but be willing to follow it. I am asking each of you as directly as I can, search your heart, search your conscience, and then decide to join us." He insisted that appropriations should come in under the 1997 spending caps, which had been violated the year before; that never really happened. His proposal for a moderate gun control bill was beaten in June 1999, and no bill passed. Then, in July 1999, he wheedled and cajoled and got the Republican $792 billion tax cut passed by 223–208; it was vetoed by Bill Clinton. In September 1999 he allowed the Shays-Meehan campaign finance bill, backed mainly by Democrats, to come to the floor; it passed but was killed by a Senate filibuster. In October 1999 Republican defectors joined Democrats to pass an HMO regulation bill; Hastert appointed conferees, most of whom disagreed. In November 1999, when he and Armey passed over a Catholic priest recommended by a plurality of a special committee for the post of House chaplain, Democrats quickly accused the Republican leaders of anti-Catholic prejudice.

But there were some successes. That fall the House passed financial services deregulation—the first major revision of the 1933 Glass-Steagall Act. Hastert channeled DeLay's energies to passing appropriations bills. Hastert engaged in businesslike negotiations (it helped that he knew White House Chief of Staff John Podesta in college) with Clinton on the budget. He allowed a foreign aid bill to go forward over DeLay's opposition and defended Republicans against charges of isolationism. He appeared with Clinton in Chicago in November 1999 in support of a "new markets" bill, originated by J.C. Watts and Jim Talent and supported by Charles Rangel and Bobby Rush, to allow tax credits and zero capital gains on investments in economically depressed urban areas; the bill was finally passed in December 2000. The chaplain controversy was ended when Hastert in March 2000 abruptly announced the appointment of another Catholic priest recommended by Chicago's Cardinal George. He backed Clinton's Plan Colombia in June 2000 and agreed in August 2000 to allow a minimum wage increase in return for tax relief for small business; in October 2000 he canceled a vote on a resolution condemning Turkey's 1915–23 massacres of Armenians in response to pleas from the White House. In the meantime he tended to local needs, channeling $832 million in transportation funds to the CTA and the suburbs' Metra, and pushing a tax exemption for the sale of an Illinois nuclear plant.

All the while, Hastert kept his eye on the 2000 elections: He effectively lobbied some Republicans in marginal seats, like Upstate New York's Amo Houghton, to stay on rather than retire; he reportedly used the tool of the Republicans' six-year term-limit on chairmanships to get those competing for spots opening up to raise money for Republican candidates; he helped the Battleground 2000 program raise some $21 million; he went fly-fishing with contributors during the Republican convention at $5,000 a head. His quiet pursuit of a modest legislative strategy let Republican candidates emphasize their own local issues—a far cry from Gingrich's nationalized Contract With America campaign in 1994. As the election approached, Republican chances improved, and by late October Hastert sent an appropriation to the White House knowing that Clinton would veto it because it overrode the administration's proposed ergonomics regulations; he evidently thought that he could negotiate on better terms after the election if House Republicans and George W. Bush won. His Republicans did hold their majority, narrowly, on November 7—"he beat the point spread," said political scientist Jack Pitney—and when the House came back after settlement of the Florida controversy in December the negotiations mostly went Hastert's way.

After the 1994 elections, Gingrich had appointed committee chairmen, often bypassing senior members. After the 2000 elections, Hastert exerted control more subtly. Would-be chairmen were interviewed by the Republican Steering Committee, whose selections were ratified by the Conference. Seniority was not always followed. Billy Tauzin got Commerce over Mike Oxley, who had more seniority as a Republican; Oxley got a beefed-up Financial Services Committee over its ranking member Marge Roukema; the senior House Republican, Philip Crane, was passed over for Ways and Means by Bill Thomas, with whom Hastert had worked closely on health issues. This is the first time that a Republican speaker has dealt with a Republican president since 1953–54. Hastert, like every speaker starting with Tip O'Neill, has relied almost entirely on his own party to pass bills; Bush seems likely to proceed as he did in Texas, to seek support from various Democrats on each of his priority issues. Still, Hastert established himself in the difficult circumstances of the 106th Congress as a successful and competent leader with a gift for holding a narrow majority together. This former wrestling coach, who commutes home to Yorkville every weekend where his wife still teaches school and where he drives a pickup truck and carves duck decoys, will surely be a major policymaker and political operator. Certainly he will have no trouble winning re-election; redistricting will slightly reduce the size of his district.

Cook's Call   *Safe.* Dennis Hastert represents one of the fastest growing districts in the state. While his district will have to contract some in redistricting, he will have no trouble winning in this solidly Republican district. Hastert and Democratic Representative Bill Lipinski authored the incumbent friendly bipartisan redistricting plan signed by Governor George Ryan in June 2001.

THE PEOPLE: Pop. 2000: 720,663; Pop. 1990: 571,540, up 26.1% 1990–2000. 83.4% White, 4.5% Black, 2.5% Asian, 0.3% Amer. Indian, 1.9% Two+ races, 7.5% Other; 17.5% Hispanic Origin.

2000 Presidential Vote

Bush (R)	144,357	(55%)
Gore (D)	109,947	(42%)
Nader (Green)	6,211	(2%)
Others	1,848	(1%)

1996 Presidential Vote

Dole (R)	103,773	(48%)
Clinton (D)	89,939	(41%)
Perot (I)	22,148	(10%)

Rep. J. Dennis Hastert (R)

Elected 1986, 8th term; b. Jan. 2, 1942, Aurora; home, Yorkville; Wheaton Col., B.A. 1964, N. IL U., M.A. 1967; Protestant; married (Jean).

Elected Office: IL House of Reps., 1980–86.

Professional Career: High schl. teacher & coach, 1965–80.

DC Office: 2369 RHOB 20515, 202-225-2976; Fax: 202-225-0697; Web site: www.house.gov/hastert.

District Office: Batavia, 630-406-1114.

Committees: *Speaker of the House.*

Group Ratings and Key Votes: Speaker does not usually vote.

Election Results

2000 general	J. Dennis Hastert (R)	188,597	(74%)	($2,299,072)
	Vern Deljonson (D)	66,309	(26%)	
2000 primary	J. Dennis Hastert (R)	unopposed		
1998 general	J. Dennis Hastert (R)	117,304	(70%)	($971,137)
	Robert A. Cozzi Jr. (D)	50,844	(30%)	($24,152)

FIFTEENTH DISTRICT

South from Chicago, the Illinois Central Railroad heads to the city of New Orleans on a railbed elevated a few feet above the rich black soil of the Illinois prairie, topsoil reaching down not just inches but feet. This land dazzled its first settlers, who were used to land that had to be cleared of trees and stumps before it could be plowed; this treeless prairie could be cultivated almost immediately, and with bounteous results. Today this remains farming country, made up not of small family farms but of large commercial operations, typically of 1,000 acres or more. Cultivating this soil is a business, requiring informed decisions about crop selection, maximizing yields, proper pesticides, marketing decisions, watching farm export prospects and, until the 1996 Freedom to Farm Act, taking advantage of government programs. The landscape on the prairies of eastern Illinois is marked by only a few towns, the largest of which, Champaign-Urbana and Bloomington-Normal, are the sites of universities (the University of Illinois and Illinois-Normal). Politically, these prairie lands have been Republican, often very Republican; they incline much more to the party of former House Speaker Joseph Cannon, a Republican from the manufacturing city of Danville east of Urbana, than to that of Vice President Adlai Stevenson, a Democrat from Bloomington, who served under *laissez-faire* Democrat Grover Cleveland and was the grandfather of the Adlai Stevenson nominated by Democrats for president in 1952 and 1956.

The 15th Congressional District of Illinois occupies much of this prairie, beginning 60 miles from Chicago, where the Illinois Central heads toward Kankakee, and moving over 150 miles of prairie to the courthouse town of Monticello. It includes Bloomington, Champaign-Urbana and Danville, and runs south almost to the National Road and U.S. 40, traditionally the line between northern Republican and southern Democratic Illinois. Today, the area is strongly Republican and has been represented for years by Republicans who have been active in local businesses, civic affairs and state legislative politics.

The congressman from the 15th is Tim Johnson, a Republican elected in 2000. Born in Champaign, Johnson earned his undergraduate and law degrees from the nearby University of Illinois in 1969 and 1972, respectively. He was elected to the Urbana City Council while still in law school and served there four years before winning election to the Illinois state House in 1976. In the legislature, Johnson worked his way up to deputy majority leader. His highlights included helping to eliminate the sales tax on food and medicine, crafting tougher drunk-driving laws, and playing important roles in passing welfare reform, educational improvements, truth-in-sentencing laws and initiatives to help businesses. He is a trial lawyer and manages a small local farm operation.

Johnson unexpectedly prevailed in what became a nasty Republican primary after Republican Tom Ewing announced his retirement in October 1999. Ewing and Speaker Dennis Hastert had been close friends in Congress and previously in the state House, and Ewing was part of the team that backed Hastert for speaker and then closely advised him in his early months. But Hastert was angered when Ewing appeared to delay his retirement announcement until his 29-year-old son Sam could move back to the district from Texas to begin his own candidacy. The speaker endorsed state Representative Bill Brady, the scion of a prominent real-estate family from Bloomington—after Hastert's deputy chief of staff Mike Stokke, who had managed Tom Ewing's first House campaign, decided against running. Johnson had some advantages of his own. He had more political experience and was a ferocious campaigner: "I've been a precinct committeeman involved in the affairs of my party more years than [Sam Ewing has] been alive." He also had the support of Governor George Ryan, who remained influential within the party despite low popularity ratings. The primary results broke down heavily on regional lines. Brady won his base of McLean County, 62%–20% over Johnson. In Champaign, the district's other large county, Johnson led Brady, 61%–28%. Ewing could not even win his family's home county of Livingston, trailing Brady there, 38%–36%. Johnson rolled up the vote elsewhere, especially in the southern part of the district, taking 7 of the 11 counties; he won 44%, while Brady finished second with 36% and Ewing was third with 17%.

In the general, Johnson faced Illinois State University instructor Mike Kelleher, who gained union support and won the Democratic primary, 53%–47%, over former state representative Laurel Prussing, who had lost the two previous campaigns to Tom Ewing. Kelleher dredged up a 1980 photo of a paper clip-rigged device Johnson had used to hold down the "yes" button on his desk in the legislature, enabling him to vote while being absent. Johnson said such tactics were "accepted practice" at the time and called it a "silly little red herring" raised by a desperate candidate. The voting pattern was similar to the primary: Kelleher won his home of McLean County, 53%–47%, while Johnson again took Champaign, 52%–48%, and 9 of the 11 counties, winning 53%–47% overall. Although Johnson's vote was smaller than that received by Ewing, he outperformed George W. Bush in the district's population centers.

Johnson's district will gain parts of the 19th District in 2002, which will give him a net increase of 58,000; most of the counties just beyond the current district lines are heavily Republican. Kelleher was planning another run against Johnson in March 2001.

Cook's Call   *Potentially Competitive.* Redistricting will certainly take a toll here, as chunks of Democrat David Phelps' 19th District will be merged with the 15th. Still, this new district will retain a healthy Republican registration advantage and Johnson would be favored over Phelps in a 2002 contest.

THE PEOPLE: Pop. 2000: 595,833; Pop. 1990: 571,292, up 4.3% 1990–2000. 85.5% White, 8.8% Black, 2.6% Asian, 0.2% Amer. Indian, 1.4% Two+ races, 1.4% Other; 3% Hispanic Origin.

2000 Presidential Vote

Bush (R)	125,902	(52%)
Gore (D)	105,836	(44%)
Nader (Green)	7,014	(3%)
Others	1,903	(1%)

1996 Presidential Vote

Clinton (D)	100,016	(45%)
Dole (R)	98,926	(45%)
Perot (I)	19,478	(9%)

Rep. Tim Johnson (R)

Elected 2000, 1st term; b. July 23, 1946, Champaign; home, Sidney; U. of IL, B.A. 1969; U. of IL, J.D. 1972; Assembly of God; divorced.

Elected Office: Urbana City Council, 1971–76; IL House of Reps., 1976–2000.

Professional Career: Practicing atty., Johnson, Frank, Frederick & Walsh.

DC Office: 1541 LHOB 20515, 202-225-2371; Fax: 202-226-0791.

District Office: Champaign, 217-403-4690.

Committees: *Agriculture* (21st of 27 R): General Farm Commodities & Risk Management. *Science* (20th of 25 R): Research (Vice Chmn.). *Transportation & Infrastructure* (33d of 42 R): Aviation; Highways & Transit.

Group Ratings and Key Votes: Newly Elected

Election Results

2000 general	Tim Johnson (R)	125,943	(53%)	($1,760,128)
	Mike Kelleher Jr. (D)	110,679	(47%)	($953,233)
2000 primary	Tim Johnson (R)	31,485	(44%)	
	Bill Brady (R)	26,004	(36%)	
	Samuel Y. Ewing (R)	12,526	(17%)	
	Other	2,155	(3%)	
1998 general	Tom Ewing (R)	104,255	(62%)	($546,599)
	Laurel Lunt Prussing (D)	65,054	(38%)	($140,733)

SIXTEENTH DISTRICT

The far northwest corner of Illinois is one of the heartlands of the Republican Party. Here in the town square of Freeport, some 15,000 people came to hear Abraham Lincoln and Stephen Douglas in one of their seven debates, and on terrain most partial to Lincoln. Settled by New England Yankees, northern Illinois was one of the strongest Republican constituencies in 1860 and for years after. Not far away, on a little river once navigable by Mississippi River steamboats, is Galena, one of the earliest settlements in northern Illinois, the home of Ulysses S. Grant before he became general and then president; not far away are Tampico and Dixon, birthplace and boyhood home of Ronald Reagan. Farther up on the Rock River is Rockford, settled by Swedes as well as Yankees, one of America's leading furniture manufacturers at one time, then a major center for machine tools. Politically, northern Illinois, perhaps inspired by Democratic Chicago, remained steadfastly Republican; it backed Herbert Hoover in 1932, Barry Goldwater in 1964 and George Bush in 1992 when most of America and Illinois were going the other way.

The 16th Congressional District consists of much of northwest Illinois, which extends west to the hilly, almost mountainous country around Galena and the Mississippi River, and east to McHenry County, full of new subdivisions surrounding old towns, where Motorola has been opening new cellular phone plants to supply Japan, and affluent young families make their way up through free enterprise and have conservative cultural values; McHenry's 42% growth in the 1990s was the most for any Illinois county. Rockford is a big exporter of machine tools, and Caterpillar, one of the nation's leading exporters, is headquartered nearby and has many subcontractors here.

The congressman from the 16th District is Donald Manzullo, a Republican first elected in 1992. He grew up in Rockford, where his father ran a grocery store, and his brother owns Manzullo's Drive-In Restaurant and Italian Villa. While in college in Washington in the mid-1960s he worked for Republican candidates and he has practiced law in Illinois since 1970. He lives on a cattle-breeding farm, writes poetry and books on constitutional law, and ran a radio talk show; he and his wife home-school two of their three children and started the Northern Illinois Crisis

Pregnancy Center. Manzullo ran for Congress in 1990 and lost the primary 54%–46% to a moderate, who after revelations of personal problems then lost the general to Democrat John Cox. Cox favored increased taxes, opposed capital punishment and was hurt when ultra-Republican McHenry County was added in redistricting. Manzullo ran again and, with support from conservative Christians, beat a moderate 56%–44% in the primary, attacking him for supporting gasoline, cigarette and computer software tax increases in the legislature. Cox campaigned for higher taxes; Manzullo for a 10% across-the-board income tax cut. Manzullo lost narrowly in Rockford and Winnebago County but he won nearly 2–1 in McHenry County and won overall with 56%.

Manzullo is now chairman of the Small Business Committee and a strong supporter of free trade. He supported NAFTA, GATT, the WTO and PNTR for China in the belief that "opening new markets benefits the United States." But he joined many protectionists in arguing against an FTC proposal to reduce the percentage of U.S. content to 75% in goods labeled "Made in U.S.A." He favors eliminating the estate tax and creating individual investment accounts for Social Security. In 1998 and 1999 he sponsored a simplified bill to relieve firms of Y2K liability. He amended the Clean Air Act to make its carpooling provisions voluntary. He got the Navy to stop giving away deactivated ships to allies; it now leases or sells them, generating $600 million in revenue. Prompted by a case in which a 38-year-old McHenry County teacher took a 14-year-old girl to a health clinic for an anti-pregnancy drug, he pressed to require federally funded health clinics to notify parents before dispensing birth control devices or contraceptives; this was passed in October 1998 (too late for Senate action) by 224–220. He has attacked Fannie Mae for what he considered its misleading direct mail campaign against the bill pressed by Financial Services Committee colleague Richard Baker. He says his top priority is Gulf War syndrome, and has called for recognition of the disease if veterans have two of the common symptoms associated with it. He has worked on local projects, including $9 million for the Routes 31 and 62 bypass in Algonquin and a new veterans' outpatient center in McHenry County. He entered Illinois's airport wars by arguing that any third Chicago-area airport should be based in Rockford, which—as he points out—is close to two of the state's fastest-growing counties.

Manzullo has been re-elected easily every two years, running well ahead of George W. Bush in this Republican area in 2000. He gained the Small Business chairmanship over New York's Sue Kelly in January 2001: Manzullo had more seniority, but many lobbyists thought that the more moderate and consensus-minded Kelly would be more productive; but Manzullo was more persuasive to the Republican Steering Committee. Small Business actually has a very limited legislative jurisdiction, but has often been used as a platform for spotlighting innovative and original proposals of the sort Manzullo has produced.

Cook's Call *Safe.* Though this northern Illinois district has a Democratic core in Rockford, it is still pretty safe Republican territory, and Manzullo is well entrenched here. Heavy growth in this suburban county means that Manzullo needs to shed about 40,000 residents. It is likely that McHenry County, now wholly contained in the 16th, will be split between the 16th and Phil Crane's 8th District.

THE PEOPLE: Pop. 2000: 691,356; Pop. 1990: 571,488, up 21% 1990–2000. 88.9% White, 5.1% Black, 1.3% Asian, 0.2% Amer. Indian, 1.4% Two+ races, 2.9% Other; 6.9% Hispanic Origin.

2000 Presidential Vote

Bush (R) 149,917 (54%)
Gore (D) 117,840 (43%)
Nader (Green) 6.878 (2%)
Others 1,958 (1%)

1996 Presidential Vote

Dole (R) 111,641 (47%)
Clinton (D) 99,397 (42%)
Perot (I) 24,153 (10%)

The *Almanac* is now on the Web

with updates!

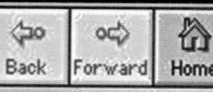

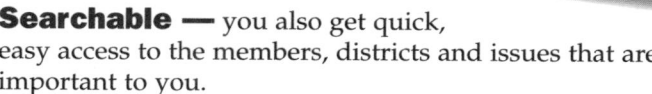

Rep. Donald Manzullo (R)

Elected 1992, 5th term; b. Mar. 24, 1944, Rockford; home, Egan; American U., B.A. 1967, Marquette U., J.D. 1970; Baptist; married (Freda).

Professional Career: Practicing atty., 1970–92; author.

DC Office: 409 CHOB 20515, 202-225-5676; Fax: 202-225-5284; Web site: www.house.gov/manzullo.

District Offices: Crystal Lake, 815-356-9800; Rockford, 815-394-1231.

Committees: *Financial Services* (21st of 37 R): Financial Institutions & Consumer Credit; International Monetary Policy & Trade. *Small Business* (Chmn. of 19 R).

Group Ratings

	ADA	ACLU	AFS	LCV	CON	ITIC	NTU	COC	ACU	NTLC	CHC
2000	5	36	0	7	83	100	67	90	95	94	93
1999	15	—	0	6	70	—	73	96	92	—	—

National Journal Ratings

	1999 LIB	—	1999 CONS		2000 LIB	—	2000 CONS
Economic	24%	—	72%		0%	—	94%
Social	32%	—	66%		26%	—	71%
Foreign	9%	—	91%		39%	—	57%

Key Votes of the 106th Congress

1. Patient Bill of Rights	N	5. Bar RU-486 $ for FDA	Y	9. NATO War in Serbia	N
2. Accelerate Min. Wage	N	6. Display 10 Commandments	Y	10. Perm. Trade with China	Y
3. Strike Ban on Ergo. Stnd.	N	7. Gun Show Bkgrnd. Checks	N	11. Debt Relief for 3rd World	N
4. Ovrd. Estate Tax Veto	Y	8. Ban Part.-Birth Abortion	Y	12. Drop Cuba Econ. Embargo	N

Election Results

2000 general	Donald Manzullo (R)	178,174	(67%)	($674,125)
	Charles W. Hendrickson (D)	88,781	(33%)	($54,882)
2000 primary	Donald Manzullo (R)	unopposed		
1998 general	Donald Manzullo (R)	unopposed		($439,914)

SEVENTEENTH DISTRICT

Illinois's western prairies are some of America's richest agricultural land. They were first settled by Yankees coming overland from northern Indiana and Ohio and Upstate New York. After 1848 Germans left their homeland in search of better opportunities and settled this land that in so many ways resembles the flat, orderly plains of northern Germany. All these migrants farmed quarter-sections and built small towns, with banks and stores, community churches and libraries. In time, investors built farm machinery factories, and the Quad Cities of the Mississippi—Davenport and Bettendorf, Iowa, and Rock Island and Moline, Illinois—became one of the nation's biggest agricultural equipment manufacturing centers. These plants were unionized in the 1930s and 1940s, and in post-World War II America their wages went up as the demand for ever more sophisticated machines rose among the Midwest's government-subsidized farmers. But eventually the cost of subsidies rose too high and the market had its revenge. In the early 1980s farm profits vanished, land values declined and orders for new machinery and equipment dried up. The result was a depression in western Illinois and neighboring Iowa, and a political swing toward the Democrats and away from the Republicans who had been the ancestral party in most of this area. In the 1990s the Democratic tide receded a bit, but this was still one of the few parts of rural America carried by Al Gore in 2000.

The 17th Congressional District includes most of Illinois' Mississippi River border with Iowa plus half a dozen more prairie counties to the east. For years its Democratic base in the Quad Cities was outvoted by Republican counties elsewhere. But for most of the last 20 years this has been a Democratic district. Its demographics are changing as a wave of Hispanics have been drawn to places like the Rock River industrial town of Sterling; they now comprise 19% of its 15,000 residents.

The congressman from the 17th District is Lane Evans, a Democrat elected in 1982 and now the ranking minority member on the Veterans Affairs Committee. Evans grew up in Rock Island, the son of a union firefighter. He joined the Marine Corps in 1969 after high school and served two years, then went to college and law school and worked as a legal services lawyer. In 1982, he ran for Congress—a seemingly quixotic race against longtime incumbent Republican Tom Railsback. But Railsback lost his primary to a conservative and the economically hard-pressed district voted 53% for Evans. He calls himself a "populist" rather than a liberal; by most standards his voting record is solidly liberal and one of the most pro-union in the House. He was a strong opponent of NAFTA, GATT and permanent trade relations with China. He fervently favored higher agricultural subsidies during his five-year tenure on the Agriculture Committee, but left that post to take a seat on Armed Services in 1988, even as farm subsidies were cut back in 1985, 1990 and 1996. Evans is co-chairman of the Alcohol Fuels Caucus; he helped the ethanol tax credit get extended from 2000 to 2007 in the 1998 transportation bill. He was one of 31 Democrats who voted for the Republicans' impeachment inquiry in October 1998, though he later voted solidly against impeachment.

Evans has devoted much time to veterans' issues. He worked hard for years to get compensation for veterans who claimed they were harmed by exposure to Agent Orange, and ultimately succeeded. In 1994 he began to investigate what he and others have characterized as Gulf war syndrome. In 1996 Evans passed a bill providing benefits to children of Vietnam veterans exposed to Agent Orange who were born with spina bifida—the first entitlement for children of veterans.

On Armed Services, Evans worked on finding alternatives to tritium production; he also questioned how much export controls should be relaxed on critical weapons materials. His major cause on the committee has been a ban on land mines, which continue to injure thousands years after wars are over. In 1996 he passed a one-year moratorium, to begin in 1999, but it was repealed by Congress in 1998. In 1997 he co-sponsored, with Republican Jack Quinn, a total ban along the lines championed by Canada and agreed to by many other nations; his ban would include "smart" mines, those which remain explosive for only a limited time and, after a 12-year exemption, all mines in South Korea. This approach was rejected by the Clinton administration, which wanted to keep mines in South Korea to repel any attack by North Korea.

In the years of agricultural unrest and high unemployment in western Illinois, Evans was re-elected by wide margins. But in recent years his margins have been narrower. In 1994 against an underfunded candidate he won with 55%. In the last three elections he faced Mark Baker, a TV anchor until 1996 in Quincy, in the southern end of the district. In 1996 Evans won 52%–47%, carrying Rock Island and the central part of the district, but losing the northern end and the area around Quincy by wide margins. In 1998 the race was targeted early on by Republicans and Baker raised more PAC money than any other House challenger. In May 1998 Evans announced he had Parkinson's disease, which was diagnosed in 1995; he said he could not stand long without pain or smile easily, but could still jog and that he had lost weight under doctor's orders. Evans ultimately raised and spent almost $1.3 million and appealed strongly to the 38,000 Farm Bureau members in the district; he depended heavily on organized labor and liberal volunteers. The result was almost exactly the same as in 1996: Evans won 52%–48%. He increased his percentages in Rock Island County and the counties immediately east and south; Baker increased his percentages in the north and south parts of the district.

In 2000 Baker ran again, but this time the race was not as high on the Republican target list and Evans had a money advantage. Baker had primary opposition from retired surgeon Harold Bayne, but won 65%–28%; Bayne supported Evans in the fall. Baker attacked Evans for taking "bunny money" from *Playboy* founder Hugh Hefner and ran ads showing him with union members. Evans spent much of his ad budget talking about his Parkinson's disease; one showed him jogging and saying, "If you hear someone say they're worried about Lane Evans, tell them you saw him running today and he's doing just fine." This time Evans widened his margin to 55%–45%, once again winning big in Rock Island County and losing counties in the southern and northern ends of the district. This was a party-line race: the two candidates' percentages closely paralleled those of Al Gore and George W. Bush. Because it needs to add 85,000 people, redistricting will change the boundaries of the 17th at least slightly for 2002, which might tilt the district a little away from Evans since almost all the adjacent counties are Republican.

Cook's Call   *Competitive*. This competitive Quad Cities district will never be an easy one for Evans to hold onto. After surviving four tight races, however, it is hard to see what more Republicans can try to do to knock him out. If Evans decides to leave (his health may be a factor), Republicans have a good shot of picking it up.

THE PEOPLE: Pop. 2000: 567,712; Pop. 1990: 571,585, down 0.7% 1990–2000. 92.2% White, 3.7% Black, 0.7% Asian, 0.2% Amer. Indian, 1.2% Two+ races, 1.9% Other; 4.6% Hispanic Origin.

2000 Presidential Vote		
Gore (D)	126,987	(51%)
Bush (R)	113,520	(46%)
Nader (Green)	4,836	(2%)
Others	2,280	(1%)

1996 Presidential Vote		
Clinton (D)	119,918	(51%)
Dole (R)	89,447	(38%)
Perot (I)	23,176	(10%)

Rep. Lane Evans (D)

Elected 1982, 11th term; b. Aug. 4, 1951, Rock Island; home, Rock Island; Augustana Col., B.A. 1974, Georgetown U., J.D. 1978; Catholic; single.

Military Career: Marine Corps, 1969–71.

Professional Career: Practicing atty., 1978–82.

DC Office: 2211 RHOB 20515, 202-225-5905; Fax: 202-225-5396; Web site: www.house.gov/evans.

District Offices: Galesburg, 309-342-4411; Moline, 309-793-5760.

Committees: *Armed Services* (4th of 28 D): Military Procurement; Military Readiness. *Veterans' Affairs* (RMM of 14 D): Benefits.

Group Ratings

	ADA	ACLU	AFS	LCV	CON	ITIC	NTU	COC	ACU	NTLC	CHC
2000	95	79	100	93	46	44	20	38	8	19	0
1999	100	—	100	94	17	—	17	16	0	—	—

National Journal Ratings

	1999 LIB	—	1999 CONS		2000 LIB	—	2000 CONS
Economic	84%	—	12%		77%	—	22%
Social	76%	—	24%		72%	—	26%
Foreign	89%	—	8%		77%	—	21%

Key Votes of the 106th Congress

1. Patient Bill of Rights	Y	5. Bar RU-486 $ for FDA	N	9. NATO War in Serbia	Y
2. Accelerate Min. Wage	Y	6. Display 10 Commandments	N	10. Perm. Trade with China	N
3. Strike Ban on Ergo. Stnd.	Y	7. Gun Show Bkgrnd. Checks	Y	11. Debt Relief for 3rd World	Y
4. Ovrd. Estate Tax Veto	N	8. Ban Part.-Birth Abortion	N	12. Drop Cuba Econ. Embargo	Y

Election Results

2000 general	Lane Evans (D)	132,494	(55%)	($1,230,267)
	Mark Baker (R)	108,853	(45%)	($984,857)
2000 primary	Lane Evans (D)	unopposed		
1998 general	Lane Evans (D)	100,128	(52%)	($1,203,109)
	Mark Baker (R)	94,072	(48%)	($1,306,748)

EIGHTEENTH DISTRICT

Old vaudeville bookers, presented with a new act, used to ask, "Will it play in Peoria?" The implication was that if an act went over in this small city on the bluffs above the Illinois River, 154 miles from Chicago and 171 miles from St. Louis, it would go over just about anywhere. In the first half of this century, Peoria did seem pretty typical of America. If its citizens were mostly of British or German descent, with a small percentage of blacks, that was the image of ordinary America that prevailed up through the 1960s, despite the great immigrations of 1880–1924 and the northward urban migrations of southern rural blacks of 1940–1965. But Peoria's economy, arguably typical at mid-century, is less so today. This is still a heavy manufacturing town, dominated by big plants that produce farm machinery and earth-moving equipment. Its biggest employer is Caterpillar, the world's leading producer of earth-moving and construction equipment, and one of America's major exporters. There are more than just memories here of the sharp divide between blue collar and white collar, union and management, Democrat and Republican—the basis of the class warfare politics that was the norm in the heavy industrial metropolises of the Great Lakes region for three or four decades starting with the sit-down strikes of the late 1930s. But the blue-collar workers now are not as numerous and the unions not as strong. The Peoria area went through terrible times in the 1980s, as big farm machinery plants laid off workers and even closed down. Then Caterpillar, struck by the United Auto Workers in 1992, hired replacement workers and continued to operate—not without some friction and inefficiency, but profitably—something unheard of a dozen or more years before. Not until March 1998 did union members approve a settlement, pretty much on the company's terms. The net effect helps to explain why the population dropped by a few hundred in the 1990s, and Peoria slipped from 3rd to 5th among the largest cities in Illinois.

Illinois' 18th Congressional District, variously configured, has been the Peoria district since the 1940s. It has been represented by two national Republican leaders: from 1933–49 by Everett McKinley Dirksen, who was elected senator in 1950 and was Senate Republican leader from 1959–69, and Robert Michel, congressman from 1957–95 and Republican House leader from 1981–95. The 18th's boundaries have changed considerably over that time; currently they extend south along the Illinois River and to the northern edge of Springfield, away from historically Republican Peoria toward the historically marginal counties of central Illinois. It is the home of Eureka College, which dedicated the Ronald Reagan Peace Garden in honor of its 1932 graduate and the end of the Cold War that he helped to achieve.

The congressman from the 18th District is Ray LaHood, a Republican elected in 1994. LaHood grew up in Peoria, the grandson of an immigrant from Lebanon and son of a restaurant manager. He worked his way through school, spent six years teaching in Catholic schools, then moved to Rock Island, where he worked with delinquent teens and became a staffer for Congressman Tom Railsback. He served in the Illinois House in 1982 (when the speaker was George Ryan, now governor), then worked for Congressman Robert Michel in Peoria and, from 1990–94, as his chief of staff in Washington. Michel, a pleasant and decent man who could be a tough partisan on occasion but always maintained amicable relations with Democratic leaders, opposed Newt Gingrich's election as minority whip in March 1989. Gingrich pointedly declined to rule out running against Michel for Republican leader after the 1994 election; Michel, faced with a December 1993 filing deadline, decided to retire. LaHood ran to replace his boss, and in the Republican primary beat state Representative Judy Koehler, 50%–40%, carrying the Peoria area but running behind in the rest of the district. In the general, LaHood's Democratic opponent was Douglas Stephens, a labor lawyer and small businessmen, who held Michel to 52% in 1982 and 55% in 1988. Stephens favored school prayer, term limits and abortion restrictions, and called for House members to debate and vote from their districts via interactive television. He put on an energetic campaign, but in this Republican year LaHood carried all but one county and won 60%–39%.

LaHood's voting record has been toward the middle of the House. An odd man out under Speaker Gingrich, LaHood became one of its most visible members in Gingrich's final days as speaker. He was one of only three Republicans who did not sign the Contract with America; he had reservations about voting for tax cuts until the budget was balanced. He worked on the 1996 Freedom to Farm Act, which phased out most farm subsidies, and went after food stamp fraud as well. But he disliked the Republicans' confrontational strategy in the 1995–96 budget crisis. During those years, decrying the angry tone of House debate, LaHood and Democrat David Skaggs started the Bipartisan Retreat at Hershey, Pennsylvania, "to foster a Congress that is more civil and to create better communication among members." He also gained a niche by probably presiding over the House more often than any other member in the past half-decade. With his experience in monitoring the floor for Michel, LaHood's evenhanded rulings, his surefooted mastery of parliamentary procedure and his determination to maintain decorum were widely appreciated. He was called on often to preside when controversial issues were debated: the partial-birth abortion ban, the Medicare overhaul, and the impeachment of Bill Clinton. Even when LaHood had self-evident sentiments about the issue himself—he had called on Clinton to pay the $4.4 million cost of the Monica Lewinsky investigation—few if any complained about his fairness; as he said, "People recognize that I have the ability to handle controversial matters but do it in a very fair way." Democratic Representative Tom Barrett praised his "evenhandedness," and during the impeachment debate he even received applause from Democrats.

With Gingrich's ouster and replacement by new Speaker Dennis Hastert, LaHood suddenly was well placed with House leaders. After the 2000 election he made a concerted effort to take the Illinois slot on the Appropriations Committee that was opened by retiring John Porter; with Hastert's support, he was successful and won a seat on the Budget Committee as well. He welcomed the disputed 2000 presidential election count in Florida as an opportunity to advance his long-time advocacy of abolishing the Electoral College and replacing it with a national popular-vote count. For years, his proposal barely got attention, other than a single hearing day in 1997 from the House Judiciary Committee, where chairman Henry Hyde of Illinois voiced his opposition. Now, LaHood said, Hastert promised that the proposal would get a full airing, despite the formidable odds against constitutional ratification.

LaHood has worked for district interests. He says that he has supported Caterpillar 90% of the time and in 1998 worked to lift duties off four chemicals used to produce herbicides at DuPont's request. With neighbor Tom Ewing he won enactment of an extension of the ethanol tax credit from 2000 to 2007. He has been willing to tangle with colleagues on behalf of local interests. He wants to promote the Illinois River, for both transportation and recreation; he bristled when the 20th District's John Shimkus came out against its designation as an American Heritage River. And when the 11th District's Jerry Weller got Joliet's new veterans' cemetery named after Abraham Lincoln, LaHood got a sentence in an appropriations bill revoking that, for fear of confusion with Springfield's Oak Ridge Cemetery, where Lincoln is buried.

LaHood has been re-elected by wide margins throughout his district. Needing to add 56,000 persons, the lines of the 18th will change again in redistricting, possibly by moving closer to Chicago, but it's not likely to threaten LaHood.

Cook's Call *Safe*. Though this district is not as Republican as it once was, it retains a good Republican core. LaHood has carved out a moderate, pragmatic image that the voters in this Peoria-based district have appreciated in their congressmen for years. The city of Peoria has lost some population and this district will need to pick up some territory during redistricting.

THE PEOPLE: Pop. 2000: 597,447; Pop. 1990: 572,238, up 4.4% 1990–2000. 90.9% White, 6.4% Black, 0.9% Asian, 0.2% Amer. Indian, 1% Two + races, 0.6% Other; 1.5% Hispanic Origin.

2000 Presidential Vote				1996 Presidential Vote		
Bush (R)	147,884	(55%)		Dole (R)	118,572	(47%)
Gore (D)	115,818	(43%)		Clinton (D)	112,678	(44%)
Nader (Green)	4,878	(2%)		Perot (I)	20,975	(8%)
Others	1,900	(1%)				

Rep. Ray LaHood (R)

Elected 1994, 4th term; b. Dec. 6, 1945, Peoria; home, Peoria; Canton Jr. Col., 1963–65, Bradley U., B.S. 1971; Catholic; married (Kathy).

Elected Office: IL House of Reps., 1982.

Professional Career: Jr. High Schl. Teacher, 1971–77; Dir., Rock Island Youth Svcs., 1972–74; Chief Planner, Bi-state Planning Comm., 1974–76; Dist. A.A., U.S. Rep. Tom Railsback, 1977–82; Dist. A.A., U.S. Rep. Bob Michel, 1983–90, Chief of Staff, 1990–94.

DC Office: 1424 LHOB 20515, 202-225-6201; Fax: 202-225-9249; Web site: www.house.gov/lahood.

District Offices: Jacksonville, 217-245-1431; Peoria, 309-671-7027; Springfield, 217-793-0808.

Committees: *Appropriations* (32d of 35 R): Agriculture, Rural Development, & FDA; The Legislative Branch. *Budget* (17th of 24 R). *Permanent Select Committee on Intelligence* (6th of 11 R): Human Intelligence, Analysis & Counterintelligence; Intelligence Policy & National Security (Vice Chmn.).

Group Ratings

	ADA	ACLU	AFS	LCV	CON	ITIC	NTU	COC	ACU	NTLC	CHC
2000	15	21	0	21	75	94	57	95	72	73	93
1999	15	—	33	19	59	—	59	84	66	—	—

National Journal Ratings

	1999 LIB	—	1999 CONS		2000 LIB	—	2000 CONS
Economic	43%	—	56%		44%	—	55%
Social	40%	—	59%		43%	—	55%
Foreign	28%	—	70%		45%	—	53%

Key Votes of the 106th Congress

1. Patient Bill of Rights	N	5. Bar RU-486 $ for FDA	Y	9. NATO War in Serbia	N
2. Accelerate Min. Wage	Y	6. Display 10 Commandments	Y	10. Perm. Trade with China	Y
3. Strike Ban on Ergo. Stnd.	N	7. Gun Show Bkgrnd. Checks	N	11. Debt Relief for 3rd World	N
4. Ovrd. Estate Tax Veto	Y	8. Ban Part.-Birth Abortion	Y	12. Drop Cuba Econ. Embargo	Y

Election Results

2000 general	Ray LaHood (R)	173,706	(67%)	($974,251)
	Joyce Harant (D)	85,317	(33%)	($86,262)
2000 primary	Ray LaHood (R)	unopposed		
1998 general	Ray LaHood (R)	unopposed		($489,326)

NINETEENTH DISTRICT

Southern Illinois is a land of prairies, of flat, treeless land sloping imperceptibly down to the Ohio and Mississippi rivers. It was settled almost entirely from the south by farmers coming overland from Kentucky, such as Abraham Lincoln's family. Just beyond the Ohio River, they found hilly terrain, some of which turned out to have coal deposits. To the north they must have been astonished, after miles of thick forest, to see the great American prairie stretch before them, a vast sea of empty land extending past the horizon. The prairie lands proved wondrously rich, and were soon crisscrossed by rail lines taking their produce away and bringing in products of industrial civilization from St. Louis, Chicago and points east. About the same time, vast coal deposits were found in southern Illinois, producing one mining town after another: This was the home turf of John L. Lewis, the imperious leader of the United Mine Workers for half a century and, in the late 1930s and early 1940s, one of the most powerful and eloquent figures in American politics.

   The 19th Congressional District covers most of the eastern half of southern Illinois. Mostly it is south of the old National Road, which became U.S. 40 and is paralleled by Interstate 70, the traditional boundary between the part of Downstate Illinois settled by Southerners and that settled by Yankees—a boundary also between traditional Democrats and traditional Republicans. North of that line, the 19th includes Decatur, a small city that's been known as home of the giant Archer

Daniels Midland Company, a major processor of corn and soybeans and the major producer and promoter of government-subsidized ethanol. Decatur got unwanted attention in late 1999 when a brawl at a local high school football game led to expulsions of several black students, protests by Rev. Jesse Jackson, and a federal court ruling upholding school officials. More negative publicity came a year later when it was revealed that defective Bridgestone/ Firestone tires were produced in a local factory. About a third of the 19th is prairie, straddling or south of the National Road; the other third is far Downstate, the Egypt region as it is called, where people speak with what Yankees regard as Southern accents and Southern mores prevail, including an attachment to a conservatively inclined Democratic Party.

The congressman from the 19th District is David Phelps, a Democrat elected in 1998 to replace Glenn Poshard, who after 10 years in the House ran for governor, won the Democratic nomination, but lost the general election. Phelps grew up in Eldorado, about 20 miles from Kentucky, and graduated from Southern Illinois University. His family always led the singing at the General Baptist Church and David, the youngest son, developed a good tenor and a gift for songwriting. With his brothers he formed the Phelps Brothers Gospel Singing Group; they had offers to tour nationally but instead sang in southern Illinois. But they did travel to Nashville—much closer in every way to this part of Illinois than Chicago—to cut records, and their songs were performed by the Oak Ridge Boys. Phelps was twice elected Saline County clerk and recorder; in 1984 he was elected to the Illinois House, beating a five-term Republican incumbent. His voting record there was anti-abortion, anti-gun control and for the death penalty; he worked to improve health care and education in rural areas.

In his first House campaign, Phelps stressed his similarities to Poshard: "I grew up 15 miles from Glenn Poshard. We go way back. We taught together. We came to Springfield together, with the same agenda." This certainly helped; Poshard's nomination for governor meant that there would be a strong Democratic turnout in November. Republicans nominated Evangelical minister and attorney Brent Winters, the party's nominee in the last two elections, but he had little money left after his primary. Phelps had support from the Blue Dogs and New Democrats, and plenty of money from party sources; national Republicans discounted Winters' chances. Winters tried to raise the impeachment issue in August, when Phelps said he was "disappointed," but still supported Clinton. In November, Winters carried six counties around his home base of Charleston and in the middle of the district. But Phelps won by a solid margin in the northern area around Decatur and carried the southern counties in and near his state legislative district by more than 2–1 margins, for a 58%–42% win overall. Meanwhile, Poshard—weak in the suburbs and northern Downstate—carried the district over George Ryan 70%–30%, while losing 51%–47% statewide.

In the House, Phelps joined the Blue Dogs and stayed away from Beltway insider circles. He continued to oppose abortion and gun control and supported term limits. He has sought more federal money to his district for economic development, highways and bridges, quality schools, and improved health care. Perhaps his toughest vote as a freshman was on permanent normal trade relations with China, with Phelps torn between his labor backers and his pro-trade farmers and Archer Daniels Midland. He received personal lobbying from President Clinton and researched the issue at length but turned down an administration offer to join a delegation to China. In the end, Phelps said, he opposed the deal because of China's human rights record and its failure to keep its past promises. He called the debate overly polarized, with undue optimism from business and fear from labor. As for local businesses, he said that they already were doing business in China and would continue to do so. Meanwhile, he stayed active with the Phelps Brothers Quartet, performing before 15,000 their "The Lord Will Make a Way, Somehow" at a gospelsinging concert at Southern Illinois University.

Phelps was re-elected easily in 2000, carrying all but two counties. With virtually no population change in the 1990s, the 19th will need to add 75,000 persons.

Cook's Call   *Competitive.* With the state forced to lose a seat, this Downstate district fell victim to the redistricting knife. The final bipartisan plan by House Speaker Dennis Hastert and Democrat Bill Lipinski chopped up this rural district and merged it with the 15th. Other parts of the 19th are parceled out to the 12th and 20th Districts as well. Phelps will likely be forced to run against 15th District Representative Tim Johnson in a Republican leaning district.

THE PEOPLE: Pop. 2000: 575,769; Pop. 1990: 571,390, up 0.8% 1990–2000. 93.6% White, 4.6% Black, 0.4% Asian, 0.2% Amer. Indian, 0.8% Two+ races, 0.3% Other; 1% Hispanic Origin.

2000 Presidential Vote

Bush (R)	136,984	(54%)
Gore (D)	107,984	(43%)
Nader (Green)	4,214	(2%)
Others	2,468	(1%)

1996 Presidential Vote

Clinton (D)	113,635	(47%)
Dole (R)	97,977	(41%)
Perot (I)	28,653	(12%)

Rep. David Phelps (D)

Elected 1998, 2d term; b. Oct. 26, 1947, Eldorado; home, Eldorado; S. IL U., B.S. 1969; Baptist; married (Leslie).

Elected Office: Saline Cnty. Clerk & Recorder, 1980–84; IL House of Reps., 1984–98.

Professional Career: Gospel singer/songwriter; Public schl. teacher & Asst. Principal, 1969–73; Small Businessman, 1973–80.

DC Office: 1523 LHOB 20515, 202-225-5201; Fax: 202-225-1541; Web site: www.house.gov/phelps.

District Offices: Charleston, 217-345-9166; Decatur, 217-425-8819; Effingham, 217-342-7220; Eldorado, 618-273-8203; Lawrenceville, 618-943-6036; Marion, 618-997-6004; West Frankfort, 618-937-6402.

Committees: *Agriculture* (15th of 24 D): Conservation, Credit, Rural Development & Research; General Farm Commodities & Risk Management. *Small Business* (10th of 17 D): Regulatory Reform Oversight; Rural Enterprises, Agricultural and Technology.

Group Ratings

	ADA	ACLU	AFS	LCV	CON	ITIC	NTU	COC	ACU	NTLC	CHC
2000	50	29	85	43	59	56	37	57	32	15	47
1999	60	—	100	63	63	—	21	28	32	—	—

National Journal Ratings

	1999 LIB	—	1999 CONS		2000 LIB	—	2000 CONS
Economic	67%	—	32%		59%	—	41%
Social	40%	—	59%		30%	—	68%
Foreign	57%	—	43%		61%	—	38%

Key Votes of the 106th Congress

1. Patient Bill of Rights	Y	5. Bar RU-486 $ for FDA	Y	9. NATO War in Serbia	N
2. Accelerate Min. Wage	Y	6. Display 10 Commandments	Y	10. Perm. Trade with China	N
3. Strike Ban on Ergo. Stnd.	Y	7. Gun Show Bkgrnd. Checks	N	11. Debt Relief for 3rd World	Y
4. Ovrd. Estate Tax Veto	Y	8. Ban Part.-Birth Abortion	Y	12. Drop Cuba Econ. Embargo	Y

Election Results

2000 general	David Phelps (D)	155,101	(65%)	($300,056)
	James Eatherly (R)	85,137	(35%)	($25,378)
2000 primary	David Phelps (D)	unopposed		
1998 general	David Phelps (D)	122,430	(58%)	($642,177)
	Brent Winters (R)	87,614	(42%)	($424,347)

TWENTIETH DISTRICT

Springfield, the capital of Illinois, has changed rather little since its great moment in history—when it was the home of Abraham Lincoln, lawyer, unsuccessful candidate for re-election to Congress and 16th president of the United States. Today, beyond the suburban fringe, the prairie countryside outside Springfield is still mostly farmland with few towns. Farming technology has changed vastly, but the patterns of cultivation, the contours of the land, even the shape of the ribbons of back country roads, cannot be entirely different from what Lincoln saw as a lawyer making his way from one county seat to another on the circuit. Nor has downtown Springfield changed as much since Lincoln's time as have downtown Columbus or Indianapolis or even Des Moines. If most of the office fronts and houses captured in the old photographs are gone, some remain; and the scale has not changed utterly. Lincoln's clapboard house is still in Springfield, and so is the courtroom where he argued cases before federal judges; the Greek revival downtown block where Lincoln & Herndon kept their law offices is open for inspection, as is the state Capitol building built here in 1839. Much of today's Springfield is tawdry, but unlike other state capitals it has not lost its 19th Century scale.

The 20th Congressional District of Illinois is one of only 19 that can claim to be the lineal descendant of a district whose representative also became a president of the United States. It includes the southern half of Springfield and much of the Downstate Illinois prairie, which in 1846 elected a 37-year-old railroad lawyer and Whig opponent of the Mexican War named Abraham Lincoln to his single term in the House. Lincoln's denunciation of the Mexican War was so strong that he gave up any chance of a second term, for the countryside south and west of Springfield, straddling the National Road and along the Illinois River, both avenues of migration from the South, was strongly supportive of that war. Similar sentiments—a cultural conservatism, strong national pride—are still apparent here today.

The congressman from the 20th District is John Shimkus, a Republican elected in 1996. Shimkus grew up in Collinsville, a county seat in Madison County, on the other side of the Mississippi River from St. Louis; he is of Lithuanian descent, as is his House predecessor, Democratic Senator Richard Durbin. Shimkus graduated from West Point, trained in the Army as a ranger and paratrooper, studied in California, then came back to Collinsville to teach high school. Almost immediately he began running for local office. In 1988 he ran for the Madison County Board, and lost; in 1989 he was elected Collinsville Township Trustee; in 1990, at 32, he beat a 12-year incumbent and was elected Madison County treasurer, the only Republican countywide officer, and was re-elected in 1994. In 1992 he ran against Congressman Richard Durbin, and, though heavily outspent ($921,000 to $278,000), held him to a 57%–43% victory. In 1995, when Durbin decided to run for the Senate seat being vacated by Paul Simon, Shimkus decided to run for Congress again. In a field of eight candidates, he easily won the Republican primary with 51%. In the general election he faced state Representative Jay Hoffman. Both were anti-abortion, anti-gun control, and pro-balanced budget amendment. But Shimkus took and Hoffman refused to take Americans for Tax Reform's pledge not to raise taxes. Hoffman raised more money and had the benefit of AFL-CIO ads, but Shimkus won by 50.3%–49.7%, a margin of 1,238 votes. Hoffman carried the Democratic counties between Springfield and Madison County and the coal country in the southeast; Shimkus, campaigning in a Winnebago with his wife and two infant sons, did well in the farthest rural corners of the district and, critically, carried both Madison County and Springfield.

In the House, Shimkus got a seat on the Commerce Committee—a feat for a freshman—and used it to sponsor one small but locally important piece of legislation. This was his amendment that qualified the soybean-diesel fuel blend B-20 for the alternative fuels program. This would make vehicles able to use B-20 qualify for the federal environmental quotas, and the Clinton administration opposed it, arguing that any standard diesel fuel engine would qualify. But Shimkus, working with Democrat Karen McCarthy, got it enacted. On other commerce issues, he supported financial services deregulation, reducing Superfund litigation and reducing the FCC's regulatory power. He opposed further restrictions on tobacco advertising, for fear it would raise a constitutional issue. He is a strong advocate of permanent normal trade status for China: "I truly believe this is the best way to free the Chinese people. Trade is the best way to create religious freedom and the best way to aid the persecuted." He voted for the Shays-Meehan campaign finance bill. He took the lead among House Republicans in passing a $1 hourly increase in the minimum wage, which became entangled in a Clinton vs. Congress conflict over tax cuts on the eve of the 2000 election.

For a junior member, Shimkus has encountered more than his share of controversy. He was a member of the bipartisan task force to select a new House chaplain, which prompted a bitter fight when Democrats said that Republican leaders overruled the task force's recommendation of Father Timothy O'Brien, a Roman Catholic priest from Milwaukee. Although Shimkus said that he had supported O'Brien, he defended the decision of Speaker Dennis Hastert and Majority Leader Dick Armey to select the Reverend Charles Parker Wright, a Presbyterian. Shimkus called the conflict "the worst thing that has happened" to him as a member of Congress. Eventually, Hastert selected a Catholic priest from Chicago. Later, Shimkus found himself in perhaps an even more unusual conflict: an internal feud over Lincoln among Illinois Republicans. When Governor George Ryan sought federal funding for an Abraham Lincoln presidential library in Springfield, Senator Peter Fitzgerald objected that the state's contracting procedures were inadequate to prevent favoritism and that federal guidelines should be used. That infuriated not only Ryan but also House Republicans, including Hastert, who accused Fitzgerald of grandstanding. Shimkus sought to broker a deal by calling for a panel to review contracts for the state project. But that did not satisfy Fitzgerald, who filibustered the appropriation bill for several more days until he was apparently satisfied that he had made his point. Shimkus had a more rewarding experience when he joined several colleagues on Representative John Lewis's commemoration of his 1965 civil rights march to Selma, Alabama. He said that the event would not score him points in his district, but that it was a "statement to me" in remembrance of sacrifices that others had made.

Despite competitive challengers, Shimkus has twice won re-election with more than 60% of the vote—winning all 19 counties in 2000—bigger wins than might have been expected given the district's recent history.

Cook's Call   *Safe.* This is the most marginal of the Downstate districts, but Democrats have been unable to find a credible challenger since coming close in 1996; that has helped Shimkus to establish a pretty good hold on this seat. Like the rest of Downstate, this district needs to gain population in redistricting (about 52,000 people). The congressional map passed in 2001 pushes the 20th District further south and west into parts of what is now the 19th District.

THE PEOPLE: Pop. 2000: 601,341; Pop. 1990: 571,138, up 5.3% 1990–2000. 92.4% White, 5.6% Black, 0.5% Asian, 0.2% Amer. Indian, 0.9% Two+ races, 0.4% Other; 1.1% Hispanic Origin.

2000 Presidential Vote		
Bush (R)	135,727	(52%)
Gore (D)	119,161	(45%)
Nader (Green)	4,909	(2%)
Others	2,268	(1%)

1996 Presidential Vote		
Clinton (D)	117,775	(47%)
Dole (R)	101,634	(41%)
Perot (I)	26,431	(11%)

Rep. John M. Shimkus (R)

Elected 1996, 3d term; b. Feb. 21, 1958, Collinsville; home, Collinsville; West Point Military Acad., B.S. 1980, Christ Col., Teaching Cert., 1990, S. IL U., M.B.A. 1997; Lutheran; married (Karen).

Military Career: Army 1980–85; Army Reserves, 1985-present.

Elected Office: Collinsville Township Trustee, 1989–93; Madison Cnty. Tres., 1990–96.

Professional Career: High schl. teacher, 1986–90.

DC Office: 513 CHOB 20515, 202-225-5271; Fax: 202-225-5880; Web site: www.house.gov/shimkus.

District Offices: Collinsville, 618-344-3065; Springfield, 217-492-5090.

Committees: *Energy & Commerce* (16th of 31 R): Commerce, Trade & Consumer Protection; Energy & Air Quality; Environment & Hazardous Materials (Vice Chmn.); Telecommunications & The Internet.

Group Ratings

	ADA	ACLU	AFS	LCV	CON	ITIC	NTU	COC	ACU	NTLC	CHC
2000	10	14	14	14	59	89	58	80	80	79	87
1999	15	—	16	0	28	—	53	96	80	—	—

National Journal Ratings

	1999 LIB	—	1999 CONS		2000 LIB	—	2000 CONS
Economic	30%	—	64%		34%	—	64%
Social	10%	—	85%		37%	—	62%
Foreign	15%	—	81%		33%	—	62%

Key Votes of the 106th Congress

1. Patient Bill of Rights	N	5. Bar RU-486 $ for FDA	Y	9. NATO War in Serbia	N
2. Accelerate Min. Wage	Y	6. Display 10 Commandments	Y	10. Perm. Trade with China	Y
3. Strike Ban on Ergo. Stnd.	N	7. Gun Show Bkgrnd. Checks	N	11. Debt Relief for 3rd World	N
4. Ovrd. Estate Tax Veto	Y	8. Ban Part.-Birth Abortion	Y	12. Drop Cuba Econ. Embargo	Y

Election Results

2000 general	John M. Shimkus (R)	161,393	(63%)	($645,920)
	Jeffrey S. Cooper (D)	94,382	(37%)	($233,699)
2000 primary	John M. Shimkus (R)	unopposed		
1998 general	John M. Shimkus (R)	121,103	(61%)	($677,009)
	Rick Verticchio (D)	76,475	(39%)	($245,796)

★ INDIANA ★

Every Memorial Day the nation's eyes turn to Indianapolis, the center of a state with the nation's most distinctive nickname—Hoosier—and some of its least distinctive borders, for a sports spectacle celebrating the knack for tinkering and the taste for powerful machines that make the Midwest the nation's manufacturing center: the Indianapolis 500. This combination of sports and manufacturing is symbolic of Indiana's strengths and successes. The image of its manufacturing base and sports heritage seems as antique as the bricks with which the Indianapolis Speedway was originally paved, though all but one yard at the start/finish line has long since been asphalted. Indiana's manufacturing economy, after rough years in the early 1980s, is now humming: high-skill, high-employment and high-tech. The Speedway is literally at the center of American manufacturing: Almost precisely half the country's manufacturing jobs are east of Indiana and the other half west, almost half are north and half south. Indiana itself has the nation's second-highest percentage of workers in manufacturing and is the number one steel producer with its giant, heavily automated steel mills on the south shore of Lake Michigan. Indiana leads the nation in making elevators, refrigerators, engines, engine-electrical equipment, recreational vehicles, mobile homes, and truck and bus bodies. It gave the world canned pork and beans, tomato juice, the Coca-Cola bottle and Alka-Seltzer.

Nor are Indiana's days of innovation over. Just as it has attracted new teams and events to Indianapolis's sports facilities, the small factories set amidst farm landscape or at the edge of small cities have become centers of advanced manufacturing innovation. Indiana's job growth was slow in the 1980s as it shed low-wage, low-skill jobs. Today, its income levels are slightly less than the national average and well below those not only of the coasts but also of the Chicago area just over the state line. But housing and health care costs are also lower than average, and the tax burden lower and tort laws are generally less onerous. Indiana's economy is export-oriented, and it has more Japanese companies than any states but California and Ohio; it cheered the opening of trade to China. But its manufacturing sector is vulnerable to downturns in the economy and high oil prices, and some of its business leaders worry that too many of its high school and college graduates leave Indiana for larger metropolitan areas.

Culturally, Indiana is like an older America; it retains some of the old norms that in the 1920s and 1930s brought sociologists Robert and Helen Lynd in their search for the typical American place to "Middletown" (actually Muncie). There was little controversy over a law allowing the Ten Commandments to be posted in schools, courts and other public buildings. Ethnically, Indiana seems older too: Except for the steel area around Gary—really an extension of the Chicago metropolitan area—Indiana has relatively few descendants from the 1840–1924 wave of immigration and only a small flow of recent Hispanic or Asian migrants. The major metropolitan area, India-

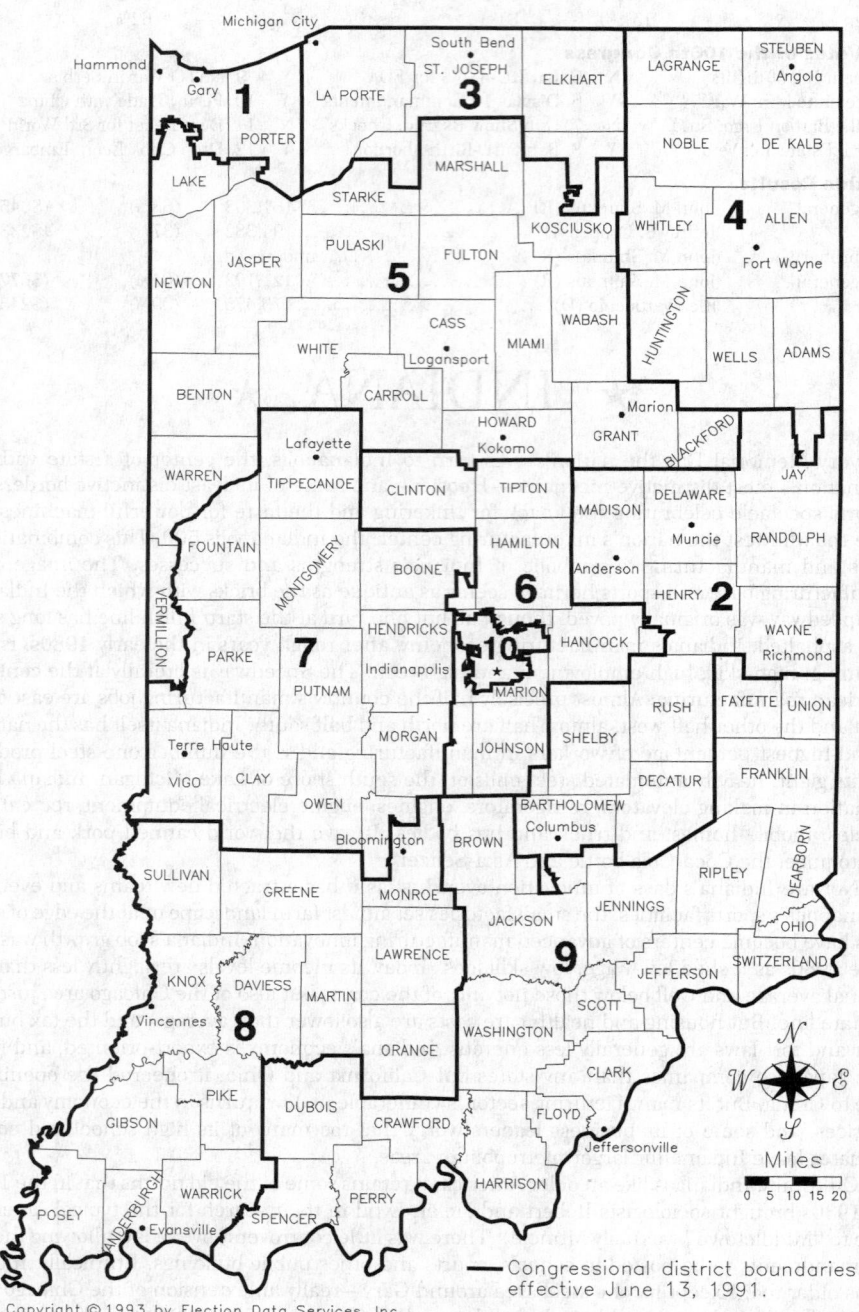

Michigan City

Hammond

Gary **1**

PORTER

LAKE

LA PORTE

STARKE

NEWTON JASPER

PULASKI **5**

South Bend
ST. JOSEPH **3**

MARSHALL

ELKHART

KOSCIUSKO

FULTON

CASS

LAGRANGE

NOBLE

WHITLEY

STEUBEN
Angola

DE KALB

4 ALLEN

Fort Wayne

HUNTINGTON

WHITE

Logansport

CARROLL

MIAMI

WABASH

WELLS ADAMS

BENTON

WARREN

Lafayette

TIPPECANOE

FOUNTAIN

MONTGOMERY

CLINTON

BOONE

HOWARD
Kokomo

TIPTON

HAMILTON

Marion

GRANT

MADISON

Muncie

Anderson

BLACKFORD

JAY

DELAWARE

RANDOLPH

HENRY **2**

VERMILLION

PARKE

7

PUTNAM

HENDRICKS

Indianapolis

10

MARION

MORGAN

JOHNSON

Terre Haute

VIGO

CLAY

OWEN

Bloomington

6

HANCOCK

SHELBY

RUSH

DECATUR

Richmond

WAYNE

FAYETTE UNION

FRANKLIN

SULLIVAN

GREENE

MONROE

BROWN

BARTHOLOMEW
Columbus

RIPLEY

DEARBORN

KNOX

Vincennes

DAVIESS

MARTIN

8

GIBSON PIKE

DUBOIS

POSEY

VANDERBURGH
Evansville

WARRICK SPENCER

LAWRENCE

ORANGE

CRAWFORD

PERRY

JACKSON

WASHINGTON

JENNINGS

9

SCOTT

JEFFERSON

CLARK

FLOYD

Jeffersonville

HARRISON

SWITZERLAND

OHIO

N
W E
S

Miles
0 5 10 15 20

————— Congressional district boundaries
effective June 13, 1991.

napolis, now has 1.5 million people but still doesn't have the big singles and gay neighborhoods of larger cities. What it does have is one of the nation's largest foundations, the Lilly Endowment (which gives much of its money locally) and a willingness to create and innovate. In the 1980s the Lilly Endowment urged Indianapolis to make itself a sports center. The city attracted the Colts professional football team to the Hoosier Dome (now the RCA Dome). In the late 1990s, Indianapolis's downtown filled with new construction projects: the pro basketball Pacers' Conseco Fieldhouse, the new NCAA headquarters, a conservatory and the Indiana State Museum; while the Convention Center and Eiteljorg Museum of Native American Art were expanded and the Circle Center Mall filled with shoppers. Longtime Indianapolis Mayor Stephen Goldsmith, a Republican, pioneered the privatization of city services for everything but police, fire and zoning. He reduced costs by nearly one-quarter and the public work force by one-third, while taxes were cut some $240 million. In the state Capitol four blocks away, Governors Evan Bayh and Frank O'Bannon, both Democrats, also cut taxes. Government has been not a drain on the private economy, but a booster.

The last decade has seen innovation in Indiana's government. But its partisan politics sometimes seems typical of an older America, with preferences anchored in the Civil War era and a small overlay of change from the union-organizing days of the 1930s. Indiana's cultural conservatism has kept it Republican in presidential elections for the last generation, but it was a crucial state from the Civil War to the New Deal in the struggles between Republicans and Democrats. Party identification was handed down like religious affiliation—the Lynds noted that Presbyterians had little to do with Methodists, but that was nothing next to divisions between Republicans and Democrats—in a state still peopled largely by descendants of its original settlers, Yankees from Ohio and New England and "Butternuts" (as they were called in the Civil War years) from Kentucky and the South.

Most Yankees became Republicans and most Butternuts Democrats, and that split has persisted over generations and can still be seen in election returns today. Of the 26 Indiana counties carried by Bill Clinton in 1996, 18 are south of Indianapolis, most near the Ohio River. The others are clustered around industrial towns that were organized by the CIO unions, the United Steelworkers and the United Auto Workers, in the 1930s. In the 1920s the Lynds, liberal academics influenced by Marx's idea that political beliefs were determined by economic interests, were puzzled why the factory workers in "Middletown" didn't vote against the bosses; in the 1930s and since in some parts of industrial Indiana they have. But this is not so in other cities, including Indianapolis, which is by far the largest. Why not? One answer is that cultural identity and personal values tend to be permanent and so have usually been the critical determinants of political allegiance in an America where economic status can often be changeable. Another is that the economic interests of Indiana's high-skill workers and its small and large factory owners are not nearly as adversarial as academics and Washington liberals suppose.

Indiana's partisan allegiances have remained remarkably steady. There is an historic base here large enough to allow Democrats to win: Evan Bayh broke a 20-year Republican hold on the governorship in 1988, with his strongest support from southern Indiana and the far northwest industrial zone. His successor, Democrat Frank O'Bannon—from a Butternut base near the Ohio River—with similar moderate policies beat Indianapolis' Stephen Goldsmith 52%–47% in 1996 and Congressman David McIntosh—one of the most active of the freshmen elected in 1994—by 57%–42% in 2000, with voting patterns much the same as in 1988. But some Hoosier politicians have been able to transcend the ancient allegiances. Richard Lugar, the only five-term senator in Indiana's history, was re-elected by 2–1 margins in 1988, 1994 and 2000; Evan Bayh was re-elected governor in 1992 and won election to the Senate in 1998 by nearly as much.

Governor   Frank O'Bannon, elected governor in 1996, grew up in the old town of Corydon, near the Ohio River, went to Indiana University, served in the Air Force, and then went to law school. He returned to Corydon, practiced law and published weekly newspapers. In 1970, at 40, he was elected to the state Senate from an Ohio River district; from 1979 he was Democratic floor leader. In 1988 he was elected as Evan Bayh's lieutenant governor and was given serious responsibilities as head of the state departments of Agriculture and Commerce. He worked on training programs and attracting business and hailed the creation of 370,000 new jobs in Indiana and the sharp drop in welfare rolls while he and Bayh were in office.

In 1996 Bayh retired after his two terms and O'Bannon ran. The early favorite was Republican Mayor Stephen Goldsmith of Indianapolis, one of the nation's leading innovators in privatizing government and cutting spending and taxes. But Goldsmith had a primary opponent who campaigned against the big city of Indianapolis, and Goldsmith won by only 54%–37%. Goldsmith's call for startling change did not go over as well as O'Bannon's pledge, as a "compassionate conservative," to continue Bayh's highly popular policies at a time when most voters believed Indiana was moving in the right direction. O'Bannon won 52%–47%, carrying Indianapolis.

As governor, O'Bannon has had to deal with budget surpluses generated by a booming economy. In four years he produced $1.5 billion in tax cuts and set up a new community college system; the welfare rolls have continued to fall, though more slowly. He has had some frustrations. His campaign finance reform plan was beaten by labor Democrats in 1997, and the Democratic teachers' unions in 1998 opposed his education proposals: an academic standards commission, paying high school students to take college entrance exams, tutoring of 10th graders who fail graduation tests, and increasing the number of credits needed for high school graduation. In 1999 the Republican state Senate rejected his proposal for full-day kindergarten. But Indiana does have testing, and scores have improved. O'Bannon was accused of mismanagement in handling a fish kill in the White River and a decertified facility for the developmentally disabled in Muscatatuck. But he had some popular successes in election year of 2000. In March O'Bannon signed a bill to use tobacco settlement money for anti-smoking measures and a prescription drug benefit for low-income seniors. He signed another bill to allow the Ten Commandments to be displayed in schools, courts and other public buildings (although a federal judge in June barred the construction of a Ten Commandments monument on the Statehouse lawn—the state has appealed the injunction). When gas prices spiked in June 2000, O'Bannon declared two 60-day moratoriums on the state gas tax, the first governor to do so. After warning legislators against new spending early in the year, he later used some of a higher-than-expected surplus for a property tax credit for homeowners, more highway spending and shoring up pension funds. In July he even urged legislators to override two of his vetoes.

O'Bannon drew a spirited opponent in Congressman David McIntosh, a former aide to Vice President Dan Quayle.. McIntosh began running in July 1999, spending little time in Washington. His campaign centerpiece was a 25% cut in property taxes, to be paid for by holding spending increases to inflation levels except for education and law enforcement; he promised not to run for reelection if he failed to put it into effect. On education, he called for block grants, merit pay for teachers, textbook funding and replacing the state test with shorter annual tests. In May 2000 he beat a primary opponent who toured all 92 counties in a red school bus by 71%–29%. He called O'Bannon a "good man," but added, "He wants to keep all that surplus for big government spending. He sounds a lot like Bill Clinton." McIntosh cited his record of tax cuts and new programs, and counted on his reputation for conservatism (he was supported by the National Rifle Association and challenged EPA rulings as harmful to Indiana industry). He said he would make sure that every child learns to read by the third grade and backed $150 million in block grants for student readiness, which school districts could use for full-day kindergarten.

In a more Democratic state, the liberals dominating the Democratic party would probably not have allowed a Democratic governor to compile a record as conservative as O'Bannon's (or Bayh's before him). But in Indiana, where many Democrats are conservative and others understand that liberal policies would be politically damaging, O'Bannon was able to provide a consensus politics which appealed to voters more than McIntosh's hard-edged promises of tax cuts. O'Bannon won decisively, 57%–42%, carrying all but 15 heavily Republican counties; he ran especially far ahead of Al Gore's losing performance in smaller counties, except those in McIntosh's 2d District. O'Bannon's challenges now include dealing with a divided legislature, trying to achieve his goals of full-day kindergarten and more rigorous testing, and dealing with a court-imposed deadline of March 2002 for changing property tax assessments.

Senior Senator   Richard Lugar, still running 5K races at the annual Dick Lugar Run and Walk in Indianapolis, has a career in public life going back to the late 1950s, when as a young

Navy officer he prepared intelligence briefings for Chief of Naval Operations Arleigh Burke and briefed President Eisenhower over closed-circuit television. Now he is the first Indiana senator ever elected to a fourth and fifth term and a powerful voice on both agriculture and foreign policy. Lugar grew up in Indianapolis, near his family's farm and food machinery firm, which was founded in 1893. He was an Eagle Scout, straight-A student and Rhodes scholar. After the service Lugar returned to the family business, was elected to the school board in 1964, then was elected mayor of Indianapolis in 1967, at 35. As mayor he consolidated the city and county into Unigov, which brought in tax resources and suburban voters, keeping the city both solvent and Republican (until 1999, when a Democrat was finally elected mayor). In the late 1960s Lugar bucked fashion and called for fewer rather than more federal programs and became known as Richard Nixon's favorite mayor; not a political asset in 1974, when Lugar ran against Senator Birch Bayh, father of his new junior colleague, and lost 51%–46%. But in the more favorable climate of 1976 and against a weaker Democratic incumbent, Vance Hartke, Lugar won 59%–40%.

Throughout his public life Lugar's strength has been that he has followed where his stubborn convictions and his considerable intellect led, regardless of political risk or reward: He has plenty of accomplishments but also some disappointments to show for it. His lone course has served him well in Indiana, but has had mixed results in the Senate and in the national arena. He is a conservative on some, but not all, of the hot-button issues of today's conservative activists; he is solidly anti-abortion but voted for background checks at gun shows in 1999. He was an internationalist even in the mid- 1990s when the president's attention to foreign issues was episodic and some in Lugar's own party were tempted to revert to isolationism. Lugar started off in the Senate leading the 1978 filibuster to defeat the AFL-CIO's labor law reform bill, although unions were then big in Indiana. He voted against the Civil Rights Act of 1990, saying it imposed racial quotas. He strongly supported NAFTA in 1993, in a Midwestern state where many thought foreigners were taking their jobs. In 1994, he doggedly raised questions about the ethical conflict posed by the investment in Lloyds of London by Supreme Court nominee Stephen Breyer. He ran for president in 1996 on his own platform and without any concessions to the political shorthand or the TV sensibility of the day, but his candidacy made little impact. Lugar based his campaign on "nuclear security and fiscal sanity"—deterring nuclear terrorism and backing a 17% national sales tax. But he got little coverage, and finished 7th in Iowa and 5th in New Hampshire and soon left the race.

Lugar's great interest is foreign policy. For 1985–86 he was chairman of the Foreign Relations Committee, where he quickly took command over a committee sharply divided between Jesse Helms—inclined to conduct his own foreign policy—and liberal Democrats. Lugar was in the middle, backing Contra aid and favoring sanctions on South Africa. He took the lead on the Philippines, quickly concluding that Ferdinand Marcos's 1986 election "victory" over Corazon Aquino was fraudulent and, at a decisive point, called on Marcos to leave office. After Republicans lost control of the Senate in 1986, Helms invoked seniority to take the ranking minority position on Foreign Relations, and after 1994 became chairman. Helms left Lugar off conference committees and seldom communicated with Lugar; their relations remain at best frosty. In April 1997 Lugar led the fight to ratify the Chemical Weapons Agreement over Helms' opposition, and won. He criticized Helms for blocking a vote on William Weld's appointment as ambassador to Mexico. If Helms is not re-elected in 2002, Lugar would return to the top spot at Foreign Relations, after a hiatus of 16 years.

Lugar favored the INF treaty in 1988, START I in 1992 and START II in 1996. He supported NATO expansion and U.S. payment of U.N. dues. But in October 1999 he voted against the Comprehensive Test Ban Treaty, arguing that the U.S. must keep testing to maintain its nuclear arsenal. Beginning in 1991 he developed the Nunn-Lugar Cooperative Threats Reduction program to pay Russia, Ukraine and Belarus to dismantle and destroy their nuclear weapons and some chemical and biological weapons as well, to prevent them from falling into the hands of hostile powers or terrorists. By 2000, 5,014 nuclear warheads had been dismantled, 384 ICBMs had been destroyed and 256 SLBM launchers had been dismantled, at a total cost of $4.5 billion— surely a bargain. In August 2000 Lugar and Nunn were nominated for the Nobel Peace Prize for their work. Meanwhile, Lugar has kept a vigilant eye on Iraq: Since August 1990 he has called for an end to Saddam Hussein's regime and said that Saddam might have to be killed and U.S. ground troops needed to accomplish that. He warned that the December 1999 Seattle WTO meeting could injure biotech and world trade. In early 2000 he warned against European protectionism on agricultural products: "Bit by bit we are being blockaded by an irrational import policy set by the Europeans."

Lugar played a key role in the passage in 1996 of the Freedom to Farm Act, which purported to phase out over seven years the farm subsidies of which he had long been a critic—though he continues to farm himself on a 600-acre spread outside Indianapolis. He was especially proud of its environmental provisions: $200 million for the Everglades, an expansion of the Conservation Reserve Program for wetlands, and an incentive program for waste containment facilities. He also sponsored a Tropical Forest Conservation Act, which would allow developing countries to swap external debt for setting up trust funds to protect rain forests. But in 1998 low crop prices sparked demands for a return to subsidies, and the crop insurance program ballooned and disaster relief was voted. In 1999 he criticized the crop insurance program for encouraging production on marginal lands, including bottomlands where runoff pollutes rivers. In fall 2000 he said he would work on a farm bill re-write in 2001, but probably wouldn't finish until 2002, when it expires.

Lugar has used his Agriculture seat for other causes. With Indianapolis Congresswoman Julia Carson, he passed in May 2000 a law allowing mothers to enroll in the CHIPS health program when they sign up for Women with Infant Children funds. With Patrick Leahy, he fought in fall 2000 to increase the deduction for donations of food by businesses and farmers to organizations that feed the hungry. He and Congressman John Boehner sponsored a law to allow farmers to income-average and fully deduct health insurance. In response to high gas prices in 2000, he sought to get rid of the requirement that gasoline use the additive MTBE in the winter. Lugar keeps an eye on scientific advances. He supported beefing up the Plum Island, Long Island, lab to study foreign animal and plant diseases. In June 2000 his bill passed to authorize a six-year $300 million program to develop fuel from biomass—stalks, shells, hulls, husks, and other vegetable products that are usually just discarded. With former CIA Director James Woolsey, Lugar argued in *Foreign Affairs* that biomass could provide a renewable source of energy, without need of subsidy, which could reduce American dependence on oil from abroad. Other Lugar causes include opposition to gambling (he co-sponsored the National Gambling Impact Study Commission), free trade, allowing future trading on individual stocks (he has co-sponsored that with Phil Gramm) and deregulating the derivatives markets.

In Indiana Lugar has remained vastly popular. His most recent victory margins have been 68%–32% in 1988, 67%–31% in 1994 and 67%–32% in 2000. The last was won against a respectable opponent, who could raise little money, whom Lugar nevertheless agreed to meet in three Lincoln-Douglas style debates.

Junior Senator   Evan Bayh was elected in 1998 to the Senate seat his father Birch Bayh first won in 1962 when Evan was just 6. He grew up mostly in Washington, graduated from Indiana University and the University of Virginia Law School, then returned to Indiana to practice law—and politics. His father, a charismatic candidate, beat three serious opponents: incumbent Senator Homer Capehart in 1962, later-Deputy Attorney General William Ruckelshaus in 1968, and future Senator Richard Lugar in 1974. But in 1980, with Evan helping run the campaign, he lost to Dan Quayle. In 1986, at 30, Evan Bayh was elected secretary of State, an office that is often a steppingstone. In 1988, at 32, he ran for governor. Republicans had controlled the office, and most of Indiana state government, for 20 years. However, their smoothly run machine had grown sluggish: The Republican nominee promised innovation, but Bayh was a young and fresh face.

Unlike his father's mostly liberal Senate voting record, Bayh has been quite a conservative Democrat. He calls himself "pragmatic" and says he wants to find "the sensible center." As governor, he balanced the budget, cut taxes and piled up a $1.6 billion budget surplus. He trimmed a deficit in state pension plans and sliced Medicaid spending. He claimed credit for the creation of 350,000 jobs, as Indiana's manufacturing economy revived. He did less to reform education and other government services, but he was immensely popular and left office with high job ratings, more than $1.3 million in his campaign treasury and a lead in the polls over incumbent Senator

Dan Coats, who had won Quayle's seat and was coming up for reelection in 1998. But in December 1996 Coats announced his retirement.

Everyone knew Bayh would run—the only question was whether the Republicans could find a strong candidate. The strongest turned out to be Fort Wayne Mayor Paul Helmke, whose father had declined to run for the House seat Quayle won in 1976. Helmke was the moderate in the field, with kind words even for the Clintons, whom he had known since law school. He narrowly won the primary with 35% against two more conservative candidates. Helmke was not uncritical of Bayh. "Evan still comes across a little the empty suit. He looks good. He sounds good. But there's a sense that he's trying to be all things to all people." It was the Republican, however, whose record included tax increases, and at mid-year Bayh had a $3.7 million war chest compared to Helmke's $64,000. Bayh said he wanted to maintain a balanced budget, save Social Security, raise education standards and move to a "fairer, flatter" tax. He ran ads showing his wife extolling his accomplishments, saying he "cracked down on deadbeat dads, sponsored Indiana's fatherhood initiative, . . . worked to make our schools safer and drug-free and to move people from welfare to work." Bayh's record as governor cinched his victory; though one might reflect that if Birch Bayh had not beaten Homer Capehart by 10,000 votes in 1962, Evan Bayh would have never been elected governor at 32 or senator at 42. Bayh won 64%–35%, carrying 88 of Indiana's 92 counties.

In his first years in the Senate Bayh compiled one of the most conservative voting records among Democrats. His first bill, co-sponsored with Pete Domenici, was a fatherhood initiative, with grants to promote an awareness of the importance of fatherhood, to encourage community-based fatherhood programs and to remove barriers for fathers by revising welfare-to-work guidelines and improving child support. (Domenici is the father of 8, Bayh the father of twins.) In February 2000 he helped form a New Democrat Coalition, with nine Senate Democrats, though they remained on good terms with Minority Leader Tom Daschle, always eager to hold together his caucus. Bayh submitted his own bill to end the marriage penalty in the tax code in April 2000. He managed to irritate some Democratic constituency groups, voting reluctantly for PNTR for China in 2000 and voting to ban partial-birth abortions in 1999; he says he opposes abortion personally but in most instances doesn't want to impose his religious beliefs on others, and as governor vetoed a 18-hour waiting period. He was one of two Democrats and one of only 21 senators to vote against allowing the importing of foreign price-controlled prescription drugs in July 2000. This was portrayed as truckling to Eli Lilly, one of Indiana's biggest employers and on whose board Bayh served in 1997–98; but his stand was vindicated when HHS Secretary Donna Shalala declined to enforce the law later in the year. His first major bill was passed in November 2000, a measure to protect senior citizens from fraud.

In May 2000 Bayh and Joseph Lieberman sponsored a revision of the basic federal aid to education act, which would increase spending by $35 billion over five years, target poor-performing school districts, foster English proficiency among immigrants, promote public school choice and demand accountability of teachers and students. It represented a sharp change from the 35-year-old ESEA, which Bayh and Lieberman emphasized by holding unofficial hearings—conspicuously bypassing the Health, Education, Labor and Pensions Committee—featuring former Clinton aide William Galston and former Republican Education Secretary William Bennett. The Bayh-Lieberman bill was very similar to the education bill George W. Bush promoted on the campaign trail and submitted to Congress in January 2001; indeed some New Democrats accused Bush of plagiarism.

In July 2000 Bayh was on Al Gore's short list of vice presidential possibilities. His moderate-to-conservative record, his vote-getting prowess in a usually Republican state, his attractive demeanor and family (*People* put him on its list of the 50 most beautiful people in the world in May 1999) all made him an appealing candidate. Despite his low-key style, Bayh has fine political skills, and had already been busy raising money for Democratic Senate candidates. But the heads of feminist organizations opposed him openly because of his partial-birth abortion vote. "I think Bayh is very bad," said NOW's Patricia Ireland. And it might have seemed odd to have a ticket including two candidates who attended the same private secondary school, St. Albans in Washington, D.C. For whatever reasons, Gore picked Joseph Lieberman, whom Bayh replaced as chairman of the Democratic Leadership Council.

In January 2001, Bayh took the trouble of writing an op-ed in *The Washington Post* to announce he would vote against John Ashcroft's nomination to be attorney general—a sure sign to many that he wanted to meet the litmus tests of the feminist and civil rights organizations that oppose him. Bayh remains, with just a few others, a plausible Democratic presidential candidate for the future; he announced in June 2001 that he would not run for president in 2004 when his Senate seat comes up.

Presidential politics   Indiana has not voted for a Democratic presidential candidate since 1964. It has been close, though not suspenseful, only in 1976, when Gerald Ford beat Jimmy Carter here by 53%–46%, and in 1996, when Bob Dole beat Bill Clinton 47%–42%. In 2000 George W. Bush won 57%–41%; he lost only 6 of 92 counties and—a bad sign for Democrats—carried voters under 30 by 64%–34%. So Indiana sees little of presidential candidates in election year autumns. Nor does it see much of them in spring or summer: Indiana's May presidential primary has not been influential since 1968. Only if Evan Bayh is on the Democratic ticket is Indiana likely to be seriously contested in 2004.

Congressional districting   Indiana lost one congressional district in the 2000 Census, and that required significant changes in district lines that had stayed pretty much the same for 20 years. This was a surprise; as one legislator put it, "Basically, we have to create nine new districts." And much larger districts: the average size had to increase from 554,000 in the 1990s to 676,000. After General Assembly could not reach consensus, by Indiana law, the new lines were decided on by a commission to which each house (the Democratic House and Republican Senate) appointed two members and the governor (a Democrat) one. Hence, Democrats controlled by 3–2, and the vote for the new map was strictly party-line. There was a push to compromise, the more so since 3d District Democrat Tim Roemer announced in January 2001 that he would not run again. The Democratic state Representative who drew up the new map felt that it would result in four safe Republican seats, two safe Democratic and three up for grabs. Basically, Stephen Buyer's 5th District was erased, placing him in a newly drawn 4th District which now stretches from his home base in White County south to Lawrence County in southern Indiana. Republican John Hostettler's 8th District has been expanded north and now takes in current 7th District Republican freshman Brian Kern's home base of Vigo County; but Kerns says he will move to the new 4th, setting up what is sure to be an intense primary against Buyer. One of the seats considered to be a "toss up" by the Democratic line drawers is Tim Roemer's old 3rd District, now renamed the 2d, which extends further south—way down to Kokomo; Chris Chocola, the Republican nominee who came close to beating Roemer in 2000, has announced he will run there even though his home base is now next door in the new 3rd District, currently held by Mark Souder who keeps a safe Republican seat. Democrat Julia Carson's 10th District now becomes the 7th, which had no choice but to expand into heavier Republican suburban territory. The old 6th District becomes the 5th, but loses Clinton County to the west, and bypasses Kokomo to take in Miami County to the north. The 2d District becomes the 6th, but now takes in Fayette, Union and Franklin Counties from the 9th –which remains the 9th District.

THE PEOPLE: Pop. 2000: 6,080,485; Pop. 1990: 5,544,159, up 9.7% 1990–2000. 2.2% of U.S. total, 14th largest; 87.5% White, 8.4% Black, 1% Asian, 0.3% Amer. Indian, 1.2% Two+ races, 1.6% Other; 3.5% Hispanic Origin. 3.2% Unemployment. 2000 Voting age pop.: 4,506,089. 2000 Turnout: 2,199,305; 49% of VAP. Registered voters (2000): 4,000,809; no party registration.

POLITICAL LINEUP: Governor, Frank O'Bannon (D); Lt. Gov., Joseph E. Kernan (D); Secy. of State, Sue Anne Gilroy (R); Atty. Gen., Steve Carter (R); Treasurer, Tim Berry (R); Auditor, Connie Kay Nass (R); Superintendent of Education, Suellen Reed (R); State Senate, 50 (18 D, 32 R); Senate Pres. Pro Tempore, Robert Garton (R); Majority Leader, Joseph Harrison (R); State House, 100 (53 D, 47 R); House Speaker, John Gregg (D). Senators, Richard G. Lugar (R) and Evan Bayh (D). Representatives, 10 (4 D, 6 R).

ELECTIONS DIVISION: 317-232-3939; **FILING DEADLINE FOR U.S. CONGRESS:** February 22, 2002.

2000 Presidential Vote

Bush (R) 1,245,836 (57%)
Gore (D) 901,980 (41%)
Others 51,489 (2%)

1996 Presidential Vote

Dole (R) 1,006,632 (47%)
Clinton (D) 887,454 (42%)
Perot (I) 224,280 (11%)

2000 Republican Presidential Primary

Bush (R) 330,095 (81%)
McCain (R) 76,569 (19%)

2000 Democratic Presidential Primary

Gore (D) 219,604 (75%)
Bradley (D) 64,339 (22%)
LaRouche (D) 9,229 (3%)

Gov. Frank O'Bannon (D)

Elected 1996, term expires Jan. 2005, 2d term; b. Jan. 30, 1930, Louisville, KY; home, Corydon; IN U., B.A. 1952, J.D. 1957; Methodist; married (Judy).

Military Career: Air Force, 1952–54.

Elected Office: IN Senate, 1971–88; IN Lt. Gov., 1989–96.

Professional Career: Practicing atty., 1957–88; Dir. & Chmn., O'Bannon Publishing Co., 1970–88.

Office: 206 State House, Indianapolis, 46204, 317-232-4567; Fax: 317-232-3443; Web site: www.state.in.us.

Election Results

2000 general	Frank O'Bannon (D)	1,232,525	(57%)
	David McIntosh (R)	908,285	(42%)
	Other	38,458	(1%)
2000 primary	Frank O'Bannon (D)	unopposed	
1996 general	Frank O'Bannon (D)	1,087,128	(52%)
	Stephen Goldsmith (R)	986,982	(47%)
	Others	35,937	(2%)

Sen. Richard G. Lugar (R)

Elected 1976, seat up 2006, 5th term; b. Apr. 4, 1932, Indianapolis; home, Indianapolis; Denison U., B.A. 1954, Rhodes Scholar, Oxford U., M.A. 1956; Methodist; married (Charlene).

Military Career: Navy, 1957–60.

Elected Office: Indianapolis Bd. of Schl. Commissioners, 1964–67; Indianapolis Mayor, 1968–75.

Professional Career: Mgr., family farm; V.P. & Treas., Thomas L. Green & Co., 1960–67; Prof., U. of Indianapolis, 1976.

DC Office: 306 HSOB, 20510, 202-224-4814; Fax: 202-228-0360; Web site: www.senate.gov/~lugar.

State Offices: Evansville, 812-465-6313; Ft. Wayne, 219-422-1505; Indianapolis, 317-226-5555; Jeffersonville, 812-288-3377; Merrillville, 219-736-9084.

Committees: *Agriculture, Nutrition & Forestry* (RMM). *Foreign Relations*: East Asian & Pacific Affairs; European Affairs; Western Hemisphere, Peace Corps, Narcotics Affairs. *Intelligence (Select)*.

Group Ratings

	ADA	ACLU	AFS	LCV	CON	ITIC	NTU	COC	ACU	NTLC	CHC
2000	10	14	0	29	26	100	72	100	84	94	92
1999	5	—	0	33	26	—	76	100	88	—	—

National Journal Ratings

	1999 LIB —	1999 CONS		2000 LIB —	2000 CONS
Economic	29% —	70%		27% —	68%
Social	42% —	55%		47% —	52%
Foreign	48% —	49%		48% —	48%

Key Votes of the 106th Congress

1. Educ. Savings Accts.	Y	5. Review Movie Violence	Y	9. NATO War in Serbia	Y
2. Prescrip. Drug Benefit	N	6. Gun Show Bckgrnd. Checks	Y	10. Table Cuba Travel Ban	N
3. Delay Ergonomic Standards	Y	7. Ban Part.-Birth Abortion	Y	11. Nuclear Test-Ban Treaty	N
4. Phase Out Estate Tax	Y	8. Broaden Hate Crimes List	Y	12. Perm. Trade with China	Y

Election Results

2000 general	Richard G. Lugar (R)	1,427,944	(67%)	($4,251,603)
	David L. Johnson (D)	683,273	(32%)	($1,179,029)
	Other	33,992	(1%)	
2000 primary	Richard G. Lugar (R)	unopposed		
1994 general	Richard G. Lugar (R)	1,039,625	(67%)	($4,688,326)
	James Jontz (D)	470,799	(31%)	($472,788)
	Others	33,144	(2%)	

Sen. Evan Bayh (D)

Elected 1998, seat up 2004, 1st term; b. Dec. 26, 1955, Shirkieville; home, Indianapolis; Indiana U., B.A. 1978, U. of VA, J.D. 1982; Episcopalian; married (Susan).

Elected Office: IN Secy. of State, 1986–89; IN Gov., 1989–97.

Professional Career: Practicing atty., 1981–86, 1997–98; Visiting Prof., Indiana U., 1997–98.

DC Office: 463 RSOB, 20510, 202-224-5623; Fax: 202-228-1377; Web site: www.senate.gov/~bayh.

State Offices: Evansville, 812-465-6500; Fort Wayne, 219-426-3151; Gary, 219-884-8528; Indianapolis, 317-554-0750; Jeffersonville, 812-218-2317.

Committees: *Aging (Special). Banking, Housing & Urban Affairs*: Financial Institutions; International Trade & Finance (Chmn.); Securities & Investment. *Energy & Natural Resources*: Energy Research, Development, Production & Regulation; Forests & Public Land Management; National Parks, Historic Preservation & Recreation. *Intelligence (Select)*.

Group Ratings

	ADA	ACLU	AFS	LCV	CON	ITIC	NTU	COC	ACU	NTLC	CHC
2000	80	33	85	100	85	93	17	60	16	3	23
1999	90	—	100	67	93	—	19	59	12	—	—

National Journal Ratings

	1999 LIB —	1999 CONS		2000 LIB —	2000 CONS
Economic	59% —	37%		64% —	34%
Social	62% —	36%		66% —	21%
Foreign	56% —	40%		72% —	15%

Key Votes of the 106th Congress

1. Educ. Savings Accts.	N	5. Review Movie Violence	Y	9. NATO War in Serbia	Y
2. Prescrip. Drug Benefit	Y	6. Gun Show Bckgrnd. Checks	Y	10. Table Cuba Travel Ban	Y
3. Delay Ergonomic Standards	N	7. Ban Part.-Birth Abortion	Y	11. Nuclear Test-Ban Treaty	Y
4. Phase Out Estate Tax	N	8. Broaden Hate Crimes List	Y	12. Perm. Trade with China	Y

Election Results

1998 general	Evan Bayh (D)	1,012,244	(64%)	($3,914,375)
	Paul Helmke (R)	552,732	(35%)	($642,784)
	Others	23,641	(1%)	
1998 primary	Evan Bayh (D)	unopposed		
1992 general	Daniel R. Coats (R)	1,267,972	(57%)	($3,802,077)
	Joseph H. Hogsett (D)	900,148	(41%)	($1,584,173)
	Others	43,306	(2%)	

FIRST DISTRICT

At the southernmost shore of Lake Michigan is a part of America made by steel. Here, in the northwest corner of Indiana, where the water highway of the Great Lakes comes closest to the rail highway of the transcontinental railroads, America's leading capitalists nearly a century ago recognized an ideal site for manufacturing steel. On empty sand dunes United States Steel, then the nation's largest corporation, founded Gary in 1906 and named it for the company's chairman, Chicago Judge Elbert Gary. For nearly 70 years the steel mills attracted a diverse work force, like Chicago and quite unlike the rest of Indiana: Irish, Poles, Czechs, Ukrainians and blacks from the American South. Politics here has always been turbulent, from the Communist-led long and unsuccessful steel strike of 1919 to the racially polarized politics of the 1960s and 1970s. The tone of public life—the clash between union stewards and management foremen, between blacks and eastern European ethnics, between the stalwarts of different factions vying for control of Gary's massive City Hall—was always abrasive, like the clash of steel on steel.

Steel brought sudden growth and sudden depression to northwest Indiana. The massive storefronts built on Gary's aptly named Broadway bear witness to the confidence and exuberance of the 1920s. But today they stand vacant—vandalized, whole blocks burned down—witness to the steel layoffs and crime waves of the 1970s. The steel mills went cold during the Depression of the 1930s, but were thronged with workers during World War II, and in the years afterward their massiveness helped create the illusion that life in the steel towns of Gary, Hammond and East Chicago would go on forever just like it was in the 1950s. But technological advances inevitably replaced increasingly expensive workers with increasingly efficient machines. And the efforts to seal off the U.S. steel market from the world inevitably failed. The oil crunch of 1979 was the catalyst for change, reducing the demand for large-sized autos, the biggest customer for steel. Steel employed 70,000 workers in northwest Indiana in 1979, and just 35,000 a few years later. Obsolete mills were closed, old mills modernized and new ones built which cut the number of man-hours needed by two-thirds. Just-in-time methods were introduced, management and high-skill workers cooperated to engineer higher-quality, less expensive steel to meet customers' needs. For the last decade Indiana has been the number one steel-producing state. But trouble arose in 1998, when recession-stricken steel-producing countries—Russia, Japan and others—were selling steel at distress prices, and American steel producers called for import quotas.

As the steel industry was changing, Gary was falling almost into ruins. As long ago as 1967, Gary elected a black mayor, Richard Hatcher, who was determined to use city government to cure poverty. But high crime rates produced a flight to the suburbs. In 1993, 1995 and 1996 Gary was the nation's murder capital. In 1995 majority-black Gary responded by electing a white Democrat mayor, Scott King, with 78% of the vote. There are now some signs of revival: murders are down (though King's nephew was shot), riverboat (actually, lakeboat) casinos owned by Donald Trump are bringing in visitors, the airport has commercial flights (to Orlando and to Portsmouth, New Hampshire). The Miss USA Pageant has come to town. But most of northwest Indiana's people have long since scattered out from Gary to suburbs and countryside, making it part of the greater Chicago area, distinctive mainly for its lower sales tax.

Indiana's 1st Congressional District stretches from Gary and Hammond along the Lake Michigan shore, east almost to Michigan City. It includes Valparaiso, known locally as Valpo, notable for its annual Popcorn Festivals, honoring longtime resident (till his death in 1995) and developer of 300 popcorn hybrids Orville Redenbacher. Politically, northwest Indiana has been a heavily Democratic area since the Depression of the early 1930s and the United Steelworkers' organizing drives of the late 1930s. It is the most Democratic part of mostly Republican Indiana.

The congressman from the 1st District is Pete Visclosky, a Democrat first elected in 1984. Visclosky grew up in northwest Indiana (his father was Mayor of Gary in the early 1960s), went to college there and law school at Notre Dame, not far away. He practiced law, then worked for six years for 1st District Congressman Adam Benjamin. Benjamin died suddenly in 1982 and Visclosky returned to Indiana. In 1984 he ran against Katie Hall, a black state senator who had been given the 1982 nomination—and thus the election, in this area—by Mayor Richard Hatcher, then district party chairman. But Hall was able to win only 33% of the 1984 primary vote; Visclosky had 34% and another white candidate 31%. Visclosky beat Hall again 57%–35% in 1986 and 51%–30% in 1990. He has not had serious opposition since.

Visclosky has a fairly liberal voting record and concentrates much of his effort on projects to help the local economy. He has a solid pro-union voting record, as one might expect. He is vice chair of the 114-member Congressional Steel Caucus and expressed alarm at the 1998 surge in steel imports. He pushed an October 1998 resolution asking the president to conduct quick 10-day scrutiny of 10 steel-producing countries and punish offenders with a one-year ban on imports, and was not satisfied with the anti-dumping penalties imposed on Japan, Brazil and Russia. In March 1999 his bill to require the Commerce Department to limit steel imports to the average monthly levels of 1994–97 was passed by a big 289–141 margin; but some may have supported expecting (as indeed happened) that the Senate would take no action; critics charged it would raise steel prices and would save relatively few jobs. In September 1999 Visclosky and Republican Robert Ney sponsored a resolution to oppose any changes in anti-dumping rules at the December WTO conference in Seattle; the House leadership prevented it from coming to a vote. In October 2000 he called for an International Trade Commission investigation of steel imports and said the White House promise of a report the next spring—when a new administration would be in office—was insufficient. Later that month he and Republican Ralph Regula inserted an amendment to the State-Commerce-Justice appropriation expanding Commerce's monthly steel import report by requiring breakdowns of carbon, alloy and stainless steel import levels.

Visclosky is the only Hoosier on Appropriations and in 1999 became ranking Democrat on the Subcommittee on Energy and Water Development. There he has pushed for $32 million in flood control and harbor reconstruction for the Little Calumet River, Burns Harbor, Cady Marsh Ditch and Mondaldi Barons; $2.2 million for beach renourishment at the Indiana Dunes National Lakeshore; $15 million for beach erosion at Ogden Dunes; $2 million for wastewater infrastructure improvements in the Gary Sanitary District; and brownfield grants for Gary, East Chicago and Hammond. He pushed through an exception to the Johnson Act, making Lake Michigan waters eligible for gambling and thus allowing riverboat casinos for Gary. He worked to fund a 760-job postal encoding facility in Gary and to stop the FAA from closing its air tower at Gary Regional Airport. Alarmed by crime in Gary, he got northwest Indiana declared a High Intensity Drug Trafficking Area, bringing in the National Guard to tear down crack houses. Stunned that crack dealers had bulletproof vests and policemen did not, Visclosky co-sponsored the Bulletproof Vest Partnership Grant Act, passed in June 1998, with funding increased to $50 million a year in 2000.

In heavily Republican 1994, with an opponent who spent more than $100,000, Visclosky lost some conservative suburbs and won by just 56%–44%. Since then he has won without difficulty; in 2000 local Republicans failed to make contact with their nominee who listed his address as a town 170 miles outside the district. Visclosky won 72%–27%. Democrats have the potential to control redistricting, and Visclosky would surely like to see some or all of Democratic LaPorte County taken from the current 3rd and added to the 1st.

Cook's Call *Probably Safe.* Visclosky has had little trouble winning in this heavily Democratic district for the last 16 years. Redistricting will move his seat further south to pick up population (taking in all or part of 5 counties now instead of three). But, politically, this district retains a good Democratic edge.

THE PEOPLE: Pop. 2000: 571,747; Pop. 1990: 554,514, up 3.1% 1990–2000. 71% White, 21.6% Black, 0.9% Asian, 0.3% Amer. Indian, 1.8% Two+ races, 4.4% Other; 11.2% Hispanic Origin.

2000 Presidential Vote		
Gore (D)	126,433	(59%)
Bush (R)	82,397	(39%)
Others	3,972	(2%)

1996 Presidential Vote		
Clinton (D)	116,355	(58%)
Dole (R)	62,595	(31%)
Perot (I)	19,530	(10%)

Rep. Peter J. Visclosky (D)

Elected 1984, 9th term; b. Aug. 13, 1949, Gary; home, Merrillville; IN U. Northwest, B.S. 1970, U. of Notre Dame, J.D. 1973, Georgetown U., LL.M. 1982; Catholic; divorced.

Professional Career: Practicing atty., 1973–76, 1983–84; Aide, U.S. Rep. Adam Benjamin, 1976–82.

DC Office: 2313 RHOB 20515, 202-225-2461; Fax: 202-225-2493; Web site: www.house.gov/visclosky.

District Offices: Gary, 219-884-1177; Portage, 219-763-2904; Valparaiso, 219-464-0315.

Committees: *Appropriations* (9th of 29 D): Defense; Energy & Water Development (RMM); Treasury, Postal Service & General Government.

Group Ratings

	ADA	ACLU	AFS	LCV	CON	ITIC	NTU	COC	ACU	NTLC	CHC
2000	75	71	100	71	87	39	22	33	12	16	20
1999	95	—	100	88	98	—	29	4	12	—	—

National Journal Ratings

	1999 LIB —	1999 CONS		2000 LIB —	2000 CONS
Economic	73% —	26%		75% —	24%
Social	70% —	29%		61% —	38%
Foreign	54% —	46%		80% —	16%

Key Votes of the 106th Congress

1. Patient Bill of Rights	Y	5. Bar RU-486 $ for FDA	N	9. NATO War in Serbia	N
2. Accelerate Min. Wage	Y	6. Display 10 Commandments	N	10. Perm. Trade with China	N
3. Strike Ban on Ergo. Stnd.	Y	7. Gun Show Bkgrnd. Checks	Y	11. Debt Relief for 3rd World	Y
4. Ovrd. Estate Tax Veto	N	8. Ban Part.-Birth Abortion	Y	12. Drop Cuba Econ. Embargo	Y

Election Results

2000 general	Peter J. Visclosky (D)	148,683	(72%)	($390,320)
	Jack Reynolds (R)	56,200	(27%)	($12,457)
	Other	2,907	(1%)	
2000 primary	Peter J. Visclosky (D)	31,507	(81%)	
	Sandra K. Smith (D)	6,098	(16%)	
	Other	1,229	(3%)	
1998 general	Peter J. Visclosky (D)	92,634	(73%)	($277,447)
	Michael Petyo (R)	33,503	(26%)	($31,151)
	Others	1,617	(1%)	

SECOND DISTRICT

Muncie, Indiana, became famous as the "Middletown" that sociologists Robert and Helen Lynd lived in and reported on in 1924–25 and again in 1935, and where a team of sociologists investigated again in 1976–78. The Lynds were attracted to Muncie by its typicalness—"every small city from Maine to California," said *Life* magazine. But it wasn't exactly: It was a factory town in a country still almost half rural, it was almost entirely Protestant and Northern in a country one-quarter Catholic and one-third Southern. Muncie was more typical in being culturally homogeneous but economically riven. In the 1920s Muncie celebrated its common values and was loath to admit its economic disparities; in the 1930s the latter came out into the open when Muncie, like most of the industrial Midwest, was unionized in what were sometimes violent uprisings. Workers who were joining CIO unions and voting for Democrats fiercely opposed the business elite—local bankers, merchants, executives at General Motors and the Ball family's glass company. Partisan politics took on the sharp, bitter tone of a struggle for wealth between two rival classes whose claims seemed irreconcilable.

Echoes of this class-warfare politics reverberate only faintly today. They grow louder with local economic distress, as Muncie suffered years ago in layoffs at GM and more recently when the Ball headquarters moved to Colorado. And there are higher Democratic percentages in towns with union traditions, like Muncie and Anderson, than in others such as Richmond and Kokomo. But Indiana's late 1990s prosperity, based on high-skill manufacturing, brought something like a political consensus here for tax cuts, holding down budgets and quiet support of traditional values, with strong support for candidates of either party who agree.

The 2d Congressional District covers most of east-central Indiana. It includes Muncie and Anderson, with their big GM factories, in the north; Richmond, founded by a major branch of American Quakers and the home of their Earlham College; and Columbus, the home of Cummins Engine, whose longtime head J. Irwin Miller paid major international architects to design most of the town's important buildings, public and private. The 2d leans Republican in presidential politics and is a swing district in Indiana races.

The congressman from the 2d District is Mike Pence, a Republican first elected in 2000. Pence, an evangelical Christian who was the Republican nominee for this same seat in 1988 and 1990 against veteran (1974–94) Democratic Congressman Philip Sharp, wrote an article after the second contest called "Confessions of a Negative Campaigner," in which he apologized for running negative advertisements. A native of Columbus, Pence graduated from Hanover College and Indiana University Law School, and two years later made his first run for Congress. From 1991 to 1993, he was president of the conservative Indiana Policy Review Foundation, a think tank based in Fort Wayne. In 1992 he began broadcasting the "Mike Pence Show," a conservative talk-radio program that was syndicated statewide beginning in 1994 until he began his 2000 campaign.

The seat became open when three-term Republican Congressman David McIntosh announced in July 1999 that he would challenge Governor Frank O'Bannon. In the relatively sedate six-candidate Republican primary in May 2000, Pence led the second-place finisher, state Representative Jeff Linder, by a solid 44%–24%. Pence won seven of 11 counties, running strongest in the Muncie and Anderson areas. Robert Rock, Anderson lawyer and son former Lieutenant Governor Robert Rock, had a closer contest in the Democratic primary, defeating former congressional aide Ronald Gyure, 30%–23%. The general became complicated when Bill Frazier, a former Republican state Senator and four-time losing nominee against Sharp, entered the race as an independent after the primary. All three candidates opposed abortion rights and gun control and supported increased military spending. But Frazier—who owns a mobile home business—tried to tap into populist sentiment by attacking free trade agreements, supporting a minimum wage increase, touting American energy independence and offering to donate his congressional salary to fund college scholarships: a sort of Pat Buchanan candidacy. Rock, a former Marine, attacked Pence for not serving in the military and supported tax cuts for middle-income families. Pence called for across-the-board tax cuts, including repeal of the marriage penalty and estate tax, as well as reform of Medicare financing. When Buchanan's candidacy seemed viable, there were predictions that Frazier would split the Republican vote, and he did—but not enough to determine the result. Pence won 51% to 39% for Rock and 9% for Frazier. Pence won Madison County (Anderson) by 617 votes and Rock won Delaware County (Muncie) by about double that margin, but Pence won more than 60% in the counties in the southern part of the district.

When he got to Congress, Pence sponsored a bill calling for $400 billion more in tax cuts than those proposed by President Bush. But redistricting will surely be Pence's biggest problem for 2002. Democrats have the upper hand in the process, one district must be eliminated and

Pence, as a freshman and something of a political outsider, cannot expect much help from legislators.

Cook's Call *Probably Safe.* Every district in Indiana felt the repercussions of losing one seat, but Pence's seat did not experience the dramatic restructuring that some other districts did. Renumbered the 6th, this sprawling central eastern Indiana district now reaches further northeast and south. It retains a Republican lean, so Pence should be safe in 2002.

THE PEOPLE: Pop. 2000: 567,204; Pop. 1990: 554,321, up 2.3% 1990–2000. 93.3% White, 4.3% Black, 0.6% Asian, 0.2% Amer. Indian, 1% Two+ races, 0.6% Other; 1.3% Hispanic Origin.

2000 Presidential Vote			1996 Presidential Vote		
Bush (R)	118,948	(57%)	Dole (R)	97,406	(45%)
Gore (D)	87,314	(42%)	Clinton (D)	89,038	(42%)
Others	4,049	(2%)	Perot (I)	26,483	(12%)

Rep. Mike Pence (R)

Elected 2000, 1st term; b. June, 7, 1959, Columbus; home, Elwood; Hanover Col., B.A. 1981; IN U., J.D. 1986; Protestant; married (Karen).

Professional Career: Practicing atty., 1986–91; Pres., IN Plcy. Review Fndt., 1991–93; Radio broadcaster, Network Indiana, 1992–99; Host, Pub. Affairs TV, UPN-23, 1995–99.

DC Office: 1605 LHOB 20515, 202-225-3021; Fax: 202-225-3382; Web site: hillsource.house.gov/mikepence/.

District Offices: Anderson, 765-640-2919; Muncie, 765-747-5566.

Committees: *Agriculture* (23d of 27 R): General Farm Commodities & Risk Management; Livestock & Horticulture. *Science* (22d of 25 R): Space & Aeronautics. *Small Business* (11th of 19 R): Regulatory Reform Oversight (Chmn.); Rural Enterprises, Agricultural and Technology.

Group Ratings and Key Votes: Newly Elected

Election Results

2000 general	Mike Pence (R)	106,023	(51%)	($1,106,140)
	Robert W. Rock (D)	80,885	(39%)	($364,888)
	Bill Frazier (I)	19,077	(9%)	($398,999)
	Other	2,422	(1%)	
2000 primary	Mike Pence (R)	21,582	(44%)	
	Jeffrey M. Linder (R)	11,615	(24%)	
	Luke Messer (R)	10,075	(21%)	
	Brad D. Steele (R)	2,819	(6%)	
	David M. Campbell (R)	1,913	(4%)	
	Other	513	(1%)	
1998 general	David McIntosh (R)	99,608	(61%)	($714,843)
	Sherman Boles (D)	62,452	(38%)	($124,185)
	Others	2,236	(1%)	

THIRD DISTRICT

When Notre Dame University was founded in 1842, Catholics were still a rarity in most of America and certainly rare on the limestone-bottomed plains of northern Indiana. This was still farm country and South Bend no more than a crossroads on the St. Joseph River. But by the 1920s, both had grown. Notre Dame, thanks to its football team, "the Fighting Irish," was the most famous Catholic university in the land, and South Bend was a significant industrial city, home of Studebaker and Bendix and dozens of other factories. In the last 50 years Notre Dame has grown in size and reputation, but South Bend has had the experience of many Midwestern industrial cities: In the 1960s Studebaker went out of business, in the early 1980s there were big layoffs at big factories, and in the early 1990s there were well-publicized layoffs in nearby Elkhart. But more important than these high-visibility job losses was the largely invisible creation of jobs in small factories throughout the region. The work here requires more skill than did the old assembly lines, and the products—Elkhart is the recreational vehicle capital of America—must be more responsive to just-in-time prime contractors or computer-inventory retailers. By the late 1990s unemployment in northern Indiana was down to 3% and below, many employers had trouble filling job openings, and the economic base was more secure than when it depended on the fate of two or three big companies.

The 3d Congressional District of Indiana has centered on South Bend for decades. This is an industrial and ethnic city—with the nation's largest percentage of Hungarian-Americans—that has long been Democratic; so is LaPorte County around Michigan City. Elkhart County, in contrast, is heavily Republican, as is Kosciusko County, part of which is in the 3rd, just to the south.

The congressman from the 3d District is Tim Roemer, a Democrat first elected in 1990 who announced in January 2001 that he would not seek reelection. Roemer grew up in South Bend and went to college in San Diego, then received a masters and Ph.D. from Notre Dame; he worked for veteran (1958–82) 3d District Congressman John Brademas and Arizona Senator Dennis DeConcini, and is married to the daughter of former Louisiana Senator Bennett Johnston. Roemer returned to South Bend and ran for Congress in 1990, raised more PAC money than Republican incumbent John Hiler, and sounded outsider themes with insider skill.

Roemer is one of the House's most visible moderate Democrats, a co-chair of the New Democrats group formed in 1997, which was designed to govern by consensus and claims 70 members for the 107th Congress. "We think that Big Government isn't the answer, but we don't believe in blowing up the Department of Education either," he told *The Indianapolis Star.* Not surprisingly, his voting record has been virtually in the middle of the House. Roemer opposed both NAFTA and fast track, but was a vigorous supporter of PNTR with China—calling the latter "a no-brainer" because it would increase access for American goods and services. He supported military action against Iraq in 1998, though he had voted against the Gulf war resolution in 1991. In September 1998 he called for censure of Bill Clinton, but declined to call for his resignation; he voted against all counts of impeachment.

Roemer has not been afraid to be a maverick. He challenged and nearly defeated the space station in the early 1990s, but his efforts gradually lost support. He supported the balanced budget amendment, votes against pork barrel projects and voted for much of the Contract With America. In 1996 he supported welfare reform and was one of 37 House Democrats who wrote Bill Clinton urging him to sign the Welfare Reform Act. He voted with Republicans to override Clinton's veto of bills eliminating the marriage penalty and estate and gift taxes. On education, Roemer has bucked teachers' unions by devising bills to use federal funds to encourage charter schools and to change credentialing by allowing lateral entry into teaching jobs. With bipartisan support in 1999, he won enactment of his "ed-flex" proposal to give school districts flexibility to waive certain regulations in return for adopting high academic goals. He was miffed when Minority Leader Dick Gephardt refused to appoint him to the House-Senate conference committee on the bill.

Following George W. Bush's victory, Roemer was out front in promoting bipartisanship. Citing "frustration with not accomplishing enough," he helped to organize a new centrist coalition in the House with opportunities on issues such as health care, taxes, education and campaign finance regulation. He was one of the members invited to Austin for a session on education with the President-elect in December 2000, and was briefly was mentioned as a potential member of the Bush cabinet.

Roemer has run well ahead of his party in a district that has long been marginal. But he had a tougher time in 2000 against Chris Chocola, a businessman with impressive fundraising skills and conservative stands on taxes, abortion and gun control. Chocola criticized Roemer as a career politician living with his family in suburban Virginia, not Indiana. Roemer responded that he wanted to spend time at home with his four young children during the week. Roemer criticized his opponent's call to eventually privatize the entire Social Security system. Despite Chocola's success in business—his grandfather invented the first motorized chicken feeder—the Chamber of Commerce and Business Roundtable endorsed Roemer. Roemer won about 60% in St. Joseph (South Bend) and LaPorte Counties, while Chocola won 60% in Elkhart County. Bush carried the district, with 68% in Elkhart County and only narrow losses in St. Joseph and LaPorte. Roemer's 52%–47% victory was the first time in three decades that an incumbent survived the "zero year hex"—Hiler lost in 1990 and Brademas in 1980.

Roemer's announcement that he would not run for re-election in 2002, when he turns 46, came as a surprise to many. But a 2002 race would have been risky in any case, because of his close margin in 2000, and even more so because of redistricting. Indiana lost a seat in the 2000 Census, and so the 3d District would have to add considerable new territory; and the territory all around, with one significant exception, is heavily Republican (Kosciusko County, the smaller part of which is in the 3rd, voted 76% for George W. Bush). The exception is marginal Porter County to the west; but that is in Democrat Pete Visclosky's 1st District, and he would surely fight any attempt to take it away.

Cook's Call *Highly Competitive.* Roemer's narrow win in 2000 highlights just how competitive this South Bend-based district really is. With Roemer retiring, Democrats are going to have a tough time keeping this seat in their column. Redistricting pushes the district further south into the former 5th, and it is now numbered the 2nd District. A number of candidates have already expressed interest in running, including 2000 Republican nominee Chris Chocola and former 4th District Democratic Representative Jill Long. Look for a very competitive race in this swing district in 2002.

THE PEOPLE: Pop. 2000: 610,182; Pop. 1990: 554,482, up 10% 1990–2000. 85.3% White, 8.4% Black, 1% Asian, 0.3% Amer. Indian, 1.8% Two+ races, 3.2% Other; 5.8% Hispanic Origin.

2000 Presidential Vote

Bush (R)	116,354	(56%)
Gore (D)	88,272	(43%)
Others	2,778	(1%)

1996 Presidential Vote

Dole (R)	91,427	(46%)
Clinton (D)	86,715	(43%)
Perot (I)	20,374	(10%)

Rep. Tim Roemer (D)

Elected 1990, 6th term; b. Oct. 30, 1956, South Bend; home, South Bend; U. of CA at San Diego, B.A. 1979, U. of Notre Dame, M.A., 1981, Ph.D. 1985; Catholic; married (Sally).

Professional Career: Staff Asst., U.S. Rep. John Brademas, 1980; Legis. Advisor, U.S. Sen. Dennis DeConcini, 1985–89; Instructor, American U., 1988.

DC Office: 2352 RHOB 20515, 202-225-3915; Fax: 202-225-6798; Web site: www.house.gov/roemer.

District Office: South Bend, 219-288-3301.

Committees: *Education & the Workforce* (7th of 22 D): Education Reform; Select Education (RMM). *Permanent Select Committee on Intelligence* (5th of 9 D): Intelligence Policy & National Security.

Group Ratings

	ADA	ACLU	AFS	LCV	CON	ITIC	NTU	COC	ACU	NTLC	CHC
2000	45	36	66	71	85	88	42	68	37	35	60
1999	80	—	83	63	89	—	26	60	36	—	—

National Journal Ratings

	1999 LIB	—	1999 CONS		2000 LIB	—	2000 CONS
Economic	55%	—	44%		55%	—	44%
Social	50%	—	50%		51%	—	49%
Foreign	52%	—	48%		63%	—	36%

Key Votes of the 106th Congress

1. Patient Bill of Rights	Y	5. Bar RU-486 $ for FDA	Y	9. NATO War in Serbia	N
2. Accelerate Min. Wage	Y	6. Display 10 Commandments	Y	10. Perm. Trade with China	Y
3. Strike Ban on Ergo. Stnd.	Y	7. Gun Show Bkgrnd. Checks	N	11. Debt Relief for 3rd World	N
4. Ovrd. Estate Tax Veto	Y	8. Ban Part.-Birth Abortion	Y	12. Drop Cuba Econ. Embargo	*

Election Results

2000 general	Tim Roemer (D)	107,438	(52%)	($734,206)
	Chris Chocola (R)	98,822	(47%)	($1,088,166)
	Other	2,050	(1%)	
2000 primary	Tim Roemer (D)	22,823	(88%)	
	Steven W. Osborn (D)	3,008	(12%)	
1998 general	Tim Roemer (D)	84,625	(58%)	($489,658)
	Daniel A. Holtz (R)	61,041	(42%)	($270,523)

FOURTH DISTRICT

The northeast corner of Indiana, in the center of a flat agricultural area, can claim to be the center of Middle America. Its first settlers were of New England Yankee stock, establishing orderly communities with public schools and even colleges; they were joined by German immigrants, who built tidy farms and their own civic institutions. In the northern part of the state there are hills and lakes, and the strange swamp that is the central focus of Gene Stratton Porter's children's classic, *Girl of the Limberlost*. The one large city here, Fort Wayne, was built on the flat terrain along the Maumee River that flows to Toledo, Ohio; it grew as a factory town, surging ahead and then falling back as large factories, often tied to the auto industry, opened and closed over the years; today it has more white-collar jobs.

The 4th Congressional District consists of nine counties in northeast Indiana, plus a bit of Jay County. It includes Fort Wayne, Huntington and Columbia City but not North Manchester. Politically this area is ancestrally Republican since the Civil War years. Since the New Deal, it has sometimes veered Democratic in times of economic distress. This part of Indiana is also a cradle of vice presidents: Thomas Marshall, Woodrow Wilson's vice president, was born in North Manchester and practiced law in Columbia City; Dan Quayle spent his high school years and later practiced law in Huntington. Quayle won this seat in 1976 and represented the district for two terms.

The congressman from the 4th District is Mark Souder, a Republican first elected in 1994. Souder grew up in Grabill, 10 miles from Fort Wayne, where his Amish great-great-grandfather's family settled. There the family started Souder's of Grabill in 1907, originally a harness shop and now a furniture store and manufacturer of store fixtures. As an undergraduate at the University of Indiana, he wore a button, "I'm proud to be a square." Souder worked in the furniture business, returned to Grabill, then went to work in 1984 for Congressman Dan Coats, Quayle's successor, as minority staff director of the Select Committee on Children, Youth and Families. He moved with Coats to the Senate in 1989, where he served as his legislative director and deputy chief of staff. In 1993 he returned to Fort Wayne and started running against Jill Long, a Democrat elected to replace Coats. With a moderate record and a farm background, she was not an easy target. But Souder raised more money and won a six-candidate primary with 40%; the state Republican ticket was also running far ahead of the Democrats in the 4th District. The result was a 55%–45% Souder victory.

Despite his Washington experience, Souder has continued to be something of a rebel in the House, even—or especially—against his own party's leaders. Souder says that he is "most defined by the fact that I'm an evangelical Christian." His independence frequently leaves Republican leaders muttering. Majority Leader Dick Armey once said, "Tell Souder I always assume that if there's trouble, it's him." As a leader of the Conservative Action Team, Souder has frequently challenged House appropriators for excessive spending—including the close-to-home matter of House members' office allowances. He voted against the balanced budget amendment because it did not require a supermajority to raise taxes. When Souder and John Hostettler cast two of the 17 votes against a continuing resolution in January 1996, Speaker Newt Gingrich announced that he would not appear at fundraisers for them. Said Souder, "This is a test of whether you can vote your conscience." In November 1997, even before the Monica Lewinsky scandal became public, he called for the impeachment of Bill Clinton for his "systematic abuses of office." But in November 1998, when impeachment was looming, he announced he would vote against; in December he voted for the third article and against the others.

Souder has been active on drug issues and blamed Bill Clinton's "half-hearted" anti-drug message for increased drug use by teens. Frustrated that the House would not do so, Souder imposed drug testing on his own staff. He proposed a bill pre-empting state laws that allow marijuana for medicinal purposes. He helped manage the drug-free workplace law and sponsored an amendment to require that students with drug convictions are ineligible for loans for a period of time based on the severity of the offense; with that adopted, he voted for the Higher Education Act. On other education issues, Souder sponsored a High Hopes program with Democrat Chaka Fattah sending letters to low-income sixth and seventh graders informing them of the availability of aid for college. He also sponsored a five-year test of IRA-type savings accounts for low-income families, to be used for first homes, higher education, emergency medical service and business capitalization. He opposed Permanent Normal Trade Relations with China because trade should be "a leverage in foreign policy." Souder's initiative with the greatest foresight may have been his continuing effort to assure that faith-based programs remain eligible for federal funds. Even though civil libertarians have raised concerns of church-state conflict, this effort has become an element of President Bush's "compassionate conservatism."

Souder has been comfortably re-elected since 1994 against poorly funded opponents. Redistricting is controlled by Democrats, but they will have a hard time giving Souder problems; his district is in a corner of the state and just about all the adjacent territory which could be added is heavily Republican.

Cook's Call *Probably Safe.* Renamed the 3rd District, this northeastern Indiana seat was not altered all that much in redistricting. It was pushed more to the east while dropping a couple southern counties to the newly drawn (and named) 6th District. It will remain a safe district for Souder.

THE PEOPLE: Pop. 2000: 619,891; Pop. 1990: 554,577, up 11.8% 1990–2000. 89.6% White, 6.2% Black, 0.9% Asian, 0.3% Amer. Indian, 1.3% Two+ races, 1.7% Other; 3.5% Hispanic Origin.

2000 Presidential Vote			1996 Presidential Vote		
Bush (R)	135,865	(63%)	Dole (R)	110,538	(53%)
Gore (D)	73,855	(34%)	Clinton (D)	75,185	(36%)
Others	4,994	(2%)	Perot (I)	19,641	(9%)

Rep. Mark Souder (R)

Elected 1994, 4th term; b. July 18, 1950, Ft. Wayne; home, Ft. Wayne; IN U., B.S. 1972, Notre Dame U., M.B.A. 1974; Protestant; married (Diane).

Professional Career: Furniture salesman, 1976–83; Staff Dir., U.S. House Select Cmte. on Children, Youth & Families, 1984–89; Legis. Dir., U.S. Sen. Dan Coats, 1989–91, Dep. Chief of Staff, 1991–93.

DC Office: 1227 LHOB 20515, 202-225-4436; Fax: 202-225-3479; Web site: www.house.gov/souder.

District Office: Ft. Wayne, 219-424-3041.

Committees: *Education & the Workforce* (11th of 27 R): 21st Century Competitiveness; Education Reform. *Government Reform* (10th of 24 R): Census; Civil Service & Agency Organization; Criminal Justice, Drug Policy & Human Resources (Chmn.). *Resources* (20th of 28 R): Forests & Forest Health; National Parks, Recreation & Public Lands.

Group Ratings

	ADA	ACLU	AFS	LCV	CON	ITIC	NTU	COC	ACU	NTLC	CHC
2000	10	14	14	14	41	67	63	71	88	79	93
1999	5	—	0	0	23	—	64	80	80	—	—

National Journal Ratings

	1999 LIB	—	1999 CONS		2000 LIB	—	2000 CONS
Economic	16%	—	78%		25%	—	72%
Social	19%	—	79%		33%	—	66%
Foreign	15%	—	81%		0%	—	88%

Key Votes of the 106th Congress

1. Patient Bill of Rights	N	5. Bar RU-486 $ for FDA	Y	9. NATO War in Serbia	N
2. Accelerate Min. Wage	N	6. Display 10 Commandments	Y	10. Perm. Trade with China	N
3. Strike Ban on Ergo. Stnd.	N	7. Gun Show Bkgrnd. Checks	N	11. Debt Relief for 3rd World	N
4. Ovrd. Estate Tax Veto	Y	8. Ban Part.-Birth Abortion	Y	12. Drop Cuba Econ. Embargo	N

Election Results

2000 general	Mark Souder (R)	131,051	(62%)	($288,827)
	Mike D. Foster (D)	74,492	(35%)	($30,285)
	Other	4,887	(3%)	
2000 primary	Mark Souder (R)	28,710	(62%)	
1998 general	Mark Souder (R)	93,671	(63%)	($221,310)
	Mark J. Wehrle (D)	54,286	(37%)	($6,932)

FIFTH DISTRICT

Across the plains of northern Indiana runs the Hoosier Heartland Corridor: The HHC, a publicist's name for U.S. 24 as it runs west from Fort Wayne along the Wabash River through Wabash, Peru and Logansport, and then overland toward the Illinois prairie. Scattered on the major east-west railroad and highway lines that connect the East Coast and Chicago, the Hoosier Heartland's small cities and large towns display a geometric order and heartland American values. It is also an economically creative place: In Kokomo, Elwood Haynes built one of the first gas-powered automobiles and invented stainless steel. This area was hit hard by recession in the early 1980s, but it has rebounded: There are sill large factories, like Delco and Daimler-Chrysler, and its small manufacturers have proved high-skill and adaptive. This is a part of America with little immigrant heritage from the early waves of immigration, relatively few blacks, and only a handful of the more recent Latin and Asian immigrants. Basic values have not been shaken so much here as in other parts of the nation: This area has one of the nation's highest percentages of households with families, married couples and children. It is also a place that has given America such icons as James Dean, who grew up in Fairmount, and Cole Porter, who grew up in Peru.

The 5th Congressional District of Indiana occupies most of the land on either side of the HHC. There are no big cities within the district; it just skirts Indianapolis, Fort Wayne, South Bend and Gary. Though farming is important here, factories large and small employ many more people; this is one of the centers of American manufacturing. Since the Civil War, this has mostly been Republican country, and the western part of the district was the home base of House Minority Leader (1959–65) Charles Halleck. But in much of the 1970s and 1980s, Democrats were competitive.

The 5th District's congressman is Steve Buyer (pronounced *BOOyer*), a Republican elected in 1992. Buyer grew up in White County, graduated from The Citadel, served in the Army, worked in Indianapolis and started a family law practice in Monticello, where he joined all the civic organizations. A lieutenant colonel in the Army reserve, he was called to active duty in fall 1990, serving as legal adviser at a prisoner-of-war camp in the Persian Gulf. Buyer was enraged that two-thirds of House Democrats, including the 5th District's Democratic Congressman Jim Jontz, voted against the war. After he returned to Indiana, where he was White County Republican vice chairman, he began making speeches around the Hoosier Heartland attacking Jontz on his Gulf war stand. In October 1991 Buyer met with all of Jontz' former opponents, then launched his own campaign. In 1992 he focused on the House bank and post office scandals and called for term limits and application of laws passed by Congress to Congress itself, an anticipation of the Contract with America. Jontz was a skilled politician, but Buyer won 51%–49%, carrying the Hoosier Heartland but losing counties at the edge of the district. He hasn't been below 60% since.

Buyer has made far more of a legislative mark than one would have expected back in 1993 for a conservative-to-moderate Republican in a then-Democratic House. On the Veterans' Affairs Committee, he has spent much time on "Gulf war syndrome." Since his return from the Gulf, Buyer has suffered from flu, pneumonia, spastic colon, kidney infection, bronchitis and a constant cough. He investigated and discovered there may have been chemical weapons in a bunker destroyed by U.S. Army troops at Khamisiyah, Iraq. In 1994 he successfully co-sponsored legislation that allows the VA to compensate Gulf war veterans suffering from chronic disabilities resulting from undiagnosed illnesses that became manifest to a degree of 10% or more within a year of the Gulf war—a real departure in veterans' law. Buyer supports continued investigation of Gulf war syndrome.

As chairman of the Military Personnel Subcommittee of Armed Services, he sponsored a resolution with fellow Gulf war veteran Paul McHale saying that U.S. deployment should not be a requisite for a peace agreement; it passed 315–104. But after visiting Bosnia with Bill Clinton and Bob Dole in December 1997, he agreed—at Newt Gingrich's urging—to sponsor a deployment bill, but with strings to set measurable objectives for implementing the Dayton accords and authorize U.S. partial or total withdrawal if they are not met. He also held hearings on sexual misconduct in the military, bringing to light problems with recruit housing and training. Just before the 2000 election, he won enactment of what military officials term the greatest expansion of health care benefits for military retirees in at least three decades. The so-called Tricare for Life program gives all retirees the menu of health care options available to federal civilian employees and makes the benefit a permanent entitlement. "This is keeping America's promise to our veterans." For the 107th Congress, Buyer gave up his military panel chair for a seat on the Energy and Commerce Committee.

Buyer is best known nationally for his work on the Judiciary Committee on the impeachment of Bill Clinton. He used his time for questions to compare Clinton's conduct with military standards. "Should we ask the members of the armed forces to accept a code of conduct that is higher for troops than for the commander-in-chief?" And he criticized advocates of civil rights who seemed prepared to condone perjury in civil rights cases. He got into one military appropriations bill an amendment that would subject the president and civilian Pentagon officials to military standards on lying and adultery, but it was not binding. A year after impeachment, he told a statewide radio interviewer that Hillary Rodham Clinton was running for the Senate because it was her best way to avoid a federal indictment and stay out of jail. But he can also be candid about his own party. When John McCain was riding high in Republican presidential primaries, Buyer said, "clearly I cannot support him" because of their differences on military legislation and because it can be "very exhausting" to work with him. During the post-election recount in Florida, he was so angry about Democrats' attempts to throw out absentee ballots by U.S. soldiers that he flew there to investigate and voice his outrage.

His 2000 challenger, Greg Goodnight, a past president of the United Steelworkers local in Kokomo, was well funded and actively promoted by Democrats. He complained that Congress was filled with too many lawyers and millionaires and that Buyer hadn't done enough to promote prescription drug coverage for seniors. Buyer highlighted federal money he had brought home: $1.2 billion to finish the Hoosier Heartland Industrial Corridor between Fort Wayne and Lafayette, and $30 million for Superfund clean-up of a former steel plant in Kokomo. Buyer won handily, 61%–38%, taking all but one small county.

The only threat to Buyer's tenure is redistricting. Even so, within the bounds of any conceivable district George W. Bush trounced Al Gore in 2000, and Buyer would carry the advantages of incumbency into any such contest.

Cook's Call   *Highly Competitive*. With the state losing one seat, and Democrats controlling the process in the state, Buyer's district fell victim to the redistricting pen. The district will be split into four surrounding districts, with his home county in the new 4th District. This new 4th District is also home to seven counties currently represented by Republican Brian Kerns.

Both Kerns and Buyer have indicated that they will run in the newly drawn 4th District, though some Republican leaders have encouraged Buyer to move north into the new 2nd District, which is an open seat. Still, regardless of who wins the primary, this is likely to stay safely in Republican control in 2002.

THE PEOPLE: Pop. 2000: 585,988; Pop. 1990: 554,240, up 5.7% 1990–2000. 94.4% White, 2.4% Black, 0.4% Asian, 0.4% Amer. Indian, 1.1% Two+ races, 1.3% Other; 3% Hispanic Origin.

2000 Presidential Vote		
Bush (R)	134,887	(61%)
Gore (D)	80,928	(37%)
Others	4,980	(2%)

1996 Presidential Vote		
Dole (R)	105,906	(50%)
Clinton (D)	78,270	(37%)
Perot (I)	27,469	(13%)

Rep. Stephen Buyer (R)

Elected 1992, 5th term; b. Nov. 26, 1958, Rensselaer; home, Monticello; The Citadel, B.S. 1980, Valparaiso U., J.D. 1984; Methodist; married (Joni).

Military Career: Army, 1984–87, 1990–91 (Persian Gulf); Army Reserves, 1980–84, 1987–present.

Professional Career: IN Dep. Atty. Gen., 1987–88; Vice Chmn., White Cnty. Repub. Party, 1988–90; Practicing atty., 1988–92.

DC Office: 2443 RHOB 20515, 202-225-5037; Fax: 202-225-2267; Web site: www.house.gov/buyer.

District Offices: Kokomo, 765-454-7551; Monticello, 219-583-9819.

Committees: *Energy & Commerce* (25th of 31 R): Commerce, Trade & Consumer Protection; Environment & Hazardous Materials; Health. *Veterans' Affairs* (6th of 17 R): Oversight & Investigations (Chmn.).

Group Ratings

	ADA	ACLU	AFS	LCV	CON	ITIC	NTU	COC	ACU	NTLC	CHC
2000	5	21	14	0	19	83	60	85	84	72	93
1999	10	—	0	6	3	—	56	88	91	—	—

National Journal Ratings

	1999 LIB —	1999 CONS		2000 LIB —	2000 CONS
Economic	22%	77%		6%	85%
Social	4%	91%		0%	79%
Foreign	42%	57%		25%	69%

Key Votes of the 106th Congress

1. Patient Bill of Rights	N	5. Bar RU-486 $ for FDA	Y	9. NATO War in Serbia	Y
2. Accelerate Min. Wage	N	6. Display 10 Commandments	Y	10. Perm. Trade with China	N
3. Strike Ban on Ergo. Stnd.	N	7. Gun Show Bkgrnd. Checks	N	11. Debt Relief for 3rd World	N
4. Ovrd. Estate Tax Veto	Y	8. Ban Part.-Birth Abortion	Y	12. Drop Cuba Econ. Embargo	N

Election Results

2000 general	Stephen Buyer (R)	132,051	(61%)	($720,714)
	Greg Goodnight (D)	81,427	(38%)	($451,647)
	Other	3,507	(2%)	
2000 primary	Stephen Buyer (R)	unopposed		
1998 general	Stephen Buyer (R)	101,567	(63%)	($457,278)
	David F. Steele III (D)	58,504	(36%)	($69,541)
	Others	2,317	(1%)	

SIXTH DISTRICT

Indianapolis is one of America's most symmetrical cities, sited in almost the exact center of Indiana, centered on Monument Circle with eight avenues radiating like wheel spokes, with the city occupying the nearly square Marion County. In the seven surrounding suburban counties, the irregularities of the physical landscape and the asymmetries of the original settlers' boundaries intrude, but a respected order has been established here. The more affluent areas are typically farther out, starting on the north side somewhere north of the home of Benjamin Harrison, Indiana's one president, and the 1920s-era Governor's Mansion built on North Meridian Street by the man who more or less invented the gas station. Here are comfortable in-town neighborhoods built in the 1940s and 1950s, the cul-de-sac subdivisions and condominiums of the 1970s and 1980s, and 1990s and 2000s developments set out on hills in the once rural counties, where towns like Fishers and Carmel more than doubled their populations and quintupled their office square footage in the last decade.

The 6th Congressional District of Indiana includes most of the suburban territory around the core of Indianapolis, which forms the 10th District. The exception is to the west of the city, where most of Hancock and Boone Counties are in the 7th District. But the 6th includes the north side of Indianapolis and the affluent Hamilton County suburbs of Carmel and Fishers; it includes Hancock County to the east and the county seat of Greenfield, where the U.S. Lawn Mower Racing Association's championship is held every September, and it takes in the less affluent but still conservative suburban territory to the south. This is by far the most Republican district in Indiana and indeed one of the most Republican districts in the country.

The congressman from the 6th District is Dan Burton, an active and enthusiastic Republican who was first elected to the House in 1982. He has been running for office since he was in his 20s. He had a horrific childhood: His father was abusive and left the family, his mother worked as a waitress and bought the kids' clothes at Goodwill, his father ultimately kidnapped his mother and went to jail, and the kids were sent to the county home. "Looking back on my life, I think one of the reasons I'm so aggressive is because all through my childhood we were looked upon as second-class citizens," he has said. Burton earned money as a teenager shining shoes and at 18 enlisted in the Army. He never finished college but made his way up as a real estate broker and insurance salesman. He also ran for public office, often unsuccessfully. He was elected to the Indiana House in 1966, 1976 and 1978 then to the Indiana Senate in 1968 and 1980; he lost races for Congress in 1970 and 1972 and finally won when the Republican legislature created this heavily Republican suburban seat.

For years Burton was regarded by many Democrats as a nut, excitably pursuing lost causes. He opposed sanctions on South Africa, backed UNITA in Angola and Renamo in Mozambique, offered dozens of spending cuts that were overwhelmingly defeated, and pushed for universal mandatory AIDS testing. He has sometimes challenged health experts: In February 2000 he filed a bill to allow a four-year-old Texas boy to be treated by a Houston doctor using nontoxic drugs not approved by the FDA, and in April 2000 he asked the Health and Human Services Department whether MMR vaccine could cause autism; he has an autistic granddaughter. But he has also been vindicated by events for some stands that were widely scorned, from his hard-line opposition to the Soviet Union to his lonely vote against the later-repealed Catastrophic Health Care Act of 1988.

Burton has had some significant legislative achievements. He co-sponsored the V-chip legislation with Massachusetts Democrat Edward Markey, passed as part of the 1996 Telecommunications Act, over the strong objection of the broadcast lobby. In the 105th Congress Burton steered to passage the Results Act, which requires federal agencies to set specific performance goals and to report on their progress—or lack of it—in meeting them. His biggest achievement was the Helms-Burton Act. It was a response to the shooting down of the Brothers to the Rescue planes by the Cuban Air Force and stated that foreign companies could be sued in American courts if, as part of business deals with Fidel Castro's regime, they took over property expropriated from American owners. Helms-Burton passed both houses in fall 1995 and was signed by Bill Clinton, but Clinton then delayed its full implementation.

As chairman of the Government Reform Committee (it dropped "Oversight" from its title in 1999), he conducted tumultuous hearings on the Clinton-Gore campaign finance scandals from 1997 to 2000. Many Republicans were queasy about having Burton conduct the hearing; they felt he was too excitable and vulnerable to attack by Democrats and remembered with dismay his

1994 speech questioning whether White House counsel Vincent Foster had been murdered and his body moved. Burton promised a bipartisan approach but encountered early and fierce opposition; ranking Democrat Henry Waxman, one of the brainiest Democrats in the House, set the tone, calling it "a partisan witch hunt." Burton helped that impression along when, in reference to Clinton, he told *The Indianapolis Star* editorial board in April 1998, "This guy's a scumbag. That's why I'm after him." Democrats yelped, and the *New York Times* demurely refused to print the epithet.

More damaging was the partial release of taped conversations between Webster Hubbell and his wife in a prison visiting room. Democrats said they were unfairly edited and a violation of privacy. But Burton said they were evidence that Hubbell was anticipating being paid off, through legal retainers for no work, and that prisoners have no rights of privacy. Regardless, Burton was forced to fire his investigator, David Bossie. In fact, Burton was facing what shows every sign of being a cover-up: Some 90 witnesses took the Fifth Amendment or left the country, and there was no cooperation from the likes of John Huang, Charlie Trie or James Riady. In July 1997 the FBI subpoenaed Burton's finance records of his House campaigns. In August 1998 Burton recommended holding Attorney General Janet Reno in contempt for refusing to produce memos from FBI Director Louis Freeh and her own adviser Charles LaBella on campaign finance, who recommended appointment of an independent counsel to investigate the Clinton-Gore finances; Reno bowed to pressure and handed over the memos. In October 1999 the committee granted immunity to Huang, whose testimony proved to have little value, perhaps because the government never sought a prison sentence for his millions in illegal contributions. In November 1999 the committee reported that Clinton granted clemency to Puerto Rican terrorists after discussions about giving political help to Al Gore and other Democrats. In May 2000, when it was revealed that White House emails from 1996–98 sought in the investigation had been erased, Burton angrily sought an investigation and an independent counsel and sent a criminal referral to the Justice Department; the email stonewall continued until the end of the Clinton presidency. In June 2000 Burton charged that Reno had been obstructing justice, and said he was considering sending criminal referrals against Reno, Clinton and Gore to the Justice Department in the next administration.

On International Affairs, Burton has bucked the tide on several issues. He opposed normalization of relations with Vietnam. He opposed cutting off aid to Turkey. He moved to reduce aid to India, because of its treatment of the Sikhs and Kashmiris, whose American counterparts contributed heavily to his 1996 campaign. Some of these stands have led Burton to campaign finance troubles. He had to return contributions to Sikh temples in April 1997 and to a lobbyist for Zaire President Mobutu Sese Seko a month later. And, as his hearings on Clinton-Gore were about to start, he was accused by a former lobbyist for Pakistan of threatening to cut off his access to other Republicans unless he raised $5,000 for Burton's campaign; Burton denied making any threats and was never charged with wrongdoing. In January 2000 Burton issued a subpoena for six-year-old Elian Gonzalez—an attempt to keep the boy in the United States.

For all the pasting Burton took from the national press, he has never been in trouble for reelection. Not even when it was revealed in 1998 that he had fathered an illegitimate son some 15 years before: Burton had not been notified by the woman until her companion, long presumed to be the father, left her five years later. Burton took a blood test and afterward paid child support. In 1998, against a male opponent, disowned by the Democrats, who made calls around town impersonating a female Indianapolis judge and a Hollywood actress, Burton won 72%–17%, with 11% for the Libertarian candidate. In 2000, against a Democrat who rode around on a palomino, Burton won 70%–26%; the Libertarian got only 3% this time. Redistricting poses little threat.

Cook's Call   *Safe.* Although the state's redistricting plan was not yet finalized by May 2001, the new map has taken Burton's suburban Indianapolis district and essentially lengthened it at both ends so that it goes as far north as Wabash County and as far south as Lawrence County, jogging around center city Indianapolis. This district will remain safely Republican and Burton will have no trouble winning here in 2002.

THE PEOPLE: Pop. 2000: 724,143; Pop. 1990: 553,865, up 30.7% 1990–2000. 94.2% White, 2.3% Black, 1.5% Asian, 0.2% Amer. Indian, 0.9% Two+ races, 0.8% Other; 1.9% Hispanic Origin.

2000 Presidential Vote		
Bush (R)	200,333	(69%)
Gore (D)	84,589	(29%)
Others	6,469	(2%)

1996 Presidential Vote		
Dole (R)	168,497	(63%)
Clinton (D)	75,285	(28%)
Perot (I)	22,404	(8%)

Rep. Dan Burton (R)

Elected 1982, 10th term; b. June 21, 1938, Indianapolis; home, Indianapolis; IN U., 1958–59, Cincinnati Bible Seminary, 1959–60; Protestant; married (Barbara).

Military Career: Army, 1956–57, Army Reserves, 1957–62.

Elected Office: IN House of Reps., 1966–68, 1976–80; IN Senate, 1968–70, 1980–82.

Professional Career: Real estate broker; Founder, Dan Burton Insurance Agency, 1968.

DC Office: 2185 RHOB 20515, 202-225-2276; Fax: 202-225-0016; Web site: www.house.gov/burton.

District Offices: Greenwood, 317-882-3640; Indianapolis, 317-848-0201.

Committees: *Government Reform* (Chmn. of 24 R). *International Relations* (6th of 26 R): Europe; Middle East & South Asia.

Group Ratings

	ADA	ACLU	AFS	LCV	CON	ITIC	NTU	COC	ACU	NTLC	CHC
2000	5	23	16	0	43	72	66	89	91	94	100
1999	5	—	0	0	26	—	61	83	95	—	—

National Journal Ratings

	1999 LIB	—	1999 CONS		2000 LIB	—	2000 CONS
Economic	23%	—	76%		6%	—	85%
Social	15%	—	84%		0%	—	79%
Foreign	9%	—	90%		31%	—	68%

Key Votes of the 106th Congress

1. Patient Bill of Rights	N	5. Bar RU-486 $ for FDA	Y	9. NATO War in Serbia	N
2. Accelerate Min. Wage	N	6. Display 10 Commandments	Y	10. Perm. Trade with China	N
3. Strike Ban on Ergo. Stnd.	N	7. Gun Show Bkgrnd. Checks	N	11. Debt Relief for 3rd World	N
4. Ovrd. Estate Tax Veto	Y	8. Ban Part.-Birth Abortion	Y	12. Drop Cuba Econ. Embargo	*

Election Results

2000 general	Dan Burton (R)	199,207	(70%)	($622,401)
	Darin Patrick Griesey (D)	74,881	(26%)	($9,123)
	Joe Hauptmann (LIB)	9,087	(3%)	($13,529)
2000 primary	Dan Burton (R)	54,399	(79%)	
	George Thomas Holland (R)	14,106	(21%)	
1998 general	Dan Burton (R)	135,250	(72%)	($902,183)
	Bob Kern (D)	31,472	(17%)	
	Joe Hauptmann (Lib)	21,032	(11%)	($11,741)

SEVENTH DISTRICT

Of the railroad passenger trains that used to run on the lines criss-crossing the township grids of the Midwest, none had a more romantic name than the *Wabash Cannonball* that rumbled along the Wabash River, across the rolling farmland of northern Indiana on its way from Detroit to St. Louis, crossing the old National Road, now U.S. 40, which runs in a nearly straight line from Indianapolis to St. Louis. The landscape here is some of the most prosaic in the United States, mostly flat, with neat farms and frame-bungalowed towns, looking unchanged from years ago. Today the *Cannonball* no longer runs: People bounce around the Midwest on commuter airlines from small city to hub, and the National Road and U.S. 40 have been replaced for through traffic by Interstate 70.

The 7th Congressional District covers much of the routes of the *Wabash Cannonball* and the National Road in western Indiana, starting from the Indianapolis city limits. Its two largest towns are quite different in character. Terre Haute is an old manufacturing town and is the boyhood home of Socialist Eugene Debs. It now has a Sony compact disc plant and made a bid for its third federal prison; the city already hosts a maximum-security penitentiary, which includes the only federal death chamber and an accompanying 50-bed cellblock. The town has lost population in recent years and tends to vote Democratic—a lonely stand in central Indiana. The other major town is Lafayette, where the main business is Purdue University, Indiana's land-grant college and the alma mater of C-SPAN founder Brian Lamb. Growing and prosperous, Lafayette tends to vote Republican. Even more Republican are the small counties and the suburban territory in Hendricks and Boone Counties outside Indianapolis.

The congressman from the 7th District is Brian Kerns, a Republican elected in 2000 to succeed Edward Pease, his former boss, who succeeded John Myers, Kerns' father-in-law. Kerns has spent his life in western Indiana and lives on a small farm south of Prairieton. He earned a bachelor's degree in political science and a master's of public administration from Indiana State University. His political career began with internships in the Indiana State Senate and the House Ethics Committee, of which Myers was a senior member. Kerns worked as director of publications and public relations at St. Joseph's College in Rensselaer, a reporter and photographer at WTWO Television in Terre Haute, and public information specialist for Indiana's Department of Natural Resources. As Pease's chief of staff, Kerns also served on the National Republican Congressional Committee's chief of staff executive committee.

When Pease unexpectedly announced in January 2000 he wanted to return home after two terms because he was suffering heart pains, Kerns was the logical successor. The contest in this solidly Republican district was essentially decided in the May primary. Kerns suffered some negative publicity in the primary when *The Indianapolis Star* reported allegations by former female aides to Pease that he verbally abused them and ordered them to perform political tasks during official work hours in 1997. Kerns denied that he broke the law and declined to comment further. Against seven other candidates, Kerns won with 39% of the vote, but he had close competition from financial planner Bob Griffiths, who swept his home base of Lafayette and Tippecanoe County to win 32%. Support from the Republican organization and his own $135,500 loan to the campaign probably made the difference. In the general election Kerns defeated a Democrat who had beaten the party favorite in the primary, apparently on the strength of 60 four-feet square wooden signs that he and his family spent hours painting; but he spent only $5,000 in the general. Kerns promised he would never vote to raise taxes and would reduce the size of federal government; the former staffers' charges did not resurface. Kerns won 65%–32%, losing only Vermillion County, which was the district's only county to vote for Al Gore. He expects to carry on Pease's work, fighting for elimination of the marriage tax penalty and the federal estate tax plus lower taxes on Social Security.

Kerns sought a seat on the Appropriations Committee, where Myers had become ranking minority member, and then was passed over for the chairmanship by incoming Speaker Newt Gingrich. But he ended up instead on Transportation. He could be on the way to a long career—this seat has been in the Republican column for 34 years—if he survives redistricting. Indiana must lose a seat, so it is possible that this central Indiana district will disappear and Kerns will be forced into a primary against another Republican.

Cook's Call   *Highly Competitive.* Kerns district will now be enveloped by both the 8th and 4th districts. Though his home is in the 8th District, he has made it clear that he intends to move into the 4th (where more than 50% of his current counties will be located) and may face Republican Steve Buyer who has also been redistricted into the 4th. Kerns has ruled out the option of challenging John Hostettler in the 8th District.

THE PEOPLE: Pop. 2000: 633,484; Pop. 1990: 554,500, up 14.2% 1990–2000. 94.1% White, 2.2% Black, 1.5% Asian, 0.3% Amer. Indian, 1% Two+ races, 0.9% Other; 2% Hispanic Origin.

2000 Presidential Vote		
Bush (R)	133,818	(62%)
Gore (D)	78,231	(36%)
Others	4,561	(2%)

1996 Presidential Vote		
Dole (R)	111,500	(52%)
Clinton (D)	75,150	(35%)
Perot (I)	25,773	(12%)

Rep. Brian Kerns (R)

Elected 2000, 1st term; b. May 22, 1957, Terre Haute; home, Prairieton; IN St. U., B.S. 1991, M.P.A. 1992; Episcopalian; married (Lori).

Professional Career: Reporter, WTWO TV, 1984–89; Pub. Info., IN Dept. of Nat. Resources, 1994–95; Pub. Rel., St. Joseph's Col., 1995–96; Press Secy., Dist. Dir., Chief of Staff, U.S. Rep. Edward Pease, 1997–2000.

DC Office: 226 CHOB 20515, 202-225-5805.

District Offices: Danville, 317-718-0307; Lafayette, 765-423-1661; Terre Haute, 812-238-1619.

Committees: *International Relations* (25th of 26 R): Africa. *Transportation & Infrastructure* (33d of 42 R): Highways & Transit; Water Resources & Environment.

Group Ratings and Key Votes: Newly Elected

Election Results

2000 general	Brian Kerns (R)	135,869	(65%)	($479,291)
	Michael Douglas Graf (D)	66,764	(32%)	($11,302)
	Other	7,032	(3%)	
2000 primary	Brian Kerns (R)	22,766	(39%)	
	Bob Griffiths (R)	18,792	(32%)	
	Alex Gatzimos (R)	7,233	(12%)	
	Bryan L. Donaldson (R)	2,869	(5%)	
	Matt Branam (R)	2,156	(4%)	
	Other	4,470	(8%)	
1998 general	Ed Pease (R)	109,712	(69%)	($489,357)
	Samuel (Dutch) Hillenberg (D)	44,823	(28%)	
	Others	4,779	(3%)	

EIGHTH DISTRICT

"Evansville," wrote John Bartlow Martin in 1947, "is the capital of a tri-state area comprising the neglected tag ends of Indiana, Kentucky and Illinois." It was a factory town then, building car parts and refrigerators, drawing workers from Kentucky, Tennessee and the picturesque but not very fertile hills of southern Indiana. It has seen hard times, such as the terrible flood of March 1997, but it has also been buzzing with small-employer job growth and a certain amount of civic spirit: It has the state's first riverboat casino and claims to have the nation's second largest street festival, second only to New Orleans's Mardi Gras celebration.

Evansville is one of two major focuses of the 8th Congressional District of Indiana, which, within irregular borders, covers most of the southwest corner of the state. The other is Bloomington, quite a different place, the home of Indiana University and a limestone-quarrying center. This southwest corner of Indiana was the first part of the state settled by whites. Vincennes, now a small town on the banks of the Wabash River, was once the metropolis of Indiana, and Scottish philanthropist and visionary Robert Owen established the town of New Harmony downstream. Owen's son was the first congressman from the area, elected in 1842 and 1844. Southern Indiana is ancestrally Democratic, just as northern Indiana is ancestrally Republican; these southern counties were hostile to the Civil War and southern Indiana's Senator Jesse Bright was expelled by the Senate for "acknowledging Jefferson Davis as 'President of the Confederate States' and support of the rebellion." In New Deal times workers in Evansville moved toward the Democrats; in the 1960s and 1970s the university community in Bloomington trended Republican even as rural counties trended Republican.

The result has been a very close political balance, and this district has become known as the "Bloody Eighth" for its close congressional races. At one point in the 1970s it elected four different congressmen in four successive elections, the only district in the country to do so in that decade. In 1984 the state counted the Republican the winner by exactly 34 votes, but the result was overturned by the Democratic House, in a fight that left many House Republicans bitterly aggrieved. In the 1990s it was as fiercely contested as ever, and in presidential politics as well: Bill Clinton carried it by 2% in 1992 and 1996.

The congressman from the 8th District is John Hostettler, a Republican elected in 1994, an ingenuous and idealistic man who seems miscast in politics. Hostettler is from Posey County, just west of Evansville; he went to Rose-Hulman Institute of Technology in Terre Haute and in 1983 became a Southern Indiana Gas & Electric Company engineer. He had never run for office, but in 1994, at 33, he was one of six Republican candidates vying to run against 12-year incumbent Democrat Frank McCloskey. Hostettler's great strength was his support from anti-abortion and Christian fundamentalist groups; he also had regional strength in the western edge of the district, along the Wabash. He won the primary with 35%, to 23% for his next competitor. In the general, Hostettler refused to take PAC money; his biggest fundraiser was a $100-per-family fried chicken dinner with Marilyn Quayle. Hostettler attacked McCloskey on taxes, gay rights, gun control, the environment, school prayer, his 65 overdrafts at the House bank, and constantly referred to him as "Frank McClinton." McCloskey accused Hostettler of wanting to outlaw all abortions and called him "John McGingrich." McCloskey carried Evansville and Bloomington by microscopic margins, but Hostettler carried most of the rural counties and won 52%–48%.

In the House, Hostettler has been a conservative willing to buck conventional political wisdom and his party leadership. He and fellow Indiana freshman Mark Souder were the only two Republicans to vote against the balanced budget amendment in 1995 because it did not require a supermajority to raise taxes. He opposed term limits out of opposition to amending the Constitution except where there is no alternative. In January 1996 he was one of 15 Republican members to vote against the continuing resolution to reopen the federal government; in response Newt Gingrich canceled his appearance at a Hostettler fundraiser, so in January 1997 Hostettler voted "present" for speaker. In May 1998 he opposed proposing the Ohio River for inclusion in Bill Clinton's American Heritage Rivers program, for fear of threatening private property rights. The mayors of Evansville and Mount Vernon, who favored it, complained they had not been consulted, but the Ohio didn't make the list.

In 2000 Hostettler opposed Speaker Dennis Hastert's compromise minimum wage and was one of three members to vote against the Violence Against Women Act in September; the other two weren't running for reelection. In May 2000 he sponsored a flurry of amendments to stop the Clinton administration accord on gun safety with Smith & Wesson—even though anti-gun control forces didn't want to raise the issue. "This is a terrible precedent to set, that any time the president can't get his legislative agenda he will legislate through litigation." He got the Armed Services Committee to bar the Defense Department from preferring any gun manufacturer that entered the accord, but was beaten on the floor; Hastert did not want the amendment on any appropriation bill, lest it be vetoed, and Hostettler's amendments to appropriations bills were beaten by narrow margins on the floor. He also sponsored a bill to require the IRS to assign taxpayer ID numbers to children whose parents for religious reasons did not want them to get Social Security numbers, and he worked to encourage public postings of the Ten Commandments. Opposed to "hate crimes" legislation, he asked, "What crime is motivated out of love? We should not create a federal thought police."

One federal project Hostettler does favor is the construction of a Canada-to-Mexico highway by extending I-69 from Indianapolis southwest, through Bloomington and Evansville, to Laredo, Texas. The current road has 259 intersections and several stop signs and rail crossings in its 100 miles. Hostettler formed the Interstate 69 Mid-Continent Highway Caucus, with 25 congressmen and 11 senators, and is co-chairman with Tom DeLay. To those who say his efforts to earmark $27 million for I-69 in southern Indiana are inconsistent with his philosophy, he responds, "Read the Constitution: It talks about roads."

Hostettler has faced serious Democratic opposition in 1996, 1998 and 2000. Refusing to raise PAC money, he had only a narrow money advantage in 1996 and was outspent in 1998 and 2000. In 1996 he faced former McCloskey aide Jonathan Weinzapfel, who was helped by $100,000 of AFL-CIO TV ads, but Hostettler eked out a 50%–48% victory. In 1998 Evansville Councilwoman Gail Riecken, with the support of EMILY's List and other national feminist groups, blamed Hostettler for Congress's failure to pass HMO regulation reform. In a low turnout election, Hostettler won 52%–46%. In 2000 Hostettler had a different kind of opponent. The Democratic favorite was John Hamilton, nephew of longtime 9th District Congressman Lee Hamilton. But he was upset in the May primary by Paul Perry, an Evansville orthopedic surgeon who had never run for office, by a 57%–38% margin. "Put a doctor in the House," Perry cried, and campaigned heavily on his support of HMO regulation, the so-called patient's bill of rights. Perry insisted that he opposed abortion and gun control as stoutly as Hostettler and campaigned vigorously, spending $350,000 of his own money. Hostettler seemed an obvious target on HMO regulation: He voted against both the Republicans' and the Democrats' versions of the bill as a federal intrusion, and supported instead medical savings accounts, association health plans and tax credits for those who buy their own health insurance. Perry's bill, he charged, would impose Canadian-style bureaucracy and amounted to "HillaryCare."

There was heavy spending by outside groups here, by the AFL-CIO for Perry and by the Health Benefits Coalition (corporate and insurance groups) for Hostettler. But there was also plenty of vigorous campaigning by both candidates in the Bloody Eighth. Perry declared he didn't want Al Gore or Joseph Lieberman campaigning in the district, though he did bring in Congressmen Steny Hoyer and Patrick Kennedy. This was one of several districts in which Kennedy, as head of the Democratic Congressional Campaign Committee, backed culturally conservative candidates who tried to use the HMO regulation and prescription drug issues to beat conservative Republicans. It was a shrewd strategy, but it failed to work. The undertow of the Democrats' national ticket in this rural and small town area was strong. Bill Clinton carried the district twice in three-way races, with 42% and 45% of the vote. But Al Gore could not even achieve those percentages, as George W. Bush carried the Bloody Eighth by 56%–41%. Hostettler won 53%–45%, carrying everything but Bloomington and one rural county—not a landslide by any means, but his best performance in four races, and against a candidate not vulnerable on cultural issues. HMO regulation and prescription drugs turned out not to be killer issues.

Now Hostettler must deal with redistricting. This is a corner district, and therefore not as susceptible to manipulation as those in the center of the state. The likelihood is that the Bloody Eighth will keep its current identity—and marginal status.

Cook's Call *Competitive.* For the last three cycles, Democrats have put Hostettler high on their target list, only to come up short each time. While Hostettler is probably too conservative for this marginal district, Democrats just can't find the magic combination of factors needed to knock him off. Plus, this district, especially Vanderburgh County (Evanston) has become more Republican over the last few years. The new redistricting plan crafted by Democrats has pushed this southeastern Indiana seat further north to take in Democratic leaning Terre Haute.

THE PEOPLE: Pop. 2000: 590,205; Pop. 1990: 554,347, up 6.5% 1990–2000. 93.7% White, 3.5% Black, 1.1% Asian, 0.2% Amer. Indian, 1% Two+ races, 0.4% Other; 1.1% Hispanic Origin.

2000 Presidential Vote			1996 Presidential Vote		
Bush (R)	126,011	(56%)	Clinton (D)	100,171	(45%)
Gore (D)	92,112	(41%)	Dole (R)	96,956	(43%)
Others	6,371	(3%)	Perot (I)	23,905	(11%)

Rep. John Hostettler (R)

Elected 1994, 4th term; b. July 19, 1961, Evansville; home, Wadesville; Rose-Hulman Inst. of Tech., B.S. 1983; Baptist; married (Elizabeth).

Professional Career: Mechanical Engineer, S. IN Gas & Electric Co., 1983–94.

DC Office: 1507 LHOB 20515, 202-225-4636; Fax: 202-225-3284; Web site: www.house.gov/hostettler.

District Offices: Bloomington, 812-334-1111; Evansville, 812-465-6484.

Committees: *Armed Services* (14th of 32 R): Military Installations & Facilities; Military Research & Development. *Judiciary* (16th of 21 R): Courts, the Internet & Intellectual Property; The Constitution.

Group Ratings

	ADA	ACLU	AFS	LCV	CON	ITIC	NTU	COC	ACU	NTLC	CHC
2000	15	36	28	0	93	61	71	76	88	88	87
1999	15	—	33	13	67	—	68	83	96	—	—

National Journal Ratings

	1999 LIB	—	1999 CONS		2000 LIB	—	2000 CONS
Economic	43%	—	57%		44%	—	55%
Social	23%	—	76%		0%	—	79%
Foreign	3%	—	92%		12%	—	78%

Key Votes of the 106th Congress

1. Patient Bill of Rights	N	5. Bar RU-486 $ for FDA	Y	9. NATO War in Serbia	N
2. Accelerate Min. Wage	N	6. Display 10 Commandments	Y	10. Perm. Trade with China	N
3. Strike Ban on Ergo. Stnd.	N	7. Gun Show Bkgrnd. Checks	N	11. Debt Relief for 3rd World	N
4. Ovrd. Estate Tax Veto	Y	8. Ban Part.-Birth Abortion	Y	12. Drop Cuba Econ. Embargo	N

Election Results

2000 general	John Hostettler (R)	116,879	(53%)	($743,755)
	Paul E. Perry (D)	100,488	(45%)	($1,543,521)
	Other	4,342	(2%)	
2000 primary	John Hostettler (R)	unopposed		
1998 general	John Hostettler (R)	92,785	(52%)	($658,886)
	Gail Riecken (D)	81,871	(46%)	($799,118)
	Others	3,401	(2%)	

NINTH DISTRICT

The southeastern corner of Indiana, in the national eye only during the awful flood of March 1997, was a busy place when settlers rafted down the Ohio River in the early 19th Century. They were mostly Southerners, "Butternuts," from across the river in Kentucky or over the mountains in Virginia, and they built the first large Indiana settlements. Today, you can see their work in the marvelous old buildings of Madison, now quiet but once one of the busiest ports on the Ohio River. Farther down the river is Corydon, from 1816–25 the state capital, the hometown of Governor Frank O'Bannon. The early 19th Century buildings here have been well preserved because these towns were bypassed first by the railroads, then by U.S. routes and interstate highways, and they certainly are remote from major airports. The river is still an artery of commerce, but utilitarian barges have replaced steamers, except for riverboat casinos.

Butternut Indiana retained its affection for things Southern into the Civil War and beyond. Local politician Jesse Bright was expelled from the U.S. Senate in 1862 for "supporting the rebellion." To this day, the hills along the Ohio River typically vote Democratic, as do the Indiana suburbs of Louisville. But to the east Indiana is now filling up with migrants from Cincinnati—a

Yankee and German abolitionist bastion in Jesse Bright's time, an overwhelmingly Republican stronghold in ours—who are moving the southeast corner of Indiana away from its ancestral party.

The 9th Congressional District of Indiana is made up of most of the state's Ohio River counties and an oddly shaped collection of lightly populated counties to the north. It is ancestrally Democratic and culturally conservative and recently trending Republican. For 34 years this was the district represented by Lee Hamilton, a Democrat who chaired the Foreign Affairs Committee. Hamilton was temperamentally inclined to a bipartisan foreign policy but frequently opposed Reagan and Bush administration policies; he was seriously considered for the vice presidential nomination in 1988 and 1992.

The congressman from the 9th is Baron Hill, a Democrat elected in 1998. Hill grew up in Seymour, the small town of John Mellencamp's song "Small Town." He played basketball for Furman, which later won him induction into the Indiana Basketball Hall of Fame with the more famous Larry Bird. He returned home to a family insurance business. In 1982, at 29, he was elected to the state House and served eight years. In 1990 he ran against Senator Dan Coats and, despite a huge money disadvantage, held him to a 54%–46% win. Governor Evan Bayh appointed Hill to head the state student assistance agency; then he worked for Merrill Lynch. When Hamilton announced his retirement in 1997, Hill plunged into the race. His opponent was Jean Leising, a former state senator who held Hamilton to a surprisingly low 52%–48% margin in 1994 and then lost 56%–42% in 1996. Leising campaigned as an opponent of all abortions and all gun control and a proponent of welfare reform. In 1998 she had primary opposition from Michael Bailey, who attracted media attention in earlier campaigns by trying to run ads showing aborted fetuses. The media gave him more heed than the voters: Leising won the primary 67%–25%. She began the campaign ahead, presumably because she was better known. She featured Charlton Heston in TV ads and called in national Republicans to campaign. Hill raised nearly twice as much money, including more from PACs and party committees. In his 1990 Senate race he had walked the state, from the Ohio River to Lake Michigan; this time he walked 400 miles through all 21 counties of the district starting in July. Hill was behind in polls in late October, but he unleashed two ads that may have made the difference. In one he said Leising wanted to abolish federal education funding (she said she wanted the money to go to local schools without strings), in the other he said she wanted to privatize Social Security (Leising said she was looking for ways for young people to invest a portion of Social Security taxes). Helped by last minute campaigning from Hamilton and O'Bannon and a good get-out-the-vote campaign, Hill won 51%–48%.

In the House, Hill sponsored a $45 million appropriation provision for physical changes at high schools to permit smaller class sizes—"schools within schools." He was denounced by a United Steelworkers local for his vote in favor of Permanent Normal Trade Relations with China, which he said would benefit Indiana farmers and autoworkers. He also voted for the partial-birth abortion ban. On local projects, he took credit for the first construction money for the seven-mile Ohio River Greenway project of parkway, trails and overlooks. And he helped to secure a $10 million bonus for the widening of Interstate 65 through Clark County.

Given his close victory in 1998, Hill was high on the House Republicans' 2000 target list. They worked with Indiana Republicans to recruit Kevin Kellems, a former aide to Senator Richard Lugar, whom they were convinced would be a strong challenger. But Kellems met an unexpected obstacle. Perhaps because he won the endorsement of Indiana's Right to Life Committee, he seemed to completely overlook his primary opponent Michael Bailey, who returned with his graphic ads. On primary night, Kellems took a strong early lead in the suburban counties along the river, and Bailey even conceded early in the evening. But when all of the rural votes were tallied and with a low turnout, Kellems lost 14 of the district's 21 counties and Bailey won, 51%–49%. A surprised and embarrassed National Republican Congressional Committee removed the district from its target list; Speaker Dennis Hastert now called it "a second-tier race." But Bailey did not give up. Remaking himself as a populist, he seized on Hill's voting to style himself as an opponent of free trade and sought support from unions, winning a local Teamsters endorsement. Hill was aided by the National Rifle Association's support. He won, 54%–44%, though he lost seven counties in the Cincinnati and Indianapolis metro orbits.

With that close contest against what Republicans viewed as a weak challenger, they remained confident that Hill could be defeated. Redistricting may well be critical. Democrats would probably like to extend Hill's district west along the Ohio River, which might put him in a contest with 8th District Republican John Hostettler; Republicans would probably like to place him in a district extending north into the heavily Republican Indianapolis suburbs. The best solution from Hill's point of view would be to slough off a few of the northern counties he didn't carry in 2000 and add the college town of Bloomington and Monroe County.

Cook's Call *Competitive.* The fact that Baron Hill took just 54% against a lackluster Republican in 2000 indicates how marginal this district is. To help shore up Hill, Democratic line drawers took Democratic-leaning Bloomington from the 8th District and put it into the 9th District. They also removed areas in the northern part of the district (burgeoning Cincinnati suburbs) that were trending more Republican and put them into the 6th. Still, this district will not be a Democratic stronghold and could be very competitive, if Republicans can find a better candidate than they have put up the last two cycles.

THE PEOPLE: Pop. 2000: 608,430; Pop. 1990: 554,516, up 9.7% 1990–2000. 96.1% White, 2% Black, 0.4% Asian, 0.2% Amer. Indian, 0.8% Two+ races, 0.6% Other; 1.3% Hispanic Origin.

2000 Presidential Vote			1996 Presidential Vote		
Bush (R)	136,878	(58%)	Clinton (D)	101,434	(44%)
Gore (D)	94,990	(40%)	Dole (R)	99,915	(44%)
Others	4,776	(2%)	Perot (I)	26,154	(11%)

Rep. Baron Hill (D)

Elected 1998, 2d term; b. June 23, 1953, Seymour; home, Seymour; Furman U., B.A. 1975; Christian; married (Betty).

Elected Office: IN House of Reps., 1982–90.

Professional Career: The Hill Agency (insurance), 1975–90; Exec. Dir., IN Student Assistance Comm., 1990–94; Financial analyst, Merrill Lynch, 1994–98.

DC Office: 1208 LHOB 20515, 202-225-5315; Fax: 202-226-6866; Web site: www.house.gov/baronhill.

District Office: Jeffersonville, 812-288-3999.

Committees: *Agriculture* (18th of 24 D): General Farm Commodities & Risk Management; Specialty Crops & Foreign Agriculture Programs. *Armed Services* (23d of 28 D): Military Personnel; Military Readiness. *Veterans' Affairs* (11th of 14 D): Oversight & Investigations.

Group Ratings

	ADA	ACLU	AFS	LCV	CON	ITIC	NTU	COC	ACU	NTLC	CHC
2000	70	36	85	79	94	83	24	60	16	15	47
1999	75	—	100	50	82	—	23	56	16	—	—

National Journal Ratings

	1999 LIB —	1999 CONS		2000 LIB —	2000 CONS
Economic	60% —	39%		72% —	28%
Social	55% —	44%		55% —	45%
Foreign	66% —	34%		77% —	21%

Key Votes of the 106th Congress

1. Patient Bill of Rights	Y	5. Bar RU-486 $ for FDA	N	9. NATO War in Serbia	Y
2. Accelerate Min. Wage	Y	6. Display 10 Commandments	N	10. Perm. Trade with China	Y
3. Strike Ban on Ergo. Stnd.	Y	7. Gun Show Bkgrnd. Checks	N	11. Debt Relief for 3rd World	N
4. Ovrd. Estate Tax Veto	N	8. Ban Part.-Birth Abortion	Y	12. Drop Cuba Econ. Embargo	Y

Election Results

2000 general	Baron Hill (D)	....	126,420	(54%)
	Michael E. Bailey (R)	....	102,219	(44%)
	Other	....	4,644	(2%)
2000 primary	Baron Hill (D)	....	42,235	(85%)
	James R. McClure Jr. (D)	....	5,264	(11%)
	Lendall B. Terry (D)	....	1,921	(4%)
1998 general	Baron Hill (D)	....	92,973	(51%)
	Jean Leising (R)	....	87,797	(48%)
	Others	....	2,406	(1%)

The dollar amounts appearing to the right:

($981,802)
($218,270)
($1,009,101)
($647,330)

TENTH DISTRICT

Indianapolis, radiating outward from the Soldiers and Sailors statue in Monument Circle, is precisely at the center of Indiana, dominating it as few other cities do a state. It is the political and governmental capital, industrial and financial center, and the intellectual center of Indiana as well. It is symmetrically laid out: Just to the west of the circle is the state Capitol, to the north is the American Legion headquarters, to the east is the City-County building, and to the south is the Circle Center mall, and the RCA Dome (formerly Hoosier Dome). Farther out are some classic and some new Indianapolis institutions: the Indiana University Medical Center, the Convention Center, the Eiteljorg Museum of Native American and Western Art and the new Indiana State Museum, Conseco Fieldhouse and NCAA headquarters. In the 1980s Indianapolis became the nation's amateur sports capital; it has also become one of the most popular places for religious conventions. Eli Lilly and Co. has been expanding its already large corporate presence. And the city has the world's biggest children's museum and is home to the Hudson Institute, a conservative think tank.

Politically, Indianapolis has long had robust competition in national as well as local races. Republicans held the mayor's office from 1967, when Richard Lugar won it, until 1999, when Stephen Goldsmith retired and became a top adviser to George W. Bush; they made Indianapolis a national innovator in privatization of services. By putting services up for bid, they saved taxpayers money and spurred many incumbent city employees to come up with innovations. Lugar expanded Indianapolis's city limits to include all of Marion County, which made it a solidly Republican constituency then. But more recently, affluent young people have been moving to counties farther out, and Marion County is trending Democratic. That trend was evident in November 1999 when Democrat Bart Peterson, a former chief of staff to Governor Evan Bayh, was elected mayor, 52%–41%, over Secretary of State Sue Anne Gilroy, and in 2000, when Marion County voted for George W. Bush by only a 50%–48% margin, even as six surrounding suburban counties gave Bush 70% to 75% of their votes.

Indiana's 10th Congressional District includes most but not all of Indianapolis and Marion County. It includes all of Center Township, with its large black population, and does not include much of the affluent, Republican northern edge of the county. It extends west toward Speedway, where the Indianapolis 500 is held, and southward and east to modest neighborhoods. Within these boundaries, the 10th District leans Democratic, and it gave Bill Clinton (twice) and Al Gore solid margins.

The congresswoman from the 10th District is Julia Carson, a Democrat elected in 1996. Carson was born to an unmarried teenage mother and grew up in poverty, working as a waitress, newspaper deliverer and summer farm laborer; she can remember going to the welfare office for a ration of cornmeal and lard. As a divorced mother she raised two children and then two grandchildren. In 1965 she was hired away from her job as a secretary at UAW Local 550 by newly elected Congressman Andy Jacobs to do casework in his Indianapolis office. When his election prospects looked dim in 1972 (he did lose, but won the seat back two years later), he encouraged Carson to run for the state House; she won, then was elected to the state Senate in 1976. In 1990 she ran for Center Township trustee, the position responsible for running welfare in central Indianapolis; the agency was $17 million in debt and accused of mismanaging taxpayer funds and mistreating welfare applicants. As trustee, she instituted a workfare program, requiring recipients to work cleaning the streets, highways and riverbanks. The debt was paid off and property taxes lowered and welfare rolls reduced; the Republican Marion County auditor said, "Julia Carson wrestled that monster to the ground."

In 1996, when Jacobs retired, Carson decided to run. She won Jacobs's endorsement and that of the local Democratic organization. She was outspent by former prosecutor and party chairman Ann DeLaney, but won the primary 49%–31%. The Republican nominee was Virginia Blankenbaker, a stockbroker and state senator from 1980–92. In this race between two grandmothers, both were also more liberal than many in their parties, pro-choice on abortion and against the death penalty. Carson cited her work as Center Township trustee and said she supported welfare reform, though not the 1996 act; she was for "universal" health care but not "nationalized" medicine. Many commentators wondered whether a black Democrat could beat a white Republican in this 30% black district, but Carson raised and spent almost as much as Blankenbaker and won 53%–45%. As she said later, "This is a wonderful city. A lot of people see you beyond the color of your skin. That becomes passe."

Carson, who was sworn into office from her hospital bed after heart surgery in January 1997 and was hospitalized in December 1999 with a serious case of pneumonia, has compiled a very liberal voting record. She sponsored a law to require trigger locks on guns and to penalize adults who let children have access to loaded guns without supervision; she obtained a $518,000 grant for the city to work on domestic violence. She worked with Senator Lugar to enact a bill wiping away bureaucratic roadblocks to child health insurance. She cried at the Capitol ceremony when President Clinton gave the Congressional Gold Medal to civil-rights pioneer Rosa Parks, pursuant to a bill that Carson authored. One of the last House members to decide how to vote on Permanent Normal Trade Relations with China, she spent the final hours before the vote chatting with Clinton for 45 minutes at the White House (but refusing to tell him how she would vote), listening to union officials, and then talking to CNN. When it finally was time to vote, Carson recounted, she saw Indianapolis jobs in her mind's eye, she told *The Indianapolis Star.* "I said, 'Julia, don't be AGAINST something. That's not what supporting this bill is about. Be FOR something. This bill is trying to accomplish something.'" Her vote left organized labor steaming, but its Indiana officials supported her reelection because they liked her overall record.

Carson has had two competitive re-election challenges and has won handily each time. In 2000, her Republican opponent was Butler University sociology professor Marvin Scott, making his fourth bid for the seat. But Scott received little national party support, and Carson won 59%–40%. Three weeks into the presidential-vote deadlock in Florida, she became one of the first Democratic defectors when she publicly advised Al Gore to "take the high ground and hand it over," which caused some grumbling among Democrats. Redistricting could pose some difficulty for Carson. The 10th must add about 100,000 new residents, and most of the adjacent precincts in Indianapolis are mildly to heavily Republican, so the 10th must be made at least marginally less Democratic.

Cook's Call *Probably Safe.* This Indianapolis-based district was one of the slowest growing in the state and, as such, will be forced to expand further into suburban Marion County. Republicans are hoping that will help make this a more competitive seat, but it is likely to retain its Democratic edge. Plus, Carson should not be underestimated: She has been dubbed vulnerable before, only to wipe the floor with her competition.

THE PEOPLE: Pop. 2000: 569,211; Pop. 1990: 554,797, up 2.6% 1990–2000. 59.7% White, 34.3% Black, 1.3% Asian, 0.3% Amer. Indian, 1.9% Two+ races, 2.5% Other; 4.8% Hispanic Origin.

2000 Presidential Vote		
Gore (D)	95,245	(59%)
Bush (R)	60,407	(38%)
Others	4,819	(3%)

1996 Presidential Vote		
Clinton (D)	89,851	(54%)
Dole (R)	61,892	(37%)
Perot (I)	12,547	(8%)

Rep. Julia Carson (D)

Elected 1996, 3d term; b. July 8, 1938, Louisville, KY; home, Indianapolis; Baptist; divorced.

Elected Office: IN House of Reps., 1972–76; IN Senate, 1976–90; Marion Cty. Center Township Trustee, 1991–96.

Professional Career: Secy., UAW, 1962–63; Legis. Aide, U.S. Rep. Andy Jacobs, 1965–72.

DC Office: 1339 LHOB 20515, 202-225-4011; Fax: 202-225-5633; Web site: www.house.gov/carson.

District Office: Indianapolis, 317-283-6516.

Committees: *Financial Services* (13th of 32 D): Financial Institutions & Consumer Credit; Housing & Community Opportunity; International Monetary Policy & Trade. *Veterans' Affairs* (5th of 14 D): Health.

Group Ratings

	ADA	ACLU	AFS	LCV	CON	ITIC	NTU	COC	ACU	NTLC	CHC
2000	90	85	85	86	34	72	24	40	4	16	0
1999	95	—	100	81	61	—	23	18	0	—	—

National Journal Ratings

	1999 LIB —	1999 CONS	2000 LIB —	2000 CONS
Economic	88%	0%	71%	28%
Social	87%	0%	94%	0%
Foreign	89%	11%	80%	20%

Key Votes of the 106th Congress

1. Patient Bill of Rights	Y	5. Bar RU-486 $ for FDA	N	9. NATO War in Serbia	Y
2. Accelerate Min. Wage	Y	6. Display 10 Commandments	*	10. Perm. Trade with China	Y
3. Strike Ban on Ergo. Stnd.	Y	7. Gun Show Bkgrnd. Checks	*	11. Debt Relief for 3rd World	Y
4. Ovrd. Estate Tax Veto	N	8. Ban Part.-Birth Abortion	N	12. Drop Cuba Econ. Embargo	Y

Election Results

2000 general	Julia Carson (D)	91,689	(59%)	($340,203)
	Marvin B. Scott (R)	62,233	(40%)	($82,504)
	Other	2,780	(2%)	
2000 primary	Julia Carson (D)	22,891	(90%)	
	Ralph Spelbring (D)	1,639	(6%)	
	Bobby Hidalgo (D)	956	(4%)	
1998 general	Julia Carson (D)	69,682	(58%)	($773,835)
	Gary A. Hofmeister (R)	47,017	(39%)	($773,589)
	Others	2,737	(2%)	

★ IOWA ★

As Americans were surging westward in the 1840s, Iowa was filling up with Yankee farmers and German immigrants, watching as wagon trains headed to the Oregon Trail and the Mormon thousands mustered by Brigham Young headed from the Mississippi across the rolling hills to Council Bluffs on the Missouri and then west. Iowa was a young state then, proud of its hundreds of schools and dozens of colleges, sending more than its share of young men back east to fight for the cause of the Union. After that war Iowans built a solid civilization based on farming, farm-machine making and meat processing that resisted the blandishments of William Jennings Bryan's populism and cheap money, and Iowa became one of the most solidly Republican states in the nation.

But starting around 1900, Iowa grew old. "Build it and they will come" was the theme from the movie *Field of Dreams*, set in Iowa, and in the 19th Century Iowans built a model society. But for most of the 20th Century very few people came. Iowa's commercial and financial center remained stuck in the railroad hub of Chicago, its economy failed to diversify and develop the dense manufacturing base of the Great Lakes states, and its young people started to move away to make their fortunes. Iowa's population, up from 674,000 in 1860 to 2.2 million in 1900, increased only slowly, and has not reached 3 million to this day: In 1900 Iowa had 11 congressional districts and California 7; in 2002 Iowa will have five and California 53. Its solid Capitol and courthouses, its sturdy but mostly old housing stock, give testimony to Iowa's strengths but also bespeak its lack of dynamism. Even its great economic achievement—the development of high-tech, ever more-productive, but also less labor-intensive agriculture—has made this a state that did not grow much.

Indeed, for much of the 20th Century, Iowa has been a culturally and politically counter-cyclical state, headed in just the opposite direction of the rest of the nation—determinedly, with confidence in its own chipper rectitude, unembarrassedly out of step. In the industrial New Deal era, it stayed mostly agricultural and Republican, even as one-time Des Moines radio announcer Ronald Reagan became an enthusiastic Roosevelt Democrat and headed to Hollywood. It partook little of postwar economic growth. It was dovish during the Vietnam war and after. In the 1980s, as Reagan, now a conservative Republican, became president, Iowans watched helplessly as farm prices and land values plummeted downward, farm implement factories closed, and 7% of its citizens left; its population fell more than any other state except West Virginia. Self-pity became the dominant note of Iowa's politics, as voters sought protection from the vagaries of the market even as commercial real estate and stock prices boomed elsewhere. By 1988 once-Republican Iowa had become one of the most Democratic states, sending presidential caucus winner Dick Gephardt's politics solidly to the left and producing the second-highest percentage for Michael Dukakis in November.

In the 1990s Iowa and the nation converged. If its economic rebellion against America's move toward free markets failed in the 1980s, its cultural qualms about America's move away from traditional values may have set an example for the rest of the country in the 1990s. For Iowa has managed to combine over the years steady habits and tolerance of diversity. The farm population continued to drop in the 1990s; from 1982 to 1997, the number of Iowans whose principal occupation was farming dropped from 86,000 to 56,000. Nor are the farm subsidies remaining after the Freedom to Farm Act likely to reverse that trend; half of the $2 billion in 1996–98 subsidies went to just 12% of farms, many of them corporate operations, and most farmers received no more than $6,000 each. But Iowa has grown in other ways. Iowans' high level of literacy and good work habits have produced white-collar and high-tech growth in and around its pleasant small cities, especially in Des Moines and Cedar Rapids, even as many old factories have closed. Iowa's unemployment rate is among the nation's lowest—2.1% in early 2000—and median incomes in 1998–99 rose more than in all but one other state. As *The Washington Post's* Thomas Edsall wrote, "Iowa has diversified into a powerful manufacturing and insurance hub and a key developer of agribusiness products." The state's population fell 4.7% in the 1980s but grew by 5.4% in the 1990s, the biggest percentage increase since the 1910s. And

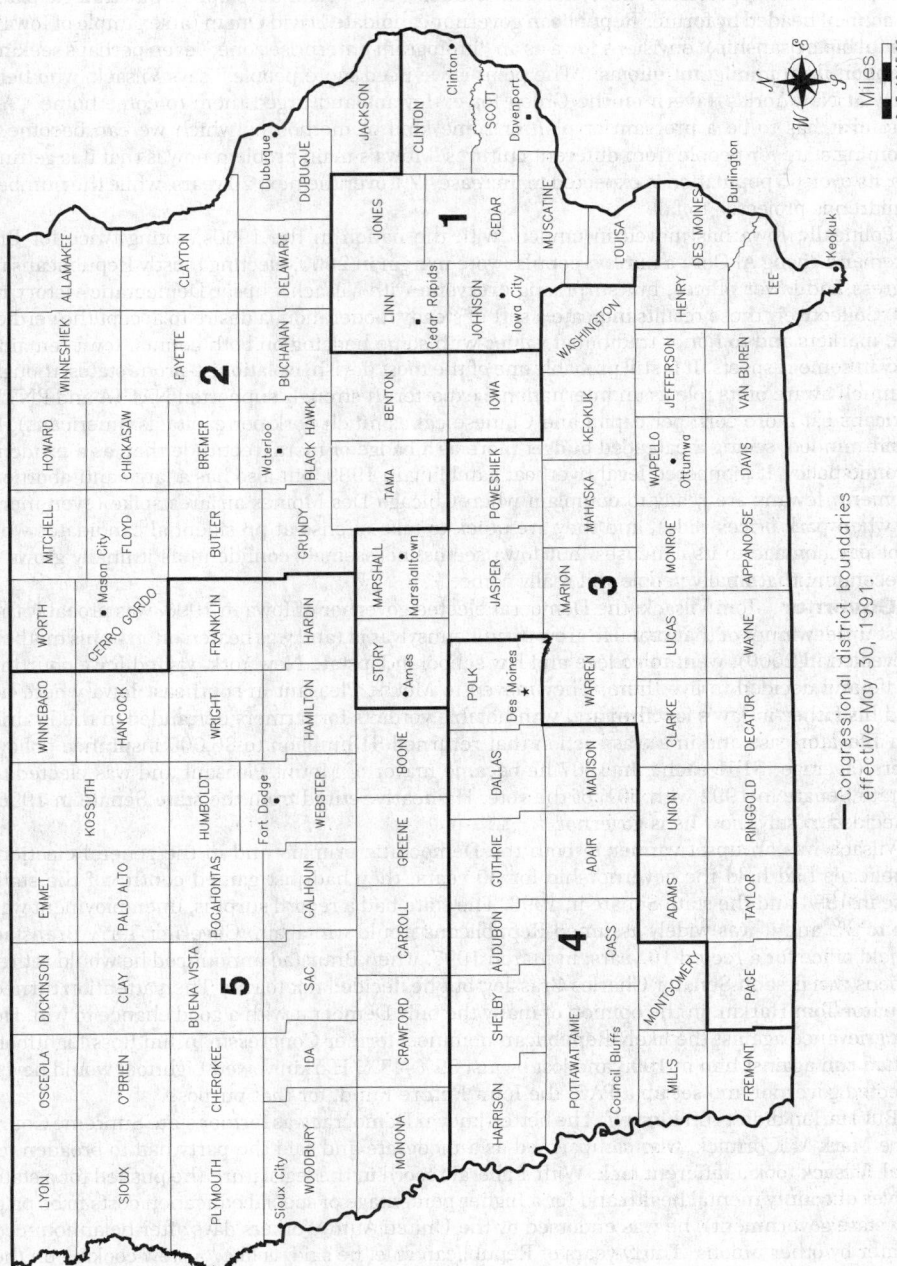

Congressional district boundaries effective May 30, 1991.

if educated young Iowans still often leave the state, immigrants are coming in—Mexicans to work in the big new meatpacking factories, Serbian and Bosnian refugees who find jobs and stay. This can lead to problems—some complain about "Mexican meth" in meatpacking towns—but it can also represent an opportunity. Governor Tom Vilsack's 2010 plan, developed by a strategic planning council headed by former Republican governor candidate David Oman (an example of Iowa's cheerful bipartisanship), envisions Iowa as an "immigrant enterprise zone," even perhaps seeking exemption from immigrant quotas. "The point is we need more people," says Vilsack, who held a party at New York's Tavern on the Green for ex-Iowans and urged them to come home. "An aspect of it has to be a program or plan or some kind of method by which we can become a welcoming state for people from different cultures." Iowa's main problem now is that it is getting older: its over-65 population is expected to increase 47% over the next 20 years, while the number of children is projected to fall.

Politically, Iowa has moved in tandem with the nation in the 1990s, voting twice for Bill Clinton and giving Al Gore a narrow popular-vote margin in 2000, electing mostly Republicans to Congress and lower offices, but surprising everyone with Vilsack's upset Democratic victory in 1998. Collectively these results indicate a sort of steady moderation, a desire to accept the verdict of the markets and to honor traditional values with some hedging on both counts. Iowa remains quirky in some respects. It is still probably one of the most dovish, isolationist-prone states, though very much aware of its role as an international exporter: It strongly supported NAFTA and PNTR (Mexicans eat more corn per capita and Chinese eat as much pork per capita as Americans). It is thrift-minded, seeing a balanced budget more as a badge of moral rectitude than as a prudent economic policy. It pioneered legal riverboat gambling in 1989, but also has a large anti-abortion movement. Iowans are ready to complain when Chicago-Des Moines airfares spike (even more than when pork prices slide), and they are quick to take offense at presidential candidates who do not pay homage to its caucuses, but Iowa seems increasingly confident, as it finally grows a new economy, that finally people will really come.

Governor   Tom Vilsack, the Democrat elected governor of Iowa in 1998, was probably the biggest upset winner of that year. He grew up in Pennsylvania (and was beaten often by his mother, he revealed in 2000), went to college and law school in Upstate New York, visited Iowa courting his wife and decided to live there. They moved to Mount Pleasant in southeast Iowa where he joined his father-in-law's law firm and won notable verdicts for farmers defrauded in the Prairie Grain Elevator case and in a class action that returned $13 million to 86,000 insurance policyholders (average: $151 each). In 1987 he became mayor of Mount Pleasant and was elected to the state Senate in 1992 with 50% of the vote. He nearly retired from the state Senate in 1996, but decided to stay; now he is governor.

Vilsack was an upset winner in both the Democratic primary and in the general election. Republicans had held the governorship for 30 years; they had just gained control of the state House in 1994 and the state Senate in 1996. The state had a record surplus, unemployment was down to 3% and it was widely assumed Republicans would win again. Governor Terry Branstad had held office for a record 16 years; in March 1997, when Branstad announced he would retire, the focus was first on Senator Charles Grassley, but he decided not to run. Then attention turned to Senator Tom Harkin, in the opinion of many the only Democrat with a good chance to win. He had a grievance against the likely Republican nominee, former Congressman Jim Ross Lightfoot, who had run against him in 1996 and lost by just 52%–47%; Harkin vowed Lightfoot would never be elected governor and set up a PAC, the Iowa Future Fund, for that purpose.

But Harkin didn't run himself. The better-known Democrat was former state Supreme Court Justice Mark McCormick, who campaigned as a moderate and said the party had to broaden its appeal. Vilsack took a different tack. With a liberal record in the legislature (he pushed for a state takeover of county mental health and for a higher percentage of special education costs to be paid for by state government), he was endorsed by the United Auto Workers days after he announced and later by other unions. Thirty years of Republican rule, he said, is like "a stew cooking on the stove. You need to stir it once in a while; otherwise it will burn at the bottom." In a light turnout he beat McCormick 51%–48%, while Lightfoot received almost as many votes in the three-candidate Republican primary as both Democrats put together. Vilsack carried Cedar Rapids and

Davenport, but lost Des Moines and the university towns of Iowa City and Ames, as well as most small counties. But the counties wholly or partly within his state Senate district, one of 50, cast 6% of the state's votes, which Vilsack carried 87%–13%, or by 5,400 votes, enough to offset Mc-Cormick's 2,220-vote margin in the rest of the state.

For the general election campaign, Lightfoot raised more money and promised a major tax cut. Vilsack called for upgrading education and attracting agribusinesses to make Iowa "the Silicon Valley of food." Lightfoot, who even aides admitted disliked campaigning, ran mainly on the tax cut and ended with ham-handed negative ads. But Harkin probably played the key role in the election. He insisted that he was against Lightfoot on issues rather than personal grounds: "His beliefs are narrow, they're constricted and they're not in keeping with the beliefs of the people of Iowa." Harkin helped raise $300,000 of Vilsack's $2.3 million treasury and Harkin himself campaigned for the last two weeks all over the state. Vilsack ran a 23-city bus caravan and advanced steadily in polls, from a 53%–35% deficit in an early October Mason-Dixon poll to a 47%–42% deficit in the last week of the month. On election night Vice President Al Gore called Vilsack to tell him he'd won; Vilsack was watching *All the President's Men* instead of the televised results. His margin was 52%–47%, the same margin by which Harkin beat Lightfoot in 1996 and just slightly better than Al Gore's 49%–48% Iowa margin in 2000.

In his first year, Vilsack worked amicably with the Republican legislature, and in his first 100 days, he was able to sign into law two campaign promises: a law on methamphetamine addiction and a reduction in class sizes in early grades. In 2000 relations between Vilsack and the legislature grew testier. Republicans charged that Vilsack's budget didn't follow the law and spent too much money, though they agreed on a 4% education spending increase. In April the legislature repealed Vilsack's order banning discrimination in state employment against gays, lesbians and transsexuals; Vilsack vetoed that and in the fall 22 legislators sued, charging he exceeded his powers—a state judge declared Vilsack's order invalid. Vilsack vetoed a waiting period for abortions and signed a health insurance regulation law without the right to sue as he had sought.

Perhaps most controversial was the recommendation, embraced by Vilsack, of a bipartisan commission headed by former Republican governor primary candidate David Oman that Iowa needs to recruit 310,000 foreign workers to settle in the state. Vilsack projected that Iowa's elderly population, already the third highest in the country, would increase to 20% by 2010; already Iowa's unemployment rate is one of the lowest in the nation, and more workers are needed to keep its economy growing. Vilsack has gone on trips to New York, Chicago and Los Angeles to encourage former Iowans to return home; he has set up "welcome centers" for Mexicans and others who have come to work in the state's meatpacking factories. Recruiting immigrants, even making the state an "immigration enterprise zone," struck Vilsack as a rational response; as Oman said, "We're not talking about hordes of people coming; we're talking about recouping our population losses." Initial polls showed the proposal unpopular. But Iowa has welcomed newcomers before: in the 1970s it resettled 10,000 Vietnamese refugees.

Despite the controversies with the legislature and the immigration proposal, Vilsack's approval rating remained very high. But when he campaigned to elect Democratic majorities in the legislature in November 2000, he came up short; Republicans retained their 30–20 and 56–44 majorities in the Senate and House. One factor cited by Republicans was Vilsack's opposition to the bill making English the official language; another was a desire to hold down spending. As Vilsack said, "Iowans essentially were interested in maintaining the status quo and a bipartisan approach to government at this time. The message I take from this is that the people want us to work together." In early 2001 Vilsack seemed in fairly strong shape for re-election in 2002. Possible candidates were state Representative Steve Sukud and engineer Bob Van der Platts, both little known—but then so was Vilsack in early 1998. Vilsack has made only a few forays into national politics—he lobbied for ethanol in Washington and went down to Florida for Al Gore—but if re-elected he will be an important national figure, as Democratic presidential candidates vie for his support. He may, as in 2000, stay neutral, though everyone noticed that his wife campaigned for Gore.

Cook's Call *Probably Safe*. Vilsack seems well positioned for re-election despite the fact that Al Gore just barely eked out a win here. No first-tier Republican has emerged; the party's attention will likely be on trying to unseat Senator Tom Harkin and hold on to the open seat Des Moines-based congressional district. But Iowa is competitive enough by nature that this race could get interesting.

Senior Senator   Charles Grassley is an unquestionably honest and preternaturally thrifty Republican who was first elected to the Senate in 1980. He grew up on a farm in Butler County near Waterloo; his parents switched parties when Franklin Roosevelt ran for a third term in 1940, and Grassley ran for the state legislature in 1956 and lost by 70-some votes. While in graduate school he ran for the state House in the Democratic year of 1958 and was elected, at 25; he won an U.S. House seat in the Democratic year of 1974 and a Senate seat by beating a strong incumbent, John Culver, in 1980. Grassley combines political shrewdness with a seeming naivete that at some level is surely genuine. He describes himself as "just a hog farmer from New Hartford," and says, "I don't know how you're going to have a strong farm economy if we don't have some farmers in Congress. I can't tell you how many people I have to tell that food doesn't grow on grocery shelves." Starting in 1997 he led the Senate in consecutive roll call votes; the last one he missed came when he was inspecting flood damage in Iowa in 1993. He goes back home to Iowa every weekend, helps his son run the family farm and holds open meetings in every one of Iowa's 99 counties each year.

Grassley's early record in Congress was guided by three issues: thrift, agriculture and dovishness on defense; he is ever alert for abuse of power. His first major legislation was the 1986 Federal False Claims Act, which authorizes suits for fraud on behalf of the government; he says it has brought in $1.8 billion. He long sponsored the bill to apply to Congress the laws it applies to others, and was the chief sponsor of the Congressional Accountability Act of 1995. He is a strong supporter of free trade and has worked from Washington to Seattle to open up markets for agricultural products; he strongly supported permanent normal trade relations with China. Grassley supported both the Freedom to Farm Act of 1996 and subsequent emergency payments and loan provisions for farmers. In 1991 he was one of two Republicans to vote against the Gulf war resolution. He does not echo other Republicans' calls for more defense spending and is quick to seize on Pentagon outrages. In 1999 he held up the nomination of UN Ambassador Richard Holbrooke because he thought the State Department unfairly reassigned a whistleblower at the UN Mission. With Ron Wyden, he has sought disclosure of the heretofore anonymous holds senators have been able to put on legislation and appointments; they have not gotten that, but in 1999 Trent Lott and Tom Daschle agreed that senators putting on holds must notify committee chairmen and the sponsor of the measure or nomination.

Grassley ascended to the top Republican spot in Finance after William Roth was defeated in 2000. There he had worked for the child care tax credit, enacted in 1997, and to reinstate the deductibility of interest on student loans. He was chief sponsor of the wind energy production tax credit of 1992 and seeks favorable treatment for ethanol and biomass. In 1998 he got the ethanol tax credit extended to 2007. He spent years highlighting abuses by the IRS and helped pass the IRS reforms of 1998. In 1999, with Judd Gregg, John Breaux and Bob Kerrey, he presented a Social Security reform bill with individual investment accounts. He sponsored or co-sponsored measures in the 2000 tax cut bill, including increasing portability of pensions, tax-deferred savings accounts for farmers to allow them to weather changes in crop prices, a deduction for long-term care insurance and a credit for costs assumed by family caregivers of the elderly, and—long a Grassley preoccupation—changing the Medicare reimbursement rates for rural hospitals and promoting telemedicine. In 2000 he also passed the breast and cervical cancer treatment bill sought by the late John Chafee. With Edward Kennedy, he sponsored a bill to retain Medicaid eligibility for families with disabled children.

On the Judiciary Committee Grassley was the chief sponsor of bankruptcy reform, which passed with a veto-proof majority in December 2000 but was never signed into law by Bill Clinton. The legislation was criticized by some as unduly harsh on debtors, but its reauthorization of Chapter 12, applying to farmers, would allow them to reorganize without creditors' consent. On the issue that seems to be agitating increasingly white-collar Iowa even more than farm prices—airline competition—he worked successfully with colleague Tom Harkin to provide more competition by eliminating grandfathered slots at O'Hare and other airports and opening them up to smaller, budget and startup airlines. He has also worked to stop agribusiness mergers, and for requiring the Agriculture Department to review them. Grassley has criticized federal judges for what he considers lavish spending and called for full disclosure of their financial interests. With Charles Schumer, he has tried to bring television to federal courts. They urged Chief Justice Rehnquist to let in the cameras when the court was considering the Florida cases in December 2000; the Court said no, but did release audiotapes immediately after oral argument.

From 1997 to 2001 Grassley chaired the Aging Committee. He conducted extensive hearings, often with witnesses from Iowa—"I have come to the conclusion that I will never have to visit Iowa in order to meet half of Iowa," said ranking Democrat John Breaux. Grassley highlighted such issues as nursing home quality, hospice care, Medicare reimbursement rules, rural health care and funeral home practices.

For more than 20 years Grassley has been the most popular politician in Iowa. As he once said, "I think I've established credibility with the people of Iowa that they know I'm going to use a common-sense approach to government." In 1986 he became the first Iowa senator to win re-election in 20 years, with a record 66%. In 1992 he broke the record when he won 70%–27%, carrying all 99 counties. In 1998, against a Democrat who campaigned by taking trips down Iowa rivers, he fell back to 68%–30%, carrying all 99 counties again, from Johnson County and its college town Iowa City (53%–45%) to heavily Dutch-American Sioux County (91%–9%). A January 2001 poll showed him with a 73% positive job rating. In August 1999 he said he expected to run again in 2004. At that point, he will have tied Bourke Hickenlooper for the second-longest tenure of an Iowa senator; he will beat the record set by William B. Allison if he serves until June 2016, three months before he turns 83.

Junior Senator Tom Harkin, first elected to the Senate in 1984, is an accomplished veteran of Capitol Hill who still brings the attitude of the aggrieved outsider to his work. Harkin grew up poor in a rural town, where his father was a coal miner and his mother, a Slovenian immigrant, died when he was 10. His desire to use government to help those who are struggling comes not from academic theory but from tough personal experience. He worked his way through college and law school, spent five years in the Navy during the 1960s, ferrying planes from Vietnam for repair. Returning there in 1970 as an aide to Congressman Neal Smith, he discovered the infamous "tiger cages" prison cells. After a narrow loss in 1972, Harkin ran for Congress again in 1974 and invented "work days," a campaign technique widely imitated since: he spent a day working at each of a dozen or so local jobs. He won solidly and held the seat with good percentages. Well before the 1984 election, he cornered the Democratic nomination to run against Senator Roger Jepsen. This was in the midst of Iowa's farm depression of the 1980s and Harkin was elected with 55% of the vote.

Harkin is now the chairman of the Agriculture Committee and has one of the most liberal voting records in the Senate. His biggest disappointment surely has been on farm policy. He came to the Senate as a self-styled populist, eager to expand government farm programs. His big initiative was the 1987 Harkin-Gephardt supply management farm bill, which would have raised overall food costs in order to benefit small farmers. But it was a nonstarter even in the 1980s, when Iowa farmers were hurting, and farm policy has moved on, to the Freedom to Farm Act, which was intended to phase out subsidies in seven years. In 2000 Harkin sought to make conservation payments an entitlement, with higher payments to those in a "higher tier" of conservation; he has promoted the use of ethanol and alcohol fuels. Farm exports are important to Iowa, and Harkin, despite his warm feelings for labor unions, voted, apparently with some reluctance, for NAFTA in 1993 and PNTR for China in 2000.

Harkin's greatest impact has probably been on health policy. Two of his sisters died from breast cancer and one brother of thyroid cancer; another brother became deaf at age nine. He insisted on having a sign language interpreter present for his brother for his swearing-in in 1985, and when he left the 1992 presidential race he spoke partly in sign language at Gallaudet University in Washington, D.C., a noted school for the hearing impaired. His interest in deafness prompted him and Senator Jennings Randolph to bring the first closed-caption TV to the Carter White House; in 1991 he passed a law requiring close-captioning on all 13-inch-plus TVs starting in 1995—useful, he notes, not only for the deaf but for a senator watching debate on C-SPAN while making phone calls. Harkin was a key player in shaping the Americans with Disabilities Act of 1990. This was a great achievement, one that required overcoming resistance based on cost and qualms about the real-world effect of regulations, to build up a bipartisan coalition with the Bush administration. As chairman and ranking Democrat on the Labor-HHS Appropriations Committee Harkin worked creatively and determinedly to double the budget for the National Institutes of Health over five years—strengthening one of America's greatest research institutions in a way that may be remembered gratefully 50 or 100 years from now. He has also used that post to to establish grants for "assistive technology" for the handicapped and set up a new NIH Institute on Deafness and Other Communication Disorders and a National Center for Alternative and Complementary Medicine. With Arlen Specter, he prepared a bill to address medical errors in 2000. He was one of the lead sponsors of the unsuccessful tobacco legislation in 1998 and 1999, and had a bill to give the FDA authority to regulate tobacco in 2000.

On other domestic issues, Harkin has weighed in against cash-balance pension plans, which vastly reduce the pensions of longtime employees. He has long decried what he considers the high-interest-rate policies of Federal Reserve Chairman Alan Greenspan. In 1996 he delayed Greenspan's confirmation until June, extending his term to June 2000, thus giving Bill Clinton little option but to reappoint him; when he did Harkin was one of four senators to vote against confirmation. Harkin and Iowa colleague Charles Grassley successfully moved to eliminate the limited slots at four major airports, including O'Hare and Reagan National; high airfares are an issue in increasingly white-collar Iowa, and the Iowa senators wanted more competition from small, budget and startup airlines. In November 1999 Harkin sponsored a resolution honoring Shoeless Joe Jackson, the baseball hero who in the movie comes to the Field of Dreams in Dyersville, Iowa.

On foreign policy, Harkin's views seem to have been shaped by the Vietnam war. He was a vocal opponent of Contra aid in the 1980s and of the Gulf war resolution in 1991, bringing a lawsuit aganst President Bush to try to prevent him from using force without congressional approval. But he favored the threat of force in Haiti in 1994. He is on the lookout for excessive military perks, in 2000 opposing unsuccessfully the leasing of nine executive jets for admirals and generals (don't the services already have a lot of planes?). He has taken on a crusade against child labor, in this country and abroad, trying to get rid of exceptions to current laws and double penalties; he has spotlighted abusive child labor in such distant countries as Nepal and Pakistan.

Harkin has never had strong bipartisan support in Iowa, but he has beaten four incumbent Republican members of Congress—Bill Scherle in his first House race, Senator Roger Jepsen in 1984 and Congressmen Tom Tauke in 1990 and Jim Ross Lightfoot in 1996. He ran for president in 1992. In angry phrases, with a Trumanesque zest, Harkin preached that George Bush and the Republicans helped only the rich and that government must get involved to help the poor and middle class. But organized labor withheld an early endorsement despite his 90%-plus AFL-CIO voting record—a great tactical victory for Bill Clinton. Harkin's sweep of the Iowa caucuses February 10, actually an impressive testimonial to his home state popularity, was mostly discounted by the media. He finished with only 10% in New Hampshire; though he won the Minnesota and Idaho caucuses March 3, he got only 7% in South Carolina March 7 after campaigning there with Jesse Jackson. In debt and ineligible for matching funds, Harkin quit the race. He went on to campaign gamely for Clinton, and in 1996 and 2000 he campaigned heartily for Clinton and for Al Gore. He supported Clinton fervently during impeachment, calling the House managers' case "a pile of dung" and made the only objection during the trial, arguing that senators should not be called "jurors" because their duties went beyond those of jurors and they were not limited by the Constitution or the Federalist Papers to just a narrow finding of fact; Chief Justice William Rehnquist, presiding over the trial, agreed. In 2000 Harkin endorsed Gore in the Iowa precinct caucuses and appeared with him all over the state—an important factor in Gore's smashing victory. Harkin was mentioned in July 2000 as a possible vice presidential nominee and was interviewed twice by Warren Christopher. Harkin strongly supported Gore in the Florida recount; afterwards, he and Arlen Specter sponsored a bipartisan commission to study elections.

Harkin's 1996 victory over Lightfoot came after a hot campaign, and was —by only a 52%–47% margin—his closest race yet. In 1998, Lightfoot ran for governor, and Harkin made it a personal project to defeat him, raising $300,000 for little-known Democrat Tom Vilsack and sending his topnotch political consultants into the campaign; Vilsack won a 52%–47% upset victory. Harkin comes up for re-election in 2002, and he is likely to get a strong challenge from Republican Congressman Greg Ganske. Harkin tends to polarize the electorate, and in early 2001 Ganske was running even with him in his home district where he is well known. In a year when most senators of both parties seem utterly safe, this could be one of the more seriously contested races in the country. Others mentioned as possible opponents are Congressman Roger Latham and farmer Bill Salier, a young conservative. But anyone who takes on Harkin will have a fight, as four former Republican members of Congress from Iowa can attest.

Cook's Call   *Highly Competitive.* Republican Congressman Greg Ganske's challenge to Harkin sets up one of the best races of this cycle. But Harkin has beaten tough opponents before. Though Ganske is a moderate and well positioned for the race, he will have to work to avoid getting pushed too far to the right, a tactic Harkin has used successfully in the past against other moderates.

Presidential politics   On a frosty evening in late January or early February, about 150,000 Iowans troop to caucuses in some 2,131 precincts and begin the process of choosing a president of the United States. The precinct caucuses were scheduled early in the cycle for 1972 by Democratic doves who wanted more leverage for their views, and that year they started George McGovern on his way to the Democratic nomination. But the caucuses have had other, unanticipated consequences. In 1976 Jimmy Carter's strategist Hamilton Jordan determined that intensive campaigning could produce a surprise victory that could make a little-known candidate a national contender: Without Iowa and the next-week New Hampshire primary, Carter would never have become president.

Then, for 20 years, the Iowa caucuses were less nomination-determinative. In 1980 George Bush's intensive campaigning gave him a victory among Republicans, while Carter, still profiting from his 1976 contacts, trounced Edward Kennedy. But Bush lost the nomination to Ronald Reagan, and Carter lost in November. In 1984 Democratic favorite Walter Mondale won 49% of the "delegate strength" (Democrats don't compute the actual number of votes), but the momentum went to the 17% second place finisher Gary Hart, though Mondale did win the nomination. In 1988, Iowa failed to pick the winners on either side: Dick Gephardt, dressed in a warm-up jacket and baseball cap, capitalized on Iowa's economic woes to win among Democrats, while George Bush finished in third place behind Bob Dole and televangelist Pat Robertson among Republicans—a sign of the rising strength of Christian conservatives here. But Gephardt and Dole lost in New Hampshire, and neither was nominated. In 1992 Iowa went dark: no Democrat challenged Iowa's Tom Harkin here, and Pat Buchanan began his campaign in New Hampshire. In 1996 Bob Dole had the support of leading Republicans, led by Governor Terry Branstad and Senator Charles Grassley, and farm state roots as well: Dole's very narrow victory was an omen of the weakness of his candidacy later, and the negative ads run against him by Steve Forbes and others may have contributed to his weak showing in Iowa in the fall.

But Iowa is determined to maintain its first-in-the-nation status, enshrined in national Democratic (but not Republican) rules. "Iowa is a good barometer of political candidates," argues Governor Tom Vilsack. "They have to come into our living rooms. They have to go into cafes. They have to go into coffee shops. They have to stand the test of time." In 2000 Iowa moved its caucus date back to Monday, January 24, when New Hampshire surprised everyone by scheduling its primary for Tuesday, February 1. And in 2000 Iowa turned out to be important again. The Republican favorite, George W. Bush, refused to campaign here (or anywhere else) before the Texas legislature adjourned in May 1999, but he charged into the battle for the Republicans' straw poll at Ames on August 14. Originally designed as a Republican fundraiser, the straw poll had let anyone with $25 vote up through 1996; in 2000 it limited participation to Iowans, and got much more than ever before—25,000 attended, about 30% as many as would vote in the much more convenient precinct caucuses in January. Bush won with 31%, followed by intensive campaigner Steve Forbes, with 21%; Elizabeth Dole, with 14%, and Gary Bauer, with 9%, which kept their campaigns alive. Pat Buchanan, with fewer votes from a larger crowd than in 1996, did not succeed, and not long afterwards left the Republican Party for his ill-fated Reform Party candidacy.

In January the standing was not much different. Bush won with 41% of the vote and Forbes got 30%, not the upset victory he needed. Both got a share of religious conservatives, as did Alan Keyes, who was third with 14%. In November 1999, John McCain announced he was staying out of dovish Iowa.

Democrats had only two candidates, and both Al Gore and Bill Bradley campaigned intensively. In his 1988 campaign Gore skipped what he called "madness" in "the small state of Iowa"; in June 1997 he was proclaiming, "I love Iowa," and in November 1998 he was on the phone congratulating Tom Vilsack before Vilsack himself realized he had been elected governor. Gore did not get Vilsack's support—he stayed carefully neutral—but Gore did get vigorous support from Vilsack's wife and from Senator Tom Harkin and, perhaps most important, from Iowa's labor unions. Bradley ran ahead in university towns, carrying Johnson County (Iowa City) and running even in Story County (Ames). And with support from professional-class liberals, he did not run far behind in the two biggest counties, Polk (Des Moines) and Linn (Cedar Rapids). But Gore won 70% or more in counties containing heavily unionized factory towns—Waterloo, Mason City, Fort Dodge, Marshalltown, Jasper, Keokuk, Burlington, Council Bluffs. That was dispositive since the Democratic vote is concentrated in urban areas, and Gore won in "delegate strength" with 63% to Bradley's 35%. This big victory undoubtedly gave Gore some momentum in New Hampshire, which he won by just 50%–46%. It would be five weeks until the next Democratic contest and, as eyes turned to George W. Bush's battles with John McCain, the race for the Democratic nomination was over.

No one pays close attention to Iowa's seven electoral votes in the fall, though perhaps someone should; this state came very close to the national average in 2000. Al Gore won a 48.5%–48.2% victory, carrying most of the counties east and north of Cedar Rapids plus a narrow margin in the Des Moines area; George W. Bush carried most counties in the west and south. In some ways this ran on traditional Iowa divisions: Bush carried Protestants, Gore Catholics. But it was not necessarily a harbinger of future Democratic victories. Iowa has the nation's third-highest percentage of elderly, and Gore carried those over 65 by 51%–48%, according to the VNS exit poll; of those who voted the issue of Social Security, Gore won by a surprisingly narrow 54%–43%. In contrast, Bush carried voters under 45—the future of Iowa—by 52%–45%. This is a state that should be seriously contested in any close race in the future.

Congressional districting   Iowa's congressional district lines are drawn by the nonpartisan Legislative Services Bureau and then approved by the (now Democratic) governor and (still Republican) legislature—as nonpolitical a process as in any state. In 1991 they were not drawn to the convenience of either party or of incumbent House members, and caused some scrambling; the resulting delegation has been 4–1 Republican since 1994. The new map presented to the legislature in June 2001 is sure to cause even more scrambling as it moves quite a bit of territory around for all five incumbents. It throws Republicans Jim Leach and Jim Nussle's hometowns together in a new 1st District, and leaves a Democratic-leaning 2nd without an incumbent. The state's only Democratic representative, Leonard Boswell ends up in vast new territory in western Iowa that has an almost 2–1 Republican edge. Des Moines gets lopped off from its surrounding suburbs and placed in a new 3rd District, which will also not have an incumbent since Republican Greg Ganske is running for governor. There could be a lot of moving vans crisscrossing this state, and it is hard to predict which party will be helped or hurt most with these new lines. Current incumbents have run ahead of party: Democrat Boswell's 3d District voted for George W. Bush and Republicans Leach and Nussle's 1st and 2d Districts voted for Al Gore.

THE PEOPLE: Pop. 2000: 2,926,324; Pop. 1990: 2,776,755, up 5.4% 1990–2000. 1% of U.S. total, 30th largest; 93.9% White, 2.1% Black, 1.3% Asian, 0.3% Amer. Indian, 1.1% Two+ races, 1.3% Other; 2.8% Hispanic Origin. 2.6% Unemployment. 2000 Voting age pop.: 2,192,686. 2000 Turnout: 1,328,067; 61% of VAP. Registered voters (2000): 1,741,346; 565,561 D (32%), 590,209 R (34%), 585,576 unaffiliated and minor parties (34%).

POLITICAL LINEUP: Governor, Thomas J. Vilsack (D); Lt. Gov., Sally Pederson (D); Secy. of State, Chester Culver (D); Atty. Gen., Tom Miller (D); Treasurer, Michael L. Fitzgerald (D); Auditor, Richard D. Johnson (R); Secy. of Agriculture, Patty Judge (D); State Senate, 50 (20 D, 30 R); Senate Pres. Pro Tempore, Andy McKean (R); Senate President, Mary Kramer (R); Majority Leader, Stewart Iverson Jr. (R); State House, 100 (44 D, 56 R); House Speaker, Brent Siegrist (R). Senators, Charles Grassley (R) and Tom Harkin (D). Representatives, 5 (1 D, 4 R).

ELECTIONS DIVISION: 515-281-5865; **FILING DEADLINE FOR U.S. CONGRESS:** March 15, 2002.

2000 Presidential Vote			1996 Presidential Vote		
Gore (D)	638,517	(49%)	Clinton (D)	620,258	(50%)
Bush (R)	634,373	(48%)	Dole (R)	492,644	(40%)
Nader (Green)	29,374	(2%)	Perot (I)	105,159	(9%)
Others	13,299	(1%)			

Gov. Thomas J. Vilsack (D)

Elected 1998, term expires Jan. 2003, 1st term; b. Dec. 13, 1950, Pittsburgh, PA; home, Mt. Pleasant; Hamilton Col., B.A. 1972, Albany Law Schl., J.D. 1975; Catholic; married (Christie).

Elected Office: Mt. Pleasant Mayor, 1987–92; IA Senate, 1992–98.

Professional Career: Practicing atty., 1975–98.

Office: State Capitol, Des Moines, 50319, 515-281-5211; Fax: 515-281-6611; Web site: www.state.ia.us.

Election Results

1998 general	Thomas J. Vilsack (D)	500,231	(52%)
	Jim Ross Lightfoot (R)	444,787	(47%)
	Others	11,397	(1%)
1998 primary	Thomas J. Vilsack (D)	59,130	(51%)
	Mark McCormick (D)	55,950	(48%)
1994 general	Terry E. Branstad (R)	566,395	(57%)
	Bonnie J. Campbell (D)	414,453	(42%)
	Others	16,400	(2%)

Sen. Charles Grassley (R)

Elected 1980, seat up 2004, 4th term; b. Sep. 17, 1933, New Hartford; home, New Hartford; U. of N. IA, B.A. 1955, M.A. 1956, U. of IA, 1957–58; Baptist; married (Barbara).

Elected Office: IA House of Reps., 1958–74; U.S. House of Reps., 1974–80.

Professional Career: Farmer.

DC Office: 135 HSOB, 20510, 202-224-3744; Fax: 202-224-6020; Web site: www.senate.gov/~grassley.

State Offices: Cedar Rapids, 319-363-6832; Council Bluffs, 712-322-7103; Davenport, 319-322-4331; Des Moines, 515-284-4890; Sioux City, 712-233-1860; Waterloo, 319-232-6657.

Committees: *Budget. Finance* (RMM): Health Care; International Trade; Long-Term Growth & Debt Reduction. *Judiciary*: Administrative Oversight & the Courts; Immigration; Youth Violence (RMM). *Joint Committee on Taxation* (3d of 5 Sens.).

Group Ratings

	ADA	ACLU	AFS	LCV	CON	ITIC	NTU	COC	ACU	NTLC	CHC
2000	0	29	0	0	11	100	74	100	96	97	92
1999	0	—	0	11	36	—	78	94	92	—	—

National Journal Ratings

	1999 LIB —	1999 CONS		2000 LIB —	2000 CONS
Economic	19% —	75%		32% —	64%
Social	41% —	58%		10% —	81%
Foreign	10% —	84%		27% —	67%

Key Votes of the 106th Congress

1. Educ. Savings Accts.	Y	5. Review Movie Violence	Y	9. NATO War in Serbia	N
2. Prescrip. Drug Benefit	N	6. Gun Show Bckgrnd. Checks	N	10. Table Cuba Travel Ban	Y
3. Delay Ergonomic Standards	Y	7. Ban Part.-Birth Abortion	Y	11. Nuclear Test-Ban Treaty	N
4. Phase Out Estate Tax	Y	8. Broaden Hate Crimes List	N	12. Perm. Trade with China	Y

Election Results

1998 general	Charles Grassley (R)	648,480	(68%)	($2,781,940)
	David Osterberg (D)	289,049	(30%)	($165,429)
	Others	10,378	(1%)	
1998 primary	Charles Grassley (R)	unopposed		
1992 general	Charles Grassley (R)	899,761	(70%)	($2,486,030)
	Jean Lloyd-Jones (D)	351,561	(27%)	($410,894)
	Others	40,879	(3%)	

Sen. Tom Harkin (D)

Elected 1984, seat up 2002, 3d term; b. Nov. 19, 1939, Cumming; home, Cumming; IA St. U., B.S. 1962, Catholic U., J.D. 1972; Catholic; married (Ruth).

Military Career: Navy, 1962–67; Naval Reserves, 1969–72.

Elected Office: U.S. House of Reps., 1974–84.

Professional Career: Practicing atty., 1972–74; Staff Aide, House Select Cmte. on U.S. Involvement in SE Asia, 1973–74.

DC Office: 731 HSOB, 20510, 202-224-3254; Fax: 202-224-9369; Web site: www.senate.gov/~harkin.

State Offices: Cedar Rapids, 319-365-4504; Davenport, 319-322-1338; Des Moines, 515-284-4574; Dubuque, 319-582-2130; Sioux City, 712-252-1550.

Committees: *Agriculture, Nutrition & Forestry* (Chmn.). *Appropriations:* Agriculture & Rural Development; Defense; Foreign Operations; Labor, HHS & Education (Chmn.); VA, HUD & Independent Agencies. *Health, Education, Labor & Pensions:* Employment, Safety & Training; Public Health. *Small Business.*

Group Ratings

	ADA	ACLU	AFS	LCV	CON	ITIC	NTU	COC	ACU	NTLC	CHC
2000	95	71	85	100	54	93	10	57	4	0	15
1999	100	—	100	89	68	—	6	47	4	—	—

National Journal Ratings

	1999 LIB —	1999 CONS		2000 LIB —	2000 CONS
Economic	90% —	0%		90% —	7%
Social	81% —	12%		79% —	0%
Foreign	87% —	0%		95% —	0%

Key Votes of the 106th Congress

1. Educ. Savings Accts.	N	5. Review Movie Violence	Y	9. NATO War in Serbia	Y
2. Prescrip. Drug Benefit	Y	6. Gun Show Bckgrnd. Checks	Y	10. Table Cuba Travel Ban	N
3. Delay Ergonomic Standards	N	7. Ban Part.-Birth Abortion	N	11. Nuclear Test-Ban Treaty	Y
4. Phase Out Estate Tax	N	8. Broaden Hate Crimes List	Y	12. Perm. Trade with China	Y

Election Results

1996 general	Tom Harkin (D)	634,166	(52%)	($6,070,137)
	Jim Ross Lightfoot (R)	571,807	(47%)	($2,439,679)
1996 primary	Tom Harkin (D)	unopposed		
1990 general	Tom Harkin (D)	529,571	(54%)	($5,628,242)
	Thomas J. Tauke (R)	453,273	(46%)	($5,060,104)

FIRST DISTRICT

A century and a half ago settlers surged west across the Mississippi River into the fertile, hilly lands that became Iowa. There New England and Midwestern Yankees built on the strange, open terrain their characteristic farmhouses, barns, town halls, church spires and small colleges; Germans, after crossing the ocean, stopped at the river bluffs reminiscent of their native land and built neat farmhouses and substantial towns; railroad builders, headquartered in Chicago, extended their networks of steel rails over the plains and rivers. Today some of the distinctiveness of these settlers remains in eastern Iowa, though the old ethnic folkways have faded and giant barges and riverboat casinos have replaced the old river craft. Davenport, on the hills over the Mississippi River still has the look of the city where Ronald Reagan got his first radio job more than 60 years ago; in order to maintain its riverfront heritage, the city has refused to erect flood walls along the Mississippi which brought the ire of FEMA Director Joseph Allbaugh during the April 2001 flood season. Cedar Rapids, a couple of counties west of the river, looks more contemporary, with big high-tech employers; it has been booming in the 1990s, and per capita income, adjusted for the local cost of living, is among the nation's highest. Iowa City, to the south, is a university town complete with trendy bookstores and vegetarian eateries; the University of Iowa is known for its Writer's Workshop and for graduate programs in audiology, printmaking, creative writing, speech-language pathology, nursing service administration—all rated number one by *U.S. News & World Report* in 2000. Rural Cedar County, the birthplace of Herbert Hoover, reported a tie on election night, the only county in the nation to do so; a recount gave Al Gore a 4,033–4,031 vote lead.

Eight counties in eastern Iowa, with Davenport in one corner and Cedar Rapids in another, make up the 1st Congressional District. Historically Republican, it trended Democratic in the 1970s and 1980s and is now by some measures the most Democratic district in the state.

The congressman from the 1st District, however, is Jim Leach, a Republican first elected in 1976, and chairman of the House Banking Committee from 1995 to 2001. Leach grew up in Davenport, where his family owned propane gas and wholesale businesses, attended Princeton, studied Soviet politics at Johns Hopkins and the London School of Economics. He became a Foreign Service officer in 1968, worked for Donald Rumsfeld at the Office of Economic Opportunity, then was assigned to the Arms Control and Disarmament Agency and served in the United Nations when George Bush was U.S. ambassador there. In 1973 Leach resigned after Richard Nixon fired special prosecutor Archibald Cox and returned to the family businesses in Davenport; in 1976 he ran for the House and beat incumbent Democrat Edward Mezvinsky. A believer in free enterprise with hands-on experience in a regulated business, Leach remains market-oriented on most economic issues. On cultural issues, he looks with some favor on international family planning and affirmative action. On foreign policy, like many Iowa Republicans, he has shown caution about asserting U.S. military power, but supported the Gulf war resolution in 1991, continued deployment of troops in Bosnia in 1997, and additional loan dollars for the International Monetary Fund in 1998.

On the Banking Committee Leach has often been ahead of his time in pointing to problems. He was one of the few who predicted the S&L crisis of the late 1980s: Leach warned early on that allowing the states to liberate their savings and loans from investment limits while maintaining federal deposit insurance and not increasing capital requirements would lead to trouble. His greatest achievement was the passage in November 1999 of financial services deregulation, tearing down the 1933 Glass-Steagall Act wall between commercial and investment banks, authorizing financial holding companies and allowing them to own insurance companies. It also contained dozens of other detailed provisions, many negotiated out after months of wrangling between various financial interests and between the Clinton Treasury and the Federal Reserve. This bill was the focus of most of his chairmanship; his efforts were blocked by the insurance industry in 1996 and his bill was yanked from the floor by the leadership in March 1998. Progress came in 1999 as Leach reached agreements with Senate Banking Chairman Phil Gramm and Commerce Chairman Thomas Bliley. When the bill finally passed by lopsided votes, he said, "This is an historic day. The landscape for delivery of financial services will now surely shift." On other Banking Committee issues, Leach was proud that debt relief for the poorest nations and the World Banks AIDS Trust Fund was passed in 1999. He sponsored a bill to protect the privacy of bank customers' medical and health information, another to hinder money-laundering by prohibiting banks from providing accounts for unregulated offshore banks and a third bill to bar Internet gambling firms from accepting credit card payments.

Leach is one of the least partisan of congressmen. But in July 1995, when he chaired hearings on Whitewater, he was confronted by a barrage of loud partisan objections from Democrats, who then tried to discredit the hearings as partisan—the Democratic modus operandi, it became clear, whenever Republicans attempted to investigate Clinton wrongdoing. At home Leach was re-elected without difficulty from 1978 to 1994. In 1996, after the Whitewater hearings, he had spirited opposition from former state Senator Bob Rush, who got a late-campaign appearance by Bill Clinton. Rush charged that Leach had become more conservative and partisan. Leach's race was made more difficult by his refusal to accept contributions over $500, from outside Iowa or from PACs. Thus, the chairman of the Banking Committee was outraised by his challenger, $370,000 to $420,000. The 1st District went solidly for Clinton in 1996 as it had in 1992, and Leach won only narrowly, 53%–46%. In disproof of Rush's charges, Leach in January 1997 was the second Republican to announce he would not vote for Newt Gingrich for speaker and said that Gingrich's defense against ethics charges was "simply inadequate for a maker of laws." In 1998, Leach beat Rush by a more comfortable margin, 57%–42%, benefiting from the pro-incumbent tide of 1998; he carried Scott County and Davenport by better than 2–1 and Linn County and Cedar Rapids as well.

In 2000 Leach faced an underfinanced opponent and readily agreed with him to not run television ads. He won by a solid 62%–36% margin, carrying every county. Before the election, he had come out in favor of electing presidents by popular vote, with a runoff if no candidate gets over 40% of the vote. Leach lost the Banking chairmanship under House Republican's six-year term limit. The International Relations chairmanship went to Henry Hyde; Hyde had asked to retain the Judiciary chairmanship and, denied that, campaigned harder for International Relations. Redistricting has significantly changed the boundaries here, putting both his and 2nd District Representative Jim Nussle's hometowns together; Leach may decide to run in the new 2nd. But this is still a pretty Democratic and it might very well be won by a Democrat.

Cook's Call *Potentially Competitive*. The June 2001 map drawn by the non-partisan Legislative Services Bureau has shaken up the state's five districts rather significantly. Nowhere is that more apparent than this district. The map has the 1st District move north to take in parts of the old 2nd, including the home of 2nd District Representative Jim Nussle. There may be a showdown between the two incumbents or, Leach may move down into the newly drawn 2nd District (which contains much of his old 1st), where he could face former 3rd District Democrat Leonard Boswell in a Democratic leaning district.

THE PEOPLE: Pop. 2000: 603,837; Pop. 1990: 555,229, up 8.8% 1990–2000. 92% White, 3.2% Black, 1.7% Asian, 0.3% Amer. Indian, 1.5% Two+ races, 1.3% Other; 3.2% Hispanic Origin.

2000 Presidential Vote			1996 Presidential Vote		
Gore (D)	147,279	(53%)	Clinton (D)	135,839	(54%)
Bush (R)	118,268	(43%)	Dole (R)	92,207	(37%)
Nader (Green)	8,074	(3%)	Perot (I)	19,027	(8%)
Others	2,160	(1%)	Others	4,409	(2%)

Rep. Jim Leach (R)

Elected 1976, 13th term; b. Oct. 15, 1942, Davenport; home, Davenport; Princeton U., B.A. 1964, Johns Hopkins U., M.A. 1966, London Schl. of Econ., 1966–68; Episcopalian; married (Elisabeth).

Professional Career: Staff Asst., U.S. Rep. Donald Rumsfeld, 1965–66; U.S. Foreign Svc., 1968–69, 1971–72 (Arms Control & Disarmament Agency); A.A. to Dir., U.S. Office of Econ. Opp., 1969–70; Pres., Flamegas Co., 1973–76; Chmn. of the Bd., Adel Wholesalers, Inc., 1973–76; Dir., Fed. Home Loan Bank Bd., Midwest Reg., 1975–76.

DC Office: 2186 RHOB 20515, 202-225-6576; Fax: 202-226-1278; Web site: www.house.gov/leach.

District Offices: Cedar Rapids, 319-363-4773; Davenport, 319-326-1841; Iowa City, 319-351-0789.

Committees: *Financial Services* (2d of 37 R): Domestic Monetary Policy, Technology & Economic Growth (Vice Chmn.). *International Relations* (3d of 26 R): East Asia & the Pacific (Chmn.); Europe.

Group Ratings

	ADA	ACLU	AFS	LCV	CON	ITIC	NTU	COC	ACU	NTLC	CHC
2000	30	43	0	79	11	94	54	80	58	58	60
1999	55	—	33	56	26	—	57	76	48	—	—

National Journal Ratings

	1999 LIB	—	1999 CONS		2000 LIB	—	2000 CONS
Economic	45%	—	55%		46%	—	54%
Social	54%	—	45%		55%	—	44%
Foreign	40%	—	59%		58%	—	40%

Key Votes of the 106th Congress

1. Patient Bill of Rights	Y	5. Bar RU-486 $ for FDA	N	9. NATO War in Serbia	N
2. Accelerate Min. Wage	Y	6. Display 10 Commandments	Y	10. Perm. Trade with China	Y
3. Strike Ban on Ergo. Stnd.	N	7. Gun Show Bkgrnd. Checks	Y	11. Debt Relief for 3rd World	Y
4. Ovrd. Estate Tax Veto	Y	8. Ban Part.-Birth Abortion	Y	12. Drop Cuba Econ. Embargo	Y

Election Results

2000 general	Jim Leach (R)	164,972	(62%)	($335,143)
	Bob Simpson (D)	96,283	(36%)	($28,536)
	Other	5,564	(2%)	
2000 primary	Jim Leach (R)	unopposed		
1998 general	Jim Leach (R)	106,419	(57%)	($673,673)
	Bob Rush (D)	79,529	(42%)	($468,465)
	Others	2,260	(1%)	

SECOND DISTRICT

Northeast Iowa, along the Mississippi River and westward, has some of the loveliest landscape in America. Here the Mississippi flows past green bluffs, then broadens out in great quiet pools and flows past picturesque German-style towns. Inland from the river are the rolling hills portrayed with surprisingly little exaggeration in the paintings of Iowa's Grant Wood. These lands were settled by immigrants in the 19th Century. German Catholics settled Dubuque, whose giant Victorian courthouse looks down on the Mississippi and up at the Fenelon Place Elevator that rides up the bluff. Just west of Dubuque is Dyersville, where *Field of Dreams* was filmed in 1989 and to which baseball buffs now repair. Farther west is Waterloo, which grew rapidly after 1900 as the John Deere tractor factory expanded and the eight-floor Rath factory became the largest meat-packing plant in the world; Rath closed in 1984 and Deere had thousands of layoffs, but Waterloo has rebounded somewhat with new businesses from a dog track to telemarketing to a high-tech Iowa Beef Processing (IBP) factory. To the northwest is Mason City, a place remembered in Meredith Willson's *Music Man*. To the south are the Amana colonies, settled in the 1850s by the Community of True Inspiration, German pietists who have retained many of their old customs even as they have built the Amana appliance business.

The 2d Congressional District covers most of northeast Iowa, including Dubuque and Waterloo, Dyersville and Mason City and the Amana colonies. There is considerable political variation here. Dubuque, heavily German Catholic, was for years Iowa's most Democratic city, and still often is unless abortion is the issue. But the rural counties along the river and farther west—more German Protestant, Scandinavian and Yankee—were traditionally Republican. Waterloo, originally Republican, trended sharply Democratic in the troubled 1980s.

The congressman from the 2d District is Jim Nussle, first elected in 1990, at 30 the youngest member of the 102nd Congress. Nussle grew up in Chicago, then moved back to his native Iowa to attend a Lutheran college (he is Danish-American and speaks Danish; he has a Great Dane PAC) and law school. In the small town way, he soon became Delaware County attorney, known for prosecuting a local day care employee for child abuse. He coupled his anti-abortion stance with support for helping expectant mothers with the expenses of parenthood. When Republican Congressman Tom Tauke ran for the Senate in 1990, Nussle ran for his seat, narrowly winning the Republican primary and then facing a better-financed Democrat. Nussle emphasized his experience in law enforcement, called for more informed parental involvement in the drug war as well as in choosing day care. This was enough for him to win 50%–49%, one of the closest margins in the country that year.

Nussle quickly became one of the leaders of the nascent Republican revolution. He was one of the Gang of Seven, a group of freshman Republican reformers who attacked the Democratic leadership. In October 1991 he made national news by donning a paper bag over his head on the House floor to protest Democratic leaders' refusal to make full disclosure of House bank overdrafts. He voted against agricultural appropriations, to the dismay of senior Iowa Democrats, and moved to cut congressional salaries 5% every year the federal budget is not balanced. For 1992, redistricting put Nussle into a district with incumbent Dave Nagle, a Democrat who had helped organize the defense of Speaker Jim Wright against Newt Gingrich's charges in 1989. Nagle had represented more of the new district's territory, but Nussle won again by 50%–49%. In 1994 Nagle tried again, and Nussle won more easily, 56%–43%.

After the election, Gingrich appointed Nussle chairman of the transition to Republican rule: from paper bag to power in just three years. Nussle froze hiring, demanded detailed accountings, and supervised an overhaul of House administration. He also got a seat on Ways and Means. But Nussle had an unexpectedly tough time of it in the 1996 election. He vastly outspent Democrat Donna Smith, a 17-year Dubuque County supervisor, but she hammered home his closeness to Gingrich, and attacked "Georgia Jim" for supporting big hog feedlots. Nussle won by just 53%–46%, losing Dubuque County and Waterloo's Black Hawk County.

After that election Nussle sounded a much less revolutionary note. He was passed over by Gingrich for the chair of the Republicans' campaign committee and in July 1997 he ran for Conference vice chairman against Jennifer Dunn, Gingrich's choice, but lost 129–85. Nussle turned to issues with local appeal. He became the loudest House supporter of extending the ethanol tax credit beyond 2000 and, though he was barred from taking that to the House floor, he was the lead House conferee on the committee that adopted Senator Charles Grassley's move to extend it to 2007.

Since then Nussle has spent much time on budget issues. Working with Democrat Ben Cardin, Nussle produced a proposal to change the budget process; it would make the budget resolution law, to be signed by the president; call for automatic continuing resolutions, to prevent government shutdowns; and set up a five-year budget for emergencies, to eliminate supplemental appropriations. It did not include the two-year budget sought by Senate leaders. Nussle and Cardin brought this to the floor in May 2000, where it was opposed by leading Appropriations and Transportation Committee members. On a bipartisan vote, it was defeated 250–166. Nussle's response: "We are going to try again. Just about everybody admits the process is broken." In July 1999, when John Kasich announced his retirement from the House, Nussle said he would run for Budget chairman. He had been on the committee for eight years, the Republican limit, and he quickly picked up the support of Majority Leader Dick Armey, whom he supported in the 1998 leadership fight. Nussle said his major goals were to mitigate partisanship and reduce the national debt. The House leadership in January 2001 picked Nussle, who now occupies one of its most visible positions.

On other issues, Nussle served four years as co-chairman of the Rural Health Coalition, and claims some of the credit for a more favorable Medicare reimbursement formula, the Critical Access program to keep rural hospitals open, expanded Medicare reimbursement for nurse practitioners and physician's assistants, and increased access to telemedicine. With Senators Charles Grassley and Tom Harkin, he wants to ban MBTE in gasoline, a competior of Iowa's ethanol. With Grassley he wants to require more energy-efficient washing machines and refrigerators: appliance manufacturers Maytag, Amana and Frigidaire have Iowa factories. One of his children is a special education student, and he wants to increase IDEA funding. In the dovish Iowa tradition, he wants to end the Selective Service, which has not had much work since the draft was abolished in 1973. He has obtained funds to expand the Effigy Mounds National Monument in Allamakee County.

After his weak showing in 1996, Nussle had serious competition in 1998 from Rob Tully, former head of the Iowa Trial Lawyers Association, who moved from Des Moines to his native Dubuque to run. Nussle won 55%–44%, losing Dubuque and Black Hawk Counties by very narrow margins and winning elsewhere. In 2000 Donna Smith ran again, once again denouncing the Freedom to Farm Act, once again with little money. But farm subsidies are no longer a hot issue in Iowa and, although Al Gore carried the 2d District, Nussle again won by a 55%–44% margin, for the first time carrying every county.

Cook's Call   *Potentially Competitive.* The non-partisan Legislative Services Bureau (the redistricting body in the state) drew a new congressional map that combines parts of Nussle's current 2nd District (including his home area of Dubuque), with parts of the 1st District represented by longtime Representative Jim Leach. Leach and Nussle could challenge each other in a Republican primary, one could retire or could move to another district.

THE PEOPLE: Pop. 2000: 568,857; Pop. 1990: 555,494, up 2.4% 1990–2000. 95.5% White, 2.1% Black, 0.5% Asian, 0.3% Amer. Indian, 0.8% Two+ races, 0.6% Other; 1.4% Hispanic Origin.

2000 Presidential Vote		
Gore (D)	132,318	(51%)
Bush (R)	117,021	(45%)
Nader (Green)	5,607	(2%)
Others	2,469	(1%)

1996 Presidential Vote		
Clinton (D)	129,148	(53%)
Dole (R)	91,155	(37%)
Perot (I)	21,377	(9%)

Rep. Jim Nussle (R)

Elected 1990, 6th term; b. June 27, 1960, Des Moines; home, Manchester; Luther Col., B.A. 1983, Drake U., J.D. 1985; Lutheran; divorced.

Elected Office: Delaware Cnty. Atty., 1986–90.

Professional Career: Practicing atty., 1985–86.

DC Office: 303 CHOB 20515, 202-225-2911; Fax: 202-225-9129; Web site: www.house.gov/nussle.

District Offices: Dubuque, 319-557-7740; Manchester, 319-927-5141; Mason City, 641-423-0303; Waterloo, 310-235-1109.

Committees: *Budget* (Chmn. of 24 R). *Ways & Means* (10th of 24 R): Trade.

Group Ratings

	ADA	ACLU	AFS	LCV	CON	ITIC	NTU	COC	ACU	NTLC	CHC
2000	15	21	0	14	50	95	62	95	84	79	100
1999	20	—	0	0	44	—	63	100	80	—	—

National Journal Ratings

	1999 LIB	—	1999 CONS		2000 LIB	—	2000 CONS
Economic	16%	—	78%		28%	—	71%
Social	29%	—	69%		0%	—	79%
Foreign	23%	—	73%		56%	—	42%

Key Votes of the 106th Congress

1. Patient Bill of Rights	N	5. Bar RU-486 $ for FDA	Y	9. NATO War in Serbia	N
2. Accelerate Min. Wage	N	6. Display 10 Commandments	Y	10. Perm. Trade with China	Y
3. Strike Ban on Ergo. Stnd.	N	7. Gun Show Bkgrnd. Checks	N	11. Debt Relief for 3rd World	Y
4. Ovrd. Estate Tax Veto	Y	8. Ban Part.-Birth Abortion	Y	12. Drop Cuba Econ. Embargo	Y

Election Results

2000 general	Jim Nussle (R)	139,906	(55%)	($907,935)
	Donna L. Smith (D)	110,327	(44%)	($92,477)
	Other	2,288	(1%)	
2000 primary	Jim Nussle (R)	unopposed		
1998 general	Jim Nussle (R)	104,613	(55%)	($902,684)
	Rob Tully (D)	83,405	(44%)	($687,083)
	Others	1,556	(1%)	

THIRD DISTRICT

As the pioneers did a century and a half ago, the rolling farmland of southern Iowa heads west, from the railroad towns perched below the bluffs on the Mississippi River to the dusty plains above the Missouri River looking over to Nebraska and the West. The southern two tiers of Iowa's counties have none of the state's large cities; the accent here sounds a bit like rural Missouri. Population here has been declining for many years, as the numerous children of large farm families seek opportunity elsewhere, since mechanization and technology require fewer people to work the land.

The 3d Congressional District covers 27 counties in southern Iowa, including almost all of the southern tier, from the Mississippi River border with Illinois almost to the Missouri River border with Nebraska. The 3d also juts north as far as Ames, the home of Iowa State University and the quadrennial "straw poll" fundraising event that now kicks off the Republican presidential contest. There are dozens of notable towns here: Pella, home of the Pella window firm; Newton, home of Maytag appliances; Grinnell, with Grinnell College; and Fairfield, the home of Maharishi University and national headquarters of the Natural Law Party, whose 2000 presidential nominee John Hagelin got 15% of the vote in surrounding Jefferson County. The historical preference here is mostly Republican, but there are traditionally Democratic counties as well, around Ames, along the Mississippi and just north of Missouri.

The congressman from the 3d District is Leonard Boswell, a Democrat elected in 1996, the only new Iowa Democrat elected to the House since 1986. He was not the stereotypical freshman, however. Boswell grew up on farms in Ringgold and Decatur Counties, near the Missouri border. He was drafted in 1956, at 22, and was a private in the Army. He re-enlisted, graduated first in his class in both fixed wing and helicopter flying school, served two years in Vietnam, and retired as a lieutenant colonel in 1976. Boswell settled down on his farm in Decatur County and became head of the local Farmers' Co-op. He managed to keep it out of bankruptcy during the farm depression of the 1980s and decided to go into politics. He was elected state senator from a six-county Republican district in 1984, served as chairman of Appropriations and, after 1992, Senate president; he was the Democratic nominee for lieutenant governor in 1994.

In 1996, when 3d District conservative Republican Congressman Jim Ross Lightfoot ran for the Senate, Boswell ran for the House. The general election with Poweshiek County attorney Mike Mahaffey was very much a contest of nice guys. Boswell flew his four-seater Piper Comanche 250 around the district and called for balancing the budget, higher education aid and protections against Medicare reductions, all to be financed with Pentagon cuts and elimination of Medicare waste. Mahaffey ran as a moderate Republican, budget-balancer and term-limits advocate. Boswell drew on his experience: "I'm a farmer, he's a lawyer. I have experience in budgeting. I've been there, done it." But Boswell was not a political naif. He was endorsed by the Farm Bureau, which usually backs Republicans. He raised more money than Mahaffey and, like other Democrats, ran ads attacking Newt Gingrich and the Republican Medicare plan. Mahaffey ran well ahead of Lightfoot's showing in the Senate race in the eastern and northern part of the district. But Boswell ran nearly 20 points ahead of Senator Tom Harkin's showing in his old state Senate district. The result was a 49%–48% Boswell victory.

Boswell got a seat on Agriculture and, amid dropping farm prices, continued to support the Freedom to Farm Act. He wants the next farm bill to help raise farmers' prices; his suggestions include increased use of conservation to reduce production and increase federal payments to farmers. Along with all of the delegation's Republicans, he voted for PNTR with China, the world's biggest market for pork. With the district's large population of seniors, he has been a vocal advocate of prescription-drug coverage in Medicare; an ad campaign by pharmaceutical firms against his position had little impact. He voted for the partial-birth abortion ban and for $18 billion in IMF loans. He was the only Iowan to vote for hate crime legislation, noting that he had seen discrimination against gay children of friends.

Boswell did not neglect Iowa issues. On the Transportation Committee he worked for continuation of the ethanol subsidy and got $33 million in road projects, including Highway 330 near Marshalltown, known as "The Ho Chi Minh Trail" because of its high death toll. He helped to form the Mississippi River Caucus to seek consensus on commercial uses of the river and its environmental protection.

In his first re-election, Boswell was one of the Republicans' top 10 incumbent targets. State Senator Larry McKibben, who raised nearly as much money as Boswell, attacked him for not voting for the fast track trade bill and for not backing drug sanctions against Mexico. But Boswell did not present a partisan image. In September 1998 he declined campaign help from Bill Clinton, who had been so helpful in 1996. In October 1998 he was one of 31 Democrats to vote for the Republicans' impeachment inquiry. In a year when most voters' mood was positive, Boswell seemed a comforting figure. Boswell won 57%–41%, carrying 22 of 27 counties. In 2000, he had token opposition and won 63%–34%. Iowa's bipartisan redistricting commission could sharply change the boundaries of this district, as it did last time, in which case Boswell would face the challenge of extending his personal popularity into new territory.

Cook's Call   *Potentially Competitive.* The non-partisan commission responsible for drawing the Iowa congressional lines drew a map that put Boswell's home in the new western 5th District, an overwhelming Republican stronghold. It is expected that Boswell will move into the adjoining 2nd District (which is made up of parts of the current 3rd and 1st) where he may face 1st District Republican Jim Leach. But, this newly created district will have a good Democratic underpinning.

THE PEOPLE: Pop. 2000: 573,674; Pop. 1990: 555,299, up 3.3% 1990–2000. 95.5% White, 1.1% Black, 1.3% Asian, 0.2% Amer. Indian, 0.9% Two+ races, 0.9% Other; 2% Hispanic Origin.

2000 Presidential Vote		
Bush (R)	125,784	(49%)
Gore (D)	122,176	(47%)
Nader (Green)	5,636	(2%)
Others	3,758	(1%)

1996 Presidential Vote		
Clinton (D)	123,246	(50%)
Dole (R)	95,308	(39%)
Perot (I)	21,408	(9%)
Others	4,576	(2%)

Rep. Leonard L. Boswell (D)

Elected 1996, 3d term; b. Jan. 10, 1934, Harrison Cnty., MO; home, Davis City; Graceland Col., B.A. 1969; Reorganized Latter Day Saints; married (Dody).

Military Career: Army, 1956–76 (Vietnam).

Elected Office: IA Senate, 1984–96, Pres., 1992–96.

Professional Career: Farmer.

DC Office: 1039 LHOB 20515, 202-225-3806; Fax: 202-225-5608; Web site: www.house.gov/boswell.

District Office: Osceola, 641-342-4801.

Committees: *Agriculture* (14th of 24 D): General Farm Commodities & Risk Management; Livestock & Horticulture. *Permanent Select Committee on Intelligence* (8th of 9 D): Human Intelligence, Analysis & Counterintelligence (RMM); Technical & Tactical Intelligence. *Transportation & Infrastructure* (23d of 34 D): Aviation; Highways & Transit.

Group Ratings

	ADA	ACLU	AFS	LCV	CON	ITIC	NTU	COC	ACU	NTLC	CHC
2000	55	36	71	57	43	83	41	65	41	27	47
1999	70	—	100	50	60	—	21	50	32	—	—

National Journal Ratings

	1999 LIB	—	1999 CONS		2000 LIB	—	2000 CONS
Economic	59%	—	40%		56%	—	43%
Social	56%	—	43%		59%	—	40%
Foreign	65%	—	34%		53%	—	47%

Key Votes of the 106th Congress

1. Patient Bill of Rights	Y	5. Bar RU-486 $ for FDA	N	9. NATO War in Serbia	Y
2. Accelerate Min. Wage	Y	6. Display 10 Commandments	Y	10. Perm. Trade with China	Y
3. Strike Ban on Ergo. Stnd.	Y	7. Gun Show Bkgrnd. Checks	N	11. Debt Relief for 3rd World	Y
4. Ovrd. Estate Tax Veto	Y	8. Ban Part.-Birth Abortion	Y	12. Drop Cuba Econ. Embargo	Y

Election Results

2000 general	Leonard L. Boswell (D)	156,327	(63%)	($710,518)
	Jay Marcus (R)	83,810	(34%)	($198,403)
	Other	8,677	(3%)	
2000 primary	Leonard L. Boswell (D)	unopposed		
1998 general	Leonard L. Boswell (D)	107,947	(57%)	($1,041,955)
	Larry McKibben (R)	78,063	(41%)	($847,794)
	Others	3,742	(2%)	

FOURTH DISTRICT

Iowa, which today seems very much in the middle of the country, was once part of the West. It was not only the home of sober farmers and pious burghers, but also the eastern terminus of the first Transcontinental Railroad, a waystop for people in a hurry to get across the Great Plains to the Rockies and the Pacific Northwest. Those who stayed behind were determined to use the wealth accumulated by methodical husbandry of their fertile farmlands to implant firmly the glories of Western civilization. You can feel that impulse today in Des Moines when you look across the river from downtown at the Victorian Capitol, its gold dome above a Corinthian pediment, or Terrace Hill, the beautifully restored governor's mansion, atop a hill overlooking the Raccoon River. The nearby Living History Farms, which recreate Indian villages, frontier towns and turn-of-the-century farms, show the effort the new settlers made to put their imprint on the environment. The same civilizing impulse can be seen farther west, in the city of Council Bluffs, in the mansion of General Grenville Dodge, who in 1859 lobbied Illinois lawyer Abraham Lincoln on the need for a transcontinental railroad; Lincoln got it through Congress in 1863, Dodge became its chief engineer, and Council Bluffs became its eastern terminus when it was completed in 1869.

Today, Iowa is, as one voter said with satisfaction, "in the heart of middle America." Around 1987, after nearly a decade of farm depression, Iowa's economy started to grow again—mostly in and around its cities, especially Des Moines, now spreading into the countryside even as farm counties' population continues to decline. Insurance and printing and service businesses are expanding in office centers downtown and at freeway interchanges; Iowans are driving 100 miles or more to fill the shopping malls at cities' edges. Missing perhaps is the heady confidence of Iowans when they were pushing the frontier west; but missing also is the bedraggled feeling of the 1980s: Des Moines is leading Iowa deliberately into the future. It ranked 10th among 219 metropolitan areas in per capita income when adjusted for the local cost of living.

The 4th Congressional District of Iowa includes Des Moines and most of its expanding suburban fringe, into fast-growing Dallas County and even into Madison County, site of the famous novel and movie. It also proceeds west to Council Bluffs and the Missouri River, along the interstate where communities are growing again. Historically, Des Moines, with its unionized workers and in the midst of corn and hog country and the liberal *Des Moines Register* setting the tone, yearned after farm subsidies and voted heavily Democratic; in the early 1990s it trended mildly toward the Republicans, though it voted for Governor Tom Vilsack in 1998 and, narrowly, for Al Gore in 2000. Council Bluffs, surrounded by beef grazing territory, where federal intrusion has long been resented, looks west to Omaha, taking on the culturally more conservative tone of Nebraska and the conservative politics of the *Omaha World-Herald*.

The congressman from the 4th District is Greg Ganske, a Republican first elected in a stunning upset in 1994. Ganske grew up in Manchester, where he worked in his father's grocery store, earning his way through the University of Iowa. After medical school he served in the Army Reserves and started a plastic surgery practice in Des Moines, specializing in reconstructive surgery for birth defects and victims of accidents, burns and crimes. Ganske and his wife, a physician, made plenty of money, raised a family and bought a farm. In 1994, he decided to run against Neal Smith, a Democrat first elected in 1958, chairman of an Appropriations subcommittee, who had not had strong opposition for years. Ganske put his own money, ultimately $618,000, into the campaign and, at Newt Gingrich's suggestion, bought a rusty beige 1958 DeSoto, made in the year Smith first won, and drove it around the district with a sign reading, "'58 Nealmobile—WHY is it still running?" Ganske opposed the Clinton health care plan and attacked Smith for "logrolling," saying, "What do 36-year career politicians like Neal Smith always do? They blame each other, spend more money and then raise your taxes." Smith spent more than $1 million, but Ganske won 53%–46%, winning 65% in Council Bluffs and 62% in rural counties, and losing to Smith in the Des Moines area by only 48%–51%.

In the House, Ganske got a seat on the Commerce Committee and compiled a moderate voting record. In Iowa fashion, he condemned plans to build a new Seawolf submarine and plans for NASA to send a monkey into space. In spring 1995 he and Pat Roberts assembled 105 Republicans to sign a letter calling for reducing the upper limit on the $500 per child tax credit from $200,000 to $95,000. After expressing some concern about the Republican Medicare plan, he successfully fought to include higher rural reimbursement rates for health plans, and voted for the bill. In 1996 he had serious competition from former nurse and Des Moines weathercaster Connie McBurney, and was a target of the AFL-CIO's barrage of TV ads; in the summer Ganske was trailing in polls. During the August 1996 recess he traveled to Peru, not to junket, but to do charity medical work, operating on children with cleft palates and other disfigurements. In the process he contracted post-viral encephalitis, and was hospitalized in Des Moines and off the campaign trail for weeks. It became difficult to portray him as a picture of greed or indifference. He regained the lead in polls, and won 52%–47%.

Ganske has become a major legislator on health issues. With Charlie Norwood, a dentist, he was one of the early and enthusiastic Republican supporters of the HMO regulation favored by most Democrats, which would allow patients to sue insurers. He was clearly influenced by experience. He showed pictures of disfigured children and said that hundreds of patients had HMO coverage denied for surgery as "cosmetic." Gingrich appointed him to the bipartisan Medicare Commission, but when it became known in July 1998 that he was going to appear with Bill Clinton in support of the Democrats' HMO bill, other Republicans protested, and Ganske resigned, apparently without rancor or retaliation. Ganske had already joined Norwood and Democrat John Dingell in seeking a discharge petition for their HMO bill; it was brought to the floor in July 1998 and defeated 217–212, and a Republican alternative passed 216–210. In the 106th Congress, Ganske and his allies continued to push for the measure. It passed the House on a much wider 275–151 margin, but Republican leaders stalled the House-Senate conference committee for the next year. The delay tactic appeared to work as Democrats shifted their focus to prescription-drug legislation and some large HMOs relaxed restrictions on patients' dealings with their physicians. But in February 2001 George W. Bush was unable to persuade Ganske to remove his name as a co-sponsor of the reintroduced legislation (though he did persuade Norwood).

On other issues, Ganske in the 106th Congress was one of six Republicans to break with their party on campaign finance reform and one of four to oppose the party's tax cut. After the Supreme Court ruled that the FDA lacked the authority to regulate tobacco, he sponsored a bill with Senator Tom Harkin to give them that power. Despite previous opposition to trade with China, he backed PNTR, citing economic benefit to Iowa. On impeachment, Ganske was considered an uncertain vote but ended up in favor.

Ganske welcomes his status as political maverick. News stories reported—erroneously—that he was contemplating a party switch. But he wasn't shy about attacking his party for being "in the HMOs' pockets." And he balked at House Republican leaders plan to assess him $100,000 to promote the team's effort to retain the majority in the 2000 campaign. Even before his own easy re-election that year, Ganske voiced interest in challenging Harkin in 2002, and he announced his candidacy in March 2001. A September 2000 poll showed Harkin ahead but running only even in the 4th District, the only part of the state where Ganske is well known—an indication that this could be a seriously contested race. Redistricting could change the shape of this district greatly, as it did 10 years ago, when Des Moines and Council Bluffs were for the first time put into one district. The Des Moines district for 2002 will be numbered the 3rd, and the tightness of the 2000 presidential race in increasingly upscale metro Des Moines—Al Gore won by just 51%–47%—suggests that this will be a closely contested seat.

Cook's Call　*Highly Competitive.* The decision by Ganske to run for the U.S. Senate has opened up one of the most marginal seats in the state and both sides have a number of anxious candidates ready to run. The non-partisan commission responsible for drawing the congressional lines in the state recently drew a map that pushed this western/central Iowa district further east and north to take in parts of the current 3rd District. Des Moines will still dominate the district and it remains evenly divided politically. The race for this district will be one of the most competitive in the country.

THE PEOPLE: Pop. 2000: 621,351; Pop. 1990: 555,276, up 11.9% 1990–2000. 91.8% White, 3.1% Black, 1.7% Asian, 0.3% Amer. Indian, 1.3% Two+ races, 1.8% Other; 3.7% Hispanic Origin.

2000 Presidential Vote			1996 Presidential Vote		
Bush (R)	140,535	(50%)	Clinton (D)	127,250	(49%)
Gore (D)	134,668	(48%)	Dole (R)	107,359	(42%)
Nader (Green)	5,372	(2%)	Perot (I)	20,296	(8%)
Others	2,091	(1%)			

Rep. Greg Ganske (R)

Elected 1994, 4th term; b. Mar. 31, 1949, New Hampton; home, Des Moines; U. of IA, B.S. 1972, M.D. 1976; Catholic; married (Corrine).

Military Career: Army Reserves, 1986–present.

Professional Career: Farmer; Surgeon, 1976–present.

DC Office: 1108 LHOB 20515, 202-225-4426; Fax: 202-225-3193; Web site: www.house.gov/ganske.

District Offices: Council Bluffs, 712-323-5976; Des Moines, 515-284-4634.

Committees: *Energy & Commerce* (13th of 31 R): Energy & Air Quality; Environment & Hazardous Materials; Health.

Group Ratings

	ADA	ACLU	AFS	LCV	CON	ITIC	NTU	COC	ACU	NTLC	CHC
2000	15	21	14	36	65	61	59	80	73	59	60
1999	35	—	50	25	82	—	48	45	44	—	—

National Journal Ratings

	1999 LIB —	1999 CONS	2000 LIB —	2000 CONS
Economic	51%	48%	49%	50%
Social	51%	49%	47%	52%
Foreign	23%	73%	56%	42%

Key Votes of the 106th Congress

1. Patient Bill of Rights	Y	5. Bar RU-486 $ for FDA	N	9. NATO War in Serbia	N
2. Accelerate Min. Wage	Y	6. Display 10 Commandments	Y	10. Perm. Trade with China	Y
3. Strike Ban on Ergo. Stnd.	N	7. Gun Show Bkgrnd. Checks	Y	11. Debt Relief for 3rd World	Y
4. Ovrd. Estate Tax Veto	Y	8. Ban Part.-Birth Abortion	Y	12. Drop Cuba Econ. Embargo	Y

Election Results

2000 general	Greg Ganske (R)	169,267	(61%)	($715,588)
	Michael L. Huston (D)	101,112	(37%)	($125,658)
	Other	5,164	(2%)	
2000 primary	Greg Ganske (R)	unopposed		
1998 general	Greg Ganske (R)	129,942	(65%)	($1,364,326)
	Jon Dvorak (D)	67,550	(34%)	($45,003)
	Others	1,904	(1%)	

FIFTH DISTRICT

Sioux City, one of the oldest market towns on the Great Plains, is situated picturesquely, nestled below and running up the loess bluffs above the Missouri River. Although still the largest city on the Plains west of Des Moines and north of Omaha, Sioux City has not grown much in the past five decades. Its original economic base has become obsolete, and so has some of the city itself: The waterfront, once raucous with boatmen and stockyard workers, is now quiet; stockyards have been replaced by IBP's modern (and low-wage) beef factory across the river in Dakota City, Nebraska; downtown stores have been replaced by shopping malls at the edge of town where people will still drive for 100 miles to spend a day doing a season's shopping. Yet many neighborhoods still look as they did during the childhood days of the Friedman twins, Eppie and Popo, better known these last 40-some years as Ann Landers and Abigail Van Buren. In recent years, Sioux City leaders have worked on cooperation and economic development with counterparts in South Sioux City, Nebraska, and North Sioux City, South Dakota. Boone County—the birthplace of Mamie Doud Eisenhower—had big economic growth in the 1990s, with a 53-acre business park and many commuters to Des Moines and Ames.

Sioux City is the largest city in the 5th Congressional District of Iowa, which covers most of northern and northwest Iowa, politically an area that, on balance, is a few points more Republican than the rest of the state. Its biggest population centers are Sioux City and Fort Dodge, northwest of Des Moines. The counties on the gently rolling landscape in between are an ethnic melange: Irish Catholics in Palo Alto, Dutch in Sioux (the most heavily Republican county in Iowa; George W. Bush won 83%–15% here); and the descendants of the English lords who built huge cattle ranches around Le Mars in Plymouth County.

The congressman from the 5th District is Tom Latham, a Republican first elected in 1994. Latham grew up on a farm in Franklin County, near Alexander (population 168) where his family has owned a seed company—a very Iowa business!—since 1947. For years Latham was active in Republican politics, attending the national convention and serving as a farm adviser to Congressman Fred Grandy. In 1994 Grandy ran against Governor Terry Branstad and lost a close primary; Latham fared more happily. Running as an opponent of the Clinton health care plan and supporting Contract with America principles before the Contract existed, Latham outpolled Democrat Sheila McGuire, 61%–39%. She had been one of 47 medical care professionals selected to sit on a White House advisory panel to review Clinton's program. "Professor McGuire helped write the Clinton health care plan that would put a bureaucrat between you and your doctor, raise your taxes and close many rural hospitals," a Latham ad said.

In the House Latham has a solidly conservative record. He served one term on the Agriculture Committee and supported the Freedom to Farm Act, which phased out subsidies for most crops. In 1997 he got a seat on the Appropriations Committee and its Agriculture Subcommittee. He protested against an amendment to place a 14 million acre limit on enrollments in the Conservation Reserve Program. With the support of independent producers seeking fair pricing, he won a requirement that packers report prices they pay for livestock. Rare for this usually quiet member who has avoided the national spotlight, he took the lead in 2000 on an amendment that opens Cuba to U.S. farm exports by lifting the sanctions on food sales—though, in a bow to the Cuban-American lobby, tightening restrictions on financing and travel. To combat methamphetamines—a big problem in rural Iowa—he has sponsored a media-intensive anti-drug initiative called the Latham project, and proposed permitting drug users to sue dealers on product liability grounds. He fought to reduce Iowa's notoriously high air fares. He helped rally 800 letters of protest when the Federal Trade Commission threatened to order Nestle to sell the Friskies pet food plant in Fort Dodge; the agency demurred. He strongly opposed legislation to permit states to allow physician-assisted suicide: Referring to his 87-year-old father with Alzheimer's, he told the House, "We could question what the value of that life is, but to my mother . . . that is her life every day, is to go to the home, visit my father, and there is extraordinary quality there."

Latham has been re-elected easily three times. Mike Palecek, his 2000 opponent who was jailed three times for civil disobedience at an Air Force base as a former disciple of Vietnam war activist Daniel Berrigan, called himself "probably not the sharpest tool in the shed." Latham won 69%–29%. In early 2001 it was generally expected that the 4th District's Greg Ganske would be the Republican nominee against Senator Tom Harkin in 2002. But in October 2000 Latham said, "I am not ruling out any possibilities at all."

Cook's Call   *Probably Safe.* Latham currently represents the most Republican district in the state. The non-partisan commission responsible for drawing the congressional lines in the state recently drew a map that pushed this sprawling district further west so that it would encompass the entire western third of the state. But, this newly drawn map put Latham's home in the newly drawn 4th District, which is more politically marginal than the newly drawn 5th. As of early June 2001, Latham had not indicated in which district he would run. But it is possible that he will avoid a serious contest in 2002.

THE PEOPLE: Pop. 2000: 558,605; Pop. 1990: 555,457, up 0.6% 1990–2000. 95.2% White, 0.8% Black, 0.9% Asian, 0.5% Amer. Indian, 0.9% Two+ races, 1.7% Other; 3.7% Hispanic Origin.

2000 Presidential Vote
Bush (R)	132,765	(55%)
Gore (D)	102,076	(42%)
Nader (Green)	4,685	(2%)
Others	2,821	(1%)

1996 Presidential Vote
Dole (R)	106,615	(45%)
Clinton (D)	104,775	(44%)
Perot (I)	23,051	(10%)

Rep. Tom Latham (R)

Elected 1994, 4th term; b. July 14, 1948, Hampton; home, Alexander; Wartburg Col., 1966–67, IA St. U., 1967–70; Lutheran; married (Kathy).

Professional Career: Farmer; Bank Teller/Bookkeeper, 1970–72; Independent Insurance Agent, 1972–74; Hartford Insurance Mktg. Rep., 1974–76; Co-Owner, Latham Seed Co., 1976–present.

DC Office: 440 CHOB 20515, 202-225-5476; Fax: 202-225-3301; Web site: www.house.gov/latham.

District Offices: Ft. Dodge, 515-573-2738; Orange City, 712-737-8708; Sioux City, 712-277-2114; Spencer, 712-262-6480.

Committees: *Appropriations* (24th of 35 R): Agriculture, Rural Development, & FDA; Commerce, Justice & State; Energy & Water Development.

Group Ratings
	ADA	ACLU	AFS	LCV	CON	ITIC	NTU	COC	ACU	NTLC	CHC
2000	5	15	0	0	45	94	63	95	88	72	100
1999	5	—	0	0	31	—	57	96	88	—	—

National Journal Ratings
	1999 LIB —	1999 CONS		2000 LIB —	2000 CONS
Economic	0% —	84%		25% —	72%
Social	29% —	71%		0% —	79%
Foreign	20% —	78%		47% —	51%

Key Votes of the 106th Congress
1. Patient Bill of Rights	N	5. Bar RU-486 $ for FDA	Y	9. NATO War in Serbia	N
2. Accelerate Min. Wage	N	6. Display 10 Commandments	Y	10. Perm. Trade with China	Y
3. Strike Ban on Ergo. Stnd.	N	7. Gun Show Bkgrnd. Checks	N	11. Debt Relief for 3rd World	Y
4. Ovrd. Estate Tax Veto	Y	8. Ban Part.-Birth Abortion	Y	12. Drop Cuba Econ. Embargo	Y

Election Results
2000 general	Tom Latham (R)	159,367	(69%)	($375,152)
	Mike Palecek (D)	67,593	(29%)	($5,933)
	Other	4,792	(2%)	
2000 primary	Tom Latham (R)	22,516	(90%)	
	Thomas D. Hall (R)	2,458	(10%)	
1998 general	Tom Latham (R)	unopposed		($450,391)

★ KANSAS ★

"Like everyone else," James Dickenson writes of his grandmother Mary Phipps, who lived her 91 years in Kansas, "she was taught that the earth and the other planets circled the sun, but deep down she had the feeling that the sun and the rest of the cosmos really revolved around western Kansas. . . . She took as the First Principle that bread, the staff of life, was one of the bases of existence itself, along with air and water. From this flowed the inescapable conclusion that wheat farmers were truly engaged in the Lord's work." These words open the book *Home on the Range*, in which Dickenson, for three decades a top national political reporter, starts with his own family and boyhood in Rawlins County to explain how Kansas came to be what it was, and how it is ceasing to be that and becoming something else.

But Kansas has always been quintessentially American, which is not to say entirely placid or entirely unflavorful. In 1989, when Russia's Yevgeny Primakov wanted to see "real Americans," he flew out with Bob Dole to Dodge City, to visit Boot Hill Museum and the Long Branch Saloon. Kansas, like so much of Russia, may look quiet, full of solid farmers who work hard and have deep roots in the soil, the place around which the cosmos revolves. But Kansas's history, like Russia's, has also been punctuated by uprisings, intellectual and violent, by moments of anger and rage sweeping through the tall sheaves like a tornado wind. The difference, of course, is that Russian traditions of law and liberty, culture and civility are weak, while in Kansas, as in all America, they are remarkably strong.

Kansas literally began in a moment of violence, the Bleeding Kansas of the 1850s that led proximately to the terrible war that split the whole nation. The trigger was the Kansas-Nebraska Act of 1854, which left to local settlers the question of whether this new Kansas Territory would be a free or slave state. Pro-slavery "bushwhackers" rode over the line from Missouri, stealing elections and writing a pro-slavery constitution. But much larger numbers of free-soil "jayhawkers" from New England and the New England-Yankee-settled Great Lakes states put down roots and, despite the massacres of the mad John Brown, prevailed and established their own law and order. The effect on national politics was tumultuous: The Democratic Party was split, the Republican Party was created, the nation was plunged into Civil War. The effect on Kansas was calming: The anti-slavery majority bent the soil to the plow and built small towns thick with schools, churches and colleges, to the point that in the 1939 color movie, *Wizard of Oz*, the Kansas scenes were shot in dreary black and white as the image of dull, prim, old-fashioned Middle America. But the rebellious impulse did not totally die out. Kansans' livelihoods were always at risk: hailstorms, grasshopper invasions, dry seasons or a drop in world farm prices could mean disaster for thousands. The high-rainfall 1880s attracted hundreds of thousands of new settlers to Kansas; the low-rainfall 1890s produced a bust and a populist rebellion. "What you farmers should do," said orator Mary Ellen Lease, "is to raise less corn and more hell." For a few years in the 1890s, and then in farm rebellions of the 1930s, 1950s and 1970s, Kansans did, but afterwards always returned to jayhawker Republicanism.

Kansas remains Republican in the 21st Century, but not in quite the same old way. Its most famous politician, Bob Dole, still returns occasionally to his small hometown of Russell, out on the plains. But Kansas' population is increasingly metropolitan. A majority of Kansans live in or within easy reach of metropolitan Kansas City, which has a booming diverse economy which is by no means dependent on farming. While small towns on the plains see their city halls and post offices padlocked, new office complexes and corporate headquarters are rising amidst the affluent suburbs of Johnson County, which has one of the highest job growth rates in the country. The smaller metropolitan area of Wichita, while less diversified, has an economy built on its role as the world's leading producer of small airplanes: here Boeing, Cessna, Bombardier, Raytheon and other manufacturers make 69% of the general aviation aircraft in the world, and 40% of its aviation sales are exports. Kansas is wired to the world, its unemployment rate is low (Hispanics are flocking to work in meatpacking factories in towns like Dodge City, whose Hispanic percentage in the 1990s rose from 18% to 43%), its population growth among the highest of Midwestern states. There is no warrant today for shooting the Kansas scenes in a movie in black and white.

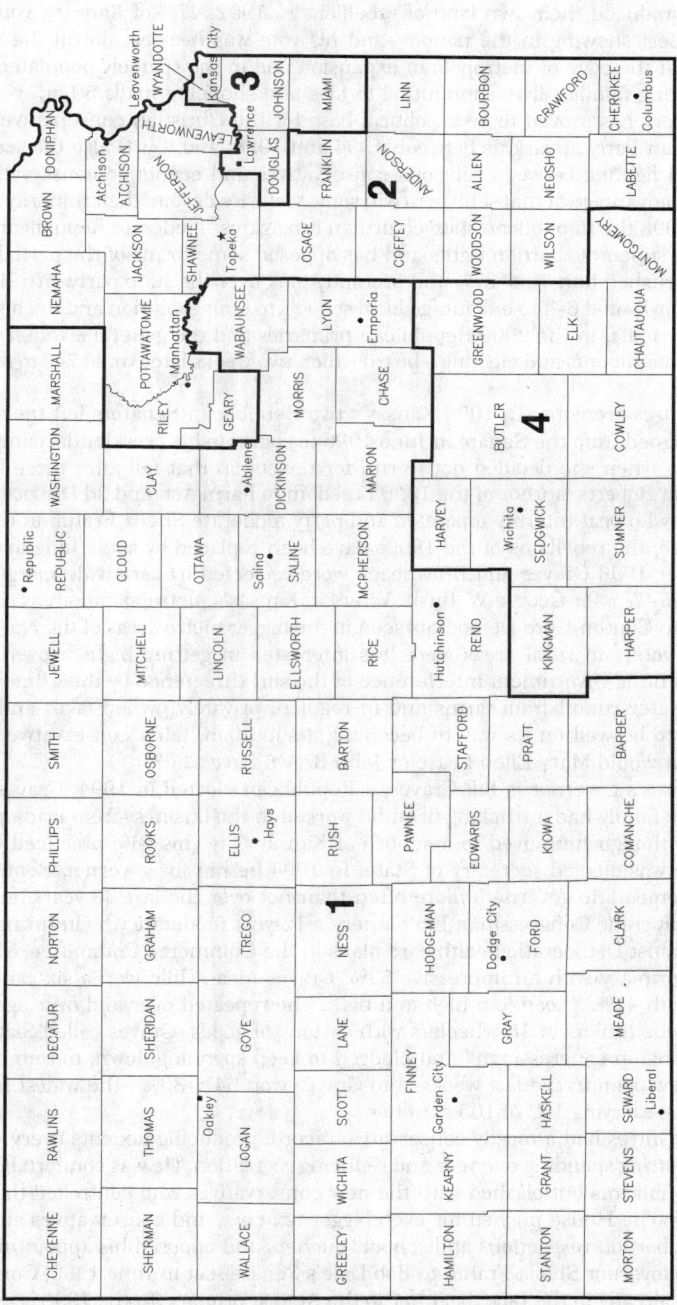

— Congressional district boundaries
effective June 3, 1992.

This transformation has had political consequences. Some 39% of Kansas's votes in 2000 were cast in the mostly suburban counties from Kansas City west to Topeka, and another 15% in Wichita's Sedgwick County. If rural Kansas once produced farm rebellions, these urban and suburban Kansans have produced their own kind of rebellion. In 1992, 27% of Kansans voted for Ross Perot—his fifth best showing in the nation—and his vote was heaviest not in the wheat country but from just at the edge of metropolitan expansion and in the sparsely populated Flint Hills, places where young families live, commuting to jobs and shopping malls 50 or even 100 miles away. This territory has proved to be a political base for the Christian conservatives who took over the Republican Party apparatus between 1994 and 1998, and it was also the scene of bitter intra-Republican fighting between religious conservatives and economic conservatives—with Democrats taking advantage of that schism to win some victories despite their minority status in the legislature. In 1998 the Republican state chairman ran against moderate Republican Governor Bill Graves, who supports abortion rights and has opposed some forms of the partial-birth abortion ban. Graves crushed him 73%–27% and promptly took over the state party. In 1999 the elected state school board voted 6–4 to encourage local schools to omit evolution and the big bang theories from their curricula; in the 2000 Republican primaries and the general election voters responded by ousting incumbents and electing a board which two weeks later voted 7–3 to reverse the decision.

Some familiar figures are gone. In 1996 Kansas's two Republican Senators left the scene: Bob Dole when he resigned from the Senate in June 1996 to spark up his presidential campaign, and Nancy Kassebaum when she decided not to run for reelection that fall after three terms. Replacing them was Pat Roberts, author of the 1996 Freedom to Farm Act, and 2d District freshman Sam Brownback, who beat interim appointee and party moderate Sheila Frahm in the primary. In elections since, the rebellions of the 1990s have been replaced by something like contentment. In November 1998 Graves and Brownback were reelected by very wide margins. In 2000 Kansas voted 58%–37% for George W. Bush. Voters in Kansas's metropolitan areas showed little of the allegiance to Clinton-Gore Democrats seen in the bigger metro areas of the Northeast and West Coast, and voters in rural areas were less interested in getting higher government subsidies than in preventing government interference of the sort threatened by the Clinton EPA plan to regulate the water runoff from farms and to regulate privately owned lakes and farm ponds. Kansas seems to be well on its way to becoming a suburban, fairly conservative, quite Republican state. What would Mary Ellen Lease or John Brown have said?

Governor   Kansas's governor is Bill Graves, a Republican elected in 1994. Graves grew up in Salina, where his family had a trucking firm; he worked in the business from loading dock to management, even though he moved to a suburb of Kansas City (his wife practiced law in Missouri). In 1986 he was elected secretary of State. In 1994 he ran for governor. Republican Kansas has elected Democratic governors more often than not over the last 30 years, and the initial favorite was Democratic Congressman Jim Slattery, a 12-year moderate who in spring 1994 cast a decisive vote against Democratic health care plans in the Commerce Committee. Slattery won a five-candidate primary with an impressive 53%. Graves meanwhile won a six-candidate Republican primary with 41%. "Load 'em high and tight," he repeated over and over again, as his family had loaded the trailers of 18-wheelers with cartons of goods. Graves called Slattery a "double-dealing Washington congressman" and pledged to keep spending down, to rein in government. The race blew open in the last weeks, and Graves won 64%–36%—the widest margin in more than 20 years—carrying 102 of 105 counties.

In his first term, Graves had a mostly conservative record, producing tax cuts every year—$1.8 billion in total—cutting spending one year and reducing regulation. He was comfortable with business-oriented Republicans but clashed with the new conservatives who controlled the state House and state party. The House pushed for even bigger tax cuts, and conservatives attacked Graves' opposition to abortion restrictions and school vouchers and opposed his appointment of moderate Lieutenant Governor Sheila Frahm to Bob Dole's Senate seat in June 1996; Congressman Sam Brownback, already in the race, beat her in the August primary. In the 1998 legislative session Graves sought to mollify critics, even as his job rating soared to 75%. He signed a partial-birth abortion ban and a law to regulate hog lots. He signed a campaign finance law that requires identification of organizations that "expressly advocate" the election or defeat of "clearly identified candidates"; this was aimed at the Triad group that supported Brownback in 1996. When the two houses disagreed on which tax cut to back, Graves compromised by backing both, for a $247 million cut. In May 1998 conservative Republican party Chairman David Miller jumped into the race to end "moral free fall." Evidently he assumed he could turn activist support into votes. But in a climate of contentment, Graves won 73%–27%. Graves carried all 105 counties; Miller came closest where the issue was not abortion but hog lots. The Democratic candidate, a 12-year state legislator, was heavily outspent. Graves won 73%–23%, carrying every county and winning the highest percentage for governor in Kansas' history.

In 1999 Graves pushed for a four-year phaseout of the car tax and pushed for restructuring of higher education. But his biggest initiative was in the opposite direction: a $12.6 billion highway and transportation program, to be funded by a four-cent increase in the gas tax. In the meantime, Republican leaders were outflanked by an alliance of Democrats and conservative Republicans, which increased state funding for mental health and children's services in exchange for killing a campaign finance disclosure bill. In 2000 the budget was balanced with the help of revenue windfalls, and the legislature required lobbyist registration and increased the number of charter schools. Democrats fought Graves' proposal for a one-year suspension of contributions to the state employees' pension fund. Graves fought against the water-quality standards proposed by EPA in response to a suit brought by environmentalists that would require immense paperwork by the state and regulation of 164 lakes and 1,292 streams designated as of secondary importance. Graves opposed proposals by an Oklahoma tribe to build a gambling casino across the street from Kansas City's City Hall. As George W. Bush swept 103 of Kansas's 105 counties, Republicans gained seats in the legislature. But Graves took a cue less from his party's legislators than from a 21st Century Vision task force, tentatively supporting a tax increase for education, and he continued to oppose school vouchers.

Graves is term-limited and cannot run for reelection in 2002. The almost certain Democratic candidate is Insurance Commissioner Kathleen Sebelius, daughter of former Ohio Governor John Gilligan and daughter-in-law of former Kansas Congressman Keith Sebelius. She has a reputation as a moderate, but Democrats have had a hard time winning except against unpopular incumbent Republican governors. One possible Republican candidate is 4th District Congressman Todd Tiahrt, from the conservative wing of the party but a quiet supporter of Graves in the 1998 primary and one who has taken care to work with moderates. Another is state House Speaker Kent Glasscock, whose wife is Graves' chief of staff; he is a supporter of vouchers. Others include state Attorney General Carla Stovall, Treasurer Tim Shallenberger, and Lieutenant Governor Gary Sherrer

Cook's Call *Probably Safe.* Now that Graves is stepping down because of term limits, Democrats hope that state Treasurer Kathleen Sebelius will make the race and that she will take advantage of a Republican party divided between conservative ideologues, who put a special emphasis on social and cultural concerns, and the mainstreamers, who care more about economic issues. But Bush won Kansas by 21 points, making this a difficult climb for any Democrat.

Senior Senator Sam Brownback grew up on a farm in Anderson County, some 50 miles from Kansas City, was student body president at Kansas State University and briefly was a farm broadcaster. After law school, Brownback practiced law for four years in Manhattan, Kansas, in the 1980s; he was appointed secretary of the state Board of Agriculture in 1986 and served until it was abolished in 1993. He claims credit for encouraging the use of wheat to make plastics and cattle hides to make wound dressings. He was a White House Fellow, working from 1990–91 for U.S. Trade Representative Carla Hills. In March 1994 he announced for Congress, condemning "a welfare system that discourages the work ethic and encourages the disintegration of families and a government that can't say no to spending or yes to reform." Brownback won the three-way House primary 48%–35%–16%. In the general he faced John Carlin, governor from 1978–86. Brownback won 66%–34%, carrying every county.

Brownback was one of the enthusiastic 1994 freshmen who tried to shake up the House. He was put in charge of selling off a House annex building, which proved harder than expected. He pushed successfully to reduce Congress' own budget. He headed a group of "New Federalists," which sought to abolish three cabinet departments. He pushed hard for the gift ban rule, which Republicans, after hesitating, passed. He backed the McCain-Feingold campaign finance bill and in 1995 spoke at Ross Perot's United We Stand convention denouncing "influence peddling" in Washington. On immigration he played a key role in separating the legal and illegal immigration issues, which led to passage of a tough measure against illegal immigrants but no major reductions in the number of legal immigrants.

On May 15, 1996, Bob Dole surprised just about everyone when he announced he was resigning from the Senate on June 11. On May 17, Brownback said he would seek the seat, noting, "They are size 25 shoes that even Michael Jordan couldn't fill." Governor Bill Graves' choice to fill the vacancy, Lieutenant Governor Sheila Frahm, delayed ten days before accepting. Though both were labeled conservative, Frahm and Brownback presented a strong contrast in the subsequent primary. She was pro-choice on abortion, he anti-abortion. Brownback accused her of voting as a state legislator to raise taxes $500 million; she criticized his "slash and burn" approach to federal spending. Graves and Senator Nancy Kassebaum endorsed Frahm; William Bennett of Empower America and James Dobson of Focus on the Family endorsed Brownback. In the August primary, Brownback won 55%–42%.

In the general election for the remaining two years of Dole's term, Brownback faced a Democrat with a great political name, Wichita stockbroker Jill Docking, wife of a former lieutenant governor whose father and grandfather both served as governor. Docking promised "Kansas common sense" likened herself to Kassebaum. Brownback campaigned on the 3 Rs: "Reduce, reform and return. Reduce the size and scope of the federal government. Reform the Congress. Return to the basic values that built the country: work and family and the recognition of a higher moral authority." He promised to serve only two terms—presumably two full terms. Both candidates spent liberally, and some fall polls showed the race close. But Brownback won by the convincing though not overwhelming margin of 54%–43%.

Brownback brought his strong-minded politics to the Senate—he has had a near-perfect conservative voting record—but has modulated some stands. From his seat on Foreign Affairs' Near Eastern and South Asian Affairs Subcommittee, he traveled to visit Middle East leaders and co-sponsored the law to aid opponents of Saddam Hussein. He criticized the Clinton administration strongly for discouraging UNSCOM inspections in Iraq. He led the effort to present the Congressional Gold Medal to Mother Teresa, which was done in June 1997. He returned from a trip to India in 1999 determined to do something about the international sex trade; he had visited a sanctuary in Nepal for teenage girls rescued from involuntary prostitution in the Middle and Far East. Working with liberal Paul Wellstone, he sponsored a bill to curb the sex trade into the United States; it became law in October 2000. In the process, he focused as well on the continued existence of slavery in Sudan and other countries. The trip to India also made Brownback more determined to end U.S. sanctions automatically imposed on India after its nuclear tests in May 1998. He and Kansas colleague Pat Roberts sponsored a law passed in October 1999 authorizing the president to lift the embargo; but Bill Clinton, determined to get India to sign the Comprehensive Test Ban Treaty which the Senate had rejected that same month, refused. In October 2000 he held hearings and criticized Vice President Al Gore for allowing Russia to sell arms to Iran without penalty.

Brownback has criticized the entertainment industry for its violent and vulgar products. He held hearings on entertainment violence in May 1999 and in June 1999 he called for an FTC investigation of the marketing of movies, music and video games to children; Bill Clinton agreed, and the resulting effort won wide publicity in 2000. In 1999 Brownback tried to get a special Senate committee created to examine the issue, but no consensus could be reached on its agenda. He worked closely with Joseph Lieberman on this issue and also on bills to do something about religious persecution in Sudan and other countries. After Lieberman was nominated for vice president, Brownback explained their joint efforts: "Senator Lieberman and I are part of a political alliance that is quite logically emerging between theologically orthodox Christians and Jews. . . . We share a belief in universal Truths, in a moral order ordained by God and discovered, not created, by man." At home Brownback hosted a marriage summit in Topeka in August 1999, to discourage divorce, and in 2000 he worked with Topeka Mayor Joan Wagnon on a Faith Works-Jobs Partnership venture to help former welfare recipients.

Brownback was a sponsor of the bill, passed but vetoed by Clinton, to end the marriage penalty. He opposed the FCC ruling that forbade noncommercial broadcasters from counting religious material as part of their educational content. He has led the opposition to NIH proposals to use human stem-cells in research, a practice he compared to Nazi medicine and called "illegal, immoral and unnecessary." In 2000 he and John McCain sponsored a bill to ban betting on amateur sports, legal now only in Nevada, but encouraged nationally by the publication of Las Vegas oddsmaker point spreads. Amid the Florida controversy, Brownback and Charles Schumer called for a $10 million study by the Federal Election Commission of election procedures, plus $250 million in matching grants to states to improve them.

On Kansas-related issues, Brownback has worked for conservation payments to farmers who employ carbon-storing practices like planting alfalfa, wind buffers to prevent erosion and refor-estation—steps that can decrease the carbon dioxide in the air. He objected to the taxation of Conservation Reserve Program payments. He protested EPA's water-quality standards for Kansas as obtrusive and ineffective. He would ease requirements that local telephone companies open themselves up to competition if they improve broadband access.

Brownback was elected to a full six-year term in 1998 by a 65%–32% margin after well-known candidates declined to run. Campaign finance did cause him some embarrassment. In March 1997 the *Kansas City Star* ran stories revealing that Brownback's in-laws gave $32,500 to seven PACs which promptly gave his campaign $31,500. All involved denied any earmarking. Then it was revealed that an organization called Triad directed money into Kansas conservatives' 1996 campaigns and also ran issue ads boosting Brownback in October 1996. There was no proof of wrongdoing, but an articulate opponent might have made something of it. Brownback was careful to stay neutral in the August 1998 primary between Governor Bill Graves and conservative David Miller. But in 2000 he made endorsements in fractious primaries in the Kansas City suburbs, backing Linda Holloway, a supporter of de-emphasizing evolution, in her race for renomination to the state school board, and legislator Phill Kline for the nomination to face Democratic Congressman Dennis Moore; Graves was on the other side. Holloway lost and Kline won; some questioned whether the endorsements might hurt Brownback among suburban moderates when he comes up for re-election in 2004. Brownback and his wife, with three children already, adopted infants from Guatemala and China in 1999. And in 2000 the Capitol Hill apartment building where Brownback makes his Washington residence burned down; he tried to put out the fire and helped rescue other tenants.

Junior Senator   Pat Roberts is from a fine Kansas Republican background: His aboli-tionist great-grandfather founded Kansas' second-oldest newspaper, and his father, Wes Roberts, was briefly Republican National Committee chairman during the Eisenhower years. Pat Roberts has spent most of his adult life preparing for the place he is in now. After four years in the Marine Corps and five years running an Arizona newspaper, he worked for two years as an aide to Senator Frank Carlson and 12 years as chief aide to 1st District Congressman Keith Sebelius. When Sebelius retired in 1980, Roberts won the seat with 56% in a three-candidate Republican primary. For 14 years, in the minority in the House, he concentrated on farm issues, learning their intri-cacies and minutiae, traveling in a van to keep in touch with constituents in a district so large that it took two weeks to visit every county seat. His voting record was moderate, and he looked after Kansas interests: raising Medicare payments for rural areas and changing wetlands law that protect "some low spot in your field where no self-respecting duck would ever land."

In January 1995 Roberts became chairman of the House Agriculture Committee. He had long believed that the huge subsidies of the early 1980s would never return: "Farm programs have declined an average of 9% since 1986 and are going to go on declining." Faced with Repub-lican budget parameters, Roberts fashioned a Freedom to Farm bill which would phase out sub-sidies over seven years. In September 1995 his bill failed in committee when Southern Republi-cans eager to protect cotton, rice and peanut subsidies voted against it. But in November 1995, Roberts persuaded Agriculture conferees to include most of his bill in the 1996 budget reconcil-iation bill, which Clinton vetoed. He agreed to maintain cotton and rice marketing loans and managed to preserve the Conservation Reserve Program, which is popular in Kansas. But overall this was the biggest change in agriculture policy since the New Deal act of 1933. Roberts' new bill passed the Agriculture Committee 29–17 in January 1996, the full House in February, and became law in April. There was tension with appropriators Bob Livingston and Joe Skeen, who resented Roberts' mandatory payments, and he resented their budget limits; but the reform passed.

Amid this furious legislative activity, one of Kansas' Senate seats came open when Nancy Landon Kassebaum announced her retirement in November 1995. At first Roberts said he was too busy working on the farm bill and declined to run. When the bill's fortunes improved, he announced his candidacy in January 1996; the law would remove much of the power of the committee, and under new Republican rules he was limited to three terms as chairman. He won the August primary with an overwhelming 78% in a four-way race. In the general election he faced state Treasurer Sally Thompson and won easily, 62%–34%, carrying 104 counties and losing one (Wyandotte County, which contains Kansas City). Thus Roberts became the first House member to give up a committee chairmanship to run for the Senate since Lister Hill in 1938 (and Hill got appointed to his Senate seat).

Roberts is on the Senate Agriculture Committee and has spent much time on farm issues. The Freedom to Farm Act worked well in 1997, and farmers seemed pleased to be able to decide what crops to plant without getting government approval. But in 1998 crop prices plunged—in line with the long-run trend of falling prices for basic commodities—and some demanded a return to the old system. Roberts resisted that, and bills were passed to give temporary aid and accelerate $4.5 billion in payments and give farmers an extra $4 billion in disaster assistance. In 1999, with prices still low, federal aid to farmers totaled $23 billion including subsidies to crop insurance, CRP payments, drought relief and direct payments to make up for low world prices and world demand. In 2000 the pattern continued: Roberts argued that increased subsidies for crop insurance would mean less need for yearly assistance and argued that limiting production would not raise prices because the U.S. accounts for less than one-fifth of world production. The problem seems intractable. The number of family farmers continues to fall in places like western Kansas, where farm communities are tending to disappear, yet prices are not sufficient to maintain many operations.

The Freedom to Farm Act comes up for reauthorization in 2002, and Roberts will surely play a major part in rewriting farm laws, presumably taking a middle position between Richard Lugar, who is hostile to subsidies, and Tom Harkin, who would like to revive the old system if he could. Roberts seems to be looking at different approaches: "Access to markets I think is one of the crucial things we're going to have to guarantee them." Roberts has tried to encourage farm exports in several ways, opposing cargo preferences, urging passage of fast track for trade agreements and replenishment of IMF funds. Roberts was a lead sponsor of the 2000 law to end the embargo on food to Cuba, and he and Kansas colleague Sam Brownback sponsored the 1999 law allowing the president to lift the embargo on India and Pakistan and in 2000 sought to end food sanctions altogether. Roberts has also obtained funding for research (some of it to be done at the University of Kansas and Kansas State University) on carbon sequestration—farming techniques like planting alfalfa, building wind buffers to prevent erosion, reforestation that seem to absorb carbon dioxide from the air. He did not sign on to Brownback's bill to provide incentives for no-till techniques, but is evidently trying to lay the groundwork for such a program, which would also provide the United States with additional leverage in international bargaining with Europeans and others on reducing carbon dioxide emissions.

Roberts has become involved in food labeling issues, sponsoring the bill to preempt state labeling, like California's health warnings on ephedra and another requiring French wine labels to read "dried animal blood is occasionally used as a clarifying agent in French wines"—presumably twitting the French for their demands for labeling of genetically modified foods. He has worked to prevent the lowering of levels in Kansas lakes to help Missouri barge traffic, and to beef up science education with more experienced teachers serving as mentors, summer institutes for teachers, and tax credits for math and science teachers' college loan repayments. He has procured funding for a $1.5 million food safety consortium at Kansas State, a new veterans' cemetery at Fort Riley and the Hoglund Brain Imaging Center in Kansas City.

Roberts's voting record is moderate on some issues. He opposed temporary repeal of the gas tax in 2000 and called for removing (the often unhonored) federal budget caps in May 2000. In June 2000 he called for a waiver of the requirement to use cleaner-burning reformulated gasoline. He serves on the Armed Services Committee and was critical of American involvement in Kosovo. He has warned of the dangers of information and biological warfare: "not a matter of if, but when." In hearings on the explosion of the U.S.S. Cole in October 2000, he said that "red flags" were ignored when the ship was ordered to Aden for refueling. In November 1999, when Bob Smith became chairman of the Environment and Public Works Committee, Roberts took on the thankless task of assuming the top Republican slot on the Ethics Committee.

Roberts comes up for re-election in 2002. Asked in October 2000 if he was running, he said, "It's too early to make that statement—but yes." In early 2001 no one was being mentioned as an opponent.

Cook's Call   *Safe.* Democrats are more likely to focus on trying to win the open gubernatorial seat next year than in trying to unseat Roberts. He should have close to a free ride.

Presidential politics   Except for 1964, when it narrowly favored Lyndon Johnson over Barry Goldwater, Kansas has voted Republican for president throughout the last 60 years. It was also one of Ross Perot's best states in 1992. In 2000 George W. Bush carried 103 of its 105 counties, losing only those containing the old industrial city of Kansas City and the university town of Lawrence. Things are only likely to get better for Republicans. Kansans under 30 voted 68%–28% for Bush according to the VNS exit poll.

In 1996 and 2000 the state legislature voted to cancel the April presidential primary; if Kansans want a look at presidential candidates, they are well advised to look up into the sky as they jet over on their way to more marginal states.

Congressional districting   Republicans have full control of redistricting in Kansas for the first time since the 1960s. They could seriously undermine the state's one Democratic congressman, Dennis Moore of the suburban 3d District, by subtracting the university town of Lawrence and surrounding Douglas County and adding Leavenworth County instead. That would make the 2d District slightly more Democratic, but incumbent Republican Jim Ryun has won by overwhelming margins. Otherwise boundary changes are likely to be slight, with little political effect.

THE PEOPLE: Pop. 2000: 2,688,418; Pop. 1990: 2,477,574, up 8.5% 1990–2000. 1% of U.S. total, 32d largest; 86.1% White, 5.7% Black, 1.7% Asian, 0.9% Amer. Indian, 2.1% Two + races, 3.4% Other; 7% Hispanic Origin. 3.7% Unemployment. 2000 Voting age pop.: 1,975,425. 2000 Turnout: 1,092,716; 55% of VAP. Registered voters (2000): 1,623,623; 449,445 D (28%), 735,435 R (45%), 438,743 unaffiliated and minor parties (27%).

POLITICAL LINEUP: Governor, Bill Graves (R); Lt. Gov., Gary Sherrer (R); Secy. of State, Ron Thornburgh (R); Atty. Gen., Carla Stovall (R); Treasurer, Tim Shallenburger (R); Commissioner of Insurance, Kathleen Sebelius (D); State Senate, 40 (10 D, 30 R); Senate President, Dave Kerr (R); Majority Leader, Lana Oleen (R); State House, 125 (46 D, 79 R); House Speaker, Kent Glasscock (R). Senators, Sam Brownback (R) and Pat Roberts (R). Representatives, 4 (1 D, 3 R).

ELECTIONS DIVISION: 785-296-4561; **FILING DEADLINE FOR U.S. CONGRESS:** June 10, 2002.

2000 Presidential Vote			1996 Presidential Vote		
Bush (R)	622,332	(58%)	Dole (R)	583,245	(54%)
Gore (D)	399,276	(37%)	Clinton (D)	387,659	(36%)
Nader (Green)	36,086	(3%)	Perot (I)	92,639	(9%)
Others	14,522	(1%)			

Gov. Bill Graves (R)

Elected 1994, term expires Jan. 2003, 2d term; b. Jan. 9, 1953, Salina; home, Salina; KS Wesleyan U., B.A. 1975, U. of KS, 1976–79; Methodist; married (Linda).

Elected Office: KS Secy. of State, 1986–94.

Professional Career: Graves Truck Line; KS Deputy Secy. of State, 1980–84; KS Asst. Secy of State, 1984–85.

Office: State Capitol, 2d Fl., Topeka, 66612, 785-296-3232; Fax: 785-296-7973; Web site: www.accesskansas.org.

Election Results

1998 general	Bill Graves (R)	544,882	(73%)
	Tom Sawyer (D)	168,243	(23%)
	Others	29,540	(4%)
1998 primary	Bill Graves (R)	225,782	(73%)
	David Miller (R)	84,368	(27%)
1994 general	Bill Graves (R)	526,113	(64%)
	Jim Slattery (D)	294,733	(36%)

Sen. Sam Brownback (R)

Elected 1996, seat up 2004, 1st term; b. Sept. 12, 1956, Garnett; home, Topeka; KS St. U., B.S. 1978, U. of KS, J.D. 1982; Methodist; married (Mary).

Elected Office: U.S. House of Reps., 1994–96.

Professional Career: Radio broadcaster, KKSU, 1978–79; Practicing atty., 1982–86, 1993; Prof., KS St. U. Law Schl., 1982–86; Ogden & Leonardville City Atty., 1983–86; KS Secy. of Agriculture, 1986–93; White House Fellow, Office of USTR, 1990–91.

DC Office: 303 HSOB, 20510, 202-224-6521; Fax: 202-228-1265; Web site: www.senate.gov/~brownback.

State Offices: Garden City, 316-275-1124; Overland Park, 913-492-6378; Pittsburg, 316-231-6040; Topeka, 785-233-2503; Wichita, 316-264-8066.

Committees: *Commerce, Science & Transportation*: Aviation; Communications; Consumer Affairs, Foreign Commerce & Tourism; Manufacturing & Competitiveness; Science, Technology & Space (RMM); Surface Transportation & Merchant Marine. *Foreign Relations*: African Affairs; International Operations & Terrorism; Near Eastern & South Asian Affairs (RMM). *Judiciary*: Antitrust, Business Rights & Competition; Immigration (RMM); Youth Violence. *Joint Economic Committee* (7th of 10 Sens.).

Group Ratings

	ADA	ACLU	AFS	LCV	CON	ITIC	NTU	COC	ACU	NTLC	CHC
2000	0	29	0	14	26	100	75	100	100	100	100
1999	5	—	0	33	29	—	79	94	95	—	—

National Journal Ratings

	1999 LIB —	1999 CONS		2000 LIB —	2000 CONS
Economic	0%	— 83%		27%	— 68%
Social	12%	— 87%		0%	— 90%
Foreign	23%	— 67%		17%	— 75%

Key Votes of the 106th Congress

1. Educ. Savings Accts.	Y	5. Review Movie Violence	Y	9. NATO War in Serbia	N
2. Prescrip. Drug Benefit	N	6. Gun Show Bckgrnd. Checks	N	10. Table Cuba Travel Ban	Y
3. Delay Ergonomic Standards	Y	7. Ban Part.-Birth Abortion	Y	11. Nuclear Test-Ban Treaty	N
4. Phase Out Estate Tax	Y	8. Broaden Hate Crimes List	N	12. Perm. Trade with China	Y

Election Results

1998 general	Sam Brownback (R)	474,639	(65%)	($1,719,612)
	Paul Feleciano Jr. (D)	229,718	(32%)	($39,500)
	Others	22,879	(3%)	
1998 primary	Sam Brownback (R)	unopposed		
1996 general	Sam Brownback (R)	574,021	(54%)	($2,269,550)
	Jill Docking (D)	461,344	(43%)	($1,125,844)
	Others	29,351	(3%)	

Sen. Pat Roberts (R)

Elected 1996, seat up 2002, 1st term; b. Apr. 20, 1936, Topeka; home, Dodge City; KS St. U., B.A. 1958; United Methodist; married (Franki).

Military Career: Marine Corps, 1958–62.

Elected Office: U.S. House of Reps., 1980–96.

Professional Career: Co-owner, editor, *The Westsider* (AZ newspaper) 1962–67; A.A., U.S. Sen. Frank Carlson, 1967–68; A.A., U.S. Rep. Keith Sebelius, 1968–80.

DC Office: 302 HSOB, 20510, 202-224-4774; Fax: 202-224-3514; Web site: www.senate.gov/~roberts.

State Offices: Dodge City, 316-227-2244; Prairie Village, 913-648-3103; Topeka, 785-295-2745; Wichita, 316-263-0416.

Committees: *Agriculture, Nutrition & Forestry*: Marketing, Inspection & Product Promotion; Production & Price Competitiveness (RMM). *Armed Services*: Airland Forces; Emerging Threats & Capabilities (RMM); Readiness & Management Support. *Ethics (Select)* (RMM). *Health, Education, Labor & Pensions*: Aging; Public Health. *Intelligence (Select)*.

Group Ratings

	ADA	ACLU	AFS	LCV	CON	ITIC	NTU	COC	ACU	NTLC	CHC
2000	0	29	0	0	36	100	71	100	92	94	92
1999	0	—	0	0	8	—	73	94	88	—	—

National Journal Ratings

	1999 LIB —	1999 CONS		2000 LIB —	2000 CONS
Economic	37% —	60%		14% —	75%
Social	21% —	77%		0% —	90%
Foreign	34% —	65%		17% —	75%

Key Votes of the 106th Congress

1. Educ. Savings Accts.	Y	5. Review Movie Violence	Y	9. NATO War in Serbia	N
2. Prescrip. Drug Benefit	N	6. Gun Show Bckgrnd. Checks	N	10. Table Cuba Travel Ban	N
3. Delay Ergonomic Standards	Y	7. Ban Part.-Birth Abortion	Y	11. Nuclear Test-Ban Treaty	N
4. Phase Out Estate Tax	Y	8. Broaden Hate Crimes List	N	12. Perm. Trade with China	Y

Election Results

1996 general	Pat Roberts (R)	652,677	(62%)	($2,305,898)
	Sally Thompson (D)	362,380	(34%)	($659,066)
	Others	37,243	(4%)	
1996 primary	Pat Roberts (R)	245,411	(78%)	
	Tom Little (R)	25,052	(8%)	
	Thomas L. Oyler (R)	23,266	(7%)	
	Richard L. Cooley (R)	20,060	(6%)	
1990 general	Nancy Landon Kassebaum (R)	578,605	(74%)	($521,140)
	Dick Williams (D)	207,491	(26%)	($16,627)

FIRST DISTRICT

"A prairie is not any old piece of flatland in the Midwest," writes Kansas-born reporter Dennis Farney. "No, a prairie is wine-colored grass, dancing in the wind. A prairie is a sun-splashed hillside, bright with wild flowers. A prairie is a fleeting cloud shadow, the song of the meadowlark. It is the wild land that has never felt the slash of the plow." This prairie once covered almost all of Kansas. Now only a little virgin prairie can still be found, in the Flint Hills region west and south of Topeka, where the waist-deep sea of grass still waves in the wind as it did when the pioneers on the Santa Fe Trail went west through here some 150 years ago; the Tallgrass Prairie National Preserve was created in 1996 to protect this unique landscape. Much of it was grazing land, first for buffalo, then for the cattle driven to Kansas railheads like Abilene and Dodge City in the 1870s and 1880s, a brief moment in history recaptured with varying accuracy in movies over a much longer span, and commemorated in Dodge City's Boot Hill Museum.

Then, after the harsh winter of 1886–87 wiped out the cattle herds, came the plow and barbed wire (commemorated in LaCrosse's Barbed Wire Museum), which enabled farmers to keep livestock out of their wheat fields. The farmers also brought to this vacant landscape Yankee civilization, with its schools and churches, and some foreign traditions as well, like the Cathedral of the Plains built by German Catholics. Now this civilization is threatened. "My great-grandparents and grandparents were part of the stream of settlers who migrated to western Kansas after the Civil War to become wheat farmers," writes James Dickenson in his elegiac *Home on the Range*. "They broke the virgin sod, erected houses, barns, schools, churches and towns, and made the area one of the most agriculturally productive in the world. A little more than a century later, the population has ebbed away from this area and many of the farms, schools, churches and towns lie vacant, dilapidated and boarded up like old boomtowns."

The 1st Congressional District consists of most of this expanse of Kansas, almost everything from the Flint Hills and Abilene west. Its 66 counties (only the Nebraska 3d and South Dakota at-large districts have more) increased from 76,000 people in 1870 to 570,000 in 1890; then growth slowed to 666,000 in 1940 and dropped to 637,000 in 2000. Kansas now has more "frontier counties," defined as between two and six people per square mile, than it did in 1890. For years young people left here and community institutions were threatened by slow growth; but at this latest turn of the century, unemployment was low and burgeoning meatpacking plants and commercial dairies—cows here have plenty of forage to graze on—attracted Latinos from Texas and California to fill jobs. With the increased farming demands, the availability of water has become a problem. Politically, the 1st remains heavily Republican; it voted 67%–28% for George W. Bush in 2000.

The congressman from the 1st District is Jerry Moran, a Republican elected in 1996. Moran grew up in Plainville in Rooks County and got his start in politics as an intern for Representative Keith Sebelius, where Moran's predecessor, now Senator Pat Roberts, was a long-time aide. Moran worked as a banker for four years before attending the University of Kansas law school. He was elected to the state Senate in 1988 where he fought to cut taxes and, as chairman of Judiciary, pushed to give judges greater flexibility on juvenile crime. In 1995 he became state Senate majority leader, succeeding Sheila Frahm, who became lieutenant governor and then the appointed U.S. senator from June to November 1996 when Bob Dole quit to run for president. When Roberts announced in January 1996 that he would run for the other Senate seat, Moran stepped into the 1st District race and, with the help of other Republicans, avoided serious primary competition. He won 76% of the vote in the primary, which was tantamount to election; in November he was elected 73%–24%.

His voting record has been moderate on economic and cultural issues, and he has pursued district causes. He argued that Medicare's Interim Payment System imposed too great a burden on rural home health care agencies, and wants greater reimbursement. He called for government help in transporting grain and guaranteed loans for short line railroads as the newly merged Union Pacific seemed unable to carry Kansas's record harvests in 1997 and 1998. He sponsored laws to allow farmers ousted from the Conservation Reserve Program to let land lie fallow one more season if they had not planted winter wheat. He complained when the Agriculture Department reported that $20 million of its funds intended to help farmers limit flooding and soil erosion had been diverted to urban projects—"for gardens," Moran said. He voted against the November 1999 omnibus spending bill, he said, because it spent too much money and "the process was wrong," including the fact that members had little time to digest the conference report that was filed at

3 a.m. before they voted the next morning. He helped to prepare a disaster relief bill for drought-stricken farmers in 2000. And despite opposition from Republican leaders, he won passage of his amendment to bar the Treasury Department from enforcing sanctions against the sale of food and medicine to Cuba. House Speaker Dennis Hastert appointed Moran to the Dwight D. Eisenhower Memorial Commission to plan for an appropriate District of Columbia monument to the Abilene native—only the fifth such tribute authorized by Congress. "What I do in Congress does not change dramatically from year to year," Moran said in 1999. "It's a goal of keeping Kansas communities and the people who live there viable."

During summer recesses, Moran annually has logged 5,000 miles around the district (people here expect to see their congressman without driving to the next county over). He was rewarded at election time 1998 with a record 81% of the vote and had no Democratic opponent in 2000. He explored the possibility of running for governor in 2002, but as of spring 2001 seemed unlikely to do so. The 1st District will have to grow a bit after redistricting but, whether or not Moran runs, it will remain safely Republican.

Cook's Call *Safe.* Republicans shouldn't have to worry much about a district that gave Bush 67% in 2000 and has never given Moran less than 73% in his three runs for the seat. Moran's name has been bandied about as a potential gubernatorial candidate, but, even if he should decide to run, Republicans will have no trouble holding onto this district.

THE PEOPLE: Pop. 2000: 637,670; Pop. 1990: 619,371, up 3% 1990–2000. 89.8% White, 1.4% Black, 0.9% Asian, 0.5% Amer. Indian, 1.6% Two+ races, 5.8% Other; 11.1% Hispanic Origin.

2000 Presidential Vote
Bush (R)	170,296	(67%)
Gore (D)	72,334	(28%)
Nader (Green)	8,539	(3%)
Others	3,542	(1%)

1996 Presidential Vote
Dole (R)	167,237	(62%)
Clinton (D)	75,840	(28%)
Perot (I)	25,055	(9%)

Rep. Jerry Moran (R)

Elected 1996, 3d term; b. May 29, 1954, Great Bend; home, Hays; U. of KS, B.S. 1976, J.D. 1981; Methodist; married (Robba).

Elected Office: KS Senate, 1988–96, Majority Ldr., 1995–97.

Professional Career: Operations Officer, Consolidated State Bank, 1975–77; Mgr., Farmers State Bank & Trust Co., 1977–78; Practicing atty., 1981–96; Instructor, Ft. Hays St. U., 1986.

DC Office: 1519 LHOB 20515, 202-225-2715; Fax: 202-225-5124; Web site: www.house.gov/moranks01.

District Offices: Hays, 785-628-6401; Hutchinson, 620-665-6138.

Committees: *Agriculture* (9th of 27 R): Conservation, Credit, Rural Development & Research; Department Operations, Oversight, Nutrition & Forestry; General Farm Commodities & Risk Management. *Transportation & Infrastructure* (20th of 42 R): Aviation; Highways & Transit; Railroads. *Veterans' Affairs* (9th of 17 R): Health (Chmn.).

Group Ratings
	ADA	ACLU	AFS	LCV	CON	ITIC	NTU	COC	ACU	NTLC	CHC
2000	0	36	0	14	83	94	61	90	92	76	93
1999	20	—	16	13	75	—	63	88	84	—	—

National Journal Ratings
	1999 LIB —	1999 CONS	2000 LIB —	2000 CONS
Economic	37% —	61%	6% —	85%
Social	37% —	61%	23% —	74%
Foreign	10% —	86%	12% —	78%

Key Votes of the 106th Congress

1. Patient Bill of Rights	Y	5. Bar RU-486 $ for FDA	Y	9. NATO War in Serbia	N
2. Accelerate Min. Wage	N	6. Display 10 Commandments	Y	10. Perm. Trade with China	Y
3. Strike Ban on Ergo. Stnd.	N	7. Gun Show Bkgrnd. Checks	N	11. Debt Relief for 3rd World	N
4. Ovrd. Estate Tax Veto	Y	8. Ban Part.-Birth Abortion	Y	12. Drop Cuba Econ. Embargo	N

Election Results

2000 general	Jerry Moran (R)	214,328	(89%)	($358,597)
	Jack Warner (Lib)	25,581	(11%)	
2000 primary	Jerry Moran (R)	unopposed		
1998 general	Jerry Moran (R)	152,775	(81%)	($295,696)
	Jim Phillips (D)	36,618	(19%)	($10,165)

SECOND DISTRICT

The green plains of eastern Kansas have seen more than their share of American history. Here, on bluffs above the Missouri River, Fort Leavenworth was built in 1827, famous in later years for its war college and military prison and now the oldest U.S. fort west of the Mississippi. In the 1850s, newly founded towns along the Kansas River and along the Missouri line were the centers of Bleeding Kansas, where the pro-slavery bushwhackers set up a state capital in tiny Lecompton and anti-slavery New Englanders set up their stronghold down the river at Lawrence. Farther up the river is Fort Riley, once an outpost against the Indians, now a major Army base often threatened with closure, and Manhattan, home of Kansas State University. Topeka, the state capital, sits here on a low bluff above the river; it was this city whose system of legal segregation was overturned in the 1954 landmark case, *Brown v. Board of Education*. Farther south, on the Missouri border, are the hills called "the Balkans." Here coal miners, often of Eastern European origin, lived in and near towns like Pittsburg and Girard, once a center of American socialism, where Clarence Darrow and Upton Sinclair made pilgrimages, and its paper, *Appeal to Reason*, had a nationwide 750,000 circulation. In the 1990s, while Topeka had little growth and struggled to find new business, the areas surrounding Shawnee County have had double-digit increases.

These disparate areas, Topeka and Manhattan, Fort Riley and Fort Leavenworth, wheat-growing counties and the Balkans—most of eastern Kansas except the Kansas City metropolitan area—make up the 2d Congressional District. The heritage here has been Republican ever since the jayhawks defeated the bushwhackers once the votes were counted honestly in the 1850s. Yet Democrats in recent decades have been competitive here in state and local races, especially in Topeka. For 20 of the 24 years from 1970–94, Democrats were elected to fill the 2d District seat. But in the last four elections it has voted for strongly conservative Republicans by increasingly solid margins.

The congressman from the 2d is Jim Ryun, famous more than 20 years before he ran for Congress. He grew up in Wichita, where in 1965 he was the first high-schooler to break the four-minute mile; his 3:55.3 time remained the world record for high schoolers until May 27, 2001, when an unassuming Reston, Virginia, student, Alan Webb, finished the mile in 3:53. He was a star runner at the University of Kansas, and ran in the Olympics of 1964, 1968 and 1972, winning a silver medal, and set world records for the 880-yard and the 1500-meter runs. After his competitive athletic career, he operated a sports camp, was a motivational speaker for corporations and Christian groups, wrote two books, started a sports management firm and worked with a hearing aid company that produced a "Sounds of Success" program to help hearing-impaired children achieve their potential.

In May 1996, when 2d District freshman Sam Brownback decided to run for the Senate seat suddenly vacated by Bob Dole, Ryun decided to run for the House. He was opposed by former Topeka Mayor Douglas Wright and Cheryl Brown Henderson, whose father was the plaintiff in *Brown v. Board*. Wright called Ryun an "extremist" and proclaimed, "This is clearly a battle over the direction of the Republican Party in Kansas," predicting that Ryun couldn't win the general. Ryun campaigned for tax cuts and opposed abortion rights. While the press treated Ryun as something of an oddity, Republican primary voters didn't: he won 62%. In the general, Ryun was outspent by trial lawyer John Frieden. Democrats circulated "Courtship Makes a Comeback," written by Ryun and his wife for Focus on the Family. It recounted their practice that any young man wanting to date Ryun's daughters has to call him and ask permission. Again there was ridicule, with the press calling Dr. Ruth to mock the Ryuns' practices. However absurd these beliefs may seem to Manhattan or Malibu sophisticates, they were not political poison in Kansas. Ryun won 52%–45%, losing Topeka and Shawnee County 52%–46%, but carrying the rest of the district 55%–43%.

In the House, Ryun has a very conservative voting record. He claimed credit for the $500 per child tax credit. He proposed elimination of a 17-page form that home-care providers must submit to Medicare every two months. On the Armed Services Committee, he backed increased military spending and was pleased that an Army National Guard division moved its headquarters to Fort Riley. The House passed his amendment designed to protect nuclear secrets by preventing the Energy Department safety and security managers from also working for the new National Nuclear Security Administration. During the 2000 presidential campaign, Ryun said that Democrats have "woefully neglected" military needs—cutting troops by one-third while increasing deployments by 300%. Funding levels must be increased, he warned. Ryun has also worked to funnel federal money for local projects: $500,000 to solve Topeka's red water problem by replacing rusty pipes.

After his own initial close contest, Ryun has twice breezed to re-election, most recently beating a trial lawyer 67%–29% in 2000. Kansas Republicans control redistricting, and may very well move Lawrence and Douglas County—one of two Kansas counties to vote for Al Gore—from the 3d to the 2d district. This would weaken Dennis Moore in the 3d while, but—considering his big recent margins—would not much hurt Ryun.

Cook's Call   *Safe.* Although this district is not the most Republican in the state, it still has a good Republican core (Bush won here by 13%). Ryun, who has avoided a serious challenge since his first race in 1996, seems pretty well settled here.

THE PEOPLE: Pop. 2000: 641,387; Pop. 1990: 619,385, up 3.6% 1990–2000. 87.9% White, 5.9% Black, 1% Asian, 1.3% Amer. Indian, 0.1% Hawaiian, 2.2% Two+ races, 1.7% Other; 4.1% Hispanic Origin.

2000 Presidential Vote

Bush (R)	139,325	(54%)
Gore (D)	103,739	(41%)
Nader (Green)	8,925	(3%)
Others	4,061	(2%)

1996 Presidential Vote

Dole (R)	125,087	(49%)
Clinton (D)	100,110	(39%)
Perot (I)	27,748	(11%)

Rep. Jim Ryun (R)

Elected 1996, 3d term; b. May 29, 1947, Wichita; home, Topeka; U. of KS, B.A. 1970; Presbyterian; married (Anne).

Professional Career: U.S. Olympian, Track & Field, 1964, 1968, 1972; Founder & Dir., Jim Ryun Running Camps, 1976–present; Rancher, 1983–present.

DC Office: 330 CHOB 20515, 202-225-6601; Fax: 202-225-7986; Web site: www.house.gov/ryun.

District Offices: Pittsburg, 316-232-6100; Topeka, 785-232-4500.

Committees: *Armed Services* (20th of 32 R): Military Personnel (Vice Chmn.); Military Procurement. *Budget* (8th of 24 R). *Financial Services* (18th of 37 R): Capital Markets, Insurance & Government Sponsored Enterprises; Financial Institutions & Consumer Credit; International Monetary Policy & Trade.

Group Ratings

	ADA	ACLU	AFS	LCV	CON	ITIC	NTU	COC	ACU	NTLC	CHC
2000	0	21	0	0	73	100	70	90	100	97	100
1999	0	—	0	0	73	—	68	84	96	—	—

National Journal Ratings

	1999 LIB	—	1999 CONS		2000 LIB	—	2000 CONS
Economic	0%	—	84%		0%	—	94%
Social	4%	—	91%		0%	—	79%
Foreign	15%	—	81%		12%	—	78%

Key Votes of the 106th Congress

1. Patient Bill of Rights	N	5. Bar RU-486 $ for FDA	Y	9. NATO War in Serbia	N
2. Accelerate Min. Wage	N	6. Display 10 Commandments	Y	10. Perm. Trade with China	Y
3. Strike Ban on Ergo. Stnd.	N	7. Gun Show Bkgrnd. Checks	N	11. Debt Relief for 3rd World	N
4. Ovrd. Estate Tax Veto	Y	8. Ban Part.-Birth Abortion	Y	12. Drop Cuba Econ. Embargo	N

Election Results

2000 general	Jim Ryun (R)	164,951	(67%)	($284,064)
	Stanley Wiles (D)	71,709	(29%)	
	Others	8,099	(3%)	
2000 primary	Jim Ryun (R)	unopposed		
1998 general	Jim Ryun (R)	108,527	(61%)	($540,653)
	Jim Clark (D)	69,521	(39%)	($116,031)

THIRD DISTRICT

Though its central city is in Missouri, one-third of metropolitan Kansas City's residents now live west of the state line in Kansas. Some are in Kansas City, Kansas, where the low-lying land near the Missouri River used to house one of the nation's largest stockyards. This is still a working-class town with a few dilapidated looking streets and lots of modest frame houses, the largest black neighborhood and oldest Catholic ethnic neighborhoods in Kansas, and old Democratic machine politics. Its older neighborhoods are separated from the affluent Kansas City, Missouri, neighborhood around the old Country Club Plaza shopping center by just a single small street; the newer neighborhoods are arrayed along the interstates, and have grown to the point that Overland Park, Olathe, Shawnee and Lenexa—unfamiliar names to most Kansans—are among the largest municipalities in the state. These suburbs are not just residential; Sprint's headquarters is in Johnson County, and a J.C. Penney catalogue center, as well as lots of thriving small businesses, are located there. Politically, Johnson County has long been heavily Republican, but with plenty of voters moderate or even liberal on cultural issues plus small but growing Asian and Latino populations.

The 3d Congressional District consists of Johnson County, Kansas City and surrounding Wyandotte County, the Douglas County town of Lawrence, which is the home of University of Kansas, and one rural county to the south. But 69% of the votes are cast in Johnson County. The most hard-fought struggle here has been between conservative and moderate Republicans. At first the conservatives made great strides, taking over the Republican Party apparatus and leadership positions in the legislature in 1994. In 1996 they showed across-the-board strength in Kansas, electing three conservative freshmen congressmen as well as Senator Sam Brownback. But in 1998 the moderates rebounded. A conservative challenge to Republican Governor Bill Graves was beaten nearly 3–1 in the Republican primary, and in the 3d District conservative freshman Congressman Vince Snowbarger was one of six House incumbents defeated for re-election.

The congressman from the 3d now is Dennis Moore, a Democrat first elected in 1998 with a long political pedigree who developed an appeal across party lines. Moore grew up in Wichita, and his father Warner Moore ran for Congress in the 4th District and lost the general by only 50.3%–49.7% in 1958—which had also been the last year a Democrat won in the 3d. Moore went to college and law school in Kansas, served in the Army and practiced law in Johnson County. In 1976, at 31, he was elected Johnson County district attorney and re-elected in 1980 and 1984. There he claims credit for starting a Consumers Protection Division and a Victims Assistance Unit and for prosecuting a national oil company. He went into private law practice in 1993 and was elected to the local community college board in 1997.

His election wins made Moore a natural when national Democrats were recruiting a candidate to oppose a vulnerable Snowbarger, who had earned a reputation as a strong conservative.

Though Snowbarger had no primary opposition in 1998, Moore took advantage of the turbulence between conservative and moderate Republicans. He got the support of a local Mainstream Co-alition formed, it seems, to do in Snowbarger and his like. Snowbarger made "trust" his major theme, but ran few if any ads on what he'd done positively. The contest attracted big independent expenditure campaigns, with the Sierra Club and the AFL-CIO spending heavily on TV ads, mailings and phone banks to elect Moore. Moore won 52%–48%, carrying Kansas City and Lawrence by wide margins, but his key wins came in northeast Johnson County, in the affluent, long-settled, elderly suburbs around Mission Hills, Roeland Park, Merriam and the north half of Overland Park. That was enough to hold Snowbarger to a 53%–47% margin in Johnson County. Snowbarger was deserted by the Republican establishment; Johnson County lawns sprouted signs for Moore next to those for Governor Bill Graves. But it also must be said that Moore showed considerable popularity and great fundraising skills.

In the House, Moore emulated earlier moderate Democrats who sought to straddle party lines. He joined Senator John McCain at a press conference to complain about tax-exempt Section 527 groups that raised undisclosed campaign funds. He got bipartisan support for his proposal to close a loophole that allows some convicts to have guns. To the dismay of organized labor, he voted for permanent normal trade relations with China. He brought federal pork back home, including $22 million for projects in Wyandotte County—compared to only $3.5 million for Johnson County; Moore aides explained the disparity by saying that previous congressmen had shortchanged Wyandotte.

All that did not diminish Republican hopes of taking out Moore in November 2000. But they hurt themselves by repeating their divisions of two years earlier. The Republican primary was a contest between tax-cutting conservative state Representative Phill Kline and Greg Musil, an Overland Park councilman and the founder of a medical relief agency. Kline was endorsed by Senator Sam Brownback and conservative leaders. Musil was endorsed by Governor Bill Graves and moderates, and had the backing of National Republican Congressional Committee chairman Tom Davis. Kline won the primary 50%–37%, with conservative physician Gary Morsch taking 13%. In the general, Kline did a more effective job than Snowbarger had in rallying moderate Republican leaders behind him. But Moore appealed to moderate Republicans by portraying himself as a fiscal conservative and a crime-fighter. Kline contended that Moore was "an enemy of the taxpayer" and, in TV ads late in the campaign, that he had supported a 1984 bill that reduced the sentence for aggravated incest. Moore responded that Kline belonged to the "farthest right of the far right" and that his votes in the legislature weakened education. Although the Teamsters opposed his re-election, Moore got a boost from the Business Roundtable's endorsement and the Chamber of Commerce's neutrality. In a result similar to 1998, Moore won 50%–47%; he led in Douglas and Wyandotte 64%–33%, while Kline took Johnson County by only 52%–45%, while it was voting 60%–36% for George W. Bush.

For 2002, Republicans have another weapon against Moore: redistricting. With large majorities in the state legislature, they could move Douglas County out of the 2d District and into the 3d, and substitute Leavenworth County or other Republican territory. But the still need to find a challenger who can unify their party and contend with the politically adroit Moore.

Cook's Call   *Highly Competitive.* There is little doubt that Dennis Moore will be a top Republican target in 2002. Moore is a political anomaly in a district that has a serious Republican edge. With Republicans in control of the redistricting process in the state, Moore could also see his district altered enough to make it even more challenging in 2002. This district was the fastest growing in the state and needs to lose about 90,000 people. But, Moore, now in his third term, is not to be underestimated. Republicans need to avoid a prolonged primary battle and must find a better caliber candidate than the ones they picked in 1998 and 2000.

THE PEOPLE: Pop. 2000: 733,606; Pop. 1990: 619,445, up 18.4% 1990–2000. 83.5% White, 8.3% Black, 2.5% Asian, 0.7% Amer. Indian, 2% Two+ races, 2.9% Other; 6.4% Hispanic Origin.

2000 Presidential Vote

Bush (R)	164,334	(53%)
Gore (D)	130,841	(42%)
Nader (Green)	11,446	(4%)
Others	3,064	(1%)

1996 Presidential Vote

Dole (R)	144,924	(50%)
Clinton (D)	121,152	(42%)
Perot (I)	18,176	(6%)

Rep. Dennis Moore (D)

Elected 1998, 2d term; b. Nov. 8, 1945, Anthony; home, Lenexa; U. of KS, B.A. 1967; Washburn U. Law Schl., J.D. 1970; Protestant; married (Stephene).

Military Career: Army, 1970; Army Reserves, 1971–73.

Elected Office: Johnson Cnty. Dist. Atty., 1976–88.

Professional Career: Asst. KS Atty. Gen., 1971–73; Practicing atty., 1973–76, 1989–98.

DC Office: 431 CHOB 20515, 202-225-2865; Fax: 202-225-2807; Web site: www.house.gov/moore.

District Offices: Kansas City, 913-621-0832; Lawrence, 785-842-9313; Overland Park, 913-383-2013.

Committees: *Budget* (14th of 20 D). *Financial Services* (21st of 32 D): Capital Markets, Insurance & Government Sponsored Enterprises; Financial Institutions & Consumer Credit; Oversight & Investigations. *Science* (21st of 22 D): Research; Space & Aeronautics.

Group Ratings

	ADA	ACLU	AFS	LCV	CON	ITIC	NTU	COC	ACU	NTLC	CHC
2000	65	64	57	93	19	78	35	66	24	24	27
1999	100	—	100	81	63	—	15	52	12	—	—

National Journal Ratings

	1999 LIB	—	1999 CONS		2000 LIB	—	2000 CONS
Economic	61%	—	39%		58%	—	41%
Social	67%	—	33%		65%	—	35%
Foreign	65%	—	34%		58%	—	40%

Key Votes of the 106th Congress

1. Patient Bill of Rights	Y	5. Bar RU-486 $ for FDA	N	9. NATO War in Serbia	Y
2. Accelerate Min. Wage	Y	6. Display 10 Commandments	N	10. Perm. Trade with China	Y
3. Strike Ban on Ergo. Stnd.	Y	7. Gun Show Bkgrnd. Checks	Y	11. Debt Relief for 3rd World	Y
4. Ovrd. Estate Tax Veto	Y	8. Ban Part.-Birth Abortion	N	12. Drop Cuba Econ. Embargo	Y

Election Results

2000 general	Dennis Moore (D)	154,505	(50%)	($1,759,414)
	Phill Kline (R)	144,672	(47%)	($1,054,489)
	Others	9,533	(3%)	
2000 primary	Dennis Moore (D)	unopposed		
1998 general	Dennis Moore (D)	103,376	(52%)	($986,688)
	Vince Snowbarger (R)	93,938	(48%)	($1,003,694)

FOURTH DISTRICT

Wichita is the largest Kansas-only metropolitan area, smaller than million-plus metro Kansas City, but a Great Plains metropolis of the magnitude of Omaha or Tulsa. It began as a farm market town and grew with local oil and gas discoveries in the 1920s. But its real impetus came during World War II and the years just after, when aircraft factories sprouted up here on the Kansas plains and Wichita suddenly became the nation's major producer of small planes. Today the big three—Cessna, Raytheon Aircraft, Bombardier—are all located here. In the early 1990s, general aviation was hurt by the recession and by suits which held manufacturers liable for planes they had produced years, even decades, before. But now Wichita has recovered: The demand for small planes is robust, and a federal limit on liability pushed through by, among others, its former Congressman Dan Glickman, has enlivened the industry. Wichita has also become a regional health center in the common Great Plains pattern, as rural counties are unable to attract new doctors or maintain hospitals, and people from miles around come to the metropolis for treatment.

Kansas' 4th Congressional District is centered around Wichita, covering wheat-growing areas to the east and west, but with most of its people in Wichita and Sedgwick County. Politically, it has voted Republican most years, even in the 1990s.

The congressman from the 4th District is Todd Tiahrt, a Republican first elected in 1994. He grew up on a farm in South Dakota, went to the same high school as South Dakota Senator Tim Johnson, played football for the South Dakota School of Mines and Technology and graduated from Evangel College. In 1976 he moved to the Wichita area to be closer to his wife's family and worked at Zenith as a project engineer and at Boeing as a proposal manager on the Space Station, Air Force One, KC-135, B-52, B-1, B-2, A-67, YF-22 and Comanche helicopter programs. In 1990 he went to the courthouse to file to run for the Kansas House and decided he was a Republican; he lost that race by only 8 votes. His grandfather had raised him to be a Democrat, but he found his strong religious views—"to me, liberty is the freedom to do the right thing, not the freedom to do anything"—were more in line with Republicans. In 1992 he was elected to the Kansas Senate, where his great cause was a concealed weapons law allowing law-abiding citizens on application to carry firearms.

In 1994 Tiahrt got it into his head to run against Dan Glickman, a task all the more daunting because Glickman seemed to be having a good ninth term. Tiahrt ran ads showing Glickman's face morphing into Bill Clinton's, and attacked him for voting for gun control in the 1994 crime bill. With his base among Wichita's numerous religious conservatives, who had taken over the local Republican Party, he assembled a corps of 1,800 volunteers, many from church contacts. Glickman spent $694,000 to Tiahrt's $200,000. Glickman ran relatively well, as he had for years, in high-income Republican precincts; but he suffered unexpectedly serious losses in middle-income areas in Wichita and Sedgwick County. Tiahrt won a solid 53%–47% victory, and Glickman went on to become secretary of Agriculture.

In the House, Tiahrt was an enthusiastic supporter of the Contract with America and boasted that he voted with Newt Gingrich 97% of the time. He is a deputy in Tom DeLay's Whip organization. He proposed eliminating the Department of Energy and transferring nuclear weapons storage and waste disposal to the Pentagon, to no effect. He tried to zero out—and later to reduce—AmeriCorps, as "largely inefficient and ineffective," but with no success. He was more successful in introducing the Adoption Promotion and Stability Act of 1996, which gave tax breaks for adoptive parents and ended the ban on transracial adoptions; introduced by Republicans, it was embraced by Clinton and passed nearly unanimously. A solid economic conservative, Tiahrt kept his eye on local economic issues, sponsoring an amendment to allow USDA money to be used for value-added products like wheat flour, and building up the Winfield and Arkansas City levees. Not surprisingly, he was targeted by Democrats in 1996, but won 50%–47%, a downtick from the 1994 result.

Tiahrt returned to take a seat on Appropriations, where he sponsored the ban on needle exchanges in the District of Columbia and called for a felony investigation of District officials who continued to fund abortions after Congress banned that in 1995. He sponsored a plan to allow parents access to their children's school files. He amended a foreign aid bill to block funding to governments that force women to be sterilized, have abortions or use contraceptives. Following the oil-price spike, he resumed his criticism of the Energy Department and the lack of a national energy policy.

Democrats continue to run well-financed opponents against Tiahrt, who has not quite locked up the district. In 2000, Wichita attorney and former Glickman aide Carlos Nolla ran a tougher-than-expected challenge against him. Tiahrt won 54%–42%, sweeping all 12 counties, but winning only 52%–45% in Sedgwick County, which cast two-thirds of the vote. Tiahrt has set up a statewide fundraising committee and has voiced interest in running for governor in 2002. Redistricting will not likely change the boundaries of the 4th, but this could be a battleground district again in 2002 as Nolla in February 2001 announced his intent to run again.

Cook's Call   *Probably Safe.* Tiahrt's 54% showing against an unknown Democrat in 2000 reminds political watchers that this Wichita-based seat has been the site of competitive contests earlier in the decade. The fact that he ran 5% behind Bush, is another sign that Tiahrt may not be as solidly planted as he seemed in 1998 when he won with 58%. He is reportedly taking a look at running for governor in 2002, and if he does, this seat could be competitive, though it would still retain a Republican edge.

THE PEOPLE: Pop. 2000: 675,755; Pop. 1990: 619,373, up 9.1% 1990–2000. 83.6% White, 6.8% Black, 2.4% Asian, 1.2% Amer. Indian, 2.6% Two+ races, 3.3% Other; 6.5% Hispanic Origin.

2000 Presidential Vote

Bush (R)	148,040	(59%)
Gore (D)	91,670	(37%)
Nader (Green)	7,145	(3%)
Others	3,841	(2%)

1996 Presidential Vote

Dole (R)	145,997	(56%)
Clinton (D)	90,557	(35%)
Perot (I)	21,660	(8%)

Rep. Todd Tiahrt (R)

Elected 1994, 4th term; b. June 15, 1951, Vermillion, SD; home, Goddard; Evangel Col., B.A. 1975; SW MO St. U., M.B.A. 1989; Assembly of God; married (Vicki).

Elected Office: KS Senate, 1992–94.

Professional Career: Project Engineer, Zenith Corp., 1976–84; Proposal Mgr., Boeing Co., 1985–94.

DC Office: 401 CHOB 20515, 202-225-6216; Fax: 202-225-3489; Web site: www.house.gov/tiahrt.

District Office: Wichita, 316-262-8992.

Committees: *Appropriations* (22d of 35 R): Defense; Transportation; Treasury, Postal Service & General Government.

Group Ratings

	ADA	ACLU	AFS	LCV	CON	ITIC	NTU	COC	ACU	NTLC	CHC
2000	0	29	0	7	50	83	64	95	91	85	100
1999	5	—	0	0	56	—	64	88	95	—	—

National Journal Ratings

	1999 LIB —	1999 CONS		2000 LIB —	2000 CONS
Economic	0% —	84%		0% —	94%
Social	19% —	79%		0% —	79%
Foreign	20% —	80%		32% —	67%

Key Votes of the 106th Congress

1. Patient Bill of Rights	N	5. Bar RU-486 $ for FDA	Y	9. NATO War in Serbia	N
2. Accelerate Min. Wage	N	6. Display 10 Commandments	Y	10. Perm. Trade with China	Y
3. Strike Ban on Ergo. Stnd.	N	7. Gun Show Bkgrnd. Checks	N	11. Debt Relief for 3rd World	N
4. Ovrd. Estate Tax Veto	Y	8. Ban Part.-Birth Abortion	Y	12. Drop Cuba Econ. Embargo	N

Election Results

2000 general	Todd Tiahrt (R)	131,871	(54%)	($854,357)
	Carlos Nolla (D)	101,980	(42%)	($313,524)
	Steven A. Rosile (Lib)	8,732	(4%)	
2000 primary	Todd Tiahrt (R)	unopposed		
1998 general	Todd Tiahrt (R)	94,785	(58%)	($635,508)
	Jim Lawing (D)	62,737	(39%)	($28,869)
	Others	5,171	(3%)	

★ KENTUCKY ★

Kentucky is a state that in many ways remains close to its beginnings. This is, literally, a Jeffersonian commonwealth: It is one of four commonwealths (the others are Virginia, Pennsylvania and Massachusetts) and when the first settlers came here, in the years Thomas Jefferson was writing his *Notes on Virginia*, it was part of Virginia. Kentucky was admitted to the Union in 1792, when Jefferson was secretary of State; and when Jefferson was aroused at the Federalists' anti-sedition acts, he ghost-wrote the Kentucky Resolutions in 1798. Kentucky's one large county is named after Jefferson and its one large city after the monarch to whom he was credentialed as ambassador to France, Louis XVI. To this day, Kentucky still has a constitution informed by a Jeffersonian jealousy of power. Its one-term limit on governors was raised to two only in 1995, and the current governor, Paul Patton, was the first eligible for a second consecutive term; it has strict limits on when the legislature can meet, so that much important business gets done in special sessions; every governor must swear that he or she has not participated in a duel (remember what Jefferson thought of Aaron Burr). Kentucky also has long favored the Democratic Party, which can trace its ancestry at least tenuously back to Jefferson; Republicans have made gains recently in federal elections, and George W. Bush carried the state handily in 2000, but in the 1990s Kentucky voted twice, though by diminishing margins, for William Jefferson Clinton.

The agrarian Jefferson would approve of Kentucky's demography, which is still largely rural, with under half its population in the big metropolitan areas of Louisville, Lexington and the Northern Kentucky area across the Ohio River from Cincinnati; only three counties have populations over 100,000. And the tobacco planters who once presided over what one historian called "the alcoholic republic" might not entirely disapprove of a Kentucky economy that remains heavily dependent on century-old industries such as tobacco (Kentucky is the nation's number two producer after North Carolina, and it has the largest number of tobacco farms), whiskey (Bourbon County, where the beverage was invented in the 18th Century, is in Kentucky) and coal. Many of the buildings here are old: the small-town 19th Century courthouses, the cabins in the coal mining Appalachians, the unpainted houses in the soggy lowlands beneath the levees by the Mississippi River. Kentucky is the home of some of the nation's oldest traditions, from bourbon to bluegrass music to religious revivals (the Disciples of Christ got their start in the enormous revival at Cane Ridge in 1801); it was the home of the inventor of Mother's Day in 1887 and a Louisville restaurant claims credit for inventing the cheeseburger. Some things have changed. Satellite dishes and four-lane highways have brought modern civilization into hollows and lowland farms that lacked indoor plumbing and electricity within living memory and farmers have begun to diversify their crops; Kentucky is now the nation's leading producer of ginseng. But people in this state still have a strong attachment to place and family; the continuity is real. Kentucky's population has grown just 42% over the past 50 years; few outsiders have moved in, though the number increased in the 1990s, so today's Kentuckians are mostly descendants of settlers who poured over the mountains in the 40 years after Daniel Boone made his way through the Cumberland Gap in 1775, when Kentucky's population rose from 73,000 in the Census of 1790 to 564,000 in 1820.

There has long been hearty, though lopsided, political competition here, with most of the 120 counties voting today as they did in the Civil War era. The eastern mountains were pro-Union and remain Republican, except for counties where coal miners were organized by the United Mine Workers in the 1930s; the Bluegrass region and the western end of the state were slave-holding territory and Democratic. Louisville, with many German immigrants, was an anti-slavery town, and for years flirted with Republicans, though now it mostly supports Democrats. These patterns, which have more or less prevailed for more than 100 years, were apparent in the returns for governor in 1995, senator in 1996 and 1998, and president in 1992 and 1996. For years, all this meant control by the Democratic Party, with the real battle in the primary. For nearly half a century there was almost a two-party system within the dominant party, with factions going back to the 1938 primary when Senate Majority Leader (and later Vice President) Alben Barkley was challenged by Governor (and later Senator and Baseball Commissioner) Happy Chandler. Barkley's faction was later led by Governor (1959–63) Bert Combs and Chandler's by Governor

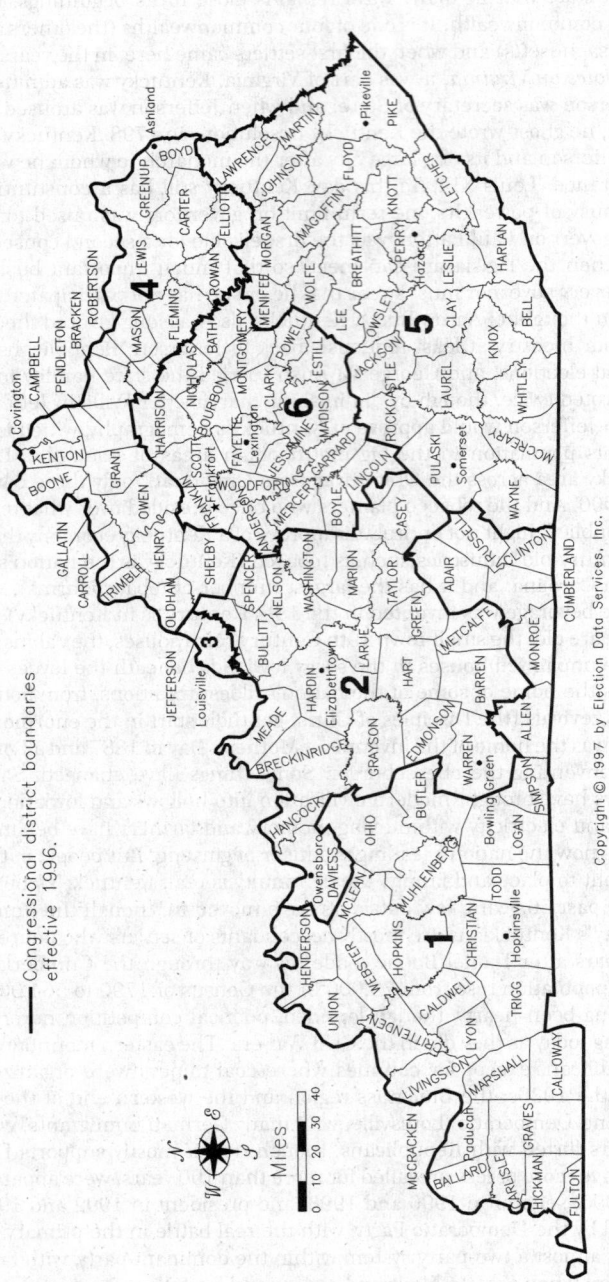

Congressional district boundaries
effective 1996.

(1971–74) and Senator (1974–99) Wendell Ford. But as Louisville *Courier-Journal* reporter Al Cross notes, factional gave way to money, with rich candidates elected governor over most of the last 20 years—John Y. Brown Jr. in 1979, Wallace Wilkinson in 1987 and Brereton Jones in 1991. But lineage still has its claims: Ben Chandler, Happy Chandler's grandson, was elected attorney general in 1995 and 1999.

But in the last 10 years there have been some changes in these patterns. Democratic Governor Paul Patton, a narrow winner in 1995, was re-elected by a wide margin over a hapless Republican in 1999. At the same time, Republicans have won near-total control of Kentucky's congressional delegation—albeit in some cases by narrow margins initially. Much of this has been the work of Senator Mitch McConnell, first elected in 1984. McConnell helped line up candidates who carried the formerly Democratic 1st, 2nd and 3rd Congressional Districts in 1994 and 1996; he provided key support for Senator Jim Bunning's 6,766-vote win in 1998 and helped capture the 6th District vacated by Bunning's opponent that year as well. Now only the 4th District is represented by a Democrat, a conservative who often votes with Republicans. In July and August 1999 party switches gave Republicans a 20–18 margin in the state Senate, where they were outnumbered 30–8 at the beginning of the decade; the state House is still heavily Democratic. The biggest triumph came in the 2000 presidential race. Al Gore initially targeted Kentucky, which is just north of his home state of Tennessee and which the Clinton-Gore ticket carried twice. But Kentucky was part of the rural trend away from Clinton Democrats and toward Republicans in the 1990s, and Gore had taken stands seen as hostile to the state's leading industries—tobacco, coal and automobiles (there are big assembly plants in Louisville and Toyota has a plant near Lexington). Early polls showed Bush far ahead, and Gore took his ads off Kentucky stations and took the state off his schedule. Bush swept the state, 57%–41%; in 50 of the 120 counties he won a higher percentage than Ronald Reagan had in his landslide re-election victory in 1984. Moreover, the popularity of his issue positions and cultural stance helped defeat Democrats the party had considered itself lucky to recruit in the 1st, 3rd and 6th congressional districts. If Bush's politics of decentralized government and confident nationalism can be called Jeffersonian, then Kentucky in 2000 voted in line with its Jeffersonian roots.

Governor   There is no question who stands at the apex of Kentucky politics: the governor. The governor's appointment powers are wide: The legislature meets in regular session for only 60 days in even-numbered years and, since 2001, 30 days in odd-numbered years; after that the governor can shift around line items in the state budget and call special sessions. Kentucky's governor, elected in 1995, is Paul Patton, a Democrat from the eastern Kentucky coal fields. He grew up in Lawrence County on the West Virginia border in a house converted from a silo. He was a 1959 graduate of the University of Kentucky's College of Engineering, and ran a coal company from 1962 to 1978. He began his public service career as deputy state Transportation secretary from 1979–80, chaired the state Democratic Party and in 1982 was elected judge-executive of Pike County, at the far eastern extremity of the state. In 1991 he was elected lieutenant governor and worked on a law granting tax credits to firms that create jobs. The 1995 gubernatorial race was an uphill battle. In the Democratic primary, Patton won 45%, with 24% for Secretary of State Bob Babbage, and 21% for legislator John "Eck" Rose. In the general, he faced Republican Larry Forgy, who campaigned hard against the Kentucky Education Reform Act, passed in 1990 after the state Supreme Court outlawed school finance laws. KERA vastly raised per pupil spending, moved toward equalizing spending in districts, mandated ungraded classes for kindergarten through third grade, and a teacher assessment system based on written portfolios; test scores at the decade mark have generally risen, although most schools are far short of targets set for 2014. Patton won 51%–49%, the Democrats' first major success in stalling Republican advances since Bill Clinton took office; Democrats all over the country took heart.

In his first years as governor, Patton took a conservative tack. When the Clinton administration threatened to regulate tobacco as a drug, Patton supported a lawsuit opposing the FDA rules, lit up a cigarette, and said he wouldn't support Clinton in 1996 if the FDA acted. On state policy, Patton's first major initiative in December 1996 was workmen's compensation reform. After extensive research, Patton decided workmens' comp rates were 20% above other states and were hurting Kentucky business. Patton mastered the details, worked hard and assembled a bipartisan majority for his reform: a four-year limit on re-opening cases, evaluation by state-paid doctors with American Medical Association guidelines on disability, and lower attorney's fees. This stirred great opposition in Patton's eastern Kentucky base and among the unions who had supported him strongly in 1995, and they and former Governor Brereton Jones called for a special session to change the law in 1997 and 1998, but Patton refused.

Patton's next big cause was higher education reform, splitting 13 junior colleges from the University of Kentucky and making the latter a major research university. He wanted more concrete goals for the community colleges together with deregulation and decentralization of the schools. Again, he immersed himself in detail and amassed a coalition, and overcame powerful lobbies. In October 1997, he tried another session, this time on health care. Patton argued that the health care system created in 1994 was unworkable because all but one private insurer had fled Kentucky; he created a high-risk pool with premiums up to 150% of the market standard, in order to preserve guaranteed portability. But the state House opposed his plan, with many backing a play-or-pay plan in which insurers would be obliged to cover high-risk people or pay an assessment to companies who would. None of the bills passed. In 1998 Patton's budget passed, and so did federally subsidized health insurance for children of the working poor. But he antagonized state employee unions in September when he forced them to switch to managed care in 1999.

Heading into 1999, the first year in which a Kentucky governor could seek a four-year term, Patton still had some criticism from former union allies, but his job approval rating was in the 65% range, the highest of any recent Kentucky governor, and one after another potential opponent declined to run. The May 1999 Republican primary had the lowest turnout ever; the winner, by a 51%–49% margin, publicist Peppy Martin, proved to be a bizarre candidate. She made unsubstantiated charges against Patton and in an October debate charged that 80% of sheriffs and 30% of state police were "bootlegging hard drugs." Senator Mitch McConnell and state Senate Republican leader David Williams endorsed Patton. He won with 61% of the vote, to 22% for Martin and 15% for Gatewood Galbraith, an independent who backed legalization of marijuana. Patton carried 113 counties; the seven he lost were in eastern Kentucky, evidently because of anger over his workmen's comp changes.

In his second term Patton moved to the left. He lobbied the legislature for tax reform and a gas tax increase; the latter was a nonstarter and the former was killed by Republicans in the state Senate. The tax on long distance phone calls was increased and the unemployment tax on employers was cut. Patton signed an early childhood development bill, funded by tobacco settlement money and designed by a commission headed by his daughter Nikki Patton. Workmen's comp was liberalized, as Patton said he had gone too far in his 1996 reform. There was bipartisan support for a law calling for schools to post the Ten Commandments and for giving the governor 553 tickets to the Kentucky Derby—distributed usually to fundraisers and heads of businesses that might bring jobs to Kentucky. But there were also bitter partisan disputes. Patton said that David Williams promised to help pass a gas tax increase, then reneged; Williams said that Patton was "mouthy drunk" at the time; Patton said that anything the legislature accomplished was despite the Republicans, and campaigned hard for Democratic state Senate candidates. But in November, as George W. Bush was carrying the state 57%–41%, the Republicans held their 20–18 seat lead. Patton had backed Gore, but was sometimes critical of him; Bush appeared in the state frequently and raised money for Republican state Senate candidates.

Patton said he would wait for the 2002 session to work on tax reform and waste management, and launched a health insurance plan for high risk patients. His job rating remained high. Already some were focusing on the 2003 governor's race. Possible Democratic candidates included House Speaker Jody Richards, former Governor Brereton Jones, Lieutenant Governor Steve Henry (who married a former Miss America in October 2000 but soon after was under investigation for Medicare fraud), Attorney General Ben Chandler and self-financing businessman Charlie Owen. Possible Republicans included RNC Treasurer Mike Duncan, Congressman Hal Rogers ("presumptive nominee," David Williams said), Williams, Congresswoman Anne Northup and Jefferson County Judge-Executive Rebecca Jackson. (the Jefferson County and Lousville governments are scheduled to merge in 2003). Patton is widely considered a likely candidate against Senator Jim Bunning in 2004.

Senior Senator   Mitch McConnell is Kentucky's senior senator, the architect of its 7–1 Republican congressional delegation and a major leader on several national issues. Yet his origins were modest and his rise anything but inevitable. He grew up in Alabama, where he overcame polio, and after age 13 moved to Louisville. He has been in politics almost his whole career: He was an intern for Senator John Sherman Cooper in 1964 and, after finishing law school, became a staffer for Senator Marlow Cook. He moved back to Louisville and in 1977, at 35, won by a narrow margin the office that had been Cook's political stepping stone, Jefferson County judge-executive. In 1981 he was re-elected, again narrowly. In 1984 he ran for the Senate, against incumbent Dee Huddleston. McConnell ran ads showing bloodhounds sniffing for Huddleston in vacation locales where he had collected fees for speeches while the Senate was in session. McConnell won by 5,169 votes of 1.2 million cast, the only challenger to beat an incumbent that year.

In the Senate, McConnell has a mostly conservative record and high party loyalty. Yet he was willing to penalize a fellow Republican when as Ethics Committee chairman in 1995 he led the investigation of Bob Packwood for sexual harassment; the committee recommended expulsion, and Packwood ultimately resigned. McConnell has been a strong backer of product liability and medical malpractice reform, and is a lead sponsor of the auto choice plan that would let car owners pay less for insurance by disclaiming pain and suffering damages. He has been the Senate sponsor of so-far unsuccessful measures to ban racial quotas and preferences. McConnell served on Foreign Relations until 1992, then switched to Appropriations and in 1994 became chairman of the Foreign Operations Subcommittee. He has strongly supported aid to Israel and has been skeptical about aid to Russia. He has faced questions about his and wife Elaine Chao's Chinese connections since she took over as Labor Secretary for the Bush Administration.

McConnell has spent much time on tobacco issues. In June 1998 he split with retiring Democrat Wendell Ford and backed an $18 billion tobacco program that would end price supports and provide mandatory buyouts of tobacco farmers. Ford and Jim Bunning, then a Republican congressman and candidate for the Senate, backed a $28 billion bailout with voluntary buyouts and continuing price supports. It was the first time in 60 years, Ford said, that Kentucky senators disagreed on tobacco. Later that month, the tobacco settlement bill died in the Senate, and McConnell, stung by criticism from tobacco farmers, reversed his previous desire to end price supports. In September he persuaded conferees to drop a provision that would have required tobacco companies to pay for tobacco price supports; they would take it out of the hide of farmers, he said. In August 1999 he got unanimous consent of a bill to overcome legal obstacles and get quicker payment of $112 million to tobacco farmers. In October 2000 he got burley tobacco growers released from repaying loans of $509 million and got disposal of 250 million pounds of surplus drought-damaged tobacco. McConnell has frequently used his seat on Appropriations to insert riders that help Kentucky. They include a transfer of mineral rights in eastern Kentucky from TVA, $1 million to study new coal technologies at a Capitol Hill power plant, $2 million to study impoundments that hold coal waste, $11 million for environmental cleanup and worker health testing at the Paducah uranium plant. He remained silent when his wife proposed transferring the Paducah program to the Justice Department, although Senator Jim Bunning and Representative Ed Whitfield objected.

McConnell's greatest expertise is on campaigns and elections. He has fought one battle after another against campaign finance bills that in his view limit free speech and vigorous electoral competition. "Spending is speech," he says. "The First Amendment denies government the power to determine that spending to promote one's political views is wasteful, excessive or unwise." He disputes the notions that campaign ads are some kind of pollution and that too much is spent on them. In 1994 he spoke all night to filibuster a campaign finance bill, "the only true all-night filibuster in the last 12 years," he said in 1999. In October 1999, with more than 40 senators on his side, he killed a version of the McCain-Feingold campaign finance bill. In 1999 Bill Clinton broke with tradition and refused to nominate Bradley Smith for FEC commissioner, the law professor picked by Senate Republicans, who opposed much campaign finance regulation as a violation of the First Amendment. McConnell got Clinton to nominate Smith by putting a hold on the nomination of Richard Holbrooke to be UN Ambassador. In March 2001, after Democrats picked up four seats in the 2000 election, John McCain insisted on bringing campaign finance forward again, and despite McConnell's efforts managed to pass his measure. But as McConnell pointed out, it did not include many provisions in previous McCain-Feingold bills, including public subsidies for candidates and voluntary spending limits. And the sweeping provisions against independent advertising inserted by an amendment by Paul Wellstone (which McConnell voted for) seemed likely to be ruled unconstitutional. McCain's bill was also amended by a doubling of the limit on individual contributions.

McConnell ran for chairman of the National Republican Senatorial Committee and lost to Phil Gramm in 1990 and in 1992 by one vote; he won the post in November 1996. But he was not able to get Republican senators to contribute as much to campaigns as Democratic senators for 1998, and he was criticized for contributing heavily to Mark Neumann of Wisconsin, who ran against Russ Feingold, and for skimping on Washington state's Linda Smith, a McCain-Feingold backer. He responded that polls showed Neumann's chances were better, and indeed Neumann won a higher percentage, but both lost. So did enough Republican hopefuls that the party gained no seats. After the election, Chuck Hagel of Nebraska ran for the post, but McConnell won 39–13. In the 2000 cycle he had tougher sledding. The death of Paul Coverdell in July 2000 cost Republicans one crucial seat. The death of Missouri Democrat Mel Carnahan in a plane crash in October 2000 resulted in the candidacy of his widow and the narrow defeat of John Ashcroft, who might have won if the crash had not occcurred. Republicans lost most of the close races, and the result was a 50–50 split. But McConnell did not seem to be getting much blame. He relinquished the post in December 2000 since his seat is up in 2002.

McConnell has had more success in building up Kentucky's chronically ailing Republican Party. He oversaw Ron Lewis's capture of the 2d District House seat in a May 1994 special election. He helped Ed Whitfield pick up the 1st District and Republican legislative candidates win in western Kentucky in 1994. He backed Anne Northup in her win in Louisville's 3d District in 1996. In 1998 McConnell strongly backed Jim Bunning's candidacy for the Senate. But when Democrat Paul Patton was narrowly elected governor in November 1995, Democrats sensed McConnell might be in trouble. He had won a second term in 1990 over former Louisville Mayor Harvey Sloane 52%–48%. The 1996 Democratic nominee, former Lieutenant Governor Steve Beshear, attacked McConnell for stopping campaign finance reform, for seeking to delay voting on the minimum wage increase and for supporting NAFTA. McConnell charged that Beshear was a lobbyist, a political insider and, worst, a fox hunter; on the campaign trail Beshear was followed by a character dressed in fox-hunting regalia. McConnell put Beshear on the defensive when Bill Clinton proposed that the FDA regulate tobacco as a drug. McConnell spent $5 million to Beshear's $2 million and, after early polls showed a close race, won 55%–43%. He carried the Louisville and Lexington areas, won 2–1 in northern Kentucky, and lost only handfuls of counties in the eastern mountains and in the far western end of the state.

In the 2000 election, McConnell helped the Bush campaign target and carry Kentucky; he backed the successful merger of the Jefferson County and Louisville city governments. After the election, he and Bob Torricelli, the Democrats' 2000 Senate campaign committee chairman, proposed a bipartisan four-member commission to study elections and make recommendations to state and local governments, with $100 million in federal grants to states.

McConnell comes up for re-election in 2002. In February 2001 Lois Combs Weinberg, daughter of former (1959–63) Governor Bert Combs, announced she was running. Bert Combs was one of the leading Kentucky politicians of the 20th Century. Weinberg has served on education boards but never before sought elective office, but her announcement was attended by state House Majority Leader Greg Stumbo and former Governors Martha Layne Collins and Edward Breathitt; she seemed unlikely to have competition for the Democratic nomination, except perhaps from self-financing (and 1998 Senate candidate) Charlie Owen. Weinberg called McConnell "the poster boy of the privileged and the powerful" and promised to attack him for his opposition to campaign finance election. Of that issue, McConnell said in 2001, "I can still confidently state that there has never been an election in American history decided on this issue one way or another, either for or against a candidate." The 2002 election may be a test of that proposition.

Cook's Call   *Safe.* Although Kentucky leans slightly Democratic, McConnell is as good a strategist and tactician as one can find on Capitol Hill. Lois Combs Weinberg, the daughter of former Governor (1959–63) Bert T. Combs, is likely to be the Democratic nominee, but millionaire Charlie Owen could challenge her. While Weinberg might provide an interesting contrast to McConnell, she is clearly an underdog.

Junior Senator   Jim Bunning, a Republican elected to the Senate in 1998, is the first and so far only member of the Baseball Hall of Fame to serve in Congress. Bunning grew up in Northern Kentucky, just across the Ohio River from Cincinnati. He started in minor league baseball in 1950, but at his father's insistence finished high school and college. He made the majors in 1956 and the next year became the only pitcher to strike out Ted Williams three times in one game. Bunning threw a no-hitter for the Detroit Tigers in 1958 and pitched a perfect game for the Philadelphia Phillies in 1964; he also played for the Pittsburgh Pirates and the Los Angeles Dodgers. He retired in 1971 with a 224–184 record, a 3.24 ERA, 2,855 strikeouts and one of the highest totals in baseball history for hitting batters; he was the second pitcher (Cy Young was the first) to achieve 1,000 strikeouts and 100 wins in both the American and the National Leagues. He was inducted into the Baseball Hall of Fame in August 1996. He is a family man, with nine children (two sets of twins) and at last count 35 grandchildren; his son David was considered for a federal judicial nomination in 2001. The skill, energy and aggressiveness he showed in baseball he brought to politics in his native northern Kentucky. He was elected to the Fort Thomas City Council in 1977, to the state Senate in 1979, and won a respectable 44% against Martha Layne Collins in the 1983 race for governor (the best showing for a Republican gubernatorial candidate between 1971 and 1995). When incumbent 4th District Congressman Gene Snyder retired in 1986, Bunning won the seat with 55% of the vote.

Bunning showed great impatience with ways of doing business in the Democratic House. He served six years on the ethics committee, starting off in March 1992 by leading the charge against the House bank overdraft scandal, and ending in January 1997 by resigning from the committee out of disgust with the partisanship of ranking Democrat Jim McDermott. In September 1993 he called Bill Clinton "the most corrupt, the most amoral, the most despicable person I've ever seen in the presidency." As Republicans became the majority, Bunning had achievements as a legislator. He chaired the Finance Social Security Subcommittee for two terms, and sponsored two major changes—raising the earnings limit for Social Security recipients up to $30,000 by 2002, and the 1994 law making the Social Security Administration an independent agency. He sponsored a disability reform, which would make it easier for recipients to return to work by granting them two years of Medicare benefits; it passed the House and, in another version, became law in 2000. He is, incidentally, in favor of repealing the antitrust exemption for baseball.

By early 1997 Bunning, with typical aggressiveness, was making plans to run for the Senate seat held by four-term Democrat Wendell Ford; in February 1997, Ford announced he would retire. Three Democrats ran serious campaigns for the nomination. Louisville businessman Charlie Owen spent $7 million of his own money and ran ads attacking the other two. Lieutenant Governor Steve Henry spent $500,000 of his own money and counted on his Louisville base and Owensboro roots. The third candidate was Lexington Congressman Scott Baesler, who had less money but other advantages: He was popular in his Republican-leaning 6th District, he is a tobacco farmer and he was still known as a star on one of Adolph Rupp's University of Kentucky basketball teams in the early 1960s. Baesler, with big margins in the Lexington media market, won the May primary with 34% of the vote, to 29% for Owen, who carried most of eastern and northern Kentucky, and 28% for Henry who carried Louisville and much of western Kentucky.

Baesler emerged from the primary ahead of Bunning in the polls but out of money; Bunning, with extensive help from Senator Mitch McConnell, had plenty of money. Baesler tried to take advantage of McConnell's support for an end to tobacco price supports, but Bunning opposed McConnell's stand, and both candidates had to agree there were no differences between them on tobacco. Ads paid for by McConnell's senatorial campaign committee highlighted Bunning's role as chairman of the Social Security Subcommittee. Bunning ran an ad showing actors thanking Baesler, in Spanish and (with subtitles) Chinese, for voting for NAFTA and MFN status for China. Baesler ads stressed campaign finance reform—a dig at McConnell, its leading opponent—and went back and attacked Bunning votes not only in the House but in the Kentucky legislature.

Baesler criticized Bunning for criticizing UK basketball coach Rick Pitino for welcoming Bill Clinton to Lexington in the last days of the 1996 campaign—an appearance that may have swung Kentucky's eight electoral votes. This was perhaps the country's closest race for months. And, despite Kentucky's early poll closing times and rapid count, it was not until late in the evening that Bunning was declared the winner. His margin was 49.7%–49.2%, or 6,766 votes. Baesler carried normally Republican Lexington, but only by 54%–46%. Bunning carried the three counties of northern Kentucky by 70%–29%; his margin there was 34,791 votes, more than five times his statewide margin, and more than Baesler's Lexington and Louisville margins put together.

Bunning has compiled one of the most conservative voting records in the Senate. His bill allowing disabled people to continue getting Medicaid or Medicare after getting a job was passed. He cautioned Alan Greenspan against quenching the flames of the economy ("Don't become so frightened by success that you throw wet blankets on a fire that isn't burning") and supported a guest worker program for Mexican workers in the United States. He worked on many Kentucky issues, sponsoring a bill to distribute $1.2 billion from the Abandoned Mine Reclamation Fund directly to Kentucky and other coal mining states and passing a bill to compensate TVA for mineral rights transferred to the Daniel Boone National Forest; this prevented coal mining in forest lands. He tussled with Tennessee's two Republican senators when he sponsored a bill to prohibit TVA from selling power throughout the country until it reduced its debt to $13 billion, half its current level. He helped to get $90 million earmarked for the troubled Paducah Gaseous Diffusion Plant after criticizing Energy Secretary Richardson for failing to carry out promises to install a Vortec incinerator there. With Mitch McConnell, he helped pass an amendment to reaffirm racetracks' right to offer interstate simulcast gambling. He dropped his bill to honor Louisville-born Muhammad Ali with the Congressional Gold Medal after some conservatives objected because of Ali's refusal of military service in the 1960s. In early 2001 he got a seat on Armed Services—to protect Fort Knox, Fort Campbell and the Bluegrass Army Depot, he said—and became chairman of the Economic Policy Subcommittee of Banking.

Bunning's seat comes up again in 2004, and everyone expects he will face Governor Paul Patton, who leaves office at the end of 2003. The relationship between the two seems to resemble those between Henry Clay and some of his rivals which ended up in duels. In 1996, Bunning said he shooks hands with Patton as he became governor "just out of respect for the office." "That's where he directly, personally insulted me or the office," said Patton. In 1998 Patton aided Scott Baesler to the Senate; Bunning vowed to work against Patton in 1999. In August 1999, when Patton, running for re-election, announced he wouldn't run against Senator Mitch McConnell in 2002, he complained that Bunning cancelled a meeting with him; Bunning said that no meeting had been scheduled. Patton's 1999 Republican opponent, Peppy Martin, was widely considered a risible candidate, and McConnell endorsed Patton; Bunning, however, endorsed Martin. While a Republican endorsing a Republican is ordinarily unremarkable, Patton said Bunning was acting out of "personal animosity" and called him "just a mean individual." Bunning said, "One of Paul Patton's problems is that he refuses to stand on any kind of principle." In March 2001 Bunning said his staff had been hearing about calls that said he was sick and dying; he accused Patton of spreading false rumors. In 2004 Bunning turns 73 and Patton 67, but the animosity between the two suggests there will be a high-spirited campaign.

Presidential politics   Kentucky's solid 57%–41% margin for George W. Bush in 2000 was all the more remarkable, because Kentucky has usually been a competitive state when Democrats run a Southerner or two on its ticket, as in such widely separated years as 1952, 1976, 1980, 1992 and 1996. But it was a continuation of a trend apparent in 1996, when Bill Clinton carried the state only by increasing his vote in the Lexington and Louisville areas and in Northern Kentucky, while falling behind his 1992 showing in the rural counties. In 2000 Gore carried Louisville's Jefferson County 50%–48% and won the usually Democratic state capital of Frankfort; he lost Lexington's Fayette County 52%–45% and trailed far behind in Northern Kentucky. Otherwise, he won only nine coal counties in the east and four ancestrally Democratic counties in the west. Gore carried only the very lowest income voters (below $15,000), and he was especially weak among younger voters (under 30s went 62%–35% for Bush)—not good signs for national Democrats here.

Kentucky was part of the Super Tuesday primary in March 1988, but switched back to a May date in 1992, so that state and presidential contests can be held on the same day. It has had no effect on the outcome of the presidential contest.

Congressional districting   Kentucky's current redistricting plan, drawn after the state lost one House seat in the 1990 Census, was intended to protect Democratic incumbents, but instead has produced a delegation that is 5–1 Republican. Democrats would control the process again this time, except that Republicans held on to their 20–18 majority in the state Senate in the 2000 election—a nice dividend of George W. Bush's strong run here. That means that both parties have a veto. That usually tends to produce minor changes in district lines, and in fact the current districts' variance from the population average is small enough that that would be easily feasible. Demography helps Republicans in one critical area: the district that needs to add the most population is the Louisville-based 3rd, and any extension outward into the suburbs will help Republican Anne Northup. The large 6th District must lose some counties, presumably to the 2nd; the boundaries of the 1st and 2nd may be smoothed out, though Republicans might resist that. Of course there is always the possibility that redistricting may end up in court, with unpredictable consequences.

THE PEOPLE: Pop. 2000: 4,041,769; Pop. 1990: 3,685,296, up 9.7% 1990–2000. 1.4% of U.S. total, 25th largest; 90.1% White, 7.3% Black, 0.7% Asian, 0.2% Amer. Indian, 1.1% Two+ races, 0.6% Other; 1.5% Hispanic Origin. 4.1% Unemployment. 2000 Voting age pop.: 3,046,951. 2000 Turnout: 1,568,058; 51% of VAP. Registered voters (2000): 2,556,815; 1,539,562 D (60%), 846,621 R (33%), 170,630 unaffiliated and minor parties (7%).

POLITICAL LINEUP: Governor, Paul E. Patton (D); Lt. Gov., Steven Henry (D); Secy. of State, John Y. Brown III (D); Atty. Gen., Albert B. (Ben) Chandler III (D); Treasurer, Jonathon Miller (D); Auditor, Ed Hatchett (D); Commissioner of Agriculture, Billy Ray Smith (D); State Senate, 38 (18 D, 20 R); Senate Pres. Pro Tempore, Richard L. Roeding (R); Senate President, David L. Williams (R); Majority Leader, Dan Kelly (R); State House, 100 (66 D, 34 R); House Speaker, Jody Richards (D). Senators, Mitch McConnell (R) and Jim Bunning (R). Representatives, 6 (1 D, 5 R).

ELECTIONS DIVISION: 502-573-7100; **FILING DEADLINE FOR U.S. CONGRESS:** January 29, 2002.

2000 Presidential Vote
Bush (R)	872,520	(57%)
Gore (D)	638,923	(41%)
Nader (Green)	23,118	(1%)
Others	9,465	(1%)

1996 Presidential Vote
Clinton (D)	636,614	(46%)
Dole (R)	623,283	(45%)
Perot (I)	120,396	(9%)

2000 Republican Presidential Primary
Bush (R)	75,783	(83%)
McCain (R)	5,780	(6%)
Other	5,423	(6%)
Keyes (R)	4,337	(5%)

2000 Democratic Presidential Primary
Gore (D)	156,966	(71%)
Bradley (D)	32,340	(15%)
Uncommitted	26,046	(12%)

Gov. Paul E. Patton (D)

Elected 1995, term expires Dec. 2003, 2d term; b. May 26, 1937, Fallsburg; home, Pikeville; U. of KY, B.S. 1959; Presbyterian; married (Judi).

Elected Office: Pike Cnty. Judge Exec., 1982–91; KY Lt. Gov., 1991–95.

Professional Career: Coal Co. Exec., 1959–79; KY Dpty. Transportation Secy., 1979–80; KY Dem. Party Chmn., 1981–83; KY Economic Develop. Secy., 1991–95.

Office: Office of the Governor, State Capitol, Frankfort, 40601, 502-564-2611; Fax: 502-564-2735; Web site: www.state.ky.us.

Election Results

1999 general	Paul E. Patton (D)	352,099	(61%)
	Peppy Martin (R)	128,788	(22%)
	Gatewood Galbraith (Ref)	88,930	(15%)
	Other	6,934	(1%)
1999 primary	Paul E. Patton (D)	unopposed	
1995 general	Paul E. Patton (D)	500,787	(51%)
	Larry Forgy (R)	479,227	(49%)
1995 primary	Paul E. Patton (D)	152,203	(45%)
	Bob Babbage (D)	81,352	(24%)
	John (Eck) Rose (D)	71,740	(21%)
	Gatewood Galbraith (D)	29,039	(9%)

Sen. Mitch McConnell (R)

Elected 1984, seat up 2002, 3d term; b. Feb. 20, 1942, Sheffield, AL; home, Louisville; U. of Louisville, B.A. 1964, U. of KY, J.D. 1967; Baptist; married (Elaine Chao).

Elected Office: Jefferson Cnty. Judge Exec., 1977–84.

Professional Career: Chief Legis. Asst., U.S. Sen. Marlow Cook, 1967–70; Dpty. Asst. U.S. Atty. Gen., 1974–75.

DC Office: 361-A RSOB, 20510, 202-224-2541; Fax: 202-224-2499; Web site: www.senate.gov/~mcconnell.

State Offices: Bowling Green, 270-781-1673; Ft. Wright, 859-578-0188; Lexington, 859-224-8286; London, 606-864-2026; Louisville, 502-582-6304; Paducah, 270-442-4554.

Committees: *Agriculture, Nutrition & Forestry*: Forestry, Conservation & Rural Revitalization; Production & Price Competitiveness; Research, Nutrition & General Legislation (RMM). *Appropriations*: Agriculture & Rural Development; Commerce, Justice, State & Judiciary; Defense; Energy & Water Development; Foreign Operations (RMM). *Judiciary*: Constitution, Federalism & Property Rights; Technology, Terrorism & Government Information; Youth Violence. *Rules & Administration* (RMM).

Group Ratings

	ADA	ACLU	AFS	LCV	CON	ITIC	NTU	COC	ACU	NTLC	CHC
2000	5	29	0	0	11	89	74	92	100	97	92
1999	0	—	0	0	8	—	75	88	84	—	—

National Journal Ratings

	1999 LIB	—	1999 CONS		2000 LIB	—	2000 CONS
Economic	0%	—	83%		0%	—	86%
Social	23%	—	72%		22%	—	73%
Foreign	46%	—	52%		5%	—	86%

Key Votes of the 106th Congress

1. Educ. Savings Accts.	Y	5. Review Movie Violence	Y	9. NATO War in Serbia	Y
2. Prescrip. Drug Benefit	N	6. Gun Show Bckgrnd. Checks	N	10. Table Cuba Travel Ban	Y
3. Delay Ergonomic Standards	Y	7. Ban Part.-Birth Abortion	Y	11. Nuclear Test-Ban Treaty	N
4. Phase Out Estate Tax	Y	8. Broaden Hate Crimes List	N	12. Perm. Trade with China	Y

Election Results

1996 general	Mitch McConnell (R)	724,794	(55%)	($5,031,293)
	Steven L. Beshear (D)	560,012	(43%)	($2,073,794)
	Others	22,240	(2%)	
1996 primary	Mitch McConnell (R)	88,620	(89%)	
	Tommy Klein (R)	11,410	(11%)	
1990 general	Mitch McConnell (R)	478,034	(52%)	($5,229,296)
	G. Harvey I. Sloane (D)	437,976	(48%)	($2,929,641)

Sen. Jim Bunning (R)

Elected 1998, seat up 2004, 1st term; b. Oct. 23, 1931, Campbell Cnty.; home, Southgate; Xavier U., B.S. 1953; Catholic; married (Mary).

Elected Office: Ft. Thomas City Cncl., 1977–79; KY Senate, 1979–83; U.S. House of Reps., 1986–98.

Professional Career: Pro baseball player, 1950–71; Investment broker & agent, 1960–86.

DC Office: 312 HSOB, 20510, 202-224-4343; Fax: 202-228-1373; Web site: www.senate.gov/~bunning.

State Offices: Ft. Wright, 859-341-2602; Hazard, 606-435-2390; Hopkinsville, 270-885-1212; Lexington, 859-219-2239; Louisville, 502-582-5341; Owensboro, 270-689-9085.

Committees: *Armed Services*: Airland Forces; Readiness & Management Support; Seapower. *Banking, Housing & Urban Affairs*: Economic Policy (RMM); Financial Institutions; Securities & Investment.

Group Ratings

	ADA	ACLU	AFS	LCV	CON	ITIC	NTU	COC	ACU	NTLC	CHC
2000	5	29	14	0	19	56	75	78	100	100	100
1999	0	—	0	0	58	—	77	82	100	—	—

National Journal Ratings

	1999 LIB	—	1999 CONS		2000 LIB	—	2000 CONS
Economic	0%	—	83%		0%	—	86%
Social	8%	—	88%		0%	—	90%
Foreign	0%	—	94%		5%	—	86%

Key Votes of the 106th Congress

1. Educ. Savings Accts.	Y	5. Review Movie Violence	Y	9. NATO War in Serbia	N
2. Prescrip. Drug Benefit	N	6. Gun Show Bckgrnd. Checks	N	10. Table Cuba Travel Ban	Y
3. Delay Ergonomic Standards	Y	7. Ban Part.-Birth Abortion	Y	11. Nuclear Test-Ban Treaty	N
4. Phase Out Estate Tax	Y	8. Broaden Hate Crimes List	N	12. Perm. Trade with China	N

Election Results

1998 general	Jim Bunning (R)	569,817	(50%)	($3,746,540)
	Scotty Baesler (D)	563,051	(49%)	($3,841,950)
	Others	12,546	(1%)	
1998 primary	Jim Bunning (R)	152,493	(74%)	
	Barry Metcalf (R)	52,798	(26%)	
1992 general	Wendell H. Ford (D)	836,888	(63%)	($2,321,131)
	David L. Williams (R)	476,604	(36%)	($335,304)

FIRST DISTRICT

The point where the Ohio River flows into the Mississippi—the intersection Huckleberry Finn and Jim missed in the fog—must have struck early settlers as a site for a great city. But no Pittsburgh or St. Louis grew up on this fertile black soil. Instead, the Kentucky land west of the dammed-up Tennessee and Cumberland rivers, bought from the Chickasaw Indians by General Andrew Jackson and Governor Isaac Shelby in 1818—the Jackson Purchase, it is still called—was settled by farmers. Most people here today are the descendants of these farmers, with memories of earlier generations living in family lore. Just to the east of the Tennessee and the Cumberland rivers is the Pennyrile (after pennyroyal, a common variety of local wild mint), a land of low hills and small farms, where you find the west Kentucky coal fields, the site of much strip mining in recent years. Here is Lyon County, founded by Matthew "Spitting" Lyon, who earned his epithet while a congressman from Vermont, and who later represented western Kentucky from 1803–1811.

The 1st Congressional District is made up of the Jackson Purchase and much of the Pennyrile, plus a line of counties stretching some 200 miles east of the Mississippi along the Tennessee border. There is a distinctive Southern atmosphere here—in the crops that are grown, in historically low wage levels, and in the fact that the big city people look to is more often Nashville than Louisville. The Jackson Purchase and the Pennyrile have long been Democratic; Paducah produced one of the most enduring Democratic politicians of this century, Alben Barkley, whose career from 1912–56 included 14 years in the House, 24 in the Senate and four as vice president; he was Senate majority and minority leader, keynoted four Democratic National Conventions, and died while delivering the peroration at Washington and Lee University's mock political convention in 1956. But the hills far from the Mississippi are Republican country and this, combined with the Republican trend that reached north from Dixie to Paducah, made the 1st District seriously contested territory in 1990s—and one of the longtime Democratic rural areas solidly for George W. Bush in 2000.

The congressman is Ed Whitfield, a longtime Democrat who turned Republican. Whitfield grew up in Hopkinsville and Madisonville, in a family with Pennyrile roots going back before 1800. He served in the Army, practiced law in Hopkinsville, and was elected to the legislature in 1973 as a Democrat where he was something of an insider; former Governor (1963–67) Edward Breathitt was best man at his wedding. After one term in Frankfort, Whitfield ran an oil distributorship in the west Kentucky coal fields, then in 1979 moved to Washington to become an executive for the Seaboard and CSX railroads. He was legal counsel to the chairman of the then-Interstate Commerce Commission from 1991–93, when he returned to west Kentucky and ran for Congress as a Republican.

He was returning to a district that since Barkley's time had been represented by quiet, long-serving, conservative Democrats. But the incumbent, Tom Barlow, was a free-spirited supporter of the Clinton Administration. In 1994, with help from Senator Mitch McConnell, Whitfield raised enough money to put on a serious campaign and attacked Barlow's vote for the Clinton budget and tax increase. He won 70% in the counties added after redistricting, but also carried traditionally Democratic areas around Hopkinsville in the Pennyrile, and Murray in the Jackson Purchase, for a 51%–49% win.

In the House, Whitfield has a moderate-to-conservative voting record and a seat on the Energy and Commerce Committee. In his first term he co-sponsored the "lock box" amendment on Medicare, prohibiting savings from being used for other purposes; this was to blunt Democratic attacks on Republican Medicare "cuts." In 1996 Whitfield was opposed by lawyer Dennis Null. The AFL-CIO ran a barrage of TV ads attacking Whitfield on tax cuts, pension security, and Medicare. But Whitfield had nearly a 2–1 money advantage and he attacked the Clinton Administration proposal for FDA regulation of tobacco. Whitfield carried 18 of the district's 31 counties, including Paducah, which he lost in 1994, and won overall 54%–46%.

One of Whitfield's big issues has been the Land Between the Lakes recreation area. In 1999, Congress decided to terminate TVA funding for the area, but Whitfield won agreement for the Forest Service to take over management. Another major concern has been the health of workers exposed to radiation at the nuclear weapons plant in Paducah; overriding the appropriators' initial objection, Whitfield on the eve of the 2000 election won $150,000 lump sum payments and medical benefits for thousands of affected workers. He also regained funding for the Kentucky Lock on the Tennessee River and secured $54 million for improvements at Fort Campbell. In response to complaints from local farmers, he filed a bill to prevent migrant workers from suing farmers in courts outside the states where they were employed. He voted for permanent trade relations with China after the Chinese agreed to lower tariffs on imported tobacco.

Whitfield steadily increased his victory margins. In 1998, Tom Barlow ran again, this time with a "grass roots" campaign that was at a huge money disadvantage. Whitfield won 55%–45%. In 2000, former U.S. Marshall Brian Roy ran a better-funded challenge emphasizing the issues of preserving Social Security and providing a prescription drug Medicare benefit. In many ways Roy, a former county sheriff and federal marshall opposed to gun control and abortions, seemed well fitted to the district. But Whitfield criticized him, curiously for a Republican, for an allegedly poor record of tax collections as sheriff, as well as for having Patrick Kennedy speak at a local fundraiser. Whitfield won 58%–42%, his biggest margin yet, and took 22 of the 31 counties, including for the first time several in the far western corner; his vote tracked closely with George

W. Bush's winning run. The biggest threat to Whitfield would be for redistricters to remove the Republican-leaning counties that were added to his eastern edge and replace them with geographically-closer and Democratic-leaning Owensboro in Daviess County; but Republicans control the state Senate and will presumably prevent that. Even if they don't, Whitfield carried the rest of the district, and Republicans won solidly in Daviess County in 2000. In May 2001, Klint Alexander, a Hopkinsville attorney whose father is the president of Murray State University, announced he would challenge Whitfield in 2002.

Cook's Call   *Probably Safe*. While this sprawling western Kentucky district still has Democratic roots, it has elected Whitfield by increasing margins since his first victory. Democratic attorney Klint Alexander has announced his candidacy against Whitfield. But, after easily disposing with the strongest Democratic challenger he had ever faced in 2000 with 58% and with rural districts like these trending more Republican over the last few years, Whitfield is favored to hold on here in 2002.

THE PEOPLE: Pop. 2000: 652,338; Pop. 1990: 614,265, up 6.2% 1990–2000. 90.2% White, 7.5% Black, 0.4% Asian, 0.2% Amer. Indian, 0.1% Hawaiian, 1% Two+ races, 0.6% Other; 1.5% Hispanic Origin.

2000 Presidential Vote			1996 Presidential Vote		
Bush (R)	142,082	(58%)	Clinton (D)	105,150	(47%)
Gore (D)	99,887	(41%)	Dole (R)	96,356	(43%)
Nader (Green)	2,309	(1%)	Perot (I)	22,727	(10%)
Others	1,645	(1%)			

Rep. Edward Whitfield (R)

Elected 1994, 4th term; b. May 25, 1943, Hopkinsville; home, Hopkinsville; U. of KY, B.S. 1965, J.D. 1969; Methodist; married (Connie).

Military Career: Army Reserves, 1967–73.

Elected Office: KY House of Reps., 1973–75.

Professional Career: Practicing atty., 1969–79; Owner, Rhodes Oil Co., 1975–79; Cnsl., Seaboard System Railroad, 1979–83; V.P., CSX, 1983–91; Cnsl., Interstate Commerce Comm., 1991–93.

DC Office: 236 CHOB 20515, 202-225-3115; Fax: 202-225-3547; Web site: www.house.gov/whitfield.

District Offices: Henderson, 270-826-4180; Hopkinsville, 270-885-8079; Paducah, 270-442-6901; Tompkinsville, 270-487-9509.

Committees: *Energy & Commerce* (12th of 31 R): Commerce, Trade & Consumer Protection; Energy & Air Quality; Health; Oversight & Investigations (Vice Chmn.).

Group Ratings

	ADA	ACLU	AFS	LCV	CON	ITIC	NTU	COC	ACU	NTLC	CHC
2000	0	29	0	14	29	94	59	90	87	67	87
1999	10	—	16	13	2	—	55	100	80	—	—

National Journal Ratings

	1999 LIB —	1999 CONS		2000 LIB —	2000 CONS
Economic	30% —	64%		17% —	83%
Social	10% —	85%		26% —	71%
Foreign	37% —	62%		25% —	69%

Key Votes of the 106th Congress

1. Patient Bill of Rights	N	5. Bar RU-486 $ for FDA	Y	9. NATO War in Serbia	N
2. Accelerate Min. Wage	N	6. Display 10 Commandments	Y	10. Perm. Trade with China	Y
3. Strike Ban on Ergo. Stnd.	N	7. Gun Show Bkgrnd. Checks	N	11. Debt Relief for 3rd World	N
4. Ovrd. Estate Tax Veto	Y	8. Ban Part.-Birth Abortion	Y	12. Drop Cuba Econ. Embargo	N

Election Results

2000 general	Edward Whitfield (R) 132,115	(58%)	($1,495,305)
	Brian Roy (D) 95,806	(42%)	($716,066)
2000 primary	Edward Whitfield (R) 12,013	(84%)	
	David Lynn Williams (R) 2,317	(16%)	
1998 general	Edward Whitfield (R) 95,308	(55%)	($608,491)
	Tom Barlow (D) 77,402	(45%)	($144,088)

SECOND DISTRICT

In the 1770s and 1780s, Americans began settling the limestone-soiled country of central Kentucky, staking out towns like Bardstown and Elizabethtown and starting academies and colleges; they were well-settled when Stephen Foster wrote "My Old Kentucky Home" just before the Civil War. That conflict tore deeply here: This part of Kentucky gave birth to both Abraham Lincoln and Jefferson Davis, and in the Civil War it lost thousands of soldiers, Union and Confederate; it would suffer disproportionate casualties in the 20th Century wars as well. This area is the home of several Kentucky landmarks—Fort Knox, the nation's gold depository; some of the nation's largest bourbon distilleries; and Mammoth Cave, the world's largest accessible cavern, near Bowling Green.

The 2d Congressional District consists of much of the territory south and southwest of Louisville, starting with the southern Jefferson County suburbs and proceeding south to Bowling Green and west along the Ohio River to Owensboro, the home of the International Bluegrass Music Museum. This is rural and small-town country, where most people have family roots that go back generations and a connection with the past not often found in big metropolitan areas. Civil War loyalties are reflected in the election returns here; Kentucky was deeply split on secession, and a color-coded map of the current 2d District would show various splotches of counties pro-South and splotches pro-Union. But the bits of color would only hint at the deep and often bitter feelings caused by the splits over the War—feelings of which current partisan preferences are a persistent reflection, but growing dimmer. For many years, the balance of opinion here favored the Democrats; in the 1990s opinion moved toward the Republicans.

The congressman from the 2d District is Ron Lewis, a Republican first elected in a 1994 special election that had national implications. Lewis was born in a log cabin and raised in eastern Kentucky; he worked his way through Morehead State as a laborer at Armco Steel. He worked in the highway department, at a state hospital, then served in the Navy. In 1980, he became a Baptist minister; in 1985 he started a Christian book store in Elizabethtown, two counties south of Louisville; he was the opposite of a political insider. Then, in March 1994, Democratic Congressman William Natcher died. He was chairman of the Appropriations Committee and a politician of a very old school, so hard-working and conscientious that he never missed a roll call vote in 41 years. Though the district voted for George Bush in 1992, Democratic leaders assumed they would win: they hand-picked former state Senate President Joe Prather; before the election, Prather even flew to Washington to go apartment hunting. But this failed to account for the national and local conservative trend. The National Republican Congressional Committee contributed $200,000 for the May 1994 special. Prather belatedly raised campaign money and asserted that he was quite a different sort of Democrat than Clinton. Lewis won a solid 55%–45% victory, carrying Bowling Green heavily and running ahead in Owensboro and outside Louisville.

In the House, Lewis made news in August 1994 when he attended a smokers' rights rally where Hillary Rodham Clinton was burned in effigy. Many Democrats assumed that Lewis's victory was aberrational and that Democratic Owensboro Mayor David Adkisson would win in November. But Lewis projected sincerity, and his strong religious views and opposition to the Clinton tax increase and health care plan were pluses. Lewis won by a resounding 60%–40% margin, even carrying Owensboro's Daviess County.

Lewis has a solidly conservative voting record but is attentive to local concerns. He co-sponsored the 1998 emergency farm relief act and pushed for precision agriculture research; he co-sponsored with Bernie Sanders a 17% increase in federal payments in lieu of taxes. He backed the Lugar tobacco buyout plan, phasing out tobacco price supports and providing a mandatory buyout of tobacco farmers' entitlements. With Senator Mitch McConnell, he won approval of a requirement that states ensure that low-income seniors are aware of federal assistance. He unsuccessfully led the fight against Henry Waxman's amendment to permit Bill Clinton's Justice Department to raise money from other federal agencies to finance its tobacco suit. He worked with other social conservatives on behalf of Dr. James Dobson's Christian-right agenda. In 1998, Lewis reversed his 1994 campaign pledge to serve no more than four full terms, announcing he had changed his mind. "I came to believe that if those of us who believe in term limits limit ourselves, then we're a dying breed." But he said he would still vote for term limits. Breaking the pledge caused barely a ripple back home. His little-known challenger in 2000 criticized Lewis for putting tobacco companies ahead of farmers and advocated stricter campaign-finance laws. Lewis won 68%–31%, carrying all 22 counties.

With a seat on the Ways and Means Committee, Lewis seems headed for a long career in the House, where he can work on his promises to cut the capital gains tax to 15%, end the marriage penalty and set aside the budget surplus for Social Security. Redistricting may shuffle the boundaries, but is not likely to pose a threat.

Cook's Call   *Safe*. Lewis, who sits in the second most Republican district in the state (Bush won here in 2000 by 26%), has not come close to losing this district in four elections, and probably never will. His district is the second largest in population in the state and will have to contract a bit in the next round of redistricting.

THE PEOPLE: Pop. 2000: 706,978; Pop. 1990: 615,131, up 14.9% 1990–2000. 92% White, 5.2% Black, 0.7% Asian, 0.2% Amer. Indian, 0.1% Hawaiian, 1.1% Two+ races, 0.6% Other; 1.5% Hispanic Origin.

2000 Presidential Vote

Bush (R)	165,232	(62%)
Gore (D)	94,915	(36%)
Nader (Green)	3,125	(1%)
Others	1,513	(1%)

1996 Presidential Vote

Dole (R)	113,923	(49%)
Clinton (D)	95,530	(41%)
Perot (I)	22,021	(9%)

Rep. Ron Lewis (R)

Elected May 1994, 4th term; b. Sept. 14, 1946, South Shore, KY; home, Cecilia; U. of KY, B.A. 1969, Morehead St. U., M.A. 1981; Baptist; married (Kayi).

Military Career: Navy OCS, 1972.

Professional Career: Heavy Equip. Sales Rep., 1975–80; Baptist Minister, 1980–present; Prof., Watterson Col., 1980–85; Owner, Alpha Christian Bookstore, 1985–94.

DC Office: 2418 RHOB 20515, 202-225-3501; Web site: www.house.gov/ronlewis.

District Offices: Bowling Green, 270-842-9896; Elizabethtown, 270-765-4360; Owensboro, 270-688-8858.

Committees: *Government Reform* (16th of 24 R): Government Efficiency, Financial Management & Intergovernmental Relations (Vice Chmn.); National Security, Veterans' Affairs & Intl. Relations. *Ways & Means* (21st of 24 R): Human Resources; Select Revenue Measures; Social Security.

Group Ratings

	ADA	ACLU	AFS	LCV	CON	ITIC	NTU	COC	ACU	NTLC	CHC
2000	0	21	0	14	5	100	60	90	96	85	100
1999	5	—	0	6	6	—	55	100	92	—	—

National Journal Ratings

	1999 LIB —	1999 CONS		2000 LIB —	2000 CONS
Economic	16%	—	78%	6%	— 85%
Social	0%	—	96%	0%	— 79%
Foreign	20%	—	78%	12%	— 78%

Key Votes of the 106th Congress

1. Patient Bill of Rights	N	5. Bar RU-486 $ for FDA	Y	9. NATO War in Serbia	N
2. Accelerate Min. Wage	N	6. Display 10 Commandments	Y	10. Perm. Trade with China	Y
3. Strike Ban on Ergo. Stnd.	N	7. Gun Show Bkgrnd. Checks	N	11. Debt Relief for 3rd World	N
4. Ovrd. Estate Tax Veto	Y	8. Ban Part.-Birth Abortion	Y	12. Drop Cuba Econ. Embargo	N

Election Results

2000 general	Ron Lewis (R)	160,800	(68%)	($225,008)
	Brian Pedigo (D)	74,537	(31%)	
	Other	2,125	(1%)	
2000 primary	Ron Lewis (R)	unopposed		
1998 general	Ron Lewis (R)	113,285	(64%)	($335,500)
	Bob Evans (D)	62,848	(35%)	
	Others	1,833	(1%)	

THIRD DISTRICT

At the falls of the Ohio River, Americans more than 200 years ago founded one of their first inland metropolises, the river port and industrial city of Louisville (pronounced *LOOuhv'l*). The city has always retained an air of the South; when Kentucky decided not to secede in 1861, the decision was not unanimous, and the culture of tidewater Virginia is still visible in the Louisville lawn party. Steamboats are tied up in front of Louisville's downtown, primed to follow the channel around the falls of the Ohio that prompted George Rogers Clark to found the town in 1778. Mint juleps are served on the verandas of mansions, especially (but not only) during Kentucky Derby week in May; horse racing is a preoccupation throughout the year. Although the Ohio River is crossed with many bridges and the accent across the river in Indiana may sound the same to outsiders, Louisville partakes of the cavalier culture that second sons of big landowners from England brought to Virginia in the 17th Century and their heirs brought over the Appalachians to the valleys of Kentucky in the 18th Century.

Though Louisville's economy is not particularly Southern, tobacco and cigarettes are a major business here, and so is distilling whiskey. Louisville still specializes in assembling large, clunky things like appliances and automobiles, and Louisville airport is a big hub for UPS. Politically, Louisville has always had some un-Southern aspects and has often voted against the rest of Kentucky; if its elite were Virginia cavaliers, many of its burghers were Germans and Pennsylvanians who made this river town a Republican and anti-slavery island in a secessionist and pro-slavery sea. In the 1990s Louisville and Jefferson County's two-party politics, which propelled Republican County Judge-Executive Mitch McConnell into the U.S. Senate in 1984, has gone more Democratic lately, though not always by wide margins; as most of Kentucky trended Republican in 2000, Louisville's Jefferson County gave a 50%–48% margin for Al Gore. At the same time, voters by a 54%–46% margin agreed to a merger of the Jefferson County and Louisville city governments, to take effect in January 2003.

The 3d Congressional District includes all of Louisville and almost all of the Jefferson County suburbs—the strip highway zone running south toward Fort Knox, the blue-collar factory zones south of Churchill Downs and the affluent suburbs in the hills to the east heading out toward Bluegrass country. Louisville's historic Republican tradition made this a closely contested district back in 1958–64 and again in 1970; today it votes for Democrats for most offices and was Bill Clinton's and Al Gore's strongest district in Kentucky. But in the last three House elections it has gone Republican.

The congresswoman from the 3d District is Anne Northup. She grew up in a large Catholic family in Louisville—she has nine sisters and one brother—and has raised six children of her own. Her husband is a small business owner and she volunteered and served on the boards of many charities and associations. In 1986 she was elected to the Kentucky House, where she worked for holding down taxes and also for Kentucky's 1990 education reform, and where she became the number one critic of tobacco in the capital of the nation's number two tobacco state.

In 1996 she decided to run for Congress, against freshman Democrat Mike Ward, an "old Democrat" who won the seat by 425 votes in 1994, when 12% voted for an anti-abortion third candidate. In a year when almost all Democrats and most Republicans ran cookie-cutter campaigns, Northup showed originality in strategy and tactics. First, she outraised the incumbent, with an amazing $868,000 coming from individuals; she spent $1,182,000 to Ward's $880,000. Second, she started TV spots in August three weeks before Ward got on the air. Third, she used unusual issues, such as Ward's vote against making English the official language. Both candidates opposed FDA regulation of tobacco, but her criticisms of tobacco companies— "I'm very disappointed that the Republicans have not been more forthcoming about kids not smoking"—moderated her image. Ward ran behind his party ticket and Northup won 50.3%–49.7%, a margin of 1,299 votes.

In Washington, Northup was singled out by the leadership and was one of two Republican freshmen to get a seat on Appropriations. Her voting record is somewhat moderate on economic and foreign issues and conservative on cultural issues. She staunchly defended the Republicans' $500 per child tax credit and voted against the Religious Freedom Act. At home she formed an association with two black ministers and got $3 million in funding for their projects. When the Lewinsky scandal broke, Northup appeared on *Meet the Press* and criticized feminists for their silence on Clinton's behavior. She opposes abortion and claims the district is "more pro-life than pro-choice." She joined most Democrats in supporting the 72-hour check for sales at gun shows. She strongly supported the Republican version of HMO regulation. At one point in May 2000 she obtained a private vote in the Republican Conference, which persuaded the Rules Committee to block the Democrats' version from the floor. On Appropriations she passed an amendment in June 2000 barring OSHA from issuing a final ergonomics standard. This was dropped from the bill in December at the insistence of the Clinton administration, which issued an ergonomics standard in its final hours. But the House and Senate voted to disapprove the regulation in March 2001. Alerted by a constituent, Northup sponsored a 2000 law putting up a plaque near the Lincoln Memorial where Martin Luther King, Jr., delivered his "I Have a Dream" speech in August 1963.

Despite her votes against spending generally, Northup has used her seat on Appropriations to bring in what she estimated in 2000 as "approaching $500 million" into her district—a "fair share" she called it. Projects include $75 million for two defense contracts at the old Naval Ordnance Station, $3 million to TARC for hybrid-electric buses, $18 million for improvements on the McAlpine Locks and Dam on the Ohio River, $2.5 million for the University of Louisville's Early Childhood Research Center and $500,000 for its Center for the Study and Prevention of Violence in Urban Schools, $11 million for the American Printing House for the Blind and $500,000 for flood control along Beargrass Creek.

In this Democratic-leaning district Northup attracted serious competition in 1998 and 2000. In 1998 former Attorney General and County Commissioner Chris Gorman ran. Gorman was almost born into politics; his mother was secretary to Governors Bert Combs and Edward Breathitt and he has spent almost all his life in the public sector. Gorman attacked Northup for voting with Newt Gingrich 95% of the time and attacked her vote for the Republican version of HMO regulation. Northup said the Democratic version would raise insurance rates sharply and she campaigned on education, Social Security and local projects. Northup once again showed her fundraising prowess, and was aided by many House colleagues: she raised over $1.6 million, almost three times as much as Gorman. She won 52%–48%, with a margin of 7,825 votes, not much, but more than four times the combined margins in the district in 1994 and 1996.

In 2000 Northup was opposed by state Representative Eleanor Jordan, from the heavily black west side of Louisville. Jordan began adult life as an unwed mother on welfare, supported her family waiting tables and eventually became the only black woman in the Kentucky Assembly. Patton persuaded her main Democratic opponent Ched Jennings to withdraw a month before the May primary. Northup campaigned on her "balanced approach" and the projects she had won for the district, but also capitalized deftly on Jordan's mistakes. She ran an ad showing Jordan in Frankfort urging colleagues to finish action quickly because "I have a fundraiser at six o'clock and I want to get out of here." In September 2000, on a radio interview show, Jordan admitted that she didn't know the cost of the Medicare prescription plan she supported and declined to comment on high gas prices; Northup quickly put her words on the air in an ad. This seemed to overpower Jordan's emphasis on health care and education; she lost ground in public polls. This was a very big-spending race, targeted by both sides. Northup, outdoing previous efforts, spent $2.9 million. Jordan, with help from EMILY's List and other liberal supporters, raised and spent $1.7 million. The U.S. Chamber of Commerce and the AFL-CIO, the Sierra Club and the National Federation of Independent Business spent money on dueling ads. Altogether, some $5.8 million was spent on Louisville TV, which was not cluttered with other political ads since neither Indiana nor Kentucky was a presidential target state. Northup won 53%–44%, her biggest victory yet. She carried the white working class districts Gorman had carried two years before; Jordan won in only heavily black legislative districts.

Northup has been less successful in party leadership elections. After the 1998 election she ran for vice chairman of the House Republican Conference, but lost to Tillie Fowler. She dropped out of the race for Conference Vice-Chairman after Deborah Pryce got in it in April 2000, and dropped out of the race for Conference Secretary in November 2000. She has been mentioned as a possible candidate for governor in 2003; asked about it, she said, "I'd probably assess it. I think it is very important that we have a strong candidate." Meanwhile, the 3rd District will have to undergo redistricting. The district has to add 47,000 people, and the good news for Northup is that almost all the surrounding territory in Jefferson County or in adjoining counties is more heavily Republican than the current district. Although Democrats would again like to avoid a primary, several expressed interest in running, including Deputy Cabinet Secretary Jack Conway, lawyer Craig Greenberg, and 2000 primary candidate Ched Jennings.

Cook's Call   *Competitive.* This Democratic-leaning district (the only one in the state won by Gore) will never be entirely safe territory for a Republican, but Northup's phenomenal fundraising ability and strong political skills have helped her to keep a hold of this Louisville-based seat. Insiders speculate that this district, which needs to grow slightly, will have to move into more Republican leaning suburbs, which could make it a little safer for Northup. As of May 2001, two Democrats—Jack Conway, a deputy secretary in the governor's Executive Cabinet, and Craig Greenberg, an attorney and venture capitalist—have announced their intentions to run against Northup in 2002.

THE PEOPLE: Pop. 2000: 626,676; Pop. 1990: 613,266, up 2.2% 1990–2000. 75.7% White, 20.5% Black, 1.4% Asian, 0.2% Amer. Indian, 1.5% Two+ races, 0.7% Other; 1.8% Hispanic Origin.

2000 Presidential Vote		
Gore (D)	139,039	(51%)
Bush (R)	125,184	(46%)
Nader (Green)	5,485	(2%)

1996 Presidential Vote		
Clinton (D)	134,975	(53%)
Dole (R)	101,977	(40%)
Perot (I)	17,230	(7%)

Rep. Anne Northup (R)

Elected 1996, 3d term; b. Jan. 22, 1948, Louisville; home, Louisville; St. Mary's Col., B.A. 1970; Catholic; married (Robert).

Elected Office: KY House of Reps., 1986–96.

DC Office: 1004 LHOB 20515, 202-225-5401; Fax: 202-225-5776; Web site: www.house.gov/northup.

District Office: Louisville, 502-582-5129.

Committees: *Appropriations* (25th of 35 R): Labor, HHS & Education; Treasury, Postal Service & General Government; VA, HUD & Independent Agencies.

Group Ratings

	ADA	ACLU	AFS	LCV	CON	ITIC	NTU	COC	ACU	NTLC	CHC
2000	0	21	0	14	17	94	58	95	72	64	87
1999	5	—	0	0	6	—	58	100	68	—	—

National Journal Ratings

	1999 LIB	—	1999 CONS		2000 LIB	—	2000 CONS
Economic	0%	—	84%		18%	—	76%
Social	42%	—	56%		43%	—	55%
Foreign	36%	—	63%		33%	—	62%

Key Votes of the 106th Congress

1. Patient Bill of Rights	N	5. Bar RU-486 $ for FDA	Y	9. NATO War in Serbia	N
2. Accelerate Min. Wage	N	6. Display 10 Commandments	Y	10. Perm. Trade with China	Y
3. Strike Ban on Ergo. Stnd.	N	7. Gun Show Bkgrnd. Checks	N	11. Debt Relief for 3rd World	N
4. Ovrd. Estate Tax Veto	Y	8. Ban Part.-Birth Abortion	Y	12. Drop Cuba Econ. Embargo	N

Election Results

2000 general	Anne Northup (R)	142,106	(53%)	($2,916,818)
	Eleanor Jordan (D)	118,785	(44%)	($1,700,171)
	Other	7,804	(3%)	
2000 primary	Anne Northup (R)	unopposed		
1998 general	Anne Northup (R)	100,690	(52%)	($1,772,613)
	Chris Gorman (D)	92,865	(48%)	($702,866)
	Others	1,881	(1%)	

FOURTH DISTRICT

The commonwealth of Kentucky has gone to court more than once to assert its claim to all of the Ohio River up to its northern bank: This is one of the northernmost extensions of the South. The Ohio sees many different parts of Kentucky. Ashland, near the West Virginia border, is industrial, the home of ancestral Ashland Oil; the river here is bound in by tight hills that hold smoke and soot close in the air. Farther down the river, the country is more bucolic: Here Eliza fled across the ice floes in Harriet Beecher Stowe's *Uncle Tom's Cabin*. Farther west, between Louisville and Cincinnati, are counties that still look like they're in the 19th Century. But metropolitan growth obtrudes. Oldham County, just upriver from Louisville, has some of Kentucky's oldest homes, but the horse country is also sprouting affluent subdivisions. And the three northern Kentucky counties across the river from Cincinnati saw rapid population growth and a sharp rise in incomes in the 1990s. Overlooking the suspension bridge built by John Roebling 16 years before the Brooklyn Bridge, new buildings on the Covington waterfront rise while Newport, once known for its gambling, is sprucing up, and office buildings and new subdivisions are rising on the hills above.

The 4th Congressional District spans all these variations of Ohio River country; it also includes lightly populated counties just inland. Economically, it runs the gamut from coal mining towns to rich suburbs. Politically, it has some of the most Democratic counties in America, like mountain-bound Elliott County (64%–35% for Al Gore in 2000), and some of the most Republican territory in Kentucky, like Oldham County with its new affluent migrants from Louisville (67%–31% for George W. Bush). The three northern Kentucky counties across the river from Cincinnati cast nearly half the district's votes, and they too have become very heavily Republican; Bush won here, 61%–37%.

The congressman from the 4th District is Ken Lucas, a conservative Democrat elected in 1998. Lucas grew up on a farm in northern Kentucky, worked his way through the University of Kentucky on a tobacco farm, and became a financial planner. In the manner of local businessmen, he served two terms on the Florence Council and two years on the Boone County Board of Commissioners in the 1970s and 1980s. In 1992 he was appointed Boone County judge-executive, and was re-elected twice. In 1998 he ran for the House, stressing that he was a very conservative Democrat, "common sense conservative, pro-life, pro-gun and pro-business." He pledged to fight crime, Internet pornography and welfare fraud, and said he would limit himself to three terms. He backed NAFTA and the Religious Freedom Act.

Lucas was not the favorite when the campaign started; it looked like the race would be determined in the Republican primary. The contenders were state Senator Gex Williams and lawyer Rick Robinson, a longtime supporter of 4th District Congressman Jim Bunning, who was running for the Senate. Williams was backed by Dr. James Dobson; his political consultant was former Christian Coalition head Ralph Reed. Robinson was backed by almost all local Republican politicians and was funded by a host of business PACs. The outsider Williams, a computer consultant, showed the greater political skills. He won the primary 51%–41%, and leaders of the religious right across the nation pointed to him as one of their future leaders. But in the general, everything went wrong for Williams and right for Lucas. Williams was accused of making campaign phone calls from the Kentucky Statehouse; an investigation found no significant violation, but only after the election. Lucas raised more money and ran hard-hitting ads. Lucas, staying true to his conservative themes, refused to appear at the Cincinnati airport, which is in Boone County, when Bill Clinton came there September 27. The result was a stunning 53%–47% victory for Lucas. Williams carried northern Kentucky by only 52%–48%, while Bunning was carrying the area 70%–29%.

In the House, Lucas joined the Blue Dogs and became one of the most conservative Democrats, on issues generally and on abortion, guns and tobacco especially. Republicans urged him to switch parties, but he said he had no intention of doing so. He took Democratic positions on some domestic issues, notably education. But he was one of 11 Democrats to vote for the Republicans' health care alternative to give various tax breaks. And when Republicans passed their big domestic spending bill before the 2000 election, he was one of four Democrats in favor. He made a point of skipping the Democratic convention in Los Angeles, and said that he would abstain in the presidential election because of Al Gore's views on abortion, guns and tobacco. "A Democratic convention should be a time for party unity, and in no way do I want to be a distraction from that," he said.

In 2000 Gex Williams considered a rematch but decided against it. Lucas was opposed by Don Bell, a retired Secret Service agent and perennial candidate who called himself the true conservative in the contest and said that Lucas was "a man without a party." Bell won Oldham and Shelby counties outside of Louisville 56%–41%, but Lucas won the district 54%–44%. After the election, he was an early advocate of the new Centrist Coalition to end what he called "the partisan grandstanding and gridlock." In 2001, he was one of 10 Democrats who voted for the Bush tax cut.

This is now the only Kentucky district that sends a Democrat to Congress, and keeps alive Kentucky's string of electing at least one Democrat every year since the party was founded by Andrew Jackson in 1828. Redistricting is a puzzle. Democrats have the governorship and a big majority in the state House; Republicans have a 20–18 margin in the Senate. The course of least resistance might be to keep the district pretty much as it is. That would likely result in a Lucas victory in 2002, but if he keeps his term limit promise this would be very promising territory for Republicans thereafter.

Cook's Call   *Competitive.* Lucas' 54% showing against a lackluster opponent in 2000 shows just how Republican this northern Kentucky district is. Bush took 61% here, but it is not clear if Republicans will be able to recruit a top-flight candidate to run against Lucas. Lucas is not an easy target: His conservative views and penchant for bucking the Democratic leadership will help to keep him in good stead.

THE PEOPLE: Pop. 2000: 691,720; Pop. 1990: 602,896, up 14.7% 1990–2000. 95.3% White, 2.6% Black, 0.5% Asian, 0.2% Amer. Indian, 0.9% Two+ races, 0.5% Other; 1.3% Hispanic Origin.

2000 Presidential Vote

Bush (R)	156,327	(61%)
Gore (D)	95,069	(37%)
Nader (Green)	4,381	(2%)
Others	1,781	(1%)

1996 Presidential Vote

Dole (R)	115,187	(49%)
Clinton (D)	95,070	(41%)
Perot (I)	20,733	(9%)

Rep. Ken Lucas (D)

Elected 1998, 2d term; b. Aug. 22, 1933, Kenton Cnty.; home, Richwood; U. of KY, B.S. 1955, Xavier U., M.B.A. 1970; Christian; married (Mary).

Military Career: Air Force, 1955–57; Air Natl. Guard, 1957–67.

Elected Office: Florence City Cncl., 1967–74; Boone Cnty. Commissioner, 1974–82; Boone Cnty. Judge Exec., 1992–98.

Professional Career: Financial planner, Sagemark Consulting, 1967–98; Pres., Boone St. Bank, 1971–86; Dir., Drees Co., 1980-present; Chmn., Fifth Third Bank, 1986–97.

DC Office: 1237 LHOB 20515, 202-225-3465; Fax: 202-225-0003; Web site: www.house.gov/kenlucas.

District Offices: Ashland, 606-324-9898; Ft. Mitchell, 859-426-0080.

Committees: *Agriculture* (16th of 24 D): General Farm Commodities & Risk Management; Specialty Crops & Foreign Agriculture Programs. *Financial Services* (27th of 32 D): Capital Markets, Insurance & Government Sponsored Enterprises; Financial Institutions & Consumer Credit.

Group Ratings

	ADA	ACLU	AFS	LCV	CON	ITIC	NTU	COC	ACU	NTLC	CHC
2000	25	8	57	43	21	94	43	80	60	52	87
1999	40	—	60	19	16	—	33	88	64	—	—

National Journal Ratings

	1999 LIB	—	1999 CONS		2000 LIB	—	2000 CONS
Economic	51%	—	49%		48%	—	52%
Social	10%	—	85%		0%	—	79%
Foreign	55%	—	45%		45%	—	53%

Key Votes of the 106th Congress

1. Patient Bill of Rights	Y	5. Bar RU-486 $ for FDA	Y	9. NATO War in Serbia	Y
2. Accelerate Min. Wage	N	6. Display 10 Commandments	Y	10. Perm. Trade with China	Y
3. Strike Ban on Ergo. Stnd.	Y	7. Gun Show Bkgrnd. Checks	N	11. Debt Relief for 3rd World	Y
4. Ovrd. Estate Tax Veto	Y	8. Ban Part.-Birth Abortion	Y	12. Drop Cuba Econ. Embargo	N

Election Results

2000 general	Ken Lucas (D)	125,872	(54%)	($779,740)
	Don Bell (R)	100,943	(44%)	($59,994)
	Others	5,148	(2%)	
2000 primary	Ken Lucas (D)	unopposed		
1998 general	Ken Lucas (D)	93,485	(53%)	($1,065,956)
	Gex Williams (R)	81,547	(47%)	($874,701)

FIFTH DISTRICT

The mountains of eastern Kentucky have been a special place since Daniel Boone came through the Cumberland Gap in 1775. As Virginians poured through and created their version of a Tidewater civilization in the Bluegrass country, the people who settled the mountain counties and the Cumberland Plateau, most of them of Irish Protestant or Border Scot descent, brought different values—an assertive egalitarianism, loyalty to family and community, and passionate willingness to settle differences by feuds or violence. Most of the people in the mountains today are descendants of families who settled there in the two or three generations after Boone. Handed down are living memories of the old ways of doing things from the time not so far distant when there was little contact here with the outside world and the ties to the rest of American civilization were secured mainly by school primers and the King James Bible.

Only when people's lives have been changed and uprooted by outside events and institutions have their basic political attitudes been changed—and with a lasting imprint. The first agent of such change here was the Civil War; the second was the great United Mine Workers organizing drives in the coal mines around the 1930s. The Civil War made the mountains and the Cumber-

Kentucky

land Plateau a stronghold of the Republican Party. This was never slave territory—hardly any blacks have ever lived here, yet communities and families were riven by the rebellion of the South. People have not forgotten: The counties around Somerset and Corbin in south central Kentucky cast some of the highest Republican percentages in the nation, election after election.

Then came coal. Early in this century, vast seams of coal were discovered under the Kentucky mountains; representatives of eastern capitalists (including the young Franklin D. Roosevelt) began prowling through these hills, hiring town lawyers to buy up mineral rights from unsuspecting farmers, building industrial slum towns in hollows and creek beds beneath glowering, heavily forested mountainsides. Coal mining was harsh and deadly work: Mine accidents, black lung disease and simple exhaustion killed tens of thousands of miners, while low wages and company stores kept them poor. Then John L. Lewis's United Mine Workers came in and something like open warfare followed, with neither mine operators nor union organizers loath to use violence and threats. The union mostly won in eastern Kentucky and in the short run raised wages and built hospitals for miners and their families; in the longer run, the UMW phased out many jobs in the mines in return for job security and health benefits, as use of oil expanded. Today there are less than 500 mines in Kentucky, a drop from over 2000 25 years ago. Politically, the UMW counties in the eastern part of the state became heavily Democratic. In the mid-1960s Lyndon Johnson came to eastern Kentucky and cited the poverty here in pushing for his Appalachian and anti-poverty bills. The high energy prices of the 1970s sparked strip mining, and eastern Kentucky's economy moved upward; the lower energy prices of the 1980s and 1990s were something of a setback, but life here today is much closer to the ordinary American standard of living than it was in Johnson's time. There is less insularity and less defensiveness, and more celebration of heritage, as in the Hillbilly Days Festival which draws 100,000 people every June to Pikeville, which is proud of its big hospital and osteopathic medical college. But there is still tragedy: The Martin County coal slurry spill of October 2000 poured more than 20 times as much sludge into Coldwater Creek as went into the Gulf of Alaska in the Exxon *Valdez* oil spill of 1989.

The 5th Congressional District of Kentucky includes much of the Cumberland Plateau and most of the eastern mountains, a mixture of heavily Republican and heavily Democratic territory. There are huge political differences here between counties separated by just a mountain ridge or two, evidence of the depth of Civil War and United Mine Workers political loyalties, and only somewhat modulated by the trend toward George W. Bush in the coal country in 2000. Jackson County, which Bill Clinton visited on his "poverty tour" in 1999, voted 84%–14% for Bush in 2000; a few counties over, Knott County voted 67%–31% for Al Gore. The 5th District, created in the 1991 redistricting, spans these lines and combines most of two former districts, one heavily Democratic and the other heavily Republican. But in 2000 at least this was a heavily Republican district.

The congressman from the 5th District is Harold Rogers, a Republican first elected in 1980. Rogers grew up in Wayne County, went off to the University of Kentucky and served in the National Guard, then practiced law in Somerset; in 1969, at 34, he was elected Pulaski-Rockcastle commonwealth's attorney. In 1979 he was the Republican nominee for lieutenant governor. In 1980, when the 5th District congressman retired, he was one of 11 Republicans in the primary; he won 23% in the primary and then easily in November. His toughest race came in 1992, with redistricting. At first his likely opponent was 7th District incumbent Chris Perkins, Carl Perkins's son; but then Perkins retired at 37, before it was revealed he had 514 overdrafts on the House bank. Rogers ended up facing state Senator John Doug Hays of Pike County, whose grandfather Doug "Sawloggin" Hays was state senator before him. Hays attacked Rogers for supporting trickle-down economics and argued that as a Democrat he could get more money for the district. Rogers countered by pointing to his ongoing efforts to build the $250 million Cumberland Gap twin tunnels and Harlan County flood projects. Rogers won with 55%. He had 71% in his old 5th District, which cast 52% of the new district's votes; he had 36% in the old 7th District.

Rogers is now the fourth ranking Republican on the Appropriations Committee. His voting record is mostly, but not always, conservative. Representing a low-income district, he is sympathetic to some spending bills; he was one of three Republicans to vote for the Clinton stimulus package in March 1993. Rogers pressed for many years for reform of the budget and "bloated and patronage-ridden" payrolls at the United Nations; in 2000 he held up funding for UN peace-keeping, seeking assurance that the U.S. wouldn't spend more than $500 million on it. He sharply criticized Attorney General Janet Reno in 1997. "Agencies under your command have been guilty of gross violations of the public trust," he said—citing the speedy dispatch of FBI files to the Clinton White House, sloppy procedures at the FBI's forensic labs and the naturalization of criminals in time for the 1996 election. He blocked the transfer of $20 million from other departments to bring the Clinton administration's tobacco lawsuit, but was overridden by the full House in 2000. Rogers has been just as sharply critical of the Immigration and Naturalization Service, and in 1998 and 1999 co-sponsored a bill with Lamar Smith and Silvestre Reyes (the only former INS agent in Congress) to split the agency into two units, one to enforce immigration laws and the other to dole out benefits. In June 1999 he was shocked at "sheer INS incompetence" when the agency set free a suspected serial killer, and charged that the INS was "unable to provide effective service to prospective legal immigrants, to enforce the growing tide of illegal immigration and it is apparently unable to protect the public from violent criminal aliens. It is the duty of Congress to fix this broken agency." He opposed sampling in the 2000 Census, withholding money in 1998 until the authorizing committee could address the issue and appropriating funds for the agency in 1999 only until March 31; in 1999, after the Supreme Court agreed that sampling could not be used to apportion House seats among the states, he agreed to back $1.7 billion in emergency funding over the $2.8 billion regular budget.

Rogers represents a district which has long been hungry for federal aid, and does not have a uniformly conservative record on economic issues. He supported most of the Contract with America, but prevented the zeroing out of several programs—the Appalachian Regional Commission, the Legal Services Corporation—by straightforwardly negotiating deals, then sticking to them. And of course he has worked on projects for eastern Kentucky. In 1997, Rogers and Kentucky state official James Bickford set up Kentucky PRIDE, a long-term project to clean up rivers and streams of sewage and garbage and to end illegal trash dumps ("holler dumps"); by 2000, $70 million in federal money was spent, 1,996 dumps were mapped and 377 eliminated. In October 2000 he claimed credit for $150 million in targeted funding for southern and eastern Kentucky. In addition, he cited $22 million for targeted highway projects in eastern Kentucky, including building an extension of I-66 between London and Somerset, safety improvements on the Daniel Boone Parkway and $900,000 for the Cumberland Gap Tunnel Project. Over the years he has worked to provide $162 million to protect the solvency of the funds for the United Mine Workers Combined Benefit Fund. In December 2000 he managed to reaffirm racetracks' right to offer interstate simulcast wagering and, after the Martin County coal slurry spill, got $2 million for a study of the impoundment of coal waste.

Since 1992, Rogers has been re-elected by overwhelming margins, carrying even the most Democratic counties. In 2000 he was re-elected 74%–26%. After the election, thanks to the Republicans' six-year term limit on Appropriations subcommittee chairmanships, he switched to become chairman of the Transportation Subcommittee. In the 1990s this lost clout as Transportation Chairman Bud Shuster got a secured revenue stream of gasoline tax money, but Shuster retired abruptly in January 2001 and Rogers may get some authority back; he will likely work to improve highways in Kentucky and confront the problem of national airline delays. Rogers says he has given thought to running for governor of Kentucky in 2003; he has been urged on by Senator Jim Bunning ("We can change the governor's race in 2003. I'm looking at you, Harold Rogers," he said at a delegation meeting) and state Senate Republican leader David Williams (who called Rogers the "presumptive nominee"). But that race is a long time away and Rogers, if Republicans maintain control of the House, may determine that he has more power in his present position. Redistricting should cause him no problems.

Cook's Call *Safe.* Rogers does not represent the most Republican district in the state, but he is arguably the safest member of the Kentucky delegation. He should have no problem winning his 12th election in 2002.

THE PEOPLE: Pop. 2000: 648,751; Pop. 1990: 624,837, up 3.8% 1990–2000. 97.7% White, 1.1% Black, 0.2% Asian, 0.2% Amer. Indian, 0.6% Two+ races, 0.1% Other; 0.7% Hispanic Origin.

2000 Presidential Vote

Bush (R)	127,418	(57%)
Gore (D)	92,964	(42%)
Nader (Green)	1,866	(1%)
Others	1,512	(1%)

1996 Presidential Vote

Clinton (D)	95,633	(47%)
Dole (R)	87,692	(43%)
Perot (I)	18,260	(9%)

Rep. Harold Rogers (R)

Elected 1980, 11th term; b. Dec. 31, 1937, Barrier; home, Somerset; U. of KY, B.A. 1962, J.D. 1964; Baptist; married (Cynthia).

Military Career: Army Natl. Guard, 1957–64.

Professional Career: Practicing atty., 1964–69; Pulaski-Rockcastle Commonwealth's Atty., 1969–80.

DC Office: 2406 RHOB 20515, 202-225-4601; Fax: 202-225-0940; Web site: www.house.gov/rogers.

District Offices: Hazard, 606-439-0794; Pikeville, 606-432-4388; Somerset, 606-679-8346.

Committees: *Appropriations* (4th of 35 R): Commerce, Justice & State; Energy & Water Development; Transportation (Chmn.).

Group Ratings

	ADA	ACLU	AFS	LCV	CON	ITIC	NTU	COC	ACU	NTLC	CHC
2000	5	14	14	7	7	67	58	76	80	70	93
1999	5	—	0	6	21	—	53	88	80	—	—

National Journal Ratings

	1999 LIB	—	1999 CONS		2000 LIB	—	2000 CONS
Economic	16%	—	78%		18%	—	76%
Social	4%	—	91%		0%	—	79%
Foreign	15%	—	81%		0%	—	88%

Key Votes of the 106th Congress

1. Patient Bill of Rights	N	5. Bar RU-486 $ for FDA	Y	9. NATO War in Serbia	N
2. Accelerate Min. Wage	N	6. Display 10 Commandments	Y	10. Perm. Trade with China	N
3. Strike Ban on Ergo. Stnd.	N	7. Gun Show Bkgrnd. Checks	N	11. Debt Relief for 3rd World	N
4. Ovrd. Estate Tax Veto	Y	8. Ban Part.-Birth Abortion	Y	12. Drop Cuba Econ. Embargo	N

Election Results

2000 general	Harold Rogers (R)	145,980	(74%)	($459,993)
	Sidney Jane Bailey (D)	52,495	(26%)	
2000 primary	Harold Rogers (R)	unopposed		
1998 general	Harold Rogers (R)	142,215	(78%)	($377,729)
	Sidney Bailey-Bamer (D)	39,585	(22%)	

SIXTH DISTRICT

With its white picket fences, horse farms and Georgian brick house-filled small towns, the Bluegrass country almost plumb in the middle of Kentucky is the part of interior America longest settled by English speakers: Lexington was founded in 1775; the town of Hopewell was renamed Paris in 1789 out of gratitude for French help during our Revolution and in a salute to theirs (though the county name remained Bourbon even after Louis XVI was guillotined). Tobacco farming started here in the 1770s, horse racing in 1787, and the first whiskey distillery, in Bourbon County, was built in 1790. Tobacco, whiskey and race horses remained the staples of the Bluegrass economy for six generations until 1956, when IBM built its typewriter plant and headquarters in Lexington. IBM's arrival "really was the beginning of Lexington's industrial revolution," as University of Kentucky historian Carl Cone put it. You imagine a Kentucky colonel sitting on the porch, dressed in a white suit and string tie sipping a mint julep, as IBM engineers in their dark suits and white shirts file into their offices. But capitalism, as Joseph Schumpeter wrote, is a process of creative destruction. The typewriter was eventually outclassed by the PC, and the IBM plant put on the block. Meanwhile, in the 1980s, Toyota, lured by generous subsidies, built a $2 billion assembly plant in Georgetown, a town with early 19th Century houses and lush countryside, just one county north of Lexington and west of Paris. Other businesses came in, and Lexington today continues to be a focus of innovation and certainly of economic growth.

The 6th Congressional District includes Lexington and the counties all around—a natural unit, unlike some other Kentucky districts. Lexington casts about one-third of the votes. Lexington was the home base of the Whig Party's great leader Henry Clay, but in the 150 years since his death, the Bluegrass country had been mostly Democratic. Although George Bush edged out Bill Clinton here in 1992 (there was a strong Perot vote), Clinton bought Lexington TV heavily and picked up the 6th in 1996. But in 2000 Al Gore wrote off Kentucky early on, and the 6th District voted for George W. Bush. Its history of closely divided contests may have changed in the congressional race as well.

The congressman from the 6th District is Ernie Fletcher, a Republican elected in a close race in 1998. Fletcher grew up in Mount Sterling, got an engineering degree from the University of Kentucky, was an Air Force pilot for five years, intercepting Soviet aircraft; then he went to medical school, practiced medicine, and was CEO of a company that managed medical practices. He did volunteer medical work in India and was a lay minister. In 1994 he was elected to the Kentucky House. In 1996 he won the Republican primary, by exactly four votes, and ran against Democratic Congressman Scott Baesler, a tobacco farmer and onetime University of Kentucky basketball star. With help from national Republicans, Fletcher raised and spent nearly as much as the incumbent and ran a spirited campaign. He lost 56%–44%, but kept his taste for campaigning. When Baesler announced he was running for the Senate, Fletcher decided to run for the House again, and this time had no serious primary competition. The winner of the seven-candidate Democratic primary was Ernesto Scorsone, a criminal defense lawyer who had defended drug dealers. Scorsone, a state legislator, claimed credit for managing Governor Paul Patton's tough anti-crime bill and he supported the partial-birth abortion ban; but overall his record was liberal. Scorsone said that Fletcher was carrying water for insurance companies; Fletcher said Scorsone played a key role in the health care reform that drove companies from the state and increased insurance premiums and favored trial lawyers, and said that as a physician he could better handle the issue. Fletcher ran one ad showing a woman whose breast cancer he had treated and another featuring a rape victim who said Scorsone represented her assailant and helped him avoid prison time. Fletcher spent about $1.3 million to Scorsone's $1 million. Fletcher won by just 53%–46%; he won Lexington 50%–49% and carried all but two counties in the rest of the district.

In the House, Fletcher was named a freshman representative to the party leadership and he became an activist legislator. Unlike other recent Republican doctors elected to the House who have taken on HMOs, he worked with John Boehner to craft the Republican alternative on HMO regulation. He was a leading advocate of the successful ed-flex bill to give the states greater flexibility in education spending. On another education issue, he secured approval of character programs designed to reflect the values of parents and local communities. He voted for Permanent Normal Trade Relations with China after George W. Bush telephoned him on his Chinese human-rights commitment. On local issues, Fletcher won an amendment to destroy chemical munitions such as those stored in the local Bluegrass Army Depot. He won $24 million to repair and upgrade Lock and Dam No. 10 on the Kentucky River, plus $2 million for LexTran.

Democrats were optimistic when Scott Baesler decided to seek his old seat and at first this seemed likely to be one of the nation's closest races in 2000. The contest became ground zero for various interest groups of many persuasions. Pharmaceutical firms spent more than $500,000 on ads against Baesler, and the managed care industry supported Fletcher as well. The American Medical Association, which supported the Democrats' version of HMO regulation, was disappointed with this doctor-congressman and refused to endorse him. Baesler was hurt when Republican objections caused local TV stations to remove DCCC ads after deciding they were wrong in accusing Fletcher of voting to "cut" education spending. But the HMO issue, which national Democrats expected to be a big vote-winner, failed to work for Baesler here. Polls showed him falling behind, and in the final days of the campaign, he took the curious step of emphasizing gun control in a district that had never shown much enthusiasm for it. Fletcher won by the impressive margin of 53%–35%, winning all 19 counties; he won Lexington 48%–37%. Reform Party candidate Gatewood Galbraith took 12%, with his idiosyncratic agenda that included repeal of existing gun laws, legalization of hemp and pullout from the United Nations.

Fletcher's surprisingly strong victory puts him in god shape to withstand redistricting, in which his interests will presumably be looked after by the 20–18 Republican state Senate.

Cook's Call　*Potentially Competitive.* This marginal, but conservative district is never going to be a slam-dunk for either party, but there are signs that it, like so many rural southern districts, is trending more Republican. Clinton won the seat in 1996 by one point, but in 2000 Bush won here by 14%. Fletcher's drubbing of former 6th District Representative and University of Kentucky basketball star Scotty Baesler, undoubtedly the strongest candidate Democrats could put forward, should give even the most optimistic Democrat some misgivings about taking on Fletcher in 2002.

THE PEOPLE: Pop. 2000: 715,306; Pop. 1990: 614,901, up 16.3% 1990–2000. 88.8% White, 7.9% Black, 1.1% Asian, 0.2% Amer. Indian, 1.2% Two+ races, 0.8% Other; 2% Hispanic Origin.

2000 Presidential Vote			1996 Presidential Vote		
Bush (R)	156,249	(56%)	Clinton (D)	110,256	(46%)
Gore (D)	117,024	(42%)	Dole (R)	108,148	(45%)
Nader (Green)	6,026	(2%)	Perot (I)	19,425	(8%)
Others	1,748	(1%)			

Rep. Ernie Fletcher (R)

Elected 1998, 2d term; b. Nov. 12, 1952, Mt. Sterling; home, Lexington; U. of KY, B.S. 1974, M.D. 1984; Baptist; married (Glenna).

Military Career: Air Force, 1974–80.

Elected Office: KY House of Reps., 1994–96.

Professional Career: Practicing physician, 1984-present; CEO, St. Joseph Medical Foundation, 1997–99.

DC Office: 1117 LHOB 20515, 202-225-4706; Fax: 202-225-2122; Web site: www.house.gov/fletcher.

District Office: Lexington, 859-219-1366.

Committees: *Agriculture* (19th of 27 R): Specialty Crops & Foreign Agriculture Programs. *Budget* (10th of 24 R). *Education & the Workforce* (18th of 27 R): Education Reform; Employer-Employee Relations (Vice Chmn.).

Group Ratings

	ADA	ACLU	AFS	LCV	CON	ITIC	NTU	COC	ACU	NTLC	CHC
2000	5	29	0	14	5	94	58	80	84	76	100
1999	0	—	0	6	8	—	58	96	84	—	—

National Journal Ratings

	1999 LIB —	1999 CONS		2000 LIB —	2000 CONS
Economic	0% —	84%		18% —	76%
Social	22% —	78%		0% —	79%
Foreign	23% —	73%		12% —	78%

Key Votes of the 106th Congress

1. Patient Bill of Rights	N	5. Bar RU-486 $ for FDA	Y	9. NATO War in Serbia	N
2. Accelerate Min. Wage	N	6. Display 10 Commandments	Y	10. Perm. Trade with China	Y
3. Strike Ban on Ergo. Stnd.	N	7. Gun Show Bkgrnd. Checks	N	11. Debt Relief for 3rd World	N
4. Ovrd. Estate Tax Veto	Y	8. Ban Part.-Birth Abortion	Y	12. Drop Cuba Econ. Embargo	N

Election Results

2000 general	Ernie Fletcher (R)	142,971	(53%)	($2,300,940)
	Scotty Baesler (D)	94,167	(35%)	($1,484,436)
	Gatewood Galbraith (Ref)	32,436	(12%)	($12,094)
2000 primary	Ernie Fletcher (R)	unopposed		
1998 general	Ernie Fletcher (R)	104,046	(53%)	($1,285,412)
	Ernesto Scorsone (D)	90,033	(46%)	($1,025,395)
	Others	1,839	(1%)	

★ LOUISIANA ★

Louisiana often seems to be America's banana republic, with its charm and inefficiency, its communities interlaced by family ties and its public sector laced with corruption, with its own indigenous culture and its tradition of fine distinctions of class and caste. It is a state with an economy uncomfortably like that of an underdeveloped country, based on pumping minerals out of soggy ground and shipping grain produced in the vast hinterland drained by its great river, an economy increasingly dependent on businesses typical of picturesque Third World countries—tourism (now the second largest industry) and gambling. Its politics too has a Third World quality, with its own peculiar election laws and a heritage of no-holds-barred conflict and demagoguery no other state can match: what other state has produced a Huey Long or an Edwin Edwards? Louisiana has a hereditary rich class and a large low-wage working class. It has conservative cultural attitudes: Louisiana and Utah have the most restrictive abortion laws in the U.S.—its partial-birth abortion ban and optional "Choose Life" license plates have been ruled illegal by federal courts—and Louisiana in 1997 became the first state to offer covenant marriages, in which spouses would agree not to be covered by no-fault divorce laws. But Louisiana also has a lazy tolerance of rule-breaking, and feels more like the Caribbean or the Mediterranean than the North Atlantic or the Pacific Rim. This is not an entirely original observation. Four decades ago, A. J. Liebling described Louisiana as an outpost of the Levant along the Gulf of Mexico. Most of the United States faces east toward the vast Atlantic Ocean or west toward the vast Pacific; Louisiana faces south, to the Gulf of Mexico and the steamy heat and volatile societies of Latin America.

New Orleans preserves the look and feel it had as a French and Spanish outpost in the New World. Traditions of centralized control and easygoing corruption—classic traits of colonialism—are part of this heritage. The *dirigiste* tradition comes from the fact that Louisiana is the only state whose law is based not on the common law of England but on the Napoleonic Code of France; the concept of civil liberties has shallower roots in Louisiana than in the other 49 states. Here abstract ideals have been overshadowed by the practical need for centralized action. This Delta land—much of it below sea level, soggy, swampy, laced with tributaries and offshoots of the Mississippi and other major rivers like the Atchafalaya—requires vast capital expenditures for levees and drainage and causeways. Even today, houses in New Orleans don't have basements, people are buried in above-ground cemeteries in grandiose crypts, and swamp lands begin abruptly at the edges of subdivisions where people find alligators in their backyards.

The economy that grew up in these rich Delta lands has always been based on raw materials. Antebellum Louisiana produced and exported sugar, rice and cotton in enough abundance to generate the wealth which built grand plantation houses behind alleys of oaks running in from the Mississippi, and to make New Orleans the nation's fifth largest city by the time of the Civil War. Then came oil, found in the great Spindletop strike just over the Texas line in 1901 and in salt domes in Louisiana not long after, followed by the huge Baton Rouge refinery that became the training ground for generations of top oil executives. When energy prices boomed after the oil shocks of 1973 and 1981, Louisiana, like an oil-rich Third World country, boomed too, reaching up toward national income levels, generating 500,000 new jobs between 1972 and 1981. But it lost 150,000 jobs in the next six years as oil prices crashed and the rig count dropped by two-thirds and energy taxes fell from 41% of state government revenues in 1982 to 9% in 1996.

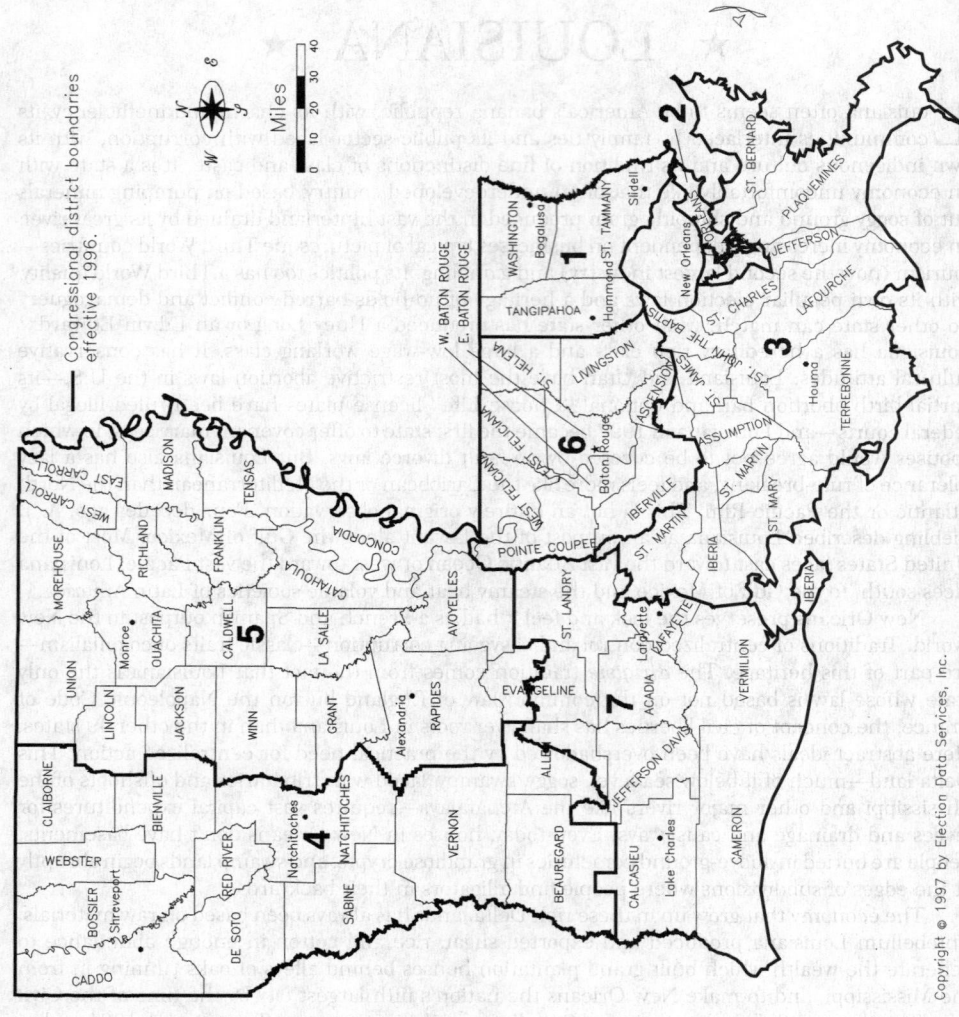

Louisiana's economy has never regained much forward momentum. Gambling, legalized in 1991, has produced less revenue than expected, and nothing like the boom that some promised.

Louisiana has high rates of cancer, early death rates, a high incidence of AIDS; in 1998 the Center for Disease Control declared that New Orleanians were the fattest Americans and they consume more sugar per capita than any other major metropolitan area. In the early 1990s New Orleans had horrendous crime rates; happily, they have been falling after a new police superintendent was appointed, the force was beefed up and New York's crime-fighting tactics were copied. The income disparities here are greater than almost anywhere else in the United States. New Orleans's rich are notoriously unventuresome and tight-knit, determined to hold on to their wealth against the grasp of the impecunious and unlearned masses.

The most enduringly famous politician here, and by far the most talented, was Huey P. Long, who in less than a single term each as governor (1928–32) and senator (1932–35), left an imprint on the state's public life and imposed an organization to its politics that have faded into history only in the last decade. Long's genius was not that he promised to tax the rich to help the poor— hundreds of idealists and demagogues in America have done that—but that, to an amazing extent, he actually delivered. He dominated the legislature so thoroughly that, as governor, he roamed the floors of both chambers at will, bringing to the podium bills he insisted be passed without changing a comma—and they were. He was ready to use bribery, intimidation and physical violence. He built a new skyscraper Capitol, a new Louisiana State University, and more miles of roads than any state but rich New York and huge Texas. He also built a national following, and by 1935, he was planning to run for president on the platform of "Share the wealth, every man a king," when he was assassinated at age 42 in the hallway of the Capitol, where the bullet holes can still be seen in the marble.

For America, the Long threat may have moved Franklin Roosevelt to embrace the liberal programs—the Wagner Labor Act, social security, steeply graduated taxes—of the second New Deal. For Louisiana, Long delivered a political structure that revolved around him even after he was dead—and a class of political leaders who, lacking his talents, treated the state as Long's incompetent doctors had treated his fatal wound, leaving Louisiana without either a fully developed economy or a fully competent public sector. For 50 years, until Huey's son Senator Russell Long retired in 1986, Longs and Long proteges held high political office in Louisiana and elections were run along pro- and anti-Long lines. The Long experience has strengthened Louisiana's already strong predispositions—tolerance of corruption, disinterest in abstract reform, and taste for colorful extremists regardless of their short-term means or long-term ends—in a way that helps explain the rise and fall of such unlikely politicians as the four-term Governor Edwin Edwards and the onetime Ku Klux Klan leader and state legislator David Duke.

Louisiana has natural political divides. One divide is by religion: Catholic Cajun parishes cast about 30% of the state's vote, the New Orleans area casts around 25% or so, and about 45% are cast in Protestant parishes from Baton Rouge on north. White Protestants for years have wanted nothing to do with national Democrats, while Cajuns tend to mull it over. Another divide is by race: Blacks are overwhelmingly Democratic, whites split in seriously contested elections. A third divide is by income: Low- and high-income whites vote very differently and are much less influenced than voters in most other states by candidates' cultural values, marital status, lifestyles and the like. As a result, Louisiana politics since Huey P. Long's time has often been a struggle between reformist and conservative forces on one side and roguish populists on the other, a struggle waged in lavishly financed campaigns and with grandiloquent rhetoric.

For a quarter century, the lead role was played by Edwin Edwards as the roguish populist, with a number of Republican rivals as reformist conservatives. Edwards was elected governor in 1971 and 1975 and was not eligible to run in 1979. In 1983 he beat incumbent Republican David Treen; in 1987 he lost to Buddy Roemer, a Democratic congressman who later switched parties. For much of this third term, Edwards faced corruption charges, until he was acquitted by a jury in 1986. In 1991 he ran again, and this time an even odder character surfaced. David Duke was an active Nazi sympathizer up through 1989, but he also had a knack for speaking to mainstream political issues in attractive political language. In 1989 he was narrowly elected to the state legislature from a district in suburban Jefferson Parish as a nominal Republican—a victory that got enormous national publicity. Immediately he ran for senator in 1990 against incumbent Bennett Johnston, and lost by the unnervingly narrow margin of 54%–44%, making major inroads into the non-affluent white vote, both Cajun and Protestant. Then in 1991, Duke ran for governor, against Roemer and Edwards. (Louisiana has a unique primary system, invented by Edwards: candidates of all parties run in a single primary; any candidate who gets 50% is elected; otherwise, the top two finishers, regardless of party, have a runoff. In December 1997 the Supreme Court ruled that this system violates a federal law requiring all congressional elections to be held on the same day in November; as a result in 1998 the first primary was held on November 3, with runoffs, which proved unnecessary that year and in 2000, scheduled for December 5.) Roemer, now a Republican, was unpopular for raising taxes after promising not to do so, and finished third with 27%; Edwards, unpopular because many thought he was a crook, had few voters except blacks faithful to his populism, but received 34%; Duke made the runoff by finishing second with 32%. All articulate opinion in Louisiana moved to Edwards's side, and Republicans from George Bush on down endorsed Edwards, who won 61%–39%. But Duke won enormous attention, even as his electoral career spun into decline; he ran for president in 1992, and got only 9% in the Louisiana primary.

In 1995 conservative Republican Mike Foster zoomed out of nowhere to win the governorship, on an anti-gambling, anti-tax platform; yet in office the local-option gambling referenda that he promised resulted in approval of riverboat gambling in most parishes. In 1996, with those referenda on the ballot and pro-gambling forces boosting turnout in black precincts, Democrat Mary Landrieu narrowly defeated Republican Woody Jenkins for the Senate—although Jenkins claimed the results were tainted by vote fraud. In November 1998 Edwin Edwards was indicted for extortion; he was convicted in May 2000 and sentenced to ten years without parole, but was set free on appeal. He was not alone: Louisiana's last three Insurance Commissioners were all convicted of crimes, Sherman Barnard in 1993, Doug Green in 1991 and James Brown in 2001. But there are happier Louisiana traditions, recalled by the death of Governor Jimmie Davis, elected in 1943 and 1959, who died in November 2000 at 101; he is best remembered around the country as the writer and singer of "You Are My Sunshine."

Governor   Louisiana's governor is Mike Foster, a Republican elected in November 1995 and re-elected in November 1999. Foster grew up in Franklin, in St. Mary Parish, in the Cajun country near the Gulf; he served in the Air Force and founded a contracting firm and served as president of Sterling Sugars. He is a large landowner who loves duck hunting, piloting helicopters and riding tractors; a critic of trial lawyers, he started taking law school classes in August 2000, at 70. He was elected to the state Senate in 1987, and in 1991 was appointed chairman of the Commerce Committee. He portrays himself as an amateur in politics, convincingly, given his penchant for blunt, impolitic statements; bald, with a mustache, he campaigned as "not just another pretty face." But he had a political pedigree: His grandfather Murphy Foster was governor from 1892–1900 and played a part in abolishing Louisiana's graft-ridden lottery.

Foster ran in 1995 as a not very well-known candidate in a large field; he switched parties in mid-campaign. A gambling opponent, he pledged to hold a referendum on video poker (operators had been caught bribing legislators), riverboat gambling (allowed in many parishes) and the New Orleans land-based casino. At first he attracted little attention. Former Governor Buddy Roemer seemed to be the leading Republican, brandishing a Contract with Louisiana and criticizing New Orleans as "Cape Fear." Congressman Cleo Fields was the one well-known black candidate, but New Orleans Mayor Marc Morial, who is black, endorsed both Fields and Democratic State Treasurer Mary Landrieu. Landrieu, whose father was once mayor of New Orleans, called for cleaning up Louisiana; she was running ahead of Lieutenant Governor Melinda Schwegmann, whose family owned New Orleans's biggest supermarket chain. Foster surged ahead in fall campaigning, and in the October 21 primary led with 26%. There was almost a three-way tie for second place. Fields edged into second place with 19%, to 18.4% for Landrieu (who ran for the Senate in 1996 and won) and 17.8% for Roemer. In the runoff against Fields, Foster called for a vast consolidation of state agencies and reform of state education and welfare. Fields said he would get tough on juvenile crime and accused Foster of "race baiting" after Foster referred to "that jungle in New Orleans." Foster won 64% to Fields's 36% and took 84% of the white vote, while Fields took 96% of the black vote.

In his first term, Foster pushed through a food tax cut and a $25 per child tax credit; he increased teacher salaries and initiated a school-based accountability system. He supported the TOPS program for public college tuition for students who finished at or above the statewide level on the ACT. In 1998 he called for selling off the state's share of the tobacco settlement and using the cash to pay off debt and raise teacher salaries some more. He increased jobless pay and cut unemployment taxes, signed bills requiring mental health coverage in employer-provided health insurance and stopping New Orleans's lawsuit against gun manufacturers, and allowed measures extending gambling to become law without his signature. New laws approved verbal prayer in schools, helmetless motorcycle riding and addressing teachers as "sir" and "ma'am."

Foster's job rating for three years hovered around 75%, and he has taken his own political course at every turn. He has pushed for initiatives and referenda, unpopular with just about every other Louisiana official. Endorsed by Patrick Buchanan in October 1995, he announced he was voting for Buchanan just before the February 1996 caucus, in which Buchanan won his upset victory. Foster declined in 1995 to disclaim his endorsement by David Duke; it was revealed in May 1999 that his campaign purchased Duke's mailing list for $150,000, for which it was fined $20,000. Foster's actions do not always produce the results he wants: the gambling referenda he sponsored in November 1996 resulted in approval of all proposed casinos and a big New Orleans turnout which may have elected Landrieu to the Senate.

Foster entered election year 1999 an overwhelming favorite. His only well-known opponent was New Orleans Congressman Bill Jefferson, who raised $2.2 million but who, as an urban black with a liberal voting record, was not well positioned. Foster won the October primary with 62% of the vote, well over the 50% required to win; Jefferson had 30%, carrying New Orleans and one rural parish. In the new year he faced fiscal problems, a shortfall in revenue and no apparent way to keep his promises to raise teacher's pay to the regional average and to alleviate poverty with early childhood education and job training. In April 2000 he persuaded the legislature to accept his plans to renew a temporary 3 cent sales tax on food and utilities and to convert the state economic development commission to a private agency, but it was rejected 68%–32% by voters in November. In May he proposed a net $700 million tax increase, with new business taxes; legislative leaders were aghast, and instead passed a fourth cent on the sales tax on food and utilities. Foster's job approval plummeted from 69% in April to 55% in June.

In November 2000 voters rejected Foster's two-pronged tax package, which would have eliminated the 4 cent tax and raised most income taxes. Scrambling for revenue to raise pay for teachers, who were refusing to show up for work, Foster made a deal with Harrah's Casino; the state would lower its $100 million minimum tax payment (Harrah's threatened to close down otherwise) combined with a tax on riverboat casinos which would fund a $2,000 raise for teachers and college professors. This passed, and two crises were at least temporarily averted; voters also seemed pleased with the plan, Foster's job approval rating had bounced back to 62% in April 2001.

Foster is not eligible under current law to run again in 2003. In April 2001 he asked legislators who were sponsoring a ballot proposal to end term limits on legislators to include the governor too.

Senior Senator John Breaux is one of the most influential members of the 107th Congress. He grew up in the politically fertile soil of the Acadia Parish seat of Crowley in Cajun country, the only child of a dressmaker and an oil field worker who spoke French before he spoke English. After graduating from LSU Law School, he practiced law for a year, then got a job with a young congressman from Crowley named Edwin Edwards. When Edwards was elected governor in 1972, Breaux ran for Congress and won the seat, at 28. Quietly in the House, more publicly in the Senate, he became a natural dealmaker, with contacts developed everywhere from the tennis court (he is one of Congress's best players) to the Democratic Leadership Council (where he followed Bill Clinton as chairman in 1992) to Mardi Gras in New Orleans (where he performs every year playing a washboard). His views on issues have a Louisiana Cajun accent: market-oriented with populist twists on economics, culturally conservative strongly anti-abortion in the Louisiana mode. He has encouraged people to think of him as a cynical dealmaker: "I'd always rather have half of something than 100% of nothing," he likes to say. But over time it has become apparent that he does have a core of belief and has developed strong principles on issues he has worked hard on.

After serving 14 years in the House, Breaux took the political gamble of his life and ran for the Senate. These were the Reagan years, and Republicans were advancing in the House, and the Republican candidate, Congressman Henson Moore, was ahead in polls and led in the all-party primary. But Breaux held him under 50% and then overtook him in the runoff. In the Senate, Democrats had regained the majority, and Breaux compiled a middle-of-the-road voting record and a bent toward bipartisan coalitions. He was chosen chief deputy whip in 1993 and was mentioned as a candidate for majority leader when George Mitchell retired in 1994; instead he supported Tom Daschle. He was less successful in influencing Clinton administration. He opposed the 1993 Clinton stimulus package and the Btu tax, and helped defeat both. In 1994 he was the chief Senate sponsor of Tennessee Congressman Jim Cooper's managed care health care bill and struggled to come up with bipartisan compromises. As the administration moved to the center after the 1994 elections, Breaux had more successes.

In 1998 Breaux became a major force for reform of entitlements and health care. He and Charles Grassley sponsored a bill to reduce home health care costs. With Judd Gregg he introduced the CSIS Social Security reform, with 2% of income in individual investment accounts. In January 1998 he was named chairman of the bipartisan commission on Medicare, and labored for more than a year with Republican Bill Thomas and others to come up with a bipartisan plan. Breaux modeled his approach on the Federal Employees Health Benefit Plan; he would allow Medicare recipients to choose from an array of choices of competitive health care plans and provide them with a specific amount of "premium support" to buy into a plan; most plans would include prescription drug benefits. He got bipartisan support, from the Republican appointees and Senator Bob Kerrey, but was one vote short of the 11 required for an official recommendation to Congress.

On Medicare, Breaux is at his most uncynical. "The good news is that people are living longer. The bad news is that people are living longer. It's a challenge. And if we don't figure out how to handle it, it becomes a problem." With Republican Bill Frist he prepared two legislative versions of his Medicare Commission proposal, in 1999 and 2000. In January 2000 he proposed a tax credit for the uninsured. Breaux opposed a stand-alone prescription drug benefit as unworkable; in June 2000 he was the only Democratic senator who voted against the Democrats' drug benefit, saying it was "good politics but bad policy." In the 2000 campaign George W. Bush endorsed something very much like Breaux-Frist as the centerpiece of his Medicare proposal, but Breaux criticized it harshly, opposing Bush's proposal for aid to state prescription drug benefit plans and arguing that the Bush tax cut would take up funds needed for Medicare changes.

After the November 2000 election, Breaux was the first Democrat who went to Austin to talk with George W. Bush. He urged him not to start off emphasizing Medicare or Social Security, but to start with education reform, on which the parties could get used to working together. Meanwhile, Breaux convened a group of 10 Democratic and 10 Republican senators, much as the late John Chafee used to, to "work across party lines." At the same time, he voted with Bush and Republicans on several key issues. In January he was one of eight Democrats to vote to confirm John Ashcroft; in February he was chief co-sponsor with Frank Murkowski of the bill to allow oil drilling in the Arctic National Wildlife Refuge; in March he was one of six Demcorats to vote to kill the Clinton ergonomics rule and one of three Democrats who opposed the McCain-Feingold campaign finance bill, arguing openly that it would hurt Democratic chances. But on taxes he stayed obdurately centrist. With 15 other senators, including a couple of Republicans, he resisted Bush's $1.6 trillion tax cut which failed by one vote; then he and others agreed on a $1.25 trillion cut, which passed 65–35. Some Democrats would have gone higher; Breaux kept the cut down.

In the meantime, quiet preparations were being made for changes in entitlements. In February Finance Committee Chairman Charles Grassley said that he would use Breaux-Frist as his starting point; and Breaux with his seat on Finance is well-positioned to move it forward. On Social Security Breaux seems likely to give Bush key support on an individual investment account plan, although he predicted a Bush commission's chances of moving a Social Security reform plan would be "zero to none." But on these issues he may have his sticking points and, judging from his manuevering on the tax cut, he may be able to prevail on them.

Breaux has stayed busy on less high-profile issues. In the House he used his committee seats to get money to battle coastal wetlands erosion and defeat the Law of the Sea Treaty. He continues to work on wetlands: the Breaux Act, providing $40 million a year to protect and rebuild wetlands, funded by user fees on small boat engines and motor fuel, was reauthorized for one year in November 1999. And he takes an interest in other oceanic issues, supporting a ban on longline fishing on the south Atlantic coast, favoring incentives for U.S. shipbuilders, trying to overcome an appropriator's ban on allowing NOAA to move into a $13 million laboratory in Lafayette. He was the lead sponsor of a pipeline safety bill passed unanimously by the Senate in 2001 but opposed in the House by John Dingell.

Breaux has been re-elected twice without serious opposition. The 1998 race was pretty much over by August 1997, when Congressman Richard Baker declined to run and Congressman Billy Tauzin, a Democrat-turned-Republican, said "I don't think John can be defeated. I'll never say a bad thing about John Breaux." (They were roommates at LSU Law School and godfathers of each other's children.) Breaux outspent his Republican opponent Jim Donelon by more than 10–1 and after the campaign still had $1.5 million cash on hand. He beat Donelon 64%–32%, carrying every parish but one (St. Tammany, the New Orleans suburbs north of Lake Pontchartrain). Breaux has been mentioned as a candidate for governor in 2003, and could probably win easily, but it seems doubtful that he would want to relinquish the critical position he holds in national policymaking.

Junior Senator   Mary Landrieu was first elected in 1996. Landrieu grew up in New Orleans, the oldest of nine children of Moon Landrieu (all with names starting with M), mayor of New Orleans in the 1970s. She was educated at Ursuline Academy and LSU and in 1979, at 23, became the youngest woman ever elected to the Louisiana state legislature, where she was sometimes the object of undue ridicule. In 1987 she was elected state treasurer; she opened bond contracts for bid and restructured the state investment portfolio; she was a sharp critic of Governor Edwin Edwards and opposed gambling as "political cancer." In 1995 she ran for governor, and in the September primary finished third, just 1% and 8,983 votes behind second-place finisher Congressman Cleo Fields. She immediately started running for the Senate seat held by Bennett Johnston, who was retiring 24 years after he was elected to the Senate after a narrow loss in a governor's race.

With a well-known name and a moderate platform—for a balanced budget amendment and capital gains tax cut, promising to make education a top priority—Landrieu shared a lead in the polls with Attorney General Richard Ieyoub, also a Democrat; under Louisiana law if they finished in the top two in the September primary, they would meet in a November runoff, and Democrats would be guaranteed a win no matter what. This was an alarming situation for Republicans, who had no such well-known candidate and who believed that they could win the seat if they could get someone into the runoff. Stepping forward to fill the gap was Woody Jenkins, a 25-year state legislator and strong abortion opponent, who had run twice for the Senate as a Democrat, losing in primaries to Bennett Johnston in 1978 by 59%–41% and to Russell Long in 1980 by 58%–39%. In August he claimed the party endorsement, but Congressman Jimmy Hayes from the Cajun country argued that he was more electable and should have party support. In early September Congressman Bob Livingston, worried that a runoff might include two Democrats or David Duke, rallied other Republicans around Jenkins and abandoned Hayes. Meanwhile, the National Republican Senatorial Committee started running ads attacking Ieyoub on ethics charges for past campaign spending practices. Jenkins surged in the polls, and led the September 21 primary with 26%, to 22% for Landrieu and 20% for Ieyoub; Duke got 12%.

At this point Jenkins looked like the favorite; Republican candidates had won 55% of the total votes and Democrats only 44%. But he had little money left, and Landrieu, who ultimately outspent him, ran ads attacking him as an extremist. Jenkins attacked her for opposing abortion restrictions and supporting gay rights, while she attacked him for never voting for a tax in 25 years. Landrieu had to spend much time getting support from blacks, since many were unhappy that she had given only nominal support to Cleo Fields for governor in 1995. Gambling interests, who were busy trying to increase black turnout in New Orleans and elsewhere for their gambling referenda, also threw their support to Landrieu. At the end of October—in uncustomary fashion—Archbishop Philip Hannan basically came out for Jenkins, saying if "a person actually believes in Catholic doctrine, then I don't see how they can vote for Landrieu without a feeling of sin."

The result was an exceedingly close election. Landrieu carried New Orleans by more than 100,000 votes and heavily Protestant northwest Louisiana around Shreveport; Jenkins carried his home base around Baton Rouge only narrowly, but also won in the heavily Catholic but often Democratic Cajun country. The official results showed Landrieu ahead by 5,788 votes, 50.2%–49.8%. Jenkins filed a lawsuit claiming vote fraud, but withdrew it, and submitted his case to the Senate. At the behest of Majority Leader Trent Lott, whose Mississippi home town is just east of New Orleans, the Senate seated Landrieu "without prejudice" to Jenkins's challenge. To the Senate Rules Committee Jenkins submitted evidence that more votes were counted in many New Orleans precincts than the number of voters who signed in, and that campaign operatives ferried in ineligible voters. But in June, it was revealed that one of Jenkins's witnesses was a convicted felon, and several others retracted their testimony. Democrats protested, and Landrieu was bitter, but Rules Chairman John Warner continued the hearings. Finally in October 1997 the committee voted unanimously to end the inquiry. While concluding that "isolated instances" of voter fraud did occur, Warner said there was no evidence to prove that there was a "widespread effort to illegally affect the outcome of this election," or that Landrieu had any involvement in the violation of election laws.

In the Senate, Landrieu has a generally moderate voting record, a little more liberal than that of colleague John Breaux. Her first bill was for a $5 million block grant for adoption services; her two children are adopted. She backs adoption tax credits and wants higher breaks for those who adopt special needs or foster children. She was the lead co-sponsor of the law providing for speedy citizenship for foreign-born children adopted by U.S. citizens; when it went into effect it created the largest number of new U.S. citizens ever on a single day. Early on she called for a "fair share" diversion of offshore oil revenues to the states, which would net Louisiana some $200 million annually, a measure attacked by environmental groups. In the 106th Congress a massive version of this Conservation and Reinvestment Act passed the House, but despite Landrieu's efforts it was vastly reduced in the Senate; when Clinton appointee George Frampton endorsed the reduction in October 2000, she put a hold on his nomination and joined Congressman John Dingell in moving to zero out his agency's appropriation. Landrieu opposed the Clinton administration's attempts to increase oil royalties on federal lands, opposed the administration as well by voting for nuclear waste storage in Nevada and attacked the administration for blocking off mineral exploration in too large a portion of federal lands.

Landrieu was part of the Centrist Democratic Caucus that first met in February 2000. "A growing number of Democrats in our caucus believe that governing from the center out works." But its first project, an education bill sponsored by Landrieu and Breaux, was defeated 84–13 in May 2000: the extremes moving in. But in the closely divided Senate of the last few years, Landrieu cast some very critical votes. She was one of four Democrats voting for the $792 billion Republican tax cut in July 1999, and one of eight to vote for marriage penalty repeal in July 2000. She voted for the $1.25 trillion compromise tax cut in April 2001. Landrieu was one of six Democrats voting in March 2001 to repeal the Clinton ergonomics rule. But she voted against the confirmation of John Ashcroft in February 2001 and, with criticism of the Bush administration, sponsored an amendment to spend $100 billion to improve the quality of life for members of the armed services in April 2001. She was one of three Democratic co-sponsors of Chuck Hagel's campaign finance bill in March 2001, but also voted for McCain-Feingold.

In January 2001 Landrieu snagged a seat on the Appropriations Committee. This gives her a chance to aid worthy Louisiana projects, which should help when she runs for re-election in 2002. In early 2001 she seemed to be running hard; she took a contribution from Harrah's Casino PAC despite her earlier stands against gambling. She was identified as a key Republican target, because of the closeness of her margin in 1996 and because George W. Bush carried Louisiana in 2000, but she seemed undefensive. As she told the Louisiana AFL-CIO in March 2001, "I'm ready for whoever wants to run. I'm very proud of my record. I most certainly didn't expect to run unopposed and I'm looking forward to the issues." In early 2001 5th District John Cooksey, who promised not to run for more than three terms in the House, seemed likely to run against her; he begins relatively unknown, especially in the New Orleans area, but has shown good campaign skills. Landrieu, he said, has to "decide if she is going to vote like the extreme liberal groups want her to, or go with the good conservative people of Louisiana." An April 2000 poll showed Landrieu leading him 49%–18%, a solid lead but one showing her hovering at the crucial 50% level. Another possible candidate is former New Orleans Councilwoman Suzanne Haik Terrell, who in November 1999 defeated none other than Woody Jenkins for the elective position of Commissioner of Elections. Also mentioned is state Senator James David Cain.

Cook's Call   *Competitive.* Landrieu's slim margin victory over an unattractive and very conservative opponent in 1996 has made her a Republican target. But the party may first have to deal with a primary between Congressman John Cooksey, a moderately conservative ophthalmologist from northeast Louisiana, and state Elections Commissioner Suzanne Haik Terrell, who is from Landrieu's New Orleans base. Landrieu has worked hard to build bridges with the business community; whether those bridges can hold up to a mainstream Republican opponent will be the real test here.

Presidential politics   Louisiana's presidential politics is racially polarized. In 2000 it voted 53%–45% for George W. Bush, with whites voting 72%–26% for Bush and blacks 92%–6% for Al Gore. One reason is that Louisiana's black percentage is the second highest in the country, after Mississippi, and rising: The state's white population increased 1% in the 1990s and its black population increased 12%, as many blacks living in the North returned to their southern roots. An estimated 29% of Louisiana voters were black in 2000; if that percentage had been 35%, with the same balance between the candidates, Gore would have carried the state. Gore's campaigning in Louisiana and his Louisiana-born campaign manager Donna Brazile's and New Orleans Mayor Marc Morial's efforts to get out black votes did not produce a victory in 2000, but similar efforts might in 2008 or 2012.

Louisiana has never played a significant role in presidential primaries and caucuses—with one odd exception. That was in 1996, when Republican allies of Phil Gramm set up a pre-Iowa-and-New-Hampshire February 6 caucus. The aim was to jump-start Gramm's campaign; instead the caucuses killed it. Gramm, relying on polls of active Republicans, was cocksure that he would win. But Pat Buchanan crisscrossed the bayous and upcountry parishes, meeting with voters, talking on cell-phones with any radio show that would have him. Only 20,000 Republicans showed up at 42 voting sites voted (as compared to 100,000 at 2,000 sites in Iowa), and Buchanan won more votes than Gramm and took 13 of the 21 delegates. Gramm's campaign in Iowa faltered, and he left the race before New Hampshire voted.

In January 1999 state Republican chairman Mike Francis got the party to schedule another pre-Iowa caucus. But in December 1999 Governor Mike Foster got the state central committee to cancel the caucuses and hold a March primary. He cited the low turnout in 1996 and the fact that only Orrin Hatch, Gary Bauer and Alan Keyes were competing in Louisiana. George W. Bush, Foster's candidate, won in March and Francis lost his seat on the party committee.

Congressional districting   Louisiana has had three sets of congressional district lines based on the 1990 Census. For 1992, the state produced two black-majority districts, one compact district in New Orleans, the other a Z-shaped monstrosity trekking from the Atchafalaya swamp to the northern edge of the state and black precincts in Shreveport. That plan was ruled unconstitutional in federal court in December 1993. In April 1994 the legislature passed a plan with a new 4th extending from the Mississippi River parishes south of Baton Rouge northwest to Shreveport; that was disallowed by a federal court in July 1994 but kept in effect for the 1994 elections. In January 1996 a federal court came up with the current plan, adopted by the legislature, that cut through few parish boundaries and had much more regular lines; it was upheld by the Supreme Court in June 1996; this has only one black-majority district, the 2d in New Orleans.

Neither party controls redistricting for 2002: Democrats control the legislature, but Republican Governor Mike Foster has a veto. In practice, neither side is very partisan, and the likely result is to change the lines marginally, which should not be difficult: no district has a population more than 7% more or less than the statewide average. The New Orleans-based 2d District will probably expand into increasingly black precincts in suburban Jefferson Parish; the 4th and 5th districts will likely creep southward; the 6th, the largest district in population, will likely contract around its Baton Rouge-Livingston Parish core. No incumbent seems likely to be discommoded, though there could be a seriously contested race in the 5th District, whose incumbent, Republican John Cooksey, in early 2001 said he would run against Senator Mary Landrieu.

THE PEOPLE: Pop. 2000: 4,468,976; Pop. 1990: 4,219,973, up 5.9% 1990–2000. 1.6% of U.S. total, 22d largest; 63.9% White, 32.5% Black, 1.2% Asian, 0.6% Amer. Indian, 1.1% Two+ races, 0.7% Other; 2.4% Hispanic Origin. 5.5% Unemployment. 2000 Voting age pop.: 3,249,177. 2000 Turnout: 1,765,656; 54% of VAP. Registered voters (2000): 2,730,380; 1,665,863 D (61%), 590,416 R (22%), 474,101 unaffiliated and minor parties (17%).

POLITICAL LINEUP: Governor, Murphy J. (Mike) Foster (R); Lt. Gov., Kathleen B. Blanco (D); Secy. of State, W. Fox McKeithen (R); Atty. Gen., Richard P. Ieyoub (D); Treasurer, John Kennedy (D); Commissioner of Insurance, Jim Brown (D); Commissioner of Agriculture & Forestry, Bob Odom (D); Commissioner of Elections, Suzanne Haik Terrell (R); State Senate, 39 (25 D, 14 R); Senate Pres. Pro Tempore, Louis J. Lambert (D); Senate President, John J. Hainkel Jr. (D); State House, 105 (70 D, 34 R, 1 vacancy); House Speaker, Charlie DeWitt (D). Senators, John Breaux (D) and Mary L. Landrieu (D). Representatives, 7 (2 D, 5 R).

ELECTIONS DIVISION: 225-925-7885; **FILING DEADLINE FOR U.S. CONGRESS:** August 23, 2002.

2000 Presidential Vote
Bush (R)	927,871	(53%)
Gore (D)	792,344	(45%)
Nader (Green)	20,473	(1%)
Others	24,968	(1%)

1996 Presidential Vote
Clinton (D)	927,836	(53%)
Dole (R)	712,586	(40%)
Perot (I)	123,292	(7%)

2000 Republican Presidential Primary
Bush (R)	86,038	(84%)
McCain (R)	9,165	(9%)
Keyes (R)	5,900	(6%)

2000 Democratic Presidential Primary
Gore (D)	114,942	(73%)
Bradley (D)	31,385	(20%)
LaRouche (D)	6,127	(4%)
Other	5,097	(3%)

Gov. Murphy J. (Mike) Foster (R)

Elected 1995, term expires Jan. 2004, 2d term; b. July 11, 1930, Shreveport; home, Franklin; LA St. U., B.S. 1951; Episcopalian; married (Alice).

Military Career: Air Force, 1952–55 (Korea), Air Force Reserves, 1955–59.

Elected Office: LA Senate, 1987–95.

Professional Career: Farmer; Pres., M.J. Foster Inc.; Pres., Sterling Sugars, Inc.; Partner, Maryland Corp.; Owner, Oaklawn Manor.

Office: State Capitol, P.O. Box 94004, Baton Rouge, 70804, 504-342-7015; Fax: 504-342-7099; Web site: www.state.la.us.

Election Results
1999 primary	Murphy J. (Mike) Foster (R)	805,203	(62%)
	William J. Jefferson (D)	382,445	(30%)
	Others	107,557	(8%)
1995 general	Murphy J. (Mike) Foster (R)	984,499	(64%)
	Cleo Fields (D)	565,861	(36%)
1995 primary	Murphy J. (Mike) Foster (R)	385,267	(26%)
	Cleo Fields (D)	280,921	(19%)
	Mary L. Landrieu (D)	271,938	(18%)
	Buddy Roemer (R)	263,330	(18%)
	Phil Preis (D)	133,271	(9%)
	Melinda Schwegmann (D)	71,288	(5%)
	Others	69,881	(5%)

Sen. John Breaux (D)

Elected 1986, seat up 2004, 3d term; b. Mar. 1, 1944, Crowley; home, Lafayette; U. of SW LA, B.A. 1964, LA St. U., J.D. 1967; Catholic; married (Lois).

Elected Office: U.S. House of Reps., 1972–87.

Professional Career: Practicing atty., 1967–68; Legis. Asst. & Dist. Mgr., U.S. Rep. Edwin W. Edwards, 1968–72.

DC Office: 503 HSOB, 20510, 202-224-4623; Fax: 202-228-2577; Web site: www.senate.gov/~breaux.

State Offices: Baton Rouge, 225-248-0104; Lafayette, 318-262-6871; Monroe, 318-325-3320; New Orleans, 504-589-2531.

Committees: *Aging (Special)* (Chmn.). *Commerce, Science & Transportation*: Aviation; Communications; Oceans & Fisheries; Science, Technology & Space (Chmn.); Surface Transportation & Merchant Marine. *Finance*: Health Care; Social Security & Family Policy (Chmn.); Taxation & IRS Oversight. *Rules & Administration*.

Group Ratings

	ADA	ACLU	AFS	LCV	CON	ITIC	NTU	COC	ACU	NTLC	CHC
2000	50	29	28	43	46	82	25	86	40	20	46
1999	80	—	83	0	40	—	21	56	17	—	—

National Journal Ratings

	1999 LIB —	1999 CONS		2000 LIB —	2000 CONS
Economic	55%	— 44%		53%	— 46%
Social	52%	— 47%		49%	— 46%
Foreign	62%	— 29%		72%	— 15%

Key Votes of the 106th Congress

1. Educ. Savings Accts.	Y	5. Review Movie Violence	Y	9. NATO War in Serbia	Y
2. Prescrip. Drug Benefit	Y	6. Gun Show Bckgrnd. Checks	Y	10. Table Cuba Travel Ban	Y
3. Delay Ergonomic Standards	Y	7. Ban Part.-Birth Abortion	Y	11. Nuclear Test-Ban Treaty	Y
4. Phase Out Estate Tax	Y	8. Broaden Hate Crimes List	Y	12. Perm. Trade with China	Y

Election Results

1998 primary	John Breaux (D)	620,502	(64%)	($3,858,472)
	Jim Donelon (R)	306,616	(32%)	($364,073)
	Others	42,047	(4%)	
1992 primary	John Breaux (D)	616,021	(73%)	($2,007,675)
	Jon Khachaturian (I)	74,785	(9%)	($94,919)
	Lyle Stockstill (R)	69,986	(8%)	($34,711)
	Nick Accardo (D)	45,839	(6%)	
	Fred Clegg Strong (R)	36,406	(4%)	

Sen. Mary L. Landrieu (D)

Elected 1996, seat up 2002, 1st term; b. Nov. 23, 1955, Arlington, VA; home, New Orleans; LA St. U., B.A. 1977; Catholic; married (Frank Snellings).

Elected Office: LA House of Reps., 1979–88; LA Treasurer, 1987–96.

DC Office: 724 HSOB, 20510, 202-224-5824; Fax: 202-224-9735; Web site: www.senate.gov/~landrieu.

State Offices: Baton Rouge, 225-389-0395; Lake Charles, 337-436-6650; New Orleans, 504-589-2427; Shreveport, 318-676-3085.

Committees: *Appropriations*: District of Columbia (Chmn.); Foreign Operations; Labor, HHS & Education; Military Construction; Treasury & General Government. *Armed Services*: Emerging Threats & Capabilities (Chmn.); Readiness & Management Support; Seapower. *Energy & Natural Resources*: Energy Research, Development, Production & Regulation; Forests & Public Land Management; National Parks, Historic Preservation & Recreation. *Small Business*.

Group Ratings

	ADA	ACLU	AFS	LCV	CON	ITIC	NTU	COC	ACU	NTLC	CHC
2000	80	43	71	71	31	90	21	73	16	17	25
1999	95	—	83	22	18	—	14	59	4	—	—

National Journal Ratings

	1999 LIB	—	1999 CONS		2000 LIB	—	2000 CONS
Economic	56%	—	42%		68%	—	31%
Social	73%	—	26%		61%	—	36%
Foreign	77%	—	22%		66%	—	31%

Key Votes of the 106th Congress

1. Educ. Savings Accts.	N	5. Review Movie Violence	N	9. NATO War in Serbia	Y
2. Prescrip. Drug Benefit	Y	6. Gun Show Bckgrnd. Checks	Y	10. Table Cuba Travel Ban	N
3. Delay Ergonomic Standards	N	7. Ban Part.-Birth Abortion	Y	11. Nuclear Test-Ban Treaty	Y
4. Phase Out Estate Tax	Y	8. Broaden Hate Crimes List	Y	12. Perm. Trade with China	Y

Election Results

1996 general	Mary L. Landrieu (D)	852,945	(50%)	($2,504,815)
	Louis (Woody) Jenkins (R)	847,157	(50%)	($1,878,242)
1996 primary	Louis (Woody) Jenkins (R)	322,244	(26%)	
	Mary L. Landrieu (D)	264,268	(22%)	
	Richard P. Ieyoub (D)	250,682	(20%)	
	David Duke (R)	141,489	(12%)	
	Jimmy Hayes (R)	71,699	(6%)	
	Bill Linder (R)	58,243	(5%)	
	Others	119,934	(10%)	
1990 primary	J. Bennett Johnston (D)	752,902	(54%)	($5,389,624)
	David Duke (R)	607,391	(44%)	($2,615,267)
	Others	35,820	(3%)	

FIRST DISTRICT

New Orleans, founded in 1718, the nation's fifth largest city at the outbreak of the Civil War, is ancient for an American metropolis; yet it is still closely girded by the peculiar wilderness of the mushy Delta lands of the sluggish Mississippi River. Climb the levee overlooking the Mississippi and you will see an expanse of water with untidy clumps of trees and disorganized-looking, seemingly abandoned docks—what Mark Twain had in his mind's eye while writing *Life on the Mississippi* in the 1870s. Or drive just past the last block of a suburban subdivision, and you are in unreclaimed swamp, vegetation and wetness, thick with herons and alligators, flat as far as the eye can see. For years the river funneled the products of half a continent down to a single port with an international heritage and flair; the New Orleans metropolitan area is still living off that geography and history, with an inward-looking elite preoccupied with who is in which Mardi Gras krewe and interested more in old families' genealogy than in Oil Patch geology. The old buildings of New Orleans are finely proportioned and its old neighborhoods charming, like those in France; and its early 20th Century improvements, like Olmstead's City Park, are grand. But its middle and late 20th Century streetscapes and subdivisions, like those of France, are without ornament or charm, utilitarian works of man made to master the below-sea-level environment.

The 1st Congressional District includes much of the newer part of the New Orleans metropolitan area, spread over the soggy lands of the lower Mississippi and Lake Pontchartrain. Most of its people live in affluent white neighborhoods in New Orleans and the vast suburb of Metairie in Jefferson Parish, divided by slanting grids and elevated only where bridges jut out over the many canals. The boundaries have been drawn so that the next-door 2nd District has a black majority; the black percentage in the 1st, 14%, is the lowest of any Louisiana district. The 1st extends across the 26-mile Lake Pontchartrain Causeway to include St. Tammany Parish, the state's fastest-growing, with old towns lush with trees and clusters of new growth around giant intersections, and north and west to Washington and Tangipahoa parishes, still mostly rural country. This is the most upscale, affluent, highly educated district in Louisiana, and also the most Republican, supportive of political reform and against economic redistribution.

The congressman from the 1st District is Republican David Vitter, who won a special election in May 1999. He grew up in the New Orleans area, graduated from Harvard, was a Rhodes Scholar, and graduated from Tulane Law School. Vitter was elected in 1991 to the first of two terms in the state House, where he became prominent for passing a term-limits bill through a reluctant state legislature in 1995. Slim and boyish-looking, he is noted for his ability to irritate other politicians; many reacted with rage at his crusade for term limits, and a popular suburban sheriff whose ethics Vitter criticized sued him three times.

The chance to run for Congress came suddenly. Congressman Bob Livingston, first elected in a 1977 special, became chairman of the Appropriations Committee in 1995. When Newt Gingrich was forced to retire as speaker three days after the 1998 election, Livingston quickly rounded up the votes and became speaker-designate. On December 17, as the House was approaching the impeachment vote, Livingston disquieted some colleagues by confessing that he had had affairs; on December 19, while speaking in the debate on impeachment, he stunned everyone by announcing that he was resigning, even as he called on Bill Clinton to do so. Governor Mike Foster set the special election for May 1, with a runoff, if no candidate received a majority, May 29: two Saturdays, one when Jazz Fest began, the other in Memorial Day weekend, seemed likely to produce low turnout.

Many Republicans jumped into the race, but the chief preoccupation of the national press, and the chief fear of Louisiana and national Republicans, was that former Ku Klux Klansman and Hitler sympathizer David Duke would run and make it into the runoff. This seemed a bit farfetched, since his career peaked almost a decade before, and his 1998 book *My Awakening* that asserted, "belief in racial equality is the modern equivalent of believing the earth is flat," gathered dust on the shelves. The establishment choice was David Treen, who ran for the House as long ago as 1962 (and gave Democrat Hale Boggs a scare in 1964) and won four terms in the House starting in 1972. In 1979 he was elected governor when Edwin Edwards was term-limited. At 70, he pledged to serve only the short term and one more and argued that his experience in the House would help the district. In contrast, Vitter said, "We need a younger congressman like me, so we can start building up the seniority we lost when Bob Livingston resigned." Perhaps the most attention-grabbing candidate was Monica Monica, an ophthalmologist, who spent more than $1.4 million including at least $900,000 of her own money, and in mid-February became the first candidate to go up with TV ads. She was encouraged to run by the 5th District's John Cooksey, also an ophthalmologist. On the Democratic side was Bill Strain, the second-most senior member of the Louisiana House, first elected in 1972. Treen, with 25%, and Vitter, with 22%, advanced to the runoff. Duke came unnervingly close to making the runoff, but finished third with 19%, followed by Monica with 16%; Strain, with 11%, died two months later. Duke asserted he would have advanced to the runoff if Strain, the conservative Democrat, had not been in the race.

Subtle differences emerged between Vitter and Treen during the runoff: Vitter denounced all forms of gun control; Treen said he supported some restrictions on more sophisticated automatic or semiautomatic weapons, and would require dealers at gun shows to perform background checks. Both opposed racial quotas and preferences but Treen also said the federal government should not prevent colleges and universities from deciding their own racial admission policies. Treen was endorsed by Livingston, Foster and several prominent local politicians, but may have been hurt when he stopped campaigning in the final week to help search for his grandson, who disappeared while hiking in Oregon; the young man was found three days before the election. But low turnout was probably a bigger factor, as Vitter rallied his troops and won the seat, 51%–49%. Treen carried his home base of St. Tammany Parish, but not enough to overcome Vitter's home advantage in Jefferson Parish.

In the House, Vitter has compiled a conservative voting record and worked on local projects.

He won House inclusion of Lake Pontchartrain in the National Estuary Program. He secured $1 million for research by Southeastern Louisiana University. He filed a bill to limit the number of doctors who could prescribe the RU-486 abortion drug. After enactment in 2000 of the bill to require more disclosure of political activity by "Section 527" tax-exempt groups, Vitter sought to relax the new rules, arguing they were burdensome at the state and local level. He became a vigorous advocate of a national missile defense. He called for prescription-drug coverage for military retirees and supported the HMO regulation bill supported mostly by Democrats. After the House passed his amendment to block the Chinese government's purchase of land near the Pentagon, which Vitter feared could become a "spy tower," the Chinese dropped their plans. He showed his maverick tendencies when he sought a new regional authority to replace the city's control of the New Orleans International Airport—causing an angry battle within the Louisiana delegation on the House floor. In January 2001, Vitter won a seat on the Appropriations Committee.

Vitter easily won re-election with 80% of the vote against four challengers. Redistricting should be no problem. The 2nd District needs to be expanded, and presumably will be given some precincts in Jefferson County which gained more black residents in the 1990s.

Cook's Call   *Safe.* Democrats have little reason to put this suburban New Orleans district on their target list. After all, in 2000 this district gave Bush his biggest winning margin in the state (34%) and Vitter took 80%. As one of the fastest growing districts in the state, it will have to contract a bit in redistricting.

THE PEOPLE: Pop. 2000: 666,747; Pop. 1990: 602,867, up 10.6% 1990–2000. 81.6% White, 13.7% Black, 1.6% Asian, 0.3% Amer. Indian, 1.4% Two+ races, 1.3% Other; 4.8% Hispanic Origin.

2000 Presidential Vote			1996 Presidential Vote		
Bush (R)	186,076	(66%)	Dole (R)	152,655	(57%)
Gore (D)	89,777	(32%)	Clinton (D)	100,655	(37%)
Nader (Green)	4,168	(1%)	Perot (I)	16,325	(6%)
Others	2,675	(1%)			

Rep. David Vitter (R)

Elected May 1999, 1st term; b. May 3, 1961, New Orleans; home, Metairie; Harvard U., A.B. 1983, Rhodes Scholar, Oxford U., B.A. 1985, Tulane Law Schl., J.D. 1988; Catholic; married (Wendy).

Elected Office: LA House of Reps., 1991–99.

Professional Career: Practicing atty., 1988–99; Adjunct Law Prof., Tulane U. & Loyola U., 1995–98.

DC Office: 414 CHOB 20515, 202-225-3015; Fax: 202-225-0739; Web site: www.house.gov/vitter.

District Offices: Hammond, 504-542-9616; Metairie, 504-589-2753.

Committees: *Appropriations* (34th of 35 R): Commerce, Justice & State; District of Columbia; Military Construction.

Group Ratings

	ADA	ACLU	AFS	LCV	CON	ITIC	NTU	COC	ACU	NTLC	CHC
2000	0	14	0	7	48	100	62	85	88	85	100
1999	5	—	0	0	14	—	50	88	83	—	—

National Journal Ratings

	1999 LIB —	1999 CONS		2000 LIB —	2000 CONS
Economic	*	*		6% —	85%
Social	15% —	85%		0% —	79%
Foreign	20% —	80%		0% —	88%

Key Votes of the 106th Congress

1. Patient Bill of Rights	Y	5. Bar RU-486 $ for FDA	Y	9. NATO War in Serbia	*
2. Accelerate Min. Wage	N	6. Display 10 Commandments	Y	10. Perm. Trade with China	Y
3. Strike Ban on Ergo. Stnd.	N	7. Gun Show Bkgrnd. Checks	N	11. Debt Relief for 3rd World	N
4. Ovrd. Estate Tax Veto	Y	8. Ban Part.-Birth Abortion	Y	12. Drop Cuba Econ. Embargo	N

Election Results

2000 primary	David Vitter (R)	191,379	(80%)	($1,604,204)
	Michael A. Armato (D)	29,935	(13%)	
	Cary J. Deaton (D)	10,982	(5%)	
	Other	5,514	(2%)	
1999 runoff	David Vitter (R)	61,661	(51%)	($807,505)
	David Treen (R)	59,849	(49%)	($494,789)
1999 primary	David Treen (R)	36,719	(25%)	
	David Vitter (R)	31,741	(22%)	
	David Duke (R)	28,059	(19%)	
	Monica Monica (R)	22,928	(16%)	
	Bill Strain (D)	16,446	(11%)	
	Rob Couhig (R)	9,295	(6%)	

SECOND DISTRICT

Founded by the French in 1718, ruled by the Spanish from 1763 to just days before the French took over to sell it to the United States in 1803, New Orleans was a Creole city—part French, a bit Spanish, more than a touch Caribbean—when the American flag was raised over what is now Jackson Square. The statue of Andrew Jackson still seems an alien intrusion in a square set off by a French Market, the Cabildo, the Presbytere, the Pontalba apartments and Cathedral St. Louis. New Orleans was the fifth largest American city from 1840 until the Civil War and the only sizable city in the South; yet even as it was sending southern cotton out to the mills of Lancashire, it was an alien cultural force in both the nation and region. Urbanized, yet poor and in many ways primitive, New Orleans had yellow fever epidemics late in the 19th Century, even as it was installing electric lights; it had a riot in which Italian immigrants were massacred, even as it was laying streetcar tracks and telephone lines. This was one of the most corrupt American cities during Reconstruction and the Gilded Age, when its votes were regularly bid for and bought; like other Southern cities, it became rigidly segregated after 1890.

For a time during the 1970s oil boom, New Orleans seemed to be a fast-growing Sun Belt city; then starting in the middle 1980s it reverted to its rougher traditions and was beset by woes big and small. Its port lost business—oil to Houston and Latin American trade to Miami. But in the mid-1990s New Orleans took a turn for the better. Under Mayor Marc Morial, the notoriously corrupt police force was cleaned up, increased in size and adopted New York's crime-fighting methods. Crime plummeted and no longer depressed the tourism business. The city's land-based casino went broke in 1995 even before the permanent building was finished; Harrah's Casino was opened in 1999, but in 2001 it threatened to close down unless the state lowered its minimum tax payment (the state did). But people come to New Orleans for other things than gambling. They want to see the gaudy bars of Bourbon Street and the restored houses there and in the Garden District. They want to see Mardi Gras and the krewes that parade for weeks before. And they want to dine in New Orleans's array of restaurants, with a cuisine all New Orleans's own, spicy and rich and unaffected by today's taste for low-fat food. *The Wall Street Journal* reported that the federal government had determined that New Orleanians "are the fattest people in America, the most likely to contract lung cancer and among the shortest lived, with an average lifespan roughly equal to the citizens of Mauritius, North Korea and Uzbekistan."

The 2d Congressional District includes almost all of the city of New Orleans, everything except a few affluent white neighborhoods, plus the west bank towns of Jefferson Parish—Gretna, Harvey, Westwego, Waggaman—industrial enclosures between levee and swamp. Here is the French Quarter—the *Vieux Carre*—its 19th Century homes still intact because the Americans who moved here after 1803 wanted to stay away from the snobbish Creoles and then built a new downtown across Canal Street. North of the Quarter is the site of Storyville, where prostitution was legal until 1918 and where jazz was probably first played; the old frame houses have long since been torn down and replaced by half-empty and crime-ridden housing projects. But many similar neighborhoods remain, where blacks and some working-class whites live in rickety frame houses which are not always strong enough to keep the rain out and never tight enough to protect against the summer humidity or the damp winter chill, along the vividly named streets—Elysian Fields, Spain, Desire, Arts—that go north from the river wharves. South of the quarter is the downtown flecked with skyscrapers and the ominous Superdome, and to the east is the old slum known as the Irish Channel—a reminder that New Orleans had more foreign immigrants than any other part of the South; a community of more than 10,000 Vietnamese refugees has grown, apparently comfortable in the hot and swampy environs. Up St. Charles Avenue is the Garden District. This was the home of rich early American settlers, and its antebellum homes are still covered with vines and Spanish moss. Quaintly named trolley cars still roll out St. Charles to Tulane University and Audubon Park. New Orleans, for many years a speckled black-and-white city, now has a 67% black majority, and the 2d District is overwhelmingly Democratic.

The congressman from the 2d District is Bill Jefferson, a Democrat first elected in 1990 after the retirement of Lindy Boggs, a charming Louisiana lady with perfect political pitch, who won majorities from blacks and whites alike and became Bill Clinton's Ambassador to the Vatican. Jefferson grew up in the northeast corner of Louisiana in Lake Providence. After attending Southern University, he went to Harvard Law School, clerked for a respected federal judge, worked for Senator Bennett Johnston and finally settled in New Orleans to set up what became the largest black law firm in the South; he received an LL.M. from Georgetown while serving in Congress. Jefferson was elected to the state Senate in 1979; he twice ran for mayor and lost. In 1990, when Boggs retired, Jefferson was endorsed by then-Mayor Sidney Barthelemy, and in the primary won 25% of the vote to 22% for Marc Morial, whose father was New Orleans's first black mayor and who was elected mayor himself in 1994 and 1998. In the November runoff, charges flew: Jefferson was dogged by reports of defaults on outstanding loans and mortgages, while Morial admitted he was the father of an eight-year-old girl living in the Ivory Coast. Jefferson won with 52% and became the first Louisiana black elected to Congress since Reconstruction.

In the House Jefferson has shown impressive political skills with a moderate voting record among Democrats. He was active in the Democratic Leadership Council and got to know its chairman, a young southern governor named Bill Clinton. In November 1991, he and Mississippi Congressman Mike Espy endorsed Clinton and provided early, and crucial, black support. From his seat on Ways and Means, he has expressed doubts about Social Security individual investment accounts and has also questioned reliance on the payroll tax: "We know it is regressive. I wonder if it's a good idea to have the payroll tax as the only thing to rely on" for Social Security's financial base. He wants to expand the availability of Individual Retirement Accounts. In 2000, he won approval of an amendment requiring health-care plans to notify beneficiaries of cheaper generic-drug options. He opposed the proposed Shintech polyvinyl chloride plant farther up the Mississippi River because it was sited near a black community; the company decided to build a smaller plant near Baton Rouge instead. Jefferson co-sponsored the Africa free trade bill that was enacted in 2000, and made several trips to Africa himself. In a speech he advised African leaders to reform their often-corrupt legal systems because businesses would shun them unless they were confident they would be treated fairly.

Jefferson has recalled that on election night 1990 he was standing next to Lindy Boggs. "I said, 'Lindy, I'm so glad this is over; I can stop running.' She looked at me and said, 'Honey, in this job you never stop running.'" Evidently he has run well, and without serious opposition. But he has also eyed other offices. In 1991, he filed to run for governor, but withdrew; in 1995, he began running for governor again, but withdrew in favor of Cleo Fields, and said he would run for Senate; in May 1996 he bowed out of that race. In January 1999 Republican Mike Foster and other statewide officials met at the Governor's Mansion and promised not to oppose each other regardless of party. Jefferson was evidently peeved and days later circulated a letter of protest and said he was running for governor. He hoped to become the first black candidate to win a statewide office since Reconstruction. Raising more than $2.2 million, he challenged Foster's claims of improving the state's economy and schools, and said that too many poor people and too many children were still being left behind. He pledged to raise teacher pay, reduce class sizes, rebuild public schools and push for tougher education standards. But voting ran pretty much along racial lines, and Foster won by a 62%–30% margin. But Jefferson may run for statewide office again, or for mayor, although Morial has been trying to repeal New Orleans's two-term limit, petitioning the City Council in May 2001 to schedule a referendum on the question.

The 2nd district's population declined 2% in the 1990s, and some 48,000 people will have to be gained to get it up to the population standard. Presumably that will be done by adding precincts in Jefferson County which gained increasing numbers of black residents in the 1990s.

Cook's Call   *Safe.* As the most heavily minority (67% black) and strongest Democratic district in the state (Gore carried this district by 56%), Bill Jefferson has few worries here and is very safe. This seat has not grown as quickly as others in the state and will need to pick up some population in redistricting.

THE PEOPLE: Pop. 2000: 590,824; Pop. 1990: 602,830, down 2% 1990–2000. 27.8% White, 66.9% Black, 2.5% Asian, 0.3% Amer. Indian, 1.3% Two+ races, 1.1% Other; 3.6% Hispanic Origin.

2000 Presidential Vote			1996 Presidential Vote		
Gore (D)	161,382	(77%)	Clinton (D)	169,930	(79%)
Bush (R)	43,347	(21%)	Dole (R)	40,739	(19%)
Nader (Green)	2,818	(1%)	Perot (I)	5,400	(2%)
Others	1,372	(1%)			

Rep. William J. Jefferson (D)

Elected 1990, 6th term; b. Mar. 14, 1947, Lake Providence; home, New Orleans; Southern U., B.A. 1969, Harvard U., J.D. 1972, Georgetown U., LL.M. 1996; Baptist; married (Andrea).

Military Career: Army Reserves, 1969–78, Army Judge Advocate Corps, 1975.

Elected Office: LA Senate, 1979–90.

Professional Career: Law clerk, U.S. Dist. Judge Alvin Rubin, 1972–73; Legis. aide, U.S. Sen. Bennett Johnston, 1973–75; Practicing atty., 1975–90.

DC Office: 240 CHOB 20515, 202-225-6636; Fax: 202-225-1988; Web site: www.house.gov/jefferson.

District Office: New Orleans, 504-589-2274.

Committees: *Ways & Means* (12th of 17 D): Select Revenue Measures; Trade.

Group Ratings

	ADA	ACLU	AFS	LCV	CON	ITIC	NTU	COC	ACU	NTLC	CHC
2000	70	67	71	79	45	83	25	66	13	6	15
1999	75	—	100	63	55	—	11	40	4	—	—

National Journal Ratings

	1999 LIB —	1999 CONS		2000 LIB —	2000 CONS
Economic	68% —	32%		67% —	32%
Social	75% —	25%		68% —	32%
Foreign	85% —	12%		74% —	24%

Key Votes of the 106th Congress

1. Patient Bill of Rights	Y	5. Bar RU-486 $ for FDA	N	9. NATO War in Serbia	Y
2. Accelerate Min. Wage	Y	6. Display 10 Commandments	N	10. Perm. Trade with China	Y
3. Strike Ban on Ergo. Stnd.	Y	7. Gun Show Bkgrnd. Checks	Y	11. Debt Relief for 3rd World	Y
4. Ovrd. Estate Tax Veto	*	8. Ban Part.-Birth Abortion	Y	12. Drop Cuba Econ. Embargo	Y

Election Results

2000 primary	William J. Jefferson (D)	unopposed		($563,238)
1998 primary	William J. Jefferson (D)	102,247	(86%)	($495,522)
	David Reed (D)	10,803	(9%)	
	Don-Terry Veal (D)	5,899	(5%)	($1,609)

THIRD DISTRICT

Below sea level, veined with bayous and creeks and wide streams of water, crossed by only an occasional road or railroad, the wetlands of southern Louisiana are one of America's unique landscapes. Technically, most of this waterlogged land rests on islands in a broad river mouth, through which the waters of the Mississippi and its tributaries drain into the Gulf of Mexico. It is rich with animal life, herons and egrets, shrimp and crawfish, muskrats and alligators. Yet it supports more people than one might think, in surprisingly sturdy small towns, with shopping malls on high ground, and in cabins along the bayous and crossroad towns where Cajun French remains the first language and roadside diners feature crawfish etouffe. But the steep-roofed Cajun houses are not the only structures: Here and there, jutting out of the swampy land, are huge elaborate metal sculptures—refineries and petrochemical plants, processing the oil and natural gas trapped under these wetlands and the shallow continental shelf of the Gulf, and released through 20th Century oil rig technology. In the 1960s and 1970s, the oil industry, by providing good jobs for young people here, helped preserve Cajun culture and built a Cajun pride that was seldom articulated a generation ago. Then oil payrolls plummeted and the wetlands were threatened by coastal erosion and battered by Hurricane Andrew in August 1992. But now offshore drilling is booming again, unemployment is low, and the outlook for the Cajun country looks good.

The 3d Congressional District of Louisiana includes about half the Cajun country, plus St. Bernard and Plaquemines parishes downriver from New Orleans. It then spreads west over the swamplands, covering Houma, where seven bayous converge; St. Charles, St. John the Baptist, St. James and Ascension parishes on both sides of the Mississippi, once the greatest sugar producers in America, now studded with refineries and petrochemical plants; roughneck Morgan City, which services many offshore oil rigs; and Iberia Parish, the home of McIlhenny's Tabasco sauce. Behind the Mississippi's western levee, hunkered side by side in Vacherie in St. James Parish, are twin reminders of the region's grandeur and pain: the stately Oak Alley plantation, whose stunning vista stood in for the home of a fictional, aristocratic governor in the 1998 movie *Primary Colors;* and the Laura Plantation, believed to be the original home of the famous Br'er Rabbit stories, and whose current owners are preserving and displaying the plantation's slave cabins to remind visitors of the facts many would prefer to forget. The ancestral language here is French, mainly Cajun but also Creole; the ancestral religion is Roman Catholic and the ancestral politics Democratic, though very conservative.

The congressman from the 3d District is Billy Tauzin, first elected as a Democrat and now a Republican, who is now chairman of the Energy and Commerce Committee. Tauzin grew up in Chackbay, worked on an oil rig to put himself through Nicholls State University and LSU Law School, where he was a roommate of Senator John Breaux. He was first elected to the legislature in 1971, at 28; he won the 3d District seat in a May 1980 special election. Tauzin ran for governor in 1987, but was doomed when Edwin Edwards entered the race, squeezing him out in Cajun country; he finished fourth, with 10%. In 1989, Tauzin inherited a Merchant Marine subcommittee chairmanship, just in time to handle legislation inspired by the Exxon *Valdez* oil spill in Alaska. In 1990 he drew up plans to allow a drawdown of the Strategic Petroleum Reserve in southern Louisiana to help pay for the Gulf war and then got the reserve built back up afterward. Tauzin is both knowledgeable and eloquent. His floor speech for a 1992 Cable Act amendment allowing wireless cable companies access to cable-originated programming carried 338–68 over the opposition of Democratic leaders and the Bush White House. He was a co-sponsor of the securities litigation reform that was passed in 1996 over Bill Clinton's veto. He can also be wily. Defeated in the committee and on the House floor, he and Senator Bennett Johnston inserted in conference committee on the Alaska Oil Export Act of 1995 a provision for royalty relief for deep-water oil drilling; that, plus advances in technology, led to the resurgence in offshore drilling in 1996.

Tauzin's party switch in was not a complete surprise. He was one of two Democrats who supported all provisions of the Contract with America and in February 1995 he and 22 other Democrats formed The Coalition, a conservative group. In August 1995 he finally became a Republican. He was expected to run for Johnston's Senate seat in 1996, but Tauzin bowed out after being promised by the Republican leadership the chair of the Telecommunications and Finance Subcommittee. Mike Oxley, the next Republican in line, objected, and, as a compromise, Telecommunications lost its Finance jurisdiction to Oxley's subcommittee. Tauzin wants to eliminate the long-distance tax and wants cable companies to give consumers a wider range of options (including low-cost service with few channels) and has passed an anti-slamming bill through the House. He and his Senate counterpart John McCain worked to allow satellite TV to broadcast local stations and compete with cable. Tauzin opposes auctioning the digital TV spectrum, regulating liquor advertising and any campaign finance bill giving free or discounted air time to candidates (in his view, unconstitutional, unfair and ineffective). Tauzin passed 264–159 a bill barring the FCC from ruling that religious material did not count as instructional programming on educational stations owned by religious broadcasters (reacting to a rescinded 1999 FCC ruling). He also passed a bill barring telemarketers from blocking caller ID, and handled technical matters with great economic impact—how telecom companies compensate each other for connecting calls, determining the incidence of state and local taxes on wireless telephone calls.

Tauzin supported the Telecommunications Act of 1996 but afterwards criticized the Clinton FCC for blocking the regional Bells from the long-distance business; George W. Bush's FCC chairman, Michael Powell, shares his view. In the 106th Congress Tauzin cannily built a coalition to allow the regional Bells to provide broadband Internet connections. He accumulated a "digital divide" coalition of members from rural districts and from poor urban areas, members of the Black and Hispanic Caucuses and conservatives wary of federal broadband subsidies. He met with regional Bell lobbyists in weekly sessions and got the endorsement of committee ranking Democrat John Dingell. In June 2000 he announced he had 218 co-sponsors, a majority of the House, but declined to bring the bill forward because of the opposition of Commerce Chairman Thomas Bliley; but Bliley was term-limited as chairman and had already announced his retirement from the House. As chairman in 2001, Tauzin got subcommittee chairman Fred Upton to sign on to what was now Tauzin-Dingell, which seemed to have impressive steam behind it; his committee approved the bill 32–23 in May 2001, although with more difficulty than many expected.

As subcommittee and committee chairman, Tauzin has held memorable hearings. In September 2000 he dominated the hearings on Firestone tires that had blown out on Ford Explorers, and proposed legislation which passed the House under suspension of the rules in October 2000 and was accepted in full by the Senate, without the criminal penalties Senate Commerce Chairman John McCain wanted. In February 2001 he held hearings on network news coverage of the 2000 elections, in which he found no evidence that networks tried to influence the outcome, but concluded that VNS's flawed models produced "a bias that consistently tended to favor Democrats." Tauzin and Louisiana Democrat Chris John negotiated a generous version of the CARA legislation allotting offshore oil royalties to coastal states, which passed the House by a wide margin; but it was cut way back in the Senate.

An undercurrent in all this was the race between Tauzin and Mike Oxley to succeed Bliley as full committee chairman. Oxley had more seniority as a Republican, Tauzin more seniority if you (as Gingrich did) count his years as a Democrat; but House Republicans do not necessarily follow seniority, and each raised about $500,000 for Republican colleagues. Tauzin ran an especially lavish Cajun party at the Republican National Convention. The contest was settled by an intricate deal, much as the Telecommunications Subcommittee chairmanship had been settled four years before. Tauzin became chairman of what he renamed the Energy and Commerce Committee. Oxley became chairman of the newly-named Financial Services Committee, essentially the old Banking Committee with Oxley's subcommittee jurisdiction added; the loser in this was Marge Roukema, the ranking Republican on Banking. As chairman, Bliley had taken tight control of subcommittees but had not aggressively asserted the committee's jurisdiction. Tauzin followed the opposite strategy, as John Dingell had during his years as chairman from 1981–95. He also granted Democrats, i.e., Dingell, more staff and funding. Under Tauzin, Energy and Commerce may take a major role in reshaping Medicare (Tauzin is an obvious ally of Breaux on this issue) and energy legislation. But Tauzin also has his own agenda—the Tauzin-Dingell broadband bill, banning of human cloning, encouraging digital television, holding down cable TV rates. Confronted with complaints of rising cable TV rates and expensive sports packages, Tauzin warned, "My message to the industry is, 'Don't let it happen.' I don't want to have to deal with it."

Tauzin has had no difficulty getting re-elected, indeed he had no Democratic opposition since 1992. In September 1996 he became the only party-switcher to be re-elected without opposition. He was unopposed in 1998. In 2000, against two Independents and a Libertarian, he was re-elected with 78% of the vote. Redistricting is unlikely to be a problem.

Cook's Call　*Safe.* By the numbers, this district is one of the more marginal seats in the state. Bush took his lowest winning percentage here in 2000 (52%). But, Tauzin, who switched parties in 1994, has never had a tight race, regularly racking up winning margins in the 70s (he was unopposed in 1996 and 1998).

THE PEOPLE: Pop. 2000: 637,359; Pop. 1990: 602,814, up 5.7% 1990–2000. 70.2% White, 25.3% Black, 1.2% Asian, 1.6% Amer. Indian, 1.2% Two+ races, 0.6% Other; 2.1% Hispanic Origin.

2000 Presidential Vote		
Bush (R)	135,313	(52%)
Gore (D)	115,179	(45%)
Nader (Green)	2,788	(1%)
Others	5,146	(2%)

1996 Presidential Vote		
Clinton (D)	153,925	(52%)
Dole (R)	120,605	(41%)
Perot (I)	22,182	(7%)

Rep. W. J. (Billy) Tauzin (R)

Elected May 1980, 11th term; b. June 14, 1943, Chackbay; home, Chackbay; Nicholls St. U., B.A. 1964, LA St. U., J.D. 1967; Catholic; married (Cecile).

Elected Office: LA House of Reps., 1971–79.

Professional Career: Practicing atty., 1968–70.

DC Office: 2183 RHOB 20515, 202-225-4031; Fax: 202-225-0563; Web site: www.house.gov/tauzin.

District Offices: Chalmette, 504-271-1707; Gonzales, 225-621-8490; Houma, 504-876-3033; New Iberia, 318-367-8231.

Committees: *Energy & Commerce* (Chmn. of 31 R). *Resources* (3d of 28 R): Energy & Mineral Resources; Fisheries Conservation, Wildlife & Oceans.

Group Ratings

	ADA	ACLU	AFS	LCV	CON	ITIC	NTU	COC	ACU	NTLC	CHC
2000	0	21	0	14	8	100	60	85	84	76	93
1999	5	—	0	0	2	—	53	100	84	—	—

National Journal Ratings

	1999 LIB —	1999 CONS		2000 LIB —	2000 CONS
Economic	0% —	84%		15% —	83%
Social	25% —	72%		0% —	79%
Foreign	15% —	85%		0% —	88%

Key Votes of the 106th Congress

1. Patient Bill of Rights	N	5. Bar RU-486 $ for FDA	Y	9. NATO War in Serbia	N
2. Accelerate Min. Wage	N	6. Display 10 Commandments	Y	10. Perm. Trade with China	Y
3. Strike Ban on Ergo. Stnd.	N	7. Gun Show Bkgrnd. Checks	N	11. Debt Relief for 3rd World	N
4. Ovrd. Estate Tax Veto	Y	8. Ban Part.-Birth Abortion	Y	12. Drop Cuba Econ. Embargo	N

Election Results

2000 primary	W. J. (Billy) Tauzin (R)	143,446	(78%)	($1,194,679)
	Edwin J. Albares (I)	16,908	(9%)	
	Anita W. Rosenthal (I)	13,488	(7%)	
	Dion Bourque (LIB)	10,118	(6%)	
1998 primary	W. J. (Billy) Tauzin (R)	unopposed		($770,827)

FOURTH DISTRICT

Northwestern Louisiana, south of Arkansas and just east of Texas, is part of the Deep South. The overwhelming majority of people here are Protestants, not Catholics, often very tradition-minded, with names that are English or Scottish, not French. The tone is set not by wide-open New Orleans—which was not accessible by interstate until 1996, when the last chunk of I-49 was completed—but by the much smaller Shreveport, which could be just another East Texas oil town. The countryside is agricultural, though there are few vestiges of large riverfront plantations and backward farm country. Shreveport was discovered when Captain Henry Miller Shreve, with the Army Corps of Engineers, in the 1830s dispatched a young deputy named Robert E. Lee to break up a 100-mile blockade of logs in the Red River, moving the region's epicenter upriver to a new town, which was named after him.

Oil provided the basis for much of the economic growth of the 20th Century; defense facilities also helped; more recently there has been some high-tech and local entrepreneurship as Shreveport has encouraged economic revival with a convention center and downtown entertainment district. Politically, northern Louisiana voters, for more than 100 years, have been voting against cosmopolitan New Orleans and the Catholic Cajun south, sometimes for riproaring populists, and more often, as the economy grows more sophisticated, for market-oriented Republicans. The local Mardi Gras was revived in 1990 and is a more sedate, family-oriented affair compared to the Big Easy.

The 4th Congressional District consists of the northwest quadrant of the state. More than half the votes here are cast in Caddo and Bossier Parishes in the far corner around Shreveport, with the rest scattered around rural areas, picturesque old towns like Natchitoches and strip-highway towns like Leesville near the Army's giant Fort Polk. This area seemed to be trending Republican in the 1980s, but in the middle 1990s it went the other way: Both Bill Clinton and Senator Mary Landrieu carried the district in 1996, a critical factor in her narrow 5,788-vote statewide margin. But in 2000 George W. Bush carried the area by a comfortable margin, 54%–43%.

The congressman from the 4th district is Jim McCrery, a Republican first elected in 1988. McCrery grew up in Leesville, graduated from Louisiana Tech in Ruston (next door to Grambling, site of the football-famous, historically black college) and LSU Law School, and practiced law in Leesville and Shreveport. In 1981 he worked for Congressman Buddy Roemer, then a Democrat; later he joined Georgia Pacific. When Roemer was elected governor in 1987, McCrery ran as a Republican and won the special election 51%–49%. McCrery's toughest re-election race was in 1992, when the creation of the new black-majority 4th District put him in the 5th District with 16-year incumbent Jerry Huckaby, a conservative Democrat. But the district, with few black voters, was heavily Republican and Huckaby had 88 overdrafts on the House bank. McCrery weathered some negative personal attacks, led in the October primary 44%–29% and won the November runoff 63%–37%.

McCrery has compiled a mostly conservative voting record and has worked on major legislation from his seat on the Ways and Means Committee. Armed with the intuition that made him one of only 72 House members to vote against the disastrous 1988 catastrophic health care bill, he advanced a Republican alternative to the Clinton health care plan in 1994, capping deductibility of health insurance, opposing the Democrats' cost control measures, limiting medical malpractice and instituting medical savings accounts. Seven years later, he continued his innovative approach when he joined with liberal Democrat Jim McDermott of Ways and Means on a sweeping plan to replace employer-provided health insurance with a system for all individuals to find private insurance, coupled with mandatory pay increases to assist them and subsidies for the poor. "If we don't address escalating costs, we will end up with a government-run health-care system," McCrery warned. "I'm doing this to avoid a government takeover of health care, which is where I think we're headed." He worked on the Republicans' Medicare and prescription-drug alternatives and on the party task force to craft HMO reform. He favors individual investment accounts for Social Security. He has worked on local projects like completing I-49 and promoting I-69, the proposed Michigan-to-Mexico interstate, which is supposed to come through the northwest corner of Louisiana.

After running in four different districts in four elections, local politics settled down after 1996 and he has not faced serious opposition. McCrery became more active in national Republican campaigns, as vice chairman for incumbent retention at the National Republican Congressional Committee. Only four incumbents, three of them in left-leaning California, were defeated in November 2000, for which he may be due some credit.

When Bill Thomas became Ways and Means chairman in January 2001, McCrery, as one of his strong backers, was named chairman of the revived Subcommittee on Select Revenue Measures. Its wide-ranging jurisdiction permits McCrery to serve as a trouble-shooter, including liaison to fellow Louisianan Billy Tauzin, chairman of Energy and Commerce in what are likely to be serious turf fights between the two committees.

Redistricting will require the district to grow slightly larger, but will not make much difference politically.

Cook's Call _Safe._ On paper, this Shreveport-based district looks like it could be competitive. Clinton rolled up large margins here in 1992 and 1996 while Bush won the district in 2000 with 54%. But McCrery has a solid hold on this district and will be extremely difficult to dislodge. As one of the slower growing districts in the state, it will need to pick up some population in redistricting.

THE PEOPLE: Pop. 2000: 616,120; Pop. 1990: 602,692, up 2.2% 1990–2000. 62.4% White, 34% Black, 0.7% Asian, 0.8% Amer. Indian, 0.1% Hawaiian, 1.3% Two + races, 0.7% Other; 2.1% Hispanic Origin.

2000 Presidential Vote
Bush (R)	124,956	(54%)
Gore (D)	99,592	(43%)
Nader (Green)	1,866	(1%)
Others	3,342	(1%)

1996 Presidential Vote
Clinton (D)	122,729	(53%)
Dole (R)	92,741	(40%)
Perot (I)	17,525	(8%)

Rep. Jim McCrery (R)

Elected Apr. 1988, 7th term; b. Sept. 18, 1949, Shreveport; home, Shreveport; LA Tech. U., B.A. 1971, LA St. U., J.D. 1975; Methodist; married (Johnette).

Professional Career: Practicing atty. 1975–78; Asst. Shreveport City Atty., 1979–80; Legis. Dir., U.S. Rep. Buddy Roemer, 1981–84; Regional Mgr., Georgia-Pacific Corp., 1984–88.

DC Office: 2104 RHOB 20515, 202-225-2777; Fax: 202-225-8039; Web site: www.house.gov/mccrery.

District Offices: Leesville, 337-238-0778; Shreveport, 318-798-2254.

Committees: _Ways & Means_ (7th of 24 R): Health; Human Resources; Select Revenue Measures (Chmn.).

Group Ratings
	ADA	ACLU	AFS	LCV	CON	ITIC	NTU	COC	ACU	NTLC	CHC
2000	5	7	0	7	11	95	57	95	83	64	93
1999	0	—	0	0	21	—	53	96	80	—	—

National Journal Ratings
	1999 LIB —	1999 CONS		2000 LIB —	2000 CONS
Economic	0% —	84%		18% —	76%
Social	16% —	82%		32% —	67%
Foreign	23% —	73%		12% —	78%

Key Votes of the 106th Congress

1. Patient Bill of Rights N	5. Bar RU-486 $ for FDA Y	9. NATO War in Serbia N
2. Accelerate Min. Wage N	6. Display 10 Commandments Y	10. Perm. Trade with China Y
3. Strike Ban on Ergo. Stnd. N	7. Gun Show Bkgrnd. Checks N	11. Debt Relief for 3rd World N
4. Ovrd. Estate Tax Veto Y	8. Ban Part.-Birth Abortion Y	12. Drop Cuba Econ. Embargo N

Election Results

2000 primary	Jim McCrery (R)	122,678	(71%)	($574,127)
	Phillip R. Green (D)	43,600	(25%)	
	Other	7,689	(4%)	
1998 primary	Jim McCrery (R)	unopposed		($666,860)

FIFTH DISTRICT

Northeast Louisiana is perhaps the least known part of the state. Along the Mississippi River and the Red River and their dozens of tributaries, it was plantation country before the Civil War, with black majorities still in many parishes. Away from the larger rivers, it is hill country, places where small farmers scratched out a living on land connected to parish courthouses by dusty lanes. Such was Winn Parish, where Huey P. Long, the pivotal figure in modern Louisiana politics, was born in 1893, and from which he began his meteoric political career—elected governor in 1928, senator in 1930, a national figure threatening both parties when he was assassinated in 1935 in the new high-rise Capitol he built in Baton Rouge.

The 5th Congressional District contains much of this country, from the river parishes to the hills of Winn Parish. The biggest urban areas here, with fewer than 100,000 people each, are Monroe in the north and Alexandria in the south. Alexandria in Rapides Parish sits at the northernmost extension of Cajun, Catholic Louisiana, while Monroe is heavily WASP and Baptist; it is home to one of the world's leading Bible collections, assembled by an heir to an early Coca-Cola bottler. The district also includes East Carroll Parish, which is hemmed in by the Arkansas border to the north and the Mississippi River to the east; USA Today reported that more than half of parish residents lived in poverty in the mid-1990s, with an even higher rate in the parish's biggest town, Lake Providence.

This district was newly created for the 1996 election; the 1992 and 1994 districting plans each had a black-majority 4th District whose boundaries jutted here and there throughout northern Louisiana. This new 5th District has geographically regular boundaries and a black population of 33% in 2000. Politically, it has trended Republican, but there are pockets of Democratic strength in rural as well as urban areas. In 1996 it produced a small margin for Bill Clinton; in 2000 it voted by a larger margin for George W. Bush.

The congressman from the 5th District is John Cooksey, a Republican elected in 1996. Cooksey grew up next to his father's sawmill in Olla, and claims to have lived all his life within a mile of U.S. 165, which runs north and south through the district. He got undergraduate and medical degrees from LSU, served in the Air Force and was sent to northern Thailand during the Vietnam war. After a year of medical residency in New Orleans, he moved to Monroe in 1972 and practiced as an ophthalmologist. He traveled on medical missions five times to Kenya and raised money to set up an eye clinic there. He was a politically active Republican for years, but never ran for office until the new 5th District was created in 1996. It had no incumbent: Jim McCrery chose to run in the 4th, and Cleo Fields, at one time Louisiana's youngest legislator and the youngest member of Congress when he was elected in 1992, decided not to run. Two other serious candidates ran. Clyde Holloway, a Republican elected narrowly to the House three times in an Alexandria-based district, carried the area around Alexandria and got 27% of the vote in the September primary. Veteran state Representative Francis Thompson, a Democrat, carried the heavily black Mississippi River parishes, and got 28%; Cooksey carried Monroe and the northern parishes inland from the river, and won 34%. With two-thirds of the primary vote going to Republicans, Cooksey was obviously the favorite in the November runoff. While supporting most conservative positions, he took some original stands—tax credits to encourage people to buy American-made products, business tax credits for developing and creating vocational and technical training programs. Cooksey spent $107,000 of his own money and won 58%–42%, carrying every parish except those near the river and winning especially big margins in Monroe and Alexandria.

In the House, Cooksey has a mostly conservative voting record, though rather moderate on cultural issues; his distinctive stands often reflect his background as a physician. He refused to support the tobacco industry settlement and rejected the argument that Louisiana must support tobacco to get others to help sugar and rice. He supported the Norwood-Dingell patients' bill of rights, and was a proponent of the bill to waive antitrust laws to permit doctors and nurses to bargain collectively with health plans over their fees and coverage provisions, so that they can provide better services to patients. He filed his own proposal to give the medically uninsured a refundable tax credit to purchase health insurance. Although he called for cutting spending generally, he was not bashful about widening U.S. 165. On cultural issues, he showed his moderation when he voted against a ban on sales of sexually explicit or violent materials to children and against posting the Ten Commandments in public schools. He disliked the partisan tone of the House: "There's always going to be some partisan politics. . . . But some of the partisan politics has become too aggressive, too vindictive and too mean."

In 1996 Cooksey pledged to limit himself to three terms in the House. In early 1999, perhaps already thinking about a statewide race, he recruited New Orleans area ophthalmologist Monica Monica to run for Bob Livingston's House seat. In late 2000, Cooksey began campaigning against Senator Mary Landrieu, running newspaper ads across the state to increase his name recognition and fundraising, though he ruled out contributions from tobacco and gambling interests. He criticized Landrieu for siding with the National Organization for Women and the American Civil Liberties Union in opposing the confirmation of Attorney General John Ashcroft and for her criticism of George W. Bush's tax package.

Cooksey's departure from the House, combined with redistricting, makes it entirely possible that this district will be seriously contested by the Democrats in 2002. Marjorie McKeithen, granddaughter of Governor John McKeithen and daughter of longtime Secretary of State Fox McKeithen, who nearly defeated the 6th District's Richard Baker in 1998, has been mentioned as a candidate. Redistricting can make some difference here. The two northern Louisiana districts must both be expanded, and the parishes directly south of the current 5th lean Democratic. That means the 5th is likely to be at least a little bit more Democratic-leaning in 2002.

Cook's Call *Competitive.* Cooksey's decision to challenge Mary Landrieu leaves open a seat that could be seriously contested in 2002. By the numbers, this seat leans Republican: Bush got 59% here. But redistricting (this seat will need to pick up some population) could add some more Democratic leaning areas to the district. Already, Cooksey's Chief of Staff Lee Fletcher has announced he's running. Other Republicans include former Representative Clyde Holloway and state Senator Robert Barham. Democrat Charlie DeWitt, the speaker of the state House is also taking a look at the race.

THE PEOPLE: Pop. 2000: 610,398; Pop. 1990: 602,928, up 1.2% 1990–2000. 65.3% White, 32.6% Black, 0.5% Asian, 0.4% Amer. Indian, 0.7% Two+ races, 0.4% Other; 1.2% Hispanic Origin.

2000 Presidential Vote

Bush (R)	141,167	(59%)
Gore (D)	91,518	(38%)
Nader (Green)	1,997	(1%)
Others	5,081	(2%)

1996 Presidential Vote

Clinton (D)	132,407	(49%)
Dole (R)	113,846	(42%)
Perot (I)	22,994	(9%)

Rep. John Cooksey (R)

Elected 1996, 3d term; b. Aug. 20, 1941, Alexandria; home, Monroe; LA St. U., B.S. 1962, M.D. 1966, U. of TX, M.B.A. 1994; Methodist; married (Ann).

Military Career: Air Force, 1967–69 (Vietnam); Air Natl. Guard, 1969–72.

Professional Career: Ophthalmologist, 1972–96.

DC Office: 113 CHOB 20515, 202-225-8490; Fax: 202-225-5639; Web site: www.house.gov/cooksey.

District Offices: Alexandria, 318-448-1777; Monroe, 318-330-9998.

Committees: *Agriculture* (13th of 27 R): Department Operations, Oversight, Nutrition & Forestry. *International Relations* (17th of 26 R): Europe; Middle East & South Asia. *Transportation & Infrastructure* (17th of 42 R): Aviation; Economic Development, Public Buildings & Emergency Management.

Group Ratings

	ADA	ACLU	AFS	LCV	CON	ITIC	NTU	COC	ACU	NTLC	CHC
2000	0	50	0	14	19	94	53	87	73	73	73
1999	15	—	0	6	6	—	56	91	62	—	—

National Journal Ratings

	1999 LIB —	1999 CONS		2000 LIB —	2000 CONS
Economic	29%	71%		33%	66%
Social	48%	52%		36%	64%
Foreign	46%	54%		0%	88%

Key Votes of the 106th Congress

1. Patient Bill of Rights	Y	5. Bar RU-486 $ for FDA	Y	9. NATO War in Serbia	Y
2. Accelerate Min. Wage	*	6. Display 10 Commandments	N	10. Perm. Trade with China	Y
3. Strike Ban on Ergo. Stnd.	N	7. Gun Show Bkgrnd. Checks	N	11. Debt Relief for 3rd World	N
4. Ovrd. Estate Tax Veto	Y	8. Ban Part.-Birth Abortion	Y	12. Drop Cuba Econ. Embargo	*

Election Results

2000 primary	John Cooksey (R)	123,975	(69%)	($508,238)
	Roger Beall (D)	42,977	(24%)	
	Sam Houston Melton Jr. (D)	7,186	(4%)	
	Other	5,335	(3%)	
1998 primary	John Cooksey (R)	unopposed		($537,985)

SIXTH DISTRICT

Baton Rouge is the central node of Louisiana, on the boundary between the French-speaking, Catholic Cajun country and the heavily Baptist Deep South, its skyscraper Capitol and Exxon refinery sitting just beyond the levees that line the Mississippi River. Baton Rouge still bears the impress of the man who dominated Louisiana politics for much of the 20th Century, Huey P. Long. Here Long became governor at 36 in the old (and still-standing) Gothic Capitol, when Baton Rouge had only 30,000 people, and was assassinated in 1935 in the hallway of the 34-story Art Deco Capitol he built, next door to the Governor's Mansion, which he also built. To the south are the buildings of Louisiana State University, much of which he built, in an amazingly short time. Today Baton Rouge is the center of a metro area of 600,000, almost all on the east bank of the Mississippi, and reaching far inland to Livingston Parish; it is the home of the new Louisiana Technology Park, built by the state for $40 million in Huey-Long-like record time. Baton Rouge tries to maintain all of Louisiana's traditions; according to Clinton adviser James Carville, who comes from nearby Carville in Iberville Parish (where three generations of his family served as postmaster), it has "the best restaurants per capita of any city in the United States."

The 6th Congressional District of Louisiana is centered on Baton Rouge, running south to the "petroleum alley" parishes along the Mississippi and east to the Florida parishes—so called because, even after the United States purchased Louisiana, they were part of the West Florida colony retained by Spain until it was annexed in 1810. And it includes plantation parishes north along the Mississippi, with high black populations. Historically, all of this territory was Democratic. Baton Rouge in the 1980s moved toward the Republicans, and the Baton Rouge area has been politically marginal in the middle 1990s; in 1996 it voted for Bill Clinton and in 2000 for George W. Bush.

The congressman from the 6th District is Richard Baker, a Republican first elected in 1986. Baker has spent most of his adult life in public office. He came to Baton Rouge to attend LSU, then in 1972, at 23, was elected as a Democrat to the Louisiana House from a blue-collar district in Baton Rouge. He became a Republican in 1985, and in 1986, when Baton Rouge Republican Congressman Henson Moore ran for the Senate, Baker ran for the House and beat a Democratic state senator 51%–46%. In 1992 he was redistricted in the same district with Republican Congressman Clyde Holloway and was opposed as well by the Democratic mayor of Alexandria. The new district lines put Baker at a disadvantage, and he trailed 37%–33% in the September primary. But he won the November runoff 51%–49%, with 71% in his home territory of East Baton Rouge and Livingston parishes.

Baker has a conservative voting record and is chairman of the Capital Markets and Insurance Subcommittee of the Financial Services Committee. He worked on financial services deregulation, one of the most heavily lobbied issues in the 1990s; the issue was how, under what terms and conditions, to dismantle the wall separating banks and other institutions created by the Glass-Steagall Act of 1933. Baker generally favored deregulation, and served on the conference committee that finally reached agreement in November 1999. His conclusion: "We repealed the laws of the 1930s and got to about 1985. . . . We haven't quite gotten to 1999 yet." He has called for disclosure of exposure to risk by banks investing in hedge funds, but no direct regulation; he wants to prevent duplicate regulation of over-the-counter derivatives on commodities exchanges. He wants to reduce TVA's debt level. On local issues, he has worked to fund the Comite River Diversion Canal project and create the Cat Island National Wildlife Refuge in West Feliciana Parish.

Baker's greatest legislative enterprise has been to change the operation of the government-sponsored enterprises (GSEs) Fannie Mae and Freddie Mac, which purchase and securitize home mortgages. These are for-profit enterprises, indeed hugely profitmaking in recent years, yet the fact that they each have $2.25 billion lines of credit with the U.S. Treasury creates an impression in the marketplace that the government will bail them out if they become insolvent. Baker admits that they are well-managed and not at risk now, and argues that that is the best time for reform. The GSEs, he told *National Journal*, "claim to be sufficiently well capitalized, with no threat of any potential failure . . . If that's the case, you shouldn't have it both ways. You shouldn't have a conditional line of credit [from the Treasury], which creates the presumption in the market that you're backed by the full faith and credit of the United States government, when at the same time you're arguing that you're so safe and sound you don't need any regulatory oversight." In February 2000 Baker introduced legislation to create a new regulatory agency for the GSEs and terminate their line of credit, increase disclosure requirements, toughen capital mandates and give regulators more say in approving new activities.

Fannie Mae and Freddie Mac vigorously opposed the bill and predicted it would never pass. In a March hearing a Treasury undersecretary testified in favor of much of the bill, including repeal of the lines of credit. Sometimes tumultuous negotiations followed. In October they reached agreement. Fannie Mae and Freddie Mac agreed to increase their equity capital and subordinated debt to 4% of assets and to disclose more information to investors. By February 2001 Fannie Mae CEO Franklin Raines was praising Baker, but they still disagreed: Baker still wanted an independent regulator, while Raines was opposed. But it was clear that this obscure subcommittee chairman had made major policy changes affecting enormous capital markets.

All the while Baker was involved in another struggle. Banking Committee Chairman Jim Leach would reach the end of the three-term limit on his chairmanship after the 2000 election, and in late 1999 Baker announced that he would seek the chairmanship though he had less seniority than Financial Institutions Subcommittee Chairman Marge Roukema. Unusually, he got the support of Senate Banking Chairman Phil Gramm. But in the days after the November 2000 election, Baker presented a fallback position to the Republican leadership. An even bigger chairmanship struggle was going on in the Commerce Committee, between Louisiana's Billy Tauzin and Mike Oxley. Baker would support Oxley for the Banking Committee chairmanship, with Commerce's jurisdiction over securities and insurance transferred to Banking. Baker would keep his Financial Services subcommittee chair plus the securities jurisdiction; Roukema would get another subcommittee. And so it happened: Baker was in a position to continue his work on the GSEs, and to work on regulation of insurance companies, securities firms and capital markets.

Baker almost missed his chance at this legislative activity in the election of 1998. He was challenged then by Democrat Marjorie McKeithen, the granddaughter of former Governor (1964–72) John McKeithen, whom she joined in law practice in 1995, and daughter of Secretary of State Fox McKeithen, whose first campaign she managed at 20 in 1986. Strongly opposed to gun control and abortion, McKeithen knocked on 40,000 doors and charmed voters with her north Louisiana accent. She criticized Baker for voting to raise his own pay $30,000 while voting against increases in the minimum wage. Baker attacked her for being a trial lawyer and for not voting consistently in local elections. Baker raised $1.4 million, McKeithen almost half that. In the end, Baker squeaked by, winning 50.7%–49.3%. He lost the outlying parishes, with their large black percentages, but carried East Baton Rouge and Livingston Parishes with 53% and 57%.

McKeithen quickly let it be known she would probably run again, and Baker seemed to face another tough race. Then she decided not to run, and Democrats had trouble finding another candidate. Baker, now more visible in the district, beat a little-known Democrat 68%–30%. Redistricting is unlikely to hurt him, though the legislature is controlled by Democrats and Republican Governor Mike Foster has little in the way of partisan instinct. The 6th is now the state's largest district, in need of shedding 45,000 people. The likeliest parishes to go are Pointe Coupee, West Baton Rouge and Iberville, where McKeithen won big majorities; Baker is likely to do well as the district contracts to East Baton Rouge and Livingston Parishes and just a few parishes beyond.

Cook's Call *Potentially Competitive.* Baker dodged a bullet in 2000 when Democrat Marjorie McKeithen decided not to challenge him. As the fastest growing district in the state, it will have to contract some in redistricting. But Baker, who has survived redistricting in 1992 and 1996 (which significantly increased the black population here), is no stranger to tough races.

THE PEOPLE: Pop. 2000: 683,536; Pop. 1990: 602,764, up 13.4% 1990–2000. 63.6% White, 33.6% Black, 1.3% Asian, 0.2% Amer. Indian, 0.8% Two+ races, 0.4% Other; 1.6% Hispanic Origin.

2000 Presidential Vote			1996 Presidential Vote		
Bush (R)	150,887	(54%)	Clinton (D)	142,156	(50%)
Gore (D)	123,241	(44%)	Dole (R)	121,851	(43%)
Nader (Green)	3,269	(1%)	Perot (I)	19,222	(7%)
Others	3,124	(1%)			

Rep. Richard H. Baker (R)

Elected 1986, 8th term; b. May 22, 1948, New Orleans; home, Baton Rouge; LA St. U., B.A. 1971; United Methodist; married (Kay).

Elected Office: LA House of Reps., 1972–86.

Professional Career: Real estate developer, 1972–86.

DC Office: 341 CHOB 20515, 202-225-3901; Fax: 202-225-7313; Web site: www.house.gov/baker.

District Office: Baton Rouge, 225-929-7711.

Committees: *Financial Services* (5th of 37 R): Capital Markets, Insurance & Government Sponsored Enterprises (Chmn.); Financial Institutions & Consumer Credit; International Monetary Policy & Trade. *Transportation*

& Infrastructure (14th of 42 R): Aviation; Highways & Transit; Water Resources & Environment. *Veterans' Affairs* (14th of 17 R): Health.

Group Ratings

	ADA	ACLU	AFS	LCV	CON	ITIC	NTU	COC	ACU	NTLC	CHC
2000	0	14	0	7	20	100	59	85	75	73	93
1999	0	—	0	0	2	—	57	96	80	—	—

National Journal Ratings

	1999 LIB	—	1999 CONS		2000 LIB	—	2000 CONS
Economic	0%	—	84%		18%	—	76%
Social	10%	—	85%		23%	—	74%
Foreign	10%	—	86%		0%	—	88%

Key Votes of the 106th Congress

1. Patient Bill of Rights	N	5. Bar RU-486 $ for FDA	Y	9. NATO War in Serbia	N
2. Accelerate Min. Wage	N	6. Display 10 Commandments	Y	10. Perm. Trade with China	Y
3. Strike Ban on Ergo. Stnd.	N	7. Gun Show Bkgrnd. Checks	N	11. Debt Relief for 3rd World	N
4. Ovrd. Estate Tax Veto	Y	8. Ban Part.-Birth Abortion	Y	12. Drop Cuba Econ. Embargo	N

Election Results

2000 primary	Richard H. Baker (R)	165,637	(68%)	($916,205)
	Kathy J. Rogillio (D)	72,192	(30%)	
	Other	5,649	(2%)	
1998 primary	Richard H. Baker (R)	97,044	(51%)	($1,444,171)
	Marjorie McKeithen (D)	94,201	(49%)	($664,611)

SEVENTH DISTRICT

More than 200 years ago, French-speaking settlers were forced to leave their land of Acadie, which the British had taken over and renamed Nova Scotia, and make their way to the wetlands of southern Louisiana. Here, without much notice, they built steep-roofed houses to slough off non-existent snow and adapted French cuisine to the crawfish and muskrat they found in abundance in the pelican-tended swamps. The heart of the Cajun country is around Lafayette, just west of the Atchafalaya Basin, where Mississippi waters pour through bayous and canals, with only occasional bits of solid land visible on the 30-mile section of Interstate 10 built on elevated stilts. For half a century the Cajun country thrived, thanks to the oil and gas plentiful here and just off shore in the Gulf of Mexico; oil rigs are common, and every once in a while the swampy foliage parts to reveal a giant refinery or petrochemical plant. In the past two decades, Cajun pride has grown: Cajun French is surviving decades of efforts to eliminate it, Cajun music—and its black-influenced variant, zydeco—are popular here and nationally, while spicy Cajun cooking has become a tourist attraction here and, in watered-down form, familiar all over the United States. Both Cajun culture and the oil business are particularly evident in Lafayette, with its Acadian Village and plethora of oil exploration firms. Lafayette features its annual *Festivals Acadiens* to celebrate music, food and crafts. Unlike New Orleans, its Mardi Gras reveries do not require anti-discrimination statements; the result has been an all-white parade and an all-black parade.

The oil price crash of the middle 1980s hit the Cajun country hard. Rising expectations, and the giddy sense that the oil industry promised lasting prosperity, suddenly collapsed, leaving borrowers overextended and ordinary homeowners unable to maintain the standard of living they expected. Politically, the Cajun country seemed to move then toward national Democrats, whom it had shunned because their cultural liberalism seemed alien to the Cajun tradition of respecting the authority of Church and state while tolerating a certain amount of *laissez les bons temps rouler* spirit. The Cajun country voted for Bill Clinton in 1992 and 1996, as it had voted for Louisiana's foremost Cajun politician, Edwin Edwards, who was elected governor four times. But George W. Bush won easily here, perhaps benefiting from his neighboring-state affinity, or from his opposition to abortion, which is anathema in heavily Catholic Acadiana.

The 7th Congressional District of Louisiana covers much of the Cajun country, from Lafayette and the Atchafalaya west along I-10 to Lake Charles and the Texas border. Redistricted three times in the 1990s, its boundaries have smoothed out. It is the descendant of the district represented from 1965–86 by Edwin Edwards and then John Breaux, both from the small city of Crowley in Acadia Parish, who became governor and senator respectively.

The congressman from the 7th District now is Chris John, a Democrat elected in 1996. John grew up in Crowley, which seems to have produced more prominent politicians per capita than any other place in America. After graduating from LSU he went into the family trucking business. In 1987, at 27, he was elected to the seat in the Louisiana House his father had once held, and served two four-year terms, chairing the Acadiana delegation. In 1996 the 7th District seat opened when Jimmy Hayes, a 10-year incumbent who had switched to the Republican Party in December 1995, ran for the Senate; he ended up a distant fifth in the primary.

A field of eight candidates ran in the open primary to replace Hayes. John's chief opponents turned out to be Republican David Thibodaux, an English professor at the University of Southwestern Louisiana who called for abolishing the Internal Revenue Service and the Department of Education, and Democrat Hunter Lundy, a maritime lawyer from Lake Charles and an anti-abortion religious conservative. John campaigned as tough on crime and in the first round, he led with 26%. Thibodaux seemed to come in second, 29 votes ahead of Lundy, but a recount gave second place to Lundy by 8 votes; Thibodaux protested and filed suit, to no avail. This meant that Democrats knew they had picked up one House seat even before the voters went to the polls in November. Neither candidate showed much support for national Democratic principles. John was endorsed by the House Blue Dog Democrats and in the closing days by Jimmy Hayes and Billy Tauzin, both former Democrats. The result came down to geography. Lundy led 63%–37% in the parishes west of the Mermenteau River, but they cast only 36% of the district's votes, and John led 62%–38% in the parishes to the east, for a 53%–47% win.

John has been a Blue Dog Democrat with a moderate voting record. On the Agriculture Committee he sought to encourage exports and looked after rice farmers (his family owns two rice farms); on Resources, he worked to protect estuaries, fishlands and marshlands. He sponsored Outer Continental Shelf revenue-sharing, soon backed by the entire Louisiana delegation; to get more support it included the Great Lakes. He helped to broker the Resources Committee's bipartisan deal for an expanded CARA conservation fund; that bill died in 2000 but it led to significantly enhanced appropriations for a similar purpose. John worked with John Dingell—a fellow sportsman—to weaken gun-control proposals. He opposed fast track trade negotiating authority, months after Fruit of the Loom closed some local plants and moved production abroad, but he later voted for permanent normal trade relations with China. He opposed impeachment because he believed Bill Clinton "had not breached national security," and added that "the 7th District is a mixed bag of philosophic thought." In January 2001, John won a seat on the Commerce Committee, where he is likely to work closely with his neighbor, Chairman Billy Tauzin, and became co-chairman of the Blue Dogs, which he hoped would be a broker for bipartisanship. In March 2001 he opposed George W. Bush's income tax cut but voted for the final budget resolution in May, and with Republicans to repeal Bill Clinton's ergonomics regulations.

Redistricting must remove 25,000 people from the district, and some Republicans were arguing that removal of part of heavily Democratic St. Landry Parish could jeopardize John's hold on the seat. But any change is likely to be very marginal. As one of only two Democratic congressmen in Louisiana, John has been mentioned as a candidate for governor in 2003.

Cook's Call *Safe.* Though this district is by no means a slam-dunk for a Democrat (Bush won the district in 2000 by 13%, though Clinton won here easily in 1992 and 1996), John is a good match for the district and will be tough to beat. When the seat opens up, however, it will certainly be heavily contested.

THE PEOPLE: Pop. 2000: 663,992; Pop. 1990: 603,078, up 10.1% 1990–2000. 72.7% White, 25% Black, 0.7% Asian, 0.3% Amer. Indian, 0.8% Two+ races, 0.4% Other; 1.5% Hispanic Origin.

2000 Presidential Vote

Bush (R)	146,125	(55%)
Gore (D)	111,656	(42%)
Nader (Green)	3,567	(1%)
Others	4,228	(2%)

1996 Presidential Vote

Clinton (D)	106,034	(54%)
Dole (R)	70,149	(36%)
Perot (I)	19,644	(10%)

Rep. Chris John (D)

Elected 1996, 3d term; b. Jan. 5, 1960, Crowley; home, Crowley; LA St. U., B.A. 1982; Catholic; married (Payton).

Elected Office: Crowley City Cncl., 1983–87; LA House of Reps., 1987–95.

Professional Career: Co-owner, John N. John Truckline, 1983–96.

DC Office: 1504 LHOB 20515, 202-225-2031; Fax: 202-225-5724; Web site: www.house.gov/john.

District Offices: Lafayette, 337-235-6322; Lake Charles, 337-433-1747.

Committees: *Energy & Commerce* (25th of 26 D): Commerce, Trade & Consumer Protection; Energy & Air Quality; Oversight & Investigations.

Group Ratings

	ADA	ACLU	AFS	LCV	CON	ITIC	NTU	COC	ACU	NTLC	CHC
2000	30	21	28	29	8	94	36	90	41	24	67
1999	45	—	83	0	18	—	19	83	50	—	—

National Journal Ratings

	1999 LIB	—	1999 CONS		2000 LIB	—	2000 CONS
Economic	53%	—	47%		53%	—	46%
Social	36%	—	63%		23%	—	74%
Foreign	59%	—	41%		62%	—	38%

Key Votes of the 106th Congress

1. Patient Bill of Rights	Y	5. Bar RU-486 $ for FDA	Y	9. NATO War in Serbia	*
2. Accelerate Min. Wage	Y	6. Display 10 Commandments	Y	10. Perm. Trade with China	Y
3. Strike Ban on Ergo. Stnd.	N	7. Gun Show Bkgrnd. Checks	N	11. Debt Relief for 3rd World	Y
4. Ovrd. Estate Tax Veto	Y	8. Ban Part.-Birth Abortion	Y	12. Drop Cuba Econ. Embargo	*

Election Results

2000 primary	Chris John (D)	152,796	(83%)	($627,685)
	Michael P. Harris (LIB)	30,687	(17%)	
1998 primary	Chris John (D)	unopposed		($287,732)

★ MAINE ★

M aine is a state with a distinctive personality—ornery, contrary-minded, almost bullheaded, rough-hewn. It is the state closest geographically to Europe, but it was not heavily settled until the mid-19th Century, and then by people coming from the south and west—the opposite of America's usual pattern. In an urbanizing and rapidly changing country, Maine was famous for its pointed firs and steady habits, with a few dozen small factory and mill towns but nothing like a major metropolis. Maine grew in a rush and then mostly stopped: There were 600,000 people here in 1860 and its population did not top 1 million until the 1970s. Then, the tremors of the New England high-tech booms of the 1980s and 1990s reverberated up I-95 and shook Maine. The simple, back-to-nature Yankee style came into vogue. The antique dockside buildings on Portland's waterfront were restored and an old-style Public Market was constructed; the Maine Mall expanded and saw office parks spring up nearby, a miniature edge city; real estate prices rose by hundreds of percents, not just in vacation coves, but in Portland and small towns that had never considered themselves picturesque. The L.L. Bean headquarters in Freeport, open 24 hours a day, 365 days a year, symbolized the boom: the two chaste initials and the Anglo-Saxon mono-syllable suggesting the dry understatement of Down East Yankees; the 24-hour-a-day schedule recalling the hard work needed to eke out a living from the cold waters of the North Atlantic to the pine-covered north woods; the commercial success of the enterprise a prime example of Maine's unexpected 1980s boom.

In the process Maine's economy was transformed. It lost jobs in shoes, chicken processing, papermaking and timber, but gained in call centers, tourism and high-tech. By mid-2000 unemployment was down to 3.6%, and 1.7% in Portland's Cumberland County; $8 an hour jobs were going begging. Shoe factory employment fell from 17,000 to 6,000 from 1983 to 1999, while telephone call center employment rose from zero to 10,000. The Grand Banks and lobster grounds have been overfished, and scratching small Maine boiling potatoes out of the soil of Aroostook County has become harder: The nation's top potato producer 50 years ago, Maine fell to eighth place in the 1990s, even as national consumption rose by 15%. By the late 1990s biotech out-produced lobster fishing and potato harvesting combined. Paper mill towns like Millinocket now stand half empty, while intersections around Portland are jammed with cars waiting for the green arrow so they can turn into the mall. Tourism continues to be the biggest business here, and Bath Iron Works, long the state's largest private employer, has a long-term contract to build 21 *Arleigh Burke* Class Naval destroyers, the work partly of former Senator and Defense Secretary William Cohen. But it is the new economy that undergirds Maine's flannel-shirt lifestyle and its fierce pride.

Up through 1958, Maine held state elections in September, a date originally chosen because it followed the state's early harvest; in the days before polls, the results here were taken as a gauge of national partisan movement—hence the saying, "As Maine goes, so goes the nation." However, in September 1936, Maine voted 56% for Republican Governor Lewis Barrows and in November only Maine and Vermont voted for Alf Landon over Franklin Roosevelt, prompting Roosevelt's campaign manager to observe, "As Maine goes, so goes Vermont." Maine's adherence to flinty Yankee Republicanism and Prohibition was echoed almost nowhere else in the nation. Since then, it has voted for the loser in the close presidential elections of 1948, 1960, 1968, 1976 and 2000—a record equalled by no other state. In the recession years, Maine distinguished itself by casting the nation's highest percentages for Ross Perot, 30% in 1992 and 14% in 1996, and in 1994 and 1998 it elected independent (and former Democrat) Angus King governor. This was not without precedent: Maine elected another independent governor, James Longley, in 1974.

If Maine's tradition-minded Yankees kept the state Republican long after the nation embraced the New Deal, the sons and daughters of its ethnics—Irish, French Canadian, Greek and Arab immigrants have come to equal the numbers of pure WASPs (though these new Mainers in many ways share traditional Yankee traits and values)—made the Democrats competitive, perhaps even dominant, here in the 1980s as they were losing ground in the rest of the nation. But as the economy changed, these differences became less important. Ticket-splitting is very much the

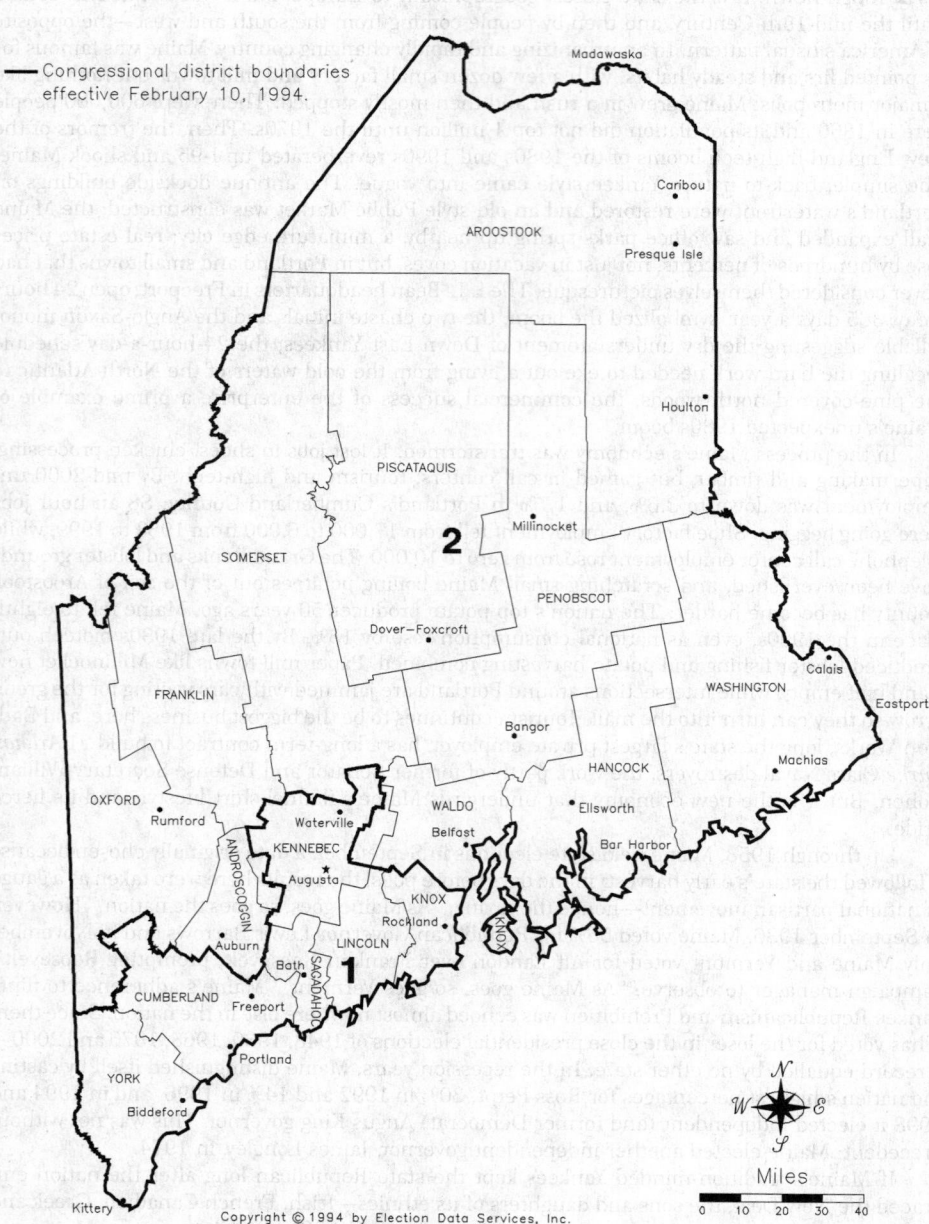

Congressional district boundaries
effective February 10, 1994.

Madawaska

Caribou

AROOSTOOK

Presque Isle

Houlton

PISCATAQUIS

Millinocket

SOMERSET

PENOBSCOT

Dover—Foxcroft

2

Calais

FRANKLIN

WASHINGTON

Eastport

Bangor

Machias

HANCOCK

OXFORD

WALDO

Rumford

Waterville

Belfast

Ellsworth

Bar Harbor

ANDROSCOGGIN

KENNEBEC

Augusta

KNOX

Auburn

Rockland

KNOX

LINCOLN

SAGADAHOC

Bath

1

CUMBERLAND

Freeport

Portland

YORK

Biddeford

Kittery

N
W　　E
S

Miles

0　10　20　30　40

norm here. In 2000 Maine voted 49%–44% for Al Gore, 69%–31% for Republican Senator Olympia Snowe and 66%–32% Democratic in its two House races. Democrats gained seats in the state House, Republicans in the state Senate; in the 1990s Maine has had more partisan turnover in its state legislative seats than any other state; in its small seats (average population of a state House seat is 8,461) Mainers vote for the person, not the party. Protestants gave Bush a 6% margin; Catholics gave Gore a 5% margin: the old religious polarization is gone. Who owns the future? Those with more education voted for Gore, a good sign for Democrats in an increasingly educated country. But voters under 30 were carried by Bush, a good sign for Republicans. Maine is up for grabs.

As the economy changed, Maine moved toward a consensus on how to balance economic growth and preserve the environment. Maine's environment-conscious newcomers have made this a good market for natural toothpaste, organic baby food and canvas bags rather than paper or plastic at the supermarket. It was the first state to ban the juicebox as insufficiently biodegradable and recycles liquor bottles. In 1996 and 1997 Maine voters rejected ballot propositions, one sponsored by environmentalists and one by paper companies, to ban clearcutting of forests and to limit clearcutting and set up 10,000 acres of public land for conservation. But private interests have moved as the political process stumbled. In December 1998 the Nature Conservancy bought 185,000 acres from International Paper for $35 million, just a week after conservationists purchased 300,000 acres in New Hampshire, Vermont and northern New York: moves to protect the Northern Appalachian Boreal Forest. In March 2001 the Pingree family agreed to sell conservation easements on 762,000 acres (more land than Rhode Island) to the New England Forestry Foundation for $28 million; King passed a $50 million bond issue, to be matched by $25 million in private contributions, to buy land. In November 1997 the tiny Edwards Dam on the Kennebec River was ordered removed, one of the first decisions to dismantle a hydroelectric dam to protect fish. On cultural issues, Maine voters have been wary of change. By narrow margins they rejected gay rights initiatives in 1998 and 2000; in 1999 they rejected a partial-birth abortion ban but endorsed medical marijuana; in 2000 they rejected physician-assisted suicide. Some change must come: King has set up a commission to force counties to change geographic place names which include the word "squaw"; for reasons not clear, Piscataquis County substituted "moose." And history has its claims. Maine and New Hampshire headed to court to decide which owns the Portsmouth Naval Shipyard, which sits on a mid-river island between the states; the Supreme Court's decision was based on a decree entered by King George II in 1740 that the New Hampshire-Maine border is in the middle of the Piscataqua River, which puts the shipyard within Maine's boundary.

Governor Angus King, elected governor of Maine in 1994 and 1998, grew up in Virginia, moved to Maine after law school to work for Pine Tree Legal Assistance in Skowhegan, worked for Senator William Hathaway in the 1970s, then practiced law and started his own energy conservation business, which he sold for $20 million in January 1994. For 18 years he hosted Maine Public Television's "MaineWatch." So he was as well-positioned to run as any independent could be: familiar with issues, capable of heavily self-financing a campaign, experienced at projecting his message over television. For several years Maine politics centered on deadlocks between Republican Governor John McKernan and Democratic legislators. King, originally a Democrat, had come to believe that "sometimes the best thing the government can do is get out of the way." He attacked high taxes, clumsy government meddling in business, and called for specific cuts. He spent $750,000 of his own money and raised about as much from others. He overshadowed Republican nominee (now Senator) Susan Collins, a former aide to then-Senator William Cohen, and he contrasted sharply with the partisan Democrat Joseph Brennan, who was elected governor in 1978 and 1982 and lost narrowly in 1990. King pulled even in the polls and won with 35% to Brennan's 34%, Collins's 23% and 6% for a Green Party candidate. King ran stronger with Republicans than Democrats and did well among Perot voters; he ran his best with high-education and high-income voters.

King is a high-energy, high-tech governor, wearing a pager and working on his laptop while on the road. He says he spends 50% to 75% of his time on economic development: "That's why I ran. I saw the Maine economy going down the tubes. And I didn't think traditional political solutions were going to fix it." He calls for more infrastructure and lower taxes, better education and no new forms of gambling: "It's a tax on the poor. It sucks money out of the economy." He cut the state budget and work force, reduced the cost of workmen's compensation and reduced environmental permit delays from nine months to 45 days, helping to attract employers like National Semiconductor. He accepted Republicans' future income tax cut in return for a property tax exemption for business machinery and equipment. He backed a children's health care plan which reduced the percentage of uninsured children to 6%. He opposed a plan for free tuition for freshmen in state colleges and backed cheaper college loans from the non-profit Maine Education Services. He backed a big increase giving Maine the nation's fourth-highest cigarette tax.

On the environment, King staked out positions between extremes with varying success. He opposed the ban on clearcutting, but his attempts in 1997 and 1998 to bring experts together on compromise measures were rejected 53%–47%, by a coalition of Greens and property rights advocates. In June 1997 he signed a bill imposing tight controls on paper mills' dioxin discharges into rivers and celebrated by jumping fully clothed into the Kennebec River. He opted out of an EPA plan for reducing vehicle emissions and barred the use of MTBE in gasoline. In 1999 he pushed a $50 million bond issue, to be matched by $25 million in private contributions, to buy up land.

In 1998 King campaigned for "The Maine Agenda" including a community college system and $25 million a year for research and development. His job approval rating ranged up to 86% and he won easily, with 59% of the vote, to 19% for the Republican, 12% for the Democrat (the same character who revealed George W. Bush's 24-year-old drunk driving arrest the Friday before the 2000 election), 7% for the Green Party candidate and 4% for the Taxpayers Party candidate. In prosperous southern and western counties, King won between 61% and 65% of the vote; in less prosperous northern and eastern counties, he won between 45% and 54%.

Perhaps the most notable legislation of King's next two years was the law to have the state leverage its buying clout to negotiate lower prices on prescription drugs for people without Medicaid or private health insurance, and impose price caps if companies don't comply by 2003. It was overturned by a federal judge in October 2000, but the state won an appeal in May 2001. King rejected a version which would have pegged prices the same as in Canada. Legislators also passed a bill allowing patients to sue health insurers. King pressed for a $50 million endowment to buy laptop computers for every Maine seventh-grader; legislators hated the idea, but he got a $30 million endowment for school technology with the possibility of $20 million more. He vetoed a Democratic bill to tax Social Security pensions. He proposed a five cent gas tax increase and got three. He challenged the EPA listing of Maine salmon as an endangered species, on the grounds that it is not a separate species. King is not eligible to run for a third term in 2002.

Cook's Call *Competitive.* Congressman John Baldacci is seen as the Democratic frontrunner, while Republicans appear likely to host a crowded primary. In keeping with Maine's tradition of political independence, Central Maine Power President David Flanagan and state Senator Mayor John Jenkins have been exploring third-party bids. While Maine has Democratic leanings giving them the edge going into the race, it should be competitive .

Senior Senator Olympia Snowe is a Republican elected in 1994. Snowe grew up in Auburn and worked as a legislative staffer after college; in 1973, after her husband, state Representative Peter Snowe, died in an auto accident, she was elected to his seat. In 1978, when then-Congressman William Cohen ran for the Senate, she ran for the House in the northern 2d District, and won handily. She had a moderate record and won by large margins in the 1980s but more narrowly in the 1990s; in 1989 she married Governor John McKernan, her former House colleague. Her voting record has been around the middle of the Senate; she is one of the Republicans who votes fairly often with Democrats, on issues including campaign finance, the minimum wage, missile defense and gun control. When Senator George Mitchell announced his retirement in March 1994, Snowe decided instantly to run. Immediately she went on the attack against her obvious Democratic opponent, 1st District Congressman Tom Andrews, whose winning margin two years before had been 107,000 votes, while hers was only 22,000. Snowe attacked him hard for voting for the bill that closed Loring Air Force Base in northern Maine and for opposing the balanced budget amendment. She won 60%–36%, carrying every county, losing only the cities of Portland and Lewiston and a few mill towns.

In the Senate she was the least conservative of the 11 freshman Republicans elected in 1994. She has supported Republican positions on many economic issues, but also has backed abortion rights and family leave. Her record on foreign and defense issues has been solidly conservative. She was one of the few Republicans to support the Clinton administration EPA's air-quality standards. On campaign finance in March 1998, she advanced a proposal to regulate ads that mention a candidate's name 60 days before a general election, but she insisted on the provision, an anathema to Democrats, to ban unions from spending their members' dues money on politics without their permission. On impeachment, she supported Republican positions on most issues, and worked with Democrats to come up with a compromise; she and Maine colleague Susan Collins proposed that the Senate vote first on a "finding of fact" describing Clinton's conduct and then separately on whether he should be removed from office. It was not successful, and Snowe voted against impeachment. In November 1999 she and Louisiana Democrat John Breaux tried to revive the Centrist Coalition. "Everything up here is very separate, very divided. There's no instrument to break down those walls of separateness. It is degrading the Senate. I hear it at home. It has not gone unnoticed by the public."

Snowe has taken a lead role on many women's health care issues. In July 2000 she sponsored a $200 million appropriation for women's health research, with $175 million for breast cancer, $12 million for ovarian cancer and $6 million for osteoperosis. She and Dianne Feinstein have sponsored the special stamp for breast cancer funding. In 1998 she co-sponsored with Harry Reid a bill that would require insurance companies to pay for women's contraceptives. In 1999 she pushed a bill to allow mastectomy patients to remain in the hospital as long as a doctor prescribes. In 2000 she sponsored a bill to extend osteoperosis screening to all Medicare recipients. With Edward Kennedy, she worked in 2000 to extend prescription drug coverage to military retirees through the military Tricare program. Child support enforcement is one of Snowe's major causes, and on the welfare bill she called for retaining some federal role in Medicaid, and helped insert a provision requiring states to spend at least 80% of their old budgets and some $3 billion for child care programs.

Since 1997 Snowe has served on Armed Services. She took the lead in opposing the recommendation of the commission headed by former Senator Nancy Kassebaum Baker to end gender-integrated basic training. She has been a backer of missile defense and the resolution she introduced with Democrat Mary Landrieu declaring it U.S. policy to deploy a ballistic missile system as soon as "technologically possible" was passed 99–0 in March 1999. She has championed the DDG-51 built at the Bath Iron Works and has worked to make available to a local building authority the former Cutler Navy base. For the 107th Congress, Snowe moved from Armed Services to the Finance Committee.

She has worked on many local issues, establishing a pilot $25 million fishing vessel buyback, passing a "Maine Lights" program to preserve historic Maine lighthouses, working to ban lobster dragging. In 2000 she worked for $10 million for fishermen who voluntarily agree to stop fishing in depleted waters and, with Collins, got $5 million for Atlantic salmon habitat protection. But she opposed the designation of the Atlantic salmon as an endangered species on the grounds that Maine rivers have been restocked so often that the fish there are no longer endangered. She and Vermont's Patrick Leahy sponsored a bill for controlling mercury pollution, a pressing issue in some parts of Maine.

Snowe approached the 2000 campaign with very high job approval ratings. She received vigorous opposition from state Senate President Mark Lawrence, who campaigned in support of Maine's prescription drug law and charged that Snowe had voted against a bill which would have provided $97 million for school construction in Maine. But it was no contest. Snowe was reelected 69%–31%, this time carrying even Portland and Lewiston, and trailing only in a few small isolated communities.

Junior Senator Susan Collins, Maine's junior Republican senator, was elected in 1996, the first time she won elective office. She grew up in Caribou, in potato-growing Aroostook County, about as far northeast as you can get in the United States, closer to the capitals of New Brunswick and Quebec than to the capital of Maine. Her family is in the lumber business, and also in politics: Her father was a state senator, her mother a mayor and her uncle a state Supreme Court justice. Right after college, she got a job as an intern with William Cohen, then a congressman on the Judiciary Committee who voted to impeach Richard Nixon. She was a Cohen staffer for 12 years and served as the staff director for the Senate Subcommittee on Oversight of Government Management on Governmental Affairs, which Cohen chaired from 1981–87. After Republicans lost their majority, Collins returned to Maine to work five years for Governor John McKernan as a financial regulation commissioner. In 1992 she was New England administrator of the Small Business Administration, and by 1994 she had announced her candidacy for governor. It was a disastrous campaign: She won the Republican nomination, but was overshadowed by independent Angus King, and ran third, with only 23% of the vote. She then became the executive director of the Husson College Center for Family Business.

Then in January 1996 Cohen surprised almost everybody by announcing he would retire from the Senate—almost as big a surprise as his selection as Defense secretary by Bill Clinton a year later. But there was a precedent in Maine for a third-place gubernatorial finisher to be elected senator: George Mitchell was similarly humiliated in 1974, then, after being appointed senator in 1980, won smashing victories in 1982 and 1988. The most visible candidate in the Republican primary was Robert Monks, an entrepreneur and business owner who had run losing races against two senators, Margaret Chase Smith in the 1972 primary and Edmund Muskie in the 1976 general. In 1996 he spent $2.1 million—a huge sum for a Maine primary—but got nowhere. Collins promoted her similarity to Olympia Snowe and Cohen, and called for a balanced budget amendment, line-item veto and term limits (and pledged to serve no more than two terms). She won the primary with 56%, carrying at least 50% in every county, to 31% for John Hathaway and only 13% for Monks.

The other familiar face belonged to Democrat Joseph Brennan, a product of working class Portland, first elected to the legislature in 1964, elected governor in 1978 and 1982, then to Congress in 1986 and 1988. But he lost races for governor in 1990 and 1994, with 44% and 34% of the vote, and he was called, somewhat unfairly, "an old-time, backroom Democratic politician" by a Democratic activist. The going was uphill: More votes were cast in the Republican primary than the Democratic for the first time since 1982; Democrats had topped 50% in governor races only once since 1966; Governor Angus King's independent platform in 1994 was much more Republican than Democratic. Brennan attacked Collins for backing only a 50-cent minimum wage increase, wanting to increase estate tax exemptions from $600,000 to $1 million, and for favoring repeal of the assault weapons ban. Collins responded by reiterating her stands and citing her experience, and added, "The next time you hear Joe speak, just close your eyes and ask yourself what year you're in. It could be 1964, the year he first ran. The world has changed, but Joe Brennan's ideas haven't." Collins raised much more money and won 49%–44%, losing very narrowly the counties around Portland, Lewiston, and Augusta, and carrying everything else. Interestingly, she led among men and he led among women; Brennan ran strongly among the elderly, Collins among college graduates—suggesting that she was more the wave of the future.

Collins has compiled a middle-of-the-Senate voting record; she has joined most Democrats on issues including the 1999 tax cut, campaign finance regulation and the partial-birth abortion ban. She has generally been quieter than Olympia Snowe, but their records are much the same, and Collins was if anything more visible during the impeachment process. She read history and constitutional law, coming up with an obscure article that argued the Senate could vote on findings of fact separately from removal; she and Snowe pushed a plan to have such separate votes, to no avail. She said that much of the evidence weighed against Clinton, but in the end voted against removal. Her first great cause in the Senate was campaign finance reform; she was beaten by a millionaire in 1994, faced two of them in the 1996 primary and had only meager finances herself "When I ran for the Senate, I seriously debated whether I could afford to keep my $160-a-month health insurance," she said. She said that limitations on self-financing candidates were a "cornerstone" of any reform for her. These limits weren't included in the bill (they are plainly unconstitutional under *Buckley v. Valeo*), but Russ Feingold persuaded her to vote for the campaign finance bill he was sponsoring with John McCain, despite heavy pressure from Majority Leader

Trent Lott. "I do consider myself to be a good Republican," she said at one point. "I'm just one of those troublesome New England Republicans."

Troublesome to the tobacco industry, at least: In 1997 she and Richard Durbin sponsored an amendment that made settlement costs non-deductible, costing the industry $50 billion. And troublesome to both parties: She insisted that investigations of campaign finances should look at misdeeds of both parties, though there was evidence of far more violations by the Clinton-Gore campaign; at the Fred Thompson hearings on campaign finance, she also probed deftly at some of those, spotlighting the Buddhist temple fundraiser. Right off she became chairwoman of Governmental Affairs' Permanent Subcommittee on Investigations and probed into Medicare fraud, investment scams, unsafe food, Internet ripoffs and fraudulent telephone billing—slamming and cramming—day trading, direct mail sweepstakes, property flipping, lead paint. Collins sponsored with Jay Rockefeller a bill for better counseling and communication for patients in advanced stages of disease, endorsed by Rosalynn Carter. Collins has backed the Republican version of HMO reform, and has sponsored her own version with John Breaux, arguing for leaving "treatment decisions in the hands of doctors, not lawyers," with internal and external appeals processes to resolve complaints. She has sought to change the Medicare rules to allow more home health care payments, to reform the evaluation of organ procurement organizations and to set up a National Registry on Juvenile Diabetes. She co-sponsored a law with the late John Chafee to help older foster children move toward independence and passed an amendment to keep vocational education funding separate from other education programs. Her proposal for deductions for the first $2,700 of interest paid on college loans made it, in modified form, into the 1997 tax cut, and she passed a law in 2000 banning distribution over the Internet of computer programs to make fake IDs.

Collins has worked on local issues—for limiting giant trawlers from fishing for herring and mackerel, for national weather bouys, for low-income heating assistance, against Canadian potato easements and Chilean salmon trade restrictions, against alleged dumping of apple juice concentrate and for USDA purchases of blueberries, for tax deductions for fishermen buying safety gear. She sought a National Weather Service office for Caribou, pointing out that since it is surrounded by Canada it does not receive weather warnings from adjacent Weather Service offices as most other American communities do. With others in the Maine delegation, she protested the designation of Atlantic salmon as an endangered species. She got fishermen included in Chapter 12 of the Bankruptcy Act, which covers farmers. Maine is a border state, and Collins tends to border issues. She protested when the Justice Department threatened to assign assistant U.S. attorneys in Maine to states on the Mexican border, and she has called for increasing Canada's $50 limit on duty-free purchases in the United States.

Collins's visible role in impeachment and her response speech to Bill Clinton's 2000 State of the Union address (his longest ever; she had to wait) have made her more visible than many freshman senators. She is up for re-election in 2002, one of only two Republican senators running in a state carried by Al Gore in 2000 (the other is Gordon Smith of Oregon). Mentioned as possible opponents are state Treasurer Dale McCormick, Bob Dunfey, former head of the New England GSA Office, Democratic Senator Chellie Pingree, sponsor of the state's controversial prescription drug law, and Chris Harte, former President of the Portland *Press Herald*. If Pingree or McCormick is the Democratic nominee it will be the first Maine all-woman general since 1960.

Cook's Call   *Potentially Competitive.* Although Collins' poll numbers do not rival those of her Senate colleague Olympia Snowe, there is not much evidence that any vulnerability she might have extends beyond the political demographics of the state. Former state Senator Chellie Pingree is running and businessman Chris Harte is contemplating a bid. Either may be able to give Collins a spirited race, but she starts as the clear favorite.

Presidential politics   Maine turned out to be a target state in the 2000 presidential election, with the lead see-sawing back and forth in polls. Indeed, Maine has been unstable in recent presidential voting, casting majorities for Republican George Bush in 1988 and Democrat Bill Clinton in 1996 and producing a virtual three-way tie in 1992, with Clinton in first place and Bush, who spent nearly every summer of his life in Maine, finishing third. In 2000 Gore won by a 49%–44% margin. Maine is one of two states (Nebraska is the other) which gives one elector to the winner in each congressional district. Bush lost the 2d district by only a 47%–46% margin; with 1% more there he would have won 272 electoral votes instead of 271.

Maine held its first-ever presidential primary on March 5, 1996, in an attempt to generate an early contest to which candidates would pay attention. But they didn't, much. Clinton had no competition and Bob Dole had clinched the Republican nomination three days earlier in South Carolina. In 2000 Maine got lost in the crush of states voting on Super Tuesday, March 7, though the results were close. George W. Bush beat John McCain 51%–44%, the one Bush victory in New England, and Al Gore beat Bill Bradley 54%–41%.

Congressional districting   Redistricting has never been controversial in Maine. Since the state lost its third congressional district in the 1960 Census, the lines have been almost exactly the same, though party control has shifted. Forty years ago, the Republican legislature wanted to split areas of Democratic strength; the result is that there is not much partisan difference between the southern 1st District and the northern 2d. Now control is split between a state Democratic House, an evenly divided state Senate and an Independent governor. The likelihood is that there will be only minor changes in the district lines, with the 2d district gaining some territory.

THE PEOPLE: Pop. 2000: 1,274,923; Pop. 1990: 1,227,928, up 3.8% 1990–2000. 0.5% of U.S. total, 40th largest; 96.9% White, 0.5% Black, 0.7% Asian, 0.6% Amer. Indian, 1% Two+ races, 0.2% Other; 0.7% Hispanic Origin. 3.5% Unemployment. 2000 Voting age pop.: 973,685. 2000 Turnout: 651,817; 67% of VAP. Registered voters (2000): 947,189; 297,405 D (31%), 278,228 R (29%), 371,556 unaffiliated and minor parties (39%).

POLITICAL LINEUP: Governor, Angus S. King Jr. (I); Secy. of State, Dan A. Gwadosky (D); Atty. Gen., G. Steven Rowe (D); Treasurer, Dale McCormick (D); Auditor, Gail Chase (D); State Senate, 35 (17 D, 17 R, 1 I); Senate Pres. Pro Tempore, Richard A. Bennett (R); Senate President, Michael H. Michaud (D); Majority Leader, Beverly Daggett (D); State House, 151 (89 D, 61 R, 1 I); House Speaker, Michael V. Saxl (D). Senators, Olympia Snowe (R) and Susan Collins (R). Representatives, 2 (2 D).

ELECTIONS DIVISION: 207-624-7734; **FILING DEADLINE FOR U.S. CONGRESS:** TBA.

2000 Presidential Vote

Gore (D)	319,951	(49%)
Bush (R)	286,616	(44%)
Nader (Green)	37,127	(6%)
Others	8,123	(1%)

1996 Presidential Vote

Clinton (D)	312,788	(53%)
Dole (R)	186,378	(32%)
Perot (I)	85,970	(15%)

2000 Republican Presidential Primary

Bush (R)	49,308	(51%)
McCain (R)	42,510	(44%)
Other	4,806	(5%)

2000 Democratic Presidential Primary

Gore (D)	34,725	(54%)
Bradley (D)	26,520	(41%)
Uncommitted	2,634	(4%)

Gov. Angus S. King, Jr. (I)

Elected 1994, term expires Jan. 2003, 2d term; b. Mar. 31, 1944, Alexandria, VA; home, Brunswick; Dartmouth Col., A.B. 1966, U. of VA Law Schl., J.D. 1969; Episcopalian; married (Mary).

Professional Career: Staff Atty., Pine Tree Legal Assistance, 1969–72; Chief Cnsl., U.S. Sen. William Hathaway, 1972–75; Practicing atty., 1975–83; TV talk show host, 1975–93; Vice Pres. & Gen. Cnsl., Swift River/Hafslund Co., 1983–89; Founder & Pres., Northeast Energy Management Inc., 1989–94.

Office: State House, Sta. 1, Augusta, 04333, 207-287-3531; Fax: 207-287-1034; Web site: www.state.me.us.

Election Results

1998 general	Angus S. King Jr. (I)	246,772	(59%)
	James B. Longley Jr. (R)	79,716	(19%)
	Thomas J. Connolly (D)	50,506	(12%)
	Patricia H. Lamarche (I)	28,722	(7%)
	Others	15,293	(4%)
1998 primary	Angus S. King Jr. (I)	unopposed	
1994 general	Angus S. King Jr. (I)	180,829	(35%)
	Joseph E. Brennan (D)	172,951	(34%)
	Susan M. Collins (R)	117,990	(23%)
	Jonathan K. Carter (Green)	32,695	(6%)

Sen. Olympia Snowe (R)

Elected 1994, seat up 2006, 2d term; b. Feb. 21, 1947, Augusta; home, Auburn; U. of ME, B.A. 1969; Greek Orthodox; married (John McKernan).

Elected Office: ME House of Reps., 1973–76; ME Senate, 1976–78; U.S. House of Reps., 1978–94.

Professional Career: Dir., Superior Concrete Co., 1969–78; Auburn Bd. of Voter Registration, 1971–73.

DC Office: 154 RSOB, 20510, 202-224-5344; Fax: 202-224-1946; Web site: www.senate.gov/~snowe.

State Offices: Auburn, 207-786-2451; Augusta, 207-622-8292; Bangor, 207-945-0432; Biddeford, 207-282-4144; Portland, 207-874-0833; Presque Isle, 207-764-5124.

Committees: *Budget. Commerce, Science & Transportation*: Aviation; Communications; Oceans & Fisheries (RMM); Surface Transportation & Merchant Marine. *Finance*: Health Care (RMM); International Trade; Taxation & IRS Oversight. *Small Business*.

Group Ratings

	ADA	ACLU	AFS	LCV	CON	ITIC	NTU	COC	ACU	NTLC	CHC
2000	30	29	0	43	26	80	60	73	80	71	31
1999	45	—	16	67	21	—	50	59	60	—	—

National Journal Ratings

	1999 LIB —	1999 CONS		2000 LIB —	2000 CONS
Economic	53% —	46%		48% —	50%
Social	50% —	49%		49% —	46%
Foreign	36% —	63%		48% —	48%

Key Votes of the 106th Congress

1. Educ. Savings Accts.	Y	5. Review Movie Violence	Y	9. NATO War in Serbia	Y
2. Prescrip. Drug Benefit	N	6. Gun Show Bckgrnd. Checks	N	10. Table Cuba Travel Ban	Y
3. Delay Ergonomic Standards	Y	7. Ban Part.-Birth Abortion	N	11. Nuclear Test-Ban Treaty	N
4. Phase Out Estate Tax	Y	8. Broaden Hate Crimes List	Y	12. Perm. Trade with China	Y

Election Results

2000 general	Olympia Snowe (R)	437,689	(69%)	($1,981,504)
	Mark Lawrence (D)	197,183	(31%)	($727,655)
2000 primary	Olympia Snowe (R)	unopposed		
1994 general	Olympia Snowe (R)	308,244	(60%)	($2,041,834)
	Thomas H. Andrews (D)	186,042	(36%)	($1,482,060)
	Others	17,447	(3%)	

Sen. Susan Collins (R)

Elected 1996, seat up 2002, 1st term; b. Dec. 7, 1952, Caribou; home, Bangor; St. Lawrence U., B.A. 1975; Catholic; single.

Professional Career: Legis. Aide, U.S. Sen. Bill Cohen, 1975–87; Staff Dir., Oversight of Gov. Mgmt. Subcmte., 1981–87; Professional & Financial Regulation Comm., 1987–92; New England Regional Dir., U.S. Small Business Admin., 1992; ME Dpty. Treas., 1993; Exec. Dir., Ctr. for Family Business, Husson Col., 1994–96.

DC Office: 172 RSOB, 20510, 202-224-2523; Fax: 202-224-2693; Web site: www.senate.gov/~collins.

State Offices: Augusta, 207-622-8414; Bangor, 207-945-0417; Biddeford, 207-283-1101; Caribou, 207-493-7873; Lewiston, 207-784-6969; Portland, 207-780-3575.

Committees: *Aging (Special). Armed Services:* Emerging Threats & Capabilities; Personnel; Seapower. *Governmental Affairs:* Government Management, Restructuring and the District of Columbia; International Security, Proliferation & Federal Services; Investigations (Permanent) (RMM). *Health, Education, Labor & Pensions:* Children & Families; Public Health.

Group Ratings

	ADA	ACLU	AFS	LCV	CON	ITIC	NTU	COC	ACU	NTLC	CHC
2000	25	43	0	43	42	80	63	80	76	80	31
1999	25	—	0	67	21	—	58	76	64	—	—

National Journal Ratings

	1999 LIB	—	1999 CONS		2000 LIB	—	2000 CONS
Economic	50%	—	49%		48%	—	50%
Social	51%	—	48%		49%	—	46%
Foreign	16%	—	77%		48%	—	48%

Key Votes of the 106th Congress

1. Educ. Savings Accts.	Y	5. Review Movie Violence	Y	9. NATO War in Serbia	N
2. Prescrip. Drug Benefit	N	6. Gun Show Bckgrnd. Checks	N	10. Table Cuba Travel Ban	Y
3. Delay Ergonomic Standards	Y	7. Ban Part.-Birth Abortion	N	11. Nuclear Test-Ban Treaty	N
4. Phase Out Estate Tax	Y	8. Broaden Hate Crimes List	Y	12. Perm. Trade with China	Y

Election Results

1996 general	Susan Collins (R)	298,422	(49%)	($1,621,475)
	Joseph E. Brennan (D)	266,226	(44%)	($976,805)
	Others	42,129	(7%)	
1996 primary	Susan Collins (R)	53,339	(56%)	
	W. John Hathaway (R)	29,792	(31%)	
	Robert A.G. Monks (R)	12,943	(13%)	
1990 general	William S. Cohen (R)	319,167	(61%)	($1,628,292)
	Neil Rolde (D)	201,053	(39%)	($1,630,894)

FIRST DISTRICT

The 1st District stretches from southernmost Kittery and nearby Kennebunkport to the craggy-shored ancestrally Republican counties to the east. The historic center is Portland, Maine's largest city, home to the yuppies and lawyers that have revived and renovated its downtown landmarks. Most voters in the 1st District, except those far Down East, live within a couple hours drive of the Maine Mall—just off the Maine Turnpike and I-295 and near the airport—the state's heaviest concentration of retail and office space. Lobsters remain an important resource, with an annual state harvest of 19 million pounds. Politically, the 1st votes very much like the state as a whole, quirkily, often for independents, splitting tickets with abandon. From 1968–96 it elected three Democrats and three Republicans, with each side serving 14 years.

The congressman from the 1st District now is Tom Allen, a Democrat first elected in 1996. Allen is a native of Portland, where his grandfather and father served on the city council. He was class president in high school and college, and at Bowdoin was captain of the football team and challenged fraternities because they wouldn't admit blacks. He was a Rhodes Scholar in Oxford the same years as Bill Clinton (who struck him as "one of the nicest, warmest people I ever knew"), Robert Reich and Strobe Talbott, and when he returned he got a job on the staff of Edmund Muskie. But he dropped out of politics, went to law school, practiced in Portland, and worked on charities and community service. In 1989 he was elected to the Portland City Council, and in 1991 rotated into the position of mayor; he started a program of low-interest loans to businesses locating downtown. In 1994 he ran for governor, finishing a distant second to former Governor Joseph Brennan in the Democratic primary, with 24%.

The 1st District race was an obvious next step, and an attractive opportunity. Freshman Republican James Longley had a well-known name as son of the independent governor elected in 1974, and he had won the 1994 race 52%–48%, though heavily outspent. But Longley's moderate record was overshadowed by his support for the Contract with America and more than $1 million in ads run by the AFL-CIO. Allen, with heavy support from Portland, won a 52%–48% primary victory over state Senator Dale McCormick, who is openly lesbian and brought her partner and their daughter to the podium at the state Democratic convention. Allen called for "incremental steps" toward a single-payer health care system. The candidates disagreed on capital punishment, partial-birth abortions, term limits and the balanced budget amendment. Allen called for scaling back Republicans' $10 billion increase in defense spending; Longley pointed out it included a Navy destroyer to be built at the Bath Iron Works; Allen backtracked and said he would of course support Maine defense contracts. Allen won 55%–45%.

Allen has a very liberal voting record, with a few exceptions on economic issues. His first major initiative was the freshman campaign finance bill, co-sponsored by Republican Asa Hutchinson, which would have banned soft money contributions by unions and corporations, index contribution limits (the $1,000 limit was enacted in 1974) and require disclosure by groups spending more than $25,000. In April 1998, after Allen launched a discharge petition, Speaker Newt Gingrich switched and allowed the freshman bill to come to the floor as the vehicle for campaign finance bills. Allen was pleased when the more stringent Shays-Meehan bill passed the House in August 1998; he subsequently became an active proponent.

Allen was an early supporter of Henry Waxman's bill to make prescription drugs available to seniors at the lowest price paid by federal government (the government would end up controlling the price of 40% of the prescription drug market). He initiated a separate bill to require that such drugs for the elderly be sold at bulk-rate prices. He introduced to Washington 78-year-old Florence "Flo" Dube of Augusta as evidence of why all seniors should have coverage: Her $15 monthly Medicaid fee covers her $310 in medications; without Medicaid, her medicine cabinet would be empty. When a federal judge before the 2000 election overturned Maine's landmark prescription-drug law, Allen promised to change federal law to reinstate the local law. On other issues, he pushed to require power plants and trash incinerators to cut mercury emissions 95% and sponsored the compact to allow Maine and Vermont to dump nuclear waste in Sierra Blanca, Texas, near the Mexico border, a measure Paul Wellstone called "environmental racism." He helped to secure $2.8 billion for three Aegis destroyers with construction work divided by Bath Iron Works and Ingalls Shipyards in Mississippi, plus funds for projects at Saco Defense, Brunswick Naval Air Station, and Portsmouth Naval Shipyard at Kittery. He launched a House Ocean Caucus to focus on environmental, fishing and other topics that affect Maine's 4500-mile shoreline. He has promoted stronger ties with Taiwan, which could produce market opportunities for Bath Iron Works.

Bowdoin political scientist Chris Potholm describes the swing voters in this district as "cruel yuppies," attracted to candidates who reflect their trendy values and negativity toward taxes. Allen seems to have won their allegiance. In 1998 he won 60%–36%. In 2000, against state senator Jane Amero, who attacked Allen for his opposition to tax cuts, he won with a virtually identical 60%–37%. Redistricting is likely to move a small part of the 1st to the slower-growing 2d District.

Cook's Call   *Probably Safe.* While this Portland and Augusta-based district has deep blue-collar (read: Democratic) roots, it also has a serious independent streak, which makes it competitive. And, Allen, ranked by *National Journal* as one of the most liberal members of Congress, has compiled a voting record that tilts more to the left than the district. But, Allen projects a moderate image and has avoided high-profile controversy that might put him in political danger. A good candidate could make this a race, but Allen would be favored. There have been rumblings that he may run for the Senate in 2002. If so, this seat should be seriously contested.

THE PEOPLE: Pop. 2000: 666,936; Pop. 1990: 613,960, up 8.6% 1990–2000. 96.8% White, 0.7% Black, 0.9% Asian, 0.3% Amer. Indian, 1% Two+ races, 0.2% Other; 0.8% Hispanic Origin.

2000 Presidential Vote				1996 Presidential Vote			
Gore (D)	176,293	(51%)		Clinton (D)	165,053	(54%)
Bush (R)	148,618	(43%)		Dole (R)	100,851	(33%)
Nader (Green)	20,297	(6%)		Perot (I)	39,845	(13%)
Others	3,743	(1%)				

Rep. Tom Allen (D)

Elected 1996, 3d term; b. Apr. 16, 1945, Portland; home, Portland; Bowdoin Col., B.A. 1967, Rhodes Scholar, Oxford U., B. Phil. 1970; Harvard J.D. 1974; Protestant; married (Diana).

Elected Office: Portland City Cncl., 1989–95; Portland Mayor, 1991.

Professional Career: Staff, U.S. Sen. Edmund Muskie, 1970–71; Practicing atty., 1974–94; Chmn., ME Clinton-Gore Campaign, 1992; Public Policy Consultant, 1995.

DC Office: 1717 LHOB 20515, 202-225-6116; Fax: 202-225-5590; Web site: www.house.gov/allen.

District Office: Portland, 207-774-5019.

Committees: *Armed Services* (11th of 28 D): Military Procurement; Military Research & Development. *Government Reform* (15th of 19 D): Criminal Justice, Drug Policy & Human Resources; National Security, Veterans' Affairs & Intl. Relations.

Group Ratings

	ADA	ACLU	AFS	LCV	CON	ITIC	NTU	COC	ACU	NTLC	CHC
2000	85	86	85	93	24	72	21	52	4	12	7
1999	95	—	100	81	18	—	14	28	0	—	—

National Journal Ratings

	1999 LIB	—	1999 CONS		2000 LIB	—	2000 CONS
Economic	84%	—	12%		92%	—	5%
Social	87%	—	0%		91%	—	6%
Foreign	95%	—	0%		92%	—	6%

Key Votes of the 106th Congress

1. Patient Bill of Rights	Y	5. Bar RU-486 $ for FDA	N	9. NATO War in Serbia	Y
2. Accelerate Min. Wage	Y	6. Display 10 Commandments	N	10. Perm. Trade with China	Y
3. Strike Ban on Ergo. Stnd.	Y	7. Gun Show Bkgrnd. Checks	Y	11. Debt Relief for 3rd World	Y
4. Ovrd. Estate Tax Veto	N	8. Ban Part.-Birth Abortion	N	12. Drop Cuba Econ. Embargo	Y

Election Results

2000 general	Tom Allen (D)	202,823	(60%)	($639,119)
	Jane Amero (R)	123,915	(37%)	($478,817)
	J. Frederic Staples (LIB)	12,356	(4%)	
2000 primary	Tom Allen (D)	unopposed		
1998 general	Tom Allen (D)	134,335	(60%)	($689,694)
	Ross J. Connelly (R)	79,160	(36%)	($527,330)
	Eric R. Greiner (I)	9,182	(4%)	

SECOND DISTRICT

The 2d District covers the northern three-quarters of the acreage of Maine. The population is not evenly distributed, however: The district dips south to include the heavily Democratic mill town of Lewiston and reaches to Belfast on Penobscot Bay. There are several different Maines here: the bays of coastal Maine, with their small fishing towns; the potato fields of far northern Aroostook County; the mill towns on the fast-running streams of western Maine, penned in between mountains. This was one of America's frontiers in the 1850s, when Bangor on the Penobscot River was the lumber capital of the world; today it is the largest city in the district. This part of Maine has had its economic troubles: Potato production is only half what it was in 1980; Loring Air Force Base was closed in 1994, though new businesses have sprouted to replace its civilian jobs; logging—though the largest single contributor to Maine's economy—has run into environmental critics and the industry fought a proposed national park in the north woods. (Opponents' bumper stickers read: "If you don't like cutting trees, try using plastic toilet paper.") To attract tourism, Bangor plans a $184 million redevelopment of its former industrial waterfront. Politically this is protest country. This was Ross Perot's strongest district in the United States in 1992 and 1996.

The congressman from the 2d District is John Baldacci, a Democrat elected in 1994, indeed one of only four Democrats elected to replace a Republican that year (in his case, Olympia Snowe, who was elected to the Senate). Baldacci has deep local roots. He grew up in Bangor, where his family ran Momma Baldacci's, a restaurant started by his grandparents in 1933; he is of Italian and Lebanese descent, distantly related to former Senator George Mitchell, and the family restaurant used to get a daily delivery of rolls from former Senator William Cohen's father's bakery. Baldacci followed his father on the Bangor City Council in 1978, at 23; in 1982, he was elected to the state Senate, where he often dissented from Democrats, chairing the tax committee. He is unassuming, unbombastic, earnest; he campaigned for the House seat in 1994 by holding spaghetti dinners at $2 a head (children under 12 free) around the district. In a seven-candidate primary, with lots of support around Bangor, Baldacci won with 27% to 23% for former Democratic state chairman James Mitchell, George Mitchell's nephew. The Republican nominee was Richard Bennett, who won 30% in a four-way primary with a base in western Maine. Baldacci opposed the Clinton health care plan; Bennett was iffy about the Contract With America's defense spending increase; both were pressed by Green Party and independent candidates, who ended up winning 5% and 9% respectively. Baldacci pledged to oppose any new taxes and was proud of running no negative ads. He won with 46% to Bennett's 41%. Bennett carried the western area and much of the coast, but Baldacci won solidly in Aroostook and carried the Bangor area as well.

In the House, Baldacci has compiled a mostly but not entirely, liberal record; he voted for versions of the balanced budget amendment, line-item veto and term limits. He helped lead the effort to retain the "e-rate," the FCC-ordered tax on telephone calls to finance the wiring of schools and libraries for the Internet. He sponsored bills for Rural Enterprise Communities and improved rural health care. He was a leader in passing the legislation to allow drugs to be reimported from other nations (notably, Canada), which Health and Human Services Secretary Donna Shalala decided not to implement. He would require insurance companies to make co-payments and length of hospital stays the same for mental health as for other conditions. He fought the Federal Reserve's interest rate increases. With Olympia Snowe, he pushed to get Canadian drilled lumber reclassified under the U.S.-Canadian Softwood Lumber Agreement; previously, even a tiny drilled hole removed the lumber from the agreement's quota. He opposed permanent trade relations with China because its alleged dumping of apple juice concentrate led at least one Maine orchard to shut down. He fought a Fish and Wildlife Service proposal to place the Atlantic salmon on the endangered species list. He worked on local projects: a second pier for Eastport, the Bates Complex in Lewiston, a magnet school at Loring, more Agriculture Department purchases of frozen wild blueberries. He brought the Agriculture Committee to Aroostook County for a hearing after Maine farmers blocked the border to protest subsidized Canadian potato exports. Later, he successfully opposed similar shipments pending review of scientific data of possible warts in the spuds.

Baldacci has been reelected three times with more than 70% of the vote. In 1994 he promised to serve only four terms. After the 2000 election, he confirmed that he will not run again for the House. He announced he will run for governor in 2002, and his House majorities suggest he would be a very strong candidate. This district could be very seriously contested; in 2000 it was carried by Al Gore by only a 47%–46% margin. Redistricting will add some territory to the 2d, but the political balance will not be changed much.

Cook's Call *Competitive.* The decision by Baldacci to run for governor has opened up a competitive House district for 2002. Already at least 12 candidates have expressed interest in running for a seat that has been open only twice in the last 22-years. More marginal than the Portland-based 1st, Gore won this sprawling northern Maine district by just 2% in 2000.

THE PEOPLE: Pop. 2000: 607,987; Pop. 1990: 613,968, down 1% 1990–2000. 97.1% White, 0.4% Black, 0.5% Asian, 0.9% Amer. Indian, 1% Two+ races, 0.2% Other; 0.7% Hispanic Origin.

2000 Presidential Vote
Gore (D) 143,658 (47%)
Bush (R) 137,998 (46%)
Nader (Green) 16,830 (6%)
Others 4,380 (1%)

1996 Presidential Vote
Clinton (D) 147,735 (53%)
Dole (R) 85,527 (31%)
Perot (I) 46,125 (17%)

Rep. John Baldacci (D)

Elected 1994, 4th term; b. Jan. 30, 1955, Bangor; home, Bangor; U. of ME, B.A. 1986; Catholic; married (Karen).

Elected Office: Bangor City Cncl., 1978–81; ME Senate, 1982–94.

Professional Career: Restaurateur.

DC Office: 1740 LHOB 20515, 202-225-6306; Fax: 202-225-2943; Web site: www.house.gov/baldacci.

District Offices: Bangor, 207-942-6935; Lewiston, 207-782-3704; Madawaska, 207-728-6160; Presque Isle, 207-764-1036.

Committees: *Agriculture* (10th of 24 D): Conservation, Credit, Rural Development & Research; Department Operations, Oversight, Nutrition & Forestry. *Transportation & Infrastructure* (27th of 34 D): Aviation; Railroads.

Group Ratings

	ADA	ACLU	AFS	LCV	CON	ITIC	NTU	COC	ACU	NTLC	CHC
2000	85	79	100	64	50	61	19	40	8	12	7
1999	100	—	100	88	12	—	16	24	4	—	—

National Journal Ratings

	1999 LIB	—	1999 CONS		2000 LIB	—	2000 CONS
Economic	84%	—	12%		80%	—	19%
Social	79%	—	20%		70%	—	29%
Foreign	78%	—	17%		73%	—	26%

Key Votes of the 106th Congress

1. Patient Bill of Rights	Y	5. Bar RU-486 $ for FDA	N	9. NATO War in Serbia	Y
2. Accelerate Min. Wage	Y	6. Display 10 Commandments	N	10. Perm. Trade with China	N
3. Strike Ban on Ergo. Stnd.	Y	7. Gun Show Bkgrnd. Checks	Y	11. Debt Relief for 3rd World	Y
4. Ovrd. Estate Tax Veto	N	8. Ban Part.-Birth Abortion	N	12. Drop Cuba Econ. Embargo	Y

Election Results

2000 general	John Baldacci (D) 219,783	(73%)	($508,966)
	Richard Campbell (R) 79,522	(27%)	($69,343)
2000 primary	John Baldacci (D) .... unopposed		
1998 general	John Baldacci (D) 146,202	(76%)	($437,247)
	Jonathan Reisman (R) 45,674	(24%)	($14,455)

★ MARYLAND ★

Just south of the Mason-Dixon line and just north of the line between the Union and the Confederacy, the midpoint of the 13 colonies, Maryland has always been betwixt and between. It has a claim to be the typical American state, yet stands out for its particularities. This was the only one of the 13 colonies founded by Roman Catholics—the Calvert family—and its embrace of religious tolerance came less from abstract principle than from the Calverts' desire to protect their property from Protestant monarchs: a harbinger of Maryland's practical-mindedness. Similarly, although hot-blooded Baltimoreans wanted to secede in 1861 ("Maryland, My Maryland" condemns Abraham Lincoln's suppression of pro-Confederate rioters), practical heads prevailed.

The puritan impulse was never lively here: Prohibition was enforced only laxly in Baltimore, to the delight of its great journalist-cum-lexicographer H.L. Mencken; slot machines were legal in the rural counties of the Western Shore; horse-racing has long thrived here. An old state law guaranteeing blacks equal access to public accommodations specifically excluded the Eastern Shore. By not pursuing any one course rigorously, Maryland could be many things at once: Northern as well as Southern, moralistic as well as libertine, industrial as well as rural, leaving people to their own devices yet with a heavy government presence. Perhaps as a result, much of Maryland's political history reads like a chronicle of rogues, from Luther Martin, the drunken haranguer at the Constitutional Convention, to the Annapolis lobbyist convicted of fraud who in 1998 continued to conduct business from the jail pay phone; a judge sentencing another lobbyist in 2000 condemned "a culture of corruption that has been tolerated by lobbyists, legislators, and the citizens of Maryland."

Maryland's genial tolerance may have given it a little too savory a history, but this state cherishes its sense of uniqueness. The Chesapeake Bay, for example, is the nation's largest estuary, with water saltier than a river but fresher than the ocean and with unique watermen and shellfish. The terrapin and Chesapeake oyster are rare today; oystermen harvested 20 million bushels in 1900 but only 100,000 in 1995. Rockfish and Chesapeake Bay blue crabs are much scarcer too, and a microbe called *Pfiesteria* killed many fish in 1997. An August 1999 *Washington Post* series documented how runoff of waste from Eastern Shore and Delaware chicken farms was polluting the Bay and killing crabs. But countermeasures are being taken. The Maryland, Virginia, and Pennsylvania state governments entered a Chesapeake Bay restoration agreement in June 2000 to increase oyster production tenfold, set harvest goals for crabs, and limit development which produces more runoff. Rockfish populations are increasing and the Chesapeake Bay Foundation is building vertical oyster reefs.

Maryland also has some reason to be proud of the economy, or economies, it has built over the years. Half a century ago, half the state's population lived in the city of Baltimore and only one-fifth in the suburbs. Now the proportions are the other way around, and then some: 12% Baltimore, 76% in the ever-growing suburbs. The Census Bureau classifies Washington-Baltimore as a single metropolitan area, the nation's fourth largest, with more than 7.6 million people. But Baltimore and Washington are not fraternal twins like Dallas and Fort Worth or Minneapolis and St. Paul; they are two quite separate cities, with different economic bases and different attitudes toward public life. Baltimore started off as a port and an industrial city, and has managed to stay diversified and successful as it spread out into the countryside from its new central core at the Inner Harbor and the solidly built edifices of its downtown grid streets. Baltimore has raised private money to rebuild the 146-year-old *U.S.S. Constellation*; it makes spices and writes insurance; it is home to the power-tool maker Black & Decker and the investment bank DB Alex. Brown & Sons. It has big government offices, the headquarters of the Social Security Administration and, quietly down the road, the National Security Agency. It is home to the Orioles in their popular Oriole Park at Camden Yards, the first of the new-old ballparks of the 1990s, and to Johns Hopkins University, with its Georgian buildings along the affluent corridor that runs directly north from downtown all the way to the developing edge city of Hunt Valley. Baltimore suffered from horrifying crime and population loss in the 1990s. But Mayor Martin O'Malley, elected in 1999 with over

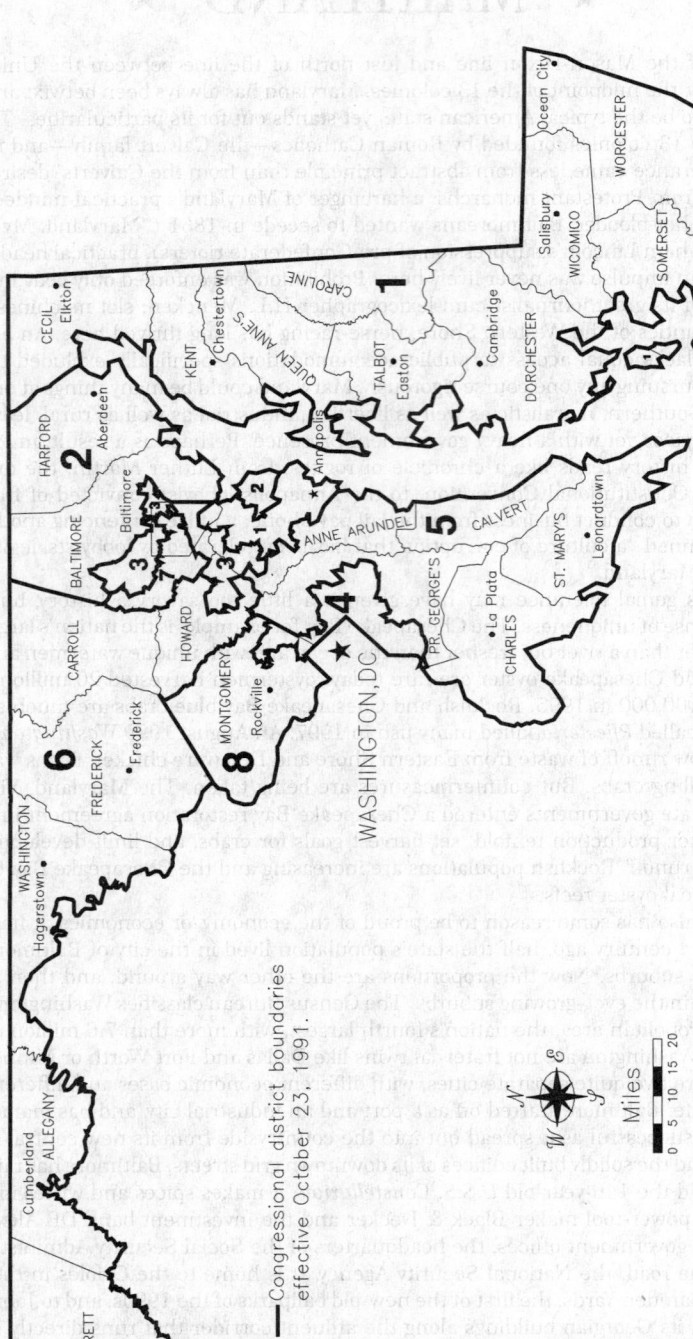

—Congressional district boundaries
effective October 23, 1991.

Miles

0 5 10 15 20

50% in the Democratic primary in a majority-black city against two black opponents, has imported Rudolph Giuliani's "zero tolerance" anti-crime policies, and crime rates seem to be on the decline.

Baltimore remains the focus of Maryland's public life, for 47% of Marylanders still live in its metropolitan area, and its influence is far greater than Washington's on the Eastern Shore and in the western counties. For years most of Maryland's successful statewide politicians came from Baltimore; today both senators live there and commute to Washington. But Governor Parris Glendening is a notable exception, something of a distrusted stranger in Baltimore; he grew up in Florida, and, in a political culture that loves gambling, he loathes it. But he is from the Washington suburbs, without whose votes he would not have been elected in 1994 nor re-elected in 1998, and many residents there have their focus elsewhere. Montgomery County has a very large percentage of people from all over the nation, who moved there to be near the nation's capital and for whom residence in Maryland is a convenience, not a commitment; Prince George's County has more high-income black residents than any other county in America, most with roots in Washington. The Eastern Shore and the counties south of Annapolis, in contrast, remain as fixated on things Maryland-ish as they are addicted to steamed crabs with characteristic Chesapeake spices. The uplands of the western counties, in contrast, are becoming difficult to distinguish from adjacent parts of Pennsylvania, Virginia and West Virginia.

Maryland is by most measures one of the nation's most Democratic states. In 2000 it voted 57%–40% for Al Gore, his fourth-best percentage, after Rhode Island, Massachusetts and New York, and an improvement over Bill Clinton's margins of 54%–39% in 1996 and 50%–36% in 1992. In statewide elections, Democrats have not lost a contest for senator or governor since liberal Republican Senator Charles Mathias won his last race in 1980. One reason for this is that some 28% of Marylanders are black, the highest percentage in any state outside the Deep South; even the prosperous blacks of Prince George's County still vote overwhelmingly Democratic. Another overlapping reason is that this state and neighboring Virginia have by far the two highest percentages of federal and public employees, natural backers of the party of government. They help to keep the Washington suburbs solidly Democratic. The Eastern Shore and the western counties may go Republican, whites in the Baltimore metropolitan area sometimes favor Republicans, but the Democratic margins among blacks and in the Washington suburbs have been big enough to put Maryland in the Democratic column. Inklings of a Republican revival, apparent in Ellen Sauerbrey's near-win for governor in 1994, were overwhelmed by the swing toward Clinton and Gore in the suburbs and the growing black vote. Governor Parris Glendening raised his victory margin from 50.2%–49.8% in 1994 to 55%–45% in 1998, with turnout up 9%; Republicans are heavily outnumbered in the legislature and seldom win the post of county executive in large counties. In no other state but Hawaii are Democrats as surely, if not entirely serenely, in control.

Governor   Parris Glendening grew up in Florida in an impoverished, dysfunctional household—his mother sometimes using food money to play bingo. He worked his way up by studying hard, got a Ph.D. in political science in 1967 at Florida State University, and began teaching at the University of Maryland in College Park. He married a former graduate student whose father was a state senator. In 1974 he was elected to the Prince George's Council; in 1982 he was elected Prince George's County Executive. Prince George's grew during these years, developed a strong economy, and dealt with school busing by developing an innovative magnet school plan.

Glendening ran for governor in 1994 in a crowded field and despite the hostility of Democratic Governor William Donald Schaefer, a dominant figure in Maryland politics since his election as mayor of Baltimore in 1971. Glendening won the ordinarily dispositive Democratic primary with 54% of the vote to 18% for his closest rival; he won 75% of the vote in the Washington suburbs and 44% elsewhere. His opponent was Ellen Sauerbrey, House of Delegates minority leader for eight years, who won an upset 52%–38% primary victory over Congresswoman Helen Delich Bentley. Sauerbrey surged in October, and was beaten only after some extraordinary—some say illegal—acts by Democrats: a purging of affluent white voters from the rolls in Baltimore City and a suspiciously timed reporting of 9,000 votes in Baltimore on election night. Sauerbrey cried foul, but investigations found no evidence of orchestrated wrongdoing. Glendening won with 50.2% of the vote, winning 63% in the Washington suburbs while losing metro Baltimore and the rest of the state, and becoming the first governor from the Washington suburbs since 1869.

In office Glendening has puzzled voters and infuriated fellow politicians by changing positions and reneging on commitments. When Maryland race track owners wanted slot machines to compete with Delaware tracks, Glendening said he was opposed in February 1996, then weeks later said he would review the alternatives, told Baltimore Mayor Kurt Schmoke (who wanted the money for education) in July he would support them, then in August said he would veto them. He went back and forth on the intercounty connector proposed for the Washington suburbs. After harshly criticizing Sauerbrey's proposed tax cut during the election, he backed a 2% cut in 1997 and a 5% cut in 1998. When longtime Controller Louis Goldstein died in summer 1998, he first said he would appoint former Congressman Michael Barnes, then backed down and appointed former Governor Schaefer, who at 76 was eager to get back into office. He pointedly refused to appear with Bill Clinton at a September 1998 Montgomery County event, then eagerly appeared with him in October.

On other issues, Glendening was steadier. He proposed a ban on workplace smoking, which passed in 1995 with an exception for restaurants. He backed a $170 million Rural Legacy program to buy up open space, which has purchased 150,000 acres and closed them to development. He closed fishing on the Pockomoke River and other Chesapeake Bay tributaries when *Pfiesteria* was found to be killing fish in September 1997; the legislature in April 1998 passed a scaled-down version of his proposal to limit the use of farm fertilizers and improve monitoring of poultry operations. He provided state financing for the Ravens football stadium in Baltimore and the Redskins stadium in Prince George's County.

In early 1998 Glendening seemed to be in trouble for re-election. Sauerbrey had never stopped running, and some prominent Democrats were hostile. But two opponents abruptly withdrew two months before the September primary, and he finally won grudging endorsements from Schmoke and Prince George's County Executive Wayne Curry. Sauerbrey was running a soft-focus campaign, talking about growing up in a Baltimore rowhouse, the daughter of a steelworker, and of her work as a biology teacher. Her tax cut message partially adopted by Glendening, she now emphasized cutting taxes on seniors. For most of the fall she ran about even with Glendening in the polls; both had high negatives. But in late October Glendening ran an ad accusing Sauerbrey of "a civil rights record to be ashamed of"—she had voted with many Democrats against a bill for racial quotas and preferences—and pulled ahead and won 55%–45%.

In his second term Glendening has set a steadier course, though he did wobble on the intercounty connector, suggesting he would back a parkway with few interchanges, then in September 1999 opposing it as "an environmental disaster" and ordering the sale of property obtained for it. He lobbied strongly for a bill banning discrimination against gays, but it was bottled up in the state Senate. He called for a $1 a pack cigarette tax increase, but the legislature reduced it to 30 cents; he moved to channel tobacco settlement money to education and health. He called for spending $1 billion by 2002 to build and improve schools and in 2000 obtained higher pay for teachers, but said little about tougher testing or accountability. He approved repeal of the inheritance tax. He lobbied hard, threatening legislators' pet projects, to pass a requirement that handguns be sold with built-in trigger locks, though he backed down on requiring so-called smart guns, which opponents said were unavailable. Glendening has called for "smart growth" policies, focusing state spending and projects on established communities in designated growth areas, most inside the Capital and Baltimore Beltways. His proposal for a regional transportation commission with Virginia went nowhere; Montgomery County politicians oppose building a new bridge across the Potomac, to connect the Dulles Airport area with upcounty Montgomery. He did get a federal commitment to pay $600 million for a new Woodrow Wilson Bridge, connecting Prince George's with Alexandria. But this could prove an open-ended commitment: The total cost of the project will be over $2 billion, and Maryland must bear most of that since it owns the Potomac; Glendening added to the cost by signing a union contract, a move rejected out of hand by Virginia Governor James Gilmore, who has sought to limit his state's outlay.

Glendening is term-limited, and in political circles in Maryland there is much buzzing about who will be elected in 2002. The clear favorite is Lieutenant Governor Kathleen Kennedy Townsend, the oldest grandchild of Joseph P. Kennedy, who campaigned hard for Glendening in 1998 and for Al Gore in 2000. She styles herself a moderate Democrat and has been given responsibility for criminal justice issues, on which she takes some tough-minded stands. But she was embarrassed at least a little in December 1999, when a Baltimore *Sun* series showed how teenage inmates at the boot camps she had championed had been treated violently, and how they were unsupervised when put on probation and committed more crimes. The heads of the program were fired and Townsend set up a commission calling for changes in the boot camps in September 2000. Other possible Democrats include three county executives: Douglas Duncan of Montgomery, Wayne Curry of Prince George's, and Dutch Ruppersberger of Baltimore. The strongest Republican candidate would probably be 2d District Congressman Bob Ehrlich, well known and popular in the Baltimore suburbs. But the 1998 and 2000 statewide election results suggest that Maryland has become more Democratic than ever. After watching Al Gore sweep the state, Ehrlich told *The Sun*, "I have a lot of crossover appeal. Is that good enough statewide? I don't know."

Cook's Call   *Safe.* Townsend has been running for this seat for four years and has nearly sewn up the Democratic nomination. Republicans hope that Congressman Bob Ehrlich will run. If he doesn't, Townsend would trounce a second- or third-tier candidate.

Senior Senator   Paul Sarbanes, now the longest-serving Maryland senator in history, was first elected to the Senate in 1976. His liberalism is rooted in his experience growing up in Salisbury on the Eastern Shore, the son of a Greek immigrant, who owned the Mayflower Grill and taught himself enough on the side to discuss philosophy with his son's Princeton professors. Sarbanes was always interested in politics: As a Princeton student in 1952 he went up to Manhattan with a "Princeton for Adlai" sign and got into the candidate's hotel suite, and as a big firm lawyer in Baltimore he worked on the city Charter Revision Commission. Working with small groups, organizing liberal supporters, he ran for office as an insurgent, and always won. He was first elected to the Maryland House of Delegates in 1966. In 1970 he challenged an incumbent in the primary and was elected to the U.S. House; another incumbent retired rather than run against him after redistricting in 1972. In 1976 he defeated former Senator Joseph Tydings in the Democratic primary and incumbent Senator Glenn Beall in the general by 59%–41%.

Since then Sarbanes has been one of the most durable champions of liberal politics: on the Banking Committee, on which he has been ranking Democrat since 1995, on the Joint Economic Committee, which he chaired from 1991–95, and on Foreign Relations. He was one of just 21 senators who voted against the 1996 Welfare Reform Act. On the financial services deregulation bill, he sponsored an amendment to allow states to issue tougher laws protecting the privacy of depositors and credit card holders than those in the federal bill: "It's quite simple—a fundamental right of privacy should be accorded every American who entrusts his or her highly sensitive and confidential information to a financial institution." He introduced new legislation to strengthen financial privacy for consumers in January 2001. He called in October 2000 for investigations of lenders to low-income homeowners who require single-premium credit life insurance. His own approach to investing is conservative: He purchased his first mutual fund in 2000 and since entering Congress has not owned stock.

He is the second ranking Democrat on the Foreign Relations Committee, where he has tilted toward aid for Greece and away from Turkey; he has supported the resolution condemning the Turks for genocidal treatment of Armenians in World War I. He worked successfully to prevent elimination of AID as a separate agency and opposes weapons sales to countries with poor human rights records. In June 2000 he was one of 19 senators to vote to cut most of the funding for the Clinton administration's military assistance to Colombia. He was the only senator to vote against the bill authorizing payment of the U.S.'s United Nations dues; he argued that it was wrong to impose conditions on the UN in repayment for payment of dues that were owed: "It's simply unacceptable that the richest nation on earth is also the biggest debtor to the United Nations." He and his Maryland colleague were two of the 15 senators who voted against Permanent Normal Trade Relations with China in September 2000.

Closer to home, Sarbanes has sponsored projects like the Chesapeake Bay Gateways and Watertrails Network, a special conservation reserve for buffer zones along Chesapeake Bay, and a project to restore the eroding Poplar Island using material dredged from the port of Baltimore's shipping channels. In 2000 he sponsored the reauthorization of the Chesapeake Bay Restoration Act, which doubled federal spending to $40 million. To help drought-stricken Maryland farmers, he sponsored in 2000 an increase in market loss payments from $75,000 to $150,000. In 2000 he also pushed through a bill to roll back federal employee benefit contribution rates to 1998 levels.

Sarbanes is not a senator who courts publicity; he sponsors few bills and sends out few press releases. He enjoys working on the mechanics of government, but returns every night to his home in Baltimore. He has been re-elected without great difficulty four times. His smallest margin was in the Republican year of 1994, when he beat former Tennessee Senator Bill Brock (who beat Albert Gore Sr. in 1970) by a solid 59%–41% margin. At one point it looked like Sarbanes might face Republican Congressman Bob Ehrlich in 2000. But Ehrlich, after seeing how handily Governor Parris Glendening beat Republican Ellen Sauerbrey in 1998, decided not to run. Sarbanes' opponent was Paul Rappaport, former Howard County police chief and unsuccessful candidate for statewide office in 1994 and 1998, who said Sarbanes was an "ultra-liberal." Sarbanes did not bother to run TV ads until five days before the election and still won 63%–37%, running 6% ahead of Al Gore's strong showing. As Rappaport said on election night, "Maybe the state is more liberal than I thought it was."

Junior Senator   Barbara Mikulski is a senator with deep roots in immigrant, urban America and with a fascination for the new technology and jobs growing in edge cities and beyond, a person who doesn't look anything like a traditional politician but who has become a savvy Senate insider. Her roots are in east Baltimore, where her Polish immigrant parents ran a bakery, and she still lives in the city and commutes to Washington. Mikulski got her start in politics as a social worker, organizing to stop a highway from going through Highlandtown. She won, and in the process was elected to the Baltimore City Council in 1971. She ran for the Senate in 1974, and got a respectable 43% against incumbent Charles Mathias; when Paul Sarbanes ran for the other Senate seat in 1976, Mikulski ran for his 3d District House seat and won. Ten years later, she gave up that seat for what seemed like a chancy Senate race, and won handily, with 50% in the primary to 31% for Montgomery County Congressman Michael Barnes and 14% for Governor Harry Hughes. In the general, she beat, 61%–39%, Linda Chavez, who George W. Bush originally nominated as Labor secretary in 2001.

Mikulski is loud and brash, humorous and warm, brusque and aggressive when she feels it is necessary, curious and thoughtful when encountering another new part of the world. One such world was the Senate. "The House is a scrappy body, and I was scrappy in the body," she explained later. "I knew the Senate was a different institution. I needed to know the rules." In her first term she won a seat on the Appropriations Committee; within two years she was chairman of a subcommittee, handling housing, space and veterans' programs; she was elected Democratic Caucus secretary in 1994. She is also the Senate's chief superintendent of the space program and an enthusiast for space exploration. An ardent backer of the manned space station *Freedom* (often attacked by other liberals), she has battled to keep it alive despite her sympathy for veterans' and housing programs also funded by her subcommittee, which tend to compete for funds. She has also strongly supported the Hubble space telescope. In February 2000, when the Near Earth Asteroid Rendezvous went into orbit around an asteroid, she and NASA Administrator Daniel Goldin high-fived each other. It does not hurt that some NASA facilities are in Maryland—the Goddard Space Center in Greenbelt and the Wallops Island flight facility—but she also keeps an eye on others. She has worked to fund Maryland defense spending, including the Patuxent River Naval Air Station, Curtis Bay Coast Guard Yard and an anti-missile jamming system assembled in Linthicum.

On domestic policy, Mikulski is a liberal who insists that "where there are rights there are responsibilities" and has criticized fellow Democrats for being "angst-addicted." She supported workfare in the 1980s and voted for the Welfare Reform Act of 1996. She voted for the Defense of Marriage Act. She also worked for the 1997 FDA reform, which updated and streamlined the approval process for drugs and medical devices and encouraged safety and efficacy testing on children. With Charles Grassley she sponsored a 2000 law to extend long-term care insurance for 13 million federal employees, military and their dependents. She sponsored a bill to give patients' rights to longer hospital stays, greater access to specialists and, for women, choice of obstetricians and gynecologists. In January 2000 she sponsored a digital divide bill, to fund e-villages in public housing, expand programs creating community technology centers with Internet access and provide tax incentives to businesses that donate technology or training to schools. She is capable of righteous indignation: During the hearings on Firestone tires in September 2000, she asked executives, "Where was your sense as a human being, as well as a corporation, to say, 'Look out, America, these tires are coming apart'?" She is not afraid to cast lonely votes. She was one of eight senators to vote against financial deregulation in November 1999, one of 19 to vote to cut most of the money for Plan Colombia in June 2000 and one of 15 to vote against Permanent Normal Trade Relations with China in September 2000.

Mikulski is the senior woman in the Senate and convenes meetings of women senators. She has pushed many of what might be called women's issues—mammography clinic standards and homemaker IRAs, retaining a guaranteed benefit with inflation protection in Social Security reform. She was the chief Senate co-sponsor with John Chafee and his son and successor Lincoln Chafee of the 2000 breast cancer bill, providing Medicaid financing of mammograms and Pap tests; but she was denied a White House signing ceremony because the chief House sponsor was Rick Lazio, Hillary Rodham Clinton's opponent in the New York Senate race. She defended Anita Hill, opposed the retirement of a four-star admiral because of the Tailhook scandal, blocked reappointment of the architect of the Capitol, condemned former Oregon Senator Bob Packwood as a member of the Ethics Committee, and journeyed to Aberdeen Proving Grounds—in each case pursuing charges of sexual harassment. But she had little to say about Bill Clinton's treatment of White House intern Monica Lewinsky until in late August 1998, when she called his behavior "very disappointing" and his actions "wrong."

Mikulski's skills are not just political. She co-authored *Capitol Offense* and *Capitol Virtues* with Marylouise Oates, mystery novels describing freshman Senator Eleanor Gorzack of Pennsylvania, who is "somewhat younger, somewhat slimmer, but no less politically savvy than I am"—and also 5'4", five inches taller than the 4'11" Mikulski.

Mikulski's toughest Senate election was her first, which she won fairly easily after strong initial competition. In 1992 and 1998 she was re-elected with 71%, first against Alan Keyes, a former Reagan appointee who has since run for president twice, and then against Ross Pierpont, a genial 81-year-old physician who had run for office and lost 14 times.

Presidential politics   In the 1990s Maryland became one of the most Democratic states in presidential elections. It was Bill Clinton's third-best state in 1992 and fifth-best in 1996 and Al Gore's fourth-best in 2000. Whites voted 51%–46% for George W. Bush, but blacks, casting one-quarter of the total, voted 92%–7% for Al Gore

Since 1992 Maryland has held its presidential primaries a week before Super Tuesday to try to get noticed, with limited success. The one notable result: In 1992, Paul Tsongas beat Bill Clinton 41%–33%, with all his margin and more coming from suburban Baltimore and Montgomery County.

Congressional districting   Maryland's convoluted district lines result from an attempt to protect most incumbents and to create two black-majority districts, one in and near Baltimore, the other including most of Prince George's County. These seats drain Democratic votes from adjacent districts, and Republicans have managed to hold four of the eight seats since 1992. Democrats control the redistricting process for 2002, and will probably draw lines to weaken Connie Morella in the Washington suburbs and Bobby Ehrlich in the Baltimore suburbs.

THE PEOPLE: Pop. 2000: 5,296,486; Pop. 1990: 4,781,468, up 10.8% 1990–2000. 1.9% of U.S. total, 19th largest; 64% White, 27.9% Black, 4% Asian, 0.3% Amer. Indian, 2% Two+ races, 1.8% Other; 4.3% Hispanic Origin. 3.9% Unemployment. 2000 Voting age pop.: 3,940,314. 2000 Turnout: 2,036,455; 52% of VAP. Registered voters (2000): 2,715,366; 1,547,117 D (57%), 805,894 R (30%), 362,355 unaffiliated and minor parties (13%).

POLITICAL LINEUP: Governor, Parris N. Glendening (D); Lt. Gov., Kathleen Kennedy Townsend (D); Secy. of State, John T. Willis (D); Atty. Gen., J. Joseph Curran, Jr. (D); Treasurer, Richard Nixon (D); Comptroller, William Schaefer (D); State Senate, 47 (34 D, 13 R); Senate Pres. Pro Tempore, Ida G. Ruben (D); Senate President, Thomas V. Mike Miller Jr. (D); Majority Leader, Clarence Blount (D); State House, 141 (106 D, 35 R); House Speaker, Casper R. Taylor Jr. (D). Senators, Paul S. Sarbanes (D) and Barbara A. Mikulski (D). Representatives, 8 (4 D, 4 R).

ELECTIONS DIVISION: 410-269-2840; **FILING DEADLINE FOR U.S. CONGRESS:** July 1, 2002.

2000 Presidential Vote

Gore (D)	1,145,782	(57%)
Bush (R)	813,797	(40%)
Nader (Green)	53,768	(3%)
Others	12,133	(1%)

1996 Presidential Vote

Clinton (D)	966,208	(54%)
Dole (R)	681,530	(39%)
Perot (I)	115,812	(7%)

2000 Republican Presidential Primary

Bush (R)	211,439	(56%)
McCain (R)	135,981	(36%)
Keyes (R)	25,020	(7%)

2000 Democratic Presidential Primary

Gore (D)	341,630	(67%)
Bradley (D)	144,387	(28%)
Uncommitted	16,935	(3%)

Gov. Parris N. Glendening (D)

Elected 1994, term expires Jan. 2003, 2d term; b. June 11, 1942, Bronx, NY; home, University Park; FL St. U., B.A. 1964, M.A. 1965, Ph.D. 1967; Catholic; married (Frances).

Elected Office: Hyattsville City Cncl., 1973–74; Prince George's Cnty. Cncl., 1974–82; Prince George's Cnty. Exec., 1982–94.

Professional Career: Prof., U. of MD, 1967–94.

Office: State House, Annapolis, 21401, 410-974-3901; Fax: 410-974-2542; Web site: www.gov.state.md.us.

Election Results

1998 general	Parris N. Glendening (D)	846,972	(55%)
	Ellen Sauerbrey (R)	688,357	(45%)
1998 primary	Parris N. Glendening (D)	296,863	(70%)
	Eileen M. Rehrmann (D)	56,806	(13%)
	Terence McGuire (D)	46,124	(11%)
	Lawrence K. Freeman (D)	23,752	(6%)
1994 general	Parris N. Glendening (D)	708,094	(50%)
	Ellen Sauerbrey (R)	702,101	(50%)

Sen. Paul S. Sarbanes (D)

Elected 1976, seat up 2006, 5th term; b. Feb. 3, 1933, Salisbury; home, Baltimore; Princeton, A.B. 1954, Rhodes Scholar, Oxford U., B.A. 1957, Harvard, LL.B. 1960; Greek Orthodox; married (Christine).

Elected Office: MD House of Delegates, 1966–70; U.S. House of Reps., 1970–76.

Professional Career: Law Clerk, Judge Morris A. Soper, U.S. 4th Circuit Crt. of Appeals, 1960–61; Practicing atty., 1961–62, 1965–70; A.A., Pres. Kennedy's Cncl. of Econ. Advisers, 1962–63; Exec. Dir., Baltimore Charter Revision Comm., 1963–64.

DC Office: 309 HSOB, 20510, 202-224-4524; Fax: 202-224-1651; Web site: www.senate.gov/~sarbanes.

State Offices: Baltimore, 410-962-4436; Cobb Island, 301-259-2404; Cumberland, 301-724-0695; Salisbury, 410-860-2131; Silver Spring, 301-589-0797.

Committees: *Banking, Housing & Urban Affairs* (Chmn.). *Budget. Foreign Relations*: European Affairs; International Economic Policy, Export & Trade Promotion (Chmn.); Near Eastern & South Asian Affairs. *Joint Economic Committee* (3d of 10 Sens.).

Group Ratings

	ADA	ACLU	AFS	LCV	CON	ITIC	NTU	COC	ACU	NTLC	CHC
2000	95	71	100	100	63	60	12	40	12	6	15
1999	100	—	100	89	51	—	4	35	4	—	—

National Journal Ratings

	1999 LIB —	1999 CONS	2000 LIB —	2000 CONS
Economic	90%	0%	96%	0%
Social	88%	0%	79%	0%
Foreign	87%	0%	66%	31%

Key Votes of the 106th Congress

1. Educ. Savings Accts.	N	5. Review Movie Violence	N
2. Prescrip. Drug Benefit	Y	6. Gun Show Bckgrnd. Checks	Y
3. Delay Ergonomic Standards	N	7. Ban Part.-Birth Abortion	N
4. Phase Out Estate Tax	N	8. Broaden Hate Crimes List	Y

9. NATO War in Serbia — Y
10. Table Cuba Travel Ban — N
11. Nuclear Test-Ban Treaty — Y
12. Perm. Trade with China — N

Election Results

2000 general	Paul S. Sarbanes (D)	1,230,013	(63%)	($1,837,286)
	Paul H. Rappaport (R)	715,178	(37%)	($146,866)
2000 primary	Paul S. Sarbanes (D)	384,748	(83%)	
	George English (D)	45,984	(10%)	
	Sidney Altman (D)	31,502	(7%)	
1994 general	Paul S. Sarbanes (D)	809,125	(59%)	($2,767,187)
	William Brock (R)	559,908	(41%)	($3,201,650)

Sen. Barbara A. Mikulski (D)

Elected 1986, seat up 2004, 3d term; b. July 20, 1936, Baltimore; home, Baltimore; Mt. St. Agnes Col., B.A. 1958, U. of MD, M.S.W. 1965; Catholic; single.

Elected Office: Baltimore City Cncl., 1971–76; U.S. House of Reps., 1976–86.

Professional Career: Social worker, Baltimore Dept. of Social Svcs., 1965–70; Chmn., DNC Delegate Selection Comm., 1972; Adjunct prof., Loyola Col., 1972–76.

DC Office: 709 HSOB, 20510, 202-224-4654; Fax: 202-224-8858; Web site: www.senate.gov/~mikulski.

State Offices: Annapolis, 410-263-1805; Baltimore, 410-962-4510; Greenbelt, 301-345-5517; Hagerstown, 301-797-2826; Salisbury, 410-546-7711.

Committees: *Democratic Conference Secretary. Appropriations:* Commerce, Justice, State & Judiciary; Foreign Operations; Transportation; Treasury & General Government; VA, HUD & Independent Agencies (Chmn.). *Health, Education, Labor & Pensions:* Aging (Chmn.); Public Health.

Group Ratings

	ADA	ACLU	AFS	LCV	CON	ITIC	NTU	COC	ACU	NTLC	CHC
2000	95	71	100	86	79	63	11	46	8	6	15
1999	100	—	100	67	32	—	6	59	4	—	—

National Journal Ratings

	1999 LIB —	1999 CONS		2000 LIB —	2000 CONS
Economic	84% —	13%		84% —	11%
Social	88% —	0%		79% —	0%
Foreign	87% —	0%		85% —	14%

Key Votes of the 106th Congress

1. Educ. Savings Accts.	N	5. Review Movie Violence	N	9. NATO War in Serbia	Y
2. Prescrip. Drug Benefit	Y	6. Gun Show Bckgrnd. Checks	Y	10. Table Cuba Travel Ban	N
3. Delay Ergonomic Standards	N	7. Ban Part.-Birth Abortion	N	11. Nuclear Test-Ban Treaty	Y
4. Phase Out Estate Tax	N	8. Broaden Hate Crimes List	Y	12. Perm. Trade with China	N

Election Results

1998 general	Barbara A. Mikulski (D)	1,062,810	(71%)	($3,014,312)
	Ross Z. Pierpont (R)	444,637	(30%)	($297,768)
1998 primary	Barbara A. Mikulski (D)	349,382	(84%)	
	Ann L. Mallory (D)	43,120	(10%)	
	Kauko H. Kokkonen (D)	21,658	(5%)	
1992 general	Barbara A. Mikulski (D)	1,307,610	(71%)	($3,623,974)
	Alan L. Keyes (R)	533,688	(29%)	($1,175,682)

FIRST DISTRICT

Chesapeake Bay, technically not a bay but an estuary, was the central focus of the most thickly settled of the 13 colonies, and today remains a central focus for much of modern Maryland and a backwater where an older civilization lives on. The first British here were amazed at the Chesapeake's oysters and terrapin turtles and crabs and rockfish; despite pollution and vastly depleted populations of crabs and oysters, watermen still make hardy livings bringing them to shore. This was an estuary civilization in colonial days, with every little hamlet tied together by the highways of bays and creeks and inlets off the Chesapeake. The streets and docks of Chestertown, Oxford, St. Michaels and Cambridge still look much as they did when George Washington slept there. On the Western Shore, Annapolis was laid out as a capital in 1694, with one circle planned for the Statehouse and one for the Church; the marble-halled Statehouse, built in 1772, where the Continental Congress ratified the Treaty of Paris, is the oldest state capitol in continuous use. Annapolis is the home of the United States Naval Academy and its waterfront, though gentrified, is a waterman's as well as a yachter's port.

In post-colonial times, when most Americans were caught up in the romance of westward movement, these estuaries and peninsulas were mostly forgotten, off the main lines of railroads and highways, left behind by thousands moving west. In the 160 years between 1790 and 1950, the Eastern Shore counties of Maryland only doubled in population, perhaps the slowest growth rate on the Eastern Seaboard. Today much of the Chesapeake has changed beyond recognition. Annapolis is now a distinctive part of the mostly booming Baltimore metropolitan area, and the Eastern Shore has been growing vigorously in the 1980s and 1990s with second-home buyers and commuters across the Chesapeake Bay Bridge. This is a land of genteel estates fronting the water and of Frank Perdue's chicken empire around Salisbury, of Easton's Waterfowl Festival and the swarms of motorboats and sailing ships making their way up and down the inlets or under the twin spans of the Bay Bridge. People are attracted by its continuity with the past and closeness to nature. But recent economic growth also has forced people along the Bay to address modern-day environmental and cultural problems.

The 1st Congressional District of Maryland includes all of the Eastern Shore and, across the Bay, Annapolis and a strip of four-lane highway suburbs up to the southern tip of Baltimore. In national elections, this is a solidly Republican area, voting against Bill Clinton twice and against Al Gore in 2000.

The congressman from the 1st District is Wayne Gilchrest, a Republican with an unusual political history and some unusual political views that stamp him as an independent thinker, both on national and local issues. Gilchrest served in the Marine Corps in Vietnam, taught high school for 13 years and painted houses in the summer. In 1988 he ran for Congress and lost to incumbent Democrat Roy Dyson 50.4%–49.6%; Dyson spent vastly more money but was embarrassed by a *Washington Post* story on his personnel practices. In 1990, Gilchrest ran again, was again vastly outspent, but won 57%–43%. In 1992 redistricting placed him in the same district with Democratic incumbent Tom McMillen, former Rhodes Scholar pro-basketball player. McMillen raised vastly more money, but Gilchrest won 52%–48%, carrying 60% on the Eastern Shore.

Gilchrest's voting record in recent years has been almost precisely at the midpoint of the House, making him a crucial vote on many issues. His specialty, helpfully in a district centered on the Chesapeake Bay, is the environment. His committee assignments—Resources and Transportation, with the chairmanship of the Fisheries and Oceans Panel on Resources—give him some leverage on these issues. In 1995 he took issue with Western Republicans when they sought to relax the Endangered Species Act, even threatening to resign his committee post when a subcommittee chairman wouldn't let him invite scientists to testify in favor of the law at field hearings in the 1st District. He was the only Maryland member to vote for D.C. statehood, and he opposed the National Rifle Association and John Dingell in 1999 on their amendment to weaken restrictions on gun show sales—in a district where many are strongly opposed to gun control. Although he has not been outspoken on foreign policy issues, he was an early supporter of deploying NATO troops to Kosovo.

He also has been a maverick to the point of being courageous—and occasionally effective—in taking on local economic and political powers. He braved local opinion by calling for Ocean City to pay some of the cost of rebuilding Assateague Island, which has eroded because of ocean movements caused by a jetty that protects the Ocean City beach. He attacked large poultry producers for running roughshod over local chicken growers. And, as detailed in a *Washington Post* series in 2000 on the Army Corps of Engineers, he opposed efforts backed by the Port of Baltimore to dredge the Chesapeake and Delaware Canal, which links the Chesapeake and Delaware bays; his objections to the risk of increased pollution outraged powerful Marylanders. In January 2001 the Corps abandoned the plan but will review it in three years.

The independent streak extended to breaking with the Maryland Republican establishment and chairing the Maryland campaign of Senator John McCain in 2000; the two had known each other as members of the Naval Academy's Board of Visitors. "I just want someone in there who has the guts and the brains to do the right thing," Gilchrest said during the primary. Even so, Bush carried the 1st District in the primary.

In his own elections Gilchrest has easily turned back challenges from both left and right. He does not accept PAC contributions, but even so he has regularly outspent his Democratic opponents, and he has won the endorsements of the Sierra Club and League of Conservation Voters. Against five primary opponents in 1996, he won with 65%. He was re-elected with 69% in 1998. He was opposed by a member of the House of Delegates in 2000, and this time Gilchrest won 64%–35%. With his solid base in the Eastern Shore and Annapolis—and the likelihood that no adjacent Democrat will want these areas—Gilchrest is a good bet to survive redistricting.

Cook's Call   *Probably Safe.* Although this Eastern Shore district is not the most Republican in the state (Bush won by 9 %), Gilchrest has had little trouble holding onto this seat. His pro-environment record not only makes sense in this Chesapeake Bay district, but it also makes it difficult for Democrats to paint him as too extreme. However, redistricting could be a problem for Gilchrest if Democrats, who control the redistricting process here, start to play around with this seat. But Gilchrest looks to be in good shape.

THE PEOPLE: Pop. 2000: 682,770; Pop. 1990: 597,821, up 14.2% 1990–2000. 81% White, 15.1% Black, 1.5% Asian, 0.3% Amer. Indian, 1.3% Two+ races, 0.8% Other; 2.2% Hispanic Origin.

2000 Presidential Vote			1996 Presidential Vote		
Bush (R)	140,217	(53%)	Dole (R)	107,122	(48%)
Gore (D)	117,820	(44%)	Clinton (D)	97,338	(43%)
Nader (Green)	7,081	(3%)	Perot (I)	20,779	(9%)
Others	1,841	(1%)			

Rep. Wayne T. Gilchrest (R)

Elected 1990, 6th term; b. Apr. 15, 1946, Rahway, NJ; home, Kennedyville; Wesley Col., A.A. 1971, DE St. Col., B.A. 1973, Loyola Col., 1984; Methodist; married (Barbara).

Military Career: Marine Corps, 1964–68 (Vietnam).

Professional Career: High schl. teacher, 1973–86; Natl. Forest Service worker, Bitterroot Natl. Forest, 1986.

DC Office: 2245 RHOB 20515, 202-225-5311; Fax: 202-225-0254; Web site: www.house.gov/gilchrest.

District Offices: Annapolis, 410-263-6321; Chestertown, 410-778-9407; Salisbury, 410-749-3184.

Committees: *Resources* (8th of 28 R): Fisheries Conservation, Wildlife & Oceans (Chmn.); National Parks, Recreation & Public Lands. *Science* (19th of 25 R): Environment, Technology & Standards. *Transportation & Infrastructure* (6th of 42 R): Coast Guard & Maritime Transportation; Water Resources & Environment.

Group Ratings

	ADA	ACLU	AFS	LCV	CON	ITIC	NTU	COC	ACU	NTLC	CHC
2000	15	18	0	57	6	94	52	80	58	61	43
1999	50	—	0	56	6	—	54	72	52	—	—

National Journal Ratings

	1999 LIB	—	1999 CONS		2000 LIB	—	2000 CONS
Economic	48%	—	50%		46%	—	54%
Social	55%	—	45%		56%	—	43%
Foreign	43%	—	55%		49%	—	49%

Key Votes of the 106th Congress

1. Patient Bill of Rights	Y	5. Bar RU-486 $ for FDA	N	9. NATO War in Serbia	Y
2. Accelerate Min. Wage	Y	6. Display 10 Commandments	Y	10. Perm. Trade with China	Y
3. Strike Ban on Ergo. Stnd.	N	7. Gun Show Bkgrnd. Checks	Y	11. Debt Relief for 3rd World	Y
4. Ovrd. Estate Tax Veto	Y	8. Ban Part.-Birth Abortion	Y	12. Drop Cuba Econ. Embargo	N

Election Results

2000 general	Wayne T. Gilchrest (R)	165,293	(64%)	($225,166)
	Bennett Bozman (D)	91,022	(35%)	($52,487)
2000 primary	Wayne T. Gilchrest (R)	unopposed		
1998 general	Wayne T. Gilchrest (R)	135,771	(69%)	($266,395)
	Irving Pinder (D)	60,450	(31%)	($68,504)

SECOND DISTRICT

The spokes of Baltimore's avenues spread out in all directions from the downtown centered on the Inner Harbor, connecting the central city with the suburbs where most residents of metropolitan Baltimore now live. The streets reach east to Dundalk and Essex, industrial suburbs where the tone of life was set for years by the giant Sparrows Point steel mill, long the biggest in the country. Northeast they extend to modest working class suburbs and the small towns of the Baltimore and Harford County countryside which are now speckled with suburban developments: Bel Air, Joppatowne, Aberdeen, Edgewood; the last two near the Aberdeen Proving Grounds and Edgewood Arsenal military installations. Straight north from downtown are higher-income suburbs and the pleasant county seat of Towson.

The 2d Congressional District of Maryland includes most of this territory. The Sparrows Point area's political tradition is union-Democratic, but that has been tempered lately. The northeast suburbs are ancestrally Democratic, but culturally rather conservative; the suburbs to the north are as solidly Republican as any part of Maryland.

The congressman from the 2d District is Bob Ehrlich, a Republican first elected in 1994. Ehrlich grew up in a rowhouse in the modest suburb of Arbutus, the son of a car salesman. A six-footer at 13, he got a football scholarship to the elite Gilman School in Baltimore and then to Princeton, where he was a linebacker; he went to law school at Wake Forest, working part-time as assistant football coach, then practiced law in Baltimore. Ehrlich volunteered in Republican campaigns and in 1986, at 28, was elected to the Maryland House of Delegates. There he worked on tough sentencing and child pornography laws, but also opposed some bills as unneeded or unconstitutional. When 2d District Congresswoman Helen Delich Bentley ran for governor in 1994 (only to be upset in the primary by anti-tax legislator Ellen Sauerbrey), Ehrlich ran for the House. He campaigned as an opponent of over-regulation, as a military hawk and a libertarian, and beat an anti-abortion candidate in the primary, 57%–38%. In the fall contest, he campaigned against the House Democratic leadership and signed the Contract With America, though he opposed term limits. He was enthusiastic about tax cuts. He ran ads showing the rowhouse where he grew up and said the most important lessons he learned were around the dining room table. The result was a solid 63%–37% Ehrlich victory.

Initially, Ehrlich showed a willingness to cast tough votes, as when he opposed the minimum wage hike and argued that it "will make some marginal workers happier and put a little money in their pockets, but you cost the other marginal workers their jobs. That's not the group we should do harm to." He also opposed gun control and supported property rights. He supported the partial-birth abortion ban, though he does not back a ban on all abortions. In June 1998 he got a majority of Republican members to sign his letter requesting the Steering Committee to take into account votes on procedural issues when determining committee assignments and naming committee and subcommittee chairmen—an idea obnoxious to (and perhaps aimed at) his 1st District neighbor Wayne Gilchrest. But he eventually broke with the Republican leadership on other social issues, such as displaying the Ten Commandments in public schools, and he has praised the Consumer Product Safety Commission for keeping kids safe. And he voted against Permanent Normal Trade Relations with China, siding with local unions. He worked on local projects like protecting Baltimore's Home Port status and teaching hospitals Baltimore County.

Ehrlich has won re-election easily and has had his eye on statewide office but has been dismayed by the strong Democratic margins in the state. In 1998 he gave some thought to running against Senator Paul Sarbanes in 2000, but after Governor Parris Glendening's solid re-election victory in November 1998, he decided not to run. Before the 2000 election, he admitted interest in running for governor, a contest in which he likely would face the popular Lieutenant Governor Kathleen Kennedy Townsend (who ran in the 2d District and lost to Bentley in 1986). Ehrlich has made hundreds of appearances across Maryland and set up a PAC to contribute to Republicans running for the House of Delegates. Like Ellen Sauerbrey, their conservative nominee in 1994 and 1998, Ehrlich urges tax cuts. He also criticizes Democratic prosecutors as weak on tracking down criminals carrying guns. But the poor performance of George W. Bush in Maryland—he lost 57%–40%—made a statewide race seem a formidable challenge. Yet Democratic redistricters have sent clear signals that Ehrlich's district faces major surgery, as it probably becomes a mostly Baltimore County seat. That could be tailor-made for popular Baltimore County Executive Dutch Ruppersberger, a Democrat who also has explored running for governor against Townsend. Other parts of Ehrlich's district probably would be merged with that of Wayne Gilchrest.

Cook's Call *Potentially Competitive.* Centered in Baltimore County suburbs, the 2nd District has been quite friendly to Republicans. Bush won the district with 55% in 2000 and Ehrlich has never dipped below 62% in his four runs for the seat. But Democrats, who control the redistricting pen, are anxious to try to draw Ehrlich out of this seat. Perhaps seeing the writing on the wall, Ehrlich has also been contemplating a run for governor. Still, Ehrlich, a smart and very savvy politician, will not be easy to beat.

THE PEOPLE: Pop. 2000: 652,938; Pop. 1990: 597,450, up 9.3% 1990–2000. 87.2% White, 8.2% Black, 2.4% Asian, 0.3% Amer. Indian, 1.3% Two+ races, 0.5% Other; 1.7% Hispanic Origin.

2000 Presidential Vote			1996 Presidential Vote		
Bush (R)	148,962	(55%)	Dole (R)	119,178	(50%)
Gore (D)	111,627	(41%)	Clinton (D)	95,112	(40%)
Nader (Green)	7,724	(3%)	Perot (I)	22,412	(9%)
Others	1,716	(1%)			

Rep. Robert L. Ehrlich, Jr. (R)

Elected 1994, 4th term; b. Nov. 25, 1957, Arbutus; home, Mays Chapel; Princeton U., B.A. 1979, Wake Forest U., J.D. 1982; Methodist; married (Kendel).

Elected Office: MD House of Delegates, 1986–94.

Professional Career: Practicing atty., 1982–94.

DC Office: 315 CHOB 20515, 202-225-3061; Fax: 202-225-3094; Web site: www.house.gov/ehrlich.

District Offices: Bel Air, 410-838-2517; Dundalk, 410-284-6828; Essex, 410-780-3911; Lutherville, 410-337-7222; Pasedena, 410-225-6983.

Committees: *Energy & Commerce* (24th of 31 R): Environment & Hazardous Materials; Health; Telecommunications & The Internet.

Group Ratings

	ADA	ACLU	AFS	LCV	CON	ITIC	NTU	COC	ACU	NTLC	CHC
2000	20	36	14	21	66	78	60	85	88	84	86
1999	20	—	0	25	47	—	57	83	83	—	—

National Journal Ratings

	1999 LIB —	1999 CONS		2000 LIB —	2000 CONS
Economic	22% —	77%		41% —	58%
Social	52% —	47%		47% —	52%
Foreign	40% —	60%		12% —	78%

Key Votes of the 106th Congress

1. Patient Bill of Rights	N	5. Bar RU-486 $ for FDA	N	9. NATO War in Serbia	N
2. Accelerate Min. Wage	N	6. Display 10 Commandments	N	10. Perm. Trade with China	N
3. Strike Ban on Ergo. Stnd.	N	7. Gun Show Bkgrnd. Checks	N	11. Debt Relief for 3rd World	N
4. Ovrd. Estate Tax Veto	Y	8. Ban Part.-Birth Abortion	Y	12. Drop Cuba Econ. Embargo	N

Election Results

2000 general	Robert L. Ehrlich Jr. (R)	178,556	(69%)	($871,393)
	Kenneth T. Bosley (D)	81,591	(31%)	
2000 primary	Robert L. Ehrlich Jr. (R)	unopposed		
1998 general	Robert L. Ehrlich Jr. (R)	145,711	(69%)	($487,110)
	Kenneth T. Bosley (D)	64,474	(31%)	

THIRD DISTRICT

Baltimore, one of America's major cities since the Revolution, in the 1990s suddenly became one of America's star cities. Its Inner Harbor and new ballpark at Camden Yards became national models. Its cuisine—steamed crabs with Chesapeake spices, crab cakes—became known beyond the watershed of the Chesapeake Bay. The central city of Baltimore has terrible problems—high crime, abandoned neighborhoods, poor schools—but the greater Baltimore that has grown far beyond the city and county lines retains a distinctive character. There is a patina of age, as on its 1829 Washington Monument and the townhouses of Mount Vernon Square, and an atmosphere of tolerance and diversity nurtured by Maryland's founding Catholics in search of liberty; the nation's first Catholic diocese and cathedral were built here when America was overwhelmingly and militantly Protestant. This is a city built solidly on commerce, and one that has always known how to reap its pleasures.

The 3d Congressional District of Maryland is centered on Baltimore and consists of three portions that extend outward like spokes of a wheel from the focus of the Inner Harbor, with boundaries designed to build a black-majority 7th District next door. One spoke extends northeast out into the Polish Highlandtown neighborhood and the mostly white Catholic northeast precincts and close-in suburbs of Overlea and Parkville. Another extends northwest to the heavily Jewish suburbs of Pikesville and Owings Mills, past the array of temples and synagogues on Park Heights Avenue to Jewish subdivisions. A third spoke extends southwest, past the old rowhouse neighborhoods overlooking Fort McHenry and out past Arbutus and Lansdowne into Linthicum and Fort Meade in Anne Arundel County and Elkridge and Columbia in Howard County, at the cusp of the invisible boundary between metro Baltimore and metro Washington. The 3d District is ancestrally Democratic and remains loyal to Democrats in most elections. Pikesville and Columbia are solidly liberal on most issues; the close-in areas are culturally more conservative.

The congressman from the 3d is Benjamin Cardin, former speaker of the Maryland House of Delegates and one of the many bright politicos produced by the Jewish neighborhoods of northwest Baltimore. He was elected to the House of Delegates in 1966, at 23, the first time he was eligible to run; he became speaker in 1979, at 35; and was easily elected to Congress in 1986 when Barbara Mikulski ran for the Senate. In the House, Cardin got a seat on Ways and Means in his second term and has been a productive and creative legislator. He supported NAFTA despite union opposition, backed a cap on medical malpractice damages despite trial lawyers' opposition, and voted for Permanent Normal Trade Relations with China after securing for local consumption a rider designed to crack down on international dumping of subsidized steel in U.S. markets.

More than any Democrat at Ways and Means—and perhaps more than any Democrat in the House—he has worked skillfully on bipartisan legislation at a time when few were sufficiently clever or independent to pursue such initiatives. Few House members of either party "can match his stature as legislative architect and master of bipartisan lawmaking," The Baltimore *Sun* editorialized. "Being a member of Congress is about working with Democrats and Republicans and crafting legislation. From reforming the IRS to protecting pensions, members need to work together," Cardin has said. Such has been his record, occasionally to the dismay of more partisan Democrats. His bill to restore the tax deduction for health insurance for the self-employed was quickly passed in the Republican Congress in 1995. He was co-sponsor with Rob Portman of the 1998 IRS reform law, the first major reform in four decades, which shifted the burden of proof away from the taxpayer and toward the government, established greater oversight of the agency, and encouraged electronic filing and updated technology. Again with Portman, he crafted in 2000 major bipartisan legislation to expand 401(k) savings and other retirement plans. In May 2001 the House overwhelmingly approved his and Portman's measure to increase the maximum IRA contribution from $2000 to $5000 annually as well as limits on 401(k) contributions. He worked with Nancy Johnson to expand child support for single parents seeking to work their way off welfare. On Social Security, too, he has shown willingness to seek bipartisan reform: "Ultimately we should look carefully at the possibility of permitting younger working Americans to direct some part of their FICA taxes into private retirement-saving accounts." Other Ways and Means Democrats were irritated when he cosponsored on the eve of the 2000 election Clay Shaw's plan to improve Social Security management, even though his own party had made Shaw one of its top targets for defeat. Cardin could become a key legislator—perhaps the key legislator—on Social Security reform.

Cardin has also been a work horse on health care. He helped draft the Democrats' version of managed care reform, including the provision that guarantees patients the right to an external process to appeal adverse health insurance decisions. On prescription drugs for seniors, he opposed Republicans' plans for private insurance coverage. To support beleaguered teaching hospitals, like Baltimore's Johns Hopkins and the University of Maryland, he proposed a 1% fee on health insurance premiums to finance medical education. He also has worked across the aisle at Ways and Means with Bill Thomas to protect the privacy of medical records.

Now in his fourth decade as a legislator, Cardin takes an institutional focus. He and Jim Nussle proposed a budget process reform to move to biennial budgeting, force earlier agreement between the president and Congress, avoid government shutdowns and impose more discipline on routine spending. But their proposal became the victim of attacks from both sides of the aisle in 2000 and it lost 217–201 in a preliminary vote, with opponents saying it would create more problems than it would solve. He was ranking Democrat on the Ethics subcommittee that painstakingly investigated the charges and resulted in sanctions against then-Speaker Newt Gingrich. In a more partisan—though futile—effort, he was deputized by Dick Gephardt to prepare the House Democrats' transition plan for running the House if they had won control in the 2000 election.

Cardin has been mentioned many times as a candidate for governor, and in 1997 canvassed support. But few politicians were willing to back him publicly, and—as in the 1980s—he cautiously deferred to party loyalty. With no foreseeable opportunity to take a Senate seat, he is left with the satisfaction of being a major policy-maker even as an increasingly senior member of the minority party. Maryland's Democratic redistricters will surely see that he has a congenial district in 2002, and he will surely continue to be re-elected easily.

Cook's Call   *Safe.* Cardin is well entrenched in this heavily Democratic Baltimore-based district. Population loss in Baltimore means that his district will have to move further out from the city. But Cardin's district is only short by about 18,000 people, while Elijah Cummings' inner city Baltimore district will need to pick up more than 120,000 people.

THE PEOPLE: Pop. 2000: 643,935; Pop. 1990: 597,712, up 7.7% 1990–2000. 66.5% White, 26.8% Black, 3.2% Asian, 0.3% Amer. Indian, 2% Two+ races, 1.1% Other; 2.8% Hispanic Origin.

2000 Presidential Vote		
Gore (D)	149,644	(63%)
Bush (R)	80,250	(34%)
Nader (Green)	7,376	(3%)
Others	1,462	(1%)

1996 Presidential Vote		
Clinton (D)	123,532	(58%)
Dole (R)	72,017	(34%)
Perot (I)	13,872	(7%)

Rep. Benjamin Cardin (D)

Elected 1986, 8th term; b. Oct. 5, 1943, Baltimore; home, Baltimore; U. of Pittsburgh, B.A. 1964, U. of MD, LL.B., J.D. 1967; Jewish; married (Myrna).

Elected Office: MD House of Delegates, 1966–86, Speaker, 1979–86.

Professional Career: Practicing atty., 1967–86.

DC Office: 2267 RHOB 20515, 202-225-4016; Fax: 202-225-9219; Web site: www.house.gov/cardin.

District Office: Baltimore, 410-433-8886.

Committees: *Ways & Means* (6th of 17 D): Human Resources (RMM); Social Security.

Group Ratings

	ADA	ACLU	AFS	LCV	CON	ITIC	NTU	COC	ACU	NTLC	CHC
2000	90	86	85	93	78	72	23	42	8	18	13
1999	100	—	100	88	63	—	14	28	0	—	—

National Journal Ratings

	1999 LIB	—	1999 CONS		2000 LIB	—	2000 CONS
Economic	67%	—	32%		85%	—	11%
Social	79%	—	20%		94%	—	0%
Foreign	85%	—	12%		66%	—	33%

Key Votes of the 106th Congress

1. Patient Bill of Rights	Y	5. Bar RU-486 $ for FDA	N	9. NATO War in Serbia	Y
2. Accelerate Min. Wage	Y	6. Display 10 Commandments	N	10. Perm. Trade with China	Y
3. Strike Ban on Ergo. Stnd.	Y	7. Gun Show Bkgrnd. Checks	Y	11. Debt Relief for 3rd World	Y
4. Ovrd. Estate Tax Veto	N	8. Ban Part.-Birth Abortion	N	12. Drop Cuba Econ. Embargo	N

Election Results

2000 general	Benjamin Cardin (D)	169,347	(76%)	($564,687)
	Colin Harby (R)	53,827	(24%)	
2000 primary	Benjamin Cardin (D)	unopposed		
1998 general	Benjamin Cardin (D)	137,501	(78%)	($441,950)
	Colin Harby (R)	39,667	(22%)	

FOURTH DISTRICT

In 1696 the proprietors of the colony of Maryland created a new county between the Potomac and Patuxent Rivers and named it after the husband of the heir to the throne, Prince George of Denmark. For 300 years Prince George's County has not often won national fame—maybe briefly when investigators chased the plotters of Abraham Lincoln's murder here—but it should now. Historically Prince George's was tobacco country, rural and heavily settled, with blacks and Catholics and big property-owners who pretty much ran things. Today Prince George's is—or should be known as—the home of America's largest black middle class, a place that gives a hopeful glimpse of the future. Prince George's is affluent by national standards, with over 70% of women working, one of the highest percentages in the nation; with office and shopping mall growth, it has proved itself a far more commercially vibrant and culturally constructive community—including substantial home-schooling—than adjacent parts of the District of Columbia. New economic projects include the building of a 12-lane span across the Potomac, which will replace the deteriorating Wilson Bridge, plus a huge new hotel and conference center near the bridge. Prince George's has always had many black residents, since the first tobacco crop was planted, but that population grew as middle-class blacks moved out of Washington into modest suburbs at the county's edge and affluent subdivisions far to the east. The black percentage here increased from 14% in 1970 to 37% in 1980, and nearly 65% by 2000. The county's median household income of more than $55,000 compares favorably with the national median of about $43,000 and is double the national median for black households.

The 4th Congressional District of Maryland includes most of Prince George's County and a portion of Montgomery County to the west; it is mostly, but not entirely, inside the Capital Beltway. The biggest industry here is still government: It has highest percentage of federal government employees than any congressional district in the nation.

The congressman from the 4th District is Albert Wynn, a Democrat effectively chosen in the 1992 primary. Wynn grew up in Prince George's County, attending all-black schools there until integration began in his sophomore year. He went to the University of Pittsburgh on a debate team scholarship and received a law degree from Georgetown University. He served a decade in the Maryland legislature, first as a member of the House and later the Senate, where he was deputy majority whip. Twenty candidates—13 Democrats and seven Republicans—ran for the seat when it was created in 1992; the two best known were Wynn and Prince George's State's Attorney Alex Williams. But Wynn was better funded, and his "put America first" platform, emphasizing domestic issues and attacks on George Bush, overshadowed Williams' proclamation that he would be "a strong, independent voice for Congress." Wynn was endorsed by the *Prince George's Journal* and *The Washington Post* and won the primary with 28% of the vote, to 26% for Williams. He has had no close contest since then.

"I consider myself a team player," Wynn has said, a loyal member of the Democratic Caucus who campaigned heartily for Bill Clinton, Al Gore and Governor Parris Glendening when each was beleaguered. One of his causes has been racial discrimination in the federal government. On behalf of the American Federation of Government Employees and its opposition to privatization, he took the lead in seeking to halt contracting-out of federal jobs until Congress could improve its monitoring. He worked with Republican John Mica to streamline the Equal Employment Opportunity complaint process and reduce the backlog of EEO cases. As head of the Congressional Black Caucus's minority business task force, he has pushed for more federal contracting with black businesses and, more generally, with small businesses, raising the goal from 20% to 23% and trying to restrict bundling (contract consolidation), which he says put contracts beyond the reach of small businesses; he received the SBA's first "Administrator's Leadership Award" in 1998. A non-racial issue that has gained his attention at the Commerce Committee is his call to ban automatic dialing systems to send recorded telephone messages.

Wynn lost the race for caucus vice chairman in November 1998 but continues to serve as a deputy whip and represents the Black Caucus in the Democratic Leadership Council. At home Wynn sponsors an annual jobs fair, bringing together 9,000 jobseekers and over 200 employers. He has won re-election without difficulty, though he has been the target of nasty attack from his little-known Republican opponent, John Kimble, who once offered to pose naked for *Playgirl* magazine, saying "I'll do whatever it takes to win the election." In one of the more creative features of the 2000 campaign, Kimble transmitted a 20-second telephone message from Wynn's former wife Jessie, which said that the congressman "does not respect black women. He left me for a white woman," and urged support for Kimble, who is white. She also criticized her ex-husband for failing to provide adequate financial support. None of it seems to have much impact. Wynn won again, with 87%.

Cook's Call   *Safe.* Wynn has one of the safest Democratic seats in the country. Gore won this majority black district with 84%. As such, Democratic line drawers have discussed taking some parts of this district, such as heavily Democratic Takoma Park, and placing them into the 8th District held by Republican Connie Morella. This would make Morella's already Democratic-leaning district even more unfriendly territory for her.

THE PEOPLE: Pop. 2000: 648,764; Pop. 1990: 597,791, up 8.5% 1990–2000. 22.1% White, 64.7% Black, 4.9% Asian, 0.3% Amer. Indian, 0.1% Hawaiian, 3.1% Two+ races, 4.9% Other; 10% Hispanic Origin.

2000 Presidential Vote			1996 Presidential Vote		
Gore (D)	178,977	(84%)	Clinton (D)	152,396	(81%)
Bush (R)	28,438	(13%)	Dole (R)	30,071	(16%)
Nader (Green)	4,380	(2%)	Perot (I)	5,591	(3%)

Rep. Albert Wynn (D)

Elected 1992, 5th term; b. Sept. 10, 1951, Philadelphia, PA; home, Largo; U. of Pittsburgh, B.S. 1973, Howard U., 1973–74, Georgetown U. Law Schl., J.D. 1977; Baptist; divorced.

Elected Office: MD House of Delegates, 1982–87; MD Senate 1987–92.

Professional Career: Exec. Dir., Prince Georges Cnty. Consumer Protection Comm., 1977–81; Chmn., Metro Wash. Cncl. of Consumer Agencies, 1980–81; Practicing atty., 1981–92.

DC Office: 434 CHOB 20515, 202-225-8699; Fax: 202-225-8714; Web site: www.house.gov/wynn.

District Offices: Oxon Hill, 301-839-5570; Silver Spring, 301-588-7328; Springdale, 301-773-4094.

Committees: *Energy & Commerce* (16th of 26 D): Energy & Air Quality; Health.

Group Ratings

	ADA	ACLU	AFS	LCV	CON	ITIC	NTU	COC	ACU	NTLC	CHC
2000	85	79	85	71	37	65	19	57	12	3	8
1999	100	—	100	81	56	—	13	22	4	—	—

National Journal Ratings

	1999 LIB —	1999 CONS		2000 LIB —	2000 CONS
Economic	83%	17%		72%	28%
Social	75%	25%		83%	17%
Foreign	88%	12%		74%	24%

Key Votes of the 106th Congress

1. Patient Bill of Rights	Y	5. Bar RU-486 $ for FDA	N	9. NATO War in Serbia	Y
2. Accelerate Min. Wage	Y	6. Display 10 Commandments	N	10. Perm. Trade with China	N
3. Strike Ban on Ergo. Stnd.	Y	7. Gun Show Bkgrnd. Checks	Y	11. Debt Relief for 3rd World	Y
4. Ovrd. Estate Tax Veto	N	8. Ban Part.-Birth Abortion	N	12. Drop Cuba Econ. Embargo	Y

Election Results

2000 general	Albert Wynn (D)	172,624	(87%)	($465,471)
	John B. Kimble (R)	24,973	(13%)	
2000 primary	Albert Wynn (D)	60,873	(88%)	
	Richard Rosenthal (D)	8,217	(12%)	
1998 general	Albert Wynn (D)	129,139	(86%)	($529,177)
	John B. Kimble (R)	21,518	(14%)	

FIFTH DISTRICT

Southern Maryland was first settled by Catholics, the Calvert family of the Lords Baltimore, who founded St. Marys in 1634, not long after Jamestown and Plymouth Rock. Maryland became one of the two great Chesapeake tobacco colonies, and plantation houses were built on every inlet off the broad Potomac and Patuxent Rivers. For years, none of these towns grew much, and even today many people here are directly descended from the old families. But tobacco farming is nearing an end here as 70% of the state's 950 remaining tobacco farmers have applied for a state buyout offered by Governor Parris Glendening. The biggest growth came from government installations like the Civil War Point Lookout prisoner-of-war camp and the Patuxent River Naval Complex, where many astronauts got their first training. This was never puritanical country: liquor flowed even during Prohibition and slot machines were specifically allowed for years by Maryland law.

The 5th Congressional District includes the three counties of southern Maryland, now attracting people who grew up in metro Washington and Baltimore, plus large slices of suburban Prince George's and Anne Arundel counties between Washington and Annapolis. Its lines were drawn to make the adjacent 4th District in Prince George's majority-black, though with blacks moving outward in Prince George's and southern Maryland's historic black population, the 5th was 29% black in 2000. Many of its people live north of Washington, in College Park, home of the University of Maryland, and in Hyattsville, Greenbelt, Beltsville and Laurel. The 5th also includes southern Prince George's, from Clinton south, and the suburbs of Bowie, Crofton and Davidsonville just west of Annapolis. Historically, this is a Democratic area. As blacks move to places like Bowie, the median household income has increased, but so has racial tension.

The congressman from the 5th District is Steny Hoyer, a veteran Democrat and one of his party's leaders in the House, who was first elected in 1981. Hoyer was elected to the Maryland Senate in 1966, at 27, just after graduating from law school. He was Senate president from 1975–78, the youngest in Maryland history; he made a misstep running for lieutenant governor on a losing ticket in 1978. But when the 5th District, then entirely in Prince George's, was declared vacant in 1981—after incumbent Gladys Spellman went into an irreversible coma—Hoyer won the special election by edging out Spellman's husband and several other Democrats in the primary and beating a well-financed, competent Republican candidate in the general.

Interestingly, Hoyer is of Danish descent, like the original Prince George. He has fine political instincts, works hard and can speak in an old-fashioned patriotic style that is genuinely moving.

A fast riser in Maryland politics, he was also a fast riser in Congress. He excelled at constituency service and soon won a seat on the Appropriations Committee, where he became a key player for the whole D.C. metropolitan area. When Democrats had control, Hoyer chaired the Treasury, Postal Service and General Government Appropriations Subcommittee, which oversees several major components of the federal work force and the White House budget. He used the panel to get $6 million for flexiplace telecommuting centers, to encourage buyouts when payrolls are reduced, to kill a Republican proposal to require federal employees to pay fair market value for parking, to get a 4.8% raise for all federal employees in 1999 with a formula that increased it in the Washington area to 4.94%, and to roll back benefit contribution rates for federal employees to 1998 levels in 2001. He has pushed for funding for Chesapeake Bay cleanup and dredging the Bay for Baltimore harbor; he got into a dispute with Wayne Gilchrest over whether dredging spoils should be dumped near the Bay Bridge. He got money for *Pfiesteria* research, adding acreage to the Patuxent wildlife reserve, buying a 5,500-acre parcel along the Potomac, which includes a Civil War encampment and North America's largest ship graveyard, and starting the Chesapeake Bay Oyster Recovery Project. He got the proposed National Harbor resort exempted further federal review in 1999. Hoyer has worked indefatigably and shrewdly to maintain and increase jobs at the Goddard Space Flight Center in Greenbelt, the Patuxent River Naval Air Station, and the Naval Surface Warfare Center at Indian Head. He uses his Appropriations seat to fund programs and to see that local facilities are suited for them. In summer 2000 he added to the Clinton budget $3 million for the Joint Strike Fighter, $2.5 million for Force Operational Readiness Combat Simulator, and $7.5 million for a Navy Remote Emitter Simulator. He helped get the Marine Corps chemical and biological warfare team moved to Indian Head in 2000. "This is a business," he says, "where you're either growing or you're going."

Hoyer's voting record is fairly liberal, though less so than when he represented a near-black-majority district in the late 1980s. He broke with party lines by supporting the balanced budget amendment in 1995, but worked hard in 1996 to support Democratic stands on the minimum wage and health insurance portability; he backed NAFTA, GATT, fast track and Permanent Normal Trade Relations with China. He was the chief House sponsor of the Americans with Disabilities Act of 1990. He opposes the partial-birth abortion ban and called the Republican bill "an outrageous, partisan political approach." He backs the Shays-Meehan campaign finance bill. In June 1999 he helped launch dozens of motions against the legislative appropriation, arguing that the Republican leadership unilaterally rewrote the appropriation bill. He defended raising the president's salary to $400,000 on the ground that the current value of George Washington's salary was $4.6 million. He begged Speaker Dennis Hastert to lobby for the resolution supporting the Bosnia bombing in April 1999, which was defeated 213–213—"one of the most shameful things the House has done since I was a member." In 2000 he supported a bill to allow local zoning decisions to be appealed to federal court. In February 2001 Hoyer offered a bill to provide $434 million to phase out punch-card ballots. In March 2001 he was one of 10 Democrats urging President Bush to end preferential treatment for Smith & Wesson.

In 1989 Hoyer was elected chairman of the Democratic Caucus, a term-limited position he left in 1994. When he tried to move up in June 1991, he was beaten for majority whip by David Bonior, who had the support of liberals and committee chairmen, 160–109. He then became chairman of the Democratic Steering Committee and was parliamentarian at the 2000 Democratic National Convention. During much of 2000 he conducted a campaign for majority whip against Nancy Pelosi, all premised on the notion that Democrats would win control of the House. He ran as the candidate with the more moderate voting record: "I represent the kind of district we need to win if we're going to win back and keep the House." He acknowledged Pelosi's appeal as a woman and a Californian, but insisted, "If the objective is to have the most effective whip, then I think I can do the best job of bringing the caucus together." The contest became academic when Democrats failed to win a majority in November 2000. But with the possibility of a Democratic majority next time far from remote, the race may continue through 2001 and 2002.

After the 1992 redistricting, Hoyer had some serious Republican competition. In 1992, against Lawrence Hogan Jr., whose father was a Prince George's congressman, Hoyer won 53%–44%, thanks to a 60%–38% margin in Prince George's. In 1994, against Donald Devine, director of OPM in the first Reagan term, he spent $1.3 million and won 59%–41%. He won by much wider margins in 1998 and 2000. Redistricting poses no terrors. Though he may lose some of Prince George's to the black-majority 4th District, he has shown he can carry southern Maryland and Anne Arundel; and redistricting is controlled by friendly Democrats who don't want to lose his clout on Capitol Hill.

Cook's Call   *Safe.* With Democrats controlling the redistricting process in Maryland in 2001, Hoyer is likely to see this district shored up for him. It was one of the fastest growing in the state.

THE PEOPLE: Pop. 2000: 714,886; Pop. 1990: 597,573, up 19.6% 1990–2000. 62.9% White, 29.1% Black, 3.7% Asian, 0.4% Amer. Indian, 0.1% Hawaiian, 2.2% Two+ races, 1.7% Other; 3.9% Hispanic Origin.

2000 Presidential Vote

Gore (D)	149,191	(55%)
Bush (R)	112,510	(42%)
Nader (Green)	6,257	(2%)
Others	1,589	(1%)

1996 Presidential Vote

Clinton (D)	117,345	(51%)
Dole (R)	95,737	(42%)
Perot (I)	14,546	(6%)

Rep. Steny H. Hoyer (D)

Elected May 1981, 10th term; b. June 14, 1939, New York, NY; home, Mitchellville; U. of MD, B.S. 1963, Georgetown U., J.D. 1966; Baptist; widowed.

Elected Office: MD Senate, 1966–78, Pres., 1975–78.

Professional Career: Practicing atty., 1966–80; MD Bd. of Higher Educ., 1978–81.

DC Office: 1705 LHOB 20515, 202-225-4131; Fax: 202-225-4300; Web site: www.house.gov/hoyer.

District Offices: Greenbelt, 301-474-0119; Waldorf, 301-843-1577.

Committees: *Democratic Steering Committee Co-Chair. Appropriations* (5th of 29 D): Labor, HHS & Education; The Legislative Branch; Treasury, Postal Service & General Government (RMM). *House Administration* (RMM of 3 D).

Group Ratings

	ADA	ACLU	AFS	LCV	CON	ITIC	NTU	COC	ACU	NTLC	CHC
2000	80	86	85	79	69	65	23	47	12	15	13
1999	90	—	100	69	73	—	14	20	8	—	—

National Journal Ratings

	1999 LIB —	1999 CONS		2000 LIB —	2000 CONS
Economic	71% —	28%		75% —	24%
Social	79% —	20%		91% —	6%
Foreign	74% —	23%		58% —	40%

Key Votes of the 106th Congress

1. Patient Bill of Rights	Y	5. Bar RU-486 $ for FDA	N	9. NATO War in Serbia	Y
2. Accelerate Min. Wage	Y	6. Display 10 Commandments	N	10. Perm. Trade with China	Y
3. Strike Ban on Ergo. Stnd.	Y	7. Gun Show Bkgrnd. Checks	Y	11. Debt Relief for 3rd World	Y
4. Ovrd. Estate Tax Veto	N	8. Ban Part.-Birth Abortion	N	12. Drop Cuba Econ. Embargo	N

Election Results

2000 general	Steny H. Hoyer (D)	166,231	(65%)	($1,268,702)
	Tim Hutchins (R)	89,019	(35%)	($64,208)
2000 primary	Steny H. Hoyer (D)	46,599	(81%)	
	Bruce M. Ross (D)	11,163	(19%)	
1998 general	Steny H. Hoyer (D)	126,792	(65%)	($916,632)
	Robert B. Ostrom (R)	67,176	(35%)	($235,004)

SIXTH DISTRICT

America's first frontier was in western Maryland, where the Appalachian ridges that cross the state diagonally from northeast to southwest cut through the long green sloping fields. These wheat fields were settled first by Pennsylvania Dutch and Scots-Irish hill people, not Chesapeake Bay tobacco growers. Maryland is where the fall line comes closest to an ocean port, where the 19th Century's great paths to the interior were staked out: The National Road, and then the nation's first railroad, the Baltimore & Ohio, crossed the wide valleys of bounteous farms and climbed over the Catoctin Mountains. Towns grew up on narrow streets lined with rowhouses that today are overhung with telephone and streetcar wires, overlooking long vistas of cornfields, pastureland and mountains of ancient stone rising above the plains. Across this placid land moved vast armies during the Civil War. In Frederick, city officials paid Confederates $200,000 not to burn down the town, and near Sharpsburg, blue- and gray-clad soldiers fought the Battle of Antietam, on the bloodiest day in American military history. Today, there is a new rush of settlement in Carroll and Howard Counties, long parts of metro Baltimore, and Frederick County, which is classified as part of metro Washington.

The 6th Congressional District of Maryland includes all of western Maryland, and runs east to Carroll County northwest of Baltimore and the old town of Ellicott City in Howard County. The political tradition in most of this area, unlike the rest of Maryland, is Republican. This was Union country in the Civil War and has been mostly Republican ever since. The new rush of settlement seems to come from those seeking respite from metropolitan crime, strengthening the area's already conservative leanings. The 6th voted solidly for Bob Dole in 1996 and George W. Bush in 2000.

The congressman from the 6th District is a Republican who matches its current mood, Roscoe Bartlett. "I represent my district well. I essentially never have to vote to violate my conscience," he says. He is an interesting character, a descendant of a signer of the Declaration of Independence and a Seventh Day Adventist with 10 children; he grew up in poverty in Pennsylvania, but his family would not take welfare. He invented life-support equipment for pilots, astronauts and fire fighters, ran his own business and taught at Frederick Community College. When Bartlett first ran for Congress in 1992, he was a 65-year-old retired University of Maryland physiology professor who seemed to have no chance of winning. Democrat Beverly Byron had represented the district for 14 years, had a conservative voting record, but was upset in the primary by Delegate Thomas Hattery, a liberal who favored national health insurance and abortion rights. Bartlett's conservative views and his attacks on Hattery for legislative perks won him a 54%–46% victory. That unlikely background explains why fellow conservative Bob Stump of Arizona said Bartlett views his job as "almost like a retirement thing."

Bartlett has proved a surprisingly durable, though iconoclastic, politician. He has one of the most conservative voting records in the House and was the only Marylander to vote for all 10 provisions of the Contract With America. Camp David is in the 6th District, and in May 1994 it was Bartlett who drew attention to a local newspaper photograph showing Clinton aide David Watkins boarding a White House helicopter at a Frederick County golf course. He carries a copy of the Constitution and consults it frequently. He voted against Permanent Normal Trade Relations with China in September 2000 because of Chinese human rights abuses and threats to American national security, he said; he has voted no on various big-spending budget bills.

Bartlett was gratified by November 2000 enactment of his bill to end the Pentagon's practice of euthanizing military working dogs at the end of their useful career. "These military dogs deserve a dignified retirement in loving homes in return for their unique and irreplaceable service to our country," he said. He has been less successful in pushing the recommendation of a commission headed by former Senator Nancy Kassebaum-Baker that men and women should be separated for basic training; he could not even get a roll call on this politically incorrect proposal. He stirred criticism when he backed the decision by Carroll County Republicans to raffle a gun, a decision denounced by Governor Parris Glendening and some Republicans. "Crime has nothing to do with guns," Bartlett responded. His fiscal prudence was reflected in his opposition to expanded federal funds for the local Interstate highway. Possibly inconsistent with his principles, Bartlett approved of the government paying for 30% of winter feed for western Maryland farmers with 35% crop loss due to drought; but he says they should buy crop insurance.

Bartlett has been re-elected by solid margins. In 2000, a veteran House Democratic staffer raised more than $200,000 and campaigned against Bartlett as "a mismatch for the district from the beginning." But Bartlett maintained his low profile and won 61%–39%. Democrats control redistricting, and might cause Bartlett mischief. But they will be hard pressed to move the district close enough to Baltimore or Washington suburbs to cause him problems.

Cook's Call   *Safe.* This western Maryland district is the most Republican in the state, and this once rural district is experiencing a tremendous amount of suburban growth, especially along the I-270 corridor. It was the fastest growing district in the state. Even with Democrats controlling redistricting, Bartlett has little to worry about since they are targeting more marginal districts in Montgomery and Baltimore Counties. Even Democrats acknowledge that this district is likely to remain a Republican stronghold.

THE PEOPLE: Pop. 2000: 723,196; Pop. 1990: 597,660, up 21% 1990–2000. 89.4% White, 6.1% Black, 2.5% Asian, 0.2% Amer. Indian, 1.2% Two+ races, 0.6% Other; 1.6% Hispanic Origin.

2000 Presidential Vote		
Bush (R)	169,879	(58%)
Gore (D)	112,214	(38%)
Nader (Green)	7,588	(3%)
Others	1,973	(1%)

1996 Presidential Vote		
Dole (R)	130,321	(52%)
Clinton (D)	96,185	(38%)
Perot (I)	21,205	(8%)

Rep. Roscoe G. Bartlett (R)

Elected 1992, 5th term; b. June 3, 1926, Moreland, KY; home, Frederick; Columbia Union Col., B.A. 1947, U. of MD, M.S. 1949, Ph.D. 1952; Seventh Day Adventist; married (Ellen).

Professional Career: Farmer; Prof., U. of MD, 1948–52; Asst. Prof., Loma Linda Schl. of Medicine, 1952–54; Asst. Prof., Howard U. Medical Schl., 1954–56; Research scientist, N.I.H., 1956–58; Research scientist, U.S. Naval Aerospace Medical Inst., 1958–62; Research scientist, Johns Hopkins U., 1962–67; Research Mgr., IBM, 1967–74; Pres., Roscoe Bartlett & Assoc., 1974–86.

DC Office: 2412 RHOB 20515, 202-225-2721; Fax: 202-225-2193; Web site: www.house.gov/bartlett.

District Offices: Cumberland, 301-724-3105; Frederick, 301-694-3030; Hagerstown, 301-797-6043; Westminster, 410-857-1115.

Committees: *Armed Services* (10th of 32 R): Military Readiness; Military Research & Development. *Science* (10th of 25 R): Energy (Chmn.); Space & Aeronautics. *Small Business* (4th of 19 R): Regulatory Reform Oversight; Rural Enterprises, Agricultural and Technology.

Group Ratings

	ADA	ACLU	AFS	LCV	CON	ITIC	NTU	COC	ACU	NTLC	CHC
2000	5	21	14	7	75	67	65	71	100	94	93
1999	10	—	0	6	40	—	67	84	96	—	—

National Journal Ratings

	1999 LIB	—	1999 CONS		2000 LIB	—	2000 CONS
Economic	16%	—	78%		0%	—	94%
Social	10%	—	85%		21%	—	78%
Foreign	10%	—	86%		0%	—	88%

Key Votes of the 106th Congress

1. Patient Bill of Rights	N	5. Bar RU-486 $ for FDA	Y	9. NATO War in Serbia	N
2. Accelerate Min. Wage	N	6. Display 10 Commandments	Y	10. Perm. Trade with China	N
3. Strike Ban on Ergo. Stnd.	N	7. Gun Show Bkgrnd. Checks	N	11. Debt Relief for 3rd World	N
4. Ovrd. Estate Tax Veto	Y	8. Ban Part.-Birth Abortion	Y	12. Drop Cuba Econ. Embargo	N

SEVENTH DISTRICT

At the junction of North and South, terminus of America's first railroad and the East Coast port closest to the great West, Baltimore is one of the few American cities to have had large numbers of both blacks and European immigrants throughout its history. Its black community has a notable history: The *Afro-American* newspaper has been published here for more than 100 years and there was once a black symphony orchestra. Eubie Blake, the famous black musician and one of the founders of ragtime music, grew up here and now has a museum to honor him on Charles Street. Near downtown on the west side is the childhood home of Babe Ruth and the home of H.L. Mencken, two great white westside Baltimoreans. For years this side of town had a biracial, bipartisan politics in which Democrats like Governor Albert Ritchie and Republicans like Mayor and Governor Theodore McKeldin competed zestfully for black and white votes.

Baltimore has been a black-majority city since the late 1970s, and most of its westside neighborhoods are heavily black. Black Republicanism has long since died out, and William Donald Schaefer, who carried west Baltimore for mayor as late as 1983, left city politics for the governorship in 1986. Then serving 12 years as mayor was Kurt Schmoke; he was capable and his good intentions sparked hopes he could help Baltimore lessen the pathologies of violent crime, single parenthood and labor force non-participation that plague cities elsewhere. But his calls for consideration of drug legalization and policing policies resulted in large parts of the city being controlled by criminal gangs. When he retired in 1999, voters chose Martin O'Malley, a white former prosecutor who vowed to "build a new Baltimore," with "zero tolerance" of crime while still promoting racial diversity. Downtown, with Harbor Place and its two stadiums, remained vital, and there were hopes that the city was on the rebound; but the verdict is still out.

Maryland's 7th Congressional District includes almost all of Baltimore City's black neighborhoods and extends into the heavily black suburbs running west from the city, Catonsville along the old Baltimore National Pike and Randallstown out Liberty Heights Avenue. From 1987 to February 1996 the congressman here was Kweisi Mfume, former councilman and radio talk show host, who became chairman of the Congressional Black Caucus in 1992, then resigned in February 1996 to become president of the NAACP. The current congressman is Elijah Cummings, who succeeded Mfume in an April 1996 special election.

Cummings grew up in Baltimore, graduated from Howard University and the University of Maryland Law School, practiced law in Baltimore, and in 1982, at 31, was elected to the Maryland House of Delegates. Two years later he was chairman of the Legislative Caucus, the youngest in its history, and he became known as a consensus builder and effective speaker. He chaired the governor's Commission on Black Males and founded the Maryland Bootcamp Aftercare program to address the self-sufficiency of former youth offenders. Cummings was one of 27 (!) Democrats to jump into the race to succeed Mfume; there were five Republicans as well—probably one of the largest congressional fields in history. Cummings's main competition came from the Reverend Frank Reid III, stepbrother of Mayor Schmoke, who raised $255,000; Reid won 24% of the vote. Cummings had support from community development organizations and from businessmen, lobbyists and state House Speaker Casper Taylor. He raised $450,000 and won 37% of the vote.

Cummings still lives in west Baltimore, where he has had more than his share of personal struggles. In a two-year period he was robbed at shotgun point, had his home burglarized four times and his car broken into seven times. He has endured extensive financial problems, including unpaid taxes, court enforcement of child-support payments, and other debts. "When you begin slipping financially, it can become like going down a mountain of ice," he told The Baltimore *Sun*. Cummings explained that he spent so much time helping other people that he failed to spend enough time on his own life. Those urban realities have made him a crusader against drug abuse and a death-penalty foe. As a witness to the effects of crime and drugs—he says he attends about 50 funerals a year for youths murdered or killed by overdoses—he favors strict gun control and has introduced a bill to establish a Commission on National Drug Policy. His voting record is very liberal; he was the only Marylander to oppose the 1996 Welfare Reform Act.

He also has had some struggles in his political career. He lost a ranking minority slot on the Government Reform subcommittee to Vermont Socialist Bernard Sanders, after a protest. He later won the top Democratic post on the civil service subcommittee, where he tends to the interests of his many federal employees. With his seat on Transportation and Infrastructure, he supported Chairman Bud Shuster's big spending bill and got three highway projects worth $40 million. He has explored more influential committee assignments. Cummings is first vice chair of the Congressional Black Caucus. After the group met with newly installed Attorney General John Ashcroft in February 2001, Cummings said, "It was definitely not a love-in."

Cummings has a safe Democratic seat and can only be threatened in the primary. Redistricting likely will give him new voters outside the city.

Cook's Call *Safe.* Taking in inner city Baltimore and western Baltimore County, the 7th is the most heavily minority district in the state (75% black) and a Democratic stronghold (Gore took 84% here). Population loss in Baltimore means that this district will have to pick up about 122,000 more people in redistricting, but the district will remain solidly Democratic. About the only thing Cummings may have to worry about would be a primary challenge in a heavily reconfigured district.

THE PEOPLE: Pop. 2000: 539,439; Pop. 1990: 597,701, down 9.7% 1990–2000. 21.3% White, 74.6% Black, 2% Asian, 0.2% Amer. Indian, 1.4% Two+ races, 0.4% Other; 1.3% Hispanic Origin.

2000 Presidential Vote			1996 Presidential Vote		
Gore (D)	140,865	(84%)	Clinton (D)	127,850	(81%)
Bush (R)	23,215	(14%)	Dole (R)	23,757	(15%)
Nader (Green)	3,910	(2%)	Perot (I)	5,207	(3%)

Rep. Elijah Cummings (D)

Elected April 1996, 3d term; b. Jan. 18, 1951, Baltimore; home, Baltimore; Howard U., B.S. 1973, U. of MD, J.D. 1976; Baptist; separated.

Elected Office: MD House of Delegates, 1982–96, Speaker Pro-Tem, 1995–96.

Professional Career: Practicing atty., 1976–96.

DC Office: 1632 LHOB 20515, 202-225-4741; Fax: 202-225-3178; Web site: www.house.gov/cummings.

District Offices: Baltimore, 410-496-2010; Baltimore, 410-367-1900; Catonsville, 410-719-8777.

Committees: *Government Reform* (9th of 19 D): Civil Service & Agency Organization; Criminal Justice, Drug Policy & Human Resources (RMM). *Transportation & Infrastructure* (18th of 34 D): Highways & Transit; Railroads.

Group Ratings

	ADA	ACLU	AFS	LCV	CON	ITIC	NTU	COC	ACU	NTLC	CHC
2000	85	86	100	86	15	56	19	47	4	9	0
1999	100	—	100	100	35	—	17	21	0	—	—

National Journal Ratings

	1999 LIB —	1999 CONS		2000 LIB —	2000 CONS
Economic	88% —	0%		95% —	0%
Social	87% —	0%		94% —	0%
Foreign	95% —	0%		84% —	15%

Key Votes of the 106th Congress

1. Patient Bill of Rights	Y	5. Bar RU-486 $ for FDA	N	9. NATO War in Serbia	Y
2. Accelerate Min. Wage	Y	6. Display 10 Commandments	N	10. Perm. Trade with China	N
3. Strike Ban on Ergo. Stnd.	Y	7. Gun Show Bkgrnd. Checks	Y	11. Debt Relief for 3rd World	*
4. Ovrd. Estate Tax Veto	N	8. Ban Part.-Birth Abortion	N	12. Drop Cuba Econ. Embargo	Y

Election Results

2000 general	Elijah Cummings (D)	134,066	(87%)	($444,442)
	Kenneth Kondner (R)	19,773	(13%)	
2000 primary	Elijah Cummings (D)	unopposed		
1998 general	Elijah Cummings (D)	112,699	(86%)	($339,883)
	Kenneth Kondner (R)	18,742	(14%)	

EIGHTH DISTRICT

Along an old road, down which colonial farmers rolled barrels of tobacco to the port of Georgetown 200 years ago, has grown one of America's most affluent and best-educated communities. The old road, now called Wisconsin Avenue and Rockville Pike, is the commercial spine of Montgomery County. And this suburban jurisdiction just northwest of Washington, D.C., has for several decades ranked at or near the top of the list of counties in income and education. Today's Montgomery County is in large part a creation of the federal government, which has put huge facilities there— Bethesda Naval Hospital, the National Institutes of Health, the Food and Drug Administration, the National Institute of Standards and Technology—and it has become the center of America's biotech industry, the home of firms like Celera and Human Genome Sciences which, in parallel with the Human Genome Project, are pioneering the study of the human gene. With the growth of private sector science, the percentage of government workers has been declining sharply, to about 15% in the mid-1990s—a figure only a percentage point or two above the national average.

Wisconsin Avenue and Rockville Pike have become strip highways, with 1950s commercial development and 1960s shopping centers like so many in the country. But the stores are upscale, some *very* upscale, and the new skyscrapers of downtown Bethesda are genuinely impressive. Author David Brooks mocked Bethesdans as "urban exiles" who frequent "anti-chain chain stores . . . that cater to people who consider themselves too refined and individualistic to shop at the mall or the mass-market big-box stores." Not all of Montgomery County is exclusively high-income: There are some modest neighborhoods in Silver Spring and Wheaton, and one of the nation's largest Asian populations—some, hard-working store owners; others, educated professionals with high incomes. Historically, the typical Montgomery County voter was a high-ranking civil servant, but as private employment outpaces government work, the picture has changed. The fastest-growing parts of the county, out past Rockville in Gaithersburg and Germantown, are filling up with Republicans and conservatives as much as Democrats and liberals.

The congresswoman from the 8th District is Connie Morella, a Republican first elected to an open seat in 1986. Morella grew up in Massachusetts and taught school in Montgomery County in the 1950s. She raised nine children, six of them her late sister's, and at the same time earned a master's degree and taught English at American University and Montgomery College. In 1978, she was elected to the Maryland House of Delegates. After two four-year terms, she ran for Congress, and won with 53% against nursing home millionaire Stewart Bainum, who spent $1.5 million of his own money. She is hard working, cooperative with colleagues, congenial with constituents, energetic enough to tend to almost 700,000 constituents who are a local phone call and a few miles away.

Morella is, by some distance, the most liberal Republican in the House. She voted against seven of 10 items in the Contract With America in 1995 and frequently has been more liberal on cultural and foreign issues than the average Democrat. On abortion rights, gun control, campaign finance reform, health care, and the environment, she has voted against most Republicans and with most Democrats. She sits on the Science Technology Subcommittee and claims credit for increases in NIH funding, which has thrived under Republicans, and for expedited commercialization of technology created in federal laboratories. On the Government Reform Committee, where she chairs the D.C. Subcommittee, she looks out for federal workers, sponsoring the recent expansion of long-term care insurance for civil servants and retirees. She also has been a leading supporter of the Violence Against Women Act, which targets family violence and child abuse.

But she has come under attack in a county that has trended increasingly Democratic. Between 1996 and 1998, when most incumbents of both parties saw their percentages rise, hers fell, to 60%. In 2000, she had her closest race yet. Two well-known liberal legislators, state Delegate Mark Shriver and state Senator Chris Von Hollen, declined to run, but Terry Lierman, a wealthy businessman and Schering-Plough lobbyist, spent more than $1.4 million of his own money. His aggressive advertising focused on Morella's Republican affiliation, and he attacked Morella as "irrelevant" because she was out of sync with House Republican philosophy. Lierman might actually have won the contest if not for a self-inflicted wound in the final days of the campaign, when *The Washington Post* revealed that he had given northern Virginia Democratic Congressman Jim Moran a $25,000 personal loan with generous terms that might not have passed ethical muster. Lierman defended the action as help to a long-time friend in financial duress. After the *Post* ran the page-one story, Moran quickly repaid the loan; but the political damage had been done. Morella survived, 52%–46%.

Following the election, Morella seemed to be feeling the heat. In an act of party apostasy, she said that local sentiment left her "obligated" to vote for Al Gore if the House were forced to vote for president, although she retreated a bit afterwards, and in any case Maryland's vote would not have been dispositive because Republicans had majorities in 28 of the 49 other states. Her seat seems to be in jeopardy in 2002. Lierman's strong run could easily persuade better-known Democrats—in a county full of Democratic officeholders—to run. And the Democrats who control redistricting could easily make this district more Democratic by adding strongly Democratic parts of Montgomery County's southeast corner and subtracting precincts from the Republican-leaning northern part of the county. Morella had been touted as a potential candidate for governor, but in June 2001 said she would run for reelection.

Cook's Call   *Highly Competitive*. Although this district has strong Democratic underpinnings, Democrats have not had much luck trying to oust six-term Morella. Democratic line drawers have publicly indicated their desire to move parts of heavily Democratic Silver Spring into the 8th District. At least three Democrats, state Senators Mark Shriver and Chris Van Hollen and trade attorney Ira Shapiro have announced their intention to run. There is no doubt that this race will be one of the most competitive in the country next year.

THE PEOPLE: Pop. 2000: 690,558; Pop. 1990: 597,760, up 15.5% 1990–2000. 70.3% White, 10.6% Black, 11.3% Asian, 0.3% Amer. Indian, 3.2% Two+ races, 4.3% Other; 10.5% Hispanic Origin.

2000 Presidential Vote			1996 Presidential Vote		
Gore (D)	183,670	(60%)	Clinton (D)	156,450	(57%)
Bush (R)	110,356	(36%)	Dole (R)	103,327	(38%)
Nader (Green)	9,452	(3%)	Perot (I)	12,200	(4%)
Others	1,744	(1%)			

Rep. Constance A. Morella (R)

Elected 1986, 8th term; b. Feb. 12, 1931, Somerville, MA; home, Bethesda; Boston U., A.B. 1954, American U., M.A. 1967; Catholic; married (Anthony).

Elected Office: MD House of Delegates, 1978–86.

Professional Career: Teacher, Montgomery Cnty. Pub. Schls., 1956–60; Instructor, American U., 1968–70; Prof., Montgomery Col., 1970–86.

DC Office: 2228 RHOB 20515, 202-225-5341; Fax: 202-225-1389; Web site: www.house.gov/morella.

District Office: Rockville, 301-424-3501.

Committees: *Government Reform* (3d of 24 R): Civil Service & Agency Organization; District of Columbia (Chmn.). *Science* (3d of 25 R): Environment, Technology and Standards.

Group Ratings

	ADA	ACLU	AFS	LCV	CON	ITIC	NTU	COC	ACU	NTLC	CHC
2000	60	79	42	86	75	94	49	71	29	27	7
1999	80	—	83	88	82	—	26	42	12	—	—

National Journal Ratings

	1999 LIB	—	1999 CONS		2000 LIB	—	2000 CONS
Economic	56%	—	43%		56%	—	44%
Social	76%	—	23%		79%	—	21%
Foreign	63%	—	36%		68%	—	32%

Key Votes of the 106th Congress

1. Patient Bill of Rights	Y	5. Bar RU-486 $ for FDA	N	9. NATO War in Serbia	Y
2. Accelerate Min. Wage	Y	6. Display 10 Commandments	N	10. Perm. Trade with China	Y
3. Strike Ban on Ergo. Stnd.	N	7. Gun Show Bkgrnd. Checks	Y	11. Debt Relief for 3rd World	Y
4. Ovrd. Estate Tax Veto	Y	8. Ban Part.-Birth Abortion	N	12. Drop Cuba Econ. Embargo	N

Election Results

2000 general	Constance A. Morella (R)	156,241	(52%)	($1,154,410)
	Terry Lierman (D)	136,840	(46%)	($2,217,488)
2000 primary	Constance A. Morella (R)	unopposed		
1998 general	Constance A. Morella (R)	133,145	(60%)	($884,238)
	Ralph G. Neas (D)	87,497	(40%)	($810,258)

★ MASSACHUSETTS ★

I t would be a city on a hill, John Winthrop wrote of the Massachusetts Bay colony his Puritans were building, an example to the entire world. And Massachusetts, in the nearly four centuries since, has always assumed it has a lot to teach others. The New World Puritans' austere creed taught that only the select would be saved and that they must extirpate the forces of Satan— Indians, Papists, tolerationists. For 150 years, New England was partial to learning, but also insular, hostile to outsiders and economically stagnant. Then, after the American Revolution, the international war between royal Britain and revolutionary and Napoleonic France allowed New England ship owners to cross enemy lines to become the world's leading merchants. They made vast profits and plowed the money into textile mills, then railroads, then coal mining and steel-making: This was the capital that made industrial America.

Massachusetts made a new America in other ways. Intellectually, New England flowered in the 19th Century: A few writers from Boston and Concord—Ralph Waldo Emerson, Henry Wadsworth Longfellow, Henry David Thoreau, John Greenleaf Whittier, Nathaniel Hawthorne—created an American literary genre and popularized an American philosophy, more than 200 years after Plymouth Rock. Demographically, New England Yankees surged across the continent: Long blocked from Upstate New York by mountains and the British-Iroquois alliance, they only reached Syracuse in the 1820s; by the 1850s they were in Iowa and Kansas and Oregon's Willamette Valley; by the 1880s they had settled Los Angeles. They helped start the Republican Party and did much to start—and win—the Civil War. They planted their economic system and their values, articulated in the *McGuffey Readers*, across the continent.

In the meantime, Massachusetts itself and Boston, the hub of the universe, were being remade. The potato famine of the 1840s and an economy that continued imploding for decades sent Irishmen across the Atlantic, and many came to Boston, looking for work in the mills, docks and factories. Yankee Protestants had seen Catholics as their great political and cultural enemy for 200 years and felt their commonwealth was under siege. As the Irish became a majority, first in Boston and then statewide, Protestants feared the Irish would use their political clout to ladle out government jobs and benefits to their own. And the Irish had a much better flair for politics than instinct for commerce. But they encountered such bigotry and rejection by the Yankees that

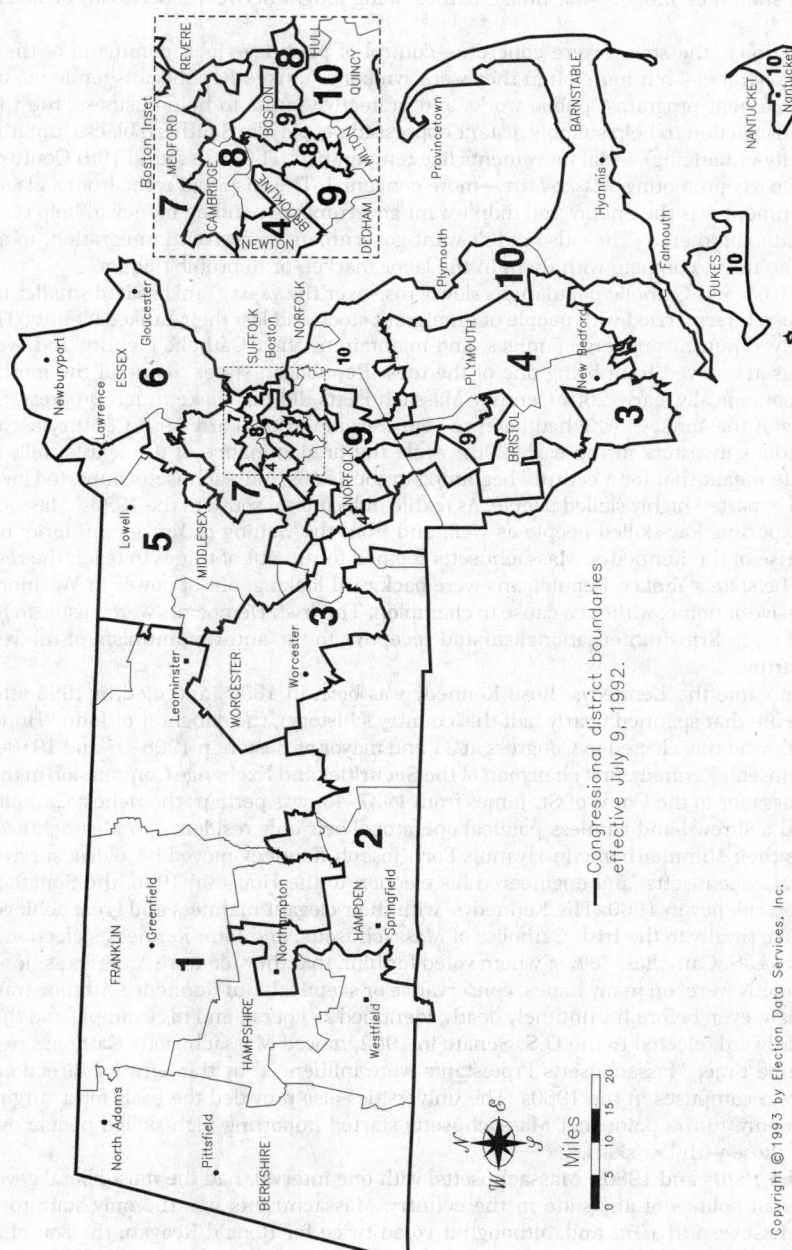

Congressional district boundaries
effective July 9, 1992.

Copyright © 1993 by Election Data Services, Inc.

even as successful an Irish Catholic as Joseph Kennedy felt obliged to move from Boston to New York in 1927. Politics in Massachusetts for years was a kind of culture war between Yankee Republicans and Irish Democrats, an argument not so much over the distribution of income or the provision of services as over whose vision of Massachusetts should be honored, and whose version of history should be taught—not unlike battles being fought between liberals and conservatives today.

Sometimes, the stakes were concrete—control of patronage jobs, command of the Boston Police Department—but more often they were symbolic. Yankee Republicans tended to back activist government programs: public works and protective tariffs to help business, the Civil War and Reconstruction to help suitably distant oppressed people like Southern blacks, uplifting (and productivity-enhancing) social movements like temperance. The Irish found 19th Century Democrats—a party promoting *laissez-faire*—more congenial. The Irish had come from a place where the government was the enemy and didn't want government spending money to help the rich or to stimulate commerce. They also didn't want government to restrict immigration, to advance blacks, who might compete with them in the labor market, or to prohibit liquor.

The Irish and Catholic populations slowly rose over the years. Yankees had smaller families, moved west, intermarried with people of immigrant stock and lost their Yankee identity. The Irish mostly stayed put, raising large families, and maintaining their Catholic identity, and eventually Massachusetts moved from being one of the most Republican states to one of the most Democratic. Economically, early 20th Century Massachusetts did not make much progress. The descendants of the Yankees who had been so venturesome in the early 19th Century became the most cautious investors in the early 20th, while the predominance of the textile mills in their home state meant that for a century beginning in the 1820s, Massachusetts imported low-skilled labor and exported highly skilled people. As textile mills moved south in the 1920s, Massachusetts started exporting low-skilled people as well; and from the waning of Yankee authority until the national rise of the Kennedys, Massachusetts seemed to run out of things to teach the rest of the nation. The state's Yankee Republicans were backward-looking, out of power in Washington, on the defensive at home, without a cause to champion. The Irish Democrats were hostile to Franklin Roosevelt's pro-British internationalism and receptive to the anti-Communism of the very Irish Joe McCarthy.

Then came the Kennedys. Rose Kennedy was born in 1890 (and died in 1995 after a remarkable life that spanned nearly half this country's history), the daughter of John "Honey Fitz" Fitzgerald, who was elected to Congress at 31 and mayor of Boston in 1906–07 and 1910–14; her husband Joseph Kennedy, first chairman of the Securities and Exchange Commission in the 1930s and ambassador to the Court of St. James from 1937–40, was perhaps the richest Catholic in the world and a shrewd and ruthless political operator. Their only residence in Massachusetts after 1927 was their summer home in Hyannis Port. Joseph Kennedy moved his oldest surviving son, John, to Massachusetts, and engineered his election to the House in 1946, the Senate in 1952 and the presidency in 1960. The Kennedys, with their elegant manners and great achievements, seemed like royalty to the Irish Catholics of Massachusetts, and John Kennedy's election in 1960 certified to U.S. Catholics, 78% of whom voted for him, that they too were Americans. Joseph and John Kennedy were, on many issues, conservative or skeptical. But Kennedy's Administration was increasingly, even before his untimely death, identified as liberal, and his example and that of his brother, Edward, elected to the U.S. Senate in 1962, moved Massachusetts Catholics to the left. At the same time, Massachusetts Protestants were influenced by the leftward direction on the state's great campuses in the 1960s. The universities also provided the basis for a surging high-tech economy, to the point that Massachusetts started importing high-skilled people even as it exported those with low skills.

In the 1970s and 1980s, Massachusetts, with one interval, had the most liberal governance and national politics of any state in the country. Massachusetts was the only state to vote for George McGovern in 1972 and, although it voted twice for Ronald Reagan, the son of an Irish Catholic, its Democratic percentage in presidential contests from 1968–88 was 53%, just 0.4% behind Rhode Island and well ahead of every other state. The state's senators included Edward Kennedy, liberal Republican Edward Brooke, and Democrats Paul Tsongas and John Kerry. Liberal governors such as Republican Francis Sargent and Democrat Michael Dukakis vastly increased spending and endorsed the inexplicable policies that sunk Dukakis's 1988 presidential campaign, notably the fact that prisoners sentenced to life without parole were given weekend furloughs. As historian David Hackett Fischer points out in *Albion's Seed*, the mindset of the original settlers remains strong even when the ethnic origin of current residents is far different, and the spirit of the Puritans, the faith that they had much to teach the rest of the world, is strong in Massachusetts liberals: in both the quietly smug liberalism of Michael Dukakis and the hearty and combative liberalism of Edward Kennedy. Then, in the early 1990s, Massachusetts had a momentary political revolution. The 1980s "Massachusetts miracle" had turned into a nightmare, as the state's economy sagged badly, as the defense cutbacks long sought by Massachusetts politicians sent unemployment rising and high-tech firms like Wang and Digital withered and Cambridge-based Lotus's software was eclipsed by Redmond, Washington-based Microsoft's. The Northeast real estate bubble burst and Massachusetts banks foundered. The state government essentially went bankrupt. In 1990, as Dukakis retired, voters embraced big tax cuts and elected Republican William Weld in his place.

Weld envisioned a government that taxes and spends lightly, that is friendly to feminism and gay rights, that exerts some effort to protect the environment and that is tough on crime. He cut spending and taxes sharply in his first years, and the state's economy began recovering. But Weld had few followers and Massachusetts liberalism persisted unembarrassed. The state voted heavily for Bill Clinton in 1992 and 1996; in 1994 it reelected Senator Edward Kennedy, after a momentary scare at the hands of Republican Mitt Romney, by a solid margin; it eliminated Republicans from its congressional delegation in 1996 and voted in veto-proof Democratic majorities in the legislature. Weld, after thinking about running for president, ran against Senator John Kerry in 1996. The contest endlessly fascinated Boston writers and got probably as much coverage in the national press as all other Senate races that year combined. But it ended predictably: This Democratic state, however much it approved Weld as governor, decided it wanted to keep two Democratic senators, and it voted 52%–45% for Kerry. Weld, bored with the governorship, resigned in July 1997; his nomination by Bill Clinton to be Ambassador to Mexico was killed by Foreign Relations Chairman Jesse Helms that fall; in 1999 he moved to New York City.

Massachusetts voted 61%–28% for Bill Clinton in 1996, his biggest margin in the nation; in 2000 it voted 60%–33% for Al Gore, his biggest margin except for Rhode Island. Only a pathetic 32 towns voted for George W. Bush. With tax increases now unthinkable, Massachusetts is now solidly Democratic on every other issue. That has not quite been the case in state elections, for it is not unthinkable that a Democratic governor and an overwhelmingly Democratic legislature might expand government again. Paul Cellucci, advanced from lieutenant governor to governor in July 1997, was challenged in the Republican primary by Treasurer Joe Malone, and won by just 59%–41% in a contest in which only 232,000 voted. The Democratic nominee, Attorney General Scott Harshbarger, was a strong liberal, and Cellucci eked out a 51%–47% win, perhaps a retrospective endorsement of Weld. Turnout was just 1.9 million, lower than in every nonpresidential year but one (1986) in the last 50 years. Similarly, turnout in 2000, when there were no seriously contested congressional races, was 2,691,000, lower than in 1992, and only 8% higher than in 1960. If you listen in to conversations at the Parker House bar you might suppose that politics is still the great preoccupation of Bay Staters as it was during the Yankee-Irish culture wars and the ascendancy of the Kennedys. But these days not many voters seem interested.

Massachusetts still has lessons to teach the rest of the country, but they are not necessarily those taught by its successful politicians. Massachusetts is the site of the Big Dig, the building of a new underground freeway to replace the tangle of overhead highway and tunnel bottlenecks in downtown Boston, first approved in 1987 and the largest public works project in American history—more expensive than the Panama Canal and Hoover Dam combined. But in April 2000 Cellucci had to fire the project's head who, according to a federal report, had intentionally concealed $1.4 billion of cost overruns. In April 2001 Attorney General Thomas Reilly opened a criminal probe into both Weld's and Cellucci's handling of the project to determine if state officials sought to coverup massive cost overruns. The total cost, projected in 1992 at $7.7 billion, was projected in November 2000 to be $14.1 billion, and who knows if it will be completed by the promised date of 2004.

Massachusetts's education system is also in a broil. In 1998 fully 59% of applicants wishing to teach public school flunked a simple entrance exam—a sharp contrast with the excellence of Massachusetts's private sector. The state board of education in 1999 set the passing grade for student 4th, 8th, and 10th grade tests at the lowest available threshold; but even at that rate some 50% of students would not be eligible to graduate as will be required in 2003. Meanwhile, the failed experiment of the Boston school-busing program, which sent Boston into turmoil in the 1970s, was quietly dropped in July 1999. In 2000 voters passed a referendum dropping the state income tax from 5.85% to 5% over three years, despite opposition from Democrats and teachers' unions. They also voted 3–1 to establish a charitable deduction; Massachusetts was one of only eight states without one, and in 2000 ranked dead last among states in charitable giving in the Urban Institute's Generosity Index. Voters also defeated a referendum which would have established universal health care; it was opposed vigorously by the state's great teaching hospitals. Massachusetts has some of the nation's toughest gun laws, passed not by the legislature but by administrative order of the state attorney general; yet in 2000 voters rejected lesser penalties for minor drug dealers. And in June 2000 the U.S. Supreme Court overturned a Massachusetts law boycotting companies that do business in Myanmar, on the grounds that foreign policy is the business of the federal government. Liberalism governs in Massachusetts, but sometimes messily.

Governor   Jane Swift, a Republican, became governor in April 2001, when Paul Cellucci resigned to become President Bush's Ambassador to Canada. She is the first woman to hold that position, and—as media stories endlessly noted—took office, at age 36, when she was seven months pregnant with twins. Swift grew up in North Adams, a small mill town in the northwest corner of Massachusetts; that makes her the first governor from the Berkshires since 1903, when the job was held by Winthrop Crane—a Republican and an heir to the paper-making family that was long a pillar of the state party. Swift has a decidedly different personal background: Her father was a plumber, and her mother has taught religion at a Catholic school in Pittsfield; her grandparents worked on the assembly line of the General Electric plant in Pittsfield. After graduating from the local high school, where she was remembered as a tenacious forward on the school's basketball team, Swift went to Trinity College in Hartford and got her bachelors degree in American studies. She worked briefly for the G. Fox department store in Danbury, Connecticut, then returned home to become an aide to state Senator Peter Webber, a Republican from Pittsfield. When Webber retired in 1990, Swift ran for his seat and, at age 25, was elected to the state Senate. As a legislator for six years and as part of a Republican minority that was large enough to sustain his vetoes, she usually was a close ally of Governor William Weld. Like Weld, she viewed herself as a fiscal conservative who supported tax cuts and trims in welfare spending, and a social liberal who supported abortion and gay rights. She favored school choice, term limits for Senate leaders, stronger penalties for drug charges and fare increases for the Boston area's MBTA transit. She also was fiercely loyal to her district, casting the only Senate vote against Weld's budget in 1994 because she said that it favored the eastern part of the state. "Jane gave me more grief than any other Republican senator," Weld told the *Boston Globe*. "She was constantly in my face, constantly reading me the riot act. And she got everything she wanted."

In 1996, Swift opposed Democratic Representative John Olver for the seat that had been held for 33 years by liberal Republican Silvio Conte. She raised an impressive sum ($693,000); business groups also targeted Olver with ads. Swift lost 53%–47%, winning most towns in the Berkshires and running even around Fitchburg, but Olver won big majorities in the Pioneer Valley. Following that campaign, Weld named her to two posts at the Massachusetts Port Authority. When Weld resigned as governor in July 1997 after President Clinton nominated him to be ambassador to Mexico, Cellucci became acting governor and named Swift as running mate for his 1998 ticket. Although the two of them became close in the campaign, Swift managed to offend some Republicans who thought that they were better suited for her job plus some aides to Cellucci who apparently resented her assertiveness. Swift gave birth to her first child two weeks before the general election.

In the contest for governor, Cellucci was challenged by Scott Harshbarger, the state Attorney

General for eight years, who was seen by many as an elitist liberal, deaf to the values of the middle-income, middle-class Catholics who are the descendants of the party's historic constituency. Still, the graduate student elite is large enough in Massachusetts—28% of the electorate in 1998—to have made the election close. Cellucci won 51%–47% in a turnout that was 19% below that of 1990. Turnout declined since 1990 by as much as one-third in the mill and factory towns that were, three or four decades ago, the Democratic base. Harshbarger's base was in the university and college towns, where turnout was down less. He carried Cambridge 74%–24%, Amherst 76%–23% and Northampton 66%–32% and carried the string of academic-heavy towns running out Route 2 from Cambridge to Concord; he won in the college-heavy Pioneer Valley and in the left-leaning towns at the tip of Cape Cod. Cellucci carried middle-income and working-class towns, which have many more votes and which had been the heart of the Democratic constituency since John Kennedy beat Henry Cabot Lodge Jr. in 1952.

After the election, the Cellucci-Swift duo continued to press for tax cuts and the death penalty. The governor prevailed over Democrats in November 2000 when he supported Question 6, which cut the income tax from 5.85% to 5%. But both were beset with bad publicity. Cellucci's Massport head Peter Blute resigned in August 1999 after stories about a "booze cruise" in Boston harbor. Swift was criticized for using her staff for babysitting and for using a state police helicopter to travel to her Berkshire County home. "I owe an apology to the people of Massachusetts. I made some mistakes and I am sorry for them," she said after the state ethics commission ruled in August 2000 that the baby-sitting was a violation and later fined her $1,250; she also quit a teaching job at Suffolk University that paid well but required little work. The worst news came out of the Big Dig. A federal report in April 2000 charged that state managers intentionally concealed cost overruns to the tune of $1.4 billion—big money even in this biggest public works project in American history and Cellucci had to fire Masspike Chairman James Kerasiotes. Approved in 1987, budgeted at $7.7 billion in 1992, the Big Dig's price tag had risen to $14.1 billion by November 2000. Cellucci called it an "engineering marvel," crucial to the state's economy. But with the federal government trying to cap its share of the cost, Massachusetts taxpayers may have to come up with billions.

Cellucci's job rating suffered from the problems with the Big Dig; in October 2000 he trailed Joe Kennedy, though he led other lesser-known Democrats. When Bush was elected, Cellucci eagerly sought an appointment that would provide a graceful exit from Beacon Hill. When Bush named him as his first ambassadorial appointment, Cellucci responded, "I love being governor . . . but when the president of the United States calls, and it's an important part of his strategy for this hemisphere and this country, it's important that you serve the country."

When she took over, Swift had had little opportunity to make a positive impression and she suffered from low poll ratings. She had to defend her living arrangement, in which her husband Charles Hunt took care of their toddler daughter at their home in Williamstown 130 miles from the State House; Hunt, a former dairy farmer and retired contractor who had no political interest and suffered from chronic kidney disease, married Swift in 1993 and became a stay-at-home dad. Unlike most other states, Massachusetts does not give its governor a place to live. So Swift responded that she wanted her family to keep to its usual routine, and she frequently took the state limousine across the state to her home in the evening, only to return to Boston the next morning. Cellucci said that Swift was suffering from "gender bias" in the media, which created a double standard with her personal life. After she was sworn in as governor in an April 10 ceremony, she moved quickly to put her stamp on the office—and to raise money for what was expected to be a tough campaign in 2002. She sought to reduce toxic emissions at the state's worst polluting power plants, which Weld and Cellucci had exempted from air-pollution rules because they might be closing.

As she prepared for re-election, Swift got some good news—just as Cellucci did four years earlier—when Joe Kennedy announced in March 2001 that he would not run for governor. That opened the way to another expected brawl for the Democratic nomination, while Swift faced a possible primary with Blute. Republican prospects did not appear bright, but were no worse perhaps than when Weld and Cellucci first ran for the governor's office, which Republicans have now held since 1991. In mid-May Swift was hospitalized for early contractions and she attempted to hold the weekly Council meeting by speakerphone from her hospital bed. Councilman Edward F. O'Brien, father of the state treasurer, said the meeting was illegal since the presiding officer wasn't present and questioned Swift's availabililty to perform her job. Swift gave birth by caesarean section to daughters Lauren and Sarah May 15, 2001, a month early; she planned to take an eight-week "working" maternity leave.

Cook's Call   *Probable Democratic Pick Up.* If she decides to seek her own term in office, the embattled Swift will begin the race as an underdog, hampered by missteps early in her tenure as lieutenant governor. Her prospects, though, have improved somewhat in the wake of the birth of twin daughters in May. If Swift opts not to run, whoever seeks the Republican nomination would have an uphill fight. The likely Democratic candidates include former Democratic National Committee Co-chairman Steve Grossman, state Senator Tom Birmingham, Secretary of State William Galvin, state House Speaker Tom Finneran, state Treasurer Shannon O'Brien and Congressman Marty Meehan. Even with a late primary, Massachusetts' strong Democratic leanings will give the eventual nominee a cushion.

Senior Senator   Edward Kennedy is approaching his fifth decade as a national celebrity and effective politician. He has had the highs and lows of his personal life followed by millions and criticized vitriolically by many; he has been a presidential candidate and, while still in his 30s, was widely assumed to be the next president. He is third in seniority in the Senate, behind Strom Thurmond and Robert Byrd. His reputation as an idealistic champion of the poor has been burnished by the praise of first-rate celebrators that no American political family has attracted before, and the nation has watched him cope impressively time and again with family tragedy, most recently when his nephew John Kennedy Jr. died in July 1999. To others, he is a symbol of personal immorality and unpunished criminal behavior, a man who has gotten away with things that would have ended the public career of almost anyone else. There is some basis for both views, but neither is an entirely fair picture of this politician, who was re-elected without much fuss in 2000, after a term in which he did much to set national policy even while Republicans controlled the Congress.

The luster of the Kennedys has worn off, in America and even in Massachusetts, and the percentage of Americans who look to the Kennedys for political leadership has grown small; most voters can't remember, or never knew, what made the Kennedys so exciting. Still, there was little in the early life of this youngest of the Kennedy siblings to suggest he would be a major politician, much less for so long. He grew up in Bronxville, New York, a rich suburb with many other rich Catholics, was thrown out of Harvard for cheating on a Spanish exam and served in the Army, returned to earn degrees at Harvard and Virginia Law School, and married a Bronxville girl who never developed a taste for politics. Then his brother was elected president of the United States at 43, and the 28-year-old Edward Kennedy was a national celebrity. His father insisted that he run for the Senate; a JFK college roommate was found to hold the seat until he reached the constitutional age of 30, in 1962. His family money and the enthusiasm among Massachusetts Catholics for this seeming royalty enabled him to beat strong candidates with good political names: Attorney General Edward McCormack, nephew of Speaker John McCormack, in the Democratic primary; George Cabot Lodge, son and great-grandson of senators, in the general. "He can do more for Massachusetts" was his slogan, as had been John Kennedy's 10 years before.

After his brothers' assassinations, Edward Kennedy was seen by many as their natural heir, and he could have been nominated for president in 1968, at 36, or in 1972 had he chosen to run. Instead, in the latter year, he gave the first of several stirring convention speeches promoting his trademark liberalism. In 1979 he did run for president, and began the race against incumbent Jimmy Carter far ahead in the polls. But he was unable to articulate his reasons for running, and his candidacy was greeted with adverse reaction to him personally as well as to his policies. It ended in a crushing defeat, relieved only by another stirring convention speech, after which he pointedly refused to raise Carter's hand on the podium. In retrospect, it is plain that Edward Kennedy's presidential chances were ended in July 1969, with the accident at Chappaquiddick. But he has been re-elected with solid margins in Massachusetts, though he did have a closer than usual call against Republican venture capitalist Mitt Romney in 1994.

Kennedy has been a hardworking and practical politician who, after his brothers' deaths, took up the liberal causes and attention to the poor, which had been the focus of Robert Kennedy in the last years of his life. He has worked hard for a quarter century on their behalf without the friendship of a Democratic administration, until the election of Bill Clinton, and since 1994 without the backing of a Democratic majority. As chairman of the Health, Education, Labor and Pensions Committee from 1987–94, Kennedy supported teachers' unions; on the Judiciary Committee, he supported pro-choice and feminist groups with energy and enthusiasm. He immediately pounced on Judge Robert Bork's nomination in 1987, but played a lesser role in the Clarence Thomas hearings, which came shortly after an incident when his nephew William Kennedy Smith was arrested and charged with rape in Palm Beach.

In 1992 Kennedy supported Bill Clinton happily and basked as Clinton gave repeated homage to the Kennedy family. Legislatively, Kennedy was productive, though not as much as he wished. He worked to pass direct student loans, AmeriCorps, Goals 2000 and the School-to-Work Opportunity Act. He again sponsored the Family and Medical Leave Act which George Bush had vetoed and which was the first law Bill Clinton signed. He also passed a bill making it illegal to block access to abortion clinics. But he was frustrated on other issues. He sought to prevent states from regulating abortions and to ban the death penalty when imposed disproportionately on criminals of different races; both efforts failed. On health care, a longtime Kennedy cause, he backed a Canadian-style single-payer system. In May 1994 he got a health care bill resembling Clinton's through committee, but that was as far as it went.

After the hard-fought 1994 election, Kennedy returned to a Republican Senate and shifted his focus from expanding government to protecting it from downsizing. In 1995 he defended Medicare and Medicaid from reductions and opposed changes in labor laws. He led the effort to block a limited school choice experiment in Washington, D.C.—taking the side of teachers' unions which wanted to keep children in the D.C. school system. In 1996 he went on the offensive. He pushed the Kassebaum-Kennedy health care bill, an incremental measure to provide portability of health insurance and to limit exclusions for pre-existing conditions; he worked to keep Medical Savings Accounts out, and the bill passed. He tried to add to the Defense of Marriage Act a provision to prohibit job discrimination against gays; this was rejected by only a narrow margin, indicating there may be a majority in the Senate for a gay rights bill some time soon. In 1996, Kennedy strongly supported Clinton, even after the president embraced a balanced budget and signed the Welfare Reform Act, and Kennedy had the pleasure of watching Clinton win and run strongest in Massachusetts. In joint appearances in Boston and New Hampshire, he issued a strong endorsement of Al Gore in January 2000 when he seemed in a close race with Bill Bradley.

Kennedy has continued to be active on health issues, opposing Republican measures and sponsoring some bipartisan initiatives of his own. His bill to allow disabled people to work without losing their health care benefits was passed with wide support in 1999. In March 1999 he opposed the bipartisan "premium support" reform proposed by John Breaux's Medicare commission as the "privatization of Medicare." He supported the Dingell-Norwood bill regulating HMOs and called the Republican version of HMO regulation "a minimalist bill that only the insurance industry could love." He worked unsuccessfully to pass a prescription drug benefit and to fashion a bipartisan medical errors bill. With HELP Chairman James Jeffords, he sponsored a law to protect consumers from counterfeit drugs purchased over the Internet. Kennedy has continued to press for increases in the minimum wage and in Pell grants. He has opposed tuition savings accounts as a threat to public schools. In 2000 he proposed "hate crimes" legislation, primarily, he said, because it would allow federal law enforcement officers to work with state and local authorities. He was a floor manager for the 1965 immigration law, which opened the doors to millions of immigrants, and in 2000 pressed for amnesty for illegal aliens in the United States since 1986 and for giving Central American and Haitian refugees the same refugee status as Cubans.

A decade ago there was talk that Kennedy would relinquish his seat to let his nephew Joe Kennedy run; nothing has been heard about that since the latter left the governor race in August 1997. In September 1999 Kennedy announced that he would run for re-election in 2000 and again in 2006. Serious opposition failed to materialize. Former Governor William Weld declined to run, and moved to New York. Former Treasurer Joe Malone, who ran against Kennedy in 1988, made no moves toward a rematch. Kennedy's 1994 opponent, Mitt Romney, moved to Utah for a three-year stint heading the troubled Salt Lake City Olympic organizing committee. One Republican did arise, Jack E. Robinson, who claimed to be a successful entrepreneur and who lived in Greenwich, Connecticut. But in March 2000 it was revealed that a former girlfriend had obtained a restraining order against him, and soon afterward he was charged his driving away from the scene of an accident on Boston's Jamaicaway. Governor Paul Cellucci made it clear he would not support Robinson, and his petitions were rejected by the secretary of State for insufficient signatures. Robinson denied the charges, and the Supreme Judicial Court put him on the ballot in July 2000. But his hapless candidacy went nowhere. Kennedy won with 73% of the vote, to 13% for Robinson and 12% for Libertarian Carla Howell. In an October 2000 poll voters were evenly split on whether Kennedy should run again in 2006, when he turns 74. But there seems little doubt that he can be re-elected then if he wants to. If he serves out that term, he will have served 50 years in the Senate, more than anyone else in history, assuming that Robert Byrd (who beat Kennedy for majority whip in January 1969) does not reach that milepost before him.

Junior Senator   John Kerry has been a national political figure since he was one of the organizers of Vietnam Veterans Against the War in 1971. He attracted attention then because of his background, unusual for a Vietnam veteran (he went to Yale, and his mother is from the Brahmin Forbes family) and because of his record of genuine heroism in combat. "How do you ask a man to be the last to die for a mistake?" he asked in congressional testimony—a good question, and one which also suggested his future political ambitions. Yet his political career did not proceed straight ahead. He ran for Congress in 1972, after some widely observed district-shopping, and lost in a district carried by George McGovern. Chastened, Kerry went to law school, worked for a prosecutor, was elected lieutenant governor on the Dukakis ticket in 1982, and ran for senator in 1984; in both races, he upset a favored rival for the Democratic nomination. In 1982, Kerry won the general as part of a tied ticket with Dukakis; in the 1984 general, he beat Raymond Shamie, a businessman and state Republican chairman, 55%–45%.

Kerry came to the Senate with a reputation as a strong liberal. He has a similar voting record to fellow Senator Edward Kennedy, but there have been differences of nuance and interest: Kerry has been more respectful of economic free markets and moved earlier than Kennedy toward supporting an expansive U.S. foreign and military policy. In the majority, Kerry made a name as an investigator, spending some time up blind alleys with klieg lights but also producing some important information. He used his Foreign Relations Western Hemisphere, Peace Corps, Narcotics and Terrorism Subcommittee chairmanship to investigate the infamous Bank of Credit & Commerce International scandal. He also brought forward evidence that Manuel Noriega of Panama was involved with drug-dealing.

Kerry's other great investigation was as chairman of the Select Committee on POW/MIA Affairs, on whether Americans were left behind in Vietnamese hands in 1973. Kerry and Republican Bob Smith of New Hampshire went to Vietnam and attempted to turn up new evidence. He concluded that there is evidence "that indicates the possibility of survival, at least for a small number," after 1973, but also said, "There is at this time no compelling evidence that any American remains alive in captivity in southeast Asia." By May 1995, Kerry and fellow Vietnam veteran Senator John McCain were convinced that Hanoi was fully cooperating and, aware they had standing on this issue that Bill Clinton conspicuously lacked, they got him to normalize relations with Vietnam. Kerry has traveled a number of times to Vietnam, and he and McCain pushed successfully for the appointment of the first U.S. ambassador there. Kerry has also worked to extend Fulbright scholarships to Vietnam. He was the lead negotiator with the State Department and the United Nations to create an international tribunal to hold hearings on genocide and war crimes in Cambodia.

Kerry has remained close with McCain and other Vietnam veterans in the Senate. Like McCain, he spoke out strongly in favor of the bombing of Bosnia in April 1999. "One of the lessons of Vietnam is: If you are going to send American forces into harm's way, you don't do it in a limited way. You don't do it tying your hands behind your back ahead of time. You don't ask people to give their lives for something less than the prospect of success." He has also spoken out against the constitutional amendment to allow punishment for flag desecration, arguing that only countries like Iran, Iraq, Libya, and North Korea have such laws. "Is this what our soldiers fought and died for . . . so that we could join this list of dictatorial, authoritarian and discredited regimes?"

Kerry has taken some interesting positions on several issues. In June 1998 he decried the "implosion" of public education and said it was caused not just by overcrowded classrooms but also by the "stifling bureaucracy" of school systems. His list of reforms, co-sponsored with Republican Gordon Smith, included some strongly opposed by the teachers' unions—important backers of the Democratic Party—ending teacher tenure, changing certification requirements to end the education school monopoly and allow lateral entry into teaching. He has worked with Republican Christopher Bond to allow direct grants to charities, including faith-based organizations, for early childhood education of at-risk children. With McCain and Spencer Abraham, he sponsored a bill to require websites to disclose their privacy policies, and with Sam Brownback and Tim Hutchinson a bill to get employers to accommodate workers' religious practices absent "undue hardship." He opposed unions and supported expansion of H1-B visas. He urged the Clinton Administration to lift export barriers on encryption and high performance computers. He favored Permanent Normal Trade Relations with China and led the floor fight against the Thompson-Torricelli amendment which would have required review of China's human rights practices. He sponsored a bill to commit $100 million yearly to a fund to fight the spread of AIDS in Africa.

Kerry has long called for campaign finance reform and has refused to take PAC contributions. In May 1995 he married Teresa Heinz, widow of Republican Senator John Heinz of Pennsylvania, who inherited his fortune of more than $600 million; *Roll Call* in 1999 rated Kerry the richest member of Congress, with $675 million, but he has said he would not spend it on his campaigns. "It's my wife's money, not mine." Indeed, she maintains her residence in Pennsylvania, where her foundations are based, and where, as some critics cavil, income tax rates are lower than in Massachusetts; when Kerry took out a $1.9 million loan for his 1996 race, it was against his own personal assets.

That year Kerry faced a major challenge from Governor William Weld, who had been re-elected two years before with 71% of the vote. Earlier, the two had worked together on some state problems and emphasized the similarity of their views—both pro-choice on abortion, even against the partial-birth abortion ban; both for gay rights; both supported the deployment of U.S. troops in Bosnia. But the campaign inevitably produced disagreements and some gentlemanly acrimony. Weld called Kerry a "tax-and-spend liberal who is soft on crime." Kerry charged that Weld would vote for budget cuts that would hurt Medicare, Medicaid, education and the environment. They held seven debates altogether, literate rounds of accusations and one-liners. They both spent liberally—Kerry, $12.6 million, the second highest of any Senate candidate for 1996; Weld, $8 million. Most polls showed Kerry ahead, some showed Weld leading, but most were within the margin of error, with both candidates usually between 40% and 45%. In the last debate, Kerry framed the issues his way by asking Weld what programs he would cut; Weld declined to answer.

In the end Kerry won 52%–45%: just as heavily Republican states like Wyoming and Nebraska were refusing to elect popular Democratic governors to the Senate, so heavily Democratic Massachusetts did not want to elect a Republican. The electorate was not split along historic lines: Catholics voted only 56%–40% for Kerry, Protestants by only 53%–42% for Weld, numbers a world away from what exit polls would have shown when John Kennedy beat Henry Cabot Lodge Jr. in 1952. The real split was along cultural lines. Jews and those voters with no religion voted about 75% for Kerry; and there was no significant bloc of conservative Protestants to balance them off. Kerry's biggest margins among education groups was among those with graduate degrees, who gave him a 62%–35% margin: teachers, social workers, lawyers, doctors and other credentialed professionals. Kerry got his biggest percentages in Boston and university towns like Cambridge and Amherst, and he carried—but not by large margins—old mill towns like Lowell and Lawrence.

Kerry has obviously long had ambitions for national office, but he lacks the warm personal demeanor of a Bill Clinton. Even his supporters on the *Boston Globe* editorial page once wrote, "His coolness can approach frost with great rapidity, and his fellow pols do not cut him the sort of slack allotted to more demonstrative personalities." He does not have an obvious common touch. But he is able and hard-working and has shown some originality on public policy, and could surely be a plausible presidential candidate. After his 1996 victory, he could be pretty sure of holding his Senate seat, and he started making trips to New Hampshire. But after opposing impeachment—like most northeast Democrats, thought it was frivolous to remove Clinton from office for his offenses—he announced in February 1999 that he would not run for the 2000 nomination. Eighteen months later he was apparently one of the two finalists for the Democratic vice presidential nomination and was obviously disappointed when Al Gore chose Joseph Lieberman. His Senate seat comes up in 2002, and seems to be in no jeopardy, and this war hero and experienced politician could very well be a serious candidate for president in 2004.

Cook's Call   *Safe.* Massachusetts Republicans will be extraordinarily lucky just to hold onto the governorship in 2002, let alone make the Senate race competitive. As of spring 2001, the only name being floated as a potential challenger to Kerry was scandal-plagued businessman and 2000 Senate nominee Jack E. Robinson, but Republicans are not likely to embrace his candidacy. Kerry will probably have the luxury of using the campaign season to position himself for a 2004 White House bid.

Presidential politics   Over the last eight presidential elections, Massachusetts has been the most Democratic state, giving Democratic nominees an average margin of 53%–39%, just ahead of next-door Rhode Island's 53%–40%. It was Bill Clinton's best state in 1996 and Al Gore's second best, after Rhode Island, in 2000. There was something approaching unanimity for Al Gore in 2000 among many groups: He carried women 67%–28%, those with graduate school educations 60%–29% (with 9% for Ralph Nader), 62%–32% among Catholics.

Massachusetts's presidential primary has long been in early March and was once the scene of great commotion. It produced victories for native sons in 1988 and 1992, Democrats Michael Dukakis and Paul Tsongas and Republican George Bush. In 2000 it voted solidly for Al Gore and John McCain, as many independents reregistered as Republicans. Candidates contesting New Hampshire always buy time on Boston TV stations, which reach much of the Granite State and the cost of which does not have to be charged against the low limit on spending in New Hampshire, and so their ads are widely seen in Massachusetts. But they don't usually bother campaigning here.

Congressional districting   Massachusetts's convoluted congressional district lines deserve their own biographer, someone with a sure political instinct and a touch of whimsy. The state lost one seat in each of the last two reapportionments; it survived the 2000 Census without losing another. That probably means another round of pro-incumbent redistricting, although it was rumored in early 2001 that 5th District Congressman Martin Meehan, who ran again in 2000 despite a 1992 pledge to serve only four terms, may run for governor.

THE PEOPLE: Pop. 2000: 6,349,097; Pop. 1990: 6,016,425, up 5.5% 1990–2000. 2.3% of U.S. total, 13th largest; 84.5% White, 5.4% Black, 3.8% Asian, 0.2% Amer. Indian, 2.3% Two+ races, 3.7% Other; 6.8% Hispanic Origin. 2.6% Unemployment. 2000 Voting age pop.: 4,849,033. 2000 Turnout: 2,734,006; 56% of VAP. Registered voters (2000): 4,008,796; 1,460,881 D (36%), 546,333 R (14%), 2,001,582 unaffiliated and minor parties (50%).

POLITICAL LINEUP: Governor, Jane Swift (R); Secy. of the Commonwealth, William Galvin (D); Atty. Gen., Thomas Reilly (D); Treasurer, Shannon O'Brien (D); Auditor, Joseph DeNucci (D); State Senate, 40 (34 D, 6 R); Senate President, Thomas F. Birmingham (D); Majority Leader, Linda Melconian (D); State House, 160 (135 D, 22 R, 3 I); House Speaker, Thomas Finneran (D). Senators, Edward Kennedy (D) and John F. Kerry (D). Representatives, 10 (10 D).

ELECTIONS DIVISION: 617-727-2828; **FILING DEADLINE FOR U.S. CONGRESS:** June 4, 2002.

2000 Presidential Vote

Gore (D)	1,616,487	(60%)
Bush (R)	878,502	(33%)
Nader (Green)	173,564	(6%)
Others	32,389	(1%)

1996 Presidential Vote

Clinton (D)	1,571,755	(61%)
Dole (R)	718,104	(28%)
Perot (I)	226,787	(9%)
Others	39,347	(2%)

2000 Republican Presidential Primary

McCain (R)	324,708	(65%)
Bush (R)	159,534	(32%)
Other	17,709	(4%)

2000 Democratic Presidential Primary

Gore (D)	341,586	(60%)
Bradley (D)	212,452	(37%)
Other	16,036	(3%)

Gov. Jane Swift (R)

Assumed office, Apr. 2001, term expires Jan. 2003, 1st term; b. Feb. 24, 1965, North Adams; home, Williamstown; Trinity College, B.A., 1987; Catholic; married (Charles Hunt).

Elected Office: MA Senate, 1991–95.

Professional Career: Dir., Regional Airport Devel., MA Port Authority, 1996–97; Dir., MA Ofc. of Consumer Affairs & Bus. Reg., 1997.

Office: State House, Boston, 02133, 617-727-3600; Fax: 617-727-9725; Web site: www.state.ma.us.

Election Results

1998 general	Paul Cellucci (R)	967,160	(51%)
	Scott Harshbarger (D)	901,843	(47%)
	Others	34,333	(2%)
1998 primary	Paul Cellucci (R)	136,258	(59%)
	Joseph D. Malone (R)	95,963	(41%)
1994 general	William Weld (R)	1,533,380	(71%)
	Mark Roosevelt (D)	611,641	(28%)

Sen. Edward Kennedy (D)

Elected 1962, seat up 2006, 7th term; b. Feb. 22, 1932, Boston; home, Hyannis Port; Harvard U., B.A. 1956, The Hague Intl. Law Schl., 1958, U. of VA, LL.B. 1959; Catholic; married (Vicki).

Military Career: Army, 1951–53.

Professional Career: Western states coord., John F. Kennedy Pres. Campaign, 1960; Asst. Dist. Atty., Suffolk Cnty., 1961–62.

DC Office: 315 RSOB, 20510, 202-224-4543; Fax: 202-224-2417; Web site: www.senate.gov/~kennedy.

State Office: Boston, 617-565-3170.

Committees: *Armed Services*: Emerging Threats & Capabilities; Personnel; Seapower (Chmn.). *Health, Education, Labor & Pensions* (Chmn.): Employment, Safety & Training; Public Health (Chmn.). *Judiciary*: Administrative Oversight & the Courts; Constitution, Federalism & Property Rights; Immigration (Chmn.). *Joint Economic Committee* (2d of 10 Sens.).

Group Ratings

	ADA	ACLU	AFS	LCV	CON	ITIC	NTU	COC	ACU	NTLC	CHC
2000	90	71	85	71	84	78	12	40	12	0	15
1999	95	—	100	89	38	—	7	47	4	—	—

National Journal Ratings

	1999 LIB —	1999 CONS		2000 LIB —	2000 CONS
Economic	90% —	0%		96% —	0%
Social	80% —	19%		79% —	0%
Foreign	78% —	13%		72% —	15%

Key Votes of the 106th Congress

1. Educ. Savings Accts.	N	5. Review Movie Violence	Y	9. NATO War in Serbia	Y
2. Prescrip. Drug Benefit	Y	6. Gun Show Bckgrnd. Checks	Y	10. Table Cuba Travel Ban	N
3. Delay Ergonomic Standards	N	7. Ban Part.-Birth Abortion	N	11. Nuclear Test-Ban Treaty	Y
4. Phase Out Estate Tax	N	8. Broaden Hate Crimes List	Y	12. Perm. Trade with China	Y

Election Results

2000 general	Edward Kennedy (D)	1,889,494	(73%)	($3,662,652)
	Jack E. Robinson III (R)	334,341	(13%)	($150,430)
	Carla A. Howell (LIB)	308,860	(12%)	($1,055,186)
	Other	66,725	(3%)	
2000 primary	Edward Kennedy (D)	unopposed		
1994 general	Edward Kennedy (D)	1,265,997	(58%)	($11,493,735)
	W. Mitt Romney (R)	894,000	(41%)	($7,624,491)

Sen. John F. Kerry (D)

Elected 1984, seat up 2002, 3d term; b. Dec. 11, 1943, Denver, CO; home, Boston; Yale U., A.B. 1966, Boston Col., LL.B. 1976; Catholic; married (Teresa Heinz).

Military Career: Navy, 1966–70 (Vietnam), Naval Reserves, 1972–78.

Elected Office: MA Lt. Gov., 1982–84.

Professional Career: Organizer, Vietnam Veterans Against the War; Asst. Dist. Atty., Middlesex Cnty., 1976–81; Practicing atty., 1981–82.

DC Office: 304 RSOB, 20510, 202-224-2742; Fax: 202-224-8525; Web site: www.senate.gov/~kerry.

State Offices: Boston, 617-565-8519; Fall River, 508-677-0522; Springfield, 413-785-4610; Worcester, 508-831-7380.

Committees: *Democratic Steering Committee Chairman. Commerce, Science & Transportation*: Communications; Oceans & Fisheries (Chmn.); Science, Technology & Space; Surface Transportation & Merchant Marine. *Finance*: Health Care; International Trade; Social Security & Family Policy. *Foreign Relations*: East Asian & Pacific Affairs (Chmn.); International Operations & Terrorism; Western Hemisphere, Peace Corps, Narcotics Affairs. *Small Business* (Chmn.).

Group Ratings

	ADA	ACLU	AFS	LCV	CON	ITIC	NTU	COC	ACU	NTLC	CHC
2000	90	71	85	86	63	83	13	53	12	3	15
1999	95	—	100	100	45	—	11	53	0	—	—

National Journal Ratings

	1999 LIB —	1999 CONS		2000 LIB —	2000 CONS
Economic	80% —	17%		84% —	11%
Social	81% —	12%		66% —	21%
Foreign	78% —	13%		70% —	28%

Key Votes of the 106th Congress

1. Educ. Savings Accts.	N	5. Review Movie Violence	Y	9. NATO War in Serbia	Y
2. Prescrip. Drug Benefit	Y	6. Gun Show Bckgrnd. Checks	Y	10. Table Cuba Travel Ban	N
3. Delay Ergonomic Standards	N	7. Ban Part.-Birth Abortion	N	11. Nuclear Test-Ban Treaty	Y
4. Phase Out Estate Tax	N	8. Broaden Hate Crimes List	Y	12. Perm. Trade with China	Y

Election Results

1996 general	John F. Kerry (D)	1,334,135	(52%)	($12,619,152)
	William Weld (R)	1,143,120	(45%)	($8,002,123)
	Others	78,687	(3%)	
1996 primary	John F. Kerry (D)	unopposed		
1990 general	John F. Kerry (D)	1,321,712	(57%)	($8,040,970)
	Jim Rappaport (R)	992,917	(43%)	($5,177,801)

FIRST DISTRICT

The stony hills and green-clad mountains of western Massachusetts, with more trees today than when Henry David Thoreau was writing in the 1840s, where stone wall fencing once bounded one working farm from another, probably does not look much different from 300 years ago. This was the frontier in the 17th Century, where Puritan preachers formed new towns in the wilderness, farming the stony soil and preaching against declension. This was also the site of the Indian uprising known as King Philip's War in 1676, and the Indian raid, supported by the French from Quebec, at Deerfield in 1704. This was Yankee New England's western frontier for nearly 200 years. In the 19th Century, western New England was the home of writers and artists, Emily Dickinson lived quietly in Amherst, Edith Wharton grandly on her estate in Lenox, "The Mount," and the sculptor Augustus Saint Gaudens lived not far from where the Boston Symphony plays at the Tanglewood Festival each summer. There were mill towns here as well, jammed in mountain crevasses or along the wide Connecticut River; but as the 20th Century went on, and trees grew up on stony land once farmed, western Massachusetts came to look less settled, except near giant factories like General Electric's now-closed electric transformer plant in Pittsfield and the Crane paper factory in nearby Dalton. In an innovative restoration in North Adams, the abandoned Sprague Electric Company mill has been converted to the large Museum of Contemporary Art.

Western Massachusetts has also changed politically. For many years it was one of the heartlands of the Republican Party—flinty, thrifty and chilly just like the area's most famous politician, Calvin Coolidge. But by the 1980s, western Massachusetts contained some of the most left-wing parts of America. Stockbridge attracted liberal artist Norman Rockwell (a solid New Dealer and peacenik) and baby boom radical Arlo Guthrie, whose Alice's Restaurant was there. The concentration of colleges and universities in the Pioneer Valley, around Amherst, Northampton and South Hadley, brought together a critical mass of liberal scholars and an even more leftish graduate student proletariat. The results show up in the election returns: Hampshire County, dominated by those college towns, voted 56%–28% for Al Gore in 2000; he carried Amherst, home of the University of Massachusetts, 60%–14% over George W. Bush; the runner-up, with 25%, was Ralph Nader.

The 1st Congressional District, like most Massachusetts districts, has convoluted boundaries that defy easy description. It covers much but not all of western Massachusetts and stretches far to the northeast. It includes all of Berkshire and Franklin Counties and much of the Pioneer Valley: Amherst is in the 1st and so is the mill town of Holyoke on the Connecticut River, but Northampton and South Hadley are in the 2d District. This is a Democratic district in most elections, but not uniformly. The Democratic base is split among the Amherst radicals, low-income factory workers of Holyoke and the descendants of ethnic mill and blue-collar workers in places like Pittsfield and Fitchburg. Remnants of the Republican base are even more scattered, among the small towns in the hills.

The congressman from the 1st is John Olver, a Democrat chosen in a special election in June 1991 after longtime Republican Congressman Silvio Conte died. Olver was educated at Tufts and MIT and came to UMass as a chemistry professor in 1961, at 25; his wife Rose is a professor of psychology and women's and gender studies at Amherst College. In 1968, he was elected to the state House; he was elected in 1972 to the state Senate, where he served 18 years. In the special election to replace Conte, his Pioneer Valley base helped him win 31% in the fragmented Democratic primary. In the general he faced Steven Pierce, former state House Republican leader and Governor William Weld's conservative opponent in the 1990 primary. With Massachusetts' liberalism in grave disrepute, the contest was close and Weld scheduled it after students' summer vacation began. But Olver eked out a 50%–48% win.

Olver has one of the most liberal voting records in the House. He opposed NAFTA and Permanent Normal Trade Relations with China, and favors Canadian-style single-payer health insurance. He has attacked the IRS for not collecting enough of taxes owed. He told a local labor group, "We need a positive program, a jobs strategy, a national minimum wage, a guarantee of jobs, increased money for research and development, universal health care and portability of health insurance." But he has had little opening to pursue these social democratic goals in the Republican House. Instead he has worked to fund local projects on the Appropriations Committee. With his unlikely assignment as the Military Construction subpanel's senior Democrat, he directed $14 million to Westover Air Force Base in Chicopee for a Marine reserve training facility and dormitory renovations.

Olver does not seem a natural politico: He likes to rock climb, a solitary and meticulous business. In a delegation filled with publicity hounds, Olver is notably shy with the press. Some Massachusetts Democrats have said that as the state's only Appropriations member, he hasn't done much for their districts. "Everyone kind of works around him," the 9th District's Joe Moakley told *The Boston Herald* in unusually harsh criticism. "He's a nice guy, bright enough, but he's not collegial." Still, the perks of seniority dictate that Olver will keep the Appropriations slot as long as he wants it.

For a conscientious Democrat in a basically Democratic district, Olver has not always had dazzling electoral performance. In 1992, he won his first re-election, 52%–43. In 1996 he faced state Representative—and now Governor— Jane Swift, a 31-year-old moderate, who spent $693,000. Olver won by only 53%–47%. In his two most recent elections Olver has won by big margins, with 68% in 2000, which amazingly enough was the lowest percentage among the state's 10 Democratic incumbents. The 1st District's position at one end of the state means that redistricting will probably be no great problem for him, though he likely will gain additional territory.

Cook's Call   *Probably Safe.* Olver has held this Western Massachusetts district for 10 years, but his tenure has been a little schizophrenic, winning by narrow margins one year, only to be unopposed the next. Olver's less than triumphant victories in the past certainly make him an intriguing target, and may explain why Olver is interested in picking up heavily Democratic Northampton (now in the 2nd District) in 2001 redistricting. One of the slower growing districts in the state, it needs to pick up about 25,000 new people. Still, Olver should be fine in 2002.

THE PEOPLE: Pop. 2000: 610,522; Pop. 1990: 601,721, up 1.5% 1990–2000. 91.1% White, 1.9% Black, 1.7% Asian, 0.2% Amer. Indian, 1.7% Two + races, 3.3% Other; 6.5% Hispanic Origin.

2000 Presidential Vote

Gore (D)	144,553	(57%)
Bush (R)	83,969	(33%)
Nader (Green)	22,755	(9%)
Others	4,352	(2%)

1996 Presidential Vote

Clinton (D)	151,531	(61%)
Dole (R)	63,998	(26%)
Perot (I)	29,116	(12%)
Others	4,718	(2%)

Rep. John W. Olver (D)

Elected June 1991, 5th term; b. Sept. 3, 1936, Honesdale, PA; home, Amherst; Rensselaer Polytechnic Inst., B.S. 1955, Tufts U., M.S. 1956, M.I.T., Ph.D. 1961; no religious affiliation; married (Rose).

Elected Office: MA House of Reps., 1968–72; MA Senate, 1972–91.

Professional Career: Prof., U. of MA, Amherst, 1961–69.

DC Office: 1027 LHOB 20515, 202-225-5335; Fax: 202-226-1224; Web site: www.house.gov/olver.

District Offices: Fitchburg, 978-342-8722; Holyoke, 413-532-7010; Pittsfield, 413-442-0946.

Committees: *Appropriations* (14th of 29 D): District of Columbia; Military Construction (RMM); Transportation.

Group Ratings

	ADA	ACLU	AFS	LCV	CON	ITIC	NTU	COC	ACU	NTLC	CHC
2000	90	86	100	93	78	44	20	38	4	9	0
1999	95	—	100	100	68	—	19	13	0	—	—

National Journal Ratings

	1999 LIB —	1999 CONS		2000 LIB —	2000 CONS
Economic	80% —	18%		85% —	11%
Social	87% —	0%		94% —	0%
Foreign	95% —	0%		92% —	6%

1. Patient Bill of Rights	Y	5. Bar RU-486 $ for FDA	N	9. NATO War in Serbia	Y
2. Accelerate Min. Wage	Y	6. Display 10 Commandments	N	10. Perm. Trade with China	N
3. Strike Ban on Ergo. Stnd.	Y	7. Gun Show Bkgrnd. Checks	Y	11. Debt Relief for 3rd World	Y
4. Ovrd. Estate Tax Veto	N	8. Ban Part.-Birth Abortion	N	12. Drop Cuba Econ. Embargo	Y

Election Results

2000 general	John W. Olver (D)	169,375	(68%)	($646,363)
	Peter J. Abair (R)	73,580	(30%)	($151,633)
	Other	5,246	(2%)	
2000 primary	John W. Over (D)	unopposed		
1998 general	John W. Olver (D)	121,863	(72%)	($569,967)
	Gregory L. Morgan (R)	48,055	(28%)	($28,828)

SECOND DISTRICT

As American as apple pie, the place where basketball was invented, the city where the Webster's unabridged dictionaries (2d and 3d editions) were edited and published, the site of the armory where M-1 rifles were manufactured during World War II: This is Springfield, Massachusetts. Springfield is the third largest city in the Bay State, but far from Boston; the second-largest city in the Connecticut River Valley, but overshadowed by Hartford; a medium-sized American city built by New England Yankees, where immigrants from a dozen different countries have worked their way up. Like other New England cities, its downtown has emptied; business leaders have tried to use a new state law to create a business improvement district, but progress has been slow.

Springfield is the largest city in the 2d Congressional District, whose irregular boundaries stretch north to South Hadley and Northampton, college towns of the Pioneer Valley, and east across stony hills and the antique center of Brimfield to the factory towns of the Blackstone Valley just north of Woonsocket, Rhode Island. Historically, this was a Yankee Republican district for much of the 20th Century, then a solidly Catholic Democratic district; now it is more diverse culturally but still solidly Democratic.

The congressman from the 2d District is Richard Neal, mayor of Springfield from 1984–88. Neal grew up in Springfield, went to work for the mayor in 1973, was elected to the Council in 1978, while teaching high school and college history. As mayor himself, Neal boasted of both downtown rehabilitation and neighborhood revitalization. He was essentially bequeathed the House seat by his predecessor, 36-year incumbent Edward Boland, a longtime friend of Tip O'Neill. In 1988, Boland announced his retirement just before the filing deadline, and after Neal had been making the rounds of the district for a year. Unopposed in the Democratic primary, Neal won 80% in the general.

Neal has a generally liberal voting record but has favored enough moderate initiatives to separate himself from more ideological Massachusetts colleagues. He voted for the final version of welfare reform, the partial birth abortion ban and the Defense of Marriage Act and refused to support the Clinton health care plan. He voted for NAFTA and GATT and—after considerable hand-wringing—for Permanent Normal Trade Relations with China. He serves on Ways and Means, where he decries the complications of the tax code and has a bill that would allow tax-payers to claim the child tax credit without calculating the alternative minimum tax; the bill would eliminate 200 lines from federal tax forms. When other Ways and Means Democrats cut a bipartisan deal to expand pensions and retirement incentives, Neal filed an alternative targeted more to blue-collar workers. With Barney Frank and Jim McGovern, he sought to preserve a state drug mandate for Medicare patients by repealing a federal exemption.

Neal tends to local matters, hailing extension of the Quinebaug-Shetucket River Valley Heritage Corridor from Connecticut to Massachusetts and pushing the Defense Center for Financial Management and Training at Southbridge. Like many other Irish Catholic brethren over the years, he has encouraged American attempts at reconciliation in Northern Ireland. In 1980, when he was a city council member, he sponsored a plank at the Democratic National Convention for the unification of Ireland. In 1993 he started one-hour special orders sessions on Irish issues; in 1994 he personally lobbied Bill Clinton to grant a visa for Gerry Adams of Sinn Fein to visit the United

States, though Adams would not condemn IRA bombing; in April 1998 Neal attended Sinn Fein's convention in Ireland; in September 1999, he proposed a reduction in the force and weaponry of the Royal Ulster Constabulary.

Neal had serious primary challenges in 1990 and 1992, but won by satisfactory margins. Republicans have never mounted credible opposition. His 1996 Republican opponent had been convicted of arson in 1991 (Massachusetts is the only state that allows convicted felons to run for office); in the two most recent elections, he faced no opposition at all.

Cook's Call   *Safe.* Richard Neal, one of the more culturally conservative members of the all-Democratic, and relatively liberal Massachusetts delegation, has represented this district since 1988. During his tenure, Neal has won re-election rather easily, though it was a bumpy road early on. Like the sprawling 1st District, this western Massachusetts district has also been losing population and needs to pick up about 20,000 people. But today, Neal's biggest opponent may be his Democratic colleague, John Olver, who is interested in taking heavily Democratic Northampton from the 2nd and placing it back in the 1st (where it was before 1990 redistricting). Neal remains a safe incumbent.

THE PEOPLE: Pop. 2000: 615,557; Pop. 1990: 601,490, up 2.3% 1990–2000. 85.3% White, 6% Black, 1.3% Asian, 0.2% Amer. Indian, 0.1% Hawaiian, 1.9% Two+ races, 5.2% Other; 9.5% Hispanic Origin.

2000 Presidential Vote

Gore (D)	145,544	(58%)
Bush (R)	85,475	(34%)
Nader (Green)	16,209	(6%)
Others	2,944	(1%)

1996 Presidential Vote

Clinton (D)	147,670	(61%)
Dole (R)	66,344	(27%)
Perot (I)	25,252	(10%)

Rep. Richard E. Neal (D)

Elected 1988, 7th term; b. Feb. 14, 1949, Springfield; home, Springfield; Amer. Intl. Col., B.A. 1972, U. of Hartford, M.A. 1976; Catholic; married (Maureen).

Elected Office: Springfield City Cncl., 1978–83; Springfield Mayor, 1984–88.

Professional Career: Staff Asst., Springfield Mayor William C. Sullivan, 1973–78; High Schl. & Col. teacher, 1978–83.

DC Office: 2133 RHOB 20515, 202-225-5601; Fax: 202-225-8112; Web site: www.house.gov/neal.

District Offices: Milford, 508-634-8198; Springfield, 413-785-0325.

Committees: *Ways & Means* (10th of 17 D): Select Revenue Measures; Trade.

Group Ratings

	ADA	ACLU	AFS	LCV	CON	ITIC	NTU	COC	ACU	NTLC	CHC
2000	80	57	85	86	66	74	21	38	8	12	13
1999	95	—	100	94	67	—	13	32	4	—	—

National Journal Ratings

	1999 LIB — 1999 CONS		2000 LIB — 2000 CONS	
Economic	84% —	12%	78% —	20%
Social	68% —	32%	64% —	36%
Foreign	89% —	8%	80% —	16%

Key Votes of the 106th Congress

1. Patient Bill of Rights	Y	5. Bar RU-486 $ for FDA	N	9. NATO War in Serbia	Y
2. Accelerate Min. Wage	Y	6. Display 10 Commandments	N	10. Perm. Trade with China	Y
3. Strike Ban on Ergo. Stnd.	Y	7. Gun Show Bkgrnd. Checks	Y	11. Debt Relief for 3rd World	Y
4. Ovrd. Estate Tax Veto	N	8. Ban Part.-Birth Abortion	Y	12. Drop Cuba Econ. Embargo	Y

Election Results

2000 general	Richard E. Neal (D) .... unopposed		($369,098)
2000 primary	Richard E. Neal (D) 20,253	(87%)	
	Joseph R. Fountain (D) 3,149	(13%)	
1998 general	Richard E. Neal (D) .... unopposed		($250,407)

THIRD DISTRICT

Worcester (its name still pronounced with a particularly pungent Massachusetts accent making it sound as if it had no Rs), although technically the second-largest city in Massachusetts, is often overlooked. People may drive in for concerts at the Centrum, but otherwise they zoom by on I-495 or the Turnpike. Worcester is one of the few major industrial cities not located on a river, lake or sea coast, and far from a major airport. A high-tech manufacturing haven before the term was invented, for 200 years the city has been one of the nation's centers of tinkering, contriving and inventing. But it hasn't always been smooth going; 50 years ago, Worcester's biggest industries were wire-making, textiles, grinding wheels and envelopes: not on the cutting edge then and certainly not now. Its blue-collar tradition survives in its dozen or so retro diners. But in the 1970s and 1980s, electronics and computer firms sprouted along I-495—the circumferential highway 20 miles east of Worcester, as they had earlier around Route 128, closer to Boston. The high-tech boom brought prosperity, labor shortages, new residents and higher housing prices to central Massachusetts. Then, in the early 1990s, the minicomputer industry slumped, bringing recession and a collapse of real estate values. But Worcester's ingenious entrepreneurs and skilled labor force have hustled, local leaders have set up a Biotechnology Research Institute and the local economy again is perking up. Single-family home values plunged nearly 30% in the early 1990s; they're on the rebound now, but still far lower than in the Boston area.

The 3d Congressional District, grotesquely shaped, has Worcester as its largest city though not its geographic center. A little more than half its people live in Worcester and a cluster of towns all around. The other population cluster is 60 miles away, in and around the old textile mill town of Fall River, east of Rhode Island, and Dartmouth and Westport on Buzzards Bay. The two are connected by a string of towns in some places only a few miles wide. Thus has the 3d District, if not quite Worcester, been made a seaport. The I-495 corridor and the towns around Worcester are Republican; Worcester itself is Democratic, and Fall River and the area around it even more so.

The congressman from the 3d District is Jim McGovern, a Democrat elected in 1996. McGovern grew up in Worcester, where his parents owned a package store on West Boylston Street. He went to American University in Washington, and while in graduate school worked in the office of former South Dakota Senator George McGovern (no relation). He ran McGovern's 1984 campaign in the Massachusetts presidential primary, where he finished third with 21% of the vote, and nominated him at the San Francisco convention. After that he got a job in Boston Rep. Joe Moakley's office and became chief of staff as Moakley moved up to Rules Committee chairman. McGovern then got into the spotlight himself, leading a 1989 investigation of the murders of six Jesuits and two lay women in El Salvador, which led to a cutoff of aid. In 1994 he ran for the House and lost in the Democratic primary 38%–30%. In 1996 he ran again, this time with no primary opposition. In the general election, two-term Republican Congressman Peter Blute stressed his "independence" from the House leadership and attacked McGovern for liberal stands on abortion and Cuba. The AFL-CIO targeted the district with TV ads, and McGovern ran a humorous spot that asked, "If you wouldn't vote for Newt, why would you ever vote for Blute?" Blute outspent McGovern, but McGovern outraised him among PACs—an example of how well Democrats on the Hill can use that system. McGovern won 53%–45%.

McGovern made several visits to Cuba and has called for easing sanctions against Fidel Castro's regime. When Elian Gonzalez sparked a tempest in Miami, McGovern worked with the boy's father to arrange their return to Cuba. But despite his liberal views, he has handled some issues on a bipartisan basis. With Republican Tom Coburn, he worked successfully to restore some home health care benefits cut in the Balanced Budget Act of 1997. He called for increasing grant awards for college freshmen and sophomores who were in the top 10% of their high school classes. He got a seat on the Transportation and Infrastructure Committee in time to work on the big 1998 highway bill, the only New England House member on the conference committee. In the bill, Worcester got $11.5 million for Union Station, $6 million for the Blackstone Valley bike path and $1.8 million for Main Street. And he helped to bail out Boston's "Big Dig" highway-funding fiasco with a $549 million annual commitment. After a fire disaster killed six Worcester firefighters, he sponsored a bill for grants to local fire departments. "This to me is a no-brainer," he said. "It shouldn't take a tragedy to move people." In August 1998 he made headlines when he invited Bill Clinton to interrupt his vacation for a carefully controlled appearance in Worcester, just 10 days after Clinton admitted he lied about Monica Lewinsky. "Worcester is not a city of fair-weather friends . . . and you, Mr. President, through your policies, have been a true friend to Worcester," he proclaimed.

At that point McGovern was facing a serious challenge from Republican Matt Amorello, who had won a Democratic state Senate seat in 1990. Amorello attacked McGovern for voting against the balanced budget amendment, the partial-birth abortion ban and the ban on needle exchanges. McGovern attacked Amorello for favoring privatization of Social Security and for his support from conservative Republican leaders. In this pro-incumbent year, the result was not particularly close: McGovern won 57%–41%. In the new spirit of bipartisanship, McGovern invited Speaker Dennis Hastert to Worcester in January 1999; he did not accept. Republicans may have given up on the district: despite having held the seat four years earlier, they ran no challenger in 2000.

Cook's Call   *Safe.* Sophomore Jim McGovern's strong showing in 1998 and the fact that he went unopposed in 2000 suggests that he has found a way to hold onto this Democratic leaning but culturally conservative district. McGovern's liberal voting record could still cause him some problems, but he is a savvy politician who has used his position as the only Massachusetts member on the Transportation Committee to bring federal highway dollars home to this economically struggling district. This district needs to shed about 20,000 people in redistricting but that is unlikely to change the make-up.

THE PEOPLE: Pop. 2000: 655,701; Pop. 1990: 601,852, up 8.9% 1990–2000. 89.7% White, 2.7% Black, 2.8% Asian, 0.2% Amer. Indian, 1.8% Two+ races, 2.7% Other; 5.5% Hispanic Origin.

2000 Presidential Vote

Gore (D)	160,936	(58%)
Bush (R)	96,290	(35%)
Nader (Green)	15,453	(6%)
Others	3,339	(1%)

1996 Presidential Vote

Clinton (D)	154,915	(60%)
Dole (R)	76,413	(29%)
Perot (I)	24,690	(9%)
Others	4,096	(2%)

Rep. James McGovern (D)

Elected 1996, 3d term; b. Nov. 20, 1959, Worcester; home, Worcester; American U., B.A. 1981, M.P.A. 1984; Catholic; married (Lisa).

Professional Career: Aide, U.S. Sen. George McGovern, 1977–80; Sr. Aide, U.S. Rep. John Joseph Moakley, 1982–96.

DC Office: 430 CHOB 20515, 202-225-6101; Fax: 202-225-5759; Web site: www.house.gov/mcgovern.

District Offices: Attleboro, 508-431-8025; Fall River, 508-677-0140; Worcester, 508-831-7356.

Committees: *Resources* (20th of 25 D): National Parks, Recreation & Public Lands. *Transportation & Infrastructure* (24th of 34 D): Highways & Transit; Water Resources & Environment.

Group Ratings

	ADA	ACLU	AFS	LCV	CON	ITIC	NTU	COC	ACU	NTLC	CHC
2000	100	79	100	100	38	56	26	33	0	9	0
1999	100	—	100	100	56	—	23	20	0	—	—

National Journal Ratings

	1999 LIB	—	1999 CONS	2000 LIB	—	2000 CONS
Economic	88%	—	0%	95%	—	0%
Social	83%	—	13%	91%	—	6%
Foreign	78%	—	17%	97%	—	0%

Key Votes of the 106th Congress

1. Patient Bill of Rights	Y	5. Bar RU-486 $ for FDA	N	9. NATO War in Serbia	Y
2. Accelerate Min. Wage	Y	6. Display 10 Commandments	N	10. Perm. Trade with China	N
3. Strike Ban on Ergo. Stnd.	Y	7. Gun Show Bkgrnd. Checks	Y	11. Debt Relief for 3rd World	Y
4. Ovrd. Estate Tax Veto	N	8. Ban Part.-Birth Abortion	N	12. Drop Cuba Econ. Embargo	Y

Election Results

2000 general	James McGovern (D)	unopposed		($550,240)
2000 primary	James McGovern (D)	unopposed		
1998 general	James McGovern (D)	108,613	(57%)	($1,312,181)
	Matthew Amorello (R)	79,174	(41%)	($680,809)
	Others	3,091	(2%)	

FOURTH DISTRICT

The political transformation of Massachusetts is nowhere better illustrated than in the Boston suburbs of Brookline and Newton. These were Yankee enclaves a century ago, with avenues built to resemble the sweep of Haussmann's Grand Boulevards in Paris, and villages of giant clapboard houses clustered within a few blocks of commuter railroad stations. Brookline was where The Country Club (the very first one) was established in 1882, and where Joseph Kennedy, an Irish Catholic 20-something banker seeking respectability, moved his family in 1914. Brookline and Newton then were solidly Republican in politics, the political base of leading politicians like Christian Herter, governor of Massachusetts and U.S. secretary of State in the 1950s; as late as 1960, Brookline and Newton and adjacent wards of Boston were electing a Republican congressman. Then came the transformation, personified by the election in 1962 of Michael Dukakis at 29 to the Great and General Court (the legislature). As Massachusetts's university-educated classes became more liberal, and as Brookline's and Newton's Jewish populations grew, and as young liberal-minded families refurbished the graceful old houses, these towns became Democratic bastions. By the 1970s, the Brookline Town Meeting was opening each year with debates over whether they should recite the Pledge of Allegiance. Brookline and Newton, even more than Boston, are the liberal heart of Massachusetts: They voted 75%–20% for Bill Clinton in 1996 and 73%–19% for Al Gore in 2000—even better than Gore's 72%–20% lead in Boston.

The 4th Congressional District includes Brookline and Newton, which are the political home bases for its congressman, Barney Frank. But they cast only 24% of the district's votes, and this grotesquely shaped district is not all of one piece. The shape results from successive redistrictings: In 1982, Frank's district was extended south to the old textile mill city of Fall River; in 1992, it lost much of Fall River and gained New Bedford, a great 19th Century whaling port and still home to one of the largest fishing fleets in the United States, with the largest percentage of Portuguese-Americans in the nation. The 4th also curves north to the interior of Plymouth County around old towns like Bridgewater. This is a Democratic district in national politics, but not nearly so Democratic nor as uniformly culturally liberal as Brookline and Newton. There is a bit of most kinds of America here: high-income WASPy Wellesley, French-Canadian mill-worker Fall River, Foxboro with its football stadium, Sharon with a middle-income Jewish population and countrified Dover.

Barney Frank, elected in 1980, is one of the intellectual and political leaders of the Democratic Party in the House—political theorist and pit bull all at the same time. He grew up in Bayonne, New Jersey, and went to Harvard, where he got to know local politicians as well as political scientists. In 1967, he went to work for newly elected Boston Mayor Kevin White; in 1971, he went to Washington to work for Congressman Michael Harrington. In 1972, Frank was elected to the Massachusetts House from the Back Bay of Boston, then just starting to be a liberal singles neighborhood. In 1980, when Congressman Robert Drinan retired after Pope John Paul

II commanded Jesuits to leave elective office, Frank moved to Brookline and ran in the 4th District. With a strong base in Brookline and Newton, he won; keeping them together as redistricting moved the seat down to Fall River; he beat Republican Margaret Heckler 60%–40% in 1982. He has been re-elected by wide margins since.

In the House, Frank soon gained a reputation as one of the smartest talkers and best debaters in the chamber—maybe one of the best of all time. Frank listens to others' arguments and engages them in his inimitable rapid-fire delivery. While he stands at the left end of the American electoral spectrum, there is an element of solid small-c conservatism beneath him. "Democratic positions are fully consistent with the values of patriotism, free enterprise, working hard for one's self and one's family, and holding people to a standard of behavior fully respectful of the person and property of others," he wrote in his 1992 book *Speaking Frankly*. More recently he said he is for "capitalism plus," that is, market capitalism with welfare state protections, and he has expressed unease at what he considers increasing isolationism in Congress, though he also believes in "tens of billions" in cuts for defense spending and has tried to tear down the firewalls around defense and domestic spending, arguing that defense should not be exempt from cuts.

Frank has worked hard, often behind the scenes, on many substantive issues. He has shaped immigration acts since 1986, working to expand legal immigration, to allow HIV-positive people to enter the country, to bar states from excluding children of illegal aliens from school and, most recently, to change the 1996 law that required mandatory deportation of immigrants convicted of a crime carrying a one-year sentence even if the offense occurred many years ago; this had been hurting Azorean and Cape Verdean immigrants in New Bedford. As ranking Democrat on the Courts and Intellectual Property Subcommittee of Judiciary, he helped build a bipartisan coalition that in the 105th Congress linked two related issues, the World Intellectual Property Organization treaties and the protection of intellectual property on the Internet. In addition, the term of copyright was extended by 20 years. After the 1998 election Frank left the ranking position on Intellectual Property and took the ranking position on Banking's Housing Subcommittee. He worked to maintain the Section 8 rental subsidy program and to block a Republican attempt to raise the 30% income cap on public housing rents. Frank argues that there is a housing crisis in Massachusetts, where property values have soared. "We've got to get some new forms of construction. We'll probably have to wait for the Democrats to take over to get some more of that."

He has also had some bipartisan successes. With Banking Committee Republican Spencer Bachus he worked hard for debt relief for very poor countries. He has worked with conservatives Frank Wolf and Christopher Smith on human rights abuses in East Timor and China; he voted against Permanent Normal Trade Relations with China in September 2000. With conservatives Henry Hyde and Bob Barr, he worked to modify the harsh federal confiscation laws enacted as part of the war against drugs; the measure passed the House by a wide margin in 1999. With Republican Charles Canady, he managed the Lobbying Disclosure Act, barring all amendments so that the House would pass the Senate bill and no conference committee would be necessary. He also passed a law, vital for the biotech industry, allowing companies to receive patents for processes for artificially manufacturing substances which exist naturally. In 1998, after years of trying, he got passed an amendment limiting the American financial contribution for the expansion of NATO; in celebration, he voted for the defense bill for the first time in years.

But not until the impeachment hearings of 1998 was Frank able to overshadow another aspect of his career. In May 1987, in a seemingly casual answer to a reporter's question, Frank said he is gay. Then in August 1989, the conservative *Washington Times* reported that Frank had employed as a personal aide a male prostitute and convicted drug possessor, Steve Gobie, and let him live in his apartment. When faced with a scandal that threatened to end his career, Frank took the course Bill Clinton did not in 1998: He told the truth. He admitted paying Gobie, but was careful never to use official or campaign funds; he denied that he tolerated prostitution in his apartment and said he had thrown the man out when he suspected it was going on. Frank called on the ethics committee to investigate. It did and dismissed all but two minor charges. The committee recommended a reprimand but not censure; Frank agreed in a contrite appearance before the House in July 1990; the House voted 287–141 against censure (moved by Newt Gingrich); the vote for reprimand was 408–18. "I think members will agree that I have always had a

reputation for honesty, not always tact or tolerance," Frank said to the House. That reputation
was one reason he survived and has thrived in the House; his brains, liberal stands, hard work
and constituency service helped him not only survive but be overwhelmingly popular in the 4th
District.

Frank has been the House's leading legislator on gay rights issues. One was the issue, raised
in the 1992 campaign by Bill Clinton and not by Frank or by gay advocacy groups, of gays in the
military. To the disappointment of many in the gay community, Frank admitted that allowing open
homosexuals to serve in the military would not be accepted by most in Congress or the Pentagon.
Taking Senator Sam Nunn's "Don't Ask, Don't Tell" compromise a step further, Frank suggested
that gays be allowed to conduct an openly gay lifestyle when off-base without fear of reprisal; but
Clinton eventually declined to go so far. In the years since, Frank has criticized the administration
and the military because the number of service members discharged for homosexuality has actually increased, and he helped persuade Al Gore to come out against "Don't ask, Don't tell" in
1999. Frank and Republican Christopher Shays have sponsored a bill to prohibit employment
discrimination on account of sexuality, and it appears to be heading toward majority support, even
in a Republican House. Frank is also the sponsor of a bill to make domestic partners of federal
employees eligible for health insurance and of the bill which would provide federal penalties for
hate crimes, which passed the House in September 2000. He spoke at a gay pride celebration at
the CIA in June 2000. "People increasingly understand that the prejudice against gay people is
silly."

After the Republican victory in November 1994, Minority Whip David Bonior asked Frank
to be the Democrats' point man in floor debates. During the Contract With America debate, Frank
prowled the floor, ready to take up a microphone and deliver stinging attacks on Republicans'
hypocrisy. His strong and orderly mind, his ability to argue abstract principles in rapid-fire but
comprehensible words, were on display—and made him the most feared adversary by the Republican side. But his belief that the Republicans' positions would prove unpopular and cost them
their majority has not, or at least not yet, proven true.

Frank also emerged, well before the impeachment crisis, as a defender of Bill Clinton against
charges of scandal. He came at these issues as a civil libertarian who is attentive to defendants'
rights. On the Banking Committee in 1994 he defended Clinton with attack-dog intensity against
Whitewater charges; on the Judiciary Committee in October 1997 he and William Delahunt
peppered Janet Reno with questions and made tough arguments when Republicans were trying
to pressure her to appoint more independent counsels. Frank acknowledged that Clinton lied in
his deposition in the Paula Jones case but he also ridiculed the case against him. When Republicans argued that Frank's preferred result, censure, would be trivial, he seized on his own experience and said, "I am struck by those who argued that censure is somehow an irrelevancy, a
triviality, something of no weight. I would tell you that having been reprimanded by this House of
Representatives, where I'm so proud to serve, was no triviality."

Through all his work on national issues, Frank has not neglected the home front. He has
worked especially hard on projects in Fall River and, after it was added to the district after the
1990 Census, New Bedford, for which he obtained the creation of a national park commemorating
the whaling industry, the funding for a new Route 18 and assistance to the fishing industry. He
got Portugal, from which many in New Bedford have emigrated, added to the list of countries for
which the United States does not require visas for visitors. He has worked for the fishing and
cranberry industries and has sought funding for the cleanup of the Muddy River in Brookline and
preservation of the Corson building in New Bedford. Frank campaigned for Al Gore in 2000 and
attacked Green Party candidate Ralph Nader for never speaking on abortion rights, gay rights, or
gun control. He recovered smartly from heart surgery in 1999, and in 2000 said he hoped to serve
in the House "another 15 years or so." He went on, "I'd still rather be here than anywhere else.
There isn't anything I'd rather do."

Cook's Call   *Safe.* A well-known fixture in the Washington political scene, Barney Frank
is securely entrenched in this heavily Democratic Boston suburban district. Since winning this
seat in 1980, Frank has never dropped below 60% in his re-election contests. This district
shouldn't be altered much in redistricting, as it needs to lose only about 4,000 people.

THE PEOPLE: Pop. 2000: 639,072; Pop. 1990: 601,392, up 6.3% 1990–2000. 89.5% White, 2.2% Black, 3.2% Asian, 0.2% Amer. Indian, 2.1% Two+ races, 2.7% Other; 3.1% Hispanic Origin.

2000 Presidential Vote

Gore (D)	176,225	(63%)
Bush (R)	85,173	(30%)
Nader (Green)	15,160	(5%)
Others	3,234	(1%)

1996 Presidential Vote

Clinton (D)	169,078	(64%)
Dole (R)	69,548	(26%)
Perot (I)	22,782	(9%)

Rep. Barney Frank (D)

Elected 1980, 11th term; b. Mar. 31, 1940, Bayonne, NJ; home, Newton; Harvard U., B.A. 1962, J.D. 1977; Jewish; single.

Elected Office: MA House of Reps., 1972–80.

Professional Career: Exec. Asst., Boston Mayor Kevin White, 1967–71; A.A., U.S. Rep. Michael Harrington, 1971–72; Lecturer, Harvard JFK Schl. of Govt., 1978–80.

DC Office: 2252 RHOB 20515, 202-225-5931; Fax: 202-225-0182; Web site: www.house.gov/frank.

District Offices: Bridgewater, 508-697-9403; Fall River, 508-674-3551; New Bedford, 508-999-6462; Newton, 617-332-3920.

Committees: *Financial Services* (2d of 32 D): Domestic Monetary Policy, Technology & Economic Growth; Housing & Community Opportunity (RMM); International Monetary Policy & Trade. *Judiciary* (2d of 17 D): Immigration & Claims; The Constitution.

Group Ratings

	ADA	ACLU	AFS	LCV	CON	ITIC	NTU	COC	ACU	NTLC	CHC
2000	95	86	100	93	81	42	29	33	12	19	0
1999	100	—	100	88	65	—	27	21	0	—	—

National Journal Ratings

	1999 LIB	—	1999 CONS		2000 LIB	—	2000 CONS
Economic	75%	—	23%		73%	—	26%
Social	87%	—	0%		94%	—	0%
Foreign	65%	—	34%		85%	—	10%

Key Votes of the 106th Congress

1. Patient Bill of Rights	Y	5. Bar RU-486 $ for FDA	N	9. NATO War in Serbia	N
2. Accelerate Min. Wage	Y	6. Display 10 Commandments	N	10. Perm. Trade with China	N
3. Strike Ban on Ergo. Stnd.	Y	7. Gun Show Bkgrnd. Checks	Y	11. Debt Relief for 3rd World	Y
4. Ovrd. Estate Tax Veto	N	8. Ban Part.-Birth Abortion	N	12. Drop Cuba Econ. Embargo	Y

Election Results

2000 general	Barney Frank (D)	200,638	(75%)	($471,381)
	Martin D. Travis (R)	56,553	(21%)	($24,553)
	David J. Euchner (LIB)	10,553	(4%)	($8,613)
2000 primary	Barney Frank (D)	unopposed		
1998 general	Barney Frank (D)	unopposed		($345,272)

FIFTH DISTRICT

The Merrimack River Valley at the northern edge of Massachusetts has had an erratic history: high-tech boom, bust, boom, bust, boom. When Massachusetts was a kind of maritime republic in the 19th Century, with a few farmers struggling to scratch out a living from the stony soil, a few clever Yankees used their profits from the sea trade to try to tame the rapidly flowing Merrimack and build cotton-spinning mills. Creating the cities of Lowell and Lawrence, they built model dormitories and recreation programs for their women workers. This was the center of America's textile industry for more than a century, long after the maritime industry faded. But in the 1920s, the price of labor rose and newly built mills in the Carolinas—much closer to the cotton supply—decimated the industry that Lawrence and Lowell built. Many residents—by then rather elderly—waited forlornly for an upturn in the local economy.

It came eventually, largely due to an unexpected source. High-tech industry drove the growth, beginning in the 1960s around MIT, then moving out to the Route 128 ring road and then I-495, which passes through Lowell and Lawrence. Wang, headquartered in Lowell, grew spectacularly, and Congressman and then Senator Paul Tsongas spearheaded a national historical restoration of the old mill area. This was the Massachusetts miracle of the early 1980s. Then came the bust: Wang's word processors and minicomputers slumped as businesses purchased personal computers and hooked them together in networks. But Lowell revived again. Its new immigrants—mostly from Cambodia and Puerto Rico—provide vitality and entrepreneurial creativity; the old Wang buildings are filled with health care, banking, telecommunications and Internet companies. Tsongas died in January 1997, but lived long enough to see Lowell on the move again, rehabbing the River Place Towers, renovating the Bon Marche and building the Paul Tsongas Arena.

The 5th Congressional District includes Lawrence and Lowell, which along with next-door towns account for about half the district's population. The remainder of the district includes the high-tech corridor south on I-495, running from the stony hills of Lawrence and Lowell to Maynard and Marlborough. The district also includes fancy suburbs like Concord, aging mill towns like Ayer and the mountains along the New Hampshire state line. Except for Lowell and Lawrence, it is ancestrally Yankee Republican. It is culturally liberal and trended toward the Democrats in the early 1970s. But in the 1980s and 1990s, amid the high-tech boom, it went Republican in national and even statewide elections: a kind of Baja New Hampshire. In 1992 it gave Bill Clinton his lowest percentage in the state, while a big vote went to high-tech pioneer Ross Perot; in 1996 and 2000, unnerved by the Republican revolutionaries, it went heavily Democratic.

The congressman from the 5th District is Martin Meehan, a Democrat elected in 1992. Meehan grew up in Lowell, one of seven children of a 43-year Lowell *Sun* typesetter. As a child, he memorized President Kennedy's speeches from long-playing records, kept a scrapbook on Robert Kennedy, and idolized Edward Kennedy, who was elected to the Senate when Meehan was 5. He is a lifelong politico: He was an aide to Congressman James Shannon while working on his masters degree, worked in the Massachusetts secretary of state's office after law school, and was first assistant district attorney in Middlesex County from 1990 until he ran for Congress in 1992. He took on eight-year incumbent Democrat Chester Atkins, who had grown highly unpopular in the district. Meehan beat Atkins by the astonishing margin of 65%–35%, winning the Lowell-Lawrence area 75%–25%. In the general, Meehan faced former Republican Congressman. Paul Cronin, who beat John Kerry in 1972 (the only open seat carried by George McGovern to also elect a Republican to the House), but lost to Paul Tsongas in 1974. Meehan called for a 50% defense cut, targeted capital gains tax cuts, income tax increases, and backed the balanced budget amendment and term limits; he won 52%–38%.

Meehan—sometimes labeled a maverick—combines a mostly liberal voting record with distinctive stands on issues. One of his crusades is against tobacco; his father, a smoker, had heart surgery when Marty was 11. He prepared a 111-page memo urging prosecution of tobacco companies, and later joined with Utah Republican James Hansen to sponsor a bill with a $1.50 a pack tax and a target of cutting youth smoking by 80%.

His other great cause is campaign finance reform. In 1997, with Christopher Shays and Senators Russ Feingold and John McCain, Meehan co-sponsored the campaign finance plan to outlaw soft money, subject non-candidate ads to disclosure and contribution limit requirements, strengthen FEC enforcement powers, require posting of forms on the Internet, and create a commission to recommend more reforms. House Republican leaders continued to oppose action, but agreed under pressure from Meehan and others; it passed in August 1998, 252–179, with 61 Republican votes, and by a nearly identical vote in September 1999. But the Senate filibustered each bill, and soft-money spending continued to escalate in presidential and congressional campaigns. Meehan and allies did achieve a modest victory of sorts when Congress approved before the 2000 conventions, a bill to require tax-exempt "Section 527" groups to disclose their receipts and spending.

Meehan serves on the Armed Services Committee and has generally moved to cut defense spending; although he boosts local Raytheon operations and its upgrades of the Patriot missile, he sided with its workers during a bitter five-week strike in 2000. Over the years, his voting record seems to have drifted left: He voted for NAFTA in 1993 and against fast track in 1997. But he was one of only two House Democrats from Massachusetts to vote in 2000 to normalize trade relations with China, arguing that it would bring benefits to U.S. workers and businesses.

When Meehan ran in 1992, he pledged to serve no more than four terms. In 1999 he changed his mind, arguing that, with the failure of term limits nationally, keeping the pledge would disadvantage his constituents. This miffed term-limit advocates and some Massachusetts colleagues, who were irritated by his support of campaign finance reform (though on the record they're for it) and for other maverick tendencies, such as introducing Republican Governor Paul Cellucci as "a friend" at a women's issues forum he hosted for Hillary Rodham Clinton in Lowell. Despite some bluster from foes, he amazingly ran unopposed in the 2000 general election and had nominal primary opposition; potential opponents were intimidated by his nearly $2 million campaign fund. Days after the election, he said that he was thinking about running for governor in 2002.

Cook's Call   *Probably Safe.* Meehan's decision whether or not he will run for governor will determine just how competitive this race will be in 2002. If Meehan does run for governor, expect a crowded primary and a potentially competitive general election. Though this district has a serious Democratic edge (Gore won here with 56%), it is by no means the most Democratic in the state. If Meehan stays put, it is hard to see him lose in 2002.

THE PEOPLE: Pop. 2000: 644,869; Pop. 1990: 601,527, up 7.2% 1990–2000. 83.7% White, 2.1% Black, 5.4% Asian, 0.2% Amer. Indian, 2.3% Two+ races, 6.1% Other; 11.1% Hispanic Origin.

2000 Presidential Vote				1996 Presidential Vote		
Gore (D)	149,854	(56%)		Clinton (D)	143,122	(58%)
Bush (R)	96,713	(36%)		Dole (R)	76,605	(31%)
Nader (Green)	16,288	(6%)		Perot (I)	24,079	(10%)
Others	3,871	(1%)		Others	4,070	(2%)

Rep. Martin T. Meehan (D)

Elected 1992, 5th term; b. Dec. 30, 1956, Lowell; home, Lowell; U. of MA, B.S. 1978, Suffolk U., M.A. 1981, J.D. 1986; Catholic; married (Ellen Murphy).

Professional Career: Staff Asst., U.S. Rep. James Shannon, 1979–81; Research analyst, MA Legislature's Joint Cmte. on Elections, 1982–84; MA Dpty. Secy. of State for Securities & Corps., 1985–90; Middlesex Cnty. 1st Asst. Dist. Atty., 1990–92.

DC Office: 2447 RHOB 20515, 202-225-3411; Fax: 202-226-0771; Web site: www.house.gov/meehan.

District Offices: Lawrence, 978-681-6200; Lowell, 978-459-0101; Marlborough, 508-460-9292.

Committees: *Armed Services* (7th of 28 D): Military Research & Development (RMM). *Judiciary* (11th of 17 D): Courts, the Internet & Intellectual Property; Crime; Immigration & Claims.

Group Ratings

	ADA	ACLU	AFS	LCV	CON	ITIC	NTU	COC	ACU	NTLC	CHC
2000	90	86	85	100	99	78	25	45	12	22	0
1999	100	—	100	100	100	—	25	20	0	—	—

National Journal Ratings

	1999 LIB	—	1999 CONS		2000 LIB	—	2000 CONS
Economic	88%	—	0%		90%	—	8%
Social	87%	—	0%		79%	—	17%
Foreign	85%	—	15%		84%	—	15%

Key Votes of the 106th Congress

1. Patient Bill of Rights	Y	5. Bar RU-486 $ for FDA	N	9. NATO War in Serbia	Y
2. Accelerate Min. Wage	Y	6. Display 10 Commandments	N	10. Perm. Trade with China	Y
3. Strike Ban on Ergo. Stnd.	Y	7. Gun Show Bkgrnd. Checks	Y	11. Debt Relief for 3rd World	Y
4. Ovrd. Estate Tax Veto	N	8. Ban Part.-Birth Abortion	N	12. Drop Cuba Econ. Embargo	Y

Election Results

2000 general	Martin T. Meehan (D)	unopposed		($508,730)
2000 primary	Martin T. Meehan (D)	16,394	(73%)	
	Thomas P. Tierney (D)	4,253	(19%)	
	Joseph F. Osbaldeston (D)	1,687	(8%)	
1998 general	Martin T. Meehan (D)	127,418	(71%)	($283,239)
	David E. Coleman (R)	52,725	(29%)	

SIXTH DISTRICT

The North Shore of Massachusetts Bay has a number of times been at the leading edge of the nation's economy. In 1640, the Saugus Iron Works was built here—the beginning of American heavy industry. When Europe's great powers were convulsed in international war from 1792 to 1815, American ship owners suddenly became the richest in the world and traders from Boston accumulated the capital needed to build textile mills and railroads and to finance much of the American industrial revolution. From the small port of Salem, ships left for China, bringing back porcelain and artifacts, which helped change American styles forever. Salem, first settled in 1626, had the nation's first millionaire, Elias Hasket Derby; in 1900 it was the richest city per capita in the nation. But the North Shore is a quiet place, from Boston harbor north to the mouth of the Merrimack River, a collection of ethnic factory towns from Lynn on up through next-door Peabody to Newburyport, alternating with the high-income enclaves of Marblehead with its yachts and Beverly with its estates, artsy Rockport and the fishing port of Gloucester. Although the ports have been hard hit by overfishing of mackerel and herring in the 1970s and cod in the 1990s, pleasure boating surged in the past decade. Lynn is the largest town and its General Electric jet engine plant is the largest employer, though with far fewer jobs than during the defense buildup of the 1980s and with payrolls threatened by offset deals to produce some engines in the countries purchasing them.

The 6th Congressional District includes the North Shore from Lynn onward, plus towns and cities inland. It is a varied area demographically and politically: Its high-income Yankee towns are liberal Republican, while Lynn, Salem, Peabody and the Merrimack mill towns are still Irish working-class Democratic. The 6th has been a Democratic district on balance since the 1960s; but in the 1980s and in the early 1990s only marginally so. While this district is the site of the original gerrymander—named after Elbridge Gerry—the current 6th District boundaries are less grotesque and politically determined than those of any other Massachusetts district.

The congressman from the 6th District is John Tierney, a Democrat elected in 1996 after coming close in 1994. Tierney grew up in Salem in modest circumstances; he worked his way through Salem State College and Suffolk University Law School as a janitor on the night shift and clerk in a Boston law firm. For nearly 20 years he practiced law in Salem. In 1994 he spied a political opening and ran for Congress. The incumbent, Peter Torkildsen, was a Republican elected in 1992 by beating veteran Democrat Nicholas Mavroulas, who had been indicted for tax evasion and bribery; the district had been safely Democratic since liberal Michael Harrington won a special election in 1969. In 1994, Tierney won a closely contested primary with 34%; Tierney attacked Torkildsen for voting against the crime bill. But in a Republican year, Torkildsen won 51%–47%.

In 1996 Tierney ran again. His ads, along with the AFL-CIO's, assailed Newt Gingrich and Republican Medicare "cuts." He called for greater educational opportunities, health care insurance for children, aid to college students and criticized Torkildsen for not bringing enough defense dollars to the district. Torkildsen raised and spent $1.1 million, while keeping his promise to accept no PAC money, and led in early polls. Tierney held his spending—$776,000 in total—mostly until the end. The result was one of the closest races in the country. Tierney led narrowly in initial returns; after several recounts, which stretched into December, he won by only 371 votes.

In the House, Tierney has been a solid ally of the unions on Education and the Workforce. He made a splash early by calling for combining the Senate and House investigations of Clinton-Gore campaign finances. He has been a leader among Democrats seeking to reduce prescription-drug costs for seniors; the House defeated his amendment to shift $74 million from national missile to health programs. But he has worked with Republicans to get aid for the district—with Jerry Lewis to get $2 million for sewer aid for Essex County, with Frank Wolf to get $1 million to study an extension of the Blue Line T from East Boston to Beverly (opposed by the MBTA as too expensive). After working to revise terms, he joined with William Delahunt and New Jersey Republican Jim Saxton to support a ban on big fishing trawlers from Georges Bank.

The 1998 campaign was another rematch. Tierney attacked Torkildsen on familiar themes: "Whenever Newt Gingrich needed him to cut an education program, he was there." Tierney emphasized his fight against Republican efforts to cut funding for summer jobs and literacy programs, and said Torkildsen's votes would endanger Social Security. Torkildsen hit Tierney for opposing the Republicans' $80 billion tax cut and for blocking a probe of the Teamsters Union after taking $30,000 from them in campaign contributions. But this was the first time that Tierney, with help from PAC money, outspent the Republicans. Even as Republican Governor Paul Cellucci easily carried the district, Tierney won 55%–42%, a marked improvement over 1996. In 2000, against a weak opponent, he was re-elected with 71% of the vote.

Cook's Call *Probably Safe.* Tierney's strong showing in 1998 against former Republican Congressman Peter Torkildsen and his 71% win in 2000 show that he has a pretty good hold of this Democratic-leaning, but still marginal district. Redistricting will force it to contract a bit (it needs to lose about 17,000 people). Tierney and 7th District Rep. Ed Markey (whose district needs to gain about 17,000 people) are discussing ways to swap population. A top-flight Republican candidate could make this a good race in 2000, but, in a district that Gore took by 22 %, this will never be an easy sell.

THE PEOPLE: Pop. 2000: 652,455; Pop. 1990: 601,811, up 8.4% 1990–2000. 90.9% White, 2.3% Black, 2.5% Asian, 0.2% Amer. Indian, 1.6% Two+ races, 2.5% Other; 5% Hispanic Origin.

2000 Presidential Vote		
Gore (D)	172,668	(57%)
Bush (R)	107,145	(36%)
Nader (Green)	17,370	(6%)
Others	3,942	(1%)

1996 Presidential Vote		
Clinton (D)	166,037	(59%)
Dole (R)	86,306	(31%)
Perot (I)	26,273	(9%)

Rep. John F. Tierney (D)

Elected 1996, 3d term; b. Sept. 18, 1951, Salem; home, Salem; Salem St. U., B.A. 1973, Suffolk U., J.D. 1976; no religious affiliation; married (Patrice).

Professional Career: Practicing atty., 1976–96.

DC Office: 120 CHOB 20515, 202-225-8020; Fax: 202-225-5915; Web site: www.house.gov/tierney.

District Offices: Haverhill, 978-469-1942; Lynn, 781-595-7375; Peabody, 978-531-1669.

Committees: *Education & the Workforce* (13th of 22 D): 21st Century Competitiveness; Employer-Employee Relations. *Government Reform* (13th of 19 D): Energy Policy, Natural Resources and Regulatory Affairs (RMM); National Security, Veterans' Affairs & Intl. Relations.

Group Ratings

	ADA	ACLU	AFS	LCV	CON	ITIC	NTU	COC	ACU	NTLC	CHC
2000	95	86	100	93	81	28	30	28	4	18	0
1999	100	—	83	94	68	—	27	12	4	—	—

National Journal Ratings

	1999 LIB —	1999 CONS	2000 LIB —	2000 CONS
Economic	73%	26%	78%	20%
Social	87%	0%	94%	0%
Foreign	67%	33%	80%	16%

Key Votes of the 106th Congress

1. Patient Bill of Rights	Y	5. Bar RU-486 $ for FDA	N	9. NATO War in Serbia	Y
2. Accelerate Min. Wage	Y	6. Display 10 Commandments	N	10. Perm. Trade with China	N
3. Strike Ban on Ergo. Stnd.	Y	7. Gun Show Bkgrnd. Checks	Y	11. Debt Relief for 3rd World	Y
4. Ovrd. Estate Tax Veto	N	8. Ban Part.-Birth Abortion	N	12. Drop Cuba Econ. Embargo	Y

Election Results

2000 general	John F. Tierney (D)	205,234	(71%)	($426,934)
	Paul McCartney (R)	83,501	(29%)	($53,528)
2000 primary	John F. Tierney (D)	unopposed		
1998 general	John F. Tierney (D)	117,132	(55%)	($998,475)
	Peter G. Torkildsen (R)	90,986	(42%)	($882,595)
	Others	6,588	(3%)	

SEVENTH DISTRICT

The Yankee Protestants and Irish Catholics who settled Massachusetts arrived by boat, the Yankees to a cold stony land with a few Indians, the Irish to a crowded city with Yankees who seemed even less welcoming. The Yankees whose ancestors once farmed the soil had, by the early 20th Century, founded suburbs filled with solid brick and white frame houses, furnished in Early American furniture. As the years went on, their local public schools were emptied as young people with children moved out, and attendance at Protestant churches went down. The Irish, for decades heavily concentrated in the crowded wards of Boston, started moving out into the Yankee suburbs 50 years ago. There were other ethnic groups here and there (Jews, Italians, French-Canadians) but the major conflict—fought out in neighborhood playgrounds, in school committee meetings and not least in political campaigns—was between Protestant Yankee Republicans and Catholic Irish Democrats.

The 7th Congressional District is made up of Boston's northern and western suburbs, where vestiges of this conflict can still be seen. Geographically, it forms an arc around Boston, starting with the clapboard beach towns of Winthrop and Revere just beyond Logan Airport, going north as far as Wakefield, west past working-class Woburn and Medford, home of Tufts University, to the patriot town of Lexington, and Waltham, home of Brandeis University, through high-income Lincoln and Weston to modest-income Natick and Framingham. Most of these towns were Yankee Republican through the 1950s, but by the late 1960s they were solidly Democratic; the high-tech suburbs trended Republican again in the 1980s but swung against Republicans in the 1990s. The highest income areas seem to run across the grain of their ethnic experience: Weston, with many Catholics, often votes Republican, though it went 50%–43% for Al Gore in 2000. Lincoln, with Yankees like Thomas Boylston Adams and George H. W. Bush's sister Nancy Ellis, has been liberal Democratic since it voted for George McGovern in 1972; it voted 60%–29% for Gore in 2000.

The congressman in the 7th District is Edward Markey, elected in 1976 at age 30, and now one of the most powerful Democrats in the House. He grew up in Malden, where his father was a milkman; he went to Malden Catholic High, Boston College and Boston College Law, then immediately to the state House, at 26. In 1976, he ran for the House and won a 12-candidate primary with 22% of the vote; he had never been to Washington. Markey made a name as a fierce opponent of nuclear power. In 1983 he was the leading political crusader for the nuclear freeze. Critics said it would have given away America's technological edge just as the defense buildup was starting to destabilize the Soviets' evil empire; by the 1990s, the freeze—and the Soviets—had become historical relics.

Seniority and events put Markey in position to be a serious legislator, and he has long since become one of the House's most legislatively productive and creative members. With help from Speaker Tip O'Neill, he got on the Commerce Committee; impressed by the high-tech boom around Route 128, he joined the old Communications Subcommittee early. Then, after only eight years in the House, he became chairman of the Energy Conservation and Power Subcommittee; after the 1986 election, with help from Chairman John Dingell, who liked aggressive and loyal younger Democrats, Markey became chairman of the Telecommunications Subcommittee. This is one of the plum positions in the House, with fabulous possibilities for campaign fundraising (Markey doesn't take PAC money, but owners and executives of regulated companies can and do contribute), and with subject matter that is intellectually more demanding (and in lobbying terms more fiercely contested) than almost anything else in Congress. Markey raised $591,000 in the 2000 cycle and could easily raise four times that if he wanted. Following a news report that he raised $33,500 at a Colorado fundraiser hosted by the chief executive of a satellite TV company five weeks after Markey passed a bill that benefits the firm, chief aide David Moulton responded, "We're not denying people who give us money have an interest in telecom issues. But the position we take is always the one that helps the consumer most."

Markey has been a major shaper of public policy, often working with Republicans, often coming up with original initiatives, knowledgeable about the workings of these industries and inclined often toward deregulation, but also casting himself as the defender of consumers. He combined his penchant for regulation with political shrewdness to produce the 1992 cable TV reregulation bill on which both houses overrode President Bush's veto—the only bill passed over his veto in his four-year term. Another achievement was the 1993 law reallocating from the public to the private sector 200 megahertz of the radio frequency spectrum, allocated by the most lucrative auction in history.

Markey's influence was not greatly reduced when he became ranking minority member; bills in these areas are hard to pass without bipartisan consensus, and he was in a key position to create or withhold it. In 1995, Markey amended Republican Jack Fields's bill to restrict cross-ownership of broadcast and cable outlets in the same market and to establish the V-chip. After Markey objected to the networks' coding, he succeeded in getting new codes, written with input from parents, with specific references to sex, violence and language; since January 2000, V-chips have been installed in all TV sets sold in the United States. Markey and then-Commerce Chairman Tom Bliley passed through the House a bill to demonopolize the satellite communications industry, which became law in March 2000. Markey and Republican Mike Oxley moved a bill to stop stock exchanges from denominating prices in 1/8s and to use dollars and cents instead; when it passed, the exchanges decided to do this on their own. Markey and Lindsey Graham stopped the Clinton Administration plan to bail out the Bellefonte nuclear reactor by producing tritium for nuclear bombs. On telephone issues, *Congress Daily* reported, Markey has been a key figure in "an unusual and little-known [bipartisan] coalition that has reshaped the telecom marketplace, hindered the Bells and aided their friends in the long-distance industry."

In the 106th Congress, Markey's chief legislative accomplishment was the privacy package that he and Republican Joe Barton added to the financial-services deregulation law. Designed to meet the challenge of the Information Age, the provisions limits the sharing of personal financial information with unaffiliated third parties. Determined to move beyond the compromise, Markey promised further rules to protect consumer privacy. Without action, he warned, "there will be such a fundamental challenge to the integrity of the family that we will have a revolt" among consumers; his new focus includes online privacy and medical data.

On other Commerce Committee issues, Markey has worked with conservative Republicans to demonopolize the electric power industry, a proposal that he admits is "a multidimensional chess game, with many parties on different sides taking different stands on different issues." Following the Firestone/Ford Explorer debacle, he was an architect of the law to provide limited additional powers to federal highway-safety regulators. On non-commerce issues, Markey has backed sanctions on China for ignoring nuclear export controls and opposed Permanent Normal Trade Relations with China.

At the start of the 107th Congress, Markey faced the dilemma of whether to retain his position as ranking Democrat on the Telecommunications panel —which he termed the best subcommittee in Congress—or fill his party's vacancy atop the Resources Committee, where his long-standing interests have included protecting the Arctic National Wildlife Refuge from oil and gas drilling. He stuck with Telecommunications, but he's likely to remain active at both committees.

The 7th District is not quite as safely Democratic as it once was: Governor Paul Cellucci failed to carry it over Democrat Scott Harshbarger by only 300 votes in 1998. But Markey has been easily re-elected, without opposition in 2000. Redistricting may change the lines, but not his secure position.

Cook's Call   *Safe*. The Democratic nature of the district (Gore won here by 34%) combined with Markey's high-profile role in telecommunications and high tech issues (key in a district that boasts a substantial high-tech corridor), help to keep Markey safely ensconced in this district. Markey will need to pick up some population in redistricting, but it should not alter his district significantly.

THE PEOPLE: Pop. 2000: 616,542; Pop. 1990: 601,476, up 2.5% 1990–2000. 86.3% White, 3.5% Black, 5.5% Asian, 0.1% Amer. Indian, 2.3% Two+ races, 2.2% Other; 4.8% Hispanic Origin.

2000 Presidential Vote		
Gore (D)	175,220	(63%)
Bush (R)	81,450	(29%)
Nader (Green)	16,551	(6%)
Others	3,684	(1%)

1996 Presidential Vote		
Clinton (D)	171,125	(64%)
Dole (R)	72,823	(27%)
Perot (I)	19,374	(7%)

Rep. Edward J. Markey (D)

Elected 1976, 13th term; b. July 11, 1946, Malden; home, Malden; Boston Col., B.A. 1968, J.D. 1972; Catholic; married (Susan Blumenthal).

Military Career: Army Reserves, 1968–73.

Elected Office: MA House of Reps., 1973–76.

DC Office: 2108 RHOB 20515, 202-225-2836; Fax: 202-226-0092; Web site: www.house.gov/markey.

District Offices: Framingham, 508-875-2900; Medford, 781-396-2900.

Committees: *Energy & Commerce* (3d of 26 D): Commerce, Trade & Consumer Protection; Energy & Air Quality; Telecommunications & The Internet (RMM). *Resources* (3d of 25 D): Energy & Mineral Resources.

Group Ratings

	ADA	ACLU	AFS	LCV	CON	ITIC	NTU	COC	ACU	NTLC	CHC
2000	85	86	100	79	79	47	23	29	4	9	0
1999	100	—	100	100	93	—	25	16	0	—	—

National Journal Ratings

	1999 LIB —	1999 CONS		2000 LIB —	2000 CONS
Economic	88%	0%		95%	0%
Social	87%	0%		84%	15%
Foreign	78%	17%		80%	16%

Key Votes of the 106th Congress

1. Patient Bill of Rights	Y	5. Bar RU-486 $ for FDA	N	9. NATO War in Serbia	Y
2. Accelerate Min. Wage	Y	6. Display 10 Commandments	N	10. Perm. Trade with China	N
3. Strike Ban on Ergo. Stnd.	*	7. Gun Show Bkgrnd. Checks	Y	11. Debt Relief for 3rd World	Y
4. Ovrd. Estate Tax Veto	N	8. Ban Part.-Birth Abortion	N	12. Drop Cuba Econ. Embargo	Y

Election Results

2000 general	Edward J. Markey (D) .... unopposed			($584,630)
2000 primary	Edward J. Markey (D) .... unopposed			
1998 general	Edward J. Markey (D) 137,178	(71%)		($390,660)
	Patricia H. Long (R) 56,977	(29%)		($5,262)

EIGHTH DISTRICT

A long generation ago, Cambridge, Massachusetts, was a plainly aging city, with a grayness in the air matching its gray winter skies. Its two great universities, Harvard and MIT, were closely hemmed in by a not very friendly town of Irish Catholics, Italians and a few Portuguese, living generation after generation in three-decker houses with cracked walls letting in the cold in the long winters. Boston was the nation's slowest-growing metropolitan area, economically stagnant, still caught in a 17th Century Puritan-Papist rivalry. Students from suburbs across the country, exploring Boston from their dormitories and campuses, felt they were pawing through the living remnants of 1920s America, a quaint place where people called traffic circles "rotaries" and milk shakes "frappes." Massachusetts has since changed, and nowhere more than in Cambridge. As universities and high tech have become driving forces of economic growth, Cambridge has gone glitzy, with trendy restaurants and high-priced hotels, boutiques and upscale condominiums. Greater Boston may well have the heaviest concentration of graduate students and post-graduate hangers-on of any major city, and this graduate student proletariat's world is centered on Cambridge, with outposts in lower-income Somerville, tenured-faculty haven Belmont, Boston's Back Bay, and Allston and Brighton near the Harvard Business School. Although new problems have emerged, such as how to operate a sometimes-risky biotech industry in an urban center, Harvard president Neil Rudenstine showed unprecedented "town-gown" sensitivity with his 1999 "Investing in the Future" report of the University's $2 billion annual impact on the local economy.

Cambridge is the center, and the rest of these communities are part, of Massachusetts's 8th Congressional District, a district with great historic sites, from the gold dome of the State House on Beacon Hill to the frigate *U.S.S. Constitution* in the Charlestown docks; the district, with MIT and the software concentration in Cambridge's once downscale Lechmere Square, is one of the high-tech capitals of America. The 8th also includes the impoverished suburb of Chelsea and much of the Roxbury black ghetto in Boston, now with many Puerto Rican and other Hispanic residents as well. This is by far the most Democratic district in Massachusetts, and one of the nation's most solid.

The congressman from the 8th District is Michael Capuano, the winner of a 10-candidate primary in 1998. It could be said that over the last 50-odd years this district has been represented alternatively by townies and Kennedys: James Michael Curley, the scampish five-term mayor of Boston and one-term governor; followed by John F. Kennedy in 1946, then from 1952, Tip O'Neill, the most successful House speaker of this half-century; succeeded on his retirement in 1986 by Joe Kennedy; and now Capuano. Capuano was born and raised in Somerville; his paternal grandfather immigrated from Italy, and his father was the first Italian-American elected official in Somerville; his mother is the granddaughter of Irish immigrants. Capuano graduated from Dartmouth and Boston College Law School. He returned to Somerville to raise his family, practice law and get into politics. By day, he worked for the legislature's Joint Committee on Taxation and practiced law; in off-hours, he served as alderman in the 5th Ward, like his father before him; he was elected alderman-at-large from 1985–89. In November 1989 he was elected mayor of Somerville in the city's closest race; he was re-elected five times.

Somerville is packed with three-deckers, giving it the densest population in the United States outside Manhattan and Hudson County, New Jersey; for years an Irish and Italian town, in the 1990s it has attracted many grad students and yuppies. Capuano seems to have been the right politician for this mix, with deep Somerville roots and a penchant for innovation and reform. He got the city's fiscal house in order, promoted recycling and created nine new parks, increasing open space by more than 15 acres (a big deal here). He built new schools and boasted the smallest class-size (19) in the Boston area; he authored a tough ethics code. So, Capuano had a solid base to run for the 8th District seat in 1998 when, everyone expected, Joe Kennedy would run for governor. But Kennedy announced in August 1997 that he wasn't running for governor and would run for re-election; after his brother Michael Kennedy died in a skiing accident in December 1997, Joe Kennedy announced three months later that he wouldn't run for re-election after all. This gave Capuano, and many others, a chance to prepare for the September 1998 primary that would determine who would represent this safe Democratic seat, probably for many years to come.

There was no lack of competitors for the Democratic nomination. Six were far out on the left wing of the Democratic Party, and between them won 49% of the votes. The four more moderate candidates split the remaining 51%, and Capuano got a near-majority of that. His total of 23% led the runner-up, former Boston Mayor (1983–93) Ray Flynn, who had 17%.

Capuano is still well to the left on the national political spectrum: for gay marriage, against the partial-birth abortion ban and opposed to the flag-burning amendment. After arriving in Washington, he moved quickly to establish his presence. During the post-Columbine debate on guns and juvenile justice, he won House agreement on his amendment to fund state and local juvenile witness assistance programs. Later, he raised one of those issues that affects virtually everyone but few of us think about, proposing that the Federal Communications Commission study the rapid disappearance of available telephone area codes. Back home, Capuano sided with opponents of a new runway at congested Logan Airport—a popular position in local neighborhoods—but he coupled that position with support for the growing movement for a second Boston-area airport in Bedford.

Capuano won re-election without opposition in the 2000 primary and general but only after John O'Connor, the millionaire environmentalist who finished fourth in the 1998 primary for the seat, spent months exploring a possible challenge. Capuano called on, among others, his new friends in the state delegation to pressure O'Connor not to run. Those tactics bordered on "political thuggery," O'Connor complained to the *Boston Globe* before making his decision. Capuano apparently has settled in comfortably.

Cook's Call   *Safe.* Arguably the most liberal district in the state, and the country, this Cambridge/Boston district is so heavily Democratic that Capuano should never have any problems in a general election. This district does need to pick up about 15,000 people who may come from retiring Rep. Joe Moakley's 9th District. The addition of cities like Roxbury and Jamaica Plain would increase the minority population in a district that is already 40% minority (and the least white district in the state). As such, Capuano could face a challenge in the Democratic primary. But, at this point, he looks well positioned.

THE PEOPLE: Pop. 2000: 620,372; Pop. 1990: 602,396, up 3% 1990–2000. 59.5% White, 20.7% Black, 7.6% Asian, 0.4% Amer. Indian, 0.1% Hawaiian, 4.5% Two+ races, 7.3% Other; 14.5% Hispanic Origin.

2000 Presidential Vote			1996 Presidential Vote		
Gore (D)	141,221	(72%)	Clinton (D)	139,383	(77%)
Bush (R)	34,184	(17%)	Dole (R)	28,253	(16%)
Nader (Green)	18,790	(10%)	Perot (I)	7,928	(4%)
Others	1,342	(1%)	Others	4,557	(3%)

Rep. Michael Capuano (D)

Elected 1998, 2d term; b. Jan. 9, 1952, Somerville; home, Somerville; Dartmouth Col., B.A. 1973, Boston Col., J.D. 1977; Catholic; married (Barbara).

Elected Office: Somerville Alderman Ward 5, 1977–79; Somerville Alderman-At-Large, 1985–89; Somerville Mayor, 1989–98.

Professional Career: Chief Legal Cnsl., MA Legislature Taxation Cmte., 1978–84; Practicing atty., 1984–90.

DC Office: 1232 LHOB 20515, 202-225-5111; Fax: 202-225-9322; Web site: www.house.gov/capuano.

District Office: Cambridge, 617-621-6208.

Committees: *Budget* (15th of 20 D). *Financial Services* (24th of 32 D): Capital Markets, Insurance & Government Sponsored Enterprises; Domestic Monetary Policy, Technology & Economic Growth; Housing & Community Opportunity; Oversight & Investigations.

Group Ratings

	ADA	ACLU	AFS	LCV	CON	ITIC	NTU	COC	ACU	NTLC	CHC
2000	100	86	100	93	78	33	24	33	0	16	0
1999	100	—	100	100	73	—	28	16	0	—	—

National Journal Ratings

	1999 LIB —	1999 CONS		2000 LIB —	2000 CONS
Economic	88%	0%		95%	0%
Social	87%	0%		94%	0%
Foreign	89%	8%		90%	9%

Key Votes of the 106th Congress

1. Patient Bill of Rights	Y	5. Bar RU-486 $ for FDA	N	9. NATO War in Serbia	Y
2. Accelerate Min. Wage	Y	6. Display 10 Commandments	N	10. Perm. Trade with China	N
3. Strike Ban on Ergo. Stnd.	Y	7. Gun Show Bkgrnd. Checks	Y	11. Debt Relief for 3rd World	Y
4. Ovrd. Estate Tax Veto	N	8. Ban Part.-Birth Abortion	N	12. Drop Cuba Econ. Embargo	Y

Election Results

2000 general	Michael Capuano (D)	unopposed		($387,340)
2000 primary	Michael Capuano (D)	unopposed		
1998 general	Michael Capuano (D)	99,603	(82%)	($633,746)
	Philip Hyde (R)	14,125	(12%)	
	Others	8,159	(7%)	

NINTH DISTRICT

The "Hub of the Universe," is what the elder Oliver Wendell Holmes called Boston in the 19th Century, and so it seems again sometimes: when you reflect that Fidelity mutual funds and so many other big financial outfits are headquartered in modern towers built on streets originally laid out as 17th Century cowpaths; when you walk on the streets where Samuel Adams and Paul Revere plotted revolution or track down the sites of rallies and headquarters of the various Kennedy campaigns; when you walk on Beacon Street past the Bull and Finch Pub, the original setting for the TV show *Cheers* (and whose name is a play on the architect of the state House, Thomas Bulfinch). Today's Boston is a different city from the Boston of John Kennedy's time. Boston then was a gray city with no new buildings and dust on every windowsill; the sky was dark with pollution and the air was thick with ancient Yankee and Irish animosity. The old office buildings were full of Yankees seeking safe investments for their antique family fortunes; the State House and City Hall were full of Irishmen, scampering after good patronage jobs and regaling each other with political battle stories. Today that Boston is mostly gone. The new skyscrapers are full of venture capitalists, lawyers and management consultants, many working for high-tech companies radiating from Cambridge out into the countryside; the advertising slogans crackle with a sauciness and *double entendre* you can find only here and maybe in New York and London.

Most of Boston's neighborhoods have changed. There are still vestiges of the old Irish neighborhoods, but even South Boston, long the center of Irish Boston, is starting to gentrify, and the central city is increasingly populated by blacks and young singles. Responding to a serious need, Fannie Mae spread $1.7 billion in five years to finance affordable housing for 35,000 Boston families; another step toward more livability has been the plan by private groups and the city to spend millions to beautify the extensive "Emerald Necklace" public parks, and add another 27 acres of open space that will become available after completion of Big Dig. The city's population is down from 801,000 in 1950 to 589,000 in 2000; more than 80% of the metropolitan area is in the suburbs. The 9th Congressional District, historically anchored in Boston, has followed the move, and today only one-third of its residents are in Boston, mostly in still-Irish areas of South Boston, Hyde Park and West Roxbury. From there, the 9th heads southwest to Easton and the old Patriots Stadium; southeast to Braintree, ancestral home of the presidential Adamses; Brockton, the old shoe manufacturing town; and the old textile mill town of Taunton. Ethnically, it is probably the nation's most heavily Irish congressional district. Politically, it has been represented by only three members, all of them Democrats, for more than 75 years, and one served only a single term.

The congressman from the 9th, Joe Moakley, was elected in 1972 as an independent, but was very much a Democrat. Moakley was a son of South Boston who lived in the 7th Ward all his life; after a battle with leukemia, he met his death in May 2001. He was a high school football star who volunteered for the Navy in 1943, at 15; went to college in Miami after the war, then went to Suffolk law school in Boston; in 1952, at 25, he was elected to the Massachusetts House. He was elected to the state Senate in the splendidly Democratic year of 1964, then to the Boston Council in 1971. He ran for the House when Speaker John McCormack retired in 1970 after 42 years of service, and lost the primary to Louise Day Hicks, the anti-busing chairman of the Boston School Committee. In 1972 he ran again, this time as an independent; in the six-candidate primary, opposition to Hicks was split, and she won with 37%, but Moakley won the general by 5,000 votes. In the House, Moakley got his pal Tip O'Neill's former seat on the Rules Committee in his second term. He moved up quickly in seniority and became chairman when Claude Pepper died in June 1989. In that position, Moakley worked closely with Speaker Tom Foley and Majority Leader Dick Gephardt; he helped David Bonior, another Catholic deeply opposed to U.S. Central American policy, win his party whip post. Under their lead, Rules increasingly passed closed rules, limiting amendments and debate, to the fury of the Republicans. Moakley's one headline cause was El Salvador. Acquainted with several nuns and priests murdered there in 1989, he sponsored a commission to look into their deaths; its top staffer was Jim McGovern, now the 3rd District congressman. It found that high-ranking Salvadoran military officials were involved, and Moakley led a fight to cutoff U.S. aid and claims credit today for El Salvador's transition to democracy.

Moakley made sure to keep flowing the federal funds which have made Boston's Big Dig—the relocation of the Central Artery expressway to a tunnel—the nation's most expensive public works projects ever. As a product of old-style politics, he occasionally had trouble with modern-day niceties. When then-Governor Paul Cellucci was planning to name his 34-year-old chief of staff Virginia Buckingham to the powerful position as director of Massport, Moakley dismissed her as "some girl sitting in the next office;" he quickly corrected himself, but the criticism was inevitable. When John Brockelman, the youthful state Republican Party executive director, criticized the all-Democratic House delegation's "serious clout power outage," Moakley responded, "This kid doesn't know his ass from third base." All of this understandably created tension with Cellucci, to whom Moakley provided tacit re-election support in 1998 and gave vital help in securing federal dollars for Big Dig cost overruns.

Usually a humorous and gentle man, he loathed Newt Gingrich and his Republican revolutionaries: "When O'Neill left [in 1986], the fun went out of this business, and the walls started to be built in that middle aisle." After 1994, he often found himself criticizing Republicans' restrictions on House debate, though arguably not as tight as the ones that he had backed—"I don't say we were fair and open all the way," he conceded. Personal problems also struck. In June 1995 he stayed in South Boston to care for his wife, who was dying of a brain tumor; the next month, he had a liver transplant. Soon after that, he was about to announce his retirement but decided to run instead. "As long as I'm in good health I will continue to serve. . . . I've been in the political business for over 40 years. And to be totally truthful, I have loved every minute of it." Moakley returned to the House, and he got involved in other projects—from visiting Cuba and calling for an end to the trade embargo to blocking New England Patriots' owner Robert Kraft's plans for a stadium in South Boston by talking the Army into refusing to turn over a key land parcel.

Capitol Hill was hit by sad news in February 2001, when Moakley announced that doctors told him that he had an incurable form of leukemia; his survival was expected to be a matter of months. His doctor advised him, "Don't buy any green bananas," Moakley joked. He was hailed in a round of tributes from Boston to Washington—including President Bush's first Rose Garden bill signing at which he enacted the naming of Boston's new federal court house for Moakley. Moakley died at the Bethesda Naval Hospital May 28, 2001.

Several Democrats expressed interest in the race, after Moakley announced in February that he would not seek re-election The most prominent was Max Kennedy, son of Robert and Ethel

Kennedy, but his campaign never gathered any traction and polls showed him even with his lesser known opponents. When Kennedy bowed out of the race in June 2001, the front runner seemed to be state Senator Steve Lynch who had a large base in South Boston and strong union ties. Other potential candidates included state Senators Brian Joyce and Marc Pacheco. But with Kennedy's withdrawal, a host of other Democrats could run. The primary—which will be tantamount to election in this district—is set for September 11, and the general set for October 18.

Cook's Call   *Safe.* Longtime Representative and dean of the Massachusetts delegation Moakley's decision to retire due to medical problems means that this Boston-based district will be competitive for the first time in 18 years. A number of candidates have lined up for this potential once-in-a-political-lifetime shot at this seat. Redistricting means that some potential candidates may find their hometown drawn into another congressional district, but this seat will remain one of the most solidly Democratic in the state.

THE PEOPLE: Pop. 2000: 630,499; Pop. 1990: 601,250, up 4.9% 1990–2000. 77.4% White, 10.5% Black, 4.7% Asian, 0.2% Amer. Indian, 3% Two+ races, 4.1% Other; 6.2% Hispanic Origin.

2000 Presidential Vote			1996 Presidential Vote		
Gore (D)	166,503	(63%)	Clinton (D)	158,967	(62%)
Bush (R)	82,263	(31%)	Dole (R)	76,202	(30%)
Nader (Green)	15,397	(6%)	Perot (I)	19,168	(7%)
Others	1,847	(1%)			

Rep. Joe Moakley (D)

Elected 1972, 15th term; b. Apr. 27, 1927, Boston; died May 28, 2001; home, Boston; U. of Miami, Suffolk U., LL.B. 1956; Catholic; widowed.

Military Career: Navy, 1943–46 (WWII).

Elected Office: MA House of Reps., 1952–62, Majority Whip, 1957; MA Senate, 1964–70; Boston City Cncl., 1971–72.

Professional Career: Practicing atty., 1957–72.

DC Office: 235 CHOB 20515, 202-225-8273; Fax: 202-225-3984; Web site: www.house.gov/moakley.

District Offices: Boston, 617-428-2000; Brockton, 508-586-5555; Taunton, 508-824-6676.

Committees: not assigned as of June 1, 2001

Group Ratings

	ADA	ACLU	AFS	LCV	CON	ITIC	NTU	COC	ACU	NTLC	CHC
2000	80	57	100	93	72	59	22	30	16	9	27
1999	90	—	100	94	47	—	15	24	4	—	—

National Journal Ratings

	1999 LIB —	1999 CONS		2000 LIB —	2000 CONS
Economic	88% —	0%		92% —	5%
Social	63% —	36%		62% —	37%
Foreign	74% —	23%		72% —	27%

Key Votes of the 106th Congress

1. Patient Bill of Rights	Y	5. Bar RU-486 $ for FDA	N	9. NATO War in Serbia	Y
2. Accelerate Min. Wage	Y	6. Display 10 Commandments	N	10. Perm. Trade with China	N
3. Strike Ban on Ergo. Stnd.	Y	7. Gun Show Bkgrnd. Checks	Y	11. Debt Relief for 3rd World	Y
4. Ovrd. Estate Tax Veto	N	8. Ban Part.-Birth Abortion	Y	12. Drop Cuba Econ. Embargo	Y

Election Results

2000 general	Joe Moakley (D)	193,020	(78%)	($1,127,856)
	Janet E. Jeghelian (R)	48,672	(20%)	($19,796)
	Other	7,064	(3%)	
2000 primary	Joe Moakley (D)	unopposed		
1998 general	Joe Moakley (D)	unopposed		($919,465)

TENTH DISTRICT

The South Shore of Massachusetts Bay, from Boston southward to Plymouth and then down Cape Cod (there is a lot of dispute about which way is up and down on the Cape), is Massachusetts's oldest-settled territory. The Pilgrims landed here at Plymouth Rock in 1620; this stony land was farmed by John Adams's father, who was anything but the aristocrat some later members of the Adams family would have you believe. Daniel Webster lived in the South Shore town of Marshfield, today a high-income suburb of Boston far out on the usually clogged Southeast Expressway. Joseph P. Kennedy used to summer with his young family on Nantasket Beach in Hull, before moving out of Massachusetts when the Yankees wouldn't let them into their beach club in Cohasset in the 1920s; but the Kennedys continue to summer at their Hyannisport compound. The Plymouth area and Cape Cod were originally farming country, with some industry. Provincetown, at the tip of the Cape, is still a fishing port, and also one of the major gay vacation areas in the country; the islands of Martha's Vineyard and Nantucket, rich whaling ports in the early 19th Century, are now favored summer resorts for the trendy liberal rich of New York and Washington. Cape Cod is the site of the bogs that still produce half of America's cranberries, but it is also filled increasingly with retirees and, to the dismay of some, is the fastest-growing part of Massachusetts. Some year-round residents complain that they can't afford housing-rental rates in the summer.

The 10th Congressional District, with grotesque boundaries like most other Bay State districts, follows the South Shore from Quincy to the Cape, jutting inland near Brockton, and including Martha's Vineyard and Nantucket. The South Shore and the Cape were once exclusively Protestant and Yankee, but in the Massachusetts way they have changed over the years, with Irish and Italian surnames as common as Yankee ones, and the descendants of Portuguese-Azorean fishermen have fanned out into the countryside. Trendy liberal politics, well established on the Vineyard and Nantucket, have spread inland as well.

The congressman from the 10th District is William Delahunt, a Democrat elected in 1996. Delahunt is a lifelong resident of Quincy, who went to college at Middlebury and Boston College Law School and served in the Coast Guard. He practiced law and was elected to the Quincy Council. In 1972 he was elected to the state House; in 1975 Governor Michael Dukakis appointed him district attorney of Norfolk County. He was prompted to run for Congress in 1996 when 12-term Congressman Gerry Studds retired. Delahunt had serious primary competition from former state Representative Philip Johnston and self-financed environmentalist Ian Bowles. Johnston carried most of the Cape and Plymouth County; Bowles carried Martha's Vineyard and Falmouth; Delahunt, the favorite, ran up very big margins in Quincy and next-door Weymouth. The initial results of the September 17 primary showed 38% each for Delahunt and Johnston, with Johnston ahead by 266 votes. A recount declared Johnston still ahead by 175 votes. But Delahunt sued, and on October 4, a judge ruled that more than 900 punch card votes in Weymouth had not been properly tabulated. In shades of another election challenge four years later, the judge ordered a recount of every ballot with an indentation, dimple or other mark: Only in this district and in 14 counties in Texas had dimpled chads ever been counted as votes in the United States until the Broward, Palm Beach and Miami-Dade County canvassing boards started counting them in November 2000. On October 10, Delahunt was declared the winner by 108 votes, even as Johnston was being hailed at a Quincy rally by Ted Kennedy and Hillary Rodham Clinton. (Subsequently, Massachusetts eliminated punch-card voting, and Delahunt voiced support for hand recounts of punch cards elsewhere.) Johnston called the result a "travesty," and Delahunt had less than a month to campaign for the general. Conservative state House Minority Leader Edward Teague had won the Republican primary. Both ran million dollar campaigns, but Teague had been running ads against Johnston. Eight years earlier, George Bush carried this district over Michael Dukakis, but reaction here to the new Republican majority in the House was hostile, and Delahunt won 54%–42%.

Delahunt has been an active legislator, including his pledge to wear Cape Cod ties in the House and hand them out to colleagues of both parties. With Roy Blunt, he convened a bipartisan freshman task force on Social Security. On the Judiciary Committee, he worked with Republicans to pass the Citizens Protection Act, which binds federal prosecutors to the same ethical standards as members of the bar. He supported House approval of cameras in federal courtrooms and a moratorium on Internet taxes. As the father of an adopted daughter who escaped Vietnam in the 1975 Operation Babylift, he has written laws to ease international adoptions. His positions on abortion are part of the story of Massachusetts's move to the left: In 1974 as a state legislator he called *Roe v. Wade* "a tragic decision," but switched to a pro-abortion rights position before running for the House and in 1997 voted against the partial-birth abortion ban. He has joined the bipartisan coalition to make more use of DNA technology to prevent unwarranted use of the death penalty. His experience with contested elections later made him an enthusiast for abolishing the Electoral College.

Delahunt also has worked on local projects, including the Cape Cod land bank, the Salt Pond visitors' center at the National Seashore entry in Eastham, and conversion of the former Camp Edwards National Guard training site to a federal wildlife refuge. He helped pass a moratorium on giant trawlers fishing for herring and mackerel. He got approval, after nearly five years, of a land transfer to Provincetown for solid waste disposal. He wrote a law requiring large ships entering Massachusetts' waters to notify the Coast Guard, so they could be warned away from endangered right whales; the International Maritime Organization approved this in December 1998.

Delahunt's greatest visibility came on the Clinton impeachment. On the polarized Judiciary Committee he was one of the few members who sat down in bipartisan breakfasts to discuss procedures, with Howard Berman, Asa Hutchinson and Lindsey Graham. But he ended up siding completely with impeachment opponents. He took the lead in framing a Democratic motion to censure Clinton and protested bitterly when Judiciary Chairman Henry Hyde would not allow it to be heard: "I think there is a fundamental unease out in the land right now about those who would tell us what is right and what is wrong. There's overtones of the Inquisition." Following that experience, the former state prosecutor explored further steps to rein in the authority of federal prosecutors and to protect defendants' rights.

In both of his re-election bids, Delahunt won easily. The initial Republican challenger in 2000 was Tom Tavener, the nephew of long-time Ohio conservative Congressman John Ashbrook, who criticized Delahunt on impeachment. But he failed to file for the primary. Against his 1998 opponent Delahunt won 70%–30%—no need to count dimpled chads. With the Cape's population growth, redistricting likely will reduce his district, but it's not likely to give much hope for a Republican revival.

Cook's Call   *Safe.* Based on Delahunt's strong showing in 1998 and 2000 it is hard to believe that this is one of the most marginal seats in the state. But, marginal is a relative term in Democratic-leaning Massachusetts. Gore won the district by 55%, his worst showing in the state. This district was also the fastest growing district in the state and needs to lose about 28,000 people in redistricting.

THE PEOPLE: Pop. 2000: 663,508; Pop. 1990: 601,510, up 10.3% 1990–2000. 91% White, 2.7% Black, 2.8% Asian, 0.3% Amer. Indian, 1.8% Two+ races, 1.4% Other; 1.7% Hispanic Origin.

2000 Presidential Vote

Gore (D)	180,450	(55%)
Bush (R)	125,522	(38%)
Nader (Green)	19,891	(6%)
Others	3,919	(1%)

1996 Presidential Vote

Clinton (D)	169,927	(56%)
Dole (R)	101,612	(33%)
Perot (I)	28,125	(9%)

Rep. William D. Delahunt (D)

Elected 1996, 3d term; b. July 18, 1941, Quincy; home, Quincy; Middlebury Col., B.A. 1963, Boston Col., J.D. 1967; Catholic; divorced.

Military Career: Coast Guard, 1963; Coast Guard Reserves, 1963–71.

Elected Office: Quincy City Cncl., 1971; MA House of Reps., 1972–75.

Professional Career: Practicing atty., 1967–75; Asst. Clerk, Norfolk Superior Court, 1969–71; Norfolk Cnty. Dist. Atty., 1975–96.

DC Office: 1317 LHOB 20515, 202-225-3111; Fax: 202-225-5658; Web site: www.house.gov/delahunt.

District Offices: Brockton, 508-584-6666; Hyannis, 508-771-0666; Quincy, 617-770-3700.

Committees: *International Relations* (14th of 23 D): Europe; Western Hemisphere. *Judiciary* (12th of 17 D): Courts, the Internet & Intellectual Property; Crime.

Group Ratings

	ADA	ACLU	AFS	LCV	CON	ITIC	NTU	COC	ACU	NTLC	CHC
2000	85	79	83	93	76	37	32	47	8	19	0
1999	100	—	100	94	84	—	27	24	0	—	—

National Journal Ratings

	1999 LIB —	1999 CONS	2000 LIB —	2000 CONS
Economic	72%	27%	70%	29%
Social	82%	17%	84%	15%
Foreign	93%	5%	90%	9%

Key Votes of the 106th Congress

1. Patient Bill of Rights	Y	5. Bar RU-486 $ for FDA	N	9. NATO War in Serbia	Y
2. Accelerate Min. Wage	Y	6. Display 10 Commandments	N	10. Perm. Trade with China	N
3. Strike Ban on Ergo. Stnd.	Y	7. Gun Show Bkgrnd. Checks	Y	11. Debt Relief for 3rd World	Y
4. Ovrd. Estate Tax Veto	Y	8. Ban Part.-Birth Abortion	N	12. Drop Cuba Econ. Embargo	*

Election Results

2000 general	William D. Delahunt (D)	234,675	(74%)	($231,526)
	Eric V. Bleicken (R)	81,192	(26%)	($1,146)
2000 primary	William D. Delahunt (D)	unopposed		
1998 general	William D. Delahunt (D)	164,917	(70%)	($242,576)
	Eric V. Bleicken (R)	70,466	(30%)	($7,286)

★ MICHIGAN ★

Michigan has surged into the 21st Century much as it surged into the 20th: a state transformed in a few years by a creative, dynamic economy and a burst of political reform. Today, Michigan is one of America's premier laboratories of innovation, busy expanding high-skill manufacturing while rethinking and downsizing government programs, just as it was once busy inventing the mass-production factory economy and then developing the giant industrial labor union and its version of the American welfare state. The latest experiment, like the earlier one, seems to be a success: Michigan's unemployment rate was below the national average from early 1995 to March 2001, it has led the nation in the number of new factories and expansions and the quality of Michigan products is vastly better than that of a generation ago. Michigan's achievement since the Big Three auto companies foundered in the late 1970s has been to move from an industrial to a post-industrial economy, from domination by big units—big business, big labor, big government—to growth increasingly driven by small units—small businesses, individual workers, flexible government.

Michigan is arguably going back to its roots in the Tocquevillian decade of the 1830s. These two peninsulas, explored and named by French explorers (which explains why Mackinac is pronounced with a silent final *c* and Michigan with a *ch* pronounced like *sh*), were settled in a rush by Yankee migrants from Upstate New York, who cut down trees and built farms and neat New Englandish towns complete with schools and colleges. Politically, Michigan was full of reformers who hated slavery, manned the Underground Railroad, promoted temperance and in 1855 gave Michigan a constitution that banned (as it does to this day) capital punishment. Michigan was one of the birthplaces of the Republican Party, which was founded in Jackson in 1854 (Ripon, Wisconsin, also stakes a claim as the party's birthplace) and swept the state in the elections later that year. Until 1929, Michigan was one of the most Republican states in the nation.

Michigan also developed an industrial economy. Its Lower Peninsula was mostly covered with trees, and lumber was the first boom industry on which Michigan over-relied; forests were clear-cut or swept by blazes like the 1881 fire that burned out half the Thumb. In the late 1800s, huge copper deposits were discovered on the Keweenaw Peninsula, which juts from the Upper Peninsula into icy Lake Superior; immigrants from Italy and Finland, Cornwall and Croatia came to work in the mines. Then came the auto industry. A combination of accident and shrewdness, of bankers willing to finance auto startups and the prickly genius of Henry Ford, ensured that America's fastest-growing industry of the first 30 years of the 20th Century was centered in Michigan. Detroit became a boomtown—the nation's fastest-growing metropolitan area after Los Angeles—zooming from 426,000 in 1900 to 2.2 million in 1930. The auto industry drew labor from the Outstate Michigan areas beyond Detroit, from southern Ontario and from the farms of Ohio and Indiana. During World War II and after, it brought whites from the Kentucky and Tennessee mountains and blacks from Alabama and Mississippi. It attracted Poles and Italians, Hungarians and Belgians, Greeks and Jews. This influx of a polyglot proletariat eventually changed Michigan's politics. The catalyst was the Great Depression of the 1930s and the company managers' desire to use machines efficiently, treating employees as extensions of machines and with great distrust. The results were the 1937 sit-down strikes organized by the new United Auto Workers (UAW); management and labor fought, sometimes literally, for pieces of what both sides feared was a shrinking pie. The UAW won and organized most of the companies after Democratic Governor Frank Murphy refused to send in troops to break the illegal strikes. In the years that followed, auto workers became a heavily Democratic voting bloc.

Michigan politics became a species of class warfare, conducted with a bitterness that split families and neighbors. The union mostly won, because demographics benefited the Democrats: auto workers and post-1900 immigrants produced more children than did Outstate Yankees or management. After Walter Reuther's election as UAW president in 1947, voters elected young, liberal G. Mennen Williams governor in 1948. By 1954, the Democrats, closely tied to the UAW, seemed to have become the natural majority in the state. And as growth continued, economic issues became less bitter; by the early 1960s, the class-warfare atmosphere had dissipated. A

Congressional district boundaries
effective April 6, 1992.

Miles
0 10 20 30 40

Republican former auto executive, George Romney, was narrowly elected governor in 1962, and Henry Ford II joined Reuther in backing Lyndon Johnson in 1964. Romney and his successor, William Milliken, accepted the welfare-state policies endorsed by the UAW leadership and the Democrats. The state government was one of the nation's most generous, and not just to the poor and the unemployed: it supported one of the nation's most distinguished and extensive higher education systems, built state parks and recreation areas, and pioneered efforts to end racial discrimination.

This system, which had seemed eternal, came crashing down with the collapse of the domestic auto industry after the oil shock of 1973. Union-management relations had been static since 1941, and there had been no major technological changes in American autos since the automatic transmission in 1940. Michigan incomes had grown as Americans grew more affluent; the one-car household became the two-car household, and consumers enjoyed the tail fins and chrome of new car styling. But in 1979, this big-unit economy went bust. It became startlingly clear that the Big Three and the UAW did not have a captive market, Americans did not have to buy a new full-sized American-made car every two or three years, and foreign competitors were producing better and cheaper cars more responsive to changes in gas prices and consumer preference. Big business and labor, so well adapted for growth in the quarter century after World War II started, proved poorly adapted for the quarter century that followed. Auto employment in Michigan fell from 437,000 in October 1978 to 289,000 in October 1982. Chrysler nearly went bankrupt, Ford was in financial distress, General Motors had its first losses in years.

The collapse of the big-unit economy after 1979 forced the state to experiment. The first to try was Governor James Blanchard, a Democrat elected in 1982 with a record of supporting big units. His major achievement in eight years in Congress was managing the Chrysler bailout in the House. Blanchard worked to build a small-unit economy; he was proud of his efforts to stimulate high-skill, capital-intensive, flexible manufacturing, and he used $750 million of state pension funds as venture capital for manufacturers of items from tape drives for microcomputers to fiberglass coffins. Dodging his traditional labor allies, Blanchard made it clear that Michigan must learn how to nurture growth and that workers, instead of seeking more vacation and earlier retirement, would have to hustle and work harder than ever before.

The second, and for the moment more successful, experiment came from John Engler, the Republican who beat Blanchard in 1990 and was resoundingly re-elected in 1994 and 1998. Engler believes in less government activism and industrial policy; he cut or held the line on every state program but education. In three terms he cut taxes more than 30 times; welfare rolls were cut by more than two-thirds. Engler pressed for public school choice and charter schools, changing state pensions from defined benefits (which produce huge liabilities for the state and a sense of entitlement in employees) to defined contributions (which reduce the state's future expenses and empower employees to act as investors). Throughout the second half of the 1990s the economy boomed. The auto industry, once an employer of thousands of low-skill workers, became high-tech; the number of unionized auto workers fell from to 250,000 in 2000, but jobs required much higher skills and auto workers' earnings averaged $60,000. With the auto companies requiring high standards and speedy turnaround from subcontractors, Michigan became the home of almost all the nation's auto parts engineering centers and of much of the nation's large-scale manufacturing experts.

Historically, politics divided Michigan between labor and management, and between the Detroit metro area and Outstate: in 1960, John Kennedy carried metro Detroit 62%–38% and Richard Nixon carried Outstate 60%–39%. Now the balance is different. Engler won reelection by wide margins in 1994 and 1998, and his Republicans won control of the state legislature in 1994, 1998 and 2000 and of the state Supreme Court since 1998. But in national politics Michigan has moved toward the Democrats. George Bush carried the state 54%–46% in 1988, a margin almost precisely at the national average. But in 2000 Al Gore beat George W. Bush 51%–46%. The big change came mainly in Oakland and Macomb Counties, just north of Detroit. This was part of a national trend: Clinton-Gore Democrats made their biggest gains in the largest metropolitan areas, where incomes and wealth surged during the prosperous 1990s and where Democrats' liberal stands on cultural issues were in tune with the views of relatively secular suburbanites. Macomb County, once heavily blue collar, was a central focus for Democratic pollster Stanley Greenberg; it went 3–2 for Reagan and Bush in the 1980s, but—now more white collar and affluent—went narrowly for Clinton and Gore in 1996 and 2000. Oakland County, even more affluent, has been a key part of Engler's Republican constituency; but it too voted for Clinton and Gore in 1996 and 2000. Outstate Michigan is now contested political ground as well. Metro Grand Rapids, heavily Dutch and with many conservative Christians, is solidly Republican, but it is balanced off by the factory corridor from Flint through Saginaw and Bay City, and Lansing, like many other capitals full of state employees, has become a Democratic stronghold as well.

The success of Michigan's experiments cannot be evaluated until the nation's economy goes through the business cycle, and in 2000 storm clouds seemed to be hovering over Michigan. General Motors's profits have been low and it closed its Oldsmobile division, Ford was threatened by the failure of Firestone tires on its SUVs and Chrysler, taken over by Germany's Daimler, posted big losses in 2000. Unemployment remained low, and state revenues kept surging: but Michigan's new economy seemed about to undergo a test. But Michigan approaches a downturn in much better shape than it did 20 years ago. Detroit, devastated by riots in 1967 and by vast crime during the administration of liberal Mayor Coleman Young from 1973 to 1993, is now seeing new businesses and new development; even Pontiac, 30 miles north, with new stores and shops is partaking in the economic growth of surrounding Oakland County. Across the state, welfare rolls are on the decline, charter schools proliferate, once empty old factories are full of new machine tools and high-skill workers, and Detroit's airport (its hideous terminal is thankfully to be replaced by a midfield terminal in July 2001) sends out 747s every day direct to London, Tokyo and Beijing.

Governor John Engler sits astride Michigan politics and government like a colossus, the last governor to win a third term (term limits go into effect after him), with a Republican-controlled legislature and state Supreme Court. Engler grew up on a farm near Mount Pleasant, drove 60 miles south to go to Michigan State in East Lansing, then was elected to the state legislature in 1970, at 22, and remained there for 20 years: this downsizer of government has spent almost all his adult life in the public sector. He came to the fore in 1983, when Republicans, reacting to Governor Jim Blanchard's tax increase, used recalls to win control of the state Senate; at 33 Engler became the state's most visible Republican. In a climate where liberals controlled most institutions, Engler was a skillful political player, capable of keeping on civil terms with opponents even as he gathered ideas from conservative think tanks and marshaled a fine political organization run by Spencer Abraham, later U.S. Senator and Energy Secretary, and Pete Secchia, George Bush's ambassador to Italy. In 1990 Engler ran for governor and lagged behind Blanchard in the polls. But his call for increasing education spending and cutting property taxes was popular, and he won 50%–49%.

From that narrow margin Engler has become one of the major policy innovators in the United States. In his first years in office Engler challenged liberal conventional wisdom and ploughed ahead despite vitriolic criticism, and eventually succeeded in moving the fulcrum point of the political balance. He ended general assistance (welfare for able-bodied non-parents) and aid to the arts; he privatized services and started seeking federal waivers for welfare reform. Democrats and the *Detroit Free Press* habitually called him "mean-spirited." His crucial first-term victory was cutting property taxes; when Democratic state Senator (now U.S. Senator) Debbie Stabenow moved to zero out the current system of financing schools, Engler accepted the dare and pushed through his own plan—a major cut in property taxes plus a sales tax increase—to a 70%–30% victory in a March 1994 referendum, with help from Detroit Mayor Dennis Archer. By 1994, Michigan's new small-unit economy was growing faster than the nation's, and Engler campaigned on the theme, "Promises made, promises kept." Against liberal former Congressman Howard Wolpe, Engler won 61%–38%.

In his second term, with a Republican legislature, Engler stepped up the pace of reform. More taxes were cut or abolished, education spending rose and charter schools were authorized, and a welfare reform requiring work was passed; welfare rolls fell from 238,000 in 1994 to 74,000 in 2000, the lowest in 30 years. As head of the Republican Governors Association, Engler spent time in Washington helping to write the Republican welfare reform bill, which was passed on its third attempt in August 1996. Engler also sponsored a Clean Michigan Initiative—a bond issue to spend money on environmental cleanup, especially on lakefronts and riverfronts, improving water quality and building infrastructure in state parks. But Engler had some setbacks. Democrats won control of the state House in 1996 and jettisoned Engler's call for state takeover of failing school districts and a three-fifths supermajority for raising taxes.

In 1998 the Democrats' primary contest appeared to be between union-backed Larry Owen and New Democrat Doug Ross. But then a surprise candidate entered: Geoffrey Fieger, a very successful trial lawyer with family roots in the left wing of the Democratic Party, known best for defending assisted-suicide advocate and practitioner Dr. Jack Kevorkian in four widely-publicized trials. Fieger was brash, self-assured, shrewd in manipulating juries; but his controversial statements and vitriol ultimately worked against him. He won the primary with 41% of the vote, with heavy support from black voters in Detroit. Suddenly the spotlight was on Fieger, and it was not an attractive sight. Engler, he said, was "fat," a "moron," a "racist," the product of barnyard miscegenation. He criticized his fellow Democrats as well. At a unity breakfast, he said they were "a party of wimps and oatmeal"; he called Detroit Mayor Dennis Archer "a slow learner." He called Catholic Archbishop Adam Maida a "nut" and when Council of Orthodox Rabbis called assisted suicide murder, he said "They are closer to Nazis than they think they are." Congressmen Bart Stupak and Sander Levin declined to endorse him; when Al Gore appeared at a Democratic rally, Fieger was not present and Gore did not refer to him. Fieger did have a program—cutting the sales tax and property taxes and repealing the gas tax and single-business tax—and spent $5.7 million of his own money on his campaign, but despite his contempt for others' intelligence, showed no mastery of state issues. Engler refused to debate Fieger and ran ads calling for drug tests of welfare recipients and attacking Fieger's ethical lapses. The outcome was never in doubt. Engler won 62%–38%, winning 27% of an expanded black voter turnout; Republicans won back control of the state House.

In 1999 Engler got most of his program through the legislature, including an income tax cut from 4.4% to 3.9% over five years, drug tests for welfare recipients, fingerprinting of juveniles who commit serious crimes, expulsion of students who assault teachers and the establishment of $2,500 Michigan Merit Awards for high schoolers with high test scores. Control of the Detroit school board was turned over from an elective board to Mayor Dennis Archer. The state overturned city residency requirements for employees, including police officers and fire fighters. A $1 billion program was passed to link three major state universities and the new Van Andel Medical Institute in Grand Rapids: a life sciences corridor, Engler called it. In 2000 Engler called for $1,000 bonuses in each of 160 schools with high test scores and laptop computers for all 90,000 public school teachers. He set up education savings accounts that would be deductible from parents' state taxes. Electricity deregulation was passed, to be phased in by 2003, and he called for easing the restrictions on oil drilling in the Great Lakes that he had imposed in 1997. Also the legislature passed a bill requiring health insurers to provide abortion coverage only under a separate, optional rider, one of many measures backed by Engler and Michigan Right To Life that helped reduce abortions in the state from 49,000 in 1987 to 26,000 in 1999.

But Engler also had his problems. In June 1999 he got a law setting a Republican presidential primary for February 22, 2000, the earliest of any large state. But despite his considerable efforts he was not able to produce a win for George W. Bush; some 250,000 self-identified Democrats, with no primary of their own and no party registration, voted in the contest and gave the victory to John McCain. In November Engler was not able to buck the trend toward presidential Democrats in Michigan, and despite his best efforts Al Gore carried the state 51%–46%. November 2000 also saw the defeat of Senator Spencer Abraham and the defeat of Proposal 1, which would have provided $3,300 vouchers for students in seven failing school districts. This proposal was the special project of Dick and Betsy DeVos, longtime Republican activists and Engler allies; but Engler opposed it in 1999, and Betsy DeVos resigned as state Republican chairman.

Engler entered his 29th year in state office still in a powerful position, with a Republican legislature ready to redistrict the state and a Republican state Supreme Court likely to approve redistricting plans. He was in line to chair the National Governors Association in 2001–02. But he is term-limited, and it was not at all clear that he would be able to pass the governorship to his obvious choice, Lieutenant Governor Dick Posthumus, a farmer from the Grand Rapids area and a 16-year state legislator. In early 2001 three well-known Democrats were exploring the possibility of running for governor, and seemed to run well ahead of the lesser-known Posthumus in public polls. Posthumus may also face competition from state senator John Schwartz, a leading McCain primary supporter. Geoffrey Fieger has expressed interest in a third-party candidacy.

Cook's Call   *Highly Competitive.* A Democratic primary may be inevitable as former Governor Jim Blanchard, state Attorney General Jennifer Granholm, House Minority Whip David Bonior and state Representative Alma Wheeler Smith all seem intent on running. On the Republican side, Lieutenant Governor Dick Posthumus, a close friend of Engler, is the frontrunner for the nomination, but he might also face primary opposition. Expect a very close general election.

Senior Senator   Carl Levin, first elected in 1978, is a durable and likable liberal Democrat, a member of one of Michigan's most respected political families. He is rumpled, unfashionable, speaks articulately but without apparent political artifice and takes unpopular stands on issues he cares about. He grew up in Detroit, worked for the state civil rights commissioner and the appellate public defender's office, and was elected to Detroit's city council in 1969 and 1973, with substantial support from both blacks and whites. In 1978 he ran for the Senate and was helped when incumbent Robert Griffin got out of the race and then back in; Levin won 52%–48%. In 1984 he won by a similar margin against a former astronaut who had given a public testimonial for his Japanese car; in 1990 and 1996 he was re-elected by wide margins.

Levin has been ranking Democrat on the Senate Armed Services Committee since 1997 and became chairman when Democrats took the majority in 2001. Levin brought to the Senate the skepticism about defense spending and military involvements common among Democrats in the 1970s, an attitude that seldom has a majority on Armed Services. He chaired the confirmation hearings of Donald Rumsfeld, speaking cordially but making it clear that he took a very different approach on some important defense issues. He characterizes his approach as supportive of basic, reliable weapons systems and conventional forces and skeptical of strategic weapons systems. He supports full funding of the Nunn-Lugar program for buying up and disassembling nuclear weapons from the former Soviet Union. On a trip to Kosovo in July 1999, after the bombing campaign, he predicted that Slobodan Milosevic would not stay in power for another year. In 2000 he opposed a measure to cut off funds for troops in Kosovo by July 2001.

The Senate's most persistent opponent of missile defense systems, Levin led the September 1998 filibuster that prevailed by just one vote, when he argued that missile defense would undermine chances of Russian approval of the 1993 START II treaty and that the nature of the missile threat was not clear. He frequently wrote Bill Clinton about the cost and technology of missile defense and ordered the CBO study which pegged the cost of Clinton's proposed system, based on land in Alaska, at $60 billion. In January 2001 he warned that a missile defense system would irritate our allies and provoke countermeasures from Russia and China. "Missile attack is a threat," he said, "but it is one we have successfully deterred." Since the last federal base closing round in 1995, he has joined John McCain in seeking new base closing legislation; but they have been frustrated by Republicans' (and some Democrats') disgust at Bill Clinton's political manipulation of the process in 1995 and even in June 2000, when it was apparent that any base closing round could not take place until after Clinton left office, their proposal was defeated 63–35. Interestingly, McCain, campaigning for the Republican nomination for president in Michigan in November 1999, praised Levin's intellect and knowledge and said that if elected he would ask him to join a small group to help him review the state of the world.

As chief sponsor of the lobbying disclosure bill that passed the Senate in 1993 and, after Republicans took control of Congress, the House in 1995, Levin has spent much of his time on process issues. He also was the chief sponsor of the Senate gift rule, setting a limit of $50 on gifts to senators and staffers; this of course did not apply to the gifts Senator-elect Hillary Rodham Clinton accepted in December 2000. He was the prime mover in re-enacting in 1994 the independent counsel law, opposed by many Republicans and signed, to his later regret, by Bill Clinton. But Levin was very displeased with Independent Counsel Kenneth Starr. He tried to get Starr disqualified when he was first appointed, and in October 1998 he charged that Starr violated the law by failing to follow Justice Department guidelines, failing to disclose conflicts of interest and advocating impeachment. The law expired in June 1999, and Levin sought to renew it with modifications; but that went nowhere. He opposed Republicans' plans to reorganize the Energy Department in 1999 by taking power away from Secretary Bill Richardson. After hearings on money laundering in 1999, he sponsored a law to make it a crime to falsify or conceal the identity of a bank customer.

Levin generally has one of the most liberal records in the Senate. He opposed NAFTA and has complained about Japanese auto-parts and Korean car trade restrictions. One issue on which he is passionate is capital punishment (abolished in Michigan in 1855), and he has often led the fight against it, calling for a moratorium on the federal death penalty in 2000. He sought to compensate Michigan apple growers after their crops were destroyed by fire blight and to stop dumping of apple juice by China. He worked for a new Coast Guard icebreaker in the Great Lakes.

Levin's reputation for candor and hard work, and his rumpled persona have given him great political strength in Michigan. In 1996 Republicans had a spirited primary out of which the 52%–48% winner, Ronna Romney, emerged with little money. The result was not in doubt: Levin won 58%–40%, a bit better than his 57%–41% margin in 1990; he carried Outstate Michigan as well as the Detroit metro area. In February 2001, he announced he would seek a fifth term in 2002; polls showed him leading possible opponents by wide margins. In 2002 he will have served longer than any other Michigan senator in history.

Cook's Call   *Probably Safe.* Now that Levin has put rumors to rest that he might retire in 2002, Republican interest in this race is waning. Their attention will be focused on retaining the governorship and congressional redistricting. Given the expense of running a competitive statewide race in Michigan, Republicans probably won't make much of an effort here.

Junior Senator   Michigan's junior senator is Deborah Ann Stabenow, usually called Debbie, a Democrat elected in 2000. Stabenow grew up in the small Outstate town of Clare, where her father was an Oldsmobile dealer and her mother a nurse. She went to Michigan State, where she got a master's degree in social work and made money singing folk songs in coffeehouses. She marched in antiwar rallies and volunteered for George McGovern in 1972, when her husband ran an unsuccessful race for Ingham County Commissioner. Provoked when the commission closed a nursing home, she ran for the commission two years later and, at 24, beat an incumbent who referred to her as "that young broad." She was elected to the state House in 1978, at 28, making a record in family law and child abuse; she was elected to the state Senate in 1990. In 1994, while running for governor, she was at the storm center of state politics and policy. In response to Republican Governor John Engler's call for education finance reform, she proposed to zero out the property tax and start over, apparently calculating that he would reject such a drastic tax cut. Instead he accepted her proposal and passed a plan reducing property taxes vastly and increasing the sales tax, which was approved by voters 70%–30% in March 1994. In the August 1994 primary for governor, Stabenow was opposed by the major forces in the Democratic Party: the Michigan Education Association, the UAW and AFL-CIO. Stabenow won 30% of the vote, ahead of Larry Owen's 26% but behind former Congressman Howard Wolpe's 35%. Perhaps it is best she lost; she was chosen as Wolpe's running mate, but the ticket lost to Engler by a 61%–38% margin.

Undaunted, Stabenow almost immediately began running for Congress. The 8th District seat, which included Lansing's Democratic Ingham County and heavily Republican Livingston County to the east, was held by Republican Dick Chrysler. For the 1996 race, Stabenow raised more than $1 million in individual contributions, a tribute to her industriousness and the fundraising prowess of the feminist left; overall each spent $1.5 million. On national issues Stabenow struck a thematic note similar to Bill Clinton, calling for "balancing the budget in a way that does not shift the burden to middle class families," equipping schools with computers, and encouraging job creation by new-tech small businesses. She won impressively, 54%–44%.

In the House Stabenow had a fairly liberal voting record; she was sought out by the moderate Democratic Blue Dogs but did not join. She spent much energy encouraging unions and business to donate labor and old computers so that every local school can have access to the Internet. She got some tax breaks to that end in the 1997 tax law. She called for a study of the impact on women of Social Security reform, while conceding that the current program on average gives women smaller monthly checks than men. She opposed fast track and the partial-birth abortion ban. In

March 1999 she announced she was running against Senator Spencer Abraham in 2000; the same day Abraham ran full-page ads calling her a liberal.

This turned out to be one of the critical races in the 2000 Senate cycle. Abraham, a former state Republican chairman and deputy chief of staff to Vice President Dan Quayle, had been elected in 1994 by a 52%–43% margin over Congressman Bob Carr. The grandson of immigrants from Lebanon, his greatest achievement in the Senate was to squelch proposals to reduce the number of legal immigrants allowed in each year; Abraham put together an alliance of conservatives and liberals that beat subcommittee chairman Al Simpson, and the basic immigration laws remained unchanged. In 2000 Abraham secured near-unanimous approval for an increase in H1-B immigration visas for high-tech workers—one of the chief legislative goals of the high-tech industry. Abraham was also a strong supporter of tax cuts. But he kept a relatively low profile in Washington. The good news for Abraham and Stabenow was that neither had primary opposition; the bad news was that neither was known in any depth by most Michigan voters.

The first barrage of ads in the race came not from either candidate or party, but from the Federation for American Immigration Reform, which in early 2000 spent $700,000 attacking Abraham for his stands on immigration and charging that his stands cost Michigan workers jobs. These ads were attacked by many, including some Abraham critics, as unfair and bigoted; Stabenow declined to comment on them. But in 1999 Abraham's voting record became more moderate than before, and in July 2000 he called for a suspension of the federal gas tax until November, a move beaten in the Senate 59–40. In summer 2000 Abraham used his money advantage—he ultimately spent nearly $13 million, to Stabenow's nearly $8 million—to run ads spotlighting his own program for prescription drugs for seniors and attacked Stabenow as a free-spending liberal favoring increased bureaucracy and opposing tax cuts, opposing welfare reform and supporting more lenient sentences for criminals. He set up a liberaldebbie.com website, and faced threats of a lawsuit from the makers of Little Debbie cakes. He ran ads featuring John McCain, who said, "There are show horses and work horses. Spence Abraham is a work horse." Stabenow resisted pressure and hoarded her money for an October ad buy.

This proved to be a good strategy: Stabenow was down by 17% in one mid-October poll but, after several weeks of equal advertising by each, wound up winning by 1%. Stabenow answered charges that she was a liberal by citing her votes for a balanced budget and ending the marriage penalty; she kept herself in the good graces of labor by voting against permanent normal trade relations with China. Stabenow said Abraham was beholden to corporations and special interests and attacked his stands on prescription drug and HMO regulation. "My opponent calls himself the work horse. The question is, who is he working for?" Abraham charged that Stabenow's prescription drug plan would require a $600 annual fee and would give government rather than seniors the choice in drugs. He pointed to his votes for a balanced budget, welfare reform and highway funds for Michigan and talked of "the total absence of congressional achievements of Debbie Stabenow." This race was light on debates— the two had just one televised debate—and heavy on ads by outside groups—the Sierra Club, Peace Action and EMILY's List for Stabenow, the Chamber of Commerce, Business Roundtable, Americans for Job Security, National Rifle Association and Michigan Right to Life for Abraham.

This was the most expensive Senate race in Michigan history, and the first since 1942 in which neither candidate won a majority of the vote. Stabenow won 49%–48%; she said that after the campaign Bill Clinton "told me all along that next to Hillary's, mine was the race he was most proud of." Abraham won Outstate Michigan 56%–42%, but in the metro Detroit area Stabenow led 57%–40%. Stabenow carried only 13 of the state's 83 counties, but she ran essentially even in critical Oakland and Macomb Counties. There was a 10% gender gap; Abraham carried voters under 45 and Stabenow voters over 45. In the Senate Stabenow got seats on the Banking, Agriculture and Budget Committees. Abraham was named secretary of Energy, a department he had three times tried to abolish on the grounds that it had "no core mission." Stabenow criticized President Bush's tax cut, claiming it would not leave enough money for a prescription drug plan, and joined a bipartisan group of moderates to call for linking cuts with debt reduction.

Presidential politics   In 1984, 1988 and 1992 Michigan voted within 1% of the national average for all major presidential candidates. But it has lost its bellwether status: in 1996 it voted

52%–38% for Bill Clinton and in 2000 51%–46% for Al Gore, 3% more Democratic than the nation. In those two elections Clinton and Gore carried suburban Oakland and Macomb Counties, the latter a special target for Democrats. Macomb was heavily Democratic in the 1950s and 1960s, then trended Republican in the 1970s, and now has swung back some distance toward the Democrats. Some of the Democratic trend here may represent a resurgence in union support of Democrats. The United Auto Workers in bargaining with the Big Three automakers obtained a paid day off on election day 2000—"the largest single corporate contribution in American history," Governor John Engler called it. Union voters were a larger share of the electorate in 2000 than in 1996, reversing a long trend. But the UAW is no longer the only important union in Michigan; just as politically active, and in some ways arguably more effective, is the Michigan Education Association, whose membership of 157,000 is dispersed more evenly around the state. Incidentally, Al Gore's statement in *Earth in the Balance* that the internal combustion energy is "a mortal threat to the security of every nation that is more deadly than that of any military enemy we are ever again likely to confront" did not prevent tickets he was on from carrying the state three times. Michigan politics is not just about autos.

Michigan has had problems setting up a presidential primary; one reason is that it does not have party registration, which violates Democratic Party rules. In 2000, Republicans held their primary February 22. Governor John Engler hoped to deliver the state's delegates to George W. Bush, whose candidacy he had backed early on. But John McCain, aroused after his defeat in South Carolina February 19, contested the state vigorously and caught many voters' imaginations. In a stinging rebuke to Engler, McCain won 51%–43%. This was hailed by his admirers in the national press as a great breakthrough. But it turned out to be atypical and an augury of nothing. Turnout was a huge 1.3 million, far higher than the 524,000 of 1996 or the 437,000 of 1992; indeed, even Bush got more votes than were cast for all candidates in those primaries. But the VNS exit poll showed that 18% of the votes were cast by self-identified Democrats (almost double the percentage in any other primary that year) and only 47% by self-identified Republicans. Bush won solidly among Republicans, as he did everywhere except in a few Northeast states, but lost by 2–1 among self-identified Independents and 8–1 among Democrats. Nothing barred Democrats from voting; when Democrats held caucuses in March, only 22,000 bothered to vote or mail in ballots. The McCain vote was really an anti-Engler vote: The man had beaten them time and again, and seemed to be successful in his policy goals, and now there was a way to get back at him. They did so by voting for McCain and by carrying the state for Al Gore in November; Engler, though able and an early Bush backer, did not get an appointment in the new administration.

Congressional districting   Michigan has now lost four seats in the last three censuses—one after the 1980 Census, two after the 1990 Census, another one after the 2000 Census. For the first time since the 1950s, redistricting is controlled by Republicans, who have majorities in both houses of the legislature and whose governor, John Engler, is determined to use the power to erase the Democrats' current 9–7 edge in the House delegation. One obvious target is David Bonior, whose 10th district could be rendered much more Republican by slicing off the southernmost three or four miles and adding them to population-losing Detroit districts; in early 2001 Bonior, the number two Democrat in the House after 25 years there, announced that he was running for governor. Republicans may also target Democrats Sander Levin (by moving his district northward) and Lynn Rivers (by eliminating her district altogether); they will surely not disturb the dean of the House, John Dingell, who is a bulwark for the auto industry in Washington. They will surely also try to strengthen freshman Mike Rogers, elected in the 8th district by 160 votes. But there are limits on how much the Republicans can do for themselves; it will be hard, perhaps impossible, to turn a 9–7 deficit to anything better than an 8–7 edge.

THE PEOPLE: Pop. 2000: 9,938,444; Pop. 1990: 9,295,297, up 6.9% 1990–2000. 3.5% of U.S. total, 8th largest; 80.2% White, 14.2% Black, 1.8% Asian, 0.6% Amer. Indian, 1.9% Two+ races, 1.3% Other; 3.3% Hispanic Origin. 3.6% Unemployment. 2000 Voting age pop.: 7,342,677. 2000 Turnout: 4,279,299; 58% of VAP. Registered voters (2000): 6,859,332; no party registration.

POLITICAL LINEUP: Governor, John M. Engler (R); Lt. Gov., Dick Posthumus (R); Secy. of State, Candice Miller (R); Atty. Gen., Jennifer Granholm (D); Treasurer, Mark Murray; State Senate, 38 (15 D, 23 R); Senate Pres. Pro Tempore, Philip Hoffman (R); Majority Leader, Dan DeGrow (R); State House, 110 (52 D, 57 R, 1 vacancy); House Speaker, Rick Johnson (R). Senators, Carl Levin (D) and Deborah Ann Stabenow (D). Representatives, 16 (9 D, 7 R).

ELECTIONS DIVISION: 517-373-2540; **FILING DEADLINE FOR U.S. CONGRESS:** May 14, 2002.

2000 Presidential Vote

Gore (D)	2,170,418	(51%)
Bush (R)	1,953,139	(46%)
Nader (Green)	84,165	(2%)
Others	24,779	(1%)

1996 Presidential Vote

Clinton (D)	1,989,683	(52%)
Dole (R)	1,481,572	(39%)
Perot (I)	336,681	(9%)

2000 Republican Presidential Primary

McCain (R)	650,805	(51%)
Bush (R)	549,665	(43%)
Keyes (R)	59,032	(5%)

Gov. John M. Engler (R)

Elected 1990, term expires Jan. 2003, 3d term; b. Oct. 12, 1948, Mt. Pleasant; home, Mt. Pleasant; MI St. U., B.A. 1971, Cooley Law Schl., J.D. 1981; Catholic; married (Michelle).

Elected Office: MI House of Reps., 1970–76; MI Senate, 1978–90, Majority Ldr. 1984–90, Chmn., Natl. Governor's Assn., 2001-present.

Office: Olds Plaza, 111 S. Capitol, Lansing, 48933, 517-373-3400; Fax: 517-335-6863; Web site: www.state.mi.us.

Election Results

1998 general	John M. Engler (R)	1,883,005	(62%)
	Geoffrey Fieger (D)	1,143,574	(38%)
1998 primary	John M. Engler (R)	477,628	(90%)
	Gary Artinian (R)	55,453	(10%)
1994 general	John M. Engler (R)	1,899,101	(61%)
	Howard Wolpe (D)	1,188,438	(38%)

Sen. Carl Levin (D)

Elected 1978, seat up 2002, 4th term; b. June 28, 1934, Detroit; home, Detroit; Swarthmore Col., B.A. 1956, Harvard U., LL.B. 1959; Jewish; married (Barbara).

Elected Office: Detroit City Cncl., 1969–77, Pres., 1973–77.

Professional Career: Practicing atty., 1959–64, 1971–73, 1978–79; MI Asst. Atty. Gen. & Gen. Cnsl., MI Civil Rights Comm., 1964–67; Detroit Chief Appellate Defender, 1967–69.

DC Office: 269 RSOB, 20510, 202-224-6221; Fax: 202-224-1388; Web site: levin.senate.gov.

State Offices: Alpena, 989-354-5520; Detroit, 313-226-6020; Escanaba, 906-789-0052; Grand Rapids, 616-456-2531; Lansing, 517-377-1508; Saginaw, 989-754-2494; Traverse City, 231-947-9569; Warren, 810-573-9145.

Committees: *Armed Services* (Chmn.). *Governmental Affairs*: International Security, Proliferation & Federal Services; Investigations (Permanent) (Chmn.). *Intelligence (Select)*. *Small Business*.

Group Ratings

	ADA	ACLU	AFS	LCV	CON	ITIC	NTU	COC	ACU	NTLC	CHC
2000	90	71	85	86	73	90	11	66	12	0	15
1999	95	—	100	78	75	—	7	53	4	—	—

National Journal Ratings

	1999 LIB	—	1999 CONS		2000 LIB	—	2000 CONS
Economic	87%	—	10%		78%	—	20%
Social	88%	—	0%		79%	—	0%
Foreign	87%	—	0%		72%	—	15%

Key Votes of the 106th Congress

1. Educ. Savings Accts.	N	5. Review Movie Violence	N	9. NATO War in Serbia	Y
2. Prescrip. Drug Benefit	Y	6. Gun Show Bckgrnd. Checks	Y	10. Table Cuba Travel Ban	N
3. Delay Ergonomic Standards	N	7. Ban Part.-Birth Abortion	N	11. Nuclear Test-Ban Treaty	Y
4. Phase Out Estate Tax	N	8. Broaden Hate Crimes List	Y	12. Perm. Trade with China	Y

Election Results

1996 general	Carl Levin (D)	2,195,738	(58%)	($6,223,409)
	Ronna Romney (R)	1,500,106	(40%)	($3,208,968)
	Others	66,731	(2%)	
1996 primary	Carl Levin (D)	unopposed		
1990 general	Carl Levin (D)	1,471,753	(57%)	($7,066,832)
	Bill Schuette (R)	1,055,695	(41%)	($2,417,705)

Sen. Deborah Ann Stabenow (D)

Elected 2000, seat up 2006, 1st term; b. Apr. 29, 1950, Gladwin; home, Lansing; MI St. U., B.A. 1972, M.S.W. 1975; United Methodist; divorced.

Elected Office: Ingham Cnty. Comm., 1975–78, Chair, 1976–78; MI House of Reps., 1978–90; MI Senate, 1990–94; U.S. House of Reps 1996–2000.

Professional Career: Consultant & Co-founder, MI Leadership Inst., 1995–96.

DC Office: 702 HSOB, 20510, 202-224-4822; Fax: 202-228-0325; Web site: stabenow.senate.gov.

State Offices: Detroit, 313-964-7342; E. Lansing, 517-203-1760; Flint, 810-720-4172; Grand Rapids, 616-975-0052; Marquette, 906-228-8756; Traverse City, 231-929-1031.

Committees: *Aging (Special)*. *Agriculture, Nutrition & Forestry*: Forestry, Conservation & Rural Revitalization; Research, Nutrition & General Legislation. *Banking, Housing & Urban Affairs*: Financial Institutions; Housing & Transportation; Securities & Investment. *Budget*.

Group Ratings

	ADA	ACLU	AFS	LCV	CON	ITIC	NTU	COC	ACU	NTLC	CHC
2000	90	64	100	86	29	71	27	47	16	24	13
1999	95	—	100	81	70	—	14	44	4	—	—

National Journal Ratings

	1999 LIB	—	1999 CONS		2000 LIB	—	2000 CONS
Economic	64%	—	36%		63%	—	36%
Social	66%	—	33%		74%	—	24%
Foreign	68%	—	30%		64%	—	34%

Key Votes of the 106th Congress

1. Patient Bill of Rights	Y	5. Bar RU-486 $ for FDA	N	9. NATO War in Serbia	Y
2. Accelerate Min. Wage	Y	6. Display 10 Commandments	Y	10. Perm. Trade with China	N
3. Strike Ban on Ergo. Stnd.	Y	7. Gun Show Bkgrnd. Checks	Y	11. Debt Relief for 3rd World	Y
4. Ovrd. Estate Tax Veto	N	8. Ban Part.-Birth Abortion	N	12. Drop Cuba Econ. Embargo	N

Election Results

2000 general	Deborah Ann Stabenow (D)	2,061,952	(49%)	($7,892,518)
	Spencer Abraham (R)	1,994,693	(48%)	($13,028,636)
	Others	111,040	(3%)	
2000 primary	Deborah Ann Stabenow (D)	unopposed		
1994 general	Spencer Abraham (R)	1,578,770	(52%)	($4,437,038)
	Bob Carr (D)	1,300,960	(43%)	($3,040,416)
	Jon Coon (Lib)	128,393	(4%)	($303,369)

FIRST DISTRICT

Michigan's Upper Peninsula, commonly known as the UP, is a land apart. Surrounded on three sides by frigid Lake Superior and Lake Michigan, it has its own flora, including the world's largest known living object, a giant fungus that lives under 37 acres of a forest floor and is 1,500 years old. Although the UP is no farther north than Montreal or Seattle, it has one of the coldest climates in settled parts of North America. "In October, usually, the first snow falls steady on the north-land," writes Dixie Lee Franklin in *A Most Superior Land*, "whispering teasing promises of more to come"—for eight months more. Far away from any major city, with ground too frozen and a growing season too short for most crops, the Upper Peninsula was explored by French voyagers more than 300 years ago but was never thickly settled until prospectors found rich veins of ore here. The mineral veins of the Keweenaw Peninsula produced 13.3 billion pounds of copper; the Marquette, Menominee and Gogebic iron ranges have more than one billion tons of iron ore. Starting in the 1880s, immigrants flocked here to work the mines: Irish, Italians, Swedes, Nor-wegians, miners' sons from Wales and Cornwall, and most prominently Finns, who must have found this cold land with its lakes and hills much like their home. By 1900, the UP was a northern industrial belt, with a few bosses and some absentee overlords and a work force disposed to radical ideas and union movements.

A major strike in 1913–14 and falling ore prices after World War I—events that would be long forgotten elsewhere—are remembered in the UP as the beginning of its decline: The UP's population peaked at 332,000 in 1920. The copper veins were mostly depleted by then, mining iron ore became less labor-intensive, and lumber and farming provided only a few thousand jobs. In the last half century, there has been great migration to Detroit, Chicago and the West Coast; the UP's population has hovered around 300,000, rising to 318,000 in 2000. But "Yoopers"—who some say have their own dialect, "Yoopanese"—remain devoted to their land.

The 1st Congressional District of Michigan includes the Upper Peninsula and 13 northern-tier counties in the Lower Peninsula. About half the people live in the UP; the other half live south of the breathtaking Mackinac Bridge. This is a vast area, geographically the second-largest district east of the Mississippi and smaller than only 26 farther west; it is a 450-mile drive from Ironwood at the western end of the UP to the Sleeping Bear Dunes towering over Lake Michigan. The Lower Peninsula counties have two different personalities. On Lake Huron—the sunrise side—are smaller industrial towns and resorts that grew in the 1990s. On Lake Michigan are affluent resort areas around Petoskey and Charlevoix, long summer places for people from Chicago (this is Ernest Hemingway's "up in Michigan"), and the boom area around Traverse City, with its burgeoning condominiums, resorts and more than two dozen wineries. Politically, the UP has long been Democratic, some parts more than others; but this is one part of Michigan that does not like Al Gore's environmental stands, and the UP went for George W. Bush in 2000. The Lake Michigan shore of the Lower Peninsula is heavily Republican, the sunrise side marginal.

The congressman from the 1st District is Bart Stupak, a Democrat and a "Yooper" from Menominee on the Wisconsin border. He was a police officer in Escanaba, then became a Michigan state trooper in 1974 and also earned a law degree; in 1984 he was injured in the line of duty and retired from the force. In 1988 he was elected to the Michigan House; in 1990 he lost a race for the state Senate. Stupak got into the 1992 House race when incumbent Republican Bob Davis, with 878 overdrafts on the House bank, decided to drop out. In the general he beat Republican Philip Ruppe, who had represented the district from 1966–78, by 54%–44%.

In the House Stupak has paid great attention to local issues. Angered by the closing of K.I.

Sawyer Air Force Base, the biggest employer in Marquette County, he threatened to vote against the 1993 Clinton budget and tax package; after some muscling, he voted for it. He opposed Clinton on NAFTA and the 1994 crime bill. He formed the Law Enforcement Caucus and has sought to ban mail-order sales of body armor. When a Sault Ste. Marie, Ontario, firm tried to sell Lake Superior water to China, he sponsored a resolution to prevent sale of any Great Lake water to a foreign country—at least until federal standards were in place. He has sought to ban directional drilling for oil and gas under the Great Lakes. When the Energy Department wanted to transport plutonium fuel rods from Los Alamos to Ontario, he led opposition to the route through Michigan; ultimately, the shipment proceeded, without incident. He is strongly opposed to abortion, and spoke out against it at the 1996 Democratic National Convention; when invited to speak at the 2000 convention, he discussed his district.

Stupak has become well known in the House for his unpredictability and for taking his time making decisions on issues. "Stupak is a good dancer, a notoriously good dancer," wrote Kevin Merida of the *Washington Post*. "He studies, he frets, he waits. He is a methodical hedger." He showed that independence in 1999, when he bucked the National Rifle Association by voting for tighter background checks at gun shows, calling it a safety measure that would not affect hunters.

All this has served him well in elections. Since 1992, he has had competitive contests but none has been serious enough to jeopardize his seat. In 1998 he had well-financed opposition from Traverse City area state Representative Michelle McManus, whose strategy was to associate Stupak with two presumably unpopular figures, Bill Clinton and gubernatorial candidate Geoffrey Fieger. Stupak's indecision on both lured her into what turned out to be traps. Stupak typically delayed deciding on whether he favored a Clinton impeachment investigation until the final days before the October vote. Initially, Stupak said that Clinton's behavior was "immoral and unacceptable and he should be held accountable." When Clinton's numbers rose after the release of the Starr report, Stupak supported the Democratic version of the investigation, and suddenly the Clinton card was working for him; he voted against impeachment. As for Fieger, Stupak refused for six weeks after the primary to say whether he would support him for governor or not. McManus ran spots attacking Stupak and asked Michigan Right to Life to withdraw its endorsement. When Stupak said he would not endorse Fieger; McManus had lost the Fieger card as well. Meanwhile, Democrats peppered her with criticism for handing in faulty filing petitions. Stupak won 59%–40%, carrying the UP by 2–1.

On Mother's Day 2000, Stupak suffered a personal tragedy, which for a time raised questions about his political future. His 17-year-old son B.J., a high school football player, killed himself on the morning after his prom; more than 60 House members attended the funeral in Menominee. In coping with the aftermath, Bart and his wife Laurie eventually focused on their son's use of Accutane, a prescription-drug for acne treatment; the Food and Drug Administration had issued warnings about adverse psychological effects, including suicide attempts. In October, Stupak went public with his concerns and he later organized a House hearing about Accutane. In the meantime, there was talk that Stupak was considering retirement, and he cancelled fundraising events. Following a request from campaign committee chairman Patrick Kennedy, dozens of House Democrats gave more than $100,000 to his campaign. Before the tragedy, Stupak was facing a vigorous challenge from Chuck Yob, a longtime Republican National committeeman known for his frank and pungent comments. Yob also criticized Stupak for taking more than 80% of his campaign money from special interest groups; the National Rifle Association endorsed Yob. But Stupak argued that voters favored common-sense gun laws, and voters seemed to be in no mood for controversy after the Stupaks' tragedy. Stupak won 58%–40%, losing only one county, though the race was about even in the Traverse City area.

Republicans control redistricting in Michigan, but there is probably little they can do to defeat Stupak, whose appeal crosses party lines.

Cook's Call   *Probably Safe.* Michigan Republicans continue to be stymied by Stupak's resilience in this conservative, rather marginal district. This year, Republicans control the redistricting process in the state, which could cause Stupak some headaches. One rumor has a Republican map placing most of the 1st in with fellow Democrat Jim Barcia's 5th. But, barring any major changes to the map, Stupak should be fine here. He has proven that he can weather difficult political environments.

THE PEOPLE: Pop. 2000: 639,161; Pop. 1990: 581,006, up 10% 1990–2000. 94% White, 1.1% Black, 0.4% Asian, 2.7% Amer. Indian, 1.5% Two+ races, 0.3% Other; 1% Hispanic Origin.

2000 Presidential Vote		
Bush (R)	156,812	(53%)
Gore (D)	126,568	(43%)
Nader (Green)	8,523	(3%)
Others	1,801	(1%)

1996 Presidential Vote		
Clinton (D)	125,135	(47%)
Dole (R)	107,577	(40%)
Perot (I)	31,184	(12%)

Rep. Bart Stupak (D)

Elected 1992, 5th term; b. Feb. 29, 1952, Milwaukee, WI; home, Menominee; NW MI Comm. Col., A.A. 1972, Saginaw Valley St. Col., B.S. 1977, Thomas Cooley Law Schl., J.D. 1981; Catholic; married (Laurie).

Elected Office: MI House of Reps., 1988–90.

Professional Career: Escanaba Police Officer, 1972–73; MI St. Trooper, 1974–84; Practicing atty., 1981–1992.

DC Office: 2348 RHOB 20515, 202-225-4735; Fax: 202-225-4744; Web site: www.house.gov/stupak.

District Offices: Alpena, 517-356-0690; Crystal Falls, 906-875-3751; Escanaba, 906-786-4504; Houghton, 906-482-1371; Marquette, 906-228-3700; Traverse City, 231-929-4711.

Committees: *Energy & Commerce* (13th of 26 D): Health; Oversight & Investigations; Telecommunications & The Internet.

Group Ratings

	ADA	ACLU	AFS	LCV	CON	ITIC	NTU	COC	ACU	NTLC	CHC
2000	65	57	100	64	82	50	30	30	22	21	43
1999	85	—	100	75	69	—	20	16	16	—	—

National Journal Ratings

	1999 LIB —	1999 CONS		2000 LIB —	2000 CONS
Economic	88% —	0%		70% —	29%
Social	56% —	44%		57% —	43%
Foreign	73% —	27%		67% —	32%

Key Votes of the 106th Congress

1. Patient Bill of Rights	Y	5. Bar RU-486 $ for FDA	Y	9. NATO War in Serbia	Y
2. Accelerate Min. Wage	Y	6. Display 10 Commandments	Y	10. Perm. Trade with China	N
3. Strike Ban on Ergo. Stnd.	Y	7. Gun Show Bkgrnd. Checks	Y	11. Debt Relief for 3rd World	Y
4. Ovrd. Estate Tax Veto	N	8. Ban Part.-Birth Abortion	Y	12. Drop Cuba Econ. Embargo	Y

Election Results

2000 general	Bart Stupak (D)	169,649	(58%)	($971,337)
	Chuck Yob (R)	117,300	(40%)	($691,468)
	Other	3,620	(1%)	
2000 primary	Bart Stupak (D)	40,601	(89%)	
	Sven Johnson (D)	5,051	(11%)	
1998 general	Bart Stupak (D)	130,129	(59%)	($672,773)
	Michelle McManus (R)	87,630	(40%)	($474,199)
	Others	4,037	(2%)	

SECOND DISTRICT

Lining the eastern shoreline of Lake Michigan, where the lake winds temper the frigid Michigan winters, are some of the nation's longest and highest sand dunes. In the late 19th Century, this shoreline was America's greatest lumber country; the ports on the small rivers were choked with logs and full of lumbermen from Norway and Sweden, Ireland and Scotland, Quebec and New England. During the lumber boom, the shoreline just to the south was the locus of America's largest migration from the Netherlands and still has the nation's largest concentration of Dutch-Americans. Wooden shoes are now seen only in the Tulip Festival in Holland, but here conscientious Dutch work habits have produced some of the most highly skilled workers in America, and major companies have grown up, like Gerber Foods in Fremont and Herman Miller furniture in Zeeland.

The 2d Congressional District of Michigan occupies the Lake Michigan shoreline counties, plus a tier of counties inland, from the lumber country around Manistee south to Holland and the resort town of Saugatuck. Some 25% of people here claim Dutch ancestry. Politically, the district is one of Michigan's two most Republican (the other is the Grand Rapids 3d). Its first Yankee settlers were part of the original Republican Party, and Dutch-Americans with their innate conservatism vie with Cuban-Americans for the title of America's most heavily Republican ethnic group (though there is little similarity in their cultural style). Holland and surrounding Ottawa County voted 85% for Governor John Engler in 1998; despite that, in the nation's first such referendum, the town in 2000 voted against a proposal from Christian conservative groups to bar access to obscene materials on the public library's computers.

The congressman from the 2d is Peter Hoekstra (pronounced *HOOKstra*), who emigrated from the Netherlands at 3, graduated from Hope College in Holland (with a semester in Washington during Watergate) and got an MBA at the University of Michigan. Hoekstra went to work at Herman Miller, where he helped develop the "Equa Chair" seat and became a vice president. In 1992, he decided to run what seemed an improbable campaign for Congress against Guy Vander Jagt, 26-year incumbent and chairman of the National Republican Congressional Committee since 1975. Hoekstra saved up vacation time and took a county-by-county bicycle tour of the district. With an earnestness that rang true, Hoekstra called for citizen, not career, politicians; refused PAC money and supported abolishing PACs; advocated 12-year term limits; and promised to uphold family values and to oppose abortion. Hoekstra spent only $55,600 to Vander Jagt's $725,000. But on primary day, he carried the heavily Dutch Ottawa and Allegan Counties, 53%–31%; they cast 59% of the primary vote, and so Hoekstra won 46%–40%. He won the general election easily and has not been threatened since.

Hoekstra brought to Washington a mistrust of government—he says he is "working to re-establish a rational federal government"—and a desire to apply the participatory management ideas he had developed at Herman Miller. In early 1994 he was asked by Newt Gingrich to plan how to manage a Republican House, something few others thought they would live to see. After his proposals were stalled in March 1996, he had an angry confrontation with Gingrich. Only a few of his reforms were adopted: the House barred former members from lobbying on the floor, and it passed (though the Senate didn't) a ban on pensions to former members convicted of a felony. Hoekstra backed Gingrich for re-election only after much mulling in January 1997. But he walked out of an anti-Gingrich coup meeting.

In 1995, Hoekstra got the chair of the Oversight and Investigations Subcommittee of the Education and Workforce Committee. In summer 1997 he started on two major assignments from the leadership, with a special $1.4 million budget. The first was an investigation of labor law. Republican leaders hoped he would investigate the role of unions in the 1996 campaigns, but instead he conducted what he called the American Worker at a Crossroads project. Eschewing spectacular hearings, except for a look at the garment industry and union oppression of workers in April 1998, he held closed-door meetings with executives from companies like Boeing and Microsoft and later with some union leaders as well. He argued that the workplace has changed since federal labor laws were written and that they stifle cooperation, innovation and employee participation. Democrats charged that Hoekstra had a pre-set agenda and was not holding open hearings; Republicans grumbled that he was missing a chance to publicize union abuses and had no clear legislative focus. Another assignment was investigating the Teamsters Union. Once again there were clear abuses: The 1996 election of Teamsters president Ron Carey had to be set aside in 1997 and the union treasury was found depleted of $150 million. But the Teamsters were unforthcoming with evidence and subpoena problems delayed the probe until 1998 when the requirement of subcommittee approval for every deposition and subpoena was dropped. Hoekstra would not hold publicized hearings: "I don't want to grandstand. It's the wrong thing to do." In early 1999 the leadership took the issue away from Hoekstra and gave it to committee chairman Bill Goodling. After he agreed with new president James P. Hoffa at a hearing that the Justice Department should lift its control of the union's operations, the Teamsters endorsed Hoekstra for reelection in the 2000 campaign; some Republicans were not amused. On other committee issues, he opposed the House's "straight A's" education bill in 1999 as more "big government" and not enough local control. And he showed up at Education Secretary Richard Riley's office to demand explanation of the Department's "slush fund." In 2001, Hoekstra took over the Select Education Subcommittee.

Hoekstra sponsored a law to insure federal funding for medical schools that refuse to teach abortion. And the House passed his bill to require that workers' W-2 forms list employers' payments for Social Security and Medicare. On foreign policy, he sometimes tends toward the liberal: he has voted against missile defense. Despite Chamber of Commerce local radio ads, he opposed permanent normal trade relations with China. Some of his proposals are quixotic: He has proposed a constitutional amendment to establish recall for members of Congress, nonbinding national referenda on issues and a "none of the above" choice in elections.

Hoekstra has remained active in Republican leadership politics. In November 1998 he ran for vice chairman of the House Republican Conference. But many Republicans wanted to have a woman in a leadership position, and he was eliminated on the second ballot. He was a leading supporter of J.C. Watts's successful bid for the Conference chairmanship, which resulted in Hoekstra getting the assignment to craft their House message for the next two years. After the 2000 election, he sought the chairmanship of the Education and the Workforce Committee, but he lost to John Boehner in the closed-door meetings of the Republican Steering Committee. During those discussions, Hoekstra unsuccessfully urged that the committee be divided into two parts with Hoekstra taking the education panel, so that it would be better prepared to handle George W. Bush's agenda; but party leaders were not keen on creating a new House committee. Earlier, he voiced interest in replacing John Kasich as Budget Committee chairman. Outside the House, Hoekstra voiced interest in running statewide in 2002. But a challenge of Senator Carl Levin would be uphill. Republican redistricters are likely to draw a similar, and still heavily Republican, Lake Michigan district.

Cook's Call *Safe.* As one of the most Republican districts in the state (Bush took 59% here) there is little competition for this seat from Democrats. Reverberations from the loss of one Michigan district will be felt throughout the state, but this seat is unlikely to change drastically.

THE PEOPLE: Pop. 2000: 686,086; Pop. 1990: 581,017, up 18.1% 1990–2000. 90.1% White, 4.4% Black, 1% Asian, 0.6% Amer. Indian, 1.6% Two+ races, 2.3% Other; 5% Hispanic Origin.

2000 Presidential Vote			1996 Presidential Vote		
Bush (R)	178,789	(59%)	Dole (R)	133,022	(50%)
Gore (D)	115,014	(38%)	Clinton (D)	108,242	(41%)
Nader (Green)	5,627	(2%)	Perot (I)	23,512	(9%)

Rep. Pete Hoekstra (R)

Elected 1992, 5th term; b. Oct. 30, 1953, Groningen, Netherlands; home, Holland; Hope Col., B.A. 1975, U. of MI, M.B.A. 1977; Reformed Church of America; married (Diane).

Professional Career: Furniture Exec., Herman Miller Co., 1977–92.

DC Office: 1124 LHOB 20515, 202-225-4401; Fax: 202-226-0779; Web site: www.house.gov/hoekstra.

District Offices: Cadillac, 231-775-0050; Holland, 616-395-0030; Muskegon, 616-722-8386.

Committees: *Budget* (3d of 24 R). *Education & the Workforce* (5th of 27 R): Employer-Employee Relations; Select Education (Chmn.). *Permanent Select Committee on Intelligence* (8th of 11 R): Human Intelligence, Analysis & Counterintelligence; Technical & Tactical Intelligence.

Group Ratings

	ADA	ACLU	AFS	LCV	CON	ITIC	NTU	COC	ACU	NTLC	CHC
2000	10	43	14	14	90	83	70	90	88	91	93
1999	5	—	0	6	79	—	68	88	88	—	—

National Journal Ratings

	1999 LIB —	1999 CONS		2000 LIB —	2000 CONS
Economic	0%	— 84%		29%	— 67%
Social	39%	— 60%		33%	— 66%
Foreign	10%	— 86%		39%	— 57%

Key Votes of the 106th Congress

1. Patient Bill of Rights	N	5. Bar RU-486 $ for FDA	Y	9. NATO War in Serbia	N
2. Accelerate Min. Wage	N	6. Display 10 Commandments	Y	10. Perm. Trade with China	N
3. Strike Ban on Ergo. Stnd.	N	7. Gun Show Bkgrnd. Checks	N	11. Debt Relief for 3rd World	N
4. Ovrd. Estate Tax Veto	Y	8. Ban Part.-Birth Abortion	Y	12. Drop Cuba Econ. Embargo	N

Election Results

2000 general	Pete Hoekstra (R)	186,762	(64%)	($291,642)
	Bob Shrauger (D)	96,370	(33%)	($171,728)
	Other	6,793	(2%)	
2000 primary	Pete Hoekstra (R)	unopposed		
1998 general	Pete Hoekstra (R)	146,854	(69%)	($210,118)
	Bob Shrauger (D)	63,573	(30%)	($98,380)
	Others	3,195	(2%)	

THIRD DISTRICT

Grand Rapids is Michigan's second-largest city, the center of its most prosperous and confident metropolitan area. The city's roots are in trees: It grew as a center for processing and turning into furniture the hardwood forests of northern Michigan. By the early 20th Century, Grand Rapids was the leading furniture manufacturer in the nation. But the Depression knocked the bottom out of the residential furniture market, and many manufacturers moved to cheaper-labor North Carolina. So Grand Rapids had to reinvent itself, and did. It went into office furniture, and today, three of the nation's largest office furniture manufacturers (Steelcase, Haworth and Herman Miller) are located in or near here. It capitalized also on a knack for retailing. Rich DeVos and Jay Van Andel started Amway, the direct sales empire, which now has half of its sales abroad, and Frederik and Hendrik Meijer started Meijer's Thrifty Acres, combining supermarkets with discount stores in a way that even Wal-Mart has not been able to equal. Grand Rapids is also the center of a machine tool empire. Fifty years ago Grand Rapids and its up-and-coming businesses were outshined by Detroit and the auto industry. Today, the Grand Rapids region has been growing rapidly and has been a major engine in Michigan's surging economy.

One ingredient in Grand Rapids' success is its unique ethnic mix. It was founded by New England Yankees, but much of its character was set by the Dutch immigrants who began arriving in western Michigan in the 1870s, and are still coming today; 23% of people here claim Dutch ancestry (probably no other city has as high a proportion of "V" pages in the phone book). The Dutch brought with them a piety witnessed in their Reform and Christian Reform churches, and a culture of hard work and precision craftsmanship; their cultural conservatism and belief in market economics runs deep. Dutch tradition and entrepreneurial success have been the ingredients of a civic activism that has given Grand Rapids a host of creative civic institutions that are the match of any city in the country.

Politically, Grand Rapids has been the center of Michigan Republicanism for most of the century. It has also produced national Republican leaders. Arthur Vandenberg, originally a newspaper editor, was U.S. senator from 1928–51; a one-time isolationist, he provided key support for the bipartisan internationalist foreign policies of Franklin Roosevelt and Harry Truman. Another was Gerald Ford, who rose to House Republican leader in 1965, vice president in 1973, and then president after Richard Nixon resigned in 1974. Nixon got a bit of a nudge from the Grand Rapids district when, in an early 1974 special election, it voted to replace Ford with a Democrat, a clear sign that the Republican heartland was turning on the president. Since then, however, the area became more Republican than ever; in 2000 Grand Rapids and Kent County voted 59% for George W. Bush.

The 3d Congressional District of Michigan includes all of Grand Rapids and Kent County, plus one and a half smaller counties east and southeast. It is the most Republican district in Michigan, indeed one of the most Republican in the Midwest, and has produced many Michigan Republican leaders—Lieutenant Governor Dick Posthumus, the party's likely candidate for governor in 2002, and Betsy DeVos, former state party chairman and sponsor of the school vouchers Proposal 1 in 2000.

The congressman from the 3d District is Vern Ehlers, chosen in a December 1993 special election. Ehlers grew up in small-town Minnesota, the son of a Christian Reform minister, attended Calvin College in Grand Rapids, got a Ph.D. in physics at Berkeley and then returned to Calvin to teach for 17 years. In 1974, concerned about local waste management, he was elected Kent County commissioner; in 1982 he won a seat in the state House and in 1986 the state Senate. After Congressman Paul Henry died in July 1993, Ehlers ran to succeed him, as he had in both houses of the legislature. In the November primary, Ehlers won with 33%; a month later he whipped the Democrat 67%–23%.

Ehlers brought to House Republicans, then entering their 40th year in the minority, a majority mindset. That brought him to the attention of Newt Gingrich, who named him to his transition team after the 1994 election. He assigned Ehlers, the first research physicist in Congress, to lead efforts to revamp the House's computer system. In 1995 Ehlers responded with a system making available vote tallies, public hearing transcripts and texts of amendments and bills. His religious faith and scientific training have left Ehlers with a middle-of-the-House voting record. He opposed Republicans' EPA riders on appropriations bills, opposed setting aside part of the Mojave National Reserve for hunting, and opposed the auto companies' proposal to freeze CAFE standards. As co-chairman of the Great Lakes Task Force, he called attention to water loss and diversion threats. As vice chairman of the Science Committee, he produced "Unlocking Our Future," the first major report on federal support of science in half a century, calling for "substantial and stable" science funding. He told Fermi Lab physicists, "It's a real indictment of the physics community that more of us haven't gotten involved." The House passed his bill to stop CB radios from operating beyond prescribed power so that they interfere with radio, television or cordless phones. He was named chairman in 2001 of the Science Subcommittee on Environment, which oversees the EPA and NOAA.

Ehlers has a penchant for compromise. As head of a three-member task force on Robert Dornan's challenge to his 984-vote defeat in 1996, Ehlers looked over the evidence and announced that it showed "a large amount" of vote fraud but not enough to vacate the seat. That may help explain why Speaker Dennis Hastert bypassed him and selected Bob Ney to chair the House Administration Committee after the 2000 election.

Ehlers refuses to take more than 30% of his campaign money from outside the district. He has been re-elected by very wide margins. Redistricting will not likely pose serious problems.

Cook's Call   *Safe.* This Grand Rapids-based district has been staunchly Republican for years. In fact, this was one of Bush's best performing districts in the state (he won by 21 %). One redistricting plan has 8th District Rep. Mike Rogers biting into eastern portions of this district to help make the 8th more reliably Republican. Still, this seat will stay safely in Republican hands and Ehlers will have no troubles winning in 2002.

THE PEOPLE: Pop. 2000: 662,041; Pop. 1990: 580,874, up 14% 1990–2000. 84.5% White, 8.2% Black, 1.7% Asian, 0.5% Amer. Indian, 0.1% Hawaiian, 2.1% Two+ races, 3% Other; 6.4% Hispanic Origin.

2000 Presidential Vote		
Bush (R)	169,928	(59%)
Gore (D)	109,736	(38%)
Nader (Green)	5,757	(2%)
Others	1,478	(1%)

1996 Presidential Vote		
Dole (R)	135,759	(53%)
Clinton (D)	99,698	(39%)
Perot (I)	17,583	(7%)

Rep. Vernon J. Ehlers (R)

Elected Dec. 1993, 4th term; b. Feb. 6, 1934, Pipestone, MN; home, Grand Rapids; Calvin Col., 1952–55; U. of CA at Berkeley, A.B. 1956, Ph.D. 1960, U. of Heidelberg, Germany, 1961–62; Christian Reformed; married (Johanna).

Elected Office: Kent Cnty. Comm., 1975–82, Chmn., 1978–81; MI House of Reps., 1982–86; MI Senate, 1986–93, Pres. Pro Tem, 1990–93.

Professional Career: Prof., Calvin Col., 1966–82.

DC Office: 1714 LHOB 20515, 202-225-3831; Fax: 202-225-5144; Web site: www.house.gov/ehlers.

District Office: Grand Rapids, 616-451-8383.

Committees: *Education & the Workforce* (16th of 27 R): 21st Century Competitiveness; Education Reform. *House Administration* (2d of 6 R). *Science* (11th of 25 R): Energy; Environment, Technology and Standards (Chmn.). *Transportation & Infrastructure* (10th of 42 R): Aviation; Water Resources & Environment.

Group Ratings

	ADA	ACLU	AFS	LCV	CON	ITIC	NTU	COC	ACU	NTLC	CHC
2000	20	29	0	64	34	94	63	80	64	59	87
1999	20	—	0	38	63	—	69	96	60	—	—

National Journal Ratings

	1999 LIB —	1999 CONS		2000 LIB —	2000 CONS
Economic	0%	—	84%	46%	—	52%
Social	46%	—	54%	49%	—	51%
Foreign	46%	—	53%	51%	—	47%

Key Votes of the 106th Congress

1. Patient Bill of Rights	N	5. Bar RU-486 $ for FDA	Y	9. NATO War in Serbia	N
2. Accelerate Min. Wage	Y	6. Display 10 Commandments	Y	10. Perm. Trade with China	Y
3. Strike Ban on Ergo. Stnd.	N	7. Gun Show Bkgrnd. Checks	N	11. Debt Relief for 3rd World	Y
4. Ovrd. Estate Tax Veto	Y	8. Ban Part.-Birth Abortion	Y	12. Drop Cuba Econ. Embargo	N

Election Results

2000 general	Vernon J. Ehlers (R)	179,539	(65%)	($302,826)
	Timothy Steele (D)	91,309	(33%)	($26,024)
	Other	5,415	(2%)	
2000 primary	Vernon J. Ehlers (R)	unopposed		
1998 general	Vernon J. Ehlers (R)	146,364	(73%)	($346,312)
	John Ferguson Jr. (D)	49,489	(25%)	($10,406)
	Others	4,398	(2%)	

FOURTH DISTRICT

Flat and treeless for miles, the central reaches of Michigan's Lower Peninsula are farm country, exposed to bitter winds and snow drifts in winter and shining sun for precious weeks in summer. Like the steppes of Eastern Europe, these are farmlands that produce hearty crops: potatoes, navy beans, sugar beets. The little cities here are often small factory towns, with neat tree-lined streets on a grid layout that suddenly end and turn to bare fields. Each city has some distinction. Midland in 1891 was a declining lumber town when Herbert Dow perfected an electrolytic process to extract chemicals from northern Michigan's extensive brine wells; that was the start of Dow Chemical, still headquartered in this now upscale town. Owosso in 1902 was the birthplace of Thomas E. Dewey, later New York governor and Republican candidate for president in 1944 and 1948. It was also the home of novelist James Oliver Curwood and his Curwood Castle writing studio; today it hosts the Curwood Festival, lovingly chronicled by Thomas Mallon in *Rockets and Rodeos*, and is the site of Mallon's novel *Dewey Defeats Truman*. Mount Pleasant, to the north, is the site of Central Michigan University; it is the home base of Governor John Engler.

The 4th Congressional District of Michigan includes much of this territory north of Lansing and Grand Rapids and west of Flint and Saginaw. It stretches north up the freeways, where thousands drive in fall to hunt and in winter to ski, into the rolling country around Houghton Lake, once lumber country and now a retirement and resort area, with trailers and condominiums between knotty-pine cottages clustered around icy green lakes. It has the most farms of any district in Michigan. Politically, it remains mostly Republican territory, though retirees from the Detroit area and commuters to Flint and Saginaw have brought in some Democratic tendencies. The district gave small pluralities to Bill Clinton in 1992 and 1996, but voted more solidly for George W. Bush in 2000.

The congressman from the 4th District is Dave Camp, a Republican first elected in 1990. Camp grew up in Midland and returned there after school to practice law. In 1984 he managed the successful congressional campaign of his boyhood friend Bill Schuette; in 1990 Schuette unsuccessfully ran against Senator Carl Levin, and Camp ran for Congress. His key victory was in the Republican primary, where with 62% in Midland County he beat former legislator and Pat Robertson supporter Al Cropsey, 33%–30%. He has won since without difficulty.

Camp has a generally conservative voting record and is influential on the Ways and Means Committee, where he has been an ally of new chairman Bill Thomas. He played a key role in passing welfare reform in 1996, helping to write the two bills vetoed by Bill Clinton. In July 1996 he and Nevada freshman John Ensign circulated a letter signed ultimately by about 100 Republicans urging that they separate their welfare and Medicaid reforms, which had been passed as one bill, and vote on welfare reform alone, daring Bill Clinton to sign it and make history, or veto it and make it a campaign issue. Newt Gingrich and the Republican leadership decided to do this, essentially disengaging House Republicans from the fate of the flagging Bob Dole presidential campaign. The bill passed, Clinton signed it, and the incumbent president and incumbent congressional Republicans got credit in November.

Camp has worked on other issues. He co-sponsored the 1996 Adoption and Safe Families Act, making the safety and best interests of the child paramount to family preservation, and helping foster children gain adoption. In 2000, he continued that work by gaining enactment of the Intercountry Adoption Act, which designates the State Department to help adoptive parents in dealing with officials in other nations. "We have a responsibility to establish international standards," said Camp, who handled adoptions as an attorney. He authored the Organ Donor Card Insert Act, under which 70 million taxpayers received organ donor information with their income tax refunds. Medicare reforms enacted in 2000 included his provisions to provide permanent drug coverage for transplant recipients and to improve reimbursement for kidney dialysis patients. He pushed for tax breaks for electric cars and against the designation of Lake Champlain as a Great Lake. The Water Resources Development Act in 2000 included Camp's provision to ensure that sales of Great Lakes water will remain under state management. With Democrat Tim Roemer, he has led unsuccessful efforts to defund the space station: "The space station is simply a floating lemon that will cost 24 times its weight in pure gold." But he and Roemer won House approval to dedicate to debt reduction any unused funds from its members' office accounts. On the ethics committee, he chaired the investigation into Representative Corinne Brown financial dealings with an African businessman, which concluded that she used "poor judgment" but dropped the inquiry because of an inability to obtain evidence from the foreigners.

Camp has had minimal opposition in the 4th District. Redistricting could give him pieces of current Democratic districts, but it's not likely to threaten Camp.

Cook's Call *Safe.* While not the most Republican district in the state (Bush won by 8 %), Dave Camp has had little trouble racking up big margins of victory here. Camp has never won with less than 63%.

THE PEOPLE: Pop. 2000: 651,347; Pop. 1990: 580,890, up 12.1% 1990–2000. 94.9% White, 1.7% Black, 0.6% Asian, 0.7% Amer. Indian, 1.3% Two + races, 0.7% Other; 2.2% Hispanic Origin.

2000 Presidential Vote		
Bush (R)	147,302	(53%)
Gore (D)	124,554	(45%)
Nader (Green)	5,700	(2%)
Others	1,528	(1%)

1996 Presidential Vote		
Clinton (D)	112,625	(47%)
Dole (R)	98,215	(41%)
Perot (I)	28,350	(12%)

Rep. Dave Camp (R)

Elected 1990, 6th term; b. July 9, 1953, Midland; home, Midland; Albion Col., B.A. 1975, U. of San Diego Law Schl., J.D. 1978; Catholic; married (Nancy).

Elected Office: MI House of Reps., 1988–90.

Professional Career: Practicing atty., 1978–90; MI Special Asst. Atty. Gen., 1980–84; A.A., U.S. Rep. Bill Schuette, 1984–87.

DC Office: 137 CHOB 20515, 202-225-3561; Fax: 202-225-9679; Web site: www.house.gov/camp.

District Offices: Houghton Lake, 517-422-7792; Midland, 517-631-2552; Owosso, 517-723-6759.

Committees: *Ways & Means* (8th of 24 R): Health; Human Resources; Trade.

Group Ratings

	ADA	ACLU	AFS	LCV	CON	ITIC	NTU	COC	ACU	NTLC	CHC
2000	5	38	0	7	27	100	59	90	84	76	79
1999	15	—	0	0	17	—	58	96	79	—	—

National Journal Ratings

	1999 LIB —	1999 CONS		2000 LIB —	2000 CONS
Economic	29%	70%		18%	76%
Social	29%	69%		34%	65%
Foreign	28%	70%		25%	69%

Key Votes of the 106th Congress

1. Patient Bill of Rights	N	5. Bar RU-486 $ for FDA	Y	9. NATO War in Serbia	N
2. Accelerate Min. Wage	N	6. Display 10 Commandments	Y	10. Perm. Trade with China	Y
3. Strike Ban on Ergo. Stnd.	N	7. Gun Show Bkgrnd. Checks	N	11. Debt Relief for 3rd World	N
4. Ovrd. Estate Tax Veto	Y	8. Ban Part.-Birth Abortion	Y	12. Drop Cuba Econ. Embargo	N

Election Results

2000 general	Dave Camp (R)	182,128	(68%)	($1,026,361)
	Lawrence Hollenbeck (D)	78,019	(29%)	($6,099)
	Other	7,672	(3%)	
2000 primary	Dave Camp (R)	unopposed		
1998 general	Dave Camp (R)	155,343	(91%)	($654,061)
	Dan Marsh (Lib)	10,404	(6%)	
	Others	4,362	(3%)	

FIFTH DISTRICT

Saginaw Bay, the inlet of Lake Huron that separates Michigan's Thumb (people really call it that) from the mitten of its Lower Peninsula, was for a moment in the 1870s the site of the greatest flow of lumber in the United States. There were 36 sawmills in Bay City then, and logs were piled high along both banks of the Saginaw River for miles. Bay City and Saginaw, 15 miles upstream, handled logs from the wide area on both sides of Saginaw Bay drained by the Saginaw River and its tributaries. Saginaw was also a center of precision machinery manufacturing, one reason General Motors put its huge power steering plants here. But starting in 1979 GM payrolls fell, and for a while the Saginaw area foundered. More recently, small high-skill manufacturing operations have grown up in old factory buildings once considered worthless; this is part of southern Michigan's industrial belt with the expertise to sustain just-in-time manufacturing. There also is agriculture here: The flat, broad fields around Saginaw Bay that once held so many trees are the nation's leading producer of navy beans (the official ingredient of U.S. Senate bean soup) and among the leaders in sugar beets, though sugar beet producers recently have plowed under part of their crops because of surpluses from Canada.

The 5th Congressional District of Michigan includes Saginaw and Bay City and lands on both sides of Saginaw Bay. To the north it goes up past Oscoda on Lake Huron, where the 1993 closing of Wurtsmith Air Force Base resulted in a local economic boom rather than a bust as new employers were attracted and property sold readily. To the east it includes most of the Thumb. To the south it reaches to the city limits of Flint, including both black and white working-class townships just north of the city. Bay City, with its large Polish population, has long been Democratic and, since the auto industry woes of the 1980s, so are Saginaw and the Flint suburbs. While the 5th has been trending Democratic, the Thumb remains among the most Republican parts of Michigan: Al Gore won the district 53%–45% in 2000, but George W. Bush carried the four Thumb counties 55%–42%.

The congressman from the 5th District is Jim Barcia, a Democrat elected in 1992. Barcia grew up in Bay City, went to Saginaw Valley State College, and has always lived in the area. He held political staff jobs and was elected to the state House in 1976, at age 24, and the state Senate in 1982. Barcia was known in the legislature for his whistleblower protection law, and he was not an automatic vote for unions or management. In 1992 he had opposition from state Senator John Cherry of Saginaw, who had strong backing from organized labor, and from Don Hare, district staffer for incumbent Bob Traxler, who was retiring. Barcia, with 72% in Bay County, won overall with 46%, to 29% for Cherry and 25% for Hare. Barcia won the general 60%–38%.

Barcia has a moderate, middle-of-the-House voting record that places him among the more conservative Democrats, although he has not been vocal in his independence. He supported the balanced budget constitutional amendment and the line-item veto; he opposed the 1994 Clinton health care plan, NAFTA and permanent normal trade relations with China. (This has long been a protectionist area: Saginaw Congressman "Sugar Beet Joe" Fordney sponsored the nation's highest tariffs ever in 1922.) He voted to override Bill Clinton's veto of the estate tax repeal.

Barcia serves on Transportation and Infrastructure, and supported the huge transportation bill of 1998; he worked with Vern Ehlers to change the funding formula and increase Michigan's share from $512 million to $825 million. He included water supply infrastructure earmarks for the town of Bad Axe, defending against charges of pork barrel spending by saying, "If this is pork, pass the platter." He attacked EPA for giving grants to a Flint group that also was trying to stop a new 200-job steel mill. Outraged by attacks on constituents, he got approval of a resolution urging all states to keep violent offenders in prison for at least 85% of their sentences. With Republican Steve Chabot, he cosponsored the "victims' rights" constitutional amendment to allow victims to confront defendants and seek restitution. An avid hunter, he opposes additional gun restrictions. As a leading House opponent of abortion, Barcia organized 1999 meetings with the National Right to Life Committee that left lingering anger among Democrats; he also sought to rescind a Health and Human Services Department ruling to permit federally-financed research on human embryonic stem cells.

Barcia has been re-elected by wide margins; in 2000 he won 83% of the vote in Bay County.

Republicans control redistricting, and Michigan has lost one House seat. Barcia can easily hold in general elections any district that includes Bay City and Saginaw, but he could face a problem if redistricters combine those two with Flint, the home base of 9th District Democrat Dale Kildee, whose record is somewhat more liberal but who also opposes abortion. Another alternative, which also would cause problems for Barcia, would be for redistricters to merge Bay City and its environs with Bart Stupak's 1st District.

Cook's Call *Potentially Competitive.* Jim Barcia, who has never been elected with less than 60%, may have his first tough contest since he won this Democratic leaning seat in 1992: Republicans control the redistricting process in the state and Barcia's district is one of the slowest growing (it needs to pick up about 75,000 people). One scenario has Barcia's Saginaw-based seat drawn in with David Bonior's 10th District. Another plan has Genesse and parts of Saginaw combined in one district that would force Barcia to run against 9th District Democrat Dale Kildee.

THE PEOPLE: Pop. 2000: 587,031; Pop. 1990: 580,981, up 1% 1990–2000. 87.3% White, 8.6% Black, 0.5% Asian, 0.5% Amer. Indian, 1.6% Two+ races, 1.5% Other; 3.8% Hispanic Origin.

2000 Presidential Vote			1996 Presidential Vote		
Gore (D)	136,936	(53%)	Clinton (D)	155,995	(57%)
Bush (R)	117,214	(45%)	Dole (R)	90,107	(33%)
Nader (Green)	4,668	(2%)	Perot (I)	27,477	(10%)

Rep. Jim Barcia (D)

Elected 1992, 5th term; b. Feb. 25, 1952, Bay City; home, Bay City; Saginaw Valley St. U., B.A. 1974; Catholic; married (Vicki).

Elected Office: MI House of Reps., 1976–82, Majority Whip, 1979–82; MI Senate, 1982–92.

Professional Career: Staff Asst., U.S. Sen. Philip Hart, 1971; Comm. Svc. Coord., MI Comm. Blood Ctr., 1974–75; A.A., MI Rep. Donald Albosta, 1975–76.

DC Office: 2419 RHOB 20515, 202-225-8171; Fax: 202-225-2168; Web site: www.house.gov/barcia.

District Offices: Bay City, 517-667-0003; Flushing, 810-732-7501; Saginaw, 517-754-6075.

Committees: *Science* (4th of 22 D): Environment, Technology and Standards (RMM). *Transportation & Infrastructure* (12th of 34 D): Coast Guard & Maritime Transportation; Economic Development, Public Buildings & Emergency Management; Highways & Transit.

Group Ratings

	ADA	ACLU	AFS	LCV	CON	ITIC	NTU	COC	ACU	NTLC	CHC
2000	40	43	71	50	38	56	46	57	56	40	67
1999	55	—	100	50	47	—	18	52	52	—	—

National Journal Ratings

	1999 LIB —	1999 CONS		2000 LIB —	2000 CONS
Economic	58%	41%		54%	46%
Social	44%	55%		37%	62%
Foreign	49%	50%		58%	40%

Key Votes of the 106th Congress

1. Patient Bill of Rights	Y	5. Bar RU-486 $ for FDA	Y	9. NATO War in Serbia	Y
2. Accelerate Min. Wage	Y	6. Display 10 Commandments	Y	10. Perm. Trade with China	N
3. Strike Ban on Ergo. Stnd.	N	7. Gun Show Bkgrnd. Checks	N	11. Debt Relief for 3rd World	Y
4. Ovrd. Estate Tax Veto	Y	8. Ban Part.-Birth Abortion	Y	12. Drop Cuba Econ. Embargo	Y

Election Results

2000 general	Jim Barcia (D)	184,048	(74%)	($202,688)
	Ronald Actis (R)	59,274	(24%)	($18,089)
	Other	4,415	(2%)	
2000 primary	Jim Barcia (D)	unopposed		
1998 general	Jim Barcia (D)	135,254	(71%)	($183,629)
	Donald Brewster (R)	51,442	(27%)	($7,220)
	Others	3,275	(2%)	

SIXTH DISTRICT

The southwest corner of Michigan is at the western end of the overland trail from Detroit, where the state's two southern tiers of counties were settled by New England Yankees and Upstate New Yorkers in the 1830s and 1840s. They built small towns with schools and churches and colleges, supported temperance and opposed capital punishment, and in 1854 started the Republican Party. There are towns in southwest Michigan that still recall proudly their past as termini of the Underground Railroad, and black families with ancestors who made their way north out of slavery to freedom. Later, big industries transformed some of the small towns into significant cities: Kalamazoo, started by Dutch-Americans who introduced celery to this country, became the home of Upjohn pharmaceuticals; Benton Harbor and St. Joseph, twin towns on Lake Michigan originally known for cherry and peach orchards, became the home of Whirlpool appliances. This southwest corner is where the influence of Michigan recedes: People here watch Chicago television and root for the Cubs or White Sox rather than the Tigers.

The 6th Congressional District of Michigan occupies this southwest corner of the state, with Kalamazoo and Benton Harbor-St. Joseph its two major urban areas, and three smaller counties besides. It was for many years arch-Republican territory, represented by a succession of congressmen who deplored federal spending and welfare state measures: New Deal opponent Clare Hoffman (1935–63), Nixon defender Edward Hutchinson (1963–77), and pork barrel critic and later Reagan Office of Management and Budget Director David Stockman (1977–81). More recently, Kalamazoo trended toward the Democrats, and the 6th cast small pluralities for Bill Clinton in 1992 and 1996. But George W. Bush and Senator Spencer Abraham won here in 2000, despite losing statewide.

The current congressman from the 6th District is Fred Upton. The grandson of one of the founders of Whirlpool, Upton grew up in St. Joseph, attended the University of Michigan and worked for David Stockman, first on his House staff, then from 1981–85 at OMB. He returned home and challenged Congressman Mark Siljander, a conservative and evangelical Christian, in the 1986 Republican primary, and won 55%–45%. Upton is less like the congressional David Stockman, a scourge of federal spending, and more like the OMB Stockman, who rued the Reagan tax cuts. He has a moderate voting record and an impulse toward bipartisanship. He voted for the Brady bill and the national service bill, and in January 1993 resigned as deputy whip. He worked for bipartisan bills on interstate waste shipments, Superfund and health care, and with John Dingell on nuclear waste; their bill for an interim central waste disposal site in Nevada passed the House and Senate, but died in 2000 when the Senate fell just short of overriding Bill Clinton's veto.

Upton has been anything but a team player in the Republican House. He has sought, with limited success, to use his leverage to reduce the size of tax cuts. He called for making Republican tax cuts in 1995 contingent on certification by the Clinton OMB that the budget was on a realistic path toward being balanced in 2002; as it turned out, the budget was balanced four years earlier than that target, at which point Upton based his tax-cutting caution on the need to pay down the debt. He voted against some Republican environmental bills and called for a lifetime ban on former members' lobbying for foreign governments. Looking back at his experience with Stockman, Upton said, "We don't want to make the historic mistake we made in the '80s." Referring to the moderate Republicans Tuesday Group, he said, "Our group was responsible for the positive agenda" at the end of 1996 on welfare reform and the Safe Drinking Water Act.

After that election, Upton decried the "shut-down, dark ages" approach taken by Republicans and said his party had come to be seen as "narrow" and "intolerant." He spoke out against John Kasich's proposed budget cuts in 1998. He backed the bill named for Mo Udall, earmarking $100 million for Parkinson's disease research; Muhammad Ali, who testified for it, has lived in Berrien Springs in the district. He got money for dredging the St. Joseph River and, showing an old "I drive U.S. 31—pray for me" bumper sticker, money for completing the U.S. 31 freeway in Berrien County. In December 1998, the Clinton White House hoped Upton would vote against impeachment, but in the final days he decided to vote for it.

Seniority increased Upton's prominence at the renamed Energy and Commerce Committee. In the 106th Congress, he chaired the Oversight and Investigations Subcommittee, where his topics of inquiry ranged from the exposing the funding scandal of the Salt Lake City Olympic games to the Firestone-Bridgestone tire scandal, on which he worked with Billy Tauzin to pass a modest package of safety reforms. Following the 2000 election, he became chairman of the Telecommunications Subcommittee, though he preferred to take the Health Subcommittee. He planned to focus on education and workplace issues: technology in the classroom and community, and keeping America competitive. He endorsed the Tauzin-Dingell bill to allow regional telephone operators to provide broadband service more easily. He opposed a tax on broadcasters who delay converting to digital service, but he did support a revamped e-rate to wire all classrooms. Meanwhile, Upton pressed his efforts at bipartisanship, helping to organize a new House coalition of moderates from each party. Conservatives were unhappy that he opposed the Michigan school-choice referendum in 2000.

Upton considered but rejected running for the Senate in 1994 and 1996. He had one serious primary challenge from a conservative in 1990, but otherwise has won re-election easily. Stuck in a corner of the state, he's not likely to see big change in redistricting.

Cook's Call *Safe*. This district has deep Republican heritage, electing a Republican to the House since the 1930s. Still, this is not the most Republican district in the state as Bush won with just 52% here. Upton, who has never won with less than 62%, should have no troubles in 2002.

THE PEOPLE: Pop. 2000: 610,640; Pop. 1990: 580,973, up 5.1% 1990–2000. 85.2% White, 9.6% Black, 1.2% Asian, 0.5% Amer. Indian, 1.9% Two+ races, 1.6% Other; 3.6% Hispanic Origin.

2000 Presidential Vote			1996 Presidential Vote		
Bush (R)	125,796	(52%)	Clinton (D)	103,454	(46%)
Gore (D)	111,217	(46%)	Dole (R)	99,975	(44%)
Nader (Green)	5,910	(2%)	Perot (I)	19,967	(9%)

Rep. Fred Upton (R)

Elected 1986, 8th term; b. Apr. 23, 1953, St. Joseph; home, St. Joseph; U. of MI, B.A. 1975; Protestant; married (Amey).

Professional Career: Project coord., U.S. Rep. David Stockman, 1975–80; Legis. Affairs, O.M.B., 1981–83, Dir., 1984–85.

DC Office: 2333 RHOB 20515, 202-225-3761; Fax: 202-225-4986; Web site: www.house.gov/upton.

District Offices: Kalamazoo, 616-385-0039; St. Joseph, 616-982-1986.

Committees: *Education & the Workforce* (14th of 27 R): 21st Century Competitiveness; Education Reform. *Energy & Commerce* (4th of 31 R): Commerce, Trade & Consumer Protection; Health; Telecommunications & The Internet (Chmn.).

Group Ratings

	ADA	ACLU	AFS	LCV	CON	ITIC	NTU	COC	ACU	NTLC	CHC
2000	25	7	0	29	83	94	61	85	60	76	80
1999	25	—	0	44	85	—	65	92	68	—	—

National Journal Ratings

	1999 LIB —	1999 CONS	2000 LIB —	2000 CONS
Economic	0% —	84%	41% —	58%
Social	42% —	56%	53% —	46%
Foreign	23% —	73%	53% —	45%

Key Votes of the 106th Congress

1. Patient Bill of Rights	N	5. Bar RU-486 $ for FDA	N	9. NATO War in Serbia	N
2. Accelerate Min. Wage	Y	6. Display 10 Commandments	Y	10. Perm. Trade with China	Y
3. Strike Ban on Ergo. Stnd.	N	7. Gun Show Bkgrnd. Checks	Y	11. Debt Relief for 3rd World	N
4. Ovrd. Estate Tax Veto	Y	8. Ban Part.-Birth Abortion	Y	12. Drop Cuba Econ. Embargo	Y

Election Results

2000 general	Fred Upton (R)	159,373	(68%)	($620,512)
	James Bupp (D)	68,532	(29%)	
	Other	6,735	(3%)	
2000 primary	Fred Upton (R)	unopposed		
1998 general	Fred Upton (R)	113,292	(70%)	($600,617)
	Clarence J. Annen (D)	45,358	(28%)	($14,943)
	Others	2,977	(2%)	

SEVENTH DISTRICT

The small cities and towns spotting the southern-tier farmland counties of Michigan have been incubators of innovation since they were settled by Yankees from New England 150 years ago. The state's public school system was established by two politicians from Marshall, whose hopes to make it the state capital were dashed. A few miles away, in Battle Creek, sanitarium operator W.K. Kellogg invented corn flakes as a health food; he and his one-time patient, C.W. Post, both established factories in the late 19th Century and created the American breakfast cereal industry. To the south is Hillsdale, where Hillsdale College has been proudly admitting blacks and women since the 1850s and refusing all federal aid; but it was touched by scandal in 1999 when college president George Roche resigned after the suicide of his daughter-in-law with whom he was having an affair. Politically, this area has been Republican territory since 1854, when the party was founded in the manufacturing and prison town of Jackson as a kind of reformist institution out of the same activist impulse that produced local support for women's rights and Prohibition and opposition to the death penalty. Southern Michigan mostly rejected New Deal tinkering and was hostile to the UAW, but the people here were receptive to moral claims made by later 20th Century reformers challenging racial segregation, the Vietnam war and the Watergate coverup.

The 7th Congressional District of Michigan covers all of six counties and parts of two others in Michigan's southern tier. It typically votes Republican, but not always: Bill Clinton carried the district by small pluralities in 1992 and 1996, but it returned to the ancestral fold and voted for George W. Bush in 2000.

The congressman from the 7th District is Nick Smith, a Republican who won the seat in 1992 after it was greatly altered by redistricting. Smith is a dairy farmer in Hillsdale County who was elected to the Somerset Township Board in 1962 after his wife "told me to get involved or stop complaining." He was elected to the state House in 1978 and state Senate in 1982. In 1992, the 7th had a brawling primary between Smith and fellow state Senator John Schwarz of Battle Creek. Smith boasted of his 1992 property tax freeze and anti-abortion record and attacked Schwarz for raising money in Washington and from PACs while he took no PAC money. Smith won 43%–36%.

In the House Smith has worked on agriculture and local issues but has been most prominent as an advocate of Social Security reform. Back in 1995 he came forward, a self-starter, with a plan to allow workers to put 2.3% of their 12.4% payroll tax into a private account that could be invested in stocks, and to raise the retirement age in steps to 69. Around his district and to anyone in Washington who would listen, Smith showed his Social Security proposal charts. He persevered after Bill Clinton in early 1999 torpedoed efforts at Social Security reform and was buoyed by the availability of budget surpluses to pay for transition costs. When Smith started talking about Social

Security reform, his was a lonely and obscure voice. But others, including some Democrats, have taken up the cause, and in 2000 George W. Bush made his own similar plan one of his major campaign issues. Now it is possible that Smith's initiative, or something very much like it, could become law.

On most issues Smith has taken a conservative stand, but he sometimes casts lonely votes on principle. He backed the Freedom to Farm Act and supported a bipartisan agriculture research program in 1998. In the bankruptcy reform bill he put a provision preventing parents from evading their child support debts to governments and in 2000 he sponsored renewal of Chapter 12, the bankruptcy provision for farmers, when the larger bankruptcy reform bill was foundering because of Bill Clinton's veto threat. He has sought to make commodities-hedging more accessible to farmers. He was one of 10 House Republicans to vote against the Republican prescription drug bill in June 2000 and one of four House members to vote against allowing futures contracts on individual stocks in October 2000. He voted against the railroad retirement act in September 2000, on the grounds that it was too big an item to be considered on suspension calendar. Such independence may be one reason he got nowhere in his attempt to win the Budget Committee chairmanship in December 2000.

Smith chairs the Research Subcommittee of the Science Committee. In April 2000 he issued a "Seeds of Technology" report on genetically modified organisms (GMOs), which are hugely controversial in Europe. He pointed out that biotechnology products include insulin, growth factors in bone marrow transplants, products for treating heart attacks, diagnostic tests for AIDS and hepatitis and enzymes used in food production, and concluded, "Biotechnology has incredible potential to enhance nutrition, feed a growing world population, open up new markets for farmers and reduce the environmental impact of farming." He argues that the risks of GMOs are no greater than those for similar plants bred by traditional methods, and that current FDA procedures are sufficient to ensure safety.

Smith has had some serious competition in the 7th District. In 1996 his Democratic opponent outspent him on television, and held him to a 55%–43% victory, much less than expected. In 1998 he was challenged by state Senator Jim Berryman, who attacked Smith's Social Security reform. Joining in the chorus were AFL-CIO ads calling for saving Social Security first, before any tax cuts. Smith won 57%–40%, a better showing than in 1996, and carried every county including, by a narrow margin, Berryman's home base. In 2000, against weaker opposition, Smith was re-elected 61%–36%. Redistricting could alter the shape of the 7th District and, though Republicans are in control, could weaken Smith's position. The reason is that the neighboring 8th District is exceedingly closely divided; Republican freshman Mike Rogers won there by just 160 votes in 2000. Taking some of heavily Democratic Lansing out of the 8th and putting it in the 7th would greatly strengthen Rogers, and probably would not endanger Smith. But it might stimulate stronger opposition for Smith than he received in 2000.

Cook's Call   *Probably Safe.* While this conservative district is about as Republican as the neighboring 6th District (Bush won here by 5%), Smith has not racked up the large margins of victory as Fred Upton, though he has never dropped below 55%. Smith's southern Michigan district needs to pick up about 40,000 people and he remains the favorite in 2002.

THE PEOPLE: Pop. 2000: 620,053; Pop. 1990: 581,005, up 6.7% 1990–2000. 89.7% White, 6.1% Black, 0.7% Asian, 0.5% Amer. Indian, 1.7% Two+ races, 1.3% Other; 3.3% Hispanic Origin.

2000 Presidential Vote

Bush (R)	129,858	(51%)
Gore (D)	115,670	(46%)
Nader (Green)	5,210	(2%)
Others	1,512	(1%)

1996 Presidential Vote

Clinton (D)	105,185	(46%)
Dole (R)	99,518	(43%)
Perot (I)	24,501	(11%)

Rep. Nick Smith (R)

Elected 1992, 5th term; b. Nov. 5, 1934, Addison; home, Addison; MI St. U., B.A. 1957, U. of DE, M.S. 1959; Congregationalist; married (Bonnalyn).

Military Career: Air Force, 1959–61.

Elected Office: Somerset Township Trustee, 1962–68, Supervisor, 1966–68; Hillsdale Cnty. Bd. of Supervisors, 1966–68; MI House of Reps., 1978–82; MI Senate, 1982–92, Pres. Pro-Tem, 1983–90.

Professional Career: Businessman, farmer; Hillsdale Cnty. Repub. Chmn., 1966–68; MI Chmn., Agricultural Stabilization and Conservation Svc., 1969–72; Natl. Energy Dir., U.S. Dept. of Agriculture, 1972–74; MI Occup. Safety Standards Comm., 1975.

DC Office: 2305 RHOB 20515, 202-225-6276; Fax: 202-225-6281; Web site: www.house.gov/nicksmith.

District Offices: Battle Creek, 616-965-9066; Jackson, 517-783-4486.

Committees: *Agriculture* (5th of 27 R): General Farm Commodities & Risk Management. *International Relations* (20th of 26 R): Europe; Western Hemisphere. *Science* (9th of 25 R): Environment, Technology and Standards; Research (Chmn.).

Group Ratings

	ADA	ACLU	AFS	LCV	CON	ITIC	NTU	COC	ACU	NTLC	CHC
2000	10	14	20	7	69	94	68	84	91	88	73
1999	10	—	0	19	87	—	64	79	84	—	—

National Journal Ratings

	1999 LIB	—	1999 CONS		2000 LIB	—	2000 CONS
Economic	0%	—	84%		33%	—	66%
Social	37%	—	61%		35%	—	64%
Foreign	31%	—	66%		25%	—	69%

Key Votes of the 106th Congress

1. Patient Bill of Rights	N	5. Bar RU-486 $ for FDA	Y	9. NATO War in Serbia	N
2. Accelerate Min. Wage	N	6. Display 10 Commandments	Y	10. Perm. Trade with China	Y
3. Strike Ban on Ergo. Stnd.	*	7. Gun Show Bkgrnd. Checks	N	11. Debt Relief for 3rd World	N
4. Ovrd. Estate Tax Veto	Y	8. Ban Part.-Birth Abortion	Y	12. Drop Cuba Econ. Embargo	N

Election Results

2000 general	Nick Smith (R)	147,369	(61%)	($112,467)
	Jennie Crittendon (D)	86,080	(36%)	($3,753)
	Other	7,561	(3%)	
2000 primary	Nick Smith (R)	unopposed		
1998 general	Nick Smith (R)	104,656	(57%)	($605,528)
	Jim Berryman (D)	72,998	(40%)	($458,229)
	Others	4,473	(2%)	

EIGHTH DISTRICT

Lansing is Michigan's state capital, chosen in 1847 because of its geographic position halfway between Lake Huron and Lake Michigan and in ignorance of the fact that it has fewer days with sunshine than any place else in the state. But it is a tidy and pleasant city with more than its share of amenities. It has a beautifully restored Capitol and a fine state history museum and is neighbor to Michigan State University in East Lansing, started in 1855 as America's first land-grant college. Its Oldsmobile plant stimulated growth in the first half of the 20th Century, and state government did the same in the second half. GM in December 2000 announced it would close the Olds line with the 2002 Bravada sports utility vehicle, but two new GM assembly plants have been under construction in the Lansing area and the Oldsmobile name will remain alive at two local museums and a baseball stadium for the Lansing Lugnuts. Lansing has tended to go with the party controlling state government. When the legislature was apportioned to stay Republican, as it was until 1964, the Lansing area was usually Republican; Democrats have had majorities in the state House in 28 of the 38 years since and Lansing has voted mostly Democratic. Grateful for the local support, Bill Clinton's farewell campaign tour stopped at the Michigan State campus.

The 8th Congressional District of Michigan includes Lansing and Ingham County but not the Lansing suburbs just across the line in Republican-leaning Clinton and Eaton Counties, which are, respectively, in the 4th and 7th Districts. The 8th has two other very different population centers. One is the suburban fringe southwest of Flint, an area long Democratic and in deep trouble in the past two decades with the General Motors shutdown there. The other is Livingston County, where I-96 crosses U.S. 23. Strewn with lakes and hills, this has been one of the fastest-growing counties in Michigan; its many new residents left the Detroit area because they disliked the crime, high taxes and liberal politics they found there. Livingston is very conservative and Republican, though becoming a bit less so as the population grows: in 1992 and 1996 it was Clinton's second and third worst county in Michigan, and it was Al Gore's sixth worst in 2000. Such politically disparate areas leave the 8th District closely balanced, and it has switched parties in three of the last four elections.

The congressman from the 8th District is now Mike Rogers, a Republican elected in 2000. He grew up in Brighton in Livingston County, and earned a Bachelor's degree in sociology and criminal justice from Adrian College, a small liberal arts school in Southeastern Michigan. He was commissioned by the ROTC as commander of an Army rapid deployment unit. Next, he graduated from the FBI Academy, and became a special agent in Chicago for six years before returning to Michigan in 1994 and winning election to the state Senate. In 1999 he was selected to be majority floor leader, where he handled pieces of John Engler's legislative program. He continued his interest in law enforcement, passing his bill to increase the penalty for using the Internet to facilitate sex crimes. Rogers also founded a business, E.B.I. Builders, along with his brothers and father in 1994.

When Democrat Debbie Stabenow gave up the 8th District seat to run successfully for the Senate, Rogers and Democrat Dianne Byrum, a fellow state senator, waged one of the closest and most-watched open-seat campaigns in the country: forecaster Charlie Cook predicted that this could be the closest race in the country, and it was. The race remained tight throughout the campaign and polls consistently showed the contest within the margin of error. Each candidate raised about $2 million; neither faced primary opposition. Because Michigan was also a presidential and senatorial battleground, the two candidates had plenty of outside help; in the final two weeks alone, Lansing campaigners included Laura and Barbara Bush, Bob Dole, John McCain, and Tipper Gore. Byrum had something of an advantage in that her state Senate district in Ingham County included nearly half of the 8th District, while Rogers's Senate seat in Livingston covered less than a third.

In the end, this contest was closer than the presidential race in Florida and it took even longer to count the final tally. Byrum conceded on December 15, and Rogers won by 160 votes. But the race was anything but even in the different parts of the district. Byrum carried her base of Ingham County by a 58%–40% margin and won by 53%–45% in Genesee County. Rogers carried his base of Livingston County by 64%–34%, running 5% ahead of George W. Bush, and led 51%–45% in the three partial outlying counties. Rogers apparently benefited from a state law he sponsored requiring college students to vote at the address on their driver's license; that prevented many Michigan State students from voting in East Lansing. Rogers won points for his promise to build coalitions with Democrats and avoid partisan bickering. This attitude led Democrat Sylvia McCollough, his 1998 state Senate opponent, to endorse him. Rogers describes his political philosophy as consistent with George W. Bush's "compassionate conservatism." He pledged to work to improve education by making schools more accountable to parents and allowing more local control. He also promised to work to improve health care by pushing a patients bill of rights and holding HMOs more accountable to patients. He refused to endorse John McCain's campaign-finance bill, worried that it might disrupt the President's agenda.

Redistricting will be critical here in 2002. Republicans control the redistricting process, and will surely try to make this a more Republican district. One way would be to pare off part of

Lansing or Ingham County and to remove the Genessee portion as well. Another would be to move the district eastward into Oakland County townships that lean Republican. But there are limits on what Republicans can do, and Republican incumbents in the 4th and 7th Districts will not want to have too many Lansing Democratic precincts in their districts. This could easily be a seriously contested district again in 2002.

Cook's Call   *Competitive.* One of the biggest goals for Republicans, who control the line drawing process here, is to help shore up freshman Republican Mike Rogers in this very marginal district. Rogers won this Lansing-area seat by just 160 votes and Gore carried the district by 3 %. Regardless of how the new lines are drawn, however, Rogers is not an easy target. The affable, politically savvy Rogers defeated the best candidate Democrats had to offer in 2000.

THE PEOPLE: Pop. 2000: 658,695; Pop. 1990: 581,072, up 13.4% 1990–2000. 87.7% White, 6.2% Black, 2.3% Asian, 0.5% Amer. Indian, 2% Two+ races, 1.3% Other; 3.4% Hispanic Origin.

2000 Presidential Vote			1996 Presidential Vote		
Gore (D)	153,417	(50%)	Clinton (D)	135,653	(49%)
Bush (R)	143,575	(47%)	Dole (R)	111,811	(40%)
Nader (Green)	7,237	(2%)	Perot (I)	25,949	(9%)
Others	1,908	(1%)			

Rep. Mike Rogers (R)

Elected 2000, 1st term; b. June 2, 1963, Livingston Cnty.; home, Brighton; Adrian Col., B.A. 1985; Methodist; married (Diane).

Military Career: Army, 1985–88.

Elected Office: MI Senate, 1995–2000, Maj. Floor Ldr., 1999–2000.

Professional Career: Co-founder, E.B.I. Builders, 1985; FBI Spec. Agent, 1988–94.

DC Office: 509 CHOB 20515, 202-225-4872; Fax: 202-225-5820; Web site: www.house.gov/mikerogers.

District Office: Lansing, 517-702-8000.

Committees: *Financial Services* (36th of 37 R): Capital Markets, Insurance & Government Sponsored Enterprises; Financial Institutions & Consumer Credit; Housing & Community Opportunity. *Transportation & Infrastructure* (28th of 42 R): Economic Development, Public Buildings & Emergency Management; Highways & Transit.

Group Ratings and Key Votes: Newly Elected

Election Results

2000 general	Mike Rogers (R)	145,179	(49%)	($2,195,500)
	Dianne Byrum (D)	145,019	(49%)	($2,093,216)
	Other	7,335	(2%)	
2000 primary	Mike Rogers (R)	unopposed		
1998 general	Deborah Ann Stabenow (D)	125,169	(57%)	($996,148)
	Susan Grimes Munsell (R)	84,254	(39%)	($125,971)
	Others	8,617	(4%)	

NINTH DISTRICT

General Motors was formed in 1908 as a merger of several smaller car companies; headquartered in Detroit, it had plants in small cities in Michigan and Ohio. Foremost among these cities were Flint and Pontiac, two industrial county seats on the old Woodward Avenue route that led northwest from Detroit. Pontiac, named for the 18th Century Indian chief who sparked a rebellion that spread all the way to what is now Pittsburgh, produced Pontiacs and GMC Trucks; Flint, named for the flint from which Indians made arrowheads, produced Buicks and Chevrolets. For five decades after 1918, Flint and Pontiac grew lustily, attracting new workers from the mountains of Kentucky and Tennessee and the Black Belt of Alabama; country and black music and Southern accents became common in towns originally settled by Yankees. There was turmoil, too. Flint was the scene in January 1937 of the great sitdown strike that, when Governor Frank Murphy refused to send the National Guard to enforce a court order, forced GM to recognize the United Auto Workers as the bargaining agent for all its workers. Yet in many ways these GM company towns built good lives for their citizens. The UAW-GM contracts produced the world's highest wages for industrial workers and lavish fringe benefits, including a generous health care plan. The Mott Foundation, started by GM's largest shareholder, Charles Stewart Mott, funded schools, including a university branch in Flint, and historical exhibitions—an exemplary plowing-back of money into a one-industry town.

Disaster struck starting in the late 1970s. Auto sales plummeted with the oil shock of 1979, and imports, especially from Japan, that were higher-quality and lower-price than American cars, were taking an increasing share of the market. GM managers and UAW leaders assumed that increased labor costs could be passed along to consumers, that buyers were indifferent to quality and eager for new models. Those assumptions proved vitally wrong: not even the cleverest advertising could persuade Americans to buy a new American car every two years. In 1979 GM employed more than 70,000 workers in its Flint plants, a huge share of the labor force in a metro area of 430,000 people; by the early 1990s GM employment was down significantly and the old Buick City assembly plant was closed in 1999. Over the years thousands left Flint and by 2000 the GM payroll was down to 22,000. Those who stayed found their real estate values—the store of wealth for most Americans—stagnant, and government attempts to develop an upscale shopping mall, a Hyatt hotel and the AutoWorld theme park went bankrupt. Flint is fighting for self-esteem again, the *Chicago Tribune* wrote in May 2000. "It has taken the last two decades of auto plant closings and double-digit unemployment rates, of population loss and white flight, of dwindling tax coffers and diminished philanthropic funding, for it to work through its grief."

Pontiac was also hurt in the late 1980s and early 1990s when GM closed plants there, but Pontiac has some advantages. The Detroit metro area has expanded, and surrounding Oakland County gained over 140,000 jobs in the 1980s, mainly in services and retail. Chrysler built its new headquarters along I-75 in Auburn Hills just east of Pontiac, GM converted its truck and coach plant into research offices and I-75 became the main street for a newly lean and efficient auto industry and its nimble just-in-time suppliers.

The 9th Congressional District of Michigan runs from Flint to Pontiac and takes in diverse political territory. It includes the city of Flint and its suburbs to the southeast; this Genesee County portion has about one-third of the district's people and is heavily Democratic. Pontiac, about half black, is heavily Democratic but is only 12% of the district. Lake-strewn Waterford Township to the west, where many Pontiac whites moved when a school busing plan was ordered in the 1970s, has grown and leans Republican. Auburn Hills and Rochester Hills east of Pontiac are high-income and heavily Republican. Clarkston and other burgeoning communities to the north, are heavily Republican. Lapeer County, north of Pontiac and east of Flint, also has been growing and has long been Republican. That means that about half the district is solidly Democratic, with a long union heritage; the other half is Republican, in some places very much so.

The congressman from the 9th District is Dale Kildee, a Democrat first elected in 1976. Kildee grew up in Flint, studied for the priesthood, taught at a Catholic high school in Detroit and at Flint Central. His door-to-door campaigning got him elected to a state legislative seat in 1964, at 35, and enabled him to beat a 26-year veteran of the state Senate in 1974. He won the House seat in 1976, when it was solidly Democratic, without a primary opponent and held it easily until the 1990s. Kildee has an intensity of conviction derived from the liberal tradition lively in the American Catholic church—a tradition with little regard for market economics and a strong sense of obligation to care for the needy. He is always pro-union and he is against abortion and something of a stickler on ethics and attendance. In late October 2000, he unintentionally broke his string of 8,141 consecutive votes, the longest in the House, while he worked on details of an education deal; his previous missed vote was in October 1985 when he had a bleeding ulcer.

Kildee is now a senior member of the Education and the Workforce and Resources Committees. He is a strong ally of teachers' unions, a backer of increased federal aid for education and an opponent of school choice. He and Buck McKeon in 1998 cooperated in lowering interest rates on student loans from 7.8% to 7% for students. He worked with Education ranking member George Miller on the Democratic education proposal in 2001, which would increase funding and school accountability, but did not include any funds for private schools. He has fought against reducing federal standards on special education students.

On other issues, Kildee was the first House member to argue imported minivans should be subject not to the 2.5% tariff for cars but to the 25% tariff for trucks, and was a strong opponent of NAFTA. With John Dingell he opposed the FTC proposal to reduce to 75% the American content required for a Made in U.S.A. label. On Resources, he has concentrated on Indian issues. Kildee can remember as a child traveling to the Grand Traverse reservation, where his grandfather had traded with Indians, and hearing his father talk of the Indians' plight. He took to visiting reservations and noting how the Bureau of Indian Affairs spruced them up for his visits; Kildee carries with his copy of the Constitution a copy of the 1832 Supreme Court decision that recognized Indian sovereignty. He set up with J.D. Hayworth of Arizona a Native American Caucus with more than 80 members. In 1999, he worked to narrowly defeat a House amendment to prevent the Interior secretary from arbitrating alternative procedures for gaming compacts between tribes and states.

Kildee has had serious challenges in the new 9th District, in which 60% of the votes are cast in Oakland County. Against former Bush/Quayle advance staffer Megan O'Neill, whom he vastly outspent, Kildee won by just 54%–45% in 1992 and 51%–47% in 1994. His margins have rebounded since then. In 2000 he won 61%–36%, carrying Genesee County 80%–19% and Oakland County 52%–44%. But now that he has become solidly entrenched, the lines are bound to be changed by redistricting. Republicans control the redistricting process, and Michigan lost one House seat in the 2000 Census. One option for redistricters would be to combine Kildee's Flint base with the Bay City-Saginaw base of the 5th District's Jim Barcia. This would pit two Democrats against each other in a heavily Democratic seat, and leave the outlying territory in Republican-leaning seats. Kildee has vowed to run again from his base in Flint, which would make him a strong contender in just about any conceivable district.

Cook's Call *Potentially Competitive.* After a number of close calls following redistricting in 1991, Kildee looks to have solidified his hold here. But, redistricting in 2001 could once again put Kildee in the hot seat: one scenario has Kildee's district pushed together with Jim Barcia's 5th. Still, the 71-year old Kildee has indicated that he intends to run, regardless of where the lines are drawn.

THE PEOPLE: Pop. 2000: 633,553; Pop. 1990: 580,908, up 9.1% 1990–2000. 76.9% White, 17.3% Black, 1.9% Asian, 0.4% Amer. Indian, 2% Two+ races, 1.4% Other; 3.8% Hispanic Origin.

2000 Presidential Vote
Gore (D) 142,311 (52%)
Bush (R) 123,236 (45%)
Nader (Green) 4,792 (2%)
Others 1,874 (1%)

1996 Presidential Vote
Clinton (D) 95,473 (46%)
Dole (R) 89,538 (43%)
Perot (I) 21,567 (10%)

Rep. Dale E. Kildee (D)

Elected 1976, 13th term; b. Sept. 16, 1929, Flint; home, Flint; Sacred Heart Seminary, B.A. 1952, U. of MI, M.A. 1961, Rotary Fellow, U. of Peshawar, Pakistan; Catholic; married (Gayle).

Elected Office: MI House of Reps., 1964–74; MI Senate, 1974–75.

Professional Career: High schl. teacher, 1954–64.

DC Office: 2107 RHOB 20515, 202-225-3611; Fax: 202-225-6393; Web site: www.house.gov/kildee.

District Offices: Flint, 810-239-1437; Pontiac, 248-373-9337.

Committees: *Education & the Workforce* (2d of 22 D): Education Reform (RMM); Employer-Employee Relations. *Resources* (4th of 25 D): Forests & Forest Health; National Parks, Recreation & Public Lands.

Group Ratings

	ADA	ACLU	AFS	LCV	CON	ITIC	NTU	COC	ACU	NTLC	CHC
2000	75	57	100	79	38	44	20	42	20	9	33
1999	90	—	100	94	37	—	20	20	12	—	—

National Journal Ratings

	1999 LIB —	1999 CONS	2000 LIB —	2000 CONS
Economic	88%	— 0%	81%	— 16%
Social	55%	— 44%	56%	— 43%
Foreign	63%	— 36%	58%	— 40%

Key Votes of the 106th Congress

1. Patient Bill of Rights	Y	5. Bar RU-486 $ for FDA	Y	9. NATO War in Serbia	Y
2. Accelerate Min. Wage	Y	6. Display 10 Commandments	N	10. Perm. Trade with China	N
3. Strike Ban on Ergo. Stnd.	Y	7. Gun Show Bkgrnd. Checks	Y	11. Debt Relief for 3rd World	Y
4. Ovrd. Estate Tax Veto	N	8. Ban Part.-Birth Abortion	Y	12. Drop Cuba Econ. Embargo	N

Election Results

2000 general	Dale E. Kildee (D)	158,184	(61%)	($307,376)
	Grant Garrett (R)	92,926	(36%)	($104,366)
	Other	7,818	(3%)	
2000 primary	Dale E. Kildee (D)	unopposed		
1998 general	Dale E. Kildee (D)	105,457	(56%)	($394,037)
	Tom McMillin (R)	79,062	(42%)	($209,050)
	Others	4,006	(2%)	

TENTH DISTRICT

Macomb County, Michigan, on the billiard-table-flat shore of Lake St. Clair just northeast of Detroit, has been one of the nation's most closely watched political battlegrounds, a place where the electoral fate of Michigan and even the entire country might be determined. But its reputation is no longer quite accurate: more people hold white-collar jobs than blue-collar these days and far fewer work in auto plants than in earlier generations; there are plenty of affluent subdivisions—the average new house prices is around $240,000—and boat ownership may well be the highest in the country. Macomb County is the product of the post-World War II boom: With just over 107,000 people in 1940, many in the old sulphur-water spa town of Mount Clemens, Macomb passed the 400,000 mark in 1960 and 600,000 by 1970; in 2000 it reached 788,000. Many people came here from Detroit: Polish-Americans marching out Van Dyke from Hamtramck to Warren; Italian-Americans heading out Gratiot from Detroit's east side to Roseville and Clinton Township; Belgian-Americans from the Mack corridor moving out farther to St. Clair Shores. These new suburbanites were heavily Catholic, often blue-collar, at least modestly affluent and ancestrally Democratic. They accepted the New Deal as part of their natural heritage but resented the efforts of Detroit politicians to tax them to pay for welfare, and they were fearful of the high crime rates in Detroit's black neighborhoods. Indeed, the suburb of East Detroit voted to change its name to Eastpointe to avoid any implication it was part of the central city.

In 1960, Macomb County was the most Democratic major suburban county in the United States, voting 63% for America's first Catholic president, John F. Kennedy. For three decades afterwards Macomb was moving away from the national Democrats—in 1962 because they would let Detroit tax suburbanites, in 1972 because they didn't vehemently oppose a metropolitan school busing plan. From 1976 through 1992, no Democratic presidential candidate got more than 40% of the vote here. In 1996, after great effort and with the advice of his sometime pollster Stan Greenberg, who has studied Macomb closely, Bill Clinton carried Macomb County by a 49%–39% margin; in 2000 Al Gore carried it by 50%–48%—pretty close to the national average. At the same time, Republican Senator Spencer Abraham, who carried the county 56%–36% in 1994, lost here to his successor Debbie Stabenow 49%–48%. But if Democrats have made gains, Macomb is still competitive country. Democrats still hold most county and legislative offices in Macomb, but not all.

The 10th Congressional District of Michigan includes most of Macomb County (all but the southwest corner) and takes in Port Huron and St. Clair County to the northeast. In the House it has been represented for a quarter-century by David Bonior, the Democratic whip since 1991. Bonior grew up in East Detroit (as it then was called), the grandson of Polish and Ukrainian immigrants; he became a seminarian in high school, had an athletic scholarship to the University of Iowa where he played football, worked as a probation officer and social worker in Mount Clemens and served in the Air Force stateside in the Vietnam era (he came to oppose the war). His father was a printer and auto worker who became mayor of East Detroit; it is his loss of that office in 1967 that Bonior refers to as his family's brush with unemployment. Bonior never became a priest, but he remains in accord with liberal strains of Catholic thought and liberation theology; he is against abortion, though he has voted with most Democrats against the anti-abortion "gag rule" and for fetal tissue research. In 1972 he was elected to the Michigan House, and in 1976, when Congressman James O'Hara ran for the Senate, Bonior ran for the U.S. House. He had a knack for symbolism: that winter an ice storm killed many Macomb County trees, and in response he gave out thousands of pine seedlings as a campaign gimmick. This struck a chord with gun-toting sportsmen and baby-boomer environmentalists alike, and by now he has handed out more than 400,000 seedlings.

Bonior brings to his work a great intensity and passion. Like many Catholic admirers of liberation theology, he opposed aid to the Nicaraguan Contras and El Salvador government. It was Bonior's deep convictions and determination that got him appointed chief deputy whip in 1986. He did not move up the leadership ladder immediately: William Gray beat him for whip in June 1989, 134–97, after Speaker Jim Wright and Whip Tony Coelho resigned. But when Gray retired in June 1991, Bonior beat Maryland's Steny Hoyer 160–109. And after Speaker Thomas Foley lost his House seat in 1994, Dick Gephardt became minority leader and Bonior won the minority whip post by 145–60 over Charles Stenholm. One of Bonior's great crusades was against Newt Gingrich. He led Democrats to file over 70 ethics charges against Gingrich, some arguably serious, many entirely without merit. After Gingrich left the House in early 1999, Bonior seemed a bit abashed at the negative image he had gained after his Ahab-like chase of Gingrich. He reached out to Blue Dog Democrats, traveled to campaign and fundraise for colleagues (as far as Guam!), worked on advancing the minimum wage bill, a measure that united Democrats and split Republicans, and established a good working relationship with Speaker Dennis Hastert, even though Minority Leader Dick Gephardt and Hastert were not speaking for most of 2000.

Bonior sees himself representing a forgotten and scorned blue-collar working class at home. With Marcy Kaptur of Ohio, he was one of the most passionate opponents of NAFTA, arguing it was "basically the sellout of [American] workers." He opposed fast-track trade authority despite the pleadings of Bill Clinton, and called for more labor and environmental protections in trade agreements. He led the fight against permanent normal trade relations with China in 2000; "I care deeply about labor rights and the environment. I've built my whole career around these principles, and human rights," he said. "The advocates of this trade deal tell us that prosperity is a precondition for democracy. And with all due respect, they're wrong. They have to grow together." Bonior has also taken a principled stand against the use of secret evidence by the INS against alleged terrorists and others; in December 2000 he called on Attorney General Janet Reno to resign because she detained two men for years based on secret evidence, Bonior called her actions "Gestapo-like tactics." He proposed a bill to bar such use of secret evidence, with John Conyers and Republicans Tom Campbell and Bob Barr. He worked with an even more unlikely colleague, Republican Dan Burton, in urging appointment of an envoy to broker the Kashmir conflict, a move hailed by Pakistani-Americans. Bonior was the co-sponsor with Jim Rogan of a resolution condemning the Turks' massacre of Armenians during World War I; Rogan got a commitment from Hastert to bring it to the floor in October 2000, but Hastert reneged after phone calls from Bill Clinton, Madeleine Albright, William Cohen and General Hugh Shelton, who feared a rupture of relations with Turkey.

Bonior's principled stands and political crusades have put him at risk in a district that has often voted Republican for other offices. In 1996, state Republican Susy Heintz attacked Bonior as a "whiny, wacky, wimpy, wasteful, worn-out, washed-up, windbag whip." With a huge financial advantage, Bonior won 54%–44%. In 1998, against self-made businessman Brian Palmer, and again with a 2–1 financial advantage, Bonior won 52%–45%. In 2000 Republican Governor John Engler made great efforts to run a strong opponent against Bonior. Secretary of State Candice Miller agreed in August 1999, and was leading Bonior in 46%–36% in one poll. But she dropped out of the race nine days later. Engler tried to recruit others, with no luck. With only nuisance opposition, Bonior won 64%–33%.

But on the same day Engler's Republicans held onto control of the state House, and thus control the redistricting process for 2002. Engler was widely believed to have Bonior as his first target. It would be easy to make the 10th District significantly more Republican: Just remove the Macomb suburbs from the Detroit city limit at Eight Mile Road up to Eleven or Twelve Mile Road and add them to one of Detroit's population-losing districts, and you will have removed most of the 10th District's heavily Democratic precincts. In May 2001 Bonior announced he was running for governor in 2002. "I can say there's been a generally favorable and encouraging response to it so far," he said, but also admitted that redistricting was a factor in his decision; "I can't say that it had no impact." It started off looking like an uphill race. Bonior is less well-known statewide than two other possible candidates, former Governor Jim Blanchard and Attorney General Jennifer Granholm. But he can expect strong support from Michigan's unions and has good relations with Arab Americans, who form a larger percentage of the population in Michigan than in any other state. He said he will finish his term as minority whip; that will presumably lead to a race between Nancy Pelosi (a Bonior ally) and Steny Hoyer, who were both planning to run for majority whip if the Democrats had won a majority in the House in November 2000. As for the 10th District, the outcome depends on redistricting, but whether Bonior runs for re-election or not this could well be a Republican gain.

Cook's Call *Highly Competitive.* Bonior has been a burr under the saddle for Republicans for years. Although this district is very marginal (Bush and Gore tied here with 49%), and Republicans have attempted a number of all out assaults to try and oust Bonior, he continues to survive. But Bonior's decision to run for governor in 2002 and the fact that Republicans control the line drawing process in the state, gives Republicans a huge opportunity to finally get their hands on this seat. Insiders say that Republicans will be working hard to create a district that is tailor-made for Republican Secretary of State Candice Miller who flirted with running in this district in 2000.

THE PEOPLE: Pop. 2000: 671,306; Pop. 1990: 580,974, up 15.5% 1990–2000. 93.9% White, 2.8% Black, 1% Asian, 0.4% Amer. Indian, 1.4% Two+ races, 0.5% Other; 1.8% Hispanic Origin.

2000 Presidential Vote			1996 Presidential Vote		
Bush (R)	144,587	(49%)	Clinton (D)	120,921	(49%)
Gore (D)	143,675	(49%)	Dole (R)	96,592	(39%)
Nader (Green)	5,343	(2%)	Perot (I)	27,083	(11%)
Others	2,288	(1%)			

Rep. David E. Bonior (D)

Elected 1976, 13th term; b. June 6, 1945, Detroit; home, Mt. Clemens; U. of IA, B.A. 1967, Chapman Col., M.A. 1972; Catholic; married (Judy).

Military Career: Air Force, 1968–72.

Elected Office: MI House of Reps., 1972–76.

Professional Career: Probation officer, adoption caseworker, 1967–68.

DC Office: 2207 RHOB 20515, 202-225-2106; Fax: 202-226-1169; Web site: davidbonior.house.gov.

District Offices: Mt. Clemens, 810-469-3232; Port Huron, 810-987-8889.

Committees: *Minority Whip.*

Group Ratings

	ADA	ACLU	AFS	LCV	CON	ITIC	NTU	COC	ACU	NTLC	CHC
2000	100	64	100	93	55	28	16	23	8	12	27
1999	90	—	100	100	12	—	13	16	4	—	—

National Journal Ratings

	1999 LIB —	1999 CONS	2000 LIB —	2000 CONS
Economic	88%	0%	95%	0%
Social	66%	33%	66%	33%
Foreign	89%	8%	80%	16%

Key Votes of the 106th Congress

1. Patient Bill of Rights	Y	5. Bar RU-486 $ for FDA	N	9. NATO War in Serbia	Y
2. Accelerate Min. Wage	Y	6. Display 10 Commandments	N	10. Perm. Trade with China	N
3. Strike Ban on Ergo. Stnd.	Y	7. Gun Show Bkgrnd. Checks	Y	11. Debt Relief for 3rd World	Y
4. Ovrd. Estate Tax Veto	N	8. Ban Part.-Birth Abortion	Y	12. Drop Cuba Econ. Embargo	Y

Election Results

2000 general	David E. Bonior (D)	181,818	(64%)	($2,312,101)
	Tom Turner (R)	93,713	(33%)	($21,123)
	Other	6,738	(2%)	
2000 primary	David E. Bonior (D)	31,835	(89%)	
	Mario Fundaro (D)	2,137	(6%)	
	Anthony America (D)	1,708	(5%)	
1998 general	David E. Bonior (D)	108,770	(52%)	($1,477,749)
	Brian Palmer (R)	94,027	(45%)	($734,291)
	Others	4,727	(2%)	

ELEVENTH DISTRICT

Oakland County, Michigan, long considered just a suburban adjunct of Detroit, is now the center of a giant, spread-out, affluent urban area. It is only minutes on the Lodge Freeway from the empty, abandoned blocks of inner-city Detroit; but suddenly, north of the Eight Mile Road boundary, there are giant office buildings and multiplying small businesses, expensive houses on large lots and one shopping mall after another, high education levels and low crime rates. Even physically there is a distinction between the two areas: Detroit is on almost perfectly flat land, while many of the Oakland County suburbs run along a line of hills and lakes that marks the southernmost advance of an Ice Age glacier. Southfield, in southern Oakland County, is Michigan's largest office space center, far ahead of Detroit; Troy is another big office center, with upscale malls that compete with high-income Birmingham; new development proliferates around Novi and Northville, north of Eight Mile Road. In 1950, Detroit had 1.9 million people and Oakland County 396,000. In 2000, Oakland had 1.2 million and Detroit 951,000. Oakland County Executive Brooks Patterson, one of the state's most prominent Republicans, complains that Oakland supplies much of the state's economic growth but gets back less than 75 cents for each dollar it pays in state taxes.

The 11th Congressional District of Michigan includes almost half of Oakland County plus the comfortable Wayne County suburbs of Redford Township and Livonia, west of Detroit. This is mostly high-income Republican territory, where people generally believe in free market economics and fiercely oppose higher taxes. It is also home to most of the Detroit area's Jewish community, which has moved out the Lodge first to Southfield and then to West Bloomfield and scattered in most of these suburbs. Jewish voters and affluent blacks who have moved to Southfield and other suburbs, form the district's chief Democratic bloc and hold down the Republican percentages. Voters here tend to support gun control and abortion rights—positions shared by few Michigan Republicans. Those issues and new Democratic voters enabled Bill Clinton to carry the 11th District in 1996 and Al Gore to carry Oakland County by 49%–48% in 2000. To be sure, that was a narrow margin; but without a good-sized margin in Oakland, Republicans cannot hope to carry Michigan.

The congressman from the 11th District is Joe Knollenberg, a Republican first elected in 1992. Knollenberg grew up the fifth child in a family of 13 on a farm in Downstate Illinois, went to college in Illinois and became an insurance agent. He moved to Oakland County in 1967 and became involved in civic affairs and Republican politics. When Republican William Broomfield retired in 1992 after 36 years in office—all in the minority—Knollenberg ran. With Broomfield's support and that of Michigan Right To Life, he was able to win the primary with 43% of the vote. He won the general election easily.

Knollenberg entered the House as a junior member of the minority. But in two years, with a change in control, he became a member of Appropriations advancing some cutting-edge ideas. He moved to zero out funding for the statistics required for CAFE standards and managed to zero out funding for implementation of the 1997 Kyoto treaty until it is ratified by the Senate. He argues that the treaty is "fatally flawed" and based on "immature science," and notes that the exemption for developing nations will put Michigan at a disadvantage in trade. Knollenberg has been a strong supporter of NAFTA, fast track and PNTR for China; Michigan is the fourth-largest exporter among states. He calls for Social Security reform, by using a portion of the budget surplus to establish individual investment accounts.

Knollenberg is chief sponsor of the Plumbing Standards Improvement Act, to repeal the 1992 law which reduced the waterflow in toilets from 3.5 to 1.6 gallons per flush; toilet makers, eager for more sales and uniformity among states, supported that law, but Knollenberg points out that the new toilets often do not perform adequately and require extra flushing, which sort of defeats the purpose. In April 2000 the bill was beaten 13–12 in subcommittee, when two Republicans from water-thirsty districts defected. Later that year Knollenberg objected to the Energy Department's proposed regulations on washing machines, which would outlaw inexpensive top-loading washers. Knollenberg has used his seat on Appropriations to legislate on other issues. In 1999 he got EPA nitrous oxide regulations delayed until litigation on the issue is complete. He charged that the 1994 Agreed Framework on nuclear energy with North Korea is being violated. In 1999 he provided for early disbursement of aid to Israel and added $60 million for resettlement of refugees there; in 2000 he called for $250 million to rebuild south Lebanon. He has pointed out that 20% of U.S. electricity comes from nuclear power and says, "The prospect of new nuclear construction in the not-too-distant future is no longer just wishful thinking." He backed efforts to use U-223 isotopes in Alpha Particle Immunotherapy cancer research.

On local issues, he and John Dingell co-sponsored the $10 million National Automobile Heritage Area in southeast Michigan. In 1998 he sponsored a bill to recognize the Swan Creek Black River Confederated Ojibwa Indians as a tribe separate from the Saginaw Chippewa tribe, which owns a big casino. "This bill is about justice that has been put off for over 100 years," he said, although opponents argue that its goal is to set up a casino in Hazel Park Harness Raceway in southern Oakland County. He has helped obtain $580,000 to repair the embankment on the Rouge River in Southfield and $450,000 for Detroit River projects.

Knollenberg was re-elected easily three times. In 2000 against a vigorous but lightly-financed opponent who campaigned for gun control, abortion rights and HMO regulation, he won by only

56%–41%, a sharp decline from other elections. But any problems he has may be solved by Republican redistricters, who could shape the district much more to his favor by adding Southfield to one of the Detroit districts and adding heavily Republican Plymouth and Northville in Wayne County. After the election Knollenberg became chairman of the District of Columbia Appropriations Subcommittee, and thus a member of the House's college of cardinals.

Cook's Call   *Safe.* Although Knollenberg has never had a tough race here, this district, like so many former Republican stronghold suburban districts, has been trending toward Democrats over the last 10 years. Though Bush won the district by 10% in 1992, Clinton won the district by one point in 1996 and Gore tied with Bush here in 2000 with 49%. With Republicans in control of the redistricting process in the state, look for some line drawing that will help to shore up Knollenberg.

THE PEOPLE: Pop. 2000: 640,548; Pop. 1990: 580,934, up 10.3% 1990–2000. 84.7% White, 8.9% Black, 4.1% Asian, 0.2% Amer. Indian, 1.7% Two+ races, 0.4% Other; 1.6% Hispanic Origin.

2000 Presidential Vote

Gore (D)	157,533	(49%)
Bush (R)	156,635	(49%)
Nader (Green)	5,612	(2%)
Others	2,156	(1%)

1996 Presidential Vote

Clinton (D)	134,344	(46%)
Dole (R)	131,571	(46%)
Perot (I)	19,322	(7%)

Rep. Joseph Knollenberg (R)

Elected 1992, 5th term; b. Nov. 28, 1933, Mattoon, IL; home, Bloomfield Township; E. IL U., B.S. 1955; Catholic; married (Sandie).

Military Career: Army, 1955–57.

Professional Career: Insurance agent, 1958–92.

DC Office: 2349 RHOB 20515, 202-225-5802; Fax: 202-226-2356; Web site: www.house.gov/knollenberg.

District Offices: Farmington Hills, 248-851-1366; Livonia, 734-425-7557.

Committees: *Appropriations* (15th of 35 R): District of Columbia (Chmn.); Foreign Operations & Export Financing; VA, HUD & Independent Agencies.

Group Ratings

	ADA	ACLU	AFS	LCV	CON	ITIC	NTU	COC	ACU	NTLC	CHC
2000	0	21	0	0	6	94	60	90	80	61	87
1999	5	—	0	0	37	—	55	92	80	—	—

National Journal Ratings

	1999 LIB	—	1999 CONS		2000 LIB	—	2000 CONS
Economic	0%	—	84%		6%	—	85%
Social	25%	—	72%		23%	—	74%
Foreign	49%	—	50%		25%	—	69%

Key Votes of the 106th Congress

1. Patient Bill of Rights	N	5. Bar RU-486 $ for FDA		9. NATO War in Serbia	Y
2. Accelerate Min. Wage	N	6. Display 10 Commandments	Y	10. Perm. Trade with China	Y
3. Strike Ban on Ergo. Stnd.	N	7. Gun Show Bkgrnd. Checks	N	11. Debt Relief for 3rd World	N
4. Ovrd. Estate Tax Veto	Y	8. Ban Part.-Birth Abortion	Y	12. Drop Cuba Econ. Embargo	N

Election Results

2000 general	Joseph Knollenberg (R)	170,790	(56%)	($1,104,909)
	Matthew Frumin (D)	124,053	(41%)	($207,948)
	Other	11,459	(4%)	
2000 primary	Joseph Knollenberg (R)	unopposed		
1998 general	Joseph Knollenberg (R)	144,264	(64%)	($992,746)
	Travis M. Reeds (D)	76,107	(34%)	($16,294)
	Others	5,433	(2%)	

TWELFTH DISTRICT

The flat expanse of land just north of Eight Mile Road, Detroit's northern city limit, was mostly vacant in the years just after World War II. A string of suburbs in Oakland County ran along Woodward Avenue, Detroit's main street, where Henry Ford drove his first prototype in 1896, and which led to the Shrine of the Little Flower church in Royal Oak. There, in the 1930s, Father Charles Coughlin made his radio broadcasts backing and then opposing Franklin Roosevelt and denouncing bankers and Jews. In the 1950s and 1960s Woodward was one of America's greatest cruising highways, where teenagers drove big Detroit cars up and down the eight lanes where the lights were timed at 42 miles per hour and zoomed into its drive-in restaurants—an era commemorated annually since 1994 with the Woodward Dream Cruise of old cars, which drew 1.2 million people in 1999. To the east in Macomb County was some industrial development along Van Dyke, but this was mostly empty land, too; Detroit's population was heading toward two million. Today, these areas are well-settled suburbs, long since built up, a few neighborhoods edging toward seediness, many others continually renovated and restored. Almost half of metro Detroit's population is now north of Eight Mile, in communities drawing on old traditions but crackling with economic creativity.

The 12th Congressional District of Michigan is in this suburban territory, with its population roughly divided in the two suburban counties. On the Oakland County side are Royal Oak and other Woodward Avenue suburbs, now attracting singles and gays as well as families; Oak Park, heavily Jewish in the 1950s and now perhaps the only small city in America with sizable numbers of Jews, Arabs and blacks; Hazel Park and Madison Heights, mostly peopled with descendants of the Appalachian migrants of a few decades ago; and Troy, once barren fields and now a major office center, with the Kmart world headquarters across from the upscale Somerset Malls on Big Beaver Road. On the Macomb County side are Warren and Sterling Heights, the destination often of Polish-Americans moving out from Hamtramck and the East Side of Detroit, and site of the General Motors Technical Center, a big Chrysler plant and the now-privatized M-1 tank plant. Historically, Macomb County was Democratic, and Oakland Republican, but both voted by similar percentages for Bill Clinton in 1996 and for Republican John Engler in 1994 and 1998; both voted by narrow margins—51%–47% in Macomb, 49%–48% in Oakland—for Al Gore in 2000.

The congressman from the 12th District is Sander Levin, a Democrat first elected in 1982 and a member of one of Michigan's most respected political families; he is the older brother of Senator Carl Levin. Levin grew up in Detroit, settled in the Woodward Avenue suburb of Berkley after school and was elected state senator in 1964; in 1970 and 1974 he ran for governor and lost narrowly each time to Republican William Milliken. In the Carter Administration he was a top appointee at the Agency for International Development. In 1982 a House seat suddenly opened up in redistricting. Levin won a spirited primary and held the seat without difficulty through 1990. The 1992 redistricting moved him east, into Macomb County, and placed him in the same district with Democrat Dennis Hertel, who decided to retire; Levin easily won the Democratic nomination.

Levin is a hard worker, a details man, willing to spend endless hours with others working out solutions. He seems always to be seeking the mean between two extremes; he likes negotiations and dislikes issues that divide opponents on stark lines of principle. On Ways and Means, he has played an important role on major issues. On the Health Subcommittee in 1994 he withheld his vote for the Democrats' health care bill until they agreed to remove Chairman Pete Stark's payroll tax increase and substituted smaller, health-related levies. On welfare reform, Levin opposed the

1995 bills passed by Republicans but helped shape the bill passed in August 1996. He was willing to end the welfare entitlement but insisted on health insurance guarantees and child care support for welfare recipients who work. In 2000 he worked with Republican Mark Foley to encourage Medicare "wellness" programs for health promotion.

Amid great controversy, Levin has been at the center of trade debates. He favored the Free Trade Agreement with Canada, which was shaped in large party by auto manufacturers and the United Auto Workers. But he was wary of Japanese trade barriers and pushed unsuccessfully for stringent measures on Japanese minivans. He was a strong opponent of NAFTA in 1993, arguing that Mexican environmental and labor standards were so far below those of the United States that the side agreements did not make sense. He supported GATT but opposed fast track. In January 1999 he replaced the pro-NAFTA Robert Matsui as ranking Democrat on the Trade Subcommittee. He wants trade agreements to contain provisions on workers' rights, fair ways of settling workers' disagreements and environmental provisions. But he opposed quotas on steel: "I think the issue in the United States is whether and to what extent we shape globalization." He spent much of the next two years pressuring the Clinton administration to demonstrate that its agreement for permanent normal trade relations with China—which was required for the U.S. to deal with China as a World Trade Organization member—was credible in its labor and environmental claims. In spring 2000 he worked with Republican Doug Bereuter to fashion an amendment that would provide a legislative-executive branch commission to monitor China's actions on human rights and trade, with power to give rewards and exact penalties. The provision passed and helped to provide the key votes to pass PNTR in the House, 237–197, in May 2000—a result that seemed uncertain only a few weeks before. Levin was criticized by union leaders and many fellow Democrats and his provision was not welcomed by many free trade Republicans. But his initiative made a major difference in public policy and was in line with his general approach: "A key part of economic life is rolling up your sleeves on a daily basis to work it out and avoid the extremes."

The 1992 redistricting removed much of metro Detroit's Jewish community from Levin's district and added unfamiliar territory in Macomb County, and at first he had serious Republican competition. In three elections he faced Republican John Pappageorge, a retired Army colonel and M-1 tank executive. In the anti-incumbent atmosphere of 1992, Levin outspent Pappageorge by $1.18 million to $190,000 and won by just 53%–46%. In 1994, when Clinton was affirmatively unpopular and John Engler was running strong, Levin again outspent the competition, $1.5 million to $470,000, and won by 52%–47%. In the much more pro-incumbent environment of 1996, Levin emphasized his work on welfare reform and making college tuition deductible; he outspent Pappageorge with similar figures and won by a larger 57%–41%.

In 1998 Levin was embarrassed by Democratic governor nominee Geoffrey Fieger and shied away from endorsing him. Republicans recruited Leslie Touma, a former Engler and Pentagon aide who ran a Michigan coalition for NAFTA and worked for the Southfield defense contractor Lear Corporation; she became the first Republican to buy Detroit TV against Levin but he still outspent her by $700,000. She backed Social Security individual investment accounts; he accused her of wanting to "let Wall Street investors gamble your retirement, eliminating the guarantee of a Social Security check." Levin won 56%–42%—by 57%–41% in Oakland, 54%–44% in Macomb—calling it "the sweetest victory of my career." Against weaker opposition in 2000 Levin won 64%–32%.

But redistricting poses a threat for 2002. Michigan lost one seat in the 2000 Census, and Republicans control the redistricting process. The 12th District, in the middle of the Detroit metropolitan area, could be the seat squeezed out; then Levin would have a choice between running in a more Republican 10th District in Macomb or against Republican Joe Knollenberg in the 11th. Even if the seat is not eliminated, redistricters could remove the most Democratic portions at its southern end—Southfield, Hazel Park, southern Warren—and attach them to population-losing Detroit districts, which would make the 12th more Republican and perhaps give Levin tough competition again. But Levin seems determined on continuing the legislative career to which he seems so well suited and has shown no sign of wanting to retire.

Cook's Call   *Potentially Competitive.* Levin is no stranger to tough races. He survived redistricting in 1991 that essentially slashed his district, the 1994 Republican tsunami and a solid, well-financed opponent in 1998. But, 2001 could be another test for Levin: A lot of shuffling in and around Oakland and Macomb Counties during redistricting could change the shape and texture of this district once again.

THE PEOPLE: Pop. 2000: 574,950; Pop. 1990: 580,987, down 1% 1990–2000. 86.5% White, 6% Black, 4.5% Asian, 0.3% Amer. Indian, 2.2% Two+ races, 0.4% Other; 1.4% Hispanic Origin.

2000 Presidential Vote			1996 Presidential Vote		
Gore (D)	138,838	(54%)	Clinton (D)	128,820	(52%)
Bush (R)	111,692	(43%)	Dole (R)	95,071	(38%)
Nader (Green)	5,197	(2%)	Perot (I)	20,612	(8%)
Others	2,087	(1%)			

Rep. Sander M. Levin (D)

Elected 1982, 10th term; b. Sept. 6, 1931, Detroit; home, Royal Oak; U. of Chicago, B.A. 1952, Columbia U., M.A. 1954, Harvard U., LL.B. 1957; Jewish; married (Vicki).

Elected Office: Oakland Bd. of Supervisors, 1961–64; MI Senate, 1964–70.

Professional Career: Practicing atty., 1957–64, 1970–76; Fellow, Harvard JFK Schl. of Govt., 1975; A.A., Agency for Intl. Devel., 1977–81.

DC Office: 2300 RHOB 20515, 202-225-4961; Fax: 202-226-1033; Web site: www.house.gov/levin.

District Office: Sterling Heights, 810-268-4444.

Committees: *Ways & Means* (5th of 17 D): Human Resources; Trade (RMM).

Group Ratings

	ADA	ACLU	AFS	LCV	CON	ITIC	NTU	COC	ACU	NTLC	CHC
2000	90	86	85	86	50	74	20	52	8	12	0
1999	95	—	100	94	49	—	17	24	4	—	—

National Journal Ratings

	1999 LIB —	1999 CONS		2000 LIB —	2000 CONS
Economic	78%	—	21%	78%	—	20%
Social	83%	—	13%	91%	—	6%
Foreign	78%	—	17%	77%	—	21%

Key Votes of the 106th Congress

1. Patient Bill of Rights	Y	5. Bar RU-486 $ for FDA	N	9. NATO War in Serbia	Y
2. Accelerate Min. Wage	Y	6. Display 10 Commandments	N	10. Perm. Trade with China	Y
3. Strike Ban on Ergo. Stnd.	Y	7. Gun Show Bkgrnd. Checks	Y	11. Debt Relief for 3rd World	Y
4. Ovrd. Estate Tax Veto	N	8. Ban Part.-Birth Abortion	N	12. Drop Cuba Econ. Embargo	N

Election Results

2000 general	Sander M. Levin (D)	157,720	(64%)	($1,054,666)
	Bart Baron (R)	78,795	(32%)	($36,158)
	Other	8,654	(4%)	
2000 primary	Sander M. Levin (D)	unopposed		
1998 general	Sander M. Levin (D)	105,824	(56%)	($1,638,901)
	Leslie A. Touma (R)	79,619	(42%)	($1,188,234)
	Others	3,985	(2%)	

THIRTEENTH DISTRICT

From Detroit's Metro Airport west to Ann Arbor runs what was once a key artery in the "arsenal of democracy." Now the I-94 expressway, it was built in 1942 so workers from Detroit could drive to the huge Willow Run bomber plant 30 miles west; later it was known by travelers for its pothole-pocked pavement and the giant Goodyear tire over the billboard with the digital counter showing the year's (American) car production. Today, it is still a key link between factories and suppliers, workers and workplaces, between the blue-collar neighborhoods of southwest Wayne County and Ann Arbor, home of the diversity-minded University of Michigan. But over the past two decades I-94 has seen a profound shift in Michigan's industrial economy: from that of many low-skill jobs assembling high-style but low-tech cars, to one with fewer but higher-skill jobs in higher-tech manufacturing, requiring precision work and computerized tools.

The 13th Congressional District of Michigan covers much of this unpicturesque landscape from the airport—where, thankfully, Northwest Airlines scheduled the opening of a much needed midfield terminal for July 2001—to Ann Arbor. A few of its suburbs are distinctly downscale, like Romulus, where poorer residents have worked a little at a time to build their own houses, on land so flat it oozes water after a rain. Others are proudly middle-income, like Westland, which was named after a shopping center, and Canton Township, which has been growing robustly in recent years; Plymouth and Northville just to the north are high-income and fast-growing. Southwest Wayne County has been Democratic since the UAW forced an unwilling Henry Ford to sign a collective bargaining contract in 1941, but as working-class wages went up and working-class consciousness declined it has become less so. In Washtenaw County, the district's largest city, Ann Arbor has a Republican history going back to its beginnings as a haven for German veterans of the failed revolutions of 1848; but undergraduates in the 1970s and graduate students in the 1980s swung it sharply to the left, making it one of the most dependably Democratic (and feminist) parts of Michigan. Ypsilanti, working class and home to Eastern Michigan University, is also Democratic. On balance the 13th leans Democratic but with pockets of Republican strength.

The congresswoman from the 13th District is Lynn Rivers, a Democrat first elected in 1994. Her story is an unusual one for an American politician. She was married and became a mother at 18; she worked her way through school as her kids grew and got a bachelor's degree at the University of Michigan in 1987 and a law degree in 1992. 'I understand what families are struggling with," she says now. "I know what it's like to go without health insurance, not to be able to buy a home, and to have more bills than money." She entered politics as "a mom who got mad at the system" and was elected to the Ann Arbor school board in 1984. In 1992 she was elected to the state House. In 1994, Congressman William Ford decided to retire after 30 years in the House. Rivers, with strong support from the liberal Democrats who dominate politics in Ann Arbor, easily won the Democratic primary. In the general election, with generous support from local and national unions as well as feminists, she outraised her Republican opponent, a Bush administration appointee, and won 52%–45% in a heavily Republican year.

Entering a House with 73 mostly conservative Republican freshmen, Rivers stood out; her voting record has been consistently liberal. She spoke out strongly against the partial birth abortion ban. She served on the Science Committee, where she promised to expose "junk science" used to justify repeal of environmental protections. But she also worked with Republicans on some issues. With Steve LaTourette of Ohio, she restored funding for the Great Lakes Environmental Research Laboratory in Ann Arbor and supported more research in ridding the Great Lakes of the zebra mussel. Continuing to uphold her grass-roots background, she sought tougher gift bans, wanted to abolish many congressional perks, including pensions and automatic pay raises, and sought to require members of Congress to pay out of their office allowance for special orders speeches—the last, an odd position for one whose politics has long been associated with vigorous defense of free expression. She has sent her pay raise back to the Treasury and opposed a measure to pay legal fees of congressmen who are cleared by juries. She favors immediate disclosure of campaign contributions. Making the case for more funding of mental illness, Rivers publicly discussed her 20-year battle with manic depression and said that politicians ought to stop keeping the disease in the closet.

After spirited challenges in 1996 and 1998, she had an easy time in 2000, winning 65%–32%. But Michigan lost one House seat in the 2000 Census, and Republicans control the redistricting process; and they will certainly want to give John Dingell of the neighboring 16th District a safe seat. That raises the possibility, though not the likelihood, that the 13th District could get squeezed out or could become more Republican. But Ann Arbor may prove to be Rivers's trump card: no Republican will want it in his district, and it will provide her with a strong base even in a more Republican-leaning district.

Cook's Call   *Potentially Competitive.* Since her first win in 1994, Rivers has not had much of a fight to hold onto this Ann Arbor-based district. But redistricting could make this seat a real barnburner in 2002. With the state slated to lose one district and a lot of shuffling in and around the Detroit area, no Democratic incumbent should feel safe. One scenario has Rivers' district merged with dean of the Michigan delegation, John Dingell.

THE PEOPLE: Pop. 2000: 628,363; Pop. 1990: 580,882, up 8.2% 1990–2000. 78.4% White, 13.1% Black, 5% Asian, 0.4% Amer. Indian, 2.3% Two+ races, 0.8% Other; 2.4% Hispanic Origin.

2000 Presidential Vote		
Gore (D)	151,388	(58%)
Bush (R)	99,366	(38%)
Nader (Green)	6,471	(2%)
Others	1,850	(1%)

1996 Presidential Vote		
Clinton (D)	135,250	(58%)
Dole (R)	76,165	(33%)
Perot (I)	16,954	(7%)
Others	3,990	(2%)

Rep. Lynn Rivers (D)

Elected 1994, 4th term; b. Dec. 19, 1956, Au Gres; home, Ann Arbor; U. of MI, B.A. 1987, Wayne St. U., J.D. 1992; Protestant; divorced.

Elected Office: Ann Arbor Schl. Bd., 1984–92; MI House of Reps., 1992–94.

DC Office: 1724 LHOB 20515, 202-225-6261; Fax: 202-225-3404; Web site: www.house.gov/rivers.

District Office: Ypsilanti, 734-485-3741.

Committees: *Education & the Workforce* (10th of 22 D): 21st Century Competitiveness; Employer-Employee Relations. *Science* (7th of 22 D): Environment, Technology and Standards; Research.

Group Ratings

	ADA	ACLU	AFS	LCV	CON	ITIC	NTU	COC	ACU	NTLC	CHC
2000	95	92	100	100	91	50	29	38	8	26	0
1999	85	—	83	63	83	—	39	28	12	—	—

National Journal Ratings

	1999 LIB —	1999 CONS	2000 LIB —	2000 CONS
Economic	60% —	39%	90% —	8%
Social	81% —	18%	86% —	12%
Foreign	53% —	46%	80% —	20%

Key Votes of the 106th Congress

1. Patient Bill of Rights	Y	5. Bar RU-486 $ for FDA	N	9. NATO War in Serbia	Y
2. Accelerate Min. Wage	Y	6. Display 10 Commandments	N	10. Perm. Trade with China	N
3. Strike Ban on Ergo. Stnd.	Y	7. Gun Show Bkgrnd. Checks	Y	11. Debt Relief for 3rd World	Y
4. Ovrd. Estate Tax Veto	N	8. Ban Part.-Birth Abortion	N	12. Drop Cuba Econ. Embargo	Y

Election Results

2000 general	Lynn Rivers (D)	160,084	(65%)	($408,014)
	Carl Berry (R)	79,445	(32%)	($11,926)
	Other	7,992	(3%)	
2000 primary	Lynn Rivers (D)	unopposed		
1998 general	Lynn Rivers (D)	99,935	(58%)	($432,084)
	Thomas Hickey (R)	68,328	(40%)	($308,030)
	Others	3,624	(2%)	

FOURTEENTH DISTRICT

Detroit's early auto factories—Packard, Hudson, Ford Highland Park, Dodge Main, Briggs, Ford Rouge, Cadillac, Kelsey-Hayes, Chrysler, Plymouth, DeSoto—were built between 1905 and 1925 in an arc about five miles from the city's center, in green fields at what was then the edge of urban development. Almost instantly the flat farmlands all around were platted in grid streets and filled with wooden bungalows and brick prairie-style houses, often with a driveway at the side and a single elm in front. Commercial strips lined the mile-square and radial main streets, stretching straight as far as the eye could see. Detroit's neighborhoods filled up with factory workers and civil servants, professionals and maintenance men, corner store owners and management personnel, Catholics and Protestants and Jews: a middle-class melting pot. With one exception: Detroit in those days had few blacks; they did not begin their big migrations here from the South, especially Alabama, until around 1940, when defense plants began hiring in large numbers.

The history of black Detroit is one of conflict and uplift, inspiration and tragedy. The wartime mixture of Appalachian mountain whites and Deep South blacks proved volatile: there was a violent race riot in June 1943. During the war years, blacks were pent up in a few severely overcrowded neighborhoods like the Black Bottom, which is now the Chrysler Freeway. After 1945, when blacks began moving outward, real estate agents played on racial fears, and in the 1950s whole square miles of Detroit changed racial composition in months. In the 1960s there was hope that the civil rights movement, encouraged by Walter Reuther's UAW, and antipoverty programs would improve blacks' lot, and in fact many black Detroiters found good jobs and made good incomes, bought their own homes and built community institutions. Then came the riot of July 1967, followed by extensive white flight and terrible increases in crime. Detroit's first black mayor, Coleman Young, elected in 1973, responded with policies that may have seemed appropriate in the 1960s but had disastrous results in the 1970s and 1980s: He pressured major employers like the Big Three auto companies to build facilities in Detroit, raised taxes to support a vast army of city employees, and attributed city problems to white racism. Violent crime became a part of everyday life and arson became common.

Detroit took on a garrison atmosphere. Crime reduced the value of residential real estate to near zero, and the city's population dropped from 1.7 million in 1960 to 951,000 in 2000. Thousands of houses were abandoned to arsonists and drug dealers. In political dialogue, most black politicians called for, and most black voters seemed to support, an ever-increasing public sector. Yet the existing public sector, which took a larger share of residents' income than almost anywhere else in the country, served citizens very poorly. Turnaround came agonizingly late in the 1990s, as Mayor Dennis Archer, elected in 1993, worked to fight crime and encourage private-sector growth. Detroit made headlines when General Motors bought the Renaissance Center downtown for its headquarters. But more important is that crime rates are falling, housing values are rising and commercial activity is starting to pick up.

The 14th Congressional District of Michigan consists of the northern half of Detroit, including most neighborhoods just beyond the auto plants. It includes adjacent suburbs from high-income Grosse Pointe Woods and more modest Dearborn Heights to Highland Park, an enclave within the city, which had 52,000 people and fine city services in 1930 and 17,000 people and an essentially defunct government today. There are some solid neighborhoods here, including high-income Palmer Woods, Sherwood Forest and Rosedale Park. On many blocks homeowners bravely install the big front-lawn lights Detroit Edison sells and patrol their streets, trying to discourage thugs that have dominion over most blocks nearby. Politically, this is one of the most Democratic areas in the nation, with many precincts turning in percentages between 90% and 98%.

The congressman from the 14th District is John Conyers, the second most senior member of the House, first elected in 1964. He is a founder of the Congressional Black Caucus, and ranking Democrat on the House Judiciary Committee. The son of a left-wing operative in the UAW, he grew up in Detroit, served in the Army in Korea, practiced law and worked as a staffer for a young congressman named John Dingell. Conyers was first elected to Congress in 1964—one of six blacks in the House at the time and the only one to take a militant approach to politics; he won his primary, in which 60,000 votes were cast, by less than 150 votes. His response to the 1967 riots was to introduce the first bill for a guaranteed annual income. He first sponsored a Martin Luther King holiday bill days after the civil rights leader was murdered in 1968, and persevered until it passed in 1983. Since 1989 he has sponsored bills to establish a commission to examine slavery and its lingering effects, and for consideration of whether reparations should be paid to descendants of slaves. It is "just a question," he says. "We ask questions about everything. But this one has been studiously avoided." He opposed most controversial parts of the crime bills of the past three decades and welfare reform in the 1990s. He has one of the most liberal voting records in the House, calling for single-payer health plans and massive public works projects.

Conyers remains alert to evidence of racism. He has pushed bills to collect racial statistics on traffic stops, in the belief that many blacks are stopped for DWB (driving while black). In 1998 he criticized the tobacco companies for targeting blacks, and he joined the criticism on a proposed plastics plant in Louisiana as environmental racism. In 2000 he called for a Justice Department investigation of the killing of a man, whose daughter was accused of shoplifting by a security guard in Fairlane Mall in Dearborn; he said it was an example of racial profiling, though the security guard as well as the suspect were black. He criticizes Republicans bitterly, but not only Republicans. He criticized the Clinton administration on Haiti until it weighed in on the side of Jean-Bertrand Aristide, and in an investigation of the Branch Davidian deaths in Waco he told Attorney General Janet Reno she did "the right thing" by offering to resign. On some civil liberties issues he has joined forces with Judiciary Committee conservatives. He and Chairman Henry Hyde sponsored the rollback of civil forfeiture laws in April 2000, and in October 2000 Conyers and Hyde worked to kill the bill, inserted into other legislation by Senator Richard Shelby, which would have made it a crime to divulge anything that had been classified, even if it was a newspaper clipping: an official secrets act, in effect.

Conyers is the only member of Congress ever to have served on two committees handling presidential impeachment. In May 1972, a month before the Watergate burglary, he called for impeaching Richard Nixon because of his conduct of the Vietnam war. He was a strong supporter of Nixon's impeachment on other grounds when the Judiciary Committee voted for it in July 1974. In 1988 and 1989 he led the fight to impeach Alcee Hastings, then federal judge, now a congressman from Florida; in 1997, when an investigation found that an agent lied in that case, he moved to reopen it. As the hearings on Bill Clinton's impeachment opened in 1998, some Democrats were queasy about Conyers, sharing the judgment of Judiciary Republican George Gekas that he was "predictably unpredictable." But Conyers performed ably. For all his criticisms of Clinton, Conyers rallied behind him, following the Democrats' strategy of partisanizing the investigation and then claiming it was partisan; he managed to craft an alternative investigation resolution that Republicans wouldn't accept, the start of partisan divisions on the issue. His own speeches and interventions were competent, and he kept some sense of humor; at one point he said, "This is my 15 minutes of fame. I have about six minutes left." But he is still ranking member and has not abandoned hopes of becoming chairman. Interestingly, he did not back reauthorization of the independent counsel law which he strongly supported in 1994.

Over the years, Conyers has mostly been re-elected without difficulty. He made two runs for mayor of Detroit, in 1989 and 1993. But he ran a desultory campaign the first time and almost no campaign the second, and came in far behind. Perhaps because of that he had two serious primary opponents in 1994, but finished well ahead of both with 51% of the vote. In 1996 and 1997, he had serious cost overruns in his office, and had to cut back staff salaries sharply. His defenders argue that he keeps large staffs to keep in touch with Detroit's problems; one of his staffers for many years has been civil rights pioneer Rosa Parks. Redistricting may add suburbs in Macomb or Oakland County to the district, but it will remain overwhelmingly Democratic, and Conyers should have no difficulty winning re-election.

Cook's Call   *Safe*. Sitting in an extremely Democratic district that Gore won by 88 % in 2000, Conyers has never had any trouble winning this seat for the last 36 years. But, Detroit's hefty population loss means that this district will need to move into more suburban areas to make up for lost population. Still, Voting Rights Act ensures that this district remains majority black.

THE PEOPLE: Pop. 2000: 550,599; Pop. 1990: 580,977, down 5.2% 1990–2000. 16.8% White, 78.9% Black, 1.3% Asian, 0.3% Amer. Indian, 2.2% Two+ races, 0.5% Other; 1.2% Hispanic Origin.

2000 Presidential Vote		
Gore (D)	169,068	(88%)
Bush (R)	21,836	(11%)
Nader (Green)	1,481	(1%)

1996 Presidential Vote		
Clinton (D)	160,009	(86%)
Dole (R)	20,915	(11%)
Perot (I)	4,772	(3%)

Rep. John Conyers, Jr. (D)

Elected 1964, 19th term; b. May 16, 1929, Detroit; home, Detroit; Wayne St. U., B.A. 1957, LL.B. 1958; Baptist; married (Monica).

Military Career: National Guard, 1948–50; Army, 1950–54 (Korea), Army Reserves, 1954–57.

Professional Career: Legis. Asst., U.S. Rep. John Dingell, 1958–61; Practicing atty., 1959–61; Referee, MI Workmen's Comp. Dept., 1961–63.

DC Office: 2426 RHOB 20515, 202-225-5126; Fax: 202-225-0072; Web site: www.house.gov/conyers.

District Office: Detroit, 313-961-5670.

Committees: *Judiciary* (RMM of 17 D): Courts, the Internet & Intellectual Property; The Constitution.

Group Ratings

	ADA	ACLU	AFS	LCV	CON	ITIC	NTU	COC	ACU	NTLC	CHC
2000	95	86	100	93	65	47	29	30	0	15	0
1999	100	—	100	94	90	—	30	17	8	—	—

National Journal Ratings

	1999 LIB	—	1999 CONS		2000 LIB	—	2000 CONS
Economic	88%	—	0%		84%	—	15%
Social	87%	—	0%		94%	—	0%
Foreign	83%	—	17%		95%	—	4%

Key Votes of the 106th Congress

1. Patient Bill of Rights	Y	5. Bar RU-486 $ for FDA	N	9. NATO War in Serbia	Y
2. Accelerate Min. Wage	Y	6. Display 10 Commandments	N	10. Perm. Trade with China	N
3. Strike Ban on Ergo. Stnd.	Y	7. Gun Show Bkgrnd. Checks	Y	11. Debt Relief for 3rd World	Y
4. Ovrd. Estate Tax Veto	N	8. Ban Part.-Birth Abortion	N	12. Drop Cuba Econ. Embargo	Y

Election Results

2000 general	John Conyers Jr. (D)	168,982	(89%)	($554,892)
	William Ashe (R)	17,852	(9%)	
	Other	3,143	(2%)	
2000 primary	John Conyers Jr. (D)	unopposed		
1998 general	John Conyers Jr. (D)	126,321	(87%)	($256,651)
	Vendella M. Collins (R)	16,140	(11%)	
	Others	2,844	(2%)	

FIFTEENTH DISTRICT

Few central cities in America have as vibrant a 20th Century history, and as sad a recent past, as Detroit. This was America's first automobile city, not just because it manufactured so many of the nation's cars but also because it was built to automobile scale. Detroit started the century as a second-rank city, no bigger than Milwaukee, with less than half a million people and extending no farther than four or five miles out from the site where the French built Fort Pontchartrain on the Detroit River in 1701. As the Motor City boomed, it grew outward along wide avenues and freeways; the auto companies put their factories and headquarters near the edge of urban settlement. As early as 1954, the nation's first big suburban shopping center, with parking for 10,000 cars, was drawing retail trade from downtown. Metro Detroit expanded to four million people, each generation moving out the roadways rapidly in many directions, leaving behind the previous generation's neighborhoods and civic institutions.

Today, that rapid movement has left large parts of Detroit literally empty. The central city had nearly 1.9 million people in 1950, but not even the help of a city bureaucracy detailed to round up uncounted residents could keep the total from falling below 1 million in 2000. The reason is obvious: crime. For 30 years Detroit had a murder rate drastically higher than in the suburbs, and naturally those who could afford to leave did so. Downtown, the giant Hudson's department store has been torn down and several skyscrapers are all but empty; GM bought for $72 million the 70-story Renaissance Center, built in the 1970s for $350 million. Beyond downtown, some of the city's jewels have been maintained: the Detroit Institute of Arts, the hospital center, the old Fox Theater. New baseball and football stadiums are being opened nearby and three gambling casinos have opened as well, and residential and commercial projects have risen on the once-neglected riverfront. But beyond these well-policed enclaves lie acres of vacant fields and half-empty blocks where there were once five-story apartments or brick houses; once vital neighborhoods are now home to pheasants.

Detroit's fate is all the more tragic because it comes in a city where liberal reformers hoped to create model anti-poverty and anti-discrimination programs. Instead, they seem to have undermined the sense of individual responsibility and confidence in the legitimacy of institutions. With auto sales booming, metro area jobs rose from 1.5 million at the trough of the 1980s to over 2 million in the 1990s; the problem is not so much a lack of jobs as the fact that too many people lived by crime instead. Detroit's mayor for 20 years from 1973 to 1993, Coleman Young, spent his energy on courting the Big Three, bulldozing the viable Poletown neighborhood for a new Cadillac plant. Dennis Archer, elected mayor in 1993 but unexpectedly retiring in 2001, took a more constructive and intelligent approach, and the city has been turning around, with lower crime, more jobs, new housing permits and a start at a growing private sector. But much of Detroit is still achingly vacant.

The 15th Congressional District of Michigan includes the southern half of Detroit, plus a few adjacent suburbs, from affluent Grosse Pointe Farms on Lake St. Clair to the Downriver industrial town of Ecorse. The district also includes Hamtramck, America's fastest-growing city between 1910–20, the Polish-American enclave around the now demolished Dodge Main plant. The district leads the nation in infant mortality and welfare dependency, and is among the top in crime and unemployment. Politically, the 15th is overwhelmingly Democratic, but voter turnout is low—158,000 in the House race in 2000, barely half the 306,000 in the high-income 11th District.

The congresswoman from the 15th District is Carolyn Cheeks Kilpatrick, a Democrat elected in 1996. She was raised in Detroit, became a teacher in Detroit public schools, and was elected to the state House in 1978. There she got a seat on the Appropriations Committee and worked on local projects, notably the highly successful River Place hotel and office complex in the old Stroh headquarters. (Her son Kwame, a former all-American football player, won her House seat and soon rose to Democratic leader in Lansing; with Archer's retirement, he became, at age 30, a leading contender to become mayor in 2001.) Kilpatrick lost a race for the Detroit City Council, but won the 15th District in the August 1996 Democratic primary by a solid 51%–31% margin against her one-time political ally, incumbent Barbara-Rose Collins. Collins, an ally of Coleman Young, was accused of campaign finance violations and misuse of campaign and office funds and had the third highest absentee rate in 1995.

In her first term, Kilpatrick attained one of the most liberal voting records in the House. She made a point of visiting the suburbs in her district, meeting local officials and assigning staffers to work with them—a contrast to Collins. She got an $8 million earmark in the Transportation bill for an intermodal freight terminal. She started studying the advertising industry and encouraging more contracts for minority ad agencies. She fought the elimination of the Low Income Heating Assistance Program and called for lifting of sanctions on Iraq. She was one of 16 members to vote against a ban on federal funds for assisted suicides. She wants to increase the availability of the dependent care tax credit for the elderly. On Appropriations since 1999, she has taken credit for funding Detroit-area projects for pre-college engineering, enrichment public television programming for kids, and improved rehabilitation services at the Detroit Medical Center. Following visits to Africa, she has sought increased foreign-aid funding for needy areas. She chaired the board of the Black Caucus's political action committee.

Kilpatrick has had no primary or general-election problems since she was first elected. Redistricting is controlled by Republicans, who are sure to maintain Detroit's two black-majority districts despite population losses; the contours of this district may change and it will likely include more suburbs, but its basic political leanings will remain the same.

Cook's Call   *Safe*. Kilpatrick's Detroit-based district is one of the most Democratic in the state but it is also the slowest growing. This district will need to pick up 131,000 new people, most likely from the surrounding Detroit suburbs. The Voting Rights Act ensures that this minority-majority district will remain intact, but with so many new people added to the district, Kilpatrick could find herself in a competitive primary contest in 2002.

THE PEOPLE: Pop. 2000: 531,634; Pop. 1990: 580,933, down 8.5% 1990–2000. 21.6% White, 69.9% Black, 1.1% Asian, 0.4% Amer. Indian, 2.7% Two+ races, 4.2% Other; 8.2% Hispanic Origin.

2000 Presidential Vote		
Gore (D)	142,600	(87%)
Bush (R)	18,829	(12%)
Nader (Green)	1,585	(1%)

1996 Presidential Vote		
Clinton (D)	146,357	(87%)
Dole (R)	17,275	(10%)
Perot (I)	3,723	(2%)

Rep. Carolyn C. Kilpatrick (D)

Elected 1996, 3d term; b. June 25, 1945, Detroit; home, Detroit; Ferris St. U., 1968–70, W. MI U., B.S. 1972, U. of MI, M.S. 1977; African Methodist Episcopal; divorced.

Elected Office: MI House of Reps., 1978–96.

Professional Career: Teacher, Detroit public schls., 1970–78.

DC Office: 1610 LHOB 20515, 202-225-2261; Fax: 202-225-5730; Web site: www.house.gov/kilpatrick.

District Office: Detroit, 313-965-9004.

Committees: *Appropriations* (26th of 29 D): Foreign Operations & Export Financing; Transportation.

Group Ratings

	ADA	ACLU	AFS	LCV	CON	ITIC	NTU	COC	ACU	NTLC	CHC
2000	85	86	100	79	69	53	19	42	8	10	0
1999	100	—	100	94	79	—	19	16	0	—	—

National Journal Ratings

	1999 LIB —	1999 CONS		2000 LIB —	2000 CONS
Economic	88%	—	0%	81%	—	16%
Social	87%	—	0%	89%	—	10%
Foreign	95%	—	0%	85%	—	10%

Key Votes of the 106th Congress

1. Patient Bill of Rights	Y	5. Bar RU-486 $ for FDA	N	9. NATO War in Serbia	Y
2. Accelerate Min. Wage	Y	6. Display 10 Commandments	N	10. Perm. Trade with China	N
3. Strike Ban on Ergo. Stnd.	Y	7. Gun Show Bkgrnd. Checks	Y	11. Debt Relief for 3rd World	Y
4. Ovrd. Estate Tax Veto	N	8. Ban Part.-Birth Abortion	N	12. Drop Cuba Econ. Embargo	Y

SIXTEENTH DISTRICT

One of America's great heavy-industry corridors is along the Detroit River, the choke point of the Great Lakes, in the Downriver communities below Detroit. Steel and chemical plants line the water, their dark and rusted hulks glaring across at Canada. A little ways up the sluggish Rouge River, in Dearborn, stands the giant Rouge complex, built by Henry Ford for $1 billion in the 1910s to take loads of iron ore, coal, limestone, and sand from Great Lake freighters and railroad cars and convert them into automobiles in 48 hours. This swampy, low-lying land, along the nation's most heavily trafficked waterway and within easy reach of the great East-West rail lines, was a natural place for industry in the early 20th Century. Around the older factories and well within range of their sulfurous odors, residential neighborhoods with neat, tightly packed houses were home to migrants who came for work—Polish, Hungarian, black, Italian, and more recently Mexican and Arab; the Detroit area has the largest Arab American community in the country and Dearborn has a higher Arab percentage than any other city. Dearborn is also home to Ford head-quarters and Greenfield Village, established by Henry Ford. This area is also part of "automation alley," one of the nation's greatest centers of manufacturing expertise, and it has also recovered from hard times as smaller manufacturers are picking up the slack resulting from layoffs by corporate giants.

The 16th Congressional District of Michigan covers Dearborn and the Downriver commu-nities, plus Monroe County directly to the south. The political tradition has been Democratic since the New Deal days, and while there is some cultural conservatism seen in top-of-the-ticket races, the basic preference remains much more Democratic here than in increasingly upscale Macomb County.

The congressman from the 16th District is John Dingell, the senior member of the House of Representatives. His father, John Dingell, Sr., was elected to the House in 1932, from a district created as a result of the Detroit area's auto boom. The first Congressman Dingell was one of the most productive urban liberals of his day, a sponsor of Social Security and, starting in 1943, of national health insurance. John Dingell Jr. has been around Capitol Hill almost as long. He was a House page from 1938–43. After his father died, Dingell was elected to succeed him in Decem-ber 1955, at 29, from a district with large Polish, black and Jewish populations. He still uses his father's office furniture and every session continues to introduce as H.R. 16 (the number matches the district) the national health insurance bill his father co-sponsored in 1943. He is the only member of the House who served in the 1950s; indeed only four others served in the 1960s (John Conyers, Patsy Mink, Philip Crane and David Obey). Dingell has had one really serious contest, because of redistricting, in 1964, against a fellow Democrat who opposed the Civil Rights Act. Although most of the district was new to Dingell, he won and has been re-elected easily since. He has an interesting personal life, raising his children after his divorce (his son Christopher was elected to the Michigan Senate in 1986) and marrying in 1981 a granddaughter of one of General Motors' Fisher brothers. Debbie Dingell is head of the General Motors Foundation and a Demo-cratic National committeewoman, and an encourager of bipartisan amity as well; she also headed Al Gore's 2000 presidential campaign in Michigan, and is given much credit for his 51%–46% win there.

From 1981–95 Dingell was chairman of the Energy and Commerce Committee and of its Investigative and Oversight Subcommittee, one of the most powerful and effective chairmen ever. It had wide jurisdiction, handled up to 40% of all House bills, and had the largest budget and staff of any House committee. As institutions will, the committee took on the character of its leader, widely known as "the truck": bright, aggressive, domineering, determined. Dingell and his committee superintended the breakup of AT&T and the sale of Conrail by public offering; Commerce's cable reregulation law of 1992 was the only bill on which Congress overrode George Bush's presidential veto. After a decade of sparring over clean air legislation, Dingell worked together with Health Subcommittee Chairman Henry Waxman to produce the 1990 Clean Air Act. But for all his efforts he could not put together a majority on the committee for a health care bill with an employer mandate, and in June 1994 conceded that Commerce was hopelessly deadlocked on the issue. Similarly, he was stymied in October 1994 when Superfund reform was killed under time pressure and House-passed telecommunications reform went down in the Senate.

On other issues, Dingell backed organized labor's agenda against NAFTA and other trade agreements. An avid outdoorsman (he hunts deer, elk, caribou and moose, because "that has a certain class and elegance"), he long opposed gun control but voted for the 1994 crime bill and resigned from the National Rifle Association board. In many ways, he is an old-fashioned Franklin Roosevelt Democrat, supporting big government and strenuous regulation, taking a conservative line on some cultural issues and backing an assertive foreign policy; he was the only Michigan Democrat to vote for the Gulf war resolution.

When the Republican majority took over, many expected Dingell to sulk or to launch bitter attacks on the other side. But he did neither. As the senior House member, he swore in Newt Gingrich with good grace and proceeded to work with Republicans and produce legislation. He opposed repeal of the Glass-Steagall Act in the 104th and 105th Congresses, but saw it pass in the 106th. He worked with new Commerce Chairman Thomas Bliley to pass the Safe Drinking Water Act of 1996—though he voted against it to protest the addition of too much pork—and to work out provisions in the pesticide regulation bill repealing the Delaney clause. In 1997 he helped build consensus on the FDA bill. Years before, he had pushed wildlife refuge legislation; he worked with Resources Chairman Don Young and ranking Democrat George Miller to produce a revision, which passed in June 1997 by 407–1, that protected wildlife and recognized hunting and recreation as a priority. He helped stall federal electricity deregulation in 1999 by insisting the bill be read in committee; he says it is unnecessary. "Why? The states are doing it." He and then-Telecommunications Subcommittee Chairman Billy Tauzin sponsored a bill to amend the 1996 Telecommunications Act by allowing broadband access regardless of a company's historical mission; with Tauzin now at the helm of the Commerce Committee, they re-introduced the bill in 2001.

Dingell has also been successful in forging Democratic positions that prevailed in the Republican House. He proposed the health care portability legislation that passed in somewhat different form in August 1996. He introduced a patient's bill of rights to regulate HMOs in February 1998 and then joined with Republican Greg Ganske. It lost 217–212 and a Republican alternative passed 216–210. The Senate never acted. But in July 1999 Dingell came back, allied with Ganske and Republican Charlie Norwood, and in October 1999 the renamed Dingell-Norwood bill passed 275–151, with 68 Republicans voting yes. The bill imposed uniform national standards for health insurance, including guaranteed access to emergency care and medical specialists, appeals of coverage decisions to an independent board, a prohibition on HMOs retaliating against doctors and a right to sue HMOs in state courts. "This was as fine a piece of work as I've ever seen in Congress," he said. The Senate again didn't act, but Dingell helped set the stage for certain passage if Al Gore was elected and likely passage if George W. Bush was. Dingell can cite anecdote as well as argument: In August 2000, after his insurer tried to force him to have ankle surgery as an outpatient, he said, "If they can kick me around like this, imagine what happens to a guy who has no connections." Dingell's goal remains national health insurance; asked what is a desirable system, he says, "Canada's, right across the river." He strongly opposed John Breaux's premium support plan for changing Medicare, and is likely to be one of the strongest opponents of George W. Bush's Medicare reforms in Congress.

Dingell is willing to work against positions held by most Democrats, notably on gun control. In June 1999, two months after the Columbine murders, the House was poised to pass a requirement of a three-day background check on sales at gun shows. Dingell, working with Republican Whip Tom DeLay, proposed a 24-hour background check and got 46 Democrats to vote for it—

thus stifling the Clinton and Democratic leadership plans. Dingell was being consistent. He had criticized the administration for not implementing the instant criminal background check that the 1994 Brady bill required to be established, and he is convinced that support of overstretching gun control legislation cost Democrats their majority that year. Also, "It was the position of my dad. He spent years in Congress doing exactly the same things that I am doing." Dingell took on the Clinton administration on other issues. In 1998 he opposed the Kyoto global warming treaty, calling it "the most asinine treaty I've ever seen." He pointed out that the burdens were on the United States, because Europeans dependent on nuclear power or natural gas would not have to shut down plants and China, India and underdeveloped countries refused to be bound. In 2000 he and Senator Mary Landrieu sought to abolish the Council of Environmental Quality that a Dingell bill established in 1969 because acting director George Frampton agreed to water down the pending Conservation and Reinvestment Act. And against Michigan's two senators, he opposed a 1998 Customs Service ruling that the importation from Canada of a syrup of molasses, water and sugar by Heartland By-Products, from which the company extracted the molasses and sold as sugar, was subject to the 7,000% sugar tariff; with consumer advocates, he prevailed.

1999 was a great year for Dingell; he prevailed on guns and on Dingell-Norwood, beating the leaderships of both parties. "I've had a very good year and I'm very grateful. The stars have assembled in proper constellation. In a nutshell, everything is going right," he said. But he still grimaced at Republican control; asked what he had learned about being in the minority, he said, "Avoid it at all costs." On his successes, he said, "I win more than I should. I work like hell. I've got a lot of experience. I'm reasonably smart. That doesn't make me a miracle worker, but that makes me an effective member of the House." He clearly relishes the idea of being in the majority again. He insisted that he had run the committee in a bipartisan fashion, and would again; he said he was for reinstituting proxy voting, getting rid of term limits on chairmen and holding more oversight hearings—with the EPA, FCC, Comptroller of the Currency and the FDA in his gunsights. In January 2001 he strongly opposed stripping the Commerce Committee of jurisdiction over insurance and the securities industry, which was part of a Republican plan to make Mike Oxley the chairman of Banking, a committee Dingell accused of "incompetence and indifference." If Democrats win control in 2002, look for Dingell to try to get that jurisdiction back.

He has been easily re-elected. Some have suggested he might retire, and perhaps pass the seat along to his wife or his son; on retirement, he said in May 2000, "The time is coming. I don't know when it is. Of course, it's coming for everybody." But Dingell seems to be in fine health and fine fettle, and the time is likely not coming for him soon; he stands to become the longest-serving member of the House ever in February 2009. Redistricting will not be a problem. Republicans control the process, but Dingell's positions on Commerce issues are very highly valued by the auto companies and Michigan manufacturing interests generally, and redistricters are likely to hand him an utterly safe district. It will not be the 16th District any more; Michigan will have only 15 districts in the 108th Congress. But that was the number of the district from which John Dingell Sr. was elected in 1932.

Cook's Call   *Safe.* Dean of the Michigan delegation John Dingell may find himself in a seriously altered district in 2001. Sixty-thousand people need to be added, and there is talk that the district's Monroe County portion may get merged with parts of Democrat Lynn Rivers' 13th District. Still, there is little doubt that if Dingell were to run for re-election, he would win easily.

THE PEOPLE: Pop. 2000: 592,437; Pop. 1990: 580,884, up 2% 1990–2000. 92.2% White, 2.5% Black, 1.2% Asian, 0.4% Amer. Indian, 2.9% Two+ races, 0.8% Other; 3.3% Hispanic Origin.

2000 Presidential Vote			1996 Presidential Vote		
Gore (D)	131,830	(54%)	Clinton (D)	122,522	(54%)
Bush (R)	107,676	(44%)	Dole (R)	78,461	(34%)
Nader (Green)	5,054	(2%)	Perot (I)	24,125	(11%)
Others	1,523	(1%)			

Rep. John D. Dingell (D)

Elected Dec. 1955, 23d term; b. July 8, 1926, Colorado Springs, CO; home, Dearborn; Georgetown U., B.S. 1949, J.D. 1952; Catholic; married (Deborah).

Military Career: Army, 1944–46 (WWII).

Professional Career: Practicing atty., 1952–55; Wayne Cnty. Asst. Prosecuting Atty., 1953–55.

DC Office: 2328 RHOB 20515, 202-225-4071; Web site: www.house.gov/dingell.

District Offices: Dearborn, 313-846-1276; Monroe, 734-243-1849.

Committees: *Energy & Commerce* (RMM of 26 D).

Group Ratings

	ADA	ACLU	AFS	LCV	CON	ITIC	NTU	COC	ACU	NTLC	CHC
2000	80	64	100	64	50	53	22	33	16	12	20
1999	80	—	100	81	33	—	15	24	12	—	—

National Journal Ratings

	1999 LIB	—	1999 CONS		2000 LIB	—	2000 CONS
Economic	88%	—	0%		70%	—	29%
Social	63%	—	37%		59%	—	40%
Foreign	71%	—	27%		69%	—	28%

Key Votes of the 106th Congress

1. Patient Bill of Rights	Y	5. Bar RU-486 $ for FDA	N	9. NATO War in Serbia	Y
2. Accelerate Min. Wage	Y	6. Display 10 Commandments	N	10. Perm. Trade with China	N
3. Strike Ban on Ergo. Stnd.	Y	7. Gun Show Bkgrnd. Checks	N	11. Debt Relief for 3rd World	Y
4. Ovrd. Estate Tax Veto	N	8. Ban Part.-Birth Abortion	Y	12. Drop Cuba Econ. Embargo	N

Election Results

2000 general	John D. Dingell (D)	167,142	(71%)	($1,048,787)
	William Morse (R)	62,469	(27%)	
	Other	5,906	(3%)	
2000 primary	John D. Dingell (D)	unopposed		
1998 general	John D. Dingell (D)	116,145	(67%)	($867,718)
	William Morse (R)	54,121	(31%)	
	Others	4,091	(2%)	

★ MINNESOTA ★

Minnesota has long been a distinctive commonwealth, set far in America's frozen North, a state which in commerce, culture and politics has set one example after another for the rest of the nation. It is the node of transcontinental railroads that linked the winter wheat fields of the northern prairies to the greatest grain milling center in the world and the great Pacific ports of Puget Sound. It is also the birthplace of Scotch Tape, Betty Crocker, Target and the Mall of America, the home base of chroniclers of small town America from Sinclair Lewis to Garrison Keillor. Politically, Minnesota over the last half century provided the nation with some of its most articulate and honorable leaders—Harold Stassen, Hubert Humphrey, Eugene McCarthy, Walter Mondale—and with traditions of probity, civic-mindedness and innovation which are second to none. Yet while commercially and culturally Minnesota has never been stronger, its recent political history often seems to be one antic episode after another. Its two political parties, with their distinctive names—Democratic-Farmer-Labor and (from 1975 until 1995) Independent Republican—have been dominated by activists of left and right stubbornly out of touch with ordinary voters. The senators Minnesota has elected since 1990 have come from the extreme wings of their respective parties, former Carleton College political science professor Paul Wellstone and Dayton Hudson heir Mark Dayton on the Democratic-Farmer-Labor left and former KMSP-TV news anchor Rod Grams on the Independent-Republican right. And in 1998, Minnesota elected a former professional wrestler and suburban mayor, Jesse "The Body" Ventura, as governor. The bald, blunt-spoken Ventura, with his strong Midwestern accent and gift for pithy phrases, quickly became a national celebrity, a possible trend-setter as a political libertarian on most cultural issues and market oriented on economics. But his election may simply be an indication that when a competent state lets its ideological party activists have too much influence over its politics, voters will recoil against party politicians altogether, in a Lake Wobegon backlash against foolishness and toward common sense.

Minnesota's distinctive traditions come from a distinctive history. The far northern states were ignored by most Yankee immigrants, who headed straight west into Iowa, Nebraska and Kansas. But others saw opportunity in Minnesota's icy lakes and ferocious winters. James J. Hill, the builder of the Great Northern Railroad ("You can't interest me in any proposition in any place where it doesn't snow"), and others operating out of Minneapolis and St. Paul—already twin cities by 1860—worked to attract Norwegian, Swedish and German migrants who would find the terrain and climate congenial. By 1890, the Twin Cities—rivals that year in a Census competition—were the nerve center of a sprawling and rich agricultural empire stretching west from Minnesota through the Dakotas and into Montana and beyond. Minneapolis and St. Paul became the termini of its rail lines and the site of its grain-milling companies.

The Twin Cities also became the center of a three-party politics and an economic radicalism reminiscent of the politics of Scandinavia. For our American regions seem a mirror image of the geography of Europe, with the East Coast resembling the British Isles and France, the industrial Midwest reminiscent of Germany and Poland, the relatively poor and always hawkish South a Baptist Mediterranean, and the Upper Midwest of Minnesota, Wisconsin and North Dakota as North American versions of Scandinavia. Like Scandinavia, these Upper Midwestern commonwealths pioneered their continent's welfare states, with an effect on public policy far out of proportion to their numbers. Alarmed by the unprecedented concentration of economic power and wealth into the hands of just a few identifiable millionaires who lived on St. Paul's Summit Avenue or the hill above Minneapolis's Hennepin Avenue, the immigrants drew on their native traditions of cooperative activity and bureaucratic socialism.

As in Wisconsin and North Dakota, a strong third party developed here in the years after the Populist era. This Farmer-Labor Party elected senators in the 1920s and dominated state politics in the 1930s. Hurt by their ties to Communists, the Farmer-Laborites were beaten by Harold Stassen's Republicans in 1938. But this was still a New Deal state, and by 1944 the bedraggled local Democrats were merged with the anti-Communist faction of Farmer-Laborites to form the Democratic-Farmer-Labor Party. A key role was played by Hubert Humphrey—mayor of Minne-

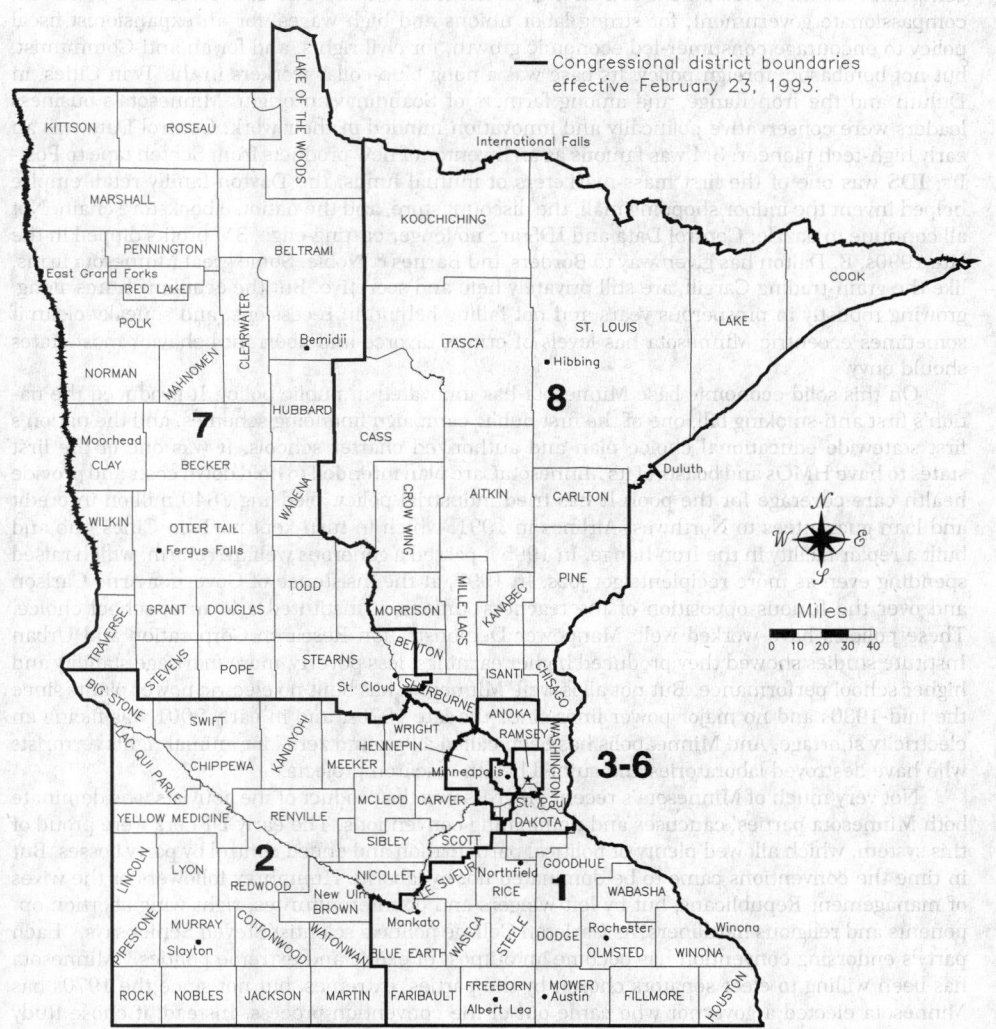

Congressional district boundaries
effective February 23, 1993.

KITTSON
ROSEAU
LAKE OF THE WOODS
International Falls

MARSHALL

KOOCHICHING

PENNINGTON
BELTRAMI
COOK

East Grand Forks
RED LAKE
CLEARWATER
POLK
Bemidji
ITASCA
ST. LOUIS
LAKE

NORMAN
MAHNOMEN
HUBBARD
Hibbing

7
Moorhead
BECKER
CASS
8
CLAY
WADENA
CROW WING
AITKIN
CARLTON
Duluth

WILKIN
OTTER TAIL
Fergus Falls
TODD
MILLE LACS
PINE

GRANT
DOUGLAS
MORRISON
KANABEC

TRAVERSE
STEVENS
POPE
STEARNS
BENTON
ISANTI
CHISAGO
St. Cloud
SHERBURNE
ANOKA
WASHINGTON

BIG STONE
SWIFT
KANDIYOHI
WRIGHT
RAMSEY
3-6
LAC QUI PARLE
CHIPPEWA
MEEKER
HENNEPIN
Minneapolis
St. Paul
DAKOTA

YELLOW MEDICINE
RENVILLE
McLEOD
CARVER
SCOTT

LINCOLN
LYON
REDWOOD
SIBLEY
NICOLLET
LE SUEUR
RICE
GOODHUE
Northfield
WABASHA

2
New Ulm
BROWN
Mankato
WASECA
STEELE
DODGE
OLMSTED
Rochester
Winona
WINONA

PIPESTONE
MURRAY
COTTONWOOD
WATONWAN
BLUE EARTH
1

Slayton

ROCK
NOBLES
JACKSON
MARTIN
FARIBAULT
FREEBORN
Albert Lea
MOWER
Austin
FILLMORE
HOUSTON

N
W E
S

Miles
0 10 20 30 40

apolis in 1945, and the dazzling advocate of the civil rights plank at the 1948 Democratic National Convention. Humphrey's DFL—clean, idealistic, closely tied to labor, backed by many farmers—attracted dozens of talented politicians, including Eugene McCarthy, Orville Freeman and Walter Mondale. In 1948 Humphrey's speech helped put the Democrats on record for civil rights, and he was elected to the Senate at age 37.

In the years following, the DFL dominated Minnesota politics, while a series of progressive companies led the development of a strong, diversified economy. The DFL stood for a generous, compassionate government, for strong labor unions and high wages, for an expansionist fiscal policy to encourage consumer-led economic growth, for civil rights, and for an anti-Communist, but not bombastic, foreign policy. Its base was among blue-collar workers in the Twin Cities, in Duluth and the Iron Range, and among farmers of Scandinavian origin. Minnesota's business leaders were conservative politically and innovation-minded in their work: Control Data was an early high-tech pioneer; 3M was famous as an inventor of new products from Scotch tape to Post-Its; IDS was one of the first mass-marketers of mutual funds; the Dayton family retail empire helped invent the indoor shopping mall, the discount store, and the national bookstore chain. Not all continue to dazzle: Control Data and IDS are no longer cutting-edge, 3M profits dipped in the late 1990s, B. Dalton has given way to Borders and Barnes & Noble. Some great Minnesota firms, like the grain-trading Cargill, are still privately held and secretive. But the economy hums along, growing robustly in prosperous years and not falling behind in recessions, and squeaky-clean if sometimes eccentric Minnesota has levels of crime, divorce and aberrant behavior most states should envy.

On this solid economic base Minnesota has innovated in public policy. It produced the nation's first anti-smoking bill, one of the first public campaign financing schemes, and the nation's first statewide educational choice plan and authorized charter schools. It was one of the first states to have HMOs and boasts of its MinnesotaCare plan intended to hold down costs and provide health care coverage for the poor. It has tried industrial policy, pledging $840 million in credit and loan guarantees to Northwest Airlines in 1991, which in turn kept its Twin Cities hub and built a repair facility in the Iron Range. In 1995 it passed a generous welfare reform, which raised spending even as more recipients got jobs. In 1997, at the insistence of Governor Arne Carlson and over the furious opposition of the teachers' unions, it instituted a form of school choice. These policies have worked well: Manpower Demonstration Research Corporation and Urban Institute studies showed they produced higher earnings, less poverty, more marriage stability and higher school performance. But not all is well. Minnesota has built no electric power plants since the mid-1980s and no major power lines since the late 1970s, and in early 2001 was facing an electricity shortage. And Minneapolis has been called a "ground zero" for animal rights terrorists who have destroyed laboratories and ruined health research projects.

Not very much of Minnesota's recent progress was the product of the activists who dominate both Minnesota parties' caucuses and nominating conventions. The early DFLers were proud of this system, which allowed plenty of political participation and ended control by party bosses. But in time the conventions came to be dominated not by laborite Humphrey followers or the wives of management Republicans, but by left-wingers and counterculturites, right-wing abortion opponents and religious hardliners. As Carleton College political scientist Steven Schier says, "Each party's endorsing convention has become an outpost of exotic and extreme politics." Minnesota has been willing to elect senators chosen by the parties' extremes, but not since the 1970s has Minnesota elected a governor who came out of the convention process. Instead, it chose Rudy Perpich, a DFL maverick from the Iron Range, in 1982 and 1986; Arne Carlson, a moderate Republican who didn't even bother to seek convention endorsement for reelection, in 1990 and 1994; and then of course Jesse Ventura, running as the nominee of the Reform Party in 1998. At the beginning of that year, the pundits focused on which of the three sons of DFL heroes—Attorney General Skip Humphrey, former state Senator Mike Freeman or former state Senator Ted Mondale—would be the DFL governor nominee, and on whether DFLer-turned-Republican Norm Coleman, the mayor of St. Paul, would be accepted by the Republican Party. But the real gainer was Ventura, who scored in the low teens in most polls but who produced a turnout surge in November and won with 37%, to 34% for Coleman and only 28% for Humphrey—less than half the 60% his father won in his first electrifying election for senator exactly 50 years earlier.

It was, literally, a new Minnesota that elected Ventura. In the Twin Cities core, Hennepin and Ramsey Counties, with one-third of the vote, it was an almost even three-way race, with Ventura leading narrowly with 36%, to 32% for Coleman and 31% for Humphrey. In the one-third of Minnesota beyond the range of Minneapolis-St. Paul TV stations on which Ventura concentrated his meager TV buy, Ventura finished third, with 29%, to 37% for Coleman and 33% for Humphrey. Coleman carried the ancestral Republican base—heavily German counties in southern Minnesota and the heavily Norwegian counties north and west of St. Cloud—and Humphrey carried the far north with pluralities plus Austin, site of the bitter Hormel strike. Ventura's breakout came in the counties outside the Twin Cities core but within the Twin Cities media market. In this one-third of the state, turnout was actually up 2% from the presidential year of 1996, and up a whopping 31% from the last off-year of 1994. This is the youngest part of Minnesota, with many young families moving out from the Twin Cities core; Minnesota allows Election Day registration, and the bulk of the new voters went for Ventura. He carried absolute majorities in six of these counties, and above 40% in all but two others.

Governor   Jesse Ventura, elected in 1998, is America's most distinctive governor: 6-foot-4, bald, a former professional wrestler who won as the candidate of the Reform Party and now governs as a member of the Independence Party. Ventura grew up in Minneapolis, the son of a steamfitter and a nurse-anesthetist; his legal name is still James George Janos. On graduating from high school, he joined the Navy and served as a SEAL in Vietnam. On returning home he went to community college and for 11 years was a professional wrestler—essentially a form of acting, but one that requires a good physique and some considerable athletic skill; he picked the name Ventura from a map of California (wisely rejecting nearby Oxnard and Santa Barbara). He also worked as a bodyguard for the Rolling Stones. In the mid-1980s he became a broadcaster, later a talk radio host and a movie actor; he appeared in *Predator* with Arnold Schwarzenegger and uttered the line, "I ain't got time to bleed." He entered politics after a Disney series he was scheduled to act in was canceled; he returned home and got elected mayor of Brooklyn Park, a middle-income suburb northwest of Minneapolis, and served from 1991–95.

Some time in 1995 Ventura got into his head the improbable idea of running for governor, as a candidate for Ross Perot's Reform Party. There was a certain shrewdness here. As he put it later, "I believe the Republicans and the Democrats have reached levels of extreme, where they're out there representing 15% extreme left and 15% extreme right. And the 70% of us who are more centrist have to then choose the lesser of two evils." The endorsement conventions and primaries would keep the two major parties busy until September, while Ventura, well known from talk radio, could set out his platform. Moreover, Minnesota's high-minded public finance system would limit the major party nominees to $2.1 million each, giving Ventura the opportunity to raise enough money to get matching funds and be reasonably competitive in spending.

In the meantime, candidates of the two major parties tried to set forth their competing visions; it was as if each represented a ring on a tree, representing a decade of Minnesota politics. They included "my three sons," the sons of revered DFL politicians. Former legislator Mike Freeman was a kind of 1940s liberal, a strong backer of labor unions who relied on union support and won the party endorsement at the June convention. Attorney General Hubert Humphrey III, universally known as Skip, was mostly famous for the large settlement he reached with the tobacco companies; otherwise he was a 1950s liberal, recalling his father's ebullience. Former state Senator Ted Mondale, who antagonized unions by supporting workmen's comp reform and called for a program of HOPE scholarships, was a 1980s New Democrat. A fourth Democrat, department store heir and former Auditor (and now U.S. Senator) Mark Dayton, recalled the era of 1960s liberalism, opposed to the Vietnam war and inspired by the civil rights movement. Competing for the Republican nomination were Lieutenant Governor Joanne Benson, a 1970s Gerald Ford moderate; Allen Quist, a 1980s abortion opponent; and St. Paul Mayor Norm Coleman, a 1990s party-switcher. Coleman, an abortion opponent himself, had tangled with public employee unions and left the Democratic Party in 1996; after a battle at the Republican Party convention, he won its endorsement and faced only token primary opposition. In the September primary, Humphrey's name-identification prevailed: He won with 37% of the vote, to 19% for Freeman, 19% for pro-life Iron Range state Senator Doug Johnson, 18% for Dayton and 7% for Mondale.

Post-primary polls showed Humphrey leading with about half the vote, with Ventura around 10%; taking note, Humphrey insisted that Ventura be included in all debates. Ventura hired the admaker who produced the humorous spots that helped elect Paul Wellstone senator in 1990. This time, the ads used the sound track from the movie *Shaft*, showed Ventura in the pose of Rodin's "The Thinker," and pitted a Jesse Ventura action figure fighting "Evil Special Interest Man." There was also substance. Ventura is solidly pro-choice on abortion and said that he would consider legalization of drugs and prostitution. But he was also for cutting taxes. He was irked at the state's $50 tax for personal watercraft (he owns five) and proposed a rebate of the state budget surplus: "I'll fight to get those Democrats and Republicans to return the $4 billion in excess taxes they took from you. That's $1,000 for every person in Minnesota." Ventura called for restricting college loans to two years, on the grounds that many students do nothing but drink beer and party. By mid-October, the polls showed Humphrey and Coleman even at around 35%, and Ventura with a promising 21%. His advertising, concentrated in the Twin Cities media market that covers two-thirds of the state, won over many young voters and erstwhile non-voters.

In a year when turnout nationally mostly sagged, turnout surged in Minnesota, especially in the outer counties of the Twin Cities media market; in many counties turnout rose 40% or more from the last off-year election, and was even above the presidential year of 1996. This was the area where Ventura ran best, with 45%, to 34% for Coleman and only 21% for Humphrey. Inter-estingly, the new voters seemed to go heavily Republican in legislative races, enabling the Repub-licans to win control of the state House. Ventura also carried the Twin Cities core counties of Hennepin and Ramsey narrowly over Coleman and Humphrey, and ran behind, but not by much, in the rest of the state, where his exposure was much less. Overall, Ventura won with 37%; Coleman, holding much of the Republican core despite switching parties, won 34%; Humphrey, with the old DFL constituency atrophying far more than almost anyone expected, had 28%. Ven-tura won largely because of his support from young voters, and from young men in particular. The VNS exit poll showed Ventura running 39%–39% with Coleman among men, while Humphrey edged Ventura 36%–34% among women. Ventura led Coleman 46%–36% with voters under 30, with only 16% for Humphrey; among voters 30 to 44, Ventura led Coleman 43%–33%. Only among the elderly, many with fond memories of his father's career, did Humphrey lead, 40%–39% over Coleman, with 21% for Ventura. Ventura's was not an elite coalition: Voters with $100,000-plus incomes widely favored Coleman, and those with graduate school degrees narrowly favored Hum-phrey; Ventura's best income group was $50,000-$75,000 and his best education groups were high school graduates and those with some college.

Ventura charmed almost everyone on election night by saying that his wife would continue running her riding school on their Maple Grove horse farm and he would continue as volunteer football coach, as he had for 11 years, at Champlain High School. He chose as chief of staff a longtime top aide to former Congressman Tim Penny, a fiscally conservative Democrat. Repub-lican Congressman Jim Ramstad's sister became commissioner of Corrections. Ventura struck a few false notes at first, suggesting that his wife be paid $25,000 a year and obtaining a permit to carry a handgun. But his dramatic inauguration and State of the State speech were well received. "I stand before you as governor willing to say what too many politicians at all levels of government have been scared to say: The free ride is over." Ventura has appeared on national television, hosted well-publicized visits with Al Gore in spring and summer 2000, and has made some embarrassing mistakes. He speaks the demotic English of middle American Minnesota, with double negatives and mispronunciations; he told David Letterman that "drunken Irishmen" laid out the crooked streets of St. Paul; his service as a referee at a World Wrestling Federation match in 1999 and his Saturday night commentary job for the now-defunct XFL football league were widely criticized. In a fall 1999 interview in *Playboy* he said, "Organized religion is a sham and a crutch for weak-minded people who need strength in numbers. It tells people to go out and stick their noses in other people's business." He does not love the press: Ventura riled state capitol reporters by issuing credential badges identifying each journalist as an "official jackal," but scrapped them after the media loudly complained. Nevertheless, his job rating in Minnesota hovered just over 70%.

For all his lack of polish, he has a serious plan for governance and has gone about putting it into effect shrewdly and with limited but significant success. He scaled down his proposals for a sales tax rebate, but checks have gone out to every household every summer since he has been governor. He called for massive tax cuts, and got smaller ones. With his veto he has opposed restrictions on abortion. He has backed the Hiawatha light rail line and, against opposition, broke ground on it in 2001. For all his support of abortion and gay rights, he is willing to challenge liberal conventional wisdom on other cultural issues. In April 1999 he said the Columbine shootings justified concealed-carry legislation and in October 2000 he opposed enhanced penalties for "hate crimes." "They're no more dead because it was a hate crime or it was a robbery and a shooting," he reasoned. "Murder is murder." Some of Ventura's proposals have been quixotic. He pressed for a unicameral legislature in 2000, to no avail. His proposal for the legislature to meet just once every two years is not going to happen. As his communications director said, "The governor stands alone. He has no allies in the legislature. A lot of people are pleased that he is willing to stand up to the two parties." When the legislature seemed deadlocked on the budget in 2000, Democratic Senate Majority Leader Roger Moe proposed that Ventura and each house could spend $175 million as each wished: Ventura lowered the license plate fee (to a maximum of $189 in the second year of ownership and $99 thereafter), the Senate Democrats increased spending on education and the House Republicans cut taxes. Something for the political scientists: an experiment in tripartite government.

Naturally the national press speculated about Ventura's role in national politics. Could he be elected president? he was asked in 2000. "Everyone says I can't, but I believe sure I could," he said. "This is America. And I proved it here. If you look at one California poll, I have an 80% recognition rate already, so I don't have to buy name recognition." At the July 1999 Reform Party national convention he said he would not run for president, and pressed for the election of Jack Gargan as Reform Party chairman over a candidate backed by Ross Perot; Gargan won. In fall 1999, when Perot was toying with Patrick Buchanan as a presidential nominee, Ventura tried to recruit New York developer Donald Trump. In February 2000 Ventura resigned from the Reform Party (calling it "hopelessly dysfunctional"); the next day Perot-Buchanan supporters removed Gargan, and Trump soon dropped out; Perot's inevitable split with Buchanan came later. Of course the Reform Party was always more a plaything of Perot's than a party, and Ventura's Independence Party, though it ran candidates in Minnesota in 2000, didn't win anything (although one Democratic legislator switched to it in 2001). Ventura also got into a bit of a feud with Senator Paul Wellstone. When rumors appeared that Wellstone might run for governor, Ventura said "Bring him on." Wellstone responded tartly, "Jesse Ventura has made a career of provoking and intimidating his opponents. Unfortunately, as governor, he hasn't been able to leave those tactics behind. One more reason not to take him seriously."

In 2001, even as economic growth was slowing, Ventura set out an ambitious program. He called for sharply reducing property taxes, lowering the sales tax rate from 6.5% to 6% but extending it to services, cutting the income tax, lowering license plate fees to $75 and, of course, sending out another rebate. He called for campaign finance legislation to reduce "special interest" influence, and for ending subsidies to rural telephone companies. He called on state agencies to identify reductions (a "challenge pool") in order to get increases in other programs. He called for increased education funding for districts that link teacher pay to student performance, and for partnership benefits for gay and lesbian state employees. In February 2000 Ventura said of the state legislature, "If they give me my initiatives and I come out very positive on all of them, I won't seek reelection. If they fight me tooth and nail, they're going to get four more years of me if the people of Minnesota want to give it to them. I'm very serious." On that basis, he seems likely to run—but no one can be entirely sure: in February 2001 he said that if he did, "I'm not going to raise a dollar and I'm not going to spend a dollar." In the meantime the DFL and the Republicans will probably have nomination fights at their state party conventions, with their extreme left and right dominating the news coverage, putting Ventura in a fine position to win—and leaving the national press to wonder out loud what he will do in 2004.

Cook's Call   *Competitive.* Ventura and his unorthodox approach to the office and to politics continue to be a thorn in the side of both parties, although the governor remains popular with rank and file voters. The Democratic field has not yet gelled, but the party is likely to produce a first-tier nominee. On the Republican side, businessman Brian Sullivan has announced his candidacy while state House Majority Leader Tim Pawlenty and some statewide officeholders are looking at the race. Ventura starts with an advantage, but this race will get interesting.

Senior Senator   Paul Wellstone was first elected to the Senate in 1990, in one of the great upsets of the decade. He grew up in northern Virginia, the son of immigrants from Russia, more interested in wrestling than politics. He married young, earned a Ph.D. at North Carolina, then went to teach at Carleton College in Minnesota in 1969. He was a "rock-the-boat professor" at Carleton, where he published little and taught the politics of protest. He made a name for himself in local politics by leading protesters in sympathy with Hormel meatpacker strikers in Austin and getting arrested while picketing a bank that had foreclosed on local farmers; he ran for state auditor and co-chaired Jesse Jackson's 1988 presidential campaign in Minnesota.

Then in 1990 Wellstone ran for the Senate seat held by Republican Rudy Boschwitz. In the primary Wellstone beat Agriculture Commissioner Jim Nichols, a populist on economics but anti-abortion, 60%–34%. In the general, he traveled around the state in a green bus and ran shrewd and humorous TV ads proclaiming that viewers wouldn't be seeing him as often as they saw Boschwitz (because he didn't accept PAC money) and made cute appeals ("I'm better looking"). In a takeoff on the film *Roger and Me*, one ad showed Wellstone in pursuit of a confrontation-shy Boschwitz; like the film, this was not entirely honest, since Boschwitz had agreed to debate. But the ad's cleverness and the candidate's charm created an almost cuddly impression, while Boschwitz responded hamhandedly, needlessly involving himself in controversy over the Republican gubernatorial nominee and switching his stand on the Voting Rights renewal. Wellstone won 50%–48%, carrying metro Twin Cities 54%–45% while losing outstate Minnesota 51%–47%. This happy warrior of the campus left became "the first 1960s radical elected to the U.S. Senate," in *Mother Jones*'s words.

Wellstone has one of the most liberal voting records in Congress. "I still believe that government can be a force for good in people's lives," he says. At first he seemed awkward in the Senate, demanding roll call votes on all appropriations. But in time he learned to use Senate rules to achieve results. He successfully led opposition to the 1991 energy bill that would have opened the Arctic National Wildlife Refuge to oil drilling. He worked hard on lobbying reform and the gift ban, then finally got a vote on them in 1996 by threatening to attach the issue to telecommunications reform. He opposed U.S. military action in the Gulf war and, showing consistency, he criticized Bill Clinton for sending troops to Haiti without the consent of Congress. He and Pete Domenici pushed successfully in 1996 for mental health coverage in health insurance. And in March 1996 he seized an opportune parliamentary moment to force a vote on a minimum wage increase.

In 1996 Wellstone once again faced Boschwitz, who seemed interested in revenge. Republican ads called Wellstone "embarrassingly liberal and decades out of touch" and "Senator Welfare" for his vote against the 1996 Welfare Reform Act. Wellstone responded exuberantly, invoking Minnesota DFL tradition: "I am a Hubert Humphrey senator. I go to the floor of the Senate, and I fight for children, I fight for senior citizens, I fight for health care. I'm a Minnesota senator!" Unlike 1990, he did not limit himself to $100 contributions, but proved himself a master of the current campaign finance system even as he denounced it, raising and spending $7.4 million, far more than Boschwitz's $4.3 million. His welfare vote proved not to be disabling; he received more flak from his own supporters for voting for the Defense of Marriage Act. Boschwitz, evidently in desperation, ran ads citing issues on which he agreed with Bill Clinton, who was cruising to an easy victory in Minnesota. Wellstone won 50%–41%, carrying the Twin Cities heavily, 52%–39%, and running a bit ahead in the rest of the state, 49%–45%. Reform Party candidate Dean Barkley, who would go on to help manage Jesse Ventura's campaign in 1998, took 7%. Wellstone said that he was limiting himself to two terms.

Wellstone's focus has become increasingly national. In 1997 he embarked on a trip to the poorest parts of America, like Tunica County, Mississippi (with its poor farmers but also gleaming casinos), echoing a trip Robert Kennedy took in 1967. "The Democratic Party has lost some of its soul," he proclaimed. He opposed a ban on human cloning, for fear it would stop useful medical research, and called on the Clinton administration to criticize China's human rights record. "We need more strong, authentic populist candidates to fight back against big money and their friends in Congress and focus on the kitchen table issues central to the lives of working families," he said and prepared to run for president himself. In July 1998 he said he was almost certain to run; Wellstone for President paraphernalia appeared at a coffee shop in the self-declared nuclear-free zone of Takoma Park, Maryland. He became the first to set up an exploratory committee. But in January 1999 he surprised and disappointed a crowd at the state Capitol in St. Paul by announcing that he would not run because his injured back couldn't sustain the trauma of campaigning. In April 1999 he endorsed Bill Bradley and, with his much more moderate colleague Bob Kerrey, campaigned exuberantly for him in primary and caucus states.

Wellstone is one of those senators who cares more about advancing principles that he hopes will some day triumph than in winning easy victories in the short run. In his 2001 book *The Conscience of a Liberal; Reclaiming the Compassionate Agenda,* Wellstone wrote, "I feel as if 80% of my work as a senator has been playing defense, cutting the extremist enthusiasms of the conservative agenda (much of which originates in the House) rather than moving forward on a progressive agenda." He was one of three senators to oppose national missile defense legislation in March 1999. To the 1999 gun control bill he tried to add a study of why disproportionate numbers of minority youth are incarcerated. He cast the Senate's only vote against the ed-flex bill in April 1999, and sponsored a bill in April 2000 to require states to let students graduate even if they don't pass state-mandated tests (he had scored below 800 on his SAT). In July 2000 he was the only Senate Democrat to vote against the Democratic version of estate tax repeal. He opposed permanent normal trade relations with China; his amendments to tie PNTR to improvements in human rights and to limit prison labor were beaten 69–28 and 68–29 in September 2000, even with the support of Jesse Helms, his ideological opposite. He spoke out long and often against the bankruptcy reform bill as "anti-consumer, anti-women, anti-children and anti-working people." On a visit to Colombia is December 2000, he was accidentally sprayed with herbicide and two land mines were found near a town he visited; he opposed Plan Colombia because of the Colombian government's human rights record. He spoke out strongly for campaign finance changes, and his amendment, of dubious constitutionality in the opinions of many, to ban independent spending in the 60 days before elections passed 51–48 in March 2001. In April 2001 he passed an amendment that reduced the Bush tax cut by $17 billion over ten years to boost funding for veterans' programs.

On health care, Wellstone has attacked pharmaceutical company profits as "obscene" and supports single-payer insurance. In 1999 he and Pete Domenici sought to extend their 1996 mental health law by requiring "parity" in treatment of "severe biologically-based mental illnesses." He and Jim Ramstad introduced bill expanding medical coverage for recovering addicts. On an issue of major interest to Minnesota farmers, Wellstone wants to repeal the Freedom to Farm Act and threatened a filibuster to get a vote on his 18-month moratorium on agribusiness mergers; it failed 71–27 in November 1999. He threatened a filibuster against the Northeast Dairy Compact that month, but it passed anyway. His bill passed unanimously in October 2000 to allow Hmong war widows to take the U.S. citizenship exam in Hmong.

Governor Jesse Ventura and Wellstone have not gotten along smoothly. Wellstone has been critical of Ventura's proposed education budget, and the governor in turn harshly criticized Wellstone for failing to get more federal funding for special education (amendments he had sponsored to do so failed in 1991, 1994, 1998 and 2000). In December 2000 Ventura said he might run against Wellstone for senator in 2002; five days later he said he had no interest in the job. But others do. In January 2001 Wellstone went back on his 1990 and 1996 promise to seek only two terms, citing the 50–50 split in the Senate and explaining that "so much has changed and so much is at stake." Two January 2001 polls showed that over 50% of Minnesota voters believed he had a moral obligation not to run. Possible Republican candidates include former St. Paul Mayor and 1998 governor candidate Norm Coleman (who was backed by Vice President Dick Cheney in April 2001, a move that dissuaded state House Majority Leader Tim Pawlenty from running), former Senator Rod Grams, Congressman Gil Gutknecht and Secretary of State Mary Kiffmeyer.

Cook's Call　*Highly Competitive.* Wellstone's liberal voting record, his broken promise to serve just two terms, and evidence that the state may be trending away from Democrats combine to pique Republican interest in this race. It is not entirely clear just how vulnerable Wellstone may be, but Republican St. Paul Mayor Norm Coleman, a party switcher with the ability to attract moderates, will give the incumbent a difficult race.

Junior Senator   Mark Dayton, elected to the Senate in 2000, grew up in Minnesota, the son of Bruce Dayton, head of Dayton Hudson, one of the nation's major and most innovative retailers (it is now called Target Corporation, and in 2001 changed the name of Dayton's in Minnesota to Marshall Field's). Mark Dayton graduated from Yale in the student-rebellion year of 1969 and taught 9th grade science in a New York public school in the Bowery for two years, then worked as a counselor and administrator for a Boston crisis center for teenage runaways. He was active in the anti-Vietnam war movement and his name found its way—presumably because of his family and that of his wife, a Rockefeller—to Richard Nixon's enemies list. In 1975 and 1976 he worked for then-Senator Walter Mondale; in 1977 he returned to Minnesota and worked for then-Governor Rudy Perpich. In 1979, after Perpich lost a re-election bid, Dayton funded with $400,000 a nonprofit agency to spur development in rural Minnesota.

In 1982 Dayton ran for the Senate, and spent the then-enormous sum of $7 million of his own money. He beat former Senator Eugene McCarthy's quixotic campaign by 69%–24% in the DFL primary, but lost 53%–47% to Republican Senator David Durenberger. Between 1983 and 1986 he was Perpich's commissioner of Energy and Economic Development. In 1990 he was elected state auditor; in 1994 decided not to run for reelection. Such statewide offices give incumbents helpful name identification, but their duties are often perfunctory; presumably Dayton felt he could purchase name identification whenever he wanted, and was seeking more useful work. In a flourish, he attempted to give back $1 million of unspent funds to the state treasury. In 1998 he ran in the Democratic primary for governor, but spent only $2 million of his own money, and finished fourth, far behind the winner, Skip Humphrey, with 18% of the vote. In 1999 and 2000 he was finance chairman for Senator Paul Wellstone.

In 2000 he stepped up to run against Senator Rod Grams, with a tattered resume in the view of some critics, but also arguably with a wealth of experience in government and community affairs. Grams was the most obviously vulnerable Republican senator up that year. A former Minneapolis-St. Paul TV news anchor, he had won in the Republican year of 1994 by only 49%–44% against an under-funded, little-known and left-wing candidate, Ann Wynia, who had served just one term in the House from a suburban Twin Cities district. Grams' very conservative voting record—as different from his colleague Paul Wellstone's as those of any two senators from the same state have been for more than half a century—was out of line with Minnesota opinion on many issues, and he had no signal legislative accomplishments.

Grams attracted seven DFL opponents before Dayton entered the race. Dayton first gave it thought in January, when he realized his second marriage had broken up. He gave it more thought in March 2000, when former Congressman Tim Penny, a fiscally conservative Democrat, surprised everyone by dropping out of the race. Dayton kept thinking about Penny's withdrawal as he went training that month near Churchill, Manitoba, for a North Pole expedition. "I saw a political vacuum. Politics, like nature, abhors a vacuum," he said later, and decided to forego the North Pole for a Senate race. He announced on April 3, got several longtime staffers to run the campaign and hired national consultants. He steered clear of the nominating convention, which chose state Senator Jerry Janezich, owner of a bar in the Iron Range. Instead, Dayton came up with innovative campaign ideas. He borrowed from a Senate candidate from Montana the idea of accompanying busloads of senior citizens to Canada to buy prescription drugs at lower prices than in the United States; this Rx Express got plenty of publicity. He set up a Healthcare Hotline for people having disputes with their HMOs, which are very common in Minnesota. He performed menial jobs across the state—the work days strategy pioneered by Iowa Senator Tom Harkin in 1974. He spent his own money liberally, but so did trial lawyer Mike Ciresi; his firm received $427 million for working on Minnesota's $6.1 billion tobacco lawsuit and he spent some $5 million on the primary. But Ciresi went off the air in mid-June while Dayton, who spent $5.2 million on the primary, had the airwaves to himself from June 17 to August 1. In the September 12 primary, Dayton won 41%, to 22% for Ciresi, 21% for Janezich and 15% for construction executive Rebecca

Yanisch. Ciresi's vote was heaviest in the Twin Cities core, Hennepin and Ramsey Counties; Janezich ran best in the Iron Range and the third of the state outside the Twin Cities media market; Dayton, with his saturation TV campaign, won 40% or more and carried the Twin Cities core, the rest of the Twin Cities media market and the rest of the state.

The two major-party nominees presented the voters with a clear contrast on the issues. Dayton was for universal government-run health insurance (a position most of whose ardent backers are self-financing millionaires: Dayton, Jon Corzine, Jay Rockefeller, Edward Kennedy), while Grams was for medical savings accounts. Grams favored individual investment accounts in Social Security, while Dayton argued that the current system would be sound until 2037. Dayton would have the government lower the price of prescription drugs; Grams' prescription drugs program would cover low-income seniors. Grams called for eliminating the estate tax and the marriage penalty and replacing the income tax with a flat tax; Dayton called for doubling the $500 per child tax credit (co-sponsored by Grams) and expanding the childcare dependent tax credit. But much of the campaign was dominated by negative charges and driven by Dayton's financial advantage. Dayton spent $11.9 million, almost all of it his own money, doubling the previous Minnesota record (set by himself in 1982); Grams spent only $6 million. He attacked Dayton as a "drug lord" for owning pharmaceutical stock; Dayton said he thought he had sold all such stock in April and in September sold his entire portfolio. Grams was hurt by publicity about two arrests of his 22-year-old son. It was revealed in December 1999 that his son had been stopped by police in July, after Grams called the Anoka County sheriff's office and asked that he be found; marijuana charges were filed against Grams' son in December and he was found guilty in January 2000. Then in September his son was arrested in New Mexico on charges of possession of firearms and a stolen vehicle. Grams, who was divorced in 1996, was also dogged by rumors of an affair between him and his aide Christine Gunhus (they married the weekend after the election); in September 2000 four emails criticizing DFL candidate Mike Ciresi and sent to 100 DFL officials were traced to Gunhus' home telephone number—she plead no contest in June to a misdemeanor complaint alleging she sent them. In response Grams ran an ad showing his mother saying, "Have you ever had someone spend a million dollars a week telling lies about someone you love?" and dismissing Dayton with the Norwegian expression "Uff-da!"

Given all this, the result must be considered fairly close. Dayton won 49%–43%, with 6% for Jim Gibson, enough to give the Independence Party major-party status for 2002—a help to Jesse Ventura. Dayton ran best in the Twin Cities core, leading there 54%–36%. In the remainder of the Twin Cities media market, the part of the state that voted heavily for Jesse Ventura two years before, Grams led 48%–44%. In Minnesota beyond the Twin Cities media market Dayton led 50%–45%. Dayton, unlike Al Gore, carried the youngest voters; otherwise the divisions were similar to those in the presidential election: Dayton ran 1% ahead of Gore, Grams 3% behind George W. Bush.

Minnesota now has two Democratic senators for the first time since 1978, yet no candidate of either party has won a Senate race with more than 50.4% of the vote since 1988. Dayton was a bit embarrassed in December 2000 when he wondered out loud whether his promise to take a salary of only $1 a year might be fulfilled if he did that in just his first year in the Senate; he said his net worth, which he estimated at the beginning of the campaign at $17 to $22 million, was down substantially. But he quickly thought better of it and agreed to work for $1 a year for the whole term; he is donating the rest to the Minnesota Senior Foundation, which operates prescription drug trips to Canada. Ranked number 100 in seniority, Dayton got seats on the Armed Services, Agriculture and Rules Committees.

Presidential politics Minnesota has the longest consecutive streak of voting Democratic for president of any state: the last time it voted Republican was in 1972, and even then it gave Richard Nixon his lowest percentage margin over George McGovern. But in 2000 Minnesota was seriously contested, and in the end gave Al Gore only a 48%–46% victory over George W. Bush. It was a vivid contrast to 1988, when Bush's father first ran and lost the state to Michael Dukakis by 53%–46%. What changed in the meantime? First, Ross Perot detached many voters from their ancestral allegiance. He won 24% of the vote here in 1992 and 12% in 1996, more in each case than any other state this large. The second factor was the Ventura victory. The VNS exit poll showed that Ventura voters preferred Gore over Bush, but counties around the Twin Cities where Ventura's percentage was highest and turnout went up most in 1998 voted for Bush in 2000, even though they had mostly voted Democratic for president in the past. Bush carried voters under 30, a good omen for Republicans. Al Gore bettered Dukakis's margins in the Twin Cities core. But starting in the suburbs and increasingly in the rural west and north, George W. Bush led by wider margins (or trailed by less) than his father had; he carried five of the eight congressional districts. In farm country and the north woods he carried many counties that had long voted DFL. If the major metro movement toward Democrats in the 1990s so visible on the East and West Coasts was far more visible in Minnesota, the countervailing rural movement toward Republicans was even more prominent. The result is that Minnesota must be counted as competitive in the next close presidential race.

Minnesota has a tradition of selecting national convention delegates in caucuses. But caucus turnout has been low: in the 1998 DFL caucuses, an average of 4.4 voters showed up in each precinct, and in one-fourth of the precincts no one showed up at all. DFL leaders, reeling from their party's third-place finish in the 1998 gubernatorial race, tried to encourage turnout and attract more voters in the March 2000 presidential precinct caucuses by moving them from Tuesday night to Saturday and by holding a presidential preference vote, with national convention delegates assigned proportionately. It made little difference: by the time Minnesotans caucused, the nomination was already clinched.

Congressional districting   Minnesota's current district lines were drawn by a state court and put in place for the 1994 election. Population shifts in the state in the 1990s were not drastic, so theoretically only minor adjustments would be necessary. The central-city 4th and 5th Districts could be expanded outward and the suburban 3d and 6th Districts contracted a bit. Republicans have a 69–65 margin in the state House, and in early 2001 passed a plan combining the central cities of Minneapolis and St. Paul into one heavily Democratic district, in the hopes they could carry three adjacent suburban districts. But the state Senate, controlled by Democrats, passed a plan preserving each city's district. Governor Jesse Ventura has said he would like to maximize the number of competitive districts; but four of the current eight districts are already competitive. The issue might have to be settled, as it was in the 1990s, in the courts.

THE PEOPLE: Pop. 2000: 4,919,479; Pop. 1990: 4,375,099, up 12.4% 1990–2000. 1.7% of U.S. total, 21st largest; 89.4% White, 3.5% Black, 2.9% Asian, 1.1% Amer. Indian, 1.7% Two + races, 1.3% Other; 2.9% Hispanic Origin. 3.3% Unemployment. 2000 Voting age pop.: 3,632,585. 2000 Turnout: 2,457,156; 68% of VAP. Registered voters (2000): 3,265,324; no party registration.

POLITICAL LINEUP: Governor, Jesse Ventura (Ind); Lt. Gov., Mae Schunk (Ref); Secy. of State, Mary Kiffmeyer (R); Atty. Gen., Mike Hatch (DFL); Treasurer, Carol Johnson (DFL); Auditor, Judith Dutcher (R); State Senate, 67 (39 DFL, 27 R, 1 I); Senate President, Don Samuelson (DFL); Majority Leader, Roger Moe (DFL); State House, 134 (65 DFL, 69 R); House Speaker, Steve Sviggum (R). Senators, Paul Wellstone (DFL) and Mark Dayton (DFL). Representatives, 8 (6 DFL, 2 R).

ELECTIONS DIVISION: 651-215-1440; **FILING DEADLINE FOR U.S. CONGRESS:** July 16, 2002.

2000 Presidential Vote			1996 Presidential Vote		
Gore (D)	1,168,266	(48%)	Clinton (D)	1,120,279	(51%)
Bush (R)	1,109,659	(46%)	Dole (R)	766,476	(35%)
Nader (Green)	126,696	(5%)	Perot (I)	257,704	(12%)
Others	34,064	(1%)	Others	48,425	(2%)

Gov. Jesse Ventura (Ind)

Elected 1998, term expires Jan. 2003, 1st term; b. July 15, 1951, Minneapolis; home, Maple Grove; N. Hennepin Commun. Col., 1975.; Lutheran; married (Terry).

Military Career: Navy, 1969–73 (Vietnam), Naval Reserves, 1973–75.

Elected Office: Brooklyn Park Mayor, 1990–95.

Professional Career: Professional wrestler, 1973–84; Actor, 1984–97; Radio talk show host, 1995–98.

Office: 130 State Capitol Bldg., Aurora Ave., St. Paul, 55155, 651-296-3391; Fax: 651-296-0039; Web site: www.state.mn.us.

Election Results

1998 general	Jesse Ventura (Ref)	773,713	(37%)
	Norm Coleman (R)	717,350	(34%)
	Hubert Humphrey III (DFL)	587,528	(28%)
	Others	13,175	(1%)
1998 primary	Jesse Ventura (Ref)	unopposed	
1994 general	Arne H. Carlson (IR)	1,094,165	(62%)
	John Marty (DFL)	589,344	(33%)
	Others	82,081	(5%)

Sen. Paul Wellstone (DFL)

Elected 1990, seat up 2002, 2d term; b. July 21, 1944, Washington, D.C.; home, St. Paul; U. of NC, B.A. 1965, Ph.D. 1969; Jewish; married (Sheila).

Professional Career: Prof., Carleton Col., 1969–90.

DC Office: 136 HSOB, 20510, 202-224-5641; Fax: 202-224-8438; Web site: www.senate.gov/~wellstone.

State Offices: St. Paul, 651-645-0323; Virginia, 218-741-1074; Wilmar, 320-231-0001.

Committees: *Foreign Relations*: European Affairs; International Economic Policy, Export & Trade Promotion; Near Eastern & South Asian Affairs (Chmn.). *Health, Education, Labor & Pensions*: Children & Families; Employment, Safety & Training (Chmn.). *Indian Affairs. Small Business. Veterans' Affairs.*

Group Ratings

	ADA	ACLU	AFS	LCV	CON	ITIC	NTU	COC	ACU	NTLC	CHC
2000	100	86	100	100	39	60	18	20	4	3	0
1999	90	—	100	89	78	—	19	24	8	—	—

National Journal Ratings

	1999 LIB	—	1999 CONS		2000 LIB	—	2000 CONS
Economic	72%	—	25%		96%	—	0%
Social	81%	—	12%		79%	—	0%
Foreign	62%	—	29%		89%	—	5%

Key Votes of the 106th Congress

1. Educ. Savings Accts.	N	5. Review Movie Violence	N	9. NATO War in Serbia	Y
2. Prescrip. Drug Benefit	Y	6. Gun Show Bckgrnd. Checks	Y	10. Table Cuba Travel Ban	N
3. Delay Ergonomic Standards	N	7. Ban Part.-Birth Abortion	N	11. Nuclear Test-Ban Treaty	Y
4. Phase Out Estate Tax	N	8. Broaden Hate Crimes List	Y	12. Perm. Trade with China	N

Election Results

1996 general	Paul Wellstone (DFL)	1,098,493	(50%)	($7,459,878)
	Rudy Boschwitz (R)	901,282	(41%)	($4,385,982)
	Dean Barkley (Ref)	152,333	(7%)	($37,240)
1996 primary	Paul Wellstone (DFL)	194,699	(86%)	
	Dick Franson (DFL)	16,465	(7%)	
	Ed Hansen (DFL)	9,990	(4%)	
	Others	4,180	(2%)	
1990 general	Paul Wellstone (DFL)	911,999	(50%)	($1,338,708)
	Rudy Boschwitz (IR)	864,375	(48%)	($6,221,133)
	Others	29,820	(2%)	

Sen. Mark Dayton (DFL)

Elected 2000, seat up 2006, 1st term; b. Jan. 26, 1947, Minneapolis; home, Minneapolis; Yale U., B.A. 1969; Presbyterian; divorced.

Elected Office: Dem. nominee, U.S. Senate, 1982; MN Auditor, 1990–94.

Professional Career: Teacher, NYC public schools, 1969–71; Counselor & administrator, social service agency, Boston, MA, 1971–75; Legis. asst., U.S. Sen. Walter Mondale, 1975–76; Aide, MN Gov. Rudy Perpich, 1977–78; MN Comm. of Economic Development, 1978–82; MN Comm. of Energy & Economic Development, 1983–86; Founder & Pres., Vermillion Investment Co., 1987–90, 1995–97.

DC Office: 346 RSOB, 20510, 202-224-3244; Fax: 202-228-2186; Web site: dayton.senate.gov.

State Office: Ft. Snelling, 612-727-5220.

Committees: *Agriculture, Nutrition & Forestry*: Forestry, Conservation & Rural Revitalization; Marketing, Inspection & Product Promotion. *Armed Services*: Airland Forces; Emerging Threats & Capabilities; Readiness & Management Support. *Rules & Administration*.

Group Ratings and Key Votes: Newly Elected

Election Results

2000 general	Mark Dayton (DFL)	1,181,553	(49%)	($11,957,114)
	Rod Grams (R)	1,047,474	(43%)	($6,024,866)
	Jim Gibson (I)	140,583	(6%)	
	Others	49,910	(2%)	
2000 primary	Mark Dayton (DFL)	178,972	(41%)	
	Mike Ciresi (DFL)	96,874	(22%)	
	Jerry R. Janezich (DFL)	90,074	(21%)	
	Rebecca Yanisch (DFL)	63,289	(15%)	
	Others (DFL)	4,190	(1%)	
1994 general	Rod Grams (IR)	869,653	(49%)	($2,439,798)
	Ann Wynia (DFL)	781,860	(44%)	($2,659,423)
	Dean M. Barkley (I)	95,400	(5%)	($24,266)

FIRST DISTRICT

The Mississippi River runs majestically southeast from Minneapolis and St. Paul, cutting a path through rolling hills and, where it widens, forming calm lakes lapping at the bottomlands: one of the finest river landscapes of North America. This far north, the westward tide of Yankee migrants thinned out. After the Civil War, most settlers following the railroads on the flood plains west of the river were Germans and Scandinavians, bringing their families to this terrain so much like the Rhine, and to the rolling uplands beyond which resemble the northern European plain. Southeastern Minnesota is a borderland between Yankee and German settlements—politically, between

Civil War Republicans and Farmer-Laborites favoring interventionist economic and isolationist foreign policies.

The 1st Congressional District occupies Minnesota's southeastern corner. Within its compact bounds is considerable diversity. Rochester has been home of the Mayo Clinic since it was founded in 1863, when English-born physician William Mayo set up a practice to examine inductees into the Union Army—early government involvement in medicine. Today, Rochester, with its large professional population, is prosperous and growing, with several new projects at Mayo. Austin, a county away, is headquarters of the Hormel meatpacking firm that beat a bitter strike in the 1980s; the huge meatpacking plant here produces Spam, Hormel chili, Dinty Moore stew and, say critics, too much ammonia-loaded waste; this is one place where class warfare politics seems alive. Rochester has long been a Republican stronghold; Austin has long been solidly DFL. But this was the one part of Minnesota outside the Twin Cities core that trended toward Democrats in the 1990s; George W. Bush won by only a small margin in Rochester and barely carried the 1st District in 2000. The 1st District extends north to new subdivisions spreading out from the Twin Cities, the stomping grounds of Jesse Ventura and his Reform Party candidacy in 1998, and to Northfield, home of former Carleton College professor Paul Wellstone, now senator. It also includes the river towns of Red Wing, Wabasha and Winona, with their 19th Century stone storefronts and mountain-like rock outcroppings that overlook the river; this is dairy farming and small industrial country.

The congressman from the 1st District is Gil Gutknecht, a Republican elected in 1994. The name, he likes to explain, means "good hired hand," though "good indentured servant" might be closer to the mark. He grew up in Iowa, son of a union member, worked nine years as a school supply salesman, then became an auctioneer, eventually handling large real estate auctions. He was elected to the legislature in 1982 from Rochester and became Republican floor leader. Partisan, ebullient, he once told Iron Range DFLers that the state motto *L'etoile du Nord* did not mean "send the money north." He had intended to run for the Senate in 1994, but 1st District Congressman Tim Penny, the very popular moderate Democrat who co-sponsored the Penny-Kasich budget cuts of 1993 and 1994, decided to retire, and Gutknecht instead ran for the House. In the Republican primary, Gutknecht argued that he was the more conservative candidate and beat former two-term Congressman Arlen Erdahl, 57%–36%. In the general against Mankato state Senator John Hottinger, who backed a single-payer health care system, Gutknecht called himself "the Minnesota equivalent of Newt Gingrich." Hottinger carried Austin and ran even in Mankato. But Gutknecht won big in Rochester and in the river counties, for a 55%–45% victory.

Gutknecht was an enthusiastic member of the new Republican majority who proudly talked of listening to Gingrich's lecture tapes, and he has a mostly conservative voting record. He has paid heed to district interests, sponsoring a Medicare formula that would pay more to rural hospitals, seeking to reduce pharmaceutical prices by permitting reimportation from other nations of U.S.-made medicines (which Health and Human Services Secretary Donna Shalala blocked after Congress enacted the change), and opposing changes in the sugar program (Minnesota is sugar beet country.) He supported fast track and sought to increase farm exports. With a seat on the Agriculture Committee, he sponsored a bill requiring that packers disclose the prices they pay to hog farmers and promised to "push for a better 'shock absorber' that protects farm income." When the 1999 catch-all spending bill favored dairy farmers in the Northeast at the expense of those from the upper Midwest, Gutknecht angrily sent a letter to Speaker Dennis Hastert resigning his post as one of Tom DeLay's regional Whips rather than continue on a leadership team "that has trampled on the interests of thousands of Minnesota dairy farmers." He sponsored—and went on the talk radio circuit to boost—a 12-year limit on congressional pension accrual. On the Budget Committee, he took some credit for locking away Social Security and Medicare surpluses. By the end of the Clinton era though, he conceded that the hype of a Republican revolution was "greatly exaggerated" and that Gingrich had been "a disappointment to everybody" in thinking he could run the nation as speaker.

Gutknecht continued to attract active opposition in a district with a strong DFL base and a Democratic trend. In 1996 he was targeted by AFL-CIO ads and had serious competition from Winona State economics professor Mary Rieder. She said she was a fiscal conservative like Penny, and she raised enough money to be competitive. Bill Clinton carried the district with a plurality and Rieder's vote tracked his closely. But that left the Democrat with 47% to Gutknecht's 53%. In 1998, state Senator Tracy Beckman, with Tim Penny as his campaign chairman, focused on Gutknecht's support for the Freedom to Farm Act together with the year's sharp drop in crop prices. Gutknecht wobbled a bit, voting against a Republican tax cut, and running ads saying he "listens to farmers" and "has been pushing the administration to enforce our trade agreements." Gutknecht had a big money advantage, and won 55%–45%. He had a rematch in 2000 against Rieder, but Gutknecht won this time with a more comfortable 56%–42%, losing only Austin's Mower County, and that by 49%–48% (while Al Gore was winning it, 58%–37%). Although redistricting prospects are wide open across the state, Gutknecht's recent stronger performances leave him less exposed as a Democratic target. He has been mentioned as a possible candidate against Senator Paul Wellstone in 2002.

Cook's Call *Probably Safe.* After a couple of close races, it looks like Gutknecht may have finally found his footing in this district. If he runs for governor or senator in 2002, this marginal district could produce a competitive race. Clinton won here by 11% in 1996 while Bush won by 2% in 2000. If Gutknecht runs for re-election, which is considered likely, he will be a safe bet for 2002.

THE PEOPLE: Pop. 2000: 594,864; Pop. 1990: 546,881, up 8.8% 1990–2000. 94.7% White, 1.2% Black, 1.7% Asian, 0.3% Amer. Indian, 1% Two+ races, 1.1% Other; 2.7% Hispanic Origin.

2000 Presidential Vote
Bush (R)	137,562	(48%)
Gore (D)	132,727	(46%)
Nader (Green)	13,904	(5%)
Others	4,144	(1%)

1996 Presidential Vote
Clinton (D)	127,730	(48%)
Dole (R)	97,050	(37%)
Perot (I)	35,408	(13%)

Rep. Gil Gutknecht (R)

Elected 1994, 4th term; b. Mar. 20, 1951, Cedar Falls, IA; home, Rochester; U. of N. IA, B.A. 1973; Catholic; married (Mary).

Elected Office: MN House of Reps. 1982–94.

Professional Career: Sales Rep., Latta School Supply Co., 1973–82; Real Estate Auctioneer, 1979–94.

DC Office: 425 CHOB 20515, 202-225-2472; Fax: 202-225-3246; Web site: www.gil.house.gov.

District Office: Rochester, 507-252-9841.

Committees: *Agriculture* (14th of 27 R): General Farm Commodities & Risk Management; Livestock & Horticulture. *Budget* (5th of 24 R). *Science* (Vice Chmn. of 25 R): Environment, Technology and Standards; Research.

Group Ratings
	ADA	ACLU	AFS	LCV	CON	ITIC	NTU	COC	ACU	NTLC	CHC
2000	5	21	0	29	75	94	60	80	92	85	87
1999	15	—	0	6	67	—	67	96	92	—	—

National Journal Ratings
	1999 LIB	—	1999 CONS		2000 LIB	—	2000 CONS
Economic	16%	—	78%		29%	—	67%
Social	4%	—	91%		0%	—	79%
Foreign	0%	—	97%		39%	—	57%

Key Votes of the 106th Congress
1. Patient Bill of Rights	N	5. Bar RU-486 $ for FDA	Y	9. NATO War in Serbia	N
2. Accelerate Min. Wage	N	6. Display 10 Commandments	Y	10. Perm. Trade with China	Y
3. Strike Ban on Ergo. Stnd.	N	7. Gun Show Bkgrnd. Checks	N	11. Debt Relief for 3rd World	N
4. Ovrd. Estate Tax Veto	Y	8. Ban Part.-Birth Abortion	Y	12. Drop Cuba Econ. Embargo	N

Election Results

2000 general	Gil Gutknecht (R) 159,835	(56%)	($969,598)
	Mary Rieder (DFL) 117,946	(42%)	($372,636)
	Other 5,440	(2%)	
2000 primary	Gil Gutknecht (R) .... unopposed		
1998 general	Gil Gutknecht (R) 131,233	(55%)	($948,385)
	Tracy L. Beckman (DFL) 108,420	(45%)	($323,895)

SECOND DISTRICT

West of the Mississippi and Minnesota rivers, where the plains rise above the gorges that the rivers have cut through them, is the great farming country of southwestern Minnesota. This is where Laura Ingalls Wilder's family came on the way west from their little house in the big woods in Wisconsin to the "Little House on the Prairie" in South Dakota, and stopped by the shores of Plum Creek, near Walnut Grove, Minnesota, not long after the Indians were forced out by U.S. troops following the Dakota rebellion of 1862. The creeks and rivers cut crevasses into these plains, spotted with occasional hills and towns settled more than 100 years ago by Yankee, German and Scandinavian farmers. This is a hard place to make a living; Laura's family, after all their struggles, left the farm for town as soon as they could. Even in the 1990s, farmers still toiled against the elements to make a profitable living, and even their successes hurt; with higher productivity, fewer people lived on the land or even in town.

The 2d Congressional District takes in roughly the southwestern quadrant of Minnesota. The farm counties slowly have become depopulated, as young people move into small towns and, more often, to the Twin Cities or other big metro areas. But a vibrant German heritage remains in communities such as New Ulm, where the Concord Singers—30 men decked out in lederhosen, red vests and white shirts—are described as one of the best male choruses in the nation. The 2d District's boundaries take in outlying counties and townships of the Twin Cities metro area. Scott and Carver County, southwest of Minneapolis, are among the nation's top 50 high-income counties, and solidly Republican. Others, farther out, like Waverly where Hubert Humphrey had his lakeside home, are more humble—places where modest-income young families are moving into what was once open countryside punctuated by small villages. The city of St. Michael in Wright County more than tripled its population in the 1990s. This outlying part of the Twin Cities metro area and media market was the heartland of support for Jesse Ventura's Reform Party candidacy for governor in 1998 and now casts about half of the district's votes. Three-fourths of the state legislators from the area are Republicans.

The new congressman from the 2d District is Mark Kennedy, a Democrat elected in 2000. He was born in Benson and grew up in Murdock and Pequot Lakes; his great-grandfather was a Swift County commissioner and his grandfather was mayor of Murdock. Kennedy graduated from St. John's University in 1978 and University of Michigan Business School in 1983. He was a CPA with Arthur Andersen before becoming financial director of Pillsbury. His path up the corporate ladder led him to Cincinnati as treasurer of Federated Department Stores, to Green Bay as chief financial officer of ShopKo, and finally back to Minneapolis as a senior vice president at Department 56, before he ran for Congress in 2000—his first bid for elected office. During those years he did political work for Senator Rudy Boschwitz and he served in 1998 as state Republican platform co-chairman. Like Boschwitz, Kennedy is energetic and often wears plaid shirts. With his strong business background and the slogan "Mark Kennedy means business," he said that he could help the district market its farm products abroad and bring more businesses to its small towns.

Kennedy challenged incumbent David Minge, a "common sense Democrat," as Minge puts it, who was first elected in 1992 by 569 votes after Republican Vin Weber decided not to run. Kennedy campaigned on opening foreign markets to Minnesota's farm products, repealing the marriage penalty and the estate tax, and improving the district's roads. He dismissed Minge's connection with the House's Blue Dog Democrats, of which Minge was a founder, and identified himself with "80%" issues with which most Republicans agree and most Democrats disagree. Although this is a swing district and Minge had had close contests, the national parties did not focus seriously on it until the final weeks of the campaign. Minge, who had formed an exploratory committee to challenge Senator Rod Grams in 2000 before ruling it out because of the prospect of a divisive primary, appeared to some Democrats to have lost some enthusiasm for campaigning; unwisely, he remained in Washington for much of October as adjournment was repeatedly delayed and his opponent was busy at home. Kennedy kept on fundraising and was among the few members of the 107th Congress who benefited from the coattails of George W. Bush, who won this district by a solid 54%–40% margin. This was an example of the Republican trend in rural areas: Bill Clinton had carried the district twice with pluralities, and Bush's father won it by only 52%–48% in 1988. Following the initial count, Kennedy had a lead of 155 votes. Minge dropped a recount challenge on December 12—the day that the Supreme Court ended the presidential recount in Florida—with Kennedy's lead at 148 votes and 300 contested ballots remaining, so the 155-vote margin stood as the official tally. With the contest close across the district, his margin of victory came from the three counties surrounding Minneapolis, where Kennedy won 51%–45%.

Kennedy achieved his goal of seats on the Agriculture and Transportation and Infrastructure Committees. Redistricting could have a huge impact—positive or negative. But the local Republican heritage and the suburban growth give him a good chance of surviving in 2002.

Cook's Call   *Potentially Competitive.* In one of the biggest upsets of the 2000 cycle, businessman Mark Kennedy defeated four-term Democratic Representative David Minge by less than 200 votes. Despite the closeness of the 2000 contest, Kennedy should be in pretty good shape in 2002: This rural district has never been particularly friendly territory for Democrats. Clinton narrowly won it in 1992 and 1996, but in 2000 Bush won this district by 14%. A strong challenger could give Kennedy a race, but he looks well positioned.

THE PEOPLE: Pop. 2000: 613,816; Pop. 1990: 546,890, up 12.2% 1990–2000. 95.6% White, 0.5% Black, 0.9% Asian, 0.5% Amer. Indian, 0.1% Hawaiian, 0.8% Two + races, 1.7% Other; 3.3% Hispanic Origin.

2000 Presidential Vote

Bush (R)	158,071	(54%)
Gore (D)	118,432	(40%)
Nader (Green)	12,113	(4%)
Others	5,131	(2%)

1996 Presidential Vote

Clinton (D)	120,652	(45%)
Dole (R)	105,205	(39%)
Perot (I)	38,117	(14%)

Rep. Mark Kennedy (R)

Elected 2000, 1st term; b. Apr. 11, 1957, Benson; home, Watertown; St. John's U. (MN) B.A. 1978; U. of MI, M.B.A. 1983; Catholic; married (Debbie).

Professional Career: CPA, Arthur Anderson, 1978–81; Dir. of Finance, Pillsbury Co., 1983–87; Treas., Federated Dept. Stores, 1987–92; CFO, Shopko Stores, 1992–95; CFO Dept. 56, Inc., 1995–2000.

DC Office: 1415 LHOB 20515, 202-225-2331; Fax: 202-225-6475; Web site: markkennedy.house.gov.

District Office: Buffalo, 763-684-1600.

Committees: *Agriculture* (27th of 27 R): Conservation, Credit, Rural Development & Research; General Farm Commodities & Risk Management. *Transportation & Infrastructure* (39th of 42 R): Aviation; Highways & Transit.

Group Ratings and Key Votes: Newly Elected

Election Results

2000 general	Mark Kennedy (R)	138,957	(48%)	($886,650)
	David Minge (DFL)	138,802	(48%)	($848,795)
	Others	9,212	(3%)	
2000 primary	Mark Kennedy (R)	13,779	(79%)	
	Joe Wagner (R)	3,598	(21%)	
1998 general	David Minge (DFL)	148,933	(57%)	($631,766)
	Craig Duehring (R)	99,490	(38%)	($291,322)
	Stan Bentz (Ref)	12,319	(5%)	

THIRD DISTRICT

Over the past half century, Minnesota's great twin metropolis has spread out from the neat streets inside the city limits of Minneapolis and St. Paul into the countryside all around. People have sorted themselves out geographically. In the lower lands along the Mississippi and Minnesota rivers, where rail lines fan out from the Twin Cities heading toward the great farmlands of America, are the blue-collar suburbs, with neat modest houses on grid streets and warehouses and factories near the tracks. Inland, around the lakes Minnesota is so proud of, in subdivisions with curved streets hugging the hills, are the Twin Cities' more affluent neighborhoods, quiet and unflashy in the Minnesota way, but comfortable whether blanketed with snow or when the lake is glinting in the summer sun. In between are the freeway interchanges where some of the Twin Cities' great innovations can be seen—Southdale Shopping Center in Edina, the first enclosed mall and site of the first B. Dalton store, the beginning of national book chains; and now the giant Mall of America, with its 4.2 million square feet, 520 stores, 49 restaurants, 14 theaters and 13,000 employees, plus expansion plans to add 5.6 million square feet, a 5,000 seat performing arts center and a rail connection to downtown Minneapolis.

The 3d Congressional District of Minnesota takes in Hennepin County suburbs north, south and west of Minneapolis. On the northside is working-class Brooklyn Park, long a DFL stronghold but more famous now for its former mayor, Governor Jesse Ventura; on the south is middle-income Bloomington, home of the Mall of America; to the west are Edina, Plymouth, Wayzata and other towns around Lake Minnetonka, all heavily Republican. This is the largest lake and these are the most affluent communities in the Twin Cities area. The area is home to the headquarters of such diverse companies as Cargill and Radisson Hotels. The 3d also takes in fast-growing Burnsville across the Minnesota River from the airport and still vacant land northwest of Minneapolis. Historically Republican, this area trended Democratic in the 1990s, and Bill Clinton twice won pluralities; in 2000 George W. Bush carried the district, but only by 50%–45%, not a robust margin in what not long ago was the most Republican district in Minnesota.

The congressman from the 3d District is Jim Ramstad, a Republican elected in 1990. He has been in politics since childhood: Raised in North Dakota, he used to go with his grandfather to visit Republican Senator Milton Young. He saw President Eisenhower in 1956 and met President Kennedy in 1963 at the same Rose Garden ceremony where a young Bill Clinton was photographed shaking Kennedy's hand (Ramstad is in the background of the now-famous photo). He worked as an intern to Young and a staffer to Congressman Tom Kleppe while in his 20s. He moved to Minnesota and in 1980, at 34, he beat a Democratic state senator (spending the then record-breaking sum of $77,932) and worked on issues like chemical dependency in young people, crack babies and the handicapped, while favoring mandatory minimum sentences for drug dealers and boot camps for drug offenders. He used to spend time with police on all-night rounds.

In 1990, when 3d District Congressman Bill Frenzel retired after 20 years, Ramstad ran for the House. The crucial contest was the Republican convention. Ramstad was pro-choice on abortion while most delegates were anti-abortion, but he had good endorsements, from Senator Rudy Boschwitz and Congressman Vin Weber, both anti-abortion, and won at the party convention on the eighth ballot.

Ramstad's voting record has been squarely in the middle of the House. He has taken on some environmental causes—trying to stop the Advanced Liquid Metal Reactor and scale down the proposed bridge over the St. Croix River—and voted against some appropriations riders weakening environmental regulations. His task force on legal reforms helped produce the securities litigation bill that passed over Bill Clinton's veto, but he worked with the Clinton White House to restore full funding to the Legal Services Corporation. The House passed his Missing Children Tax Fairness Act, which allows families of abducted children to continue to claim a dependency exemption. Ramstad has taken his market economics to the Ways and Means Committee. He has backed 401(k)-type pensions for public employees, employee stock ownership plans and exemptions for state health insurance risk pools; he sponsored an exemption for survivor benefits for spouses of police and fire officers killed in the line of duty. He worked on the Taxpayer Bill of Rights and on Medicare and hospital funding formulas. He pushed to increase the availability of new medical technology to Medicare patients. He argues that the current tax system is too complex, too costly and too invasive, and hopes that prospects for reform improve under the Bush administration. He has been a strong supporter of free trade, whipping votes for NAFTA, fast track and permanent normal trade relations with China.

Ramstad has been a recovering alcoholic since 1981, when he awoke in jail after a night of drinking ended in a brawl, and he has backed measures for both discipline and therapy for substance abusers. He opposed SSI cash benefits for alcoholics ("Cash benefits only make the problem of alcoholism worse," he says) and drug tests for released federal prisoners. With Senator Paul Wellstone, he sponsored a bill to require insurance coverage for alcohol and drug addiction programs; they got the backing of Gerald and Betty Ford. He argues that alcoholism costs society $90 billion a year, and that his program would save $7 for every dollar spent; the increase in premiums, he says, would be no more than the price of a cup of coffee. But when Ramstad later called for programs to emphasize abstinence and discourage treatment with narcotics, that caused a split with Wellstone. He has counseled House colleagues with a drinking problem, including Philip Crane of Ways and Means. On other issues, Ramstad co-sponsored with the late Bruce Vento a bill to waive English language and residency requirements for U.S. citizenship for Hmong and Laotians recruited into pro-U.S. guerrilla units between 1961–75. He opposed holding the Clinton impeachment debate while U.S. planes were bombing Iraq, but voted for impeachment.

Ramstad has been easily re-elected every two years in this high-turnout district in high-turnout Minnesota. Redistricting should pose no major problems.

Cook's Call　*Safe.* Although this district is not the most Republican in the state (Bush won here by just 5 %), Ramstad's moderate profile has proven to be a good fit. Heavy growth in the Twin Cities means that this district will have to shed about 25,000 residents in redistricting.

THE PEOPLE: Pop. 2000: 642,053; Pop. 1990: 546,796, up 17.4% 1990–2000. 88.7% White, 4% Black, 4.3% Asian, 0.4% Amer. Indian, 1.7% Two+ races, 0.9% Other; 2% Hispanic Origin.

2000 Presidential Vote			1996 Presidential Vote		
Bush (R)	170,412	(50%)	Clinton (D)	141,109	(47%)
Gore (D)	154,997	(45%)	Dole (R)	125,019	(41%)
Nader (Green)	14,094	(4%)	Perot (I)	31,021	(10%)
Others	2,731	(1%)	Others	5,532	(2%)

Rep. Jim Ramstad (R)

Elected 1990, 6th term; b. May 6, 1946, Jamestown, ND; home, Minnetonka; U. of MN, B.A. 1968, George Washington U., J.D. 1973; Protestant; single.

Military Career: Army Reserves, 1968–74.

Elected Office: MN Senate, 1980–90.

Professional Career: Special Asst., U.S. Rep. Tom Kleppe, 1970; Practicing atty., 1973–80; Adjunct Prof., American U., 1975–78.

DC Office: 103 CHOB 20515, 202-225-2871; Fax: 202-225-6351; Web site: www.house.gov/ramstad.

District Office: Bloomington, 952-881-4600.

Committees: *Ways & Means* (9th of 24 R): Health; Trade.

Group Ratings

	ADA	ACLU	AFS	LCV	CON	ITIC	NTU	COC	ACU	NTLC	CHC
2000	30	7	0	86	85	100	67	90	68	79	67
1999	40	—	16	75	95	—	70	80	72	—	—

National Journal Ratings

	1999 LIB —	1999 CONS		2000 LIB —	2000 CONS
Economic	39%	59%		42%	57%
Social	52%	48%		54%	45%
Foreign	10%	86%		53%	45%

Key Votes of the 106th Congress

1. Patient Bill of Rights	N	5. Bar RU-486 $ for FDA	N	9. NATO War in Serbia	N
2. Accelerate Min. Wage	N	6. Display 10 Commandments	Y	10. Perm. Trade with China	Y
3. Strike Ban on Ergo. Stnd.	N	7. Gun Show Bkgrnd. Checks	Y	11. Debt Relief for 3rd World	Y
4. Ovrd. Estate Tax Veto	Y	8. Ban Part.-Birth Abortion	Y	12. Drop Cuba Econ. Embargo	Y

Election Results

2000 general	Jim Ramstad (R)	222,571	(68%)	($747,976)
	Sue Shuff (DFL)	98,219	(30%)	($22,824)
	Others	8,272	(3%)	
2000 primary	Jim Ramstad (R)	unopposed		
1998 general	Jim Ramstad (R)	203,731	(72%)	($766,951)
	Stan J. Leino (DFL)	66,505	(23%)	($13,098)
	Derek W. Schramm (TXP)	12,823	(5%)	

FOURTH DISTRICT

Above the Mississippi River bluffs, forested when the first settlers arrived in the 1850s and one of America's great urban vistas today, stand the two great landmarks of St. Paul: the Minnesota Capitol and Archbishop Ireland's Cathedral. This is the older and smaller of the Twin Cities, settled mainly by Catholic Irish and German immigrants, while Minneapolis was attracting Protestant Swedes and Yankees. St. Paul became a major transportation hub, a railroad center and river port, while Minneapolis, farther up river at the Falls of St. Anthony, became the nation's largest grain milling center. St. Paul has a vibrant core. Beneath the Capitol and the cathedral, its skywalk-linked downtown is home to the Ordway Music Theater, the headquarters of Minnesota Public Radio and an active pop music industry. Beyond the cathedral is Summit Avenue, on which capitalists like the Great Northern Railway's James J. Hill built grandiose Romanesque houses, and which, with Monument Avenue in Richmond and Meridian Street in Indianapolis, remains one of America's grand 19th Century residential boulevards. In more modest neighborhoods are sturdy houses lined up on grid streets, and beyond are the close-in suburbs with more irregular street patterns and shopping nodes.

Minnesota's 4th Congressional District is made up of St. Paul, the Ramsey County suburbs to the north, West St. Paul and South St. Paul (which are right next to each other) to the south, and Lake Elmo and Woodbury to the east. St. Paul was one of the most Democratic parts of Minnesota even before the Democratic-Farmer-Labor Party was formed in 1944, and it remained proudly DFL for a half-century. The area has become home to tens of thousands of Hmong veterans, who had been recruited by the CIA and U.S. special forces during the Vietnam war and eventually resettled here after Laos fell to the Communists in 1975, bringing their strong sense of community. The 4th District has been held by the DFL since 1948, when it elected Eugene McCarthy.

The congresswoman from the 4th District is Democrat Betty McCollum, first elected in 2000. She grew up in North St. Paul and graduated from the College of St. Catherine. For 11 years she taught high school social studies and then she was a retail sales manager for 14 years. "Retail teaches you to listen to people," she said. After her daughter was hurt on the slide in a city park, McCollum ran and was elected in 1986 to the North St. Paul City Council. She served on the council until 1992, when she was elected to the state House of Representatives after defeating incumbents in both the primary and general (it was a redistricting year). Her accomplishments there included a comprehensive school bus safety law, constitutional amendments that allow citizens to recall elected officials for wrongdoing, and bonuses to Gulf war veterans.

The 4th District had been represented since the 1976 election by Bruce Vento, a Democrat with an almost perfectly liberal voting record and strong environmental record. In February 2000 Vento announced he would not seek reelection and that he had malignant mesothelioma, a pernicious lung cancer that medical researchers said is caused by inhaling asbestos fibers; he could have contracted the disease at any of several blue-collar jobs he had held or during his 10 years as a public school teacher. Despite surgery to remove one of his lungs, Vento died on October 10, 2000.

In the September primary, McCollum, who was endorsed by Minnesota's Democratic-Farmer-Labor Party and EMILY's List, faced three opponents. Although she called herself "a little more conservative than my [state House] caucus sometimes wants," she had been assistant majority leader for six years. The primary at first appeared wide open, but in this race, unlike statewide contests, the DFL convention endorsement counted for something, and McCollum won easily with 50% to 23% for state Senator Steve Novak and 19% for St. Paul City Council member Chris Coleman.

Republicans nominated state senator Linda Runbeck, a vigorously anti-abortion candidate. This was not a two-way but a three-way race, thanks to the candidacy of former Ramsey County prosecutor Tom Foley, a long-time DFLer who had been named to the National Indian Gaming Commission by Bill Clinton in 1995, now running on the ticket of Governor Jesse Ventura's Independence Party. Foley called McCollum and Runbeck "puppets" of their national parties. Once again, the contest was hard-fought and appeared close. McCollum supporters feared that she could lose if Foley won 20% of the vote. McCollum backed prescription-drug coverage under Medicare and opposed large tax cuts before Congress paid down the debt. Runbeck, who opposed gun controls and took conservative positions on health care and education, attacked McCollum and her Democratic allies for running "hateful, vicious attack ads" that distorted her positions on guns. McCollum conceded at a debate the she was "very disappointed in my own party for sending out distasteful images" on her behalf. Once again, McCollum won unexpectedly easily, 48%–31%, with 21% for Foley. She was the first woman elected to the House from Minnesota since Coya Knutson was famously called home by her estranged husband in 1958 (see 7th District).

Cook's Call   *Probably Safe.* This St. Paul-based district has a Democratic core but is certainly more conservative than the neighboring Minneapolis-based 5th District: Gore won here by 20% but won the 5th by 34%. Republicans are hoping that as this St. Paul-centered district continues to push out to the suburbs (it will need to add about 37,000 people in redistricting), it will become more marginal politically. But McCollum looks well positioned for 2002.

THE PEOPLE: Pop. 2000: 577,077; Pop. 1990: 547,061, up 5.5% 1990–2000. 79% White, 7% Black, 8% Asian, 0.8% Amer. Indian, 0.1% Hawaiian, 2.8% Two+ races, 2.5% Other; 5.4% Hispanic Origin.

2000 Presidential Vote			**1996 Presidential Vote**		
Gore (D)	157,582	(56%)	Clinton (D)	152,555	(58%)
Bush (R)	101,741	(36%)	Dole (R)	77,704	(30%)
Nader (Green)	17,315	(6%)	Perot (I)	23,566	(9%)
Others	3,009	(1%)	Others	7,688	(3%)

Rep. Betty McCollum (DFL)

Elected 2000, 1st term; b. July 12, 1954, Minneapolis; home, N. St. Paul; Col. of St. Catherine, B.S. 1986; Catholic; married (Doug).

Elected Office: N. St. Paul City Cncl., 1986–92; MN House of Reps., 1992–2000.

Professional Career: Teacher; Retail sales & management.

DC Office: 1029 LHOB 20515, 202-225-6631; Fax: 202-225-1968; Web site: www.house.gov/mccollum.

District Office: St. Paul, 651-224-9191.

Committees: *Education & the Workforce* (22d of 22 D): 21st Century Competitiveness; Select Education. *Resources* (24th of 25 D): Forests & Forest Health; National Parks, Recreation & Public Lands.

Group Ratings and Key Votes: Newly Elected

Election Results

2000 general	Betty McCollum (DFL)	130,403	(48%)	($1,090,046)
	Linda Runbeck (R)	83,852	(31%)	($900,795)
	Tom Foley (Ind)	55,899	(21%)	($267,287)
	Other	1,285	(0%)	
2000 primary	Betty McCollum (DFL)	35,911	(50%)	
	Steven G. Novak (DFL)	16,332	(23%)	
	Chris Coleman (DFL)	13,555	(19%)	
	Cathie Hartnett (DFL)	5,454	(8%)	
1998 general	Bruce F. Vento (DFL)	128,726	(54%)	($599,905)
	Dennis Newinski (R)	95,388	(40%)	($370,060)
	Others	15,632	(7%)	

FIFTH DISTRICT

From almost nowhere in Minneapolis today can you see the geographic feature that put the city here—the Falls of St. Anthony, the head of navigation on the Mississippi River, where waters rush in rapids beneath low downtown bridges. In olden days, every riverboat had to stop here, and the waterpower generated by the falls was the energy source first for pioneers' grist mills and then for the giant grain mills that processed the wheat of the northern Great Plains into food for the United States and the world. By 1890 Minneapolis and St. Paul made up one of America's largest urban areas, living mainly off grain. Today, Minneapolis is a center of high-tech industry, banking and finance. It is a regional railroad center and the nerve center of an economic region that extends almost 1,000 miles west to the Rocky Mountains in Montana.

The city of Minneapolis, plus a few of its older suburbs directly west and south, make up the 5th District of Minnesota. In the southwest corner are part of the suburb of Edina and the gracefully aged Minneapolis neighborhoods around Lake Calhoun and Lake Harriet—affluent areas, long built-up and proudly maintained, not far from Minneapolis's skywalk-laced downtown skyscrapers and museum quarter up on the hill above Hennepin Avenue. But most of the 5th District is lower on the income scale. There are few blocks here as abandoned and ruined by crime as are some square miles of Chicago or Detroit. But many of the working-class neighborhoods of small frame houses on grid streets with ample parks are now kept up by elderly homeowners, while new immigrants have built small communities of their own. North of the Mississippi is the University of Minnesota; to the northeast, behind the railroad and warehouse district along the Mississippi, is the home of many Hmongs from Laos. The 5th District is solidly Democratic. Minneapolis's political liberalism is drawn from the Yankee tradition of clean government, the Scandinavian tradition of cooperative enterprise and the industrial labor tradition of economic redistribution. To this has been added in recent years, by feminists and the graduate student proletariat, an antic cultural liberalism notable for its ignorance not only of any conservative heritage but of many of the liberal traditions here as well.

The congressman from the 5th District is Martin Olav Sabo, son of Norwegian immigrants, a DFL leader who has spent all his adult life in politics. He was elected to the Minnesota legislature in 1960 at age 22, was the minority leader at 30, and speaker at 34. In 1978 he was elected to the House and in his first year got a seat on the Appropriations Committee. It began as a quiet career: Sabo can be articulate, even humorous, and certainly is knowledgeable and averse to the cheap shot. But he pursued his career with a certain Scandinavian reticence and aversion to national publicity—except perhaps for his role as coach and second baseman for the Democrats in the annual House baseball game. Sabo also served on the Budget Committee, where he wrote the 1990 budget summit agreement's "firewalls" between defense and domestic spending, intended by liberals as an attempt to save domestic programs and by conservatives as a way of protecting the Pentagon. After Leon Panetta was appointed OMB director in January 1993, Sabo ran for Budget chairman, and won by 149–112 over the more moderate John Spratt of South Carolina. In that position it fell to Sabo to defend the first Clinton budget, which eventually passed by 218–216. Sabo then fought against the spending cut packages proposed by his Minnesota colleague Tim Penny and his successor as Budget chairman, Republican John Kasich.

After the 1996 election Sabo rotated off Budget and concentrated more on Appropriations, where he is an ally of ranking Democrat David Obey. Sabo is ranking member on the Transportation Subcommittee. Although that put him at odds with Bud Shuster, the power-grabbing chairman until 2001 of the Transportation and Infrastructure Committee, Sabo nevertheless came out in the 1998 transportation bill with $37.2 million in projects for the Twin Cities, including $12 million for light rail along Hiawatha Avenue (the direct route from downtown to the airport), $10.5 million for new buses on I-35W, $7.7 million for bus stops and other facilities on University Avenue (the direct route from downtown Minneapolis to downtown St. Paul) and $6 million for the Minnesota Guidestar: a reflection of Sabo's penchant for mass transit. In the 2000 spending bill, he got an additional $50 million to assure construction of the Hiawatha light rail transit line, plus $13.5 million for Metro buses and facilities.

On other issues, Sabo pursues goals both practical and visionary. He calls himself a "liberal decentrist," which means he supports liberal social causes but believes that the federal government should intervene only when local governments can't or need help. He endorsed the 1997 Blue Dog Medicare plan, partly because he believed the old formula had short-changed Minnesota. He joined then Democratic Congressional Campaign Committee Chairman Martin Frost in defending soft money. But he has a bill, not likely to pass soon, limiting CEO pay to 25 times the pay of the lowest-paid full-time worker or taxing the corporation at a higher rate. He has another bill for public financing of House general election campaigns. He wants to guarantee Medicare benefits for divorcees and is against raising the Medicare age, as the Social Security age is scheduled to be raised, to 67. He opposed the moratorium on Internet taxes, calling it "grossly unfair" to Main Street merchants. He opposed permanent trade relations with China, despite the importunings of Minnesota's 3M, Honeywell and Cargill.

Continuing to practice old-fashioned political door-knocking that he began when he campaigned for Adlai Stevenson in 1956, Sabo has been reelected by wide margins of 2–1 or more. The locals concede that his Norwegian habits leave little conversation; it's simply good to see him, he maintains. Republican redistricters have discussed the unlikely step of combining Minneapolis and St. Paul, but Democrats plan to stoutly resist this ahistorical combination, and Sabo's daughter as a state senator is in a position to defend his interests.

Cook's Call   *Safe.* This Minneapolis-based seat is the most Democratic district in the state. While Minneapolis had its first population gain in 50 years, this district will still need to pick up about 57,000 people. Sabo will have no trouble winning another term.

THE PEOPLE: Pop. 2000: 557,819; Pop. 1990: 546,858, up 2% 1990–2000. 72.3% White, 13.8% Black, 5.3% Asian, 1.7% Amer. Indian, 0.1% Hawaiian, 3.6% Two+ races, 3.3% Other; 6.2% Hispanic Origin.

2000 Presidential Vote

Gore (D)	170,176	(63%)
Bush (R)	76,389	(28%)
Nader (Green)	23,073	(8%)
Others	2,625	(1%)

1996 Presidential Vote

Clinton (D)	159,018	(62%)
Dole (R)	62,507	(25%)
Perot (I)	20,499	(8%)
Others	12,636	(5%)

Rep. Martin Olav Sabo (DFL)

Elected 1978, 12th term; b. Feb. 28, 1938, Crosby, ND; home, Minneapolis; Augsburg Col., B.A. 1959; Lutheran; married (Sylvia).

Elected Office: MN House of Reps., 1960–78, Minority Ldr., 1968–72, Speaker, 1972–78.

DC Office: 2336 RHOB 20515, 202-225-4755; Fax: 202-225-4886; Web site: www.house.gov/sabo.

District Office: Minneapolis, 612-664-8000.

Committees: *Appropriations* (4th of 29 D): Defense; Interior; Transportation (RMM). *Standards of Official Conduct* (2d of 5 D).

Group Ratings

	ADA	ACLU	AFS	LCV	CON	ITIC	NTU	COC	ACU	NTLC	CHC
2000	100	86	100	86	90	50	24	38	0	16	0
1999	95	—	83	94	54	—	20	13	0	—	—

National Journal Ratings

	1999 LIB —	1999 CONS		2000 LIB —	2000 CONS
Economic	69% —	31%		75% —	24%
Social	83% —	13%		94% —	0%
Foreign	95% —	0%		97% —	0%

Key Votes of the 106th Congress

1. Patient Bill of Rights	*	5. Bar RU-486 $ for FDA	N	9. NATO War in Serbia	Y
2. Accelerate Min. Wage	Y	6. Display 10 Commandments	N	10. Perm. Trade with China	N
3. Strike Ban on Ergo. Stnd.	Y	7. Gun Show Bkgrnd. Checks	Y	11. Debt Relief for 3rd World	Y
4. Ovrd. Estate Tax Veto	N	8. Ban Part.-Birth Abortion	N	12. Drop Cuba Econ. Embargo	Y

Election Results

2000 general	Martin Olav Sabo (DFL)	176,629	(69%)	($467,849)
	Frank Taylor (R)	58,191	(23%)	($51,941)
	Rob Tomich (Ind)	11,323	(4%)	
	Others	9,002	(4%)	
2000 primary	Martin Olav Sabo (DFL)	unopposed		
1998 general	Martin Olav Sabo (DFL)	145,535	(67%)	($414,554)
	Frank Taylor (R)	60,035	(28%)	($14,788)
	Others	12,042	(6%)	

SIXTH DISTRICT

The earliest settlers to the Twin Cities of Minneapolis and St. Paul came up the Mississippi River, or up the rail lines which were soon built on the bottomlands beside. They lived within walking distance of the mills and factories and railyards; as first streetcars and then automobiles allowed them to live farther from work, they spread out in St. Paul and Minneapolis and then over the lake-strewn countryside all around. The flatlands are bleak here when the winter sun struggles to shine through gray clouds. The lakes are often surrounded by, sometimes indistinguishable from, swamps. The old lumber mill towns which pioneers built, like Stillwater on the St. Croix, were for years economic backwaters, their antique structures ill-tended. But the creativity and productivity of Minnesotans have turned this not especially attractive environment into some of the most pleasant suburbs in the world. They have taken maximum advantage of their lakes and have refurbished old towns and farmhouses and have built comfortable homes in new subdivisions. Here live today's typical American families. Busy at home and at the workplace, communicating with each other by Post-it notes (invented at St. Paul's 3M), exhausted at the end of each day, winning through their efforts a material standard of living that would have dazzled their grandparents but at a price that might have given them pause.

The 6th Congressional District of Minnesota includes much of the Twin Cities metropolitan area, suburbs and townships north, east and south of St. Paul and Minneapolis. To the northwest, the Anoka County suburbs along the Mississippi River have attracted blue collar families. Incomes are below the high metro average, and politically this has long been a DFL area. Stillwater, facing Wisconsin on hills above the St. Croix River, with Victorian buildings from its days as a lumber port when it nearly became Minnesota's capital, and surrounding Washington County have attracted a mix of people and are politically marginal; voters in Washington County, which has the 19th highest-income in the nation, narrowly rejected in 2000 an open-space referendum to allow landowners to sell the county their development rights while retaining ownership. South of St. Paul, the Dakota County towns along the Mississippi are blue collar and DFL; the newer, fast-growing Eagan and Apple Valley to the southwest are quite affluent and tend to vote Republican.

Altogether, this is Minnesota's fastest growing and perhaps most volatile district. In 1998 it was in the 6th District, more than any other, that elected Jesse Ventura governor of Minnesota. Ventura's hometown is just across the Mississippi River west of Anoka, and he clearly appealed to the hard-working young families of these suburbs. Turnout in 1998 in the 6th District was up 31% from 1994, and was even up 1% over the presidential year of 1996. Ventura carried the district solidly, with 44% of the vote, to 34% for Democrat-turned-Republican Norm Coleman, the mayor of St. Paul, and only 21% for the DFL nominee, Skip Humphrey. In 2000, although most Ventura voters told VNS exit pollsters that they supported Al Gore, the 6th District for all its DFL roots delivered a 48%–46% plurality to George W. Bush, a better performance that when his father ran 12 years before and the district split 50%–50%.

The congressman from the 6th District is Bill Luther, a Democrat elected in 1994. He grew up near Fergus Falls on a dairy farm owned by his family since 1882, went to college and law school at the University of Michigan, then was elected to the state House in 1974 at 29, and to the state Senate in 1976; his wife has been a member of the state House since 1992. He ran once before for Congress, in 1982, and lost the DFL endorsement to fellow legislator Gerry Sikorski, whose 697 overdrafts on the House bank ended his career in 1992. The seat was then won by Republican newscaster Rod Grams; when the district lines were altered for 1994, making it less Republican, Grams ran for the Senate and won; he lost that seat in 2000. Luther in his 20 years in the legislature worked hard, kept a low profile, developed shrewd strategies and was strongly partisan. He was assistant majority leader in the state Senate, wrote the state's campaign finance laws, promoted an anti-drug initiative for children. He had been eyeing the 6th District since Grams won it, and when the boundaries changed he moved his residence from Brooklyn Park (of which Jesse Ventura was then mayor) to Stillwater. His Republican opponent, Tad Jude, was another career politician, recently switched from DFL to Republican, with a residence outside the new district lines. The Luther-Jude matchup was an expensive and fierce campaign: Luther spent $1.1 million and Jude $699,000. Luther painted Jude as an extremist on abortion; Jude attacked Luther for voting against longer sentences for violent rapists and criminals who attacked seniors. Luther won by 550 votes, carrying Washington and Anoka counties and losing Dakota.

In the House Luther has a moderate record on economics and is more liberal on cultural and foreign issues. In 1997 he was rated number two in the House by Taxpayers for Common Sense, which tends to give Democrats higher ratings than Republicans, and number one among Democrats by the National Taxpayers Union, which tends to give Republicans higher ratings. He has been a persistent, though largely unsuccessful, foe of the Trident D-5 submarine-launched missile program, calling the subs "cumbersome relics of the Cold War." He voted against fast track and school vouchers, for welfare reform in 1996 and the balanced budget agreement in 1997.

Prompted by a letter from 14-year-old Alicia Sarrazin of Hastings, he sponsored a resolution to urge Hollywood to stop portraying cigarette smoking as glamorous; he sponsored another to make the export and advertising of tobacco products abroad subject to U.S. restrictions. He called for tire companies to report to U.S. regulators the foreign recalls of their products. He opposed permanent normal trade relations with China, preferring to retain annual reviews.

Luther is a critic of the federal campaign finance laws and an admirer of the Minnesota laws, which he helped write, which limit total spending; but he is also a prodigious fundraiser, able and willing to raise more than $1 million each cycle under the federal rules he dislikes. In 1996, again facing Tad Jude, Luther won 56%–44%, running well ahead of Bill Clinton. In 1998 he opposed John Kline, a retired Marine colonel, who served in Vietnam and Somalia and as one of the military aides who held the nuclear "football" for Presidents Carter and Reagan. Kline campaigned for tax cuts and against abortion, for more military spending and the resignation of Bill Clinton. He spent only $283,000 in all; but Luther, who raised $1.1 million in the cycle, spent only $412,000. That might have become a mistake. In a turnout swelled with new voters supporting Jesse Ventura, Republicans did well in these suburban counties, electing Republican legislators who helped their party win control of the state House. Luther won by only 50%–46%. Kline hardly stopped running; more experienced and better financed for 2000, he made the rematch one of the nation's high-profile House contests. He received fundraising boosts from Senator John McCain, the pharmaceutical industry and the NRA. Unlike some Democrats in marginal districts, Luther did not try to fudge all the differences between them: he opposed repeal of the marriage penalty and estate and gift taxes, and any privatization of Social Security. The result was closer across the board than in 1998, but not what Republicans had expected. Luther won 50%–48%, winning Anoka County 51%–47% and Washington 50%–48%, while losing Dakota 50%–48%. A discouraged Kline said that he was not likely to try a third time.

Redistricting in Minnesota could easily add new complications for Luther, who knows quite a bit about the process because of the key role he played in the state Senate during the 1991 cycle. But his experience in tough races, ample fundraising from his seat on Energy and Commerce, plus his capacity for hard work have shown he is not an easy mark.

Cook's Call *Potentially Competitive.* Despite his standing as one of the most prolific fundraisers in the House, Luther has had two brushes with political death, winning by just 50% in 1998 and 2000. This suburban Twin Cities district has become increasingly marginal over the last few years with Bush actually winning here by 2 % in 2000. Luther could once again be a Republican target in 2002, but the decision by 1998 and 2000 Republican nominee John Kline to take his name out of consideration leaves Republicans without a top-flight candidate. As the fastest growing district in the state, it will need to shed about 106,000 residents, many of whom will likely end up in the St. Paul-based 4th District.

THE PEOPLE: Pop. 2000: 720,995; Pop. 1990: 546,807, up 31.9% 1990–2000. 93.2% White, 1.8% Black, 2.2% Asian, 0.5% Amer. Indian, 1.6% Two+ races, 0.7% Other; 1.9% Hispanic Origin.

2000 Presidential Vote		
Bush (R)	176,703	(48%)
Gore (D)	169,478	(46%)
Nader (Green)	16,132	(4%)
Others	3,791	(1%)

1996 Presidential Vote		
Clinton (D)	154,333	(51%)
Dole (R)	107,560	(35%)
Perot (I)	37,111	(12%)
Others	5,201	(2%)

Rep. William P. (Bill) Luther (DFL)

Elected 1994, 4th term; b. June 27, 1945, Fergus Falls; home, Stillwater; U. of MN, B.S. 1967, J.D. 1970; Catholic; married (Darlene).

Elected Office: MN House of Reps., 1974–76; MN Senate, 1976–94.

Professional Career: Clerk, 8th Circuit U.S. Court of Appeals, 1970–71; Practicing atty., 1971–92.

DC Office: 117 CHOB 20515, 202-225-2271; Fax: 202-225-3368; Web site: www.house.gov/luther.

District Office: Woodbury, 651-730-4949.

Committees: *Energy & Commerce* (22d of 26 D): Energy & Air Quality; Environment & Hazardous Materials; Telecommunications & The Internet.

Group Ratings

	ADA	ACLU	AFS	LCV	CON	ITIC	NTU	COC	ACU	NTLC	CHC
2000	95	64	100	100	98	67	33	42	16	36	20
1999	100	—	100	88	100	—	33	27	8	—	—

National Journal Ratings

	1999 LIB	—	1999 CONS	2000 LIB	—	2000 CONS
Economic	65%	—	35%	70%	—	29%
Social	64%	—	36%	72%	—	26%
Foreign	88%	—	12%	77%	—	21%

Key Votes of the 106th Congress

1. Patient Bill of Rights	Y	5. Bar RU-486 $ for FDA	N	9. NATO War in Serbia	Y
2. Accelerate Min. Wage	Y	6. Display 10 Commandments	N	10. Perm. Trade with China	N
3. Strike Ban on Ergo. Stnd.	Y	7. Gun Show Bkgrnd. Checks	Y	11. Debt Relief for 3rd World	Y
4. Ovrd. Estate Tax Veto	N	8. Ban Part.-Birth Abortion	N	12. Drop Cuba Econ. Embargo	Y

Election Results

2000 general	William P. (Bill) Luther (DFL)	176,340	(50%)	($2,597,244)
	John Kline (R)	170,900	(48%)	($1,200,309)
	Other	8,584	(2%)	
2000 primary	William P. (Bill) Luther (DFL)	unopposed		
1998 general	William P. (Bill) Luther (DFL)	148,728	(50%)	($412,541)
	John Kline (R)	136,866	(46%)	($283,348)
	Others	12,107	(4%)	

SEVENTH DISTRICT

The lake-strewn country along the upper stretches of the Mississippi River, settled by Norwegian and German immigrants, is the source of some prime American literary and political traditions. Here a century ago in the town of Sauk Centre grew up Sinclair Lewis, whose *Main Street* and *Babbitt* were greeted as the definitive satires of small-town life, though on rereading they show surprising affection for their subjects. Not far north of Sauk Centre is Little Falls, the boyhood home of Charles Lindbergh, whose father was a progressive and isolationist congressman who opposed declaring war on Germany in 1917. In those years this seemingly placid country was seething with rage, as WASPy nationalists banned German from schools, renamed sauerkraut liberty cabbage, and boycotted German-American businesses. The rage simmered and became the source of the bitter isolationism of the 1930s and 1940s, of which Lindbergh was a national leader, and of the bitter anti-Communism of the 1950s. This part of Minnesota is probably also the home—though the actual location has somehow disappeared from the map, and Garrison Keillor himself says he was inspired by small towns in Stearns County that were evenly divided between German Catholics and Norwegian Lutherans—of Lake Wobegon, whose history has an authentic ring: founded by New England Yankees as New Albion in 1852, renamed when Norwegians got a majority on the council in 1880, where the Norwegian flag still flies on holidays but where no one has seen a German flag fly since 1917.

The 7th Congressional District, covering the northwest corner of Minnesota, includes just about all this territory. It takes in the wheat-farming plains up near North Dakota and the German Catholic country, strewn with farm villages named for saints, around Sauk Centre and St. Cloud. There are many political traditions here: some wheat counties are heavily DFL; heavily Norwegian Otter Tail County leans Republican; St. Cloud and Stearns County are volatile, dovish and anti-abortion. The 7th's political history reads like something out of *Lake Wobegon Days*. Back in 1958, Congresswoman Coya Knutson lost re-election when her husband Andy issued a plaintive statement urging her to come home and make his breakfast again; she was the only incumbent Democrat to lose in heavily Democratic 1958. Other Scandinavian names followed: Republican Odin Langen, Democrat Bob Bergland (later Jimmy Carter's secretary of Agriculture), Republican Arlan Stangeland. None except Bergland won by any great margin. For most of the last 40 years this has been one of America's prime marginal districts.

The congressman from the 7th District today is Collin Peterson, who has run for this seat ten times and won six times, and has convincingly removed the 7th from the marginal column. Peterson grew up here, went to Moorhead State College across the Red River of the North from Fargo, North Dakota, then started a CPA office in Detroit Lakes. In 1976 he was elected to the state Senate, passing a 16% farm property tax reduction in 1985 and starting the Chickadee Checkoff, which raises $900,000 a year for a non-game wildlife fund. He also started running for the House. He lost a DFL caucus in 1982; he lost to Stangeland in 1984 and 1986 (by only 121 votes the second time; he declared victory and went to Washington to set up an office); he lost the DFL primary again in 1988. But in 1990, when the *St. Cloud Times* reported that Stangeland made 341 credit card calls to a woman not his wife, Peterson won with a robust 54%. In office, he continued to do things his way, wearing cowboy boots and playing guitar in a country rock band called the Recess Renegades, acting as his own campaign consultant and pilot on flights within the district. He has a small staff, with community economic development professionals rather than Washington policy wonks. He opposes abortion and gun control, backs farm subsidies and labor unions, and opposed the 1993 Clinton budget, NAFTA and permanent trade relations with China. He pulled Florida Secretary of State Katherine Harris out of a snowbank during an Aspen ski vacation in 1991; the two dated for a while and remain friends.

Peterson's political fortune has been bolstered by the Republican victory of 1994, which made him a visibly different kind of Democrat. In 1995, while voting for some parts of the Contract with America, Peterson and Gary Condit founded the Blue Dog Democrats for "common sense legislation that embraces the ideas and values of mainstream America." He has sided with Republicans on their prescription-drug and HMO legislation. With John Linder, he has cosponsored "FairTax," a national sales tax of 23% that would replace all income, payroll, corporate and estate taxes. He was one of 10 House Democrats to vote for the Bush tax cut in March 2001. Peterson is the opposite of many middle-of-the-House Republicans, who favor heavy environmental restrictions; he takes the view of his constituents, who hunt and fish as a way of life and see environmentalists' policies as hindrances. Peterson once said, presumably with a sigh, or perhaps an expletive, "City people have no understanding of the rural way of life. Still, they always come up there and try to tell us how to live." He is co-chairman of the Congressional Sportsmen's Caucus and wants to require that federal lands be open to hunting and fishing except when there is a good reason not to (as in national parks). But he unexpectedly found himself on the side of the animal-huggers—not by choice, he said—when he sponsored a bill to close a loophole that permits shipment in interstate commerce of birds for cockfighting, which is legal only in New Mexico, Louisiana and Oklahoma; Peterson said he was trying to help law enforcement officials.

In 1998 Minnesota farmers dumped wheat and attempted to blockade the border, charging that under NAFTA, Canadian-subsidized wheat had an unfair advantage over U.S. wheat. Five years of wet weather and plummeting world wheat prices marginalized the value of farm property in northwest Minnesota, and Peterson struggled to respond. He had expressed reservations about the 1996 Freedom to Farm Act and predicted low prices: "Farmers are going to be in Washington asking for help. And we'll help them. We always do." Not exactly, it turned out. In summer 1998 he pushed for raising the commodity loan rate, but it lost in the Senate. The number of farmers in northwest Minnesota seems to be continuing its historic decline, as commodity prices continue their historic trend downward. "I don't know how to fix it," Peterson admitted. "We're in a box. The world is awash in wheat. There's too much barley. Commodity prices show it."

Peterson's politics have been a smash hit with 7th District voters and an irritant to local DFL activists. He has not had a close contest since 1994. In January 1999 Peterson was mentioned as a candidate for state natural resources director and had an interview with Governor Jesse Ventura. But he said, "I did not get the vibes I would have needed to even consider" the job. He also turned down Ventura's offer to support him for the Senate in 2000: not all mavericks are alike. Two years later, after he urged Al Gore to stop the Florida recount (he had called Harris to offer support), there were rumors that he would join the Bush administration. But he apparently likes where he is.

Cook's Call   *Safe.* After some very close races in the early 1990's, Peterson has not been seriously contested in years and has solidified himself in this conservative swing district. Republicans seem more interested in wooing Peterson to switch parties (Bush won his district by 15 %) than finding a Republican opponent. The 7th needs to pick up about 26,000 people in redistricting. Peterson looks safe for 2002, but when he leaves, this district will be tough for Democrats to keep.

THE PEOPLE: Pop. 2000: 588,825; Pop. 1990: 547,011, up 7.6% 1990–2000. 94.2% White, 0.5% Black, 0.8% Asian, 2.7% Amer. Indian, 1.1% Two+ races, 0.7% Other; 1.6% Hispanic Origin.

2000 Presidential Vote

Bush (R)	149,830	(54%)
Gore (D)	108,950	(39%)
Nader (Green)	13,477	(5%)
Others	6,964	(2%)

1996 Presidential Vote

Clinton (D)	115,996	(45%)
Dole (R)	103,336	(40%)
Perot (I)	33,577	(13%)
Others	4,079	(2%)

Rep. Collin C. Peterson (DFL)

Elected 1990, 6th term; b. June 29, 1944, Fargo, ND; home, Detroit Lakes; Moorhead St. U., B.A. 1966; Lutheran; divorced.

Military Career: Army Natl. Guard, 1963–69.

Elected Office: MN Senate, 1976–86.

Professional Career: Accountant, 1966–90.

DC Office: 2159 RHOB 20515, 202-225-2165; Fax: 202-225-1593; Web site: www.house.gov/collinpeterson.

District Offices: Detroit Lakes, 218-847-5056; Red Lake Falls, 218-253-4356; Waite Park, 320-259-0559.

Committees: *Agriculture* (3d of 24 D): Conservation, Credit, Rural Development & Research; General Farm Commodities & Risk Management; Livestock & Horticulture (RMM). *Permanent Select Committee on Intelligence* (9th of 9 D): Intelligence Policy & National Security.

Group Ratings

	ADA	ACLU	AFS	LCV	CON	ITIC	NTU	COC	ACU	NTLC	CHC
2000	60	21	71	43	88	67	37	52	32	22	67
1999	40	—	83	38	96	—	36	72	52	—	—

National Journal Ratings

	1999 LIB	—	1999 CONS		2000 LIB	—	2000 CONS
Economic	53%	—	46%		57%	—	42%
Social	35%	—	64%		30%	—	68%
Foreign	27%	—	72%		69%	—	28%

Key Votes of the 106th Congress

1. Patient Bill of Rights	N	5. Bar RU-486 $ for FDA	Y	9. NATO War in Serbia	N
2. Accelerate Min. Wage	Y	6. Display 10 Commandments	Y	10. Perm. Trade with China	N
3. Strike Ban on Ergo. Stnd.	Y	7. Gun Show Bkgrnd. Checks	N	11. Debt Relief for 3rd World	Y
4. Ovrd. Estate Tax Veto	Y	8. Ban Part.-Birth Abortion	Y	12. Drop Cuba Econ. Embargo	Y

Election Results

2000 general	Collin C. Peterson (DFL)	185,771	(69%)	($207,292)
	Glen Menze (R)	79,175	(29%)	($59,446)
	Other	5,550	(2%)	
2000 primary	Collin C. Peterson (DFL)	unopposed		
1998 general	Collin C. Peterson (DFL)	169,907	(72%)	($271,794)
	Aleta Edin (R)	66,562	(28%)	($35,751)

EIGHTH DISTRICT

In the 1860s, prospectors in the Arrowhead region of the new state of Minnesota, northwest of Lake Superior in the low hills of the Mesabi Range, happened upon the nation's largest veins of iron ore; they moved on, looking for gold. But in the 1880s, Duluth banker George Stone and Philadelphia financier Charlemagne Tower started mining the Iron Range and created the northern end of the lifeline of American heavy industry. South from the Range run rail lines to the port of Duluth nestled on dramatic bluffs over the always cold and, for long months every winter, frozen waters of Lake Superior—one of the most beautiful settings for a city in North America. Duluth was a grain-shipping rival of Chicago and the premier iron-ore port. Its city plan was drawn up by Daniel Burnham and its splendid turn-of-the-century buildings still celebrate the triumph of technology and civilization over wilderness and the elements. Millions of tons of ore have been dug out of the Range, loaded into rail cars for the ride to Duluth, and into Great Lakes freighters for shipment to Cleveland, Gary, Detroit, Chicago, Pittsburgh and Buffalo.

For most of the last century, in this land where the Arctic winds blow down over the Canadian Shield's thousands of inland lakes, about 100,000 people have lived on the Iron Range and another 100,000 in Duluth, most of them the products of America's 1880–1924 wave of immigration: Italians, Poles, Serbs and Croats, Jews, Swedes and Finns. In this punishing environment, they worked to the point of exhaustion, built solid houses with staunch central heating, and wore layers of warm clothing to survive the winter. Life was rough: the work was hard, the hours long, and the pay low. The churches, a separate one for each ethnic group, were the main community institutions. Living conditions improved vastly in the decades of great economic growth after World War II, but life remains rough-hewn today, and there is still economic distress. As iron mines and steel factories got more efficient they needed fewer workers; employment is still well below its 1970s peak. As water fills abandoned open-pit mines and factories close and mines are shut down, the Iron Range looks bleaker. Duluth's population was down to 86,000 in 2000, and the Iron Range's was about the same. But all is not moribund. Northwest Airlines, with an $840 million investment from state government in 1993, has built a repair facility in Duluth and a reservations center in the Iron Range. Fiber-optic cable is being laid all over the Range. The port of Duluth still ships large quantities of grain, and in the late 1990s a new taconite and steelmaking factory was built—the first big new plant in more than 20 years. Duluth has set up Soft Center Duluth, a center for education in business and banking modeled after a center in its sister city Vaxjo in Sweden. And Gene Nicolelli has set up a Greyhound Museum in Hibbing, where in 1914 an entrepreneur started transporting people in unsaleable open-air Hupmobiles, an enterprise which eventually became the Greyhound Bus Company.

The 8th Congressional District of Minnesota includes Duluth and the Iron Range, plus much of the north woods and lake country to the west and south; it moves all the way south to the boundaries of the Twin Cities metro area, to Isanti and Chisago counties, where young families are building new homes near pleasant old lakeside towns. This district has been the bulwark of Minnesota's Democratic-Farmer-Labor Party since it was formed in 1944, and is ordinarily safe Democratic today; but there are signs of change. With big turnout increases in the southern counties, which are in the Twin Cities media market, Jesse Ventura actually carried the 8th in

1998, with 34%, to 33% for the DFL's Skip Humphrey and 32% for Republican Norm Coleman. In 2000, cultural issues like gun control and environmental restrictions here moved opinion toward the Republicans; and George W. Bush lost the 8th District to Al Gore by only 49%–44%, a much smaller margin than his father's 60%–40% loss 12 years earlier.

The congressman from the 8th District is Jim Oberstar, a Democrat first elected in 1974— "part scholar and part Iron Range street fighter, part pothole-filling ward healer and part workaholic," in the words of St. *Paul Pioneer Press*. Oberstar grew up in the Iron Range city of Chisholm, where his father was an iron miner and union official, who sent him off to St. Thomas College with $2,500 saved in quarters at the Slovenian National Benefit Society; Oberstar has been known to sing polka songs in Slovenian at a House Democratic retreat. He studied French in college and in Belgium; for four years he was a civilian employee of the U.S. Naval Mission to Haiti, teaching French and Creole to Marines, and French and English to Haitians (he also speaks Serbo-Croatian, Italian and Spanish). Then, in 1963, at 29, he landed a job as chief of staff to Congressman John Blatnik in Washington: he has been working for the 8th District for going on four decades. When Blatnik retired in 1974, Oberstar won a primary over Tony Perpich, brother of Governor Rudy Perpich. He won tough primaries in 1980 and 1984, the latter after briefly running for the Senate.

Oberstar's views are in the liberal Catholic tradition: "I believe you will be measured by how you respond to the neediest among you," he says. He believes in an economically active government and has little faith in economic markets. He was long dubious about American military involvement abroad, especially in Central America, but favored the 1994 deployment in Haiti. He is an opponent of abortion and a backer of adoption, sponsoring bills to insure family and medical leave and dependent deductions for families in the process of adopting; when he first proposed a $1,500 adoption tax deduction in the 1970s he was laughed out of Ways and Means, but now, thanks in large part to his effort, there is a $5,000 tax credit. With Henry Hyde, he sponsored a bill to ban the use of drugs in assisted suicides. With Collin Peterson and Dave Minge, he proposed that the Veterans Department provide care for any veteran with hepatitis C, to which many veterans were exposed in Vietnam and whose symptoms are not apparent for years.

From this North Country district, Oberstar has been a supporter of local hunting and fishing activities and of the steel industry. He opposed creation of the Boundary Waters Canoe Area Wilderness—a raging issue in these parts—and after a 1993 ruling outlawed motorized portage (using trucks to take boats between lakes) he pushed to reinstate it. In a 1998 compromise with Bruce Vento, Oberstar got motorized portages restored at the Moose Lake-Basswood portage and between Vermilion and Trout lakes; in return, he acceded to a ban on motorboats in Seagull Lake and two smaller lakes. Nonetheless, in May 2000, when Vento was dying of cancer, he proposed naming Eagle Mountain, Minnesota's highest peak, after him. On steel, he favored retaliation against what he considered dumping by Russia and East Asian countries in 1998. When permanent national trade relations for China came before the House, he tried to get an amendment of the 1974 trade act that would treat steel slab imports as a direct threat to taconite miners; when the administration wasn't interested, he voted against PNTR. In December 2000, after LTV Steel announced a mine closure, he sought a Section 201 investigation of steel imports: "This is a simple case of supply and demand—other countries are illegally dumping their excess steel supply in the U.S. marketplace, which has saturated the demand for domestic steel." He called for keeping the border closed against Mexican trucks.

Since October 1995 Oberstar has been ranking Democrat on Transportation and Infrastructure—a position of real power, even in a Republican Congress. This committee (long known as Public Works) has a long tradition of bipartisanship, and of sponsoring members' roads (and, since 1994, other transportation) projects; it has 75 members, the largest in the House. For six years Oberstar and Chairman Bud Shuster worked to make it more powerful than ever. Their great monument was the May 1998 transportation bill, with $217 billion in spending, including $10 billion in projects earmarked by members. This came just a year after the Republican leadership managed to stop, by only 216–214, Shuster's and Oberstar's attempt to take transportation spending off budget; they had to break through projected budget limits to win. Earmarking was done by formula: Committee members received $40 million for specific projects in their districts, with more for high-seniority members; other members of the House received $15 million. Shuster, Oberstar, and the chairman and ranking member of the Surface Transportation Subcommittee, Tom Petri and Nick Rahall, each could veto anyone's earmark. Back when Oberstar's boss John Blatnik was chairman, the committee's power was threatened by an alliance of environmentalists and fiscal conservatives; by 1998 it was carrying all before it. Another reason: the 1991 ISTEA, of which 1998's TEA-21 was the reauthorization, included spending for mass transit, bicycle trails and pollution control research, at the option of states or House members. This has helped win the support of many liberals; Oberstar himself is a bicycling enthusiast, proud of logging 2,000 miles a year in Washington, Duluth, on the Range and in the Tour de Frog in St. Cloud. He stoutly opposed a temporary cut in the gas tax in April 2000; this would have decreased revenue for transportation projects. And he resisted successfully Jim Nussle's proposal to make the budget resolution have the force of law; this would reduce the committee's ability to control spending. In January 2001, in accordance with the Republicans' six-year term limit on chairmanships, Shuster lost that post and immediately announced he was resigning from Congress. Oberstar's response: "I said, 'I want a recount. Don't go.' I just can't conceive of doing the work of our committee without him present." But it is likely that he will get along with the new chairman, who also represents the frozen north, Don Young of Alaska

Oberstar once chaired Transportation's Aviation Subcommittee and remains involved in aviation issues. He worked hard for the state investment in Northwest Airlines, but in recent years has criticized the company harshly, opposing presidential intervention in the summer 1998 pilots' strike and criticizing Northwest for opposing regulations intended to help small startup airlines. As if in response to pressure, the airline instituted jet service from its Detroit hub to Duluth in October 1998. In September 1999 he called on the administration to oppose the European Union ban on "hush-kitted" airliners—retrofitted in 1990 to be less noisy—as trade discrimination. He has been critical of big airline mergers. In June 2000 he charged that the spinoff from the proposed United-USAirways merger of routes to a company headed by Black Entertainment Network founder Robert Johnson would form an unviable competitor with "plantation" status; he quickly apologized for using that term. He also criticized American Airlines' proposed purchase of TWA.

Oberstar's one political setback came in 1984, when he ran for the Senate but was denied endorsement by the liberal DFL convention. In the 8th District he has been re-elected by very wide margins; longtime DFL voters may be moving away from Democrats higher up on the ticket, but they have been faithful to Oberstar. In 2000 he won 68%–26%, running nearly 20% ahead of Al Gore.

Cook's Call   *Safe.* Not as Democratic as the Minneapolis-St. Paul districts, this rural Iron Range district still has deep DFL roots and has elected Oberstar to Congress without much fanfare for the last 26 years. But once he leaves, this district could be competitive.

THE PEOPLE: Pop. 2000: 624,030; Pop. 1990: 546,795, up 14.1% 1990–2000. 95.3% White, 0.5% Black, 0.4% Asian, 2.3% Amer. Indian, 1.1% Two+ races, 0.2% Other; 0.9% Hispanic Origin.

2000 Presidential Vote

Gore (D)	155,924	(49%)
Bush (R)	138,951	(44%)
Nader (Green)	16,588	(5%)
Others	5,669	(2%)

1996 Presidential Vote

Clinton (D)	148,886	(53%)
Dole (R)	88,095	(31%)
Perot (I)	38,405	(14%)
Others	6,147	(2%)

Rep. James L. Oberstar (DFL)

Elected 1974, 14th term; b. Sept. 10, 1934, Chisholm; home, Chisholm; St. Thomas Col., B.A. 1956, Col. of Europe, Bruges, Belgium, M.A. 1957; Catholic; married (Jean).

Professional Career: Navy civilian language teacher, Haiti, 1959–63; A.A., U.S. Rep. John Blatnik, 1963–74; A.A., U.S. House Public Works Cmte., 1971–74.

DC Office: 2365 RHOB 20515, 202-225-6211; Fax: 202-225-0699; Web site: www.house.gov/oberstar.

District Offices: Brainerd, 218-828-4400; Chisholm, 218-254-5761; Duluth, 218-727-7474; Elk River, 612-241-0188; North Branch, 651-277-1234.

Committees: *Transportation & Infrastructure* (RMM of 34 D).

Group Ratings

	ADA	ACLU	AFS	LCV	CON	ITIC	NTU	COC	ACU	NTLC	CHC
2000	75	64	100	71	68	44	27	25	8	9	27
1999	75	—	100	75	91	—	29	23	12	—	—

National Journal Ratings

	1999 LIB —	1999 CONS		2000 LIB —	2000 CONS
Economic	88%	0%		90%	8%
Social	56%	43%		62%	37%
Foreign	95%	0%		97%	0%

Key Votes of the 106th Congress

1. Patient Bill of Rights	Y	5. Bar RU-486 $ for FDA	Y	9. NATO War in Serbia	Y
2. Accelerate Min. Wage	Y	6. Display 10 Commandments	N	10. Perm. Trade with China	N
3. Strike Ban on Ergo. Stnd.	Y	7. Gun Show Bkgrnd. Checks	N	11. Debt Relief for 3rd World	Y
4. Ovrd. Estate Tax Veto	N	8. Ban Part.-Birth Abortion	Y	12. Drop Cuba Econ. Embargo	Y

Election Results

2000 general	James L. Oberstar (DFL)	210,094	(68%)	($1,032,070)
	Bob Lemen (R)	79,890	(26%)	($22,253)
	Mike Darling (Ind)	19,667	(6%)	
2000 primary	James L. Oberstar (DFL)	unopposed		
1998 general	James L. Oberstar (DFL)	173,734	(66%)	($696,670)
	Jerry Shuster (R)	69,667	(26%)	($7,616)
	Stan (The Man) Estes (Ref)	15,137	(6%)	($3,588)
	Others	4,725	(2%)	

★ MISSISSIPPI ★

Mississippi bears the weight of a tragic history as it takes quickening steps toward the future. This green land was settled in a rush in Jacksonian America, mostly by small farmers heading west from Georgia and south from Tennessee—and also by a few big planters, who made vast gains and great losses, built grand mansions and sent their sons to fight in the Civil War. For a century afterward, even as industrial farmers drained the Delta lands, Mississippi with its racial segregation, subsistence farmers and sharecroppers and low wages, lived apart from most of America. Faulkner's Mississippi never knew the Homestead Act, the giant factories, the rushes of immigration, the rise of suburbs that were the indispensable backdrop of most of 20th Century American life. Mississippi never developed great cities—its two commercial metropolises are just outside its borders, Memphis and New Orleans. But if it did not excel at commerce, it did produce great art. Mississippi gave us the music of the blues and Elvis Presley. It gave the world William Faulkner and Eudora Welty, Walker Percy and Shelby Foote. Their work was informed by a sense of the tragic missing or forgotten in most of America, where life is a triumphant sales pitch or a labor-saving invention. As Anthony Walton, born in Illinois to Mississippi-born parents, put it, "In Mississippi I have learned to stop trying to evade and forget what I have seen and heard and understood and now must know, but rather to embrace the ghosts and cradle the bones and call them my own." Ghosts and cradles and bones: The writer Willie Morris, who chronicled his success in New York in *North Toward Home*, returned to live in Mississippi and, when he died in August 1999, lay in rest at the Old Capitol and then was buried in the cemetery in Yazoo City where he walked as a child where "I learned more about the town's past here, the migrations, the epidemics, the old forgotten tragedies, than I could ever have learned in the library. Sometimes we would take our lunch."

Mississippi has made much progress in the last three decades, but the past still hangs heavy. For years no other state had such a painful contrast between image and reality, between an ideal sincerely strived for and the tawdry facts of everyday life. Magnolia trees on the lawns of antebellum mansions, golden-haired young women in white dresses on the veranda, faithful black servants and retainers: this was once the ideal. And behind it stood loose-jointed frame houses and unpainted back-country stores, cabins without indoor plumbing and poor white crossroads clustered with askew advertising signs. This is a state, writes David Sansing, with "two souls, two hearts, two minds. We have the highest rate of illiteracy and the largest number of Pulitzer Prize winners in literature. We at one time have the scent of magnolias and the smell of burning crosses." Mississippi for years ranked 50th, and a very low 50th, among states in income, literacy, health and education levels, despite the best efforts of civic, political and business leaders. As William Faulkner said of his state, "You don't love because: you love despite."

Today Mississippi still ranks 50th on many scales, but the gulf between Mississippi and the rest of America has narrowed enormously in the last half-century. In 1940, Mississippi had an economy based on low-wage, subsistence or sharecropper agriculture and a system of racial segregation enforced often by violence. If history is, as Sir Henry Maine wrote, the story of the progress from status to contract, then old Mississippi was still at the beginning, for status—race—meant just about everything. In the years since, Mississippi has moved, not always willingly, from status to contract, in its economy and in race relations. Per capita income in Mississippi was 36% of the national average in 1940; in 1999, it was 72%, well below average but, given the lower cost of living here, a level recognizably American. Mississippi is home to a giant corporation, WorldCom, which bought MCI in 1997; it has the nation's second largest furniture industry, around Tupelo; it has a $930 million Nissan plant going up in Canton. Daily life, thanks to cheap gas and air conditioning, national brands and the mechanization of farming, has changed drastically. Most Mississippians of 50 years ago would be astonished by the physical comforts and mechanical marvels their grandchildren take for granted today: Every classroom in the state is air-conditioned and the governor wants to wire them all up to the Internet. They would be astonished as well by relations between blacks and whites. As *The Washington Post's* William Raspberry, a Mississippi native, wrote, "There is an easiness to relationships, a mutual respect and a will-

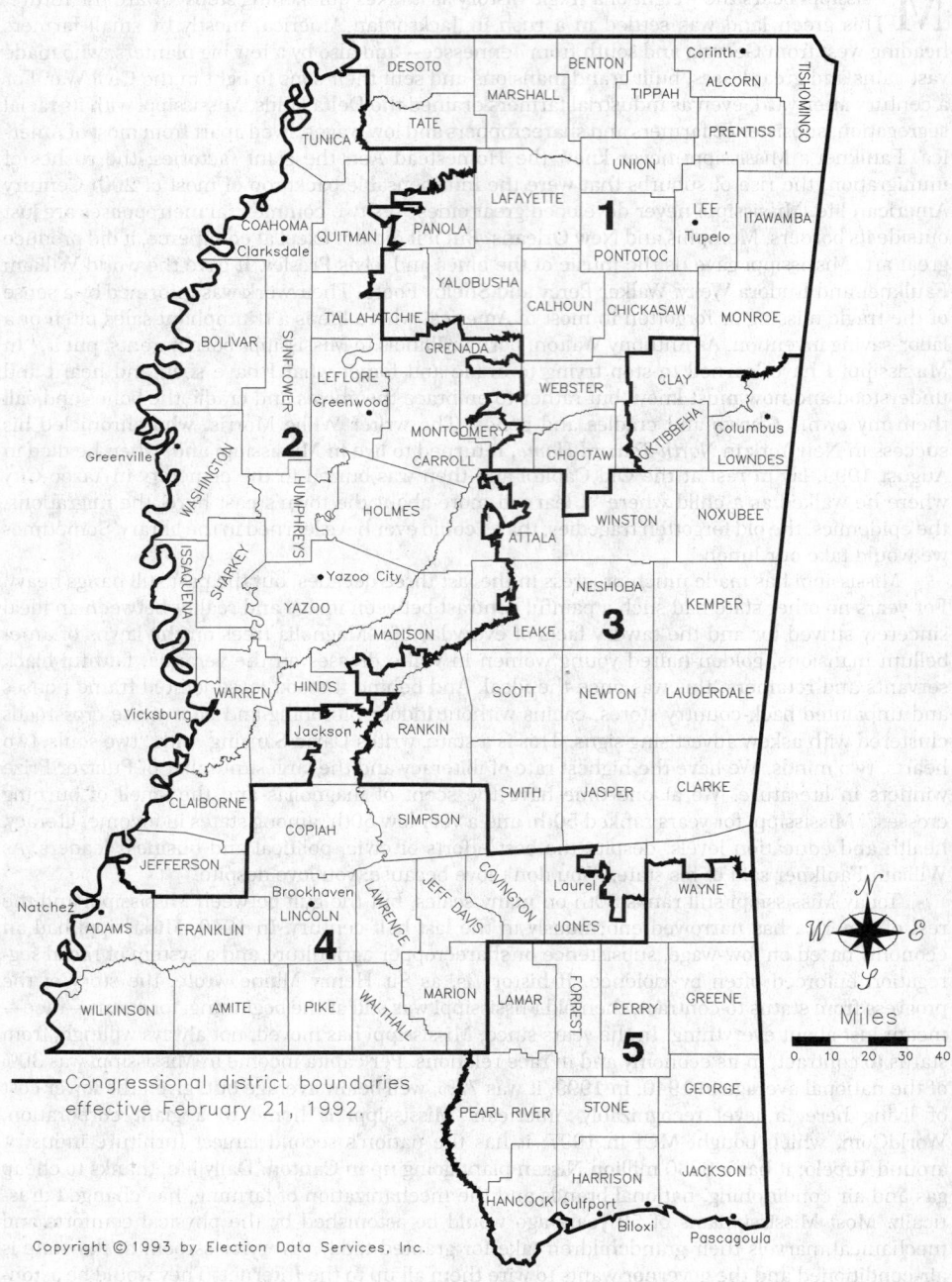

Congressional district boundaries
effective February 21, 1992.

Miles
0 10 20 30 40

ingness to move beyond race that, quite frankly, didn't exist during my years in the state. Mississippi is finally a good place to be." In June 2000, after a 17-year-old black hanged himself in the town of Kokomo, Jesse Jackson charged that he was the victim of a lynching. But there was no evidence for this, and the charge was rejected by most Mississippians. Robert McElvaine, a liberal historian at Millsaps College, noted that Mississippi prosecutors in 1994 secured the conviction of the killer of civil rights leader Medgar Evers, murdered in 1963, and said that if a lynching had occurred, "State officials and the vast majority of the citizens of Mississippi would be appalled and would insist that the perpetrators be arrested and convicted." The Mississippi traditions of friendliness and courtesy seem to be trumping the historical tradition of racism: Mississippi may rank 50th in incomes, but it ranks number one in per capita charitable giving.

One way Mississippi has improved is in education. Governor William Winter, elected in 1979, finally made kindergarten mandatory and raised the dropout age to 14; Governor Ray Mabus, elected in 1987, proposed a major school reform policy. But the uncomfortable fact is that most high taxpayers are white and most public school children are black (Jackson's student body is 88% black), because many white children attend private academies. About 40% of state spending goes to education, but those who oppose higher spending or taxes can point to the fact that there is no demonstrated correlation between higher spending and improved test scores and learning. But test scores are rising and dropout rates are falling. Another way Mississippi has improved is by encouraging small businesses and service industry. This was the strategy of Governor Kirk Fordice, a Republican elected in 1991 and 1995, who also called for tougher action against crime; Mississippi's prison population more than doubled between 1994 and 2000. From 1992 to 1997, the number of manufacturing jobs here dropped 10,000 to 241,000, but the number of service jobs increased by 72,000, to 180,000, and the new jobs tended to pay higher wages. In the 1990s the percentage of children living with working parents rose to 69%, well above the national average of 55%.

But the biggest driver of growth has been gambling. Mississippi approved riverboat gambling in 1989, and Mississippi now has 31 casinos, 11 in Harrison County on the Gulf coast and 10 in once-impoverished Tunica County, just south of Memphis, and the rest scattered along the Mississippi River border. Mississippi is number three in gambling revenues, behind Nevada and New Jersey; gambling has produced 40,000 service jobs, at above-average wages. But this is not an alloyed good. The original riverboats Mark Twain described in *Life on the Mississippi* were working vehicles, sooty and dangerous, taking chances on the treacherous river; but their captains showed how hard work could get people ahead. Mississippi's riverboat casinos are a form of entertainment, a diversion from gainful economic activity, which teaches the lesson that getting ahead depends on luck rather than talent and hard work. Popular culture hurts in other ways. Greenville, which produced authors Hodding Carter (*Main Street Meets the River*) and William Alexander Percy (*Lanterns on the Levee*), and where Shelby Foote and Walker Percy went to high school together, is now the nation's top media market in which people watch television more hours a day than any other.

Politically, Mississippi is a conservative state, carried by Republicans in the last six presidential elections. But Mississippi Democrats with good old boy personas have become competitive. Democrat Gene Taylor was elected to Senator Trent Lott's old House seat in 1989, Democrat Ronnie Shows was elected to an open House seat in 1998, and in 1999 Democrat Ronnie Musgrove was elected governor; he failed to win 50% of the popular vote, but under Mississippi law he was installed by the legislature, which remains overwhelmingly Democratic. Nor do Mississippians dislike these old-time politicians: In 1995 and 1999 they rejected term limits for state legislators—the only state to have voted them down. The legislators, politically canny, handed the hottest of hot potatoes back to the voters in 2001. Since 1894, the Mississippi flag has included a Confederate emblem in the top left corner. But in May 2000 the state Supreme Court ruled it was not the legal flag, since the 1894 law was not included in the full codification of state laws in 1906. Black politicians and many white businessmen wanted to replace it, and Musgrove appointed a commission headed by former Governor Winter, which presented a new design in January 2001 with a circle of 20 white stars (rather like those in the European Union flag) replacing the Confederate cross. Musgrove supported the change, but legislators decided to leave the decision up to the voters in a referendum on April 17, 2001. Many admited that the legislators would have kept the old flag and many feared—or hoped—that a large majority of white voters would choose that in the privacy of the voting booth. They did, by a 64%–36% margin. The old design won in 63 of 83 counties, and the new design won more than 60% in only five counties. Apparently the economic argument did not convince Mississippians: Shelby Foote noted, " I think a lot of people like me think that flag represents something they stand for . . . never mind its definitions of slavery. I think the people who want a new flag are worried about tourists. I never cared much for tourists myself."

Governor   Ronnie Musgrove was elected governor by the Mississippi House of Represen-tatives in January 2000, after leading the popular vote in November 1999 by a 49.6%–48.5% margin. Musgrove grew up in Tocowa, in Panola County; he can remember political discussions at the dinner table with his father, a state highway worker, who died when he was 7. Musgrove says he wanted to become a lawyer because his father had spoken well of the profession. He is the first Mississippi governor not to have lived as an adult during the searing years of the civil rights revolution; the protests when James Meredith integrated the University of Mississippi in 1962, the murder of Medgar Evers in 1963, the murders of three civil rights workers in 1964—all happened when he was no older than 8. Musgrove went to college and law school at Ole Miss, where he was a classmate and friend of the novelist John Grisham—and where his nickname was Governor, "because Musgrove knew everybody," Grisham says. He worked his way through school selling encyclopedias. After school he practiced law in Batesville. Musgrove was elected to the state Senate in 1987, at 31, and re-elected in 1991. During legislative sessions he was well known for eschewing whiskey for soft drinks and for refereeing high school and community college bas-ketball games. In 1995 he ventured to run for lieutenant governor, and with his strong Southern drawl, elaborate courtesy and high-pitched laugh, and with his emphasis on education and family values beat Republican incumbent Eddie Briggs. In his second month in office, February 1996, he suffered a mild brain injury in an auto accident; for a time it seemed his life was in danger, but he recovered fully.

Musgrove was obviously on the road to running for governor, but the road had some obstacles. Incumbent Republican Governor Kirk Fordice had worked to lower taxes and encourage new business, and Mississippi was enjoying economic growth, an increase in jobs and state budget surpluses. But Fordice also had his problems—bad relations with the legislature and the much publicized breakup of his marriage. In 1996 he had been injured in an auto accident while re-turning from a lunch with his junior high school sweetheart in Memphis while his wife was in Europe. In 1999 he bought a new house outside Jackson that his wife said "wasn't for me," and then sued for divorce, while she remained in the governor's mansion. Fordice and Musgrove had not gotten along well, and the Republican trend in voting worked against Musgrove. But he cam-paigned hard and effectively. In the August 1999 Democratic primary, still the primary of choice of the large majority of voters, he won with 57% of the vote in an eight-candidate field. But the Republican primary, between three former Democrats, failed to produce the expected runoff, as former Congressman Mike Parker won with 51% to 28% for Musgrove's 1999 opponent Eddie Briggs.

Polls showed the race about even. Parker ran folksy ads featuring endorsements from his relatives, including a distant cousin named Loretta Musgrove, who was shown shelling peas. Musgrove attacked Parker's record in the acrimonious House and spotlighted education. Mus-grove pledged to raise teacher pay to the Southeastern state average, to put an Internet-connected computer on the desk of every pupil in every grade and to lower class size in kindergarten through third grade from 24 to 15. "We're starting to make the connection between a good education and a good way of life. People want conservative values that are progressive and will move us forward." He opposed abortion and any new gun control law, but did not abandon the Democratic base entirely; he had lots of support from trial lawyers and accompanied Bill Clinton on his July 1999 tour of the Mississippi Delta. John Grisham, who once served in the Mississippi House, came from his home in Charlottesville, Virginia (Faulkner had moved there too), to campaign for Mus-grove. "If you're looking for trustworthiness in a public official, they come no cleaner than Mus-grove."

The election turned out to be the closest in Mississippi history. Musgrove won 49.6% of the vote, Parker 48.5%. Musgrove ran far ahead of national Democrats in northeast Mississippi, where he carried most counties, and he held down Republican margins in the Gulf Coast impressively. The Delta and the Jackson area split much as they do in national elections, with huge majorities of blacks voting Democratic and huge majorities of whites Republican. But winning the popular vote was not decisive under a Mississippi law passed in 1890 to prevent blacks from winning statewide elections with pluralities. With neither candidate winning the popular vote, the law said the winner would be determined by which candidate won the most state House districts. After the tedious tabulation, the result was that 61 districts voted for Musgrove and 61 for Parker. Under the 1890 law, the decision then went to the state House of Representatives. Democrats had a big margin there, but Parker refused to concede and Musgrove did not choose agency heads or set the details of his legislative agenda. On January 4, 2000, Musgrove was finally elected by a margin of 86–36.

In his first legislative session, Musgrove achieved his biggest goal, a six-year, $338 million teacher pay raise, up to the Southeastern state average. But he had to make some concessions: the first raise comes in the 2001–02 school year, and raises are contingent on 5% growth in state revenues—a provision insisted on by Lieutenant Governor Amy Tuck and the state Senate. To avoid antagonizing legislators, Musgrove let pass into law a bill giving them a better retirement system than any other state employees; voters screamed, and Musgrove called a special session to repeal the law. Musgrove also called an August special session to reshape state job development efforts as the "Advantage Mississippi" initiative. Musgrove's program to put computers on every desk in every classroom passed and the first were installed in February 2001. He appointed blacks to head the prison system, the Department of Human Services, the Medicaid agency and the Highway Patrol. But in July he replaced the interim Medicaid director without first notifying black legislators and in December 2000 he fired the DHS head, which again angered the black community. The legislature required drivers to carry insurance and banned adoptions by gays. Laws were passed giving scholarships to medical students who promise to work in the Delta. Musgrove was pleased to announce that Nissan was building a $930 million plant in Canton, just north of Jackson. The state finally settled for $500 million a suit brought in 1975 regarding higher education desegregation; the settlement will pay for extra spending for its three historically black colleges.

Some problems remain. State government revenues in late 2000 were below projections, and Musgrove called for uniform spending cuts and dipped into the state's reserves. Musgrove sought to sell a $120 million, 12-year settlement from a lawsuit against computer software makers and use the $93 million for current spending; House Speaker Tim Ford was opposed. The issue of the Mississippi flag was kindled in May 2000, when the state Supreme Court ruled that the flag, which features a Confederate emblem in the upper left corner, was not legally the state flag, because the 1894 law authorizing it was not included in the full codification in state laws in 1906. Musgrove appointed a commission headed by former Governor William Winter to design a new flag which he and four other statewide officials endorsed, but the legislators decided to send the issue to voters in a referendum April 17, 2001. Most blacks and many business leaders support the new design, but there was vocal opposition from many whites, and many feared—or hoped— that a large majority of white voters would choose that in the privacy of the voting booth. The new flag design was defeated by a resounding 65%–36%.

Senior Senator   Thad Cochran was elected to the House in 1972 and the Senate in 1978, where he sits at Jefferson Davis' old desk. He grew up in small towns in northern Mississippi, the son of a principal and a teacher, graduated with high grades from Ole Miss (where he was a cheerleader, which was a very big deal) and its Law School, served in the Navy, spent a year abroad and practiced law in Jackson. In 1972, as Richard Nixon was sweeping Mississippi, he was elected as a Republican to the House from the Jackson-area district with a plurality against a white Democrat and black independent. After three terms, he was ready to step down, when Senator James Eastland retired; Cochran ran, and once again won with a plurality over a white Democrat and a black independent. In the House and in the Senate he has managed to amass a generally conservative record with little controversy or acrimony. His pleasant personal demeanor, his refusal to engage in racial politics and his Republican Party label, in a state where most whites have been voting Republican for president for three decades, have made him broadly acceptable to voters. His toughest race came in 1984, when he was opposed by popular former Governor William Winter. Winter could make a case for himself but not against Cochran; Cochran outraised him $2.7 million to $738,000, and won 61%–39%.

Cochran is the number two Republican on the Appropriations Committee where he has the top slot on the Agriculture Subcommittee; he also serves on the Agriculture Committee. In 1996 he played a major role on the Freedom to Farm Act. He supported the move to phase out most crop subsidies over seven years, but insisted on maintaining the cotton marketing loan plan which he largely wrote in 1985. He worked with Vermont's James Jeffords on the complex dairy program and wrote the Senate version of the Wildlife Habitat Incentives Program. More recently he has played a key role in fashioning each year's emergency farm rescue package—essentially, a substitute for the subsidies that are being phased out. He has tried to double transition payments and loan deficiency payments, and has added in extra money for tobacco, dairy and cotton farmers. He also created new uncapped certificates that cotton farmers can accept instead of regular cash payments.

Cochran has used his Appropriations seat to legislate on many other issues. He has been the Senate's leading proponent of missile defense. In March 1999, after the implications of the July 1998 Rumsfeld report and the August 1998 North Korean three-stage missile launching sunk in, his missile defense resolution passed by 97–3. He defended missile defense after the test failure in January 2000. "We test because we expect to find problems and try to solve them. This technology is not just within our reach, but is actually in our grasp now." He has supported the construction of a land-based missile defense system on an Aleutian Island in Alaska, and in January 2001 opposed phasing that out in favor of developing sea-based or space-based systems—a stand that may put him in conflict with the Bush administration. "To change direction at this point . . . would unnecessarily delay deployment and cause us to be vulnerable for a long time." He serves on the Defense Appropriations Subcommittee and, working with Mississippi colleague Trent Lott, has worked to fund projects big and small which are based in Mississippi—the DDG-51 Aegis destroyers, two of them to be built at Ingalls Shipyard in Pascagoula, the LHD-8 helicopter carrier, additional AN/APG-73 radars for the F-18 Hornet, $2 million for Mississippi State University's research center where superfast computers do undersea modeling of Navy projects, $2 million for University of Mississippi computer labs receiving information from orbiting satellites. He has pushed for a $51 million fishery research vessel for NOAA likely to be built at Halter Marine in Moss Point.

Timely amendments to appropriations making major policy are a Cochran specialty. To the bill allowing reimportation of prescription medicines in July 2000 Cochran added an amendment to require the FDA to certify lack of risk to public health and safety; HHS Secretary Donna Shalala was unable to so certify, and the law became a dead letter. An October 2000 amendment delaying the imposition of regulations on the treatment of rats, mice and birds in research laboratories prevented a big increase in the cost of medical research. Smaller issues attract Cochran's attention: he tried to get the government to pay the legal fees of former Congressman and Agriculture Secretary Mike Espy, he wants to make the Congressional Research Service separate from the Library of Congress, he wants to repay federal employees placed through no fault of their own in the wrong retirement system. He authored the Mississippi Wilderness Act, worked for grants for historically black colleges and for vocational training for the disabled, added Emerald Mound, the second largest Indian mound in the United States, to the Natchez Trace Parkway, and sought to let the entrepreneurial Choctaw Tribe in Neshoba County add newly purchased land to its reservation.

Going into the 107th Congress, Cochran and Trent Lott have combined congressional service of 56 years; both were first elected to the House in 1972. Their relations have not always been harmonious. They clashed over judgeships and vied for White House favor in the 1980s and mixed it up in leadership fights in the 1990s. In 1990 Cochran challenged the more moderate John Chafee of Rhode Island for the chairmanship of the Senate Republican Conference, the number three leadership position, and won 22–21. When Trent Lott challenged Al Simpson for majority whip, the number two position, Cochran pointedly endorsed Simpson; Lott won anyway, with the support of junior conservatives, and thus leapfrogged Cochran. When Bob Dole announced in May 1996 that he would resign from the Senate in June, Cochran and Lott both entered the race for majority leader; Lott had the contest sewed up, but Cochran stayed in and lost 44–8. In January 2001, Cochran appeared by John McCain's side as a new co-sponsor of the latest version of the McCain-Feingold campaign finance bill; this has been strongly opposed by Lott, and Cochran's vote made the bill apparently filibuster-proof and gave McCain leverage in his drive to get it early consideration.

Cochran holds what seems to be one of the safest seats in the Senate. In 1990 he was unopposed and for 1996 he was re-elected 71%–27% over a Democrat who spent half of his $4,700 on gas for a borrowed car. He seems sure to be re-elected in 2002.

Cook's Call   *Safe.* There is no reason to think that Cochran is vulnerable or that Democrats will put any effort into attempting to defeat him.

Junior Senator   Trent Lott, first elected to the Senate in 1988 and now minority leader, was for exactly five years majority leader, from June 1996 until June 2001 when Vermont Senator James Jeffords defected from the Republican Party. Lott grew up in Pascagoula, the son of a shipyard worker and a teacher, went to Ole Miss (where he was a cheerleader, like his Mississippi colleague Thad Cochran) and worked his way through law school by running the Ole Miss alumni affairs office, accumulating good contacts along the way. After a year of law practice, he got a job with Democratic Gulf Coast Congressman William Colmer, chairman of the Rules Committee. When Colmer retired in 1972, Lott ran for the House seat with Colmer's encouragement and endorsement—as a Republican. He was elected with 55% in what was the strongest Nixon district in the country that year. In 1974, Lott was the youngest member of the Judiciary Committee, loyally defending Richard Nixon in the impeachment hearings. In 1980, he was elected Republican whip, and he ran the Republican National Convention's platform committees in 1980 and 1984. In the House he was an ally of Jack Kemp and Newt Gingrich. He supported Kemp for president in 1988, and his decision to run for the Senate that year opened the way for Gingrich's rise: Lott was succeeded as whip by Dick Cheney; when Cheney became Defense secretary in March 1989, Gingrich was elected whip 87–85.

There is a discernible hard core of beliefs in Lott's career, and yet he is less the hard-edged ideologue that Washington insiders presumed than he is an instinctive deal-maker, not much interested in quixotic gestures, an orderly and well-organized man who is dismayed by the dilatoriness of others. His beliefs are reminiscent of the mostly unarticulated beliefs of the coalition of Southern conservative Democrats and small-town conservative Northerners which had controlled the House for most of the 35 years previous to when he arrived there: against increased taxes, hostile to federal regulation of business and local government, for an assertive foreign policy and strong defense, for the traditional rules of moral conduct; on one issue, civil rights, he moved as seamlessly as he changed parties, from Colmer's support for racial segregation to the small town Republicans' backing for equal rights. He can be sharp in debate, aggressively partisan and combative, but he is gregarious and personable, striving to keep on good terms with most other members and careful to cultivate those whose support he needs.

In the Senate Lott moved quickly into the leadership. After the 1992 election, he ran for Conference secretary, the number four leadership post, and won, with 20 votes to 14 for Christopher Bond and 5 for Frank Murkowski. In 1993 he was chosen the Republican point man on Clinton appointments, but he mostly avoided confrontations. In 1994, after he had been re-elected 69%–31%, he challenged Republican Whip Al Simpson. Majority Leader Bob Dole and most Republican moderates backed Simpson, but Lott won most of the younger conservatives elected in 1992 and 1994 and won 27–26—the first Republican ever elected whip in both houses. In the process he leapfrogged over his Mississippi colleague Thad Cochran, who held the number three leadership position. Lott's comment was typically unsentimental. "There comes a time in life, in politics as in baseball, when you seize the moment or it's gone forever. I ran and he didn't."

As whip for 17 months, Lott was careful not to usurp the prerogatives of Dole, who kept many decisions close to the chest. Then in May 1996 Dole surprised almost everyone when he announced he would resign from the Senate in June. Lott immediately began canvassing for votes for majority leader and found himself far ahead of Cochran, who ran anyway and lost 44–8. During the summer, Lott moved adroitly, pushing for a vote on welfare reform, disposing of the minimum wage issue, pushing for the compromise health care bill and the Safe Drinking Water Act. He gave Senate Republicans a solid record to run on—but left Dole with fewer issues on which to attack Clinton. He established a smooth working relationship with Democratic Leader Tom Daschle.

After Dole lost and Gingrich faced ethics charges that threatened to topple him, Lott was suddenly the most visible Republican leader in Congress. After sending conciliatory signals that he would wait for Clinton to come forward with a budget in early 1997, he moved relentlessly in closed-door negotiations that led to the May bipartisan agreement to balance the budget and passage of the budget in July. But at times he angered colleagues. His insistence on investigating the Louisiana Senate race results infuriated Democrats. Conservatives were angry when he worked with the Clinton Administration, and against Foreign Relations Chairman Jesse Helms, to secure ratification of the Chemical Weapons Treaty in April 1997. Democrats were furious that he sidelined their campaign finance bill in October 1997 by presenting an amendment to require union members to give their authorization before union leaders could use their dues money for political purposes. Lott encountered—or engendered—more controversy in 1998. He tasked Commerce Chairman John McCain with getting a committee consensus on a tobacco bill; McCain did and Lott brought it forward. But most Republicans opposed it as a tax increase, and Lott ordered it pulled from the calendar in June 1998.

Then came impeachment, which tested his influence among Republican senators and his close working relationship with Tom Daschle. In December 1998 after the House voted, Lott encouraged the Gorton-Lieberman plan to allow four days of argument in the impeachment trial, to be followed by a vote on whether the charges, if true, would justify impeachment; if that fell short of the two-thirds required for removal, as everyone assumed it would, the trial would be adjourned. House Judiciary Chairman Henry Hyde, the leader of the House managers, wrote an angry letter and Senate conservatives howled; Lott retreated. Democrats remained furious about the prospect of a lengthy, salacious trial, and raised the specter of partisanship which most senators, after the House debate and in line with Senate tradition, wanted to avoid. On January 7, Lott tagged along with Daschle for a scheduled press conference, and they agreed to an all-senators closed caucus the next day. In that extraordinary meeting, senators agreed to a suggestion by Phil Gramm and Edward Kennedy to postpone the issue of calling witnesses and go on with the trial. There was giddy delight at this demonstration of senatorial comity, though the House managers were furious and the Clinton defense team still wary. The trial proceeded in orderly fashion; the verdict went as expected, mostly along partisan lines, with Lott and most Republicans preventing a vote on censure until after the verdict, at which point Democrats weren't much interested.

In the 106th Congress Lott tried to bar non-germane amendments on appropriations bills, arguing that Democrats were using them to hurt Republicans in elections and that it was better procedure to have "clean votes" on issues. He took to filing cloture petitions when he brought bills to the floor and filed lots of amendments himself, to preclude others. Democrats were immensely irritated, and in spring 2000 relations between Lott and Daschle turned very sour; Daschle said Lott was resorting to "a Senate version of dictatorship that I think is unacceptable." In September 1999 Lott did accede to Democrats' loud demands for a vote on the Comprehensive Test Ban Treaty. Then, when Democrats belatedly discovered that Republicans were united against it, they demanded that the treaty be pulled; Lott kept to his earlier commitment and it was defeated. In February and March 2000, Lott allowed some votes on Clinton judicial nominees, to the anger of some Republicans. He supported the move to temporarily suspend the gas tax, which failed by a wide margin, and held up a supplemental appropriation on Kosovo and Colombia, to the wrath of Appropriations Chairman Ted Stevens. In June 2000 Nebraska's Chuck Hagel said there could be changes in the leadership if Republicans lost seats in November; Hagel had contemplated running against Lott after the November 1998 elections, and ran unsuccessfully against campaign chairman Mitch McConnell instead. In July 2000 Lott steered estate tax repeal through, but at the cost of allowing votes on many Democratic amendments. In fall 2000 Lott followed a "no veto" strategy and tried to negotiate with the Clinton administration on appropriations; this was opposed by House Republican Whip Tom DeLay, who wanted to set clear conservative markers and get members out of town. The result was relatively high spending, and a delay in many appropriations until after the November elections and, as seemed sensible, after the Florida recounts as well.

By late 2000, almost everyone seemed angry with Lott for one reason or another. "I don't feel unappreciated, and I don't feel exceedingly appreciated," he said. But no one—not even Majority Whip Don Nickles, a frequent critic—moved to run against him, though Lott ally Larry Craig was challenged for his leadership position and kept it by only a 26–24 vote. Lott had lost some of his closest confidants in the Senate—Connie Mack retired, Paul Coverdell died in July 2000 and Slade Gorton, after a long recount, was defeated for re-election. That left the Senate divided 50–50. Democrats demanded equal numbers of members on each committee; some Republican conservatives strongly opposed that, though some committee chairmen offered equal membership. "Look, we got the high ground," Lott said. "We took the leap of faith." On January 5, 2001, after negotiations with Daschle, Lott surprised many by agreeing to equal membership. There was a strong theoretical argument for that—committee membership should reflect the balance on the floor—but even stronger practical arguments; plus not insisting on every ounce of partisan advantage was probably prudent. Democrats, many angry about Florida, were of a mood to filibuster the organizational resolution, which would probably have prevented confirmation of Bush appointees; and Lott wanted to make sure that no Democratic senator would challenge the Florida electoral votes on January 6, and thereby trigger debate on that issue. And there was also the possibility that control could shift to the Democrats. Most observers pointed to 98-year-old Strom Thurmond as one senator who might leave office, but there were 45 senators with governors of a different party, 26 Democrats and 19 Republicans, whose departure could change party control. While there was some hope that Georgia's Zell Miller—much paraded about as a Democratic backer of Bush's tax cut—might cross the aisle and strengthen this fragile majority, it was not much suspected in May 2001 that James Jeffords would defect and unravel it. The visibly angry Lott called it a "coup of one" and said, "The decision of one man has—however else you describe it—trumped the will of the American people."

The fact is that the position of Senate majority leader carries little institutional power. The majority leader can take the lead in scheduling business—as Lott did when he got John McCain to wait two months, until March 2001, to debate his campaign finance bill—but such decisions can often require unanimous consent and can usually be overturned by majorities. With a Republican president, Lott will be less often the national spokesman for his party, as he was many times from 1996 to 2000; he will be spending more time, as minority leader, trying to get the Bush programs through. The day before the Senate balance of power was officially to change hands, Lott remarked: "There's something liberating about being in the minority . . . You're freer to advocate positions and amendments you really think should be adopted."

In the meantime he will surely keep tending to Mississippi interests. Working often with colleague Thad Cochran, who ranks second on Appropriations, Lott has pressed hard for $375 million for the LHD-8 helicopter carrier, to be manufactured in Pascagoula's Ingalls Shipyards, a ship not sought by the Navy; he has gotten $72 million for projects at the Raytheon plant in Forest; he has worked for $2 million for Mississippi State University's research center where superfast computers do undersea modeling of Navy projects and $2 million for University of Mississippi computer labs receiving information from orbiting satellites; he got $5 million for an electronic targeting system at the Army Reserves' Camp Shelby near Hattiesburg. He got Madison County designated as a "renewal community" on the grounds that it is "right on the edge of" the impoverished Mississippi Delta; but the county is filling up with affluent Jackson suburbanites and can probably use to designation to pave the way for a $930 million auto plant Nissan is planning to build there.

Lott gave up a safe House seat to run for the Senate in 1988, and he had something of a fight for it against Democratic Congressman Wayne Dowdy. But Lott raised plenty of money and beat Dowdy by a 61%–39% margin in the Jackson area, the Gulf Coast and other counties where turnout had increased 10% since 1980; in the rest of the state, Dowdy won only 51%–49%, giving

Lott a 54%–46% win overall. In 1994 and 2000 Lott did not have serious competition and won easily, 69%–31% and 66%–32%. The 2000 VNS exit poll shows Lott carrying whites 88%–9% and losing blacks 88%–10%, but the latter figure seems dubious. He carried Hinds County, whose population is 61% black, with 51% of the vote, and ran even in the black-majority Delta; his efforts to win black Mississippians' votes seem to have borne some fruit.

Presidential politics Mississippi voted 58%–41% for George W. Bush in 2000—almost the same as the 60%–39% margin by which his father carried the state in 1988. There is no way of avoiding the conclusion that this is a racially polarized electorate: whites voted 82%–17% for Bush, blacks 96%–3% for Gore. Yet it should also be said that Mississippi's majority does not seek a return of racial segregation, but lines up with Republicans on a whole raft of issues—defense, crime, cultural attitudes, taxes—just as blacks line up with Democrats on the same issues. Mississippi holds a presidential primary on Southern Super Tuesday; in 2000 both parties' contests were effectively over.

Congressional districting Mississippi lost one of its five House districts in the 2000 Census; this will be the first decade in which Mississippi has just four congressmen since the 1840s. Democrats, with the governorship and large majorities in the legislature, control the process; a joint redistricting committee, made up of 19 Democrats and five Republicans, is expected to draw the lines. Geography and the Supreme Court's rulings on racial redistricting will have much influence on the plan.

First, geography: Because Mississippi's Gulf Coast counties have nearly enough population for a district, the current 5th District will probably just be extended northward (and renumbered) to include either Laurel or Meridian. In an open seat election, this would be a strongly Republican district. But Gene Taylor, the independent-minded Democratic incumbent, is hugely popular; he won 79%–18% in 2000. Republican Chip Pickering of the 3rd District grew up in Laurel, but even before redistricting he moved his residence to the heavily Republican suburbs of Rankin County, just east of Jackson, which he carried 83%–16% in 2000; he presumably will not run against Taylor.

Mississippi was the first state to get a redistricting plan dominated by the Supreme Court's interpretation of the Voting Rights Act in 1984; this 2d District was won in 1986 by black Democrat Mike Espy, later Bill Clinton's secretary of Agriculture. Bennie Thompson, the current Democratic incumbent, would probably prefer a district similar to the current 2nd, which combines the black-majority counties of the Delta with black-majority precincts in Jackson's Hinds County; he won there 65%–31% in 2000. But Democratic redistricters must add territory to get the district up to the required population, and there was speculation in early 2001 that they would add either Rankin County or DeSoto County, the heavily Republican county just south of Memphis, to the 2nd. The theory would be that Thompson would still be able to win, that the Republican in the adjoining district would be weakened and that the district would be easier to defend than the current 2nd against charges of racial gerrymandering given the Supreme Court's latest interpretation of the Voting Rights Act that race cannot be the sole factor in creating districts. But the Democratic percentage in a 2nd-plus-Rankin district would be cut to 55%–41%, too close perhaps for Thompson's comfort, and such a plan might be resisted by black legislators whose votes Democrats need for approval of the district lines.

Probably the likeliest result is that Thompson would emerge with a 2nd District similar to the current one, Republican Roger Wicker would have a reasonably safe 1st District in north and northeast Mississippi, and 4th District Democrat Ronnie Shows and 3rd District Republican Chip Pickering would fight it out in a district with areas of strength for both candidates—rural counties for Shows, Rankin County for Pickering.

THE PEOPLE: Pop. 2000: 2,844,658; Pop. 1990: 2,573,216, up 10.5% 1990–2000. 1% of U.S. total, 31st largest; 61.4% White, 36.3% Black, 0.7% Asian, 0.4% Amer. Indian, 0.7% Two+ races, 0.5% Other; 1.4% Hispanic Origin. 5.7% Unemployment. 2000 Voting age pop.: 2,069,471. 2000 Turnout: 994,184; 48% of VAP. Registered voters (2000): 1,759,092; no party registration.

POLITICAL LINEUP: Governor, Ronnie Musgrove (D); Lt. Gov., Amy Tuck (D); Secy. of State, Eric Clark (D); Atty. Gen., Mike Moore (D); Treasurer, Marshall Bennett (D); Commissioner of Insurance, George Dale (D); Auditor, Phil Bryant (R); Commissioner of Agriculture & Commerce, Lester Spell Jr. (D); State Senate, 52 (34 D, 18 R); Senate Pres. Pro Tempore, Travis Little (D); Senate President, Amy Tuck (D); State House, 122 (86 D, 33 R, 3 I); House Speaker, Timothy A. Ford (D). Senators, Thad Cochran (R) and Trent Lott (R). Representatives, 5 (3 D, 2 R).

ELECTIONS DIVISION: 601-359-6357; **FILING DEADLINE FOR U.S. CONGRESS:** April 5, 2002.

2000 Presidential Vote
Bush (R)	572,844	(58%)
Gore (D)	404,614	(41%)
Nader (Green)	8,122	(1%)
Others	8,604	(1%)

1996 Presidential Vote
Dole (R)	439,833	(49%)
Clinton (D)	394,020	(44%)
Perot (I)	52,221	(6%)

2000 Republican Presidential Primary
Bush (R)	101,042	(88%)
Keyes (R)	6,478	(6%)
McCain (R)	6,263	(5%)

2000 Democratic Presidential Primary
Gore (D)	79,408	(90%)
Bradley (D)	7,621	(9%)

Gov. Ronnie Musgrove (D)

Elected 1999, term expires Jan. 2004, 1st term; b. Jul. 29, 1956, Tocowa; home, Batesville; B.A. 1978, J.D. 1981 U. of MS; Southern Baptist; separated.

Elected Office: MS Senate, 1987–95; MS Lt. Gov., 1995–99.

Professional Career: Atty., Smith, Musgrove & McCord, 1981–99.

Office: State Capitol, P.O. Box 139, Jackson, 39205, 601-359-3100; Fax: 601-359-3741; Web site: www.state.ms.us.

Election Results
1999 general	Ronnie Musgrove (D)	379,034	(49.6%)
	Mike Parker (R)	370,691	(48.5%)
	Others	14,213	(2%)
1999 primary	Ronnie Musgrove (D)	309,519	(57%)
	James Roberts Jr. (D)	142,617	(26%)
	Richard Barrett (D)	32,383	(6%)
	Others	61,036	(11%)
1995 general	Kirk Fordice (R)	455,261	(56%)
	Dick Molpus (D)	364,210	(44%)
1995 primary	Kirk Fordice (R)	117,907	(94%)
	George (Wagon Wheel) Blair (R)	4,919	(4%)
	Others	2,956	(2%)

Sen. Thad Cochran (R)

Elected 1978, seat up 2002, 4th term; b. Dec. 7, 1937, Pontotoc; home, Jackson; U. of MS, B.A. 1959, J.D. 1965, Rotary Fellow, Trinity Col., Ireland, 1963–64; Baptist; married (Rose).

Military Career: Navy, 1959–61.

Elected Office: U.S. House of Reps., 1972–78.

Professional Career: Practicing atty., 1965–72.

DC Office: 326 RSOB, 20510, 202-224-5054; Fax: 202-224-9450; Web site: www.senate.gov/~cochran.

State Offices: Gulfport, 228-867-9710; Jackson, 601-965-4459; Oxford, 662-236-1018.

Committees: *Agriculture, Nutrition & Forestry*: Marketing, Inspection & Product Promotion; Production & Price Competitiveness. *Appropriations*: Agriculture & Rural Development (RMM); Defense; Energy & Water Development; Interior; Labor, HHS & Education. *Governmental Affairs*: Government Management, Restructuring and the District of Columbia; International Security, Proliferation & Federal Services (RMM); Investigations (Permanent). *Rules & Administration.*

Group Ratings

	ADA	ACLU	AFS	LCV	CON	ITIC	NTU	COC	ACU	NTLC	CHC
2000	0	14	0	0	36	97	74	100	92	94	92
1999	0	—	0	0	8	—	74	88	84	—	—

National Journal Ratings

	1999 LIB —	1999 CONS	2000 LIB —	2000 CONS
Economic	35%	63%	0%	86%
Social	23%	72%	10%	81%
Foreign	37%	60%	36%	58%

Key Votes of the 106th Congress

1. Educ. Savings Accts.	Y	5. Review Movie Violence	Y	9. NATO War in Serbia	*
2. Prescrip. Drug Benefit	N	6. Gun Show Bckgrnd. Checks	N	10. Table Cuba Travel Ban	Y
3. Delay Ergonomic Standards	Y	7. Ban Part.-Birth Abortion	Y	11. Nuclear Test-Ban Treaty	N
4. Phase Out Estate Tax	Y	8. Broaden Hate Crimes List	N	12. Perm. Trade with China	Y

Election Results

1996 general	Thad Cochran (R)	624,154	(71%)	($1,305,680)
	James W. Hunt (D)	240,647	(27%)	
	Others	13,861	(2%)	
1996 primary	Thad Cochran (R)	138,813	(95%)	
	Richard O'Hara (R)	6,762	(5%)	
1990 general	Thad Cochran (R)	unopposed		($691,865)

Sen. Trent Lott (R)

Elected 1988, seat up 2006, 3d term; b. Oct. 9, 1941, Grenada; home, Pascagoula; U. of MS, B.A. 1963, J.D. 1967; Baptist; married (Tricia).

Elected Office: U.S. House of Reps., 1972–88.

Professional Career: Practicing atty., 1967–68; A.A., U.S. Rep. William Colmer, 1968–72.

DC Office: 487 RSOB, 20510, 202-224-6253; Fax: 202-224-2262; Web site: lott.senate.gov.

State Offices: Greenwood, 662-453-5681; Gulfport, 228-863-1988; Jackson, 601-965-4644; Oxford, 662-234-3774; Pascagoula, 228-762-5400.

Committees: *Minority Leader. Commerce, Science & Transportation*: Aviation; Communications; Science, Technology & Space; Surface Transportation & Merchant Marine. *Finance*: International Trade; Social Security & Family Policy; Taxation & IRS Oversight. *Rules & Administration*.

Group Ratings

	ADA	ACLU	AFS	LCV	CON	ITIC	NTU	COC	ACU	NTLC	CHC
2000	5	14	0	0	11	91	74	93	100	97	92
1999	0	—	0	0	8	—	74	82	96	—	—

National Journal Ratings

	1999 LIB	—	1999 CONS		2000 LIB	—	2000 CONS
Economic	0%	—	83%		36%	—	63%
Social	18%	—	79%		10%	—	81%
Foreign	23%	—	67%		5%	—	86%

Key Votes of the 106th Congress

1. Educ. Savings Accts.	Y	5. Review Movie Violence	Y	9. NATO War in Serbia	N
2. Prescrip. Drug Benefit	N	6. Gun Show Bckgrnd. Checks	N	10. Table Cuba Travel Ban	Y
3. Delay Ergonomic Standards	Y	7. Ban Part.-Birth Abortion	Y	11. Nuclear Test-Ban Treaty	N
4. Phase Out Estate Tax	Y	8. Broaden Hate Crimes List	N	12. Perm. Trade with China	Y

Election Results

2000 general	Trent Lott (R)	654,941	(66%)	($3,663,052)
	Troy Brown (D)	314,090	(32%)	($40,349)
	Others	25,113	(3%)	
2000 primary	Trent Lott (R)	unopposed		
1994 general	Trent Lott (R)	418,333	(69%)	($2,516,189)
	Ken Harper (D)	189,752	(31%)	($345,379)

FIRST DISTRICT

The university town of Oxford, the center of William Faulkner's fictional Yoknapatawpha County, sits on a divide between the hill country of Mississippi and the flat farmlands of the Mississippi Delta. The mostly white-hill counties run up to where the Tennessee River nicks the northeast corner of Tishomingo County. The Tennessee Valley Authority brought electricity here, the Tennessee-Tombigbee Waterway provided construction jobs for years and a new shipping canal when it was completed in 1985. The focus, though, is different in the hill-country metropolis, Tupelo, which is a stronghold of private enterprise and traditional values. It excels at corporate recruitment, attracting new jobs without giving away the store—"probably the best small city in the South" at it, says one corporate recruiter; the upholstered furniture industry here accounts for the largest manufacturing sector in the state. Elvis Presley was born in Tupelo in 1935, in a two-room house that is open to visitors, as is the Elvis Presley Museum with a modest collection of memorabilia. West of Oxford is Mississippi's Delta, the swampy land pioneered by large planters around the turn of the century, with large black work forces little removed—in the conditions of their daily lives or long-term economic chances—from slavery. Oxford, home of Ole Miss, is also the home today of the Center for the Study of Southern Culture.

The 1st Congressional District includes most of the hill country and a little bit of the Delta plus the Memphis suburbs of DeSoto County. This was the district represented by Jamie Whitten, the longest-serving House member in history, from his special election victory in November 1941 until January 1995: 53 years and two months. This territory still shows some signs of allegiance to Whitten's party: the 1st District was carried solidly by George W. Bush in 2000, but it also voted solidly for Democratic Governor Ronnie Musgrove in 1999.

The congressman from the 1st District today is Roger Wicker, a Republican elected in 1994. He grew up in Pontotoc, 20 miles from Tupelo, the son of a state senator and circuit judge, attended public schools and was a House page in 1967: the first of the 1994 freshmen to get on the floor of the House. He is a fifth cousin once removed of Senator Fred Thompson, who grew up not far across the state line in Lawrenceburg, Tennessee. Wicker went to college and law school at Ole Miss, where he was student body president, served in the Air Force, and in 1980 became a staffer to Trent Lott on the House Rules Committee. In 1987, at 36, he was elected as a Republican to the state Senate and chaired the Elections, and Public Health and Welfare committees, where he sponsored a 24-hour waiting period for abortions and helped to write the state's welfare reform law. In 1994, when Whitten retired, Wicker was one of six Republicans and three Democrats to run for the seat. Wicker, carrying his home base around Tupelo, led in the first primary 27%–19% over Grant Fox, former aide to Senator Thad Cochran. In the runoff, Wicker campaigned as a conservative, but Fox, just 27, hit him hard for voting to override Governor Fordice's sales tax increase veto. Wicker won by 53%–47%. Defeating House Speaker Tim Ford, State Representative Bill Wheeler was the Democratic nominee with support from blacks, unions and teachers' unions, an advantage in the primary but not the general. The result wasn't even close: a district held for 53 years by a Democratic leader voted 63%–37% for the Republican.

In the House Wicker was elected president of the 73-member freshman class, one of the largest in the 20th Century. He also won Whitten's old seat on the Appropriations Committee. Wicker had a conservative voting record, and rallied the freshman to support the budget even after Newt Gingrich capitulated to Clinton in January 1996. He sponsored a "litigation fairness" proposal to specify the rules for government-sponsored lawsuits. He became part of "The Group," an informal network of Speaker Dennis Hastert's close legislative advisers. Yet in some ways Wicker has acted like an old-style Democrat. He worked on local projects and backed measures which helped local industries. He fought to preserve the Appalachian Regional Commission and the Economic Development Administration, to support funding of the Natchez Trace Parkway, started in the 1930s but never completed, and for Yalobusha River flood control. After winning approval in 1998 of a study of flame-retardant chemicals that blocked further regulation of upholstered furniture companies by the Consumer Product Safety Commission, Wicker claimed complete vindication two years later when scientists for the National Research Council found little or no health risk from the chemicals. On national issues, he has vigorously advocated additional health care research and heart-disease prevention strategies; the state has the nation's highest death rate from cardiovascular disease, especially among blacks. In the old style, Wicker has used that focus to bring research dollars to Mississippi universities. He has worked on a global eradication campaign for polio.

Wicker has consistently been re-elected by better than 2–1 margins. His 2000 campaign opponent, state representative Joey Grist, had his convenience store shut down because of failure to pay sales taxes. Although he has a far different ideology than his predecessor, Wicker has shown that the nation's consensus-minded mood has reached even the rebel hills of northern Mississippi. "There's too much partisanship in Congress. I served in the Mississippi legislature where we had to work with people from both sides of the aisle. It's far different in Washington." Democrats control the redistricting process, and Mississippi lost one House seat in the 2000 Census. Theoretically, redistricters could remove DeSoto County and add some Delta counties to the district, which would make it much less Republican. But that would not please 2nd District Democratic Bennie Thompson and would probably be resisted by black legislators. So the likelihood is that the 1st District will be extended southward and will remain a safe seat for Wicker.

Cook's Call *Probably Safe.* Wicker has had little trouble, or little competition, since winning this conservative Republican-leaning district in 1994. But, redistricting could cause Wicker some problems. The state is slated to lose one seat and Democrats, who control the line-drawing process in the state, may decide to combine this seat with Republican Rep. Chip Pickering's 3rd District.

THE PEOPLE: Pop. 2000: 607,229; Pop. 1990: 515,196, up 17.9% 1990–2000. 75.8% White, 22.4% Black, 0.4% Asian, 0.2% Amer. Indian, 0.6% Two + races, 0.6% Other; 1.5% Hispanic Origin.

2000 Presidential Vote			1996 Presidential Vote		
Bush (R)	129,119	(60%)	Dole (R)	90,604	(48%)
Gore (D)	81,640	(38%)	Clinton (D)	78,894	(42%)
Nader (Green)	1,929	(1%)	Perot (I)	13,695	(7%)
Others	1,418	(1%)	Others	3,864	(2%)

Rep. Roger Wicker (R)

Elected 1994, 4th term; b. July 5, 1951, Pontotoc; home, Tupelo; U. of MS, B.A. 1973, J.D. 1975; Baptist; married (Gayle).

Military Career: Air Force, 1976–80; Air Force Reserves, 1980–present.

Elected Office: Tupelo City Judge Pro Tem, 1986–87; MS Senate, 1987–94.

Professional Career: Staff, U.S. House Rules Cmte., 1980–82; Practicing atty., 1982–94; Lee Cnty. Public Defender, 1984–87.

DC Office: 206 CHOB 20515, 202-225-4306; Fax: 202-225-3549; Web site: www.house.gov/wicker.

District Offices: Southaven, 662-342-3942; Tupelo, 662-844-5437.

Committees: *Appropriations* (19th of 35 R): Energy & Water Development; Foreign Operations & Export Financing; Labor, HHS & Education.

Group Ratings

	ADA	ACLU	AFS	LCV	CON	ITIC	NTU	COC	ACU	NTLC	CHC
2000	0	21	0	0	29	94	60	85	84	73	100
1999	0	—	0	0	21	—	54	96	92	—	—

National Journal Ratings

	1999 LIB —	1999 CONS		2000 LIB —	2000 CONS
Economic	0%	84%		6%	85%
Social	4%	91%		23%	74%
Foreign	23%	73%		25%	69%

Key Votes of the 106th Congress

1. Patient Bill of Rights	N	5. Bar RU-486 $ for FDA	Y	9. NATO War in Serbia	N
2. Accelerate Min. Wage	N	6. Display 10 Commandments	Y	10. Perm. Trade with China	Y
3. Strike Ban on Ergo. Stnd.	N	7. Gun Show Bkgrnd. Checks	N	11. Debt Relief for 3rd World	N
4. Ovrd. Estate Tax Veto	Y	8. Ban Part.-Birth Abortion	Y	12. Drop Cuba Econ. Embargo	N

Election Results

2000 general	Roger Wicker (R)	145,967	(70%)	($1,283,515)
	Joey Grist (D)	59,763	(29%)	
	Other	3,310	(2%)	
2000 primary	Roger Wicker (R)	unopposed		
1998 general	Roger Wicker (R)	66,738	(67%)	($288,354)
	Rex N. Weathers (D)	30,438	(31%)	
	Others	2,157	(2%)	

SECOND DISTRICT

"The Mississippi Delta," wrote Delta native David Cohn, "begins in the lobby of the Peabody Hotel in Memphis and ends on Catfish Row in Vicksburg." For centuries, the flooding Mississippi and Yazoo Rivers left their sediments here, producing a fertile dark soil. Ironically, what may well be America's richest agricultural land has been home for more than a century to many of its poorest people. The Delta, criss-crossed by rivers and famously disease-ridden, wasn't much settled until after the Civil War; the tradition here is not of paternal masters and gracious mansions, but of sharp, profit-seeking operators who used 19th Century technology to drain the land, line the river with levees and build railroads on tracks above the rise of the river. Black sharecroppers and field hands worked here in conditions almost of bondage. From this episode of industrial farming came both great misery and great art: Clarksdale in Coahoma County was the home of W.C. Handy and Muddy Waters, the real birthplace of blues music; Greenville on the Mississippi has produced writers of the caliber of Walker Percy and Shelby Foote. Now Vicksburg's antebellum mansions, battlefield monuments and riverboat gambling bring in 1.5 million tourists annually from around the country.

Twentieth Century technology changed life in the Delta. The mechanical cotton-picking machine, invented in 1944, came along just as northern factories were seeking low-wage workers; the great exodus to Chicago and Memphis began, and the Delta's population has been declining ever since. Income levels remain very low, poverty is over 50% in some areas and infant mortality is at Third World levels; the crime and drugs of urban Chicago have been brought back by Delta migrants returning home. There are signs of hope: Soybeans have become a big dollar crop here, although there is more acreage still in cotton; poultry farms have become a major enterprise, and the Delta produces 62% of the nation's catfish. Riverboat gambling was approved in 1992 in Tunica County, by some measures the nation's poorest county, which had been perhaps best known for its Sugar Ditch, the open sewer in the town's black section. In 2000, 10 million people arrived in Tunica's casinos, which now have more square footage than Atlantic City's, and plans are under-way for a regional airport that will further expand the tourist trade. There is still a gulf between the races, culturally and economically, but also positive signs: when Ku Klux Klansmen demon-strated in Greenwood and Clarksdale in 1994, they were promptly arrested and attracted no support. Still, the Delta has been slow to develop the self-propelling market economy that has brought growth to most of the nation. During his 1999 tour to focus on the nation's poorest communities, Bill Clinton stopped in Clarksdale to listen to local stories of deprivation. Clinton was boosting his plan to create the Delta Regional Authority, encouraging economic development in portions of seven states. In November 2000 came another positive development when Nissan announced a $930 million pickup truck factory in heavily black Canton, in an area 15 miles north of Jackson. The new factory will sit on one of the old South's most enduring symbols: a cotton field.

The 2d Congressional District occupies the entire Mississippi Delta region, indeed the whole riverfront from Tunica almost to Natchez, plus black neighborhoods of Jackson. It is Mississippi's one black-majority district, first created as such in 1984, with modest changes in boundaries for 1992. Thirty years ago, when blacks were not allowed to vote in Mississippi, politics here was the domain of the big plantation owners, symbolized by James Eastland, Senate Judiciary chairman from 1955–79, an unyielding segregationist and conservative. Even after blacks got the vote, black registration was low and habits of deference in some places prevailed. In 1986, the district elected its first black congressman since Reconstruction, Mike Espy, whose grandfather and father built a chain of funeral homes and were among the biggest landowners in the state. He worked on farm issues, opposed gun control and courted white voters; in 1993, Bill Clinton tapped him as secretary of Agriculture.

The congressman from the 2d District is Bennie Thompson, who grew up in Bolton, in Hinds County outside Jackson, graduated from Tougaloo College and received a masters from Jackson State. He was elected alderman in Bolton in 1969, at 21, and mayor four years later; he was the first person in Mississippi to get a street named after Martin Luther King Jr. In 1980 he became a Hinds County supervisor. He worked to encourage other blacks to run for office; Mississippi now has more than 850 black officeholders; he was lead plaintiff in a suit charging that the state underfunded historically black state colleges. In the March 1993 all-party primary, he won 28% to 20% for Henry Espy, Mike Espy's brother and mayor of Clarksdale. But the leader, with 34%, was Republican Hayes Dent, a 31-year-old aide to Governor Kirk Fordice. In the April runoff voting was mostly along racial lines, and Thompson won 55%–45%. Most of his margin came from Jackson and Hinds County.

Unlike Espy, Thompson initially made no particular attempt to win white votes and had a solidly liberal voting record, making as few concessions across the racial divide as had Eastland in his day. He worked for the empowerment zone which Bill Clinton established in six Delta counties and for the Delta Regional Authority; he got money for restoring buildings at Tougaloo and Rust colleges; he got the Jackson and Ruleville post offices named for Medgar Evers and Fannie Lou Hamer. He successfully sought restitution for black farmers who lost land because of Agriculture Department discrimination. He was a lead plaintiff in the suit against the state in a 26-year-old case to increase funding for black colleges, settled in 2001. In time he reached out to the white community, including a meeting with the Clarksdale-area Chamber of Commerce in October 2000. He also met with some large farmers. "Delta planters have gradually warmed up to Thompson, with a few even hosting political fund-raisers on his behalf," the *Clarksdale Press-Register* reported.

Thompson chaired the Congressional Black Caucus's Tobacco Working Group, which worked to make sure minority groups got a share of public health spending in the tobacco settlement. He sponsored the law to award the Congressional Gold Medal to the nine students who integrated Little Rock's Central High School. In the 107th Congress, he sought the Black Caucus chairmanship with a pledge to work more closely with business interests, but he lost by one vote to Eddie Bernice Johnson.

Thompson has won re-election by wide margins. He provided important help in turning out black voters for Ronnie Musgrove's narrow 1999 win for governor. Mississippi lost one House seat in the 2000 Census, so districts will have to grow. Democrats control the redistricting process, with black legislators casting critical votes, and the Voting Rights Act under prevailing interpretations requires the creation of black-majority districts if they are geographically compact, as this district is. There may be an attempt to include in the 2nd either Rankin or DeSoto Counties, both heavily white and Republican, to weaken Republicans in an adjacent district. Thompson probably will resist such efforts, and even then the 2nd would be left with a solid Democratic majority.

Cook's Call   *Safe.* This majority-black district is the safest Democratic seat in the state. It was also the slowest growing district in the state and will need to pick up almost 195,000 people. But, the Voting Rights Act ensures that this district (the black population increased here by 2%) will remain majority black.

THE PEOPLE: Pop. 2000: 517,345; Pop. 1990: 514,469, up 0.6% 1990–2000. 33.4% White, 65.2% Black, 0.4% Asian, 0.1% Amer. Indian, 0.5% Two+ races, 0.3% Other; 1.2% Hispanic Origin.

2000 Presidential Vote				1996 Presidential Vote			
Gore (D)	105,104	(59%)		Clinton (D)	104,639	(62%)	
Bush (R)	69,229	(39%)		Dole (R)	58,177	(34%)	
Others	2,596	(1%)		Perot (I)	5,714	(3%)	

Rep. Bennie G. Thompson (D)

Elected Apr., 1993, 4th term; b. Jan. 28, 1948, Bolton; home, Bolton; Tougaloo Col., B.A. 1968, Jackson St. U., M.S. 1972; Methodist; married (London).

Elected Office: Bolton Bd. of Aldermen, 1969–73; Bolton Mayor, 1973–79; Hinds Cnty. Supervisor, 1980–93.

DC Office: 2432 RHOB 20515, 202-225-5876; Fax: 202-225-5898; Web site: www.house.gov/thompson.

District Offices: Bolton, 601-866-9003; Greenville, 662-335-9003; Greenwood, 662-455-9003; Marks, 662-326-9003; Mound Bayou, 662-741-9003.

Committees: *Agriculture* (9th of 24 D): General Farm Commodities & Risk Management; Specialty Crops & Foreign Agriculture Programs. *Budget* (3d of 20 D).

Group Ratings

	ADA	ACLU	AFS	LCV	CON	ITIC	NTU	COC	ACU	NTLC	CHC
2000	90	79	100	64	15	60	25	50	8	23	7
1999	100	—	100	88	63	—	17	17	0	—	—

National Journal Ratings

	1999 LIB —	1999 CONS		2000 LIB —	2000 CONS
Economic	88% —	0%		68% —	32%
Social	78% —	22%		79% —	17%
Foreign	88% —	11%		74% —	24%

Key Votes of the 106th Congress

1. Patient Bill of Rights	Y	5. Bar RU-486 $ for FDA	N	9. NATO War in Serbia		*
2. Accelerate Min. Wage	Y	6. Display 10 Commandments	N	10. Perm. Trade with China	N	
3. Strike Ban on Ergo. Stnd.	Y	7. Gun Show Bkgrnd. Checks	Y	11. Debt Relief for 3rd World	Y	
4. Ovrd. Estate Tax Veto	N	8. Ban Part.-Birth Abortion	N	12. Drop Cuba Econ. Embargo	Y	

Election Results

2000 general	Bennie G. Thompson (D)	112,777	(65%)	($409,852)
	Hardy Caraway (R)	54,090	(31%)	
	Others	6,440	(4%)	
2000 primary	Bennie G. Thompson (D)	unopposed		
1998 general	Bennie G. Thompson (D)	80,284	(71%)	($281,858)
	William G. Chipman (Lib)	32,533	(29%)	

THIRD DISTRICT

Mississippi, old and new: The old Mississippi is the Neshoba County fair, held every August since 1892 in the town of Philadelphia. This is traditionally the place where Mississippi politicians announce their candidacies, with the crowds watching to take their measure. When Ronald Reagan came here in 1980 and Michael Dukakis in 1988, neither mentioned what Philadelphia and Neshoba County are best known for in history, nor is there any memorial except engraved stones at two black churches: It was here during the "Freedom Summer" of 1964 that three civil rights workers, two white and one black, were murdered for the crime of urging black American citizens to register and vote. The new Mississippi is some 80 miles away, in Rankin and Madison County east and north of Jackson, where subdivisions and shopping centers are sprouting up on lands which only a few years ago seemed out in the country.

The 3d Congressional District includes the Rankin and the Madison County suburbs of Jackson and Neshoba County. It stretches north to Starkville, home of Mississippi State University, and south to Laurel, an hour's drive from the Gulf Coast. In the middle is Meridian, a small city that may go down in history as the site of departures of two White House chiefs of staff: Nixon informed Bob Haldeman that he was out as chief of staff in April 1973 and in December 1991 John Sununu penned his letter of resignation to President Bush. The political tradition here is Southern Democratic, but the area's recent preference has been Republican: Mississippi, old and new.

The congressman from the 3d District is Chip Pickering, a Republican elected in 1996. He grew up in Laurel where he worked on the family dairy and catfish farm and attended public schools; his father was a state senator and state Republican chairman and is now a federal judge. Pickering was more interested in football than politics at college, and he next spent 17 months as a Southern Baptist missionary in then-Communist Hungary. He was at the Agriculture Department in the Bush administration, and a staffer for Senator Trent Lott, working primarily on telecommunications issues. In fall 1995, Sonny Montgomery, congressman from the 3d District, a Democrat who mostly voted with Republicans, announced that he would retire after 30 years; Pickering returned to Mississippi and started running for Congress.

He faced competition; nine Republicans and three Democrats ran. Pickering used his old party ties: His father's executive director at the state party had been Haley Barbour, Republican National Committee chairman from 1993–97, and Pickering's campaign manager was his nephew Henry Barbour. In the primary Pickering ran first in 13 of 19 counties, though in neither of the big population centers, and won 27% of the vote. In second was former state Representative Bill Crawford from Meridian, with 24%, who Pickering attacked strongly for supporting Democratic gubernatorial candidate Ray Mabus in 1987; Pickering won the runoff 56%–44% with big margins in the Jackson suburbs. The general election was a battle between 32-year-old Pickering and 29-year-old John Arthur Eaves Jr., son of a well-known lawyer and Democratic politician. Eaves spent $542,000 of his own money, and sounded some Republican themes. Pickering spent more than $1 million, boasted of his Republican label and won in this heavily Republican district 61%–36%.

In the House, Pickering has a very conservative voting record and with his Capitol Hill contacts picked up key assignments. As vice chairman of the Surface Transportation Subcommittee, he helped to preside over the huge 1998 transportation bill. In 1999, he passed bills to halt FCC regulation of religious programming and force schools to fiter the Internet; librarians and civil activists challenged the bill in court. He filed a bill limiting the FCC's ability to review telecommunications mergers. As co-chairman of the Congressional Wireless Caucus, he sought increased focus on the industry's concerns: competition, public safety, privacy and the spectrum. He sought to protect hunters with a bill to establish federal recognition of the value of hunting for recreation and wildlife management. On local issues, he sponsored legislation to develop a vaccine for disease in catfish and he sought funds for a new support facility at the Meridian Naval Air Station.

Pickering seems headed for a long and influential House career, and is a likely prospect for the Senate if Thad Cochran or Trent Lott should choose to retire—if he survives redistricting in 2002. Mississippi lost one House seat in the 2000 Census, and Democrats control the redistricting process. Given the population data, it is likely that Pickering's home town of Laurel will be placed in the Gulf Coast district; this is a heavily Republican district in most elections, but Democratic Congressman Gene Taylor is hugely popular—he won 79%–18% in 2000—and Pickering, evidently unwilling to run against him in mostly unfamiliar territory, has moved his residence to Rankin County. There has been speculation that this heavily Republican county will be placed in the black-majority 2nd District, but the incumbent there, Democrat Bennie Thompson, will probably resist that. Most likely Pickering will be placed in the same district with Democrat Ronnie Shows, a district including much of southwest Mississippi, some but not all the counties in Pickering's 3rd District, plus white areas of Jackson and Rankin County. Within these bounds, George W. Bush ran well ahead of Al Gore in 2000, but Shows has strong appeal in rural southwestern Mississippi, so this would be a tough fight. Pickering after the 2000 election had nearly $500,000 in his campaign treasury, and has the capacity to raise much more.

Cook's Call *Competitive.* Since his win here in 1996, Pickering has never had a tough general election in this conservative Republican stronghold. But with Mississippi slated to lose one district in 2001 redistricting and Democrats in control of the process in the state, this district has a big target on it. The most talked about redistricting scenario has this seat drawn in with Democratic Representative Ronnie Shows' 4th District. Republican influence, on where Republican leaning Rankin County (suburban Jackson) ends up, will determine just how competitive Republicans can be in a combined 3rd/4th CD.

THE PEOPLE: Pop. 2000: 588,915; Pop. 1990: 515,225, up 14.3% 1990–2000. 65% White, 32.1% Black, 0.6% Asian, 1.2% Amer. Indian, 0.6% Two+ races, 0.5% Other; 1.4% Hispanic Origin.

2000 Presidential Vote			1996 Presidential Vote		
Bush (R)	139,789	(66%)	Dole (R)	107,292	(58%)
Gore (D)	69,304	(33%)	Clinton (D)	66,027	(36%)
Nader (Green)	1,351	(1%)	Perot (I)	9,733	(5%)

Rep. Charles (Chip) Pickering (R)

Elected 1996, 3d term; b. Aug. 10, 1963, Laurel; home, Laurel; MS Col., 1981–82, U. of MS, B.A. 1986, Baylor U., M.B.A. 1988; Baptist; married (Leisha).

Professional Career: Baptist missionary, Budapest, Hungary, 1986–87; Spec. Asst. to the Admin. & Asst. Coord., East European & Soviet Secretariat, U.S. Dept. of Agriculture, 1989–90; Legis. Aide, U.S. Sen. Trent Lott, 1990–94.

DC Office: 427 CHOB 20515, 202-225-5031; Fax: 202-225-5797; Web site: www.house.gov/pickering.

District Offices: Columbus, 662-327-2766; Meridian, 601-693-6681; Pearl, 601-932-2410.

Committees: *Agriculture* (20th of 27 R): General Farm Commodities & Risk Management; Livestock & Horticulture. *Energy & Commerce* (19th of 31 R): Energy & Air Quality; Health; Telecommunications & The Internet.

Group Ratings

	ADA	ACLU	AFS	LCV	CON	ITIC	NTU	COC	ACU	NTLC	CHC
2000	0	14	0	7	69	88	62	90	100	78	100
1999	0	—	0	6	56	—	56	88	92	—	—

National Journal Ratings

	1999 LIB	—	1999 CONS		2000 LIB	—	2000 CONS
Economic	0%	—	84%		6%	—	85%
Social	0%	—	96%		0%	—	79%
Foreign	10%	—	86%		12%	—	78%

Key Votes of the 106th Congress

1. Patient Bill of Rights	N	5. Bar RU-486 $ for FDA	Y	9. NATO War in Serbia	N
2. Accelerate Min. Wage	N	6. Display 10 Commandments	Y	10. Perm. Trade with China	Y
3. Strike Ban on Ergo. Stnd.	N	7. Gun Show Bkgrnd. Checks	N	11. Debt Relief for 3rd World	N
4. Ovrd. Estate Tax Veto	Y	8. Ban Part.-Birth Abortion	Y	12. Drop Cuba Econ. Embargo	N

Election Results

2000 general	Charles (Chip) Pickering (R)	153,899	(73%)	($519,957)
	William Thrash (D)	54,151	(26%)	($1,349)
	Other	2,313	(1%)	
2000 primary	Charles (Chip) Pickering (R)	unopposed		
1998 general	Charles (Chip) Pickering (R)	84,785	(85%)	($517,249)
	Charles T. Scarborough Jr (Lib)	15,465	(15%)	

FOURTH DISTRICT

A few decades ago, Jackson was a small town centered on the grand Beaux Arts 1901 state Capitol. Today, Jackson is clearly the metropolis of Mississippi, the pivot point between the Delta and the hills, the rivers flowing sluggishly to New Orleans and the Gulf of Mexico and the highways running north to Memphis and Chicago. Like Mississippi generally, it is racially divided, with a black, not-affluent south side and a white affluent north side. In its new subdivisions of pleasant, large colonial houses under huge, overhanging trees, you can get a sense of what growth has meant to Jackson—especially when you consider that at least some of the people in these neighborhoods came from humble, rural Mississippi beginnings. This newer Mississippi contrasts with Natchez, where the finest collection of antebellum mansions sits on the bluffs overlooking the Mississippi River. Natchez had white millionaires and half the state's free blacks before the Civil War; it was content enough to oppose secession, and was spared major damage in the war because it was of no military importance. More recently, both Jackson and Natchez endured an ugly decade during the civil rights revolution: Mississippi blacks were murdered for registering to vote or for seeking higher-paying jobs. Today, both cities are more open, with more social contact between the races than in most northern metropolitan areas, but there is still yearning for economic growth and high-skill jobs.

The 4th Congressional District includes most of Jackson (excluding most black areas, which are in the black-majority 2d) and all of Natchez; it extends east to Laurel and south to the Louisiana line. This is an area that has trended Republican in national and statewide elections, as newly affluent white Mississippians vote for a party they associate with economic growth and assertive foreign policy, while blacks remain pretty solidly Democratic. But in local contests, Democrats still win many races.

Indeed, the congressman from the 4th District, Ronnie Shows, is a Democrat elected in 1998. Shows grew up on a farm in Jones County, went to two junior colleges and graduated from the University of Southern Mississippi—the first college graduate in his family. He taught in junior high and elementary schools and two private academies. In 1976, at 29, he was elected Jefferson Davis County Clerk; he moved up twice by winning elections to fill vacancies, to the state Senate in 1980 and as southern district transportation commissioner in 1988. The latter job gave him lots of opportunity to make friends in an area that covers most of the 4th District, even as he stayed in his two-bedroom house in tiny Bassfield. He was as well positioned as anyone to run when in Congressman Mike Parker, elected as a Democrat in 1988 and a switcher to the Republicans in 1995, prepared to run for governor in 1999.

Republicans were favored to hold this district, which voted twice against Bill Clinton, and the Republican primary outdrew the Democrats, with 59% of the votes. But just as Democrats in the old days bruised themselves and sapped their energy in vigorously contested primaries and runoffs, so did Republicans here. Shows won his primary in June, with 54% against two black candidates. The initial favorite for the Republican nod was Art Rhodes, Parker's chief of staff, but the leader in Jackson and Hinds County, which cast 39% of the district's votes was Delbert Hosemann, a tax lawyer with Jackson's largest firm, who had served on many civic boards but had not run for office before. Also competitive were Phil Davis from Simpson County; Pike County District Attorney Dunn Lampton; and Heath Hall, former press secretary to Governor Kirk Fordice. All five were running within close range of each other, when odd mailings started to appear in the last days before the primary—what looked like a letter from the ACLU endorsing Rhodes because he was against school prayer and what looked like a letter from Hall promising to move into the district if he was elected. Hosemann accused Davis of violating federal law; the FBI started investigating. Hosemann ran first in the primary, with 21%. Davis was second, with 18%. In the three weeks before the runoff, Hosemann ran an ad on the subject: "Dirty tricks, negative phone calls, false mailings and an FBI investigation. Mr. Davis, we deserve better. We demand an answer." Hosemann won the runoff 56%–44%, chiefly because of his 62%–38% margin in Hinds County. (In March 1999, Davis was indicted for violating the Watergate-era law, apparently never before used in a prosecution, banning misidentifying the source of a campaign mailing.)

In the general Shows displayed greater political skills and strength. From his work as highway commissioner, he started off with more name identification. He was heavily outspent, and Hosemann attacked him for liberal votes in the legislature on taxes and education. Shows campaigned in his good ole boy manner, and charged that Hosemann was a wealthy big city lawyer out of touch with rural areas. He was endorsed by the Blue Dog Democrats in Washington. In a 41% black district, he did not take black voters for granted, but appeared constantly in black churches. Shows won a solid 53%–45% victory, all the more impressive because he was outspent more than 2–1.

Shows joined the Blue Dog Democrats and had a voting record in the middle of the House, though more conservative on social issues. When Republicans initially pushed for big tax cuts in 1999, he said in his down-home way that the money would be better used mostly to reduce the federal debt. But when the talk later shifted to more targeted cuts of the marriage penalty and estate taxes, Shows sided with the Republicans. He became the Democratic whip in the Pro-Life Caucus. He was a leading supporter of the House-passed resolution that calls for all federal buildings to display the motto, "In God We Trust." Said Shows: "The values we teach at home and church are universal and should not be left outside the schoolhouse door, or outside of where we work and play every day." But he also talked up Democratic priorities, including prescription-drug coverage for seniors and more federal support for education.

For the 2000 campaign, Republicans nominated local prosecutor Dunn Lampton, who finished fourth in the 1998 primary. The candidates traded charges of unfair campaign ads, including the claim by Shows that Lampton incorrectly accused him of taking a contribution in 1998 from a convicted narcotics violator. Senator John McCain made a late-campaign appearance for Lampton, citing his service to country and law enforcement; Shows responded by criticizing McCain for missing a Senate vote. Shows benefited from raising more than twice as much money as the challenger. He won by an unexpectedly large margin, 58%–40%, winning 14 of the 15 counties.

Shows faces another threat with redistricting. Mississippi lost one seat in the 2000 Census, and one incumbent must go. But redistricting is controlled by Democrats, who will surely try to help Shows. The easiest way to do so would be to place black-majority Jackson precincts or Delta counties into his district, but that will presumably be resisted by Bennie Thompson of the black-majority 2nd District and by black legislators. The likelihood is that Shows will end up in the same district with 3rd District Republican Chip Pickering. (Interestingly, they are both natives of Jones County which, given the numbers, is likely to end up in the Gulf Coast district.) Redistricters will probably see that most of the new district comes from the current 4th, which will give Shows an advantage. But the district is likely also to include heavily Republican Rankin County, now in Pickering's 3rd District. This could be one of the most strongly contested races in the country, and an important one for both parties.

Cook's Call   *Competitive.* Shows' strong showings in 1998 and 2000 belie the serious Republican nature of this district. Bush won here by 10% in 2000 and Dole won it in 1996 by 2%. Shows' conservative voting record and down-home, good-old-boy style make him a solid fit for this mostly rural district. But, with the state slated to lose one seat in redistricting, this seat, like every other district in the state, will feel the impact. There is serious talk about combining the Shows' district with Republican Rep. Chip Pickering in the 3rd. Still, Shows should get some help from state Democrats who control redistricting and will try to ensure that this district retains a black base (it is 47%).

THE PEOPLE: Pop. 2000: 530,679; Pop. 1990: 513,715, up 3.3% 1990–2000. 51.6% White, 46.9% Black, 0.4% Asian, 0.1% Amer. Indian, 0.6% Two+ races, 0.3% Other; 0.9% Hispanic Origin.

2000 Presidential Vote			1996 Presidential Vote		
Bush (R)	107,213	(54%)	Dole (R)	86,880	(48%)
Gore (D)	87,200	(44%)	Clinton (D)	83,425	(46%)
Nader (Green)	1,349	(1%)	Perot (I)	9,648	(5%)
Others	2,337	(1%)			

Rep. Ronnie Shows (D)

Elected 1998, 2d term; b. Jan. 26, 1947, Moselle; home, Bassfield; Jones Cnty. Jr. Col., SE Baptist Col., U. of S. MS, B. A. 1971; Baptist; married (Johnnie Ruth).

Elected Office: Jefferson Davis Cnty. Circuit Clerk, 1976–80; MS Senate, 1980–88; MS Southern Dist. Transportation Comm., 1988–98.

Professional Career: High schl. teacher & coach, 1971–76.

DC Office: 1408 LHOB 20515, 202-225-5865; Fax: 202-225-5886; Web site: www.house.gov/shows.

District Offices: Jackson, 601-352-1355; Laurel, 601-425-4999; Natchez, 601-446-8825.

Committees: *Agriculture* (24th of 24 D): General Farm Commodities & Risk Management. *Financial Services* (28th of 32 D): Capital Markets, Insurance & Government Sponsored Enterprises; Financial Institutions & Consumer Credit; Oversight & Investigations. *Veterans' Affairs* (9th of 14 D): Health.

Group Ratings

	ADA	ACLU	AFS	LCV	CON	ITIC	NTU	COC	ACU	NTLC	CHC
2000	35	7	71	21	29	56	40	61	69	42	73
1999	55	—	83	31	28	—	19	56	52	—	—

National Journal Ratings

	1999 LIB —	1999 CONS		2000 LIB —	2000 CONS
Economic	57% —	43%		52% —	47%
Social	23% —	76%		29% —	71%
Foreign	56% —	43%		39% —	57%

Key Votes of the 106th Congress

1. Patient Bill of Rights	Y	5. Bar RU-486 $ for FDA	Y	9. NATO War in Serbia	Y
2. Accelerate Min. Wage	Y	6. Display 10 Commandments	Y	10. Perm. Trade with China	N
3. Strike Ban on Ergo. Stnd.	N	7. Gun Show Bkgrnd. Checks	N	11. Debt Relief for 3rd World	N
4. Ovrd. Estate Tax Veto	Y	8. Ban Part.-Birth Abortion	Y	12. Drop Cuba Econ. Embargo	Y

Election Results

2000 general	Ronnie Shows (D)	115,732	(58%)	($1,120,105)
	Dunn Lampton (R)	79,218	(40%)	($568,409)
	Others	4,084	(2%)	
2000 primary	Ronnie Shows (D)	unopposed		
1998 general	Ronnie Shows (D)	73,252	(53%)	($654,887)
	Delbert Hosemann (R)	61,551	(45%)	($1,462,310)
	Others	2,396	(2%)	

FIFTH DISTRICT

The strand where Mississippi faces the Gulf of Mexico has gone through several transformations. French explorers here founded Biloxi in 1699, before New Orleans or St. Louis, and made it the capital of an empire extending to Yellowstone Park. Two hundred years later, rich people from New Orleans came to this Gulf Coast in summer to get away from yellow fever and to rest on Victorian verandas; six American presidents have vacationed here. More recently the Gulf Coast, with the help of riverboat casinos since 1992, has been growing more than any other part of Mississippi; along much of the strand, new 1,000-room hotels are rising as part of Mississippi's boom and about 50,000 jobs were created during the past decade. Biloxi's Keesler Air Force Base is one of the four largest in the country. Pascagoula, once a small town, is now home of the 11,000-employee Ingalls Shipyard, whose gray hangar-like buildings and skeletons of ships under construction loom over the flat landscape. To the west is the Stennis Space Center named for longtime (1947–89) Senator John Stennis, where Lockheed Martin has established an advanced propulsion center.

This is the heart of the 5th Congressional District, some 60% of whose people live on the Gulf Coast; the rest are inland, in farm counties or around Hattiesburg. This was mostly scrub land, not much good for plantations. With its low black percentage and mostly booming economy, the 5th District has become prime Republican territory. It gave Richard Nixon his highest percentage in all 435 districts in 1972, it voted five times against fellow Southerners Jimmy Carter, Bill Clinton and Al Gore, and it was represented for 16 years in the House by Trent Lott until he was elected to the Senate in 1988.

The congressman from the 5th District is Gene Taylor, a Democrat first chosen in an October 1989 special election. Taylor graduated from Tulane and served in the Coast Guard Reserves as skipper of a search and rescue boat for 10 years. He was elected to the Bay St. Louis Council in 1981 and in 1983, at 30, was elected to the state Senate. In 1988, when Lott left the House to run for the Senate, Taylor ran for Congress, won the Democratic primary, but lost to Republican Larkin Smith 55%–45%. Smith died in an August 1989 plane crash, and Lott brushed aside Smith's widow and backed his own longtime aide Tom Anderson, who had spent little time in the district and proved to be an abrasive candidate. Taylor, combining a barely reined-in aggressiveness with a down-home manner, won the special 65%–35%.

In the House, Taylor has a conservative voting record and has criticized the leadership of his own party and the Republicans. When asked to vote for the October 1998 omnibus budget, he characteristically remarked, "One of the people who is asking us to trust him is now being studied to see if he committed perjury. Another of the people who says trust us admitted lying to the ethics committee. That's not a very good place to start." Taylor is a peppery populist ("what Mississippians think is usually the right answer") with a reasonably consistent view on issues. He is against abortion, gun control, free trade and foreign aid. He is strongly pro-defense and boasts of bringing defense contracts to the area. As ranking Democrat on an Armed Services subcommittee dealing with military installations, he is a firm believer in improving pay and benefits. He was a leading proponent of the major expansion in 2000 of health benefits for military retirees.

Feisty to the point of being belligerent, he opposes any U.S. military commitment that stops short of assured and total victory: He voted against the Gulf war resolution, lifting the arms embargo on Bosnia, sending troops to Haiti, and favored limits on forces in Colombia. But when faced with apparently ineffective American military involvement in Serbia in April 1999, he called for a declaration of war. He is a protectionist, loudly opposing NAFTA, GATT and permanent normal trade relations with China. If anything holds his record together, it is boats. He promotes Ingalls and other shipyards, he succeeded in widening and deepening the Gulfport shipping channel, he champions the seafood industry, and he wants to prohibit foreign-flag ships from conducting passenger "voyages to nowhere" from U.S. ports. He supports the federal shipbuilding program and revitalizing the Merchant Marines; he objects to waivers to the Jones Act, which requires coastal shipping to be conducted in U.S.-made ships; he backed the skipper of the USS Cole, when it returned to Pascagoula for repairs following its bombing by terrorists in Yemen; he was pleased by the purchase of Cat Island for inclusion in the Gulf Islands National Seashore. For some time, his Washington residence was a 34-foot boat on the Anacostia River.

He is hardly ever a reliable Democratic vote. Taylor voted "present" rather than vote for Dick Gephardt for speaker in 1995 and he voted for Jack Murtha in 2001, without explanation. He voted against disciplining Newt Gingrich in 1997, because he opposed the $300,000 "penalty" the ethics committee had concocted. There was little doubt about his vote for impeachment. When White House chief of staff Erskine Bowles asked a group of Blue Dog Democrats what they thought the president should do, Taylor's hand shot up first. "I think he should resign." He was one of five Democrats to vote for two counts of impeachment. But Taylor has rebuffed all importunings to switch parties. "I personally would feel like a prostitute. I still believe the average working person's best interest is best served by the Democratic Party." When Republican National Chairman Haley Barbour offered a $1 million reward to anyone who could prove Republicans had "cut" Medicare, Taylor laid claim to it. He voted for the Republican-passed welfare reform: "It's this or nothing. And this is better than nothing." Sometimes, he finds himself a lonely vote: He was one of only four House members to vote against an electronic-signatures bill and a measure to permit an expansion of futures trading contracts. Facing possible House action in the event of an Electoral College deadlock in 2000, he said that he would vote for George W. Bush to reflect the views of his constituents.

Taylor has seldom had much serious opposition, except in 1996, when he was opposed by Republican Dennis Dollar, a party-switcher himself in the legislature, who matched Taylor's spending. But Taylor won with a solid 58%–40%, even as Bob Dole was carrying the district by a similar margin. He won the last two elections with 78% and 79% of the vote. Mississippi lost one House seat in the 2000 Census. But redistricting is controlled by Democrats, and geography favors creation of another Gulf Coast district, extended north to Laurel or perhaps Meridian. This would bring into the (renumbered) 5th the original home counties of both Republican Chip Pickering of the 3rd District and Democrat Ronnie Shows in the 4th, but surely neither would like to take on Taylor.

Cook's Call　*Safe.* Although this district votes for Republicans on the national level, they are also quite comfortable electing Democrat Gene Taylor year after year. Once Taylor decides to leave the House, his very conservative district will likely fall into Republican hands. The district was one of the faster growing in the state, but it will still need to pick up about 100,000 people.

THE PEOPLE: Pop. 2000: 600,490; Pop. 1990: 514,611, up 16.7% 1990–2000. 76% White, 20.4% Black, 1.4% Asian, 0.4% Amer. Indian, 1.2% Two+ races, 0.6% Other; 1.9% Hispanic Origin.

2000 Presidential Vote		
Bush (R)	128,636	(66%)
Gore (D)	63,625	(32%)
Nader (Green)	2,741	(1%)
Others	1,310	(1%)

1996 Presidential Vote		
Dole (R)	96,880	(56%)
Clinton (D)	61,035	(35%)
Perot (I)	13,431	(8%)

Rep. Gene Taylor (D)

Elected Oct., 1989, 6th term; b. Sept. 17, 1953, New Orleans, LA; home, Bay St. Louis; Tulane U., B.A. 1974; Catholic; married (Margaret).

Military Career: Coast Guard Reserves, 1971–84.

Elected Office: Bay St. Louis City Cncl., 1981–83; MS Senate, 1983–89.

Professional Career: Sales rep., Stone Container Corp., 1977–89.

DC Office: 2311 RHOB 20515, 202-225-5772; Fax: 202-225-7074; Web site: www.house.gov/genetaylor.

District Offices: Gulfport, 228-864-7670; Hattiesburg, 601-582-3246; Ocean Springs, 228-872-7950.

Committees: *Armed Services* (5th of 28 D): Military Installations & Facilities; Military Procurement (RMM). *Transportation & Infrastructure* (16th of 34 D): Coast Guard & Maritime Transportation; Water Resources & Environment.

Group Ratings

	ADA	ACLU	AFS	LCV	CON	ITIC	NTU	COC	ACU	NTLC	CHC
2000	45	7	57	43	96	44	31	38	52	33	67
1999	50	—	50	38	73	—	35	68	72	—	—

National Journal Ratings

	1999 LIB —	1999 CONS		2000 LIB —	2000 CONS
Economic	52%	— 48%		58%	— 41%
Social	10%	— 85%		26%	— 71%
Foreign	41%	— 58%		45%	— 53%

Key Votes of the 106th Congress

1. Patient Bill of Rights	Y	5. Bar RU-486 $ for FDA	Y	9. NATO War in Serbia	N
2. Accelerate Min. Wage	Y	6. Display 10 Commandments	Y	10. Perm. Trade with China	N
3. Strike Ban on Ergo. Stnd.	N	7. Gun Show Bkgrnd. Checks	N	11. Debt Relief for 3rd World	N
4. Ovrd. Estate Tax Veto	N	8. Ban Part.-Birth Abortion	Y	12. Drop Cuba Econ. Embargo	Y

Election Results

2000 general	Gene Taylor (D)	153,264	(79%)	($287,750)
	Randy McDonnell (R)	35,309	(18%)	
	Others	5,822	(3%)	
2000 primary	Gene Taylor (D)	unopposed		
1998 general	Gene Taylor (D)	78,661	(78%)	($233,630)
	Randy McDonnell (R)	19,341	(19%)	($7,980)
	Others	3,093	(3%)	

★ MISSOURI ★

When Meriwether Lewis and William Clark set out on their expedition to the Pacific, they embarked from St. Louis in 1804. On high ground just below the point where the Missouri River swirls into the Mississippi, St. Louis was at the time the one well-established city in America's interior, with an aristocracy of French merchants, a brawling bourgeoisie of Yankee and Southern frontiersmen and fur traders and a proletariat of black slaves. Part of the Louisiana Purchase in 1803, St. Louis by 1821 was part of the new state of Missouri, and for decades St. Louis and Missouri were the gateways to the frontier. In Missouri, Daniel Boone finally found elbow room. Here were the eastern termini of the Pony Express, in St. Joseph, and the Santa Fe Trail, in Westport, now part of Kansas City; here were railroads reaching across the continent, connecting the farmers of vast prairies with their markets. Here also were the Mississippi River steamboats, and the boyhood home of their great chronicler, Mark Twain.

For Missouri was not just the gateway to the frontier; it was also the focus of the furious battle over slavery. Missouri was the northernmost slave state at mid-century; it was Missouri ruffians crossing the border and killing antislavery settlers in the Kansas Territory that led prox- imately to the Civil War. In the 1860s, Missouri had its own mini- civil war in the hilly counties along the Missouri River. Throughout the 19th Century, both before and after the Civil War, Americans turned away from their oceans and headed inward to settle the great interior of the continent. They found Missouri at its heart, with farmland and mines, rivers and railroads, a major manufacturing state—and in the days before tractors, the nation's leading breeder and trader of mules. In 1874 the Eads Bridge opened, one of very few across the Mississippi, and St. Louis' Cupples Station was the largest rail hub in the world. At the turn of the 20th Century, Missouri was the fifth-largest state. St. Louis was the fourth-largest city, site of the 1904 World's Fair, and one of the few cities with two major league baseball teams, the Cardinals and the Browns; Missouri after the 1900 Census had 16 congressional districts.

Today, Missouri does not loom as large in the national consciousness, yet it is in some sense still central. In the 20th Century, Americans—like the Browns who moved to Baltimore in the 1950s and the football Cardinals who moved to Phoenix in the 1980s—increasingly headed to the coasts, to the big cities of the East and to California, and eventually to Florida and Texas. Missouri has had below-average population growth since 1900, and today it is the 17th largest state, with just nine congressional districts. But Missouri is the geographic center of the nation's population in the 2000 Census: an imaginary, flat map of the United States population, if everyone weighed the same, would balance near Edgar Springs in Phelps County, Missouri. Missouri started perking up demographically in the 1990s, growing by 9% (its greatest decennial increase in a century); growth was particularly strong in the outer suburbs of St. Louis and Kansas City and in the Ozarks, but dozens of rural counties that have been losing population for most of the 20th Century started growing again. The state economy, long sluggish, was showing signs of solid growth. And Missouri has again captured Americans' imaginations: if Americans in 1904 flocked to St. Louis on the banks of the Mississippi, in the 1990s their vans and buses were jamming the two-lane road through the Ozarks to Branson, population 6,050, one of America's top tourist destinations (with 7 million visitors a year), with country music stars and soft rock veterans, country violinist Shoji Tabuchi, nearly 50 theaters and more seats than on Broadway, and more seats for regularly sched- uled music concerts than anywhere else in America.

For most of the 20th Century, Missouri was one of America's political bellwethers: it has voted for every presidential winner but one (Eisenhower in 1956) since 1900. From the 1960s to the 1990s it mirrored national trends by moving its congressional politics from pretty solidly Dem- ocratic to leaning Republican. In the excruciatingly close presidential year of 2000, the results in Missouri were exquisitely close as well. George W. Bush carried the state by a 50%–47% margin. But at the same time, Missourians gave Democrats narrow margins for governor and senator— 49%–48% for Governor Bob Holden and 51%–48% for the late Mel Carnahan over Senator John Ashcroft. But the patterns of support were very different from those in the recent past. For most of the 20th Century Missouri's ancient Civil War political divisions still held: Little Dixie in the

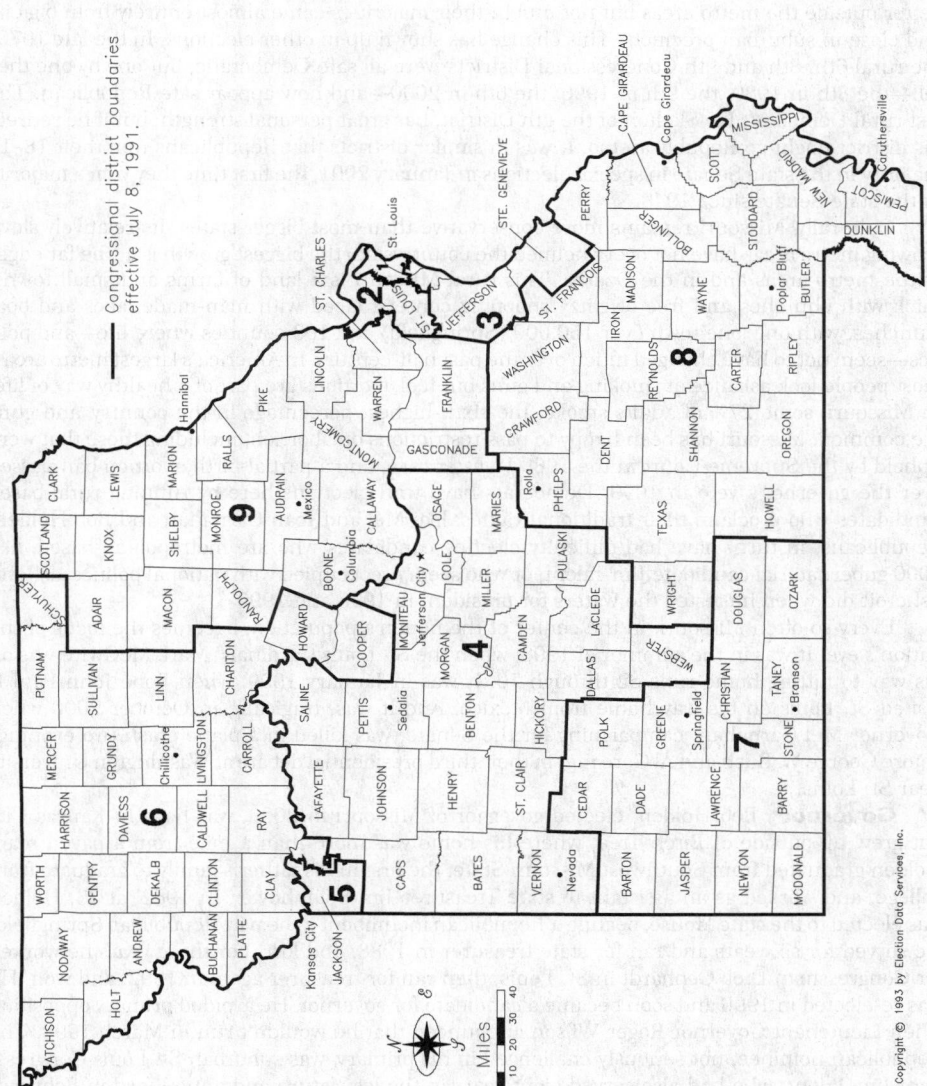

Congressional district boundaries
effective July 8, 1991.

northeast, first settled by Virginians, and the northwest, settled by Southerners, voted Democratic; the Ozarks in the southwest, which was pro-Union, was unusually Republican; the southeast was split, like next-door Downstate Illinois. But in 2000 the real divide was between the state's two big metropolitan areas and the rural remainder of Missouri. The St. Louis metro area voted 53%–45% for Al Gore; metro Kansas City, about half as big, voted 54%–43% for Gore. But the rest of Missouri, casting 44% of the votes, was 58%–39% for George W. Bush. Of the 103 counties outside the two big metro areas, Bush carried 95 and Gore eight. The other Democrats did a little better outside the metro areas but not much: their majorities came almost entirely from big city and close-in suburban precincts. This change has shown up in other elections. In the late 1970s the rural 6th, 8th and 9th Congressional Districts were all safe Democratic, but one by one they fell—the 8th in 1980, the 9th in 1996, the 6th in 2000—and now appear safe Republican. The last rural Democrat, Ike Skelton of the 4th District, has great personal strength; but if he retired, his district might go Republican too. It was in similar districts that Republicans won their 18–16 majority in the state Senate in special elections in January 2001, the first time they won a majority in the state Senate since 1948.

Culturally, Missouri remains more conservative than most bigger states. Its relatively slow-growing metro areas have not overwhelmed the countryside; the biggest growth is at the far edges of the metro areas and in the Ozarks. This rural Missouri is a land of farms and small towns, thick with churches and free of glitzy shopping centers, laced with man-made lakes and boat launches, with only one town over 150,000 (Springfield) and 103 counties where life—and politics—seem not to have changed much over the past half-century. In America's largest metro areas, most people look askance at smoking and guns but feel abortions are part of a healthy way of life. In Missouri, some 27% of adults smoke, the sixth-highest percentage in the country, and guns are common. Missouri has been happy to pass restrictions on abortion, including those that were upheld by the Supreme Court in the 1989 *Webster* case, and a partial-birth abortion ban passed over the governor's veto in 1999. Democrats have won elections here by running rural-based candidates who proclaim their traditional values, like Mel and Jean Carnahan and Bob Holden. Republicans, in turn, have had difficulty electing candidates who are metropolitan-based, like 2000 gubernatorial candidate Jim Talent, or who seem preoccupied with national politics, as John Ashcroft did when he tested the waters for president in 1998 and 1999.

Every so often Missouri, in the center of the nation's population, becomes the focus of the nation's eye. It was in the summer of 1998, when the St. Louis Cardinals' Mark McGwire was on his way to hitting home runs 62 through 70. It was in January 1999, when Pope John Paul II visited St. Louis on his way home from Mexico. And it was, tragically, in October 2000 when Governor Mel Carnahan, campaigning for the Senate, was killed in a plane crash two evenings before George W. Bush and Al Gore met in their third presidential debate at Washington University near St. Louis.

Governor   Bob Holden, elected governor of Missouri in 2000, was born in Kansas City but grew up outside of Birch Tree, where his home was more than a mile from a paved road. Holden graduated from Southwest Missouri State, the first in his father's family to graduate from college, and worked as an assistant to state Treasurer Jim Spainhower. In 1982, at 33, Holden was elected to the state House, beating a Republican incumbent in heavily Republican Springfield. He served for six years and ran for state treasurer in 1988, and lost. For three years he worked for Congressman Dick Gephardt in St. Louis, then ran for treasurer again in 1992, and won. He was re-elected in 1996 and soon became a candidate for governor. He avoided primary opposition when Lieutenant Governor Roger Wilson announced that he wouldn't run in March 1998. The Republican nominee, not seriously challenged in his primary, was suburban St. Louis Congressman Jim Talent, who had also served eight years in the legislature and announced in February 1999. This was the most expensive gubernatorial race in Missouri history, by far; the candidates took advantage of a court ruling overturning the limit on individual contributions to raise some $3 million in over-limit money, until the U.S. Supreme Court upheld the Missouri law in January 2000.

In many ways this race was a referendum on the eight-year governorship of Democrat Mel Carnahan, who was not eligible for a third term and was running against his predecessor, Senator

John Ashcroft. Back in 1993, Carnahan passed a $315 million tax increase to pay for a new school funding plan; he strongly supported capital punishment though he commuted one sentence in 1999 at the request of Pope John Paul II on his visit to St. Louis; he pushed through a children's health plan; he helped to defeat a proposal to allow law-abiding citizens to get permits to carry concealed weapons in 1998; his 1999 veto of a partial-birth abortion ban was overturned. "The question is, do you want to keep Missouri moving forward, or do you want to radically change course?" asked Holden. He promised to use tobacco settlement money to provide prescription drugs for the elderly and health insurance to more low-income people; he said he would raise education spending, provide more accountability and reduce class sizes. Talent, though he represented affluent suburbs, had been one of the Republican leaders, with J.C. Watts, of the community renewal legislation targeted on troubled central cities. He called for resuscitating a 1992 rural highway building program which had been abandoned in 1998; he promised to deliver all gambling revenue to education, and called for school vouchers for parents of children in failing schools. "My opponent represents a failed establishment that can't change the status quo and ridicules people who believe that our state government can do what other state governments have done for years," Talent said.

The race took a tragic turn when Mel Carnahan was killed in a plane crash October 16, the night before the third presidential debate in St. Louis. All candidates agreed to pull negative ads, though some Talent spots still ran—despite his efforts, he said. Carnahan's eulogies naturally recalled his service in positive terms, and probably made Talent's anti-status quo theme less appealing. Negative themes—Talent's talk of crumbling roads and kids not learning to read, Holden's attacks on Talent's backing of school vouchers and charges that highway bonds would bankrupt the state—must have sounded out of line. This was one of the closest races in the country, and one of three top-of-the-ticket races that turned out to be very close in Missouri. On election night, St. Louis Democrats got a state judge to order the polls remain open three extra hours because of alleged shortages of ballots and booths; 45 minutes later the order was reversed on appeal, but Republicans from Senator Christopher Bond on down argued that Democrats got illegitimate votes, and no one defended the competence of St. Louis's election procedures.

Holden won by 21,000 votes, 49%–48%. Talent ran ahead of other Republicans, George W. Bush and John Ashcroft, in his native St. Louis area, losing there by just 51%–46%. But he lost by a wide 57%–41% margin in the Kansas City area, more than Bush. And his support of rural highways did not prevent Holden from carrying 30 counties outside the two big metro areas (while Al Gore was carrying eight); Talent carried rural Missouri by just a 53%–45% margin. Rural Missouri has never cared much for St. Louis; the last St. Louis-based governor was Republican Forrest Donnell, elected in 1940.

Once in office Holden, like many governors, confronted a possible deficit as the economy slowed down. There were also unanticipated expenses from well-intended government programs: a stipend to grandparents acting as foster parents had been extended to other relatives and increased from $1.4 million to $22.4 million; a tax credit for seniors buying prescription drugs expected to cost $20 million turned out to cost $89 million. Holden's first efforts to persuade legislators to use tobacco settlement money to prevent a budget deficit were rejected in February 2001. In March 2001 he proposed $620 million for transportation, subject to the approval of voters. Holden replaced all members of the controversial St. Louis election board in April 2001.

Senior Senator Christopher Bond was first elected to statewide office in 1970 and was first elected to the Senate in 1986. Bond grew up in the town of Mexico, Missouri, where his family were part owners of the largest business, A.P. Green, makers of heat-resistant bricks, which was sold to another firm in 1998. He graduated from Princeton and the University of Virginia Law School, then ran for Congress in 1968, at age 29, and narrowly lost. He was elected state auditor in 1970 and was elected governor at 33 in 1972, and became one of the youngest governors in the nation's history. He lost in an upset to Democrat Joseph Teasdale in 1976 and won a comeback victory against Teasdale in 1980. As governor, Bond pushed reorganization, open meetings, merit hiring and campaign finance in his first term; he wrestled with fiscal problems, crime control and early childhood education in his second term. He still touts his Parents As Teachers program, and made it the basis of a federal law; in 2001 he sponsored legislation to allocate $5 million for the Parents As Teachers National Center and $50 million for groups like the YMCA and YWCA, Boy Scouts and Girl Scouts and Boys and Girls Club to encourage parents to read to their children. After two years in private life he ran for the Senate against Harriett Woods, who had come close to beating Bond's longtime ally, then-Senator John Danforth, in 1982. Woods ran a three-part ad showing a farmer breaking into tears as he and his wife told Woods about their foreclosure and named Bond as a board member of the insurance company that foreclosed; evidently this struck voters as either demagoguery or an invasion of privacy, and Woods fell in the polls. Bond won, 53%–47%.

Bond has a moderate voting record in the Senate. He has usually worked behind the scenes, trying to forge bipartisan consensus. He was the chief Republican sponsor of the Family and Medical Leave Act, vetoed by George Bush and signed by Bill Clinton. He has been the lead Republican senator on housing, starting on the Banking Committee and now as chairman of the VA-HUD Appropriations Subcommittee. He supervised Henry Cisneros's downsizing and decentralizing of HUD, passed legislation to allow demolition of public housing projects, worked to reduce looming Section 8 multi-family housing program costs, supported locally based community development organizations that build housing, and fought to allow elderly housing that excludes youngsters. He got into disagreements with former HUD Secretary Andrew Cuomo, opposing his $130 million settlement with the Puerto Rico Public Housing Administration and his attempts to take over control of funding for homeless programs. In 2000 Bond sponsored a bill to stop HUD aid to Indians building smoke shops to sell cigarettes. He worked to pass a law with $2 billion in preferences for small businesses located in poor neighborhoods that hire local residents. He has ranged afield on other issues, co-sponsoring a ban on human cloning in early 1998, funding research on the plant genome process and passing a law on birth defect prevention. He has criticized ADM and Frito-Lay for encouraging farmers not to plant and sell genetically altered seed and opposes labeling of genetically modified foods.

Bond opposed the Clinton administration plan to release water at Gavins Point Dam in Yankton, South Dakota, to create a spring rise in the Missouri River; the idea is to imitate the flow of water before the river was heavily dammed, in order to protect the endangered species such as the least tern and pallid sturgeon. Bond argues that a spring rise risks floods, and holding back water in the summer threatens the flow of barge traffic. In 2000 Bond inserted a rider in an appropriation preventing the Corps from spending its funding if the Missouri flows were altered; in September 2000 Bill Clinton announced he would veto the bill unless the amendment was removed. So it was, but with political cost: This controversy, invisible nationally, was big news in Missouri and may have had something to do with the fact that Al Gore lost the state to George W. Bush. Bond has also tried to block funding for an outlet on swollen Devils Lake in North Dakota for fear it would take water from the Missouri River. He worked to stop the Clinton administration from banning lead and zinc mining in Mark Twain National Forest. But Bond has his environmental side. He led the fight for the Wild Horse Act, and was dismayed when wild horses were shot in November 2000 in the Ozarks National Scenic Riverways. An avid fisherman, he sponsored a law to encourage voluntary activity to clean up rivers; it would create watershed councils which would give grants to help farmers establish buffer zones, fence off livestock, and reduce runoff of fertilizers and farm chemicals without onerous regulations.

On Missouri defense projects, Bond is a hawk, keeping close tabs on Boeing's McDonnell Douglas fighter planes built in St. Louis County. He pushed the Air Force to complete purchases of F-15s for which he had obtained appropriations; he promoted the Hornet on a visit to South Korean President Kim Dae Jung and denounced U.S. diplomats in Prague for recommending another fighter to the Czechs. On other Missouri issues, he sponsored a Good Samaritan Food Donation Act and a new Cape Girardeau Bridge, both named after the late Congressman Bill Emerson. Bond promotes barge traffic on the Mississippi and Missouri rivers and brought together the barge industry and the anti-barge American Rivers organization to agree on a $50 million program for the rivers. He has used his seat on Appropriations to aid Missouri projects—$600,000 to Children's Mercy Hospital in Kansas City, $3.6 million for the Donald Danforth Plant Science in Creve Coeur, $8 million for renovation of the Truman Library in Independence. Bond's Senate suite includes Truman's old Senate office.

Bond got his political start as part of a group of young reform Republicans—his former Senate colleague John Danforth was another—working against the Democratic political establishment in Missouri, and he can be a strong partisan on occasion. After he was re-elected 52%–45% in 1992, a year in which Missouri Republicans lost every other major race, he spent two years raising $750,000 for the party. In 1998 he faced a tough partisan opponent in state Attorney General Jay Nixon. Nixon had lost 68%–32% to Danforth in 1988 but had been elected attorney general in 1992 after canoeing the length of the Missouri River and was re-elected 57%–39% in 1996. Nixon had gotten great publicity for cleaning up the second injury fund and prosecuting consumer fraud and attacking telecom and insurance fraud. Nixon pledged to serve only two terms and opposed Bond's stands on tobacco, the minimum wage and HMO reform. But he was dogged by controversy over his actions on the St. Louis school desegregation cases. Both St. Louis and Kansas City schools were laboring under 1970s court orders which required massive busing and ordered the state government to spend large sums. When Nixon, like previous Republican attorneys general, moved for a settlement with sharply reduced state payments, black leaders protested vehemently. St. Louis Congressman Bill Clay denounced Nixon in vitriolic terms and the NAACP threatened to mount a picket line when Bill Clinton came in for a Nixon fundraiser. In the meantime, Bond built on the ties he had developed with black leaders over many years of working on housing programs and sought their support or neutrality. Nixon also made mistakes; early attacks on Bond turned out to be based on simple factual errors, and his attacks on Bond for commuting sentences of violent criminals when he was governor seemed to be dredging up the past. Bond attacked Nixon for paying private trial lawyers a fee on the order of $350 million in the state's tobacco suit, and for opposing Auditor Margaret Kelly's lawsuit seeking an additional $120 million tax refund from state revenues from riverboat admission fees. Bond campaigned hard, traveling across the state pointing to projects he had funded, and outspent Nixon. He won 53%–44%, winning 33% among black voters—outstanding for a Republican—and sweeping non-metropolitan Missouri by a wide margin.

Bond's standing among black politicians and perhaps among black voters has suffered since. He joined John Ashcroft in opposing the judicial nomination of Justice Ronnie White, because of the judge's strained dissent in a horrifying capital murder case. Bond was furious when St. Louis Democrats persuaded a state judge to order the polls opened three extra hours in the city; an appeals court overturned the order within 45 minutes, but Bond, who charged that Democrats tried to keep the St. Louis polls open till midnight to defeat him in 1972, said the election had been stolen, and indeed Republicans Jim Talent and John Ashcroft lost by narrow margins. Certainly there were irregularities in St. Louis; Democratic Governor Bob Holden removed its entire election board in April 2001. Bond charges that the motor voter act has installed and kept on the rolls many names of those not entitled to vote; he filed a bill to require mail-in registrants to vote in person the first time they vote and to drop from the rolls people whose address cards are returned as "undeliverable."

Bond comes up for reelection in 2004. His attempt to win a place in the leadership failed in December 2000 when he lost the chairmanship of the Senate Republican Conference to Rick Santorum by a vote of 30–20.

Junior Senator   Jean Carnahan was named to the Senate in 2000 under unusual and tragic circumstances. She grew up in Washington, D.C., in the Anacostia section southeast of the Capitol. She graduated from George Washington University and married, at 20, a fellow student she had met in high school, Mel Carnahan from Birch Tree, Missouri. Carnahan married into politics: her husband's father, A.S.J. Carnahan, was a Democratic congressman from Missouri (1945–47, 1949–61) and then ambassador to Sierra Leone. The younger Carnahans returned to Missouri and Jean Carnahan worked closely with her husband as he served in public office—as a municipal judge in their hometown of Rolla in 1960, as a state representative from 1962–66, as Missouri treasurer in 1980–84 and lieutenant governor in 1988–92. In that job Carnahan had a distant relationship with the Republican governor, John Ashcroft. In 1992 Mel Carnahan was elected governor.

Ineligible to run for a third term as governor, Mel Carnahan announced in November 1998 that he would run against John Ashcroft for the Senate. Ashcroft, meanwhile, was launching what looked very much like a campaign for president. With a strong conservative voting record and good rapport with religious conservatives, he hoped to emerge as the favorite of one wing of the Republican party while remaining acceptable to others. He was one of the first to say that the Lewinsky scandal might warrant impeachment, he sponsored repeal of the marriage penalty, he opposed Surgeon General nominee David Satcher and opposed the Clinton national educational testing program. But Republicans' failure to make gains in the November 1998 elections and the fact that only 34% of Missouri voters said he would be a good president in the VNS exit poll tended to undercut Ashcroft's candidacy. Carnahan argued that Ashcroft posed as a tax-cutter, while as governor he had pressed for tax increases, and criticized him for taking an anti-government line while he had spent most of his adult life in politics and government. In January 1999 Ashcroft pulled out of the presidential race, and became part of what may well have been the most closely and bitterly contested 2000 Senate race between two men who had each twice been elected governor and had nine statewide victories between them.

Then, on the night of October 16, Mel Carnahan, together with his son Randy and aide Chris Sifford, were killed in a plane crash. It brought back memories of another plane crash in a Missouri Senate race, in August 1976, when Democratic primary winner Jerry Litton and his family were killed on primary night. The third presidential debate went on in St. Louis on October 17, but Ashcroft announced that he was suspending his campaign, and Carnahan's campaign manager told staffers they were free to leave. After a memorial service for Carnahan October 20, many leading Democrats were talking about what to do next. It was too late to reprint ballots, and a write-in candidacy seemed daunting. Many of them talked about Jean Carnahan running in his place, and some mentioned the possibility to her. If more people voted for Carnahan than Ashcroft, under state law the new governor, Roger Wilson, would have to name someone to serve two years of the term. On October 23, Wilson called Jean Carnahan and offered to nominate her to the Senate if Carnahan won. On October 30 Carnahan agreed.

Ashcroft began campaigning again, running positive ads about his accomplishments and experience, plus an ad showing John Danforth criticizing the *St. Louis Post-Dispatch* for its negative coverage. Democrats handed out "Still with Mel" buttons and Jean Carnahan appeared, head-on, in one 60-second spot pledging to carry on her husband's work. Naturally, in the wake of his death, only positive feelings were brought forward; any Carnahan negatives disappeared. Polls showed the race very close throughout: Mel Carnahan won, 51%–48%. Some Republicans urged Ashcroft to challenge the result, on the ground that the Constitution requires that a senator be a citizen of his state when elected. But he declined and said, "I believe the will of the people has been expressed with compassion, and I believe the people's voice should be respected and heard." On December 4, Wilson appointed Jean Carnahan to the vacancy beginning January 3.

In the Senate, Jean Carnahan lined up with most of her fellow Democrats on issues in early 2001. She was one of the 42 Democrats to vote against the confirmation of Ashcroft as attorney general; she said he was "too divisive." But she was also one of the 12 Democrats to vote for the $1.3 trillion compromise tax cut in May 2001. She introduced a $50 billion education bill in February 2001, based on her husband's proposals. In early 2001 she said she had not decided whether to run in 2002 for the four years remaining in the term, though she did set up a re-election committee. In early 2001 former Congressman Jim Talent was expected to announce his candidacy.

Cook's Call   *Highly Competitive*. Given the hotly contested nature of this state and the unique circumstances under which Carnahan got to the Senate, this seems destined to be a competitive contest. As of spring 2001 Carnahan had not yet said whether she would run in the special election to fill the remaining four years of the term. The likely Republican candidate is former Congressman Jim Talent, who was the party's 2000 gubernatorial nominee. If she opts to step aside, the open seat contest would be a toss up.

Presidential politics   Missouri's peculiar balance of North and South, urban and rural, has helped to make it a presidential bellwether and explains its one deviation in the 20th Century: it voted for Adlai Stevenson in 1956, who capitalized on farmer discontent and whose lukewarmness about civil rights helped him carry traditional Southern Democrats. In the 1990s Missouri saw the two countervailing national trends—toward Democrats in major metropolitan areas, toward Republicans in rural areas—but in different proportions: the rural areas count for more here. Bill Clinton carried Missouri by 10% in 1992 and by 7% in 1996. In 2000 Al Gore could carry only a handful of counties outside Missouri's two big metropolitan areas, and lost by a 3% margin. Issues like gun control and abortion, which worked for him in the largest states, worked against him in Missouri. Women voted for Gore by just a 51%–47% margin, while men voted 54%–43% for George W. Bush. Blacks voted 84%–14% for Gore—a lesser margin than in many states—while white Protestants voted 59%–39% and white Catholics 56%–43% for Bush.

Missouri joined the Super Tuesday primary for 1988, then went back to multi-tiered caucuses to elect delegates in 1992 and 1996. In 2000 Missouri went back to the Super Tuesday primary, in which George W. Bush and Al Gore won easy victories, even though Gore's rival Bill Bradley grew up in Jefferson County, Missouri.

Congressional districting Missouri did not lose any seats in the 1990 or 2000 Censuses, but in both cases falling population in the central cities of St. Louis and Kansas City hurt Democrats. Republicans now have a 5–4 edge in the delegation, and a say in redistricting, since in January 2001 they won control of the state Senate by an 18–16 margin. The chief problem area for Democrats is St. Louis. Fifty years ago the city of St. Louis had 856,000 people, enough for almost three congressional districts; in 2000 it had 348,000 people, enough for barely more than half a district.

In early 2001 an open fight broke out between 1st District Democrat Lacy Clay and 3d District Democrat Dick Gephardt. It hardly seemed an even match: Gephardt is House minority leader, Clay a freshman; but Clay succeeded his father Bill Clay who held the seat for 32 years. The 1st District is currently 60% black, but it lost population in the 1990s and must add 107,000 people. The most heavily black areas nearby are in the 3d, and in April 2001 Clay was demanding all of St. Louis south to I-44. Gephardt resisted, and seemed to get Clay to agree to use the farther north I-40 as a boundary, not far from the current line. But in May 2001 it was not clear whether that agreement would hold, or whether it would be honored by state Senate Republicans. They might prefer to extend Gephardt's district west into heavily Republican St. Louis County suburbs; in the current district he has been held under 60% of the vote since 1992, and a new seat might threaten his tenure, or at least tie him down and keep him from helping other Democrats—or it might persuade him to retire and set out to run for president in 2004.

The 5th District in Kansas City and Jackson County must be extended outward as well, but that could be done fairly easily. Redistricting outside the two big metro areas does not seem likely to be controversial.

THE PEOPLE: Pop. 2000: 5,595,211; Pop. 1990: 5,117,073, up 9.3% 1990–2000. 2% of U.S. total, 17th largest; 84.9% White, 11.2% Black, 1.1% Asian, 0.4% Amer. Indian, 0.1% Hawaiian, 1.5% Two+ races, 0.8% Other; 2.1% Hispanic Origin. 3.5% Unemployment. 2000 Voting age pop.: 4,167,519. 2000 Turnout: 2,359,892; 57% of VAP. Registered voters (2000): 3,860,672; no party registration.

POLITICAL LINEUP: Governor, Bob Holden (D); Lt. Gov., Joe Maxwell (D); Secy. of State, Matt Blunt (R); Atty. Gen., Jay Nixon (D); Treasurer, Nancy Farmer (D); Auditor, Claire McCaskill (D); State Senate, 34 (16 D, 18 R); Senate Pres. Pro Tempore, Peter Kinder (R); Majority Leader, Bill Kenney (R); State House, 163 (86 D, 74 R, 3 vacancies); House Speaker, Jim Kreider (D). Senators, Christopher S. Bond (R) and Jean Carnahan (D). Representatives, 9 (4 D, 5 R).

ELECTIONS DIVISION: 573-751-2301; **FILING DEADLINE FOR U.S. CONGRESS:** March 26, 2002.

2000 Presidential Vote

Bush (R)	1,189,924	(50%)
Gore (D)	1,111,138	(47%)
Nader (Green)	38,515	(2%)
Others	20,315	(1%)

1996 Presidential Vote

Clinton (D)	1,025,935	(48%)
Dole (R)	890,014	(41%)
Perot (I)	217,219	(10%)

2000 Republican Presidential Primary

Bush (R)	275,366	(58%)
McCain (R)	167,831	(35%)
Keyes (R)	27,282	(6%)

2000 Democratic Presidential Primary

Gore (D)	171,562	(65%)
Bradley (D)	89,092	(34%)

Gov. Bob Holden (D)

Elected 2000, term expires Jan. 2005, 1st term; b. Aug. 8, 1949, Kansas City; home, Jefferson City; S.W. MO St. U., B.S. 1973.; Disciples of Christ; married (Lori).

Military Career: MO Natl. Guard, 1971–77.

Elected Office: MO House of Reps., 1982–88; MO Treasurer, 1992–2000.

Professional Career: Asst., MO Treasurer James Spainhower, 1976–81; St. Louis A.A., U.S. Rep. Richard Gephardt, 1989–91.

Office: State Capitol Bldg., Jefferson City, 65101, 573-751-3222; Fax: 573-751-1495; Web site: www.state.mo.us.

Election Results

2000 general	Bob Holden (D)	1,152,752	(49%)
	Jim Talent (R)	1,131,307	(48%)
	Other	62,771	(3%)
2000 primary	Bob Holden (D)	unopposed	
1996 general	Mel Carnahan (D)	1,224,801	(57%)
	Margaret Kelly (R)	866,268	(40%)
	Others	51,449	(2%)

Sen. Christopher S. Bond (R)

Elected 1986, seat up 2004, 3d term; b. Mar. 6, 1939, St. Louis; home, Mexico; Princeton U., B.A. 1960, U. of VA, LL.B. 1963; Presbyterian; divorced.

Elected Office: MO Auditor, 1970–72; MO Gov., 1972–76, 1980–84.

Professional Career: Practicing atty., 1964–69, 1977–80; MO Asst. Atty. Gen., 1969–70.

DC Office: 274 RSOB, 20510, 202-224-5721; Fax: 202-224-8149; Web site: www.senate.gov/~bond.

State Offices: Cape Girardeau, 573-334-7044; Jefferson City, 573-634-2488; Kansas City, 816-471-7141; Springfield, 417-864-8258; St. Louis, 314-725-4484.

Committees: *Appropriations*: Agriculture & Rural Development; Defense; Foreign Operations; Transportation; VA, HUD & Independent Agencies (RMM). *Budget. Environment & Public Works*: Fisheries, Wildlife & Water; Transportation & Infrastructure. *Health, Education, Labor & Pensions*: Aging; Children & Families. *Small Business* (RMM).

Group Ratings

	ADA	ACLU	AFS	LCV	CON	ITIC	NTU	COC	ACU	NTLC	CHC
2000	0	14	0	0	36	100	73	100	92	91	92
1999	0	—	0	0	8	—	70	94	84	—	—

National Journal Ratings

	1999 LIB —	1999 CONS		2000 LIB —	2000 CONS
Economic	19%	—	75%	0%	—	86%
Social	23%	—	72%	22%	—	73%
Foreign	33%	—	66%	27%	—	67%

Key Votes of the 106th Congress

1. Educ. Savings Accts.	Y	5. Review Movie Violence	Y	9. NATO War in Serbia	N
2. Prescrip. Drug Benefit	N	6. Gun Show Bckgrnd. Checks	N	10. Table Cuba Travel Ban	N
3. Delay Ergonomic Standards	Y	7. Ban Part.-Birth Abortion	Y	11. Nuclear Test-Ban Treaty	N
4. Phase Out Estate Tax	Y	8. Broaden Hate Crimes List	N	12. Perm. Trade with China	Y

Election Results

1998 general	Christopher S. Bond (R)	830,625	(53%)	($6,229,649)
	Jay Nixon (D)	690,208	(44%)	($2,568,879)
	Others	56,024	(4%)	
1998 primary	Christopher S. Bond (R)	213,569	(87%)	
	Others	32,274	(13%)	
1992 general	Christopher S. Bond (R)	1,221,901	(52%)	($5,048,333)
	Geri Rothman-Serot (D)	1,057,967	(45%)	($1,112,187)
	Others	75,048	(3%)	

Sen. Jean Carnahan (D)

Appointed Nov. 2000, seat up 2002, 1st term; b. Dec. 20, 1933, Washington, DC; home, Rolla; George Washington U., B.A. 1955; Baptist; divorced.

Professional Career: Public speaker; Author.

DC Office: 517 HSOB, 20510, 202-224-6154; Fax: 202-228-0043; Web site: carnahan.senate.gov.

State Offices: Jefferson City, 573-636-1070; Kansas City, 816-421-1639; Springfield, 417-831-2735; St. Louis, 314-436-3416.

Committees: *Aging (Special)*. *Armed Services*: Airland Forces; Personnel; Seapower. *Commerce, Science & Transportation*: Aviation; Consumer Affairs, Foreign Commerce & Tourism; Science, Technology & Space; Surface Transportation & Merchant Marine. *Governmental Affairs*: Government Management, Restructuring and the District of Columbia; International Security, Proliferation & Federal Services; Investigations (Permanent).

Group Ratings and Key Votes: Newly Elected

Election Results

2000 general	Mel Carnahan (D)	1,191,812	(51%)	($8,800,864)
	John Ashcroft (R)	1,142,852	(48%)	($9,378,581)
	Others	26,922	(1%)	
2000 primary	Mel Carnahan (D)	323,841	(78%)	
	Ronald W. Wagganer (D)	90,251	(22%)	
1994 general	John Ashcroft (R)	1,060,149	(60%)	($4,063,927)
	Alan Wheat (D)	633,697	(36%)	($3,505,701)
	Bill Johnson (Lib)	81,264	(5%)	

FIRST DISTRICT

For a century or more, St. Louis seemed the center of America: the starting point for the Lewis and Clark expedition in 1804; the locus half a century later of the *Dred Scott* case, a Supreme Court ruling that helped split the nation; the site of the 1904 World's Fair that introduced the hot dog and the ice cream cone and got 19 million people to *Meet Me in St. Louis*. Its 630-foot-high Gateway Arch is just below the point where the waters of the Missouri surge into the Mississippi, about halfway between New Orleans and Lake Superior, the Atlantic and the Pacific. St. Louis was once again a great gathering place in 1999, when Pope John Paul II visited here, recalling the *Dred Scott* decision and speaking out for life and against abortion and capital punishment.

This first major American city west of the Mississippi River was the final resting place of Daniel Boone and for many years was Chicago's rival as the transportation hub of America. In 1904 St. Louis already had the Eads Bridge, one of America's first suspension bridges, the Wainwright Building, one of Louis Sullivan's first skyscrapers, and Union Station, the world's largest passenger train station when it opened in 1894; some 600,000 people lived in densely-packed brick houses on old street grids radiating outward from downtown. This was a heavily German city, with a Teutonic solidity and orderliness which distinguished it from the surrounding Southern-accented rural terrain; and from Mitteleuropa came the founders of St. Louis's great businesses—the Anheuser-Busch brewery, May Company department stores, Joseph Pulitzer's *St. Louis Post-Dispatch*—and its first great politician and a friend of Abraham Lincoln, Senator and Interior Secretary Carl Schurz. There is almost a European aura to Forest Park, the site of the 1904 fair, and the dozen mansion-lined private streets nearby, like Portland Place.

St. Louis is still one of the nation's 20 largest metro areas, but today it does not occupy as central a place in the national consciousness, and the central city itself has largely emptied out. The German order that made so many people comfortable living in close quarters and commuting by streetcar seems to have yielded to an American desire for Daniel Boone's wide open (suburban) spaces and the less restrictive automobile. St. Louis' population peaked at 856,000 in 1950; it was down to 348,000 in 2000, far less than the 1 million in suburban (and juridically separate) St. Louis County. Downtown St. Louis has been spruced up admirably: the Gateway Arch was finished in 1965; Union Station has been redeveloped; Laclede's Landing is stocked with shops. But most of St. Louis's old factories have closed and many of its once tight neighborhoods are only a memory.

Missouri's congressional districts have followed the people out of St. Louis. The 1st District, historically based on the north side of the city, has most of its votes cast in suburban St. Louis County. It includes most of central and north St. Louis, the affluent and racially integrated suburbs of University City and Clayton just west of Forest Park, and the mostly black and mixed-race suburbs from the city limits north to Bellefontaine Neighbors, Florissant and the airport. In 2000 the district was 60% black; it is easily the most Democratic in the state.

The congressman from the 1st District is Lacy Clay, a Democrat elected in 2000 to the seat that his father Bill Clay had held for 32 years. Lacy Clay's whole life bears the imprint of his father's politics. Born in St. Louis, he moved to the Washington, D.C. area after his father's 1968 election and grew up there as a congressman's son. He attended Silver Spring, Maryland public schools and then the University of Maryland, studying by night for seven years while he worked as a House staffer by day. He had started law classes at Howard University when a special election for a state House race in 1983 drew him back to St. Louis, and he was appointed the Democratic nominee by party leaders. Eight years later, Lacy Clay was again picked by party leaders to run in a special election for a vacant, safely Democratic state Senate seat, after incumbent John Bass was given a job with a congressional subcommittee.

When his father decided in 1999 not to run again after having helped to enact many labor and education laws, Clay had a somewhat more serious contest than in the past, but not much. His most credible opposition in the Democratic primary was from St. Louis Councilman Charlie Dooley. Dooley raised nearly $400,000 and, though African American, had a base of support in the mostly white suburbs of St. Louis County. Dooley campaigned that the office should not be "inherited" and he attacked Clay's old-style tactics of political threats and bossism. To educate voters that he was not challenging the incumbent, Dooley's unusual billboards read: "Congressman Bill Clay is retiring this year." The St. Louis Labor Council and Missouri AFL-CIO, long allied to Clay Sr., declined to endorse his son, but he won endorsements from more than 30 locals. With many voters still thinking the two Clays were the same person, Clay Jr. played up his father's name and revved up the still reliable machine. He won the six-candidate primary 61%–28% over Dooley, winning the city 76%–12% and the county—where twice as many votes were cast—49%–39%. The general election was no contest. Lacy Clay won 75%–22%, which was better than his father had done in recent elections. Some of those city precincts became the target of Republican complaints and calls to investigate voting irregularities in the tight statewide contests on Election Day. Clay was one of the Democrats who persuaded a state judge to order the polls kept open an extra three hours. That order was reversed by an appeals court 45 minutes later, but Republicans charged that there were great irregularities in the voting in St. Louis, and in April 2001 Governor Bob Holden, a Democrat, dismissed the entire St. Louis city election board.

In Washington, Clay became president of the Democrats' freshman class. He serves on different committees than his father—Financial Services and Government Reform. His chief re-election threat is redistricting. The 1st District lost population in the 1990s, and must add 107,000 more people to meet the population standard. The most ready supply of additional black precincts is in the 3d District, represented by House Minority Leader Dick Gephardt, and in early 2001 Clay called for adding all of St. Louis City north of I-44 in the 1st. Gephardt objected vehemently: this would remove the most Democratic precincts from his district, and he has not won as much as 60% of the vote since 1992. But in May 2001 an agreement was reached to use I-40, farther north, as the boundary, not far from the current line.

Cook's Call   *Safe.* As the slowest growing district in the state, this St. Louis-based district needed to spread further into St. Louis County to pick up more than 100,000 people. A newly drawn congressional map essentially keeps this district safely Democratic and Clay should be in good shape in this heavily Democratic district in 2002.

THE PEOPLE: Pop. 2000: 514,264; Pop. 1990: 568,472, down 9.5% 1990–2000. 36.6% White, 59.9% Black, 1.3% Asian, 0.2% Amer. Indian, 1.6% Two + races, 0.5% Other; 1.2% Hispanic Origin.

2000 Presidential Vote

Gore (D)	156,288	(78%)
Bush (R)	39,990	(20%)
Nader (Green)	2,982	(1%)
Others	1,130	(1%)

1996 Presidential Vote

Clinton (D)	145,586	(74%)
Dole (R)	38,505	(20%)
Perot (I)	9,721	(5%)

Rep. William Lacy Clay, Jr. (D)

Elected 2000, 1st term; b. July 27, 1956, St. Louis; home, St. Louis; U. of MD, B.S. 1983; Catholic; married (Ivie).

Elected Office: MO House of Reps., 1983–90; MO Senate, 1991–2000.

Professional Career: Paralegal, 1982–2000; Real estate agent, 1986–2000.

DC Office: 415 CHOB 20515, 202-225-2406; Fax: 202-225-1725; Web site: www.house.gov/clay.

District Offices: St. Louis, 314-367-1970; St. Louis, 314-890-0349.

Committees: *Financial Services* (30th of 32 D): Domestic Monetary Policy, Technology & Economic Growth; Housing & Community Opportunity; Oversight & Investigations. *Government Reform* (17th of 19 D): Census (RMM); National Security, Veterans' Affairs & Intl. Relations.

Group Ratings

	ADA	ACLU	AFS	LCV	CON	ITIC	NTU	COC	ACU	NTLC	CHC
2000	80	86	100	79	40	59	20	46	5	9	0
1999	100	—	100	100	36	—	18	22	0	—	—

National Journal Ratings

	1999 LIB —	1999 CONS		2000 LIB —	2000 CONS
Economic	88%	0%		75%	25%
Social	87%	13%		83%	16%
Foreign	84%	16%		94%	6%

Key Votes of the 106th Congress

1. Patient Bill of Rights	Y	5. Bar RU-486 $ for FDA	N	9. NATO War in Serbia	*
2. Accelerate Min. Wage	Y	6. Display 10 Commandments	N	10. Perm. Trade with China	N
3. Strike Ban on Ergo. Stnd.	*	7. Gun Show Bkgrnd. Checks	Y	11. Debt Relief for 3rd World	*
4. Ovrd. Estate Tax Veto	N	8. Ban Part.-Birth Abortion	N	12. Drop Cuba Econ. Embargo	*

Election Results

2000 general	William Lacy Clay Jr. (D)	149,173	(75%)	($679,776)
	Dwight Billingsly (R)	42,730	(22%)	($3,787)
	Others	6,444	(3%)	
2000 primary	William Lacy Clay Jr. (D)	34,398	(61%)	
	Charlie Dooley (D)	15,612	(28%)	
	Eric E. Vickers (D)	3,543	(6%)	
	Others	3,250	(6%)	
1998 general	William (Bill) Clay (D)	90,840	(73%)	($270,118)
	Richmond A. Soluade Sr. (R)	30,635	(25%)	
	Others	3,576	(3%)	

SECOND DISTRICT

Just as the U.S. population's geographic center has slowly crept westward into the center of Missouri, the greater St. Louis area continues to move farther west from the Gateway Arch on the Mississippi River. The fulcrum now rests in St. Louis County, established in 1876 when the city, tired of paying for dusty back roads, separated itself from the sticks. There were then about 350,000 people in the city and 31,000 in the county. In 2000, the city, which once had 856,000 people, dropped below its 1876 level, while the county exceeded 1 million. By the 1960s, the center of office employment had moved from downtown across the county line to Clayton; now even many Clayton office buildings seem dated, and the focus is fast moving out the Daniel Boone Expressway (U.S. 40) to Chesterfield, west of the I-270 ring road.

The 2d Congressional District of Missouri is made up of central and western St. Louis County, plus some St. Charles County suburbs northwest across the Missouri River. It includes the blue-collar areas around the Ford plant, the airport and Boeing's McDonnell Douglas in North County and the Chrysler plant in South County; these are mostly Democratic areas. It has fast-growing suburbs in and beyond St. Charles and historic suburbs like Webster Groves and Kirkwood; these are pretty solidly Republican. And in the center of St. Louis County, along the Daniel Boone Expressway, are elite Ladue and high-income Creve Coeur, Town and Country, Manchester and Chesterfield: all Republican, even more so in the newer family-oriented subdivisions than in the leafy precincts of the old rich.

The congressman from the 2d District is Todd Akin, a Republican elected in 2000. He has continued to live in his boyhood home, a 50-year-old farmhouse that rests in what has become an upscale neighborhood of Town and Country. He graduated from Worcester Polytechnic Institute and got a divinity degree at Covenant Seminary. After service as an Army combat engineer, he worked for IBM in the Boston area and then at Laclede Steel in Alton, the same company where his father once worked. He was elected to the state House in 1988. During the next 12 years, as part of the Republican minority, he passed few of his bills. Undaunted, he took to the courts, filing one lawsuit to stop a tax increase intended to fund education improvements and another to stop riverboat gambling on barges moored in artificial ponds; the former case failed but the latter succeeded, forcing the gambling industry to spend millions on a referendum which changed the law in its favor. Akin's idealism derives from his avid study of American history and the Constitution, on which he lectures at various public and private institutions. "Today we've gotten confused and we think there's no room for faith in the area of civil government, and that's not where our founders came from," he says . While a state legislator, he sold standardized tests to parents who home school their children; he and his wife have home schooled their six children. State House reporters noted that he sometimes played gospel tunes on his guitar in the Capitol late at night.

When Republican Congressman Jim Talent announced in early 1999 that he was running for governor, Akin ran for the House. He started off as the underdog to Gene McNary, the former Bush Administration INS commissioner and well known from his 15 years as St. Louis County executive and as a candidate for U.S. Senate in 1980 and twice for governor. A third candidate, former state Senate Minority Leader Franc Flotron, ran as a conservative and charged that McNary had shown favoritism while at INS. Akin called himself "a conservative with a soft edge," who tries to work as a team player. He emphasized that he had never voted to raise taxes, and he had strong support from religious conservatives, and he may have benefited from staying above the personal attacks. In a low-turnout, rainy-day Republican primary, Akin rallied his committed cadre to win the five-candidate contest by 56 votes. Akin won St. Louis County by 293 votes over McNary; in St. Charles County, both narrowly trailed Barbara Cooper, who was Talent's former district director, but she was much weaker in St. Louis County and finished fourth overall.

Democrats were hopeful that the Republicans' sharply contested primary would give an opening to their unopposed nominee, state Senator Ted House, a former aide to Congressman Ike Skelton. House gained national attention when he led the successful effort to override Governor Mel Carnahan's veto of a ban on partial-birth abortions. Akin focused on his differences with House on taxes, including his vote for a 1993 education tax increase which Republicans had unsuccessfully challenged in court. House depicted Akin as a narrow ideologue who was an ineffective legislator. House, whose TV ads did not identify himself as a Democrat, cited a report by a liberal activist group that Akin had written a supportive letter read at a militia rally in 1995 that focused on the right to bear arms; Akin responded that he had turned down an invitation to speak. Akin won 55%–42%. House won 50%–48% in St. Charles County, his home base, but that was only 21% of the total vote; Akin won the St. Louis County vote 57%–40%.

In the House, Akin won seats on the Armed Services, Science and Small Business Committees. He joined Senator Christopher Bond in urging the Bush administration not to tighten ozone standards for the St. Louis area. He also urged the Navy not to cut back its production of Super Hornet aircraft at Boeing's local plant. Redistricting seems likely to push this district further out into Republican suburbs, where the only threat might be in the primary. Akin might gladly give up his eastern part of St. Charles County to either Lacy Clay or Dick Gephardt, whose districts need additional people.

Cook's Call   *Probably Safe.* Like the rest of the St. Louis area, this district has not grown as quickly as the north and western parts of the state. In redistricting, the 2nd District picked up Lincoln County and part of southern St. Louis County. This seat should stay safely Republican for 2002.

THE PEOPLE: Pop. 2000: 610,984; Pop. 1990: 568,449, up 7.5% 1990–2000. 90.4% White, 5.1% Black, 2.7% Asian, 0.2% Amer. Indian, 1.1% Two+ races, 0.5% Other; 1.6% Hispanic Origin.

2000 Presidential Vote			**1996 Presidential Vote**		
Bush (R)	165,257	(55%)	Dole (R)	138,401	(49%)
Gore (D)	130,722	(43%)	Clinton (D)	115,698	(41%)
Nader (Green)	4,965	(2%)	Perot (I)	22,791	(8%)
Others	1,866	(1%)			

Rep. Todd Akin (R)

Elected 2000, 1st term; b. July 5, 1947, New York, NY; home, Town and Country; Worcester Polytech Inst. (MA), B.S. 1971; Covenant Theological Seminary (MO), M. Div. 1984; Presbyterian; married (Lulli).

Military Career: Army Reserves 1972–80.

Elected Office: MO House of Reps., 1988–2000.

Professional Career: Marketing Mgr., IBM, 1974–78; Mgmt. Dir., Laclede Steel, 1977–80; Instructor, Maryville U.

DC Office: 501 CHOB 20515, 202-225-2561; Fax: 202-225-2563; Web site: akin.house.gov.

District Offices: St. Charles, 636-949-3832; St. Louis, 314-878-0513.

Committees: *Armed Services* (31st of 32 R): Military Personnel; Military Research & Development. *Science* (20th of 25 R): Energy; Research. *Small Business* (17th of 19 R): Regulatory Reform Oversight; Tax, Finance & Exports.

Group Ratings and Key Votes: Newly Elected

Election Results

2000 general	Todd Akin (R)	164,926	(55%)	($1,015,568)
	Ted House (D)	126,441	(42%)	($858,204)
	Others	6,695	(2%)	
2000 primary	Todd Akin (R)	14,911	(26%)	
	Gene McNary (R)	14,855	(26%)	
	Francis E. Flotron Jr. (R)	12,362	(22%)	
	Barbara Cooper (R)	10,538	(18%)	
	Jack Jackson (R)	4,955	(9%)	
1998 general	James M. Talent (R)	142,313	(70%)	($926,361)
	John Ross (D)	57,565	(28%)	
	Others	3,381	(2%)	

THIRD DISTRICT

Middle America, it could be said, lies somewhere on the south side of metropolitan St. Louis. The geographical center of the country's population was here in 1980, just south of St. Louis in once rural and now mostly suburban Jefferson County; while that point has moved about 100 miles southwest, St. Louis is still the metro area nearest the midpoint of a country most of whose people live in million-plus metro areas. Geographically, this is a node where some of the nation's main arteries come together. The Missouri River flows into the Mississippi a few miles north of St. Louis's Gateway Arch; the National Road and its successors, U.S. 40 and Interstate 70, cross the Mississippi just below the Arch. And the great tides of Southerners migrating west up the Mississippi and Germans migrating overland met here to create one of the nation's largest and most bustling cities out of a town founded by the French before the Revolutionary War. The south side of St. Louis is famous for its tight-knit, neat neighborhoods and pleasant parks; its most famous symbols are the Anheuser-Busch brewery just south of downtown and Grant's Farm, where Ulysses S. Grant lived in the 1850s and where Anheuser-Busch now keeps the Budweiser Clydesdales. But many more people now live in the suburbs heading out all directions, well into Jefferson County to the south.

The 3d Congressional District of Missouri consists of the south side of St. Louis City, the southern St. Louis County suburbs, Jefferson County, and rural Ste. Genevieve County on the Mississippi to the south, the site of Missouri's oldest permanent settlement, founded near a salt mine in 1730. It is the descendant of districts dominated by St. Louis voters, but now the city casts less than 25% of its votes, fewer than Jefferson County; almost half are cast in St. Louis County. Ethnically, this has been a heavily German-American area since the mid-19th Century. Politically, it has been Democratic since the New Deal of the 1930s.

The congressman from the 3d District is Dick Gephardt, first elected in 1976, the leader of the Democratic Party in the House, presidential candidate in 1988 and perhaps again in 2004. Gephardt grew up on the south side of St. Louis, the son of a milk truck driver who worked himself up into the middle class. A bit too old to be part of the generation of Vietnam-era student rebels, Gephardt returned home from law school in 1965 to work in a large downtown law firm, but was clearly intent on a traditional political career; he moved to the south side and was elected alderman in 1971. In 1976, when 3d District Congresswoman Leonor Sullivan announced her retirement, Gephardt jumped into the race as an anti-establishment candidate. He beat a labor union official in the primary and a former board of aldermen president in the general. Gephardt started off in the House as one of the newer breed of Democrats who did not automatically favor big government and higher taxes. With the help of Missouri's Richard Bolling, Gephardt got a seat on the Ways and Means Committee—rare for a freshman. He voted for the 1981 Reagan tax cut and was the House co-sponsor of New Jersey Senator Bill Bradley's bill that was the basis of the 1986 tax reform. Gephardt was one of the founders of the moderate Democratic Leadership Council and opposed many popular Democratic causes such as abortion, busing and raising the minimum wage.

But around the mid-1980s he began to shift, perhaps reflecting the increasingly liberal tenor of the Democratic Caucus, of which he was elected chairman over David Obey in 1984. Gephardt has always been a superb caucus politician and a good listener. He is a hard-working detail man, eager to absorb information, with a gift for molding compromises, and for coming up with positions that hold together the often unruly and fissiparous Democratic Caucus. When Gephardt started running for president in 1986 he had the enthusiastic support of dozens of House colleagues as he spent 144 days in Iowa campaigning for the February 1988 caucuses. Gephardt adjusted to this new arena, sometimes to the dismay of his former allies. He played little role in the 1986 tax reform he had originally co-sponsored; he changed his stand on abortion to pro-choice. In Iowa, he supported mandatory agricultural production controls, a non-starter even in a Democratic Congress. Even more prominently, he went on the offensive on trade issues. The United Auto Workers is a major factor in Iowa caucuses, and Gephardt, who had opposed the UAW's domestic content bill, came up with his amendment requiring retaliation against countries (read: Japan) running large trade surpluses with the United States. Gephardt won the Iowa caucuses with 31% of the vote, to 27% for Paul Simon and 22% for Michael Dukakis. In New Hampshire, Gephardt found himself under attack for switching positions in a fast-growing and prosperous state that hates taxes and government regulation; he finished second with 20% to Dukakis's 36%. On Super Tuesday, Gephardt had run out of money, won only Missouri and was out of the race.

Back in the House, Gephardt rebounded when another leadership position came his way. In June 1989 Speaker Jim Wright and Majority Whip Tony Coelho resigned, and as Thomas Foley was elected speaker, Gephardt ran for majority leader and defeated Georgian Ed Jenkins 181–76. Gephardt went to work creating a sense of camaraderie in a dispirited caucus. In the 1990 budget summit talks, Gephardt used OMB Director Richard Darman's desire for agreement to frame the issue as a choice between the Democrats' plan to tax the rich more and Bush's refusal to do so— a contrast that at least momentarily hurt Republican candidates and prevented them from making gains in the November 1990 elections. In September 1990 Gephardt supported George Bush's dispatch of troops to the Persian Gulf, but in January 1991 he led the opposition to the Gulf war resolution and uncharacteristically stumbled by threatening to cut off funds for U.S. troops there.

In the first Clinton years, Gephardt combined ardent support for the administration on most issues with carefully calibrated dissent on others. He fought for the Clinton economic stimulus plan and for the spending cuts and tax increase package which passed with exactly 218 votes in August 1993. His major dissent was on trade. He held off opposing NAFTA for several months as he sought more concessions from administration officials and he eventually came out against it. In December 1993 Gephardt endorsed GATT; in February 1994 he came up with his own plan to force Japan to meet numerical goals in opening its markets or face retaliation. Gephardt vigorously supported the Clinton health care plan in 1994 and tried to put together his own bill combining the Clinton and Ways and Means plans; but it was tough slogging and no bill came to the floor. Then in August 1994 the leadership lost the vote on the crime bill rule. To hold together the caucus, gun control amendments as well as tougher penalties were included; but gun control repelled too many moderate Democrats and Chairman Jack Brooks' high-handedness antagonized many moderate Republicans, and the rule failed.

Clinton had shaped his two major initiatives—the 1993 budget and tax increase and the 1994 health care bill—along the lines recommended by House Democratic leaders. In November 1994 they were all stunningly repudiated. Democrats lost 52 seats and control of the House. Speaker Thomas Foley was defeated, and Gephardt lost his post as majority leader and became minority leader instead. The strategy followed by Speakers Tip O'Neill, Jim Wright and Foley— hold the Democratic Caucus together enough to produce 218 votes—was now obsolete: there weren't 218 Democrats any more. Gephardt pushed aside a challenge by North Carolina's Charlie Rose for the party leadership, 150–58. But the day he handed over the gavel to Speaker Newt Gingrich, Gephardt later said, "was one of the worst days of my life." In the debates on the Contract with America, Gephardt was far less visible than the strongly anti-Gingrich Democratic Whip David Bonior.

Times got better for Democrats as support for Republicans and Gingrich plummeted during the government shutdown. Gephardt created a House Democratic Policy Committee to serve as a forum for developing a Democratic alternative to the Contract. By June 1996 Gephardt and Senate Minority Leader Tom Daschle came up with a united Democratic "Families First" platform, including tax deductions for child care, health insurance and higher education, a balanced budget and tough anti-crime measures. And House Democrats scored a rousing success when they forced a vote on, and passage of, a minimum-wage increase in summer 1996. But the surging Clinton-Gore campaign ignored Gephardt and, though most polls started showing Democrats ahead of Republicans in the generic vote, ignored Democrats' efforts to win a majority in the House. Clinton never mentioned Families First, but instead unveiled a package of "little things" himself. When Gephardt spoke to the Democratic National Convention in August, the obedient crowd chanted "Four more years!" Clinton and Gore each devoted one sentence in their accep-tance speeches to the need for Democratic majorities in Congress. Gephardt's hopes to become speaker came crashing down in November 1996, as Democrats won only 207 House seats and Republicans 227, despite Gingrich's unpopularity, despite the AFL-CIO $35 million ad campaign, and despite Clinton's victory.

Over the next two years Gephardt's fortunes and strategies oscillated widely. Forging major-ities with moderate Republicans was difficult because Democratic leaders had mostly refused to deal with them when they had a majority. Holding together the Democrats is always hard; they have always tended to be a divided party, an uneasy alliance of disparate elements. Most of the Black Caucus and perhaps 40 other members are dedicated social democrats, dismayed at the acceptance of the goal of a balanced budget, frustrated with downward pressure in discretionary spending, and determined not to give up the fading strength of the Medicare or Social Security issues. And then there are 20-some Blue Dogs, moderate on cultural issues, generally conservative on economics, supportive of some Republican stands. And there are the many Democrats moti-vated most strongly by liberal views on cultural issues like abortion.

Meanwhile, major budget issues had been settled by negotiations between House Republicans and the White House, from which Gephardt was ostentatiously shut out. He opposed the balanced budget agreement ("a budget of many deficits—a deficit of principle, a deficit of fairness, a deficit of tax justice and, worst of all, a deficit of dollars") reached in principle in May 1997 and sealed in legislation in August; 132 House Democrats supported it anyway. House Democrats looked to be as split and forlorn as House Republicans were after the budget deal of 1990. In December 1997 Gephardt made a speech at Harvard's Kennedy School, celebrating "core Democratic val-ues," calling for the party to reject small-bore ideas and speak boldly to the needs of working people in the United States and around the world: *cri de coeur* against the Clinton administration. For that Gephardt was criticized by many House Democrats. He continued to receive great ap-plause from AFL-CIO audiences, happy with his opposition to NAFTA and normal trade relations status with China, and angry at Al Gore's stands in favor.

Then came the Lewinsky scandal. Suddenly Clinton was finding his strongest defenders among the left wing of the congressional party; he began making concessions with them and, as his poll numbers stayed high, confronting them on budget issues. After Clinton's disastrous August 17 speech, Gephardt, whose personal life is exemplary, called the president's conduct "reprehen-sible" and said impeachment was possible. He said he would decline to take a partisan role in defending Clinton, and began the impeachment inquiry process in a statesmanlike joint appear-ance with Gingrich. But he still saw no tension between that stance and with relying on Clinton to raise money for Democratic candidates: "We don't have a choice. We have to have the money." Clinton was more than happy to put Democrats in his debt and raised funds for them as never before. On December 13 Gephardt assailed Clinton's character and reliance on polls—and said he would vote against impeachment. On the day of the vote, December 19, speaking just after Bob Livingston made his breathtaking announcement that he would step down, Gephardt junked his previous draft and made an eloquent speech. "The politics of slash and burn must end," he said. "We need to stop destroying imperfect people at the altar of an unobtainable majority." Yet, after Clinton was impeached, he joined the Democratic members that bused over to the White House for a kind of celebration of the president almost all of them had agreed had dishonored his office.

One reason for Democratic unity is that the party actually gained seats in the 1998 off-year election, as Republican core voters were turned off by the tepid compromises the party's leaders accepted in the October 1998 omnibus budget and Democrats were energized by their support of Clinton. "We won!" proclaimed Gephardt on election night, as Democrats gained five House seats, the first such gain for a president's party in off-year elections since 1934. "Their problem is that the far right dominates their party," he said. "What I see is a unified Democratic Party that can work with moderate Republicans to get a lot of things done." Gephardt's gift is holding a caucus together, and House Democrats in early 1999 seemed absolutely convinced that they would win the six seats they needed for control, and more, in the 2000 elections. Sensing that Democrats had a real chance for a majority, and deterred perhaps by the Clinton White House's all-out support of Al Gore, Gephardt in February 1999 announced—in a press conference emblazoned with "Speaker Gephardt" signs—that he would not run for president. "I want to take this House back to what really matters," he said. As the year went on, the Clinton-Gore team took stands in line with Gephardt's, in rejecting Social Security reform, which obviously had a latent majority in the Congress, in rejecting the Medicare reform worked out by Democrats John Breaux and Bob Kerrey, in resisting broad-based tax cuts for the targeted tax cuts favored by Clinton. In the meantime, Gephardt's strategy of trying to build coalitions with moderate Republicans was frustrated by the fact that House rules allow the majority party, if it stays together, to schedule issues and set the terms of debate. Speaker Dennis Hastert instead reached across the lines to propitiate enough Democrats to win large bipartisan majorities on issues like EdFlex, missile defense, bankruptcy reform and Y2K liability. Democrats retaliated by demanding votes on issues on which they could amass bipartisan majorities—campaign finance, the minimum wage, education spending increases. But in the process Gephardt's relationship with Hastert frayed. Gephardt had a poor working relationship with Gingrich, something which might be explained by the former speaker's mercurial temperament; but with the phlegmatic Hastert his relations were no better. During 2000 they barely spoke, although Hastert was willing to negotiate with Minority Whip David Bonior.

Gephardt seemed to be concentrating instead on winning back a majority in the House. He appointed Patrick Kennedy as chairman of the Democratic Congressional Campaign Committee, not for his psephological skills but for his ability to raise money: Democrats all over the country will pay money to see a Kennedy. Gephardt staffers were installed at the DCCC, and did a fine job of targeting weak Republicans and fielding good candidates in open seats. And there were more Republican than Democratic open seats, because Gephardt worked hard to convince senior Democrats and Democrats whose personal popularity was critical in their districts to run for reelection rather than retire or run for other office. He personally raised at least $37 million for Democrats, and overall matched House Republicans in dollars—an impressive achievement. House Democrats developed attractive positions on prescription drugs for seniors and HMO regulation on which Democrats in all districts could run. It is hard to think of what else Gephardt could have done, yet on election day Democrats fell heartbreakingly short of their goal, as Republicans won 221 seats—three more than a 218 majority. It turned out that 2000, like 1998 and 1996, were incumbents' years, times in which discontent was low and satisfaction with incumbent members was high; most of the Republican open seats turned out to be safe Republican, and in some Republicans by narrow margins outhustled Democrats. The gun control issue, on which Democrats had counted, may have hurt in some rural and conservative districts; it did help Democrats overall, but by 2000 they had already gained most of the seats where the issue was a plus. Nor did Al Gore's candidacy help much; as Gephardt said later, "In retrospect, if we had a little wind at the top of the ticket, it would have helped some of those close races."

After the election Kennedy, with his own problems, decided to step down as campaign committee chairman; Gephardt tried to get him to reconsider, and then appointed Nita Lowey in his place; with great energy and her own contacts in feminist circles, she also had good fundraising potential. Gephardt, though undoubtedly greatly disheartened, worked hard as always on fundraising and seemed cautiously optimistic: "In essence the election was a tie. And if the economy keeps going, I think we deserve some of the credit for putting it in the right place. If it doesn't, I think Bush will bear the brunt of the burden." The non-presidential party, after all, usually wins seats in the off-year election. But redistricting will probably benefit Republicans on balance, and it may be harder for Gephardt to persuade members again not to retire or to refrain from running for statewide office. In early 2001 Gephardt cultivated his relations with Iowa Governor Tom

Vilsack and New Hampshire Governor Jeanne Shaheen. Some Washington observers concluded that he was looking toward a second run for the presidency in 2004, and certainly he did not seem as confident as he had in early 1999 that in two years he would be speaker.

In the House Gephardt reestablished a speaking relationship with Hastert after the election, and together they opposed a move by California members to give congressmen a $165 tax-free per diem, as California legislators get. But for all of George W. Bush's talk of bipartisanship, Gephardt did not find House Republicans any more bipartisan that they had been in 1999 and 2000. After Senate Democrats got a 50–50 split on committee memberships, Gephardt sought 49% of committee places for House Democrats, but gained only a few seats here and there. He demanded equal membership on a bipartisan election reform commission, and when he didn't get it named Maxine Waters as chair of an all-Democratic panel—the fiery Waters was the last Democrat with whom Republicans would work. Gephardt complained bitterly in March 2001 when Republicans in two days repealed the Clinton ergonomics rule and then passed their own $1.6 trillion tax cuts; in the following weekend, only about one-third of members showed up at the bipartisan retreat at the Greenbrier. "Bipartisanship is over—not that it ever began," said Gephardt. George W. Bush may assemble some bipartisan coalitions in the House in the 107th Congress, but not through working with the Democratic leadership; this most partisan of the branches of government is likely to remain crunchily partisan at least through 2002.

Back home, Gephardt worked hard to keep the National Imagery and Mapping Agency in Jefferson County, he earmarked $30 million for rebuilding Route 21 (the most dangerous road in Missouri, he said), he pumped in money to keep the Ste. Genevieve levee on schedule instead of 10 years behind as the Army Corps of Engineers proposed, he got money for a new sewage treatment plant at the confluence of the Meramec and Mississippi Rivers and for a levee between Festus and Crystal City, he got $3.5 million for wetlands protection for the Meramec River. He has worked hard to keep McDonnell Douglas's F-15 production line running, securing $400 million for five F-15s in July 2000 and urging South Korean leaders to purchase F-15s in December 2000.

But the 3d District has been trending Republican, and Gephardt, despite spending millions of dollars every campaign year, has not topped 60% since 1992. In 1998 Republican William Federer, operating with only $196,000, held him to a 56%–42% margin. In 2000 Federer ran again; this time George W. Bush's uncle William Bush chaired his finance committee, and Federer spent $2.3 million. He launched sharp attacks on Gephardt on issues like gay rights, and Democrats punched back sharply. A Gephardt worker charged him with assault when he tried to stop him from videotaping a parade in early October, and in late October the St. Louis County prosecutor, a Democrat, said he was investigating charges that the Federer campaign wrongfully pocketed proceeds from sale of a book originally published by a church. Gephardt won 58%–40%, an uptick from 1998, but not an overwhelming victory.

Another problem looms: redistricting. The 3d District had below-average population growth in the 1990s and must expand by 25,000 people. But the next-door, 60% black 1st District lost even more population, and must expand by 107,000. In early 2001 freshman 1st District Congressman Lacy Clay urged that the 1st District be extended southward into the 3d down to I-44, to pick up precincts with many black voters. But these are also the most heavily Democratic precincts in the 3d District, and Gephardt resisted, arguing that I-40, near the current boundary, would be a fairer border. A compromise plan agreed to by 8 of the 9 House members—only Todd Akin dissented—was approved by legislature in May. This slightly strengthened Gephardt's district while somewhat weakening Clay's and making Akin's 2d District a bit more Democratic.

Cook's Call *Safe.* One of the slower growing districts in the state, this district needed to pick up approximately 25,000 residents. Gephardt picked up more portions of St. Louis city, which will give this district more of a Democratic base. Though he has not broken 58% since 1992, it will be exceedingly tough to beat the well-financed minority leader in 2002.

THE PEOPLE: Pop. 2000: 596,066; Pop. 1990: 568,105, up 4.9% 1990–2000. 90% White, 6.4% Black, 1.4% Asian, 0.3% Amer. Indian, 1.4% Two+ races, 0.6% Other; 1.7% Hispanic Origin.

2000 Presidential Vote

Gore (D)	130,055	(51%)
Bush (R)	118,593	(46%)
Nader (Green)	5,442	(2%)
Others	2,046	(1%)

1996 Presidential Vote

Clinton (D)	115,141	(48%)
Dole (R)	93,190	(39%)
Perot (I)	25,643	(11%)
Others	3,604	(2%)

Rep. Richard A. Gephardt (D)

Elected 1976, 13th term; b. Jan. 31, 1941, St. Louis; home, St. Louis; Northwestern U., B.S. 1962, U. of MI, J.D. 1965; Baptist; married (Jane).

Military Career: Air Natl. Guard, 1965–71.

Elected Office: St. Louis City Alderman, 1971–76; Dem. Presidential Candidate, 1988.

Professional Career: Practicing atty., 1965–77.

DC Office: 1236 LHOB 20515, 202-225-2671; Fax: 202-225-7414; Web site: www.house.gov/gephardt.

District Offices: Festus, 636-937-6399; St. Louis, 314-894-3400.

Committees: *Minority Leader.*

Group Ratings

	ADA	ACLU	AFS	LCV	CON	ITIC	NTU	COC	ACU	NTLC	CHC
2000	90	69	100	93	15	50	20	28	13	12	7
1999	100	—	100	94	28	—	12	24	0	—	—

National Journal Ratings

	1999 LIB —	1999 CONS		2000 LIB —	2000 CONS
Economic	83% —	17%		84% —	15%
Social	78% —	21%		68% —	32%
Foreign	78% —	17%		66% —	33%

Key Votes of the 106th Congress

1. Patient Bill of Rights	Y	5. Bar RU-486 $ for FDA	N	9. NATO War in Serbia	Y
2. Accelerate Min. Wage	Y	6. Display 10 Commandments	N	10. Perm. Trade with China	N
3. Strike Ban on Ergo. Stnd.	Y	7. Gun Show Bkgrnd. Checks	Y	11. Debt Relief for 3rd World	Y
4. Ovrd. Estate Tax Veto	N	8. Ban Part.-Birth Abortion	Y	12. Drop Cuba Econ. Embargo	N

Election Results

2000 general	Richard A. Gephardt (D)	147,222	(58%)	($5,580,964)
	William J. Federer (R)	100,967	(40%)	($2,319,819)
	Others	6,350	(2%)	
2000 primary	Richard A. Gephardt (D)	unopposed		
1998 general	Richard A. Gephardt (D)	98,287	(56%)	($3,340,959)
	William J. Federer (R)	74,005	(42%)	($196,061)
	Others	3,807	(2%)	

FOURTH DISTRICT

Missouri was the first state settled west of the Mississippi, and the folks who settled it were a picture of pioneer diversity. Virginians and other Southerners made their way to counties north of the Missouri River, while Germans settled around the still small capital city of Jefferson City. A taste of that diversity can be found in the Capitol, with its mural by Thomas Hart Benton, great-grandnephew and eponym of Missouri's first senator, who championed hard money and westward expansion for 30 years and lost his seat for opposing the expansion of slavery. The painting shows dance hall girls, black coal miners and a mother diapering an infant—all reminders that pioneer life was less homogeneous than many imagine.

The 4th Congressional District occupies much of this early-settled part of central and western

Missouri. It penetrates Kansas City's Jackson County and its metro overflow in Cass County, but the overall atmosphere here is rural and small-town, with political traditions dating back to the community's early days. The rural counties around Kansas City were full of pro-slavery-expansion Bushwhackers who rode across the Kansas line to thwart the Yankee Jayhawks, and these areas today vote Democratic. The German area around Jefferson City was anti-slavery and remains among the most Republican parts of Missouri, and the new resort areas around Lake of the Ozarks are mixed. Party Cove, at the lake's western end, is an archetypical example of deregulation—no curfew, speed or size limits for boats on the water. Growth in the Lake of the Ozarks area has been rapid in the 1990s. Much of this region is Truman country: Harry Truman was born just south of the district and lived just northwest of it, spanning the gaps between country and city, South and North; Truman's mother could remember her house being attacked by Yankee soldiers, and she remained pro-Confederate even when her son was in the White House.

The congressman from the 4th District is Ike Skelton, who in many ways can be called a Truman Democrat; his father met Truman in 1928, when he was Lafayette County prosecutor and the future president was Jackson County judge, and they remained friends for life. Ike Skelton grew up in Lexington, where he returned after college and law school to practice law; he became county prosecutor in 1957, at 25, and was elected to the Missouri Senate in 1970. In 1976 he ran for Congress and won rather easily. Skelton looks and votes like an old-fashioned rural Missouri Democrat: his voting record puts him near the midpoint of this Republican House on economics and foreign issues, slightly to the right on cultural issues. He supports the same expansive, assertive foreign and defense policies the preponderance of Democrats supported in the days of Truman.

Skelton is the ranking Democrat on the Armed Services Committee where he has made great contributions to policy. He has long called for better strategic training in the armed services, particularly in the war colleges, and for improving the higher-level military educational programs. Since the end of the Cold War, he has warned of the perils of further cuts in military spending. "If our nation, as the world's only superpower, chooses to go without a strong military, we are inviting global instability and conflict," he once said. Armed Services is one of the House's least partisan committees; most members are strong defense supporters and it usually reports bills with bipartisan support. Skelton is greatly respected by Republicans as well as Democrats on the committee. But the House as a whole is not always of the same opinion on military issues. "I have detected a growing cultural gap between military and civilian America," Skelton noted in 1997. "Fewer people today have direct contact with the military. I can tell you that as fewer sons and daughters wear the uniforms of our country, members of Congress receive less encouragement from voters in their districts to support a substantial military for our nation." Skelton's work over the years has helped transform the American military into the high-performance force evident in the Gulf war. But he remained cautious about military engagement and wary of the strain the stepped-up operational tempo of the Clinton years has put on the military. He was reluctant to support sending troops to Bosnia in September 1995, and passed a resolution, 287–141, which called for strict neutrality in the peacekeeping effort. He supported the air war in the former Yugoslavia in March 1999. Displeased that George W. Bush froze the military budget despite campaign rhetoric that "help is on the way"; Skelton in early 2001 called for an immediate supplemental appropriation. He takes a strict view of the services' separation from politics; he opposed the decision to ship weapons for display at the former Philadelphia Naval Shipyard during the Republican National Convention and said he would oppose sending them to Los Angeles for the Democratic Convention. And he takes a long view of history. He was one of the co-sponsors of the measure that restored the stars of Admiral Husband Kimmel and Lieutenant General Walter Short, which were taken away after Pearl Harbor.

The 4th District includes the Army's giant Fort Leonard Wood and, in Skelton's home county, Whiteman Air Force Base, from which B-2s took off to bomb Serbia and Kosovo and returned the same day. But, as he points out, they are both major bases with unique functions unlikely to be shuttered by any base closing commission. Indeed, in 1999, when other Missourians were trying to keep the F-15 line open in St. Louis County, Skelton said that he doubted any more F-15s would be built; he opposed ordering them in appropriations bills when they hadn't been authorized by Armed Services. In 2000 he arranged for a 22,000-pound Navy anchor to be placed on display at Whiteman, for a Naval Reserve unit. "These anchors are really a symbol of continued jointness between the services," he said, adding with a smile, "You have to have some fun along the way." He also worked for 10 years for the aircraft carrier the *U.S.S. Harry S Truman*, commissioned in July 1998, and with Missourian Roy Blunt co-sponsored the 2000 law naming the State Department building after Truman.

Skelton has voted for some Republican measures, like the balanced budget amendment, the 1996 welfare reform and estate tax repeal. But he criticized Republican proposals for Medicare and tax cuts. In October 1998 he was one of 31 Democrats who voted for the Republican impeachment inquiry resolution. But he strongly criticized the Republicans for going ahead with the impeachment vote while Clinton's bombing of Iraq was going on, and voted against impeachment after being one of the last Democrats to announce his position.

Skelton's toughest race came in 1982, when he was redistricted in with a Republican incumbent; he won 55%–45%. He has won by very large margins in recent years, and is greatly respected; in 1999 citizens in Lexington and Lafayette Counties began raising money to build the Ike Skelton Museum of the American Armed Forces. Redistricting could remove the Jackson County portion of the district, but Skelton seems safe regardless. His real goal is to become chairman of the Armed Services Committee, which will require 217 other Democrats to win in 2002.

Cook's Call   *Safe.* Skelton's solid winning margins here over the past 24 years belie the fact that this is a rather marginal district. Republican presidential nominees have won this district since 1992. This district, like the 3rd, could be a real trouble spot for Democrats once it opens up.

THE PEOPLE: Pop. 2000: 659,533; Pop. 1990: 569,295, up 15.9% 1990–2000. 93.4% White, 3.1% Black, 0.6% Asian, 0.5% Amer. Indian, 0.1% Hawaiian, 1.4% Two+ races, 0.8% Other; 2% Hispanic Origin.

2000 Presidential Vote

Bush (R)	162,746	(58%)
Gore (D)	110,947	(40%)
Nader (Green)	3,818	(1%)
Others	2,681	(1%)

1996 Presidential Vote

Dole (R)	111,172	(46%)
Clinton (D)	99,975	(41%)
Perot (I)	29,011	(12%)

Rep. Ike Skelton (D)

Elected 1976, 13th term; b. Dec. 20, 1931, Lexington; home, Lexington; Wentworth Military Acad. Jr. Col., 1949–51, U. of MO, A.B. 1953, LL.B. 1956; Disciples of Christ; married (Susie).

Elected Office: MO Senate, 1971–76.

Professional Career: Lafayette Cnty. Prosecuting atty., 1957–60; MO Special Asst. Atty. Gen., 1961–63; Practicing atty., 1963–76.

DC Office: 2206 RHOB 20515, 202-225-2876; Web site: www.house.gov/skelton.

District Offices: Blue Springs, 816-228-4242; Jefferson City, 573-635-3499; Lebanon, 417-532-7964; Sedalia, 660-826-2675.

Committees: *Armed Services* (RMM of 28 D): Military Procurement.

Group Ratings

	ADA	ACLU	AFS	LCV	CON	ITIC	NTU	COC	ACU	NTLC	CHC
2000	40	15	57	57	24	83	34	66	40	30	67
1999	55	—	100	38	63	—	22	52	41	—	—

National Journal Ratings

	1999 LIB	—	1999 CONS		2000 LIB	—	2000 CONS
Economic	57%	—	42%		59%	—	41%
Social	31%	—	68%		39%	—	60%
Foreign	74%	—	23%		53%	—	45%

FIFTH DISTRICT

Kansas City, Missouri, named after a state it isn't in and a river that doesn't touch it, is the center of one of America's large metro areas, the biggest on the central Great Plains. The first pioneers here started little towns on the bluffs above the Missouri River—Independence, Kansas City, Westport—which coalesced a few decades later. Here the Santa Fe Trail set out to cross the Sand Hills of Kansas and reach Mexican territory; here Jayhawks and Bushwhackers set out to fight for control of Bleeding Kansas. It was a rail center and had one of the largest stockyards in the country, a major commercial center with lean skyscrapers and the Country Club Plaza, the first shopping center in America, in the 1920s. It is famous for Harry Truman, who grew up on a farm now in the suburb of Grandview and who lived in his wife's family's house in Independence, the old county seat just to the east. It is famous also for its black community, and jazz musicians like Scott Joplin, Charlie Parker and Count Basie, and for its much-praised barbecue.

The 5th Congressional District of Missouri includes most of Kansas City in Jackson County, plus Grandview and the bulk of Independence; most of the city's landmarks, including the Truman home, are here. It includes all of Kansas City's black neighborhoods and was 26% black in 2000. About half its voters are in Kansas City, half in the suburbs. Politically, it is solidly Democratic.

The congresswoman from the 5th is Karen McCarthy, a Democrat first elected in 1994. She moved to Kansas City to teach school, and shortly thereafter, in 1976, at 29, was elected to the Missouri House. She served there 18 years, rising to become chairwoman of Ways and Means in 1983 and president of the National Conference of State Legislators in 1994, working also as a government affairs consultant. In 1994 Congressman Alan Wheat ran for the Senate, and ultimately lost to John Ashcroft. McCarthy ran for his House seat and managed the not inconsiderable feat of winning 41% in an 11-candidate primary; the next two finishers also were women. McCarthy was supported by unions, environmentalists, black organizations and Kansas City Mayor Emanuel Cleaver; she raised more than $350,000 for the primary. The Republicans had a serious candidate, Ron Freeman, an African American who played professional football in the short-lived United States Football League and then worked with the Fellowship of Christian Athletes, and who attacked "a government which has refused to be accountable to the citizenship." McCarthy stressed her conciliatory skills. She was supported by business leaders and had a $250,000 edge in PAC money. She won 57%–43%, carrying Kansas City 2–1 but losing the suburban half of the district. She has not been seriously challenged since.

McCarthy calls herself a New Democrat and supported the balanced budget amendment, a capital gains tax cut and opposed unfunded federal mandates. Her voting record has been more moderate on economic issues than on cultural and foreign policy. She has been pro-gun control, pro-choice on abortion, against the flat tax and school vouchers. In the Missouri House she sponsored an energy policy act that encouraged alternative fuels; she has supported mixing diesel fuel with beef tallow for Kansas City buses. "This is the fuel of the future, and we're going to prove it right here in our community," she said, though she might have said the same of the soybean oil used before. She attended the 1997 Kyoto conference on climate change and praised Al Gore's speech there as "a shot in the arm" that "resuscitated" the talks.

After delaying long enough to include herself in the "anxiety caucus," she opposed permanent normal trade relations with China because of reservations about the World Trade Organization. On the Commerce Committee she has been a supporter of prescription-drug coverage for Medicare, and she has encouraged arts education in public schools. McCarthy has promoted many local projects—a $100 million court house, $5 million to replace the 110-year-old Chouteau Bridge, $5 million in high-tech grants to local schools to use computers to study the Santa Fe Trail and put Truman Library documents on the Internet, $12 million in the 1998 transportation bill for Jackson County Roadway, Strother Road in Lee's Summit and Missouri 150, and $8 million in 2000 to renovate the Truman Library. She advocated the interests of an important local company when she urged the Justice Department in 1999 to abandon its plan to end the tradition of donating Hallmark greeting cards to millions of prison inmates during the Christmas season; the department maintained the tradition. McCarthy was the only Missouri member to support Bill Clinton's veto of the 2000 energy and water spending bill, which included a provision to prevent the Missouri River from being raised occasionally to protect endangered species upstream in South Dakota.

Cook's Call *Safe.* This Kansas-City based district is the second most Democratic in the state after the 1st District in St. Louis. Like so many urban districts, this seat grew slowly during the 1990's and needed to pick up about 44,000 new residents in 2001. Her newly redrawn district pushes the 5th into Cass County. McCarthy should have no problem winning in 2002.

THE PEOPLE: Pop. 2000: 577,050; Pop. 1990: 569,289, up 1.4% 1990–2000. 66.8% White, 26.1% Black, 1.4% Asian, 0.5% Amer. Indian, 0.2% Hawaiian, 2.4% Two+ races, 2.7% Other; 5.8% Hispanic Origin.

2000 Presidential Vote		
Gore (D)	141,980	(62%)
Bush (R)	81,637	(36%)
Nader (Green)	4,327	(2%)
Others	1,825	(1%)

1996 Presidential Vote		
Clinton (D)	127,691	(58%)
Dole (R)	71,453	(33%)
Perot (I)	17,489	(8%)

Rep. Karen McCarthy (D)

Elected 1994, 4th term; b. Mar. 18, 1947, Haverhill, MA; home, Kansas City; U. of KS, B.A. 1969, M.B.A. 1986, U. of MO, M.A. 1976; Catholic; divorced.

Elected Office: MO House of Reps., 1976–94.

Professional Career: High schl. teacher, 1969–76; Financial analyst, 1984–86; Govt. affairs consultant, Marion Merrill Dow, 1986–94; Pres., Natl. Conf. of State Legislatures, 1994.

DC Office: 1330 LHOB 20515, 202-225-4535; Fax: 202-225-4403; Web site: www.house.gov/karenmccarthy.

District Offices: Independence, 816-833-4545; Kansas City, 816-842-4545.

Committees: *Budget* (13th of 20 D). *Energy & Commerce* (18th of 26 D): Energy & Air Quality; Environment & Hazardous Materials; Telecommunications & The Internet.

Group Ratings

	ADA	ACLU	AFS	LCV	CON	ITIC	NTU	COC	ACU	NTLC	CHC
2000	95	85	100	86	65	67	20	52	4	12	8
1999	95	—	100	81	94	—	20	44	0	—	—

National Journal Ratings

	1999 LIB —	1999 CONS		2000 LIB —	2000 CONS
Economic	65%	34%		92%	8%
Social	83%	13%		86%	12%
Foreign	92%	8%		85%	10%

Key Votes of the 106th Congress

1. Patient Bill of Rights	Y	5. Bar RU-486 $ for FDA	N	9. NATO War in Serbia	Y
2. Accelerate Min. Wage	Y	6. Display 10 Commandments	N	10. Perm. Trade with China	N
3. Strike Ban on Ergo. Stnd.	Y	7. Gun Show Bkgrnd. Checks	Y	11. Debt Relief for 3rd World	Y
4. Ovrd. Estate Tax Veto	N	8. Ban Part.-Birth Abortion	N	12. Drop Cuba Econ. Embargo	Y

Election Results

2000 general	Karen McCarthy (D)	159,826	(69%)	($331,907)
	Steve Gordon (R)	66,439	(29%)	($10,060)
	Others	5,872	(3%)	
2000 primary	Karen McCarthy (D)	35,071	(85%)	
	Charles Lindsey (D)	6,013	(15%)	
1998 general	Karen McCarthy (D)	101,313	(66%)	($316,001)
	Penny Bennett (R)	47,582	(31%)	($29,620)
	Others	4,790	(3%)	

SIXTH DISTRICT

The rolling, surging fields along the Missouri River in northwest Missouri were settled in a rush in the late 19th Century and have been losing people ever since. Fewer hands are needed on farms than half a century ago, far fewer than at the turn of the century. In 1940, this area had one of the largest meatpacking operations in the world, but the meatpacking business for years generated no new jobs, and St. Joseph, the biggest town here, has fewer people than in 1900. The counties of northwest Missouri, aside from those in the Kansas City metro area, had 508,000 people in 1900, 452,000 in 1940 and 318,000 in 1900. But in the 1990s, the local economy began to perk up a little, and the number climbed to 330,000; some counties that had been losing population since 1900 started to gain.

All these counties plus part of metro Kansas City—Clay and Platte counties and a small portion of Jackson County east of Independence—make up Missouri's 6th Congressional District. Over the years greater Kansas City has gained people almost precisely to the extent that northwest Missouri has lost them. The Kansas City area casts about half the district's votes. The historic political tradition here is mostly Democratic, but has been tempered by dislike for national Democrats' cultural liberalism. This was strong Perot country in 1992: he got 27% of the vote in the 6th District, and Bill Clinton carried it with a 40%–32% plurality; Clinton won again in 1996 by a narrower 46%–42%. But as the rural vote across the nation moved toward Republicans in 2000, George W. Bush won 53%–44%.

The congressman from the 6th District is Sam Graves, a Republican first elected in 2000. A lifelong resident of the small town of Tarkio, he began his career in agriculture, the issue which defines much of his politics. He graduated from the University of Missouri as an agronomist and soon after, in 1987, joined the Farm Bureau. The 1980s farm crisis drew Graves into politics. He ran for the state House in 1992 and beat a longtime Democratic incumbent; two years later he was elected to the state Senate. He led a successful push to lighten automobile inspection requirements. He attracted attention in 1998 with a five-hour filibuster, when he nearly derailed the legislature over a school desegregation bill he called slanted against rural districts like Tarkio, though the bill eventually passed.

Graves got his opportunity to run for the House when Congresswoman Pat Danner, 22 minutes before the May 23 state deadline and without a public announcement, delivered to the secretary of State a statement of withdrawal from her campaign for reelection. She had surgery for breast cancer in January, but had described her prognosis as excellent. Not by accident, the immediate favorite to succeed her was her son, state Senator Steve Danner. House Republican leaders in Washington thought they had a good opportunity to win this district, but their intervention on Graves' behalf became awkward because of the candidacy of Teresa Loar, a moderate Republican on the Kansas City Council who favored abortion rights and had filed before Pat Danner's retirement. Loar blasted Graves as the darling of extremist and sexist party leaders, while Graves countered by criticizing her travel expenses while on the council and running a pro-family message. Graves rolled over Loar 68%–17%, with especially big margins in rural counties.

Against three weak Democratic alternatives, Steve Danner was held to 56%—a bad omen for November.

In the general, Danner called himself a conservative Democrat and the candidates agreed on some issues: the death penalty, repeal of the marriage-penalty tax, and trade relations with China. But they had plenty of differences, including education funding, abortion rights, gun control and the performance of Bill Clinton. Graves called Danner a "tax and spend liberal" and said that when his acorn fell from the tree (his mother), "it rolled to the left." Danner attacked Graves for opposing a bill to lower the maximum blood-alcohol level for drivers, and toughen nursing home regulations. Loar endorsed Danner, but Graves ran a more aggressive and better-financed campaign. Surprisingly, Danner made little use of his mother or her record during the campaign. The contrast, in the end, may have come down to personality. In an editorial in favor of Graves, *The Kansas City Star* said that Danner's campaign switch on abortion policy showed that he "engaged in raw opportunism at the slightest opportunity," with his central principle of "me first." Graves won 51%–47%, as he took 20 of the 27 counties. Danner's strongest counties were in the Kansas City area, but Graves kept Danner's metro-area lead to 192 votes of nearly 135,000 cast.

With seats on Agriculture, Transportation and Infrastructure, and Small Business, Graves has the opportunity to tend to local issues and entrench himself. Redistricting should not have a significant political effect.

Cook's Call   *Competitive.* As a freshman Republican representing a district that has been held by a Democrat for the last eight years and who won his 2000 race with just 51%, Graves should be a top target for Democrats in 2002. But Graves will be tough to take out. This district has been trending more Republican over the years (Bush won by 9%) and Graves, who defeated the son of the popular Democratic incumbent in 2000, knows how to win difficult races.

THE PEOPLE: Pop. 2000: 635,835; Pop. 1990: 568,823, up 11.8% 1990–2000. 93.9% White, 2.8% Black, 0.8% Asian, 0.4% Amer. Indian, 0.1% Hawaiian, 1.3% Two+ races, 0.7% Other; 2.3% Hispanic Origin.

2000 Presidential Vote

Bush (R)	146,265	(53%)
Gore (D)	122,997	(44%)
Nader (Green)	4,799	(2%)
Others	2,736	(1%)

1996 Presidential Vote

Clinton (D)	115,342	(46%)
Dole (R)	105,084	(42%)
Perot (I)	29,302	(12%)

Rep. Sam Graves (R)

Elected 2000, 1st term; b. Nov. 7, 1963, Tarkio; home, Tarkio; U. of MO (Columbia), B.S. 1986; Baptist; married (Lesley).

Elected Office: MO House of Reps., 1992–94; MO Senate 1994–2000.

Professional Career: Farmer.

DC Office: 1407 LHOB 20515, 202-225-7041; Fax: 202-225-8221; Web site: www.house.gov/graves.

District Offices: Liberty, 816-792-3976; St. Charles, 816-233-9818.

Committees: *Agriculture* (25th of 27 R): Conservation, Credit, Rural Development & Research; General Farm Commodities & Risk Management. *Small Business* (14th of 19 R): Regulatory Reform Oversight. *Transportation & Infrastructure* (37th of 42 R): Aviation; Highways & Transit.

Group Ratings and Key Votes: Newly Elected

2000 general	Sam Graves (R)	138,925	(51%)	($1,115,338)
	Steve Danner (D)	127,792	(47%)	($811,060)
	Others	6,484	(2%)	
2000 primary	Sam Graves (R)	30,014	(68%)	
	Teresa Anne Loar (R)	7,493	(17%)	
	Jeff Bailey (R)	4,575	(10%)	
	Others	2,023	(5%)	
1998 general	Pat Danner (D)	136,774	(71%)	($53,708)
	Jeff Bailey (R)	51,679	(27%)	
	Others	4,324	(2%)	

SEVENTH DISTRICT

One of the biggest tourist destinations in America today is Branson, Missouri—a fact almost no one predicted 20 years ago. Even today Branson has only 6,050 residents, is served by two-lane roads, is nowhere near a major airport; but it thrives, paralleling the surging popularity of country and western music. Branson was put on the map early in the century by Harold Bell Wright's novel, *The Shepherd of the Hills*, about the hardy people of the mountains, hills and meadows of southwest Missouri, just north of Arkansas. More tourists came in with completion of the Ozark Beach Dam that created Bull Shoals Lake in 1913, lured by the native bass and stocked trout. Then in the 1960s, new lakes were formed, a Shepherd of the Hills pageant and Silver Dollar City were started, and entertainers—the five Maybe brothers performing as "The Baldknobbers" and Box Car Willie from the Grand Ole Opry—started performing. They were followed by others— Roy Clark, Glen Campbell, Charlie Pride, Mel Tillis, Louise Mandrell and the violinist Shoji Ta- buchi. Today Branson has 7 million visitors a year and more than two dozen theaters with 55,000 seats—more than Broadway. Workers come in from as far away as Springfield, the biggest city in southwest Missouri, and headquarters of such middle American institutions as the Mid-America Dairymen, the nation's largest milk producers' cooperative; the Bass Pro Shops Outdoor World, probably the nation's largest fishing equipment store; and the Assemblies of God, one of the nation's and the world's largest and fastest-growing Protestant denominations. What do people like about Branson? The non-stop entertainment and fishing and boating; country music and family style entertainment; plenty of shopping and a safe atmosphere. These are also things that have made southwest Missouri the fastest growing part of the state in the last 20 years, generating new businesses and attracting retirees as well as vacationers.

The 7th Congressional District includes Branson and Springfield and most of southwest Missouri. Historically, this area has been Republican since it opposed secession in 1861: pro- Union Springfield changed hands several times as Missouri's staged its own civil war. Its conser- vative response to the big-spending government of the 1960s and cultural liberalism of the 1970s reinforced its allegiance, and now this is the most Republican part of Missouri.

The congressman from the 7th District is Roy Blunt, a Republican first elected in 1996. Blunt grew up on a dairy farm in southwest Missouri, in a political family; his father was a state representative from a district near Springfield. He taught high school and college history and government. Roy Blunt got his start in politics by volunteering for John Ashcroft's unsuccessful campaign for Congress in 1972, and in 1973, at 23, he became Greene County (Springfield) clerk. In 1984, at 34, he was elected Missouri secretary of State and was re-elected with 60% in 1988. In 1992 he ran for governor and lost the Republican primary to William Webster, 44%–39%. (Webster was defeated and disgraced, sent to jail because of his improper administration of the Second Injury Fund.) Blunt became president of his alma mater, Southwest Baptist University in Bolivar. In 1996 Congressman Mel Hancock kept his pledge to serve only four terms and retired. In the primary Blunt faced Gary Nodler, businessman and one-time staffer to Congressman Gene Taylor. Nodler carried his home area around Joplin and Carthage, but Blunt carried everything else and won 56%–44%. There were 75,000 votes cast in the Republican primary and only 16,000 in the Democratic primary: a harbinger of the general election, which Blunt won 65%–32%, running ahead of the Republican ticket and carrying every county with at least 62% of the vote. He has been re-elected easily since.

Blunt has shown great political skills and has become part of the Republican House leadership. His political adeptness was first apparent in his committee assignments: Agriculture, International Relations, Transportation and Infrastructure. On Agriculture, he supported the Clinton administration's proposal to reduce the number of federal milk marketing orders from 31 to 11 and to include southern Missouri in the southeast region—a position also supported by Mid-America Dairymen—and he opposed food embargoes. On International Relations, he supported the bill to penalize countries that practice or allow religious persecution—a concern of denominations like the Assemblies of God, which has more members abroad than in the United States. He was on Transportation during passage of the 1998 transportation bill, which increased Missouri's funding $213 million. He and Asa Hutchinson from the adjoining Arkansas district made U.S. 71 from Kansas City to Shreveport a "high-priority corridor," a step on the way to upgrading it to interstate status. Blunt also took up important conservative causes. He co-sponsored the bill to zero out the tax code by December 2000. When tobacco became a headline issue, he proposed yanking the licenses of teenage drivers for 60 days if they were caught with tobacco, and with Hutchinson he moved to earmark tobacco settlement funds not used for anti-smoking programs for debt reduction and tax cuts. He was part of Majority Whip Tom DeLay's "free speech" team proposing bills to undermine the Shays-Meehan campaign finance bill. Blunt was not inattentive to fellow members. He supported a cost-of-living pay increase for House members in 1997, despite local flak. In the 1998 campaign cycle he raised and contributed $250,000 to other incumbent Republicans.

Three weeks after the 1998 election Blunt won a seat on the Commerce Committee. Then in January 1999 Tom DeLay plucked him from the ranks of 48 deputy whips and appointed him Chief Deputy Whip, the position Dennis Hastert held until his astonishing elevation to speaker. On a number of issues Blunt was given the job of making more palatable to core Republicans measures that were going through in any case. In September 1999 he brokered a deal to tie business tax cuts to the minimum wage increase. In September 2000 he brokered a deal on food sales to Cuba: Miami's two Cuban-Americans got a ban on U.S. credits for sales, but the export-minded George Nethercutt got third-party financing. In October 2000 Blunt helped orchestrate a 315–98 override of a Bill Clinton veto of a water projects bill; at issue was a Clinton proposal to allow spring rises (floods, said opponents) of the Missouri River to protect endangered species upstream. Blunt supported George W. Bush early, in March 1999, and was named the Bush campaign's liaison to House members, a busy position and a sensitive one given Bush's pointed criticisms of House Republicans in 1999. He also formed his own leadership PAC, Rely on Your Beliefs Fund, or the RoyB Fund. Blunt is the only House Republican who has served as a state chief elections officer, and in February 2001 Hastert named him the Republican chairman of a bipartisan select committee on elections. But it turned out to be neither bipartisan nor a committee, as Dick Gephardt and Hastert could not reach an agreement.

Blunt has also worked on local issues. He and Missouri colleague Ike Skelton co-sponsored the law that named the State Department building after Missouri's Harry Truman. And the political tradition in his family goes on. His son Matt Blunt in 1998 was elected, at 27, to the state House and in 2000 was elected to his father's old position as secretary of State.

Cook's Call   *Safe.* Blunt should have no trouble winning a fourth term in this strongly Republican district that gave Bush 62% in 2000. This district has grown faster than any other in the state has.

THE PEOPLE: Pop. 2000: 695,069; Pop. 1990: 568,017, up 22.4% 1990–2000. 94.4% White, 1.2% Black, 0.6% Asian, 1% Amer. Indian, 0.1% Hawaiian, 1.7% Two+ races, 1% Other; 2.4% Hispanic Origin.

2000 Presidential Vote		
Bush (R)	173,741	(62%)
Gore (D)	97,730	(35%)
Nader (Green)	4,288	(2%)
Others	2,737	(1%)

1996 Presidential Vote		
Dole (R)	129,249	(51%)
Clinton (D)	93,537	(37%)
Perot (I)	27,580	(11%)

Rep. Roy Blunt (R)

Elected 1996, 3d term; b. Jan. 10, 1950, Niangua; home, Strafford; SW Baptist U., B.A. 1970, SW MO St. U., M.A. 1972; Baptist; married (Roseann).

Elected Office: MO Secy. of State, 1984–93.

Professional Career: High schl. teacher, 1970–73; Greene Cnty. Clerk, 1973–85; Adjunct Instructor, Drury Col., 1976–82; Pres., SW Baptist U., 1993–96.

DC Office: 217 CHOB 20515, 202-225-6536; Fax: 202-225-5604; Web site: www.house.gov/blunt.

District Offices: Joplin, 417-781-1041; Springfield, 417-889-1800.

Committees: *Chief Deputy Majority Whip. Energy & Commerce* (21st of 31 R): Energy & Air Quality; Telecommunications & The Internet.

Group Ratings

	ADA	ACLU	AFS	LCV	CON	ITIC	NTU	COC	ACU	NTLC	CHC
2000	0	29	0	0	65	94	64	90	96	79	93
1999	10	—	16	0	28	—	55	96	87	—	—

National Journal Ratings

	1999 LIB —	1999 CONS		2000 LIB —	2000 CONS
Economic	24%	72%		6%	85%
Social	9%	91%		0%	79%
Foreign	15%	81%		0%	88%

Key Votes of the 106th Congress

1. Patient Bill of Rights	N	5. Bar RU-486 $ for FDA	Y	9. NATO War in Serbia	N
2. Accelerate Min. Wage	N	6. Display 10 Commandments	Y	10. Perm. Trade with China	Y
3. Strike Ban on Ergo. Stnd.	N	7. Gun Show Bkgrnd. Checks	N	11. Debt Relief for 3rd World	N
4. Ovrd. Estate Tax Veto	Y	8. Ban Part.-Birth Abortion	Y	12. Drop Cuba Econ. Embargo	N

Election Results

2000 general	Roy Blunt (R)	202,305	(74%)	($1,177,456)
	Charles Christup (D)	65,510	(24%)	
	Others	6,122	(2%)	
2000 primary	Roy Blunt (R)	62,711	(86%)	
	Mike Harman (R)	9,856	(14%)	
1998 general	Roy Blunt (R)	129,746	(73%)	($567,315)
	Marc Perkel (D)	43,416	(24%)	
	Others	5,639	(3%)	

EIGHTH DISTRICT

Mark Twain might not recognize life on the Mississippi below St. Louis today, where the land flattens out and the river is hidden behind levees, which ordinarily—except during the terrible flood of 1993—screen small towns and river roads from the sight of rows of barges tethered together, full of coal or soybeans. The Mississippi today is an industrial waterway. But it was never really all that romantic. Twain's steamboats, as he was at pains to point out, were dangerous, noisy contraptions, forever blowing up or getting embedded in roots and branches in the swirling river currents. This is one of the older-settled parts of the United States: French settlers founded Missouri towns like Cape Girardeau in the late 1700s. But the big influx started just a few years after the 1811 earthquake centered on New Madrid; the spongy Mississippi valley land is also seismically very active, and this was the site of one of the most devastating earthquakes in U.S. history.

Outwardly, the southeast quadrant of Missouri—the river valley and the hills to the west, with coal and lead mines (the area produces most of the world's lead) with their miles of tunnels, plus the Bootheel that hangs down in the far southeast—hasn't changed much in 50 years. For years there has been a big population outflow from the Bootheel, as machines replace low-wage farm workers, and the only big growth here has been around Cape Girardeau and along the route of I-44; in the 1990s growth rates picked up slightly, as people sought lives in small communities.

The 8th Congressional District covers this southeast corner of Missouri. The political heritage is mixed. The Bootheel was as solidly Democratic as the Mississippi Valley around Memphis used to be, and some of the mining counties are Democratic. Cape Girardeau, the boyhood home of Rush Limbaugh and also the starting point of the 1996 Clinton-Gore bus tour, votes solidly Republican, as do surrounding counties. For many years this was a safe Democratic district; since 1980 it has been represented by Republicans.

The congresswoman from the 8th District is Jo Ann Emerson, elected in 1996 to replace her late husband Bill Emerson, who was first elected in 1980 and died in June 1996. Jo Ann Emerson grew up in the Washington suburb of Bethesda, Maryland, in a Republican family (her father was executive director of the Republican National Committee) but next door to Democrats Hale and Lindy Boggs, who served in Congress over a period of 50 years; their daughter, Cokie Roberts, babysat Jo Ann. In 1975 she married Republican Bill Emerson, then a Washington lobbyist with Capitol Hill experience. In 1979, spotting the personal vulnerability of the Democratic incumbent, Bill Emerson went back home to Missouri to run, and won with 55%. In 1995 he was diagnosed with cancer, but missed few votes during radiation therapy. Two pieces of legislation passed in 1996 memorialized him: the Bill Emerson Good Samaritan Food Donation Act, setting national standards to encourage donations of unused food, and the Bill Emerson Bridge across the Mississippi at Cape Girardeau.

After Bill's death, Jo Ann Emerson decided to run. "I was so totally focused on a mission to keep the seat and make it a living memorial to Bill," she said. She had political experience of her own: she worked for the American Insurance Association and National Restaurant Association and had been a press aide at the National Republican Congressional Committee. Her views are conservative—for the balanced budget amendment, against gun control, for abortion restrictions, for property rights—and she was quickly endorsed by leading state and national Republicans. But she could not run for the Republican nomination in the August 6 primary: Missouri law bars reopening the filing deadline for new candidates if an incumbent dies less than 11 weeks before the primary, so Emerson ran as an independent in the general. Democrats had a serious candidate, Emily Firebaugh, a timber company owner and lifelong area resident, who attacked Emerson as a product of the Washington suburbs. Firebaugh eventually spent the impressive sum of $831,000, more than Emerson's $806,000. The Republican nominee Richard Kline was less trouble: In 1995 he had used pepper spray to try to place a Veterans Administration doctor under citizen's arrest. Bill Emerson's record, Jo Ann Emerson's conservative views on issues, and the poignancy of the situation all worked in the same direction: toward an Emerson victory. She received 50% of the votes, with 37% for Firebaugh and 11% for Kline.

In the House, Emerson secured funding for local projects, including $8 million for the Bill Emerson Bridge. A property rights supporter, she got her portion of the district excluded from the American Heritage Rivers project which she later opposed as an abuse of executive power to tighten environmental rules along rivers in order to save wetlands. In 1999 Emerson joined Appropriations and its Agriculture Subcommittee. Her priority was addressing low prices for farm commodities. She worked with other members from farm districts to open Cuba-to-U.S. agricultural trade. With Democrat Eva Clayton of North Carolina, she revived the Congressional Rural Caucus. She also helped to organize the House's bipartisan civility retreat in 1998.

Emerson has won re-election without difficulty. In early 2001 many Republicans urged her to run in 2002 against Senator Jean Carnahan, appointed to the post after her late husband Mel Carnahan ran ahead of Senator John Ashcroft in the 2000 Senate race. Some thought her own experience of being elected as a widow would balance out the sympathy Missourians felt for the Senator. But Emerson said that she was disinclined to run, and seems likely to run for re-election, and win. Redistricting is not likely to significantly affect this corner seat.

Cook's Call   *Safe.* After a competitive 1996 contest, Emerson has not had to break a sweat to hold onto this southeastern Missouri district. She has been mentioned as a potential Senate candidate, but she is unlikely to run. Even if Emerson were to leave this seat, it would be a tough one for Democrats to recapture. This rural district, once a Democratic stronghold, has been trending Republican over the last 10 years.

THE PEOPLE: Pop. 2000: 611,537; Pop. 1990: 568,385, up 7.6% 1990–2000. 93% White, 4.4% Black, 0.4% Asian, 0.6% Amer. Indian, 1.2% Two+ races, 0.3% Other; 1% Hispanic Origin.

2000 Presidential Vote			1996 Presidential Vote		
Bush (R)	139,318	(59%)	Clinton (D)	101,339	(45%)
Gore (D)	92,043	(39%)	Dole (R)	96,457	(43%)
Nader (Green)	2,660	(1%)	Perot (I)	25,089	(11%)
Others	2,699	(1%)			

Rep. Jo Ann Emerson (R)

Elected 1996, 4th term; b. Sept. 16, 1950, Washington, DC; home, Cape Girardeau; Ohio Wesleyan U., B.A. 1972; Presbyterian; married (Ron Gladney).

Professional Career: Deputy Communications Dir., Natl. Repub. Cong. Cmte., 1984–91; Dir., State Relations & Grassroot Programs, Natl. Restaurant Assn., 1991–94; Sr. Vice Pres., Pub. Affairs, American Insurance Assn., 1994–96.

DC Office: 326 CHOB 20515, 202-225-4404; Web site: www.house.gov/emerson.

District Offices: Cape Girardeau, 573-335-0101; Farmington, 573-756-9755; Rolla, 573-364-2455.

Committees: *Appropriations* (27th of 35 R): Agriculture, Rural Development, & FDA; Energy & Water Development; Transportation.

Group Ratings

	ADA	ACLU	AFS	LCV	CON	ITIC	NTU	COC	ACU	NTLC	CHC
2000	0	21	14	0	30	89	59	80	80	61	93
1999	10	—	16	6	68	—	54	80	80	—	—

National Journal Ratings

	1999 LIB —	1999 CONS		2000 LIB —	2000 CONS
Economic	30% —	64%		18% —	76%
Social	9% —	91%		0% —	79%
Foreign	37% —	62%		31% —	69%

Key Votes of the 106th Congress

1. Patient Bill of Rights	N	5. Bar RU-486 $ for FDA	Y	9. NATO War in Serbia	N
2. Accelerate Min. Wage	N	6. Display 10 Commandments	Y	10. Perm. Trade with China	Y
3. Strike Ban on Ergo. Stnd.	N	7. Gun Show Bkgrnd. Checks	N	11. Debt Relief for 3rd World	N
4. Ovrd. Estate Tax Veto	Y	8. Ban Part.-Birth Abortion	Y	12. Drop Cuba Econ. Embargo	N

Election Results

2000 general	Jo Ann Emerson (R)	162,239	(69%)	($794,800)
	Bob Camp (D)	67,760	(29%)	
	Others	4,067	(2%)	
2000 primary	Jo Ann Emerson (R)	unopposed		
1998 general	Jo Ann Emerson (R)	104,271	(63%)	($1,084,449)
	Anthony J. (Tony) Heckemeyer (D)	59,426	(36%)	($375,093)
	Others	2,827	(2%)	

NINTH DISTRICT

Little Dixie, the swath of northeast Missouri along the Mississippi River, was settled by Southerners from Kentucky and Virginia. Its most famous native son is Mark Twain, born Sam Clemens in Hannibal, then as now a little town on bluffs overlooking the river. Hannibal was the thinly disguised St. Petersburg of Tom Sawyer and Huckleberry Finn, lovingly created years later complete with Pike County and other dialect by Twain, then living in New England. Little Dixie was pro-Confederate during the Civil War; Callaway County declared its independence from the Union. Twain's view of politics was different, both darker and more optimistic: he created a vision of America that transcended region and a view of antebellum society that identified slavery as an evil without ever saying so; Twain himself was a Republican and close friend of Union General and President Ulysses S. Grant. But whatever the author's feelings for his birthplace, Hannibal loves Twain; some quarter-million tourists pour in to visit his boyhood home each year. For many years faithfully Democratic, Little Dixie has reared some notable politicians as well. One was Champ Clark, speaker of the House from 1911–19 and presidential candidate in 1912; another was Clarence Cannon, author of the definitive text on the House's parliamentary procedures and chairman of the House Appropriations Committee until his death in 1964.

The 9th Congressional District of Missouri is the descendant of the Little Dixie districts that elected Clark and Cannon, but declining population expanded it far to the south. Now it extends to Columbia, home of the University of Missouri, and Fulton, home of Westminster College, where in 1946 Winston Churchill, accompanied by President Harry Truman, told the world that "from Stettin on the Baltic to Trieste on the Adriatic, an iron curtain has descended across the continent." To the east the 9th includes Franklin County and half of St. Charles County, now increasingly suburbanized, with population up more than 30% in the 1990s. These suburban areas, which lean Republican, now cast nearly 40% of the district's votes, and another one-third are cast in Columbia and adjoining counties, leaving less than one-third for the formerly dominant and no longer quite so Democratic Little Dixie.

The congressman from the 9th District is Kenny Hulshof, a Republican first elected in 1996. He grew up on a farm in far southeast Missouri, near the confluence of the Mississippi and Ohio rivers. After law school he joined the public defender's office in Cape Girardeau. In 1989 he became a special prosecutor for the Missouri attorney general's office, and from his home in Columbia traveled to 53 counties, getting 60 violent felony convictions and seven death sentences. In the midst of this, in 1994, he became the Republican nominee for the 9th District. This was a surprise: challenger Rick Hardy had held Democratic Congressman Harold Volkmer to a 48%–46% victory in 1992 and was running again; but after the primary filing deadline, he withdrew from the race due to depression and exhaustion. In August, party leaders named Hulshof as Hardy's replacement. He was far outspent, but even so made a respectable showing, carrying Columbia and Boone County, and trailing 50%–45% overall.

In January 1996 Hulshof resigned as special prosecutor and started to run again. Volkmer's combative temperament and irritation with the new Republican majority made him one of its most persistent antagonists on the floor. His close races, and the fact that a LaRouche follower got 28% in the primary against him, suggested weakness. But Hulshof had competition in the primary. Ophthalmologist Harry Eggleston moved to St. Charles County, spent $806,000, and carried St. Charles and Franklin counties with big margins and ran slightly ahead in Little Dixie. But Hulshof won big in and around Columbia capturing the party's line by only 168 votes out of 38,000 cast. The general election was sharply contested. Volkmer ran an ad showing Hulshof in a Porsche driven by Newt Gingrich attacking him for signing away his independence in the Contract with America. Hulshof replied that his Porsche was a used car sitting under a tarp in his yard. Hulshof charged that Volkmer had voted to raise taxes 20 times in 20 years and had voted for 40% pay raises. The key moment came in October, when Volkmer, in response to a question, said voters were not overtaxed and that he would not mind paying $1 million in taxes. Hulshof ran radio ads quoting Volkmer all over the district. Volkmer carried Little Dixie 53%–46%, but Hulshof carried the Columbia area 54%–39% and St. Charles and Franklin Counties 49%–48%, for a 49%–47% win.

In the House, Hulshof was elected president of the Republican freshman class and quickly sounded the note of consensus that voters yearned for: he decried "partisan bickering" 15 days after taking office, helped organize the civility retreat in Hershey, backed Shays-Meehan campaign reform and, with Democratic freshman president Jim Davis, supported the 1997 balanced budget agreement. The Republican leadership gave him a prized seat on Ways and Means as a freshman.

This gave him a platform for backing proposals like repeal of the estate tax, exemption of the first $400 of dividend and interest income from the income tax, and FARRM accounts to allow farmers to income-average over five years; it also gave him a fine base for fundraising. But Ways and Means presented perils. One of Hulshof's major causes was preserving the favorable tax treatment of ethanol. But after his amendment was defeated in committee, he voted for the Republican tax bill immediately. Missouri Democrats quickly charged: "Hulshof abandons support of ethanol." To his rescue eventually came Gingrich, who put Hulshof and Iowa's Jim Nussle on the committee that preserved the ethanol credit. He has called for a permanent agricultural negotiator in the office of the United States Trade Representative. On local projects, he secured $12 million to widen Highway 63 in Randolph County and he supported funds for biotech research at the University of Missouri.

When Hulshof was elected, Democrats looked forward to giving him a tough challenge. But his success at fundraising, his shrewdness at spotting issues and the generally pro-incumbent trend have given him two comfortable reelections. Also, the 1990s trend toward Republicans in rural America worked in Hulshof's favor: in 2000 George W. Bush carried every single county in Little Dixie, and Hulshof won by a 59%–38% margin. Redistricting poses something of a threat for Hulshof: the 9th District must lose 73,000 people. But Hulshof seems capable of holding this seat.

Cook's Call *Safe.* Although a Democrat represented this northeastern Missouri district for 26 of the last 30 years, Republican Kenny Hulshof has had little trouble winning re-election to this seat, never dipping below 59% since his defeat of Democratic Harold Volkmer in 1996. With the addition of four Republican-leaning counties (Maries, Miller, Osage and Crawford) in the new state map, this Republican trending district has been shored up a bit for Hulshof, which leaves him pretty well entrenched here and tough to beat.

THE PEOPLE: Pop. 2000: 694,873; Pop. 1990: 568,238, up 22.3% 1990–2000. 93.2% White, 4% Black, 0.9% Asian, 0.3% Amer. Indian, 1.2% Two+ races, 0.4% Other; 1.2% Hispanic Origin.

2000 Presidential Vote			1996 Presidential Vote		
Bush (R)	161,889	(54%)	Clinton (D)	111,626	(44%)
Gore (D)	127,994	(43%)	Dole (R)	106,503	(42%)
Nader (Green)	5,224	(2%)	Perot (I)	30,593	(12%)
Others	2,592	(1%)			

Rep. Kenny Hulshof (R)

Elected 1996, 3d term; b. May 22, 1958, Sikeston; home, Columbia; U. of MO, B.S. 1980, U. of MS, J.D. 1983; Catholic; married (Renee).

Professional Career: Asst. Pub. Defender, 32nd Judicial Circuit, 1983–86; Asst. Prosecuting Atty., Cape Girardeau, 1986–89; Special Prosecutor, MO Atty. General, 1989–96.

DC Office: 412 CHOB 20515, 202-225-2956; Fax: 202-225-5712; Web site: www.house.gov/hulshof.

District Offices: Columbia, 573-449-5111; Hannibal, 573-221-1200; Washington, 636-239-4001.

Committees: *Ways & Means* (19th of 24 R): Oversight; Social Security.

Group Ratings

	ADA	ACLU	AFS	LCV	CON	ITIC	NTU	COC	ACU	NTLC	CHC
2000	5	29	0	7	78	95	63	85	96	79	93
1999	25	—	16	31	79	—	63	88	84	—	—

National Journal Ratings

	1999 LIB —	1999 CONS	2000 LIB —	2000 CONS
Economic	28% —	71%	6% —	85%
Social	32% —	66%	0% —	79%
Foreign	19% —	80%	12% —	78%

Key Votes of the 106th Congress

1. Patient Bill of Rights	*	5. Bar RU-486 $ for FDA	Y	9. NATO War in Serbia	N
2. Accelerate Min. Wage	N	6. Display 10 Commandments	Y	10. Perm. Trade with China	Y
3. Strike Ban on Ergo. Stnd.	N	7. Gun Show Bkgrnd. Checks	N	11. Debt Relief for 3rd World	N
4. Ovrd. Estate Tax Veto	Y	8. Ban Part.-Birth Abortion	Y	12. Drop Cuba Econ. Embargo	N

Election Results

2000 general	Kenny Hulshof (R)	172,787	(59%)	($1,202,235)
	Steven R. Carroll (D)	111,662	(38%)	($360,765)
	Others	7,161	(2%)	
2000 primary	Kenny Hulshof (R)	unopposed		
1998 general	Kenny Hulshof (R)	117,196	(62%)	($963,984)
	Linda Vogt (D)	66,861	(36%)	($157,869)
	Others	4,248	(2%)	

★ MONTANA ★

"Montana is what America used to be," says former Governor Marc Racicot. Physically, it is America's Big Sky Country, a land of great empty vistas, with mountains in the west and vast expanses of plateaus and plains in the east—the 4th largest state in area and 44th in population. Almost nowhere in the state are wilderness and empty land out of sight. Parts of Montana are losing population and being left behind, but parts are also growing. This is a place where you'll come across the Old West of 19th Century cowboys but also, thanks to 21st Century electronic communications, financial advisors communicating via modem with clients all across the country. You can see 1920s Montana in Butte's dimly lit bars and lonely ranch houses, but you can also see 2000s Montana in the ubiquitous coffee houses and gambling parlors across the state.

Montana sits atop America, spanning the Rockies so that on I-15 you can cross the Continental Divide three times. Here in the mountains are the headwaters of the Missouri, from its source in Beaverhead County to its mouth in the Gulf of Mexico the longest river in North America. The beauty of the Clark Fork, which flows into the Columbia and eventually the Pacific, hides the fact that is contaminated with more than century's worth of toxic mining waste. Not far away, at Egg Mountain near Choteau on the Deep Teton River, is the world's most plenteous source of dinosaur remains. But Montana's recorded history is recent: At its 1989 centennial, the son of one of its original cattleman-settlers watched 105 cowboys drive 4,000 cattle with 300 covered wagons trailing behind.

Statehood came less than a century after the first white Americans came here as agents of the government—the Lewis and Clark expedition in 1805. Next came the mountain men, seeking fur, and then came the miners seeking gold, silver, copper—sudden riches that would make them kings not of this barren land but of the metropolises back East. Raucous mining towns sprang up, complete with outlaws and vigilantes. The mining economy gave Montana a radical, class warfare politics. On one side was the Anaconda Mining Company, which until 1959 owned five of Montana's six daily newspapers, many of its utilities, and many of its politicians, and had strong allies in the Stockmen's Association and the Farm Bureau. On the other side were progressives like Senators Thomas Walsh, who exposed the Teapot Dome scandal, and Burton Wheeler, a New Dealer who broke with Franklin Roosevelt over court packing and isolationism, the labor unions (Montana has no right-to-work law and is the most pro-union state in the Rockies), and pork barrel beneficiaries (for a while in the 1930s, Montana received more federal money per capita than almost any other state). The locus of all this was Butte, with its gold and copper mines on

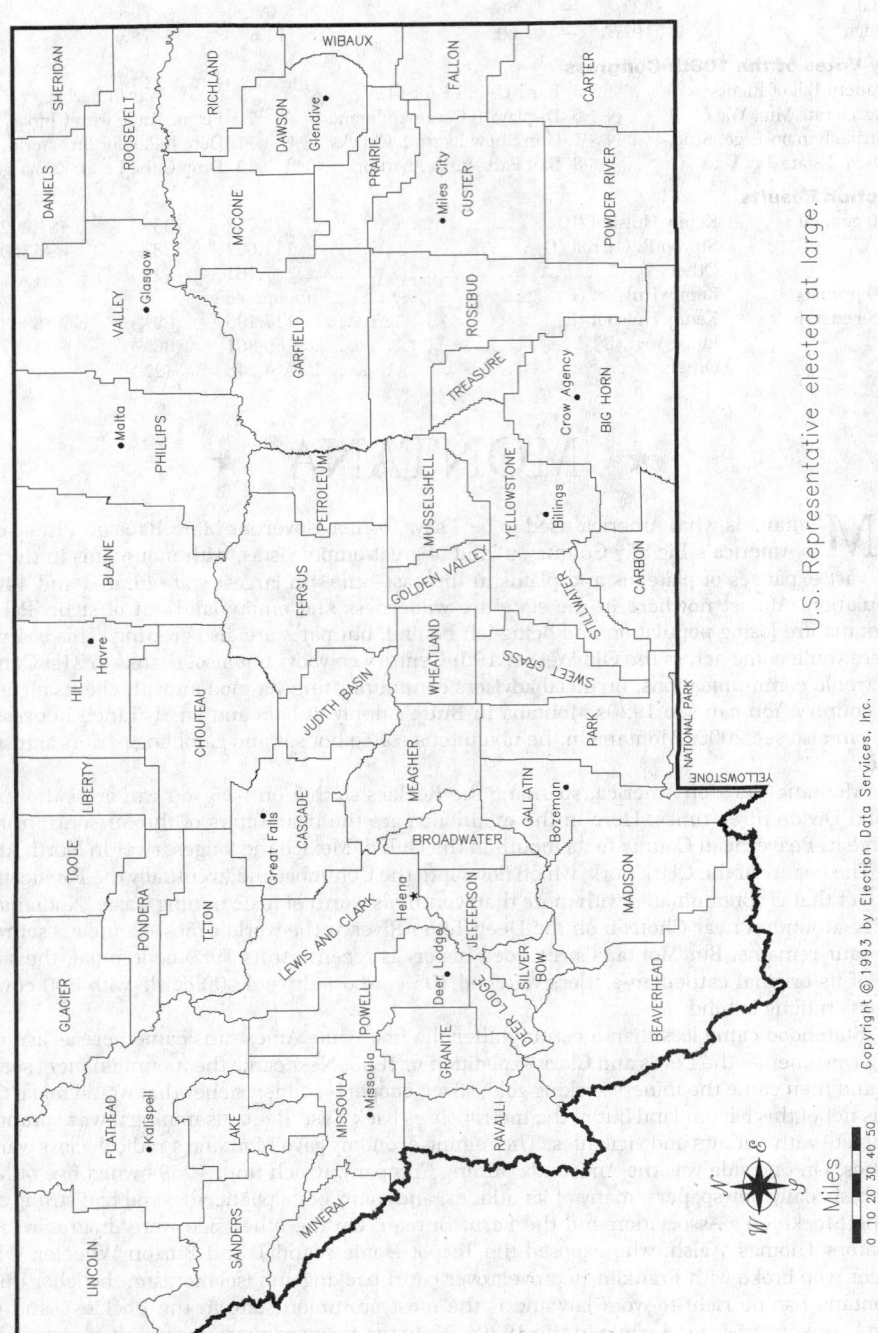

"The Richest Hill on Earth," with its gamblers and bootleggers, company goons and union thugs, IWW organizers and Socialist mayor and millionaires who bought seats in the U.S. Senate. Today the mines are closed, the ore depleted, and the stone temples of commerce and grim, looming mineheads are being restored to a cleanliness they never enjoyed in the boom days.

Butte's population peaked in 1920, mines gradually closed all over the state, and agriculture—wheat growing and cattle grazing—became the mainstays of the economy and class warfare died down. Other towns grew, though none is over 100,000 yet: Billings with its agricultural marketing in the east, the university town of Missoula, Great Falls just east of the Rockies, Kalispell near Lake Flathead, the university and resort town of Bozeman, and the state capital of Helena. The muscular tone of a land settled by ranch hands, miners and railroad workers, of cowboy hats, boots and blue jeans, of men who do hard physical work and relax hard afterwards, remains a link with Montanans going back to the mountain men, miners and cowboys who drove herds of Texas longhorns across the open range. And there is still the sense of space. Hunting and fishing are never far away; development in the small cities and resort areas has not been enough to drive the game away.

In the late 1970s, Montana started attracting affluent second home buyers, and by the mid-1990s they came in a rush, movie stars and Wall Street magnates but also just ordinary people buying small spreads near Big Sky or McLeod, near Bozeman, or around Flathead Lake or Big Timber or the Big Mountain ski resort in Whitefish, where grizzlies come down to forage and the bars hold mouse races. Many newcomers, from California and other urban states, set down roots here, as computers, modems and fax machines make it possible for small businessmen and entrepreneurs to work in Montana, far from their customers and clients, but in an environment they love. These new Montanans have added a spark of energy and inventiveness to a state much of which consisted of those left behind when others moved elsewhere. In the 1990s Montana's population grew rapidly, even though the eastern plains lost population. Montana lost its second congressional district after the 1990 Census, and is now the nation's largest district in population and second largest (after Alaska) in size. Despite gaining more than 100,000 residents in the 1990s, Montana was about 8,000 people short of gaining back its second congressional seat.

Politically, Montana is the most Democratic of the Rocky Mountain states—which means pretty Republican by national standards. It voted narrowly for Bill Clinton in 1992 and for Bob Dole in 1996, but in 2000 it went 58%–33% for George W. Bush, with 6% for Ralph Nader. The results were closer in races for senator, congressman-at-large, and governor, but Republicans won all three narrowly. In these races Democrats carried old mining towns like Butte and Anaconda, Indian reservations, old railroad towns like Great Falls and Havre, university towns like Missoula and Bozeman, and the state capital of Helena. Republicans carried everything else, including fast-growing Billings, Kalispell, and the Bitteroot Valley.

Framing the issues were controversies over the intersection of wilderness and civilization. In August much of western Montana was swept by 31 wildfires burning on almost one million acres. Racicot criticized Clinton administration support of controlled burns and opposition to logging which, many Montanans said, would remove much combustible timber. Vocal Montanans also opposed Clinton proposals to make the Upper Breaks of the Missouri River a national monument and to reintroduce grizzly bears into the Bitterroot Mountains (which Bush Interior Secretary Gail Norton is reconsidering), and a federal court decision barring bank stabilization on the Yellowstone River. Many were disturbed when EPA suddenly announced that a closed asbestos plant in Libby, Racicot's hometown, was responsible for asbestos-related illnesses resulting in 200 deaths. Most voters here seem to be part of what conservative activist Grover Norquist calls the "Leave-Us-Alone Coalition." In the 1990s the legislature stoutly resisted tax increases, even when proposed by the popular Racicot, and when the state Supreme Court decision ordered the legislature to pass a speed limit, it set it at 75 miles per hour.

Governor   Judy Martz, elected governor in 2000, was born in Big Timber, on the plains beneath the Absaroka Range, and spent most her life in Butte. An amateur athlete, she was crowned Miss Rodeo Montana at 20 and represented the U.S. as a speed skater in the 1964 Winter Olympics. She worked for Republican candidates in the 1960s and in the 1970s became more involved in politics after her husband set up a garbage disposal company in Butte. In 1990 she became a field representative for Senator Conrad Burns. She served on a Butte hospital board, chaired the local Chamber of Commerce, and helped build a high altitude speed skating center in Butte. She worked to clean up mining tailings and build baseball fields on the site.

Martz always wears a turtle pin on her blouse to illustrate a favorite saying: "Behold the turtle. He only goes forward when his neck's stuck out." In 1995 Lieutenant Governor Dennis Rehberg started running for the Senate (he lost in 1996, but was elected congressman-at-large in 2000), and Governor Marc Racicot (pronounced *roscoe*) was looking for a new running mate. Martz stuck out her neck and called him up and asked him for the job. After two extensive interviews, he made her his running mate. Racicot's job approval was around 75%, and his re-election was not in doubt. The Racicot-Martz ticket won with 79% of the vote.

As lieutenant governor, she chaired a drought advisory council and co-chaired the Montana-Alberta Boundary Advisory Commission (Montana abuts three Canadian provinces, the only state to do so). In 1999 she began running for governor. She said the state needed to be made more attractive to businesses, and supported the law to phase out the 3% business equipment tax in 2003. She emphasized a 21-point JOBS program to encourage public-private partnerships and supported Racicot's Vision 2005 program to double agricultural output. She favored five-year tax credits to high-tech companies. "I'm still a small business person. I worked the garbage route for 13 years. I took my turns at the graveyard shift."

It was a crowded field. In the primary Martz faced University of Montana law professor Rob Natelson, an anti-tax crusader who won 24% against Racicot in the 1996 primary and sponsored a 1998 ballot measure to require voter approval for new taxes and fees, which passed but was overturned by the state Supreme Court. Martz won 57%–43%; Natelson carried Great Falls, Kalispell, Missoula and the Bitterroot Valley. The Democratic primary was a contest between three term-limited statewide officials. The best known at the start was probably Attorney General Joe Mazurek. But state Auditor Mark O'Keefe organized early and spent $240,000 of his own money; he is married to Dayton-Hudson heir Lucy Dayton, whose brother Mark Dayton spent liberally of his own money and was elected to the U.S. Senate in Minnesota in 2000. O'Keefe won with 48%, to 36% for Mazurek and 16% for Secretary of State Mike Cooney.

O'Keefe served an Army paratrooper in Vietnam, came to Montana in 1977 and worked in Glacier National Park and state government. In 1983 he started a business guiding tours in and near Glacier National Park. In 1988 he was elected to the legislature; in 1992 he won the hitherto sleepy office of state auditor, and compiled a record regulating insurance companies and securities businesses. O'Keefe argued that the key to encouraging economic growth in Montana was education, and he proposed increasing state funding of public schools to 70%. He said scornfully, "I don't think she's prepared to be governor. She doesn't understand the policy implications of her proposals. She wants to further cut taxes on wealthy taxpayers and out-of-state corporations, but she doesn't realize that those cuts are going to be devastating to education, schools and kids in this state." He said he would retain the 3% business property tax and use the money for property tax relief for homeowners.

Martz attacked O'Keefe as an ambitious, big-spending liberal. "If he spends taxpayers' money the way he spends the millions of his wife, then Montana is in trouble." She claimed his economic development and education policies would require $183 million in new spending and higher taxes. She kept repeating that the Consumer Federation of America gave O'Keefe a D on insurance regulation; he blamed it on insufficient funding from Racicot and the legislature.

Polls showed an even race for much of the year. O'Keefe spent $2.2 million of his own money, and far outspent Martz. In September a group called People for Montana financed by 10 large corporations spent ads attacking O'Keefe's policies as harmful to Montana's economy. He responded, "I may indeed be their worst nightmare," and said they were supporting Martz "because she's promised to lower their biggest tax to zero—that's right, ZERO—which will put even more of our tax burden on the backs of homeowners." Racicot appeared in TV spots for Martz, and on November 1 he asked the attorney general to investigate whether O'Keefe improperly helped Montanans to invest in a venture capital fund while he also regulated securities.

The result was close, and perhaps George W. Bush's strong showing here made the difference. Martz won 51%–47%, carrying most of the state's counties. O'Keefe carried the mining towns, counties with large Indian populations, plus Missoula, Great Falls, and Helena. Martz is Montana's first woman governor (although the state elected a woman to the U.S. House as long ago as 1916) and one with not much in the way of pretention. As she said during the campaign, "I am what you see, and I will not promise you the world."

Senior Senator Max Baucus, now in his fourth term, is from a well-known Montana ranching family; his great-grandfather Henry Sieben started the huge Sieben Ranch in 1897. Baucus grew up on a 125,000-acre ranch near Helena, graduated from college and law school at Stanford, then worked at the SEC in Washington, returned home in 1971 and was executive director of the state constitutional convention in 1972. In 1973 he served in the state House. In 1974, at 32, he won the western House seat (Montana had two House seats until 1992) by walking 600 miles along highways through the district and beating three past or future holders of it (Democrats Pat Williams and Arnold Olsen in the primary and Republican Richard Shoup in the general). He won his Senate seat in 1978 by easily beating an appointed senator in the primary and a conservative Republican investment adviser in the general. He has had a moderate to liberal voting record.

With his 22 years of seniority and the retirement of Daniel Patrick Moynihan, Baucus has become the chairman of the Senate Finance Committee. He is also the second ranking Democrat on the Environment and Public Works Committee, which he chaired in 1993–94. On Finance he has taken a lead role on trade issues. He has been a leading advocate of normal trade relations with China, a potentially huge market for Montana wheat. He stresses that Montana does business all over the world: Corporate Air in Billings contracts for FedEx in the Philippines; Montana State University's TechLink is selling locust control products for plague in Madagascar. In 2000 he led the fight for approval of permanent normal trade relations (PNTR) with China. In the spring he worked against the Taiwan Security Enhancement Act as an obstacle to PNTR, and in September fought against the Thompson-Torricelli amendment, which would have penalized Chinese companies that traffic in nuclear, chemical and biological weapons and would have required an annual review of Chinese weapon proliferation. "It's too strong, too draconian and aimed too narrowly on China alone," he said; the amendment lost 65–32. PNTR was soon approved, and Baucus responded by calling, with Pat Roberts of Kansas, for an end to the trade embargo on Cuba. In March 2001 he and Sander Levin called for a free trade pact with Jordan.

On taxes, Baucus has favored some tax cuts but has had problems with Republican proposals. He worked for a tax credit for small domestic oil and gas producers in September 2000. But he opposed the Abraham amendment to suspend gas taxes in July 2000. In March 2000 he opposed the Republican marriage penalty tax cut as overly broad. In June 2000 he supported a prescription drug plan sponsored by Democrat Bob Graham and Republican Lincoln Chafee. In February 2001 he and top Finance Republican Charles Grassley said they would not act on President's Bush's campaign proposal to restructure Medicare but instead try to add prescription drug benefits to the program; "We really mean it when we say we want to work together," said Baucus of their relationship. Early in the 107th Congress, the Finance chairman and the ranking minority member co-sponsored legislation to create permanent tax deductions for student loan payments as well as a multibillion-dollar package to promote retirement savings. After being targeted by Republican ad campaigns—as well as being lobbied on a personal visit by Bush—Baucus in April 2001 was one of 15 Senate Democrats to vote for a $1.3 trillion tax cut.

Baucus has been a pivotal player on key issues. In March 1993, he opposed the Clinton proposal to raise grazing fees and impose a 12.5% mining royalty on federal land and Clinton eventually buckled. After initial qualms, he supported the Republican welfare reform in 1996. In the runup to the 1996 election, he switched and supported the balanced budget amendment. He worked successfully for education tax credits in 1998, for the first $1,000 and half the second $1,000 of college costs. In 1999 he opposed the Clinton government-invested USA accounts and proposed his own Y2Save private accounts instead. In April 2000 he spoke against proposed restrictions on dissemination of EPA data on toxic chemicals. In September 2000 he and Republican Bob Smith moved for one-year study of independent reviews by the Army Corps of Engineers. In March 2001 he was one of six Democrats to vote to kill the Clinton administration's rule on ergonomics and was one of six to support the Frist-Breaux proposal to remove the soft-money ban from McCain-Feingold.

When Baucus came to the Senate, there were six Democratic and eight Republican senators from the Rocky Mountain states; today he is one of only three Democrats from the region. The increasing conservatism of Montana voters and resentment at Clinton environmental policies have put him in an uncomfortable position. He supported the Clinton Administration moratorium on mining in the Rocky Mountain Front north of Helena. He was the only Senate Democrat to oppose a resolution calling for gun control legislation by Memorial Day 2000. Baucus was neutral on the Clinton proposal to give national monument status to the 149-mile Missouri River Breaks area, which Republican Conrad Burns strongly opposed. He sponsored a federal study of a Clinton proposal to stop anti-erosion efforts on the Yellowstone River, which Burns also opposed. In May 2000 he said a proposed ban on snowmobiles in national parks "goes too far" and is "a bit premature." On the 1998 transportation bill, he worked for a funding formula much more favorable to Montana than the House version; it gave Montana a 60% increase. He tried unsuccessfully in September 2000 to block Christopher Bond's efforts to prevent an increase in the springtime flow of the Missouri River.

Baucus has campaigned vigorously across Montana—in 1995–96 he walked 820 miles across the state and shook thousands of hands; he makes a practice of working a full day at a different job every month. He was re-elected by wide margins in 1984 and 1990, but in 1996, as the state seemed to be moving right, he was targeted by Republicans. His opponent, then-Lieutenant Governor Dennis Rehberg, called for term limits and attacked Baucus for voting for the 1993 tax increase and the assault weapons ban (he voted for the 1994 crime bill). "Max takes three sides of a two-sided issue," he said. Baucus responded that Rehberg was a "special interest" candidate backing billions in tax breaks for the rich and that the Republican balanced budget would produce "cuts" in Medicare and student loans. Polls showed Baucus in the lead throughout, hovering around 50%, and he benefited from a huge money advantage: $4.2 million to Rehberg's $1.3 million. But in the end Baucus won by just 50%–45%, his closest showing ever.

Baucus comes up for re-election in 2002. His position on the Finance Committee will likely be an asset. But he may encounter serious opposition. Some have speculated that a sexual harassment lawsuit brought against him by a former top aide may hurt him, but it was "dismissed with prejudice" in March 2001 by a federal judge.

Cook's Call   *Competitive.* Montana keeps getting tougher and tougher for Democrats—Gore won only 33% here—and early polls suggest that Baucus' support is dangerously thin. Baucus has survived strong challengers in the past, but Republicans are working hard to recruit a first-tier opponent. If they succeed, this race has the potential to become one of the closest in the cycle.

Junior Senator   Conrad Burns cuts the figure of a stereotypical Westerner, picking his teeth with a pocketknife, chewing tobacco, sporting pellets in his arm from a hunting accident, telling deadpan jokes. He grew up in northwest Missouri, joined the Marines after two years of college, worked for two airlines, then became a livestock fieldman and auctioneer and field representative of the *Polled Hereford World* and moved to Billings; when he was reassigned back east (to Des Moines), he quit so he could stay in Billings. He set up a farm news radio network, which grew from four radio stations in 1975 to 29 radio and six TV stations in 1988. Piqued at a local politician, Burns ran for Yellowstone County commissioner in 1986 and won; two years later, he ran against Democratic Senator John Melcher. Burns attacked him as "a liberal who is soft on drugs, soft on defense and very high on social programs." Melcher was hurt by a Reagan veto of a Melcher wilderness bill and by public opposition to the "let-it-burn" policy that resulted in the Yellowstone fires of summer 1988. Burns, who ended every speech with a Western "You bet!" won 52%–48%. In 1994 he faced law professor Jack Mudd, who was poorly funded; Burns won 62%–38%, the first time Montana voters have ever re-elected a Republican senator.

Burns has a solidly conservative voting record in the Senate. In 1997 he became chairman of the Communications Subcommittee, one of the key regulatory posts in Congress. There this former broadcaster has generally favored deregulation and encouragement of Internet commerce. He wrote Section 706 of the 1996 Telecommunications Act, which provided incentives for broadband data networks. In January 1999 Burns announced his "Digital Dozen" of telecom proposals. One was to force the FCC to spend more to implement Section 706; Burns argues that in states like Montana laying fiber-optic cable is uneconomic, so that he seeks more broadband capacity through regional and small telephone companies and low-power television stations. In Montana, one-third of households are satellite TV subscribers; Burns wants commercial network stations to be available on satellite TV. He has worked with Phil Gramm of the Banking Committee for a loan guarantee program for rural satellite TV; he was angry when his Montana colleague tried to get a similar measure through the Agriculture Committee. Burns's bill to replace the Intelsat monopoly with competition in the international satellite business became law in March 2000. He supported the Children's Online Privacy Protection Act included in the October 1998 omnibus budget, and wants to expand it to protect the privacy of adults. He pushed to passage a national wireless telephone 911 number, which passed in October 1999. He has pushed to allow encrypted software to be exported, to allow commercial transactions to be conducted confidentially in bills labeled PROTECT and Pro-CODE (Burns or some staffer has a penchant for snappy names). He supported a bill to provide for electronic authentication of online contracts and user identities became law in June 2000. A bill to protect low-power TV stations from losing spectrum to digital TV was put in the 2000 omnibus spending bill.

Burns has opposed the 3% "e-rate" telephone tax imposed by the FCC on long-distance calls to fund Internet access in schools, and would cut it to 1% and use general funds for the e-rate program. He is against requiring free air time to be given to political candidates and against banning liquor ads on broadcasts, though he wants broadcasters to continue not to run them voluntarily. With Ernest Hollings, ranking Democrat, he opposed Deutsche Telekom's purchase of purchase of VoiceStream in July 2000, because a foreign government owned the acquiring company. He questioned the Time Warner-AOL merger in March 2000 because he feared that it would limit instant messaging to one Internet provider.

On Montana issues Burns is often critical of environmentalists. He opposed reintroduction of grey wolves into Yellowstone National Park, estimating the cost at $1.8 million per wolf. He has blocked Democrats' plans for a Montana wilderness bill and they have blocked his. He co-sponsored Orrin Hatch's property rights bill and with Richard Shelby sponsored a sportsmen's bill of rights. He opposed Clinton proposals for national monument status for the 149-mile Missouri Breaks region. He opposed a proposed ban on snowmobiles in national parks. He says, "I think the people who live on the land, and who have their culture on the land, usually make the best decisions for the land." As the new chairman of the Appropriation Subcommittee on the Interior in the 107th Congress, Burns was looking forward to working with Bush's Interior Secretary Gale Norton.

As a Republican senator in a Republican state, Burns was expected to be in good shape for re-election in 2000. Back in 1988 he had promised to serve only two terms; in February 1999 he broke that pledge, saying that he had risen to positions where he had much to do: "I still support the idea of term limits, but I don't want to risk the position of Montana." That same month, speaking before a Montana group, he referred to Arabs as "ragheads" and had to make a quick apology—his penchant for quips had gone too far.

The next month he got a tough opponent when Brian Schweitzer, a Whitefish rancher who raises cattle, mint and dill, and used to export bull semen, got into the race. Schweitzer had some political connections—he was a Clinton appointee to the Farm Service Agency—but, driving a Dodge pickup with a cracked windshield, he effectively portrayed himself as nonpolitical: "This is an experiment to see if a farmer from Whitefish, an average guy with good ideas, who is not a politician, can go to Washington." Schweitzer once worked on irrigation projects in the Middle East, and charged that Montana had a third-world economy, exporting raw materials and exporting educated young people. Schweitzer was the first candidate in the 1999–2000 cycle to call for a prescription drug benefit, and in fall 1999 he organized the first busload of seniors to Canada to buy drugs at lower prices: "I got in my truck and drove around. I literally flagged people down. And what I found was that a lot of people were cutting their pills in half. . . . If you can get the same pill in Canada—made by an American pharmaceutical company—for half the price? I could do something about this. We could rewrite the laws and allow those drugs to be sold in the United

States." Burns responded ineptly. At one point he said that many Montanans elect to be uninsured and suggested that some seniors like to go to the doctor to have "somebody to visit with. There's nothing wrong with them."

Another issue that played a role was asbestos. There was heavy publicity about the asbestos-related illnesses and deaths in the town of Libby, where children played in tailings from a closed verimculite plant. In January 2000 a trial lawyer-financed group attacked Burns for supporting a bill that would limit compensation to those who had asbestos-related disease and shut down the giant asbestos tort cases; it showed a Libby resident accusing Burns of "standing up for the people who made me sick and killed my father." In March Burns withdrew his support of the bill and pushed for $3.5 million for a Libby hospital and $8 million for local economic development. Also a group backed by the U.S. Chamber of Commerce and an asbestos company ran ads showing relatives of an asbestos victim blaming "asbestos lawyers" for clogging the courts and preventing them from getting compensation. Later, another group backed by pharmaceutical companies ran ads saying Schweitzer favored "Canadian-style government controls on prescription medicine." On the defensive, Burns in April voted for a Democratic resolution to bar tax cuts until a prescription drug benefit was passed. In May he switched his vote at the last minute to back a Republican bill for background checks at gun shows, and in June voted with John McCain and Democrats to require disclosure by Section 527 campaign groups.

Burns outspent Schweitzer by 2–1, and in ads talked about bringing $1 billion of federal money to Montana and linked Schweitzer to Al Gore. Polls in the closing weeks showed the race close, and Burns won by only 51%–47%—a margin similar to that by which Republicans won the races for congressman-at-large, governor and secretary of state. After the election, Burns said he did not rule out running for a fourth term in 2006.

Representative-At-Large Dennis Rehberg, a Republican elected in 2000, is a rancher from Billings who raises 500 cattle and 600 cashmere goats on his family ranch and who has been involved in politics most of his adult life. After college, he worked in real estate and then on the Washington staff of Congressman Ron Marlenee. He returned to Montana in 1982 and was elected to the state House in 1984, at 29; he managed Marlenee's campaign in 1986 and Conrad Burns' first campaign for the Senate in 1988. He served as Burns' state director for two years, then was appointed lieutenant governor by Republican Stan Stephens, and was elected to that post on the ticket headed by Marc Racicot in 1992. In 1996 he ran against Senator Max Baucus. Rehberg backed term limits and promised to forego pay increases and attacked Baucus for backing the 1993 tax increase and the assault weapons ban. Baucus called Rehberg a "special interest" candidate backing billions in tax cuts for the rich and argued against Republican Medicare "cuts." Rehberg was outspent by $4.2 million to $1.3 million, but made it a close race: Baucus won 50%–45%.

In mid-1999 the House race appeared to be a close contest between incumbent Republican Rick Hill and Democratic Superintendent of Public Instruction Nancy Keenan. Keenan worked in a copper smelter and was a special education teacher in Anaconda who was elected to the state House in 1982 and as superintendent in 1988. In May Hill was criticized when he said he was a better candidate because he was married and had children and attacked the "lifestyle" of Keenan, who has never married and has no children. Hill had won re-election in 1998 by only 53%–44% and polls showed the 2000 race close. In September Hill announced he would not run because of complications from eye surgery which made it impossible for him to read. Several Republicans were mentioned as possible candidates, but Rehberg, well known from his 1996 Senate race, was the only one who ran.

This was a classic contest between a liberal Democrat and a conservative Republican, but there was also some consensus. Both decried Montana's low-wage economy. Rehberg said, "If you take a look at the statistics, indications are that no one in America works as hard and has less to show for it than Montana working families. We lead the country in the percentage of people with multiple jobs and we're close to the bottom in per capita income. That's a bad combination for Montana working families and I know moms and dads would like to spend more time with their kids." Keenan said, "Today, Montana workers are at the very bottom of the nation in average wages. Our family farmers and ranchers, our Main Street businesses, our working men and women are just struggling to survive. It is abundantly clear to me that there is much work, collaboration and cooperation to be done if we are going to get the state moving in the right direction." But it was not clear what either would do about it. Rehberg and Keenan also agreed on opposing gun control, repealing the marriage penalty and letting patients sue HMOs.

But naturally there was more discussion of their disagreements—on abortion rights, on inheritance taxes (Rehberg was for repeal, Keenan for raising the cap), a prescription drug benefit (Rehberg favored it for the needy, Keenan for all), individual investment accounts in Social Security. Rehberg favored a minimum wage increase only if it includes tax breaks for small business and a ban on soft money only if it would cover unions; he opposed taxes on Internet commerce. Keenan emphasized education, opposing vouchers and favoring small class sizes, safe and drug-free schools and more money for special education.

In February Keenan, perhaps remembering Hill's remarks, said, "I think the tone at times is going to get hysterical and vicious." Not at first: Keenan accepted Rehberg's challenge to a series of 90-minute single-issue debates. But the tone got testier, partly because of the involvement of outside groups. It has been estimated that total political spending in Montana, with less than one million people, was $20 million; organizations like the AFL-CIO, the NEA, the Chamber of Commerce and the NFIB each spent $100,000 and more in this state with seriously contested races for Senate and House; also weighing in were abortion rights supporters and EMILY's List. Some may have had it in mind that the representative from this one state would be able to cast the same vote for president as the 52 representatives from California if the presidential election ended up in the House. Rehberg ran ads with strong endorsements from Governor Marc Racicot and often showing his family, especially his two-year-old daughter. By the end of the campaign, Rehberg was accusing Keenan of being a social liberal favoring big government, more taxes and more spending, while Keenan called Rehberg a dirty politician whose positions would hurt education and deny essentials for the elderly. Spending was almost even: $2.1 million for Rehberg, $1.9 million for Keenan.

The result was close too. Rehberg won 51%–46%, almost precisely the same margin, with almost the same results county by county, by which Senator Conrad Burns beat Democrat Brian Schweitzer and by which Republican Judy Martz was elected governor over Democrat Mark O'Keefe. All the Republicans were surely helped by George W. Bush's 58%–33% margin over Al Gore. Looming over his House service is the question whether Rehberg will seek a rematch against Senator Max Baucus in 2002.

Cook's Call   *Potentially Competitive.* Although this at-large district has seen its fair share of competitive races since it was created in 1991, the increasingly conservative bent of the state means that it is getting tougher and tougher for Democrats to win here. Rehberg has a good profile for the state (he is a rancher) and has avoided stepping into controversy like his Republican predecessor Rick Hill often did. Brian Schweitzer, the Democratic nominee for the Senate in 2000, is contemplating a run in 2002 and would give Rehberg a serious run for his money.

Presidential politics   Montana, with its few electoral votes, doesn't see much of presidential candidates. Its presidential primary is in early June, far too late to affect any results. But in 1992 and 1996 Montana was closely divided, as Ross Perot got some of his highest percentages here—26% in 1992 and 13.6% in Montana in 1996, just under Maine's 14.2% for his best showing. Almost all those votes seem to have gone for Bush in 2000, as he carried the state by a wider margin than Ronald Reagan or Richard Nixon in the Republican landslide years of 1984 and 1972.

THE PEOPLE: Pop. 2000: 902,195; Pop. 1990: 799,065, up 12.9% 1990–2000. 0.3% of U.S. total, 44th largest; 90.6% White, 0.3% Black, 0.5% Asian, 6.2% Amer. Indian, 0.1% Hawaiian, 1.7% Two+ races, 0.6% Other; 2% Hispanic Origin. 4.9% Unemployment. 2000 Voting age pop.: 672,133. 2000 Turnout: 417,916; 62% of VAP. Registered voters (2000): 698,260; no party registration.

POLITICAL LINEUP: Governor, Judy Martz (R); Lt. Gov., Karl Ohs (R); Secy. of State, Bob Brown (R); Atty. Gen., Mike McGrath (D); Auditor, John Morrison (D); Super. of Public Instruction, Linda McCulloch (D); State Senate, 50 (19 D, 31 R); Senate Pres. Pro Tempore, Walter McNutt (R); Senate President, Tom Beck (R); Majority Leader, Fred Thomas (R); State House, 100 (42 D, 58 R); House Speaker, Dan McGee (R). Senators, Max Baucus (D) and Conrad Burns (R). Representative, 1 R at-large.

ELECTIONS DIVISION: 406-444-2034; **FILING DEADLINE FOR U.S. CONGRESS:** TBA.

2000 Presidential Vote

Bush (R)	240,178	(58%)
Gore (D)	137,126	(33%)
Nader (Green)	24,437	(6%)
Others	9,245	(2%)

1996 Presidential Vote

Dole (R)	179,652	(44%)
Clinton (D)	167,922	(41%)
Perot (I)	55,229	(14%)

2000 Republican Presidential Primary

Bush (R)	88,194	(78%)
Keyes (R)	20,822	(18%)
No Preference	4,655	(4%)

2000 Democratic Presidential Primary

Gore (D)	68,420	(78%)
No Preference (D)	19,447	(22%)

Gov. Judy Martz (R)

Elected 2000, term expires Jan. 2005, 1st term; b. July 28, 1948, Big Timber; home, Helena; E. MT Col.; Christian; married (Harry).

Elected Office: MT Lt. Gov., 1996–2000.

Professional Career: Field Ofc. Rep., Sen. Conrad Burns, 1989–95; Owner, Martz Disposal, 1965-present.

Office: Office of the Governor, State Capitol, Helena, 59620, 406-444-3111; Fax: 406-444-4151; Web site: www.state.mt.us.

Election Results

2000 general	Judy Martz (R)	209,135	(51%)
	Mark O'Keefe (D)	193,131	(47%)
	Other	7,926	(2%)
2000 primary	Judy Martz (R)	64,278	(57%)
	Rob Natelson (R)	48,738	(43%)
1996 general	Marc Racicot (R)	320,768	(79%)
	Judy Jacobson (D)	76,471	(19%)
	Others	7,936	(2%)

Sen. Max Baucus (D)

Elected 1978, seat up 2002, 4th term; b. Dec. 11, 1941, Helena; home, Helena; Stanford U., B.A. 1964, LL.B. 1967; Protestant; married (Wanda).

Elected Office: MT House of Reps., 1973–74; U.S. House of Reps., 1974–78.

Professional Career: Staff atty., Civil Aeronautics Bd., 1967–69; Legal Asst., Securities & Exchange Comm., 1969–71; Practicing atty., 1971–74.

DC Office: 511 HSOB, 20510, 202-224-2651; Fax: 202-224-1974; Web site: www.senate.gov/~baucus.

State Offices: Billings, 406-657-6790; Bozeman, 406-586-6104; Butte, 406-782-8700; Great Falls, 406-761-1574; Helena, 406-449-5480; Kalispell, 406-756-1150; Missoula, 406-329-3123.

Committees: *Agriculture, Nutrition & Forestry*: Marketing, Inspection & Product Promotion (Chmn.); Production & Price Competitiveness. *Environment & Public Works*: Fisheries, Wildlife & Water; Transportation & Infrastructure (Chmn.). *Finance* (Chmn.): International Trade (Chmn.); Long-Term Growth & Debt Reduction; Taxation & IRS Oversight. *Joint Committee on Taxation* (Vice Chmn. of 5 Sens.).

Group Ratings

	ADA	ACLU	AFS	LCV	CON	ITIC	NTU	COC	ACU	NTLC	CHC
2000	85	57	85	57	73	100	13	46	16	6	15
1999	95	—	100	78	75	—	7	59	4	—	—

National Journal Ratings

	1999 LIB	—	1999 CONS		2000 LIB	—	2000 CONS
Economic	75%	—	20%		80%	—	18%
Social	59%	—	40%		56%	—	43%
Foreign	87%	—	0%		72%	—	15%

Key Votes of the 106th Congress

1. Educ. Savings Accts.	N	5. Review Movie Violence	N	9. NATO War in Serbia	Y
2. Prescrip. Drug Benefit	Y	6. Gun Show Bckgrnd. Checks	N	10. Table Cuba Travel Ban	N
3. Delay Ergonomic Standards	N	7. Ban Part.-Birth Abortion	N	11. Nuclear Test-Ban Treaty	Y
4. Phase Out Estate Tax	N	8. Broaden Hate Crimes List	Y	12. Perm. Trade with China	Y

Election Results

1996 general	Max Baucus (D)	201,935	(50%)	($4,280,747)
	Dennis Rehberg (R)	182,111	(45%)	($1,358,165)
	Becky Shaw (Reform)	19,276	(5%)	
1996 primary	Max Baucus (D)	unopposed		
1990 general	Max Baucus (D)	217,563	(68%)	($2,568,899)
	Allen C. Kolstad (R)	93,836	(29%)	($747,661)
	Others	7,937	(2%)	

Sen. Conrad Burns (R)

Elected 1988, seat up 2006, 3d term; b. Jan. 25, 1935, Gallatin, MO; home, Billings; U. of MO, 1952–54; Lutheran; married (Phyllis).

Military Career: Marine Corps, 1955–57.

Elected Office: Yellowstone Cnty. Comm., 1986–88.

Professional Career: TWA and Ozark Airlines, 1958–61; Field rep., *Polled Hereford World*, 1962; Mgr., Billings Livestock Show, 1968; Radio & TV broadcaster, 1968–86.

DC Office: 187 DSOB, 20510, 202-224-2644; Fax: 202-224-8594; Web site: www.senate.gov/~burns.

State Office: Billings, 406-252-0550; Bozeman, 406-586-4450; Butte, 406-723-3277; Glendive, 406-365-2391; Great Falls, 406-452-9585; Helena, 406-449-5401; Kalispell, 406-257-3360; Missoula, 406-329-3528.

Committees: *Aging (Special)*. *Appropriations*: Agriculture & Rural Development; Energy & Water Development; Interior (RMM); Military Construction; VA, HUD & Independent Agencies. *Commerce, Science & Transportation*: Aviation; Communications (RMM); Consumer Affairs, Foreign Commerce & Tourism; Science, Technology & Space; Surface Transportation & Merchant Marine. *Energy & Natural Resources*: Energy Research, Development, Production & Regulation; Forests & Public Land Management; National Parks, Historic Preservation & Recreation. *Small Business*.

Group Ratings

	ADA	ACLU	AFS	LCV	CON	ITIC	NTU	COC	ACU	NTLC	CHC
2000	5	29	0	0	78	100	72	93	87	94	92
1999	0	—	0	0	70	—	73	88	96	—	—

National Journal Ratings

	1999 LIB	—	1999 CONS		2000 LIB	—	2000 CONS
Economic	19%	—	75%		44%	—	55%
Social	3%	—	94%		35%	—	64%
Foreign	16%	—	77%		36%	—	58%

Key Votes of the 106th Congress

1. Educ. Savings Accts.	Y	5. Review Movie Violence	Y	9. NATO War in Serbia	N
2. Prescrip. Drug Benefit	Y	6. Gun Show Bckgrnd. Checks	N	10. Table Cuba Travel Ban	Y
3. Delay Ergonomic Standards	Y	7. Ban Part.-Birth Abortion	Y	11. Nuclear Test-Ban Treaty	N
4. Phase Out Estate Tax	Y	8. Broaden Hate Crimes List	Y	12. Perm. Trade with China	Y

Election Results

2000 general	Conrad Burns (R)	208,082	(51%)	($4,337,961)
	Brian Schweitzer (D)	194,430	(47%)	($2,033,530)
	Other	9,089	(2%)	
2000 primary	Conrad Burns (R)	unopposed		
1994 general	Conrad Burns (R)	218,542	(62%)	($3,518,574)
	Jack Mudd (D)	131,845	(38%)	($1,107,591)

Rep. Dennis Rehberg (R)

Elected 2000, 1st term; b. Oct. 5, 1955, Billings; home, Billings; WA St. U., B.A. 1977; Episcopalian; married (Jan).

Elected Office: MT House of Reps., 1984–90; MT Lt. Gov., 1990–96.

Professional Career: Leg. Asst., U.S. Rep. Ron Marlenee, 1979–81; Rancher, 1982-present.

DC Office: 516 CHOB, 20515, 202-225-3211; Fax: 202-225-5687; Web site: wwwa.house.gov/rehberg.

District Office: Billings, 406-256-1019; Great Falls, 406-454-1066; Helena, 406-443-7878; Missoula, 406-543-9550.

Committees: *Agriculture* (24th of 27 R): Department Operations, Oversight, Nutrition & Forestry; General Farm Commodities & Risk Management; Specialty Crops & Foreign Agriculture Programs. *Resources* (27th of 28 R): Energy & Mineral Resources. *Transportation & Infrastructure* (34th of 42 R): Aviation; Highways & Transit; Water Resources & Environment.

Group Ratings and Key Votes: Newly Elected

Election Results

2000 general	Dennis Rehberg (R)	211,418	(51%)	($2,125,364)
	Nancy Keenan (D)	189,971	(46%)	($1,932,099)
	Other	9,132	(2%)	
2000 primary	Dennis Rehberg (R)	unopposed		
1998 general	Rick Hill (R)	175,748	(53%)	($1,228,097)
	Dusty Deschamps (D)	147,073	(44%)	($705,914)
	Others	8,730	(3%)	

★ NEBRASKA ★

"The sea of Nebraska" is what the first settlers coming west called the Platte River—not actually a single river but a braid of streams that weaves a silver chain around sandbars and islands, flooding the level floor of the great plain—a mile wide, as the saying goes, and six inches deep. Nebraska was formed in one rush of settlement in the 1880s, when its population increased from 452,000 to 1,062,000; it has increased just a bit more than that (to 1,711,000 in 2000) in the 110 years since. In the 1880s Omaha became a major railroad center, Lincoln the state capital, and farming and food products the main businesses. And for about 100 years, Nebraska remained pretty much that way. This is not what its founders intended: They hoped Nebraska would develop a diversified farming, industrial and commercial economy like Ohio, Illinois, Missouri or Minnesota. But while the 1880s were a time of plentiful rain here, the 1890s were a decade of drought, and Nebraska stopped growing. Many rural counties, and even Omaha, lost population and Nebraska exported for 100 years: 48% of Nebraskans in 1890 were children; in 2000, only 26% were. For a long time the creative energies in the economy seem to have skipped over the Great Plains and moved far to the West.

The sudden boom of the 1880s and the bust of the 1890s produced the most colorful—and atypical—politics of Nebraska's history: the populist movement and William Jennings Bryan, the "silver tongued orator of the Platte." Bryan was only 36 when he delivered the famous Cross of Gold speech at the 1896 Democratic National Convention and was swept to the Democratic nomination. He was thought so radical that Democratic President Grover Cleveland wouldn't support him, but he still won 47% of the popular vote in the first of three attempts at the presidency. Since Bryan's time, Nebraska's most notable politician has been George Norris, who led the House rebellion against Speaker Joseph Cannon in 1911, and in the 1930s pushed through the Norris-LaGuardia Anti-Injunction Act, the first national pro-union legislation, and the Tennessee Valley Authority. But most Nebraskans were repelled by the New Deal, which seemed to threaten their way of life. Although it often elects Democratic governors and senators, Nebraska over the past half-century has been the most Republican state in presidential elections.

In the 1990s Nebraska started to grow robustly for the first time in decades. Its population grew 8% between 1990 and 2000, less than the national average but more than Nebraska has grown since the 1910s. To be sure, most rural counties lost population: in tiny county seats stores are closing, across the plains farmhouses are shuttered up, small school buildings are half-empty. But metro Omaha and Lincoln grew smartly; so did the northeast corner of the state and the counties strung along the Platte River and I-80 from Omaha to Lexington. Omaha is the home base of the fast-growing ConAgra food combine, of the giant Peter Kiewit construction company and of mega-investor Warren Buffett, whose down-home wit complements his knack for picking stocks that go up hundreds of percents. The nearby Strategic Air Command base brought the world's most advanced phone system to the Omaha area 40-odd years ago; starting in the 1980s hotel chains, credit card companies and telemarketers set up operations, making this the world's leading telemarketing center. Computers and fiber optics have made Nebraska, as one mayor said, "just another suburb of Chicago." Nebraska ranks number one in combine manufacturing, with a big new plant opening in Grand Island; it is one of the leaders in meatpacking, with a big IBP plant across the Missouri River from Sioux City, Iowa; new ethanol plants are going up.

Nebraska's unemployment rate, 3.0% in 2000, is the 10th lowest in the country. Its aging population has not been producing enough young people to fill its jobs, and for the first time in a century there has been migration into the state. Latinos have been coming from Texas and Mexico to work in meatpacking factories: The Hispanic percentage rose from 2% to 6% in the 1990s, and 8% of the state's children are Hispanic. Hispanic percentages are highest in the counties around Lexington (25%), South Sioux City (23%), Scottsbluff (17%) and Grand Island (14%). Nebraska business leaders are even recruiting Nigerian professionals. Businesses and the state spent $70 million to create the Peter Kiewit Institute of Information Sciences, Technology and Engineering; First Data donated the old Ak-Sar-Ben (try spelling it backward) race track as the site for the new building. Demographically, Nebraska increasingly looks like a Rocky Mountain state, with popu-

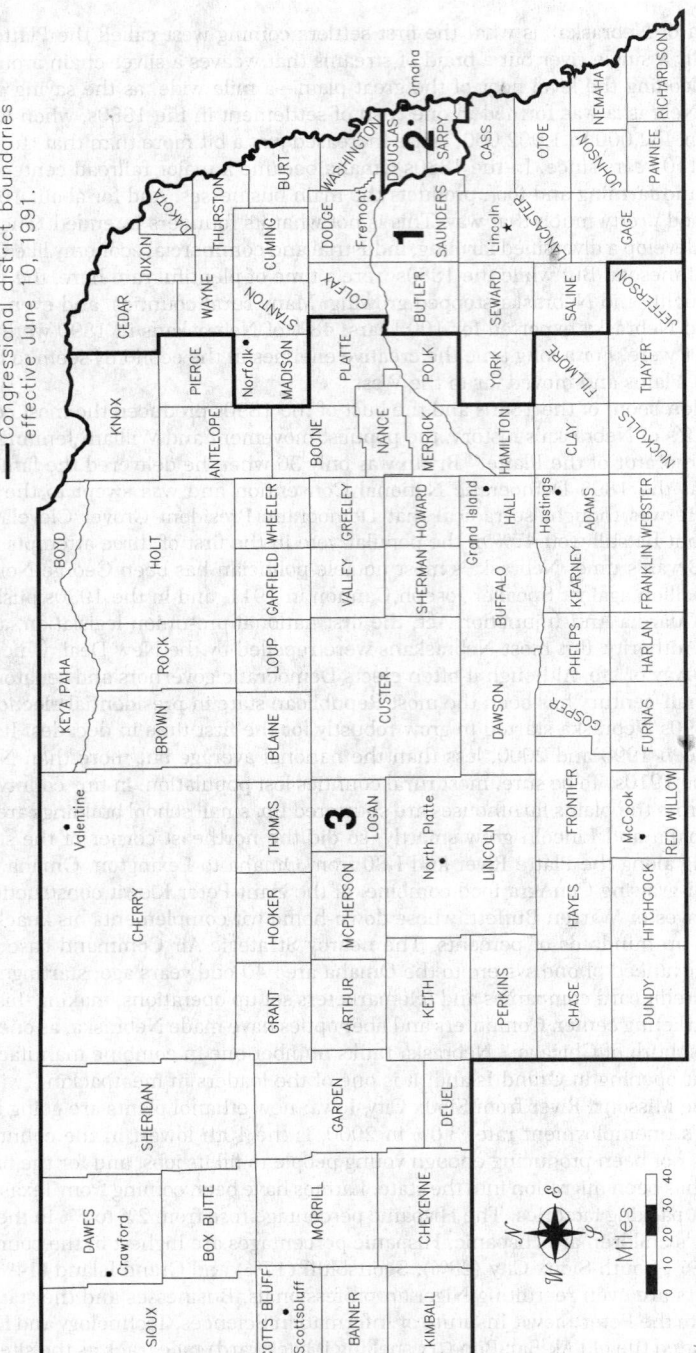

— Congressional district boundaries effective June 10, 1991.

lation concentrated in two cities and several smaller factory towns, with relatively few people spread out over farmlands.

Politically, Nebraska for the last three decades has remained a heavily Republican state that nonetheless often elects Democratic governors and senators—the same individuals. Jim Exon, elected governor in 1970 and 1974, won the first of three Senate terms in 1978; Bob Kerrey, elected governor in 1982, won the first of two Senate terms in 1988. Both retired undefeated. Ben Nelson, governor during most of the 1990s, had a tax-cutting record and some of the highest job ratings in the nation. He lost his first Senate bid to Republican Chuck Hagel in 1996 by 56%–42%. But in 2000 he ran again, and beat Republican Attorney General Don Stenberg by 51%–49%. Republicans recaptured the governorship in 1998, but Mike Johanns won by just a 54%–46% margin in a competitive race. There was nothing close about the 2000 presidential race: George W. Bush won Nebraska by a 62%–33% margin, his fourth best showing, after Wyoming, Idaho and Utah. Bush carried all 93 counties, and dipped below 60% in just seven, though two of those were the counties including Omaha and Lincoln. In the past, low farm prices and the drought which prevailed in summer 2000 would have moved the Nebraska farm vote toward the Democrats. But rural voters with their conservative cultural values were nearly unanimous for Bush, and the booming metro areas and factory towns went his way as well. Nebraska is not just a farm state any more.

Governor   Mike Johanns was elected governor of Nebraska in 1998. He was born in Iowa, grew up on a dairy farm, went to college in Minnesota, then got a law degree at Creighton University in Omaha and clerked there for one year. He practiced law in O'Neill, in the vast plains of Holt County, then in Lincoln; he was elected to the Lancaster County Board of Commissioners in 1982 and to the Lincoln City Council in 1989. These were nonpartisan offices; Johanns was a Democrat until 1988. He was elected Lincoln mayor in 1991 and re-elected without opposition in 1995; his wife is a former state senator (a nonpartisan office in Nebraska, which is unicameral). He helped establish a work empowerment program for Lancaster County inmates and a Handi-Van service for seniors in rural Lancaster County. In 1995 he began his campaign for governor and traveled all over the state, ultimately visiting all 93 counties (some with only a few hundred voters).

There was vigorous competition in the Republican primary. State Auditor John Breslow spent $2.5 million of his own money, and 2nd District Congressman Jon Christensen had strong religious conservative support. All supported Initiative 413, which would limit state spending increases based on the rate of inflation plus population growth; all favored property tax relief. There was a rush of negative ads. Breslow ran a spot showing animated peas (we are not making this up) saying that Johanns and Christensen were both tax-and-spend liberals. Then Christensen ran an ad attacking Johanns for opposing Ronald Reagan in the 1980s (he did; he was a Democrat then) and for supporting Bill Clinton's 1993 budget package and tax increase and attending the signing of the bill. Actually, Johanns had traveled with other mayors to endorse the outline of Clinton's soon-dead stimulus package and budget resolution in March 1993, but was not present at the bill signing in August 1993. A week before the May primary, Christensen's campaign distributed flyers attacking Johanns for allowing obscene and racist broadcasts to air on Lincoln's public access cable channel. In fact Johanns had tried to stop the broadcasts, but was foiled by the city council. On the Saturday before the primary, Senator Chuck Hagel called the flyer "absolute trash" and said, "Nobody in the Republican Party of Nebraska can be proud of Jon Christensen's conduct." This was a high-spending contest—Breslow spent $3.8 million altogether, Christensen $1.8 million, Johanns $1.7 million—and turnout was up 14% from the last seriously contested Republican primary for governor. Johanns won with 40% of the vote, to 30% for Breslow and 28% for Christensen. Christensen carried his congressional district by only 36%–34% over Johanns, while Johanns won with 61% in Lincoln's Lancaster County and his travels to all 93 counties paid off in rural areas. Meanwhile, the winner in the much quieter Democratic primary was Bill Hoppner, longtime aide to former Governor and Senator Jim Exon and former Governor and current Senator Bob Kerrey, who had lost the 1990 primary to Ben Nelson by only 42 votes.

Hoppner based much of his campaign on the plausible charge that Initiative 413 would make property tax relief impossible. But in early July Johanns switched and came out against 413.

Hoppner argued that Johanns couldn't be trusted to keep his word. Hagel again came to his rescue, saying Johanns "gave good, solid reasons for his decision and showed leadership by being willing to change his position." The campaign was conducted civilly, but with major differences on issues, with Johanns taking crisp conservative positions. Johanns won 54%–46%. Hoppner carried Lancaster County (always an opponent of state spending cuts) but Johanns carried the Omaha area and got nearly 60% in central and western Nebraska. At the same time, Initiative 413 lost by a wide margin.

As governor, Johanns proved to be low-key, non-confrontational, outgoing; by August 2000 he had traveled to all 93 counties again. Nebraska is the only state with a unicameral legislature, the Senate, often called the Unicam, adopted by referendum at the urging of George Norris in 1934. The Senate is capable of taking the initiative. In March 1999 it overrode a Johanns veto by a 39–7 margin and Johanns agreed to back property tax relief through a school aid increase of $90 million. They also agreed on a $1,000 incentive to adopt state wards and funding for 12 [!] more state troopers. Johanns continued his predecessor Ben Nelson's child care subsidy, despite a $30 million cost overrun, and approved more money for special education. He vetoed a moratorium on the death penalty. Johanns rattled some cages when he refused to issue a proclamation for Earth Religion Awareness Day requested by a Wiccan group; 140 angry emails and calls came in. In 2000 the Senate rejected Johann's proposals for a wilderness camp and a parole revocation facility. He vetoed 26 bills, the most in 10 years, including a measure raising elected officials' salaries and his own salary from the nation's lowest, $65,000; that veto was overridden 46–1. He got passed a $10 million bill for tax credits and entrepreneurship grants to firms that open businesses in rural areas and a voluntary meatpacking workers' bill of rights, to be published in English and Spanish. He and most Nebraskans were disappointed when the Supreme Court in *Carhart v. Stenberg* overturned the state's ban on partial-birth abortion; Johanns strongly backed the law, and opposed the use of fetal tissue obtained from elective abortions in medical research.

In September 2000, Johanns' job rating was 81% positive, a record. In early 2001 he pushed for $10 million for juvenile justice facilities and mental health treatment and called for a $51 million increase in funding for the University of Nebraska; his overall budget raised spending 7.4% a year. He said he was open to discussing a state supplement of teacher's pay, but would not allow an income tax increase. He sought to allocate two cents of the 34 cent tobacco tax for relocation of Abbott Drive in Omaha and Antelope Valley redevelopment in Lincoln. Nebraska's last three Republican governors were all defeated for second terms because of tax increases or fiscal problems. In early 2001 Johanns seemed to have no such problems and appeared in strong shape for re-election in 2002.

Cook's Call *Safe.* Bush won Nebraska by 29 points, illustrating just how difficult it is for Democrats to get a toehold here. Democrat Ben Nelson's Senate victory last year is more the exception than the rule. Making things even tougher, Johanns has not made any real mistakes and continues to be popular with voters. He should win a second term easily.

Senior Senator Chuck Hagel, elected in 1996, is now Nebraska's senior senator. Hagel grew up in the Sand Hills and small towns of Nebraska; his father died when he was 16; he became a radio DJ, then with his younger brother Tom volunteered for service in Vietnam. Promoted to sergeant because so many were dying, Chuck and Tom served together; in March 1968, when their armored personnel carrier was hit by a mine, Chuck, his body on fire, dragged Tom from the APC to safety. Chuck Hagel returned home, worked his way through the University of Nebraska, then got a job in Omaha Congressman John McCollister's office. He rose to administrative assistant; after McCollister lost a Senate race in 1976, Hagel became a lobbyist for Firestone. He got the number two position in the Reagan Veterans' Affairs Administration, but resigned after only one year. He was one of two main speakers at the 1982 groundbreaking of the Vietnam Veterans' Memorial. Then he made his great break, using all of his savings—$5,000—and starting Vanguard Cellular Systems, which became the second largest independent cell phone company in the nation; Hagel traveled on business to 60 countries and installed cell phone systems in Costa Rica, Saudi Arabia and Britain. Then he went back into government, as head of World USO and then deputy director of the 1990 G-7 Summit. In 1992 he returned to Omaha, to work in investment banking—and to prepare to run for the Senate.

In 1995 he started running for the Senate, very much the underdog. In his first ad in January 1996, he said, "I fought in Vietnam where my brother and I were wounded. I served President Reagan. I started my own business, creating hundreds of new jobs. Now I'm running for the United States Senate because we don't need more career politicians in Washington. We need lower taxes, less government, a balanced budget and more personal responsibility." His platform was solidly conservative, sometimes riskily so: he backed school choice, opposed racial quotas and preferences, backed the Freedom to Farm Act ("less government and more open markets"), opposed the estate tax. In the primary he called state Attorney General Don Stenberg a "career politician"; Stenberg hit him for living 20 years in Virginia and for contributing to Bob Kerrey's 1992 presidential campaign. Hagel won the May primary 62%–37%. In the general he faced Governor Ben Nelson, who had won re-election in 1994 by a 73%–26% margin and had a record of tax-cutting and supported the balanced budget amendment and other conservative causes. Nelson led consistently in polls, though by lower margins in the fall. Nelson raised far more PAC money—$909,000, nearly half of his campaign funds—but Hagel spent $1 million of his own money and $3.5 million altogether. Hagel resisted advice from Republican campaign committee head Alfonse D'Amato to go negative; Nelson in the last weeks charged that Hagel had engaged in fraudulent franchising practices with Vanguard. Newspapers hit Nelson, and Hagel responded, "This is a guy who lies. This is a guy who cheats. This is a guy who will do anything." Hagel won 56%–42%, carrying all but five counties.

In the Senate Hagel sought a seat on Foreign Relations and got it—because no one else wanted it. He quickly became, in David Broder's words, "the freshman who probably has made the deepest impression on his colleagues of both parties." From a historically isolationist state, but one now heavily dependent on exports, Hagel has become a leading internationalist. Trent Lott made him the lead man on the $18 billion IMF funding. Hagel negotiated with Treasury Secretary Robert Rubin and Federal Reserve Chairman Alan Greenspan and came up with conditions that were widely acceptable; in March 1998 the Senate passed his IMF measure 84–16. Hagel also took the lead among Republicans against the 1997 Kyoto global warming treaty. In July 1997 he and Democrat Robert Byrd sponsored a resolution disapproving the treaty if all nations were not subject to its emissions reductions standards; the resolution passed 95–0. Ever since Kyoto has been treated as a live issue by European leaders and American media, though it is plain that it will never be ratified by the United States.

Hagel's impulse is toward a bipartisan foreign policy, when possible. Hagel called on his military experience in 1997 to support the treaty against land mines, opposed by the Clinton administration; he spoke for the chemical weapons treaty ratified by the Senate in 1997 over the objections of Foreign Relations Chairman Jesse Helms; he voted against the Comprehensive Test Ban Treaty in October 1999 but joined Democrats and the administration in trying to prevent the vote. He supported the bombing of Serbia in spring 1999, but decried the Clinton policy of ruling out the use of ground troops. In May 2000, when most Senate Republicans wanted to set a deadline for withdrawal of U.S. troops from Kosovo, Hagel was the first senator to consult George W. Bush, even though he had been campaigning for John McCain two months before, and ask his opinion; Bush, like the Clinton administration, opposed the deadline, and the measure never passed.

In his first two years in the Senate, Hagel was a favorite of the Republican leadership. But in 1999 and 2000, on foreign policy and other issues, he grew caustically critical of the leadership, in public. The first rift came when he echoed his friend John McCain and attacked pork barrel spending in the October 1998 omnibus spending bill. In November 1998 he criticized the leadership in a letter calling for biennial budgets and a mechanism to cut pork barrel spending. After the 1998 elections he launched a campaign to head the Senate Republican campaign committee; he recalled his resistance to D'Amato's negative campaign advice, scathingly attacked "demonizing" ads and called for a more positive focus. But incumbent Chairman Mitch McConnell had the votes and won 39–13. In spring 1999, when his bill to exclude food and medicine from future economic sanctions—a popular measure in food-producing Nebraska—was dropped, he said Majority Leader Trent Lott "screwed up." When in July 1999 Lott and others put holds on the nomination of Richard Holbrooke to be UN Ambassador he said that was "an irresponsible way to govern." He called the leadership budget devices "silly" and "a charade" in fall 1999. In June 2000, he said, "If we lose the Senate, I don't think it's too difficult to imagine that we're going to change leadership."

Some of this critical attitude may have rubbed off from John McCain. He and Hagel and other Vietnam veterans in the Senate often meet together and have developed a strong bond. When McCain told him he wasn't running for president, Hagel in 1998 seemed intent on endorsing George W. Bush; but when McCain entered the race Hagel endorsed him in March 1999. He was one of only four senators who did so (the others were Fred Thompson, Mike DeWine and Arizona's Jon Kyl). Hagel traveled frequently on McCain's Straight Talk Express and made appearances for him in Iowa, New Hampshire, South Carolina and other states; in the first half of 2000 he appeared on Sunday interview programs more often than any other member of Congress but McCain. He sharply criticized George W. Bush's campaign tactics in South Carolina, but he also was one of the few who would talk back to McCain—and to whom McCain always listened. After McCain lost, Hagel was on George W. Bush's short list of vice presidential prospects. Though he did not get that nomination, the McCain campaign, plus Hagel's own work on foreign policy, made him a national figure.

Other issues Hagel has worked on often have a Nebraska angle. His bills to exclude food from economic sanctions and to retaliate against the European Union for its exclusion of hormone-treated beef obviously have appeal in a state of food and beef producers. He has a bill to require EPA to use hard scientific evidence, not just risk factors gathered from research data, in deciding whether to ban pesticides. He has sponsored bills to increase crop insurance and to better combat meth labs. He introduced a prescription drug bill to give seniors access to discounts and capping the amounts they pay, depending on their income. On campaign finance, he has differed from his great friend McCain. He came out with his own approach in May 2000, putting a $60,000 cap on but not eliminating soft money, raising the individual contribution limit from $1,000 to $3,000 (about what the $1,000 limit was worth when it was enacted in 1974) and requiring disclosure of officers of groups making independent expenditures. During the campaign finance debate in March 2001 he advanced this as an alternative to McCain-Feingold; it was attacked by Democrats as fraudulent reform and was defeated, though the disclosure section passed unanimously. Through the debate Hagel and McCain chatted amicably and their friendship emerged intact. Incidentally, one backer of Hagel's amendment was his new Nebraska Democratic colleague, and 1996 opponent, Ben Nelson.

Hagel is now a national figure, one who gets mentioned when people are asked about future presidential candidates, though in George W. Bush's first months in office that future seemed quite distant. He gets foreign policy advice from Henry Kissinger and breakfasts regularly with Alan Greenspan. In Nebraska his job approval rating in September 2000 was 76%. He is up for re-election in 2002, and seems sure to win by a wide margin. He would come up for re-election in 2008, the next time the Republican presidential nomination seems likely to be open. He may not be averse to running. Once, when Nebraska schoolchildren asked him if he would like to be president, he said, "Maybe." And he is certainly not daunted by the risks. As he said when he started running for the Senate and was asked whether he feared rejection, "I used to kid people, saying, 'What are you going to do? Send me to Vietnam?' I mean, I've been to hell, so I never saw anything I've done as a risk."

Cook's Call   *Safe.* Under special circumstances, such as an extraordinarily strong Democrat against an unusually weak Republican, Democrats can win in Nebraska. But Hagel is an uncommonly strong Republican, giving Democrats essentially no chance of defeating him.

Junior Senator   Ben Nelson, two-term Democratic Governor of Nebraska, was elected to the Senate in 2000 in his second try. Nelson grew up in McCook, the home town of Senator George Norris and novelist Willa Cather; his high school principal, Ralph Brooks, a Democrat, was elected governor in 1958, by a 50.2%–49.8% margin. Nelson went to the University of Nebraska, practiced law, served as state insurance director and headed a major insurance company. He has collected several hundred clocks and is an avid hunter of turkeys and bears. In 1990 he ran for governor, taking on former Bob Kerrey staff aide Bill Hoppner in the primary, and won by all of 42 votes. In the general he beat Governor Kay Orr 50%–49%, because she raised taxes and her political consultants failed to place many of her paid-for TV spots in October. Nelson pledged to serve "one Nebraska," spreading economic growth outward from Omaha and Lincoln, and to cut property taxes. He cut spending increases by two-thirds and used his line-item veto to cut appropriations. In 1992 he got the Senate to pass and voters to approve a lottery, with proceeds to go to creative education and environmental projects. He built more prisons, reformed workmen's comp and reorganized the human services department. Nationally, he was a leader against unfunded federal mandates. He pushed an Employment First welfare reform. He cut property taxes and reduced the income and sales taxes. He promoted a statewide "university without walls." His record won him high job ratings and re-election by a 73%–26% margin in the Republican year of 1994. When he ran for the Senate in 1996, he led in polls most of the way, but then fell behind in October and lost to Republican Chuck Hagel by a 56%–42% margin.

In 2000 Nebraska's other Senate seat came up. Everyone expected easy re-election for Senator Bob Kerrey, one of the Democratic Party's national stars—recipient of the Congressional Medal of Honor for service in Vietnam, popular governor of Nebraska in the 1980s, elected to the Senate in 1988, presidential candidate in 1992. But Kerrey is not a captive of politics. In 1986 he did not run for re-election as governor. And in January 2000 he shocked Democrats and just about everyone else when he said that he would not run for reelection that fall. Nelson, a lawyer in Omaha with an interest in a public affairs firm in Washington, was obviously the strongest possible Democratic nominee and entered the race a month later. Six Republicans ran in the May primary. The winner was Attorney General Don Stenberg, with 50% of the vote, well ahead of Secretary of State Scott Moore's 22% and agribusinessman David Hergert's 17%.

Nelson and Stenberg agreed on some issues; both were against abortion and for tax cuts. But there were significant differences in style and a considerable history of partisan differences between the two in the 1990s. Nelson never mentioned his Democratic Party affiliation, unless asked directly about it. Instead he noted, "Nebraska has always supported a bipartisan approach to things and the independent-minded approach, or we wouldn't continue to have a nonpartisan legislature." Stenberg ran as part of the "Bush-Hagel-Stenberg Team," sometimes bringing in Governor Mike Johanns as well. To which Nelson responded, "My opponent hasn't given us a single reason to vote for him apart from his party registration and the fact that he's associated with two people who are more popular than he is." Then there is style: Nelson is gregarious, has a good sense of humor, seems to enjoy campaigning; Stenberg is described as serious and studious—not a natural meeter-and-greeter. There were some serious differences on issues. Stenberg was for individual investment accounts as part of Social Security; Nelson was against. And the two sparred over which of them was responsible for Nebraska's parlous position in a lawsuit brought by the four other states in a five-state compact to build a radioactive waste disposal site in Boyd County which Nebraska regulators blocked. Nelson led always in the polls, by 24% in May and by 20% in mid-September, and raised and spent more money; the big difference here was PAC contributions, of which the Democrat received three times as much as the Republican. Nelson was helped also by active campaigning by Bob Kerrey; George W. Bush, in a close national race, couldn't afford to spend time in locked-up (for him) Nebraska.

But Nelson's poll leads narrowed in October, to 12% in the *Omaha World-Herald*, and memories went back to 1996, when Nelson's poll leads vanished altogether. This time that didn't happen, quite. Nelson won 51%–49%. Nelson carried the Omaha area 54%–46% and the Lincoln area 60%–39%; he lost the remaining half of the state 54%–46%. Nelson ran 16% ahead of Al Gore in the Omaha area, 18% in the Lincoln area and 19% ahead in the rest of the state—just enough to win. Nelson serves on the Agriculture, Armed Services and Veterans Affairs Committee; he said that the Freedom to Farm Act hasn't worked and has a bill to require ethanol be used as a fuel additive. He was one of eight Democrats to support the nomination of John Ashcroft and one of three to support Chuck Hagel's campaign finance bill. He accompanied George W. Bush to Nebraska in February—the state's second presidential visit in two months—and got a Bush nickname, "Nellie"; he wrote back, "How about something more macho, like 'Tiger' or 'Killer?' I need to preserve my image." But he didn't vote for the Bush version of the budget resolution in April 2001, but voted for the trimmed down version of $1.35 trillion in May.

Presidential politics   Over the last 50 years, Nebraska has voted more Republican in presidential elections than any other state—61.0% to Utah's second-place 60.67%. It was appropriate, perhaps, that this was the last state Bill Clinton visited as president, in December 2000. Greater Omaha usually goes Republican, while Lincoln is more closely divided; rural western counties are heavily Republican—Bush's percentages there ranged up to 86%. In the VNS exit poll no statistically significant demographic group came close to voting for Al Gore. Nebraska law allows its electoral votes to be split, with one going to the winner of each congressional district and two to the statewide winner. This has never made any difference; in 2000 the closest district was the 2nd, which Bush carried 57%–38%.

Nebraska has a presidential primary in May which once attracted attention; the whole national press followed Robert Kennedy and Eugene McCarthy out here in 1968 and took note when Frank Church won in 1976. No more: Nominations are now sewn up long before May, and Nebraska votes as unnoticed then as in November.

Congressional districting   Nebraska has had three congressional districts since the 1960s. Redistricting made only marginal changes for the 1990s, and is not likely to make major changes after the 2000 Census. The western 3rd District, which gained only 2% in population, will have to be moved several counties east; the 2nd District's portion of Cass County and 15,000 people in either Sarpy or Douglas County will have to be snipped off. No Democrat has been elected from a Nebraska district since 1992.

THE PEOPLE: Pop. 2000: 1,711,263; Pop. 1990: 1,578,385, up 8.4% 1990–2000. 0.6% of U.S. total, 38th largest; 89.6% White, 4% Black, 1.3% Asian, 0.9% Amer. Indian, 1.4% Two+ races, 2.8% Other; 5.5% Hispanic Origin. 3% Unemployment. 2000 Voting age pop.: 1,261,021. 2000 Turnout: 707,223; 56% of VAP. Registered voters (2000): 1,085,272; 392,344 D (36%), 537,605 R (50%), 155,268 unaffiliated and minor parties (14%).

POLITICAL LINEUP: Governor, Mike Johanns (R); Lt. Gov., Dave Maurstad (R); Secy. of State, John A. Gale (R); Atty. Gen., Donald Stenberg (R); Treasurer, David Heineman (R); Auditor, Kate Witek (R); Unicameral Legislature, 49 (no party affiliation); Legislature Speaker, Doug Kristensen (R). Senators, Chuck Hagel (R) and Benjamin Nelson (D). Representatives, 3 (3 R).

ELECTIONS DIVISION: 402-471-3229; **FILING DEADLINE FOR U.S. CONGRESS:** February 15, 2002.

2000 Presidential Vote
Bush (R)	433,862	(62%)
Gore (D)	231,780	(33%)
Nader (Green)	24,540	(4%)
Others	6,837	(1%)

1996 Presidential Vote
Dole (R)	363,467	(54%)
Clinton (D)	236,761	(35%)
Perot (I)	71,278	(11%)

2000 Republican Presidential Primary
Bush (R)	145,176	(78%)
McCain (R)	28,065	(15%)
Keyes (R)	12,073	(7%)

2000 Democratic Presidential Primary
Gore (D)	73,639	(70%)
Bradley (D)	27,884	(26%)
Other	3,748	(4%)

Gov. Mike Johanns (R)

Elected 1998, term expires Jan. 2003, 1st term; b. June 18, 1950, Osage, IA; home, Lincoln; St. Mary's Col., B.A. 1971; Creighton U., J.D. 1974; Catholic; married (Stephanie).

Elected Office: Lancaster Cnty. Bd. of Comm., 1982–88; Lincoln City Cncl., 1989–90; Lincoln Mayor, 1991–98.

Professional Career: Law clerk, Hon. Hale McCown, 1974–75; Practicing atty., 1975–91.

Office: State Capitol, P.O. Box 94848, Lincoln, 68509, 402-471-2244; Fax: 402-471-6031; Web site: www.state.ne.us.

Election Results

1998 general	Mike Johanns (R)	293,910	(54%)
	Bill Hoppner (D)	250,678	(46%)
1998 primary	Mike Johanns (R)	88,173	(40%)
	John Breslow (R)	65,806	(30%)
	Jon Christensen (R)	62,107	(28%)
	Others	4,229	(2%)
1994 general	Benjamin Nelson (D)	423,270	(73%)
	Gene Spence (R)	148,230	(26%)

Sen. Chuck Hagel (R)

Elected 1996, seat up 2002, 1st term; b. Oct. 4, 1946, North Platte; home, Omaha; U. of NE, B.A. 1971; Episcopalian; married (Lilibet).

Military Career: Army, 1967–68 (Vietnam).

Professional Career: Newscaster & Talk Show Host, KBON & KLNG Radio, 1969–71; Admin. Asst., U.S. Rep. John Y. McCollister, 1971–77; Mgr., Govt. Affairs, Firestone Tire & Rubber Co., 1977–80; Dpty. Admin., Veterans' Admin., 1981; U.S. Dpty. Commissioner General, World's Fair, 1982; Pres., Collins, Hagel & Clarke Inc., 1983–84; Co-founder, Dir. & Exec. V.P., Vanguard Cellular Systems Inc., 1984–87; Pres. & CEO, World USO, 1987–90; Pres. & CEO, Priv. Sector Cncl., 1990–92; Pres., McCarth & Co., 1992–95.

DC Office: 250 RSOB, 20510, 202-224-4224; Fax: 202-224-5213; Web site: www.senate.gov/~hagel.

State Offices: Kearney, 308-236-7602; Lincoln, 402-476-1400; Omaha, 402-758-8981; Scottsbluff, 308-632-6032.

Committees: *Banking, Housing & Urban Affairs*: Housing & Transportation; International Trade & Finance (RMM); Securities & Investment. *Budget. Energy & Natural Resources*: Energy Research, Development, Production & Regulation; National Parks, Historic Preservation & Recreation; Water & Power. *Foreign Relations*: East Asian & Pacific Affairs; European Affairs; International Economic Policy, Export & Trade Promotion (RMM).

Group Ratings

	ADA	ACLU	AFS	LCV	CON	ITIC	NTU	COC	ACU	NTLC	CHC
2000	0	14	0	0	36	100	75	100	88	97	100
1999	5	—	0	11	87	—	84	100	88	—	—

National Journal Ratings

	1999 LIB	—	1999 CONS		2000 LIB	—	2000 CONS
Economic	0%	—	83%		0%	—	86%
Social	18%	—	79%		22%	—	73%
Foreign	55%	—	44%		43%	—	53%

Key Votes of the 106th Congress

1. Educ. Savings Accts.	Y	5. Review Movie Violence	N	9. NATO War in Serbia	Y
2. Prescrip. Drug Benefit	N	6. Gun Show Bckgrnd. Checks	N	10. Table Cuba Travel Ban	N
3. Delay Ergonomic Standards	Y	7. Ban Part.-Birth Abortion	Y	11. Nuclear Test-Ban Treaty	N
4. Phase Out Estate Tax	Y	8. Broaden Hate Crimes List	N	12. Perm. Trade with China	Y

Election Results

1996 general	Chuck Hagel (R)	379,933	(56%)	($3,564,316)
	Benjamin Nelson (D)	281,904	(42%)	($2,159,653)
	Others	14,952	(2%)	
1996 primary	Chuck Hagel (R)	112,953	(62%)	
	Don Stenberg (R)	67,974	(37%)	
1990 general	James Exon (D)	349,779	(59%)	($2,410,097)
	Hal Daub (R)	243,013	(41%)	($1,452,681)

Sen. Benjamin Nelson (D)

Elected 2000, seat up 2006, 1st term; b. May 17, 1941, McCook; home, Lincoln; U. of NE, B.A. 1963, M.A. 1965, LL.B. 1970; Methodist; married (Diane).

Elected Office: NE Gov., 1990–98.

Professional Career: Gen. Cnsl., Central Natl. Group Insurance, 1972–74, Pres. & CEO, 1977–81; NE Insurance Dir., 1975–76; Exec. V.P., Natl. Assn. of Insurance Commissioners, 1982–85; Practicing atty., 1985–90.

DC Office: 720 HSOB, 20510, 202-224-6551; Fax: 202-228-0012; Web site: www.senate.gov/~bennelson.

State Offices: Central Nebraska, 308-345-2043; Lincoln, 402-437-5246; Omaha, 402-391-3411; Western Nebraska, 308-260-2278.

Committees: *Agriculture, Nutrition & Forestry*: Marketing, Inspection & Product Promotion; Research, Nutrition & General Legislation. *Armed Services*: Airland Forces; Readiness & Management Support; Strategic Forces. *Veterans' Affairs.*

Group Ratings and Key Votes: Newly Elected

Election Results

2000 general	Benjamin Nelson (D)	353,093	(51%)	($2,794,887)
	Don Stenberg (R)	337,977	(49%)	($1,795,402)
2000 primary	Benjamin Nelson (D)	105,661	(92%)	
	Al Hamburg (D)	8,482	(7%)	
1994 general	Bob Kerrey (D)	317,297	(55%)	($5,009,792)
	Jan Stoney (R)	260,668	(45%)	($1,821,778)

FIRST DISTRICT

The eastern half of Nebraska, between the Missouri River and the 98th parallel, was laid out in relentless Midwestern mile-square grids and became some of America's prime farmland in the single decade of the 1880s. The land here has contours just regular enough and weather just favorable enough to make farming economically viable. The plains here have completed most of their gentle decline from the Rockies to sea level; above the river bottoms the land is open to the winds. This land was settled by Yankee-descended Midwestern farmers and German immigrants. Politically it has long been Republican in national elections, but votes Democratic in seriously contested state races.

The 1st Congressional District includes 25 counties in eastern Nebraska. Omaha and its suburbs are separate, in the 2nd District; the 1st District's large city is Lincoln, the state capital and home of the University of Nebraska Cornhuskers. Lincoln, with the state government, the university and telemarketing, has been growing rapidly; it is affluent, with above-national-average incomes and unemployment that is among the lowest in the United States. In smaller towns there are significant farm equipment and meatpacking factories; population growth here was robust in the 1990s. Politically, Lincoln is fond of moderate Democrats but is still on balance Republican in national contests; the district voted 59%–36% for George W. Bush in 2000.

The congressman from the 1st District is Douglas Bereuter (pronounced *BEEwriter*), a Republican first elected in 1978. He grew up in Utica, in Seward County, graduated from the University of Nebraska, served in the Army, then got degrees in planning and public policy from Harvard. He was one of the young aides to Governor Norbert Tiemann in the late 1960s and worked as a planning consultant and part-time professor in Lincoln in the 1970s. He was elected to the Nebraska legislature in 1974, and when Congressman Charles Thone was elected governor in 1978, Bereuter ran for the House, winning the primary 52%–48% and the general 58%–42% in what was then an expensive campaign ($167,000). He was elected the same year as Newt Gingrich, but his approach was different. "Partisanship is not a compelling motive for service for me. I'm more interested in legislation." He is cautious, well-prepared, with a stately manner more typical of House members when he arrived than today.

Bereuter has been a hard-working member of the International Relations Committee, and his main cause has been eliminating trade barriers and opening up more markets for agricultural exports. He was one of the leaders in the annual fight to maintain most favored nation status for China, and for renaming the designation to the more accurate normal trade relations. He worked on the China Policy Act of 1995 and in March 1996 toned down the resolution committing U.S. troops to defend Taiwan if attacked. In 1997 he proposed granting PNTR to China as soon as it is admitted to the World Trade Organization: That proposal became permanent normal trade relations, and Bereuter played a key role in getting it through the House in May 2000. Weeks before, PNTR was far short of the votes needed for passage; it was opposed by labor unions, by critics of China's human rights record, by advocates of a harder line policy against China's menacing military buildup. Bereuter, then chairman of the Asia and Pacific Subcommittee of International Relations, had traveled widely in China and East Asia and had been in top-level discussions with its leaders; in April 1999 Chinese Premier Zhu Rongji, evidently convinced that he could play a key role on PNTR, requested a private meeting with Bereuter in Washington. In fall 1999 Bereuter began working on amendments to address PNTR opponents' concerns while still passing the measure. Also working in that direction was Sander Levin, the ranking Democrat on the Ways and Means Trade Subcommittee; he and Bereuter had met on a congressional trip to Eastern Europe in 1984, and in early 2000 they began working together. They wrote an amendment that would create a congressional-executive commission to evaluate human rights in China, impose tough protections against import surges, create task forces on prison labor exports and rule of law and provide for the entry of Taiwan into the WTO after China entered. Bereuter and Rules Committee Chairman David Dreier convinced the Republican leadership to support the Bereuter-Levin amendment and it was combined with the PNTR bill, which passed 294–136 in May 2000. Without it, PNTR would probably not have passed, as it did a few days later. Bereuter has long wanted to exclude agricultural products from economic sanctions, and he supported the June 2000 measure to allow sale of food and medicine to Cuba. On other foreign issues, he supported expanding NATO and has worked for aid programs that encourage sustainable agriculture in the poor countries of Africa. He has been a strong critic of stationing ground forces in the former Yugoslavia, expressed deep skepticism on the 1998 air strikes against Iraq and was opposed to the bombing campaign against Serbia.

Though not on the Agriculture Committee, Bereuter has come up with proposals to aid farmers. In the 107th Congress, with David Minge he sponsored a Flexible Fallow bill, to allow farmers to idle 30% of their land for higher loan rates. He had a Habitat Enhancement Rotation Option (HERO), to promote short-term reserves of land from productions. He wants to phase out MTBE and use ethanol instead. On the Banking Committee he fashioned a single-family home loan guarantee program, which has provided $10 billion in financing since 1991. He succeeded in getting out of Appropriations the first two installment on a $42 million hospital project for the Winnebago Tribe. He got an amendment keeping Norfolk eligible for an Agriculture Department housing program though its population went over the 20,000 limit in the 2000 Census. One of his favorite projects has been promoting hiking trails, notably the 6,357-mile American Discovery Trail from Cape Henlopen, Delaware, to Point Reyes, California, running from Omaha west along the Platte River Valley through Nebraska. He has also promoted bridges across the Missouri, including the Standing Bear Bridge, named after a Ponca chief, connecting Niobrara and Springfield, South Dakota, necessary for Indians to reach a South Dakota health center. When Bellevue, just south of Omaha, wanted a new bridge and Plattsmouth, in the 1st District, wanted its Missouri bridge replaced, he and the 2d District's Jon Christensen came up with a compromise: build both. He has voted to take the transportation trust fund off-budget, and in 1999 the leadership gave him a seat on Transportation and Infrastructure.

Bereuter has been re-elected easily. From a small state, popular in his district, he seemed for many years to be a logical candidate for statewide office. But he has decided four times not to run for the Senate, most recently in January 2000, when Bob Kerrey announced his retirement. One reason was that he hoped to become chairman of the International Relations Committee;

Ben Gilman, chairman since 1995, would have to step down in 2001 because of House Republicans' six-year term-limit on chairmen. When he was pondering running for Kerrey's seat in 2000, Speaker Dennis Hastert gave him "every assurance that he possibly could that he wanted me to be the next chairman." Then it seemed he would have competition from Jim Leach, term-limited as Banking chairman; Leach and Bereuter, unlike competitors for other chairmanships refused to start leadership PACs to raise money to give to Republican colleagues or campaign committees. But Bereuter was foiled in his ambition. In December 2000 Henry Hyde, chairman of Judiciary and senior to Bereuter on International Relations, made a heartfelt plea for an exemption; he had lost two years of legislating, he said, for the distasteful responsibility of handling impeachment. Many strong conservatives backed Hyde. But Hastert turned him down. At the Steering Committee's closed meeting there was feeling that Hyde would prevail in a full Conference vote, and the Steering Committee gave the International Relations chairmanship to Hyde. Bereuter, deeply disappointed, announced that he would take a subcommittee chairmanship on Financial Services, even though he had probably been the hardest working International Relations subcommittee chairman. In late January 2001 Hastert found a consolation prize. Bereuter was appointed to the Intelligence Committee, on which he had served before. The rule allowing only one tour of duty on that committee was waived, and Bereuter was named vice chairman. Chairman Porter Goss had already announced he would retire from Congress in 2002; it was assumed that Bereuter was promised he would become chairman in January 2003. Then he could serve four years and be eligible to be chairman of International Relations when Hyde's six years was over. Of course, all this assumes that Republicans would continue to be the majority party in the House after the next three elections—a far from certain proposition. But even in the minority, Bereuter can look forward to a long stretch of important responsibility and serious legislating on foreign policy.

   Cook's Call   *Safe.* This Lincoln-based district has a solid Republican core that ensures 22-year incumbent Bereuter remains a safe bet for re-election year after year. He should have no trouble winning again in 2002.

THE PEOPLE: Pop. 2000: 581,488; Pop. 1990: 526,291, up 10.5% 1990–2000. 92.1% White, 1.4% Black, 1.6% Asian, 1.2% Amer. Indian, 0.1% Hawaiian, 1.3% Two+ races, 2.2% Other; 4.2% Hispanic Origin.

2000 Presidential Vote			1996 Presidential Vote		
Bush (R)	142,347	(59%)	Dole (R)	114,563	(50%)
Gore (D)	86,907	(36%)	Clinton (D)	87,712	(38%)
Nader (Green)	10,208	(4%)	Perot (I)	25,974	(11%)
Others	2,426	(1%)			

Rep. Douglas K. Bereuter (R)

Elected 1978, 12th term; b. Oct. 6, 1939, York; home, Cedar Bluffs; U. of NE, B.A. 1961, Harvard U., M.C.P. 1966, M.P.A. 1973; Lutheran; married (Louise).

Military Career: Army, 1963–65.

Elected Office: NE Legislature, 1974–78.

Professional Career: Urban planner, U.S. Dept. of HUD, 1965–66; Div. Dir., NE Econ. Devel. Dept., 1967–68; Dir., NE Office of Planning, 1968–70.

DC Office: 2184 RHOB 20515, 202-225-4806; Fax: 202-225-5686; Web site: www.house.gov/bereuter.

District Offices: Fremont, 402-727-0888; Lincoln, 402-438-1598.

Committees: *Financial Services* (4th of 37 R): Financial Institutions & Consumer Credit; Housing & Community Opportunity; International Monetary Policy & Trade (Chmn.). *International Relations* (4th of 26 R): Europe. *Permanent Select Committee on Intelligence* (Vice Chmn. of 11 R): Intelligence Policy & National Security (Chmn.). *Transportation & Infrastructure* (23d of 42 R): Highways & Transit; Water Resources & Environment.

Group Ratings

	ADA	ACLU	AFS	LCV	CON	ITIC	NTU	COC	ACU	NTLC	CHC
2000	10	21	0	36	88	90	52	90	64	55	73
1999	35	—	16	38	42	—	49	92	62	—	—

National Journal Ratings

	1999 LIB	—	1999 CONS		2000 LIB	—	2000 CONS
Economic	39%	—	59%		45%	—	54%
Social	42%	—	56%		43%	—	55%
Foreign	40%	—	60%		25%	—	69%

Key Votes of the 106th Congress

1. Patient Bill of Rights	N	5. Bar RU-486 $ for FDA	Y	9. NATO War in Serbia	N
2. Accelerate Min. Wage	N	6. Display 10 Commandments	Y	10. Perm. Trade with China	Y
3. Strike Ban on Ergo. Stnd.	N	7. Gun Show Bkgrnd. Checks	Y	11. Debt Relief for 3rd World	N
4. Ovrd. Estate Tax Veto	N	8. Ban Part.-Birth Abortion	Y	12. Drop Cuba Econ. Embargo	N

Election Results

2000 general	Douglas K. Bereuter (R)	155,485	(66%)	($380,036)
	Alan Jacobsen (D)	72,859	(31%)	($107,256)
	Others	6,354	(3%)	
2000 primary	Douglas K. Bereuter (R)	unopposed		
1998 general	Douglas K. Bereuter (R)	136,058	(73%)	($214,449)
	Don Eret (D)	48,826	(26%)	($14,746)

SECOND DISTRICT

Omaha, the commercial metropolis of Nebraska, the largest city on the Great Plains north of Kansas City and west of Minneapolis, got its start from government: Abraham Lincoln picked it as the eastern terminus of the Union Pacific railroad, from which emerged the stockyards and livestock exchange that made it a top livestock town. Over the years, Omaha filled up with cattle hands from the West and European immigrants, especially Germans and Czechs; it developed fine civic institutions from the Joslyn Art Museum to the Boys Town, founded by Father Flanagan in 1917, the subject of a 1938 movie and today still innovative and thriving in its promotion of traditional values. Though a major city by the 1880s, Omaha has remained small enough (and famous on Wall Street as the place where Warren Buffett lives and works) to be readily comprehensible; you don't feel distant, physically or psychologically, from the other side of town, and you usually know people from a broader range of backgrounds than you would in a large homogeneous neighborhood within a big metropolitan area. The older, less affluent part of Omaha is near the river and Iowa; to the west, the city has been quietly booming, with affluent neighborhoods and new shopping malls; downtown and the riverfront are in a construction boom, the Tower at First National Center going up, the tallest structure between Minneapolis and Denver. Omaha's economy has been changing. It still has many processors of food products, like the hard-charging ConAgra company, and the giant Peter Kiewit construction firm; but it is also the nation's telecommunications center, handling 20 million '800' and '900' calls a day and employing more than 20,000 people in over two dozen telemarketing centers. Its civic institutions are thriving as well: an opera company, museums, a children's theater, a zoo with the country's largest indoor jungle west of Chicago.

The 2d Congressional District is metropolitan Omaha: Douglas County with Omaha and its western suburbs; Sarpy County with suburbs to the south and the old Strategic Air Command headquarters at Offutt Air Force Base; and a sliver of Cass County just to the south. Politically, Omaha has long had competitive politics, with Democrats strong on the south side around the stockyards and the northeast and Republicans strong in the area west of 72d Street. But as Omaha and Nebraska have boomed, they have become more Republican, and increasingly it is the Republican primary that decides elections here.

The congressman from the 2d District is Lee Terry, a Republican elected in 1998. Terry grew up in Omaha, and became interested in politics at 14 when his father, TV anchor Lee Terry Sr., ran for the House in 1976; a confrontational conservative, he lost 55%–45% to 31-year-old Democrat John Cavanaugh. Terry Sr. remained a prominent local commentator on politics; Terry Jr. went off to college and law school, practiced law, and was elected to the Omaha Council from an affluent west side district in 1991, at 29. There he worked to stop teenage cruising on Dodge Street and collaborated with private enterprise to build the Moylan-Tranquillity IcePlex skating rink at 125th Street and West Maple Road. He contemplated not running for re-election in 1997, but stayed on.

Then in September 1997, 2d District Congressman Jon Christensen announced he was running for governor—a surprise, since he had touted his seat on Ways and Means and had been appointed the National Republican Congressional Committee's recruiting director. Christensen had strong support from Christian conservatives and a record of odd political utterances and bizarre controversy; he ended up finishing third in the May 1998 primary after a last-minute flyer critical of Mike Johanns was attacked as unfair by Senator Chuck Hagel and his two House colleagues. Terry announced at the IcePlex. He decried frivolous lawsuits, the Department of Education and "corporate welfare," and said he would apply the lessons he learned in city government and devolve power to local government.

Terry had primary competition from Brad Kuiper, owner of a pest control business in west Douglas County, and Steve Kupka, former chief of staff to Mayor Hal Daub (who served four terms in the House in the 1980s) and an official in the Reagan-David Stockman OMB. The contrast between the three was less on issues—they were all for lower taxes and against abortion— than on style and approach. Kuiper, with less money than the other two, targeted religious conservatives and emphasized cultural issues—much as Christensen had done here and was doing in the gubernatorial primary. Kupka assembled Washington endorsements and, spending the most money, went on the attack. He criticized Terry for not opposing a 1991 garbage fee (actually, Terry favored the legislature giving the city authority to impose the fee, but voted against it) and said Terry had added $1 million to the city budget over two years.

Terry's approach was more in line with the consensus-minded mood that pervaded the country in 1998. He stressed his work building consensus on the Council, and his ads trumpeted that and his support of lower taxes, including a flat tax with mortgage and charity deductions. He counted on strong support from his council district, which included 20% of Republican primary voters, and from his greater name identification. The dynamic was much the same as in the governor's race, in which Mike Johanns won with 40% to 30% for John Breslow and 28% for Christensen. The results in the 2d District primary were almost identical: 40% for Terry, 30% for Kupka and 26% for Kuiper.

The general election was anticlimactic. Democrats were competitive in this district the last four times it has been open, in 1970, 1976, 1980 and 1988, and won in 1976 and 1988. Terry won 66%–34% against Democrat Michael Scott. In April 1999 he reneged on his promise to serve only three terms.

In Washington Terry did not get on the committees he wanted and did not sponsor major legislation. He attracted attention in October 1999 when he purposely bundled Clinton tax increases and user fees into one $19 billion bill and brought it to the floor; it lost 419–5. In April 2000 he did it again, with $116 billion; that lost 420–1. He proposed to abolish all questions asked by the Census on the long form except for those on the short form. Between 1999 and 2000 he switched on mandatory trigger locks for guns, supporting them in 2000: "probably the correct middle ground after a year of reflection." Much of his focus was one local matters, like making sure impact aid continues; it provided 20% of the school budget of Bellevue, impacted by Offutt Air Force Base. He complained that Agriculture Department investigators lied to the owners of three Omaha stores who were fined for illegally selling Mexican avocadoes. He threatened to cut off funding of the INS unless he got a straight answer on whether it would replace its overcrowded Omaha office; a day later the agency wrote that it planned to buy land and build a facility "on an expedited basis" in the next fiscal year. The two cases are testimony to the impact of immigration on the Omaha area.

Terry had surprisingly vigorous opposition in the 2000 general from Democratic state Senator Shelley Kiel, who campaigned strenuously and spent $345,000. But Terry won 66%–31%. In

January 2001 he got a seat on the Commerce Committee; evidently he has given up on getting a seat on Ways and Means. Redistricting must clip the district back a bit.

Cook's Call   *Safe.* Although this district gave Bush his lowest winning percentage in the state, it is by no means fertile territory for Democrats. Bush still won this district with 57% and Terry rolled up a 66% win himself. This Omaha-based district grew the fastest of any in the state and must drop about 20,000 people. With Republicans controlling the process (and Bush winning the state by 29% in 2000), it is hard to see how Democrats gain any advantage here.

THE PEOPLE: Pop. 2000: 594,207; Pop. 1990: 526,573, up 12.8% 1990–2000. 82.9% White, 9.9% Black, 1.7% Asian, 0.6% Amer. Indian, 0.1% Hawaiian, 1.8% Two+ races, 3% Other; 6.1% Hispanic Origin.

2000 Presidential Vote
Bush (R)	131,700	(57%)
Gore (D)	89,014	(38%)
Nader (Green)	8,502	(4%)
Others	2,063	(1%)

1996 Presidential Vote
Dole (R)	116,889	(52%)
Clinton (D)	84,667	(38%)
Perot (I)	18,934	(9%)

Rep. Lee Terry (R)

Elected 1998, 2d term; b. Jan. 29, 1962, Omaha; home, Omaha; U. of NE at Lincoln, B.A. 1984; Creighton U., J.D. 1987; Methodist; married (Robyn).

Elected Office: Omaha City Cncl., 1991–98, Pres., 1995–96.

Professional Career: Practicing atty., 1988–98.

DC Office: 1513 LHOB 20515, 202-225-4155; Fax: 202-226-5452; Web site: www.house.gov/terry.

District Office: Omaha, 402-397-9944.

Committees: *Energy & Commerce* (31st of 31 R): Commerce, Trade & Consumer Protection; Environment & Hazardous Materials; Telecommunications & The Internet.

Group Ratings
	ADA	ACLU	AFS	LCV	CON	ITIC	NTU	COC	ACU	NTLC	CHC
2000	5	21	0	14	85	94	64	95	96	85	100
1999	5	—	16	13	59	—	69	88	83	—	—

National Journal Ratings
	1999 LIB	—	1999 CONS		2000 LIB	—	2000 CONS
Economic	30%	—	64%		39%	—	60%
Social	19%	—	79%		21%	—	78%
Foreign	31%	—	66%		12%	—	78%

Key Votes of the 106th Congress
1. Patient Bill of Rights	N	5. Bar RU-486 $ for FDA	Y	9. NATO War in Serbia	N
2. Accelerate Min. Wage	N	6. Display 10 Commandments	Y	10. Perm. Trade with China	Y
3. Strike Ban on Ergo. Stnd.	N	7. Gun Show Bkgrnd. Checks	N	11. Debt Relief for 3rd World	N
4. Ovrd. Estate Tax Veto	Y	8. Ban Part.-Birth Abortion	Y	12. Drop Cuba Econ. Embargo	N

Election Results
2000 general	Lee Terry (R)	148,911	(66%)	($844,465)
	Shelley Kiel (D)	70,268	(31%)	($345,347)
	Others	7,101	(3%)	
2000 primary	Lee Terry (R)	unopposed		
1998 general	Lee Terry (R)	106,782	(66%)	($868,153)
	Michael Scott (D)	55,722	(34%)	($94,939)

THIRD DISTRICT

West of Grand Island, Nebraska is wheat and livestock country. For miles on end you can see nothing but rolling brown fields, sectioned off here and there by barbed wire fences, and in the distance a grain elevator towering over a tiny town and its miniature railroad depot. The winds and rain and tornadoes that come suddenly out of the sky remind you that the original settlers likened this part of the country to an ocean and thought themselves in their wooden wagons almost as helpless as passengers at sea in a rowboat. Settlers passed through here on the Oregon Trail in the 1840s, then set down roots in the 1880s, but the rain they hoped for fell too unreliably, and wheatlands gave way to pasture and open range. It is a beautiful but hard land, exacting much from its people, as the novels of western Nebraska's Willa Cather make poignantly clear. Dozens of small counties today have fewer people than they did in 1940 or 1900. And the frontier may even be moving back. In November 2000 140 head of pure-bred Texas longhorn cattle were driven from the Fort Niobrara National Wildlife Refuge to Fort Robinson State Park: It was the last true Texas longhorn drive in Nebraska, made necessary because the refuge needed more room for elk, bison and bighorn sheep.

The 3d Congressional District has 31% of the state's people spread out over 82% of its acreage. Except along the interstate and around Scottsbluff, the 3d has been losing population for decades; these 66 counties had 608,000 people in 1940, and gained virtually no people during the 1990s, having 536,000 people in 2000. Geographically and politically, the 3d District is where the Midwest becomes the West. For years people here welcomed farm subsidies even as they angrily opposed federal interference. Politically, it is heavily Republican and sometimes ornery: George Bush and Bob Dole easily carried the district in the 1990s, and in 1992 Ross Perot got more votes than Bill Clinton. George W. Bush carried the district 71%–25%.

The congressman from the 3rd District is Tom Osborne, a Republican elected in 2000, a man who had never run for office before but who was better known than most congressmen are after serving 20 years. He grew up in Hastings and excelled at basketball, football and track in high school and at the University of Nebraska. Osborne graduated in 1959 and played professional football for three years in Washington and San Francisco. Then Osborne returned to NU to work as a graduate assistant in the football program. He stayed for 36 years, working first under coach Bob Devaney, then becoming coach himself in 1973; he also got a master's degree and doctorate in educational psychology. He was head football coach for 25 years, at first compared unfavorably to Devaney, but over the whole period exceedingly successful. He won three national championships before retiring in 1998; he had perfect seasons in 1994, 1995 and 1997; his record was 87–11–1 in the 1990s and 60–3 over his last five years. After retiring he was inducted into the College Football Hall of Fame in 1999; the three-year waiting period was waived, for only the second time. At the ceremony he mused on his experiences. "Some of the players tried you, stressed you. But it's gratifying to see them at 22 or 27 or even 35 do a U-turn. Whether or not they end up doing well, they were still your players. They're still your young men, and you have a responsibility to them, no matter what happens."

In March 1999, 3rd District Congressman Bill Barrett announced that he was retiring; he had served 10 years and had compiled a solidly conservative record. In January 2000 Osborne announced he was running. He had been urged to run for the Senate seat being vacated by Bob Kerrey, but declined; he said he did not want to commit to serve the six-year term. It was apparent from the beginning that Osborne was going to win. Nevertheless, he campaigned hard. He traveled 60,000 miles and made more than 650 scheduled stops during the campaign; he often drove alone hundreds of miles to events to save the cost of paying a staffer to drive. At first he was uncomfortable shaking hands and asking for votes, but enjoyed talking to people in small groups; Nebraskans were delighted to meet him. He won the May primary with 71% of the vote against two candidates with solid political backgrounds, former Nebraska Republican Chairman and now secretary of State John Gale and state Board of Education member Kathy Wilmot. His Democratic opponent, Rollie Reynolds, was a distant relative who called Osborne "my hero" and "everybody's hero." This was a positive campaign all around, with relatively low levels of spending. Osborne refused to take PAC money; Reynolds got $250 from PACs, though one wonders why. Osborne won 82%–16%.

After the election, Osborne, as promised, held eight meetings around the state at which 16 farmers were elected to meet in December at Kearney and come up with a farm policy that was a consensus of eight regions in the state. After they produced their policy, Osborne said, "Now we'll see where this meshes with the people in Washington. We're not going to reformulate a national farm policy, but we may be able to move people in our direction." He also pledged to complete the Heartland Expressway and to exclude food exports from embargoes. He said the U.S. has a "very bad" energy policy, and should make more use of ethanol and soy diesel fuel: "It's a no-brainer." He had varying luck in Washington. Apprised that a freshman would be unlikely to get on Appropriations, he sought seats on the Agriculture, Education and Resources Committees, where he can work on reauthorization of the Freedom to Farm Act and promote the kind of mentoring programs he has worked on in Nebraska. But in the House freshman office lottery, he drew number 39 of 39, and found himself in Room 507 of the Cannon House Office Building, known as "Siberia."

Redistricting added territory to the already physically huge 3rd District, which grew much less rapidly than the rest of the state. This will only give Osborne a few hundred more miles to drive.

Cook's Call   *Safe.* Even if Tom Osborne, the former coach of the University of Nebraska football team, were not one of the most recognized and respected figures in the state, he would still have no trouble holding onto this sprawling district. The most Republican district in the state (Bush won here by 46%), any Republican could hold onto this seat without breaking a sweat. The new congressional map, completed in early June, moved Saline and York counties from Bereuter's 1st CD into the 3rd district.

THE PEOPLE: Pop. 2000: 535,568; Pop. 1990: 525,521, up 1.9% 1990–2000. 94.3% White, 0.3% Black, 0.5% Asian, 0.8% Amer. Indian, 1% Two + races, 3.1% Other; 6.2% Hispanic Origin.

2000 Presidential Vote			1996 Presidential Vote		
Bush (R)	159,815	(71%)	Dole (R)	132,015	(59%)
Gore (D)	55,859	(25%)	Clinton (D)	64,382	(29%)
Nader (Green)	5,960	(3%)	Perot (I)	26,370	(12%)
Others	2,350	(1%)			

Rep. Tom Osborne (R)

Elected 2000, 1st term; b. Feb. 23, 1937, Hastings; home, Lemoyne; Hastings Col., B.A. 1959; U. of NE, M.A. 1963; U. of NE, Ph.D. 1965; Methodist; married (Nancy).

Military Career: Army Natl. Guard, 1960–66.

Professional Career: Pro Football Player, Natl. Football League, 1959–62; Football Coach, U. of NE, 1962–97, Head Coach 1973–97.

DC Office: 507 CHOB 20515, 202-225-6435; Fax: 202-226-1385; Web site: www.house.gov/osborne.

District Offices: Grand Island, 308-381-5555; Scottsbluff, 308-632-3333.

Committees: *Agriculture* (22d of 27 R): Conservation, Credit, Rural Development & Research; Livestock & Horticulture. *Education & the Workforce* (26th of 27 R): 21st Century Competitiveness; Education Reform. *Resources* (25th of 28 R): Water & Power.

Group Ratings and Key Votes: Newly Elected

Election Results

2000 general	Tom Osborne (R)	182,117	(82%)	($484,797)
	Roland E. Reynolds (D)	34,944	(16%)	($12,857)
	Others	5,032	(2%)	
2000 primary	Tom Osborne (R)	52,436	(71%)	
	Jonh A. Gale (R)	12,553	(17%)	
	Kathy Wilmot (R)	9,127	(12%)	
	Other	26	(0%)	
1998 general	Bill Barrett (R)	149,896	(84%)	($160,275)
	Jerry Hickman (Lib)	27,278	(15%)	

★ NEVADA ★

A pyramid rising from the desert, New York skyscrapers across the street from the sphinx-like lion, a not-too-miniature Eiffel Tower and the gondolas of Venice, a flaming pirate ship next door to Roman ruins: this is what you see as the plane approaches the runway at Las Vegas. All these surrealistic monuments, and miles of spreading subdivisions, are set in one of North America's most forbidding landscapes, a bowl-shaped desert valley rimmed by barren peaks. Nature provided nothing here to encourage human settlement—Las Vegas is far from the lodes of gold and silver which attracted the first settlers of Nevada. Today's Nevada is wholly the creation of post-industrial, post-modern man. Its existence as a state is happenstance: The discovery of the Comstock Lode silver mine in 1859—$500 million worth was taken out in 20 years—brought settlers, and Abraham Lincoln's Republicans made it a state in 1864, even though Nevada did not meet the population requirement for statehood, because Republicans thought they needed an extra three electoral votes. But Nevada was not really a viable state; its population dropped by the early 20th Century, and in the early 1930s there were only 91,000 Nevadans and the state government was about to go bankrupt. So Nevada decided to roll the dice. The state reduced its residency requirement for divorce to six weeks and legalized gambling. Catering to what most Americans considered sin—casinos, pawnshops, divorce mills, quick wedding chapels, even legal brothels—turned out to be good business. Nevada has been America's fastest-growing state since 1960; in the 1990s it grew 66%, from 1.2 million to 2 million

Las Vegas, a mere spot on the map when gambling was legalized, now is the center of a metro area of more than 1.5 million; Henderson, on the road southeast toward Hoover Dam, was the fastest-growing American city in the 1990s. Reno, known as "the biggest little city in the world," now has, together with Lake Tahoe and the capital of Carson City, another 470,000. Gaming—the Nevada word for gambling—generates most of this growth: Las Vegas's 124,000 hotel rooms (as of early 2001) house more than 35 million visitors who spend $31.5 billion a year, Reno's nearly 5 million tourists spend almost $4 billion, and not just in casinos and hotels but in increasingly upscale restaurants and malls. They come from all over the United States and from foreign countries, especially Japan. Though at least one form of gambling is now available in 47 states, Las Vegas has made itself a destination; it has twice as much convention exhibit space as the number two city, Chicago. This is a service economy: of the more than 1 million people employed, nearly 90% produce services rather than goods. The 6.25% gambling receipts tax generates enough revenue so that Nevada has no income, corporate or inheritance tax, and the cost of living is low; housing is inexpensive, and many people moving here from California in the 1990s couldn't find a house that cost as much as the one they sold.

From mining to gaming, Nevada has been a second chance state, a place for outcasts to succeed and misfits to rebound. Nine out of every 1,000 Nevadans get divorced each year, the highest rate in the nation. Nevada has been an avenue of success for ethnic groups who faced roadblocks elsewhere. The four owners of the Comstock Lode—MacKay, Fair, Flood, O'Brien—were Irishmen; the first big hotel on the Las Vegas strip, the Flamingo, was built in 1946 by Jewish gangster Bugsy Siegel, later gunned down in his Beverly Hills home; most of the big casinos were owned by mobsters until Howard Hughes—a different kind of outcast—bought them up in the

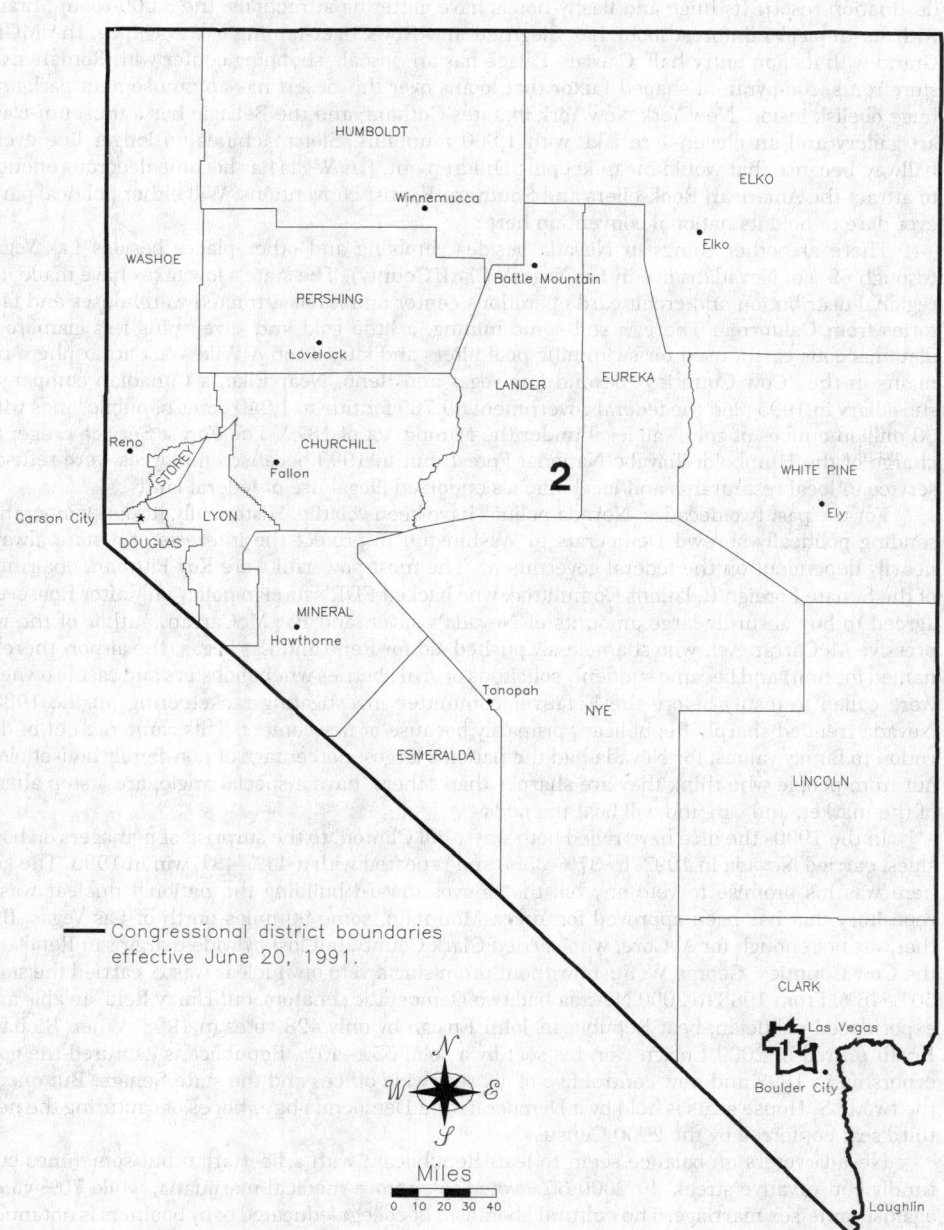

Congressional district boundaries
effective June 20, 1991.

Miles
0 10 20 30 40

late 1960s. In the 1990s Latinos moved here in large numbers, attracted by the plentiful jobs; Nevada was 20% Hispanic in 2000. For years, the casinos catered to older tastes in entertainment, from Frank Sinatra to girlie shows, and depended on gamblers for all their trade. But in the early 1990s, as riverboat and Indian casinos opened in many states, Las Vegas became a family-friendly destination resort. Its huge and flashy hotels have glittering attractions: the 3,000-room Mirage with its tropical rainforest lobby has Siegfried and Roy's tiger-taming extravaganza, the MGM Grand with its lion entry-hall, Caesars Palace has an upscale shopping center with Roman-style storefronts, the pyramid-shaped Luxor that looms over this desert has an amusement park and huge obelisk inside, New York New York imitates Gotham, and the Bellagio has a museum-class art gallery and an eleven-acre lake with 1,000 fountains. Slot machines no longer line every hallway, because that would mean keeping children out. Las Vegas has become decorous enough to attract the American Booksellers and Southern Baptist conventions. Will either political party ever dare to hold its national convention here?

There are other things in Nevada besides gambling and other places besides Las Vegas (though 69% of Nevadans live in Las Vegas's Clark County). The state's low taxes have made it a regional distribution and credit card operations center and it has attracted warehouses and factories from California. There is still some mining, a little gold and silver, plus less glamorous diatomaceous earth, used for swimming pool filters and kitty litter. A Wild West atmosphere remains in the "Cow Counties" beyond Las Vegas and Reno. Near Elko, a Canadian company's subsidiary in 1995 paid the federal government $9,765 for title to 1,949 acres of public lands with 30 million ounces of gold—all legal under the Mining Act of 1872. The Forest Service ranger in charge of the Humboldt-Toiyabe National Forest quit in 1999 because employees were refused service in local restaurants and local officials endorsed illegal use of federal lands.

For the past two decades, Nevada politics have been volatile. Historically, it was Democratic, sending politically shrewd Democrats to Washington to protect the interests of a state always heavily dependent on the federal government. The most powerful were Key Pittman, chairman of the Senate Foreign Relations Committee, who backed FDR's foreign policy only after Roosevelt agreed to buy absurdly large amounts of Nevada's silver, and Pat McCarran, author of the repressive McCarran Act, who shamelessly pushed aid for Reno and Las Vegas (the airport there is named for him) and became suddenly solicitous of civil liberties when mobsters and casino owners were called to testify before the Kefauver committee investigating racketeering. In the 1980s Nevada trended sharply Republican, primarily because of newcomers. This came not out of devotion to family values, for Nevada had the nation's largest percentage of non-family households, but from people who think they are sharper than others, have a special angle, are a step ahead of the market, and can and will beat the odds.

In the 1990s the dice have rolled both ways. Bill Clinton, to the surprise of managers on both sides, carried Nevada in 1992, by 37%–35%, and repeated with a 44%–43% win in 1996. The key here was his promise to veto any bill that moves toward building the national nuclear waste repository that has been approved for Yucca Mountain, some 90 miles north of Las Vegas. But that was not enough for Al Gore, who carried Clark County, but lost by wide margins in Reno and the Cow Counties; George W. Bush, without promising a veto on nuclear waste, carried the state 50%–46%. From 1988 to 2000 Nevada had two Democratic senators, but Harry Reid, an able and experienced politician, beat Republican John Ensign by only 428 votes in 1998. When Richard Bryan retired in 2000 Ensign won his seat by a solid 55%–40%. Republicans captured the governorship in 1998 and now control five of six statewide offices and the state Senate. But one of the two U.S. House seats is held by a Democrat, and Democrats have hopes of capturing the new third seat conferred by the 2000 Census.

Nevada voters on balance seem to lean Republican, with a libertarian but sometimes culturally conservative streak. In 2000 65% voted to approve medical marijuana, while 70% voted against same-sex marriage. The cultural liberalism of college-educated baby boomers is not much in evidence here: One reason that Gore lost the state is that he didn't win the margins here that he did in other states among unmarried people without children, people who never attend church and people with graduate degrees. This is the libertarianism not of Bob Dylan but of Wayne Newton (who has an unprecedented 10-year contract on the Strip). Another unique feature of

Nevada politics: since 1975 voters can vote for "none of these candidates." "None" finished second in the 1998 Democratic primary for lieutenant governor and has occasionally finished first in races for minor offices, but the law is toothless: even when there is a plurality for "none of the above," the top-running candidate wins.

Special issues are more important in Nevada than political parties. Republican Kenny Guinn may have succeeded Democrat Bob Miller as governor, but that did not produce any major shift of policy: both were supported strongly by the gaming industry. And the unions which have successfully organized Las Vegas casinos and hotels have no more been challenged by Guinn than they were by Miller. Indeed, a local court cooperatively removed a payroll protection initiative from the ballot in 1998. Nevada politicians worked together to blunt the recommendations of the National Gambling Impact Study Commission, which in a June 1999 report called for more research and treatment programs for problem gamblers, a moratorium on gambling expansion, standardizing the minimum gambling age at 21, banning Internet gambling, and banning political contributions to state and local campaigns by gambling companies. But the commission also said that the vast majority of Americans "experience no measurable side effects related to their gambling, or they choose not to gamble at all," and it noted the industry's powerful economic impact on "sleepy backwaters" and "once-fading tourist areas." "The verdict is in and the accused has been exonerated," said American Gaming Association President Frank Fahrenkopf, former chairman of the Republican National Committee.

The other raging Nevada issue is the proposed Yucca Mountain nuclear waste repository. It was chosen by Congress in 1987, when the Nevada delegation was unusually weak: Harry Reid was in his first year in the Senate and Republican Chic Hecht seemed to be facing sure defeat. The plan is to bury the waste deep within the mountain, 1,300 feet above the water table, in reinforced steel containers in a 1,400-acre maze with 100 miles of storage tunnels. Many in Nevada argue that rainwater will flush the radioactive material out of the depository and into the water table; a December 1998 Energy Department study found no evidence that would happen. But Nevada opinion is strongly opposed to the repository. Nevadans in Congress have tried to stop the project and, with crucial help from Bill Clinton's vetoes, have succeeded in delaying it. But outside of Nevada support for Yucca Mountain has accumulated as nuclear waste has piled up in 72 sites in 31 states, and the key issue now is whether to build a temporary repository at the Nevada Test Site, next to Yucca Mountain; the expectation is that once the waste is in Nevada, Congress will never vote to ship it elsewhere. Idaho Senator Larry Craig, whose state agreed to temporarily take government nuclear waste, got 63 votes in 1995, 65 in 1997 and 64 in 2000—just a couple of votes short of a veto-proof majority—for the temporary Nevada site, and similar measures have won veto-proof margins in the House. But in June 1998 Speaker Newt Gingrich pulled it off the calendar to help the John Ensign's Senate candidacy. In April 2000 a veto override on a measure to ship waste starting in 2007 failed in the Senate by 64–35. George W. Bush in 2000 pledged not to place a temporary storage site in Nevada. But Bush refrained from promising to veto a permanent repository, saying that his decision would be based on "sound science and not politics." The permanent site, under existing law, is not supposed to open until 2010, but the political battles are far from over. Other states will still want to be relieved of their nuclear waste, while Nevadans will argue that it is safer to keep the waste at nuclear plant sites over the next 100 years than to transport it: a strategy to postpone the controversy for a century.

Governor   Kenny Guinn was elected governor of Nevada in 1998 in his first race for elective office. He grew up in the Central Valley of California, due west of Las Vegas but separated by Death Valley and Mount Whitney; he majored in physical education at Fresno State and got an education doctorate at Utah State. In 1964 he moved to Las Vegas to work for the Clark County School District; he became school superintendent in 1969. Later he went to work for the S&L that became PriMerit Bank and became chairman in 1987, then went to Southwest Gas Corporation and became chairman in 1993. In 1994 he spent a year as interim president of the University of Nevada at Las Vegas, then recovering from a basketball scandal, and donated his salary to the schools scholarship fund. In the process he accumulated much civic renown. In February 1996 he started running to replace term-limited Governor Bob Miller; immediately he picked up much of the support from the gaming industry Miller had, though he is a Republican and Miller a Democrat. He was christened "The Anointed One" by political analyst Jon Ralston.

But if the Anointed One had widespread support, he also had opposition. In the September 1998 primary he faced Aaron Russo, a former Hollywood producer who moved to Las Vegas in 1996. Russo refused casino money, leaving a $1,000 check from Donald Trump on his desk ostentatiously uncashed, and called for increasing the 6.25% tax on casinos' gross. Guinn retaliated by playing in his ads a video Russo had made in 1994 when he formed a Ross Perot-like Constitution Party; it showed Russo in long hair and a dangling earring ranting in protest at politicians. Russo got within 7% in an August poll, but Guinn won handily, 58%–26%.

The Democratic nominee was Las Vegas Mayor Jan Laverty Jones. She had become locally famous in the 1980s as a costumed pitchman in television commercials for her then-husband's car dealerships; then she ran for mayor in 1991, and won. In 1994 she had run against Governor Bob Miller in the primary, and lost 63%–28%. Jones announced on filing day, only a few months after breast cancer surgery, and while still undergoing chemotherapy and radiation; she was utterly open about this and showed great vigor. Jones boasted about hiring hundreds more policemen, a 9% property tax rebate in 1997, and creating a MASH homeless shelter and the Fremont Street Experience. In July 1998 she was brought before the state ethics committee on charges of favoring political allies in a zoning dispute, her seventh such charge since 1994; in August 1998 she was absolved, as she had been in each case before. The general election campaign was not very eventful. Guinn charged Jones with raising property taxes; Jones charged Guinn with raising gas rates. Russo endorsed Jones. Guinn won 52%–42%, carrying the Las Vegas and Reno areas by almost identical majorities and winning by 59%–34% in the Cow Counties.

Nevada's 63 citizen-legislators meet only four months every two years; they get $60 for postage and have no staff except secretaries. Nonetheless, the 1999 legislature proved productive. It passed Guinn's proposal for Millennium Scholarships, to allow B students in core subjects to go to college almost for free; that got 40% of the state's tobacco settlement money, with 60% going to health programs. Guinn succeeded in privatizing the state workmen's comp insurer and strengthening the ethics code. The legislature expanded charter schools and the concealed weapons law; it banned job discrimination against gays, required students to say the Pledge of Allegiance and declared that parents have a right to spank children. It also provided tax breaks for those who purchase and display fine art: casino owner Steve Wynn keeps his museum-quality collection on display in a casino gallery. Guinn came out for a sales tax on Internet transactions. He and the legislature backed electricity deregulation in 1999, but in 2001, facing high prices because of California's botched deregulation, he said deregulation should be abandoned for the rest of his term and called for price caps on electricity. He sharply opposed a teachers' union proposal to place a 4% tax on business; it was yanked off the ballot by the courts.

Guinn pledged to do anything he could to stop the storage of nuclear waste at Yucca Mountain or a temporary site in Nevada. In September 2000 he called for banning the import of water into the state to build Yucca Mountain, with fines of $1 million a gallon. In January 2001 he proposed a $5 million fund to lobby against the project and persuade other states that it would be dangerous to transport nuclear waste over their roads.

Guinn succeeded in passing a prescription drug program for seniors much like the one Republicans passed in the House in 2000. But only one insurer bid on the contract, and in 2000 Democratic Congresswoman Shelley Berkley said it "crashed and burned." Guinn responded that she was "mean-spirited" and said he would "do everything I can to work against her." In 2001 he moved to expand coverage. The Anointed One comes up for reelection in 2002.

Cook's Call   *Safe.* Although Democrats are competitive here, Guinn has not left them many openings to challenge him next year. He should have little trouble winning reelection.

Senior Senator   Harry Reid, a Democrat first elected in 1986, has held high office in Nevada for most of the last 30 years. He grew up in Searchlight, Nevada, in the scorching desert south of Las Vegas, and hitchhiked 40 miles to high school in Henderson, where his civics teacher and boxing coach Mike O'Callaghan became his political mentor. Reid was elected to the Assembly in 1968, at age 28; in 1970 Callaghan was elected governor and Reid, running separately, was elected lieutenant governor. In 1974 he came within 624 votes of beating Paul Laxalt in the race for senator, lost for mayor of Las Vegas in 1976, and then became head of the Gaming Commission from 1977–81—as sensitive a post as any in Nevada. In 1982, when Nevada got two House seats for the first time and Congressman-at-Large Jim Santini ran for the Senate, Reid ran in the Las Vegas-based 1st District and won. Laxalt retired in 1986 and Reid ran for the Senate again; his opponent turned out to be Santini, who had switched parties at the last minute and was running as a Republican. Reid's ads depicted him as David to Santini's Goliath, and he won 50%–45%.

Reid is now the Democratic whip in the Senate, the number two man in the party's leadership, a constant presence on the floor and one of the reasons why Senate Democrats have managed to be a major force. He is soft-spoken and frank, far from an eloquent debater; he has managed to develop good working relations with Republican leaders while remaining a tough and persevering partisan. He strongly supported Al Gore in 2000 (he was one of the few members of Congress to support Gore's campaign for president in 1988) and after George W. Bush appeared at Bob Jones University, Reid and Bob Torricelli introduced a resolution to condemn the institution; at the Democratic convention he was ready with plenty of harsh criticism of Bush. He has a conservative record on some issues: He is against abortion, was one of the few Democrats to vote for the Gulf war resolution, and has opposed environmental groups consistently on mining issues. But he is also a party man: for the 1993 budget and tax increase, for the 1994 crime bill with its gun control provisions, casting a decisive vote against the balanced budget amendment in 1993. After the 1994 election, he said, "We have to all swallow a little bit of our pride and go toward the middle." In December 1998, after months of rounding up votes, he was elected minority whip, even after winning re-election by only 428 votes.

On national issues, Reid has taken some distinctive positions: he worked for the Taxpayers Bill of Rights in 1988 and the IRS reform of 1998; he has demanded prosecution of IRS officials who encouraged or tolerated collection quotas; he wants to remove J. Edgar Hoover's name from the FBI Building in Washington. He has sponsored an air travelers' bill of rights and an increase in fines for passengers who assault flight attendants. He has worked to speed up the timeline for changing export controls on computer equipment and launched the Senate Democrats' High-Tech Working Group. Although Reid opposes abortion, he stalled the adjournment of the Senate in October 1998 to protest the killing of an amendment to provide contraceptive insurance to federal workers, and he co-sponsored a resolution disapproving of George W. Bush's reinstatment of the Mexico City policy to deny funding for international organizations that pay for abortions.

Although he has opposed environmental groups on mining issues, Reid has opposed other Republican-backed riders. On the Environment and Public Works Committee, he co-sponsored a brownfields bill to increase annual federal funding for the cleanup of contaminated former industrial sites from $92 million to $200 million; this passed the Senate 99–0 in April 2001. With Nevada colleague John Ensign, he sponsored a bill to provide $750 million annually to help small communities build water-treatment systems to reduce arsenic levels. He has strongly opposed steps to build the 1987-approved Yucca Mountain permanent nuclear waste repository in Nevada and to build a temporary storage site in the state. He assembled enough votes to uphold Bill Clinton's veto of a temporary site in 1997 and then, with Nevada colleague Richard Bryan, prevented a vote in 1998 and 1999; when the bill passed in April 2000 there were again enough votes to prevent an override. "We have 34 votes, and we will always have 34 votes," he said triumphantly. George W. Bush in 2000 pledged not to support a temporary site, but Bush also refrained from promising to veto a permanent one, saying that his decision would be based on "sound science and not politics."

Reid has worked on a host of other Nevada issues. He has strongly supported the gaming industry, and in December 2000 he and Ensign announced that their number one priority was to oppose the bill, backed by John McCain and others, to prohibit betting on college and amateur sports. Nevada is the only state to allow this form of wagering. In 2000 Reid supported giving permanent resident status to immigrants who have been in the United States illegally since 1986, with a five-year rolling registry; Nevada's population in 2000 was 20% Hispanic. He pushed through a "source tax" amendment barring states from taxing the state pensions of retirees who move to another state—as many have to Nevada. Through two years of negotiation he produced an agreement on allocating water from Lake Tahoe and the Truckee River between Nevada and

California; Reid got the Pyramid Lake Paiute Indians to agree to return their fisheries to the state for $25 million, plus $40 million in economic aid. He got $121 million for the Western Shoshones to settle their land claims. He got a grant for a Suicide Prevention Center at the University of Nevada's medical school—Nevada's suicide rate is the nation's highest—and opposed lowering the blood alcohol level for DWIs—a measure disliked by owners of hotels and bars. He co-sponsored with Dianne Feinstein the Lake Tahoe cleanup law passed in 2000. The Senate also passed Reid's bill to let Clark County buy 6,500 acres of federal land in the Ivanpah Valley to build a second airport.

Despite all this, Reid has never won a Senate election with more than 51% of the vote. He was elected in 1986 by 50%–45%. In the 1992 primary he won 53%–39% over Charles Woods, a businessman badly wounded and scarred in World War II; in the general he beat rancher Demar Dahl 51%–40%. In the 1998 race his opponent was 1st District Congressman John Ensign, who had run and won high-spending races in the Las Vegas area in 1994 and 1996. Reid in his feisty way attacked Ensign harshly as an "extremist" who called environmentalists "socialists," and would gut Social Security. "You send Ensign to the Senate, you send nuclear waste to Nevada," he proclaimed; an assertion Ensign vehemently disputed. He argued that Reid voted for higher taxes in the Senate. But Reid, the father of five and grandfather of nine, ran an ad showing his wife saying, "For me, Harry Reid's greatest accomplishment is being a devoted husband and father who helped raise five exceptional children. His being a senator is great, but having the love and respect of your family is the ultimate accomplishment."

This was Nevada's most expensive Senate campaign ever. Reid put ads up on the air in April 1998, Ensign in May. Eventually they spent $4.9 million and $3.5 million respectively; both were supported by the gaming and mining industries. The League of Conservation Voters and the Sierra Club spent $400,000 on ads to help Reid. The Foundation for Government spent $300,000 against Reid because of his opposition to triple-trailer trucks. The AFL-CIO ran a "ground war" campaign costing perhaps $300,000. That in many observers' views made the difference, but Reid believes he won because of his inroads with Republican voters in Reno and Washoe County from his work on local projects; he lost the usually Republican area by only 48%–46%. Ensign did better in the Cow Counties, winning 59%–36%. In Las Vegas' Clark County, both candidates' home base, Reid won 53%–44%. The election night tally showed Reid ahead by 459 votes; Ensign called for a recount, and it turned out that the Washoe County ballots had been misprinted, preventing some from being read by machines. The hand count there took weeks, and Ensign finally conceded December 9, with Reid ahead by 428 votes.

After the election Reid reshuffled his local staff. But Nevada is still attracting hundreds of thousands of newcomers, and he may have a serious challenge again in 2004, possibly from Congressman Jim Gibbons. In the meantime he remains a formidable member of the Senate.

Junior Senator John Ensign was elected to the Senate in 2000, in his second try for the office. He succeeded moderate Democrat Richard Bryan, who retired in 2000 after a long career in politics: Bryan had been elected to the Nevada legislature in 1968, won the first of two terms as governor in 1982 and defeated Republican Senator Chic Hecht in 1988 by 50%–46%. Ensign grew up in northern Nevada and moved to Las Vegas at 16. For a time his mother was a change girl at a Reno casino, supporting three children with no help from her ex-husband. Then she married Mike Ensign, who became a top executive at Circus Circus and is now head of the Mandalay Resort Group. John Ensign graduated from Oregon State in 1981 and went to veterinary school at Colorado State, where he became a born-again Christian. He built a successful veterinary practice in Las Vegas, managed a family hotel, became involved in civic affairs and at his wife's suggestion became active in The Promise Keepers. Disturbed at trends in national life, they decided he would run for the House in 1994, against 1st District incumbent James Bilbray. This was the more Democratic of Nevada's then two seats, and Bilbray was a 8-year incumbent. But 1994 was also a Republican year, and with the help of Ensign's stepfather's connections in the gaming industry he was able to raise substantial funds. On election night, Bilbray claimed victory, but when the votes came in Ensign had won by 1,436 votes. In the House Ensign compiled a generally conservative voting record and got a seat on the Ways and Means Committee. In the summer of 1996 he and colleague David Camp persuaded Newt Gingrich to separate the welfare and Medicaid issues and present Bill Clinton with a welfare reform bill, which he signed 11 weeks before the election; Ensign can reasonably claim to be one of the fathers of the 1996 Welfare Reform. He was re-elected in 1996 by 50%–44%.

Ensign decided to run against Senator Harry Reid in 1998. This was a hard-fought, high-spending race, targeted by both national parties and fought with intensity by the candidates; Reid spent $4.9 million and Ensign $3.5 million. Reid attacked Ensign harshly as an "extremist" who called environmentalists "socialists," and would gut Social Security. "You send Ensign to the Senate, you send nuclear waste to Nevada," he proclaimed. Ensign responded, "Does Reid think that Dick Bryan is going to give up the fight? Bryan's a Democrat who works with Republicans, and I'm a Republican who works with Democrats." Reid ran behind only 48%–46% in Reno's usually Republican Washoe County; Ensign ran well ahead in the Cow Counties, 59%–36%. In Las Vegas' Clark County, both candidates' home base, Reid won 53%–44%. The election night tally showed Reid ahead by 459 votes; Ensign called for a recount, and it turned out that the Washoe County ballots had been misprinted, preventing some from being read by machines. The hand count there took weeks, and Ensign finally conceded December 9, with Reid ahead by 428 votes.

Then just two months later, in February 1999, Bryan announced that he would not run for re-election in 2000. Ensign, who had said he would not run against Bryan, announced his candidacy the next day. Democrats tried to enlist their strongest candidate, Bob Miller, who had just completed eight years as governor, but he preferred to remain in the private sector in Las Vegas. Then Attorney General Frankie Sue Del Papa launched her candidacy; an April poll showed Ensign with a narrow 45%–40% lead, but he was much farther ahead in money: $1.1 million to $250,000 by the end of June. In September Del Papa abruptly withdrew from the race, as she had withdrawn from the 1998 race for governor, citing difficulties in fundraising; her bad relations with Las Vegas unions did not help. Democratic efforts to recruit Brian Greenspun, owner of the *Las Vegas Sun*, failed. What appears to have happened is that the gaming industry, developers and other leading funders in Las Vegas, who had supported Miller and then, in the local term, anointed Republican Kenny Guinn to succeed him, decided that Ensign was on the road to victory and that it might suit their interests to have one Democratic and one Republican senator.

That left the Democratic banner in the hands of Ed Bernstein, a personal injury lawyer who had run ads on Las Vegas TV for years. Bernstein put in $1.1 million of his own money and said, "I will stand up for working families against the special interests"; his ads attacking Ensign signed off with the phrase, "He goes too far." Bernstein's main issues were prescription drugs for seniors and abortion. The candidates engaged in six debates; one highlight came when Ensign quizzed Bernstein about a water project in northern Nevada of which Bernstein obviously had never heard. Naturally both candidates promised to fight nuclear waste storage in Nevada; Ensign was careful to return a contribution from a Yucca Mountain contractor. In a September interview with a Pahrump TV station, Ensign was asked whether an 11-year-old rape victim should be allowed to have an abortion, and answered, "I believe that helping them find a home for the baby is the best thing for them psychologically. And that's why, even with my own daughter, I would do the same. . . . And I would hope that's exactly the choice she would choose." The national Democrats responded with an ad that said, "Ensign even said an 11-year-old rape victim and her family should have no choice." Ensign ran an ad with his wife and Governor Kenny Guinn's wife charging that Democrats were misrepresenting his views. Bernstein managed to tighten the race for a while, but Ensign ended up winning by a large 55%–40%. Ensign carried Las Vegas and Clark County 51%–45%, Reno and Washoe County 58%–35% and the Cow Counties 68%–27%.

Ensign and Reid, rivals in 1998, quickly became cooperative colleagues. In December 2000 they announced that their first priority was blocking the move by John McCain and Sam Brownback to prohibit betting on college and amateur sports—they argue that sports books are well regulated by Nevada state authorities—and Ensign tried to gut the bill in the Commerce Committee in May 2001 but his amendment to do so failed 10–10. They also seemed ready to work against the Yucca Mountain waste repository and, fortified with a pledge from George W. Bush, against any temporary nuclear storage site in Nevada. Ensign announced that he would "continue to consult with Senator Reid" on appointments of federal judges and the U.S. attorney in Nevada—a closer level of cooperation than in many other states. In March 2001 Ensign sought to add "high-growth grants" to the Bush education program; Clark County school enrollment has been growing at 6% per year. Ensign's seat does not come up until 2006.

Presidential politics   In the 1940s Nevada was a Democratic state; in the 1960s it was divided much as the nation was, voting narrowly for John Kennedy in 1960 and Richard Nixon in 1968. In the 1980s it was heavily Republican, twice giving more than 60% to Ronald Reagan and 59%–38% for George Bush in 1988. In the 1990s it voted twice for Bill Clinton; critical to his margin was his pledge to veto bills moving nuclear waste to Yucca Mountain or temporary storage sites. But the basic Republican proclivity of the state produced a 50%–46% margin for George W. Bush, who promised only to block a temporary storage site. Nevada, like other Rocky Mountain states, received a big influx of white middle-aged Californians in the 1990s, an exodus that made California more Democratic and the Rocky Mountain states more Republican.

Nevada's late March presidential primary has attracted little attention; efforts to join a proposed Western states primary set for Friday, March 10, 2000, were defeated by Democrats in the Nevada House in June 1999.

Congressional districting   Nevada has had two congressional districts since the 1980s Census; the 2000 Census gave it a third seat for 2002. Redistricting in the past has been simplicity itself: the 1st District is the inner part of Clark County (the "hole in the bagel," says Congresswoman Shelley Berkley), politically marginal and won by both parties in the 1990s; the 2d District is the rest of the state, heavily Republican. For 2002 the demographic realities seem pretty clear. Clark County, with 69% of the state's population, is entitled to two whole districts and a small part of a third, which would also include the rest of the state. The issue—despite some proposals to create three districts each containing part of Clark County—is how to divide up the Las Vegas area.

Control of redistricting is divided between the Democratic state Assembly, Republican state Senate and Republican Governor Kenny Guinn. But in Nevada things are not always decided on party lines. In 1996 a bipartisan group was assembled to support Guinn for governor—"the anointed one." In early 2001 a similar group seemed to have been formed to support 28-year-old Clark County Commissioner Dario Herrera, a Democrat, for Congress; a fundraiser invitation included the names of leading gaming leaders, developers, labor union heads, Hispanic and black politicians, Las Vegas Mayor Oscar Goodman, Attorney General Frankie Sue Del Papa, etc., etc. An obvious aim here is to meet the political demands of Hispanics, who formed 20% of Nevada's population in 2000, and are obviously going to be an important part of the electorate in years to come.

The 2001 map ended up with a new "T" shaped 3d District centered just below Las Vegas, taking in mostly suburban territory. The Republican and Democratic Party registration is about dead even here, and the Hispanic population is 16%—the same as in the 2d District but not nearly as high as the 1st District's 28%. Republican state Senator Jon Porter, who helped shape the district, would be a formidable candidate against Herrera should he decide to run. Berkley's home fell outside of the newly drawn 1st District, but in June 2001 she had already sold her old house and was looking for a new one in the 1st.

THE PEOPLE: Pop. 2000: 1,998,257; Pop. 1990: 1,201,833, up 66.3% 1990–2000. 0.7% of U.S. total, 35th largest; 75.2% White, 6.8% Black, 4.5% Asian, 1.3% Amer. Indian, 0.4% Hawaiian, 3.8% Two+ races, 8% Other; 19.7% Hispanic Origin. 4.1% Unemployment. 2000 Voting age pop.: 1,486,458. 2000 Turnout: 613,360; 41% of VAP. Registered voters (2000): 898,347; 372,889 D (42%), 374,196 R (42%), 151,262 unaffiliated and minor parties (17%).

POLITICAL LINEUP: Governor, Kenny Guinn (R); Lt. Gov., Lorraine Hunt (R); Secy. of State, Dean Heller (R); Atty. Gen., Frankie Sue Del Papa (D); Treasurer, Brian Krolicki (R); Controller, Kathy Augustine (R); State Senate, 21 (9 D, 12 R); Senate Pres. Pro Tempore, Lawrence Jacobsen (R); Majority Leader, William Raggio (R); State Assembly, 42 (27 D, 15 R); Assembly Speaker, Richard Perkins (D). Senators, Harry Reid (D) and John Ensign (R). Representatives, 2 (1 D, 1 R).

ELECTIONS DIVISION: 775-684-5705; **FILING DEADLINE FOR U.S. CONGRESS:** May 15, 2002.

2000 Presidential Vote

Bush (R) 301,575 (50%)
Gore (D) 279,978 (46%)
Nader (Green) 15,008 (2%)
Others 12,409 (2%)

1996 Presidential Vote

Clinton (D) 203,974 (44%)
Dole (R) 199,244 (43%)
Perot (I) 43,986 (9%)
Others 17,130 (4%)

Gov. Kenny Guinn (R)

Elected 1998, term expires Jan. 2003, 1st term; b. Aug. 24, 1936, Garland, TX; home, Las Vegas; Fresno St. U, B.A. 1957, M.A. 1958; Utah St. U., Ph.D. 1970; Non-denominational; married (Dema).

Professional Career: Planning Specialist, Clark Cnty. Schl. Dist., 1964–69; Superintendent, Clark Cnty. Schl. Dist., 1969–78; Nevada Savings & Loan, 1978–80; Pres. & COO, PriMerit Bank, 1980–85; CEO, 1985–87; Pres. & COO Southwest Gas Corp., 1987–93; Chairman & CEO 1988–93; Interim Pres., U.N.L.V., 1994–95.

Office: Executive Chambers, Capitol Bldg., Carson City, 89710, 775-687-5670; Web site: www.state.nv.us.

Election Results

1998 general	Kenny Guinn (R)	223,892	(52%)
	Jan Laverty Jones (D)	182,281	(42%)
	Others	27,457	(6%)
1998 primary	Kenny Guinn (R)	76,953	(58%)
	Aaron Russo (R)	34,251	(26%)
	Lonnie Hammargren (R)	13,410	(10%)
	Others	1,956	(1%)
1994 general	Bob Miller (D)	200,026	(53%)
	Jim Gibbons (R)	156,875	(41%)
	Others	22,775	(6%)

Sen. Harry Reid (D)

Elected 1986, seat up 2004, 3d term; b. Dec. 2, 1939, Searchlight; home, Searchlight; S. UT St. Col., A.S. 1959, UT St. U., B.S. 1961, George Washington U., J.D. 1964, U. of NV, 1969–70; Mormon; married (Landra).

Elected Office: NV Assembly, 1968–70; NV Lt. Gov., 1970–74; U.S. House of Reps., 1982–86.

Professional Career: Practicing atty., 1969–82; Henderson City Atty., 1964–66; Chmn., NV Gaming Comm., 1977–81.

DC Office: 528 HSOB, 20510, 202-224-3542; Fax: 202-224-7327; Web site: www.senate.gov/~reid.

State Offices: Carson City, 775-882-7343; Las Vegas, 702-388-5020; Reno, 775-686-5750.

Committees: *Majority Whip. Aging (Special). Appropriations*: Defense; Energy & Water Development (Chmn.); Interior; Labor, HHS & Education; Transportation. *Ethics (Select)* (Chmn.). *Indian Affairs.*

Group Ratings

	ADA	ACLU	AFS	LCV	CON	ITIC	NTU	COC	ACU	NTLC	CHC
2000	90	29	100	86	54	70	12	40	12	6	46
1999	90	—	100	67	51	—	5	35	12	—	—

National Journal Ratings

	1999 LIB	—	1999 CONS	2000 LIB	—	2000 CONS
Economic	90%	—	0%	84%	—	11%
Social	56%	—	42%	54%	—	44%
Foreign	62%	—	29%	62%	—	34%

Key Votes of the 106th Congress

1. Educ. Savings Accts.	N	5. Review Movie Violence	N	9. NATO War in Serbia	Y
2. Prescrip. Drug Benefit	Y	6. Gun Show Bckgrnd. Checks	Y	10. Table Cuba Travel Ban	Y
3. Delay Ergonomic Standards	N	7. Ban Part.-Birth Abortion	Y	11. Nuclear Test-Ban Treaty	Y
4. Phase Out Estate Tax	N	8. Broaden Hate Crimes List	Y	12. Perm. Trade with China	N

Election Results

1998 general	Harry Reid (D)	208,650	(48%)	($4,939,010)
	John Ensign (R)	208,222	(48%)	($3,490,256)
	Others	18,918	(4%)	
1998 primary	Harry Reid (D)	unopposed		
1992 general	Harry Reid (D)	253,150	(51%)	($3,259,802)
	Demar Dahl (R)	199,413	(40%)	($471,371)
	Others	43,333	(9%)	

Sen. John Ensign (R)

Elected 2000, seat up 2006, 1st term; b. Mar. 25, 1958, Roseville, CA; home, Las Vegas; OR St. U., B.S. 1981, CO St. U., D.V.M. 1985; Christian; married (Darlene).

Elected Office: U.S. House of Reps. 1994–98.

Professional Career: Veternarian, 1987–93; Gen. Mgr., Gold Strike Hotel, 1991–93.

DC Office: 364 RSOB, 20510, 202-224-6244; Web site: www.senate.gov/~ensign.

State Offices: Carson City, 775-885-9111; Las Vegas, 702-388-6605; Reno, 775-686-5770.

Committees: *Aging (Special). Banking, Housing & Urban Affairs*: Economic Policy; Financial Institutions; Housing & Transportation. *Commerce, Science & Transportation*: Aviation; Communications; Consumer Affairs; Foreign Commerce & Tourism; Manufacturing & Competitiveness (RMM); Surface Transportation & Merchant Marine. *Small Business*.

Group Ratings and Key Votes: Newly Elected

Election Results

2000 general	John Ensign (R)	330,687	(55%)	($4,872,176)
	Ed Bernstein (D)	238,260	(40%)	($2,449,093)
	Other	31,303	(5%)	
2000 primary	John Ensign (R)	95,904	(88%)	
	Richard Hamzik (R)	6,202	(6%)	
	Other	6,833	(6%)	
1994 general	Richard H. Bryan (D)	193,804	(51%)	($3,021,834)
	Hal Furman (R)	156,020	(41%)	($845,340)
	Others	30,706	(8%)	

FIRST DISTRICT

After spending the 1990s successfully selling a more wholesome, family-oriented image in its lavish resorts, Las Vegas turned to the future with an appeal to its old ways: sex, gambling, whatever the visitors want and whenever they want it. "We're bringing back the sex appeal of Las

Vegas. That's part of the sizzle and the sell," MGM Grand president Bill Hornbuckle told *The Wall Street Journal* in January 2001. After an 18-month study by the local convention authority revealed that visitors were nostalgic for the Las Vegas of the 1970s, promoters brought back ads with scantily-clad women and an appeal to the emotions that Las Vegas fulfills in ways unlike any other American city. But some things have changed. On the Strip, only two hotels offered showgirl productions with lots of song, skin and special effects. The allure of the statuesque performers in sparkling costumes has been replaced by different kinds of performers—young women dancing nude at the hotels and strip clubs, or glitzy and over-the-top spectacles for parents and kids. Las Vegas has become home to real people with families who have established comfortable lives in the desert. Big houses in gated communities have become the heart of the nation's fastest-growing metropolis, which has been growing at the rate of 6,000 people a month and has made Nevada the nation's fastest-growing state in the 1990s. Oscar Goodman, a lawyer who had once represented Meyer Lansky and other mobsters, was elected mayor of Las Vegas in June 1999 and announced plans for improving local services and reviving the downtown area.

The 1st District of Nevada consists of Las Vegas and its close-in suburbs. It grew 56%—one of the highest rates in the country—but the 2d grew by an even greater 77%. Something like a nervously drawn circle in the center of Clark County, the 1st takes in all of Las Vegas, most of majority Hispanic and black North Las Vegas, just a bit of the Las Vegas Colony Indian Reservation, plus suburban Henderson—which nearly tripled in population to 175,000 during the 1990s. It also includes most of the Democratic precincts in the state.

The congresswoman from the 1st District is Shelley Berkley, a Democrat elected in 1998 and the winner of two close contests. Berkley moved to Las Vegas at 11; her father worked at the Sands and rose to maitre d'; she waited tables and was a keno runner as she made her way through the University of Nevada at Las Vegas, where she was student body president, and the University of San Diego Law School. "My roots in this community run very, very deep," she says, and she has worked for many of its major institutions. She was chairman of the Nevada Hotel and Motel Associations, government and business affairs vice president at the Sands, in-house counsel at Southwest Gas (of which Governor Kenny Guinn was once chief executive). She was elected to one term in the state House, in 1982, and in 1990 was appointed to the University of Nevada Board of Regents by Governor Bob Miller. After Republican Congressman John Ensign was re-elected in 1996 by only 50%–44% despite spending $1.9 million, she decided to run for the 1st District seat. In September 1997 House Democratic Leader Dick Gephardt endorsed her and promised her a seat on Ways and Means. Brassy, direct, effusive, she seemed headed for victory after Ensign decided to run against Senator Harry Reid.

Indeed, Republicans lacked a serious candidate until filing day in May 1998. Lieutenant Governor Lonnie Hammargren ran for governor instead of Congress (he got 10% in the Republican primary), and 15 minutes before the deadline Judge Donald Chairez, who had switched his registration to Republican, resigned his post and filed for the seat. Then in June came a bombshell. The *Las Vegas Review-Journal* reported on tapes of Berkley's May 1997 telephone conversations to a friend and texts of a memo Berkley sent the Sands' owner Sheldon Adelson when he was seeking approvals for his Venetian mega-hotel. They showed her advising him to make campaign contributions to local judges to curry favor, to grant Clark County Commissioner Yvonne Atkinson Gates a daiquiri concession and to hire the uncle of County Commissioner Erin Kenny in the hopes of getting their votes for approval. "Those suggestions were at best unethical and at worst illegal," said the Sands' President Bill Weidner, and Adelson fired Berkley in May 1997. Berkley quickly apologized, and the Clark County District Attorney saw no cause for prosecution. But Chairez made his slogan, "Fairness not favors!" And the Republican campaign committee eventually ran six ads featuring the charges. Berkley raised other issues, arguing for affordable college tuition, adequate classrooms and computers; both candidates supported the gaming industry and opposed the temporary nuclear storage site. The Democratic Congressional Campaign Committee ran ads criticizing Chairez' rulings in controversial cases. With strong support from the gaming industry, Berkley outspent Chairez by $1.2 million to $554,000. She won more narrowly, by 49%–46%.

In the House, Berkley's voting record places her in the center of House Democrats. She did not get the promised seat on Ways and Means; because they remained in the minority, Democrats had only one vacancy in 1999 and it went to Lloyd Doggett of Texas, while the vacant seat in 2001 went to Earl Pomeroy of North Dakota. But she kept a close watch on the interests of the gaming industry: she led opposition to a proposal by the National Collegiate Athletic Association to bar Nevada casinos from accepting bets on college sports. As an alternative to storing nuclear waste at Yucca Mountain, she sponsored a House-approved plan for Energy Department research into decontaminating the waste at reactor sites. As a loyal Democrat, she backed prescription drug coverage for seniors and criticized pharmaceutical companies for excessive prices. She opposed permanent normal trade relations with China. But she voted in 2001 for Republican proposals to repeal the marriage penalty and estate taxes. Although she called herself a card-carrying member of the American Civil Liberties Union, she voted for the constitutional amendment to bar flag-burning. After her new husband, physician Larry Lehrner, diagnosed that she was suffering from advanced stages of osteoporosis, she began urging visitors to her office to drink milk and consume calcium tablets.

Berkley had a tough re-election campaign against state Senator Jon Porter of Henderson, who revived the 1998 controversy by attacking her for failing to apologize for her conversations and notes to Adelson; "my opponent thinks justice is for sale in Nevada," Porter charged. After Berkley said that the state's prescription drug plan "crashed and burned," Governor Kenny Guinn said that he would do everything he could to defeat her. Porter demanded that Berkley apologize to Guinn. She refused and called Guinn "a friend for 30 years." Both candidates spent heavily on ads, with Porter helped by additional hundreds of thousands from pharmaceutical firms. Berkley won 52%–44%.

Nevada gained a House seat from the 2000 Census, and Clark County, which grew by 86% in the 1990s, has 69% of the state's population, thus making it likely that it will contain two whole congressional districts. Berkley has called the current 1st District the "hole in the bagel," and came out for a plan giving her a smaller district including Las Vegas and North Las Vegas, which would be more Democratic than the current 1st. Porter favors a similar plan, which would also create a Republican-leaning encircling district for him to run in.

Cook's Call   *Competitive.* Berkley has yet to get a solid hold of this Las Vegas-based district. Berkley faced a lackluster candidate in 2000 and was once again one of the strongest fundraisers in the House, yet she still won with just 52%. Redistricting may help Berkley's fortunes in the 2002 election. Berkley's 1st District will gain about four percent more registered Democrats than it had before.

THE PEOPLE: Pop. 2000: 936,104; Pop. 1990: 601,042, up 55.7% 1990–2000. 68.9% White, 9.6% Black, 5.3% Asian, 0.8% Amer. Indian, 0.5% Hawaiian, 4.4% Two+ races, 10.5% Other; 26.6% Hispanic Origin.

2000 Presidential Vote			1996 Presidential Vote		
Gore (D)	127,697	(54%)	Clinton (D)	91,307	(51%)
Bush (R)	99,199	(42%)	Dole (R)	65,990	(37%)
Nader (Green)	5,157	(2%)	Perot (I)	15,949	(9%)
Others	3,773	(2%)	Others	5,811	(3%)

Rep. Shelley Berkley (D)

Elected 1998, 2d term; b. Jan. 20, 1951, South Fallsburg, NY; home, Las Vegas; U.N.L.V., B.A. 1972; U. of San Diego Law Schl., J.D. 1976; Jewish; married (Larry Lehrner).

Elected Office: NV Assembly, 1982–84; Regent, U. Commun. Col. System of NV, 1990–98.

Professional Career: Cnsl., SW Gas Corp., 1977–82; VP, Sands Hotel, 1989–98; Chair, NV Hotel & Motel Assn., 1994.

DC Office: 439 CHOB 20515, 202-225-5965; Fax: 202-225-3119; Web site: www.house.gov/berkley.

District Offices: Elko, 775-777-7920; Las Vegas, 702-220-9823; Reno, 775-686-5760.

Committees: *International Relations* (20th of 23 D): Middle East & South Asia. *Transportation & Infrastructure* (30th of 34 D): Aviation; Highways & Transit. *Veterans' Affairs* (10th of 14 D): Health.

Group Ratings

	ADA	ACLU	AFS	LCV	CON	ITIC	NTU	COC	ACU	NTLC	CHC
2000	65	71	85	86	9	72	43	57	28	30	20
1999	100	—	100	75	59	—	16	36	4	—	—

National Journal Ratings

	1999 LIB —	1999 CONS		2000 LIB —	2000 CONS
Economic	70%	— 29%		57%	— 42%
Social	73%	— 26%		76%	— 24%
Foreign	71%	— 27%		56%	— 42%

Key Votes of the 106th Congress

1. Patient Bill of Rights	Y	5. Bar RU-486 $ for FDA	N	9. NATO War in Serbia	Y
2. Accelerate Min. Wage	Y	6. Display 10 Commandments	N	10. Perm. Trade with China	N
3. Strike Ban on Ergo. Stnd.	Y	7. Gun Show Bkgrnd. Checks	Y	11. Debt Relief for 3rd World	Y
4. Ovrd. Estate Tax Veto	Y	8. Ban Part.-Birth Abortion	N	12. Drop Cuba Econ. Embargo	N

Election Results

2000 general	Shelley Berkley (D)	118,469	(52%)	($2,062,803)
	Jon Porter (R)	101,276	(44%)	($1,386,081)
	Other	9,490	(4%)	
2000 primary	Shelley Berkley (D)	unopposed		
1998 general	Shelley Berkley (D)	79,315	(49%)	($1,295,091)
	Don Chairez (R)	73,540	(46%)	($554,983)
	Others	8,227	(5%)	

SECOND DISTRICT

Nevada's 2d Congressional District is the more Republican of Nevada's two districts and one of the most distinctive in the nation. It includes all of the state except the urban core of Las Vegas. With 99.8% of the state's land area, it is the nation's third-largest district in area; with 1.06 million people, up 77% in the 1990s, it is the nation's most-populous district and the one with the highest population growth in the past decade. In that time subdivisions have been sprouting up in the desert in Clark County; there are more people in the 2d District's portion of Clark County than in all of Reno's Washoe County. Washoe County grew by 33% in the 1990s, which would be awesome growth in most states; Reno has always been the more Republican of Nevada's two major cities. The remaining 14 Cow Counties are sparsely populated, with 14% of the state's residents—down from 17% in 1990—and more than 87% of its land owned by the federal government, including the Humboldt-Toiyabe National Forest, the largest in the lower 48 states and a source of constant friction with local officials, ranchers, loggers and miners. In 2000 George W. Bush trailed Al Gore in Clark County 51%–45%, but he led in Washoe County 52%–43% and in the Cow Counties 64%–30%

The congressman from the 2d District is Jim Gibbons, a Republican elected in 1996. Gibbons grew up near Reno, went to the University of Nevada and served in the Air Force in Vietnam. He went to law school and has practiced law, but he also was a mining geologist, a hydrologist, a pilot for Delta and Western Airlines and became vice commander of the Nevada Air National Guard. In 1988 he was elected to the Assembly; in 1990 he was called up to active duty in the Gulf war. While he was flying unarmed air reconnaissance missions, his wife took his place in the legislature. After his celebrated return, he proposed a ballot initiative to require a two-thirds supermajority to raise any state tax; it passed with more than 70% of the votes in 1994 and by 1996 became law. In 1994 Gibbons ran for governor. He beat Secretary of State Cheryl Lau 52%–32% in the primary, but lost the general to Bob Miller, 53%–41%.

In 1996, after Congresswoman Barbara Vucanovich retired, Gibbons ran for the 2d District seat. He had serious competition in the primary from Lau, who returned from more than a year as counsel to the U.S. House, and Patty Cafferata, a former state treasurer and Vucanovich's daughter. Gibbons carried the Reno area and Las Vegas suburbs to win with 42%, to 24% each for Lau and Cafferata. Meanwhile, in the Democratic primary, former state senator and former head of the state Ethics Commission Spike Wilson beat former Mustang Ranch brothel worker Jessi Winchester 62%–21%. In the general Gibbons won solidly, 59%–35%.

Gibbons has said, "Nevadans are a fiercely proud citizenry who believe they know more about the education of their children than Washington does, that they know how to solve their problems, whether it's crime, pollution or what have you, than Washington." He opposes what he regards as federal intrusion on local rights. He sponsored legislation to allow Clark County to buy 6,500 acres of dry lake bed in the Ivanpah Valley from the federal government for development of southern Nevada's second major airport—Bill Clinton signed the bill in October 2000—and he has tried to allow Elko and Winnemucca to buy surrounding federal lands. The House in May 2000 defeated his amendment to give local counties more control over the disposal of unwanted property that had been owned by the Bureau of Land Management.

His independence frequently has left him voting against Republican dogma in the House. He strongly opposes the nuclear repository at Yucca Mountain and the proposed temporary storage site at the Nevada Test Site—both in the district. Working with House Democrats, he led a coalition in March 2000 that unsuccessfully opposed a Republican-sponsored nuclear waste storage bill—Clinton vetoed the measure. Despite their frequent conflicts, he joined Shelley Berkley in urging the Bush administration to move from the Justice Department to the Labor Department control of the program to compensate workers who were exposed to radiation at nuclear weapons plants. He also joined Democrats in bucking his party leadership by supporting the patients' bill of rights and opposing permanent normal trade relations with China. Gibbons strongly supports the gaming industry, proposing a bill to stop the IRS from taxing free meals eaten by gaming employees and opposing the Interior Department plan to allow the Interior secretary to approve Indian casinos without the consent of the states.

Gibbons has been re-elected easily. His 2000 Democratic opponent, a teacher who named her daughter Kennedy because of her political allegiance, conceded she had as much chance of winning "as a snowball in Las Vegas." Gibbons won 65%–30%. But he has come up short in his efforts to win a seat on Ways and Means—an important panel for the gaming industry. He has continued to express interest in running for statewide office, perhaps against Senator Harry Reid in 2004. With Nevada gaining a seat, redistricting likely will leave Gibbons with a district that is most of the state outside Clark County.

Cook's Call   *Safe.* Under a newly drawn congressional map, Gibbons' sprawling 2nd District will remain a good Republican stronghold. Gibbons, who has not dipped below 59 percent of the vote since winning here in 1996, can hold onto this northern Nevada seat for as long as he likes.

THE PEOPLE: Pop. 2000: 1,062,153; Pop. 1990: 600,791, up 76.8% 1990–2000. 80.7% White, 4.3% Black, 3.8% Asian, 1.8% Amer. Indian, 0.4% Hawaiian, 3.3% Two+ races, 5.7% Other; 13.6% Hispanic Origin.

2000 Presidential Vote

Bush (R)	202,376	(55%)
Gore (D)	152,281	(41%)
Nader (Green)	9,851	(3%)
Others	6,801	(2%)

1996 Presidential Vote

Dole (R)	133,254	(47%)
Clinton (D)	112,667	(39%)
Perot (I)	28,037	(10%)
Others	11,319	(4%)

Rep. Jim Gibbons (R)

Elected 1996, 3d term; b. Dec. 16, 1944, Sparks; home, Reno; U. of NV, B.S. 1967, M.S. 1973, Southwestern U., J.D. 1979; Protestant; married (Dawn).

Military Career: Air Force, 1967–71 (Vietnam), NV Air Natl. Guard, 1975–96 (Persian Gulf).

Elected Office: NV Assembly, 1988–94.

Professional Career: Pilot, Western Airlines, 1979–87, Delta Airlines, 1987–96.

DC Office: 100 CHOB 20515, 202-225-6155; Fax: 202-225-5679; Web site: www.house.gov/gibbons.

District Offices: Elko, 775-777-7920; Las Vegas, 702-255-1651; Reno, 775-686-5760.

Committees: *Armed Services* (22d of 32 R): Military Procurement; Military Readiness. *Permanent Select Committee on Intelligence* (5th of 11 R): Human Intelligence, Analysis & Counterintelligence (Chmn.); Intelligence Policy & National Security; Technical & Tactical Intelligence (Vice Chmn.). *Resources* (19th of 28 R): Energy & Mineral Resources; National Parks, Recreation & Public Lands. *Veterans' Affairs* (11th of 17 R): Health.

Group Ratings

	ADA	ACLU	AFS	LCV	CON	ITIC	NTU	COC	ACU	NTLC	CHC
2000	30	29	14	14	46	71	66	61	88	88	100
1999	15	—	0	13	56	—	56	68	84	—	—

National Journal Ratings

	1999 LIB	—	1999 CONS	2000 LIB	—	2000 CONS
Economic	41%	—	57%	41%	—	58%
Social	37%	—	61%	42%	—	57%
Foreign	9%	—	91%	12%	—	78%

Key Votes of the 106th Congress

1. Patient Bill of Rights	Y	5. Bar RU-486 $ for FDA	N	9. NATO War in Serbia	N
2. Accelerate Min. Wage	Y	6. Display 10 Commandments	Y	10. Perm. Trade with China	N
3. Strike Ban on Ergo. Stnd.	N	7. Gun Show Bkgrnd. Checks	N	11. Debt Relief for 3rd World	N
4. Ovrd. Estate Tax Veto	Y	8. Ban Part.-Birth Abortion	Y	12. Drop Cuba Econ. Embargo	N

Election Results

2000 general	Jim Gibbons (R)	229,608	(65%)	($320,019)
	Tierney Cahill (D)	106,379	(30%)	
	Other	19,982	(6%)	
2000 primary	Jim Gibbons (R)	68,917	(88%)	
	Mitchell T. Tracy (R)	7,986	(10%)	
1998 general	Jim Gibbons (R)	201,623	(81%)	($236,465)
	Christopher Horne (AI)	20,738	(8%)	
	Louis R. Tomburello (Lib)	18,561	(7%)	
	Others	7,841	(3%)	

★ NEW HAMPSHIRE ★

New Hampshire, in an odd corner of the country, with four-tenths of 1% of the nation's population, with unusual public policies—now in flux—becomes every four years the epicenter of the political universe, the site where the contest for the presidency of the most powerful nation in the history of the world is temporarily centered, where every vote is avidly sought and where members of the political press vie for access to candidates and for tables at the latest cycle's most fashionable bars and restaurants. New Hampshire has done much to change the political world—not just the United States, but the entire world: It gave a huge boost to Dwight Eisenhower's candidacy in 1952, it prompted the retirement of Lyndon Johnson in 1968, it sent on his way to power first Jimmy Carter in 1976, then Ronald Reagan in 1980 and George Bush in 1988. The lever by which this small state moves the world is New Hampshire's first-in-the-nation presidential primary, a device first contested in the 1950s, then sanctioned by Democratic reformers in the 1970s, and exploited by Republicans in the 1980s. And New Hampshire did all this when its public policies were atypical of the nation and its political terrain unusual if not eccentric. This is one of the few states which over the last half century has had more registered Republicans than Democrats, and of all the states this has been arguably the one with the most antipathy to taxes. Yet in the last dozen years, New Hampshire has changed. The last two presidents have both lost the New Hampshire primary, though Bill Clinton avoided the sting of defeat by proclaiming himself "the comeback kid" on primary night and George W. Bush recovered quickly enough to win decisively in South Carolina. And New Hampshire in November is no longer one of the most Republican states and seems to be moving, with lurches and bellows of protest, toward a tax regime more like that of most of the other 49 states: In 2000 it voted for a governor who did not "take the pledge" to oppose an income or sales tax.

New Hampshire's distinctiveness started early. In a country that prides itself on its feistiness and freedom from outside direction, it has always been even feistier and less fettered by authority. Before the Revolutionary War, New Hampshire was almost an outlaw colony, its great fortunes made by poachers in the king's forests and smugglers avoiding taxes. It was the first colony with an independent government and was fighting the British before the Minutemen stood at Lexington and Concord. In this environment, 19th Century entrepreneurs built textile mills along fast-flowing rivers; the Amoskeag Mills in Manchester, lining the Merrimack River for a mile, were once the largest cotton mills on the globe, employing 17,000 people and producing enough cloth every two months to put a band around the world. Around the mills grew a city of red brick dormitories and three-family frame houses filled with immigrants from Quebec, Ireland, Poland and Greece, set down amid dirt-roaded villages of flinty Yankee farmers and mechanics. New Hampshire held to its traditions of local government and little external control, and for years its refusal to join most other states and enact an income or sales tax, or to provide statewide guidance of schools and social services, seemed to doom it to continued backwardness.

But low taxes instead proved to be New Hampshire's fortune. Starting in the 1960s, New Hampshire has had the fastest growth in the Northeast, attracting businesses from Massachusetts and other high-tax states. It became a location of choice for entrepreneurs and high-tech innovators, attracting an increasing number of people skeptical of government programs. From 1965–2000, Massachusetts grew from 5.5 million to 6.3 million, up 15%; New Hampshire grew from 676,000 to 1,236,000, up 83%. The bedraggled New Hampshire of 50 years ago, of poor Yankee farmers and French Canadian mill hands, has largely disappeared, and in its place one of the nation's most prosperous economic communities has arisen. The low taxes that spurred New Hampshire's growth would probably have been raised in the late 1960s or early 1970s, as they were in so many states at the time, but for the far from gentle advocacy of the Manchester *Union Leader* and its owner William Loeb. The *Union Leader* insisted that governors and legislators "take the pledge" to vote for no sales or income tax and, from 1970 to 1998, almost all did, and the two who didn't were defeated. That meant keeping education and welfare as local responsibilities and holding down spending. At the same time, New Hampshire boasted the highest SAT scores in the country and had the brainpower to participate fully in New England's high-

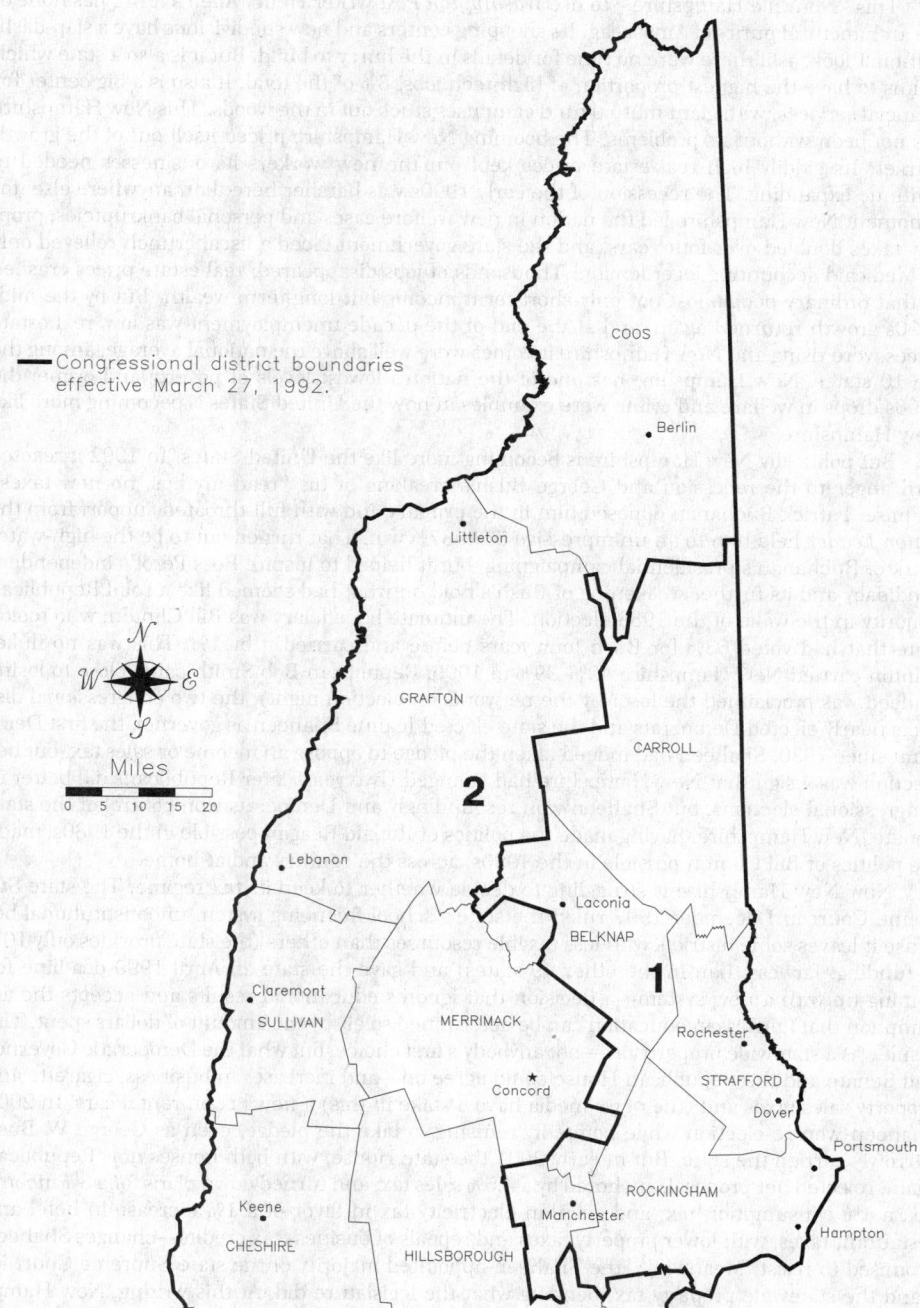

Congressional district boundaries
effective March 27, 1992.

COOS

Berlin

Littleton

GRAFTON

CARROLL

N W E S

Miles
0 5 10 15 20

2

Lebanon

Laconia

BELKNAP

1

Claremont

SULLIVAN

MERRIMACK

Rochester

STRAFFORD

Concord

Dover

Portsmouth

ROCKINGHAM

Keene

Manchester

Hampton

CHESHIRE

HILLSBOROUGH

Nashua

tech boom. The old Amoskeag Mills were converted to offices, and once grimy Manchester is now a high-tech center.

This "Nouvelle Hampshire," to use *Washington Post* writer Henry Allen's term, has none of the architectural purity of Amoskeag: Its shopping centers and new subdivisions have a slap-dash, half-built look, as if there were no time for details in the hurry to build. But it is also a state which claims to have the highest proportion of high-tech jobs, 8% of the total. It also is a big center for financial services, with giant mutual fund campuses stuck out in the woods. This New Hampshire has not been without its problems. The booming New Hampshire priced itself out of the growth market: Its giddily high real estate prices kept out the new workers its businesses needed to continue expanding. The recession of the early 1990s was harsher here than anywhere else: for a moment New Hampshire led the nation in new welfare cases and personal bankruptcies; property taxes doubled over four years, and the state government faced a fiscal crunch relieved only by Medicaid accounting legerdemain. Thousands of jobs disappeared; real estate prices crashed so that ordinary people lost not only short-term income but long-term wealth. But by the mid-1990s growth returned again, and at the end of the decade unemployment was low, real estate prices were rising and New Hampshire incomes were well above the national average, among the top 10 states. New Hampshire has one of the nation's lowest levels of poverty and crime: the 1990s drops in welfare and crime were examples in how the United States is becoming more like New Hampshire.

But politically New Hampshire is becoming more like the United States. In 1992 it reacted with anger to the recession and George Bush's breaking of his "read my lips, no new taxes" promise. Patrick Buchanan opposed him in the primary and with full-throated support from the *Union Leader* held him to an unimpressive 53%–37% win. That turned out to be the high-water mark of Buchanan's presidential campaigning, but it helped to inspire Ross Perot's independent candidacy and its further weakening of Bush's hold on what had seemed like a solid Republican majority in the wake of the 1988 election. The ultimate beneficiary was Bill Clinton, who took a state that had voted 63% for Bush four years before and carried it by 1%. This was no fluke: Clinton carried New Hampshire 49%–39% in 1996, Republican Bob Smith came close to losing (indeed was proclaimed the loser by the networks on election night), the two congressional districts nearly elected Democrats and the state elected Jeanne Shaheen as governor, the first Democrat since 1980. Shaheen had indeed taken the pledge to oppose an income or sales tax, but her election was a sign that New Hampshire had changed. Two years later Republicans did better in congressional elections, but Shaheen won resoundingly and Democrats won control of the state Senate. New Hampshire, having made the politics of Ronald Reagan possible in the 1980s, made the politics of Bill Clinton possible in the 1990s, across the country and at home.

Now New Hampshire is struggling to decide whether to keep its tax regime. The state Supreme Court in December 1997 ruled the state's school financing system unconstitutional because it leaves some districts with less taxable resources than others (the state provides only 10% of funding, far less than in the other 49 states) and gave the state an April 1999 deadline for coming up with a new system—a decision that ignores educational results and accepts the assumption that fairness in education can be determined solely by the amount of dollars spent. The result was a statewide property tax—not anybody's first choice, but what the Democratic Governor and Senate and the Republican House could agree on—and increases in business, cigarette and property sales taxes and (the news media have a stake in this) a new tax on rental cars. In 2000 Shaheen won re-election while pointedly refusing to take the pledge, even as George W. Bush narrowly carried the state. But in early 2001 the state House, with both houses now Republican again, rejected her proposal, anchored by a 2.5% sales tax, and turned down plans for a 3% income tax, a 1% consumption tax, and even an electricity tax in favor of a 1% increase in hotel and restaurant taxes, with lower property taxes and repeals of business tax credits—changes Shaheen promised to resist. Meanwhile, the Shaheen-appointed majority of the state Supreme Court let stand the statewide property tax, pending what the legislature did. At this writing, New Hampshire's political and fiscal future is uncertain.

Governor   Jeanne Shaheen, the governor of New Hampshire is, like many in this state's politics, from somewhere else: she was born in Missouri, went to college in Pennsylvania and graduate school in Mississippi. She moved to New Hampshire in 1973, taught school, ran a silver and leather business with her husband and got into politics. She worked in Jimmy Carter's campaigns in 1976 and 1980 and managed Gary Hart's campaign here in 1984—three winners in a row. In 1990 she ran for the state Senate and served three terms. There she worked on New Hampshire's pioneering effort to open up electric utilities to competition and sponsored health care laws—stabilizing insurance rates, barring rejection for pre-existing conditions, and trying to stop managed care insurers from denying access to physicians of choice.

In April 1996 Republican Governor Steve Merrill announced he was retiring from office, and Shaheen decided to run for governor. Up through the September primary, most eyes were on rival Republicans—1st District Congressman Bill Zeliff, an economic-issues conservative, and state Board of Education Chairman Ovide Lamontagne, strongly against abortion and endorsed by the Manchester *Union Leader*. After a petition-signature dispute knocked Zeliff off the ballot temporarily, Lamontagne won 47%–43%, largely from his margin in Manchester. Shaheen suited much better the mood of a contented, pro-incumbent year. "I think most people would agree I'm less confrontational than some of my predecessors have been." She took the anti-tax pledge and campaigned for expanding kindergarten (only 119 of 154 New Hampshire school districts had them), cutting electric rates through deregulation and promoting tourism. As Bill Clinton was carrying the state 49%–39%, Shaheen won 57%–40%.

In 1997 Shaheen bargained with the legislature and increased kindergarten aid from $500 to $750 per pupil; she also signed a needle exchange pilot program (but no community asked for the money) and a gay rights measure; she pleased teachers' unions by vetoing teacher tenure reform and limited school vouchers. Shaheen's greatest problem was the state Supreme Court decision in the Claremont cases outlawing local-based school financing. The court in December 1993 and again in December 1997 ruled against the state. The next month Shaheen proposed an "ABC" funding reform, with a statewide property tax rate and supplemental aid for districts unable to meet state-determined minimum costs from their own tax bases; the money would come from taxes on video slot machines at race tracks and a 23 cent tobacco tax increase. Most Republicans were opposed and called for a constitutional amendment to overturn the Claremont ruling; but they could never get the three-fifths necessary in the state House to get the issue on the ballot. In May the state Senate requested an advisory opinion from the state Supreme Court and in June the court said ABC was unconstitutional. In November 1998, after Shaheen was re-elected, the Supreme Court restated its April 1, 1999, deadline for legislative change and said that local school property taxes would afterwards be illegal. The obvious effect, and perhaps the intent, was to force a statewide tax, although at least 60% of voters oppose any of the three proposed—income, sales, property.

In that uncertain environment, Shaheen was given a vote of confidence in November 1998, as she beat a conservative Republican 66%–31%. Democrats gained a 13–11 majority in the state Senate. Again she had taken the pledge, and as the April 1999 deadline approached she promised to veto any plan that included a state income tax. In late April 1999 the state House and Senate finally agreed on a compromise plan which did include a statewide property tax, other tax increases and one-time revenue sources, and Shaheen signed it within hours. In late 1999 and early 2000 New Hampshire was preoccupied with the presidential primary; Shaheen's husband was Al Gore's state campaign chairman, and she played an important role in Gore's nomination-winning 50%–46% win over Bill Bradley. Shaheen succeeded in getting the legislature to pass an HMO bill requiring review by independent boards but could not get an increase in the cigarette tax; she vetoed repeal of the inheritance tax and vetoed a bill repealing capital punishment (New Hampshire has a very low crime rate and its last execution was in 1939). With the governors of Maine and Vermont, Shaheen started a tri-state pool to buy prescription drugs at discount. But looming ahead was a budget deficit and uncertainty about how the state would finance school aid. Shaheen appointed a blue-ribbon commission to come up with a plan in December 2000, and announced that she would no longer pledge to oppose a broad-based tax. "This year I can't make that promise. Because my first priority is to make sure that all children, wherever they live, get the education they deserve, I will not rule out any potential solution."

But first she needed to get re-elected, and she had tough competition in both the Democratic primary and the general election. Many liberal Democrats, angry at her opposition to an income tax and support of the death penalty, supported her primary challenger, state Senator Mark Fernald, who called for a 3.5% income tax; he was backed by the largest teachers' union. In the September primary she won by only a 61%–38% margin; she lost the western part of the state and towns hit hard by the statewide property tax. In the general election she faced former Senator Gordon Humphrey, who stepped down in 1990 in line with his pledge to serve only two terms. Shaheen started off well ahead and, citing some of his Senate votes, called him a "right-wing extremist." Humphrey took the pledge on taxes and attacked Shaheen for deferring any decision until the conveniently timed commission report in December. "What's your plan, Governor?" his signs said, and he picked up support by charging that she would back an income tax. Shaheen won, but by a margin unimpressive for someone who a few months before had made one of the shorter lists for Al Gore's vice presidential nomination: 49%–44%, with 6% for pro-income tax Independent Mary Brown. Republicans got a 13–11 majority in the state Senate and gained in the House. Still, it was the first time a candidate who refused to take the pledge had been elected since 1970.

New Hampshire elects its legislators from tiny districts and pays them $100 a year; as a result the state House, with 400 members, is filled with retirees, students and eccentrics. As the legislature assembled in January 2001, controversy arose over Tom Alciere, elected a Republican state Representative from Nashua, who turned out to be an aficionado of cop-killer websites; "I view cops an enemy officers," he said, until he was quickly persuaded to resign. But even as electricity deregulation was going to court, the chief issue was taxes to finance schools. In Febuary Shaheen proposed a 2.5% sales tax, but it was rejected by the House in April. Legislators also rejected Shaheen's longtime favorite revenue source, video slot machines at race tracks. In April Republicans introduced a plan to eliminate business tax credits, reimpose a tax on nuclear power plants, increase by 1% a tax on meals and hotel rooms and maintain some of the statewide property tax; Shaheen said she would veto it. But in May 2001 the state Supreme Court reduced some of the pressure on the legislature and governor by overturning a lower court decision overturning the statewide property tax. At this writing, it is not clear how, or whether, this problem will be resolved.

New Hampshire is one of the last two states (the other is Vermont) with two-year terms for its governor, and it has never elected a governor to four two-year terms. In early 2001 it was generally assumed that Shaheen would not run for re-election, and she seemed likely to run for the Senate seat held by Republican Bob Smith. A January 2001 poll showed her leading Smith 48%–38%, a strong showing against an incumbent. But in spring 2001 many Republicans were urging Congressman John Sununu to challenge Smith in the primary, and polls showed him leading both Smith in that contest and Shaheen in a general election. In any case, Shaheen's standing in November 2002 is likely to depend on the school financing issue.

Cook's Call   *Competitive.* If Shaheen runs for Senate, there is a long line of Democratic hopefuls. Regardless of the opponent, Republicans will likely have a strong nominee given the ongoing battle over taxes. An influx of new residents, however, has made New Hampshire considerably less conservative and Republican than it was a decade ago, which greatly increases the chances for a competitive open-seat race.

Senior Senator   Senator Bob Smith grew up in New Jersey, worked his way through college, then served in the Navy, including a year in the Gulf of Tonkin. He moved to Wolfeboro, New Hampshire, taught high school history and coached baseball, then managed Yankee Pedlar Real Estate. In 1980 he ran for the House and lost the primary; in 1982 he ran and lost the general 55%–45%; in 1984 he ran again, won a four-candidate primary with 42% and beat Democrat Dudley Dudley 59%–40%. In 1990, when Senator Gordon Humphrey honored a promise to retire after two terms, Smith won the Republican nomination over a pro-choicer, 65%–29%, and in the general beat feisty former (1975–80) Senator John Durkin, who attacked the big oil companies as he had in the 1970s and called for $10 billion in new spending programs. Smith won 65%–32%.

In the Senate Smith has one of the most conservative voting records and has taken on a variety of issues. In 1991 he became vice chairman of the Select Committee on POW/MIA Affairs, chaired by Massachusetts Senator John Kerry, also a Vietnam veteran; in 1993 Smith signed the final report concluding that there was "no compelling evidence" that POWs or MIAs left behind in Vietnam are now in Southeast Asia, but the investigation brought to light disturbing evidence that some may have been left behind and could not rule out the possibility that some are still there against their will. In 1994, he opposed the Clinton administration's lifting of the economic embargo against Vietnam. He has investigated Gulf war syndrome and opposed putting U.S. troops in Bosnia in 1995 and Kosovo in 1998. Smith is a strong opponent of abortion and once used an anatomically correct doll to explain partial-birth abortion on the Senate floor; he sponsored the first ban on the procedure in 1994.

In an amazing sequence, Smith was re-elected with the narrowest of margins in New Hampshire in 1996 and promptly started preparing to run for president in 1997. His Senate opponent was Dick Swett, elected to the 2d District House seat in 1990 and 1992 and defeated 51%–46% in 1994. Swett only narrowly won the primary, but ultimately spent more than $1.5 million, much of it raised with the help of his father-in-law California Congressman Tom Lantos. Smith had only a narrow lead in most polls and was behind in some; he perhaps suffered from his heavy campaigning for Phil Gramm, who ended up withdrawing from the presidential campaign before he got to New Hampshire. In the end, Smith won by just 49%–46%; he had a near-political-death experience on election night when the VNS exit poll declared him the loser (New Hampshire exit polls have leaned Democratic since 1988).

Not many months later Smith was traveling to Iowa (where he spent 42 days in 1997) and Louisiana, exploring a presidential race. What prompted him to think he would make a plausible candidate is not clear: he had had no executive experience in government and no major legislative achievement. His standing with New Hampshire voters was shaky and support from his colleagues was nonexistent. But he formed a Live Free or Die PAC and went on the circuit to belt out, with good-natured articulateness, his message of strong conviction and steadiness under pressure. Smith became the first candidate to formally announce for the presidency in February 1999. Much of the buzz in New Hampshire was hostile, and many feared his presence would drive out other presidential contenders, and thus reduce the importance of New Hampshire's first-in-the-nation primary. A Channel 9 poll on whether he should run came out 59%–25% against.

In July 1999 Smith rose on the Senate floor and made a 50-minute speech announcing that he was leaving the Republican Party and would run for president as an independent or third party candidate. He said that the Republican commitment to the rights of gun owners and the unborn "is a fraud and everyone knows it." But Senate Republican leaders, fretful of their small majority, allowed him to keep his committee seats and seniority. Then on October 24, 1999, John Chafee died; he was chairman of the Environment and Public Works Committee and Smith held the next-ranking Republican seat. Four days later Smith abandoned his presidential candidacy, saying he could not raise enough money, and on November 1 he announced he was a Republican again. A day later he became chairman of the Environment Committee. Previously, his record on the committee had been solidly conservative, while his efforts as a subcommittee chairman to change the troubled Superfund program had gone nowhere. But he had also sought full funding for the Land and Water Conservation Fund and was a lead sponsor of the North American Wetlands Conservation Act. Now he took up the cause of the $7.8 billion Everglades Restoration Act, which had strong bipartisan support in Florida and nationally; he held hearings in January and the Senate passed the bill in September. In March 2000 he came out against oil drilling in the Arctic National Wildlife Refuge. In July 2000 he supported a ban on the gasoline additive (and pollutant) MTBE. He worked for the Estuaries and Clean Water Act of 2000. He sought to delay EPA runoff pollution standards pending a National Academy of Sciences study and agreed to a one-year study of the Army Corps of Engineers. His ratings from liberal environmental groups had been very low, but their leaders now warmed to Smith, who insisted he was a "Teddy Roosevelt Republican" who favored "traditional conservation." In early 2001 he assembled bipartisan sponsors for a brownfield development bill, proposed new market-based limits on emissions from power plants and sought tax credits for energy-efficient buildings for homeowners, home builders and architects.

Smith still took some quixotic conservative stands, and has maintained a mostly conservative voting record. He temporarily blocked the nomination of Joseph Prueher to be ambassador to China in 1999; he filibustered gun control provisions in a 1999 juvenile justice bill and was voted down 77–22; he was an aggressive defender of the Miami relatives of Elian Gonzalez. But the response to his presidential candidacy weakened his already shaky standing with New Hampshire voters, as he approached the 2002 election. A January 2001 poll showed him trailing Governor Jeanne Shaheen by a 48%–38% margin—an extraordinarily weak showing for an incumbent in a state which has long favored his party. In February 2001 columnist Robert Novak reported that "national Republican leaders" regarded Smith as a "hopeless case" and were urging 1st District Congressman John Sununu to run for the seat. Vice President Dick Cheney assured Smith that the White House supported all incumbent Republican senators, and Trent Lott and Senate Republican campaign chairman Bill Frist came to New Hampshire for Smith fundraisers in March 2001. But there was speculation that the leadership would be neutral in a primary and that the committee would not contribute to Smith in a primary—a serious problem in a state where the primary is in September, less than two months before the general election. Polls in March and April showed Sununu leading Smith in primary pairings, and Sununu running better than Smith against Shaheen. New Hampshire Republicans of all stripes—liberal former Senator Warren Rudman, establishment conservative former Governor Steve Merrill, maverick conservative former Congressman Chuck Douglas—were all reported to be leaning to Sununu. National conservative leader Grover Norquist said, "Bob Smith betrayed the conservative movement by whoring after the environmentalists, and he doesn't have the candlepower to realize that they're not going to lift a finger for him." Smith insisted that he was running, and that Shaheen's standing could be damaged by the then unresolved school financing controversy. But rumors continued that he would be offered a presidential appointment, and his re-election in early 2001 seemed problematic. There is in any case something of a two-term tradition in New Hampshire: The last New Hampshire senator to win a third full term was Norris Cotton in 1968.

Cook's Call *Highly Competitive.* Smith may be the most vulnerable incumbent of either party seeking re-election in 2002. New Hampshire is far less conservative and Republican then it was when he was first elected to the Senate. But to make matters worse for Smith, he may have a primary challenge from Congressman John Sununu. The eventual nominee is likely to face sitting Democratic Governor Jeanne Shaheen in the general. Although she has plenty of political problems herself, Shaheen would give either Smith or Sununu a tough race.

Junior Senator Judd Gregg, New Hampshire's junior senator, grew up in Nashua and in politics. His father, Hugh Gregg, was elected governor in 1952 and was a power in presidential primary politics up through 1988, when he backed George Bush. Judd Gregg was a student at Columbia during the student riots of 1968, but stayed true to New Hampshire Republicanism; after law school, he returned to Nashua and practiced law. In 1978 he was elected to the Executive Council, which dates to the colonial era and approves state appointments and expenditures. In 1980 he was elected to the House, where he was an eager participant in the Reagan revolution. In 1988, he ran for governor and won handily; he was easily re-elected in 1990.

In 1992, Gregg ran for the Senate when Warren Rudman retired, and in his taciturn way seemed sure he would win. But the New Hampshire economy had turned sour, and the race turned close. In the September primary he beat a construction company owner by only 50%–38%. In the general, he faced retired businessman John Rauh, who backed the line-item veto and balanced budget amendment and attacked Gregg for opposing abortion. Gregg was also attacked for having received a draft deferment in 1969 for bad knees, sleepwalking and severe acne. He won by an unimpressive 48%–45% margin.

In the Senate Gregg has a moderate to conservative voting record. He has been chief deputy majority whip since June 1996 and became an Appropriations subcommittee chairman in 1999, but has made his greatest impression by taking the lead on some controversial issues. He served on the 1994 Entitlements Commission and in 1995 headed the Senate Republicans' working group on entitlement reform; he drafted a Medicare reform to give seniors more choices, including the current system. In 1998 he served on the CSIS National Commission on Retirement Policy and co-sponsored its Social Security reform, which would put 2% of payroll taxes into mandatory investment accounts, lift minimum benefits levels, raise the retirement age and means-test affluent workers. In 2001 he and Democrat John Breaux proposed a 12-member Social Security commission, with Democratic members picked by Republicans and Republican members by Democrats.

On environmental issues Gregg has backed reform of the 1872 Mining Act and higher grazing fees. In 1998 he and Vermont's Patrick Leahy sponsored the Northern Forest Stewardship Act, to preserve mostly privately owned forests from Maine west to Upstate New York. He opposed the 1999 Clinton order closing off 30% of the White Mountain National Forest, and has argued that local communities should have more of a say in forest use. He has procured federal money to buy land to preserve Lake Tarleton, expand the Hubbard Brook Experimental Forest, purchase a conservation easement in the Ossipee Mountains and to preserve Great Bay in Portsmouth. He has also used his seat on Appropriations to fund other New Hampshire projects—$4 million for the New Hampshire Institute of Politics at St. Anselm's College, $15 million in counterterrorism research at Dartmouth, $10.5 million for New Hampshire law enforcement. He used an appropriations rider to seek patent protection on a drug owned by his alma mater, Columbia, and in a hand-written amendment got $1.4 million for the Advisory Commission on Electronic Commerce. With Herb Kohl, he sponsored a bill to establish that out-of-state businesses are not responsible for state sales tax collection on Internet transactions, and in 2001 he sponsored a ban on Internet sale of Social Security numbers.

On the HELP Committee Gregg has been a supporter of greater federal funding of special education. He has sponsored bills to protect teachers from civil suits over school discipline. In early 2001 he was the point man for the Bush administration on education reform, working with Republicans across the spectrum and with moderate Democrats to get a bill to the floor. Gregg has taken a hand in foreign policy as well, using his power as an appropriator to hold up or deliver funds for UN peacekeeping missions. In May 2000, for example, he allowed funds to be spent on operations in Kosovo; in June 2000, when he decided that the Clinton administration had abandoned the Lome accord, he released funds for Sierra Leone; other countries affected were East Timor and Congo.

Gregg has maintained a network of supporters in New Hampshire, but the Gregg organization that was so effective for George Bush in 1988 was unable to deliver a victory for George W. Bush in 2000. Gregg played Al Gore in candidate Bush's debate preparation; whether he anticipated Gore's loud sighs in the first debate is not clear. Gregg's standing in New Hampshire seems strong. In 1998 potential serious challengers—Dick Swett, John Rauh and his wife Mary—decided not to run, and Gregg was opposed by a low-spending Democrat who called him a "draft dodger" and a "wimp" and who said at one rally that he would like to get Gregg between a dog and a fire hydrant. Gregg won 68%–28%.

Presidential politics Since 1920, New Hampshire has had the first-in-the-nation primary, and since 1952, when candidates' names were first put on the ballot, it has had extraordinary influence on the presidential selection process—a fact that will surely strike future political scientists as bizarre. To be sure, there are arguments for having early contests in small states which provide a venue for "retail politics," in which candidates meet voters in person, listen and talk to them, exchange ideas and allow them to gauge their character. In-person contact was one of the things that saved Bill Clinton in 1992, after the Gennifer Flowers charges, and John McCain's jampacked town meetings showed a moving rapport between candidate and voter. New Hampshire is small enough physically (unlike Iowa) that candidates can efficiently meet voters; everything except the lightly populated north country is within an hour's drive of Manchester, and for all the state's abstract dislike of government, New Hampshire does an excellent job of keeping its roads clear of snow. New Hampshire's retail politics offers little-known candidates the ability to propel themselves into the national spotlight, though over the last 20 years none of those candidates—Gary Hart in 1984, Paul Tsongas and Patrick Buchanan in 1992, John McCain in 2000—has gone on to win their party's nominations. The last to do so were George McGovern and Jimmy Carter in the 1970s.

In any case, New Hampshire retains its first-in-the-nation status not on its merits but because of threats. Democrats tried in the 1970s to confine primaries to a "window" period in which New Hampshire would have competition. But New Hampshire, with its outlaw tradition, insisted it would hold its primary before the window if necessary, confident that candidates and reporters would pay it heed even if its tiny delegation were threatened with not being seated at the national convention. Republicans made no such rules, but in 1996 let Iowa Governor Terry Branstad and New Hampshire Governor Steve Merrill, both Republicans, threaten voter retaliation against candidates who took part in caucuses or primaries held before their states' or even during the week afterwards. Democratic Governor Jeanne Shaheen continued the tradition in December 1998, demanding candidates take a pledge not to participate in such contests. In fact New Hampshire tries to ban contests that come too soon *after* it votes. New Hampshire considers it an affront that Delaware holds its primary four days *after* New Hampshire, and its threats to shun candidates who campaign in Delaware have led candidates to plead that the only time they went there was riding on the Metroliner. In 2000 the Democrats imposed a *five-week* window of no contests after New Hampshire, which made Al Gore's 50%–46% victory here decisive; Bill Bradley's candidacy effectively died through inattention before he could reach Super Tuesday. Fortunately for George W. Bush, the *laissez faire* Republicans did not restrict other states as much as the rule-bound Democrats, and he could recover 19 days later in South Carolina. John McCain's smashing 49%–30% victory here, unexpectedly large and proof that New Hampshire voters are no longer necessarily fixated on low taxes, knocked the wind out of the Bush campaign for about a week, but it turned out to be a template not for contests in other states, but for other contests in New England. Only there did registered and self-identified Republicans, as in New Hampshire, prefer McCain to Bush, and in Arizona (his home state) and Michigan (where 20% of voters were self-identified Democrats and 35% self-identified independents) was McCain able to duplicate his New Hampshire victory beyond the bounds of New England.

A word should be said about New Hampshire media. The Manchester *Union Leader* has one of the nation's sharpest conservative tongues. Its editorials, even now after the deaths of William Loeb and his widow Nackey, scold Republicans who stray from its gospel, which these days includes Pat Buchanan's opposition to free trade. Its insistence that politicians take the anti-tax pledge for years set the course for New Hampshire state politics and government. But the *Union Leader* cannot automatically deliver votes on primary day—Buchanan won in 1996, but with just 27% of the votes—and its news coverage is more objective than that of many left-leaning national media outlets. New Hampshire's other great medium is Manchester's WMUR-TV, Channel 9, which also provides tons of information to a winter-bound audience. Channel 9's rule is to cover every candidate every day he or she is in New Hampshire, allowing each to present views and make arguments without the overlay of opinionated commentary that national network reporters use; the new WNDS, Channel 50 seems to provide similar coverage.

Despite Democrats' recent successes here, New Hampshire is one of the few states with substantially more registered Republicans than Democrats—just another way in which it is not typical of the nation. The Republican heart of the state is the Merrimack Valley, with the two biggest cities of Manchester and Nashua. Old Yankee towns farther north are also heavily Republican, and so are the suburbs just north of the Massachusetts line. More Democratic is the western edge of the state along the Connecticut River, which partakes a bit of the Ben & Jerry's Vermont liberalism, and Portsmouth and smaller former mill towns along the Maine border. The highest Democratic percentages in New Hampshire often come from Hanover, home of Dartmouth College; the highest Republican percentages from Dixville Notch in the far north, whose 29 voters troop in at one minute after midnight and cast the nation's first recorded votes every presidential year.

Where New Hampshire proved crucial in 2000 was, surprisingly, in the general election. Usually its motel rooms are abandoned by the national press the morning after the primary and its diners remain unpatrolled by TV camera crews all fall. But New Hampshire proved to be closely contested. New Hampshire and Maine were the two Northeastern states which the Bush and Gore campaigns targeted and where the candidates made forays from Middle America to campaign in. The result was exceedingly close, but outside of recount range: Bush won 48%–47%, with a popular vote margin of 7,211 votes, just a bit larger than the 6,395 votes by which Al Gore beat Bill Bradley. How Gore won that close primary and how Bush won that close general election—something few national reporters covered closely—turned out to be more crucial than how

John McCain, thronged by congenial reporters on his Straight Talk Express, established the rapport which gave him his impressive primary victory.

Congressional districting   With only slight changes, New Hampshire's two congressional districts basically have had the same boundaries since 1881, neatly separating the Merrimack River mill towns of Manchester and Nashua, the state's largest cities. That was done originally to split the Catholic Democratic vote, but now both cities are high-tech Republican towns. If the split now gives Republicans an edge in both districts, it also gives Democrats a chance for upset victories in both. With a Democratic governor and a Republican legislature, there is not likely to be a major change in the lines for 2002; some 7,500 people have to be moved from the 1st to the 2nd district. Incidentally, both of New Hampshire's congressmen and one of its senators are the son or grandson of governors.

THE PEOPLE: Pop. 2000: 1,235,786; Pop. 1990: 1,109,252, up 11.4% 1990–2000. 0.4% of U.S. total, 41st largest; 96% White, 0.7% Black, 1.3% Asian, 0.2% Amer. Indian, 1.1% Two+ races, 0.6% Other; 1.7% Hispanic Origin. 2.8% Unemployment. 2000 Voting age pop.: 926,224. 2000 Turnout: 578,656; 62% of VAP. Registered voters (2000): 854,695; 224,295 D (26%), 301,844 R (35%), 328,556 unaffiliated and minor parties (38%).

POLITICAL LINEUP: Governor, Jeanne Shaheen (D); Secy. of State, William M. Gardner (D); Atty. Gen., Philip McLaughlin (D); Treasurer, Georgie A. Thomas (R); State Senate, 24 (11 D, 13 R); Senate President, Arthur P. Klemm Jr. (R); Majority Leader, Gary R. Francoeur (R); State House, 400 (139 D, 256 R, 1 I, 4 vacancies); House Speaker, Gene Chandler (R). Senators, Bob Smith (R) and Judd Gregg (R). Representatives, 2 (2 R).

ELECTIONS DIVISION: 603-271-3242; **FILING DEADLINE FOR U.S. CONGRESS:** June 14, 2002.

2000 Presidential Vote

Bush (R)	273,559	(48%)
Gore (D)	266,348	(47%)
Nader (Green)	22,188	(4%)
Others	5,700	(1%)

1996 Presidential Vote

Clinton (D)	246,166	(49%)
Dole (R)	196,486	(39%)
Perot (I)	48,387	(10%)
Others	8,014	(2%)

2000 Republican Presidential Primary

McCain (R)	115,606	(49%)
Bush (R)	72,330	(30%)
Forbes (R)	30,166	(13%)
Keyes (R)	15,179	(6%)
Other	4,925	(2%)

2000 Democratic Presidential Primary

Gore (D)	76,897	(50%)
Bradley (D)	70,502	(46%)
Other	7,240	(5%)

Gov. Jeanne Shaheen (D)

Elected 1996, term expires Jan. 2003, 3d term; b. Jan. 28, 1947, St. Charles, MO; home, Madbury; Shippensburg U., B.A. 1969, U. of MS, M.A. 1973; Protestant; married (William).

Elected Office: NH Senate, 1990–96.

Professional Career: Teacher, 1969–71; A.A., U. of NH, 1973–74; Parents' Assoc. Program Coord., 1982–86; Mgr., seasonal retail business, 1973–76; Campaign Mgr., Carter/Mondale NH Pres. Campaign, 1979–80; Hart NH Pres. Campaign, 1983–84; McEachern NH Gov. Campaign, 1986–88.

Office: State House, Concord, 03301, 603-271-2121; Fax: 603-271-2130; Web site: www.state.nh.us.

Election Results

2000 general	Jeanne Shaheen (D)	275,038	(49%)
	Gordon Humphrey (R)	246,952	(44%)
	Mary Brown (I)	35,904	(6%)
2000 primary	Jeanne Shaheen (D)	45,249	(61%)
	Mark Fernald (D)	28,488	(38%)
1998 general	Jeanne Shaheen (D)	210,769	(66%)
	Jay Lucas (R)	98,473	(31%)
	Others	9,698	(3%)

Sen. Bob Smith (R)

Elected 1990, seat up 2002, 2d term; b. Mar. 30, 1941, Trenton, NJ; home, Tuftonboro; Trenton Jr. Col., A.A. 1963, Lafayette Col., B.A. 1965, Long Beach St. Col., 1968–69; Catholic; married (Mary Jo).

Military Career: Navy, 1965–67 (Vietnam); Naval Reserves, 1962–65, 1967–69.

Elected Office: Chmn., Gov. Wentworth Schl. Bd., 1978–83; U.S. House of Reps., 1984–90.

Professional Career: High schl. teacher, 1975–84; Real estate agent, 1975–84.

DC Office: 307 DSOB, 20510, 202-224-2841; Fax: 202-224-1353; Web site: www.senate.gov/~smith.

State Offices: Manchester, 603-634-5000; Portsmouth, 603-433-1667.

Committees: *Armed Services*: Emerging Threats & Capabilities; Seapower; Strategic Forces. *Environment & Public Works* (RMM).

Group Ratings

	ADA	ACLU	AFS	LCV	CON	ITIC	NTU	COC	ACU	NTLC	CHC
2000	10	29	14	14	26	69	79	73	100	97	100
1999	5	—	0	0	87	—	84	82	96	—	—

National Journal Ratings

	1999 LIB —	1999 CONS		2000 LIB —	2000 CONS
Economic	0% —	83%		14% —	75%
Social	0% —	97%		0% —	90%
Foreign	16% —	77%		0% —	95%

Key Votes of the 106th Congress

1. Educ. Savings Accts.	Y	5. Review Movie Violence	Y	9. NATO War in Serbia	N
2. Prescrip. Drug Benefit	N	6. Gun Show Bckgrnd. Checks	N	10. Table Cuba Travel Ban	Y
3. Delay Ergonomic Standards	Y	7. Ban Part.-Birth Abortion	Y	11. Nuclear Test-Ban Treaty	N
4. Phase Out Estate Tax	Y	8. Broaden Hate Crimes List	N	12. Perm. Trade with China	N

Election Results

1996 general	Bob Smith (R)	242,257	(49%)	($1,929,468)
	Dick Swett (D)	227,355	(46%)	($1,558,563)
	Ken Blevens (Lib)	22,261	(5%)	
1996 primary	Bob Smith (R)	85,223	(97%)	
	Others	2,354	(3%)	
1990 general	Bob Smith (R)	189,792	(65%)	($1,419,127)
	John A. Durkin (D)	91,299	(32%)	($319,879)
	Others	10,302	(3%)	

Sen. Judd Gregg (R)

Elected 1992, seat up 2004, 2d term; b. Feb. 14, 1947, Nashua; home, Rye; Columbia U., A.B. 1969, Boston U., J.D. 1972, LL.M. 1975; Protestant; married (Kathleen).

Elected Office: NH Exec. Cncl., 1978–80; U.S. House of Reps., 1980–88; NH Gov., 1988–92.

Professional Career: Practicing atty., 1976–80.

DC Office: 393 RSOB, 20510, 202-224-3324; Fax: 202-224-4952; Web site: www.senate.gov/~gregg.

State Offices: Berlin, 603-752-2604; Concord, 603-225-7115; Manchester, 603-622-7979; Portsmouth, 603-431-2171.

Committees: *Appropriations*: Commerce, Justice, State & Judiciary (RMM); Defense; Foreign Operations; Interior; Labor, HHS & Education. *Budget. Governmental Affairs*: International Security, Proliferation & Federal Services; Investigations (Permanent). *Health, Education, Labor & Pensions* (RMM): Children & Families (RMM); Employment, Safety & Training; Public Health.

Group Ratings

	ADA	ACLU	AFS	LCV	CON	ITIC	NTU	COC	ACU	NTLC	CHC
2000	0	40	0	14	93	89	76	86	100	97	91
1999	0	—	0	44	71	—	81	76	91	—	—

National Journal Ratings

	1999 LIB	—	1999 CONS		2000 LIB	—	2000 CONS
Economic	30%	—	68%		37%	—	62%
Social	31%	—	68%		10%	—	81%
Foreign	6%	—	90%		5%	—	86%

Key Votes of the 106th Congress

1. Educ. Savings Accts.	Y	5. Review Movie Violence	Y	9. NATO War in Serbia	N
2. Prescrip. Drug Benefit	N	6. Gun Show Bckgrnd. Checks	N	10. Table Cuba Travel Ban	Y
3. Delay Ergonomic Standards	Y	7. Ban Part.-Birth Abortion	*	11. Nuclear Test-Ban Treaty	N
4. Phase Out Estate Tax	Y	8. Broaden Hate Crimes List	N	12. Perm. Trade with China	Y

Election Results

1998 general	Judd Gregg (R)	213,477	(68%)	($904,448)
	George Condodemetraky (D)	88,883	(28%)	($28,547)
	Others	12,596	(4%)	
1998 primary	Judd Gregg (R)	63,729	(86%)	
	Phil Weber (R)	10,784	(14%)	
1992 general	Judd Gregg (R)	249,591	(48%)	($875,675)
	John Rauh (D)	234,982	(45%)	($1,109,467)
	Katherine Alexander (Lib)	18,214	(4%)	
	Others	15,629	(3%)	

FIRST DISTRICT

The 1st Congressional District of New Hampshire includes Manchester, its suburbs and the seacoast—the e-coast some are now calling it. Manchester was once a heavily French Canadian textile mill town, which also had the nation's largest percentage of Greek-Americans; in the 1980s it became a fast-growing, high-tech city. There are new shopping malls here and in towns on the Massachusetts border. Portsmouth has restored its downtown to some of its historic splendor; and the successful redevelopment of Pease Air Force Base into the Pease International Tradeport is driving the seacoast economy with new jobs. There is a Democratic heritage, especially in Manchester, but in general elections this is usually Republican territory.

The congressman from the 1st District is John E. Sununu, a Republican elected in 1996, one of eight children of former New Hampshire Governor and White House Chief of Staff John

H. Sununu. The younger Sununu grew up in Salem, became an engineer, worked for a microwave manufacturer, a high-tech consulting firm, the building automation manufacturer Teletrol and as a consultant for JHS Associates. In April 1996, when Congressman Bill Zeliff announced for governor, Sununu and seven other Republicans got into the House race. The best known was four-term Manchester Mayor Raymond "The Wiz" Wieczorek, builder of the new airport and endorsee of the Manchester *Union Leader*. But Wieczorek was 67 and did not carry much punch outside of Manchester. Sununu called for tax simplification and a capital gains tax cut and a devolution of education programs to the states. This was an exceedingly close race: Sununu won with 28%, Wieczorek had 27% and Jack Heath, news director of WMUR-TV, took 26%. In the general Sununu faced Joe Keefe, former Democratic state chairman, who had run twice before in the district and who, with help from PACs, raised more money than Sununu. This also was a close race: Keefe carried the eastern part of the district around Portsmouth, Rochester and Durham, and also won in Manchester, but Sununu won big in the Manchester suburbs and the north country, winning overall 50%–47%.

In the House Sununu has compiled a conservative voting record and has climbed to important committee spots. He favors school vouchers and a 17% flat tax and voted against the Shays-Meehan campaign finance bill. With Democrat Rob Andrews, he sponsored a successful amendment to end subsidies to auto makers for research in making cars more efficient. In November 1998, when Bob Livingston was Speaker-designate, he put Sununu on the Appropriations Committee, where his mastery of budget numbers impressed the leadership. In 2000 Speaker Dennis Hastert urged him to seek the chairmanship of the Budget Committee; it went to Jim Nussle, but Hastert named Sununu vice-chairman. He was also named vice-chairman of the Treasury Subcommittee of Appropriations. He has worked on many local projects, getting $100,000 for upgraded radio equipment for rescue personnel in Tuckerman Ravine in the Presidential Range, $1 million for the University of New Hampshire Bedrock Bioremediation Center, $4.9 million to upgrade the waterfront crane at Portsmouth Naval Shipyard and National Wild and Scenic River status for a 12-mile stretch of the Lamprey River in Epping.

Sununu was re-elected 67%–33% in 1998; against a spirited challenge from Portsmouth state Representative Martha Fuller Clark, he won 53%–45% in 2000. His father served three terms as governor in the 1980s, but in March 2001 he announced he would not run for governor, but would give serious consideration to running for the Senate seat held by Republican Bob Smith, whose standing was hurt by his dramatic resignation from the Republican Party in July 1999 and his quixotic presidential candidacy over the next three months. Polls taken in March and April showed Sununu leading Smith in primary pairings and running ahead of Jeanne Shaheen, the likely Democratic candidate, in general election pairings. While Vice President Dick Cheney and Trent Lott said they supported Smith, New Hampshire Republicans of all stripes—liberal former Senator Warren Rudman, establishment conservative former Governor Steve Merrill, maverick conservative former Congressman Chuck Douglas—were all reported to be leaning to Sununu.

If Sununu does run for the Senate, a host of Republicans have been mentioned as possible candidates in the 1st district—former Congressman Bill Zeliff, Ovid Lamontagne (who beat Zeliff in the 1996 primary for governor), state housing finance director Clara Monier, former Executive Councilor William Cahill, Belknap County Commissioner Chris Boothby, state Representatives Fran Wendelboe and Jeb Bradley. Sununu's 2000 opponent, Martha Fuller Clark, said she never stopped running and, given her 45% showing, this could be a seriously contested race in November 2002.

Cook's Call *Competitive.* Sununu's surprisingly poor showing against an unknown Democrat in 2000 underscores the marginal nature of this district. Bush won here in 2000 by just 3% and Clinton won here in 1996 by 8%. If Sununu runs for the Senate, this open seat would be highly targeted by both sides in 2002.

THE PEOPLE: Pop. 2000: 625,527; Pop. 1990: 554,303, up 12.8% 1990–2000. 96.1% White, 0.8% Black, 1.2% Asian, 0.2% Amer. Indian, 1.1% Two+ races, 0.5% Other; 1.6% Hispanic Origin.

2000 Presidential Vote

Bush (R)	142,114	(49%)
Gore (D)	132,760	(46%)
Nader (Green)	10,833	(4%)
Others	2,722	(1%)

1996 Presidential Vote

Clinton (D)	121,602	(48%)
Dole (R)	101,295	(40%)
Perot (I)	23,898	(10%)
Others	3,937	(2%)

Rep. John E. Sununu (R)

Elected 1996, 3d term; b. Sept. 10, 1964, Boston, MA; home, Bedford; M.I.T., B.S. 1986, M.S. 1987, Harvard U., M.B.A. 1991; Catholic; married (Kitty).

Professional Career: Design Engineer, Remec, Inc., 1987–89; Mgr. & Operations Specialist, Pittiglio, Rabin, Todd & McGrath, 1990–92; C.F.O. & Dir. of Operations, Teletrol Systems Inc., 1993–95; Consultant, JHS Associates, 1995–96.

DC Office: 316 CHOB 20515, 202-225-5456; Fax: 202-225-5822; Web site: www.house.gov/sununu.

District Offices: Dover, 603-743-4813; Manchester, 603-641-9536.

Committees: *Appropriations* (28th of 35 R): Foreign Operations & Export Financing; Treasury, Postal Service & General Government; VA, HUD & Independent Agencies. *Budget* (Vice Chmn. of 24 R).

Group Ratings

	ADA	ACLU	AFS	LCV	CON	ITIC	NTU	COC	ACU	NTLC	CHC
2000	10	31	0	21	95	100	71	85	96	97	92
1999	0	—	0	19	87	—	69	88	100	—	—

National Journal Ratings

	1999 LIB —	1999 CONS		2000 LIB —	2000 CONS
Economic	0% —	84%		34% —	64%
Social	31% —	69%		0% —	79%
Foreign	0% —	97%		39% —	57%

Key Votes of the 106th Congress

1. Patient Bill of Rights	N	5. Bar RU-486 $ for FDA	Y	9. NATO War in Serbia	N
2. Accelerate Min. Wage	N	6. Display 10 Commandments	Y	10. Perm. Trade with China	Y
3. Strike Ban on Ergo. Stnd.	N	7. Gun Show Bkgrnd. Checks	N	11. Debt Relief for 3rd World	Y
4. Ovrd. Estate Tax Veto	Y	8. Ban Part.-Birth Abortion	Y	12. Drop Cuba Econ. Embargo	N

Election Results

2000 general	John E. Sununu (R)	150,609	(53%)	($578,633)
	Martha Fuller Clark (D)	128,387	(45%)	($1,055,513)
	Other	5,713	(2%)	
2000 primary	John E. Sununu (R)	unopposed		
1998 general	John E. Sununu (R)	104,430	(67%)	($536,509)
	Peter Flood (D)	51,783	(33%)	($26,812)

SECOND DISTRICT

The 2d Congressional District includes Nashua, the state's second largest city, and Salem, both right on the Massachusetts line and solidly conservative: people came here to get away from "Taxachusetts." These are boom areas, mushrooming with high-tech industries and financial services offices, growing lustily in the 1990s as in the 1980s. The 2d also includes, farther from Boston and readier for taxes and government services, the state capital of Concord and towns in the Connecticut River Valley, from Keene near Mount Monadnock north to Hanover, home of Dartmouth College, an area of artists' retreats. The 2d runs to the farthest north country: Dixville Notch and the paper mill town of Berlin, with its new Northern Forest Heritage Park, the Mount Washington Hotel and cog railway and the resort of Bretton Woods where the world monetary system, and the basis for post-World War II prosperity, was established in a conference in 1944. Far above is Mount Washington, with its spectacularly violent weather, with winds measured up to 231 miles per hour.

The congressman from the 2d District is Charles Bass, who has a long political pedigree: His grandfather Robert Bass was elected governor in 1910 and his father Perkins Bass served in the House from 1955–63. Charles Bass, after graduating from Dartmouth, worked for Maine Congressmen William Cohen and David Emery, then returned to New Hampshire to run for Congress in 1980; he finished third in the primary, with 22%, to 34% for now-Senator Judd Gregg and 25% for liberal Susan McLane. He ran a factory making architectural products with his two brothers and served in the state legislature—in the House from 1982 and the Senate from 1988—where he wrote the state's voluntary campaign spending law, which called on U.S. House candidates to observe the $500,000 total limit for both primary and general elections.

In 1994 Bass ran in the Republican primary for the right to oppose two-term Democratic Congressman Dick Swett. Bass ran as a moderate—pro-choice on abortion, but also as a fiscal conservative, a supporter of welfare cuts and tougher sentencing. Bass ran only a few points better in the primary than in 1980, but his 29% this time was enough to beat former NRA consultant Mike Hammond, who had 24%. Bass attacked Swett for voting with Bill Clinton 90% of the time and for raising most of his money out of state, much of it generated by his father-in-law, California Congressman Tom Lantos. Swett spent over $1 million, while Bass adhered to the voluntary spending limits and spent $448,000; Bass won 51%–46%. Swett carried Concord, Hanover and other towns on the Connecticut River, the Keene area and the mill town of Berlin, but Bass carried practically everything else.

In the House Bass has a conservative record on economics and a moderate record on cultural and foreign issues; he has emphasized environmental issues. He is a sponsor of the Northern Forest Stewardship Act, which encourages states and private owners to preserve the massive forests from Maine west to Upstate New York. He also backed the Conte Refuge Eminent Domain Protection Act, the Androscoggin River Valley Heritage Act and protecting the area around Lake Tarleton. In 1999 he tried to end the federal coyote killing program, "cowboy welfare" in his words. He wants to stop the use of MTBE in gasoline. On two environmental issues he opposes the Bush administration: He came out against oil drilling in the Arctic National Wildlife Refuge in 2000, and in March 2001 he criticized Bush for going back on his one-sentence campaign promise to vastly reduce the level of carbon dioxide in the air. He was also one of only three Republicans to vote against the budget resolution in May 2001. On the Transportation Committee he got $810 million for New Hampshire in the 1998 transportation bill, plus $9 million for winter ice storm cleanup and Superfund money to clean up the Nashua Manville asbestos site; he got $1 million to buy a conservation easement around the Pond of Safety in Randolph and Jefferson. He supported the Shays-Meehan campaign finance bill and sponsored a bill against "slamming"— the switching of long-distance phone carriers without customer notice. He supports fully funding special education by 2006. In February 2001 he got a seat on the Energy and Commerce Committee.

Most incumbent congressmen cruise to re-election without much more than a murmur of opposition; Bass has had spirited opposition three times. In the 1996 general election he was pressed hard by Deborah "Arnie" Arnesen, who outspent him and matched him in September polls. Bass recalled how she backed a 6% state income tax in 1992; she said Bass was no longer the moderate that used to vote with her in the state Senate. Bass won 51%–43%. In fall 1998 he was opposed by Mary Rauh, former head of New England Planned Parenthood, wife of 1992 and 1996 Senate candidate John Rauh. She took no PAC money and limited her contributions to $250, a more stringent regimen than that of Bass, who kept to his New Hampshire law and, for the first time, outspent his Democratic opponent. Polls from February to September showed Bass with well under 50%, a danger sign for an incumbent. But he pulled away to lead by early October and won 53%–45%. In 2000 Democrat Barney Brannen ran a spirited campaign, with ads distinguishing him from Barney Rubble and the purple Barney and attacking Bass on prescription drugs for seniors; he raised and spent $872,000, $60,000 more than Bass. But Bass attacked him for his support from trial lawyers and labor unions and ran ads with an endorsement from John

McCain. An anonymous mailing pointed out that as a lawyer Bannon had represented a Vermont man convicted of three attacks on women. Al Gore, though he narrowly lost the state, carried the 2nd District 48%–47%. But Bass ran 9% ahead of George W. Bush and won 56%–41%.

Cook's Call   *Potentially Competitive*. For the first time in four runs for this office, Bass looks like he has finally taken hold of this swing district. After turning in lackluster performances since 1994, Bass defeated a well-funded Democrat in 2000 with a solid 56%. Bass's big win in 2000 and his moderate profile, critical in a district that Democratic presidential nominees have won since 1992, make him a tough target in 2002.

THE PEOPLE: Pop. 2000: 610,259; Pop. 1990: 554,949, up 10% 1990–2000. 95.9% White, 0.7% Black, 1.4% Asian, 0.3% Amer. Indian, 1.1% Two+ races, 0.7% Other; 1.7% Hispanic Origin.

2000 Presidential Vote

Gore (D)	133,588	(48%)
Bush (R)	131,445	(47%)
Nader (Green)	11,355	(4%)
Others	2,978	(1%)

1996 Presidential Vote

Clinton (D)	124,564	(50%)
Dole (R)	95,191	(38%)
Perot (I)	24,489	(10%)
Others	4,077	(2%)

Rep. Charles Bass (R)

Elected 1994, 4th term; b. Jan. 8, 1952, Boston, MA; home, Peterborough; Dartmouth Col., A.B. 1974; Episcopalian; married (Lisa).

Elected Office: NH House of Reps., 1982–88; NH Senate, 1988–92.

Professional Career: Field worker, U.S. Rep. William Cohen, 1974; Legis. Asst., U.S. Rep. David Emery, 1975–76, Chief of Staff, 1976–79; Vice Pres., High Standard Inc., 1980–93; Chmn., Columbia Architectural Products, 1980–93.

DC Office: 218 CHOB 20515, 202-225-5206; Fax: 202-225-2946; Web site: www.house.gov/bass.

District Offices: Concord, 603-226-0249; Keene, 603-358-4094; Littleton, 603-444-1271; Nashua, 603-889-8772.

Committees: *Budget* (4th of 24 R). *Energy & Commerce* (27th of 31 R): Commerce, Trade & Consumer Protection; Environment & Hazardous Materials; Oversight & Investigations.

Group Ratings

	ADA	ACLU	AFS	LCV	CON	ITIC	NTU	COC	ACU	NTLC	CHC
2000	20	36	0	57	24	100	56	90	75	79	47
1999	20	—	0	38	15	—	58	88	68	—	—

National Journal Ratings

	1999 LIB —	1999 CONS		2000 LIB —	2000 CONS
Economic	0% —	84%		42% —	57%
Social	52% —	48%		53% —	47%
Foreign	28% —	70%		22% —	76%

Key Votes of the 106th Congress

1. Patient Bill of Rights	N	5. Bar RU-486 $ for FDA	N	9. NATO War in Serbia	N
2. Accelerate Min. Wage	N	6. Display 10 Commandments	Y	10. Perm. Trade with China	Y
3. Strike Ban on Ergo. Stnd.	N	7. Gun Show Bkgrnd. Checks	N	11. Debt Relief for 3rd World	N
4. Ovrd. Estate Tax Veto	Y	8. Ban Part.-Birth Abortion	Y	12. Drop Cuba Econ. Embargo	N

Election Results

2000 general	Charles Bass (R)	152,581	(56%)	($812,727)
	Barney Brannen (D)	110,367	(41%)	($872,115)
	Other	8,392	(3%)	
2000 primary	Charles Bass (R)	unopposed		
1998 general	Charles Bass (R)	85,740	(53%)	($547,937)
	Mary Rauh (D)	72,217	(45%)	($330,690)
	Others	3,419	(2%)	

★ NEW JERSEY ★

New Jersey has been overshadowed for years by the metropolises of New York and Philadelphia—"a valley of humility between two mountains of conceit," its neighbor Benjamin Franklin called it. It was named by King James II, then Duke of York, for the Channel Island on which he was sheltered during the English Civil War. New Jersey was plagued in its early years by rival claims from its neighbors and took to the Supreme Court its argument with New York over who owns the Statue of Liberty and Ellis Island; New Jersey got most of the land, but New York got the immigrant museum and Great Hall. But New Jersey has much to say for itself. It is "a sort of laboratory in which the best blood is prepared for other communities to thrive on," Woodrow Wilson said when he was governor, just a tad defensively.

Today, New Jersey is the nation's ninth most populous state: It boomed in the 1980s, suffered sharply in the early 1990s recession, and now has come back more strongly than its neighbors: unemployment sank to the national average in the late 1990s. High-tech has led the resurgence: New Jersey's pharmaceutical firms, like Merck and Johnson & Johnson, anchor the "Jersey Research Corridor," while firms like Lucent also help make the state a leader in telecommunications. Within its close boundaries is great diversity, geographically from beaches to mountains, demographically from old Quaker stock to new Hispanics, economically from inner city slums to hunt country mansions. Though New York writers are inclined to look on New Jersey as a land of 1940s diners and 1970s shopping malls, this state much more closely resembles the rest of America than does Manhattan, even if some of its traffic signals are arrayed horizontally rather than vertically and its accents can sometimes be incomprehensible to outsiders. The Jersey City row houses seen on emerging from the Holland Tunnel, many renovated by Wall Street commuters and Latin immigrants, give way within a few miles to the lonely skyscrapers of Newark and comfortably packed middle-income suburbs. Farther out are the horse country around Far Hills, the university town of Princeton, old industrial cities like Paterson, and dozens of suburban towns and small factory cities where people work and raise families over generations; an hour from Philadelphia and two hours from Manhattan is Atlantic City, with gambling revenues in 2000 ($4.3 billion) that nearly matched the Las Vegas strip ($4.7 billion).

In the last two decades, a new New Jersey has sprouted. The oil tank farms and swamplands of the Jersey Meadows have become sports palaces and office complexes; the intersection of I-78 and I-287 has become a major shopping and office edge city; U.S. 1 north from Princeton to North Brunswick has become one of the nation's high-tech centers; the flat vegetable fields once dotted with gas station junctions now have tourist attractions like Great Adventure amusement park. Despite former Governor Christine Todd Whitman's $1 billion open space preservation act, open land is being gobbled up by big office centers and new subdivisions. Even some of New Jersey's long-ailing central cities are perking up. Jersey City's waterfront is sprouting shopping malls, apartment complexes, and the *New York Daily News* printing plant; Newark is graced with a sparkling Performing Arts Center and new subdivisions; Trenton, after many years of being the only state capital without a major hotel, is getting a Marriott. New Jersey increasingly has an identity of its own. It is the home of big league football, basketball and hockey franchises and of the world's longest expanse of boardwalks on the Jersey Shore from Cape May to Sandy Hook.

State government played an important role in building New Jersey identity and pride. Governor Brendan Byrne in the 1970s started the Meadowlands sports complex and got casino gambling legalized in Atlantic City. Governor Tom Kean in the 1980s started education reforms and promoted the state shamelessly. The revolt against Governor Jim Florio's tax increase in 1990 was led by the first all-New Jersey talk radio station and took on national significance. In the late 1990s crime was dropping—9% in 1998, 6% in 1999—and welfare rolls tumbled 43% between 1997 and 1999; in 2000, auto insurance rates fell 15%, but still were the highest in the nation. All these were reasons for contentment, and there were even reasons for pride. For the first time since Woodrow Wilson, New Jersey has produced politicians of national stature—Bill Bradley, who retired from the Senate in 1996 after three terms and ran for president in 2000; Christine Todd Whitman, who gave Bradley a scare in 1990, beat Florio in 1993, and became George W. Bush's

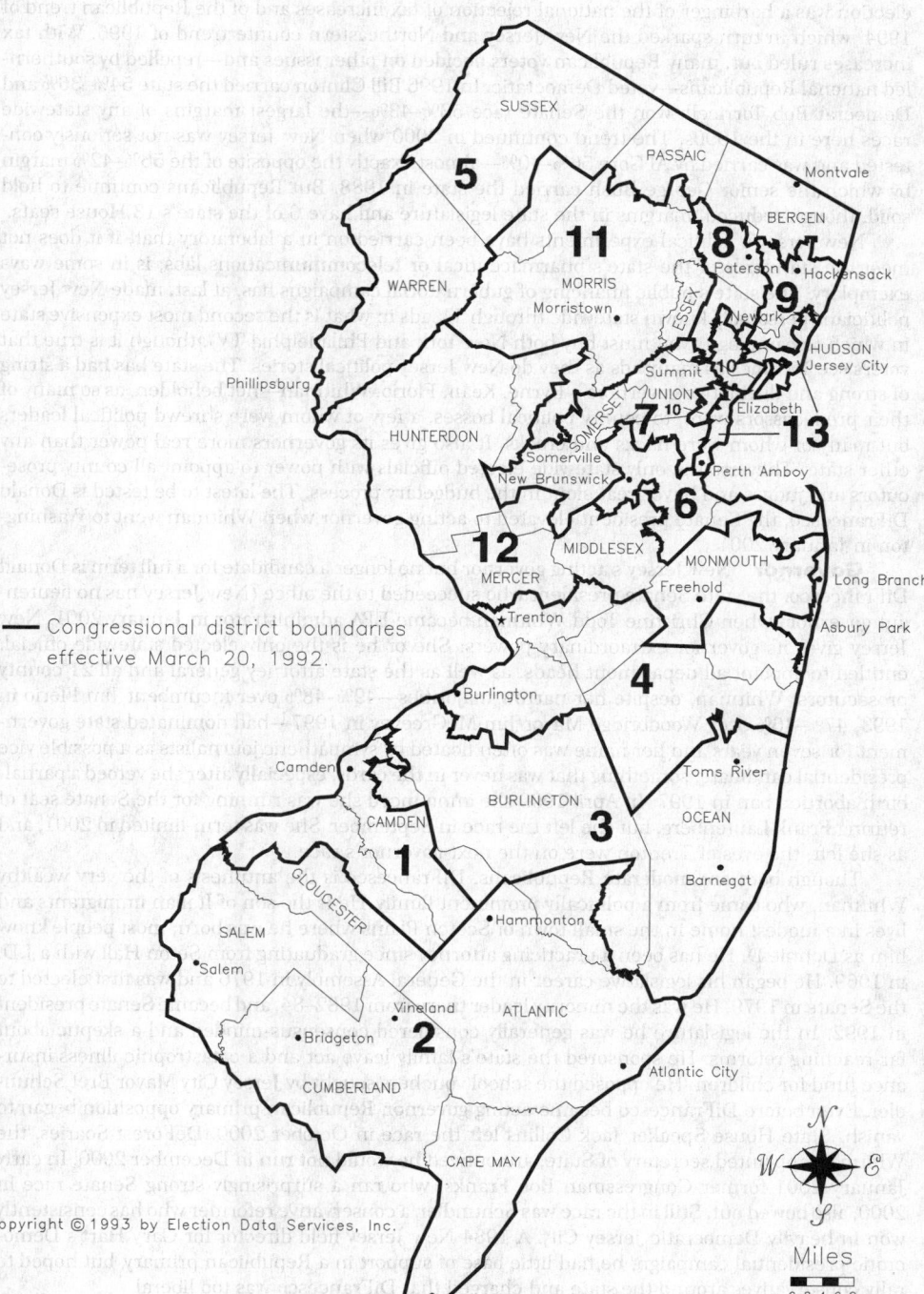

SUSSEX

PASSAIC

Montvale

5

BERGEN

11

8

Paterson • Hackensack

WARREN

MORRIS

Morristown

9

Newark

ESSEX

HUDSON
Jersey City

Summit

10

Phillipsburg

UNION

7

10

HUNTERDON

Elizabeth

13

SOMERSET

Somerville

Perth Amboy

New Brunswick

6

12

MIDDLESEX

MONMOUTH

MERCER

Freehold

Long Branch

★ Trenton

Asbury Park

— Congressional district boundaries
effective March 20, 1992.

4

Burlington

Camden

Toms River

BURLINGTON

OCEAN

CAMDEN

1

Barnegat

GLOUCESTER

3

Hammonton

SALEM

• Salem

Vineland

ATLANTIC

2

• Bridgeton

Atlantic City

CUMBERLAND

CAPE MAY

N
W   E
S

Miles

0 2 4 6 8

Cape May

EPA administrator in 2001; publisher Steve Forbes, who helped prepare Whitman's tax cut package in 1993 and then used his own money to run for president in 1996 and 2000. Whitman's election was a harbinger of the national rejection of tax increases and of the Republican trend of 1994, which in turn sparked the New Jersey and Northeastern countertrend of 1996. With tax increases ruled out, many Republican voters decided on other issues and—repelled by southern-led national Republicans—voted Democratic. In 1996 Bill Clinton carried the state 54%–36% and Democrat Bob Torricelli won the Senate race 53%–43%—the largest margins of any statewide races here in the 1990s. The trend continued in 2000 when New Jersey was not seriously contested and was carried by Al Gore 56%–40%—almost exactly the opposite of the 56%–42% margin by which the senior George Bush carried the state in 1988. But Republicans continue to hold solid, though reduced, margins in the state legislature and have 6 of the state's 13 House seats.

New Jersey's political experiments have been carried on in a laboratory that, if it does not meet the standards of the state's pharmaceutical or telecommunications labs, is in some ways exemplary. The state's public financing of gubernatorial campaigns has, at last, made New Jersey politicians personally known statewide through TV ads in what is the second most expensive state in which to campaign (you must buy both New York and Philadelphia TV), though it is true that voters see 10 times as many ads as they do New Jersey political stories. The state has had a string of strong and distinctive governors—Byrne, Kean, Florio, Whitman—not beholden, as so many of their predecessors were, to county political bosses, a few of whom were shrewd political leaders but many of whom were hacks and crooks. It also gives its governors more real power than any other state. They are the only statewide elected officials with power to appoint all county prosecutors and judges and have great clout in the budgetary process. The latest to be tested is Donald DiFrancesco, the Senate president elevated to acting governor when Whitman went to Washington in January 2001.

Governor   New Jersey's acting governor but no longer a candidate for a full term is Donald DiFrancesco, the state Senate president who succeeded to the office (New Jersey has no lieutenant governor) when Christine Todd Whitman became EPA administrator in January 2001. New Jersey gives its governor extraordinary powers: She or he is the only elected statewide official, entitled to appoint all department heads, as well as the state attorney general and all 21 county prosecutors. Whitman, despite her narrow majorities—49%–48% over incumbent Jim Florio in 1993, 47%–46% over Woodbridge Mayor Jim McGreevey in 1997—had dominated state government for seven years and her name was often floated by sympathetic journalists as a possible vice presidential candidate, something that was never in the cards, especially after she vetoed a partial-birth abortion ban in 1997. In April 1999 she announced she was running for the Senate seat of retiring Frank Lautenberg, but she left the race in September. She was term-limited in 2001, and as she left, the eyes of Trenton were on the next governor's race.

Though both are moderate Republicans, DiFrancesco is the antithesis of the very wealthy Whitman, who came from a politically prominent family. He is the son of Italian immigrants and lives in a modest home in the small town of Scotch Plains where he was born; most people know him as Donnie D. He has been a practicing attorney since graduating from Seton Hall with a J.D. in 1969. He began his legislative career in the General Assembly in 1976 and was first elected to the Senate in 1979. He was the minority leader there from 1982–84, and became Senate president in 1992. In the legislature he was generally considered consensus-minded and a skeptic about far-reaching reforms. He sponsored the state's family leave act and a catastrophic illness insurance fund for children. He opposed the school vouchers sought by Jersey City Mayor Bret Schundler. Even before DiFrancesco became acting governor, Republican primary opposition began to vanish. State House Speaker Jack Collins left the race in October 2000. DeForest Soaries, the Whitman-appointed secretary of State, announced he would not run in December 2000. In early January 2001 former Congressman Bob Franks, who ran a surprisingly strong Senate race in 2000, also bowed out. Still in the race was Schundler, a conservative reformer who has consistently won in heavily Democratic Jersey City. A 1984 New Jersey field director for Gary Hart's Democratic presidential campaign, he had little base of support in a Republican primary, but hoped to rally conservatives around the state and charged that DiFrancesco was too liberal.

DiFrancesco's tenure became a disaster soon after he was sworn in as governor on January

31. Ethical practices that were common for state legislators became unacceptable for the state's chief executive, especially someone who entered the office without a contest and was preparing for his first statewide campaign. His initial problem was a series of disclosures of favorable financial deals that he received from friends and close family members whom he helped win state jobs and contracts, plus possible conflicts of interests in his concurrent job as the town lawyer for Scotch Plains. Then, he was forced to abandon Isabel Miranda, his choice for state treasurer, when his former Senate colleagues wanted to learn more about the circumstances of her firing by Citibank, where she had used her expense account for personal travel. DiFrancesco compounded that problem when it was learned that, rather than resign, Miranda had taken an unpaid leave from her job at U.S. Trust Company of New Jersey after he tapped her as treasurer; the firm was a potential trustee for billions of dollars of state funds. The unfavorable media coverage left Republicans worried that DiFrancesco could not win in November. On April 25, he decided that he had enough. "I've had it," he told reporters. "These past several weeks have—almost seemed like several years, quite frankly—have really dealt a blow to me and my family, and I think it's too difficult."

That left him in the still-unique position of acting governor and Senate president for the remainder of 2001, but it jolted the November contest for a new governor. Even before DiFrancesco formally announced his withdrawal, Bob Franks had rallied support from most of the state's Republican county chairmen. With that powerful political base, he declared his candidacy for governor with an only-in-New-Jersey pledge to "shake up the political process" as a reformer favoring term limits, an elected auditor general, plus citizen initiatives. "Honest and effective public service" became the campaign theme for Franks, whose 14 years in the Assembly and service as state Republican chairman in the pre-Whitman years made him knowledgeable about state government and politics before he was elected to Congress from the suburban 7th District in 1992. Meanwhile, the Legislature voted a three-week delay of the primary until June 26, which also accommodated a separate federal court review of redistricting changes for the Legislature; and lawmakers extended the deadline for candidates to replace DiFrancesco on the primary ballot. All this was an outrage to Schundler, who accused Republican bosses of changing the rules in the middle of the election to thwart him. But the state Supreme Court threw out his challenge to the election changes, and another judge allowed DiFrancesco to transfer his $720,000 kitty to Franks. Although he emphasized the themes of school choice, lower taxes and controls on suburban sprawl, Schundler's pro-gun, anti-abortion views were greeted skeptically by many party insiders. As a fresher and more soothing face in Trenton, Franks became the strong favorite to win the Republican nomination.

The turmoil raised doubts about the well-laid plans for an insurgent campaign by the usually fissiparous Democrats who, after some commotion, agreed in early 2001 on their nominee. The initial conflict was caused by Senator Robert Torricelli, who in early July 2000 said that he would run for governor. Three weeks later, after many Democrats including Newark Mayor Sharpe James said they would support McGreevey, Torricelli ended his candidacy. McGreevey had already gotten many commitments from Democrats and labor leaders and raised $3.2 million for the state Democratic Party. In mid-November, McGreevey presided over a unity rally where he was endorsed by Torricelli and Democratic leaders in 20 of 21 counties. McGreevey decried "seven years of rudderless government" and attacked Whitman for a botched emissions testing system and cost overruns on installing E-ZPass. But not only was Whitman gone, so was DiFrancesco, the Republican insiders in Trenton. With Franks having spent most of the Whitman years in Washington pursuing a moderate voting record in Congress, he sought to distance himself from those problems.

Whitman left behind one legacy unchallenged: New Jersey has one of the nation's most liberal activist state Supreme Courts; in recent years it has ruled that the Boy Scouts can't exclude gays (that was overturned by the U. S. Supreme Court), struck down parental notification abortion laws, upheld the right of political activists to campaign in privately-owned shopping malls, and ruled that a lesbian who helped raise children has visitation rights after breaking up with the mother.

Cook's Call   *Highly Competitive.* In the battle for the Republican nomination, Congressman Bob Franks is the favorite against conservative Jersey City Mayor Brent Schundler. On the Democratic side, Woodbridge Mayor Jim McGreevey—who has been running for the post since 1997, when he narrowly lost to Whitman—has locked up the nomination. The general election should be close.

Senior Senator　Bob Torricelli, a Democrat elected to the Senate in 1996, grew up in Franklin Lakes in North Jersey, graduated from Rutgers and the Kennedy School at Harvard and in 1975, at 24, became an aide to New Jersey Governor Brendan Byrne. Three years later he was working for Vice President Walter Mondale; he managed the decisive Carter-Mondale victory over Edward Kennedy in the 1980 Illinois primary and argued party rules with Kennedy's Harold Ickes at the convention. He is aggressive, adversarial, articulate and politically savvy. In 1982, at 31, he returned home to New Jersey, raised lots of money and beat an incumbent Republican congressman in the 9th District. In the House, he took politically beneficial committee assignments: International Relations (many of his ethnic constituents had particular interests in Israel, Greece, Korea, the Philippines and Cuba) and Science (North Jersey has big pharmaceutical and hightech firms). In the Senate, he outmaneuvered several other Democrats following the 2000 election to win a seat on Finance. He can be a tough party loyalist: He was one of Bill Clinton's most outspoken defenders in 1998. But he can also take an independent stand: He was one of the most vocal supporters of the Gulf war resolution in 1991 and he sharply criticized Clinton's Kosovo policy in 1999; he said that Clinton had no clear strategy and that the White House advisers were terrible. He chaired the Democrats' Senate campaign committee in 1999–2000 and helped produce the 50–50 split that few had thought possible. In December 2000, he was one of the first Democrats to call on Al Gore to concede and praised the nomination of John Ashcroft as attorney general, though he voted against his confirmation a few weeks later; and he angered Democrats in a private meeting with his commendations of Supreme Court Justice Antonin Scalia after the election deadlock.

When Bill Bradley announced in August 1995 he would not run for another term in the Senate, Torricelli rushed into the race. He cleared away any Democratic opposition and raised money at a record-setting pace, spending $9 million. Torricelli had serious opposition from 12th District Republican Congressman Dick Zimmer, who maneuvered former Governor Tom Kean out of the race and spent $8 million. Zimmer was solidly conservative on taxes, more moderate on cultural issues—pro-choice on abortion, for environmental protection of undeveloped land. The campaign was classically hard-hitting. Torricelli hit Zimmer for supporting the assault weapons ban, Medicare "cuts," changes in student loans, renewal of ocean dumping and constantly brought up Newt Gingrich. Torricelli was going with the flow: Opinion in New Jersey was clearly hostile to the Gingrich Republicans, and moving sharply toward Bill Clinton, who got 43% of the vote here in 1992 and 54% in 1996. Torricelli won 53%–43%, losing the western suburbs and the Jersey Shore, but piling up large margins in the counties within an hour's drive of New York and Philadelphia.

Torricelli can be highly partisan, but he has also had one of the most moderate voting records among Senate Democrats, with some initiatives well chosen for New Jersey—one of the highest-income states, but one where few people consider themselves rich. With Republican Paul Coverdell he sponsored the bill for $2,000 per year per child tax-free savings accounts for children's education, which could be used for private schools, colleges or trade schools. It passed the Senate twice, but was vetoed by Clinton in 1998. In May 2001, he was one of four Finance Committee Democrats to buck Tom Daschle and vote for the tax cuts prepared by Chuck Grassley and Max Baucus, including the phase-out of the estate tax and lower income-tax rates for the wealthy; in exchange, the committee included Torricelli's plan to make college tuition deductible. "Nobody told me when I became a Democrat that that involved opposition to lower taxes." He supported a bill to reduce the waiting time and the costs of asbestos suits and supported a patent extension for Schering-Plough's Claritin, both of which were attacked by Democratic Senate candidates in the 2000 cycle. He has sponsored Internet privacy bills requiring websites to get consumers' permission before releasing personal information; with Patrick Leahy, he passed an amendment to protect privacy of personal information held by firms filing for bankruptcy.

He has kept a high profile on foreign issues. He has taken a consistent hard line against Fidel

Castro's Cuba, supporting the Helms-Burton Act, and opposing an end to the embargo. He co-sponsored with Jesse Helms a bill to strengthen the 1979 Taiwan Relations Act. In September 2000, he and Fred Thompson sought to amend permanent normal trade relations with an amendment penalizing Chinese companies that sell nuclear, chemical or biological weapons and long-range missiles and requiring an annual presidential decision on the issue; it was beaten 65–32.

Torricelli became chairman of the Democratic Senate Campaign Committee when no one else wanted the job and few thought that Democrats could win control. He set out to raise $104 million, to spend more soft money on ads and to recruit candidates. It was Torricelli who on *Meet the Press* in January 1999 first mentioned, without asking her permission, that Hillary Rodham Clinton was thinking about running for the Senate in New York; he thought she was the only Democrat who could beat Rudolph Giuliani. When his New Jersey colleague Frank Lautenberg announced his retirement in February 1999, Torricelli exacerbated their bitter feud. He gave great offense to Congressmen Bob Menendez and Frank Pallone and former Governor James Florio when he pushed forward Goldman Sachs chairman Jon Corzine, who had the money to self-finance his campaign. He spotted the weakness of incumbent Republicans in Delaware, Michigan, Minnesota, Missouri, and Washington; all lost, the largest number of incumbents to lose in years. Columnist Robert Novak wrote that Torricelli "is often called the most disliked member of the Senate," and Democratic colleagues resent his conservativism on many issues on which a liberal stand would be unpopular in New Jersey. To which Torricelli says, "I will accept criticism of my loyalty to the Democratic Party from anyone who has recruited more candidates, raised more money, or defeated more Republicans."

The Democrats' big gains in the 2000 Senate races were a big victory for Torricelli; "he's earned redemption," said the New Jersey Democratic chairman. His conciliatory post-election attitude extended to legislation. In addition to supporting Bush's tax cut, he joined Republican Mitch McConnell in calling for a bipartisan commission to make recommendations on election procedures. He rallied Democratic support for the confirmation of Christie Whitman as EPA Director. Torricelli played a major rule during the two-week Senate debate on McCain-Feingold in March 2001; he also won passage of an amendment to require broadcasters to provide discounted TV advertising rates for political commercials in prime time.

Torricelli has made political missteps. In July 2000 he announced that he was running for governor in 2001, and tried to elbow aside Jim McGreevey, who had been campaigning nonstop since losing to Christie Whitman by only 47%–46%. Most prominent Democrats rallied to McGreevey, and Torricelli bowed out by the end of the month. At the same time was besieged by the Justice Department investigation of his political activity. The inquiry, in which seven people had been convicted and three of his top aides were targeted, initially dealt with illegal contributions to his 1996 campaign. But it expanded to include his relationship with New Jersey businessman David Chang, a major fundraiser for his campaign plus the Senate campaign committee, who allegedly gave Torricelli numerous gifts—including clothing, jewelry, antiques and cash—and may have benefited from Torricelli's contacts with federal agencies on his behalf. Torricelli denied any wrongdoing, and said that the gifts were permissible because Chang was a friend. He was also, unusually for a senator, an active stock trader, with 112 transactions, many on high-tech stocks, in 1999. Reports of a possible indictment fueled speculation that Torricelli might resign or, at least, not seek reelection in 2002.

Running against Torricelli has presented stiff challenges, but his legal problems raised Republican prospects. Possible contenders included state Senator William Gormley, who lost the primary narrowly to Bob Franks in the 2000 primary, Essex County Executive James Treffinger, Congressman Frank LoBiondo, investment banker and Port Authority Chairman Lewis Eisenberg, and publisher and former presidential candidate Steve Forbes. Still, if he survives the investigation, a Senate seat may not be the limit of Torricelli's ambitions. Asked in October 1999 whether he would run for president, he said, "It's certainly something that I've never said I either would do or wouldn't do. It obviously depends on the circumstances."

Cook's Call *Potentially Competitive.* Torricelli begins his re-election bid in strong financial shape and New Jersey is trending increasingly Democratic, but an ongoing investigation of his 1996 campaign finances and allegations of ethics violations have fueled Republican interest in this race. Republican polls indicate some softness in Torricelli's approval ratings and overall support, and a long line of Republican hopefuls has started to form. Although Torricelli's problems improve Republican chances, statewide campaigns in New Jersey are notoriously expensive and defeating an incumbent is no easy task.

Junior Senator   Jon Corzine, former chairman of Goldman Sachs, was elected senator from New Jersey in 2000 after waging the most expensive campaign in American history. Corzine grew up on a family farm in Downstate Illinois, far from New Jersey; he went to college at the University of Illinois and business school at the University of Chicago and served six years in the Marine Corps Reserve. In 1975 Corzine joined Goldman Sachs in New York; his entry-level position included fetching coffee for his superiors. "The coffee must have been great," *National Journal's* Gideon Berger writes: in 1980 Corzine was made a general partner in the investment bank. In 1994 he became co-chairman and CEO. In May 1999 Goldman Sachs went public, and the $3.66 billion initial offering netted Corzine more than $300 million; he retired in 1999 after a management shakeup. For all his wealth, Corzine has continued to live in the pleasant but far from pretentious suburb of Summit, New Jersey. Aside from contributing to Democratic (and some Republican) candidates, he was not involved in politics, indeed did not vote in primary elections from 1988 to 1998 or in the 1991, 1995 and 1998 general elections; in 1997 he co-chaired a presidential commission on increasing investment in technology, infrastructure and schools.

In early 1999 a Senate race was probably the farthest thing from Corzine's mind. Then, in February 1999, Senator Frank Lautenberg announced he would not run again in 2000; Lautenberg, also a self-made millionaire who spent liberally on his campaigns, was instrumental in, among other things, outlawing smoking on planes and reducing the legal blood alcohol limit for drunk driving to .08%. Plunging immediately into the race was former Governor Jim Florio, still unpopular for the $2.8 billion tax increase he secured in 1990; Democrats lost control of the legislature in 1991 and Florio was defeated in 1993. In April Governor Christie Whitman, presumably the strongest possible Republican candidate, announced she was running. Many Democratic insiders, including Senator Bob Torricelli, feared that Whitman would win the seat, and scurried around to find other contenders. In June Congressman Frank Pallone left the race.

Then Torricelli and North Jersey Democratic insiders found Corzine, with $300 million and without a job. He started running, going around the state to meet leaders of the county Democratic organizations, who are considered vital in the primary, and, it was revealed much later, contributing generously to them and to community organizations. He quickly cornered organization support outside Florio's home area in South Jersey and, like most local Democratic insiders, endorsed Al Gore over New Jersey's Bill Bradley. Meanwhile, Corzine's great wealth and his willingness to spend it, cleared the field. Whitman withdrew in September; former Governor Tom Kean said he would not run in October; former Democratic state Chairman Tom Byrne, Republican Congressman Frank LoBiondo and Republican Port Authority Chairman Lewis Eisenberg left the race in November. Corzine's money talked even while most New Jersey voters had never heard of him.

Still Florio, backed by Camden County Democratic leader George Norcross and some labor unions, campaigned aggressively. He attacked Corzine's inexperience and spotty voting record. He said Corzine represented "Wall Street values" and was attempting a "hostile takeover of the Democratic Party." He seized on Corzine's casual remark in March 2000 to an Italian-American construction company owner, "Oh, you make cement shoes." He charged that under Corzine Goldman Sachs floated a bond issue for a company that invests in Sudan, with its terrible human rights record. Even so, New Jersey Democratic leaders dreaded that Florio would lose to even the little-known candidates running for the Republican nomination. In March, three months before the primary, Corzine went up with TV ads in the New York and Philadelphia markets. He set forth his liberal stands on issues—for a universal health care system, for government payment of tuition to college or vocational or technical school for students with at least a B average, to end discrimination against women "globally," for gun control, for abortion rights. "I want to invest in America," as he said at one point. "That's what this campaign is about." Corzine's investment—he spent $35 million up to the June primary—paid off. Florio won in South Jersey by a 67%–33%

margin, but South Jersey cast only 23% of the votes. In North Jersey Corzine led 65%–35%, for an overall 58%–42% victory.

After the primary, Corzine cut back on spending—for a while. The Republican primary, with a pathetically low turnout, was won by 7th District Congressman Bob Franks—amazingly, a member of the same church as Corzine. With North Jersey support, Franks narrowly (36%–34%) edged state Senator William Gormley, who had a big financial advantage thanks to support from Atlantic City casino interests. Corzine's ads talked about his big-government positions in appealing terms, but he almost made a political neophyte's mistakes that got him bad publicity. In early September he told the Sierra Club he had voted for an open space referendum in 1998; but in 1998 he had not voted at all. Still stuck below 50% in the polls, he started running negative ads against Franks two weeks later. He had been refusing to make his income tax returns public, on the ground they violated a confidentiality agreement with Goldman Sachs. Then in mid-September he released records showing that in 1996–99 he made $145 million, paid $43 million in taxes and gave $25 million to charity. But when reporters started investigating which charities, they found that he had stepped up giving to New Jersey groups in 1999, and that he gave hundreds of thousands to groups whose leaders and sponsors later endorsed him. He gave $30,000 to a dinner honoring Lautenberg, who later endorsed him; he gave $50,000 to Operation Rainbow/PUSH, and Jesse Jackson endorsed him the night before the primary; he gave $25,000 to St. Matthew's A.M.E. Church in Orange and was endorsed by the Black Ministers Alliance of New Jersey. When he was asked whether he had contributed to any of the churches, he said no; it turned out his family foundation made the contribution.

Franks, like Florio, argued that Corzine was trying to buy a Senate seat and attacked him for failing to disclose the tax returns and for backing "universal" government programs that were unrealistic and too costly. When Corzine's numbers stalled because of his mistakes, Franks held onto his money and spent $2.5 million in the last two and a half weeks, when he also benefited from endorsements by the *New York Times* and the *Philadelphia Inquirer*. Corzine spent $7.4 million on turnout efforts including, embarrassingly, busing in residents of Philadelphia homeless shelters and halfway houses to work on his campaign. In the end Corzine spent more than $63 million, the all-time record. He won 50%–47%, with big margins in central cities—the turnout effort delivered. But that trailed the generic vote in increasingly Democratic New Jersey.

Corzine fills the expanding ranks of left-wing Democratic senators, including Hillary Rodham Clinton of New York and Mark Dayton of Minnesota. Interestingly, many of the Senate's strongest supporters of government-provided universal health care are very rich men who self-financed at least their first campaigns—Corzine, Dayton, Jay Rockefeller, Edward Kennedy.

Presidential politics For most of the twentieth century New Jersey was a close state in close presidential elections, giving small margins to winners in 1960 and 1968 and losers in 1948 and 1976; but no more. In the 1980s the vast suburban expanses of New Jersey leaned toward the Republicans; since 1995 they have leaned to the Democrats. This is a state with relatively few strong-belief Christians and with a high number of seculars and Jews; sophisticated and cynical, it reacted strongly against the Southern-accented Republicans of Newt Gingrich's revolution. The 1996 results and polls in 1999 and 2000 showed New Jersey so heavily Democratic that neither party made it a target state—to the relief of fundraisers, who no longer had to raise money to buy New York TV. As it turned out, Bush carried white Protestants and white Catholics by narrow margins, but was far behind among blacks, Jews and, by lesser margins, Hispanics, and Gore won as easily as expected.

For years, New Jersey's June presidential primary was overshadowed by California's on the same day. In 1996 California voted in March, and New Jersey did not get to the polls until two months after the nominations were sewed up. In 1998 the state Senate refused to move the primary to March 7, and so it stayed in June—far, far too late to provide a needed victory for New Jersey's Bill Bradley, as it turned out. In any case, most of the state's Democratic establishment signed up with Al Gore.

Congressional districting New Jersey's population rose 9% between the 1990 and 2000 Censuses, the most of any Northeastern state except Delaware and New Hampshire, so it will not lose a House seat in 2002 as it did 10 years before. New Jersey has a 10-member commission, equally divided between the parties, which is supposed to agree on new lines, with a previously selected arbitrator choosing a tie-breaker. In the likely event that the commission disagrees, the tie-breaker can produce a compromise plan and see if it gets a majority of the commission; if not the tie-breaker picks one of the two parties' plans. In 1991 the tie-breaker picked the Republican plan, with grotesquely-shaped districts. But given New Jersey's post-1994 Democratic trend, by 2000 it yielded the Republicans only 6 of the state's 13 seats. It is possible, but far from certain, that the parties will agree on an incumbent-protection plan. Overall, the Republicans' advantage is that the fastest growth in the state has come in heavily Republican areas; the Democrats' advantage is that, given New Jersey's Democratic trend, there aren't so many heavily Republican areas as there were 10 years ago.

THE PEOPLE: Pop. 2000: 8,414,350; Pop. 1990: 7,730,188, up 8.9% 1990–2000. 3% of U.S. total, 9th largest; 72.6% White, 13.6% Black, 5.7% Asian, 0.2% Amer. Indian, 2.5% Two + races, 5.4% Other; 13.3% Hispanic Origin. 3.8% Unemployment. 2000 Voting age pop.: 6,326,792. 2000 Turnout: 3,293,378; 52% of VAP. Registered voters (2000): 4,710,768; 1,179,577 D (25%), 876,386 R (19%), 2,654,805 unaffiliated and minor parties (56%).

POLITICAL LINEUP: Governor, Donald T. DiFrancesco (R); Secy. of State, DeForest B. Soaries Jr. (I); Atty. Gen., John J. Farmer Jr. (R); Treasurer, Peter Lawrence (R); State Senate, 40 (15 D, 25 R); Senate President, Donald T. DiFrancesco (R); Majority Leader, John Bennett (R); State Assembly, 80 (35 D, 44 R, 1 vacancy); Assembly Speaker, Jack Collins (R). Senators, Robert G. Torricelli (D) and Jon Corzine (D). Representatives, 13 (7 D, 6 R).

ELECTIONS DIVISION: 609-292-3760; **FILING DEADLINE FOR U.S. CONGRESS:** TBA.

2000 Presidential Vote			1996 Presidential Vote		
Gore (D)	1,788,850	(56%)	Clinton (D)	1,651,019	(54%)
Bush (R)	1,284,173	(40%)	Dole (R)	1,102,577	(36%)
Nader (Green)	94,554	(3%)	Perot (I)	261,932	(9%)
Other	19,649	(1%)	Others	59,424	(2%)

2000 Republican Presidential Primary			2000 Democratic Presidential Primary		
Bush (R)	201,209	(84%)	Gore (D)	358,951	(95%)
Keyes (R)	39,601	(16%)	LaRouche (D)	19,321	(5%)

Actg. Gov. Donald T. DiFrancesco (R)

Assumed office Jan. 2001, term expires Jan. 2002, 1st term; b. Nov. 20, 1944, Scotch Plains; home, Scotch Plains; PA St. U., B.S. 1966; Seton Hall U., J.D. 1969; Catholic; married (Diane).

Elected Office: NJ General Assembly, 1976–79; NJ Senate 1979-present, Min. Leader 1982–84, President 1992-present.

Professional Career: Practicing atty., 1969–2001.

Office: State House, 125 W. State St., #CN-001, Trenton, 08625, 609-292-6000; Fax: 609-292-3454; Web site: www.state.nj.us.

Election Results

1997 general	Christine Todd Whitman (R)	1,133,394	(47%)
	Jim McGreevey (D)	1,107,968	(46%)
	Murray Sabrin (L)	114,172	(5%)
	Others	65,099	(2%)
1997 primary	Christine Todd Whitman (R)	unopposed	
1993 general	Christine Todd Whitman (R)	1,236,124	(49%)
	Jim Florio (D)	1,210,031	(48%)
	Others	59,809	(2%)

Sen. Robert G. Torricelli (D)

Elected 1996, seat up 2002, 1st term; b. Aug. 26, 1951, Paterson; home, Englewood; Rutgers U., B.A. 1974, J.D. 1977, Harvard JFK Schl. of Govt., M.P.A. 1980; United Methodist; divorced.

Elected Office: U.S. House of Reps., 1982–96.

Professional Career: Asst., NJ Gov. Brendan Byrne, 1975–77; Cnsl., Vice Pres. Walter Mondale, 1978–81; Practicing atty., 1981–82.

DC Office: 113 DSOB, 20510, 202-224-3224; Fax: 202-224-8567; Web site: www.senate.gov/~torricelli.

State Offices: Bellmawr, 609-933-2245; Newark, 973-624-5555.

Committees: *Finance*: Health Care; International Trade; Taxation & IRS Oversight. *Foreign Relations*: East Asian & Pacific Affairs; International Economic Policy, Export & Trade Promotion; Near Eastern & South Asian Affairs. *Governmental Affairs*: Government Management, Restructuring and the District of Columbia; International Security, Proliferation & Federal Services; Investigations (Permanent). *Rules & Administration*.

Group Ratings

	ADA	ACLU	AFS	LCV	CON	ITIC	NTU	COC	ACU	NTLC	CHC
2000	75	71	57	100	1	77	33	57	29	20	15
1999	95	—	83	89	43	—	16	41	8	—	—

National Journal Ratings

	1999 LIB —	1999 CONS	2000 LIB —	2000 CONS
Economic	59%	37%	56%	43%
Social	64%	31%	79%	0%
Foreign	56%	40%	53%	46%

Key Votes of the 106th Congress

1. Educ. Savings Accts.	Y	5. Review Movie Violence	N	9. NATO War in Serbia	Y
2. Prescrip. Drug Benefit	Y	6. Gun Show Bckgrnd. Checks	Y	10. Table Cuba Travel Ban	Y
3. Delay Ergonomic Standards	N	7. Ban Part.-Birth Abortion	N	11. Nuclear Test-Ban Treaty	Y
4. Phase Out Estate Tax	Y	8. Broaden Hate Crimes List	Y	12. Perm. Trade with China	Y

Election Results

1996 general	Robert G. Torricelli (D)	1,519,154	(53%)	($9,134,854)
	Dick Zimmer (R)	1,227,351	(43%)	($8,238,181)
	Others	136,961	(5%)	
1996 primary	Robert G. Torricelli (D)	unopposed		
1990 general	Bill Bradley (D)	977,810	(50%)	($12,444,283)
	Christine Todd Whitman (R)	918,874	(47%)	($801,660)
	Others	41,770	(2%)	

Sen. Jon Corzine (D)

Elected 2000, seat up 2006, 1st term; b. Jan. 1, 1947, Taylorville, IL; home, Summit; U. of IL (Urbana-Champaign), B.A. 1969; U. of Chicago, M.B.A. 1973; Christian; married (Joanne).

Military Career: Marine Corps Reserves, 1969–75.

Professional Career: Officer, Continental IL Natl. Bank, 1970–73; Asst. V.P., BancOhio, 1973–75; Goldman Sachs, Bond Trader 1975–80, Partner 1980–99, Chmn. & CEO 1994–99.

DC Office: 502 HSOB, 20510, 202-224-4744; Fax: 202-228-2197.

State Offices: Barrington, 856-757-5353; Newark, 973-645-3030.

Committees: *Banking, Housing & Urban Affairs*: Economic Policy; Housing & Transportation; Securities & Investment. *Environment & Public Works*: Clean Air, Wetlands, Private Property & Nuclear Safety; Fisheries, Wildlife & Water; Superfund, Waste Control & Risk Assessment. *Joint Economic Committee* (5th of 10 Sens.).

Group Ratings and Key Votes: Newly Elected

Election Results

2000 general	Jon Corzine (D)	1,511,237	(50%)	($63,209,506)
	Bob Franks (R)	1,420,267	(47%)	($6,389,936)
	Other	84,158	(3%)	
2000 primary	Jon Corzine (D)	251,216	(58%)	
	Jim Florio (D)	182,212	(42%)	
1994 general	Frank Lautenberg (D)	1,033,487	(50%)	($8,217,716)
	Garabed (Chuck) Haytaian (R)	966,244	(47%)	($5,110,378)
	Others	55,156	(3%)	

FIRST DISTRICT

Across the Delaware River from Philadelphia's skyline, Camden, New Jersey, with its closely built streets was jammed with immigrants in the 19th Century, when poet Walt Whitman lived here. In 1894, a Camden machinist named Eldridge Johnson produced the Victor Talking Machine—the birth of the company that became RCA Victor in 1929. In 1897, Camden was the site of the invention of condensed soup, and the Campbell Soup Company was founded soon afterwards. Thus Camden became a major industrial locus on the Jersey side of the Delaware River, not the broadest and certainly not the most picturesque of our Atlantic estuaries, but probably the East Coast's premier industrial waterway, with a concentration of steel factories, chemical plants and oil tank farms equal to any in the country. The flat lands of South Jersey all around, ignored in the 19th Century, had easy access to cheap water transport and plenty of skilled labor from the Philadelphia area. For a quarter-century starting in the 1940s, they became one of the country's fastest-growing industrial areas.

Now, Camden has tended to empty out, many of its factories closed, its neighborhoods beset by crime, its local government so incompetent that its mayor was convicted for doing favors for Philadelphia's organized crime leaders and the state is paying for two-thirds of the nearly-bankrupt city's budget. But as Republican national convention delegates discovered when they crossed the Ben Franklin Bridge, the city offers a few attractions: The local Cooper's Ferry Development Corporation has developed a riverfront park, with the New Jersey Aquarium and the Sony Music/Pace amphitheater, that takes advantage of Camden's site and attracts multiracial crowds; an aerospace complex and a Campbell Soup office tower have gone up. Still, city government and crime remain major impediments to Camden making additional strides.

The 1st Congressional District is, more or less, greater Camden, the Delaware riverfront from Riverton south to a point across from the Delaware state line, and suburbs running southeast to the flat vegetable fields of South Jersey. Its boroughs and townships retain their separate identities; right next to Camden is Collingswood, with its middle-class porches still freshly painted and its shops prosperous. The district includes some underclass poor, but most people here are at some level of upward mobility from the grinding working-class life of 50 years ago, living in comfortable communities, worried that the petrochemical plants which have helped many of them move up may also be poisoning their land, water and air. Politically, this is an area with a Democratic heritage, the most Democratic district in South Jersey.

The 1st District is represented by Rob Andrews, first elected in 1990. Andrews grew up in Bellmawr, the son of a shipyard worker, made a splendid record in college and law school, returned home and with then-Congressman Jim Florio's support was elected to the Camden County Board of Chosen Freeholders (wonderful name!) before he was 30. When Florio left Congress to become governor in January 1990, he postponed the special election to replace him until November; he supported Andrews, though Andrews was silent on his state tax increase. Andrews had other help. He spent $541,000 on his campaign, and he had a Republican opponent who switched positions on abortion and claimed to have attended a college he hadn't. Even so, in the anti-Florio climate, Andrews won by only 54%–43%.

Andrews became one of the Democrats' most aggressive and independent-minded reformers. One big initiative was direct student loans. Andrews felt banks were making college loans inefficiently and that direct government loans would "save money for students, families, schools and the federal treasury." Against strong lobbying opposition, he got the House to approve direct loan demonstration projects, got candidate Bill Clinton to endorse the idea in 1992 and then got it passed into law in 1993. He argues that it is one of the major achievements of the Clinton administration. He has a rather conservative record on economics and foreign policy but is more liberal on cultural issues. He voted against tax increases, including the Clinton budget package of 1993 and announced early opposition to the Clinton health care program. To some of Andrews's Democratic critics, he is a grandstander who would cut needed government programs. But his record shows that he supports government that is vigorous and serves real needs—but insists on pruning government that isn't working and on not forcing voters to pay more in taxes for the same low level of services they've been getting.

In the Republican House Andrews has had less opportunity for such initiatives but he has remained active, often by working with Republicans. As the ranking Democrat on the Employer-Employee Relations Subcommittee, he worked with chairman John Boehner to expand the panel's focus on pension and retirement issues. Unlike most Democrats, he advocates the national missile defense system. He joined Senator Joe Lieberman and several Republicans in The Empowerment Network, which has sought to renew America's families. He reduced $126 million from one of Al Gore's favorite initiatives for federal development of a new generation of fuel-efficient vehicles. Back home, he joined the three other south Jersey representatives—all Republicans—in seeking to split the state into two federal judicial districts. And he opposed the Army Corps of Engineers plan to dredge the Delaware River to permit ships to carry more freight to Philadelphia and Camden. But Andrews has been a leader among regular Democrats on several key party initiatives, including expanded health insurance, HMO reform, and education funding.

After the November 1996 election he announced he was running for governor; he managed to get the endorsements of Jim Florio and Hudson County Executive Bob Janiszewski, who were both mentioned as candidates themselves. Andrews was initially favored to win the primary, but he ran into stiff competition from then-state Senator James McGreevey, who had the backing of more Democratic county organizations in North Jersey plus key elements of organized labor. Andrews swept South Jersey and took Hudson County, but McGreevey's big margins in Middlesex, Essex and Union Counties gave him a tight 39%–37% win.

Andrews has been re-elected to the House by overwhelming margins and has continued to live in Haddon Heights, commuting by train to the Capitol and occasionally sleeping overnight in his office. Despite his split with the Camden County Democratic organization, which began in 1995 and widened to open rupture in 1998, his House seat seems safe as long as he wants it. His close loss in the gubernatorial primary and his $1 million campaign surplus suggest he may be thinking of another statewide race. In the House, Andrews joined the Armed Services Committee in 1999, a belated move that sacrificed his seniority.

Cook's Call   *Safe.* Don't look for a competitive race in this solidly Democratic district. Since winning a special election here in 1990, Andrews has never dipped below 54% and regularly racks up wins in the mid-70s.

THE PEOPLE: Pop. 2000: 609,847; Pop. 1990: 594,494, up 2.6% 1990–2000. 73.3% White, 17.4% Black, 2.7% Asian, 0.3% Amer. Indian, 1.9% Two+ races, 4.4% Other; 8.5% Hispanic Origin.

2000 Presidential Vote

Gore (D)	148,265	(64%)
Bush (R)	76,386	(33%)
Nader (Green)	7,048	(3%)

1996 Presidential Vote

Clinton (D)	132,715	(59%)
Dole (R)	61,294	(27%)
Perot (I)	25,052	(11%)
Others	5,122	(2%)

Rep. Robert Andrews (D)

Elected 1990, 6th term; b. Aug. 4, 1957, Camden; home, Haddon Heights; Bucknell U., B.A. 1979, Cornell U., J.D. 1982; Episcopalian; married (Camille).

Elected Office: Camden Cnty. Bd. of Chosen Freeholders, 1987–90.

Professional Career: Practicing atty., 1982–90; Adjunct Prof., Rutgers Law Schl., 1985–86, 1989–90.

DC Office: 2439 RHOB 20515, 202-225-6501; Fax: 202-225-6583; Web site: www.house.gov/andrews.

District Offices: Haddon Heights, 856-546-5100; Woodbury, 856-848-3900.

Committees: *Armed Services* (22d of 28 D): Military Personnel; Military Research & Development. *Education & the Workforce* (6th of 22 D): 21st Century Competitiveness; Employer-Employee Relations (RMM).

Group Ratings

	ADA	ACLU	AFS	LCV	CON	ITIC	NTU	COC	ACU	NTLC	CHC
2000	75	64	85	100	46	56	33	38	20	21	27
1999	95	—	100	94	18	—	19	25	20	—	—

National Journal Ratings

	1999 LIB	—	1999 CONS		2000 LIB	—	2000 CONS
Economic	64%	—	35%		66%	—	33%
Social	71%	—	28%		70%	—	29%
Foreign	55%	—	44%		49%	—	49%

Key Votes of the 106th Congress

1. Patient Bill of Rights	Y	5. Bar RU-486 $ for FDA	N	9. NATO War in Serbia	N
2. Accelerate Min. Wage	Y	6. Display 10 Commandments	N	10. Perm. Trade with China	N
3. Strike Ban on Ergo. Stnd.	Y	7. Gun Show Bkgrnd. Checks	Y	11. Debt Relief for 3rd World	Y
4. Ovrd. Estate Tax Veto	Y	8. Ban Part.-Birth Abortion	N	12. Drop Cuba Econ. Embargo	N

Election Results

2000 general	Robert Andrews (D)	167,327	(76%)	($405,723)
	Charlene Cathcart (R)	46,455	(21%)	($7,162)
	Other	5,830	(3%)	
2000 primary	Robert Andrews (D)	unopposed		
1998 general	Robert Andrews (D)	90,279	(73%)	($332,906)
	Ronald L. Richards (R)	27,855	(23%)	($8,796)
	Others	5,208	(4%)	

SECOND DISTRICT

The builders of the Camden & Atlantic Railroad in 1852 may not have known it, but when they extended their line to the little inlet town of Absecon, they were starting America's biggest beach resort, Atlantic City. Like all resorts, it was a product of developments elsewhere: of industrialization and spreading affluence, of railroad technology and the conquest of diseases which used to make summer a time of terror for parents and doctors. In the years after the Civil War, first Atlantic City and then the whole Jersey Shore from Brigantine to Cape May became America's first seaside resort, and Atlantic City developed its characteristic features: the Boardwalk in 1870, the amusement pier in 1882, the rolling chair in 1884, salt water taffy in the 1890s, Miss America in 1921. By 1940, when 16 million Americans visited every summer, Atlantic City was a common man's resort of old traditions; it declined in the years after World War II as people could afford nicer vacations. By the early 1970s, Atlantic City was grim, with a bedraggled convention hall (site of the 1964 Democratic National Convention), empty hotels and bleak streets of rowhouses built in the ugliest Philadelphia style.

Then in 1977, New Jersey voters legalized casino gambling in Atlantic City and gleaming new hotels sprang up, big name entertainers came in and Atlantic City became more glamorous than it had been in 90 years. But not for all of its residents: Casino and hotel jobs tend to be low-wage, and the slums begin just feet from the massive parking lots of the casinos. In the 1990s Atlantic City's gambling business was thriving—casinos came out ahead $4.3 billion in 2000—and huge new casinos were built on both Boardwalk and bayside. Meanwhile, city fathers planned to build 600 new much-needed townhouses for local residents. Now listed among the top 10 House districts nationwide for tourist economies, Atlantic City is growing into what Las Vegas has become, not just a collection of gaudy casinos but a gaggle of theme parks, with entertainment for the family as well as adults.

The Jersey Shore south of Atlantic City is a string of different resorts. There is the old Methodist town of Ocean City, where Gay Talese grew up the son of Italian immigrants, as he tells movingly in *Unto the Sons*. There is Wildwood, with its gritty boardwalk, and Cape May, with its beautifully preserved Victorian houses. Together, wrote columnist Michael Kelly, these beaches provide a paradise of "uplifting egalitarianism" for eager eaters. "The Jersey diet takes the most fattening foods that each ethnicity offers, puts them all on the same menu and double sizes them." Behind the Shore are swamp and flatland, the Pine Barrens and vegetable fields that gave New Jersey the name "Garden State." Growth has been slow in these small towns and gas station intersections, communities in whose eerie calmness in the summer you can hear mosquitoes whining. In the flatness, you can also find towns clustered around low-wage apparel factories or petrochemical plants on the Delaware estuary; the Northeast high-tech service economy has not reached this far south in Jersey yet.

This part of South Jersey makes up the 2d Congressional District. Politically, it has strong Democratic presences in the chemical industry towns along the Delaware River and in Vineland and a strong Republican presence in Cape May; Atlantic City often votes Democratic but has an antique Republican machine that goes back generations. Democrats carried the area in all 1990s statewide elections and won easily in the 1996 and 2000 presidential races. This is prime marginal territory, off the beaten track of Northeast politics.

The congressman from the 2d District is Frank LoBiondo, a Republican elected in 1994. He grew up in Vineland, went to college in Philadelphia and worked for the family trucking firm, LoBiondo Brothers Motor Express, which originally carried produce from Jersey farms. In 1987 he was elected to the Assembly, where he stoutly opposed new taxes. LoBiondo also opposes gun control, and was backed by the National Rifle Association. In 1992 LoBiondo ran unsuccessfully against veteran Congressman William Hughes, and lost 56%–41%. After Hughes decided to retire in 1994. LoBiondo ran again and in the primary faced Atlantic County state Senator William Gormley; LoBiondo attacked him as a taxer and NRA ads called him "a liberal in Republican clothing." LoBiondo won 54%–35%, an impressive margin inasmuch as Gormley went on to carry the area in the primaries for governor in 1993 and senator in 2000. LoBiondo then easily won the 1994 general, 65%–35%.

In the House, LoBiondo has compiled a moderate voting record, especially on economic issues. He was one of six Republicans to vote against Newt Gingrich's Medicare plan in October 1995 (four were from New Jersey); he voted against a veterans' appropriation as having insufficient medical care and against exempting small businesses from the minimum wage. He is a founder and co-chair of the Congressional Gaming Caucus. He won House passage of in 1999 of the Honesty in Sweepstakes Act, to make clear that no purchase of merchandise is necessary to enter contests. He and Peter Visclosky won nearly unanimously passage of a bill to provide $25 million in funding for bulletproof vests for police officers. And he won enactment of his Coastal Heritage Trail Route. With his background in small business, he has become a senior member of the Small Business Committee, where he advocates the needs of entrepreneurs such as Jersey farmers, including elimination of the estate tax. He remains a friend of the NRA—one of two House members from New Jersey to vote for John Dingell's amendment that gutted the gun-control bill.

LoBiondo has had three easy reelections. His 2000 opponent was 82 years old. LoBiondo considered a run for the open Senate seat in 2000, but bowed out of the race in November 1999, evidently deterred by the deep pockets of Democrat Jon Corzine. He has given renewed thought to seeking Bob Torricelli's Senate seat in 2002.

Cook's Call   *Safe.* Based on past Democratic performance on the presidential level (Gore won this seat by 12%), this district should be a prime target for Democrats. But LoBiondo, who has easily won here since 1994, has turned this swing district into rather safe territory for himself. When he leaves (in May 2001 he was taking a look at running for Senate) the seat will be very competitive, but for now, it remains safely in LoBiondo's hands.

THE PEOPLE: Pop. 2000: 652,730; Pop. 1990: 594,723, up 9.8% 1990–2000. 75.3% White, 14.8% Black, 2.5% Asian, 0.4% Amer. Indian, 2.1% Two+ races, 4.9% Other; 10.3% Hispanic Origin.

2000 Presidential Vote		
Gore (D)	135,600	(55%)
Bush (R)	105,464	(43%)
Nader (Green)	6,290	(3%)

1996 Presidential Vote		
Clinton (D)	117,526	(50%)
Dole (R)	84,043	(36%)
Perot (I)	27,589	(12%)
Others	4,464	(2%)

Rep. Frank A. LoBiondo (R)

Elected 1994, 4th term; b. May 12, 1946, Bridgeton; home, Vineland; St. Joseph's U., B.A. 1968; Catholic; married (Jan).

Elected Office: Cumberland Cnty. Bd. of Chosen Freeholders, 1985–88; NJ Assembly, 1987–94.

Professional Career: Operations Mgr., LoBiondo Bros. Motor Express Inc., 1968–94.

DC Office: 225 CHOB 20515, 202-225-6572; Fax: 202-225-3318; Web site: www.house.gov/lobiondo.

District Office: Mays Landing, 609-625-5008.

Committees: *Small Business* (5th of 19 R): Tax, Finance & Exports; Workforce, Empowerment & Government Programs. *Transportation & Infrastructure* (19th of 42 R): Aviation; Coast Guard & Maritime Transportation (Chmn.).

Group Ratings

	ADA	ACLU	AFS	LCV	CON	ITIC	NTU	COC	ACU	NTLC	CHC
2000	20	14	42	71	54	61	54	57	64	85	80
1999	40	—	50	44	15	—	56	68	80	—	—

National Journal Ratings

	1999 LIB	—	1999 CONS		2000 LIB	—	2000 CONS
Economic	45%	—	55%		50%	—	49%
Social	29%	—	69%		47%	—	52%
Foreign	10%	—	86%		33%	—	62%

Key Votes of the 106th Congress

1. Patient Bill of Rights	Y	5. Bar RU-486 $ for FDA	Y	9. NATO War in Serbia		N
2. Accelerate Min. Wage	Y	6. Display 10 Commandments	Y	10. Perm. Trade with China		N
3. Strike Ban on Ergo. Stnd.	Y	7. Gun Show Bkgrnd. Checks	N	11. Debt Relief for 3rd World		N
4. Ovrd. Estate Tax Veto	Y	8. Ban Part.-Birth Abortion	Y	12. Drop Cuba Econ. Embargo		N

Election Results

2000 general	Frank A. LoBiondo (R)	155,187	(66%)	($779,831)
	Edward G. Janosik (D)	74,632	(32%)	($75,622)
	Other	4,040	(2%)	
2000 primary	Frank A. LoBiondo (R)	unopposed		
1998 general	Frank A. LoBiondo (R)	93,248	(66%)	($382,050)
	Derek Hunsberger (D)	43,563	(31%)	
	Others	4,703	(3%)	

THIRD DISTRICT

The Pine Barrens of New Jersey are one of the last vacant spots on the eastern seaboard; not quite *terra incognita*, but still not thickly populated. Encroached by the Philadelphia suburbs of

South Jersey on the west and burgeoning retirement developments of the Jersey Shore on the east, they are crossed even today mostly by narrow two-lane roads; there are only a few small towns here, plus Fort Dix and McGuire Air Force Base. For years, the Barrens were seen as a barrier to civilization; only recently have environment-minded Jerseyites come to see them as a natural treasure.

The 3d Congressional District spans the Pine Barrens. Most of its residents live in the South Jersey suburbs of Philadelphia, in the spread-out suburb of Cherry Hill with its 1960s and 1970s shopping centers, or in the older towns along the Delaware River and newer ones inland toward McGuire. This is comfortable, but not hugely affluent, suburban country. East of the Pine Barrens is Ocean County, including the barrier islands from Normandy Beach south to Little Egg Harbor, with older beachfront communities and larger clusters of new subdivisions and condominium complexes inland. Ocean County grew rapidly in the 1980s and 1990s, a kind of frost belt Florida, with many retirees from New York and North Jersey eager to leave the big cities' high crime and high taxes. The two big military bases have remained active, with Fort Dix providing medical treatment for Kosovo refugees. Both the west and east ends of this district have been traditionally Republican, though the district was carried by Bill Clinton and Al Gore.

The congressman from the 3d District is James Saxton. He grew up in South Jersey, worked as a teacher for three years, then became a real estate broker. In 1975 he was elected to the New Jersey Assembly, when Republicans were struggling to stop Governor Brendan Byrne's income tax. In 1984 he ran to fill a vacancy in the House, won the Republican primary 45%–41%, easily won the general and had no serious challenge until 2000.

In the House Saxton has compiled a moderate to conservative voting record. He co-sponsored the ocean dumping law of 1988, when medical wastes were washing up against the Jersey Shore. In 1995, he became chairman of the Fisheries Conservation, Wildlife and Oceans Subcommittee. With Republican Wayne Gilchrest, Saxton came up with a proposal for tax incentives for land-owners who help protect endangered species before they are listed. He supported a revision of the Safe Drinking Water Act in 1996, and with Democrat Henry Waxman authored a "right to know" provision requiring water utilities to disclose pollutants. He backed legislation to clean up 28 "nationally significant" local estuaries and has won millions of dollars to study high childhood cancer in Toms River. He won support for protecting coral reefs, which provide habitat for hundreds of fish species.

Saxton is a supporter of strong anti-terrorism efforts and of aid to Israel. He chaired a task force to study the threat of terrorism, concluding that the nation needed prompt action to combat the risk of biological weapons. After the 1998 bombings of U.S. embassies in Kenya and Tanzania, he criticized the "lack of determination" to punish terrorists. He sponsored a bill that allowed a local couple to successfully sue Iran for their daughter's death in a 1995 Gaza Strip bombing; that apparently was the first time that a U.S. citizen won damages in federal court from a foreign government in a terrorism case. In April 1999 he went to Belgrade and met with the foreign minister, to the surprise of the White House, but failed to secure release of three soldiers captured by the Serbians or further any negotiations.

On the Joint Economic Committee, he worked with Dick Armey to question the Clinton administration's request for an additional $18 billion to the IMF. His efforts pressured IMF officials to open their operations to greater public view; after months of delay, the House agreed that some Asian and Latin American nations might go bankrupt and in October 1998 approved the full amount. He has backed a tax change to limit the capital gains taxes that millions of mutual-fund investors must pay. With a seat on Armed Services he has worked to save local bases. When Fort Dix ended up on the 1991 base closing list, Saxton turned much of it into a federal prison and state police training center. When McGuire Air Force base was on the 1993 list, Saxton convinced the commission the base needed to be expanded as the East Coast air mobility hub for the armed forces. In 2001, he took over the locally useful chairmanship of the Military Installation and Facilities Subcommittee.

Democrats targeted Saxton early in the 2000 campaign with strong support for 12-year Cherry Hill Mayor Susan Bass Levin. With a local appearance and recorded phone calls from President Clinton, Levin was well-funded and sought to depict Saxton as too conservative and out of the mainstream locally. But he was helped by his endorsement from the local Sierra Club and New Jersey Environmental Federation and by staff resignations and other disarray in Levin's campaign. Levin carried her home area narrowly, but lost the rest of the district by solid margins, and Saxton won 57%–41%. If redistricting produces another similar ocean-to-Delaware-River district, his 2000 performance may deter serious competition in the future.

　　Cook's Call　*Safe.* The fact that Saxton easily defeated his best known and best funded Democratic opponent in years by a whopping 57% shows just how well situated the 16-year incumbent is in this swing district. Though this south central New Jersey district has been voting for Democrats at the presidential level since 1996, voters here are also very comfortable supporting Saxton. He is unlikely to face serious competition in 2002.

THE PEOPLE: Pop. 2000: 647,095; Pop. 1990: 594,667, up 8.8% 1990–2000. 86.3% White, 8.3% Black, 2.7% Asian, 0.2% Amer. Indian, 1.5% Two+ races, 1% Other; 3.6% Hispanic Origin.

2000 Presidential Vote

Gore (D)	151,560	(53%)
Bush (R)	123,301	(43%)
Nader (Green)	8,606	(3%)

1996 Presidential Vote

Clinton (D)	134,326	(50%)
Dole (R)	101,100	(38%)
Perot (I)	28,212	(11%)
Others	4,914	(2%)

Rep. Jim Saxton (R)

Elected 1984, 9th term; b. Jan. 22, 1943, Nicholson, PA; home, Mt. Holly; E. Stroudsburg St. Col., B.A. 1965, Temple U., 1967–68; United Methodist; divorced.

Elected Office: NJ Assembly, 1975–82; NJ Senate, 1982–84.

Professional Career: Jr. High schl. teacher, 1965–68; Real estate broker, 1968–84.

DC Office: 339 CHOB 20515, 202-225-4765; Fax: 202-225-0778; Web site: www.house.gov/saxton.

District Offices: Cherry Hill, 856-428-0520; Mt. Holly, 609-261-5800; Ocean County, 732-914-2020; Toms River, 908-914-2020.

Committees: *Armed Services* (7th of 32 R): Military Installations & Facilities (Chmn.); Military Research & Development. *Resources* (4th of 28 R): Fisheries Conservation, Wildlife & Oceans (Vice Chmn.). *Joint Economic Committee* (Chmn. of 10 Reps.).

Group Ratings

	ADA	ACLU	AFS	LCV	CON	ITIC	NTU	COC	ACU	NTLC	CHC
2000	20	14	42	64	31	72	52	61	56	64	80
1999	25	—	33	63	2	—	51	68	68	—	—

National Journal Ratings

	1999 LIB	—	1999 CONS		2000 LIB	—	2000 CONS
Economic	50%	—	50%		50%	—	50%
Social	21%	—	78%		47%	—	52%
Foreign	35%	—	64%		33%	—	62%

Key Votes of the 106th Congress

1. Patient Bill of Rights	Y	5. Bar RU-486 $ for FDA	Y	9. NATO War in Serbia	N
2. Accelerate Min. Wage	Y	6. Display 10 Commandments	Y	10. Perm. Trade with China	N
3. Strike Ban on Ergo. Stnd.	Y	7. Gun Show Bkgrnd. Checks	N	11. Debt Relief for 3rd World	N
4. Ovrd. Estate Tax Veto	Y	8. Ban Part.-Birth Abortion	Y	12. Drop Cuba Econ. Embargo	N

Election Results

2000 general	Jim Saxton (R)	157,053	(57%)	($2,143,518)
	Susan Bass Levin (D)	112,848	(41%)	($1,760,625)
	Other	4,182	(2%)	
2000 primary	Jim Saxton (R)	unopposed		
1998 general	Jim Saxton (R)	97,508	(62%)	($535,528)
	Steven J. Polansky (D)	55,248	(35%)	($2,738)
	Others	4,483	(3%)	

FOURTH DISTRICT

New Jersey, a state long thought to be split between a North Jersey that is an appendage of New York City and a South Jersey that has the distinctive accent of Philadelphia, is becoming a state with its own identity. In the 1980s, it bubbled over with pride at its growth and new civic institutions; in 1990, it raged with anger at Governor Jim Florio's tax increases. This showed a new unity: for the great medium of protest was the first New Jersey-oriented talk radio station, begun in Trenton in 1989, and the symbolic event was the Hands Across New Jersey demonstration on a route approximating I-195, from the Jersey Shore west to the State House in Trenton overlooking the Delaware River. Trenton is an old manufacturing city ("Trenton Makes, The World Takes," the sign proclaims over the rooftops) where John Roebling of Brooklyn Bridge fame started making wire in 1848, and Walter Scott Lenox started making dishes in 1889. It is now the anomalously gritty capital—for years the only state capital with no large downtown hotel—of a mostly white-collar state.

The 4th Congressional District covers approximately the same span as Hands Across New Jersey, from Trenton to the Jersey Shore, roughly following I-195 to the Shore communities of Manasquan and Point Pleasant and Mantoloking. It includes the old colonial town of Burlington on the Delaware River and the Great Adventure Safari and Entertainment Park in the Pine Barrens. This is one part of America where population movement has been eastward, from the old neighborhoods of Trenton and its close-in suburbs to the new subdivisions of Ocean County and Wall Township. Trenton has long been a solidly Democratic town, but its suburbs are much less so, with the Jersey Shore parts of the district solidly Republican.

The congressman from the 4th District is Christopher Smith, a youthful-looking Republican with great seniority who has applied strong moral principles to practical politics with impressive results. Smith grew up in the Trenton area, worked in his family's sporting goods business, and was executive director of the New Jersey Right to Life Committee in the 1970s. In 1980 he ran for the House in a more Trenton-centered 4th District and beat 26-year incumbent Frank Thompson, a convicted Abscam defendant. A fluke, it seemed: but Smith proceeded to beat several additional serious Democrats, winning more than 60% each time. His motivation comes from religion. "Christ said it in Matthew 25: 'Whatsoever you do to the least of my brethren, you do likewise to me.' That was my motivating scripture through all of my years in Right to Life, and it continues to be," he has said. He is concerned about children and about victims of human rights violations.

On abortion, Smith got the House in 1995 to reinstate the ban, overturned by the Clinton administration, on federal health insurance paying for abortion except when the woman's life is in danger, and he has worked to stop abortions in military hospitals. Smith worked for years to reinstate the Reagan-era restrictions that would deny federal funds to family planning organizations that promote abortions abroad. The ensuing struggle lasted more than two years, with Smith leveraging his opposition to the family planning money to prevent passage of the Clinton administration's high-priority efforts to reorganize the State Department, pay U.S. dues to the United Nations and provide $18 billion for the International Monetary Fund. Smith finally was forced to yield in 1998 and 1999 omnibus spending bills, but he won in return White House agreement to restrict support for international abortion advocacy—which angered some Clinton loyalists. By executive order, President George W. Bush restored the family-planning restrictions his first full day in office. Smith also was a prime mover of legislation to ban partial-birth abortions; the House voted to override Clinton's vetoes, but Smith's side fell a few votes short of the two-thirds needed in the Senate.

At a time when few lawmakers focus on events overseas, Smith works on problems that bring him little reward at home. As chairman of the International Operations and Human Rights Subcommittee, Smith criticized China for its forced sterilizations and abortions and its persecution of Christians and other religious minorities, and opposed Permanent Normal Trade Relations. He has won passage of House resolutions condemning the killing of a human-rights activist in Northern Ireland, abortion-rights groups seeking to limit the status of the Holy See at the United Nations, anti-Semitic statements by members of the Russian Duma, and violations of individual freedoms by the new states of central Asia. Just before the 2000 election, he won passage of $95 million to protect women who had become victims of the international sex trade.

On domestic issues, his expansive view of federal spending is a contrast to many anti-abortion Republicans. He filed legislation to raise the 1996 welfare law's family cap so that states can provide extra benefits to women who have babies while on welfare, with the hope that they will be less likely to seek an abortion. This proposal created an unusual coalition with the National Organization for Women and the American Civil Liberties Union. Smith also opposes the death penalty. "Politicians holding the consistent life-life position are as rare as they are gutsy," Andrew Sullivan wrote about Smith in *The New York Times Magazine*.

At the start of the 107th Congress, Smith made known his interest in filling the top post at the International Relations panel. But that went to Henry Hyde, also a longtime abortion opponent, and Smith instead became chairman of the Veterans Affairs Committee, where he increased the VA budget by 12%. Back home, some Democrats continue to view him as a target in his independent district, but Smith has a reputation for tending to constituent problems and has been re-elected by impressive margins, 63%–35% in 2000. Redistricting could alter the lines of this center-of-the-state district sharply, but Smith has shown the capacity to carry Democratic precincts.

Cook's Call   *Safe.* Like the rest of the state, this central New Jersey district has little trouble splitting its ticket. Since 1996, voters here have overwhelmingly supported Democrats running for president while also voting for Republican Chris Smith. He should be safe in 2002.

THE PEOPLE: Pop. 2000: 674,193; Pop. 1990: 594,673, up 13.4% 1990–2000. 80.4% White, 12.5% Black, 2.1% Asian, 0.2% Amer. Indian, 0.1% Hawaiian, 1.8% Two+ races, 3% Other; 7.8% Hispanic Origin.

2000 Presidential Vote			**1996 Presidential Vote**		
Gore (D)	139,646	(52%)	Clinton (D)	127,489	(51%)
Bush (R)	119,249	(45%)	Dole (R)	92,845	(37%)
Nader (Green)	8,451	(3%)	Perot (I)	26,880	(11%)
			Others	4,709	(2%)

Rep. Christopher H. Smith (R)

Elected 1980, 11th term; b. Mar. 4, 1953, Rahway; home, Washington Township; Trenton St. Col., B.S. 1975; Catholic; married (Marie).

Professional Career: Sales exec., family-owned sporting goods business, 1975–80; Exec. Dir., NJ Right to Life, 1976–78.

DC Office: 2373 RHOB 20515, 202-225-3765; Fax: 202-225-7768; Web site: www.house.gov/chrissmith.

District Offices: Hamilton, 609-585-7878; Whiting, 732-350-2300.

Committees: *International Relations* (5th of 26 R): East Asia & the Pacific; International Operations and Human Rights. *Veterans' Affairs* (Chmn. of 17 R): Benefits.

Group Ratings

	ADA	ACLU	AFS	LCV	CON	ITIC	NTU	COC	ACU	NTLC	CHC
2000	30	31	57	86	43	63	56	47	64	85	100
1999	40	—	33	75	6	—	52	64	79	—	—

National Journal Ratings

	1999 LIB —	1999 CONS		2000 LIB —	2000 CONS
Economic	48%	52%		51%	48%
Social	39%	61%		45%	54%
Foreign	40%	60%		47%	51%

Key Votes of the 106th Congress

1. Patient Bill of Rights	Y	5. Bar RU-486 $ for FDA	Y	9. NATO War in Serbia	Y
2. Accelerate Min. Wage	Y	6. Display 10 Commandments	*	10. Perm. Trade with China	N
3. Strike Ban on Ergo. Stnd.	Y	7. Gun Show Bkgrnd. Checks	Y	11. Debt Relief for 3rd World	Y
4. Ovrd. Estate Tax Veto	Y	8. Ban Part.-Birth Abortion	Y	12. Drop Cuba Econ. Embargo	N

Election Results

2000 general	Christopher H. Smith (R)	158,515	(63%)	($611,785)
	Reed Gusciora (D)	87,956	(35%)	($115,392)
	Other	4,339	(2%)	
2000 primary	Christopher H. Smith (R)	unopposed		
1998 general	Christopher H. Smith (R)	92,991	(62%)	($317,824)
	Larry Schneider (D)	52,281	(35%)	($37,604)
	Others	4,305	(3%)	

FIFTH DISTRICT

The northern edge of New Jersey was first settled three centuries ago by the Dutch, for whom this plateau of land behind the Hudson River Palisades seemed a natural part of Nieuw Amsterdam. The Dutch influence is seen in old steep-roofed farmhouses and in many of the place names—Bergen County, Cresskill, Closter. But overall, northernmost New Jersey has the well-settled look of so many northeastern suburbs, with touches both of affluence and small town hominess, criss-crossed at its edges with limited access highways lined with shopping centers—with five million square feet in Paramus, the headquarters of Toys "R" Us. Not far away are Saddle River, with million-dollar houses on multi-acre lots, and Park Ridge, with office buildings and condominiums. This area may look like WASP suburbia on the surface, but in fact it is home to successful people of all ethnic groups, many descended from those who first saw the Statue of Liberty from the steerage deck and passed through the inspection queues at Ellis Island.

The 5th Congressional District consists of most of northern Bergen County, plus a swath of North Jersey stretching west to the hill-enclosed upper reaches of the Delaware, crossing one ridge of mountains after another, running south along I-78. Three-fifths of its population is clustered in Bergen; to the west, little subdivisions set amid the lakes of western Passaic County are filling up with young families; farther west are once rural, now more or less suburban Sussex and Warren counties. Politically, this area has long been solidly Republican, although like all of New Jersey it moved toward Democrats in the 1990s; it was one of the state's two districts carried by Bob Dole in 1996 and George W. Bush in 2000.

Since 1980, the congresswoman from this district has been Marge Roukema, a Republican whose Dutch name and Italian descent tell much of the district's ethnic history. She grew up in West Orange, settled with her psychiatrist husband in Ridgewood. She was a teacher who gave up her job to raise her children and was involved in community activities before becoming a candidate; she brings to politics experience in the actual workings of civic institutions. She first ran for the House in 1978, against liberal Democrat Andrew Maguire, because she was convinced only a moderate Republican could win. She lost that time but won in 1980; redistricting has given her a safe Republican district since 1982, but she has been challenged by conservatives in the primary seven times. She has a moderate, middle-of-the-House, but sometimes liberal, voting record, and has not been shy about dissenting vocally from the Republican leadership—on gun control, abortion, campaign finance, HMO regulation. She did not agree to support the leadership's $792 billion tax cut until a "marathon meeting" in July 1999, in which she and others extracted the concession that deficit reduction would have priority over tax relief.

Roukema was the lead Republican sponsor of the Family and Medical Leave Act, vetoed by George Bush in 1990 and 1992 and signed by Bill Clinton in February 1993. After Republicans took control of Congress, she frequently opposed items on Speaker Newt Gingrich's agenda, including faster missile defense research, small business exemptions from the minimum wage, term limits and the 1996 Welfare Reform Act, though she sponsored its child support provisions. She was the lead House sponsor of the 1996 health care portability bill to ban insurance rejections for pre-existing conditions, but was the only Republican to vote against it because of leadership-added malpractice liability limitations and Medical Savings Account provisions. As a senior member of the Banking Committee, she worked hard on the financial services deregulation bill that passed in November 1999; she helped to resolve the struggle between the Treasury and the Federal Reserve that was holding up the bill. She has worked to combat money laundering, backing the requirement that Western Union offices and cash-checking stores register with the government.

On other issues she supported the Democrats' HMO regulation and with New Jersey Democrat Frank Pallone sponsored her own prescription drug benefit bill. She wants to equalize insurers' limits on physical and mental health coverage and to require hospitals to use needle-less syringes whenever possible. She and Carolyn McCarthy led the debate for gun-controllers against the Dingell amendment in June 1999. She favors repealing the law requiring gender equity in school sports. On local issues, she has worked to fund protection of Sterling Forest, sought first drought and then flood relief in summer 1999. She sponsored a bill for $400 million to buy up flood-prone homes and businesses and a campus fire safety bill after the deadly fire at Seton Hall University. She got $2.3 million to repave I-287 from Oakland to the New York line to replace the noisy grooved pavement.

Roukema had serious primary opposition in June 1998 and June 2000 from state Assemblyman E. Scott Garrett of Sussex County. In 1998 he attacked her for supporting abortion rights and gun control; she pointed to her conservative votes on economic issues and received money from Republican leaders. Garrett carried the western part of the district, and Roukema won by only 52%–48%. Garrett ran again in 2000, this time with support of the Washington-based Club for Growth, which argued that a district this Republican should have a more conservative representative. The Club for Growth generated some $250,000 for Garrett and he was supported by pro-life groups and the National Rifle Association. Roukema, with support from banks and insurance companies and from House Republican leaders, spent $532,000 and had support from the moderate Republican Leadership Council. Once again Roukema won 52%–48%, carrying Bergen County 63%–37% and losing the western counties, which cast nearly half the votes, 58%–42%. Her comment: "The message here is that our Republican Party has got to pull together to start beating the Democrats, and not listen to some outside group who comes in trying to tell us what to do." In both years she won the general election easily.

She was not so successful in her campaign to win the chairmanship of the Banking Committee. Republicans' six-year term limit barred Chairman Jim Leach, and Roukema was next in seniority. But she was opposed by conservative Richard Baker, who raised $1.6 million for colleagues. Roukema decried the appearance of buying a chairmanship and said she was reluctant to play "the gender card," but added, "I do think in the background there's a political question that will be raised by others. Do you really want to pass over a Republican woman who is clearly qualified?" But in January 2001, when the Republican Steering Committee met, both Roukema and Baker were passed over. The leadership shifted the Commerce subcommittee on securities regulation to Banking and renamed the committee Financial Services, and gave the chairmanship to Mike Oxley, who had seniority as a Republican on Commerce but was opposed by Billy Tauzin. Speaker Dennis Hastert called Roukema and offered her the honorific job of Treasurer of the United States, as well as president of the Government National Mortgage Association; she declined but said she would consider something more substantial and became chair of the Housing Subcommittee on Financial Services.

Her failure to win the chairmanship and the possibility that redistricting may alter the district, tilting the primary electorate away from her, raise the question of whether Roukema will run for reelection in 2002. But she is tenacious and a hard fighter, and no one should count her out.

Cook's Call *Safe.* The biggest threat to Roukema's tenure in this wealthy and Republican leaning district comes not from Democrats but from conservative Republicans who are unhappy with her moderate voting record. It is conceivable that Roukema will once again get a challenge from her right in 2002. This was Bush's second-best performing district in the state in 2000 (he won it by 6%).

THE PEOPLE: Pop. 2000: 638,669; Pop. 1990: 594,581, up 7.4% 1990–2000. 89.8% White, 1.5% Black, 6.2% Asian, 0.2% Amer. Indian, 1.3% Two+ races, 1.1% Other; 4.4% Hispanic Origin.

2000 Presidential Vote

Bush (R)	150,686	(51%)
Gore (D)	134,051	(45%)
Nader (Green)	9,464	(3%)

1996 Presidential Vote

Dole (R)	127,286	(47%)
Clinton (D)	115,060	(42%)
Perot (I)	23,642	(9%)
Others	5,090	(2%)

Rep. Marge Roukema (R)

Elected 1980, 11th term; b. Sept. 19, 1929, W. Orange; home, Ridgewood; Montclair St. Col., B.A. 1951, Rutgers U.; Protestant; married (Richard).

Elected Office: Ridgewood Board of Ed., 1970–73.

Professional Career: High schl. teacher, 1951–55; Co-founder, Ridgewood Sr. Citizens Housing Corp., 1973.

DC Office: 2469 RHOB 20515, 202-225-4465; Fax: 202-225-9048; Web site: www.house.gov/roukema.

District Offices: Hackettstown, 908-850-4747; Ridgewood, 201-447-3900.

Committees: *Education & the Workforce* (3d of 27 R): Education Reform; Employer-Employee Relations. *Financial Services* (3d of 37 R): Financial Institutions & Consumer Credit; Housing & Community Opportunity (Chmn.); International Monetary Policy & Trade.

Group Ratings

	ADA	ACLU	AFS	LCV	CON	ITIC	NTU	COC	ACU	NTLC	CHC
2000	15	14	0	71	86	100	60	76	68	76	67
1999	45	—	33	63	81	—	54	72	60	—	—

National Journal Ratings

	1999 LIB —	1999 CONS		2000 LIB —	2000 CONS
Economic	46% —	53%		42% —	57%
Social	52% —	48%		57% —	42%
Foreign	34% —	65%		25% —	69%

Key Votes of the 106th Congress

1. Patient Bill of Rights	Y	5. Bar RU-486 $ for FDA	N	9. NATO War in Serbia	N
2. Accelerate Min. Wage	N	6. Display 10 Commandments	Y	10. Perm. Trade with China	Y
3. Strike Ban on Ergo. Stnd.	N	7. Gun Show Bkgrnd. Checks	Y	11. Debt Relief for 3rd World	N
4. Ovrd. Estate Tax Veto	Y	8. Ban Part.-Birth Abortion	Y	12. Drop Cuba Econ. Embargo	N

Election Results

2000 general	Marge Roukema (R)	175,546	(65%)	($1,005,148)
	Linda A. Mercurio (D)	81,715	(30%)	($65,607)
	Other	11,263	(5%)	
2000 primary	Marge Roukema (R)	23,043	(52%)	
	Scott Garrett (R)	21,051	(48%)	
1998 general	Marge Roukema (R)	106,304	(64%)	($760,098)
	Mike Schneider (D)	55,487	(33%)	($62,440)
	Others	5,027	(3%)	

SIXTH DISTRICT

For generations great transportation arteries have brought people out of the huge central cities of New York and Philadelphia and into the long-empty flatlands and hills of New Jersey—to vacation, to raise families and to work toward affluence and build communities. The railroads of the late 19th Century created the towns of the Jersey Shore, from 1874, when the first train from New York City reached Long Branch, which quickly became the summer home of presidents from

Grant to Wilson (Garfield, convalescing after he was shot, died there in 1881) and of New York race horse owners and socialites. The great freight rail lines in the New York-Philadelphia corridor sparked big electrical and chemical industries here—building on the inventions of Thomas Edison, many produced in his Menlo Park laboratory just off the rail lines. The same corridor was the site of America's first cloverleaf intersection, at the junction of U.S. 1 and U.S. 9, and the intersection of two of America's great post-World War II highways, the New Jersey Turnpike and the Garden State Parkway. The Turnpike, now 12 lanes wide, roars past oil tank farms and petrochemical plants, major rail lines and Newark Airport and the oily waters of Raritan Bay; the Parkway links leafy affluent suburbs a dozen miles west of the Hudson with the Jersey Shore.

The 6th Congressional District ties together these great transportation nodes and the upward mobility and economic progress that have taken place around them. It includes the central core of Middlesex County—New Brunswick and Edison Township and the surrounding communities— a heavy industry area that also, since the time of Thomas Edison, has housed some of America's great research and development facilities. Here, immigrant factory workers in modest frame houses have raised their families in small towns that seem as far removed from Manhattan as any place in the Midwest. The 6th District also includes a strip of territory overlooking Lower New York Bay, with spacious estates on highlands above little port towns from Sandy Hook south to Sea Girt, the site of a federal "beach nourishment" project to restore the eroding beach: Asbury Park, once the vital center of this beachfront; and Ocean Grove, founded in 1869 as a Methodist resort "free from the dissipation and follies of fashionable watering places," still for teetotalers who throng to its 10,000-seat 1894 Great Hall. The Shore has remained a summer vacation area that attracts millions, but also has year-round communities, with their own upward-striving families.

The congressman from the 6th District is Frank Pallone, a Democrat who overcame severe challenges to hold the seat. Pallone is the son of a disabled Long Branch policeman; he has been an environmentalist since 1969, when as a college freshman in Vermont he worked for that state's first-in-the-nation bottle deposit law. He was elected to the Long Branch City Council in 1982, at 31, and to the New Jersey Senate in 1983, where he did not always follow party lines and concentrated on environmental issues. When Congressman Jim Howard, chairman of the Transportation and Infrastructure Committee, died in March 1988, Pallone ran for the House. The district leaned Republican, but was angry about untreated sludge, plastic containers and medical waste washing up on the beach. Pallone's bumper sticker, without mentioning his party affiliation, said, "Stop Ocean Dumping." That, combined with his conservative stands on taxes and crime, helped him to a 52% win.

In the House, Pallone continued to be a maverick, distancing himself from Governor Jim Florio's 1990 tax increase. Redistricting nearly ended Pallone's career. For 1992, the new 6th combined much of Pallone's Shore district in Monmouth County with large parts of the former Middlesex County seat; Pallone won the primary with only 55% against a Middlesex opponent. In the general, Pallone depended on a huge money advantage and Bill Clinton's edge in the district to win 52%–45%. New Jersey has since trended Democratic, and Pallone won in three of the next four campaigns with at least 60% of the vote.

Pallone has continued his moderate-to-liberal voting record, while adding a more partisan edge after Democrats lost control of the House. Pallone had supported single-payer health insurance in the 1992 campaign, but steered clear of the Clinton health care plan in 1994, helping to stymie its progress through John Dingell's Commerce Committee. In the minority, Pallone opposed repealing retroactive liability in Superfund and worked on the Safe Drinking Water Act. He became an active member of the Democrats' floor team—known as The Message Group—that frequently engaged in late-night attacks to trumpet his party's latest initiative and dump on the latest Republican scheme. He has focused lately on the need for a prescription drug benefit under Medicare, accusing Republicans and pharmaceutical firms of playing a "cruel hoax" on Americans. With many Indian-Americans in the district (the most in the country, he says), he formed the Congressional Caucus on India and Indian-Americans with Republican Bill McCollum; although he supported sanctions against India after its nuclear tests, he welcomed President Clinton's India travels and his chilly visit to Pakistan. At home, Pallone's environmental focus turned to the ever-lively border war with New York, opposing off-shore dumping near Sandy Hook of highly contaminated dredge material from New York City port terminals; the Army Corps of Engineers, he complained, failed to respond to New Jersey objections. He also opposed a South Amboy firm that sought to mine sand from the from the ocean bed, claiming it could have irreversible effects on fish and coastal erosion.

Pallone's political career remains rocky and his ambition unfulfilled. He has sought opportunities to run statewide, but Rutgers political scientist Ross Baker told the *Asbury Park Press*, "His personal style is not one that commands respect. . . . It's hard for people to see him as a Senator or governor. They see him as a representative." When Senator Frank Lautenberg announced his retirement in February 1999, Pallone formed an exploratory committee for a Senate bid, leading forces opposed to Jim Florio. But when Jon Corzine, with the $300 million he made at Goldman Sachs, entered the race, Pallone withdrew in June. He considered running for governor in 2001, only to bow out when Jim McGreevey wrapped up support from party leaders, though he said he still wants to run statewide. In the House, he had a stormy re-election campaign in 1998 against 28-year-old Republican Michael Ferguson, an education reformer close to former Governor Thomas Kean. An insurance group unhappy with Pallone's support for Clinton's managed-care bill of rights plan spent nearly $2 million in an independent expenditure campaign. But Ferguson's $1 million spending did not help him much in a pro-incumbent year: Pallone beat him 57%–40%. In 2000, Ferguson was elected in the neighboring 7th district: district lines in central New Jersey are evidently pretty porous.

In 1999, Dick Gephardt named Pallone chairman of the Democrats' Health Care Task Force, and a co-chairman of the Democratic Congressional Campaign Committee—after tapping Patrick Kennedy instead of Pallone to chair the committee. Pallone won easily in 2000, defeating 68%–30% the man he ousted from the state Senate in 1983. Still, this district in the center of the state could be greatly altered in redistricting, which Pallone surely will be watching closely.

Cook's Call   *Probably Safe.* For most of the early 1990s, Pallone held onto this district by his fingernails, never winning by more than 52% from 1988–94. But, since then, he seems to have turned the political corner, posting solid wins, including a 57% showing in 1998 against a well-funded Republican. Pallone is well settled here and should not be a top target in 2002.

THE PEOPLE: Pop. 2000: 632,202; Pop. 1990: 594,650, up 6.3% 1990–2000. 71.9% White, 12.2% Black, 9.4% Asian, 0.2% Amer. Indian, 2.4% Two+ races, 3.9% Other; 10.6% Hispanic Origin.

2000 Presidential Vote			1996 Presidential Vote		
Gore (D)	128,967	(58%)	Clinton (D)	122,851	(54%)
Bush (R)	85,336	(38%)	Dole (R)	74,937	(33%)
Nader (Green)	8,747	(4%)	Perot (I)	22,192	(10%)
			Others	5,968	(3%)

Rep. Frank E. Pallone (D)

Elected 1988, 7th term; b. Oct. 30, 1951, Long Branch; home, Long Branch; Middlebury Col., B.A. 1973, Fletcher Schl. of Law & Diplomacy, M.A. 1974, Rutgers U., J.D. 1978; Catholic; married (Sarah).

Elected Office: Long Branch City Cncl., 1982–88; NJ Senate, 1983–88.

Professional Career: Asst. prof., Rutgers U., 1979–80; Practicing atty., 1981–83; Instructor, Monmouth Col., 1984–86.

DC Office: 420 CHOB 20515, 202-225-4671; Fax: 202-225-9665; Web site: www.house.gov/pallone.

District Offices: Hazlet, 732-264-9104; Long Branch, 732-571-1140; New Brunswick, 732-249-8892.

Committees: *Energy & Commerce* (7th of 26 D): Environment & Hazardous Materials (RMM); Health. *Resources* (9th of 25 D): Fisheries Conservation, Wildlife & Oceans; National Parks, Recreation & Public Lands.

Group Ratings

	ADA	ACLU	AFS	LCV	CON	ITIC	NTU	COC	ACU	NTLC	CHC
2000	85	71	100	93	47	50	23	30	12	25	20
1999	95	—	100	100	49	—	24	24	8	—	—

National Journal Ratings

	1999 LIB	—	1999 CONS		2000 LIB	—	2000 CONS
Economic	75%	—	23%		78%	—	22%
Social	74%	—	25%		72%	—	26%
Foreign	67%	—	33%		61%	—	38%

Key Votes of the 106th Congress

1. Patient Bill of Rights	Y	5. Bar RU-486 $ for FDA	N	9. NATO War in Serbia	Y
2. Accelerate Min. Wage	Y	6. Display 10 Commandments	N	10. Perm. Trade with China	N
3. Strike Ban on Ergo. Stnd.	Y	7. Gun Show Bkgrnd. Checks	Y	11. Debt Relief for 3rd World	Y
4. Ovrd. Estate Tax Veto	N	8. Ban Part.-Birth Abortion	N	12. Drop Cuba Econ. Embargo	N

Election Results

2000 general	Frank E. Pallone (D)	141,698	(68%)	($836,362)
	Brian T. Kennedy (R)	62,454	(30%)	($32,021)
	Other	5,700	(2%)	
2000 primary	Frank E. Pallone (D)	unopposed		
1998 general	Frank E. Pallone (D)	78,102	(57%)	($1,144,629)
	Michael Ferguson (R)	55,180	(40%)	($1,069,603)
	Others	3,730	(3%)	

SEVENTH DISTRICT

The transportation arteries beneath the curve of the First Watchung Mountain are one of New Jersey's historic lines of development. The rail lines of the late 19th Century opened up commuter suburbs; in the 1940s the four lanes of U.S. 22 created an automobile civilization; and finally I-78, completed in the mid-1980s, put Newark only an hour's distance from the Pennsylvania line. Interstate-78 stimulated the development of an Edge City called Bridgewater Commons, where a huge shopping mall and office developments that included the new headquarters of AT&T rose up amid horse country around Far Hills and Bernardsville, where the likes of Malcolm Forbes and Charles Engelhard owned huge estates.

The 7th Congressional District covers these several generations of suburban development. It begins just west of Elizabeth, taking in affluent railroad commuter towns like Short Hills and Summit. It also includes more modest suburbs along U.S. 22, like Union and Westfield and the old city of Plainfield, with its large black community, plus the working class suburbs of Woodbridge and South Plainfield in Middlesex County. It then follows I-78 and the Watchung Mountains far into the countryside to the fields of Somerset County. Once this was all solidly Republican; now the closer-in suburbs are fairly solidly Democratic, while the farther-out Edge City areas are moving away from their Republican leanings. The 7th District was carried solidly by Bill Clinton and Al Gore, but has been represented in the House by Republicans for many years.

The congressman from the 7th is Michael Ferguson, an education reformer close to one-time Education Secretary William Bennett. After graduating from Notre Dame, he taught history as an unpaid volunteer and coached basketball at Mount St. Michael Academy in the Bronx. He served as executive director of the Catholic Campaign for America and the Better Schools Foundations in Washington, which was founded by Lamar Alexander and Paul Coverdell; during that time, he focused on education issues while earning a master's degree in public policy from Georgetown. He returned to New Jersey to found Strategic Education Initiatives, an education consulting firm, and became an ally of Jersey City's Republican mayor Bret Schundler. In 1998, Ferguson challenged Frank Pallone in the 6th District, spending $1 million but losing 57%–40%. When Bob Franks decided to give up the neighboring 7th District seat and run for the Senate in 2000, Ferguson moved to the district and entered the contest. But he faced serious opposition in a four-way primary. While Ferguson raised the most money and focused on fiscal issues, such as cutting taxes, Tom Kean Jr.—son of the popular former governor—had the highest name recognition and the most early endorsements, but he suffered from political inexperience. State Assemblyman Joel Weingarten, the only candidate previously elected to office, suffered from his votes for higher taxes. The fourth candidate was Patrick Morrissey, a former House Commerce Committee aide who advocated simplifying federal health services. Ferguson won with 41% of the vote, to 28% for Kean, who narrowly carried Union County, and 23% for Weingarten, who won an absolute majority in his home area in Essex County.

In the general, Ferguson faced Fanwood Mayor Maryanne Connelly, a retired AT&T human resources executive who in 1998 gave Franks his closest race. In the Democratic primary, she overcame support for her opponent Michael Lapolla, the Union County manager, from local party officials and the Democratic Congressional Campaign Committee. Connelly's 294-vote primary win was aided by adverse reaction to Lapolla's radio ad lampooning her for going "which way the political winds are blowing." Connelly accused him of sexism, and the party split was exacerbated when 8th District Congressman Bill Pascrell blasted the DCCC for endorsing Lapolla without consulting the divided delegation. While barely mentioning his conservative views—favoring school prayer and a constitutional amendment banning abortion—Ferguson emphasized centrist positions, including a waiting period for gun purchases and mandatory trigger locks. He stressed the need for limiting sprawl and preserving open space, and generally agreed with Connelly on prescription drug coverage under Medicare plus patients' rights in dealing with HMOs. His campaign centerpiece, not surprisingly, was education reform. He strongly advocated school vouchers and urged increased accountability for public schools. Against the 55-year-old Connelly, a widow without children, Ferguson highlighted his youthfulness and two children. Connelly criticized Ferguson for wrongly claiming endorsements from the American Medical Association and American Hospital Association, and claimed she better understood local needs. But she suffered when the Newark *Star-Ledger* said she was in the running for "New Jersey's sleaziest candidate," even though she later won the newspaper's endorsement. Al Gore carried the district solidly, but Ferguson won by 52%–46%, with a big margin in Somerset County, out by Bridgewater Commons, while running about even in the older suburbs.

Ferguson's re-election prospects depend heavily on redistricting. He could benefit from picking up Republican precincts in neighboring districts held by Democrats Rush Holt and Frank Pallone.

Cook's Call   *Competitive.* The fact that Ferguson won here by just 52% in 2000 would be reason enough for Democrats to target him in 2002. This district, once a Republican stronghold, has been trending more Democratic over the last 10 years with Gore winning here in 2000 by 11%. Still, Ferguson has shown he can run and win in a tough district in a less than hospitable political climate. His moderate approach to issues like the environment and gun control will also help to insulate him.

THE PEOPLE: Pop. 2000: 642,715; Pop. 1990: 594,844, up 8% 1990–2000. 74.2% White, 11.7% Black, 8.7% Asian, 0.1% Amer. Indian, 2.1% Two+ races, 3.1% Other; 9.3% Hispanic Origin.

2000 Presidential Vote		
Gore (D)	137,790	(54%)
Bush (R)	108,862	(43%)
Nader (Green)	7,692	(3%)

1996 Presidential Vote		
Clinton (D)	129,773	(51%)
Dole (R)	101,538	(40%)
Perot (I)	19,769	(8%)
Others	4,710	(2%)

Rep. Michael Ferguson (R)

Elected 2000, 1st term; b. July 22, 1970, Ridgewood; home, Warren; U. of Notre Dame, B.S. 1992; Georgetown U., M.P.P. 1994; Catholic; married (Maureen Malloy).

Professional Career: H.S. teacher, Mount St. Michael Acad., 1992–93; Exec. Dir., Better Schools Fndt., 1994; Dir., Save Our Schoolchildren, 1994; Exec. Dir., Catholic Campaign for America, 1995–97; Adjunct Prof., Brookdale Com. Col., 1997–2000; Founder & Pres., Strategic Educ. Initiatives, 1997-present.

DC Office: 214 CHOB 20515, 202-225-5361; Fax: 202-225-9460; Web site: www.house.gov/ferguson.

District Office: Union, 908-686-5576.

Committees: *Financial Services* (35th of 37 R): Capital Markets, Insurance & Government Sponsored Enterprises; Financial Institutions & Consumer Credit; International Monetary Policy & Trade. *Small Business* (12th of 19 R): Workforce, Empowerment & Government Programs. *Transportation & Infrastructure* (36th of 42 R): Highways & Transit; Railroads.

Group Ratings and Key Votes: Newly Elected

Election Results

2000 general	Michael Ferguson (R)	128,434	(52%)	($2,294,820)
	Maryanne Connelly (D)	113,479	(46%)	($1,837,766)
	Other	7,086	(3%)	
2000 primary	Michael Ferguson (R)	10,748	(41%)	
	Tom Kean Jr. (R)	7,358	(28%)	
	Joel M. Weingarten (R)	6,089	(23%)	
	Patrick Morrisey (R)	2,284	(9%)	
1998 general	Bob Franks (R)	77,751	(53%)	($802,120)
	Maryanne Connelly (D)	65,776	(44%)	($199,576)
	Others	4,515	(3%)	

EIGHTH DISTRICT

Paterson, New Jersey, is one of few American cities that has turned out pretty much as planned. The planner was Alexander Hamilton, who in the 1790s journeyed 20 miles from Manhattan into the interior of New Jersey to the Great Falls of the Passaic River. Watching the water surge down 72 feet—the highest falls along the East Coast—he predicted an industrial city would rise on this site. He formed the Society for Establishing Useful Manufactures, which opened a calico factory in 1794, and got Pierre L'Enfant, the designer of Washington, D.C., to design Paterson (named after then-Governor William Paterson). In 1836, Samuel Colt began manufacturing revolvers here; the first locomotive, the Sandusky, was built here in 1837; a walkout of Paterson cotton workers in 1828 was America's first factory strike. Paterson ultimately became America's "Silk City," employing 25,000 silk mill workers before the great strike of 1913 led by the radical Industrial Workers of the World. Paterson kept producing locomotives and, after the silk mills started closing down following another unsuccessful strike in 1924, became a cloth-dying center. Throughout, it attracted immigrants from England, Ireland and, after 1890, Italy and Poland. But now Paterson is a kind of misfit in time and place: still a manufacturing center in a service-dominated economy, a blue-collar city set amid dozens of white-collar suburbs. The city also has lost touch with its own citizens, say Paterson officials who sought in the 2000 Census to avoid a repeat of 1990, when they claimed an undercount of 25,000.

The 8th Congressional District includes Paterson as its largest city, plus much suburban territory west and south of Paterson and north and west of Newark. It includes the mixed factory and middle-class towns south of Paterson on the Passaic River—Clifton, Passaic, Nutley, Belleville. On higher ground are Bloomfield and, up on a ridge with views of New York City, part of Montclair. An affluent part of the Oranges is also included, as well as Wayne Township west of Paterson. The political heritage of the 8th District is Democratic, partly from its radical past, but more from the allegiances of its immigrant groups. In the 1980s, the central cities were outvoted by the increasingly Republican suburbs, and the district was closely divided; but it swung heavily to Bill Clinton in 1996 and Al Gore in 2000.

The congressman from the 8th District—the fourth the district chose in the 1990s—is Bill Pascrell, a Democrat elected in 1996. He grew up in Paterson, the grandson of Italian immigrants, graduated from Fordham, served in the Army, then taught high school for 14 years. From there he went into politics, first on the Paterson Board of Education, then in 1987 to the New Jersey Assembly. In 1990 he was elected mayor of Paterson, but continued to serve in the Assembly—a common practice in New Jersey. In these offices Pascrell showed a flair for innovation. He sponsored a health program with preventive medicine and child immunizations and a housing program with new construction and help for first-time home-buyers. To stop drug dealers, he required permits for new pay phones and personally ripped out phones without permits.

Meanwhile, he watched as the 8th District seat changed hands. After Public Works Committee chairman Robert Roe retired in 1992, liberal Democrat Herb Klein won, only to be replaced by Bill Martini in the Republican sweep two years later. Pascrell attacked him in 1996 as the puppet of an "extremist" Republican leadership—one ad even showed Martini's face on a puppet operated by Speaker Newt Gingrich. Despite Martini's support from the Sierra Club and some labor unions, Pascrell rode the coattails of the Clinton-Gore campaign. In a district that went 58% for Clinton, Pascrell won 51%–48%.

In the House Pascrell has compiled a liberal record on economics, more moderate on cultural and foreign issues. He called it "my proudest day" in Congress when he won approval for authorizing $400 million in federal aid to local fire departments, a provision that curiously was included in the military-spending measure. He advocated President Clinton's plan for aid to local school construction. After joining other North Jersey Representatives in unsuccessfully opposing a 90-mile natural gas pipeline for their region, he then demanded new safety measures. He has voted for the partial-birth abortion ban and for parental-notification requirements when a minor travels to another state to end her pregnancy. Pascrell gave new meaning to the "all politics is local" view by leading a move to give Italy a permanent seat on the United Nations Security Council. When he voted to condemn Palestinians for inciting Mideast violence, local Muslims held a rally to protest his vote.

Pascrell has had ambitions for statewide office. In 1999 he voiced interest in running for governor in 2001. But his support for Jim Florio in the 2000 Senate primary against Jon Corzine left him on the losing side of the North Jersey party establishment, and in early 2001 Woodbridge Mayor Jim McGreevey, who lost by only 47%–46% to Christie Whitman in 1997, had the governor nomination sewed up. The results in the 8th district have shown Pascrell's strength as well as the Democratic trend in the nation's largest metropolitan areas. In 2000 he won 67%–30% against Anthony Fusco, an attorney whose clients have ranged from local police officers to heavyweight Mike Tyson in his unsuccessful bid to regain a New Jersey boxing license.

Cook's Call   *Safe.* Not too long ago this northeast New Jersey district was one of the most volatile in the state. Today, Pascrell looks like he has solidified his hold on this seat, which has been performing much more like a Democratic stronghold than a swing district. Clinton won this district by just 3% in 1992, but eight years later Gore won here by a whopping 25%.

THE PEOPLE: Pop. 2000: 640,015; Pop. 1990: 594,912, up 7.6% 1990–2000. 63.2% White, 13.9% Black, 5.1% Asian, 0.3% Amer. Indian, 3.8% Two + races, 13.6% Other; 25.8% Hispanic Origin.

2000 Presidential Vote		
Gore (D)	132,379	(61%)
Bush (R)	78,933	(36%)
Nader (Green)	5,779	(3%)

1996 Presidential Vote		
Clinton (D)	123,856	(58%)
Dole (R)	73,731	(34%)
Perot (I)	12,864	(6%)
Others	4,095	(2%)

Rep. Bill Pascrell, Jr. (D)

Elected 1996, 3d term; b. Jan. 25, 1937, Paterson; home, Paterson; Fordham U., B.A. 1959, M.A. 1961; Catholic; married (Elsie).

Military Career: Army, 1961; Army Reserves, 1962–67.

Elected Office: Pres., Paterson Bd. of Ed., 1979–82; NJ Assembly, 1987–97, Minority Ldr. Pro-Tem; Paterson Mayor, 1990–97.

Professional Career: High Schl. teacher, 1960–74; Dir., Paterson Dept. of Public Works, 1974–77; Dir., Paterson Dept. of Policy, 1977–87.

DC Office: 1722 LHOB 20515, 202-225-5751; Fax: 202-225-5782; Web site: www.house.gov/pascrell.

District Office: Paterson, 973-523-5152.

Committees: *Small Business* (4th of 17 D): Regulatory Reform Oversight; Tax, Finance & Exports (RMM). *Transportation & Infrastructure* (22d of 34 D): Aviation; Highways & Transit; Water Resources & Environment.

Group Ratings

	ADA	ACLU	AFS	LCV	CON	ITIC	NTU	COC	ACU	NTLC	CHC
2000	75	50	85	100	29	47	28	35	20	12	27
1999	95	—	100	100	28	—	16	25	18	—	—

National Journal Ratings

	1999 LIB —	1999 CONS	2000 LIB —	2000 CONS
Economic	73%	26%	70%	29%
Social	61%	38%	66%	33%
Foreign	61%	37%	56%	42%

Key Votes of the 106th Congress

1. Patient Bill of Rights	Y	5. Bar RU-486 $ for FDA	N	9. NATO War in Serbia	Y
2. Accelerate Min. Wage	Y	6. Display 10 Commandments	N	10. Perm. Trade with China	N
3. Strike Ban on Ergo. Stnd.	Y	7. Gun Show Bkgrnd. Checks	Y	11. Debt Relief for 3rd World	Y
4. Ovrd. Estate Tax Veto	N	8. Ban Part.-Birth Abortion	Y	12. Drop Cuba Econ. Embargo	N

Election Results

2000 general	Bill Pascrell Jr. (D)	134,074	(67%)	($1,081,808)
	Anthony Fusco Jr. (R)	60,606	(30%)	($279,545)
	Other	5,452	(3%)	
2000 primary	Bill Pascrell Jr. (D)	unopposed		
1998 general	Bill Pascrell Jr. (D)	81,068	(62%)	($968,274)
	Matthew Kirnan (R)	46,289	(35%)	($289,910)
	Others	3,231	(2%)	

NINTH DISTRICT

The George Washington Bridge, one of several wondrous suspension bridges completed in America in the 1930s, strides the Hudson, its west tower almost up against the green cliff of New Jersey's Palisades. It is one of the glories of modern engineering, enabling people and goods to be transported through the irregular terrain of metropolitan New York—tidal rivers and cliffs and broad expanses of swamp. For a century the dramatic beauty of the Palisades contrasted with the ugly sprawl of the Hackensack River Valley and the Jersey Meadowlands. This giant swamp was the image of New Jersey for many—a landscape of gas station signs, oil tank farms, truck terminals and 12 lanes of New Jersey Turnpike—a smelly, ugly place that meant you were still not where you wanted to go, full of garbage and pig farms, briefly famous when Secaucus tavern owner Henry Krajewski ran for president in 1956 and commemorated in today's New Jersey Garbage Museum. But the Meadowlands were the largest hunk of empty real estate near such a huge city center, and eventually they were developed. In the 1970s, the state built the Meadowlands Sports Complex—Giants Stadium (where the Giants and Jets play now), the Meadowlands Racetrack, the Brendan Byrne Arena (later Continental Airlines Arena, home of the Nets and Devils). Private development followed—hotels, warehouses, light industry—in what became a small city.

The 9th Congressional District includes much of the Palisades and the Meadowlands. It runs from the high-rise towers of Fort Lee and Cliffside Park, where apartment houses brag about their views of New York City, west and north to the leafy suburbs of Englewood and Teaneck, and southwest to the high land overlooking the Meadowlands and the Passaic River in old small towns like Rutherford, with Polish-, German- and Italian-Americans. Hackensack, an old industrial town and the Bergen County seat, and much of Fair Lawn, a planned town with a large Jewish population, also are in the 9th. This area grew in the 1950s and 1960s, as New Yorkers moved out of the City; it lost population in the 1970s and 1980s, as young people moved farther out and left empty nesters behind. Now the population in some towns is rising, with new immigrants: Englewood's schoolchildren are mostly black, Fort Lee's mostly Asian, many of Hackensack's are Hispanic. This was Republican country in the New Deal years, an area of white-collar enclaves. But the conservative families who grew up in Bergen County are now being replaced by heavily Democratic immigrants and "tower dwellers."

The congressman from the 9th District is Steve Rothman, a Democrat elected in 1996. Rothman grew up in Englewood and Tenafly, went off to school at Syracuse University and Washington University law school in St. Louis, then practiced law. From 1983–89 he was mayor of Englewood, where he claims to have cut taxes, reduced crime and led an economic renaissance. In 1993 he became a judge in the Bergen County Surrogate's Court. When 14-year Congressman Bob Torricelli ran for the Senate in 1996, Rothman resigned his judgeship and ran for the House. With the party endorsement, Rothman faced Kathleen Donovan—Bergen County clerk, former assemblywoman, and from 1994–95 chairman of the New York-New Jersey Port Authority, who was endorsed by the Sierra Club, New Jersey Education Association and Cuban-American leader Jorge Mas Canosa. But this part of New Jersey was swinging sharply to the Democrats in the wake of the Republican takeover of the House and the 1995–96 budget struggle; the 9th District was 47%–40% for Clinton in 1992 and 60%–31% in 1996. Rothman won by a solid 56%–42%.

In the House Rothman moved to form a juvenile crime task force and won enactment of the "Secure Our Schools Act," to keep guns out of schools with the installation of metal detectors, cameras and trained personnel. He called for Israel to be grouped with the Western European bloc at the United Nations so it might have a chance for a Security Council seat—which the U.N. accepted in 2000—and he blamed Yasser Arafat for Mideast violence following the 2000 Camp David talks. He cited human rights violations in opposing Permanent Normal Trade Relations with China. On local issues, he objected to noise and congestion problems at the Teterboro airport, and he won an Internal Revenue Service apology when an internal report found that 8,500 New Jersey taxpayers were the victims of an overzealous IRS office.

But his big moment in the spotlight came during the Judiciary Committee impeachment hearings. After Independent Counsel Kenneth Starr sent his report to the House, Rothman initially expressed unhappiness with Clinton's behavior and studied the charges intently. But as public opinion turned against impeachment, so did Rothman. He actively supported Clinton on television talk shows and complained that Republicans were ignoring the few moderate Democrats like himself. The divisive process left him more partisan and, Rothman said, "heartsick." In January 2001, he won a seat on Appropriations, a favorable omen for a lengthy career.

Rothman twice won easy re-election, with majorities almost as good as Torricelli's best showings. Redistricting could pose some risk by moving him farther out into less Democratic suburbs.

Cook's Call *Safe.* Since winning this district in 1996 with a healthy 56%, Rothman has held the seat rather easily. It is hard to see why he would be a target for Republicans in 2002.

THE PEOPLE: Pop. 2000: 647,240; Pop. 1990: 594,790, up 8.8% 1990–2000. 70.9% White, 7.2% Black, 11.3% Asian, 0.2% Amer. Indian, 3.5% Two+ races, 6.9% Other; 18.9% Hispanic Origin.

2000 Presidential Vote			1996 Presidential Vote		
Gore (D)	136,458	(63%)	Clinton (D)	138,242	(60%)
Bush (R)	72,574	(34%)	Dole (R)	71,741	(31%)
Nader (Green)	5,760	(3%)	Perot (I)	17,012	(7%)

Rep. Steven R. Rothman (D)

Elected 1996, 3d term; b. Oct. 14, 1952, Englewood; home, Fair Lawn; Syracuse U., B.A. 1974, Washington U., J.D. 1977; Jewish; divorced.

Elected Office: Englewood Mayor, 1983–89; Bergen Cnty. Surrogate Court Judge, 1993–96.

Professional Career: Practicing atty., 1977–93.

DC Office: 1607 LHOB 20515, 202-225-5061; Fax: 202-225-5851; Web site: www.house.gov/rothman.

District Offices: Hackensack, 201-646-0808; Jersey City, 201-798-1366.

Committees: *Appropriations* (29th of 29 D): Foreign Operations & Export Financing; Treasury, Postal Service & General Government.

Group Ratings

	ADA	ACLU	AFS	LCV	CON	ITIC	NTU	COC	ACU	NTLC	CHC
2000	90	71	100	86	34	30	20	38	12	16	13
1999	100	—	100	94	16	—	16	28	4	—	—

National Journal Ratings

	1999 LIB	—	1999 CONS		2000 LIB	—	2000 CONS
Economic	73%	—	26%		81%	—	16%
Social	69%	—	31%		72%	—	28%
Foreign	78%	—	17%		55%	—	45%

Key Votes of the 106th Congress

1. Patient Bill of Rights	Y	5. Bar RU-486 $ for FDA	N	9. NATO War in Serbia	Y
2. Accelerate Min. Wage	Y	6. Display 10 Commandments	N	10. Perm. Trade with China	N
3. Strike Ban on Ergo. Stnd.	Y	7. Gun Show Bkgrnd. Checks	Y	11. Debt Relief for 3rd World	Y
4. Ovrd. Estate Tax Veto	N	8. Ban Part.-Birth Abortion	N	12. Drop Cuba Econ. Embargo	N

Election Results

2000 general	Steven R. Rothman (D)	140,462	(68%)	($880,283)
	Joseph Tedeschi (R)	61,984	(30%)	($30,099)
	Other	4,325	(2%)	
2000 primary	Steven R. Rothman (D)	unopposed		
1998 general	Steven R. Rothman (D)	91,330	(65%)	($1,120,409)
	Steve Lonegan (R)	47,817	(34%)	($598,958)
	Others	2,312	(2%)	

TENTH DISTRICT

Newark has been the hollow core of New Jersey, the city to which main transportation arteries once led and whose corporate headquarters buildings were the tallest in the state. In 1930, 442,000 people lived here, one of every nine in New Jersey; in 2000, 273,000 did, one in 30. Recently Newark's core has been perking up; new office buildings have joined the Prudential and Public Service Electric & Gas headquarters and the New Jersey Performing Arts Center has been a big hit. There has been industrial development around Newark Airport, and immigrant neighborhoods like the Ironbound district are showing new vitality. What hurt Newark for so many years was high crime; large parts of the city were dominated by criminals and deserted by most law-abiding residents who could get out. Now crime rates have been going down, and life is coming back to deserted streets. There may even be hope for the Newark public schools, taken over by the state in 1994, which had some of the nation's lowest test scores and the highest spending per pupil.

The 10th Congressional District is made up of most of Newark—the Central, South and West Wards—plus Irvington, most of the Oranges and part of Montclair to the west, and much of Elizabeth, Rahway, and Linden to the south. The 10th was 61% black in 2000, and overwhelmingly

Democratic; its boundary lines wiggle around to include blacks in Jersey City, Montclair and Elizabeth, and leave Hispanics in the next-door 13th District.

The congressman from the 10th is Donald Payne, a Democrat elected in 1988. He grew up in Newark, was a teacher, worked for Prudential, served on the Essex Board of Chosen Freeholders in the 1970s and was vice president of Urban Data Systems for 13 years. In 1980 and 1986, he ran against Congressman Peter Rodino, chairman of the House Judiciary Committee when it voted to impeach President Richard Nixon; Payne lost, even as an African American in a district with a black majority. But when Rodino retired in 1988, Payne got 73% in the Democratic primary and easily won the general.

Payne has an impeccably liberal voting record. He served as chairman of the Congressional Black Caucus in 1995 and 1996, just as Republicans were defunding the caucuses (the Black Caucus has raised enough money on its own to remain a vigorous force) and as senior Democrats had to relinquish chairmanships to Republicans. Payne struggled to save affirmative action and racial quota programs as they were under attack, with varying success. He could not stop a law that eliminated race preferences in broadcast licenses nor could he stop the House from passing a bill outlawing "social investments" for pension funds. But he was successful in urging Bill Clinton not to abandon racial quotas and preferences and in urging Newt Gingrich not to bring such measures to the floor.

Payne saved the Africa Subcommittee from abolition when Republicans won the majority, and attacked cuts in aid to African countries. But he did not lionize all of Africa's leaders. He sponsored a resolution to cut off new investment in Sudan because of its practice of slavery—though he criticized as "unconscionable" the pullout from Sudan of international private-aid agencies. He traveled on Clinton's spring 1998 trip to Africa, which Payne praised as a "sea change" for viewing African issues and leaders as equals to those of other continents. In 1999, he gained from fellow New Jerseyan Robert Menendez the ranking Democratic slot on the Africa Subcommittee. Half the bills he filed in the 106th Congress dealt with Africa. But he criticized foreign-aid spending levels of the needs for United Nations peacekeeping operations.

Nationally, Payne was a leader in passage of legislation to protect churches and other places of worship from burnings. He worked to drum up money for a revolutionary war memorial for African Americans on Washington's Mall. He has become a leading Democrat on education policy. He unsuccessfully fought a Republican initiative to lower the threshold for local eligibility for special-education funding of schools in poor areas. But he won approval for forgiving student loans to students who choose careers as public defenders.

On local issues, Payne has worked to bring millions of dollars in federal housing grants to his district, supported the Newark Riverfront project and secured grants to hire more police officers in Newark and Jersey City. He continues to win reelection overwhelmingly against token opposition. Redistricting likely will expand the district boundaries, but it's not likely to cause problems for Payne.

Cook's Call *Safe.* Payne is sitting in the most Democratic district in New Jersey and one of the most Democratic districts in the entire country. His district was the slowest growing in the state and will need to pick up about 50,000 people. But it will retain its overall Democratic nature.

THE PEOPLE: Pop. 2000: 597,384; Pop. 1990: 593,876, up 0.6% 1990–2000. 25.5% White, 60.9% Black, 3% Asian, 0.3% Amer. Indian, 0.1% Hawaiian, 4% Two+ races, 6.4% Other; 15.8% Hispanic Origin.

2000 Presidential Vote

Gore (D)	140,241	(85%)
Bush (R)	22,446	(14%)
Nader (Green)	2,567	(2%)

1996 Presidential Vote

Clinton (D)	138,128	(82%)
Dole (R)	21,911	(13%)
Perot (I)	5,774	(3%)

Rep. Donald M. Payne (D)

Elected 1988, 7th term; b. July 16, 1934, Newark; home, Newark; Seton Hall, B.A. 1957; Baptist; widowed.

Elected Office: Essex Cnty. Bd. of Chosen Freeholders, 1972–78, Dir. 1977–78; Newark Municipal Cncl., 1982–89.

Professional Career: Elem. & High Schl. teacher, 1957–64; Exec., Prudential Insurance Co., 1964–72; Pres., YMCAs of the U.S., 1970; Vice Pres., Urban Data Systems Inc., 1975–88.

DC Office: 2209 RHOB 20515, 202-225-3436; Fax: 202-225-4160; Web site: www.house.gov/payne.

District Offices: Elizabeth, 908-629-0222; Newark, 973-645-3213.

Committees: *Education & the Workforce* (4th of 22 D): Education Reform; Employer-Employee Relations. *International Relations* (5th of 23 D): Africa (RMM); Western Hemisphere.

Group Ratings

	ADA	ACLU	AFS	LCV	CON	ITIC	NTU	COC	ACU	NTLC	CHC
2000	95	86	100	79	63	45	26	33	0	12	0
1999	100	—	100	100	51	—	27	21	0	—	—

National Journal Ratings

	1999 LIB	—	1999 CONS		2000 LIB	—	2000 CONS
Economic	88%	—	0%		95%	—	0%
Social	87%	—	0%		84%	—	15%
Foreign	95%	—	0%		97%	—	0%

Key Votes of the 106th Congress

1. Patient Bill of Rights	Y	5. Bar RU-486 $ for FDA	N	9. NATO War in Serbia	Y
2. Accelerate Min. Wage	Y	6. Display 10 Commandments	N	10. Perm. Trade with China	N
3. Strike Ban on Ergo. Stnd.	Y	7. Gun Show Bkgrnd. Checks	Y	11. Debt Relief for 3rd World	Y
4. Ovrd. Estate Tax Veto	N	8. Ban Part.-Birth Abortion	N	12. Drop Cuba Econ. Embargo	Y

Election Results

2000 general	Donald M. Payne (D)	133,073	(88%)	($347,319)
	Dirk B. Weber (R)	18,436	(12%)	
2000 primary	Donald M. Payne (D)	unopposed		
1998 general	Donald M. Payne (D)	82,244	(84%)	($414,705)
	William Stanley Wnuck (R)	10,678	(11%)	
	Others	5,572	(6%)	

ELEVENTH DISTRICT

New Jersey's Morris County, west of the Watchung Mountain ridges, was one of the first settled parts of the interior United States west of the seaboard. It has long been a place of comparative affluence, the home of skilled craftsmen during the Revolutionary War, with plenty of water mills and iron forges by the 19th Century. But only in the late 20th Century has it come into its own, as one of the wealthiest areas in the United States. And it is not just a collection of country estates with huddled small towns for the servants to live in, but a well-rounded community with all the appurtenances of urbanity except high crime and poverty rates. The very rich have lived here for some time, connected to Manhattan by commuter rail lines. But starting in the 1970s, new residents rushed out the newly completed I-80 and I-280 or the ring road I-287. Prompted by court-required zoning changes, old farms and woods have been cleared to make way for new subdivisions. And it is not just a bedroom community. New office complexes and corporate headquarters have been rising; much of New Jersey's economic energy, entrepreneurial creativity and research expertise are out here.

The 11th Congressional District includes all of Morris County plus similar adjacent areas. It is one of the most affluent districts in the country. It is family territory, with relatively few singles; not a strongly cultural conservative area, but not aggressively liberal either. Politically, it is the most Republican district in New Jersey, and one of the most Republican in the Northeast. It was one of only two New Jersey districts to vote for George W. Bush in 2000.

The congressman from the 11th District is Rodney Frelinghuysen, a Republican and member of one of New Jersey's most durable political families, which moved from Germany near the Dutch border in 1720 and settled in Rodney's current district. Four Frelinghuysens served as senator from New Jersey, starting in 1793 and as recently as 1923; Theodore Frelinghuysen was Whig presidential nominee Henry Clay's running-mate in 1844 (leading to the memorable slogan, "Hurrah! Hurrah! The country's risin'/ For Henry Clay and Frelinghuysen"); Frederick Frelinghuysen was Chester Arthur's secretary of State; Peter Frelinghuysen, Rodney's father, was elected to the House in 1952 and served until his retirement in 1974. As a child, Rodney Frelinghuysen lived in the large brick house on Georgetown's N Street now owned by former *Washington Post* editor Ben Bradlee and his wife Sally Quinn, and he attended St. Albans school with Al Gore. After college, the congressman's son was drafted and served in the Army in Vietnam, where he built roads in the Mekong Delta. In 1972 he was appointed an aide by then-Morris County Free-holder (and later 11th District congressman) Dean Gallo; he served as a freeholder himself from 1974–83 and was elected to the Assembly in 1983. As chairman of the Appropriations Committee, he worked to control spending and roll back taxes as an ally of Governor Christie Whitman.

Frelinghuysen ran for Congress in 1990 in what is now the 12th District, when its boundaries were different, and lost the primary to Dick Zimmer. In August 1994, after that year's primary, Gallo retired because of illness; he died two days before the election. Frelinghuysen was chosen to be the Republican nominee at a September party convention and was elected with 71% of the vote.

He showed his insider skills as a freshman by winning a seat on the Appropriations Committee, where Gallo had served. On Appropriations Frelinghuysen worked to cut spending on many programs, including the Tennessee Valley Authority, while maintaining a moderate voting record and concentrating on New Jersey projects. He supported funds for "Urban Core" and "Midtown Direct" mass transit lines. He helped push Sterling Forest preservation into the 1996 parks bill President Clinton signed, and got $1 million to expand the Great Swamp National Wildlife Refuge by 79 acres. He helped to add 295 acres to the Wildcat Refuge and he accelerated Superfund clean-up of the former Dow Chemical toxic-waste site in Boonton. He showed moderate stripes in 1998 as one of five Appropriations Republicans to join Democrats in preserving the National Endowment for the Arts. In 2000, he won unanimous House passage of his "Know Your Caller" bill, which bars telemarketers from interfering with caller-ID systems of customers seeking to avoid such solicitations. When he voted to impeach Clinton, he was the third Freling-huysen with a similar distinction: his great-great-grandfather Frederick voted to convict Andrew Johnson in 1868, and his father Peter, after the revelations of July 1974, would have voted to impeach Nixon if the president had not resigned.

Frelinghuysen was re-elected by 68%–30% margins in 1998 and 2000. Redistricting may change the boundaries somewhat, but the adjacent areas are almost all heavily Republican.

Cook's Call *Safe.* Frelinghuyesen sits in the most Republican district in the state and has no reason to be worried about his re-election prospects.

THE PEOPLE: Pop. 2000: 665,932; Pop. 1990: 594,526, up 12% 1990–2000. 87.6% White, 2.7% Black, 6.4% Asian, 0.1% Amer. Indian, 1.5% Two+ races, 1.7% Other; 6.8% Hispanic Origin.

2000 Presidential Vote		
Bush (R)	156,876	(53%)
Gore (D)	127,285	(43%)
Nader (Green)	9,020	(3%)

1996 Presidential Vote		
Dole (R)	135,972	(49%)
Clinton (D)	116,225	(42%)
Perot (I)	21,376	(8%)
Others	5,240	(2%)

Rep. Rodney Frelinghuysen (R)

Elected 1994, 4th term; b. Apr. 29, 1946, New York City; home, Morristown; Hobart Col., B.A. 1969; Episcopalian; married (Virginia).

Military Career: Army, 1969–71 (Vietnam).

Elected Office: Morris Cnty. Bd. of Freeholders, 1974–83; NJ Assembly, 1983–94.

Professional Career: Aide, Morris Cnty. Bd. of Freeholders, 1972–74.

DC Office: 2442 RHOB 20515, 202-225-5034; Fax: 202-225-3186; Web site: www.house.gov/frelinghuysen.

District Office: Morristown, 973-984-0711.

Committees: *Appropriations* (18th of 35 R): Defense; Energy & Water Development; VA, HUD & Independent Agencies.

Group Ratings

	ADA	ACLU	AFS	LCV	CON	ITIC	NTU	COC	ACU	NTLC	CHC
2000	25	29	0	71	24	94	56	71	56	61	47
1999	40	—	16	56	44	—	54	68	48	—	—

National Journal Ratings

	1999 LIB	—	1999 CONS		2000 LIB	—	2000 CONS
Economic	24%	—	72%		45%	—	54%
Social	58%	—	40%		61%	—	38%
Foreign	50%	—	48%		33%	—	62%

Key Votes of the 106th Congress

1. Patient Bill of Rights	Y	5. Bar RU-486 $ for FDA	N	9. NATO War in Serbia		Y
2. Accelerate Min. Wage	Y	6. Display 10 Commandments	N	10. Perm. Trade with China		Y
3. Strike Ban on Ergo. Stnd.	N	7. Gun Show Bkgrnd. Checks	Y	11. Debt Relief for 3rd World		N
4. Ovrd. Estate Tax Veto	Y	8. Ban Part.-Birth Abortion	Y	12. Drop Cuba Econ. Embargo		N

Election Results

2000 general	Rodney Frelinghuysen (R)	186,140	(68%)	($557,937)
	John P. Scollo (D)	80,958	(30%)	($9,161)
	Other	6,740	(3%)	
2000 primary	Rodney Frelinghuysen (R)	unopposed		
1998 general	Rodney Frelinghuysen (R)	100,910	(68%)	($418,522)
	John P. Scollo (D)	44,160	(30%)	
	Others	3,901	(3%)	

TWELFTH DISTRICT

It was once the main East Coast arterial highway, carrying the nation's highest volume of truck traffic. Today it is crowded with cars taking high-salaried workers and clerical help to one of the East Coast's thickest concentrations of office buildings in one of the bigger edge cities spawned in the 1980s. This is U.S. 1, which once just connected the industrial cities of Trenton and New Brunswick on its way from Philadelphia to New York; now it is better thought of around here as connecting the university towns around Princeton and Rutgers, and is a locus of telecommunications and pharmaceutical research. This had been empty bucolic country, looked out on by F. Scott Fitzgerald's undergraduates from their Gothic Princeton towers; now it is filled with postmodern office campuses and hotels and restaurants clamoring for attention.

The 12th Congressional District extends several dozen miles on either side of U.S. 1. To the west, it takes in the rolling country of Hunterdon County, around the old county seat of Flemington, once the site of the Lindbergh kidnapping trial, now an outlet store center with many young families, affluent if not elite, anxious at growing suburban sprawl even while causing it. On the other side of U.S. 1, the 12th takes in modest-income suburbs like East Brunswick in Middlesex County and much of Monmouth County, almost to the beach resorts of the Jersey Shore. Some of these communities are long-settled, others are spanking new. Politically, the Princeton area and Middlesex County, in the center of the district, are Democratic. The two ends of the district—Monmouth County near the Shore and Hunterdon County inland—are usually Republican. This is a district that trended Democratic in the 1990s. In 1992 it voted for George Bush 43%–40%; in 1996 it voted for Bill Clinton 48%–42%, and in 2000 it voted for Al Gore **51%–46%**.

The congressman from the 12th District is Rush Holt, a Democrat elected in 1998 with an unusual political pedigree. His father Rush D. Holt—a favorite of United Mine Workers' leader John Lewis—was elected as the "boy senator" from West Virginia in 1934 at 29; he could not take his seat until June 1935 when he turned 30. But he clashed early and often with Franklin Roosevelt and lost the Democratic primary to Harley Kilgore in 1940. After his father died, when young Rush was age 6, he grew up in Washington, D.C., where his mother Helen—who had been West Virginia secretary of State—became a top official with the Federal Housing Agency. He went off to Carleton College in Minnesota and to New York University, where he earned master's and doctorate degrees in physics, eventually becoming assistant director of the Princeton Plasma Physics Laboratory, which studies fusion. He also was an arms-control expert for the State Department.

Rush Holt entered politics in 1996, when Republican Dick Zimmer's unsuccessful Senate run opened his House seat. Holt finished third in the Democratic primary with 24% of the vote, trailing David Del Vecchio, mayor of Lawrenceville, who had 45%, and Princeton Town Committeeman Carl Mayer with 31%. The Republican primary victory of cultural conservative Mike Pappas gave Democrats an opening, and Pappas won by only 50%–47%. Pappas immediately became a top Democratic target in 1998. Holt decided early in the year that Clinton's State of the Union message gave him an agenda to appeal to suburban voters. The wealthy and self-financed Mayer—an investment attorney and former Ralph Nader aide—decided to run again, but national and local Democrats favored Holt, who won the endorsements of all five country Democratic organizations plus all of Mayer's former colleagues on the Princeton Town Committee, and took the primary by 64%–36%. Then, in July, Pappas took to the House floor to recite a poem: "Twinkle, Twinkle Kenneth Starr, now we see how brave you are. We could not see which way to go, if you did not lead us so." New Jersey was pro-Clinton, anti-impeachment territory, and Pappas's ditty—replayed on network newscasts and incorporated into a Holt TV spot—proved a great liability. Holt emphasized gun control, abortion rights, the environment and preserving Social Security. Holt won a 50%–47% upset victory.

Holt immediately became a Republican target. After flirting with another Senate bid, Zimmer declared he would run for his old House seat in 2000; soon, Pappas did too. But Holt was undeterred. He compiled a generally liberal voting record, well tailored to the district. He voted to override Clinton's veto of the marriage penalty and estate tax repeal. He concentrated on education and environmental issues popular locally. As the second research physicist in the House, he worked with Republican Vern Ehlers to promote science education, barring spending reductions in math and science courses and trying to give science equal standing with reading and math in Title I. He sponsored a bill to provide $30 million for open space preservation—a hot issue in growing central New Jersey. He sponsored bills to give government preference to gun makers that adopt Smith & Wesson's "safety and dealer responsibility standards," to raise the minimum age for purchasing handguns from 18 to 21, to fund "smart gun" research, to more than double funding for bulletproof vests for police and—this one attracted no co-sponsors—to require licensing and registration of all handguns. He sponsored a bill to ban sending ads to wireless phones. He got $18 million for a district road, dredging and bike path projects. He promoted a survey aimed at making New Jersey a National Heritage Area because of its Revolutionary War battlefields. With Frank Pallone he worked to keep the Navy from moving four ships and 2,000 sailors from the Earle Naval Weapons Station.

The June Republican primary was fiercely contested. Dick Zimmer had support from Governor Christie Whitman, former Governor Tom Kean, Speaker Dennis Hastert, Senator John McCain and campaign Committee Chairman Tom Davis; Mike Pappas was supported by former presidential candidate Steve Forbes, Majority Leader Dick Armey and Majority Whip Tom DeLay. Zimmer won convincingly, 62%–38%, carrying all parts of the district. He immediately became the target of some $2 million of Democratic Congressional Campaign Committee negative ads.

Zimmer got one, charging he never voted for an education bill, withdrawn for inaccuracy; another, charging that he didn't support women's health measures, he attacked as unfair since his mother and three sisters all had breast cancer. These controversies put Holt on the defensive; so, a little, did his old nemesis Carl Mayer, now running as the Green Party candidate, charging that Holt was "marinated in PAC money."

Holt did indeed raise the prodigious sum of more than $2.6 million and ran ads emphasizing his stands on education, the environment and gun control. He was accompanied for a day of campaigning in August by Bill Clinton—a political plus in this district. In his ads, Zimmer referred to himself as "Congressman" and cited his record of opposition to spending and support of abortion rights and gun control—a winning platform here in the early 1990s: "I'm not running toward the middle. I've always been in the middle." But the political terrain had changed; as Zimmer said during the primary, "There's a cultural divide between the Northeast and what's become the Republican base. The world looks different from suburban New Jersey than it does from Texas."

This turned out to be one of the closest races in the nation. At one point on election night Zimmer was declared the winner, and in the days after Holt's lead was 172 votes. Zimmer charged that Democrats cynically collected the votes of patients in psychiatric hospitals and there was a dispute over 423 paper ballots in Mercer County. Holt was declared the winner by 653 votes and on November 17 claimed victory. Zimmer called for a recount. When it showed Holt's lead widening, Zimmer conceded on November 29.

Though Holt has shown impressive skill in winning twice, the current 12th District cannot be called a safe seat for anybody, and no one can be sure what it will look like after redistricting. The happiest scenario for Holt, whose district must lose 63,000 people, would be to gain heavily Democratic Trenton, now in Republican Chris Smith's 4th District, and lose Republican territory in either the western or eastern ends of the current 12th.

Cook's Call *Competitive.* Though Holt has never had a particularly easy time with this swing district, with two wins now under his belt, he is certainly in better political shape than he was just two years ago. Republicans are likely to target Holt again in 2002, but the Holt has proven to be a tenacious and savvy campaigner who should not be underestimated. This suburban district was the fastest growing in the state and will need to drop more than 50,000 residents in redistricting. How the lines are redrawn here will also impact just how competitive this race will be in 2002.

THE PEOPLE: Pop. 2000: 709,867; Pop. 1990: 594,577, up 19.4% 1990–2000. 84.1% White, 5.3% Black, 7.8% Asian, 0.1% Amer. Indian, 1.5% Two + races, 1.1% Other; 4.1% Hispanic Origin.

2000 Presidential Vote			1996 Presidential Vote		
Gore (D)	159,473	(51%)	Clinton (D)	139,252	(48%)
Bush (R)	142,855	(46%)	Dole (R)	120,913	(42%)
Nader (Green)	10,909	(3%)	Perot (I)	23,159	(8%)
			Others	6,716	(2%)

Rep. Rush Holt (D)

Elected 1998, 2d term; b. Oct. 15, 1948, Weston, WV; home, Hopewell Township; Carleton Col., B.S. 1970, N.Y.U., PhD. 1981; Protestant; married (Margaret Lancefield).

Professional Career: Prof., Swarthmore Col., 1981–89; Asst. Dir., Princeton Plasma Physics Lab., 1989–98.

DC Office: 1630 LHOB 20515, 202-225-5801; Fax: 202-225-6025; Web site: www.house.gov/rholt.

District Office: Princeton Junction, 609-750-9365.

Committees: *Budget* (18th of 20 D). *Education & the Workforce* (19th of 22 D): 21st Century Competitiveness; Select Education. *Resources* (19th of 25 D): Forests & Forest Health; National Parks, Recreation & Public Lands.

Group Ratings

	ADA	ACLU	AFS	LCV	CON	ITIC	NTU	COC	ACU	NTLC	CHC
2000	80	79	85	100	45	61	38	47	16	22	13
1999	95	—	83	100	96	—	24	24	4	—	—

National Journal Ratings

	1999 LIB	—	1999 CONS		2000 LIB	—	2000 CONS
Economic	75%	—	23%		60%	—	39%
Social	79%	—	20%		77%	—	22%
Foreign	78%	—	22%		80%	—	16%

Key Votes of the 106th Congress

1. Patient Bill of Rights	Y	5. Bar RU-486 $ for FDA	N	9. NATO War in Serbia	Y
2. Accelerate Min. Wage	Y	6. Display 10 Commandments	N	10. Perm. Trade with China	N
3. Strike Ban on Ergo. Stnd.	Y	7. Gun Show Bkgrnd. Checks	Y	11. Debt Relief for 3rd World	Y
4. Ovrd. Estate Tax Veto	Y	8. Ban Part.-Birth Abortion	N	12. Drop Cuba Econ. Embargo	Y

Election Results

2000 general	Rush Holt (D)	146,612	(49%)	($2,566,080)
	Dick Zimmer (R)	145,511	(49%)	($2,196,588)
	Other	8,269	(3%)	
2000 primary	Rush Holt (D)	unopposed		
1998 general	Rush Holt (D)	92,528	(50%)	($919,905)
	Michael Pappas (R)	87,221	(47%)	($889,475)
	Others	4,861	(3%)	

THIRTEENTH DISTRICT

The Statue of Liberty, standing in New York Harbor since 1886, has been the great symbol of America welcoming immigrants to its shores. Actually, the statue is on the New Jersey side of the harbor, and so (as the Supreme Court ruled in 1998) is most of Ellis Island, where they were processed. The towns sitting on the granite and gneiss ridge of Hudson County, overlooking the harbor, have in particular been immigrant territory. When immigration was shut off in 1924, many children and grandchildren of the Irish and Italian immigrants stayed in Hudson County, living in the same neighborhoods, working on the same docks or factories and voting the dictates of the same political machine.

Hudson County was the setting of one of America's classic political machines, undisciplined by any metropolitan elite. From 1917–49, the boss of Hudson County was Frank ("I am the law") Hague; his machine chose governors and U.S. Senators, prosecutors and judges, and had influence in the White House of Franklin D. Roosevelt. Hague collected high taxes from industries clustered here—who then passed them on to consumers everywhere—and in return gave them an orderly city, free of most crime and vice, and a work force insulated against racketeers and militant unions. Hague's successor, John V. Kenny, was boss from 1949–71—continuous power for 54 years. But Hudson County began changing again, in ways little noticed by either the local machine or Manhattan sophisticates. New immigrants were coming in—refugees from Castro's Cuba, other Latinos and Asians after the 1965 immigration law changed the rules. Union City became predominantly Cuban, Jersey City neighborhoods became heavily Latino. Upscale young singles looking for lower rents moved into Hoboken's five-story Victorian apartments that sparkle with light off the Hudson, and are a quick commute through the PATH tubes to Wall Street or Greenwich Village. Starting in the 1980s, huge new condominium and office developments went up in Jersey City—Port Liberte, Newport, Liberty Place—and going up now are more—Port Imperial South, a 45-story Goldman Sachs tower, back-office buildings for Chase Bank, Merrill Lynch, Paine Webber, U.S. Trust. Aiding this private sector growth is reform of the public sector, notably by Jersey City's Republican mayor, Bret Schundler, a former Wall Streeter elected in 1992 after the incumbent went to jail, who was elected to full terms in 1993 and 1997 and ran for governor in 2001. Meanwhile, new immigrants are coming in. Union City is less Cuban today, as middle class Cubans move to Bergen County suburbs, and more Colombian, Ecuadoran, Peruvian and Dominican. Old rail lines long embedded in pavement are being dug up and used for the new Hudson-Bergen light rail lines, and new ferry terminals are being built on the Hudson.

The 13th Congressional District of New Jersey includes most of Hudson County plus most of the immigrant entry ports along the water. It was designed in 1992 to be an "Hispanic influence" district; 48% of its residents in 2000 were Hispanic and 13% were black. With most of Jersey City and all of Union City and West New York and Weehawken, it also includes 105,000 people in the old Ironbound area of Newark, a neighborhood kept alive during Newark's bad days by Portuguese and Brazilian immigrants, now buzzing with crowded stores and schools and new $300,000 houses. And it proceeds south past Port Newark, now highly mechanized and employing only one-tenth as many longshoremen as a generation ago, to include the port sections of Elizabeth and Perth Amboy, with its own new waterfront developments.

The congressman from the 13th is Robert Menendez, a Democrat elected in 1992. He is of Cuban descent and grew up in Union City, America's most densely populated city (in 2000 it had 60,000 people in 1.3 square miles), and got into politics early. He was elected to the school board in 1974, at 20. He worked for Union City Mayor William Musto in the 1970s, but quit and testified against Musto in a corruption trial, and ran against him and lost in 1982. Menendez was elected mayor in 1986 and to the legislature in 1987, serving in both jobs (a common practice in New Jersey) until his 1992 election to Congress. When new district lines were created and incumbent Frank Guarini retired, Menendez won the primary 68%–32% and the general 64%–31%.

In the House, Menendez serves on the International Relations Committee where he became ranking minority member on the Western Hemisphere Subcommittee in 2001. He has been a strong supporter of anti-Castro legislation—the 1992 Cuban Democracy Act, the 1996 Helms-Burton Act. He criticized the Clinton administration for not enforcing Helms-Burton and taking steps to relax the trade embargo. When Elian Gonzalez was assaulted by federal agents, he said grimly, "I think that the use of armed agents with automatic weapons, in the pre-dawn hours on the morning of the holiest weekend of the year, is, in my mind, something we would see in Fidel Castro's Cuba, not in the democracy of the United States." In 1999 he protested against the Baltimore Orioles' trip to Cuba and kept charter flights to Cuba out of Newark Airport. But his concerns are not limited to Cuba. He supported the Caribbean Basin Initiative and the proposal to allow Central American and Haitian refugees long in this country to remain. He denounced the "total disregard of the United States Navy for the people of Vieques." He was chief sponsor of a 1999 resolution to withhold money from the IAEA because it was helping Iran build a nuclear power plant.

Noting, perhaps, the increasing importance of the financial services industry in Hudson County, he broke with many Democrats to support bankruptcy reform and financial services deregulation; one Blue Dog Democrat called him "the pro-business member of the leadership." He has pressed for more set-asides for minority contractors and Senate confirmation of Hispanic judges. Noting that almost all immigrants are eager to learn English, he says "English-only is a solution to a problem that does not exist."

On local issues, he helped to secure $733 million to deepen the main channel of Newark Bay from 40 to 45 feet by 2004 to accommodate larger cargo ships to the container port. He seeks a cleanup of the Passaic River and wants Hudson dredging pollution standards to be based on "sound science and thoughtful review, not rhetoric." He got $12 million for a ferry terminal near the Port Imperial South projects, whose owner is a key financial backer. "If he ends up, along with everybody else, being a beneficiary of what I'm advocating, what can I say?" He has obtained funding for Hudson-Bergen and Newark-Elizabeth light rail and for Hope VI grants to transform public housing in Jersey City, Elizabeth and Newark.

Menendez has shown fine political skills. In 1997, after replacing Bill Richardson as chief deputy minority whip, he aggressively supported Loretta Sanchez against the election challenge brought by Robert Dornan. In November 1998 Democrats elected him vice chairman of the Caucus; on the second ballot he beat Cal Dooley of California 124–81. When Senator Frank Lautenberg announced his retirement in February 1999, Menendez was widely expected to run for the Senate. But support was not forthcoming from New Jersey Senator Bob Torricelli, the Democratic Senatorial Campaign Committee Chairman, who wanted a deep-pockets candidate and found him in Jon Corzine, whom Menendez endorsed in November 1999; in July 2000, after Torricelli announced he was running for governor, Menendez choreographed an endorsement by many Hudson County Democrats of Jim McGreevey, which helped persuade Torricelli ignominiously to withdraw from the race. Menendez does not forget. In 1978 he had bucked Hudson County Democratic leaders and backed Bill Bradley for the Senate; when he asked for Bradley's endorsement in his own 1992 primary, Bradley refused—"a very disappointing moment"—and in 1999 Menendez endorsed Al Gore for president. Another reason that Menendez decided not to run for the Senate is that Minority Leader Dick Gephardt urged him to stay in the House, arguing that as a leader of a Democratic majority he could be more important than a junior senator. He is still in the minority, but he is eight years, seven months younger than those higher on the leadership ladder. In 2000 he was mentioned briefly as a possible vice presidential nominee and following the election went to Miami to help Al Gore, at the risk of offending Republican Cuban-Americans who have been big contributors.

They are not the only ones: in 2000 Menendez had $1.7 million in his campaign treasury, although he has had no serious competition for his seat since 1992. Redistricting will likely preserve this Hispanic-influence district in pretty much its current form.

Cook's Call   *Safe.* This Jersey City-based district gave Gore his biggest winning margin in the state in 2000 (47%) and will not give Menendez any worries in 2002. Conventional wisdom held that this district was losing population and would have to be altered significantly in redistricting, but it was actually one of the faster growing in the state and needs to shed about 10,000 residents.

THE PEOPLE: Pop. 2000: 656,461; Pop. 1990: 594,875, up 10.4% 1990–2000. 55.7% White, 12.9% Black, 6% Asian, 0.5% Amer. Indian, 0.1% Hawaiian, 5.8% Two+ races, 19% Other; 47.2% Hispanic Origin.

2000 Presidential Vote		
Gore (D)	117,047	(72%)
Bush (R)	41,102	(25%)
Nader (Green)	3,770	(2%)

1996 Presidential Vote		
Clinton (D)	115,576	(71%)
Dole (R)	35,266	(22%)
Perot (I)	8,411	(5%)
Others	2,764	(2%)

Rep. Robert Menendez (D)

Elected 1992, 5th term; b. Jan. 1, 1954, New York, NY; home, Union City; St. Peter's Col., B.A. 1976, Rutgers Law Schl., J.D. 1979; Catholic; married (Jane Jacobsen-Menendez).

Elected Office: Union City Board of Ed., 1974–82; Union City Mayor, 1986–92; NJ Assembly, 1987–91; NJ Senate, 1991–92.

Professional Career: Practicing atty., 1980–92.

DC Office: 2238 RHOB 20515, 202-225-7919; Fax: 202-226-0792; Web site: menendez.house.gov.

District Offices: Bayonne, 201-823-2900; Jersey City, 201-222-2828; Perth Amboy, 908-324-6212; Union City, 201-558-0800.

Committees: *Democratic Caucus Vice Chairman. International Relations* (6th of 23 D): International Operations and Human Rights; Western Hemisphere (RMM). *Transportation & Infrastructure* (10th of 34 D): Aviation; Water Resources & Environment.

Group Ratings

	ADA	ACLU	AFS	LCV	CON	ITIC	NTU	COC	ACU	NTLC	CHC
2000	95	79	100	93	61	55	19	38	8	12	20
1999	100	—	100	100	28	—	12	24	4	—	—

National Journal Ratings

	1999 LIB	—	1999 CONS		2000 LIB	—	2000 CONS
Economic	78%	—	21%		92%	—	5%
Social	76%	—	23%		72%	—	26%
Foreign	65%	—	34%		61%	—	38%

Key Votes of the 106th Congress

1. Patient Bill of Rights	Y	5. Bar RU-486 $ for FDA	N	9. NATO War in Serbia	Y
2. Accelerate Min. Wage	Y	6. Display 10 Commandments	N	10. Perm. Trade with China	N
3. Strike Ban on Ergo. Stnd.	Y	7. Gun Show Bkgrnd. Checks	Y	11. Debt Relief for 3rd World	Y
4. Ovrd. Estate Tax Veto	N	8. Ban Part.-Birth Abortion	N	12. Drop Cuba Econ. Embargo	N

Election Results

2000 general	Robert Menendez (D)	117,856	(79%)	($1,713,018)
	Theresa de Leon (R)	27,849	(19%)	($19,822)
	Other	3,893	(3%)	
2000 primary	Robert Menendez (D)	unopposed		
1998 general	Robert Menendez (D)	70,308	(80%)	($964,145)
	Theresa De Leon (R)	14,615	(17%)	($35,252)
	Others	2,900	(3%)	

★ NEW MEXICO ★

America's oldest settlements and its newest technologies can be found, in surrealistic proximity, in New Mexico. For the oldest permanently inhabited city in the United States is not Plymouth, Massachusetts, or Jamestown, Virginia, or even St. Augustine, Florida, it is probably Acoma, New Mexico. Probably, because Acoma, inhabited by the Anasazi, "an agricultural, settled and architecturally sophisticated people," wrote historian Roger Kennedy in *Rediscovering America*, had perhaps 1,000 years of unrecorded history before Spanish conquistadors came upon them in 1540. Some 460 years later, much of what makes New Mexico distinctive derives from the people found here by the first European explorers—something true of no other state but Hawaii. While the Pilgrims built flimsy wood houses, the Indians in New Mexico were living in extensive dwellings hundreds of years old, made with the adobe that is still the characteristic building material here.

Other state cultures are generally based on what early white settlers brought to the land; natives have mostly disappeared or been killed off by diseases contracted from the first white settlers. Not in New Mexico. The English-speaking culture here is superimposed, at times rather lightly, on a society whose written history dates back to the Spanish settlement of Santa Fe in 1609, and to centuries long past when the Pueblo Indians set up stable agricultural societies on the sandy, rocky lands of northern New Mexico, using small pebbles as mulch to retain scarce moisture. Pueblo culture is still celebrated in the Indian pottery that commands premium prices in Santa Fe and in the annual Gathering of Nations pow-wow in Albuquerque which attracts 100,000 people. Today, a very substantial minority of New Mexicans are descendants of these Indians or the Spanish, or both. New Mexico had the highest percentage of Hispanics (42%) in the U.S. after the 2000 Census. Nearly one-third of the people in this state speak Spanish in everyday life, and relatively few are recent migrants from Mexico. The Hispanic roots go very deep, as witnessed by the discovery of Hebrew symbols left on Christian gravestones by the *conversos*, Jews who hid their religion after it was outlawed by the Spanish in 1492; there are families here who have secretly maintained Jewish practices for centuries.

New Mexico is the northernmost salient of the great Indian-Spanish civilizations of the Cordillera, which extend along the mountain chain through Mexico and Central and South America, to the southern tip of Chile and Argentina. Yet New Mexico also is a civilization built on modern technology. It was to a remote mesa called Los Alamos that General Leslie Groves brought his Manhattan Project scientists during World War II to build a secret town and develop a secret weapon that would in two explosions end World War II and change the course of history. Los Alamos, which remains a government high-tech laboratory, made news in early 1999 when it was revealed that Chinese spies had obtained hundreds of computer files from there. New Mexico has other high-tech sites as well—the White Sands Missile Range near Alamogordo, where the first atomic bomb was detonated, and the Sandia Laboratories near Albuquerque, run by Lockheed-Martin for the government, a non-nuclear high-tech weapons research facility, with one of

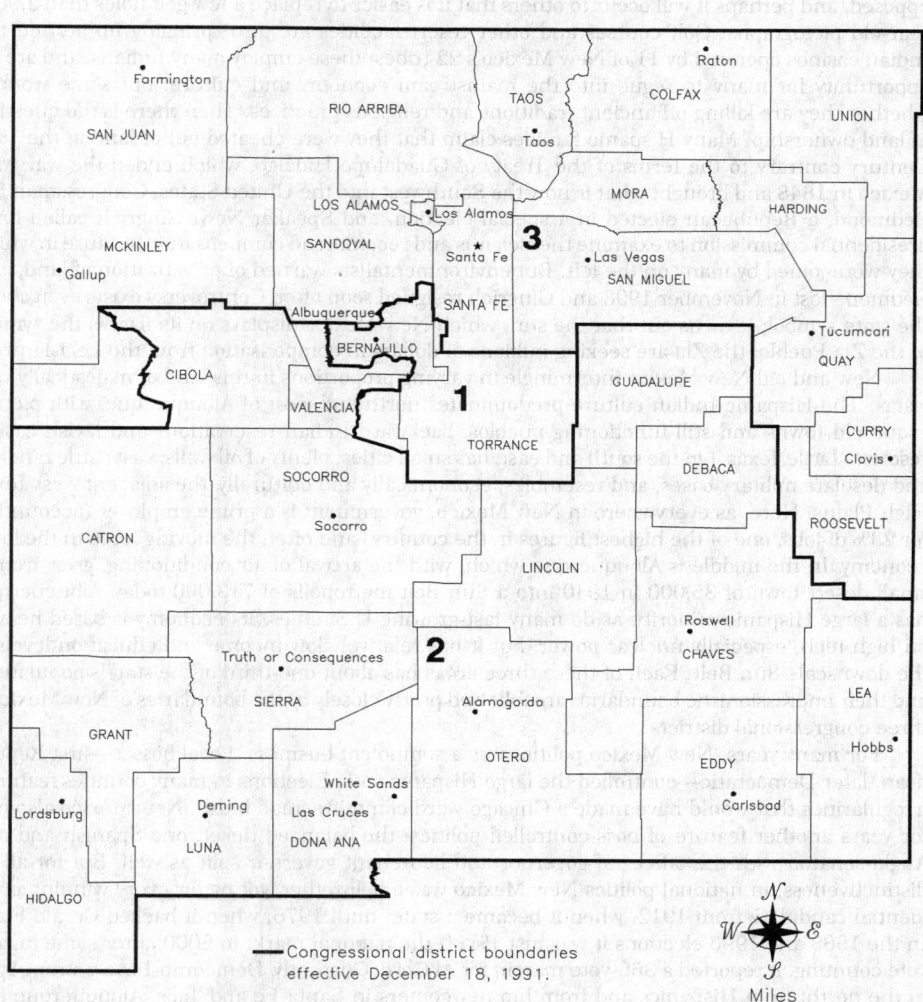

Congressional district boundaries
effective December 18, 1991.

Miles
0 10 20 30 40

the fastest computers in the world, used to simulate nuclear explosions. Near Carlsbad is the federal Waste Isolation Pilot Plant (WIPP), where the Energy Department deposits transuranic radioactive waste; after many delays, the first waste from the Idaho National Engineering and Environmental Laboratory arrived here in March 1999.

But the past intrudes on this new high-tech New Mexico. West of Albuquerque, developers and most local politicians want to build a highway through 8.5 acres of the 7,231-acre Petroglyph National Monument, filled with black volcanic rock with ancient mysterious carvings; a proposal to put the road through a nearby golf course was nixed. But Albuquerque Mayor Jim Baca is opposed, and perhaps it will occur to others that it is easier to replace a few golf holes than 2,000-year-old pictographs. Golf courses and other resort facilities are also springing up around the Indian casinos operated by 11 of New Mexico's 22 tribes; these employ many Indians, and are an opportunity for many to segue into the mainstream economy and culture; but some wonder whether they are killing off ancient traditions and religious practices. Then there is the question of land ownership: Many Hispanic families claim that they were cheated out of land in the 19th Century contrary to the terms of the Treaty of Guadalupe Hidalgo, which ended the war with Mexico in 1848 and brought what is now the Southwest into the United States. Congressman Bill Redmond, a Republican elected in a special election, and Speaker Newt Gingrich called for a presidential commission to examine their claims and recommend compensation, a cause in which they were joined by many on the left. But environmentalists warned of privatization of land, and Redmond lost in November 1998 and Gingrich resigned soon after. Controversy exists even about the state symbol; it turns out that the sun, which New Mexico displays on its flag, is the symbol of the Zia Pueblo; the Zia are seeking millions of dollars in compensation from the Legislature.

New and old New Mexico intermingle in varying proportions in this land of majestically vast vistas. The Hispanic-Indian culture predominates north and west of Albuquerque, with pictur-esque old towns and still-functioning pueblos, backward Indian reservations and lavish casino resorts. "Little Texas," in the south and east, has small cities, plenty of oil wells, vast cattle ranches and desolate military bases, and resembles, economically and culturally, the adjacent west Texas High Plains. Here, as everywhere in New Mexico, government is a prime employer (accounting for 23% of jobs, one of the highest figures in the country) and often the moving force in the local economy. In the middle is Albuquerque which, with the arrival of air conditioning, grew from a small desert town of 35,000 in 1940 into a Sun Belt metropolis of 713,000 today. Albuquerque has a large Hispanic minority, as do many fast-growing U.S. cities. Its economy is based heavily on high tech, especially nuclear power; but it has relatively low income and education levels—the downscale Sun Belt. Each of these three areas has about one-third of the state's population, and their impressionistic boundaries are followed pretty closely by the boundaries of New Mexico's three congressional districts.

For many years, New Mexico politics was a somnolent business. Local bosses—first Repub-lican, later Democratic—controlled the large Hispanic vote. Elections in many counties featured irregularities that would have made a Chicago ward committeeman blush. New Mexico also had for years another feature of boss-controlled politics: the balanced ticket, one Spanish and one Anglo senator, with the offices of governor and lieutenant governor split as well. But for all its distinctiveness, in national politics New Mexico was a bellwether, voting for every winning pres-idential candidate from 1912, when it became a state, until 1976, when it backed Gerald Ford. In the 1988 and 1996 elections it was just 1% off the national mark; in 2000, after some ragged vote counting, it reported a 366-vote margin for Al Gore. Currently, Democrats have a strong base in the north, from Hispanics and from hip newcomers in Santa Fe and Taos. Albuquerque has been politically marginal; its migrants have been conservative culturally but liberal on economics. Southeast New Mexico is as conservative and Republican as west Texas. Southwest New Mexico, around Las Cruces and Silver City, is more Hispanic and marginally Democratic.

New Mexico politics also has its peculiarities. In the 1990s a Green Party formed, in protest against the practical-minded and sometimes corrupt politics of many Democratic wheelhorses; the Green candidate for governor won 10% of the vote in 1994, and Republican Gary Johnson might well have not been elected otherwise. Johnson is also a new political force—the first strongly conservative Republican to win major office in many years, and one of the few Republicans to come out for drug legalization; he has been ferociously opposed by the Democrats who control the legislature. But he won re-election without any third party candidacies in 1998, against a strong candidate, former Albuquerque Mayor Martin Chavez, and his Republicans have reduced the Democrats' margin in the legislature. New Mexico continues to have two long-serving senators, Republican Pete Domenici and Democrat Jeff Bingaman. But two of its three House members were first elected in 1998. And the Green Party was downgraded by the state to minor-party status, after Ralph Nader's lackluster showing of 3.5% on the 2000 presidential ballot.

Governor   The governor of New Mexico is Gary Johnson, a Republican elected in 1994 and 1998. Johnson moved to Albuquerque when he was in junior high; his father was a teacher and his mother worked for the Bureau of Indian Affairs. In 1974, at 21, while still a student at the University of New Mexico, he started a construction business, and built a door-to-door solicitation business into Big J Enterprises, one of the largest construction companies in the state with 900 employees. He sees his success as a typical product of hard work: "Anybody that wants to be an entrepreneur in this country can make an absolute fortune." Johnson served on civic boards, sponsored children's athletic events and is himself a competitor: He won the 1993 Bump, Bike and Bolt competition in Taos, completed a triathlon in Hawaii in October 1993, and ran a 100-mile race partly backward after pulling a muscle. He still runs and excels at triathlons and begins his workouts every morning at 4:45 a.m. He exercises on a point system, with one point each for a mile run, a quarter-mile swim, three miles of biking and 10 minutes of weightlifting; he logs (except when recovering from a fractured vertebrae in January 2001) 77 points a week.

In 1994, Johnson ran for governor, on vague slogans—"people before politics," "citizen service"—and on promises to hold the line on government growth and to roll back a six-cent gas tax increase. He won the Republican primary by only 34%–33% over Dick Cheney (not the vice president), and in the general election faced Governor Bruce King, elected in 1970, 1978, and 1990. But King had won the Democratic primary by only 39%–36% over his lieutenant governor, Casey Luna, with 25% for former Clinton Interior official Jim Baca, now mayor of Albuquerque. And there was also a Green Party candidate, former Lieutenant Governor Roberto Mondragon, who won 10% of the vote. Johnson beat King 50%–40%.

In his first term, Johnson faced bitter opposition from Democratic legislative leaders. He vetoed 388 bills, cut the state budget unilaterally, reduced state workforce by 1,200 and limited state budget growth to 4.2% a year, down from nearly 10% in the previous decade. He did not get his proposed income tax cut and prescription tax abolition, but he did get the six-cent gas tax repealed and claimed to reduce taxes by $106 million a year. In 1998 he cut the top personal income tax rate, instituted a low income tax rebate, and a gross receipts tax cut that included prescription drugs. He pushed successfully for two new prisons, to be privately built, and established a tough prison regime—frequent drug tests, mandatory hard labor, deprivation of body-building equipment, and 23-hour solitary confinement for misbehaving gang members. Johnson called for school vouchers, charter schools and testing of students every year. He also raised teachers' salaries sharply. He supported Indian gambling and signed a bill banning drive-through alcohol sales.

Johnson was not afraid of a fight. He vetoed the legislature's 1997 welfare reform bill and instituted his own Progress plan, counting federal housing subsidies and incomes of everyone in a house to determine eligibility and instituting tough work requirements. Welfare rolls fell from 34,900 in November 1994 to 16,500 in November 1997. But the Progress plan was rejected by the feds, and Johnson was held in indirect civil contempt by the state Supreme Court and ordered to reinstate the old AFDC system in December 1997. Eventually Johnson got a welfare reform approved—the last in the nation—with a mandatory work requirement, but the rolls rose to 23,700 in September 1998. Johnson's Republicans picked up legislative seats in 1996 even as Bill Clinton carried the state. Still, Democrats had fond hopes of beating Johnson in 1998. They took special care to propitiate the Green Party, to prevent a candidacy like those that hurt them in 1994 and in the May 1997 3d District special election. Their strongest candidate was Martin Chavez, state senator from 1989–93 and mayor of Albuquerque from 1993–97. In the June 1998 primary, Chavez beat state Representative Gary King, son of Bruce King, by 48%–30%. Chavez promised full-time kindergarten and criticized Johnson for not getting along with the legislature. Johnson argued that Chavez couldn't fulfill his promises without raising taxes. The two candidates participated, mostly civilly, in 24 debates. Johnson led most of the way, and won 55%–45%; he carried the Anglo vote 2–1, while losing Hispanics 2–1. He won an impressive 58% in Albuquerque and Bernalillo County, and carried Little Texas 2–1. Chavez carried Santa Fe County 2–1, but next-door Sandoval County, once rural, Hispanic and Democratic, was now filling up with suburbanites spreading north from Albuquerque, and Johnson carried it 60%–40%.

Johnson signed two bills allowing more charter schools in April 1999. He vetoed an extension of the public employees collective bargaining act. His big highway-building program, to make every town of 15,000 reachable by four-lane highways, was approved. In 2000 he signed a partial-birth abortion ban and a law limiting property tax increases to 3%; he vetoed a minimum wage increase and higher Medicaid spending. In 2001 Democrats elected new, more conciliatory legislative leaders. But the legislature killed Johnson's school vouchers proposal and his $72 million tax cut; he vetoed their $27 million tax cut and rebates and killed $95 million in spending with line-item vetoes.

But Johnson attracted the most attention, in New Mexico and nationally, with his proposals for drug decriminalization. In the summer of 1999, safely re-elected and barred from a third term, Johnson suddenly endorsed legalization of heroin and marijuana. He argued that drug laws were ineffective on a cost-benefit analysis; the country was spending $40 billion on them, without good results, and that that money would be better spent for drug treatment. "Half of what we spend on law enforcement, half of what we spend on the courts and half of what we spend on prisons is drug-related. Our current policies on drugs are perhaps the greatest problem the country has." He recounted his own use of marijuana in his 20s, and said that he had twice tried cocaine, but stopped because he liked it too much. He told college students in Washington that marijuana was "cool," and gave interviews on the issue to *Penthouse* and *Playboy*. The response was furious. His chief law enforcement officer quit, one local sheriff called him an "idiot," and his job approval rating fell. National drug czar Barry McCaffrey said his ideas were "goofy thinking," and the New Mexico Senate, on a motion introduced by his fellow Republicans, condemned his stand by a 37–4 vote margin. In 2000 he backed away from heroin legalization, and emphasized legalization of marijuana and advocated "harm reduction" strategies for other drugs. In 2001 he introduced eight drug bills. Only three passed: non-prosecution of pharmacists for selling clean syringes, $24 million for drug treatment and immunity for administering opioid antagonists to reverse the effects of heroin and opium overdoses.

Johnson gave speeches around the state and across the country on drug legalization. He also endorsed Steve Forbes for president in July 1999, while New Mexico's other leading Republicans backed George W. Bush. A local group tried to draft him as the Libertarian candidate for president; he declined. When Ralph Nader endorsed legalization of marijuana, Johnson said he should be included in presidential debates. Johnson is term-limited in 2002, and there is no Senate seat he could run for up until 2006. With his views on drugs, he is unlikely to be nominated for a post in the Bush administration. The most prominent potential candidate to succeed him is former Congressman, Ambassador to the UN and Energy Secretary Bill Richardson.

Cook's Call　*Highly Competitive.* New Mexico has become a swing state: Gore won here by less than 400 votes, while Democrats hold one Senate seat and one of the three House seats. Among Democrats, state Attorney General Patricia Madrid and Gary King, whose father was governor, are running, while former Congressman and Clinton administration Energy Secretary Bill Richardson are exploring bids. On the Republican side, Lieutenant Governor Walter Bradley, state Senator Ramsay Gorham and businessman Larry Willard are looking at the race.

Senior Senator　Pete Domenici is in his third decade in the Senate and is beginning his third decade as chairman of—or ranking Republican on—the Senate Budget Committee. Certainly he is the giant political figure in New Mexico. Domenici grew up in Albuquerque, the son of Italian immigrants who ran a grocery wholesale business. He played baseball for the Albuquerque Dukes, practiced law, was elected to the city commission in 1966; he ran for governor in 1970, and lost to Bruce King. In 1972, when a Senate seat opened up in a Republican year, he ran and won, beating a Democrat named Jack Daniels. Ever since he has been re-elected by wide margins.

Domenici's great work in the Senate is on the budget. He got a seat on the Budget committee in 1973, his first year in the Senate. In 1990 he turned down the ranking minority position on Energy and Natural Resources, an important committee for New Mexico, in order to stay on the Budget Committee; he is also a senior member of Appropriations. For years Domenici was frustrated there. He was genuinely appalled at the deficits of the 1980s and was ready to recommend the bitterest of medicine—entitlement cuts, tax increases. But Democrats fought spending cuts and Republicans fought tax increases, so Domenici's victories were few and hard won. In May 1985, Domenici and Bob Dole got Republican senators to pass a freeze on Social Security cost-of-living adjustments; then Ronald Reagan dropped the COLA freeze in a compromise with House Speaker Tip O'Neill, and Senate Republicans, left exposed, lost their majority in 1986. Domenici backed the 1987 Gramm-Rudman Act, whose mechanisms, along with Reagan Budget Director Jim Miller's fixation on holding down spending, cut the deficit by about half; he backed the 1990 budget summit tax increase with its domestic and defense spending caps; like all other Republicans, he opposed the Clinton budget and tax package in 1993.

Domenici did not get his way after Republicans won majorities in 1994. His own preference was a plan with $476 billion in tax cuts, $1.4 trillion in spending cuts over 10 years and a consumption tax to replace the income tax. The pace was set by Speaker Newt Gingrich and House Budget Chairman John Kasich in the 1995–96 confrontation with Bill Clinton. But the tax increase he opposed in 1993 and the spending standstill in the budget eventually passed in early 1996 put the deficit on a downward trajectory. In this setting Domenici was the impresario in the negotiations that produced the May 1997 balanced budget agreement. In 1998 he opposed Kasich's and Gingrich's proposal for a large tax cut and effectively scuttled it. In January 1999, with the budget now officially balanced, Domenici took a different tack. He accepted Bill Clinton's proposal to reserve 62% of the surplus for Social Security, but argued that much of the rest should be devoted to tax cuts; he called also for increased spending on defense and elementary and secondary education. "We're beginning a period that I never could have imagined when I began doing this more than 20 years ago, a period of surpluses." He helped to shape the budget resolutions in 1999 and 2000, but as an appropriator helped work out the arrangements that resulted in exceeding the budget caps. In February 2001 he worked to pass the $1.6 trillion Bush tax cut and charged that Democrats had "anti-tax cut fever." In March he recognized that there were not quite 50 votes for either the $1.6 trillion tax cut or Bush's 4% lid on discretionary spending, but supported them anyway. He supported frontloading the tax cut but criticized Democratic proposals for a $300 rebate. Shy one vote in the Senate, Republicans did not end up reaching Bush's goals on the budget resolution. But they came close, and would have ended up much further away if Domenici had been lukewarm about the Bush plan.

Generally, Domenici is a passionate moderate, with a middle-of-the-road record. He has argued strongly for including coverage of mental illness in health insurance, and talked of the severe mental illness of one of his daughters. Working with Democrat Paul Wellstone, he got the Senate to include mental illness in the 1996 health care bill and got the conference committee to accept coverage with a low cap. Domenici cited evidence that mental health treatments are increasingly rigorous and efficacious; opponents feared high and uncontrollable costs. In 1999 and 2000 he co-sponsored bills to bar insurers from limiting hospital stays and outpatient visits at clinics for people suffering mental illness, to train medical professionals about mental health treatment and to increase HMO reimbursement for mental illness. In early 2001 he was working on reauthorization of the 1996 bill, due to expire in September 2001.

As a member of the Appropriations Committee, Domenici battled House Transportation Committee Chairman Bud Shuster's attempts to take the highway and aviation trust funds off budget. In 1998 Shuster succeeded in getting firewalls around highway trust fund spending. But in a December 1999 conference committee, Domenici beat his attempt to do the same for the aviation trust fund, by offering a conciliatory-sounding compromise which he knew Shuster would not accept. In late 1999 Domenici was also the chief sponsor of the Republicans' minimum wage increase, combining it with tax cuts for small business. Domenici pays close attention to New Mexico's Los Alamos and Sandia National Laboratories. After the controversy over security lapses at Los Alamos, he sponsored the creation of a new Undersecretary of Energy for Nuclear Stewardship, taking much of the power away from Energy Secretary Bill Richardson; this was approved 96–1. He worked to double federal spending on basic research over 10 years and to prevent big cuts in nuclear weapons programs; he favors more use of nuclear energy to generate power, opening of an interim nuclear waste storage facility in Nevada, a reduction in nuclear weapons stockpiles and irradiation of food. Domenici uses his Appropriations seat to help New Mexico projects, notably the $101 million purchase of the Baca Ranch in Sandoval County, finally accomplished after four failed attempts in July 2000. This ranch occupies 95,000 acres in the giant bowl of the Valles Caldera, the remains of an exploded volcano that was once higher than Mount Everest; Domenici insisted that the government operate it as a working ranch. He has supported grazing rights on federal lands, threatening a filibuster in 1993 against a proposed 85% increase in grazing fees and demanding that grazing permits be renewed even if federal agents haven't completed environmental reviews in 1999. He made sure that the Senate passed $500 million for compensation for damages in the May 2000 forced burn fire that spread to Los Alamos and a nine-month extension for income tax filing for those affected. He opposed the Fish and Wildlife Service's attempt to ban use of Rio Grande water to save the silvery minnow. He was seeking in early 2001 to extend the program compensating nuclear facility workers suffering from radiation-produced disease. In February 2001 he introduced a bill to void Bill Clinton's last-minute change in the federal arsenic standard which, he said, would require New Mexico communities to spend $424 million to meet a standard "lacking a foundation of sound science."

Domenici has not been successful in seeking Senate leadership positions. He lost the majority leadership to Bob Dole in 1984 and the post of Republican Policy Committee Chairman to Don Nickles by 23–20 in November 1990. In December 2000 he made a last-minute race against Policy Committee Chairman Larry Craig; this was taken as a criticism of Majority Leader Trent Lott, although Domenici said it wasn't; in any case he lost 26–24. He has remained highly popular in New Mexico and has won re-election easily, most recently in 1996. But he has sometimes gotten involved in local politics. In the June 1998 special election in New Mexico's 1st District, he campaigned heavily for Republican Heather Wilson, who won. His Pete's Political Action Committee contributed more than $80,000 to Hispanic congressional and state candidates in New Mexico, Texas and California in 2000. In March 2001 his amendment to the McCain-Feingold campaign finance bill to allow increases in the contribution limit by candidates opposed by self-financers passed 70–30. That same month he criticized state Republican Chairman John Dendahl after a press conference in which he supported Governor Gary Johnson's drug decriminalization bills. Domenici's seat comes up again in 2002.

Cook's Call   *Safe.* As long as Domenici runs, Democrats will be hard-pressed to recruit a top-tier challenger. As of spring 2001, Federal Communications Commission member Gloria Tristani appeared to be the likely Democratic nominee. In the unlikely event that Domenici retires, this race would be very competitive and former Energy Secretary and Democratic Congressman Bill Richardson would have to be considered the presumptive favorite.

Junior Senator   Jeff Bingaman, a Democrat first elected in 1982, is New Mexico's junior senator. He has a good political lineage: His father was a professor at Western New Mexico University in Silver City, and his uncle was campaign manager for longtime Senator Clinton Anderson. He graduated from Harvard and Stanford Law School, then returned to New Mexico; a year out of law school, Bingaman was counsel to the state constitutional convention; later he went into law practice in Santa Fe with former Governor Jack Campbell. Bingaman's wife, Anne, started a highly successful law practice of her own that helped finance his first campaigns; she was assistant attorney general for antitrust in the first Clinton term. In a small state, bright young people like Jeff Bingaman can rise fast. He ran for attorney general in 1978 and won; in 1982, he ran against Senator Harrison Schmitt, the former astronaut, also from Silver City, and won with 54%, partly because it was a recession year, but also because of Schmitt's misleading and negative ads.

Bingaman has followed a course in the Senate much like that of Clinton Anderson, who used his influence behind the scenes to great effect but shunned national publicity—so much so that one New Mexico magazine called him "the invisible senator." He is not well known in most of Washington, but has a close relationship with Democratic Leader Tom Daschle and stays on good terms with many senators of both parties. He got seats on two committees of great importance to the state, Armed Services and Energy. On Armed Services he became a protege of Sam Nunn, who created a subcommittee tailored to his interests; in 1997, Bingaman traded his ranking position there for one on the Strategic Forces Subcommittee. From these seats Bingaman has had lots of say over New Mexico's Los Alamos and Sandia labs, which he has encouraged to enter into partnership with private firms. He sponsored a $1.6 billion defense conversion package that passed in 1992 and $100 million in seed money for regional partnerships of small technology firms. Behind the scenes he helped to get Kirtland Air Force Base off the 1995 base-closing list.

On the Energy Committee, he became the top-ranking Democrat in 1999. He supported the CARA bill in 2000 to expand spending on state environmental projects, while Domenici opposed it because it bypassed the appropriations process; it was passed in fall 2000, but scaled back from $45 billion to $12 billion and from 15 years to six years. In July 1998 he proposed spending $420 million to restock the Strategic Petroleum Reserve; he argued that the government had been selling oil to raise cash, and it made more sense to buy oil when the price was low. He sponsored the Radiation Exposure Act of 1990, to compensate uranium miners and workers; he has continued to work to see that workers with radiation-caused illnesses are compensated. In May 1999, just after the Columbine murders, he got the Senate to pass a bill to provide $10 million for a Safe School Technology Center at the Sandia Lab; in 2000 he and Domenici sponsored an amendment creating a single Joint Technology Office under terms that made it clear it would be located at Kirtland Air Force Base in Albuquerque.

Bingaman voted for reorganization of the Energy Department in September 1999, to take direct control of nuclear security programs from New Mexico's Bill Richardson, then Energy secretary, but said he didn't see how the new agency would improve security. On electricity deregulation, Energy Chairman Frank Murkowski in May 2000 wanted to reduce FERC jurisdiction, while Bingaman wanted to give the agency vast new powers; they could not agree on that and so combined to produce an electricity reliability bill in June 2000. In 2000 Bingaman introduced an underground pipeline safety bill, part of which was included in a bill that was one of the first to pass the new Senate in February 2001. In early 2001 Bingaman opposed oil drilling in the Arctic National Wildlife Refuge and sponsored an energy bill concentrating on energy conservation and more federal R&D money for solar and wind energy.

In 1997 Bingaman set out to get the government to purchase the Baca Ranch, which occupies 95,000 acres in Sandoval County in the giant bowl of the Valles Caldera, the remains of an exploded volcano that was once higher than Mount Everest. At first Domenici opposed this, but switched after Bingaman agreed that the ranch would be managed not by the Interior Department but by a board of trustees and would be maintained (and financed) as a working ranch. In 1999 and 2000 the two worked together, and the $101 million purchase was completed in July 2000. Bingaman and Domenici also worked together and, after the disastrous planned burn fire in Los Alamos in May 2000, got approval of $240 million to thin dense national forests near settled communities; they worked in early 2001 to exempt fire compensation payments from the income tax.

Bingaman's voting record is moderate to liberal, with efforts at bipartisanship. He has been creative in coming up with projects to improve education—grants for technology in schools, grants to encourage education schools to train teachers in the subjects they will teach, grants to enable low-income students to take the SAT for free, a 1997 law to discourage dropouts (the dropout rate is high in New Mexico). In early 2001 he supported the Bush education program except for vouchers, and got several of his amendments added to it—promoting anti-dropout programs, requiring poor schools to inform parents about teachers' qualifications. He sponsored a bill to pay up to $125,000 of doctors' loans, to attract specialists to states like New Mexico. His bill providing grants for fluoridation and dental sealant services to low-income area became law in October 2000. He passed a law providing $75 million for electricity for the Navajo, and sponsored the granting of Congressional Gold Medals to the 29 Navajo Code Talkers, who in World War II used their native language to send *en clair* messages which the Germans and Japanese could not understand.

Bingaman faced his most serious challenge in the Republican year of 1994, when Republican Colin McMillan, a rancher and former assistant Defense secretary, spent over $1 million of his own money and attacked Bingaman's vote for Clinton's 1993 tax increase and for what McMillan said was a vote to increase grazing fees. Bingaman ads boasted of his work on defense conversion, national education standards and education technology. The race tightened up in October, and Bingaman won 54%–46%, decisive but not overwhelming. In 2000 he faced former Congressman Bill Redmond, who won the heavily Democratic 3rd District in a special election in 1997 and then lost to Tom Udall in 1998. Redmond, a former minister with working class roots, called for tax cuts and charged that Bingaman should have worked for forest-thinning earlier. Bingaman talked about bringing high-wage jobs to the state, improving education and expanding access to health care. And people heard more of what Bingaman was saying: he spent $2.56 million, Redmond only $639,000. Bingaman had wide leads in the polls, and won 62%–38% on election day; he lost only six counties and ran 14% ahead of Al Gore, who after all managed, barely, to carry the state.

In January 2001 Bingaman gave up his long-held seat on Armed Services for one on Finance.

Presidential politics   New Mexico's near-bellwether status seems more accidental than anything else; it's hard to think of a state more atypical of the nation, yet it keeps on voting at or near the national average. It voted Republican for president in the 1980s, Democratic in the 1990s and gave Al Gore a 366-vote margin in 2000. Unlike most Rocky Mountain states, New Mexico's demographic trends favor Democrats: conservative Little Texas gained little population in the 1990s, while the Hispanic percentage rose, and George W. Bush's popularity among Latinos in Texas didn't transfer at all to New Mexico's very different Hispanic voters. Whites here voted 58%–37% for Bush, Hispanics 66%–32% for Gore. The vote counting here in 2000 was as ragged as in Florida, or more so. In Bernalillo County, where one-third of the state's votes were cast, the optical scanning machine used for counting the 66,000 absentee and early ballots was misprogrammed; also, an envelope with 257 ballots was lost in the warehouse. When these glitches were finally fixed, George W. Bush ended up leading the state count by exactly 4 votes. Then someone discovered that a "620" had been misread as "120" in Dona Ana County, costing Al Gore 500 votes. Republicans declined to ask for a recount because that was Bush campaign policy and New Mexico's electoral votes didn't matter. But who knows who really won?

New Mexico is one of the four states that still has a presidential primary in June, long after every major party nomination since 1984 has been settled.

Congressional districting   The boundaries of New Mexico's three congressional districts have been substantially the same since 1982, and may continue that way. The Democratic legislature would surely like to redraw the Albuquerque-based 1st District to make it more Democratic, but Republican Governor Gary Johnson, who has vetoed many of their bills, would surely veto such a plan. But it is less likely that he will be able to persuade the legislature to add Rio Rancho to the 1st, which would greatly help incumbent Republican Heather Wilson. In spring 2001 a 16-member redistricting committee was created to make recommendations to a September 2001 special session of the legislature.

THE PEOPLE: Pop. 2000: 1,819,046; Pop. 1990: 1,515,069, up 20.1% 1990–2000. 0.6% of U.S. total, 36th largest; 66.8% White, 1.9% Black, 1.1% Asian, 9.5% Amer. Indian, 0.1% Hawaiian, 3.6% Two+ races, 17% Other; 42.1% Hispanic Origin. 4.9% Unemployment. 2000 Voting age pop.: 1,310,472. 2000 Turnout: 615,607; 47% of VAP. Registered voters (2000): 969,251; 505,272 D (52%), 317,223 R (33%), 146,756 unaffiliated and minor parties (15%).

POLITICAL LINEUP: Governor, Gary E. Johnson (R); Lt. Gov., Walter Bradley (R); Secy. of State, Rebecca Vigil-Giron (D); Atty. Gen., Patricia Madrid (D); Treasurer, Michael A. Montoya (D); Auditor, Domingo Martinez (D); State Senate, 42 (24 D, 18 R); Majority Leader, Tim Jennings (D); State House, 70 (42 D, 28 R); House Speaker, Ben Lujan (D). Senators, Pete V. Domenici (R) and Jeff Bingaman (D). Representatives, 3 (1 D, 2 R).

2000 Presidential Vote

Gore (D)	286,783	(48%)
Bush (R)	286,418	(48%)
Nader (Green)	21,251	(4%)
Others	4,154	(1%)

2000 Republican Presidential Primary

Bush (R)	62,161	(83%)
McCain (R)	7,619	(10%)
Keyes (R)	4,850	(6%)

1996 Presidential Vote

Clinton (D)	273,495	(49%)
Dole (R)	232,751	(42%)
Perot (I)	32,271	(6%)
Others	17,566	(3%)

2000 Democratic Presidential Primary

Gore (D)	98,715	(75%)
Bradley (D)	27,204	(21%)
Other	6,361	(5%)

Gov. Gary E. Johnson (R)

Elected 1994, term expires Jan. 2003, 2d term; b. Jan. 1, 1953, Minot, ND; home, Santa Fe; U. of NM, B.A. 1975; Lutheran; married (Dee).

Professional Career: Pres. & CEO, Big J Enterprises Inc., 1976–present.

Office: State Capitol, #417, Santa Fe, 87503, 505-827-3000; Fax: 505-827-3026; Web site: www.state.nm.us.

Election Results

1998 general	Gary E. Johnson (R)	271,948	(55%)
	Martin Chavez (D)	226,755	(45%)
1998 primary	Gary E. Johnson (R)	unopposed	
1994 general	Gary E. Johnson (R)	232,945	(50%)
	Bruce King (D)	186,686	(40%)
	Roberto Mondragon (Green)	47,990	(10%)

Sen. Pete V. Domenici (R)

Elected 1972, seat up 2002, 5th term; b. May 7, 1932, Albuquerque; home, Albuquerque; U. of NM, B.S. 1954, Denver U., LL.B. 1958; Catholic; married (Nancy).

Elected Office: Albuquerque City Comm., 1966–70, Mayor Ex-Officio, 1967–70.

Professional Career: Practicing atty., 1958–72.

DC Office: 328 HSOB, 20510, 202-224-6621; Fax: 202-228-0900; Web site: www.senate.gov/~domenici.

State Offices: Albuquerque, 505-346-6791; Las Cruces, 505-526-5475; Roswell, 505-623-6170; Santa Fe, 505-988-6511.

Committees: *Appropriations*: Commerce, Justice, State & Judiciary; Defense; Energy & Water Development (RMM); Interior. *Budget* (RMM). *Energy & Natural Resources*: Energy Research, Development, Production & Regulation; Forests & Public Land Management; National Parks, Historic Preservation & Recreation. *Governmental Affairs*: Government Management, Restructuring and the District of Columbia; International Security, Proliferation & Federal Services; Investigations (Permanent). *Indian Affairs*.

Group Ratings

	ADA	ACLU	AFS	LCV	CON	ITIC	NTU	COC	ACU	NTLC	CHC
2000	0	14	0	0	77	100	73	100	95	88	92
1999	5	—	0	0	8	—	68	94	88	—	—

National Journal Ratings

	1999 LIB	—	1999 CONS		2000 LIB	—	2000 CONS
Economic	19%	—	75%		40%	—	59%
Social	36%	—	59%		36%	—	62%
Foreign	23%	—	67%		42%	—	57%

Key Votes of the 106th Congress

1. Educ. Savings Accts.	Y	5. Review Movie Violence	Y	9. NATO War in Serbia	N
2. Prescrip. Drug Benefit	N	6. Gun Show Bckgrnd. Checks	N	10. Table Cuba Travel Ban	Y
3. Delay Ergonomic Standards	Y	7. Ban Part.-Birth Abortion	Y	11. Nuclear Test-Ban Treaty	N
4. Phase Out Estate Tax	Y	8. Broaden Hate Crimes List	N	12. Perm. Trade with China	Y

Election Results

1996 general	Pete V. Domenici (R)	357,171	(65%)	($3,435,164)
	Art Trujillo (D)	164,356	(30%)	($155,213)
	Abraham J. Gutmann (Green)	24,230	(4%)	($12,025)
1996 primary	Pete V. Domenici (R)	unopposed		
1990 general	Pete V. Domenici (R)	296,712	(73%)	($2,250,086)
	Tom R. Benavides (D)	110,033	(27%)	($38,510)

Sen. Jeff Bingaman (D)

Elected 1982, seat up 2006, 4th term; b. Oct. 3, 1943, El Paso, TX; home, Santa Fe; Harvard U., B.A. 1965, Stanford U., LL.B. 1968; United Methodist; married (Anne).

Military Career: Army Reserves, 1968–74.

Elected Office: NM Atty. Gen., 1979–82.

Professional Career: NM Asst. Atty. Gen., 1969; Practicing atty., 1970–78.

DC Office: 703 HSOB, 20510, 202-224-5521; Fax: 202-224-2852; Web site: www.senate.gov/~bingaman.

State Offices: Albuquerque, 505-346-6601; Las Cruces, 505-523-6561; Las Vegas, 505-454-8824; Roswell, 505-622-7113; Santa Fe, 505-988-6647.

Committees: *Energy & Natural Resources* (Chmn.). *Finance*: Health Care; Social Security & Family Policy; Taxation & IRS Oversight. *Health, Education, Labor & Pensions*: Children & Families; Public Health. *Joint Economic Committee* (4th of 10 Sens.).

Group Ratings

	ADA	ACLU	AFS	LCV	CON	ITIC	NTU	COC	ACU	NTLC	CHC
2000	85	71	85	71	46	97	15	64	16	6	15
1999	100	—	100	67	18	—	9	59	4	—	—

National Journal Ratings

	1999 LIB	—	1999 CONS		2000 LIB	—	2000 CONS
Economic	63%	—	36%		66%	—	33%
Social	75%	—	20%		66%	—	21%
Foreign	62%	—	29%		72%	—	15%

Key Votes of the 106th Congress

1. Educ. Savings Accts.	N	5. Review Movie Violence	N	9. NATO War in Serbia	N
2. Prescrip. Drug Benefit	Y	6. Gun Show Bckgrnd. Checks	Y	10. Table Cuba Travel Ban	N
3. Delay Ergonomic Standards	N	7. Ban Part.-Birth Abortion	N	11. Nuclear Test-Ban Treaty	Y
4. Phase Out Estate Tax	N	8. Broaden Hate Crimes List	Y	12. Perm. Trade with China	Y

Election Results

2000 general	Jeff Bingaman (D)	363,744	(62%)	($2,568,649)
	Bill Redmond (R)	225,517	(38%)	($639,424)
2000 primary	Jeff Bingaman (D)	unopposed		
1994 general	Jeff Bingaman (D)	249,989	(54%)	($3,652,899)
	Colin R. McMillan (R)	213,025	(46%)	($1,537,563)

FIRST DISTRICT

The future and the past of New Mexico come together in its single metropolis, Albuquerque. Its Spanish and Indian past is memorialized in its name (for a 17th Century Spanish grandee) and age (founded in 1706) and its quaint Old Town; its high-tech future is symbolized by Sandia Laboratories and Kirtland Air Force Base, the government installations that are the city's biggest employers. When rocket scientist Robert Goddard moved here in 1930 and nuclear scientist J. Robert Oppenheimer reconnoitered the site in 1940, Albuquerque was still a town of 35,000 sitting at the junction of the Rio Grande and the old U.S. 66 that paralleled the Santa Fe Railroad—"a dirty red sod-hut tortilla desert highway city," Tom Wolfe wrote. Since then, Albuquerque has grown more than any place in New Mexico and its metro population has more people (712,000 in 2000) than all New Mexico did when the scientists first arrived. Albuquerque's prosperous neighborhoods have climbed the gently rising heights to the east; poorer residents have spread north and south along the Rio Grande. Hemmed in by mountains and federal installations, growth is now moving west, across the Rio Grande, and to the north, especially to the new town of Rio Rancho, with Intel, Olympus, U.S. Cotton and Pepsico installations. Albuquerque is counted as part of the Sun Belt, but its climate is closer to that of the High Plains of west Texas: hot in the summer, sometimes very cold in the winter, with high winds most of the time. Nor is its economy like that of other Sun Belt cities. It has lower income levels, and its recent growth has lagged behind: metro Albuquerque grew 21% in the 1990s, compared to 30% for metro Denver and 45% for metro Phoenix. Albuquerque has some white-collar job growth and diversification and has become something of a tourist center (it is home of the International Balloon Fiesta every October), but it still depends heavily on government.

The 1st Congressional District includes the city of Albuquerque and some of its suburbs. It includes most of Bernalillo County and stretches out into the desert to include largely empty Torrance County. But it does not include rapidly growing Corrales and Rio Rancho just to the north in Sandoval County, nor does it include Isleta and Las Lunas just to the south in Valencia County. Albuquerque is one Sun Belt city which is not solidly Republican, but not solidly Democratic either; it voted for Ronald Reagan and George Bush in the 1980s and for Bill Clinton in the 1990s. In 2000 Bernalillo County voted narrowly for Al Gore, Sandoval and Valencia Counties, with their new suburbanites, for George W. Bush: overall the 1st district was narrowly for Gore.

The congresswoman from the 1st District is Heather Wilson, a Republican and the winner of two elections in 1998 against the second-highest spender in the history of House campaigns. She grew up in New Hampshire, graduated from the Air Force Academy, then became a Rhodes Scholar at Oxford. She served in the Air Force until 1989, then worked two years on the National Security Council in charge of NATO and European affairs. In 1991 she moved to New Mexico, to marry her former Air Force Academy law instructor; she started a consulting firm, and then Governor Gary Johnson appointed her secretary of the Children, Youth and Families Department.

In January 1998, just 12 days before the filing deadline, Congressman Steven Schiff announced he would not run again; he had not returned to the House after cancer surgery in April 1997 and died in March 1998. In January, Senator Pete Domenici, usually loath to intervene in local politics, backed Wilson strongly; after the county Republican chairman filled vacancies by appointing Wilson backers, she beat a conservative state senator for the state central committee endorsement by winning 55 votes, the exact minimum required. The Democratic nomination was captured by Phil Maloof, a young state senator from a wealthy family that made its fortune through beer distribution, casinos, banking interests, hotels and professional sports franchises; a statue of his late father stands in Albuquerque's Civic Plaza. Also running was Green Party candidate Bob Anderson; fresh in everyone's mind was the fact that the Green candidate had won 17% in the 3rd District special election in May 1997 and helped Republican Bill Redmond to an upset 43%–40% win.

Because Republicans had held the seat for nearly 30 years despite its marginal character, this was a key race for both parties. Wilson's slogan was "fighting for our families," and her first ad showed her two-year-old daughter running into her arms; she concluded speeches by talking about reading to her four-year-old son on the roof of their house. She called for a dollars-to-classroom program, with less money for bureaucracy, and for a pilot program of school vouchers. She also called for eliminating the marriage penalty and reducing estate and gift taxes. Maloof favored raising the minimum wage, opposed school vouchers, and ran soft-focus ads playing on his family's 100-year history in New Mexico (next to Wilson's seven).

But in the three-month campaign, the tone quickly turned negative. The toughest ads came when Maloof ran a spot showing footage of a 1996 KOAT-TV report alleging that Wilson, while commissioner of Children, Youth and Families, "abused her position of power" by removing a state foster-family file about her, her husband and their foster son. The charge at first cut into Wilson's small lead in polls; she countered that she ordered the file sequestered, and did not read it herself, to keep it away from those who might use it politically. Maloof spent $3.1 million, almost all of it his own, in the special. Wilson won 45% of the vote, Maloof 40% and Anderson won 15%, though he spent less than $10,000. Local analysts said that the Green vote included not just left-wing environmentalists but also voters disgruntled with the negative campaigns of both major parties. All three candidates ran again in November. Maloof tried to appeal to environmentalists; he switched to oppose the road proposed to cut through 8.5 acres of the Petroglyph National Monument, and Anderson's former campaign manager endorsed him. But the margin was similar: Wilson 48%, Maloof 42%, Anderson 10%.

Wilson thus became the first woman veteran to serve in Congress. Her voting record has been moderate, especially on cultural issues. She won a seat on the Commerce Committee, a fine perch for legislating and fundraising. Her work there included a bill to enable computers users to opt out of receiving junk e-mail, or "spam." When she voiced strong opposition to air strikes, Speaker Dennis Hastert used her as his point person on Kosovo; she led two Kosovo discussions in the Republican Conference and gave the party's response to Bill Clinton's radio address on the situation. On occasion she showed independence, as when she voted against the amendment to prevent adoptions by gays in the District of Columbia. And she complained when Republicans planned to bring a bill to the House floor that would have moved the nuclear-weapons program from the Energy Department to the Pentagon; the leaders pulled the bill and made changes. She pushed for increased spending on science research and federal wildfire suppression and prevention. On local issues, she enacted a bill to preserve the old U.S. 66, which ran down Albuquerque's Central Avenue and which some have called America's Main Street.

In the 2000 campaign, she ran into another well-financed challenger— John Kelly, the former U.S. Attorney for New Mexico and a friend of Bill Clinton since both were undergraduates at Georgetown. It was Kelly's office which did much to botch the prosecution of atomic scientist Wen Ho Lee. The campaign was filled with controversial advertising tactics by outside groups— including a spot by Citizens for Better Medicare on behalf of Wilson and an AFL-CIO ad for Kelly, both of which focused on prescription drug coverage for seniors. Wilson won 50%–43%, with 6% to Green Party candidate Daniel Kerlinsky. Republican leaders rewarded Wilson with an unusual second major committee assignment to Armed Services.

Redistricting must add 13,000 people to the district. The Democratic legislature would undoubtedly like to excise Republican neighborhoods and add heavily Democratic areas from the 3rd and 1st Districts; Republican Governor Gary Johnson would undoubtedly like to add Republican suburbs in Sandoval and Valencia Counties and excise Democratic precincts. Johnson has been unafraid to veto the legislature's bills, and has enough Republican votes to uphold a veto: this is one that could end up in court. Wilson has won three races by 5%, 6% and 7%—not quite enough to remove her from Democratic target lists.

Cook's Call *Competitive.* Wilson has yet to get her feet firmly planted in this Albuquerque-based seat, and she has never won by more than 50%. What's more, her less than solid showings were against sub-par Democratic challengers. Wilson's predecessor, the late Republican Steve Schiff, never took less than 57% in his four re-election bids. But, Wilson, a tenacious campaigner and a strong fundraiser, will be tough to beat.

THE PEOPLE: Pop. 2000: 592,911; Pop. 1990: 505,329, up 17.3% 1990–2000. 71% White, 2.6% Black, 1.8% Asian, 3.5% Amer. Indian, 0.1% Hawaiian, 4.2% Two+ races, 16.8% Other; 42.8% Hispanic Origin.

2000 Presidential Vote
Gore (D)	104,634	(48%)
Bush (R)	101,143	(47%)
Nader (Green)	8,723	(4%)
Others	1,432	(1%)

1996 Presidential Vote
Clinton (D)	93,178	(48%)
Dole (R)	82,613	(43%)
Perot (I)	9,520	(5%)
Others	7,212	(4%)

Rep. Heather Wilson (R)

Elected June 1998, 2d term; b. Dec. 30, 1960, Keene, NH; home, Albuquerque; U.S. Air Force Acad., B.S. 1982, Rhodes Scholar, Oxford U., M.A. 1984, Ph.D. 1985; Methodist; married (Jay Hone).

Military Career: Air Force, 1982–89.

Professional Career: Dir., European Defense Policy & Arms Control, White House NSC, 1989–91; Pres. Keystone Intl. Inc., 1991–95; NM Secy. of Children, Youth & Families, 1995–98.

DC Office: 318 CHOB 20515, 202-225-6316; Fax: 202-225-4975; Web site: www.house.gov/wilson.

District Office: Albuquerque, 505-346-6781.

Committees: *Armed Services* (24th of 32 R): Military Personnel; Military Procurement. *Energy & Commerce* (17th of 31 R): Energy & Air Quality; Environment & Hazardous Materials; Health; Telecommunications & The Internet.

Group Ratings
	ADA	ACLU	AFS	LCV	CON	ITIC	NTU	COC	ACU	NTLC	CHC
2000	10	36	0	29	9	100	53	80	80	64	80
1999	15	—	0	6	2	—	51	88	68	—	—

National Journal Ratings
	1999 LIB	—	1999 CONS		2000 LIB	—	2000 CONS
Economic	37%	—	61%		34%	—	64%
Social	46%	—	54%		43%	—	55%
Foreign	38%	—	61%		44%	—	56%

Key Votes of the 106th Congress
1. Patient Bill of Rights	Y	5. Bar RU-486 $ for FDA	N	9. NATO War in Serbia	Y
2. Accelerate Min. Wage	Y	6. Display 10 Commandments	N	10. Perm. Trade with China	Y
3. Strike Ban on Ergo. Stnd.	N	7. Gun Show Bkgrnd. Checks	N	11. Debt Relief for 3rd World	N
4. Ovrd. Estate Tax Veto	Y	8. Ban Part.-Birth Abortion	Y	12. Drop Cuba Econ. Embargo	N

Election Results
2000 general	Heather Wilson (R)	107,296	(50%)	($2,203,322)
	John J. Kelly (D)	92,187	(43%)	($1,445,633)
	Daniel Kerlinsky (Green)	13,656	(6%)	
2000 primary	Heather Wilson (R)	unopposed		
1998 general	Heather Wilson (R)	86,784	(48%)	($1,121,676)
	Phillip J. Maloof (D)	75,040	(42%)	($5,379,249)
	Robert L. Anderson (Green)	17,266	(10%)	($14,773)

SECOND DISTRICT

The plains of southern and eastern New Mexico are about as disparate a landscape as can be imagined: miles of sagebrush-strewn acreage, and then, suddenly, 9,000-foot mountain peaks rising in the distance. The eastern part of this region, Little Texas, is an extension of the Texas civilization that filled up empty counties when irrigation was developed. Oil has long been the economic mainstay here; cattle ranching is common; cotton is grown on irrigated land. The little cities are full of people with Texas twangs, not the lilt of northern New Mexico. One of the larger towns is Roswell, the alien capital of the world, the site of a supposed flying saucer landing in

1947 and home of the International UFO Museum and Research Center. West from Clovis and Portales, Lovington and Hobbs, the towns become fewer and farming mostly disappears. The scrub land shades into desert, and people are crammed into small cities, protected from an environment that is burning hot in the summer and sometimes deathly cold in winter. Here the major center is Las Cruces, now New Mexico's second largest city, with migrants from Mexico coming up the Rio Grande from million-plus El Paso, Texas, and Juarez, Chihuahua, just 45 miles south.

The 2d Congressional District of New Mexico includes the entire southern half of the state—most of Little Texas, plus the desert on either side of the Rio Grande and the mining territory in the mountains just north of the Mexican border and just short of the Arizona line. These places today vote the opposite of their partisan tradition: Little Texas, settled by Yellow Dog Democrats from the Lone Star state, is now solidly Republican; Las Cruces, long leaning Republican, has moved Democratic. The district has the highest Hispanic percentage of any in New Mexico, 48% in 2000, but many are recent immigrants and Latino turnout is below that in the long-settled Spanish-speaking communities of northern New Mexico. This is usually the most Republican of New Mexico's three districts, and was carried solidly by George W. Bush in 2000.

The congressman from the 2d District is Republican Joe Skeen. Skeen served in the Navy, graduated from Texas A&M and worked as a soil and water conservation officer on the Zuni Pueblo and Navajo Reservation. He has been a sheep rancher for more than 40 years, since he bought his grandmother's 15,000-acre Buckhorn Ranch near Picacho. He was elected to the New Mexico Senate in 1960, at 33; he ran for lieutenant governor on a ticket with Pete Domenici and narrowly lost in 1970, and ran for governor in 1974 and 1978, losing by 1% each time. He was elected to the House in 1980, the hard way, as a write-in, with 61,000 votes, when Democratic incumbent Harold "Mud" Runnels died and the Democrats put Governor Bruce King's nephew on the ballot. Skeen got 38% of the vote to 34% for King and 28% for Runnels's widow, also a write-in. He has been re-elected ever since, and in January 2001 became the longest-serving New Mexico House member ever.

When Skeen became minority leader of the state Senate in 1965, there were only three other Republicans there. Now he is part of the majority, and a member of the House Appropriations Committee's "college of cardinals," as chairman of the Agriculture Subcommittee from 1995 to 2001 and (because of House Republicans' six-year term limit on chairmen) now chairman of the Interior Subcommittee. Skeen has a conservative voting record but has also backed many local projects. "We're doing the job people tell us they want us to do. Get government out of their lives as much as possible, get good jobs for them and a good place to live in. That's what people want."

Skeen has staunchly opposed efforts to increase grazing fees for livestock producers, so far successfully. He has worked for a lamb and wool checkoff program to promote sheep products and proposed a uniform national policy for fossil collecting on federal lands. He blocked the designation of the Rio Grande as an American Heritage River. He has opposed the reintroduction of wolves into New Mexico, and criticized an accusative questionnaire sent out by the feds after a wolf killing; he supports subsidies for predator control. Of wolf reintroduction advocates, he says, "These individuals are trying to put ranchers out of business." He helped pass an October 1999 law imposing New Mexico water law on federal purchases of Rio Grande water, which environmentalists wanted to stop to protect the Rio Grande silvery minnow; he filed a brief against the government's designation of much of New Mexico as the critical habitat for the fish. When the Forest Service's planned burn went out of control and fire spread to Los Alamos in May 2000, he wrote Bill Clinton, "The federal government is the culprit in this fire and is directly responsible for the cost and damages caused by the fire." He does not oppose all land protection measures: He voted for the $101 million Baca Ranch purchase, and got $2 million to help the Nature Conservancy buy a 442-acre parcel near the Dripping Springs Nature Area in the Organ Mountains east of Las Cruces. In June 2000 his proposal to transfer 5,200 acres of oil-rich lands to the Carlsbad Irrigation District became law. His first work as Interior Subcommittee chairman was to look into last-minute public lands actions of the Clinton administration.

Skeen has worked to fund many New Mexico projects. He has worked to save the High Energy Laser Systems Test Facility at White Sands Missile Range, where short-range rockets, of the type fired by guerrillas around the world, are shot down with lasers. He has worked for the WIPP nuclear waste disposal site in Carlsbad, finally licensed in May 1998, over the opposition of Attorney General, now Congressman Tom Udall. In 1999 he helped produce $920 million in defense spending in New Mexico, up 27% from the year before.

Skeen has been re-elected by solid but not overwhelming margins in the last three elections. In 1997 he announced that he had Parkinson's disease, but in 2000 said he has not been impaired. "I live by myself, I drive myself, I walk myself. I've maintained one of the highest voting records in Congress: 98%." In 1996 he beat Democrat Shirley Baca by 56%–44%, losing Las Cruces. He evidently worked the area, and in 1998 carried it while beating Baca 58%–42%. In 2000 two well-known Democrats queued up to run against him, both from the Albuquerque suburb of Los Lunas, at the northern edge of the district. One was Mike Runnels, son of Skeen's predecessor, whom Skeen beat in 1986 by 63%–37%. The other was state Treasurer Michael Montoya. Shortly before the June primary Montoya was embarrassed when his brother came under investigation for embezzling $630,000 from a subsidized housing venture (the brother was officially charged in August). Montoya was so upset that he spent the weekend before the primary walking the streets of El Paso, Texas, and Juarez, Mexico. Still, he won 52%–48%; the vote seemed to fall on Anglo-Hispanic lines, and Hispanics seem more numerous in the Democratic primary. In the general Skeen would not comment on Montoya's brother's problem; there were charges that the allegedly embezzled money was funneled into Montoya's campaign, but no proof: Montoya spent $143,000 of his own money and raised $147,000 more, but was outspent by more than 2–1. Skeen won 58%–42%, running 6% ahead of George W. Bush and carrying Las Cruces again; he ran far ahead in Little Texas and carried two of three Hispanic-majority counties.

Some territory needs to be added to the 2nd District in redistricting, and Skeen might welcome a shuffling of counties with 3rd District Democrat Tom Udall; heavily Indian Cibola County and heavily Hispanic Guadalupe County might be added to the 3rd, while the Little Texas counties of Roosevelt, Curry and Quay might be added to the 2nd, strengthening both incumbents. But there is a good chance of deadlock between the Democratic legislature and Republican Governor Gary Johnson, and the outcome may be decided by the courts. In February 2001 former Republican legislator Phelps Anderson, a Roswell rancher and son of former Arco Chairman Robert Anderson, announced that he would run in 2002; was he anticipating Skeen's retirement?

Cook's Call *Probably Safe.* In an open seat situation, this marginal district would be up for grabs. Clinton won this district in 1992 and 1996 by one point, while Bush won here in 2000 by 11%. But, beating the well-entrenched 11-term incumbent Skeen is not easy.

THE PEOPLE: Pop. 2000: 596,790; Pop. 1990: 504,767, up 18.2% 1990–2000. 69.8% White, 1.9% Black, 0.6% Asian, 4.2% Amer. Indian, 0.1% Hawaiian, 3.4% Two+ races, 20.2% Other; 48% Hispanic Origin.

2000 Presidential Vote		
Bush (R)	95,513	(54%)
Gore (D)	75,752	(43%)
Nader (Green)	4,219	(2%)
Others	1,320	(1%)

1996 Presidential Vote		
Clinton (D)	80,572	(46%)
Dole (R)	77,634	(45%)
Perot (I)	12,149	(7%)
Others	3,149	(2%)

Rep. Joe Skeen (R)

Elected 1980, 11th term; b. June 30, 1927, Roswell; home, Picacho; TX A&M, B.S. 1950; Catholic; married (Mary).

Military Career: Navy, 1945–46 (WWII), Air Force Reserves, 1949–52.

Elected Office: NM Senate, 1960–70, Minority Ldr., 1965–70.

Professional Career: Sheep rancher; Engineer, Zuni & Ramah Navajo Indian Reservations, 1950–51.

DC Office: 2302 RHOB 20515, 202-225-2365; Fax: 202-225-9599; Web site: www.house.gov/skeen.

District Offices: Las Cruces, 505-527-1771; Roswell, 505-622-0055.

Committees: *Appropriations* (5th of 35 R): Defense; Interior (Chmn.); Military Construction.

Group Ratings

	ADA	ACLU	AFS	LCV	CON	ITIC	NTU	COC	ACU	NTLC	CHC
2000	0	36	0	7	11	94	59	90	84	61	80
1999	10	—	0	6	21	—	53	88	83	—	—

National Journal Ratings

	1999 LIB	—	1999 CONS		2000 LIB	—	2000 CONS
Economic	22%	—	77%		18%	—	76%
Social	29%	—	69%		23%	—	74%
Foreign	37%	—	62%		12%	—	78%

Key Votes of the 106th Congress

1. Patient Bill of Rights	N	5. Bar RU-486 $ for FDA	Y	9. NATO War in Serbia	Y
2. Accelerate Min. Wage	N	6. Display 10 Commandments	Y	10. Perm. Trade with China	Y
3. Strike Ban on Ergo. Stnd.	N	7. Gun Show Bkgrnd. Checks	N	11. Debt Relief for 3rd World	Y
4. Ovrd. Estate Tax Veto	Y	8. Ban Part.-Birth Abortion	Y	12. Drop Cuba Econ. Embargo	N

Election Results

2000 general	Joe Skeen (R)	100,742	(58%)	($699,299)
	Michael A. Montoya (D)	72,614	(42%)	($292,955)
2000 primary	Joe Skeen (R)	unopposed		
1998 general	Joe Skeen (R)	85,077	(58%)	($557,221)
	E. Shirley Baca (D)	61,796	(42%)	($298,176)

THIRD DISTRICT

"The dancing ground of the sun," the Pueblo Indians called the land of northern New Mexico, where the long, empty vistas stretch for miles, the mountains in the distance detailed in pinpoint clarity in the cold light and clear air. For 100 years, artists have been coming here, attracted by the scenery and by a unique civilization that is part Indian, part Spanish, only a little Mexican (northern New Mexico was Mexican only briefly, from 1821–46), part Anglo-American. The Spanish language, Indian pottery and dances, and the adobe pueblos give the impression that life on this rocky desert soil has gone on for centuries in much the same way. Actually, the civilization hasn't been so stable. The pueblos were built in sudden spurts; the Spanish conquistadors and priests brought the Catholic religion, the baroque accents of the adobe buildings and the Spanish language in a rush; successive waves of American settlement have changed New Mexico in different ways. The Indian crafts which thrive today nearly died out in the 1880s, and the Palace of the Governors, built in Santa Fe in 1610, had its Victorian balustrade torn off in 1913 to restore its original appearance. Yet up the back roads in Rio Arriba or Taos counties, one can find a religion that mixes Catholicism with adaptations of Indian festivals, buildings not that much different from the old pueblos, and a standard of living reminiscent of the Indian past—quite a contrast to Santa Fe, with its thousands of affluent, bohemian migrants, its 200-plus restaurants, its local book publishers and the third-largest art market in the country.

The politics of northern New Mexico is a unique blend. For years, debate was conducted and votes bartered in Spanish, not by separatists, but by Republican and Democratic politicos, often cynically, sometimes corruptly; loyalties ran to families and communities more than to principles or parties. In the back country, you can still find more than just vestiges of the old communities and the old politics—though no one is going to let you in on them, even if you speak good Spanish. In Santa Fe and Taos, the affluent and hippie migrants have produced a politics of the cultural and environmental left, while high-tech havens—the atomic laboratory town of Los Alamos, the mining country around Farmington, the huge new suburb of Rio Rancho, north of Albuquerque and centered on an Intel installation—favor free-market politics.

The 3d Congressional District contains most of the state's historic Spanish-speaking and Indian parts. In 2000 its Hispanic population was 36%, the lowest of the state's three districts, but in the central part of the district it ranged from 49% in Santa Fe County to 82% in Mora County. Another 20% of the population is Indian, mostly in and around the Navajo Reservation in the west. The district's largest and dominant city is Santa Fe, but the district runs from the High Plains along the Texas border, past the haunting Sangre de Cristo Mountains, through the vast ridges and isolated buttes in the center, to the windy and dusty desert-like plains, dotted occasionally by mountains. Although the Little Texas counties, the Albuquerque suburb of Rio Rancho and the mineral prospecting country in the San Juan Basin around Farmington tend to vote Republican, this is on the whole a Democratic district; both Hispanics and Indians are very Democratic, and migrants to Santa Fe and Taos tend to be downright leftish. The congressman from the 3rd for 14 years was Bill Richardson, a Democrat of Mexican background, who became Bill Clinton's ambassador to the United Nations in 1997 and Energy secretary in August 1998; he was considered a possible nominee for vice president in 2000 until he became embroiled in controversy over security at the Los Alamos Laboratory.

The congressman from the 3d District now is Tom Udall, a Democrat elected in 1998, the son of Arizona Congressman (1955–61) and Interior Secretary (1961–69) Stewart Udall, nephew of Arizona Congressman (1961–91) Morris Udall, first cousin of Colorado Congressman Mark Udall, also elected in 1998, and distant cousin of Oregon Senator Gordon Smith, the only Republican in the bunch. Tom Udall grew up in Tucson and McLean, Virginia, went to college in Arizona, got a degree at Cambridge University in England, and went to law school in New Mexico. He worked as a federal law clerk, then as a counsel in New Mexico state government, and went into private law practice. Politics was obviously on his mind: he ran for Congress in 1982 when the 3d District was newly created, and finished last among four candidates, with 13%; in 1988 he ran in the open Albuquerque-based 1st District, won the Democratic nomination but lost the general to Steven Schiff 51%–47%. In 1990 he was elected state attorney general, where he later took on energy companies. In 1997, when Richardson resigned and opened the 3d District seat, he didn't run—a prudent decision, it now seems.

That election was won in a stunning upset by Republican Bill Redmond, son of a Chicago tool and die maker and a self-styled "blue-collar person," an independent Christian minister from Los Alamos, who got just 31% against Richardson in 1996. The Democratic nomination, which was widely considered tantamount to election, was decided by 89 members of the Democratic central committee; in January the Democratic chairmen in the district's 11 counties declared that Eric Serna, Rio Arriba County politico and member of the state Corporation Commission since 1981, had the votes locked up. This was an unfortunate choice. Charges were well known that Serna had raised money from firms with interests before his Commission. Redmond attacked his "seamy past" and said it was "no secret that Eric Serna is a corrupt politician." Carol Miller, a public health care consultant and candidate of the Green Party, seized on these charges and built on a base of support in Santa Fe and Taos counties' feminist communities. But Redmond courted Navajos in McKinley, Cibola and San Juan Counties and ran organizing drives in the high-tech areas. The result was a shocker: Redmond beat Serna 43%–40%, with 17% for Miller. The four most heavily Hispanic counties, once the political heart of the district, voted 62%–26% for Serna over Redmond; but they cast only 16% of the district's votes.

Redmond had a sometimes moderate voting record and worked hard to appeal to the district, but back at home Udall was working to consolidate the Democratic vote. Drawing on lawyers, the arts community and friends of the Udall family, he raised daunting sums. In the primary, he outspent Serna, his main opponent, by better than 2–1, and won the primary 44%–36%. Though he lost the Hispanic counties, he moved to propitiate the Hispanic constituency, and was helped by the distaste of active politicians for Redmond. The Sierra Club and the League of Conservation Voters criticized Redmond and ran waves of ads against him. Udall's own platform was not much more than a restatement of Clinton-Gore campaign slogans on Social Security, HMOs and education. Udall criticized the campaign finance laws fiercely and at the same time took better advantage of them than the Gingrich-backed Redmond: He spent $1.59 million to Redmond's $1.39 million.

As for the third party threat, Udall said, "I intend to make peace with the Greens." He was utterly successful. When confronted with the specter of a Republican congressman who agreed with the religious right on many issues, and presented with the alternative of a Udall who was not a traditional politico like Serna, the trust funders, feminist left and others of similar persuasion decided to vote Democratic. Udall won 53% of the vote, Redmond, for all his efforts to attract various constituencies, won the same 43% he had won 18 months before, while Carol Miller saw her 17% evaporate to 4%. Udall carried the leftish Santa Fe and Taos counties 69%–26. Redmond carried the high-tech counties 56%–40%, but this was down from the 60%–28% he had carried them before. Redmond improved his standing in the Hispanic counties to 34%, but they only cast 15% of the vote. And the Indian counties were 64%–34% for Udall.

In the House, Udall has had a moderate-to-liberal voting record and rarely bucks his party leaders. He has a seat on the Resources Committee, on which his father served and which his uncle once chaired. He reintroduced Redmond's bill to create a commission to examine land grants; the new Republican leadership had little interest in taking this up for a Democratic congressman. In 2000, he helped to enact the locally popular bill to buy the 95,000 acre Baca Ranch in the Jemez Montains for $101 million. He chaired the House campaign finance task force and has been a vocal advocate of the Shays-Meehan bill. He called for opening the presidential debates to third-party candidates. He was easily re-elected and faces little threat from redistricting; he would be helped by a reshuffling of boundaries sending some of his Little Texas territory to the 2nd district and adding heavily Democratic territory in Cibola and Guadalupe Counties.

Cook's Call *Safe.* Since defeating a Republican incumbent in 1998 to win this Santa Fe-based district, Udall has won re-election easily, taking 67% in 2000. He should be safe from a tough challenge in the future. This district, while it has some Republican and independent leanings, is the most solidly Democratic in the state.

THE PEOPLE: Pop. 2000: 629,345; Pop. 1990: 504,973, up 24.6% 1990–2000. 59.9% White, 1.2% Black, 0.8% Asian, 20.3% Amer. Indian, 0.1% Hawaiian, 3.4% Two+ races, 14.3% Other; 35.7% Hispanic Origin.

2000 Presidential Vote		
Gore (D)	106,397	(52%)
Bush (R)	89,762	(44%)
Nader (Green)	8,309	(4%)
Others	1,402	(1%)

1996 Presidential Vote		
Clinton (D)	99,745	(52%)
Dole (R)	72,504	(38%)
Perot (I)	10,602	(6%)
Others	7,205	(4%)

Rep. Tom Udall (D)

Elected 1998, 2d term; b. May 18, 1948, Tucson, AZ; home, Santa Fe; Prescott Col., B.A. 1970; Cambridge U., B.L. 1975; U. of NM, J.D. 1977; Mormon; married (Jill Cooper).

Elected Office: NM Atty. Gen., 1990–98.

Professional Career: Law clerk, 10th Circuit Court of Appeals, 1977; Asst. U.S. Atty., 1978–81; Practicing atty., 1981–83, 1985–90; Chief Cnsl., NM Health & Environment Dept., 1983–84.

DC Office: 502 CHOB 20515, 202-225-6190; Fax: 202-226-1331; Web site: www.house.gov/tomudall.

District Offices: Clovis, 505-763-7616; Farmington, 505-324-1005; Gallup, 505-863-0582; Rio Rancho, 505-994-0499; Santa Fe, 505-984-8950.

Committees: *Resources* (17th of 25 D): Forests & Forest Health; National Parks, Recreation & Public Lands. *Small Business* (7th of 17 D): Rural Enterprises, Agricultural and Technology (RMM). *Veterans' Affairs* (12th of 14 D): Oversight & Investigations.

Group Ratings

	ADA	ACLU	AFS	LCV	CON	ITIC	NTU	COC	ACU	NTLC	CHC
2000	80	79	100	93	53	47	23	35	9	19	7
1999	95	—	100	88	77	—	19	24	0	—	—

National Journal Ratings

	1999 LIB —	1999 CONS		2000 LIB —	2000 CONS
Economic	75% —	23%		92% —	5%
Social	76% —	23%		67% —	32%
Foreign	78% —	17%		90% —	10%

Key Votes of the 106th Congress

1. Patient Bill of Rights	Y	5. Bar RU-486 $ for FDA	N	9. NATO War in Serbia	Y
2. Accelerate Min. Wage	Y	6. Display 10 Commandments	Y	10. Perm. Trade with China	N
3. Strike Ban on Ergo. Stnd.	Y	7. Gun Show Bkgrnd. Checks	Y	11. Debt Relief for 3rd World	Y
4. Ovrd. Estate Tax Veto	N	8. Ban Part.-Birth Abortion	N	12. Drop Cuba Econ. Embargo	Y

Election Results

2000 general	Tom Udall (D)	135,040	(67%)	($340,174)
	Lisa L. Lutz (R)	65,979	(33%)	($39,120)
2000 primary	Tom Udall (D)	49,585	(83%)	
	Francesca Lobato (D)	10,441	(17%)	
1998 general	Tom Udall (D)	91,248	(53%)	($1,591,017)
	Bill Redmond (R)	74,266	(43%)	($1,390,159)
	Others	6,135	(4%)	

★ NEW YORK ★

New York is a state of extremes, of miracles and disasters, wealth and poverty, hope and despair. For three decades New York State has had sluggish growth—18.2 million people lived here in 1970, 19.0 million in 2000—yet it still has America's largest city, its financial capital, its center of arts and letters and media, and its largest immigrant destination. Neither New York's successes nor its shortcomings were inevitable. They happened because New Yorkers—and not least those people from elsewhere who opted to become New Yorkers—worked to make them happen. They did it in a city that has a certain enduring character which goes back to its birth as the 17th Century Dutch colony of Nieuw Amsterdam. Simon Schama's *The Embarrassment of Riches* paints a picture of the old world Amsterdam: the richest city in the world; full of people who work hard all day and stay up late at night, smoke too much tobacco and drink too much coffee and gin, but are dazzlingly smart and shrewd; people who know their way around every corner of the globe and can make fine aesthetic discriminations, but are attached to their uncomfortable, crowded, bad-smelling city; merchants and manipulators with no aristocratic pedigree, welcoming any religious or ethnic group who can achieve and accumulate and show good taste, cherishing education and culture but indifferent to credentials. Probably fewer than 2% of today's New Yorkers are descended from the Dutch of Nieuw Amsterdam, but the character of the place endures in daily life and in the workings of its great institutions, and helps explain its miraculous growth. Combine Amsterdam and America: Dutch character with British-born political freedoms and American military invulnerability and you have the opportunity to build a city-state that can lead the world.

New York was not always the nation's leader. In 1776 it was the seventh most populous colony. Only in the 19th Century did the descendants of Dutch patroons, Huguenot refugees, British West Indies traders and Yankee farmers become the nation's most successful merchants and capitalists, forging the first routes to the great American interior through the valleys of the Hudson and the Mohawk, and building grand brownstone mansions on broad midtown Manhattan avenues. That early diversity provides one clue to New York's success: if New York has been cynical, ready to cooperate with Loyalists and Revolutionaries, depending on who was ahead, it has also been tolerant, ready to accept anyone smart or rich enough to be counted a success. It has been propelled upward at each stage—forging ahead of London as a financial and manufacturing center by the first World War, and staying ahead of surging Chicago—by incorporating every wave of immigrants and consistently rewarding intelligence and hard work, with no concern about preserving hierarchies.

New York's success has been a product not only of market economics, but of government—and politics. The Iroquois, the most deeply-rooted and militarily strong Native Americans, kept in place for 100 years by an alliance with British troops, were driven out of Upstate New York by the Revolution. The Erie Canal, which connected western New York State with the Hudson River, was the project of Governor DeWitt Clinton's state government. And New York led the nation in

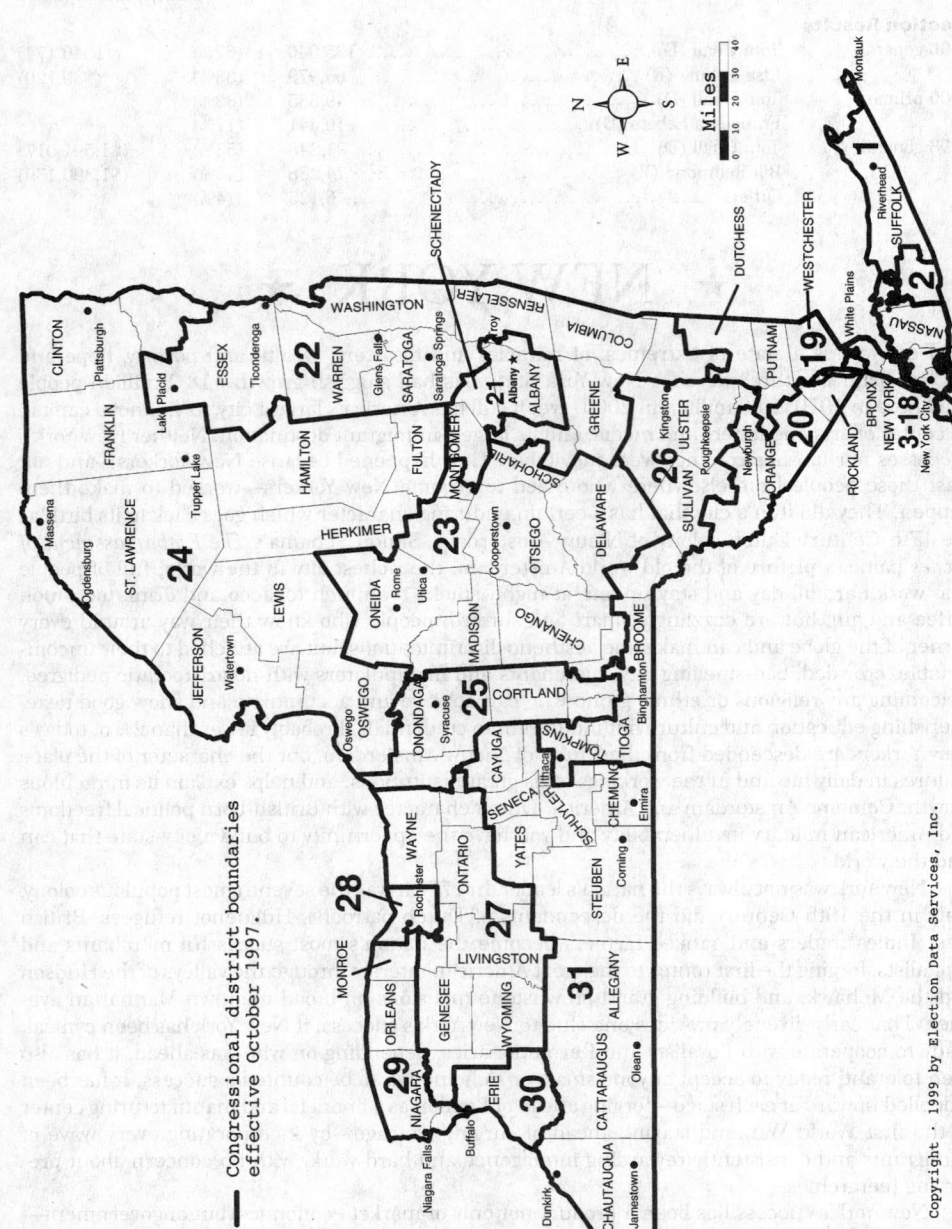

Congressional district boundaries
effective October 1997.

political innovation: Martin Van Buren's Albany Regency was the first state political machine, an ally of New York City's Tammany Hall; Van Buren invented or institutionalized the Democratic Party, the national convention and the inaugural parade. His adversaries, Thurlow Weed and William Seward, formed the Whig Party and ultimately became Republicans; noting that Van Buren's Democrats were winning large margins from Irish Catholics and other immigrants, they too made bids for the newcomers' votes. Both parties served the function of mediating between the divergent interests of the New York City masses and Upstate New York's farmers and burghers, a conflict still evident in New York between city and country, immigrant and native, Catholic and Protestant, the Big Apple and the apple-knockers.

Both parties also worked to protect New Yorkers against the untrammeled workings of free economic and political markets. Old-line Democrats embarked on an unprecedented, labor-intensive building of infrastructure, of bridges and tunnels that made Greater New York possible, from the time of Mayor Abram Hewitt, elected in 1886 over the single-taxer Henry George and the young Theodore Roosevelt, up through the time of Governor Al Smith in the 1920s and his protege Robert Moses, who built bridges and tunnels and highways and beaches and two World's Fairs up through the 1960s. Mugwump Republicans, from Theodore Roosevelt through Elihu Root and Henry Stimson, worked to create civil service laws and bureaucratized purchasing and spending to protect taxpayers from corrupt party machines. The Democratic Tammany machine led by Charles F. Murphy and the talented young men he advanced, Al Smith and Robert Wagner, responded to the shocking 1911 Triangle Shirtwaist fire (when hundreds of women jumped 11 floors to their death because fire escapes were blocked) by passing labor and safety measures. The results included minimum wages, maximum work hours, working-conditions regulations, encouragement of unions and state-owned electric utilities—the prototype 20 years later of the New Deal and the first American welfare state. In years after, New York pioneered public housing and fair housing laws, industry-wide unions (in the garment trades), increased minimum wages, rent control and dairy price controls to help both New York City tenants and Upstate farmers.

Statewide elections were exceedingly close, with Democrats carrying the New York City Catholic vote and Republicans winning Protestants Upstate. Swing votes were cast by the 2 million Jewish immigrants and their children, who supported a generous welfare state but mistrusted the Tammany machine and valued civil rights. The politician who combined these appeals most cannily was Fiorello LaGuardia: a nominal Republican but almost a socialist, an Episcopalian who was half-Jewish and as well as Italian, and who, as mayor of New York City from 1933–45, built much of the public housing and many of the civic monuments that still stand. But both parties produced politicians whose positions appealed to these swing voters, politicians who became nationally prominent and often presidential candidates at a time when the national media was much more concentrated in Manhattan than today: Democrats Al Smith, Robert Wagner, Franklin Roosevelt and Averell Harriman; Republicans Thomas Dewey, Wendell Willkie, Dwight Eisenhower (a New Yorker as president of Columbia University when he was elected president in 1952) and Nelson Rockefeller.

The polity that these men built was productive, generous, tolerant and closely regulated. In an America where people were becoming used to working in big units—employed by big corporations, represented by big unions, regulated by big government—this kind of New York was a natural leader. The financial dominance of Wall Street and the big banks was protected by federal regulation. The high-tech thrust of America in the mid-20th Century was directed by big companies headquartered in New York's suburbs or Upstate: General Electric and IBM, Eastman Kodak and Xerox. This New York took for granted the productivity of its thousands of entrepreneurs and the high skills of its largely immigrant-born, public and Catholic school-educated work force. It was blase about its own miraculous infrastructure—the bridges and subways, electronic cables and electric wires connecting it better than any place else with every corner of the world.

But in the last quarter of the 20th Century New York's public strengths became weaknesses. The state which was clearly the national leader of a big-unit America lost the leadership of a country where growth now occurs in small economic units, where flexibility and adaptability are more important than centralized planning. The institutions and practices and infrastructure which helped produce its successes became ossified and brittle and in decline. Welfare-state benefits became too expensive, measures meant to protect against corruption stifled innovation, and both failed to achieve their objectives—ghettos throbbed with the pains of disorganization, and payoffs and rackets remained part of the everyday cost of doing business in New York as in no other place in the country. The noble aim of creating a public sector which would guarantee cheap rents, top-notch public schools and colleges, and public hospitals, instead guaranteed that none of these will be readily available: Rent control kept housing scarce, school bureaucracies stifled good teaching, public hospitals rationed care down toward nothing. The attempt to create a fail-safe government produced a government that was sure to fail. The government that intended to aid growth seemed to be cutting it off—not completely, but enough to explain why New York state, which grew 32% in population from 1940–65, grew only 2% from 1965–97, while California was growing about 74% and Texas about 87%, making both larger now than New York.

People and businesses started voting with their feet, especially during the terms of Mayor John Lindsay, a liberal Republican hailed when he was elected in 1965 by the powerful New York-based liberal media of the day as the next John Kennedy, though about all he shared with Kennedy was good looks. Lindsay denounced Democrats for being too cozy with municipal unions, but gave up more to them than any mayor before or since. He institutionalized the practice of borrowing against next year's revenues to pay this year's bills, bringing city government to the brink of bankruptcy, which came two years after he left office. He convinced New York's minorities that he cared about them, while allowing the institutions that had taught previous generations' immigrants to embrace middle-class values, to scorn those values. "The confluence of radical spite, absurd legal extrapolations and liberal disdain for white ethnics that led to forced busing, the bloating of welfare rolls and the mau-mauing of white teachers broke the spine of New York's civic culture," writes liberal Jim Sleeper in *The Closest of Strangers*. Antagonized middle-class New Yorkers fled not just to the suburbs, but by the hundreds of thousands to (then) low-tax New Jersey, Connecticut and Florida. In the 1970s, the population of New York, city and state, dropped by 1 million—an unprecedented hemorrhage of talent and productivity, a flight of the middle class away from a polity that seemed to be dying.

Retrenchment followed the mid-1970s bankruptcy crisis. Private financiers and the state government took control of city government, cut spending and negotiated cutbacks in jobs and salaries with public employees' unions. Wall Street boomed in the 1980s and Manhattan once again brimmed over with confidence. Two highly competent Democrats headed the city and state government, Edward Koch for 12 years after he was first elected mayor in 1977, Mario Cuomo for 12 years after he was first elected governor in 1982. Some taxes were cut, bureaucracy was for a time reined in, rational management was installed. But institutional problems remained. New York's legislature—"the worst governmental institution in the western world," writes former city official William Stern—remained unusually tightly controlled by the two chambers' leaders, with the Assembly dominated by New York City Democrats and the state Senate by suburban and Upstate Republicans engaged in classic political logrolling, lavishing taxpayers' dollars on each other's pet projects, with no incentives to hold spending down or deliver services. Public employee unions re-established their stranglehold. The mild recession of the early 1990s struck New York with great force: A private sector that had grown little if at all outside Wall Street could no longer finance the countercyclically growing demands of its oversized welfare state, while big companies Upstate—Xerox, Kodak, IBM—suffered serious reverses.

By the end of the 1990s New York seemed to have adapted and changed. Leading the way to reform are two Republican executives, elected on similar government-cutting platforms, though not at all as political allies, Mayor Rudolph Giuliani, who beat David Dinkins in 1993, and Governor George Pataki, who beat Mario Cuomo in 1994. Both are unsentimental men of little eloquence, without illusions, ambitious politicians who have unhesitatingly elbowed others aside, navigating with a clear eye on a lodestar of principle but willing to maneuver course to avoid political shoals and rapids. Giuliani was elected by just 51%–48%, a reversal of his 50%–48% defeat in 1989 against Dinkins. Pataki won 49%–45% after falling behind in the polls, watching Giuliani endorse Cuomo, being snubbed by the patronage-rich Nassau County Republicans and being dismissed by most of the media, led by *The New York Times*, which cheered for "our governor." Both victories represented a judgment that what Cuomo and *New York Times* writers called "the

New York tradition" was destroying jobs, communities and neighborhoods. The New York version of the welfare state, for all the attractiveness of its champions, was repudiated.

Now, after nearly a decade of reform, it is clear that public policies—and life on the ground—in New York have greatly improved. In New York City, Giuliani and his police commissioners employed the "broken windows" police tactics urged by James Q. Wilson and George Kelling: aggressively enforcing and prosecuting perpetrators of small crimes—the graffiti vandals, turnstile jumpers, squeegee men, aggressive panhandlers. Giuliani used computers to keep track of crimes every day and to send in police to stop them, and he used accountability, demoting police precinct commanders whose numbers went up. The result is a department where patrolmen believe the mayor will know if there is a crime increase on their beats; a department that is focused not on making arrests or avoiding complaints but on stopping crime. Violent crime has been cut in half in New York City, the streets everywhere are visibly safer and churning with new life: a result which liberal criminologists had declared impossible and which even Giuliani himself declined to predict. Liberal media and protesters like Al Sharpton focused on a few widely publicized abuses, or alleged abuses, by police to delegitimize Giuliani's achievements. In fact under Giuliani the use of violence by police has sharply decreased. It is true that black voters remain hostile to Giuliani, and voted against him even as he was re-elected 58%–40% in 1997. But they are also living in safer, more economically vibrant neighborhoods as a result of his policies. And he hacked away at bureaucracy and taxes, with little regard to the log-rolling Democratic majority on the city council or the constantly demonstrating public employee unions.

Giuliani's reforms had national ramifications. His drive against crime set an example followed in dozens of other cities and destroyed the myth that crime is something city-dwellers just have to endure. He has improved the quality of everyday life for Americans in the 1990s more than any other politician in the nation. This conservative reformer showed that a smaller government, held accountable to the mayor and the voters, could be more vigorous and competent than the flabby, oversized government built by his predecessors. His time in office is coming to an end. In early 2000 he was running for the Senate against Hillary Rodham Clinton, then withdrew in May 2000 while undergoing treatment for prostate cancer; term limits prevented him from running for a third term. None of the four Democrats running to succeed him—City Controller Alan Hevesi, Bronx Borough President Fernando Ferrer, Council Majority Leader Peter Vallone and Public Advocate Mark Green—nor Michael Bloomberg, the media billionaire who in early 2001 was preparing to run as a Republican, share all of Giuliani's views or have his relentless and aggressive energy, and a *Daily News* poll showed that even Bill Clinton running for mayor would beat any of them by a whopping margin. But whoever is elected, New York has already changed—or has recovered some of its traditional strengths and character. "New York," wrote James Traub in the *New York Times Magazine*, in the wake of the first subway series since 1956, "feels like a magnet again."

The City still has problems. Its surging economy is uncomfortably dependent, even more than in the 1980s, on a surging Wall Street: The securities industry, which supplied 2% of city jobs and 4% of wages in 1975, provided 21% of the city's employment and 40% of its income growth during the boom of the late 1990s. As historian Fred Siegel says, "The growth in Wall Street wages has masked the continued weaknesses of most other sectors of the economy." In contrast, as Siegel points out, the outer boroughs are increasingly dependent on public sector jobs—not a growth industry in these times—with one-third of jobs in Brooklyn and half in the Bronx directly dependent on the city or state governments. It took five years of Giuliani to return to New York City the number of jobs it had at the beginning of Dinkins' administration. But even beyond Manhattan there are signs of revival. Large swaths of the south Bronx are now livable again, and neighborhoods in Brooklyn and Queens have been revived. Immigrants have been streaming into outer borough neighborhoods, creating new businesses, churches and neighborhood institutions—Caribbean blacks in Flatbush, Chinese in Flushing and Borough Park, Colombians in Corona, Pakistanis in Jackson Heights, Greeks in Astoria, Russians in Brighton Beach. For a quick look at the future, go and see the crowds of young people of dozens of ethnic backgrounds studying every day at the main Queens Library in Jamaica. The question is whether the outer boroughs will develop the private sector jobs and housing as New York did in the earlier

20th Century surge of immigration and whether immigrants will be helped to assimilate into American society as they were then or shunted off into multicultural ghettos.

But if in state politics New York seems to be a Republican state, in national politics it is more Democratic than ever. In the 1980s the tax issue still worked for Republicans; many voters in this high-income, high-living-cost state feared (correctly) that national Democrats would raise taxes, so much so that in 1988 the older George Bush lost New York to Michael Dukakis by only 51%–48%. But when Bush broke his read-my-lips promise, his percentage here dropped to 34% in 1992. Then taxes were increased, but the surging prosperity of the 1990s, especially the surge in the wealth of many ordinary people, made higher federal taxes seem bearable, and New Yorkers—increasingly liberal on cultural issues, and profoundly uneasy about the prominence of Southerners and Christian conservatives in the Republican Party—became more Democratic than ever. Bill Clinton carried New York by 61%–31% in 1996, and in 2000 Al Gore's percentage was actually higher, for a 60%–35% win. George W. Bush carried only four of 31 congressional districts, all Upstate. Gore carried New York City 78%–18%—a bigger margin than Lyndon Johnson's over Barry Goldwater in 1964. Bush in turn seems to have as little use for New York as it does for him. He is from a New York family: Both his parents grew up in New York suburbs, where Manhattan was always the central focus of attention. But the younger Bush's only trips to Manhattan during the general campaign were to appear at the Al Smith dinner and on the David Letterman program.

Governor   George Pataki was elected governor of New York in 1994 and 1998; he began the 1990s as a politically obscure minority-party assemblyman and ended it as a major national political figure. He grew up in Peekskill, a small industrial city on the Hudson in northern Westchester County, at the cusp of metropolitan New York City and Upstate New York. His father was the son of Hungarian immigrants, his mother is of Italian and Irish ancestry; his parents had a farm in Peekskill and built it into a business; those years are the primary subject of his autobiography *Pataki*. Pataki went to Yale and Columbia Law School, where he was an unabashed conservative in the late 1960s; he practiced law with a big Wall Street firm, then moved to a Westchester firm in 1974. In 1982 he was elected mayor of Peekskill, where he converted tax-exempt property to taxpaying housing, held taxes down, opened an industrial plant and approved 1,000 new housing units. In 1984 he ran against an incumbent Democratic assemblyman and won. In 1992, after eight years as a member of a powerless minority, he challenged an incumbent Republican state senator and beat her by 558 votes. In the state Senate he chafed at the leadership of Nassau County's Ralph Marino and voted against the budget—an almost unheard of rebellion in lockstep-party-voting Albany. In all this he showed ambition, ruthlessness, a penchant for cutting government; but few were paying attention.

In 1993, the almost unknown Pataki began running for governor, taking on one of America's best-known politicians, Mario Cuomo. For all his national fame, and his feints at running for president in 1987 and 1991, Cuomo was in trouble in New York: he cut the top tax rates but also created other taxes and increased spending robustly; he claimed credit for a workfare program but tended to support the public employee unions. Pataki provided a clear contrast on the issues, and he also showed political skill. He got the support of Senator Alfonse D'Amato, fresh from reelection in 1992 and in control of the state Republican Party apparatus. Pataki easily won the May 1994 convention and prevented a primary challenge and a Conservative Party candidacy. In the general election, Cuomo attacked Pataki for having raised taxes in Peekskill and Democrats charged that he was a puppet of D'Amato. But Pataki led in polls until New York City Mayor Rudolph Giuliani in late October endorsed Cuomo and bitterly criticized Pataki. Cuomo went into the lead, gaining votes in New York City and in Nassau County, with its revenue-hungry Republican machine. Thomas Golisano, a Rochester businessman, was spending millions as an independent, advised by pro-Perot pollster Gordon Black; Perot endorsed him and polls showed him with 8%. But Golisano's share of the vote fell to 4%, and Cuomo got 45%, about where he was running in polls. Pataki won 49% of the vote, losing New York City 70%–28% but carrying the suburbs 54%–43% and Upstate (where Giuliani's endorsement hurt Cuomo) 59%–32%.

As governor, Pataki showed determination and even ruthlessness in seeking his goals. After the election, he declined to take a congratulatory phone call from Giuliani for three weeks and engineered a coup ousting Marino as Senate leader that was executed while the governor was on vacation in Florida. Pataki proposed cuts in taxes and in spending and, after bruising negotiations with Democratic Assembly Speaker Sheldon Silver, got much of what he wanted. Pataki signed the death penalty into law in March. In 1996 he got reform of workmen's comp. With D'Amato and almost all leading New York Republicans except Giuliani, he endorsed Bob Dole for the Republican nomination; but when the Dole campaign went nowhere in New York he coolly said in November, "I wasn't involved in the campaign."

Instead he spent much effort on a $1.75 billion environmental bond issue, citing his longtime admiration for Theodore Roosevelt and gathering support from business, labor and environmental groups. He also switched and supported the partial state takeover of the Long Island utility Lilco, agreeing in early 1997 to issuing $7 billion in bonds. In early 1997 Pataki unveiled his welfare reform plan, cutting benefits to recipients who do not find work by 45% over four years; he called for a three-year phaseout of estate and gift taxes, which send many affluent New Yorkers to Florida; he pushed his STAR school tax relief plan to rebate taxes and give more aid to schools. He stayed aloof from Senate President Joseph Bruno's crusade to end state-wide rent controls, brokering a compromise which left controls intact in Manhattan. Pataki's budgets in 1997 and 1998 had above-economic-growth spending increases; he established who was in control, however, by line-item-vetoing $1.6 billion from the legislature's budget in April 1998. All this left Pataki in strong shape for reelection in 1998. He got the support of Giuliani and former Mayor Edward Koch; potentially strong opponents like then-Congressman Charles Schumer and Comptroller Carl McCall declined to run. The Democratic nomination was won by New York City Council Speaker Peter Vallone, a competent and constructive veteran widely admired in knowledgeable circles. But he was scarcely known outside New York City, and never had a chance against the well-financed Pataki. Pataki won 54%–33%, losing New York City by 60%–33%—a slight improvement over 1994—but carrying the suburbs 62%–29% and Upstate by 64%–18%; 13% of the vote there went to Golisano, running a third-party candidacy.

In his second term Pataki again tightened up on spending and continued to press for tax cuts, but took liberal stands on many issues. He has long supported abortion rights and welfare for legal immigrants. Since 1999 he has proposed changing the Rockefeller drug laws, with their mandatory minimum sentences. In 1999 he passed a Family Health Plus program for those without insurance, financed by a 55-cent increase in the cigarette tax, and criticized the Clinton administration for not granting waivers for it. He also subjected cigarettes to fire-safety laws. He pushed through innovative gun-control laws in 2000, including requiring ballistic fingerprinting of every gun sold. He met a major demand of public employees unions by signing in July 2000 a cost of living adjustment for public employee retiree pensions. He signed a hate-crimes law and set up a DNA review commission in 2000, plus laws for tougher sentences for sex offenders.

Pataki lives in a large house overlooking the Hudson Highlands—some of the most gorgeous scenery in America—and has supported many environmental measures. He imposed strict pollution limits on old power plants and in 1999 signed auto-emissions standards as tough as California's. In 1999 the state purchased an easement on 110,000 acres of the Adirondacks owned by Champion International Company. In 2000 he signed a ban on the gas additive MBTE and called for dredging of the Hudson to remove the PCBs discharged there by General Electric many years ago. He brags that New York now recycles more than 40% of its trash and that sturgeon are now plentiful in the Hudson River.

Through all this Pataki maintains a closed-mouth, lockstep control of his administration and his party, and is not afraid of getting into a scrap. He and New Jersey Governor Christie Whitman had a major disagreement about the bi-state Port of New York Authority, resolved in June 2000 when Pataki agreed to allow a $200 million cargo terminal to be built in Port Elizabeth-Newark in return for $250 million on projects in New York. He has opposed the claims of the Oneida, Cayuga, Mohawk, Seneca and Onondaga tribes on thousands of acres of Upstate lands, and criticized the Clinton administration for giving in to the Indians. His relationship with Giuliani has often been edgy. Pataki has opposed Giuliani's plans for a stadium for the Yankees on the West Side of Manhattan and he signed a bill exempting suburban commuters from the city's income tax. In early 1999 both had half an eye on a presidential race. In May 1999 Pataki endorsed

George W. Bush, with Giuliani, who later did so too, pointedly not at his side; in August 1999 he endorsed Giuliani for the Senate seat being vacated by Daniel Patrick Moynihan, brushing aside Congressman Rick Lazio, whom he had earlier encouraged to consider the race. Pataki's Republican chairman used the state's convoluted ballot access laws to try to keep John McCain off the March 7 primary ballot; a court ordered him on, but Bush won anyway, and a few days later Pataki blithely called for reforming the ballot laws.

In 1994 Pataki pledged to serve only two terms, but he reneged on that in 1998, and in early 2001 he was obviously running for a third term. He called for consolidation of state aid to schools—a dicey issue, since legislators have been creating programs to give their constituents special advantages for years—and for more local control, plus property tax cuts for farmers and seniors and a doubling of "empire zones" to encourage investment in high-risk areas. His outlook for 2002 was good at the beginning of 2001. And it appeared that Democrats would have a contentious September 2002 primary. In January 2001 former HUD Secretary Andrew Cuomo, Mario Cuomo's son, returned to New York and announced he was running for governor; he was to have made the announcement at the apartment of Denise Rich, former wife of pardoned fugitive and accused tax evader Marc Rich, but switched it at the last minute to the flagship store of his brother-in-law Kenneth Cole. A few days later Comptroller Carl McCall announced that he was running; he is the first black elected to statewide office in New York, and appeared to have the support of most Democratic politicians and labor leaders. Cuomo and McCall started off by denouncing Pataki, but their primary contest could become a bitter one.

Cook's Call   *Highly Competitive.* As desire for reform has abated and New York's strong economy slowed down, Pataki's poll numbers have dipped, which suggests a very close race is in the offing. Democrats look headed for a bruising primary between state Comptroller Carl McCall and former HUD Secretary Andrew Cuomo. Cuomo has good name identification, but there are signs that many of his father's key backers are sitting this one out. Race may also be a factor, since McCall would be the first black major party gubernatorial nominee in the Empire State. Regardless of who wins the nod, the general election will be competitive.

Senior Senator   Charles Schumer, New York's senior senator, is a Democrat elected in 1998 in what was the most expensive Senate race ever in which neither candidate self-financed his campaign—at least it was until the 2000 New York Senate race (a short-lived notoriety). Schumer grew up in Flatbush, Brooklyn, and graduated first in his class at James Madison High School, alma mater of Justice Ruth Bader Ginsburg and many other notables. He graduated from Harvard College and Law School and, with the latter diploma fresh in his hand in June 1974, immediately began running for an open Assembly seat. He won, at 23. In 1980 he was elected to the House from an open Brooklyn seat, just before he turned 30. Through energy, imagination, hard work, good humor and a certain amount of chutzpah, he became a skilled legislator, and one noted—and sometimes resented—for his knack for getting publicity: Bob Dole said that the most dangerous place in Washington was in between Schumer and a television camera. As soon as he got to Congress he raised a campaign treasury of over $1 million, lest he and Brooklyn neighbor Stephen Solarz be redistricted together in 1982, but they weren't and both coexisted for a decade. By 1992 he had $2 million in the bank, again for fear of a primary race against Solarz; but Solarz ran and lost in the neighboring Hispanic-majority 12th District.

From the unlikely venue of the Banking Committee, a panel that most talented members lobby to get off of, Schumer spotted the perverse incentives set up by the combination of deposit insurance and letting S&Ls make risky investments. He called early on for higher capital requirements, and helped shape the 1989 S&L bailout bill. He also worked on housing programs, building on the success of the Nehemiah projects in Brooklyn. On Judiciary and, eventually, as chairman of its Crime Subcommittee, he ranged far afield, contributing key provisions to immigration acts in 1986 and 1990, leading with free marketeer Dick Armey attacks on farm subsidies, and with Florida Republican Dan Miller a nearly successful assault on sugar programs. Other Schumer causes included the Violence Against Women Act and a federal law against impeding access to abortion clinics. Schumer sponsored the 1994 crime bill and got the House to pass the Brady bill, with its waiting period for handgun purchases, over strong opposition from the National Rifle Association.

The idea of running for statewide office was surely never far from his mind. Had Mario Cuomo retired in 1994, Schumer would probably have run for governor, and in 1995 and 1996 he was considering running against Governor George Pataki. But in April 1997 Pataki's strong job rating, and especially his overwhelming strength Upstate, led Schumer to switch and use his $5 million treasury to run for Alfonse D'Amato's senate seat instead. It was by no means obvious that he would win. D'Amato was known for his assiduous constituent service and for his ability to win the tabloid wars that dominate campaigning in metropolitan New York. Although some of his stands—against abortion and gun control—and his aggressive investigation of Whitewater in 1995 were unpopular in New York, he also achieved results in popular crusades—for breast cancer research, against Swiss banks withholding money from Holocaust survivors, for gay rights. D'Amato was chairman of the Banking Committee and excelled at raising money; his early support did much to make Pataki governor. Schumer started off largely unknown outside his district (which starting in 1992 included part of Queens as well as Brooklyn) and faced serious primary opposition from 1984 vice presidential nominee Geraldine Ferraro and Mark Green, New York City public advocate and D'Amato's opponent in 1986. By summer Schumer was leading in polls and was much better financed, and in September he won the primary with 51% of the vote, to 26% for Ferraro and 19% for Green.

Schumer immediately launched an attack on D'Amato, saying he had told "too many lies for too long"; it echoed D'Amato's attacks on earlier opponents as "too liberal for too long." Schumer claimed he was tougher on crime, citing his support for longer sentences, limiting death row appeals, expanding capital punishment and broadening wiretap authority; he emphasized his support of abortion rights and gun control. D'Amato concentrated heavily on Schumer's missed votes while running for Senate, but the implication that Schumer was lazy was implausible. Still, by mid-October, Schumer's poll leads were mostly less than the statistical margin of error. On October 20, D'Amato scored coups by winning endorsements from the Human Rights Campaign and former Democratic Congressman Floyd Flake of Queens. But in a closed meeting before a Jewish group D'Amato called Schumer a "putzhead"; when that became public, he denied it, then backtracked unconvincingly after his own supporter, former Democratic Mayor Edward Koch, confirmed it. D'Amato lost confidence and momentum, and by early November was sagging in polls. Schumer, who announced in October that he would vote against impeachment though he believed Bill Clinton lied under oath, was the beneficiary of two visits from Clinton and no less than four from Hillary Rodham Clinton (the rousing reception she got may have been what convinced her to run for the Senate in New York). Though outspent, Schumer won 55%–44%, winning 74%–25% in a big turnout in New York City and losing the suburbs by only 51%–49%. He lost Upstate by only 53%–45%. Jewish voters, about 40% of whom voted for D'Amato in 1986 and 1992, now went 76%–23% for Schumer; voters with graduate degrees, the most heavily Democratic educational group in New York, went 69%–31% for Schumer.

In the Senate Schumer has a solidly liberal voting record and has not yet matched his legislative productivity in the House; but even in his first year he appeared 14 times on Sunday interview programs, sixth most of all senators. He got to vote twice on impeachment: against it in the House in December 1998, against conviction in the Senate in February 1999. He lobbied successfully to get approval for JetBlue to fly from Kennedy to Buffalo, Rochester and Syracuse—high air fares is a perennial Upstate complaint—and he pressed for more money for New York's teaching hospitals. He helped to broker agreement between Banking Chairman Phil Gramm and the Clinton administration on Community Reinvestment Act disclosure, the last obstacle to enactment of financial services deregulation in October 1999. An ally of the securities industry on both the House and Senate Banking Committees, Schumer has called for making electronic communications networks subject to the same regulations as stock exchanges and for making the New York Stock Exchange a profit-making corporation. He opposed the Clinton administration by calling for mandatory, not discretionary, penalties against offshore banks involved in money laundering. He opposed the bankruptcy reform bill and passed an amendment making penalties for assaults on abortion clinics undischargeable in bankruptcy.

Schumer serves on Judiciary, where he was one of the most vocal opponents of the confirmation of Attorney General John Ashcroft. He was one of the leading advocates for gun control measures after the Columbine shootings of April 1999, and in 2000 sponsored bills to require ballistic fingerprinting, licensing and registration of all handguns and cracking down on gun dealers who sell to straw purchases; he sponsored studies showing that many guns used in crimes were sold illegally. With conservative Bob Barr, he sponsored a bill to require employers to tell employees if employers can read their email. He and John McCain sponsored a bill to speed approval of generic drugs. In 2000 he called early for release of oil from the Strategic Petroleum Reserve to combat OPEC price increases. He has a bill to reclassify SUVs as cars, not trucks, and subject them to higher fuel efficiency requirements. In 1999 he called for the Navy to leave the Puerto Rican island of Vieques and worked against restrictions on the import of antiquities from Italy—both, in their way, New York issues. The two New York and two California senators threatened a filibuster when Richard Shelby tried to limit states to 12.5% of federal transit spending. He has worked to get $170 million for the Brookhaven National Laboratory on Long Island, for vintage designation for Long Island, for disaster relief for a lobster killoff in Long Island Sound, for shutting down a federal halfway house in Manhattan's Washington Heights neighborhood. After the 2000 election, he and Sam Brownback of Kansas sponsored a bill to create a commission, with eight members appointed by Congress, plus experts and state and local officials, to recommend upgrades in voting machines and to provide $2.5 billion in federal matching grants for states to carry out its recommendations. On the pardon of Marc Rich he was not, like his colleague Hillary Rodham Clinton, silent: "The pardoning of fugitives stands our criminal justice system on its head."

Schumer faces the prospect of a long Senate career: No Democratic incumbent senator has been defeated in New York since direct election of senators began (though seven incumbent Republicans have lost). He knew that he would become the state's senior senator soon, since three days after the 1998 election Daniel Patrick Moynihan announced his retirement. There is much speculation that he may resent being in the shadow of his new junior colleague, who also has the prospect of a long Senate career ahead of her if she wants. But Schumer is resourceful, energetic and creative enough—and unbashful enough—to find plenty of work and get some publicity for it.

Junior Senator Hillary Rodham Clinton was elected in November 2000 while she was first lady of the United States. Clinton grew up in Park Ridge, Illinois; her father owned and ran a drape and curtain factory. She excelled at her studies and was elected to student government at Maine South High School. Park Ridge is a solidly Republican Chicago suburb, near O'Hare Airport, and the young Hillary Rodham was a Goldwater girl in 1964. She went to Wellesley College, where she became a Democrat in the turbulent election year of 1968: she wrote her senior thesis (kept under lock and key by the college since 1993) on applying the theories of radical Chicago organizer Saul Alinsky and argued that antipoverty programs did not give enough power to the poor. She was elected student government president, in which she pushed successfully for admission of more black students and admission of men to women's dorms. At the 1969 commencement she gave a speech which got notice in *Life* magazine. She went on to Yale Law School, where she worked with the attorney for Black Panthers accused of murder and clerked for a summer with Communist attorney Robert Treuhaft in Berkeley. At Yale she met Bill Clinton, and they became partners for life.

Bill Clinton was anything but reticent about his political ambitions in his native Arkansas. He showed her around the state and together they went to Austin in 1972 to run the McGovern campaign. After graduation in 1973, Bill Clinton moved to Fayetteville to teach law at the University of Arkansas. In 1974 Hillary Rodham moved to Washington to work for the House Judiciary Committee's special counsel John Doar on the impeachment of Richard Nixon; Bill Clinton, at 28, ran against Republican Congressman John Paul Hammerschmidt and nearly beat him. After Nixon resigned, she returned to Arkansas to teach law, and in October 1975 she and Clinton were married. In 1976 he was elected attorney general of Arkansas; she worked for Jimmy Carter's campaign. After that she worked for the Rose Law Firm in Little Rock and in 1977 was appointed to part-time chairman of the Legal Services Corporation. Under her leadership the Legal Services budget increased dramatically, including contributions to local political campaigns and conducting campaigns against ballot propositions. In 1978 Bill Clinton ran for governor, and after he won the

Democratic nomination, tantamount to victory that year, Hillary Rodham invested $1,000 in commodities future and with the help of a friend who was general counsel of Tyson Foods, one of the state's biggest businesses, saw that turned into $100,000.

In 1980 Bill Clinton was defeated for re-election. He promptly took up a more moderate line and his wife began to call herself Hillary Clinton; in 1982 he beat the incumbent and became governor again. Hillary Clinton continued her law practice and service on the board of the Children's Defense Fund and other organizations. She chaired the Arkansas Education Standards Committee in 1983–84 and former Arkansas Advocates for Children and Families. She served on the boards of Wal-Mart, TCBY and in 1988 and 1991 was named by the *National Law Journal* as one of the 100 most influential lawyers in the country. It was in these years also that she and her husband invested in the Whitewater real estate project and that she performed legal work for the Morgan Guaranty Savings and Loan, which invested in the project and whose failure cost the federal government $73 million. Whitewater later became the subject of congressional hearings and an independent counsel investigation, both of which were impeded when Rose Law Firm billing records were subpoenaed in July 1994 but were not found until they turned up in the residential quarters of the White House in January 1996. Independent Counsel Robert Ray in September 2000 ended the investigation, saying he could not prove that the Clinton had been involved in criminal activity or that they concealed information from investigators or obstructed justice: "The evidence was insufficient to prove to a jury beyond a reasonable doubt."

In 1991 Bill Clinton ran for president. It was widely rumored that he had had many extramarital affairs; at a Washington press breakfast the Clintons admitted that their marriage had not been without problems. After the election, Clinton announced that the leader of his task force on health care reform would be the first lady, Hillary Rodham Clinton—the first time her maiden name was featured. The task force under her direction and that of Ira Magaziner met secretly and without input from members of Congress; a complicated plan was finally produced after a couple of deadlines were not met. Clinton eventually did testify before Congress; there and in other public forums she was crisp, articulate, knowledgeable. But she was unable to persuade Congress to adopt her plan. It never came to the floor in either house, and was abandoned in September 1994. In the meantime, the first lady had problems with scandals. In May 1993 the members of the White House Travel Office were fired, and director Billy Ray Dale was later prosecuted—and acquitted by a jury within minutes. Clinton denied that she had any role in the firings, or in apparent plans to replace the charter service with one owned by Clinton friends and Hollywood producers Harry Thomason and Linda Bloodworth-Thomason. In June 2000 Independent Counsel Robert Ray concluded that Clinton had given "factually false" testimony in a sworn depositon, but declined to prosecute her.

Clinton persevered through the humiliations of the health care fiasco and the scandals with an aplomb that showed great discipline and determination. She worked on lesser, but nonetheless worthy projects, helping to shape the CHIP children's health insurance program, seeking funding for breast cancer and other women's health problems, producing the bipartisan Adoption and Safe Family Act of 1997. She wrote *It Takes a Village* and donated the proceeds to children's hospitals. In January 1998, when Bill Clinton denied the charge that he had had an affair with then-White House intern Monica Lewinsky, Hillary Rodham Clinton flew to New York to appear on the *Today* show and charge that the allegations were the product of "a vast right-wing conspiracy." She continued to support him, though with obvious frostiness, when he was forced to admit in August 1998 that the charges were true.

Meanwhile, she campaigned gamely for Democratic candidates in the 1998 elections, and was particularly moved by the warm applause she received in her four appearances in New York for Senate candidate Charles Schumer. In October 1998 New York Congressman Charles Rangel told her that she should run for the Senate from New York herself: "She said, 'Who would want me to run here?' But she had a twinkle in her eye. And I knew then this was more than a joke for her." Three days after the 1998 election, Senator Daniel Patrick Moynihan announced that he would not run for re-election in New York in 2000. Moynihan, the nation's best thinker among politicians since Lincoln and its best politician among thinkers since Jefferson, a man whose public career extends back into the 1950s and includes many prescient warnings and original insights, who had served four terms in the Senate after serving in the cabinet or subcabinets of four successive presidents, obviously was not going to be replaced by a politician of similar magnitude; there aren't any. But there also weren't any obvious Democratic successors. Moynihan himself suggested state Controller Carl McCall; Congresswoman Nita Lowey of Westchester County was interested in the race; but it was not clear that either had the stature to beat the likely Republican nominee, New York City Mayor Rudolph Giuliani. In early 1999 Bob Torricelli, the aggressive head of the Senate Democrats' campaign committee, called for Clinton to run. She said she was giving "careful thought" to it. She started making more trips to New York, and Lowey said she would be glad to step aside if Clinton ran. In July 1999 she appeared at Moynihans' Upstate farm and then began a "listening tour" across Upstate New York. Giuliani responded with an appearance in Arkansas.

Clinton's early campaign was not without troubles. There was widespread ridicule of the idea of someone with no previous connection with the state running for senator from New York. Her claims that she had always been a New York Yankees fan were met with disbelief, and her claim that she had often driven through Upstate New York on childhood vacations (her family often summered near her father's home town of Scranton, Pennsylvania, not far away) seemed a pathetic reach. In August 1999 Bill Clinton granted clemency to four Puerto Rican terrorists who never expressed remorse for their violent crimes—an obvious pitch for the Puerto Rican vote and a foreshadowing of the pardons he would issue in January 2001. Embarrassed, she came out against the move, without giving a heads-up to Puerto Rican leaders. That same month the Clintons left their favorite vacation spot, fashionable Martha's Vineyard, for a sojourn in Skaneateles, a pleasant town in the Finger Lakes they would never have visited otherwise. In October the Clintons bought a house in woodsy Chappaqua in Westchester County and were then embarrassed because they borrowed most of the purchase price from Democratic fundraiser Terry McAuliffe; later they got more conventional financing. In November1999 on a trip to Israel Clinton embraced and kissed the wife of Yasir Arafat after a speech in which she lambasted the Israelis; Clinton explained later that she was acting in a diplomatic capacity, but her act brought back memories of her endorsement of an independent Palestinian state when that was not yet U.S. policy. In February 2000 she formally announced her candidacy, with her husband standing silently by, from a venue in Westchester. By that point her poll ratings had slipped, and she was running no better than even with Giuliani.

Carpetbagging is not necessarily a political crime in New York. Voters there in 1964 elected Robert Kennedy, though he lived in Virginia and had a technical residence in Massachusetts. Robert Kennedy won in 1964 not just because of Lyndon Johnson's coattails, but because he ran virtually even in usually Republican Upstate New York; national celebrities may be commonplace in New York City, but when they show up in small Upstate towns and cities it is noted and appreciated. Hillary Rodham Clinton's strategy was similar. With her usual hard work, perseverance and intensity, she criss-crossed Upstate New York, listened to its voters' many complaints, learned about local issues and adopted appealing positions on them: the same slogging persistence she had shown in the dreary days in Arkansas and the tumultuous days after the health care fiasco and scandal charges in Washington. And she waited for the opposition to make mistakes, which it did. In March 2000 Giuliani was under attack when police officers shot an unarmed man in Manhattan; the liberal New York press seized on this opportunity, and the mayor helped them by releasing the victim's juvenile crime record. In April Giuliani announced that he had prostate cancer; in May he announced that he was seeking a separation from his wife, days after she announced she was appearing in the *Vagina Monologues*. Days later, in a dramatic press conference, he announced he was leaving the Senate race.

Within 24 hours the Republicans had another candidate, Long Island Congressman Rick Lazio. He had talked of running in summer 1999, until Governor George Pataki announced suddenly in August that he was backing his longtime rival Giuliani. Lazio had a moderate voting record in the House; like Giuliani he backed abortion rights; he also had a genuine legislative achievement, enactment of major reforms of public housing, passed in October 1998. He raised plenty of money: Hillary haters from all over the country sent in contributions large and small, and he ended up spending $40 million. But his campaign was less than perfect. He was dogged for a while by an SEC investigation of a 1997 option trade which netted him far less than Clinton's commodities trades; though the complaint was dismissed without action in August, this was similar to HUD's attempt to take away control of public housing from Giuliani and the Civil Rights Commission's negative report on police practices in New York—attempts to abuse the powers of the federal government to further the first lady's candidacy. He was vulnerable to attacks, made often by Clinton, that he had supported Newt Gingrich, a *bete noire* to most New York voters. And there were unforced errors. In the first debate on September 13, Lazio walked over to Clinton and presented her a paper with a pledge to eschew soft money ads. In a time when voters were eager for consensus, Lazio was providing them with confrontation, and this in-your-face behavior was especially repugnant to women. Nine days later they both agreed to not run ads financed by soft money, that is, contributions to parties; but this was unenforceable, since parties and others can spend what they want to, and the assumption of Lazio strategist Mike Murphy—a key advisor in John McCain's campaign—that campaign finance was a vote-moving issue proved ill-founded. In the second debate, Lazio declined to say that he would vote for any Supreme Court nominee who opposed the key abortion rights decision of *Roe v. Wade*, a defensible position intellectually, but one difficult to sustain politically in New York, and Clinton pounded him on it. Lazio was also embarrassed by phone calls paid for by the state Republican Party, which under Pataki's leadership has a penchant for in-your-face tactics, that attacked Clinton for accepting $50,000 in June from the Muslim Alliance, one of whose leaders, the ad said accurately, "openly brags about its support for a Mideast terrorism group—the same kind of terrorism that killed our sailors on the *U.S.S. Cole*." To voters this seemed a stretch, and the ads put Lazio on the defensive for the last two weeks of the campaign.

For a race that was close almost all the way in the polls, this Senate election—surpassing the 1998 New York Senate race as the most expensive in history not involving a self-financing candidate—was decided by a surprisingly wide margin. Clinton won 55%–43%, almost the same as Schumer's 55%–44% two years earlier. "Sixty-two counties, 16 months, three debates, two opponents and six black pantsuits later—here we are!" exulted Clinton on election night. She was helped, of course, by the fact that Al Gore was carrying New York 60%–35%. But she ran well on her own. Robert Kennedy had won 53%–43% when Lyndon Johnson was carrying the state 69%–31%; the coattails were smaller in 2000, and Clinton's margin slightly greater. She carried New York City by 74%–25%, the same margin as Schumer's in 1998. She trailed in the suburbs by only 53%–45%, despite Lazio's suburban provenance; he carried his Long Island base, but she carried her now native Westchester. And Lazio won Upstate by only 51%–47%; Clinton carried most of the large counties there, and her percentages in county after county, not usually 50% but seldom under 40%, are impressive evidence of her hard work in campaigning and mastering Upstate issues. Clinton carried the Jewish vote, according to the VNS exit poll, by only 53%–45%, which would usually mean disaster for a Democrat in New York, and she did far less well than Schumer and other Democrats among those with graduate degrees, a large percentage of whom are Jewish. But she carried Upstate women by 55%–43%, an excellent showing for a Democrat: the work paid off.

A few days after the election, Clinton took a victory lap around Upstate New York and had a harmonious meeting in Albany with Governor George Pataki. She called for abolition of the Electoral College—a position her senior colleague Schumer shares, but he notes that it will never be ratified by a majority of state legislature. But her standing fell in the months after the election. In December 2000 she signed a book contract with Simon & Shuster for $8 million—$4.5 million more than the book contract for which Newt Gingrich was so roundly attacked in 1995. In departing the White House, the Clintons took $190,000 in gifts—far above the Senate's $50 limit—and many had to be returned when it was revealed that they included items donated to the White House, not the Clintons. Among the gifts were $7,375 worth of coffee tables and chairs donated by Denise Rich, former wife and advocate of Marc Rich, the fugitive financier pardoned by Bill Clinton on his last day in office, despite the opposition of New York U.S. Attorney Mary Jo White. Hillary Rodham Clinton said she had no opinion on the pardon. Nor, she said, did she have any role in the pardon of four Hasidic Jews from the Rockland County community of New Square who were convicted of fleecing the federal government of millions of dollars—a pardon White also opposed. But Clinton had visited New Square in August 2000, had won the community's vote by a margin of 1,400 to 12 and had been present at a White House Map Room meeting between their leaders and Bill Clinton on December 21, 2000, where they asked for the pardons. She said she had no knowledge as well that her brother Hugh Rodham had, while living at the White House, pushed for and obtained the pardon of two other felons for which he had been paid $400,000. In the Senate, Clinton was greeted courteously for the most part, but she did not receive the Super A committee assignment she sought, and instead got seats on Budget, Health and Education, and Environment and Public Works. She joined the New Democrats and introduced bills designed to revive the Upstate economy and called for an ending to military exercises on the Puerto Rican island of Vieques. Clinton's prospects for a long Senate career are good; no New York Democratic senator has been defeated for re-election since direct election of senators became part of the Constitution. But what is surely her ultimate goal although she denied it—her election as president in her own right—seemed in early 2001 considerably more distant than it did on election night 2000.

Presidential politics In the first half of the 20th Century, New York was the most pivotal—indeed, sometimes it seemed the dominant—state in presidential politics. It had the most electoral votes—45 from 1912–28, 47 from 1932–48, 45 from 1952–60—and of all the large states it was usually the most evenly divided between the two parties. But New York had just 33 electoral votes in 2000 and will have just 31 in 2004, and is among the largest states the most heavily Democratic. How has this come to pass? One reason is that Jewish voters, who did not identify strongly with either major party in the first half of the 20th Century, became strong Democrats—arguably the core of the Democratic Party—in the second. Increases in the percentage of black and Puerto Rican voters raised the Democratic percentage. White Catholic voters, very conservative on cultural issues half a century ago, can now take solidly liberal stands on issues like abortion and gun control. And, now that national Democrats seem less determined to increase the size and scope of the federal government, they have even greater appeal to New Yorkers who do not want it scaled back. Al Gore, who met with Al Sharpton at his daughter Karenna Gore Schiff's Upper East Side apartment during the campaign, made a splendid showing in New York: he won the state 60%–35%, carrying New York City 78%–18%, the suburbs 56%–40% and historically Republican Upstate New York 49%–45%.

For years New York had bossed politics, and it never had a presidential primary until 1968. Turnout is low. Democratic turnout was 1.1 million in 2000, well below the peak of 1.5 million in 1988, when Mayor Ed Koch's shrill support of Al Gore won him few votes as Michael Dukakis beat Jesse Jackson; on March 7, 2000, Gore won by a 2–1 margin. As for the Republican primary, the rules for qualifying for the ballot are so convoluted that no one but party insiders can master them; there were no contests here in the 1980s and Steve Forbes qualified in 1996 only after spending $1 million. In 2000 Republican state Chairman William Powers manuevered to keep John McCain off the ballot, to give an uncontested victory to Governor George Pataki's candidate, George W. Bush. But McCain went to court and got on the ballot. Then the Pataki forces ran harsh ads against McCain, including one attacking him for not supporting breast cancer funding which drew protests from Mayor Rudolph Giuliani even though he too was supporting Bush. But voting was limited to registered Republicans, and McCain did not have the appeal here he showed in New England; he carried affluent parts of Manhattan and the suburbs, but Bush won just about everywhere else. Voters voted for delegates, not presidential candidates; Bush delegates got 50% of the vote, McCain delegates 44%.

New York's minor parties no longer much matter. The Liberal Party and its predecessor, the American Labor Party, were founded to give Jewish garment workers a line on which to vote for Franklin Roosevelt and against local Tammany Hall candidates; the Liberal line was a help to Giuliani in the 1993 and 1997 mayoral elections. The Conservative Party was founded to withhold votes from liberal Republicans like Nelson Rockefeller and John Lindsay and encourage the Republican Party to nominate more conservative candidates. Lack of the Conservative line was a problem for Giuliani when he was running for senator, but the party did support the not-very-conservative Rick Lazio. It is quite comfortable with George Pataki, the first Conservative-backed governor.

Congressional districting When John Kennedy was elected president in 1960, New York elected 43 congressmen and California 30. In the next House election, New York will elect 29 and California 53. This is what happens when one state grows rapidly and another grows not at all. Redistricting is carnage time: New York lost five districts in the 1980 Census, another three in 1990 and two more in 2000. In 1992 New York produced the latest and most convoluted redistricting plan of any state. There was further litigation which changed the boundaries of the heavily Hispanic 12th District which snakes through Brooklyn and Queens and takes in part of Manhattan's Lower East Side.

It is generally expected that the plan for 2002 will cut one Democratic district in New York City and one Republican district Upstate. The key decisions will be made by three people, Governor George Pataki, Republican state Senate President Joseph Bruno and Democratic Assembly Speaker Sheldon Silver. Sure to be protected are Ways and Means ranking Democrat Charles Rangel and the three other black Democrats and two Hispanic Democrats; Republicans close to Pataki, like John Sweeney and Tom Reynolds, are unlikely to be endangered. Some members are protected by geography: There is almost sure to be a Republican-leaning district at the east end of Long Island for freshman Felix Grucci, a Staten Island-based district for Republican Vito Fossella and an Albany-based district for Democrat Michael McNulty. Amory Houghton has been lobbying to protect his Southern Tier district, less for himself (he is one of the wealthiest members of Congress and has been considering retiring) than for the communities he represents.

THE PEOPLE: Pop. 2000: 18,976,457; Pop. 1990: 17,990,455, up 5.5% 1990–2000. 6.7% of U.S. total, 3d largest; 67.9% White, 15.9% Black, 5.5% Asian, 0.4% Amer. Indian, 3.1% Two+ races, 7.1% Other; 15.1% Hispanic Origin. 4.6% Unemployment. 2000 Voting age pop.: 14,286,350. 2000 Turnout: 6,960,215; 49% of VAP. Registered voters (2000): 11,262,816; 5,243,617 D (47%), 3,171,044 R (28%), 2,848,155 unaffiliated and minor parties (25%).

POLITICAL LINEUP: Governor, George E. Pataki (R); Lt. Gov., Mary Donohue (R); Secy. of State, Randy Daniels (D); Atty. Gen., Eliot Spitzer (D); Comptroller, H. Carl McCall (D); State Senate, 61 (25 D, 36 R); Majority Leader, Joseph Bruno (R); State Assembly, 150 (99 D, 51 R); Assembly Speaker, Sheldon Silver (D). Senators, Charles E. Schumer (D) and Hillary Rodham Clinton (D). Representatives, 31 (19 D, 12 R).

ELECTIONS DIVISION: 518-474-1953; **FILING DEADLINE FOR U.S. CONGRESS:** TBA.

2000 Presidential Vote

Gore (D)	4,107,697	(60%)
Bush (R)	2,403,374	(35%)
Nader (Green)	244,030	(4%)
Others	66,898	(1%)

1996 Presidential Vote

Clinton (D)	3,756,565	(61%)
Dole (R)	1,932,900	(31%)
Perot (I)	503,356	(8%)

2000 Republican Presidential Primary

Bush (R)	1,102,850	(51%)
McCain (R)	937,655	(43%)
Keyes (R)	71,196	(3%)
Forbes (R)	49,817	(2%)

2000 Democratic Presidential Primary

Gore (D)	639,417	(66%)
Bradley (D)	326,038	(33%)

Gov. George E. Pataki (R)

Elected 1994, term expires Jan. 2003, 2d term; b. June 24, 1945, Peekskill; home, Garrison; Yale U., B.A. 1967, Columbia U. Law Schl., J.D. 1970; Catholic; married (Libby).

Elected Office: Peekskill Mayor, 1982–84; NY Assembly, 1984–92; NY Senate, 1992–94.

Professional Career: Practicing atty., 1970–89.

Office: Executive Chamber, State Capitol, Albany, 12224, 518-474-8390; Web site: www.state.ny.us.

Election Results

1998 general	George E. Pataki (R-C)	2,571,991	(54%)
	Peter F. Vallone (D-WF)	1,570,317	(33%)
	B. Thomas Golisano (Ind)	364,056	(8%)
	Others	228,872	(5%)
1998 primary	George E. Pataki (R)	unopposed	
1994 general	George E. Pataki (R-C)	2,538,702	(49%)
	Mario M. Cuomo (D-L)	2,364,904	(45%)
	B. Thomas Golisano (Ind)	217,490	(4%)
	Others	82,666	(2%)

Sen. Charles E. Schumer (D)

Elected 1998, seat up 2004, 1st term; b. Nov. 23, 1950, Brooklyn; home, Brooklyn; Harvard U., B.A. 1971, J.D. 1974; Jewish; married (Iris).

Elected Office: NY Assembly, 1974–80; U.S. House of Reps., 1980–1998.

DC Office: 313 HSOB, 20510, 202-224-6542; Fax: 202-228-3027; Web site: www.senate.gov/~schumer.

State Offices: Albany, 518-431-4070; Binghamton, 607-772-8109; Buffalo, 716-846-4545; Manhattan, 212-486-4430; Rochester, 716-263-5866; Syracuse, 315-423-5471.

Committees: *Banking, Housing & Urban Affairs:* Economic Policy (Chmn.); Housing & Transportation; Securities & Investment. *Energy & Natural Resources:* Energy Research, Development, Production & Regulation; Forests & Public Land Management; National Parks, Historic Preservation & Recreation. *Judiciary:* Administrative Oversight & the Courts (Chmn.); Antitrust, Business Rights & Competition; Immigration. *Rules & Administration.*

Group Ratings

	ADA	ACLU	AFS	LCV	CON	ITIC	NTU	COC	ACU	NTLC	CHC
2000	95	71	85	100	50	87	16	53	12	6	15
1999	100	—	100	100	19	—	8	53	4	—	—

National Journal Ratings

	1999 LIB	—	1999 CONS		2000 LIB	—	2000 CONS
Economic	80%	—	17%		84%	—	11%
Social	88%	—	0%		79%	—	0%
Foreign	87%	—	0%		72%	—	15%

Key Votes of the 106th Congress

1. Educ. Savings Accts.	N	5. Review Movie Violence	N	9. NATO War in Serbia	Y
2. Prescrip. Drug Benefit	Y	6. Gun Show Bckgrnd. Checks	Y	10. Table Cuba Travel Ban	N
3. Delay Ergonomic Standards	N	7. Ban Part.-Birth Abortion	N	11. Nuclear Test-Ban Treaty	Y
4. Phase Out Estate Tax	N	8. Broaden Hate Crimes List	Y	12. Perm. Trade with China	Y

Election Results

1998 general	Charles E. Schumer (D-Ind-L)	2,551,065	(55%)	($16,671,877)
	Al D'Amato (R-C-RTL)	2,058,988	(44%)	($24,195,287)
	Others	60,752	(1%)	
1998 primary	Charles E. Schumer (D)	388,701	(51%)	
	Geraldine A. Ferraro (D)	201,265	(26%)	
	Mark Green (D)	145,819	(19%)	
	Others	28,493	(4%)	
1992 general	Al D'Amato (R-C-RTL)	3,166,994	(49%)	($11,550,958)
	Robert Abrams (D-L)	3,086,200	(48%)	($6,408,981)
	Others	205,632	(3%)	

Sen. Hillary Rodham Clinton (D)

Elected 2000, seat up 2006, 1st term; b. Oct. 26, 1947, Chicago, IL; home, Chappaqua; Wellesley Col., B.A. 1969; Yale U., J.D. 1973; Methodist; married (William).

Professional Career: Atty., Children's Defense Fund, 1973–74; Council, U.S. House of Reps. Judiciary Committee, 1974; Asst. professor, U. of AR School of Law, 1974–77, 1979–80; Practicing atty., 1977–92; Chair, Pres. Task Force on Health Care Reform, 1993.

DC Office: 476 RSOB, 20510, 202-224-4451; Fax: 202-228-0282; Web site: clinton.senate.gov.

State Offices: Albany, 518-431-0120; Buffalo, 716-854-9725; New York City, 212-688-6262; Syracuse, 315-448-0470.

Committees: *Budget. Environment & Public Works*: Clean Air, Wetlands, Private Property & Nuclear Safety; Fisheries, Wildlife & Water; Superfund, Waste Control & Risk Assessment. *Health, Education, Labor & Pensions*: Aging; Public Health.

Group Ratings and Key Votes: Newly Elected

Election Results

2000 general	Hillary Rodham Clinton (D-L-WF)	3,747,310	(55%)	($41,469,898)
	Rick Lazio (R-C)	2,915,730	(43%)	($40,576,273)
	Others	116,799	(2%)	
2000 primary	Hillary Rodham Clinton (D)	565,353	(82%)	
	Mark S. McMahon (D)	124,315	(18%)	
1994 general	Daniel Patrick Moynihan (D-L)	2,646,541	(55%)	($6,705,482)
	Bernadette Castro (R-C)	1,988,308	(42%)	($1,581,901)
	Others	155,487	(3%)	

FIRST DISTRICT

Long Island—the Island to most New Yorkers—is America's largest, most populous and in some ways most troubled island: 103 miles long, 12 to 20 miles wide, with gentle hills and cliffs above Long Island Sound and sandspit beaches fronting the Atlantic Ocean. Some 7.4 million people live here, more than in all but nine states, 4.7 million in the New York City boroughs of Brooklyn and Queens and 2.7 million in the suburban counties of Nassau and Suffolk. Brooklyn, at the western end of the island, is urban and thickly settled, while the Hamptons at the east end are carefully manicured countryside, preserved by a stylish New York elite. The Hamptons and the old whaling village of Sag Harbor, originally settled by New Englanders, were left behind in the rush of westward migration; today they appear more comfortable than grand, a shingled and windmilled portion of middle America kept more pristine than workaday middle America ever was.

Demographically, the Hamptons are only a small (though growing) part of Long Island. More important are the (no longer growing) suburbs created in the rush eastward into what was once farmland after World War II. Developers looked for cheaper land for aircraft factories and shopping centers, subdivisions and office parks, and found them first in Nassau County just east of Queens, and then in Suffolk County. Suffolk attracted young families, of Irish and Italian descent more often than Jewish or black, looking for more ground and trees and less crime and tension than in their city neighborhoods. Politically, Suffolk County was long one of the most conservative parts of New York, though not very conservative today by national standards. It has also become turbulent political territory, as life in Long Island turned sour in the past decade. Defense plants shut down and jobs evaporated as the defense buildup and then the Cold War ended. The Long Island Lighting Company, the local electric utility, had cost overruns on its nuclear plant in Shoreham, and then went into bankruptcy after Governor Mario Cuomo shut the plant down, giving Long Island the nation's highest electric rates. The partial state takeover of Lilco, brokered by Governor George Pataki, was designed to cut rates, but they are still among the nation's highest.

The 1st Congressional District covers eastern Suffolk County, running east from Smithtown on the North Shore and Patchogue on the South Shore. It includes the Hamptons but, more important politically, the Brookhaven National Laboratory and the defense plants in the center of the Island. Politically, this is a Republican area where Democrats have sometimes been competitive.

The congressman from the 1st District is Felix Grucci, a Republican elected in 2000. A native of Bellport, Long Island, Grucci began working at Fireworks by Grucci—his family's business—straight out of high school in 1970. Felix became its president after a devastating accident at the company in 1983, and transformed it from a small, hometown business to an international pyrotechnic entertainment firm that set off fireworks at the Reagan, Bush, Clinton and Bush inaugurals, the centennial celebrations of the Statue of Liberty and the Brooklyn Bridge, and the 2000 New Year's celebration on the Washington Mall. Grucci was elected supervisor of the Town of Brookhaven, which includes 62% of the district's population, in 1995 and re-elected in 1997 and 1999, never receiving less than 62% of the vote. Meanwhile, other Suffolk Republican bosses were the target of criminal investigations: the party's former county leader John Powell was convicted in December 1999 of extortion and racketeering in connection with stolen trucks and illegal trucking fees at the Brookhaven landfill.

The tale of Grucci's election to the House is intertwined with the bizarre odyssey of his predecessor, Michael Forbes, who was first elected a Republican in 1994. Then a New York-area staffer for the U.S. Chamber of Commerce, Forbes defeated Democratic Congressman George Hochbrueckner by promising a balanced budget and tax incentives for small business and jobs. Forbes initially had close relations with Republican leaders but also a middle-of-the-House voting record. His 10-year acquaintance with Newt Gingrich helped him win a seat on Appropriations—unusual for a freshman—where he built a good relationship with Chairman Bob Livingston. But in December 1996, he was the first House Republican to announce he would not vote for Gingrich for speaker on January 7. Democrats and the press treated this as the beginning of the end for Gingrich; Republican leaders muttered that it was just personal ambition. Against an underfunded Democrat in 1998, Forbes was easily re-elected, 64%–36%. In early December, Livingston, then Speaker-designate, named him an "assistant to the speaker." But both came on hard times. Under attack for an extramarital affair, Livingston resigned. Forbes was attacked by some Republicans for giving money to two Democratic colleagues, Bill Pascrell and Loretta Sanchez. And, after being widely mentioned as a vote against impeachment, he came out for it, leaving many Democrats and Hamptons denizens angry.

In July 1999, Forbes became the first House member to switch from Republican to Democrat since Donald Riegle in 1973. It was summer, when rich liberals from New York are thick on the ground in the Hamptons: this is one part of the country where the rich are Democrats and the (relatively) poor are Republicans. After discussions with New York Democrats Gary Ackerman and Eliot Engel and promises of political and financial support from Dick Gephardt and Bill Clinton, Forbes announced he was switching parties, and fired a blast at the Republicans for having "become defined through the actions of extremists in the House." The next day—sitting with his wife Barbara, whom he married in Bob Dole's office with Alfonse D'Amato as best man—he told *The New York Times,* "I was too miserable. I didn't want to be part of it anymore." Not surprisingly, House Republicans immediately targeted Forbes for defeat and attacked what Republican campaign committee chairman Tom Davis called a pattern of "inconsistent and erratic actions." Although national Democratic leaders embraced Forbes as a vital stepping-stone to retaking the House majority, the local Democrats who had campaigned against him in three House races were hostile. Forbes's only opponent in the September 2000 primary was Regina Seltzer, a 71-year-old retired school librarian and a member of the Brookhaven council in the 1970s. But Davis's committee, without much fanfare, released embarrassing video outtakes of old Forbes campaign commercials and photos—including Newt Gingrich—and sent a mailing to Democratic voters portraying Forbes as an arch-conservative. Seltzer won a court ruling halting state Democratic Party ads that she said illegally interfered with the primary by helping Forbes; she campaigned gamely as "the real Democrat." In the low-turnout September 12 contest that took a week to recount, she won by 35 votes, 6,077 to 6,042, despite getting outspent by almost $1 million—stunning herself, Forbes and Democratic leaders who had organized no turnout effort, but not Davis' stealth operatives. She immediately became an underdog against Grucci.

In the brief general campaign, Democrats were slow to overcome their shock. Among other problems, Forbes, though he said he supported Seltzer, remained the nominee of the Working Families party, whose line was led by Al Gore and Hillary Rodham Clinton; he ended up with 3% of the vote. Democrats had been planning to attack Grucci for alleged toxic poisoning to 11 drinking-water wells caused by his fireworks factory and for using taxpayer money for a campaign event with John McCain, but they did not run anything like the serious campaign they had planned on the assumption that Forbes would be their nominee. For national Democrats, to whom every seat was vital and the Forbes seat a year earlier was the keystone to their House takeover, this was a debacle. Grucci won 56%–41%—not overwhelming but evidence of the district's continuing Republican tilt.

On redistricting, geography works Grucci's way. It's hard to avoid creating a Republican-leaning district at the east end of Long Island.

Cook's Call *Potentially Competitive.* A bizarre set of circumstances helped Grucci cruise to an easy 56% win in this normally competitive Long Island district in 2000. Incumbent Michael Forbes, who had switched parties, lost the September Democratic primary in to a little known opponent Regina Seltzer; Seltzer lacked the money or national party support to launch a serious campaign against Grucci, and he won without breaking much of a sweat. But, in a district that Clinton won in 1996 by 15% and that Gore won by 9% in 2000, Democrats could be competitive here in 2002.

THE PEOPLE: Pop. 2000: 642,032; Pop. 1990: 580,076, up 10.7% 1990–2000. 89.1% White, 4.3% Black, 2.4% Asian, 0.3% Amer. Indian, 1.7% Two+ races, 2.1% Other; 7.6% Hispanic Origin.

2000 Presidential Vote			1996 Presidential Vote		
Gore (D)	140,275	(52%)	Clinton (D)	118,187	(52%)
Bush (R)	114,126	(43%)	Dole (R)	83,956	(37%)
Nader (Green)	9,224	(3%)	Perot (I)	25,850	(11%)
Others	3,832	(1%)			

Rep. Felix Grucci (R)

Elected 2000, 1st term; b. Nov. 25, 1951, Brookhaven; home, E. Patchogue; Catholic; married (Madeline).

Elected Office: Brookhaven Town Council, 1993–95; Brookhaven Town Supervisor, 1995–2000.

Professional Career: Pres., Fireworks by Grucci, 1984–2000.

DC Office: 1505 LHOB 20515, 202-225-3826; Fax: 202-225-3143; Web site: www.house.gov/grucci.

District Office: Patchogue, 631-758-4600.

Committees: *Financial Services* (32d of 37 R): Domestic Monetary Policy, Technology & Economic Growth; Financial Institutions & Consumer Credit; Housing & Community Opportunity. *Science* (23d of 25 R): Environment, Technology and Standards (Vice Chmn.); Research. *Small Business* (16th of 19 R): Rural Enterprises, Agricultural and Technology; Workforce, Empowerment & Government Programs.

Group Ratings and Key Votes: Newly Elected

Election Results

2000 general	Felix Grucci (R-Ind-C-RTL)	133,020	(56%)	($1,565,346)
	Regina Seltzer (D)	97,299	(41%)	($338,158)
	Others	9,285	(4%)	
2000 primary	Felix Grucci (R)	unopposed		
1998 general	Michael P. Forbes (R-C-Ind-RTL)	99,460	(64%)	($874,633)
	William G. Holst (D-HMO)	55,630	(36%)	($50,454)

SECOND DISTRICT

In the years after World War II, hundreds of thousands of New York City residents—people who had trouble imagining they would live anywhere but the close-packed city streets—moved to what had been the potato fields of central Long Island. The highways that Robert Moses built to connect Jones Beach with the city masses were the routes of that migration—and often the daily commuter paths back into New York—as young veterans and their families found they could afford to leave the row-house neighborhoods where they had grown up for the single-family houses of Levittown and other Long Island subdivisions. The first wave of postwar migration moved into Nassau County, and it was largely a cross-section of all but the poorest New Yorkers: about half Catholic, with the other half split almost evenly between Jews and Protestants. As Long Island developed its own employment base, another wave moved farther east into Suffolk County. This group was more Catholic and less Jewish than the first, and more blue-collar. It was ancestrally Democratic, but firmly traditional and culturally conservative. This was the best constituency in the state for the successful Conservative party candidacy of Senator James Buckley in 1970. Since that time, issues have changed; crime is down and the liberalism of New York Mayor John Lindsay has vanished, and on the cultural issues of the 1990s, abortion and gun control, voters in Suffolk County are, like those throughout the New York metro area, more attuned to northern-accented Democrats than southern-accented Republicans.

The 2d Congressional District of New York includes most of western Suffolk County. The bulk of the district's population is concentrated in the South Shore townships of Babylon and Islip, with dozens of suburbs in each. There are some spacious houses with views of the Great South Bay and, across the bay lie the beaches of Fire Island, where many homes are weekend retreats owned by affluent New York City residents. But, for the most part, the 2d is the lower-income part of Long Island, beyond the more fashionable and expensive commuter suburbs to the west and well south of the picturesque North Shore. This area filled up in the 1950s and 1960s but has grown little since then. However, with some of the lowest-priced housing on the Island, it attracts some young families. More than 15% of the 2d is Hispanic, the largest percentage of any of the Long Island districts.

The congressman from the 2d District is Steve Israel, a Democrat elected in 2000. He grew up in Wantagh and graduated from George Washington University in 1983. While in college, he worked full-time on Capitol Hill, first as a constituent correspondent for Robert Matsui of California, then as a legislative assistant on foreign policy and national security for Richard Ottinger of New York. After college Israel returned to Long Island, where he was Suffolk director for the American Jewish Congress, fundraising director for Touro Law School from 1985–88, assistant for intergovernmental relations to Suffolk County executive Patrick Halpin for three years, then ran his own public relations and marking firm. He also was president and CEO of the Institute on the Holocaust and the Law. In 1993 Israel was the only Democrat elected to the Huntington Town Council, where he forged a reputation as a bipartisan leader who helped revive the finances of the then-strapped town; he eventually became majority leader. Israel had not been planning to run in early 2000. Republican Rick Lazio, who won the seat by beating Democrat Tom Downey in 1992, had been reelected by wide margins. But in May 2000 Rudolph Giuliani suddenly dropped out of the Senate race against Hillary Rodham Clinton, a race Lazio had considered entering until Governor George Pataki endorsed Giuliani in August 1999. One day later Lazio announced he was running for the Senate, and the House race was suddenly open.

The September primary was fiercely contested by Israel and Suffolk County Legislator David Bishop, who was better-known and a slight favorite. Bishop initially had the support of local Democratic leaders and hoped that a convention selection could avoid an expensive primary. But Israel insisted on a primary. Bishop accused Israel of giving raises to Huntington employees who had volunteered for his campaign and questioned Israel's credentials and environmental record. Israel said the raises were deserved and had bipartisan support, and added that he worked to pass a $15 million bond to preserve open space in the township and that he had given Bishop his first job in politics—a claim Bishop denied. Israel was endorsed by both *The New York Times* and

Newsday for his broader experience and bipartisan skills. Each candidate raised more than $350,000 for the primary but Israel squeaked out a 45%–41% victory.

In the general, Republican Joan Johnson had an appealing story. As a 66-year old black woman, who grew up in segregated Florida and moved to New York to become a school teacher, she would have been the first black Republican woman elected to Congress. In addition, as the elected town clerk since 1991 of Islip (which includes 51% of the 2nd District), she had the Suffolk County party's supposed organizational muscle behind her. But, despite running with help from Lazio, Johnson turned out to be a disappointing candidate. She was forced to pull a TV ad attacking Israel for voting to raise taxes after Israel protested that he had opposed tax hikes. Israel said that he wanted to protect Social Security while Johnson wanted to privatize it, and that he wanted to pass a bill that protects senior citizens from HMOs. Johnson was hurt by the candidacies of Richard Thompson on the Conservative line and Robert Walsh on the Right to Life line; both criticized her on abortion. Even some Republicans criticized her limited campaign skills and sparse public appearances. Israel won by a surprisingly easy 48%–35%, with 6% for Walsh, 6% for Thompson and 4% for Bishop, whose name appeared on three lines on the ballot.

Israel showed an early sign of his connections and knowledge of House politics when he was elected as the freshman on the Democratic Steering Committee and was appointed to the Financial Services Committee. Now he faces a test of his Albany connections, as he faces redistricting. It is possible that the district will be little changed: control of redistricting is split between the parties, and eastern Long Island is not easy to combine with any other part of the state.

Cook's Call *Competitive.* Israel's election in 2000 marked the first time in 8 years that Democrats have won this swing district. This seat has an underlying Democratic edge (Clinton won here in 1996 by 20% while Gore took it by 16% in 2000), but it is by no means a safe Democratic seat. To beat Israel in 2002 Republicans will need to recruit a better candidate than their 2000 choice.

THE PEOPLE: Pop. 2000: 612,961; Pop. 1990: 580,303, up 5.6% 1990–2000. 77.5% White, 11.1% Black, 2.4% Asian, 0.3% Amer. Indian, 2.7% Two+ races, 6% Other; 15.4% Hispanic Origin.

2000 Presidential Vote

Gore (D)	125,111	(56%)
Bush (R)	89,583	(40%)
Nader (Green)	6,143	(3%)
Others	3,715	(2%)

1996 Presidential Vote

Clinton (D)	108,598	(55%)
Dole (R)	68,710	(35%)
Perot (I)	20,419	(10%)

Rep. Steve Israel (D)

Elected 2000, 1st term; b. May 30, 1958, Brooklyn; home, Dix Hills; George Wash. U., B.A. 1983; Jewish; separated.

Elected Office: Huntington Town Bd., 1993–2000, Maj. Ldr., 1997–2000.

Professional Career: Legis. Asst., U.S. Rep. Richard Ottinger, 1980–83; Fundraising Dir., Touro Law Ctr., 1985–88; Pres., Steve Israel Assoc., Inc., 1992–98; Pres. & CEO, Inst. on Holocaust and Law, 1998–2000.

DC Office: 429 CHOB 20515, 202-225-3335; Fax: 202-225-4669; Web site: www.house.gov/israel.

District Office: Bay Shore, 631-665-7333.

Committees: *Financial Services* (31st of 32 D): Capital Markets, Insurance & Government Sponsored Enterprises; Housing & Community Opportunity. *Science* (20th of 22 D): Research.

Group Ratings and Key Votes: Newly Elected

Election Results

2000 general	Steve Israel (D)	90,438	(48%)	($1,055,977)
	Joan B. Johnson (R)	65,880	(35%)	($1,015,225)
	Robert T. Walsh (RTL)	11,224	(6%)	($47,609)
	Richard N. Thompson (C)	10,824	(6%)	($38,967)
	David A. Bishop (Ind-Green-WF)	10,266	(5%)	($350,653)
2000 primary	Steve Israel (D)	6,004	(45%)	
	David A. Bishop (D)	5,449	(41%)	
	Ghenya B. Grant (D)	1,785	(13%)	
1998 general	Rick A. Lazio (R-C)	85,089	(66%)	($1,451,458)
	John C. Bace (D)	37,949	(30%)	
	Others	5,400	(4%)	

THIRD DISTRICT

It was a pivotal moment in American suburban history: in September 1947, 300 families moved into 300 tiny 750-square-foot houses, built in record time by mass production. They sold for $6,990, with no down payment for veterans. This was Levittown, and by the time the last new house was sold for $9,500 in November 1951, the name had become a synonym for rapid suburban development. Developer William Levitt recognized that many young veterans and their families were eager to move out of crowded New York City neighborhoods, so he bought a Nassau County potato field, planted trees, designed floor plans to allow easy additions and built a community of 65,000 people. A half-century later, few of the original four-room bungalows could be found, but homes are still affordable. And if school enrollment has dropped here, and retiree workshops have cropped up, it only reflects Nassau's trend toward empty nesters. In 1940 the county population was 450,000; by 1960 it was 1.3 million and 1.4 million in 1970; then it went back to around 1.3 million in 1990 and stayed there in 2000 as youngsters moved out.

Nassau County also is home to what may have been the nation's premier county Republican machine. It was the creation of Nassau Republican Chairman J. Russell Sprague before the post-war population boom. Sprague managed to carry the county for Alf Landon in 1936 and that same year persuaded the voters to adopt a county executive form of government in which control of political patronage would center in one man, responsible to the county Republican chairman. The result became one of the most high-salaried, high-spending local governments in America, and a Republican political machine that vied in size and power with the Democratic big city machines of old. But the old-time apparatus came on hard times in the late 1990s, as the county's credit rating dipped to near junk-bond status—even with the nation's highest sales tax rate and commercial property taxes that were higher than in New York City; Gail Collins of the *New York Times* called the county "possibly the worst-run political institution in the country." Business conditions were bad enough that Chase Manhattan Bank moved two customer service centers from Nassau to Texas. Voters rebelled in November 1999, giving Democrats for the first time a majority in the county legislature. In June 2000 the state legislature passed a $105 million bailout for Nassau County, one of the most affluent parts of the state.

The 3d Congressional District includes nearly half of Nassau County. Most of the people in the district live in towns strung along either side of Sunrise Highway or just off the Southern or Northern State Parkways from Levittown and Hicksville, east to the county line. The district also includes Bethpage, home to the old Grumman aircraft company, once a big employer here and now part of Northrop Grumman. The northern geographic half of the district, with about one-fifth of the population, includes the old estate areas around Oyster Bay, Old Westbury and Man-hasset. Not many of greater New York's wealthiest live in the 3d, but the overall level of affluence is high, and the district in 1990 had the third-highest median income of any in the nation, just behind the New Jersey 11th and Maryland 8th. The 3d was once pretty solidly Republican, but Democrats have become competitive here, and it was carried easily by Bill Clinton in 1996 and Al Gore in 2000. In the 2000 Senate race Suffolk County neighbor Rick Lazio defeated Hillary Rodham Clinton in Nassau County, 52%–44%—a win, but far below the margins that Republicans once rolled up here.

The congressman from the 3d District is Peter King, a Republican first elected in 1992. King grew up in Sunnyside, Queens; his parents were Irish immigrants and Democrats, his father an NYPD detective. He went to St. Francis College and law school at Notre Dame, and clerked one summer at Richard Nixon's law firm with a Long Islander named Rudolph Giuliani. After school he followed the trek to the suburbs and became part of the Nassau County Republican machine. He started working as a lawyer and staffer in county government in 1972, at 28; in 1981 he became county comptroller. When 22-year incumbent Republican Congressman Norman Lent announced his retirement in June 1992, King ran and won the Republican primary 2–1. In the general—facing a Democrat who spent $700,000 of his own money and ran as a reformer and supporter of abortion rights—King ran as a political insider, fiscal conservative and abortion opponent; he won by just 50%–46%. He has not faced a close reelection since then.

King has a middle-of-the-House voting record, more conservative on cultural issues, but with distinctive interests and accents. He is against abortion, racial quotas and preferences, bilingual education, gun control and the National Endowment for the Arts. He denounced the hiring of Louis Farrakhan's groups to police public housing projects. He is for English-only laws and against aid to illegal immigrants. He sponsored a bill to deduct from foreign aid 110% of the amount owed by foreign countries on New York City parking tickets. He is unapologetic about being a machine politician—he wrote a college paper on ousted New York Mayor Jimmy Walker—and seethes against proposals for campaign finance reform.

He came to the House as one of the country's strongest supporters of the Irish Republican Army; within days of his election in 1992 he flew to Belfast to meet with leaders of Sinn Fein, the IRA's political arm. He urged the Clinton administration to drop travel and fundraising restrictions on Sinn Fein leader Gerry Adams. In the 1998 negotiations finale, King carried messages between the IRA and the Irish government. In August 1998 Clinton took him on *Air Force One* to Russia and Ireland and had a long late-night conversation with him. On impeachment King was torn by party loyalty and his closeness to Clinton and support of his Northern Ireland policy. He played a visible but not pivotal role—voting for an impeachment inquiry in October, but in December worked for a censure with a financial penalty. He contended that "reform politics," which included the independent counsel law, had produced a situation that made little sense and threatened to make Republicans a minority again. He said publicly that as many as 20 Republicans were prepared to vote against impeachment; in the end only four, including King, voted against all four counts. Later, he was a rare Republican backing Clinton's military campaign in Kosovo.

King often seems more comfortable with Democrats and labor leaders—the kind of people he dealt with in Nassau County, than with Southern or Western Republicans, for whom he seems to have no more affinity than Ulster Protestants. In 1997 he criticized Peter Hoekstra's investigation of labor unions; three years later, he escorted Teamsters president James Hoffa to the Republican convention. He called for Newt Gingrich to step down after the 1996 elections and in March 1997 wrote in the *Weekly Standard*, "As roadkill on the highway of American politics, Newt Gingrich cannot sell the Republican agenda. So instead of replacing Newt, the Republican leadership has replaced the agenda. . . . Congressional Republicans are adrift." But he did not support the July 1997 coup against Gingrich, on the ground that it made no sense to change leaders in mid-term. And he criticized a 1999 Clinton administration investigation of job statistics in New York, which he said was designed to promote Hillary Rodham Clinton's Senate candidacy. In early 2001, he warned President Bush not to pick fights with labor after he threatened to intervene in a Northwest Airlines strike threat.

Over the years, King became a provocative presence on broadcast chat shows. He gained additional attention with a novel, *Terrible Beauty*, about politics in Belfast. He sought, but with little success, to push his candidacy for Daniel Patrick Moynihan's Senate seat. And his efforts to secure a post in George W. Bush's Cabinet went nowhere: not surprising, given King's support of John McCain in the primary, when he called Bush "politically tone-deaf" in his dealings with McCain. (His support for McCain had a curious tone, given King's previous criticism of McCain's "self-righteousness" in pushing campaign reform.) After the 2000 election, he criticized New York Republican leaders for working harder to keep McCain off the ballot than trying to elect Rick Lazio. "There is no grass-roots democracy in the party," King said.

In the House, King suffered little visible retribution for his apostasy. "There's a small majority, so the Republicans will have to deal with the cards they're dealt, and I'm one of the cards," he said. "Hope I'm not the joker." Apparently not. In the 107th Congress, he became chair of the reorganized Financial Services Subcommittee on Domestic Monetary Policy, Technology and Economic Growth—a good platform for a representative for New York who also enjoys high-visibility ratings. Redistricting is not likely to be a problem.

Cook's Call *Safe.* Though this Long Island district has been steadily trending away from Republicans over the last 10 years, King is safely ensconced in this seat. But redistricting will impact just about every member of the delegation. This district was the slowest growing Long Island-based seat.

THE PEOPLE: Pop. 2000: 588,611; Pop. 1990: 580,468, up 1.4% 1990–2000. 89.8% White, 2.6% Black, 3.9% Asian, 0.1% Amer. Indian, 1.5% Two+ races, 2.2% Other; 6.9% Hispanic Origin.

2000 Presidential Vote

Gore (D)	152,108	(55%)
Bush (R)	115,123	(41%)
Nader (Green)	7,329	(3%)
Others	2,864	(1%)

1996 Presidential Vote

Clinton (D)	136,505	(54%)
Dole (R)	97,034	(38%)
Perot (I)	18,975	(8%)

Rep. Peter T. King (R)

Elected 1992, 5th term; b. Apr. 5, 1944, Manhattan; home, Seaford; St. Francis Col., B.A. 1965, U. of Notre Dame, J.D. 1968; Catholic; married (Rosemary).

Military Career: Army Natl. Guard, 1968–73.

Elected Office: Hempstead Town Cncl., 1977–81; Nassau Cnty. Comptroller, 1981–92.

Professional Career: Practicing atty., 1968–72, 1978–81; Dep. Atty., Nassau Cnty., 1972–74; Exec. Asst., Nassau Cnty. Exec., 1974–76, Gen. Cnsl., 1977.

DC Office: 436 CHOB 20515, 202-225-7896; Fax: 202-226-2279; Web site: www.house.gov/king.

District Office: Massapequa Park, 516-541-4225.

Committees: *Financial Services* (8th of 37 R): Domestic Monetary Policy, Technology & Economic Growth (Chmn.); Housing & Community Opportunity; Oversight & Investigations. *International Relations* (12th of 26 R): Europe; Middle East & South Asia.

Group Ratings

	ADA	ACLU	AFS	LCV	CON	ITIC	NTU	COC	ACU	NTLC	CHC
2000	15	21	57	29	2	65	53	55	64	58	100
1999	30	—	33	31	2	—	52	54	75	—	—

National Journal Ratings

	1999 LIB —	1999 CONS		2000 LIB —	2000 CONS
Economic	48% —	50%		49% —	50%
Social	37% —	61%		42% —	57%
Foreign	52% —	47%		39% —	57%

Key Votes of the 106th Congress

1. Patient Bill of Rights	Y	5. Bar RU-486 $ for FDA	Y	9. NATO War in Serbia	Y
2. Accelerate Min. Wage	Y	6. Display 10 Commandments	Y	10. Perm. Trade with China	N
3. Strike Ban on Ergo. Stnd.	Y	7. Gun Show Bkgrnd. Checks	Y	11. Debt Relief for 3rd World	N
4. Ovrd. Estate Tax Veto	Y	8. Ban Part.-Birth Abortion	Y	12. Drop Cuba Econ. Embargo	N

FOURTH DISTRICT

Garden City is one of America's first suburbs, created more than a century ago by New York retailer A.T. Stewart at a time when reformers wanted to maintain the commercial vitality and social interaction of the city, but in a setting that preserved the healthful openness of the country-side. Garden City's wide avenues and single-family homes, connected to New York City by the Long Island Railroad, were intended to be middle-income territory, but its amenities have made it one of the highest-income parts of Long Island. In the century after its founding, the rest of Nassau County has changed from almost entirely rural to almost entirely suburban. The big rush came after World War II, as one town ran into another, freeways replaced strip highways, and shopping centers sprang up at intersections. Today, many of the middle- and upper-income residents of the 4th Congressional District still depend on the Long Island Railroad to get them to jobs in New York City. Garden City now sits amid Nassau County's civic institutions just south of the county seat of Mineola and the site of Roosevelt Field, where Charles Lindbergh took off for Paris. Almost 60 years later, Roosevelt Field is a large suburban shopping center, with the Nassau Coliseum—home to hockey's New York Islanders—nearby.

The 4th District includes Garden City and the civic center of Nassau County. It includes half of Levittown and the neat and conservative suburbs along the Queens line from New Hyde Park to Valley Stream; it takes in the "Five Towns"—Lawrence, Inwood, Cedarhurst, Hewlett and Woodmere—near Kennedy Airport's flight paths. Nassau County has traditionally been Republican, and Garden City and heavily Catholic suburbs like East Meadow are solidly Republican. But about one-third of the residents here are either black or Hispanic, and the Five Towns are heavily Democratic. The 4th District has voted mostly Republican in local and state politics, but it also voted twice for Bill Clinton and also for Al Gore. Its congressional politics proved to be a bit quirky, as it elected four people to the House in the 1990s.

The congresswoman from the 4th District is Carolyn McCarthy, elected as a Democrat in 1996. She was born in Brooklyn, trained as a nurse, married and raised a family on Long Island; originally, she was a Republican. In 1993 her husband was killed and her son seriously injured in the "Long Island Railroad Massacre," when a black gunman opened fire on passengers as the train crossed the Nassau County line (he said he did not want to kill anyone in New York City lest he embarrass Mayor David Dinkins). McCarthy spoke movingly at Colin Ferguson's trial and her strength in tragedy won many admirers. "You took away my husband," she said directly to Ferguson. "You took away my best friend." She began campaigning for gun control, and in 1995 lobbied her Congressman Daniel Frisa to vote against repeal of the assault weapons ban, unsuccessfully. McCarthy inquired about running against Frisa in the primary, but Nassau County Republicans discouraged this. But Democrats had been eyeing the seat for some time and recruited her. McCarthy initially knew little about politics. When told that Minority Leader Dick Gephardt wanted to meet her, she reportedly asked, "Who's Dick Gephardt?" But she learned quickly. As the Democratic nominee, she called for gun control and attacked Frisa as too close to Newt Gingrich. The political tide was going her way, Frisa disappeared in the campaign's final week, did not show up at his election night party and never made a concession statement. McCarthy won 57%–41%.

In the House, McCarthy has compiled a moderately liberal voting record and sponsored gun control measures. She called for childproof locks on handguns, and fines for parents if a child gets a handgun and shows it in public and jail terms if a crime is committed with it. She beat

Jack Murtha's 1997 amendment to allow import of World War II-era firearms and sought to ban the sale of guns to temporary visitors to the United States. She worked hard and surprised people on some votes, opposing the partial-birth abortion ban and backing the Republicans' impeachment investigation resolution. In May 1998 a TV movie of McCarthy's story was broadcast; the National Rifle Association said it was inaccurate and Nassau County Republican Chairman Joseph Mondello said, "That's one hell of a campaign advertisement." But she declined a contract to write a book in time for the movie.

Republicans thrashed around to line up opposition: Frisa ran ads in early 1998 but withdrew from the race in July 1998; Mondello even pondered running. The ultimate Republican nominee was 16-year state Assemblyman Gregory Becker, from an ancestral Long Island Republican family: his grandfather moved to Lynbrook in 1905 and served in the House from 1953–65, his father was mayor of Lynbrook, his uncle is a district leader who feuded with Mondello. This turned out to be a closer election than most expected. McCarthy won in this pro-incumbent year by just 53%–47%.

As she gained experience, McCarthy broadened her portfolio, taking an interest in education and health-care issues. She worked on HMO reform with John Dingell, who opposed her on some gun issues. She helped to reverse Medicare cutbacks for New York hospitals. She released a study showing that Long Island women with breast cancer pay excessive prices for their medication. Although Congress failed to approve serious gun-control proposals, even after the extended debate following the Littleton Colorado school shootings, McCarthy had some success elsewhere. She backed the Justice Department's agreement with Smith & Wesson on marketing and safety measures. She shared the stage with George Pataki and praised him when he signed a wide-ranging package of state controls.

After becoming the first incumbent since 1990 re-elected to this seat, she had an easier time in 2000, again running against Becker. He spent about the same amount as in 1998; she spent more than twice her earlier totals—just less than $2 million. She also had the advantage of Al Gore and Joe Lieberman at the top of the ticket, instead of the locally popular Pataki. She won 61%–39%. Redistricting is not likely to be a problem.

Cook's Call *Potentially Competitive.* After a less than impressive win in 1998, McCarthy's 61% showing in 2000 was a definite improvement. McCarthy's personal story is her biggest asset, but the former nurse has acquired a better grasp of her role in Congress and seems to understand that she can no longer simply rely on her outsider appeal to win races. McCarthy has also been helped by the fact that Republicans have yet to put up a well-funded candidate to face her. This socially conservative district will never be a slam-dunk for McCarthy, but she will be tough to dislodge.

THE PEOPLE: Pop. 2000: 611,953; Pop. 1990: 580,492, up 5.4% 1990–2000. 68.1% White, 18.8% Black, 5% Asian, 0.2% Amer. Indian, 2.7% Two + races, 5.2% Other; 13.3% Hispanic Origin.

2000 Presidential Vote		
Gore (D)	147,864	(59%)
Bush (R)	94,318	(38%)
Nader (Green)	6,032	(2%)
Others	3,022	(1%)

1996 Presidential Vote		
Clinton (D)	131,825	(57%)
Dole (R)	83,750	(36%)
Perot (I)	14,493	(6%)

Rep. Carolyn McCarthy (D)

Elected 1996, 3d term; b. Jan. 5, 1944, Brooklyn; home, Mineola; Glen Cove Nursing Schl., L.P.N. 1964; Catholic; widowed.

Professional Career: Nurse, 1964–93; Gun control activist, 1993–96.

DC Office: 1224 LHOB 20515, 202-225-5516; Fax: 202-225-5758; Web site: www.house.gov/carolynmccarthy.

District Office: Hempstead, 516-489-7066.

Committees: *Education & the Workforce* (12th of 22 D): Education Reform; Employer-Employee Relations.

Group Ratings

	ADA	ACLU	AFS	LCV	CON	ITIC	NTU	COC	ACU	NTLC	CHC
2000	65	69	71	86	2	83	37	65	24	33	21
1999	90	—	100	81	19	—	17	44	8	—	—

National Journal Ratings

	1999 LIB —	1999 CONS	2000 LIB —	2000 CONS
Economic	61%	38%	57%	42%
Social	70%	30%	74%	24%
Foreign	71%	27%	60%	39%

Key Votes of the 106th Congress

1. Patient Bill of Rights	Y	5. Bar RU-486 $ for FDA	N	9. NATO War in Serbia	Y
2. Accelerate Min. Wage	Y	6. Display 10 Commandments	N	10. Perm. Trade with China	N
3. Strike Ban on Ergo. Stnd.	Y	7. Gun Show Bkgrnd. Checks	Y	11. Debt Relief for 3rd World	Y
4. Ovrd. Estate Tax Veto	Y	8. Ban Part.-Birth Abortion	N	12. Drop Cuba Econ. Embargo	Y

Election Results

2000 general	Carolyn McCarthy (D-Ind-WF)	136,703	(61%)	($1,923,299)
	Gregory R. Becker (R-C-RTL)	87,830	(39%)	($269,062)
	Others	1,222	(1%)	
2000 primary	Carolyn McCarthy (D)	unopposed		
1998 general	Carolyn McCarthy (D-Ind)	90,256	(53%)	($896,128)
	Gregory R. Becker (R-C-RTL)	79,984	(47%)	($298,760)
	Others	1,343	(1%)	

FIFTH DISTRICT

The North Shore of Long Island is "Gatsby country," where peninsulas jutting out into the Sound are covered with vast green lawns leading to the mansions of America's great capitalists. Nineteenth Century millionaires commuted by steam yacht from Manhattan to their estates in what now are Queens and Nassau County. In the early 20th Century the richest people in business and entertainment spent their leisure time here, playing croquet while their servants unloaded bootleggers' boats at their private docks during Prohibition. Inland, behind the expansive lawns, Long Island was still farm country, with little villages clustered at railroad stations, occasional colonial era houses, and acres of billboard-strewn wasteland on the highways to New York City. But The City grew out. Affluent neighborhoods developed in Douglaston and Bayside on the water, just beyond the middle-class Flushing area of Queens inland. The Great Neck peninsula became a very affluent, mostly Jewish suburb. Farther out, on Sands Point and Oyster Bay, old estates alternated with more modest homes, originally built for servants, and newer subdivision mansions. Further east, in Suffolk County, affluent subdivisions grew up on hilly land above the bays and points.

The 5th Congressional District ties together a disparate collection of New York City neighborhoods and suburbs on or within a few miles of the North Shore. At several points the district is connected across open water, and any candidate promising to walk the district had better be a good swimmer. About one-third of its votes are cast in Suffolk County, where the political leanings are conservative on cultural and economic issues. In the middle, with about one-quarter of the votes, are the North Shore communities of Nassau: the Jewish areas Democratic and liberal, the WASPy areas Republican but also culturally liberal. Roughly half the district's population and about 40% of its voters are in the borough of Queens. Here along the Sound are the affluent double-house Bayside neighborhood, and higher-income Douglaston and Little Neck, next to the Nassau border—all Republican territory. A few blocks inland is Flushing, an old Dutch settlement from the 17th Century, with the Queens numbered-street grid superimposed on old Dutch trails. Once heavily Jewish, this is the cultural and business heart of Queens and has become one of the biggest Chinese (mostly Taiwanese) communities in the country, where business people may venture from Kennedy airport without setting foot in Manhattan; the new Flushing branch of the Queens library is the busiest branch of the nation's busiest city library system. The 5th also goes south almost to the Long Island Expressway, to pleasant homeowner neighborhoods like Fresh Meadows and Oakland Gardens. But even here, far from Manhattan and in relatively affluent areas, there are plenty of high-rises.

The congressman from the 5th District is Gary Ackerman, a Democrat first elected in a March 1983 special election. Ackerman grew up in Flushing, taught junior high school, ran an advertising agency, started the weekly *Queens Tribune* in 1970 and sold it to publisher Jerry Finkelstein in 1978. That same year he was elected to the New York Senate, where Democrats seem permanently in the minority. He won his seat in the House, from a district centered in the heavily Jewish apartment complexes in central Queens. Ackerman is a colorful character, who always wears a white carnation and lives on a houseboat in Washington (the *Unsinkable II*, successor to the *Unsinkable I*, which sunk); he hosts an annual "Taste of New York" fundraiser, featuring pastrami sandwiches and stuffed cabbage, with waiters imported from New York. Acerbic but humorous, he is a pungent speaker, with a humor that makes even opponents smile. On recent roll calls for speaker, Ackerman has been second in alphabetical order after Neil Abercrombie of Hawaii; after both voted for Dick Gephardt, he has yelled, "Close the roll!" During the impeachment inquiry debate, frustrated by time limits, he rose and said, "I move that when the House adjourn, we do so to Salem, a quaint village in the Commonwealth of Massachusetts whose history beckons us thence."

Ackerman has a solidly liberal voting record and a penchant for taking on worthy but neglected causes. He has been active on the International Relations Committee, devoting much attention to rescuing Ethiopian Jews and relieving government-caused famines in Ethiopia and Sudan. As chairman of the Asia and the Pacific Subcommittee, he was one of the first Americans to meet with North Korean dictator Kim Il Sung. As chairman of the congressional India Caucus, he has encouraged the growing interest and support for that nation. He led a congressional letter-writing criticism of Burger King for removing its franchise from an Israeli settlement, under threat of an Arab boycott. On AIDS issues he joined with Oklahoma Republican Tom Coburn ("one of the leaders of those people we used to call wackos," he said) to pass the "Baby AIDS" bill requiring HIV testing of newborns and disclosure of the results to the mother; the bill also bars insurers from terminating coverage because of AIDS test results. This measure had been opposed by Manhattan liberals, although many HIV-positive newborns can be saved if identified in time; it took some courage for Ackerman to brave the wrath of New York's left wing. He and Coburn also worked to stop the Center for Disease Control from opposing this and secured funding to assist states in AIDS testing.

Ackerman has also looked after North Shore issues. He opposed the inane postal regulation that requires Queens zip codes to be labeled only Jamaica, Long Island City, Flushing or Far Rockaway rather than the dozens of other community names or simply Queens. He opposed expansion of slots at LaGuardia airport. With Republicans, he secured a $2 million increase for the Merchant Marine Academy at Kings Point. He worked to direct disaster aid to Long Island Sound lobstermen suffering from a depleted supply.

The 1992 redistricting switched Ackerman to this less-Democratic North Shore district in which two other incumbents also lived. But both retired, and Ackerman has made this a safe district. The next redistricting poses another threat, since Ackerman has few friends in Albany and this long, thin district could easily be sliced up among its neighbors; the head of Governor George Pataki's New York City office ostentatiously moved into Great Neck in 1998. But both Nassau and Suffolk Counties have enough population for two districts, with a little more left over in each case. The district could be shifted farther into Queens, making it more Democratic; but it could put Ackerman into a primary against the 7th District's Joseph Crowley, with the winner assured of an easy general election.

Cook's Call *Safe*. Although he had a couple of tight races in the early 1990s when his district was heavily altered, he has made it into a safe seat. Of course, redistricting could alter this seat again in 2002. With the state losing two seats in redistricting, just about every member of the state delegation will feel the impact.

THE PEOPLE: Pop. 2000: 615,731; Pop. 1990: 581,073, up 6% 1990–2000. 72.2% White, 3.5% Black, 18.7% Asian, 0.1% Amer. Indian, 2.5% Two+ races, 3% Other; 9.2% Hispanic Origin.

2000 Presidential Vote		
Gore (D)	148,740	(62%)
Bush (R)	83,305	(35%)
Nader (Green)	6,724	(3%)
Others	1,961	(1%)

1996 Presidential Vote		
Clinton (D)	132,588	(61%)
Dole (R)	71,194	(33%)
Perot (I)	13,354	(6%)

Rep. Gary L. Ackerman (D)

Elected Mar. 1983, 9th term; b. Nov. 19, 1942, Brooklyn; home, Jamaica Estates; Queens Col., B.A. 1965; Jewish; married (Rita).

Elected Office: NY Senate, 1978–83.

Professional Career: Jr. High schl. teacher, 1966–70; Editor & publisher, *Queens Tribune*, 1970–78; Pres., advertising agcy., 1972–78.

DC Office: 2243 RHOB 20515, 202-225-2601; Fax: 202-225-1589; Web site: www.house.gov/ackerman.

District Offices: Bayside, 718-423-2154; Huntington, 631-423-2154.

Committees: *Financial Services* (9th of 32 D): Capital Markets, Insurance & Government Sponsored Enterprises; Financial Institutions & Consumer Credit. *International Relations* (3d of 23 D): East Asia & the Pacific; Middle East & South Asia (RMM).

Group Ratings

	ADA	ACLU	AFS	LCV	CON	ITIC	NTU	COC	ACU	NTLC	CHC
2000	80	86	85	86	73	79	21	41	13	13	0
1999	100	—	100	100	21	—	15	29	0	—	—

National Journal Ratings

	1999 LIB —	1999 CONS	2000 LIB —	2000 CONS
Economic	88% —	0%	89% —	10%
Social	87% —	0%	91% —	6%
Foreign	83% —	17%	72% —	27%

Key Votes of the 106th Congress

1. Patient Bill of Rights	Y	5. Bar RU-486 $ for FDA	N	9. NATO War in Serbia	Y
2. Accelerate Min. Wage	Y	6. Display 10 Commandments	N	10. Perm. Trade with China	Y
3. Strike Ban on Ergo. Stnd.	Y	7. Gun Show Bkgrnd. Checks	Y	11. Debt Relief for 3rd World	Y
4. Ovrd. Estate Tax Veto	N	8. Ban Part.-Birth Abortion	N	12. Drop Cuba Econ. Embargo	N

SIXTH DISTRICT

New York City's largest middle-class black neighborhoods are not in Harlem or Brooklyn, but in the southeast corner of Queens. Here, in block on block of frame and brick one- and two-family houses built mostly from the 1920s to the 1950s, are the neighborhoods of Springfield Gardens and Laurelton, St. Albans and Rosedale, Cambria Heights and Queens Village, near Kennedy Airport and the tidal marsh of Jamaica Bay, just west of the Nassau County line. There was a small black community in South Jamaica half a century ago, and since then many black families have bought houses and raised their families in neighborhoods on the streets fanning east from Jamaica. They fought to maintain the relatively spacious streets, relishing unrefracted light in their windows, enjoying safe schools and good neighborhood stores.

The 6th Congressional District contains all of these southeast Queens neighborhoods, plus others less affluent and orderly, in southern Queens, roughly south of the Grand Central and renamed Jackie Robinson Parkways, including half of the 11-mile Rockaway Peninsula—a ghost city across Jamaica Bay that paradoxically has remained impervious to development in a city with an acute housing shortage. It includes white ethnic Richmond Hill and Ozone Park as well as the heavily black neighborhoods in the southeast. In 2000, 53% of the people here were black, 18% Hispanic, 10% Asian and 18% non-Hispanic white. While there are pockets of poverty, the district is mostly middle-class country: in 1990, the median income was $36,200, far ahead of the $19,000 to $27,000 of New York's other black-majority districts—indeed ahead of the $30,300 of the Queens-Bronx white-majority 7th District. Economically, Jamaica has gained an $82 million shopping center and it may benefit from the opening of the long-sought AirTrain light rail taking passengers from Kennedy to Jamaica Station in eight minutes. Politically, it is heavily Democratic, though one black-majority assembly district voted for Republican Mayor Rudolph Giuliani in 1997.

The congressman from the 6th District is Gregory Meeks, a Democrat elected in February 1998 to replace 11-year incumbent Floyd Flake, who resigned to devote more time to his church. Meeks grew up in Harlem, in public housing projects. After graduating from college and law school, he moved to Far Rockaway and pursued a public sector career. He became an assistant district attorney in 1978, a staffer for the Committee on Investigations in 1984, a workmen's comp judge in 1985; after losing a race for City Council in 1991, was elected assemblyman in 1992. Like most members there, he voted along party lines; he voted to help livery cab drivers and against Megan's law, and worked to clean up the Dubos Point Wildlife Sanctuary in Arverne. He became an ally of Flake, an extraordinary minister who built his Allen A.M.E. Church from 1,400 members in 1976 to 11,000 in 1998, built community schools and hundreds of housing units and encouraged private sector investment in the community. Flake dissented from most of his fellow Democrats by backing school choice for central city students and said of his party, "much of our leadership is still mired in the rhetoric of the 1960s and 1970s." Flake supported Giuliani for mayor in 1997 and Senator Alfonse D'Amato in 1998.

Flake supported Meeks to succeed him, though the initial favorite was state Senator Alton Waldon, who lost to Flake in the 1986 Democratic primary. At the January 1998 endorsement meetings Meeks won a bare majority of committeemen and was the Democratic nominee. Waldon ran on the Conservative and Independence lines, and spent $100,000; Assemblywoman Barbara Clark ran an independent candidacy; Republicans had a candidate as well. But Meeks had support not only from Flake but from City Comptroller Alan Hevesi, Congressman Charles Rangel, Al Sharpton and Jesse Jackson. Meeks won with 57%, to 21% for Waldon, 13% for Clark, and 9% for Republican Celestine Miller.

On winning Meeks said, "My role, as a part of a new generation of African-American leadership, is to take us to the new phase of the civil rights movement, that is, the economic development of our community." He got Flake's seat on the Banking Committee and developed a solidly liberal voting record. He was elected to a full term without opposition in November 1998. Soon, Meeks became a player. As one of the final undecideds on Permanent Normal Trade Relations to China, he was lobbied furiously by both sides. Various factors finally convinced him to support the deal: vigorous lobbying by Rangel and Bill Clinton, by United Parcel Service, a major employer at Kennedy airport, a White House-sponsored trip to China where he met with senior officials and saw first-hand the economic growth, plus a last-minute agreement by the White House and Speaker Dennis Hastert to extend tax breaks and public investment to distressed urban and rural areas.

For the 107th Congress, Meeks was selected as whip for the Congressional Black Caucus. He was again reelected without opposition, and will not likely have major redistricting changes.

Cook's Call *Safe.* Meeks will never have a problem winning a general election in this district that Gore won by 77%. His district will need to contract slightly (by about 10,000 residents), but Meeks is a sure bet here in 2002.

THE PEOPLE: Pop. 2000: 664,941; Pop. 1990: 581,812, up 14.3% 1990–2000. 18% White, 52.5% Black, 9.9% Asian, 0.7% Amer. Indian, 0.1% Hawaiian, 8.1% Two+ races, 10.6% Other; 18.1% Hispanic Origin.

2000 Presidential Vote			1996 Presidential Vote		
Gore (D)	148,658	(88%)	Clinton (D)	128,166	(86%)
Bush (R)	18,258	(11%)	Dole (R)	15,960	(11%)
Nader (Green)	2,086	(1%)	Perot (I)	4,381	(3%)

Rep. Gregory Meeks (D)

Elected Feb. 1998, 2d term; b. Sept. 25, 1953, Harlem; home, Far Rockaway; Adelphi U., B.A., 1975, Howard U., J.D., 1978; Baptist; married (Simone-Marie).

Elected Office: NY Assembly, 1992–98.

Professional Career: Asst. Dist. Atty., Queens Co., NY, 1978–84; NY St. Comm. of Investigations, 1984–85; Judge, NY St. Workers Compensation Bd., 1985–92.

DC Office: 1710 LHOB 20515, 202-225-3461; Fax: 202-226-4169; Web site: www.house.gov/meeks.

District Offices: Far Rockaway, 718-327-9791; St. Albans, 718-949-5600.

Committees: *Financial Services* (16th of 32 D): Capital Markets, Insurance & Government Sponsored Enterprises (Vice Chmn.); Domestic Monetary Policy, Technology & Economic Growth; Financial Institutions & Consumer Credit. *International Relations* (15th of 23 D): Africa; East Asia & the Pacific.

Group Ratings

	ADA	ACLU	AFS	LCV	CON	ITIC	NTU	COC	ACU	NTLC	CHC
2000	95	85	85	93	40	63	26	50	8	12	0
1999	95	—	100	81	35	—	21	29	0	—	—

National Journal Ratings

	1999 LIB	—	1999 CONS		2000 LIB	—	2000 CONS
Economic	84%	—	12%		81%	—	16%
Social	87%	—	0%		84%	—	16%
Foreign	95%	—	0%		96%	—	3%

Key Votes of the 106th Congress

1. Patient Bill of Rights	Y	5. Bar RU-486 $ for FDA	N	9. NATO War in Serbia	Y
2. Accelerate Min. Wage	Y	6. Display 10 Commandments	N	10. Perm. Trade with China	Y
3. Strike Ban on Ergo. Stnd.	Y	7. Gun Show Bkgrnd. Checks	Y	11. Debt Relief for 3rd World	Y
4. Ovrd. Estate Tax Veto	N	8. Ban Part.-Birth Abortion	N	12. Drop Cuba Econ. Embargo	Y

SEVENTH DISTRICT

The borough of Queens, home of Shea Stadium and Forest Hills Stadium, site of the 1939 and 1964 World's Fairs, the home base of national politicians Mario Cuomo and Geraldine Ferraro, doesn't get much attention or respect, even though this 2.2 million-person borough on its own would be the nation's fourth-largest city. But Queens does not have a well-known history. It started as nondescript farmland in the 17th Century, with villages growing quickly into urban nodes as the subways reached the borough. It has no obvious center, unlike downtown Brooklyn or the Grand Concourse in the Bronx. Even Queens Boulevard is just another arterial street, starting in the industrial mishmash around the Queensborough Bridge (usually referred to by its Manhattan name, 59th Street) and ending near the unimpressive brick Borough Hall, near the Grand Central Parkway overpass, across from a chain drug store.

Yet Queens is still growing with great vitality around dozens of small hubs, not from a central point outward or directly from Manhattan. More than any other area of New York City, this is a borough of neighborhoods and of immigrants. It has high-income enclaves, like the old Tudor-mansioned Forest Hills. It has old ethnic communities, like Irish Sunnyside and College Point and German Ridgewood. Astoria, on the tip of Queens near the Triborough Bridge, is Greek-American and effervescently prosperous. Flushing, once mostly Jewish, is now heavily Chinese, the terminus of the Number 7 subway line known as the Orient Express—the subway line Atlanta Brave John Rocker didn't want to ride. Indian and Pakistani immigrants own stores and restaurants, Koreans own fruit stands, Colombians and Irish and Dominicans shop in the bustling streets of Jackson Heights and Corona. Sixty years ago the small frame houses and stolid brick apartments of Queens neighborhoods adjacent to subway lines were the homes of the immigrant wave of the early 20th Century; now they are the home of early 21st Century immigrants. The 2000 Census revealed that, with its overall 11% population increase, the county had grown to 25% Hispanic, 20% Black and 18% Asian, but had dropped to less than one-third non-Hispanic white. New York's high taxes, its burdensome regulations, its housing shortage created by rent control, all impose burdens on its immigrants that were not borne by their predecessors. Woodside may be the pro-totypical neighborhood: one-fifth of a square mile along Queens Boulevard, its residents come from 49 nations and speak 34 languages; formerly "Irishtown," few children of its new wave of immigrants live in a English-speaking home. But with the aid of public schools, by no means all of which are hopeless, and the entrepreneurial-minded Queens Library with its dozens of branches, they are learning to be successful Americans, not fenced-off "multicultural" groups dependent on government for quotas and welfare.

The 7th Congressional District, loosely connected by narrow corridors, is a collection of Queens neighborhoods plus, over the Bronx-Whitestone Bridge, a salient of land running deep into the Bronx. Major landmarks include the Queensborough Bridge, habitually-delayed and comparatively tiny LaGuardia Airport, Flushing Meadow, site of the still-remembered Trylon and Perisphere rising over the 1939 World's Fair and of Shea Stadium, the graceful Bronx-Whitestone Bridge and the giant Parkchester apartment complex and Yeshiva University in the Bronx. Fifty years ago most residents of Queens referred to Manhattan as "The City," and voted Republican, against the masters of Tammany Hall. Today, many still call Manhattan "The City" and, though they vote heavily Democratic in national elections, also gave solid margins to Republican Mayor Rudolph Giuliani.

The congressman from the 7th District is Joseph Crowley, a Democrat elected in 1998 and effectively chosen by one man, his predecessor Tom Manton, who is head of the Queens County Democratic Party. Crowley grew up in Woodside, where his family was involved in politics; his uncle Walter Crowley was elected to succeed Manton on the council in 1984. When Walter Crowley died in 1985, Crowley wanted to succeed him, though he was only 23; Manton chose his chief of staff, Walter McCaffrey, instead. In 1986 Assemblyman Ralph Goldstein from Elmhurst died; Crowley ran and, with support from Manton, won at 24, fresh from Queens College. He chaired the Racing and Waging Committee, working to revive harness racing and to get the city's Off-track Betting Corporation to make a profit (only the New York public sector could produce a bookie that loses money). Crowley was interested in Irish affairs and sponsored the law that requires public school students to be taught about the Irish potato famine. He supported legalized casino gambling and higher police pay; he opposed abortion. He played guitar and sang tenor with the Budget Blues Boys, a group of assemblymen who performed on cold Albany nights.

Crowley's elevation to Congress came suddenly. In 1998, Manton filed for re-election by the July 16 filing deadline. Then at 11 a.m. on July 21, he convened a meeting of Queens Democratic committeemen, announced he was retiring and got them to vote in Crowley as the Democratic nominee. Other potential candidates were not notified ahead of time and were naturally miffed, but quickly accepted the reality. Manton was unapologetic: "After 29 years of service, I have the right to decide when I'm going to leave." He argued that Crowley, at 36, was in a good position to accumulate seniority and power in Washington. Crowley was plainly delighted: "What you're hearing is not so much about the process, but sour grapes. What happened here is simply that I was offered an ice cream cone, and I took it." His Republican opponent had no money and no chance. Crowley won in November 69%–26%.

Once elected, Crowley demonstrated his legislative experience. He served six months as the freshman Democrats' class president, which gave him entre to party leadership circles. Despite his opposition to abortion, he worked to restore $25 million in family planning funds for the United Nations. He unsuccessfully fought to preserve "slot" limits at LaGuardia but the FAA subsequently reimposed limits. The funds he brought home included $30 million to reduce aircraft noise in neighborhoods surrounding LaGuardia and Kennedy airports, plus $10 million for New York City's Housing Opportunities for People with AIDS. He sought to ban gun sales on the Internet. Following up on an initiative by Bill Clinton, he called for doubling to $2 billion U.S. support for global health initiatives. He worked with Republican Tom Coburn to pass an amendment to allow the reimportation of cheaper pharmaceutical drugs from outside the nation's borders. Recounting his crowded local schools, he was a leader in Democrats' efforts to increase funding for school construction. When George W. Bush visited Bob Jones University during the Republican primary, Crowley filed a resolution condemning the school's anti-Catholic beliefs. But he caused grumbling within the local delegation when he rushed to take credit for House approval of $10 million for Long Island Rail Road's East Side Access project.

The circumstances of his 1998 election created threats to Crowley's tenure. Several Queens Democrats threatened to challenge him in the 2000 primary. But City Councilman Walter McCaffrey, the only one to actually file, withdrew in July at the prompting of party leaders after disclosures that he had spent campaign money for personal expenses, including car service. Crowley again defeated a token Republican opponent. But redistricting looms as a major problem— not least because Manton, who remains Crowley's patron, was part of a group of politicians who unsuccessfully tried to oust Assembly Speaker Sheldon Silver. New York lost two House seats in the 2000 election, and it is generally agreed that one of them will be a Democratic seat in New York City. The convoluted 7th District is an obvious candidate for extinction. But Crowley could survive. One possibility is that he will be put in a district with 5th District Democrat Gary Ackerman, a district that will likely extend much farther into Queens than the current 5th.

Cook's Call *Potentially Competitive.* Crowley's only threat in this heavily Democratic district comes from redistricting. With the state slated to lose two seats in the redistricting process, talk has been of dismantling one seat upstate and one seat in New York City. Crowley's Queens-based seat was mentioned as the most likely to go in the city. But with census figures showing that the city significantly outpaced upstate in population growth, there has been a new call from New York City members to take both seats from upstate. In fact, this district is actually the most populated in the state and needs to shed about 30,000 people in redistricting.

THE PEOPLE: Pop. 2000: 684,573; Pop. 1990: 580,116, up 18% 1990–2000. 51% White, 9% Black, 16.8% Asian, 0.6% Amer. Indian, 0.1% Hawaiian, 6% Two+ races, 16.6% Other; 39.1% Hispanic Origin.

2000 Presidential Vote

Gore (D) 104,297 (71%)
Bush (R) 37,255 (25%)
Nader (Green) 4,141 (3%)
Others 1,003 (1%)

1996 Presidential Vote

Clinton (D) 94,661 (70%)
Dole (R) 33,352 (25%)
Perot (I) 6,601 (5%)

Rep. Joseph Crowley (D)

Elected 1998, 2d term; b. Mar. 16, 1962, Elmhurst, NY; home, Elmhurst; C.U.N.Y. Queens College, B.A. 1985; Catholic; married (Kasey).

Elected Office: NY Assembly, 1986–98.

DC Office: 312 CHOB 20515, 202-225-3965; Fax: 202-225-1909; Web site: www.house.gov/crowley.

District Offices: Bronx, 718-931-1400; Jackson Heights, 718-779-1400.

Committees: *Financial Services* (29th of 32 D): Capital Markets, Insurance & Government Sponsored Enterprises; Financial Institutions & Consumer Credit; Oversight & Investigations. *International Relations* (17th of 23 D): Europe; Middle East & South Asia.

Group Ratings

	ADA	ACLU	AFS	LCV	CON	ITIC	NTU	COC	ACU	NTLC	CHC
2000	85	57	100	93	54	65	21	38	20	12	20
1999	95	—	100	100	79	—	14	32	8	—	—

National Journal Ratings

	1999 LIB	—	1999 CONS		2000 LIB	—	2000 CONS
Economic	78%	—	21%		74%	—	26%
Social	61%	—	38%		63%	—	37%
Foreign	85%	—	12%		62%	—	37%

Key Votes of the 106th Congress

1. Patient Bill of Rights	Y	5. Bar RU-486 $ for FDA	Y	9. NATO War in Serbia	Y
2. Accelerate Min. Wage	Y	6. Display 10 Commandments	N	10. Perm. Trade with China	N
3. Strike Ban on Ergo. Stnd.	Y	7. Gun Show Bkgrnd. Checks	Y	11. Debt Relief for 3rd World	Y
4. Ovrd. Estate Tax Veto	N	8. Ban Part.-Birth Abortion	Y	12. Drop Cuba Econ. Embargo	N

Election Results

2000 general	Joseph Crowley (D)	78,207	(72%)	($657,359)
	Rose Robles Birtley (R)	24,592	(23%)	($20,776)
	Others	6,302	(6%)	
2000 primary	Joseph Crowley (D)	unopposed		
1998 general	Joseph Crowley (D)	50,924	(69%)	($99,776)
	James J. Dillon (R)	18,896	(26%)	
	Richard Retcho (C)	3,960	(5%)	

EIGHTH DISTRICT

For the last 200 years, New York has been a heavily Jewish city. New York's Dutch founders came from the European country most tolerant of Jews, and so Jews settled in Nieuw Amsterdam as they had in old. German Jews came in large numbers in the 19th Century, some insisting they were more German than they were Jewish; some founded great merchant banking dynasties and started great retail and clothing businesses. Around 1890, Ashkenazi Jews from Eastern Europe started coming from what were then the Romanov and Hapsburg empires—now Poland, Lithuania, Belarus, Ukraine, Hungary and Romania. Then, after being persecuted in the years after

World War I, as many as 400,000 Jews came past the Statue of Liberty to Ellis Island every year in the early 1920s, until a 1924 law virtually shut down immigration. Had a malapportioned, rural-dominated, nativist Congress not done that, perhaps two million of the six million who perished in the Holocaust would instead have become Americans.

Ashkenazi Jews initially lived on the Lower East Side but moved out to Brooklyn and the Bronx almost as soon as the subways were built. Their children moved up faster than any new group in memorable history, rising despite prejudice to the top of almost every profession that would let them in. They invented new businesses from the rag trade to show biz: second-caste people from third-rate countries almost immediately becoming elite in the world's foremost country. Their descendants live all over the country, but New York remains America's most heavily Jewish city and has the largest Jewish population of any city in the world.

While there are no reliable figures, as the Census does not record religion, the 8th Congressional District of New York may be the most heavily Jewish district in the nation. About three-fifths of its population is in Manhattan, two-fifths in Brooklyn. Bizarre boundaries cordon off blacks and Hispanics in nearby majority-minority districts. One big voting area is the Upper West Side from 59th Street north to Morningside Heights and Columbia University: the venerable apartments along Central Park West and West End Avenue and Riverside Drive, and the brownstones on the cross streets which house some of America's most idealistic and dedicated liberal-to-radical voters. These professional people include the wealthy, as well as the struggling who enjoy the grittiness of the Upper West Side, the almost European atmosphere of boulevarded upper Broadway, and the fierce struggle that is daily life in New York. People on the West Side took up the reform issue in the 1950s and eventually eviscerated the old Tammany Hall Democratic machine; in the 1960s they took up the struggle against the Vietnam war and helped oust a Democratic administration. By the 1980s their dominant cause was feminism, from the preservation of abortion rights against any erosion to the eradication of gender-incorrect speech. Another big voting area is Greenwich Village, America's original Bohemia in the 1910s, now a neighborhood of expensive apartments and houses interlaced with much cheaper dwellings, and long New York's most conspicuous gay community. Politically the Village has long had a taste for what it regards as radical. Then there are new Village-type residential areas to the south: SoHo, where old factory buildings have been refurbished as lofts; TriBeCa, where commercial space now houses artists; Battery Park City, the attractive modern apartments built on a landfill west of the now-crumbled West Side Highway; Chelsea, just north of 14th Street, which may be replacing the Village as New York's most vibrant gay neighborhood. After many years of decline, Manhattan's population rose in the 1990s, briskly in some of these neighborhoods—though it is still far below its peak in 1910, when the subways were starting to siphon people to the outer boroughs.

The 8th District includes two Brooklyn neighborhoods: Brighton Beach and Coney Island, with the largest concentration of Russian Jewish immigrants in New York; and Borough Park, with many culturally conservative Orthodox and Hasidic Jews, some living close to poverty. While they are connected to the heavily Jewish Manhattan neighborhoods by a narrow land bridge running along the Brooklyn waterfront and the massive Bush Terminal buildings, these areas are politically very different. The Russians favor free enterprise and are anti-socialist. Borough Park is hostile to racial preferences and favors tough police treatment of crime. Overall this is a very solidly Democratic district.

The congressman from the 8th District is Jerrold Nadler, a West Side liberal Democrat elected in 1992. He was born in Brooklyn and moved around; his father was a chicken farmer in New Jersey, ran a gas station on Long Island and owned a traveling auto parts store. At Stuyvesant High School in Manhattan he met Richard Gottfried (elected to the Assembly in 1970 at 23 and still there) and Dick Morris (pollster for Bill Clinton among others); they helped Nadler get elected student body president. At Columbia he roomed with Morris; they campaigned for Eugene McCarthy and were there during the 1968 campus riots. He worked as a legislative staffer and ran for the Assembly in 1976, at 29; in the primary he beat Ruth Messinger (Democratic nominee for mayor in 1997) by 73 votes. In the Assembly he was known as an expert on mass transit and advocate of rail freight into New York City.

In 1992 he was suddenly presented with the opportunity to run for Congress. Two incumbents were based in the new 8th District. Stephen Solarz of Brooklyn, a lead backer of the Gulf war resolution, shied away from running in leftish Manhattan and ran and lost in the Hispanic-majority 12th District. That left the 8th to Manhattan's Ted Weiss, long an Upper West Side icon. But he died the day before the September primary (which he won anyway). The nomination was decided by a convention of almost 1,000 county Democratic committee members, many of them involved in acerbic ideological and personal squabbles for decades. The key vote was procedural, for a system of weighted voting under which Nadler won 62% of the votes and Councilwoman Ronnie Eldridge 21%; opponents decried this system (after they lost), perhaps with reason. Nadler became the Democratic nominee and thus congressman. He has not been seriously challenged since.

Nadler's voting record has been among the most liberal in the House. Over the opposition of John Dingell, he pushed to passage the "Nadler rule" which restricted ranking members on full committees from taking any ranking subcommittee posts on their panels as well. He has opposed bankruptcy reform, saying the bill's tighter restrictions were "a wishlist of every big-money special interest group." He fought developer Donald Trump's attempts to alter the West Side Highway to accommodate his luxury housing projects; though the highway's fate remained up in the air, Trump won construction of a huge development on old rail yards between 59th and 72nd Streets. (In a book, Trump termed Nadler "one of the most egregious hacks in contemporary politics.") Although his district includes Wall Street, he strongly opposes individual investment accounts in Social Security. He fought to get more rail competition east of the Hudson as Conrail was being carved up by CSX and the Norfolk Southern, and worked to save Amtrak.

His greatest project is a rail-freight tunnel under the Hudson, from the 65th Street rail yard in Bay Ridge to little-used rail yards in either Bayonne, New Jersey or Staten Island. Lack of a rail-freight line means that New York gets only about 3% of its freight by rail, compared to 30% in the average large city; cheaper freight could help rebuild small manufacturing in New York and could revive the Brooklyn docks, which were abandoned by Governor Nelson Rockefeller in the 1960s when vessels began the switch to container cargo. The cost would be huge—perhaps more than $2 billion—but it could provide the manufacturing jobs New York has thoughtlessly cast away and a way upward for the city's economy and its hundreds of thousands of new immigrants. Nadler's proposal was ridiculed for years. But he persisted. In 1997 Mayor Rudolph Giuliani endorsed it, and others have come to appreciate it as well; if it is ever built, it would be an impressive monument for a career. The two also have sought to develop the waterfront. In one of Bill Clinton's final actions as president in January 2001, he embraced one of Nadler's pet projects with an executive order designating two fortresses on Governor's Island in New York harbor as national monuments, which could lead to return of the centuries-old military base to New York State

Nadler achieved more prominence during the impeachment hearings in late 1998. He was one of several Judiciary members who peppered Republicans with questions, objections, high-minded arguments and low-minded ridicule in what Nadler called a "partisan coup d'etat." Nadler seemed to take delight in interjecting comments, and perhaps irritating Chairman Henry Hyde; but he showed a fine mind, a quick wit, and an ability to make strong arguments. Nadler argued that Clinton didn't commit perjury or obstruct justice, and that even if he had, those offenses would not be impeachable. He was cheered and feted in Manhattan as never before. His verdict: "It would have been better for the country if this whole thing hadn't happened. But if it had to happen, I'm glad I was on the Judiciary Committee. After all, the reason I got into public life was to be at the center of important things." But as Clinton left office, Nadler lamented, "I'm angry at the President for giving the Republicans a target in all this."

In the 107th Congress, Nadler became ranking Democrat on the Constitution Subcommittee, which has become an ideological battleground especially as Republicans advocate constitutional amendments to overturn court rulings. He also has been a leading foe of abortion restrictions, including legislation designed to protect the human fetus. Nadler was among the handful of congressional Democrats to support Bill Bradley in the 2000 primaries, objecting to Al Gore's mixed record on abortion, among other things. He has been re-elected without difficulty. Although redistricting poses a threat and drawing a similar Manhattan-Brooklyn district poses a challenge, he has retained good connections in Albany and likely will survive.

Cook's Call *Safe.* Nadler will never be targeted in this heavily Democratic, very liberal district. But, it has not grown as quickly as others in the state and needs to expand and pick up almost 40,000 new people in redistricting.

THE PEOPLE: Pop. 2000: 618,987; Pop. 1990: 581,453, up 6.5% 1990–2000. 75.2% White, 6.5% Black, 10.4% Asian, 0.2% Amer. Indian, 0.1% Hawaiian, 3.2% Two+ races, 4.5% Other; 11.5% Hispanic Origin.

2000 Presidential Vote		
Gore (D)	170,136	(77%)
Bush (R)	37,600	(17%)
Nader (Green)	12,996	(6%)
Others	1,256	(1%)

1996 Presidential Vote		
Clinton (D)	147,864	(81%)
Dole (R)	30,141	(16%)
Perot (I)	5,142	(3%)

Rep. Jerrold Nadler (D)

Elected 1992, 5th term; b. June 13, 1947, Brooklyn; home, Manhattan; Columbia U., B.A. 1970, Fordham U., J.D. 1978; Jewish; married (Joyce Miller).

Elected Office: NY Assembly, 1976–92.

Professional Career: Legis. Asst., NY Assembly, 1972; Law Clerk, 1976.

DC Office: 2334 RHOB 20515, 202-225-5635; Fax: 202-225-6923; Web site: www.house.gov/nadler.

District Offices: Brooklyn, 718-373-3198; Manhattan, 212-367-7350.

Committees: *Judiciary* (5th of 17 D): Commercial & Administrative Law; The Constitution (RMM). *Transportation & Infrastructure* (9th of 34 D): Highways & Transit; Railroads.

Group Ratings

	ADA	ACLU	AFS	LCV	CON	ITIC	NTU	COC	ACU	NTLC	CHC
2000	95	86	100	93	58	47	28	28	4	12	0
1999	100	—	100	100	66	—	26	12	0	—	—

National Journal Ratings

	1999 LIB —	1999 CONS	2000 LIB —	2000 CONS
Economic	88% —	0%	81% —	16%
Social	87% —	0%	91% —	6%
Foreign	93% —	5%	97% —	0%

Key Votes of the 106th Congress

1. Patient Bill of Rights	Y	5. Bar RU-486 $ for FDA	N	9. NATO War in Serbia	Y
2. Accelerate Min. Wage	Y	6. Display 10 Commandments	N	10. Perm. Trade with China	N
3. Strike Ban on Ergo. Stnd.	Y	7. Gun Show Bkgrnd. Checks	Y	11. Debt Relief for 3rd World	Y
4. Ovrd. Estate Tax Veto	N	8. Ban Part.-Birth Abortion	N	12. Drop Cuba Econ. Embargo	Y

Election Results

2000 general	Jerrold Nadler (D-L-WF)	150,273	(81%)	($484,835)
	Marian S. Henry (R)	27,057	(15%)	
	Others	7,639	(4%)	
2000 primary	Jerrold Nadler (D)	unopposed		
1998 general	Jerrold Nadler (D-L)	112,948	(86%)	($336,133)
	Theodore Howard (R)	18,383	(14%)	

NINTH DISTRICT

Brooklyn. The single word used to arouse laughter in a comedian's monologue, applause when someone said that's where they were from. It evoked an accent that twisted the English language almost to non-recognition, a raucous and brusque confrontational style, a sense of humor with an edge, the chip-on-the-shoulder assertiveness of those sure they will always be in second place. Brooklyn would never be more important than Manhattan; the Dodgers would always lose the world series to the Yankees or the pennant to the Giants, and when they finally did win, in 1955, they moved to Los Angeles two years later. Brooklyn, as its Dutch name testifies, was a separate community from the 17th Century on, one of the largest cities in the country in the 19th Century, with its own celebrities (Henry Ward Beecher, Walt Whitman, John Roebling). By 1898, when the five boroughs were welded into Greater New York, one million people lived in Brooklyn, but the Brooklyn of the comedians really came into being as the subways were built in the early 20th Century. Suddenly workers in all the little Manhattan factories no longer had to live in Lower East Side tenements. They moved out the subway lines, into neighborhoods of three- to five-story apartments and four-family houses. Brooklyn grew from 1.1 million in 1900 to 1.6 million in 1910 to 2 million in 1920 and 2.6 million in 1930. The old Brooklynites were mostly Protestant—Dutch, Yankee, German—plus some Catholic Irish. The new Brooklynites were heavily Italian and Jewish, and peopled the sports and entertainment businesses for a long generation, making their home town and its impenetrable accent nationally famous. In 1940, as the nation was about to go to war, Brooklyn had 2.7 million people: one of every 49 Americans lived in this one borough.

Today, 2.46 million people—one of every 114 Americans—live in Brooklyn, and it is no longer a staple of national comedy. Some of its old neighborhoods—Jewish Brownsville, Italian East New York—have been ravaged by crime and stand empty and toothless. But there is great vitality in much of Brooklyn, among upwardly mobile Hispanic, Asian, Russian and Jewish immigrants and a hard-working black middle class, and in neighborhoods of the grandchildren of earlier Jews and Italians. The farther reaches of Ocean Parkway and the expanse of Flatlands and Canarsie, the quiet corners of Sheepshead Bay and Gerritsen are such places. Here young Orthodox Jews raise families within walking distance of school, and neighbors patrol the streets at night to keep down the crime that has wrecked neighborhoods just a few miles away.

The 9th Congressional District includes many such neighborhoods in Brooklyn and in the borough of Queens as well. Its geography is grotesque, its demography more comprehensible. This is where descendants of the 1890–1924 migrants live. In Brooklyn it extends from Prospect Park south along Ocean Parkway to Coney Island and Sheepshead Bay: still one of the most Jewish areas in the United States. It extends east over Flatlands and much of Canarsie and then across Jamaica Bay south to the Rockaway Peninsula and north to a collection of Queens neighborhoods: Howard Beach, next to Kennedy Airport; the old German neighborhoods of Glendale and Ridgewood, still orderly and spotlessly clean; Italian Woodhaven and Tudor-trimmed Forest Hills; much of the heavily Jewish high-rise area along Queens Boulevard. After the 1997 redistricting, the Queens portion was enlarged and the Brooklyn portion reduced, and the vote is now almost evenly balanced between the two. This remains a solidly Democratic district, though there are significant Republican neighborhoods in Queens and some Orthodox neighborhoods are very conservative.

The congressman from the 9th District is Anthony Weiner, a Democrat elected in 1998. Weiner grew up in Brooklyn, went to a SUNY college upstate, then returned to work in the House for the energetic Charles Schumer. In 1991 Weiner was elected to the City Council, at 27, the youngest member ever. There he worked on issues from airport regulations to fire alarm boxes and the Fire Department-EMS merger. On consumer affairs, he investigated abuses in modeling agencies and dating services. In 1997, as Schumer prepared to run for the Senate, Weiner began running for Congress. Naturally there was competition. Assemblywoman Melinda Katz, based in Forest Hills, ran with the support of the Queens Democratic organization, the Robert F. Kennedy Democratic Club and City Controller Alan Hevesi. Assemblyman Daniel Feldman, based in Sheepshead Bay, had the endorsement of the Brooklyn Democratic organization and Congressman Jerrold Nadler. Councilman Noach Dear, based in Borough Park, ran with the endorsement of Orthodox leaders; he raised $1.5 million and spent half of it on TV ads and much of the rest on videotapes sent out to 20,000 registered Democrats. Dear had a sharply more conservative record than the others; he is opposed to abortion, for example. Otherwise the differences were in emphasis: Weiner talked about public safety, Katz about health care, Feldman his sponsorship of Megan's law. This was mainly a battle of organizations and endorsements. In the last weeks, as he was sailing far ahead in the Senate primary, Schumer endorsed Weiner. That may have made the difference, though others thought it was his endorsement by a Canarsie club or door-to-door canvassing in the Rockaways. The September 15 primary was so close that the results weren't certified for two weeks. In a turnout of 45,000—not enormous in such a heavily Democratic district—Weiner won with 28.1%, to 27.5% for Katz, and 22% each for Dear and Feldman. Weiner won the general election easily.

In the House, Weiner styled himself a moderate on issues dealing with business and crime. He took conventional Democratic stances in fighting high credit card rates and fees on check bouncing; plus he called for the Federal Communications Commission to set minimum standards for cell-phone service. But, conceding his political risk, he was among the handful of labor-friendly House Democrats to back Permanent Normal Trade Relations with China. On the Judiciary Committee, he worked to expand federal DNA testing of crime scene evidence, and he sought better treatment for victims of sexual assault. He secured funds to revitalize the Gateway National Recreation Area and won funding for beach replenishment in the Rockaways. As befits a Schumer protege, he took credit for making more television appearances than any other House freshman.

In 2000 Noach Dear challenged Weiner in the Democratic primary. Some thought the race would be close, but Weiner carried almost every assembly district and won 74%–26%. Dear was on the Republican and Conservative lines in November; this time Weiner beat him 68%–32%. Redistricting could be a problem for Weiner. New York lost two House seats in the 2000 Census, and it is generally agreed that New York City will lose one Democratic seat. The three black-majority and the one Hispanic-majority districts in Brooklyn and Queens will surely be maintained; that means that Weiner will be competing for white areas sought by the 7th District's Joseph Crowley and the 8th District's Jerrold Nadler. Since Assembly Speaker Sheldon Silver has an animus against Crowley and is from Brooklyn himself, Weiner's odds of ending up with a secure Brooklyn-Queens district are pretty good.

Cook's Call *Safe.* Despite the consistent presence of Brooklyn Councilmember Noach Dear as a foe (he ran against Weiner in the 1998 primary, the 2000 primary, and as a Republican in the general election in 2000), Weiner has had no real trouble holding onto this heavily Democratic district. Dear, who has spent almost $2 million in his races for this seat, is said to be looking at running again in 2002. Weiner should be re-elected easily.

THE PEOPLE: Pop. 2000: 652,370; Pop. 1990: 579,876, up 12.5% 1990–2000. 70.5% White, 4.5% Black, 13.4% Asian, 0.3% Amer. Indian, 0.1% Hawaiian, 3.6% Two+ races, 7.6% Other; 17% Hispanic Origin.

2000 Presidential Vote			1996 Presidential Vote		
Gore (D)	120,475	(67%)	Clinton (D)	107,835	(67%)
Bush (R)	51,696	(29%)	Dole (R)	46,400	(29%)
Nader (Green)	5,429	(3%)	Perot (I)	7,884	(5%)
Others	1,003	(1%)			

Rep. Anthony Weiner (D)

Elected 1998, 2d term; b. Sept. 4, 1964, Brooklyn; home, Brooklyn; S.U.N.Y. Plattsburgh, B.A. 1985; Jewish; single.

Elected Office: NY City Cncl., 1991–98.

Professional Career: Aide, U.S. Rep. Charles Schumer, 1985–91.

DC Office: 222 CHOB 20515, 202-225-6616; Fax: 202-226-7253; Web site: www.house.gov/weiner.

District Offices: Brooklyn, 718-332-9001; Forest Hills, 718-261-7170; Rockaway, 718-318-9255.

Committees: *Judiciary* (15th of 17 D): Commercial & Administrative Law; Crime. *Science* (15th of 22 D): Environment, Technology and Standards; Space & Aeronautics.

Group Ratings

	ADA	ACLU	AFS	LCV	CON	ITIC	NTU	COC	ACU	NTLC	CHC
2000	85	67	85	93	26	70	27	40	8	10	7
1999	100	—	100	94	59	—	18	24	0	—	—

National Journal Ratings

	1999 LIB	—	1999 CONS		2000 LIB	—	2000 CONS
Economic	84%	—	12%		75%	—	24%
Social	77%	—	22%		79%	—	17%
Foreign	95%	—	0%		94%	—	5%

Key Votes of the 106th Congress

1. Patient Bill of Rights	Y	5. Bar RU-486 $ for FDA	N	9. NATO War in Serbia	Y
2. Accelerate Min. Wage	Y	6. Display 10 Commandments	N	10. Perm. Trade with China	Y
3. Strike Ban on Ergo. Stnd.	Y	7. Gun Show Bkgrnd. Checks	Y	11. Debt Relief for 3rd World	Y
4. Ovrd. Estate Tax Veto	N	8. Ban Part.-Birth Abortion	N	12. Drop Cuba Econ. Embargo	Y

Election Results

2000 general	Anthony Weiner (D-L)	98,983	(68%)	($510,247)
	Noach Dear (R-C)	45,649	(32%)	($1,521,320)
2000 primary	Anthony Weiner (D)	24,895	(74%)	
	Noach Dear (D)	8,847	(26%)	
1998 general	Anthony Weiner (D-Ind)	69,439	(66%)	($401,197)
	Louis Telano (R)	24,486	(23%)	($8,788)
	Melinda Katz (L)	5,698	(5%)	($741,921)
	Arthur J. Smith (C)	4,899	(5%)	

TENTH DISTRICT

Bedford, a century ago one of Brooklyn's fashionable neighborhoods, has given its name to half of what is Brooklyn's best known—and not most downtrodden—black neighborhood. If Bedford-Stuyvesant's brownstones looked bedraggled even before modern urban decay, they also remain solid and, on many streets, well-tended. The black community settled here well before World War II, but it was then one of the smaller of dozens of Brooklyn ethnic enclaves. It grew in the years after World War II as crime and crowding moved people out of Harlem, and busloads of blacks came north from the Carolinas in the 1950s and early 1960s. Sluggish job growth has meant less migration, but Brooklyn's black community, with some of New York's highest birth rates, has grown rapidly and far beyond the original bounds of Bedford-Stuyvesant.

The 10th Congressional District is centered on Bedford-Stuyvesant and is entirely contained within Brooklyn; there, regularity ends. Its irregular shape includes parts of gentrified Brooklyn Heights at the west end and extends east to Jamaica Bay, including much of East New York and Canarsie and Brownsville. The landscape varies widely, from utterly bombed-out blocks to secure and hardy blocks of rowhouses or high-rise, rent-supplemented apartments. The district was 61% black and 17% Hispanic in 2000, with some blocks of Italians and Hasidic Jews. Politically, it is overwhelmingly Democratic. In 1996 it gave Bill Clinton his third highest vote percentage in the country, 91%; Al Gore's 90% here in 2000 was one of his highest in the nation.

The congressman from the 10th is Ed Towns, elected in 1982. He is a black Democrat from East New York who is as experienced in government as in politics. Towns has been a teacher, social worker and hospital administrator, and he is active in the civic affairs of this changing community. He became widely popular as Brooklyn's deputy borough president for six years. In the House, Towns's two best known legislative initiatives are the Student Athlete Right-to-Know Act, which requires colleges to report the graduation rates of student athletes, and strengthening the National Health Service Corps and the Minority Health Initiative. On the Energy and Commerce Committee, he has been a mainstay of support for securities litigation reform, which was backed by Silicon Valley and other entrepreneurs, opposed by trial lawyers, vetoed by Clinton and passed over his veto in 1995—one of only two veto overrides in Clinton's presidency. In 1997 Towns backed uniform federal standards on such suits—another measure vigorously opposed by trial lawyers. He worked with other Democrats on legislation to bridge the "digital divide" by earmarking telephone excise taxes to telecommunications projects. Responding to a local tragedy, he sought to ban the sale of toy guns that resemble real guns and convinced local stores to end sales of certain models. He has worked on some local projects, notably a $430 million federal courthouse complex for Brooklyn.

The 107th Congress brought a reorganization of his subcommittee assignments, leaving Towns as the senior Democrat on the Commerce, Trade and Consumer Protection Subcommittee. Previously, he was top Democrat on the Finance and Hazardous Materials Subcommittee chaired by Mike Oxley; when Oxley took the securities issues from that panel to the Financial Services Committee, where he became the new chairman, Towns objected that the new panel had "no expertise" on securities and finance issues. Democrats had no voice in the jurisdictional switch.

For years Towns was re-elected without difficulty; but not in the past two elections. In 1997 he startled many longtime allies, notably Brooklyn Democratic Chairman Clarence Norman, by supporting Rudolph Giuliani for mayor. This took some courage; Giuliani got only 15% in two Bedford-Stuyvesant assembly districts, his worst showing in the city. In 1998 he worked with Assemblyman Tony Genovesi in backing judicial slates against Norman's; they lost (and Genovesi died in a car crash in August 1998). Norman moved to recruit primary opposition for Towns. He approached agitator Al Sharpton, who decided not to run. But there was opposition from Barry Ford, a Harvard-educated Wall Street lawyer and Democratic contributor. He was endorsed by leftish labor unions and Democratic clubs, by Public Advocate Mark Green and former Mayor David Dinkins. Towns' reply: "Most people who are mayor and serve their term then become statesmen. David seems to be very bitter, and that's unfortunate. I was very supportive of him when he was mayor." Towns' critics concentrated on the tobacco issue. His father was a tobacco sharecropper in North Carolina, and he opposed much anti-tobacco legislation on the ground it would hurt farmers: "Tobacco is bad. So is starvation. Both will kill you." The Campaign for Tobacco-Free Kids put up billboards reading, "Representative Towns: Big Tobacco or Kids?" Others called him "the Marlboro man" and attacked him for accepting $54,000 from tobacco interests over 10 years. "Tobacco money is not illegal. I don't see any problem," Towns said at first. Later he added, "I've gotten most of my money from the health care community. If you're talking about dollars to influence, then I would have to be called the health-care congressman." Towns was helped when Giuliani, in August 1998, approved an application for a Brooklyn empowerment zone—because of Towns, he said. Towns beat Ford, but by only 52%–36%, not impressive for a 16-year incumbent.

Emboldened by that result, Ford barely stopped campaigning for the next two years, while highlighting Towns's 1997 support for Giuliani, whose standing in the black community had suffered after highly-publicized police shootings of young blacks. This time, Ford was better known and he appeared to have a real prospect of ousting Towns. But the incumbent campaigned much harder. "I'm out here, and I'm focused," he told voters at subway stations. Towns defended his support for Giuliani by pointing to the Mayor's support for commercial development. He decided not to take campaign contributions from tobacco companies. The New York Times endorsed Ford as an "energetic" activist and criticized Towns for his "minimal" record and support for tobacco and other special interests. Towns won this time, 57%–43%; Ford raised his percentage, but so too did Towns.

Redistricting could be decisive in this district in 2002. The redistricters will surely preserve the two black-majority districts in Brooklyn, but they may change the boundaries between Towns's 10th and the 11th, where Major Owens had an even closer primary in 2000. Inside Brooklyn politics will probably determine the outcome.

Cook's Call   Safe. Like so many New York City-based Democratic members who sit in overwhelmingly Democratic districts (Gore won here with 90%), Towns' only challenge is a primary. He clearly does not take any challenge lightly: In 2000, he spent over $1 million to beat back a primary challenge from Barry Ford, who held him to 52% in 1998.

THE PEOPLE: Pop. 2000: 621,305; Pop. 1990: 581,311, up 6.9% 1990–2000. 20.7% White, 63.9% Black, 2.4% Asian, 0.4% Amer. Indian, 0.1% Hawaiian, 4% Two+ races, 8.6% Other; 17.1% Hispanic Origin.

2000 Presidential Vote

Gore (D)	154,372	(90%)
Bush (R)	11,999	(7%)
Nader (Green)	4,405	(3%)

1996 Presidential Vote

Clinton (D)	134,677	(91%)
Dole (R)	10,199	(7%)
Perot (I)	2,718	(2%)

Rep. Edolphus Towns (D)

Elected 1982, 10th term; b. July 21, 1934, Chadbourn, NC; home, Brooklyn; NC A&T, B.S. 1956, Adelphi U., M.S.W. 1973; Presbyterian; married (Gwendolyn).

Military Career: Army, 1956–58.

Professional Career: Baptist Minister; Social Worker; Prof., Medgar Evers Col.; NY public schl. teacher; Dpty. Hospital Admin., 1965–71; Brooklyn Dpty. Borough Pres., 1976–82.

DC Office: 2232 RHOB 20515, 202-225-5936; Fax: 202-225-1018; Web site: www.house.gov/towns.

District Offices: Brooklyn, 718-855-8018; Brooklyn, 718-272-1175; Brooklyn, 718-774-5682.

Committees: *Energy & Commerce* (6th of 26 D): Commerce, Trade & Consumer Protection (RMM); Environment & Hazardous Materials; Health. *Government Reform* (4th of 19 D): Energy Policy, Natural Resources and Regulatory Affairs.

Group Ratings

	ADA	ACLU	AFS	LCV	CON	ITIC	NTU	COC	ACU	NTLC	CHC
2000	95	85	100	86	44	72	24	50	4	9	0
1999	95	—	100	88	42	—	22	28	4	—	—

National Journal Ratings

	1999 LIB	—	1999 CONS		2000 LIB	—	2000 CONS
Economic	80%	—	18%		90%	—	8%
Social	82%	—	17%		94%	—	0%
Foreign	73%	—	27%		95%	—	5%

Key Votes of the 106th Congress

1. Patient Bill of Rights	Y	5. Bar RU-486 $ for FDA	N	9. NATO War in Serbia	*
2. Accelerate Min. Wage	Y	6. Display 10 Commandments	N	10. Perm. Trade with China	N
3. Strike Ban on Ergo. Stnd.	Y	7. Gun Show Bkgrnd. Checks	Y	11. Debt Relief for 3rd World	Y
4. Ovrd. Estate Tax Veto	N	8. Ban Part.-Birth Abortion	N	12. Drop Cuba Econ. Embargo	Y

Election Results

2000 general	Edolphus Towns (D-L)	120,700	(90%)	($1,187,226)
	Ernestine M. Brown (R)	6,852	(5%)	
	Barry Ford (WF)	5,530	(4%)	($281,004)
	Others	802	(1%)	
2000 primary	Edolphus Towns (D)	25,735	(57%)	
	Barry Ford (D)	19,040	(43%)	
1998 general	Edolphus Towns (D-L)	83,528	(92%)	($736,179)
	Ernestine M. Brown (R)	5,577	(6%)	
	Others	1,396	(2%)	

ELEVENTH DISTRICT

When Jackie Robinson suited up for the Brooklyn Dodgers in 1947, becoming the first black major league baseball player, the borough didn't have many blacks. Manhattan's Harlem was the center of black life and entertainment in New York, though Brooklyn's Bedford-Stuyvesant, not far from Ebbets Field, had a scattering of blacks in modest apartments. Then a subway line, built to replace the El, connected Bed-Stuy with Harlem, and inspired Duke Ellington's "Take the A Train."

In later years Harlem lost population and dozens of blocks were emptied out, their brownstone townhouses vacant or vanished. But Brooklyn's black neighborhoods have grown and to some degree have prospered. Many of New York's black families came from the South, but large numbers, particularly in Flatbush, the area south of the Hasidic Jewish outposts in Crown Heights, come from what New Yorkers call "the Islands"—Jamaica, Haiti, the Dominican Republic, Barbados, Trinidad and Tobago. Speaking deeply accented English, French, Spanish or various forms of Creole, they bring spiced bread, peanut punch, Matouk's Special Hot Calypso Sauce, reggae and calypso music. These Caribbean immigrants tend to stay in family units more often than low-income American-born blacks; they work hard, are commercially inclined and civic-minded. Coming from places where life and property are not always respected by governments, they work, like so many other immigrants to America, to build new communities.

The 11th Congressional District extends from the edge of downtown Brooklyn, across Crown Heights—the scene of violent clashes between blacks and Hasidic Jews—and centers on Flatbush; it also picks up most of Brownsville and parts of East Flatbush, the home of the Hatikva Jewish Identity Center— the surviving anti-Arab splinter group of the late Rabbi Meir Kahane, which the State Department has called a foreign terrorist group. This area had the largest concentration of Jews in America from the 1920s to the 1960s. For the 1990s it was one of the highest black percentage districts in the country, with probably as many blacks with roots in the Islands as in the American South. Like depopulated Brownsville, some neighborhoods here are in dreadful shape, while others, like much of Flatbush, seem to have considerable vitality.

The congressman from the 11th is Major Owens, a Democrat first elected in 1982, who claims to be the first librarian elected to Congress. Owens grew up in Memphis, went to Morehouse College and Atlanta University and became a librarian. He worked in the Brownsville Community Council and with the Congress of Racial Equality, and served in Mayor John Lindsay's administration from 1968–73 as commissioner of the city's Community Development Agency; critic Charles Morris called Owens "the most capable and canny" of New York's anti-poverty program directors. It was a high-pressure job with few guidelines, and Owens may have been relieved when he was elected to serve in the antique chamber of the New York Senate in 1974. When Congresswoman Shirley Chisholm, an immigrant from Barbados and presidential candidate in 1972, announced her retirement, Owens entered the primary to succeed her and beat Chisholm's choice. Until 2000, Owens had no serious electoral competition.

Owens has one of the most liberal voting records in the House. When Democrats last controlled the House, he chaired the then-Education and Labor's Subcommittee on Select Education and Civil Rights; in 2001, he became senior Democrat on the Workforce Protections subcommittee. He supported Tony Hall's resolution apologizing for slavery. "We think so much more is needed than an apology, but it's a good place to begin. We've been asking for much more for a long time." He often makes long, vigorous floor speeches after the House has finished work for the day—speaking passionately of the need to support libraries, vital institutions in immigrant communities of New York's outer boroughs. He has been outspokenly critical of the Republican majority in the House, which he said has left black lawmakers "simply shellshocked." On the Education and the Workforce Committee, he has strongly opposed the Republicans' plan to give employees the option of taking compensatory time rather than overtime pay; he opposed their school-vouchers plan as deceptive and dishonest, and said that the solution is to restore faith in public schools. He opposed increasing the number of H-1B visas for high-skill workers, saying that might take jobs from Americans. But he favored the Republicans' plan to expand stock-option programs for workers. Following the Elian Gonzalez affair, which he called "a window of opportunity for the reform of the cruel and inhuman provisions in the present immigration law," Owens responded to his community's concerns with a bill giving naturalized citizen status to an alien child on American soil who is less than 12 and without a parent and prohibiting deportation of an alien parent of an American-born child less than 18. He called for enhanced U.S. trade with Caribbean Basin nations. At the start of 2001, he was angered when Republicans moved oversight of historically black colleges to the Select Education Subcommittee.

Owens had opposition in the 2000 Democratic primary from City Councilwoman Una Clarke, his Jamaican-born former protege. Although they had long been close friends and he had helped her win the Council seat, their relationship became rancorous and she accused Owens of being ineffective and anti-immigrant. He accused Clarke—whose council seat was term-limited—of betraying their friendship. Most local party officials endorsed Owens because of his seniority. Despite Clarke's strong showing in the Caribbean precincts, Owens won 54%–46%. But the close margin may mean another heated primary in 2002. Much will depend on redistricting. The redistricters will surely preserve the two black-majority districts in Brooklyn, but they may change the boundaries between Owens's 11th and the 10th district of Ed Towns, who also had a serious primary challenge in 2000. Neighborhood politics will probably determine the outcome.

Cook's Call   *Safe.* In a district that gave Gore 89%, Owens' only concern in this central Brooklyn district is a competitive primary, which he had in 2000 against his former protege, City Councilwoman Una Clarke. As this district increases in diversity (there has been an influx of Caribbean immigrants), a new form of ethnic politics has emerged. Term limits on New York City councilmembers also means that ambitious politicians will continue to be tempted to challenge Owens in a primary. Clarke, who was termed out of her city council seat, has indicated that she may run again. As one of the slowest growing districts in the city, the 11th needs to pick up almost 70,000 new residents.

THE PEOPLE: Pop. 2000: 586,819; Pop. 1990: 582,332, up 0.8% 1990–2000. 19.3% White, 68.6% Black, 3.4% Asian, 0.3% Amer. Indian, 3.9% Two+ races, 4.6% Other; 10.8% Hispanic Origin.

2000 Presidential Vote		
Gore (D)	140,287	(89%)
Bush (R)	11,607	(7%)
Nader (Green)	4,808	(3%)

1996 Presidential Vote		
Clinton (D)	116,439	(92%)
Dole (R)	8,926	(7%)
Perot (I)	1,878	(1%)

Rep. Major R. Owens (D)

Elected 1982, 10th term; b. June 28, 1936, Memphis, TN; home, Brooklyn; Morehouse Col., B.A. 1956, Atlanta U., M.L.S. 1957; Baptist; married (Maria).

Elected Office: NY Senate, 1974–82.

Professional Career: Librarian; Brooklyn Public Library, 1958–65, Community Coord., 1964–65; V.P., Metro. Cncl. of Housing, 1964; Chmn., Brooklyn Congress on Racial Equality; Exec. Dir., Brownsville Community Cncl., 1966–68; NYC Community Devel. Agency, Comm., 1968–73, Dpty. Admin., 1972–74; Dir., Community Media Library Program, Columbia U., 1973–74.

DC Office: 2309 RHOB 20515, 202-225-6231; Fax: 202-226-0112; Web site: www.house.gov/owens.

District Offices: Brooklyn, 718-940-3213; Brooklyn, 718-773-3100.

Committees: *Education & the Workforce* (3d of 22 D): Education Reform; Workforce Protections (RMM). *Government Reform* (3d of 19 D): Civil Service & Agency Organization; Government Efficiency, Financial Management & Intergovernmental Relations.

Group Ratings

	ADA	ACLU	AFS	LCV	CON	ITIC	NTU	COC	ACU	NTLC	CHC
2000	90	86	100	93	80	53	30	42	0	14	0
1999	100	—	100	100	56	—	26	21	0	—	—

National Journal Ratings

	1999 LIB	—	1999 CONS		2000 LIB	—	2000 CONS
Economic	80%	—	18%		95%	—	0%
Social	87%	—	0%		94%	—	0%
Foreign	89%	—	8%		96%	—	3%

Key Votes of the 106th Congress

1. Patient Bill of Rights	Y	5. Bar RU-486 $ for FDA	N	9. NATO War in Serbia	Y
2. Accelerate Min. Wage	Y	6. Display 10 Commandments	N	10. Perm. Trade with China	N
3. Strike Ban on Ergo. Stnd.	Y	7. Gun Show Bkgrnd. Checks	Y	11. Debt Relief for 3rd World	Y
4. Ovrd. Estate Tax Veto	N	8. Ban Part.-Birth Abortion	N	12. Drop Cuba Econ. Embargo	Y

Election Results

2000 general	Major R. Owens (D-WF)	112,050	(87%)	($548,071)
	Susan Cleary (R-SCH)	8,406	(7%)	($22,790)
	Una S. T. Clarke (L)	7,366	(6%)	($265,208)
	Others	962	(1%)	
2000 primary	Major R. Owens (D)	25,962	(54%)	
	Una S. T. Clarke (D)	21,769	(46%)	
1998 general	Major R. Owens (D-L)	75,773	(90%)	($120,197)
	David Greene (R-C)	7,284	(9%)	
	Others	1,144	(1%)	

TWELFTH DISTRICT

Amid a vast wave of migration that seemed destined to make Puerto Ricans the majority in New York, Leonard Bernstein in 1957 wrote his musical, *West Side Story*, with Romeo as an Italian-American and Juliet as a Manhattan Puerto Rican. But New York never became majority Puerto Rican, as Bernstein may have expected. The inflow and outflow of Puerto Ricans balanced out by the early 1960s, and in the late 1990s the number of Puerto Ricans in New York was declining, as many young people of Puerto Rican descent born in New York were moving to Puerto Rico. But starting in the late 1960s, New York has had a vast influx of Hispanics from places not under the U.S. flag, and today most New York Hispanics are not Puerto Rican. The largest new group is the Dominicans, and there are many Colombians, Mexicans, Panamanians and Peruvians.

The 12th Congressional District was designed to join these diverse people together. As drawn for the 1992, 1994 and 1996 elections it was a serpentine-shaped entity called by many the "Bullwinkle" district, because of its alleged resemblance to the cartoon character. Stitched together, often by the thinnest of threads, were the heavily Puerto Rican Sunset Park neighborhood in Brooklyn and on the other side of the borough, Bushwick. The Dominican neighborhood of East Elmhurst and Corona, Queens were put in the 12th, as were the Colombian areas several blocks west in Jackson Heights, plus some black neighborhoods in East New York. It also jumped across the Manhattan Bridge to include Puerto Rican parts of the Lower East Side. The district is connected by cemeteries or parks in at least three places. Not too surprisingly, after two Supreme Court rulings overturning district lines drawn using race as the predominant factor, a lawsuit was brought challenging the 12th District. In February 1997 a federal court ordered redrawing of the "Bullwinkle" district, because race was the predominant factor, though Hispanicness technically is not a race; it added that there was no need for New York to create a seventh "majority-minority" district, especially one with such erose lines. The legislature complied and passed a new plan. The new 12th dropped the farther Queens portions of the district and added the Williamsburg neighborhood in Brooklyn, with many Hasidic and Polish voters. Otherwise the lines were smoothed out a bit in Brooklyn and Manhattan. In 2000, Hispanics were 49%, Asians 16% and blacks 13%.

The congresswoman from the 12th is Nydia Velazquez, chosen by a narrow margin in the 1992 primary and re-elected ever since. She was born in Puerto Rico, taught at the University of Puerto Rico in the 1970s and at Hunter College in the 1980s, worked for Congressman Ed Towns in 1983 and served on the New York City Council in 1984. Then she worked for Puerto Rico's government offices in New York. She was one of three major contenders when the district was created in 1992. One was liberal Elisabeth Colon and another was incumbent Stephen Solarz, chairman of the Asia Subcommittee and a major force on foreign policy; he decided to run here rather than in the Manhattan-dominated 8th or in the 9th District in which Charles Schumer had a heavy advantage. Velazquez got the endorsements of then-Mayor David Dinkins and of Jesse Jackson, and in a light turnout beat Solarz 34%–28%, with 26% for Colon. Had it been included in the district then, Williamsburg would probably have swung the race to Solarz. After the primary, confidential hospital records were leaked to a New York tabloid showing that in September 1991, Velazquez had attempted suicide, was hospitalized and later underwent counseling. Evidently, that was of little concern to voters: she won in November with 77%.

In the House she has a solidly liberal voting record. She used her seat on the Banking Committee to try to require credit bureaus to let people talk with live operators and to provide consumers with a free copy of their credit report after information is corrected. In 1997 she complained about the lack of Hispanic appointees in the Clinton Administration. She tried to give the INS the discretion to make exceptions to the draconian requirement that all immigrants must be deported for any crimes, no matter how trivial or how long ago they were committed. She was a sponsor of the Clinton administration proposals to stop money laundering in 1999, and with Republican James Talent she helped pass a bill creating 40 new renewal zones eligible for tax breaks in 2000.

Since, 1998, Velazquez has been ranking Democrat on the Small Business Committee. Velasquez sponsored studies that showed that small businesses' share of federal contracts fell from $6.4 billion in 1997 to $4.9 billion in 1999. In response she sponsored a bill which passed the House easily to closely monitor contract bundling—federal agencies' practice of putting small contracts together in one large package, which usually results in the contract going to a large business. Citing the 2 million minority-owned and 9 million woman-owned businesses, she spoke out for repeal of the estate tax in June 2000 and voted for it. But when Bill Clinton vetoed the bill, she voted to uphold his veto after a phone call from him. She has worked on district projects, including a $1.6 million grant in 2000 for education and housing for the homeless and a long-awaited new post office in Bushwick, which opened in August 2000.

Velazquez has been a major voice on issues relating to Puerto Rico. She used to favor independence, a cause favored by less than 5% of voters in Puerto Rico; by 1997 she favored continuation of the current commonwealth status (more accurately described in the Spanish term, *estado liberado asociado*, free associated state). She attacked the March 1998 bill setting the terms for a referendum on status—always the number one issue in Puerto Rico—as "a one-sided bill that is biased in favor of Puerto Rican statehood" that shows "a lack of respect for the people of Puerto Rico." She said its definition of commonwealth was biased, because it did not guarantee U.S. citizenship to future generations of Puerto Ricans (citizenship is now based not on the Fourteenth Amendment, but on a law passed by Congress in 1917, which could be repealed). She has strongly opposed the Navy's bombing range on the island of Vieques and in May 2000 she was one of more than 200 protesters evicted from Vieques, along with Illinois Congressman Luis Gutierrez. Velasquez strongly advocated clemency for members of the FALN terrorist group—which was responsible for the deaths of six people—who had been imprisoned for 19 years after being convicted on seditious conspiracy and weapons charges and had not expressed regret. When Bill Clinton granted clemency in August 1999 conditioned on a renunciation of violence, she said that the clemency should have been unconditional. When the grant was opposed by Hillary Rodham Clinton, then contemplating a run for the Senate, Velasquez said she should have come to the community and listened to the people; she was dismayed when the House condemned the clemency by a 311–41 vote. After violence during New York's Puerto Rican Day parade in June 2000, she said, "I am outraged. Some bad apples have tarnished the reputation of the entire New York community."

Velazquez called the ruling overturning the old 12th District lines in 1997 "a sad day for equal justice for communities of color." But it did not turn out to be a sad political day for her. Brooklyn Democratic Chairman Clarence Norman sought candidates to run against her in 1998, but failed. In 2000 Velazquez did have primary opposition, but won with 77% of the vote. New York City's big increases in the Hispanic population in the 1990s will make it easier for redistricters to create a heavily or majority Hispanic district based in Brooklyn than it was 10 years ago. In the 2000 Census, Queens had a much higher Hispanic population than Brooklyn. This suggests that the bulk of the new Hispanic district will be in Queens, especially if the 7th district represented by Joseph Crowley is eliminated. Nor does this guarantee Velasquez a safe seat. Few of the newcomers, especially in Queens, are Puerto Rican and share her preoccupation with Puerto Rican issues.

Cook's Call *Safe.* Minor line changes here in 1997 had little impact on Velazquez as she has continued to win this seat easily. This heavily Democratic district will never give Velazquez much trouble. Redistricting will alter the lines here again somewhat, as this district needs to pick up about 30,000 people in redistricting.

THE PEOPLE: Pop. 2000: 620,677; Pop. 1990: 577,757, up 7.4% 1990–2000. 36.8% White, 12.6% Black, 16.4% Asian, 0.8% Amer. Indian, 0.1% Hawaiian, 6% Two+ races, 27.3% Other; 48.6% Hispanic Origin.

2000 Presidential Vote		
Gore (D)	103,110	(81%)
Bush (R)	16,575	(13%)
Nader (Green)	7,399	(6%)
Others	772	(1%)

1996 Presidential Vote		
Clinton (D)	89,535	(85%)
Dole (R)	12,874	(12%)
Perot (I)	3,161	(3%)

Rep. Nydia M. Velazquez (D)

Elected 1992, 5th term; b. Mar. 28, 1953, Yabucoa, PR; home, Brooklyn; U. of PR, B.A. 1974, N.Y.U., M.A. 1976; Catholic; married (Paul Bader).

Elected Office: NY City Cncl., 1984–86.

Professional Career: Instructor, U. of PR, 1976–81; Adjunct prof., Hunter Col., 1981–83; Special Asst., U.S. Rep. Edolphus Towns, 1983; Migration Dir., PR Dept. of Labor & Human Resources, 1986–89; Secy., PR Dept. of Community Affairs in the U.S., 1989–92.

DC Office: 2241 RHOB 20515, 202-225-2361; Fax: 202-226-0327; Web site: www.house.gov/velazquez.

District Offices: Brooklyn, 718-599-3658; Brooklyn, 718-222-5819; Manhattan, 212-673-3997.

Committees: *Financial Services* (7th of 32 D): Capital Markets, Insurance & Government Sponsored Enterprises; Financial Institutions & Consumer Credit; Housing & Community Opportunity; International Monetary Policy & Trade. *Small Business* (RMM of 17 D).

Group Ratings

	ADA	ACLU	AFS	LCV	CON	ITIC	NTU	COC	ACU	NTLC	CHC
2000	90	85	85	100	53	56	31	40	4	6	0
1999	100	—	100	94	54	—	26	24	4	—	—

National Journal Ratings

	1999 LIB —	1999 CONS	2000 LIB —	2000 CONS
Economic	71% —	28%	81% —	16%
Social	87% —	0%	79% —	21%
Foreign	89% —	8%	85% —	10%

Key Votes of the 106th Congress

1. Patient Bill of Rights	Y	5. Bar RU-486 $ for FDA	N	9. NATO War in Serbia	Y
2. Accelerate Min. Wage	Y	6. Display 10 Commandments	N	10. Perm. Trade with China	N
3. Strike Ban on Ergo. Stnd.	Y	7. Gun Show Bkgrnd. Checks	Y	11. Debt Relief for 3rd World	Y
4. Ovrd. Estate Tax Veto	N	8. Ban Part.-Birth Abortion	*	12. Drop Cuba Econ. Embargo	Y

Election Results

2000 general	Nydia M. Velazquez (D-WF)	86,288	(87%)	($437,579)
	Rosemary Markgraf (R)	10,052	(10%)	($11,078)
	Others	2,740	(3%)	
2000 primary	Nydia M. Velazquez (D)	15,894	(77%)	
	Mildred Rosario (D)	4,713	(23%)	
1998 general	Nydia M. Velazquez (D)	53,269	(84%)	($359,402)
	Rosemarie Markgraf (R)	7,405	(12%)	($1,620)
	Others	3,032	(5%)	

THIRTEENTH DISTRICT

Staten Island is part of New York City, yet a land apart; it is closer geographically to New Jersey, separated only by narrow Arthur Kill and Kill van Kull, than to Brooklyn, over the 5-mile-long span of the Verrazano Narrows Bridge. Its inclusion in Greater New York in 1898 was something of an afterthought, and for two-thirds of a century it was connected to the rest of the City only by ferry or through Bayonne, New Jersey, until the Verrazano was opened in 1965. It is far less densely populated than the rest of New York: with about as much acreage as Brooklyn has for 2.46 million people, Staten Island has some 440,000—and that's after recent robust population growth that's the most rapid of the five boroughs. Ethnically, Staten Island is the second most heavily Italian part of the United States, after Providence, Rhode Island; the signs on coffee shops here read *Caffe* and on delicatessens *Salumeria*.

Not so long ago you could still find some cows on Staten Island, and there still is much empty space. It has the highest point on the eastern seaboard, Todt Hill, and the vast Fresh Kills dump, whose motto symbolizes the local psyche: "Don't dump on us." Culturally, Staten Islanders are deeply conservative—more so than in most of New York's suburbs—quite a contrast from Manhattan at the other end of the ferry. New York City income taxes, the highest in the nation, pay for many programs opposed by most Staten Islanders; in November 1993, Staten Island voted for secession, but the legislature never acted; that same year Staten Islanders provided the margin of victory for Mayor Rudolph Giuliani whose record—cutting crime and welfare rolls in half—has made them less interested in breaking away. The crime reduction has been especially pronounced on Staten Island: if it were counted on its own, it would have the lowest crime rate of any city in the nation with more than 100,000 population. The Giuliani years also produced an economic boon, with a new ferry terminal, additional shops and hundreds of new homes near cleaned-up beaches, Plus, the biggest victory: Fresh Kills finally was shut down in March 2001.

The 13th Congressional District of New York is made up of Staten Island plus a couple of adjacent neighborhoods over the Verrazano Narrows Bridge in Brooklyn. The largest of these is Bay Ridge, heavily Catholic and Italian, mostly middle-class though with an increasing number of new immigrants, with thick New York accents and resentment of high New York taxes and welfare payments: large single-family houses and small apartment buildings by the looming towers of the Bridge. The 13th also includes most of heavily Italian Bensonhurst, where you can still see old men playing bocci, and has more police officers than any other district in America.

The congressman from the 13th District is Vito Fossella, a Republican elected in November 1997. Fossella comes from a political, and Democratic, Staten Island family: his great-grandfather, James O'Leary, was a New Deal congressman from 1935–44, elected from Staten Island and the Wall Street tip of Manhattan; his father, Vito Fossella Sr., chaired the city's Board of Standards under Mayor Edward Koch; his uncle, Frank Fossella, was elected to the City Council in 1981 and in 1985 he was beaten by Republican Susan Molinari, Vito Fossella Jr.'s predecessor in Congress. Despite the party difference, the families became close. Vito Fossella graduated from Penn and Fordham Law School and became a Republican in 1990, at 25, because of his conservative philosophy; he switched from pro-choice to pro-life in 1995, after the birth of his son. He worked on the campaigns of Susan Molinari, who succeeded her father in the House. In April 1994, Fossella, less than a year after finishing law school, was elected to the City Council to fill a vacancy, winning 47% in a six-candidate nonpartisan election, with the help of the Molinaris. On the council he worked for increased school and transportation funding for Staten Island and, most important, passed a bill mandating the closing of the Fresh Kills dump by 2001.

Fossella was elected to Congress after the surprise resignation of Susan Molinari. She was married to Congressman Bill Paxon, part of the leadership until he was part of the unsuccessful coup against Newt Gingrich in July 1997 and announced he wasn't seeking re-election. She didn't lose her political touch, however: she timed her resignation for August, which meant that the Republican nomination would go to the party committeemen, dominated by her father; they rejected the pleas of two other contenders and chose Fossella. This turned out to be a high visibility contest. Democrats picked Eric Vitaliano, a 15-year assemblyman from the conservative mid-Island district, an abortion opponent and sponsor of New York's death penalty. Vitaliano criticized Fossella as inexperienced and constantly tried to link Fossella with Gingrich. Fossella hit Vitaliano for supporting higher taxes and needle exchanges, and for not taking Americans for Tax Reform's anti-tax-raise pledge. "Eric Vitaliano: Talks like us but votes like an Albany liberal." Two other factors helped Fossella. One was a $750,000 independent expenditure by the national Republican Party, attacking Vitaliano for supporting tax increases, and a group called Victory 97, which paid for posters depicting Vitaliano's silly spending programs: snow-making equipment in Ulster

County, a state Museum of Cheese. The other was the re-election campaign of Giuliani, in a district where few local Democrats would admit they supported their liberal nominee Ruth Messinger. On election day Giuliani carried the district 3–1 and Fossella won 61%–39%. He won 59% in Staten Island and 67% in Brooklyn. "The message is that the government works for the people and not the other way around," he said.

In the House, Fossella has a more conservative voting record than Molinari, one of the most conservative in the New York delegation. He worked on interstate waste issues and pushed for rerouting Newark Airport flights away from Staten Island. He amended the Shays-Meehan campaign finance bill to ban contributions from foreigners, even if they reside in the U.S. He voted for Permanent Normal Trade Relations with China. Republican leaders looked to him to reach out to Catholic voters: he sponsored the Congressional Gold Medal for New York's Cardinal John O'Connor shortly before his death. When Bill Clinton granted clemency to members of the Puerto Rican FALN terrorist group which was responsible for fatal local bombings, Fossella led the opposition, demanding that Clinton provide more details of his deliberations and sponsoring a resolution to rebuke the President; it passed the House 311–41. In the 2000 presidential primary, he broke with Guy Molinari to support George W. Bush. That helps to explain why at the Republican convention in Philadelphia, Fossella was tapped as a featured speaker advocating personal investment accounts for Social Security. "Today, 80 million Americans are investors. My friends, 80 million Americans can't be wrong." Following their post-election reorganization, he held seats on both the Energy and Commerce, and Financial Services Committees, both locally useful slots.

Fossella has been re-elected easily. Assuming he keeps his Brooklyn precincts in redistricting—rather than regaining parts of Lower Manhattan—he should remain strongly entrenched.

Cook's Call *Safe.* Don't look for Democrats to post a serious challenge here in 2002. As one of the fastest growing districts in the state, this Staten Island seat needs to shed about 16,000 people in redistricting.

THE PEOPLE: Pop. 2000: 670,006; Pop. 1990: 579,521, up 15.6% 1990–2000. 76.3% White, 6.7% Black, 9.6% Asian, 0.2% Amer. Indian, 3.2% Two+ races, 3.9% Other; 11.1% Hispanic Origin.

2000 Presidential Vote

Gore (D)	103,603	(53%)
Bush (R)	86,342	(44%)
Nader (Green)	5,413	(3%)
Others	1,250	(1%)

1996 Presidential Vote

Clinton (D)	92,612	(52%)
Dole (R)	72,228	(41%)
Perot (I)	12,093	(7%)

Rep. Vito Fossella (R)

Elected Nov. 1997, 2d term; b. Mar. 9, 1965, Staten Island; home, Staten Island; U. of PA., B.S. 1993, Fordham U., J.D. 1994; Catholic; married (Mary Pat).

Elected Office: NY City Cncl., 1994–97.

Professional Career: Practicing atty., 1994.

DC Office: 1239 LHOB 20515, 202-225-3371; Fax: 202-226-1272; Web site: www.house.gov/fossella.

District Offices: Brooklyn, 718-630-5277; Staten Island, 718-356-8400.

Committees: *Energy & Commerce* (20th of 31 R): Energy & Air Quality; Environment & Hazardous Materials; Telecommunications & The Internet. *Financial Services* (29th of 37 R): Capital Markets, Insurance & Government Sponsored Enterprises; Domestic Monetary Policy, Technology & Economic Growth; Oversight & Investigations.

Group Ratings

	ADA	ACLU	AFS	LCV	CON	ITIC	NTU	COC	ACU	NTLC	CHC
2000	0	31	0	29	78	100	63	80	80	88	100
1999	15	—	0	31	56	—	63	91	83	—	—

National Journal Ratings

	1999 LIB	—	1999 CONS		2000 LIB	—	2000 CONS
Economic	29%	—	71%		29%	—	67%
Social	42%	—	56%		39%	—	61%
Foreign	31%	—	69%		38%	—	61%

Key Votes of the 106th Congress

1. Patient Bill of Rights	N	5. Bar RU-486 $ for FDA	Y	9. NATO War in Serbia	N
2. Accelerate Min. Wage	N	6. Display 10 Commandments	Y	10. Perm. Trade with China	Y
3. Strike Ban on Ergo. Stnd.	N	7. Gun Show Bkgrnd. Checks	N	11. Debt Relief for 3rd World	N
4. Ovrd. Estate Tax Veto	Y	8. Ban Part.-Birth Abortion	Y	12. Drop Cuba Econ. Embargo	N

Election Results

2000 general	Vito Fossella (R-C-RTL)	109,806	(65%)	($767,582)
	Katina M. Johnstone (D-WF)	57,603	(34%)	($39,475)
	Others	2,653	(2%)	
2000 primary	Vito Fossella (R)	unopposed		
1998 general	Vito Fossella (R-C-RTL)	76,138	(65%)	($1,591,057)
	Eugene V. Prisco (D-L)	40,167	(34%)	($14,858)
	Others	1,245	(1%)	

FOURTEENTH DISTRICT

Hardly any remnant can be found of early 19th Century New York, the city that diarists Philip Hone and George Templeton Strong said was continually being torn down and rebuilt, its earlier structures expendable after a generation or so on the high-priced real estate of this small, compact island. Yet the mayor of this quintessentially 20th Century city lives and works in two buildings of early 19th Century scale: City Hall, built in 1803–11, where his ground floor office, dwarfed by the Municipal and Woolworth Buildings, overlooks City Hall Park; and Gracie Mansion, built in 1799, which looks across East End Avenue to high-rise apartments and over the East River to the Triborough Bridge. In contrast are the gleaming postmodern skyscrapers in Manhattan and the high-priced storefronts of the 1990s. But most of Manhattan has an early or mid-20th Century look; its enduring landmarks—the Empire State Building, the Woolworth Building, Rockefeller Center—are the product of the first half of the century, and some of its infrastructure is now dilapidated and crumbling, despite fixups during the administration of Mayor Rudolph Giuliani.

The 14th Congressional District covers most of the East Side of Manhattan, running irregularly from 14th Street north to 96th street, plus small salients on the Lower East Side and Upper West Side of Manhattan; it also includes parts of the Queens neighborhoods of Astoria and Long Island City. This is the direct descendant of the famous Silk Stocking district, originally created in 1918, then consisting of the few blocks east of Fifth Avenue along Central Park. In the years since, rich and articulate Manhattan, with its securities, publishing, advertising, entertainment, broadcasting and communications industries, has spread from this narrow enclave and taken over the greater part of the island, with robust population increases in the 1990s. Meanwhile, the political leanings of this larger upper class—defined partly by income, but also by tastes in the arts, fashion, letters, all the things in which New York remains clearly the nation's capital—have changed, from elite Republican to culturally liberal.

Historically, the Silk Stocking tradition was elite Republican, cosmopolitan and international-minded, confident in its duty to lead the nation and mistrustful of the city's (usually Democratic) immigrant masses—the politics of Theodore Roosevelt and the old *New York Herald Tribune* and Henry Luce's *Time* magazine. While it did not trust union leaders and Democratic Party politicians, it accepted much of the New Deal. This district believed the nation should be led by the well-educated Protestant gentlemen one saw strolling down Madison Avenue to their clubs, who held high government posts from Theodore Roosevelt's day and past Franklin's. But the district changed during the tenure of John Lindsay, congressman from 1959–65 and mayor from 1966–73. Lindsay changed from being a liberal Republican to a leftish Democrat. While mayor, he ran up huge debts that led the city to the brink of bankruptcy in 1975, while neighborhoods deteriorated and the city lost 1 million people in the 1970s. He was succeeded as congressman and ultimately as mayor by Edward Koch, whose political travels were the reverse: Koch started as a liberal reform Democrat and became more conservative, and in the process lost the support of Manhattan by backing capital punishment, opposing racial quotas and questioning poverty programs. Attitudes have now changed: the high crime and visible deterioration in the mayoralty of David Dinkins led Manhattanites to back Giuliani, and they applauded his successes in cutting crime and welfare and taxes. But Manhattan would have nothing to do with the Republican party of Newt Gingrich and Bob Dole and George W. Bush: Bush lost the borough of Manhattan by 80%–14% in 2000.

Thus does the Silk Stocking district prove that economics is not necessarily the basis of American politics. In 1997, its residents had the highest average household income in America, $74,780, but they also are solidly Democratic. Its 10021 ZIP code on the Upper East Side, termed the "urban gold coast" with many graduate degrees but few automobiles or children, was a favored source of campaign contributions for Bill Clinton and Al Gore. While the district is affluent, it also is full of gays, singles and others who consider anything past the canyons of Manhattan's east-west grid streets and the Hudson hostile country. In youth-thronged clubs and Park Avenue dinner parties, in chic restaurants and in high-fashion stores, nary a good word is to be said for the national leaders of the party that once was led by Manhattan's upper crust.

The congresswoman from the 14th district is Carolyn Maloney, a liberal Democrat elected in 1992. Born and educated in North Carolina, she visited New York in 1970 at the age of 22, loved it and "just stayed." She worked on welfare education programs during the 1970s, and from 1977–82 she was a legislative staffer in Albany. She was elected to the New York City Council in 1982; one observer of her time there described her as "a little spacey" until she found a cause, but then she became "a pit bull." For 1992, redistricting created a Silk Stocking district even more Democratic than its predecessor and Maloney ran against liberal Republican Bill Green, a thoughtful legislator who shared Manhattan's cultural liberalism but could not compete with the enthusiasm of a Democratic Party dominated by the feminist left for a woman candidate. And he was poorly positioned to appeal to voters in the outer borough neighborhoods, who liked Republicans conservative on cultural issues and liberal on economics. Green won the Manhattan part of the district, but only by 50%–44%; Maloney carried the outer borough portions with 62%, for a 50%–48% upset win.

Maloney started off in the House with a certain naivete but stayed to make serious contributions on important issues. With John Dingell she sponsored a campaign finance commission, whose result would have to be approved or rejected as a whole by Congress. But when Republican leaders allowed a vote on that in 1998, she backtracked, lest it get more votes than Shays-Meehan and under the rule supersede it. On the Banking Committee, she worked to keep banks from controlling other businesses, has proposed regulation of hedge funds with assets over $1 billion, and has sought more oversight of the Federal Reserve. With Republican Richard Baker, she sponsored a "Kiddie Mac" bill for mortgage guarantees to lenders who financed child-care centers. With an eye to Astoria, she helped found the Congressional Caucus on Hellenic Issues; with an eye to Manhattan radicals, she protested Peru's imprisonment of Lori Berenson for participating in the Tupac Amaru revolutionary groups; with an eye to the corporate suites, she voted for Permanent Normal Trade Relations with China. She secured $3 million for a study of the long-proposed but never-built Second Avenue subway line. Maloney opposes the Arab boycott of Israel and worked on a law to disclose Nazi war crime records. A leader of the Women's Caucus, she criticized Defense Secretary William Cohen's refusal to discharge General Joseph Ralston for adultery. She opposed separating men and women in basic training. She put a provision for annual Medicare mammograms in the 1998 omnibus budget and won approval a year later for a mother's right to breast-feed her child on federal property.

In 1997 she became the ranking Democrat on the new Census Subcommittee. She was a fervent backer of Census sampling; the 1990 undercount in New York City, she said, was 244,000, and the city was being deprived of needed federal funds. She backed the Clinton administration plan to present one Census result determined by sampling rather than the head count, which she called "the civil rights issue of this decade." After the Supreme Court ruled in January 1999 that the Constitution required an actual enumeration for apportionment of House seats among the states, she backed the administration's plan to produce two figures, one from an enumeration for reapportionment and another from sampling to be used for redistricting and funding formulas. But she was rebuffed in March 2001 when Census Bureau professionals recommended against using sample numbers because they could not determine whether they were more accurate than the head count. When Commerce Secretary Donald Evans made the final decision to report only the head count numbers, she led the protests and criticized the Bush administration for putting "politics over people." Maloney has called for a special census of Americans living abroad in 2003 as a blueprint for the 2010 census. But the Census is no longer her preoccupation; in 2001 she switched off Census to become ranking Democrat on the Domestic Monetary Policy Subcommittee.

Any doubts that Maloney had a firm lock on the district were dispelled in the Republican year of 1994. Manhattan Councilman Charles Millard spent almost $1 million against her; but the 14th District was voting 78% for Mario Cuomo and Maloney won 64%–35%. Redistricting could be a problem. New York lost two House seats in the 2000 Census, and it is likely that Maloney will end up with a district that extends farther into ethnic and immigrant neighborhoods in Queens, geographically near but culturally very different from the core of her constituency on the Upper East Side.

Cook's Call *Safe*. Like most New York City members, Maloney's greatest threat comes not from a Republican challenge but a 2002 redistricting map. Her district is about 50,000 people below the required population, and she could find it seriously altered in 2002.

THE PEOPLE: Pop. 2000: 608,017; Pop. 1990: 578,639, up 5.1% 1990–2000. 77.4% White, 4.6% Black, 9.3% Asian, 0.2% Amer. Indian, 0.1% Hawaiian, 3.7% Two+ races, 4.7% Other; 12.2% Hispanic Origin.

2000 Presidential Vote

Gore (D)	173,003	(71%)
Bush (R)	55,349	(23%)
Nader (Green)	12,855	(5%)
Others	1,355	(1%)

1996 Presidential Vote

Clinton (D)	146,811	(73%)
Dole (R)	47,084	(23%)
Perot (I)	6,593	(3%)

Rep. Carolyn B. Maloney (D)

Elected 1992, 5th term; b. Feb. 19, 1948, Greensboro, NC; home, Manhattan; Greensboro Col, A.B. 1968; Presbyterian; married (Clifton).

Elected Office: NY City Cncl., 1982–92.

Professional Career: NYC Bd. of Ed., 1970–77; Legis. aide, NY Assembly & NY Senate, 1977–82.

DC Office: 2430 RHOB 20515, 202-225-7944; Fax: 202-225-4709; Web site: www.house.gov/maloney.

District Offices: Manhattan, 212-860-0606; Queens, 718-932-1804.

Committees: *Financial Services* (5th of 32 D): Domestic Monetary Policy, Technology & Economic Growth (RMM); Financial Institutions & Consumer Credit; International Monetary Policy & Trade. *Government Reform* (7th of 19 D): Census; Government Efficiency, Financial Management & Intergovernmental Relations. *Joint Economic Committee* (8th of 10 Reps.).

Group Ratings

	ADA	ACLU	AFS	LCV	CON	ITIC	NTU	COC	ACU	NTLC	CHC
2000	90	86	85	93	26	78	22	45	12	42	7
1999	100	—	100	63	21	—	17	36	4	—	—

National Journal Ratings

	1999 LIB	—	1999 CONS		2000 LIB	—	2000 CONS
Economic	77%	—	23%		73%	—	26%
Social	82%	—	17%		79%	—	17%
Foreign	78%	—	17%		74%	—	24%

Key Votes of the 106th Congress

1. Patient Bill of Rights	Y	5. Bar RU-486 $ for FDA	N	9. NATO War in Serbia	Y
2. Accelerate Min. Wage	Y	6. Display 10 Commandments	N	10. Perm. Trade with China	Y
3. Strike Ban on Ergo. Stnd.	Y	7. Gun Show Bkgrnd. Checks	Y	11. Debt Relief for 3rd World	Y
4. Ovrd. Estate Tax Veto	N	8. Ban Part.-Birth Abortion	N	12. Drop Cuba Econ. Embargo	N

Election Results

2000 general	Carolyn B. Maloney (D-L)	148,080	(74%)	($802,053)
	C. Adrienne Rhodes (R)	45,453	(23%)	($28,382)
	Others	6,815	(3%)	
2000 primary	Carolyn B. Maloney (D)	unopposed		
1998 general	Carolyn B. Maloney (D-Ind-L)	111,072	(77%)	($592,788)
	Stephanie E. Kupferman (R)	32,458	(23%)	($96,902)

FIFTEENTH DISTRICT

Harlem, for many years America's most famous black ghetto, is now recovering from three decades of grim times. For a long moment Harlem was a center of writers and professionals and entertainers; the rosters of the Apollo Theater on 125th Street in the 1920s and 1930s were filled with the names of great artists still remembered today. This Harlem was a wondrous place: "To whites seeking amusement," the *WPA Guide* wrote in the late 1930s, Harlem "is an exuberant, original and unconventional entertainment center; to Negro college graduates, it is an opportunity to practice a profession among their own people; to those aspiring to racial leadership, it is a domain where they may advocate their theories unmolested; to the mass of Negro people, it is the spiritual capital of Black America." Harlem was almost new then: it was one of the last parts of Manhattan to be developed; early critics of Central Park questioned the necessity of setting aside open land when picnickers could always go to Harlem. The five-story tenements of solid brownstone were built about 100 years ago for working-class whites: Black Harlem expanded from its nucleus around Lenox Avenue and 125 Street in the years that followed even as the Italian neighborhood, later "Spanish Harlem," expanded from a nucleus at 116th Street and Pleasant Avenue. Starting with the summer 1964 riot, Harlem had three decades of deterioration and population loss. Hundreds of brownstones were abandoned, many pulled down; as successful black families moved outward, to Springfield Gardens in Queens or Williamsbridge in the Bronx or to Jersey suburbs, Harlem was increasingly left with welfare mothers and criminal gangs; its population dropped by one-third between 1970 and 1990. Drugs, crime, AIDS infection and infant mortality rose to horrifying levels. The near-disappearance of manufacturing jobs in New York City and the poor quality of the area's public schools meant that public payrolls were the only way up. Antipoverty money was channeled to a tight group of successful politicians, with few results except for the enrichment of the well-connected.

But in the 1990s things turned up. The huge drop in crime under Mayor Rudolph Giuliani made Harlem real estate now worth something again. Brownstones have been renovated, neighborhood schools upgraded (notably in East Harlem's District 4), commercial frontage repaired. Giuliani sold off city-owned buildings, often vacant, to private owners. Community development corporations, often linked to churches, encouraged home ownership. The Empowerment Zone headed by Deborah Wright, an appointee of Governor George Pataki, has produced private as well as public sector growth: the state office building on 125th Street has been joined by Disney, Cineplex Odeon, Old Navy, HMV, Starbucks. A private developer has plans to build a shopping center, with a Home Depot and Costco and 2,000 jobs, at the old Washburn Wire factory at 116th Street and East River Drive, and Pathmark built a supermarket on 125th Street in 1999. The federal government appropriated $1 million to start a National Jazz Museum in Harlem. The heavily Dominican neighborhood in Washington Heights, northwest of central Harlem, hit hard by the crack epidemic in the late 1980s and early 1990s, once again has the vitality typical of immigrant centers, with dozens of bodegas and vastly reduced crime. And in February 2001, when he was criticized for seeking to rent ultraexpensive office space in the Carnegie Hall Tower in midtown Manhattan, Bill Clinton made the move uptown and established his postpresidential office at 55 West 125th Street in Harlem.

Politically, Harlem has been heavily Democratic since blacks shifted from the Republican Party of Abraham Lincoln to the Democratic Party of Franklin Roosevelt in the 1930s. Oddly, Harlem did not get its own congressional district until 1944; the lines, previously drawn in 1918, were based on the 1910 Census, when Harlem had far fewer people. The new congressman was Adam Clayton Powell Jr. minister at the Abyssinian Baptist Church, a brilliant orator who became the most famous (and infamous) black politician of his time: chairman of the Education and Labor Committee when it passed the Great Society programs in 1965, excluded from Congress (illegally, the Supreme Court ruled) in 1967 for refusing to honor a New York decree in a libel case brought by a woman he called a "bag woman."

The current 15th Congressional District includes all of Harlem, indeed almost all of northern Manhattan, from approximately East 96th Street and West 91st Street on up. It includes some of the white-liberal Upper West Side and the precincts around Columbia University; the once Jewish and now Dominican Washington Heights and the once Irish and now Dominican Inwood to the north; East Harlem, Italian in the days of Fiorello LaGuardia, now Puerto Rican and Latino. Overall the district is 37% black and 51% Hispanic—figures testifying to black flight from Harlem and the continuing inrush of Western Hemisphere immigrants.

The congressman from the 15th is Charles Rangel, first elected in 1970. Rangel is now the senior member of the New York delegation and ranking Democrat on Ways and Means. He grew up in Harlem and served in the Army in Korea, where he rescued 40 men from behind the lines in Kunu-ri and was awarded the Bronze Star; he returned to Korea in June 2000 for the 50th anniversary of the outbreak of the war. "I know that nothing is ever going to happen to me in life that I'm going to complain about after Kunu-ri." He graduated from New York University and St. John's University Law School, served as legal counsel in several government agencies and was elected to the Assembly in 1966; in 1970 he challenged Powell in the Democratic primary and narrowly won. Like most Harlem politicians, he has long argued that government aid and racial preferences are needed to solve Harlem's problems. Yet much in his own career suggests otherwise. Rangel's main emphasis for a decade was denunciation of the drug trade. From 1983 until it was abolished in 1993 with the other House select committees, Rangel chaired the Select Committee on Narcotics Abuse and Control, and seldom missed a chance to relate other problems to drugs; after all, he has seen how they can destroy a community. Rangel wants money spent on rehabilitation programs as much as interdiction and police work, but he also worked with the Justice Department's Weed and Seed program, combining intensive law enforcement with social services. He has sharply criticized Mayor Rudolph Giuliani's police policies and in April 2000 called for a federal investigation of whether Giuliani defamed the victims three highly-publicized police shootings. Recently Rangel has called for reconsideration of mandatory sentences for first-time drug offenders. "The so-called war against drugs has been a war against people. It has warehoused our young," he said in August 2000. "It has denied us the opportunity to educate."

On Ways and Means Rangel worked, with success, to protect state and local income tax deductibility in the 1986 tax reform and for years was a prime defender of Section 936, the tax exemption that created many jobs in Puerto Rico. To a bill extending the research and development tax credit he attached an amendment giving Puerto Rico and the Virgin Islands a bigger share of import taxes on rum. He is an author of the Federal Empowerment Zone demonstration, the Low Income Housing tax credit (which he says financed 90% of affordable housing from 1984–94) and the Targeted Jobs tax credit. He helped pass the renewal zones legislation in December 2000, establishing zones with zero capital gains taxes. All those are aimed at turning around places like Harlem.

Rangel combines political shrewdness with a winning personality, but when Republicans took control of the House he indulged in some extravagant rhetoric. When a bipartisan majority voted to end racial preferences in broadcasting in 1995, Rangel lashed out in a letter to Ways and Means Chairman Bill Archer: "Mr. Chairman, in America we cannot afford to be colorblind. Just like under Hitler, people say they don't mean to blame any particular individuals and groups, but in the U.S. those groups always turn out to be minorities and immigrants." This of course was inaccurate—Hitler did single out Jews and other specific groups for persecution—but it also coarsened political discourse. Archer refused to speak to Rangel except in public committee meetings and refused to meet with him in private until June 1999, when Archer and Rangel were working on Social Security reform. He defended Bill Clinton against impeachment with great vigor, but he did not always get along with Clinton. He resented it when the administration negotiated directly with Republicans, leaving congressional Democrats out of the loop. He lobbied vigorously and successfully against cuts in New York's Medicaid payments in 1999 and 2000.

Since January 1997 Rangel has been ranking Democrat on Ways and Means; if Democrats win in 2002, he would be its first New York City chairman since Fernando Wood in 1877–81. Rangel remembered how he had been beaten for House whip in 1986 by Tony Coelho, a champion Democratic fundraiser, and decided for the first time to become a major fundraiser himself: of course it helped that with only a few more Democratic seats he would chair Ways and Means. In the 1997–98 cycle he raised more than $1.3 million for Democratic candidates, drawing on successful black entrepreneurs like Robert Johnson of Black Entertainment Television. In 1999–2000 he even more actively solicited contributions from and shared his views on issues with leading corporate and financial executives. In 1999 he raised $2.3 million for the campaign committee, more than anyone else except Minority Leader Dick Gephardt and committee Chairman Patrick Kennedy; and he raised another $4 million in 2000. In October 1998, campaigning with Hillary Rodham Clinton in New York, he suggested she should run for the Senate there. "She said, 'Who would want me to run here?' But she had a twinkle in her eye. And I knew then this was more than a joke for her."

Amid all this politicking, Rangel still found time for legislating. With Republican Nancy Johnson he fashioned a tax credit for school modernization bonds, but was unable to get it enacted. He worked hard for a bill to cut tariffs on apparel and other imports from sub-Saharan Africa, and also from the Caribbean and Central America. His chief partners in this were Republicans Ed Royce and Tom DeLay; it was opposed by unions and textile interests, and also by Jesse Jackson Jr. and other members of the Congressional Black Caucus; Jackson said it would help only multinational corporations and "African elites." But it passed the House 309–110 in May 2000. Said Rangel, "We are on the brink of history. Why don't we give the African people a chance? They may not be in the major leagues, but by God let them in the ball game." On Permanent Normal Trade Relations with China Rangel kept silent for many months, torn between union opponents and Clinton administration proponents. In May 2000 he finally came out in favor—the key vote to many observers. At that point, Tom DeLay said, "Okay, Mr. Future Chairman of Ways and Means, get the votes for passage." Rangel did: 73 Democrats joined 164 Republicans to pass it through what had been a very uncertain House. Rangel favors eliminating all sanctions on trade with Cuba; he favors allowing Haitian and Dominican immigrants into the United States on the same basis as refugees from Cuba.

Rangel has seldom had serious primary opposition. In 1994 he was opposed by the son of his predecessor, the Puerto Rican-raised Adam Clayton Powell IV (Adam Clayton Powell III, another son, is a respected media expert). Rangel spent $1.4 million and won 61%–33%. In 2000 he beat a primary challenger 82%–18%. Redistricting will not affect his tenure.

Cook's Call *Safe.* One of the most recognizable faces and voices in Congress, Rangel is an institution in this Harlem-based district where he has served for 30 years. This district will need to pick up about 50,000 people in redistricting, but Rangel will have no trouble winning a 17th term in 2002.

THE PEOPLE: Pop. 2000: 607,324; Pop. 1990: 580,354, up 4.6% 1990–2000. 24.4% White, 36.7% Black, 2.7% Asian, 0.9% Amer. Indian, 0.1% Hawaiian, 6.1% Two+ races, 29% Other; 50.5% Hispanic Origin.

2000 Presidential Vote

Gore (D)	150,560	(90%)
Bush (R)	10,136	(6%)
Nader (Green)	6,179	(4%)
Others	893	(1%)

1996 Presidential Vote

Clinton (D)	135,845	(93%)
Dole (R)	7,658	(5%)
Perot (I)	2,377	(2%)

Rep. Charles B. Rangel (D)

Elected 1970, 16th term; b. June 11, 1930, New York City; home, Manhattan; N.Y.U., B.S. 1957, St. John's U., LL.B. 1960; Catholic; married (Alma).

Military Career: Army, 1948–52 (Korea).

Elected Office: NY Assembly, 1966–70.

Professional Career: Asst. U.S. Atty., S. Dist. of NY, 1961; Legal Cnsl., NYC Housing & Redevel. Bd., Neighborhood Conservation Bureau, 1963–68; Gen. Cnsl., Natl. Advisory Comm. on Selective Svc., 1966.

DC Office: 2354 RHOB 20515, 202-225-4365; Fax: 202-225-0816; Web site: www.house.gov/rangel.

District Offices: Manhattan, 212-348-9630; Manhattan, 212-663-3900.

Committees: *Ways & Means* (RMM of 17 D): Trade. *Joint Committee on Taxation* (4th of 5 Reps.).

Group Ratings

	ADA	ACLU	AFS	LCV	CON	ITIC	NTU	COC	ACU	NTLC	CHC
2000	90	86	85	64	44	83	23	41	4	12	0
1999	90	—	100	100	44	—	21	29	0	—	—

National Journal Ratings

	1999 LIB	—	1999 CONS		2000 LIB	—	2000 CONS
Economic	84%	—	12%		92%	—	8%
Social	87%	—	0%		94%	—	0%
Foreign	89%	—	8%		95%	—	5%

Key Votes of the 106th Congress

1. Patient Bill of Rights	Y	5. Bar RU-486 $ for FDA	N
2. Accelerate Min. Wage	Y	6. Display 10 Commandments	N
3. Strike Ban on Ergo. Stnd.	Y	7. Gun Show Bkgrnd. Checks	Y
4. Ovrd. Estate Tax Veto	N	8. Ban Part.-Birth Abortion	N

9. NATO War in Serbia	Y
10. Perm. Trade with China	Y
11. Debt Relief for 3rd World	Y
12. Drop Cuba Econ. Embargo	Y

Election Results

2000 general	Charles B. Rangel (D-L-WF)	130,161	(92%)	($2,032,835)
	Jose Agustin Suero (R-Ref)	7,346	(5%)	($410)
	Others	4,157	(3%)	
2000 primary	Charles B. Rangel (D)	33,526	(82%)	
1998 general	Charles B. Rangel (D-L)	90,424	(93%)	($1,051,333)
	David E. Cunningham (R)	5,633	(6%)	
	Others	1,082	(1%)	

SIXTEENTH DISTRICT

It may not quite be "the beautiful Bronx," as borough historian Lloyd Utlan calls it, but The Bronx seems to be coming back. The beautiful days were in the 1930s and 1940s, when Presidents Roosevelt and Truman rode down 138th Street, when Babe Ruth and Lou Gehrig and Joe Di-Maggio hit home runs in Yankee Stadium, when Art Deco apartment buildings went up along the Grand Concourse, when shoppers thronged Tremont Avenue stores and New Yorkers from all over flocked to the Bronx Zoo. This Bronx was built in a trice, starting in 1906 when the first subway came in, bringing the children of immigrants from dimly lit Lower East Side tenements to more spacious apartments flooded with light. The Bronx's population grew from 200,000 in 1900 to 430,000 in 1910, 732,000 in 1920, and 1.3 million in 1930. The Bronx's population peaked at nearly 1.5 million in 1950, then fell to 1.2 million in 1990. Now it is up again, to 1.3 million in 2000, as new immigrants revive neighborhoods that had been given up for dead.

The Bronx fell rapidly in the dozen years after John Lindsay was elected mayor in 1965. One reason was rent control, insisted on by tenants, which guarantees that owners of low-rent property won't maintain it: The result is empty vandalized shells and venues for drug deals. Another was the drop in low-income, low-skill jobs in Manhattan and The Bronx, abetted by high union and minimum wages, restrictive work rules and the tolls exacted by organized crime. A third reason was the disintegration of family structure. Stable, law-abiding males became scarce in these parts. Most important was crime. With no community institutions and little parental supervision, poor teenagers here committed an alarming number of crimes, with seeming impunity. Arson became increasingly common, perpetrated by kids for kicks or on behalf of landlords who wanted to get insurance money for rent-controlled buildings. A vicious cycle was created: Crime drove away jobs, which drove away fathers, which produced more crime. A section of the South Bronx with 476,000 people in 1960 and 460,000 in 1970 dropped to 233,000 in 1980, a stunning change. As people left, presidents and presidential candidates came in—Jimmy Carter in 1977, Ronald Reagan in 1980—promising help.

Now the South Bronx seems to have turned around. It is still one of the lowest-income parts of America, but low-income families are finding it possible to work their way up. Government has helped, particularly former Democratic Mayor Edward Koch's housing subsidies and Republican Mayor Rudolph Giuliani's police tactics. Rent control was phased out, criminals were held in prison longer, pocket parks were built, graffiti painted over, crime vastly reduced. Citizens did much of the work, forming community development groups called Banana Kelly or Mid-Bronx Desperadoes (now MBD Housing) to build single-family pastel bungalows and small-scale apartment projects for the elderly, single-parent families and former homeless. Local institutions, notably Bronx-Lebanon Hospital, employed area residents and became a strong force for neighborhood stability; warehousing and truck terminals opened up as the streets became safer; with community policing, homicides dropped by two-thirds from 1994 to 1999. Population rose in the South Bronx more than almost anywhere else in New York City; immigrants moved in from Ecuador and Ghana and Bangladesh. Charlotte Street, which Jimmy Carter and Ronald Reagan once visited as the worst of the slums, is now Charlotte Gardens, with owner-occupied homes exceeding $180,000.

The 16th Congressional District includes most of the Bronx south of the Bronx Zoo. It includes the Art Deco apartments of the Grand Concourse and the narrow commercial strips of Westchester Avenue, Boston Road and the Hub. It includes the industrial flatlands of Bruckner Boulevard and Hunts Point and the hard-rock ridges through which the original subways bore. This is still a low-income district, with more residents below the poverty line than any other in the nation in 1990, with the lowest median family income, the second lowest per capita income and the third lowest median household income of any congressional district. "There has been a serious drug and gun problem here for 25 years," Borough president Fernando Ferrer conceded. The people here are 63% Hispanic; this has long been New York's largest concentration of Puerto Ricans, but an increasing percentage of Hispanics here now are from other parts of Latin America. Politically, this was the most Democratic district in the country in 1996, 95% for Bill Clinton and 4% for Bob Dole. George W. Bush didn't do much better; he got 6% to Al Gore's 93%—again, the nation's most Democratic district.

The congressman from the 16th District is Jose Serrano, chosen in a March 1990 special election. A native of Mayaguez, Puerto Rico, who grew up in the Millbrook project in the South Bronx, Serrano moved up while other Bronx politicians fell by the wayside because of corruption. He was elected to the New York Assembly in 1974 and chaired its Education Committee beginning in 1983; in 1985, he ran for Bronx borough president, bucking the Democratic organization, and nearly won. Two years later the winner was forced out because of scandal. Then in January 1990, South Bronx Congressman Robert Garcia was convicted for accepting money from the minority contractor Wedtech; his resignation (his conviction was later reversed) opened the way to Serrano's election to the House.

Serrano has one of the most liberal voting records in the House. He is now ranking Democrat on the Appropriations Subcommittee on Commerce, Justice, State and the Judiciary; he has used that position to redress past injustices by the FBI. In 1997, when Bill Richardson resigned from the House to become U.N. Ambassador, Minority Leader Dick Gephardt passed over Serrano for the less senior Robert Menendez of New Jersey—a better fundraiser, with his Cuban-American connections—to be chief deputy whip. In 1998 Serrano ran for Democratic Caucus vice-chairman as "the candidate who refuses to raise money to buy your vote for leadership." But he withdrew in favor of Menendez. At a March 2001 hearing, he told Justices Anthony Kennedy and Clarence

Thomas the Supreme Court "broke my heart by getting involved with a political decision" in the Florida presidential recount.

Serrano is known as Fidel Castro's greatest champion in the House. He says he admires Castro and has sought repeal of economic sanctions and the Helms-Burton Act; he argued for admitting Cuban baseball players without requiring they renounce the Castro regime. He led efforts to overturn the four-decade embargo of Cuba—emerging as a vocal defender of Castro's regime during the Elian Gonzalez affair. He calls Puerto Rico an American "colony," and strongly backs statehood. He supported Don Young's bill authorizing a statehood referendum, which passed the House by one vote in 1998. Serrano's amendment to allow the 2.7 million Puerto Ricans on the mainland to vote as well as the 3.7 million Puerto Ricans on the island was defeated; but he helped to defeat an amendment requiring English to be used in government and schools of a state of Puerto Rico. In December 1998, the pro-statehood Puerto Rico government conducted its own referendum, in which statehood won 46.5%, the same as in the 1993 referendum, and "none of the above," supported by backers of the current commonwealth status and of independence, got 50.3%. "You can't reject statehood without presenting an alternative," Serrano grumbled. But the move toward statehood stalled. Serrano strongly defended Clinton's 1999 clemency for Puerto Ricans members of the FALN terrorist group as an example of reconciliation. In May 2000, he was arrested for blocking passage at the White House to protest the Navy's bombing at Vieques, Puerto Rico. In the December 2000 budget deal, he won reforms of procedures for 400,000 undocumented immigrants who had been denied amnesty under the 1986 immigration act. That budget also included $10.9 million to improve the riverbanks along the Bronx River and restore parkland in the Hunts Points area.

In New York politics, Serrano takes stubbornly liberal positions. He has battled Ferrer and Bronx Democratic Chairman Roberto Ramirez. He backed Al Sharpton for mayor in 1997 and Mark Green for senator in 1998; both lost their primaries. In November 1997 he told colleagues he would run for mayor in 2001, but later said he was not interested. Meanwhile, Serrano was alert to affronts from other quarters. He called an amendment to channel bilingual education money to programs that teach English in two years an attempt "to beat up on immigrants and gain votes from the far right." He attacked the Census undercount, allegedly larger here than in any other congressional district. When owner George Steinbrenner threatened to move his team out of the South Bronx's Yankee Stadium, he called on Bill Clinton to declare it a national landmark; but as Steinbrenner's spokesman pointed out, landmark status would prevent the changes needed to make the stadium profitable and structurally sound. Serrano achieved one goal when he persuaded the House to award a Congressional Gold Medal to Frank Sinatra, whose work he has long admired.

Serrano has held the seat without difficulty, and faces little threat from redistricting.

Cook's Call   *Safe*. A district that gave Bush just 6% is not a place where Democrats should have any troubles. Serrano's district was one of the faster growing in the city.

THE PEOPLE: Pop. 2000: 647,437; Pop. 1990: 581,053, up 11.4% 1990–2000. 21.2% White, 36% Black, 1.9% Asian, 1.1% Amer. Indian, 0.1% Hawaiian, 6.6% Two+ races, 33.1% Other; 62.9% Hispanic Origin.

2000 Presidential Vote		
Gore (D)	122,663	(93%)
Bush (R)	7,965	(6%)
Nader (Green)	826	(1%)
Others	663	(1%)

1996 Presidential Vote		
Clinton (D)	117,624	(95%)
Dole (R)	4,825	(4%)
Perot (I)	1,862	(1%)

✓ YES! send me *The Almanac of American Politics 2002.*

—— Copies of the softcover *Almanac 2002* for $56.95 per copy $ _____

—— Copies of the hardcover *Almanac 2002* for $75.95 per copy $ _____

Add 10% shipping and handling $ _____

Add sales tax: DC (5.75%), CA (7.25%) or VA (4.5%) $ _____

TOTAL $ _____

☐ **Check Enclosed**   ☐ **Bill me**   *P.O. #:* _____

☐ **Charge:**   ☐ Visa   ☐ Mastercard   ☐ American Express

_____   _____

Acct. #   *Exp. Date*

Signature

Name: _____ Title: _____

Organization: _____

Address: _____

City/State/Zip: _____

Phone: _____ Fax: _____

E-mail: _____

For even faster service, or special discounts on 10 or more
Call Toll Free 1-800-356-4838

✓ YES! I want six free issues of National Journal

The leading weekly on politics, policy and government

Please complete all information.

Name: _____ Title: _____

Organization: _____

Address: _____

City/State/Zip: _____

Phone: _____ Fax: _____

E-mail: _____

Mail this postage-paid card today, or for faster service
Call Toll Free 1-800-424-2921

NO POSTAGE
NECESSARY
IF MAILED
IN THE
UNITED STATES

BUSINESS REPLY MAIL
FIRST-CLASS MAIL   PERMIT NO. 1338   WASHINGTON DC

POSTAGE WILL BE PAID BY ADDRESSEE

NATIONAL JOURNAL GROUP
P O BOX 96157
WASHINGTON DC 20078-7509

NO POSTAGE
NECESSARY
IF MAILED
IN THE
UNITED STATES

BUSINESS REPLY MAIL
FIRST-CLASS MAIL   PERMIT NO. 1338   WASHINGTON DC

POSTAGE WILL BE PAID BY ADDRESSEE

NATIONAL JOURNAL GROUP
P O BOX 96157
WASHINGTON DC 20078-7509

Rep. Jose Serrano (D)

Elected Mar. 1990, 6th term; b. Oct. 24, 1943, Mayaguez, PR; home, Bronx; Lehman Col.; Catholic; married (Mary).

Military Career: Army Medical Corps, 1964–66.

Elected Office: Dist. 7 Schl. Bd., 1969–74; NY Assembly, 1974–90.

Professional Career: Banker, 1961–69.

DC Office: 2342 RHOB 20515, 202-225-4361; Fax: 202-225-6001; Web site: www.house.gov/serrano.

District Office: Bronx, 718-538-5400.

Committees: *Appropriations* (11th of 29 D): Commerce, Justice & State (RMM); Transportation.

Group Ratings

	ADA	ACLU	AFS	LCV	CON	ITIC	NTU	COC	ACU	NTLC	CHC
2000	90	86	85	86	79	71	16	42	0	10	0
1999	95	—	100	100	61	—	17	12	4	—	—

National Journal Ratings

	1999 LIB —	1999 CONS		2000 LIB —	2000 CONS
Economic	88%	0%		95%	0%
Social	87%	0%		94%	0%
Foreign	57%	42%		97%	0%

Key Votes of the 106th Congress

1. Patient Bill of Rights	Y	5. Bar RU-486 $ for FDA	N	9. NATO War in Serbia	Y
2. Accelerate Min. Wage	Y	6. Display 10 Commandments	N	10. Perm. Trade with China	Y
3. Strike Ban on Ergo. Stnd.	Y	7. Gun Show Bkgrnd. Checks	Y	11. Debt Relief for 3rd World	Y
4. Ovrd. Estate Tax Veto	N	8. Ban Part.-Birth Abortion	N	12. Drop Cuba Econ. Embargo	Y

Election Results

2000 general	Jose Serrano (D-L)	103,041	(96%)	($210,037)
	Aaron Justice (R)	3,934	(4%)	
	Others	571	(1%)	
2000 primary	Jose Serrano (D)	unopposed		
1998 general	Jose Serrano (D-L)	67,367	(95%)	($71,281)
	Others	3,213	(5%)	

SEVENTEENTH DISTRICT

The Bronx, a product almost entirely of the first half of the 20th Century, was originally a collection of middle-class neighborhoods clustered around subway stops, a borough where children of immigrants left gloomy Manhattan for the sunlight of wide avenues and the vistas of a city where the street grid bent to adapt to nature's ridges and hills. Different ethnic groups were clustered here and there: Irish in Kingsbridge, in the valley between Riverdale and the Grand Concourse; Italians in Bedford Park, north of Fordham University and Bronx Park; well-to-do WASPs and Jews in Riverdale, on the palisades above the Hudson River; Jews with less education and advantages originally in the Art Deco apartments on the Grand Concourse, then in a rush to Co-op City, the giant union-built apartment complex, with 35 35-story buildings, built in 1965 on marshland between the Hutchinson River Parkway and I-95.

The 17th Congressional District includes much of these Bronx neighborhoods plus several in the Westchester County suburbs just to the north. Co-op City is one anchor, and perhaps the largest political bloc in the district. Just to the west is the heavily black, middle-income neighborhood of Williamsbridge. The 17th's portions of Yonkers, Mount Vernon and New Rochelle in Westchester are carefully drawn to include most blacks there. The district also dips south along the Harlem River to take in some housing projects in the South Bronx. The 17th is, in Voting Rights Act argot, a minority-influence district, 44% black and 36% Hispanic in 2000.

Eliot Engel, the congressman from the 17th District, is a son of the Bronx and long a resident of Co-op City (though now he lives in Riverdale), a political junkie who memorized the names of all 100 senators when he was a boy. He was a teacher and guidance counselor who has won office (like Jose Serrano in the next-door 16th District) when incumbents have been struck by scandal. He was elected to the New York Assembly in a special election in March 1977, at 30, to replace a convicted incumbent, and to the House in 1988 to replace Democrat Mario Biaggi, once the most decorated member of the New York Police Department, after he was convicted in two tawdry bribery cases. Engel beat Biaggi in the Democratic primary 48%–26% and in the general, in which Biaggi was the Republican nominee, by 56%–27%.

Engel has one of the most liberal voting records in the House. On the International Relations Committee, he made his name as the backer of one ethnic cause after another; members of just about any ethnic group can be found in the Bronx. He has been a prime sponsor of the resolution to recognize Jerusalem as the capital of Israel and criticized proposals to dismantle West Bank settlements. He met with Sinn Fein leader Gerry Adams, proposed legislation to oppose the British in Northern Ireland, and supported Bill Clinton's efforts to seek peace there. He has sponsored designation of October as Italian American Culture and Heritage Month and called for investigation of the internment of Italian nationals and other harsh restrictions during World War Two. Engel is not a 1970s-style dove: He supported the Gulf war resolution in 1991 and the bombing of Serbia to get a settlement in Bosnia. He heads the Congressional Albanian Issues Caucus and keeps an eye on Albanian rights in the Former Yugoslav Republic of Macedonia. He called for air strikes after the 1998 Yugoslav crackdown and got a U.S. Information Office set up in Pristina. He strongly supported Clinton's military campaign in Kosovo.

He used the disputed 2000 presidential election to advocate Electoral College reform. His separate proposals would award a state's electoral votes based on the proportion of the popular vote received by each candidate, or allocate electoral votes based on the results in each congressional district, with two votes to the winner of each statewide vote. He called suggestions for a direct vote that would abolish the Electoral College "foolhardy." He also called for financial incentives to the states to update their voting machines, calling punchcard technology "antiquated" and prone to human error. An Engel tradition: Since 1989 he has staked out an aisle seat hours before each State of the Union speech, so that he can shake the president's hand.

At home, Engel is a relentless constituency service congressman, with five district offices in this geographically tiny district. In June 1996 *The Wall Street Journal* profiled him as "Revenge of a Nerd," telling how he is known as "the mayor" in the north Bronx because of his persistent attention to local problems from broken traffic lights to congested subway trains. He picketed a local motel because of concerns that it was a locale of prostitution. When stories broke about alleged arson of southern black churches, Engel held an arson protection conference for local churches and synagogues.

The major political threat to Engel is the rising percentages of blacks and Hispanics in the district. In 1994 he was opposed by salsa singer Willie Colon, who was supported by Al Sharpton and Assemblyman Larry Seabrook. Engel won 61%–39%, not an entirely reassuring margin. In 1998 Seabrook, who is black and had become a state senator, made no secret he was running. Engel was endorsed unanimously by Democrats in heavily black Mount Vernon; in May he got a 69% endorsement vote from the Black Democrats of Westchester County. Democratic County Chairman Roberto Ramirez spoke to Seabrook, making vague promises about working on voter registration, and Seabrook bowed out of the 1998 race. Finally in the September 2000 primary, there was the showdown between Engel and Seabrook. Seabrook argued that the district needed "real leadership" and attacked Engel for living in suburban Maryland. Ramirez and the Bronx Democratic organization backed Seabrook this time; he had a meeting with Congressional Black Caucus members, which brought angry comments from other Jewish members who argued that all Democrats should support their incumbent colleagues. When Seabrook produced a campaign button that said, "Vote First African-American Congressman," Engel objected to the use of race in the campaign. The contest turned uglier when a page-one story in the New York *Daily News* said that Seabrook secretly divorced his wife in 1993 but continued to sign joint tax returns in violation of the law. Seabrook accused Engel of leaking sealed court documents, which Engel denied, but refused to provide copies of his tax returns. Engel responded with criticisms of Seabrook's high absenteeism and improper travel reimbursements in the state senate. In the end Engel won by a 50%–41% margin, with 9% for a candidate named Sonny Zayas.

Engel's Democratic primary problems highlighted the jeopardy that he faces in redistricting. It is generally agreed that New York City will lose one Democratic seat. Some Bronx politicians would like to see a black-majority seat based in The Bronx, but they would presumably not want to eliminate the heavily Hispanic 16th. The Bronx, thanks to an unexpected population gain, has enough people for two full districts with a few left over. Although there are now far more Hispanics than blacks in the borough, drawing a district with a black percentage higher than the current 17th is possible. So the likelihood is that will happen, and Engel will face the choice for another decade of representing a gloriously multiracial, multiethnic constituency—or, perhaps, taking a shot at a Westchester-based district.

Cook's Call *Probably Safe.* Engel's only threat in this solidly Democratic district has been from Democrats. He has had a primary challenge ever since he was elected in 1988, but his 2000 contest against black state Senator Larry Seabrook was the most competitive of his career. As the black and Hispanic population in the district continues to rise, Engel will likely see himself in more competitive primary contests.

THE PEOPLE: Pop. 2000: 627,566; Pop. 1990: 578,424, up 8.5% 1990–2000. 28.6% White, 43.6% Black, 3.5% Asian, 0.7% Amer. Indian, 0.1% Hawaiian, 5.5% Two+ races, 18.1% Other; 35.9% Hispanic Origin.

2000 Presidential Vote		
Gore (D)	138,512	(87%)
Bush (R)	17,511	(11%)
Nader (Green)	2,922	(2%)
Others	1,119	(1%)

1996 Presidential Vote		
Clinton (D)	126,787	(86%)
Dole (R)	16,238	(11%)
Perot (I)	3,844	(3%)

Rep. Eliot L. Engel (D)

Elected 1988, 7th term; b. Feb. 18, 1947, Bronx; home, Bronx; Hunter-Lehman Col., B.A. 1969, C.U.N.Y., Lehman Col., M.A. 1973, NY Law Schl., J.D. 1987; Jewish; married (Patricia).

Elected Office: NY Assembly, 1977–88.

Professional Career: Teacher, guidance counselor, NYC public schl., 1969–77.

DC Office: 2303 RHOB 20515, 202-225-2464; Fax: 202-225-5513; Web site: www.house.gov/engel.

District Offices: Bronx, 718-796-9700; Bronx, 718-652-0400; Bronx, 718-320-2314; Mt. Vernon, 914-699-4100; Yonkers, 914-423-0700.

Committees: *Energy & Commerce* (14th of 26 D): Health; Telecommunications & The Internet. *International Relations* (13th of 23 D): Europe; Middle East & South Asia.

Group Ratings

	ADA	ACLU	AFS	LCV	CON	ITIC	NTU	COC	ACU	NTLC	CHC
2000	85	86	100	93	36	53	22	38	22	20	0
1999	95	—	100	94	35	—	9	24	0	—	—

National Journal Ratings

	1999 LIB —	1999 CONS		2000 LIB —	2000 CONS
Economic	88%	0%		81%	19%
Social	82%	17%		88%	11%
Foreign	78%	17%		74%	24%

Key Votes of the 106th Congress

1. Patient Bill of Rights	Y	5. Bar RU-486 $ for FDA	N	9. NATO War in Serbia	Y
2. Accelerate Min. Wage	Y	6. Display 10 Commandments	N	10. Perm. Trade with China	N
3. Strike Ban on Ergo. Stnd.	Y	7. Gun Show Bkgrnd. Checks	Y	11. Debt Relief for 3rd World	Y
4. Ovrd. Estate Tax Veto	N	8. Ban Part.-Birth Abortion	N	12. Drop Cuba Econ. Embargo	N

Election Results

2000 general	Eliot L. Engel (D-L)	115,093	(90%)	($1,028,928)
	Patrick McManus (R-C)	13,201	(10%)	
2000 primary	Eliot L. Engel (D)	24,159	(50%)	
	Larry B. Seabrook (D)	19,629	(41%)	
	Sonny A. Zayas (D)	4,115	(9%)	
1998 general	Eliot L. Engel (D-L)	80,947	(88%)	($364,459)
	Peter Fiumefreddo (R-C-Ind)	11,037	(12%)	($16,043)

EIGHTEENTH DISTRICT

The great granite ridges that form the spine of Manhattan and the Bronx move north into the thin peninsula of land between Long Island Sound and the Hudson River that is lower Westchester County. Blessed with some of America's loveliest scenery, easily accessible to Manhattan by train since the mid-19th Century, this became some of the country's first suburban terrain, with grand estates built by great millionaires, like Jay Gould's Gothic revival Lyndhurst or John D. Rockefeller's spectacular Kykuit, with villages for retainers clustered around the railroad stations.

Today, Westchester still looks suburban, perhaps more than ever now that it has a nice patina of age. It has little commuter railroad stations across from faux Tudor drugstores, soda fountains and cobblestone post offices; it also has shopping malls and galleries and corporate headquarters. The county does have its share of homeless and racial ghettos, its seedy neighborhoods if not slums. But intensive development has not proceeded too far north of White Plains, for just to the north Westchester is crossed by the first of several mountain ridges—the closest the Appalachians come to the ocean. More than Nassau or Suffolk counties or northern New Jersey, it has attracted liberal-minded professionals, often Jewish, who have made very high-income places like Scarsdale Democratic strongholds. In addition, blue-collar voters and blacks in southern Westchester make this a mixed constituency. Historically Republican, Westchester votes a lot like the comfortable central city neighborhoods it physically resembles—Cambridge's Brattle Street, Philadelphia's Chestnut Hill, Washington's Cleveland Park—which is to say, solidly Democratic.

The 18th Congressional District contains the heart of suburban Westchester County but actually has less than half the county's population; it also includes a little territory in the Bronx and widely scattered areas in Queens. Politics, as one might expect, is at work here; this is a district designed for Congresswoman Nita Lowey, a Democrat first elected in 1988 and a favorite of then-Governor Mario Cuomo. The 18th includes most of southern Westchester, but not the black neighborhoods of Yonkers, Mount Vernon and New Rochelle, which are in the minority-influence 17th District. It includes the rich suburbs of Pelham, Eastchester, Bronxville and Scarsdale, a convenient 30-minute trip to Grand Central on Metro North, plus some of the Long Island Sound towns, once mostly Republican but now solidly liberal. The 18th also contains the southern half of White Plains, the county seat-corporate headquarters-shopping mall center. From there the 18th goes on its odyssey, picking up a few thousand people in Bronx communities facing the Sound and the urban resort of City Island. Then it crosses the Throgs Neck Bridge and is connected by a block-wide land-bridge through Flushing to two distinct areas of Queens. One is Lefrak City and other high-rise apartments in Rego Park, along Queens Boulevard, where the first condominium conversion in New York took place in 1966; this area is heavily Jewish and very Democratic. The other is the heavily Italian neighborhoods around St. John's University, including the longtime home of its most famous alumnus, Mario Cuomo, in the pleasant winding streets of Holliswood, a more politically mixed area. In 2000, its non-Hispanic white population had dropped to 63%, with 15% Hispanic, 11% Asian, and 8% Black.

Nita Lowey was born in the Bronx, raised her family in Queens, and now lives in upper-crust Harrison in Westchester. She went to work for Cuomo in 1975, after he was appointed secretary of state by Governor Hugh Carey; she was an assistant secretary of state when she decided to run for Congress in 1988. In the primary, she faced Hamilton Fish III, son and grandson of Republican Hudson River congressmen, and as a former publisher of *The Nation* considerably more liberal than Lowey; she won 44%–36%. Her opponent in the general was Joseph DioGuardi, a two-term incumbent who trumpeted his experience as a CPA but was dogged by charges of illicit contributions; she won 50%–47%. Each spent over $1 million, with Lowey spending $657,000 of her own money.

In the House, Lowey has a fairly solid liberal record. She was a Clinton loyalist when it was tough to be so, voting for the 1993 budget and tax package in this high-income district, splitting with most New York Democrats and organized labor to support both NAFTA and permanent normal trade relations with China. She helped to originate the plan for federal aid for school construction; it was dropped from the 1997 budget agreement, but later revived by Clinton as a major Democratic initiative. Much of Lowey's legislative work has been done on Appropriations, and much has been connected with feminist issues. In 1994 she organized 72 members, mostly Democrats, who pledged not to vote for a health care plan that did not cover abortions. She was a leading backer of funds for international family planning, and led the unsuccessful opposition to George W. Bush's reversal of the policy when he took office. She achieved a rare feminist victory in Congress by getting into the 1998 omnibus bill a provision requiring federal employee health plans that cover prescriptions to include contraceptives; reluctantly she agreed to an exclusion for plans and physicians with religious objections. She criticized Bill Clinton's decision to require a national registry of doctors permitted to prescribe the drug when the Food and Drug Administration agreed to allow sale of the RU-486 abortion pill. Working with Henry Hyde, she expanded coverage of the Children's Health Insurance Program for prenatal benefits. With Rosa DeLauro and Nancy Pelosi, she worked for increased funding for breast and cervical cancer screening. She also was a leader in the lengthy fight to reduce from .10% to .08% the blood-alcohol limit on drivers that states must set to continue to receive their entire federal highway aid allocation; it was enacted in October 2000.

Lowey has been a strong supporter of the National Endowment for the Arts. She opposed a 15% cap on state NEA grants: "Artistic excellence is not spread evenly around the country. Other states produce corn and soybeans; our tremendous contribution to the United States is our artistic areas, among other things." On local matters, she got money to restore Beaver Swamp Brook in Westchester and Willow Lake in Queens, dredge Mamaroneck Harbor and clean up the Long Island Sound watershed. Calling the number of flights airlines scheduled "excessive and unrealistic," she called for a moratorium on new flights into LaGuardia Airport.

Since Lowey first won, the 18th District has been moving left and she has proved a prodigious fundraiser, never spending less than $878,000 on a campaign. In 1992, DioGuardi came back for a rematch; she won 71% in the Queens portion just added to the district and won overall 56%–44%. Since then, she has become entrenched. In November 1998, when Senator Daniel Patrick Moynihan announced he would retire in 2000, Lowey was mentioned as one of several Democrats interested in the seat; several others dropped out and Lowey stayed in. When rumors of a Hillary Rodham Clinton candidacy began, Lowey stepped aside and said she would support the First Lady.

Her party loyalty and avid fundraising led to Minority Leader Dick Gephardt's decision in January 2001 to appoint Lowey to chair the Democratic Congressional Campaign Committee. With Patty Murray of Washington chairing its Senate Democratic counterpart, they are the first two women to head party campaign committees. "We've come a long way," Lowey said. "There was a time when women couldn't raise the money they needed for campaigns." But she faced a difficult task in leading the Democrats' bid to regain House control in 2002. Democrats will have to propitiate fundraisers who remember their assurances that they would win in 2000, they will have to overcome the fact that this is the first cycle in 50 years in which Republicans have the advantage in redistricting and they may have to face a large number of their own members retiring and leaving open seats which may be difficult to defend. She will also have to face her own redistricting problem. It is generally conceded that New York City must lose one seat. But if, as some insiders expect, that seat is the 7th District, that would leave a lot of territory in Queens that could still be attached by a narrow corridor in the Bronx to the mostly white and solidly Democratic towns of southern Westchester.

Cook's Call *Safe.* Since defeating a Republican incumbent here in 1988, Lowey has not had much trouble holding onto this Democratic-leaning seat. Redistricting could make this seat, which stretches from Westchester County to parts of Queens and the Bronx, more marginal if

Lowey were pushed further into Republican leaning Westchester County and out of the boroughs of New York City. Her district will need to pick up about 30,000 people in redistricting.

THE PEOPLE: Pop. 2000: 620,213; Pop. 1990: 581,021, up 6.7% 1990–2000. 70.6% White, 8.5% Black, 11.1% Asian, 0.2% Amer. Indian, 3.6% Two+ races, 6% Other; 15.3% Hispanic Origin.

2000 Presidential Vote

Gore (D)	133,229	(60%)
Bush (R)	81,783	(37%)
Nader (Green)	6,316	(3%)
Others	1,604	(1%)

1996 Presidential Vote

Clinton (D)	121,501	(59%)
Dole (R)	73,399	(36%)
Perot (I)	10,215	(5%)

Rep. Nita M. Lowey (D)

Elected 1988, 7th term; b. July 5, 1937, Bronx; home, Harrison; Mt. Holyoke Col., B.A. 1959; Jewish; married (Stephen).

Professional Career: Asst. for Econ. Devel. & Neighborhood Preservation, NY Secy. of State; Dep. Dir., Division of Econ. Opportunity, 1975–85; NY Asst. Secy. of St., 1985–87.

DC Office: 2329 RHOB 20515, 202-225-6506; Fax: 202-225-0546; Web site: www.house.gov/lowey.

District Offices: Rego Park, 718-897-3602; White Plains, 914-428-1707.

Committees: *DCCC Chairman. Appropriations* (10th of 29 D): Foreign Operations & Export Financing (RMM); Labor, HHS & Education.

Group Ratings

	ADA	ACLU	AFS	LCV	CON	ITIC	NTU	COC	ACU	NTLC	CHC
2000	75	79	85	79	63	78	26	52	9	16	7
1999	100	—	100	94	71	—	19	16	4	—	—

National Journal Ratings

	1999 LIB —	1999 CONS		2000 LIB —	2000 CONS
Economic	88% —	0%		74% —	25%
Social	75% —	24%		91% —	6%
Foreign	78% —	22%		96% —	3%

Key Votes of the 106th Congress

1. Patient Bill of Rights	Y	5. Bar RU-486 $ for FDA	N	9. NATO War in Serbia	Y
2. Accelerate Min. Wage	Y	6. Display 10 Commandments	N	10. Perm. Trade with China	Y
3. Strike Ban on Ergo. Stnd.	Y	7. Gun Show Bkgrnd. Checks	Y	11. Debt Relief for 3rd World	Y
4. Ovrd. Estate Tax Veto	N	8. Ban Part.-Birth Abortion	N	12. Drop Cuba Econ. Embargo	Y

Election Results

2000 general	Nita M. Lowey (D)	126,878	(67%)	($1,055,962)
	John G. Vonglis (R-C)	58,022	(31%)	
	Others	3,747	(2%)	
2000 primary	Nita M. Lowey (D)	unopposed		
1998 general	Nita M. Lowey (D)	91,623	(83%)	($932,342)
	Daniel McMahon (C)	12,594	(11%)	
	Others	6,485	(6%)	

NINETEENTH DISTRICT

The great interior of America can be said to begin where the Hudson River squeezes through the chain of Appalachian ridges at the Hudson Highlands. This choke point was the barrier to British military power during the Revolutionary War, when American forces built a chain across the river to keep the British from sailing north. It was over control of this part of the Hudson that Benedict Arnold betrayed his country, and it was here that the new nation built its Military Academy high on the cliffs at West Point. The Hudson was the impetus for the builders of the Erie Canal and the water-level New York Central Railroad, the great projects that made New York City the port of the American interior, as well as the builders of the Croton Aqueduct not far away, which provided the water without which New York could not grow—and also provided a way for the first cockroaches to reach the city. Some distant day the great aqueduct may crumble. But the cockroaches will remain.

The lower Hudson was Dutch territory, with Washington Irving country in Tarrytown and ancient estates like the now-restored Philipsburg Manor. In the late 19th Century, the ridges east of the Lower Hudson were first the site of great estates of New York's very rich and then became high-income suburbs: colonial-style Bedford, woodsy Chappaqua, John Cheever's Ossining. And in the mid-20th Century, these hills became home to some of America's leading corporations. *Reader's Digest* had built its colonial-style campus north of Pleasantville as early as the 1930s; General Foods moved to the north side of White Plains in the 1950s; soon after, not far from the Cross-Westchester Expressway, IBM, Pepsico, and Texaco built headquarters. Yet as woods have grown over what used to be farmland, this country has also become wilder: overpopulating deer have been eating gardens in northern Westchester and in May 1997 a black bear was captured running loose in White Plains. Bill and Hillary Rodham Clinton, at their home in Chappaqua, may have to watch out.

The 19th District of New York covers much of the lower Hudson. It reaches south to take in part of White Plains and the corporate territory nearby, and includes northern Westchester County—now, for all its rural look, with almost as many people as the county's population-losing suburbs nearer New York City. The 19th runs north across towns filling up with middle-income public and corporate employees seeking reasonably priced housing in safe areas, up through Putnam County to Dutchess County and the old city of Poughkeepsie on the Hudson and the valleys of Millbrook and Amenia and the Innisfree gardens. It crosses the Hudson where the rebels' chain did, by West Point and the Storm King Highway, and runs inland in Orange County. IBM, with its headquarters in Armonk and research center in Yorktown Heights, has been a major area employer, and its longtime policy of lifetime employment was a mainstay here; IBM's big layoffs in the mid-1990s came as an unnerving shock. Politically, sentiments here run counter to what might be expected. The older communities, with their well-educated and liberally inclined residents, have been historically Republican but now lean more to the Democrats. The newer communities, with upwardly striving people often disgusted by the crime and cultural disorder of New York City, may be filled with ancestral Democrats but are trending Republican.

The congresswoman from this district is Sue Kelly, a Republican elected in 1994. Kelly is not a Hudson Valley aristocrat but the daughter of a Lima, Ohio, doctor. She met her husband while she was a botany researcher at Harvard; they raised their family in Katonah, where she volunteered in many organizations, worked as a patient advocate, rape crisis counselor and educator, and sang in a church choir. She had a business renovating buildings and owned and ran a florist shop. She also had political experience as campaign manager for Assemblyman Jon Fossel in the 1970s. In March 1994, Congressman Hamilton Fish, a Hudson County aristocrat, decided to retire, and Kelly decided to use the $150,000 she had saved to buy a new business to help finance a campaign for Congress instead. It was a crowded field, in which Kelly emerged as the only candidate who was both for lower taxes and "huge" budget cuts, and pro-choice on abortion. Her chief opponent in the primary was Joseph DioGuardi, twice elected in the Westchester district to the south and twice defeated there by Nita Lowey. Kelly won the primary with 23% to DioGuardi's 20%, with two other candidates at 19% and 18%. The Democratic nominee was Hamilton Fish Jr., son of the retiring congressman but as publisher of the leftish and anti-Israel *The Nation*, with quite different politics. This was expected to be a close race but with good margins in the northern counties Kelly beat Fish 52%–37%, with 10% for DioGuardi on the Conservative and Right-to-Life lines.

Kelly, with her middle-of-the-House voting record, has been whipsawed by criticism from right and left. She supported the Contract with America, which earned her howls from the left.

On environmental issues, she sponsored the 1996 Hudson River Habitat Restoration Act, supported $17.5 million for land acquisition in Sterling Forest and pushed EPA to authorize a Superfund cleanup to reduce PCBs on the Hudson. But environmental groups were furious that she supported Republican bills promoting cost-benefit analyses. In January 2001, when Con Edison made mistakes in moving too quickly to reopen the Indian Point nuclear reactor in her district, Kelly criticized the utility's "keep-the-plant-running-at-all-costs mentality." On abortion, she irritated many conservatives by being one of the few Republicans to vote against the partial-birth abortion ban in 1996. But in 1997, when the executive director of the National Coalition of Abortion Providers admitted he lied about the frequency of partial-birth abortions, she changed her mind and came out for the ban. "When you get into doing it on a healthy woman, with a healthy fetus, very late term, what are we talking about here?" she said. And in 1998 she joined other Republican women to ask why feminist Democrats were not outraged about the charges brought against Bill Clinton; she voted for two of the four impeachment counts. So when in 1999 she was chosen as the Republican co-chair of the Congressional Caucus for Women's Issues, feminists yelped in rage. Kelly stood her ground—in February 2000 calling Hillary Rodham Clinton, her new constituent, "a carpetbagger" who did not know New York or have the background to represent the state. The First Lady's spokesman responded by calling Kelly's comments "not very neighborly."

Occasionally she does something seemingly uncontroversial, like sponsoring a private immigration bill for marathoner Khalid Khannouchi, a Moroccan living in Ossining, so he could represent the United States in the 2000 Olympics. But that caused a local brouhaha when he subsequently withdrew from the Olympic trials because of leg injuries; his wife blamed the problem on political pressure on him to run in a London marathon in order to meet citizenship requirements.

Kelly's difficulty in balancing conflicting pressures became apparent when she sought to circumvent seniority and seek the House Small Business Committee chairmanship in January 2001. She offered her bipartisan approach, her appeal as a woman and her positive dealings with small-business groups. But Speaker Dennis Hastert stuck with fellow Illinoisan Don Manzullo, who was next in line for the post, and Kelly may have been hurt by her moderate voting record.

In elections she has been challenged on all sides. Not even a plea from Speaker Newt Gingrich's office could keep DioGuardi from challenging Kelly in the 1996 Republican primary. Kelly won the primary, but by a narrow 53%–42%. In the general, Kelly beat the Democrat by only 46%–39%, with 12% for DioGuardi. Her subsequent victories were by more convincing margins. Her 2000 opponent was Larry Otis Graham, author of best-selling *Our Kind of People: Inside America's Black Upper Class*. Graham, who boasted of campaign advice from his Chappaqua neighbor Bill Clinton, criticized Kelly as out of touch with her constituents; he lost, 61%–36%. Redistricting could change this district at the chokepoint of New York, with results difficult to predict. If as seems likely the district is extended northward it would become somewhat more Republican.

Cook's Call *Safe*. After beating back serious challenges by Right to Life and Conservative Party candidates in the mid-1990s, Kelly looks like she has a solid grasp of this marginally Republican district.

THE PEOPLE: Pop. 2000: 626,776; Pop. 1990: 580,386, up 8% 1990–2000. 84.3% White, 7.5% Black, 2.8% Asian, 0.2% Amer. Indian, 2% Two+ races, 3.2% Other; 9% Hispanic Origin.

2000 Presidential Vote			1996 Presidential Vote		
Gore (D)	131,977	(50%)	Clinton (D)	116,697	(49%)
Bush (R)	120,101	(45%)	Dole (R)	98,597	(42%)
Nader (Green)	10,200	(4%)	Perot (I)	20,803	(9%)
Others	2,591	(1%)			

Rep. Sue W. Kelly (R)

Elected 1994, 4th term; b. Sept. 26, 1936, Lima, OH; home, Katonah; Denison U., B.A. 1958, Sarah Lawrence Col., M.A. 1985; Presbyterian; married (Edward).

Professional Career: Owner/Mgr., Kelly & Assoc. bldg. rehab.; Researcher, Harvard U., 1958–60; Owner/Mgr., Kelly Florist, 1980–83; Prof., Sarah Lawrence Col., 1988–91.

DC Office: 1127 LHOB 20515, 202-225-5441; Fax: 202-225-3289; Web site: www.house.gov/suekelly.

District Offices: Fishkill, 845-897-5200; Mt. Kisco, 914-241-6340.

Committees: *Financial Services* (13th of 37 R): Financial Institutions & Consumer Credit; Housing & Community Opportunity; Oversight & Investigations (Chmn.). *Small Business* (6th of 19 R): Regulatory Reform Oversight. *Transportation & Infrastructure* (13th of 42 R): Aviation; Highways & Transit; Water Resources & Environment.

Group Ratings

	ADA	ACLU	AFS	LCV	CON	ITIC	NTU	COC	ACU	NTLC	CHC
2000	35	36	14	86	9	100	55	76	56	64	53
1999	50	—	16	69	11	—	53	80	56	—	—

National Journal Ratings

	1999 LIB	—	1999 CONS		2000 LIB	—	2000 CONS
Economic	45%	—	55%		44%	—	55%
Social	55%	—	44%		57%	—	42%
Foreign	50%	—	48%		51%	—	47%

Key Votes of the 106th Congress

1. Patient Bill of Rights	Y	5. Bar RU-486 $ for FDA	N	9. NATO War in Serbia	Y
2. Accelerate Min. Wage	N	6. Display 10 Commandments	Y	10. Perm. Trade with China	Y
3. Strike Ban on Ergo. Stnd.	N	7. Gun Show Bkgrnd. Checks	N	11. Debt Relief for 3rd World	Y
4. Ovrd. Estate Tax Veto	Y	8. Ban Part.-Birth Abortion	Y	12. Drop Cuba Econ. Embargo	N

Election Results

2000 general	Sue W. Kelly (R-C)	145,532	(61%)	($980,892)
	Larry Otis Graham (D-L-WF)	85,871	(36%)	($314,199)
	Others	7,748	(3%)	
2000 primary	Sue W. Kelly (R)	unopposed		
1998 general	Sue W. Kelly (R-C)	104,467	(62%)	($595,985)
	Dick Collins (D)	56,378	(34%)	($8,461)
	Others	6,987	(4%)	

TWENTIETH DISTRICT

From Sunnyside, the whimsical house that Washington Irving built in Tarrytown near the country he immortalized as Sleepy Hollow, you can see across the waters of the Tappan Zee, the widest point of the Hudson, and get a sense of how the land looked when first settled by Dutchmen. All around is Irving country—the old towns of Tarrytown, Irvington, Dobbs Ferry and Hastings-on-Hudson, now comfortably affluent suburbs. On the other side of the Tappan Zee is Rockland County, a stretch of suburbs between the Hudson and the Ramapos, the first Appalachian chain west of New York. First settled by Dutchmen, Rockland then was studded by little towns that grew up as if 1,000 miles from Gotham, but they have thrived on the actual proximity: the town of Nyack here was the home of actress Helen Hayes; and James A. Farley, Franklin Roosevelt's chief political major domo and Democratic National Committee chairman, was from Stony Point, just below the Hudson Highlands.

The 20th Congressional District spans the Tappan Zee, connecting most of the Irving suburbs with Rockland County and stepping over the Ramapos 120 miles inland to the Pennsylvania border. Past the Ramapos is most of Orange County, New York's third-fastest-growing county since 1990, where old villages between mountains and farms on the nation's biggest deposit of muck soil outside the Everglades have been flanked with new modest-income subdivisions. Farther out, past the Shawangunk Mountains, is Sullivan County and the Catskills Borscht Belt district, a Jewish resort area where huge kosher hotels were built starting in the late 19th Century; these thrived when Jews were excluded from other resorts, but fell on hard times in the late 20th century. The St. Regis Mohawk Indian tribe also planned a huge casino in Sullivan County. Politically, this area has been trending Republican, as old Upstate-minded residents are joined by newcomers fleeing the city.

The 20th's congressman, Republican Benjamin Gilman, grew up in Middletown, in Orange County; he traveled with his father to Nazi Germany in 1933, at 10, and remembers Hitler's storm troopers. After service in World War II, he became a lawyer, working for the state and bringing *habeas corpus* cases for mental hospital patients. In 1966 he was elected to the Assembly, and in 1972 to the U.S. House. Gilman is moderate on economics and cultural issues, but more conservative on foreign policy; he is pleasant and ordinarily arouses little animosity. In the 1970s he worked, often with East German lawyer Wolfgang Vogel, to arrange spy swaps. He visited Buenos Aires newspaper editor Jacobo Timmerman in jail in Argentina and helped secure his release; he championed the human rights of Pentecostals, Ukrainians, Poles and Jews in the Soviet Union.

Gilman became ranking Republican on International Relations in 1993 and chairman in 1995. Under his leadership the committee pushed and prodded the Clinton Administration, clucking disapproval helplessly sometimes, steering the course of policy at others. Gilman favored NATO expansion and air strikes against the Bosnian Serbs before Bill Clinton did. He wanted to delay full recognition of Vietnam pending a full accounting of American POWs. He urged increases in the foreign aid budget and continuation of aid to family planning programs despite the objections of most Republicans. One of Gilman's major concerns has been drugs. In 1997, he held up shipment of helicopters to Mexico, saying that the Colombian national police could make better use of them; he opposed the administration's refusal to certify that Colombia was "cooperating" even as it insisted that Mexico was "fully cooperating." He became a steadfast supporter of Colombian officials' effort to eradicate the primary source of cocaine and heroin for American youth, but second-guessed the Clinton decision to cede a "demilitarized zone" to the narco-guerrillas. In November 2000, he abruptly withdrew his support for the $1.3 billion military aid to Colombia, complaining of a history of corruption and human rights abuses; he called for shifting money to the national police.

On the Middle East, Gilman has been a supporter of Israel, and has backed aggressive stances against Iraq and Iran. He pressed the Clinton Administration to stop Chinese sales of naval cruise missiles and other weapons to Iran. He was the sponsor of the Iraq Liberation Act, which called for policies to oust Saddam Hussein, and after its passage criticized Clinton's "lethargic approach." He favored Radio Free Asia broadcasts to China and listing of Chinese military firms, is wary of the transfer of high-tech systems and weapons to China, and opposed permanent normal trade relations. Of the Kyoto climate treaty, he said, "The rest of the world ganged up on the United States" and "the administration effectively joined the gang." He demanded in June 2000 that Russia repay its debts to the United States, which the Clinton Administration had rescheduled at least five times. On impeachment, he was listed as undecided until almost the last day, then voted for it, but with four other Republicans urged senators to consider censure instead.

Gilman still works his district hard, sometimes spending Saturdays riding around in his mobile home-office. He won the seat fairly easily in 1972 against ultra-liberal John Dow, and he has had only one difficult re-election race since, in 1982 after redistricting, when he faced Republican-turned-Democrat Peter Peyser and won 53%–42%. His 1998 and 2000 opponent was the Town of Greenburgh supervisor, who set up a town matchmaking service and got the Bronx River Parkway closed Sundays for bicyclists. Each time, he beat Gilman almost 2–1 on his own turf in Westchester; Gilman won by about 2–1 west of the Hudson and was reelected by a solid margin.

Gilman objected strongly to the Republicans' three-term limit for committee chairmen, which forced him to give up the International Relations chair in 2001. He generated little interest in his bid for an exemption, but got a consolation prize as Chairman of the revived Middle East and South Asia Subcommittee. After the next election he could chair the Government Reform Committee, where he is second-ranking, but Gilman has expressed little interest in that. A more immediate problem is redistricting. Although his own district has gained population, changes elsewhere could force him closer to less-friendly Westchester or move Democrat Maurice Hinchey into the territory of Gilman, who is not well-connected in Albany. There is speculation that Gilman, who turns 80 in 2002, might retire, and that if he does a Democrat might well win a Rockland-Orange seat; Al Gore won the 20th District by 53%–42% in 2000.

Cook's Call *Safe.* Democrats continue to hope that the 77 year-old Gilman will retire: This district is one of the most Democratic in the state to be held by a Republican. Democrats have had little luck in trying to oust the 15-term incumbent, and he has never won with less than 57% since 1982. If Gilman does leave (he has made no indication that he intends to step down), expect a hotly contested race for this marginal district. If Gilman stays, don't expect a close race. He is well entrenched here.

THE PEOPLE: Pop. 2000: 635,820; Pop. 1990: 580,025, up 9.6% 1990–2000. 81% White, 8.9% Black, 4.3% Asian, 0.3% Amer. Indian, 0.1% Hawaiian, 2.3% Two+ races, 3.2% Other; 9.6% Hispanic Origin.

2000 Presidential Vote		
Gore (D)	141,972	(53%)
Bush (R)	112,232	(42%)
Nader (Green)	8,398	(3%)
Others	4,192	(2%)

1996 Presidential Vote		
Clinton (D)	130,550	(55%)
Dole (R)	89,214	(37%)
Perot (I)	18,216	(8%)

Rep. Benjamin A. Gilman (R)

Elected 1972, 15th term; b. Dec. 6, 1922, Poughkeepsie; home, Middletown; U. of PA, B.S. 1946, NY Law Schl., LL.B. 1950; Jewish; married (Georgia).

Military Career: Army Air Corps, 1942–45 (WWII); NY State Guard, 1981-present.

Elected Office: NY Assembly, 1966–72.

Professional Career: Practicing atty., 1950–72; NY Asst. Atty. Gen., 1953–55; Atty., NY Temporary Comm. on the Courts.

DC Office: 2449 RHOB 20515, 202-225-3776; Fax: 202-225-2541; Web site: www.house.gov/gilman.

District Offices: Hastings-on-Hudson, 914-478-5550; Middletown, 914-343-6666; Monsey, 914-357-9000.

Committees: *Government Reform* (2d of 24 R): Criminal Justice, Drug Policy & Human Resources (Vice Chmn.); National Security, Veterans' Affairs & Intl. Relations. *International Relations* (2d of 26 R): Europe; Middle East & South Asia (Chmn.).

Group Ratings

	ADA	ACLU	AFS	LCV	CON	ITIC	NTU	COC	ACU	NTLC	CHC
2000	35	50	60	79	7	60	48	57	43	41	40
1999	50	—	50	63	2	—	48	48	52	—	—

National Journal Ratings

	1999 LIB —	1999 CONS		2000 LIB —	2000 CONS
Economic	51% —	49%		53% —	47%
Social	58% —	40%		64% —	36%
Foreign	48% —	52%		31% —	69%

Key Votes of the 106th Congress

1. Patient Bill of Rights	Y	5. Bar RU-486 $ for FDA	N	9. NATO War in Serbia	Y
2. Accelerate Min. Wage	Y	6. Display 10 Commandments	Y	10. Perm. Trade with China	N
3. Strike Ban on Ergo. Stnd.	*	7. Gun Show Bkgrnd. Checks	N	11. Debt Relief for 3rd World	N
4. Ovrd. Estate Tax Veto	Y	8. Ban Part.-Birth Abortion	N	12. Drop Cuba Econ. Embargo	N

Election Results

2000 general	Benjamin A. Gilman (R)	136,016	(58%)	($1,177,222)
	Paul J. Feiner (D-L-Green-WF)	94,646	(40%)	($431,215)
	Others	5,371	(2%)	
2000 primary	Benjamin A. Gilman (R)	unopposed		
1998 general	Benjamin A. Gilman (R)	98,546	(58%)	($942,146)
	Paul J. Feiner (D-Ind-L)	61,753	(37%)	($258,717)
	Others	8,605	(5%)	

TWENTY-FIRST DISTRICT

Albany, as readers of its novelist laureate William Kennedy know, is within living memory an antique city. Its solid rowhouses show its 19th Century prosperity; its once teeming lumberyards and railroad car shops, old restaurants and hotels, have the patina of age and the accumulated grime of decades of coal smoke burned during six-month-long winters. Its history is traceable to 1624, when the Dutch built Fort Orange on the banks of the Hudson so seagoing ships could dock at the edge of the great gloomy forests near the confluence of the Hudson and the Mohawk—the natural crossroads of Upstate New York even before the building of the Erie Canal and the New York Central Railroad. This was one of America's early industrial centers. Troy, a few miles upriver, was a steel town rivaling Pittsburgh in the 1840s, and later the leading producer of detachable collars; Cohoes, at the junction of the Hudson and the Mohawk, became a leading textile producer; Schenectady, a few miles up the Mohawk, was the site of Charles Steinmetz's fabled General Electric laboratories and has been a big GE town ever since. Albany was one of America's biggest lumber towns as well as the state capital.

Albany continues to have one of the nation's most famed Democratic political machines, dating back to 1921, when Daniel O'Connell and his brothers and local aristocrat Edwin Corning took control of City Hall. They never really relinquished it: O'Connell died in 1977 at age 91, still boss after 56 years, and his early partner's son, Erastus Corning II, was mayor from 1942 until his death in 1983. The machine was sustained by legions of city and county employees, by a certain creativity when it came to counting votes, and by the raffish atmosphere that was found in the speakeasies of so many cities during Prohibition and lingered in Albany for decades after: read Kennedy and you are there. Curiously, the machine made possible the transformation of antique Albany into the shiny metropolis it is today. Mayor Corning provided financing for Nelson Rockefeller's monumental South Mall, expressways were built, the old Union Station was spruced up, and yuppies began buying and renovating old townhouses. These days, the Albany machine can't always control the suburbs as it once could Albany; but it clings to power in the H.H. Richardson City Hall facing the gaudy state house.

The 21st Congressional District includes all of Albany and Schenectady Counties, plus Troy on the Hudson's east bank, and the depressed factory town of Amsterdam on the Mohawk. More than half its votes are cast in Albany County, and it is a solidly Democratic district—under a solid Democratic machine.

The congressman from the 21st District is Michael McNulty, a Democrat first elected in 1988. McNulty's roots in Albany politics go back to his grandfather, who served as Albany County sheriff, as did his father, who was also a town mayor. Michael McNulty was first elected to office in 1969, at 22, and served 13 years as town supervisor and mayor in the industrial suburb of Green Island; he was elected to the Assembly in 1982, at 35. The opening to Congress came without much warning. In 1988, four days after the July filing deadline and on the last day for withdrawal, 30-year incumbent Democrat Samuel Stratton announced he was retiring for health reasons, giving the Democratic machine a chance to name a replacement, which turned out to be McNulty. Serving in Congress was a fulfillment of his family's and his own ambition. McNulty won the 1988 general election by 62%–38% against a venture capital specialist who attacked him for avoiding the issues and for having been chosen by party bosses rather than primary voters. He has not had trouble in the general election since.

McNulty is hard-working, serious, abstemious, pleasant and a conscientious campaigner. His voting record is very liberal on economics, moderate on cultural and foreign issues; he is one of a handful of New York Democrats endorsed by the Conservative, not the Liberal, Party. He is anti-abortion and for the amendment allowing penalties for desecration of the flag. He voted for much of the Contract with America in 1995, except for tax cuts and welfare reforms. He strongly opposed the 1996 welfare reform and wants to increase payments to unemployed adults, legal immigrants and families with high shelter costs. He was one of three Democrats to vote against a bipartisan Medicare bill in Ways and Means in 1997. In 1996 he had primary opposition on the left from Lee Wasserman, head of Environmental Advocates, and won by only 57%–43%, not a huge margin for an incumbent.

In 1997 McNulty endorsed the EPA's new emissions standards for ozone and particulates and criticized General Electric for not being willing to dredge the Hudson for PCBs deposited years before; three years later, when the EPA made plans to purchase local land for temporary storage and treatment of PCB sediments, he strongly objected to the lack of local consultation. He called GE "brutally impersonal" when it cut hundreds of jobs at its power systems division in Schenectady. He criticized the Army when it cut the number of jobs at the Watervliet Arsenal, and wondered whether further cuts would require closure and require dependence on foreign producers; in 2000, the facility was revived by a Navy contract for 450 cannons. "This breaks the cycle," McNulty said. "Now, maybe we can have the annual ritual of building employment, rather than announcing layoffs." On the 1998 transportation bill he got $11 million for the Amtrak station in Rensselaer, and $8.7 million for an I-90 connector near Hudson Valley Community College. He had also worked for the new Albany airport, and got funds for noise abatement and the purchase of houses near Albany airport. In 2000, he got $4.9 million for runway expansion and another $6 million for the rail station. However, he complained about high air fares on Albany flights; Upstate New York, economically ailing, has done badly by airline deregulation.

McNulty in 1998 brought Hillary Rodham Clinton to Troy to commemorate Kate Mullaney, who organized the all-female Collar Laundry Union in 1864. But his effort to make her home a labor museum bogged down at the Resources Committee and the building deteriorated. On Ways and Means, McNulty and Amo Houghton sponsored a bill to relieve David Kaczynski of taxes on the reward money he earned for turning in his brother, the Unabomber, and which he said he would distribute to his victims; it never came up for a vote. In 1999, McNulty boycotted a prayer breakfast in D.C. because Yasir Arafat was invited.

McNulty seems to have solidified his base and appears secure in redistricting; no Republican wants any part of Albany County, and any district based on Albany County should be heavily Democratic.

Cook's Call   *Safe.* The conservative McNulty is not entirely safe from a challenge from the left, but the solid Democratic underpinnings of this Albany-district make it hard to defeat him in a general election. With the state forced to lose two seats in redistricting, every member in the delegation, especially from the slow-growing upstate districts, is vulnerable. McNulty's district needs to gain 81,000 people.

THE PEOPLE: Pop. 2000: 573,294; Pop. 1990: 580,320, down 1.2% 1990–2000. 85.7% White, 8.7% Black, 2.4% Asian, 0.2% Amer. Indian, 1.8% Two+ races, 1.2% Other; 3.4% Hispanic Origin.

2000 Presidential Vote		
Gore (D)	143,668	(57%)
Bush (R)	91,996	(36%)
Nader (Green)	11,456	(5%)
Others	5,159	(2%)

1996 Presidential Vote		
Clinton (D)	151,701	(59%)
Dole (R)	79,880	(31%)
Perot (I)	26,840	(10%)

Rep. Michael R. McNulty (D)

Elected 1988, 7th term; b. Sept. 16, 1947, Troy; home, Green Island; Holy Cross Col., B.A. 1969; Catholic; married (Nancy Ann).

Elected Office: Green Island Town Supervisor, 1969–77; Green Island Mayor, 1977–82; NY Assembly, 1982–88.

DC Office: 2161 RHOB 20515, 202-225-5076; Fax: 202-225-5077; Web site: www.house.gov/mcnulty.

District Offices: Albany, 518-465-0700; Amsterdam, 518-843-3400; Schenectady, 518-374-4547; Troy, 518-271-0822.

Committees: *Ways & Means* (11th of 17 D): Oversight; Select Revenue Measures (RMM).

Group Ratings

	ADA	ACLU	AFS	LCV	CON	ITIC	NTU	COC	ACU	NTLC	CHC
2000	55	54	83	86	28	74	24	57	17	17	25
1999	90	—	100	88	35	—	15	21	8	—	—

National Journal Ratings

	1999 LIB	—	1999 CONS		2000 LIB	—	2000 CONS
Economic	84%	—	12%		68%	—	31%
Social	58%	—	42%		56%	—	43%
Foreign	61%	—	39%		60%	—	39%

Key Votes of the 106th Congress

1. Patient Bill of Rights	Y	5. Bar RU-486 $ for FDA	Y	9. NATO War in Serbia	N
2. Accelerate Min. Wage	Y	6. Display 10 Commandments	N	10. Perm. Trade with China	N
3. Strike Ban on Ergo. Stnd.	Y	7. Gun Show Bkgrnd. Checks	Y	11. Debt Relief for 3rd World	*
4. Ovrd. Estate Tax Veto	N	8. Ban Part.-Birth Abortion	Y	12. Drop Cuba Econ. Embargo	Y

Election Results

2000 general	Michael R. McNulty (D-C-Ind)	175,339	(74%)	($334,030)
	Thomas G. Pillsworth (R)	60,333	(26%)	($12,402)
2000 primary	Michael R. McNulty (D)	unopposed		
1998 general	Michael R. McNulty (D-C-Ind)	146,639	(74%)	($243,107)
	Lauren Ayers (R)	50,931	(26%)	

TWENTY-SECOND DISTRICT

The Hudson River, an avenue of commerce in colonial days, an inspiration to artists past and present, is still one of America's great sights, though it is no longer central, as it was not so long ago, in the nation's consciousness and politics. The classic mansions overlooking the river, like Clermont, whose builder Robert Livingston financed Robert Fulton's first steamboat, and Montgomery Place, built by Janet Livingston Montgomery, widow of the general who captured Quebec in 1775, are reminders of the cool serenity of the 18th Century mind and the daring nature of its spirit. Robert Livingston (whose descendants include Eleanor Roosevelt, Tom Kean of New Jersey and Bob Livingston of Louisiana) administered the first oath of office to George Washington in 1789 and helped negotiate the Louisiana Purchase in 1803. It was on a visit to his lands in the 1790s that James Madison and Aaron Burr welded the Virginia-New York alliance that set the course of American political history. The Hudson was also a center of America during the Romantic Era: From Frederick Church's Moorish mansion, Olana, you can see the still unspoiled river landscape that inspired his art and that of others of the Hudson River school of painters.

The Hudson gave birth to our passionate party politics: Nearby is Kinderhook, home of Martin Van Buren, the innkeeper's son who in alliance with Andrew Jackson invented the torchlight parade, the national party convention and, some argue, the Democratic Party itself. Later in the 19th Century, the Hudson was lined with the palaces of the nation's first great millionaires and the comfortable country houses of New York's gentry. In one of the latter, Springwood in Hyde Park, Franklin Roosevelt was born and lived; this politician, who expanded government at home and was the victorious commander-in-chief of American military forces throughout the world, was most comfortable looking out over his sloping lawn down to the river on which he remembered iceboating during the winters of the 1880s.

The 22d Congressional District includes much of the Hudson Valley, the grand river south of Albany and the smaller river, freshly fed by the Adirondacks, to the north. It extends north to include most of Essex County and Lake Placid in the Adirondacks. Much of the district, just outside the old manufacturing city of Troy and the grand 19th Century harness racing center of Saratoga Springs (which has lost 75% of its fan base in the last 30 years), is essentially suburban Albany. Despite Van Buren and Roosevelt, this has been a Republican area since the birth of the Republican Party; indeed, Roosevelt never carried his home territory except when he ran for state Senate in 1910.

The congressman from the 22d is John Sweeney, a Republican elected in 1998. Sweeney grew up in Troy, the son of a shirt factory worker active in the Amalgamated Shirt Cutters Union; he lived for a time in a housing project. He worked his way through college, then worked for the Rensselaer County government, heading a DWI project. He went to law school part time and practiced law. He caught the eye of Republican State Chairman William Powers, an ally of then-Senator Alfonse D'Amato, who made Sweeney executive director of the party in 1992. After George Pataki was elected governor in 1994, he appointed Sweeney as Labor commissioner, then in 1997 as deputy secretary to the state Executive Chamber, one of his top aides.

In April 1998, Gerald Solomon, congressman from the 22d District for 20 years and chairman of the House Rules Committee, announced he was retiring. In this heavily Republican district there was naturally a contest for the party's nomination. But it was effectively settled in a few days in May. Assemblyman John Faso, probably the best-known possibility, declined to run because he had been elected minority leader in March. Solomon had backed Roy McDonald, a township supervisor in Saratoga County, the district's largest; he said that of the nine candidates running, only Sweeney was unacceptable. Facing pressure from Powers, Saratoga County Republican Chairman Jasper Nolan announced he was not supporting McDonald, who, suddenly with no chance in the endorsement convention, withdrew from the race. Powers's message, though not public, was obvious: Pataki wanted Sweeney. Sweeney had yet to officially announce, but as Solomon said, "John Sweeney is going to be the candidate." Sweeney refused to join debates but won the September primary with 52%, to 27% for the nearest contender. In the general, Sweeney vastly outspent the Democratic nominee, Jean Bordewich, a writer, owner of a computer publishing company, and one-term council member in Red Hook in Dutchess County. Like Solomon, he opposed requiring General Electric to clean up PCBs in the Hudson—a hot local issue. He said he opposed banning abortion but backed the partial-birth abortion ban. He opposed NAFTA and GATT and said he felt strongly about the Second Amendment. Bordewich struck a conciliatory note; she said she hoped GE and EPA could somehow get together on the PCBs problem. Solomon's testimonial ad for Sweeney had greater influence. Pataki also appeared in Sweeney ads, and the Civil Service Employees Union endorsed the Republican. Sweeney won 55%–42%.

In the House he followed Solomon's earlier support for the Northeast Dairy Compact, but denied reports that his predecessor had violated federal law by lobbying him on current legislation. When the House debated campaign finance reform in 1999, it passed Sweeney's amendment requiring any candidate running for office to reimburse the government for official transportation expenses; the proposal obviously was aimed at Hillary Rodham Clinton's Senate campaign. He lobbied for Southwest Airlines to provide service to Albany, which began in May 2000. He objected to a plan announced by EPA in the closing days of the Clinton Administration charging GE $490 million to clean up the PCBs in the Hudson, mostly by dredging the sediment along 40 miles of the river. Although Pataki announced his support, Sweeney sought to delay the action until the National Academy of Sciences released a report, and he hoped that the Bush White House would be more sympathetic.

Sweeney got an Appropriation Committee seat in the 107th Congress, after having impressed Republican leaders with his fundraising skills. He's well-connected to the Bush White House: his former chief of staff Brad Card is the brother of Bush's top aide Andy Card. And Bush insiders will not forget that Sweeney was present in the Miami-Dade County board of canvassers meeting when the canvassers proposed to count the ballots out of view of observers in violation of Florida's sunshine law. "Thugs in that building are trying to hijack this election," Sweeney said. After angry but not violent protests by Republican aides, the canvassers changed their minds and shut down the Miami-Dade count.

Cook's Call *Safe.* This Republican-leaning district will not give Sweeney much trouble in a general election, but redistricting could give Sweeney some heartburn. Upstate New York is slated to lose at least one seat in redistricting which will impact every member in the area. Sweeney's district was the fastest growing in the region, however, and needs to pick up fewer new residents than many of his upstate colleagues.

THE PEOPLE: Pop. 2000: 619,548; Pop. 1990: 580,522, up 6.7% 1990–2000. 94.7% White, 2.5% Black, 0.8% Asian, 0.2% Amer. Indian, 1.1% Two+ races, 0.7% Other; 2.1% Hispanic Origin.

2000 Presidential Vote		
Bush (R)	146,322	(49%)
Gore (D)	131,774	(44%)
Nader (Green)	14,173	(5%)
Others	4,428	(1%)

1996 Presidential Vote		
Clinton (D)	117,831	(46%)
Dole (R)	105,106	(41%)
Perot (I)	34,415	(13%)

Rep. John Sweeney (R)

Elected 1998, 2d term; b. Aug. 9, 1955, Troy; home, Clifton Park; Russell Sage Col., B.A. 1981, W. New England Law Schl., J.D. 1990; Catholic; separated.

Professional Career: Practicing atty., 1990–92; Exec. Dir. & Chief Cnsl., NY State Repub. Cmte., 1992–95; NY Comm. of Labor, 1995–97; Dpty. Secy., Gov. George Pataki, 1997–98.

DC Office: 416 CHOB 20515, 202-225-5614; Fax: 202-225-6234; Web site: www.house.gov/sweeney.

District Offices: Glens Falls, 518-792-3031; Hudson, 518-828-0181; Saratoga Springs, 518-587-9800.

Committees: *Appropriations* (33d of 35 R): District of Columbia; Transportation; Treasury, Postal Service & General Government.

Group Ratings

	ADA	ACLU	AFS	LCV	CON	ITIC	NTU	COC	ACU	NTLC	CHC
2000	10	14	28	29	19	78	58	76	72	73	87
1999	25	—	16	13	23	—	58	76	72	—	—

National Journal Ratings

	1999 LIB —	1999 CONS		2000 LIB —	2000 CONS
Economic	45%	55%		29%	67%
Social	41%	58%		50%	50%
Foreign	8%	91%		33%	62%

Key Votes of the 106th Congress

1. Patient Bill of Rights	Y	5. Bar RU-486 $ for FDA	N	9. NATO War in Serbia	N
2. Accelerate Min. Wage	N	6. Display 10 Commandments	Y	10. Perm. Trade with China	Y
3. Strike Ban on Ergo. Stnd.	N	7. Gun Show Bkgrnd. Checks	N	11. Debt Relief for 3rd World	N
4. Ovrd. Estate Tax Veto	Y	8. Ban Part.-Birth Abortion	Y	12. Drop Cuba Econ. Embargo	N

Election Results

2000 general	John Sweeney (R-C)	167,368	(68%)	($807,676)
	Kenneth F. McCallion (D-Green-WF)	79,111	(32%)	($72,122)
2000 primary	John Sweeney (R)	unopposed		
1998 general	John Sweeney (R-C-Ind)	106,919	(55%)	($818,624)
	Jean P. Bordewich (D)	81,296	(42%)	($322,748)
	Others	5,051	(3%)	

TWENTY-THIRD DISTRICT

One of the first American frontiers was the Mohawk River Valley of Upstate New York—a frontier that remained static for 150 years. From the establishment of Fort Orange in 1624 in what now is Albany until the Revolutionary War, white settlers did not dare move west along the Mohawk. The British used their Iroquois allies as a buffer against the French and in return kept New England Yankees from moving westward. Only after the French were driven from the colonies in 1759 did the pressures for westward settlement prevail; the British tried to keep their word to the Indians, but once the Revolutionary War started, the Iroquois dominion ended.

This is the background of *Drums Along the Mohawk* and of James Fenimore Cooper's *Leatherstocking Tales*. But there is little in these rolling hills today to evoke the bloody violence whose conclusion made possible the digging of the Erie Canal and the building of the New York Central Railroad. As migration slowed and trade increased, the Mohawk Valley became one of the nation's early industrial centers. The little Oneida County hamlets of Utica and Rome, where the canal builders had to dig through the route's highest ground, became sizable factory towns. Even the utopian Oneida Community, with its believers in plural marriage and communal ownership, operated a stainless steel factory. First settled by New England Yankees, these towns attracted a new wave of immigration from the Atlantic coast in the early 20th Century. Today they are the most heavily Italian and Polish-American communities between Albany and Buffalo; politically, they are usually marginally Republican; Bill Clinton carried most of them in 1996 but George W. Bush's local win in 2000 restored the ancestral tradition.

The 23d Congressional District, in the Mohawk Valley, is centered on Utica and Rome in Oneida County and includes a row of more sparsely settled counties to the south. Here the hilly land has an early 19th Century cast, in places like Cooperstown, certainly one of the best-preserved small towns in America and home to the Baseball Hall of Fame, and Pindars Corners, the crossroads site of former Senator Daniel Patrick Moynihan's farm where he wrote 18 books in a 19th Century schoolhouse. Madison County here was one of the hotbeds of abolitionism in the 1850s. But this is also a part of Upstate New York that feels bypassed by more recent economic growth and in need of government assistance and sustenance.

The congressman from the 23d is Sherwood Boehlert, a Republican elected in 1982, now Chairman of the Science Committee. Boehlert grew up and went to college in Utica, served in the Army, worked briefly in industry. For 14 years he was chief of staff for his two predecessors in Congress, then was elected Oneida County executive in 1978 and won the House seat in 1982. Boehlert has one of the most liberal voting records of any Republican House member—number three in both 1999 and 2000—and has taken a lead role in defeating what he considers extreme party positions, while maintaining party loyalty on many other matters and trying to forge bipartisan consensus on some issues. Boehlert has voted for an increased minimum wage. He sided with labor in March 2001 as one of 13 Republicans to oppose the repeal of the ergonomics rule, has voted against the partial-birth abortion ban and has supported the National Endowment for the Arts. He signed the Contract With America, but voted against more of it than any other Republican except Connie Morella of Maryland. Some of Boehlert's votes have a local angle: he supports dairy subsidies (the 23d is part of New York City's milkshed), he favors baseball's antitrust exemption (Cooperstown is where baseball was supposedly invented in 1839 and Boehlert is part owner of a minor league team); he sponsored Pledge of Allegiance Day (the Pledge was written by Francis Bellamy in Rome in 1892). One great success was leading the fight against the superconducting Supercollider, a giant atom smasher that was to be built in Texas.

Boehlert has played a particularly critical role on environmental issues. His convictions here are strong. After Republicans took control in 1995 he took the lead in opposing environmental policy riders on EPA and other appropriations. In 1995 he was named by Speaker Newt Gingrich—to whom he gave crucial support when Gingrich won the whip's post by 2 votes in 1989—to head, with conservative Richard Pombo, a task force on environmental issues. This produced some results: Republicans agreed on the bipartisan Safe Drinking Water Act of 1996 and the environmental provisions of the 1996 Freedom to Farm Act. He argued that Republicans were passing more environmental laws than Democrats had, saying Democrats "feel they own the environment as an issue, but there is a sizable and growing segment of Republicans that are proving day in and day out that they are environmentally friendly." But in mid-1997 the intra-party truce broke down; after Boehlert rallied votes to water down an attempt by Western Republicans to exempt flood control projects from the Endangered Species Act, they complained bitterly to Gingrich that Boehlert had too much influence over Republican environmental policy. Boehlert persisted after Gingrich left. In February 1999 he opposed the Mandates Information Act, which would have allowed members to object to bills that would impose costs of more than $100 million on private companies, concerns that it could be used to impede environmental legislation; Boehlert's amendment failed and the bill passed the House that month. Later in 1999 he opposed power companies' attempts to stop EPA fining operators of coal-fired electric plants. In 2000 he opposed the bill to allow property rights disputes involving state and local zoning to be appealed quickly to federal court. In July 2000 he asked the Clinton administration to consider breaching the Snake River dams—a hugely unpopular idea in Idaho and eastern Oregon and Washington. In January 2001, he urged caution about overturning last-minute Clinton administration environmental regulations and orders.

On the Water Resources and Environment Subcommittee he chaired until 2001, Boehlert tried to reach bipartisan agreement on Superfund reform, but without success. He sponsored an amendment in September 2000 to exempt small businesses from Superfund if they disposed of only ordinary garbage under a procedure requiring a two-thirds vote, but it fell short of that margin. In April 2000 Boehlert said, "Before I die—before the expired Superfund taxes are reinstated—I'd like to see meaningful reform and brownfields revitalization." He argues that the Superfund provisions imposing liability on anyone ever connected with the site and which requires restoration to pristine conditions prevents the industrial and commercial development of brownfield sites, of which there are many in Upstate New York. But so far he has been frustrated.

Boehlert seems to relish the pivotal position he occupies in the House: as the Republican margin has shrunk, his voice and vote have become more important. "This is the moderate moment," he said in April 2000. "Our time has come." And his record has served him well in general elections, in which he has run ahead of party lines in an already safely Republican district, one of only four in New York which voted for both George W. Bush and Rick Lazio in 2000. But he seems to have increasing vulnerability in the Republican primary. Against two primary opponents he won 65% of the vote in 1996. In 1998, potential primary challenger David Vickers was knocked off the ballot in August when the Board of Elections threw out his petitions for violations; New York election law is particularly convoluted, which helps party insiders eliminate competition. In 2000 Vickers, a high school Spanish teacher, qualified for the ballot. Boehlert won the September primary by only 57%–43% margin—not much for an 18-year incumbent and after Vickers spent only $27,000. Boehlert carried Madison County 2–1 but ran nearly even in Oneida County, the largest in the district. Boehlert won the general election with 61% of the vote, but Vickers got 21% as the nominee of the Conservative and Right-to-Life parties. Boehlert could get primary competition again in 2002. And some of the territory in his new district may turn out to be unfamiliar. It is generally agreed that Upstate New York must lose one congressional district, and the current 23rd is right in the middle of Upstate. So it is possible that Boehlert could face another incumbent.

Cook's Call *Safe.* As one of the more out-front voices of the moderate wing of the Republican Party, Boehlert has raised the ire of some of the more conservative members of the House. He has no such problems in his home district where he has won easily since his first re-election in 1984. Boehlert's district was also one of the slowest growing in the already slow-growing region of upstate and is short 100,000 people; it will likely be altered significantly in redistricting.

THE PEOPLE: Pop. 2000: 563,385; Pop. 1990: 580,259, down 2.9% 1990–2000. 94.1% White, 3.1% Black, 0.8% Asian, 0.3% Amer. Indian, 1.2% Two+ races, 0.7% Other; 2.1% Hispanic Origin.

2000 Presidential Vote			1996 Presidential Vote		
Bush (R)	115,816	(50%)	Clinton (D)	102,854	(47%)
Gore (D)	102,751	(44%)	Dole (R)	88,120	(40%)
Nader (Green)	8,805	(4%)	Perot (I)	29,172	(13%)
Others	5,298	(2%)			

Rep. Sherwood L. Boehlert (R)

Elected 1982, 10th term; b. Sept. 28, 1936, Utica; home, New Hartford; Utica Col., B.A. 1961; Catholic; married (Marianne).

Military Career: Army, 1956–58.

Elected Office: Oneida Cnty. Exec., 1978–82.

Professional Career: P.R. Mgr., Wyandotte Chemicals Corp., 1961–64; A.A., U.S. Rep. Alexander Pirnie, 1964–72; A.A., U.S. Rep. Donald Mitchell, 1973–79.

DC Office: 2246 RHOB 20515, 202-225-3665; Fax: 202-225-1891; Web site: www.house.gov/boehlert.

District Office: Utica, 315-793-8146.

Committees: *Permanent Select Committee on Intelligence* (4th of 11 R): Human Intelligence, Analysis & Counterintelligence (Vice Chmn.); Technical & Tactical Intelligence. *Science* (Chmn. of 25 R). *Transportation & Infrastructure* (3d of 42 R): Highways & Transit; Railroads; Water Resources & Environment.

Group Ratings

	ADA	ACLU	AFS	LCV	CON	ITIC	NTU	COC	ACU	NTLC	CHC
2000	40	64	28	64	7	100	49	80	40	55	27
1999	65	—	50	75	12	—	45	60	40	—	—

National Journal Ratings

	1999 LIB	—	1999 CONS		2000 LIB	—	2000 CONS
Economic	52%	—	47%		52%	—	48%
Social	63%	—	36%		66%	—	33%
Foreign	53%	—	47%		51%	—	47%

Key Votes of the 106th Congress

1. Patient Bill of Rights	Y	5. Bar RU-486 $ for FDA	N	9. NATO War in Serbia	Y
2. Accelerate Min. Wage	Y	6. Display 10 Commandments	N	10. Perm. Trade with China	Y
3. Strike Ban on Ergo. Stnd.	Y	7. Gun Show Bkgrnd. Checks	Y	11. Debt Relief for 3rd World	Y
4. Ovrd. Estate Tax Veto	Y	8. Ban Part.-Birth Abortion	N	12. Drop Cuba Econ. Embargo	Y

Election Results

2000 general	Sherwood L. Boehlert (R-Ind)	124,132	(61%)	($808,371)
	David B. Vickers (C-RTL)	42,854	(21%)	($29,583)
	Richard W. Englebrecht (D)	38,049	(19%)	($14,129)
2000 primary	Sherwood L. Boehlert (R)	15,269	(57%)	
	David B. Vickers (R)	11,382	(43%)	
1998 general	Sherwood L. Boehlert (R)	111,242	(81%)	($551,012)
	David B. Vickers (C-RTL)	26,493	(19%)	($7,894)

TWENTY-FOURTH DISTRICT

The North Country of Upstate New York, some early 19th Century visionaries thought, was the land of the future. Financier Gouverneur Morris, French slave trader James Leray, and Dutch silver speculator David Parish bought up thousands of acres between the Adirondacks and the St. Lawrence River and tried to unload them on farmers unaware of the shortness of the growing season and the unnavigability of the river. They left behind grand mansions, but their hopes for huge profits were frustrated when the Erie Canal turned the stream of settlement westward, and Canadians built their new capital far north of the river. But northern New York was not without its business successes: It was in Watertown in 1878 that 26-year-old Frank Woolworth put a sign over a table of odds and ends that read "Any Article 5 Cents," starting America's first retail chain and inventing the concept of discount stores.

More recently, the North Country has looked to government for help. The St. Lawrence Seaway proved too small for most ocean-going freighters and remains frozen three months of the year; the locks are slow and icebreakers would wreck the shoreline. The state government has built prisons in Ogdensburg and Cape Vincent and Malone, and private developers have built big malls in Watertown and Massena (attracting Canadians, as even New York has lower taxes than Ontario). But the biggest initiative has been the enlargement of Fort Drum, near Watertown, where despite the Army's preference for warm weather training sites, a 10,000-person light infantry division was stationed in 1985.

The 24th Congressional District covers most of the North Country, from Plattsburgh on Lake Champlain along the St. Lawrence Seaway and over the Adirondacks Forest Preserve to Watertown and Oswego on Lake Ontario. Geographically one of the largest districts in the East, it is ancestrally Republican country. But it trended Democratic in the 1990s, giving a big margin to Bill Clinton in 1996 and a small margin to Al Gore in 2000.

The congressman from the 24th is John McHugh, a Republican first elected in 1992. McHugh has long been in government: he worked for the Watertown city manager in 1971; for eight years he was a staffer for state Senator Douglas Barclay; in 1984 he was elected to succeed Barclay in Albany. McHugh specialized in dairy issues (New York has long price-fixed dairy products to help farmers) and military bases—both part of the North Country's economic lifeblood. When incumbent David Martin announced his retirement in June 1992, just when the district lines were redrawn, McHugh ran, with plenty of financing plus Martin's endorsement. He won the Republican primary with 70%, then won the general 61%–24%.

McHugh combines a moderate voting record with a concern about local economic needs, not surprising given his district's dependence on federal spending. In 1993 he got a seat on Armed Services and hired none other than Martin to monitor the Defense Base Closure and Realignment Commission. In that year's base closure round, McHugh found himself pitted in a fierce lobbying battle against his colleague to the south, Republican Sherwood Boehlert. Griffiss Air Force Base, a major employer in Boehlert's district, and Plattsburgh Air Force Base, in McHugh's, were competing for a similar mission. In the end, the commission voted to close both bases. He has been a long-time advocate of a 170-mile, four-lane Rooftop Highway for the North Country, connecting Watertown and Plattsburgh, and got a $1.5 million feasibility study; he called the road vital for the timber, paper and farming interests.

After Republicans won House control, McHugh became chairman of the Government Reform subcommittee with jurisdiction over the Postal Service, a somewhat dubious honor since it gives him responsibility for one of Congress's perennial headaches. He worked on what would have been the biggest reform of Postal Service law since the 1970s. His version passed his subcommittee in 1998 but moved no further. McHugh would have given the Postal Service more flexibility in setting prices, and would allow volume discounts; this pleased big advertising mailers but displeased newspapers, who feared they would lose ads. It would have reduced the limits on first-class mail that others, like FedEx and UPS, could carry. This was a heavily lobbied measure, in which most members have little interest; it may be a while before anything passes. McHugh was more successful in winning enactment of his Semipostal Authorization Act, which allows the Postal Service to issue added-value stamps to advance causes—such as health or safety—that it considers in the public interest, with a maximum 25 per cent surcharge made available for the cause.

On impeachment, McHugh was one of the last members to announce a position and was part of nearly a dozen Republicans who came out for impeachment on December 15, four days before the vote, thus determining the outcome. He was one of the final members to announce support for Permanent Normal Trade Relations with China, deciding that benefits for dairy farmers outweighed possible job losses for General Motors. In the 107th Congress, he became chairman of the Armed Services Military Personnel Subcommittee, a useful perk for his local interests.

McHugh has been re-elected with more than 70% of the vote against token opposition each election since 1992. Redistricters will have to add territory to this district, but it is unlikely to be greatly altered.

Cook's Call   *Safe.* Although this district is not a Republican stronghold, Democrats haven't put up a whole lot of competition against McHugh, and it is unlikely that they ever will. His moderate voting record and attention to district needs makes him a tough target. Heavy shuffling of congressional lines in Upstate New York during redistricting will certainly have an impact here, but, unlike other members from Upstate, McHugh's district has not seen the most dramatic population loss.

THE PEOPLE: Pop. 2000: 582,371; Pop. 1990: 580,376, up 0.3% 1990–2000. 93.3% White, 3% Black, 0.6% Asian, 1% Amer. Indian, 1% Two+ races, 1% Other; 2.3% Hispanic Origin.

2000 Presidential Vote

Gore (D)	103,959	(47%)
Bush (R)	103,632	(47%)
Nader (Green)	7,621	(3%)
Others	6,037	(3%)

1996 Presidential Vote

Clinton (D)	102,007	(50%)
Dole (R)	72,301	(35%)
Perot (I)	30,047	(15%)

Rep. John M. McHugh (R)

Elected 1992, 5th term; b. Sept. 29, 1948, Watertown; home, Pierrepont Manor; Utica Col., B.A. 1970, S.U.N.Y. Albany, M.P.A. 1977; Catholic; divorced.

Elected Office: NY Senate, 1984–92.

Professional Career: Confidential Asst., Watertown City Mgr., 1971–76; Research & Liaison Chief, NY Sen. Douglas Barclay, 1976–84.

DC Office: 2441 RHOB 20515, 202-225-4611; Fax: 202-226-0621; Web site: www.house.gov/mchugh.

District Offices: Johnstown, 518-762-0379; Plattsburgh, 518-563-1406; Watertown, 315-782-3150.

Committees: *Armed Services* (8th of 32 R): Military Installations & Facilities; Military Personnel (Chmn.). *Government Reform* (6th of 24 R): Energy Policy, Natural Resources and Regulatory Affairs; National Security, Veterans' Affairs & Intl. Relations. *International Relations* (15th of 26 R): Middle East & South Asia.

Group Ratings

	ADA	ACLU	AFS	LCV	CON	ITIC	NTU	COC	ACU	NTLC	CHC
2000	5	14	28	21	13	94	55	80	73	56	80
1999	35	—	33	25	11	—	51	76	72	—	—

National Journal Ratings

	1999 LIB —	1999 CONS	2000 LIB —	2000 CONS
Economic	48% —	52%	44% —	56%
Social	32% —	66%	43% —	55%
Foreign	45% —	55%	25% —	69%

Key Votes of the 106th Congress

1. Patient Bill of Rights	Y	5. Bar RU-486 $ for FDA	Y	9. NATO War in Serbia	N
2. Accelerate Min. Wage	Y	6. Display 10 Commandments	Y	10. Perm. Trade with China	Y
3. Strike Ban on Ergo. Stnd.	Y	7. Gun Show Bkgrnd. Checks	N	11. Debt Relief for 3rd World	N
4. Ovrd. Estate Tax Veto	Y	8. Ban Part.-Birth Abortion	Y	12. Drop Cuba Econ. Embargo	N

Election Results

2000 general	John M. McHugh (R-C)	138,322	(74%)	($300,643)
	Neil P. Tallon (D-WF)	42,698	(23%)	
	Others	5,167	(3%)	
2000 primary	John M. McHugh (R)	unopposed		
1998 general	John M. McHugh (R-C)	116,682	(79%)	($293,655)
	Neil P. Tallon (D)	31,011	(21%)	

TWENTY-FIFTH DISTRICT

Syracuse is a middle American city in the middle of Upstate New York, halfway between Albany and Buffalo on the Erie Canal and the old New York Central Railroad, for years the nation's major east-west transportation routes. Built on a swamp that was a salt spring, Syracuse is the home of many inventions: the dental chair, Stickley mission furniture, the drive-in bank teller, the foot measuring devices used in shoe stores. It was one of the first big manufacturers of typewriters and is the site of the New York State Fair. Its agricultural hinterland is rich with specialty crops like wine grapes, and its industrial jobs are mostly high-skill. Syracuse has spread out slowly across the countryside, and growth has been sluggish here; this is one of the parts of Upstate New York that has been languishing, and that responded positively to Hillary Rodham Clinton's campaigning in 1999 and 2000.

The 25th Congressional District includes all of Syracuse and Onondaga County. It goes west to include part of Auburn, the home town of Governor, Senator and Secretary of State William Seward, and south to Cortland County and almost to Binghamton. Seward was the first great Republican politician of Upstate New York, and historically Syracuse has been heavily Republican, partly out of antipathy to New York City. But in the 1990s the Syracuse area trended sharply toward national Democrats (to bring in federal dollars) even as it voted overwhelmingly for Republican Governor George Pataki (to hold down taxes).

The congressman from the 25th District is James Walsh, a Republican elected in 1988. He grew up in Syracuse, the son of Syracuse mayor and (1973–79) Congressman William Walsh. He came to the House as almost a professional civic activist: He was a volunteer in the Peace Corps in Nepal, a social worker, then worked for New York Telephone and NYNEX, which detailed him to a local university. He was elected five times to the Syracuse Common Council, then ran for Congress in 1988 when a Republican incumbent nearly beaten two years earlier decided to retire. He won by a solid 57%–42%. Like other Republicans from economically sluggish Upstate areas, he is open to government intervention in the economy. He voted for the Clinton stimulus package in March 1993, but he also voted for the balanced budget amendment and the line-item veto.

Walsh has a seat on the Appropriations Committee, and has now been chairman of three subcommittees—part of the "college of cardinals," in House lingo. In 1995 and 1996 he chaired the District of Columbia Subcommittee, just as Marion Barry was returned to the mayor's office after serving time in prison. He worked with Northern Virginia Republican Tom Davis and District Delegate Eleanor Holmes Norton to create the financial control board to monitor District spending and to make the accountings and file the financial reports the D.C. government chronically failed to produce. Walsh also sponsored a limited school-choice experiment, to allow some small number of poor children options other than the wretched and mismanaged D.C. public schools. This aroused furious opposition from teachers' unions, and though it passed the House it was killed in the Senate. In 1997 and 1998 Walsh chaired the Legislative Branch Subcommittee, which sets Congress's own budget. He suffered the embarrassment in spring 1997 of seeing his appropriation defeated because of defections by 11 Republicans, who were determined to uphold promises to cut Congress's budget.

Since 1999 Walsh has been Chairman of the VA-HUD-Independent Agencies Subcommittee. In that capacity he got into some fights with HUD Secretary Andrew Cuomo. He attacked Cuomo for using anti-drug money to fund a gun buy-back program, and said at one point that HUD employees could be arrested. He supported setting up a Millennial Housing Commission chaired by former Congresswoman Susan Molinari and former New York developer Richard Ravitch. He worked to create the Erie Canalway National Heritage Corridor, running 524 miles from Albany to Buffalo—and through downtown Syracuse—though it was held up because Governor George Pataki wanted to name its governing commission, to keep Clinton Democrats from control; it was approved finally in December 2000 when it was clear that George W. Bush was the next president. Walsh has not been shy about supporting what some call pork barrel projects; his 1999 appropriation included 215 earmarks. Many were for the Syracuse area. "Our economy's in tough shape right now, so we're not bashful at all in helping our own state." They have included $10 million for earth sciences research at the Regional Application Center in Cayuga County, $1.5 million for water quality management in Onondaga and Cayuga Counties, $1 million for Syracuse University and $150,000 to renovate the Schine Theater in Auburn. Walsh is a sponsor of the Hunger Has a Cure Act, and a sponsor of the measure to restore food stamps for legal immigrants; he worked to increase eligibility for food stamps in 2000. As chairman of Friends of Ireland and co-chairman of the U.S.-Irish Interparliamentary Group, he accompanied Bill Clinton on his 1995 trip to

Ireland. In 1998 he sponsored the "Walsh Visas" to allow young unemployed people from Northern Ireland and adjacent counties in the Irish Republic to live and work in the United States for five years.

Walsh has mostly won re-election without difficulty. After he sponsored school vouchers in Washington, D.C., the AFL-CIO, 42% of whose members are public employees, targeted Walsh's district, ran an estimated $500,000 in TV ads against Walsh and a vigorous organizing campaign in 1996. With a late-spending and organizational surge, Walsh won 55%–45%. In 1998 and 2000 he was reelected with 69% of the vote. Redistricting could pose some risks for him. The current 25th District will have to be significantly expanded, and one Upstate district must be eliminated. Walsh will surely concentrate on holding Syracuse and Onondaga County together; if that happens, he should be in good shape, even if he has to face another incumbent.

Cook's Call *Safe.* The marginal nature of this district makes it an intriguing target for Democrats who want to make some inroads into the almost all-Republican Upstate delegation. But, after surviving an all-out assault in 1996 by a healthy 10 point margin (even as Clinton was cleaning up here), Democrats have avoided taking on Walsh. This Syracuse-based district will need to be altered significantly in redistricting, as it is almost 100,000 people short of the required district population.

THE PEOPLE: Pop. 2000: 569,864; Pop. 1990: 580,233, down 1.8% 1990–2000. 87.2% White, 7.7% Black, 1.8% Asian, 0.7% Amer. Indian, 1.8% Two + races, 0.8% Other; 2.1% Hispanic Origin.

2000 Presidential Vote			1996 Presidential Vote		
Gore (D)	132,372	(52%)	Clinton (D)	121,304	(51%)
Bush (R)	106,027	(42%)	Dole (R)	90,774	(39%)
Nader (Green)	9,661	(4%)	Perot (I)	23,516	(10%)
Others	5,261	(2%)			

Rep. James T. Walsh (R)

Elected 1988, 7th term; b. June 19, 1947, Syracuse; home, Syracuse; St. Bonaventure U., B.A. 1970; Catholic; married (Dede).

Elected Office: Syracuse Common Cncl., 1978–88, Pres. 1986–88.

Professional Career: Peace Corps, Nepal, 1970–72; Social worker, Onondaga Cnty. Social Svcs. Dept., 1972–74; Marketing exec., NYNEX, 1974–88.

DC Office: 2351 RHOB 20515, 202-225-3701; Fax: 202-225-4042; Web site: www.house.gov/walsh.

District Offices: Auburn, 315-255-0649; Cortland, 607-758-3918; Syracuse, 315-423-5657.

Committees: *Appropriations* (10th of 35 R): Agriculture, Rural Development, & FDA; Military Construction; VA, HUD & Independent Agencies (Chmn.).

Group Ratings

	ADA	ACLU	AFS	LCV	CON	ITIC	NTU	COC	ACU	NTLC	CHC
2000	20	14	0	43	13	83	52	85	56	48	73
1999	35	—	0	31	33	—	46	72	64	—	—

National Journal Ratings

	1999 LIB —	1999 CONS		2000 LIB —	2000 CONS
Economic	41% —	57%		48% —	51%
Social	35% —	64%		49% —	51%
Foreign	48% —	51%		39% —	57%

Key Votes of the 106th Congress

1. Patient Bill of Rights	Y	5. Bar RU-486 $ for FDA	Y	9. NATO War in Serbia	N
2. Accelerate Min. Wage	Y	6. Display 10 Commandments	Y	10. Perm. Trade with China	Y
3. Strike Ban on Ergo. Stnd.	N	7. Gun Show Bkgrnd. Checks	N	11. Debt Relief for 3rd World	N
4. Ovrd. Estate Tax Veto	Y	8. Ban Part.-Birth Abortion	Y	12. Drop Cuba Econ. Embargo	N

Election Results

2000 general	James T. Walsh (R-Ind-C)	151,880	(69%)		($580,767)
	Francis J. Gavin (D)	64,533	(29%)		
	Others	3,830	(2%)		
2000 primary	James T. Walsh (R)	unopposed			
1998 general	James T. Walsh (R-C)	121,204	(69%)		($311,345)
	Yvonne Rothenberg (D-L-Green)	53,461	(31%)		($143,309)

TWENTY-SIXTH DISTRICT

New York's Southern Tier is territory not often explored by today's Americans. In colonial days, the Catskills looming over the Hudson were a great barrier, a mysterious zone in which phantom Dutchmen played nine pins and Indians lurked in the days of James Fenimore Cooper. The area then became part of a great pathway west, along the Erie Lackawanna and Delaware & Hudson Railroad lines, with engines steaming over giant viaducts and along narrow river valleys through these hills and mountains. But today, this quarter of Upstate New York has little passenger rail service and is bypassed by major air travel networks. Its interstates are lightly traveled, particularly as the once-famous kosher resorts in the "Borscht Belt" of the Catskills have lost their popularity in the past quarter century.

The sprawling 26th Congressional District includes much of the Southern Tier. The district stretches from the city of Beacon on the east side of the Hudson—where commuters board the train daily for jobs in New York City—west and north across the still-mysterious Catskills, past Bethel, site of the misnamed 1969 Woodstock music festival, to the industrial city of Binghamton in Broome County on the upper Susquehanna River, and finally to the university town of Ithaca, with Cornell University looming high above Cayuga Lake's waters. Along the west bank of the Hudson in Ulster County lies Kingston, settled by Dutchmen more than 300 years ago. This was Rip van Winkle country, and in the 19th Century was the political base of Governor and Vice President George Clinton. There are two population centers, widely separated: Binghamton-Ithaca in the west has about half the district's votes, and the Hudson Valley has about one-third. Politically, the heritage is Republican, but the Ithaca area, like so many university communities, is heavily Democratic, and national Democrats have been running well in Binghamton and in the Hudson Valley.

The congressman from the 26th is Maurice Hinchey, a liberal Democrat elected in 1992. Hinchey grew up in a humble background, enlisted in the Navy at 18, labored in a cement factory for five years, then worked his way through college as a New York State Thruway toll collector. He was an analyst for the state education department; then in the Democratic year of 1974, at 36, he was elected from Ulster County to the Assembly. He served for nine terms; he was proud of the more than 600 bills he passed—on, among other things, acid rain, toxic waste, illegal dumping (and organized crime's influence over it), groundwater and wetlands protection. When he ran for Congress, Hinchey called for national health insurance, a repeal of Reagan-Bush tax cuts for the rich and corporations, and "reindustrializing America." His Republican opponent Bob Moppert, a Binghamton moving company owner, called for less government spending and bureaucracy. In a contest that was not only partisan but geographic, Hinchey beat Moppert 50%–47%. Hinchey carried Ulster and Moppert carried the Binghamton area; Ithaca and Tompkins County decided it, with a big margin for Hinchey.

Hinchey has one of the most liberal voting records in the House. One issue that caused Hinchey both political and personal discomfort was gun control. He backed the Brady Bill on handguns. But, facing in 1994 a tough re-election campaign against Moppert in a non-metropolitan district, he agonized over the assault weapons ban, deciding at the last minute to vote against it, despite a call from Bill Clinton. He survived 49%–48%. As part of the minority in the House, he has mostly taken on lost causes, lost at least for the moment. He has called for creation of Empowerment Zones in rural areas, a ban on checks for unsolicited loans, a patient's safety bill, and a stop on shifting of Veterans funds to the Sun Belt. He has opposed individual investment accounts in Social Security. He was pleased when the Hudson was named a National Heritage river and has sought to get General Electric to dredge PCBs from its bed. When the EPA announced a sweeping clean-up proposal in December 2000, Hinchey praised it; he also spoke positively about new EPA administrator Christie Whitman, who will have an important say on the final plan. He advocated the statue of Franklin Roosevelt in a wheelchair, which was unveiled on the Washington Mall. He directed $100,000 to a New Paltz apple-packing plant that was victimized by low prices and bad weather. He opposed a plan to make the Erie Canal a National Heritage Corridor because he objected that Governor Pataki would be given too much control; some alleged Hinchey was angry that Pataki had taken a partisan approach in managing the Hudson River National Heritage Corridor. The conflict was resolved after George W. Bush was elected President.

Hinchey has been a Republican target but has built impressive strength in the district. In 1996, as Bill Clinton carried the district and Hinchey spent nearly $1 million, Hinchey won 55%–42%, carrying all parts of the district. In 1997 a North American subsidiary of an Italian power plant construction company pleaded guilty in federal court of making $40,000 in illegal contributions to his 1992 campaign, and his 1992 finance director pleaded guilty to illegally funneling $27,000 from a company he controlled: The amounts together were about one-fifth of what he spent that year. But Hinchey was not implicated in either case. In 1998 the focus shifted to his opposition. The favored Republican candidate, radio station owner William (Bud) Walker, was overshadowed by Randall Terry, the Binghamton talk radio host who founded Operation Rescue in 1987 and staged anti-abortion rallies ever since. Terry raised and spent $1.2 million, most of it from abortion opponents across the country; his campaign unearthed court documents in which Walker's former wife accused him of hitting their children and failing to give them medicine. Walker won the Republican primary by an unimpressive 53%–35%, and Terry kept campaigning as the Right-to-Life nominee. Hinchey won with a solid 62% to 31% for Walker and 7% for Terry; he peaked at 10% and 12% in the two Binghamton area counties. In 2000, Moppert ran again but received little national support; Hinchey won, 62%–38%.

Hinchey might face serious redistricting problems in 2002; this is a district whose geographic shape makes it easy to slice up among its neighbors, and Hinchey might lose either his eastern or his western base. But he hired a former aide to Assembly Speaker Sheldon Silver to represent him, and he has shown impressive staying power for a member whose first victory seemed something of a fluke.

Cook's Call *Potentially Competitive.* Though Hinchey's liberal voting record made him a consistent target in this district for much of the 1990s, Republicans did not but up a serious challenger in 2000. But he is not out of the woods for 2002: Worried that redistricting will endanger his district, Hinchey has hired a lobbyist to help him curry favor with the state legislators charged with drawing the new lines. Upstate New York is the slowest growing part of the state and, with the state slated to lose two seats in redistricting, Upstate has become a very tempting target. Hinchey's district will be altered (it is short about 60,000 people), but how difficult it will be for him to hold onto the seat is unclear.

THE PEOPLE: Pop. 2000: 589,237; Pop. 1990: 580,540, up 1.5% 1990–2000. 85.8% White, 6.6% Black, 2.6% Asian, 0.3% Amer. Indian, 2.1% Two+ races, 2.6% Other; 6.6% Hispanic Origin.

2000 Presidential Vote

Gore (D)	124,913	(51%)
Bush (R)	101,426	(41%)
Nader (Green)	14,962	(6%)
Others	3,216	(1%)

1996 Presidential Vote

Clinton (D)	120,755	(53%)
Dole (R)	82,044	(36%)
Perot (I)	25,237	(11%)

Rep. Maurice D. Hinchey (D)

Elected 1992, 5th term; b. Oct. 27, 1938, New York, NY; home, Saugerties; S.U.N.Y. New Paltz, B.S. 1968, M.A. 1969; Catholic; married (Ilene).

Military Career: Navy, 1956–59.

Elected Office: NY Assembly, 1974–92.

Professional Career: Cement plant worker, 1959–64; NY St. Thruway toll collector, 1959–68; Analyst, NY St. Dept. of Educ., 1971–74.

DC Office: 2431 RHOB 20515, 202-225-6335; Fax: 202-226-0774; Web site: www.house.gov/hinchey.

District Offices: Binghamton, 607-773-2768; Ithaca, 607-273-1388; Kingston, 845-331-4466.

Committees: *Appropriations* (22d of 29 D): Agriculture, Rural Development, & FDA; Interior.

Group Ratings

	ADA	ACLU	AFS	LCV	CON	ITIC	NTU	COC	ACU	NTLC	CHC
2000	95	86	100	93	83	33	20	23	0	9	0
1999	95	—	100	81	81	—	17	16	4	—	—

National Journal Ratings

	1999 LIB	—	1999 CONS		2000 LIB	—	2000 CONS
Economic	88%	—	0%		95%	—	0%
Social	77%	—	22%		94%	—	0%
Foreign	95%	—	0%		92%	—	6%

Key Votes of the 106th Congress

1. Patient Bill of Rights	Y	5. Bar RU-486 $ for FDA	N	9. NATO War in Serbia	Y
2. Accelerate Min. Wage	Y	6. Display 10 Commandments	N	10. Perm. Trade with China	N
3. Strike Ban on Ergo. Stnd.	Y	7. Gun Show Bkgrnd. Checks	Y	11. Debt Relief for 3rd World	Y
4. Ovrd. Estate Tax Veto	N	8. Ban Part.-Birth Abortion	N	12. Drop Cuba Econ. Embargo	Y

Election Results

2000 general	Maurice D. Hinchey (D-Ind-L-WF)	140,395	(62%)	($795,829)
	Bob Moppert (R-C)	83,856	(37%)	($176,395)
	Others	2,328	(1%)	
2000 primary	Maurice D. Hinchey (D)	unopposed		
1998 general	Maurice D. Hinchey (D-Ind-L)	108,204	(62%)	($1,007,554)
	William H. (Bud) Walker (R-C)	54,776	(31%)	($770,134)
	Randall Terry (RTL)	12,160	(7%)	($1,214,416)

TWENTY-SEVENTH DISTRICT

Across the Finger Lakes of New York—the long, thin, deep-blue lakes in glacier-carved folds between rolling hillsides thick with grapevines—ran one of the first paths of westward migration. Originally cut off from white settlement by the British and the Iroquois, Upstate New York opened up after the Revolution, and streams of New England Yankees moved west. They followed the Mohawk River and the Erie Canal, dug by hand labor and finished in 1825, connecting the Hudson River and Lake Erie, the East Coast and the vast interior of America. The Finger Lakes region became one of the fastest-growing and most dynamic parts of America. Town squares here today have monuments to the enthusiasms of the 1830s and 1840s, when these new communities were full of young families on the rise, and religious revivals were so fervent that the area was known as the Burnt-Over district. Here in the village of Palmyra, near the Erie Canal, Joseph Smith had his vision of the angel Moroni and saw the golden tablets that led him to found the Mormon Church. Preachers fanned enthusiasm for abolition of slavery, greater here than anywhere else in the country. This was the birthplace of the women's movement: in Seneca Falls in 1848, Elizabeth Cady Stanton and Lucretia Mott produced a Declaration of Sentiments that started the women's suffrage movement. Upstate was also the birthplace of the temperance movement, another women's cause in those days.

The 27th Congressional District covers much of this territory, now economically less dynamic and politically calmer than in its heyday. The district starts at Aurelius, one of the many Upstate towns with classical names, and includes Seneca Falls and Palmyra, then passes south of Rochester and through Batavia and Attica to the Buffalo suburb of Amherst. Most of this is part of America's Republican heartland, though Erie County around Buffalo, with its historic industrial base, has leaned Democratic.

The congressman from the 27th is Thomas Reynolds, a Republican elected in 1998. Reynolds grew up in Springville, in southern Erie County, and became an insurance and real estate broker there. He got into politics early: in 1973 he was aide to an assemblyman and that same year, at 23, he was elected to the Town of Concord council. In 1982 he was named to a vacant seat in the Erie County Legislature. In 1988 he was elected to the Assembly and also helped run the congressional campaign of Bill Paxon, who was elected to succeed Jack Kemp. From 1990–96 he was Erie County Republican Chairman, from 1995–98 the Assembly minority leader. He chaired Dennis Vacco's successful campaign for attorney general in 1994. In early 1998 it seemed sure that he would stay in Albany, though perhaps under a cloud; the *New York Post*'s Frederick U. Dicker reported that Governor Pataki was furious with Reynolds because Assembly Republicans did not applaud loudly enough Pataki's State of the State address.

Then suddenly the 27th House seat fell open. For 10 years Paxon had been one of the rising stars in the House. He chaired the House Republicans' campaign committee, when it gained 52 seats and control of the House in 1994. Newt Gingrich told intimates that Paxon was the most talented Republican in the House. But in July 1997 Paxon played a key part in the unsuccessful coup against Gingrich; he resigned his leadership post, saying someone would have to take the blame. In February 1998, Paxon announced he would retire from Congress at the end of his term, and never run for office again. At his side in Erie County was Reynolds, who announced he was running for the House the next morning. No serious Republican opposition appeared. Democrats spent most of March and April looking for a candidate. The party reaffirmed the endorsement it made, before Reynolds's announcement, of Bill Cook, a professor at SUNY-Geneseo. It was not a suspenseful or eventful campaign. Reynolds won 57%–43% and by 51%–49% in Erie County.

In the House, Reynolds—with some help from Paxon—quickly showed he was in good repute with his party's leadership when he became only the second Republican freshman to win a seat on the Rules Committee in a century. That assignment gave him quick entry into the House's leadership circles and the Capitol's back rooms. He procured $2.7 million for Genesee County, including distance learning programs for Daemen College, the county's water system and a sewer project for the town of Clarence. Like Paxon, Reynolds proved a skillful fundraiser, gaining appointment to chair the National Republican Congressional Committee's Battleground 2000 program, which raised $21 million from House members. Many expect that he will become chairman of the House Republicans' campaign committee after the 2002 election, when Tom Davis plans to step down. In January 2001, Speaker Dennis Hastert gave Reynolds a slot on the leadership-friendly House Administration Committee, which has responsibility for campaign finance legislation. As a further sign of the leadership's gratitude to Reynolds for his campaign service and a measure of his growing influence, Hastert also secured for him a seat on the Ways and Means Committee, where he is accumulating seniority even though he is on leave while continuing to serve at Rules—perhaps awaiting the retirement at Ways and Means of Upstate neighbor Amo Houghton.

Reynolds easily won reelection in 2000. Redistricting poses a challenge. The Census numbers mean that Upstate New York must lose a seat, and Assembly Democrats will probably insist that it be a Republican seat. Western New York's population has been falling, and it would be easily to slice the long, thin 27th District into slices. But Reynolds is well connected in Albany, and determined to retain the seat. He could try to gain territory from the Southern Tier counties of the 31st District, but Houghton, one of the wealthiest members of Congress, has been lobbying hard to keep the Southern Tier together. He may lose his native territory in Erie County and will probably try to extend the district eastward, though he hopes not far enough to get into a battle with another incumbent.

Cook's Call *Safe.* Though all Upstate members should be nervous about redistricting, rising Republican star Tom Reynolds is not expected to be in much trouble. Though only a sophomore, Reynolds has already landed a seat on the exclusive Rules Committee and was appointed to serve as chair of the Executive Committee of the NRCC. As the former state House Minority Leader, Reynolds has great relationships with those in charge of drawing the new lines. His was the only district in western New York to gain population, but it still needs to pick up about 40,000 new residents in redistricting.

THE PEOPLE: Pop. 2000: 610,516; Pop. 1990: 580,317, up 5.2% 1990–2000. 93.4% White, 3% Black, 1.5% Asian, 0.3% Amer. Indian, 1.1% Two+ races, 0.7% Other; 1.9% Hispanic Origin.

2000 Presidential Vote			1996 Presidential Vote		
Bush (R)	147,221	(53%)	Clinton (D)	111,804	(44%)
Gore (D)	117,597	(42%)	Dole (R)	111,371	(44%)
Nader (Green)	10,504	(4%)	Perot (I)	28,980	(11%)
Others	4,792	(2%)			

Rep. Thomas Reynolds (R)

Elected 1998, 2d term; b. Sept. 3, 1950, Belfonte, PA; home, Springville; Springville-Griffith Inst., Kent St. U.; Presbyterian; married (Donna).

Military Career: NY Air Natl. Guard, 1970–76.

Elected Office: Concord Town Bd., 1974–82; Erie Cnty. Legislature, 1982–88; NY Assembly, 1988–98, Min. Ldr., 1995–98.

Professional Career: Real estate & insurance broker; Erie Cty. Repub. Chmn., 1990–96.

DC Office: 413 CHOB 20515, 202-225-5265; Fax: 202-225-5910; Web site: www.house.gov/reynolds.

District Offices: Victor, 716-742-1600; Williamsville, 716-634-2324.

Committees: *House Administration* (6th of 6 R). *Rules* (9th of 9 R): Rules & Organization of the House.

Group Ratings

	ADA	ACLU	AFS	LCV	CON	ITIC	NTU	COC	ACU	NTLC	CHC
2000	0	14	0	21	19	94	59	85	84	70	93
1999	15	—	0	19	6	—	54	92	79	—	—

National Journal Ratings

	1999 LIB —	1999 CONS		2000 LIB —	2000 CONS
Economic	24% —	72%		18% —	76%
Social	16% —	82%		26% —	71%
Foreign	22% —	77%		25% —	69%

Key Votes of the 106th Congress

1. Patient Bill of Rights	Y	5. Bar RU-486 $ for FDA	Y	9. NATO War in Serbia	N
2. Accelerate Min. Wage	N	6. Display 10 Commandments	Y	10. Perm. Trade with China	Y
3. Strike Ban on Ergo. Stnd.	N	7. Gun Show Bkgrnd. Checks	N	11. Debt Relief for 3rd World	N
4. Ovrd. Estate Tax Veto	Y	8. Ban Part.-Birth Abortion	Y	12. Drop Cuba Econ. Embargo	N

Election Results

2000 general	Thomas Reynolds (R-C)	157,694	(69%)	($832,254)
	Thomas W. Pecoraro (D)	69,870	(31%)	($27,587)
2000 primary	Thomas Reynolds (R)	unopposed		
1998 general	Thomas Reynolds (R-C)	102,042	(57%)	($851,862)
	Bill Cook (D-Ind-RTL)	75,978	(43%)	($60,622)

TWENTY-EIGHTH DISTRICT

Rochester, with a metro area of just over one million, is one of the major cities of Upstate New York. Located where the Erie Canal, the backbone of Upstate, crosses the Genesee River, Rochester became a major industrial city, the "Flour City," in the 1830s, as it milled the wheat produced by western New York farmers; then, a high-tech city, when a bank clerk named George Eastman began making photographic dry plates and marketed the first still camera and film for Thomas Edison's motion picture camera. Later, Bausch & Lomb developed its lens business here. Rochester, the home of Susan B. Anthony and Frederick Douglass, has lived on high-tech versions of the eye. Its great industries—Bausch & Lomb, Eastman Kodak, and Xerox, which started here as Haloid—have thrived on technical innovation, precision workmanship, high reliability and customer service, giving Rochester an affluent and well-educated population that maintains fine civic institutions and traditions. This was the city that in 1918 invented the Community Chest and has the nation's highest United Way contributions; it is also the home of Wegman's, quite possibly the nation's best supermarket chain. A *Washington Post* 1996 profile of Rochester concluded that the city's growth proves "the economic future of cities and states depends less on where the biggest companies chose to locate than where the best people chose to locate." Unhappily, Rochester's big businesses have fallen on hard times: Xerox moved many jobs out of here a decade ago, and in the past decade Kodak has been hard pressed. Unemployment here is not as high in some parts of Upstate New York, and metro Rochester did not lose population as the Buffalo and Syracuse areas did between 1990 and 2000; but Rochester has not grown much either.

The 28th Congressional District includes Rochester and most of its Monroe County suburbs—a compact district in a state where redistricting produced a dozen grotesqueries. In the 1990s, for the first time in 50 years, the heart of Monroe County wasn't separated into two districts. Traditionally Republican, the Rochester area moved toward Democrats in the 1970s and 1980s; Monroe County voted for Al Gore over George W. Bush in 2000.

The congresswoman from the 28th District is Louise Slaughter, a Democrat first elected in 1986. A coal miner's daughter and a descendant of Daniel Boone, she grew up in Kentucky and still speaks with the accent and pungent phraseology of the mountains. She is one of several notable women who came into public life after raising a family. Slaughter worked as a local staffer for Mario Cuomo when he was lieutenant governor in the 1970s and she won a seat on the Monroe County Legislature in 1976; she was elected to the New York Assembly in 1982. Four years later, she beat a one-term conservative Republican congressman 51%–49%, by charging that he did nothing to free reporter Terry Anderson, a hostage in Lebanon and Rochester native. She held the seat by tending carefully to local problems, by winning the support of area businessmen and the local *Democrat & Chronicle* newspaper—ironically, the flagship of Gannett, a chain founded by a diehard Upstate Republican. Because Rochester has moved left and her district includes all the central city, her solidly liberal voting record is not a liability.

When Democrats were in the majority, Slaughter became a member of the Rules Committee, a proponent of her party's House reforms (and a disparager of the Republicans'). She worked to get funding for the Rochester International Airport and the harbor, for the Center for Integrated Manufacturing Studies, and for a high-tech business incubator. She voted against NAFTA and fast track. A major grievance has been airline deregulation, which has hurt slow-growing areas like Upstate New York; Rochester in 1998 had the fourth-highest air fares in the nation. Slaughter's efforts at reregulation—requiring hub airlines to service smaller airports, banning temporary price cuts to drive out competition—have not prevailed. She celebrated when start-up JetBlue began service from Rochester; but travelers were bedeviled by horrifying delays and flights Upstate were cancelled. Subsequently, other small carriers moved into the Rochester market. Slaughter is a prime supporter of the National Endowment for the Arts, and finally managed a spending victory in the 2000 budget debate. She has sponsored bills for free broadcast time for candidates. And she had a bill providing $1.25 billion in matching grants for local after-school crime prevention programs. She sometimes sounds sterner notes: The House has approved her proposal for federal life-without-parole sentences for serial rapists.

Slaughter backs feminist causes and is active on health issues. In 1991 she was one of the seven women House members who marched on the Senate to protest its treatment of Anita Hill, in 1994 she sponsored the law to ban blockades of abortion clinics and in 1995 she spoke out loudly for surgeon general nominee Henry Foster. She worked for more funding for breast cancer research, sponsored a bill to require insurance companies to cover reconstructive surgery for breast cancer victims, and pushed for national screening for colon cancer. After sponsoring a law making the practice a federal crime, she sought a report on genital mutilation of women, a common practice among certain Africans. Slaughter wants to bar insurance companies from using genetic tests to deny or limit coverage to healthy people; she also contends that such data should be kept private and out of the hands of employers and health insurers.

The Lewinsky scandal and impeachment left Slaughter uncomfortable. In March 1998 she said defensively, "I have not changed a bit from my days with Anita Hill. Sexual harassment in the workplace is a terrible thing and should not be tolerated." Long resentful of Clinton's moderation and changeability on issues, and of his penchant for negotiating directly with House Republicans and leaving House Democrats out of the loop, she said in December, "I don't think you'd find a whole lot of loyalty to Bill Clinton around here. He's not the best Democrat any of us have seen." She said she was ready to call for resignation in August but backed away when she saw the videotape of his testimony in which she thought his rights were abridged; like so many other feminists, she voted Clinton's way when the time came.

Slaughter has been frustrated in seeking higher positions. In December 1994 she lost the race for vice chairman of the Democratic Caucus to Barbara Kennelly by a 93–90 margin. And she lost the December 1996 race for ranking Democrat on the Budget Committee to the more moderate John Spratt by 106–83. In 1998 she complained that House Democrats have done little to elevate women to positions of power: "There's not been an inch of progress made that I can determine."

After a close start, she has become entrenched in the district. Redistricting should not be a problem; Monroe County has enough people for one district, with a little bit left over.

Cook's Call *Potentially Competitive.* After some less than overpowering wins in the early 1990s, Slaughter seems to have caught her stride in this marginally Democratic district and has won her last three races by large margins. Redistricting could give her some heartburn in 2002: With the state slated to lose two seats, all eyes are on Upstate New York, the slowest growing portion of the state. Slaughter's Rochester-based district is short of the ideal congressional population by 62,000 residents.

THE PEOPLE: Pop. 2000: 592,533; Pop. 1990: 580,347, up 2.1% 1990–2000. 75.7% White, 16.2% Black, 2.7% Asian, 0.3% Amer. Indian, 2.1% Two + races, 2.9% Other; 6.1% Hispanic Origin.

2000 Presidential Vote

Gore (D)	133,723	(53%)
Bush (R)	105,917	(42%)
Nader (Green)	9,482	(4%)
Others	2,523	(1%)

1996 Presidential Vote

Clinton (D)	136,424	(56%)
Dole (R)	88,279	(36%)
Perot (I)	17,841	(7%)

Rep. Louise M. Slaughter (D)

Elected 1986, 8th term; b. Aug. 14, 1929, Harlan Cnty., KY; home, Fairport; U. of KY, B.S. 1951, M.S. 1953; Episcopalian; married (Robert).

Elected Office: Monroe Cnty. Legislature, 1976–79; NY Assembly, 1982–86.

Professional Career: Regional Coord., Lt. Gov. Mario Cuomo, 1976–79.

DC Office: 2347 RHOB 20515, 202-225-3615; Fax: 202-225-7822; Web site: www.house.gov/slaughter.

District Office: Rochester, 716-232-4850.

Committees: *Rules* (3d of 4 D): Rules & Organization of the House.

Group Ratings

	ADA	ACLU	AFS	LCV	CON	ITIC	NTU	COC	ACU	NTLC	CHC
2000	90	86	100	93	72	53	18	38	4	13	7
1999	100	—	100	94	17	—	18	21	4	—	—

National Journal Ratings

	1999 LIB	—	1999 CONS		2000 LIB	—	2000 CONS
Economic	82%	—	17%		78%	—	20%
Social	87%	—	0%		90%	—	10%
Foreign	67%	—	32%		80%	—	16%

Key Votes of the 106th Congress

1. Patient Bill of Rights	Y	5. Bar RU-486 $ for FDA	N	9. NATO War in Serbia	*
2. Accelerate Min. Wage	Y	6. Display 10 Commandments	N	10. Perm. Trade with China	N
3. Strike Ban on Ergo. Stnd.	Y	7. Gun Show Bkgrnd. Checks	Y	11. Debt Relief for 3rd World	Y
4. Ovrd. Estate Tax Veto	N	8. Ban Part.-Birth Abortion	N	12. Drop Cuba Econ. Embargo	Y

Election Results

2000 general	Louise M. Slaughter (D)	151,688	(66%)	($167,851)
	Mark C. Johns (R-C)	75,348	(33%)	
	Others	3,820	(2%)	
2000 primary	Louise M. Slaughter (D)	unopposed		
1998 general	Louise M. Slaughter (D)	118,856	(65%)	($456,930)
	Richard A. Kaplan (R-Ind)	56,443	(31%)	($511,083)
	Others	8,159	(4%)	

TWENTY-NINTH DISTRICT

The Niagara Frontier is the romantic name for the Buffalo metropolitan area and the northwest corner of Upstate New York facing Lake Ontario. This really was the frontier once, between the United States and British-held Upper Canada, when American troops crossed the raging Niagara River in the War of 1812 to fight the Battle of Lundys Lane. Not many years later, Niagara Falls became a prime vacation spot, a must-see sight for European tourists and American honeymooners. By the mid-20th Century, Niagara Falls vacations had become routine, and few tourists took notice of the huge water intakes farther up the river, the hydroelectric power lines strung out on giant pylons fanning out in every direction, providing cheap public power for the chemical and steel factories that made the Niagara Frontier one of the heavy industry capitals of America. The city of Niagara Falls itself has fallen on hard times. It has lost 70% of its manufacturing since the 1960s and had the nation's third lowest rate of job growth in the late 1990s. Its population has fallen from a peak of more than 100,000 to 55,000 in 2000. Urban renewal leveled most of the downtown, but redevelopment has remained an elusive dream. The latest project is for the city to build an Indian museum at the turtle-shaped Turtle, a museum operated by Tuscarora Indians that closed in 1996.

The 29th Congressional District includes the heart of the Niagara Frontier: the Falls; the Buffalo suburbs of Tonawanda and Kenmore; and the northwest one-third of Buffalo itself, with the city's downtown and its fine but financially beleaguered cultural institutions. The 29th also runs east to include towns and farm country along the southern shore of Lake Ontario to the Rochester suburb of Gates. Like most of Upstate New York, this was once Republican territory; as heavy industries declined, it trended Democratic. Its most famous congressman was William Miller, the Republican National Committee chairman from 1961–64 and Barry Goldwater's 1964 vice presidential nominee. But it hasn't elected a Republican since 1972.

The congressman from the 29th is John LaFalce, a son of Buffalo who attended Canisius College and was elected to the New York Senate in 1970, at 31, and to the Assembly in 1972. In 1974, when the Republican incumbent retired, he was elected to the House. His record is very liberal on economics, but moderate on cultural and foreign issues. Much of his work has been to get government to spur development of industrial areas. In the 1980s, LaFalce took up the banner of promoting competitiveness. He strongly backed the U.S.-Canada Free Trade Agreement, which enabled the Niagara Frontier, with its low land costs and rents, to partake of the prosperity of Ontario's Toronto-based Golden Horseshoe. But he voted against NAFTA: Niagara Falls and El Paso are connected by U.S. 62, but it's a long ride. As chairman of the Small Business Committee from 1987–95, he superintended the various Small Business Administration loan programs, which represent only a minuscule percentage of total lending to small business. LaFalce's small business interests led him to draw up his own family and medical leave, disabilities and civil rights bills, and he was a leader in the fight to repeal the Section 89 employee-benefits tax provisions that small business owners detested.

After the 1996 election, LaFalce decided to seek the ranking position on Banking by trying to oust the often autocratic and distracted 80-year-old Henry Gonzalez. But after winning support from a leadership committee, LaFalce unexpectedly dropped his challenge. It was a brilliant stroke: He won over Gonzalez's friends, including many Hispanics and blacks. In 1997 Gonzalez stopped coming to Washington, and LaFalce was named acting ranking member; in February 1998, with Gonzalez's consent, he was unanimously elected ranking member. He will be chairman if and when Democrats win a majority in the House.

On Banking LaFalce worked hard on the financial services deregulation bill finally passed in November 1999, one of the major achievements of the 106th Congress. This repealed the 1933 Glass-Steagall Act and broke down barriers between banks, brokerage firms and insurance companies, but keeps financial services companies separate from commercial firms. It requires ATM surcharge disclosures and prevents companies from sharing personal information. This was a heavily lobbied measure, which eventually passed as a consensus product. "We have a bill that brings us into the 21st century [and] protects and promotes consumer rights," LaFalce said. He has proposed bills to prevent what he regards as consumer abuses—to lower the threshold for regulation of high-cost lending, to prohibit the making of high-interest payday loans, to require disclosure of the terms of teasers in credit card agreements, to prohibit ATMs in the immediate area of gambling in casinos. In 1999 he introduced a measure to waive HUD's 2% mortgage insurance premium for borrowers who use the proceeds of an FHA reverse mortgage to purchase or make payments on long-term care insurance; this became part of a law passed in 2000 to allow seniors to get reverse mortgages. In October 2000 he and outgoing Banking Chairman Jim Leach shepherded a bill relieving bankers of 20 minor burdensome regulations, renewing banking regulatory reports and creating low-cost mortgages for teachers and other public employees.

LaFalce is capable of bipartisan good will—he was the only Democrat who spoke as the House voted the Congressional Gold Medal to Ronald and Nancy Reagan in April 2000—but he insisted that, if he got to be chairman after the 2000 elections, he would do things differently. "You surely will see a much greater emphasis on consumer rights under my chairmanship than you have under the past six years. There are a lot of abusive practices that are taking place today . . . with respect to mortgage lending, with respect to credit card [company accountability], with respect to automobile lease [term disclosures] and, of course, with respect to privacy. Privacy is an extremely important area deserving of enhanced oversight and coverage, and so we certainly would delve into these areas more aggressively than we have in the past."

LaFalce has also worked on local issues for the ailing Niagara Frontier. He helped persuade Fannie Mae to commit money, $2 billion was his estimate, to the Buffalo area over five years and worked for $120 million in improvements to the Rainbow Bridge and the Niagara Falls Air Reserve Base. With Louise Slaughter of Rochester, he sponsored measures to reregulate airlines, taking slots away from major carriers and auctioning them off; western New York has some of the nation's highest air fares. He urged regulators to guarantee competition between CSX and Norfolk Southern when they bought Conrail's lines. He called for renegotiating limits on Canadian wool imports; Rochester's Hickey-Freeman is a leading manufacturer of fine men's clothes. He called for dropping fees on small pleasure craft crossing the border and tried to change the new immigration law requirement that all aliens fill out visa forms when entering or leaving the U.S.—a surefire recipe for gridlock at Niagara Frontier bridges.

LaFalce's re-election margins fell to 55% in the early 1990s but have risen since. Against a businessman who spent $565,000 of his own money, he won 57%–41% in 1998. In 2000 he won 61%–39%. Redistricting may not be too much of a problem, though the Niagara Frontier lost population in the 1990s. It might be in the interest of both LaFalce and Republican Jack Quinn of the 30th District to swap some territory, giving LaFalce more of Buffalo, but it is not clear that legislators will go along; Democrats might want to keep the 30th heavily Democratic, so that when the locally popular Quinn retires it will go their way.

Cook's Call *Potentially Competitive.* With New York forced to lose two seats in redisricting, most insiders speculate that at least one of those seats will come from Upstate. All eyes are on western New York, which has lost the most population. LaFalce's district is more than 31,000 people short of the ideal district, and like every member of western New York's delegation, will have a seriously altered seat to contend with in 2002.

THE PEOPLE: Pop. 2000: 572,581; Pop. 1990: 579,831, down 1.3% 1990–2000. 88.9% White, 6% Black, 1% Asian, 0.8% Amer. Indian, 1.5% Two+ races, 1.8% Other; 4% Hispanic Origin.

2000 Presidential Vote			1996 Presidential Vote		
Gore (D)	126,193	(52%)	Clinton (D)	120,777	(52%)
Bush (R)	103,867	(42%)	Dole (R)	82,737	(36%)
Nader (Green)	9,988	(4%)	Perot (I)	28,015	(12%)
Others	4,598	(2%)			

Rep. John J. LaFalce (D)

Elected 1974, 14th term; b. Oct. 6, 1939, Buffalo; home, Tonawanda; Canisius Col., B.S. 1961, Villanova U., J.D. 1964; Catholic; married (Patricia).

Military Career: Army, 1965–67.

Elected Office: NY Senate, 1970–72; NY Assembly, 1972–74.

Professional Career: Law Clerk, U.S. Navy Gen. Cnsl., 1963; Lecturer, George Washington U., 1965–66; Practicing atty., 1967–74.

DC Office: 2310 RHOB 20515, 202-225-3231; Fax: 202-226-9911; Web site: www.house.gov/lafalce.

District Offices: Buffalo, 716-846-4056; Niagara Falls, 716-284-9976; Spencerport, 716-352-4777.

Committees: *Financial Services* (RMM of 32 D).

Group Ratings

	ADA	ACLU	AFS	LCV	CON	ITIC	NTU	COC	ACU	NTLC	CHC
2000	65	57	85	86	68	67	16	42	12	18	40
1999	85	—	100	88	92	—	15	24	12	—	—

National Journal Ratings

	1999 LIB —	1999 CONS		2000 LIB —	2000 CONS
Economic	88%	0%		85%	11%
Social	57%	42%		59%	41%
Foreign	78%	17%		85%	15%

Key Votes of the 106th Congress

1. Patient Bill of Rights	Y	5. Bar RU-486 $ for FDA	Y	9. NATO War in Serbia	Y
2. Accelerate Min. Wage	Y	6. Display 10 Commandments	Y	10. Perm. Trade with China	Y
3. Strike Ban on Ergo. Stnd.	Y	7. Gun Show Bkgrnd. Checks	Y	11. Debt Relief for 3rd World	Y
4. Ovrd. Estate Tax Veto	N	8. Ban Part.-Birth Abortion	Y	12. Drop Cuba Econ. Embargo	Y

Election Results

2000 general	John J. LaFalce (D-Ind-L)	128,328	(61%)	($487,016)
	Brett M. Sommer (R-C-RTL)	81,159	(39%)	($20,595)
2000 primary	John L. LaFalce (D)	unopposed		
1998 general	John J. LaFalce (D-Ind-L)	97,235	(57%)	($1,026,355)
	Chris Collins (R-C)	69,481	(41%)	($963,479)
	Others	3,813	(2%)	

THIRTIETH DISTRICT

Buffalo, New York's second city, with its massive 1920s skyscraper City Hall overlooking the Niagara River and Lake Erie, has been going through rough times. The butt of many jokes about the snow that piles up at the eastern end of Lake Erie and that supposedly keeps it immobilized half the year, Buffalo also should be credited with building a heavy industrial base in the late 19 and early 20th Centuries, as America's number one grain milling center, and as a major st producer. Today, the Lackawanna steel mills are cold, and grain milling waned after the St. La rence Seaway opened in the 1950s. Buffalo is eclipsed economically by the bigger Great Lak industrial cities of Cleveland, Detroit and Chicago, and its architecturally bold downtown sl scrapers are far overshadowed by the high-rise horizon of Toronto, not many miles away. Buff was one of the nation's 20 largest cities in 1950 when it had a population of 580,000; hal century later, it was not one of the top 50, with a population down to 292,000, less than in 19 Surrounding Erie County, once well over 1 million, was down to 950,000. Buffalo still has co siderable assets: a high-skill labor force and inexpensive real estate, including a gentrified a handsome waterfront on a now-clean Lake Erie, some marvelous cultural institutions. Rig across Buffalo's Peace Bridge is the richest part of Canada, the golden horseshoe from Niaga Falls through Hamilton to Toronto. But Buffalo's hopes of becoming Toronto's back office ha faded, as the Canadian dollar has weakened; New York's taxes have declined, but so have C tario's, and New York taxes are still high enough to leave Buffalo at a serious disadvantage.

The 30th Congressional District of New York consists of the eastern and southern two-thi of Buffalo, plus most of the Erie County suburbs east and south of the city, from working-cl Cheektowaga and the steel-mill town of Lackawanna to higher-income Hamburg on Lake E This is a solidly Democratic district, by any measure the most Democratic in Upstate New Yo although some of the suburbs are Republican. But in the early 1990s, as Buffalo struggled to gr it was politically volatile. In 1992 Buffalo gave Ross Perot 28%, his best showing in a central c anywhere, and in 1994 Mario Cuomo, who had always run well in Buffalo, lost Erie County George Pataki; Pataki carried Erie County 55%–22% in 1998. But in contests for president a senator Buffalo and Erie County have been solidly Democratic.

The congressman from the 30th District is Jack Quinn, a Republican elected in 1992. He an authentic product of Buffalo, the son of a union railroad engineer, a union member hims as a steelworker and teacher, a graduate of Siena College who became a teacher and coach Orchard Park Central High School, and the Town of Hamburg supervisor (a full-time job) fr 1983–92. When incumbent Democrat Henry Nowak retired in 1992, Quinn saw his chance run as a reformer; he created his own Change Congress Party so his name would appear und this as well as the Republican Party label; he ran on an 11-point program of congressional refor including term limits and a reduction in House staff. In a stunning upset, Quinn beat Erie Cou Executive Dennis Gorski by 52%–46%; in effect, Quinn got the Perot vote while Gorski ran sically even with Bill Clinton's 46% plurality.

Quinn, sometimes compared with Ronald Reagan, is known on Capitol Hill as well as Buffalo for his affable personality and, like Reagan, has shown that he is politically shrewd. Tagg almost immediately by Democrats as their number one target in 1994, Quinn worked to rea out to organized labor, voting against NAFTA. He was one of the few Republicans to support defeated striker replacement bill and supported family and medical leave. He favored the Clin crime bill in August 1994, proposing changes that helped attract support for the measure—me ing with Clinton once and talking with him twice on the phone. Meanwhile, local Democrats w split among several contenders, and Quinn rolled over his opponent, 67%–33%.

In the Republican Congress, Quinn did even more to demonstrate his independence of party's leadership. He was the lead Republican pushing in 1996 for an increase in the minim wage, and in 1999 he was one of only two Republicans (the other was Maryland's Connie More to vote against the Republican budget and one of four Republicans to vote against the $792 bill tax cut. He supported summer youth employment and winter home heating laws, the hate cri law, the NEA, and lobby reform. He opposed fast track and Permanent Normal Trade Relati with China, and sought quotas and other aid for the import-battered steel industry. He was a booster of the bipartisan civility meetings, and in 1998 he led 22 other Republicans to a meet with AFL-CIO president John Sweeney. In early 2001, he jousted with President Bush over decision to ban project labor agreements. Challenged once on the floor for wearing bermuda sho and a polo shirt with his coat and tie, he promised, "From now on I'm going to take my cue fr [Ohio's astonishingly dressed James] Traficant."

On local issues, Quinn worked on the Transportation and Infrastructure Committee to save Amtrak and build a new station in Memorial Auditorium. He sought to assure local competition after CSX and Norfolk Southern bought Conrail; with Senator Charles Schumer, he called for the rail companies to pay for a new bridge over the Buffalo River, where significant rail congestion has harmed shippers. He got projects ranging from $40 million seed money for U.S. 219 south of Buffalo to $300,000 for a traffic calming study on Route 5 in Hamburg. He called for lifting restrictions on imports of Canadian softwood lumber to help local home builders and lumber dealers. He told the EPA not to send to his district the Hudson River's PCB-infected sediment. Quinn helped overturn a provision in the 1996 immigration law, which would have required aliens to stop at chokepoints and be questioned by federal officers when entering and exiting the United States—a daffy law that would have tied up traffic for hours at the Peace Bridge and in Niagara Falls; the solution was the development of a new data collection system by the INS. In the 107th Congress, he became chairman of the Railroad Subcommittee, which should provide additional local benefits.

This record has helped Quinn hold this basically Democratic seat. In 1996 the AFL-CIO endorsed Democratic Assemblyman Frank Pordum and Bill Clinton carried the 30th District 59%–29%. But Quinn won 55%–45%—an impressive example of ticket-splitting.

Impeachment was a problem for Quinn. His good relations with Clinton—he watched the 1997 Super Bowl at the White House—and the Democratic leanings of the 30th District led everyone to assume he would oppose. On December 9, 1998, Clinton called Quinn from *Air Force One* and Quinn gave no sign of wavering. But as he listened to the arguments of the Judiciary Committee Republicans, he did. On December 15, four days before the vote, he announced he would vote for impeachment, and eight other Republicans followed that day, deciding the issue. What changed his mind? As he told *The Washington Post*, "It wasn't a single event; it was a gradual process. It was just a very difficult decision to make. My friendship with the president made it doubly difficult." Much local reaction was furious. The head of the Buffalo AFL-CIO Council said, "We thought he was a friend of ours. We really, really did. Let me tell you something . . . We won't forget this in two years." Clinton refused to shake Quinn's hand after the State of the Union in January, and journeyed to Buffalo for a rally the day after. Hillary Rodham Clinton, not yet contemplating a New York Senate race herself, promised to campaign for Quinn's 2000 opponent. Quinn said he was puzzled why labor leaders were so angry, since Clinton had deserted them on important issues like NAFTA and fast track and he had held fast. Quinn had it figured right. Dropping their earlier threats, state and local AFL-CIO unions again endorsed him. The Democrats did not have a strong candidate, and Quinn won 67%–33%. Redistricting will probably not be a problem. Erie County now has enough population for less than one-and-a-half districts.

Cook's Call   *Potentially Competitive.* Although this Buffalo-based district has a serious Democratic tilt to it (Gore won here by 24%), Quinn's moderate record and pro-labor stances have insulated him from charges that he is out of step with his constituency. Since winning here in 1992, he has never dropped below 52%, but redistricting could deal him a huge blow. Quinn's district, which lost over 17,000 people in the 1990s, is now the smallest congressional district in the state and needs to pick up almost 100,000 new people. His district could be seriously altered in redistricting.

THE PEOPLE: Pop. 2000: 563,256; Pop. 1990: 580,818, down 3% 1990–2000. 78.3% White, 18.4% Black, 0.8% Asian, 0.6% Amer. Indian, 1.2% Two+ races, 0.8% Other; 2.2% Hispanic Origin.

2000 Presidential Vote

Gore (D)	145,545	(59%)
Bush (R)	85,906	(35%)
Nader (Green)	9,384	(4%)
Others	3,961	(2%)

1996 Presidential Vote

Clinton (D)	137,557	(59%)
Dole (R)	69,341	(29%)
Perot (I)	28,166	(12%)

Rep. Jack Quinn (R)

Elected 1992, 5th term; b. Apr. 13, 1951, Buffalo; home, Hamburg; Siena Col., B.A. 1973, S.U.N.Y. Buffalo, M.A. 1978; Catholic; married (Mary Beth).

Elected Office: Hamburg Town Supervisor, 1983–92.

Professional Career: Teacher & coach, Orchard Park Central Schl., 1973–83.

DC Office: 2448 RHOB 20515, 202-225-3306; Fax: 202-226-0347; Web site: www.house.gov/quinn.

District Office: Buffalo, 716-845-5257.

Committees: *Transportation & Infrastructure* (9th of 42 R): Aviation; Highways & Transit; Railroads (Chmn.). *Veterans' Affairs* (7th of 17 R): Benefits.

Group Ratings

	ADA	ACLU	AFS	LCV	CON	ITIC	NTU	COC	ACU	NTLC	CHC
2000	15	21	57	36	1	78	55	70	70	52	67
1999	50	—	83	44	15	—	33	72	60	—	—

National Journal Ratings

	1999 LIB	—	1999 CONS		2000 LIB	—	2000 CONS
Economic	50%	—	49%		52%	—	48%
Social	41%	—	59%		50%	—	50%
Foreign	42%	—	57%		25%	—	75%

Key Votes of the 106th Congress

1. Patient Bill of Rights	Y	5. Bar RU-486 $ for FDA	Y	9. NATO War in Serbia	*
2. Accelerate Min. Wage	Y	6. Display 10 Commandments	Y	10. Perm. Trade with China	N
3. Strike Ban on Ergo. Stnd.	Y	7. Gun Show Bkgrnd. Checks	Y	11. Debt Relief for 3rd World	N
4. Ovrd. Estate Tax Veto	Y	8. Ban Part.-Birth Abortion	Y	12. Drop Cuba Econ. Embargo	N

Election Results

2000 general	Jack Quinn (R-C-Ind)	138,452	(67%)	($615,608)
	John Fee (D-L-Green-WF)	67,819	(33%)	($162,267)
2000 primary	Jack Quinn (R)	unopposed		
1998 general	Jack Quinn (R-C-Ind)	116,093	(68%)	($405,825)
	Crystal D. Peoples (D)	55,199	(32%)	($48,613)

THIRTY-FIRST DISTRICT

The Southern Tier of New York is one of the nation's forgotten stretches of territory, yet it has an interesting and distinctive history. Elmira was the hometown of Mark Twain's beloved wife, Olivia, and where Twain is buried. On Lake Chautauqua, not far from Lake Erie, a training camp for Methodist Sunday school teachers was founded in 1874, where in summers, on wide green lawns and on porches and in gazebos decorated with Victorian gingerbread, some 25,000 people heard educational talks and inspirational lectures from the likes of Ralph Waldo Emerson and William Jennings Bryan; Chautauqua lecture programs still thrive today. Corning is the headquarters of Corning Glass Works, one of America's long-successful and also artistically distinguished manu-facturing companies; the company sold off its famed kitchenware unit and now specializes in high-tech products and has significantly added local workers. In between are two small Indian reservations, miles and miles of dairy farms, and much of New York's wine country. Sheltered by hills, the lands at the edge of Upstate's deep lakes are the nation's largest grape-growing area outside California, and the leader in Concord grapes, with headquarters of prime New York State wineries and Welch's grape juice.

The Southern Tier's western half forms the 31st Congressional District. Politically, this has been Republican country since the party's founding. The towns and countryside are no longer homogeneously Protestant, but they remain solidly Republican in most elections—though occasionally willing to consider a Democrat. Bill Clinton carried the district in 1996, but it voted for George W. Bush and Rick Lazio in 2000.

The 31st District's congressman carries his familiar name with considerable grace: He is Amory Houghton, scion of the very rich family that owns the Corning Glass Works, founded in 1851. He was a top executive at Corning for 25 years and had considered retiring to be a missionary in Africa, but instead ran for Congress. The Houghtons are not just rich folks in a small town, they are charter members of the American establishment: Houghton's father was ambassador to France; his grandfather, a congressman in the 1920s, built one of the biggest mansions on Washington's Embassy Row; his family endowed the rare books library at Harvard; and this latest Houghton sat on boards of companies like IBM, Citicorp, and Procter and Gamble. Cheerful, articulate, used to being in comfortable command, Amo Houghton ran a chipper and well-financed campaign in 1986; he chatted with voters, competed with a serious Democratic opponent and won 60% of the vote. Houghton is not just a leader. He joined the Marine Corps in 1945, at 18, and in his campaigns did "work days" as a disc jockey at an Elmira radio station, as a cook at the Texas Hots restaurant in Wellsville, and as a man-on-the-street reporter for the *Olean Times-Herald*. He has been re-elected by wide margins.

Houghton is one of only two former CEOs of a Fortune 500 company in Congress, and he brings that perspective to government—he generally finds it wasteful and foolish, but also wants to preserve some programs with little public support. He dislikes adversariness (CEOs tend to hear little but praise) but is ready to listen to complaints (the up-to-date CEO had better know if the organization is not working). If he was not a typical freshman congressman in the 1980s, he may be more what the Founding Fathers had in mind than the politically adept youngsters who win in so many districts. By one estimate, he is the richest member of Congress, with more than $700 million; but he says that includes the wealth of many members of his rather large family. Anyway, he pays for his foreign travel out of personal funds. He seems to have the unassuming nature of one to whom much is given, who has been living up to his responsibilities and has mostly enjoyed himself in the process. "a wealthy Brahmin with a social conscience, a moderate congressman of grace with a spiritual bent," *The New York Times* profiled him.

Houghton's voting places him among the dozen most liberal Republicans on issues. He was an early supporter of the Shays-Meehan campaign finance bill; he delivered a passionate speech against the school prayer amendment in 1998. In early 1997 he organized the Mainstreet Coalition, which he sees as a counterpart to the Democratic Leadership Council, a think tank for Republican moderates though it has yet to produce work of the volume or rigor as the DLC. It hired as chief staffer former Congressman Steve Gunderson, who is gay; when that choice was criticized, he said, "We went with the best person. That might bother some people, but I don't know why it should. This never bothered people who went to a Cole Porter musical." A contributor to the arts for many years, he is a staunch advocate of the National Endowment for the Arts, though not a total defender; when a Buffalo area arts group wanted to fund a proposal by two women who had created a video called, "We're Talking Vulva," he responded sensibly, "Why should they fund that? It doesn't have anything to do with elevating the spirit." He demanded that his party leaders reduce the ceiling for families who could take advantage of the $500 per-child tax credit. He was one of four Republicans to vote against all four articles of impeachment, preferring that Congress approve a strongly-worded censure. Following the 2000 election, he helped to organize a bipartisan centrist coalition in the House to seek common ground on major issues.

On Ways and Means, he chairs the Oversight Subcommittee. He used that position to enact the only campaign-reform measure during the 106th Congress: a requirement that "Section 527" tax-exempt political advocacy groups, an increasingly popular funding loophole, disclose their contributors and spending. He helped to enact, with Philip Crane and Charles Rangel, the African Growth and Opportunity Act, which authorizes free trade agreements with African countries, and encourages additional private investment. Although he is not an unvarnished free-trader, he supported Permanent Normal Trade Relations with China. He was chief sponsor of the bill to award Nelson Mandela a Congressional Gold Medal. On local issues, he got a change in the Medicare reimbursement formula for the Southern Tier and a $1 million grant to start a business development center near Salamanca. After his initial reservation, he gained approval for converting Route 17 to Interstate 86, the Southern Tier Expressway.

The only threat to Houghton's tenure is redistricting. He has been so fearful that legislators in Albany would eliminate the Southern Tier district that he rejected plans to retire in 2000 and began vigorous lobbying and making campaign contributions to state legislators to preserve the seat, rather than see it absorbed into districts centered around Buffalo and Rochester, as local leaders have expected. He wasn't certain that he would succeed, and some New Yorkers predicted that, at 76, he ultimately would retire in 2002. But he vowed that Republicans will take seriously his district and the surviving traces of rural America.

Cook's Call *Potentially Competitive.* Initially, it looked highly likely that Houghton's sprawling district would be one of two districts to be eliminated in 2002. He has talked publicly of retiring, and the 8-term incumbent will turn 75 in August 2001. But, in 2001, Houghton has been active in trying to save his district. Still, it is unlikely that this district will not feel the pinch of redistricting, as it lost population in the last decade and needs to pick up more than 78,000 new residents.

THE PEOPLE: Pop. 2000: 575,753; Pop. 1990: 580,400, down 0.8% 1990–2000. 94% White, 2.6% Black, 0.7% Asian, 0.6% Amer. Indian, 1.1% Two+ races, 0.8% Other; 2.1% Hispanic Origin.

2000 Presidential Vote		
Bush (R)	124,681	(52%)
Gore (D)	99,722	(42%)
Nader (Green)	8,507	(4%)
Others	5,444	(2%)

1996 Presidential Vote		
Clinton (D)	98,244	(45%)
Dole (R)	91,208	(42%)
Perot (I)	30,268	(14%)

Rep. Amo Houghton (R)

Elected 1986, 8th term; b. Aug. 7, 1926, Corning; home, Corning; Harvard U., B.A. 1950, M.B.A. 1952; Episcopalian; married (Priscilla).

Military Career: Marine Corps, 1945–46 (WWII).

Professional Career: Exec., Corning Glass Works, 1951–86, Chmn. & CEO, 1964–86.

DC Office: 1111 LHOB 20515, 202-225-3161; Fax: 202-225-5574; Web site: www.house.gov/houghton.

District Offices: Auburn, 800-562-7431; Corning, 607-937-3333; Jamestown, 716-484-0252.

Committees: *International Relations* (14th of 26 R): Africa. *Ways & Means* (5th of 24 R): Oversight (Chmn.); Trade.

Group Ratings

	ADA	ACLU	AFS	LCV	CON	ITIC	NTU	COC	ACU	NTLC	CHC
2000	20	50	16	43	59	100	56	85	52	45	29
1999	45	—	16	44	9	—	48	87	40	—	—

National Journal Ratings

	1999 LIB	—	1999 CONS		2000 LIB	—	2000 CONS
Economic	45%	—	54%		45%	—	55%
Social	70%	—	30%		59%	—	41%
Foreign	55%	—	45%		49%	—	49%

Key Votes of the 106th Congress

1. Patient Bill of Rights	N	5. Bar RU-486 $ for FDA	N	9. NATO War in Serbia	Y
2. Accelerate Min. Wage	Y	6. Display 10 Commandments	*	10. Perm. Trade with China	Y
3. Strike Ban on Ergo. Stnd.	N	7. Gun Show Bkgrnd. Checks	*	11. Debt Relief for 3rd World	N
4. Ovrd. Estate Tax Veto	Y	8. Ban Part.-Birth Abortion	Y	12. Drop Cuba Econ. Embargo	N

★ NORTH CAROLINA ★

North Carolina, in its third century as a state, has become one of the leading-edge parts of the nation, a state whose growing economy, booming demography and vibrant culture are in many ways typical of the way the nation is going—or would like to go. This was mostly unanticipated. Few people 20 years ago picked North Carolina as a state that would chart a path to the future. It had no great central city, no Atlanta primed to become another Chicago or Los Angeles, but rather a series of small metropolitan areas spaced out over thickly settled countryside. It did not have what seemed to be cutting-edge industries: the biggest employer was textiles, typically an underdeveloped nation's first industry, and the other two were stolid furniture and soon-to-be-disfavored tobacco. Geographically, it seemed to be off the nation's main lines of commerce—too steamy to be businesslike in the summer, too cold to be a resort in the winter. It did not seem socially advanced, with a population made up almost entirely of native-born Anglo-Saxons and African-Americans and with an attachment to traditional and sometimes fundamentalist religion.

Yet North Carolina has emerged as one of America's leading growth states. Its population grew by 37% from 1980 to 2000, from 5.9 million to 8 million; it ranks just behind also-fast-growing Georgia as the 11th largest state. Its economy has diversified and grown steadily. The number of textile and tobacco jobs is down, but Research Triangle Park, between Raleigh, Durham and Chapel Hill, has become one of the world's leading pharmaceutical and high-tech research centers. Charlotte has become one of the nation's leading banking centers, the headquarters of Bank of America (formerly NationsBank and NCNB) and First Union; another big rival, Wachovia, is based in Winston-Salem. Charlotte and Raleigh-Durham have national sports franchises and huge hub airports, and the state's three big metro areas, spreading out into formerly rural counties, now have nearly half the state's population.

Not all of North Carolina is upscale. The state is the nation's number two hog producer, and the waste from big hog lots has polluted the state's rivers, most spectacularly when Hurricane Floyd drove the rivers upstream in November 1999; big national trial lawyers are now targeting the hog industry. Some people are worried about the state's decline in manufacturing jobs, as low-wage factories are closed and work moved to lower-wage factories in less affluent states or abroad. North Carolina, number one in the percentage of workers in manufacturing jobs in 1993, was number six in 2000. But manufacturing job losses have been overwhelmed by the rise in service jobs, and the unemployment rate is low enough that so many Latinos moved into North Carolina seeking entry-level jobs they more than doubled the state's Hispanic population during the 1990s. Yet for all its metropolitan growth, life in North Carolina has not lost its rural tone. This has always been thickly settled rural land, and if one is never out of sight of others there is also plenty of green space and reminders of rural roots, from barbecue stands to country Baptist churches to stock car tracks: North Carolina was the home of beloved NASCAR driver Dale Earnhardt, who died in a horrific crash at the Daytona 500 in February 2001. Tarheels can live surrounded by forests or farms and yet be within an hour's drive of huge shopping centers and thousands of workplaces.

Change has not been directed from any single establishment; the forces that have produced it are diverse and sometimes hostile. North Carolina does have a small and articulate elite, which looks for guidance from the University of North Carolina at Chapel Hill and the historically progressive editors of the state's newspapers, most prominently the Raleigh *News & Observer* and

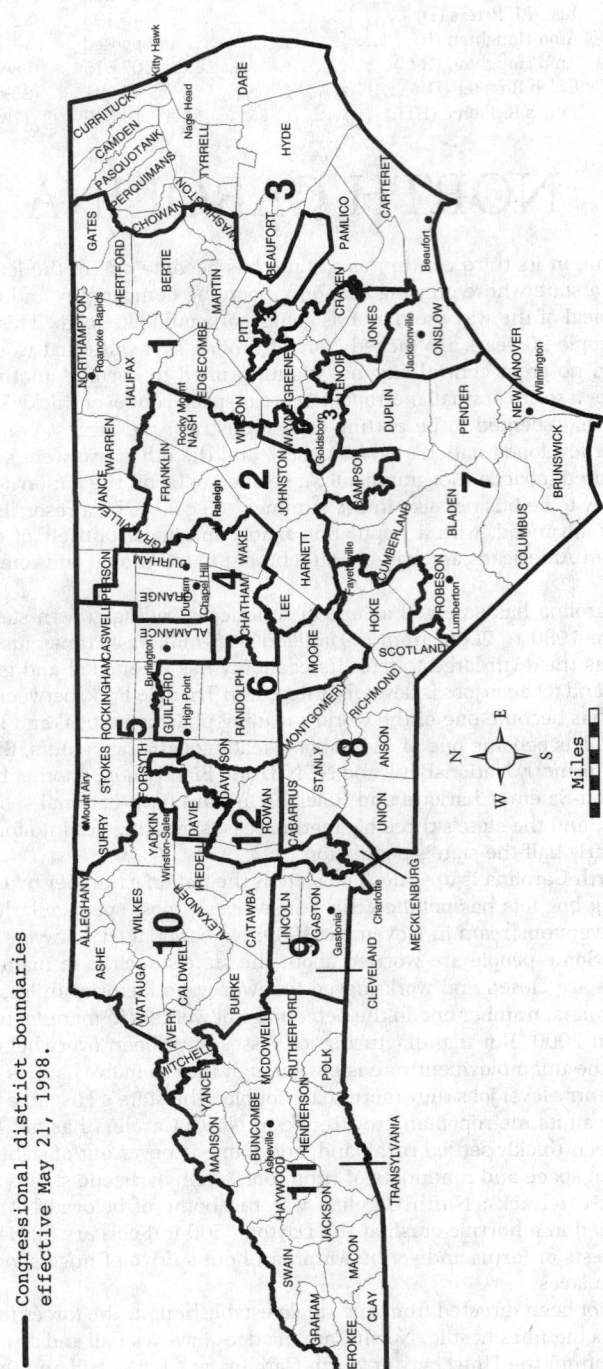

Congressional district boundaries
effective May 21, 1998.

Copyright · 1999 by Election Data Services, Inc.

the *Charlotte Observer*. Quite different attitudes are nurtured by tradition-minded churches in a state where churchgoing is deeply ingrained, endorsed for years through Sunday blue laws and strengthened periodically by religious revivals. North Carolina's Billy Graham remains a strong voice for revealed religion; he all but endorsed George W. Bush in 2000, and his son Franklin Graham delivered the invocation at Bush's inauguration. In the economically backward state North Carolina was when infant mortality was common and indoor plumbing was not, religion was a fountain of hope and a source of discipline; and it is still, perhaps even more, in this now bustling air-conditioned, cable- and computer-wired commonwealth, a place whose governor in 1999 declared eliminating outhouses one of his top priorities.

North Carolina has grown with the aid of both its progressive and tradition-minded citizens, and in spite of—sometimes because of—the polarized politics that has developed between the two sides. North Carolina's professionals tend to share progressive values; its businessmen and conservative Protestants tend to share tradition-minded values. Both groups have contributed to the state's economic dynamism and cultural energy. Liberal progressivism has provided an impetus toward building good schools and universities and highways and amenities like the nation's first state-funded symphony and state high schools for science and mathematics and the arts. North Carolina's education reforms, including stringent testing and bonuses for teachers in high-performing schools, made it one of the two states (the other was Texas) with the biggest gains in reading and math test scores in first half of the 1990s. And in 2000 the state voted 73% for $3 billion in higher education bonds.

From these two strands of North Carolina tradition developed a polarized, increasingly party-line politics that is pretty evenly balanced, waged partly on economic issues but even more on cultural attitudes. It is a politics in which Democrats and Republicans have been distinctive, sometimes bitter in their rivalries, for years not overlapping in their ideas but by the mid-1990s converging on at least some issues. This politics was built on historic partisan patterns: coastal North Carolina settlers tended to be British Anglicans who became Methodists, slaveholders who supported the Confederacy and voted Democratic; Piedmont settlers tended to be Scots-Irish Presbyterians with a scattering of Germans sects, Union men in 1861 and Republicans ever after. The most effective paladins of both traditions for the last quarter century, Republican Senator Jesse Helms and Democratic Governor Jim Hunt, were each elected to statewide office five times over 25 years, and in 1984 waged what was then the most expensive Senate race in U.S. history; once bitter rivals, they have since reconciled, and work together on some issues. Now they may be departing the scene: Hunt retired from the governorship after four non-consecutive terms in 2000, and Helms may not run for re-election in 2002 when he turns 81.

Most elections here have been decided by relatively narrow margins. Bill Clinton lost North Carolina twice, by less than 1% in 1992 and by 5% in 1996; in 2000, this was not a seriously contested state, yet George W. Bush beat Al Gore by just 56%–43%. Helms was re-elected over Democrat Harvey Gantt in 1990 and 1996 with just 53%. Hunt won his last term as governor in 1996 with 56% and was succeeded in 2000 by Democrat Mike Easley, who beat Republican Richard Vinroot 52%–46%. In 1994 Republicans took control of the North Carolina House; in 1998 Democrats took it back, and elected John Edwards senator over incumbent Republican Lauch Faircloth. Now Democrats control both the governorship and the legislature.

North Carolina's electorate breaks along cultural, not economic lines. In the 2000 exit poll blacks were overwhelmingly Democratic (90% for Al Gore), while white Protestants were heavily Republican (72% for George W. Bush). Those with non-Christian or no religion voted 64%–31% for Gore, but made up only a small proportion of the electorate. Geographically, this means the centers of the Piedmont urban areas, filling up with professionals and with significant black populations, have trended Democratic; the counties farther out, filling up with middle-income families working in decentralized businesses, have switched from historic Democratic preferences to solid Republican ones. Coastal east Carolina, once overwhelmingly Democratic, is now mixed; smaller counties in and near the western mountains are heavily Republican. The result is a close balance between two cultural and political blocs which have contributed to North Carolina's unanticipated growth—though neither is inclined to give the other much credit.

Governor The election of Mike Easley as governor in 2000 was the first time that a

Democrat has won the governorship three times in a row since 1968. He entered office in many ways overshadowed by Jim Hunt, who was elected in 1976 and 1980 and again in 1992 and 1996; Hunt ran against Senator Jesse Helms in 1984 and lost by a narrow margin after a fiercely contested campaign. Hunt's accomplishments were many—huge increases in both education spending and test scores, tough anti-crime policies, welfare reform, a "conceal and carry" weapons law; during his 2000 campaign, George W. Bush pointed to Hunt as a Democratic governor who had achieved great results. In 2000, barred from running again for governor, Hunt discouraged talk of a vice presidential nomination and said he would not run for Helms's Senate seat in 2002.

Easley grew up in Rocky Mount, 50 miles east of Raleigh, and graduated from the University of North Carolina and North Carolina Central University Law School. He has spent his whole adult life in government. He served as an assistant district attorney and in 1982, at 31, became district attorney in three southeast counties. There he attracted attention for programs against rape and sexual abuse, counseling child abuse victims and prosecuting drug traffickers. In 1992 he took a big step upward by winning election statewide as attorney general. In that office he won publicity by fighting a cap on prison populations imposed by a federal court, creating a task force on environmental crimes, working to protect abortion clinics and supporting weapon-free school zones. He took part in the national tobacco settlement and got some compensation for North Carolina tobacco farmers. He appeared in $1 million worth of public service ads, many warning about predatory lending to old people; his constant appearances irritated Republicans, who pushed through a law banning such appearances in election years.

Re-elected in 1996, Easley started running for governor in 1999, obviously a strong candidate but by no means the favorite. His main Democratic primary opponent, Lieutenant Governor Dennis Wicker, was endorsed by teachers' unions, feminist groups and black leaders. But Easley won the May primary by 59%–36%. Meanwhile, the Republican nomination went to former Charlotte Mayor Richard Vinroot—supported by former Governor Jim Martin and former UNC basketball coach Dean Smith—who beat legislator Leo Daughtry, who was supported by the Christian Coalition and the National Rifle Association, 45%–37% (North Carolina requires a runoff only when no candidate gets 40% of the vote). Easley called for prescription drugs for seniors and a patient's bill of rights, improvements in public schools and for a lottery to fund education. He avoided the national Democratic Party and didn't attend the convention in Los Angeles. Vinroot opposed the lottery but said he would allow a referendum; he pledged not to raise taxes and called for school vouchers for low-income children in failing schools. There was a negative tone to the campaign: the 6'7" Vinroot, a basketball player at UNC, got lots of notice when he referred to the 5'10" Easley as the "little fellow."

For most of the campaign Easley ran about 10% ahead in polls. Then, when the presidential candidates debated at Wake Forest University in Winston-Salem on October 11, Vinroot tied Easley to Al Gore. One ad called Easley an "Al Gore liberal"; another said, "Don't be fooled. Mike Easley, like Al Gore, will say anything to get elected." Easley attacked Vinroot for his support of vouchers and opposition to a lottery. Easley had more money, and in the last week ran an ad with an endorsement from North Carolina's Andy Griffith. That helped portray him as a down home, rural Carolinian, running against a city slicker. Even as George W. Bush was carrying North Carolina, Easley won 52%–46%. He carried east Carolina and the rural areas as a whole; he carried the Raleigh-Durham area by nearly 3–2 and ran even in the Greensboro-Winston-Salem area, running behind only in Vinroot's home turf in metro Charlotte.

As Easley took office in January 2001, the state appeared to face a budget shortfall. But he moved ahead to get approval of a lottery to provide funds for education and hoped to pay for a prescription drugs program for seniors with money from the tobacco settlement.

Senior Senator No American politician is more controversial, beloved in some quarters and hated in others, than Jesse Helms, now finishing his fifth term in the Senate. Helms grew up the son of the police chief of Monroe, North Carolina, 15 miles from the birthplace of Andrew Jackson—a breeding ground, it seems, for true-believing, contentious leaders. With Jacksonian tenacity he has stuck to his early convictions—respect for elders and law and order, traditional religious faith and moral principles, patriotism, the order imposed by racial segregation—with the exception of the last, and his abandonment of it in earlier years seemed grudging and halfhearted.

Helms has always seemed more an advocate than a doer, yet he has had a considerable effect on events over the years, and has become a major force, respected internationally perhaps even more than at home, in shaping American foreign policy. If he has not restored America to the state of the Monroe of his youth, he has succeeded in moving the country in a different direction from what his liberal critics optimistically and he pessimistically believed was inevitable 30 years ago. And he has done so with little or no surrender of principle; as Fred Barnes wrote in *The Weekly Standard*, "Helms follows a simple formula: Implacability equals strength. It works. He can't be buffaloed—or ignored. . . . The point here is Helms has gained strange, new respect not as many conservatives have—by moving left. Helms has earned it the hard way—by not moving at all."

Helms attended Wingate College and Wake Forest but did not graduate. He served in the Navy in World War II and became a journalist in Raleigh, worked for two U.S. senators from 1951–53, headed the state Banker's Association, served on the Raleigh Council and from 1960–72 was a commentator on Raleigh TV and the Tobacco Radio Network. So he was a familiar voice and a seasoned political operator when he ran for the Senate in 1972, and upset a moderate Democrat 54%–46%. Helms made then and makes now no attempt to win over everyone; he has a solidly conservative voting record, and can state his views pungently. He has had vigorous opposition every time he has run for reelection and his percentages have been in a narrow range: 54%, 55%, 52%, 53%, 53%.

In his first 20 years in the Senate, Helms—nicknamed Senator No—was mostly in the posture of opposition; since the mid-1990s he has been pursuing his own reform policies, with some success. He has long served on the Agriculture Committee, and chaired it in the 1980s; he supported tobacco programs there, but had to be bailed out of difficulties managing farm bills in the 1980s by Bob Dole. Helms was happier obtaining roll call votes on cultural issues: abortion and the fetal tissue research ban, school busing, Japanese American redress, AIDS funding, and the National Endowment for the Arts. He has been a strong supporter of the anti-flag-burning and school-prayer amendments.

Helms has used his seat on Foreign Relations to conduct something like his own foreign policy. His great cause in the 1970s was to defeat the Panama Canal treaties—a cause which helped defeat a dozen liberal senators and kept alive Ronald Reagan's candidacy when it threatened to die prior to the North Carolina primary in 1976. In the Reagan and Bush years, Helms and aides James Lucier, Christopher Manion and Deborah DeMoss developed their own sources and influenced State Department appointments to help the Contras in Nicaragua and rightists in El Salvador. Helms promised not to take the Foreign Relations chairmanship in his 1984 campaign, and in 1985 and 1986 the committee was chaired by Richard Lugar. But after Republicans lost their majority in 1986, Helms did not feel bound by his promise not to seek the ranking minority position, and citing his greater seniority beat Lugar in the Republican Conference. That put him in position to become chairman when Republicans won back the majority in 1994.

As chairman, Helms did not always prevail, but was a force to reckon with. He favored lifting the arms embargo on Bosnia; he opposed the U.S. military intervention in Haiti; he opposed the use of U.S. troops as peacekeeping forces in the Golan Heights; he was leery of the U.S. agreement with North Korea. Helms had some notable achievements. One was passage of the Helms-Burton Act after Fidel Castro's air force shot down two Brothers to the Rescue planes in February 1996; it codified the U.S. trade embargo against Cuba and allowed lawsuits against foreign companies who benefited from American property expropriated by Castro's Communist dictatorship. Helms was pleased to see Madeleine Albright, then ambassador to the United Nations, denounce the plane attack as "cowardice" and, later in the year, maneuver to block Boutros Boutros-Ghali from a second term as UN secretary general. Helms welcomed her appointment as secretary of State and on a trip to North Carolina in March 1997 she presented him with a T-shirt ("Someone in the State Department Loves Me") and he gave her some barbecue for the flight home.

Another Helms achievement was reorganization of the State Department. In 1995, after the Clinton White House rejected Secretary of State Warren Christopher's proposal to reorganize foreign policy agencies, Helms presented a similar plan of his own, holding up 18 ambassador nominations and approval of the START II and Chemical Weapons treaties; he ultimately passed $1.7 billion in spending cuts from State Department agencies over five years. Clinton vetoed the reorganization, but Helms persevered. Working with Democrat Joseph Biden, Helms ultimately prevailed, and in October 1998 the Arms Control Disarmament Agency and U.S. Information Agency were abolished and their functions were folded into the State Department. Under the reorganization plan, the U.S. Agency for International Development remained an independent agency, but its administrator started reporting to the secretary of State.

Helms has used the Senate's confirmation power to block appointments. In 1995 he vetoed Robert Pastor, a former Carter administration Latin American expert, as ambassador to Panama. In 1997 he balked at the nomination of Massachusetts Governor William Weld to be ambassador to Mexico. Helms complained that Weld supported medical marijuana and had a poor record of drug prosecutions as a U.S. attorney in the 1980s. He may also have minded that Weld, during his unsuccessful campaign for the Senate in 1996, declined to say he would vote for Helms for Foreign Relations chairman. Helms refused to allow the nomination to go forward, and Weld, who had resigned as governor, dropped out. In 1999 Helms opposed the nomination of former Senator Carol Moseley-Braun, who had met with Nigerian dictator Sani Abacha, to be ambassador to New Zealand; senatorial courtesy gave her overwhelming support, and he let the nomination come to the floor where it was approved 96–2. In 2000 he opposed the nomination of Larry Pope to be ambassador to Kuwait; as an aide to the Central Command, Pope had not supported the Iraqi liberation force which the Iraq Liberation Act of 1998 encouraged. Helms opposed Clinton judicial appointees to the Fourth Circuit Court of Appeals, although North Carolina has no judges there, citing the circuit's chief judge who has said that new appointees are not needed; critics have fastened onto the fact that two Clinton appointees are black.

Many criticize Helms' use of the confirmation process as mischievous. But it has sometimes had positive results. In 1999 Helms held up the confirmation of Richard Holbrooke as ambassador to the United Nations until he received commitments on the sticky issue of the United States' UN dues—and until Holbrooke acknowledged that he had violated federal lobbying laws in 1996. The dues had long been in arrears, and Helms, along with Biden, opposed payment until the UN reformed its huge and inefficient bureaucracy and until the U.S. share of total dues was reduced. Holbrooke vowed to negotiate such an agreement. These two unlikely partners worked closely together. Holbrooke arranged for Helms to speak to the UN Security Council in January 2000. Helms' message was blunt: "A United Nations that seeks to impose its presumed authority on the American people, without their consent, begs for confrontation and—I want to be candid with you—eventual U.S. withdrawal." But he also spoke directly with each member's representative, and hosted the Security Council to a meeting in the Capitol in March 2000. Holbrooke eventually secured an agreement that called for the U.S. to pay $926 million in back dues while reducing the U.S. share of the UN administrative budget from 25% to 22% and of UN peacekeeping forces from 31% to 26%. Helms accepted the agreement and praised Holbrooke; Biden, in an unusual tribute, hailed Helms for keeping his word and solving a long-festering problem.

The Foreign Relations Committee's power to send treaties to the floor, or not, has been used by Helms to help determine U.S. policy. He hailed the Clinton administration for its refusal to endorse the land mines treaty in September 1997. His opposition to the International Criminal Court treaty, negotiated but not endorsed by Clinton in 1998, has kept it a dead letter; in 2000 Helms sponsored a bill to bar U.S. cooperation with such a tribunal which, in his view, could subject U.S. military personnel to prosecution. In April 2000, six weeks before a Clinton visit to Russia, Helms promised to block approval of any arms control agreements negotiated by the lame duck president. Helms supported some Clinton initiatives, including the December 1998 air strikes against Iraq launched when Clinton faced the impeachment vote, and the spring 1999 bombing campaign against Serbia; but in each case he pressed for sponsoring democratic change, which came in Serbia but not Iraq. He opposed permanent normal trade relations with China, and with liberal Democrat Paul Wellstone (who on becoming a senator said that he "detested" Helms) sponsored a series of amendments to highlight China's suppression of human rights. He called for an investigation of Baltimore Orioles owner Peter Angelos when Angelos refused to hire baseball players who had fled Communist Cuba. He wants to funnel all U.S. foreign aid not through government but through private charities such as World Vision, Save the Children, Hadassa, Catholic Relief Services and Samaritan's Purse.

Helms has taken an insouciant attitude toward winning re-election. The 1984 contest between Helms and Jim Hunt was the most expensive Senate race in history then. In 1990 and 1996 Helms faced Harvey Gantt, former mayor of Charlotte and who in his youth had, amid much publicity and no little danger, desegregated Clemson University. The 1990 race was especially closely fought and closely watched. Gantt did a fine job of framing the issues, dismissing Helms' preoccupation with the NEA and abortion as unimportant. But Helms, armed with money raised by a nationwide direct mail campaign, ran ads attacking racial quotas and accusing Gantt of taking financial advantage of a law providing for racial preference in broadcast licenses. Gantt fell in the polls and Helms won 53%–47%. In 1996 Helms ran a sort of stealth campaign, refusing to debate, not announcing his public schedule and communicating with the press mostly by fax. He won 53%–46%, in a near carbon copy of the 1990 results; Gantt—in an interesting note for those who insist that whites won't vote for blacks—ran ahead of Bill Clinton.

Will Helms run again in 2002, when he turns 81? Washington reporters have focused on his health: He has had double knee replacement surgery, suffered from Paget's bone disease in his hip and has peripheral neuropathy, a loss of sensation in his feet, which impairs his balance and requires him to ride a motorized scooter. But he still has plenty of energy and determination. Few Democrats seem eager to run against him, though many might run for an open seat; names mentioned include Secretary of State Elaine Marshall, former state House Speaker Dan Blue, Richard Vinroot and Congressman Bob Etheridge. On the Republican side, Congressman Richard Burr has been traveling the state and seems likely to run, but only if Helms retires. Other possible Republican candidates include House members Robin Hayes, Sue Myrick and Walter Jones Jr.

Cook's Call *Competitive*. It isn't clear whether Republicans are better off with or without Helms, who may, or may not, retire. In all likelihood there will be a competitive contest with the potential to be one of the top races in the country.

Junior Senator John Edwards is a Democrat elected in 1998 to a seat that has been under a kind of jinx: No one has been re-elected to it since 1968, and it has switched back and forth from party to party in each election since 1980; in his three decades in the Senate, Jesse Helms has had six different colleagues. Edwards was born in South Carolina and grew up there and in Robbins, in Moore County, where his father was a supervisor in a textile mill and his mother ran a furniture refinishing business. He was the first in his family to go to college, at North Carolina State, then went to the University of North Carolina Law School. He started off defending recording companies accused of pirating Elvis Presley records, then moved to Raleigh in 1981 and became a plaintiff's personal injury lawyer, working hard to prepare cases (he was one of the first trial lawyers here to use focus groups) and fluently and persuasively presenting them in down-home style to juries. He was good at it, winning verdicts of $152 million; with 30% or more going to the lawyer, this enabled him to amass a fortune variously estimated at $20 million to $50 million. In January 1997 he won $25 million in compensatory damages for a nine-year-old girl from Cary horribly injured by a faulty swimming pool drain—the largest personal-injury verdict in North Carolina history.

At about this time Edwards began thinking about running for the Senate. He had not run for office before, had not even voted in every election, and said he could not remember whether he had first registered as a Democrat or Republican. But he did have strong views on some issues, and proved to have acute judgment in spotting the political weakness of incumbent Republican Senator Lauch Faircloth. In the years since his surprise victory in 1992, Faircloth, a wealthy hog farmer and long-time insider in Democratic politics, had a voting record as conservative as Jesse Helms' and had been a strong critic of the Clintons in various investigations. Some better-known Democrats dropped out of the race, and Edwards' main rival in the May 1998 Democratic primary was D.G. Martin, former lobbyist for the University of North Carolina and a nearly successful House candidate in 1984 and 1986. "I am prepared to raise and spend whatever is necessary," Edwards said in February 1997, and spent $3.2 million of his own money and ran ads about his background and views. He promised to be a "people's senator, someone who speaks for all the people of North Carolina, not the special interests," and he refused to take money from PACs or Washington lobbyists. The ads were criticized for suggesting that he was born in North Carolina and that he worked his way through college loading UPS trucks (he worked there for six months). But Edwards outspent Martin 4–1 and, needing 40% to avoid a runoff, won 51%–28%.

The contrast between Edwards and Faircloth was vivid. Edwards was articulate, charming, young (45 and a three-time marathon finisher); Faircloth was wrinkled with his 70 years, the embodiment of an older, rural, conservative North Carolina that many natives and newcomers wanted to leave behind. Faircloth, recognizing the threat, ran ads against Edwards in the primary, saying that he was a trial lawyer who earned millions suing doctors and driving up health care costs. He continued the negative approach, despite the voters' contented, pro-incumbent mood, throughout the campaign. Edwards proposed they pool their money and, instead of running ads, buy time for televised debates; Faircloth, less than eager for debates with a highly competent trial lawyer, would not even allow photographs one of the few times their paths crossed on the campaign trail. Edwards ran positive ads, and called for hiring teachers, building schools, an HMO patients' bill of rights, fixing Social Security. Occasionally his inexperience showed. He said credit unions should be taxed like banks, then backed off; he refused to say how he'd vote on tobacco bill, then later said he would have voted to kill it. But as former political consultant and *Hotline* founder Doug Bailey said, "Edwards is an extremely effective television-age communicator. This is a guy who has very gifted communications skills and a mind behind the skills." This was a big-spending race: Edwards spent $8.3 million, nearly three-quarters of it his own money; Faircloth spent nearly $9.4 million, including $1.7 million of his own. Faircloth started to slip in the polls and even changed pollsters in October; Edwards edged to a lead, and won 51%–47%. In this race, as in Helms', the Democrat carried younger voters, the Republican carried the elderly; Edwards won 55%–44% in the Raleigh-Durham area and ran well in traditionally Democratic east Carolina counties.

In the Senate, Edwards' voting record is mostly liberal, but in February 2000 he joined the moderate Senate New Democrat Coalition. On the Banking Committee he worked on privacy issues, and at Tom Daschle's request worked for a compromise on HMO reform. After Hurricane Floyd in September 1999, he pushed hard for disaster aid, threatening to hold up Senate proceedings in November; in time the state got more than $250 million. He did not announce his position on permanent normal trade relations with China until the last minute in September 2000; he was evidently worried about the effect on the textile industry, but recognized that North Carolina could gain export jobs in pork, poultry, furniture, telecommunications and software and ultimately voted for it. On the proposal to build jetties at Oregon Inlet in the Outer Banks, he opposed then-Governor Jim Hunt and Senator Jesse Helms, who wanted the Army Corps of Engineers to build it, and with the Clinton administration favored keeping the land under the Interior Department. He was leery of the United Airlines-USAirways merger. He brought in long-time University of North Carolina basketball coach Dean Smith to testify for his bill to outlaw betting on college and other amateur sports. Edwards made an immediate favorable impression in the impeachment debate: He was one of three Democrats to preside over the depositions of Monica Lewinsky, Vernon Jordan and Sidney Blumenthal, and his floor speeches were rated by many as the most effective during the debate.

There was little in Edwards' brief Senate record to make him a national figure, yet he was Al Gore's runner-up choice for the vice presidential nomination. The reason is his appealing manner. Though he is now rich—he sold his law practice for $5 million and bought a $2.2 million house in Washington near Hillary Rodham Clinton's—he still has a common touch. He has an appealing family, touched by tragedy: his 16-year-old son was killed in a car crash in 1996 (a consolation call came from Jesse Helms, who had been impressed by the young man in an awards ceremony in Washington). For all Edwards' charm he is also persuasive and capable of making complex arguments understandable and undercutting an opponent's; as one Republican senator says, "Never yield the floor to John Edwards." Political consultants Bob Shrum and Tad Devine pressed Gore to pick Edwards for VP; after he was passed over he spoke to the national convention delegations from Massachusetts, New York and California—filled with big contributors—and Iowa as well. He declined the chair of the Senate Democratic Campaign Committee and declined to be chief spokesman for the Gore campaign in Florida. And he was abashed when in November 2000 he was named as the sexiest politician in *People's* "Sexiest Man Alive" issue. Three months ater, Edwards was in Iowa addressing the Drake University Law School's annual dinner in Des Moines. In February 2001, he co-sponsored John McCain's patients' bill of rights legislation, a high-profile stance perhaps taken to enhance his national image.

Election year 2004 presents Edwards with some difficult choices. His seat comes up in North Carolina, and there is little doubt that he will be a strong candidate for reelection, but he may also be running for president. He has an obvious fundraising base in trial lawyers and a moderate record and demeanor that may be appealing to many Democrats, though he could compete for that constituency with his sometime jogging partner, Indiana Senator Evan Bayh. In the meantime, Edwards has seats on the Commerce and the Health, Education, Labor and Pensions Committees, and may have an opportunity to show legislative skills he has had little chance to display.

Presidential politics   North Carolina was the scene of one of the most crucial moments in the 2000 presidential campaign, when the second debate was held at Wake Forest University in Winston-Salem in October. Otherwise the state saw little of the candidates. Bill Clinton's and Al Gore's crusade against tobacco helped to put North Carolina out of reach for the Democrats, and neither campaign targeted this now fairly expensive state. Gore ran no better than even in the Raleigh-Durham metro area, and lost the Charlotte and Greensboro-Winston Salem areas by nearly 3–2 margins. In February 2001, the Democratic legislature, presumably giving up on the hope of a national Democratic candidate carrying the state, was considering whether to award 3 of the state's 15 electoral votes to the winner in each congressional district; that would guarantee the Democrats at least three more electoral votes—enough to have elected Al Gore in 2000.

North Carolina's presidential primary has been crucial only once, in 1976, when after five straight losses, Ronald Reagan started denouncing the Panama Canal Treaty and won his first victory over Gerald Ford. It has been part of the Super Tuesday primary since 1988, but has been overshadowed by the even larger states which vote that day.

Congressional districting   North Carolina won a 12th House seat in the 1990 Census and, quite unexpectedly, a 13th seat in the 2000 Census. It beat out Utah for the latter by just 856 people, and because its apportionment population includes some 18,000 U.S. troops and diplomats who claim North Carolina as their home, Utah filed a lawsuit arguing that its apportionment population should be credited with Mormon missionaries overseas who claim Utah as their home. But in April 2001 a three-judge federal panel ruled unanimously against Utah; the state has appealed that ruling to the U.S. Supreme Court but it is unlikely to be overturned.

Redistricting in the 1990s led to a legal controversy which has gone up to the U.S. Supreme Court four times. In 1992 the Justice Department, under the prevailing interpretation of the Voting Rights Act, required the state to create two black-majority districts—difficult because North Carolina has no concentrations of blacks as large as those in Georgia or Texas. So the Democratic legislature drew a plan with a jagged-boundaried 1st District in east Carolina and a 12th extending, sometimes just along the median strip of I-85, from Gastonia through Charlotte, Winston-Salem and Greensboro to Durham. In June 1993 the Supreme Court in *Shaw v. Reno*, focusing on the 12th, ordered the plan re-examined. On remand a three-judge federal panel upheld the plan in August 1994. But in June 1996 the Supreme Court declared the 12th unconstitutional and sent it back to the three-judge panel, which ruled it had to be redrawn by April 1997. In March 1997 the legislature agreed to a new plan which smoothed out the lines but, in a spirit of bipartisan compromise, left the districts much as they were. The 1st and 12th Districts, both formerly 57% black, were now 50% and 47% black, respectively (measuring by the 1990 Census). That plan was thrown out by a different three-judge panel in April 1998. In May 1998 the legislature passed a third plan which further reduced the size of the 12th District: In the first plan it stretched from Gastonia to Durham, in the second from Charlotte to Greensboro, in the third from Charlotte to Winston-Salem. The state appealed to the Supreme Court and argued for adoption of the 1997 plan. In May 1999 the Supreme Court remanded the case for trial, and in March 2000 the district court ruled that the 1997 districts were unconstitutional. That order was stayed by the Supreme Court, and the 2000 elections were held under the 1998 plan. Three weeks after the election, the Supreme Court heard argument on the case again, and in April 2001 ruled 5–4 that the 1997 districts could stand. The issue was arguably academic in North Carolina, since new lines will be drawn for the 2002 election, based on the 2000 Census, which gave the state 13 rather than 12 districts. But Justice Stephen Breyer's majority opinion that race is not an illegitimate consideration in redistricting as long as it is not the "dominant and controlling" factor provided breathing room to state legislatures across the nation grappling with redistricting, as well a warning to federal judges not to confuse political considerations with racial issues.

Control over redistricting for 2002 is in the hands of the Democratic legislature and governor. They would obviously like to change the Republicans' current 7–5 advantage in the delegation, and to create a new Democratic seat. But they will also want to safeguard the seats of the current Democratic incumbents, and doing that leaves little heavily Democratic territory left over. The seats of the two black incumbents, Eva Clayton's 1st District and Mel Watt's 12th, will surely by protected—within the limits set by the April Supreme Court decision, *Easley v. Cromartie*.

THE PEOPLE: Pop. 2000: 8,049,313; Pop. 1990: 6,628,637, up 21.4% 1990–2000. 2.9% of U.S. total, 11th largest; 72.1% White, 21.6% Black, 1.4% Asian, 1.2% Amer. Indian, 1.3% Two+ races, 2.3% Other; 4.7% Hispanic Origin. 3.6% Unemployment. 2000 Voting age pop.: 6,085,266. 2000 Turnout: 3,015,964; 50% of VAP. Registered voters (2000): 5,122,123; 2,588,137 D (51%), 1,765,476 R (34%), 768,510 unaffiliated and minor parties (15%).

POLITICAL LINEUP: Governor, Michael F. Easley (D); Lt. Gov., Beverly Perdue (D); Secy. of State, Elaine Marshall (D); Atty. Gen., Roy A. Cooper III (D); Treasurer, Richard Moore (D); Commissioner of Insurance, James Long (D); Auditor, Ralph Campbell Jr. (D); Super. of Public Instruction, Michael E. Ward (D); Commissioner of Agriculture, Meg Scott Phipps (D); Commissioner of Labor, Cherie K. Berry (R); State Senate, 50 (35 D, 15 R); Senate Pres. Pro Tempore, Marc Basnight (D); Majority Leader, Tony Rand (D); State House, 120 (62 D, 58 R); House Speaker, James B. Black (D). Senators, Jesse Helms (R) and John Edwards (D). Representatives, 12 (5 D, 7 R).

ELECTIONS DIVISION: 919-733-7173; **FILING DEADLINE FOR U.S. CONGRESS:** February 4, 2002.

2000 Presidential Vote
Bush (R)	1,631,163	(56%)
Gore (D)	1,257,692	(43%)
Others	26,135	(1%)

1996 Presidential Vote
Dole (R)	1,213,819	(49%)
Clinton (D)	1,098,297	(44%)
Perot (I)	167,465	(7%)

2000 Republican Presidential Primary
Bush (R)	253,485	(79%)
McCain (R)	35,018	(11%)
Keyes (R)	25,320	(8%)
Other	8,694	(3%)

2000 Democratic Presidential Primary
Gore (D)	383,696	(70%)
Bradley (D)	99,796	(18%)
No Preference	49,905	(9%)
Other	11,525	(2%)

Gov. Michael F. Easley (D)

Elected 2000, term expires Jan. 2005, 1st term; b. Mar. 23, 1950, Rock Mount; home, Raleigh; U. of N.C. (Chapel Hill), B.A. 1972; N.C. Central U., J.D 1976; Catholic; married (Mary).

Elected Office: NC Atty. Gen., 1992–2000.

Professional Career: Asst. D.A., N.C. 13th Dist., 1976–78, 1979–82; N.C Dist. Atty., 1982–90; private practice, 1978–79, 1990–92.

Office: State Capitol, Raleigh, 27603, 919-733-4240; Fax: 919-733-5166 Web site: www.state.nc.us.

Election Results

2000 general	Michael F. Easley (D)	1,530,324	(52%)
	Richard Vinroot (R)	1,360,960	(46%)
	Others	50,778	(2%)
2000 primary	Michael F. Easley (D)	330,764	(59%)
	Dennis A. Wicker (D)	203,723	(36%)
	Others	27,453	(5%)
1996 general	James B. Hunt Jr. (D)	1,436,638	(56%)
	Robin Hayes (R)	1,097,053	(43%)

Sen. Jesse Helms (R)

Elected 1972, seat up 2002, 5th term; b. Oct. 18, 1921, Monroe; home, Raleigh; Wingate Col., Wake Forest U.; Baptist; married (Dorothy).

Military Career: Navy, 1942–45 (World War II).

Elected Office: Raleigh City Cncl., 1957–61.

Professional Career: City Editor, *Raleigh Times*; A.A., U.S. Sen. Willis Smith, 1951–53; A.A., U.S. Sen. Alton Lennon, 1953; Exec. Dir., NC Bankers Assn., 1953–60; Exec. V.P., WRAL-TV & Tobacco Radio Network, 1960–72.

DC Office: 403 DSOB, 20510, 202-224-6342; Fax: 202-228-1339; Web site: www.senate.gov/~helms.

State Offices: Hickory, 828-322-5170; Raleigh, 919-856-4630.

Committees: *Agriculture, Nutrition & Forestry*: Marketing, Inspection & Product Promotion; Production & Price Competitiveness; Research, Nutrition & General Legislation. *Foreign Relations* (RMM): East Asian & Pacific Affairs; International Operations & Terrorism; Western Hemisphere, Peace Corps, Narcotics Affairs. *Rules & Administration*.

Group Ratings

	ADA	ACLU	AFS	LCV	CON	ITIC	NTU	COC	ACU	NTLC	CHC
2000	5	29	14	0	32	67	82	76	100	100	100
1999	0	—	0	0	62	—	77	82	100	—	—

National Journal Ratings

	1999 LIB —	1999 CONS		2000 LIB —	2000 CONS
Economic	19%	75%		25%	73%
Social	8%	88%		0%	90%
Foreign	0%	94%		5%	86%

Key Votes of the 106th Congress

1. Educ. Savings Accts.	Y	5. Review Movie Violence	Y	9. NATO War in Serbia	N
2. Prescrip. Drug Benefit	N	6. Gun Show Bckgrnd. Checks	N	10. Table Cuba Travel Ban	Y
3. Delay Ergonomic Standards	Y	7. Ban Part.-Birth Abortion	Y	11. Nuclear Test-Ban Treaty	N
4. Phase Out Estate Tax	Y	8. Broaden Hate Crimes List	N	12. Perm. Trade with China	N

Election Results

1996 general	Jesse Helms (R)	1,345,833	(53%)	($14,589,266)
	Harvey B. Gantt (D)	1,173,875	(46%)	($7,992,980)
1996 primary	Jesse Helms (R)	unopposed		
1990 general	Jesse Helms (R)	1,088,331	(53%)	($17,761,579)
	Harvey B. Gantt (D)	981,573	(47%)	($7,811,520)

Sen. John Edwards (D)

Elected 1998, seat up 2004, 1st term; b. June 10, 1953, Seneca, SC; home, Raleigh; NC St. U., B.S. 1974, U. of NC at Chapel Hill, J.D. 1977; Methodist; married (Elizabeth).

Professional Career: Practicing atty., 1978–98.

DC Office: 225 DSOB, 20510, 202-224-3154; Fax: 202-228-1374; Web site: www.senate.gov/~edwards.

State Offices: Asheville, 828-285-0760; Charlotte, 704-344-6154; Greensboro, 336-333-5311; Greenville, 252-931-1111; Raleigh, 919-856-4245.

Committees: *Commerce, Science & Transportation*: Aviation; Communications; Consumer Affairs, Foreign Commerce & Tourism; Science, Technology & Space. *Health, Education, Labor & Pensions*: Aging; Public Health. *Intelligence (Select)*. *Small Business*.

Group Ratings

	ADA	ACLU	AFS	LCV	CON	ITIC	NTU	COC	ACU	NTLC	CHC
2000	85	67	85	100	88	90	12	40	12	9	15
1999	90	—	100	78	92	—	15	41	8	—	—

National Journal Ratings

	1999 LIB	—	1999 CONS		2000 LIB	—	2000 CONS
Economic	58%	—	41%		90%	—	7%
Social	81%	—	12%		66%	—	21%
Foreign	71%	—	24%		72%	—	15%

Key Votes of the 106th Congress

1. Educ. Savings Accts.	N	5. Review Movie Violence	Y	9. NATO War in Serbia	Y
2. Prescrip. Drug Benefit	Y	6. Gun Show Bckgrnd. Checks	Y	10. Table Cuba Travel Ban	Y
3. Delay Ergonomic Standards	N	7. Ban Part.-Birth Abortion	N	11. Nuclear Test-Ban Treaty	Y
4. Phase Out Estate Tax	N	8. Broaden Hate Crimes List	Y	12. Perm. Trade with China	Y

Election Results

1998 general	John Edwards (D)	1,029,237	(51%)	($8,331,382)
	Lauch Faircloth (R)	945,943	(47%)	($9,375,771)
	Others	36,963	(2%)	
1998 primary	John Edwards (D)	277,468	(51%)	
	D. G. Martin (D)	149,049	(28%)	
	Ella Scarborough (D)	55,486	(10%)	
	Robert Ayers Jr. (D)	22,477	(4%)	
	Others	35,551	(7%)	
1992 general	Lauch Faircloth (R)	1,297,892	(50%)	($2,952,102)
	Terry Sanford (D)	1,194,015	(46%)	($2,486,380)
	Others	85,984	(3%)	

FIRST DISTRICT

Eastern North Carolina in colonial days was a smaller version of the Chesapeake Bay colonies of Virginia and Maryland—a fertile land laced by dozens of rivers and inlets, with tobacco plantations and farms with docks on the water accessible to the ocean and so to London. North Carolina was settled later than the Chesapeake colonies, and was poorer, with smaller landholdings. But vestiges of its 18th Century past can still be seen in New Bern with its Tryon Palace, the governor's house when this was the capital, and the tiny well-preserved town of Edenton on Albemarle Sound. Today, east Carolina is still tobacco country, indeed the major tobacco-producing land in the United States. It is inhabited almost entirely by the descendants of the original white settlers and black slaves of 250 years ago. They live in small towns and cities and in some of the most thickly settled rural land in the United States. Tobacco is a labor-intensive crop which can produce yields of

$4,000 an acre. A family can make a living off 40 acres of tobacco land and, with a tobacco allotment, many here do. But fewer so than in the past. No-smoking laws and anti-smoking campaigns have cut cigarette sales, and many old east Carolina tobacco fields are now planted with cucumbers, sweet potatoes and blueberries.

The 1st Congressional District of North Carolina, as redrawn in May 1998 and upheld in March 2000, covers much of the tobacco country of inland east Carolina. It touches Albemarle and Pamlico Sounds in the east and juts inland to reach black neighborhoods in Greenville and Goldsboro. Although the court that ordered the lines did not rule that the 1st District was unconstitutional, the lines of every district were changed, and about 30% of the residents of the 1st were new to the district. The new lines are less irregular than those of 1992–96, and the district's percentage of blacks was reduced from 57% to 51%. Politically, some white voters here have been attracted to the Republicanism of Jesse Helms, but overall this remains a solid Democratic district.

The congresswoman from the 1st District is Eva Clayton, a Democrat first elected in 1992. Part of the black middle class who have worked their way up in or close to government, she grew up in Savannah, Georgia. In the mid-1970s, she was director of the North Carolina Soul City Foundation, civil rights leader Floyd McKissick's attempt to form a black "new town." That foundered, but Clayton backed Jim Hunt in 1976 and became an assistant secretary for community development in his first term as governor. She was elected to, and served as chairman of, the Warren County Board of Commissioners from 1982–90. She also ran her own consulting firm and in 1992 ran for the 1st District seat. The incumbent, 78-year-old Walter Jones Sr., was retiring, and died in September 1992. His son, state legislator Walter Jones Jr., ran and won 38% in the Democratic primary, just 2% less than the 40% which under North Carolina law would have given him the nomination; Clayton was second with 31%. Clayton won the runoff 55%–45%, and she won in November with 67%. (One of Jesse Jackson's crusades in the 1980s was to abolish runoffs; if he had succeeded, Clayton would have lost.) Thus she and 12th District Congressman Mel Watt became the first blacks elected to Congress from North Carolina since George White in 1898.

In her campaigns, Clayton backed more public investment and job training and lower defense spending to cut the deficit; in office she earned one of the most liberal voting records in the House. Freshman Democrats elected her to chair their class. She was proud of working for WIC and food stamps extension, for crop disaster assistance, for the Section 515 affordable housing program. She amended the food stamps proposal in 1996 to reduce the 20-hour work requirement for those who receive food stamps worth less than what they would earn working 20 hours at the minimum wage. To urban Black Caucus members seeking her support for bills, she responds, "Does it include rural areas?" In 1998 she successfully moved to lift the statute of limitations to allow farmers to sue the Agriculture Department for racial discrimination; Agriculture soon settled with hundreds of black farmers' claims of racial discrimination in the past distribution of loans. With Jo Ann Emerson, she revived the bipartisan Rural Caucus with more than 100 members pledged to expand the agricultural safety net and narrow the digital divide in rural areas. With Mel Watt, she organized a summit to generate 1 million new black homeowners by 2005.

Clayton bucked the Clinton administration on trade; she voted against both the Africa trade bill and permanent normal trade relations with China, saying each would take jobs from her district. "Must eastern North Carolina lose in order for the Research Triangle to win?" she asked. But in negotiations on the China bill, she won White House promises to sell China more tobacco. She said she would support a tobacco bill if it was balanced and included protection for tobacco farmers. In something of a surprise but a comment on the measure's support in rural communities, she joined 52 other House Democrats in a failed attempt to override Clinton's veto of the estate-tax repeal. She has been alert to district interests, including defense contracts and bases outside district lines which employ many district residents, like the Newport News shipyard. In the aftermath of the devastating Hurricane Floyd of 1999, which left parts of the area under 14 feet of water for weeks, she got $1.5 million to study the dike along the Tar River in Princeville; in 1885 it was the nation's first town to be chartered and governed solely by blacks. She won then-Agriculture Secretary Dan Glickman's support for $12.3 million to extend water lines to more than 2,200 families in Vance, Warren and Wilson counties.

Clayton disagreed with the court decision which set the lines for 1998, and she had primary opposition for the first time since 1992. But with far more money and a visit from Tipper Gore, she beat State Representative Linwood Mercer 67%–33%. She won the general election easily, 66%–33%. After the 2000 election the Federal Election Commission said Clayton was the House tardiest member in filing routine campaign finance reports. Democratic redistricters will undoubtedly create another black-majority (or black-influence) district in east Carolina.

Cook's Call   *Safe.* As the slowest growing district in the state, Clayton's sprawling eastern North Carolina district will have to expand in 2002 redistricting. Still, Clayton should be safe. She was able to survive a 1998 redraw that added over 100,000 new residents to the district and dropped the black population by 7%.

THE PEOPLE: Pop. 2000: 587,830; Pop. 1990: 553,426, up 6.2% 1990–2000. 45.9% White, 50.5% Black, 0.4% Asian, 0.7% Amer. Indian, 0.8% Two+ races, 1.6% Other; 3% Hispanic Origin.

2000 Presidential Vote		
Gore (D)	109,118	(56%)
Bush (R)	85,802	(44%)

1996 Presidential Vote		
Clinton (D)	100,650	(57%)
Dole (R)	66,342	(38%)
Perot (I)	8,295	(5%)

Rep. Eva M. Clayton (D)

Elected 1992, 5th term; b. Sept. 16, 1934, Savannah, GA; home, Littleton; Johnson C. Smith U., B.S. 1955, NC Central U., M.S. 1962, U. of NC Law Schl., 1967–68; Presbyterian; married (Theaoseus).

Elected Office: Chmn., Warren Cnty. Comm., 1982–90.

Professional Career: Exec. Dir., Soul City Foundation, 1974–76; NC Asst. Secy., Community Development, 1977–81; Pres. & Owner, Technical Resources Intl. Inc., 1981–92.

DC Office: 2440 RHOB 20515, 202-225-3101; Fax: 202-225-3354; Web site: www.house.gov/clayton.

District Offices: Greenville, 252-758-8800; Norlina, 252-456-4800.

Committees: *Agriculture* (5th of 24 D): Conservation, Credit, Rural Development & Research; Department Operations, Oversight, Nutrition & Forestry (RMM). *Budget* (6th of 20 D).

Group Ratings

	ADA	ACLU	AFS	LCV	CON	ITIC	NTU	COC	ACU	NTLC	CHC
2000	70	86	85	71	34	72	21	61	16	12	7
1999	100	—	100	81	95	—	20	21	0	—	—

National Journal Ratings

	1999 LIB —	1999 CONS		2000 LIB —	2000 CONS
Economic	80% —	18%		64% —	36%
Social	87% —	0%		94% —	0%
Foreign	92% —	7%		69% —	28%

Key Votes of the 106th Congress

1. Patient Bill of Rights	Y	5. Bar RU-486 $ for FDA	N	9. NATO War in Serbia	Y
2. Accelerate Min. Wage	Y	6. Display 10 Commandments	N	10. Perm. Trade with China	N
3. Strike Ban on Ergo. Stnd.	Y	7. Gun Show Bkgrnd. Checks	Y	11. Debt Relief for 3rd World	Y
4. Ovrd. Estate Tax Veto	Y	8. Ban Part.-Birth Abortion	N	12. Drop Cuba Econ. Embargo	Y

Election Results

2000 general	Eva M. Clayton (D)	142,171	(66%)	($450,199)
	Duane E. Krazter Jr. (R)	62,198	(33%)	
	Other	2,799	(1%)	
2000 primary	Eva M. Clayton (D)	unopposed		
1998 general	Eva M. Clayton (D)	85,125	(62%)	($644,157)
	Ted Tyler (R)	50,578	(37%)	($27,880)
	Others	1,044	(1%)	

SECOND DISTRICT

The coastal plain of North Carolina was long bypassed by history. It was settled after Virginia and South Carolina, and only filled in with English settlers as Scots-Irish families were streaming down the valley of Virginia to the western Piedmont. This has always been tobacco country, with life organized around a crop high-yield enough that a 40-acre plot of land can support a family (if it has a tobacco allotment). Tobacco was an important colonial crop, even more so after James B. Duke created Bull Durham tobacco and Lucky Strike cigarettes. But this was long a backward area. Its small farms and little cities were homes mainly to tenant farmers and mill hands, people raising families in thin-walled frame houses often with no electricity or running water.

Today, life is much better in the coastal plain. Not just because incomes are up, but because this is now part of, or just adjacent to, one of America's fastest-growing metropolitan areas: Raleigh-Durham. Its dynamic economy has generated tens of thousands of jobs, and subdivisions have sprouted up all over Wake County and in the once rural counties beyond. Textile mills have closed and tobacco plots have become just supplementary income sources. The city has become a tourist hub, combining glitzy new museums with Big Ed's City Market Restaurant serving up country-cured ham, collards and other local dishes. West of Raleigh, around Durham and the Research Triangle, pharmaceuticals, high-tech and universities have become the biggest employers; this area has one of the lowest unemployment rates and largest totals of Ph.D.s of any part of the nation, and has been moving left politically despite rising incomes. The counties, east, south and north of Raleigh, in contrast, are not quite as upscale, and have filled up with people with family roots and church affiliations in east Carolina. That is true of once-rural Wake County as well, and in the 1990s these were the fastest-growing counties in North Carolina, except for the small coastal area around Wilmington. Politically these counties have trended Republican, casting big margins for George W. Bush in 2000.

The 2d Congressional District of North Carolina, as redrawn by the legislature in May 1998, covers much of the coastal plain in a semi-circle around Raleigh. It stretches as far east as Rocky Mount, goes south into hog-producing Sampson County, spreads west to Sanford. This is a fast-growing area: in the 1990s, Wake County's population rose 48%, Johnston County 50% and Harnett County 34%. Up through the 1996 election, the 2d included Durham, which is heavily Democratic; that is now removed, but added was about half of Raleigh's Wake County including many black precincts in Raleigh. As a result, the district's black percentage rose from about 22% to 27%.

The congressman from the 2d District is Bob Etheridge, a Democrat elected in 1996. His biography seems tailored to the district: He was born in the hamlet of Turkey in Sampson County, grew up in Johnston County, went to Campbell University in Harnett County and owned a hardware store in Lillington, the county seat. He is a tobacco farmer, the only one currently in Congress, a pillar of his community and member of many boards; he served four years on the Harnett County Commission in the 1970s, was elected to the North Carolina House in 1978 and served 10 years, eventually chairing the Appropriations Committee. In 1988 and 1992 he was elected state superintendent of Public Instruction. In the mid-1990s Governor Jim Hunt called for abolishing the superintendent post and transferred 300 employees to the state Board of Education. Etheridge, spying an opportunity, decided to run for the House in 1996 against freshman David Funderburk, a longtime ally of Jesse Helms. Funderburk had a solid conservative voting record and the district seemed politically favorable; in 1996 under the old district lines it voted 52%–42% for Bob Dole. Funderburk tried to tie Etheridge to Bill Clinton's approval of FDA Commissioner David Kessler's announcement that tobacco could be regulated as a drug. Etheridge responded by citing his own tobacco credentials: "I own tobacco allotments and have for years. I'd like to know how many days Mr. Funderburk spent priming tobacco, setting tobacco, and how many days he spent under the hot sun in the tobacco fields." Etheridge won 53%–46%.

In the House, Etheridge has compiled a moderate voting record, just a bit to the left of center. Etheridge bellowed his opposition to all attempts to regulate tobacco: he voted against the 1997 budget because it included a cigarette tax increase; he opposed eliminating crop insurance for tobacco farmers; he was the first House member to denounce the McCain tobacco bill; he led the fight in 2000 for a $125 million bailout for tobacco farmers whose surplus did not sell on the open market, including a few thousand dollars for his own farm. After China agreed to drop its ban on tobacco products, he voted for permanent normal trade relations; Research Triangle exports to China had previously doubled in five years. He defended another area crop when the Transportation Department proposed peanut-free rows on airlines to protect those with allergies to peanuts, saying, "This nutty rule is clearly an overreaction to a serious, but limited, problem faced by a fraction of the population." He pushed through a provision of the Higher Education Reorganization Act to teach values in public schools, supported the flag burning amendment and partial-birth abortion ban, and voted to override Clinton's veto of the estate-tax repeal. Named by Dick Gephardt to co-chair a party task force on education, Etheridge's special cause was school construction, especially in growing areas like those around Raleigh. When the Republicans' education bill called for giving states flexibility, Etheridge said, "This is just another way to cut the money for the public schools."

Republicans hoped to regain this seat, and their 1998 candidate was 32-year-old Dan Page, a state Senator who supported a flat tax and school vouchers and opposed Etheridge's education stand. A week before Clinton admitted he lied about Monica Lewinsky, Page ran the nation's first ad trying to link a Democratic candidate with the Clinton scandals. It said, "His is the most corrupt administration in American history. Dishonoring our heritage. And who stands with Bill Clinton, even now? Liberal Bob Etheridge. Applauding Clinton's values, not ours." Etheridge replied, "Mr. Page is confused. He's running against me, not Bill Clinton. Last time I checked, my name was on the ballot." Etheridge professed disgust for Clinton's actions and voted for the Republicans' impeachment inquiry resolution in October 1998. But he also appeared with Clinton at a Rose Garden ceremony that month. Etheridge won 57%–42%, not overwhelming but an impressive margin in this district. He had an easier time in 2000, after Raleigh Mayor Tom Fetzer decided not to run and conservative education reformer Doug Haynes sought to tie his campaign to George W. Bush. Etheridge won every county except Wilson in his 58%–41% victory.

Redistricting will undoubtedly change the shape of the district, particularly if the new 13th District is created in the fast-growing Research Triangle area. The Democratic legislature will probably try to fashion lines that will favor a conservative Democrat like Etheridge, but should he not run a Republican could be very competitive in this area.

Cook's Call　*Potentially Competitive.* Etheridge's big wins here in 1998 and 2000 belie the underlying marginal nature of this district. Bush won this district in 2000 by 11%. One of the fastest growing districts in the state this district will need to shed over 100,000 people and will undergo serious changes. There are also rumors that Etheridge will run for the Senate in 2002. All this volatility makes for a potentially competitive contest in 2002. Even if Etheridge does stay put, his moderate voting record and strong fundraising ability make him a difficult Democrat to unseat.

THE PEOPLE: Pop. 2000: 730,266; Pop. 1990: 552,529, up 32.2% 1990–2000. 66.4% White, 26.9% Black, 1.1% Asian, 0.5% Amer. Indian, 1.3% Two + races, 3.7% Other; 6.5% Hispanic Origin.

2000 Presidential Vote

Bush (R)	138,766	(55%)
Gore (D)	110,757	(44%)
Others	2,089	(1%)

1996 Presidential Vote

Dole (R)	104,762	(49%)
Clinton (D)	97,055	(45%)
Perot (I)	12,215	(6%)

Rep. Bob Etheridge (D)

Elected 1996, 3d term; b. Aug. 7, 1941, Turkey; home, Lillington; Campbell U., B.S. 1965; Presbyterian; married (Faye).

Military Career: Army, 1965–67.

Elected Office: Harnett Cnty. Comm., 1973–76, Chmn., 1975–76; NC House of Reps., 1978–88; NC Superintendent of Public Instruction, 1988–96.

Professional Career: Farmer, 1965–present; Vice Pres. Sales, Sorensen Industries, 1968–87; Owner, Layton Hardware, 1973–90; Co-owner, WLLN Radio, 1979–91.

DC Office: 1533 LHOB 20515, 202-225-4531; Fax: 202-225-5662; Web site: www.house.gov/etheridge.

District Offices: Lillington, 910-814-0335; Raleigh, 919-829-9122.

mmittees: *Agriculture* (13th of 24 D): Livestock & Horticulture; Specialty Crops & Foreign Agriculture grams. *Science* (10th of 22 D): Research; Space & Aeronautics.

oup Ratings

	ADA	ACLU	AFS	LCV	CON	ITIC	NTU	COC	ACU	NTLC	CHC
)0	60	36	57	71	11	88	36	66	28	27	47
19	85	—	100	75	79	—	20	48	24	—	—

tional Journal Ratings

	1999 LIB	—	1999 CONS		2000 LIB	—	2000 CONS
onomic	59%	—	40%		58%	—	42%
ial	60%	—	40%		60%	—	40%
eign	61%	—	37%		64%	—	34%

y Votes of the 106th Congress

'atient Bill of Rights	Y	5. Bar RU-486 $ for FDA	N	9. NATO War in Serbia	Y
\ccelerate Min. Wage	Y	6. Display 10 Commandments	Y	10. Perm. Trade with China	Y
itrike Ban on Ergo. Stnd.	Y	7. Gun Show Bkgrnd. Checks	N	11. Debt Relief for 3rd World	Y
)vrd. Estate Tax Veto	Y	8. Ban Part.-Birth Abortion	Y	12. Drop Cuba Econ. Embargo	N

•ction Results

)0 general	Bob Etheridge (D)	146,733	(58%)	($911,578)
	Doug Haynes (R)	103,011	(41%)	($266,976)
	Other	2,094	(1%)	
)0 primary	Bob Etheridge (D)	unopposed		
)8 general	Bob Etheridge (D)	100,550	(57%)	($1,106,220)
	Dan Page (R)	72,997	(42%)	($349,939)
	Others	1,647	(1%)	

HIRD DISTRICT

arly 500 years ago, Giovanni da Verrazano sailed past the Gulf Stream and landed on a sandspit ınd he thought was the outer edge of China. He was wrong. It was the Outer Banks of North rolina. These are probably America's most unstable barrier islands, constantly changing shape d cut by new inlets as they are battered by the ocean currents and storm winds. They were tled early by Europeans: Sir Walter Raleigh's Roanoke colony was founded here in 1587, then ished shortly thereafter; Edward Teach—Blackbeard—and other pirates lurked in Pamlico d Albemarle sounds behind the islets. History is still very much alive on the Outer Banks: an ique form of English is spoken on Ocracoke Island, reachable only by ferry; the 208-foot thouse on Cape Hatteras, America's tallest, looks out on some of the most treacherous currents the Atlantic which have claimed hundreds of ships; the sands along Kitty Hawk, with their istant winds, are where the Wright Brothers made mankind's first heavier-than-air flight in cember 1903. Today, the Outer Banks have become vacation and retirement country, with uent beachfront communities around Kitty Hawk, Nags Head and Duck and, much farther ith, around Beaufort (*BOWfort*, not *BEWfort* as in South Carolina) and Morehead City. Inland, amid swamps, are some of America's biggest military bases, the Marine Corps' Camp Lejeune the Army's Fort Bragg and Seymour Johnson Air Force Base. The flat lands of east Carolina have long been tobacco- and peanut-growing country, and now also hog-raising land.

The 3d Congressional District of North Carolina covers the Outer Banks and much of the coastal plain. Though less so since the May 1998 redistricting, this remains an irregularly shaped district, with fingers of land going inland to include mostly white voters around Greenville and Goldsboro while leaving black majority areas in the 50% black 1st District; in both cases the district was about 20% black.

The congressman from the 3d District is Walter Jones, a Republican elected in 1994. He grew up in eastern North Carolina, attended North Carolina State and Atlantic Christian College and served in the National Guard. His father, Walter Jones Sr., was a Democratic congressman from the 1st District, which included most of northeast North Carolina, from 1966 until his death in 1992. The younger Jones was elected in 1982 to the state House, where he voted to oust the Democratic speaker and often broke with Democratic leaders. In 1992 he ran in the new black majority 1st District after his father decided to retire, winning 38% in the Democratic primary just 2% shy of the 40% needed to avoid a runoff, then losing the runoff to Eva Clayton 55%–45%.

In April 1993, Jones switched to the Republican Party, and in May 1994 announced he was running for Congress in the 3d District: "My old party has changed and so has the world. Sadly in my opinion, both are not for the best in far too many circumstances." This pitted Jones against four-term Congressman Martin Lancaster, a Democrat who had worked hard on local projects. But Lancaster had voted for the Clinton budget and tax package in 1993 and the crime bill in 1994, and hadn't been able to persuade the Clintons to drop the cigarette tax from their health care package. Jones ran an ad showing Lancaster jogging with Bill Clinton: "How'd Martin Lancaster get so out of touch? Well, look who he's running around with in Washington." Jones won 53%–47%, running especially strong in Greenville and Kinston and carried the areas around Camp Lejeune and Morehead City.

In the House, Jones got seats on Armed Services and on Resources, which absorbed his father's old Merchant Marine and Fisheries panel. His voting record has been consistently conservative. He posted the Ten Commandments in his Capitol Hill office. In his first term one of his bills became law, the War Crimes Act of 1996, which authorizes future American prisoners of war to bring lawsuits against those who commit war crimes; this provides an enforcement mechanism for the Geneva Convention. Jones has opposed gays and lesbians in the military and favored more defense spending; he sponsored a bill for a $500 tax credit for military personnel on food stamps. He has argued for sending U.S. troops abroad only when "there is a clear mission and an achievable goal," and "only under the flag and command of the United States." He opposed permanent normal trade relations because of the inability to trust China, which he said, "steals technology and sells it our enemies, steals our nuclear secrets and tries to influence our election process." When an Osprey helicopter crashed in April 2000, Jones—who has taken a demonstration flight in the aircraft—defended it as "the fighting machine that the Marines say they need."

Jones has pursued environmental issues of local import. He passed laws protecting a herd of wild horses on Shackelford Banks and providing for a coin and commemorative ceremonies honoring the Wright brothers' first flight at Kitty Hawk. He opposes oil drilling on the North Carolina coast and won victory of a sort when Conoco gave up its federal leases for drilling on the Outer Banks, where the Gulf Stream and Labrador Current meet. To protect the Cape Hatteras lighthouse, which was built 1,500 feet from the sea and is now only 120 feet away, he got approval for moving the lighthouse a quarter-mile inland. He helped to get $3 million to combat *pfiesteria piscicida* outbreaks on the Neuse River. He won $1.8 billion to fight North Carolina beach erosion in a water projects bill passed just before the 2000 election. But he defends beach driving along the shore, criticizing a proposed National Parks ban of off-road driving as "short sighted" and harmful to tourism. With Democrat Bob Clement, he has sponsored a new wetland protection act.

Jones has easily won re-election three times, apparently cementing the district's partisan transition. In 2000 Leigh McNairy, a conservative former school teacher, criticized Jones for not doing enough to assist local recovery following the devastation of Hurricane Floyd and for breaking

is pledge to return a congressional pay raise. Although she spent more than $1.2 million, in-
luding $600,000 of her own money, McNairy was unable to dent Jones's popularity and lost
1%–37%, with Jones winning all but three counties in the northern part of the district. Although
)emocrats control redistricting, they will find it difficult to threaten the only Republican district
1 east Carolina. Jones has been mentioned as a candidate for the Senate, but he might be at a
1ndraising disadvantage compared to urban-based Republicans.

Cook's Call *Probably Safe.* Though a Democrat represented it as recently as 1994, the
rd District, like so many southern districts, has trended more Republican over the years. Bush
on here by 23% in 2000. This district has grown steadily over the last 10 years and could be
ltered by redistricting. Still, Jones looks in good shape.

HE PEOPLE: Pop. 2000: 615,614; Pop. 1990: 551,918, up 11.5% 1990–2000. 75.1% White, 19.5% Black, 1%
sian, 0.5% Amer. Indian, 0.1% Hawaiian, 1.6% Two+ races, 2.2% Other; 4.2% Hispanic Origin.

000 Presidential Vote			1996 Presidential Vote		
ush (R)	119,576	(61%)	Dole (R)	86,289	(54%)
ore (D)	73,727	(38%)	Clinton (D)	62,941	(39%)
thers	1,608	(1%)	Perot (I)	11,550	(7%)

Rep. Walter B. Jones (R)

Elected 1994, 4th term; b. Feb. 10, 1943, Farmville; home, Farmville; NC St.
U., 1962–65, Atlantic Christian Col., B.A. 1967; Catholic; married (Joe Anne).

Military Career: NC Natl. Guard, 1967–71.

Elected Office: NC House of Reps., 1982–92.

Professional Career: Mgr., Walter B. Jones Office Supply Co., 1967–73;
Salesman, Dunn Assoc., 1973–82; Pres., Benefit Reserves Inc., 1989–94;
Pres., Judson Co., 1990–94.

DC Office: 422 CHOB 20515, 202-225-3415; Fax: 202-225-3286; Web site:
www.house.gov/jones.

District Office: Greenville, 252-931-1003.

ommittees: *Armed Services* (18th of 32 R): Military Readiness; Military Research & Development. *Financial
rvices* (22d of 37 R): Capital Markets, Insurance & Government Sponsored Enterprises; Financial Institutions
Consumer Credit; Oversight & Investigations. *Resources* (14th of 28 R): Fisheries Conservation, Wildlife &
ceans; National Parks, Recreation & Public Lands (Vice Chmn.).

roup Ratings

	ADA	ACLU	AFS	LCV	CON	ITIC	NTU	COC	ACU	NTLC	CHC
)00	5	31	14	14	75	71	67	61	96	94	100
)99	15	—	0	25	90	—	71	72	100	—	—

ational Journal Ratings

	1999 LIB —	1999 CONS		2000 LIB —	2000 CONS
conomic	36%	63%		6%	85%
)cial	0%	96%		0%	79%
)reign	0%	97%		0%	88%

ey Votes of the 106th Congress

Patient Bill of Rights	Y	5. Bar RU-486 $ for FDA	Y	9. NATO War in Serbia	N
Accelerate Min. Wage	N	6. Display 10 Commandments	Y	10. Perm. Trade with China	N
Strike Ban on Ergo. Stnd.	N	7. Gun Show Bkgrnd. Checks	N	11. Debt Relief for 3rd World	N
Ovrd. Estate Tax Veto	Y	8. Ban Part.-Birth Abortion	Y	12. Drop Cuba Econ. Embargo	N

2000 general	Walter B. Jones (R)	121,940	(61%)	($1,266,7
	Leigh Harvey McNairy (D)	74,058	(37%)	($1,176,1
	Other	2,457	(1%)	
2000 primary	Walter B. Jones (R)	unopposed		
1998 general	Walter B. Jones (R)	83,529	(62%)	($626,2
	Jon Williams (D)	50,041	(37%)	($303,8
	Others	1,342	(1%)	

FOURTH DISTRICT

Back in the 1950s, few people would have predicted that the countryside around Raleigh a Durham, North Carolina, would be one of America's high-tech boom areas. But Governor Lut Hodges did, when he started Research Triangle Park as an R&D industrial park between musty state capital of Raleigh, the Lucky Strike-manufacturing city of Durham and the tiny v versity town of Chapel Hill. With the drawing power of three universities (North Carolina S in Raleigh, Duke in Durham and the University of North Carolina in Chapel Hill), Resea Triangle Park slowly began attracting big research outfits like Glaxo-Wellcome, IBM, North Telecom and the federal Environmental Protection Agency; today it has more than 40,000 pec working for more than 100 major companies, stimulating hundreds of small startups and serv businesses. Raleigh-Durham airport, which had four gates in the early 1970s, became a ma national hub. The metro area grew by nearly 39% in the 1990s, to more than 1.2 million, fastest metropolitan growth north and east of Atlanta, and for years has had one of the low unemployment rates in the nation.

The 4th Congressional District of North Carolina includes most of the Research Trian Starting with the 1992 election, it included all of Raleigh's Wake County and Chapel Hill's Ora County, plus rural Chatham County; the May 1998 redistricting removed the eastern half of W County and added Durham and the Research Triangle Park itself. Politics here revolves arou cultural issues. The two Democratic bases here are the black community and whites with p graduate degrees. The big Republican base is whites with traditional religious beliefs. The bala in the 4th District, unlike that in North Carolina as a whole, has usually gone the Democr way, even though it is only 20% black; the post-graduate liberals tend to outvote tradition-min whites. But the balance is closer, and the Democrats' margins narrower, than in high-tech distr in northern California or New England.

The congressman from the 4th District now is David Price, a Democrat first elected in 19 lost his seat in 1994 and regained it in 1996. Price grew up in east Tennessee, the son of a sch principal and an English teacher. He is an interesting blend of political scientist, practical po cian, and a lay Baptist preacher. He came to North Carolina to go to college at Chapel Hill, ear a degree in divinity and a Ph.D. in political science at Yale and taught there for four years, t became a political science professor at Duke in 1973. He was executive director of the N Carolina Democratic Party in the 1980 election cycle and chairman from 1983–84—both effect, appointments of Governor Jim Hunt; he helped develop North Carolina's robust strai ticket politics. In 1986 he ran for the House and beat a Republican who won in the 1984 swe In 1994 Price lost 50.4%–49.6% to Fred Heineman, a former New York City cop and Rale police chief in the 1970s. In 1996 Heineman made some unforced errors and was outspen Price, who regained the seat 54%–44%. He has written several books, including one, *The C gressional Experience*, about his observations on Congress, which he updated in 2000.

During his first tour in the House, Price helped pass laws increasing the percentage home's value the FHA can insure, aiding technical education at community colleges, funding EPA Research Triangle lab and raising the Falls Lake dam to ensure Raleigh's water supply. Wl he returned after 1996, Price rejoined the Appropriations Committee on which, had he not in 1994, he would have had enough seniority to be ranking minority member of a subcommit His Education Affordability Act, "my personal centerpiece," on which he had been working f dozen years, was folded into the 1997 Balanced Budget Act; it made interest on student loans deductible and allowed penalty-free withdrawals from IRAs for education expenses. His r priority on education is for building more classrooms. With Bob Etheridge, who represents the remainder of Wake County, he has pushed a federal initiative to hire 100,000 teachers to reduce class size nationwide. His Teaching Fellows program would give states incentives to encourage top students into teaching careers.

In the appropriations process, Price has nurtured local projects: $272 million for a new EPA complex in Research Triangle Park, $35 million for Raleigh's Outer Loop, $40 million for the Triangle Transit Authority to develop a regional rail line, $30 million for a high-tech state criminal tracking system, nearly $1 million for North Carolina Central University to study the environmental effects of landfills on minority communities, and $4 million for hog waste research by North Carolina State University; ironically, Citizens Against Government Waste has featured Price in its "pig book" for pork-barrel spending. With Republican Steve Horn, a fellow political scientist in the House, Price has sponsored a "stand by your ad" bill to require candidates to appear in the full frame of TV ads reading their disclaimers on the air, so they would more likely be held responsible for negative ads. Parts of that bill have been incorporated into the House-passed campaign-reform bill; a similar proposal took effect in North Carolina in 2000. Responding to Research Triangle urging, he was one of four North Carolina House members to vote for permanent trade relations with China.

After a competitive contest in 1998 against former Wake County Republican chairman Tom Roberg, which Price won by a solid but not overwhelming 57%–42% victory, he coasted to reelection in 2000 62%–37%. In the days following the 2000 election, the political scientist Price sought to alert House colleagues about possible Electoral College machinations in the presidential contest. Price's prospects for continued re-election are good, but depend on redistricting.

Cook's Call   *Probably Safe.* North Carolina will be picking up one new seat in redistricting and there has been a lot of talk about centering the new seat in the fast growing Research Triangle area. In fact, this district was the fastest growing in the state and will need to shed more than 140,000 people. With Democrats controlling redistricting in the state, Price should be well taken care of during the line drawing process.

THE PEOPLE: Pop. 2000: 765,876; Pop. 1990: 552,441, up 38.6% 1990–2000. 71.9% White, 19.9% Black, 3.7% Asian, 0.3% Amer. Indian, 1.6% Two+ races, 2.5% Other; 5.3% Hispanic Origin.

2000 Presidential Vote		
Gore (D)	168,356	(51%)
Bush (R)	157,568	(48%)
Others	4,163	(1%)

1996 Presidential Vote		
Clinton (D)	142,650	(51%)
Dole (R)	121,839	(44%)
Perot (I)	13,356	(5%)

Rep. David Price (D)

Elected 1996, 3d term; b. Aug. 17, 1940, Erwin, TN; home, Chapel Hill; U. of NC, B.A. 1961, Yale U., B.D. 1964, Ph.D. 1969; Baptist; married (Lisa).

Elected Office: U.S. House of Reps., 1986–94.

Professional Career: Legis. Aide, U.S. Sen. Bartlett, 1963–67; Prof., Yale U., 1969–73, Duke U., 1973–present; Exec. Dir., NC Dem. Party, 1979–80, Chmn., 1983–84; Staff Dir., DNC Comm. on Pres. Nominations, 1981–82.

DC Office: 2162 RHOB 20515, 202-225-1784; Fax: 202-225-2014; Web site: www.house.gov/price.

District Offices: Chapel Hill, 919-967-7924; Durham, 919-688-3004; Raleigh, 919-789-8771.

Committees: *Appropriations* (17th of 29 D): Treasury, Postal Service & General Government; VA, HUD & Independent Agencies. *Budget* (7th of 20 D).

Group Ratings

	ADA	ACLU	AFS	LCV	CON	ITIC	NTU	COC	ACU	NTLC	CHC
2000	85	86	71	86	55	83	20	61	4	15	20
1999	95	—	100	81	51	—	14	40	4	—	—

National Journal Ratings

	1999 LIB	—	1999 CONS		2000 LIB	—	2000 CONS
Economic	64%	—	36%		63%	—	36%
Social	75%	—	24%		70%	—	29%
Foreign	71%	—	27%		92%	—	6%

Key Votes of the 106th Congress

1. Patient Bill of Rights	Y	5. Bar RU-486 $ for FDA	N	9. NATO War in Serbia	Y
2. Accelerate Min. Wage	Y	6. Display 10 Commandments	N	10. Perm. Trade with China	Y
3. Strike Ban on Ergo. Stnd.	Y	7. Gun Show Bkgrnd. Checks	Y	11. Debt Relief for 3rd World	Y
4. Ovrd. Estate Tax Veto	N	8. Ban Part.-Birth Abortion	N	12. Drop Cuba Econ. Embargo	Y

Election Results

2000 general	David Price (D)	200,885	(62%)	($686,476)
	Jess Ward (R)	119,412	(37%)	($41,009)
	Other	5,573	(2%)	
2000 primary	David Price (D)	56,886	(89%)	
	John Winters (D)	6,919	(11%)	
1998 general	David Price (D)	129,157	(57%)	($1,229,519)
	Tom Roberg (R)	93,469	(42%)	($452,724)
	Others	2,284	(1%)	

FIFTH DISTRICT

From the coastal plain of North Carolina, the terrain rises slowly through modest hills cut by rivers in the Piedmont, until finally the first mountain ridges appear, their mysterious blue haze filling the crevasse valleys or clinging to the steep hillsides. The Piedmont, in between the plain and the mountains, was first settled by independent-minded Scots-Irish farmers and by followers of British and German sects like the Moravians. This was hardscrabble farm country at the time of the Civil War, with few slaves. By the late 19th Century, it was becoming industrialized, with textile mills alongside streams, furniture factories not far from hardwood forests and the R. J. Reynolds cigarette factories in Winston-Salem (the only city to be honored by the name of two cigarette brands). This Piedmont economy was hailed as the basis of a progressive New South, although textile mills paid low wages and tobacco employed fewer workers. In fact, North Carolina's present day affluence owes more to pharmaceuticals, banking and high-skill Piedmont factories like the country's most advanced tire recycling plant in Winston-Salem and a custom furniture-making operation in Kernersville.

All these are within the boundaries of the 5th Congressional District, which sweeps along the northern edge of North Carolina across the Piedmont to the Blue Ridge, stopping along the way to include the northern fringe of Greensboro and most of the Winston-Salem area. About half the district's votes are cast in and around Winston-Salem; the rest are sprinkled across the countryside and in small industrial cities like Reidsville, Eden and Mt. Airy (the setting for the fictional town of Mayberry in the *Andy Griffith Show*). The legislature's May 1998 redistricting excised the 5th's eastern and western extremities, making it somewhat more compact but not changing the political balance; most of the black sections of Winston-Salem remain in the 12th District.

The congressman from the 5th District is Richard Burr, a Republican elected in 1994. Burr grew up in Winston-Salem, was a star football player at Reynolds High and Wake Forest, then worked for a wholesaling firm. In 1992 Burr ran against Congressman Steve Neal, a Democrat first elected in 1974, who usually won by close margins; Burr was outspent 3–1 and lost 53%–46%. Neal retired in 1994 and Burr ran again. His Democratic opponent was state Senator Sandy Sands, a rural trial lawyer who attacked Burr for using Jerry Falwell's Liberty University studios to produce his 1992 ads. Burr supported the Contract with America, promised to make defense of tobacco his number one issue, and worked hard to tie Sands to the Clinton administration. Burr won a solid 57%, carrying all but two counties and taking the Winston-Salem area by nearly 2–1. He has not had a serious challenge since then; state Democratic officials said that it wasn't worth the money to challenge him in 2000.

In the House Burr has a mostly conservative voting record and, with help from Greensboro's Howard Coble, won a seat on the Commerce Committee. His main cause there has been streamlining the FDA drug and medical device approval process, which he claims has kept valuable and life-saving products from patients. By the mid-1990s the FDA was moving so slowly that it took more than 10 years and $350 million to move a prescription drug from idea to market, and 773 days to approve a medical device. He at first took a radical approach that aroused much opposition, but then for over two years worked with the agency, doctors, patients, consumer groups and the pharmaceutical industry to come up with a consensus. The FDA Modernization Act was enacted with broad bipartisan support in 1997. The new law requires the FDA to establish protocol guidelines before extensive research is begun, to review applications in a more timely manner, to use due process to determine scientific disputes and to create a scientific advisory panel; it was criticized by some on the left but praised by HHS Secretary Donna Shalala. As a bonus, the FDA approved the Sensor Pad, a device to help breast self-examination, which had been a Burr crusade. He worked to change the Medicaid formula, which got $900 million more for North Carolina over seven years, and was a leading proponent of the Republicans' prescription drug coverage plan. As oversight subcommittee vice-chairman, Burr defended Bridgestone-Firestone officials and federal regulators during the investigation of defective tires. He sought a crackdown on illegal textile imports, routed by China through other countries to evade quotas, and he opposed PNTR. He strongly backed the United Airlines merger with US Airways (United has a reservations system in Winston-Salem and USAirways has a major hub in Charlotte).

Burr's next big cause has been electricity deregulation. He sponsored a bill to give states the ability to design deregulation if they want; it barred mandatory power purchases but continued current contracts, and allowed rural cooperatives to compete wherever investor-owned utilities can. He has sponsored bills to allow satellite TV providers to include local network stations, and to delay EPA's new air-quality standards. Burr strongly opposed tobacco legislation and when Clinton called for the Justice Department to sue the tobacco companies, Burr said, "This is an administration whose policy is to drive the industry out." Burr unexpectedly became a celebrity with an appearance on the "Imus" radio show when, while testifying in opposition to the law requiring that toilets made in the United States use no more than 1.6 gallons of water per flush, he read his testimony from a roll of toilet paper.

Burr has worked his district aggressively, holding women's health and electricity summits in Winston-Salem, and employing a 30-cup rule: he buys a cup of coffee everywhere he stops to talk to constituents and says he has bought as many as 30 in a day. But his ambitions have turned statewide. After Raleigh Mayor Tom Fetzer, a longtime friend, dropped out of the gubernatorial race in January 1999, Burr considered running but decided he didn't have "the fire in my belly." He added that his sights were set on running for the Senate in 2002, if Jesse Helms retires, or 2004; that would be in line with his 1994 promise to serve no more than five terms in the House. Regardless of his plans, it's likely that a Winston-Salem-based district will continue to elect a Republican to the House; the only nearby big source of Democratic votes, the black neighborhoods of Winston-Salem, will presumably remain in the heavily black 12th District.

Cook's Call *Safe.* Regardless of whether Burr stays put or runs for the Senate, the 5th District seat is likely to retain a serious Republican edge.

THE PEOPLE: Pop. 2000: 637,158; Pop. 1990: 552,337, up 15.4% 1990–2000. 81.2% White, 14.3% Black, 0.8% Asian, 0.3% Amer. Indian, 1% Two+ races, 2.4% Other; 4.7% Hispanic Origin.

2000 Presidential Vote			1996 Presidential Vote		
Bush (R)	152,470	(62%)	Dole (R)	134,379	(57%)
Gore (D)	90,981	(37%)	Clinton (D)	86,437	(36%)
Others	1,908	(1%)	Perot (I)	16,203	(7%)

Rep. Richard Burr (R)

Elected 1994, 4th term; b. Nov. 30, 1955, Charlottesville, VA; home, Winston-Salem; Wake Forest U., B.A. 1978; Methodist; married (Brooke).

Professional Career: Natl. Sales Mgr., Carswell Distributing, 1978–94; NC Taxpayers United, Co-Chmn., 1993–present.

DC Office: 1526 LHOB 20515, 202-225-2071; Fax: 202-225-2995; Web site: www.house.gov/burr.

District Office: Winston-Salem, 336-631-5125.

Committees: *Energy & Commerce* (Vice Chmn. of 31 R): Energy & Air Quality; Health; Oversight & Investigations. *International Relations* (16th of 26 R): East Asia & the Pacific; Europe. *Permanent Select Committee on Intelligence* (9th of 11 R): Human Intelligence, Analysis & Counterintelligence; Technical & Tactical Intelligence.

Group Ratings

	ADA	ACLU	AFS	LCV	CON	ITIC	NTU	COC	ACU	NTLC	CHC
2000	5	36	14	14	32	72	63	80	88	87	93
1999	5	—	16	0	79	—	65	84	87	—	—

National Journal Ratings

	1999 LIB	—	1999 CONS		2000 LIB	—	2000 CONS
Economic	24%	—	72%		6%	—	85%
Social	10%	—	85%		26%	—	71%
Foreign	28%	—	70%		0%	—	88%

Key Votes of the 106th Congress

1. Patient Bill of Rights	N	5. Bar RU-486 $ for FDA	Y	9. NATO War in Serbia	N
2. Accelerate Min. Wage	N	6. Display 10 Commandments	Y	10. Perm. Trade with China	N
3. Strike Ban on Ergo. Stnd.	N	7. Gun Show Bkgrnd. Checks	N	11. Debt Relief for 3rd World	N
4. Ovrd. Estate Tax Veto	Y	8. Ban Part.-Birth Abortion	Y	12. Drop Cuba Econ. Embargo	N

Election Results

2000 general	Richard Burr (R)	172,489	(93%)	($421,060)
	Steven Francis LeBoeuf (Lib)	13,366	(7%)	
2000 primary	Richard Burr (R)	unopposed		
1998 general	Richard Burr (R)	119,103	(68%)	($575,327)
	Mike Robinson (D)	55,806	(32%)	($9,702)
	Others	1,382	(1%)	

SIXTH DISTRICT

For more than half a century, furniture store managers and owners from all over the country twice a year have converged on the huge Furniture Mart in High Point, the center of the U.S. furniture business, for the giant trade show put on by manufacturers. High Point sits amidst rolling farmland originally settled by Quakers, the site of the Battle of Guilford Courthouse in the Revolutionary War, then slaveholding country in the years before the Civil War. The furniture business grew here early in the 20th Century because of the hardwoods in the mountains not far west and the abundance of low-wage labor in the flatlands not far east. Soon it was said of High Point that there were so many factories, "only a wise man knows his own factory whistle." Today, employment in furniture continues to grow, unlike in textiles and tobacco, and wages have risen. Race relations are now outwardly pleasant in Greensboro, where in 1960 black students at North Carolina A&T started the first lunch counter sit-in at a local five-and-dime.

The 6th Congressional District of North Carolina covers most of Greensboro and High Point in Guilford County, Quaker-settled Randolph County and golf-course-sprinkled Moore County to the south and part of furniture-manufacturing Davidson County to the west. The May 1998 redistricting took black precincts in Guilford County away from the 12th District and placed them back in the 6th; the result is that the 6th's black percentage increased from 7% to 11%.

The congressman from the 6th District is Howard Coble, a Republican first elected in 1984. He grew up in Guilford County, went to Guilford College, then after wrecking his father's car joined the Coast Guard, in which he started off collecting garbage and served for five years. He was an insurance claims representative, went to law school and became an assistant U.S. attorney, state revenue commissioner and served in the state House from 1968–70 and 1978–84. In 1984 Coble was elected to Congress in what was then a swing district; it was the third time the 6th had changed parties in three elections. Coble won reelection in 1986 by just 79 votes—in a contest that Democrats complained was decided by the Guilford County election board's refusal to hold a recount. But his personal popularity and the 1992 redistricting made this a safe seat; the later addition of black precincts posed no jeopardy.

Coble is a friendly man who asks visitors if they mind if he smokes his cheap cigars; he likes bluegrass music and eats pork brains and eggs for breakfast. He is solidly conservative, with interesting twists. He is tightfisted, and since his first term he has tried to pass legislation to abolish congressional pensions; he boycotts that program himself, but hasn't found many co-sponsors. Like many of his constituents, he is leery of free trade. He opposed fast-track for NAFTA, but finally voted for it in 1993 (without visiting the White House or selling his vote, he said); but he opposed GATT and permanent normal trade relations with China. Unsurprisingly, he opposes FDA regulation of tobacco.

"I see my role more as one of keeping bad legislation off the books," Coble once said. But as a subcommittee chairman he became legislatively productive. In 1995 he became chairman of the panel with jurisdiction over the Coast Guard, and steered to House passage bills replacing the maritime cartel with free markets and closing down Coast Guard stations; but they went nowhere in the Senate. In 1997 he became chairman of the Courts and Intellectual Property Subcommittee of Judiciary. Suddenly this cigar-chomping and suspender-wearing Tar Heel hayseed found himself sought out by Hollywood and Nashville stars: he dined with Billy Joel and had office visits from Johnny and June Carter Cash, Michael J. Fox and Paul Reiser. Arguing that copyright industries produce more GDP than manufacturing and that patent protection is essential to technological progress, Coble supports greater protection for intellectual property—to consumerists' dismay. He passed a bill to extend the term of copyright by 20 years. (Otherwise Mickey Mouse would have gone out of copyright by 2004.) He introduced measures to make it illegal to circumvent encryption technology used to protect copyrighted material and to remove digital author codes from copyrighted material, to protect creative work transmitted over the Internet. This law, signed in October 1998, conforms U.S. law to World Intellectual Property Organization treaties.

Coble concedes that he is not computer literate, but says that has not been an obstacle to dealing with the digital revolution and that he has come to appreciate the developers of the Internet. His bill to impose criminal penalties for unauthorized use of materials in electronic data bases generated fierce opposition; critics complained that it would permit the stock exchanges to prevent publication of stock prices. In the 106th Congress, Coble became the center of added controversy after he slipped a four-line amendment to the copyright law into an unrelated bill on home satellites; his "work for hire" provision, which recording companies requested, extended their control of recorded music past 35 years after its release; Coble thought that he was merely formalizing what already was common practice. Following strong objections from prominent musicians such as rock star Don Henley (who wrote a song complaining about the unfairness) and bluegrass banjoer Earl Scruggs—and, not incidentally, from fellow subcommittee member Mary Bono, widow of Sonny—Coble before the 2000 election agreed with ranking Democrat Howard Berman to repeal the earlier measure. Still, he enacted more than a dozen bills after taking over the copyright subcommittee and remained popular with colleagues. In the 107th Congress, Coble was named chairman of the revamped Internet and Intellectual Property subcommittee.

On other court-related issues, Coble sponsored the law that established a commission to consider realignment of the federal appeals courts, especially the cumbersomely large and often-reversed 9th Circuit. He proposed cutting the fees that finance the Patent and Trademark office, whose surplus the Clinton administration was raiding. When former Congressman Robert Drinan said Republicans were seeking "vengeance" against Clinton, Coble replied, "We're going about our business, and if anybody thinks that vengeance is involved, I'll meet 'em in the parking lot later on tonight." No such meetings took place. Coble—who became a friend in the Coast Guard with fellow Tarheel Erskine Bowles, Clinton's chief of staff in 1997 and 1998—voted to impeach but declined to become a House manager, because of his father's illness.

Coble was the only North Carolinian on the Transportation and Infrastructure Committee as it put together the huge highway bill in 1998. The highway formula was shifted very much to his state's advantage, and Coble brought home some bacon: $22 million for the Greensboro Outer Loop, $22 million to build the U.S. 311 expressway in High Point, $6.6 million for a Greensboro Intermodal Center at the old train station and $3.3 million for new Greensboro buses and vans.

Coble has had no Democratic opponent in three of four contests since 1994. Democratic redistricters may make the district more Democratic, not so much with the hope of defeating Coble as making it a winnable district if he retires.

Cook's Call _Safe._ Coble has had little competition here since 1986, and he is not likely to see any action in 2002 either. This district needs to shed about 70,000 residents in 2002 redistricting, but it is unlikely to undermine the Republican-leaning nature of this district. He is safely situated here.

THE PEOPLE: Pop. 2000: 689,529; Pop. 1990: 552,663, up 24.8% 1990–2000. 84.1% White, 10.9% Black, 1.3% Asian, 0.4% Amer. Indian, 1.1% Two + races, 2.2% Other; 4.4% Hispanic Origin.

2000 Presidential Vote			1996 Presidential Vote		
Bush (R)	169,105	(64%)	Dole (R)	105,779	(50%)
Gore (D)	92,116	(35%)	Clinton (D)	88,812	(42%)
Others	1,970	(1%)	Perot (I)	15,484	(7%)

Rep. Howard Coble (R)

Elected 1984, 9th term; b. Mar. 18, 1931, Greensboro; home, Greensboro; Appalachian St. U., 1949–50, Guilford Col., A.B. 1958, U. of NC, J.D. 1962; Presbyterian; single.

Military Career: Coast Guard, 1952–56, 1977–78, Coast Guard Reserves, 1960–81.

Elected Office: NC House of Reps., 1968–70, 1978–84.

Professional Career: Asst. U.S. Atty., NC Middle Dist., 1969–73; Commissioner, NC Dept. of Revenue, 1973–77; Practicing atty., 1979–83.

DC Office: 2468 RHOB 20515, 202-225-3065; Fax: 202-225-8611; Web site: www.house.gov/coble.

District Offices: Asheboro, 336-626-3060; Greensboro, 336-333-5005; High Point, 336-886-5106.

Committees: _Judiciary_ (4th of 21 R): Courts, the Internet & Intellectual Property (Chmn.); Crime. _Transportation & Infrastructure_ (4th of 42 R): Coast Guard & Maritime Transportation; Highways & Transit; Railroads.

Group Ratings

	ADA	ACLU	AFS	LCV	CON	ITIC	NTU	COC	ACU	NTLC	CHC
2000	15	36	14	7	31	75	63	76	86	91	100
1999	15	—	0	6	51	—	71	78	100	—	—

National Journal Ratings

	1999 LIB —	1999 CONS		2000 LIB —	2000 CONS
Economic	36% —	64%		40% —	60%
Social	22% —	77%		0% —	79%
Foreign	0% —	97%		12% —	78%

Key Votes of the 106th Congress

1. Patient Bill of Rights	Y	5. Bar RU-486 $ for FDA	Y	9. NATO War in Serbia	N
2. Accelerate Min. Wage	N	6. Display 10 Commandments	Y	10. Perm. Trade with China	N
3. Strike Ban on Ergo. Stnd.	N	7. Gun Show Bkgrnd. Checks	N	11. Debt Relief for 3rd World	N
4. Ovrd. Estate Tax Veto	Y	8. Ban Part.-Birth Abortion	Y	12. Drop Cuba Econ. Embargo	N

Election Results

2000 general	Howard Coble (R)	195,727	(91%)	($301,790)
	Jeffrey Dean Bentley (Lib)	18,726	(9%)	($4,885)
2000 primary	Howard Coble (R)	unopposed		
1998 general	Howard Coble (R)	112,740	(89%)	($401,604)
	Jeffrey Dean Bentley (Lib)	14,454	(11%)	

SEVENTH DISTRICT

Southernmost North Carolina, where the state boundary dips down along the Atlantic coast, has been economically dependent on tobacco for more than 200 years. Tobacco can be cultivated profitably in only a few places in the world; it is labor-intensive, requiring close tending and serial picking (one leaf on a stalk matures before the one above it); and it is valuable enough that North Carolina farmers today, if they have one of the tobacco allotments handed out in the 1930s or have bought the rights to one, can make a living off 40 acres. Tobacco produces more voters per federally assisted acre than any other crop. This tobacco country, it should be added, is racially diverse, the home of many blacks as well as the Lumbee Indians, whose origins have been lost in antiquity, but who were treated by state segregation laws—and still are treated by continuing custom—as a race distinct from whites and blacks; each race makes up about one-third of the population of Robeson County around Lumberton.

Southernmost North Carolina is also military country. The port city of Wilmington is home of the World War II battleship *U.S.S. North Carolina*. Wilmington and the nearby beach towns were the second-fastest growing part of North Carolina in the 1990s. Eastward, in swampland, is Camp Lejeune, home base of one-fifth of the Marine Corps. Inland, near Fayetteville, is the huge complex of Fort Bragg and Pope Air Force Base, whence 39,000 troops left for the Persian Gulf in 1990. As the site of one of the biggest bases in the country, Fayetteville has developed the strip highway to an art form, with strip joints, fast food galore and the world's first Putt-Putt golf course.

North Carolina's 7th Congressional District covers much of this territory. Starting in 1992 it had astonishingly jagged boundaries and took in Camp Lejeune and Fort Bragg; the 1998 redistricting removed the two bases but retained Fayetteville, which is so dependent on them. Politically, the 7th consists of three areas: the coastal area around Wilmington, with hundreds of affluent condo-dwellers, now trending Republican; the area around Fayetteville, pretty evenly divided between the parties; and the Lumbee Indian country in and around Robeson County, very heavily Democratic. This was for many years a solidly Democratic district, but is now more marginal; in 2000 it was carried by George W. Bush and Democratic Governor Mike Easley.

The congressman from the 7th District is Mike McIntyre, a Democrat elected in 1996. McIntyre grew up in Lumberton, in Robeson County, graduated from college and law school at Chapel Hill and practiced law in Lumberton, where his family has been prominent for 200 years. In 1974 he was an intern in the office of Congressman Charlie Rose, then in his first term, and whispered to his father he would like one day to run for Rose's seat. McIntyre was active in civic affairs and in his church and was often asked to run for office. In 1995, four months before Rose announced his retirement, McIntyre decided to run. He was not alone: seven Democrats and four Republicans filed. McIntyre's chief opposition in the primary was Rose Marie Lowry-Townsend, a Lumbee and a liberal, who had support from the National Education Association, labor PACs and national women's groups; nearly half of her contributions came from outside North Carolina. Lowry-Townsend led McIntyre 30%–23% in the first contest. McIntyre called for smaller government and cited his close ties to the district and involvement in community activities. He won the runoff 52%–48%, carrying the Lumbee country and Fayetteville and trailing on the coast. Against Republican nominee Bill Caster, a retired Coast Guard officer and New Hanover County commissioner, McIntyre's platform was almost as conservative as Caster's—on some things, more so. He was moved by state labor leaders to withdraw his support for a national right-to-work law, but continued to favor right-to-work in North Carolina. Caster ridiculed McIntyre's emphasis on his community ties: "While it's all well and good to coach Little League, that doesn't mean you're ready to go to Congress." Caster carried the coastal counties; McIntyre carried the Fayetteville area and had a huge majority in Robeson County. Overall, he won the district 53%–46%, even as Clinton was losing it 48%–44%.

McIntyre immediately joined the conservative Blue Dog Democrats and got seats on Armed Services and Agriculture. His voting record—conservative among Democrats—stands at the middle of the House. He voted for the anti-flag burning amendment, the partial-birth abortion ban, and sunset of the tax code, and he posted the Ten Commandments in his office. But he supported racial quotas and preferences and opposed school vouchers. In the 107th Congress he voted to repeal the Clinton administration's new ergonomics rules and was in favor of the Bush tax cut. He was one of 31 Democrats to vote for the Republicans' impeachment inquiry.

"I firmly believe that the people who elected you are first and foremost the people to whom you owe your allegiance," McIntyre said. "Projects in the district are of paramount importance to us." He fought the proposal to end crop insurance for tobacco farmers and prevailed. "It would punish small farmers, the ones who could least afford to lose it," he said. He got money for hurricane relief and a new postal processing center in Wilmington, and promoted deepening of the Wilmington port for an improved shipping channel along the Cape Fear River. He pushed to reopen the Lockwood Folly River's original outlet to the sea and partially block the man-made inlet with a dike. He co-chaired the Rural Health Care Coalition, where he secured Medicare funding relief, and he backed efforts to create a Carolinas Caucus. He opposed permanent normal trade relations with China and he sought to impose a higher tariff on new imports of Caribbean Basin footware; Converse's plant west of Lumberton was once the largest shoe factory in the United States. He sought federal recognition of the Lumbees as an Indian tribe to give them "the dignity they deserve."

McIntyre has won endorsements from the U.S. Chamber of Commerce and Gary Bauer's Campaign for Working Families. "I wish Mike McIntyre would make it official and switch over to the Republican Party," said a North Carolina Republican spokesman. "He's voted with the Republicans quite a bit and is one of their most conservative members in Congress." But McIntyre has not been interested in switching. He has been re-elected twice without serious opposition. Democrats control the redistricting process and will undoubtedly make sure that McIntyre retains his base.

Cook's Call　*Safe.* As an open seat, this rural, marginal district will be tough for Democrats to defend. Bush won here in 2000 by 6%. But the conservative McIntyre is well suited for this district, and Republicans have not put up a serious fight here since McIntyre won the seat in 1996.

THE PEOPLE: Pop. 2000: 690,054; Pop. 1990: 552,037, up 25% 1990–2000. 65.6% White, 23% Black, 0.6% Asian, 6.8% Amer. Indian, 0.1% Hawaiian, 1.3% Two+ races, 2.4% Other; 4.4% Hispanic Origin.

2000 Presidential Vote			**1996 Presidential Vote**		
Bush (R)	121,965	(52%)	Clinton (D)	93,133	(47%)
Gore (D)	108,919	(47%)	Dole (R)	90,785	(46%)
Others	1,540	(1%)	Perot (I)	13,699	(7%)

Rep. Mike McIntyre (D)

Elected 1996, 3d term; b. Aug. 6, 1956, Lumberton; home, Lumberton; U. of NC, B.A. 1978, J.D. 1981; Presbyterian; married (Dee).

Professional Career: Practicing atty., 1981–96.

DC Office: 228 CHOB 20515, 202-225-2731; Fax: 202-225-5773; Web site: www.house.gov/mcintyre.

District Offices: Fayetteville, 910-323-0260; Lumberton, 910-671-6223; Wilmington, 910-815-4959.

Committees: *Agriculture* (12th of 24 D): General Farm Commodities & Risk Management; Specialty Crops & Foreign Agriculture Programs. *Armed Services* (17th of 28 D): Military Procurement; Military Readiness.

Group Ratings

	ADA	ACLU	AFS	LCV	CON	ITIC	NTU	COC	ACU	NTLC	CHC
2000	35	21	57	29	31	61	38	66	48	36	67
1999	55	—	83	38	67	—	32	52	52	—	—

National Journal Ratings

	1999 LIB	—	1999 CONS		2000 LIB	—	2000 CONS
Economic	55%	—	44%		53%	—	46%
Social	32%	—	66%		35%	—	64%
Foreign	54%	—	45%		33%	—	62%

Key Votes of the 106th Congress

1. Patient Bill of Rights	Y	5. Bar RU-486 $ for FDA	Y	9. NATO War in Serbia	Y
2. Accelerate Min. Wage	Y	6. Display 10 Commandments	Y	10. Perm. Trade with China	N
3. Strike Ban on Ergo. Stnd.	N	7. Gun Show Bkgrnd. Checks	N	11. Debt Relief for 3rd World	N
4. Ovrd. Estate Tax Veto	Y	8. Ban Part.-Birth Abortion	Y	12. Drop Cuba Econ. Embargo	N

Election Results

2000 general	Mike McIntyre (D)	160,185	(70%)	($428,263)
	James R. Adams (R)	66,463	(29%)	
	Other	3,018	(1%)	
2000 primary	Mike McIntyre (D)	63,520	(93%)	
	Randy Crow (D)	4,440	(7%)	
1998 general	Mike McIntyre (D)	124,366	(91%)	($392,316)
	Paul Meadows (Lib)	11,924	(9%)	

EIGHTH DISTRICT

From Atlanta to Durham in the Carolina Piedmont, along Interstate 85, is the thickest concentration of America's textile industry—so thick you can almost see the lint. Within North Carolina, I-85 passes past Salisbury, Concord and Kannapolis—named for its founding company, Cannon Mills. East Carolina was settled by Englishmen from the coast. This Piedmont land was settled primarily by Scots and diverse groups like Quakers and Moravian sects, coming down the Blue Ridge from Pennsylvania through Virginia. These migratory patterns were reflected in Civil War divisions and continue in current voting habits. The coastal counties all the way up through the Sand Hills were Confederate and are now Democratic. The textile mill towns along I-85 were anti-secession and are now Republican.

The 8th Congressional District of North Carolina combines the area around Kannapolis and Concord with Sand Hill counties extending east to Fayetteville. In the district lines in effect for 1992, nearly two-thirds of the population was in the textile country or the expanding Charlotte suburbs in fast-growing Union County. Under the May 1998 redistricting plan, the textile counties of Rowan and Iredell were removed, as was Moore County, and heavily Democratic precincts in the east were added. This raised the black percentage from 23% to 26% and the Democratic registration to over 68%—a significant political shift in a closely balanced constituency.

The congressman from the 8th District is Robin Hayes, a Republican elected in 1998. He grew up in Concord, the grandson of Cannon Mills founder Charles Cannon; he graduated from Duke and returned to Concord, where he ran several businesses—selling Mack trucks, building highways, running the Mt. Pleasant Hosiery Mills. He coached football at a local college and worked in the Prison Fellowship movement. He was elected a Concord alderman, and in 1991 he switched to the Republican Party. In 1992 Hayes was elected to the North Carolina House, and became majority whip; there he sponsored the 1995 bill requiring schools to teach abstinence as the primary method of birth control and supported parental consent for abortion, caps on punitive damages and a big income tax cut. In 1996 he ran for governor, won the Republican primary, but lost the general to Jim Hunt 56%–43%.

In November 1997 Hayes announced he was running against 8th District Congressman Bill Hefner, a singer elected to the House in 1974 and winner of many close races since. In January 1998 Hefner surprised just about everyone by announcing that he would retire. No Republican moved to oppose Hayes, and Democrats had a hard time coming up with a candidate. Former Lieutenant Governor Bob Jordan said no in January 1998; in March former state Senator Glenn Jernigan, who had run third in the 1996 7th District primary, bowed out because of his wife's illness. That left as the sole Democratic candidate Mike Taylor, a Stanly County lawyer with an attractive biography but little name recognition. He was the grandson of a Baptist preacher who lived to 106 and son of Baptist missionaries to Africa; he served in the Navy in Vietnam's Mekong Delta; he had a Harvard Ph.D. in classical archaeology.

Hayes campaigned on a standard conservative platform, stressing the issues he had pushed in the legislature and calling for "top-to-bottom comprehensive tax reform." His personal wealth made his candidacy appear formidable to political insiders, but he spent only $127,000 of his own money and instead spent much time on fundraising, ultimately spending $1.22 million. He was the recipient of many visits from Republican luminaries: Bob Dole, Charlton Heston, Jesse Helms, Oliver North, Dan Quayle, Dick Armey. Taylor soldiered on, calling for building more classrooms, more discipline in schools, mastering of skills before promotion, zero tolerance of violence and drugs. His military record helped him win the endorsement of the VFW, and he spent $367,000. But Hayes outspent Taylor by 3–1, and Taylor was a nonpresence in the Charlotte media market. Hayes did not make much of a dent on central North Carolina's ancestral political loyalties. He carried the textile counties 61%–38%, but after the May 1998 redistricting they cast only 36% of the votes in the district. He carried Union County even more heavily, 65%–34%. But the counties to the east voted in some cases more than 2–1 Democratic, and cast 43% of the district's votes; Taylor carried them overall 64%–35%. Hayes won by a close 51%–48%.

In the House, Hayes has compiled a conservative voting record, but devoted much of his energy to getting federal money for the state and district. This included $3 million for North Carolina State and Georgetown to investigate whether tobacco plants can help cure cervical cancer, and $340 million for tobacco farmers ($100 million in North Carolina) in the May 2000 farm bailout. Occasionally there were snafus: he got $50,000 for the town of Hamlet to demolish the Imperial Foods chicken plant where 25 workers died in a 1991 fire, but the town council refused to spend the money because of concerns about liability.

Early in 1999, Taylor started running again. National Democrats, convinced he would have won in 1998 with more money, this time raised more. He spent twice as much and went up on Charlotte TV. But Hayes fought back. When Minority Leader Dick Gephardt appeared in Concord for Taylor, Hayes greeted him and shook his hand while he was being interviewed for local television. A bizarre fillip: In January 2000 the American Dairy Association ran ads showing two candidates, "Hayes" and "Taylor," labeling the hypothetical Hayes as "no Gouda" and reporting the hypothetical Taylor as saying, "I love cheese": just a coincidence, the ADA said. Hayes traveled the campaign trail with a four-foot-wide reusable blank check signed "Uncle Sam." At each stop he took a felt-tip pen and wrote in the federal money he had brought in: $650,000 to extend water lines to a school in Stanly County, $258,000 for a pilot housing program in Troy, $4 million for two airports. Taylor campaigned for a prescription drug program for seniors and benefited from

Sierra Club ads. Hayes' campaign made this scarcely a test of conservatism. Instead, the vote once again broke down on historic lines; Hayes ran about as well as George W. Bush. He carried the textile counties 66%–33% and Union County by 67%–32%; Taylor carried the eastern counties 60%–40%. Overall Hayes won 55%–44%.

But this may not be a safe Republican seat in 2002. Democrats control redistricting, and they could move the district to the east, excising Republican areas and adding Democratic ones. There is also a possibility that Hayes will run for Jesse Helms' Senate seat.

Cook's Call *Potentially Competitive.* After narrowly winning one of the most unexpectedly close races in the country in 1998, Hayes proved that he could nail down this district when he defeated his 1998 Democratic opponent with 55% in the 2000 rematch. With redistricting on the horizon, it is far too early to predict what could happen, but there is the potential for a competitive contest here in 2002.

THE PEOPLE: Pop. 2000: 661,112; Pop. 1990: 552,039, up 19.8% 1990–2000. 65.1% White, 26.4% Black, 1.2% Asian, 2.7% Amer. Indian, 0.1% Hawaiian, 1.7% Two+ races, 2.7% Other; 5.9% Hispanic Origin.

2000 Presidential Vote

Bush (R)	115,927	(56%)
Gore (D)	88,679	(43%)
Others	1,754	(1%)

1996 Presidential Vote

Dole (R)	77,564	(46%)
Clinton (D)	77,269	(46%)
Perot (I)	12,729	(8%)

Rep. Robin Hayes (R)

Elected 1998, 2d term; b. Aug. 14, 1945, Concord; home, Concord; Duke U., B.A. 1967; Presbyterian; married (Barbara).

Elected Office: Concord Bd. of Alderman, 1978–81; NC House of Reps., 1992–96, Majority Whip, 1995–96.

Professional Career: Businessman, 1967-present; Owner, Mt. Pleasant Hosiery Mill, 1988-present.

DC Office: 130 CHOB 20515, 202-225-3715; Fax: 202-225-4036; Web site: www.house.gov/hayes.

District Offices: Concord, 704-786-1612; Rockingham, 910-997-2070.

Committees: *Agriculture* (18th of 27 R): General Farm Commodities & Risk Management; Specialty Crops & Foreign Agriculture Programs. *Armed Services* (23d of 32 R): Military Installations & Facilities (Vice Chmn.); Military Research & Development. *Transportation & Infrastructure* (26th of 42 R): Aviation; Highways & Transit.

Group Ratings

	ADA	ACLU	AFS	LCV	CON	ITIC	NTU	COC	ACU	NTLC	CHC
2000	5	14	14	14	21	72	56	76	76	85	100
1999	5	—	0	13	6	—	59	88	96	—	—

National Journal Ratings

	1999 LIB —	1999 CONS		2000 LIB —	2000 CONS
Economic	16% —	78%		18% —	76%
Social	4% —	91%		0% —	79%
Foreign	36% —	63%		0% —	88%

Key Votes of the 106th Congress

1. Patient Bill of Rights	N	5. Bar RU-486 $ for FDA	Y	9. NATO War in Serbia	N
2. Accelerate Min. Wage	N	6. Display 10 Commandments	Y	10. Perm. Trade with China	N
3. Strike Ban on Ergo. Stnd.	N	7. Gun Show Bkgrnd. Checks	N	11. Debt Relief for 3rd World	N
4. Ovrd. Estate Tax Veto	Y	8. Ban Part.-Birth Abortion	Y	12. Drop Cuba Econ. Embargo	N

Election Results

2000 general	Robin Hayes (R)	119,950	(55%)	($1,942,592)
	Mike Taylor (D)	89,505	(44%)	($773,202)
	Other	2,009	(1%)	
2000 primary	Robin Hayes (R)	unopposed		
1998 general	Robin Hayes (R)	67,505	(51%)	($1,224,344)
	Mike Taylor (D)	64,127	(48%)	($366,624)
	Others	1,492	(1%)	

NINTH DISTRICT

"An agreeable village but in a damn rebellious country," recorded General Cornwallis when, before the unpleasantness at Yorktown, he visited Charlotte, North Carolina. "A veritable nest of hornets." This town, settled by Scots-Irish and German colonists who came down the Blue Ridge from Pennsylvania, is now a metropolitan area of 1.4 million people. Before the California gold rush, Charlotte was the gold mining capital of the country. Now, it is the headquarters of two of the nation's biggest banks: Bank of America, formed from the September 1998 merger of NationsBank and San Francisco's BankAmerica, and First Union; with nearly $1 trillion in assets, Charlotte is the second-largest financial center in the nation, behind only New York. It is the center of the nation's biggest textile manufacturing region and an airline hub for USAirways. It has become home to the NBA Hornets and NFL Panthers. Across from Bank of America's 60-story tower is a $50 million performing arts center. The rebelliousness Cornwallis noted can still be seen in this home of one of the nation's biggest stock car race tracks; just up the road is Mooresville, home of the late Dale Earnhardt. Charlotte has also built a boosterish pride in its capacity for accommodation. It is proud that it responded amicably to a busing order approved in a landmark Supreme Court case in 1971; that it uncovered the shenanigans of its nearby South Carolina neighbors Jim and Tammy Faye Bakker; that it elected Harvey Gantt, who is black, mayor two times and then replaced him with Sue Myrick, a Republican woman whose grievance wasn't race but traffic.

The 9th Congressional District of North Carolina includes about half of Charlotte and Mecklenburg County—the central and northern parts are in the 12th District—and extends west to Gaston, Cleveland and Lincoln Counties, with their many textile mills. Mecklenburg County is politically marginal, but the 9th has the more Republican part. So this is a heavily Republican district, though one which sometimes votes out of sync with the rest of North Carolina; people in Charlotte think the state's politics is dominated by politicians from eastern North Carolina—Jesse Helms, Jim Hunt—and that not enough attention is paid to the state's largest metropolis.

The congresswoman from the 9th District is Sue Myrick, a Republican first elected in 1994. Myrick grew up and went to college in Ohio, raised her family in Charlotte, owned an advertising agency and Amway distributorship. In 1981 she ran for the Charlotte Council and lost. She ran again and won in 1983, ran for mayor and lost in 1985, then beat Harvey Gantt in 1987. Despite nasty personal charges, she was reelected in 1989; she is proud of making infrastructure improvements, bringing the NFL Carolina Panthers to Charlotte, and preventing property tax increases for four years. Myrick ran for the Senate in 1992, but was beaten by Lauch Faircloth in the primary 48%–30%. In 1994 Charlotte Congressman Alex McMillan, passed over for the ranking position on Budget, retired. In the 1994 primary, against State House Minority Leader David Balmer, a 31-year-old ambitious politician, Myrick led in the first primary by just 34%–28%. But before the runoff three weeks later, it was revealed that Balmer had falsely claimed on his resume to have graduated in the top 20% of his law school class and to have played varsity soccer. Myrick won 68%–32%, then easily won the general.

Myrick was one of the proud leaders of the 1994 Republican freshman class. She served on Newt Gingrich's transition team and was first freshman- and then sophomore-class liaison to the leadership. But she was in communications with the unsuccessful coup against Gingrich in July 1997, and later that month lost the post of Conference secretary by 110–65 to Deborah Pryce, whom Gingrich backed. Myrick got a seat on the Budget Committee in 1995 and co-chaired a task force on privatizing HUD functions, supported a flat-rate income tax and sponsored a bill for civil monetary penalties for making false statements in political ads. She has been a strong backer of Republicans' flex-time bill to give workers a choice between overtime pay or time off. After the 1996 election, which she won easily, she was named to the Rules Committee; she took "on-leave" status on Banking, where she cannot vote but can build seniority.

Myrick has taken a lead role on many Republican initiatives. She sponsored the 1998 bill to outlaw taking a child out of state to get an abortion to avoid a state parental notification law. She sponsored the law passed in October 1998 to impose mandatory additional sentences for criminals convicted of using a firearm to commit a crime of violence or drug trafficking, and, motivated by a hideous crime in Charlotte, proposed making it a federal crime to take an officer's firearm and kill him with it. She sponsored Kristen's Act, passed in 2000, inspired by the disappearance of a young Charlotte woman in San Francisco; it sets up a national database for tracking missing adults believed to be in danger. She had surgery for breast cancer in December 1999 and underwent chemotherapy and radiation treatment; she was a sponsor of the 2000 law provide Medicaid coverage for low-income women for mammograms and Pap smears, and was critical when Bill Clinton signed it in private in October 2000 in order to deny a photo opportunity to co-sponsor Rick Lazio. Representing a prosperous and growing district, she turned down the Transportation Committee's offer of $15 million for Charlotte's outerbelt because she felt the transportation bill would bust the budget: "I said when I ran for this job, 'If you want somebody to bring home the bacon, don't send me.' We get a balanced budget agreement for the first time in 30 years, and now they do this?" But she is willing to help others: in fall 1999 she set up a database so that Charlotte residents could help those in east Carolina recover from Hurricane Floyd.

After the 1998 election Myrick ran for vice chair of the Republican Conference, the fifth-ranking leadership position, but on the first ballot her 38 votes were far behind Tillie Fowler's 90 and just behind Anne Northup's 43 and Pete Hoekstra's 39. She was more successful in 2000, when she was named one of two vice chairs of the Republican platform committee; under her experienced gavel, the proceedings on the foreign policy planks proceeded briskly. "It's a very visionary, proud, positive, inclusive document," she said. Myrick has been mentioned as a possible candidate for Jesse Helms' Senate seat should he retire in 2002, but as of early 2001 she was making no moves to run. Redistricting is unlikely to be much of a problem for Myrick. The Democratic redistricters will want to give the 12th District's Mel Watt another heavily black district, which will leave a seat dominated by the heavily white and heavily Republican areas of Charlotte.

Cook's Call   *Safe.* Even though she lost some parts of her Charlotte-based district in the 1998 remap, Myrick still represents a strongly Republican district. Heavy growth in Mecklenburg County means that this district will once again have to be altered in redistricting. But, Myrick should have little trouble winning here in 2002.

THE PEOPLE: Pop. 2000: 693,042; Pop. 1990: 552,490, up 25.4% 1990–2000. 79.9% White, 14.8% Black, 2.2% Asian, 0.3% Amer. Indian, 1.2% Two+ races, 1.6% Other; 4.1% Hispanic Origin.

2000 Presidential Vote

Bush (R)	158,848	(60%)
Gore (D)	104,236	(39%)
Others	2,146	(1%)

1996 Presidential Vote

Dole (R)	124,907	(57%)
Clinton (D)	81,994	(37%)
Perot (I)	13,839	(6%)

Rep. Sue Myrick (R)

Elected 1994, 4th term; b. Aug. 1, 1941, Tiffin, OH; home, Charlotte; Heidelberg Col., 1959–60; Methodist; married (Ed).

Elected Office: Charlotte City Cncl., 1983–85; Charlotte Mayor, 1987–91.

Professional Career: Pres. & CEO, Myrick Advertising, 1985–94; Pres. & CEO, Myrick Enterprises, 1992–94.

DC Office: 230 CHOB 20515, 202-225-1976; Fax: 202-225-3389; Web site: www.house.gov/myrick.

District Offices: Charlotte, 704-362-1060; Gastonia, 704-861-1976.

Committees: *Rules* (7th of 9 R): The Legislative & Budget Process.

Group Ratings

	ADA	ACLU	AFS	LCV	CON	ITIC	NTU	COC	ACU	NTLC	CHC
2000	0	21	0	14	79	100	63	90	95	90	100
1999	5	—	0	6	89	—	69	84	91	—	—

National Journal Ratings

	1999 LIB	—	1999 CONS		2000 LIB	—	2000 CONS
Economic	0%	—	84%		18%	—	82%
Social	21%	—	78%		0%	—	79%
Foreign	0%	—	97%		43%	—	56%

Key Votes of the 106th Congress

1. Patient Bill of Rights	N	5. Bar RU-486 $ for FDA	Y	9. NATO War in Serbia	N
2. Accelerate Min. Wage	N	6. Display 10 Commandments	Y	10. Perm. Trade with China	Y
3. Strike Ban on Ergo. Stnd.	N	7. Gun Show Bkgrnd. Checks	N	11. Debt Relief for 3rd World	N
4. Ovrd. Estate Tax Veto	Y	8. Ban Part.-Birth Abortion	Y	12. Drop Cuba Econ. Embargo	N

Election Results

2000 general	Sue Myrick (R)	181,161	(69%)	($959,304)
	Ed McGuire (D)	79,382	(30%)	($71,375)
	Others	3,677	(1%)	
2000 primary	Sue Myrick (R)	unopposed		
1998 general	Sue Myrick (R)	120,570	(69%)	($721,459)
	Rory Blake (D)	51,345	(29%)	($29,048)
	Others	2,167	(1%)	

TENTH DISTRICT

Wreathed in the haze that gave them the name "Smoky," the heavily wooded mountains of North Carolina seem placid and ancient. Geologically, they are some of the oldest ranges in the world; economically, they are churning with activity. The North Carolina counties where the hills of the Appalachians rise from the Piedmont are not just countryside. Nestled in their valleys is perhaps the largest concentration of furniture factories in the world, where skilled craftsmen create, from the hardwoods of Carolina forests, both high quality and mass-market furniture. Other industries are here—textiles, though not as much as in the I-85 corridor in the Piedmont, and chickens in Wilkes County, once (and perhaps still) one of the moonshine capitals of America. There is high-tech as well: The Catawba Valley is home to three large fiber-optic cable manufacturers, Comm-Scope, Alcatel and Siecor.

The 10th Congressional District of North Carolina covers much of this hill and mountain country, roughly west of I-77 and north of Hickory and Morganton. The district lines for 1992, 1994 and 1996 were very irregular; the May 1998 redistricting smoothed out the lines and leaves the district more compact. Politically, this is a very Republican area, though the Republicans here tend not to be Jesse Helms fans, but rough-hewn hill Republicans, unsympathetic to government regulators, from factory inspectors to revenuers on the lookout for illegal stills.

The congressman from the 10th District is Cass Ballenger, a Republican elected in 1986. Ballenger grew up in Hickory, enlisted in the Navy at 18, went to school in the East and headed a paper box company. In 1957 he founded Plastic Packaging Inc. to make plastic wrappings for J.C. Penney underwear. He served on the Catawba County Board of Commissioners for eight years and in the state legislature for 12. In 1986, after Congressman James Broyhill was appointed to the Senate (he lost in November), Ballenger ran for the House. He promised to be a "Broyhill Republican" and beat a primary opponent backed by Helms. Ballenger has consistently won general elections by large margins.

Ballenger combines a moderate-to-conservative voting record with a sense of civic responsibility. He and his wife have organized humanitarian trips to Central and South America, delivering donated medical supplies and second-hand fire engines; Plastic Packaging sent a half-million plastic bags to Haiti to be used to grow eucalyptus seedlings to reforest the barren hills. When Democrats were in control of Congress, he opposed the Clinton health care plan, family and medical leave and striker replacement; he amended an OSHA law by exempting employers when violations are caused by employees breaking company work rules. When Republicans gained control, Ballenger became chairman of the Workforce Protections Subcommittee but had to give it up for the 107th Congress due to term limits—he now chairs the Western Hemisphere Subcommittee on International Relations.

On the workforce protections panel Ballenger saw his job as updating labor laws that are out of line with today's flexible management and family-conscious employees. One response was the comp-time (or flex-time) bill, which would allow employees who work overtime to choose whether to receive overtime pay or compensatory time within the next year; federal employees have had this option since 1985. "Working parents need more flexibility as they try to deal with family needs and the demands of the job," Ballenger said. Comp-time passed the House in July 1996 but was fiercely opposed by the AFL-CIO, which argues that employers will coerce employees to take leave time. It passed the House again, 222–210, in March 1997, but was not acted on in the Senate.

Another major initiative has been OSHA reform. Ballenger started off pressed between subcommittee Republicans who would like to abolish the agency altogether and Democrats and labor leaders resisting any change. In 1997 he introduced a package of eight OSHA reforms; one feature was an increase from 16% to 50% of OSHA funds which must be spent on assisting businesses in complying with OSHA standards. "We ought to change the attitude of OSHA from being a Gestapo to being a teacher," he said. Two of his proposals were enacted into law and signed in July 1998, the first free-standing changes in OSHA since it was established in 1970. One codified OSHA's own consultation program operated by the states; businesses could get advice without inviting adversarial proceedings. The second bars enforcement quotas and using enforcement activities as performance measures. In 2000 Ballenger led the battle against OSHA's proposed ergonomic standards, arguably the most burdensome regulations on business ever. The Febuary 2000 draft regulations, he argued, did not identify the hazards being regulated nor what employers needed to do to control or eliminate the hazards; he urged that the regulations be delayed until publication of a National Academy of Sciences study due in 2001. The Clinton administration went ahead anyway, putting the standards into effect four days before Clinton left office; but in March 2001 the House voted to repeal them. Ballenger continues to argue that OSHA should not use employers' safety audits as evidence in the enforcement process, on the grounds it discourages employers from improving safety on their own.

Ballenger has spoken out against bills which he believes would bust the budget caps. He eschews the traditional protectionism of textile areas, now that western North Carolina is developing other strong industries. He wants to extend NAFTA to Central and South America and supported fast track in November 1997 and PNTR for China in 2000. In 2000 he urged the use of $1.8 million Huey helicopters instead of $12.8 million Blackhawks in Plan Colombia, which he supported. He has traveled extensively in Latin America, and objected in January 2000 when a 14-seat jet was yanked from a congressional delegation investigating Venezuela mudslides and drug trafficking in Central America and given to Hillary Rodham Clinton for a campaign trip to Buffalo.

Cook's Call   *Safe.* Since capturing this seat in 1986, Ballenger has never won by less than 61%. Redistricting will alter his district a bit (he needs to shed about 36,000 people), but this should not be enough to make this heavily Republican district any more competitive.

THE PEOPLE: Pop. 2000: 655,413; Pop. 1990: 552,303, up 18.7% 1990–2000. 89.5% White, 6% Black, 1.4% Asian, 0.2% Amer. Indian, 0.1% Hawaiian, 0.9% Two+ races, 1.8% Other; 4% Hispanic Origin.

2000 Presidential Vote			1996 Presidential Vote		
Bush (R)	162,784	(66%)	Dole (R)	120,378	(56%)
Gore (D)	79,991	(33%)	Clinton (D)	74,648	(35%)
Others	2,106	(1%)	Perot (I)	18,365	(9%)

Rep. Cass Ballenger (R)

Elected 1986, 8th term; b. Dec. 6, 1926, Hickory; home, Hickory; U. of NC, Amherst Col., B.A. 1948; Episcopalian; married (Donna).

Military Career: Naval Air Corps, 1944–45.

Elected Office: Catawba Cnty. Bd. of Commissioners, 1966–74, Chmn. 1970–74; NC House of Reps., 1974–76; NC Senate, 1976–86.

Professional Career: Businessman; Pres., Hickory Paper Box Co., 1948–70; Founder & Pres., Plastic Packaging Inc., 1957–present.

DC Office: 2182 RHOB 20515, 202-225-2576; Fax: 202-225-0316; Web site: www.house.gov/ballenger.

District Office: Hickory, 828-327-6100.

Committees: *Education & the Workforce* (4th of 27 R): Employer-Employee Relations; Workforce Protections. *International Relations* (9th of 26 R): International Operations and Human Rights; Western Hemisphere (Chmn.).

Group Ratings

	ADA	ACLU	AFS	LCV	CON	ITIC	NTU	COC	ACU	NTLC	CHC
2000	0	21	0	14	32	90	64	94	91	85	87
1999	5	—	0	6	44	—	59	84	80	—	—

National Journal Ratings

	1999 LIB —	1999 CONS		2000 LIB —	2000 CONS
Economic	0% —	84%		6% —	85%
Social	32% —	66%		34% —	65%
Foreign	27% —	72%		0% —	88%

Key Votes of the 106th Congress

1. Patient Bill of Rights	N	5. Bar RU-486 $ for FDA	Y	9. NATO War in Serbia	N
2. Accelerate Min. Wage	N	6. Display 10 Commandments	Y	10. Perm. Trade with China	Y
3. Strike Ban on Ergo. Stnd.	N	7. Gun Show Bkgrnd. Checks	N	11. Debt Relief for 3rd World	N
4. Ovrd. Estate Tax Veto	Y	8. Ban Part.-Birth Abortion	Y	12. Drop Cuba Econ. Embargo	N

Election Results

2000 general	Cass Ballenger (R)	164,182	(68%)	($266,557)
	Delmas Parker (D)	70,877	(29%)	
	Other	5,599	(2%)	
2000 primary	Cass Ballenger (R)	unopposed		
1998 general	Cass Ballenger (R)	118,541	(86%)	($201,489)
	Deborah Garrett Eddins (Lib)	19,970	(14%)	

ELEVENTH DISTRICT

Western North Carolina, the protrusion of the Tarheel state deep into the fastness of the eastern United States' highest and oldest mountains, is a land of long and ornery traditions. First settled by whites not long after the Revolutionary War, it still has tiny Indian communities and hollows where people are descended from the first white settlers. Its biggest city, Asheville, is memorialized in Thomas Wolfe's novels and was a retreat for lung patients in the early 20th Century. It was also the home of the brilliant eccentric George Vanderbilt, who built the chateau-like Biltmore mansion, and its vast forests, on which he pioneered scientific forestry. More recently, these mountains are presumably the hiding place of Eric Rudolph, the bomber of Atlanta's Centennial Olympic Park in 1996 and an Alabama abortion clinic in 1998, who was last seen here in 1998. Over a ridge is the Great Smoky Mountains National Park, the nation's most heavily visited, 20 degrees cooler in the summer than the lowland towns an hour or so away. The climate and the forested, green, fog-wisped mountains have attracted millions of tourists and thousands of retirees to this area.

The 11th Congressional District is made up of the western end of North Carolina; its jagged boundaries in effect in 1992, 1994 and 1996 were smoothed out by the May 1998 redistricting plan. The orneriness of the mountain country has come out in its politics. This part of the state was reluctant to secede in the Civil War. There were few slaves and many small farmers loyal to the Union, and those who took up the Confederate cause did so out of loyalty to Governor Zebulon Vance, an Asheville native and reluctant secessionist. Ancestral party loyalties remain strong; local notables, like the Ponder family of Madison County, held power for years; the retirees in the mountains south of Asheville haven't tipped things much. The partisan balance here has been close, and for a dozen years the 11th was one of the nation's most closely contested districts, throwing out incumbents in five of six elections between 1980 and 1990. But in the last decade the tilt has gone to the Republicans.

The congressman from the 11th District is Charles Taylor, a Republican elected in 1990. He grew up in Brevard, where he has been a tree farmer and one of the biggest private landholders in the area; his net worth is estimated at somewhere between $12 million and $57 million. He served in the legislature from 1966–74, and ran for Congress in 1988 and narrowly lost. In 1990 he ran again and won. Taylor has a very conservative voting record and has spent much energy on district projects. He worked to delay drawdowns of area lakes each year by the Tennessee Valley Authority until August 1, and later until October 1, to keep waters high for tourist season. He worked to get the Asheville veterans' hospital refurbished and obtained funding for the I-26 highway. He has worked for years on what he calls the Magnet Triangle economic development plan, to build three federal facilities which he says will double tourism in the area: the Blue Ridge Parkway headquarters, the Cradle of Forestry interpretive center near Brevard, and the Oconaluftee museum and visitors' center. He ran a western North Carolina workforce consortium, to encourage training in skills needed in high-tech jobs.

Early in his House career Taylor was one of the members of 1991's Gang of Seven, Republican freshmen who pushed for full disclosure of overdrafts on the House bank and other congressional reforms. In the 104th Congress the House passed his property-rights protection amendments to the National Biological Survey and the Montana Wilderness Act. Also passed was his amendment to stop EEOC guidelines he believed would promote religious harassment in workplaces; in 1996 he sought to protect religious radio stations from unfair FCC licensing practices. He sponsored the Congressional Gold Medal for Ruth and Billy Graham, residents of western North Carolina, which was awarded in May 1996. Taylor got a seat on Appropriations in 1993, and in 1997 became chairman of the District of Columbia Subcommittee. He started off with the conviction that District spending was out of control, and tried to take more city functions away from Mayor Marion Barry and give them to the Congress-created Control Board. Now Taylor is chairman of the Legislative Branch Subcommittee, which handles Congress's own budget.

In 2000 Taylor received an unexpectedly strong challenge and responded with unexpected strength. In February he roused controversy when he refused to provide federal funding to purchase lands around Lake Logan; the proposal was insufficiently detailed, he said. The Clean Water Management Trust Fund and the Boy Scouts supplied the money instead. In May and August two counties threatened to garnish Taylor's congressional pay for unpaid property taxes. Taylor paid $18,466 to one county and $29,658 to the other, and his lawyer said the dispute arose because Taylor claimed a forestry tax break the counties denied. "I have always paid the property taxes I owe. But I don't believe in paying property taxes I don't owe," Taylor said in an ad. North Carolina newspapers reported that a federal grand jury was investigating $1 million in loans from a bank controlled by Taylor to a supporter that were never repaid, and that Taylor had extended high-interest loans to a former KGB officer for construction of apartments and commercial buildings in Russia. And for the first time in several elections Taylor had articulate opposition from lawyer Sam Neill, former head of the University of North Carolina governing board. A Neill ad showed Taylor's large house and said, "Congressman Charles Taylor. He cheats on his local taxes, then blames everyone else." But Neill's positive ads were amateurish and his campaign relied on attacks on Taylor.

Taylor ran his own negative ads too. After the Sierra Club ran ads against him, Taylor accused them of favoring using taxpayer money to take private property, banning hunting, raising gasoline taxes and using "your tax dollars for involuntary forced abortions in China." He claimed that a woman who delivered a Sierra Club letter to Taylor headquarters drove a car with Vermont license plates and a bumper sticker for Vermont's socialist Congressman Bernie Sanders. But Taylor also made a case for himself. In July 2000 he called for a GAO study of pollution in the Great Smokies National Park and introduced a bill to force the TVA to reduce sulfur dioxide and nitrogen oxide emissions 75% from 1997 levels by 2005; environmental groups called this a "complete charade" and Neill asked why Taylor had not aiming at pollution before. In September Taylor obtained $4 million funding to help the Foothills Conservancy protect land around Lake James. In October he got $2.5 million for the Asheville Regional Airport and funding to extend the "road to nowhere" north of Lake James to provide access to a cemetery blocked since the TVA flooded the area to create the Fontana Dam in 1943. In October 2000 Bill Cosby laid the groundwork for a Deliver the Dream retreat for families of seriously ill children, on 200 acres donated by Taylor and his family.

Taylor won 55%–42%, carrying all but one county. This was behind George W. Bush's winning margins; Democrats have made it possible to vote a straight ticket only by voting for president first, and then marking a straight ballot. Taylor's margin was down only slightly from his 57%–42% in 1998 and 58%–40% in 1996. There have been rumors that Taylor might retire—he suffered a stroke in 1997 and for a time his speech was slurred—but his vigorous response to Neill's challenge suggests that he will run again. Democratic redistricters cannot do much to change the shape of this district, which sits at one end of the state; the adjacent territory is even more Republican.

Cook's Call *Potentially Competitive.* From 1994–98, Taylor did not have to work up much of a sweat to win this Asheville-based district by large margins. In 2000, however, Taylor's own political and personal problems gave Democrats a tremendous opportunity to win this seat. The fact that Taylor won by 55% is a testament to the Republican-leaning nature of the district, Taylor's own deep base of support here and a less than stellar Democratic nominee. This western North Carolina district, like most in the state, is overpopulated and will need to shed some people in redistricting.

THE PEOPLE: Pop. 2000: 656,619; Pop. 1990: 552,497, up 18.8% 1990–2000. 91.1% White, 4.8% Black, 0.5% Asian, 1.5% Amer. Indian, 1% Two+ races, 1% Other; 2.6% Hispanic Origin.

2000 Presidential Vote			1996 Presidential Vote		
Bush (R)	158,394	(59%)	Dole (R)	109,629	(48%)
Gore (D)	106,829	(40%)	Clinton (D)	95,273	(42%)
Others	4,673	(2%)	Perot (I)	21,255	(9%)

Rep. Charles H. Taylor (R)

Elected 1990, 6th term; b. Jan. 23, 1941, Brevard; home, Brevard; Wake Forest U., B.A. 1963, J.D. 1966; Baptist; married (Elizabeth).

Elected Office: NC House of Reps., 1966–72, Minority Ldr., 1968–72; NC Senate, 1972–74, Minority Ldr., 1972–74.

Professional Career: Tree farmer.

DC Office: 231 CHOB 20515, 202-225-6401; Web site: www.house.gov/charlestaylor.

District Offices: Asheville, 828-251-1988; Hendersonville, 828-697-8539; Murphy, 828-837-3249; Rutherfordton, 828-286-8750; Waynesville, 828-456-7559.

Committees: *Appropriations* (11th of 35 R): Commerce, Justice & State; Interior; The Legislative Branch (Chmn.).

Group Ratings

	ADA	ACLU	AFS	LCV	CON	ITIC	NTU	COC	ACU	NTLC	CHC
2000	5	21	16	0	13	71	63	72	92	82	100
1999	5	—	0	6	46	—	60	78	100	—	—

National Journal Ratings

	1999 LIB — 1999 CONS		2000 LIB — 2000 CONS	
Economic	0% —	84%	0% —	94%
Social	0% —	96%	0% —	79%
Foreign	15% —	81%	12% —	78%

Key Votes of the 106th Congress

1. Patient Bill of Rights	N	5. Bar RU-486 $ for FDA	Y	9. NATO War in Serbia	N
2. Accelerate Min. Wage	N	6. Display 10 Commandments	Y	10. Perm. Trade with China	N
3. Strike Ban on Ergo. Stnd.	N	7. Gun Show Bkgrnd. Checks	N	11. Debt Relief for 3rd World	N
4. Ovrd. Estate Tax Veto	Y	8. Ban Part.-Birth Abortion	Y	12. Drop Cuba Econ. Embargo	N

Election Results

2000 general	Charles H. Taylor (R)	146,677	(55%)	($1,555,039)
	Sam Neill (D)	112,234	(42%)	($851,434)
	Other	7,466	(3%)	
2000 primary	Charles H. Taylor (R)	unopposed		
1998 general	Charles H. Taylor (R)	112,908	(57%)	($826,274)
	David Young (D)	84,256	(42%)	($344,066)
	Others	2,259	(1%)	

TWELFTH DISTRICT

"This is perhaps the Negro's temporary farewell to Congress," said George White, a Tarboro, North Carolina lawyer and Republican, in his last days in the House of Representatives in 1901. Segregation was being imposed by law, and blacks informally but effectively were being stricken from the voting rolls in the rural South. It was 28 years until another black candidate was elected to Congress and 70 years until another black won in the South. In North Carolina, although blacks have been politically influential since the Voting Rights Act of 1965, White's prophecy was not overturned until 1992, when two blacks were elected. One, Eva Clayton, was from the mostly rural and small-town 1st District—the kind of country where most blacks lived in White's day. The other, Melvin Watt, represents the new 12th District, whose original boundaries connected blacks in several different cities, and which were ruled unconstitutional by the Supreme Court.

The 12th District has been the most litigated district in the country during the 1990s. The boundaries in effect for the 1992, 1994 and 1996 elections were the most egregious example in the nation of the interpretation, urged by blacks and Republicans, that the 1982 revisions of the Voting Rights Act require the maximization of black percentages in congressional districts. It was called the I-85 district, because it consists of a series of urban black areas connected by a narrow line in some places no wider than I-85, splitting adjacent districts in two. It stretched from Gastonia, west of Charlotte, through Winston-Salem and Greensboro all the way to Durham. A lawsuit was brought, and in June 1993 the Supreme Court in *Shaw v. Reno*, focusing on the 12th, ordered the plan re-examined.

On remand a three-judge federal panel upheld the plan in August 1994. But in June 1996 the Supreme Court declared the 12th unconstitutional and sent it back to the three-judge panel, which ruled it had to be redrawn by April 1997. In March 1997 the legislature drew new lines, cutting off the Durham and Gastonia extremes but leaving the district much the same. That plan was thrown out by a different three-judge panel in April 1998. In May 1998 the legislature passed a third plan which included the central and northern section of Charlotte and Mecklenburg County (45% black) and black neighborhoods in Winston-Salem and Forsyth County (61% black), connected by textile mill territory in Iredell, Rowan and Davidson counties (14% black). This was used in 1998, with the primary delayed until September. But the state appealed to the Supreme Court and argued for adoption of the 1997 plan. In May 1999 the Supreme Court remanded the case for trial, and in March 2000 the district court ruled that the 1997 districts were unconstitutional. That order was stayed by the Supreme Court, and the 2000 elections were held under the 1998 plan. Three weeks after the election, the Supreme Court heard argument on the case again, and in April 2001 ruled 5–4 that the 1997 districts could stand. The issue was arguably academic in North Carolina, since new lines will be drawn for the 2002 election, based on the 2000 Census, which gave the state 13 rather than 12 districts. The practical effect of these decisions can be seen in the fact that the 12th District in 1992–96 was 53% black, the 12th District in the 1998 election was 33% black and the 12th District in the 2000 election was 45% black.

The congressman from the 12th District since it was created in 1992 has been Mel Watt, a Democrat. Watt grew up in a place called Dixie outside Charlotte, now overgrown with woods, in a tin-roofed house with no electricity or running water. His dream was to attend the University of North Carolina, and he was one of the first black students there; he made a fine academic record, went on to Yale Law School, and then to a civil rights law practice in Charlotte. Today he owns an elderly care facility and is part owner of McDonald's Cafeteria and Hotel in Charlotte—and has been starting pitcher on the House Democrats' baseball team. He served one term in the state Senate, then decided not to seek office again until his sons completed high school. He managed Harvey Gantt's campaigns for city council and mayor in the 1980s and for the U.S. Senate in 1990.

In 1992 Watt decided to run in the 12th District. The contest turned out to be the kind of friends-and-neighbors Democratic primary common in the old segregated South. Watt took 47% of all votes in a four-way race, well over the 40% necessary for victory without a runoff in North Carolina; his base in Charlotte was bigger than those of his rivals, and he made inroads in other counties as well. He won the general election easily, and on election night said he was "saddened that it took 92 years" to elect another black member from the state, "and I'm disappointed, because I know that thousands and thousands of people, but for the color of their skin, would have been just as qualified to fill this office."

In the House Watt has compiled a liberal voting record. On one issue after another he has risked unpopular stands to defend principle. He refused to oppose the tobacco tax in the Clinton health care plan (though he asked Clinton not to increase it in 2000) and backed a Canadian-style single-payer system. He has voted against crime bills because of their death penalty provisions, against gun bans in urban housing projects, against increased prison sentences for crimes against children because he said it would interfere with the U.S. Sentencing Commission's autonomy. He vehemently opposed the 1996 Welfare Reform Act. On the partial-birth abortion ban, he wanted to put the burden of proving a woman's life in danger on the state. In 1996 he cast the only vote in the House against Megan's Law requiring registration of convicted sex offenders. As a member of the Judiciary Committee, Watt was a vehement opponent of the impeachment of Bill Clinton. Angry that Senator Jesse Helms has blocked all appointees to the 4th Circuit Court of Appeals, Watt said that the lack of black judges on the circuit was "outrageous and inexplicable." Watt was host to the 1999 Raising the Roof summit of black officials in Charlotte aimed at generating 1 million new black homeowners by 2005. During summer recess he has a practice of "trading places," working at jobs ranging from UPS delivery to handling crisis line calls to serving lunch at a mission.

Watt had his toughest race since the 1992 primary in the 1998 general, when the 12th District extended only from Charlotte to Winston-Salem. The Republican nomination was won by Scott Keadle, a Rowan County dentist and property developer, who attacked Watt as an "extreme liberal" and called for major tax cuts. Then Keadle concentrated on Watt's vote against Megan's Law. A Keadle TV ad showed a little girl skipping down a sidewalk, then a sinister looking man coming out from behind a tree. "Mel Watt—the only vote against our children," it said. In their third and final debate, Watt defended his vote by saying, "Would the next step be to register everyone who commits a murder?" But later he conceded that his vote had been wrong and said that he twice voted for funding for state compliance with the law. Watt won 56%–42%, a decisive margin though far below what he had received in the old district. He ran well ahead of racial lines, winning 75% in Forsyth County, 69% in Mecklenburg County and 36% in the other three counties, which usually vote Republican. "There are still whites who under no circumstances will vote for a black person," Watt has said. "They're never going to touch me, they're never going to be in a room with me. As far as they're concerned, I'm not their congressman." Undoubtedly that is true. But he was also right when he said, "I'd like to think it's an indication that race is becoming less of a factor as we go along." In the more favorable lines used in 2000, which included black areas in Greensboro and High Point as well as Charlotte and Winston-Salem, Watt won 65%–33%.

For 2002, the Democratic legislature is likely to create another Charlotte-to-Greensboro district in which Watt can win easily.

Cook's Call *Safe.* Watt's oddly shaped district has been in litigation from 1993 until the recent Supreme Court decision on April 18, 2000, that upheld the district's lines. Even after the district was dramatically altered for the 1998 election, Watt has been able to win easily here. The Supreme Court decision may help to ensure that Watt's district stays out of the courts in 2002, but even so, with all the growth in and around Charlotte, his district will have to be altered in the newest round of redistricting.

THE PEOPLE: Pop. 2000: 666,800; Pop. 1990: 551,957, up 20.8% 1990–2000. 47.6% White, 44.6% Black, 2.3% Asian, 0.4% Amer. Indian, 1.6% Two+ races, 3.4% Other; 6.8% Hispanic Origin.

2000 Presidential Vote			1996 Presidential Vote		
Gore (D)	123,981	(58%)	Clinton (D)	97,435	(54%)
Bush (R)	89,951	(42%)	Dole (R)	71,166	(40%)
Others	1,340	(1%)	Perot (I)	10,475	(6%)

Rep. Melvin Watt (D)

Elected 1992, 5th term; b. Aug. 26, 1945, Mecklenburg; home, Charlotte; U. of NC at Chapel Hill, B.S. 1967, Yale U., J.D. 1970; Presbyterian; married (Eulada).

Elected Office: NC Senate, 1984–86.

Professional Career: Practicing atty., 1971–92; Co-owner, East Town Manor nursing home, 1989–present; Campaign Mgr., Harvey Gantt Senate Campaign, 1990.

DC Office: 2236 RHOB 20515, 202-225-1510; Fax: 202-225-1512; Web site: www.house.gov/watt.

District Offices: Charlotte, 704-344-9950; Salisbury, 704-797-9950; Winston-Salem, 336-721-9950.

Committees: *Financial Services* (8th of 32 D): Financial Institutions & Consumer Credit; Housing & Community Opportunity; International Monetary Policy & Trade. *Judiciary* (7th of 17 D): Commercial & Administrative Law (RMM); The Constitution. *Joint Economic Committee* (9th of 10 Reps.).

Group Ratings

	ADA	ACLU	AFS	LCV	CON	ITIC	NTU	COC	ACU	NTLC	CHC
2000	85	86	100	86	40	35	25	45	8	6	0
1999	100	—	100	88	96	—	17	12	0	—	—

National Journal Ratings

	1999 LIB —	1999 CONS		2000 LIB —	2000 CONS
Economic	88%	0%		65%	34%
Social	87%	0%		84%	15%
Foreign	85%	12%		92%	6%

Key Votes of the 106th Congress

1. Patient Bill of Rights	Y	5. Bar RU-486 $ for FDA	N	9. NATO War in Serbia	Y
2. Accelerate Min. Wage	Y	6. Display 10 Commandments	N	10. Perm. Trade with China	N
3. Strike Ban on Ergo. Stnd.	Y	7. Gun Show Bkgrnd. Checks	Y	11. Debt Relief for 3rd World	Y
4. Ovrd. Estate Tax Veto	N	8. Ban Part.-Birth Abortion	N	12. Drop Cuba Econ. Embargo	Y

Election Results

2000 general	Melvin Watt (D)	135,570	(65%)	($361,869)
	Chad Mitchell (R)	69,596	(33%)	($25,254)
	Other	3,978	(2%)	
2000 primary	Melvin Watt (D)	unopposed		
1998 general	Melvin Watt (D)	82,305	(56%)	($641,416)
	John "Scott" Keadle (R)	62,070	(42%)	($381,065)
	Others	2,713	(2%)	

★ NORTH DAKOTA ★

For more than a century after statehood, North Dakota remained as close to its roots as any other state. Yet in its second century there are signs of change ahead. North Dakota was settled and its farm economy developed in a short generation. There are North Dakotans alive today who knew the men and women that settled this land and saw the state enter the Union in 1889. As children, they walked in the ruts left by the early settlers' wagon trains; they saw the Indians, recently defeated, herded onto reservations; they saw still shining new the rails that brought the world's commerce to these desolate prairies. This was the frontier to which Teddy Roosevelt came in 1884, determined to shoot one of the fast-disappearing buffalo, a place where settlers were only then breaking the sod and plowing under the natural prairies that are still preserved in a few places. This was some of the best wheat land in the world, empty by then of Indians and buffalo, connected to markets by rail, ready to become a cog in the industrial world being created by entrepreneurs and to raise its living standards to unparalleled heights.

And so, in a sudden rush of settlement during the 20 years before World War I, North Dakota filled up pretty much its present population. There were 632,000 people here in 1920 and in counts since, the number has fluctuated between 617,000 and 680,000. In the 2000 Census it was 642,000, and cumulatively it is the state with the lowest growth rate since 1950. Wheat is not the only crop here, there are also pinto beans and soybeans, and as the plains become more arid to the west, ranching and livestock grazing—along with strip mining and oil and natural gas production—are important, and hardy root crops like potatoes and sugar beets grow as well. But wheat is still number one. Typically the state produces about one-tenth of the U.S. crop, and a fair percentage of the world's; its durum wheat is the main ingredient of American pasta.

This dependence on agriculture shaped North Dakota's politics. Farmers, as much as they like to extol their way of life, are seldom content with the workings of the market. When prices are high, it is often because of low production; when they are low, farmers seek protection. The boosterish optimism of the first settlers was soon followed by cries reverberating with varying intensity for government protection against market forces. Since commodity prices tend to fall during periods of economic growth, there has been a countercyclical element in North Dakota politics, a tendency to vote against the national trends, and a radical strain going back to the 1910s

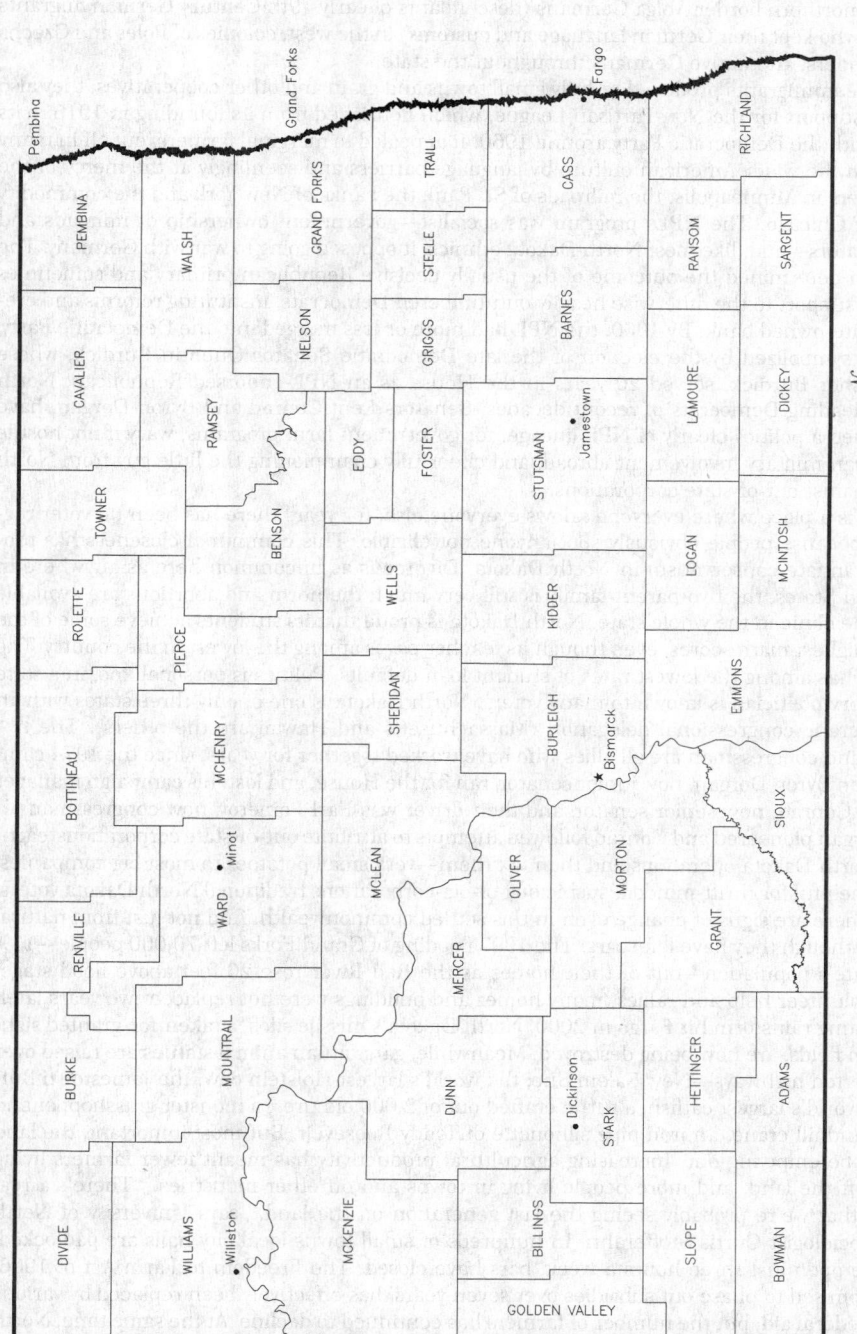

U.S. Representative elected at large.

and still lively in recent years. That radical strain also owes much to the immigrant origins of so many of North Dakota's early settlers: Norwegians in the eastern part of the state, Canadians along the northern border, Volga Germans (descendants of early 19th Century German migrants to Russia who kept their German language and customs) in the west, colonies of Poles and Czechs and Icelanders, and native Germans throughout the state.

These immigrants produced orderly small towns and grain and other cooperatives; they also provided support for the Non-Partisan League, which flourished from its founding in 1915 to its alliance with the Democratic Party around 1960. It appealed to marginal farmers, cut off in many cases from the wider American culture by language barriers and seemingly at the mercy of the grain millers in Minneapolis, the railroads of St. Paul, the banks of New York and the commodity traders of Chicago. The NPL's program was socialist—government ownership of railroads and grain elevators—and, like most North Dakota ethnics, it opposed going to war with Germany. The NPL often determined the outcome of the usually decisive Republican primary and sometimes swung its support to the otherwise heavily outnumbered Democrats, instituting reforms and creating a state-owned bank. By 1960, the NPL had more or less merged into the Democratic Party, a merger symbolized by the election of the late Democratic Senator Quentin Burdick, whose father, Usher Burdick, served 20 years in the House as an NPL-endorsed Republican. North Dakota's leading Democrats of recent decades, Senators Kent Conrad and Byron Dorgan, have championed a politics clearly of NPL lineage: for government farm programs, wary if not hostile to American military involvement abroad, and cheerfully championing the little guy from North Dakota against out-of-state corporations.

This is a place where everyone knows everyone else; for years there has been no voter registration because people obviously spot anyone not eligible. This communal closeness has produced an innate conservatism in North Dakota. Divorce is as uncommon here as anywhere in the United States, the two-parent family is still very much the norm and abortions are available in only one clinic in the whole state. North Dakota is proud that its students achieve some of the nation's highest math scores, even though its teacher pay is among the lowest in the country. The state also has among the lowest rates of student loan defaults. Politics is personal, too, in a state where every politician is known to many voters. North Dakota is one of only three states with an all-Democratic congressional delegation (Massachusetts and Hawaii are the others). The two senators and congressman are all allies who have worked together for years, since the 1974 campaign when Byron Dorgan, now junior senator, ran for the House, and lost; his campaign manager was Kent Conrad, now senior senator, and their driver was Earl Pomeroy, now congressman-at-large. Dorgan pioneered and Conrad followed attempts to attribute out-of-state corporations' earnings to North Dakota operations and then tax them—very small potatoes to most big companies, but very helpful for thrift-minded, suspicious-of-big-corporations traditional North Dakota voters.

Yet there are signs of change even in this settled commonwealth. And not just from natural disasters, though they have left scars. The 1997 flooding of Grand Forks left 70,000 people—11% of the state's population—out of their homes as the Red River rose 26 feet above flood stage; despite volunteer help and rallies, many homes and buildings were not replaced two years later. A devastating rainstorm hit Fargo in 2000. North Dakota's missile silos, a taken-for-granted sight in its farm fields, are now being destroyed. Meanwhile, gargantuan animal statues are raised over near-deserted highways—New Salem Sue, the world's largest Holstein cow; the Jamestown Buffalo, the world's largest catfish, a turtle crafted out of 2,000 old tires, a monster grasshopper and a giant sandhill crane, an iron pipe silhouette of Teddy Roosevelt. But most important, the land seems to be emptying out. Increasing agricultural productivity has meant fewer farmers living directly off the land, and more people living in towns and off other industries. "There's a real concern that we're probably seeing the last generation on the land," says University of North Dakota sociologist Curtis Stofferahn. In hundreds of small towns local city halls are padlocked, banks are open just three hours a week, bars have closed. The Freedom to Farm Act of 1996, which promised to phase out subsidies over seven years, has effectively been replaced by various kinds of federal aid; but the number of farmers has continued to decline. At the same time, North Dakota's small cities have grown. The state's four biggest counties, containing Fargo, Grand Forks, Bismarck and Minot, grew from 134,000 in 1930 to 317,000 in 2000, while the state's other 49 counties dropped from 546,000 to 325,000; in 2000 these four counties cast half the state's votes. Unemployment there is extremely low, and if wages tended to be low and home ownership dropped, these were still not the prerequisites to the old style of farm rebellion. Politicians still pay homage to family farmers, but as their numbers decline, they no longer seem to have the critical mass to drive politics; there is less talk of helping farmers and more demands for better airline connections. Instead the movement is toward what some academics call "the Buffalo Commons." Bison have been reintroduced on Indian reservations and ranches, and North Dakota has the nation's only meatpacking plant specializing in buffalo. In effect North Dakota is developing the demographics of the Rocky Mountain states, with population concentrated in a few cities and towns.

On balance these developments tend to undermine the state's radical tradition. If the typical elderly North Dakotan is a hard-working retired farmer, with fond memories of NPL agitation and a belief in government programs, the typical young North Dakotan is a family person with a college education (49% of the state's households have college graduates) more trusting of markets and the private sector. They may have noticed that nearby South Dakota has attracted white-collar jobs with low tax rates and that North Dakota, with its higher taxes and pro-government traditions, is the Great Plains state with the lowest population growth in the 1990s—up 3,400 people, or 0.5%. This is a state which Bill Clinton did not come close to carrying, and George W. Bush won here in 2000 by a 61%–33% margin. At the same time, Republican John Hoeven was elected governor over the strong candidacy of Democrat Heidi Heitkamp by a 55%–45% margin. To be sure, Democratic Senator Kent Conrad and Congressman Earl Pomeroy were re-elected, but Republicans won most statewide offices and made gains in the legislature. That trend is likely to continue: voters over 60 vote Democratic, but those under 60 vote Republican; interestingly, more women than men voted for Bush. It's too soon to say that North Dakota has moved away from its radical political roots, but a conservative strain in its heritage is asserting itself.

Governor   John Hoeven, the governor of North Dakota, is a Republican elected in 2000. He was born in Bismarck and grew up in Minot; he graduated from Dartmouth College and received an MBA from Northwestern, and in 1981 entered the family business, First Western Bank in Minot; he became executive vice president and was active in many civic endeavors. In 1993 he was chosen to be head of the state-owned Bank of North Dakota—a Non-Partisan League creation—by a board that included his predecessor as governor, Republican Ed Schafer, and his 2000 Democratic opponent, Attorney Genreal Heidi Heitkamp. Under Hoeven's stewardship, the bank's worth rose from $990 million to $1.6 billion and its loan portfolio increased from $200 million to $1 billion; it returns $50 million into the state's biannual budget. Hoeven was not always a Republican; in 1996, as a Democrat, he thought out loud about running against Schafer. He gave serious consideration to running in 2000 only when Schafer announced in October 1999 he would not run again.

Schafer, whose family started one of North Dakota's few big businesses, Gold Seal Wax, had a record of lowering taxes, "right-sizing" government and trying to stimulate economic growth with, among other things, a North Dakota telecommunications network, was widely popular and had been re-elected overwhelmingly in 1996. Republicans were worried that they had no good candidate to run against the popular Heitkamp. In November Hoeven, who had never won elective office, announced his candidacy, promising to take up where Schafer left off.

This was a generally civil campaign, between two candidates who knew each other well, although at one point Heitkamp criticized Hoeven for taking away bank documents when he left the Bank of North Dakota. Bismarck is a small town, where officeholders can scarcely avoid each other, and North Dakotans are a civil people. Hoeven cited his work in attracting jobs by founding Minot's Magic Fund, a city sales tax used for business development, and by organizing to keep Minot Air Force Base off the base-closure list, as well as his work at the Bank of North Dakota. He called for economic development with high-paying jobs in technology and said that education was crucial in preparing future workers; he pledged more money for teacher training and salaries. He also called for a bigger federal safety net for farmers and for farmers to produce value-added goods. Heitkamp, who grew up in the town of Mantador (population 77), was elected tax commissioner in 1984 and 1988 and attorney general in 1992 and 1996. She was known for her "big red hair" and her work in the tobacco lawsuit and settlement. She said she would try to keep young people in the state through a recruitment and mentoring program, by reinstating a living wage for employees of companies receiving financial assistance and by giving tax incentives to companies guaranteeing high-wage jobs. She said she would "demand a domestic farm policy that works for family farms" and "fight back against unfair foreign competition." She called for the state to participate in the federal children's health insurance program, which the legislature rejected in 1999.

These were two attractive candidates running on similar, though not identical, platforms. They both raised over $1 million, Hoeven getting more from business interests, Heitkamp from labor unions and tobacco case lawyers. They were running about even in polls when, in September 2000, Heitkamp announced that she had breast cancer. She underwent a mastectomy September 25, and Hoeven suspended his ads for two days. Quickly she returned to the campaign trail. For several weeks, Heitkamp had a small lead in the polls.

Then momentum went back to Hoeven, and he won 55%–45%. He carried the state's largest counties 57%–43%; she carried only 12 rural counties. There was not much of a gender gap; Heitkamp ran only 4% better among women than men. Voters over 60 backed the Democrat, voters under 60 the Republican. At the same time Republicans won seven of nine of the statewide offices and increased their majorities in the legislature to 32–17 in the state Senate and 69–29 in the state House. North Dakota's skyscraper Capitol, towering over neatly-kept Bismarck and the rolling plains beyond, now houses more Republicans in high office than at any time since the NPL allied with the Democrats. Hoeven began his term by working to combine several state agencies into a Department of Commerce and to begin Phase 2 of the North Dakota Telecommunications Network. He called for a 20% tax credit on investments up to $50,000 in new or expanding businesses and elimination of the sales tax on farm equipment.

Senior Senator Kent Conrad, North Dakota's senior senator, was first elected in 1986. He grew up in North Dakota; his parents were killed in an auto accident when he was five, and he was raised by his grandparents. One grandfather owned a bi-weekly newspaper in Bismarck and had been North Dakota chairman for Progressive Robert LaFollette in 1924; another was the physician for longtime Governor and Senator William Langer: it was a family full of connections in the small world of North Dakota politics. Kent Conrad graduated from Stanford, then returned in 1974 to work on Byron Dorgan's unsuccessful House campaign. When Dorgan ran for Congress again in 1980, Conrad ran for tax commissioner and won; when Dorgan declined the opportunity again, in 1986 Conrad ran against Senator Mark Andrews, and won 50%–49%. In 1986 Conrad earnestly promised not to run again unless "the federal deficit, the trade deficit and real interest rates will be brought under control." By 1992 the latter two arguably were, and he could argue that he had worked to cut the budget deficit. Early 1992 polls showed Conrad well ahead, but in April 1992, after ruminating on the issue and after his wife had been mugged and dragged down the street near their Capitol Hill home, Conrad announced he was retiring because he had not kept his pledge, and Dorgan ran for his seat.

Then in September 1992, the elderly Senator Quentin Burdick, no ally of Dorgan and Conrad, died. State law said a special election had to be held after November but before January, so Conrad ran for this seat while serving his last month in the other. This was awkward, but Conrad's earnestness, on display in more than 1,000 town meetings over six years, helped. He was nominated unanimously at the Democratic state convention. His Republican opponent called for an absurdly expensive $5 per bushel wheat program, and an anti-abortion independent lambasted Conrad; but he had far more money and won easily, 63%–34%. For a few hours in December 1992, Conrad held both Senate seats: he was sworn in December 14 to fill Burdick's term, and a few hours later Dorgan was sworn in to fill his. In 1994 this seat came up again. Republican Ben Clayburgh, 70-year-old former head of the state medical association, accused Conrad of voting most of the time with Bill Clinton; Conrad responded with an ad saying he voted with Bob Dole more than 50% of the time. Dole endorsed Clayburgh, but Conrad won by a reduced margin of 58%–42%.

Conrad has often taken popular positions on issues that are in tension with each other, then agonizingly resolving them when they come into conflict. Foremost among them is the balanced budget amendment. Conrad voted for it in 1994, but when Dorgan pushed an amendment taking Social Security out of deficit calculations, Conrad negotiated first in the Republican and then in the Democratic cloakroom, emerging to cast the decisive vote against the amendment in March 1995; he voted against it again in February 1997. On the 1996 Welfare Reform Act, he supported block grants to states for welfare programs, but passed an amendment to keep food aid a federal program.

For years North Dakota senators tended closely to the details of farm bills, especially wheat subsidies, and then often voted against the every-four-year farm bills as insufficiently generous. But in 1995 Republicans proposed to phase out farm subsidies over seven years. Conrad naturally opposed this, as he opposed NAFTA on farm issues. But Freedom to Farm passed anyway. In 1997, as North Dakota was battered by floods and by thunderstorms in calving season, Conrad pushed successfully for $500 million in flood relief and various farm relief measures—indemnity relief for those affected by freakish bad weather and speedier availability of crop insurance. A pattern emerged. For each year of farm woes, whether from low prices as in 1998 or major flooding as in 2000, crop insurance subsidies were increased and billions appropriated for disaster relief— $8.7 billion in October 1999, with about $300 million for North Dakota. Conrad has had little success with his other agriculture policy initiatives—trying to duplicate here the farm subsidies of the European Union and trying to oppose agribusiness mergers (antitrust chief Joel Klein testified that they didn't raise prices). The delegation did get $300,000 for sunflower research in 2000; North Dakota produces 85% of U.S. sunflowers.

North Dakota sits astride North America's longest river, the Missouri, and Conrad has spent much time on water issues. He has urged that the Army Corps of Engineers give more attention to upstream users, by maintaining high levels in Lake Sakakawea, and less to downstream users, by maintaining high enough levels for barges in Missouri; here he has had fierce opposition from Missouri's senators. He and Dorgan, after compromising with the Missourians, pushed a Dakota Water Resources Act through in an appropriation; this would authorize diversion of Missouri River water to the Red River Valley in eastern North Dakota, and is opposed by Canada, Minnesota and many environmentalists. Conrad proposed a $200 million trust fund to prevent silt from accumulating in a delta on the south side of Bismarck. He was "outraged" in June 2000 when the Army Corps refused to build an emergency outlet for Devils Lake. This body of water, nearly dry in 1993, is in a closed basin (like the Great Salt Lake); its waters have risen 25 feet in recent years, and flooded 120,000 acres. If it rises 12 feet more, it will flood into the nearby Sheyenne River, something which has happened four times in 4,000 years. The Army Corps says the diversion of water through an outlet would not be enough to be worth the cost, and environmentalists say the salty Devils Lake water would pollute the Red River of the North. But Conrad used his senatorial prerogative of holding up all promotions in the Army Corps to get it to change its mind.

Conrad has a seat on the Senate Finance Committee, and has voted with other moderate Democrats there on issues like the prescription drug benefits and Medicare. He voted against repealing the marriage penalty and the estate tax in 2000. He wants to cut the depreciation period on building improvements from 39 years to 10. Conrad could be a key vote on taxes, Medicare and Social Security in the 107th Congress. No other Democratic senator represents a state which cast a higher percentage for George W. Bush in 2000, and in January 2001 the Republican Leadership Council ran ads in North Dakota asking him to vote for the Bush tax cut, but Conrad opposed it in May 2001.

Conrad worked to keep Grand Forks and Minot Air Force Bases operational. North Dakota is the nation's one missile defense site authorized by the Anti-Ballistic Missile treaty; in July 2000 he opposed the Clinton plan for a missile defense site in Alaska, and proposed that Alaskans and Hawaiians who could not be protected by the North Dakota site could be compensated by generous payments.

Conrad entered the 2000 election with a good job rating. His Republican opponent was a surprise candidate: Duane Sand, Annapolis graduate and 15-year Navy veteran, returned to North Dakota and set out running for senator—or rather walking across the state, in January 2000. In March he won an upset victory over a state legislator at the Republican nominating convention. Starting in May, he campaigned door-to-door in every city and town with a post office, about 300 in all. Sand campaigned against what he characterized as Conrad's liberal voting record and said his farm bills have "languished in committee." He showed great persistence, and John McCain campaigned for him in October. But Conrad spent far more money, $2.3 million, while Sand was ignored by the Republican campaign committee and raised less than $400,000. Conrad won 62%–38%, carrying every demographic group and all but three small counties.

Junior Senator   Byron Dorgan, who first held statewide office in 1969 and has often had the highest popularity ratings in North Dakota, was elected to the Senate in 1992. Dorgan grew up in Regent, North Dakota, where his family had a farm equipment and petroleum business and raised cattle and horses. After college and business school he worked for a Denver aerospace firm, then in 1969, at 26, was appointed state tax commissioner. His politics are very much out of the Non-Partisan League tradition: he has a strong mistrust of economic markets, a deep belief that government should intervene to protect the family farmer and small businessman, and a capacity to frame issues in a popular and unthreatening way. His first big issue, as tax commissioner, was taxing out-of-state corporations, which struck a chord in a state always hostile to big out-of-state money. To his work Dorgan brought the zest and cornball good humor that New Deal enthusiasts liked to summon up when liberals thought they represented the ordinary, inarticulate little guy, in contrast to the conservatives seen as old stuffed shirts. On the House Ways and Means Committee, he called for more tax audits, opposed intangibles write-offs for corporate takeovers, and opposed the use of high-yield bonds for corporate takeovers. He has always fought for farm subsidies, especially payments to farmers when prices are low; he vigorously attacked the 1996 Freedom to Farm Act.

Dorgan ran for the House in 1974, and lost to Republican Mark Andrews. In 1980, when Andrews ran for the Senate, Dorgan was elected to the House. His lowest percentage in a House race was 65%, against Ed Schafer, who was elected governor two years later. Dorgan declined to challenge Andrews for the Senate in 1986, a race his successor as Tax Commissioner Kent Conrad won, and he declined to take on 80-year-old fellow-Democrat Quentin Burdick in 1988. Only with Conrad's surprise decision not to run for re-election in 1992 did he finally run for the Senate. He and his Republican opponent both backed Most Favored Nation trade status for China (a major buyer of North Dakota wheat), but remained wary of free trade otherwise and opposed the regulations which have classified hundreds of seasonal puddles in North Dakota as protected wetlands. Dorgan won by a solid 59%–39% margin.

In the Senate, Dorgan's voting record has been almost exactly the same as Conrad's; this is one case where senators of the same party from the same state have worked harmoniously together. Dorgan strongly backed fellow Dakotan Tom Daschle for Senate Democratic leader in 1994, and became an assistant floor leader; he considered running for whip against Harry Reid four years later, but withdrew and in December 1998 he became co-chairman of the Democratic Policy Committee. Dorgan continues to be a champion of family farms, even as their numbers fall: "This isn't just about dollars and cents. The country will lose something very important. Family values roll from family farms to small towns to big cities." He backed the big crop insurance and disaster relief packages in 1998, 1999 and 2000. He has sought a ban on Canadian wheat imports, then a requirement that they all come in through one border crossing; he rejoiced when the special trade representative started investigating Canadian practices in October 2000.

As a champion of the family farmer, Dorgan opposes high interest rates and mergers, but does not see taxes as such a threat. He has often criticized Alan Greenspan—"he continues to search in closets and under beds for inflation," he said after one interest rate increase—and was one of four senators to vote against his reconfirmation as Federal Reserve chairman in February 2000. He opposed financial services deregulation in 1999—"that which is true in the 1930s is true in 2010"—and wants the SEC to regulate derivatives. He opposed the FCC's loosening of rules on multiple ownership of TV and radio stations in August 1999, sponsored a bill with an 18-month moratorium on agribusiness mergers in October 1999, opposed all railroad mergers in March 2000 and criticized airline mergers in June 2000. But his results have been at the micro level. He pressured airlines for more seats on Bismarck-Denver flights in 1999 and helped get Necco, the makers of the Clark Bar, from keeping Mandan candy maker Debbie Kruger from producing her Lewis & Clark Bar in 2000.

Dorgan was ranked number two on TechCentralStation.com's list of top 10 "tech-savvy legislators" in 2000. He has promoted low-interest loans to deploy broadband technology in North Dakota and other rural states, and passed unanimously a bill for every cell phone to have a primary service area. But he has not favored the moratorium on Internet taxes. Instead, he has a bill calling on states to simplify their tax structures so that they can collect sales taxes that are rarely collected: "a mechanism for allowing people to pay a tax that they already owe." He abandoned his usual non-interference with the District of Columbia to oppose a tax cut there in 1999, on the grounds that the District didn't jail a violent parolee who failed a drug test. He opposes individual investment accounts for Social Security and opposed full repeal of the estate tax. With a career based on taxing out-of-staters, he has proposed a tax on foreign airline overflights and sought to eliminate tax deductions for companies that build plants abroad. Dorgan threatened to tie up the Senate floor in June 1999 to get a vote on the Democrats' HMO regulation, but the Republican plan passed instead. He co-sponsored the October 2000 law to allow prescription drugs to be reimported from Canada and other nations where prices are lower; but HHS Secretary Donna Shalala ruled it was unenforceable in December.

On foreign policy, Dorgan has been a prime mover in scaling back the embargo on Cuba. "To continue such an embargo only hurts U.S. family farmers." In 2000 he got the Senate to lift the embargo on food and medicine and to prevail against a House version which he said would limit financing of sales to Cuba. He has been skeptical about missile defense. After a test failure in July 2000 he said, "It's hard to see how they can recommend a deployment decision of a missile system that doesn't work." He was a strong but not successful supporter of the Comprehensive Test Ban Treaty which Bill Clinton submitted to the Senate in September 1997. Frustrated because Jesse Helms was keeping the treaty in the Foreign Relations Committee, Dorgan in September 1999 said "I intend to plant myself on the floor like a potted plant" and hold up proceedings till it was considered. A month later Joseph Biden and the Clinton administration took up his cause, and Majority Leader Trent Lott agreed on debate and a floor vote. But Dorgan and his allies didn't realize that Arizona Republican Jon Kyl had been quietly persuading Republicans to oppose the treaty; he had long since put together the 34 hard votes needed to deny it two-thirds approval and by September had nearly every Republican opposed. Dorgan's "potted plant" speech made it too embarrassing for Democrats to withdraw the treaty, and it was defeated 51–48 in October 1999.

On North Dakota issues, Dorgan has sometimes disappointed environmental groups. He opposed the Forest Service's encouragement of prairie dogs in 1999. "We're certainly not short on prairie dogs in North Dakota. What we're short on is farmers and ranchers." And he refused to recommend a larger wilderness area than the Forest Service recommended in 2000. In September 2000 he threatened to block EPA nominations unless North Dakota farmers were allowed to import a pesticide from Canada. Dorgan worked closely with Kent Conrad on water issues. They worked to limit the drawdown on Lake Sakakawea in the Missouri River and fought Missouri's senators who wanted more water let out to keep the barges floating on the river in their state. They succeeded in December 2000 in getting the $631 million Dakota Water Resources Act included in an appropriation; this would authorize diversion of Missouri River water to the Red River Valley in eastern North Dakota, and is opposed by Canada, Minnesota and many environmentalists.

Dorgan was easily re-elected in 1998. His first opponent was a Fargo nudist rights advocate Crystal Dueker who said she would "be the sacrificial virgin." She added, "I fight to win. I know how to kick a man where it hurts." But she bowed out in March after Fargo police had her hospitalized for psychiatric evaluation. The eventual Republican nominee, state Senator Donna Nalewaja, called on Dorgan to observe the limits of the McCain-Feingold campaign finance bill he supported. No go: she spent only $152,000; he had $200,000 on hand after the campaign. Dorgan won 63%–35%, carrying every county but one; the vote in Sheridan County was 423–423. His vote was highest among elderly North Dakotans, but he carried every demographic group by wide margins. His seat comes up in 2004.

Representative-At-Large Earl Pomeroy, North Dakota's single House member, is a Democrat first elected in 1992. Pomeroy grew up in Valley City, and after college served as Byron

Dorgan's driver during the 1974 campaign, then went to law school and practiced law in Valley City. In 1980, when Dorgan and Conrad won statewide elections, Pomeroy at 28 won a seat in the legislature; in 1984 and 1988 he was elected insurance commissioner (his brother Glenn Pomeroy followed him in the office). In 1992, he was planning to retire from politics and serve in the Peace Corps in Russia; then Dorgan ran for Conrad's seat in the Senate and Pomeroy ran for Dorgan's seat in the House. Articulate, cheerful and sincere, a critic of insurance companies yet unabrasive, he was the obvious choice for the House seat and was nominated unanimously by the Democratic convention. He won the general 57%–39%, almost exactly Dorgan's margin in the Senate race.

Pomeroy has compiled a moderate to liberal voting record, defending North Dakota interests and working with Republicans as well as Democrats on many issues. He served on the Budget Committee in his first term, and voted for both the Clinton budget and the Penny-Kasich spending cuts in 1993 and opposed the Clinton health care plan. In the Republican Congress he supported the Blue Dog budget and the Republican balanced budget in 1997. He strongly supported the adoption tax credit and brought his two-year-old daughter, adopted from Korea, onto the floor for the vote. He formed a bipartisan, bicameral committee to seek consensus on retirement and pension issues; Pomeroy, with his experience as insurance commissioner, wants to help people with their lifelong project of accumulation of wealth. He has sponsored bills to help small businesses set up pension plans, to allow employees moving from non-profit to for-profit employers to shift money from 403(b)s to 401(k)s and to allow employees to begin collecting part of their pension while still working after age 59 or after 30 years on the jobs ("the private sector equivalent of lifting the Social Security earnings limit"). He supported the March 1999 Clinton Social Security plan: investing 15% of the Social Security trust fund in private equities. He argues that such government investment would amount to only 4% of the entire stock market and that it would be insulated from political manipulation by an independent oversight board and by competition between private fund managers, who would invest in broad market index funds. He argues that individual retirement accounts would have high administrative costs and would not provide survivor benefits for women or disability coverage. With, finally, a seat on Ways and Means (one Democratic aide said that "many people have been promised the seat, but Pomeroy has been promised it the most"), he could play a key role on Social Security reform.

Pomeroy is co-chairman of the House Rural Caucus. Though not averse to all change in farm programs, he opposed the Freedom to Farm Act, though he helped write its wetlands reform provisions. He has supported the crop insurance and disaster relief bills which have provided the rough equivalent of the old subsidies which the Freedom to Farm Act promises to phase out by 2003. He wants to raise the federal loan rate on crops to 96% of the cost of production. Like other North Dakotans, he has decried what he calls Canadian wheat "dumping" and has sought government action against it; but he wants to allow North Dakota farmers to buy chemicals from Canada that are presently banned in the U.S. He opposed the Forest Service grasslands management plan in 2000 and presented petitions with 13,500 signatures protesting it.

During the devastating Grand Forks flooding in April 1997, he helped man the dikes and slept in a nearby Air Force shelter in order to help residents deal with the disaster; later he worked and got nearly $500 million in flood relief, and has worked for a $300 million system of levees and walls to prevent future floods. He has worked to get a study of an emergency outlet for Devils Lake, whose water level has been rising and has inundated 120,000 acres. But he has had some difficulty in the Republican House. In 2000 House Majority Whip Tom DeLay flew over Devils Lake with Pomeroy's Republican opponent. In an unusually acerbic criticism of a colleague, DeLay told reporters, "We will help Devils Lake. We will get this done in spite of Earl Pomeroy. But you ought to have a representative who knows how to work the system." He added, "He played partisan politics last year. Why should we lift a finger this year for him?" Pomeroy's response: "To have the majority whip say they were unhappy with me on previous votes so they took it out on the people of Devils Lake is sad."

Pomeroy worked on the children's health insurance bill in 1997, and in 2000 criticized the North Dakota legislature for not funding it. He sponsored a bill to encourage schools to teach students about finance, and called on the entertainment industry to follow FTC recommendations against marketing adult movies, video games and records to children. He was a vigorous supporter of PNTR for China in 2000. As co-chairman in 1999 of the committee to recommend the selection of a new House chaplain, he was caught up in the controversy that followed when Speaker Dennis Hastert passed over the committee's plurality choice, a Roman Catholic priest. He said in February 2000 that he passed on the relative support for the different candidates to Hastert and Minority Leader Dick Gephardt. "I don't think they were picking on Catholics, but I do think they walked away from an opportunity to have a consensus chaplain."

Pomeroy has had serious challenges every two years. In 1994 businessman Gary Porter used his own money to match the incumbent's spending. Pomeroy won 52%–45%, carrying the four largest counties by only 50%–48%. In 1996 and 1998 he was opposed by state Economic Development and Finance Director Kevin Cramer. In 1996, with $604,000 in PAC contributions, Pomeroy outspent him by more than 2–1 and increased his margin to 55%–43%. In 1998 Cramer peppered Pomeroy with negative ads and attacked him for seeking to invest Social Security funds in the stock market. In a pro-incumbent year, Pomeroy increased his percentage to 56%–41%.

Pomeroy and his family moved from the Washington suburbs to Bismarck in early 1997, and some thought he might run for governor in 2000. But he ran for re-election and had vigorous opposition from state House Majority Leader John Dorso. Dorso said Pomeroy was "ineffective," that he had failed to get full funding for special education and had not gotten an emergency outlet for Devils Lake. Dorso portrayed himself as more aggressive and pugnacious, though Pomeroy proved his own mettle when he wrestled and subdued a man brandishing a broken bottle at a House hearing in May 2000. Dorso attacked Pomeroy for supporting the Medicare cuts in the 1997 budget agreement and attacked the Clinton administration plans to move the nation's one missile defense site from North Dakota to Alaska. Pomeroy argued that his sobriety and thoughtfulness helped bring $1 billion into North Dakota. Pomeroy won 53%–44%, carrying the four big counties 52%–45%, a result almost identical with the 1994 results, and a downtick from 1996 and 1998. "These have not been easy years, but they've been tremendously interesting," he said on election night.

In the 107th Congress only a handful of Democrats represent a district which cast a higher percentage for George W. Bush than North Dakota's 61%. Four days after the election, Pomeroy said that if the election went to the House, he would vote for Bush—a vote that would not have made a difference, since a majority of state delegations were controlled by Republicans, but it would have meant that his one vote would have cancelled out the vote of the 32 House Democrats from California. Pomeroy will probably have to reckon with serious opposition again in 2002. When he came to the House, Democrats held most statewide offices in North Dakota and controlled the legislature: a strong bench. But now Republicans hold most of the statewide offices and large majorities in the legislature: there is a bench full of prospective candidates for the House.

Cook's Call   *Probably Safe.* No Democrat can feel entirely safe in this conservative leaning state, but Pomeroy has won here rather handily, despite a couple close calls. He has publicly flirted with retiring in the past; if he does retire, this seat will be up for grabs.

Presidential politics   Massachusetts and Hawaii, the other states with all-Democratic congressional delegations, are heavily Democratic in presidential elections; North Dakota is heavily Republican. In olden days, North Dakota veered toward Democrats when farm prices fell; in 2000, though prices were low, it voted heavily Republican.

With a tiny delegation, an out-of-the-way location and frigid weather in the early primary season, North Dakota does not loom large in choosing presidential nominees. In 2000 the Republicans' February 29 caucuses attracted 9,100 North Dakotans; George W. Bush got 14 of the 19 delegates. A week later the Democrats caucused, and Al Gore won 14 of 22 delegates.

THE PEOPLE: Pop. 2000: 642,200; Pop. 1990: 638,800, up 0.5% 1990–2000. 0.2% of U.S. total, 47th largest; 92.4% White, 0.6% Black, 0.6% Asian, 4.9% Amer. Indian, 1.2% Two+ races, 0.4% Other; 1.2% Hispanic Origin. 3% Unemployment. 2000 Voting age pop.: 481,351. 2000 Turnout: 292,249; 61% of VAP. No state voter registration.

POLITICAL LINEUP: Governor, John Hoeven (R); Lt. Gov., Jack Dalrymple (R); Secy. of State, Alvin Jaeger (R); Atty. Gen., Wayne Stenehjem (R); Treasurer, Kathi Gilmore (D); Commissioner of Insurance, Jim Poolman (R); Auditor, Robert R. Peterson (R); Tax Commissioner, Rick Clayburgh (R); Superintendent of Education, Wayne G. Sanstead; Commissioner of Agriculture, Roger Johnson (D); State Senate, 49 (17 D, 32 R); Majority Leader, Gary Nelson (R); State House, 98 (29 D, 69 R); House Speaker, Leroy G. Bernstein (R). Senators, Kent Conrad (D) and Byron Dorgan (D). Representative, 1 D at large.

ELECTIONS DIVISION: 701-328-4146; **FILING DEADLINE FOR U.S. CONGRESS:** April 12, 2002.

2000 Presidential Vote			1996 Presidential Vote		
Bush (R)	174,852	(61%)	Dole (R)	125,050	(47%)
Gore (D)	95,284	(33%)	Clinton (D)	106,905	(40%)
Nader (Green)	9,486	(3%)	Perot (I)	32,515	(12%)
Others	8,634	(3%)			

Gov. John Hoeven (R)

Elected 2000, term expires Jan. 2005, 1st term; b. March 13, 1957, Bismarck; home, Bismarck; Dartmouth, B.A. 1979; Northwestern U., Kellogg Grad. Schl., M.B.A. 1981; Catholic; married (Mical).

Professional Career: Exec. V.P., First Western Bank, 1986–93; Pres. & CEO, Bank of ND, 1993–2000.

Office: State Capitol, 600 E. Boulevard, Bismarck, 58505, 701-328-2200; Fax: 701-328-2205; Web site: www.state.nd.us.

Election Results

2000 general	John Hoeven (R)	159,255	(55%)
	Heidi Heitkamp (D)	130,144	(45%)
2000 primary	John Hoeven (R)	unopposed	
1996 general	Edward T. Schafer (R)	174,937	(66%)
	Lee Kaldor (D)	89,349	(34%)

Sen. Kent Conrad (D)

Elected 1986, seat up 2006, 2d term; b. Mar. 12, 1948, Bismarck; home, Bismarck; Stanford U., B.A. 1971, George Washington U., M.B.A. 1975; Unitarian; married (Lucy Calautti).

Elected Office: ND Tax Commissioner, 1981–86.

Professional Career: Asst., ND Tax Commissioner, 1974–80; Dir., Mgmt. Planning & Personnel, ND Tax Dept., 1980.

DC Office: 530 HSOB, 20510, 202-224-2043; Fax: 202-224-7776; Web site: www.senate.gov/~conrad.

State Offices: Bismarck, 701-258-4648; Fargo, 701-232-8030; Grand Forks, 701-775-9601; Minot, 701-852-0703.

Committees: *Agriculture, Nutrition & Forestry*: Marketing, Inspection & Product Promotion; Production & Price Competitiveness (Chmn.); Research, Nutrition & General Legislation. *Budget* (Chmn.). *Finance*: International Trade; Long-Term Growth & Debt Reduction; Taxation & IRS Oversight (Chmn.). *Indian Affairs*.

Group Ratings

	ADA	ACLU	AFS	LCV	CON	ITIC	NTU	COC	ACU	NTLC	CHC
2000	85	43	85	71	26	81	15	42	29	12	31
1999	90	—	100	56	81	—	7	53	16	—	—

National Journal Ratings

	1999 LIB —	1999 CONS	2000 LIB —	2000 CONS
Economic	68% —	29%	70% —	29%
Social	56% —	42%	57% —	39%
Foreign	62% —	29%	56% —	43%

Key Votes of the 106th Congress

1. Educ. Savings Accts.	N	5. Review Movie Violence	Y	9. NATO War in Serbia	Y
2. Prescrip. Drug Benefit	Y	6. Gun Show Bckgrnd. Checks	Y	10. Table Cuba Travel Ban	N
3. Delay Ergonomic Standards	N	7. Ban Part.-Birth Abortion	Y	11. Nuclear Test-Ban Treaty	Y
4. Phase Out Estate Tax	N	8. Broaden Hate Crimes List	Y	12. Perm. Trade with China	Y

Election Results

2000 general	Kent Conrad (D)	176,470	(62%)	($2,312,543)
	Duane Sand (R)	110,420	(38%)	($399,584)
2000 primary	Kent Conrad (D)	unopposed		
1994 general	Kent Conrad (D)	137,157	(58%)	($1,927,866)
	Ben Clayburgh (R)	99,390	(42%)	($941,192)

Sen. Byron Dorgan (D)

Elected 1992, seat up 2004, 2d term; b. May 14, 1942, Dickinson; home, Bismarck; U. of ND, B.S. 1965, U. of Denver, M.B.A. 1966; Lutheran; married (Kimberly).

Elected Office: ND Tax Commissioner, 1969–80; U.S. House of Reps., 1980–92.

Professional Career: Martin-Marietta Exec. Develop. Prog., 1966–68; ND Dpty. Tax Commissioner, 1968–69.

DC Office: 713 HSOB, 20510, 202-224-2551; Fax: 202-224-1193; Web site: www.senate.gov/~dorgan.

State Offices: Bismarck, 701-250-4618; Fargo, 701-239-5389; Minot, 701-852-0703.

Committees: *Democratic Policy Committee Co-Chairman. Appropriations*: Agriculture & Rural Development; Defense; Energy & Water Development; Interior; Treasury & General Government (Chmn.). *Commerce, Science & Transportation*: Aviation; Communications; Consumer Affairs, Foreign Commerce & Tourism (Chmn.); Science, Technology & Space; Surface Transportation & Merchant Marine. *Energy & Natural Resources*: National Parks, Historic Preservation & Recreation; Water & Power (Chmn.). *Indian Affairs*.

Group Ratings

	ADA	ACLU	AFS	LCV	CON	ITIC	NTU	COC	ACU	NTLC	CHC
2000	90	57	85	71	26	83	12	46	16	9	31
1999	95	—	100	78	82	—	7	35	12	—	—

National Journal Ratings

	1999 LIB —	1999 CONS	2000 LIB —	2000 CONS
Economic	75% —	20%	72% —	27%
Social	58% —	41%	57% —	39%
Foreign	60% —	38%	95% —	0%

Key Votes of the 106th Congress

1. Educ. Savings Accts.	N	5. Review Movie Violence	Y	9. NATO War in Serbia	Y
2. Prescrip. Drug Benefit	Y	6. Gun Show Bckgrnd. Checks	Y	10. Table Cuba Travel Ban	N
3. Delay Ergonomic Standards	N	7. Ban Part.-Birth Abortion	Y	11. Nuclear Test-Ban Treaty	Y
4. Phase Out Estate Tax	N	8. Broaden Hate Crimes List	Y	12. Perm. Trade with China	Y

Election Results

1998 general	Byron Dorgan (D)	134,747	(63%)	($1,681,842)
	Donna Nalewaja (R)	75,013	(35%)	($152,183)
	Others	3,598	(2%)	
1998 primary	Byron Dorgan (D)	unopposed		
1992 general	Byron Dorgan (D)	179,347	(59%)	($1,124,512)
	Steve Sydness (R)	118,162	(39%)	($498,107)
	Others	6,448	(2%)	

Rep. Earl Pomeroy (D)

Elected 1992, 5th term; b. Sept. 2, 1952, Valley City; home, Valley City; U. of ND, B.A. 1974, J.D., 1979; Presbyterian; married (Laurie Kirby).

Elected Office: ND House of Reps., 1980–84; ND Insurance Commissioner, 1984–92.

Professional Career: Practicing atty., 1979–84; Natl. Assn. of Insurance Commissioners., Vice Pres. 1989, Pres. 1990.

DC Office: 1110 LHOB, 20515, 202-225-2611; Fax: 202-226-0893; Web site: www.house.gov/pomeroy.

District Offices: Bismarck, 701-224-0355; Fargo, 701-235-9760.

Committees: *Ways & Means* (17th of 17 D): Oversight; Social Security.

Group Ratings

	ADA	ACLU	AFS	LCV	CON	ITIC	NTU	COC	ACU	NTLC	CHC
2000	85	50	85	57	69	89	21	57	8	15	40
1999	85	—	100	56	77	—	21	44	12	—	—

National Journal Ratings

	1999 LIB	—	1999 CONS		2000 LIB	—	2000 CONS
Economic	59%	—	41%		85%	—	11%
Social	58%	—	42%		64%	—	36%
Foreign	85%	—	12%		96%	—	3%

Key Votes of the 106th Congress

1. Patient Bill of Rights	Y	5. Bar RU-486 $ for FDA	N	9. NATO War in Serbia	Y
2. Accelerate Min. Wage	Y	6. Display 10 Commandments	N	10. Perm. Trade with China	Y
3. Strike Ban on Ergo. Stnd.	Y	7. Gun Show Bkgrnd. Checks	Y	11. Debt Relief for 3rd World	Y
4. Ovrd. Estate Tax Veto	N	8. Ban Part.-Birth Abortion	Y	12. Drop Cuba Econ. Embargo	Y

Election Results

2000 general	Earl Pomeroy (D)	151,173	(53%)	($1,052,831)
	John Dorso (R)	127,251	(45%)	($448,823)
	Others	7,234	(3%)	
2000 primary	Earl Pomeroy (D)	unopposed		
1998 general	Earl Pomeroy (D)	119,668	(56%)	($775,948)
	Kevin Cramer (R)	87,511	(41%)	($321,242)
	Others	5,709	(3%)	

★ OHIO ★

O hio was the first entirely American state, and one which ever since has seemed an epitome of American normalcy. The original 13 states started as British colonies, and the next three, Vermont, Kentucky and Tennessee, were spun off from them. But Ohio sprung Athena-like from the head of Congress, as the first state formed from the Northwest Territory of 1787. The Northwest Ordinance established 6 by 6 mile square townships, which imposed geometric order on diverse American landscapes west to the Pacific; it set aside one square mile per township for public schools, and the landscape was soon peppered with schoolhouses and small colleges, the foundation stones of a literate republic. The Ordinance prohibited slavery, opening the way for free labor to clear fields, raise crops, build mills and factories, and in less than half a century, make this wilderness one of the most productive parts of western civilization. Ohio, in the years after the Civil War, became one of the great industrial states, the longtime headquarters of John D. Rockefeller's Standard Oil, the site of major steel mills along the narrow and languidly flowing Cuyahoga and Mahoning Rivers, and home of the biggest soap companies, machine tool makers, tire manufacturers and producers of safety glass. Settled by Virginians in the southwest around Cincinnati, by New Englanders in the northeast in the Western Reserve around Cleveland, Ohio has always been split between cultures: between the Southern-accented counties south of the National Road and U.S. 40 and the Northern-accented cities and towns to the north; between Butternut and Copperhead territory that didn't want to fight the Civil War and Yankee territory that fiercely prosecuted the War and Reconstruction afterwards.

This split heritage made Ohio politically a closely divided state—and a nationally pivotal one. A century ago Ohio produced the candidate and campaign manager—Governor and former Ways and Means Chairman William McKinley and iron and coal industrialist Mark Hanna; McKinley won the presidency in 1896 and 1900 and inaugurated a 34-year period of Republican national majorities. McKinley's Republicans were for high tariffs and hard money, had a friendly regard for workers and even some unions, but no patience with large union combinations and nascent socialism. They preached a nationalist Americanism tempered by a wariness about making major commitments abroad. Republicans were the majority in this increasingly industrial Ohio, losing rural Butternut counties but carrying the big industrial cities of the north.

Then came the Depression of the 1930s, and Ohio became the scene of something like class warfare, with sit-down strikes and victories for the CIO industrial unions in autos, steel and tires. CIO cities—Cleveland, Akron, Youngstown, Toledo—moved sharply toward the Democrats, while places with few CIO members—Cincinnati, Columbus, the dozens of small factory towns dotting the flat limestone plains of northern Ohio—stayed Republican. The political fighting was fierce and the stakes seemed high. CIO leaders hoped to organize the entire work force and build a Scandinavian-style welfare state; Republican leaders like Ohio's Senator Robert Taft feared union control of business would imperil freedoms and throttle the economy. In the 1930s and 1940s the unions made great gains. But Taft held them off, reducing union power with the Taft-Hartley Act of 1947, his own reelection to the Senate in 1950, and the election of his rival Dwight Eisenhower as president in 1952.

In the years since, Ohio has oscillated and been courted by national campaigns. In the 1970s it seemed to swing toward the Democrats. Jimmy Carter won crucial electoral votes by carrying Ohio by 11,000 votes and Democrats controlled the state House throughout the 1970s and 1980s. In the 1990s Ohio swung to the Republicans. Bill Clinton did carry the state twice, but by the narrowest of his margins in any large state—40%–38% in 1992, 47%–41% in 1996—and Al Gore lost here 50%–46% in 2000. Ohio Republicans won smashing victories in 1994 and 1998 and held their own in 1996 and 2000. The leading figure was George Voinovich, elected governor in 1990 by 56%–44%, reelected in 1994 by 72%–25%—by far the biggest margin since 1826, when neither Republican nor Democratic parties existed—and elected senator by 56%–44% in 1998. But this has not just been a personal victory. From 1976–94 Ohio was represented by two Democrats in the Senate, but when they retired they were replaced by Republicans: Mike DeWine, who won 53%–39% in 1994, and Voinovich, both of whom had run unsuccessfully for the Senate before.

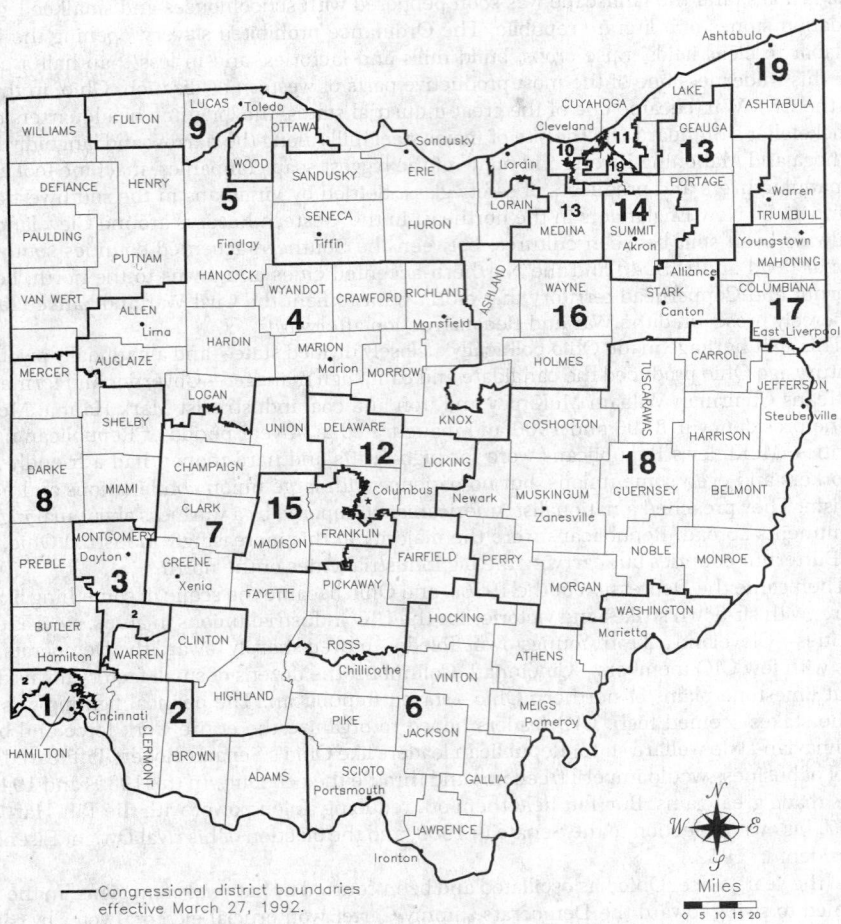

WILLIAMS · FULTON · LUCAS *Toledo* — **9**
OTTAWA
Sandusky · CUYAHOGA · LAKE · Ashtabula
Cleveland · **19**
GEAUGA · ASHTABULA

DEFIANCE · HENRY · WOOD — **5**
SANDUSKY · ERIE · Lorain · **11**
10 · **19**
13 · PORTAGE

PAULDING · PUTNAM · SENECA
Findlay · *Tiffin* · HURON · LORAIN
Warren
TRUMBULL

VAN WERT · ALLEN · HANCOCK
WYANDOT · CRAWFORD · RICHLAND · **13** · MEDINA · **14** · SUMMIT · *Akron*
Alliance
Youngstown
MAHONING

Lima · HARDIN · MARION
Mansfield · WAYNE · STARK · *Canton* · COLUMBIANA · **17**
East Liverpool

MERCER · AUGLAIZE · LOGAN · *Marion* · MORROW
16 · HOLMES
CARROLL · JEFFERSON
Steubenville

SHELBY · UNION · DELAWARE · KNOX · COSHOCTON · TUSCARAWAS · HARRISON

CHAMPAIGN · **12** · LICKING
18 · GUERNSEY · BELMONT

DARKE · **8** · MIAMI · CLARK · **7** · **15** · FRANKLIN · *Columbus* · *Newark* · MUSKINGUM · *Zanesville* · NOBLE · MONROE
MADISON
MONTGOMERY · *Dayton* · GREENE · *Xenia*

PREBLE · **3** · FAIRFIELD · PERRY · MORGAN · WASHINGTON · *Marietta*
FAYETTE · PICKAWAY

BUTLER · WARREN · CLINTON · ROSS · HOCKING · ATHENS
Hamilton · *Chillicothe* · VINTON

2 · **1** · *Cincinnati* · **2** · HIGHLAND · PIKE · **6** · JACKSON · MEIGS · *Pomeroy*
HAMILTON · CLERMONT · BROWN · ADAMS · SCIOTO · GALLIA
Portsmouth
LAWRENCE
Ironton

—Congressional district boundaries
effective March 27, 1992.

Miles
0 5 10 15 20

N
W E
S

And in 1998 Republican Bob Taft, bearer of a great Ohio name, was elected governor over Democrat Lee Fisher by 50%–45%. Until Taft's victory, Ohio's governorship had been passed back and forth between the two parties, with neither holding it for more than eight years, since George K. Nash won in 1899. Republicans hold every downballot statewide office, most of which were held by Democrats between 1970–94, and they have large and seemingly impervious margins in both houses of the legislature. Republicans have an 11–8 edge in the U.S. House delegation, a 21–12 margin in the state Senate and 59–40 in the state House.

Is this is a short-term blip or a long-run trend, a return to a McKinley-type Republican majority or a momentary interruption of New Deal voting patterns? It is a question of national significance, for in income levels, urban-rural balance, and ethnic mix, as well as presidential percentages, Ohio is not very far from the national average. One place to look for answers is in north-and-east Ohio, the traditionally Democratic area along Lake Erie and reaching south to the coal-mining counties across the Ohio River from West Virginia. This was the heartland of the CIO unions, the United Steelworkers in Youngstown and Cleveland, United Rubber Workers in Akron, United Mine Workers in the coal country, and United Auto Workers in Toledo and the Cleveland area. It is heavily ethnic, with hundreds of thousands of Poles, Hungarians, Slovaks, Serbs and Croatians streaming in throughout the early 20th Century. When its auto, steel, rubber and glass factories lost hundreds of thousands of jobs in the five years after the oil shock of 1979, north-and-east Ohio was one of the most Democratic parts of the country; as a separate state, it would have come as close to voting against Ronald Reagan in 1980 and 1984 as Massachusetts or New York. It voted solidly for Michael Dukakis in 1988 (54%–46%) and Bill Clinton in 1992 (47%–31%). But as the shock of the early 1980s wore off and it became clear that CIO industries' high-wage, low-skill jobs were gone for good, attitudes began changing. Voters gave up on trying to recreate the old factory economy and began building a new, more supple and adaptable manufacturing economy, with smaller factories, less rigid management and fewer union members, fewer low-skill jobs with high wages and more medium-skill, high-flexibility jobs with chances for advancement. They mostly gave up on restricting trade, as steel and auto import quotas lapsed and NAFTA was approved, and began manufacturing goods for export markets. And so Ohio began to grow again. Cleveland's new downtown is gleaming, Akron is proud of the polymer technologies which have replaced tire manufacturing, the Cuyahoga River is clean, and the valleys carved by rivers in the limestone are a source of pride.

George Voinovich, long familiar to the Cleveland TV market, carried north-and-east Ohio by a small margin when he was elected governor in 1990; in 1994, against a little-known opponent, he won 69%–29%, the kind of Republican margin not seen in this area of Ohio since the 1920s; Mike DeWine carried this area over Democrat Joel Hyatt 47%–45% in the 1994 Senate race. In the late 1990s, as the AFL-CIO revived its moribund political operations, north-and-east Ohio moved some distance back to its Democratic roots. In 1998 Voinovich and Bob Taft lost the area, albeit by modest margins, 51%–49% and 53%–42%. Bill Clinton, running strong in metro Cleveland as he did in most of the nation's major metro areas, carried north-and-east Ohio 54%–33% in 1996. And in 2000, Al Gore carried the area 56%–41%, a better percentage, but a smaller margin. Significantly, union members voted 67%–30% for Gore. But in neither case was the Democrats' margin here enough to produce a statewide majority. The politics of union-management struggle has not entirely died out in one of its old strongholds, but it is not as strong as it once was.

The rest of Ohio has long been a Republican area, a stronghold for James Rhodes, governor for 16 of the 20 years from 1962–82, who favored low taxes in order to attract jobs and who died in March 2001 at 91. In the 1980s and 1990s, this larger part of Ohio's cultural conservatism and patriotic nationalism, plus faith in a growing economy, made it heavily Republican: In their losing races, George Bush carried it 44%–35% in 1992 and Bob Dole 47%–42% in 1996; and winning Republicans have won big majorities here—in 1998, Voinovich won 61%–39% and Taft 55%–39%. In 2000 this part of Ohio cast 54% of the state's votes, and George W. Bush carried it 58%–39%. There has been a countervailing trend in the 1990s to the Democrats' gains in major metro areas, and that has been Republican gains in rural and small town areas; and in Ohio that was enough to produce 21 precious electoral votes for Bush. There are only a few pockets of

Democratic strength in this rest-of-Ohio, in the central cities of Cincinnati, Columbus and Dayton and in a few lightly populated Butternut counties south of U.S. 40, and with the exception of Columbus, the population in such areas has been declining.

The economy in both parts of Ohio proved to be surprisingly robust in the 1990s. The unemployment rate, long high, fell below the national average; household incomes are up sharply; more than half a million jobs were created since 1991. Ohioans' high-skill manufacturing has been booming, and small entrepreneurs have created thousands of jobs in the shadows of huge steel mills long since shut down. Signs of a slowdown were apparent in early 2001, but no signs that it would be as devastating as the industrial recessions of 1958, 1970 or the early 1980s. The state's population increased 5% in the 1990s, well below the national average yet significantly above Ohio's anemic growth in the 1970s and 1980s. Central city populations were mostly down, especially in Cincinnati, which declined 9%, an augury perhaps of the nasty riot of April 2001; the 2000 Census counted 478,000 people in Cleveland, its lowest number since 1900 and barely half the 914,000 in 1950. But population rose robustly in Columbus and in suburban and once-rural counties outside the big cities; Ohioans are using their prosperity to live in communities more to their liking.

The 1998 and 2000 elections posed a test of where Ohio stands in history. Is it New Deal Ohio, with ethnic factory workers ranged against small town businessmen, ethnic Catholics versus rural Protestants, all engaged in a contest to see how far and in what ways government should be enlarged? Or is it McKinley's Ohio, with mechanical tinkerers and can-do manufacturers, adaptive businessmen and employees, striving to work hard, raise families and serve communities that feel little class conflict or economic envy? The answer, by a small but decisive margin, is that it is McKinley's Ohio, but it is not clear whether this consensus and political dominance can be sustained for a long generation as it was by McKinley and Hanna and their political heirs.

Governor Bob Taft, elected governor in 1998, is from a famed Ohio family. His great-grandfather William Howard Taft was elected president in 1908 and appointed chief justice in 1921. His grandfather, Robert A. Taft, was elected senator in 1938, 1944 and 1950; a strong and principled conservative known as "Mr. Republican," he ran for president and lost the Republican nomination in 1940 and 1952, and was Senate Majority Leader when he died in 1953. His father, Robert Taft Jr., was elected to the House in 1962, 1966 and 1968 and to the Senate in 1970, then lost to Howard Metzenbaum in 1976. The increasing informality of 20th Century politics can be gauged by the style of the Tafts' names: President Taft used three full names, the first Senator Taft an initial, the second Senator Taft a Jr. and this latest Taft calls himself simply Bob—and didn't make reference to his illustrious family in his campaign ads. He grew up in Cincinnati, graduated from Yale, served two years in the Peace Corps in East Africa, got a masters degree at Princeton and worked four years as a budget officer in Illinois state government. Then he returned to Cincinnati, graduated from the University of Cincinnati law school, and was elected to the state House in 1976. In 1981 he was elected Hamilton County commissioner. In 1990 he started to run for governor, then was persuaded by Republican National Chairman Lee Atwater in one of his last political acts to step aside for George Voinovich and run for secretary of state instead; he was elected to that office, critical for redistricting the state legislature, in November.

The common expectation was that Taft would run for governor in 1998, when Voinovich would be ineligible for a third term. At first he looked to have primary opposition from Treasurer Kenneth Blackwell, but Blackwell agreed in January 1998 to run for secretary of State instead (he won, too, and has indicated he will run for governor in 2006). But Taft had strong Democratic opposition: Lee Fisher, elected attorney general in 1990, defeated by a narrow margin in heavily Republican 1994, who from his base in the Cleveland suburbs raised nearly as much money as the Republican. On primary day, voters rejected Issue 2, a one-cent sales tax for schools and property tax relief, written in response to a court decision requiring more school funding. Both Taft and Fisher supported it, and had to scramble to come up with new ways to address the number one issue, education, without a tax increase. Fisher promised to cut property taxes by 15% over two years; Taft proposed much smaller tax cuts, a homestead exemption and a $2,500 college tuition deduction for families with incomes under $50,000. Much of the ruckus of the campaign came over attacks for backing previous tax increases: Fisher attacked Taft for backing

11 tax increases in Hamilton County; Taft attacked Fisher for backing 27 tax increases in Columbus. The newspapers made much of supposed Taft gaffes (one ad just read "Bob Taft Governor") and Fisher accused Taft of dodging debates (Taft insisted on having the two minor candidates participate). There was the obvious difference in background. As Fisher put it, "My great-grandfather was an immigrant sheet-metal worker from Russia, and I am running against a man whose great-grandfather was president of the United States." He might have added that Taft's great-grandfather vetoed a bill to restrict immigration. Taft won 50%–45%, losing 53%–42% in north-and-east Ohio and winning 55%–39% in the rest of the state. Taft carried all income groups over $30,000 and got about 57% among both Catholics and white Protestants, and Fisher's lead in union households was only 54%–40%: the old bright lines between Ohioans have become blurred.

In his first year in office Taft fulfilled many of his campaign promises. Working with the Republican legislature, he required students to take reading tests in the fourth grade to be academically promoted, created School Safety Zones, the college tuition deduction, the homestead tax cut, tougher penalties for juvenile criminals and cheats who exploit the elderly. He got approval of bonding for school construction. He started his Ohio Reads program (recruiting more than 13,000 volunteers to teach children to read), reduced the estate tax and made other state tax cuts, and got voter approval of a $400 million environmental bond issue. He stood firm on giving the schools a larger share of the tobacco settlement, but backed down before the legislature on the right to sue HMOs and requiring safe storage of firearms. His major problem was criticism of his use of a box at Ohio State football games to raise campaign money and of his unsuccessful attempt to defeat state Supreme Court Justice Alice Robie Resnick. Even organized labor was not unhappy; he had kept his pledge not to seek anti-union legislation.

But in early 2001 Taft faced more difficulties. Because of term limits, the legislature included many new members and some new leaders. Tax revenues, which had increased at a spritely pace in 2000, increased very little in 2001. The state Supreme Court had set a June 15 deadline for a new school finance program, and Taft, Senate President Richard Finan and new House Speaker Larry Householder all had different approaches. Meanwhile, Medicaid costs were skyrocketing, and Democrats criticized Taft for seeking only minimal increases in some departments and for his plan to close 56 unemployment offices. A further problem: the Jobs and Family Services Department withheld $8 million intended for child support payments; the director resigned and Taft hired a pro-choice moderate as interim director, which sparked criticism by conservatives. Courts caused other difficulties. The Sixth Circuit Court of Appeals ruled in December 2000 that Cleveland's school vouchers were unconstitutional; that case will probably go to the Supreme Court. And in April 2000 a three-judge panel of the Sixth Circuit ruled 2–1 that Ohio's motto, "With God, all things are possible," was unconstitutional; the full court reversed that 9–4 in March 2001. Why the slogan should be unobjectionable is unclear: even atheists concede that if the motto's premise is true, its conclusion must follow; their quarrel is with the premise that we are "with God."

For all his problems in early 2001, Taft still seemed well positioned for re-election in 2002. In May 2001 the state House passed a Republican budget devoting $1.4 billion for school funding over the next two years using revenue from video lottery as well as the state's savings account; the Senate seemed likely to follow suit. Taft's job rating held and Democrats did not have a well-known challenger. Congressman Sherrod Brown, threatened with unfavorable districting, said that if his district were abolished he might run; he could be a serious candidate but did lose to Taft for secretary of State in 1990.

Cook's Call   *Safe.* Taft has high approval ratings and a hefty war chest while Democrats are faced with a shallow bench. Congressman Sherrod Brown may run if his district is eliminated, and former Cuyahoga County Commissioner Tim Hagan is also exploring a bid. While both would be credible candidates, the race is Taft's to lose.

Senior Senator   Michael DeWine is a Republican elected in 1994 and though often underestimated in his career he was resoundingly re-elected in 2000. DeWine grew up in Yellow Springs, the home of liberal Antioch College, where his family owned a successful seed business; after finishing school DeWine and his wife moved to nearby Cedarville, in a part of the state with rolling hills, winding creeks and covered bridges, where they now host an annual ice cream social.

There DeWine was elected Greene County prosecutor at 29, where he resisted plea bargaining, and in order to nail a drug dealer, once put up the collateral to get $50,000 cash to stage a buy. In 1980, at 33, he was elected to the Ohio Senate; two years later he won a six-candidate Republican primary with 69% and was elected to a U.S. House seat. He worked for tougher drunk driving penalties, mandatory sentencing, and aid to child crime victims, with more success in Republican Columbus than on Democratic Capitol Hill. Elected lieutenant governor in 1990, DeWine sought better and more responsive teenage offender facilities and an Ohio DNA analysis lab. In 1992 he ran against Senator John Glenn. It was a hard-hitting campaign: He attacked Glenn for his part in the Keating Five case. In September 1992 Glenn was below 50% in the polls. But Democrats brought up DeWine's 31 overdrafts on the House bank and the time he fell asleep at the Iran-Contra hearings. Glenn won 51%–42%, his closest general election margin ever; he needed his 58%–35% margin in north-and-east Ohio, because DeWine carried the rest of the state 47%–45%.

In 1994 DeWine decided to run for the Senate again. This time the incumbent, Howard Metzenbaum, was retiring, and hoped to be succeeded by his son-in-law, Joel Hyatt, founder of the storefront Hyatt Legal Services chain. But in the May primary, Hyatt defeated Cuyahoga County Commissioner Mary Boyle by only 47%–43%, while DeWine won by 53%–32% over Bernadine Healy, former director of the National Institutes of Health. From then on, DeWine had solid leads in most polls. He spent much time in the Cleveland area, cutting into the Democrats' base. DeWine's anti-crime planks, his backing of term limits and the line-item veto helped him. Also, DeWine's support of NAFTA did not hurt; in an exit poll voters thought it was good for Ohio by a 26%–23% margin, and in fact Ohio exports to Mexico and Latin America have boomed since NAFTA was ratified. The 23% of voters in union households split evenly, while the 29% who were gun owners voted 58%–31% for the almost always plaid-shirt-clad DeWine. DeWine won statewide 53%–39%, by 47%–45% in north-and-east Ohio, and 58%–35% in the rest of the state.

The common motif that runs through DeWine's career is a concern for children and the championing of legislation often prompted by tragedy striking a particular child, including his own: his daughter Becky died in an auto accident in 1993, at 22, and he and his wife decided to donate her organs; DeWine spends much effort on organ donor programs and awareness. He was one of the chief backers of the .08% blood-alcohol limit. With Jay Rockefeller, he sponsored a law to change the family preservation emphasis in social work, and helped pass a law requiring the best interest of the child as paramount in custody cases involving abusive or drug-problem parents. He came out early for banning hospitals from discharging mothers in the 48 hours after delivery. Prompted by the death of a 13-year-old Greene County girl, he has crusaded for school bus safety and put incentives for the states to promote it in an appropriations bill. With Herb Kohl, he pushed through a law making it a felony to cross state lines to avoid paying child support in cases after one year or more than $5,000 in arrears. In the recesses of the Senate's impeachment trial, he made calls to try to get medical benefits for a Middletown five-year-old with xeroderma pigmentosum, a disease so rare it is not on the Social Security Administration's list of covered treatments. He took over the chairmanship of the District of Columbia Appropriations Subcommittee—generally regarded as a thankless task—with a determination to reform the District's child welfare system, which he described as "wrought with dysfunction, chaos and tragedy." He recalled that 150 complaints of sexual abuse had not been investigated for more than a year and said that he became physically ill after reading about the January 2000 death of Brianna Blackmond, a girl placed in the custody of a violent and negligent mother through the inattention and indifference of foster care workers.

On such issues DeWine has worked with Democrats. Similarly, as chairman of the Employment and Training Subcommittee, he assembled bipartisan support for a sweeping rewriting of job training laws, with more flexibility for cities and counties; it passed in 1998. He worked with Democrats Tony Hall of Dayton and Maryland's Paul Sarbanes to pass the Africa Seeds of Hope Act. To the Higher Education Act DeWine added provisions helping to repay college loans of those who work in early childhood education or day care, encouraging alternative certification of teachers, and creating public-private partnerships to train teachers. He successfully sponsored a Nazi War Crimes Disclosure Act, to make public the response of the U.S. government to the Holocaust.

In 2000 he succeeded in reauthorizing the Older Americans Act, which had expired in 1995, setting guidelines for services from free meals to employment assistance, with a new $125 million caregiver support program.

DeWine also worked on the Western Hemisphere Drug Elimination Act, pushing for tougher interdiction of drugs; he favors drug courts and making powdered cocaine penalties as severe as those for crack. He has traveled to Colombia three times and was one of the framers of the Plan Colombia legislation in June 2000, which pledged nearly $1.3 billion in aid to that country to stop drug production in guerrilla-held areas. As chairman of the Antitrust Subcommittee, he called for opposition to all telephone mergers unless they clearly benefited consumers in September 1998, and urged the FTC to hold off approval of the BP-Amoco merger in December 1998. In November 2000 he held a hearing on baseball, featuring such experts as columnist George Will, broadcaster Bob Costas and former Senator George Mitchell. Representing a state with some of the smaller franchises, the Cleveland Indians and the Cincinnati Reds, he said, "The status quo is simply unacceptable. Unless something is done to correct the payroll and revenue disparities among the teams—unless we untie the stranglehold around the small- and medium-market teams by increasing competition—baseball cannot survive." In March 2001 he questioned the proposed USAirway-United Airlines merger.

DeWine has worked on various Ohio issues, usually but not always to local satisfaction. Ohio's two senators are the only state's who have a joint office handling constituency services. He got a Cleveland federal courthouse named after the late Mayor Carl Stokes, brother of former Congressman Louis Stokes, and passed a law naming the Cleveland area NASA research center after his onetime opponent and retired colleague John Glenn. He has worked to secure funding for the Port Columbus air traffic control tower, Cleveland Hopkins Airport improvement and the Cincinnati riverfront transportation center. He worked to get $11 million for the Franklintown floodwall in Columbus. More controversially, he supports creation of the Little Darby Creek Refuge in Madison and Union Counties, west of Columbus; the idea is to provide green space in an area that may soon become suburban and to prevent runoff pollution into the river. The Fish and Wildlife Service would buy land only from willing sellers, and not condemn property; but many local residents are strongly opposed, and the controversy has reached the point that this small project got mentioned in the 2000 campaign.

When DeWine was first elected, Democrats predicted that they would be able to beat him in six years. Later they thought that his visible role in impeachment—Trent Lott put him, with Fred Thompson and Orrin Hatch, in charge of screening senators' questions for Chief Justice William Rehnquist and he was also asked to monitor the testimony of Monica Lewinsky—would hurt him. But potential opponents who might have put up a serious contest kept dropping out: Congress members Sherrod Brown, Ted Strickland and Marcy Kaptur, 1998 gubernatorial candidate Lee Fisher, former Congressman Dennis Eckhart, and most spectacularly, talk show host and former Cincinnati Mayor Jerry Springer. DeWine spent much of late 1999 and early 2000 campaigning for John McCain in Ohio and elsewhere; he was one of only four senators who endorsed McCain (the others were Jon Kyl, Chuck Hagel and Fred Thompson). DeWine's Democratic opponent turned out to be Ted Celeste, a real estate agent in Grandview Heights and former Ohio State Board of Trustees chairman, and brother of former Governor Richard Celeste. DeWine spent $5.7 million, much of it on television. Celeste spent $477,000, and put up one ad on the Internet which focused on prescription drug prices. DeWine won 60%–36%, the first Ohio Republican senator to be re-elected since John Bricker in 1952, and with the largest margin for a Republican senator here since Theodore Burton in 1928. He won 23% of the votes of blacks and 24% of Democrats and lost union members by only 55%–44%, and those who had not graduated from high school by 52%–43%; otherwise he carried all sexes, ages, income groups and demographic categories. He won 83 of 88 counties, losing only the two Mahoning County steel counties, two eastern Ohio coal counties and usually Republican Madison County, the site of Little Darby Creek.

In 2001 DeWine lost out on a seat on the Finance Committee to Jon Kyl, who has the same Senate and House seniority but won a luck-of-the-draw contest in 1995. In March 2001 he got offered an amendment to the McCain-Feingold campaign finance bill that passed 70–30 setting higher contribution limits for candidates opposed by self-financers.

Junior Senator   George Voinovich, elected to the Senate in 1998, is now the junior colleague of the man elected as his first lieutenant governor in 1990, Mike DeWine. Voinovich is of Serbian and Slovenian descent and grew up in heavily ethnic Cleveland; he practiced law, then was elected to the legislature in 1966, at 30. He was elected county auditor in 1971, county commissioner in 1977, and lieutenant governor in 1978. In 1979, after Mayor Dennis Kucinich bankrupted Cleveland, Voinovich ran for mayor. It was a strenuous campaign, running as a Republican in a heavily Democratic city, and one touched by tragedy: his daughter was killed in an auto accident at the time. In 10 years in office, he fixed the budget and sparked the city's renaissance. His one defeat came in 1988, when he lost 57%–43% to Senator Howard Metzenbaum.

In 1990 Voinovich ran for governor and beat Attorney General Anthony Celebrezze Jr., 56%–44%; in 1994 he was re-elected by the spectacular margin of 72%–25%. Voinovich got the state government's fiscal house in order, with the help of a tax increase in 1992; he helped to encourage the growth of small businesses, which got Ohio's economy humming by the middle 1990s; he cut welfare rolls and helped welfare recipients get jobs. He increased school funding and wiring of schools for the Internet and spent much of his last years grappling with court decisions attacking the state's education funding formula. He sponsored a managed health care plan, OhioCare, for Medicaid recipients and the uninsured. He is opposed to abortion but recognizes *Roe v. Wade* as the law and says, "Let's deal in the real world." Voinovich also worked with Bob Dole and Newt Gingrich in early 1995 on the successful Republican move to limit unfunded mandates on the states, and at the same time urged a balanced budget amendment. He was the first governor to endorse Bob Dole for president; he was mentioned for the vice presidential nomination but took himself out of the running.

In February 1997 Senator John Glenn announced he would retire in 1998, and Voinovich, not eligible to run for re-election as governor, was the obvious favorite; he led in polls for nearly two years. His Democratic opponent was another Clevelander (as a boy Voinovich delivered newspapers to her family's house), Cuyahoga County Commissioner Mary Boyle, who lost the 1994 Senate primary but this time had no competition. Boyle campaigned on education, blaming Voinovich for allowing Ohio schools to decline; she called for HMO regulation and a minimum wage increase. She also attacked him for supporting the tax increase which voters rejected in the May primary. Voinovich mostly ignored her attacks and outspent her by almost 3–1, running ads that highlighted his record as governor. He was endorsed by the National Education Association, and proclaimed, "If I get into the Senate, I will probably know more about domestic policy that any member of the Senate." The results showed Voinovich a bit weaker than he had seemed when Glenn announced his retirement. An unknown won 28% against him in the May primary, and in November his margin over Boyle was a decisive but not overwhelming 56%–44%. He lost his home turf in north-and-east Ohio by 51%–49%, though he had won it in 1990, but he had a solid 61%–39% in the rest of Ohio. He won 30% among blacks—a fine showing for a Republican—and carried all income groups above $30,000 and lost by only 56%–42% in union households—not much class warfare there. He won more than 60% among Catholics and white Protestants—no trace of religious wars, either.

Voinovich's work in the Senate bears the clear imprint of his experience as governor and mayor. The governor who raised taxes in 1992 to balance his budget refused to cut them in 1999 and 2000 for fear of not balancing one. In July and August 1999, Voinovich voted against the Republicans' $792 billion tax cut, against the smaller Democratic tax cut, against the bipartisan moderates' compromise tax cut. "I'm an old war horse and I'm running out of time. I've been through the mill . . . 33 years," he said. "I've had to deal with real budgetary problems. I think I understand them as well as most, and my logic tells me you just don't do this." To arguments that government should return money to taxpayers because there was a surplus, he said, "There's an old saying that most of us learned as children that goes, 'If it sounds too good to be true, then it is.'" He was the only Republican to vote in November 1999 against the Republican minimum wage bill, with its tax cuts for small businessmen. In April 2000 he was one of two Republicans to vote against the Republican budget. In July 2000 he was one of four Republicans to vote against estate tax repeal and the only Republican to vote against marriage penalty relief. With Utah Governor Mike Leavitt, he led a group of other Republicans seeking to tax Internet sales; his attempt to get a fix on how much they cost states misfired when the GAO came in with an estimate varying from $300 million to $3.8 billion—i.e., they had no idea at all.

Voinovich is interested not only in maintaining government's revenue flow, but in how government works. As chairman of the Government Reform subcommittee on Government Management, Restructuring and the District of Columbia, he gave some mentoring advice to incoming Washington Mayor Anthony Williams and worked with him to end the operations of the control board which had run government during Marion Barry's last years as mayor. He prepared questions for incoming cabinet and subcabinet officers on management—how would they provide incentives to employees, would they use performance pay, how would they motivate subordinates? In September 1999 he raked OMB deputy director-designate Sally Katzen over the coals for a directive on one of his favorite subjects, federalism, which the Clinton administration had issued in 1998 without consultation with state or local government officials.

Local officials like to say there is no Republican or Democratic way to lay sewer pipes, and that is a subject in which Voinovich has much interest. As an Environment and Public Works subcommittee chairman, he steered to passage in September 2000 a giant energy and water authorization, which included the $1.1 billion Everglades restoration project estimated to eventually cost $7.8 billion. But a month later he voted against a water and power appropriation, which included many Ohio projects, arguing that it spent too much money: authorizing committee members like to keep appropriators on a short leash. In February 2001 Voinovich and Congressman John Dingell announced a WATER-21 program to spend $57 billion on water pipes and sewage treatment facilities; he has argued that federal regulators shouldn't penalize state and local governments for polluting waterways if the federal government hasn't providing financing for proper sewer facilities.

After Congress's late 2000 spending spree Voinovich appears to have concluded that the major obstacle to balancing the budget is not too little revenue but too much spending. In January 2001 he and Democrat Russ Feingold wrote an article decrying the workings of the budget process. They noted that in 2000 the Congress and the president exceeded the budget caps by $92 billion, exceeded Congress's own spending priorities by $34 billion and exceeded Bill Clinton's budget by $11 billion. In March 2001 Voinovich enthusiastically embraced the Bush budget and tax cut package.

Voinovich is the only Serbian-American in the Senate, and as a college freshman wrote a paper on how the United States sold out Yugoslavia at the February 1945 Yalta conference; in 1991 his Serbian relatives were forced out of their homes in the newly independent Croatia. In March and April 1999 he strongly opposed the bombing of Serbia, but he has called Slobodan Milosevic a "war criminal" and tried to convince the State Department to support forces to depose him. In July 1999 he placed a hold on the nomination of Richard Holbrooke to be ambassador to the UN because of his role in the Balkans. He refused to visit Serbia while Milosevic was in power, but went there in December 2000 and was impressed by the new leaders of the Serbian government.

Voinovich's term comes up in 2004. In spring 2000 Cleveland civic leaders urged him to run for mayor again, but he was not interested.

Presidential politics With 21 electoral votes and a tradition of close partisan competition, Ohio is a crucial state in presidential politics. It matched the national average in 1984 and 1988, came close to doing so in 1996 and was only 2 points off in 2000. No Republican has ever been elected president without carrying Ohio; no Democrat, in today's electoral vote arithmetic, can be sure of winning without it. In 2000 George W. Bush, despite holding narrow leads in polls, made Ohio a priority state from start to finish, while the Gore campaign, looking to opportunities elsewhere, pulled out much of its advertising in mid-October, only to put more money in at the end of the month. But Ohio still went to Bush, by a 50%–46% margin. Of the large industrial states—Pennsylvania, Ohio, Michigan, Illinois—Ohio has been consistently the most Republican for 50 years, with the single exception of 1976, when Jimmy Carter ran well in the Southern-accented counties below U.S. 40 and carried the state by 11,000 votes. In recent years this has been because Ohio's metropolitan areas have not generated as large a percentage of culturally liberal high-education voters. In 2000 Bush carried college graduates and those with post-graduate degrees; the latter went heavily for Gore in states like New York and California. There were still traces of New Deal economic voting behavior—those with incomes over $100,000 were 65%–32% for Bush while union members were 67%–30% for Gore. But there are more high-income people and fewer union members than a generation or two ago. Working women were 56%–40% for Gore, but women not working outside the household were 54%–42% for Bush: the feminist left is weaker here than in other big states.

In 1996 Ohio switched its presidential primary from May to March 19, and voted on the same day as Illinois, Michigan and Wisconsin. But even then, just four weeks after New Hampshire, the race was already over. In May 1999 the state legislature voted to move the date to March 7, and Ohio was again seriously contested. Bush and Gore, with serious organizational support, won overwhelming victories as they clinched their parties' nominations.

Congressional districting   Ohio lost two districts in the 1990 Census and one in the 2000 Census; this state that elected 24 congressmen in 1970 will elect 18 in 2002. The current convoluted district lines, with at least three grotesque barbell-shaped districts, are the product of a bipartisan compromise in 1992. But for 2002 Republicans are in firm control of redistricting for the first time in 40 years, and seem determined to alter the district lines for their party's benefit. In early 2001 the member who seemed most likely to lose his seat was Democrat Sherrod Brown of the 13th District; the district was one of only four that exceeded the statewide average, but its barbell shape might have made it a candidate for elimination by nonpartisan redistricters. Brown resisted by threatening to run against Governor Bob Taft; they faced off before, in 1990 for secretary of state, and Taft won, but Taft would surely prefer to face an inarticulate unknown than the energetic and aggressive Brown, whose last name has been a ticket to statewide office in Ohio since the 1950s. Another target is Democrat Ted Strickland of the 6th District, which was originally designed to combine two Republican seats; by chopping off some Democratic territory and adding Republican counties things could get difficult for Strickland, and he too threatened to run for statewide office. Republicans will also surely try to strengthen some of their incumbents: The Ohio delegation currently consists of 11 Republicans and 8 Democrats; after the 2002 election, it could be 12 Republicans and 6 Democrats.

THE PEOPLE: Pop. 2000: 11,353,140; Pop. 1990: 10,847,115, up 4.7% 1990–2000. 4% of U.S. total, 7th largest; 85% White, 11.5% Black, 1.2% Asian, 0.2% Amer. Indian, 1.4% Two + races, 0.8% Other; 1.9% Hispanic Origin. 4.1% Unemployment. 2000 Voting age pop.: 8,464,801. 2000 Turnout: 4,795,989; 57% of VAP. Registered voters (2000): 7,537,822; 1,021,214 D (14%), 1,422,767 R (19%), 5,093,841 unaffiliated and minor parties (68%).

POLITICAL LINEUP: Governor, Bob Taft (R); Lt. Gov., Maureen O'Connor (R); Secy. of State, J. Kenneth Blackwell (R); Atty. Gen., Betty D. Montgomery (R); Treasurer, Joseph Deters (R); Auditor, James Petro (R); State Senate, 33 (12 D, 21 R); Senate Pres. Pro Tempore, Bruce E. Johnson (R); Senate President, Richard Finan (R); State House, 99 (40 D, 59 R); House Speaker, Larry Householder (R). Senators, Mike DeWine (R) and George Voinovich (R). Representatives, 19 (8 D, 11 R).

ELECTIONS DIVISION: 614-466-2585; **FILING DEADLINE FOR U.S. CONGRESS:** February 21, 2002.

2000 Presidential Vote

Bush (R)	2,350,363	(50%)
Gore (D)	2,183,628	(46%)
Nader (Green)	117,799	(3%)
Others	50,208	(1%)

1996 Presidential Vote

Clinton (D)	2,148,309	(47%)
Dole (R)	1,860,768	(41%)
Perot (I)	483,277	(11%)

2000 Republican Presidential Primary

Bush (R)	810,369	(58%)
McCain (R)	516,790	(37%)
Keyes (R)	55,266	(4%)

2000 Democratic Presidential Primary

Gore (D)	720,311	(74%)
Bradley (D)	241,688	(25%)
Other	16,513	(2%)

Gov. Bob Taft (R)

Elected 1998, term expires Jan. 2003, 1st term; b. Jan. 8, 1942, Boston, MA; home, Cincinnati; Yale U., B.A. 1963, Princeton U., M.A. 1967, U. of Cincinnati, J.D. 1976; Protestant; married (Hope).

Elected Office: OH House of Reps., 1976–81; Hamilton Cnty. Commissioner, 1981–90; OH Secy. of State, 1991–98.

Professional Career: Peace Corps, East Africa, 1963–65; State Dept., Vietnam, 1967–69; Budget Officer & Asst. Dir., IL Budget Bureau, 1969–73.

Office: Office of the Governor, 77 S. High St., 30th Fl., 43215, 614-466-3555; Fax: 614-644-0951; Web site: www.state.oh.us.

Election Results

1998 general	Bob Taft (R)	1,678,721	(50%)
	Lee Fisher (D)	1,498,956	(45%)
	Others	176,536	(5%)
1998 primary	Bob Taft (R)	unopposed	
1994 general	George Voinovich (R)	2,401,572	(72%)
	Robert L. Burch, Jr. (D)	835,849	(25%)
	Others	108,817	(3%)

Sen. Mike DeWine (R)

Elected 1994, seat up 2006, 2d term; b. Jan. 5. 1947, Springfield; home, Cedarville; Miami U. of OH, B.S. 1969, OH Northern U., J.D. 1972; Catholic; married (Frances).

Elected Office: Greene Cnty. Prosecuting atty., 1977–81; OH Senate, 1980–82; U.S. House of Reps., 1982–90; OH Lt. Gov., 1990–94.

Professional Career: Practicing atty; Greene Cnty. Asst. Prosecuting atty., 1973–75.

DC Office: 140 RSOB, 20510, 202-224-2315; Fax: 202-224-6519; Web site: www.senate.gov/~dewine.

State Offices: Cincinnati, 513-763-8260; Cleveland, 216-522-7272; Columbus, 614-469-5186; Marietta, 740-373-2317; Toledo, 419-259-7536; Xenia, 937-376-3080.

Committees: *Appropriations*: District of Columbia (RMM); Labor, HHS & Education; Military Construction; Treasury & General Government. *Intelligence (Select)*. *Judiciary*: Antitrust, Business Rights & Competition (RMM); Immigration; Technology, Terrorism & Government Information.

Group Ratings

	ADA	ACLU	AFS	LCV	CON	ITIC	NTU	COC	ACU	NTLC	CHC
2000	10	14	0	29	42	85	69	93	80	91	92
1999	10	—	0	11	8	—	70	82	84	—	—

National Journal Ratings

	1999 LIB	—	1999 CONS		2000 LIB	—	2000 CONS
Economic	49%	—	50%		45%	—	53%
Social	46%	—	52%		34%	—	65%
Foreign	40%	—	56%		43%	—	53%

Key Votes of the 106th Congress

1. Educ. Savings Accts.	Y	5. Review Movie Violence	Y	9. NATO War in Serbia	Y
2. Prescrip. Drug Benefit	Y	6. Gun Show Bckgrnd. Checks	Y	10. Table Cuba Travel Ban	Y
3. Delay Ergonomic Standards	Y	7. Ban Part.-Birth Abortion	Y	11. Nuclear Test-Ban Treaty	N
4. Phase Out Estate Tax	Y	8. Broaden Hate Crimes List	Y	12. Perm. Trade with China	Y

Election Results

2000 general	Mike DeWine (R)	2,665,512	(60%)	($5,699,889)
	Ted Celeste (D)	1,595,066	(36%)	($477,176)
	Others	188,223	(4%)	
2000 primary	Mike DeWine (R)	1,029,860	(80%)	
	Ronald Dickson (R)	161,185	(12%)	
	Frank Cremeans (R)	104,219	(8%)	
1994 general	Mike DeWine (R)	1,836,556	(53%)	($6,084,663)
	Joel Hyatt (D)	1,348,213	(39%)	($4,921,223)
	Joseph J. Slovenec (I)	252,031	(7%)	($192,867)

Sen. George Voinovich (R)

Elected 1998, seat up 2004, 1st term; b. July 15, 1936, Cleveland; home, Columbus; Ohio U., B.A. 1958, Ohio St. U., J.D. 1961; Catholic; married (Janet).

Elected Office: OH House of Reps., 1966–71; Cuyahoga Cnty. Auditor, 1971–76; Cuyahoga Cnty. Commissioner, 1977–78; OH Lt. Gov., 1978–79; Cleveland Mayor, 1979–89; OH Gov., 1990–98.

Professional Career: OH Asst. Atty. Gen., 1963–64.

DC Office: 317 HSOB, 20510, 202-224-3353; Fax: 202-228-1382; Web site: www.senate.gov/~voinovich.

State Offices: Cincinnati, 513-684-3265; Cleveland, 216-522-7095; Columbus, 614-469-6697; Toledo, 419-259-3895.

Committees: *Environment & Public Works*: Clean Air, Wetlands, Private Property & Nuclear Safety (RMM); Transportation & Infrastructure. *Ethics (Select)*. *Governmental Affairs*: Government Management, Restructuring and the District of Columbia (RMM); Investigations (Permanent).

Group Ratings

	ADA	ACLU	AFS	LCV	CON	ITIC	NTU	COC	ACU	NTLC	CHC
2000	10	33	14	14	99	80	68	80	64	68	85
1999	20	—	16	11	99	—	67	82	88	—	—

National Journal Ratings

	1999 LIB —	1999 CONS		2000 LIB —	2000 CONS
Economic	44% —	55%		51% —	48%
Social	42% —	55%		38% —	60%
Foreign	35% —	64%		34% —	64%

Key Votes of the 106th Congress

1. Educ. Savings Accts.	Y	5. Review Movie Violence	N	9. NATO War in Serbia	N
2. Prescrip. Drug Benefit	N	6. Gun Show Bckgrnd. Checks	Y	10. Table Cuba Travel Ban	*
3. Delay Ergonomic Standards	Y	7. Ban Part.-Birth Abortion	Y	11. Nuclear Test-Ban Treaty	N
4. Phase Out Estate Tax	N	8. Broaden Hate Crimes List	Y	12. Perm. Trade with China	Y

Election Results

1998 general	George Voinovich (R)	1,922,087	(56%)	($6,756,712)
	Mary O. Boyle (D)	1,482,054	(44%)	($2,236,137)
1998 primary	George Voinovich (R)	539,424	(72%)	
	David McCollough (R)	207,135	(28%)	
1992 general	John H. Glenn, Jr. (D)	2,444,419	(51%)	($4,974,109)
	Mike DeWine (R)	2,028,300	(42%)	($3,053,156)
	Martha Kathryn Grevatt (I)	321,670	(7%)	

FIRST DISTRICT

From its seven hills, Cincinnati, dubbed the Queen City of the West in the 19th Century, looks down on the curves of the Ohio River. Ohio's first major metropolis, this was the nation's fourth-largest city at the outbreak of the Civil War, a heavily German beehive of riverboats and sausage factories, known in the 1850s as Porkopolis. Cincinnati has long given off an air of the recent past; Mark Twain said he'd like to be there for the apocalypse because everything in Cincinnati is 20 years behind. Growing slowly over many decades, Cincinnati has long-settled good looks and an urbanity somehow consistent with its natural terrain: the bottomlands along the river, the hills and rolling terrain above. In the middle of Cincinnati is Mill Creek, lined with factories; on the hills to the west, above the restored Union Terminal with the children's, historic, and natural history museums, are the modest streetcar suburbs of the 19th Century and the early years of the 20th. On Mount Adams and toward the northeast are set a string of affluent neighborhoods, with stately mansions like the William Howard Taft house, and the comfortable Tudors and co-lonials of the 20th Century bourgeoisie—Reform Jewish as well as WASP and German. But there are also slums, like the Over-the-Rhine district, where blacks rioted and attacked white motorists after a police officer shot a young man in April 2001.

Cincinnati was the site of great innovations: the first iron suspension bridge, in 1867, con-necting Cincinnati to northern Kentucky and designed by John Roebling, who later built the Brooklyn Bridge; the first baseball team, the Red Stockings, in 1869; the country's leading Reform Jewish seminary, Hebrew Union College, in 1875. And if over the past century Cincinnati has not had the growth spurts of cities like Cleveland or Houston, neither has it had their sharp contrac-tions. It has spawned not flashy but solid industries, like the Procter & Gamble soap business, now headquartered in a striking two-towered office complex at the edge of downtown, and it has America's biggest concentration of machine tool makers. Downtown Cincinnati's spruced-up Fountain Square shows off the well-maintained skyscrapers of the past, and its first-class restau-rants still attract a dressy clientele. Old ethnic neighborhoods, crowded with brick row houses on steep hills, keep their thick local accents and special local foods, from German sauerbrauten to Cincinnati chili (try it "four way," served with spaghetti, onions and grated cheese).

The 1st Congressional District of Ohio includes almost all of Cincinnati, except for its affluent eastern edge, plus the middle-class suburbs that cling to the woody hills north and west, all the way to North Bend, the home of President William Henry Harrison, and the Indiana border. Ancestrally Republican, Cincinnati was a German anti-slavery island in a Southern-stock pro-Confederate sea. City elections here were for years competitive between old-line Republicans and a combination of Democrats and Charterites (the latter started by Charles Taft, liberal brother of Senator Robert Taft Sr.). Council members here become celebrities throughout the entire media market. One or both Cincinnati-area congressional districts were represented for decades by former Cincinnati council members, with the understandable exception of Robert Taft Jr. Tradi-tionally, Cincinnati has been a Republican stronghold, and culturally conservative, though the suburbs now are much more Republican than the city. In the 1990s Cincinnati's population declined by the startling amount of 9%, with many whites leaving for suburban counties, which grew rapidly; left behind were poor blacks. The result is a "doughnut effect," said a local demog-rapher: people drive downtown for work but are sick of paying high taxes for poor local services. The 1st District lost 5% of its population in the 1990s and in 2000 was 34% black.

The congressman from the 1st District is Steve Chabot, a Republican first elected in 1994. Like so many other congressmen here, he grew up in Cincinnati and served on the city council. After college he taught elementary school for a year, then went to law school and had a small family-law practice; he was elected to the council in 1985, at 32, and to the Hamilton County Commission in 1990. Chabot stepped forward to run in 1994 amid an odd set of circumstances. In 1992, first-termer Charles Luken (son of longtime incumbent Tom) retired suddenly after the June primary; he is now the mayor of Cincinnati. In the special primary to replace him, moderate Democratic Councilman David Mann defeated liberal state Senator William Bowen, 33%–32%, by 416 votes. In the general, Mann beat by 51%–43% a Republican who ran as an independent because no Republican had made it on the ballot. In the House, Mann voted against the Clinton tax package and for NAFTA, and infuriated local unions; Bowen ran again in 1994 and this time Mann won 49%–48%, by 667 votes. In the fall, Chabot backed the balanced budget amendment, strongly opposed abortion, and attacked Mann's support of Bill Clinton. Chabot won comfortably, 56%–44%.

Chabot has a conservative voting record in the House. He has shown himself willing to take political risks for principle. He voted against the Appalachian Regional Commission, which gives money to southern Ohio, against a $2 million study of light rail in the Cincinnati area, and against a broader bill with $6 million for the National Underground Railroad Freedom Center in the city. Chabot believes Cincinnati should look for ways to solve problems with local resources and not depend on Washington. He opposed farm subsidies and his tight-fistedness created unusual alliances with environmentalists fighting "wasteful" spending. He opposed the 1998 omnibus budget, objecting that it neither cut taxes nor saved Social Security. But he worked with Democrat Zoe Lofgren to allow counties as well as cities to apply for federal anti-crime aid. On the Judiciary Immigration Subcommittee, Chabot played a major role on the 1996 immigration bill. He opposed Chairman Lamar Smith's procedure for employers to verify all employees' immigration status: "The goal of the scheme's backers is to prohibit any employee from holding his or her job unless the federal government has signed off on the arrangement," which Chabot called "1–800-Big-Brother." As a House manager during the Clinton impeachment trial, Chabot pressed Judiciary Chairman Henry Hyde's futile demand for witnesses in the Senate. Chabot had no regrets about his role. "It didn't turn out the way we wanted, but I'm satisfied," he told *The Cincinnati Enquirer*. "I did my best. We were fair." With increased seniority, Chabot in January 2001 became chairman of Judiciary's Constitution Subcommittee—perennially a forum for bitter ideological debate but little legislative action. With Democrat Nick Lampson of Texas, he became a leader on behalf of children who are abducted by a relative, seeking to improve both domestic and international enforcement. He sponsored a bill to allow video recording of proceedings in federal courtrooms. He has been a House leader for a constitutional amendment to protect the rights of crime victims.

Back home, Chabot has been a prime Democratic target. In 1996 the AFL-CIO spent over $1 million, running nearly 2,000 television ads against him. A light moment came in October when Democratic challenger Mark Longabaugh, a top aide in Dick Gephardt's 1988 presidential campaign, ran an ad showing Chabot's yellow pages listing and noting that he took clients in DUI cases; Chabot responded with an ad showing the white pages and asking, "Where's Mark Longabaugh been listed for 15 years? Not here!" Chabot won 54%–43%. In 1998 Chabot was opposed by Cincinnati Mayor (and Council member) Roxanne Qualls. This was one of the hardest fought races in the country, and one of the most expensive: Chabot spent $1.5 million, Qualls $1.2 million. Qualls argued that Chabot's views were too conservative for the district. Chabot called for broad-based tax cuts, and cuts in pork barrel projects and corporate welfare. They disagreed on the partial-birth abortion ban and school vouchers. Impeachment also became an issue. But Chabot won 53%–47%, just a bit closer than his earlier elections. In 2000, after Qualls decided against another run, Chabot defeated 26-year-old lawyer John Cranley 53%–44%, even as Al Gore narrowly carried the district; the contest received little Democratic money and its chief national attention was a post-election MTV special on young candidates.

That may have been Democrats' last serious chance to defeat Chabot for a while. Republicans are in firm control of redistricting, and the 1st District needs to add 88,000 people. Redistricters will undoubtedly add heavily Republican suburbs and perhaps remove some central city precincts to make the district safely Republican.

Cook's Call *Probably Safe*. Chabot's conservative voting record and the marginal nature of this Cincinnati-based district have made him an attractive target for Democrats for the last six years. But Chabot has proven to be an impressive campaigner and has never won with less than 53% of the vote, even as Democratic presidential nominees have racked up wins in his district (Clinton won here in 1996 by 7%, Gore won by 3% in 2000). With Republicans controlling redistricting in the state, Chabot may receive a friendlier district for 2002.

THE PEOPLE: Pop. 2000: 542,618; Pop. 1990: 571,052, down 5% 1990–2000. 62.5% White, 34% Black, 1.3% Asian, 0.2% Amer. Indian, 1.5% Two+ races, 0.5% Other; 1.1% Hispanic Origin.

Rep. Steve Chabot (R)

Elected 1994, 4th term; b. Jan. 22, 1953, Cincinnati; home, Cincinnati; William & Mary Col., B.A. 1975, N. KY U., J.D. 1978; Catholic; married (Donna).

Elected Office: Cincinnati City Cncl., 1985–90; Hamilton Cnty. Comm., 1990–94.

Professional Career: Elem. Schl. teacher, 1975–76; Practicing atty., 1978–94.

DC Office: 129 CHOB 20515, 202-225-2216; Fax: 202-225-3012; Web site: www.house.gov/chabot.

District Office: Cincinnati, 513-684-2723.

Committees: *International Relations* (13th of 26 R): East Asia & the Pacific; Middle East & South Asia. *Judiciary* (8th of 21 R): Commercial & Administrative Law; Crime; The Constitution (Chmn.). *Small Business* (7th of 19 R): Tax, Finance & Exports.

Group Ratings

	ADA	ACLU	AFS	LCV	CON	ITIC	NTU	COC	ACU	NTLC	CHC
2000	5	21	0	21	97	95	76	76	100	97	100
1999	10	—	0	38	95	—	80	84	96	—	—

National Journal Ratings

	1999 LIB —	1999 CONS		2000 LIB —	2000 CONS
Economic	0% —	84%		6% —	85%
Social	4% —	91%		0% —	79%
Foreign	3% —	92%		39% —	57%

Key Votes of the 106th Congress

1. Patient Bill of Rights	N	5. Bar RU-486 $ for FDA	Y	9. NATO War in Serbia	N
2. Accelerate Min. Wage	N	6. Display 10 Commandments	Y	10. Perm. Trade with China	Y
3. Strike Ban on Ergo. Stnd.	N	7. Gun Show Bkgrnd. Checks	N	11. Debt Relief for 3rd World	N
4. Ovrd. Estate Tax Veto	Y	8. Ban Part.-Birth Abortion	Y	12. Drop Cuba Econ. Embargo	N

Election Results

2000 general	Steve Chabot (R)	116,768	(53%)	($1,099,555)
	John Cranley (D)	98,328	(45%)	($465,561)
	Other	5,332	(2%)	
2000 primary	Steve Chabot (R)	unopposed		
1998 general	Steve Chabot (R)	92,421	(53%)	($1,623,706)
	Roxanne Qualls (D)	82,003	(47%)	($1,229,276)

SECOND DISTRICT

The most Republican major metro area in the nation over the longest time span has been Cincinnati. Back in the 1850s, when Harriet Beecher Stowe wrote *Uncle Tom's Cabin* here, Cincinnati was an island of German, pro-Union, Republican sentiment in a Southern, Democratic, pro-slavery sea. Later Cincinnati attracted fewer southern and eastern European immigrants than Great Lakes industrial cities like Cleveland, Detroit and Chicago; its ethnic character (like its physical appearance) and its political preference have remained pretty well fixed. Even many of the Appalachians here are Republicans, from Civil War Republican counties in the hills. Democratic constituencies here never got very large: economically, it was never a strong CIO town;

culturally, it is home to a strong anti-pornography movement that, among other things, was the site of obscenity charges filed against *Hustler* publisher Larry Flynt. The local Republican record remains intact: It was the only million-plus metro area that George Bush and Bob Dole carried by more than 50% in 1992 and 1996; George W. Bush won Hamilton County handily, and he got more total votes here than in much-larger Cuyahoga and Franklin counties.

For 140 years after 1852, Cincinnati and surrounding Hamilton County were divided by a north-south line into two congressional districts. After the 1990 Census, redistricters created one mostly urban district that leaned a bit to the Democrats and a mostly suburban district that spread out into the countryside and was heavily Republican. Ohio's 2d Congressional District includes the affluent eastern suburbs around elite Indian Hill and newer Montgomery, plus a few prosperous precincts of Cincinnati itself; it includes recent growth areas like northeastern Hamilton County and Anderson Township south of the Little Miami River, plus the far west part of Hamilton County, all heavily Republican; it heads east along the Ohio River to include Clermont County, a fast-growth area for 20 years, plus two rural counties and an oddly-shaped sliver of Warren County between Cincinnati and Dayton. Clermont and Warren Counties grew rapidly in the 1990s, even as Cincinnati's population fell by 9%. The 2d District is heavily Republican; it was George W. Bush's best district in Ohio in 2000.

The congressman from the 2d District is Rob Portman, a Republican first elected in May 1993, who quickly became one of the most important legislators in the House. Portman has good connections both at home and in Washington. He grew up in Cincinnati, campaigned for his predecessor Bill Gradison before turning 21, went to work after law school for Patton Boggs & Blow in Washington and then for a Cincinnati law firm. In 1989 he worked in the Bush White House, first in the counsel's office and then in legislative affairs; in 1992 he was U.S. representative to the United Nations Human Rights Council. He was back in Cincinnati in January 1993 when Gradison unexpectedly resigned from Congress to become head of the Health Insurance Association of America. Portman ran for the seat with Gradison's endorsement and impressive financial backing from the Cincinnati establishment. In the primary he faced former Congressman Bob McEwen, who had represented the 6th District to the east for 12 years and then lost it after a contentious primary in 1992, and businessman Jay Buchert, president of the National Association of Home Builders, who ran a vitriolic campaign against both Portman and McEwen. With help from a radio ad by Barbara Bush, Portman won with 36% of the vote, to 30% for McEwen, who carried counties he had once represented, and 25% for Buchert. Portman won the general with 70%. He has had no re-election problems since then.

In the House, Portman made himself a rising star and an expert on several issues. As part of the Contract with America, he helped floor-manage in early 1995 the unfunded mandates bill—a large responsibility for one who hadn't even been a member two years. This measure, signed by Bill Clinton, required unfunded mandates over $50 million for local governments to be subject to a point of order in the House or Senate, which can be overridden only by majority vote. Other bills he authored or co-authored that were signed by Clinton included the Drug Demand Reduction Act to streamline the federal anti-drug bureaucracy; the Tropical Forest Conservation Act to write off part of the debt to the United States from less-developed countries in exchange for them committing to protect their forests; the National Underground Railroad Network to Freedom Act to preserve those sites within the National Park Service; and a measure protecting state and local employee pension plans from raids by local governments. With a seat on Ways and Means, Portman became active on several causes. He shepherded, as co-chairman with Senator Bob Kerrey of the National Commission on Restructuring the Internal Revenue Service, a bipartisan package to define taxpayer rights and make the 100,000-plus employee agency more user friendly. With Democrat Ben Cardin, he filed a bill to make pensions more portable, permit increased savings, and relax federal restrictions; the House passed their bill 401-25 in 2000, and it was passed again in May 2001 by 407–24 and seemed headed for enactment. With Bob Matsui, he won broad support to repeal the 3% excise tax on telephone service, which critics derided as the "Spanish-American War tax" because of it was instituted as a temporary measure to finance that war, which ended in 1898.

Portman's far-flung activities made him a close ally of Chairmen Bill Archer and later, Bill

Thomas, at Ways and Means, and of Speaker Dennis Hastert, who named him to the influential post as chairman of the Republican leadership. Adding to this web of alliances was a tight relationship with George W. Bush: It began during the early 1990s when Portman worked for the older Bush, and continued during Governor Bush's presidential campaign, when Portman served quietly but actively as an adviser to Bush and his top staff on Washington policies and politics and when he coached Bush and Dick Cheney for their debates. There were rumors—not denied by Portman—that Bush inquired whether he would serve as White House chief of staff and he was offered the directorship of the Office of Management and Budget, but Portman decided that he could be more helpful to Bush and to his own career by becoming a presidential trouble-shooter and continuing his move up the House's leadership ladder.

At home, Portman sponsored a community-based anti-drug effort, urging schools, businesses, churches, and local media to discourage drug abuse; he boasts that it takes no federal money. He takes no contributions from political action committees. Redistricting will change the boundaries of the district. The 2d make take in some central Cincinnati precincts, to make the 1st District safer for Republican Steve Chabot, but for the most part it will probably move west, to remove part of the 6th District represented by Democrat Ted Strickland, who is likely to be one of the Republican redistricters' prime targets.

Cook's Call   *Safe.* Drawn to be the more Republican of the Cincinnati-based districts, the 2d is actually about the most Republican in the state; Bush won the district by 34% in 2000. Portman has had no trouble racking up big margins here in the past and should not have much to worry about in 2002.

THE PEOPLE: Pop. 2000: 634,061; Pop. 1990: 570,779, up 11.1% 1990–2000. 94.5% White, 2.6% Black, 1.4% Asian, 0.2% Amer. Indian, 0.9% Two+ races, 0.3% Other; 1% Hispanic Origin.

2000 Presidential Vote		
Bush (R)	188,484	(65%)
Gore (D)	91,344	(32%)
Nader (Green)	6,010	(2%)
Others	2,192	(1%)

1996 Presidential Vote		
Dole (R)	153,627	(58%)
Clinton (D)	90,571	(34%)
Perot (I)	19,894	(7%)

Rep. Rob Portman (R)

Elected May 1993, 4th term; b. Dec. 19, 1955, Cincinnati; home, Terrace Park; Dartmouth Col., B.A. 1979, U. of MI, J.D. 1984; Methodist; married (Jane).

Professional Career: Practicing atty., 1984–88; Assoc. Cnsl., White House, 1989; Dpty. Asst. & White House Legis. Affairs Dir., 1990–91; Alternate U.S. Rep. to UN Human Rights Comm., 1992.

DC Office: 238 CHOB 20515, 202-225-3164; Web site: www.house.gov/portman.

District Offices: Batavia, 513-732-2948; Cincinnati, 513-791-0381.

Committees: *Republican Leadership Chairman. Budget* (16th of 24 R). *Standards of Official Conduct* (2d of 5 R). *Ways & Means* (14th of 24 R): Oversight.

Group Ratings

	ADA	ACLU	AFS	LCV	CON	ITIC	NTU	COC	ACU	NTLC	CHC
2000	0	8	0	36	86	100	63	85	87	70	100
1999	5	—	0	25	81	—	69	92	76	—	—

National Journal Ratings

	1999 LIB —	1999 CONS		2000 LIB —	2000 CONS
Economic	0% —	84%		29% —	67%
Social	29% —	69%		26% —	71%
Foreign	39% —	60%		33% —	62%

Key Votes of the 106th Congress

1. Patient Bill of Rights	*	5. Bar RU-486 $ for FDA	Y	9. NATO War in Serbia	Y
2. Accelerate Min. Wage	N	6. Display 10 Commandments	Y	10. Perm. Trade with China	Y
3. Strike Ban on Ergo. Stnd.	N	7. Gun Show Bkgrnd. Checks	N	11. Debt Relief for 3rd World	N
4. Ovrd. Estate Tax Veto	Y	8. Ban Part.-Birth Abortion	*	12. Drop Cuba Econ. Embargo	N

Election Results

2000 general	Rob Portman (R)	204,184	(74%)	($406,952)
	Charles Sanders (D)	64,091	(23%)	($12,599)
	Other	9,266	(3%)	
2000 primary	Rob Portman (R)	unopposed		
1998 general	Rob Portman (R)	154,344	(76%)	($359,922)
	Charles W. Sanders (D)	49,293	(24%)	($9,174)

THIRD DISTRICT

Dayton, once a medium-sized city known as the home of the typical American voter, became the name of the international peace agreement reached in November 1995 that stopped the slaughter in the former Yugoslavia. The 21 days of negotiating took place at Wright-Patterson Air Force Base, outside the city limits, but the people of Dayton played a role. "From the time we landed at the airport," wrote U.S. negotiator Richard Holbrooke, "until the time we left, we felt that we were in a community that was literally praying for us. People were lighting candles in their windows, there were signs all over the airport and on the byways. That would never have happened in New York or in Washington. And it made a tremendous impression on people."

Dayton has made a difference in people's lives in America and around the world for many years. Here, just south of the old National Road that spans the Midwest, was the home of James Ritty, who in 1879 invented the cash register—that indispensable instrument of mass retail trade—and of John Henry Patterson, who bought it from Ritty for $6,500 in 1884 and established the National Cash Register company (NCR). It was home of a former Patterson subordinate, Tom Watson Sr., who feuded with him and went off to found IBM. It was in Dayton in the 1890s that Wilbur and Orville Wright, tinkering in their bicycle shop and observing the horseless carriages driven through Dayton's streets, experimented with kites and gliders and constructed the first wind tunnel in the world and the first heavier-than-air flying machine, which they took to everwindy Kitty Hawk, North Carolina, to fly in December 1903. A few years later, Dayton's Charles Kettering invented the automatic starter for cars. In the 1970s and 1980s, Dayton's economy seemed to be sputtering. General Motors, the area's largest employer, was in trouble; NCR was overtaken in a merger. But by the mid-1990s Dayton's unemployment rate was below the national average and its economic growth faster. There are now more scientists, engineers, computer specialists and technicians here than GM workers. The area's small manufacturers and suppliers have shown that Dayton's spirit of tinkering and innovation, practical organization and mechanical dreaming, are still thriving, as much as its neighborliness and compassion. But the population here, as elsewhere in Ohio, is spreading out from the city centers to the countryside. In the 1990s Dayton had a 9% population loss and Montgomery County lost 3%.

Politically, the Dayton area has been known as a bellwether since Richard Scammon and Ben Wattenberg's *The Real Majority* of 1970 profiled the Dayton housewife. Since then, the area has mostly voted for statewide and national winners, leaning just a bit more Democratic than Ohio as a whole; Al Gore beat George W. Bush in Montgomery County 50%–48%. Ohio's 3d Congressional District includes Dayton and all but a small corner of the surrounding county.

The congressman from Dayton is Tony Hall, a Democrat first elected in 1978. Hall grew up in Dayton, where his father was once mayor; in 1966 and 1967 he served in the Peace Corps in Thailand, while the Vietnam war was raging not far away. He returned home and in 1968, at 26, was elected to the state legislature, where he served for a decade. When the 3d District came open in 1978, he easily won in a generally Republican year. In the early 1980s Hall became a born-again Christian. He opposes abortion, but his number one cause has been to alleviate world hunger. When Texas Congressman Mickey Leland died in a plane crash in Ethiopia, Hall succeeded him as chairman of the Select Committee on Hunger, and decried the civil wars and infrastructural deficiencies that obstructed food delivery throughout much of Africa (he talks less about how African socialism has reduced food supplies). He has traveled to such places as Somalia, Haiti, Uganda, Rwanda, North Korea and the former Yugoslavia, and has been deeply moved by those suffering from hunger. At home he has started "gleaning" programs to use leftover hotel and restaurant food to feed the poor; he also applied these programs elsewhere—including the Atlanta Olympics and both parties' national convention cities. He set up the first 800 telephone number for food emergency assistance. In 2000, he picketed diamond stores, describing how battles for the mines promoted civil wars in Africa.

In the House, Hall has suffered setbacks, but he has been effective in getting results. In 1993 the House responded to pressure from freshman Democrats to trim the institution and voted not to reauthorize the Select Committee on Hunger, and Hall embarked on a 22-day fast. Then in 1995 the Republican House voted to eliminate all funded caucuses, including his Hunger Caucus. But Hall's dedication, hard work, and obvious sincerity have probably made more difference than a staff structure. His 15-year-old son died of leukemia in July 1996, after a bone marrow transplant. But Hall worked on, urging the Democratic National Convention to adopt "tolerance language" recognizing and welcoming those Democrats like Hall who oppose abortion; in 2000, Al Gore talked with him several times about hunger issues. That year, Hall took a two-day "hunger tour" of Appalachia. He was among the first American officials to visit North Korea, where he nearly moved doctors to tears when he carried 10 boxes of medicine to a hospital that conducts surgery without adequate anesthesia and no antibiotics. Following a visit to Iraq in 2000, he said that sanctions should remain in place against Saddam Hussein's regime because of its continued threat of proliferation of nuclear weapons. With co-sponsorship from civil-rights hero John Lewis, Hall filed a resolution apologizing for slavery and said that he was "stunned" by the controversy it aroused. When George W. Bush pushed for "faith-based" initiatives, Hall signed on early and he joined House Republican Conference Chairman J.C. Watts in sponsoring a bill embracing several tax changes to promote that goal.

In his district, Hall fights hard to maintain Wright-Pat as the center for Air Force research and development and has saved the Dayton Aviation Heritage National Historic Park. He made sure the federal government took responsibility for cleaning up the Energy Department's former Mound Nuclear Weapons Plant, which is being converted to a high-tech industrial park. For more than 20 years, Hall has easily won reelection. There were rumors in early 2001 that Hall would receive an appointment from the Bush administration, perhaps to head the Peace Corps, but as of May 2001 he had not. Nevertheless, Republican redistricters, who have to add 75,000 people to the district, can hardly help making it more Republican. This is not likely to threaten Hall's hold on the district, but it could make it a more desirable district for a Republican if Hall does not run.

Cook's Call *Potentially Competitive.* Although this district can be rather competitive on the presidential level (Gore won here by just 2% in 2000), Tony Hall has had little trouble holding onto this Dayton-based seat for the past 20 years. But redistricting could be Hall's toughest challenge yet: With the state slated to lose one seat in redistricting, some are suggesting that this seat may be the one to go. There is also talk that Hall may retire. Either way, this district will have to be altered significantly for 2002 election.

THE PEOPLE: Pop. 2000: 556,039; Pop. 1990: 570,913, down 2.6% 1990–2000. 76.4% White, 20% Black, 1.3% Asian, 0.2% Amer. Indian, 1.5% Two+ races, 0.5% Other; 1.3% Hispanic Origin.

2000 Presidential Vote

Gore (D)	114,125	(50%)
Bush (R)	108,896	(47%)
Nader (Green)	4,671	(2%)
Others	1,895	(1%)

1996 Presidential Vote

Clinton (D)	115,168	(50%)
Dole (R)	95,003	(41%)
Perot (I)	18,194	(8%)

Rep. Tony P. Hall (D)

Elected 1978, 12th term; b. Jan. 16, 1942, Dayton; home, Dayton; Denison U., A.B. 1964; Presbyterian; married (Janet).

Elected Office: OH House of Reps., 1968–72; OH Senate, 1972–78.

Professional Career: Peace Corps, Thailand, 1966–67; Real estate broker, 1968–78.

DC Office: 1432 LHOB 20515, 202-225-6465; Web site: www.house.gov/tonyhall.

District Office: Dayton, 937-225-2843.

Committees: *Rules* (2d of 4 D): Rules & Organization of the House (RMM).

Group Ratings

	ADA	ACLU	AFS	LCV	CON	ITIC	NTU	COC	ACU	NTLC	CHC
2000	75	21	100	79	79	65	23	52	21	18	57
1999	80	—	100	75	40	—	15	25	12	—	—

National Journal Ratings

	1999 LIB —	1999 CONS		2000 LIB —	2000 CONS
Economic	66%	— 34%		69%	— 30%
Social	50%	— 50%		50%	— 50%
Foreign	74%	— 23%		63%	— 36%

Key Votes of the 106th Congress

1. Patient Bill of Rights	Y	5. Bar RU-486 $ for FDA	Y	9. NATO War in Serbia	Y
2. Accelerate Min. Wage	Y	6. Display 10 Commandments	Y	10. Perm. Trade with China	N
3. Strike Ban on Ergo. Stnd.	Y	7. Gun Show Bkgrnd. Checks	Y	11. Debt Relief for 3rd World	Y
4. Ovrd. Estate Tax Veto	N	8. Ban Part.-Birth Abortion	Y	12. Drop Cuba Econ. Embargo	Y

Election Results

2000 general	Tony P. Hall (D)	177,731	(83%)	($192,835)
	Regina Birch (NL)	36,516	(17%)	
2000 primary	Tony P. Hall (D)	unopposed		
1998 general	Tony P. Hall (D)	114,198	(69%)	($122,866)
	John S. Shondel (R)	50,544	(31%)	($20,726)

FOURTH DISTRICT

Central Ohio looks mostly like farmland to the traveler. Yet this is manufacturing country, indeed one of America's premier manufacturing areas, where most people make their living in factories in small towns and on rural highways. These places seem far from anywhere important, yet are on one of the great east-west routes—the old rail lines and newer highways—that cross the country. They seem old-fashioned and rooted in an older technological time, yet here, in Wapakoneta, a typically Ohioan-Indian name, is the hometown of Neil Armstrong, first man on the moon. Politically, this crossroads on the flat limestone plains of northern Ohio is one of the Republican heartlands of the United States. On the B&O tracks from Dayton to Toledo that intersect the east-west rail lines used by Richard Nixon in 1968, Ronald Reagan in 1984, George Bush in 1992 and Bill Clinton in 1996 to make whistle-stop campaign tours, one can summon up memories of past campaign styles and loyalties.

Much of central Ohio makes up the 4th Congressional District, oddly regular in shape for an Ohio district. It includes Wapakoneta; Lima, whose name was pulled from a hat; Findlay, where a museum holds the captain's bathtub from the *U.S.S. Maine*, sunk in the Havana harbor in 1898; Marion, where young Socialist-to-be Norman Thomas delivered newspapers edited by President-to-be Warren Harding; and Mansfield, home of John Sherman, one of Ohio's great 19th Century Republican statesmen, and his brother General William Tecumseh Sherman, who marched his troops through Georgia for the Union and refused to be considered for president. This has been a Republican stronghold since the Civil War, industrial since the late 19th Century, quietly prosperous most of the years since World War II, though shaken by the collapse of the auto-steel-coal industries after the oil shock of 1979. It gave solid margins to Bob Dole in 1996 and George W. Bush in 2000.

The congressman here is Mike Oxley, first elected in June 1981, now chairman of the Financial Services Committee. Oxley grew up in Findlay, worked for his Republican congressman, served three years in the FBI after law school, then came home and was elected to the legislature in 1972, at 28. After the incumbent died, Oxley ran for the House and won the special during the heyday of Reagan popularity by the surprisingly narrow margin of 378 votes. Since then he has been reelected without difficulty.

In 1983 Oxley got a seat on the Energy and Commerce Committee, which under Chairman John Dingell had a broad and expanding jurisdiction over complex regulatory issues. Although in the minority for 14 years, Oxley played a significant role in major legislation, able to unite his own Republicans and work with Democrats across the aisle. He was a major player on the 1990 Clean Air Act, working with Ohioans of both parties to protect that state's high-sulfur power plants and big factories from being saddled with high costs. On the Commerce Telecommunications Subcommittee, over opposition from Democrats, he required new frequencies of the radio spectrum to be allocated not by lottery but by auction; the resulting auctions for personal communications systems, cell phones, and pagers have been the largest in history and have supplied the Treasury with billions in revenue. He took a major part in the 1996 Telecommunications Act. As he earlier proposed, the act permits regional Bell companies to enter long distance and manufacturing services, and allows long distance carriers into local phone service; when a federal court overturned its ban of indecency on the Internet, he crafted a new provision that was inserted in the omnibus 1998 spending bill to restrict minors' access to adult material. Oxley has also worked to open foreign markets to U.S. telecom manufacturers and to let foreigners own U.S. telephone and broadcasting companies. He is a supporter of the Resource Conservation and Recovery Act, regulating interstate transport of solid waste, and has worked to give states more power to ban the import of out-of-state garbage (much New York garbage is trucked to Ohio).

In late 1996 Oxley fought with Louisiana's Billy Tauzin for the chairmanship of the Commerce Telecommunications and Finance Subcommittee. Speaker Newt Gingrich had promised the spot to Tauzin when he switched parties in August 1995 and Tauzin, who was first elected in May 1980, has 13 months' more seniority. The solution was to split the subcommittee, whose jurisdiction was perhaps greater than that of any other in Congress. Tauzin got first choice and took Telecommunications, Trade and Consumer Protection; Oxley got Finance and Hazardous Materials. He played an important role in the landmark financial services deregulation passed in November 1999, which broke down the walls between banks, securities firms and insurance companies. Although regarded as pro-business, and although he has raised vast sums from regulated industries, Oxley has often taken stands they have vigorously opposed. He and Democrat Edward Markey pushed successfully for stock exchanges to list prices in dollars and cents rather than eighths of a dollar; this means more money for investors and less for brokers. With John Dingell, Oxley moved to require mutual funds to give investors quarterly information about fees. Oxley has taken quick action to reverse regulators when convinced they are wrong. When the FCC ruled in December 1999 that a religious broadcaster with a noncommercial license must present instructional broadcasting 50% of the time, and that proselytizing did not qualify, Oxley sponsored a bill to reverse the ruling and got 50 co-sponsors; in January 2000 the FCC reversed itself 4–1. Oxley opposed the Clinton FCC plan to license hundreds of low-power FM stations on the grounds it would interfere with existing stations, and got Dingell's support; his bill passed 274–110 in April 2000. His bill to reform boxing—a longtime interest—passed the House by voice vote in May 2000; it would limit promoters' contracts to one year and bar them from having a financial interest in a boxer. His bill to give the Army Corps of Engineers authority to relocate a school as a cleanup option passed 353–63 in May 2000; it would enable the Corps to move the River Valley school in Marion County.

For much of 1999 and 2000 Oxley was involved in a complex behind-the-scenes fight with

Tauzin over the chairmanship of the Commerce Committee. Republicans' six-year term limit on chairmen was clicking in on Thomas Bliley, who was retiring; Gingrich's decision to count Tauzin's years as a Democrat gave him the edge in seniority but Oxley proclaimed that he had spent "14 long years in the minority." As early as 1999 some members were thinking about a fallback position: Tauzin would get Commerce and Oxley Banking, with enlarged jurisdiction. The passage of financial services deregulation that fall gave power to a process argument, that it no longer made sense to have one committee with jurisdiction over securities and insurance and another with jurisdiction over banking. Oxley nonetheless pressed hard for Commerce, but lost in the Republican Steering Committee. Speaker Dennis Hastert persuaded Republicans to expand Banking's jurisdiction and rename it Financial Services. The leadership was not unhappy with passing over senior Banking Republican Marge Roukema, and the other Republican seeking that chairmanship, Richard Baker, supported Oxley and the jurisdiction switch. So in January 2001 Oxley became chairman of Financial Services, with all of Banking's jurisdiction plus securities and insurance. The committee is now the second largest in the House, with 70 members. In February 2001 Oxley announced that he would seek to revise the securities laws in a deregulatory manner, would reduce SEC fees (which are supposed to fund the agency, but bring in $2 billion while the SEC budget is only $377 million), modernize laws governing financial institutions and promote agency-sharing to track down fraudulent brokers.

Cook's Call *Safe.* Oxley has had little trouble winning in this solidly Republican district and has never won with less than 61% in 10 re-election contests. Like most of the Ohio delegation, Oxley will feel the impact of redistricting (his district is about 40,000 people short). But with Republicans calling the shots on line drawing, Oxley should be well protected for 2002.

THE PEOPLE: Pop. 2000: 591,795; Pop. 1990: 570,917, up 3.7% 1990–2000. 92.5% White, 5.2% Black, 0.5% Asian, 0.2% Amer. Indian, 1.1% Two+ races, 0.5% Other; 1.2% Hispanic Origin.

2000 Presidential Vote			1996 Presidential Vote		
Bush (R)	149,495	(62%)	Dole (R)	118,298	(50%)
Gore (D)	83,642	(35%)	Clinton (D)	88,758	(37%)
Nader (Green)	5,232	(2%)	Perot (I)	28,248	(12%)
Others	2,719	(1%)			

Rep. Michael G. Oxley (R)

Elected June 1981, 10th term; b. Feb. 11, 1944, Findlay; home, Findlay; Miami U. (OH), B.A. 1966, OH St. U., J.D. 1969; Lutheran; married (Patricia).

Elected Office: OH House of Reps., 1972–81.

Professional Career: FBI Spec. Agent, 1969–71; Practicing atty., 1972–1981.

DC Office: 2233 RHOB 20515, 202-225-2676; Web site: www.house.gov/oxley.

District Offices: Findlay, 419-423-3210; Lima, 419-999-6455; Mansfield, 419-522-5757.

Committees: *Financial Services* (Chmn. of 37 R).

Group Ratings

	ADA	ACLU	AFS	LCV	CON	ITIC	NTU	COC	ACU	NTLC	CHC
2000	0	21	0	0	31	100	63	95	81	68	80
1999	5	—	0	0	44	—	58	96	76	—	—

National Journal Ratings

	1999 LIB —	1999 CONS		2000 LIB —	2000 CONS
Economic	0%	84%		6%	85%
Social	25%	72%		32%	67%
Foreign	45%	54%		33%	62%

Key Votes of the 106th Congress

1. Patient Bill of Rights	N	5. Bar RU-486 $ for FDA	Y	9. NATO War in Serbia	Y
2. Accelerate Min. Wage	N	6. Display 10 Commandments	Y	10. Perm. Trade with China	Y
3. Strike Ban on Ergo. Stnd.	N	7. Gun Show Bkgrnd. Checks	N	11. Debt Relief for 3rd World	N
4. Ovrd. Estate Tax Veto	Y	8. Ban Part.-Birth Abortion	Y	12. Drop Cuba Econ. Embargo	N

Election Results

2000 general	Michael G. Oxley (R)	156,510	(67%)	($790,624)
	Daniel Dickman (D)	67,330	(29%)	($29,528)
	Ralph Mullinger (LIB)	8,278	(4%)	
2000 primary	Michael G. Oxley (R)	unopposed		
1998 general	Michael G. Oxley (R)	112,011	(64%)	($616,196)
	Paul McClain (D)	63,529	(36%)	($33,824)

FIFTH DISTRICT

Undergirded by limestone, as flat and fertile as any place in America, northwest Ohio sits astride the land routes in parts of the country that were economically the most productive in the years they were settled. Here were the "Firelands," reserved for Connecticut Yankees whose farms were burned in the Revolution, and the neat and substantial small towns built by German Protestants in the mid-19th Century. Northwest Ohio is the beginning of the great corn and hog belt that stretches through Indiana and Illinois into Iowa, and was long a heartland of the Republican party. Fremont, settled by abstemious Yankees, was the home of President Rutherford B. Hayes, whose wife Lucy served only lemonade in the White House; nearby Sandusky, settled by Germans who built big wineries and breweries, now has its own Merry-Go-Round Museum; Port Clinton, on Lake Erie, bills itself as the "Walleye Capital of the World" and drops a walleye on New Year's Eve to rival Times Square. Not far away is Milan, birthplace of the great inventor and capitalist Thomas Edison.

This is prime industrial country: its limestone, rail connections and location near the Great Lakes have spurred the growth of a factory economy that in dollar terms is far more important than agriculture. After the first settlement, northwest Ohio grew steadily for many decades, surging ahead in the 1950s and 1960s as its small factories supplied the big auto plants in Detroit and Ohio cities. Growth lagged noticeably in the early 1980s, when the domestic auto industry collapsed, but returned in the 1990s as small firms sold not only to the Big Three but to foreign customers.

The 5th Congressional District sweeps across northwest Ohio, from Grafton, just beyond the westward expansion of metropolitan Cleveland, across the limestone plains through Sandusky, its harbor on Lake Erie, and home of the giant Cedar Point amusement park—rated the top amusement park in the world in 1998, 1999 and 2000. It continues through Milan and Fremont, past part of the university town of Bowling Green and the Toledo suburb of Perrysburg, to the western Ohio towns of Defiance and Napoleon (wonderful names!). Its factories include the world's largest ketchup plant in Fremont and the largest washing machine plant in Clyde, both in Sandusky County, plus the largest baking soda plant in Old Fort. It avoids Toledo and its suburbs directly east and west. Historically, this was a solidly Republican district from the Civil War through the New Deal and up through the 1970s. In 1996 it gave only a narrow plurality to Bob Dole, but then it voted 58%–39% for George W. Bush in 2000.

The congressman from the 5th is Paul Gillmor, a Republican first elected in 1988. He grew up in northern Ohio, practiced law and was elected, at 27, to the state Senate in 1966, where he later became president. He is a professional, though not especially provocative, politician. For years Gillmor eyed this seat and waited for incumbent Delbert Latta to retire; he even passed a state law blocking the party from designating Latta's son as nominee if Latta resigned. In the 1988 primary Gillmor beat the junior Latta by exactly 27 votes out of 63,000 cast.

Gillmor focused on internal reform in his first years in the House, working to freeze committee funding, and on local issues, repealing the Coast Guard recreational boating user fees. On the now-renamed Energy and Commerce Committee, he backed limits on out-of-state solid waste and greater competition for cable TV and telephone companies. He has called for amending the

Public Utility Holding Company Act to allow utilities to offer telecom services and wants to require corporations to disclose charitable contributions. He favors cost-benefit analysis and risk assessment for federal regulations and has a solidly conservative record on economics. Reflecting his small-town economics, Gillmor wants mutual funds to more fully disclose their tax-related actions to shareholders. As chairman of a Republican task force on the Federal Communications Commission, he sought regulatory changes that would make the agency more attuned to the marketplace. "The change in technology frequently bypasses the regulatory structure that we set up," Gillmor said. He is comfortable with Republican moderates on cultural and foreign issues, and has been a member of both the Tuesday Group and the Leadership's Whip Team. In January 2001, he became chairman of the Subcommittee on Environment and Hazardous Materials. He said that he wanted to resolve long-deadlocked Superfund legislation, in part by giving more authority to the states.

On local issues, Gillmor saved the National Rifle Matches at Camp Perry by creating a private non-profit corporation to conduct them; they were imperiled by liberals in the appropriations process. He got the National Weather Service to keep a radar facility in Fort Wayne so that tornado-prone northwest Ohio would not have to rely on Cleveland. And he won funds to renovate the Rutherford B. Hayes home in Fremont.

Gillmor has been re-elected easily. Redistricting will probably push him south or east, but should not pose a problem.

Cook's Call   *Safe.* Gillmor is well entrenched in this Republican-leaning district. It will need to expand a bit in redistricting but don't look for a competitive race here in 2002.

THE PEOPLE: Pop. 2000: 589,716; Pop. 1990: 570,946, up 3.3% 1990–2000. 94.3% White, 2.3% Black, 0.4% Asian, 0.2% Amer. Indian, 1.2% Two+ races, 1.6% Other; 3.7% Hispanic Origin.

2000 Presidential Vote			1996 Presidential Vote		
Bush (R)	145,019	(57%)	Dole (R)	108,255	(44%)
Gore (D)	100,446	(40%)	Clinton (D)	102,862	(42%)
Nader (Green)	6,071	(2%)	Perot (I)	32,365	(13%)
Others	2,715	(1%)			

Rep. Paul E. Gillmor (R)

Elected 1988, 7th term; b. Feb. 1, 1939, Tiffin; home, Old Fort; Ohio Wesleyan U., B.A. 1961, U. of MI, J.D. 1964; Methodist; married (Karen).

Military Career: Air Force, 1965–66.

Elected Office: OH Senate, 1966–88.

Professional Career: Practicing atty., 1965–88.

DC Office: 1203 LHOB 20515, 202-225-6405; Web site: www.house.gov/gillmor.

District Offices: Defiance, 419-782-1996; Norwalk, 419-668-0206; Port Clinton, 419-734-1999.

Committees: *Energy & Commerce* (6th of 31 R): Environment & Hazardous Materials (Chmn.); Oversight & Investigations; Telecommunications & The Internet. *Financial Services* (15th of 37 R): Capital Markets, Insurance & Government Sponsored Enterprises; Financial Institutions & Consumer Credit.

Group Ratings

	ADA	ACLU	AFS	LCV	CON	ITIC	NTU	COC	ACU	NTLC	CHC
2000	10	14	0	14	20	94	53	80	76	56	80
1999	15	—	0	0	28	—	53	88	80	—	—

National Journal Ratings

	1999 LIB	—	1999 CONS		2000 LIB	—	2000 CONS
Economic	16%	—	78%		36%	—	63%
Social	25%	—	72%		45%	—	54%
Foreign	39%	—	60%		25%	—	69%

Key Votes of the 106th Congress

1. Patient Bill of Rights	N	5. Bar RU-486 $ for FDA	Y	9. NATO War in Serbia	N
2. Accelerate Min. Wage	N	6. Display 10 Commandments	Y	10. Perm. Trade with China	Y
3. Strike Ban on Ergo. Stnd.	N	7. Gun Show Bkgrnd. Checks	N	11. Debt Relief for 3rd World	N
4. Ovrd. Estate Tax Veto	Y	8. Ban Part.-Birth Abortion	Y	12. Drop Cuba Econ. Embargo	N

Election Results

2000 general	Paul E. Gillmor (R)	169,857	(70%)	($245,036)
	Dannie Edmon (D)	62,138	(26%)	
	Other	11,345	(5%)	
2000 primary	Paul E. Gillmor (R)	unopposed		
1998 general	Paul E. Gillmor (R)	123,979	(67%)	($264,320)
	Susan Davenport Darrow (D)	61,926	(33%)	($8,532)

SIXTH DISTRICT

Early settlers of Ohio came from the south, where the Ohio River was a superhighway through the forest. Yankees traveled down the Ohio from Pittsburgh and founded Marietta in 1788 as Ohio's first town. About the same time, George Washington procured bounty lands for Revolutionary War veterans in the Virginia Military District of Ohio between the Scioto and Miami rivers, centered on Chillicothe. In Marietta the Yankees built New England-style churches; in Chillicothe the young Virginian Thomas Worthington, who became governor of Ohio, built his home, Adena, designed by architect Benjamin Latrobe. Virginians soon outnumbered New Englanders, and their traces remain on the landscape, which is laid out in irregular-shaped parcels as in Virginia, unlike the Northwest Ordinance's checkerboard grid imposed on most of the Midwest. There have been lasting political effects too. These rolling lands south of U.S. 40 have never attracted much industry; most people here speak with an accent that sounds Southern to northern Ohioans; they retain, with conservative cultural attitudes, a Democratic heritage that manifests itself on occasion. One sign of Bill Clinton's shrewd campaign instincts was that the 1992 Clinton-Gore bus trip out of the New York convention went through this part of Ohio, and that Clinton returned in 1996, carrying Ohio both times in part because of margins he won in many southern Ohio counties. In his own campaign, Al Gore had less appeal here, losing by a solid margin.

The 6th Congressional District covers most of southern Ohio, from Marietta down the Ohio River to the gritty industrial towns of Ironton and Portsmouth; it runs across the hilly landscape to include part of Chillicothe and all of Piketon, and west over to the Warren County suburbs of Dayton and Cincinnati. It has no large central cities and mostly avoids metropolitan areas. Politically, this has been not just a battlefield but also a killing ground: During the 1990s, four incumbent congressmen were defeated in the current boundaries of the 6th District. The first two were Republicans, who were thrown together in 1992 by redistricting, Clarence Miller and Bob McEwen; the third was a Democrat elected in the wake of the Clinton bus tour, Ted Strickland; the fourth was a Republican elected in 1994, Frank Cremeans, who lost to Strickland two years later and then lost the Republican primary in 1998 and the Senate primary in 2000.

Strickland did not win this seat without trying: he ran unsuccessfully in 1976, 1978 and 1980, won in 1992, lost in 1994, and won again in 1996 (all of the last three were 51%–49% races). The son of a steelworker and eighth of nine children, Strickland is a Methodist minister, was director of a children's home, and then a prison psychologist (at Lucasville, site of a 1993 riot) and psychology professor at Shawnee State College. He and his wife have both made their way up as counseling professionals. He once described his goal as "building communities where children are nurtured and educated and protected and cared for."

In his first term Strickland voted for the Clinton budget and tax package, but against the 1994 crime bill because of its gun control provisions and against NAFTA. In the 1994 campaign he was on the defensive, under attack for supporting the tax increase. As the election neared, Strickland suggested there might be a need to increase taxes to pay for health care reform; Cremeans seized on this and ran a last-minute ad that may have made the difference in his win. Cremeans compiled a conservative voting record; he was the first member of Congress to support Steve Forbes for president. In the 1996 campaign, Strickland attacked Cremeans for Medicare "cuts" and scaling down the Earned Income Tax Credit, which he called a tax increase on the poor. Strickland won by the seemingly obligatory margin of 51%–49%, with crucial votes in the counties around Gallipolis. Back on Capitol Hill, Strickland got a seat on the Energy and Commerce Committee, where he sought a moratorium on implementation of Clean Air Act regulations that affect industries in his region. He complained in March 2001 when the Nuclear Regulatory Commission failed to challenge the planned closing of the uranium-enrichment plant in Piketon, which would eliminate more than 1,700 local jobs and leave the nation only one other such facility, in Paducah, Kentucky. Strickland has been vigilant in pursuing safety claims at the plant, which was privatized in 1998; in 2001 he complained when Labor Secretary Elaine Chao sought to transfer to the Justice Department the new program to compensate workers who suffered adverse effects at nuclear plants.

In 1998 and 2000 Strickland was re-elected by more comfortable margins. In 1998 he faced Lieutenant Governor Nancy Hollister, but she was hurt by opposition from local conservatives unhappy with her support of abortion rights and resentful that party bosses pushed her candidacy, while Strickland benefited from labor unions' on-the-ground campaign. Strickland won by the huge (for this district) margin of 57%–43%—the first time a 6th District incumbent was re-elected since 1990. In 2000, against conservative Michael Azinger, Strickland won 58%–40%. Azinger won Warren County 65%–33%, but Strickland rolled up huge majorities in Athens, Lawrence and Scioto—a combined 70%–28%.

Strickland is likely to have more trouble in 2002. Republicans control redistricting, and have made it no secret that Strickland is one of their prime targets. One possibility is that they may move more of the Ohio River counties to the heavily Republican 1st District, and make the 6th run in more of a north-south direction east of Columbus, perhaps adding Republican-leaning Fairfield and Licking Counties. Strickland has said that if he gets a heavily Republican district he may run statewide; he volunteered to run for lieutenant governor on a ticket with Sherrod Brown, another likely redistricting target, who may run for governor.

Cook's Call *Competitive.* Strickland's easy victories here in 1998 and 2000 belie the marginal nature of this sprawling southern Ohio district. Bush won here by 15% in 2000 and Clinton won by just 1% in 1996. Republicans, who control the line-drawing process, may boost their chances of winning here in 2002. This is a seat to watch.

THE PEOPLE: Pop. 2000: 620,901; Pop. 1990: 570,804, up 8.8% 1990–2000. 95.6% White, 2.2% Black, 0.6% Asian, 0.3% Amer. Indian, 1.1% Two+ races, 0.2% Other; 0.7% Hispanic Origin.

2000 Presidential Vote			1996 Presidential Vote		
Bush (R)	136,835	(56%)	Clinton (D)	106,479	(44%)
Gore (D)	99,615	(41%)	Dole (R)	101,991	(43%)
Nader (Green)	5,828	(2%)	Perot (I)	28,942	(12%)
Others	3,366	(1%)			

Rep. Ted Strickland (D)

Elected 1996, 5th term; b. Aug. 4, 1941, Lucasville; home, Lucasville; Asbury Col., B.A. 1963, M.A., 1967, U. of KY, Ph.D. 1980; Methodist; married (Frances).

Elected Office: U.S. House of Reps., 1992–94.

Professional Career: Assoc. Minister, Trinity Methodist Church, 1967–68; Dir. of Soc. Svcs., KY Methodist Home, 1968–70; Consulting psychologist, Southern OH Correctional Facility, 1985–92, 1995–96; Prof., Shawnee St. U., 1988–92, 1994–96.

DC Office: 336 CHOB 20515, 202-225-5705; Fax: 202-225-5907; Web site: www.house.gov/strickland.

District Offices: Jackson, 740-286-5199; Marrieta, 740-376-0868; Portsmouth, 740-353-5171; Wilmington, 937-382-4585.

Committees: *Energy & Commerce* (19th of 26 D): Energy & Air Quality; Health; Oversight & Investigations.

Group Ratings

	ADA	ACLU	AFS	LCV	CON	ITIC	NTU	COC	ACU	NTLC	CHC
2000	90	64	100	71	38	50	22	31	12	15	20
1999	85	—	100	69	37	—	19	20	12	—	—

National Journal Ratings

	1999 LIB	—	1999 CONS		2000 LIB	—	2000 CONS
Economic	71%	—	28%		73%	—	26%
Social	64%	—	35%		62%	—	37%
Foreign	77%	—	22%		74%	—	24%

Key Votes of the 106th Congress

1. Patient Bill of Rights	Y	5. Bar RU-486 $ for FDA	N	9. NATO War in Serbia	*
2. Accelerate Min. Wage	Y	6. Display 10 Commandments	N	10. Perm. Trade with China	N
3. Strike Ban on Ergo. Stnd.	Y	7. Gun Show Bkgrnd. Checks	N	11. Debt Relief for 3rd World	Y
4. Ovrd. Estate Tax Veto	N	8. Ban Part.-Birth Abortion	Y	12. Drop Cuba Econ. Embargo	Y

Election Results

2000 general	Ted Strickland (D)	138,849	(58%)	($544,415)
	Michael Azinger (R)	96,966	(40%)	($202,525)
	Other	4,759	(2%)	
2000 primary	Ted Strickland (D)	unopposed		
1998 general	Ted Strickland (D)	102,852	(57%)	($1,050,157)
	Nancy P. Hollister (R)	77,711	(43%)	($1,008,844)

SEVENTH DISTRICT

The hills and plains of central Ohio are dotted with towns and small cities that have been manufacturing centers almost since they were settled in the early 19th Century, when the dominant technologies were the waterwheel and the open forge. In the decades since, they have been replaced by one new technology after another, and the local manufacturing economy, sometimes with uncomfortable fits and starts, has adjusted and advanced. There were painful job losses here in the early 1980s, but small business has grown since then. As old factories shut down, new ones open that are more productive; the results are higher incomes and, though not often remembered, far less of the backbreaking hard work and drudgery that were almost everyone's lot in supposedly better times.

The 7th Congressional District is made up of a G-shaped slice of the central part of Ohio surrounding Columbus. Its largest city is Springfield, where the truck plant of Navistar, formerly International Harvester, has long been the biggest employer. To the south are the eastern suburbs of Dayton around Wright-Patterson Air Force Base, whose name recalls the Dayton-based fathers of the airplane and the cash register. In the northern end of the 7th District are Bellefontaine, site of the first concrete street in America, and a few miles away, Marysville, the site of Honda's first U.S. plant, where American workers assemble Honda Accords. The district has always been Republican territory. It backed the policies of Ohio Republican President William McKinley—tariff protection, railroad regulation, antitrust suits against monopolies, discouragement of labor unions—and of Governor James Rhodes—low taxes, promotion of new businesses and jobs. It is culturally conservative and economically mostly satisfied with free markets. It has given good margins to recent Republican presidential contenders.

The 7th District's congressman is David Hobson, a Republican from Springfield first elected in 1990 after eight years in the state Senate. Hobson sold real estate for many years and retains properties in the area. He has a moderate to conservative voting record. After a 13-year-old Ohio girl was killed when her coat drawstring was caught in a school bus door, Hobson got clothing manufacturers to voluntarily remove drawstrings longer than three inches. He works on local issues, from advocating Wright-Patterson Air Force Base as home for the Joint Strike Force research center and other Pentagon contracts, to improving the U.S. 33 bypass. He worked with Dayton Democrat Tony Hall to secure a federal waiver for the Dayton Area Health Plan and to establish Dayton's National Aviation Historic Park.

Hobson is a key member of the Appropriations Committee, where he is chairman of the

Military Construction Subcommittee—a useful slot for a representative concerned about a local Air Force base which has been suffering job losses and may be threatened in another round of base closings. He said that his top priority is to ensure that military families have the quality housing and secure work facilities they deserve; following a trip to bases in Germany and Italy, he criticized the troops' "substandard" housing there. Responding to reports of inadequate military health care, he won passage of a requirement that all military doctors hold unrestricted state medical licenses and complete education requirements. He also serves on the Appropriations Defense Subcommittee. Hobson was a force for moderation among Republicans in January 1996 after Bill Clinton's budget vetoes and the federal shutdown, when he said, "We wanted to prove to the country that we are reasonable people." He seemed more at home with the bipartisan cooperation on budget, health care, and welfare reform that later prevailed. Hobson worked on the Republican proposal for Medicare reform and sought support from the Blue Dogs. He was a lieutenant of Speaker Newt Gingrich, protecting his interests at the ethics committee and during the aborted 1997 coup. And he was a close ally of Budget Committee chairman and presidential candidate John Kasich, who represented the adjacent 12th District until he retired in 2000.

His steady demeanor and backroom skills continue to make Hobson a resource for House Republican leaders—advising them on budget issues and working with Dennis Hastert on health care legislation even before his Illinois friend became speaker. But Hobson does not seek the spotlight on Capitol Hill: When leadership meetings break up and many head for the ever-present microphones and television cameras, Hobson typically passes them by. "That isn't my style," he says. "I'm not doing this to build Dave Hobson into a national name." During the 2000 presidential recount, he served as an observer in Florida and complained that the system was "flawed" because it had no uniform standards for hand counts.

Hobson has not been seriously challenged for re-election. Redistricting may push his district to the south to pick up parts of the current 6th, where Republicans hope to oust Democrat Ted Strickland.

Cook's Call   *Safe.* Hobson has been easily re-elected to this west-central Ohio district since 1990. While redistricting will have an impact on every district in the state, Hobson is unlikely to feel much fallout in this heavily Republican area.

THE PEOPLE: Pop. 2000: 620,156; Pop. 1990: 570,939, up 8.6% 1990–2000. 92% White, 5.2% Black, 0.9% Asian, 0.3% Amer. Indian, 1.3% Two + races, 0.4% Other; 1% Hispanic Origin.

2000 Presidential Vote			1996 Presidential Vote		
Bush (R)	146,981	(58%)	Dole (R)	115,393	(47%)
Gore (D)	99,811	(39%)	Clinton (D)	100,509	(41%)
Nader (Green)	5,518	(2%)	Perot (I)	25,373	(10%)
Others	2,254	(1%)			

Rep. David Hobson (R)

Elected 1990, 6th term; b. Oct. 17, 1936, Cincinnati; home, Springfield; OH Wesleyan U., B.A. 1958, OH St. U., J.D. 1963; Methodist; married (Carolyn).

Military Career: OH Air Natl. Guard, 1958–63.

Elected Office: OH Senate, 1982–90, Majority Whip, 1986–88, Pres. Pro-Tem, 1988–90.

Professional Career: Real estate agent, 1969–90; Restaurant owner, 1977–93.

DC Office: 1514 LHOB 20515, 202-225-4324; Fax: 202-225-1984; Web site: www.house.gov/hobson.

District Offices: Lancaster, 740-654-5149; Springfield, 937-325-0474.

Committees: *Appropriations* (12th of 35 R): Defense; Military Construction (Chmn.); VA, HUD & Independent Agencies.

Group Ratings

	ADA	ACLU	AFS	LCV	CON	ITIC	NTU	COC	ACU	NTLC	CHC
2000	0	29	0	14	16	83	60	90	72	61	80
1999	20	—	16	6	37	—	56	83	80	—	—

National Journal Ratings

	1999 LIB — 1999 CONS		2000 LIB — 2000 CONS	
Economic	30%	— 64%	29%	— 67%
Social	40%	— 59%	40%	— 60%
Foreign	49%	— 50%	25%	— 69%

Key Votes of the 106th Congress

1. Patient Bill of Rights	N	5. Bar RU-486 $ for FDA	Y	9. NATO War in Serbia	Y
2. Accelerate Min. Wage	N	6. Display 10 Commandments	Y	10. Perm. Trade with China	Y
3. Strike Ban on Ergo. Stnd.	N	7. Gun Show Bkgrnd. Checks	N	11. Debt Relief for 3rd World	N
4. Ovrd. Estate Tax Veto	Y	8. Ban Part.-Birth Abortion	Y	12. Drop Cuba Econ. Embargo	N

Election Results

2000 general	David Hobson (R)	163,646	(68%)	($706,884)
	Donald Minor (D)	60,755	(25%)	
	John Mitchel (I)	13,983	(6%)	($15,695)
	Other	3,802	(2%)	
2000 primary	David Hobson (R)	unopposed		
1998 general	David Hobson (R)	120,765	(67%)	($662,103)
	Donald Minor (D)	49,780	(28%)	
	James A. Schrader (Lib)	9,146	(5%)	($13,221)

EIGHTH DISTRICT

The far west end of Ohio—where U.S. 40, the old National Road, heads straight as an arrow in its last miles across Ohio to Indiana, and the rail lines crisscross the land from Cincinnati to Dayton—has since the early 20th Century housed some of the nation's prime industrial country. Here the Great and Little Miami rivers drain south into the Ohio; U.S. 40 jogs southward twice to go over the Miami and Stillwater River dams, built after the great flood of 1913 that killed 361 people in Dayton and caused $1 billion in damage. Around Dayton and Cincinnati, in large factory towns like Middletown and Hamilton and smaller factory towns like Troy and Piqua, Ohioans, after the recession of the early 1980s, adapted to new conditions and began to produce exports to Europe, Latin America and Asia as well as for the American market. And as city centers slowly emptied out, comfortable suburban tracts were growing in what were once open fields, or near the giant year-round Traders' World flea market on I-75 between Cincinnati and Dayton.

The 8th Congressional District of Ohio covers much of this territory, including most of four counties north of Dayton and U.S. 40, Preble County west of Dayton, and Butler County between Dayton and Cincinnati. About half its people live in Butler, around Hamilton and Middletown and in suburbs north of Cincinnati—now a single metropolitan strip from northern Kentucky to U.S. 40 north of Dayton. Politically, this is solidly Republican territory.

The congressman from the 8th District, John Boehner (pronounced *bayner*), is a Republican first elected in 1990 and now chairman of the Committee on Education and the Workforce. Boehner grew up in Cincinnati, one of 12 children, and after college moved just beyond the line to Butler County; he started a plastics packaging company, served on the Union Township Board of Trustees, and in 1984, at 34, was elected to the Ohio House. He won the congressional seat in the 1990 primary, by beating not one but two of his predecessors—incumbent Buz Lukens, who inexplicably ran after he was convicted of having sex with a 16-year-old girl, and Tom Kindness, who gave up the seat to run against Senator John Glenn in 1986 and then, as Boehner put it, deserted the district to become a Washington lobbyist. Boehner won 49%, to 32% for Kindness and 17% for Lukens. Boehner has since been re-elected without difficulty.

In the House, Boehner joined the Gang of Seven, young freshman Republicans who insisted on revealing the names of all 355 members who had overdrafts at the House bank, and then went on to assail Democratic leaders and Republican go-alongers on the pay raise and the House Post

Office scandal. They also argued that members of Congress should be subject to the laws they impose on other citizens; in 1992 Boehner invited OSHA inspectors to his office, where they found what would have been 15 violations if Congress were subject to its regulations. That same month Boehner took the lead in the formal adoption of the 27th Amendment to the Constitution, proposed by James Madison with the original Bill of Rights in 1789, to prohibit Congress from varying its pay during its current term. Boehner's Gang of Seven infuriated House veterans, but they struck a chord around the nation. In the process Boehner became a top lieutenant of then-Minority Whip Newt Gingrich, raising money for Republican candidates, and managing Gingrich's campaign for Republican leader. He was a major player in drafting and championing the 10-point Contract With America. After the 1994 election, he ran for chairman of the Republican Conference and, with Gingrich's backing, beat California's Duncan Hunter 122–102.

That made Boehner number four in the Republican leadership, and he worked hard to prepare the party message and to enforce discipline on issues from repealing the assault weapons ban to fielding ethics charges against Gingrich. By any recent historic standard, Republicans held together quite well during their first term in the majority. Boehner also pushed for the Freedom to Farm bill, which phased out most subsidies—the most important farm legislation since 1933, and one that deprives farm-state Democrats of an issue on which they have long won.

The next two years were a turbulent time for Boehner. The ethics investigation on Gingrich placed Boehner in the middle of a legal altercation after a Florida couple taped Boehner's cellular telephone conversation with Republican leaders while he was driving through the state. The couple, Democratic activists, presented the tape to their congresswoman, Karen Thurman, who suggested they turn it over to Jim McDermott of Washington, the senior Democrat on the House ethics committee, who then made the contents available to *The New York Times*. In 1998 Boehner sued McDermott in federal court for invasion of privacy; the trial judge ruled that the suit would infringe First Amendment rights, but the D.C. Circuit Court of Appeals reversed the decision. McDermott appealed to the Supreme Court; it is expected to send the case back to the appeals court after issuing a ruling in a similar case in May 2001 which found that journalists may not be prevented from reporting information obtained illegally.

Boehner's leadership position became imperiled because of his role in the July 1997 attempted coup against Gingrich. Boehner's allies said that he did not back ouster efforts, while his critics contended that he was disloyal and ought to have alerted Gingrich. The incident soured their relationship and led to complaints that Boehner was failing to effectively deliver the party's message. Boehner later conceded that he underestimated the rebels' threats, which at the time "only struck me as slightly more than average." Even so, he played a key role in coordinating the House's one-vote passage of major reform of federal banking laws, and took the lead for Republicans in seeking tax cuts and debt reduction in response to the new federal surplus. Republicans' loss of five seats in the November 1998 election, plus memories of the coup, created a demand for a change in leadership. Members who thought Boehner had not produced a convincing enough Republican message united to back J.C. Watts to replace Boehner as Conference chairman. After Dick Armey was re-elected over Steve Largent's challenge, Boehner's fate was sealed: Watts won 121–93.

Many speculated that Boehner would be disheartened and retreat from legislative work. But he rebounded quickly. "I don't think there was anything more important than standing tall, smiling and being myself," he said. "It would actually allow me to heal more quickly and show people that I could get knocked down, but I could get back up and do fine." He prepared a multi-step plan of action and plunged into his role as chairman of the Employer-Employee Relations Subcommittee. By June 1999 the subcommittee passed eight bills restructuring managed care and health insurance; Speaker Dennis Hastert, pleased by Boehner's initiative and dismayed that other committees had not acted, adopted these as the Republican health care agenda. Boehner's managed care bill, which had an independent review board to resolve disputes, was eventually defeated 284–145 in October 1999, but it prevented Republicans from having no alternative to the Dingell-Norwood bill that eventually passed the House—and which went nowhere in the conference committee, on which Boehner served. With Amo Houghton, Boehner also produced a bill to allow employers to hire investment advisers for employees with 401(k) plans, and a bill making stock options more attractive to employees. Still a free market man on agriculture, Boehner co-sponsored with Senator Richard Lugar a package of trade measures and tax cuts intended to make the endangered Freedom to Farm Act work, and sponsored a bill based on one by Democrat David Obey to get rid of the Northeast Dairy Compact and provide fair competition for Midwestern dairy farmers. With John Kasich, he called for a permanent ban on Internet taxes.

In the meantime, Boehner continued to raise money, collecting $1 million and distributing $600,000 to other Republicans. Some believe he pondered seeking a leadership post after the 2000 election, but instead he sought the chairmanship of the Education and the Workforce Committee; the incumbent chairman, William Goodling, was retiring. Boehner's opponents were the second-ranking Republican, Tim Petri, and the less senior Peter Hoekstra, who had been running the seemingly stalled investigation into illegal Teamster Union contributions. Boehner got Armey's support and Hastert told him, "If I were you, I'd go ahead." He helped Ralph Regula oust Bud Shuster from his post on the Steering Committee, which in turn chose him. He quickly took charge of the committee, eliminating Hoekstra's Oversight Subcommittee (he got Select Education instead) and moving Historically Black Colleges and Universities to the 21st Century Competitiveness Subcommittee. Democrats howled in protest, because other colleges were handled by the Select Education Subcommittee and 21st Century handled juvenile delinquency and child abuse. They boycotted all subcommittee meetings for a month until Boehner and ranking Democrat George Miller agreed that legislative authority over the HBCUs would remain in 21st Century, but oversight would go to Select Education.

In March 2001 Boehner, who in 1995 sought to abolish the Department of Education, put together the House version of the Bush education program. It included early reading programs, public school choice, block grants of many education programs, a $1,500 voucher for children in failing schools and a charter state initiative (states could waive federal regulations by promising to achieve specific goals in five years). In response to conservative Republicans like Hoekstra, who mistrusted national testing, it provided for testing by NAEP of "another reliable sample of student achievement." On that issue Miller, like Bush, favored NAEP or NAEP-type tests. But Miller and other Democrats opposed vouchers. Putting together a bipartisan education package on a committee which has long been one of the most partisan in Congress—labor unions since 1958 insisted on vetting all Democratic members, and Republicans have been mostly pro-management conservatives—was a considerable achievement; it passed the House 384–45. Boehner, seemingly ousted from power in December 1998, now seems to be a more powerful member than ever, and on major substantive issues at that.

Cook's Call *Safe*. Boehner, who has never won with less than 71% since 1990, is safely ensconced in this western Ohio district. Redistricting will alter the lines here, but it should not be enough to make Boehner nervous about his re-election chances.

THE PEOPLE: Pop. 2000: 625,445; Pop. 1990: 570,837, up 9.6% 1990–2000. 94% White, 3.3% Black, 1.1% Asian, 0.2% Amer. Indian, 1% Two+ races, 0.5% Other; 1.1% Hispanic Origin.

2000 Presidential Vote

Bush (R)	167,339	(63%)
Gore (D)	89,283	(34%)
Nader (Green)	5,304	(2%)
Others	2,320	(1%)

1996 Presidential Vote

Dole (R)	125,577	(52%)
Clinton (D)	89,331	(37%)
Perot (I)	26,111	(11%)

Rep. John A. Boehner (R)

Elected 1990, 6th term; b. Nov. 17, 1949, Cincinnati; home, West Chester; Xavier U., B.S. 1977; Catholic; married (Debbie).

Military Career: Navy, 1969.

Elected Office: Union Township Bd. of Trustees, 1981–85, Pres., 1984; OH House of Reps., 1984–90.

Professional Career: Pres., Nucite Sales Inc., 1976–90.

DC Office: 1011 LHOB 20515, 202-225-6205; Fax: 202-225-0704; Web site: www.house.gov/boehner.

District Offices: Hamilton, 513-870-0300; Troy, 937-339-1524.

Committees: *Agriculture* (2d of 27 R): General Farm Commodities & Risk Management; Livestock & Horticulture. *Education & the Workforce* (Chmn. of 27 R): 21st Century Competitiveness; Employer-Employee Relations.

Group Ratings

	ADA	ACLU	AFS	LCV	CON	ITIC	NTU	COC	ACU	NTLC	CHC
2000	5	29	0	7	48	100	66	85	87	72	93
1999	10	—	16	0	44	—	61	92	91	—	—

National Journal Ratings

	1999 LIB	—	1999 CONS		2000 LIB	—	2000 CONS
Economic	0%	—	84%		0%	—	94%
Social	23%	—	76%		26%	—	71%
Foreign	42%	—	57%		31%	—	68%

Key Votes of the 106th Congress

1. Patient Bill of Rights	N	5. Bar RU-486 $ for FDA	Y	9. NATO War in Serbia	N
2. Accelerate Min. Wage	N	6. Display 10 Commandments	Y	10. Perm. Trade with China	Y
3. Strike Ban on Ergo. Stnd.	N	7. Gun Show Bkgrnd. Checks	N	11. Debt Relief for 3rd World	N
4. Ovrd. Estate Tax Veto	Y	8. Ban Part.-Birth Abortion	Y	12. Drop Cuba Econ. Embargo	N

Election Results

2000 general	John A. Boehner (R)	179,756	(71%)	($1,042,008)
	John Parks (D)	66,293	(26%)	($31,098)
	Other	7,254	(3%)	
2000 primary	John A. Boehner (R)	unopposed		
1998 general	John A. Boehner (R)	127,979	(71%)	($1,165,947)
	John W. Griffin (D)	52,912	(29%)	

NINTH DISTRICT

In the 1920s Toledo was one of America's boomtowns. This was "a decade of fabulous figures," Harlan Hatcher wrote: The Willys-Overland plant employed 25,000 workers and turned out an automobile every 30 seconds; the city built $20 million coal and iron ore docks; the Libbey-Owens-Ford merger made Toledo, with local supplies of natural gas and sand, the nation's largest glass manufacturer; the city built a new museum and transcontinental airport. Toledo had long been well-situated, where the Maumee River empties into Lake Erie, where two dozen rail lines connected it with the East Coast and Chicago and the coal fields of Kentucky and West Virginia. It was also well positioned to be a center of the brash rising auto industry, a national leader when it first produced the Jeep in the 1940s. But by the late 1970s and early 1980s auto company management had allowed the unions to bid wages and benefits too high while watching quality decline, to the point that consumers would not buy enough American-made cars for the industry to survive without vast subsidy or major shrinkage. Subsidy, beyond the temporary Chrysler loan and a few small trade barriers, was not forthcoming; so Toledo and other auto-dependent cities went through tough times. Revival was on its way, however. Toledo's small manufacturers in search of markets here and abroad showed energy and ingenuity lacking in the big auto and glass companies 20 years prior. Toledo in the 1990s produced one of America's hottest vehicles, the Jeep Cherokee; the old plant was set to close, but the city offered Chrysler $300 million in incentives to stay—a new plant was built along I-75. But the Daimler Company's purchase of Chrysler in 1998 was a mixed blessing for Toledo. In February 2001—after announcing that the new Jeep Liberty would be produced at the new assembly plant—the firm also scheduled cutbacks, including production of the Jeep Wrangler in Toledo.

Ohio's 9th Congressional District is centered on Toledo, spreading east to the flatlands of Ottawa County, south to Bowling Green State University, and west to rural Fulton County. Toledo has been heavily Democratic since CIO unions organized the plants in the late 1930s; the collapse of the auto industry so unnerved the district that in 1980 it voted for Ronald Reagan and elected a Republican congressman. In 1982, it became solidly Democratic again, and has been ever since. But like Ohio's other districts based in the old industrial cities, the 9th lost population in the 1990s; Toledo was hit with a 6% loss and has dropped more than 70,000 since 1970.

The congresswoman from the 9th District is Marcy Kaptur, a Democrat elected in 1982. The senior female House Democrat, she has called for more portraits and statues of women in the Capitol. Kaptur is fervent and principled, hard-working and dedicated, always a loyal daughter of Toledo. She grew up there in a blue-collar neighborhood, where her parents worked at local auto plants and the family operated a small grocery store, and she has spent almost her entire career in the public sector. After being the first in her family to attend college and then working eight years as an urban planner in Toledo, she got a job in the Carter White House; she was shrewd enough to return home in 1982 when no other Democrat would run for the House seat and won, although outspent by 3–1. She saw Toledo's economy nosedive, and felt intensely the pain of ordinary people who played by the rules but ended up losing because of larger economic forces.

Kaptur's great cause is trade. She has long been convinced that Toledo and places like it have lost jobs and industry because of unfair trade practices by the Japanese and low-wage competition in countries like China and Mexico. America must use its global trading power to advance democracy and the rule of law and to raise all peoples' living standards, she says. If "capitalism laughs at boundaries," as the historian Fernand Braudel wrote, Kaptur, with her faith in the public sector, has worked hard to make those boundaries stronger, and not something to be snickered at. She pressured the Japanese to buy more American auto parts, but is leery of Japanese investment in the United States. She has proposed to prohibit top government officials from representing foreign corporations for five years and foreign governments forever after they leave office; she also would ban campaign contributions by foreign individuals or corporations—a provision she got attached to the Shays-Meehan campaign finance reform bill that passed the House. She favors a constitutional amendment to permit campaign spending limits. Kaptur was probably Congress's most vocal and dedicated opponent of NAFTA. She visited the Mexican border in spring 1993, and returned home with soil and water samples to demonstrate the pollution there. She argued that 100,000 jobs had been transferred from Ohio to Mexico. She criticized Bill Clinton for doing nothing for sagging U.S. industries and for ignoring her and other Democrats opposed to NAFTA. She brought to this issue a commitment that was genuinely moving, and did not drop trade issues even after it passed. In early 1995, she argued forcefully against Clinton's proposal to bail out the Mexican peso with $40 billion of U.S. loan guarantees; Clinton was forced to abandon the legislation and proceed with an administrative rescue. Even as the two nations' economic ties boomed, Kaptur complained that the trade was one-sided toward Mexico. In 2000, she was a vocal opponent of permanent normal trade relations with China.

Kaptur opposes funding for abortion and favors the partial-birth abortion ban. She has worked on local projects, like securing a new Maumee River crossing, which has been billed as the largest bridge project in Ohio history, and was the original sponsor in 1987 of the World War II Memorial planned for the Washington Mall. She has set up the Golden Eagle Awards for exemplary companies and the Vulture Awards for poor corporate citizens. On the Appropriations Agriculture Subcommittee, where she is the ranking Democrat, Kaptur passed amendments requiring farmers to plant or conserve land in order to receive transition payments, and requiring more careful monitoring by the Agriculture Department of food aid to foreign countries. In September 1998, she expressed "sadness, anger and disgust" about the Lewinsky scandal and urged Clinton to "choose an honorable course and do what is right for our nation." She added, "If he resigned tomorrow, it wouldn't be enough in my judgment," and suggested he might perform community service.

Kaptur is exceedingly popular in Toledo, and has run far ahead of party lines in the 9th District. She has also become something of a national political figure. In August 1995 she appeared before Ross Perot's United We Stand and made a rousing speech, mostly on trade, that had delegates cheering. Perot praised her and offered his vice presidential nomination in August 1996; she turned it down. She also has also declined opportunities to run for statewide office. But her trips to Iowa in early 2001 sparked rumors of a presidential bid in 2004. She has published a book on women in Congress, has hosted a weekly radio show on nearly 100 stations, and shows no sign of discouragement in representing the workers of Toledo. Redistricting will extend Kaptur farther out from Toledo, but she is one of the few Ohio Democrats who is not a Republican target.

Cook's Call   *Safe.* Like most of northern Ohio, this Toledo-based district has lost population over the last 10 years. Kaptur's district needs to gain more than 60,000 people for 2002 and will be altered significantly in redistricting. While it is likely that Republicans will dissolve a congressional district in the northern part of the state, Kaptur's seat seems safe from elimination.

THE PEOPLE: Pop. 2000: 569,053; Pop. 1990: 570,911, down 0.3% 1990–2000. 81% White, 13.8% Black, 1.1% Asian, 0.3% Amer. Indian, 2% Two+ races, 1.8% Other; 4.5% Hispanic Origin.

2000 Presidential Vote			1996 Presidential Vote		
Gore (D)	129,057	(55%)	Clinton (D)	125,971	(55%)
Bush (R)	98,301	(42%)	Dole (R)	76,613	(34%)
Nader (Green)	5,373	(2%)	Perot (I)	22,960	(10%)
Others	1,860	(1%)			

Rep. Marcy Kaptur (D)

Elected 1982, 10th term; b. June 17, 1946, Toledo; home, Toledo; U. of WI, B.A. 1968, U. of MI, M.A. 1974, M.I.T., 1981–82; Catholic; single.

Professional Career: Urban planner, Lucas Cnty. Planning Comm., 1969–75; Urban planning consultant, 1975–77; White House Asst. Dir. for Urban Affairs, 1977–80; Dpty. Secy., Natl. Consumer Coop. Bank, 1980–81; Author.

DC Office: 2366 RHOB 20515, 202-225-4146; Fax: 202-225-7711; Web site: www.house.gov/kaptur.

District Office: Toledo, 419-259-7500.

Committees: *Appropriations* (7th of 29 D): Agriculture, Rural Development, & FDA (RMM); The Legislative Branch; VA, HUD & Independent Agencies.

Group Ratings

	ADA	ACLU	AFS	LCV	CON	ITIC	NTU	COC	ACU	NTLC	CHC
2000	75	64	100	79	53	35	24	30	18	16	20
1999	85	—	100	81	97	—	23	26	4	—	—

National Journal Ratings

	1999 LIB	—	1999 CONS		2000 LIB	—	2000 CONS
Economic	69%	—	31%		69%	—	30%
Social	64%	—	36%		66%	—	34%
Foreign	68%	—	30%		73%	—	26%

Key Votes of the 106th Congress

1. Patient Bill of Rights	*	5. Bar RU-486 $ for FDA	N	9. NATO War in Serbia	Y
2. Accelerate Min. Wage	Y	6. Display 10 Commandments	N	10. Perm. Trade with China	N
3. Strike Ban on Ergo. Stnd.	Y	7. Gun Show Bkgrnd. Checks	Y	11. Debt Relief for 3rd World	Y
4. Ovrd. Estate Tax Veto	N	8. Ban Part.-Birth Abortion	Y	12. Drop Cuba Econ. Embargo	N

Election Results

2000 general	Marcy Kaptur (D)	168,547	(75%)	($285,239)
	Dwight Bryan (R)	49,446	(22%)	($86,815)
	Other	7,335	(3%)	
2000 primary	Marcy Kaptur (D)	unopposed		
1998 general	Marcy Kaptur (D)	130,793	(81%)	($148,561)
	Edward S. Emery (R)	30,312	(19%)	($5,869)

TENTH DISTRICT

Cleveland, one of America's great cities at the beginning of the 20th Century, faced some hardships in the latter half of the century, but is on its way back in the new century. It grew as a center of heavy industry: This was the original home base of John D. Rockefeller's Standard Oil; the city's twisting and deep Cuyahoga River was the site of several of the nation's largest steel mills; great industrial fortunes here built civic institutions like the museums in Wade Park, Case Western University and the Cleveland Symphony, and financed the campaigns of northeast Ohio Republican Presidents James Garfield and William McKinley. On the old Public Square, designed like a New England town green by the Yankees who settled this Western Reserve (the northeast corner of Ohio) in the early 19th Century, the two eccentric Van Sweringen brothers, trolley magnates of the early 20th Century, built the Terminal Tower, for many years the highest skyscraper in interior America. This yeasty, ethnic city, with more than 40 nationalities—Hungarians, Czechs, Serbs, Croatians, Poles, Italians, Germans (the Hapsburg Empire and more)—and many distinct ethnic neighborhoods, produced a robust two-party politics. In the 1930s, after CIO unions organized the steel factories and auto assembly plants, Cleveland became solidly Democratic, though with some affluent Republican suburbs.

But Cleveland never led the nation as it hoped: America's fourth largest city in 1910, it was overtaken in size first by Detroit, eventually by the likes of Houston and Dallas; today, it's the center of the nation's 16th largest metropolitan area. The central city declined from 914,000 in 1950 to 478,000 in 2000, as the children who grew up in the tightly packed neighborhoods made more money and moved to the close-in suburbs and then outer-suburban counties. The 1970s were a bad decade for Cleveland, which became an object of ridicule by national sophisticates. Its heavy industries were fast declining, Lake Erie and the Cuyahoga River were badly polluted (the river caught fire in June 1969). City politics became racially polarized with the election of black Mayor Carl Stokes in 1967 and 1969, and in December 1978 the city defaulted on bank loans under Mayor Dennis Kucinich.

The city government was rescued by George Voinovich, elected mayor in 1979 and later governor and senator. And the current mayor, Michael White, who is black, broke down racial polarization and first won the mayor's office in 1989 by carrying white wards west of the Cuyahoga while losing the black wards east of the river to black machine politician George Forbes. Downtown Cleveland revived, with the second-largest theater district center in the nation at Playhouse Square, the Jacobs Field baseball stadium, a basketball arena, and the Rock and Roll Hall of Fame. Following the departure of the city's beloved Browns to Baltimore, a new football stadium has been constructed with an NFL payment, $9 million in damages from Browns' owner Art Modell for breaking his lease, and public money from a sin tax. The city took no satisfaction when Modell's Ravens won the Super Bowl for Baltimore in 2000, but it gained an expansion team in 1999, retaining the Browns name and colors. People swim in now-clean Lake Erie; restaurants and pleasure boat docks line the Cuyahoga where diners can sip Burning River pale ale. Cleveland continues to be headquarters of several of the nation's largest law firms, and some businesses, like iron-ore giant Cleveland-Cliffs, have sharply revived; the city's number one employer is now health services, and the Cleveland Clinic may be its best-known firm. The airport made plans for a new runway (though it needs to set up some rental-car-return signs). The city's population declined only 6% in the 1990s, seemingly bottoming out, while the metropolitan area grew.

The 10th Congressional District of Ohio includes most of the west side of Cleveland and the western suburbs in Cuyahoga County. Excluded is one salient of mostly black Cleveland precincts attached to the 11th District across the Cuyahoga; also several western suburbs—Brook Park,

Middleburg Heights—are in the convoluted suburban 19th District. Suburbs in the 10th include Lakewood, well-established by the 1920s and still comfortable middle-class territory, plus Rocky River and Bay Village, growing more affluent westward along the lake. Inland is Parma, a creation of the 1950s, when second- and third-generation ethnics moved out to subdivision houses set amid what was once America's densest concentration of bowling alleys. The political tradition is almost entirely Democratic, though Voinovich has won majorities from grateful voters here, and Al Gore carried the district by only 54%–41% in 2000.

The congressman from the 10th District is Dennis Kucinich, elected in 1996, still unrepentant about the day he plunged the city into default. Kucinich grew up as the oldest of seven children whose father was a truckdriver and family moved 21 times in different parts of Cleveland. He was a political prodigy who was elected to the City Council in 1969, at 23; he saw himself as the champion of the working man, eager for confrontations with Cleveland's business establishment. He was elected mayor in 1977 when the city government was in terrible financial straits. Kucinich was unwilling or unable to balance the budget and meet obligations and when bankers demanded he sell city-owned properties, he refused, and they called their loans. The public verdict was negative: Kucinich lost in 1979. He taught at Cleveland State and Case Western Reserve, hosted a radio talk show, and was a TV reporter.

In 1994 Kucinich staged a political comeback, arguing that he had saved utility ratepayers money, and was elected to the state Senate, defeating an incumbent Republican. In 1996 he ran for the House. The incumbent Martin Hoke, a Republican who made millions in business, was elected twice against Democrats with serious ethical problems. Kucinich campaigned against NAFTA and GATT (though Ohio businesses have made money on exports to Mexico) and defended his ties with labor. Democrats, many of them former Kucinich critics, rallied around him: The Cleveland City Council named a public power plant for him on the same day Bill Clinton campaigned for him in Parma. Hoke was not helped when 19th District Republican Steve LaTourette was quoted in the Cleveland *Plain Dealer* saying he didn't think Hoke would win. Actually, given the Democratic leanings of the district, Hoke did very well. Kucinich won, but by only 49%–46%.

Kucinich has sought to expand job-training programs for skilled workers and has been a vocal foe of international trade deals. He bars his staff from parking foreign cars in congressional lots and was a leader in the fight against permanent normal trade relations with China. Kucinich took on companies that produce genetically modified foods and he promoted more consumer awareness. He has been centrist on cultural issues, including opposition to abortion. He voiced local sentiments on issues as disparate as a new telephone area code and noise control at the airport. In contrast to some Rust Belt Democrats, he backed the EPA's new air-quality standards. Kucinich led a group of 25 Democrats to oppose Clinton on bombing of Kosovo and has been called the "leading Democratic dove." He questioned Al Gore's ability to motivate grassroots workers during his presidential campaign. In 2001 he was chairman of the Progressive Caucus and a proponent of Democrats who want to define differences with George W. Bush's policies.

Kucinich emphasizes his own local roots. He dedicated his Web site to polka, bowling and Kielbasa. He easily won re-election in 1998 and 2000. Ohio lost one House seat in the 2000 Census, and Republicans control redistricting. They have long targeted the 13th District's Sherrod Brown, whose home base in Lorain County may be moved into the 10th District. But it is not clear that the two Democratic incumbents will face each other in a primary.

Cook's Call *Potentially Competitive.* With Ohio slated to lose one seat, Republicans, who control redistricting, are heavily focused on the Cleveland area, where growth has been slow and where Democrats currently dominate the delegation. Kucinich's district is short almost 60,000 people and there has been talk of merging this Cleveland-centered district with parts of Sherrod Brown's 13th, perhaps setting up a primary between the two Democratic members. With new lines not expected out until early in 2002, the political future is still very murky here.

THE PEOPLE: Pop. 2000: 573,874; Pop. 1990: 570,530, up 0.6% 1990–2000. 87.8% White, 5.1% Black, 1.8% Asian, 0.2% Amer. Indian, 2.1% Two+ races, 2.9% Other; 6.3% Hispanic Origin.

2000 Presidential Vote

Gore (D)	147,562	(54%)
Bush (R)	111,565	(41%)
Nader (Green)	9,681	(4%)
Others	3,103	(1%)

1996 Presidential Vote

Clinton (D)	117,878	(51%)
Dole (R)	83,055	(36%)
Perot (I)	26,952	(12%)

Rep. Dennis Kucinich (D)

Elected 1996, 3d term; b. Oct. 6, 1946, Cleveland; home, Cleveland; Cleveland St. U., 1967–70, Case Western Reserve U., B.A., M.A., 1973; Catholic; single.

Elected Office: Cleveland City Cncl., 1970–75, 1983–85; Cleveland Mayor, 1977–79; OH Senate, 1994–96.

Professional Career: Clerk, Municipal Courts, 1976–77; Radio Talk Show Host, 1979, 1989; Lecturer, 1980–83; Consultant, 1986–94; TV Reporter, Channel 8, 1989–92.

DC Office: 1730 LHOB 20515, 202-225-5871; Fax: 202-225-5745; Web site: www.house.gov/kucinich.

District Offices: Lakewood, 216-228-8850; Parma, 440-845-2707.

Committees: *Education & the Workforce* (17th of 22 D): Education Reform; Workforce Protections. *Government Reform* (10th of 19 D): Energy Policy, Natural Resources and Regulatory Affairs; National Security, Veterans' Affairs & Intl. Relations (RMM).

Group Ratings

	ADA	ACLU	AFS	LCV	CON	ITIC	NTU	COC	ACU	NTLC	CHC
2000	80	57	100	93	57	22	30	28	16	25	27
1999	90	—	100	88	93	—	33	12	20	—	—

National Journal Ratings

	1999 LIB	—	1999 CONS		2000 LIB	—	2000 CONS
Economic	88%	—	0%		81%	—	16%
Social	58%	—	40%		56%	—	43%
Foreign	50%	—	48%		68%	—	31%

Key Votes of the 106th Congress

1. Patient Bill of Rights	Y	5. Bar RU-486 $ for FDA	Y	9. NATO War in Serbia	Y
2. Accelerate Min. Wage	Y	6. Display 10 Commandments	N	10. Perm. Trade with China	N
3. Strike Ban on Ergo. Stnd.	Y	7. Gun Show Bkgrnd. Checks	Y	11. Debt Relief for 3rd World	N
4. Ovrd. Estate Tax Veto	N	8. Ban Part.-Birth Abortion	Y	12. Drop Cuba Econ. Embargo	Y

Election Results

2000 general	Dennis Kucinich (D)	167,063	(75%)	($550,063)
	Bill Smith (R)	48,930	(22%)	($5,564)
	Other	6,762	(3%)	
2000 primary	Dennis Kucinich (D)	56,781	(93%)	
	C. River Smith (D)	4,145	(7%)	
1998 general	Dennis Kucinich (D)	110,552	(67%)	($580,626)
	Joe Slovenec (R)	55,015	(33%)	($204,276)

ELEVENTH DISTRICT

Like most great American cities, Cleveland grew in great bursts of migration, when capitalists' investments suddenly were paying off beyond their wildest dreams and low-wage workers were attracted from ready corners of the country and the world. Cleveland's greatest surge of growth started in the 1890s and lasted through the 1920s, as tens of thousands of immigrants from central and southern Europe arrived here, looking for jobs in steel, auto and other factories. Bohemians came to the tightly packed neighborhoods along Broadway, Hungarians a bit to the northeast, Jews north of University Circle along East 105th Street, and Italians to Little Italy along Mayfield Road.

As the nation's heavy industries geared up for World War II and enjoyed years of prosperous growth afterward, a second surge of immigrants came, this time blacks from the American South. From Cleveland's old ghetto, south of Carnegie Avenue downtown to East 105th, the rapidly increasing number of blacks covered most of the east side by the middle 1960s, with only a few Bohemian and Italian enclaves left east of the Cuyahoga. Migration stopped around 1965, but blacks have continued to move out beyond the city limits to the east side suburbs, including modest East Cleveland and Warrensville Heights and upper-income Shaker Heights, laid out in 1905 on broad boulevards by streetcar magnates, the Van Sweringen brothers. These surges of migration led to political changes. A string of ethnic mayors—Frank Lausche, Anthony Celebrezze, Ralph Locher—was followed by the election in 1967 and 1969 of Carl Stokes, the nation's first black big-city mayor, and Cleveland had racially polarized politics for much of the 1970s. Ironically, the city never had a black majority until the 2000 Census, in which its population was just 51% black. It elected its second black mayor, Michael White, in 1989, because white voters preferred his accommodating politics to the more polarizing ways of longtime City Council Chairman George Forbes.

The 11th Congressional District includes most of the east side of Cleveland, plus the suburbs just to the east, which together have about as many people as the city now. Some of these—East Cleveland, Warrensville Heights—are mostly black; some, notably Shaker Heights, have stable black percentages in carefully maintained neighborhoods where racial integration has succeeded. Others are the destination of blacks seeking low-crime neighborhoods and middle-class schools not often found on the city side among Cleveland's impressive museums and medical centers. This is a heavily Democratic district, with a 65% black majority; it was represented for 30 years by Louis Stokes, Carl Stokes's brother, the first black member of Appropriations, chairman of the ethics committee and later the Intelligence Committee, who retired in 1998.

The congresswoman from the 11th District is Stephanie Tubbs Jones, for all practical purposes chosen in the May 1998 primary. She grew up in Cleveland as the daughter of a Hopkins Airport skycap, graduated from college and law school at Case Western and served her entire legal career as a federal or local-government attorney. She served eight years as judge on the Court of Common Pleas of Cuyahoga County and in 1990 narrowly lost as the Democratic nominee for Ohio Supreme Court. In 1991 she was appointed by the county's Democratic Party as the first woman and first black prosecutor in Cuyahoga County; she easily won election with 79%. When Stokes announced his retirement Tubbs Jones decided to run for the House. Her chief opponents in the primary were state Senator Jeffrey Johnson and Reverend Marvin McMickle, minister of the Antioch Baptist Church, one of the city's largest black congregations. Tubbs Jones, the early favorite, campaigned in both black and white neighborhoods—unlike her opponents. Tubbs Jones faced second-guessing of her refusal to re-open the criminal investigation of Dr. Samuel Sheppard, who was convicted in a celebrated 1954 case of murdering his wife, but was later acquitted and died in 1970. Sheppard's family claimed that new DNA evidence exonerated him; Tubbs Jones said that she could not prove there had been no tampering with the evidence. Stokes was officially neutral in the campaign, but he helped Tubbs Jones raise money in Washington. Tubbs Jones won 51% of the primary vote, with Johnson and McMickle each receiving 20%. The general election was just a formality.

In the House, Tubbs Jones had a strongly liberal voting record. She quickly showed her political skills by winning appointment as the freshman on the Democratic steering committee, which makes committee assignments. She wisely sought ways to cooperate with several of the influential Republicans in the Ohio delegation. President Clinton signed the bill that she filed with Deborah Pryce that increases funding of child abuse programs. She co-sponsored Rob Portman's bill to create the National Underground Railroad Freedom Center in Cincinnati. She worked with Steve LaTourette, yet another Ohio Republican, to require Medicare HMO insurers to maintain service and benefits for at least three years. On the Financial Services Committee, she has defended Fannie Mae from conservative critics of its practices. "If it ain't broke, don't fix it," Tubbs Jones said.

Tubbs Jones was easily re-elected in 2000. A Cleveland *Plain Dealer* poll in May 2000 showed that she would defeat Mayor White 51%–28%, but she said that she was happy in Congress.

Redistricting will force her district to add 98,000 people, but the Republican redistricters will surely be careful to create a black-majority east side district which Tubbs Jones can easily carry; the problem will be for Democrats in adjacent seats.

Cook's Call *Safe.* This Cleveland-based district lost the most population of any in the state and is currently almost 100,000 people short. But the Voting Rights Act will help ensure that this majority-black district will not be eliminated in redistricting. Tubbs-Jones is a safe bet for 2002.

THE PEOPLE: Pop. 2000: 532,337; Pop. 1990: 571,295, down 6.8% 1990–2000. 31.7% White, 64.5% Black, 1.4% Asian, 0.2% Amer. Indian, 1.6% Two+ races, 0.6% Other; 1.5% Hispanic Origin.

2000 Presidential Vote

Gore (D)	149,710	(83%)
Bush (R)	26,302	(14%)
Nader (Green)	3,773	(2%)
Others	1,650	(1%)

1996 Presidential Vote

Clinton (D)	155,895	(79%)
Dole (R)	28,938	(15%)
Perot (I)	9,553	(5%)

Rep. Stephanie Tubbs Jones (D)

Elected 1998, 2d term; b. Sept. 10, 1949, Cleveland; home, Cleveland; Case Western Reserve U., B.A. 1971, J.D. 1974.; Baptist; married (Mervyn Jones).

Elected Office: Cleveland Municipal Court Judge, 1982–83; Cuyahoga Cnty. Court of Common Pleas Judge, 1983–91.

Professional Career: Asst. Gen. Cnsl. & EEO Admin., NE OH Regional Sewer Dist., 1974–76; Asst. Cuyahoga Cnty. Prosecutor, 1976–79; Equal Employment Opportunity Comm., 1979–81; Cuyahoga Cnty. Prosecutor, 1991–98.

DC Office: 1516 LHOB 20515, 202-225-7032; Fax: 202-225-1339; Web site: www.house.gov/tubbsjones.

District Office: Shaker Heights, 216-522-4900.

Committees: *Financial Services* (23d of 32 D): Capital Markets, Insurance & Government Sponsored Enterprises; Housing & Community Opportunity; Oversight & Investigations. *Small Business* (8th of 17 D): Workforce, Empowerment & Government Programs. *Standards of Official Conduct* (5th of 5 D).

Group Ratings

	ADA	ACLU	AFS	LCV	CON	ITIC	NTU	COC	ACU	NTLC	CHC
2000	100	69	100	71	52	53	19	47	0	12	0
1999	90	—	100	88	35	—	23	25	0	—	—

National Journal Ratings

	1999 LIB —	1999 CONS	2000 LIB —	2000 CONS
Economic	79% —	20%	92% —	5%
Social	87% —	0%	77% —	23%
Foreign	95% —	0%	97% —	0%

Key Votes of the 106th Congress

1. Patient Bill of Rights	Y	5. Bar RU-486 $ for FDA	N	9. NATO War in Serbia	Y
2. Accelerate Min. Wage	Y	6. Display 10 Commandments	N	10. Perm. Trade with China	N
3. Strike Ban on Ergo. Stnd.	Y	7. Gun Show Bkgrnd. Checks	Y	11. Debt Relief for 3rd World	Y
4. Ovrd. Estate Tax Veto	N	8. Ban Part.-Birth Abortion	N	12. Drop Cuba Econ. Embargo	Y

Election Results

2000 general	Stephanie Tubbs Jones (D)	164,134	(85%)	($240,018)
	James Sykora (R)	21,630	(11%)	
	Other	7,755	(4%)	
2000 primary	Stephanie Tubbs Jones (D)	67,680	(92%)	
	Gerald Henley (D)	6,286	(8%)	
1998 general	Stephanie Tubbs Jones (D)	115,226	(80%)	($425,151)
	James D. Hereford (R)	18,592	(13%)	($4,550)
	Jean Murrell Capers (Ind)	9,477	(7%)	

TWELFTH DISTRICT

Columbus is on the verge of becoming a major metropolis. With city limits stretching toward farmland at each point of the compass, Columbus is geographically the largest city in Ohio; its metropolitan area, though far less populous than Cleveland and a bit smaller than Cincinnati, is growing much more rapidly; Columbus's Franklin County has passed the 1 million mark in 2000, with an 11% increase in the 1990s. It is centrally located, not only in the center of Ohio, but a one-day truck drive from more than one-half of the nation's population. With its growing jobs base, Columbus was the only one of the 15 largest cities in Ohio to gain population in the 1990s. It has advantages of being a state capital, the home of Ohio State University, and a major white-collar employment town: It is the home of The Limited's Leslie Wexner and Wendy's Dave Thomas, of Nationwide Insurance and American Electric Power. Columbus likes to brag that its airfreight operations at Port Columbus, the airport, make it the largest in the country dedicated to cargo, and about the $43 million Wexner Center for the Visual Arts, a post-post-modern structure by architect Peter Eisenman that has evoked vast controversy. This economic base and civic infrastructure has attracted the kind of upscale, enterprising people who have produced most of America's growth in recent years.

Politically, Columbus has traditionally been a Republican city, with an even more Republican hinterland. It had few of the eastern European immigrants and CIO unions that made Cleveland so Democratic. From 1971, its mayor was a Republican with support from a machine redolent of the era of William McKinley (whose statue sits in front of the flat-domed Capitol). Then, in November 1999, Democrat Michael Coleman won a spirited contest for mayor; Coleman, who is black, built a modern coalition that crossed racial, gender and economic lines. But the suburbs remain heavily Republican and the countryside even more so. The Columbus area dominates two of Ohio's congressional districts. The 12th extends east to the small industrial town of Newark and north to fast-growing Delaware County, and includes black areas and the affluent east side of the city around Bexley; the 15th includes most of the territory within the city limits and extends south and west to include Madison County.

The congressman from the 12th District is Pat Tiberi, a Republican elected in 2000. The son of Italian immigrants, he grew up in Columbus and graduated from Ohio State. Tiberi worked as a real estate agent and then served for eight years as an assistant to Congressman John Kasich, who helped Tiberi win in 1992, at age 30, a seat in the state House. He became majority leader and was known for supporting business-friendly legislation and legal reform. In July 1999 Kasich announced his retirement, after a brief run for the presidency and six years as the politically controversial but fiscally successful House Budget Committee chairman. Tiberi won support to replace his mentor from most of the Republican establishment plus the U.S. Chamber of Commerce. He faced a noisy but not very effective primary challenge from state Senator Gene Watts, who made a term-limits pledge and sought to rally the conservative base. Tiberi won 73%–21%.

The resounding victory for the nomination gave him a big boost heading into the general election against Democrat Maryellen O'Shaughnessy, a funeral home owner and Columbus city council member. She told her personal story as the single mother of a 10-year-old son and sought to define differences with Tiberi on prescription drug benefits, campaign reform, taxes and Social Security. Tiberi played up his Columbus roots as a former member of the Ohio State marching band and attacked O'Shaughnessy for the "negative campaign" run by the state Democratic Party with ads that tagged him as the defender of insurance companies on prescription-drug pricing. He said that drug coverage should be added for seniors as part of a broader overhaul of the Medicare program to make it more efficient and solvent—an echo of themes long voiced by Kasich. This was one of the most-watched House races in the nation, with Dick Gephardt pleading that a local victory would be essential for Democrats to win the House majority. But with campaign help from Kasich, who retained his local popularity, Tiberi won 53%–44%, running 2% ahead of George W. Bush. Following in the footsteps of the mayoral race a year earlier, O'Shaughnessy won Franklin County 51%–46%. But Tiberi won 66%–31% in the outlying Delaware and Licking Counties, which cast 35% of the total vote.

In the House, Tiberi won seats on Financial Services and Education and the Workforce. He joined activist Republicans pushing to increase George W. Bush's tax cut above his original $1.6 trillion dollar plan and offered an amendment to increase flexibility for local school districts in exchange for better student performance. For redistricting, he will have something of a luxury: His district was the fastest-growing in the state in the past decade and, in their control of the process, Republicans may remove some of its Democratic precincts.

Cook's Call *Potentially Competitive.* As a freshman that won this marginal district with just 53% in 2000, Tiberi certainly looks like a potential target for Democrats in 2002. But Republicans control redistricting and they want to help shore up this district. It will need to shed about 30,000 people.

THE PEOPLE: Pop. 2000: 661,049; Pop. 1990: 571,341, up 15.7% 1990–2000. 71.8% White, 22.8% Black, 2.2% Asian, 0.3% Amer. Indian, 2.2% Two+ races, 0.8% Other; 1.8% Hispanic Origin.

2000 Presidential Vote			1996 Presidential Vote		
Bush (R)	150,411	(51%)	Clinton (D)	118,228	(47%)
Gore (D)	136,840	(46%)	Dole (R)	114,405	(46%)
Nader (Green)	6,241	(2%)	Perot (I)	16,426	(7%)
Others	2,325	(1%)			

Rep. Patrick J. Tiberi (R)

Elected 2000, 1st term; b. Oct. 21, 1962, Columbus; home, Columbus; OH St. U., B.A. 1985; Catholic; married (Denice).

Elected Office: OH House of Reps., 1992–2000, Maj. Ldr., 1999–2000.

Professional Career: Staff asst., U.S. Rep. John Kasich, 1984–92; Realtor, ReMax Achievers, 1995–2000.

DC Office: 508 CHOB 20515, 202-225-5355; Fax: 202-226-4523; Web site: www.house.gov/tiberi.

District Office: Columbus, 614-523-2555.

Committees: *Education & the Workforce* (24th of 27 R): Employer-Employee Relations; Select Education (Vice Chmn.). *Financial Services* (37th of 37 R): Financial Institutions & Consumer Credit; Housing & Community Opportunity; Oversight & Investigations.

Group Ratings and Key Votes: Newly Elected

Election Results

2000 general	Patrick J. Tiberi (R)	139,242	(53%)	($2,349,872)
	Maryellen O'Shaughnessy (D)	115,432	(44%)	($1,340,688)
	Other	8,712	(3%)	
2000 primary	Patrick J. Tiberi (R)	57,548	(73%)	
	Eugene Watts (R)	16,331	(21%)	
	Ramona Whisler (R)	3,481	(4%)	
	Other	1,469	(2%)	
1998 general	John R. Kasich (R)	124,197	(67%)	($769,107)
	Edward S. Brown (D)	60,694	(33%)	($8,545)

THIRTEENTH DISTRICT

The imprint of the westward track of New England Yankee migration is still apparent today on the shores of Lake Erie in northern Ohio. The Yankees, cooped up in New England for 200 years, shot across the country through upstate New York, west across Ohio and Michigan to Chicago, and on to Kansas and southern California in just two or three generations, providing inspiration, manpower and technical might for the Union victory in the Civil War, and leaving their imprint along the way. One place they stopped was the Western Reserve, the northeast corner of Ohio, created for the excess population of Connecticut; its towns, colleges and cultural institutions were established by Yankees mostly. A prime example of Western Reserve Yankeeism is Oberlin College, founded in 1832 as the first co-educational college in America, though no women dared apply until 1837; it accepted black students a few years later, and the town of Oberlin became a center of the Underground Railroad. Or consider Hiram, home of another college and of James Garfield, who once represented the area in Congress when it was the most Republican part of Ohio, and who was the only president elected directly from the House, in 1880.

Politically, the lands of the Yankee diaspora, with their reformist ideas and dislike of slavery and the South, were naturally Republican territory. But the great masses of immigrants lured to Cleveland and the smaller industrial cities built by Yankee capital provided a base for labor unions and Progressive politics. After the New Deal and the bloody CIO organizing drives of the late 1930s, the Western Reserve had something like class-warfare politics for 30 years, with the Democrats usually winning. Northern Ohio, like New England, moved away from the Republicans and toward the Democrats. Now the Western Reserve, like Connecticut and Massachusetts, may be moving toward a post-industrial economy. Factory employment has dropped, but total jobs are rising again; small, adaptive business units with highly skilled workers are the growth sectors. That leaves the Western Reserve, like New England, leaning Democratic—but not reliably so.

The 13th Congressional District of Ohio is grotesquely shaped—something like a barbell—with two large segments of the Western Reserve connected by a sort of land bridge between Cleveland and Akron. The western end includes the factory towns of Lorain and Elyria, plus Oberlin and Medina County, once rural and now filling up with migrants from Cleveland along I-71. The eastern, less heavily populated area includes all of Geauga County, high-income hilly townships with many reminders of New England origins, and rural parts of Trumbull and Portage counties. This end of the district tends to vote Republican, while on the west end Lorain County is Democratic and Medina County Republican. This was an ungainly product of redistricting in 1992, the home of suburban Cleveland Democratic incumbents, both of whom chose to retire.

The congressman from the 13th District is Sherrod Brown, one of Ohio Democrats' few remaining successful career politicians. He grew up in Mansfield, graduated from Yale in 1974 and won a seat in the state House of Representatives later that year (a state employee, mistaking him for an intern, gave him a dollar to get her a cup of coffee). For more than a quarter century he has never stopped running for office. In 1982 he was elected secretary of State at 30 and worked hard to increase voter registration and turnout. In 1990 he lost that office to Bob Taft, who is now governor, and in 1991 Republican redistricters took care to keep Brown's hometown of Mansfield outside the new 13th. But in 1992 Brown moved into a rented lake cottage in Medina County and faced Republican Margaret Mueller, a millionaire social worker from Geauga County. Brown showed great flair in the campaign, taking a 200-mile bicycle tour around the district; with solid labor support, he campaigned loud and hard against NAFTA and championed universal health care. He won 53%–35%, with 61% in Lorain County.

In the House, Brown has had a solidly liberal voting record and has been a politically adept member of the Energy and Commerce Committee. He supported the Clinton economic plan and a single-payer health care plan like Canada's, but he did not sign onto the Clinton plan. On trade he has been one of the most voluble liberal-labor members from the Great Lakes area attacking NAFTA, GATT and permanent normal trade relations with China; he has objected to measures to open the border to Mexican trucks, which he argues are unsafe. But he did support the balanced budget amendment and line-item veto. In the minority party, his position as ranking Democrat on the reorganized Energy and Commerce health subcommittee has given him little influence because Republicans have crafted their health care proposals mostly in party task forces. Should Democrats regain the majority and Brown retain his seat, he would be chairman of one of the most important subcommittees in the House, with the power of drawing national attention and framing the debate on important health issues. He has been a foe of pharmaceutical and insurance companies, introducing with Republican Jo Ann Emerson in May 2001 a bill to speed approval of generic drugs; he has criticized Republicans for seeking to privatize Medicare; and he has urged adoption of the Europeans' ban on farm use of growth-promoting antibiotics. On international issues, he won enactment of a bill in 1999 to require support for Taiwan in international organizations and House approval to strengthen enforcement of laws against importing goods made with slave labor. He authored *Congress from the Inside*, a book that says that House Democrats lost the majority because "we were blamed for everything the voters did not like" and takes Republicans to task for the loss of civility.

Brown had a serious Republican challenge in 1994 from Lorain County Prosecutor Gregory White, but Brown survived by 49%–46%, with the help of business and labor PAC money. Since then he has won easily, but redistricting may change things. Ohio lost a House seat in the 2000 Census, and Republicans control the redistricting process. For some time they have said that Brown is their number one target, and indeed one could make the case that the Ohio district which has the most convoluted borders and most lacks an identity as a single community is the 13th. Given population losses in northeast Ohio, it would be easy to attach much of this district to the Cleveland-based 10th and parts of the rest to the Akron-dominated 14th and the 19th. Brown threatened to run against Governor Bob Taft if he got an unfavorable district, and as of spring 2001 it was not clear whether Republicans would call his bluff; Taft has a high job-approval rating, but no politician likes to guarantee himself an articulate and politically adept opponent. In any case, Brown has the skills and perhaps the opportunity to continue to be a highly successful politician.

Cook's Call *Competitive.* If there is any member in Congress walking around with a target on his head, it is Brown. Ohio is slated to lose one seat in redistricting and most insiders in the state point to Brown's dumbbell-shaped district as the one that will go. Brown has threatened to run for governor should he be redistricted out of this seat, but it's not yet clear if that will intimidate Republicans.

THE PEOPLE: Pop. 2000: 645,068; Pop. 1990: 570,838, up 13% 1990–2000. 91.6% White, 4.7% Black, 0.7% Asian, 0.2% Amer. Indian, 1.4% Two+ races, 1.4% Other; 3.4% Hispanic Origin.

2000 Presidential Vote

Bush (R)	136,747	(50%)
Gore (D)	127,024	(46%)
Nader (Green)	8,093	(3%)
Others	3,221	(1%)

1996 Presidential Vote

Clinton (D)	116,720	(46%)
Dole (R)	98,349	(39%)
Perot (I)	35,527	(14%)

Rep. Sherrod Brown (D)

Elected 1992, 1st term; b. Nov. 9, 1952, Mansfield; home, Lorain; Yale U., B.A. 1974, OH St. U., M.A. 1979, M.A. 1981; Lutheran; divorced.

Elected Office: OH House of Reps. 1974–82; OH Secy. of State, 1982–90.

Professional Career: Prof., OH St. U. at Mansfield, 1979–81.

DC Office: 2438 RHOB 20515, 202-225-3401; Fax: 202-225-2266; Web site: www.house.gov/sherrodbrown.

District Offices: Elyria, 440-934-5100; Medina, 330-722-9262.

Committees: *Energy & Commerce* (8th of 26 D): Environment & Hazardous Materials; Health (RMM); Telecommunications & The Internet. *International Relations* (7th of 23 D): East Asia & the Pacific.

Group Ratings

	ADA	ACLU	AFS	LCV	CON	ITIC	NTU	COC	ACU	NTLC	CHC
2000	90	83	100	100	57	40	26	25	4	13	0
1999	100	—	100	94	97	—	32	0	0	—	—

National Journal Ratings

	1999 LIB —	1999 CONS	2000 LIB —	2000 CONS
Economic	88% —	0%	90% —	10%
Social	83% —	13%	90% —	9%
Foreign	77% —	22%	94% —	6%

Key Votes of the 106th Congress

1. Patient Bill of Rights	Y	5. Bar RU-486 $ for FDA	N	9. NATO War in Serbia	*
2. Accelerate Min. Wage	Y	6. Display 10 Commandments	N	10. Perm. Trade with China	N
3. Strike Ban on Ergo. Stnd.	Y	7. Gun Show Bkgrnd. Checks	Y	11. Debt Relief for 3rd World	Y
4. Ovrd. Estate Tax Veto	N	8. Ban Part.-Birth Abortion	N	12. Drop Cuba Econ. Embargo	Y

Election Results

2000 general	Sherrod Brown (D)	170,058	(65%)	($789,866)
	Rick Jeric (R)	84,295	(32%)	($28,276)
	Other	8,945	(3%)	
2000 primary	Sherrod Brown (D)	unopposed		
1998 general	Sherrod Brown (D)	116,309	(62%)	($682,041)
	Grace L. Drake (R)	72,666	(38%)	($162,341)

FOURTEENTH DISTRICT

Akron, what some Ohioans today call the Polymer Center of the Americas, formerly was known as Rubber Town. (Akron is named from the Greek word for high, the same root for Acropolis, because it sits on a ridge between the Great Lakes and Mississippi watersheds.) Thirty years ago, the city was as synonymous with tires as Detroit was with cars: Firestone, Goodyear, General Tire, and B.F. Goodrich all had their headquarters and big tire factories here; the United Rubber Workers had been the big union since the 1930s. But after the oil shocks of the 1970s, Akron's antiquated auto tire plants closed, and the last truck and airplane tire plants closed in 1984 and 1985; several big firms were sold to out-of-town companies, though Goodyear remains a leading employer. To adapt, Akron built on its expertise in shaping rubber objects and began specializing in polymers, plastics and other hydrocarbons that can be formed or shaped like rubber into useful industrial products. The first polymer, polyvinyl chloride (PVC), was invented in 1926 when B.F. Goodrich chemist Waldo Semon, looking to make synthetic rubber, found a mysterious goo in the bottom of his test tube; the company did not bother to patent it until 1933, but now PVC is everywhere, in pipes and siding, shoes and toys, car tops and stadium covers. Ohio conducts 80% of the nation's polymer research; it employs more people in the field than all states except California. Metro Akron's growth in the 1990s has not been spectacular, but it has generated new jobs and an economy at least as vital as that produced by tires.

This change in the local economy has had political effects. Akron's population is largely descended from migrants from eastern Europe and West Virginia, who thronged here in the 1910s and 1920s to snap up jobs in the tire factories for 10 or 12 hours a day at the price of smelling burning rubber for 24. In the 1930s these people joined the new United Rubber Workers union and started voting Democratic; they were courted in turn by Republicans with blue-collar backgrounds fielded by local Republican Chairman Ray Bliss, who was also Republican National Committee chairman in the 1950s and 1960s. But as the smell of rubber vanished from Akron's air, the language of class conflict has mostly passed from its politics. Now Akron has more flexible businesses and a more upscale work force. Greater Akron usually votes Democratic, it sometimes votes Republican as well.

Ohio's 14th Congressional District has long been made up of Akron and most of surrounding Summit County; currently it also includes the area around Kent (and Kent State University) just to the east. The current congressman, Tom Sawyer, has spent most of his adult life in public office. He grew up in Akron and graduated from the University of Akron. He was elected to the state House in 1976, at 31, became Akron mayor in 1984, and was elected in the 14th District when the incumbent retired in 1986. In that election and again in 1994, he survived tough competition from Summit County prosecutor Lynn Slaby.

Sawyer has a mostly liberal voting record. He has loudly denounced Republicans but also has taken on some bipartisan initiatives. With Republican David Hobson, he sponsored a common standard for electronic transmission of health care billing information, which passed in 1996. He joined The Coalition, a group of moderate Democrats, but not the Blue Dogs. Representing a district where organized labor was historically strong, Sawyer still sometimes spurns the union line. After much public agonizing, he supported NAFTA in November 1993; as a result he had opposition in the 1994 primary from plumber Kenneth Mack, whom he beat 69%–31%. In 1996 he did not oppose the Republicans' Teamwork for Employees and Management bill outright, as unions did, but proposed an amendment asserting workers' rights to independent representation. In 1997 Sawyer gave up seniority on the Education and the Workforce Committee—something no Akron Democrat would have done in the days when unions were strong—to get a seat on Energy and Commerce, where he focused on telecommunications issues and utility services. He showed his contrariness again when he was among the few Rust Belt Democrats to vote for permanent normal trade relations with China, following a Clinton visit to Akron a week before the vote. He has been the Democratic organizer of the House's bipartisan "civility" retreats. Local projects for which he secured funds include $2.8 million for the National Inventors' Hall of Fame and $100,000 for the University of Akron's Institute for Global Business. He prevailed on the Office of Management and Budget in 2000 to keep Akron outside the Cleveland metro region for Census purposes.

Despite the Teamsters Union's decision in 2000 to pull its endorsement plus the unhappiness of others in organized labor with his China vote, Sawyer continued to win re-election easily. But redistricting may make it more difficult for him in 2002. Ohio lost one seat in the 2000 Census and it is likely to come out of northeast Ohio. Republicans control the redistricting process; with one of the Democratic districts in northeast Ohio virtually certain to be eliminated, Sawyer could find himself matched against another incumbent—most likely Sherrod Brown of the 13th District, although Brown has said he may run for governor. In any event, the changes in district lines will move him into some unfamiliar territory, where organized labor could decide to support a local candidate who pledges solidarity and challenges Sawyer's independence of the union label, or where a Republican could launch a stronger challenge.

Cook's Call *Potentially Competitive.* A couple of tough, well-funded challengers kept Sawyer under 55% in 1994 and 1996, but he has never come too close to losing this Akron-based district. With the state slated to lose one seat in redistricting, Sawyer may find himself in a tough place in 2002. One scenario has Sawyer's district chopped up among three northern Ohio districts. At the very least, it will be altered significantly in 2002.

THE PEOPLE: Pop. 2000: 586,402; Pop. 1990: 570,987, up 2.7% 1990–2000. 84.5% White, 12.3% Black, 1.3% Asian, 0.2% Amer. Indian, 1.4% Two+ races, 0.3% Other; 0.9% Hispanic Origin.

2000 Presidential Vote

Gore (D)	128,790	(54%)
Bush (R)	100,397	(42%)
Nader (Green)	6,958	(3%)
Others	2,682	(1%)

1996 Presidential Vote

Clinton (D)	121,635	(53%)
Dole (R)	76,083	(33%)
Perot (I)	30,312	(13%)

Rep. Tom Sawyer (D)

Elected 1986, 8th term; b. Aug. 15, 1945, Akron; home, Akron; U. of Akron, B.A., 1968; M.A., 1970; Presbyterian; married (Joyce).

Elected Office: OH House of Reps., 1976–82; Akron Mayor, 1984–86.

DC Office: 1414 LHOB 20515, 202-225-5231; Fax: 202-225-5278; Web site: www.house.gov/sawyer.

District Office: Akron, 330-375-5710.

Committees: *Energy & Commerce* (15th of 26 D): Energy & Air Quality; Telecommunications & The Internet.

Group Ratings

	ADA	ACLU	AFS	LCV	CON	ITIC	NTU	COC	ACU	NTLC	CHC
2000	90	86	85	93	50	83	19	47	4	12	7
1999	100	—	100	100	70	—	13	24	0	—	—

National Journal Ratings

	1999 LIB	—	1999 CONS	2000 LIB	—	2000 CONS
Economic	88%	—	0%	85%	—	11%
Social	83%	—	13%	91%	—	6%
Foreign	93%	—	5%	96%	—	3%

Key Votes of the 106th Congress

1. Patient Bill of Rights	Y	5. Bar RU-486 $ for FDA	N	9. NATO War in Serbia	Y
2. Accelerate Min. Wage	Y	6. Display 10 Commandments	N	10. Perm. Trade with China	Y
3. Strike Ban on Ergo. Stnd.	Y	7. Gun Show Bkgrnd. Checks	Y	11. Debt Relief for 3rd World	Y
4. Ovrd. Estate Tax Veto	N	8. Ban Part.-Birth Abortion	N	12. Drop Cuba Econ. Embargo	Y

Election Results

2000 general	Tom Sawyer (D)	149,184	(65%)	($515,026)
	Rick Wood (R)	71,432	(31%)	($32,459)
	Other	9,472	(4%)	
2000 primary	Tom Sawyer (D)	unopposed		
1998 general	Tom Sawyer (D)	106,046	(63%)	($504,893)
	Tom Watkins (R)	63,027	(37%)	($93,311)

FIFTEENTH DISTRICT

Columbus, smack in the center of Ohio, was founded in 1812 to be the state capital. Its flat-domed Capitol at Broad and High, with the statue of William McKinley out front, is surrounded by high-rises, public and private, while the city has been growing in all directions into the country-side, and now is on the verge of becoming a large metropolis. It is the headquarters of state government and Ohio State, one of the nation's largest universities; it is the home as well of Nationwide Insurance and The Limited and Wendy's. It is the headquarters of the Batelle Memorial Institute, the think tank that helped invent compact discs, office copy machines and the universal product code; a major industry here is data retrieval. Columbus, which has kept annexing suburbs, is now Ohio's largest central city by far, with 711,000 people in 2000; Franklin County topped 1 million and the metro area extends into formerly rural counties. Columbus is rapidly building civic landmarks—the Center of Science and Industry on the riverfront, the Jerome Shottenstein Center for sports and concerts at OSU, a hockey stadium for the Columbus Blue Jackets and the nation's first stadium built for a professional soccer team, the Columbus Crew. With the nation's highest proportion of residents age 25 to 34, Columbus continues to be a prime test market for products of all kinds.

Ohio's 15th Congressional District is made up of most of Columbus, all but the east side, plus southern and western Franklin County and rural Madison County directly to the west. The 15th includes some of Columbus' black population, white working-class areas on the south side of the city and in nearby Grove City, and the Ohio State University campus. Politically, these Democratic areas are more than balanced by the heavily Republican suburb of Upper Arlington, across the Olentangy River from Ohio State, and by Republican subdivisions sprouting up in rural land between the old villages.

The 15th District is represented in the House by Deborah Pryce, a Republican first elected in 1992. Pryce grew up in Warren, graduated from law school in Columbus in 1976, worked in state government and as a city prosecutor, and was elected municipal court judge in 1985. In 1992, when incumbent Chalmers Wylie retired after 26 years, Pryce ran for the House. She was unopposed in the primary but had tough competition in the general from Democrat Richard Cordray and from anti-abortion independent Linda Reidelbach, who became angry when Pryce announced she would support a Freedom of Choice Act that would restrict states' power to limit abortions. Pryce talked much about congressional reform—term limits, rotating chairmanships, line-item veto—and called for limiting annual spending increases to 3%. She won with 44% of the vote to Cordray's 38% and Reidelbach's 18%.

In the House, Pryce has a voting record that is mostly conservative on economic and foreign issues, sometimes liberal on cultural issues. In her first term she was elected interim president of her Republican class and helped to craft the Contract with America. When Republicans won the majority in 1994, Newt Gingrich tapped her to chair a committee to examine legal ramifications of the transition, including severance pay for thousands of aides who lost their jobs. Pryce has been a leadership loyalist on the Rules Committee since 1995 and headed the House Republican task force on tobacco.

Pryce has been particularly interested in issues relating to children, adoption and cancer. Her adoptive daughter developed cancer in September 1998 and died at age nine in September 1999. Pryce and her husband started Hope Street Kids, an organization to raise funds for cancer research, using funds donated in memory of their daughter. She is co-chairwoman of the House Cancer Working Group and sponsored a bill in 2001 to require private insurers to provide coverage of routine patient costs of cancer patients who qualify to participate in a clinical trial. She has favored increasing the $5,000 adoption tax credit to $10,000, which passed in May 2001. She tried unsuccessfully to change the Indian Child Welfare Act to exempt children whose parents have no significant tribal affiliation. She sponsored the law creating the adoption stamp, which was unveiled by Wendy's founder and adoption advocate Dave Thomas. She sponsored a law signed in March 2000 giving child protective services and child welfare workers access to more court records and doubling funding for federal child abuse and domestic assistance programs to $20 million.

On other issues, Pryce was a sponsor of the privacy amendment voted into financial services deregulation by the House in July 1999; it would give consumers the right to block banks and financial institutions from selling personal data to outside firms, but would let them share it with affiliated companies. In 2000 she inserted into an appropriation $235 million for graduate medical programs at children's hospitals; Children's Hospital of Columbus stood to get $5 million. In 2001 she sponsored an "apples for teachers" bill which would grant teachers a $400 tax credit for out-of-pocket expenses. She has obtained $11 million of a projected cost of $15 million for the West Columbus Floodwall project. She got the Appropriations Committee to grant $430,000 for Columbus Mayor Michael Coleman's $20 million revolving loan fund for central-city housing initiatives.

In July 1997, Pryce was elected Republican Conference secretary when leadership positions opened up following the retirement of Conference Vice Chair Susan Molinari. Running as the moderate among the four candidates, Pryce won 110 votes on the second ballot to 65 for Sue Myrick and 42 for Duke Cunningham. In November 2000 she moved up, being elected Conference vice chair without opposition.

Pryce has won re-election easily. Redistricting is controlled by Republicans, and the 15th is one of four Ohio districts that must shed population.

Cook's Call   *Safe.* Although this district is not the most Republican in the state (Bush only won here with 52% in 2000), Pryce has had little trouble winning this suburban Columbus district. She should be safe in 2002.

THE PEOPLE: Pop. 2000: 649,980; Pop. 1990: 570,740, up 13.9% 1990–2000. 85.9% White, 7.7% Black, 3.2% Asian, 0.3% Amer. Indian, 1.8% Two+ races, 1% Other; 2.3% Hispanic Origin.

2000 Presidential Vote			1996 Presidential Vote		
Bush (R)	117,382	(52%)	Dole (R)	114,183	(48%)
Gore (D)	101,364	(45%)	Clinton (D)	105,947	(44%)
Nader (Green)	6,851	(3%)	Perot (I)	17,324	(7%)
Others	2,115	(1%)			

Rep. Deborah Pryce (R)

Elected 1992, 5th term; b. July 29, 1951, Warren; home, Columbus; OH St. U., B.A. 1973, Capital U. Law Schl., J.D. 1976; Presbyterian; married (Randy Walker).

Elected Office: Franklin Cnty. Municipal Court Judge, 1985–92.

Professional Career: Admin. Law Judge, OH Dept. of Insurance, 1976; Columbus City Asst. Prosecutor & Asst. City Atty., 1978–85; Practicing atty., 1992.

DC Office: 221 CHOB 20515, 202-225-2015; Web site: www.house.gov/pryce.

District Office: Columbus, 614-469-5614.

Committees: *Republican Conference Vice Chairman. Rules* (4th of 9 R): The Legislative & Budget Process (Chmn.).

Group Ratings

	ADA	ACLU	AFS	LCV	CON	ITIC	NTU	COC	ACU	NTLC	CHC
2000	15	31	0	14	62	100	59	90	80	65	62
1999	20	—	0	6	9	—	58	100	56	—	—

National Journal Ratings

	1999 LIB —	1999 CONS	2000 LIB —	2000 CONS
Economic	0%	84%	18%	76%
Social	53%	47%	53%	47%
Foreign	48%	52%	0%	88%

Key Votes of the 106th Congress

1. Patient Bill of Rights	N	5. Bar RU-486 $ for FDA	N	9. NATO War in Serbia	N
2. Accelerate Min. Wage	N	6. Display 10 Commandments	Y	10. Perm. Trade with China	Y
3. Strike Ban on Ergo. Stnd.	N	7. Gun Show Bkgrnd. Checks	N	11. Debt Relief for 3rd World	N
4. Ovrd. Estate Tax Veto	Y	8. Ban Part.-Birth Abortion	Y	12. Drop Cuba Econ. Embargo	N

Election Results

2000 general	Deborah Pryce (R)	156,792	(68%)	($589,675)
	Bill Buckel (D)	64,805	(28%)	($4,455)
	Scott Smith (LIB)	10,700	(5%)	
2000 primary	Deborah Pryce (R)	61,931	(88%)	
	Craig Lortz (R)	8,400	(12%)	
1998 general	Deborah Pryce (R)	113,846	(66%)	($368,958)
	Adam Clay Miller (D)	49,334	(28%)	($86,036)
	Kevin Nestor (I)	9,996	(6%)	($18,849)

SIXTEENTH DISTRICT

A little more than a century ago, Canton, Ohio, was at the center of American politics. Canton was already an industrial city then, though not with the huge steel factories built in Youngstown or Cleveland. Its high-skill workers were fashioning new kinds of plows and reapers, making watches and, beginning in 1899, roller bearings. Canton did not attract masses of immigrants. Its factories did not run on harsh stopwatch discipline; there were not the class-warfare politics here that would be seen later in other northern Ohio industrial cities. Instead Canton was united in admiring its first citizen, William McKinley, who rose to the rank of major at 22 in the Civil War, was elected congressman and governor, and chaired the House Ways and Means Committee. As Republican nominee for president in 1896, McKinley campaigned from his front porch in Canton, meeting with delegations brought in by train from all over the country. This spectacle, with its display of technological virtuosity and personal modesty, sounds an appealing and reverberating note in American politics, as does the McKinley platform—the "full dinner pail," the gold standard, the enforcement of law and order in labor relations—which has long been viewed as antiquated but still provides useful instruction.

The 16th Congressional District includes all of Stark County, plus three-and-a-half more Republican counties to the west: Wayne, site of the College of Wooster and the headquarters of Rubbermaid; Holmes, with its Amish communities; and Ashland and part of Knox. The district has been mostly Republican since McKinley's time, and has elected only Republican congressmen since 1950. Though no longer at the center of American politics, Canton and surrounding Stark County, which have voted much like the nation as a whole for the last 30 years, were the subject of a year-long series of stories by Michael Winerip in *The New York Times*. What he found in 1996 was a community still based on manufacturing—mostly high-skill, with companies like Timken, Diebold, Republic Engineered Steels, and Hoover—economically prosperous but uneasy because of downsizing and decisions by some local companies to build new plants elsewhere, politically ambivalent about both major party candidates, worried about the young House Republicans but mostly opposed to old liberal Democrats. Stark County can still be pretty close to a bellwether: in 2000 it voted 49%–47% for George W. Bush, just 1% more Republican than the national average.

The congressman from the 16th District is Ralph Regula, first elected in 1972 and one of the most senior Republicans in the House. He grew up in outer Stark County, the son of a farmer and coal mine operator; he served in the Navy in World War II, worked his way through the William McKinley School of Law while teaching elementary school, and was elected to the Ohio legislature in 1964, just before turning 40. He still has a beef farm near Canton. When the incumbent retired in 1972, Regula ran for the House and was easily elected. He is the second most senior Republican on the Appropriations Committee; from 1995 to 2001 he chaired the Interior Subcommittee, and in 2001, thanks to Republicans' six-year term limits on chairmen, began chairing the Labor-HHS Subcommittee, which oversees more domestic spending than any other.

On the Interior Subcommittee, Regula was a counterweight to the Resources Committee and its chairman, Don Young of Alaska, who added riders to Regula's appropriations strongly opposed by environmental groups and the Clinton administration. Regula resisted these, and often gave them up in end-of-session conference committees when Clinton threatened a veto. Conservative efforts to abolish the National Endowment for the Arts failed, but had some effect; in 2000 Regula increased its budget by 7% but required that all the increase must be spent on the populist Challenge America initiative. Spending caps forced Regula to cut deeply into energy research and land acquisition; he argued that it was more important to properly fund current parks rather than to designate new ones. But he makes some exceptions: one was for Everglades restoration, another for the 87-mile Ohio and Erie Canal Heritage Corridor, which he finally succeeded in authorizing in the omnibus parks bill in 1996. In 1999 he opposed Young's CARA bill, which would dedicate offshore oil royalties to states for land acquisition; he opposed it because it took the money off-budget (and out of Appropriations) and because he thought it could better be used to maintain existing parks. Young and Regula also got into a fight about Mount McKinley. In May 1999, just after Regula and a conference committee removed an amendment to allow commercial fishing near Glacier Bay National Park in Alaska, Young introduced a bill to rename the mountain Denali, an Alaska Native name. Regula replied heatedly that that controversy had already been settled in 1980, when the McKinley name stayed on the mountain but the park was renamed Denali National Park.

In 2000 the budget surplus suddenly made it possible (even though it exceeded the 1997 budget caps) to increase spending sharply, and the reductions in Young's CARA by western state senators increased the pressure—this is just one example of why domestic discretionary spending zoomed upward in 1999 and 2000. The Interior appropriation for 2001 was increased by 26%, with a 190% increase for fighting forest fires, an 88% increase in land conservation and 6% to 10% increases in other areas. Regula also added a pet measure, a ban on the Interior Department moving callers into voice mail between 7:30 a.m. and 4:30 p.m.; he had spent too much time listening to recorded messages. And he redesignated the Cuyahoga Valley National Recreation Area a national park, but exempted the national park air standards. He scuttled $1 million for land purchase at Ohio's Little Darby Creek, a pet project of Senator Mike DeWine opposed by Ohio House members, and got $500,000 for the National First Ladies' Library in Canton, which his wife founded and served as its president.

In 1999 and 2000 Regula served as chairman of the Congressional Steel Caucus. In response to an increase in steel imports, he passed $1 billion of federal loan guarantees for the steel, oil, and gas industries in August 1999. He tried but failed to zero out the $3 million economics office of the International Trade Commission after it ruled against U.S. steel firms. But he voted for permanent normal trade relations with China, as workers at a Wooster Rubbermaid factory scheduled to be moved to Mexico sent him a letter on the back of a bathmat urging him to vote no. He called on the Bush administration to order a Section 201 investigation of the effects of steel imports.

Cook's Call *Safe*. Regula is about as safely entrenched as they come. His Canton-area district needs to pick up some population in 2002 redistricting (it is about 25,000 people short), but he should have no real trouble winning a 16th term.

THE PEOPLE: Pop. 2000: 605,661; Pop. 1990: 570,705, up 6.1% 1990–2000. 92.9% White, 4.9% Black, 0.5% Asian, 0.2% Amer. Indian, 1.2% Two+ races, 0.3% Other; 0.9% Hispanic Origin.

2000 Presidential Vote

Bush (R)	128,917	(54%)
Gore (D)	101,527	(42%)
Nader (Green)	6,127	(3%)
Others	3,666	(2%)

1996 Presidential Vote

Clinton (D)	100,293	(43%)
Dole (R)	98,786	(42%)
Perot (I)	33,255	(14%)

Rep. Ralph Regula (R)

Elected 1972, 15th term; b. Dec. 3, 1924, Beach City; home, Navarre; Mt. Union Col., B.A. 1948, William McKinley Law Schl., LL.B. 1952; Episcopalian; married (Mary).

Military Career: Navy, 1944–46 (WWII).

Elected Office: OH House of Reps., 1964–66; OH Senate, 1966–72.

Professional Career: Teacher & schl. principal, 1948–52; Practicing atty., 1952–73; OH Bd. of Educ., 1960–64.

DC Office: 2306 RHOB 20515, 202-225-3876; Fax: 202-225-3059; Web site: www.house.gov/regula.

District Office: Canton, 330-489-4414.

Committees: *Appropriations* (2d of 35 R): Commerce, Justice & State; Interior; Labor, HHS & Education (Chmn.).

Group Ratings

	ADA	ACLU	AFS	LCV	CON	ITIC	NTU	COC	ACU	NTLC	CHC
2000	10	21	14	14	24	94	58	80	76	55	60
1999	25	—	16	13	37	—	54	84	64	—	—

National Journal Ratings

	1999 LIB —	1999 CONS		2000 LIB —	2000 CONS
Economic	30% —	64%		25% —	72%
Social	41% —	58%		43% —	55%
Foreign	43% —	55%		31% —	68%

Key Votes of the 106th Congress

1. Patient Bill of Rights	N	5. Bar RU-486 $ for FDA	Y	9. NATO War in Serbia	Y
2. Accelerate Min. Wage	N	6. Display 10 Commandments	Y	10. Perm. Trade with China	Y
3. Strike Ban on Ergo. Stnd.	N	7. Gun Show Bkgrnd. Checks	N	11. Debt Relief for 3rd World	N
4. Ovrd. Estate Tax Veto	Y	8. Ban Part.-Birth Abortion	Y	12. Drop Cuba Econ. Embargo	N

Election Results

2000 general	Ralph Regula (R)	162,294	(69%)	($166,663)
	William Smith (D)	62,709	(27%)	
	Other	9,397	(4%)	
2000 primary	Ralph Regula (R)	unopposed		
1998 general	Ralph Regula (R)	117,426	(64%)	($178,180)
	Peter D. Ferguson (D)	66,047	(36%)	($156,385)

SEVENTEENTH DISTRICT

For nearly a century, the Mahoning Valley, between the Lake Erie docks that unload iron ore from Great Lakes freighters and the coalfields of western Pennsylvania and West Virginia, was one of the steel capitals of the United States. The first coal mine here opened in 1826, canals followed, and in 1892 the first steel mill was built in Youngstown. The valley soon filled up with mills, converters, and furnace. Now the steel mills stand empty, smokeless and silent—except those that have been dynamited and torn down. Big steel management allowed foreign producers to gain a technological edge in the 1950s and 1960s; worldwide overcapacity in steel grew as almost every developing country decided it needed its own steel mill, while cooperation between the United Steelworkers and management after the 119-day strike in 1959 boosted wages and fringe benefits to price domestic steel out of the market. Import restrictions kept the furnaces hot for a while, but the oil shock of 1979 produced sharply higher energy prices and a collapse in the U.S. auto and steel markets. Every plant in Youngstown and the Mahoning Valley closed, and in the early 1980s metro Youngstown had one of the nation's highest unemployment rates.

Steel has since revived, but not here: in decentralized mini-mills or in huge new rolling plants in northern Indiana. The biggest business headquartered in Youngstown is now the shopping center empire of the late Edward DeBartolo. The high-wage living standard of the 1970s has vanished; young people looking for opportunities routinely leave; population has declined. Organized crime, it seems, has deeply infiltrated local government; a federal investigation has led to more than 70 convictions, including a prosecutor, a sheriff and a congressional aide. The two big counties here, Mahoning and Trumbull, saw population declines of 3% and 1% in the 1990s; Youngstown, the largest city, saw its population decline 14%.

The 17th Congressional District of Ohio includes all of the Mahoning Valley, running south from Youngstown to the Ohio River across from West Virginia and north past Warren halfway to Lake Erie. Politically, this is an area that has writhed in anger. Republican in the 1920s, solidly Democratic for years after the United Steelworkers organized the plants following sometimes bloody skirmishes in the late 1930s, the area wobbled toward Republicans in the Carter 1970s, then veered back to the Democrats in the Reagan 1980s; now it is one of the most Democratic parts of the country. In 2000 the 17th District voted 58%–38% for Al Gore, his second best district in Ohio, after the black-majority 11th.

The congressman from the 17th is Jim Traficant, a Democrat who speaks in the authentic demotic accents of the Mahoning Valley. Traficant grew up in Poland, Ohio, in Mahoning County, and was a star quarterback at the University of Pittsburgh. He directed a drug program from 1971–81, and was elected Mahoning County sheriff in 1980, where he met controversy. When he was indicted by state authorities for taking bribes, he admitted taking large bribes from mobsters to overlook local gambling, loan-sharking, drug trafficking and prostitution and argued, when presented with tapes of some of these transactions, that this was his own sting operation. Tried on criminal charges in 1983 and acting as his own lawyer, he persuaded the jury to find him not guilty; but he owed more than $100,000 after the U.S. Tax Court ruled that he owed back taxes for the bribes. In 1984 he ran for the House against Republican Lyle Williams and won 53%–46%.

In the House, Traficant is a unique figure, with his polyester flare-bottom and denim suits and a shock of hair that stands up "like a Chia pet," in the words of Lizette Alvarez of *The New York Times*. "I do my hair with a weed whacker," Traficant says. He has compiled a middle-of-the-House voting record, but a distinctive one. Like Youngstown Republicans of the 1920s, he is protectionist and isolationist: He is a vitriolic opponent to aid to Israel and voted against NAFTA and GATT. He is familiar to C-SPAN viewers for his loud speeches—tirades, some say—against foreign aid, free trade, the Federal Reserve and the oppression visited on citizens by the Internal Revenue Service; he often concludes with the *Star Trek* phrase, "Beam me up." But Traficant has some accomplishments. His "Made in America" amendments, which he offers to many spending bills, often pass. He has advanced his Taxpayer Bill of Rights measures by such tactics as standing on the floor for 10 hours and raising points of order against every section of the Treasury bill. He amended a crime bill to require a net gain in street cops, amended an immigration bill to require monitoring of federal efforts to stop illegal immigration, and amended the Taxpayer Bill of Rights to impose penalties of up to $1 million for IRS agent misconduct. Loud and abrasive on the floor, he is one of the kindest and most thoughtful members to House employees and pages.

In 1997 the local U.S. attorney's office started an investigation of corruption in the Youngstown area, with Traficant evidently as one target. Traficant in turn began attacking the Justice Department; at one point he said that Attorney General Janet Reno was an alcoholic lesbian being blackmailed by the mob. He charged that Reno let Bill Clinton get away with corruption connected with China: "Chinagate makes Watergate look like a jaywalking misdemeanor. You have evidence of the Communist Party funneling cash to influence national politics in America, and there is no investigation. There is not even a hearing in a junior high school in Oshkosh, Wisconsin." Shunned by Democrats, he became increasingly friendly with Republicans. In 1998 he campaigned for the reelection of Republican Steve Chabot in Cincinnati. He developed friendly relations with down-to-earth House Speaker Dennis Hastert (it is impossible to imagine this happening with Newt Gingrich) and the Republican leadership began helping him pass his bills. In November 1999 the House passed his bill to ban oil and gas drilling under Mosquito Creek Lake in northeast Ohio. In March 2000, over the grumbling of conservatives, House leaders pushed through his bill to raise the minimum wage by $1 in two, rather than three years. In April the Republicans allowed a floor vote on $35 million for a community center in Youngstown; it passed easily. He was one of the Democrats who voted to override Clinton's veto of the estate tax and marriage penalty repeal in September. In October Traficant's language requiring the CIA to investigate how foreign espionage affected the U.S. economy and whether China was a threat to U.S. security was put into the intelligence authorization bill.

In the meantime, Traficant was under challenge at home. Local Democrats—backed, Traficant said, by the Democratic Congressional Campaign Committee and its chairman, Patrick Kennedy—backed state Senator Robert Hagan in the March 7 Democratic primary. Hagan decried corruption: "I'm tired of dealing with this corruption. . . . I'm tired of the media showing up every time there's an indictment, and I think everyone here should be tired of it too." Hagan suggested that he and Traficant take polygraph tests administered on the 50-yard line during halftime at a Youngstown State University football game, and he volunteered to undergo electroshock treatment if his answers were found to be untrue. Some 116,000 people voted in the Democratic primary, an unusually high turnout; Traficant won 50% of the vote, to 34% for Hagan and 14% for Mahoning County Auditor George Tablack. Another 40,000 voted in the Republican primary, an unusually large number for that party; Traficant's 1998 opponent Paul Alberty beat former Congressman Lyle Williams 52%–48%.

Traficant subsequently rose on the House floor and predicted that he would be indicted. "I have nothing to hide. I have done nothing wrong," he said, and promised to "fight like a junkyard dog." Later that month, Traficant aide Charles O'Nesti pleaded guilty to perjury and racketeering charges for delivering bribes to public officials from Youngstown crime boss Leonard Strollo. In May 2000, Traficant charged that FBI agents urged one witness to commit murder and stole large sums of money and in June he charged, "FBI agents in the Northern District of Ohio have been on the payroll of the mob." In July he refused to comply with a subpoena issued in May. In October a Youngstown contractor pleaded guilty for perjury in falsifying billing records on work his firm did at Traficant's farm. At home Traficant had vocal opposition from Republican Alberty and from condominium developer Randy Walter, who spent $476,000 running as an independent. Undaunted, Traficant campaigned for endangered Republican Jay Dickey in Arkansas and walked into a TV studio without a script and cut his one spot for the campaign on the first take. In October he said that he would vote for Hastert for speaker and indicated his disdain for the Democratic leadership: "I came in here without really the control of the leadership, quite frankly, Scarlett."

("Quite frankly, Scarlett" is another common Traficant closing line.) The election results showed that Traficant was not universally regarded as a hero: He ran 8% behind Al Gore, with 50% of the vote. But the opposition was split: Alberty won 23%, Walter 22%.

In January 2001, Traficant kept his promise to vote for Hastert. Democrats responded, not unreasonably, by denying him any committee assignments. Some expected that he would join the Republican Party, surely a fatal move in the 17th district. But as Traficant put it, the Democratic leadership "didn't have the anatomy" to throw him out of the caucus, and he didn't ask the Republicans for committee assignments either. Nevertheless, in March the House passed 407–3 his bill to provide a toll-free number for consumers to get information on whether products were made in the United States; in the same month he was one of 10 Democrats to vote for the Bush tax cut and one of three Democrats to vote for the Republican budget resolution. But the federal prosecutors—still Democratic appointees, not replaced by George W. Bush—were closing in. In February a Youngstown-area horse trainer was sentenced to jail for conspiring to harm a witness about to testify about Traficant. In May 2001, 14 months after his floor-of-the-House prediction, Traficant was indicted on 10 counts of bribery and racketeering charges. They said he accepted "things of value" for political influence, that he accepted the use of a Corvette, the gift of an Avanti and the construction of a pole barn on his farm in return from those seeking political influence. The charges seemed far less severe than those that had resulted in the conviction of so many public officials in the Youngstown area; Traficant said he was innocent and that he was prepared to defend himself again in court. He added, "I'm as frightened as anyone can be. I'm going to say this to the U.S. attorneys. You'd best defeat me, because if I beat you, you'll be working in Mingo Junction." After his indictment, cooperation from Republicans abruptly ended as six Republicans on the Resources Committee voted to defeat his bill to spend $10 million on renovations to a Youngstown performing arts center.

What about Traficant's political future? He could lose a Democratic primary in 2002, and conceivably even lose the 2002 general election, given the results of the 2000 contests and changes in mind that might be produced by the indictment and any legal proceedings that followed. But it is not likely that the Mahoning Valley will lose its House seat. Republicans control the redistricting process and Ohio must lose one seat, but Republicans have shown no interest in dividing up the heavily Democratic 17th District among its neighbors. The likelihood is that the 17th will add needed population in redistricting, and that the election that will matter is the Democratic primary, in which Traficant will likely again be challenged.

Cook's Call *Potentially Competitive.* Traficant is like a man without a country. He may face a serious challenge in the 2002 Democratic primary, stemming from his May 2001 indictment on charges of racketeering, bribery and conspiracy. He intends to defend himself at his February 2002 trial, which will take place just three months before the Ohio Democratic primary. This district—and the trial—will be worth watching in 2002.

THE PEOPLE: Pop. 2000: 563,164; Pop. 1990: 570,963, down 1.4% 1990–2000. 86.8% White, 10.8% Black, 0.4% Asian, 0.2% Amer. Indian, 1.2% Two+ races, 0.6% Other; 1.9% Hispanic Origin.

2000 Presidential Vote

Gore (D)	141,091	(58%)
Bush (R)	91,762	(38%)
Nader (Green)	6,900	(3%)
Others	2,884	(1%)

1996 Presidential Vote

Clinton (D)	142,121	(58%)
Dole (R)	67,705	(28%)
Perot (I)	31,494	(13%)

Rep. James A. Traficant, Jr. (D)

Elected 1984, 9th term; b. May 8, 1941, Youngstown; home, Poland; U. of Pittsburgh, B.S. 1963, Youngstown St. U., M.S. 1973, M.S. 1976; Catholic; married (Patricia).

Elected Office: Mahoning Cnty. Sheriff, 1980–85.

Professional Career: Dir., Mahoning Cnty. Drug Program, 1971–81.

DC Office: 2446 RHOB 20515, 202-225-5261; Fax: 202-225-3719; Web site: www.house.gov/traficant.

District Offices: E. Liverpool, 330-385-5921; Niles, 330-652-5649; Youngstown, 330-743-1914.

Committees: None.

Group Ratings

	ADA	ACLU	AFS	LCV	CON	ITIC	NTU	COC	ACU	NTLC	CHC
2000	30	29	42	14	1	61	47	52	60	42	73
1999	60	—	100	19	11	—	24	36	52	—	—

National Journal Ratings

	1999 LIB —	1999 CONS	2000 LIB —	2000 CONS
Economic	58%	42%	53%	46%
Social	32%	66%	33%	66%
Foreign	39%	60%	47%	51%

Key Votes of the 106th Congress

1. Patient Bill of Rights	Y	5. Bar RU-486 $ for FDA	Y	9. NATO War in Serbia	N
2. Accelerate Min. Wage	Y	6. Display 10 Commandments	Y	10. Perm. Trade with China	N
3. Strike Ban on Ergo. Stnd.	Y	7. Gun Show Bkgrnd. Checks	N	11. Debt Relief for 3rd World	Y
4. Ovrd. Estate Tax Veto	Y	8. Ban Part.-Birth Abortion	Y	12. Drop Cuba Econ. Embargo	N

Election Results

2000 general	James A. Traficant Jr. (D)	120,333	(50%)	($285,165)
	Paul Alberty (R)	54,751	(23%)	($165,860)
	Randy Walter (I)	51,793	(22%)	($476,871)
	Lou D'Apolito (I)	9,568	(4%)	($39,788)
	Other	4,432	(2%)	
2000 primary	James A. Traficant Jr. (D)	59,415	(50%)	
	Robert Hagan (D)	40,079	(34%)	
	George Tablack (D)	16,203	(14%)	
	Other	1,988	(2%)	
1998 general	James A. Traficant Jr. (D)	123,718	(68%)	($155,897)
	Paul H. Alberty (R)	57,703	(32%)	($26,013)

EIGHTEENTH DISTRICT

From their earliest settlement in the 1790s, the hills of east central Ohio have been industrial country. The local clay was used to make pottery, the coal that lies near the surface was dug up, a green vitriol works was built, and a nail factory went into operation, all before 1814. For more than 100 years, this area has been part of the great coal and steel belt that centers on Pittsburgh and Cleveland and stretches from the coal mines of West Virginia to Lake Erie, the destination of freighters filled with iron ore from Minnesota's Mesabi Range. This area is filled with small cities, each with its little steel mill or factory, most of them old towns whose storefronts and wooden, working-class houses bear the unmistakable imprint of the early 20th Century. For a time the pay was good, but after the oil shock of 1979, the coal and steel economy collapsed; the impact here was cushioned by continuing demand for coal from electric utilities, but that has been jeopardized by the 1990 Clean Air Act amendments. Wage levels have sagged and the hopes many had of getting ahead have been disappointed.

Ohio's 18th Congressional District covers much of this land along the Ohio River, just west of West Virginia, and spreads west over hilly farmland pockmarked by strip mines, from the steel town of Steubenville on the Ohio, which was the birthplace of crooner Dean Martin and used to have the nation's worst air quality; to New Rumley, the birthplace of General George Custer; and Zanesville, the birthplace of writer Zane Grey and architect Cass Gilbert and home of a famous Y-shaped bridge. As one goes west, the territory is less industrial, but overall the 18th is, sociologically and politically, a kind of ethnic working-class neighborhood. Since the New Deal, it has leaned Democratic in most elections. But in the late 1990s it has moved toward the Republicans, voting for Governor Bob Taft and Senator George Voinovich in 1998, and giving George W. Bush a 51%–45% margin in 2000—similar to the showings he made in the coal country of West Virginia just across the Ohio River.

The congressman from the 18th District is Bob Ney, a Republican elected in 1994 in this Democratic territory. Ney grew up in Bellaire, just across the Ohio from Wheeling, West Virginia, and worked as a teacher and as safety director for the city of Bellaire. A former teacher in Iran when the Shah ruled there, he is the only House member who speaks fluent Farsi and has called for closer ties with that nation. He was elected to the state House in 1980, at 26, in quite an upset, beating Wayne Hays, the longtime congressman and power in the House who quit this seat in 1976 due to scandal and won a state House seat two years later. Ney lost that seat in the Democratic year of 1982 but in 1984 was elected to the state Senate. When Democrat Douglas Applegate announced his retirement from the U.S. House in 1994, Ney gave up his Finance Committee chair in Columbus to run. Democrats nominated state Representative Greg DiDonato, who criticized Ney for accepting honoraria from lobbyists; Ney criticized DiDonato for sharing an apartment with a cable TV lobbyist. Most unions backed DiDonato, except for teachers' unions, who backed ex-teacher Ney. His Belmont County home base turned out to be the key; only 35% for Republican Senate candidate Mike DeWine, it voted 67% for Ney, enough to clinch a 54%–46% victory.

In the House, Ney's record is often at odds with the Republican leadership and clearly aimed at the folks back home. His first legislative action came on the House Administration Committee, where he moved to cut each member's mail allowance by one-third. He worked successfully to prevent the zeroing out of the Appalachian Regional Commission and the Development Disabilities Councils. He removed language eliminating provisions of the Coal Industry Retiree Health Benefits Act that make former employers pay for retirees' health care. He helped organized labor by protecting the bargaining rights of unionized bus drivers, and he opposed Republican leaders' anti-union bills. He was a leader among House Republicans opposed to permanent normal trade relations with China. On occasion, his blue-collar initiatives have been consistent with Republican policy. He fought against what he called EPA's "overregulation" under the Clean Air Act, and won House support to cut $5 million from EPA's budget for travel and management. With John Kasich, he toughened work requirements for able-bodied food stamp recipients under 50. With other Steel Belt members, he backed quotas on foreign steel and he said the Clinton administration was "dead wrong" to put international interests ahead of "working families who have been brutalized by a flood" of steel imports. He bolstered his Republican credentials by backing tax cuts and opposing abortion rights.

In the 107th Congress, Speaker Dennis Hastert named Ney chairman of the House Administration Committee, the very panel where Wayne Hays created his power base as the mayor of Capitol Hill. By contrast, Ney was selected because of his pledge of loyalty to party leaders, who jumped over Vern Ehlers of Michigan because they feared he would be independent of their wishes. The assignment made Ney the first member of the Class of 1994 to become a committee chairman, and put him at the center of the intense debate over campaign finance regulation after the Senate passed McCain-Feingold in April 2001. Reformers said that they wanted a House vote by May, but Ney—who has opposed the bill in the past—showed his leadership credentials when he insisted that the issue would need extended hearings across the nation. With his inclination toward bipartisanship, Ney initially won a favorable response from Democrats for working closely with Steny Hoyer to increase funding for Democratic staff on House committees. His committee was given another hot political potato: reform of federal election law and voting procedures in response to the Florida presidential recount.

Ney twice won re-election against former state Senator Robert Burch, a favorite of organized labor and the 1994 Democratic nominee for governor. Burch tried to make the campaigns a referendum on Newt Gingrich. Ney's pro-labor record got him the NEA endorsement. In 1996 Ney did not run so well in Belmont County, but he gained ground elsewhere, enough for a 50%–46% win, even as Bob Dole was losing badly in the district. In 1998 he carried every county except for a tiny sliver of Columbiana, and won by an impressive 60%–40%. "I have defied the odds for years," Ney proclaimed, and so he has; after his impressive 1998 win, he got an easy ride in 2000 against a former state Representative who invited trash-TV host (and former mayor of Cincinnati) Jerry Springer to appear on his behalf; Ney won 64%–34%. Some 44,000 people need to be added to the 18th during redistricting, which is controlled by Republicans. The district could become more Democratic for 2002, but—based on past performance—still safe for Ney.

Cook's Call   *Probably Safe.* Ney has been a top target of Democrats since he won this blue-collar, Democratic-leaning district in 1994. But Ney's moderate record on labor issues and his political savvy make him a tough target. After solid wins in 1998 and 2000, Ney looks to have a pretty good hold on this seat. Some Republicans are worried that too much tinkering with other Democratic districts around the state could adversely impact the 18th, but Ney seems unlikely to be seriously targeted in 2002.

THE PEOPLE: Pop. 2000: 586,247; Pop. 1990: 570,784, up 2.7% 1990–2000. 95.7% White, 2.6% Black, 0.3% Asian, 0.2% Amer. Indian, 1% Two + races, 0.2% Other; 0.6% Hispanic Origin.

2000 Presidential Vote		
Bush (R)	122,309	(51%)
Gore (D)	107,601	(45%)
Nader (Green)	6,199	(3%)
Others	4,678	(2%)

1996 Presidential Vote		
Clinton (D)	112,851	(47%)
Dole (R)	86,305	(36%)
Perot (I)	36,143	(15%)

Rep. Bob Ney (R)

Elected 1994, 4th term; b. July 5, 1954, Wheeling, WV; home, St. Clairsville; OH St. U., B.S. 1976; Catholic; married (Elizabeth).

Elected Office: OH House of Reps., 1980–82; OH Senate, 1984–94.

Professional Career: Teacher, Iran, 1978; Program Mgr., OH Office of Appalachia, 1979; Bellaire Safety Dir., 1980.

DC Office: 1024 LHOB 20515, 202-225-6265; Fax: 202-225-3394; Web site: www.house.gov/ney.

District Offices: Bellaire, 740-676-1960; New Philadelphia, 330-364-6380; Zanesville, 740-452-7023.

Committees: *Financial Services* (11th of 37 R): Capital Markets, Insurance & Government Sponsored Enterprises (Vice Chmn.); Housing & Community Opportunity; Oversight & Investigations. *House Administration* (Chmn. of 6 R). *Transportation & Infrastructure* (15th of 42 R).

Group Ratings

	ADA	ACLU	AFS	LCV	CON	ITIC	NTU	COC	ACU	NTLC	CHC
2000	20	43	42	14	11	61	55	61	83	70	87
1999	10	—	16	0	7	—	52	92	84	—	—

National Journal Ratings

	1999 LIB —	1999 CONS		2000 LIB —	2000 CONS
Economic	41%	—	57%	39%	—	60%
Social	19%	—	79%	0%	—	79%
Foreign	20%	—	78%	12%	—	78%

Key Votes of the 106th Congress

1. Patient Bill of Rights	N	5. Bar RU-486 $ for FDA	Y	9. NATO War in Serbia	N
2. Accelerate Min. Wage	Y	6. Display 10 Commandments	Y	10. Perm. Trade with China	N
3. Strike Ban on Ergo. Stnd.	N	7. Gun Show Bkgrnd. Checks	N	11. Debt Relief for 3rd World	N
4. Ovrd. Estate Tax Veto	Y	8. Ban Part.-Birth Abortion	Y	12. Drop Cuba Econ. Embargo	N

Election Results

2000 general	Bob Ney (R)	152,325	(64%)	($725,334)
	Marc Guthrie (D)	79,232	(34%)	($223,429)
	Other	4,948	(2%)	
2000 primary	Bob Ney (R)	unopposed		
1998 general	Bob Ney (R)	113,119	(60%)	($928,302)
	Robert L. Burch (D)	74,571	(40%)	($405,010)

NINETEENTH DISTRICT

The Western Reserve—the northeast corner of Ohio that belonged to Connecticut until 1800—still bears a distinctive New England Yankee imprint. This land was on the westward trail of Yankee settlement in the years before the Civil War; here, amid the low hills that produced the steel streams of the Cuyahoga and the Mahoning, they established New England-style townships, churches and schools. This area produced some of the strongest opposition to slavery and support of the Union armies and Republican party in the nation. Its thrifty, hard-working, well-educated citizens built communities with fine schools and, with their accumulated savings, invested in what became some of the nation's leading industries. That brought great masses of immigrants to Cleveland and the other cities of northeast Ohio, which remained solidly Republican until the Great Depression and the bloody CIO organizing drives of the late 1930s; then for 30 years, the Western Reserve was Democratic during Ohio's class-warfare politics. In the early 1980s, when the auto and steel industries lost thousands of jobs, northeast Ohio went heavily Democratic; in the 1990s, as the economy diversified and recovered, it hovered between the parties.

The 19th Congressional District takes in a very irregularly shaped hunk of northeast Ohio and the old Western Reserve. It includes all of Lake County, with mixed middling-to-affluent suburbs and industrial Ashtabula County in the northeast corner of the state. It also includes a motley collection of the Cuyahoga County suburbs of Cleveland—"both polo fields and bingo halls," says its congressman. East of Cleveland are affluent Italian, Jewish and WASP suburbs: Beachwood, Pepper Pike and Chagrin Falls. Directly south of Cleveland are more working-class suburbs on either side of the Cuyahoga River gorge and west to Brook Park around the convention center and airport. Typical of suburban districts in the largest metropolitan areas, it reacted positively to Clinton-Gore Democrats in the 1990s, and voted 49%–47% for Al Gore in 2000.

The congressman from the 19th District is Steve LaTourette, a Republican elected in 1994. LaTourette grew up in the Cleveland area and went to law school at Cleveland State University; in the 1980s he worked as a public defender and a private lawyer in Lake County, and became Lake County district attorney in 1988, at 34. Well-known and well-liked, he won a three-candidate 1994 Republican primary with 54%. In the general he faced Eric Fingerhut, a 35-year-old political prodigy who in 1992 was elected to replace not one but two retiring Democratic incumbents. LaTourette attacked Fingerhut for backing the Clinton budget and tax increase, for being soft on crime, and for hypocritically using his franking privileges. LaTourette won 48%–43%, even though he did not raise nearly as much PAC money as Fingerhut; Fingerhut now represents a solidly Democratic district in the Ohio Senate.

In the House, LaTourette has a moderate voting record and shows more irreverence than one might expect from a former prosecutor or a Republican. The only bearded freshman, in his first weeks, he invited humorist Dave Barry to spend several days on his press staff, with predictably funny results. Later he was quoted as saying that being a congressman "sucks." He backs up his independence with his votes. He was one of 10 Republicans to vote against the party's balanced budget plan in 1995. He is among a handful of Republicans who bucked his party on the HMO regulation, which won LaTourette praise from the AFL-CIO. On the Banking Committee, he sponsored the 1998 credit-union membership reform bill that overturned a Supreme Court decision jeopardizing many existing credit unions. When the House passed a bill in 2000 to increase savings incentives, LaTourette made a seemingly minor change to calculate construction workers' pension benefits based on a worker's three highest years of earnings, instead of the three highest consecutive years; but that would make a big difference for workers in carpentry and plumbing, where annual income can vary widely. He broke with House Republicans to oppose permanent normal trade relations with China. In 2001 he became chairman of the Transportation Committee's Economic Development, Public Buildings, and Emergency Management Subcommittee—a mouthful of an assignment that gave LaTourette control of several slabs of pork that many House members find vital.

In 1996 the AFL-CIO ran ads against LaTourette for several months but quit in June to concentrate on defeating Martin Hoke, the Republican representing the more Democratic 10th. In 1998 Republican governor candidate Bob Taft offered LaTourette the lieutenant governor nomination; perhaps not eager for the enforced idleness of the office, he declined. LaTourette worked with Democrat James Traficant in the neighboring district to increase his comfort level with House Republicans before Traficant decided to vote for Dennis Hastert for speaker in January 2001. With Republicans in control of Ohio redistricting, it's a good bet that LaTourette will gain a more favorable district. He likely will pick up heavily Republican Geauga County from the 13th District and could lose some of the more Democratic Cleveland suburbs. When he was first elected in 1994, LaTourette said he would limit himself to four two-year terms. More recently he told Republican leaders that he would extend his service to no more than 10 years.

Cook's Call *Safe.* Despite the fact that this district is one of the most competitive in the state, LaTourette has not had much trouble winning three re-election contests. Republicans control redistricting and are interested in shoring up this district. Democrats have not targeted this race for four years, so it is unlikely that it will be targeted in 2002, when it will probably be less marginal.

THE PEOPLE: Pop. 2000: 599,574; Pop. 1990: 570,834, up 5% 1990–2000. 93.8% White, 2.9% Black, 1.6% Asian, 0.1% Amer. Indian, 1% Two+ races, 0.5% Other; 1.5% Hispanic Origin.

2000 Presidential Vote			1996 Presidential Vote		
Gore (D)	125,774	(49%)	Clinton (D)	126,926	(48%)
Bush (R)	119,191	(47%)	Dole (R)	102,099	(39%)
Nader (Green)	7,530	(3%)	Perot (I)	31,362	(12%)
Others	2,727	(1%)			

Rep. Steven C. LaTourette (R)

Elected 1994, 4th term; b. July 22, 1954, Cleveland; home, Madison Village; U. of MI, B.A. 1976, Cleveland St. U., J.D. 1979; Methodist; married (Susan).

Professional Career: Lake Cnty. Asst. Public Defender, 1980–83; Practicing atty., 1983–88; Lake Cnty. Prosecuting atty., 1988–94.

DC Office: 2453 RHOB 20515, 202-225-5731; Fax: 202-225-3307; Web site: www.house.gov/latourette.

District Office: Painesville, 440-352-3939.

Committees: *Financial Services* (20th of 37 R): Capital Markets, Insurance & Government Sponsored Enterprises; Domestic Monetary Policy, Technology & Economic Growth; Financial Institutions & Consumer Credit. *Government Reform* (12th of 24 R): Energy Policy, Natural Resources and Regulatory Affairs; National Security, Veterans' Affairs & Intl. Relations. *Transportation & Infrastructure* (12th of 42 R): Economic Development, Public Buildings & Emergency Management (Chmn.); Highways & Transit; Water Resources & Environment.

Group Ratings

	ADA	ACLU	AFS	LCV	CON	ITIC	NTU	COC	ACU	NTLC	CHC
2000	25	43	28	21	37	88	57	80	68	61	60
1999	35	—	16	25	75	—	61	79	64	—	—

National Journal Ratings

	1999 LIB	—	1999 CONS		2000 LIB	—	2000 CONS
Economic	44%	—	56%		39%	—	60%
Social	48%	—	52%		41%	—	58%
Foreign	46%	—	53%		49%	—	49%

Key Votes of the 106th Congress

1. Patient Bill of Rights	Y	5. Bar RU-486 $ for FDA	Y	9. NATO War in Serbia	Y
2. Accelerate Min. Wage	N	6. Display 10 Commandments	Y	10. Perm. Trade with China	N
3. Strike Ban on Ergo. Stnd.	N	7. Gun Show Bkgrnd. Checks	N	11. Debt Relief for 3rd World	Y
4. Ovrd. Estate Tax Veto	Y	8. Ban Part.-Birth Abortion	Y	12. Drop Cuba Econ. Embargo	Y

Election Results

2000 general	Steven C. LaTourette (R)	174,262	(69%)	($332,893)
	Dale Blanchard (D)	70,429	(28%)	
	Other	6,957	(3%)	
2000 primary	Steven C. LaTourette (R)	unopposed		
1998 general	Steven C. LaTourette (R)	126,786	(66%)	($798,114)
	Elizabeth Kelley (D)	64,090	(34%)	($128,265)

★ OKLAHOMA ★

Oklahoma, proud of its history of rising from humble beginnings, enjoying the surging prosperity of the 1990s but uneasy about whether it is keeping pace in education and high-skill employment, is in the middle of America geographically and perhaps spiritually as well. Oklahoma was in the national spotlight when the Oklahoma City federal building was bombed in April 1995, and all Americans marveled at the grace and determination with which Oklahomans went about rescuing the wounded and honoring the dead. And in early May 1999 dozens of tornadoes tore through the Oklahoma City area, killing 44 people and causing $1 billion in damage. But these are not the only catastrophes from which Oklahoma has rebounded. It has had exhilarating highs and sickening lows several times in its improbable history. Oklahoma was settled in a rush, first by the Five Civilized Tribes driven west by Andrew Jackson's troops over the Cherokees' Trail of Tears in the 1830s. Then came white settlers one morning in April 1889 when, in the great land rush memorialized in an Edna Ferber novel, the Rodgers and Hammerstein musical, and half a dozen Hollywood movies, thousands of would-be homesteaders drove their wagons across the territorial line at the sound of a gunshot, the most adventurous or unscrupulous of them literally jumping the gun—the Sooners.

The heritage of these rushes remains. Oklahoma has the second-largest Indian population in the country, after California, 273,000 in the 2000 Census, though there is just one reservation and the status of many other tribal entities is often disputed. The Cherokee Nation suffered through the late 1990s through charges of financial misconduct and brawling against its principal chief, Joe Byrd; but he was defeated by Chad Smith in the 1999 election. Some Indian tribes here have unsuccessfully sought a return of native lands and face high unemployment rates. But there has been much intermarriage over the years, and many Oklahomans proudly claim some Indian blood; assimilation into everyday life plus commemoration of historic traditions and efforts to keep the Cherokee, Choctaw, Chickasaw and Seminole languages from dying out—you can see street signs in the Cherokee alphabet in Tahlequah—seem to have provided a better life for most Native Americans here than it approaches elsewhere.

Statehood came to Oklahoma late, in 1907, at which point it filled up with farmers, rising from 1.5 million people in 1907 to 2.4 million in 1930. Oil helped: The first well was drilled here in 1897 and by 1920 Tulsa was an oil boom town. Then came a decade of bust—or dust—as soil

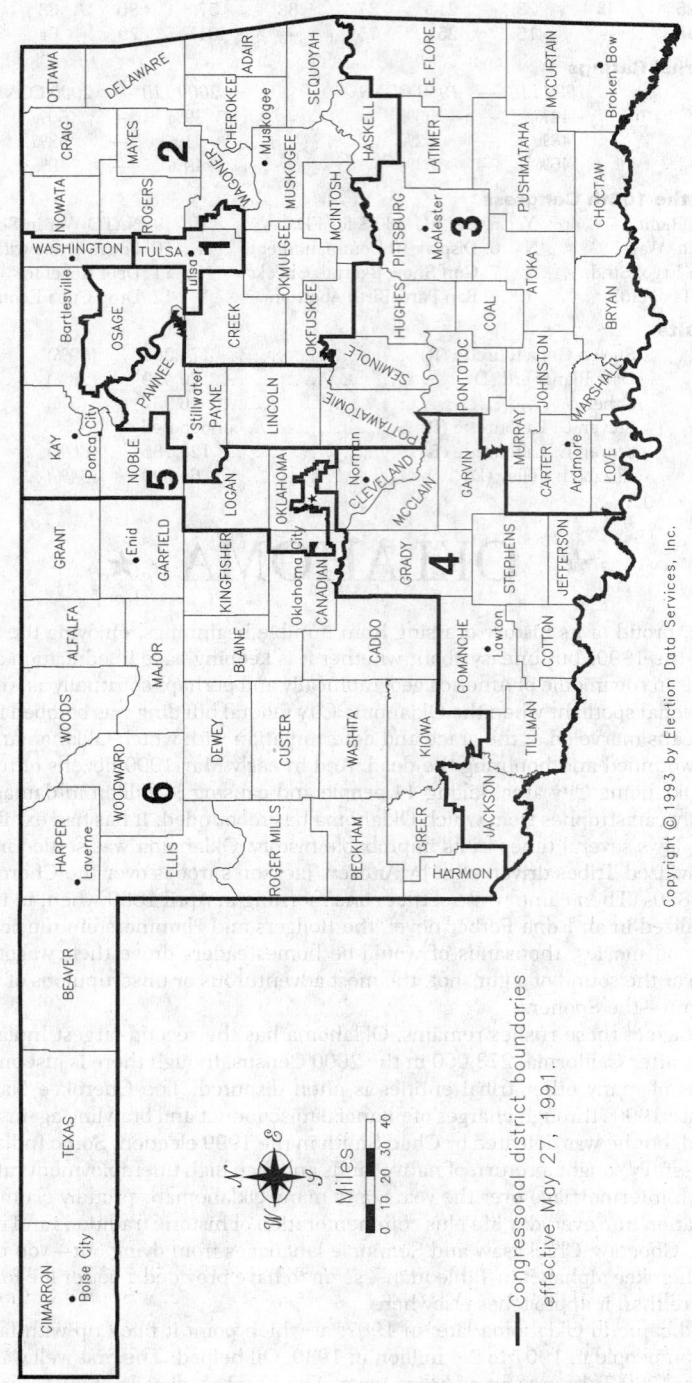

— Congressional district boundaries
effective May 27, 1991.

Miles

0 10 20 30 40

loosened by erosion was whipped into giant swirling clouds: the Dust Bowl. "On a single day, I heard, 50 million tons of soil were blown away," John Gunther reported later. "People sat in Oklahoma City, with the sky invisible for three days in a row, holding dust masks over their faces and wet towels to protect their mouths at night, while the farms blew by." Okies headed in droves west on U.S. 66 to the green land of California, and Oklahoma's population sank to 2.3 million in 1940 and 2.2 million in 1950, not to reach its 1930 level again until 1970.

Then oil brought another boom: As the oil shocks of 1973 and 1979 sent oil prices up, Oklahoma's population rose from 2.5 million in 1970 to 3 million in 1980 and 3.3 million in 1983. Then, with the collapse of oil prices and of Oklahoma's farm economy as well, it was bust again. A giddy rise was followed by a giddier fall: The rig count fell from 882 in January 1982 to 232 in February 1983, and was just 141 in February 2001; Oklahoma's oil production in 1999 fell to its lowest point in 80 years, and the rising prices of 2000 stimulated little new production. Just as the dust cloud symbolized Oklahoma's 1930s bust, so the auction of oil drilling equipment was a symbol of the 1980s calamity. The 1990 Census reported just 3.1 million Oklahomans. But in the 1990s, Oklahoma has been building a more diversified economy, with high-tech employers like WorldCom, Lucent and Williams. Population rose 10% in the decade, to 3.45 million in 2000. Tax breaks for any business located on current or "former" Indian reservation land—nearly the entire state—have brought in new jobs. But incomes have not risen much, and thousands of Indians in Oklahoma have filed a massive class-action suit against the government charging that officials have grossly mismanaged Indian trust funds. Oklahoma continues to have above-average rates of divorce, teenage pregnancy and crime, and a low rate of college graduates. Oklahoma knows it has risen far but still has some distance to go.

For most of the 1990s Oklahoma was split between a Democratic heritage, reflected by a heavily Democratic legislature and county courthouses, and a strong Republican surge, reflected by Governor Frank Keating and, for four years, an all-Republican congressional delegation. The House delegation was transformed in just three years from 4–2 Democratic to 6–0 Republican. The historical political patterns were set in the early years: most of the first settlers were Southerners and so Oklahoma leaned to the Democrats. They were especially strong in Little Dixie in the south, while the wheat counties of the northwest leaned Republican; Tulsa, originally Republican, and Oklahoma City, originally Democratic, are both now Republican. In 2000 there was an ebbing of both trends. Democrat Brad Carson won an open U.S. House seat, and Republicans made significant gains in the legislature, holding Democrats to a 53–48 edge in the House and a larger 30–18 edge in the Senate. Keating predicted Republican majorities in 2002 or 2004, when term limits will force many Democratic legislators to retire. And Democratic House Speaker Larry Adair admitted, "We're losing a lot of the young voters." The VNS exit poll showed that George W. Bush carried voters under 60 by a whopping 64%-34% margin; only among those over 60 was it close, with Bush still leading 53%–46%. Oklahoma is growing fastest in the once-rural counties around Oklahoma City and Tulsa, which are heavily Republican; losing population are the dry western counties, also heavily Republican. But old traditions have not entirely died out. Oklahoma is one of three states to allow the ancient American sport of cockfighting, and although animal rights activists gathered over 140,000 signatures to qualify for a statewide referendum, breeders successfully challenged 43,000 to disqualify it from the November 2000 ballot.

Governor Frank Keating, elected governor in 1994 and re-elected in 1998, grew up in Tulsa in comfortable circumstances. He went to Georgetown—where he overlapped with Bill Clinton—and the University of Oklahoma Law School, then in 1969 became an FBI agent, investigating new-left terrorists on the West Coast. Keating worked as a prosecutor in Tulsa and was elected to the Oklahoma House in 1972, at 28, and the state Senate in 1974. In 1981 he became U.S. attorney in Tulsa. During Ronald Reagan's second term Keating served as assistant secretary of the Treasury and then as associate attorney general under the first Bush administration; he was general counsel of HUD when Jack Kemp was its secretary. After Senate Democrats refused to act on his nomination for a federal judgeship, Keating returned to Oklahoma in 1993 and began running for governor. He was clearly the party leaders' choice and won the 1994 Republican primary 57%–29%. He presented an image of competent conservatism while the Democrats were in disarray. Incumbent David Walters, after pleading guilty of campaign finance violations, hesitated before dropping out of the race. Lieutenant Governor Jack Mildren, with 49% in the August primary, was forced into a September runoff. Former Democratic Congressman Wes Watkins, from Little Dixie, who had lost the 1990 runoff to Walters 51%–49%, ran as an independent. Keating campaigned for business and other tax cuts and won with 47% of the vote, to 30% for Mildren and 23% for Watkins.

In office Keating encountered vehement opposition from Democratic legislators, but was nevertheless able to pass much of his program. Among his successes were the largest tax cut in the state's history, a property tax cap, tort reform, a 58% cut in welfare rolls and workmen's compensation reform. He spent more money on higher education, as the University of Oklahoma blossomed under the leadership of former Governor and Senator David Boren, and Keating passed a $1 billion program to build highways and beef up Oklahoma's turnpikes. Keating performed with aplomb after the April 1995 Oklahoma City bombing, supervising the search for survivors and comforting victims and their families; his wife helped raise $7 million for them and compiled a commemorative book which made the bestseller lists. In April 1998 he pushed through a partial-birth abortion ban by prodding legislators on TV.

Despite vehement opposition from legislative Democrats, Keating had a high job rating, and in 1998 several prominent moderate Democrats declined to run. The nominee, liberal state Representative Laura Boyd, campaigned gamely, starting with an ad showing her riding a horse named Keating through a barrel race and saying that by the time the campaign is over Keating will "look like he's been rode hard and put up wet." But Keating vastly outspent her and won easily, 58%–41%. He was only the second Oklahoma governor to win two consecutive terms. His margin was up in metro Oklahoma City (66%–33%) but down in Tulsa (55%–43%); he carried ancestrally Democratic counties in south central and southwest Oklahoma, but lost most counties in eastern Little Dixie and in the heavily Indian northeast. In 1999 and 2000 Keating's relations with the legislature continued to be abrasive. But in 1999 he was able to pass a major education reform, with school choice and charter schools, summer school instead of social promotion, and high school graduation requirements of four years of English and three of math, science and social studies. Bills were passed for 10-year sentences for attackers in violent crimes and criminalizing possession of three of the seven chemicals needed to produce methamphetamines; the state gave tax credits to airlines providing nonstop flights to the East and West Coasts. Keating defended a state textbook commission ruling that biology texts must label evolution a "controversial theory." In 2000 the legislature passed Keating's $3,000 teacher pay increase plus $2,000 in merit pay. But Keating aroused controversy when he jokingly answered "homicide" to a question about teachers' unions. He failed to get action on tax cuts and was embroiled in controversy about an auto tag tax cut proposal which went on the August 2000 ballot. Altogether he vetoed 240 bills in six years. Two interesting Keating projects: He wants to cut the divorce rate in Oklahoma by one-third in 10 years, and has used state funding and a private Oklahoma Marriage Covenant Movement to change attitudes about divorce. And he raised private money to build a dome on the state Capitol; original construction stopped when funds ran out in 1915. Now it is scheduled to go up by November 2002.

In 1998 there was talk that Keating might run for president. He made no moves to do so, but as head of the Republican Governors Association endorsed George W. Bush early and in the course of 2000 campaigned for him often. He was on the short list of vice presidential prospects in July 2000, but was not chosen. After campaigning for Bush in many states in the fall, he was mentioned as a possible attorney general, but again Bush did not select him. But Keating could take satisfaction in Oklahoma's election results. The state voted heavily for Bush, and also cut the Democrats' edges in the legislature. This brought into sight one of Keating's major goals, a right-to-work law, which he believes will make Oklahoma more competitive with neighboring states; he had hopes that enough Democrats could be brought over to put the issue on the 2002 ballot. Keating also had hopes that Republicans could win legislative majorities in 2002 or, after term limits kick in, in 2004. Keating is term-limited himself, and thus will not be able to work with a Republican legislature. In early 2001 many politicians were mentioned as possible candidates. Republicans included Congressmen Steve Largent (who has said he will retire from the House in November 2001), Wes Watkins (who ran as a Democrat in 1986 and as an independent in 1990), and Jim Denny, father of two children injured in the Oklahoma City bombing. Democratic possibilities included Treasurer Robert Butkin, Auditor Clifton Scott, and state Representative Russ Roach.

Cook's Call   *Probably Safe.* Although Oklahoma retains pockets of Democratic voters, it has trended more Republican in recent years, giving the Republican a decided edge in this race. It appears that Congressman Steve Largent is the frontrunner for the Republican nomination. On the Democratic side, the roster of potential candidates includes some statewide elected officials, but it is not certain that any of them could make it a real contest.

Senior Senator   Don Nickles, the Senate minority whip, was first elected in 1980. He grew up in Ponca City, and, after his father died when he was 13, worked his way through Oklahoma State as a janitor making minimum wage; he then returned to Ponca City and helped run the family machine business. In 1978, at 29, he was elected to the Oklahoma Senate; two years later, he ran for the U.S. Senate seat being vacated by Republican Henry Bellmon. With support from Christian conservatives, he won 35% in a multi-candidate primary and 65% in the runoff; in the general he won 53%–44%, and at 31 became the youngest Republican ever elected to the Senate. It was a signal that conservative Republicanism was the prevailing current of opinion in Oklahoma, just as Nickles's rise to a Senate leadership post is a signal of conservative Republican strength there.

In the Senate Nickles has been a stalwart for conservative principles—"the keeper of the conservative flame," as *CongressDaily* put it. He ascribes his views to his experience running a small business. "I'm a strong proponent and believer in the free enterprise system. . . . I built up a business that was almost bankrupt. If I see government causing problems or doing things that interfere with personal freedom or economic freedom or religious freedom, I feel very strongly that we should get involved and try to change it." Without much notice outside Washington, he has risen to the number two position in the Republican leadership. He chaired the Republican Senate campaign committee during the 1990 cycle and, as an opponent of the 1990 budget summit tax increase, he beat the more senior Pete Domenici for Republican Conference chairman in December 1990 by 23–20. When Bob Dole resigned in June 1998, Nickles considered running for majority leader, but didn't challenge Trent Lott; both got their posts unopposed. After the November 1998 election, Nickles was urged to run against Lott, but decided not to. He said a race against Lott "would probably end one of our political careers."

There is nonetheless a tension between their approaches: Lott, though very conservative on substance, is temperamentally a deal-maker; Nickles, though personable and pleasant, is inclined to stand solid on his convictions. After the June 1997 tobacco settlement, Lott charged Nickles with putting together a tobacco bill, but he would not compromise with the tax increases sought by Orrin Hatch and Edward Kennedy. The assignment went to Commerce Chairman John McCain, whose bill Nickles opposed as "one of the worst pieces of legislation I've ever seen." In summer 1998 he coordinated a three-week filibuster which killed the bill; his own proposal is for a $1 billion program to discourage teen smoking and drug use. On HMO regulation, Lott in 1997 made Nickles head of a health care task force. In summer 1998 Nickles came up with his own HMO bill with 49 co-sponsors, and Democrats did not bring up their bill after a version of it passed the House. When Democrats got 51 votes for the House bill in 2000, Nickles continued to resist action, and it did not come to the floor. Nickles has resisted increases in the minimum wage, even when leavened by tax relief for small business. "By raising the minimum wage, politicians would yank the ladder up too high for some people to get on in the first place." He had little enthusiasm for the community renewal bill which was a 2000 project of Bill Clinton and Dennis Hastert.

In his early years in the Senate Nickles backed the successful fights to deregulate oil and natural gas prices, to repeal the windfall profits tax, and to repeal the 55-mile-per-hour speed limit. He opposed the Clinton Btu and gasoline taxes in 1993, and in 1998 sponsored an electricity deregulation law which would prohibit the states from granting electric utilities exclusive service territories. He got the Senate to go on record 76–23 in 1993 against allowing HIV-positive immigrants into the country. In 1998 he held up the nomination of Jane Henney to head the FDA until HHS Secretary Donna Shalala agreed not to seek a manufacturer for RU-486 or finance more abortions under Medicaid or Kiddiecare. He takes sometimes lonely stands—against the confirmation of Ambassador to the UN Richard Holbrooke in 1999, against $15 billion in aid to farmers and against outlawing Section 527 campaign organizations in 2000. He opposed the Conservation and Reinvestment Act as a federal power grab and called AmeriCorps a "boondoggle," though Oklahoma's Republican Governor Frank Keating supports both. His move to require congressional approval of national monument designations—a power used by Bill Clinton during the 1996 campaign and in his last year in office—failed by a 50–49 vote in July 2000. He spoke out against tapping the Strategic Petroleum Reserve in September 2000 and against giving Native Hawaiians the same status as American Indian tribes in October 2000.

On occasion Nickles has taken bipartisan initiatives. With Nevada's Harry Reid, he won Senate passage of a bipartisan regulatory reform bill in March 1995—a more realistic and effective version of the moratorium on new regulations in the House's Contract With America. Nickles was also the chief sponsor of the Republican $500-per-child tax credit included in the 1995 budget reconciliation bill vetoed by President Clinton, but passed in 1998. He sponsored the Religious Freedom Act, which passed unanimously in 1998, though without the automatic sanctions some sought. He helped to pass the Digital Millennium Copyright Act and to ratify the World Intellectual Property Organization. He and Mary Landrieu sponsored a 2000 law for automatic citizenship for foreign-born children adopted by Americans.

Nickles can be a tenacious fighter. He has long sought to bar the Cheyenne-Arapaho tribe from claiming ancestral land at Fort Reno which has been an USDA research station. This was the tribe that lobbied Bill Clinton in the White House after making a $100,000 contribution to the Democratic National Committee. In September 2000 Nickles passed an amendment blocking the land transfer, against the strong opposition of Daniel Inouye. Nickles has also worked hard to in effect repeal Oregon's 1994 assisted suicide law, by sponsoring what he calls the Pain Relief Promotion Act which would bar physicians from prescribing controlled substances for purposes of suicide. This passed the House in 1999, and Nickles worked to find a vehicle to bring it to the floor of the Senate. In the process he tangled with Oregon Democrat Ron Wyden, as he attempted to stop a vote and Nickles put holds on other Oregon legislation.

For all his commitment to cutting spending, Nickles does work to bring projects to Oklahoma, including a $12 million veterans cemetery in Fort Sill (line-item vetoed by Clinton but revived in 2000), a $3 million weather station in Norman, $40 million for the Montgomery Point Lock and Dam on the McClellan-Kerr Navigation System and the $18 million anti-terrorism institute near the site of the 1995 federal building bombing in Oklahoma City. He is a big fan of Amtrak's Heartland Flyer that runs from Oklahoma City to Fort Worth, and in August 2000 sponsored a contest for high schoolers to design a symbol for the train.

Nickles has been very popular in Oklahoma. His one tough re-election came in 1986, when he faced Tulsa Congressman Jim Jones. But Jones's ad campaign misfired and Nickles showed greater strength than many in Washington expected, winning 55%–45% in a year several other Southern Republicans elected in 1980 lost. In 1992 Nickles won easily, 59%–38%. In 1998 he had no big-name opponents. The Democratic nomination was won by Tahlequah air-conditioning contractor Don Carroll when he defeated a woman who had died a week after filing for office. Nickles carried all but one county and won 66%–31%. Does he wish to stay in the Senate as long as Strom Thurmond? Nickles professed himself "surprised I'm running for my fourth term" and suggested he might retire from office after that. But he said, two years before George W. Bush was elected, the possibility of a Republican president could get him to stay on. No one doubts that he can be re-elected in 2004, and some see him as a successor to Trent Lott as Republican leader.

Junior Senator James Inhofe, Oklahoma's junior senator, was elected to a short term in 1994 and a full term in 1996. Inhofe grew up in Tulsa, served in the Army, worked in real estate, insurance and aviation, has for years regularly flown planes and is one of Congress's few certified commercial pilots; he flew around the world following Wiley Post's route and on short notice flew into Texas military bases to check on readiness. He was elected to the Oklahoma House in 1966, at 31, and to the Oklahoma Senate in 1969; he ran for governor in 1974 and lost to David Boren, 64%–36%. In 1976, Inhofe ran for the U.S. House against Jim Jones and lost; from 1979–84 Inhofe was mayor of Tulsa. He won the heavily Republican 1st District House seat in 1986, but held it with uninspiring margins. He was hurt by negative publicity about a family business lawsuit (he eventually was awarded $3.6 million) and charges of campaign finance irregularities, leveled often by the liberal-leaning *Tulsa World*. Inhofe's great achievement in the House was reforming the arcane discharge petition rule. For years House rules kept secret the names of signers of petitions to discharge bills stuck in committees; members could say they had worked to bring legislation to the floor when they had done just the opposite. That was changed September 28, 1993, and one of the first bills to benefit from the new rules was the aviation liability reform bill, co-sponsored by Inhofe, which limited the liability of small airplane manufacturers in lawsuits resulting from crashes.

Inhofe jumped into the 1994 Senate race when his onetime opponent David Boren, a conservative Democrat who carried not only every county but every precinct in 1990, announced he was retiring to become president of the University of Oklahoma. The Democratic nominee was Dave McCurdy, congressman since 1980 from southwest Oklahoma, chairman of the moderate Democratic Leadership Council. An extrapolation from their past electoral showings would put Inhofe far behind: He had won by small margins in a heavily Republican district, while McCurdy had won by large margins in a district that gave Bill Clinton only one-third of its votes in 1992. But in Oklahoma in 1994 the Clinton burden was too heavy for even McCurdy to carry. McCurdy had voted for the 1993 Clinton budget and tax package with its original Btu tax and for the 1994 crime bill with its assault weapons ban. Inhofe won by a solid 55%–40%, carrying the Tulsa area by a higher percentage than ever before (60%–37%) and Oklahoma City by even more (61%–35%); he also bested McCurdy in the rest of Oklahoma (52%–42%). In the Senate Inhofe was president of the conservative 11-member freshman class. He had the satisfaction of seeing the Congressional Medal of Honor awarded to seven black soldiers for their service in World War II; since 1990 he had been championing the cause of Ruben Rivers, a Hotulka, Oklahoma, soldier who after being gravely wounded refused evacuation and was killed trying to save his unit. Inhofe was elected to a full six-year term in 1996 over James Boren, David Boren's cousin, by 57%–40%.

Inhofe has a very conservative voting record and has committee assignments with jurisdiction over military readiness and the Clean Air Act. Inhofe argued in early 1998 that the military was in a poor state of readiness. Military leaders disagreed, but in September 1998 hearings Joint Chiefs Chairman Henry Shelton vindicated Inhofe's concerns. In 2000 Inhofe was citing a report of unreadiness at the Field Artillery School in Oklahoma's Fort Sill as further evidence his charges were true, and in October 2000 he said that Navy cuts in at-sea refueling was maybe "partly at fault" in the bombing of the *Cole*. Inhofe has been a strong supporter of missile defense, and attacked General Shelton's August 1998 statement, made just before North Korea launched a three-stage missile over Japan, that there was no short-term threat from hostile missiles. He has constantly criticized the "no-end" American commitment in Bosnia; in November 1998 he said the U.S. should "pull out of the area entirely." He was one of the leaders of the successful fight in October 1999 to deny ratification to the Comprehensive Test Ban Treaty. When Puerto Ricans called for an end to live-fire amphibious exercises on the island of Vieques, Inhofe called for their continuation and said that if they were stopped the Navy should close its $3 billion Roosevelt Roads base in Puerto Rico. Inhofe attacked the Clinton Administration's handling of base closings as dishonest, especially the "privatization" of depot bases in electoral-vote-rich California and Texas rather than transfer of work to bases in Oklahoma, Utah and Georgia. He has worked to maintain at least 50% of Air Force repair work in Air Force bases. He has also sought to bar state-owned companies from leasing former military bases; the target here is the lease of part of Long Beach Harbor to a Chinese-owned company. He has backed a Tulsa company's proposal to develop aircraft to detect weapons of mass destruction at Oklahoma's Camp Gruber; it could be used to spot meth labs too, he says. He opposed PNTR with China: "National security must take precedence over trade."

As chairman of an environmental subcommittee, Inhofe criticized the Clinton EPA for acting without a scientific basis and without regard to cost. He said the EPA stricter air-quality standards were based on a dishonest rationale, and called for their delay; he tried to block the EPA regulations on sulfur in gasoline. With Dianne Feinstein, he sponsored an amendment to allow governors to waive the federal requirement for using reformulated gas, because it includes the harmful substance MTBE. After the death of John Chafee in fall 1999, Inhofe sought the chairmanship of the Environment Committee; this was when the only more senior Republican, Bob Smith of New Hampshire, had left the party. But Smith scampered back, and Inhofe did not get the chair.

Inhofe often casts lonely votes. He was one of the few votes against Richard Holbrooke for UN Ambassador, against the May 1997 budget deal and the October 1998 omnibus budget, against the bipartisan Everglades bill. In December 1999 he put holds on every pending judicial nomination after Bill Clinton made a recess appointment to the National Labor Relations Board without giving notice. But Orrin Hatch and Trent Lott would not throttle every nomination; they brought some forward in February and March 2000, against which Inhofe voted in vain. Inhofe has worked with others in the Oklahoma delegation to simplify the land laws applying to the Five Tribes, so that land can be developed and mineral rights exploited more easily. Another pet measure was his provision allowing pilots to appeal a license suspension by the FAA to the National Transportation Safety Board.

Inhofe comes up for re-election in 2002. In January 2001, when no other prominent Democrat came forward, former Governor David Walters said he was considering making the race, though he pleaded guilty in 1993 to one count of campaign finance law violations.

Cook's Call   *Safe.* There are few reasons to believe Inhofe is particularly vulnerable. Former Democratic Governor David Walters, who did not run for reelection in 1994 after pleading guilty to misdemeanor campaign finance violations, is gearing up for a challenge, but he is likely to be damaged merchandise in what would be a difficult race even without his past ethical problems.

Presidential politics   Oklahoma has been a solidly Republican state in presidential elections since the 1950s. There are no large blocs of voters here who back national Democrats and almost everyone finds national Republicans acceptable. Oklahoma is thus not on anyone's list of target states in October, nor is it the subject of much attention as one of the southern Super Tuesday primaries. It has voted for party nominees in the last three presidential primaries; the last time it did not was in 1988, when it voted for Al Gore (a distant relation of onetime Oklahoma Senator Thomas Gore, grandfather of writer Gore Vidal).

Congressional districting   Oklahoma lost one of its six House seats in the 2000 Census, a loss it narrowly averted 10 years before. Then the delegation was 4–2 Democratic; now it is 5–1 Republican, and was 6–0 until Brad Carson won the open 2nd District seat in 2000. The legislature is controlled by Democrats, but Republican Governor Frank Keating may veto a plan if he believes it helps their party too much. Democrats will certainly try to make sure Carson has a safe seat, which means they will also maintain heavily Republican Tulsa as the nucleus of another district. Democrats may also try to create another favorable seat by extending the 3rd District westward and perhaps by lopping off Republican Stillwater. But 3rd District Republican incumbent Wes Watkins, who previously served 14 years as a Democrat, is highly popular in the area; he wants Stillwater kept in the district and, though he has been known to consider retirement he said in November 2000, "If they make me mad, I might run anyway." That would leave a musical chairs game with three Republicans—J.C. Watts, Ernest Istook and Frank Lucas— seeking two seats. National Republicans are particularly eager to keep Watts, the party's only black member of Congress. All three represent parts of greater Oklahoma City today; the way that area is carved up may determine the outcome.

THE PEOPLE: Pop. 2000: 3,450,654; Pop. 1990: 3,145,585, up 9.7% 1990–2000. 1.2% of U.S. total, 27th largest; 76.2% White, 7.6% Black, 1.4% Asian, 7.9% Amer. Indian, 0.1% Hawaiian, 4.5% Two+ races, 2.4% Other; 5.2% Hispanic Origin. 3% Unemployment. 2000 Voting age pop.: 2,558,294. 2000 Turnout: 1,234,229; 48% of VAP. Registered voters (2000): 2,233,602; 1,234,297 D (55%), 798,149 R (36%), 201,156 unaffiliated and minor parties (9%).

POLITICAL LINEUP: Governor, Frank Keating (R); Lt. Gov., Mary Fallin (R); Secy. of State, Mike Hunter (R); Atty. Gen., Drew Edmondson (D); Treasurer, Robert Butkin (D); Commissioner of Insurance, Carroll Fisher (D); Auditor, Clifton Scott (D); Superintendent of Education, Sandy Garrett (D); Commissioner of Labor, Brenda Reneau Wynn (R); State Senate, 48 (30 D, 18 R); Senate Pres. Pro Tempore, Stratton Taylor (D); Majority Leader, Billy Mickle (D); State House, 101 (53 D, 48 R); House Speaker, Larry E. Adair (D). Senators, Don Nickles (R) and James M. Inhofe (R). Representatives, 6 (1 D, 5 R).

ELECTIONS DIVISION: 405-521-2391; **FILING DEADLINE FOR U.S. CONGRESS:** July 10, 2002.

2000 Presidential Vote

Bush (R)	744,337	(60%)
Gore (D)	474,276	(38%)
Others	15,616	(1%)

1996 Presidential Vote

Dole (R)	582,315	(48%)
Clinton (D)	488,105	(40%)
Perot (I)	130,788	(11%)

2000 Republican Presidential Primary

Bush (R)	98,781	(79%)
McCain (R)	12,973	(10%)
Keyes (R)	11,595	(9%)
Other	1,460	(1%)

2000 Democratic Presidential Primary

Gore (D)	92,654	(69%)
Bradley (D)	34,311	(25%)
LaRouche (D)	7,885	(6%)

Gov. Frank Keating (R)

Elected 1994, term expires Jan. 2003, 2d term; b. Feb. 10, 1944, St. Louis, MO; home, Oklahoma City; Georgetown U., B.A. 1966, U. of OK, J.D. 1969; Catholic; married (Catherine).

Elected Office: OK House of Reps., 1972–74; OK Senate, 1974–81.

Professional Career: FBI Agent, 1969–71; Asst. Dist. Atty., Tulsa Cnty., 1971–72; U.S. Atty., N. OK Dist., 1981–84; U.S. Asst. Secy. of Treasury, 1986–88; U.S. Assoc. Atty. Gen., 1988–89; Gen. Cnsl. & Acting Dpty. Secy. of HUD, 1989–93; Practicing atty., 1993–95; Chmn., Repub. Govs. Assn., 1998–99.

Office: 212 State Capitol Bldg., Oklahoma City, 73105, 405-521-2342; Fax: 405-521-3353; Web site: www.state.ok.us.

Election Results

1998 general	Frank Keating (R)	505,498	(58%)
	Laura Boyd (D)	357,552	(41%)
	Others	10,535	(1%)
1998 primary	Frank Keating (R)	unopposed	
1994 general	Frank Keating (R)	466,740	(47%)
	Jack Mildren (D)	294,936	(30%)
	Wes Watkins (I)	233,336	(23%)

Sen. Don Nickles (R)

Elected 1980, seat up 2004, 4th term; b. Dec. 6, 1948, Ponca City; home, Ponca City; OK St. U., B.A. 1971; Catholic; married (Linda).

Military Career: OK Natl. Guard, 1970–76.

Elected Office: OK Senate, 1978–80.

Professional Career: V. P. & Gen. Mgr., Nickles Machine Co., 1976–80.

DC Office: 133 HSOB, 20510, 202-224-5754; Fax: 202-224-6008; Web site: www.senate.gov/~nickles.

State Offices: Lawton, 580-357-9878; Oklahoma City, 405-231-4941; Ponca City, 580-767-1270; Tulsa, 918-581-7651.

Committees: *Minority Whip. Budget. Energy & Natural Resources*: Energy Research, Development, Production & Regulation (RMM); Forests & Public Land Management. *Finance*: Health Care; Social Security & Family Policy; Taxation & IRS Oversight (RMM). *Rules & Administration.*

Group Ratings

	ADA	ACLU	AFS	LCV	CON	ITIC	NTU	COC	ACU	NTLC	CHC
2000	0	29	0	0	93	100	83	86	100	100	100
1999	0	—	0	0	80	—	83	88	96	—	—

National Journal Ratings

	1999 LIB —	1999 CONS		2000 LIB —	2000 CONS
Economic	0%	83%		27%	68%
Social	13%	84%		20%	78%
Foreign	6%	90%		5%	86%

Key Votes of the 106th Congress

1. Educ. Savings Accts.	Y	5. Review Movie Violence	N	9. NATO War in Serbia	N
2. Prescrip. Drug Benefit	N	6. Gun Show Bckgrnd. Checks	N	10. Table Cuba Travel Ban	Y
3. Delay Ergonomic Standards	Y	7. Ban Part.-Birth Abortion	Y	11. Nuclear Test-Ban Treaty	N
4. Phase Out Estate Tax	Y	8. Broaden Hate Crimes List	N	12. Perm. Trade with China	Y

Election Results

1998 general	Don Nickles (R)	570,682	(66%)	($2,415,565)
	Don E. Carroll (D)	268,898	(31%)	($8,618)
	Others	20,133	(2%)	
1998 primary	Don Nickles (R)	unopposed		
1992 general	Don Nickles (R)	757,876	(59%)	($3,492,603)
	Steve Lewis (D)	494,350	(38%)	($1,455,848)
	Others	42,197	(3%)	

Sen. James M. Inhofe (R)

Elected 1994, seat up 2002, 1st term; b. Nov. 17, 1934, Des Moines, IA; home, Tulsa; U. of Tulsa, B.A. 1973; Presbyterian; married (Kay).

Military Career: Army, 1957–58.

Elected Office: OK House of Reps., 1966–69; OK Senate, 1969–77, Repub. Ldr., 1975–77; Repub. gubernatorial nominee, 1974; Tulsa Mayor, 1978–84; U.S. House of Reps., 1986–94.

Professional Career: Businessman, land developer, 1962–86.

DC Office: 453 RSOB, 20510, 202-224-4721; Fax: 202-228-0380; Web site: inhofe.senate.gov.

State Offices: Enid, 580-234-5105; McAlester, 918-426-0933; Oklahoma City, 405-608-4381; Tulsa, 918-748-5111.

Committees: *Armed Services*: Airland Forces; Readiness & Management Support (RMM); Strategic Forces. *Environment & Public Works*: Clean Air, Wetlands, Private Property & Nuclear Safety; Superfund, Waste Control & Risk Assessment; Transportation & Infrastructure (RMM). *Indian Affairs. Intelligence (Select).*

Group Ratings

	ADA	ACLU	AFS	LCV	CON	ITIC	NTU	COC	ACU	NTLC	CHC
2000	5	29	14	0	11	67	77	85	100	100	100
1999	0	—	0	0	87	—	82	94	100	—	—

National Journal Ratings

	1999 LIB —	1999 CONS		2000 LIB —	2000 CONS
Economic	26%	71%		0%	86%
Social	0%	97%		19%	80%
Foreign	0%	94%		0%	95%

Key Votes of the 106th Congress

1. Educ. Savings Accts.	Y	5. Review Movie Violence	Y	9. NATO War in Serbia	N
2. Prescrip. Drug Benefit	N	6. Gun Show Bckgrnd. Checks	N	10. Table Cuba Travel Ban	Y
3. Delay Ergonomic Standards	Y	7. Ban Part.-Birth Abortion	Y	11. Nuclear Test-Ban Treaty	N
4. Phase Out Estate Tax	Y	8. Broaden Hate Crimes List	*	12. Perm. Trade with China	N

Election Results

1996 general	James M. Inhofe (R)	670,610	(57%)	($2,510,946)
	James Boren (D)	474,162	(40%)	($301,621)
	Others	38,378	(3%)	
1996 primary	James M. Inhofe (R)	116,241	(75%)	
	Dan Lowe (R)	38,044	(25%)	
1994 general	James M. Inhofe (R)	542,390	(55%)	($1,920,227)
	Dave McCurdy (D)	392,488	(40%)	($1,872,160)
	Danny Corn (I)	47,552	(5%)	

FIRST DISTRICT

Tulsa was one of America's oil boom towns in the early 20th Century, settled not just by people from the immediate hinterland but by Midwesterners and New Englanders of Yankee stock. In the 1920s, as its skyscrapers rose in downtown on heights above the Arkansas River, it was a raw town, intent on culture. It was optimistic and ready to seek economic change, yet culturally and politically conservative, with a Yankee elite and an Indian heritage recalled today in the Gilcrease Museum—left by one-eighth Creek Indian oil millionaire Thomas Gilcrease—and an ethnic variety suggested by the Gershon & Rebecca Fenster Museum of Jewish Art. In the decades since, Tulsa has boomed and occasionally busted; it has remained cosmopolitan and conservative; it is one of America's leading petroleum centers, and also the headquarters of Oral Roberts and his university and 60-story City of Faith hospital.

The 1st Congressional District includes all of Tulsa County plus a bit of Wagoner County to the southeast: essentially metropolitan Tulsa. The political tradition here is heavily Republican, accentuated in recent decades by national Democrats' cultural liberalism and penchant for petroleum taxes. Even during the collapse of oil prices in the 1980s, Tulsa remained full of a contagious enthusiasm for new business enterprises and innovations. Ordinary people here do not resent the oil companies or the new rich; they identify with them. They see not class conflict, but a coincidence of economic interests. They see government as interfering with efforts to produce desired goods and services—although Tulsans are pleased that the federal government built the McClellan-Kerr Waterway that made nearby Catoosa suburb a seaport. Hit by the oil price collapse of the early 1980s, Tulsa has recovered smartly and is spreading out into the countryside beyond Tulsa County in fast-growing suburbs like Broken Arrow.

The congressman from the 1st District is Steve Largent, a Republican elected in 1994, one of four Republican freshmen and two football players elected from Oklahoma that year. Largent grew up in Oklahoma City and Tulsa, the son of a divorced mother and an abusive stepfather. He played football for the University of Tulsa in the mid-1970s, then went on to become a record-setting wide receiver with the Seattle Seahawks, retiring in 1989. Back in Tulsa he started an advertising and consulting firm. When Tulsa Congressman Jim Inhofe ran for the Senate, Senator Don Nickles asked Largent to run for the House. He won the Republican nomination with an impressive 51% in the six-candidate primary. His Democratic opponent spent almost as much money, but Largent won 63%–37%.

Largent is an ardent Christian conservative who is used to overcoming great obstacles; when he retired he had caught more passes than anyone in pro football history though he was only 5'11", 190 pounds and not especially fleet-footed. (His athletic abilities extend beyond football. In Congress, he has been the Republicans' usually winning pitcher in the annual baseball game between the two parties.) In early 1995 he was not only sworn in as a member of Congress but also inducted into the National Football Hall of Fame. There, he said: "I thank my Lord and Savior, Jesus Christ. Football is what He gave me the physical gifts to do for a time. But my faith really defines who I am, as a husband, a father and a man." Abandoned by a father he saw only twice in his childhood, he wants to strengthen the family and enforce child support. He was the lead sponsor of the Defense of Marriage Act and of the Parental Rights and Responsibilities Act, which would give parents more control at a time when schools distribute condoms and conduct psychological tests. He opposes abortion and gay rights measures, which he sees as validating an unhealthy lifestyle; he sponsored an amendment to bar adoptions by gay couples in the District of Columbia, but, after passing the House approval a year earlier, it was defeated 213–215 in 1999. His advocacy of family led to his unusual and angry split with other conservative activists as he cosponsored Charles Rangel's resolution stating that the United States should return Elian Gonzalez to Cuba—and his father—and should stay out of family battles. "I'm not supporting Charlie Rangel," Largent told *Roll Call*. "I'm supporting a father being reunited with his son." Later in 2000, he made an unannounced visit to Cuba. He became the center of another emotional controversy when, as a member of the bipartisan task force selecting a new House chaplain, he was accused by Democrats of asking whether a Roman Catholic priest's collar might be divisive on the House floor; Largent angrily responded that his critics were "off-base" and that the best man at his own wedding was Catholic.

In pursuing his goals, Largent has not been afraid of going against his own party's leadership. After the 1996 election he said it would be a "good idea" for Gingrich to step aside as speaker pending settlement of his ethics problems. He was one of 11 members summoned by Gingrich in March 1997 to explain their votes against a routine appropriation. "I've been in smaller rooms with bigger people, and I can't be intimidated," Largent said. "I've had linebackers who wanted to kill me." He was a leading force in the unsuccessful coup against Gingrich in July 1997. All this, despite receiving the plum committee assignment of Commerce. But Largent is not interested in pork barrel projects, he would like to see a flat tax and an eventual end to the current Social Security system, moving toward individual investment accounts instead. In April 2000 his Tax Code Termination Act again passed the House 229–187; it would end the current tax code by December 31, 2004, with the intent of a commission reporting on a new code by 2002 and forcing Congress to pass a new, flatter tax system. Democrats criticized the proposal as a public-relations gambit.

But Largent is not simply a critic; he is also a competitor. He lives in a bipartisan rooming house with several other House members, and has gathered a group of members for "accountability sessions" on Tuesday nights. In November 1998 he challenged Dick Armey for the majority leader post, banking on mistrust of Armey from the 1997 coup and calling for a more "family-friendly" schedule and more principled leadership. He finished ahead of Jennifer Dunn 58–45 in the first round. But in the second round, Armey, with his vote-counting apparatus intact and the support of the later-to-be-Speaker Dennis Hastert, won 127–95. After his defeat Largent said, "I'm not accustomed to losing. I don't like to lose."

Early in his House career Largent said he wanted his tenure in office to be "brilliant but brief"—no more than 12 years. He has been re-elected easily, by 69%–29% in November 2000. After the election, Largent shut down his congressional leadership PACs, and said that he would not seek another term. The following spring he made it clear he was running for governor in 2002 and announced he would resign from his House seat in November 2001. The early favorite to replace him was Governor Keating's wife, Cathy, who had already raised $400,000 when Largent made his announcement.

Cook's Call *Safe.* Although Largent will be leaving this district in November to prepare for a run for governor in 2002, this seat, one of the most Republican in the state, is highly unlikely to switch control. As of early June, four Republicans, including First Lady Cathy Keating had announced their intention to run in the special election.

THE PEOPLE: Pop. 2000: 586,853; Pop. 1990: 524,135, up 12% 1990–2000. 75.3% White, 10.6% Black, 1.6% Asian, 5.3% Amer. Indian, 4.4% Two+ races, 2.7% Other; 5.8% Hispanic Origin.

2000 Presidential Vote			1996 Presidential Vote		
Bush (R)	140,331	(62%)	Dole (R)	115,997	(54%)
Gore (D)	84,567	(37%)	Clinton (D)	79,518	(37%)
Others	2,983	(1%)	Perot (I)	19,087	(9%)

Rep. Steve Largent (R)

Elected 1994, 4th term; b. Sept. 28, 1954, Tulsa; home, Tulsa; Tulsa U., B.S. 1976; Protestant; married (Terry).

Professional Career: Pro football player, Seattle Seahawks, 1976–89; Owner, adv. & mktg. co., 1989–present.

DC Office: 106 CHOB 20515, 202-225-2211; Fax: 202-225-9187; Web site: www.house.gov/largent.

District Office: Tulsa, 918-749-0014.

Committees: *Energy & Commerce* (10th of 31 R): Energy & Air Quality (Vice Chmn.); Environment & Hazardous Materials; Oversight & Investigations; Telecommunications & The Internet.

Group Ratings

	ADA	ACLU	AFS	LCV	CON	ITIC	NTU	COC	ACU	NTLC	CHC
2000	0	21	0	0	94	100	74	90	95	97	100
1999	15	—	0	13	66	—	71	87	91	—	—

National Journal Ratings

	1999 LIB	—	1999 CONS		2000 LIB	—	2000 CONS
Economic	16%	—	78%		0%	—	94%
Social	9%	—	91%		0%	—	79%
Foreign	23%	—	77%		43%	—	56%

Key Votes of the 106th Congress

1. Patient Bill of Rights	N	5. Bar RU-486 $ for FDA	Y	9. NATO War in Serbia	N
2. Accelerate Min. Wage	N	6. Display 10 Commandments	Y	10. Perm. Trade with China	Y
3. Strike Ban on Ergo. Stnd.	N	7. Gun Show Bkgrnd. Checks	N	11. Debt Relief for 3rd World	N
4. Ovrd. Estate Tax Veto	Y	8. Ban Part.-Birth Abortion	Y	12. Drop Cuba Econ. Embargo	Y

Election Results

2000 general	Steve Largent (R)	138,528	(69%)	($401,666)
	Dan Lowe (D)	58,493	(29%)	($23,718)
	Others	2,984	(1%)	
2000 primary	Steve Largent (R)	38,206	(88%)	
	Evelyn L. Rogers (R)	5,355	(12%)	
1998 general	Steve Largent (R)	91,031	(62%)	($507,161)
	Howard Plowman (D)	56,309	(38%)	($119,690)

SECOND DISTRICT

The land that is now northeast Oklahoma a century ago was the Indian Territory, the place where in the 1830s the Five Civilized Tribes were driven from Georgia and Alabama over the Trail of Tears. More than one in six people here report their race as American Indian, and in some counties more than 40% claim they are at least partly of Native American descent. The Indian percentage is highest in the hilly counties just west of the Ozarks of Arkansas, where county names—Cherokee, Osage, Sequoyah—recall the Civilized Tribes; the street signs in Tahlequah, once the Cherokee capital, are written in the Cherokee script as well as English. This pleasant land of gentle hills and man-made lakes grew at a healthy pace in the 1990s, from overspill from Tulsa and also from retirees and young families moving into the land that became the home of the Civilized Tribes more than 150 years ago.

The 2d Congressional District is made up of the northeast corner of the state, minus Tulsa County. Its geographic center is Muskogee, subject of Merle Haggard's song, "Okie from Muskogee"; it includes Will Rogers's home town of Claremore in Rogers County. It reaches far northeast where the TV signal is from Joplin, Missouri and spreads west of Tulsa to include Osage County, still an Indian reservation and site of a revived tallgrass prairie where buffalo again roam. Most of this area is ancestrally Democratic, but trended Republican on cultural issues in the 1980s and early 1990s. In the late 1990s it trended toward Democrats, at least Oklahoma Democrats; Bush won the 2d 53%–46%.

The congressman from the 2d District is Brad Carson, a Democrat elected in 2000. Carson is a sixth-generation Oklahoman, Eagle Scout, and a member of the Cherokee Nation. He graduated from Baylor University and won a Rhodes scholarship to Oxford, then graduated from the University of Oklahoma Law School. Carson practiced law in Oklahoma and then worked a year at the Pentagon as an aide to Defense Secretary William Cohen—a Democrat working for a Republican in a Democratic administration. In December 1998 he moved back to Oklahoma to work for a Tulsa law firm. Undoubtedly he had an eye on running in the 2d District. The incumbent congressman, Tom Coburn, was highly popular—an obstetrician who continued delivering babies even as he bucked the Republican leadership—and just about everyone else—on issues ranging from abortion and the V-chip (he opposed each) to congressional perks and physician-assisted suicide (he opposed those, too). Against vitriolic opposition, he insisted that pregnant women at risk be given HIV tests, so their babies could be saved. Coburn could have been re-elected for years. But in 1994 he promised to serve only three terms, and in 2000 he kept his word and retired. He said he didn't want a legacy. "That's the genius of this place," he said, "when you come and you leave, nobody remembers you were here."

Ten candidates ran for the seat, three Democrats and seven Republicans. Carson, running at 33 and with no elective experience, had major opposition from Bill Settle, 62, chairman of the state House Appropriations Committee. Settle emphasized health care, focusing on his legislation to allow patients to sue HMOs, and contrasted his experience with Carson's youth. Carson sought to turn his inexperience into a plus, focusing on campaign finance reform and criticized Settle for accepting large donations from nursing homes. And for all his inexperience, he was a fluent and charming candidate, with flawless political instincts. In the August primary Carson led Settle 45%–39%; in the September runoff Carson won 57%–43%, as Settle won his Muskogee base but nothing else. The Republican primary was more one-sided. Tom Coburn actively supported car dealer Andy Ewing, a political novice who shared his views on issues and on the importance of having citizen-representatives. His chief primary opponent Jack Ross ran an ad in which a woman referred to Ewing as a "goober." That ad apparently backfired; Ewing won the nomination in the August primary by a 60%–28% margin.

In the general, Ewing benefited from Coburn's endorsement and from his name recognition after appearing for 20 years in TV ads for his car dealerships. Like Coburn, he promised to serve only three terms in office, a pledge that Carson dismissed as harmful for the district. Both candidates opposed gun control, but they disagreed on abortion, with Carson supporting abortion rights. Ewing tried to portray Carson, who moved to the district two years earlier, as an outsider and a political opportunist. But Carson has roots in the district—his mother's family migrated to Oklahoma on the Trail of Tears—and he sought to portray himself as a moderate, fresh face. And Carson benefited from Ewing's political inexperience, his unfamiliarity with many issues, his awkward phrasing; Carson in contrast spoke smoothly and knowledgeably. Health care emerged as a key issue: Carson criticized Ewing's proposal to help seniors with drug costs by stimulating competition among pharmaceutical companies and instead called for adding a prescription drug benefit for all Medicare beneficiaries. In the inexpensive Tulsa media market both national parties spent heavily on this contest; more than half of the ad money was spent by the two congressional campaign committees, on ads that both candidates admitted were too negative. The 2d District, historically Democratic, voted for liberal governor nominee Laura Boyd in 1998, and continued its Democratic trend in this race. Carson won 17 of 18 counties, and was elected by a 55%–42% margin, carrying all but one small county.

Carson has the look of a politician who is heading toward statewide office and perhaps beyond, though he is not thought likely to run for governor in 2002 and neither of Oklahoma's two Republican senators looks vulnerable at the moment. The late Mike Synar held this seat for 16 years despite a liberal record far out of line with local opinion on some issues; Carson seems likely to avoid such positions. But first Carson must get through redistricting. Oklahoma lost one House seat in the 2000 Census. As Oklahoma's only Democrat in Congress, Carson will undoubtedly be protected by the Democratic legislature; and even if such a plan is frustrated by Governor Frank Keating's veto, there is enough Democratic territory in eastern Oklahoma to produce a seat Carson should be able to carry. But there is a possibility he will end up in a district with fellow incumbent Wes Watkins, who represented the 3d District for 14 years as a Democrat, until he ran for governor in 1990, and was elected as a Republican in 1996. Watkins is the one Republican with a strong base in Little Dixie, as southeast Oklahoma is called, and Carson would have a tough race against him. But there have been rumors that Watkins will retire, in which case a district with more of Little Dixie would suit Carson very well.

Cook's Call *Competitive.* On paper, freshman Rep. Brad Carson, the only Democrat in the six-member state delegation in a Republican-leaning state, would seem like an obvious target for Republicans in 2002. But, Carson, who won this seat by 55% in 2000 even as Bush won here by 7%, is not an easy target. With Democrats controlling the redistricting process, his seat will stay relatively intact in 2002.

THE PEOPLE: Pop. 2000: 599,445; Pop. 1990: 524,389, up 14.3% 1990–2000. 70.7% White, 4.4% Black, 0.3% Asian, 17% Amer. Indian, 6.8% Two+ races, 0.8% Other; 2.2% Hispanic Origin.

2000 Presidential Vote

Bush (R)	112,070	(53%)
Gore (D)	97,891	(46%)
Others	3,454	(2%)

1996 Presidential Vote

Clinton (D)	97,284	(47%)
Dole (R)	81,558	(40%)
Perot (I)	25,928	(13%)

Rep. Brad Carson (D)

Elected 2000, 1st term; b. Mar. 11, 1967, Winslow, AZ; home, Claremore; Baylor U., B.A. 1989; Oxford U., Rhodes Scholar, M.A. 1991; U. of OK, J.D. 1994; Baptist; married (Julie).

Professional Career: Atty., 1994–99; White House Fellow, U.S. Dept. of Defense, 1997–98.

DC Office: 317 CHOB 20515, 202-225-2701; Fax: 202-225-3038; Web site: www.house.gov/bradcarson.

District Offices: Claremore, 918-341-9336; Muskogee, 918-687-2533.

Committees: *Resources* (23d of 25 D): Energy & Mineral Resources; Water & Power. *Small Business* (16th of 17 D): Rural Enterprises, Agricultural and Technology. *Transportation & Infrastructure* (31st of 34 D): Aviation; Highways & Transit.

Group Ratings and Key Votes: Newly Elected

Election Results

2000 general	Brad Carson (D)	107,273	(55%)	($1,209,242)
	Andy Ewing (R)	81,672	(42%)	($988,161)
	Others	6,467	(3%)	
2000 runoff	Brad Carson (D)	35,410	(57%)	
	Bill Settle (D)	26,981	(43%)	
2000 primary	Brad Carson (D)	39,837	(45%)	
	Bill Settle (D)	34,964	(39%)	
	James R. Wilson (D)	13,949	(16%)	
1998 general	Tom Coburn (R)	85,581	(58%)	($496,552)
	Kent Pharaoh (D)	59,042	(40%)	($123,733)
	Others	3,641	(2%)	

THIRD DISTRICT

West of Arkansas and just north of Texas, Little Dixie is the most recognizably southern part of Oklahoma. It was settled between 1889 and 1907 by white Southerners, most of them poor; some county names (Leflore, Pontotoc) were taken directly from Mississippi. It remains mostly rural today but no longer poor. A private economy that has produced jobs is one reason; another is government, which built interstate highways and turnpikes connecting many people to jobs in more vibrant metropolitan areas. Dam-made lakes have spurred the creation of resort and retirement communities. But traditional cultural attitudes are still strong here: People listen to religious radio and read the Bible twice as frequently as the average American, they serve more often in the military, they stay married longer and raise larger families. The area was reminded in May 1999 of the boom-bust cycle when a tornado ripped through Stroud; it had been a whisky town near an Indian reservation more than a century ago, went dry, enjoyed prosperous years from cotton and oil, and then saw the destruction of its chief income source—an outlet mall.

The 3d Congressional District includes most of the Little Dixie counties, and juts up into the center of the state into the old university town of Stillwater, which is Republican territory, to include enough people to meet the population standard. It has long been solidly Democratic and voted for Bill Clinton in the 1990s, but only three small counties voted for Al Gore in 2000. For 30 years, from 1947 to 1977, it was represented by Carl Albert, speaker of the House his last six years and majority leader during the Kennedy-Johnson years. Until 1996 it had never elected a Republican congressman, though its conservative cultural attitudes have been helping Republicans in other races.

The congressman from the 3d District is Wes Watkins, elected as a Republican in 1996, after serving for 14 years as a Democrat and spending six out of office. Watkins grew up in a family that moved around, from Arkansas to California and back again. He graduated from Oklahoma State, worked for the university and for a local development agency, then ran his own real estate and homebuilding firm for nine years. In 1974, at 36, he was elected to the state Senate. In 1976, when Albert retired, he ran for Congress and won the Democratic nomination by beating Albert aide Charles Ward. In the House he served on Appropriations for 10 years and concentrated on encouraging rural development, including advanced technology and international trade centers at Oklahoma State. He had a middle-of-the-House voting record and headed the House Rural Caucus and the Congressional Prayer Breakfast Group. In 1990 he ran for governor and lost the Democratic runoff to David Walters, 51%–49%. He went into private business and campaigned for Ross Perot in 1992. In 1994 he ran for governor as an independent, finishing third with a respectable 23% of the vote and carrying the 3d District.

In December 1995, when conservative Democratic Congressman Bill Brewster announced his retirement, Watkins ran as a Republican because he was for a balanced budget amendment and against gun control. "I'm the same Wes Watkins," he said, adding that he had been promised a seat on Ways and Means (which he received) and would work hard for local projects again. The Democratic nominee, state Senator Darryl Roberts, a former Carter County district attorney and Vietnam veteran, attacked Watkins for party disloyalty, flipflopping on issues and avoiding debates. Watkins said that Roberts had voted 50 times to raise taxes and fees, and a Watkins ad showed Roberts letting criminals out on the street, a reference to his support of a Specialized Supervision Program to relieve overcrowding in prisons. Watkins raised more money and won 51%–45%, with large margins in the northern counties around Stillwater, but also carried Little Dixie.

On Ways and Means, he immediately worked to support two major tax advantages for the area. One gave faster depreciation to businesses on Indian reservations and former reservations. When an Oklahoma lawyer claimed that almost all of Oklahoma was a former reservation, the IRS balked and Texas members moved to change the law. But Watkins kept it in the Code and pushed the agency to apply it fully. The other was tax incentives for stripper and low-production wells still pumping oil and gas. After securing both provisions by June 1997 Watkins said, "If I never serve another day, I feel like I was able to put something together to help Oklahoma." Although his voting record turned sharply conservative after his election as a Republican, he remained a voice for farmers. He would exempt from capital gains taxation farmers and ranchers who sell their operations, including houses. He backed agreements with China to reduce tariffs on American beef and increase the quota for wheat.

In April 1998 Watkins announced he was having spinal surgery and said he would not run again. No Republican replacement was apparent, and House Democrats counted the seat as one reason they had a good chance to regain a majority. But by mid-June Speaker Newt Gingrich persuaded Watkins to reconsider, promising help with fundraising and on Oklahoma issues. Watkins postponed a second surgery until after the election. Democrats had a spirited campaign to oppose him—nominating a different Roberts, Walt, who was a former legislator and rancher. Watkins won big, 62%–38%. In 2000, he had no major-party opposition.

2002 looms as more complex for Watkins and Oklahoma. The state lost one House seat in redistricting, and by early 2001 there was widespread speculation that Watkins would retire. In that event, the Democratic legislature might choose to divide the district, giving some of its heavily Democratic Little Dixie territory to Democrat Brad Carson's 2d District and western counties to Republican J.C. Watts's 4th District. But in November 2000 Watkins was urging that Stillwater, his current home, be kept in the 3d, and added, "If they make me mad, I might run anyway."

Cook's Call *Potentially Competitive.* The fact that Wes Watkins has been easily re-elected to this marginal district in 1998 and 2000 is a constant source of disappointment for Democrats. With the state losing a seat in redistricting and Democrats in control of the line-drawing process in the state, Watkins could find himself either without a district or in a much more competitive district in 2002.

THE PEOPLE: Pop. 2000: 565,932; Pop. 1990: 524,287, up 7.9% 1990–2000. 78.5% White, 3.8% Black, 0.7% Asian, 11.3% Amer. Indian, 4.7% Two+ races, 1% Other; 2.6% Hispanic Origin.

2000 Presidential Vote
Bush (R)	110,643	(56%)
Gore (D)	83,532	(42%)
Others	2,460	(1%)

1996 Presidential Vote
Clinton (D)	92,007	(47%)
Dole (R)	77,287	(40%)
Perot (I)	24,580	(13%)

Rep. Wes Watkins (R)

Elected 1996, 3d term; b. Dec. 15, 1938, DeQueen, AR; home, Stillwater; OK St. U., B.S. 1960, M.S. 1961; Presbyterian; married (Lou).

Military Career: OK Air Natl. Guard, 1960–62, 1964–67.

Elected Office: OK Senate, 1974–76; U.S. House of Reps., 1976–90.

Professional Career: Dir., High School Relations, OK St. U., 1963–66; Exec. Dir., Kiamichi Econ. Devel. Dist., 1966–67; Residential construction, 1967–77; Pres. & CEO, World Export Services, 1990–96.

DC Office: 1401 LHOB 20515, 202-225-4565; Fax: 202-225-5966; Web site: www.house.gov/watkins.

District Offices: Ada, 580-436-1980; McAlester, 918-423-5951; Stillwater, 405-743-1400.

Committees: *Budget* (13th of 24 R). *Ways & Means* (16th of 24 R): Human Resources.

Group Ratings
	ADA	ACLU	AFS	LCV	CON	ITIC	NTU	COC	ACU	NTLC	CHC
2000	0	21	0	0	18	100	58	95	87	79	100
1999	0	—	0	0	51	—	60	96	96	—	—

National Journal Ratings
	1999 LIB	—	1999 CONS		2000 LIB	—	2000 CONS
Economic	0%	—	84%		15%	—	83%
Social	0%	—	96%		0%	—	79%
Foreign	10%	—	86%		12%	—	78%

Key Votes of the 106th Congress
1. Patient Bill of Rights	N	5. Bar RU-486 $ for FDA	Y	9. NATO War in Serbia	N
2. Accelerate Min. Wage	N	6. Display 10 Commandments	Y	10. Perm. Trade with China	Y
3. Strike Ban on Ergo. Stnd.	N	7. Gun Show Bkgrnd. Checks	N	11. Debt Relief for 3rd World	N
4. Ovrd. Estate Tax Veto	Y	8. Ban Part.-Birth Abortion	Y	12. Drop Cuba Econ. Embargo	N

Election Results

2000 general	Wes Watkins (R) 137,826	(87%)	($288,397)
	Argus W. Yandell, Jr. (I) 14,660	(9%)	
	R.C. Sevier White (Lib) 6,730	(4%)	
2000 primary	Wes Watkins (R) .... unopposed		
1998 general	Wes Watkins (R) 89,832	(62%)	($1,220,356)
	Walt Roberts (D) 55,163	(38%)	($808,385)

FOURTH DISTRICT

In the years just after 1900, the brown hills west of Oklahoma City and north of the Red River suddenly filled up with farmers riding north from Texas, past the well-watered green lands of the east toward the bare pasture lands of the west. These were young people with large families, and in the years since, this land has emptied out, as children have grown up and moved elsewhere and fewer hands are needed for farming. People in southwest Oklahoma instead have accumulated around major government institutions: the state capital of Oklahoma City; Norman, home of the University of Oklahoma; Lawton, to the southwest, home of the Army's Fort Sill.

These are major landmarks for the 4th Congressional District, which begins a few miles from the oil-derrick-surrounded state Capitol in Oklahoma City, smack dab in the middle of the state, and proceeds south and west to cover half of Oklahoma's Red River Valley. Demographically, this district is becoming more suburban, but the cultural tone remains country. That is true even in the Oklahoma City suburbs, which stretch out over the mile-grid roads, where in new subdivisions dust may still get tracked indoors and people still prefer chicken-fried steak to stir-fried chicken (though they eat both). At the same time there is technical sophistication here, and Norman, with OU playing a big role, may be on the verge of becoming a center of high-tech creativity; the military is also a big presence, in Fort Sill and the giant depot at Tinker Air Force Base. Ancestrally, this is Democratic country, but Norman, Lawton and the Oklahoma City fringe now have voted pretty solidly Republican over the last decade.

The congressman from the 4th District is J.C. Watts, a Republican, former college and professional football player, conservative Christian and African-American. Watts grew up in Eufaula, Oklahoma (named after the largest town in the Alabama county where George Wallace grew up), son of a Baptist minister who was also a policeman and cattle trader; he was one of two children who integrated his elementary school and the first black quarterback on the high school football team. Watts was a quarterback at the University of Oklahoma and led the team to Big Eight championships and Orange Bowl wins in 1980 and 1981. From 1981–86, he played in the Canadian Football League. In Oklahoma, Watts owned real estate and petroleum marketing companies and was a youth minister at the Sunnylane Southern Baptist Church in Del City. In 1980 he heard a debate between Senate candidates and decided that he agreed more with the young Republican, Don Nickles, but he still voted for Democrats as late as Michael Dukakis in 1988. He became a Republican in 1989, because he thought the Democratic Party leadership had deserted the values he had learned growing up. In 1990 he ran for corporation commissioner, a statewide office, and won.

In 1994, when 4th District Democratic Congressman Dave McCurdy ran for the Senate and lost to Republican Jim Inhofe, Watts decided to run for Congress. He had plenty of competition. He led in the Republican primary, 49%–35%, but was forced into a runoff in which he was accused of bad debts and tardy taxes. Watts won by just 757 votes. In October, Democrat David Perryman ran an ad opening with a picture of Watts in high school with an Afro haircut, followed by Perryman as a Future Farmer of America holding a pig. Watts won by a comfortable 52%–43%; though he lost most of the rural counties, he won 60% in Norman's Cleveland County and 58% in Oklahoma County.

Watts inevitably attracted attention as one of two black Republicans in the House (Gary Franks, the other, was defeated in 1996). Newt Gingrich asked him to respond to Bill Clinton's Saturday radio address right after the election, and Watts declined to join the Congressional Black Caucus ("I didn't come to Congress to be a black leader or a white leader, but a leader.").

He disagrees with the liberal premise that government programs help blacks. "Historically, black people believe in family, church and community. It is only when they . . . allowed government to control their lives that they encountered deepening poverty, decaying families and a sick welfare system that penalizes women for wanting to marry the father of their child and mothers for saving money." In February 2000 he challenged Bob Jones University to come up with a Biblical text to justify its ban on interracial dating; the college couldn't and later changed its policy. He joined others in calling for a commemoration of the slaves who did much of the construction work on the Capitol and the White House, and set up a Republican Conference task force on HCBUs (historically black colleges and universities).

Watts's voting record has been conservative; he counseled going slow on repealing racial quotas and preferences. He has favored large pay increases for the military and wrote language on capital market development in Africa contained in the foreign aid bill. His chief legislative project, co-sponsored with Jim Talent, was called the Community Renewal Act, which targeted low-income urban and rural areas, to reduce taxes and regulations and to encourage local and faith-based problem solving. Some of its tax, regulatory and brownfields provisions were incorporated in the 1998 tax bill and some of its housing provisions were included in a 1998 housing bill. In November 1999, Bill Clinton and Speaker Dennis Hastert endorsed the idea at a meeting in Chicago, and made it their special project. It was passed in the House in July 2000 and became law in December 2000. In its final form it included a zero capital gains tax on businesses in each of 40 "renewal communities," with other tax breaks for rehabilitating buildings and the like, and it included Watts' provision allowing churches to get federal dollars for drug treatment programs.

Watts has often been placed in the national spotlight. He showed his self-assured and fluent speaking skills at the 1996 Republican National Convention ("character is simply doing right when nobody is looking") and in the response to Bill Clinton's 1997 State of the Union speech. But the old-line networks, which have run every minute of convention speeches by Jesse Jackson, covered little of Watts' 1996 speech. He was one of three co-chairmen of the 2000 Republican National Convention, and campaigned extensively, sometimes on a bus with John McCain, for Republican candidates in 2000.

In November 1998, just after the fall of Newt Gingrich, Watts ran against John Boehner for the post of House Republican Conference chairman, the number four position in the leadership, and won 121–93. His main responsibility was developing the party's message—in effect, providing daily and even hourly emails on the spin of the day. There was some grumbling with Watts' performance, and in July 1999 he threatened to quit, after Whip Tom DeLay unveiled a new program for members to do media outreach on appropriations bills (DeLay's own assignment). In time Speaker Dennis Hastert persuaded Watts to stay, and there were fewer criticisms. Amid this national prominence, Watts did not lose sight of local concerns. He turned down a seat on Appropriations in July 1999, apparently so that he could continue to work on local issues on Armed Services, and he worked to keep jobs at Tinker. He worked for $3.6 million to help build the dome on Oklahoma's Capitol, abandoned in 1915 but taken up again in 1999, and for funds to preserve old buildings on the University of Science and Arts of Oklahoma in Chickasha, founded as the Industrial Institute and College for Girls in 1908. He worked for the national weather research center in Norman and for advanced trainers for air traffic control at the FAA center in Oklahoma City. After the government threatened to confiscate Geronimo's Indian headdress when it was offered for sale at $1.2 million on the web (it contains eagle feathers, which cannot legally be sold), he called for it to be returned to Fort Sill, where Geronimo was held as a prisoner until his death in 1909.

Watts has been re-elected three times by wide margins. In 1996 Watts told voters he would not serve more than six years, and in January 2000 he considered retiring, but after discussions with Hastert, his constituents and his family he decided to run again. He was re-elected by a 65%–31% margin, and a week later re-elected Conference chairman without opposition. The 4th District could be changed by redistricting; Oklahoma lost a House seat in the 2000 Census and the Democratic legislature, unless stopped by Republican Frank Keating, may try to create two Democrat-friendly districts. But Keating and other Republicans will surely fight hard for a seat where Watts can win easily.

Cook's Call *Probably Safe.* Watts has not won here by some of the very large margins of his Oklahoma colleagues, but he has yet to find himself in a highly competitive race. There is no reason to believe that Democrats will target this Republican-leaning district in 2002, but with the state losing one seat in redistricting every district will be drastically redrawn.

THE PEOPLE: Pop. 2000: 572,589; Pop. 1990: 524,407, up 9.2% 1990–2000. 79.5% White, 7.5% Black, 1.8% Asian, 4.6% Amer. Indian, 0.1% Hawaiian, 4% Two+ races, 2.4% Other; 5.7% Hispanic Origin.

2000 Presidential Vote		
Bush (R)	119,477	(61%)
Gore (D)	73,217	(38%)
Others	2,168	(1%)

1996 Presidential Vote		
Dole (R)	92,011	(49%)
Clinton (D)	75,291	(40%)
Perot (I)	20,376	(11%)

Rep. J.C. Watts, Jr. (R)

Elected 1994, 4th term; b. Nov. 18, 1957, Eufaula; home, Norman; U. of OK, B.A. 1981; Baptist; married (Frankie).

Elected Office: OK St. Corp. Comm., 1990–94, Chmn., 1992–94.

Professional Career: Pro football player, Canadian Football League, 1981–86; Businessman, 1986–94.

DC Office: 1007 LHOB 20515, 202-225-6165; Fax: 202-225-3512; Web site: www.house.gov/watts.

District Offices: Lawton, 580-357-2131; Norman, 405-329-6500.

Committees: *Republican Conference Chairman. Armed Services* (12th of 32 R): Military Procurement; Military Readiness.

Group Ratings

	ADA	ACLU	AFS	LCV	CON	ITIC	NTU	COC	ACU	NTLC	CHC
2000	0	21	0	0	17	94	60	90	88	88	100
1999	0	—	0	0	11	—	58	100	92	—	—

National Journal Ratings

	1999 LIB — 1999 CONS		2000 LIB — 2000 CONS	
Economic	0% —	84%	6% —	85%
Social	0% —	96%	0% —	79%
Foreign	23% —	73%	0% —	88%

Key Votes of the 106th Congress

1. Patient Bill of Rights	N	5. Bar RU-486 $ for FDA	Y	9. NATO War in Serbia	N
2. Accelerate Min. Wage	N	6. Display 10 Commandments	Y	10. Perm. Trade with China	Y
3. Strike Ban on Ergo. Stnd.	N	7. Gun Show Bkgrnd. Checks	N	11. Debt Relief for 3rd World	N
4. Ovrd. Estate Tax Veto	Y	8. Ban Part.-Birth Abortion	Y	12. Drop Cuba Econ. Embargo	N

Election Results

2000 general	J.C. Watts (R)	114,000	(65%)	($1,546,659)
	Larry Weatherford (D)	54,808	(31%)	($57,455)
	Others	6,876	(4%)	
2000 primary	J.C. Watts (R)	21,960	(81%)	
	James Odom (R)	5,163	(19%)	
1998 general	J.C. Watts (R)	83,272	(62%)	($1,463,694)
	Ben Odom (D)	52,107	(38%)	($356,373)

FIFTH DISTRICT

Oklahoma City, suddenly the center of the nation's attention in April 1995 when a bomb destroyed the Alfred P. Murrah federal building, killing 168 and injuring more than 500, has for a century been the center of Oklahoma. Oklahoma City, like many state capitals, was not the spontaneous creation of commerce but the deliberate creation of government, sited in the geographic center of the state, on what turned out to be oil lands; oil rigs were pumping crude on the grounds of the domeless Capitol until 1989. The land here is browner and more eroded by creeks than the greener, rolling Oklahoma farmland farther east. From its center Oklahoma City has grown far out into the countryside, followed, as in so many southwestern cities, by expanding city limits so that it extends into five counties and four congressional districts and covers 624 square miles.

The 5th Congressional District includes most of Oklahoma City, but it is a carefully chosen part: the most Democratic sections of the city, including its black areas, were chopped off and put in the 6th District. This is a solidly Republican area as a result. The 5th proceeds north through wheat country, to the one-time state capital of Guthrie and the market town of Ponca City, areas as Republican as any similar place in nearby Kansas. Connected by a strip of mostly uninhabited Osage County is Bartlesville, headquarters of Phillips Petroleum, solidly conservative in the Oil Patch manner.

The congressman from the 5th District is Ernest Istook, first elected in 1992, in his views and attitudes a forerunner of the Republican freshmen of 1994. With heavy turnover he became in just two terms the most senior of the state's House delegation. Istook is the grandson of Hungarian immigrants; after graduating from Baylor, he was a radio reporter in Oklahoma City and went to law school at night. He attracted attention as head of Governor David Boren's alcohol control board when he refused to stop an investigation of liquor distributors. He practiced law and was elected to the Oklahoma House in 1986. In 1992 he ran for the House, taking on 16-year incumbent Republican Mickey Edwards, who had 386 overdrafts on the House bank. Edwards finished third in the primary, with 26% to 32% for Istook and 37% for 1990 gubernatorial nominee Bill Price, who harshly criticized Edwards. Istook ran on conservative issues and won the runoff 56%–44%. He won the general election by only 53%–47% over oil and gas lawyer Laurie Williams, who attacked Istook for his anti-abortion stance. He has been easily re-elected since.

Istook has a very conservative voting record and has used his seat on Appropriations to press for various controversial amendments. One was his 1995 effort to ban organizations that receive federal funds from using more than 5% of their money for lobbying: welfare reform for lobbyists. This was fought vociferously by nonprofits, eager to use taxpayers' dollars, as somehow an infringement on freedom of speech. Different forms of the Istook amendment were passed by both houses, but no limit was passed. Another amendment would have allowed states to refuse to use federal funds to pay for abortions in cases of rape and incest; again his side lost. A third Istook amendment, requiring parental notification for dispensing birth control devices to minors (as it is required for dispensing aspirin), passed 224–200 in October 1998, but was dropped in conference. He refocused his efforts on abstinence and won a 40% increase in funding for programs in the 2000 budget deal. In 1998 Istook pushed to require businesses on Indian-owned land to pay state gas, liquor and tobacco taxes; that was dropped to accommodate Wes Watkins, who did not want a vote on the issue, but Istook continued to press for it in 1999 and 2000.

Istook was the chief sponsor of the Religious Freedom amendment, which came to a vote in a revised form in June 1998; it stated, "The people's right to pray and to recognize their religious belief, heritage or tradition on public property, including schools, shall not be infringed. The government shall not require any person to join in prayer, initiate or designate school prayers, discriminate against religion, or deny equal access to a benefit on account of religion." It got 224 votes, well short of the required two-thirds, and short of the 240 a school prayer amendment got the last time it reached the floor, in 1971. But Istook has had some successes. A proposal to require schools and libraries to use softwear to screen Internet pornography was voted into a 2001 appropriation bill, but the ACLU has filed lawsuits to challenge it. He was successful in limiting direct lending to 40% of all student loans, banning Centers for Disease Control research on gunshot wounds, and (after bringing the issue to the Supreme Court) stopping the Clinton Administration's imposition of a striker replacement law that failed to pass even in the Democratic Congress.

Istook is the only Oklahoman on an appropriations committee, but has declined to use his seat to bring home pork. He refused to back J.C. Watts' attempts to get federal funds for building a dome for the Oklahoma Capitol (the state ran out of money in 1915 and is only now reembarked on the project) and he doesn't think much of Amtrak's Heartland Flyer that runs from Oklahoma City to Fort Worth (though it is a great favorite of Senator Don Nickles). He opposed the Republicans' prescription drug plan on the ground that if drugs were too expensive the government shouldn't pay such high prices. He voted for an Internet tax moratorium, but denounced it as an infringement on the rights of the states. But he did seek to invoke federal power in another area, complaining bitterly about American Airlines' non-jet service from Oklahoma City to Dallas-Fort Worth. "Like many other Americans, Oklahomans are tired of being treated like cattle on some airline flights," he said. "The link through DFW is abominable."

In 1999 Istook became chairman of the D.C. Appropriations Subcommittee, and thus a member of the "College of Cardinals." In the past he had backed riders repealing what he considered wrongful District policies, like health care benefits for gay partners of city employees. But in his first year he consulted closely with D.C. officials and with D.C. Delegate Eleanor Holmes Norton and avoided controversy. He took initiatives in adding spending for what he and District officials considered worthy programs—$25 million for drug testing of parolees, $7 million for parole violators, and $8.5 million to help 3,000 foster children find homes. But he did criticize the District's needle exchange programs and its new 2000 "Taxation Without Representation" license plates. In 2001, Istook became chairman of the Treasury-Postal Appropriations subcommittee, which supervises the White House budget. His first major project was to investigate whether taxpayers should subsidize a New York City penthouse office for President Clinton.

Cook's Call   *Safe.* Istook has never had to worry much about his re-election prospects in this district, the most Republican in the state. But, with the state losing one seat in redistricting, every seat in the state will be seriously impacted. Still, in a district that Bush won with 68% in 2000, it is hard to see how many of these new districts get any better for Democrats.

THE PEOPLE: Pop. 2000: 593,898; Pop. 1990: 523,729, up 13.4% 1990–2000. 79.9% White, 6.5% Black, 2.5% Asian, 4.1% Amer. Indian, 0.1% Hawaiian, 3.7% Two+ races, 3.2% Other; 6.7% Hispanic Origin.

2000 Presidential Vote			1996 Presidential Vote		
Bush (R)	152,850	(68%)	Dole (R)	128,792	(59%)
Gore (D)	67,853	(30%)	Clinton (D)	68,222	(31%)
Others	2,572	(1%)	Perot (I)	20,668	(9%)

Rep. Ernest J. Istook, Jr. (R)

Elected 1992, 5th term; b. Feb. 11, 1950, Ft. Worth, TX; home, Warr Acres; Baylor U., B.A. 1971, OK City U. Law Schl., J.D. 1976; Mormon; married (Judy).

Elected Office: OK House of Reps., 1986–92.

Professional Career: Political reporter, Oklahoma City KOMA Radio, 1972–73, WKY Radio, 1973–76; Dir., OK Alcohol Beverage Control Bd., 1977; Practicing atty., 1977–92.

DC Office: 2404 RHOB 20515, 202-225-2132; Fax: 202-226-1463; Web site: www.house.gov/istook.

District Offices: Bartlesville, 918-336-5546; Oklahoma City, 405-942-3636; Ponca City, 580-762-6778.

Committees: *Appropriations* (13th of 35 R): District of Columbia; Labor, HHS & Education; Treasury, Postal Service & General Government (Chmn.).

Group Ratings

	ADA	ACLU	AFS	LCV	CON	ITIC	NTU	COC	ACU	NTLC	CHC
2000	5	21	20	7	4	94	65	73	90	85	100
1999	0	—	0	0	63	—	67	83	92	—	—

National Journal Ratings

	1999 LIB —	1999 CONS		2000 LIB —	2000 CONS
Economic	30%	64%		40%	60%
Social	0%	96%		26%	74%
Foreign	3%	92%		39%	57%

Key Votes of the 106th Congress

1. Patient Bill of Rights	N	5. Bar RU-486 $ for FDA	Y	9. NATO War in Serbia	N
2. Accelerate Min. Wage	N	6. Display 10 Commandments	Y	10. Perm. Trade with China	Y
3. Strike Ban on Ergo. Stnd.	*	7. Gun Show Bkgrnd. Checks	N	11. Debt Relief for 3rd World	N
4. Ovrd. Estate Tax Veto	Y	8. Ban Part.-Birth Abortion	Y	12. Drop Cuba Econ. Embargo	N

Election Results

2000 general	Ernest J. Istook, Jr. (R)	134,159	(68%)	($520,608)
	Garland McWatters (D)	53,275	(27%)	($22,401)
	Others	8,588	(4%)	
2000 primary	Ernest J. Istook, Jr. (R)	39,976	(85%)	
	Phillip A. Hillian (R)	7,179	(15%)	
1998 general	Ernest J. Istook Jr. (R)	103,217	(68%)	($403,434)
	Mary C. Smothermon (D)	48,182	(32%)	($146,983)

SIXTH DISTRICT

First settled just a century ago, western Oklahoma is a fertile land forever at the mercy of the elements. The western plains are scorching hot under the summer sun and snow-blown in winter; this is one of the windiest parts of America. The rural counties here have far fewer people than before the dust bowl of the 1930s, and fewer than during the Anadarko basin oil and natural gas boom of the 1970s.

The 6th Congressional District is made up of the western plains of Oklahoma, plus blue-collar and black neighborhoods in Oklahoma City. A few of its counties in the south, settled by farmers crossing the Red River from Texas, have been heavily Democratic ever since. But most of these plains were settled by farmers coming south from Kansas, and these have long been heavily Republican. These divisions are as permanent as if Oklahoma had been split down the middle during the Civil War, even though there were no whites in the state at the time. The bigger fact here is depopulation: Counties wholly within the 6th Congressional District had 423,000 people in 1930 and 282,000 in 2000. Four in 10 votes in the district are cast in metropolitan Oklahoma City. But there is some new migration into the district, as Latinos move to work in hog farms and packing plants in places like Texas County in the panhandle; the county's Hispanic population more than tripled in the last decade.

The congressman from the 6th District is Frank Lucas, a Republican chosen in a May 1994 special election. Lucas's roots are in western Oklahoma; he owns a farm and cattle ranch in Roger Mills County and was elected to the Oklahoma House in 1988, at 28. He got his chance to run for Congress in 1994 because Glenn English, a 19-year conservative Democrat, resigned to head the National Rural Electric Cooperative Association. Lucas had serious competition in both the primary and general elections. In the primary he trailed 36%–34% state Senator Brooks Douglass, who campaigned from his Oklahoma City base with a Western accent. In the runoff Lucas ridiculed "some Johnny-come-lately dressed up like a drugstore cowboy" and carried all the rural areas to win 56%–44%. In the general he faced Dan Webber, 27-year-old press secretary to outgoing Senator David Boren. Lucas ran an ad showing the U.S. Capitol ("this is where Dan Webber has worked his entire adult life") and Oklahoma farmland ("this is where Frank Lucas has worked his entire adult life") and benefited from Oklahoma Taxpayers Union ads and Christian Coalition voting guides, winning 54%–46%. It was the first step in the three-year transformation of the Oklahoma House delegation from 4–2 Democratic to 6–0 Republican (it is now back to 5–1 Republican).

Lucas has one of the most conservative voting records in the House, but he has a practical bent. Representing the site of the Oklahoma City bombing, he introduced the resolution condemning it, the bill for relief spending and the bill to authorize the bombing monument and make it part of the national parks system. He supported the anti-terrorism bill and, after the Oklahoma City trial was moved to Denver, sponsored the amendments to allow closed-circuit broadcasting of out-of-town trials and to allow bombing victims, survivors and relatives to watch the trial and still testify in the sentencing hearing. On more traditional constituent service, he hailed the base-closing commission's decision to close two other maintenance depots and keep open Oklahoma

City's Tinker Air Force Base. He got the site of Custer's massacre of Chief Black Kettle's people, near Cheyenne, declared Black Kettle National Park. He delivered assistance to modern-day Indians, making it easier for seven tribes in Oklahoma to lease mineral rights to their land. The most important legislation Lucas worked on was the 1996 Freedom to Farm Act, which he backed. "We have to get Uncle Sam out of the farm business and give farmers the ability to produce for markets. This bill will help farmers, by breaking the bonds of the old and ringing in a market-oriented program which will guide us into the next century." He led a successful House effort to rehabilitate the nation's small watershed dams, which tend to deteriorate after 50 years—not a hot news topic on Capitol Hill but important to the many Americans who depend on them; of the nation's more than 10,000 dams to control flash flooding, most are on private property and almost 20% are in Oklahoma. "We don't allow our highways to crumble," Lucas said, "nor should we ignore our small watershed dams."

Lucas has been re-elected by wide margins. His 1996 and 1998 opponent Paul Barby showed courage and commitment by announcing before running that he is gay, and by spending over $500,000 of his own money. But he was not able to make much of a dent. Lucas won 65%–33% in 1998, carrying Oklahoma County by only 49%–48% but the rest of the district 72%–26%. In 2000, he faced a more experienced and financially competitive challenger: state representative and cattle rancher Randy Beutler complained that Lucas was not aggressive enough in fighting for local needs. Both described themselves as anti-abortion, pro-guns, pro-tax cuts and in favor of international trade, but Beutler would have voted against the 1996 farm bill and wasn't convinced that President Clinton committed an impeachable offense. Beutler won 59% in his base of three counties in the district's southwestern corner and he won the Oklahoma County vote 51%–47%, but that wasn't nearly enough to offset the 66% to 83% majorities Lucas won in the counties north of I-40, giving him a 59%–39% win. Redistricting is the one threat to Lucas's tenure. Oklahoma must lose one House seat, and if the Democratic legislature were to get past Republican Governor Frank Keating a plan that creates two more or less Democratic seats in northeast and southeast Oklahoma, that would probably leave Lucas, Ernest Istook and J.C. Watts, all now representing parts of metro Oklahoma City, in a three-man game of musical chairs. But that is unlikely to happen if Wes Watkins retires and his 3d District is split among its neighbors.

Cook's Call *Probably Safe.* A serious challenge by a Democratic state legislator in 2000 gave Lucas his closest race in six years. Still, Lucas won with 59%, a sign of just how Republican this district is. But Lucas, like the other five members of the state delegation, may find himself in a very different looking district in 2002. This sprawling panhandle based district, already the slowest growing in the state, needs to gain more than 150,000 people and there is some talk that Lucas' district may be merged with 5th District Republican Ernest Istook.

THE PEOPLE: Pop. 2000: 531,937; Pop. 1990: 524,638, up 1.4% 1990–2000. 73% White, 13% Black, 1.3% Asian, 4.8% Amer. Indian, 0.1% Hawaiian, 3.4% Two+ races, 4.4% Other; 8.4% Hispanic Origin.

2000 Presidential Vote		
Bush (R)	108,966	(61%)
Gore (D)	67,216	(38%)
Others	1,979	(1%)

1996 Presidential Vote		
Dole (R)	86,670	(47%)
Clinton (D)	75,783	(41%)
Perot (I)	20,149	(11%)

Rep. Frank Lucas (R)

Elected May 1994, 4th term; b. Jan. 6, 1960, Cheyenne; home, Cheyenne; OK St. U., B.S. 1982; Baptist; married (Lynda).

Elected Office: OK House of Reps., 1988–94.

Professional Career: Farmer & rancher.

DC Office: 438 CHOB 20515, 202-225-5565; Fax: 202-225-8698; Web site: www.house.gov/lucas.

District Offices: Clinton, 580-323-6232; Enid, 580-233-9224; Oklahoma City, 405-235-5311; Woodward, 580-256-5752.

Committees: *Agriculture* (7th of 27 R): Conservation, Credit, Rural Development & Research (Chmn.); General Farm Commodities & Risk Management. *Financial Services* (10th of 37 R): Capital Markets, Insurance & Government Sponsored Enterprises; Domestic Monetary Policy, Technology & Economic Growth; Financial Institutions & Consumer Credit. *Science* (16th of 25 R): Research; Space & Aeronautics.

Group Ratings

	ADA	ACLU	AFS	LCV	CON	ITIC	NTU	COC	ACU	NTLC	CHC
2000	0	23	0	7	7	100	60	85	91	76	100
1999	0	—	0	0	18	—	59	96	96	—	—

National Journal Ratings

	1999 LIB —	1999 CONS	2000 LIB —	2000 CONS
Economic	0%	84%	15%	85%
Social	9%	90%	0%	79%
Foreign	0%	97%	12%	78%

Key Votes of the 106th Congress

1. Patient Bill of Rights	N	5. Bar RU-486 $ for FDA	Y	9. NATO War in Serbia	N
2. Accelerate Min. Wage	N	6. Display 10 Commandments	Y	10. Perm. Trade with China	Y
3. Strike Ban on Ergo. Stnd.	N	7. Gun Show Bkgrnd. Checks	N	11. Debt Relief for 3rd World	N
4. Ovrd. Estate Tax Veto	Y	8. Ban Part.-Birth Abortion	Y	12. Drop Cuba Econ. Embargo	N

Election Results

2000 general	Frank Lucas (R)	95,635	(59%)	($700,850)
	Randy Beutler (D)	63,106	(39%)	($414,786)
	Others	2,435	(2%)	
2000 primary	Frank Lucas (R)	unopposed		
1998 general	Frank Lucas (R)	85,261	(65%)	($344,338)
	Paul M. Barby (D)	43,555	(33%)	($268,307)
	Others	2,455	(2%)	

★ OREGON ★

O regon is an experimental commonwealth and laboratory of reform on the Pacific Rim, a maker of national trends. It is far removed from where most Americans live, but closer in touch with the rest of America than sometimes appears: within minutes after a tree branch brushed a power line in Oregon in August 1996, the entire western power grid shut down all the way from the Canadian border to San Diego, where the Republican National Convention was opening two days later. Oregon has led the nation with bike trails and Nike sneakers, light rail trams and Pendleton shirts, with assisted suicide and mail-in ballots. Oregon is an affluent high-tech civilization where one can still see much the same land and water—and rain—that Lewis and Clark saw in 1805 when they came down the Columbia River gorge, past what is now Portland, to the vast Pacific Ocean.

This Oregon was settled by Americans when John Jacob Astor set up his fur trading post at Astoria in 1811 and when New England Yankees in the 1840s rode the Oregon Trail and floated down the Columbia to the well-watered Willamette Valley. In this remote land, nearly 2,000 miles from the Mississippi River frontier and 700 miles from the small settlements of California, they built an orderly, productive society—a kind of western New England. It grew steadily over the years, with a few booms—when timber, always its first industry, surged in 1900–10, during the war and after in the 1940s, and in the 1970s when home building skyrocketed and Oregon's natural environment began to be widely appreciated.

Today's Oregon is more confident it can live comfortably with growth. In the 1990s it was the nation's 10th fastest growing state, with its population up 20%. Its newcomers are highly educated, sparkplugs of the economic growth that leaves employers begging for workers. The newcomers fill Portland's postmodern skyscrapers and high-tech offices in Silicon Forest to the west, and they prosper and invent in the smaller cities and towns of the green Willamette Valley and the sere lands of eastern Oregon as well.

They come to a state which has a distinctive culture. Founded by New England churchmen, Oregon today is America's most unchurched state, with the lowest rate of church membership, with large numbers of believers in astrology, New Age lore and the like. To the innovations of this cultural left the public voices of Oregon's big institutions, like those of New England, have been friendly. Oregon a generation ago produced one of the first bottle-deposit laws, decriminalized marijuana, legalized most abortions before *Roe v. Wade*, and backed limits on development and use of property. It is one of two states that bans self-service gas. In the 1990s, it produced an Oregon Health Plan which rations medical care, denying specified low-priority treatments to Medicaid recipients. It legalized assisted suicide, in referenda in 1994 and 1997, to the point that doctors can prescribe but not administer lethal drugs; in 1998 15 terminally ill people were reported to have ended their lives with lethal medication. A gun control law passed banning semi-automatic weapons, and weekly betting on professional sports games was legalized. The Portland area has limited development and set aside green space, to the point that metropolitan area housing prices have risen to among the highest in the nation. As one Oregonian told *The New York Times*, "Oregonians are still in kind of a flashback to the '60s. They haven't come forward to the '90s, but that doesn't mean it's wrong or anything."

In 1996 Oregonians voted by mail only for a special U.S. Senate election; in 1998 they voted by referendum to hold all elections that way. So in November 2000 there were no polls open in Oregon on election day; voters had until that night to get their ballots to the election clerk. Unfortunately, Oregon has no statewide registry, so people could cast votes in multiple counties; also, some voters handed ballots to people standing outside clerks' offices who said they would file them—"snatching" ballots, some said. Proponents of mail-in ballots argue that they increase the percentage of eligibles who vote, which has always been high in Oregon anyway, and they give voters time to read over and think about the numerous ballot iniatiatives.

Oregon does indeed have as many ballot initiatives as any state—sometimes more. In 1998 voters approved medical marijuana, mail-in ballots and the unsealing of adoption records, and the state granted health care and other benefits to employees' domestic partners. But they rejected

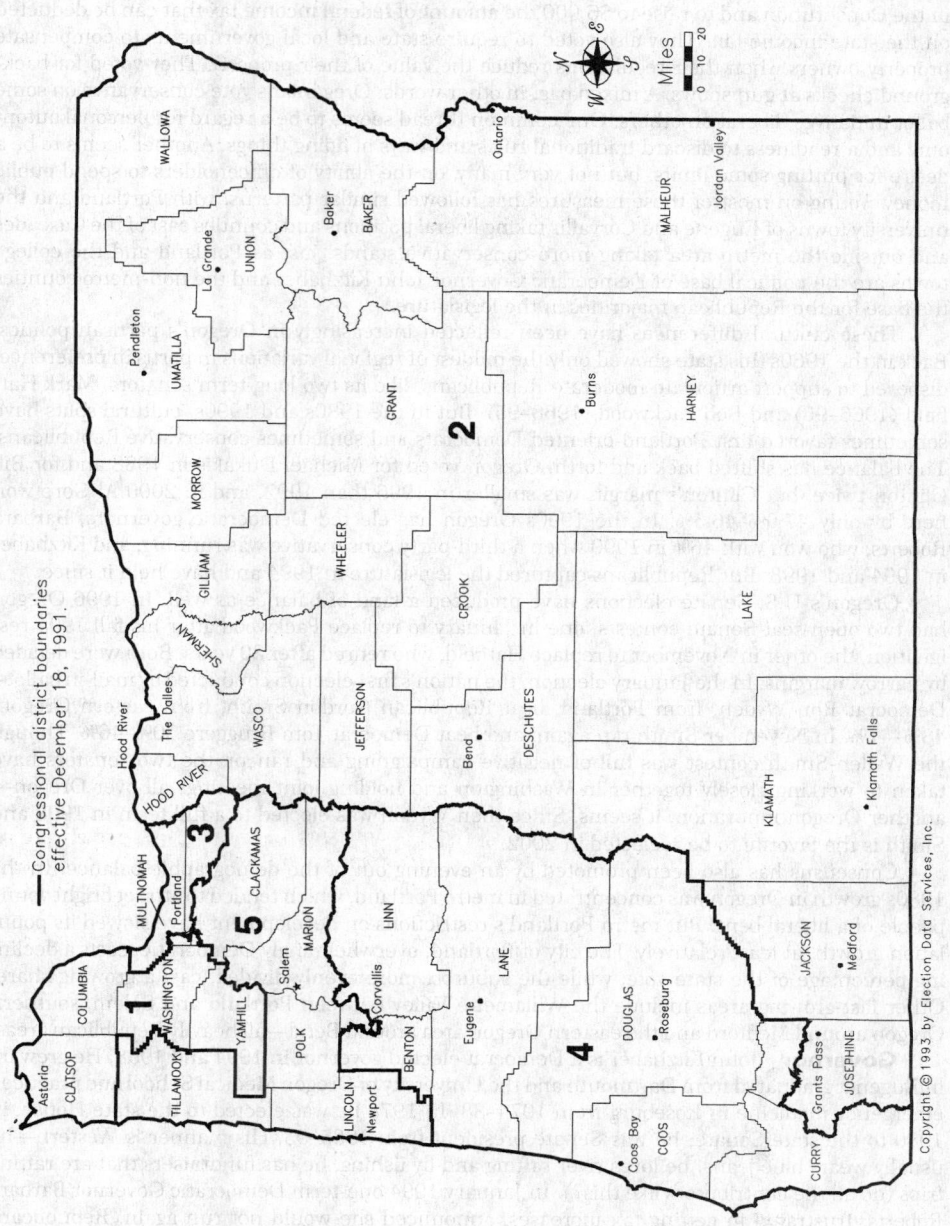

— Congressional district boundaries
effective December 18, 1991.

Copyright © 1993 by Election Data Services, Inc.

a ban on clearcut logging and required notice to property owners of proposed zoning changes. In November 2000 there were 26 initiatives on the ballot, more than in any state since North Dakota in 1932; the voters' guide ran 376 pages. Voters rejected a state spending limit, a $1 billion income tax cut, requiring votes on new taxes and fees and, by a narrow margin, a ban on teaching sanctioning homosexuality. But they voted to put the state's surplus income tax "kicker" (a refund) in the Constitution and to raise to $5,000 the amount of federal income tax that can be deducted on the state income tax. They also voted to require state and local governments to compensate property owners when their regulations reduce the value of their property. They voted for background checks at gun shows. A mixed bag, in other words: Oregonians vote conservative on some ballot initiatives, liberal on others. One common thread seems to be a regard for personal autonomy and a readiness to discard traditional rules and ways of doing things. Another seems to be a desire for putting some limits, but not very many, on the ability of officeholders to spend public money. Voting on most of these measures has followed similar patterns, with Portland and the university towns of Eugene and Corvallis taking liberal positions and counties east of the Cascades and outside the metro area taking more conservative stands, just as Portland and the college towns are the political base of Democratic Governor John Kitzhaber and the non-metro counties the base for the Republican majorities in the legislature.

These cultural differences have been reflected increasingly in Oregon's partisan politics. Back in the 1960s this state showed only the mildest of regional variations in partisan preference, disposed to support articulate moderate Republicans, like its two long-term senators, Mark Hatfield (1966–96) and Bob Packwood (1968–95). But in the 1980s and 1990s, cultural splits have sometimes favored first Portland-oriented Democrats and sometimes conservative Republicans. The balance has shifted back and forth. Oregon voted for Michael Dukakis in 1988 and for Bill Clinton twice, but Clinton's margin was smaller in 1996 than 1992, and in 2000 Al Gore won here by only 47.0%–46.5%. In the 1990s Oregon has elected Democratic governors, Barbara Roberts, who won with 46% in 1990 when a third-party conservative was running, and Kitzhaber in 1994 and 1998. But Republicans captured the legislature in 1994 and have held it since.

Oregon's U.S. Senate elections have produced a kind of balance as well. In 1996 Oregon had two open-seat Senate contests, one in January to replace Packwood after his fall 1995 resignation, the other in November to replace Hatfield, who retired after 30 years. Both were decided by narrow margins. In the January election, the nation's first election conducted by mail-in ballots, Democrat Ron Wyden, from Portland, beat Republican Gordon Smith, from eastern Oregon, 48%–47%. In November Smith ran again, and beat Democrat Tom Bruggere 50%–46%. Though the Wyden-Smith contest was full of negative campaigning and rancor, the two senators have taken to working closely together in Washington and holding joint meetings all over Oregon— another Oregon innovation, it seems. Since then Wyden was elected to a full term in 1998 and Smith is the favorite to be reelected in 2002.

Consensus has also been promoted by an evening out of the demographic balance. In the 1980s growth in Oregon was concentrated in metro Portland, which tended to attract bright young people of a liberal bent. But metro Portland's restrictions on development have slowed its population growth, at least relatively. The city of Portland, overwhelmingly Democratic, casts a declining percentage of the state vote, while the suburbs, more evenly divided, cast a growing share. Other fast-growing areas include the Willamette Valley between Portland and Salem, southern Oregon around Medford and the eastern Oregon area around Bend—all heavily Republican areas.

Governor John Kitzhaber is a Democrat elected governor in 1994 and 1998. He grew up in Eugene, graduated from Dartmouth and the University of Oregon Medical School and practiced emergency medicine in Roseburg from 1974–88. In 1978 he was elected to the state House, in 1980 to the state Senate; he was Senate president from 1985–93. His manner is Western—he usually wears blue jeans, he loves river rafting and fly fishing, he has fundraisers that are rafting trips (do all the contributors like this?). In January 1994 one-term Democratic Governor Barbara Roberts, frustrated in getting tax increases, announced she would not run again. Republicans already had a primary between former Congressman Denny Smith, son of a former governor and head of a family newspaper chain, and Craig Berkman, former state party chairman and critic of the conservative Oregon Citizens' Alliance. Kitzhaber jumped into the race and won the Democratic primary with 88% of the vote; Smith rallied conservatives and beat Berkman 50%–41%. In the general, Kitzhaber won statewide 51%–42%; he carried the Portland area and the university towns handsomely, but carried only a handful of counties in the rest of the state. At the same time, Republicans won control of the legislature.

Kitzhaber's great achievement in the legislature was was the Oregon Health Plan (the other physician-governor, Vermont Democrat Howard Dean, is a health care reformer too). Its strategy is to increase Medicaid coverage by rationing treatments. Blocked by the Bush administration, it went into effect in February 1994. Cigarette taxes were increased 10 cents per pack to pay for the plan, under which state officials drew up a list of 696 (now 743) medical treatments and ranked them by effectiveness and importance to basic health. Then based on cost estimates, the state decides how many treatments it can afford, and draws a line—originally it was at 606, in 2001 it was 574 and Kitzhaber has proposed 564. Above the line, the state will pay; below, it won't. This can raise poignant issues: Should an 18-year-old with cystic fibrosis receive a $250,000 liver and lung transplant? These questions are often avoided because the rules aren't always applied by private managed care plans which have Medicaid contracts with the state; and it is said that doctors often game the system. In the meantime costs rose from $435 million in 1993–94 to $750 million in 1999–2000, many insurers are dropping out and there are still plenty of uninsured.

The Oregon Health Plan has been characteristic of Kitzhaber's initiatives—its cool rationality, its faith in the judgment of centralized experts, its taste for complexity, its secular disregard for tradition, its willingness to use the power of the state to make decisions for others, tempered in some cases by a desire to give local government and local citizens an active role. He supports assisted suicide and denounced the U.S. House when in October 1999 it passed a bill which would have outlawed it (the bill never passed the Senate). His welfare reform plan used money from food stamps and cash benefits to subsidize employment for nine months, with employers contributing $1 an hour to education accounts. He has worked long and hard to increase Oregon's dwindling salmon stocks. He worked to develop a program of incentives for private landowners to preserve the habitat of coastal coho and steelhead salmon; despite his efforts, the federal government stepped in and listed coho as a threatened species. He sought a new bottle tax for the salmon plan and state parks; the state House nixed that. In February 2000 he called for breaching four dams on the Snake River—a measure terrifically unpopular with eastern Oregon farmers—to save the salmon, and in November he and outgoing Montana Governor Marc Racicot joined up to create a salmon recovery advisory committee for the Columbia River Basin; unfortunately the governors of Washington and Idaho and Northwest Indian tribes were opposed. In January 2000 he endorsed Bill Bradley for president because Al Gore refused to back breaching the Snake River dams (and because he liked Bradley's universal health insurance plan).

Much of Kitzhaber's time has been spent fighting the legislature on taxing and spending issues; he became known as "Dr. No" because he vetoed so many bills—69 in 1999 when he beat the record established by Governor Oswald West in 1911. Despite these battles, Kitzhaber brought a high job rating into the 1998 campaign and ended up with a weak opponent. This was Bill Sizemore, who makes a living putting conservative initiatives, mostly anti-tax, onto the ballot, some of which have passed—a property tax cut that limited increases to 3% annually—to Kitzhaber's consternation. But Sizemore had a serious problem. In April 1998 the Portland *Oregonian* ran a long and critical story on Sizemore's financial reverses. Sizemore won the May 1998 primary with only 50% of the vote against three weak opponents; his unfavorable rating was over 50%; there were rumors he was quitting the race in July. In November Kitzhaber won 64%–30%, carrying all but one county—the first Democratic governor to be re-elected here since 1906, indeed the first Oregon governor re-elected since 1982.

The wars with the legislature continued. The legislature had rejected Kitzhaber's tax based on cars' size and mileage in 1997. In 1999 they compromised on a gas tax. The legislature kept spending down, saved tax refunds due in December and killed Kitzhaber's proposed 1% income tax increase. Kitzhaber vetoed the legislature's tax cuts, many land use bills, a parental consent abortion bill and the 75 mile per hour speed limit. After much argument and outbiddings, they agreed to increase the biennial school budget 10.5%. Charter schools, not previously a Kitzhaber priority, were authorized. A law was passed to prevent parents who believe in faith healing only to bar medical treatment of their children. Under Kitzhaber the state government agreed with the Forest Service on demonstration projects for controlled burns and thinning of overcrowded forests and agreed with EPA on Superfund listing for Portland harbor; but Kitzhaber insisted on a role for state government. After a report charged that Oregon water quality was deteriorating, Kitzhaber blamed runoff from urban residents washing their cars and fertilizing their lawns. But he called for no government action: "Solutions lie not in regulations but in changing people's everyday behavior, how they live, work and play."

In the fall 2000 elections Kitzhaber raised $2.5 million from businesses and labor to campaign against the anti-tax ballot initiatives sponsored by Sizemore and others. Kitzhaber won on most, but not all. For the first time he actively raised money for Democratic legislative candidates, but was less successful. They trimmed Republican margins, but Republicans held control of the Senate 16–14 and the House 33–27. Going into the 2001 session, Kitzhaber and Republicans seemed much more in a mood to cooperate. Kitzhaber proposed no direct tax increases, and they seemed less far apart on spending; his budget had more money for schools and the Oregon Health Plan, less for police and human services. Kitzhaber is term-limited and cannot run for re-election in 2002.

Cook's Call   *Highly Competitive.* The closeness of the presidential race here—Gore won Oregon by less than 7,000 votes—suggests that the 6–2-seat Democratic advantage in the state's congressional delegation is deceptive. For the Republicans, state Labor and Industries Commissioner Jack Roberts and Portland school board member Ron Saxton are running, and the field may expand. On the Democratic side, Multnomah County Commission Chair Bev Stein, former state Treasurer Jim Hill and former Port of Portland Director Mike Thorne are almost certain to run, while Congressman Peter DeFazio and state Supreme Court Justice and 1982 gubernatorial candidate Ted Kulongoski are also possibilities.

Senior Senator   Ron Wyden grew up in California, graduated from Stanford, and came to Oregon to attend the University of Oregon Law School. After graduating in 1974 he founded the Gray Panthers, an advocacy group for the elderly; his first foray into electoral politics was sponsoring a successful referendum reducing the price of dentures. In 1980, at 31, he challenged an incumbent in the heavily Democratic 3d District, which covers most of Portland, and won the primary 60%–40%. Wyden has a genius for coming up with sensible-sounding ideas no one else has thought of and a knack for making the counter-intuitive political alliances which are so helpful in passing unfamiliar measures through the House. His achievements include a law, co-sponsored with Connecticut Republican Nancy Johnson, reducing federally funded community health clinics' malpractice insurance premiums by requiring the Justice Department to defend them in malpractice cases. He worked hard to get a waiver for John Kitzhaber's Oregon Health Plan and salmon recovery plan, and to bring the abortifacient RU-486 to the United States.

When the Senate Ethics Committee recommended the expulsion of Bob Packwood in September 1995, Wyden, who had long been eyeing the seat, decided to run in the January 1996 special election to replace him—the first election Oregon conducted by mail-in ballot. With his home base in Portland, whose TV stations cover most of the state, he had greater name identification than any competitor. But he had spirited opposition in the primary from Eugene-based Congressman Peter DeFazio. They differed on some issues and DeFazio was helped when Wyden, taking a quiz on KOIN-TV, could not name the prime minister of Canada or locate Bosnia on a globe. DeFazio carried his own district overwhelmingly, holding Wyden to a 50%–44% win. The Republican nomination was won by state Senate President Gordon Smith, a frozen vegetable tycoon from eastern Oregon who ultimately spent $2 million of his own money and beat longtime statewide official Norma Paulus 63%–25% in the primary. Most polls had the race in a dead heat as Smith adroitly avoided identification with House Republicans' intransigent stands on the budget and won the support of Senator Mark Hatfield. But organized labor and environmental groups ran heavy flights of ads against him. Wyden seemed to pick up strength the week before the January 30 deadline and won 48%–47%. This was hailed as a rejection of Newt Gingrich and a victory for abortion rights, but most voters deciding on abortion picked Smith, and Wyden, with his considerable strengths, had just barely managed to win in a state carried by Bill Clinton and Michael Dukakis.

In the Senate Wyden continued some of his crusades from the House. In April 1997 he and Republican Charles Grassley called for disclosure of the names of senators who place "holds" on legislation—a cause Wyden started working on in 1992 when a bill he backed was killed by anonymous holds. Wyden and Grassley persevered, and in March 1999 Majority Leader Trent Lott and Minority Leader Tom Daschle unveiled a new procedure: a senator putting a hold on a bill must inform the sponsor, the committee chairman and the two party leaders. "The fog of secrecy is starting to lift from the U.S. Senate," Wyden said.

Another Wyden cause was the Internet. In summer 1996 he worked with California Congressman Christopher Cox to push their amendment prohibiting government censorship of the Internet and urging online providers to offer technologies to help parents control their children's access to Internet materials. He and Cox also sponsored the three-year ban on Internet taxation that passed in October 1998; they have been trying to make it permanent. In June 2000 the bill sponsored by Wyden and Republican Spencer Abraham establishing electronic signatures as legally valid became law. Wyden has also worked on Internet privacy issues: "You can't stuff the new economy into a set of rules that were written for a smokestack economy." He worked with John McCain to produce the June 1999 Y2K liability bill, which gave businesses 90 days to handle problems and put limits on lawsuits. He wants to fund Internet access at senior centers. With McCain, he co-sponsored an airline passenger bill of rights in February 1999, to inform passengers when flights are oversold and why planes are late or flights cancelled, and to legalize back-to-back ticketing and hidden cities (means of taking advantage of low air fares). When McCain softened his bill after airlines adopted a voluntary code in June 1999, Wyden voted against it. In McCain's words: "He's very active, in fact, to the point of being a pain in the ass. I say that in a complimentary fashion. He's very tenacious about the things he believes in."

Wyden continues to be interested in health issues. He has worked on HMO regulation, to bar restrictions on physicians from mentioning alternative treatments to allowing lawsuits. He has worked to change Medicare reimbursement rates, which he claims are unfair to Oregon. In 1999 and 2000 he threatened filibusters many times to block Don Nickles's attempt to effectively repeal Oregon's assisted suicide bill. The repeal passed the House in 1999, and Nickles attached it to a tax cut bill in 2000, but Wyden, though he voted against assisted suicide in 1994 and 1997 referenda, argued that the federal government shouldn't interfere in regulating medical decisions and prevailed. With Republican Olympia Snowe, Wyden introduced a prescription drug benefit in June 1999, to be funded with tobacco settlement money, with competing private plans modified by a federal board. Pharmaceutical companies dropped their opposition in January 2000. And he worked with Congressman Bill Thomas to toward including the benefit in Medicare. In the process he pushed his proposal to require drug companies to pay a reasonable fee to NIH when they benefit from government-sponsored research. On other issues, the education flexibility bill sponsored by Wyden and Republican Bill Frist became law in April 1999. Wyden was the first senator to call on the Energy Department to swap oil from the Strategic Petroleum Reserve, a measure which helped hold down oil prices. And Wyden changed Senate tradition: In April 1997 he was blocked from bringing a blind staffer's guide dog to the floor of the Senate when Robert Byrd objected; Trent Lott quickly scurried to change the rules, and all three appeared on the floor the next day.

Ten months after Wyden was elected, his opponent Gordon Smith won the state's other Senate seat: the first time two senators were elected who had run against each other in the same year. With the departure of Bob Packwood and Mark Hatfield, Oregon had lost 56 years of Senate seniority and had gained two senators who everyone expected would be bitter enemies. But instead they became friends. They have held more than a dozen town meetings together across Oregon and meet for lunch every Thursday with their chiefs of staff. After losing a bet with Smith, Wyden answered phones for him: "Senator Smith's office; this is Ron Wyden." They began collaborating on Oregon issues, some with national application. After shooting deaths in a Springfield, Oregon, school, they sponsored a bill to require pupils who bring guns to school to be held for 72 hours and undergo psychological evaluation. Smith supported the law sponsored by Wyden and Idaho Republican Larry Craig to reimburse counties with national forests at a steady rate—fees based on logging had plummeted because of Clinton administration policies—and Wyden worked to make sure the state would send money to the counties. Wyden also worked with Oregon Republican Congressman Greg Walden to reach an agreement on protecting the environment around Steens Mountain in eastern Oregon while respecting the interests of local cattlemen; the result was the Steens Mountain Cooperative Management and Protection Area created in October 2000. With Democratic Congressman Peter DeFazio, Wyden worked to promote fish screens. With Smith and Washington's Slade Gorton, he called for the removal of the Portland INS director; the office's strip searches and hostility to foreign travelers earned it the name "Deportland."

Wyden has also set his own course on some local issues. He has opposed the sale of the Bonneville Power Administration, opposed a restart of the experimental reactor on the Hanford Reservation and cast the lone vote against a July 1999 energy bill because he feared it would permit the reopening of a nuclear reactor in Oregon. He lobbied the Chinese ambassador and got China to accept Pacific Northwest wheat for the first time in 20 years. He got national forest land transferred to the town of Sisters for a waste treatment plan and got permanent resident status for a Russian woman whose son was being treated for cerebral palsy in Portland. He attacked oil companies for zone pricing and redlining in Oregon and opposed logging at the Eagle site in Mount Hood National Forest.

This bipartisan tone helped Wyden win election to a full term in November 1998. His opponent, state Senator John Lim, who is of Korean descent, did not raise much money and Wyden had $500,000 left over after the campaign. He won 61%–34%, carrying all but one county, and improved his January 1996 showing by 10% in metro Portland, 14% in the Willamette Valley and 18% in the rest of the state. "I was bipartisan before it was p.c.," Wyden says, though not quite on everything. He voted against Bush cabinet appointees John Ashcroft and Gale Norton and, after Gordon Smith started a PAC to aid Republican candidates for the Oregon legislature in the 1998 cycle, Wyden started a PAC to help Democrats in 2000. Wyden's seat is not up until 2004. In the meantime, as Mark O'Keefe of the Portland *Oregonian* wrote in January 2000, "Whether from hard work, political acumen, raw luck or aggressive outreach to Republicans, particularly in the Oregon delegation, Wyden is enjoying the best run of his legislative career."

Junior Senator Republican Gordon Smith was born in Pendleton and grew up, after his father sold his food processing business to serve as an aide to Eisenhower Agriculture Secretary Ezra Taft Benson, in the Washington suburbs. He is a cousin of former Congressmen Morris and Stewart Udall and therefore of their sons, Congressmen Mark Udall and Tom Udall. Smith served two years as a Mormon missionary in New Zealand, then graduated from Brigham Young and from law school in Los Angeles, was a law clerk in New Mexico and practiced law in Arizona. Then he bought the family frozen vegetable processing company in Pendleton, and guided it out of debt to profitability; Smith Frozen Foods is now one of largest private label packers of frozen vegetables in the country. In 1992 he was elected to the state Senate and in 1995 became Senate president; he pushed through a law for parental notification of abortions. In 1995 and 1996 he ran for the Senate seat from which Bob Packwood resigned. He lost, after a battle of negative ads, to Ron Wyden 48%–47% in January 1996. The month before, Mark Hatfield had announced his retirement after 30 years in the Senate. At first Smith was reluctant to run again—indeed, he is the first person to run in two Senate races in the same year—but Republicans urged him to do so. Attacked during the Wyden race for being endorsed by the conservative Oregon Citizens' Alliance, Smith positioned himself closer to the center and turned down the OCA endorsement this time; when OCA head Lon Mabon ran against him in the primary, Smith beat him 78%–8%.

Smith's opponent in the general was Tom Bruggere, another self-made millionaire, who started Mentor Graphics near Portland and, like Smith, owned a Ferrari. In an ad shot in soft focus, Smith said he continued to oppose abortion, but promised not to back a constitutional amendment banning it and at the end of the campaign said he would vote for Medicaid to cover abortions in cases of rape, incest or threat to life of the mother; he promised to work for a balance of environmental protection, economic development and job creation. Bruggere ran positive ads, touting his firm's day care program and contribution of 1% of profits to charity; he attacked Smith on abortion and the environment and charged that his plant polluted the water. Smith responded with an ad attacking Bruggere for taking $2.5 million in stock options while laying off 500 employees in 1991 and 1992. The result was apparent only when Oregon's large number of absentee ballots were counted: Smith won 50%–46%, carrying every county but Portland, two university towns and two northwest counties; he lost metro Portland by 53%–43%, far less than in January, and carried the Willamette Valley 50%–45% and the rest of the state 58%–37%. Bruggere's vote closely tracked Bill Clinton's 47%, but that was not enough to win a two-way race.

Smith has compiled one of the most moderate voting records among Senate Republicans. In May 1999 he attracted attention when, after voting for Republican bills for limited background checks on sales in gun shows, he called on the leadership to change its stand. He voted for mandatory background checks and for children safety locks on guns—both reversals of previous stands. "I am proud to stand on the floor of the United States Senate and proclaim myself a defender of the Second Amendment," he said. "[But] I think it's possible to defend this consti-tutional right and also defend kids in the school cafeteria." He continued to oppose abortion, but in 2000 backed the use of stem cells in medical research; the cells are used in research to combat Parkinson's disease from which has stricken several of his relatives. He did not change his position on assisted suicide, however. While his Oregon colleague repeatedly threatened to filibuster Don Nickles's bill which would have overturned the assisted-suicide law Oregon voters supported in 1994 and 1997 referenda, Smith, after some agonizing over the issue, voted for it. He gave strong support to the prescription drug benefit bill sponsored by Wyden and Republican Olympia Snowe, and he and Barbara Mikulski sponsored a law that expanded Medicaid coverage for breast and cervical cancer. On legal issues, he sponsored a bill to give those convicted of crimes access to DNA evidence, and he co-sponsored with Edward Kennedy the amendment including gays in Kennedy's hate crimes law. With Massachusetts Democrat John Kerry, he proposed an education plan in December 1998 with $5 billion for raising teacher pay, tightening discipline and improving student health, starting second-chance schools and improving teacher training.

Smith serves on Foreign Relations and the subcommittee on Europe. Again he has steered something of a middle course; he was one of the few Republicans to vote for the Comprehensive Test Ban Treaty in October 1999. He traveled to Russia in April 1998 to investigate charges of persecution of religious minorities, and offers yearly amendments conditioning aid to Russia on lack of religious persecution. He is one of four senators on the Presidential Advisory Commission on Holocaust Assets. After the Clinton administration failed to get the backing it wanted for the bombing of Kosovo, he said, "The level of trust is at such a low ebb there is no interest in taking risks in advancing policies that are loaded with political difficulties. If the president was serious, he would find plenty of us who would respond." But he criticized the bombing of the Chinese embassy in Belgrade as a "debacle of monumental proportions" and said the Clinton policy was "half-hearted and ham-handed." In October 2000 he accused Al Gore of violating the law he had sponsored as a senator barring aid to Russia if it sells arms to Iran.

The election of Wyden in January 1996 and Smith in November 1996 was the first time two senators were elected who had run against each other in the same year. Surprisingly, considering the negative character of their campaign, they became friends. They have held more than a dozen joint town meetings across Oregon and lunch together every Thursday, and often issue joint press releases on transportation projects, the Medicare reimbursement formula and other Oregon is-sues. After shooting deaths in a Springfield, Oregon, school, they sponsored a bill to require pupils who bring guns to school to be held for 72 hours and undergo psychological evaluation. Wyden and Smith worked to expand the Little Sandy watershed protection area, from which Portland gets drinking water. Smith, Wyden and Congressman Greg Walden worked to reach an agreement on protecting the environment around Steens Mountain in eastern Oregon while respecting the interests of local cattlemen; the result was the Steens Mountain Cooperative Management and Protection Area created in October 2000. With Wyden and Washington's Slade Gorton, Smith called for the removal of the Portland INS director; the office's strip searches and hostility to foreign travelers earned it the name "Deportland."

Smith voted for the $3 billion conservation program to fund state purchases of land, despite qualms about its effect on property rights. He was a vocal opponent of Clinton administration bans on road building in national forests and, after the wildfires of summer 2000, condemned the administration for diverting money from firefighting to land acquisition. He has very strongly opposed breaching dams on the Snake River: "They'd have to take me out to take those dams out." He argues that the Columbia River has more fish now than in any year since 1938: "The basics are these: Power is not created by lifting a light switch. Gasoline doesn't come from a building. Food doesn't come from Safeway. They come from natural resources, and we all rely upon them." In 1999 he became chairman of the subcommittee with jurisdiction over the Bonneville Power Administration; he opposes selling BPA, but criticized the agency for plans to build a $1.4 billion surplus by 2006. He obtained $50 million in payments and purchases for cranberry farmers and $30.6 million for Oregon transportation projects, including radar and air traffic control upgrades for small airports and funding for Portland's light rail. He inserted into an appropriation bill language directing the Fish and Wildlife Service to return to Idaho wolves which have strayed over Oregon's border.

Smith headed George W. Bush's 2000 campaign in Oregon, and campaigned with him as he promised to oppose breaching the Snake River dams and came out against assisted suicide. Bush came within a few thousand votes of carrying the state, which his father had lost by a much wider margin in 1988. In January 2001, a Portland *Oregonian* reporter wrote that Smith "is at the top of his political game. He has carved out a comfortably moderate niche within the Republican majority in Congress, and he has the ear of President-elect Bush." He seemed certain to run for reelection, and stands to profit from the bipartisan tone that he and Wyden have set; he did not campaign against Wyden in 1998, and Wyden seems sure not to campaign against him in 2002. His best known possible opponent for 2002 is term-limited Governor John Kitzhaber; that could be a high-spending race, and one of the most seriously contested of the cycle. If Kitzhaber does not run, another possible Democrat is Secretary of State Bill Bradbury.

Cook's Call *Competitive.* Smith has not made any serious mistakes and has compiled a moderate voting record in accordance with Oregon voters, but this is a very competitive state. If Democratic Governor John Kitzhaber is in the race it will be highly competitive. If not, Smith should win without too much difficulty.

Presidential politics Oregon was once the most Republican state in the West, voting for Thomas Dewey over Harry Truman in 1948; in the 1980s and early 1990s it was one of the most Democratic. Now it seems more evenly balanced, much less Democratic than California, more Republican than the Rocky Mountain states. As compared to 1988, the 2000 Democratic percentage was flat and the Republican percentage up. One reason was the showing of Ralph Nader, who won 4% here in 1996, his best showing that year, and 5% in 2000. Oregon seems sure to be a target state in 2004.

Oregon once had an important presidential primary, scheduled in May. In 1948 Oregon ended Harold Stassen's serious presidential prospects, when he lost 52%–48% to Dewey; in 1968 Oregon gave Robert Kennedy his only defeat when it voted 44%–38% for Eugene McCarthy. Oregon in those days was part of a West Coast campaign swing, just before the California primary; at a time when campaigners were not used to flying all over the country they, like National Football League teams in the 1950s, scheduled West Coast contests together to minimize travel time. For 1992 and 1996, Oregon scheduled its primary for Super Tuesday in March, but it was overshadowed by bigger contests in the South. In 2000 the primary was held again in May. Few candidates remained. George W. Bush beat Alan Keyes and Al Gore beat Lyndon LaRouche.

Congressional districting The 1990s redistricting plan created a safe Democratic seat based in Portland, two marginal districts based in the Portland suburbs, a Democratic seat (though it went for George W. Bush in 2000) around Eugene, and a heavily Republican district in southern and eastern Oregon. Democrats currently hold four of the seats, Republicans only one. For 2002, the lines will be drawn initially by the Republican legislature, but subject to Democratic Governor John Kitzhaber's veto. The Portland, Eugene and eastern districts will probably not be much altered. The real struggle will be over the lines in the suburban 1st and 5th Districts. The Republican strategy will presumably be to pare off heavily Democratic precincts from these districts and put them in the Portland-based 3d, which will need to add people to meet the equal-population standard.

THE PEOPLE: Pop. 2000: 3,421,399; Pop. 1990: 2,842,321, up 20.4% 1990–2000. 1.2% of U.S. total, 28th largest; 86.6% White, 1.6% Black, 3% Asian, 1.3% Amer. Indian, 0.2% Hawaiian, 3.1% Two+ races, 4.2% Other; 8% Hispanic Origin. 4.9% Unemployment. 2000 Voting age pop.: 2,574,873. 2000 Turnout: 1,559,215; 61% of VAP. Registered voters (2000): 1,954,006; 765,641 D (39%), 696,657 R (36%), 491,708 unaffiliated and minor parties (25%).

POLITICAL LINEUP: Governor, John Kitzhaber (D); Secy. of State, Bill Bradbury (D); Atty. Gen., Hardy Myers (D); Treasurer, Randall Edwards (D); Super. of Public Instruction, Stan Bunn; Commissioner of Labor, Jack Roberts; State Senate, 30 (14 D, 16 R); Senate President, Gene Derfler (R); Majority Leader, David Nelson (R); State House, 60 (27 D, 33 R); House Speaker, Mark Simmons (R). Senators, Ron Wyden (D) and Gordon H. Smith (R). Representatives, 5 (4 D, 1 R).

ELECTIONS DIVISION: 503-986-1518; **FILING DEADLINE FOR U.S. CONGRESS:** March 12, 2002.

2000 Presidential Vote
Gore (D)	720,342	(47%)
Bush (R)	713,577	(47%)
Nader (Green)	77,357	(5%)
Others	22,692	(1%)

1996 Presidential Vote
Clinton (D)	649,631	(47%)
Dole (R)	538,155	(39%)
Perot (I)	121,218	(9%)
Others	68,746	(5%)

2000 Republican Presidential Primary
Bush (R)	292,522	(84%)
Keyes (R)	46,764	(13%)
Other	10,545	(3%)

2000 Democratic Presidential Primary
Gore (D)	300,922	(85%)
LaRouche (D)	38,521	(11%)
Other	15,151	(4%)

Gov. John Kitzhaber (D)

Elected 1994, term expires Jan. 2003, 2d term; b. Mar. 5, 1947, Colfax, WA; home, Eugene; Dartmouth Col., B.S. 1969; U. of OR Med. Schl., M.D. 1973; no religious affiliation; married (Sharon).

Elected Office: OR House of Reps., 1978–80; OR Senate, 1980–94, Pres., 1985–93.

Professional Career: Practicing physician, 1974–88; Health & environment consultant, 1988–93.

Office: State Capitol, Rm. 254, Salem, 97310, 503-378-3111; Fax: 503-378-6827; Web site: www.state.or.us.

Election Results
1998 general	John Kitzhaber (D)	717,061	(64%)
	Bill Sizemore (R)	334,001	(30%)
	Others	62,036	(6%)
1998 primary	John Kitzhaber (D)	271,781	(88%)
	Dave Foley (D)	23,870	(8%)
	Others	14,094	(5%)
1994 general	John Kitzhaber (D)	622,083	(51%)
	Denny Smith (R)	517,874	(42%)
	Ed Hickman (American)	58,449	(5%)
	Others	22,604	(2%)

Sen. Ron Wyden (D)

Elected Jan. 1996, seat up 2004, 1st term; b. May 3, 1949, Wichita, KS; home, Portland; Stanford U., B.A. 1971, U. of OR, J.D. 1974; Jewish; divorced.

Elected Office: U.S. House of Reps., 1980–96.

Professional Career: Co-Dir. & Co-Founder, OR Gray Panthers, 1974–80; Dir., OR Legal Svcs. for the Elderly, 1977–79; Prof. of Gerontology, U. of OR, 1976, Portland St. U., 1979, U. of Portland, 1980.

DC Office: 516 HSOB, 20510, 202-224-5244; Fax: 202-228-2717; Web site: www.senate.gov/~wyden.

State Offices: Bend, 541-330-9142; Eugene, 541-431-0229; LaGrande, 541-962-7691; Medford, 541-858-5122; Portland, 503-326-7525; Salem, 503-589-4555.

Committees: *Aging (Special). Budget. Commerce, Science & Transportation*: Aviation; Communications; Consumer Affairs, Foreign Commerce & Tourism; Manufacturing & Competitiveness (Chmn.); Surface Transportation & Merchant Marine. *Energy & Natural Resources*: Energy Research, Development, Production & Regulation; Forests & Public Land Management (Chmn.); Water & Power. *Environment & Public Works*: Fisheries, Wildlife & Water; Superfund, Waste Control & Risk Assessment; Transportation & Infrastructure. *Intelligence (Select)*.

Group Ratings

	ADA	ACLU	AFS	LCV	CON	ITIC	NTU	COC	ACU	NTLC	CHC
2000	90	71	71	100	54	91	14	60	8	9	15
1999	100	—	100	100	43	—	12	59	4	—	—

National Journal Ratings

	1999 LIB	—	1999 CONS		2000 LIB	—	2000 CONS
Economic	65%	—	34%		80%	—	18%
Social	81%	—	12%		66%	—	21%
Foreign	87%	—	0%		89%	—	5%

Key Votes of the 106th Congress

1. Educ. Savings Accts.	N	5. Review Movie Violence	Y
2. Prescrip. Drug Benefit	Y	6. Gun Show Bckgrnd. Checks	Y
3. Delay Ergonomic Standards	N	7. Ban Part.-Birth Abortion	N
4. Phase Out Estate Tax	Y	8. Broaden Hate Crimes List	Y

9. NATO War in Serbia	Y
10. Table Cuba Travel Ban	N
11. Nuclear Test-Ban Treaty	Y
12. Perm. Trade with China	Y

Election Results

1998 general	Ron Wyden (D)	682,425	(61%)	($2,866,368)
	John Lim (R)	377,739	(34%)	($413,187)
	Others	57,583	(5%)	
1998 primary	Ron Wyden (D)	283,654	(92%)	
	John Sweeney (D)	25,456	(8%)	
	Others	853	(0%)	
1996 special	Ron Wyden (D)	571,739	(48%)	($4,237,134)
	Gordon H. Smith (R)	553,519	(47%)	($5,542,482)
	Others	56,392	(5%)	
1992 general	Bob Packwood (R)	717,455	(52%)	($8,034,249)
	Les AuCoin (D)	639,851	(47%)	($2,629,397)

Sen. Gordon H. Smith (R)

Elected 1996, seat up 2002, 1st term; b. May 25, 1952, Pendleton; home, Pendleton; Brigham Young U., B.A. 1976, Southwestern U., J.D. 1979; Mormon; married (Sharon).

Elected Office: OR Senate, 1992–96, Pres., 1994–96.

Professional Career: Law Clerk, NM Supreme Court, 1979–80; Practicing atty., 1980–81; Pres., Smith Frozen Foods, 1980–96.

DC Office: 404 RSOB, 20510, 202-224-3753; Fax: 202-228-3997; Web site: www.senate.gov/~gsmith.

State Offices: Bend, 541-318-1298; Eugene, 541-465-6750; Medford, 541-608-9102; Pendleton, 541-278-1129; Portland, 503-326-3386.

Committees: *Budget. Commerce, Science & Transportation*: Aviation; Communications; Consumer Affairs, Foreign Commerce & Tourism; Oceans & Fisheries; Surface Transportation & Merchant Marine (RMM). *Energy & Natural Resources*: Forests & Public Land Management; National Parks, Historic Preservation & Recreation; Water & Power (RMM). *Foreign Relations*: African Affairs; European Affairs (RMM); Near Eastern & South Asian Affairs.

Group Ratings

	ADA	ACLU	AFS	LCV	CON	ITIC	NTU	COC	ACU	NTLC	CHC
2000	10	14	0	0	11	100	73	100	84	94	85
1999	15	—	0	33	16	—	72	94	76	—	—

National Journal Ratings

	1999 LIB	—	1999 CONS		2000 LIB	—	2000 CONS
Economic	46%	—	52%		32%	—	64%
Social	36%	—	59%		48%	—	51%
Foreign	62%	—	29%		52%	—	47%

Key Votes of the 106th Congress

1. Educ. Savings Accts.	Y	5. Review Movie Violence	Y	9. NATO War in Serbia	Y
2. Prescrip. Drug Benefit	N	6. Gun Show Bckgrnd. Checks	N	10. Table Cuba Travel Ban	Y
3. Delay Ergonomic Standards	Y	7. Ban Part.-Birth Abortion	Y	11. Nuclear Test-Ban Treaty	Y
4. Phase Out Estate Tax	Y	8. Broaden Hate Crimes List	Y	12. Perm. Trade with China	Y

Election Results

1996 general	Gordon H. Smith (R)	677,336	(50%)	($3,527,252)
	Tom Bruggere (D)	624,370	(46%)	($3,301,736)
	Others	58,524	(4%)	
1996 primary	Gordon H. Smith (R)	224,428	(78%)	
	Lon Mabon (R)	23,479	(8%)	
	Kirby Brumfield (R)	15,744	(5%)	
	Jeff Lewis (R)	13,359	(5%)	
	Others	10,490	(4%)	
1990 general	Mark O. Hatfield (R)	590,095	(54%)	($2,714,661)
	Harry Lonsdale (D)	507,743	(46%)	($1,479,099)

FIRST DISTRICT

Postmodern skyscrapers rising above the riverfront and below a range of hills: This is downtown Portland. The city—which would have been named Boston if a coin toss had gone the other way—started here, along the Willamette River just before it flows into the Columbia, and downtown was built on the narrow margin of land west of the river and below the hills, not on the flat expanse that stretches east towards the snow-capped peak of Mount Hood. Downtown Portland was once a dowdy place, proper in a New Englandish way, with a few formal buildings above the warehouses and factories. But in the last 20 years there has been an explosion of creativity here, symbolized by handsome high-rises—the pyramid-crested brick KOIN Tower, the wedge-shaped Justice Center—restored Victorian storefronts, a downtown transit trolley and a light rail line known as MAX

(Metropolitan Area Express), and just across the river the new Oregon Museum of Science and Industry. The affluent neighborhoods in the hills overlooking downtown are full of old lumber barons' mansions with splendid views.

Just over the hills are the valleys and interstices between green mountains of suburban Washington County. Not so long ago, this was farm country, with 39,000 people in 1940; now it has about 400,000 and is an integral part of metro Portland. This is an affluent area, with clusters of towns and protected forest areas that feature a high-tech, healthy-lifestyle aura; major employers here are Tektronix, Intel, Nike and Sequent Computer Systems. Like Silicon Valley, the Silicon Forest has an environment—at the foot of mountains, woodsy and even rustic but outfitted with all the comforts and services of modern civilization—that appeals to a highly skilled work force. As they say locally, wood chips have been replaced by computer chips. Economic growth has been so powerful that Washington County told Intel's officers that the company could add another 1,000 to its 4,000 employees (more than are based at its Santa Clara headquarters), but only if the company agreed to a "growth impact fee"—a $1,000 assessment for each worker over the agreed limit.

The 1st Congressional District includes downtown Portland and its western hills, plus a bit of the residential areas east of the Willamette, and all of Washington County. The 1st also proceeds northwest along the Columbia to Astoria and the Pacific Coast, and southwest to Yamhill County, where metro growth is spreading. Like Oregon, the 1st District is historically New England Republican, electing only Republican congressmen from 1892 to 1972; like New England, it then trended sharply left on cultural issues, even as its high-tech economy brought new affluence, and since 1974 it has elected liberal Democrats. But the political balance is close here: Washington County has become increasingly Republican, and no one won more than 52% of the vote in the 1st District in the 1990s. In Washington County, Al Gore led George W. Bush, 48.7%–46.3%, with Ralph Nader getting 3.8%.

The congressman from the 1st District is David Wu, a Democrat elected in 1998, the third Chinese-American to have served in Congress. He was born in Taiwan in 1955 and came to the U.S. with the rest of his family to join his father, studying at Rensselaer Polytechnic Institute in 1961, after restrictions on non-European immigration were softened. He grew up mostly in Orange County, California, went to college at Stanford, started medical school at Harvard, then switched to law school at Yale. He clerked for a federal judge in Portland and settled there; he also worked on Jimmy Carter's campaign in 1980 and Gary Hart's in 1984. He started his own law firm in 1988 and served on the Portland Planning Commission.

In June 1997, Congresswoman Elizabeth Furse, a liberal Democrat and supporter of term limits, announced she would not run again, and Wu ran. The Democratic frontrunner was Linda Peters, who was well known as Washington County Board chairwoman and had the backing of EMILY's List. Wu spent $100,000 of his own money and left his law practice. He started attacking Peters in ads for taking a personal loan from a developer and for misspending tax dollars while traveling on county business. Wu's tactic drew cries of protest from Furse, the League of Women Voters and state party leaders, but he won the primary 52%–43%. Republicans nominated 29-year-old Molly Bordonaro, whose father is a prominent real estate man in Portland. Coming out of the primary, she had more money than Wu, a more united party behind her and was running even in the polls. Yet Wu won. One reason was that, with help from national Democrats and labor unions, he caught up in fundraising. Another was that Wu established himself early as a moderate. He talked of a balanced approach to the environment, smaller government, less business regulation. He used his own life story to extol America's system of education and to call for more spending on Head Start (his wife is a Head Start teacher) and aid to college students. A mid-October poll showed the race even; in November, Wu won 50%–47%. All of his margin and much more came from the Multnomah County part of the district, which he carried 67%–30%; Bordonaro carried Washington County 51%–47%, but that was not enough.

In the House, Wu joined the centrist New Democrat Coalition and fostered a reputation as a maverick, though the closer truth is that he's usually a party regular—with a voting pattern similar to that of the Portland area's two other liberal House Democrats. On education, health care, abortion and gun control, he was a reliable Democratic voice. Displeasing local business, he voted against permanent trade relations with China because of "our commitment to American values and the sacrifices of countless families like mine." He opposed estate and gift tax repeal. Within the delegation, he caused a stir by seeking an Appropriations Committee seat, which the more senior Darlene Hooley also wanted; neither succeeded. When Al Gore appeared in Portland two weeks before the election, Wu told *The New York Times*, "sometimes the vice president's delivery has gotten in the way of his message."

Wu's Republican challenger in 2000 was Charles Starr, a state senator and Christian conservative. Despite an aggressive campaign, Starr was outspent more than 5-to-1 and had no TV advertising. Although Intel's PAC gave Starr $5,000, his total from the business community was paltry. Given that he was outpolled by Bush, Starr's outspoken conservative views may have been a burden in this suburban district. Wu won, 58%–38%. Still, he may not be secure due to redistricting.

Cook's Call *Competitive.* The fact that Wu won his first re-election bid in 2000 by 58% belies the marginal nature of this district. Gore won this district with just 51% in 2000. The fastest growing district in the state, the 1st will have to contract by about 60,000 people in redistricting. Republicans argue that the Multnomah County (Portland) portions of the district should be shed, thereby creating a much more suburban (read: marginal) district. Regardless of how the new lines look, Republicans will need to recruit a much stronger candidate than they did in 2000 if they are to be competitive here in 2002.

THE PEOPLE: Pop. 2000: 743,195; Pop. 1990: 568,501, up 30.7% 1990–2000. 85.4% White, 1.2% Black, 5% Asian, 0.8% Amer. Indian, 0.2% Hawaiian, 2.9% Two+ races, 4.5% Other; 8.9% Hispanic Origin.

2000 Presidential Vote		
Gore (D)	169,019	(51%)
Bush (R)	145,106	(44%)
Nader (Green)	14,920	(4%)
Others	4,064	(1%)

1996 Presidential Vote		
Clinton (D)	145,540	(50%)
Dole (R)	112,152	(38%)
Perot (I)	21,304	(7%)
Others	14,310	(5%)

Rep. David Wu (D)

Elected 1998, 2d term; b. Apr. 8, 1955, Taiwan; home, Portland; Stanford U., B.S. 1977; Harvard Med. Schl., 1978; Yale Law Schl., J.D. 1982; Presbyterian; married (Michelle).

Professional Career: Law clerk, 9th Circuit Court of Appeals, 1982–83; Campaign staff, Gary Hart for President, 1984; Practicing atty., 1984–98.

DC Office: 1023 LHOB 20515, 202-225-0855; Fax: 202-225-9497; Web site: www.house.gov/wu.

District Office: Portland, 503-326-2901.

Committees: *Education & the Workforce* (18th of 22 D): 21st Century Competitiveness. *Science* (14th of 22 D): Energy; Space & Aeronautics.

Group Ratings

	ADA	ACLU	AFS	LCV	CON	ITIC	NTU	COC	ACU	NTLC	CHC
2000	90	77	85	86	50	67	34	52	20	24	0
1999	100	—	100	88	85	—	26	24	4	—	—

National Journal Ratings

	1999 LIB	—	1999 CONS		2000 LIB	—	2000 CONS
Economic	71%	—	28%		65%	—	34%
Social	70%	—	29%		72%	—	26%
Foreign	73%	—	27%		53%	—	45%

Key Votes of the 106th Congress

1. Patient Bill of Rights	Y	5. Bar RU-486 $ for FDA	N	9. NATO War in Serbia	*
2. Accelerate Min. Wage	Y	6. Display 10 Commandments	N	10. Perm. Trade with China	N
3. Strike Ban on Ergo. Stnd.	Y	7. Gun Show Bkgrnd. Checks	Y	11. Debt Relief for 3rd World	Y
4. Ovrd. Estate Tax Veto	N	8. Ban Part.-Birth Abortion	N	12. Drop Cuba Econ. Embargo	N

Election Results

2000 general	David Wu (D)	176,902	(58%)	($1,437,974)
	Charles Starr (R)	115,303	(38%)	($278,345)
	Other	11,316	(4%)	
2000 primary	David Wu (D)	unopposed		
1998 general	David Wu (D)	119,993	(50%)	($1,602,063)
	Molly Bordonaro (R)	112,827	(47%)	($1,367,154)
	Others	6,676	(3%)	

SECOND DISTRICT

The Cascade Mountains that wall eastern Oregon off from the rest of the state are a magnificent chain of once (and quite possibly still) active volcanic mountains that drain almost every drop of moisture out of the air coming in from the Pacific, and thus separate green, wet western Oregon from the brown, parched east. Eastern Oregon has 70% of the state's land, but less than 400,000 of its 3.4 million people, most of whom still make their living off the land: beef and dairy cattle, timber and lumber, fish from the Columbia River and wheat from the irrigated plains. The effect of the Cascades can be felt in the one place they are breached—by the Columbia River Gorge. There, surrounded by brown hills on both sides, funneled winds pound in steadily from the west, making the confluence of the Columbia and Hood rivers the best windsurfing site in the United States. In January 2001, plans were announced to build the world's largest wind farm here; it will produce 450 windmills capable of generating electricity for 70,000 homes.

The 2d Congressional District covers all of the state east of the Cascades and the southern-most valley between the Cascades and the Coast Range. Much of this land is empty: Harney County, with a land area larger than that of nine states, has a population of 7,000. Population concentrations here are far apart: Pendleton, a genuine rodeo town amid the northeastern wheat fields; La Grande in the rich Grande Ronde Valley; The Dalles, where the Columbia River Gorge begins; Bend in the center of the state, near Crook County, which until it voted for George Bush in 1992 was the only county in the country to have voted for the winning presidential candidate in every election (it went for Bob Dole in 1996 and for George W. Bush in 2000). In the south-western corner, separated from other areas by the Cascades and the once huge volcano whose blown-off cone is now 2,000-foot deep Crater Lake, is the lumber and pear orchard country around Medford, Ashland, Klamath Falls and Grants Pass.

Politically, the 2d District has grown very Republican and often suspicious of the federal government. A few government pursuits here are considered acceptable; the Army's Umatilla Chemical Depot, near Hermiston, with 3,700 tons of chemical weapons, generated no controversy for 50 years until the Army announced it would destroy the weapons by incineration. But the federal government is more often viewed here as the owner of three-quarters of the district's land and the protector of the endangered spotted owl, which has forced timber companies increasingly onto Oregon's limited expanses of state and private land. When Interior Secretary Bruce Babbitt came to Medford in 1998 to take a ceremonial whack out of a soon-to-be-demolished dam, he was heckled mercilessly. The cultural liberalism of Portland and the East Coast isn't particularly welcomed, either; this is more a part of the leave-us-alone Rocky Mountain basin than of the culturally hip West Coast.

The congressman from the 2d District is Greg Walden, a Republican elected in 1998. He grew up on a cherry orchard near The Dalles in the Columbia gorge; his father served in the state House. Walden served as press secretary and chief of staff to Congressman Denny Smith from 1981–87, then returned to Hood River as a radio station owner. In 1988 he was elected to the state House, and in his second term became majority leader. Walden was known for cobbling together consensus on issues that divided the state, working to expand the lottery and write rules for the Oregon Health Plan. He is conservative on economic issues but more moderate on social issues; he is pro-choice but opposes federal funding of abortions.

Walden succeeded Bob Smith, who had returned to the House to serve one term as chairman of the Agriculture Committee after embarrassed Republicans decided they needed to replace Representative Wes Cooley; one of the less impressive and sometimes not so truthful members of Newt Gingrich's Class of 1994. Walden was faced with substantial primary opposition. There was lots of grumbling about outside interference, which appeared in the form of $130,000 in ads by Americans for Limited Terms and $50,000 in ads by Gary Bauer's Family Research Council. Walden, the target, was miffed: "It's such an irony to have developed such a broad base of support, and then these groups can come in from back East and nail you." Walden's wide support and the $500,000 he raised enabled him to win fairly easily, with 55% of the vote to 33% for religious broadcaster Perry Atkinson and 9% for the unembarrassable Cooley. The general election was anticlimactic. Democrat Kevin Campbell ran as a conservative but carried only his home county; Walden won 61%–35%.

In his first term, Walden's legislative highlight was enactment of his Steens Mountain Cooperative Management and Protection Act, which was a response to Interior Secretary Bruce Babbitt's threat to create 175,000 acres of wilderness in southeast Oregon. Walden's alternative created incentives for public-private management of the land. He joined other northwest Republicans on a nonbinding resolution that ruled out breaching dams as an option to save endangered runs of salmon. He worked to improve Internet access in rural areas, even bringing telephone service for the first time to Granite, Oregon (population, 20). On an issue that generated huge controversy in Oregon and beyond, Walden voiced reservations about the state's assisted suicide law, but he argued that voters should be entitled to their views rather than face federal preemption. In a novel campaign-reform plan, he introduced with Senator Ron Wyden a proposal that candidates should pay a 35% fee for running TV attack ads in which they do not appear. An enthusiastic supporter of permanent trade relations with China, he found himself in a somewhat embarrassed position as one of only four congressman who joined a dozen Clinton administration officials visiting China to make the case for support of the deal.

Walden easily won re-election in 2000 over retired teacher Walter Ponsford, 74%–26%. It was the district's first routine, non-Cooley contest in six years. He announced that he would not run for governor in 2002 to succeed term-limited John Kitzhaber. "I want to stay here [in Washington] for a while," said Walden, who gained a seat on the Energy and Commerce Committee. There is no reason to believe that he won't get his wish, including the possibility of moving onto the House leadership ladder.

Cook's Call   *Safe.* Don't look for a competitive race in this district, the most Republican in the state. The second fastest growing district in the state, this sprawling, 70,000 square mile district will need to contract in 2002 redistricting.

THE PEOPLE: Pop. 2000: 701,847; Pop. 1990: 568,437, up 23.5% 1990–2000. 89.3% White, 0.4% Black, 0.8% Asian, 2.1% Amer. Indian, 0.2% Hawaiian, 2.5% Two+ races, 4.8% Other; 8.6% Hispanic Origin.

2000 Presidential Vote			**1996 Presidential Vote**		
Bush (R)	186,784	(60%)	Dole (R)	130,408	(48%)
Gore (D)	108,210	(34%)	Clinton (D)	103,116	(38%)
Nader (Green)	13,357	(4%)	Perot (I)	30,093	(11%)
Others	5,466	(2%)	Others	10,362	(4%)

Rep. Greg Walden (R)

Elected 1998, 2d term; b. Jan. 10, 1957, The Dalles; home, Hood River; U. of OR, B.S. 1981; Episcopalian; married (Mylene).

Elected Office: OR House of Reps., 1988–94, Majority Ldr., 1991–93; OR Senate, 1994–96.

Professional Career: Press secy., U.S. Rep. Denny Smith, 1981–84, Chief of staff, 1984–86; Owner, Columbia Gorge Broadcasters Inc., 1986-present.

DC Office: 1404 LHOB 20515, 202-225-6730; Fax: 202-225-5774; Web site: www.house.gov/walden.

District Offices: Hood River, 541-386-9152; Medford, 503-326-2901.

Committees: *Energy & Commerce* (30th of 31 R): Commerce, Trade & Consumer Protection; Energy & Air Quality; Environment & Hazardous Materials. *Resources* (21st of 28 R): Water & Power.

Group Ratings

	ADA	ACLU	AFS	LCV	CON	ITIC	NTU	COC	ACU	NTLC	CHC
2000	5	29	14	7	37	100	64	90	88	70	87
1999	10	—	16	6	8	—	56	96	80	—	—

National Journal Ratings

	1999 LIB	—	1999 CONS		2000 LIB	—	2000 CONS
Economic	24%	—	72%		29%	—	67%
Social	44%	—	55%		38%	—	61%
Foreign	23%	—	73%		12%	—	78%

Key Votes of the 106th Congress

1. Patient Bill of Rights	N	5. Bar RU-486 $ for FDA	Y	9. NATO War in Serbia	N
2. Accelerate Min. Wage	N	6. Display 10 Commandments	Y	10. Perm. Trade with China	Y
3. Strike Ban on Ergo. Stnd.	N	7. Gun Show Bkgrnd. Checks	N	11. Debt Relief for 3rd World	N
4. Ovrd. Estate Tax Veto	Y	8. Ban Part.-Birth Abortion	Y	12. Drop Cuba Econ. Embargo	N

Election Results

2000 general	Greg Walden (R)	220,086	(74%)	($523,820)
	Walter Ponsford (D)	78,101	(26%)	
2000 primary	Greg Walden (R)	unopposed		
1998 general	Greg Walden (R)	132,316	(61%)	($879,010)
	Kevin M. Campbell (D)	74,924	(35%)	($86,931)
	Others	7,976	(4%)	

THIRD DISTRICT

Postmodern Portland, the Rose City set between Mount Hood to the east and the Tualatin Mountains to the west, spanning the Willamette River with its airport and industrial back to the Columbia, is still one of America's least known major cities—and one of its most distinctive. This was not always so. For most of its history Portland was a prosaic city in a magic setting; it was in many ways a muscular, blue-collar town, which piled Oregon lumber and Oregon pears into freight cars or unloaded machines from back East or autos from Japan on its docks. But in the past three decades Portland has been transformed. Out on the Pacific Rim, it increasingly makes its living on foreign trade, seeing East Asians as customers more than competitors. It has become a home of high-tech industries, particularly in the Washington County suburbs to the west—Silicon Forest. Government has also produced change. Oregon's land-use act, passed in 1973, required local governments to set geographic limits on growth; Metro, the regional government established in 1979 just as growth was accelerating, has created something of a counterweight against the endless spread outward of population into former farmland. Portland opened its first light-rail line in 1986 and has encouraged the development of high-density commercial space and housing around transit stops; bicycle paths wind throughout the metropolitan area, and downtown, west of the Willamette River, boasts proud postmodern structures amid classic masonry buildings.

In the process, the central city of Portland, like San Francisco and Seattle, has come to attract political and cultural liberals. And, like those two cities, Portland has its share of traffic congestion—it was ranked 8th worst in the nation in 2001—and high home prices. The light-rail system caused an unusually large number of casualties because it failed to build barriers to busy street traffic. But this "livable community" was rated the best city to live in by *Money* magazine in 2000 and its long-term approach to transportation, creating mixed-use neighborhoods and increasing development density, may ultimately pay off. The city dropped from the fourth-least affordable place in the nation to purchase a new home in the early 1990s to 25th by the end of the decade.

The 3d Congressional District takes in most of Portland and Multnomah County east of the Willamette River, extending over suburban plains and hills to the splendid scenery of the Bonneville Dam in the Columbia River Gorge and Mount Hood high in the Cascades. Politically, it is dominated by a cultural liberalism which sets Portland apart even from its suburbs and the rest of Oregon. In 2000 Portland's Multnomah County voted 64%–28% for Al Gore, and gave Ralph Nader 7% of the vote—the same share he received in 1996.

The congressman from the 3d District is Earl Blumenauer, elected in May 1996 to replace Ron Wyden, who was elected to the Senate in January. Blumenauer grew up in Portland, graduated from Lewis and Clark College and its Northwestern Law School. He was inspired by the civil rights and anti-Vietnam war movements while in his teens; in 1969, in college, he headed a statewide campaign to lower Oregon's voting age. He has held public office almost all his adult life. In 1972, at 23, he was elected to the Oregon House; in 1978 he was elected to the Multnomah County Board of Commissioners; in 1986 he was elected to the Portland City Council. In these offices he has championed many of the policies which have made Portland distinctive—regional light rail transit, curbside recycling, land use planning. He initiated a law taking away the cars of repeat drunk driving offenders. He encouraged bike riding and Regional Rail Summits, which try to bring neighborhood residents into the process of planning for higher densities at transit nodes. Blumenauer has had his name on the ballot 26 times and has had some setbacks, notably when he lost the 1992 mayoral race to Vera Katz. But when Wyden was elected to the Senate, Blumenauer was the obvious successor. He was supported by prominent Democrats including former Governors Neil Goldschmidt and Barbara Roberts and even by Republican Senator Mark Hatfield (Blumenauer headed "Democrats for Hatfield" in 1990). He won the special election 68%–25%.

In the House Blumenauer has a very liberal voting record and a distinctive agenda. He rides his bicycle everywhere and formed a Bicycle Caucus with more than 30 members; he fought for showers for bike commuters and boasts that he has never driven a car in Washington. But he does get around the city in other ways: He ran the Marine Corps Marathon in slightly over four hours, the best time from the Hill. He was astonished to find that the House subsidized parking for employees, but not mass transit; now employees can get $21 a month toward transit fares, and he wants to raise it to $65. To help communities address quality of life and growth issues, he promotes "Rail-Volution," a national rail conference, which last year attracted 1200 participants from more than 200 cities. He hails the 1991 ISTEA transportation act that allows communities to choose to use money for mass transit and bike paths as well as highways, and he notes that 30% of the project requests from his colleagues were for transit projects. He is interested in what seem like quixotic projects now, but may not be in a few years: an interstate highway system for bicycle paths, development of "livable communities" on the sites of Denver's closed Stapleton Airport and closed military bases.

Blumenauer sits on the International Relations' East Asia Subcommittee—a key assignment for promoting Portland's foreign trade. He was an active supporter of permanent normal trade relations with China and was part of the Clinton delegation that visited Vietnam in November 2000. After a Chinese businesswoman was strip-searched and jailed by the Portland INS, he pushed for the resignation of the director there and for more scrutiny of the Portland agency's operations. "It took a long time to get the attention of upper management of the INS about the problems in Portland, and now that we have it, we don't want to lose it," he said; his office has handled more than 1,000 INS cases in the last five years.

In Portland, he proudly terms his home a model for the future of the city, with its ample bicycle lanes, public transit and limits on sprawl. Pointing to the Green Bay Packers, he has sponsored what he calls the Give Fans a Chance Act, to encourage public ownership of sports teams by revoking the antitrust broadcast exemption for any league that prohibits public ownership. Assisting Beaverton-based Nike, he won passage of a law allowing importers to receive customs refunds when they recycle defective materials—such as old shoes. He won agreement for federal funding of a 5.6-mile extension of Portland's light-rail system to northern neighborhoods.

How popular Blumenauer's sometimes eclectic ideas become nationally, and how well their unintended consequences can be ironed out, remains to be seen. Either way, his seat seems safe. In typical Portland fashion, the most distinctive feature of his re-election in 2000 may have been the 6% of the vote that went to Green Party candidate Tre Arrow, who sat on a ledge in downtown to protest national forest logging.

Cook's Call *Safe.* Blumenauer is sitting in a solidly Democratic district and will have no trouble here in 2002. His Portland-based district needs to pick up some population in 2002 redistricting, but it is unlikely that this seat would become competitive.

THE PEOPLE: Pop. 2000: 650,092; Pop. 1990: 568,276, up 14.4% 1990–2000. 79.3% White, 5.5% Black, 5.6% Asian, 1% Amer. Indian, 0.4% Hawaiian, 4.1% Two+ races, 4.2% Other; 7.7% Hispanic Origin.

2000 Presidential Vote			1996 Presidential Vote		
Gore (D)	172,358	(61%)	Clinton (D)	147,056	(58%)
Bush (R)	87,375	(31%)	Dole (R)	72,124	(28%)
Nader (Green)	18,975	(7%)	Perot (I)	18,553	(7%)
Others	2,823	(1%)	Others	17,884	(7%)

Rep. Earl Blumenauer (D)

Elected May 1996, 3d term; b. Aug. 16, 1948, Portland; home, Portland; Lewis & Clark Col., B.A. 1970, J.D. 1976; no religious affiliation; divorced.

Elected Office: OR House of Reps., 1972–78; Multnomah Cnty. Comm., 1978–86; Portland City Cncl., 1986–96.

Professional Career: Asst. to Pres., Portland St. U., 1970–77.

DC Office: 1406 LHOB 20515, 202-225-4811; Fax: 202-225-8941; Web site: www.house.gov/blumenauer.

District Office: Portland, 503-231-2300.

Committees: *International Relations* (19th of 23 D): East Asia & the Pacific. *Transportation & Infrastructure* (19th of 34 D): Railroads; Water Resources & Environment.

Group Ratings

	ADA	ACLU	AFS	LCV	CON	ITIC	NTU	COC	ACU	NTLC	CHC
2000	90	79	83	93	84	94	32	42	0	6	0
1999	95	—	100	88	94	—	25	40	4	—	—

National Journal Ratings

	1999 LIB —	1999 CONS		2000 LIB —	2000 CONS
Economic	67% —	32%		90% —	8%
Social	82% —	17%		85% —	14%
Foreign	89% —	8%		97% —	0%

Key Votes of the 106th Congress

1. Patient Bill of Rights	Y	5. Bar RU-486 $ for FDA	N	9. NATO War in Serbia	Y
2. Accelerate Min. Wage	Y	6. Display 10 Commandments	N	10. Perm. Trade with China	Y
3. Strike Ban on Ergo. Stnd.	Y	7. Gun Show Bkgrnd. Checks	Y	11. Debt Relief for 3rd World	Y
4. Ovrd. Estate Tax Veto	N	8. Ban Part.-Birth Abortion	N	12. Drop Cuba Econ. Embargo	Y

Election Results

2000 general	Earl Blumenauer (D)	181,049	(67%)	($404,807)
	Jeffery L. Pollock (R)	64,128	(24%)	($92,005)
	Tre Arrow (Green)	15,763	(6%)	
	Other	10,221	(4%)	
2000 primary	Earl Blumenauer (D)	70,388	(88%)	
	John Sweeney (D)	9,237	(12%)	
1998 general	Earl Blumenauer (D)	153,889	(84%)	($237,571)
	Bruce Alexander Knight (Lib)	16,930	(9%)	
	Walter F. Brown (Soc)	10,199	(6%)	
	Others	2,333	(1%)	

FOURTH DISTRICT

Eugene is nestled in the southernmost bit of lowland at the end of Oregon's Willamette Valley, surrounded by mountains on three sides. It is a farming center, a lumber metropolis and, most notably, a leafy university town. Settlers first arrived here in 1846, farming in the valley and cutting timber in the hills. In 1876, the University of Oregon was established, a symbol of Oregon's strong Yankee cultural ethic and sparse settlement; its first graduating class had just five students. Thousands of miles from most Americans, Eugene and next-door Springfield, once a lumber town and now with computer chip factories, have grown steadily into the comfortable middle-sized towns in which many Americans would like to live. Eugene has bicycle paths along the river banks and on main streets and likes to bill itself as the Running Capital of the Universe; it is where Phil Knight and his former University of Oregon track coach, Bill Bowerman, started Nike—the first soles formed on a waffle iron. But there is also tragedy here. Springfield was the place where in May 1998 a 15-year-old, after killing his parents, opened fire in a school, killing two students and injuring 22 others—for "no reason," he later said with an apology, as he was sentenced to life in prison.

Beyond Eugene and Springfield, southwestern Oregon is surrounded by green-clad mountains and for years cut more timber than any other place in the country. But demand for wood is volatile, dependent on the vagaries of interest rates; East Asia increasingly wants unprocessed logs rather than milled lumber, which means fewer jobs for Oregon. The early 1980s, when recession reduced the demand for housing, were tough on southern Oregon; the late 1980s, when cutting of old-growth forests was banned to protect the endangered spotted owl, were even worse. In between, many big lumber companies switched their major operations to the pinelands of the Southeastern U.S., while sawmills ran short of work because of log exports to the Far East. In the early 1990s, it seemed federal restrictions on logging would destroy the area's economy. But, since then, an otherwise robust local economy and active job retraining have resulted in local job gains and far less unemployment than forecast.

The 4th Congressional District of Oregon includes Eugene and Springfield and surrounding Lane County; it goes south to include Roseburg in Douglas County, once perhaps the premier logging county in the United States; it extends north to Albany and part of Corvallis, home of Oregon State University; and includes the entire southern half of Oregon's stunning Pacific coastline, whose craggy seastacks and surging whitecaps were stained by oil as the cargo ship New Carissa was wrecked in Coos Bay in February 1999 and later washed up 60 miles north. Eugene is now heavily Democratic, and so is Corvallis. Roseburg and Albany tend to be Republican, but the overall balance here is toward the cultural left.

The congressman from the 4th District is Peter DeFazio, a Democrat first elected in 1986. He grew up in Massachusetts, came to Oregon for graduate school, and in 1977 went to work for 4th District Congressman Jim Weaver; in 1982, he moved to Springfield and won a seat on the county commission. When Weaver retired in 1986, DeFazio won the House seat in a three-way race. DeFazio has compiled a record that seems to satisfy both Eugene and the rest of the district— liberal on most issues, moderate or even conservative on some. An original founder of the loose-knit Progressive Caucus, he made the case that millions of Americans were suffering during the Clinton administration's booming prosperity. He has opposed NAFTA, GATT and fast-track authority and strongly criticized the Mexican financial bailout; he wants to require congressional approval for international loans over $250 million. During the World Trade Organization protests in Seattle, he spent the week marching with coalitions from organized labor and environmental activists. He criticized the WTO as a "corporate bill of rights." When the protests moved a few months later to the IMF meeting in Washington, he blamed international financiers for economic and social ills in developing nations. A leader of the fight against permanent trade relations with China, he said that supporters were "a lot of well-intentioned people . . . who think it means their salvation, and actually what it means is their destruction." He sought unsuccessfully to stop the export of oil from Alaska until the President determines that the United States no longer has a crude oil shortage.

He offered a bill, with interesting support from right and left, to allow patients greater access to alternative medical treatments and, with Republican Jack Metcalf, vigorously opposed Agriculture Department regulations on organic foods for failing to adequately protect consumers; they also sought to create special labels for genetically engineered food. He has been a harsh critic of airlines and their broken promises to consumers; a pet cause has been his advocacy of poor treatment of dogs and cats during flights. He also attacked the lack of regulations for cruise ships. Within 72 hours after the Springfield shooting, DeFazio introduced nine bills aimed at school violence, including a 72-hour hold for juveniles who bring guns to school, mandatory trigger locks, background checks of buyers at gun shows and identification of troubled dropouts. Also at home, he has advocated long-term planning to resolve conflicts in national forests; he won approval of annual federal payments to counties with tax-exempt forest lands. After the 2000 election deadlock, he and Republican Jim Leach proposed a broad study of federal election procedures, including the "historical rationale" for the Electoral College. "If Boeing built airplanes like we conduct elections, no one would ever get on an airplane again," he said.

DeFazio has won re-election by impressive margins in a district which before him was often marginal. After Senator Bob Packwood resigned in 1995, DeFazio ran to succeed him. He had far less money than Portland Congressman Ron Wyden, whom he attacked for receiving money from Packwood contributors; in an ad, DeFazio made the best of this: "[DeFazio's] '63 Dodge tells the lobbyists and special interests he's not for sale." His opposition to gun control, NAFTA and GATT provided clear contrasts with Wyden. He ran strongly in the 4th District and the two counties just to the south, leading Wyden 72%–22% there. But Wyden ran ahead 61%–32% in the rest of the state, for a 50%–44% victory, and went on to win the seat in January. Since then, he has called for public financing of campaigns. His support from progressive activists could be the base for a campaign for governor in 2002, he said.

Cook's Call *Probably Safe.* Though the 4th District is more marginal than the two Portland-based districts (Bush won here by 5% in 2000), DeFazio has had little trouble winning by large margins since his first re-election campaign in 1988. This district was the slowest growing in the state and will need to pick up about 50,000 people in redistricting. DeFazio has a good hold on the seat and will be tough to defeat. Once it opens up, however (DeFazio has been mentioned as a potential gubernatorial candidate), it is likely to be heavily contested.

THE PEOPLE: Pop. 2000: 633,335; Pop. 1990: 568,395, up 11.4% 1990–2000. 91.9% White, 0.5% Black, 1.4% Asian, 1.4% Amer. Indian, 0.2% Hawaiian, 3% Two+ races, 1.6% Other; 4.2% Hispanic Origin.

2000 Presidential Vote		
Bush (R)	145,722	(49%)
Gore (D)	129,779	(44%)
Nader (Green)	16,265	(5%)
Others	4,448	(2%)

1996 Presidential Vote		
Clinton (D)	122,392	(45%)
Dole (R)	108,780	(40%)
Perot (I)	26,826	(10%)

Rep. Peter DeFazio (D)

Elected 1986, 8th term; b. May 27, 1947, Needham, MA; home, Springfield; Tufts U., B.A. 1969, U. of OR, M.S. 1977; Catholic; married (Myrnie).

Military Career: Air Force, 1967–71.

Elected Office: Lane Cnty. Bd. of Commissioners, 1982–86.

Professional Career: Dist. Dir., U.S. Rep. James Weaver, 1977–82.

DC Office: 2134 RHOB 20515, 202-225-6416; Fax: 202-225-0032; Web site: www.house.gov/defazio.

District Offices: Coos Bay, 541-269-2609; Eugene, 541-465-6732; Roseburg, 541-440-3523.

Committees: *Resources* (5th of 25 D): Water & Power. *Transportation & Infrastructure* (5th of 34 D): Aviation; Coast Guard & Maritime Transportation; Water Resources & Environment (RMM).

Group Ratings

	ADA	ACLU	AFS	LCV	CON	ITIC	NTU	COC	ACU	NTLC	CHC
2000	90	86	100	93	84	44	35	25	8	26	0
1999	100	—	100	88	81	—	39	12	8	—	—

National Journal Ratings

	1999 LIB —	1999 CONS		2000 LIB —	2000 CONS
Economic	73%	26%		71%	29%
Social	82%	17%		74%	24%
Foreign	55%	44%		69%	28%

Key Votes of the 106th Congress

1. Patient Bill of Rights	Y	5. Bar RU-486 $ for FDA	N	9. NATO War in Serbia	Y
2. Accelerate Min. Wage	Y	6. Display 10 Commandments	N	10. Perm. Trade with China	N
3. Strike Ban on Ergo. Stnd.	Y	7. Gun Show Bkgrnd. Checks	Y	11. Debt Relief for 3rd World	Y
4. Ovrd. Estate Tax Veto	N	8. Ban Part.-Birth Abortion	N	12. Drop Cuba Econ. Embargo	Y

Election Results

2000 general	Peter DeFazio (D)	197,998	(68%)	($332,650)
	John Lindsey (R)	88,950	(31%)	($34,788)
	Other	4,117	(1%)	
2000 primary	Peter DeFazio (D)	unopposed		
1998 general	Peter DeFazio (D)	157,524	(70%)	($262,098)
	Steve J. Webb (R)	64,143	(29%)	
	Others	2,970	(1%)	

FIFTH DISTRICT

The Willamette Valley was the great promised land at the end of the Oregon Trail, shielded by the Coast Range from the cold storms of the Pacific but squeezing most of the moisture out of the clouds in the form of rain, fog and persistent mist. Here, New England Yankees planted small towns they called Salem and Albany and Oregon City, founded schools and colleges, built high-spired churches and eventually Salem's cylindrical-domed Art Deco state Capitol. This was one of the few valleys in the West which settlers found readily suitable for agriculture. The Willamette Valley's soil is fertile, the plain created by the waters of the Willamette sweeping down from the mountains is broad, and the rains everyone hears about in Oregon are dependable. Today, metro Portland is spreading south, with young people leapfrogging over the lands protected from development by and into counties to the south.

The 5th Congressional District includes much of the northern Willamette Valley. Near Portland it has the old pioneer town of Oregon City, and spreads south to the state capital of Salem (rather conservative) and Corvallis (home of Oregon State University and quite liberal). Then the district hops over the Coast Range to take in Lincoln and Tillamook counties, fishing and logging and cheesemaking communities (strongly Democratic) and also includes all of Polk

County. Historically, the Willamette Valley was Republican, like the New England whence most of its settlers came, but, also like New England, it has been trending Democratic, and now is prime marginal territory.

The congresswoman from the 5th District is Darlene Hooley, a Democrat elected in 1996. Born in North Dakota, Hooley moved with her family to Salem at age 8. She worked as a reading and physical education teacher in rural Woodburn Gervais and raised her family in West Linn, on the Willamette north of Oregon City. Angry when council members wouldn't replace the rugged asphalt after her son fell off a playground swing and cut his head, she served on the park district board and then was elected to the city Council in 1976, at 37. In 1980 she was elected to the Oregon House, where she worked on recycling, land use and equal pay laws. In 1987 she was appointed to the Clackamas County Board of Supervisors, where she worked on roads, welfare reform and crime and claimed credit for creating 10,000 private-sector jobs.

Rather late in the 1996 campaign cycle, Hooley decided to run for Congress. Incumbent Republican Jim Bunn, elected 50%–47% in 1994, combined religious conservatism with a moderate record on issues and support of the Oregon Health Plan and Portland light rail. Hooley had two Democratic primary opponents, but with help from EMILY's List had far more money. She won the three-way primary with 51% and launched into attacks on Bunn for supporting Newt Gingrich and Medicare-cuts." Ultimately, she spent $1.1 million, twice as much as the incumbent. Working most strongly against Bunn was his divorce and subsequent marriage to his 31-year-old chief of staff, whom he was paying $97,500—more than any other staffer in Oregon's House delegation. She quit as his aide, but the issue may well have kept Bunn from being re-elected. Hooley won 51%–46%, carrying all but one county, though most by narrow margins.

In the House Hooley has a mostly liberal record. She did not get the seat on Appropriations she wanted and served on the Banking Committee instead; in 1999 she got a seat on Budget and left Science. Hooley supported the Shays-Meehan campaign finance bill, sought to expand health insurance coverage for children, while also crossing party lines to support cutting the estate tax and eliminating the marriage penalty for taxpayers. She joined the moderate New Democrats, contending that she wanted to work with business in a district dependent on trade; in contrast to David Wu in the adjacent suburban district, she voted for permanent trade relations with China. She got funding for a highway interchange at Sunnyside, Portland area light rail and local after-school programs. She led the fight to preserve Oregon's assisted suicide law, using the powerful argument of states' rights.

In this marginal seat, which was represented by two Republicans and two Democrats during the 1990s, Hooley was re-elected in 2000 with 57% of the vote, her best ever, after three experienced Republicans decided not to run. Hooley was a target of the pharmaceutical industry's Citizens for Better Medicare, whose ad campaign accused her of "playing politics." First-time Republican candidate Brian Boquist emphasized his military career, and support for gun owners and private property rights—probably not the ideal profile in this district. Redistricting could make or break Hooley's career.

Cook's Call *Competitive.* Hooley is one of the luckier members of Congress. Though she sits in a very marginal district that has a history of ousting incumbents, she has won her two re-election bids easily, due in large part to the fact that Republicans have failed to recruit a top-tier challenger against her. But, redistricting could make this district even more marginal in 2002 and, if Republicans were to ever find a serious candidate, Hooley would have her hands full.

THE PEOPLE: Pop. 2000: 692,930; Pop. 1990: 568,712, up 21.8% 1990–2000. 87% White, 0.7% Black, 2% Asian, 1.3% Amer. Indian, 0.3% Hawaiian, 2.9% Two+ races, 5.9% Other; 10.4% Hispanic Origin.

2000 Presidential Vote

Bush (R)	148,568	(48%)
Gore (D)	140,959	(46%)
Nader (Green)	13,825	(4%)
Others	4,181	(1%)

1996 Presidential Vote

Clinton (D)	131,527	(47%)
Dole (R)	114,691	(41%)
Perot (I)	24,442	(9%)
Others	11,103	(5%)

Rep. Darlene Hooley (D)

Elected 1996, 3d term; b. Apr. 4, 1939, Williston, ND; home, West Linn; OR St. U., B.S. 1961; Lutheran; divorced.

Elected Office: West Linn City Cncl., 1977–80; OR House of Reps., 1980–86; Clackamas Cnty. Comm., 1987–96.

Professional Career: Teacher, 1961–75.

DC Office: 1130 LHOB 20515, 202-225-5711; Fax: 202-225-5699; Web site: www.house.gov/hooley.

District Offices: Oregon City, 503-557-1324; Salem, 503-588-9100.

Committees: *Budget* (11th of 20 D). *Financial Services* (12th of 32 D): Capital Markets, Insurance & Government Sponsored Enterprises; Domestic Monetary Policy, Technology & Economic Growth; Financial Institutions & Consumer Credit.

Group Ratings

	ADA	ACLU	AFS	LCV	CON	ITIC	NTU	COC	ACU	NTLC	CHC
2000	70	77	71	93	5	78	42	61	16	21	7
1999	100	—	100	81	73	—	19	40	4	—	—

National Journal Ratings

	1999 LIB	—	1999 CONS		2000 LIB	—	2000 CONS
Economic	64%	—	35%		63%	—	36%
Social	69%	—	30%		76%	—	23%
Foreign	78%	—	17%		69%	—	28%

Key Votes of the 106th Congress

1. Patient Bill of Rights	Y	5. Bar RU-486 $ for FDA	N	9. NATO War in Serbia	Y
2. Accelerate Min. Wage	Y	6. Display 10 Commandments	N	10. Perm. Trade with China	Y
3. Strike Ban on Ergo. Stnd.	Y	7. Gun Show Bkgrnd. Checks	Y	11. Debt Relief for 3rd World	Y
4. Ovrd. Estate Tax Veto	Y	8. Ban Part.-Birth Abortion	N	12. Drop Cuba Econ. Embargo	Y

Election Results

2000 general	Darlene Hooley (D)	156,315	(57%)	($762,764)
	Brian J. Boquist (R)	118,631	(43%)	($197,061)
2000 primary	Darlene Hooley (D)	unopposed		
1998 general	Darlene Hooley (D)	124,916	(55%)	($1,005,353)
	Marylin Shannon (R)	92,215	(41%)	($289,053)
	Others	10,526	(5%)	

★ PENNSYLVANIA ★

Pennsylvania started off as the center of America: Philadelphia was the 13 colonies' largest city when it hosted the Continental Congress in 1776 and the Constitutional Convention in 1787. This was one of the newer colonies, founded 50 years after Massachusetts and 70 years after Virginia. Under the benevolent rule of the early Penns and with its Quaker traditions, Pennsylvania soon became the major settlement in the Middle Colonies: Its tolerance attracted Englishmen of all religious sects and thousands of Germans as well. Bordermen from Scotland, Yorkshire and Northern Ireland crossed the corduroy-like ridges of the Appalachians and settled the mountainous interior where General Braddock had been beaten by the French and Indians not long before, and where a decade later George Washington would again lead troops when the Whiskey Rebellion flared up. On the banks of the wide Delaware estuary, with its thriving commerce and rich hinterland, Philadelphia was, after London and Dublin, the largest Georgian city in the late 18th Century. It seemed destined to be the London of America, the metropolis of government and commerce and culture.

But Philadelphia—and Pennsylvania—failed to hold the central position the Founders had expected. The nation's capital was put on the Potomac rather than the Delaware as part of a political deal, and the Erie Canal and the water-level railroad from the Hudson to Lake Erie channeled trade away from Philadelphia to New York. Philadelphia lost its chance to be the nation's financial capital when Andrew Jackson in righteous rage vetoed the rechartering of the Second Bank of the United States. Philadelphia's Quaker tradition, tolerant of diversity and indifferent to others' behavior, was overshadowed in intellectual life by New England's Puritan tradition, angrily intolerant and ready to use the state to impose cultural values from abolition to prohibition.

Instead, Pennsylvania became America's energy and heavy industry capital. The key was coal. Northeast Pennsylvania was the nation's primary source of anthracite, the hard coal used for home heating, and western Pennsylvania was laced with bituminous coal, the soft coal used in steel production. Connected with Philadelphia by the Pennsylvania Railroad, Pittsburgh, where the Allegheny and Monongahela rivers join to become the Ohio, was the center of the nation's steel industry by 1890. Immigrants poured in from Europe and from the surrounding hills to work in western Pennsylvania's mines and factories. Pittsburgh became synonymous with industrial prosperity, the inspiration behind the civic pride that celebrated huffing smokestacks. In 1900, Pennsylvania was the nation's second-largest state and growing rapidly. But the boom ended conclusively with the Depression of the 1930s, and in parts of Pennsylvania it has never returned. After World War II, both home heating and industry switched away from coal. John L. Lewis's United Mine Workers traded higher pay and benefits for payroll cuts. Even when coal prices boomed in the 1970s, strip mining created relatively few new jobs. Similarly, Pennsylvania steel began its decline three decades ago, when management decided not to keep up with new technology and agreed to big wage and benefit increases with the mistaken confidence they could pass the costs along. Big steel got import quotas in 1969—Pennsylvania has been the nation's most protectionist state since the first Bessemer converter furnaces were lit—but they didn't create jobs. By the time quotas lapsed in the 1990s, the industry had modernized, but mostly in huge new Indiana mills and small mini-mills scattered far from the factories that once lined the Monongahela.

The result has been the slowest population growth of any major state: There were 9.5 million Pennsylvanians in 1930, 12.3 million in 2000. Pennsylvania cast 36 electoral votes for Franklin Roosevelt in 1940 and 23 for Al Gore in 2000; it had as many congressmen as California in 1960 (30), but in the next Congress will have 19 to California's 53. People growing up here are as likely to leave the state as stay, and few out-of-staters move in. Pennsylvania looks and sounds today more like it did in the 1940s than any other major state. The 1980s and 1990s booms have produced some new Pennsylvania growth in southeast Pennsylvania, around Philadelphia, which partook of the upscale boom that was more spectacular up and down the East Coast. Center City Philadelphia sprouted new office towers and hosted the Republican National Convention in 2000,

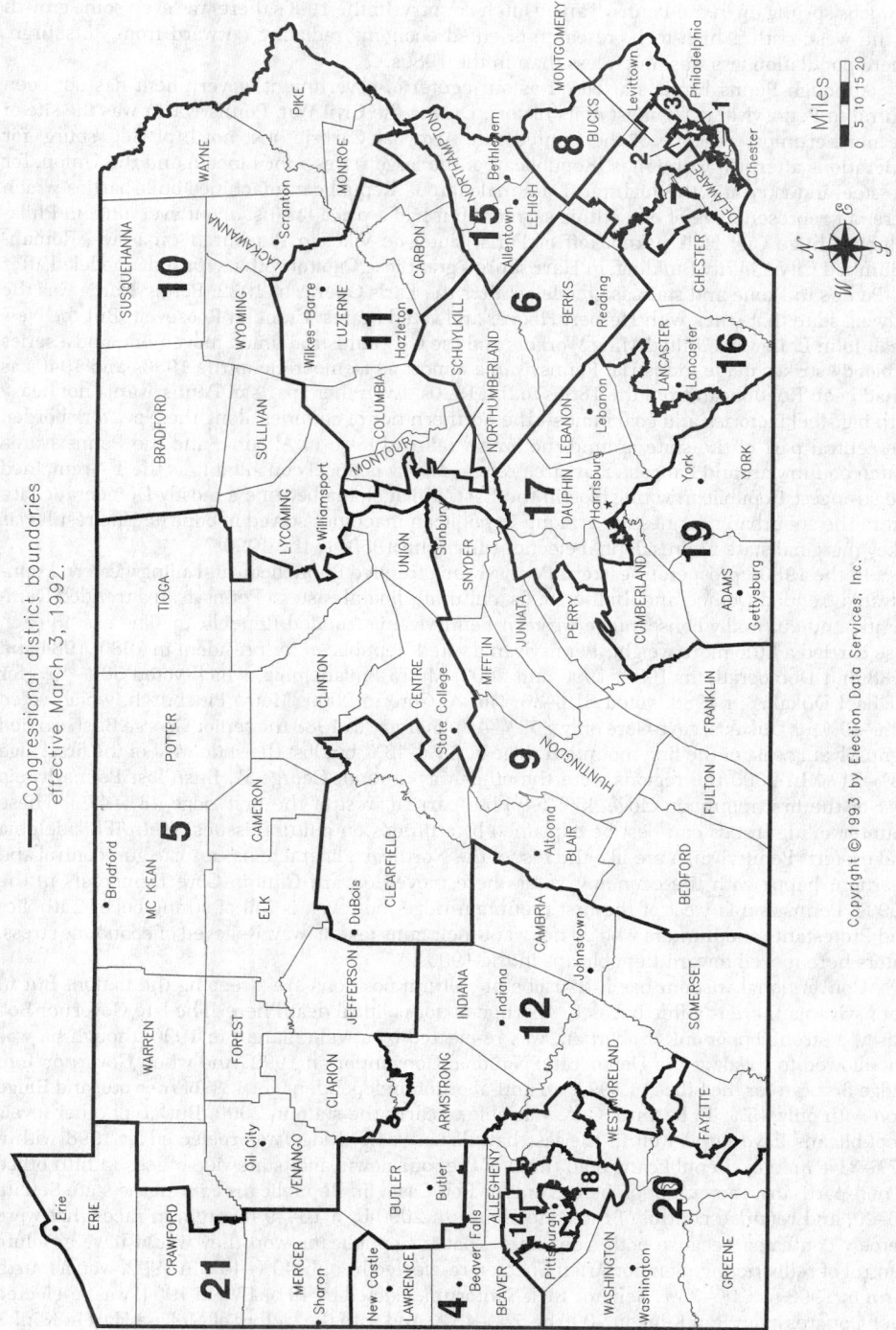

Congressional district boundaries
effective March 3, 1992.

Copyright © 1993 by Election Data Services, Inc.

the edge city around King of Prussia blossomed, and pharmaceutical and biotech jobs replaced those of the Fairless steel plant. Outlet stores proliferated around Reading and Lancaster, and new jobs sprung up in the Pennsylvania Dutch country. In the 1990s there was even some growth in the west, with a high-tech, research-oriented economy radiating outward from Pittsburgh, where population loss was much less than in the 1980s.

Although Pennsylvania started off as our center of government, government has not been central to Pennsylvania for most of its history. During the Civil War, Pennsylvania was the site of the northernmost advance of the Confederate Army, at Carlisle, just north of Gettysburg; for generations after it was the most Republican of the large states—for Lincoln and the Union, for the steel industry and the high tariff. Its malodorous Republican machines built parties which were not representative of one ethnic segment but had a place for just about everyone: in Philadelphia's huge City Hall, a knockoff of Paris' Hotel de Ville; in Pittsburgh's massive, Roman-columned City-County Building; in Harrisburg's grandiose Capitol with its rotunda modeled after St. Peter's in Rome and staircase modeled after the Paris Opera. In 1932, Pennsylvania was the only big state that stuck with Herbert Hoover and voted against Franklin Roosevelt. But the New Deal, John L. Lewis's United Mine Workers and the CIO industrial union movement, and a series of bloody strikes made industrial Pennsylvania almost as Democratic in the 1930s and 1940s as it had been Republican from the 1860s to the 1920s. Even then, parts of Pennsylvania not heavy with big steel factories and coal mines—the northern tier of counties along the New York border, the central part of the state around the Welsh railroad town of Altoona, and the Pennsylvania Dutch country around Lancaster, an area referred to by political consultants as the T—remained the strongest Republican voting bloc in the East. Philadelphia became a mostly Democratic city, but in the suburban counties the antique Republican machines stayed in control. The result was a key marginal state in presidential elections from the 1950s to the 1990s.

In the 1980s, prosperous eastern Pennsylvania trended Republican and ailing western Pennsylvania trended Democratic. In the 1990s, culturally liberal eastern Pennsylvania trended Democratic and culturally conservative western Pennsylvania trended Republican. The east in each case carried a little more weight: Pennsylvania voted Republican for president in 1980, 1984 and 1988 and Democratic in 1992, 1996 and 2000. Metro Philadelphia, which voted 50%–49% for Michael Dukakis in 1988, voted 61%–36% for Al Gore in 2000. Metro Pittsburgh, which voted 59%–40% for Dukakis, gave Gore only a 53%–44% margin. In 1988 the senior George Bush carried Pennsylvania east of the first mountain ridge by 53%–46%, but lost the state west of the first ridge 48%–51%. In 2000 the regions were the other way around. George W. Bush lost Pennsylvania east of the first mountain ridge 45%–54% but carried west of the first ridge 48%–47%. These countervailing trends can best be explained by attitudes on cultural issues. Metro Philadelphia and eastern Pennsylvania are like the rest of the Northeast, liberal on issues like gun control and abortion; happy with the economy, voters here moved toward Clinton-Gore Democrats in the 1990s. Pennsylvania west of the first mountain ridge, however, is full of strong-belief Catholics and Protestants and hunters who do not want their guns taken away. Relieved of economic stress, voters here moved toward Republicans in the 1990s.

Conventional wisdom has it that liberal cultural positions are sweeping the nation. But in Pennsylvania there is a fine balance. Abortion is not political death here: The late Governor Bob Casey, a strong opponent of abortion, was re-elected by a wide margin in 1990, though he was not allowed to speak at the Democratic National Convention in 1992. And when Governor Tom Ridge first ran for the office in 1994, an anti-abortion independent got 13% of the vote, and Ridge won with only 45%. To be sure, Gore was able to carry the state in 2000. But at all other levels Republicans have fared well in the last half dozen years. Ridge was reelected in 1998 with a 57%–31% margin. Republicans hold three of the four downballot statewide offices (a fifth office is non-partisan), the exception being Auditor Bob Casey Jr. Republicans control the state Senate 30–20, and retained control of the state House in 2000 by a 104–99 margin in races that were fiercely contested because both sides knew that if Republicans won they would have absolute control of redistricting. Senator Arlen Specter, re-elected by only 49%–46% in 1992, won a fourth term in 1998 by 61%–35%. Senator Rick Santorum, elected by 49%–47% in 1994, was re-elected over Congressman Ron Klink in 2000 by 52%–46%. And with the victory of Melissa Hart in Klink's old congressional district, Republicans have an edge, 11–10, in the state's House delegation for the first time in 40 years. In some of these races the abortion issue has done more damage to Democrats than Republicans; Klink because of his opposition to abortion could not raise enough money to make himself a strong contender. Democrats in Pennsylvania tend to be culturally more conservative than those in most states and Republicans sometimes economically more liberal; strategies that work nationally can be counterproductive in Pennsylvania. Philadelphia as host of the 2000 Republican National Convention was for four days once again the center of the nation's politics, but Pennsylvania though closely contested is not a replica of the nation politically.

Governor Tom Ridge, elected governor of Pennsylvania in 1994 and 1998, grew up in Erie, off in the far northwestern corner of the state. His father was a salesman, of Slavic descent, his mother Irish; they lived modestly, in a veterans' housing project and then in the bungalow where Ridge's mother lives today—she appeared in his campaign ads to remind him to wear his hat. He went to Harvard, spent a year at Dickinson Law School, then served in the Army as a staff sergeant in Vietnam, serving in combat and winning the Bronze Star. He finished law school, returned to Erie and practiced law, and was an assistant district attorney for a couple of years. He did a bit of work for George Bush's presidential campaign in 1980 and got to know the candidate's son George W. Bush. In 1982 he ran for the open House seat in the closely divided 21st District (now the 19th) and in a Democratic year in western Pennsylvania beat state legislator Buzz Andrezeski by 729 votes, 50.2%–49.8%. He became the first enlisted man who saw combat in Vietnam to be elected to the House. In the House he had a mixed voting record by the lights of almost every rating group—not always market-oriented on economics, sometimes dovish on defense and foreign policy, liberal on some cultural issues and tradition-minded on others. He worked on banking and home finance legislation; he favored more spending for homeless veterans and treatment of post traumatic stress disorder.

In February 1993 he announced he would run for governor in 1994. Outside his district he was hardly known, though the addition of a new county in 1992 had given him an excuse to run ads on Pittsburgh TV. This was a crowded race. With backing from party leaders, Ridge won the May primary with 35% to 29% for Attorney General Ernie Preate, 16% for Philadelphia businessman Sam Katz, and 14% for Pittsburgh legislator Mike Fisher; Katz was the Republican candidate for mayor of Philadelphia in 1999 and nearly won, and Fisher was elected attorney general in 1996 and 2000. Democrats had an even more crowded primary; Lieutenant Governor Mark Singel, who was acting governor for six months while Governor Bob Casey recovered from a heart and liver transplant, won with 31%.

In the general, Ridge campaigned for tough crime measures, citizens rights' to statewide initiatives and referenda, less-strict environmental regulation and a lower corporate tax. Both Ridge and Singel were pro-choice on abortion, which probably hurt them: Singel, because Casey was lukewarm to him; Ridge, because of the independent candidacy of anti-abortion Peg Luksik, who won 13% of the vote, with more than 20% in heavily Republican counties in central and western Pennsylvania. But the defining issue was probably crime. Ridge attacked Singel for his votes as chairman of the Pardons Board recommending the release of 55 prisoners serving life sentences. Ridge won 45%–40%, continuing Pennsylvania's 40-year practice of alternating the two parties in the governorship every eight years.

Ridge's hallmark as governor has been cutting taxes: He has pushed tax cuts in each of his seven years in office, and claims that altogether they cut taxes by more than $4 billion. In the process he cut state spending growth in half and increased the Rainy Day fund from $30 million to $1.1 billion in 2000. His first two budgets increased spending at less than the rate of inflation and he got the legislature to abolish the state tax on computer services and give a tax credit for research and development. He moved to cut the state income tax on lower-income families; there is now no state income tax on families of four with income under $28,000. Ridge tax cuts include big cuts in individual and corporate income taxes, a job creation tax credit, inheritance tax relief, a phaseout of the business franchise and capital stock taxes, a $330 million property tax rebate. Tax cuts totaled $400 million in the 1999 session and $774 million—a record—in 2000. Electricity deregulation—the 1997 Pennsylvania statute has been held up as a national model—has cut utility costs for businesses and individuals; natural gas deregulation was passed in 1999, together with the cut in utility rates Ridge estimates taxpayers will save $458 million. But the gas tax was increased to provide for more road building. Ridge set up an opportunity zones program for distressed areas and set up a program that has cleaned up 600 polluted industrial sites, by limiting landowners' liability after certain conditions were met; in contrast, the federal government's Superfund program, which relies on lawyers seeking big judgment from landowners, had cleaned up only 50 of 114 sites in Pennsylvania in nearly 20 years. Ridge has often said that his chief goal is to make Pennsylvania more welcoming to business, and has gone on trade missions to South America, Europe, East Asia and Israel; since he took office the state gained more than 400,000 jobs.

At the same time Ridge pushed for welfare, education and criminal justice reforms. His 1996 welfare reform required able-bodied recipients to work at least 100 hours a month or, if they are school-age, remain in schools; money was added for job readiness and child care, and more than 177,000 welfare recipients had left the rolls in 2000. On education, Ridge got money for computers in schools, reform of teacher tenure and sabbaticals, and creation of more charter schools. He set up an advisory commission to produce rigorous standards that were so comprehensible that "parents can hang them on the refrigerator door and discuss them with their children. No jargon, no buzz words, no educational fads." By narrow margins, Ridge's proposals for school choice vouchers have failed in the legislature; they have won support from some Philadelphia black legislators, but are opposed by some suburban Republicans. He was pleased when the legislature passed a bill to help pay for new stadiums for Pennsylvania's two baseball and two football franchises, and proudly unveiled the state's new license plates, the first to include a Website address. Ridge and the legislature have produced some original initiatives. A gun bill requiring trigger locks and banning city lawsuits against gun manufacturers was passed in 1999. Teens are required to hold a learner's permit for six months and to drive with adult supervision before getting a driver's license; crashes by teen drivers fell 25% and fatalities involving 16-year-old drivers fell 71%. Ridge signed bills making it a felony for felons to possess guns and creating a victim's bill of rights. He supported a law to allow municipalities to plan together to avoid urban sprawl. He increased aid to public libraries by $32 million. He got heavily involved in Philadelphia's negotiations with teachers' unions in fall 2000, supporting Mayor John Street's goals of increasing work hours and preventing a school shutdown.

Ridge was re-elected easily in 1998. Democrats had difficulty fielding a candidate; their nominee, longtime Pittsburgh legislator (and nuclear engineer) Ivan Itkin, was little known and had a very liberal record. Peg Luksik ran again as an anti-abortion candidate, and won 10% of the vote; Ridge beat Itkin 57%–31%; the Democrat carried Philadelphia and the Republican the other 66 counties. Ridge was mentioned as a possible nominee for vice president in 1996 and, this time much more frequently, in 1999 and 2000. As a big state ethnic, a Harvard graduate and Vietnam veteran, a successful governor in a presidentially marginal state, he had obvious appeal; plus, he had a relationship with George W. Bush that goes back to 1980. But there was one obvious problem: His support of abortion rights was anathema to a majority of Republican convention delegates, and the old-line TV networks tend to cover Republican conventions as if they were about nothing but abortion. In addition, there were sharp attacks on Ridge's congressional record in *National Review*; he had opposed the MX missile, contra aid and the Strategic Defense Initiative. Ridge was considered to be on Bush's very short list until a week before the Philadelphia convention. But then he said that he had taken himself out of contention three weeks earlier for personal reasons.

Ridge nonetheless campaigned heavily for Bush in Pennsylvania and elsewhere. After the election he said, "The most disappointment I had—I was really hoping to deliver Pennsylvania to Governor Bush." In December Ridge was mentioned as a possible nominee for secretary of Defense, and was said to have been recommended by Colin Powell; but again he was opposed by conservatives who pointed to his House record, and the nomination went to Donald Rumsfeld. In 2001 Ridge became head of the Republican Governors Association and was busy with legislation in Harrisburg. In May he signed an education reform package, in exchange for doubling legislators' pensions and increasing teachers' pensions by 25%, that includes teacher assessments and business tax credits to fund private or public school scholarships.

Pennsylvania governors are limited to two four-year terms, and since 1954 the two parties have swapped the governorship every eight years. Vying for the Democratic nomination in early 2001 were Auditor Bob Casey Jr. and former Philadelphia Mayor Ed Rendell, who served as Democratic National Chairman in 1999 and 2000. Their contest is a reprise of the 1986 battle between Rendell and the elder Casey. Rendell began this race with more money, but Casey was fundraising vigorously and got the endorsement of the United Steelworkers. On the Republican side, many were surprised when Lieutenant Governor Mark Schweiker took himself out of the race in October 2000; three months before he could have been looking forward to becoming governor if Ridge had been elected vice president. The main Republican contenders appeared to be Attorney General Mike Fisher, a solid conservative, and state Treasurer Barbara Hafer, who is seen as more moderate and as Republican nominee against Bob Casey Sr. in 1990 won 32% of the vote.

Cook's Call *Highly Competitive.* This race could host an epic battle for the Democratic nomination between former Philadelphia Mayor and Democratic National Committee Co-chairman Ed Rendell and state Auditor Bob Casey, whose late father was governor from 1986 to 1994. Rendell is a fairly liberal Democrat while Casey, who is pro-life and pro-gun, has appeal to the many Democratic voters in the western part of the state. On the Republican side, most bet that Attorney General Mike Fisher and state Treasurer Barbara Hafer will run. The general should be a closely fought and expensive contest.

Senior Senator Arlen Specter, one of the nation's most durable career politicians, has held public office and has been an important national figure off and on for most of four decades. Specter grew up in Russell, Kansas, also the home town of Bob Dole; his father was an immigrant who worked as a tailor, owned a junk yard and sent four children through college. Specter came to Philadelphia at 17 to attend the University of Pennsylvania. After college he served in the Air Force, went to Yale Law School and practiced law in Philadelphia. In 1964 he was a top staffer for the Warren Commission investigating the Kennedy assassination, where he helped develop the single-bullet theory. After the Warren Commission, he returned to his law practice, switched to the Republican Party, and was elected district attorney in Democratic Philadelphia in 1965 and again in 1969. He lost the race for D.A. in 1973, and was beaten in Republican primaries for senator in 1976 and governor in 1978, before narrowly (36%–33%) edging a former state Republican chairman in the 1980 primary and beating a low-spending Democrat 50%–48% in the general for his Senate seat. In 1986, he won re-election by a 56%–43% margin against a low-profile House Democrat; in 1992 he was re-elected 49%–46% after he became a target of feminists for his questioning of Anita Hill during the confirmation hearings of Clarence Thomas. He ran for president in 1995, but withdrew before the first caucus or primary.

Throughout this career of narrow victories and numerous defeats, Specter's assets have been brains and hard work. He is respected by colleagues and constituents, though not always well-liked. He sides with conservatives on some divisive issues, with liberals on others, building up no permanent credit with either. He is aggressive and prosecutorial, well-prepared and persuasive once he takes a stand. These traits are both his strengths and weaknesses; they explain why he was vulnerable in 1992, and why he won; why he ran for president, and why his campaign went nowhere. His voting record is almost precisely at the midpoint of the Senate, and he has played key roles on a variety of issues. Though he switched and voted to override Bill Clinton's "partial-birth" abortion veto, he is generally pro-choice on abortion—an issue he featured in his presidential campaign, infuriating many Republican activists. He pushes tough penalties for crime and supports capital punishment. On a closely divided and rancorous Judiciary Committee, he played a key role on several Supreme Court nominations. More than anyone else, he defeated Robert Bork in 1987 and, more than anyone but John Danforth, he confirmed Clarence Thomas in 1991. In 1994 his devastatingly complex chart describing the Clinton health care plan played no small part in defeating it. As chairman of the Intelligence Committee in 1995–96, he failed to reorganize intelligence agencies and to make theft of "proprietary economic information" a crime, but his sharp questioning of CIA director nominee Anthony Lake led Lake to withdraw in March 1997. As chairman of the Veterans' Affairs Committee in 1997, he called for doing more to investigate whether there is a Gulf war syndrome and what was known about chemical hazards in the region.

On impeachment, Specter took his own course. "I propose abandoning impeachment and, after the president leaves office, holding him accountable in the same way any other person would be: through indictment and prosecution for any federal crimes established by the evidence," he said in November 1998. In February 1999, in a decision he called "a lot ambiguous, maybe even a little amorphous," Specter said he would vote "not proven," citing Scottish criminal law. "I think it is important to make a distinction that I do not believe that the president is not guilty," he said. "It's a trial on which you can't really come to a verdict because of the absence of witnesses and the absence of relevant evidence."

On many issues Specter has been one of the few Republicans voting with Senate Democrats—on the Republican tax cut in August 1999, the Comprehensive Test Ban Treaty in October 1999, the minimum wage in November 1999, on the federal tobacco lawsuit in July 2000, and HMO regulation in July 2000. With Congressman Frank Wolf, he introduced in May 1997 a religious persecution bill to retaliate against countries that engage in that practice; in 1998 he revised it to try to meet the objections of the Clinton administration. In March 1998, Specter, ever the prosecutor, said that Saddam Hussein should be tried as a war criminal. In August 1998 he questioned whether Bill Clinton's order of cruise missile strikes in Afghanistan and Sudan had a "diversionary motive"; after Republican leaders declined to follow his lead, he backtracked. In July 1998 he urged the appointment of an independent counsel to investigate Clinton-Gore campaign fundraising and threatened to take Janet Reno to court if she didn't. Specter's May 1999 amendment to the defense authorization bill, invoking the War Powers Act to prevent the deployment of ground troops in the former Yugoslavia, failed 52–48. In early 1999 he supported tariffs and revisions in dumping laws to protect Pennsylvania steelmakers against Russian and East Asian imports.

Specter is quick to recognize a popular issue and to propose legislation on it. In 1999 he proposed to require sports teams to set aside 10% of their television revenues to pay for new stadiums; Pennsylvania is publicly financing two new stadiums in Philadelphia and Pittsburgh. With Edward Kennedy, he sponsored hate crimes legislation that passed the Senate in July 1999. When the Clinton administration issued a report on medical errors, he held two quick hearings in two months—one on a day when the government was closed by a blizzard—and was the first senator with legislation on the subject. He sponsored a bill to change the law on air crashes so that relatives of the victims of the 1996 TWA 800 crash could recover noneconomic damages. During the hearings on Firestone tires in September 2000, he proposed to criminalize any product "dangerous to human life and limb beyond the reasonable and accepted risk with such or similar products lacking such a flaw." He has sponsored a bill to exempt the Amish from child labor laws. Two months before the Supreme Court hearings on the Florida case, he and Joseph Biden sponsored a bill to require that Supreme Court proceedings be televised. Specter is not afraid to antagonize his colleagues. In 1999 he persuaded Majority Leader Trent Lott to name him chairman of a task force to investigate the Clinton Justice Department, a move clearly resented by Judiciary Chairman Orrin Hatch. In 2000 Specter proceeded to conduct hearings on transmission of secrets to China and the handling of the Wen Ho Lee case, the fundraising activities of Al Gore and others in the 1996 Clinton-Gore campaign, the Waco confrontation of 1993; he sought to look into Justice's handling of the Elian Gonzalez case; he was blocked by Hatch from subpoenaing FBI Director Louis Freeh.

On the Labor-HHS-Education Subcommittee of Appropriations, Specter has been a leader of the bipartisan move to double the funding of the National Institutes of Health over five years. He is not shy about using his place on the committee to funnel money into Pennsylvania, from the Philadelphia Navy Yard to Lake Erie. He has supported changes in federal organ transplant policy in 1998 (Pittsburgh has a big organ transplant hospital) and called in 1999 for research on stem cells from human embryos. In 2000 he got $3 million for the Scranton-Wilkes-Barre Airport, $1 million for the Wilkes-Barre Intermodal Center, $5 million to Mag-Lev Inc and $2 million to Pittsburgh Airborne Shuttle System for research on magnetic-levitation trains, $5 million for Pittsburgh's North Shore Connector and $10 million for SEPTA's 62-mile Schuylkill Valley corridor from Philadelphia to Wyomissing in Berks County.

Toward the Bush administration, he took a characteristically ambiguous stance. His early announcement of support for John Ashcroft's nomination as attorney general helped ensure that he would have solid Republican support. But he undercut the Bush tax cut by supporting tax triggers and by voting to reduce the tax cut to $1.25 trillion. In February 2001 he held hearings on Clinton's last-minute pardons of Marc Rich and others, and on one television news show said tantalyzingly, "I'm not suggesting it should be done, but President Clinton technically could still be impeached." But he declined to call on Clinton to testify. After Jim Jeffords defected from the Republican Party, Specter was given a leadership role to be a voice for moderates in the party.

After his tough re-election race in 1992, Specter had an easier time of it in 1998. He overcame serious health problems—he had brain tumor surgery in June 1993, underwent a radiation procedure in October 1996 and had double heart-bypass surgery in June 1998, returning to the Senate in early July—and continued to work hard getting around the state and raising money. Pennsylvania Democrats have shown little adeptness at winning Senate elections: They have won only one, the 1991 special after the death of John Heinz, since 1962. In 1997, well-known Democrats one after the other declined to run against a candidate who had won only 49% five years before. Specter's 1998 opponent was former state Representative William Lloyd, who ran third in the 1996 Democratic primary for auditor. He spent only $187,000 and put up no TV spots. Specter spent $4.5 million and ran spots showing him being praised by Philadelphia Mayor Ed Rendell, the state's most prominent Democrat. The Pennsylvania AFL-CIO endorsed Specter in July, the United Steelworkers in October. So confident was Specter that he had more than $2.6 million in cash left over. Specter won 61%–35%, carrying every county but Philadelphia and Somerset. He became the first Pennsylvania senator to be popularly elected to four terms, and if he finishes out the term he will be only nine months behind the record tenure for a Pennsylvania senator, held by Boies Penrose (1897–1921). In January 2001 a rumor circulated that Specter was going to switch parties, again. "It's ridiculous! Nothing to it." But 1st district Congressman and Philadelphia Democratic Chairman Bob Brady said, "I wish it was true."

Junior Senator Rick Santorum, a Republican elected in 1994, is the third youngest senator (Peter Fitzgerald and Blanche Lincoln are younger), elected from one of the oldest states, a strong conservative elected in a state that still has many New Deal voters. Santorum is the son of an Italian immigrant who was a clinical psychologist for the Veterans' Administration; he was born in Virginia and moved to Butler, Pennsylvania, at age 7. He started in politics working for John Heinz's first Senate campaign in 1976; he went to Penn State and Pitt business school and worked his way through Dickinson law school as a staffer for state Senate Republicans in Harrisburg; he worked for a blue chip law firm in Pittsburgh for four years. In 1990, at 32, he challenged seven-term incumbent Congressman Doug Walgren, who outspent him $717,000 to $251,000. But Santorum knocked on 25,000 doors, amassed an army of volunteers including many right-to-lifers, attacked Walgren for voting for a pay raise seven times and for living in the Washington suburbs. Santorum opposed the congressional pay raise, backed the line-item veto and came out for limits on PAC contributions. He won 51%–49%.

In the House he had a solid conservative voting record and was one of the "Gang of Seven" freshman Republicans who helped expose the House bank scandal. Redistricting gave him a seat shorn of many Republican suburbs and centered on the industrial Monongahela Valley, historically very Democratic. George Bush got only 30% in this new district, but Santorum beat a state senator 61%–38%—an astonishing victory. Brash and confident, Santorum immediately started running for the Senate. His opponent was Harris Wofford, elected in November 1991 to replace John Heinz, who died in a plane crash. Wofford was a civil rights activist in the 1960s, the adviser who persuaded John Kennedy to phone Coretta Scott King when her husband was jailed during the 1960 campaign. Appointed to the Senate by Governor Bob Casey in May 1991, he upset former Governor Dick Thornburgh 55%–45% by emphasizing health care. In the Senate Wofford was politically hurt when the Clinton health care bill failed to pass.

This was a race of sharp contrasts in issues and style: Santorum, brashly eager to chop government, backing medical savings accounts and opposing gun control; Wofford, earnestly working for government health care financing, backing the 1994 crime bill and gun control. Wofford appealed to a long liberal tradition; Santorum scoffed at him for championing 1960s ideas in the 1990s. With home town appeal, Santorum ran behind only 50%–47% in metro Pittsburgh, where Wofford had won 61% in 1991. Santorum did not go over so well in metro Phila-delphia, which Wofford carried 54%–42%. But in the rest of the state—where half the votes are cast and where gun control hurt Wofford—Santorum won 55%–41%, for a statewide victory of 49%–47%.

Santorum was not cowed by the traditions of the Senate. In his first full month there he argued about the balanced budget amendment with Robert Byrd, who was elected to the Senate the year Santorum was born. Then, when senior Republican Mark Hatfield cast a decisive vote against the amendment, Santorum called on Hatfield to be removed as Appropriations chairman. Senior senators and Washington insiders tut-tutted. Hatfield wasn't removed, but Senate Repub-licans changed the rules, limiting chairmen to six years and calling for secret ballot elections of chairmen starting in 1997. Later in 1995 Santorum took to the floor a dozen times with a "Where's Bill?" sign, asking where the President's balanced budget was; Democrats were furious. Santo-rum's reply to those who call him brash: "I don't run around looking for a fight. I just stand up for what I'm elected to do."

Santorum's voting record has grown somewhat less conservative over the years, but he still ranks among the more conservative Republicans in the Senate. But he took the lead on important legislation, and on occasion at some political risk. Santorum floor-managed welfare reform to passage three times in 1995 and 1996; the first two times it was vetoed by Bill Clinton, but in August 1996, 13 weeks before the election, Clinton signed it. Santorum has also taken the lead on the partial birth abortion ban. It passed the Senate 64–36 in May 1997—a big gain from 54–44 in 1995—and was vetoed by Bill Clinton; it passed 63–34 in October 1999, and was again vetoed. This was not just a theoretical issue for him: In 1996 he and his wife had to decide what to do when their unborn child had a fatal defect; the baby was born in October 1996 and died two hours later. Santorum was part of the Renewal Alliance: conservative Republicans who want to encourage private sector, especially faith-based, organizations to care for the poor and helpless, even as they repeal government programs originally intended to help them. In early 2001 he was the lead sponsor of George W. Bush's faith-based initiative and charitable tax deduction plan, which was not included in Bush's final tax bill.

Santorum has taken care to support some measures of great importance to labor unions. He backed minimum wage increases in the House and Senate, and supported the steel import quota bill which died in June 1999. He serves on the Agriculture Committee, and got into the 1996 farm bill an amendment helping states' farmland protection programs, which in Pennsylvania covers more than 100,000 acres; he voted for $7.4 billion in farm relief in 1999, the first time he had voted to exceed the budget ceilings. He has proposed a safety net for dairy farmers and opposed the Northeast Dairy Compact. He has sponsored bills putting a $250,000 cap on medical malpractice lawsuits; he was embarrassed in December 1999 when his wife won a $350,000 judgment against her former chiropractor. A spokesman explained, "The senator and his wife, believe it or not, disagree on some issues. This is a case between her and her attorney and her chiropractor. It has nothing to do with Senator Santorum." He supported the compromise organ transplant bill which would have sent organs to the sickest patients instead of those who live closet to the donors; Pittsburgh has one of the country's biggest organ transplant programs. He has sponsored bills to promote telecommuting and sponsored an Internet filtering amendment for libraries. In June 2000 he and Joseph Lieberman sponsored a version of the community renewal bill which would have doubled the spending of the $6 billion program backed by Bill Clinton and Speaker Dennis Hastert.

Perhaps Santorum's greatest gamble has been to propose Social Security reform; Pennsyl-vania has a high percentage of elderly. In 1999 he came forward with a plan to allow personal retirement accounts, with 4% of earnings up to $18,000 and then 2% up to the Social Security wage limit, to be invested, with limitations, in the stock market; benefits similar to the current system would be guaranteed. Santorum argues that this would enable low- and middle-income workers to accumulate wealth as upper-income workers do already. He argues that having the government invest the funds in the markets, as some Democrats have proposed, would mean that stock market increases would go to other government programs rather than individuals. Far from quailing at this issue, Santorum became co-chairman of Trent Lott's Social Security task force and spoke forcefully for his plan at the December 1998 White House conference on Social Security. While some observers of his 2000 campaign argued that he was becoming more liberal by talking about Social Security, they failed to notice that his proposal differs greatly from liberal orthodoxy—and that he was re-elected nonetheless.

Going into the 2000 campaign cycle, Santorum looked to some to be one of the most vulnerable of the Republican senators elected in 1994. Although Pennsylvania has elected a Democratic senator only once since 1962, it has not had a Republican senator as forthrightly conservative on so many, if not all, issues since the 1950s. A fair-sized field assembled to run in the April Democratic primary for the right to oppose Santorum, but there were some dropouts. Former Congressman Peter Kostmayer, then the Washington head of Zero Population Growth, decided not to run in 1999. Former Congresswoman Marjorie Margolies-Mezvinsky, who switched and cast the decisive vote for the Clinton tax increase in July 1993, left the race in January 2000. That left three major candidates: state Senator Allyson Schwartz, from the Philadelphia suburbs, who formerly headed a women's health clinic; former state Labor Secretary Tom Foley, from Hershey, who ran unsuccessfully for lieutenant governor in 1994 and auditor general in 1996; and Congressman Ron Klink, from suburban Pittsburgh and a former anchor on KDKA-TV. Schwartz had backing from feminists and from Philadelphia Mayor John Street; Foley had support from AFSCME and Harrisburg insiders; Klink got support from Allegheny County Democratic leader Leonard Bodack, the United Steelworkers and state Auditor Bob Casey Jr. But this was primarily a regional contest. Pennsylvania's two major metropolitan areas might as well be in two different states. And on cultural issues, Philadelphia area Democrats tend to be strong liberals while Pittsburgh area Democrats are strong conservatives. Klink, who opposes gun control and abortion, had great strength in his home media market; he borrowed $300,000 on his home and put most of his money into Pittsburgh TV, and put a Casey spot up in Scranton. Klink's strategy paid off. Schwartz carried metro Philadelphia with 56%, to 26% for Foley and only 9% for Klink; but the Philly area cast only 27% of the statewide vote. Metro Pittsburgh, which has fewer people but higher turnout and cast 35% of the vote, voted 73% for Klink, with 12% each for Schwartz and Foley. Foley slightly edged Klink in the rest of the state, but that was not enough: Klink won 41% of the vote, to 27% for Schwartz and 25% for Foley.

On paper Klink looked like a strong candidate, with vote-getting appeal in Santorum's home base and conservative issue stands appealing in the huge "T" between metro Philadelphia and metro Pittsburgh. Klink, referring to Santorum's brash first years in the Senate, called him "an absolute embarrassment" and attacked his "public commitments that he wanted to privatize Social Security and that he wants to raise the retirement age to 70 or higher." But Santorum was way ahead in one key respect: money. Santorum had $3.7 million cash on hand after the April primary; Klink had $119,000, with debts of $446,000. And Klink had great difficulty raising more. For Democratic moneygivers in the Philadelphia area, and for that matter in the nation generally, no issues evoke more emotional commitment than abortion and gun control, and on these issues Klink's stands were totally wrong. Not until nearly three months after the primary did Allyson Schwartz agree to be eastern Pennsylvania chairman for Klink; not until July 2000 did the indefatigable fundraiser Bill Clinton come in to make a lukewarm pitch for him. In the meantime, Santorum was running positive ads about his record, campaigning as a "compassionate conservative," emphasizing his ability to work with Democrats like Joseph Lieberman and former Philadelphia Mayor Ed Rendell. The first Klink ads did not go up until September; he went negative against Santorum, and voters never really heard a positive case for Klink. Santorum concentrated on positive spots, though near the end he ran ads in the Pittsburgh market charging that Klink had been part owner of a bar shut down for illegal gambling and had been the subject of civil lawsuits: "Trouble with the law seems to be a pattern for Klink." In all Santorum spent $10.6 million, Klink $3.6 million. Santorum won 52%–46%. He ran behind in metro Philadelphia 53%–45%, but this 8% margin was far better than Al Gore's 25% margin over George W. Bush there. He ran slightly behind his 1994 showing in metro Pittsburgh, which Klink carried 52%–46%. But in the rest of the state, which cast 46% of the votes, Santorum won a whopping 60%–37% margin, a big improvement on 1994.

Back in Washington, Santorum was elected Republican Conference chairman by a 30–20 margin over Missouri's Christopher Bond.

Presidential politics Pennsylvania, with its 23 electoral votes, has been a swing state in every close presidential election, and even some that were not close. Yet it is not typical of the country. With its older, deeply-rooted population, it tends to be culturally conservative; with its long-dying, blue-collar communities, it tends to be economically more liberal—though both tendencies are being muted with time. But it does present a problem for political strategists of both parties: Combinations of issue positions which work for Democrats on the East and West Coasts or for Republicans in the South and the Great Plains and Rocky Mountains do not work well here. Elderly voters—the New Deal generation—are Pennsylvania's strongest Democratic bloc; they voted 60%–38% for Al Gore in 2000. Voters 30 to 44—the Reagan generation—were the only age group to favor George W. Bush, 50%–47%. There are echoes in the VNS exit poll of the economic politics of the past, with under $15,000 voters 61%–35% and union members 67%–29% for Gore and over $100,000 voters 60%–36% for Bush. White Protestants continue to be heavily Republican, 60%–39% for Bush; but white Catholics, overwhelmingly for John Kennedy 40 years before, gave Gore only a 50%–46% margin.

Pennsylvania's April presidential primary has not been crucial since 1976, when Jimmy Carter clinched the Democratic nomination here by beating Henry Jackson and Morris Udall. In 1999 the legislature moved the primary date from April 25 to April 4, but it made little difference; both parties' nominations had already been cinched by then.

Congressional districting Pennsylvania lost two seats in the 2000 Census, the eighth consecutive census, starting in 1930, in which it has lost seats; it might have lost after the 1920 Census as well, but Congress then refused to reapportion House seats among the states. Pennsylvania will have 19 House members in the 108th Congress, the lowest since the 12th Congress assembled in 1811, when it had 18. Republicans, with the governorship, a 30–20 majority in the state Senate and a 104–99 majority in the state House, are in firm control of redistricting, and in early 2001 seemed determined to redraw the lines so as to increase their current 11–10 margin in the House delegation.

Early speculation was that one Democratic seat each would be eliminated in Philadelphia and in Pittsburgh's Allegheny County; both had population declines of 4% in the 1990s. That will probably happen in Pittsburgh, where the likely target is the 18th district's Mike Doyle. His former boss, state Senator Frank Pecora, switched from the Republican to the Democratic Party in 1992, and thereby gave Democrats, temporarily, control of the state Senate; elephants do not forget, and one Republican called Doyle's likely elimination "a study in patient and deferred gratification." This could be done by expanding the current underpopulated 14th District, placing more Republican suburbs in Republican freshman Melissa Hart's 4th District and perhaps by extending John Murtha's 12th District into the heavily Democratic Mon Valley. Murtha is the second ranking Democrat on Appropriations, skilled in bringing money into Pennsylvania, and the Republicans will surely try to give him a safe seat. This would leave Doyle with the choice of running against a fellow Democrat in a district most of which will be new to him, or retiring.

Republicans may not eliminate a Philadelphia seat, however. A more effective partisan course would be to extend one or two of the current Philadelphia districts into the suburban Montgomery County 13th District won by Democrat Joseph Hoeffel in 1998 and 2000. This would preserve Philadelphia's two black-majority districts and keep a seat for Robert Borski, a high-ranking member of the Transportation Committee sorely needed by Pennsylvania highway builders since the departure in 2001 of Pennsylvania's Bud Shuster, who failed to persuade Republicans to make him an exception to their six year term limit on committee chairmen. Putting heavily Jewish and other Democratic precincts in the lower county into the Philadelphia district would deprive Hoeffel of most or all of his majority, and his district could be extended into unfamiliar and Republican-leaning country in Berks County, where the cultural liberalism of the Philadelphia suburbs is not so popular. A corollary to that strategy would be to place Democrats Tim Holden of the 6th District and Paul Kanjorski of the 11th District into the same seat, while making the 10th District seat held precariously by Republican Don Sherwood more Republican. Other districts would not be as greatly changed. Such a plan is likely to produce a 12–7 Republican delegation, a gain of one for Republicans and a loss of three seats for Democrats.

In the process, the redistricters could do everyone a favor by renumbering the districts in some sensible geographic sequence. As Pennsylvania has lost seats, district numbers have been hurled across the state; Hart's district in far western Pennsylvania, once the 25th, was given the number of an abolished Philadelphia district when Pennsylvania was reduced from 25 to 23 seats after the 1970 Census.

THE PEOPLE: Pop. 2000: 12,281,054; Pop. 1990: 11,881,643, up 3.4% 1990–2000. 4.4% of U.S. total, 6th largest; 85.4% White, 10% Black, 1.8% Asian, 0.1% Amer. Indian, 1.2% Two+ races, 1.5% Other; 3.2% Hispanic Origin. 4.2% Unemployment. 2000 Voting age pop.: 9,358,833. 2000 Turnout: 4,912,185; 52% of VAP. Registered voters (2000): 7,781,997; 3,736,304 D (48%), 3,250,764 R (42%), 794,929 unaffiliated and minor parties (10%).

POLITICAL LINEUP: Governor, Tom Ridge (R); Lt. Gov., Mark Schweiker (R); Secy. of Commonwealth, Kim Pizzingrilli; Atty. Gen., D. Michael Fisher (R); Treasurer, Barbara Hafer (R); Auditor General, Robert P. Casey Jr. (D); State Senate, 50 (20 D, 30 R); Senate Pres. Pro Tempore, Robert C. Jubelirer (R); Majority Leader, David J. Brightbill (R); State House, 203 (99 D, 104 R); House Speaker, Matthew J. Ryan (R). Senators, Arlen Specter (R) and Rick Santorum (R). Representatives, 21 (10 D, 11 R).

ELECTIONS DIVISION: 717-787-5280; **FILING DEADLINE FOR U.S. CONGRESS:** February 13, 2002.

2000 Presidential Vote
Gore (D)	2,485,967	(51%)
Bush (R)	2,281,127	(46%)
Nader (Green)	103,392	(2%)
Others	41,699	(1%)

1996 Presidential Vote
Clinton (D)	2,215,819	(49%)
Dole (R)	1,801,169	(40%)
Perot (I)	430,984	(10%)

2000 Republican Presidential Primary
Bush (R)	472,398	(74%)
McCain (R)	145,719	(23%)
Other	24,968	(4%)

2000 Democratic Presidential Primary
Gore (D)	525,306	(75%)
Bradley (D)	146,797	(21%)
LaRouche (D)	32,047	(5%)

Gov. Tom Ridge (R)

Elected 1994, term expires Jan. 2003, 2d term; b. Aug. 26, 1945, Munhall; home, Erie; Harvard U., B.A. 1967, Dickinson Law Schl., J.D. 1972; Catholic; married (Michele).

Military Career: Army, 1968–70 (Vietnam).

Elected Office: U.S. House of Reps., 1982–94.

Professional Career: Practicing atty., 1972–82; Erie Cnty. Asst. Dist. Atty., 1979–81.

Office: 225 Capitol Bldg., Harrisburg, 17120, 717-787-2500; Fax: 717-772-8284; Web site: www.state.pa.us.

Election Results
1998 general	Tom Ridge (R)	1,736,844	(57%)
	Ivan Itkin (D)	938,745	(31%)
	Peg Luksik (Const)	315,761	(10%)
	Others	33,802	(1%)
1998 primary	Tom Ridge (R)	unopposed	
1994 general	Tom Ridge (R)	1,627,976	(45%)
	Mark S. Singel (D)	1,430,099	(40%)
	Peg Luksik (Const)	460,269	(13%)
	Others	67,182	(2%)

Sen. Arlen Specter (R)

Elected 1980, seat up 2004, 4th term; b. Feb. 12, 1930, Wichita, KS; home, Philadelphia; U. of PA, B.A. 1951, Yale U., LL.B. 1956; Jewish; married (Joan).

Military Career: Air Force, 1951–53.

Elected Office: Philadelphia Dist. Atty., 1965–73.

Professional Career: Practicing atty., 1955–56, 1974–80; Asst. Cnsl., Warren Comm., 1964; PA Asst. Atty. Gen., 1964–65.

DC Office: 711 HSOB, 20510, 202-224-4254; Fax: 202-228-1229; Web site: www.senate.gov/~specter.

State Offices: Allentown, 610-434-1444; Erie, 814-453-3010; Harrisburg, 717-782-3951; Philadelphia, 215-597-7200; Pittsburgh, 412-644-3400; Scranton, 570-346-2006.

Committees: *Appropriations*: Agriculture & Rural Development; Defense; Foreign Operations; Labor, HHS & Education (RMM); Transportation. *Environment & Public Works*: Superfund, Waste Control & Risk Assessment. *Judiciary*: Administrative Oversight & the Courts; Antitrust, Business Rights & Competition; Immigration. *Veterans' Affairs* (RMM).

Group Ratings

	ADA	ACLU	AFS	LCV	CON	ITIC	NTU	COC	ACU	NTLC	CHC
2000	40	43	57	29	52	58	53	53	62	60	31
1999	40	—	50	44	41	—	38	47	48	—	—

National Journal Ratings

	1999 LIB	—	1999 CONS		2000 LIB	—	2000 CONS
Economic	54%	—	45%		54%	—	45%
Social	53%	—	46%		49%	—	46%
Foreign	48%	—	49%		16%	—	83%

Key Votes of the 106th Congress

1. Educ. Savings Accts.	Y	5. Review Movie Violence	Y	9. NATO War in Serbia	Y
2. Prescrip. Drug Benefit	Y	6. Gun Show Bckgrnd. Checks	N	10. Table Cuba Travel Ban	N
3. Delay Ergonomic Standards	N	7. Ban Part.-Birth Abortion	Y	11. Nuclear Test-Ban Treaty	Y
4. Phase Out Estate Tax	N	8. Broaden Hate Crimes List	Y	12. Perm. Trade with China	N

Election Results

1998 general	Arlen Specter (R)	1,814,180	(61%)	($4,535,887)
	Bill Lloyd (D)	1,028,839	(35%)	($187,157)
	Others	114,753	(4%)	
1998 primary	Arlen Specter (R)	376,322	(67%)	
	Larry Murphy (R)	101,120	(18%)	
	Tom Lingenfelter (R)	82,168	(15%)	
1992 general	Arlen Specter (R)	2,358,125	(49%)	($10,454,793)
	Lynn Yeakel (D)	2,224,966	(46%)	($5,028,669)
	John F. Perry (Lib)	219,319	(5%)	($53,690)

Sen. Rick Santorum (R)

Elected 1994, seat up 2006, 2d term; b. May 10, 1958, Winchester, VA; home, Penn Hills; PA St. U., B.A. 1980, U. of Pittsburgh, M.B.A. 1981, Dickinson Law Schl., J.D. 1986; Catholic; married (Karen).

Elected Office: U.S. House of Reps., 1990–94.

Professional Career: A.A., PA Sen. J. Doyle 1981–86; Exec. Dir., PA Senate Local Govt. Cmte., 1981–84; Exec. Dir., PA Senate Transportation Cmte., 1984–86; Practicing atty., 1986–90.

DC Office: 120 RSOB, 20510, 202-224-6324; Fax: 202-228-0604; Web site: www.senate.gov/~santorum.

State Offices: Allentown, 610-770-0142; Altoona, 814-946-7023; Erie, 814-454-7114; Harrisburg, 717-231-7540; Philadelphia, 215-864-6900; Pittsburgh, 412-562-0533; Scranton, 570-344-8799.

Committees: *Republican Conference Chairman. Aging (Special). Armed Services:* Airland Forces (RMM); Emerging Threats & Capabilities; Readiness & Management Support. *Banking, Housing & Urban Affairs:* Financial Institutions; Housing & Transportation; Securities & Investment. *Rules & Administration.*

Group Ratings

	ADA	ACLU	AFS	LCV	CON	ITIC	NTU	COC	ACU	NTLC	CHC
2000	0	14	0	0	26	90	73	93	100	94	92
1999	5	—	0	0	61	—	74	81	88	—	—

National Journal Ratings

	1999 LIB —	1999 CONS	2000 LIB —	2000 CONS
Economic	45%	54%	0%	86%
Social	23%	72%	30%	68%
Foreign	10%	84%	15%	84%

Key Votes of the 106th Congress

1. Educ. Savings Accts.	Y	5. Review Movie Violence	Y	9. NATO War in Serbia	N
2. Prescrip. Drug Benefit	N	6. Gun Show Bckgrnd. Checks	N	10. Table Cuba Travel Ban	Y
3. Delay Ergonomic Standards	Y	7. Ban Part.-Birth Abortion	Y	11. Nuclear Test-Ban Treaty	N
4. Phase Out Estate Tax	Y	8. Broaden Hate Crimes List	N	12. Perm. Trade with China	Y

Election Results

2000 general	Rick Santorum (R)	2,481,962	(52%)	($10,616,262)
	Ron Klink (D)	2,154,908	(46%)	($3,641,167)
	Others	98,246	(2%)	
2000 primary	Rick Santorum (R)	unopposed		
1994 general	Rick Santorum (R)	1,735,691	(49%)	($6,732,849)
	Harris Wofford (D)	1,648,481	(47%)	($6,300,560)
	Others	129,189	(4%)	

FIRST DISTRICT

In Center City Philadelphia, the 1680s look out on the 1780s, 1880s and 1980s. The statue of William Penn, who founded the city in 1682, stands 37 feet high atop the 548-foot tower of the 1880s Second Empire-style City Hall at Market and Broad; east, is Independence Hall, where Americans in the 1780s drew up the nation's Constitution; west, is the tower of One Liberty Place, with its "romantic modernist" spire, the 1980s building that broke tradition to rise above City Hall. Philadelphia is built on a certain order. Earlier American colonies were settled by practical men, out to make money or replicate a farm settlement back home. But Penn was a Quaker, a member of one of those rationalizing sects of the 17th Century, who intended to impose order on his new environment, and did: no cowpath street patterns here, like those in Boston or Charleston, but a grid of numbered and named streets, with precisely spaced open squares. Penn's city of brotherly love has turned out to be a commercial and industrial metropolis that has grown steadily over the years, spreading out over the countryside. Yet there are still places in which you can see the distant past: in the restored townhouses of Society Hill and the tree-shaded public buildings around Independence Hall and, on the way to the ornate City Hall, the Federal and Greek Revival buildings and the temples of commerce, built when Philadelphia was the nation's largest city. Interspersed are I.M. Pei's modernist Society Hill Towers (though the rich in Philadelphia, unlike New York or Chicago, don't much like apartments) and the 1920s masonry-faced skyscrapers and 1970s glass-and-steel towers built around City Hall and in Center City farther west.

For all the grandness of City Hall, Philadelphia has seldom had a city government of which to be proud. Corruption has reigned here off and on for more than a century, and so has incompetence. While the city's private economy grew robustly in the 1980s, the city government—swollen with overpaid employees, committed to a costly, union-run health plan and mismanaged with ferocious ineptitude—lurched unknowingly toward bankruptcy under Mayor Wilson Goode. Then in 1991 Democrat Ed Rendell was elected mayor. Ebullient and energetic, he immediately set to work, literally scrubbing City Hall's grimy steps. He cut spending sharply, privatized government functions and faced down unions in a strike threat; at the same time, he improved performance and sponsored innovative new programs. Unfortunately, Rendell's push for reform stalled in the mid-1990s, and Philadelphia still has an inordinately expensive city government and neighborhoods wracked by crime that have emptied out over the years. His successor, John Street, elected narrowly in 1999, has had to contend with militant municipal employees and teachers' union. But there are signs of hope. Philadelphia, the home of George W. Bush's faith-based initiatives coordinator John DiIulio, has some of the nation's most vibrant and charitably active churches; its economy is vibrant enough to attract some Latino and Asian immigrants, though many fewer than New York or Chicago; and its Center City is still attractive, as it was when it was on display at the 2000 Republican National Convention.

City Hall lies at the geographic center of Pennsylvania's 1st Congressional District. The 1st runs north on both sides of the Broad Street corridor to include much of black North Philadelphia and south through most of heavily Italian South Philadelphia, where Italian families and their grocery stores and restaurants have been pressed tightly into narrow streets under a tangle of overhead wires; this is the neighborhood where the various *Rockys* were filmed and the original Philadelphia cheesesteaks are sold. The district also includes the oil tank farms where the Schuylkill River flows into the Delaware River, the Navy Yard, the Philadelphia airport, and the swath of industrial suburbs along the river to the black-majority city of Chester. This was created as a black-majority district, in the argot of the Voting Rights Act, and was 55% black and 12% Hispanic in 2000, and is overwhelmingly Democratic.

The congressman from the 1st District is Bob Brady, a Democrat elected in May 1998, who personifies the nation's old-fashioned urban politics. He grew up in Overbrook Park in West Philadelphia, with an Irish father and Italian mother, he depicts himself as a roll-up-your-sleeves guy who represents working-class voters. After high school he went to work as a carpenter and quickly rose up the ranks of the carpenter's union leadership. He entered politics in 1967, at 22, when the local ward leader wouldn't replace a burnt-out streetlight; Brady was elected to the 34th Ward Democratic Executive Committee, and in 1980 he was elected Ward leader. In 1975 he became assistant Sergeant-at-Arms of the city council; he was a consultant to the state Senate and member of the Pennsylvania Turnpike Commission and on the board of the city's Redevelopment Authority. In 1986 he became chairman of the Philadelphia Democratic Party, where he has been a close ally of talented politicians like former state Senator Buddy Cianfrani and state Senator Vincent Fumo.

In November 1997, Thomas Foglietta, 1st District congressman since 1980 and a veteran of South Philly politics, resigned after being confirmed as ambassador to Italy, and Brady ran for the seat. In other cities, this might have led to a primary fight between black politicians; in Philadelphia the Democratic nomination for the special election, held on the same day as the regular primary for the next election, was determined by the Democratic ward leaders in the district. That gave Brady a great advantage, for he seemed sure to win the committeemen's vote; former 2d District Congressman Lucien Blackwell, probably his strongest opponent, dropped out of the race even before Brady officially declared. Brady won the endorsement of many black leaders and built a strong election day organization. He won the special election with 74% of the vote and the

Democratic nomination for November, against three little-known opponents, with 64%. He easily won the general election. This was the triumph of a politician known for making "accommodations" with others—"they're always accommodations, never deals," he insists—and whose positions on national issues were not always set in stone; he decided that he was in favor of abortion rights after asking his mother.

Even after he was elected to the House, Brady's attention focused back home. In July 1998, local officials credited him with mediating an end to the 41-day strike that had shut down parts of the SEPTA transit system. He mediated the teachers' strike in 2000, and he sought common ground between the mayor and City Council on a deal for two new stadiums. His ties to City Hall and to the local unions gave him credibility with both sides. He urged shipbuilding firms around the world to do business in the city's old Naval Shipyard. During the convention, he encouraged friends to wear "Republican for a Week" T-shirts and afterwards disposed of the shirts in a bonfire. In the House, where he had a liberal voting record, Brady continued his mostly local focus. He called for a congressional housing task force. He won enactment of a study on whether firefighters and emergency medical technicians have a greater chance of contacting the Hepatitis C virus, which was an increasing concern in the Philadelphia force. He claimed credit for a casting pit modernization project at the shipyard, and he directed $11.2 million in the 2000 budget to local schools, museums and arts organizations.

Brady has said that he dreamed as a boy of becoming a U.S. senator. But it is unlikely that his machine-style politics will play well in a statewide campaign. When he announced for reelection in 2000, he noted that some in the news media had called him a "political hack." But, he added, "I think I might have proved them wrong a little." Nor is it clear whether he will have a long career in the House. That depends on redistricting. Philadelphia's population declined 4% in the 1990s, and the city, which now has almost three full districts, is only entitled to 2.3 districts under the new figures. Republicans control redistricting, and there was speculation in early 2001 that they would eliminate one of the Philadelphia districts, forcing Brady into a contest with the 3rd District's more senior Robert Borski. Another idea may be to extend the Philadelphia districts out into the Philadelphia suburbs, thus weakening 13th District Democrat Joseph Hoeffel. Such a plan would probably produce a safe district for Brady.

Cook's Call *Probably Safe*. Pennsylvania will lose two House seats in 2002, and the longstanding assumption was that Philadelphia would lose one of its three congressional districts. But Brady has cut a deal with the Republican leadership in the state legislature to help keep his seat and retain the three city districts. Whether this deal materializes remains to be seen.

THE PEOPLE: Pop. 2000: 515,560; Pop. 1990: 566,133, down 8.9% 1990–2000. 31% White, 55.4% Black, 4.2% Asian, 0.3% Amer. Indian, 2.2% Two+ races, 6.8% Other; 11.5% Hispanic Origin.

2000 Presidential Vote

Gore (D)	156,718	(85%)
Bush (R)	24,404	(13%)
Nader (Green)	2,129	(1%)
Others	1,077	(1%)

1996 Presidential Vote

Clinton (D)	148,850	(83%)
Dole (R)	21,845	(12%)
Perot (I)	7,519	(4%)

Rep. Robert Brady (D)

Elected May 1998, 2d term; b. April 7, 1945, Philadelphia; home, Philadelphia; Catholic; married (Debra).

Elected Office: 34th Ward Dem. Exec. Cmte. Mbr., 1967–present, Ward Ldr., 1980.

Professional Career: Carpenter; Real estate salesman; Philadelphia Dpty. Mayor for Labor, 1984–87; Chmn., Philadelphia Dem. Party, 1986; Legis. Rep., Metro. Regional Cncl. of Carpenters & Joiners, 1987–98; Lecturer, U. of PA, 1997-present.

DC Office: 216 CHOB 20515, 202-225-4731; Fax: 202-225-0088; Web site: www.house.gov/robertbrady.

District Offices: Chester, 610-874-7094; Philadelphia, 215-236-5430; Philadelphia, 215-389-4627.

Committees: *Armed Services* (21st of 28 D): Military Procurement; Military Readiness. *Small Business* (6th of 17 D): Regulatory Reform Oversight (RMM); Tax, Finance & Exports.

Group Ratings

	ADA	ACLU	AFS	LCV	CON	ITIC	NTU	COC	ACU	NTLC	CHC
2000	90	86	100	79	66	44	17	42	12	12	0
1999	95	—	100	81	20	—	17	20	8	—	—

National Journal Ratings

	1999 LIB	—	1999 CONS		2000 LIB	—	2000 CONS
Economic	88%	—	0%		80%	—	19%
Social	83%	—	13%		86%	—	14%
Foreign	70%	—	29%		74%	—	24%

Key Votes of the 106th Congress

1. Patient Bill of Rights	Y	5. Bar RU-486 $ for FDA	N	9. NATO War in Serbia	Y
2. Accelerate Min. Wage	Y	6. Display 10 Commandments	N	10. Perm. Trade with China	N
3. Strike Ban on Ergo. Stnd.	Y	7. Gun Show Bkgrnd. Checks	Y	11. Debt Relief for 3rd World	Y
4. Ovrd. Estate Tax Veto	N	8. Ban Part.-Birth Abortion	N	12. Drop Cuba Econ. Embargo	N

Election Results

2000 general	Robert Brady (D)	149,621	(88%)	($411,375)
	Steven N. Kush (R)	19,920	(12%)	($1,733)
2000 primary	Robert Brady (D)	28,333	(77%)	
	Andrew J. Carn (D)	6,346	(17%)	
	Timothy Hannah (D)	1,943	(5%)	
1998 general	Robert A. Brady (D)	77,788	(81%)	($333,055)
	William M. Harrison (R)	15,898	(17%)	
	Others	2,162	(2%)	

SECOND DISTRICT

Looking out over the Schuylkill River north of Center City Philadelphia, you can still see the landscape painted 100 years ago by Philadelphia artist Thomas Eakins—the tightly-packed but formidable rowhouses, the old fieldstone houses of Germantown, the gray-blue water flowing past boat houses below the small Greek temples of the Water Works and the larger temple of the Museum of Art and the skyscraper towers looming behind. On both sides of this romantic scene are some of Philadelphia's long-established black neighborhoods: West Philadelphia, across the Schuylkill on either side of Market Street; North Philadelphia, on either side of Broad Street; to the northwest, off the narrow diagonal of Germantown Avenue that ran through open fields in Benjamin Franklin's time. Its many poor neighborhoods continue to suffer neglected and abandoned housing, and the city has 550,000 fewer people today than in 1950. In an effort to clean up some of the eyesores before the arrival of the 2000 Republican Convention, bulldozers razed 957 homes sinking on an unstable landfill, in a working class swath of North Philadelphia.

The 2d Congressional District of Pennsylvania is centered on this part of Philadelphia, following the Schuylkill north and south. It includes center city skyscrapers, affluent Chestnut Hill, upper-class Rittenhouse Square, and the University of Pennsylvania. Pennsylvania never had slavery—thanks to William Penn's Quaker legacy—and Philadelphia had a large black community even before the Civil War. The John Coltrane House on North 33rd Street has been designated a national historic landmark, in celebration of the jazz innovator's early years here. Local fear of crime revived after Philadelphia *Daily News* columnist Russell Byers was murdered in his Chestnut Hill neighborhood in December 1999. Within its current boundaries, the 2d District was 64% black in 2000, and overwhelmingly Democratic.

The congressman from the 2d District is Chaka Fattah, first elected in 1994. Fattah grew up in Philadelphia, and in 1982, at 25, was elected to the state House—the youngest member ever. In 1988 he was elected to the state Senate, where he worked to fend off bankruptcy for Philadelphia. In 1991, much to everyone's surprise, 2d District Congressman William Gray resigned to become head of the United Negro College Fund. Gray was a shining star in the political firmament, chairman of the Budget Committee from 1984–88, majority whip since 1989. Local ward leaders nominated Councilman Lucien Blackwell, a former longshoreman, boxer and labor union stalwart; he attended to parochial neighborhood concerns while leaders like Gray were concerned about the world beyond. Fattah ran under the Consumer Party label and state Welfare Secretary John White ran as an independent. Blackwell won the special election with 39% to 28% for Fattah and 27% for White. In 1994 Fattah ran again, in the Democratic primary. Blackwell relied mostly on ward politicians; Fattah was endorsed by the Black Clergy of Philadelphia and Vicinity and by state Senator Hardy Williams. This time Fattah won, 58%–42%.

Fattah annually is rated among the most liberal voting records in the House and he voted against Contract with America measures more often than all but one other member. He has advocated guaranteeing Pell grants for students in poverty areas who stay in high school and maintain the necessary grades, a federal law to get states to equalize school district funding, expanding HUD lending to community development. He criticized Speaker Newt Gingrich in 1997 for dismissing as a "dead-end" gesture a resolution for a federal apology for slavery. He strongly defended Bill Clinton against impeachment charges, pointing to the benefits that he brought the black community. "Like any group, African-Americans operate from self-interest," he said. He accompanied Clinton on a trip to Nigeria to express support for democratic progress there. In January 2000, he organized at City Hall the Congressional Black Caucus's first "Town Hall Meeting on AIDS in the Black Community." Fattah was the prime sponsor of a law to support an educational program that encourages partnerships between colleges and public schools with at least 50% low-income students to put middle-school students on the track to college by promising federally funded scholarships. He served on a congressional commission studying Internet-based education, which urged President Bush to make "E-learning" the centerpiece of the nation's education policy. He got 183 votes in the 106th Congress for his bill to require each state to equalize funding for education within its borders. As an Ethics Committee member, he served on the panel that that investigated the financial dealings of Representative Corinne Brown, concluding that she used "poor judgment" but deciding not to issue formal charges.

In the 107th Congress, after an earlier setback when Pennsylvania's senior Democrat John Murtha failed to deliver him the position, he won a seat on the Appropriations Committee, a useful slot for a member who seems intent on a long House career; he said that he would use the position to push for more money for education. Since entering the House, Fattah has had no serious primary or general election challenge. He is articulate and telegenic, and could be an attractive candidate for higher office, though his liberal stands on some issues would be a handicap in a statewide race. Redistricting after 2000 is likely to retain a black-majority Philadelphia seat that Fattah can win easily.

Cook's Call *Probably Safe.* Fattah is safely settled in this solidly Democratic district, but like every Democrat in the Philadelphia delegation he has to be wary of redistricting in 2002. The Philadelphia area is expected to lose at least one district, and part of Democrat Joe Hoeffel's suburban seat could be added to Fattah's.

THE PEOPLE: Pop. 2000: 532,455; Pop. 1990: 565,242, down 5.8% 1990–2000. 29.4% White, 64.4% Black, 3.3% Asian, 0.2% Amer. Indian, 1.9% Two+ races, 0.8% Other; 2% Hispanic Origin.

2000 Presidential Vote		
Gore (D)	187,503	(88%)
Bush (R)	22,291	(10%)
Nader (Green)	2,961	(1%)

1996 Presidential Vote		
Clinton (D)	173,723	(86%)
Dole (R)	20,675	(10%)
Perot (I)	5,981	(3%)

Rep. Chaka Fattah (D)

Elected 1994, 3d term; b. Nov. 21, 1956, Philadelphia; home, Philadelphia; Community Col. of Philadelphia, U. of PA, M.A. 1986, Harvard U. Kennedy Schl. of Gov., 1984.; Baptist; married (Renee Chenault).

Elected Office: PA House of Reps., 1982–88; PA Senate, 1988–94.

Professional Career: Asst. Dir., House of Umoja, 1977–79; City of Philadelphia, Spec. Asst. to Dir. of Housing & Community Dev., 1980, Spec. Asst. to Managing Director, 1981.

DC Office: 1205 LHOB 20515, 202-225-4001; Fax: 202-225-5392; Web site: www.house.gov/fattah.

District Offices: Philadelphia, 215-848-9386; Philadelphia, 215-387-6404.

Committees: *Appropriations* (28th of 29 D): District of Columbia (RMM); VA, HUD & Independent Agencies. *House Administration* (2d of 3 D).

Group Ratings

	ADA	ACLU	AFS	LCV	CON	ITIC	NTU	COC	ACU	NTLC	CHC
2000	95	86	100	93	77	63	25	40	0	6	0
1999	95	—	100	88	54	—	19	24	0	—	—

National Journal Ratings

	1999 LIB	—	1999 CONS		2000 LIB	—	2000 CONS
Economic	88%	—	0%		92%	—	5%
Social	87%	—	0%		84%	—	16%
Foreign	93%	—	7%		91%	—	8%

Key Votes of the 106th Congress

1. Patient Bill of Rights	Y	5. Bar RU-486 $ for FDA	N	9. NATO War in Serbia	Y
2. Accelerate Min. Wage	Y	6. Display 10 Commandments	N	10. Perm. Trade with China	N
3. Strike Ban on Ergo. Stnd.	Y	7. Gun Show Bkgrnd. Checks	Y	11. Debt Relief for 3rd World	Y
4. Ovrd. Estate Tax Veto	N	8. Ban Part.-Birth Abortion	N	12. Drop Cuba Econ. Embargo	Y

Election Results

2000 general	Chaka Fattah (D)	180,021	(98%)	($296,851)
	Others	3,673	(2%)	
2000 primary	Chaka Fattah (D)	unopposed		
1998 general	Chaka Fattah (D)	102,763	(87%)	($327,896)
	Anne Marie Mulligan (R)	16,001	(13%)	

THIRD DISTRICT

North and east of Center City Philadelphia, stretching more than a dozen miles along the Delaware River and back along the parklands by Frankford, Tacony and Pennypacker Creeks, are most of the white residential neighborhoods of Philadelphia. They start off in the closely packed 19th Century homes of Kensington, where for years descendants of Irish and Italian immigrants lived in tiny frame houses; now they are being replaced by Hispanics. Farther out is Northeast Philadelphia, a more suburban area itself the size of a major city. Here, when the alley-wide streets of North and South Philadelphia and the river wards were already teeming and the Main Line suburbs were already well-settled, the workers of Philadelphia's docks, factories and Center City offices were just starting to fill up vacant land. They settled in neighborhoods like the one near Pennypack Park, where local hero Sylvester Stallone grew up. Unlike much of the city, with its high crime and struggling government, Northeast Philadelphia remains new urban territory, with more than half of its dwellings built after 1950, and still growing.

Politically the district appears to be a throwback to an earlier era, when you would expect to see ward heelers walking through the neighborhoods of Kensington and Frankford, distributing coal for the winter. Most people here are Catholic, and there are also many Jews; in the 2000 Census the district was 14% black, 11% Hispanic and 5% Asian. The houses are pleasant, but modest. Many residents are part of the hard-pressed lower middle class and are Democrats, but also are conservative on cultural issues, and there is a Republican tradition in some wards. Northeast Philadelphia voted for Mayor Frank Rizzo when he was running as a Republican in the 1980s; now it seems to have returned to its Democratic roots.

The congressman from the 3d District is Robert Borski, a Democrat first elected in 1982. He grew up in Northeast Philadelphia, and first distinguished himself as an athlete: He was captain of the Frankford High basketball and baseball teams in 1966 and became a coach after graduating from college with an athletic scholarship. Contacts made as an athlete helped him get a job as a floor manager at the Philadelphia Stock Exchange, and in 1976 he was elected to the state House of Representatives, where he served until his election to Congress. In 1982 Borski defeated Republican Charlie Dougherty, who had won in 1978 over a Democrat who had been indicted; he has won easily ever since.

Borski is a party loyalist, favorable to organized labor, with a voting record a bit to the conservative side on cultural issues. But most of all, he is concerned about Philadelphia, and about using his seat on the Transportation and Infrastructure Committee to help it. He does work on national legislation, like his bills to ban backhauling of toxic chemicals and to ban triple-trailer trucks. He objects to Republican Superfund changes on reimbursing polluters, and insists on retaining taxes on companies that created the waste dumps. He sponsored an amendment, partially drafted by the National Governors' Association, to protect wetlands, and has also sponsored a brownfields law. He sponsored a bipartisan water infrastructure caucus to urge support for new projects. In 2001, he became the ranking Democrat on the Highways and Transit Subcommittee, making him well-positioned to wield considerable influence on the next highway bill, which is due in 2003—he is now Pennsylvania's main man on the committee, since previous chairman Bud Shuster resigned in January 2001.

"I do need to be talking to the people in Philadelphia," Borski said in 1996 when he was detained in Washington on the ethics committee judging the complaint against Newt Gingrich. "I normally spend this time talking to the airport folks and the port people about what their legislative wishes are." On the Transportation Committee, he beat a provision in the Amtrak privatization law that would have required SEPTA to pay Amtrak higher fees for use of its tracks. He has superintended the Superfund toxic waste cleanup at the Metal Bank property in Tacony. His accomplishments in the 1998 highway bill included about $90 million in local improvements for I-95, a new transportation center in Frankford for SEPTA and refurbishing of the Philadelphia Airport, including its new international terminal. He is working for SEPTA's current goal of a 62-mile rail line to Reading, the "Schuylkill Valley Metro." He considers one of his greatest achievements the reversal of a base-closing commission plan to close the Aviation Supply Office in Northeast Philadelphia, which would have cost 8,000 jobs. He won passage of a new Gateway Visitors Center at Independence Park. He urged the redevelopment of the Delaware River's largely abandoned northern waterfront, with new parks, housing and office complexes.

In 2000, he easily prevailed in his third rematch with Dougherty, who has spent much time in recent years in Washington with the Cassidy and Associates lobbying firm. The chief threat to Borski's tenure is redistricting. Pennsylvania lost two House seats in the 2000 Census, and Republicans control the redistricting process. Philadelphia has had almost all of three districts, but now has only population enough for 2.3. There was speculation in 2000 that Republicans would eliminate one of the Philadelphia districts, and put Borski in the same district as the 1st District's Bob Brady. But Republicans may have another idea: to extend the Philadelphia districts out into the suburbs, to weaken 13th District Democrat Joseph Hoeffel. Such a plan would extend the

3rd out from Northeast Philadelphia into the heavily Jewish suburbs of Montgomery County. That might trigger a primary between Borski and Hoeffel, with Borski having the advantage in terrain; or Hoeffel might run in a new 13th District, extended outward into Berks County, which would leave Borski home free.

Cook's Call   *Potentially Competitive.* Although the 3rd is not as solidly Democratic as the other two Philadelphia districts, Borski has held it for 18 years. He was first elected with the help of redistricting, but this year, redistricting could ultimately cost him this seat. As with every other district in the area, the 3rd is far below ideal population. It could receive portions of fellow Democrat Joe Hoeffel's suburban Philadelphia district.

THE PEOPLE: Pop. 2000: 572,488; Pop. 1990: 565,884, up 1.2% 1990–2000. 72.4% White, 13.7% Black, 5.2% Asian, 0.2% Amer. Indian, 2.4% Two+ races, 6% Other; 10.8% Hispanic Origin.

2000 Presidential Vote		
Gore (D)	134,266	(66%)
Bush (R)	63,634	(31%)
Nader (Green)	3,756	(2%)
Others	1,369	(1%)

1996 Presidential Vote		
Clinton (D)	114,680	(61%)
Dole (R)	51,781	(28%)
Perot (I)	18,878	(10%)
Others	2,870	(2%)

Rep. Robert A. Borski (D)

Elected 1982, 10th term; b. Oct. 20, 1948, Philadelphia; home, Philadelphia; U. of Baltimore, B.A. 1971; Catholic; married (Karen).

Elected Office: PA House of Reps., 1976–82.

Professional Career: Asst. Coach, U. of Baltimore, 1971–72; Stockbroker, 1972–76.

DC Office: 2409 RHOB 20515, 202-225-8251; Fax: 202-225-4628; Web site: www.house.gov/borski.

District Offices: Philadelphia, 215-426-4616; Philadelphia, 215-335-3355.

Committees: *Transportation & Infrastructure* (3d of 34 D): Highways & Transit (RMM); Railroads; Water Resources & Environment.

Group Ratings

	ADA	ACLU	AFS	LCV	CON	ITIC	NTU	COC	ACU	NTLC	CHC
2000	75	62	100	86	24	56	20	47	16	10	33
1999	85	—	100	88	23	—	18	24	12	—	—

National Journal Ratings

	1999 LIB —	1999 CONS		2000 LIB —	2000 CONS
Economic	80% —	18%		84% —	15%
Social	57% —	42%		54% —	45%
Foreign	73% —	26%		66% —	33%

Key Votes of the 106th Congress

1. Patient Bill of Rights	Y	5. Bar RU-486 $ for FDA	Y	9. NATO War in Serbia	Y
2. Accelerate Min. Wage	Y	6. Display 10 Commandments	N	10. Perm. Trade with China	N
3. Strike Ban on Ergo. Stnd.	Y	7. Gun Show Bkgrnd. Checks	Y	11. Debt Relief for 3rd World	Y
4. Ovrd. Estate Tax Veto	N	8. Ban Part.-Birth Abortion	Y	12. Drop Cuba Econ. Embargo	N

Election Results

2000 general	Robert A. Borski (D)	130,528	(69%)	($474,626)
	Charles F. Dougherty (R)	59,343	(31%)	($106,908)
2000 primary	Robert A. Borski (D)	unopposed		
1998 general	Robert A. Borski (D)	66,270	(59%)	($514,639)
	Charles F. Dougherty (R)	45,390	(41%)	($226,280)

FOURTH DISTRICT

For a century, one of America's great industrial zones was along the banks of the Beaver and Ohio Rivers, near where they join in western-most Pennsylvania. This was steel country, with mills rising black and brooding from the bottomlands and filling the narrow river valleys with smoke. The sinewy sons of immigrant families worked hard in the hot mills. Looking down on riverscapes lined with piles of iron ore, limestone and coal, and littered with cranes, stocks and furnaces, families lived in small frame houses on the hillsides. Although not an environmentalist's idea of perfection, this was a land of opportunity for thousands whose lives were far worse before moving to steel country. For a few heady years, the high union wages and early retirement plans seemed to make working in the mills the way to affluence. But the industry crashed after the oil shock of 1979, when mills were closed and jobs vanished. Today, thousands of workers who long ago exhausted their unemployment benefits have given up and left the Beaver and Ohio valleys. Forty years ago, the western Pennsylvania steel country had 11 House Members; it now has six and it will have only five after redistricting.

The 4th Congressional District of Pennsylvania includes much of this steel country. It is shaped something like a dumbbell. In the west it includes Beaver and Lawrence County, with their steel mills, many now closed, along the Beaver and Ohio Rivers; these are usually heavily Democratic. In the east, it includes the northwest portion of Westmoreland County, hilly, even mountainous, including old industrial towns like New Kensington and newer and more upscale suburbs like Murrysville; this area was historically Democratic but has been trending Republican. Connecting the two areas are the northern tier of townships in Allegheny County and the southern tier in Butler County, a mixed area again, but including growing affluent subdivisions; this is one of the more Republican parts of the heavily Democratic Pittsburgh area. Overall, the district's heritage is Democratic, but it has been trending Republican, as it did in the 2000 election.

The congressman from the 4th District is Melissa Hart, a Republican first elected in 2000. She grew up in the Pittsburgh area, graduated from Washington and Jefferson College and the University of Pittsburgh Law School. After law school, she worked as a real estate attorney for a Pittsburgh firm. She was elected to the state Senate in 1990, defeating an incumbent Democrat, and won re-election twice. As Chairman of the Finance Committee, Hart sponsored Pennsylvania's first major tax reform in more than a century, which permits communities to reduce property taxes by implementing an earned income tax. She also worked to expand penalties for domestic violence and repeat drunk drivers, and advocated a school choice program. When Democrat Ron Klink, who had held the seat for eight years, decided to challenge Senator Rick Santorum, Hart was unopposed for the Republican nomination in this seat, which had not elected a Republican in 18 years. In the Democratic primary, state Representative Terry Van Horne from Westmoreland County unexpectedly led the eight-candidate field, with 24% of the vote; Matthew Mangino—the pro-gun, anti-abortion prosecutor in Lawrence County who had been supported by the Democratic Congressional Campaign Committee—finished second with 15%. A 20-year state representative, Van Horne is a former grocer and quintessential back-slapping politician. A key event in the campaign came the morning after the primary when the National Republican Congressional Committee eagerly drew attention to a racial slur Van Horne had used in reference to a black state Representative in 1994; committee chairman Tom Davis called him "frightening" and "unelectable." Van Horne, who had apologized on the floor of the state House after making the comment, said it had been taken out of context, and the target of the slur accepted Van Horne's apology long ago. But Jesse Jackson and several members of the Congressional Black Caucus expressed their concern when they learned of the comment.

In the general, Van Horne and Hart clashed over prescription drug plans for seniors, campaign finance and soft money, with both launching a series of attack ads. Van Horne criticized Hart for recently moving to the district and highlighted his own support for public education, organized labor, protecting Social Security and enforcing current gun laws rather than adding new ones. Democrats accused her of taking a $5,000 contribution from the National Association of Home Builders shortly before endorsing a proposed Army Corps of Engineers project for one of its members. Hart touted her labor roots and hoped that her anti-tax, anti-abortion, anti-gun control views would play well in this predominantly blue-collar district, and said that her opponent was a do-nothing lawmaker who had supported tax increases. A Republican ad said that Van Horne was a deadbeat who failed to repay nearly $200,000 on a loan from the Small Business Administration for his grocery store that failed in the 1980s. Hart had a big fundraising advantage. She won by a surprisingly large 59%–41%, carrying each of the five counties including Van Horne's home base in Westmoreland County.

Republican leaders quickly spotlighted their hard-charging newcomer, tapping her to give the party response to Bill Clinton on the Saturday after her election. She was soon mentioned as a prospective candidate for a party leadership post, or a statewide office. She hoped to use her Judiciary Committee assignment to work on an Internet anti-pornography bill, a partial-birth abortion ban, and legislation to permit women to leave unwanted newborns in "safe havens." On Financial Services, she hoped to focus on technology and privacy laws that might affect Pittsburgh's growing high-tech sector. Republicans control redistricting. If Van Horne had won, this dumbbell-shaped district might have been headed for extinction. But the Republican redistricters will try to make it safer for Hart, perhaps by eliminating all or most of Beaver County and adding Allegheny County suburbs that Hart represented in the state Senate.

Cook's Call *Potentially Competitive.* Hart's drubbing of Democrat Terry Van Horne in 2000 belies the very marginal nature of this district, which has been in Democratic hands for years. Republicans control the redistricting process and are committed to helping Hart, but it is unlikely that she will ever have a safe, heavily Republican district. The right Democrat could give her a race.

THE PEOPLE: Pop. 2000: 582,777; Pop. 1990: 565,809, up 3% 1990–2000. 95% White, 3.4% Black, 0.5% Asian, 0.1% Amer. Indian, 0.8% Two+ races, 0.2% Other; 0.6% Hispanic Origin.

2000 Presidential Vote		
Bush (R)	125,536	(50%)
Gore (D)	117,367	(47%)
Nader (Green)	4,189	(2%)
Others	2,137	(1%)

1996 Presidential Vote		
Clinton (D)	107,017	(47%)
Dole (R)	96,511	(42%)
Perot (I)	23,375	(10%)

Rep. Melissa Hart (R)

Elected 2000, 1st term; b. Apr. 4, 1962, Pittsburgh; home, Bradford Woods; Washington & Jefferson Col., B.A. 1984; U. of Pittsburgh, J.D. 1987; Catholic; single.

Elected Office: PA Senate, 1991–2000.

Professional Career: Praticing atty., 1987–2001.

DC Office: 1508 LHOB 20515, 202-225-2565; Fax: 202-226-2274; Web site: www.house.gov/hart.

District Offices: Beaver, 724-728-2378; Cranberry, 724-779-1330; New Castle, 724-654-7972; New Kensington, 724-334-4578.

Committees: *Financial Services* (33d of 37 R): Capital Markets, Insurance & Government Sponsored Enterprises; Domestic Monetary Policy, Technology & Economic Growth; Financial Institutions & Consumer Credit. *Judiciary* (20th of 21 R): Commercial & Administrative Law; Immigration & Claims; The Constitution. *Science* (24th of 25 R): Energy (Vice Chmn.); Environment, Technology and Standards; Research.

Group Ratings and Key Votes: Newly Elected

Election Results

2000 general	Melissa Hart (R)	145,390	(59%)	($1,724,048)
	Terry Van Horne (D)	100,995	(41%)	($673,346)
2000 primary	Melissa Hart (R)	unopposed		
1998 general	Ron Klink (D)	103,763	(64%)	($861,377)
	Mike Turzai (R)	58,485	(36%)	($555,368)

FIFTH DISTRICT

North central Pennsylvania—isolated from the rest of the country by chains of mountains, off the main east-west rail and highway lines until the 1970s—is one of those empty spaces that make even the northeastern states seem lightly populated to someone used to the densely packed terrain of Western Europe or East Asia. In narrow valleys, pressed tightly by mountains and fast-flowing rivers, connected by roads that switch back and wind precariously over mountains, there are few population concentrations. The largest is in the Nittany Valley, home of Pennsylvania State University, long known for its powerful football teams coached by Joe Paterno. To the west are Titusville, where Colonel Edwin Drake sank the first successful oil well in 1859, and Oil City, headquarters of Quaker State Oil from 1931 until it left for Texas in 1995. To the east, near the Susquehanna River, is Lewisburg, home of Bucknell University and the federal penitentiary. The solidly built courthouses and banks in the center of each county seat testify to the long history of hard work and thrift in this part of the country. Yet today, even with the main east-west truck line, Interstate 80, it is a low-wage area, although a few local towns saw above-average growth in the 1990s.

The 5th Congressional District of Pennsylvania includes a very wide swath of north central Pennsylvania, and has somewhat irregular boundaries. Its largest city is State College. The small towns include Punxsutawney, home of legendary groundhog Phil, who predicts the arrival of spring based on whether he sees his shadow on Groundhog Day each year. The political heritage here is Republican, with few exceptions, from the Civil War through the New Deal and Great Society, in Ronald Reagan's 1980s and Bill Clinton's 1990s.

The congressman from the 5th District is John Peterson, a Republican elected in 1996. Peterson grew up in Titusville, the son of a steelworker; he went to Penn State, served in the Army as a cook, then opened a grocery store that eventually became Peterson's Golden Dawn Supermarket chain. He served on the Pleasantville Borough Council for eight years, then in 1977, at 39, was elected to the state House. In 1984 he was elected to the state Senate, where he chaired the Public Health and Welfare Committee, concentrating on rural health issues, and working on Pennsylvania's welfare reform. In 1996 Bill Clinger announced his retirement after 18 years in the House. Peterson was an obvious candidate; his state Senate district included eight of the 5th's 17 counties. Three other Republicans ran. The one who attracted the most attention was Bob Shuster, the brother of recently-elected 9th District Congressman Bill Shuster and son of Bud Shuster, who was the influential chairman of the Transportation and Infrastructure Committee and an unashamed builder of roads in their home district. "What a one-two punch we could be for central Pennsylvania," Bud Shuster said on announcement day. But Peterson's chief competition was Daniel Gordeuk, a Centre County surgeon with strong local roots. Peterson won with 38%, to 28% for Gordeuk, and 18% for Shuster. In the general, Peterson attacked the Democratic nominee as "an old-fashioned liberal" and touted his work in the legislature, his support for a "flatter tax" and his opposition to abortion and gun control. Peterson won 60%–40%.

In the House, Peterson has been a Republican loyalist, helping to enact renewal of higher education and vocational education measures. He favors 12-year term limits and tax cuts. He emerged as a critic of environmentalists, complaining about their "push for world government" in the Kyoto treaty and opposing a proposed moratorium on roadbuilding in national forests. He chaired the health care task force of the Rural Caucus. He filed legislation requiring Hillary Rodham Clinton, as First Lady and Senate candidate, to disclose her official travel expenses. He passed a House resolution in October 2000, urging the Clinton administration to link aid to Russia to the release of Edmond Pope, a Penn State-funded naval researcher imprisoned on spy charges, who was suffering from a rare kind of cancer; when Pope was released two months later, he termed Peterson "one of the two heroes" in winning his freedom, along with his wife. On local issues, he wants federal recognition to promote the history of Titusville and Oil Creek Valley. "We need a lot more show and tell," he said. The Park Service gave preliminary approval of its feasibility. With a seat on the Appropriations Committee, he increased spending for a program that finances vocational education. On the 2000 spending bills, he won $19 million for Pentagon advanced-technology research projects at Penn State, $7.2 million for maintenance of lakes in

Tioga and Forest counties, $5 million for transportation service in his district, and $1 million for an oil drilling research project by Penn State.

Peterson had surgery to clear a blocked artery in his heart in August 1999. In his two re-election campaigns, he had no Democratic opponent. Redistricting will enlarge his district, but it should not put this seat in jeopardy.

Cook's Call *Safe.* This district has a serious Republican lean to it and Peterson is well entrenched. It will have to pick up some population in redistricting, but will remain a fundamentally Republican seat.

THE PEOPLE: Pop. 2000: 582,083; Pop. 1990: 565,736, up 2.9% 1990–2000. 96% White, 1.6% Black, 1.2% Asian, 0.2% Amer. Indian, 0.7% Two+ races, 0.3% Other; 1% Hispanic Origin.

2000 Presidential Vote			1996 Presidential Vote		
Bush (R)	122,950	(58%)	Dole (R)	91,619	(46%)
Gore (D)	80,016	(38%)	Clinton (D)	80,003	(40%)
Nader (Green)	5,443	(3%)	Perot (I)	25,687	(13%)
Others	1,990	(1%)			

Rep. John E. Peterson (R)

Elected 1996, 3d term; b. Dec. 25, 1938, Titusville; home, Pleasantville; PA St. U., 1974–76; Methodist; married (Sandy).

Military Career: Army, 1958–64.

Elected Office: Pleasantville Borough Cncl., 1969–77; PA House of Reps., 1977–84; PA Senate, 1984–96.

Professional Career: Owner, Peterson's Golden Dawn Food Market, 1958–84.

DC Office: 307 CHOB 20515, 202-225-5121; Fax: 202-225-5796; Web site: www.house.gov/johnpeterson.

District Offices: State College, 814-238-1776; Titusville, 814-827-3985; Warren, 814-726-3910.

Committees: *Appropriations* (30th of 35 R): Interior; Labor, HHS & Education; Treasury, Postal Service & General Government. *Resources* (17th of 28 R): Forests & Forest Health (Vice Chmn.).

Group Ratings

	ADA	ACLU	AFS	LCV	CON	ITIC	NTU	COC	ACU	NTLC	CHC
2000	0	15	0	0	45	93	63	90	96	67	100
1999	5	—	0	0	4	—	47	100	80	—	—

National Journal Ratings

	1999 LIB —	1999 CONS		2000 LIB —	2000 CONS
Economic	24%	76%		15%	83%
Social	0%	96%		30%	68%
Foreign	30%	69%		25%	69%

Key Votes of the 106th Congress

1. Patient Bill of Rights	N	5. Bar RU-486 $ for FDA	Y	9. NATO War in Serbia	N
2. Accelerate Min. Wage	N	6. Display 10 Commandments	Y	10. Perm. Trade with China	Y
3. Strike Ban on Ergo. Stnd.	N	7. Gun Show Bkgrnd. Checks	N	11. Debt Relief for 3rd World	N
4. Ovrd. Estate Tax Veto	Y	8. Ban Part.-Birth Abortion	Y	12. Drop Cuba Econ. Embargo	N

Election Results

2000 general	John E. Peterson (R)	147,570	(83%)	($413,790)
	Thomas A. Martin (LIB)	17,020	(10%)	
	William M. Belitskus (Green)	13,857	(8%)	
2000 primary	John E. Peterson (R)	unopposed		
1998 general	John E. Peterson (R)	99,502	(85%)	($245,311)
	William M. Belitskus (Green)	17,734	(15%)	

SIXTH DISTRICT

The gentle hills of southeastern Pennsylvania, settled in the 18th Century by Quaker townsmen, Welsh farmers, German peasants, and members of pietistic sects who became known as the Pennsylvania Dutch, were America's first polyglot interior. A diverse lot looking for tolerance in the area above Philadelphia and the Delaware River and below the first chains of the Appalachians, they found a land that yielded riches, first in crops, then in ironworking and other industry. This was the Pennsylvania John Updike described in his 1960 novel *Rabbit, Run* and its sequels. In time this civilization poured over the mountain chains, where the farmers were rough-hewn and more violence-prone, and where the towns existed solely to mine rich veins of anthracite and bituminous coal, the primary energy source of late 19th and early 20th Century America. These mountain towns were less orderly, filled with tough-talking miners and factory workers who stayed menacingly in the background unless a character stumbled into the wrong roadhouse at night or the wrong diner at dawn: This was the Pennsylvania John O'Hara grew up in and described in his 1930s and 1940s novels and stories.

These two areas were linked by the Reading Railroad in 1842 and became one of America's prime industrial sites for a century after. The anthracite country around Pottsville, nestled amid mountains, has never rebounded from the switch from coal to oil and natural gas for home heating: With a disproportionately aging population, Schuylkill County around Pottsville had 228,000 people in 1940 and 150,000 in 2000. But Reading has come back, starting in 1970, when a company called Vanity Fair began selling seconds and overruns of stockings and lingerie at wholesale prices in what had been the Berkshire Knitting Mills; this was the first of the factory outlets. Reading has become home to more than 300 outlets, selling deeply-discounted goods on the polished wood floors of converted brick mills, bringing in more than half a billion dollars a year, generating thousands of jobs and spawning 2,200 motel and hotel rooms. In the 1990s Reading and Berks County attracted a large number of Hispanics, who found jobs in a growing though not terribly affluent economy.

The 6th Congressional District includes Berks and Schuylkill Counties centered on Reading and Pottsville, plus an almost unconnected sliver of Northumberland County, an industrial area between mountains and the upper Susquehanna River. It is politically divided between the quietism of the Pennsylvania Dutch and the rough mining tradition of the anthracite country, between Republican Berks County and more Democratic Schuylkill County.

The congressman from the 6th District is Tim Holden, a Democrat first elected in 1992. Holden comes from a political family from the coal mining hamlet of St. Clair; his great-grandfather was a coal miner who founded the forerunner to the United Mine Workers, and his father served four terms as Schuylkill County commissioner. Holden gained fame as a local football player, although tuberculosis cut short his college career. In 1985, at age 28, after selling insurance and real estate for five years, he was elected Schuylkill County sheriff, and re-elected with 75%. Holden's opponent in the 1992 Congressional race was John Jones III, a lawyer who ran a family business operating golf courses: two characters out of Updike and O'Hara. Jones called Holden "clueless" and backed term limits and congressional salary cuts; Holden said he represented "the hardworking men and women" of the district. In culturally conservative but economically polarized Schuylkill County, this appeal sold, and Holden won 52%–48%.

Holden has a moderate voting record: He has consistently been near the middle of the House on economic, cultural and foreign issues. He is one of the centrist Blue Dog Democrats. "The problems our country is facing need to be solved in a bipartisan manner," he says. "There's about 70 liberals and 70 ultraconservatives still in the House. They need to be left behind." He opposed NAFTA and the Clinton health care plan, but backed welfare reform and health care portability. He opposed any tax cut or spending increase until the Treasury fully reimburses the social security trust fund, but voted in 2000 to override Bill Clinton's veto of the marriage-penalty tax repeal and favors an increase in tax thresholds for the estate tax. He is anti-abortion, and opposed the FDA's approval of the RU-486 drug. On the Agriculture Committee, Holden looks after dairy programs; he wants the government to buy more cheese, increase the flow of dairy products in international food aid and resume a dairy export subsidy program; he asked for an antitrust investigation of why milk prices remain so high. He wants to increase black lung benefits for miners and persuaded the Environmental Protection Agency to drop its proposal to declare ash from coal-burning power plants a hazardous substance. Most of all, he works the district hard, talking issues and solving constituents' problems. As the Pottsville *Republican & Evening Herald* wrote, "It would be hard to imagine a legislator more precisely in tune with his county on virtually any and every issue that has come before Congress in the past four years." Holden has won reelection easily even as the district goes Republican for other offices, as it did for George W. Bush in 2000.

Redistricting poses a serious threat to Holden's career. Pennsylvania lost two House seats in the 2000 Census, and Republicans control the redistricting process. There was wide speculation in early 2001 that Holden would be placed in the same seat with 11th District Democrat Paul Kanjorski. This would be a byproduct of the Republicans' apparent strategy in metro Philadelphia. They seem likely to extend the Philadelphia districts outward into suburban Montgomery County, removing Democratic townships from the 13th District held by Democrat Joseph Hoeffel. That would leave much of what remains from Montgomery County to be combined with a majority of Berks County in a new district—making it a significantly more Republican seat. Then, they would create a new district centered on Luzerne and Schuylkill County; it would include Holden's base, but more territory would come from Kanjorski's 11th. This would be a pretty safe Democratic seat, but would force Holden into a primary against Kanjorski in which he would probably be at a disadvantage.

Cook's Call *Potentially Competitive.* This conservative district is not friendly Democratic territory, but Holden's deep local roots and conservative voting record have made him a difficult target. Republicans, who control the redistricting process, are reportedly interested in combining his seat with fellow Democrat Paul Kanjorski's 11th District.

THE PEOPLE: Pop. 2000: 600,437; Pop. 1990: 565,923, up 6.1% 1990–2000. 90.8% White, 3.5% Black, 0.8% Asian, 0.1% Amer. Indian, 1.2% Two+ races, 3.6% Other; 6.6% Hispanic Origin.

2000 Presidential Vote			**1996 Presidential Vote**		
Bush (R)	114,826	(53%)	Dole (R)	89,695	(45%)
Gore (D)	94,419	(43%)	Clinton (D)	83,779	(42%)
Nader (Green)	5,746	(3%)	Perot (I)	25,139	(13%)
Others	2,175	(1%)			

Rep. Tim Holden (D)

Elected 1992, 5th term; b. Mar. 5, 1957, Pottsville; home, St. Clair; U. of Richmond, 1976–78, Bloomsburg St. U., B.A. 1980; Catholic; married (Gwen).

Elected Office: Schuylkill Cnty. Sheriff, 1985–92.

Professional Career: Real estate agent; Insurance broker, Holden Insurance Agency, 1980–85; Probation Officer, 1980–85.

DC Office: 2417 RHOB 20515, 202-225-5546; Fax: 202-226-0996; Web site: www.house.gov/holden.

District Offices: Pottsville, 570-622-4212; Reading, 610-371-9931.

Committees: *Agriculture* (7th of 24 D): Department Operations, Oversight, Nutrition & Forestry; Livestock & Horticulture. *Transportation & Infrastructure* (25th of 34 D): Aviation; Highways & Transit.

Group Ratings

	ADA	ACLU	AFS	LCV	CON	ITIC	NTU	COC	ACU	NTLC	CHC
2000	55	29	100	43	86	72	26	50	32	21	47
1999	65	—	100	56	68	—	25	58	28	—	—

National Journal Ratings

	1999 LIB	—	1999 CONS		2000 LIB	—	2000 CONS
Economic	56%	—	44%		62%	—	37%
Social	47%	—	53%		40%	—	59%
Foreign	59%	—	40%		51%	—	47%

Key Votes of the 106th Congress

1. Patient Bill of Rights	Y	5. Bar RU-486 $ for FDA	Y	9. NATO War in Serbia	Y
2. Accelerate Min. Wage	Y	6. Display 10 Commandments	N	10. Perm. Trade with China	N
3. Strike Ban on Ergo. Stnd.	Y	7. Gun Show Bkgrnd. Checks	N	11. Debt Relief for 3rd World	N
4. Ovrd. Estate Tax Veto	N	8. Ban Part.-Birth Abortion	Y	12. Drop Cuba Econ. Embargo	N

Election Results

2000 general	Tim Holden (D)	140,084	(66%)	($417,147)
	Thomas G. Kopel (R)	71,227	(34%)	($30,913)
2000 primary	Tim Holden (D) .... unopposed			
1998 general	Tim Holden (D)	85,374	(61%)	($602,163)
	John Meckley (R)	54,579	(39%)	($175,568)

SEVENTH DISTRICT

The close-in suburbs of the great eastern cities are homes to some of the most curious and long-lasting political machines in America. They are Republican; they conduct business in the accents of ordinary people, ethnic as well as WASP; they have a tolerance for patronage, and for what city reform liberals would call corruption, that is sharply at odds with their embodiment of middle-class morality; they are old, going back to the days when political machines were as much a part of the urban landscape as trolley lines or overhead electrical wires; and, unlike most big-city Democratic machines, a few of them are still in business. One such machine is the War Board of Pennsylvania's Delaware County. This is a diverse area, mostly but not entirely white, predominantly Catholic where it was predominantly Protestant two generations ago. Its housing is aging but well-maintained; its population is above average in income but differs from the affluent Main Line commuter towns. People here have deep roots in greater Philadelphia, but also deep fears about crime in nearby city neighborhoods.

The 7th Congressional District includes almost all of Delaware County, except for a few towns appended to Philadelphia districts, and extends north to include Main Line suburbs and King of Prussia, the edge city where the Schuylkill Expressway intersects the Pennsylvania Turnpike. For many years this has been a solidly Republican district, but in national politics it trended toward Democrats in the 1990s, voting narrowly for Bill Clinton in 1996 and Al Gore in 2000.

The congressman from the 7th District is Curt Weldon, a Republican backed by the War Board and with anything but an aristocratic pedigree. A teacher and personnel trainer, he first came to public attention as mayor of Marcus Hook, Pennsylvania's southernmost town on the Delaware River, the home of oil tank farms and a rusty-looking steel mill. Weldon was elected to the county council, ran for the House in 1984 against liberal Democrat Bob Edgar (who got to Congress when the War Board split 10 years earlier), lost by 412 votes, then ran successfully in 1986 when Edgar ran unsuccessfully for the Senate.

Weldon started off as a local congressman, and has become a major force on international issues of the greatest import. Weldon is usually a partisan Republican but not always a free-market enthusiast; like Pennsylvanian Republicans of yore, he supports trade restrictions and voted against NAFTA and fast-track legislation. Although he has supported unions on some issues, including family-leave legislation, he is a co-sponsor of Davis-Bacon reform and favors the flextime plan to permit workers to take compensatory time off rather than overtime pay. He strongly backs the partial-birth abortion ban. As a former volunteer fireman, he founded the Congressional Fire Services Caucus; he pushed in 2000 for the reopening of Engine Company No. 3 in the District of Columbia, to better protect the Capitol. In 2000 he also started an Oceans Caucus—fire and water—and asked Maine Democrat Tom Allen to lead it. Prompted by the murder of a local young woman by a man released from prison after serving only 11 years for murder, he worked for passage in 2000 of Aimee's law, with incentives for states to impose strong sentences on criminals convicted of rape, murder and child molestation. He pushed successfully for $3 million to buy lands for and maintain the Brandywine Battlefield and $1.2 million for the Paoli battlefield. Urged by Newt Gingrich to be tested, he discovered in 1996 that he has diabetes, and has become a spokesman for testing and treatment.

Weldon is now a senior member of the Armed Services Committee and has had a major impact on military policy. After he spotlighted the discovery of the Soviet radar at Krasnoyarsk, a violation of the ABM treaty, he has been for more than a decade a strong advocate of missile defense. Since 1994 he has held more than 100 briefings and hearings on the subject. In 1995 he challenged CIA estimates that there was no missile threat from rogue states; in 1996 he and 40 other members sued the Clinton administration to get appropriated funds spent; in 1997 he bluntly told the general in charge of the program, "I can't trust you." His warnings were vindicated by the July 1998 Rumsfeld report revealing that missile threats could come from rogue states without notice, and he has kept pressing hard for missile defense ever since.

Another Weldon interest is Russia. A Russian studies major in college, he initiated a U.S. Congress-Duma Study Group and meets regularly with senior Russian officials, both in Moscow and Washington. He criticized, sometimes in sharp terms, the Clinton administration for ignoring most Russian politicians and parliamentarians and basing policy excessively on relations with Boris Yeltsin and Viktor Chernomyrdin. He worries that crime, corruption and internal disintegration are so rampant in Russia that nuclear-weapons theft "seems entirely plausible." He is concerned that Russia is dumping nuclear waste in the ocean. And he harshly criticized the Clinton administration's approval of export licenses for commercial satellite sales to China that likely revealed vital weapons technology. He also criticized Clinton for weakening national defense by over-extending military forces and equipment with a record number of deployments. He has encouraged investment in Russia, supports funding a private mortgage program for Russians and invited Russian parliamentarians and others to visit the Republican National Convention in Philadelphia.

Weldon is quite possibly the House's strongest advocate of the Marine Corps's V-22 Osprey, one of whose prime contractors, the Boeing helicopter division, is located in Ridley Park in Delaware County. The plane, which flies on both rotors and wings, was cancelled by Defense Secretary Dick Cheney in 1989, but reinstated by Congress soon after. Since then, Weldon has assembled an Osprey coalition that has kept it alive despite crashes in 1991, 1992 and 2000. "We had a coalition broad and deep. We had the ex-Marines in Congress. We brought in the retired Marine reserve officers' association. I brought in the United Auto Workers and the civil aviation people." The latest crash in December 2000 and allegations that test results were rigged put the Osprey again in peril, but Weldon and his coalition vowed to "reinvigorate the debate" in 2001. He has fought as well to bring jobs to the Philadelphia Naval Shipyard after it was abandoned by the Navy. As a result of his efforts and those of others, the Navy now has a machinery systems research and development center there; the Kvaerner Philadelphia Shipyard began work in 2000 and component supplier Alstom set up shop a month later.

At the Republican convention in 2000, he set up a Congressional Village next to the First Union Center convention hall, where members of Congress could get Philadelphia cheese steaks, entertain their families, get some rest or exercise. This was part of a campaign to become chairman of the Armed Services Committee. With Floyd Spence approaching his six-year term limit, Weldon began contributing generously to other Republicans—$440,000 to the House Republican campaign committee, a total of $1.4 million to Republicans in 1999 and 2000. He campaigned in 29 districts. After the election, he ran against Bob Stump, who followed Spence in seniority. That raised some hackles. Duncan Hunter supported Stump, whom he followed in seniority, and said that he should get the chairmanship if Stump didn't. In any case, the Republican Steering Committee picked Stump. Weldon remained a subcommittee chairman but was unhappy about his setback; he initially encouraged speculation that he might take a position in the Bush Administration or run for governor, but said in April 2001 that he planned to remain in Congress.

Weldon has been reelected every two years by robust margins. Pennsylvania lost two House seats in the 2000 Census. Republicans control redistricting, and change in Delaware County does not appear part of their plans. So Weldon likely will have a similar district in which to run in 2002.

Cook's Call *Safe*. Like other suburban areas, this former Republican stronghold is trending toward Democrats at the national level. Clinton won here by 2% in 1996 while Gore won by 3% in 2000. As long as Weldon stays he is likely to win re-election.

THE PEOPLE: Pop. 2000: 587,281; Pop. 1990: 565,815, up 3.8% 1990–2000. 88.8% White, 5.8% Black, 3.9% Asian, 0.1% Amer. Indian, 1.1% Two + races, 0.4% Other; 1.3% Hispanic Origin.

2000 Presidential Vote
Gore (D)	138,511	(50%)
Bush (R)	131,554	(47%)
Nader (Green)	6,227	(2%)
Others	2,014	(1%)

1996 Presidential Vote
Clinton (D)	116,654	(45%)
Dole (R)	112,429	(44%)
Perot (I)	23,647	(9%)
Others	4,338	(2%)

Rep. Curt Weldon (R)

Elected 1986, 8th term; b. July 22, 1947, Marcus Hook; home, Aston; West Chester St. Col., B.A. 1969; Protestant; married (Mary).

Elected Office: Marcus Hook Mayor, 1977–82; Delaware Cnty. Cncl., 1982–86, Chmn. 1985–86.

Professional Career: Elem. schl. teacher & Vice principal, 1969–76; Dir., Training & Manpower Devel., CIGNA Corp., 1976–81.

DC Office: 2466 RHOB 20515, 202-225-2011; Fax: 202-225-8137; Web site: www.house.gov/curtweldon.

District Office: Upper Darby, 610-259-0700.

Committees: *Armed Services* (5th of 32 R): Military Readiness (Chmn.); Military Research & Development. *Science* (5th of 25 R): Environment, Technology and Standards; Research.

Group Ratings
	ADA	ACLU	AFS	LCV	CON	ITIC	NTU	COC	ACU	NTLC	CHC
2000	5	7	28	43	34	100	54	80	76	68	79
1999	20	—	16	25	10	—	52	68	73	—	—

National Journal Ratings
	1999 LIB —	1999 CONS		2000 LIB —	2000 CONS
Economic	47%	52%		46%	52%
Social	32%	66%		30%	68%
Foreign	37%	63%		0%	88%

Key Votes of the 106th Congress
1. Patient Bill of Rights	Y	5. Bar RU-486 $ for FDA	Y	9. NATO War in Serbia	N
2. Accelerate Min. Wage	Y	6. Display 10 Commandments	Y	10. Perm. Trade with China	Y
3. Strike Ban on Ergo. Stnd.	Y	7. Gun Show Bkgrnd. Checks	N	11. Debt Relief for 3rd World	N
4. Ovrd. Estate Tax Veto	Y	8. Ban Part.-Birth Abortion	Y	12. Drop Cuba Econ. Embargo	N

Election Results
2000 general	Curt Weldon (R)	172,569	(65%)	($618,319)
	Peter A. Lennon (D)	93,687	(35%)	($22,578)
2000 primary	Curt Weldon (R)	unopposed		
1998 general	Curt Weldon (R)	119,491	(72%)	($493,502)
	Martin J. D'Urso (D)	46,920	(28%)	($6,677)

EIGHTH DISTRICT

One of William Penn's three original settlements, Bucks County had a split personality from the start. It was a paradise of bucolic hills and creeks running into the Delaware River and, after Penn's secretary James Logan built the Durham Furnace iron works in 1727, one of the nation's major industrial sites. In the 1920s, Bucks County's well-settled farmland, old fieldstone houses and covered bridges in its northern parts captured the imagination of writers and artists, attracting the New York theatrical crowd—Oscar Hammerstein, Moss Hart, Dorothy Parker, S. J. Perelman. After World War II, its location between Philadelphia and Trenton, New Jersey, brought the industrial part of Bucks to the forefront. The ocean-navigable Delaware River and several rail lines resulted in huge new developments: U.S. Steel's Fairless Works, one of the few big postwar steel plants, down by the river, and the Levitt organization's second Levittown, in what had been farmland and swamp between U.S. 13 and U.S. 1. But now the steel mill is closed, and Bucks County's economy depends more on modern technologies.

Bucks County's political tradition was heavily Republican and protectionist; more recently it has been marginally Republican and environmentalist. This was the home of Senator Joseph Grundy, longtime head of the Pennsylvania Manufacturers Association, who opposed the 1930 Smoot-Hawley tariff as not protectionist enough. Development in Bucks came after the New Deal, unlike other suburban Philadelphia counties where most blue-collar immigration occurred years earlier, when county political organizations were ready to enroll new residents in their party. So Lower Bucks around the Fairless Works and Levittown, with its tightly-packed homes filled with blue collar workers, became Democratic. And Upper Bucks, faster-growing and still attracting trendy New Yorkers, is Republican but environment-conscious.

The 8th Congressional District includes all of Bucks County plus Horsham Township in Montgomery County. One of the few districts in the country with boundaries almost entirely unchanged for the last two decades, it was marginal in congressional elections between 1976 and 1992, and voted narrowly twice for Bill Clinton in 1992 and 1996 and gave Al Gore a slight margin in 2000. But in other elections it has remained mostly Republican.

The congressman from the 8th District is Jim Greenwood, a Republican elected in 1992. Greenwood grew up in Newtown, on the margin between Lower Bucks and Upper Bucks. After college he worked for a state legislator, then was a social worker in Langhorne. He was elected to the state House in 1980 and the state Senate in 1986. In 1992 he ran against Peter Kostmayer, an environment-minded, defense-cutting liberal, who first won the seat in 1976 and held it with one two-year exception by spotlighting environmental issues at home and raising large sums nationally from admirers of his leftish foreign and environmental stands. But Kostmayer had 50 overdrafts on the House bank and other financial problems, and Greenwood won 52%–46%.

In the House, Greenwood's voting record has been conservative on economic issues and moderate-to-liberal on cultural issues. He has worked closely with Republican leaders and was the moderate Tuesday Group's representative at Republican leadership meetings; in 1997 Speaker Newt Gingrich appointed him to head the House Republican long-term planning team after Bill Paxon resigned the post following the botched "coup" against Gingrich. On impeachment, he was undecided nearly until the vote and displayed his balancing act by voting for House charges but urging the Senate to quickly end the trial with a bipartisan rebuke of Clinton. When Dennis Hastert took over as speaker in 1999, Greenwood sought assurances that moderates would have a voice in the leadership. He sought a bipartisan health care alternative, in vain. One of his big causes has been to maintain funding of international family planning, insisting the issue wasn't abortion. "The whole planet is too fragile to support a runaway population," he says. Domestically, he wants to ensure that all private health insurance covers contraceptives. He has been among the handful of House Republicans opposing the ban on partial-birth abortions.

Greenwood is an active legislator on an array of consumer issues at Energy and Commerce. He worked to pass legislation to speed up FDA approval of drugs. He wants to give state and local governments power to control the disposal of out-of-state solid waste, and in 1999 was lead sponsor of a bill that would allow states to freeze trash imports at 1993 levels. He won committee approval of changes in the Superfund program to relieve liability from small businesses, recyclers and municipalities and to allocate more money to clean up abandoned brownfield sites. On another Commerce issue, he helped to write legislation restricting Internet pornography's availability to kids, but a federal appeals court issued an injunction against it. As the new chairman in 2001 of the Oversight and Investigations Subcommittee, he targeted rising prices by insurance and pharmaceutical companies, demanded proof that government agencies protect against computer hackers, and held hearings on human cloning. He won enactment in 2000 of a long-sought plan to designate the Delaware River through Monroe and Bucks counties as wild and scenic, which blocks spending on public works projects there. But the national Sierra Club dropped its endorsement in 2000 because his environmental voting record had slipped on issues such as wetlands protections and polluter penalties. After the 2000 election, he helped organize a bipartisan centrist coalition in the House.

Greenwood's political formula still seems to suit the 8th District well. He has been re-elected comfortably. His problem has been conservative Republicans: In the past three cycles, he had competitive primary challenges, and won with between 60% and 67% of the vote. He has said he might be interested in running for the Senate if Arlen Specter retires in 2004. Redistricting is not likely to be a problem. Pennsylvania lost two seats in the 2000 Census and many districts will be greatly reshaped. But the Republicans who control redistricting can maintain the current 8th with only the most minor of adjustments, changing the lines a bit in Montgomery County, while pursuing their other objectives; if so, this district will retain its basic shape longer than almost any other in a state with more than a few districts.

Cook's Call   *Safe*. Though this district is quite competitive on the national level (Gore won here by 4% in 2000), Greenwood is difficult to beat. His moderate voting record, especially on social issues, has insulated him from tough challenges. Redistricting in and around the Philadelphia region will have an impact here, but Greenwood should be safe in 2002.

THE PEOPLE: Pop. 2000: 624,248; Pop. 1990: 565,820, up 10.3% 1990–2000. 92.4% White, 3.3% Black, 2.4% Asian, 0.1% Amer. Indian, 1% Two+ races, 0.8% Other; 2.3% Hispanic Origin.

2000 Presidential Vote		
Gore (D)	138,605	(50%)
Bush (R)	128,022	(46%)
Nader (Green)	6,531	(2%)
Others	2,354	(1%)

1996 Presidential Vote		
Clinton (D)	107,500	(45%)
Dole (R)	99,458	(42%)
Perot (I)	25,570	(11%)
Others	4,771	(2%)

Rep. Jim Greenwood (R)

Elected 1992, 6th term; b. May 4, 1951, Philadelphia; home, Erwinna; Dickinson Col., B.A. 1973; Protestant; married (Christina).

Elected Office: PA House of Reps., 1980–86; PA Senate, 1986–93.

Professional Career: Legis. Asst., PA Rep. John Renninger, 1972–76; Social worker, Woods Schools, 1974–76; Caseworker, Bucks Cnty. Children & Youth Social Svc. Agency, 1977–80.

DC Office: 2436 RHOB 20515, 202-225-4276; Fax: 202-225-9511; Web site: www.house.gov/greenwood.

District Offices: Doylestown, 215-348-7511; Langhorne, 215-752-7711.

Committees: *Education & the Workforce* (9th of 27 R): Education Reform; Select Education. *Energy & Commerce* (7th of 31 R): Environment & Hazardous Materials; Health; Oversight & Investigations (Chmn.).

Group Ratings

	ADA	ACLU	AFS	LCV	CON	ITIC	NTU	COC	ACU	NTLC	CHC
2000	25	71	0	50	16	94	53	77	60	69	40
1999	70	—	16	50	6	—	55	76	41	—	—

National Journal Ratings

	1999 LIB —	1999 CONS		2000 LIB —	2000 CONS
Economic	46%	53%		43%	56%
Social	67%	33%		65%	35%
Foreign	47%	53%		12%	78%

Key Votes of the 106th Congress

1. Patient Bill of Rights	Y	5. Bar RU-486 $ for FDA	N	9. NATO War in Serbia	N
2. Accelerate Min. Wage	Y	6. Display 10 Commandments	N	10. Perm. Trade with China	Y
3. Strike Ban on Ergo. Stnd.	*	7. Gun Show Bkgrnd. Checks	Y	11. Debt Relief for 3rd World	N
4. Ovrd. Estate Tax Veto	*	8. Ban Part.-Birth Abortion	N	12. Drop Cuba Econ. Embargo	N

Election Results

2000 general	Jim Greenwood (R)	154,090	(59%)	($889,821)
	Ronald L. Strouse (D)	100,617	(39%)	($146,563)
	Others	5,394	(2%)	
2000 primary	Jim Greenwood (R)	25,170	(67%)	
	Tom Lingenfelter (R)	12,278	(33%)	
1998 general	Jim Greenwood (R)	93,697	(63%)	($915,287)
	Bill Tuthill (D)	48,320	(33%)	($22,681)
	Others	6,183	(4%)	

NINTH DISTRICT

Like a series of vertebrae through central Pennsylvania, the Appalachian mountain chain has been a formidable barrier throughout most of the state's history. Up close the mountains look tantalizingly low: you imagine that you could hike over them in an hour or so. But they are much more daunting than they seem. The colonials and British regulars (led by General Braddock to defeat near Pittsburgh in 1754) found it hard going, despite guidance from George Washington; 19th Century pioneers in Conestoga wagons found it not much easier, for there are few gaps in the ridges and, unless you build a tunnel, you have to climb over the top. During the 18th Century, the mountains provided Quaker Pennsylvania with a rampart against Indian attacks and allowed the commonwealth to become the richest and most populous of the colonies. But in the 19th Century, when people wanted to open up and trade with the vast interior, the mountains proved to be a barrier, and at first people traveled via New York's Erie Canal and New York Central Railroad instead. It took the aggressive capitalists who built the Pennsylvania Railroad to get trains over these ridges, and a nation facing war in 1940 to build the first highway, the Pennsylvania Turnpike, that could dependably get trucks over them. Today, the old towns look much as they did 60 years ago; the farmhouses and red barns still sit on rolling hills in the shadow of the ridges, seemingly isolated and out of touch with the pulsing rhythms of 21st Century America.

Pennsylvania's 9th Congressional District lies wholly within these mountains. This part of the Alleghenies (the term is often used interchangeably with Appalachians in Pennsylvania) was settled by poor Scottish and Ulster Irish farmers just after the Revolutionary War. They were fiercely independent and proud, as the Whiskey Rebellion demonstrated; corn was not an article of commerce out here unless distilled into easily portable, if not very potable, alcohol. The settlers worked their hardscrabble farms and built little towns. Most of the 9th is not coal country and was thus spared the boom-bust cycles of northeastern Pennsylvania and West Virginia. This was an important area for the Pennsylvania Railroad, however. Near Altoona was the railroad's famous Horseshoe Curve, and in Altoona the nation's largest car yards were built. As rail transportation became less important and the prosperous Pennsylvania Railroad became the bankrupt Penn Central, Altoona's population fell from 82,000 in 1930 to 49,000 in 2000. It has benefited in recent years from economic diversity, including growth in health-care employers, a new convention center in Blair County, and a service center for truck-based distribution operations. This part of Pennsylvania has been solidly Republican since 1860 and has not come close to electing a Democrat to Congress for decades.

The congressman from the 9th District is Bill Shuster, a Republican first elected in a special election in May 2001, which was scheduled after his father Bud Shuster, for six years the powerful Chairman of the Transportation and Infrastructure Committee, announced his resignation in January 2001, after his attempts to get an exception from the Republicans' six-year term limit on chairmanships failed. "I have been chairman of the largest and most productive committee in Congress. I have no desire to do less," he said. As Transportation Chairman, Bud Shuster was both a generous local benefactor and a serious national policymaker; his work can be seen not only in the Bud Shuster Highway (as Interstate 99 in Bedford and Blair Counties is known) but also in transportation projects sprinkled across the country in the giant May 1998 TEA-21 bill, and in the fact that Shuster guaranteed his committee a revenue stream from gas and other user taxes free from control by the Appropriations Committee. He also was the subject of an ethics committee investigation into his relationship with transportation lobbyist Ann Eppard, his former chief of staff, who had pleaded guilty in November 1999 to misdemeanor charges after being indicted for corruption and illegal payments; the committee concluded that Shuster had engaged in a "pattern and practice" that created the appearance that his official decisions might have been improperly affected.

Bill Shuster grew up in the Pittsburgh area, where his father started a successful business. After attending Dickinson College and earning an M.B.A. from American University, he moved to Blair County, where he owned the family's car dealership, Shuster Chrysler in East Freedom, near Altoona. Although he was a newcomer to politics, he had plenty of experience from observing his father. "You don't grow up in a family that has been involved in politics for 28 years and not develop an interest in it," he said.

The contest for the House seat was for all practical purposes decided at a district-wide Republican convention on February 17, when Bill Shuster won 69 of 133 votes, two more than the required majority. Facing nine other contenders, Shuster—with back-room help from his father—ran an insider campaign that took advantage of the family's years of service and favors to the district. Under state law for the special election, delegates were nominated by either the local party or party chairman, with the number of delegates based on George W. Bush's local showing in the presidential election. Although there was some local grumbling about a Shuster dynasty and a desire for new blood, opposing factions failed to coalesce behind a single candidate. In a key move, Shuster's allies obtained a state court injunction forcing a vote on a new slate of delegates for Blair County after claiming that the original slate supporting his opponent had been seated in violation of the rules; Shuster was aided by state Senate president Bob Jubelirer, who is from Blair County. At the convention, state representative Pat Fleagle finished second with 38 votes (mostly from his base in Franklin County) and Blair County commissioner John Eichelberger—a long-time adversary, whom Bud Shuster termed "unfit to hold any position of public trust"—finished third with only 10 of his home county's 28 delegates. In the general election in the heavily Republican district that had not elected a Democrat since the New Deal, Shuster ran ads touting his "hardwork, real world experience" and "conservative values." With appearances by Governor Ridge and Speaker Hastert and a radio ad by George W. Bush, he defeated H. Scott Conklin, whom the Democrats chose at their own convention; Conklin campaigned vigorously on his anti-gun control, anti-abortion views, but House Democrats had no expectation of winning this seat in a district that Bush carried by 2–1. Shuster won by a closer than expected 52%–44%, which Republicans attributed to residual intra-party ill will over his nomination. Citing the local rock-ribbed Republicanism, House Democratic leaders dismissed second-guessing that they should have invested more resources in the contest.

Although Bill Shuster will have to make his own way in the House, he began with a promise from the new Transportation Chairman, Don Young, that he could have his father's seat on the committee. Republican control in Harrisburg means that he probably won't face trouble in redistricting.

Cook's Call   *Safe.* Though Shuster had an underwhelming 52% to 44% win over Democrat Scott Conklin in the May 15 special election, it is highly unlikely that Shuster will be challenged in this heavily Republican district in 2002.

THE PEOPLE: Pop. 2000: 588,138; Pop. 1990: 565,858, up 3.9% 1990–2000. 97% White, 1.6% Black, 0.3% Asian, 0.1% Amer. Indian, 0.6% Two+ races, 0.3% Other; 0.9% Hispanic Origin.

2000 Presidential Vote

Bush (R)	138,734	(65%)
Gore (D)	69,024	(32%)
Nader (Green)	3,625	(2%)
Others	1,527	(1%)

1996 Presidential Vote

Dole (R)	102,847	(53%)
Clinton (D)	70,206	(36%)
Perot (I)	21,239	(11%)

Rep. Bill Shuster (R)

Elected May 2001, 1st term; b. Jan. 10, 1961, McKeesport; home, Hollidaysburg; Dickinson Col., B.A. 1983; American U., M.B.A. 1987; Lutheran; married (Rebecca).

Professional Career: Mgr., Goodyear Tire & Rubber Co., 1983–87; District Mgr., Bandag Inc., 1987–90; Gen. Mgr., Shuster Chrysler, 1990–2001.

DC Office: 2188 RHOB 20515, 202-225-2431.

Committees: *Small Business* (19th of 19 R). *Transportation & Infrastructure* (41st of 42 R).

Group Ratings and Key Votes: Newly Elected

Election Results

2001 special	Bill Shuster (R)	55,549	(52%)	($490,469)
	Scott Conklin (D)	47,049	(44%)	($237,971)
	Alanna Hartzok (Green)	4,420	(4%)	
2000 general	Bud Shuster (R)	unopposed		($1,150,318)
2000 primary	Bud Shuster (R)	unopposed		

TENTH DISTRICT

"Coal is the theme song of this city in the hills," the *WPA Guide* said of Scranton in the middle of the 20th Century. But as those words were written, the anthracite kingdom was dying. Demand for hard coal as a home heating fuel started falling in the 1920s and plummeted in the 1940s; the three major anthracite counties in Pennsylvania had 991,000 people in 1930 and 683,000 in 2000, with Scranton's Lackawanna County dropping from 310,000 to 213,000. In the process, the coal dust and air pollution vanished, the ethnic groups—Irish and Poles, Ukrainians and Welsh—became less distinctive, and what had been boom towns full of young families became time-worn communities of senior citizens. In the 1960s and 1970s, there was an influx of textile and apparel mills, bringing low-wage, non-union jobs to what had once been a high-wage, unionized area. But the anthracite kingdom, created by unbridled free enterprise, was looking to government for sustenance.

The 10th Congressional District is centered on Scranton and includes most of the northeast corner of Pennsylvania—green hills with little towns in crevassed river valleys, criss-crossed by giant viaducts built for the railroads linking coal and iron mines with the great cities' factories, the outer-borough New Yorkers' resorts of the Poconos and, in the three counties closest to New York and New Jersey, new subdivisions for refugees from high taxes. Traffic along the Lackawanna Trail—the once-booming back road from Scranton to Binghamton, New York—has dried up and the rural area has an abandoned feel. In the early part of the century all this territory was heavily Republican; since the 1930s Scranton and Lackawanna County have been strongly Democratic and the rest of the district strongly Republican. But for years congressional politics depended less on party than on pork. Joseph McDade, a Republican first elected in 1962, rose to become top-ranking Republican on the Appropriations Committee and worked with members of both parties to bring home the bacon on projects ranging from the $66 million Steamtown train historic site to securing Pentagon contracts for the Chamberlain Manufacturing Corporation's production of howitzer shells. But McDade did not become chairman when the Republicans gained their majority because he had been indicted on charges that he received campaign contributions and speaking fees from officials of a local company for which he helped get a Defense Department minority set-aside contract. When he was eventually acquitted in 1996, McDade became chairman of the Energy and Water Development Subcommittee.

The congressman from the 10th District is Don Sherwood, a Republican elected in 1998.

He has deep roots in Tunkhannock in Wyoming County, 40 winding miles northwest of Scranton. Sherwood became a Chevrolet dealer in 1967—at age 26, the youngest Chevy dealer in the East— and he also served on the Tunkhannock school board since 1975. He raises Belgian horses, which he shows throughout the state. When McDade announced his retirement, Sherwood ran for the seat, assembling a grass-roots organization of 1,800 volunteers and propounding an agenda that combined small business goals to cut taxes and "eliminate the IRS as we know it" with calls for a minimum wage increase and HMO reform. With a personable style and an open wallet—he ultimately spent $795,000 of his own money on the campaign—he won 43% in the eight-candidate Republican primary, well ahead of the 23% for Scranton Mayor James Connors in second place.

The general election was a tougher challenge. The Democratic nominee was Pat Casey, son of former Governor Robert Casey. Pat shared the views of his father, who died in May 2000, a strong opponent of abortion and advocate of government programs to help children, and started off with a big advantage in name identification. He appealed to the pork tradition of northeast Pennsylvania, arguing that by entering Congress at a young age he could aid the district for many years to come, and said that Sherwood's ideas on Social Security and education are "walking in lockstep with Dick Armey and Newt Gingrich." Sherwood argued that he was "a proven job creator" and that his support of a higher minimum wage showed he was alert to the district's needs. Sherwood got a big boost in the closing days when Speaker Newt Gingrich came in and pledged to assign him to fill McDade's seat on the Appropriations, but when Gingrich resigned the offer was not honored and the seat was given to John Peterson. This turned out to be one of the closest races in the nation. Sherwood won by just 515 votes, 49%–48%. Casey carried Lackawanna County by 62%–36%, but it cast only 42% of the total votes—compared to over 50% a generation ago. Sherwood carried the other counties 58%–39%.

In the House, Sherwood compiled a mostly conservative voting record. He supported a bipartisan plan for a one-dollar increase in the minimum wage. But he opposed organized labor with his vote for permanent trade relations with China. He sponsored an amendment of the Death on the High Seas Act to allow damage claims for airline crashes at sea; the victims of the TWA 800 crash off Long Island in 1996 included 21 students and chaperones from the local Montoursville High School, most of whose families had been unable to file claims because of maritime law. He won designation of the Lackawanna Valley as a national heritage area, $12 million for anthracite coal mine cleanup, and $6.7 million for a new maintenance facility at the Tobyhanna Army Depot.

Democrats again nominated Pat Casey to oppose Sherwood in 2000, and both again spent heavily. In vivid contrast to 1992, when then-Governor Casey was barred from speaking to the Democratic convention, Pat Casey paid tribute to his father from the podium of the 2000 convention in Los Angeles. He attacked Sherwood's support for tax cuts for the wealthy and privatization of Social Security. The AFL-CIO ran an ad that Sherwood sided with the pharmaceutical industry on drug coverage for seniors. Sherwood said that he was working to strengthen Medicare and that Casey would say anything to get elected and "has trouble with the truth." Sherwood won by a larger margin this time, 53%–47%, losing Lackawanna County 62%–38% and narrowly in Monroe County but piling up sizable majorities elsewhere. After the election, Republican leaders gave him the Appropriations seat that he was denied two years earlier. Republicans control redistricting, and may try to strengthen Sherwood by shifting Scranton and other parts of Lackawanna County to a new Anthracite-counties district that would lean Democratic, and adding more Republican areas from the 5th or 11th Districts; the district needs a net gain of 33,000 people.

Cook's Call *Potentially Competitive.* Sherwood improved from a 515-vote win against Democrat Pat Casey in 1998 to a 53%–47% victory in the 2000 rematch, which is certain to give pause to other ambitious Democrats. Since Republicans will also try to help shore up this marginal seat through redistricting, Sherwood looks tough to beat in 2002.

THE PEOPLE: Pop. 2000: 613,459; Pop. 1990: 565,777, up 8.4% 1990–2000. 94.9% White, 2.6% Black, 0.6% Asian, 0.2% Amer. Indian, 0.9% Two+ races, 0.8% Other; 2.1% Hispanic Origin.

2000 Presidential Vote
Bush (R)	121,947	(50%)
Gore (D)	114,029	(47%)
Nader (Green)	6,166	(3%)
Others	2,988	(1%)

1996 Presidential Vote
Clinton (D)	95,712	(45%)
Dole (R)	91,629	(43%)
Perot (I)	24,303	(11%)

Rep. Don Sherwood (R)

Elected 1998, 2d term; b. Mar. 5, 1941, Nicholson; home, Tunkhannock; Dartmouth Col., B.A. 1963; Methodist; married (Carol).

Military Career: Army, 1964–66.

Elected Office: Tunkhannock Area Schl. Bd., 1975–98, Pres., 1992–98.

Professional Career: Businessman; Auto dealer, 1967-present.

DC Office: 1223 LHOB 20515, 202-225-3731; Fax: 202-225-9594; Web site: www.house.gov/sherwood.

District Offices: Scranton, 570-346-3834; Williamsport, 570-327-8161.

Committees: *Appropriations* (35th of 35 R): Labor, HHS & Education; The Legislative Branch; Treasury, Postal Service & General Government.

Group Ratings
	ADA	ACLU	AFS	LCV	CON	ITIC	NTU	COC	ACU	NTLC	CHC
2000	10	21	14	14	5	94	56	85	75	63	93
1999	10	—	0	6	11	—	56	88	80	—	—

National Journal Ratings
	1999 LIB —	1999 CONS		2000 LIB —	2000 CONS
Economic	30%	64%		38%	62%
Social	18%	81%		35%	64%
Foreign	47%	53%		25%	69%

Key Votes of the 106th Congress
1. Patient Bill of Rights	Y	5. Bar RU-486 $ for FDA	Y	9. NATO War in Serbia	Y
2. Accelerate Min. Wage	Y	6. Display 10 Commandments	Y	10. Perm. Trade with China	Y
3. Strike Ban on Ergo. Stnd. ·	N	7. Gun Show Bkgrnd. Checks	N	11. Debt Relief for 3rd World	N
4. Ovrd. Estate Tax Veto	Y	8. Ban Part.-Birth Abortion	Y	12. Drop Cuba Econ. Embargo	N

Election Results
2000 general	Don Sherwood (R)	124,830	(53%)	($2,107,286)
	Pat Casey (D)	112,580	(47%)	($1,619,801)
2000 primary	Don Sherwood (R)	unopposed		
1998 general	Don Sherwood (R)	84,275	(49%)	($1,921,129)
	Patrick Casey (D)	83,760	(48%)	($1,287,027)
	Others	5,021	(3%)	

ELEVENTH DISTRICT

One of the major industrial centers of America grew up in the 19th Century, nestled in the valley of the East Branch of the Susquehanna River, surrounded by mountain ridges. The mountains were laced with anthracite coal, the main home-heating fuel of the time. Thousands of immigrants, attracted by the high wages paid to scrape out the coal, flocked to this valley, in the chain of little cities north and south of Wilkes-Barre, named for two backers of the American revolution. While the supply was endless—the area produced 40% of the world's hard coal—the demand was not. The peak year of anthracite production was 1917, and long strikes in 1922 and 1925 quickened the conversion to oil and gas. By the 1930s, the valley around Wilkes-Barre was in decline; surrounding Luzerne County's population, 445,000 in 1930, was 319,000 in 2000.

This is the land of Pennsylvania's 11th Congressional District, including all of Luzerne County and similar land east to the town of Jim Thorpe (named after the Olympic decathlon star and first National Football League President, and the site of his mausoleum) and the Poconos, and west almost to the Susquehanna. A large Democratic voting bloc, the miners, has been here since the 1930s, but there also were a lot of white-collar and rural Republicans. In presidential politics this was a Republican district in the 1980s, Democratic in the 1990s; it went narrowly for Al Gore in 2000. The district long has hungered for federal aid and subsidy, much of which was delivered by Congressman Daniel Flood, a theatrical Democrat who, until he resigned in 1980 amid scandal, used his seat on Appropriations to bring millions of dollars into the anthracite country.

The congressman from the 11th District now is Paul Kanjorski, first elected in 1984. Kanjorski grew up in Nanticoke, near Wilkes-Barre. As a 16-year-old page in 1954, he witnessed the shooting of five congressmen by Puerto Rican terrorists in the House gallery and he was sprayed by dust from the gunfire. After college and law school, both of which he attended but did not graduate from, he passed the bar exam and returned home to practice law; he was a workmen's compensation administrative law judge for nine years and Nanticoke city solicitor for 12. In 1984 he ran for Congress and won the May Democratic primary by pointing out the incumbent was in Central America while flood-soaked Wilkes-Barre area residents had to boil tap water because of contamination. Kanjorski has retained the seat easily ever since.

In the House, Kanjorski's voting record has been liberal on economics and moderate on cultural issues. He is anti-abortion but has voted for international family planning aid. He is skeptical about foreign commitments and Washington lobbyists. He is also a tough partisan. While chairing a subcommittee with jurisdiction over White House operations, he sharply attacked the first Bush White House for lavish spending; Bush once apologized at a breakfast meeting for the skimpy meal, blaming Kanjorski's investigations. But with Bill Clinton in the White House, Kanjorski vociferously attacked fellow Pennsylvanian Bill Clinger's investigation of the White House travel office firings, delaying issuance of the report and saying, "Like horses, we should take it out and shoot it." When Dan Burton chaired the Government Reform Committee's hearings on campaign finance abuses, Kanjorski said the panel "should be holding its meeting in a chamber with padded walls." When the House considered impeachment options in October 1998, he was one of five House Democrats who voted against all impeachment inquiry resolutions. Legislatively, Kanjorski helped to enact credit-union reforms, featuring expanded access to membership. That measure, which he termed "a victory of David over Goliath," was a setback for banks since it overturned a Supreme Court ruling that limited credit union membership to one occupational group. In 2000, he won compensation for workers who were harmed by exposure to beryllium at nuclear weapons plants, including the former facility in Hazle Township in Luzerne County. He sponsored the New Markets community renewal legislation of President Clinton and Speaker Hastert and pushed to expand its tax credits so that more people in his district could qualify. On the massive financial services deregulation bill, he opposed Senator Phil Gramm's provision to weaken the authority of the Federal Home Loan Banks. On the reorganized Financial Services Committee, he is ranking Democrat on the Capital Markets, Insurance and Government Sponsored Enterprises Subcommittee.

Most important to Kanjorski is helping his economically ailing district. *The New York Times* called him "a master of earmarking" for capturing millions of dollars for the Earth Conservancy Applied Research Center, a public-private project for developing new technologies to reclaim mine-ravaged northeastern Pennsylvania. When Bill Clinton called for 10 more National Historic Rivers, Kanjorski set the designation of the Susquehanna as his main district project. Although the river was not included on the original list, Kanjorski's intervention led Clinton to expand the list to 14—including the Susquehanna. Referring to the White House, he boasted to his local newspaper, "They know I'm a nag."

Redistricting could shake up the district lines in anthracite country. Republicans control the redistricting process, and in early 2001 seemed to be looking to combine most of Kanjorski's 11th District with much of Democrat Tim Holden's 6th District, perhaps even including some of Lackawanna County from the 10th District. That would probably mean that Kanjorski would face

Holden in a Democratic primary; the edge would go to whoever had previously represented more of the new district—probably Kanjorski. This new district would be heavily Democratic, but it would result in the election of one less Democratic congressman.

Cook's Call *Potentially Competitive.* Although this is a marginal district at the national level (Gore only won here by 3% in 2000), Kanjorski has had little trouble getting re-elected. But Republicans are discussing a redistricting plan that combines Kanjorski's district with that of Democrat Tim Holden, which would create one Democratic-leaning coal district.

THE PEOPLE: Pop. 2000: 579,470; Pop. 1990: 565,802, up 2.4% 1990–2000. 96.2% White, 1.9% Black, 0.6% Asian, 0.1% Amer. Indian, 0.7% Two+ races, 0.5% Other; 1.7% Hispanic Origin.

2000 Presidential Vote

Gore (D)	104,592	(49%)
Bush (R)	98,851	(47%)
Nader (Green)	6,091	(3%)
Others	2,696	(1%)

1996 Presidential Vote

Clinton (D)	97,393	(48%)
Dole (R)	76,969	(38%)
Perot (I)	25,597	(13%)

Rep. Paul E. Kanjorski (D)

Elected 1984, 9th term; b. Apr. 2, 1937, Nanticoke; home, Nanticoke; Temple U., 1957–61, Dickinson Law Schl., 1962–65; Catholic; married (Nancy).

Military Career: Army Reserves, 1960–61.

Professional Career: Practicing atty., 1966–85; Nanticoke City Solicitor, 1969–81; Admin. Law Judge, 1971–80.

DC Office: 2353 RHOB 20515, 202-225-6511; Fax: 202-225-0764; Web site: www.house.gov/kanjorski.

District Offices: Kulpmont, 570-373-1540; Wilkes-Barre, 570-825-2200.

Committees: *Financial Services* (3d of 32 D): Capital Markets, Insurance & Government Sponsored Enterprises (RMM); Financial Institutions & Consumer Credit; International Monetary Policy & Trade. *Government Reform* (5th of 19 D): Government Efficiency, Financial Management & Intergovernmental Relations; Technology & Procurement Policy.

Group Ratings

	ADA	ACLU	AFS	LCV	CON	ITIC	NTU	COC	ACU	NTLC	CHC
2000	65	57	100	71	50	50	19	42	16	12	33
1999	75	—	100	81	48	—	24	24	16	—	—

National Journal Ratings

	1999 LIB —	1999 CONS		2000 LIB —	2000 CONS
Economic	66%	—	34%	78%	— 20%
Social	55%	—	44%	52%	— 48%
Foreign	67%	—	33%	77%	— 21%

Key Votes of the 106th Congress

1. Patient Bill of Rights	Y	5. Bar RU-486 $ for FDA	Y
2. Accelerate Min. Wage	Y	6. Display 10 Commandments	N
3. Strike Ban on Ergo. Stnd.	Y	7. Gun Show Bkgrnd. Checks	N
4. Ovrd. Estate Tax Veto	N	8. Ban Part.-Birth Abortion	Y

9. NATO War in Serbia	Y
10. Perm. Trade with China	N
11. Debt Relief for 3rd World	Y
12. Drop Cuba Econ. Embargo	Y

Election Results

2000 general	Paul E. Kanjorski (D)	131,948	(66%)	($271,258)
	Stephen A. Urban (R)	66,699	(34%)	($18,760)
2000 primary	Paul E. Kanjorski (D)	unopposed		
1998 general	Paul E. Kanjorski (D)	88,933	(67%)	($273,588)
	Stephen A. Urban (R)	44,123	(33%)	($24,412)

TWELFTH DISTRICT

The mountains and valley within a 100-mile radius of Pittsburgh comprise one of America's most beautiful areas—and have also been one of the most economically troubled. This has been tough, hard-working country ever since Scots-Irish farmers settled here in the 1790s. Their first big product was whiskey—this was the site of the Whiskey Rebellion of 1794—but historically the most important product was bituminous coal. Discovered in the 19th Century, it was the basic energy source for the production of iron and steel, and local farmers were joined by thousands of immigrants to work the mines and blast furnaces. Politically, this was one of the most Republican parts of America from the Civil War up to the 1930s. Republican policies, including high tariffs and discouragement of labor unions, were seen as protecting jobs and increasing growth in the steel economy centered on Pittsburgh. With the coming of the New Deal, and the successes of the United Mine Workers and the United Steelworkers, the area began voting mostly Democratic. But it has not followed the national Democratic Party on all issues. As employment in coal collapsed in the 1950s and employment in steel collapsed in the 1980s, people here sought trade restrictions to protect the remaining jobs, even as Democrats elsewhere favored free trade. And they maintained their conservative views on cultural issues and foreign policy, even as Democrats elsewhere embraced various forms of liberation. Today those traditions continue in muted form, as unemployment has dropped and the area has perked up. First, Pittsburgh, and now the mountain areas all around are fighting to develop a more diverse and supple economy.

The 12th Congressional District includes much of this coal and steel country. Its best known community is Johnstown, the steel town that was ravaged by the disastrous flood of May 31, 1889, when a dam broke and a 75-foot wall of water half a mile wide swept through the town killing more than 2,200 people. The tragedy is documented at the Johnstown Flood Museum, which is designed to promote tourism and local boosterism. Johnstown had 67,000 people in 1920 and 23,900 in 2000. From Johnstown, the 12th reaches south to the West Virginia border and west to take in Armstrong and Indiana Counties northeast of Pittsburgh. It also includes the hills around Ligonier, green with prosperity, where Mellons and others of Pittsburgh's elite have vast estates. On balance this is a Democratic district, though one troubled by some of the party's tendencies.

The congressman from the 12th District is John Murtha, a Democrat first elected in a 1974 special election that signaled the political weakness of Richard Nixon. Murtha grew up in this area, served in the Marine Corps, then graduated from the University of Pittsburgh and re-enlisted in the Marines in 1966, at 34; he was the first Vietnam veteran to serve in Congress. He is a member of the Appropriations Committee and the ranking Democrat on the Defense Subcommittee, his party's key man on the defense budget. His voting record—hawkish and patriotic on foreign policy, interventionist on economics and usually tradition-minded on cultural issues—seems perfectly suited to the steel and coal country. Murtha is also one of those old-time politicians who operate best in secret, sitting in the back of the House chamber and trading gossip and votes, speaking for attribution to few national or local reporters and appearing on television only when he presided over the Democratic-majority chamber. He works on many back-room issues dear to his colleagues, including pay raises, committee assignments and—following the trial and acquittal of Scranton-based Joe McDade—a provision requiring the Justice Department to reimburse members of Congress who are indicted but subsequently acquitted. With John Dingell, he leads a faction of Democrats opposed to gun control.

On foreign issues, Murtha voted for the Gulf war resolution but opposed intervention in Bosnia and deployment in Somalia, arguing that UN officials lacked the know-how to command U.S. troops. He was embarrassed when the House voted not to support air strikes against Kosovo, and supported a supplemental spending bill for Kosovo operations and increased military readiness. He calls for "more clear rules on when the United States will intervene on humanitarian missions in other countries." He argues that we need to have a "clear national interest, achievable goals and a clear timetable and plan for getting out—before we get into any troop deployment." He has supported the Nunn-Lugar program to decommission former Soviet nuclear weapons. He favors technology that provides "force multipliers" and has focused on quality-of-life improvements for service men and women, recognizing the challenge for the military to attract and retain good volunteers. With Defense subcommittee chairman Jerry Lewis, he raised questions about production of the F-22 fighter plane, but worked on changes and testing to avoid its elimination. He opposed Permanent Normal Trade Relations with China because of its threat to use force against Taiwan. He is caught sometimes between Democratic demands for lower defense spending to make more money available for domestic programs and Republican desires to spend even more on defense, but he seeks to come up with appropriations that the House will sustain on a bipartisan basis. With Pete Stark, he was one of two House members to oppose repeal of the telephone tax. When a bipartisan group of 14 members met in Austin with George W. Bush in January 2001, Murtha urged him to reduce the tax cut to assure adequate money for the Pentagon.

In 1990 Murtha had an uncomfortably close primary race, and since then his interests in the district have taken interesting turns. He hired a press secretary who concentrated on local press, and he traveled around the district, staying days in communities. From these visits have come a more secure electoral base plus a conviction that environmental cleanup could be the key to the area's economic growth in the post-steel era. He has pushed for passive treatment systems to clean up creeks, inspired river improvement projects, and urged groups to develop processes to extract minerals from mine draining so that restoring the environment will become a business itself. Although he also has lured several defense contractors to the region, he seems to be relying less on providing federal dollars, though he does some of that, than in stimulating imaginative commercial ideas and community action. Like most other steel-district members, he has aggressively backed that industry's push for federal relief from claims of subsidized imports.

Despite the jeopardy to several Pennsylvania Democrats, Murtha appears secure in redistricting—in part, because of his local popularity: local officials named the Johnstown airport in his honor. Pennsylvania Republicans control redistricting, and western Pennsylvania will lose a district, but it will not be Murtha's; Republicans respect his ability to help the state and will give him a safe Democratic seat. One possibility is to shear off some of the Republican counties (to beef up Republican districts) and move the district west to the Pittsburgh area, including Democratic portions of Westmoreland County and perhaps even the Mon Valley southwest of Pittsburgh; the only risk is that Murtha might face a primary from another Democratic incumbent.

Cook's Call *Safe.* Republican plans to heavily alter parts of western Pennsylvania in redistricting, which will impact Murtha's district. It is unlikely that he will be in danger of losing in 2002. But this district, already quite marginal at the national level, will be very competitive once Murtha leaves office.

THE PEOPLE: Pop. 2000: 556,856; Pop. 1990: 565,760, down 1.6% 1990–2000. 97.2% White, 1.7% Black, 0.3% Asian, 0.1% Amer. Indian, 0.5% Two+ races, 0.2% Other; 0.6% Hispanic Origin.

2000 Presidential Vote			1996 Presidential Vote		
Bush (R)	110,290	(52%)	Clinton (D)	93,532	(46%)
Gore (D)	94,686	(45%)	Dole (R)	81,122	(40%)
Nader (Green)	4,009	(2%)	Perot (I)	25,755	(13%)
Others	2,004	(1%)			

Rep. John P. Murtha (D)

Elected Feb. 1974, 14th term; b. June 17, 1932, New Martinsville, WV; home, Johnstown; U. of Pittsburgh, B.A. 1962, Indiana U. of PA, 1963–64; Catholic; married (Joyce).

Military Career: Marine Corps, 1952–55, 1966–67 (Vietnam); Marine Corps Reserves, 1955–66, 1967–90.

Elected Office: PA House of Reps., 1969–74.

Professional Career: Owner, Johnstown Minute Car Wash.

DC Office: 2423 RHOB 20515, 202-225-2065; Fax: 202-225-5709; Web site: www.house.gov/murtha.

District Office: Johnstown, 814-535-2642.

Committees: *Appropriations* (2d of 29 D): Defense (RMM); Interior.

Group Ratings

	ADA	ACLU	AFS	LCV	CON	ITIC	NTU	COC	ACU	NTLC	CHC
2000	55	57	100	36	50	71	25	45	24	12	47
1999	60	—	100	38	35	—	17	43	24	—	—

National Journal Ratings

	1999 LIB	—	1999 CONS		2000 LIB	—	2000 CONS
Economic	61%	—	39%		67%	—	33%
Social	50%	—	50%		45%	—	54%
Foreign	59%	—	40%		60%	—	39%

Key Votes of the 106th Congress

1. Patient Bill of Rights	Y	5. Bar RU-486 $ for FDA	Y	9. NATO War in Serbia	Y
2. Accelerate Min. Wage	Y	6. Display 10 Commandments	Y	10. Perm. Trade with China	N
3. Strike Ban on Ergo. Stnd.	Y	7. Gun Show Bkgrnd. Checks	N	11. Debt Relief for 3rd World	Y
4. Ovrd. Estate Tax Veto	N	8. Ban Part.-Birth Abortion	Y	12. Drop Cuba Econ. Embargo	N

Election Results

2000 general	John P. Murtha (D)	145,538	(71%)	($968,531)
	Bill Choby (R)	56,575	(28%)	($8,310)
	Others	3,324	(2%)	
2000 primary	John P. Murtha (D)	unopposed		
1998 general	John P. Murtha (D)	100,528	(68%)	($742,261)
	Timothy E. Holloway (R)	46,239	(32%)	($75,395)

THIRTEENTH DISTRICT

Montgomery County, Pennsylvania, is the hinterland of Philadelphia: rolling hills cut on one side by the Schuylkill River and at intervals by the Pennsylvania and Reading Railroad lines radiating outward from Center City. Older suburbs, the rich Main Line towns and more modest places like Glenside and Ambler, grew up around rail stations, with comfortable houses within walking distance for commuters. Here and there are the old Schuylkill River factory towns, Conshohocken and Norristown and towns established 200 years ago by German sects; near the big shopping malls around King of Prussia is Valley Forge, where George Washington wintered in 1778 and Ross Perot was nominated by the Reform Party in 1996. Farther out are 18th and 19th Century villages, once surrounded by farm fields, now encroached on by subdivisions where people depend on cars, not rail lines, to get to work, and office complexes in places like Blue Bell. Statistically, Montgomery County is the most affluent part of metro Philadelphia, but as in most suburban counties there is much variety here—economically, with high income enclaves like Gladwyne, and ethnically, with Jewish suburbs out York Road.

The 13th Congressional District is made up of most of Montgomery County, but small parts of the county are nibbled off by four other districts. Historically it was a quintessentially Republican seat, where the style of politics was set for years by Ivy-educated Republican men, and where Republicans with more modest and sometimes ethnic backgrounds manned the local precincts and staffed local offices. But now the suburbs are as multi-ethnic as the central city, if not more so, and with varied cultural attitudes. By the end of the decade, the Route 202 corridor had become an Internet hot spot, with new computer-industry campuses that had a Silicon Valley feel. Montgomery County cast huge margins for Ronald Reagan and George Bush in the 1980s but voted comfortably for Bill Clinton in the 1990s and Al Gore in 2000.

The congressman from the 13th District is Joseph Hoeffel, a Democrat elected in 1998. Hoeffel grew up in the Philadelphia area and has spent most of his adult life in politics and public office. He was elected to the state House in 1976, at 26, and re-elected three times. In 1984 he challenged Republican Congressman Lawrence Coughlin and was beaten 56%–44%—a respectable showing in the Reagan landslide. Two years later he ran again and lost 59%–41%. After five years in law practice, he was elected a Montgomery County commissioner in 1991. There he forged an alliance with a Democrat to keep Jon Fox from being elected commission chairman. In 1992 Fox won the Republican nomination for Congress, but lost by 1,373 votes to Marjorie Margolies-Mezvinsky; in 1994 he beat her by 8,000 votes after her embarrassing last-minute shift provided the one-vote margin for the Clinton budget and tax increase in August 1993. In 1996 Hoeffel ran against Fox and lost by 84 votes, 48.91%–48.87%. In 1998 Hoeffel ran again, as Fox was peppered by Republican opponents from both left and right, and won only 49% of the primary votes—an obvious trouble sign for an incumbent. In both his campaigns against Fox, Hoeffel linked him to Newt Gingrich and said such a political profile does not fit the district's "moderate, progressive community." Impeachment may have had an impact on this contest. Hoeffel said he initially feared that the Lewinsky scandal would harm other Democrats, but later he argued Republicans overplayed their hand and produced a voter backlash by October. But Hoeffel did not invite Bill Clinton to make a campaign appearance in Montgomery County, nor did he attend his October Democratic fundraiser in Philadelphia. Instead, Hillary Rodham Clinton made an appearance for Hoeffel, as did Minority Leader Dick Gephardt. Hoeffel won 52%–47%.

In the House, his record has been consistently liberal. He helped win inclusion of the Schuylkill River Valley in the national heritage area program. He was torn on Permanent Normal Trade Relations with China between his claims to be a pro-trade New Democrat and the opposition from labor unions who have been crucial campaign supporters; he decided to vote no to, he said, maintain "leverage" on the Chinese. On appropriations bills, he claimed credit for $10 million for SEPTA's Schuylkill Valley MetroRail design and construction, $5 million for sound barriers along Route 309, and $2.7 million for life-long learning programs in Montgomery County. His priorities for the 107th Congress include a new veterans cemetery at Valley Forge, applying federal gun safety regulations to antique guns, and more money for local transportation projects. He wants a congressional commission to recommend cuts in corporate welfare programs.

Hoeffel started off as a top target of Republicans in 2000. In their primary, young conservative John Coffey made a spirited challenge of Stewart Greenleaf, a state Senator for 22 years; Greenleaf won by just 57%–43%. But the narrow primary margin and Greenleaf's reputation for leisurely campaigning persuaded Republicans to take the district off the top priority list. Hoeffel emphasized their differences on prescription-drug legislation and criticized Greenleaf for supporting HMOs. Greenleaf featured his support for tax cuts, including the marriage penalty and estate taxes, and partial privatization of Social Security. Hoeffel won by the relatively comfortable margin of 53%–46%, as old-line Republican politics no longer seemed to work in Montgomery County.

What may work for Republicans against Hoeffel is redistricting. Pennsylvania lost two House seats in the 2000 Census, and Republicans control redistricting. In late 2000, the strategy seemed to be to extend one or two of the Philadelphia seats out into Montgomery County. This could remove a large part of lower Montgomery County from the 13th District, possibly everything south of Conshohocken and Ambler—an area that includes most of Montgomery's heavily Jewish areas, which voted strongly for Hoeffel. The 13th would then be extended outward to include all of upper Montgomery County and much of Berks County, a Republican-leaning area around Reading. Such a plan would leave Hoeffel with two unattractive choices. One would be to run in a heavily Democratic district including much of Philadelphia, in which he would have to face another incumbent Democrat in the primary, probably Robert Borski. The other would be to run in the far less Democratic new 13th, in which he probably would have to improve his 2000 showing with independents in order to win.

Cook's Call *Highly Competitive.* Pennsylvania must lose two seats in redistricting, and Republicans are likely to chop this district up and parcel it into as many as four different ones. This could force Hoeffel to run against another Democrat, like Bob Borski. But as the first Democrat in over 80 years to be re-elected to this seat, Hoeffel clearly knows how to run and win tough races.

THE PEOPLE: Pop. 2000: 628,203; Pop. 1990: 565,663, up 11.1% 1990–2000. 85.9% White, 7.9% Black, 4.2% Asian, 0.1% Amer. Indian, 1.1% Two+ races, 0.7% Other; 2% Hispanic Origin.

2000 Presidential Vote			1996 Presidential Vote		
Gore (D)	154,996	(54%)	Clinton (D)	125,364	(50%)
Bush (R)	123,000	(43%)	Dole (R)	103,461	(41%)
Nader (Green)	5,748	(2%)	Perot (I)	19,922	(8%)
Others	1,625	(1%)	Others	4,179	(2%)

Rep. Joseph M. Hoeffel (D)

Elected 1998, 2d term; b. Sept. 3, 1950, Philadelphia; home, Abington; Boston U., B.A. 1972, Temple U. Law Schl., J.D. 1986; Protestant; married (Francesca).

Military Career: Army Reserves, 1970–76.

Elected Office: PA House of Reps., 1976–84; Montgomery Cnty. Comm., 1991–98.

Professional Career: Practicing atty., 1986–91.

DC Office: 1229 LHOB 20515, 202-225-6111; Fax: 202-226-0611; Web site: www.house.gov/hoeffel.

District Office: Norristown, 610-272-8400.

Committees: *Budget* (17th of 20 D). *International Relations* (18th of 23 D): Middle East & South Asia.

Group Ratings

	ADA	ACLU	AFS	LCV	CON	ITIC	NTU	COC	ACU	NTLC	CHC
2000	90	86	100	93	38	68	21	42	8	15	13
1999	100	—	100	94	87	—	20	20	4	—	—

National Journal Ratings

	1999 LIB —	1999 CONS		2000 LIB —	2000 CONS
Economic	84% —	12%		85% —	11%
Social	83% —	13%		79% —	17%
Foreign	74% —	23%		64% —	34%

Key Votes of the 106th Congress

1. Patient Bill of Rights	Y	5. Bar RU-486 $ for FDA	N	9. NATO War in Serbia	Y
2. Accelerate Min. Wage	Y	6. Display 10 Commandments	N	10. Perm. Trade with China	N
3. Strike Ban on Ergo. Stnd.	Y	7. Gun Show Bkgrnd. Checks	Y	11. Debt Relief for 3rd World	Y
4. Ovrd. Estate Tax Veto	N	8. Ban Part.-Birth Abortion	N	12. Drop Cuba Econ. Embargo	Y

Election Results

2000 general	Joseph M. Hoeffel (D)	146,026	(53%)	($1,772,923)
	Stewart J. Greenleaf (R)	126,501	(46%)	($1,481,942)
	Others	4,224	(2%)	
2000 primary	Joseph M. Hoeffel (D)	unopposed		
1998 general	Joseph M. Hoeffel (D)	95,105	(52%)	($1,259,326)
	Jon D. Fox (R)	85,915	(47%)	($1,921,005)
	Others	3,470	(2%)	

FOURTEENTH DISTRICT

The Golden Triangle is the inevitable focus of Pittsburgh, the tip of land where the Allegheny and Monongahela Rivers come together to form the Ohio, and has been a strategic site for more than 200 years. It was there, to Fort Duquesne in the French and Indian War, that Braddock's army was headed (with George Washington helping lead the way) when it was ambushed and defeated in 1754. A few years later, the first American city west of the Appalachian chain was carved out of the wilderness here and named after the English statesman William Pitt. Pittsburgh grew rapidly in those days when most of the nation's commerce moved over water. When traffic switched to railroads, Pittsburgh still did nicely, since rail lines run at riverside rather than scale the mountains. Then came Andrew Carnegie—and steel. A Scottish immigrant working as a telegrapher for the Pennsylvania Railroad, he saw that steel would replace iron for railroad bridges and built a steel factory in Pittsburgh—then a rail junction with large deposits of coal nearby and ready access to iron ore from the Great Lakes. With associates like Henry Clay Frick and Henry Phipps, Carnegie built his capacity to the point that when he sold out in 1901, the resulting U.S. Steel Corporation had a near-monopoly of the business.

The Pittsburgh that Carnegie and his steel men built is one of giant mills in the bottomlands along the rivers and massive buildings downtown, like the classic City-County Building next to the Richardsonian jail. There were 12 cable cars going up the Duquesne Incline and other routes, connecting mills with neighborhoods above, and the ever-present grime of coal smoke in the air. The Pittsburgh smog—a word used here before it was in Los Angeles—was so bad that street lights stayed on all day downtown; a 1947 photograph shows a midnight-like darkness at nine in the morning. In the years after World War II, Pittsburgh's business leaders and Mayor David Lawrence were determined to clean up the smog and succeeded: Pittsburgh is one of our cleaner-air cities today. They also cleaned up the riverfront and created a grand park at the junction of the three rivers. Pittsburgh ranks high, though not as high as it used to, as a headquarters of major corporations (USX, Heinz, Alcoa, Koppers, PPG) and has fine cultural institutions, from Carnegie-Mellon University and the University of Pittsburgh with its "cathedral of learning" to its public television station (home of the now-retired *Mr. Rogers' Neighborhood*) and the Andy Warhol museum. In the early 1980s, Pittsburgh formed a high-tech council to encourage start-up businesses. By the early 1990s, it had a robust high-tech, white-collar sector, replacing the manufacturing jobs that had declined in the metropolitan area from 265,000 in the mid-1970s to 140,000 in 1999. The USAirways hub at the Pittsburgh airport, privately run and one of the most attractive airports anywhere, also helped build up the local economy. The old millworker towns in the outer metro ring continued to lose population and jobs, but much of the central city still has vitality, with nearly 30,000 tech workers and yuppie-like growth of software firms in Mount Washington and Manchester, fine homes still maintained in Shadyside and Squirrel Hill, and a nationally acclaimed safety-net program to help recipients with post-welfare needs. Vacant lots with abandoned steel mills have been converted into industrial parks and residential developments. New projects include two stadiums, a convention center and office complexes.

The 14th Congressional District includes all of Pittsburgh plus suburban territory in Allegheny County to the west and north. It takes in the city's black neighborhoods and Shadyside and its depopulated white working-class areas. To the west it goes out along a new expressway to the airport; to the north, through middle-income townships and northeast along the Ohio River to some of the hilly high-income precincts of Sewickley. The 14th has its Republican neighborhoods but its Republican heritage has not been very lively since the New Deal, and this is a solidly Democratic district. It became more Democratic during the steel industry's collapse in the 1980s, while national Democrats' cultural liberalism made it somewhat less so in the 1990s.

The congressman from the 14th District is William Coyne, a Democrat first elected in 1980. He grew up in an Irish-American family in Pittsburgh, served in the Army, worked as an accountant, and graduated from Robert Morris College. With a characteristic Irish-American knack for politics, he went to the legislature in 1970, at 34, to the city council in 1973, to the chairmanship of the Democratic Party in Pittsburgh in 1978, and then to Congress when he beat his predecessor's son in the Democratic primary by a 65%–35% margin. After the 1984 election, he won a seat on the Ways and Means Committee, where he was the kind of reliable Democrat with whom then-Chairman Dan Rostenkowski was comfortable; he is now its fourth-senior Democrat and ranking on the Oversight Subcommittee.

Coyne's voting record is one of the most liberal in the House. He wants the government to spend more on transportation, education and energy conservation, which he believes will produce economic growth. He was the only western Pennsylvanian to oppose the partial-birth abortion ban and support gun control. He worked to make the earned income tax credit payable monthly rather than yearly. He has secured funding for many local projects—the Software Engineering Institute, Children's Hospital, restructuring the former Hays Ammunition Plant. In the minority, he has been less successful in seeking incentives to clean up urban brownfields, expanding workers' rights in trade agreements and making food stamps more widely available. In 1997 he worked with Republicans to reorganize the IRS and in 1999 to simplify the capital gains tax.

For years Coyne worked quietly, not seeking publicity as most congressmen do. "I am a quiet person by nature," he told a local reporter, and he said that he has never held a press conference. That modesty changed a bit in 1996, when he was challenged in the primary by 38-year-old Pittsburgh Councilman Dan Cohen. Coyne, who had never spent more than $323,000, spent $1 million this time. "Results. Not Talk," was his slogan, making his taciturnity an asset, and he knocked on 25,000 doors by the primary. He was endorsed by the local Democratic Party, the AFL-CIO, and the Sierra Club; District Attorney Bob Colville cut an ad praising Coyne's record against crime. The result was a thumping 66%–34% victory for Coyne. He was re-elected easily that fall and has had no primary opposition since.

His biggest problem may be redistricting. Pennsylvania lost two House seats in the 2000 Census, and Republicans control the redistricting process. It is generally agreed that the Pittsburgh area will lose one seat, and the Republicans' prime target appears to be Mike Doyle, of the neighboring 18th District, against whom they have an old grudge. But that could very well mean that Coyne would face Doyle in the Democratic primary, something no incumbent likes to see happen. The new district will in any case be heavily Democratic; indeed Republican townships in the current 14th will probably be given to 4th District Republican Melissa Hart.

Cook's Call   *Potentially Competitive*. For the first time in 20 years, Coyne is likely to have a very tough race. This district is expected to be merged with that of fellow Democrat Mike Doyle in 2002.

THE PEOPLE: Pop. 2000: 529,299; Pop. 1990: 565,838, down 6.5% 1990–2000. 77.3% White, 18.4% Black, 2.3% Asian, 0.2% Amer. Indian, 1.3% Two+ races, 0.5% Other; 1.1% Hispanic Origin.

2000 Presidential Vote

Gore (D)	142,879	(62%)
Bush (R)	79,877	(35%)
Nader (Green)	4,676	(2%)
Others	2,882	(1%)

1996 Presidential Vote

Clinton (D)	126,704	(59%)
Dole (R)	70,466	(33%)
Perot (I)	15,417	(7%)
Others	3,690	(2%)

Rep. William J. Coyne (D)

Elected 1980, 11th term; b. Aug. 24, 1936, Pittsburgh; home, Pittsburgh; Robert Morris Col., B.S. 1965; Catholic; single.

Military Career: Army, 1955–57.

Elected Office: PA House of Reps., 1970–72; Pittsburgh City Cncl., 1973–80.

Professional Career: Accountant, 1957–70; Chmn., Pittsburgh Dem. Party, 1978–84.

DC Office: 2455 RHOB 20515, 202-225-2301; Fax: 202-225-1844; Web site: www.house.gov/coyne.

District Office: Pittsburgh, 412-644-2870.

Committees: *Ways & Means* (4th of 17 D): Oversight (RMM).

Group Ratings

	ADA	ACLU	AFS	LCV	CON	ITIC	NTU	COC	ACU	NTLC	CHC
2000	90	86	100	93	60	50	28	30	8	9	0
1999	95	—	100	88	70	—	22	24	0	—	—

National Journal Ratings

	1999 LIB	—	1999 CONS		2000 LIB	—	2000 CONS
Economic	88%	—	0%		92%	—	5%
Social	87%	—	0%		90%	—	9%
Foreign	93%	—	5%		85%	—	10%

FIFTEENTH DISTRICT

Allentown, Pennsylvania, has long been derided by show biz songwriters, from "42nd Street" back in 1933, in which it is scorned as nowhere, the polar opposite of Broadway, to Billy Joel's "Allentown" in 1982, with its grim picture of closed factories and unemployment. Neither is an entirely fair portrait of this largest city in Pennsylvania's Lehigh Valley, though both have nuggets of truth. Allentown and next-door Bethlehem are off the Metroliner corridor that is the big population center of the Northeast, and both have suffered from industrial shutdowns—Allentown, when Mack Truck moved one of its main assembly plants to non-union South Carolina, and Bethlehem, when Bethlehem Steel announced it was shutting down its last blast furnace in the city that was its since 1857. But the rolling hills of the Lehigh Valley today are economically productive and creative, with big new installations from AT&T and Nestle, long-surviving businesses like Crayola Crayons and Dixie cups, and dozens of small startups which never get the visibility of the big closedowns but together have produced more new jobs than have been lost. Redevelopment of Bethlehem includes a convention center, hotel complex and National Museum of Industrial History. If the Lehigh Valley is off the main lines of traffic, it is connected by I-78 to New York and by the Turnpike Extension to Philadelphia, and its lower living costs and taxes make it attractive to people from both big metro areas.

The 15th Congressional District consists of the Lehigh Valley plus a small adjacent chunk of Montgomery County. This has been a marginal political area for years, the intersection of heavily Democratic industrial precincts with the Republican farmlands of the Pennsylvania Dutch Country.

The congressman from the 15th today is businessman Pat Toomey, a Republican elected in 1998. Toomey grew up in a blue-collar Rhode Island family, got enough scholarship aid to attend Harvard, then turned to a career in investment banking. After getting wealthy by creating an international financial services consulting firm, he moved to Allentown in 1990, where he invested in Rookies' Restaurants, which he helped to organize with his brothers. He entered government in 1994 as an elected member of the Allentown Government Study Commission, where he helped to author tax-limitation plans, including the requirement of a super-majority for the city council to raise taxes. In November 1997, Democratic Congressman Paul McHale announced he was retiring; McHale became the first House Democrat to call for Clinton's resignation in August 1998 and one of five Democrats to vote for impeachment. Toomey started to run for the House right after McHale's announcement. The six-candidate Republican primary included two state legislators. Toomey called for Social Security reform and a simple 17% flat tax; he pledged to serve no more than six years and promised never to vote to raise taxes. He spent heavily and won the Republican primary with 27% to 25% for realtor and Christian conservative Bob Kilbanks (who had lost to McHale 55%–41% in 1996) and 23% for state Senator Joseph Uliana.

The Democratic nominee was Allentown state Senator Roy Afflerbach. Toomey put him on the defensive early with an ad that highlighted Afflerbach's support of tax increases in the legislature, calling him "the tax man" and attacking him for voting against repeal of a tax on toothpaste and dental floss. Afflerbach criticized Toomey's tax plan as a threat to Social Security and the budget surplus. Afflerbach tried to appeal to conservative, blue-collar voters by calling Toomey an outsider: "Pat has only been in Pennsylvania for seven years and prior to that he was all over the world doing private business, while I was here doing public business." But Toomey won by the surprisingly large margin of 55%–45%. McHale's support of impeachment may have cast a pall over Democratic efforts here. Toomey's win demonstrated the growing strength of suburbs over the declining Democratic strongholds of Allentown and Bethlehem, where Afflerbach had only single-digit margins.

In the House, Toomey quickly went to work on national economic issues. He took on the task for conservative Republicans of challenging excessive spending by the Appropriations Committee and won the leadership's support for setting aside an additional $4 billion for debt reduction. "We've got three parties in Congress—Republicans, Democrats and Appropriators," Toomey complained. He led opposition among Republicans to waiving the six-year term limits for committee chairmen. After the 2000 election, he urged a larger tax cut than George W. Bush's plan, with additional savings incentives and lower capital gains taxes.

Toomey received a stronger than expected reelection challenge from Edward O'Brien, a former blast-furnace worker at Bethlehem Steel and the number-two United Steelworkers official in Pennsylvania. With strongly divergent views, the contest had elements of class warfare. Toomey backed limits on how much a patient can sue an HMO, and individual investment accounts for Social Security. O'Brien opposed each, and called for strengthening Social Security. Toomey won 53%–47%, drawing 54% in Lehigh County but only 51% in Northampton. Republicans control redistricting, and while they seem likely to keep the Lehigh Valley together, they will presumably add heavily Republican territory in adjacent counties to make the district more favorable to Toomey. He has been mentioned as a possible Senate candidate in 2004, if Arlen Specter retires.

Cook's Call *Competitive.* Toomey's 53%–47% victory in 2000 against a second-tier Democrat illustrates the marginal nature of this district. Republicans control redistricting in the state, which could help shore up this district for Toomey. In June 2001 Toomey was complaining publicly about a redistricting plan that would carve out parts of his Lehigh Valley district and give them to fellow Republican Jim Greenwood.

THE PEOPLE: Pop. 2000: 612,265; Pop. 1990: 565,818, up 8.2% 1990–2000. 89.4% White, 3.1% Black, 1.7% Asian, 0.2% Amer. Indian, 1.6% Two+ races, 4% Other; 8.2% Hispanic Origin.

2000 Presidential Vote		
Gore (D)	114,481	(49%)
Bush (R)	109,301	(47%)
Nader (Green)	6,593	(3%)
Others	2,168	(1%)

1996 Presidential Vote		
Clinton (D)	96,380	(46%)
Dole (R)	85,736	(41%)
Perot (I)	22,125	(11%)
Others	3,130	(2%)

Rep. Patrick Toomey (R)

Elected 1998, 2d term; b. Nov. 17, 1961, Providence, RI; home, Allentown; Harvard U., B.S. 1984; Catholic; married (Kris).

Elected Office: Allentown Govt. Study Comm., 1994.

Professional Career: Investment Banker, 1984–89; Financial Consultant, 1990; Restaurateur, 1990-present.

DC Office: 224 CHOB 20515, 202-225-6411; Fax: 202-226-0778; Web site: www.house.gov/toomey.

District Office: Allentown, 610-439-8861.

Committees: *Budget* (12th of 24 R). *Financial Services* (26th of 37 R): Capital Markets, Insurance & Government Sponsored Enterprises; Financial Institutions & Consumer Credit; International Monetary Policy & Trade. *Small Business* (8th of 19 R): Regulatory Reform Oversight; Tax, Finance & Exports (Chmn.).

Group Ratings

	ADA	ACLU	AFS	LCV	CON	ITIC	NTU	COC	ACU	NTLC	CHC
2000	10	36	0	7	91	100	78	80	95	94	100
1999	5	—	0	31	95	—	77	88	92	—	—

National Journal Ratings

	1999 LIB	—	1999 CONS		2000 LIB	—	2000 CONS
Economic	16%	—	78%		25%	—	72%
Social	41%	—	58%		34%	—	66%
Foreign	28%	—	70%		12%	—	78%

Key Votes of the 106th Congress

1. Patient Bill of Rights	N	5. Bar RU-486 $ for FDA	N	9. NATO War in Serbia	N
2. Accelerate Min. Wage	N	6. Display 10 Commandments	N	10. Perm. Trade with China	Y
3. Strike Ban on Ergo. Stnd.	N	7. Gun Show Bkgrnd. Checks	N	11. Debt Relief for 3rd World	N
4. Ovrd. Estate Tax Veto	Y	8. Ban Part.-Birth Abortion	Y	12. Drop Cuba Econ. Embargo	N

Election Results

2000 general	Patrick Toomey (R)	118,307	(53%)	($975,795)
	Ed O'Brien (D)	103,864	(47%)	($772,988)
2000 primary	Patrick Toomey (R)	unopposed		
1998 general	Patrick Toomey (R)	81,755	(55%)	($1,039,189)
	Roy C. Afflerbach (D)	66,930	(45%)	($562,251)

SIXTEENTH DISTRICT

The Pennsylvania Dutch Country, settled by Germans in the 18th Century when it was Pennsylvania's frontier, remains a distinctive part of America. These Germans were Amish and Mennonite, pietistic sects seeking religious liberty and determined to farm rich lands in the same intensive way they had in Germany. Today, many of their descendants—the Eisenhower family is the most famous example—have blended into mainstream America, but in the Dutch area around Lancaster, many "Plain People" still live. Tourists can still see Amish families clad in black, clattering over the back roads in horse-drawn carriages, with scrupulously tended farms set amid rolling hills, the barns decorated with hex signs. Farmers here continue to produce some of the highest per-acre yields on earth, with simple equipment and limited use of chemicals. Local business groups claim that Lancaster ranks first nationally in farm receipts for non-irrigated counties, in the number of egg-laying hens, plus its acres preserved solely for farmland. But efficient farming is not all that is happening here economically. Lancaster is the headquarters of financially-troubled Armstrong Cork and the largest stockyards east of Chicago. Nearby Hershey is where Milton Hershey built his chocolate firm in 1903; this has been the site of the bipartisan House of Representatives "civility retreats." The Dutch area also has many small firms and new outlet malls; new startups prosper, profiting from the skills and work habits of the labor force. Lancaster County has had solid growth in recent years, and so has western Chester County, technically part of metro Philadelphia, but with its own Pennsylvania Dutch communities. This was the fastest-growing part of Pennsylvania in the 1990s.

The 16th District includes most of Lancaster County and part of Chester County, ranging east from the Dutch Country through the small towns and spreading suburbs of greater Philadelphia, including America's leading mushroom-growing center around Kennett Square (fragrant with the compost needed for the crop) and on to the Wyeth country around Chadds Ford. This is one of the most Republican districts in Pennsylvania and the whole Northeast. It has favored the party of Lincoln since it abandoned the party of Pennsylvania's only president, Lancaster resident James Buchanan, just before the Civil War.

The congressman from the 16th District is Joe Pitts, a Republican elected in 1996. Pitts grew up in Kentucky, joined the Air Force after college, served three tours of duty and flew 116 B-52 combat missions in Vietnam. He returned to become a math and science teacher in Malvern, in Chester County, and later owned a nursery near Kennett Square. He and his daughter have exhibited their artwork, everything from painting to sculpture, at local galleries. In 1972, at 33, he was elected to the Pennsylvania House. Pitts became a leader in Harrisburg, a "champion of traditional values," in his words, and staunchly anti-abortion. In 1989 he became chairman of the Appropriations Committee, and was proud of balancing budgets and starting a program in which low-income neighborhood leaders met regularly with legislators to discuss how government could "support and not hinder" their organizations. He oversaw the restoration of the Pennsylvania Capitol. In December 1995, when Congressman Bob Walker, one of the conservative reformers close to Newt Gingrich who helped revolutionize the House, cited the "Pennsylvania Dutch tradition" of not serving over 20 years and said he was retiring, Pitts plunged into the primary. He spoke favorably of home-schooling and unfavorably of gambling, and ran as a "true conservative." He raised the most money and won the most votes in the five-candidate race. In the general, Pitts easily defeated newspaper publisher James Blaine, a descendant of James G. Blaine, the "Plumed Knight" and Republican presidential nominee in 1884.

In the House, Pitts has had a firmly conservative record. He advocated repeal of the estate tax, which he says breaks up family businesses and produces little net revenue, and he won House passage of an "Amish bill" to permit Amish youth an exemption from child-labor laws to work with adult supervision at sites with heavy machinery. He co-chairs the Renewal Alliance, seeking ways to encourage local and faith-based groups in low-income neighborhoods to work on the needs of the poor. He led the Pro-Life Caucus and headed the Republicans' "values action team" that worked with the Christian Coalition and other family groups to promote a pro-family agenda. And he founded two diverse groups: the religious prisoners' congressional task force, to plead for human rights around the world, and the Electronic Warfare Working Group. Responding to Armstrong's woes, he wants to limit a company's exposure to asbestos litigation. Unlike Walker, Pitts focused on earmarking local highway projects and won major improvements on U.S. 30 in Lancaster County and Route 41 in Chester County. And he has used his international advocacy to encourage overseas investors in his district.

Pitts has been re-elected easily twice. After the 2000 election, he won a seat on the Energy and Commerce Committee. Redistricting should not be a problem for him. Republicans control the redistricting process, and the 16th is the one district in Pennsylvania that exceeds the population required for new districts.

Cook's Call   *Safe.* Though only in his third term, Pitts is safely settled in this heavily Republican seat. This was also the fastest-growing district in Pennsylvania during the 1990s.

THE PEOPLE: Pop. 2000: 647,575; Pop. 1990: 565,908, up 14.4% 1990–2000. 88.7% White, 5.4% Black, 1.6% Asian, 0.2% Amer. Indian, 1.3% Two+ races, 2.7% Other; 5.9% Hispanic Origin.

2000 Presidential Vote				**1996 Presidential Vote**		
Bush (R)	147,441	(58%)		Dole (R)	114,164	(53%)
Gore (D)	97,609	(39%)		Clinton (D)	80,476	(37%)
Nader (Green)	5,327	(2%)		Perot (I)	18,010	(8%)
Others	1,670	(1%)				

Rep. Joseph R. Pitts (R)

Elected 1996, 3d term; b. Oct. 10, 1939, Lexington, KY; home, Kennett Square; Asbury Col., B.A. 1961, West Chester U., M.Ed. 1972; Protestant; married (Virginia).

Military Career: Air Force, 1963–69 (Vietnam).

Professional Career: High schl. teacher, 1969–72; PA House of Reps., 1972–96; Owner, Landscape & Nursery Co., 1974–90.

DC Office: 204 CHOB 20515, 202-225-2411; Fax: 202-225-2013; Web site: www.house.gov/pitts.

District Offices: Kennett Square, 610-444-4581; Lancaster, 717-393-0667.

Committees: *Energy & Commerce* (28th of 31 R): Commerce, Trade & Consumer Protection; Environment & Hazardous Materials; Health. *International Relations* (21st of 26 R): International Operations and Human Rights; Middle East & South Asia.

Group Ratings

	ADA	ACLU	AFS	LCV	CON	ITIC	NTU	COC	ACU	NTLC	CHC
2000	0	21	0	14	93	100	71	85	100	88	100
1999	0	—	0	6	79	—	66	92	92	—	—

National Journal Ratings

	1999 LIB	—	1999 CONS		2000 LIB	—	2000 CONS
Economic	0%	—	84%		25%	—	72%
Social	4%	—	91%		0%	—	79%
Foreign	3%	—	92%		0%	—	88%

Key Votes of the 106th Congress

1. Patient Bill of Rights	N	5. Bar RU-486 $ for FDA	Y	9. NATO War in Serbia	N
2. Accelerate Min. Wage	N	6. Display 10 Commandments	Y	10. Perm. Trade with China	Y
3. Strike Ban on Ergo. Stnd.	N	7. Gun Show Bkgrnd. Checks	N	11. Debt Relief for 3rd World	N
4. Ovrd. Estate Tax Veto	Y	8. Ban Part.-Birth Abortion	Y	12. Drop Cuba Econ. Embargo	N

Election Results

2000 general	Joseph R. Pitts (R)	162,403	(67%)	($366,418)
	Bob Yorczyk (D)	80,177	(33%)	($9,809)
2000 primary	Joseph R. Pitts (R)	unopposed		
1998 general	Joseph R. Pitts (R)	95,979	(71%)	($372,699)
	Robert S. Yorczyk (D)	40,092	(29%)	($3,686)

SEVENTEENTH DISTRICT

Through the center of Pennsylvania flows the Susquehanna, the longest river in the East if you include the Chesapeake Bay, which is actually the flooded lower Susquehanna Valley. Starting in Cooperstown, New York, emptying into the Chesapeake next to the antique town of Havre de Grace, Maryland, the Susquehanna is the one river strong enough to break through the Appalachian chains of central Pennsylvania. But few songs are written to celebrate the Susquehanna; it has not given a name to a fever (Potomac), a school of painting (Hudson) or economics (Charles), or to a state (Delaware, Connecticut, Ohio, Mississippi, Alabama, Illinois, Missouri, Colorado).

The 17th Congressional District covers much of the lower Susquehanna Valley, where the river drains the fertile plains of the Pennsylvania Dutch Country, one of colonial America's great frontiers. Its population center is Harrisburg, the central city huddled around the marvelous restored Capitol building—its dome is modeled after St. Peter's in Rome, its stairway on the Paris Opera—with the metro area spreading over various valleys, not far upstream from the Three Mile Island nuclear power plant. From there the district spreads east to the Pennsylvania Dutch Country, including Lebanon County and part of Lancaster County. Here the black buggies of the "Plain People" click-clack over the roads of some of the most fertile farmland in the world. This is a solidly Republican area. Harrisburg has been a Republican town from the days when the party seemed to conquer all in Pennsylvania; Republicans held the governorship for all but eight years from 1860 to 1934 and filled the ornate halls of the Capitol with Republican patronage hacks. The Pennsylvania Dutch Country is even more Republican.

The congressman from the 17th District is George Gekas, who as state senator from Harrisburg helped draw the district boundaries and won the seat easily in 1982. Gekas grew up in Harrisburg, went to Dickinson College in nearby Carlisle, served in the Army, graduated from Dickinson Law. Within two years he was in the public sector as Dauphin County assistant district attorney. He was elected to the Pennsylvania House in 1966, at 36, to the Pennsylvania Senate in 1976, and to the U.S. House in 1982: an example of a conservative who has spent most of his life in government.

Gekas is third-ranking Republican on the Judiciary Committee, now chairman of its Immigration and Claims Subcommittee, an active and sometimes creative legislator, with a solidly conservative voting record leavened by some moderate votes on cultural issues. For years he has sponsored the death penalty for various heinous crimes. Prompted by constituents' experiences, he enacted a proposal preventing international kidnapping of children and another preventing evictions of the elderly. He sponsored the law, which took effect in 1992, that bars congressmen from converting leftover campaign funds to personal use. He worked to keep Legal Services Corporation lawyers from taking abortion cases and proposed block-granting legal aid funds to the states and abolishing the Corporation—a solution not entirely satisfactory to House conservatives or liberals.

Gekas parted company with Judiciary Committee conservatives when he helped to sink in 1997 their attempt to end racial quotas and preferences; he feared that a national debate would be "divisive." Gekas sponsored the International Child Adoption Act signed by Bill Clinton. He is interested in biomedical research, calling for increases in funding for the National Institutes of Health. He seeks limited protection from lawsuits for suppliers of raw materials for biomedical implantation devices. Responding to the 1995 crisis, he authored the House-passed Government Shutdown Protection Act, providing enough funds if appropriations bills aren't signed to "keep the government's lights on," but the proposal died as part of a supplemental-spending bill that Clinton vetoed. He oversaw the sunsetting of the Independent Counsel law in 1999. He sponsored the bill to repeal what Republicans called the "Gore tax"—authority for federal regulators, such as the FCC, to impose a user fee. He has been the chief House sponsor of a bankruptcy-reform bill, which would make it more difficult for individuals to file for bankruptcy to erase their debts; "people use it as a tool for financial management rather than a last resort," he complained of the current law. After years of debate, Congress agreed on a measure, but Clinton pocket-vetoed it during his final weeks in office; Republicans passed the bill again in March 2001 but efforts to resolve differences with the Senate stalled.

Gekas was briefly in the national spotlight as one of the House managers during the impeachment trial during which he spoke without notes as a home-spun defender of common-sense values against Clinton's "falsehoods uttered under oath." He subsequently refused to join the managers in a political action committee to support Republican candidates on the ground it would be presumptuous to try to associate impeachment proceedings with fundraising. On local issues, Gekas has worked to save Fort Indiantown Gap military base and to clean up the Harrisburg Airport Superfund site. Gekas has been re-elected with large majorities every two years. As a one-time redistricter himself, he will probably be treated well in redistricting, which is controlled by Republicans.

Cook's Call *Safe.* Redistricting is not likely to make this heavily Republican district any better for Democrats in 2002.

THE PEOPLE: Pop. 2000: 608,390; Pop. 1990: 565,702, up 7.5% 1990–2000. 87.9% White, 7.6% Black, 1.5% Asian, 0.1% Amer. Indian, 1.3% Two + races, 1.5% Other; 3.4% Hispanic Origin.

2000 Presidential Vote		
Bush (R)	145,270	(60%)
Gore (D)	89,243	(37%)
Nader (Green)	4,743	(2%)
Others	1,635	(1%)

1996 Presidential Vote		
Dole (R)	116,473	(54%)
Clinton (D)	81,205	(37%)
Perot (I)	17,997	(8%)

Rep. George W. Gekas (R)

Elected 1982, 10th term; b. Apr. 14, 1930, Harrisburg; home, Harrisburg; Dickinson Col., B.A. 1952, Dickinson Law Schl., J.D. 1958; Greek Orthodox; married (Evangeline).

Military Career: Army, 1953–55.

Elected Office: PA House of Reps., 1966–74; PA Senate, 1976–82.

Professional Career: Asst. Dist. Atty., Dauphin Cnty., 1960–66.

DC Office: 2109 RHOB 20515, 202-225-4315; Fax: 202-225-8440; Web site: www.house.gov/gekas.

District Offices: Elizabethtown, 717-367-6731; Harrisburg, 717-541-5507; Lebanon, 717-273-1451.

Committees: *Judiciary* (3d of 21 R): Commercial & Administrative Law; Immigration & Claims (Chmn.).

Group Ratings

	ADA	ACLU	AFS	LCV	CON	ITIC	NTU	COC	ACU	NTLC	CHC
2000	0	21	0	7	43	95	60	95	87	70	93
1999	5	—	0	0	23	—	55	100	84	—	—

National Journal Ratings

	1999 LIB —	1999 CONS		2000 LIB —	2000 CONS
Economic	22% —	77%		6% —	85%
Social	32% —	66%		22% —	77%
Foreign	37% —	62%		0% —	88%

Key Votes of the 106th Congress

1. Patient Bill of Rights	N	5. Bar RU-486 $ for FDA	Y	9. NATO War in Serbia	Y
2. Accelerate Min. Wage	N	6. Display 10 Commandments	Y	10. Perm. Trade with China	Y
3. Strike Ban on Ergo. Stnd.	N	7. Gun Show Bkgrnd. Checks	N	11. Debt Relief for 3rd World	N
4. Ovrd. Estate Tax Veto	Y	8. Ban Part.-Birth Abortion	Y	12. Drop Cuba Econ. Embargo	N

Election Results

2000 general	George W. Gekas (R)	166,236	(72%)	($206,666)
	Leslye Hess Herrmann (D)	66,190	(28%)	($22,090)
2000 primary	George W. Gekas (R)	unopposed		
1998 general	George W. Gekas (R)	unopposed		($92,690)

EIGHTEENTH DISTRICT

Pittsburgh is surely the hilliest of the large metropolitan areas of the United States—indicative of the nerve of its founders who were willing to build on such steep terrain. In its years of great growth, from the mid-1800s to the early 1900s, with the steel mills lining the riverbanks, Pittsburgh and its suburbs spread up and down hills, through the interstices of river valleys and over gaps to the next nearly level spot. As growth resumed in the mid-20th Century, the spreading-out process continued. One result is that there are no clusters of rich and poor suburbs, no single middle-class zone: they are spread out around the irregular terrain. The richest Pittsburghers, for example, live in Fox Chapel and Sewickley to the northeast and northwest; there are upper-middle-income suburbs like Mount Lebanon south of the Golden Triangle, but also some north of the Allegheny; working-class enclaves, now greatly depopulated, are strung along the Monongahela River near the mostly cold steel mills, but are found in other pockets as well. Pittsburgh does not have an edge city, though there are new housing and a few office developments to the north and to the west around the airport, now a major hub for USAirways.

When John Kennedy was elected president, there were four congressional districts in Pittsburgh's Allegheny County, numbered 27 through 30; now, only two are fully in the county. One, the 14th, is made up primarily of the city of Pittsburgh; the other, the 18th, includes suburbs to the north, south and east, plus most of the industrial Mon Valley to the southeast. This is the creation of 1990s redistricting, containing much of the old Republican-leaning suburban 18th and some of the heavily Democratic Mon Valley 20th. It has become a safe Democratic district.

The congressman from the 18th is Mike Doyle, a Democrat who won in 1994 when the Republican incumbent, brash conservative Rick Santorum, was elected to the U.S. Senate. Of Irish and Italian descent, Doyle grew up in the Mon Valley town of Swissvale, worked in steel mills during summers off from Penn State, worked as an insurance agent and for a nonprofit agency and was elected to the Swissvale Borough Council in 1977, at 24. In 1978 he became chief of staff to state Senator Frank Pecora, a Republican who had switched parties, ran against Santorum in 1992, and lost 61%–38%. In the process, he briefly gave Democrats control of the state Senate—something Senate Republicans, who now have a 30–20 margin, have not forgotten. In 1994 Doyle ran as a Democrat for the House; he was one of seven Democrats and four Republicans to seek the open seat. The Democrats were close to evenly matched: each won between 10% and 20% of the vote. Doyle, who had just switched to the Democratic Party himself, was helped by endorsements from unions and community leaders; like Santorum in his first campaign, he knocked on 40,000 doors. In the general, he faced John McCarty, an aide to the late Senator John Heinz; interestingly, McCarty was pro-choice and Doyle anti-abortion. Doyle campaigned for sweeping health care reform, against the new General Agreement on Tariffs and Trade, and for rebuilding the Mon Valley's industrial base, and won in a Republican year 55%–45%.

In the House, Doyle has a mixed voting record, toward the right on cultural issues, toward the left on economics. He supported the Blue Dogs on budget, welfare and regulatory reform, and he voted with most Republicans in opposing Clinton Administration plans for national student testing. He opposed tax cuts and called for higher Medicare co-payments for high-income recipients. He worked to funnel federal dollars to the Pittsburgh Supercomputing Center, the Pittsburgh Energy Technology Center and the Oakland veterans hospital. As a Steel Caucus member he co-sponsored the industry's legislation to reduce foreign imports. He opposed the EPA's new air-quality standards for fear of further local job losses. He helped win a brownfields provision in 1997 to give tax incentives for cleaning up contaminated industrial sites. Clinton signed his proposal for a program to develop methane hydrates as a "clean" energy source. And he wants a national historic park along the Mon River as part of the local Rivers of Steel program. Doyle was easily reelected in 1998 and 2000. He lives on Capitol Hill with six other bipartisan House colleagues and is one of the dwindling number of members who drive back home after each week's final vote.

The major threat to Doyle's tenure is redistricting. Pennsylvania lost two House seats in the 2000 Census, and Allegheny County's population declined 4%. Republicans control the redistricting process, and it is generally assumed that they will eliminate one of the Pittsburgh area's seats. Doyle now calls his party switch "ancient history," but it has not been forgotten by state Senate Republicans; one Republican called Doyle's likely elimination "a study in patient and deferred gratification." This could be done by expanding the current underpopulated 14th District, placing more Republican suburbs in Republican freshman Melissa Hart's 4th District and perhaps by extending John Murtha's 12th District into the heavily Democratic Mon Valley. This would leave Doyle with the choice of running against another Democratic incumbent—most likely William Coyne in a Pittsburgh-based 14th, possibly against Frank Mascara in the successor of the southwest Pennsylvania 20th, perhaps against John Murtha in a district stretching west across unfamiliar territory to Johnstown.

Cook's Call *Potentially Competitive.* This seat is being targeted during the redistricting process by Republicans, who are likely to combine it with Bill Coyne's 14th District. This would set up a potential battle between two Democratic incumbents for a Pittsburgh-based, Democratic-leaning district.

THE PEOPLE: Pop. 2000: 535,432; Pop. 1990: 565,771, down 5.4% 1990–2000. 86.9% White, 10.5% Black, 1.2% Asian, 0.1% Amer. Indian, 1% Two+ races, 0.3% Other; 0.7% Hispanic Origin.

2000 Presidential Vote		
Gore (D)	140,905	(57%)
Bush (R)	101,147	(41%)
Nader (Green)	4,254	(2%)
Others	2,908	(1%)

1996 Presidential Vote		
Clinton (D)	119,943	(52%)
Dole (R)	89,580	(39%)
Perot (I)	19,689	(8%)

Rep. Mike Doyle (D)

Elected 1994, 4th term; b. Aug. 5, 1953, Pittsburgh; home, Swissvale; PA St. U., B.S. 1975; Catholic; married (Susan).

Elected Office: Swissvale Borough Cncl., 1977–81.

Professional Career: Insurance agent, 1975–77; Exec. Dir., Turtle Creek Valley Citizens Union, 1977–79; Chief of Staff, PA Sen. Frank Pecora, 1978–94; Co-Founder/Owner, Eastgate Insurance Agency, 1983–present.

DC Office: 133 CHOB 20515, 202-225-2135; Fax: 202-225-3084; Web site: www.house.gov/doyle.

District Offices: McKeesport, 412-664-4049; Penn Hills, 412-241-6055.

Committees: *Energy & Commerce* (24th of 26 D): Commerce, Trade & Consumer Protection; Energy & Air Quality; Environment & Hazardous Materials.

Group Ratings

	ADA	ACLU	AFS	LCV	CON	ITIC	NTU	COC	ACU	NTLC	CHC
2000	65	36	100	50	34	56	25	47	20	21	33
1999	85	—	100	56	65	—	17	32	16	—	—

National Journal Ratings

	1999 LIB —	1999 CONS		2000 LIB —	2000 CONS
Economic	63% —	36%		64% —	35%
Social	53% —	47%		52% —	48%
Foreign	57% —	43%		55% —	45%

Key Votes of the 106th Congress

1. Patient Bill of Rights	Y	5. Bar RU-486 $ for FDA	Y	9. NATO War in Serbia	Y
2. Accelerate Min. Wage	Y	6. Display 10 Commandments	Y	10. Perm. Trade with China	N
3. Strike Ban on Ergo. Stnd.	Y	7. Gun Show Bkgrnd. Checks	Y	11. Debt Relief for 3rd World	Y
4. Ovrd. Estate Tax Veto	N	8. Ban Part.-Birth Abortion	Y	12. Drop Cuba Econ. Embargo	Y

Election Results

2000 general	Mike Doyle (D)	156,131	(69%)	($421,732)
	Craig C. Stephens (R)	68,798	(31%)	($7,729)
2000 primary	Mike Doyle (D)	unopposed		
1998 general	Mike Doyle (D)	98,363	(68%)	($400,293)
	Dick Walker (R)	46,945	(32%)	($81,999)

NINETEENTH DISTRICT

The Mason-Dixon Line, the historic boundary between Maryland and Pennsylvania, runs through some of the country's most pleasant rolling farmlands, west of the Susquehanna River up through the first of the Appalachian chains. It was over this invisible line that Robert E. Lee's Confederate troops crossed and were then repulsed in the Battle of Gettysburg in July 1863. Nearby was the westernmost capital of the United States during the Revolutionary War, the small city of York, capital from September 1777 to June 1778. This is where the Continental Congress passed the Articles of Confederation, received word from Benjamin Franklin in Paris that the French would help the colonies with money and ships, and issued the first proclamation calling for a national day of thanksgiving. Little today recalls it was once frontier and later fiercely fought over: The green farmland looks peaceful, prosperous and mostly undisturbed by the current era's commercial trappings and stylistic excesses.

Some 50 miles of the Mason-Dixon Line is the southern boundary of the 19th Congressional District of Pennsylvania, which is centered on York, and includes the suburbs of Harrisburg across the Susquehanna, the old town of Carlisle with Dickinson College, the Carlisle Barracks, the U.S. Army War College, and President Eisenhower's retirement home near Gettysburg. Eisenhower was of Pennsylvania Dutch stock himself; his father migrated in the late 19th Century, with a group of Mennonite brethren, to Kansas and Texas. The district has the look of deeply contented land and has been, with occasional exceptions, heavily Republican.

The congressman from the 19th District is Todd Platts, a Republican first elected in 2000. Platts grew up in York, graduated from Shippensburg University and Pepperdine University School of Law. In 1992, at age 30, after practicing law in Lancaster, he was elected to the state House of Representatives, where he served four terms. He chaired the Subcommittee for Basic Education. He opposed public funding of stadiums and legislative pay raises. He has been active in community affairs in York, including transportation and urban planning boards. He was the first to announce his candidacy after Bill Goodling—a former public school teacher, coach and principal and author of numerous initiatives to shift school funding to local control as the term-limited chairman of the Education and the Workforce Committee—officially announced his retirement in early 1999. Platts's chief primary opponents were state representative Al Masland, attorney and Goodling-endorsee Dick Stewart and Charlie Gerow, head of the state Citizens Against Government Waste, who twice challenged Goodling in the primary—losing 55%–45% in 1996. The campaign motto for Platts, who refused contributions from political action committees and was outspent by his chief Republican rivals, was "Putting People First;" his conservative supporters apparently weren't bothered by the fact that the phrase had been the title of a book by Bill Clinton. He emphasized his views on campaign finance, education, shoring up social security, and health care issues. Platts won with 33% to 29% for Masland and 19% for Stewart, rolling up huge margins in his home base of York County; Masland had a big edge in his base of Cumberland County, but it had less than half as many votes.

The Democratic nominee was Jeff Sanders, a Towson University psychology professor. But the district had not elected a Democrat since 1964, when one upset Goodling's father. Sanders criticized Platts for voting against using the state's surplus for school funding; Platts criticized Sanders for breaking their pledge to campaign positively. Platts favored allowing individuals to invest privately some of their Social Security benefits, but opposed privatization of the entire system. Sanders had little money, and Platts won, 73%–26%, with 75% of the vote in York County. Platts's total spending was about one-third the average of first-time House winners in 2000.

In the House, Platts was elected freshman class representative on the Republican Policy Committee, and got seats on Education, Government Reform, and Transportation and Infrastructure. He said his top priority is to reform campaign finance laws and he marks education reform high on his priority list. Redistricting may shift the district's lines, but it's not likely to threaten Platts.

Cook's Call   *Safe.* This solidly Republican district was also one of the fastest growing in Pennsylvania during the 1990s. Platts should have little trouble winning re-election in 2002.

THE PEOPLE: Pop. 2000: 632,862; Pop. 1990: 565,789, up 11.9% 1990–2000. 93.5% White, 3.1% Black, 0.9% Asian, 0.2% Amer. Indian, 1% Two+ races, 1.2% Other; 2.7% Hispanic Origin.

2000 Presidential Vote			1996 Presidential Vote		
Bush (R)	147,609	(61%)	Dole (R)	112,221	(52%)
Gore (D)	85,695	(36%)	Clinton (D)	81,319	(38%)
Nader (Green)	5,243	(2%)	Perot (I)	18,972	(9%)
Others	1,969	(1%)			

Rep. Todd Platts (R)

Elected 2000, 1st term; b. Mar. 5, 1962, York; home, York; Shippensburg U., B.S. 1984; Pepperdine U., J.D. 1991; Episcopalian; married (Leslie).

Elected Office: PA House of Reps., 1993–2000.

Professional Career: Praticing atty.

DC Office: 1032 LHOB 20515, 202-225-5836; Fax: 202-226-1000; Web site: www.house.gov/platts.

District Offices: Carlisle, 717-249-0190; Gettysburg, 717-338-1919; York, 717-600-1919.

Committees: *Education & the Workforce* (23d of 27 R): Education Reform; Select Education. *Government Reform* (18th of 24 R): District of Columbia (Vice Chmn.); National Security, Veterans' Affairs & Intl. Relations. *Transportation & Infrastructure* (35th of 42 R): Highways & Transit; Railroads.

Group Ratings and Key Votes: Newly Elected

Election Results

2000 general	Todd Platts (R)	168,722	(73%)	($308,158)
	Jeff Sanders (D)	61,538	(26%)	($33,709)
	Others	2,234	(1%)	
2000 primary	Todd Platts (R)	21,448	(33%)	
	Al Masland (R)	18,674	(29%)	
	Dick Stewart (R)	11,973	(18%)	
	Charlie Gerow (R)	8,314	(13%)	
	Christopher B. Reilly (R)	3,948	(6%)	
1998 general	William F. Goodling (R)	96,284	(68%)	($458,976)
	Linda G. Ropp (D)	40,674	(29%)	($6,905)
	Others	5,531	(4%)	

TWENTIETH DISTRICT

The area south of Pittsburgh and next to the deceptively straight-edged West Virginia state line is one of the industrial backlands of America. The Scots and Irish bordermen who came here 200 years ago were wild settlers who were never tamed by townsmen in their native countries or here; this was the land of the Whiskey Rebellion of 1794. In the 19th Century, more or less continuous seams of bituminous coal were discovered under these never-ending ridges. The offspring of the original settlers were joined by immigrants from Italy, Poland and Czechoslovakia, living in little frame houses packed into the towns on interstices between hills and rivers, within walking distance of steel factories, foundries and coal mine shafts. Life was never easy here; after some prosperous years in the 1960s and 1970s, the coal country was hit hard by the recession that followed the 1979 oil shock. Young people have been leaving the area for years, and it has a disproportionate elderly population. Only in recent years has the revived high-tech economy of greater Pittsburgh radiated outward into these hills, so far with limited effect.

The 20th Congressional District consists of this southwest corner of Pennsylvania. It includes Washington, Fayette, and Greene Counties, which have been heavily Democratic since the United Mine Workers backed the New Deal and established the United Steelworkers as the bargaining agent in the steel mills. But there is political balance: The 20th also includes some high- and middle-income suburbs of Pittsburgh in Allegheny County and a corner of Westmoreland County. The Nemacolin Woodlands resort in Fayette County has been the site of House Democratic retreats, including the unprecedented February 2001 visit by George W. Bush.

The congressman from the 20th District is Frank Mascara, a Democrat who won the seat in 1994 after coming close in 1992. Mascara grew up in this rough industrial country and knows its risks personally: His father was injured and suffered for years from the aftermath of a steel mill accident in Monessen and his grandfather was killed in a mining accident in Fayette County. Frank Mascara served in the Army as a teenager and was an accountant and small businessman before being elected Washington County controller in 1973; he was elected chairman of the county board of commissioners in 1980 and held that post through 1994. There he helped create Southpointe industrial park, a magnet for business development and new communities. In 1992 he ran for Congress and lost to scandal-tarred incumbent Austin Murphy in the Democratic primary by only 36%–34%. In 1994, after Murphy retired, Mascara ran again, winning a three-candidate primary with 54%, and in the general beating financial consultant Mike McCormick by 53%–47%.

In the House Mascara has on balance a moderate voting record. He vociferously attacked the Contract with America, but he also voted for many of its provisions: the line-item veto, the unfunded mandates bill, welfare reform. He calls himself "pro-life and pro-gun." He voted to override Bill Clinton's veto of the ban on partial-birth abortion. One of the few congressmen with vivid memories of the hardships of the 1930s, when his injured father supported a family of seven as a WPA worker, he called the Republican labor plans "class warfare" and proclaimed, "I believe in workplace safety and do not want it diluted!" Not surprisingly, he firmly supports lifetime health care benefits for retired miners. Although he stuck with most Democrats in opposing repeal of estate taxes, he voted to override Clinton's veto of the bill to repeal the marriage penalty. Mascara also worked on local issues, keeping the 911th Air Wing at Pittsburgh Airport and the Charles E.

Kelly Army Support facility off the base-closing list. He helped to authorize the coin commemorating General George C. Marshall, a native of Fayette County, and he sought flexibility in meeting air quality standards. On the highway bill, Mascara won $20 million for the new Mon-Fayette Freeway. He secured $2 million to combat shoreline erosion in Point Marion along the Monongahela River.

After winning a bitterly-contested 1996 re-election against McCormick, 54%–46%, Mascara was reelected without opposition in 1998 and won 64%–36% in 2000. Redistricting may be a problem for Mascara. Western Pennsylvania must lose one House seat, and Republicans control the redistricting process. In early 2001 it seemed that their target would more likely be the 18th District's Mike Doyle, in which case Mascara might do well out of the process: if redistricters help 4th District Republican Melissa Hart by taking heavily Democratic Beaver County out of her district, they will probably put it into the 20th, which would help Mascara. But there is still the possibility that Mascara may face a primary against another Democratic incumbent. There is some speculation that, at age 72, he may choose to retire.

Cook's Call   *Safe.* Although this district is very competitive at the national level (Gore won here by only 4% in 2000), Mascara has not had a tight race since 1996. But redistricting is likely to have an impact here: Republicans may combine the two Pittsburgh-area districts (14th and 18th) into one city-based district, which would make this seat a little more Democratic.

THE PEOPLE: Pop. 2000: 570,336; Pop. 1990: 565,789, up 0.8% 1990–2000. 94.9% White, 3.4% Black, 0.7% Asian, 0.1% Amer. Indian, 0.8% Two+ races, 0.2% Other; 0.6% Hispanic Origin.

2000 Presidential Vote

Gore (D)	120,778	(51%)
Bush (R)	110,556	(47%)
Nader (Green)	4,080	(2%)
Others	2,209	(1%)

1996 Presidential Vote

Clinton (D)	109,299	(50%)
Dole (R)	85,040	(39%)
Perot (I)	23,652	(11%)

Rep. Frank R. Mascara (D)

Elected 1994, 4th term; b. Jan. 19, 1930, Belle Vernon; home, Charleroi; CA U. of PA., B.S. 1972; Catholic; married (Delores).

Military Career: Army, 1946–47.

Elected Office: Washington Cnty. Controller, 1973–80; Chmn., Bd. of Cnty. Commissioners, 1980–94.

Professional Career: Businessman & Accountant, 1956–74.

DC Office: 314 CHOB 20515, 202-225-4665; Fax: 202-225-3377; Web site: www.house.gov/mascara.

District Offices: Greensburg, 724-834-6441; N. Charleroi, 724-483-9016; Uniontown, 724-437-5078; Washington, 724-228-4326; Waynesburg, 724-852-2182.

Committees: *Financial Services* (18th of 32 D): Capital Markets, Insurance & Government Sponsored Enterprises; Financial Institutions & Consumer Credit. *Transportation & Infrastructure* (15th of 34 D): Highways & Transit; Water Resources & Environment.

Group Ratings

	ADA	ACLU	AFS	LCV	CON	ITIC	NTU	COC	ACU	NTLC	CHC
2000	65	29	100	50	34	56	24	47	28	19	50
1999	70	—	100	56	37	—	14	20	21	—	—

National Journal Ratings

	1999 LIB	—	1999 CONS		2000 LIB	—	2000 CONS
Economic	75%	—	25%		65%	—	34%
Social	49%	—	50%		43%	—	55%
Foreign	58%	—	42%		58%	—	40%

Key Votes of the 106th Congress

1. Patient Bill of Rights	Y	5. Bar RU-486 $ for FDA	Y	9. NATO War in Serbia	Y
2. Accelerate Min. Wage	Y	6. Display 10 Commandments	Y	10. Perm. Trade with China	N
3. Strike Ban on Ergo. Stnd.	Y	7. Gun Show Bkgrnd. Checks	N	11. Debt Relief for 3rd World	Y
4. Ovrd. Estate Tax Veto	N	8. Ban Part.-Birth Abortion	Y	12. Drop Cuba Econ. Embargo	N

Election Results

2000 general	Frank R. Mascara (D)	145,131	(64%)	($509,444)
	Ronald J. Davis (R)	80,312	(36%)	
2000 primary	Frank R. Mascara (D)	unopposed		
1998 general	Frank R. Mascara (D)	unopposed		($424,974)

TWENTY-FIRST DISTRICT

The best natural harbor on Lake Erie is in a state that few think of as a Great Lakes state. This is Erie, protected by the Presque Isle peninsula, up in the remotest corner of Pennsylvania, 428 miles from Center City Philadelphia. This is heavy industry country: There is farmland here, and even some woods, but this land between the Great Lakes and the basin of the Ohio River has been prime heavy industry territory for more than 100 years.

The 21st Congressional District occupies this corner of Pennsylvania. About half its people are in Erie County, where the local economy has featured tourism growth and a small cut in the giant General Electric Transportation Systems plant. To the south are the farming areas of Crawford County, the steel-producing town of Sharon in Mercer County—on the Ohio border and part of the Youngstown-Warren area—and Butler County, a faster-growing suburban area directly north of Pittsburgh. Politically this is closely balanced territory: Erie and Mercer counties usually vote Democratic, and Butler and Crawford counties usually vote Republican. The result was one of the classic marginal seats in the nation from 1964–82 and again in the middle 1990s. In between came the tenure of Tom Ridge, a Republican from a Catholic working class family in Erie, a Harvard graduate and Vietnam veteran, first elected here by a narrow margin in 1982, who then won easily until he was elected governor in 1994. The district voted for Bill Clinton in the 1990s, but voted narrowly for George W. Bush in 2000, even though he didn't put Ridge on the ticket.

The congressman from the 21st is Phil English, a Republican elected in 1994. English grew up in Erie and has worked at little else but politics and government. At 20, he was an alternate to the 1976 Republican National Convention, and he worked during the early 1980s as a Republican staffer in Harrisburg. In 1985 he became Erie controller; in 1988, he was the Republican nominee for state treasurer, losing to Democrat Catherine Baker Knoll. He has unusual experience in having worked for his current colleagues. In 1990 he helped produce Rick Santorum's upset win in the Pittsburgh-area 18th District, the first step on Santorum's path to the Senate; he went on to become chief of staff to then-state senator Melissa Hart, who later followed him to the House in the adjacent 4th District. In 1994, when Ridge ran for governor, English ran for the House and won 66% in the Republican primary. In the general, English promised to reform welfare, cut wasteful spending and create jobs for northwestern Pennsylvania with an 18-point plan for revitalizing small business and manufacturing. Three of the four counties voted on party lines. But Erie, English's home—and probably more important, Ridge's—supported the Republican, giving him a 49%–47% victory.

In the House, the obviously vulnerable English became one of the first freshman Republicans since George Bush in 1967 to win a seat on Ways and Means, an excellent spot from which to both legislate and raise money. Early on, English made a record on local issues, getting the Army Corps of Engineers to dredge and replenish the beach at Presque Isle, working to stop Korea's dumping of steel pipe and tubing (the Shenango Valley is the leading U.S. producer), preserving spending on low-income heating, and protecting Erie Forge & Steel from the IRS. While he supported the Republican leadership on most votes, he has a moderate record on economic and foreign issues and has dissented prominently on occasion. He has been one of the House Republicans most willing to support a minimum wage increase and was the only member from his party to sponsor a bill limiting the tax deduction for pay to corporate chief executives. He was among 15 Republicans in 1999 to vote against the bill to make it more difficult to file class-action lawsuits.

His policy goals include fundamental tax reform to replace individual and corporate income taxes with a consumption tax to promote savings and level the playing field for U.S. businesses and workers. He won enactment in 1998 of his innovative proposal to grant a tax break to donors to groups such as the Make-A-Wish Foundation. "No child with a severe illness should have to be careful of what they wish for," English said. He has sponsored a bill to give a tax credit of up to 20% for the deployment of broadband Internet service. He was out front on behalf of the steel industry's efforts to impose quotas on steel imports—a campaign to warn the international community that "Congress is not willing to roll over and be a patsy." He was chosen to lead the Steel Caucus in March 2001. He won House approval of $3 million for more "trade cops" to enforce U.S. laws on unfair trade practices. During the 2000 campaign, he criticized Bush for backing "free-trade generalities." When the Kosovo crisis erupted, English conceded that he was uncertain what direction U.S. policy should head and that his international interest has not spread much beyond economic issues. "Foreign policy is not really my thing," he told *The Washington Post*. "My constituents don't get too fired up about it either. They focus more on things like health care, and so do I." That perspective helps to explain why English, with Democrat Earl Pomeroy, in early 2001 filed a bill to reduce the beer tax.

English had a tough reelection challenge in 1996 from Democrat Ron DiNicola, who returned home from law practice in Los Angeles to run in Erie. "California office. California driver's license. And a great tan," English's campaign proclaimed, "Independent voice. Pennsylvania values," emphasizing his support for the minimum wage. English won 51%–49%, taking 48% in Erie County and 47% in Mercer, but carrying Butler and Crawford Counties solidly. He has had no serious challenge since. Redistricting probably does not pose great problems for him. Republicans control the redistricting process, and his corner district would be hard to slice up by even hostile redistricters. However, he and his former boss Melissa Hart may have a friendly competition to see who gets more of heavily Republican Butler County.

Cook's Call *Safe*. While this district is competitive at the nation level (Bush won here by just 1% in 2000), Democrats have not recruited a strong challenger since 1996. English could get some help from redistricting since Republicans control the process.

THE PEOPLE: Pop. 2000: 581,440; Pop. 1990: 565,806, up 2.8% 1990–2000. 93.4% White, 4.4% Black, 0.5% Asian, 0.1% Amer. Indian, 1% Two + races, 0.5% Other; 1.4% Hispanic Origin.

2000 Presidential Vote			1996 Presidential Vote		
Bush (R)	112,163	(49%)	Clinton (D)	106,080	(49%)
Gore (D)	110,146	(48%)	Dole (R)	87,448	(40%)
Nader (Green)	5,628	(2%)	Perot (I)	22,510	(10%)
Others	2,308	(1%)			

Rep. Phil English (R)

Elected 1994, 4th term; b. June 20, 1956, Erie; home, Erie; U. of PA., B.A. 1978; Catholic; married (Christiane).

Elected Office: Erie City Controller, 1985–89.

Professional Career: Staff aide, PA Senate; 1980–84; Chief of Staff, PA Sen. Melissa Hart 1990–92; Exec. Dir., PA Senate Finance Cmte., 1990–94.

DC Office: 1410 LHOB 20515, 202-225-5406; Fax: 202-225-3103; Web site: www.house.gov/english.

District Offices: Butler, 724-285-7005; Erie, 814-456-2038; Hermitage, 724-342-6132; Meadville, 814-724-8414.

Committees: *Ways & Means* (15th of 24 R): Health; Human Resources; Trade. *Joint Economic Committee* (5th of 10 Reps.).

Group Ratings

	ADA	ACLU	AFS	LCV	CON	ITIC	NTU	COC	ACU	NTLC	CHC
2000	25	36	28	21	24	95	54	76	56	73	80
1999	25	—	40	19	6	—	53	76	72	—	—

National Journal Ratings

	1999 LIB	—	1999 CONS		2000 LIB	—	2000 CONS
Economic	48%	—	52%		48%	—	52%
Social	25%	—	72%		37%	—	62%
Foreign	41%	—	58%		51%	—	47%

Key Votes of the 106th Congress

1. Patient Bill of Rights	N	5. Bar RU-486 $ for FDA	Y	9. NATO War in Serbia	N
2. Accelerate Min. Wage	Y	6. Display 10 Commandments	Y	10. Perm. Trade with China	Y
3. Strike Ban on Ergo. Stnd.	Y	7. Gun Show Bkgrnd. Checks	N	11. Debt Relief for 3rd World	Y
4. Ovrd. Estate Tax Veto	Y	8. Ban Part.-Birth Abortion	Y	12. Drop Cuba Econ. Embargo	Y

Election Results

2000 general	Phil English (R)	135,164	(61%)	($1,219,501)
	Marc A. Flitter (D)	87,018	(39%)	($306,378)
2000 primary	Phil English (R)	unopposed		
1998 general	Phil English (R)	94,518	(63%)	($1,140,104)
	Larry Klemens (D)	54,591	(37%)	($19,228)

★ RHODE ISLAND ★

The tiny little city-state with a mouthful of an official name, Rhode Island and Providence Plantations, has as turbulent a political history as any state in the Union. A successful trading community since the 1600s, a leader in manufacturing since Samuel Slater replicated from memory an English water-powered cotton textile mill in Pawtucket in 1791, Rhode Island also had its beginning as an upstart community, a refuge for religious dissenters, "the sewer of New England," as the orthodox Cotton Mather put it. Rhode Island profited from slavery (two-thirds of America's slaves arrived on ships owned by Rhode Islanders) and war (the state boomed during the Civil War), and carried its tradition of tolerating just about anything into its politics. Rhode Island refused to pay its share for the Revolutionary War, declined to send delegates to the 1787 Constitutional Convention, and delayed joining the Union until the other 12 states had, prompting George Washington to say, "Rhode Island still perseveres in that impolitic, unjust—and one might add without much impropriety—scandalous conduct, which seems to have marked all her public counsels of late." The new nation's first bank failure occurred here in 1809, when a bank capitalized at $45 issued $800,000 in bank notes. In the 1840s, conflict between hard money merchants and soft money farmers resulted in two state governments and a conflict known as Dorr's War, with the outcome determined when merchant Dorr's two ancient cannons failed to fire.

Then, in the 1930s, Rhode Island had something resembling a political revolution. Thousands of immigrants from French Canada, Ireland and Italy came to Rhode Island to work in the textile mills and this colony of dissident Protestants became the most heavily Catholic state in the nation. Yankee Republicans tried to appeal to Catholics by running French-Canadians for office. But national events—Al Smith's candidacy in 1928, when he carried Rhode Island, and Franklin Roosevelt's New Deal—moved the Catholics toward the Democrats. Then came the revolution: in 1935, the Democrats under Governor Theodore Green, although they had won only 20 of the 42 state Senate seats, refused to seat two Republicans. With the lieutenant governor's tie-breaker, they voted Democrats into the seats, and proceeded in 14 minutes to declare the state Supreme Court seats vacant, abolish state boards that controlled Democratic cities, strengthen the power of the governor and reorganize state government to purge Republicans. This ended the direct political control of Rhode Island's "Five Families"—the Browns, Metcalfs, Goddards, Lippitts and Chafees—who owned or ran many of the textile mills, the Rhode Island Hospital Trust (long the largest bank), the Providence *Journal-Bulletin*, Brown University, the Rhode Island School of

Woonsocket

CUMBERLAND

NORTH SMITHFIELD

Cumberland Hill

BURRILLVILLE

Pascoag

LINCOLN

Valley Falls

SMITHFIELD

Central Falls

GLOCESTER

Greenville

Pawtucket

PROVIDENCE

North Providence

Providence ★

East Providence

JOHNSTON

FOSTER

SCITUATE

Cranston

1

BRISTOL

Barrington

WARREN

COVENTRY

West Warwick

Warwick

KENT

Bristol

Tiverton

WEST GREENWICH

2

EAST GREENWICH

PORTSMOUTH

EXETER

NORTH KINGSTOWN

NEWPORT

MIDDLETOWN

JAMESTOWN

Newport East

RICHMOND

Newport

LITTLE COMPTON

HOPKINTON

WASHINGTON

Kingston

SOUTH KINGSTOWN

Wakefield–Peacedale

NARRAGANSETT

CHARLESTOWN

Westerly

— Congressional district boundaries
effective May 22, 1992.

— County boundaries.

2

NEW SHOREHAM
Block Island

N
W   E
S

Miles
0 1 2 3 4

Design and the state Republican Party. The Democrats have won most elections with the lion's share of votes from Rhode Island's 64% Catholic majority, starting with Green's election in 1936, at age 69, to the first of his four terms as U.S. senator. From 1940–80, Democrats won every election for U.S. House seats; its Democratic percentages in presidential elections from 1968–96 are rivalled only by Massachusetts. Republicans have won when they've been able to capitalize· on scandal or Democratic disarray, as Governor Lincoln Almond did in 1994. But the only really durable Republican politician has been John Chafee, elected governor in 1962, 1964 and 1966, senator in 1976, 1982, 1988 and 1994; and even he lost twice statewide, in 1968 and 1972.

Rhode Island has gone through a long and painful economic transformation, from blue collar to white collar, from textiles to high-tech. It suffered economic problems in the early 1990s, but has smartly recovered and entered the new century more productive and confident than it has been in decades. The Census Bureau estimated that Rhode Island's population fell below the 1 million mark in 1996, but the 2000 Census showed it up to 1,048,000, a 4% increase for the decade. The submarine factory and Navy base at Quonset Point lost thousands of jobs; employment in costume jewelry, Rhode Island's major manufacturer, fell from 32,500 in 1977 to 6,300 in 2000; overfishing has cut the lobster and winter flounder stocks sharply. But Republican Governor Lincoln Almond, elected in 1994 and 1998, persuaded the overwhelmingly Democratic legislature (44–6 in the Senate, 85–15 in the House) to gradually cut income taxes and eliminate the car tax, and Providence Mayor Buddy Cianci promoted brilliantly successful redevelopment in the state's capital and largest city. The 1995 Capital Center project opened up Providence's riverfront, where WaterFire shows attracted thousands; vacant lots and dilapidated industrial buildings were transformed into parks, plazas and new streets; the old Biltmore Hotel was renovated and a $35 million luxury condominium development built; in 1999 high-end Providence Place Mall opened; Cianci saw that over 100 restaurants got financing. "We've gone from blight to bright," Cianci said. Tourism became Rhode Island's second largest industry, and computer data processing a major part of the economy; Rhode Island's university hospitals drew a far-above-average number of federal research dollars; Rhode Island's research and development tax credit, claimed to be the largest in the nation, encouraged high-tech startups; Providence's T.F. Green Airport boomed, as a low-cost alternative to Boston's Logan. Providence, after losing population for decades, grew 8% in the 1990s, the biggest gain since 1900–10, and Latino immigrants—from the Dominican Republic and Guatemala, Peru and Ecuador—brought vitality to neighborhoods long given up for dead. As Almond said, "Our cities have grown and prospered through the contributions of new generations of immigrants. It's gratfying to see this trend continue."

There seemed to be a new sense of optimism—and fun. Tourists came to see Nibbles Woodaway, the 58-foot-long termite built by the New England Pest Control Company and the state marketed Mr. Potato Head, created in Pawtucket, as the symbol of "Rhode Island—the birthplace of fun." The television show *Providence* painted the city's booming East Side in soft and golden hues. Yet there were also problems. Cianci, mayor from 1975 to 1984, when he was convicted of assaulting and burning a man he accused of having an affair with his wife, and mayor again from 1991, was indicted in April 2001. This was the result of a federal investigation called Operation Plunder Dome; federal prosecutors brought 30 counts of bribery totaling $1.5 million, including payments to Cianci or his campaign in return for a School Department lease on a former auto body shop, property tax reductions, city jobs, tow truck contracts and a lifetime membership in the University Club. Governor Lincoln Almond and Senator Lincoln Chafee called on Cianci to resign; Senator Jack Reed said it was up to Cianci, but that the charges were serious; Congressmen Patrick Kennedy and James Langvevin said they supported the mayor. "I assure you that I am not guilty of these charges," Cianci said, and ridiculed them on Don Imus's radio talk show.

Governor Lincoln Almond, elected governor of Rhode Island, grew up in the mill town of Central Falls, not the usual venue for a Republican, and got involved in local government in Lincoln in 1963, at 26. He ran for Congress in 1968 and lost, then served as U.S. attorney from 1969–78, ran for governor in 1978 and lost, and was U.S. attorney again from 1981–93. He ran for governor again in 1994, and this time won. It was an upset not only in the general but also in the primary. The favorite was 1st District Congressman Ron Machtley, a career military veteran who in 1988 beat Banking Chairman Fernand St Germain, the man whose lax savings and loan laws led to the collapse of the industry and hundreds of billions in losses to taxpayers. But Almond rallied more party support and won the primary 58%–42%. Meanwhile, incumbent Democrat Bruce Sundlun, who had been unpopular since his first-term tax increases, lost to liberal state Senator Myrth York by a humiliating 57%–27% margin. In the general, Almond and York disputed over casino gambling: Almond was totally opposed, York said it was up to the people; the Mashantucket Pequot's Foxwoods casino in Connecticut has become a major employer of Rhode Islanders. Ultimately, Almond won by the narrow margin of 47%–44%, with 9% for Robert Healey, the bearded and long-haired candidate of the Cool Moose Party.

Almond seems oddly unpolitical; the Providence *Journal-Bulletin* called him "a man with no instinctive grasp of politics," who refuses to adjust his off-hours schedule to walk in parades, attend christenings or wakes or even fundraisers. He jousted much of the time with the overwhelmingly Democratic legislature. Yet in his first term he made progress on some fronts. He managed to reduce the number of state employees and pushed through a 9% income tax cut over five years, a R&D investment tax credit, and a new formula for distributing state educational aid. He signed a welfare reform bill requiring recipients to work after two years, a bill to deregulate electric utilities and a bill banning discrimination against gays. He pushed for passage of a $72 million bond issue to finance rail construction to Quonset Point/Davisville, where he has tried to create a container port, over the opposition of local officials. In January 1997 Democrats argued that he had no right to appoint a new lieutenant governor when incumbent Robert Weygand retired to serve in Congress; Almond appointed Bernard Jackvony anyway and the state Supreme Court upheld him. Almond remained a staunch opponent of casino gambling, despite the importunings of the Narragansett Indians.

In 1998 Almond was again opposed by York. York actually raised more money than Almond up through August, put ads up on the air first and led in many polls up through October. She argued that Almond's education spending hadn't produced any increase in test scores and called for building more classrooms and reducing class sizes in early grades. Almond claimed credit for the booming economy and increase in jobs. Almond backed a $43 million basketball arena and convocation center for the University of Rhode Island (he is the first URI graduate to become governor); York opposed the project. Healey, the Cool Moose candidate, ran again, with the slogan, "Healey for governor. Why not? You've done worse before." Almond won 51%–42%, with 6% for Healey. But Lieutenant Governor Bernard Jackvony lost 50%–44% to Democrat Charles Fogarty, and Democratic former U.S. Attorney Sheldon Whitehouse was elected Attorney General.

In his second term Almond continued to push for the container port. He approved a higher minimum wage and persuaded the legislature to cut taxes for brokers, bankers and jewelry makers. He got rid of Providence's residency requirements for teachers but vetoed a bill that failed to require teacher applicants to pass a state exam. He got the legislature to approve full-day kindergarten. He successfully sought $94 million in bonds to preserve open space and protect Narragansett Bay, but voters turned down $25 million in bonds for a Heritage Harbor Museum in Providence. He backed a Newport campus for the Community College of Rhode Island, approved by voters in November. He signed an anti-racial profiling law, a .08% blood alcohol limit and Whitehouse's bill for a mandatory ten year sentence for anyone pulling a gun while committing a crime. When several health insurers left Rhode Island, Almond's administration moved adroitly to maintain Rhode Island's highest-in-the-nation ranking in health insurance coverage. In February 2001 Almond called for more e-government, an end to the state's capital gains tax and $25 million in borrowing for affordable housing.

Almond is term-limited and cannot run for re-election in 2002. There is every prospect for a seriously and, as in the 2000 Senate race, bitterly contested Democratic primary.

Cook's Call *Potentially Competitive.* Democrats are likely to host a very hard-fought, late primary: State Attorney General Sheldon Whitehouse, Lieutenant Governor Charlie Fogarty, state Representative Tony Pires, and 1994 and 1998 gubernatorial nominee Myrth York all looking at bids. On the Republican side, former Attorney General Jeff Pine is the favorite should he run, businessman Don Carcieri and 1998 state Treasurer candidate Jim Bennett have also been mentioned.

Senior Senator Jack Reed, Rhode Island's senior Senator, was elected to the House in

1990 and the Senate in 1996. He grew up in working-class Cranston, the son of a school custodian; he graduated from West Point, served in the 82d Airborne, then taught at West Point. In 1979 he retired from the Army and went to Harvard Law School. In 1984, at 35, he beat an incumbent in the primary for state Senate, where he served for six years, was close to the party leadership, and built a good reputation. When Republican Claudine Schneider left the House to run against Senator Claiborne Pell in 1990, Reed ran for the House seat, overcoming several better known candidates in the primary, and winning with 59% over Save the Bay Executive Director Trudy Coxe in the general.

Reed compiled a substantially, though not quite totally, liberal record in the House. On the Education and the Workforce Committee he worked for the Goals 2000 Act, insisting on a requirement that states show gradual progress in meeting educational standards; on reauthorization of the Elementary and Secondary Education Act, he backed the "opportunity to learn" standards—spending requirements— backed by teachers' unions. He tried to amend the 1996 Welfare Reform Act to have block grants increase when national unemployment is more than 6%. Using his military experience, he criticized U.N. efforts in the Balkans as trying to be "all things to all people" and, before American Rangers were killed, said the Somalia mission was hampered by "poor intelligence" and "an awkward command structure." In summer 1994, after a trip to Haiti, he called for tougher economic sanctions and no military involvement; in March 1995 he said he was "pleasantly surprised" about Aristide's "apparent commitment to democratic reform." On local issues, Reed worked for the freight rail connection at the Quonset Point/Davisville port and introduced legislation to require indelible country-of-origin markings on foreign-made jewelry and jewelry boxes; Rhode Island's jewelry industry produces about a third of the costume jewelry in the United States.

When Senator Claiborne Pell announced his retirement after 36 years in the Senate, Reed almost immediately started running. Reed was easily nominated and faced state Treasurer Nancy Mayer in the general. National Republicans spent nearly $1 million on ads attacking Reed as a liberal for opposing workfare and for supporting labor unions; in liberal, unionized Rhode Island these did not hurt him and may have helped. Mayer's support for campaign finance reform and opposition to soft money were parried when Reed in debate asked her why she didn't call off the Republican soft money campaign against him. Mayer's campaign was overshadowed by Reed's: She spent $773,000 and he spent $2.7 million. His biography was his message: Reed launched his campaign in a school conference room named after his late father; he stressed how he came up from humble beginnings by hard work and called for education spending to help others rise as he had. That message, and his own pleasant, unassuming demeanor evidently touched a chord. He won 63%–35%, an impressive first Senate victory.

In the Senate, Reed has a liberal voting record. He serves on the HELP Committee and has sought to amend major bills. He restored a $35 million program cut by Appropriations which gives federal money to state programs aiding low-income college students. The 1998 Higher Education law included his TEACH program, grants to teacher colleges for partnerships with K-12 schools. He sponsored a bill in 2000 to require all schools to give parents information about their children. He has been a strong supporter of requiring continual teacher training. He believes that school libraries have been underfunded and in 2001 with Thad Cochran sponsored a bill to provide them $500 million. Reed has sponsored bills to increase spending on the National Endowments for the Arts and the Humanities and on the Energy Department's Weatherization Assistance program. He has sought to increase Medicare spending for home health care and to promote purchasing pools for health insurance. In October 2000 he put a hold on a bill granting citizenship to foreign children adopted by American parents, in an effort to get permanent refugee status for 10,000 Liberians who came to the United States, many of them to Rhode Island. In March 2001 he sought an expansion of funding for Travelers Aid, which serves the homeless. "Ultimately, the mark of our country and our society is not our prodigious economy. It's not our military prowess. It's really whether or not we have communities where people can find shelter, can find the kind of support they need to use their talents for themselves and for their families and for this great nation."

Reed is one of the few senators of his generation with military experience. He was appointed to the governing board of West Point in 1998 and got a seat on the Armed Services Committee in January 1999. He wants to consolidate the Naval War College and the Naval Undersea Warfare Center, two of the remaining Rhode Island military facilities; defense jobs in the state declined from 44,000 in 1970 to 8,000 in 1999. In January 1998 he called for extending the June 1998 deadline for withdrawal of U.S. troops from Bosnia, but with clear "milestones." When the deadline arrived he and John McCain led the fight against cutting off funds for the Bosnia deployment. In February 1999 he expressed "deep skepticism" about U.S. involvement in Yugoslavia, but he supported the air war over Serbia and Kosovo; in July 1999 he said that UN forces faced "a very challenging political situation" in Kosovo. In May 2000 he inserted language in the defense authorization requesting that the Pentagon show economical ways to expand the submarine fleet.

In Rhode Island politics, Reed has always been his own man, unentangled with the various machine politicians who come and go. He picked a non-political prosecutor to be U.S. attorney in 1998. He has helped get funding for various Rhode Island projects, including the Heritage Harbor Museum, disaster planning, health research at the University of Rhode Island and the John H. Chafee Blackstone Valley National Heritage Corridor.

This is a Senate seat whose members have had long tenures. Theodore Green, elected at 69, served 24 years; Claiborne Pell, elected at 41, served 36 years. Reed, elected just before turning 47, has the prospect of long service before him.

Cook's Call   *Safe.* There are no indications that Reed will face a credible challenger in this incredibly Democratic state.

Junior Senator   Lincoln Chafee, the junior senator from Rhode Island, was appointed to the office in November 1999, a week after the death of his father, Senator John Chafee. He was only the second son appointed to the Senate to succeed his father; the other was Harry Byrd, Jr., in 1965. Lincoln Chafee grew up in Warwick, Rhode Island, on a 20-acre estate; there he developed his love of horses. "The outside of a horse is good for the inside of a man," he likes to say. His father was elected governor when he was eight, and he remembers going to the 1964 Republican National Convention, at 11, and the hostility of the Goldwater supporters there for Rockefeller Republicans. In 1969 John Chafee became secretary of the Navy; Lincoln Chafee was at Andover, where one of his schoolmates was Jeb Bush. In 1976 John Chafee was elected to the Senate; the year before, Lincoln Chafee graduated from Brown and went off to horseshoeing school at Montana State University. For seven years he worked as a farrier at race tracks in the United States and Canada. In 1984 he returned to Rhode Island, and was elected to the City Council in Warwick in 1986, the state's second largest city. In 1992 he was elected mayor of Warwick, the first Republican in 32 years. He was re-elected three times, and as mayor privatized the solicitor's office, produced an economic development plan for the T.F. Green Airport area and left the city with a $6.6 million surplus. In March 1999, John Chafee announced that he would not seek re-election in 2000: "I want to come home," he said. The next day Lincoln Chafee announced he would run for the seat. The older Chafee was a productive legislator, who assembled bipartisan majorities for revisions of the Clean Air and Clean Water Act; he was greatly beloved in Rhode Island, respected as a member of one of Rhode Island's "Five Families" who had volunteered for the Marine Corps and served in combat in World War II and Korea, and who worked hard at public service and kept in touch with ordinary Rhode Islanders, a natural compromise-maker who could also be a tough partisan when convinced that was right.

John Chafee died in October 1999. After a week of mourning Governor Lincoln Almond appointed Lincoln Chafee to the Senate. He had not been running strong in the polls against possible Democratic opponents, and some thought he was hurt when in August 1999 he admitted he had used cocaine. In the Senate he served on his father's old committees and promised to continue in his tradition. On one of his first votes he was one of four Republicans to vote against the party's minimum wage bill. He sponsored a John Chafee fellowship in environmental education and, with Tom Harkin, a bill to allow the FDA to regulate tobacco. In 2000 he voted with Democrats on the estate tax and HMO regulation. But he said he would not switch parties—"I'm named after Abraham Lincoln"—and said that Senate Republican leaders "have been very understanding of my votes." Obviously they understood that only a Republican who often voted with Democrats, and only a Chafee, could hold this seat in the nation's most Democratic state.

Certainly he could expect Democratic competition. Senate seats don't come up often in Rhode Island: John Chafee held his for 23 years, Claiborne Pell held his for 36, John Pastore for 26, Theodore Green for 24—they, plus Jack Reed, were the only senators from Rhode Island from 1950 to 1999. Democrats were in the midst of a party feud when in spring 1999 2d District Congressman Robert Weygand announced he would campaign on early childhood programs, home health care and support for small business. Weygand got his start as a landscape architect who was shaken down by the mayor of Pawtucket and, wired by prosecutors, helped get him convicted and removed from office. He was elected lieutenant governor in 1992 and congressman in 1996. But he was also a political enemy of 1st District Congressman Patrick Kennedy who announced he would not run for the Senate but would concentrate on taking back the House as chairman of the Democratic Congressional Campaign Committee. Kennedy was initially expected to back House Speaker John Harwood, but when he didn't run backed former Lieutenant Governor Richard Licht, who had lost to John Chafee 55%–45% in 1988 (and whose uncle Frank Licht beat Chafee for governor 51%–49% in 1968). In April 2000 the state Democratic convention endorsed Licht; but Weygand got the AFL-CIO endorsement and boasted, "I'm willing to challenge my party."

The primary was not until September 12, and for five months the two Democrats battered each other with charges and countercharges. Each spent more than $1 million on the primary campaign. Licht's ads attacked Weygand for his opposition to abortion; other Democrats grumbled that he was one of the 31 Democrats who voted for the Republican version of the impeachment inquiry. Licht called Weygand a "special interest hypocrite," who took money from tobacco company lawyers; Weygand said that Licht represented "politics as usual at its worst." Weygand backers pointed out that Licht's wife and two children lived in Massachusetts, where she was a state judge; Licht said they lived together on weekends in the Rhode Island resort town of Little Compton. Weygand won the September 12 primary by a 57%–43% margin; Licht carried Little Compton and his old home town of Providence, but little else. But wounds still stung: Not until September 30 did Patrick Kennedy and Senator Jack Reed endorse Weygand.

In the meantime, the Republican Senate campaign committee was running ads praising Chafee for his independence and citing his votes against Republican positions on HMO regulation and prescription drugs. One Chafee ad accused Weygand of "embroidering the truth" in an ad about his Labrador retriever taking the arthritis drug Lodine. Weygand ran negative spots attacking Chafee's record as mayor, linking him with right-wing Republicans, depicting him as a pawn of the pharmaceutical industry. Democrats made much of a $6,000 fund Chafee used as mayor to buy presents for children of city employees and contribute to charity. Chafee actually spent less than Weygand, but of course he did not have a primary opponent. Chafee won 57%–41%, running 25% ahead of George W. Bush in Rhode Island.

After the election Chafee said he liked the tone of the Bush campaign, but he did not like many of the early Bush policies—the ban on aid to international organizations that provide abortion counseling, support of oil drilling in the Arctic National Wildlife Refuge, renunciation of the Kyoto treaty, reversal of Bush's little noticed one-sentence commitment to reduce levels of carbon dioxide. Chafee was the first Senate Republican to oppose the Bush tax cut, and said his position was not negotiable; he effectively let Democrat John Breaux negotiate for him. He voted with Democrats and John McCain on campaign finance in March 2001. In May 2001 his bipartisan brownfields bill passed unanimously; it barred EPA from regulating old industrial sites once it said they were clean. This had been held up by western Republicans in 2000 who wanted more sweeping Superfund changes; its fate in the House was unclear.

Presidential politics   Rhode Island is almost always one of the most Democratic states in presidential elections—over the last generation, the most Democratic on average: It voted 61%–32% for Al Gore in 2000. Bush carried the towns of East Greenwich and (by 6 votes) Scituate; Gore carried every other city and town. White Protestants, once the Republican base here, voted 51%–41% for Gore; white Catholics voted 59%–35% for Gore. Rhode Island's Catholic majority is heavily Democratic and, interestingly, pro-choice on abortion: In states where Catholics are beleaguered minorities they may stand together and strongly oppose abortion; here, where they're the strong majority and where the mostly Mediterranean Catholics traditionally didn't pay strict attention to the mostly Irish priests, they come out against the church position.

Rhode Island holds a presidential primary the same day as Massachusetts, usually with the lowest turnout rate in the nation. It has not won much attention. In 1992 only 66,000 of the one million Rhode Islanders voted in both parties' primaries; in 2000, when the primary was held of March 7 and the outcomes not entirely clear, 82,000 voted. Al Gore beat Bill Bradley 57%–41%— one of Bradley's better performances—and John McCain beat George W. Bush 60%–36%.

Congressional districting The boundaries of Rhode Island's two congressional districts have remained pretty much the same since 1842, except for the period from 1912 to 1932 when the state had three districts. Providence is split and both districts are overwhelmingly Democratic. For 2002, 14,000 people need to be moved from the 2nd district to the 1st; in early 2001 the state's two Democratic congressmen said they would work together on drawing new lines.

THE PEOPLE: Pop. 2000: 1,048,319; Pop. 1990: 1,003,464, up 4.5% 1990–2000. 0.4% of U.S. total, 43d largest; 85% White, 4.5% Black, 2.3% Asian, 0.5% Amer. Indian, 0.1% Hawaiian, 2.7% Two+ races, 5% Other; 8.7% Hispanic Origin. 4.1% Unemployment. 2000 Voting age pop.: 800,497. 2000 Turnout: 412,074; 51% of VAP. Registered voters (2000): 671,612; no party registration.

POLITICAL LINEUP: Governor, Lincoln Almond (R); Lt. Gov., Charles J. Fogarty (D); Secy. of State, Edward S. Inman III (D); Atty. Gen., Sheldon Whitehouse (D); General Treasurer, Paul Tavares (D); State Senate, 50 (44 D, 6 R); Majority Leader, William V. Irons (D); State House, 100 (85 D, 15 R, 1 I); House Speaker, John Harwood (D). Senators, Jack Reed (D) and Lincoln Chafee (R). Representatives, 2 (2 D).

ELECTIONS DIVISION: 401-222-2345; **FILING DEADLINE FOR U.S. CONGRESS:** June 26, 2002.

2000 Presidential Vote

Gore (D)	249,508	(61%)
Bush (R)	130,555	(32%)
Nader (Green)	25,052	(6%)
Others	3,668	(1%)

1996 Presidential Vote

Clinton (D)	233,050	(60%)
Dole (R)	104,683	(27%)
Perot (I)	43,723	(11%)
Others	8,674	(2%)

2000 Republican Presidential Primary

McCain (R)	21,754	(60%)
Bush (R)	13,170	(36%)
Other	1,196	(3%)

2000 Democratic Presidential Primary

Gore (D)	26,801	(57%)
Bradley (D)	19,000	(41%)
Other	1,043	(2%)

Gov. Lincoln Almond (R)

Elected 1994, term expires Jan. 2003, 2d term; b. June 16, 1936, Pawtucket; home, Lincoln; U. of RI, B.S. 1959, Boston U., J.D. 1961; Episcopalian; married (Marilyn).

Military Career: Naval Reserves, 1953–61.

Elected Office: Lincoln Town Admin., 1963–68; Repub. nominee for U.S. House, 1968; Repub. nominee for Gov., 1978.

Professional Career: Practicing atty., 1962–94; U.S. Atty. for RI, 1969–78, 1981–93; Pres., Blackstone Valley Land Develop. Foundation, 1982–94.

Office: The State House, Providence, 02903, 401-222-2080; Fax: 401-861-5894; Web site: www.governor.state.ri.us.

Election Results

1998 general	Lincoln Almond (R)	156,180	(51%)
	Myrth York (D)	129,105	(42%)
	Robert J. Healey (Cool Moose)	19,250	(6%)
	Others	1,910	(1%)
1998 primary	Lincoln Almond (R)	unopposed	
1994 general	Lincoln Almond (R)	171,194	(47%)
	Myrth York (D)	157,361	(44%)
	Robert J. Healey (Cool Moose)	32,822	(9%)

Sen. Jack Reed (D)

Elected 1996, seat up 2002, 1st term; b. Nov. 12, 1949, Cranston; home, Cranston; U.S. Military Acad., West Point, B.S. 1971, Harvard U., M.P.P. 1973, J.D. 1982; Catholic; single.

Military Career: Army, 1967–79; Army Reserves, 1979–91.

Elected Office: RI Senate, 1984–90; U.S. House of Reps., 1990–96.

Professional Career: Assoc. Prof., U.S. Military Acad. at West Point, 1978–79; Practicing atty., 1982–90.

DC Office: 320 HSOB, 20510, 202-224-4642; Fax: 202-224-4680; Web site: www.senate.gov/~reed.

State Offices: Cranston, 401-943-3100; Providence, 401-528-5200.

Committees: *Armed Services*: Personnel; Seapower; Strategic Forces (Chmn.). *Banking, Housing & Urban Affairs*: Financial Institutions; Housing & Transportation (Chmn.); Securities & Investment. *Health, Education, Labor & Pensions*: Children & Families; Public Health. *Joint Economic Committee* (Vice Chmn. of 10 Sens.).

Group Ratings

	ADA	ACLU	AFS	LCV	CON	ITIC	NTU	COC	ACU	NTLC	CHC
2000	95	71	85	100	63	93	12	46	12	0	15
1999	100	—	100	100	32	—	7	47	4	—	—

National Journal Ratings

	1999 LIB	—	1999 CONS		2000 LIB	—	2000 CONS
Economic	84%	—	13%		96%	—	0%
Social	88%	—	0%		79%	—	0%
Foreign	78%	—	13%		72%	—	15%

Key Votes of the 106th Congress

1. Educ. Savings Accts.	N	5. Review Movie Violence	N	9. NATO War in Serbia	Y
2. Prescrip. Drug Benefit	Y	6. Gun Show Bckgrnd. Checks	Y	10. Table Cuba Travel Ban	N
3. Delay Ergonomic Standards	N	7. Ban Part.-Birth Abortion	N	11. Nuclear Test-Ban Treaty	Y
4. Phase Out Estate Tax	N	8. Broaden Hate Crimes List	Y	12. Perm. Trade with China	Y

Election Results

1996 general	Jack Reed (D)	230,676	(63%)	($2,732,011)
	Nancy J. Mayer (R)	127,368	(35%)	($773,789)
1996 primary	Jack Reed (D)	59,336	(86%)	
	Don Gil (D)	9,554	(14%)	
1990 general	Claiborne Pell (D)	225,105	(62%)	($2,363,904)
	Claudine Schneider (R)	138,947	(38%)	($2,056,923)

Sen. Lincoln Chafee (R)

Appointed Nov. 1999, seat up 2006, 1st term; b. Mar. 26, 1953, Warwick; home, Warwick; Brown U., B.A., 1975; Episcopalian; married (Stephanie).

Elected Office: Warwick city council, 1986–92; Warwick mayor, 1992–99.

Professional Career: Farrier, 1976–83; Cranston Print Works, 1984–85; Rhode Island Forging Steel, 1985–86; Planner, General Dynamics, 1986–90; Exec. dir., Northeast Corridor Initiative, 1990–92.

DC Office: 141 RSOB, 20510, 202-224-2921; Fax: 202-228-2853; Web site: www.senate.gov/~chafee.

State Office: Providence, 401-453-5294.

Committees: *Environment & Public Works*: Fisheries, Wildlife & Water; Superfund, Waste Control & Risk Assessment (RMM); Transportation & Infrastructure. *Foreign Relations*: European Affairs; International Economic Policy, Export & Trade Promotion; Western Hemisphere, Peace Corps, Narcotics Affairs (RMM). *Joint Economic Committee* (10th of 10 Sens.).

Group Ratings (Only Served Partial Term)

	ADA	ACLU	AFS	LCV	CON	ITIC	NTU	COC	ACU	NTLC	CHC
2000	70	100	57	100	67	100	27	66	44	41	*
1999	*	—	*	*	*	—	*	*	*	*	*

National Journal Ratings (Only Served Partial Term)

	1999 LIB — 1999 CONS	2000 LIB — 2000 CONS
Economic	* — *	55% — 44%
Social	* — *	79% — 0%
Foreign	* — *	54% — 45%

Key Votes of the 106th Congress (Only Served Partial Term)

1. Educ. Savings Accts.	N	5. Review Movie Violence	*	9. NATO War in Serbia	*
2. Prescrip. Drug Benefit	Y	6. Gun Show Bckgrnd. Checks	*	10. Table Cuba Travel Ban	*
3. Delay Ergonomic Standards	Y	7. Ban Part.-Birth Abortion	*	11. Nuclear Test-Ban Treaty	*
4. Phase Out Estate Tax	N	8. Broaden Hate Crimes List	Y	12. Perm. Trade with China	Y

Election Results

2000 general	Lincoln Chafee (R)	222,588	(57%)	($2,265,221)
	Robert A. Weygand (D)	161,023	(41%)	($2,297,885)
	Others	7,742	(2%)	
2000 primary	Lincoln Chafee (R)	unopposed		
1994 general	John H. Chafee (R)	222,856	(65%)	($2,086,236)
	Linda J. Kushner (D)	122,532	(35%)	($805,867)

FIRST DISTRICT

The 1st Congressional District is the eastern half of Rhode Island, east of Narragansett Bay, a line that cuts through Providence and then proceeds west and north to the Massachusetts-Connecticut-Rhode Island border. It includes much of Providence (including elite East Side and College Hill around Brown University) and all of next-door Pawtucket whose Slater Mill is known as the birthplace of the American Industrial Revolution. The onetime textile mill towns of the Blackstone Valley, Woonsocket and Central Falls are also in the 1st, along with high-income Barrington and Bristol and, south on the ocean, the old city of Newport, with its restored 18th Century houses and the summer "cottages" that are really palaces. Newport was once home to the America's Cup races and now hosts a famous jazz festival; it is also the site of the oldest synagogue in North America, to whose congregation George Washington declared that the United States gives "to bigotry no sanction, to persecution no assistance." Ethnically, this district is the more French-Canadian and the less Italian of the two Rhode Island districts; politically, it is strongly Democratic.

The congressman from the 1st District is Patrick Kennedy, a Democrat elected in 1994. Patrick Kennedy was born in 1967, his father Edward Kennedy's fifth year in the Senate; a week after his second birthday came the terrible accident at Chappaquiddick. He grew up in McLean, Virginia, and had a somewhat troubled youth, spending time in a drug rehabilitation clinic in 1986 before enrolling at Providence College, at 20, in 1987. Almost immediately, in 1988, he ran for a seat in the state House and beat the longtime incumbent as the tiny (population 9,800) district was inundated with visits by Kennedy family members and funds raised by the Kennedy national fundraising network. He became chairman of the Rules Committee in 1992, a year after spending the now-infamous Easter weekend in Palm Beach with his father and cousin William Kennedy Smith. In 1994, when the 1st District's Congressman Ron Machtley ran for governor, Kennedy decided to run for Congress. Kennedy had an attractive and energetic Republican opponent, Kevin Vigilante, a doctor who worked with handicapped orphans in Romania and with female prison inmates infected with HIV. Vigilante was a moderate on issues and raised enough to spend $803,000. But Kennedy had the advantages of money and his family name, and won 54%–46% in a Republican year.

In the House Kennedy has a very liberal voting record and has proven an excitable if not always eloquent debater. He started off by avoiding national media and working on local issues, from the Naval Undersea Warfare Center in Newport to visas for Portuguese immigrants. He was co-founder of the Portuguese-American Caucus and brought the president of Portugal to Rhode Island and visited the former Portuguese colony of East Timor; he co-sponsored a resolution condemning violence in East and West Timor in September 2000. He sponsored a bill to fund public-private partnerships on ocean research. He voted for the partial-birth abortion ban and unsuccessfully backed casino gambling rights for the Narragansett Indians. He supported the law to make it easier to evict unruly tenants from public housing. He has been strongly opposed to Fidel Castro, whom he blames for the death of his uncle John F. Kennedy; he voted for the Helms-Burton Act and backed the 2000 bill that would have made Elian Gonzalez a U.S. citizen. He has strongly supported gun control—another issue with family reverberations—and embarrassed himself in June 1999 when he told reporters House Democrats had "written off the rural areas" because of gun control. In 1999 he sponsored a bill providing a 20% tax credit, capped at $2 million, for purchases of U.S.-built yachts and $25 million for export assistance to the boat-building industry, which is big in Rhode Island. In February 2001 he sought permanent residence status for Liberian refugees, many of whom live in Rhode Island.

After winning re-election by 69%–28% in 1996, he took on a more combative role and seemed to be eyeing a race for the Senate seat held by John Chafee. He criticized Chafee sharply for voting for the Defense of Marriage Act and for his bill, passed in 1996, blocking the Narragansett Indians from building a casino without a referendum. But Chafee fought back gamely, returning often to the state, working hard on local projects, and his standing in the polls, never weak, slowly rose. Meanwhile, the harshness of Kennedy's attacks evidently grated; his job approval fell from 62% to 44% during the year. Former Republican state Chairman John Holmes argued that Kennedy's attacks made him seem an "uncontrollable young man who is trying to grab as many headlines as possible. Rhode Islanders do not forgive you for immaturely attacking 60- and 70-year old people who have passed the test of time."

In 1998 Kennedy's career took another turn. In April he said he wanted a seat on Appropriations—not a likely goal if he intended to seek only one more term in the House. He struck up a friendship with Minority Leader Dick Gephardt, even forming a joint PAC with him to help finance their political travels; Kennedy let it be known that he would support Gephardt for president over Gore. Kennedy bristled in November 1997 when the Clinton administration threatened to put some of the Blackstone Valley National Heritage Corridor on the line-item veto list a day before fast track, which he and Gephardt opposed; he was pointedly not invited to a 1998 Rhode Island Social Security forum featuring Al Gore, though Chafee and 2d District Congressman Robert Weygand were. When Gephardt decided not to run for president, but to concentrate on helping Democrats win him a majority in the House, which would make him speaker, he enlisted Kennedy as a key ally. In November 1998, after Kennedy easily won reelection, Gephardt named him chairman of the Democratic Congressional Campaign Committee (one of the few leadership positions of either party which is appointive rather than elective). A few days later Kennedy announced what was already pretty plain, that he would not run for the Senate, whatever Chafee's decision. As he later explained, he preferred the House to the Senate, which he described as "an old white men's club, and that's not where I am most comfortable. I like the diversity of the House. I like the hurly-burly. I like the give-and-take."

As DCCC chairman, Kennedy excelled not as a strategist but as a fundraiser. "I'm prepared to devote all my time, energy and assets, which include the family name, toward retaking the House," he said in 1999. "And I'm absolutely convinced that I'm using my family name to its best ends—and that is to promote an agenda that my family fought for and died for in service to this country. And I feel spiritual about it. I really feel that I am a vehicle for my family's legacy of public service." He traveled indefatigably around the country to fundraisers, and made yeoman efforts to raise soft money, even while calling for campaign finance legislation which would outlaw it. As a result, the DCCC in 1999 and 2000 raised nearly $50 million in soft money, reaching parity with its Republican counterpart, the NRSC; the NRSC raised more hard money, but Kennedy vastly reduced the disadvantage his party labored under in the 1996 and 1998 cycles. As NRSC

Chairman Tom Davis conceded, "Patrick Kennedy did more for the DCCC than any previous chairman. He brought the DCCC to a financial level where they'd never been before."

He was less successful in other respects. In May 2000 he brought a RICO racketeering suit against Republican Whip Tom DeLay, arguing that he was extorting contributions from various groups. But some Democrats as well as many Republicans said that this was a misuse of the RICO statute, and after DeLay threatened to take depositions of every House Democrat, the suit was dropped. Nor were Democrats successful in their efforts to regain a majority in the House. They needed only a net gain of six seats, and they benefited from Gephardt's success in persuading senior Democrats and incumbents who held their districts more through personal popularity than party strength to run for one more term. But voters in 2000, as in 1998 and 1996, were in a pro-incumbent mood, and it proved hard to persuade them to oust Republican incumbents. Democrats persuaded Long Island Republican Michael Forbes to switch parties, but were caught napping when the NRSC helped another Democrat beat him in a low-turnout primary—which gave the seat to the Republican in November. Two Democratic incumbents, Sam Gejdenson and Dave Minge, who had seemed safe, were defeated. And despite Gephardt's and Kennedy's efforts to recruit locally strong candidates, Democrats won only nine of the 35 open seats. Counting the two independents with the party they support, the Democrats won 213 seats, the Republicans 222—an agonizingly close defeat for Gephardt and Kennedy. A week after the election, Kennedy announced he would not serve another term as DCCC Chairman. Gephardt tried to change his mind, but did not succeed.

Instead he seemed to be moving from national politics to concentration on Rhode Island. He sought to take back the Appropriations seat to which he had been appointed in December 1998, but from which he took a leave of absence to chair the DCCC. Other Democrats were in line also, but the death of Julian Dixon in December 2000 opened up another Appropriations seat, and Kennedy got it. On Armed Services he had already been active in seeking funding for Rhode Island military projects. He supported a law passed in 2000 granting $275 million over five years to restore wildlife habitat in marine estuaries; this was originated by Senator John Chafee, who died in October 1999, and supported by his son Lincoln Chafee, appointed to succeed him in November 1999 and elected to a full term in November 2000.

But despite this work and his 67%–33% victory in November, Kennedy saw his standing in Rhode Island decline because of a series of imbroglios. In March 2000, he shoved an airport security guard in Los Angeles, sending her backward and jostling the metal detector archway. A police complaint was filed, but the Los Angeles city attorney decided against prosecution. In an informal hearing in May 2000, Kennedy apologized to the woman. But she sued him in March 2001, and Kennedy said his insurance company would handle the suit. The insurance company, it appeared, had already been busy settling claims against Kennedy by owners of sailboats he had chartered. In August 1999 a rented boat required assistance from the Coast Guard after becoming entangled in fishing nets, and suffered several thousand dollars damage; Kennedy docked the boat and drove off, leaving his security deposit to pay for it. In July 2000, the Coast Guard was summoned to a boat Kennedy had rented in which a woman he was dating was alone; she and Kennedy had had an argument and she had called a friend in Florida who then called the Coast Guard, who took her to shore. This was not reported until November 2000, when it was also reported that Kennedy had ruined the engine and damaged the rigging. His insurance company settled the case, and one of his staffers called on the Coast Guard to bring a hoax call case against the Florida friend; the Coast Guard declined. In November 2000 his insurance company settled a claim that he had damaged a 42-foot sloop rented in Mystic, Connecticut, and abandoned it off Martha's Vineyard in August 2000.

These incidents surely did not help him in Rhode Island. For whatever reasons, Kennedy's job rating fell from 63% in early 2000 to 49% in early 2001. At the Providence Journal Follies in March 2001 Kennedy responded gamely with humor: he arrived in a white sailor's outfit with a woman on each arm and said, "Now when I hear someone talking about a Rhode Island politician whose father was a senator and who got to Washington based on his family name, used cocaine and wasn't very smart, I know there is only a 50–50 chance it's me"; the reference was to Senator Lincoln Chafee's admission in 1999 that he had used cocaine. But in April 2001 Kennedy dismissed his chief of staff and district director—momentous actions for a congressman who has always relied heavily on a talented staff. There was speculation that Governor Lincoln Almond might run against him in 2002, something Almond refused to rule out, although he turns 66 that year and he added, "Don't tell my wife." Fresh from his lead role in national politics in 1999 and 2000, Kennedy seems likely to concentrate on improving his standing in his home base; the young man who a few years before seemed to have every prospect of becoming a senator for life now seemed to be preparing to defend his House seat.

Cook's Call   *Safe*. Kennedy's recent personal and political troubles could result in a tough contest in 2002. On paper, this district should never give a Democrat any trouble. But Kennedy, who spent most of the 2000 election cycle flying across the country as the DCCC chairman, has a lot of bridges to rebuild back home.

THE PEOPLE: Pop. 2000: 510,287; Pop. 1990: 501,696, up 1.7% 1990–2000. 86.4% White, 4.2% Black, 1.8% Asian, 0.3% Amer. Indian, 2.9% Two+ races, 4.4% Other; 7% Hispanic Origin.

2000 Presidential Vote		
Gore (D)	122,864	(62%)
Bush (R)	60,613	(31%)
Nader (Green)	11,730	(6%)
Others	1,722	(1%)

1996 Presidential Vote		
Clinton (D)	114,858	(61%)
Dole (R)	48,964	(26%)
Perot (I)	20,287	(11%)
Others	4,304	(2%)

Rep. Patrick J. Kennedy (D)

Elected 1994, 4th term; b. July 14, 1967, Brighton, MA; home, Providence; Providence Col., B.A. 1991; Catholic; single.

Elected Office: RI House of Reps., 1988–94.

DC Office: 407 CHOB 20515, 202-225-4911; Fax: 202-225-3290; Web site: www.house.gov/patrickkennedy.

District Office: Pawtucket, 401-729-5600.

Committees: *Appropriations* (20th of 29 D): Commerce, Justice & State; Labor, HHS & Education.

Group Ratings

	ADA	ACLU	AFS	LCV	CON	ITIC	NTU	COC	ACU	NTLC	CHC
2000	90	79	100	93	46	44	17	15	16	16	7
1999	90	—	100	94	25	—	16	25	4	—	—

National Journal Ratings

	1999 LIB —	1999 CONS	2000 LIB —	2000 CONS
Economic	69% —	30%	85% —	11%
Social	87% —	0%	79% —	17%
Foreign	88% —	12%	56% —	42%

Key Votes of the 106th Congress

1. Patient Bill of Rights	Y	5. Bar RU-486 $ for FDA	N	9. NATO War in Serbia	Y
2. Accelerate Min. Wage	Y	6. Display 10 Commandments	N	10. Perm. Trade with China	N
3. Strike Ban on Ergo. Stnd.	Y	7. Gun Show Bkgrnd. Checks	Y	11. Debt Relief for 3rd World	Y
4. Ovrd. Estate Tax Veto	N	8. Ban Part.-Birth Abortion	Y	12. Drop Cuba Econ. Embargo	N

Election Results

2000 general	Patrick J. Kennedy (D)	123,442	(67%)	($1,263,102)
	Stephen Cabral (R)	61,522	(33%)	($8,902)
2000 primary	Patrick J. Kennedy (D)	unopposed		
1998 general	Patrick J. Kennedy (D)	92,788	(67%)	($1,023,152)
	Ronald G. Santa (R)	38,460	(28%)	($26,044)
	James C. Sheehan (Ref)	6,202	(4%)	($22,577)

SECOND DISTRICT

The 2d Congressional District is the western half of Rhode Island. While the 1st includes many mill towns, the 2d has most of its population in working- and middle-class towns like Cranston and Warwick which, despite their British names, are inhabited mostly by people with Irish, Italian, French and Portuguese surnames. The 2d also includes South County—not an official place, but the common name for Rhode Island south of East Greenwich, including the affluent suburbs to the south along Narragansett Bay and the area around Westerly, where many residents work at the Electric Boat shipyards in Groton, Connecticut. It includes Rhode Island's rolling farm land, though they do not include many acres, and the communities along the Bay and the Ocean, where many people still make their living building boats and catching fish.

The congressman from the 2d district is James Langevin, a Democrat elected in 2000. Langevin grew up in Warwick, and as a boy hoped to become an FBI agent. But in 1980, at age 16, when he was a police cadet in the Boy Scout Explorer program, he was shot by a police officer when a gun accidentally discharged. The bullet went through his upper back and throat and damaged the upper part of his spinal column; ever since, he has been a quadriplegic, getting around in a wheelchair. He received $2.2 million in a settlement with the city of Warwick and currently hires a home health care aide; it takes him two and a half hours to get dressed each morning. This tragic accident focused attention on him, at first unwanted, but he says it made him determined to make something of his life. He worked as an intern in the State House and for Senator Claiborne Pell. In 1988, while he was a student at Rhode Island College, he was elected to the state House of Representatives; his 1st District colleague Patrick Kennedy, was also elected that year to the state House as a college student, though in other respects their circumstances were different. While in the state House Langevin graduated from college and he received a master's degree from the Kennedy School at Harvard.

In 1994 Langevin was elected Rhode Island's secretary of State. He replaced lever voting machines with electronic scanners, and made Rhode Island's public records accessible through the Internet. In 1998 he issued a report called "Access Denied," exposing secret meetings held by legislators in violation of Rhode Island's open meetings laws. When he was re-elected in 1998, he said he might be interested in running for governor or for Congress; under Rhode Island's term limits law he was barred from a third term as secretary of State. In 2000, when 2d District Congressman Bob Weygand ran for the Senate, Langevin decided to run for his House seat.

It was a four-way race in the Democratic primary, and Langevin's most strenuous opposition came from Kate Coyne-McCoy, executive director of the Rhode Island Association of Social Workers. Langevin had support from many Democratic Party leaders and some unions, and won the party endorsement at the April 2000 convention, from which Coyne-McCoy angrily withdrew. But she waged an aggressive campaign, financed by unions, health care workers and EMILY's List. "There's no such thing as being too liberal," Coyne-McCoy said, and came out for a ban on the sale and manufacture of hand guns, government-run universal health insurance, an $8 minimum wage and an immediate price freeze on prescription drugs. Her ads showed her with a cartoonish character named Pill Bill, lampooned Langevin's health care plan and generally peppered him with attacks. Langevin called her positions "unrealistic and extreme." He backed non-government universal health care coverage, prescription drug coverage in Medicare and HMO regulation— the standard Democratic program that year. He favored less stringent forms of gun control and said, "No one has to tell me how dangerous weapons can be." They also clashed on abortion. Coyne-McCoy attacked Langevin for opposing abortion rights. He said, "because of what happened to me, I became aware of how precious life is . . . I'm pro-life." He spoke often of the accident that paralyzed him, and to criticisms of that he said, "To every endeavor we come to we all bring our life's experience. People are married. They have children. They have a war record, military service. John McCain was a P.O.W. These are all life experiences, and we bring them all to what we do. Certainly, being disabled is part of who I am, but it doesn't define me."

In the September 12 primary, Langevin led Coyne-McCoy 47%–29%. In third place was lawyer Angel Taveras, with 12%; he talked of how he moved from Head Start to Harvard, and nearly beat Langevin in Providence, with its many Hispanic voters. In fourth place was Cranston

City Council President Kevin McAllister, with 12%, who said many of his Cranston supporters voted for Langevin in order to beat Coyne-McCoy. In the general election, Langevin's chief opposition came not from Republican nominee Robert Tingle but from Rodney Driver, nominee of the Conscience for Congress Party, a retired mathematics professor who spent $300,000 of his retirement savings on his campaign. Langevin won with 62%, to 21% for Driver and 14% for Tingle.

In the House, Langevin seemed likely to have a solid Democratic voting record, except on abortion. As he prepared to take his seat, House staffers were busy making the chamber wheelchair-accessible; we have had a wheelchair-bound president (Franklin D. Roosevelt) and senator (Max Cleland of Georgia), but not a wheelchair-bound member of the House. He quickly began using his experience as secretary of State as the House debated election reform, favoring setting minimum federal standards, but giving ultimate responsibility to state officials.

Cook's Call *Safe.* Although this district is not as Democratic as the 1st, it still retains a healthy Democratic advantage. Langevin should have no trouble winning a second term in 2002.

THE PEOPLE: Pop. 2000: 538,032; Pop. 1990: 501,768, up 7.2% 1990–2000. 83.7% White, 4.7% Black, 2.7% Asian, 0.6% Amer. Indian, 0.1% Hawaiian, 2.5% Two+ races, 5.6% Other; 10.2% Hispanic Origin.

2000 Presidential Vote			1996 Presidential Vote		
Gore (D)	126,644	(60%)	Clinton (D)	118,192	(59%)
Bush (R)	69,942	(33%)	Dole (R)	55,719	(28%)
Nader (Green)	13,322	(6%)	Perot (I)	23,436	(12%)
Others	1,946	(1%)	Others	4,370	(2%)

Rep. James Langevin (D)

Elected 2000, 1st term; b. Apr. 22, 1964, Warwick; home, Warwick; RI Col., B.A. 1990; Harvard U., M.P.A. 1994; Catholic; single.

Elected Office: RI House of Reps., 1988–94; RI Sec. of State, 1994–2000.

DC Office: 109 CHOB 20515, 202-225-2735; Fax: 202-225-5976; Web site: www.house.gov/langevin.

District Office: Warwick, 401-732-9400.

Committees: *Armed Services* (27th of 28 D): Military Personnel; Military Research & Development. *Small Business* (14th of 17 D): Regulatory Reform Oversight; Tax, Finance & Exports.

Group Ratings and Key Votes: Newly Elected

Election Results

2000 general	James Langevin (D)	123,805	(62%)	($1,041,752)
	Rodney R. Driver (CFC)	42,625	(21%)	($274,183)
	Robert G. Tingle (R)	27,932	(14%)	
	Others	4,536	(2%)	
2000 primary	James Langevin (D)	22,955	(47%)	
	Kate Coyne-McCoy (D)	14,219	(29%)	
	Angel Taveras (D)	5,803	(12%)	
	Kevin J. McAllister (D)	5,633	(12%)	
1998 general	Robert A. Weygand (D)	110,917	(72%)	($566,499)
	John O. Matson (R)	38,170	(25%)	($39,945)
	Others	4,966	(3%)	

★ SOUTH CAROLINA ★

S outh Carolina, at times beleaguered and under attack, stands proud but not untroubled, a
state that has made much progress but still feels it has some distance to go. Within living
memory this state looked like an underdeveloped country: Beneath a thin veneer of rich people,
it was among the poorest of states, with income levels less than half the national average and with
high levels of illiteracy and disease. South Carolina was founded by planters from Barbados and
even today there are reminders of the West Indies—the semitropical climate, the lush foliage and
trademark palmettos, and the billions of damage from hurricanes. But economically and culturally,
South Carolina is now clearly part of the booming South Atlantic region from Maryland to Florida,
filling up with new retirement condominiums, factories and office buildings, giant shopping centers, growing robustly in the 1990s.

South Carolina started off with a plantation economy built on the swampy Low Country below
the Fall Line, where the great 18th and 19th Century planters built rice paddies and cultivated
exotic crops like indigo in the days before cotton was king. The great wealth of these Low Country
planters was destroyed by the Civil War which they, more than any other Southerners, provoked.
But their pride and way of life continued as did that of former slaves. As late as 1940, 43% of
South Carolinians were black, most living in conditions inconceivable today. South Carolina's
economic growth started only in the 1920s, with that lowest-wage of industries, textiles. Mills
were built in the Up Country above Columbia, hiring poor whites (never blacks) from the hardscrabble farms in the area. Politics remained a rough business, with harsh appeals to racial fear
and economic envy, and with limited participation: in 1940, just 99,000 South Carolinians voted
for president, 96% of them Democratic—the highest Democratic percentage in the nation. In the
1946 Democratic primary, the year Strom Thurmond was elected governor, only 271,000 people
voted in this state of more than two million.

Now this once underdeveloped country has joined the First World: The 2000 Census counted
4 million South Carolinians, 30% of them black, 2% Hispanic. Personal incomes are up toward
national levels; health standards are as good as those in the rest of the nation; educational achievement still lags, though not nearly so much as before. South Carolina was helped for some years
by the military bases clustered around Charleston, by the big textile mills around Greenville and
Spartanburg, and by the outmigration of Low Country blacks to big cities of the Northeast. Then,
starting in the 1970s, South Carolina became the most aggressive state in the South in attracting
new industry. It advertised its business climate (one of the lowest rates of unionization), its taxes
(low), and its willingness to meet local employers' needs (very high). It enticed French and German firms to set up major operations in the Piedmont and the Low Country, a process capped
when BMW in 1992 built its first U.S. assembly plant off I-85 in Spartanburg. From 1960–90
international investment in the state grew from $80 million to $16.4 trillion. But even more typical
are the decisions of hundreds of small employers to open plants, rent offices and create jobs in
what has become one of America's more vibrant economic environments. This has happened
even as federal support has diminished: The Pentagon closed the Charleston Navy Base in 1996,
and the Savannah River nuclear plant, including the only tritium plant in the country, closed
down in 1993. But Charleston civic leaders immediately came forward with a plan to develop the
Navy bases—there are 4,000 jobs there now—and the Aiken area around the tritium plant kept
growing. In 2000 South Carolina lost 4,400 textile and apparel jobs, but gained 35,000 jobs overall,
despite the end-of-year softening of the national economy. And these gains came not from government-subsidized big plants but from expansion of existing businesses: South Carolina now has
a self-sustaining economy.

As South Carolina's economy grew, it slowly, sometimes grudgingly, overcame its heritage of
slavery and racial segregation. Starting in the 1950s, fewer people were kept from voting by the
poll tax, and turnout surged as South Carolina became competitive in the presidential elections
of 1952, 1956 and 1960. Clemson University was peaceably desegregated during the governorship
(1959–62) of Ernest Hollings; most South Carolina whites opposed integration, but not with the
violence of Alabama and Mississippi. Then the Civil Rights Act of 1964 and the Voting Rights Act

— Congressional district boundaries
  effective March 29, 1994.

of 1965 ended legal segregation of public accommodations and workplaces and brought blacks suddenly into the electorate. This changed the political balance. Senator Strom Thurmond, who set a record filibustering a civil rights bill in 1957, started appointing black staffers and a black federal judge in the late 1960s and early 1970s. But politics still cleaved the electorate along racial lines: In 2000 whites voted 69%–27% for George W. Bush and blacks voted 91%–7% for Al Gore. And during the 2000 primary season South Carolina was still grappling with the controversy over the Confederate battle flag, flown over the state Capitol since 1962. Democratic Governor James Hodges, like the Republican governor he defeated in 1998, David Beasley, favored taking the battle flag down; the NAACP was urging a boycott of South Carolina until the flag came down; longtime Charleston Mayor Joe Riley Jr. led a 120-mile march to urge the flag come down. A compromise was fashioned in the state Senate: the battle flag would fly not from the Capitol, but from a 30-foot pole on the Capitol grounds, while an African-American history monument would rise nearby. In May 2000 the Senate voted 37–8 for this; the House followed, 66–43, though the NAACP was not satisfied with the result, but most voters evidently were; the battle flag came down from the Capitol on July 1.

In partisan politics, South Carolina has been one of the Republicans' strongest states. Strom Thurmond provided critical votes to nominate Richard Nixon at the 1968 Republican National Convention, and South Carolina spurned George Wallace and voted for Nixon in November. Republican Carroll Campbell was elected governor in 1986 and 1990, and Republicans made gains in U.S. House and state legislative states. Campbell ally Lee Atwater managed George Bush's 1988 campaign; he and Campbell set up an early South Carolina primary, on the Saturday before Southern Super Tuesday; Bush won big on Saturday and then on Tuesday cinched the nomination. In November South Carolina gave him one of his biggest majorities, 62%–38%.

But parties with big majorities can become complacent and fissiparous, while parties seemingly stuck in the minority find new leaders, develop new issues and build new coalitions. Campbell's protege Beasley won in 1994 and Republicans won six of eight downballot offices and a majority in the state House. But Beasley's switch on the Confederate battle flag undermined his base and his opposition to video poker provided financial support for Democrat Jim Hodges in 1998. Video poker had been approved by 34 of 46 counties in 1994 referendums; the business mushroomed, with 60% more machines in four years, to a $2.4 billion industry, the third biggest video poker operation in any state. Hodges supported a referendum on statewide video poker and on a lottery with proceeds to go to education, a proposal that had been highly popular in next-door Georgia. Hodges won 53%–45%, and Senator Ernest Hollings, who nearly lost six years before, was re-elected over Congressman Bob Inglis by an almost identical 53%–46%. Democrats had adapted, and made South Carolina a two-party state again. But they have not been entirely successful. In July 1999 the legislature passed a bill banning video poker unless voters decided in a referendum to keep it. But one small video poker filed a lawsuit to overturn the law—a gamble that lost big. In October 1999 the state Supreme Court upheld the ban but overturned the referendum: on July 1, 2000, video poker suddenly became illegal. In November 2000, voters approved the lottery. But George W. Bush easily carried the state 57%–41% and Republicans, after a party switch, took control of the state Senate 24–22.

For years South Carolina sent young people, black and white, to other states in large numbers. In the 1990s the state's population grew 15%, with newcomers moving to the coastal counties, and to York County outside Charlotte, North Carolina. It has been throwing off the burdens of its past, while profiting from an appreciation of its glories, as visitors to Charleston and the mansions of the Low Country can see. South Carolina is the host every year to Charleston's Spoleto Festival, to Renaissance Weekend at Hilton Head, where Bill and Hillary Rodham Clinton for years spent New Year's Eve with hundreds of friends in gatherings hosted by Phil Lader, Clinton's last Ambassador to Britain, and to the Southern 500 stock car race in Darlington, which attracts a different but no less vibrant crowd. If South Carolina has not had the spectacular growth of metropolitan Atlanta or the Piedmont of North Carolina, it is not the backwater that it seemed fated to be for many years but a state that has transformed its fighting spirit into an engine of innovation and growth.

Governor   Jim Hodges, the first Democrat elected governor of South Carolina since 1982, grew up in rural Lancaster County, near the North Carolina border. After graduating from college and law school at the University of South Carolina, he returned to Lancaster to practice law. In short order he became county attorney, and in 1986, at 29, was elected to the state House. In 1994 he became House minority leader; he had a conservative enough record to be supported by the National Federation of Independent Businesses and National Rifle Association. Meanwhile (South Carolina has a part-time legislature) he became general counsel at Springs Company, a major textile and financial services firm.

In 1998 Hodges embarked on what seemed to be a daunting race for governor. He was not Democratic leaders' first choice, but others were daunted by incumbent Republican David Beasley's lead in the polls and the might of Carroll Campbell's Republican organization. Hodges started off attacking Beasley on education, citing the state's low ranking on SAT scores, and presented detailed critiques of Beasley's record, including his opposition to all-day kindergarten; Hodges got the legislature to vote for that in 1996, and Beasley switched to support further study into it. He charged that Beasley's plan to use the Savannah River Site in Barnwell County for a nuclear waste depository was not bringing in the money Beasley promised for his need-based and Palmetto merit-based college scholarships. Hodges's solution was an adaptation of Georgia Governor Zell Miller's lottery and HOPE scholarships; Hodges called them COPE scholarships for college tuition and added that he would spend lottery proceeds on all-day kindergarten and school construction as well.

Hodges was also helped by Beasley's problems. Beasley had originally opposed removing the Confederate battle flag from the dome of the state Capitol, then in a flurry of publicity changed his mind, but did not persuade the legislature to go along; both flag supporters and opponents were unhappy. Beasley's switch in October 1998, to support a referendum on the lottery, reminded voters of the flag switch. And Beasley was the target of heavy spending by video poker operators. Hodges had opposed video poker in the legislature, but running for governor said it was an issue that should be decided by the people in a referendum. Also, Beasley was hurt by Sheriff Jimmy Metts of heavily Republican Lexington County, who announced he was running as an independent and dredged up rumors that Beasley had had an extramarital affair. Metts later withdrew from the race, but the rumors lingered. Hodges won by the solid margin of 53%–45%, carrying almost every rural county and wide margins in Charleston County and Columbia's Richland County as well. Hodges won 21% of self-identified Republicans, an unusually high percentage; Democrats won back the offices of treasurer, comptroller and education superintendent. Hodges won 92% from blacks and cut Beasley's margin among whites almost in half.

As governor, Hodges has had successes but also a few embarrassments. In July 1999 the legislature passed a bill banning video poker unless voters decided in a referendum to keep it. But one small video poker filed a lawsuit to overturn the law, and in October 1999 the state Supreme Court upheld the ban but overturned the referendum: on July 1, 2000, video poker was gone, and with it much of Hodges's financial base. In September 1999 Hodges was much criticized for ordering evacuation of Charleston and the Low Country because of Hurricane Floyd but not making I-26 one-way; traffic was jammed for hours. But Hodges played a major role in getting the legislature to vote in May 2000 to take the Confederate flag off the dome and put it up on the Capitol grounds; he also got the legislature to pass a Martin Luther King Holiday, plus a Confederate Memorial Day in May. And he appeared at the annual memorial meeting recalling the killing of black students by state police in Orangeburg in 1968. "We deeply regret what happened here on the night of February 8, 1968. The Orangeburg massacre was a great tragedy for our state." Other Hodges initiatives included a nuclear waste compact that barred the sending of waste to the Barnwell plant from any other states except Connecticut and New Jersey; the Silver Card prescription drug plan for seniors, financed by tobacco money; a three-day sales tax holiday at back-to-school time in August 2000; a package of bills designed to make South Carolina attractive to insurance companies. He signed a bill encouraging schools to get students to say "Yes, sir," and "Yes, ma'am" to teachers. He announced a plan to raise teacher salaries to the national average by 2007, and opposed tying the raises to teacher performance.

Hodges's biggest success came in November 2000 when voters approved the lottery. Some 55% of whites opposed the lottery, but 75% of blacks, despite the opposition of many black preachers, supported it. But the legislature still had to act, and Republicans ended up controlling both houses, the House by 70–54 and the Senate, after party switches, 24–22. And for a month Attorney General Charlie Condon investigated charges that Hodges was seeking $50,000 for the pro-lottery campaign from New York investment banks interested in being awarded contracts for the securitization of the state's $800 million tobacco settlement bonds; Condon, a strongly partisan Republican, said in March 2001 that he found "no hard evidence" of illegalities. Hodges's job ratings have not been as high as those of many other governors, of both parties, perhaps because of strong feelings on issues like the flag and the lottery. But in early 2001 he could boast of a surging state economy, improvement in students' SAT scores and resolution of the battle flag and video poker issues. In early 2001 several Republicans were lining up to oppose him in 2002. The first to announce was Charlie Condon; his geographical base is in the Low Country, but he also has strong support from religious conservatives in the Up Country and from proponents of the Confederate battle flag. Next to announce, in March 2001, was Mark Sanford, who stepped down after six years as Low Country congressman to fulfill a 1994 promise to serve only three terms. Sanford called himself a Teddy Roosevelt Republican, and as a fiscal conservative could appeal to business conservatives; he was a supporter of John McCain in the 2000 presidential primary, and hopes to appeal to the independents and Democrats who provided most of McCain's votes. Expected to run were Lieutenant Governor Bob Peeler and Secretary of State Jim Miles. Peeler is from the Up Country, and known for appearing in TV ads for Peeler Dairy. Miles, who was urged to run against Strom Thurmond in the 1996 primary but did not, has the support of consultant Rod Sheely, whose candidates have won several upset victories. South Carolina is not a state to oust incumbents: It has had the same two U.S. senators since 1966, and in 58 of the last 60 chances it has re-elected incumbent congressmen. But Hodges has the disadvantage of being a member of the party that is still the minority here, despite its 1998 victories.

Cook's Call *Competitive.* The Republicans seem destined to hold a competitive primary among a field of first-tier candidates including Lieutenant Governor Bob Peeler, state Attorney General Charles Condon, Secretary of State Jim Miles, and former Congressman Mark Sanford. Hodges has gotten generally good reviews but he can take nothing for granted.

Senior Senator The most enduring figure in American politics today is Strom Thurmond. The man who was elected to his eighth term in the Senate in 1996 as a Republican was elected to the South Carolina House as a Democrat in 1932. Thurmond grew up in the small town of Edgefield, was a teacher, coach and school superintendent, studied law under his father and was elected to the legislature at 31. At the age of 6 he shook hands with his father's friend "Pitchfork Ben" Tillman, South Carolina governor and senator, who was born in 1847. On June 6, 1944, Thurmond parachuted into Normandy on D-Day only after getting an exemption because he was over age. He attended the Democratic National Convention in 1932 and voted for Franklin D. Roosevelt, and he attended the Republican National Convention in 1996 and voted for Bob Dole—64 years later. Thurmond was elected governor in 1946, ran for president in 1948 as a "States' Rights Democrat" and won 39 electoral votes. He was elected senator as a write-in candidate in 1954, resigned and ran for the seat again in 1956. In March 1996, at 93, he became the oldest person ever to serve in Congress; in May 1997 he became the longest-serving senator in history. In July 2000, when Al Gore invoked the memory of Harry Truman, Thurmond issued a press release: "In Al Gore's latest reincarnation, he claims to be Truman-like, blaming Congress. Mr. Gore, I knew Harry Truman. I ran against Harry Truman. And Mr. Gore, you're no Harry Truman." In December 1999 a 32-ton statue of him was unveiled on the grounds of the South Carolina Capitol.

Thurmond switched to the Republican Party to support Barry Goldwater in 1964, which means that by 2000 he had been a Democrat 32 years and a Republican 36 years in his political career. His party switch seemed unwise at the time but proved sentient about the direction of opinion; in 1968, Thurmond provided key backing to hold the South for Richard Nixon at the Republican National Convention. Thurmond has combined a reputation for steadfastness with a flexibility and adroitness that have enabled this onetime symbol of racial segregation to prosper politically in an era of integration. In 1957, he set a record, filibustering for 24 hours and 18 minutes against a civil rights bill. But when South Carolina blacks started voting in large numbers after the Voting Rights Act of 1965, Thurmond shifted gears and became the first Southern senator to hire black staffers and appoint blacks to high positions (including a federal judgeship). He voted for renewal of the Voting Rights Act and the Martin Luther King Jr. Holiday. He gets more votes from blacks than most Republicans.

Thurmond has been a physical fitness buff all his life. His first wife was 23 years his junior; after she died, he married a South Carolina beauty queen 44 years younger; the first of his four children was born when he was 68. In January 2001 he recommended his 28-year-old son Strom Thurmond Jr. to be United States Attorney for South Carolina. In recent years Thurmond has not played a guiding role on major legislation, but has pursued pet causes about which he has strong feelings. He worked for years and finally got warning labels on alcoholic beverages in 1988; in February 1999 he moved swiftly to stop educational labeling of wine that would promote its health benefits; he has sponsored so many bills to tighten regulation and raise taxes on wine that *Wine Spectator* magazine labeled him "wine's public enemy number one." He has backed fetal tissue research and moved to oppose a ban on human cloning and cloning tissue, because one of his daughters has a medical condition for which such tissue is needed in research. He has sponsored bills for mandatory drug treatment as an alternative to prison and to withdraw the exemption of union leaders for prosecutions for union violence. In June 1999 he angrily called in military brass after the commander of Fort Hood allowed witchcraft services on the base. He has been the great patron of the Junior Reserve Office Training Corps, and has seen to it that there are JROTC chapters in every South Carolina high school that wants one. In June 2000 he grilled Energy Secretary Bill Richardson on security lapses at the Savannah River Site and, with Congressman James DeMint, asked Major League Baseball to lift the lifetime suspension of Greenville, South Carolina, native Shoeless Joe Jackson, imposed after the 1919 World Series, of which Thurmond alone of members of Congress can remember.

In July 1999 this man born before the invention of the airplane and the proliferation of the automobile signed by computer the Y2K liability bill. In January 1999 he stepped forward in full view of the country to administer the oath to Chief Justice William Rehnquist to preside over the impeachment trial of Bill Clinton. For the entire trial he sat upright in his chair and listened carefully, but bellowed out "Noooo!" when the House managers sought to have Monica Lewinsky testify on the floor of the Senate. But that same month he stepped down as chairman of the Armed Services Committee, a move he announced in December 1997. "I've been up there a long time and I've seen some . . . get in the position of chairman and serve as long as they can. . . . I think that's selfish." Thurmond's longevity and stamina have been astonishing, but in early 2001 it was apparent that he was slowing down—although after Hillary Rodham Clinton was sworn in he came over to her and asked, "Can I hug you?" He was hospitalized five times between February 2000 and February 2001, mostly for dehydration, and in February 2001 stopped his practice of opening every session of the Senate. There was much speculation in the press that the Senate's 50–50 balance would be changed if Thurmond was no longer senator and his replacement was named by Democratic Governor Jim Hodges; some recalled that in the closely divided Senate of 1953–55 nine senators died and one resigned, and party control switched a number of times. But in the 106th Congress it was the 61-year-old Paul Coverdell who died, not the then 97-year-old Thurmond; Hodges said he expected the senator to serve out his term, and that if he did not he would appoint a caretaker who would not run for the seat in 2002. Republican legislators sponsored a bill requiring the governor to appoint a person of the same party to any vacancy, but presumably Hodges would veto that. There were stories that Thurmond's wife Nancy met with Hodges and played a videotape of Thurmond offering to resign if Hodges would appoint Nancy Thurmond in his place; but nothing came of that. Thurmond turns 100 in December 2002, one month before his term ends.

Thurmond's age was an issue when he won his last term in 1996. He won a Republican primary by 61%–30% and the general election by 53%–44%—well below his usual margins. Congressman Lindsey Graham announced in February 2001 that he would run for the seat; he became highly popular in the state during his performance on impeachment, and had united support from Republicans and ran ahead of potential Democratic candidates in the polls. By June 2001, eight well-known Democrats had turned down the race.

Cook's Call *Competitive*. This seat will be open for the first time in 48 years—in fact, it has been 36 years since there was an open-seat Senate race in the Palmetto State. Congressman Lindsey Graham will be the Republican nominee. Democrats were having trouble finding a nominee. As of spring 2001, only College of Charleston President Alex Sanders seemed interested in running. Give the edge to Republicans, but under the right circumstances, Democrats could make it at least interesting.

Junior Senator Ernest Hollings has served more than one-third of a century in the Senate and is still the junior senator from South Carolina—the longest-serving junior senator in history. Hollings grew up in Charleston, in moderate but not aristocratic circumstances, graduated from The Citadel and served in the Army in World War II. Returning home, he worked as a trial lawyer and was elected to the legislature in 1948, at 26, and was a member of the leadership two years later; he was elected governor in 1958, at 36, serving as South Carolina first faced school desegregation, which thanks to his efforts proceeded in an orderly fashion—a considerable achievement at the time. Hollings then spent four years out of office until he beat another former governor in the 1966 special election Senate race. Hollings has one of the quickest and sharpest tongues in the Senate and his instinct for zeroing in on others' weaknesses can be directed at the strong as well as the weak. When twitted by ABC's Sam Donaldson for wearing imported suits when he supported trade restrictions, and asked by Donaldson where he got his suit, he replied, "The same place you bought your wig, Sam."

In the 1980s Hollings concentrated on budget issues, arguing for a budget freeze in the early 1980s. In 1983 and 1984 he ran for president; his candidacy did not get far, but when Congress after a long struggle with Bill Clinton did freeze spending for a year in 1996, balance followed not long after. In 1985 he co-sponsored the Gramm-Rudman-Hollings deficit-cutting bill, which did in fact lead to lower deficits. He strongly backed the line-item veto and was one of 19 Senate Democrats to vote for it in 1995. In 1993 he argued for a value-added tax as an alternative to the Clinton tax increases. When the May 1997 budget agreement was reached, Hollings insisted that it would not produce a surplus, since the total of government and intragovernmental debt (including Social Security's Treasury IOUs) would still be rising; he offered to jump off the Capitol dome if the Treasury ever reported a surplus. The offer evidently still stands, though in March 2001 Hollings introduced a budget that would cut taxes in the case of a surplus, defined as a reduction in gross federal debt. Overall, Hollings believes in an activist but disciplined government, disagreeing with Republicans on the former and Democrats on the latter. In the Democratic Senate, his voting record was usually middle-of-the-road.

Hollings spent much of the 1990s working on telecommunications issues, as chairman or ranking minority member on the Commerce Committee and its Communications Subcommittee. Telecom issues were probably the most intellectually demanding and certainly the most heavily lobbied issues in Congress during many of those years, and Hollings managed to keep an even keel—and to get legislation passed. Hollings's instinct is to regulate at the federal level, which puts him at odds with many trends of the times. He was the major opponent of deregulating broadcasting and a major proponent of the 1992 Cable Reregulation Act, the one law on which Congress overrode George Bush's veto. But he has also been the most persistent backer of telecommunications reform, for more competition between long distance companies and the regional Bells. He first raised the issue in the early 1990s, then worked hard as a bill passed the House in 1994; but it died in the Senate because Hollings insisted that regional Bell companies get actual competition in local service before they were permitted to enter the long distance or cable markets. In 1995 and 1996, Hollings worked with new Chairman Larry Pressler to produce a bipartisan bill, which was signed into law in February 1996.

Hollings has worked since then to superintend the deregulatory process, always working (with Ted Stevens and House members Thomas Bliley and Edward Markey) to block the regional Bells from the long distance market and Internet business. He opposed Joel Klein as head of the Antitrust Division after Klein refused to oppose the Bell Atlantic-Nynex merger. He continued to insist on FCC rather than state regulation of the rates regional Bells could charge long distance companies for interconnecting their wires, but at the same time criticized the FCC for its enforcement, or non-enforcement, of the act. He opposed Deutsche Telekom's acquisition of VoiceStream in

2000, on the grounds that the German government owned 43% of DT, more than the 25% limit set in law; his amendment to bar the FCC from waiving the 25% limit was killed in October 2000 after it was criticized by Europeans, but the German government sold off much of its DT stock. He was chief sponsor of bills in 2000 that would have required websites to get explicit permission from consumers before collecting identifying information about them and that would require the FCC to set aside hours in which violent programming would be banned from TV.

Hollings's relations with ranking Republican John McCain, Commerce chairman since 1997, have not always been warm. In May 1998 Hollings vigorously opposed the tobacco bill that McCain passed through the committee 19–1 after it was changed to phase out tobacco price supports; there are many tobacco farmers in the corner of South Carolina around Marlboro and Chesterfield counties. In early 1999 he seemed to mistrust McCain for his presidential candidacy, though he did join with him in sponsoring a bill to require software to block inappropriate material from the Internet wired up to schools under a Gore-backed FCC measure. He was one of three Democrats to oppose the McCain-Feingold campaign finance bill in April 2001, though he has long complained that because of the press for campaign funds the Senate "has been so corrupted, it can't deliberate." Twice he has sponsored amendments to the First Amendment to allow Congress to set "reasonable limits" on campaign contributions and spending. In March 1997 he had the support of Minority Leaders Tom Daschle and Dick Gephardt; the amendment lost 61–38. In March 2000 it was defeated 67–33.

Hollings has been one of the Senate's strongest opponents of free trade and one of its strongest backers of trial lawyers. On trade, he has doubtless wanted to protect textile jobs in South Carolina, even though they are in long-term decline and the state is booming anyway. He shepherded a textile bill to passage in 1990, only to see it vetoed; he opposed NAFTA and caused GATT to be postponed until after the 1994 elections over the objections of then-Majority Leader George Mitchell, and then voted against. He filibustered the Africa and Caribbean trade bill in November 1999 until cloture was voted 74–23. He delivered a long speech against permanent normal trade relations with China in September 2000 and sought to retain annual review and to drop the words "permanent" and "normal." He remembers his own days as a trial lawyer and regards plaintiff's attorneys as fighters for the rights of the little guy. He opposed the 1999 Y2K relief bill as an infringement on the right to sue. Hollings takes an interest in a variety of other issues. In early 2000 he and Judd Gregg held up international peacekeeping funds in protest against the agreement which left Foday Sankoh in the government of Sierra Leone. He sponsored the 2000 law to create an Oceans Commission. With three other senators, he co-sponsored a 2001 bill to end the yearly drug certification process for Mexico. In the controversy over Bob Jones University in February 2000, he called the school a "national embarrassment." As a member of the Appropriations Committee, he has not been shy about getting money for South Carolina projects—a $1 million bridge to Kiawah Island, $4 million for the Lake Marion Regional Water Agency, $500,000 for the Parker's Ferry Community Center, $9 million for the Charleston Border Patrol Academy, $300,000 each for shrimp research, sea turtle research, and research on the "Charleston bump," an offshore feature that attracts many fish. In the evenly divided Senate, he often casts a key vote. He was one of 42 Democrats to vote against the confirmation of former colleague John Ashcroft in February 2001 and one of six Democrats to vote to repeal OSHA's ergonomics standards in March 2001.

In increasingly Republican South Carolina, Hollings was re-elected by only 50%–47% in 1992 over former Congressman Tommy Harnett; his January 1991 vote against the Gulf war resolution probably hurt. In polls running up to the 1998 election, he trailed former Governor Carroll Campbell, but in January 1998 Campbell decided not to run. Hollings had instead vigorous competition from 4th District Congressman Bob Inglis. Inglis eschewed pork barrel spending—he said that if voters wanted a senator to go on "a looting misson of the federal treasury, then I don't want the job"—and promised to serve only 12 years, in a state whose senators then had served a total of 76 years. He asked Hollings to join him in a pledge to wage a "courteous" campaign. This is not Hollings's style; in mid-October Hollings described Inglis to the *Rock Hill Herald* in mid-October thusly: "He finesses all around. He is Jack be nimble, Jack be quick. He's all around the damn clock, so oozing and goozing and such a nice little choirboy and so pleasant, and everybody's rude, and he wants to be courteous. He is a goddamn skunk." He apologized the next day, and said he was angered by "the gross distortions of my record and the callous accusations that have been leveled against me"—obviously staff-written language, without the authentic Hollings touch. Hollings's not-so-secret weapon was money; he outspent Inglis, who promised not to take PAC money, by $4.9 million to $2.1 million. Hollings organized a turnout drive which had a major effect on election day; he also benefited from the lively campaign of gubernatorial candidate Jim Hodges, financed heavily by video poker money. Inglis in contrast was stand-offish to his state party and avoided campaign professionals. His attempts to link Hollings to Bill Clinton were unconvincing, since Hollings had made clear his contempt for Clinton many times; in 1996 he had said, "Clinton's as popular as AIDS in South Carolina," and when the president's ratings rose that same year he said, "If they reach 60%, then he can start dating again." In the first solid Democratic year in South Carolina in nearly 20 years, he won a sixth term 53%–46%. Since Strom Thurmond has promised not to run for re-election in 2002, Hollings stands to become in January 2003 the state's senior senator. In August 2000 he told a cheering South Carolina Democratic convention that he would run for re-election in 2004, when he turns 82; it is not improbable that he could win in a state that re-elected Thurmond at 82, 88 and 94.

Presidential politics South Carolina can be said to have led the South into the Republican Party. It was the only Deep South state to vote for Richard Nixon over George Wallace in 1968 and since then has voted Democratic only once, for Jimmy Carter in 1976. It was one of the top three Republican states in 1988 and 1992; it was solidly Republican in 1996 and 2000.

South Carolina also has been pivotal in Republican nomination contests. In 1987 Lee Atwater purposefully scheduled the Republican primary here for the Saturday before Super Tuesday, and in 1988 George Bush won a smashing victory over Bob Dole and Pat Robertson, forecasting the Southern sweep that clinched his nomination. In 1992 Bush won with two-thirds of the vote, squashing Pat Buchanan's claims to represent the South. In 1996 former Governor Carroll Campbell and Governor David Beasley led a grass-roots campaign that gave Bob Dole, after his disappointing showings elsewhere, an impressive 45%–29% victory over Buchanan March 9. And in 2000 Campbell and Beasley, both now ex-governors, supported the successful campaign of George W. Bush.

The South Carolina February 19 primary turned out to be, once again, the critical battle in the war for the Republican nomination. John McCain came into the state fresh from a solid victory in New Hampshire, and in county after county attracted large crowds with whom he established a moving emotional bond. But he also went negative, saying Bush "twists the truth like Clinton," and he continued to emphasize campaign finance reform instead of issues on which his positions were widely shared by Republican voters. Bush came back by proclaiming himself a "reformer with results," citing his record in Texas and emphasizing the issues he had all along. Backed by Campbell and most Republican state officeholders, he also appealed to Christian conservatives, appearing at many religious schools, including Bob Jones University; for that last visit, he was criticized because of the college's ban on interracial dating and the anti-Catholic sentiments expressed on its websites. Bush launched a series of negative attack ads, accusing McCain of pledging to run a positive campaign, but then attacking Bush; as Bush said, "you can't take the high horse and then claim the low road." The substance of Bush's message was not significantly different from what he had been saying in Iowa and New Hampshire, but the national press insisted he had moved sharply to the right. Primary turnout was more than double that in 1996, and 30% of primary voters were self-identified Independents and 10% self-identified Democrats (South Carolina does not have party registration). McCain carried the independents and Democrats by a wide margin, but Bush won among self-identified Republicans and won overall 53%–42%. McCain carried Low Country counties, which have many newcomers from the North; Bush ran especially strongly in the Piedmont around Greenville and Spartanburg. For all the press emphasis on the southern particularity of South Carolina, the results here proved to be a template for those in later contests, with Bush carrying Republicans and McCain carrying Independents and Democrats. Only where the latter voted in unusually large numbers, as in Michigan, and in his home state of Arizona did McCain win again.

McCain was helped because Democrats, complying with party rules prohibiting contests between New Hampshire and Super Tuesday, decided to hold a caucus March 9; predictably, it got little coverage.

Congressional districting South Carolina's current congressional district boundaries were the result of a plan adopted in May 1992 and revised slightly in March 1994 to comply with a U.S. Supreme Court decision. A black-majority 6th District was created, combining black precincts in Charleston, the Low Country and Columbia; the result was to make adjoining districts more Republican. Republicans have held a 4–2 edge in the delegation since 1992 and in 1994 came close to winning another seat. For 2002, control of redistricting is split between the Republican legislature and Democratic Governor Jim Hodges. In early 2001 Republicans were talking about making major shifts in lines, taking Spartanburg out of the 4th District and combining it with much of the 5th; this would be a much tougher district for 5th District Democrat John Spratt, ranking minority member of the Budget Committee. But Hodges will presumably prevent such (in his eyes, anyway) mischief, and both the legislature and the governor will presumably insist on continuing to have a black-majority district. Demographically, it would be easy to draw a plan with minimal changes in district lines. Four of the six districts are near the population average, and would need just minor tweaking. The black-majority 6th District needs to add 68,000 people and the 2nd District needs to shed 62,000; the obvious solution would be to shift more heavily black precincts in Columbia and the Low Country from the 6th to the 2nd.

THE PEOPLE: Pop. 2000: 4,012,012; Pop. 1990: 3,486,703, up 15.1% 1990–2000. 1.4% of U.S. total, 26th largest; 67.2% White, 29.5% Black, 0.9% Asian, 0.3% Amer. Indian, 1% Two+ races, 1% Other; 2.4% Hispanic Origin. 3.9% Unemployment. 2000 Voting age pop.: 3,002,371. 2000 Turnout: 1,433,533; 48% of VAP. Registered voters (2000): 2,266,199; no party registration.

POLITICAL LINEUP: Governor, Jim Hodges (D); Lt. Gov., Bob Peeler (R); Secy. of State, Jim Miles (R); Atty. Gen., Charles M. Condon (R); Treasurer, Grady Patterson Jr. (D); Comptroller General, James Lander (D); Superintendent of Education, Inez Tenenbaum (D); Commissioner of Agriculture, D. Leslie Tindal (R); Adjutant General, MGen. Stanhope S. Spears (R); State Senate, 46 (22 D, 24 R); Senate Pres. Pro Tempore, Glenn F. McConnell (R); Majority Leader, John C. Land III (D); State House, 124 (54 D, 70 R); House Speaker, David Wilkins (R). Senators, Strom Thurmond (R) and Ernest F. Hollings (D). Representatives, 6 (2 D, 4 R).

ELECTIONS DIVISION: 803-734-9060; **FILING DEADLINE FOR U.S. CONGRESS:** March 30, 2002.

2000 Presidential Vote

Bush (R)	786,892	(57%)
Gore (D)	566,039	(41%)
Nader (Green)	20,279	(1%)
Others	10,832	(1%)

1996 Presidential Vote

Dole (R)	573,458	(50%)
Clinton (D)	506,283	(44%)
Perot (I)	64,386	(6%)

2000 Republican Presidential Primary

Bush (R)	305,998	(53%)
McCain (R)	239,964	(42%)
Keyes (R)	25,966	(5%)

Gov. Jim Hodges (D)

Elected 1998, term expires Jan. 2003, 1st term; b. Nov. 19, 1956, Lancaster; home, Lancaster; U. of SC, B.S. 1979, J.D. 1982; Methodist; married (Rachel).

Elected Office: SC House of Reps., 1986–97, Minority Ldr. 1994–97.

Professional Career: Practicing atty., 1983–90; Lancaster Cnty. Atty., 1983–86; Gen. Cnsl., Springs Co., 1990–98.

Office: P.O. Box 11829, The State House, Columbia, 29211, 803-734-9818; Fax: 803-734-1598; Web site: www.state.sc.us/governor.

Election Results

1998 general	Jim Hodges (D)	574,035	(53%)
	David Beasley (R)	486,342	(45%)
	Others	16,758	(2%)
1998 primary	Jim Hodges (D)	unopposed	
1994 general	David Beasley (R)	470,756	(50%)
	Nick A. Theodore (D)	447,002	(48%)
	Others	17,128	(2%)

Sen. Strom Thurmond (R)

Elected 1956, seat up 2002, 8th term; b. Dec. 5, 1902, Edgefield; home, Aiken; Clemson U., B.S. 1923; Baptist; separated.

Military Career: Army, 1942–46 (WWII), Army Reserves, 1923–59.

Elected Office: SC Senate, 1933–38; Circuit Judge, 1938–42; SC Gov., 1947–51; States' Rights candidate for U.S. Pres., 1948; US Senate, 1954–56.

Professional Career: Teacher & coach, 1923–29; Edgefield Cnty. Supervisor of Ed., 1929–33; Practicing atty., 1930–38, 1951–55.

DC Office: 217 RSOB, 20510, 202-224-5972; Fax: 202-224-1300; Web site: www.senate.gov/~thurmond.

State Offices: Aiken, 803-649-2591; Charleston, 843-727-4282; Columbia, 803-765-5494; Florence, 843-662-8873.

Committees: *Armed Services*: Personnel; Readiness & Management Support; Strategic Forces. *Judiciary*: Administrative Oversight & the Courts; Antitrust, Business Rights & Competition; Constitution, Federalism & Property Rights (RMM). *Veterans' Affairs*.

Group Ratings

	ADA	ACLU	AFS	LCV	CON	ITIC	NTU	COC	ACU	NTLC	CHC
2000	0	14	0	0	11	92	73	86	100	100	100
1999	0	—	0	0	8	—	73	76	100	—	—

National Journal Ratings

	1999 LIB	—	1999 CONS		2000 LIB	—	2000 CONS
Economic	35%	—	63%		27%	—	68%
Social	29%	—	69%		27%	—	70%
Foreign	6%	—	90%		27%	—	67%

Key Votes of the 106th Congress

1. Educ. Savings Accts.	Y	5. Review Movie Violence	Y	9. NATO War in Serbia	N
2. Prescrip. Drug Benefit	N	6. Gun Show Bckgrnd. Checks	N	10. Table Cuba Travel Ban	Y
3. Delay Ergonomic Standards	Y	7. Ban Part.-Birth Abortion	Y	11. Nuclear Test-Ban Treaty	N
4. Phase Out Estate Tax	Y	8. Broaden Hate Crimes List	N	12. Perm. Trade with China	Y

Election Results

1996 general	Strom Thurmond (R)	619,739	(53%)	($2,632,682)
	Elliott Close (D)	510,810	(44%)	($1,913,574)
	Others	30,419	(3%)	
1996 primary	Strom Thurmond (R)	132,157	(61%)	
	Harold Worley (R)	65,670	(30%)	
	Charlie Thompson (R)	20,188	(9%)	
1990 general	Strom Thurmond (R)	482,032	(64%)	($2,333,689)
	Robert H. Cunningham (D)	244,112	(33%)	($6,232)

Sen. Ernest F. Hollings (D)

Elected 1966, seat up 2004, 6th term; b. Jan. 1, 1922, Charleston; home, Charleston; The Citadel, B.A. 1942, U. of SC, LL.B. 1947; Lutheran; married (Peatsy).

Military Career: Army, 1942–45 (WWII).

Elected Office: SC House of Reps., 1948–54, Speaker Pro-Tem, 1951–54; SC Lt. Gov., 1954–58; SC Gov., 1958–62.

Professional Career: Practicing atty., 1947–55, 1963–66.

DC Office: 125 RSOB, 20510, 202-224-6121; Fax: 202-224-4293; Web site: hollings.senate.gov.

State Offices: Charleston, 843-727-4525; Columbia, 803-765-5731; Greenville, 864-233-5366.

Committees: *Appropriations*: Commerce, Justice, State & Judiciary (Chmn.); Defense; Energy & Water Development; Interior; Labor, HHS & Education. *Budget. Commerce, Science & Transportation* (Chmn.): Aviation; Communications (Chmn.); Manufacturing & Competitiveness; Oceans & Fisheries.

Group Ratings

	ADA	ACLU	AFS	LCV	CON	ITIC	NTU	COC	ACU	NTLC	CHC
2000	85	50	85	71	50	45	9	33	20	0	23
1999	85	—	100	56	51	—	6	27	12	—	—

National Journal Ratings

	1999 LIB	—	1999 CONS		2000 LIB	—	2000 CONS
Economic	66%	—	32%		67%	—	32%
Social	74%	—	25%		66%	—	21%
Foreign	51%	—	47%		58%	—	38%

Key Votes of the 106th Congress

1. Educ. Savings Accts.	N	5. Review Movie Violence	N	9. NATO War in Serbia	N
2. Prescrip. Drug Benefit	Y	6. Gun Show Bckgrnd. Checks	Y	10. Table Cuba Travel Ban	Y
3. Delay Ergonomic Standards	Y	7. Ban Part.-Birth Abortion	Y	11. Nuclear Test-Ban Treaty	Y
4. Phase Out Estate Tax	N	8. Broaden Hate Crimes List	Y	12. Perm. Trade with China	N

Election Results

1998 general	Ernest F. Hollings (D)	563,296	(53%)	($4,968,456)
	Bob Inglis (R)	488,217	(46%)	($2,143,278)
	Others	17,444	(2%)	
1998 primary	Ernest F. Hollings (D)	unopposed		
1992 general	Ernest F. Hollings (D)	591,030	(50%)	($4,188,829)
	Tommy Hartnett (R)	554,175	(47%)	($886,816)
	Others	35,233	(3%)	

FIRST DISTRICT

Looking out across the harbor to Fort Sumter are the glorious mansions of the Battery, gazing on the same view that the hot-blooded young swells of Charleston saw in April 1861 when they fired the shots that began the Civil War. Today there are few more beautiful urban scenes in America than the pastel "single houses" of Charleston, built flush with the sidewalk, turning their shoulders to the streets, with open piazzas inside their gateways facing south to catch the breeze, lovingly restored and maintained. Charleston, founded in 1670, was blessed with one of the finest harbors on the Atlantic, at the point where, Charlestonians say, the Ashley and Cooper Rivers meet to form the Atlantic Ocean. It was one of the South's two leading cities through the Civil War. Across its docks went cargoes of rice, indigo and cotton—all cultivated by black slaves, enriching the white planters and merchants who dominated the state's economic and political life. In the years following the Civil War, Charleston became an economic backwater, enabling the old buildings to survive; now the prosperity of recent years has financed their restoration. Its heritage remains important: In 2000, local Civil War buffs successfully raised the Confederate submarine

Hunley, which had sunk 136 years earlier at the mouth of Charleston harbor; tours to visit the ship, which was 80% filled with silt but appeared relatively intact, became a hot ticket.

This old society, descended from Barbados planters and French Huguenots, Sephardic Jews and English gentry second sons, was once a leading force in American political life. The hotheads in the gallery disrupted the 1860 Democratic National Convention here so boisterously that it was adjourned and reconvened in Baltimore, while Southern Democrats split off and nominated their own candidate, enabling Abraham Lincoln to win with 38% of the popular vote. South Carolina's blacks also have a lively history. There were free blacks here before the Civil War (some even owned slaves themselves), and Charleston's historic black culture was memorialized in George Gershwin's *Porgy and Bess*. The local accent, which seems to outsiders to have a touch of New Jersey and which can be incomprehensible when rapidly spoken, is best appreciated in the speech of Charlestonian Senator Ernest Hollings.

Some 25 years ago, the Charleston area depended heavily on its Navy and Air Force bases, which accounted for 20% of regional payrolls. Since then, Charleston has lost most of the bases, but far from languishing it has built a vibrant private economy with lots of small companies. As mayor for the last 25 years, Joe Riley Jr. cut crime along with Reuben Greenberg, the only black Jewish police chief in the United States (or perhaps anywhere else), and sponsored new parks and commercial projects that respect and amplify Charleston's historic heritage, and made it a major tourist destination. Also prime spots are South Carolina beaches from the high rises of the Grand Strand around Myrtle Beach in rapidly-growing Horry County to the eponymous hammocks of Pawleys Island. Low Country South Carolina, once a backwater dependent on the military, is now one of the most gracefully growing parts of the United States.

The 1st Congressional District includes most of the Charleston area and much of the Low Country. Its lines were drawn to maximize the black population of the next-door 6th; but, given the plantation heritage here, it is still 21% black. It includes the old houses of the Battery of Charleston and the beachfront and affluent suburbs strung out on high ground in all directions. It proceeds north past Pawleys Island to the Grand Strand; it runs south to Kiawah Island, but stops short of Hilton Head. About two-thirds of the voters are in metropolitan Charleston. Politically, it is solidly Republican, the more so as more newcomers move to the Charleston area and the Grand Strand.

The congressman from the 1st District is Henry Brown, a Republican elected in 2000. He has a very different pedigree than his conservative and often iconoclastic predecessor, Republican Mark Sanford—who kept his pledge to serve only three terms, while lamenting that many of his colleagues in the Class of 1994 had been co-opted, and moved to run for governor in 2002. Brown grew up on a small farm in Cordesville, worked at the Charleston Naval Shipyard as his father had, and then spent almost 30 years at the Piggly Wiggly grocery chain, where he eventually became a vice president. In 1981, at age 45, Brown entered the world of politics when he was elected to the Hanahan City Council. In 1985, he was elected to the state House; after the 1994 elections he became chairman of the Ways and Means Committee, where he claimed credit in 1995 for enacting the largest tax cut in the state's history.

In 2000 he ran for Congress. His chief opponent Buck Limehouse, member of an old Charleston family, and better known from his time as head of the state's Transportation Commission. Brown stressed issues of concern to the district's many senior citizens: property tax relief and shoring up Social Security. To boost his name recognition, he distributed 20,000 "Oh! Henry" chocolate bars. He ran an ad criticizing a proposal from Limehouse's department to place a toll on Charleston's Cooper River bridge replacement. Brown won endorsements from many legislators and from Christian conservatives. Limehouse, a Charleston developer, spent $790,000 to Brown's $315,000 and had the support of the party establishment, including Senator Strom Thurmond and former Governor Carroll Campbell. In the six-candidate primary, Brown led 44%–34%; Brown won comfortable pluralities in four of the five counties surrounding Charleston, while Limehouse carried his base up the coast in Georgetown County. In the runoff two weeks later, Limehouse also narrowly won the Grand Strand. But Brown won Charleston County 53%–47% and his home base, Berkeley County, which had the third-largest turnout, by 70%–30%; winning overall 55%–45%. The general election was anticlimactic. Brown beat a former Hollings spokesman by 60%–36%, carrying all five counties.

In the House, Brown won seats on Budget, Veterans' Affairs, and Transportation and Infrastructure—a good combination for a legislative insider who wants to deliver back home. Although redistricting may shift some lines with the neighboring 6th District, Brown should be safe.

Cook's Call *Safe.* Though this district is not the most Republican in the state, it does have a serious Republican base that should insulate Brown. The 1st was one of the fastest growing districts in South Carolina in the 1990s and will need to shed about 20,000 residents in redistricting.

THE PEOPLE: Pop. 2000: 684,765; Pop. 1990: 581,195, up 17.8% 1990–2000. 74.9% White, 21% Black, 1.2% Asian, 0.4% Amer. Indian, 0.1% Hawaiian, 1.3% Two+ races, 1.1% Other; 2.5% Hispanic Origin.

2000 Presidential Vote			**1996 Presidential Vote**		
Bush (R)	145,961	(59%)	Dole (R)	107,221	(55%)
Gore (D)	94,647	(38%)	Clinton (D)	74,150	(38%)
Nader (Green)	4,902	(2%)	Perot (I)	11,491	(6%)
Others	2,016	(1%)			

Rep. Henry Brown, Jr. (R)

Elected 2000, 1st term; b. Dec. 20, 1935, Bishopville; home, Hanahan; The Citadel; Baptist Col.; Baptist; married (Billye).

Military Career: SC Natl. Guard, 1953–62.

Elected Office: Hanahan City Council, 1981–85; SC House of Reps., 1985–2000.

Professional Career: V.P., Piggly Wiggly Carolina Co., 1958–85.

DC Office: 1017 LHOB 20515, 202-225-3176; Fax: 202-225-3407; Web site: www.house.gov/henrybrown.

District Offices: Conway, 843-248-2660; N. Charleston, 843-747-4175.

Committees: *Budget* (21st of 24 R). *Transportation & Infrastructure* (31st of 42 R): Highways & Transit; Water Resources & Environment. *Veterans' Affairs* (16th of 17 R): Health.

Group Ratings and Key Votes: Newly Elected

Election Results

2000 general	Henry Brown Jr. (R)	139,597	(60%)	($606,776)
	Andy Brack (D)	82,622	(36%)	($485,733)
	Others	9,227	(4%)	
2000 runoff	Henry Brown Jr. (R)	21,631	(55%)	
	Buck Limehouse (R)	17,990	(45%)	
2000 primary	Henry Brown Jr. (R)	22,072	(44%)	
	Buck Limehouse (R)	17,171	(34%)	
	Van Jenerette (R)	4,269	(8%)	
	Wheeler Tillman (R)	2,627	(5%)	
	Mike Seekings (R)	2,470	(5%)	
	Charlie Thompson (R)	1,998	(4%)	
1998 general	Mark Sanford (R)	118,414	(91%)	($49,458)
	Joe Innella (NL)	11,586	(9%)	

SECOND DISTRICT

Soon after the Revolutionary War, in 1786, the South Carolina legislature decided to move the state's capital away from the Charleston aristocracy and into the Up Country interior, away from a city named after a king to a new city named after a discoverer of America: so began Columbia.

The State House was built on high ground above the Congaree River in a town of one-and-a-half story houses with first floor porticoes, dormers and raised brick basements—"Columbia cottages." In 1865, General William Tecumseh Sherman's army burned everything here but the State House. In the post-Sherman years, Columbia grew slowly, with state government and the university, the Army's Fort Jackson and local insurance companies proving steady employers. In the 1970s, it started to boom, attracting plants such as Michelin, Allied Chemical, United Technologies, FN of Belgium, DuPont and Square D. With a metro area population of 536,000, Columbia is now a confident city, not just a village-capital.

The Columbia to which Jimmy Byrnes, after years in top posts in Democratic Washington, returned as governor to lament the *Brown v. Board of Education* decision in 1954, has trended Republican in the years since. Upwardly mobile South Carolinians, transplanted from underdeveloped rural areas to comfortable subdivisions with two-car garages, preferred Republicans first in national and then in state and local elections. Columbia voted for Eisenhower in the 1950s; in the late 1960s and 1970s, blacks were usually outnumbered by increasingly Republican whites in Columbia's Richland County and fast-growing Lexington County across the river. In the 1990s, as Columbia has spread out into formerly rural areas, Richland County, with a higher black percentage, has been voting Democratic, and in 1998 even generated a large enough margin to overcome Lexington's Republican majority. In the 2000 presidential race, Al Gore won Richland 54%–43%, but George W. Bush won Lexington 70%–27%; Bush carried the metro area 54%–43%.

The 2d Congressional District of South Carolina includes most of metropolitan Columbia, except for black neighborhoods lopped off in 1992 to form part of a black-majority 6th District. It contains the city's affluent white neighborhoods and the spread-out towns of Richland and Lexington counties, with their shopping centers and many churches and the Army's huge training center, Fort Jackson. The district extends south through the horse-farm area around Aiken and several lightly populated black-majority rural counties, and then includes Beaufort and Hilton Head on the coast—the former is an old town, with wonderful mansions and a history intertwined with slave plantations and the Marine Corps's Parris Island training base; the latter has been developed with meticulous attention to its natural environment, a model now for Atlantic Coast condominium and vacation communities. Beaufort County's population rose 40% in the 1990s, the highest growth in the state. This is a solidly Republican district, though Democrats, with relatively big turnouts in black areas, were able to whittle down its Republican majority in 1998 and 2000.

The congressman from the 2d District is Floyd Spence, a Republican first elected in 1970, and former chairman of the Armed Services Committee. Spence was a star football player and student body president at the University of South Carolina; he served as an officer in the Navy and was in the Naval Reserve until 1988. When he graduated from law school in 1956, he was elected to the state House; he switched parties and became a Republican in 1962, two years before Strom Thurmond. He narrowly lost a House race that year to a Democrat who later switched parties; then Spence was elected to the state Senate as a Republican in 1966. When the incumbent ran for governor in 1970, Spence ran again for the House seat and won. He is now second in seniority among House Republicans, trailing only Philip Crane and tied with Bill Young.

Spence has a solidly conservative voting record. He was the first House member to sponsor the balanced budget constitutional amendment, in 1971; he served for 13 years as ranking Republican on the ethics committee. But his greatest energy has been devoted to military issues. He supported the defense buildup of the 1980s and called for "responsible downsizing of defense expenditures rather than drastic cuts" in the 1990s. But that downsizing went much farther than he considered wise. As chairman, Spence peppered the Clinton administration with criticism even as he has managed the complex and lengthy defense authorization bills. He argued that defense cuts were too deep, twice as deep as Clinton promised in 1992. He worried about the erosion of the nuclear stockpile. He argued that cuts jeopardized the technological superiority so apparent in the Gulf war. "Our national strategy is to be able to [simultaneously] fight and win two major regional contingencies. But we've cut back so much since Desert Storm that I don't think we could do even one," he said in 1998. Spence was particularly concerned when retention rates declined and standards for enlistment were cut. "The decline in military quality of life is approaching a state of crisis," he said, and said he would support a military draft if retention rates and readiness did not improve. He decried the administration policy of selling high-tech devices to China. He secured funding to support the troops in Iraq and Bosnia despite voicing his disapproval of the way NATO was conducting the operation of the latter. He criticized Clinton's policy toward North Korea as "appeasement and bribery."

Spence has long urged the United States to build a system of missile defense. "We don't have a defense against weapons of mass destruction, and the president has blocked all our efforts to increase national security," he said in 1998. Efforts to declare missile defense a national priority were frustrated by a Democratic filibuster that year (South Carolina's Ernest Hollings was one of four Democrats to vote to cut off the filibuster). But Spence moved missile defense significantly forward by creating the commission on missile defense headed by Donald Rumsfeld, which in July 1998 unanimously concluded that rogue states could develop missiles with the capacity of delivering nuclear weapons without our intelligence agencies knowing. This changed the conversation, and in 1999 the House passed legislation that would commit the U.S. to building a missile defense system as soon as it is technologically possible. Rumsfeld's work on the missile defense commission was one item recommending him to George W. Bush, and as Defense secretary he is in a position to move missile defense forward—a development for which Spence deserves much credit.

One change Spence has stoutly resisted is a new round of base closures. South Carolina suffered from the earlier rounds, but has recovered economically with little damage. Spence charged that more base closures won't save money for several years: "The reality of ongoing base closures is that the upfront costs, including huge bills for environmental cleanup, are enormous." Indeed, Congress has appropriated more than $1 billion for cleanup of the closed Savannah River nuclear site. His focus on military retirees led to enactment in 2000 of a huge increase in what Spence termed "permanent lifetime health care" by using Tricare, the military insurance program, as a Medicare supplement. During the presidential election recount in Florida, he voiced concern when Democrats stopped the counting of absentee military ballots without postmarks. The Republicans' three-term limit on committee chairmen forced Spence to step down in 2001, and he became chairman of Armed Services' influential procurement panel.

Spence received a double lung transplant in 1988, and in May 2000, after two months of kidney failure, he received a transplant from his oldest son. From 1990 to 1996 he did not have a Democratic opponent. In 1998 he was opposed by Beaufort County architect Jane Frederick, a self-styled "feminist" who attacked his "archaic, insensitive and unacceptable view toward women" and his stands on abortion, family leave and the minimum wage. Spence campaigned robustly around the district, but his campaign organization was rusty, and Democrats—fed by video poker money—made their best South Carolina showing in years. Spence won 58%–41%, a solid but not overwhelming margin. He ran ahead of the state ticket but, despite years of helping local black officials, lost in three black-majority counties. Frederick ran again in 2000, and the result was virtually the same: Spence won 57%–41%, winning six of 11 counties and taking Richland and Lexington counties by 38,000 votes, plus Frederick's Beaufort County base by 6,000. After losing his committee chairmanship, plus his health and local political problems, it would not be a surprise if he retired in 2002 at age 74. But South Carolina legislators have a way of surviving a long time. The district must give up 62,000 people in redistricting; the Republican legislature could move some heavily black areas in Columbia and rural counties to the neighboring 6th district, which needs to gain 68,000 people—a change that would help both incumbents.

Cook's Call *Probably Safe.* As the fastest-growing district in South Carolina during the 1990s, the 2nd will need to shed about 62,000 people. Should Spence decide to retire, this Republican-leaning district would still be tough for Democrats to win.

THE PEOPLE: Pop. 2000: 731,022; Pop. 1990: 580,636, up 25.9% 1990–2000. 68.2% White, 27.7% Black, 1.2% Asian, 0.3% Amer. Indian, 0.1% Hawaiian, 1.2% Two+ races, 1.4% Other; 3.2% Hispanic Origin.

2000 Presidential Vote
Bush (R) 165,499 (58%)
Gore (D) 114,090 (40%)
Nader (Green) 4,981 (2%)
Others 2,220 (1%)

1996 Presidential Vote
Dole (R) 117,261 (53%)
Clinton (D) 90,871 (41%)
Perot (I) 10,827 (5%)

Rep. Floyd Spence (R)

Elected 1970, 16th term; b. Apr. 9, 1928, Columbia; home, Lexington; U. of SC, A.B. 1952, LL.B. 1956; Lutheran; married (Deborah).

Military Career: Naval Reserves, 1947–88 (Korea).

Elected Office: SC House of Reps., 1956–62; SC Senate, 1966–70, Minority Ldr., 1966–70.

Professional Career: Practicing atty., 1956–70.

DC Office: 2405 RHOB 20515, 202-225-2452; Fax: 202-225-2455; Web site: www.house.gov/spence.

District Offices: Beaufort, 843-521-2530; Columbia, 803-254-5120; Estill, 803-625-3177; Orangeburg, 803-536-4641.

Committees: *Armed Services* (Vice Chmn. of 32 R): Military Procurement (Chmn.). *Veterans' Affairs* (4th of 17 R): Benefits.

Group Ratings

	ADA	ACLU	AFS	LCV	CON	ITIC	NTU	COC	ACU	NTLC	CHC
2000	5	21	14	0	18	76	59	93	85	70	93
1999	10	—	0	6	15	—	58	80	88	—	—

National Journal Ratings

	1999 LIB	—	1999 CONS		2000 LIB	—	2000 CONS
Economic	24%	—	72%		15%	—	83%
Social	4%	—	91%		0%	—	79%
Foreign	31%	—	66%		0%	—	88%

Key Votes of the 106th Congress

1. Patient Bill of Rights	Y	5. Bar RU-486 $ for FDA	Y	9. NATO War in Serbia	N
2. Accelerate Min. Wage	*	6. Display 10 Commandments	Y	10. Perm. Trade with China	N
3. Strike Ban on Ergo. Stnd.	N	7. Gun Show Bkgrnd. Checks	N	11. Debt Relief for 3rd World	N
4. Ovrd. Estate Tax Veto	Y	8. Ban Part.-Birth Abortion	Y	12. Drop Cuba Econ. Embargo	N

Election Results

2000 general	Floyd Spence (R)	153,870	(57%)	($618,718)
	Jane Frederick (D)	110,161	(41%)	($367,796)
	Others	5,914	(2%)	
2000 primary	Floyd Spence (R)	unopposed		
1998 general	Floyd Spence (R)	119,583	(58%)	($537,752)
	Jane Frederick (D)	84,864	(41%)	($202,584)

THIRD DISTRICT

The South Carolina Up Country, many days' travel by wagon from the Low Country plantations, was first settled by Scots-Irish farmers, like the family of John C. Calhoun in the years around the Revolutionary War. The pioneers wanted to make big plantations of these forests, but the land did not always cooperate; it was often too hilly for the labor-intensive rice crop grown in the Low Country and sometimes too cold for cotton. So relatively few slaves were brought here, and the land was mostly small farms owned by whites. Today, the racial and cultural tone of Up Country South Carolina shows traces of these roots. This is a mostly white part of the South, with a hell-of-a-fella tone to daily life, an economically growing and culturally tradition-minded slice of Middle America.

The 3d Congressional District covers much of this territory, following the Georgia border from the government's troubled Savannah River Site all the way north to mountains on the North Carolina border. In the southern part of the 3d are a few heavily black communities, like Edgefield, where Strom Thurmond grew up and first won public office in the 1930s. But the major population center here is the increasingly affluent suburban strip linking Aiken and Augusta, Georgia. In the northern part of this district, Calhoun had his mansion and his son-in-law founded Clemson University nearby. Here today, the Savannah River intersects Interstate 85, the main street of what was once America's textile belt and now of the booming Southeast from Raleigh-Durham to Atlanta, one of the nation's prime economic growth areas.

The politics of this area, ancestrally Democratic, has been trending Republican for years. Yankified Aiken started voting Republican for Dwight Eisenhower in the 1950s, well before Thurmond switched parties in 1964; Anderson skittered around, supporting Jimmy Carter for a while but then veering Republican again; Pickens and Oconee counties around Clemson and the mountains are heavily Republican. This is a fervently religious part of America, and the increasing secularism and hostility to religious values of many leading Democrats moved it away from its ancestral party. In presidential elections the 3d has become solidly Republican, and it voted Republican even as Democrats swept the state in 1998.

The congressman from the 3d District is Lindsey Graham, a Republican first elected in 1994. Graham grew up in Oconee County, where his parents owned a "beer joint." He was the first in his family to graduate from college and law school, then served in the Air Force as a prosecutor; in 1988 he returned home and practiced law, also serving as judge advocate at McEntire Air National Guard base. He was called up to active duty and served stateside in the Gulf war. In 1992 he was elected state representative. In 1994, with the retirement of 20-year Congressman Butler Derrick, a member of the Democratic leadership who came under tough criticism back home, Graham ran for Congress. Both parties had contested primaries, but the Republican contest attracted more voters—41,000 versus 35,000—and Graham won with 52% of the vote. In the general he faced state Senator Jim Bryan. Graham called for term limits, supported more defense spending and was against gays in the military. His attitude toward the Clinton Administration and the House Democratic leadership was unequivocal: "I'm one less vote for an agenda that makes you want to throw up." Bryan also campaigned as a conservative—pro-life, anti-gays in the military, against employer mandates in health care, against defense cuts, and boasted of his experience in the legislature. But Graham modeled his campaign after Bob Inglis's successful 1992 race in the next-door 4th District and won 60%–40%—a smashing victory in a district represented only by Democrats since Reconstruction. In 1996 he was opposed by Deborah Dorn, daughter of Derrick's predecessor William Jennings Bryan Dorn, and won by 60%–39%. Since then, he has been reelected easily.

In the House Graham has a strong though not entirely conservative voting record. He supported the Contract with America and called for lifting the tax burden on individuals and removing onerous regulations on business. But in January 1996 he was one of 15 Republicans who voted against settling the budget fight. He came to see Newt Gingrich as just another deal-making career politician. In July 1997 Graham helped organize a group of Republican leaders to plot the toppling of Gingrich, and Tom DeLay said he would vote to oust the speaker. This coup quickly foundered—it could have given Democrats control of the House—and in a Republican conference meeting when Dick Armey said no party leader was involved, Graham lunged to the microphone to contradict him. Graham also showed independence on legislation. He opposed the 1997 budget deal because it included a children's health insurance plan financed by higher tobacco taxes, and he bucked the leadership on HMO reform, arguing that patients should have the right to sue. Much of his work has been devoted to the Savannah River Site (SRS). This huge installation was once used to manufacture tritium for nuclear weapons; with as many as 35,000 jobs, it was among the largest employers in South Carolina. Now the nuclear plant is shut down and SRS is used as a holding site for nuclear waste while Washington works on developing a long-term disposal. Graham wants to make SRS a waste processing site for surplus weapons-grade plutonium and highly-enriched uranium, to keep reprocessing canyons fully used to process nuclear waste and to place a linear accelerator there; with nuclear power foe Edward Markey he sponsored an amendment to block any commercial tritium reactor that would be built elsewhere. If successful, the SRS project could cost $4 billion over 20 years. Meanwhile, Graham helped to enact in 2000 a bill giving $150,000 each to compensate workers at the former nuclear-weapons site who had become sick.

As a member of the Judiciary Committee, Graham played a major role in impeachment. When Clinton defenders quibbled about the meanings of words and insisted that Clinton's deposition testimony was "legally accurate," Graham exploded in opposition. He was especially upset with the way Clinton used the official powers of the White House to discredit Monica Lewinsky. Yet he voted against impeaching Clinton for lying in the Paula Jones deposition, on the ground that it was later ruled immaterial by the judge. In the Senate trial, Graham's folksy manner and clear description of Clinton's offenses—"Where I come from, a man who calls someone up at 2:30 in the morning is up to no good"—made him one of the most effective managers. Yet he conceded a major political point when he agreed that a reasonable person could disagree on whether Clinton should be removed. On other issues, he passed in the House in 1999 and 2001 the Unborn Victims of Violence Act, which makes it a separate crime to injure a fetus when assaulting a pregnant woman. And he moved through the Judiciary Committee a bill to ban gambling on amateur and Olympic sporting events. When the House passed a bill in 2000 to make it a hate crime to attack gays, Graham opposed it on the ground that all crimes are heinous. When Clinton left office, Graham quipped to a local reporter, "Bill Clinton probably did more for my career than I did. I'll miss him but it probably won't be for long."

Graham has continued to march to his own drummer on party matters. In the 2000 campaign, citing the need for Republicans to regain their "reform" momentum, he was a tireless and highly visible supporter of John McCain in the primary campaign. When Graham was elected in 1994, he imposed a six-term limit on himself. In February 2001, he announced he was running for Strom Thurmond's Senate seat. Local Democrats have termed Graham "the Seinfeld Congressman—all about nothing" because of his impeachment fame. But no opponent immediately stepped forward, and Graham was running well in polls. Leading Republicans quickly rallied around Graham, including three former governors and Bob Dole. When Democratic state chairman Dick Harpootlian said on the day of his announcement that he was "light in the loafers," Graham accused him of slander because the phrase is a frequently pejorative reference to homosexuality and added that such attacks would not succeed. Harpootlian, perhaps disingenuously, denied any such imputation. Among local Republicans lining up early for the 3rd District seat were state Representatives Gresham Barrett and James Klauber, businessman Michael Thompson, and former local prosecutor George Ducworth. Redistricting will likely not change the district much, leaving any Republican nominee with a big advantage in November.

Cook's Call   *Safe.* Graham's decision to run for the Senate in 2002 means that this seat will be open for only the second time in 26 years. Although a Democrat represented it as recently as 1994, the 3rd now has a serious Republican edge: Bush won here with 63% in 2000 and Graham has never dipped below 60% in his four races.

THE PEOPLE: Pop. 2000: 670,139; Pop. 1990: 580,861, up 15.4% 1990–2000. 76.7% White, 20.9% Black, 0.6% Asian, 0.2% Amer. Indian, 0.8% Two+ races, 0.8% Other; 1.9% Hispanic Origin.

2000 Presidential Vote

Bush (R)	137,336	(63%)
Gore (D)	75,993	(35%)
Nader (Green)	2,992	(1%)
Others	2,033	(1%)

1996 Presidential Vote

Dole (R)	100,390	(54%)
Clinton (D)	71,755	(39%)
Perot (I)	13,220	(7%)

Rep. Lindsey Graham (R)

Elected 1994, 4th term; b. July 9, 1955, Central; home, Seneca; U. of SC, B.A. 1977, J.D. 1981; Baptist; single.

Military Career: Air Force, 1982–88; SC Air Natl. Guard, 1989–94; Air Force Reserves, 1995–present (Operation Desert Storm).

Elected Office: SC House of Reps., 1992–94.

Professional Career: U.S. Air Forces Europe Circuit Trial Counsel, 1984–88; Asst. Oconee Cnty. Atty., 1988–92; Practicing atty., 1988–94; Judge Advocate, McEntire Air Natl. Guard Base, 1989–94; Central SC City Atty., 1990–94.

DC Office: 1429 LHOB 20515, 202-225-5301; Fax: 202-225-3216; Web site: www.house.gov/graham.

District Offices: Aiken, 803-649-5571; Anderson, 864-224-7401; Greenwood, 864-223-8251.

Committees: *Armed Services* (19th of 32 R): Military Personnel; Military Procurement (Vice Chmn.). *Education & the Workforce* (10th of 27 R): 21st Century Competitiveness; Workforce Protections. *Judiciary* (13th of 21 R): Courts, the Internet & Intellectual Property; The Constitution.

Group Ratings

	ADA	ACLU	AFS	LCV	CON	ITIC	NTU	COC	ACU	NTLC	CHC
2000	5	29	14	7	94	60	72	70	100	94	87
1999	20	—	16	6	79	—	66	50	88	—	—

National Journal Ratings

	1999 LIB	—	1999 CONS		2000 LIB	—	2000 CONS
Economic	46%	—	53%		0%	—	94%
Social	19%	—	79%		0%	—	79%
Foreign	34%	—	65%		0%	—	88%

Key Votes of the 106th Congress

1. Patient Bill of Rights	Y	5. Bar RU-486 $ for FDA	Y	9. NATO War in Serbia	N
2. Accelerate Min. Wage	N	6. Display 10 Commandments	Y	10. Perm. Trade with China	N
3. Strike Ban on Ergo. Stnd.	N	7. Gun Show Bkgrnd. Checks	N	11. Debt Relief for 3rd World	N
4. Ovrd. Estate Tax Veto	Y	8. Ban Part.-Birth Abortion	Y	12. Drop Cuba Econ. Embargo	N

Election Results

2000 general	Lindsey Graham (R)	150,176	(68%)	($725,118)
	George L. Brightharp (D)	64,920	(29%)	($41,713)
	Others	6,525	(3%)	
2000 primary	Lindsey Graham (R)	unopposed		
1998 general	Lindsey Graham (R)	unopposed		($321,502)

FOURTH DISTRICT

A century ago, Northern investors seeking sites for textile mills looked at the Up Country of South Carolina and "were attracted by the mild climate, abundant water power, proximity to the cotton fields and plenty of native [white] labor already accustomed to a low standard of living." As mills fled New England, the textile industry became concentrated along the Southern Railway and Seaboard Coast Line tracks between Charlotte and Atlanta, especially in the Piedmont of South Carolina. The textile country might look bucolic, but Greenville, Spartanburg and the dozens of mill towns thick in the surrounding countryside were as industrial as Lancashire or the Ruhr, with mills rising up on what were once twisting woodland paths.

Today, this same stretch of land along Interstate 85, which parallels the Southern Railway, remains the number one textile-producing area in the United States. But it is much more than that. The number of textile and apparel jobs has continued to steadily decline, but so many more jobs were created in the 1990s by big and small companies that the South Carolina Manufacturers Alliance dropped "textiles" from its name. Michelin's North American headquarters is near

Greenville and BMW's plant is next to the airport in Spartanburg County just off I-85. What attracts these businesses? Sometimes big tax concessions, as with BMW. More importantly, overall tax levels are low, with good state-built infrastructure—airports, interstate highways, the port of Charleston, now one of the busiest on the East Coast. Unions are almost nonexistent. Culturally this area ranges from conservative to very conservative, with strong influence from Greenville's straight-laced and nationally-controversial Bob Jones University and many evangelical and fundamentalist churches. But the culture of mainstream churches and civic boosters has a certain bedrock conservatism as well.

The 4th Congressional District of South Carolina includes all of Greenville and Spartanburg Counties, plus much smaller Union County and a sliver of Laurens County. It is a heavily Republican area in all elections; the real political divide here is between religious and economic conservatives.

The congressman from the 4th District is Jim DeMint, a Republican elected in 1998. DeMint grew up in Greenville, graduated from the University of Tennessee and Clemson Business School, and returned to Greenville to work as a paper salesman and in the advertising business. In 1983 he founded DeMint Marketing, with businesses, schools, colleges and hospitals as clients. In 1992, at age 41, he went to work for 33-year-old lawyer Bob Inglis' House campaign. As he explains, "I became increasingly concerned that the freedoms we take for granted in America are under attack in such a subtle way that no one is noticing it. I developed the feeling that I had a burden to try to change things." Inglis pledged to serve only three terms, to take no PAC money, to oppose pork barrel projects even in South Carolina; DeMint honed his message using focus groups and advertising expertise. Inglis upset an incumbent Democrat by 50%–48%, and kept his promises.

DeMint ran, with Inglis' support, for the open seat. Like Inglis, he pledged to serve only three terms and take no PAC money; on pork, he was more practical, saying that if bills were going to pass he would make sure some of the money went to South Carolina. He called for a national sales tax or flat tax, for individual retirement accounts in Social Security, for the right-to-life amendment, for the English rule (loser pays winner's attorney fees) in tort cases. Four other Republicans ran, and the favorite was Mike Fair, former University of South Carolina quarterback, 10-year state representative and first term state senator, "arguably the state's most conservative politician," according to the Columbia *State*. He opposed coed dorms at the state university, criticized sex education that advocated condom use, backed covenant marriage and fought for a ban on all abortion. In the June primary Fair led with 32%; DeMint came in second with 23%, 699 votes ahead of hospital executive Howell Clyborne. The order was the same in Greenville County; but in Spartanburg County, which cast 36% of the vote, Spartanburg lawyer Jim Ritchie led with 42%. In the runoff two weeks later, it seemed obvious that Spartanburg would determine the outcome. Fair bragged about his experience, DeMint called him a "career politician." The result was a 53%–47% upset win for DeMint. He trailed in Greenville County 51%–49%, but carried Spartanburg County by 60%–40%. In the general, Democratic state senator Glenn Reese made a game effort, but he was running uphill and was heavily outspent. DeMint won 58%–40%.

In the House, DeMint was elected president of the freshman class and quickly became a strong conservative voice. He joined other junior Republicans seeking to rein in spending by the appropriators. When party leaders scheduled a vote on the minimum wage but prevented DeMint from offering an amendment to permit states to "opt out," he complained that "conservative Republicans in the House have been pushed to the edge." But he resisted local pressures and took a more national perspective as the only South Carolina House member to vote for permanent normal trade relations with China, arguing that the best way to remedy human-rights abuses was "to export our products and principles." The libertarian Cato Institute ranked DeMint in the top 1% of "free traders" in the House; his vote was a sign that the anti-free trade textile industry no longer holds sway here. In the gun control debate following the Columbine shootings, DeMint won approval of his amendment to exempt defendants from paying both sides' attorney fees for any lawsuit claiming that a public school permitted a student's religious expression. When President Bush proposed his $1.6 trillion tax-cut package, he was among a small group who immediately pushed for more.

In 2000 DeMint was reelected without Democratic opposition. In early 2001 DeMint was lobbied not to keep his term limit pledge in 2004, and Inglis said that he planned to run again that year and would not make such a pledge again.

Cook's Call   *Safe*. This deeply conservative district is arguably the most Republican in South Carolina (Bush won here with 64% in 2000) and one of the most Republican in the South. The only thing preventing DeMint from planting himself here for a good long time is the fact that he has limited himself to three terms and pledged to leave the House in 2004.

THE PEOPLE: Pop. 2000: 670,335; Pop. 1990: 581,385, up 15.3% 1990–2000. 76.2% White, 19.8% Black, 1.3% Asian, 0.2% Amer. Indian, 1.1% Two+ races, 1.3% Other; 3.2% Hispanic Origin.

2000 Presidential Vote		
Bush (R)	152,026	(64%)
Gore (D)	78,379	(33%)
Nader (Green)	3,643	(2%)
Others	2,205	(1%)

1996 Presidential Vote		
Dole (R)	111,699	(56%)
Clinton (D)	74,208	(37%)
Perot (I)	11,496	(6%)

Rep. Jim DeMint (R)

Elected 1998, 2d term; b. Sept. 2, 1951, Greenville; home, Greenville; U. of TN, B.S. 1973, Clemson U., M.B.A. 1981; Presbyterian; married (Debbie).

Professional Career: Sales Rep., Scott Paper, 1973–75; Acct. Rep., Henderson Advertising, 1975–81; V.P., Leslie Advertising, 1981–84; Pres., DeMint Marketing, 1983-present.

DC Office: 504 CHOB 20515, 202-225-6030; Fax: 202-226-1177; Web site: www.demint.house.gov.

District Offices: Greenville, 864-232-1141; Spartanburg, 864-582-6422; Union, 864-427-2205.

Committees: *Education & the Workforce* (19th of 27 R): Education Reform; Employer-Employee Relations. *Small Business* (9th of 19 R): Tax, Finance & Exports; Workforce, Empowerment & Government Programs (Chmn.). *Transportation & Infrastructure* (22d of 42 R): Coast Guard & Maritime Transportation; Highways & Transit; Railroads.

Group Ratings

	ADA	ACLU	AFS	LCV	CON	ITIC	NTU	COC	ACU	NTLC	CHC
2000	0	21	0	7	85	100	74	90	100	94	100
1999	0	—	0	13	51	—	69	92	91	—	—

National Journal Ratings

	1999 LIB —	1999 CONS		2000 LIB —	2000 CONS
Economic	0% —	84%		0% —	94%
Social	4% —	91%		0% —	79%
Foreign	0% —	97%		22% —	76%

Key Votes of the 106th Congress

1. Patient Bill of Rights	N	5. Bar RU-486 $ for FDA	Y
2. Accelerate Min. Wage	N	6. Display 10 Commandments	Y
3. Strike Ban on Ergo. Stnd.	N	7. Gun Show Bkgrnd. Checks	N
4. Ovrd. Estate Tax Veto	Y	8. Ban Part.-Birth Abortion	Y

9. NATO War in Serbia	N
10. Perm. Trade with China	Y
11. Debt Relief for 3rd World	N
12. Drop Cuba Econ. Embargo	N

Election Results

2000 general	Jim DeMint (R)	150,436	(80%)	($303,967)
	Ted Adams (CNP)	16,532	(9%)	($15,968)
	April Bishop (LIB)	12,757	(7%)	($69,869)
	Others	9,326	(5%)	
2000 primary	Jim DeMint (R)	41,851	(77%)	
	Franklin D. Raddish (R)	12,279	(23%)	
1998 general	Jim DeMint (R)	105,264	(58%)	($453,336)
	Glenn Reese (D)	73,314	(40%)	($112,995)
	Others	3,972	(2%)	

FIFTH DISTRICT

Some of the fiercest battles of the Revolutionary War were fought in South Carolina's Up Country, on hilly lands just being settled by Scots-Irish farmers moving up from the Low Country or down the Virginia Piedmont valley. This was a country of violent passions and unclear lines; Carolinians have long argued over which side of the North and South Carolina boundary Andrew Jackson was born in 1767. Ever since, the fighting spirit and Calvinist faith of Up Country Carolinians have never wavered. This "Olde English District" remains intensely religious and pro-military. But it is no longer impoverished. For many years, the dominant industry here was textiles, traditionally the first factory enterprise of industrializing countries, with low pay and poor working conditions. But in the 1980s and 1990s the number of textile jobs declined, and small-business prosperity more recently has been barreling out the interstates from Greenville-Spartanburg and Columbia and Charlotte, to transform counties once dependent on tobacco fields and textile mills.

The 5th Congressional District consists of all or part of 13 counties, mostly in the Up Country. It includes just one small county in the Greenville metro area and fast-growing (up 25% in the 1990s) York County, part of the metro area centered on Charlotte, North Carolina. In the east, the 5th includes Dillon County, site of the pink, orange and turquoise South of the Border tourist attraction heralded on 250 billboards on I-95, and Darlington, site of the Southern 500 stock car race every Labor Day, and verges on lowland tobacco country, including Marlboro and Chesterfield counties. In the west, it includes Fort Mill and Rock Hill in York County, just south of Charlotte, the site of rapid development after a 1993 land settlement with the Catawba Indians. Politically, this homeland of Andrew Jackson is ancestrally Democratic. But Republicans are now competitive if not dominant here.

The congressman from the 5th District is John Spratt, ranking Democrat on the House Budget Committee, first elected in 1982. He comes from a prominent York County family and has degrees from Davidson, Yale Law and Oxford; he first got involved in politics in Charles Ravenel's unsuccessful 1974 campaign for governor. In 1982 the 5th District incumbent announced his retirement a week before the filing deadline; Spratt put a campaign together fast and won 38% in the primary, 55% in the runoff against a high-spending candidate, and 68% in the general. For 10 years he was re-elected easily; then in 1994 and 1996 he had tough races, winning by 52%–48% and 54%–45%, carrying the rural counties and running even in York County. It is a measure of the strength of the Republican tide of the mid-1990s that a Democrat with so many political assets could be so hard pressed. But in 1998 and 2000 Spratt won by larger margins, 58%–40% and 59%–39%; in the latter year he ran 17% ahead of Al Gore.

Spratt is the second ranking Democrat on the Armed Services Committee. In the 1980s, he worked with then-Chairman Les Aspin and, in his thick Carolina accent and with impressive knowledge of details, stitched together compromises on the MX missile, binary nerve gas weapons, the Strategic Defense Initiative, and the Savannah River Site and other nuclear plants—keeping military projects flowing through the House, many of whose members were constantly looking to cut military spending. In the early 1990s he worked on the details of defense budgets, concentrating on maintaining troop levels and equipment in good condition. Starting in the mid-1990s Spratt has been the Democrats' lead man on missile defense. He has conceded for some time that the ABM Treaty will have to be abandoned some day, but has been cautious about rapid development and deployment of missile defense. His amendment on the subject prevailed in February 1995 by 218–212, the first significant defeat of a Contract with America promise in the Republican House. In August 1998, a month after the Rumsfeld Commission report on missile defense, he joined Curt Weldon and other Republicans in support of a one-sentence bill declaring "the policy of the United States is to deploy a national missile defense." This passed the House, but Senate Democrats (except for South Carolina's Ernest Hollings and three others) filibustered against any missile defense measure in September 1998. In late May 1999 the House passed a bill that would make the construction of a national missile defense a top priority. In May 2000 Spratt argued that near-term deployment of missile defense would be a mistake, but said that missile defense tests were promising; he said that much work needed to be done diplomatically with Russia and our European allies before withdrawing from the ABM Treaty, although he prefers modification of the agreement over withdrawal.

In 1991 Spratt got a seat on the Budget Committee. His moderate voting record made him a natural point of contact between the parties, but Democrats did not see him as their leader: In their November 1992 caucus he was beaten for Budget chairman by the more liberal Martin Sabo by 149–112. He rotated off the committee in 1992, then ran for the ranking Democrat position on Budget again in December 1996, proclaiming his "determination" to balance the budget. Democrats, now in the minority, were more ready for his leadership; he was nominated by Appropriations ranking Democrat David Obey and beat the more liberal Louise Slaughter by 106–83, though he actually had fewer votes than four years before. He played a major role in putting together the May 1997 agreement to reach a balanced budget, holding together Democrats who disliked the concessions to high-income taxpayers and staying in touch with Republicans who wanted more spending cuts. In the process, he got support from Bill Archer and Al Gore against a proposed Medicaid funding cut which would have hurt South Carolina, and came up with an alternative Republican Governor David Beasley praised. Spratt continued to work with the White House, House Republicans and House Democrats in establishing the specific details of the balanced budget package, which finally were agreed on in August 1997. "My party was no longer calling the shots, but I was in the middle of the biggest game going on," he said.

The bipartisanship of that period has not continued, and Spratt offered Democratic alternatives which were beaten on party lines. His March 2000 budget resolution would have provided for more non-defense spending and less defense spending (though an increase) than Chairman John Kasich's. In early 2001 he urged George W. Bush to approach the budget as Bill Clinton did in 1997, with negotiations between leaders of both parties. But the new Budget chairman, Jim Nussle, instead offered a budget resolution based on Bush's program, with a $1.6 trillion tax cut over 10 years and a 4% increase in non-defense spending. Spratt's alternative offered a smaller tax cut, with one-third of the surplus going to tax cuts, one-third to increased spending and one-third to a "strategic reserve fund." He charged that the Republican budget would force cuts of 9% to 46% in departments other than Defense and Education; those figures compared Bush's spending levels not to previous appropriations but to CBO's inflation-adjusted baseline, which Spratt argues better represents the cost of continuing existing programs. He decried the size of the Republican tax cuts. "One of the reasons we're so skeptical of these frothy, blue-sky projections is we remember all too well 1981 and how long it has taken us to turn this big battleship around and get to surplus. We, doggone it, don't want to see us backslide into the hole we just dug ourselves out of." But the Republican budget resolution prevailed 23–19 in committee and by 221–207 on the floor of the House.

On other issues, Spratt has a moderate record, a bit to the left of the middle of the House. He voted for the line-item veto in 1995, though he thought its particular form was unconstitutional; the Supreme Court agreed. He co-sponsored the Democratic welfare alternative with Georgia's Nathan Deal in March 1995, which came close to passing; but it was overtaken by the welfare reform act Clinton signed in August 1996, for which Spratt voted. He has been co-chair of the Textile Caucus, and pressed in various ways to get the Clinton Administration to enforce rules against illegal textile imports. He criticized the FDA's attempts to regulate tobacco as unjustified by law, and sponsored a bill to prohibit FDA regulation. He sponsored the V-chip legislation adopted in 1996. He has worked to keep Shaw Air Force Base near Sumter off the base-closing list, and he settled the 15-year controversy over Catawba Indian land claims just before a 1992 deadline which would have triggered a lawsuit against 62,000 landowners. With Edward Markey he opposed building a civilian nuclear plant for tritium production; South Carolina wants the work at the Savannah River Site, and Spratt argued that a civilian plant would undermine U.S. anti-nuclear proliferation efforts. He proposed a $4 million exemption from estate taxes for family farms and family-owned business. He sponsored a bill to spend $14 million preserving and restoring buildings at seven historically women's colleges, including Winthrop University in Rock Hill.

The Republican surge in 1994 gave Spratt plenty of competition, but after his solid margins in 1998 and 2000 his seat seems safe again. The one problem he faces is redistricting. In early

2001 there was talk that the Republican legislature might split heavily Republican Greenville and Spartanburg Counties, long joined together in the 4th District. That would be done presumably by joining Spartanburg with York County, Spratt's home base, but an increasingly Republican area which he was delighted to carry by a narrow margin in 2000, and several smaller counties nearby. Such a district would be about 4% more Republican than the current 5th, and the inclusion of Spartanburg might draw a strong Republican challenger in a 2002 race. But for all those reasons, such a plan is likely to be vetoed by Democratic Governor Jim Hodges. The current 5th District's population is close to the state average, and it would be easy to maintain the current lines with just a little tweaking; that seems likely to happen, in which case Spratt will be well positioned to win again and, if Democrats win a majority, become chairman of the Budget Committee.

Cook's Call   *Probably Safe.* This is one of those Republican-trending districts that Democrats will have an excruciatingly difficult time holding on to once the popular Democratic incumbent retires. Until then, Spratt will be very tough to beat.

THE PEOPLE: Pop. 2000: 655,525; Pop. 1990: 581,174, up 12.8% 1990–2000. 66.5% White, 30.6% Black, 0.5% Asian, 0.6% Amer. Indian, 0.8% Two+ races, 0.8% Other; 1.8% Hispanic Origin.

2000 Presidential Vote		
Bush (R)	120,783	(56%)
Gore (D)	90,125	(42%)
Nader (Green)	2,334	(1%)
Others	1,643	(1%)

1996 Presidential Vote		
Dole (R)	83,273	(47%)
Clinton (D)	82,203	(46%)
Perot (I)	11,827	(7%)

Rep. John M. Spratt, Jr. (D)

Elected 1982, 10th term; b. Nov. 1, 1942, Charlotte, NC; home, York; Davidson Col., A.B. 1964, Oxford U., M.A. 1966, Yale U., LL.B. 1969; Presbyterian; married (Jane Stacy).

Military Career: Army Operations, U.S. Dept. of Defense, 1969–71.

Professional Career: Practicing atty., 1971–82; Pres., Bank of Ft. Mill, 1973–82; Pres., Spratt Insurance Agcy., 1973–82.

DC Office: 1536 LHOB 20515, 202-225-5501; Fax: 202-225-0464; Web site: www.house.gov/spratt.

District Offices: Darlington, 843-393-3998; Rock Hill, 803-327-1114; Sumter, 803-773-3362.

Committees: *Armed Services* (2d of 28 D): Military Procurement; Military Research & Development. *Budget* (RMM of 20 D).

Group Ratings

	ADA	ACLU	AFS	LCV	CON	ITIC	NTU	COC	ACU	NTLC	CHC
2000	70	36	71	71	69	53	26	52	20	16	40
1999	80	—	100	63	66	—	16	26	12	—	—

National Journal Ratings

	1999 LIB —	1999 CONS		2000 LIB —	2000 CONS
Economic	63%	37%		58%	42%
Social	61%	39%		58%	41%
Foreign	70%	30%		63%	36%

Key Votes of the 106th Congress

1. Patient Bill of Rights	Y	5. Bar RU-486 $ for FDA	N	9. NATO War in Serbia	Y
2. Accelerate Min. Wage	Y	6. Display 10 Commandments	N	10. Perm. Trade with China	N
3. Strike Ban on Ergo. Stnd.	Y	7. Gun Show Bkgrnd. Checks	Y	11. Debt Relief for 3rd World	Y
4. Ovrd. Estate Tax Veto	N	8. Ban Part.-Birth Abortion	Y	12. Drop Cuba Econ. Embargo	N

Election Results

2000 general	John M. Spratt Jr. (D)	126,877	(59%)	($1,070,965)
	Carl L. Gullick (R)	85,247	(39%)	($342,397)
	Others	3,714	(2%)	
2000 primary	John M. Spratt Jr. (D)	unopposed		
1998 general	John M. Spratt Jr. (D)	95,696	(58%)	($869,632)
	Mike Burkhold (R)	66,367	(40%)	($494,042)
	Others	2,868	(2%)	

SIXTH DISTRICT

South Carolina was first settled by planters from Barbados, bringing with them a tropical plantation economy, which they transferred to the not quite tropical climate of the Carolina coastal lowlands. Here the flat Low Country and many islands are laced with sluggish-flowing rivers and swamps, and here the planters brought thousands of slaves directly from Africa. Colonial South Carolina was one of the richest parts of North America, with dazzling Georgian architecture in Charleston and classic plantation gardens; the planters built great irrigation systems and grew rice and cotton and the dye-plant indigo, all heavily in demand in Britain and elsewhere. And of course all this wealth was built on the slave labor of thousands of African-Americans, many of them still speaking their ancestral languages, or a patois mixing them with English. A majority of colonial South Carolinians were black slaves; so were most residents of the lowlands when the Civil War started with the bombardment of Fort Sumter in Charleston Harbor, although by that time there were also many free blacks in Charleston, some of whom owned slaves themselves.

South Carolina's black heritage has left an imprint on American culture, and is still apparent in the lowlands today. The special accents and dialects of lowland blacks were long retained: Traces of Gullah and other accents still can be found on lowland islands and in the Charleston accent, which to outsiders seems often incomprehensible (how many C-SPAN watchers click on closed-caption text when Senator Ernest Hollings speaks?). The poverty that was the almost universal lot of lowland blacks after the Civil War has only in the last generation been alleviated, as development came to the coast and the long cultural isolation of its people dissipated. But many blacks who grew up here have long since left, leaving after high school graduation on the bus for New York, nicknamed "the chicken-bone special" because of the fried chicken their families packed for the journey.

The 6th Congressional District, created in 1992 to have a black majority and modified slightly in 1994, includes very little of the coast, now mostly lined with affluent condominium communities; but it does include most of the geographic expanse of Low Country South Carolina. Its erose boundaries are designed to include the black central city neighborhoods of Charleston and Columbia but leave in the adjacent 1st and 2d districts their affluent white city and suburban areas. The 6th District includes much of Orangeburg, home of the historically black South Carolina State University, and Florence, at the center of the Pee Dee tobacco-growing country in eastern South Carolina.

The congressman from the 6th is James Clyburn, a Democrat elected in 1992. Clyburn grew up in Sumter, the son of a minister. In 1960 he was one of seven young people who organized the state's first sit-ins, at a five-and-dime store in the Orangeburg town square; in February 2001, Governor Jim Hodges apologized for the massacre that took place there in 1968, when highway patrolmen killed three protestors and wounded 27 others. Clyburn worked as a teacher, in government antipoverty programs, and on the staff of Governor John West. In 1974 he became state Human Affairs commissioner, serving 18 years under Republican and Democratic governors; when criticized for working for Republican Carroll Campbell, Clyburn got him to back the state's first fair housing act. Twice he ran for secretary of State, losing narrowly. In 1992 Clyburn effectively won the 6th District seat in the Democratic primary, with 56% of the vote against four black opponents, all with serious claims for the nomination; the white Democratic incumbent in the old 6th District, Robin Tallon, at the last minute decided not to run. Clyburn, well known statewide, ran first or second in each major center and piled up 88% in his home county of Sumter.

Clyburn, the first black to represent South Carolina in Congress since 1897, has a moderate-to-liberal voting record. He has good working relationships with leading businessmen and Republicans and—like many South Carolinians before him—has focused on local priorities first. He supported the balanced budget amendment and term limits, and joined the moderate New Democrat Coalition at its inception in 1997, the only black to do so. On the Transportation Committee, he worked on local projects like airport funding and the South Carolina Heritage Corridor, pushed for funds to restore buildings at historically black colleges and universities, and won a $175 million annual increase in the state's share. He won a fight with Strom Thurmond to get the courthouse in Columbia named after Matthew Perry, South Carolina's first black federal judge, appointed by Thurmond. Against campaign finance critics in his own party, he has defended PACs as the voice of the little guy. When cigarette tax increases have been proposed, he has urged safeguards for tobacco farmers.

In 1999, he got a seat on the Appropriations Committee, where he continued his focus on local projects, including $30 million for the Cooper River bridge replacement in Charleston. When Mike Forbes switched parties to the Democrats, Clyburn agreed to take a temporary leave of absence so that Forbes could keep an Appropriations seat; Forbes lost his Democratic primary in 2000, and Clyburn returned to Appropriations in 2001. Also in 1999, he became chairman of the Congressional Black Caucus, where he showed another side to his reputation for being conciliatory and non-confrontational. He shared credit when Bill Clinton made a recess appointment in December 2000 of Roger Gregory, the first black on the 4th U.S. Circuit Court of Appeals. He urged the Democratic National Committee to become more responsive to blacks, and sought to create a Policy and Leadership Institute for the Caucus to develop new liberal positions and protect black lawmakers in redistricting. But he ran into opposition when he supported the King family's efforts to have the Library of Congress purchase Dr. Martin Luther King's papers for perhaps $20 million. After the 2000 presidential election, he was among those who complained of an "election stolen from us" by intimidation of voters in Florida.

Back home, he helped to energize voters in the 1998 campaign that resulted in the election of Governor Jim Hodges and the re-election of the seemingly endangered Hollings. Clyburn has been re-elected easily to the House, but said he would not run for the Senate seat in 2002. Redistricting requires the 6th to add 68,000 people, which could easily be done by adding black areas in Columbia and rural counties from the 2nd district, which must shed 62,000 people. Republicans control the legislature, but it is highly unlikely that they will try to eliminate South Carolina's one black-majority district, for it removes heavily Democratic precincts from the adjoining districts.

Cook's Call   *Safe.* The 6th was the slowest-growing district in South Carolina during the 1990s and will need to pick up about 70,000 new residents in redistricting. Still, this seat will be very safe for Clyburn in 2002.

THE PEOPLE: Pop. 2000: 600,226; Pop. 1990: 581,452, up 3.2% 1990–2000. 37.2% White, 60.9% Black, 0.4% Asian, 0.2% Amer. Indian, 0.7% Two+ races, 0.5% Other; 1.4% Hispanic Origin.

2000 Presidential Vote

Gore (D)	112,771	(63%)
Bush (R)	65,235	(36%)
Nader (Green)	1,426	(1%)
Others	920	(1%)

1996 Presidential Vote

Clinton (D)	113,096	(65%)
Dole (R)	53,614	(31%)
Perot (I)	5,525	(3%)

Rep. James E. Clyburn (D)

Elected 1992, 5th term; b. July 21, 1940, Sumter; home, Columbia; SC St. U., B.A. 1962; African Methodist Episcopal; married (Emily).

Professional Career: Teacher, 1962–66; Dir., Charleston Neighborhood Youth Corps, 1966–68; Exec. Dir., SC Comm. for Farm Workers, 1968–71; Asst., SC Gov. West, 1971–74; SC Human Affairs Comm., 1974–92.

DC Office: 319 CHOB 20515, 202-225-3315; Fax: 202-225-2313; Web site: www.house.gov/clyburn.

District Offices: Columbia, 803-799-1100; Florence, 843-622-1212; N. Charleston, 843-965-5578.

Committees: *Appropriations* (21st of 29 D): Energy & Water Development; Transportation.

Group Ratings

	ADA	ACLU	AFS	LCV	CON	ITIC	NTU	COC	ACU	NTLC	CHC
2000	85	79	100	86	21	56	25	57	8	16	0
1999	85	—	100	94	56	—	14	13	0	—	—

National Journal Ratings

	1999 LIB	—	1999 CONS		2000 LIB	—	2000 CONS
Economic	88%	—	0%		60%	—	40%
Social	79%	—	20%		79%	—	17%
Foreign	95%	—	0%		76%	—	23%

Key Votes of the 106th Congress

1. Patient Bill of Rights	*	5. Bar RU-486 $ for FDA	N	9. NATO War in Serbia	Y
2. Accelerate Min. Wage	Y	6. Display 10 Commandments	N	10. Perm. Trade with China	N
3. Strike Ban on Ergo. Stnd.	Y	7. Gun Show Bkgrnd. Checks	Y	11. Debt Relief for 3rd World	Y
4. Ovrd. Estate Tax Veto	N	8. Ban Part.-Birth Abortion	N	12. Drop Cuba Econ. Embargo	Y

Election Results

2000 general	James E. Clyburn (D)	138,053	(72%)	($449,439)
	Vince Ellison (R)	50,005	(26%)	($39,945)
	Others	4,322	(2%)	
2000 primary	James E. Clyburn (D)	unopposed		
1998 general	James E. Clyburn (D)	116,446	(73%)	($294,243)
	Gary McLeod (R)	41,385	(26%)	($25,108)
	Others	2,646	(2%)	

★ SOUTH DAKOTA ★

When the Census Bureau proclaimed the closing of the American frontier in 1890, one of the last places to close was the southern part of the Dakota Territory, just admitted to the Union in 1889 as the state of South Dakota. For years this land had been the home of the Oglala Sioux, one of the largest Native American tribes, who had built a buffalo hunting civilization by becoming masters of the horses the Spaniards had imported to North America 350 years earlier. It was the Sioux warrior chief Sitting Bull, now buried on a bluff above the Missouri River, who destroyed Custer at Little Big Horn in 1876; it was Oglala Sioux who were the victims at the massacre of Wounded Knee in 1890. After half a century of horrifying disease and a decade of defeat, the Sioux were a traumatized people, and still are today, living on reservations with proud traditions but in terrible poverty. They are isolated far from the mainstream economic marketplace, beset by high rates of alcoholism and suicide, with life expectancy and disease rates like those of sub-Saharan Africa. But perhaps there is a turnaround. Indian populations are now on the rise, up to 8% of the South Dakota total, and four of the top 10 counties with the greatest percentage of children under 5 are in South Dakota and home to the Sioux. Indians are in the process of getting a great monument, the late Korczak Ziolkowski's Crazy Horse sculpture, which—when and if finished—will dwarf Mount Rushmore (which was left unfinished itself at the start of World War II); by 2000 the chief's full mouth and cleft chin have begun to emerge.

Less tragic and more successful, though not without its moments of violence, has been the whites' settlement of South Dakota. It was a rapid process: the first gold strikes in the Black Hills came in 1876, and soon the mountains swarmed with settlers; Deadwood became a city of 20,000 where Calamity Jane ruled the saloons and Wild Bill Hickok was shot in the back while holding two pair—aces and eights. Ranchers, knowing that the buffalo could not be contained by barbed wire fences, massacred them so thoroughly that when Teddy Roosevelt got to the Dakota Territory in 1884, he had a hard time finding one to shoot. It was not long before the railroad came through, and then settlers, many of them German and Scandinavian immigrants recruited by the railroads, had built sodhouses, broken the land and set down enough roots to justify making both the two Dakota states.

Geographically, South Dakota has never entirely filled up. In the 25 years between statehood and World War I, the eastern third of the state, sectioned off Midwestern style into 640 acre square miles, was settled by farmers. But moving westward, before a traveler reaches the Missouri River in the middle of the state, green turns to brown, cultivation grows sparse and then stops; the plains are open grazing land, scarcely touched by the white men who were so eager to establish dominion over them a century ago. The land is punctuated, not by roads meeting every mile at precise angles, but by buttes, gullies and grasslands sweeping to the horizon with no sign of human habitation except the occasional missile silos which once pointed toward the Soviet Union, and which by 1994 were all empty.

South Dakota's political patterns were fairly well set by the early 1900s. Its early settlers were mostly Midwesterners who brought their Republicanism with them. Voters here never had much use for the Non-Partisan League, which caught on in the more Scandinavian soil of North Dakota, and there was never anything here comparable to the Farmer-Labor Party of Minnesota. But the nature of the farm economy—its dependence on the great railroads and milling companies, and on the vagaries of international markets—meant that South Dakota was subject to periodic farm revolts. It voted for Populists and William Jennings Bryan in the 1890s; it supported the early New Deal; it revolted against the Eisenhower Administration in the 1950s by electing a young congressman named George McGovern, then a professor at Dakota Wesleyan University in Mitchell, home also of the Corn Palace, built in 1892 and decorated every year with 13 murals using 275,000 ears of corn. South Dakota also shared the isolationist impulse of much of the Great Plains, and McGovern's opposition to the Vietnam war in the late 1960s was not a liability here. In the early 1970s, Democrats seemed on the verge of becoming the majority party.

Instead, South Dakota moved sharply to the Republicans. This began with the angry response to Wounded Knee in 1975. And it was perpetuated by the policies of Republican Governor William

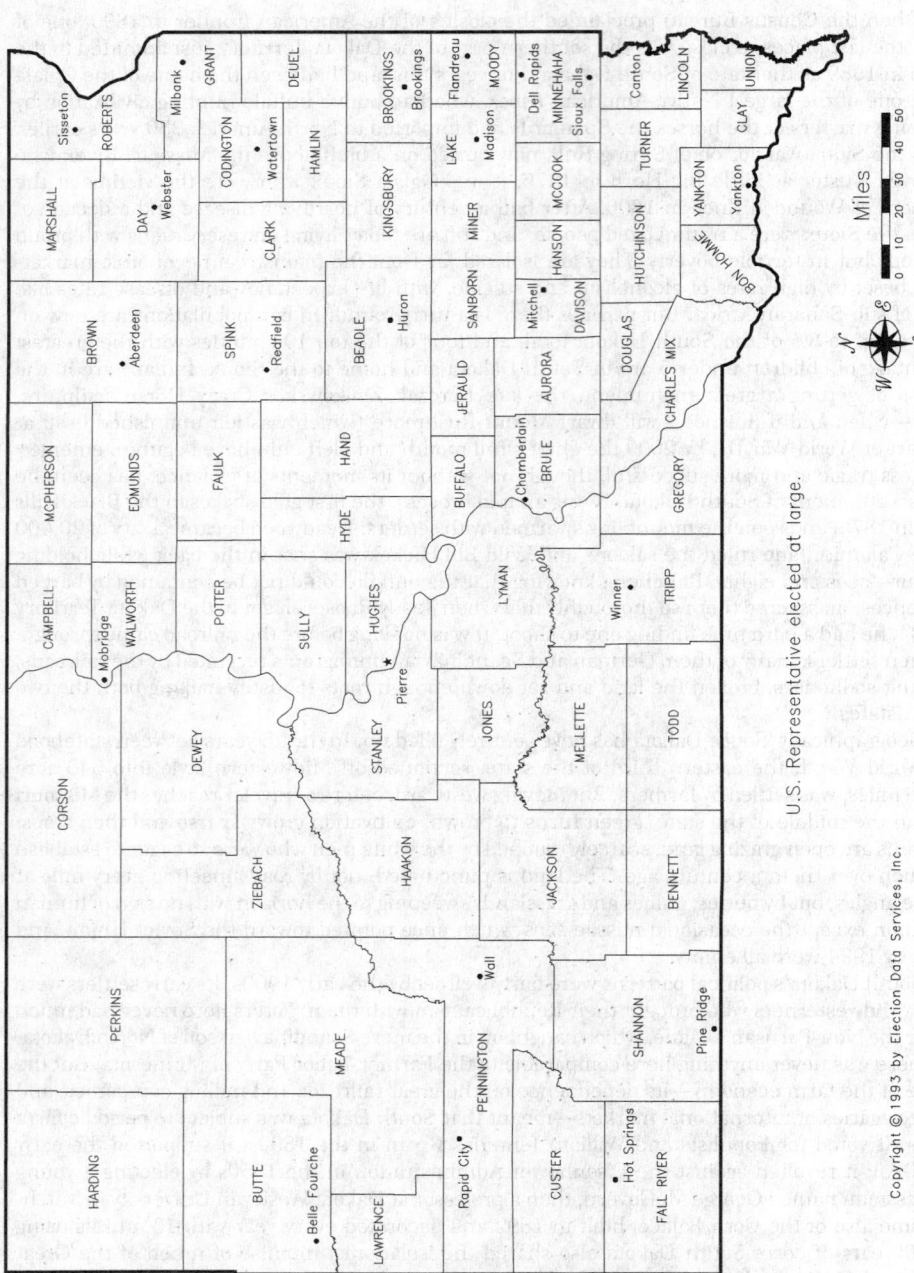

U.S. Representative elected at large.

Miles

0 10 20 30 40 50

Janklow, elected in 1978 and 1982 and then again in 1994 and 1998. It was Janklow who got the legislature to repeal the usury law in 1981 and invited Citicorp to move its credit card operations to Sioux Falls, where they could charge market interest rates and which had no state corporate or personal income taxes, and a literate low-wage work force. The Citibank operation here grew from 50 employees to 3,750 in 2001, replacing the meatpacker John Morrell as the biggest employer; other banks and telemarketing followed; some 9,000 people in the Sioux Falls area work in financial services. And new firms started up, like NordicTrak and Gateway Computer (their executive offices have moved to San Diego but most employees are still in North Sioux City). South Dakotans have proved to be an ideal work force; as Gateway's Ted Waitt says, "A lot of it has to do with the people. It basically gets back to Midwest values . . . honesty, integrity and loyalty." Some meatpacking plants have closed, but others are manned now by a largely Hispanic work force, recruited from the Southwest and beyond; 40 languages are spoken on the floor of the John Morrell plant in Sioux City. South Dakota has also worked hard to court tourists. The lure of natural attractions in the Black Hills and the huge and varyingly unfinished sculptures of Mount Rushmore and the Crazy Horse Memorial are augmented by such enterprises as gold-panning creeks and gambling casinos in Deadwood and on Indian reservations. And Wall Drug, the 46,000-square foot emporium between the Badlands and Rapid City, snares three-quarters of the freeway traffic.

As a result, South Dakota's population centers have grown, in some cases lustily, while its farm counties continue to empty out. Metro Sioux Falls grew 13% in the 1980s and 24% in the 1990s—amazing growth in a state which had often lost population between censuses—and Lincoln County, just south of Sioux Falls, was one of the nation's fastest growing counties in the 1990s. In recent years South Dakota has also had the nation's lowest unemployment rate, down to 1.4% in Sioux Falls in 1999; Rapid City, with a similar economic boost plus tourism, also grew; Watertown and Brookings, mid-sized towns on I-29, grew as well, even as most small counties lost population. Half a century ago South Dakota was indubitably a farm state, with most people living off the land; by 2001 there were only 2,500 farms left, and cattle ranching (and cattle rustling) was replacing crop growing. Population patterns on the Plains now look much like those in the Rockies, with most people concentrated around a few cities and towns, while vast acreage remains vacant, punctuated with infrequent ranches and resort areas—a landscape that would not have been totally alien to Sitting Bull. South Dakota is not a farm state any more.

Politically, this economic success has helped to re-establish South Dakota's Republican heritage. True, the state has two Democratic Senators—Tim Johnson, elected by a narrow margin in 1996, and Senate Majority Leader Tom Daschle, who won his first race for the House in 1978 by just 139 votes. (This is a fine example of a few votes making a big difference: If just 70 votes in one obscure Senate race more than 20 years ago had gone the other way, South Dakota today would probably have two Republican senators.) But the Democrats' hold may be weakened in the long run, because the farm issues which used to be their chief political asset seem less and less important: In 2001 the legislature declined extra funding for ethanol and refused to require state vehicles to use ethanol. Low farm prices did nothing to swing South Dakota voters toward Al Gore in 2000; the Republican Congress has continued sending out large sums to farmers as disaster relief, and no one seems to expect anything more. In the meantime, Republicans here have won almost everything else—the governorship and both houses of the legislature, the state's lone House seat.

Governor Bill Janklow has had more impact on state government and the South Dakota economy than any other South Dakota governor. He grew up in Chicago, then after the death of his father, a prosecutor at the Nuremberg war crimes trial, the family moved to his mother's hometown, Flandreau, South Dakota. Janklow dropped out of high school and joined the Marines; he returned in 1960, married, and without a high school diploma talked his way into the University of South Dakota. After law school he worked in the legal aid program at the Rosebud Indian Reservation. He was elected state attorney general in 1974, with 67% of the vote, getting tough on Indian violence and compiling a high conviction record. In 1978 he was elected governor with 56%; in 1982 re-elected with 71%. During this time, he attracted Citicorp to the state, reduced agricultural and residential property taxes, cut state payrolls, stimulated new business, and converted a state college into a prison. Term-limited in 1986, Janklow ran against incumbent Republican Senator Jim Abdnor and lost 55%–45% in the primary; it is a tantalizing question whether Janklow would have beaten Tom Daschle in the fall.

Janklow's successor, Republican George Mickelson, took a different course, with a revolving economic development fund financed by a temporary one-cent sales tax increase. He died in a plane crash in April 1993, and was succeeded by 67-year-old Walter Dale Miller, a rancher from near Rapid City who served 20 years in the legislature and six as lieutenant governor. Janklow challenged him in the 1994 Republican primary and won by a 54%–46% margin, carrying most of eastern South Dakota and losing much of the west. In the general election he won easily, 55%–41%, over Jim Beddow, the former president of George McGovern's alma mater, Dakota Wesleyan University.

Janklow ran promising to cut homeowners' property taxes by 30%; by the 1998 election they were down 25%, and he won approval of the last 5% in 2000. He cut the state payroll, and even cut total spending in 1996; he worked to establish state standards for student learning and give school districts the leeway to achieve them. He welcomed more new businesses including the headquarters of IBP meatpackers to South Dakota, and reduced EPA hazardous waste reporting forms from 155 pages to four. He has reduced foster care by encouraging adoption and has worked to increase child immunizations. He changed the name "correctional facility" to "prison" and "client" to "inmate." And he set up a program to use inmates for public labor, building small houses for the elderly and disabled, and day care centers, as well as wiring schools, public libraries, colleges and hospitals to the Internet; all the schools have been connected, and the $20,000 senior bungalows built by prisoners have opened up housing for young newcomers.

In March 1998 Janklow was in the hospital for 22 days for intestinal surgery. When he returned he announced he was running for an unprecedented fourth term. He continued to make unusual headlines. After the town of Spencer was destroyed by a May 1998 tornado he camped out there and superintended evacuation and recovery plans; the Oglala Sioux tribe, long critical, gave him an award for his work. In September 1998, in protest of what he considered unfair Canadian trade practices, he ordered state troopers to stop and inspect trucks carrying Canadian livestock and grain; they were to be searched and not allowed in the state if the livestock was not proved free of drugs legal in Canada but not in the U.S., and if the grain was not certified as free of disease and wild oats. The searches continued for three weeks, until Agriculture Secretary Dan Glickman promised to raise the issues with Canadian officials.

Janklow paid little attention to his 1998 Democratic opponent, state Senate Minority Leader Bernie Hunhoff. Janklow paid even less attention to Republican Senate candidate Ron Schmidt; instead Janklow continued to lavish praise on Senator Tom Daschle for using his position as minority leader on South Dakota issues. Their friendship went back to 1994, when Daschle was accused of exerting undue influence with the FAA; Janklow wrote a letter to *The New York Times* affirming his integrity, and Daschle responded with a handwritten letter. Said Janklow, "He and I philosophically are different. I jokingly say we go to different churches together. When I ask him to help us with something for South Dakota, he always says yes. He has never let us down." One example was shifting control of boat ramps and the Missouri River shoreline from the Army Corps of Engineers to the state government, which Daschle put in the October 1998 omnibus budget; for this both were later criticized by the Sioux nation, which claims ownership. Janklow was re-elected 64%–33%, and Daschle was re-elected 62%–36%. According to the VNS exit poll, 62% of Daschle voters voted for Janklow, and 60% of Janklow voters voted for Daschle.

Janklow promised that his fourth term would be devoted to education; he called for public preschool, more reading and music programs, classes in parenting skills. Noting South Dakota's high percentage of working mothers, he hired a former Democratic legislator to work on day care. He criticized the Forest Service for not removing timber downed in an April 2000 blizzard, and after an August 2000 fire, set in the Black Hills by an arsonist, renewed his criticisms and got the Forest Service to agree to let South Dakota prisoners clear the area. As voters considered outlawing video lotteries, which have been legal since 1989 and bring $95 million to the state, he said the video games were a "lousy" way to raise money but warned that outlawing them would require the biggest tax increase in state history; voters came out for the games 54%–46%. In 2001 the legislature approved a Janklow proposal to reward high school students with high grades and tough class loads.

Janklow is, once again, term limited. Despite past demurrals, he said in early 2001 that he would not rule out a bid for the Senate or the House, but made it clear he would not accept an appointment from George W. Bush.

Cook's Call   *Probably Safe.* Although he is under pressure to challenge Democratic Senator Tim Johnson in 2002, it appears that Republican Congressman John Thune has decided to run for the open gubernatorial seat instead, probably clearing the Republican field in the process. Democrats do not have much of a bench here and Bush's 22-point win can't be encouraging. The Democrats mentioned as of spring 2001 were state Senator Ron Volesky and University of South Dakota President Jim Abbott.

Senior Senator   Tom Daschle, first elected to the Senate in 1986, is the Senate majority leader. He grew up in Aberdeen, where his father was a bookkeeper at an auto parts store, and graduated from South Dakota State; he served in the Air Force in the years George McGovern was running for president. In 1973 he became a Washington staffer for Senator James Abourezk. In 1978, as Abourezk was about to retire, Daschle returned to South Dakota, ran for the eastern House district that Larry Pressler was vacating to run for the Senate, and won by exactly 139 votes over former P.O.W. Leo Thorsness, who had come close to beating McGovern for the Senate in 1974. Daschle was a generally faithful follower of the Democratic leadership in the House, trapped far behind others in seniority; his political highlight came in 1982, when South Dakota lost one of its two House seats and he ran against incumbent Republican Cliff Roberts and won 52%–48%.

Already representing the entire state, it was natural for Daschle to run in 1986 for the Senate seat held by Republican Jim Abdnor. Daschle had the additional good luck that Governor Bill Janklow was opposing Abdnor in the primary, putting Abdnor on the defensive and forcing him to use much of his money. Daschle again won 52%–48%, in one of the key victories that returned control of the Senate to the Democrats for eight years. Two years later, in January 1989, new Senate Majority Leader George Mitchell named Daschle co-chairman of the Senate Democratic Policy Committee—in effect, though not in title, the number two man in the Senate leadership. When Mitchell announced his retirement in March 1994, Daschle immediately started running for majority leader—too soon to suit some traditionalists. His opponent Jim Sasser seemed to have enough votes to win, but Sasser lost to Republican Bill Frist in Tennessee in November. That was the good news for Daschle; the bad news was that Democrats had lost enough seats that the race was for minority rather than majority leader. Connecticut's Christopher Dodd immediately entered the race, with encouragement from some older committee chairmen; but Daschle relinquished his seat on the Finance Committee to Carol Moseley-Braun of Illinois, whose vote gave him a 24–23 victory—one that brings to mind his first election to the House.

Daschle's capacity for dogged hard work, his seemingly mild manner and ability to stay unruffled, his efforts at building consensus and fellow feeling have made the Democratic Caucus more united than in many years—maybe ever—and more effective legislatively than almost anyone expected. Senator Robert Byrd, nominating him for reelection in 1996, recalled that he had opposed Daschle in 1994 because he thought him not tough enough to deal with Bob Dole: "I am here today to tell you that I was totally wrong about this young man. He has steel in his spine, despite his reasonable and modest demeanor." His first big test was on the balanced budget amendment. Daschle segued smoothly from his former support of the amendment to opposition, with the argument that any such amendment should exclude Social Security. That provided cover for him and five other Democrats who had previously supported balanced budget amendments to switch and defeat the amendment by one vote in March 1995. To this achievement he added other successes in 1996: passage of the minimum wage increase and the bipartisan health care portability bill. Congress also passed a law declaring children born with spina bifida to Vietnam veterans exposed to Agent Orange to be entitled to VA benefits—the first entitlement ever for children of veterans, and a follow-up to Daschle's long advocacy of compensation for Agent Orange victims.

For years Daschle was a "prairie populist," resisting cuts in farm subsidies, which were nonetheless cut in the farm bills of 1985 and 1990—big losses, compared to his gains in getting reformulated gas included in the 1990 Clean Air Act and subsidizing ethanol. But in 1996 he was not able to stop the Republicans and Democrats, including ranking Agriculture Committee Democrat Patrick Leahy, from supporting the Freedom to Farm Act, which promised to phase out farm subsidies for most crops over seven years. In 1998, as farm prices sagged, he helped put together a $6 billion package of emergency aid—the first of three disaster relief packages which delivered more money to farmers of favored crops than the old subsidy system.

Through all this, Daschle's soft-spoken style, about which many Democrats had qualms, proved effective on television. He maintained his generally liberal voting record; a strong backer of the Clinton health care plan in 1994, he pushed health coverage for uninsured children. Once rather skeptical of American foreign involvements, and an opponent of the Gulf war resolution, he steadily supported the Clinton administration on Bosnia and Kosovo and on permanent normal trade relations for China. After Republicans gained two seats in the 1996 election, Daschle advanced his own priorities. One was changes in campaign finance regulation: he backs a constitutional amendment to limit spending by candidates, parties and independent groups. He backed the May 1997 budget deal, and hailed the inclusion of children's health insurance and college tax credits. He came up with an alternative to the partial-birth abortion ban, which he had voted against and whose backers were running ads in South Dakota. But Daschle's version, which would have limited late-term abortions but allowed the exception for health, was beaten 64–36; Daschle switched and voted for the ban, which passed 64–36 but fell short of a veto-proof two-thirds.

Every August Daschle travels to all 66 of South Dakota's counties; he sometimes just drives by himself, dressed casually, and over coffee or at gas stations asks voters about their concerns. That—and a whole lot of money—have paid off at the polls. In 1992 he was re-elected 65%–33% over Republican Charlene Haar; he ignored Republican calls for turning down out-of-state money since the large majority of funds for Democrats here come from outside South Dakota. In 1998 Daschle ignored his Republican opponent and outspent him by more than $4.8 million to $492,000. Daschle argued that his leadership position had helped the state. "I think it clearly has made a difference in the last four years. . . . I've always said that my major responsibility in the Senate is to put South Dakota's agenda on the national agenda." Republican Governor Bill Janklow frequently chimed in to agree: "Senator Daschle is in the position he is in and the cooperative spirit that he has, has been terribly beneficial in terms of Bill Janklow and his administration's ability to work with him." Daschle won 62%–36%, while Janklow was winning 64%–33%. According to the VNS exit poll, 60% of Janklow voters voted for Daschle, and 62% of Daschle voters voted for Janklow.

On impeachment, Daschle steadily defended Bill Clinton and advanced partisan positions in a pleasant but steely manner. But as Clinton's lawyers kept trying to insist that he had not lied under oath in August 1998 about lying under oath in January 1998, Daschle called on Clinton to stop "hairsplitting" in September. During the impeachment trial, as on other issues, he stayed in close and constant touch with Majority Leader Trent Lott, which led to the 100-senator caucus in the Old Senate Chamber and a much more harmonious proceeding than had been expected.

Daschle's success in holding Senate Democrats together is accomplished not by intimidation—there is not much he can threaten them with—but dialogue. He understands that colleagues will sometimes disagree with the party position, but he asks them not to go off the reservation without talking to him first—and then often gets them to agree to delay going public. As a result, Democrats who might be publicly committed to opposing the party often end up supporting it instead: inertia works for party unity. Daschle has used the Senate rules allowing nongermane amendments to advantage, advancing to the floor Democratic proposals which test well in the polls even while using procedure to obstruct popular Republican measures to move forward. He has used such tactics on the minimum wage, prescription drugs for seniors, HMO regulation—most of which have not become law, but have advanced his party's standing. He has expressed frustration publicly only when such tactics seem not to be working. He called the rejection of the Comprehensive Test Ban Treaty in October 1999 a "terrible, terrible mistake," and was angry that Republicans would not allow the vote to be delayed; but the demands for a floor vote originally came from North Dakota Democrat Byron Dorgan and Foreign Relations ranking Democrat Joseph Biden, although neither of them (nor Daschle) had counted the votes on the floor. Similarly, in May 2000 Daschle held up Senate business for 10 days in protest against Lott's refusal to allow as many amendments as Daschle thought proper under Senate rules.

The emergence of a 50–50 Senate and the election of George W. Bush—neither of them apparent until December 2000—made Daschle one of the pivotal figures in American politics. He was majority leader for 17 days, from January 3 to January 20, 2001, when the new Senate took office and the tie-breaking vote was still cast by Vice President Al Gore. But Daschle sensibly made no move to capitalize unduly on that temporary majority. Instead, by threatening to tie up Senate business for months, he forced Trent Lott to agree on January 5 to equal membership on all committees for both parties. This agreement, much resented by some Republicans, made sense in terms of political process: committees are supposed to represent opinion on the floor—and Daschle made something of a concession by agreeing that on tied committee votes nominations and bills could be brought to the floor: both parties' ability to obstruct was reduced.

But Daschle, for all the reasonableness of his demeanor, was obviously determined to oppose most of the proposals of George W. Bush any way he could. He complained early and often that Bush's pleas for bipartisan action were not matched by any willingness to negotiate with the Democratic leadership. Instead Bush, remembering how his father had been forced to break his read-my-lips-no-new-taxes in negotiations with Daschle's predecessor, George Mitchell, sought out individual Democrats who agreed with his programs, and went behind the leadership's back. Daschle reacted sharply when Democrat Zell Miller, appointed in July 2000 to replace Republican Paul Coverdell, endorsed Bush's tax cut and backed Attorney General nominee John Ashcroft; Miller had broken Daschle's unwritten rule of not consulting with him first, and giving Daschle an opportunity to persuade him to delay any break with the party. But while Miller was unphased, few Democratic senators followed his example. Even so, Daschle had only limited success in the first months of the Bush administration. He helped to rally 42 Democrats to vote against Ashcroft, but that was not enough to defeat his nomination—although it did suggest Democrats might have the votes to filibuster Bush nominees for judgeships. He attacked the Bush tax cuts early and often, arguing that they would produce budget deficits as he said the 1981 Reagan tax cuts had, and saying that they would give rich people enough money to buy a Lexus but middle-class tax-payers only enough to buy a muffler. He held just enough Democratic votes to force Republicans to accept a lower, $1.2 trillion tax cut in the Senate in April 2001. But in May 2001 John Breaux and his bloc of Democrats and Republicans delivered agreement on a $1.3 trillion tax cut—not a full victory for Bush, but not at all Daschle's preferred outcome.

It was the tax cut, nevertheless, that led to Daschle regaining his post as majority leader. Vermont Republican James Jeffords had helped force Republicans to compromise on the tax cut, and Daschle and Democratic Whip Harry Reid reached out to Jeffords just as his relations with Republican leaders began to deteriorate. In June 2001, when Jeffords officially switched his party affiliation from Republican to become an independent who votes with the Democrats for orga-nizational purposes—much like Vermont's socialist House member Bernie Sanders—Daschle be-came majority leader in a 50–49–1 Senate. The power-sharing agreement was declared null and void, and Daschle was left to negotiate a new organizational agreement with Republicans. "At a time when Americans are evenly divided about their choices of leaders, they are unified in their demand for action," he said "We need to prove to the American people that we can overcome the lines that all too often divide us. We need to prove we can do the work the American people have sent us to do."

For all his national importance, Daschle keeps a sharp eye on South Dakota. He sponsored a bill to increase the Agriculture Department's power to bring antitrust suits and opposed the threatened purchase of IBP by Smithfield Foods and Tyson Foods. He sponsored a bill to eliminate MTBE in reformulated gas but to retain requirements to use ethanol—the Bush administration in June 2001 ruled that California had to use ethanol instead of MTBE, much to Daschle's pleasure. He helped pass a six-state pilot project to allow farmers to enroll plots of five acres and less of wetlands into the Conservation Reserve Program: good for South Dakota pheasant habitat. He favored bankruptcy reform, strongly backed by credit card companies. He worked shrewdly to get a two-year reprieve on the Clinton administration's ban on snowmobiling on federal lands. He supported the Fish and Wildlife Service and Army Corps of Engineer's proposal to allow a spring rise in the water of the Missouri River, to imitate its natural state and help preserve the endangered piping plover, least tern and pallid sturgeon; when Missouri's Christopher Bond, eager to avoid spring floods and to maintain summer river levels for barges, pushed to stop that proposal, Daschle got Bill Clinton to declare that he would veto the entire bill over the issue: this is likely to come up again in the 107th Congress. He has secured $23 million for the Eastern Dakota Expressway from I-29 to Aberdeen and $29 million for the Heartland Expressway Southeast Connector around Rapid City: it has probably not escaped his notice that almost all of South Dakota's recent growth has come in counties served by interstate highways.

Daschle comes up for reelection in 2004. He seems entirely unphased by the prospect of facing South Dakota voters in the same year as George W. Bush, who got 60% of the vote in 2000 and who, if his administration seems successful, may get even more for reelection. Or perhaps, as some think, he is thinking of running for president that year. He is not an implausible candidate, but a campaign would require him to spend much time away from the Capitol and South Dakota's 66 counties—something which, as of early 2001, he seemed disinclined to do.

Junior Senator   Tim Johnson, a Democrat, was elected to the Senate in 1996. He grew up in southeast South Dakota, went to the University of South Dakota and served briefly in the Army (he was discharged because of a hearing problem). He went to graduate school in Michigan, then returned to South Dakota to law school and a law practice. He was elected to the legislature in 1978, at 31, and served in the House and Senate until he ran for South Dakota's single House seat in 1986, when incumbent Tom Daschle ran for the Senate. Like Daschle, Johnson won his House seat by a narrow margin; he edged a fellow state senator in the primary 48%–45%, with big margins in his southeastern home area and in Sioux Falls and Rapid City. He won the general by 59%–41%, and ran even better every two years thereafter.

In the House, Johnson compiled a generally liberal voting record, though he voted for the balanced budget amendment and was the only Democrat to switch his vote to support lifting the Bosnia arms embargo. He worked on South Dakota water and public works projects and tried to maintain farm subsidies. He successfully managed reauthorization of crop insurance as a subcommittee chairman in 1994 and helped relax the "swampbuster" provisions penalizing farmers who violated wetlands regulations in the 1996 Freedom to Farm Act; but he warned that the phasing out of farm supports would hurt in drought years. Johnson opposed any cuts in or taxes on Social Security benefits and favored penalties for drug companies that charge seniors high prices for medications.

Johnson's 1996 race against Republican Senator Larry Pressler had been a long time contemplated. Pressler won election to the House in 1974 and the Senate in 1978 as a constituency-service, ear-to-the-ground Republican, in tune with South Dakota opinion. In the late 1980s, and after 1994 when he became chairman of the Commerce Committee, he became consistently more conservative. This was a high-spending, high-stakes race: Pressler spent $5.1 million, with over $1.7 million from PACs; Johnson spent almost $3 million, with $850,000 from PACs. TV ads began in August 1995, when the race was about even, and it stayed that way for 15 months. Since South Dakota TV is cheap, that meant one barrage of ads after another—plus seven debates. Pressler attacked Johnson as too liberal, going back to a 1981 vote in the legislature against workfare. Johnson attacked Pressler as a Newt-oid Medicare cutter and charged that he switched from opposition to support of maritime subsidies after receiving $29,000 from maritime PACs. Johnson was assisted by collateral attacks from others: the Sioux Falls *Argus Leader* charged that Pressler didn't properly itemize some campaign expenses. But the key role may have been played by national issues. Pressler spent much time in 1995 and 1996 on the telecommunications bill, the most-lobbied and arguably most complex bill before the 104th Congress. In negotiations he held out for deregulation, and to South Dakotans he promised lower telephone and cable TV rates. Pressler succeeded in passing the bill, the first major rewrite of communications law in 63 years, but back home Johnson was charging that phone and cable rates were going up. The final result was a 51%–49% Johnson victory, narrower than the final month's polls suggested. The state split almost precisely along the 100th meridian that is often taken as the dividing line between farm land and grazing land. Johnson carried almost every county east of the 100th, except for a couple of ethnic Republican counties; Pressler carried almost everything west of the 100th, except for a few Indian counties.

In the Senate Johnson got seats on the Agriculture, Banking, Budget and Energy Committees, presumably a gift from his South Dakota colleague, Democratic Leader Tom Daschle. His voting record has been generally liberal, except on some cultural issues—he opposes abortion and supported the partial-birth abortion ban. On farm issues, long the staple of South Dakota Democrats, he has been displeased that low crop prices have not led the Senate to revisit the Freedom to Farm Act. "Five years of declining transition payments and a pat on the back and a 'Good luck' isn't much of a farm policy, but that's what we've got right now," he said in August 1998. He pushed hard for country-of-origin labeling of imported meat; that passed the Senate but was killed in conference; he opposed a measure that would label as "Made in the U.S.A." beef from cattle that had fed in the United States for only 100 days. He also got extension of farmers' Chapter 12 of the Bankruptcy Act into the October 1998 omnibus budget. He worked on rail grain issues and a bill granting $6 billion in emergency relief for farmers; he worked to promote biodiesel and wants to make permanent the tax treatment of ethanol.

Johnson supported the transportation bill, which raised South Dakota's take from $120 million to $180 million. He secured earmarks for completing the first phase of the Heartland Expressway and the Vermillion bridge. He and Republican Craig Thomas worked to increase spending on rural transit by $500 million over five years. He has promoted a bill, similar to one passed in South Dakota, requiring prisoners to pay health care costs if they have the money. He backs Daschle's proposal to amend the First Amendment to allow limits on campaign spending and contributions. Some of his work was prompted by the terrible winter weather and floods of 1997–98 and the Spencer tornado of May 1998: $7.5 million for the National Differential Global Positioning System, $10 million for the James River Water Development District, regulatory relief for banks so they can respond quickly to disasters, expanding weather radio, funding for a tornado pilot preparedness program. He pushed through a rural water system for Fall River County, and preservation of Spirit Mound in Clay County (one of the few sights in South Dakota unchanged since Lewis and Clark saw it). He passed through the Senate a Minuteman Missile National Historic Site (much of South Dakota is laced with missile sites), worked to build Indian schools and housing, sponsored a ban on Internet gambling, and worked to maintain Great Lakes air service to Brookings and Yankton. He co-sponsored a bill prohibiting meatpackers from owning, feeding or keeping livestock. He sought to extend government-guaranteed loans for satellite local-to-local TV service to the smallest 170 media markets. He proposed a Flexible Fallow program, put together by two South Dakota farmers, to allow farmers to set aside 30% of their land for conservation and to provide higher per-bushel rates on marketing loans. He helped pass a six-state pilot project to allow farmers to enroll plots of five acres and less of wetlands into the Conservation Reserve Program: good for South Dakota pheasant habitat. He has sponsored a bill to provide drug discounts to Medicare beneficiaries, determined by the average price in Canada, France, Germany, Italy, Japan and the United Kingdom.

Johnson comes up for reelection in 2002. This is a seat that has naturally been targeted by Republicans: Johnson won it by just 51%–49% in a state that George W. Bush carried 60%–38%. He is one of the few incumbent senators in recent years who has lagged behind in polls: Republican polls showed him trailing Congressman-at-Large John Thune by 48%–41% in March 2001. But Johnson also has considerable assets. In January 2001 he got a seat on Appropriations, in time to aid South Dakota projects. In April 2001 he pressed for a $97 billion agriculture budget increase, well above the $63 billion sought by Republican Charles Grassley. Although Johnson has stuck with Democrats on some votes, opposing the confirmation of John Ashcroft, he also voted for the Republican Social Security lockbox in March 2001 and for the $1.3 trillion tax cut in May 2001. Meanwhile, Republicans have had some difficulty finding a strong candidate. In December 2000 Thune set up an exploratory committee to run for governor; that job, he said, would allow him to spend more time with his wife and daughters, who have continued living in Sioux Falls. But in his March 2001 trip to South Dakota, and in an April dinner at the White House, George W. Bush tried to talk Thune into running for the Senate. This could be one of the country's most seriously contested Senate races, in one of its smallest states.

Cook's Call　*Potentially Competitive*. There is no reason to think that Johnson is particularly vulnerable except that he is a Democrat in South Dakota. Republicans hope that Congressman John Thune will run, but he seems more interested in a gubernatorial bid. Without a particularly strong Republican, Johnson will probably sail to victory.

Representative-At-Large　South Dakota has had only one seat in the House since 1982. The congressman-at-large is John Thune, a Republican elected in 1996. He grew up in Murdo, on the dusty plains west of the Missouri River, where his father was a teacher and the family was Democratic; he went to college and business school at the University of South Dakota. As a high school freshman he met then-Congressman Jim Abdnor, when Abdnor spotted him at a grocery checkout counter and recalled that he had missed one of six free throws in the basketball game the previous night. They kept in touch and Thune got a job on by-then Senator Abdnor's staff in Washington in 1985; he stayed with Abdnor after he lost to Tom Daschle and was appointed to the Small Business Administration. As he recalls, "I was coming of age about the time that Reagan was coming on the national political scene. I just loved the way that despite what people thought or said about him, he stood by his principles and convictions." He returned to South Dakota in 1989, at 28, to become executive director of the state Republican Party. In 1991 he became state railroad director under Governor George Mickelson and in 1993 director of the state Municipal League. In his early 30s he had many contacts in Pierre, the nation's smallest state capital, and around the state.

Thune nevertheless entered the 1996 race for the House as very much an underdog. The favorite in the Republican primary was Lieutenant Governor Carole Hillard, who seemed to have Governor Bill Janklow on her side and was endorsed by the 1994 Republican nominee. A poll released in May 1996 showed her ahead of Thune 69%–15%. But Thune was escorted around main streets by Abdnor, he attracted the support of religious conservatives and presidential campaign leaders, fresh from organizing for the February 27 presidential primary. Hillard lent her campaign $140,000 but didn't raise much money, and Janklow eventually announced he was neutral. It turned out to be no contest. Thune carried 54 counties, Hillard 12; Thune won 59%–41%; it would have been more except that Hillard carried Rapid City. The Democratic nominee was Rick Weiland, a former state director for Senator Daschle, who carried 46 counties and led television executive Jim Abbott 42%–28%, well above the 35% needed in South Dakota to avoid a runoff. After the primary the Sioux Falls *Argus Leader* summarized the race: "November's option is crystal clear: choose a liberal or a conservative." Thune was for term limits, against all tax increases (and against Bob Dole's tax cut pending a balanced budget), and pledged to refuse the congressional pension; he promised to serve only three terms and had the support of Christian conservatives and cattlemen's organizations. Weiland attacked Newt Gingrich and Medicare "cuts" and called for an "impact fee" on big hog producers to build a loan fund for small hog producers. On agriculture, Thune called not for farm subsidies but for increasing exports and promoting value-added goods: "market solutions that can help keep prices high." Weiland carried only six counties (his home, a university county, and four Indian counties), and Thune won 58%–37%.

In the House, Thune has a very conservative voting record and serves on the Agriculture and Transportation committees; he was chosen the freshman class representative to the Republican leadership. In May 1997 he criticized the House leadership for attaching other issues to the bill for relief of floods that had devastated much of North Dakota and Minnesota and damaged much of South Dakota that spring. When Dakota Democrats criticized Speaker Newt Gingrich and Appropriations Chairman Bob Livingston for refusing cash payments to local communities, Gingrich asked Thune to come up with a way to do so; ultimately the House passed a $500 million amendment. In June 1998 he proposed to make it easier for the government to buy property in flood prone areas. As farm prices started plunging in 1998, Thune proposed to increase price supports, but admitted, "This is a tough pull even in the Agriculture Committee itself, not only among Republicans, but among Democrats as well." Instead he proposed a bill to allow farmers to receive the present value of Freedom to Farm Act transition payments due up to 2002. He said he was pleased with the ultimate $6 billion emergency aid package, which allowed farmers to claim 1999 payments early.

On Transportation and Infrastructure, Thune worked on the May 1998 transportation bill, which raised South Dakota's payments from roughly $120 million to $180 million. As a committee member, he got $60 million worth of earmarked projects, and put some into the Heartland Expressway Phase 1 and Eastern Dakota Expressway, and bridges in Hell Canyon, Yankton and Vermillion. He worked for the Lewis and Clark Water Project, with a total price tag of $273 million, to provide a steady water supply for fast-growing Sioux Falls and the nearby area in South Dakota, Minnesota and Iowa; it passed the House in May 2000 but with amendments which made it difficult to reconcile with the Senate version. Thune has worked for the funding of other South Dakota water projects—the Mini Wiconi project, the Mid-Dakota Rural Water system, the buyout of flooded homes in Pierre and Fort Pierre. He got House support for the six-state pilot project, backed by Senators Tom Daschle and Tim Johnson, to allow farmers to enroll plots of five acres and less of wetlands into the Conservation Reserve Program: good for South Dakota pheasant habitat. He opposed the ban on watercraft in the Missouri River on the South Dakota-Nebraska border and backed country-of-origin meat labeling for animals born, raised and slaughtered in the United States. He won reelection in 1998 and 2000 by overwhelming margins: 75%–25% and 73%–25%.

After winning reelection in 2000, Thune did not flinch from keeping his promise to run for no more than three House terms. Instead the question is whether he would run to replace Governor William Janklow or against Senator Tim Johnson. National Republicans hoped he would run for the Senate. Johnson had been elected by only 51%–49% in 1996, and Thune led him in Republican polls by 48%–41% in March 2001. But Thune's wife and daughters, after trying life in metropolitan Washington, had chosen to live in Sioux Falls, and Thune seemed to be opting for a run for governor. In December 2000 he set up an exploratory committee for the governor race, and by April it had raised $250,000—money not eligible to be used in a Senate race. But on his trip to South Dakota in March 2001 and in a White House dinner in April, George W. Bush urged Thune to run for the Senate; and in December 2000 Thune had $483,000 in his House campaign treasury, which he could use for a Senate run. Bush had carried South Dakota 60%–38%, and there were rumors that Bush associates promised Thune two October 2002 appearances in the state if he ran against Johnson. The outlook for the race for South Dakota's at-large seat are also unclear, but here there would certainly be a strong advantage for the Republican nominee.

Cook's Call   *Competitive.* Thune's decision to abide by his term-limits pledge has opened the floodgates for what could be a once-in-a-political-lifetime shot at this at-large seat. While South Dakota has a serious Republican lean at the national level (Bush won here with 60% in 2000), Democrats have been successful at the congressional level.

Presidential politics   South Dakota has voted Democratic for president just four times since statehood, in 1896, 1932, 1936 and 1964. It was reasonably close in five of the seven elections between 1972, when South Dakota's George McGovern was the Democratic nominee, and 1996, when Bill Clinton came within 3% of winning. But the cultural liberalism and environmental policies of Al Gore were far from popular here, and George W. Bush carried the state 60%–38%. Gore carried only Indians, a rising but small percentage of the electorate, and ran even among the elderly, but the percentage of voters who remember Franklin Roosevelt is on the wane. South Dakota's three electoral votes were not seriously contested in 2000 and seem unlikely to be seriously contested in 2004.

South Dakota's presidential primary for years was held in June, on the same day as California's, and eclipsed by it. Since 1988 it has been held in February, just one week after New Hampshire. So far it has been not a trendsetter, but a booster of Great Plains candidates who do not fare well elsewhere: Bob Dole and Dick Gephardt in 1988, Bob Kerrey and Tom Harkin in 1992. In 2000 the primary was moved back to June and attracted little notice.

THE PEOPLE: Pop. 2000: 754,844; Pop. 1990: 696,004, up 8.5% 1990–2000. 0.3% of U.S. total, 46th largest; 88.7% White, 0.6% Black, 0.6% Asian, 8.3% Amer. Indian, 1.3% Two+ races, 0.5% Other; 1.4% Hispanic Origin. 2.3% Unemployment. 2000 Voting age pop.: 552,195. 2000 Turnout: 322,159; 58% of VAP. Registered voters (2000): 471,152; 181,129 D (38%), 226,906 R (48%), 63,117 unaffiliated and minor parties (13%).

POLITICAL LINEUP: Governor, William J. Janklow (R); Lt. Gov., Carole Hillard (R); Secy. of State, Joyce Hazeltine (R); Atty. Gen., Mark Barnett (R); Treasurer, Richard Butler (D); Auditor, Vernon L. Larson (R); Commissioner of Schools & Public Lands, Curt Johnson (D); State Senate, 35 (11 D, 24 R); Senate Pres. Pro Tempore, Arnold M. Brown (R); Majority Leader, Barbara Everest (R); State House, 70 (20 D, 50 R); House Speaker, Scott Eccarius (R). Senators, Thomas A. Daschle (D) and Timothy P. Johnson (D). Representative, 1 R at large.

ELECTIONS DIVISION: 605-773-3537; **FILING DEADLINE FOR U.S. CONGRESS:** April 2, 2002.

2000 Presidential Vote				**1996 Presidential Vote**			
Bush (R)		190,700	(60%)	Dole (R)		150,543	(46%)
Gore (D)		118,804	(38%)	Clinton (D)		139,333	(43%)
Others		6,765	(2%)	Perot (I)		31,250	(10%)

2000 Republican Presidential Primary

Bush (R)		35,418	(78%)
McCain (R)		6,228	(14%)
Keyes (R)		3,478	(8%)

Gov. William J. Janklow (R)

Elected 1994, term expires Jan. 2003, 2d term; b. Sept. 13, 1939, Chicago, IL; home, Brandon; U. of SD, B.S. 1964, LL.B 1966; Lutheran; married (Mary Dean).

Military Career: Marine Corps, 1956–59.

Elected Office: SD Atty. Gen., 1974–78; SD Gov., 1978–86.

Professional Career: Legal Aid, Rosebud Indian Reservation, 1966–73; SD Special Prosecutor, 1973–75; Practicing atty., 1987–94.

Office: Executive Office, State Capitol, Pierre, 57501, 605-773-3212; Fax: 605-773-5844; Web site: www.state.sd.us.

Election Results

1998 general	William J. Janklow (R)	166,621	(64%)
	Bernie Hunhoff (D)	85,473	(33%)
	Others	8,093	(3%)
1998 primary	William J. Janklow (R)	unopposed	
1994 general	William J. Janklow (R)	172,515	(55%)
	Jim Beddow (D)	126,273	(41%)
	Nathan A. Barton (Lib)	12,825	(4%)

Sen. Thomas A. Daschle (D)

Elected 1986, seat up 2004, 3d term; b. Dec. 9, 1947, Aberdeen; home, Aberdeen; SD St. U., B.A. 1969; Catholic; married (Linda).

Military Career: Air Force, 1969–72, Air Force Reserves, 1975–78.

Elected Office: U.S. House of Reps., 1978–86.

Professional Career: Legis. Asst., U.S. Sen. James Abourezk, 1973–77.

DC Office: 509 HSOB, 20510, 202-224-2321; Fax: 202-224-7895; Web site: www.senate.gov/~daschle.

State Offices: Aberdeen, 605-225-8823; Rapid City, 605-348-7551; Sioux Falls, 605-334-9596.

Committees: *Majority Leader. Agriculture, Nutrition & Forestry*: Forestry, Conservation & Rural Revitalization; Production & Price Competitiveness. *Finance*: Health Care; International Trade; Social Security & Family Policy. *Rules & Administration*.

Group Ratings

	ADA	ACLU	AFS	LCV	CON	ITIC	NTU	COC	ACU	NTLC	CHC
2000	85	57	83	57	82	93	10	71	8	0	23
1999	90	—	100	56	51	—	2	56	8	—	—

National Journal Ratings

	1999 LIB —	1999 CONS	2000 LIB —	2000 CONS
Economic	90%	0%	75%	24%
Social	64%	31%	79%	0%
Foreign	87%	0%	72%	15%

Key Votes of the 106th Congress

1. Educ. Savings Accts.	N	5. Review Movie Violence	N	9. NATO War in Serbia	Y
2. Prescrip. Drug Benefit	Y	6. Gun Show Bckgrnd. Checks	Y	10. Table Cuba Travel Ban	N
3. Delay Ergonomic Standards	N	7. Ban Part.-Birth Abortion	Y	11. Nuclear Test-Ban Treaty	Y
4. Phase Out Estate Tax	*	8. Broaden Hate Crimes List	Y	12. Perm. Trade with China	Y

Election Results

1998 general	Thomas A. Daschle (D)	162,884	(62%)	($4,861,541)
	Ron Schmidt (R)	95,431	(36%)	($492,854)
	Others	3,796	(1%)	
1998 primary	Thomas A. Daschle (D)	unopposed		
1992 general	Thomas A. Daschle (D)	217,095	(65%)	($3,981,548)
	Charlene Haar (R)	108,733	(33%)	($478,421)
	Others	8,667	(3%)	

Sen. Timothy P. Johnson (D)

Elected 1996, seat up 2002, 1st term; b. Dec. 28, 1946, Canton; home, Vermillion; U. of SD, B.A. 1969, M.A. 1970, J.D. 1975, MI St. U., 1970–71; Lutheran; married (Barbara).

Military Career: Army, 1969.

Elected Office: SD House of Reps., 1978–82; SD Senate, 1982–86; U.S. House of Reps., 1986–96.

Professional Career: Budget Analyst, MI Senate, 1971–72; Practicing atty., 1975–85; Clay Cnty. Dpty. Atty., 1985.

DC Office: 324 HSOB, 20510, 202-224-5842; Fax: 202-228-5765; Web site: www.senate.gov/~johnson.

State Offices: Aberdeen, 605-226-3440; Rapid City, 605-341-3990; Sioux Falls, 605-332-8896.

Committees: *Appropriations*: Agriculture & Rural Development; Foreign Operations; Legislative Branch; Military Construction; VA, HUD & Independent Agencies. *Banking, Housing & Urban Affairs*: Financial Institutions (Chmn.); International Trade & Finance; Securities & Investment. *Budget. Energy & Natural Resources*: Energy Research, Development, Production & Regulation; Forests & Public Land Management; Water & Power. *Indian Affairs*.

Group Ratings

	ADA	ACLU	AFS	LCV	CON	ITIC	NTU	COC	ACU	NTLC	CHC
2000	80	43	85	86	26	90	11	60	16	9	23
1999	95	—	100	89	32	—	5	47	8	—	—

National Journal Ratings

	1999 LIB —	1999 CONS	2000 LIB —	2000 CONS
Economic	75%	20%	71%	28%
Social	69%	28%	57%	39%
Foreign	71%	24%	89%	5%

Key Votes of the 106th Congress

1. Educ. Savings Accts.	N	5. Review Movie Violence	Y	9. NATO War in Serbia		Y
2. Prescrip. Drug Benefit	Y	6. Gun Show Bckgrnd. Checks	Y	10. Table Cuba Travel Ban		N
3. Delay Ergonomic Standards	N	7. Ban Part.-Birth Abortion	Y	11. Nuclear Test-Ban Treaty		Y
4. Phase Out Estate Tax	N	8. Broaden Hate Crimes List	Y	12. Perm. Trade with China		Y

Election Results

1996 general	Timothy P. Johnson (D)	166,533	(51%)	($2,990,554)
	Larry Pressler (R)	157,954	(49%)	($5,138,298)
1996 primary	Timothy P. Johnson (D)	unopposed		
1990 general	Larry Pressler (R)	135,682	(52%)	($2,124,359)
	Ted Muenster (D)	116,727	(45%)	($1,323,770)

Rep. John Thune (R)

Elected 1996, 3d term; b. Jan. 7, 1961, Pierre; home, Pierre; Biola U., B.A. 1983, U. of SD, M.B.A. 1984; Protestant; married (Kimberley).

Professional Career: Legis. Asst., U.S. Sen. James Abdnor, 1985–87; Special Asst., U.S. Small Business Admin., 1987–89; Exec. Dir. SD Republican Party, 1989–91; SD Railroad Dir., 1991–93; Exec. Dir., SD Municipal League, 1993–96.

DC Office: 1005 LHOB, 20515, 202-225-2801; Fax: 202-225-5823; Web site: www.house.gov/thune.

District Offices: Aberdeen, 605-622-7988; Rapid City, 605-342-5135; Sioux Falls, 800-755-5646.

Committees: *Agriculture* (11th of 27 R): Conservation, Credit, Rural Development & Research; General Farm Commodities & Risk Management. *Small Business* (10th of 19 R): Rural Enterprises, Agricultural and Technology (Chmn.); Tax, Finance & Exports. *Transportation & Infrastructure* (18th of 42 R): Aviation; Highways & Transit.

Group Ratings

	ADA	ACLU	AFS	LCV	CON	ITIC	NTU	COC	ACU	NTLC	CHC
2000	5	21	0	14	50	94	53	85	76	76	87
1999	10	—	16	6	28	—	58	92	80	—	—

National Journal Ratings

	1999 LIB —	1999 CONS		2000 LIB —	2000 CONS
Economic	24%	72%		34%	64%
Social	19%	79%		33%	66%
Foreign	3%	92%		33%	62%

Key Votes of the 106th Congress

1. Patient Bill of Rights	N	5. Bar RU-486 $ for FDA	Y	9. NATO War in Serbia	N
2. Accelerate Min. Wage	Y	6. Display 10 Commandments	Y	10. Perm. Trade with China	Y
3. Strike Ban on Ergo. Stnd.	N	7. Gun Show Bkgrnd. Checks	N	11. Debt Relief for 3rd World	N
4. Ovrd. Estate Tax Veto	Y	8. Ban Part.-Birth Abortion	Y	12. Drop Cuba Econ. Embargo	Y

Election Results

2000 general	John Thune (R)	231,083	(73%)	($953,757)
	Curt Hohn (D)	78,321	(25%)	($115,038)
	Other	5,357	(2%)	
2000 primary	John Thune (R)	unopposed		
1998 general	John Thune (R)	194,157	(75%)	($621,024)
	Jeff Moser (D)	64,433	(25%)	($56,266)

★ TENNESSEE ★

Tennessee is a battleground state, with a fighting temperament since it was settled 200 years ago by the likes of Andrew Jackson and went on to produce so many soldiers it came to be known as the Volunteer State. This was a frontier battleground in the 1790s, from which Jackson launched his wars on the Indians and the British. It was a military battleground in the 1860s, when Yankee troops swept down the Tennessee and Cumberland Rivers on their way to Mississippi and through Chattanooga's Lookout Mountain on their way to Atlanta and the sea. It has been a cultural battleground for much of this century. On one side were the Fugitives, writers like John Crowe Ransom and Allen Tate, who contributed to "I'll Take My Stand," a manifesto calling for retaining the South's rural economy and heritage. On the other side have been business leaders and politicians who have made Tennessee the fastest-growing state of the interior South: Tennessee has given birth to the first supermarket (a Piggly Wiggly), the Holiday Inn, Federal Express and Goo-Goo Clusters.

This state has also been a marshaling ground for the music traditions that have vied for a large place in Americans' lives. East Tennessee is one of the homes of bluegrass music and mountain fiddling, with string bands and vocal harmony; Knoxville's Tennessee Barn Dance has been broadcast since 1942. Gospel music has long been centered in Nashville, which is also the nation's leading center of religious publishing. Country music got its commercial start in Nashville, with broadcasts of the Grand Ole Opry from Ryman Auditorium starting in 1925 and then the Opryland U.S.A. theme park; and Nashville remains indisputably the capital of country music. The Mississippi lowlands around Memphis, economically and culturally the metropolis of the Mississippi Delta, gave birth to the blues in the years from the 1890s to 1920; and the blues were in turn the inspiration for the jazz musicians of Beale Street in the 1920s and Elvis Presley, whose Graceland mansion is now a major tourist destination, in the 1950s and 1960s.

Tennessee is and has long been a political battleground. Its political divisions have their roots in the Civil War, and most counties today still vote their 1860s loyalties: the Union counties, mainly in the east but with a scattering to the west, vote solidly Republican, while the Confederate counties in middle and west Tennessee have long been heavily Democratic. Within the limits of these enduring party loyalties, political entrepreneurs have set the tone for the state. From the 1920s to 1948, Edward Crump, longtime mayor of Memphis, used his total control of Democratic primary votes there to elect governors and senators. The Tennessee Valley Authority and the cheap electric power it generated provided an institutional base for reform liberal Democrats Estes Kefauver and Albert Gore Sr., elected to the Senate in 1948 and 1952. They were soon national figures, with reliable enough backing from Tennessee's yellow-dog Democratic majority to vote for civil rights bills and to refuse to sign the segregationist Southern Manifesto, and still thrive electorally. Kefauver died in 1963 and Gore was defeated in 1970, but lived on to see his son twice elected vice president, before dying in December 1998. Tennessee has never had a large black population—about 16% in the 1990s, half of whom live in and around Memphis—and the state was not riven by the racial animosity that seared so much of the South in the 1950s and 1960s, thanks in large part to the actions of its leading politicians, but also to the continuing hold of ancestral partisan preferences.

Today the political balance has changed, and Tennessee has become a mostly Republican state—as witness the fact that Al Gore was beaten 51%–47% in his home state in 2000. Democrats' cultural liberalism has moved rural voters in west and middle Tennessee away from their ancestral loyalties, and the surging growth in the ring of counties around Nashville in the 1990s has created a new voting bloc conservative on both economic and cultural issues. The first movement toward the Republicans occurred in the 1960s and 1970s, symbolized by the elections of Republican Senators Howard Baker and Bill Brock in 1966 and 1970, and Republican Governor Lamar Alexander in 1978. Brock's defeat of Albert Gore Sr. is still remembered with bitterness by the circle of politicians and journalists around the Gore family. Then, as Jimmy Carter changed the image of the Democratic Party, Democrats rallied; Democrats Jim Sasser and Al Gore were elected to the Senate in 1976 and 1984, and Democrat Ned Ray McWherter was elected governor in 1986.

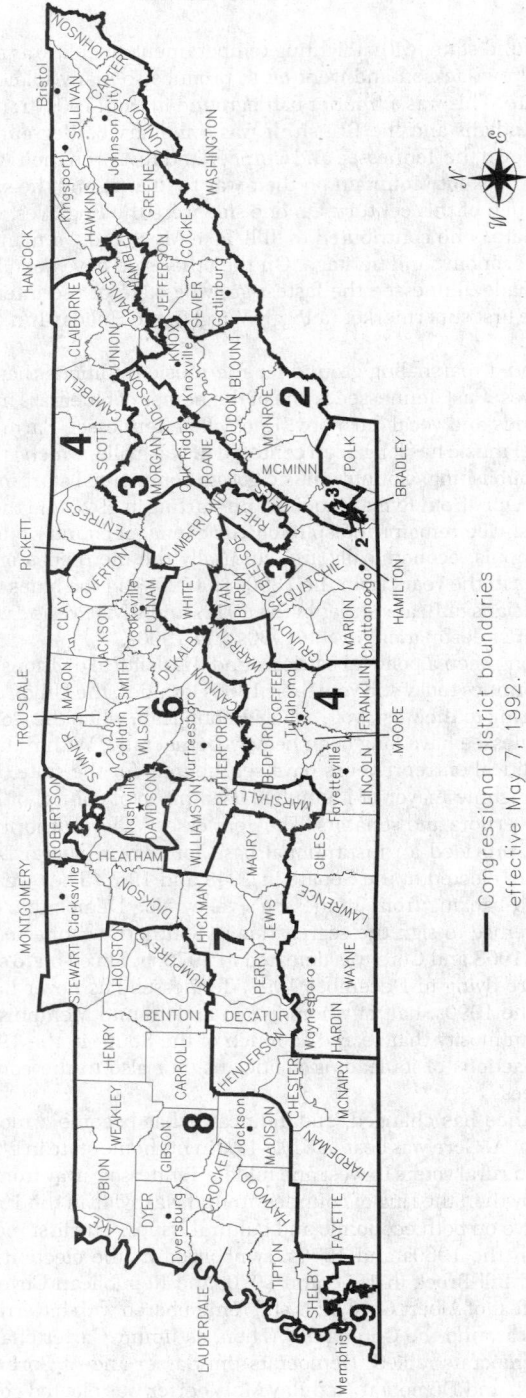

—Congressional district boundaries
effective May 7, 1992.

This movement was still strong enough for the Clinton-Gore ticket to carry Tennessee 47%–42% in 1992. But the narrowness of the margin was a warning of what was ahead. In 1994 Tennessee turned against the Clinton administration and produced a kind of political revolution. Republican Fred Thompson, famous as a Watergate investigator and movie actor, won the remainder of Gore's Senate term by a landslide, surgeon Bill Frist beat Sasser, and Republican Don Sundquist was elected governor. Republicans won a majority of the vote for the U.S. House, gaining two seats and coming close in a third. The Republican trend was strong enough in 1996 that only after extraordinary efforts—Gore made 16 appearances here and the campaign pumped in money for late ads—was the Clinton-Gore ticket able to win by a narrow 48%–46% margin. The VNS exit poll showed the vote almost even among voters under 45, with Democrats winning their biggest margin among the elderly—not a good augury for the future.

In 2000 the tide was even stronger. George W. Bush targeted the state early and worked it energetically; the Gore campaign, though headquartered in Nashville, seemed to assume it would come around in the end, and only campaigned hard here in the last few days. Bush carried the state by 51%–47% and Gore became only the third major party nominee to lose his home state in 85 years (the others were South Dakota's George McGovern in 1972 and New Jersey's Woodrow Wilson in 1916). The loss was all the more crushing since if Gore had won Tennessee's 11 electoral votes, he would have won the presidency. Gore carried Tennessee blacks 92%–8%, but Bush carried white Protestants 60%–37%. Voters over 65 voted 55%–45% for Gore, but voters under 65 voted 52%–46% for Bush. Nor did Gore's populist "people versus the powerful" theme have much appeal in a state where it once rallied voters for his father and Estes Kefauver. Gore lost six of Tennessee's nine congressional districts, carrying only the districts that included Memphis and Nashville; he even lost within the boundaries of the congressional district which had first elected him in 1976, a district so Democratic that Gore took 94% of the vote then and Republicans did not even field a candidate in 1978 and 1980. In his gracious concession speech, Gore noted that he had some fence-mending to do in Tennessee, but the problem was not that he was personally unpopular; the problem was that the issue positions and cultural tone of the Clinton-Gore administration, so appealing to voters in the great suburban expanses of the largest non-Southern metropolitan areas, was alien and grating in rural Tennessee and in the suburban subdivisions expanding from Nashville and other cities out into the countryside.

This is a Tennessee that is expanding economically but is not abandoning its cultural roots. The expansion started in the early 1980s, when Governor Lamar Alexander helped bring big auto plants to middle Tennessee—the Nissan plant in Smyrna and the Saturn plant in Spring Hill, both within an hour's drive of Nashville. The country music business boomed, and so did tourism: big attractions now are Opryland and the nearby Opry Mills mall, at the edge of the city. Nashville is also a health care center, the headquarters of Columbia/ HCA, rescued after some problems by Thomas Frist Jr., brother of Senator Bill Frist. And Nashville's banks and insurance companies have provided plenty of white-collar employment. Nashville now has teams in the National Football and National Hockey Leagues; it has a sparkling new library and the Frist Center for the Visual Arts and the Tennessee Performing Arts Center. In May 2001 Nashville opened the $37 million Country Music Hall of Fame in its newly revitalized downtown. The Nashville establishment traditionally supported Democrats in Tennessee politics. But now Nashville money has become heavily Republican: Lamar Alexander's presidential campaigns raised so much money locally that 37205 and 37215 became two of the Republicans' top five fundraising zip codes in 1996, and continued to be big contributors.

There seems to be economic change in east Tennessee as well. For years east Tennessee Republicans vied with middle Tennessee Democrats in supporting the TVA. But in 1997 TVA Chairman Craven Crowell Jr., a Clinton appointee, proposed eliminating the authority's $106 million in federal funding for non-power programs by 1999, so that TVA could concentrate on electricity sales in the increasingly competitive market and spin off its navigation and flood control functions to state or federal agencies. Tennessee has grown, attracting and spawning new businesses, in part because its institutions were mostly untouched by the labor union strife of the 1930s and the civil rights strife of the 1960s. The lack of strong unions and racial divisions attracted the many Japanese companies here, which in turn attracted General Motors. If Tennessee's economy lagged behind the nation's through much of the 20th Century, its respect for hard work and its open climate for entrepreneurism have enabled it to grow mightily in its last decades and in the first years of the 21st.

Governor   Don Sundquist is a Republican elected governor in 1994 and 1998. Unusually for a Tennessee politician, he grew up elsewhere—in Illinois, the son of a welder—was the first in his family to go to college and served in the Navy. He worked for Jostens, a college and high school jewelry maker, in Shelbyville, Tennessee, for 10 years; in 1972 he started his own graphics and printing firm in Memphis. He volunteered for Howard Baker as early as 1964, when Baker lost a Senate race, and became active in the national Young Republicans organization. In 1982 Sundquist ran for Congress from the 7th District, which stretched from Memphis all the way to Nashville; he won 51%–49% over current 5th District Congressman Bob Clement, carrying the white Memphis suburbs but losing the rural counties. Sundquist served on the Ways and Means Committee and opposed tax increases; he worked his rural counties with 100 "community days" a year. He was re-elected easily.

In 1994 Sundquist ran for governor. The Democratic nominee was Nashville Mayor Phil Bredesen, also a migrant from the North, who made a fortune in health care. Bredesen was popular in Nashville, center of the state's largest media market, and rich enough to self-finance his campaign. Moreover, the record of Democratic incumbent Ned Ray McWherter was impressive: the passage of TennCare; 21st Century Schools, with teacher salary raises and more leeway for superintendents and principals in choosing teachers; no income tax (Tennessee is one of seven states without one). Sundquist was boosted by former Governor Lamar Alexander, Baker and east Tennessee Congressman Jimmy Quillen, and won by a solid 54%–45% margin, losing Nashville but carrying the other big metro areas handily.

Sundquist worked on a bipartisan basis with the state legislature to pass a 20-bill crime package and Families First, a plan to move welfare recipients to work in 18 months; by October 1998 the rolls were down 60%. He put all children's programs in one department, launched a TNKids initiative for early intervention and prevention for children at risk, and sought to make TennCare coverage available to all uninsured children. Tennessee became the first state to connect every school and library to the Internet. His main negative publicity came when he questioned high spending at the University of Tennessee, and gave substantial raises to members of his staff. In 1998 Sundquist had the additional good fortune of being opposed by John Jay Hooker, "a half-comic caricature from the past," in the words of *The Tennessean*'s Larry Daughtrey. Hooker had run for governor twice before, losing to Buford Ellington in 1966 and Republican Winfield Dunn in 1970; he headed Minnie Pearl Chicken (renamed Performance Systems), which went bust; STP Corp. and UPI; he ran for the Senate unsuccessfully in 1976, 1994 and 1996; in his one success, he urged Ross Perot to run for president in 1992. Hooker raised no money, ran no ads, seldom ventured from Nashville and sued Sundquist twice, for libel and for not letting him use the governor's mansion for a rally. Sundquist won 69%–29%, carrying all but two counties—an astonishing feat given rural Tennessee's Civil War loyalties—and had $3 million in unspent funds.

In the months that followed Sundquist reversed some of the stands that had brought him such success. The reason was TennCare, the cost of which was rising twice as rapidly as Medicaid in other states. In February 1999 Sundquist called for a 2.5% tax on business profits and compensation paid; legislators protested that this was an income tax, which Sundquist had always said he opposed. The legislature adjourned in May 1999 after passing a budget that included more than $190 million for TennCare but without the tax measures. In October 1999 Sundquist called for a 3.5% state income tax, plus a reduction in the 6% sales tax to 3.75%, and called a special session of the legislature. There were loud protests, led by radio talk show hosts; as the legislature met, motorists honked their horns outside the Capitol. Sundquist's tax package was defeated but in 2000 he tried again. In June 2000 he vetoed the legislature's budget because it contained no income tax and balanced the state budget by changing the revenue estimate; this was the first time a Tennessee governor had ever vetoed a budget. The legislature overrode his veto by the resounding margins of 78–19 and 20–9. Democrats supported Sundquist's plan; he was booed at Republican meetings. Sundquist was obdurate: "We have missed the opportunity to do what's right for Tennessee. We have missed the opportunity to put in place a fair tax system. And we have missed the opportunity to move Tennessee forward with a tax system." The onetime tax opponent was now a solid tax booster.

After the November 2000 election, in which Republican efforts to win majorities failed, Sundquist said he would not propose an income tax again; there were predictions that the legislature would balance the budget by using windfall money from the tobacco settlement. TennCare spending was increased 13%, from $4.5 billion to $5.1 billion, in an effort to get more managed care companies to participate. Sundquist said he would support a 2002 referendum on a lottery if the proceeds were used for education. Sundquist is term-limited. In February 2001 Senator Fred Thompson said he would not run for governor. That opened up the race for many other politicians. Local strength may prove crucial if there are large fields in the primaries since Tennessee is the one former Confederate state with no runoff primary.

Cook's Call *Highly Competitive.* Although Tennessee has taken on a slight Republican tilt, the many battles that Sundquist fought may diminish the strength of the ultimate Republican nominee. There is a long line of potential candidates on both sides and both fields are expected to expand. Regardless of the nominees, expect a close race.

Senior Senator Fred Thompson, first elected to the Senate in 1994, grew up in Lawrenceburg, Tennessee, the son of a used car dealer, and worked his way through school rearing a young family. After law school at Vanderbilt, he became an assistant U.S. attorney in Nashville, handling moonshine and stolen car cases. In 1973 Howard Baker made Thompson chief Republican counsel to the Senate Watergate Committee, where he helped uncover the scandal that drove a Republican president from office. Back in Tennessee, incoming Governor Lamar Alexander appointed Thompson special counsel to investigate clemency selling by outgoing Governor Ray Blanton, who went to jail. In the process, Thompson defended parole board chairman Marie Ragghianti, whose plight was the subject of the movie *Marie;* offered the chance to play himself, Thompson accepted. He took a couple more special counsel assignments in Washington and acted in 18 movies, including box office hits like *The Hunt for Red October.* His roles included a CIA chief, FBI director, a White House chief of staff and a senator, as well as some explicit villains. But he spent most of his time practicing law and lobbying, and for years made no move to run for office.

Then Al Gore resigned his Senate seat to become vice president, and Governor Ned Ray McWherter passed over the Democrat who seemed the most likely candidate—Congressman Jim Cooper—to appoint his own aide Harlan Mathews, who did not run in the 1994 election to fill the last two years of Gore's term. Thompson and Cooper did. Cooper seemed well positioned: The son of a former governor, he had represented the elongated 4th District for 12 years and was conspicuously a New Democrat and chief sponsor of a managed care health bill, which was vigorously opposed by the Clinton White House. With a seat on Commerce, he raised plenty of money and ultimately spent slightly more than Thompson.

But Thompson found a device to symbolize his message. One of his issues, long advocated by Baker and featured by Alexander in his 1996 presidential campaign, was limiting congressional sessions to half the year and allowing lawmakers to make their livings in their home communities. To this he coupled strong advocacy of term limits. The symbol—gimmick, Democrats said—for this was the red pickup truck which Thompson leased in August 1994 and drove all around Tennessee, speaking to small groups over coffee or fried chicken. Ads also captured a personal contrast between the candidates: the six-foot-five Thompson appeared in workshirts, speaking confidently to the camera while walking up porch stairs (not so easy to do: his acting experience helped); the much shorter and youthful-looking Cooper appeared before a church in starched white shirt and tie. In early October, Thompson zoomed to a lead, and Cooper got squeezed out of the middle ground he had long worked to occupy. Tennesseans decided to vote against the Clinton administration and career politicians, and Thompson won 60%–39%.

He quickly became a political star in Washington. Bob Dole named him to respond on television to Clinton's 1994 speech urging a tax cut. Thompson's strong words and delivery made him seem the more presidential: "We welcome the president to help us lead America in a new direction, but if he will not, we will welcome the president to follow—because we are moving ahead." Thompson voted for most of the Contract with America provisions. He soft-pedaled issues like abortion, and emphasized campaign finance reform, sponsoring a measure to save the current presidential checkoff system. He brought the term limit amendment to the floor in 1995 and sponsored the 1996 amendment to freeze congressional pay.

Thompson then became chairman of the Governmental Affairs Committee, and was assigned the duty of investigating the Clinton scandals by Majority Leader Trent Lott. He started off uncertainly, asking for a $6.5 million budget without consulting Lott or the Democrats, then irritating Republicans when he promised a broad investigation of congressional and Republican campaigns as well as the Clinton-Gore operation. Ultimately, Thompson got $4.35 million and the broader mandate he had originally sought. He started the hearings in July 1997 by asserting that "high-level Chinese government officials crafted a plan to increase China's influence over the U.S. political process" by allocating "substantial sums of money" to congressional and the 1996 presidential elections. Democrats responded with outrage and obstruction. Thompson could not produce direct evidence of the Chinese efforts as key witnesses declined to testify or fled the country—though plenty of evidence has come out since. Then he focused on Clinton's and Gore's fundraising on federal property—a clear violation of the letter of the law—and called their raising and spending of vast sums of soft money a "ruse." But Democrats raised hairsplitting objections and Attorney General Janet Reno refused to call for an independent counsel.

On Government Affairs, Thompson has worked to repair the mechanics of government. With Carl Levin and Gore, he helped develop a regulatory reform package that found its way into the October 1998 omnibus budget; it set up a framework for cost-benefit analysis and risk assessment of major government regulations. He passed a vacancy reform act in October 1998, limiting acting officers to 120 days in office unless the president has submitted a permanent nomination. In early 1999 he said Reno's decisions not to call for independent counsel put "the final nail in the coffin of the independent counsel law"; it was not renewed. He helped author a bipartisan August 1999 report on how the government bungled the Wen Ho Lee prosecution. He has been willing to cast lonely votes against popular measures because on federalism grounds he believes they should be left to the states: the .08% blood alcohol level for DWI, the school gun law, limiting tort liability of volunteers. He authored a bill to allow states to go to court and argue that their laws are not preempted by federal legislation: "This fits with my longstanding concern that every time there is a news story, we run to the floor and want to federalize something." He obtained a GAO report that said that the government failed to collect $4 billion in debts and made $16 billion in overpayments to contractors, and he criticized the Clinton administration for not addressing programs that generate unpaid debts or overpayments. Decrying the status quo—"the loopholes are bigger than the laws"—he strongly supported the McCain-Feingold campaign finance bills.

On Tennessee issues, Thompson worked often with junior colleague Bill Frist. He passed a bill to protect 2,000 civilians working at Fort Campbell from paying Kentucky taxes (Tennessee has no income tax). In May 1998 he formed the Great Smoky Mountains National Park Congressional Caucus and pushed to allow the park to retain 100% rather than 80% of fees; he has said that the large number of smokestacks in the Tennessee Valley are threatening the park's air quality. He got funding for the $1 billion Spallation Neutron Source at the Oak Ridge National Laboratory and helped broker the bill to compensate uranium miners. He backed copyright extensions and opposed exempting small restaurants from paying royalties to songwriters: matters of interest in Nashville. Thompson and Frist have worked together on TVA problems. In 1998 they called for refinancing its $3.2 billion debt (much of it run up by nuclear power plants) plus a $50 million direct appropriation for non-power activities; this went into the October 1998 omnibus budget. In 2000 they prepared a TVA deregulation bill, which would allow TVA to sell power freely, not just to its current 14 non-Valley customers. With Congressman John Duncan, he passed a law giving TVA an independent inspector general. In December 2000 he and Frist got $6 million for a school of government at the University of Tennessee named after UT grad Howard Baker.

In September 2000 Thompson and Bob Torricelli sponsored an amendment to permanent normal trade relations with China that would have empowered the president to impose sanctions on Chinese companies that export nuclear, chemical or biological weapons or missiles to proliferating countries. Advocates of PNTR did not want any amendments to the measure, and this was a key test; Thompson-Torricelli lost 65–32. Thompson said he might press the issue again, and in November 2000 criticized the Clinton administration for waiving sanctions on past exports in return for a Chinese pledge to export no more.

Thompson has expressed frustrations with the pace of the Senate: "I'm not 30 years old. I don't want to spend the rest of my life up here. I don't like spending 14- and 16-hour days voting on 'sense of the Senate' resolutions on irrelevant matters." But he has made no moves to leave before his self-imposed limit of two full terms. When his seat came up in 1996, he ran an ad saying, "I want you to meet my number one adviser on Social Security and Medicare," and introduced his mother. Thompson won 61%–37%, winning nearly 1.1 million votes, more than anyone ever had in Tennessee. In March 1999 Thompson announced that he wouldn't run for president and that he would support Lamar Alexander, who was set to launch his campaign. Thompson backed Alexander until his withdrawal, then was one of the few senators backing John McCain, then spoke out at both party's conventions, on the hustings and in Florida for George W. Bush. At one point he noted tartly that Gore has "certainly not solved any of the problems at the TVA. As vice president, he has provided no advantage to Tennessee projects." As Frist said, "I think Fred has the ability to communicate a message better than anybody else in the U.S. Senate." In February 2001 Thompson stopped speculation by announcing that he would not run for governor in 2002; it was widely assumed he would run for another term, and win easily.

Cook's Call   *Safe.* As long as Thompson seeks reelection this seat is firmly in Republican hands. If the seat is open, the contest would become very competitive and House members from both parties would take a serious look at the race.

Junior Senator   Bill Frist, first elected to the Senate in 1994, grew up in Nashville, in an old Tennessee family; his father practiced medicine for 55 years and was the physician for six Tennessee governors. Frist graduated from Princeton and Harvard Medical School, studied at Mass General, in England and at Stanford, and became a heart and lung transplant surgeon, setting up the transplant program at Vanderbilt. He performed 250 transplants and wrote a book, *Transplant*, on the social and ethical issues of these surgeries; he has written more than 100 peer-reviewed articles. In 1968 his father and brother, Thomas Frist Jr., set up HCA, which through a 1994 merger became Columbia/ HCA, the world's largest hospital company; the new firm was hit with charges of Medicare violations in 1997, and Thomas Frist Jr. came back from semi-retirement to run it; he owns millions of dollars of the stock and Bill Frist has somewhere between $5 million and $25 million, put into blind trust. Frist also pilots his own airplane and runs marathons (51 seconds faster than Al Gore in 1998), and regularly does volunteer medical work on a mobile health clinic in Washington, and in Tennessee and—venturing into the war-torn "no-go zone"—in Sudan. For years Frist was unpolitical: he never voted until age 36, after he moved back to Nashville. When he was appointed by Democratic Governor Ned Ray Mc-Wherter to head a task force on Medicaid in 1992, many assumed he was a Democrat.

In 1994 Frist decided to run against Senator Jim Sasser, then Budget Committee chairman and a candidate for majority leader. He had tough primary opposition from east Tennessee businessman Bob Corker, who attacked him for not voting and for obtaining cats from animal shelters for experiments as a medical student. But Frist, spending liberally, carried the Nashville and Memphis media markets and beat Corker 44%–32%. In the general, Frist said he wanted to "give communities and individuals the freedom to solve problems and return to our basic conservative values," and backed welfare reform, federal spending cuts, school prayer and term limits; he follows Howard Baker in calling for citizen-politicians and pledged to serve just two terms—"Term limits for career politicians and the death penalty for career criminals," one ad said. Sasser emphasized school prayer, the balanced budget amendment and cracking down on illegal immigrants, and he ridiculed Frist as a bored, rich surgeon. Frist outspent Sasser, spending $3.7 million of his own money. Sasser led in polls up through October, but in November Frist won 56%–42%, carrying all the large metro areas and losing only scattered traditionally Democratic rural counties.

Frist is the first physician to serve in the Senate for 50 years; he points out that there were many more in the days of the citizen-politician. In September 1995 he resuscitated a constituent outside the Dirksen Office Building, and in July 1998 he ran over to the House and tended to those wounded in the shooting that killed two Capitol police officers. Naturally he got involved in health issues; the Senate ethics committee ruled that he is not prohibited from voting on any "legislation of general applicability to the health care industry." He played a key role on the 1996 health care bill on portability and pre-existing conditions, working to include Medical Savings Accounts. He also helped to write the provision guaranteeing insurance coverage for 48-hour hospital maternity stays. He worked to reauthorize the Ryan White CARE Act for the treatment and support of AIDS patients. He put on the income tax form a box to check off for information on organ donor cards. He worked to make sure Tennessee was not penalized for extending TennCare to uninsured children.

On some health issues Frist has worked with Democrats. With Jay Rockefeller, he sponsored a law to allow physicians and hospitals to establish service provider organizations to contract directly with Medicare. He backed the 1997 Clinton bill to ban discrimination by insurers by genetic traits and to assure privacy of genetic information. He supported Surgeon General nominees Henry Foster and David Satcher. He has supported doubling NIH funding over five years. In 2000 he worked with Ted Kennedy to forge a compromise on organ transplants, to try to reduce regional disparities; but the House, which backed the United Network of Organ Sharing, with its 62 separate geographic regions, refused to compromise. In 2000 Frist and Kennedy steered through a $919 million authorization for public health laws, including $540 million for research on bioterrorism and $180 million to refurbish Center for Disease Control labs. He passed a law with incentives for primary care physicians in rural and inner city areas, and worked to reauthorize the bone marrow registry, with recruitment of minorities. He helped get both houses to pass a 1998 law for research on women's health problems. Frist sponsored the ban on human cloning and supported the partial-birth abortion ban, "because it is needlessly risky to the woman, because it is an unnecessary procedure, because it is inhumane to the fetus, and because it is medically unacceptable and offends the very basic civil sensibilities of people all across this country."

On HMO regulation and prescription drugs, Frist has been the lead man in forging Republican positions. He served on the Medicare Commission that presented its premium support plan in March 1999. In June 2000 sponsored a Medicare reform bill with commission chairman John Breaux. Their plan would have private insurers competing to provide coverage to Medicare beneficiaries, overseen by a new government agency which would approve the content of plans; the idea is to evade the cumbersome HCFA bureaucracy in HHS. They seek to include prescription drug coverage as part of a larger reform of Medicare, with subsidies for all seniors and a progressive sliding scale of subsidies depending on income. Frist has also co-sponsored with Breaux and James Jeffords a plan to provide those uninsured and ineligible for Medicaid a tax credit, $1,000 for individuals and $2,000 for families, for amounts spent for health insurance; this would give them some of the same benefits others get for employer-provided health insurance. Frist worked on tobacco legislation with John McCain in 1998, but ended up opposing his bill; in 2000 they joined to sponsor a bill giving the FDA limited power to regulate tobacco marketing to children.

On other issues, Frist was the lead sponsor with Democrat Ron Wyden of the Ed-Flex bill which passed by a wide margin in March 1999; it would give school systems greater flexibility in return for holding them to greater accountability. He favors individual retirement accounts as part of Social Security. After a trip to Sudan, he said in 1998 that the Clinton administration's acquiescence to Sudanese government manipulation of humanitarian relief "may be a contributing factor in the horrendous prospect of widespread starvation." And in July 2000, after recounting the horrifying conditions he had seen in Sudan a week before, he got UN Ambassador Richard Holbrooke to commit to a change in U.S. policy.

Senators of the same party from the same state often have acrimonious relationships, but Frist and Fred Thompson, elected the same year, seem to get on unusually well, although they disagree on about 20% of roll call votes—many of the disagreements are what you might expect between a doctor and a lawyer. They have worked in tandem on many Tennessee issues, including the 1998 TVA bill that refinanced its debt, saving $100 million, and added $50 million for its non-power activities, like the Land Between the Lakes park. They worked in 2000 to prepare TVA for deregulation. In December 2000 they got $6 million for a school of government to be named after Howard Baker at the University of Tennessee.

Frist came up for re-election in 2000, and Democrats were eager to field a strong candidate against him in order to help Al Gore in his native Tennessee. In summer 1999, 29-year-old Congressman Harold Ford of Memphis traveled across the state and attacked Frist for his holdings in Columbia/ HCA and his opposition to the Democrats' HMO regulation bill. He told state Democrats that he would decide whether to run by Labor Day. But he announced no decision and quit barnstorming, leaving Democrats with the prospect of having as their candidate John Jay Hooker, an up-and-coming politician 30 years before but now something of a joke; he won 29% as the Democratic nominee against Governor Don Sundquist in 1998. Ford's indecision and Hooker's notoriety kept Memphis businessman John Lowery, who once said he was willing to spend $1 million of his own money, out of the race. The Democratic nomination went to computer science professor Jeff Clark, who beat Hooker by just 810 votes in the August primary, 34.2%–33.8%, in a light turnout. Clark, as he put it himself, spent "zero dollars on television, zero dollars on radio and zero dollars on direct mail." He attacked Frist for the alleged Columbia/ HCA conflict and denounced pharmaceutical companies. Frist set up organizations in all 95 counties and ran ads stressing his achievements on education and health care and featuring testimonials from constituents. Frist won 65%–32%, with the highest number of votes cast for a candidate in Tennessee history. He lost only five of the 95 counties, including Al Gore's home in Smith County.

Frist, meanwhile, delivered the Republican response to Bill Clinton's State of the Union address in January 2000. In July 2000 he was named to replace the late Paul Coverdell as the liaison between George W. Bush's campaign and Republican senators. He worked on the Republican platform and spoke Thursday night at the Philadelphia convention. He was on an early list of possible vice presidential candidates. Tennessee Democrats and Republicans speculated that he was thinking of running for president some day. In December 2000 he was elected head of the National Republican Senatorial Committee, with the assignment of bettering the party's total in a year when 20 Republican and 14 Democratic Senate seats are up.

Presidential politics Tennessee has been about evenly divided in presidential politics at several different points in the last half-century, even as its basic political leanings have switched from Democratic to Republican. It was close in the Eisenhower-Stevenson races in the 1950s, in the Carter-Reagan race of 1980 and again in 1992, 1996 and 2000. But the fact that native son Al Gore was unable to win here as the representative of the incumbent party in a time of peace and prosperity suggests that Tennessee is likely to be out of reach for presidential Democrats in the near future.

Tennessee's presidential primary is held on Super Tuesday (though Tennessee holds its state primaries on Thursdays, the only state to do so). But it is far from the biggest state to vote that day, and so receives relatively little attention from presidential candidates.

Congressional districting Despite their success at the statewide level, Republicans failed in 2000 to win majorities in either house of the Tennessee legislature, and so the Democrats will control redistricting, subject to the veto pen of Republican Governor Don Sundquist. One possible compromise is a plan that would take Republican territory from the fast-growing 6th District and add it to the slow-growing 4th District, which stretches almost all across the state; this would strengthen incumbents of both parties, although 4th District Republican Van Hilleary may run for governor. The last time an incumbent Tennessee congressman was defeated was in 1974, when a Republican lost in an increasingly black central Memphis district.

THE PEOPLE: Pop. 2000: 5,689,283; Pop. 1990: 4,877,185, up 16.7% 1990–2000. 2% of U.S. total, 16th largest; 80.2% White, 16.4% Black, 1% Asian, 0.3% Amer. Indian, 1.1% Two + races, 1% Other; 2.2% Hispanic Origin. 3.9% Unemployment. 2000 Voting age pop.: 4,290,762. 2000 Turnout: 2,100,241; 49% of VAP. Registered voters (2000): 3,181,108; no party registration.

POLITICAL LINEUP: Governor, Don Sundquist (R); Lt. Gov., John Wilder (D); Secy. of State, Riley C. Darnell (D); Atty. Gen., Paul Summers; Treasurer, Steve Adams (D); State Senate, 33 (18 D, 15 R); Senate Pres. Pro Tempore, Robert Rochelle (D); Majority Leader, Ward Crutchfield (D); State House, 99 (58 D, 41 R); House Speaker, Jimmy Naifeh (D). Senators, Fred D. Thompson (R) and Bill Frist (R). Representatives, 9 (4 D, 5 R).

ELECTIONS DIVISION: 615-741-7956; **FILING DEADLINE FOR U.S. CONGRESS:** April 4, 2002.

2000 Presidential Vote
Bush (R)	1,061,949	(51%)
Gore (D)	981,720	(47%)
Nader (Green)	19,781	(1%)
Others	12,731	(1%)

1996 Presidential Vote
Clinton (D)	909,146	(48%)
Dole (R)	863,530	(46%)
Perot (I)	105,918	(6%)

2000 Republican Presidential Primary
Bush (R)	193,166	(77%)
McCain (R)	36,436	(15%)
Keyes (R)	16,916	(7%)
Other	4,273	(2%)

2000 Democratic Presidential Primary
Gore (D)	198,264	(92%)
Bradley (D)	11,323	(5%)
Other	5,616	(3%)

Gov. Don Sundquist (R)

Elected 1994, term expires Jan. 2003, 2d term; b. Mar. 15, 1936, Moline, IL; home, Memphis; Augustana Col., B.A. 1957; Lutheran; married (Martha).

Military Career: Navy, 1957–59.

Elected Office: U.S. House of Reps., 1982–94.

Professional Career: Jostens, Inc., 1962–72; Pres. & Partner, Graphic Sales of Amer., 1972–82; Shelby Cnty. Repub. Chmn., 1976–78; Campaign Mgr., Howard Baker for President, 1979; Co-founder, Red, Hot & Blue Restaurant.

Office: State Capitol, 7th Ave. & Charlotte, Nashville, 37243, 615-741-2001; Fax: 615-741-1416; Web site: www.state.tn.us.

Election Results
1998 general	Don Sundquist (R)	669,973	(69%)
	John Jay Hooker (D)	287,750	(29%)
	Others	18,513	(2%)
1998 primary	Don Sundquist (R)	358,014	(93%)
	Shirley Beck-Vosse (R)	28,912	(7%)
1994 general	Don Sundquist (R)	807,104	(54%)
	Phil Bredesen (D)	664,252	(45%)

Sen. Fred D. Thompson (R)

Elected 1994, seat up 2002, 1st term; b. Aug. 19, 1942, Sheffield, AL; home, Nashville; Memphis St. U., B.S. 1964, Vanderbilt U. Law Schl., J.D. 1967; Protestant; divorced.

Professional Career: Practicing Atty,. 1967–94; Asst. US Atty., Middle TN Dist., 1969–72; Minority Cnsl., U.S. Sen. Watergate Cmte., 1973–74; Special Cnsl., TN Gov. Lamar Alexander, 1980; Special Cnsl., U.S. Sen. Foreign Relations Cmte., 1980–81; Special Cnsl., U.S. Sen. Intelligence Cmte., 1982; TN Appellate Court Nom. Comm., 1985–87; Author; Actor.

DC Office: 521 DSOB, 20515, 202-224-4944; Fax: 202-228-3679; Web site: www.senate.gov/~thompson.

State Offices: Chattanooga, 423-752-5337; Jackson, 901-423-9344; Knoxville, 865-545-4253; Memphis, 901-544-4224; Nashville, 615-736-5129; Tri-Cities, 423-325-6217.

Committees: *Finance*: Health Care; International Trade; Taxation & IRS Oversight. *Governmental Affairs* (RMM). *Intelligence (Select)*.

Group Ratings
	ADA	ACLU	AFS	LCV	CON	ITIC	NTU	COC	ACU	NTLC	CHC
2000	0	14	0	0	26	77	75	93	92	97	77
1999	5	—	0	0	26	—	80	71	84	—	—

National Journal Ratings

	1999 LIB	—	1999 CONS		2000 LIB	—	2000 CONS
Economic	37%	—	60%		0%	—	86%
Social	8%	—	88%		38%	—	60%
Foreign	16%	—	77%		17%	—	75%

Key Votes of the 106th Congress

1. Educ. Savings Accts.	Y	5. Review Movie Violence	N	9. NATO War in Serbia	N
2. Prescrip. Drug Benefit	N	6. Gun Show Bckgrnd. Checks	N	10. Table Cuba Travel Ban	Y
3. Delay Ergonomic Standards	Y	7. Ban Part.-Birth Abortion	Y	11. Nuclear Test-Ban Treaty	N
4. Phase Out Estate Tax	Y	8. Broaden Hate Crimes List	N	12. Perm. Trade with China	Y

Election Results

1996 general	Fred D. Thompson (R)	1,091,554	(61%)	($3,469,369)
	Houston Gordon (D)	654,937	(37%)	($795,969)
	Others	32,173	(2%)	
1996 primary	Fred D. Thompson (R)	266,549	(94%)	
	Jim F. Counts (R)	16,715	(6%)	
1994 general	Fred D. Thompson (R)	885,998	(60%)	($3,793,813)
	Jim Cooper (D)	565,930	(39%)	($3,979,425)

Sen. Bill Frist (R)

Elected 1994, seat up 2006, 2d term; b. Feb. 22, 1952, Nashville; home, Nashville; Princeton U., A.B. 1974, Harvard Med. Schl., M.D. 1978; Presbyterian; married (Karyn).

Professional Career: Practicing surgeon, 1978–94; Dir., Vanderbilt Medical Ctr. Heart-Lung Transplant Program, 1986–93.

DC Office: 416 RSOB, 20510, 202-224-3344; Fax: 202-228-1264; Web site: www.senate.gov/~frist.

State Offices: Chattanooga, 423-894-2203; Jackson, 901-424-9655; Kingsport, 423-323-1252; Knoxville, 423-602-7977; Memphis, 901-683-1910; Nashville, 615-352-9411.

Committees: *NRSC Chairman. Budget. Foreign Relations*: African Affairs (RMM); International Operations & Terrorism; Near Eastern & South Asian Affairs. *Health, Education, Labor & Pensions*: Children & Families; Public Health (RMM).

Group Ratings

	ADA	ACLU	AFS	LCV	CON	ITIC	NTU	COC	ACU	NTLC	CHC
2000	0	14	0	0	67	91	74	86	92	97	92
1999	0	—	0	0	8	—	73	100	92	—	—

National Journal Ratings

	1999 LIB	—	1999 CONS		2000 LIB	—	2000 CONS
Economic	30%	—	68%		0%	—	86%
Social	36%	—	59%		30%	—	68%
Foreign	23%	—	67%		27%	—	67%

Key Votes of the 106th Congress

1. Educ. Savings Accts.	Y	5. Review Movie Violence	Y	9. NATO War in Serbia	N
2. Prescrip. Drug Benefit	N	6. Gun Show Bckgrnd. Checks	N	10. Table Cuba Travel Ban	Y
3. Delay Ergonomic Standards	Y	7. Ban Part.-Birth Abortion	Y	11. Nuclear Test-Ban Treaty	N
4. Phase Out Estate Tax	Y	8. Broaden Hate Crimes List	N	12. Perm. Trade with China	Y

FIRST DISTRICT

Between the corduroy-like ridges of the Appalachian chains, as they bend west and then south, the valley of Virginia extends far into northeastern Tennessee. The communities of this region—a hilly patchwork of industrial centers, small farms and federal land—were largely shaped by the building of railroads in the 1850s. The land rush immediately after the Revolutionary War populated the area; here in tiny Jonesborough the early settlers established the free state of Franklin in 1784, and many pioneer cabins, federal mansions and Greek Revival churches are lovingly preserved. It was the railroads, however, that determined the winners and losers. Other Appalachian areas were cut off from the rest of America, with tracks running only to the coal mines, but the small industrial cities that had grown up here—Johnson City, Kingsport, Bristol—were on the main lines of national commerce even before the Civil War. The War had a different political effect here than in most of the South: northeast Tennessee, the home of wartime Governor and then Vice President Andrew Johnson, had few slaves and with its connection to northern industry was Union territory. It remains heavily Republican to this day.

The political continuity is all the more surprising because this area has had continuous economic growth and has developed the sort of industrial economy which produced unions and Democrats in the North. Its growth has been helped by modest wage levels, a skilled and hard-working labor force, low electric power rates because of the Tennessee Valley Authority and good transportation routes (rail lines and now Interstate 81). Its small cities boast major paper and printing plants, and have the look of comfortable, clean, 1920s factory towns. Growth has been rapid only around Sevier County, where Gatlinburg and Pigeon Forge (home of Dolly Parton's Dollywood theme park) are the main tourist centers for travelers to the Great Smoky Mountains National Park, with more than 14,000 motel and hotel rooms and numerous attractions.

The far northeastern end of Tennessee forms the 1st Congressional District, a district so heavily Republican that it has not elected a Democrat to the House for more than 100 years. Nonetheless, it has had turbulent politics on occasion. For almost 40 years (1921–61, with one four-year and one two-year hiatus), the seat was held by B. Carroll Reece, a fierce mountain politician who was Republican National chairman from 1946–48. After Reece died in 1961, and his widow was elected to fill out his term, there was a hotly contested primary in 1962. The winner, Jimmy Quillen, a bread-and-butter politician and former owner of the *Johnson City Times*, represented the 1st for the next 34 years.

The congressman from the 1st District now is Bill Jenkins, elected in 1996. Jenkins is a lawyer from Rogersville in Hawkins County, and a farmer who raises beef cattle and grows burley tobacco. He was elected to the state House in 1962, at 25. In 1969 the state House was evenly split between Democrats and Republicans, and Jenkins was elected speaker, the only Republican to serve in that position in the 20th Century. In 1971 he was named to the TVA Board of Directors; he served as commissioner of the state Department of Conservation; in 1990 he was elected Circuit Court Judge. When Quillen announced his retirement, Jenkins resigned his judgeship to run for Congress. He was one of 11 Republicans—the Quillen 11—who filed to run in the August 1996 primary. Tennessee has no runoff, and this was what political scientist V.O. Key called a "friends and neighbors" primary: there were few perceptible differences on issues, and candidates struggled to get enough votes out in their home areas to win. Jenkins won with just 18% of the votes, including 74% in Hawkins County. In second, just 331 votes behind, was state Senator Jim Holcomb, who had conservative Christian activist support. The general election was anticlimactic; Jenkins won 65%–32%.

In the House, Jenkins has a strong conservative voting record. From the start, he began tending to local needs, pressing the EPA to deny a wastewater discharge permit and variance to Champion International's paper mill just across the Pigeon River in Canton, North Carolina. He promised to look out for tobacco farmers. He wants to restore the deductibility of state sales taxes, a move that would help Tennesseans, who have no state income tax. He defended TVA from criticism of its plan to lease $70,000 worth of luxury sky boxes at the Bristol Motor Speedway. Like Quillen, Jenkins has no press secretary but, unlike Quillen, he seldom returned Tennessee reporters' phone calls. "The P.R. aspects of it are not that essential for him," a district staffer explained. That helped him to save more than $200,000 from the roughly $800,000 that House members are allotted for office expenses. "I believe that we need to set an example for others who spend money in the government," he told the *Knoxville News-Sentinel*. But he did hold many open-door sessions in the district. He was perhaps the quietest member of the Judiciary Committee in its impeachment sessions, but firmly supported impeachment.

It was obvious that the key obstacle to a second term for Jenkins would be the August 1998 Republican primary. Many of his 1996 opponents did not regard the result as final and itched to run, but one after another dropped out. But Holcomb, the second-place finisher in 1996, sharply attacked Jenkins's vote for normal trade relations with China on his radio show "There Ought to Be a Law," and announced his candidacy in March 1998. The chairman of the Sullivan County Republican Party resigned to support him. But others rallied to the incumbent: House Majority Leader Dick Armey attended a Jenkins fundraiser in April, and later that month Jimmy Quillen appeared at Jenkins' re-election announcement. Holcomb, who had not been able to raise much money, dropped out of the race in May. Jenkins was unopposed in August and won easily in November. In 2000, after getting the federal courthouse in Greeneville named after Quillen, Jenkins ran without major-party opposition.

Cook's Call *Safe.* The only thing Jenkins has to worry about in this solidly Republican district is a serious primary challenge. But as an incumbent with two good victories under his belt, it is hard to see why he would be contested.

THE PEOPLE: Pop. 2000: 628,443; Pop. 1990: 541,978, up 16% 1990–2000. 96.2% White, 2% Black, 0.4% Asian, 0.2% Amer. Indian, 0.8% Two+ races, 0.4% Other; 1% Hispanic Origin.

2000 Presidential Vote			1996 Presidential Vote		
Bush (R)	132,115	(61%)	Dole (R)	107,668	(54%)
Gore (D)	80,513	(37%)	Clinton (D)	73,681	(37%)
Nader (Green)	1,979	(1%)	Perot (I)	14,532	(7%)
Others	1,475	(1%)			

Rep. Bill Jenkins (R)

Elected 1996, 3d term; b. Nov. 29, 1936, Detroit, MI; home, Rogersville; TN Tech., B.B.A. 1957, U. of TN, J.D. 1961; Baptist; married (Kathryn).

Military Career: Army, 1960–62.

Elected Office: TN Assembly, 1962–71, Speaker, 1969–71; TN Circuit Court Judge, 1990–96.

Professional Career: Farmer, 1961–present; Practicing atty., 1961–90; Commissioner, TN Dept. of Conservation, 1971–72; Dir., TN Valley Authority, 1971–78.

DC Office: 1708 LHOB 20515, 202-225-6356; Fax: 202-225-5714; Web site: www.house.gov/jenkins.

District Office: Kingsport, 423-247-8161.

Committees: *Agriculture* (12th of 27 R): General Farm Commodities & Risk Management; Specialty Crops & Foreign Agriculture Programs. *Judiciary* (10th of 21 R): Courts, the Internet & Intellectual Property; The Constitution.

Group Ratings

	ADA	ACLU	AFS	LCV	CON	ITIC	NTU	COC	ACU	NTLC	CHC
2000	0	21	0	7	32	90	59	80	91	75	93
1999	15	—	0	13	12	—	55	84	87	—	

National Journal Ratings

	1999 LIB —	1999 CONS	2000 LIB —	2000 CONS
Economic	30%	64%	24%	75%
Social	4%	91%	26%	71%
Foreign	20%	78%	0%	88%

Key Votes of the 106th Congress

1. Patient Bill of Rights	Y	5. Bar RU-486 $ for FDA	Y	9. NATO War in Serbia	N
2. Accelerate Min. Wage	N	6. Display 10 Commandments	Y	10. Perm. Trade with China	Y
3. Strike Ban on Ergo. Stnd.	N	7. Gun Show Bkgrnd. Checks	N	11. Debt Relief for 3rd World	N
4. Ovrd. Estate Tax Veto	Y	8. Ban Part.-Birth Abortion	Y	12. Drop Cuba Econ. Embargo	N

Election Results

2000 general	Bill Jenkins (R)	unopposed		($92,463)
2000 primary	Bill Jenkins (R)	unopposed		
1998 general	Bill Jenkins (R)	68,904	(69%)	($336,612)
	Kay C. White (D)	30,710	(31%)	($39,296)

SECOND DISTRICT

Knoxville, the largest city in east Tennessee, is nestled between mountain ridges where the Holston and French Broad Rivers join to form the Tennessee River. It was established not long after the first wave of pioneers came through the gaps and down between the mountains of the Appalachian chain. During the Civil War it was Union territory, and it has remained Republican in allegiance ever since: the ancestral tug of Tennessee politics. But its Republican heritage is tempered by another tradition, that of the Tennessee Valley Authority. A venturesome program when created in the 1930s, it is now part of the fabric of life in east Tennessee, sometimes criticized as its cheap hydroelectric power capacity was filled and more of its production came from expensive and sometimes poorly functioning nuclear plants.

Both TVA and the region have been undergoing turbulent changes in recent years. TVA has cut its payroll sharply and held down rates; in a newly competitive electricity market, its director has proposed abandoning federal subsidies and spinning off navigation and flood control functions to state or federal agencies; but TVA is laboring under billions of dollars in debt mostly incurred in building nuclear power plants. In other ways Knoxville has been down on its luck. Education entrepreneur Christopher Whittle's projects fell short of financial goals, leaving his Harvard-style campus in downtown Knoxville to be sold to the federal government for a courthouse complex. The banking empire of 1982 World's Fair promoter (and 1978 Democratic governor nominee) Jake Butcher collapsed in scandal in 1983 and the remains of the World's Fair have been a 20-year embarrassment as local officials proposed more than a dozen redevelopment plans; but a new convention center is finally slated to open in July 2002. Meanwhile, a developer in April 2001 announced plans to build the Knoxville Universe, a tourist attraction-educational center to span two downtown blocks and rise 23 stories.

The 2d Congressional District of Tennessee, which includes Knoxville and several mountainous counties to the south, including fast-growing Blount County, is one of the nation's most reliably Republican districts and one of the more practical-minded.

The congressman from the district is Jimmy Duncan, a Republican elected in 1988; his father, who was senior Republican on the House Ways and Means Committee, represented the 2nd from 1964 until his death in May 1988. Duncan studied in Knoxville and Washington, practiced law and was a trial judge in the 1980s. When his father died, he won the seat despite a spirited challenge from Democrat Dudley Taylor, a scion of another prominent east Tennessee political family. Taylor attacked Duncan for signing up with the National Guard in 1970 and for his ties to Butcher, but Duncan won with 57% in the special and 56% in November. He has been re-elected easily.

For six years, Duncan chaired the Aviation Subcommittee of Transportation and Infrastructure, dealing with issues like airline ticket taxes, aviation safety and unruly airplane passengers. With committee chairman Bud Shuster, he helped to enact the AIR-21 renewal of the aviation program, including its trust fund. He sponsored bills to encourage lower air fares for small airports like ones in Knoxville and Chattanooga, including federal loan guarantees for regional jets and allotting new slots at LaGuardia, Kennedy, Reagan and O'Hare Airports for airlines that provide new service to underserved airports. He raised questions about the anticompetitive effect of the proposed merger of United Airlines and US Airways. Because of term limits, he switched in 2001 to chair the Water Resources Subcommittee. He has a conservative voting record and likes to spotlight questionable projects like NASA's $12 million to search for extraterrestrial intelligence. He called the space station "the biggest boondoggle in the history of Congress." Duncan opposed the U.S. troop deployment to Bosnia, questioned the Mexico bailout, criticized Alan Greenspan for actions to prop up Japanese banks, and opposed permanent normal trade relations with China. He showed independence from party lines when he voted against term limits and for the Shays-Meehan campaign finance bill.

Duncan voted in 1997 to end subsidies for sugar, peanuts and tobacco—not an obvious vote-winner back home. Later he questioned excessive bonuses and pensions for TVA executives and won enactment of his bill to switch the appointment of TVA's inspector general to the president, instead of the TVA board. Duncan hasn't been shy about seeking funding for other local projects, from resurfacing the Foothills Parkway in the Great Smoky Mountains National Park to a rail and trolley system for downtown Knoxville. Duncan is chief sponsor of a National Parks check-off on the income tax form, which would provide more funding for U.S. parks, including the Great Smoky Mountains National Park. He predicted that the Bush administration would approve empowerment zone funding for Knoxville.

Cook's Call *Safe*. Duncan has had little competition for this solidly Republican seat during the last seven elections. There is no reason to think that he will be challenged seriously in 2002.

THE PEOPLE: Pop. 2000: 636,383; Pop. 1990: 541,780, up 17.5% 1990–2000. 90.7% White, 6.3% Black, 1% Asian, 0.3% Amer. Indian, 1.1% Two+ races, 0.6% Other; 1.4% Hispanic Origin.

2000 Presidential Vote			1996 Presidential Vote		
Bush (R)	96,948	(58%)	Dole (R)	117,248	(51%)
Gore (D)	66,226	(40%)	Clinton (D)	95,810	(42%)
Nader (Green)	2,032	(1%)	Perot (I)	12,522	(5%)
Others	1,326	(1%)			

Rep. John J. Duncan, Jr. (R)

Elected 1988, 7th term; b. July 21, 1947, Lebanon; home, Knoxville; U. of TN, B.S. 1969, George Washington U., J.D. 1973; Presbyterian; married (Lynn).

Military Career: Army Natl. Guard & Army Reserves, 1970–87.

Professional Career: Practicing atty., 1973–81; TN St. Trial Judge, 1981–88.

DC Office: 2400 RHOB 20515, 202-225-5435; Fax: 202-225-6440; Web site: www.house.gov/duncan.

District Offices: Athens, 423-745-4671; Knoxville, 865-523-3772; Maryville, 865-984-5464.

Committees: *Government Reform* (24th of 24 R). *Resources* (6th of 28 R): Forests & Forest Health; National Parks, Recreation & Public Lands. *Transportation & Infrastructure* (5th of 42 R): Aviation; Highways & Transit; Water Resources & Environment (Chmn.).

Group Ratings

	ADA	ACLU	AFS	LCV	CON	ITIC	NTU	COC	ACU	NTLC	CHC
2000	15	14	14	14	73	44	71	71	84	88	93
1999	25	—	0	13	84	—	75	56	92	—	—

National Journal Ratings

	1999 LIB	—	1999 CONS		2000 LIB	—	2000 CONS
Economic	41%	—	57%		18%	—	76%
Social	4%	—	91%		34%	—	65%
Foreign	3%	—	92%		49%	—	49%

Key Votes of the 106th Congress

1. Patient Bill of Rights	Y	5. Bar RU-486 $ for FDA	Y	9. NATO War in Serbia	N
2. Accelerate Min. Wage	N	6. Display 10 Commandments	Y	10. Perm. Trade with China	N
3. Strike Ban on Ergo. Stnd.	N	7. Gun Show Bkgrnd. Checks	N	11. Debt Relief for 3rd World	N
4. Ovrd. Estate Tax Veto	Y	8. Ban Part.-Birth Abortion	Y	12. Drop Cuba Econ. Embargo	N

Election Results

2000 general	John J. Duncan Jr. (R)	187,154	(89%)	($342,829)
	Kevin J. Rowland (Lib)	22,304	(11%)	
2000 primary	John J. Duncan Jr. (R)	unopposed		
1998 general	John J. Duncan Jr. (R)	90,860	(89%)	($288,566)
	Robert O. Watson (I)	4,372	(4%)	
	Greg Samples (I)	4,332	(4%)	
	Others	2,938	(3%)	

THIRD DISTRICT

Through some of the most vivid scenery of the Appalachian chain, etching its way through the serrated ridges of east Tennessee, is the river that gave Tennessee its name. From Knoxville, the river cuts through a ridge and then plunges down a long valley to the city of Chattanooga at the Georgia line. There it switches course again, winding around the table-top Lookout Mountain and then moving into northern Alabama. Chattanooga, the city at the base of Lookout Mountain, was just a village when it was a Civil War battlefield; after the war, it became the industrial "Dynamo of Dixie." A quarter-century ago it was labeled America's most polluted city. But regional political leaders, prodded by the influential and civic-minded remnants of its Industrial Age aristocracy, used creative measures, such as a locally built electric shuttle bus, to reduce pollution and spruce up the city's scenic river banks. Chattanooga is now the proud home of the 12-story-high Tennessee Aquarium, the world's largest fresh water aquarium, with an exhibit in which you can follow the course of a drop of rain from the headwaters of the Tennessee until it flows out the Mississippi River into the Gulf.

The 3d Congressional District of Tennessee is centered on Chattanooga, with an irregular outline that has a political provenance. It reaches far north to take in Oak Ridge, a highly educated enclave that is still shaped by the can-do ideals of the New Deal pioneers who secretly constructed it from virgin Appalachian forest during World War II in order to house the key nuclear facility that is now called the Oak Ridge National Laboratory. From there, the district avoids heavily Republican counties as it reaches east to the North Carolina line and west to the Cumberland Plateau. In recent years, the region has pinned its hopes for growth more on the private sector and less on the public sector institutions that had heretofore shaped it. The Tennessee Valley Authority, buffeted by a changing energy market and pro-competition moves in Congress, has slashed its workforce from its 1980 peak of more than 50,000 to less than 13,500 in 1999; the Oak Ridge National Laboratory, faced with shifting priorities in the post-Cold War era, has also cut its staff. Oak Ridge officials now take pains to sponsor entrepreneurial efforts to market the lab's discoveries; further south, outside Chattanooga, the Army's enormous Volunteer TNT plant, which had been dormant since 1977, now pitches itself as a place where private businesses can set up shop. Downtown Chattanooga's revival was accomplished with a 4–1 ratio of private money to government cash.

The congressman from the 3d District is Zach Wamp, a Republican elected in 1994. Wamp left college before graduating to become a real estate developer in Chattanooga, selling $22 million in real estate in five years. In 1992 he ran a high-voltage race for Congress against 20-year Democratic incumbent Marilyn Lloyd. At the start, Wamp revealed he had used cocaine and received treatment for it 10 years earlier. Wamp carried Chattanooga and Hamilton County 51%–44%. Overall, Lloyd won by just 49%–47%, the closest margin of her career; with that, she decided to retire. In 1994 Wamp ran again as a strong conservative; one proposal was to pay members of Congress the same as a lieutenant colonel and billet them in officer housing. Democrat Randy Button won a close primary and attacked Wamp's character. Wamp accused Button of flip-flopping on issues, attacked him for taking PAC money, and, like many Republicans, ran an ad showing his opponent's face morphing into Bill Clinton's. Wamp trailed the statewide Republican ticket, but still won, carrying Hamilton County 54%–43% and losing the Oak Ridge area only narrowly, for an overall win of 52%–46%.

In the House, Wamp got a seat on the Appropriations Committee. He has a conservative record laced with locally appealing stands. He called himself "a heat-seeking missile on behalf of Tennessee and my district." He got $25 million for flood control in East Ridge, $3 million for the Chattanooga Police Department's new computer system, and funding for natural gas lines to Meigs County. He supported study of a Chattanooga-to-Atlanta high-speed rail route, secured funding to repair the deteriorating Chickamauga Lock in Chattanooga, and has sought to attract new industries to parts of the Oak Ridge reservation and Chattanooga's former Army ammunition plant. He won Bill Clinton's approval of an appropriations measure to provide additional benefits for employees with work-related illnesses at Oak Ridge, a city with a tongue-in-cheek reputation for people who "glow in the dark."

Despite his generally conservative record, Wamp has taken some maverick stances. His support for TVA, including opposition to Rodney Frelinghuysen's attempt to sell off its non-hydro power plants, annoyed many conservatives. He has never accepted PAC money and he vocally supported the McCain-Feingold campaign finance bill, a stance that irritated the Republican leadership and prompted the National Right to Life Committee to run radio ads against him, even though he is opposed to abortion; the committee feared that the bill would prevent it from running issue-advocacy ads at campaign time. He called for reforming managed health care to ensure that patients "get the treatment they need," showed little zeal to abolish racial preferences and placed preservation of Social Security above tax cuts. Among House Republicans, he unsuccessfully sought after the 2000 election to repeal the three-term limit on chairmanships. He helped to arrange a rented home on Capitol Hill with three other House Republicans and three Democrats. "My attitude toward the Congress has changed," Wamp told *The New York Times Magazine*. "We must realize public service is a great way of life. I came in with the attitude there were a bunch of thieves here. That's not true."

In 1996 he faced a spirited challenge from Chuck Jolly, the second-place finisher in the 1994 Democratic primary. With Marilyn Lloyd's endorsement, Wamp won 56%–43%, an improvement on 1994 and nearly 10 points ahead of Bob Dole. In 2000 his Democratic opponent made headlines only when, at the Democratic convention in Los Angeles, he proposed marriage to his girlfriend, a state House Democratic aide. Wamp was reelected 64%–35%. Redistricting could change the shape of the district, although probably to Wamp's liking; the Democratic legislature may want to detach some rural counties to make the adjacent 4th District more Democratic.

Cook's Call *Safe.* Wamp seems to have found the right formula to hold on to this district. While the 3rd has a deep Democratic heritage, it has been trending Republican for the last few years. Dole won here by 1% in 1996 and Bush won by 11% in 2000.

THE PEOPLE: Pop. 2000: 595,855; Pop. 1990: 542,065, up 9.9% 1990–2000. 85.2% White, 11.9% Black, 0.9% Asian, 0.3% Amer. Indian, 1.1% Two+ races, 0.6% Other; 1.5% Hispanic Origin.

2000 Presidential Vote		
Bush (R)	127,262	(55%)
Gore (D)	101,734	(44%)
Nader (Green)	2,299	(1%)
Others	1,728	(1%)

1996 Presidential Vote		
Dole (R)	93,799	(47%)
Clinton (D)	92,780	(46%)
Perot (I)	13,284	(7%)

Rep. Zach Wamp (R)

Elected 1994, 4th term; b. Oct. 28, 1957, Fort Benning, GA; home, Chattanooga; U. of NC, 1976–77, 1979–80, U. of TN, 1978–79; Baptist; married (Kim).

Professional Career: Regional Sales Super., 1981–82, Partner, Wamp Alliance Architectural Devel. Co., 1983–89; Real Estate broker, 1989–94.

DC Office: 423 CHOB 20515, 202-225-3271; Fax: 202-225-3494; Web site: www.house.gov/wamp.

District Offices: Chattanooga, 423-756-2342; Oak Ridge, 865-576-1976.

Committees: *Appropriations* (23d of 35 R): Energy & Water Development; Interior; The Legislative Branch.

Group Ratings

	ADA	ACLU	AFS	LCV	CON	ITIC	NTU	COC	ACU	NTLC	CHC
2000	10	29	14	14	81	61	59	71	87	85	87
1999	20	—	0	13	60	—	62	60	96	—	—

National Journal Ratings

	1999 LIB	—	1999 CONS		2000 LIB	—	2000 CONS
Economic	39%	—	59%		15%	—	83%
Social	23%	—	76%		23%	—	74%
Foreign	3%	—	92%		22%	—	76%

Key Votes of the 106th Congress

1. Patient Bill of Rights	Y	5. Bar RU-486 $ for FDA	Y	9. NATO War in Serbia	N
2. Accelerate Min. Wage	N	6. Display 10 Commandments	Y	10. Perm. Trade with China	N
3. Strike Ban on Ergo. Stnd.	N	7. Gun Show Bkgrnd. Checks	N	11. Debt Relief for 3rd World	N
4. Ovrd. Estate Tax Veto	Y	8. Ban Part.-Birth Abortion	Y	12. Drop Cuba Econ. Embargo	N

Election Results

2000 general	Zach Wamp (R)	139,840	(64%)	($737,216)
	William L. Callaway (D)	75,785	(35%)	($232,095)
	Others	3,315	(2%)	
2000 primary	Zach Wamp (R)	unopposed		
1998 general	Zach Wamp (R)	75,100	(66%)	($384,227)
	James M. Lewis Jr. (D)	37,144	(33%)	($27,074)

FOURTH DISTRICT

The invisible line between Civil War Republican and Civil War Democratic territory runs along the Cumberland Plateau, the westernmost upswelling of the Appalachians, west of the valley where the Tennessee River runs south from Knoxville to Chattanooga. It separates the Tennessee Valley, which had few slaves and whose economic ties were with the North, from the rolling farmlands of middle Tennessee, first settled by Andrew Jackson in the 1790s and resolutely Democratic from the time he became the first president to call himself a Democrat in the 1830s. And not only is this line invisible, it is also irregular: some counties in west Tennessee, where the Tennessee River runs north from Alabama to Kentucky, are Union Republican.

The 4th Congressional District runs across this line and crosses Tennessee northeast to southwest, from Lee County, Virginia, all the way to Tishomingo County, Mississippi. It is some 300 miles long, yet seldom more than one county wide. The district includes Sewanee, the pleasant home of the University of the South, and Dayton, where in 1925 John Scopes was prosecuted by William Jennings Bryan and defended by Clarence Darrow for teaching Darwin's theory of evolution. Jack Daniels whiskey has been made for generations in Lynchburg, which appears every bit the idealized small town that the distillery's folksy, black-and-white advertisements make it out to be.

The congressman from the 4th District is Van Hilleary, a Republican elected in 1994. Hilleary grew up in Spring City, where he helped start the family textile company; after college he served in the Air Force, went to law school and volunteered for duty in the Persian Gulf, where he flew 24 missions on a C-130. In 1992, at 33, he ran for the state Senate against 18-year incumbent Anna Belle Clement O'Brien, sister of former Governor Frank Clement, and lost by only 52%–48% despite her much greater fame and financing. In 1994, when 4th District incumbent Democrat Jim Cooper ran for the Senate, Hilleary easily won a three-way primary with 58%, arguing for term limits, welfare reform, tougher sentencing and PAC-donation limits. In the general, Hilleary faced Democrat Jeff Whorley, at 34 a veteran of campaigns since he was 18 and a one-time aide to 6th District Democrat Bart Gordon. Whorley favored a mostly a conservative platform and spent $225,000 more than Hilleary, who took no PAC money. Hilleary carried the eastern Republican counties by wide margins, and he carried the far western counties, where Whorley was hurt by a harsh primary campaign. These offset his losses in the middle Tennessee counties; overall, Hilleary won 57%–42%.

Hilleary has had a consistently conservative record. In his second full month in the House, he was in the spotlight for sponsoring a term-limit constitutional amendment—the first freshman to put an amendment to a vote since 1897. Hilleary's version, which would have limited members to 12 years or less if required by state law, was caught between advocates of six- and 12-year term limits and failed, 164–265. Hilleary was more successful on a quieter issue: an amendment to kill a $1,000 docking fee imposed by the Tennessee Valley Authority's Shoreline Management Initiative on anyone who builds or improves a dock on the TVA's lakes. Hilleary's amendment passed, but was killed in conference by pro-TVA Republican Jimmy Quillen. However, Hilleary snuck his dock deposit ban into the October 1996 continuing resolution and it became law. Writer Linda Killian focused on Hilleary as "the perfect everyman of the freshman class" in her 1998 book *The Freshmen: What Happened to the Republican Revolution?*

In the 105th Congress Hilleary got a seat on the Budget Committee and was named a deputy whip. But he still showed independence of the leadership. He refused to back reinstatement of the airline ticket tax without an offsetting tax cut; later he became involved with a group of dissident Republicans concerned about the party's "leadership vacuum." Although Hilleary later said that the group did not initiate the July 1997 coup against Speaker Newt Gingrich, as some reports indicated, he said he and his friends "talked about it quite a bit." He pushed unsuccessfully to end the U.S. troop deployment in Bosnia by December 1997 and opposed military actions in Serbia and Kosovo in 1999. He favored permanent normal trade relations with China as a boost to small family farmers.

Democrats continued to run well-funded opponents against him. In 1996 Hilleary faced Mark Stewart, whose grandfather, A. Tom Stewart, had been a U.S. senator from 1939–49. Although Bill Clinton carried the district 46%–45%, Hilleary outspent his opponent 2–1 and won 58%–41%, carrying every county but two. In 1998, Hilleary faced lumber company owner and 14-year state Senator Jerry Cooper, who had the support of Vice President Gore and former Governor Ned Ray McWherter. Hilleary, despite a continued rejection of PAC money, outspent Cooper more than 2–1 and won 60%–40%. In 2000, Hilleary had an easier contest, against an attorney who attacked him for inaction on health-care issues and was hoping for a boost from Al Gore's presidential campaign. But Gore lost the district 55%–44% and Hilleary won 66%–33%, carrying every county.

Democrats control the state legislature, and could try to make the 4th District more Democratic. In 2000 Hilleary was openly contemplating running for governor in 2002; an early poll gave him a lead in a potential Republican primary, but probably reflected the fact that neither he nor other tested candidates was widely known, and his district puts him in more media markets.

Cook's Call *Competitive.* Hilleary's big wins here in the past four elections belie the very marginal nature of this district. But with Hilleary almost certain to run for governor in 2002, Democrats see a tremendous opportunity to put this traditionally Democratic seat back into their column, especially since they control the redistricting process. Still, Tennessee continues to trend away from its Democratic roots (just ask Al Gore).

THE PEOPLE: Pop. 2000: 635,355; Pop. 1990: 541,650, up 17.3% 1990–2000. 94.1% White, 3.4% Black, 0.3% Asian, 0.3% Amer. Indian, 0.9% Two+ races, 1% Other; 2.1% Hispanic Origin.

2000 Presidential Vote			1996 Presidential Vote		
Bush (R)	159,181	(55%)	Clinton (D)	92,106	(46%)
Gore (D)	126,941	(44%)	Dole (R)	90,135	(45%)
Nader (Green)	2,248	(1%)	Perot (I)	14,816	(7%)
Others	1,903	(1%)			

Rep. Van Hilleary (R)

Elected 1994, 4th term; b. June 20, 1959, Dayton; home, Spring City; U. of TN, B.S. 1981, Samford U. Law Schl., J.D. 1990; Presbyterian; married (Meredith).

Military Career: Air Force, 1982, Air Force Reserves, 1982-present (Persian Gulf).

Professional Career: Dir., Planning & Business Devel., SSM Industries Inc., 1984–86, 1992–94.

DC Office: 114 CHOB 20515, 202-225-6831; Fax: 202-225-3272; Web site: www.house.gov/hilleary.

District Offices: Crossville, 931-484-1114; Morristown, 423-587-0396; Tullahoma, 931-393-4764.

Committees: *Armed Services* (16th of 32 R): Military Readiness; Military Research & Development (Vice Chmn.). *Budget* (6th of 24 R). *Education & the Workforce* (15th of 27 R): Education Reform; Select Education.

Group Ratings

	ADA	ACLU	AFS	LCV	CON	ITIC	NTU	COC	ACU	NTLC	CHC
2000	0	21	0	0	27	83	64	80	92	91	93
1999	15	—	0	13	44	—	65	83	96	—	—

National Journal Ratings

	1999 LIB —	1999 CONS		2000 LIB —	2000 CONS
Economic	16% —	78%		0% —	94%
Social	4% —	91%		0% —	79%
Foreign	0% —	97%		24% —	76%

Key Votes of the 106th Congress

1. Patient Bill of Rights	N	5. Bar RU-486 $ for FDA	Y	9. NATO War in Serbia	N
2. Accelerate Min. Wage	N	6. Display 10 Commandments	Y	10. Perm. Trade with China	Y
3. Strike Ban on Ergo. Stnd.	N	7. Gun Show Bkgrnd. Checks	N	11. Debt Relief for 3rd World	N
4. Ovrd. Estate Tax Veto	Y	8. Ban Part.-Birth Abortion	Y	12. Drop Cuba Econ. Embargo	N

Election Results

2000 general	Van Hilleary (R)	133,622	(66%)	($1,320,424)
	David H. Dunaway (D)	67,165	(33%)	($417,105)
	Others	2,423	(1%)	
2000 primary	Van Hilleary (R)	unopposed		
1998 general	Van Hilleary (R)	62,829	(60%)	($1,084,001)
	Jerry W. Cooper (D)	42,627	(40%)	($487,914)

FIFTH DISTRICT

Nashville is the home of country music, the buckle of the Bible Belt, and in almost every way the heart of Tennessee. This was one of the first American cities established west of the Appalachians; Andrew Jackson built his Hermitage nearby above the banks of the Cumberland River, and his political home base has remained Democratic ever since. It was the capital of Tennessee early on, just as it was, and still is, the center of the state's political life and discourse: home to *The Tennessean,* a classically partisan Democratic paper, and the state's biggest television market.

Nashville is proud of its universities and of its columned Capitol and its Parthenon; this is perhaps the greatest center of Greek Revival architecture in America. Nashville is also firmly established as the religious publishing center of the country, producing more bibles than probably any other city in the world. Country music, an art form that emerged from the hardscrabble, mountainous counties of eastern Tennessee, now constitutes a $2 billion-a-year business and is the nation's dominant radio format. The industry, run from a series of deceptively modest homes-turned-offices on what's called Music Row, congregated in Nashville because local radio station WSM possessed a clear channel from which to beam its weekly "barn dances" throughout the South in the 1920s; these later became known as the Grand Ole Opry, and features the longest continuously running radio show in the nation. The venerable institution survived its 1970s move from a downtown tabernacle to Opryland, a giant theme park on the banks of the Cumberland; nearby is the huge Opry Mills mall, a major tourist destination in its own right.

For years, both the city's Parthenon-building elite and its religious leadership resented the growing local influence of country music; the former looked down on the music's uneducated practitioners, while the latter cringed at the musicians' unwholesome travails and occasional indecorous deaths. But all three groups made their peace in the 1970s, and since then Nashville has become one of the South's boom cities—the fastest growing metropolitan area between Atlanta and Dallas-Fort Worth. New-generation industry moved in, with Nissan building a big plant in nearby Smyrna and General Motors setting up its Saturn plant in nearby Spring Hill. There were commercial and apartment real estate booms as well, though naturally followed by some busts. In the 1990s Nashville and Tennessee got their first major-league sports teams, the NFL's Titans and the NHL's Predators. An agreeable quality of life, plenty of medium-wage, high-skill labor, a central location, and absence of urban strife and militant unions have all helped Nashville boom. The dominant cultural tone remains conservative, and the fast-growing surrounding counties have become increasingly Republican, but Nashville and Davidson County remain one of the Democratic bulwarks of Republican-trending Tennessee.

The 5th District of Tennessee includes all but one precinct of Nashville and Davidson County plus the bulk of increasingly suburban Robertson County to the north. The 5th is usually reliably Democratic in statewide elections; to Congress it has long elected rather liberal Democrats—this is, after all, the home of the first Democratic president. It was also for several years the home of Al Gore, when he was a divinity student at Vanderbilt and reporter for *The Tennessean*, and has been as much his home base as his ancestral home near Carthage in Smith County: his campaign was headquartered in Nashville (although he made few visits here, perhaps too few) and the 5th was one of three Tennessee districts to vote for him in 2000.

The congressman from the 5th District is Bob Clement, a Democrat first elected in 1988. His father Frank Clement served three terms as governor of Tennessee. In 1972, at 29, Bob Clement was elected to the Public Service Commission; he served six years, went into private business, sat on the Tennessee Valley Authority board from 1979–81, and in 1982 lost a House race in the 7th District to Don Sundquist, the current governor, by 51%–49%. He then went into real estate and became president of Cumberland University. In 1987, after incumbent Bill Boner resigned one step ahead of an ethics investigation, Clement ran in a special election in the 5th, winning the Democratic primary with 40% and easily winning the special election.

In the House, Clement has compiled a moderate voting record, voting for welfare reform and English as the official language, and taking leading roles in backing the 1997 balanced budget agreement and the International Freedom from Religious Persecution Act. Although he leans toward the Democrats' conservative wing—he voted for repeal of Clinton's ergonomic rule and for Bush's tax cut, he supports most of the party's leading agenda items, from HMO regulation to more funding for local school construction. He believes that Social Security should get a higher return on its investment. He was a key sponsor of the law to criminalize the theft of another person's identity. He has supported music and arts education and has won funding for the restoration of buildings at historically black colleges and universities. He helped form the House Education Caucus, made up of former teachers and administrators in schools and colleges, and served as its co-chairman. He has proposed to eliminate soft money, saying he's "weary of the negative politics." On local issues, he steered $6 million to a commuter line from Nashville to

Lebanon and wants to permit the local system to use tracks owned by the CSX system. He got $700,000 to spruce up neighborhoods around three Nashville college campuses.

Clement has been re-elected by wide margins in the 5th District. He considered running for governor in 1994, but decided not to do so, and was not interested in running in 1998. He talked up his possible candidacy in 2002 and early polls showed him faring well, but in late May 2001 Clement again said he would not run.

Cook's Call *Safe.* Clement, who has never dipped below 60% of the vote in any of his races for this seat, is safely ensconced here. And, while the state itself continues to trend more Republican, this district was one of only three in Tennessee won by Gore in 2000.

THE PEOPLE: Pop. 2000: 607,853; Pop. 1990: 541,878, up 12.2% 1990–2000. 68.3% White, 24.9% Black, 2.2% Asian, 0.3% Amer. Indian, 0.1% Hawaiian, 1.9% Two+ races, 2.3% Other; 4.5% Hispanic Origin.

2000 Presidential Vote

Gore (D)	90,180	(59%)
Bush (R)	59,960	(39%)
Nader (Green)	2,491	(2%)
Others	876	(1%)

1996 Presidential Vote

Clinton (D)	116,987	(55%)
Dole (R)	82,053	(39%)
Perot (I)	9,727	(5%)

Rep. Bob Clement (D)

Elected Jan. 1988, 7th term; b. Sept. 23, 1943, Nashville; home, Nashville; U. of TN, B.S. 1967, Memphis St. U., M.B.A. 1968; Christ Church; married (Mary).

Military Career: Army, 1969–71, Army Natl. Guard, 1971–present.

Elected Office: TN Public Svc. Comm., 1972–78.

Professional Career: Bd. of Dir., TN Valley Authority, 1979–81; Founder & owner, Bob Clement & Assoc., 1981–83; Owner, Charter Equities real estate, 1981–83; Pres., Cumberland U., 1983–87.

DC Office: 2229 RHOB 20515, 202-225-4311; Fax: 202-226-1035; Web site: www.house.gov/clement.

District Offices: N. Nashville, 615-320-1363; Nashville, 615-736-5295; Springfield, 615-384-6600.

Committees: *Budget* (9th of 20 D). *Transportation & Infrastructure* (6th of 34 D): Highways & Transit; Railroads (RMM).

Group Ratings

	ADA	ACLU	AFS	LCV	CON	ITIC	NTU	COC	ACU	NTLC	CHC
2000	60	21	57	50	11	78	35	76	40	24	47
1999	85	—	83	44	63	—	16	68	32	—	—

National Journal Ratings

	1999 LIB	—	1999 CONS		2000 LIB	—	2000 CONS
Economic	57%	—	43%		54%	—	45%
Social	53%	—	47%		52%	—	48%
Foreign	63%	—	36%		64%	—	34%

Key Votes of the 106th Congress

1. Patient Bill of Rights	Y	5. Bar RU-486 $ for FDA	N	9. NATO War in Serbia	Y
2. Accelerate Min. Wage	Y	6. Display 10 Commandments	Y	10. Perm. Trade with China	N
3. Strike Ban on Ergo. Stnd.	N	7. Gun Show Bkgrnd. Checks	N	11. Debt Relief for 3rd World	Y
4. Ovrd. Estate Tax Veto	Y	8. Ban Part.-Birth Abortion	Y	12. Drop Cuba Econ. Embargo	Y

Election Results

2000 general	Bob Clement (D)	149,277	(73%)	($715,189)
	Stan Scott (R)	50,386	(25%)	
	Others	6,270	(3%)	
2000 primary	Bob Clement (D)	unopposed		
1998 general	Bob Clement (D)	74,611	(83%)	($282,219)
	William M. Lancaster (I)	6,162	(7%)	
	Al Borgman (I)	4,983	(6%)	
	Gary I. Wordon (I)	4,345	(5%)	

SIXTH DISTRICT

The rolling countryside of middle Tennessee, west of the Cumberland Plateau and the last chain of Appalachians, has been called "the dimple of the universe." This is hilly and fertile land, cut by deep rivers ambling along in S-curves. The terrain here was never much suited for plantation crops; this has long been a land of small farmers and small county seat towns, nestled amid what people here regard as some of the loveliest scenery on earth. Middle Tennessee has also been one of the heartlands of the Democratic Party. It was the political home base of Andrew Jackson and supported him nearly unanimously; during the Civil War, though it had very few slaves, it resisted the invading Union armies. For 140 years after Jackson, it voted solidly Democratic and elected as its congressmen some of the luminaries of the national Democratic Party: James K. Polk (1825–39), speaker of the House and later president; Cordell Hull (1907–21, 1923–31), later senator and secretary of State; Albert Gore Sr., (1939–53), later senator; and Albert Gore Jr., (1977–85), later senator and vice president.

The 6th Congressional District includes 14 middle Tennessee counties east and south of Nashville, plus one precinct of Nashville itself. The heritage here is old and rural, but economic growth has fanned out into the farmland from Nashville, evident in thousands of jobs created by Japanese companies and American startups, firms fleeing the North and entrepreneurs fleeing taxes. Many new voters here are Republican, not only in the affluent suburbs of Williamson County just south of Nashville, but in the more modest suburbs spreading to the east. The 6th District voted for the Clinton-Gore ticket by 47%–40% in 1992, a margin that would not have impressed Andrew Jackson. In 1996 it voted for the Dole-Kemp ticket 47%–45%. In 2000 it voted 52%–47% for the Bush-Cheney ticket; the margin in the four counties surrounding Nashville was 58%–42%. Back in 1976, when Al Gore was first elected to Congress, the district was so Democratic that Gore won 94% of the vote. Now the 6th District leans Republican, and is trending even more so.

The congressman from the 6th District is Bart Gordon, a Democrat first elected in 1984 when Gore gave up his House seat to run for the Senate. Gordon grew up in Murfreesboro in Rutherford County and went to Middle Tennessee State University. He practiced law and became Tennessee Democratic chairman in 1981: politics has been most of his life. In 1984, he ran a computerized fund-raising operation and voter contact system—then a novelty in this district where a personal handshake from a candidate was the norm. He won a multi-candidate primary with 28% of the vote and won the general election 63%–37%.

In the House, Gordon has used his insider skills to build a close relationship with the Democratic leadership, and got a seat on the Rules Committee in 1987. He passed new accountability provisions for the federal financial aid system in 1992 and claimed that defaults dropped from 22% of loans in 1990 to 12% in 1993—a significant saving for taxpayers. He also helped pass a proposal to ban Pell grants to prison inmates, which amazingly enough has saved between $70 million and $200 million a year. Gordon, who lost his seat on Rules and moved to Commerce when the Republicans took control of the House, has worked to limit children's access to adult material by phone, on television, and on the Internet. With a similar ear for constituents' complaints, he has opposed construction of a temporary nuclear waste dump in middle Tennessee. He also opposed Republican proposals to sell the Southeastern Power Administration, which he says will put the dam-created lakes on the Tennessee and Cumberland rivers up for auction. He secured funds for four new wetlands projects in Rutherford County and worked for the Energy

Department's release of $68 million for the Spallation Neutron Source project at Oak Ridge. On the eve of the 2000 election, he voted with House Republicans to repeal the marriage penalty and the estate tax. A notable accomplishment in the increasingly fit House: Gordon has won for several years the 5K race as the fastest member of Congress; his September 2000 time was 17 minutes, 14 seconds.

Gordon's moderate-to-liberal voting record and his ties to the Democratic leadership in this Republican-trending district caused him trouble in the 1990s. In 1994 he faced Steve Gill, a lawyer from Williamson County and a veteran of a championship basketball team at the University of Tennessee. In a good Republican year, Gill voiced anti-Clinton themes. Gordon spent $1,386,000, with $608,000 of it from PACs—more than Gill spent altogether. Gordon carried the smaller rural counties 58%–42%, for a slim overall margin of 51%–49%. After the election, neither Gill nor Gordon stopped running. Gordon courted local tobacco farmers, even as former tobacco Al Gore was pummeling the tobacco industry at the Chicago convention. Gill spent $1.1 million, but Gordon spent $1.6 million, raising—despite Republican control of the House—$743,000 from PACs. Gordon won 54%–42%, with 51% in the counties outside Nashville and 64% in the rural counties. In the pro-incumbent year of 1998 Gordon won 55%–45%. In 2000, against less well-financed opposition, Gordon won 62%–36%, winning every county but Williamson and the precinct in Nashville.

Whether Gordon can continue to hold this seat may depend on redistricting. The suburban counties around Nashville are the fastest-growing parts of Tennessee. Gordon has signaled that he is eager to dump Williamson County, perhaps in exchange for parts of the 5th District. He will likely get sympathetic treatment from the Democratic legislature, but Republican Governor Don Sundquist has a veto and therefore some leverage, and it would be possible to draw a more Republican 6th District.

Cook's Call *Potentially Competitive.* The 6th District—the fastest growing in Tennessee during the 1990s—gave Bush 52% in 2000. Gordon, however, has proven to be quite resilient and continues to win in both good and bad political climates, and Democrats will try to shore up the 6th during redistricting. While a good Republican candidate could give Gordon a tough race, beating him is still a challenge.

THE PEOPLE: Pop. 2000: 738,663; Pop. 1990: 542,002, up 36.3% 1990–2000. 91% White, 5.7% Black, 1% Asian, 0.3% Amer. Indian, 0.9% Two+ races, 1% Other; 2.2% Hispanic Origin.

2000 Presidential Vote			1996 Presidential Vote		
Bush (R)	179,812	(52%)	Dole (R)	112,827	(47%)
Gore (D)	161,845	(47%)	Clinton (D)	107,821	(45%)
Nader (Green)	3,487	(1%)	Perot (I)	15,375	(6%)
Others	1,800	(1%)			

Rep. Bart Gordon (D)

Elected 1984, 9th term; b. Jan. 24, 1949, Murfreesboro; home, Murfreesboro; Middle TN St. U., B.S. 1971, U. of TN, J.D. 1973; United Methodist; married (Leslie).

Military Career: Army Reserves, 1971–72.

Professional Career: Practicing atty., 1974–84; Chmn., TN Dem. Party, 1981–83.

DC Office: 2368 RHOB 20515, 202-225-4231; Fax: 202-225-6887; Web site: www.house.gov/gordon.

District Offices: Cookeville, 931-528-5907; Murfreesboro, 615-896-1986.

Committees: *Energy & Commerce* (9th of 26 D): Commerce, Trade & Consumer Protection; Energy & Air Quality; Telecommunications & The Internet. *Science* (2d of 22 D): Space & Aeronautics (RMM).

Group Ratings

	ADA	ACLU	AFS	LCV	CON	ITIC	NTU	COC	ACU	NTLC	CHC
2000	60	21	85	50	1	72	38	71	44	36	47
1999	70	—	100	56	31	—	25	71	36	—	—

National Journal Ratings

	1999 LIB	—	1999 CONS		2000 LIB	—	2000 CONS
Economic	54%	—	45%		53%	—	46%
Social	49%	—	51%		55%	—	45%
Foreign	55%	—	44%		47%	—	51%

Key Votes of the 106th Congress

1. Patient Bill of Rights	Y	5. Bar RU-486 $ for FDA	N	9. NATO War in Serbia	N
2. Accelerate Min. Wage	Y	6. Display 10 Commandments	Y	10. Perm. Trade with China	N
3. Strike Ban on Ergo. Stnd.	Y	7. Gun Show Bkgrnd. Checks	N	11. Debt Relief for 3rd World	Y
4. Ovrd. Estate Tax Veto	Y	8. Ban Part.-Birth Abortion	Y	12. Drop Cuba Econ. Embargo	N

Election Results

2000 general	Bart Gordon (D)	168,861	(62%)	($1,135,811)
	David Charles (R)	97,169	(36%)	($174,937)
	Others	5,869	(2%)	
2000 primary	Bart Gordon (D)	unopposed		
1998 general	Bart Gordon (D)	75,055	(55%)	($981,306)
	Walt Massey (R)	62,277	(45%)	($417,743)

SEVENTH DISTRICT

Rural Tennessee north of Mississippi is one of the most sparsely settled areas in the state. Along each side of the Tennessee River, as it flows north and widens out into Kentucky Lake amid heavy forests, are small rural communities with colorful names like Spot, Only and Bucksnort; many go back to pre-Civil War days and have not grown much since. Farther west the land is flatter and more open, a northward extension economically and demographically of the northern Mississippi farmlands, with cotton fields and a large black rural population. This mostly empty land is bounded on two sides by large metropolitan areas, Nashville to the east and Memphis to the west.

The 7th Congressional District of Tennessee spans this territory, from the Cheatham County suburban fringe of Nashville, west across the Tennessee River and south to the Mississippi border and finally to the white neighborhoods on the east side of Memphis and Shelby County. It is a mixed district politically. Most of the rural counties are traditionally Democratic, with a few Republican exceptions, while the fringe of Nashville is mixed and the 7th District's portion of Memphis is, like all white parts of Memphis, heavily Republican. The balance has usually tipped toward Republicans, though the lines in Memphis and Shelby County were altered by 1990s redistricting to help the Democrats—but with little success.

The congressman from the 7th District is Ed Bryant, a Republican elected in 1994 to replace Republican Don Sundquist, who was elected governor. Bryant is from Jackson in west Tennessee, went to school at Ole Miss, served in the Army, taught law at West Point and practiced law in Tennessee starting in 1978. In 1991, President Bush, on the recommendation of Don Sundquist, made him U.S. attorney in West Tennessee; Bryant left that post in 1993 in a dispute over jury selection in the bank fraud trial of then- Congressman Harold Ford Sr. The case was hugely visible and controversial, which gave Bryant wide celebrity. When Sundquist decided to run for governor, Bryant ran for the seat. In the Republican primary, he lost Shelby County to Germantown Mayor Charles Salvaggio. But he won in all but one of the rural counties by enough votes to win overall 35%–33%. The Democratic nomination went to Harold Byrd, a former state legislator and former aide to Senator Jim Sasser. Outside Shelby County the race was close: 51%–48% for Bryant. But Bryant carried Shelby County with 72% for a solid overall win, 60%–39%.

In the House, Bryant maintained a strongly conservative voting record. He was a visible cosponsor of the Contract with America crime bills, and also sponsored bills that doubled the penalty for prison escapes from five to 10 years, for a life-without-parole sentence in military law, and for trying federal judges in different circuits from where they served. After repeatedly struggling with the issue, Bryant supported normal trade relations status with China and then backed permanent trade relations, contending that China would benefit from exposure to trade and ideas from democratic nations. In response to a bill that sought to block the move of the NFL's Houston Oilers to Tennessee, Bryant proposed the Sports Relocation Reform Act. In 1998 he helped open a new veterans' clinic in Clarksville. He successfully sponsored legislation to repeal taxes that Tennessee residents working in Kentucky's Fort Campbell had to pay the state of Kentucky. He defended TVA from critics seeking to force a quicker reduction of its debt. When Nashville-based Bridgestone/ Firestone was accused of selling defective tires and Congress responded by toughening regulatory enforcement, Bryant advocated an amendment to make it a crime for dealers to knowingly sell recalled tires.

After a relatively quiet two terms, Bryant leapt onto the national stage as one of the managers of President Clinton's Senate impeachment trial. "He has lost his moral leadership, his moral authority that all of us expect the president to have," Bryant said in September 1998. Bryant was the House manager picked to interview former White House intern Monica Lewinsky; Bryant explained his selection by citing the rumor that his subdued style had made him the manager Lewinsky "disliked the least."

Bryant was unopposed in 1998 and reelected with 70% of the vote in 2000. He talked about running for governor in 2002 but decided against it. Redistricting could result in a primary for Bryant against 4th District Republican Van Hilleary. But there is sure to be a district anchored in the white portions of Memphis and Shelby County that will be heavily Republican.

Cook's Call *Safe*. Bryant could run for the Senate should fellow Republican Fred Thompson decide not to seek re-election. Regardless, this seat should remain in Republican hands in 2002.

THE PEOPLE: Pop. 2000: 728,956; Pop. 1990: 542,270, up 34.4% 1990–2000. 80.3% White, 15.5% Black, 1.4% Asian, 0.3% Amer. Indian, 0.1% Hawaiian, 1.4% Two+ races, 1.1% Other; 2.5% Hispanic Origin.

2000 Presidential Vote		
Bush (R)	186,707	(51%)
Gore (D)	171,203	(47%)
Nader (Green)	2,659	(1%)
Others	2,059	(1%)

1996 Presidential Vote		
Dole (R)	122,177	(54%)
Clinton (D)	92,802	(41%)
Perot (I)	10,965	(5%)

Rep. Ed Bryant (R)

Elected 1994, 4th term; b. Sept. 7, 1948, Jackson; home, Henderson; U. of MS, B.A. 1970, J.D. 1972; Protestant; married (Cyndi).

Military Career: Army, Judge Advocate General Corps, 1970–78; Instructor, West Point Military Acad., 1977–78.

Professional Career: Practicing atty., 1978–90; US Atty. for W. TN, 1991–93.

DC Office: 408 CHOB 20515, 202-225-2811; Fax: 202-225-2989; Web site: www.house.gov/bryant.

District Offices: Clarksville, 931-503-0391; Columbia, 931-381-8100; Memphis, 901-382-5811.

Committees: *Energy & Commerce* (23d of 31 R): Commerce, Trade & Consumer Protection; Energy & Air Quality; Health.

Group Ratings

	ADA	ACLU	AFS	LCV	CON	ITIC	NTU	COC	ACU	NTLC	CHC
2000	0	7	0	0	61	100	63	80	95	82	100
1999	5	—	0	6	12	—	55	92	88	—	—

National Journal Ratings

	1999 LIB	—	1999 CONS		2000 LIB	—	2000 CONS
Economic	16%	—	78%		0%	—	94%
Social	4%	—	91%		0%	—	79%
Foreign	3%	—	92%		0%	—	88%

Key Votes of the 106th Congress

1. Patient Bill of Rights	N	5. Bar RU-486 $ for FDA	Y	9. NATO War in Serbia	N
2. Accelerate Min. Wage	N	6. Display 10 Commandments	Y	10. Perm. Trade with China	Y
3. Strike Ban on Ergo. Stnd.	N	7. Gun Show Bkgrnd. Checks	N	11. Debt Relief for 3rd World	N
4. Ovrd. Estate Tax Veto	Y	8. Ban Part.-Birth Abortion	Y	12. Drop Cuba Econ. Embargo	N

Election Results

2000 general	Ed Bryant (R)	171,056	(70%)	($727,131)
	Richard P. Sims (D)	71,587	(29%)	($10,493)
	Others	3,006	(1%)	
2000 primary	Ed Bryant (R)	unopposed		
1998 general	Ed Bryant (R)	unopposed		($392,944)

EIGHTH DISTRICT

West of Nashville and the lakes along the Tennessee River and north of Memphis, the rivers roll lazily through flat or gently rolling land that almost could be the northern end of Mississippi. Cotton and soybeans are the main crops; more blacks remain in rural areas here than in any other part of Tennessee, a reminder of its old plantation economy. The towns here are small, edged in by farm fields; the river bottoms, often flooded, are heavily forested. Here is Henning, the hometown of Alex Haley, where he used to sit on his porch and listen to his aunts tell him stories about slave ships and the Civil War that became *Roots*.

The 8th Congressional District includes much of this west Tennessee farmland, from the lakes west to the Mississippi; its largest city is Jackson, but it includes the northern fringe of Memphis. Historically, this is Democratic country; Republicans haven't represented most of the counties that make up the 8th since the end of Reconstruction. The region trended Republican in national races in the 1960s and 1970s, then turned back toward the Democrats with the help of some smart local politicians. One of them is Ned Ray McWherter, first elected to the legislature from Weakley County in 1968, speaker from 1973–86, then governor until 1994. In the 1990s it trended Republican again and has been a key marginal area in Tennessee politics; rural Carroll County has been something of a bellwether, voting 50%–49% for George W. Bush over Al Gore in 2000. Enough Democratic strength remains that the 8th was one of the three Tennessee congressional districts won by Gore.

The congressman from the 8th District is John Tanner, a Democrat elected in 1988. Tanner grew up in Obion County, went to college and law school at the University of Tennessee, served four years in the Navy, then practiced law in Union City. In 1976, at 32, he successfully ran for the Tennessee House, where he served 12 years. In 1988, when the incumbent retired, Tanner ran for Congress and won with a whopping 66% in a four-candidate primary and 62% in the general.

Tanner's voting record put him solidly in the middle of the Democratic House, a little to the left of midpoint after Republicans took control. He has worked on local issues, promoting the city of Millington and then getting a grant to redevelop its Naval Air Station's surplus property. He successfully opposed a 1995 move to end federal payments to the Tennessee Valley Authority, which would have cut funding for the Land Between the Lakes park; in 1997 the TVA director called for an end to federal payments and spinning off of such functions to state governments and federal agencies, but $50 million in funding of non-power operations was voted in 1998. Tanner has sponsored research on the New Madrid Fault, which produced three great earthquakes in 1811–12.

In 1997 Tanner got a seat on Ways and Means; his 8th District predecessor Jere Cooper served there from 1932 to 1957, the last three years as chairman. He went to work on tax issues, including elimination of estate taxes on family-owned farms and small businesses and opposition to the IRS's current-year taxation of farmers' income from deferred payment contracts. In 1999 he joined Republican Jennifer Dunn in sponsoring legislation to eliminate the estate tax, on the ground it keeps most family farms and small businesses from passing to the second generation. The bill passed but was vetoed by Bill Clinton. Tanner has long supported the balanced budget amendment and line-item veto, though he has opposed some Republican versions. He supported fast-track trade authority in 1997 and permanent normal trade relations with China in 2000. With Senator Christopher Bond, he filed legislation to encourage communities to create local "watershed councils" to draw up blueprints for making local rivers and lakes more hospitable to fish—preempting EPA authority by having these councils report to the Agriculture and Interior Departments.

In 1992 Tanner could have been a senator for the asking. Governor Ned Ray McWherter was ready to appoint him to succeed Al Gore, but Tanner refused the post and chose instead to stay in the House. If he had accepted he might have become a more nationally prominent figure, but he would also have had to defend the seat against Fred Thompson in what turned out to be the very Republican year of 1994. Instead, Tanner became a major force in the House. He was a founder of a group of moderate-to-conservative Democrats called the Blue Dogs who advanced their own proposals for balancing the budget and reforming welfare. Tanner co-sponsored the Blue Dogs' welfare reform proposal, which, he claims with some legitimacy, was "the genesis for the broad welfare reform plan that Clinton signed" in August 1996. When House Republicans revived the issue in July 1996, Tanner passed amendments allowing states to provide non-cash assistance such as baby formula and diapers and providing that no one loses Medicaid because of federally imposed time limits; he also grandfathered time limits of states' currently approved reform plans, like Tennessee's bipartisan Families First. These provisions helped win the support of half the House's Democrats and became part of the 1996 welfare reform signed by Clinton.

In the 8th District Tanner has held more than 1,000 town hall meetings and has been re-elected by wide margins. In 2000 his Democratic primary opponent was backed by the United Steelworkers because of Tanner's free trade votes; Tanner won the August primary 87%–13%. The same week he won something else—a Jaguar, when he hit a hole-in-one at a golf tournament in honor of the late Commerce Secretary Ron Brown while at the Democratic Convention in Los Angeles. When columnist Robert Novak wrote that Tanner might switch parties, he was furious and responded, "it's just grotesquely irresponsible to write something like that." Novak apologized for relying on a Republican source and not checking with Tanner.

Cook's Call *Safe*. Tanner's Blue Dog voting record and down-home style have helped insulate him in this Democratic-leaning, but still marginal district. His decision to forgo a race for governor means this seat will stay in Democratic hands in 2002.

THE PEOPLE: Pop. 2000: 604,894; Pop. 1990: 541,852, up 11.6% 1990–2000. 74.1% White, 23.5% Black, 0.5% Asian, 0.3% Amer. Indian, 0.9% Two+ races, 0.7% Other; 1.6% Hispanic Origin.

2000 Presidential Vote			1996 Presidential Vote		
Gore (D)	95,961	(50%)	Clinton (D)	98,925	(50%)
Bush (R)	95,352	(49%)	Dole (R)	85,856	(44%)
Nader (Green)	1,363	(1%)	Perot (I)	10,835	(6%)
Others	1,064	(1%)			

Rep. John S. Tanner (D)

Elected 1988, 7th term; b. Sept. 22, 1944, Halls; home, Union City; U. of TN, B.S. 1966, J.D. 1968; Disciples of Christ; married (Betty Ann).

Military Career: Navy, 1968–72; TN Natl. Guard, 1974–2000.

Elected Office: TN House of Reps., 1976–88.

Professional Career: Practicing atty., 1973–88.

DC Office: 1226 LHOB 20515, 202-225-4714; Fax: 202-225-1765; Web site: www.house.gov/tanner.

District Offices: Jackson, 731-423-4848; Millington, 901-873-5690; Union City, 731-885-7070.

Committees: *Ways & Means* (13th of 17 D): Select Revenue Measures; Trade.

Group Ratings

	ADA	ACLU	AFS	LCV	CON	ITIC	NTU	COC	ACU	NTLC	CHC
2000	45	43	28	43	96	95	34	85	36	25	53
1999	70	—	83	31	70	—	20	76	29	—	—

National Journal Ratings

	1999 LIB	—	1999 CONS		2000 LIB	—	2000 CONS
Economic	53%	—	47%		55%	—	44%
Social	53%	—	46%		51%	—	49%
Foreign	58%	—	41%		69%	—	28%

Key Votes of the 106th Congress

1. Patient Bill of Rights	Y	5. Bar RU-486 $ for FDA	N	9. NATO War in Serbia	Y
2. Accelerate Min. Wage	Y	6. Display 10 Commandments	Y	10. Perm. Trade with China	Y
3. Strike Ban on Ergo. Stnd.	N	7. Gun Show Bkgrnd. Checks	N	11. Debt Relief for 3rd World	Y
4. Ovrd. Estate Tax Veto	Y	8. Ban Part.-Birth Abortion	Y	12. Drop Cuba Econ. Embargo	Y

Election Results

2000 general	John S. Tanner (D)	143,127	(72%)	($621,357)
	Billy Yancy (R)	54,929	(28%)	($3,658)
2000 primary	John S. Tanner (D)	32,078	(87%)	
	Marvin Williams (D)	4,914	(13%)	
1998 general	John S. Tanner (D)	unopposed		($369,763)

NINTH DISTRICT

Memphis, the largest city in Tennessee, is in the state's far southwestern corner, 500 miles from the Appalachian border with Virginia but only 20 miles from Mississippi's cotton fields and riverboat casinos. Metropolitan Memphis has one of the highest percentages of blacks in the country—evidence of the city's economic heritage as a capital of the Cotton Kingdom. Big Mississippi planters used to come north to sell their crop in the courtyard of the Peabody Hotel, then make financial arrangements for the next growing season.

Such facts have shaped the city's most celebrated tradition, the blues—a musical form worlds apart from Nashville's country music. Whereas country music emerged from mountainous, mainly white middle and east Tennessee, the Memphis sound originated from the self-taught musical stylings of poor, rural blacks in the Mississippi Delta. Throughout the first half of the 20th Century, the most talented black musicians migrated north to Memphis and congregated downtown on Beale Street. The blues sound was later adapted by Elvis Presley, a poor white from rural Mississippi, in pivotal sessions in July 1954 at Sam Phillips' Sun Studio in Memphis—the birth of rock 'n' roll, and the beginnings of an Elvis cult that long outlived the man. In the early 1960s Memphis once again became the crucible of a new sound, soul music, which emerged as a counterpoint to rock, its increasingly white-dominated cousin. For some years Memphis tried to live down all this musical heritage; much of Beale Street was razed and set on a misguided path towards urban renewal. But more recently, the city has come to recognize its history as an asset. Graceland, Presley's garishly decorated mansion, which attracts hordes of musical pilgrims from all over the world is perhaps the best example, and there are plans to build a Museum of American Soul Music on the site of the Stax studio, demolished in 1989, where Otis Redding, Isaac Hayes, the Staple Singers and Sam & Dave once made their records.

Music is not the city's only asset. Geographically central in the U.S., Memphis is the home of the first supermarket chain (the Piggly Wiggly, founded in 1916; its symbol, Mr. Pig, was slimmed down in 1998) and the first Holiday Inn. Home of the world's busiest cargo airport, Memphis calls itself "America's distribution center": by far its biggest employer is FedEx, which ships all of its domestic packages in and out of Memphis Airport every night, helped by the opening of a third runway in 2000. Despite such enterprises, racial discord has scarred the political life of Memphis. It is the city where Martin Luther King Jr. was assassinated in 1968; the site of the murder, the Lorraine Motel, was converted into a civil rights museum. Even today, the resurgent Beale Street is one of the few racially integrated spaces in the city, a division that holds equally true in voting. Blacks vote almost unanimously Democratic; whites vote Republican by percentages almost as high. The 9th Congressional District of Tennessee consists of most of the city of Memphis and a bit of its suburban fringe; in 2000, 66% of its residents were black.

The congressman from the 9th District is Harold Ford Jr., a Democrat elected in 1996 at age 26; his father, Harold Ford Sr., had been elected in 1974 at 29 and represented the 9th for 22 years. Harold Ford Jr. grew up in Memphis until 1979, when the family moved to Washington. He graduated from the elite St. Albans School, a classmate of Jesse Jackson's son Yusef, then graduated from the University of Pennsylvania in 1992. He worked on his father's 1992 and 1994 campaigns and on the Clinton transition team and as a special assistant in the Economic Development Administration (and thus technically worked for Commerce Secretary Ron Brown, whom he has praised as a "profound influence"). In 1993 he went off to the University of Michigan Law School.

The Fords are a large family—Harold Ford Sr. has 11 siblings and Harold Ford Jr. has 74 first cousins—from a humble background. Ford Sr. grew up in a house with no plumbing, but the family built a successful funeral home business. Harold Ford Sr. was elected to the state legislature in 1970, at 25, and there has been a Ford on the Memphis Council since 1971; other Fords have served on the county commission and in the state Senate. Harold Ford Sr.'s House career was stalled when he lost his subcommittee chairmanship after being indicted in April 1987 for receiving allegedly illegal loans from political backers; a Memphis jury hung 8–4 along racial lines for acquittal in April 1990, and a jury of 11 whites and 1 black acquitted him in April 1993, at which point he became chairman again, until Republicans won control in 1994. In 1996 Harold Ford Sr. decided to retire from Congress in favor of his son, who had cut an ad for him in 1974 at age 4, calling for "lower cookie prices." Opposition came from liberal state Senator Steve Cohen, but his campaign faltered when he lost the endorsement of public employee unions that he had always supported, and Ford rolled on to a 60%–34% primary win. In the general, "Jr."—as Ford's campaign buttons read—won 61%–37%, slightly better than the 58% his father had won during his last three general elections.

In the House, Harold Ford Jr. has taken notably more moderate positions on issues than most members of the Black Caucus, although he has the most liberal voting record in the Tennessee delegation. He says that he talks regularly with his father, but that they often disagree on issues. He joined the New Democrat Coalition in 1997 and was part of a centrist group meeting regularly in December 2000. He voted against needle exchanges, for the prayer in school and anti-flag burning constitutional amendments, for the balanced budget amendment, fast track trade authority, the capital gains tax cut, repeal of the estate tax, permanent normal trade relations with China and aid to tobacco farmers. He sought additional funding for school construction, but he also backed efforts to end "social promotion" and opposed the teaching of Ebonics, and he favored the introduction of "competition, competency and accountability" into public schools; he says he is willing to consider vouchers. In 1998 he responded sharply to House Minority Leader Dick Gephardt's criticism of New Democrats. He has sponsored bills to encourage VISTA volunteers to recruit teens to put together computer systems for schools and libraries and to give home buyers access to secret credit scoring information.

At home in Memphis, Ford's appeal has crossed racial lines. "I wouldn't have a white message and a black message," he said. "I'd have a message." He was re-elected with 79% of the vote in 1998 and was unopposed in 2000. In the summer of 1999 he crisscrossed Tennessee in preparation for running against Republican Senator Bill Frist. In sharp partisan terms he criticized Frist for voting on health care issues while owning large amounts of Columbia/ HCA stock and for opposing the Democrats' HMO regulation bill. He promised he would decide whether to run by Labor Day, but the deadline passed and, while campaigning less, he did not announce he was not running until February 2000; some Democrats groused that he had left the party without a serious candidate. But in his announcement he left little doubt that he will eventually run for statewide office when he said, "I absolutely look forward to serving the entire state of Tennessee some day." Senators Fred Thompson and Bill Frist are highly popular, but both have limited themselves to two full terms. If they fulfill those pledges, there will be open seat races for Tennessee's Senate seats in 2006 and 2008, when Ford will still be in his 30s. Though Tennessee has been trending Republican, Ford's moderate record, his articulateness and his appeal across racial boundaries could make him a very strong candidate.

His ambitions may not stop there. Al Gore, who has helped Ford's career along at several stages, chose Ford as the keynote speaker at the 2000 Democratic National Convention. In a brief speech that repays careful reading, Ford paid tribute to the black experience in America as part of the wider American experience: "I recognize that I stand here this evening because of the brave men and women, many of whom were no older than I am today, who fought and stood and oftentimes sat down to help create that more perfect union. But I also stand here this evening representing a new generation, a generation committed to the ideals of the past but inspired by an unshakable confidence in our future." It is possible to imagine this still very young-looking man as some day the first black president of the United States. In the meantime, he obviously can easily win re-election to the House.

Cook's Call   *Safe.* Ford may be contemplating a run against Senator Fred Thompson in 2002. But it is hard to see how Democrats could lose a district that gave Al Gore 77%. This majority black district was the slowest growing in Tennessee in the 1990s and will need to pick up about 120,000 people.

THE PEOPLE: Pop. 2000: 512,881; Pop. 1990: 541,710, down 5.3% 1990–2000. 30.1% White, 66.2% Black, 1.2% Asian, 0.2% Amer. Indian, 0.9% Two + races, 1.3% Other; 2.8% Hispanic Origin.

2000 Presidential Vote		
Gore (D)	87,117	(77%)
Bush (R)	24,612	(22%)
Nader (Green)	1,223	(1%)

1996 Presidential Vote		
Clinton (D)	138,234	(71%)
Dole (R)	51,767	(27%)
Perot (I)	3,862	(2%)

Rep. Harold E. Ford, Jr. (D)

Elected 1996, 3d term; b. May 11, 1970, Memphis; home, Memphis; U. of PA, B.A. 1992, U. of MI, J.D. 1996; Baptist; single.

Professional Career: Staff Aide, U.S. Senate Budget Cmte., 1992; Spec. Asst., Clinton/Gore Transition Team, 1992; Spec. Asst., DNC Chairs Ron Brown & Alexis Herman, 1993; Spec. Asst., U.S. Dept. of Commerce, 1993.

DC Office: 325 CHOB 20515, 202-225-3265; Fax: 202-225-5663; Web site: www.house.gov/ford.

District Office: Memphis, 901-544-4131.

Committees: *Education & the Workforce* (16th of 22 D): Education Reform; Employer-Employee Relations. *Financial Services* (25th of 32 D): Capital Markets, Insurance & Government Sponsored Enterprises; Financial Institutions & Consumer Credit.

Group Ratings

	ADA	ACLU	AFS	LCV	CON	ITIC	NTU	COC	ACU	NTLC	CHC
2000	60	58	71	71	34	78	25	70	24	15	23
1999	100	—	100	81	76	—	17	40	4	—	—

National Journal Ratings

	1999 LIB	—	1999 CONS		2000 LIB	—	2000 CONS
Economic	70%	—	30%		63%	—	37%
Social	72%	—	28%		68%	—	31%
Foreign	78%	—	17%		79%	—	20%

Key Votes of the 106th Congress

1. Patient Bill of Rights	Y	5. Bar RU-486 $ for FDA	N	9. NATO War in Serbia	Y
2. Accelerate Min. Wage	Y	6. Display 10 Commandments	Y	10. Perm. Trade with China	Y
3. Strike Ban on Ergo. Stnd.	Y	7. Gun Show Bkgrnd. Checks	Y	11. Debt Relief for 3rd World	Y
4. Ovrd. Estate Tax Veto	Y	8. Ban Part.-Birth Abortion	Y	12. Drop Cuba Econ. Embargo	Y

Election Results

2000 general	Harold E. Ford Jr. (D)	.... unopposed	($475,376)
2000 primary	Harold E. Ford Jr. (D)	.... unopposed	
1998 general	Harold E. Ford Jr. (D)	.... 75,428 (79%)	($521,544)
	Claude Burdikoff (R)	.... 18,078 (19%)	
	Others	.... 2,276 (2%)	

★ TEXAS ★

Texas is a nation-sized state, one of four to have been an independent republic (the others are California, Vermont and Hawaii), and the one that stuck to it the longest. It is a state with an international image and international impact. The nation has voted for president 11 times since 1960: four times it has voted for Californians, four times for Texans. These two largest states have put their stamp on national politics in our times, just as New York did before 1960, when it was the residence of five of the winners elected in the 15 contests starting in 1900. Texas has been the second largest state in area since Alaska was admitted to the Union in 1959; it became the second largest in population in 1994, when it passed New York. The key to Texas's history is that this is a society with no aristocratic past, a state not formed by plantation owners or plutocrats but by dirt farmers. Texas was founded by Southerners, mainly Tennesseans, who wanted to establish their own republic in what were empty spaces within the borders of Mexico, a republic with Anglo-Saxon freedoms and black slavery. They defended their dream to the death at the Alamo and to a bloody victory at San Jacinto; they entered the Union willingly in 1845 and left it enthusiastically in 1861. The Texas that emerged from the Civil War was still young and poor; it was only in 1901 that oil was discovered at Spindletop, and the Texas wildcatters made their first fortunes.

Without the underpinnings and burdens of tradition, 20th Century Texas has produced fabulous wealth, generously rewarding success while unforgiving of failure. It has respect for learning and style—think of its great universities, or Neiman Marcus—and it revels in rough manners and western wear. Texans are prone to wild swings in fortune—think of Sam Houston, or the great wildcatters, or Lyndon Johnson. And as the 20th Century ended, Texans, for all their history of slavery and segregation, have proved open to immigrants and friendly with their neighbors in Mexico. NAFTA, the opening up of the border and the coming together of these two countries which are at such different economic levels and have such different cultures, is a project mainly of Texans of both political parties, of President George Bush and Treasury Secretary Lloyd Bentsen, Governors Ann Richards and George W. Bush. At the same time, Texas has become a high-tech powerhouse, a country with some of the nation's most creative businesses. But its success

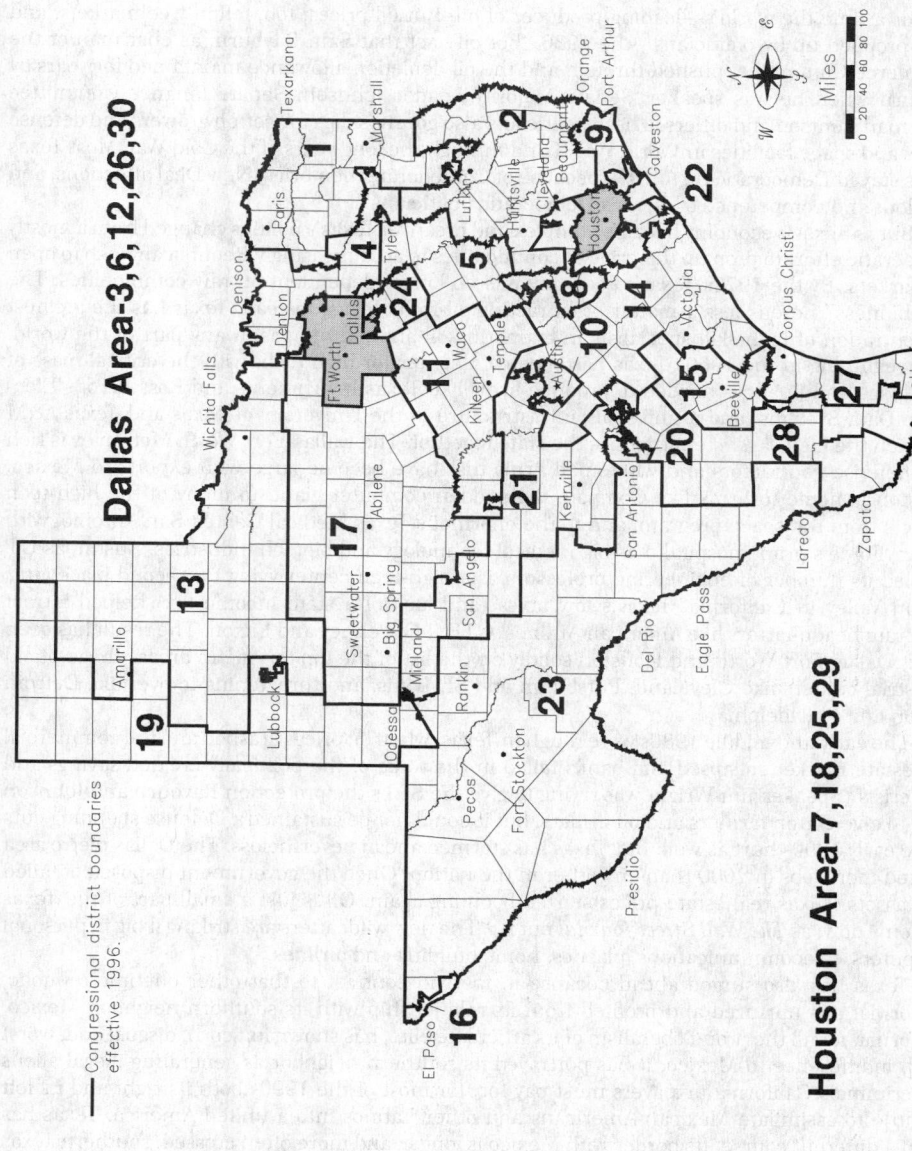

Dallas Area-3,6,12,26,30

— Congressional district boundaries
  effective 1996.

Houston Area-7,18,25,29

Copyright ©1997 by Election Data Services, Inc.

N
W   E
S

Miles

0 20 40 60 80 100

Texarkana

Marshall

1

2

Orange
Port Arthur

9

Galveston

22

Paris

Denison

Denton

Wichita Falls

Tyler

Luf...

Huntsville

Cleveland

Baumo...

4

4

5

24

Houston

Ft. Worth
Dallas

Waco

Temple

Kileen

11

8

10

14

Victoria

Corpus Christi

Harlingen

Brownsville

Austin

15

Beeville

27

Abilene

17

Big Spring

San Angelo

Kerrville

21

San Antonio

20

28

McAllen

13

Amarillo

Lubbock

3

Midland

Odessa

Rankin

23

Del Rio

Eagle Pass

Laredo

Zapata

19

Pecos

Fort Stockton

Presidio

16

El Paso

Sweetwater

is not just economic. There are large elements of heroism—some mythical, some genuine—in the Texas history that every high school student here learns. "What Texans dream, Texans can do," George W. Bush liked to say, before he set his ambitions beyond the wide horizon of Texas.

Texans' dreams, sometimes seemingly unrealistic, have taken them far. Texas started off as a marchland on the border of the Third World, with an economy based on commodities, mainly cotton, whose prices were in long-term decline. Its farmers felt like part of a colonial economy controlled by bankers and Wall Street financiers. After Spindletop, Texas became the nation's— and for a time the world's—leading producer of oil. But oil prices, too, fell in free markets, and were propped up by politicians—the 1936 "hot oil" act that Sam Rayburn, as chairman of the Commerce Committee, pushed through and the oil depletion allowance maintained for years by Rayburn when he was speaker, Senate Majority Leader Johnson, Senate Finance Committee Chairman Bentsen and others. These politicians also got subsidies for cotton growers and defense plants and space facilities in World War II and through the long years of the Cold War. Most Texas voters stayed Democratic up to 1970 because of Confederate memories, New Deal affections, and the clout and competence of Texas's Democratic politicians.

But as Texas's economy became complex and creative, Texas's politics changed from a mostly Democratic effort to prop up the price of commodities to an increasingly Republican push to open up markets. By the 1970s Texas's economy was no longer dependent on raw commodities. The "awl bidness" here is less a matter of extracting oil from Texas; instead, Texas has the greatest concentration of high-skill specialists in extracting oil and natural gas in any part of the world. Also, beginning in the 1960s Texas has become a center for high tech, with the critical mass of knowledge and finances needed to produce firms like Texas Instruments and Ross Perot's Electronic Data Systems, and a university infrastructure in the University of Texas and Texas A&M to match the highway system that ties the state together. The Dallas-Fort Worth Metroplex is rich with defense contractors and with small firms that have become large with exports to Mexico. Houston is home to firms like Compaq, the sudden computer giant, to many of the high-tech spinoffs from the space program, and to the enormous Texas Medical Center. San Antonio, with the Air Force's prime hospital, has big medical technology and biotech industries. Austin, as UT doubled its number of engineering professors, is a high-tech center vying for second place after Silicon Valley in California. Texas's low taxes (and lack of a state income tax) helped attract corporate headquarters like American Airlines, GTE, J.C. Penney and Exxon. The result has been to put Dallas-Fort Worth and Houston solidly on the list of the top ten metro areas, ahead of old industrial centers like Cleveland, Pittsburgh and St. Louis, and threatening to overtake Detroit, Boston and Philadelphia.

The early and middle 1980s were rough in Texas, when oil prices crashed and the commercial real estate market collapsed and banks failed in the wake of the politically-created savings and loan crisis (Speaker Jim Wright was trying to give the S&Ls the protection Rayburn and Johnson used to give cotton farmers and oil drillers, but it could not be sustained). Defense spending cuts in the early 1990s hurt as well. But Texas has stormed ahead nevertheless. The Dallas metro area created more jobs in 2000 than any other in the nation. Once the government disposed of failed S&L assets, Texas real estate prices started booming again. Oil is just a small part of the Texas economy now; as *The Wall Street Journal* put it, "The new wildcatters are striking it big in personal computers, telecommunications, plastics, home building and airlines."

Texas has also surged ahead because it, in vivid contrast to that other onetime republic, California, has nurtured and profited from its relationship with its southern neighbor, Mexico. California, for all the proud liberalism of its articulate elite, has shown its scorn, disgust and, worst of all, indifference to Mexico; it has portrayed its southern neighbor as generating illegal aliens and criminals California taxpayers must pay for; for most of the 1990s both its right and its left did little to assimilate Mexican-Americans and other Latinos into a united America. Texas has taken a different course. Its border with Mexico is longer, and more often crossed; southern Texas along the Rio Grande is a kind of transition zone, and Monterrey, 140 miles from Laredo, is perhaps Mexico's most America-friendly city; despite a history of racial segregation, Texas has shown a friendly face to Mexicans, while Mexican immigrants have shown they wanted to become Texans and Americans. As *Mexico Business* magazine wrote, "Texas has embraced Mexico while

California has given it the cold shoulder." Fewer Latinos have crossed the border here to take advantage of welfare programs, which are much less generous in Texas than in California. Political leadership has made a difference. California's former Governor Pete Wilson had little contact with Mexico and strongly championed Proposition 187 against services for illegal immigrants in 1994 and Proposition 209 banning racial quotas and preferences in 1996; a chilly tone was set, which has only begun to be dissipated by Wilson's successor Gray Davis. George W. Bush, like Governor Ann Richards before him, journeyed often to Mexico and invited Mexican leaders to Texas, emphasizing the positive in public and leaving any negative details to private negotiations. "You cannot wall off Mexico," said Bush. "Our cultures are completely intertwined." So increasingly are their economies. Nearly half of U.S. merchandise exports to Mexico are from Texas, significantly more than California; 70% of U.S. exports to Mexico go through Texas. The NAFTA secretariat of labor is in Dallas, the North American Development Bank is headquartered in San Antonio, the Border Environmental Cooperation Commission is in Juarez, across the Rio Grande from El Paso, and the busiest truck crossing between the countries is the World Trade Bridge between Laredo and Nuevo Laredo.

Texas stands as a model for the American future, a model admired by many and disparaged by others. Quite explicitly in the 2000 campaign George W. Bush constantly cited his Texas record; Al Gore highlighted the state's shortcomings. Texas is an open society, unpretentious, delivered from its heritage of racial and ethnic discrimination. But it also has vast income disparities, between struggling and population-losing rural counties and the surging cities, and between the gleaming affluent neighborhoods spreading out into the countryside and the poor and crime-ridden neighborhoods of rickety frame houses not far from the urban cores. Texas presents a contrast with and a challenge to the traditions of other megastates—New York which pioneered the American welfare state, California which used high taxes to build highways and schools, the Great Lakes industrial states with their big labor unions. For Texas has some of the lowest taxes in the country and some of the lowest welfare levels; it has few union members and a relatively small public sector; it has resisted court-ordered moves to equalize spending among school districts; it continues to be a violent state, with a high crime rate and the highest number of executions. For years, out-of-state elites and liberals in Texas have called on the state to become more like New York or California or Michigan. But most Texans prefer their own model. Indeed, in important respects New York and California and Michigan are choosing to become more like Texas. Low taxes and high tech, few barriers to opportunity but a less elaborate safety net, moving away from reliance on agriculture and oil, bypassing the era of big factories and big unions of the Great Lakes and eschewing the liberal cultural values of the two coasts: This is Texas's way, and increasingly the way of the other 49 states and of Mexico.

Politically, Texas is now an indisputably Republican state: George W. Bush carried it in 2000 by a 59%–38% margin, significantly larger than the 56%–43% margin his father won 12 years before. It was not always so: George W. Bush and Senators Phil Gramm and Kay Bailey Hutchison each lost an election before they started winning. One-party Democratic dominance ended in the 1960s, and for two decades Democratic victories were largely the product of Lloyd Bentsen, when he was on the ballot in 1970, 1976, 1982 and 1988 and when he exerted his influence for Ann Richards for governor in 1990. The old Democratic strength in the Texas countryside is gone— in 1998 George W. Bush carried 239 of 254 counties and in 2000 he carried 230—and the Republican hold on the big cities is solid. Bush carried the Dallas-Forth Worth Metroplex 61%–37% in 2000 and metro Houston 57%–40%; together those two areas cast 47% of Texas's votes. Texas's two Republican senators have been re-elected against weak opponents, Phil Gramm by a 55%–44% margin in 1996 after his unsuccessful presidential campaign, Kay Bailey Hutchison by a 65%–32% margin in 2000, running ahead of George W. Bush. Democrats still have a majority in the U.S. House delegation, but that is only because of the cleverest Democratic redistricting plan of the 1990s: Republicans have won the total popular vote for the House every time since 1994 but have not captured more than 13 of the 30 seats.

In races sharply contested by trial lawyers and their adversaries, Republicans have taken over the state Supreme Court and in 1998 elected Attorney General John Cornyn, who sharply criticized his predecessor's huge fees to trial lawyers in the tobacco case. Republicans won all seven downballot offices in 1998, as Bush won his second term as governor by a 68%–31% margin. Republicans have rolled toward majorities in the state legislature. The state Senate is now 16–15 Republican, the state House 78–72 Democratic; Democrats were pleased in 2000 that they suffered no losses, as they had in every election in the 1990s. Once upon a time election outcomes in Texas were determined in the Democratic primary, and as recently as 1978, the year the first Republican governor was elected, 1.8 million votes were cast in the Democratic primary and only 158,000 in the Republican. (There is no party registration, and voters can choose either primary.) In 2000 it was something like the other way around: 1.1 million voters in the Republican presidential primary, 787,000 in the Democratic. This is not just a matter of Bush's local popularity. His successor as governor is Rick Perry, the Republican elected lieutenant governor in 1998; Perry's successor in the post, an important one in Texas because its holder runs the state Senate, is Republican former state Senator Bill Ratliff.

Pockets of Democratic strength in Texas are increasingly isolated. Their best vote is in the heavily Latino Border counties, which cast 8% of the state's votes; they voted 61%–38% for Ann Richards over George W. Bush when he ran in 1994, but in 2000 Al Gore's margin was less, 56%–42%. Another traditionally Democratic area is the urban strip from San Antonio to Austin. But the cultural liberals who hang out on Austin's Sixth Street are now being joined by high-tech engineers and hard-charging entrepreneurs in the new subdivisions and office centers running north of the pink marble Capitol and the UT campus, and the Anglos in San Antonio seem more solidly Republicans than its Latinos are Democratic. In 2000 Bush carried the counties containing Austin and San Antonio and won the combined metro areas 54%–40%. Rural Texas was once the most heavily Democratic part of the state: It was supplying crucial big margins for Lyndon Johnson and Lloyd Bentsen when the two big metro areas were voting Republican. In 1976 Jimmy Carter carried Texas 51%–48% because he carried rural Texas, which then cast 36% of the vote, 53%–46%. A dozen years later, George Bush carried rural Texas 57%–42%, which was 1% above his showing in the rest of the state. By 2000 rural Texas had moved again. It voted a rousing 67%–31% for George W. Bush; although it now casts only 30% of the state's votes, it produced 49% of his statewide popular vote margin. Cultural attitudes have always been conservative here, and there is trace left of the economic populism of Sam Rayburn.

The first parts of Texas to go Republican were the big cities: Dallas first elected a Republican congressman in 1954, Houston in 1966. In the early 1990s the Dallas-Fort Worth Metroplex was politically volatile, supplying the votes that elected Ann Richards in 1990 and giving native son Ross Perot 28% of its votes in 1992, nearly as many as Bill Clinton. But even as Dallas County has become more Democratic, the rapidly-growing surrounding counties have become overwhelmingly Republican, and the Metroplex voted 61%–37% for George W. Bush in 2000. Metro Houston, slightly less Republican, voted 57%–40% for Bush. Dallas-Fort Worth and Houston have had big in-migrations of Latinos, each has large black communities and each has the nucleus of left-leaning central city neighborhoods with the values of Boston or Seattle. But there was none of the movement toward the Democrats here that was so apparent in major metro areas in other states in the 1990s. The suburban expanses, full of aggressive entrepreneurs and conservative Christians, remained very heavily Republican. Take Collin County, north of Dallas, whose population increased 86%, from 264,000 to 491,000 in the 1990s. It has long been heavily Republican, voting a nearly identical 74%–25% for George Bush in 1988 and 73%–24% for George W. Bush in 2000. But the senior Bush's popular vote margin here was 44,000 votes; the younger Bush carried it by 85,000.

Texas Democrats look like an endangered species, but they are also a game lot, and if their situation is bleak they realize that they have nowhere to go but up. George W. Bush will not be on the ballot in 2002, and Democrats have some hopes that they can seriously challenge Governor Rick Perry; in early 2001 they were encouraging banker and oil man Tony Sanchez to run, hoping that he would spend liberally of his $600 million fortune. Perry won statewide in 1998 by just 50%–48%. And that was only after he and his opponent raised $15 million for a race that was crucial to George W. Bush's candidacy, for it would have been awkward to run for president if that meant turning the governorship over to the other party; the stars at Perry's fundraisers were George and Barbara Bush. But for the moment Democrats have political control only in small enclaves, in the central city cores and the Rio Grande Valley; Texas's national political figures are all Republicans—Bush, Senators Gramm and Hutchison, House Majority Leader Dick Armey, House Majority Whip Tom DeLay. On the major issues, and on the overriding question of whether to continue Texas's traditions of cultural conservatism and minimalist government, Bush and the Republicans seem very much on the majority side in Texas, and have a chance now to extend the Texas model to the nation as well.

Governor Rick Perry, then the Republican lieutenant governor, became governor of Texas on December 21, 2000, when George W. Bush, assured of his election as president, resigned the office. Perry grew up on his family's farm in Paint Creek, near where his great-great grandfather settled after fighting in the Civil War and was elected to the Texas house in the 1890s. His family owns a 10,000-acre ranch, and his father served 28 years as a county commissioner, as a Democrat. He was an Eagle Scout and went to Texas A&M to study to be a veterinarian; that didn't pan out though he did receive a degree in animal science. But he became a yell leader—cheerleader on lesser campuses, and a coveted position at A&M. These were the years of great student rebellions, but apparently not at College Station; Perry says he never saw a war protest. After college he served five years in the Air Force, piloting C-130 transports. In 1977 he returned to work on the family ranch. In 1984 he was elected to the state House, as a Democrat; this part of West Texas was for a very long time strong Democratic territory. He got on the Appropriations Committee and was one of three young legislators known there as the "pit bulls." In 1989 he was passed over for a leadership position and switched to the Republican Party. In 1990 he ran for Agriculture commissioner against the picturesque incumbent Jim Hightower, a populist who was perhaps the most liberal Democrat ever elected to statewide office. Perry got the support of the Farm Bureau and won an upset victory even while Democrat Ann Richards was winning the governorship. In an increasingly Republican Texas, Perry was easily re-elected in 1994.

Then in 1998 Perry ran for lieutenant governor. This is an important position in Texas, more powerful than the governorship, some say; the lieutenant governor not only presides over the state Senate but controls its proceedings and appoints its committee members and chairmen. The incumbent was Bob Bullock, a grizzled veteran and glorious political fighter, the strongest Texas Democrat after Richards lost in 1994. George W. Bush took care to work closely with Bullock, and developed a close and trusting relationship with him; Bullock endorsed Bush for reelection in 1998, even though he was godfather to one of Democratic candidate Gary Mauro's children, and he predicted that Bush would be president, and a good one. Bullock retired voluntarily in 1998, and died in 1999; his widow Jan introduced Bush at the 2000 convention in Philadelphia. Governors and lieutenant governors are elected separately in Texas, and Bush and Perry ran separate campaigns; Bush's chief political adviser, Karl Rove, worked for Perry in 1990 and 1994 but not in 1998. Nevertheless there were clear signs that Bush was vitally interested in Perry's candidacy, for without a Republican lieutenant governor he would be open to criticism in a presidential campaign that he was leaving the governorship to a Democrat. Perry, interestingly, had no Republican primary opposition for a post that obviously could lead directly to the governorship. Perry and his Democratic opponent, state Comptroller John Sharp, managed to raise $15 million for the campaign; George and Barbara Bush appeared at Perry's fundraisers. Sharp was a new Democrat who had done some interesting work on government reform, and served as student body president at A&M when Perry was yell leader. Perry's 50%–48% win opened the way to the governor's office for him, and to the presidency for Bush.

As lieutenant governor, Perry—contrary to the expectations of many—followed the Bush tradition of bipartisanship, working with senators of both parties, and breaking an impasse that threatened to turn the end of the 1999 session into chaos. He helped to pass record tax cuts, a teacher pay increase and more money for public schools. He also made a few missteps. Videotape caught him angrily protesting when his driver was stopped for speeding by state police. A letter sent to lobbyists specifying minimum contributions for them and their clients inevitably became public. His relations with Democratic Speaker Pete Laney, whom he had opposed for that office in 1992, were frayed, and Laney criticized him for campaigning for Republicans running against Democratic incumbents in 2000. For five weeks after the election it was not clear, of course, whether he would become governor, but he was obviously preparing. On December 21 he was sworn in—interestingly, the first Aggie governor of Texas. In his first major policy speech in January 2001 he made little mention of some of his trademark conservative issues—school vouchers, more prison construction, opposition to hate crime bills that mention special groups. Instead he called for $300 million for college scholarships, $40 million for teacher training in math education, affordable health insurance for teachers: where Bush had emphasized reading, Perry emphasized math; where Bush had emphasized the early grades, Perry called for doing more on higher education. Perry positioned himself in the center quickly, signing a hate crimes bill and a bill to provide DNA testing for defendents and prisoners, but also vetoing a bill banning the execution of mentally retarded persons.

There is one problem Texas doesn't have: its electricity deregulation, begun in 2001, has created no California-type problems; it allows utilities to make long-term contracts and since 1995 the state has built or is building 37 new power plants. Meanwhile, the Natural Resources Conservation Commission ordered a 90% cut in nitrogen oxide emissions from refineries and factories and a 55 mile per hour speed limit on freeways in the Houston area to reduce air pollution. Perry appointed blacks to the Supreme Court and the University of Texas Board of Regents—both firsts—and named Henry Cuellar, a Hispanic, Secretary of State.

Will Perry win a full term in 2002? He was helped when Senator Kay Bailey Hutchison announced in March 2001 that she would not run. But he may face serious Democratic competition from Tony Sanchez, the largest shareholder in International Bancshares and founder of Sanchez Oil & Gas, who is said to have a $600 million fortune and to be willing to spend between $10 and $30 million on a campaign. In early 2001 prominent Democrats like John Sharp and former San Antonio Mayor Henry Cisneros were urging Sanchez to run; Sanchez had contributed to many Democrats and also to George W. Bush, who named him to the University of Texas Board of Regents. A Sanchez candidacy would likely reduce the inroads Republicans have been making among Latino voters, who were 10% of the electorate in 2000 (Perry has been taking Spanish lessons) and might raise the spirits of Texas Democrats who have had much reason to be dispirited about Texas politics.

Cook's Call *Probably Safe.* Democrats are optimistic about wealthy businessman Tony Sanchez, hoping that his ability to finance a campaign and his Hispanic surname will end the party's dry spell. However, Sanchez has been mired in controversy and may not be as effective as Democrats hope. Sanchez could make this race very interesting, but Perry starts with the advantage.

Senior Senator Phil Gramm is a Republican first elected to the House in 1978 and the Senate in 1984. He is the product of adverse circumstances who makes his own considerable success sound like a hard grind. His father was an Army sergeant who died young; his mother, as he remembered in a grim-looking 1996 presidential campaign ad, sat him and his brother around the kitchen table and decided which bills they would pay. He flunked third, seventh and ninth grades, but his mother made him work hard and he went on to earn his Ph.D. from the University of Georgia. His field was economics, the one discipline that has moved to the right since the 1960s, with the growing belief in the efficacy of free markets; and Gramm certainly is a believer in free markets. He moved to Texas in 1967 to teach economics at Texas A&M. There he met and married his second wife, Wendy Lee, granddaughter of Korean immigrants and also an economics Ph.D. In the Texas of Lyndon Johnson's time, where Democrats held almost all offices and while preaching conservatism concentrated on funneling federal money into what was then considered an underdeveloped economy, Gramm conceived political ambitions, though he had no local connections, no personal money and little to none of the good ol' boy charm which was long an ingredient of political success in the state.

Seething with energy and conviction, he started giving speeches around the state, boosting free market economics and decrying the grasping hand of government. One of his first fans was Dicky Flatt, a print shop owner in Mexia who became a staple in Gramm speeches as the hard-working American whose money the government was taking away to spend on someone else. In 1976, at 34, Gramm ran as a Democrat in the primary against Senator Lloyd Bentsen and lost 64%–28%. Undaunted, Gramm ran for an open House seat in 1978, making the runoff by 115 votes over current 11th District Congressman Chet Edwards, and then winning the primary runoff 53%–47% and easily beating the Republican in the general. One sign of future races: He spent the then very considerable sum of $480,000. Within three years, Gramm was a major national figure. He got a seat on the Budget Committee, promising Majority Leader Jim Wright to be a team player. But, while he kept attending Democratic strategy meetings, he became co-sponsor of the Gramm-Latta budget resolution, the 1981 Reagan budget cuts, which passed the House over the opposition of the Democratic leadership.

For that apostasy and because Democrats decided that they could not trust him with confidential information, Speaker Tip O'Neill kicked Gramm off the Budget Committee in 1983. But Gramm turned that to his advantage by switching parties, resigning and triumphantly running in a special election campaign that gave him exposure in both the Houston and Dallas-Fort Worth media markets. "I had to choose between Tip O'Neill and y'all," he said, showing his capacity for attractively framing issues, "and I decided to stand with y'all." He won with 55% and in 1984 easily won the Republican Senate nomination when John Tower announced his retirement from Congress. The Democratic winner in an epic three-way primary was Lloyd Doggett, then a liberal state senator from Austin and now congressman from the 10th District, whom Gramm attacked for holding a fundraiser at a gay male strip joint in San Antonio. Gramm won 59%–41%.

In his first year in the Senate Gramm had two major initiatives. First, he engineered a vacancy in the east Texas 1st District seat by securing a federal judgeship for the incumbent Democrat and, with the aid of a young operative named Lee Atwater, came close to having his Republican candidate win in that yellow dog Democratic territory. His idea was to encourage Republicans to run in rural southern districts. If he had succeeded, they might have captured the House in 1988 or 1990, rather than 1994. Gramm's second initiative, advanced immediately after his first, was the Gramm-Rudman deficit reduction law requiring automatic budget cuts if the deficit was not reduced to specific levels. Politically, Gramm-Rudman swept all before it and passed both houses. Fiscally, under the lead of OMB Director James Miller (who earned his economics Ph.D. from the University of Georgia at the same time as Gramm), it did in fact result in lowering the deficit.

Gramm was one of the Republican negotiators at the 1990 budget summit and helped negotiate the final package of budget cuts, spending caps and tax increases. In 1991, he joined with Newt Gingrich to propose a series of tax cuts; in 1992, he held up Senate business to press for the balanced budget amendment; in 1995, he saw abolition of "baseline" and "current services" budgeting, which he had long opposed. Gramm was involved not only in national policymaking but in national politics. He was elected chairman of the Senate Republicans' campaign committee for the 1992 cycle and, despite Bill Clinton's victory and the press ballyhoo about "the year of the woman" (there were no such articles when most women candidates were Republicans in 1990), Republicans picked up one seat on election day and then another weeks later in the Georgia runoff. Gramm won a second term as chairman by 20–19 over Mitch McConnell, and in the 1994 cycle had a splendid record, as Republicans gained seven seats on November 8, 1994, and an eighth a day later when Richard Shelby of Alabama switched parties, and won control of the Senate.

Gramm was also running for president, and was not shy about it. "I love raising money," he said, and put out the theory that any candidate would have to spend $20 million to win the 1996 Republican nomination. That kept several candidates out of the field. He also tried to define the terms of the debate. "I have always felt on budget issues the party that defines the parameters of the debate almost always wins the debate," he once said, and he is as good as anyone in American politics at tightly defining issues to steer the public his way. Gramm preached root-and-branch opposition to the Clinton health care plan in 1993 and 1994; he supported the House Republicans' tough line on the budget in 1995. A strong free trader, he took on Pat Buchanan on trade issues when others counseled quiet. To his presidential campaign Gramm brought a bullish aggressiveness, a strong and well-disciplined mind, a gift for pungent phrase, the ability to frame issues favorably for his cause. But he also insisted on doing things his way, even when it did not help him. His commercials and his stump speech projected an angry, even pessimistic tone; there was nothing of the geniality and uplift of his fellow party-switcher Ronald Reagan. Gramm raised vast sums of money, but also spent vast sums on staff and in contests like the August 1995 Iowa straw poll in which he tied Bob Dole. He tried to engineer contests earlier than the Iowa caucuses and

New Hampshire primary, in order to get a lead on others with lesser resources. But that infuriated the governors of Iowa and New Hampshire, and cast a pall over his campaigns in those states. Then Buchanan took up his challenge in a Gramm-engineered firehouse primary in Louisiana February 6. Gramm, confident that his party backers would triumph, spent little time there, while Buchanan criss-crossed the state, calling talk radio hosts on his cell phone and getting interviewed by country editors. Gramm predicted he would win all 21 delegates; instead Buchanan won 13, and Gramm's campaign was effectively over. He finished fifth eight days later in Iowa, and pulled out of the race two days later, when it was obvious he would get nowhere in New Hampshire. In contrast to his high visibility in 1988 and 1992, he was quiet the rest of the year; "when you lose, you sit down," he said.

Gramm was also running for re-election in Texas and, under a law written by Democrats for Lyndon Johnson and used also by Lloyd Bentsen, he was allowed to run for both offices. Two Democratic congressmen ran against him, John Bryant of Dallas and Jim Chapman of east Texas, but the lead in the March 1996 primary went to Victor Morales (with the same last name as state Attorney General Dan Morales), a civics teacher at Poteet High School in Mesquite, who campaigned driving his pickup truck around the state. Bryant carried the Dallas-Fort Worth area with 62% of the vote, but it cast only 10% of primary votes; in rural Texas Chapman had a lead of only 38%–28% over Morales; in the border counties, which cast 19% of the vote, far more than their share of population, Morales won 60% of the vote. Statewide he had 36% to 30% for Bryant and 27% for Chapman. In the runoff Morales's ingenuous stands on issues and his Hispanic name got him past Bryant 51%–49%. Gramm, re-elected six years before with 60%, now seemed beleaguered. But Morales was hurt by the fact that his wife had not repaid delinquent student loans and by his stands against the balanced budget amendment and welfare reform and for affirmative action and same-sex marriage. Gramm won 55%–44%, losing the border counties that he had carried in 1990 but winning 60% again in rural Texas.

In January 1999 Gramm became chairman of the Banking Committee: the erstwhile rebel against the leadership had become an old bull. The main legislation before the committee was financial services deregulation. There was widespread support for repealing the 1933 Glass-Steagall Act, which separated banks from investment banking and commercial firms. In October 1998 Banking Chairman Alfonse D'Amato had assembled bipartisan support for a bill that had already passed the House. But Gramm blocked passage, because he wanted to change the Community Reinvestment Act, which he regarded as a "vehicle for fraud and extortion," encouraging "crony capitalism" because it requires bankers to provide loans to low and moderate income areas. Gramm proceeded to mark up his own version of financial services deregulation, but he reopened some issues considered settled in 1998, notably by allowing banks to cross over into insurance, real estate and securities industries. He also insisted on exempting small banks from the Community Reinvestment Act. His bill passed by an 11–9 party-line vote, but ranking Democrat Paul Sarbanes strongly opposed it, and Treasury Secretary Robert Rubin threatened a presidential veto. Another problem was that it provided for regulation by the Federal Reserve of banks that merge with other financial service companies, while the House committee bill provided for regulation by the Treasury. Gramm also beat Richard Shelby's proposal for allowing banks to act through operating subsidiaries. Gramm insisted on putting all 20 Banking Committee members on the conference committee, which proved unwieldy. Gramm negotiated a compromise on consumer protection amendments (he favored less stringent privacy amendments than the House) and agreed to bar new and existing thrifts from affiliating with commercial firms. When the Clinton administration threatened a veto on the CRA provisions in October, he called its bluff. After an all-night negotiating session, Gramm got a provision requiring CRA community groups to disclose their operations, with civil and criminal penalties, but agreed to retain the provision that barred banks with unsatisfactory CRA ratings to expand services. The result was that in November 1999 financial services deregulation was passed and signed into law—arguably the biggest legislative achievement of the 106th Congress. "The world changes and we have to change with it. We have a new century coming, and we have an opportunity to dominate that century the same way we dominated this country. Glass-Steagall, in the midst of the Great Depression, came at a time when the thinking was that the government was the answer. In this era of economic prosperity, we have decided that freedom is the answer."

Gramm was active on other legislative fronts. He worked to fortify the firewalls between defense and non-defense spending in the May 2000 budget resolution. With Charles Schumer, another big-state senator with whom he has worked (and tussled) on much Banking Committee legislation over the years, he sponsored an electricity deregulation bill that would have required power providers to sell to utilities and allowed them to sell directly to consumers; in February 2001 he argued that the Clinton and Bush orders that power providers must sell natural gas to near-bankrupt California utilities was not authorized by a Korean War-era law and could subject the government to substantial liability. Also with Schumer he proposed reducing SEC fees paid by companies that register and trade stocks; the fees are supposed to finance the agency, but in 2000 they brought in $2.2 billion and the SEC budget was only $370 million. He has opposed commodities regulation of banks' swaps contracts. He worked in 2000, as in previous years, to kill what he regards as pork-barrel legislation, but his relations with his one-time partner in that enterprise, John McCain, are cool; McCain was one of the few senators who supported his presidential candidacy in 1995, but in 1999 he backed his fellow Texan George W. Bush over McCain, though Gramm reached out to McCain after he suspended his campaign. In January 2001 he opposed Trent Lott's concession of equal committee memberships to Democrats: "I hope we have not cut the baby in half here today. I hope we can make this work." His relations with Banking's new chairman, Paul Sarbanes, are not close; Sarbanes resented how he worked with other committee Democrats on financial services deregulation. Gramm and Democrat Zell Miller came out early in January 2001 for George W. Bush's tax cut, perhaps bonding because both grew up in Georgia. He worked to quickly bring to the floor the bankruptcy bill that had been vetoed by Bill Clinton.

In recent years Gramm has taken a greater interest in Mexico. Long dubious about Mexico's enforcement of drug laws, in early 2001 he co-sponsored with liberal Democrat Barbara Boxer of California a proposal to do away with the drug certification process for Mexico. He became convinced that the new Mexican President, Vicente Fox, was determined to reduce the drug trade. "The only thing wrong with our drug certification law is that when we try to apply it to Mexico, it doesn't work. Instead of stemming the influx of drugs, it forces the United States to certify something that is plainly false, or it hobbles the Mexican officials who want to join us in halting the cross-border drug trade." And he made one of his priorities a guest worker law, which Fox has called for and would allow guest workers to remain in the United States for temporary agricultural and other work but would not necessarily lead to citizenship. Gramm's characteristic contribution: retirement accounts in which Mexican workers could put in money tax-free that they could access only in their native countries. Since most such workers intend to return home and remit large sums there in the meantime, this would be a net gain for them.

Gramm comes up for re-election in 2002. There was some speculation that, his presidential hopes gone, he might enter the private sector then, but he announced for re-election in January 2001.

Cook's Call   *Safe*. Gramm is a safe bet for re-election, and even if he retired it's highly unlikely that Democrats could win an open seat.

Junior Senator   Kay Bailey Hutchison, junior senator from Texas, is a Republican who won her seat in a June 1993 special election. She is of old Texas stock, the great-great-granddaughter of Charles S. Taylor, a signer of the Texas Declaration of Independence, who was a friend and business partner of Senator Thomas Jefferson Rusk, the first person to hold this seat. She grew up in LaMarque, near the refinery town of Texas City, a prom queen who went to college and then law school at the University of Texas; unable to get a law job in 1967, she worked for a Houston TV station as a reporter. In 1972, she won a seat in the legislature, its first Republican woman. In 1976 she went to Washington to fill the number two position at the National Transportation Safety Board. She married, moved to Dallas and went into banking and became a small business owner in 1978. In 1982, she lost a House race to Steve Bartlett, later mayor of Dallas. But she stayed active in Republican politics and in 1990 was elected state treasurer, a breakthrough race for state Republicans. Hutchison began her political career when it was no advantage to be a woman and has been mocked by liberals for her tight-lipped good manners and by Washington conservatives as a "Texas pompom girl." Her response: "This is what I have faced all my life—the trivialization of me—which I have not ever let bother me. I have always been able to rise above the expectations." Indeed: She is Senator from the nation's second largest state, one of three senators in history (Dianne Feinstein and Daniel Patrick Moynihan are the others) to have been elected with 4 million votes.

Her big break came in January 1993 when Lloyd Bentsen resigned his Senate seat after 22 years to become secretary of the Treasury. To replace him, Governor Ann Richards appointed Bob Krueger, a two-term congressman in the 1970s who nearly beat Senator John Tower in 1978, then ran third in a three-way Senate primary in 1984 and was elected Railroad commissioner (actually, oil regulator) in 1990. Running against him in the May 1993 all-party primary were three Republicans, Hutchison and Congressmen Joe Barton and Jack Fields. Krueger opposed the Clinton budget and tax plan, but Democrats were so unpopular in Texas then—Clinton had a 73% negative job rating—that Krueger won only 29% of the total vote, just behind Hutchison, also with 29%; Barton and Fields won 14% each. Krueger's cause was obviously doomed, and his campaign flailed around, running absurd ads in which Krueger, dressed in an Arnold Schwarzenegger *Terminator* outfit, claimed to be a lousy politician. Meanwhile, Hutchison kept the focus on Clinton. Hutchison won the June runoff by an astonishing 67%–33%, ahead of any Senate candidate here since the 1950s, when Republicans did not put up serious candidates.

Hutchison started her Senate career articulate and pleasant but willing to be partisan: pro-choice on abortion but opposing taxpayer funding and a Freedom of Choice Act that would wipe out state parental consent laws; opposing the Clinton tax increase and supporting NAFTA; and voting with two other women senators to deny Admiral Frank Kelso retirement with his four-star rank. But immediately after her win in 1993, Austin District Attorney Ronnie Earle, a liberal Democrat, sought to indict Hutchison for using office employees for political purposes and for destroying some records. It was a rotten prosecution from the start: The law imposes limits on state elected officials that at times seem absurd, and the destroyed records were mailing lists Hutchison had purged from her Texas computer on the advice of the Democratic attorney general. Then, in February 1994, Earle dropped the charges when the trial judge refused to rule on the admissibility of evidence seized in a June 1993 raid on Hutchison's office, in effect admitting he had no case.

Hutchison's job rating had declined, but not disastrously, as she entered the race for the full term in 1994. Three serious Democrats were running. The potentially strongest candidate, moderate Houston Congressman Mike Andrews, was eliminated in the March primary. In the April runoff, former Attorney General and bitter Richards enemy Jim Mattox lost 54%–46% to Richard Fisher, a free-spending moderate who campaigned extensively in the Border counties in Spanish. Fisher's credentials seemed a bit fishy—he claimed to have been an adviser to former British Prime Minister Margaret Thatcher, though Thatcher said their acquaintance was minor—and Hutchison cruised to a solid 61%–38% victory.

Back in the Senate she worked on welfare reform, helping to write a funding formula helpful to Texas and getting funding for colonias and other border infrastructure. She supported the partial-birth abortion ban but was still the target of conservatives who wanted to keep her off the delegation to the Republican National Convention in San Diego. But as a delegate there she presented the toughest criticism of Bill Clinton, mocking his changing schedule for balancing the federal budget. She sponsored a federal anti-stalking bill and homemakers' IRAs. In a time of falling prices, she has worked to keep Texas's oil industry pumping. In May 1998 she put into the disaster relief bill an amendment to stop the government from increasing the fees oil companies pay for pumping oil on federal land. In 1999, she called for tax credits to keep marginal wells operating and a tax exemption for restarting plugged up wells; she applauded Energy Secretary Bill Richardson for diverting 100,000 barrels a day into the Strategic Petroleum Reserve when prices were low. She beat a Democratic filibuster and inserted in a September 1999 appropriation a ban on Clinton administration plans to increase oil and gas royalties on federal land. In June 2000 she called for a "summer vacation" for the federal gas tax.

Hutchison has been one of the few senators elected in the 1990s who has taken a close interest in foreign policy. She has been wary of U.S. involvement in the former Yugoslavia, calling for an eventual pullout from Bosnia, and decrying Clinton administration policy in Kosovo. She commended the Clinton administration's decision not to send troops to East Timor in September 1999, but added, "We have seen the United States stumble into a series of regional crises—displacing local powers that share our objectives and are otherwise able to act on their own. This has led to strategic missteps—a hallmark of Clinton administration foreign policy." On Mexico issues, she called for a one-year waiver of the drug certification process in August 2000 and for examination of the Mexican policy requiring drivers of U.S.-registered vehicles to pay refundable deposits of up to $800 when they travel into the interior of Mexico.

Domestically, Hutchison was the Senate lead sponsor of measures to repeal the marriage penalty in the income tax since 1997. That bill was passed by the Senate 61–38 but was quietly vetoed by Bill Clinton. She brought it forward again in early 2001, when she went farther, with a proposal to relieve the tax burden not just on two-income families, but to give tax relief to home-makers too. "We want to help all married couples, not just those with a penalty." It passed the Senate 62–38 in May 2001 as part of President Bush's tax cut proposal. On other women's issues, Hutchison sponsored an anti-stalking law and has sought, with Dianne Feinstein, to extend the breast cancer stamp, with proceeds going to cancer research.

Hutchison's battle for re-election in 2000 turned out to be no contest. The winner of the March 2000 Democratic primary was a 74-year-old lawyer named Gene Kelly who was shunned by party leaders (the director of the state Democratic Party said, "The man has never called our office") and who spent all of $4,600 on his campaign. Hutchison, long since well-financed, spent $3.5 million and had $4.6 million cash on hand after November. Hutchison won 65%–32%, car-rying 237 of 254 counties. After the election she was selected vice chairman of the Senate Re-publican Conference. Her ambitions have not always been limited to the Senate. Possibilities of running for president have been shut off by the candidacy and victory of George W. Bush. But in late 2000 and early 2001 she showed some interest in running for governor of Texas, at one point saying that she was running for her last term in the Senate and that she would run for governor if it were an open seat—i.e., if Bush lost the presidential race and did not seek re-election in 2002. Even when Bush won and Republican Lieutenant Governor Rick Perry became governor, she maintained that "There are major issues in Texas that I care about," and "I'm not going to close the door." There was speculation she was waiting to see how Perry would fare with the legislature scheduled to end in May 2001. But party leaders wanted no part of a primary, and in March 2001 Hutchison said she would not run. "The speculation has gotten out of control, and I wanted to put an end to it. It was hurting our ability to do what we needed to do in our respective offices."

Presidential politics Texas is the counterweight to New York in presidential politics. In 2004 Texas will cast 34 electoral votes for the Republican nominee and New York 31 for the Democrat; in 2000, when the electoral vote was based on the 1990 Census, Texas cast 32 and New York 33. That will give the Republican, presumably George W. Bush, a +3 electoral votes from the second and third largest states, as versus a −1 in 2000; not much difference, but help to a president who won with 271 electoral votes. Texas last voted Democratic for president in 1976, when Jimmy Carter got most of his majority by carrying rural Texas, something a Democrat is not likely to do again soon, since Bush won rural Texas 67%–31%. The test case for Democrats probably came in 1988, when Texas's Lloyd Bentsen was the Democratic nominee for vice pres-ident. Bentsen had a strong political organization in Texas; he had first won his seat, in 1970, by defeating none other than George Bush. But the best the Dukakis-Bentsen ticket could do here was 43% of the vote. Bill Clinton lost Texas twice in the 1990s, and Al Gore never had a chance in 2000. He carried black voters by 91%–5%, but among Hispanics led by only 54%–42%; whites voted 73%–24% for Bush.

Texas's presidential primary, originally in May, was moved to March for Super Tuesday in 1988. In 2000, Bush won 88% of the vote here; Al Gore won 80% in the Democratic primary. The Republican primary electorate is heavily conservative; the Democratic primary electorate is in-creasingly liberal. In 1988, Michael Dukakis won the Democratic primary here with 33% and Jesse Jackson got 25%, ahead of Al Gore, running as a southern moderate, with 20%. And that was with a turnout of 1.7 million; turnout in 2000 was 787,000, with many fewer conservative voters in rural areas.

Congressional districting Texas's current congressional districting plan was the shrewdest gerrymander of the 1990s. The original 1991 redistricting plan was the product of Bob Mansker, aide to Democratic Congressman Martin Frost, and put into law when Democrats controlled the legislature and held the governorship. While modified in 1996 by court ruling, it is still in effect for 17 of the 30 districts, and has not been much changed for the others. The plan carefully constructs Democratic districts with incredibly convoluted lines and packs heavily Republican suburban areas into just a few districts. Starting in 1994, Republicans outpolled Democrats in House races, but Democrats still have a 17–13 majority in the delegation.

In January 2003 it will be different. Texas gained two seats in the 2000 Census, and Democrats no longer control redistricting. Governor Rick Perry is a Republican, Republicans have a 16–15 margin in the state Senate, while Democrats have a 78–72 margin in the state House. But there is a strong tradition of bipartisanship in the Texas legislature; minority party members are routinely given chairmanships, and few votes are on party lines; Bush nurtured bipartisan consensus on most major issues, made easier by the fact that many Democratic legislators are conservative on many issues. House Speaker Pete Laney, a Democrat who often cooperated with George W. Bush, appointed a Republican as chairman of House redistricting committee. And it takes 21 votes to assure that a bill will come to the floor of the Senate. Democrats in early 2001 were pushing for a plan that would protect incumbents first. Republicans were seeking a plan with smoother lines where heavily Republican areas are not just concentrated in a few districts. But any compromise will leave Democrats in a less favorable situation than they have been.

Demographically, one new district should be drawn in the Dallas-Fort Worth Metroplex, and this is likely to be heavily Republican; Democrats will have to hustle to preserve a winnable 24th district for Martin Frost, probably at the cost of putting the previously Democratic 5th out of reach. Another new district could be created in the rapidly growing Austin area; this would likely lean Republican, though it would also pare back the 10th and make it more Democratic. The great plains districts will have to be moved eastward, and the current arrangements of dividing the cities of Amarillo, Lubbock, Odessa and Midland into two districts—something done to boost Democrats' chances—will probably be abandoned. The east Texas lines, rooted in history, may be smoothed out. Some Democratic incumbents—Ralph Hall, Charles Stenholm, Chet Edwards—represent districts that are heavily Republican; they may be made more so. Odds favor a majority-Republican delegation from Texas, sooner or later.

THE PEOPLE: Pop. 2000: 20,851,820; Pop. 1990: 16,986,510, up 22.8% 1990–2000. 7.4% of U.S. total, 2d largest; 71% White, 11.5% Black, 2.7% Asian, 0.6% Amer. Indian, 0.1% Hawaiian, 2.5% Two+ races, 11.7% Other; 32% Hispanic Origin. 4.2% Unemployment. 2000 Voting age pop.: 14,965,061. 2000 Turnout: 6,407,637; 43% of VAP. Registered voters (2000): 12,365,235; no party registration.

POLITICAL LINEUP: Governor, Rick Perry (R); Lt. Gov., Bill Ratliff (R); Secy. of State, Henry Cueller (D); Atty. Gen., John Cornyn (R); Comptroller, Carole Keeton Rylander (R); Commissioner of Agriculture, Susan Combs (R); Commissioner of State Lands, David Dewhurst (R); State Senate, 31 (15 D, 16 R); Senate Pres. Pro Tempore, Chris Harris (R); State House, 150 (78 D, 72 R); House Speaker, Pete Laney (D). Senators, Phil Gramm (R) and Kay Bailey Hutchison (R). Representatives, 30 (17 D, 13 R).

ELECTIONS DIVISION: 512-463-5650; **FILING DEADLINE FOR U.S. CONGRESS:** January 2, 2002.

2000 Presidential Vote

Bush (R)	3,799,639	(59%)
Gore (D)	2,433,746	(38%)
Nader (Green)	137,994	(2%)
Other	36,258	(1%)

1996 Presidential Vote

Dole (R)	2,730,085	(49%)
Clinton (D)	2,455,853	(44%)
Perot (I)	378,117	(7%)

2000 Republican Presidential Primary

Bush (R)	986,416	(88%)
McCain (R)	80,082	(7%)
Keyes (R)	43,518	(4%)
Other	16,741	(2%)

2000 Democratic Presidential Primary

Gore (D)	631,428	(80%)
Bradley (D)	128,564	(16%)
LaRouche (D)	26,898	(3%)

Gov. Rick Perry (R)

Assumed office Dec. 2000, term expires Jan. 2003, 1st term; b. Mar. 4, 1950, Paint Creek; home, Austin; Texas A&M U., B.S. 1972; United Methodist; married (Anita).

Military Career: Air Force, 1972–77.

Elected Office: TX House of Reps., 1984–90; Comm., TX Dept. of Agriculture, 1990–98; Lt. Gov., 1998–2000.

Professional Career: Farmer & rancher.

Office: State Capitol, P.O. Box 12428, Austin, 78711, 512-463-2000; Fax: 512-463-1849; Web site: www.state.tx.us.

Election Results

1998 general	George W. Bush (R)	2,550,821	(68%)
	Garry Mauro (D)	1,165,592	(31%)
	Others	21,665	(1%)
1998 primary	George W. Bush (R)	576,528	(97%)
	Others	20,311	(3%)
1994 general	George W. Bush (R)	2,350,994	(53%)
	Ann Richards (D)	2,016,928	(46%)

Sen. Phil Gramm (R)

Elected 1984, seat up 2002, 3d term; b. July 8, 1942, Ft. Benning, GA; home, College Station; U. of GA, B.A. 1964, Ph.D. 1967; Episcopalian; married (Wendy).

Elected Office: U.S. House of Reps., 1978–84.

Professional Career: Prof., TX A&M U., 1967–78.

DC Office: 370 RSOB, 20510, 202-224-2934; Fax: 202-228-2856; Web site: www.senate.gov/~gramm.

State Offices: Dallas, 214-767-3000; El Paso, 915-534-6896; Harlingen, 210-423-6118; Houston, 713-718-4000; Lubbock, 806-472-7533; San Antonio, 210-366-9494; Tyler, 903-593-0902.

Committees: *Banking, Housing & Urban Affairs* (RMM). *Budget. Finance*: Health Care; International Trade; Social Security & Family Policy.

Group Ratings

	ADA	ACLU	AFS	LCV	CON	ITIC	NTU	COC	ACU	NTLC	CHC
2000	0	29	0	0	93	100	88	86	100	100	100
1999	0	—	0	0	75	—	83	94	96	—	—

National Journal Ratings

	1999 LIB —	1999 CONS		2000 LIB —	2000 CONS
Economic	0% —	83%		41% —	57%
Social	0% —	97%		0% —	90%
Foreign	6% —	90%		17% —	75%

Key Votes of the 106th Congress

1. Educ. Savings Accts.	Y	5. Review Movie Violence	Y	9. NATO War in Serbia	N
2. Prescrip. Drug Benefit	N	6. Gun Show Bckgrnd. Checks	N	10. Table Cuba Travel Ban	Y
3. Delay Ergonomic Standards	Y	7. Ban Part.-Birth Abortion	Y	11. Nuclear Test-Ban Treaty	N
4. Phase Out Estate Tax	Y	8. Broaden Hate Crimes List	N	12. Perm. Trade with China	Y

Election Results

1996 general	Phil Gramm (R)	3,027,680	(55%)	($14,078,131)
	Victor M. Morales (D)	2,428,776	(44%)	($978,862)
1996 primary	Phil Gramm (R)	838,339	(85%)	
	David Young (R)	75,463	(8%)	
	Henry C. Grover (R)	72,400	(7%)	
1990 general	Phil Gramm (R)	2,302,357	(60%)	($12,349,397)
	Hugh Parmer (D)	1,429,986	(37%)	($1,677,087)
	Others	89,814	(2%)	

Sen. Kay Bailey Hutchison (R)

Elected June 1993, seat up 2006, 2d term; b. July 22, 1943, Galveston; home, Dallas; U. of TX, B.A. 1992, J.D. 1967; Episcopalian; married (Ray).

Elected Office: TX House of Reps., 1972–76; TX Treasurer, 1990–93.

Professional Career: Political & legal corresp., KPRC-TV, 1967–70; Vice Chmn., Natl. Transp. Safety Bd., 1976–78; V.P. & Gen. Cnsl., RepublicBank Corp., 1978–82; Owner, McCraw Candies, 1984–88.

DC Office: 284 RSOB, 20510, 202-224-5922; Fax: 202-224-0776; Web site: www.senate.gov/~hutchison.

State Offices: Abilene, 915-676-2839; Austin, 512-916-5834; Dallas, 214-361-3500; Houston, 713-653-3456; San Antonio, 210-340-2885.

Committees: *Republican Conference Vice Chair. Appropriations*: Commerce, Justice, State & Judiciary; Defense; District of Columbia; Labor, HHS & Education; Military Construction (RMM); Transportation; VA, HUD & Independent Agencies. *Commerce, Science & Transportation*: Aviation (RMM); Communications; Oceans & Fisheries; Science, Technology & Space; Surface Transportation & Merchant Marine. *Rules & Administration*.

Group Ratings

	ADA	ACLU	AFS	LCV	CON	ITIC	NTU	COC	ACU	NTLC	CHC
2000	0	29	0	0	11	91	73	93	96	100	92
1999	0	—	0	0	26	—	72	94	88	—	—

National Journal Ratings

	1999 LIB	—	1999 CONS		2000 LIB	—	2000 CONS
Economic	40%	—	57%		32%	—	64%
Social	34%	—	64%		22%	—	73%
Foreign	16%	—	77%		27%	—	67%

Key Votes of the 106th Congress

1. Educ. Savings Accts.	Y	5. Review Movie Violence	Y	9. NATO War in Serbia	N
2. Prescrip. Drug Benefit	N	6. Gun Show Bckgrnd. Checks	N	10. Table Cuba Travel Ban	Y
3. Delay Ergonomic Standards	Y	7. Ban Part.-Birth Abortion	Y	11. Nuclear Test-Ban Treaty	N
4. Phase Out Estate Tax	Y	8. Broaden Hate Crimes List	N	12. Perm. Trade with China	Y

Election Results

2000 general	Kay Bailey Hutchison (R)	4,082,091	(65%)	($3,518,862)
	Gene Kelly (D)	2,030,315	(32%)	($4,602)
	Others	164,246	(3%)	
2000 primary	Kay Bailey Hutchison (R)	unopposed		
1994 general	Kay Bailey Hutchison (R)	2,604,218	(61%)	($6,114,755)
	Richard Fisher (D)	1,639,615	(38%)	($3,360,850)

FIRST DISTRICT

Texarkana, with a population of 35,000 and a rural and small town hinterland somewhat larger, for years was noteworthy mainly because its neat grid streets cross the Texas-Arkansas state line.

The downtown post office straddles the boundary; those who work in Texarkana, Texas, and live in Texarkana, Arkansas, are exempted from the Arkansas state income tax because Texas has none. Yet this small city and its hinterland produced not one but two 1990s presidential candidates: Ross Perot grew up in Texarkana, Texas, while Bill Clinton's boyhood home of Hope, Arkansas, is only 30 miles east on Interstate 30. Both grew up in comfortable but not lavish circumstances: Perot's father was a cotton broker, Clinton's stepfather a Buick dealer. Both lived in town, where most people had electricity and indoor plumbing—a vivid contrast with those living in the countryside when Perot was growing up in the 1930s and even when Clinton was young in the late 1940s.

Did the particular atmosphere of the Texarkana area have an effect on these men's politics? Maybe. Both were taught that they had obligations to those less fortunate, even while they obliged themselves to work hard to get ahead. Texarkana was populist country then, a place where farmers producing crops felt themselves at the mercy of Dallas cotton brokers, Wall Street financiers and railroad magnates who were grabbing all the gains of their hard work. Outside Texarkana, in landscape littered with small houses amid lazily winding rivers, there was little protection from the sun and wind, and precious little ornament. The politics here has always been Democratic: Clinton, who remembers his grandfather as an FDR fan, has never been anything else, while Perot seemed more at ease with moderate Democrats Lloyd Bentsen and Ann Richards than with the Republican Bushes. And in Texarkana this politics was surely affected by Wright Patman, congressman from the 1st District from 1929 until he died in office in 1976, a populist who began his career in the House by moving to impeach Treasury Secretary Andrew Mellon, punctuated it by calling constantly for low interest rates, and ended it after 12 years as Banking Committee chairman. But culture here was always traditional: this is an area of heavy churchgoing and proud patriotism. Traces of that can be seen in Perot's military bearing and Clinton's religious cadences. Another kind of culture is recalled at Texarkana's Perot Theater—which Ross helped to restore with an $800,000 donation; featuring an Italian Renaissance design and Grecian gold-leaf trim, the stage once featured performers such as Will Rogers and Annie Oakley, and has reopened as a live theater.

The 1st Congressional District of Texas includes most of the northeastern corner of the Texas—from Texarkana west to within two counties of Dallas and south almost to Lufkin. Politically, it is traditionally Democratic but has trended toward Republicans since the 1980s, especially in statewide races. In 1985 it was the scene of an epic special election, contrived by Phil Gramm, opposed by Jim Wright and Tony Coelho; the result was a narrow 51%–49% win for Democrat Jim Chapman and a halt to Gramm's plans to take control of the House by capturing rural Southern seats—a delay in the Republican takeover for nine years until 1994.

The congressman from the 1st District is still a Democrat, Max Sandlin, elected in 1996 to replace Chapman. Sandlin grew up in East Texas, went to Baylor, practiced law in Marshall and got involved in oil and gas exploration. He was Harrison County judge, an elected administrative position, when he ran for the House in a campaign far less dramatic and politically meaningful than the 1985 contest. Despite the district's Republican strength in statewide races, the Democratic primary attracted four times as many voters—a vestige of tradition—and Sandlin led attorney Jo Ann Howard, wife of a longtime Chapman opponent, 42%–34%. In the runoff, Sandlin, spending his own money and using his oil business connections to raise more, beat Howard 56%–44%. Sandlin pointed to his local tax-cutting experience and promised to find "common sense" solutions to Medicare and education. He attacked Republican Ed Merritt, an insurance attorney with no political experience, for backing Medicare "cuts." Merritt attacked him for appearing with Bill Clinton. Overall Sandlin spent $1.7 million, including $784,000 of his own money—a total almost four times Merritt's. Sandlin won 52%–47%, losing counties only in the periphery of the district, perhaps out of range of his media buy.

In the House, Sandlin failed to get a seat on the coveted Commerce Committee, but on the Transportation and Infrastructure Committee he worked for a funding formula to bring more highway money to Texas in the 1998 transportation bill. He has a moderate voting record that carefully straddles Democratic wings, joining the centrist Blue Dogs but also taking on populist causes like the right to sue HMOs. Feeling local pain from low energy prices and lower oil rig counts, Sandlin wants to increase tax credits for marginal wells, fill the Strategic Petroleum Reserve, and take other steps to bolster domestic production. At the last minute, he decided to support Clinton on Permanent Normal Trade Relations with China, but he voted to override Clinton vetoes on repeal of the marriage penalty and estate and gift taxes.

After defeating a poorly-financed challenger 59%–41% in pro-incumbent 1998, Sandlin became an early Republican target in 2000. The National Republican Congressional Committee hyped the candidacy of political neophyte Noble Willingham, a native of Wood County who gained reknown as barkeeper C.D. Parker on the long-running TV show, *Walker, Texas Ranger.* Willingham criticized Sandlin's bringing President Clinton to the district for a fundraiser and for his support of the Democratic agenda. But Sandlin won the Chamber of Commerce endorsement and showed that "yellow dog" Democrats still prevail in east Texas. He won 56%–43%, winning all 19 counties except for Nacogdoches in the southern tip of the district and Wood. Redistricting will require that the 1st gain about 30,000 new people; Democrats envision a modest shift of a few towns with the neighboring 2nd, but Republicans want big shifts in the erose lines in East Texas—shifts that could then hurt the Democratic incumbents.

Cook's Call *Potentially Competitive.* This marginal district is not safe territory for Democrats (Bush won here in 2000 with 64%) and Sandlin has to be wary of Republican redistricting plans for 2002.

THE PEOPLE: Pop. 2000: 622,475; Pop. 1990: 565,594, up 10.1% 1990–2000. 77.1% White, 17% Black, 0.4% Asian, 0.6% Amer. Indian, 1.3% Two+ races, 3.6% Other; 7.3% Hispanic Origin.

2000 Presidential Vote		
Bush (R)	136,777	(64%)
Gore (D)	77,001	(36%)

1996 Presidential Vote		
Dole (R)	94,433	(46%)
Clinton (D)	91,721	(45%)
Perot (I)	17,237	(8%)

Rep. Max Sandlin (D)

Elected 1996, 3d term; b. Sept. 29, 1952, Texarkana; home, Marshall; Baylor U., B.A. 1975, J.D. 1978; Baptist; divorced.

Elected Office: Harrison Cnty. Judge, 1986–89; Judge, Harrison Cnty. Court at Law, 1989–96.

Professional Career: Practicing atty., 1978–96; V.P., Howell & Sandlin Inc., 1989–96; Pres., E. TX Fuels, Inc., 1992–96.

DC Office: 324 CHOB 20515, 202-225-3035; Fax: 202-225-5866; Web site: www.house.gov/sandlin.

District Offices: Marshall, 903-938-8386; New Boston, 903-628-5594; Sulphur Springs, 903-885-8682.

Committees: *Financial Services* (15th of 32 D): Capital Markets, Insurance & Government Sponsored Enterprises; Domestic Monetary Policy, Technology & Economic Growth; Financial Institutions & Consumer Credit. *Transportation & Infrastructure* (20th of 34 D): Aviation; Highways & Transit.

Group Ratings

	ADA	ACLU	AFS	LCV	CON	ITIC	NTU	COC	ACU	NTLC	CHC
2000	60	50	71	36	22	83	40	71	33	30	40
1999	70	—	100	19	28	—	17	60	24	—	—

National Journal Ratings

	1999 LIB —	1999 CONS		2000 LIB —	2000 CONS
Economic	57% —	42%		56% —	44%
Social	55% —	45%		59% —	41%
Foreign	78% —	17%		69% —	28%

Key Votes of the 106th Congress

1. Patient Bill of Rights	Y	5. Bar RU-486 $ for FDA	N	9. NATO War in Serbia			Y
2. Accelerate Min. Wage	Y	6. Display 10 Commandments	Y	10. Perm. Trade with China			Y
3. Strike Ban on Ergo. Stnd.	Y	7. Gun Show Bkgrnd. Checks	N	11. Debt Relief for 3rd World			Y
4. Ovrd. Estate Tax Veto	Y	8. Ban Part.-Birth Abortion	Y	12. Drop Cuba Econ. Embargo			Y

Election Results

2000 general	Max Sandlin (D)	118,157	(56%)	($1,147,002)
	Noble Willingham (R)	91,912	(43%)	($246,827)
	Others	1,779	(1%)	
2000 primary	Max Sandlin (D)	56,207	(85%)	
	B.D. Blount (D)	10,265	(15%)	
1998 general	Max Sandlin (D)	80,788	(59%)	($814,434)
	Dennis Boerner (R)	55,191	(41%)	($72,992)

SECOND DISTRICT

East Texas is thick with landmarks of Lone Star history. There's still an Indian reservation in Polk County, and the Big Thicket National Preserve reminds you of what this land once looked like. Near Beaumont is Spindletop, where the world's first gusher spewed out in 1901 and started the Texas oil boom. Not far away is the huge oil field that wildcatter H. L. Hunt found in 1931, the foundation of a billion-dollar fortune. Much of East Texas looks little different from the wildcat days of 50 years ago: the town squares with courthouses and churches; the stands of cheap, quick-growing pine; the rough farmland. Yet much has changed. Real incomes have tripled over 50 years, endemic diseases have been wiped out, and racial segregation has mostly been abolished. When three white men in Jasper dragged James Byrd, an African American, behind their truck to his death in June 1998, a local jury quickly returned with guilty verdicts for all three and death sentence for two. Small-town isolation has been ended by television, interstate highways and regional shopping malls; metropolitan growth, sprinting outward from Houston's loop freeways, is spreading between the pine forests and reservoirs.

The 2d Congressional District includes all or part of 19 East Texas counties, most of them still seemingly rural; it runs from the oil port of Orange past Lufkin and Nacogdoches to Jackson-ville. Political tradition here is Democratic and populist, devoted to traditional values but with a taste for military posture and a certain Texas rowdiness. This is the kind of district Democrats must carry to win Texas: Ann Richards won it in 1990 and Bill Clinton in 1992 and 1996. But it voted for George W. Bush in his narrow win in 1994, and in 2000 he carried it by a 62%–38% margin over Al Gore.

The congressman from the 2d District is Jim Turner, a Democrat elected in 1996. He grew up in East Texas, went to college and law school in Austin, served in the Army, then returned to Crockett in Houston County, practiced law and was active in church and community organizations. In 1980 he was elected to the Texas House and served four years; he was mayor of Crockett for two years; in 1990 he returned to Austin in the state Senate. His opportunity to run for the House came when Congressman Charlie Wilson decided to retire after 24 years. Turner's legislative work against crime and for patient protection against HMOs, plus Wilson's support, helped him win a three-candidate Democratic primary with 59%, carrying everything but his opponents' home counties. The Republican primary was something of a surprise. Donna Peterson, a West Point graduate who opposed Wilson three times, lost the runoff by 2–1 to Christian conservative Brian Babin. Turner outspent Babin by nearly 2–1 and won 52%–46% in a year when the district was even in the presidential race; four years later it might have gone the other way.

In the House Turner joined the conservative-leaning New Democrat Coalition and Blue Dog Democrats. When Bill Clinton announced the bipartisan deal on the budget in May 1997, Turner was there beaming right behind him in the photograph. After the murder of James Byrd, Turner spoke eloquently about "this terrible act" and joined Congressional Black Caucus members in calling for federal prosecution, which of course proved to be unnecessary. Like other skillful Texas Democrats over the years, he took on legislative tasks in the House, like promoting the Shays-Meehan campaign finance bill by filing a discharge petition in 1999. He backed legislation to reduce prescription drug costs under Medicare. And unlike his East Texas Democratic colleague Max Sandlin, Turner was a party regular who voted to sustain Clinton's vetoes of the marriage-penalty and estate and gift tax repeals. With Republican Kevin Brady and Democrat Lloyd Doggett, he proposed that Congress apply to the federal government the sunset review process used in Texas. As the Blue Dogs policy co-chair in 2001, he urged George W. Bush to devote half of the surplus to reducing the debt, one-fourth to tax cuts, and one-fourth to spending priorities. On local projects, Turner took credit for securing $9 million for a shipbuilding contract in Orange, a $450 million contract for missile construction in Lufkin, and $2 million for environmental clean-up technology development in Huntsville.

Turner won 58%–41% in a 1998 rematch. In 2000 he had no Republican challenger. His biggest long-term threat is redistricting. Democrats no longer control the process in Texas, and the convoluted boundaries of the 2nd District may be smoothed out—or a district drawn that is demographically more dominated by the heavily Republican outer suburbs of Houston.

Cook's Call *Potentially Competitive*. Turner's moderate-to-conservative voting record helps insulate him against charges that he is too liberal for this Republican-trending, conservative district. But redistricting could give Turner some trouble.

THE PEOPLE: Pop. 2000: 669,591; Pop. 1990: 565,906, up 18.3% 1990–2000. 77.6% White, 15.5% Black, 0.5% Asian, 0.5% Amer. Indian, 1.3% Two+ races, 4.6% Other; 10.1% Hispanic Origin.

2000 Presidential Vote			1996 Presidential Vote		
Bush (R)	134,320	(62%)	Clinton (D)	90,379	(45%)
Gore (D)	81,731	(38%)	Dole (R)	89,817	(45%)
			Perot (I)	19,136	(10%)

Rep. Jim Turner (D)

Elected 1996, 3d term; b. Feb. 6, 1946, Ft. Lewis, WA; home, Crockett; U. of TX, B.B.A. 1968, M.B.A. 1971, J.D. 1971; Baptist; married (Ginny).

Military Career: Army, 1970–78.

Elected Office: TX House of Reps., 1981–84; Crockett Mayor, 1989–91; TX Senate, 1991–96.

Professional Career: Practicing atty., 1978–96; Exec. Asst., Gov. Mark White, 1984–86; Practicing atty., 1986–96; Chmn., TX Comm. on Children & Youth, 1993–94.

DC Office: 208 CHOB 20515, 202-225-2401; Fax: 202-225-5955; Web site: www.house.gov/turner.

District Offices: Lufkin, 936-637-1770; Orange, 409-883-4990.

Committees: *Armed Services* (13th of 28 D): Military Procurement; Military Research & Development. *Government Reform* (14th of 19 D): Criminal Justice, Drug Policy & Human Resources; Technology & Procurement Policy (RMM).

Group Ratings

	ADA	ACLU	AFS	LCV	CON	ITIC	NTU	COC	ACU	NTLC	CHC
2000	75	14	57	50	24	89	22	61	29	18	53
1999	75	—	83	38	40	—	15	60	28	—	—

National Journal Ratings

	1999 LIB —	1999 CONS		2000 LIB —	2000 CONS
Economic	57%	42%		61%	39%
Social	42%	56%		53%	47%
Foreign	61%	39%		58%	42%

Key Votes of the 106th Congress

1. Patient Bill of Rights	Y	5. Bar RU-486 $ for FDA	N	9. NATO War in Serbia	Y
2. Accelerate Min. Wage	Y	6. Display 10 Commandments	Y	10. Perm. Trade with China	Y
3. Strike Ban on Ergo. Stnd.	N	7. Gun Show Bkgrnd. Checks	N	11. Debt Relief for 3rd World	Y
4. Ovrd. Estate Tax Veto	N	8. Ban Part.-Birth Abortion	Y	12. Drop Cuba Econ. Embargo	Y

Election Results

2000 general	Jim Turner (D)	162,891	(91%)	($138,491)
	Gary Lyndon Dye (Lib)	15,939	(9%)	
2000 primary	Jim Turner (D) .... unopposed			
1998 general	Jim Turner (D)	81,556	(58%)	($575,117)
	Brian Babin (R)	56,891	(41%)	($287,322)

THIRD DISTRICT

Dallas, a synonym in popular culture for newly-gotten riches, is actually a community with a long history, and in its early years was one of the poorest and most backward parts of the nation. Dallas was named, improbably, for the stuffy and otherwise forgotten Philadelphia lawyer who was James K. Polk's vice president. The city got its commercial start as the place where the first railroad in Texas stopped at the three forks of the Trinity River, surrounded by dirt-poor farm country. "Its wealth originally came from cotton," John Gunther wrote in 1946, "but primarily it is a banking and jobbing and distributing center, the headquarters of railroads and utilities." In the 1960s Dallas was at the cutting edge of high-tech, the home of Texas Instruments and Ross Perot's EDS and of many defense contractors. The defense business is not as robust as it was in the 1980s, and the high-tech cutting edge of the 1990s can be found in other metropolitan areas. But the Dallas-Fort Worth Metroplex thrived in the 1990s, with growth from corporate headquarters re-located from less business-friendly precincts, from small businesses growing quickly in an entre-preneur-friendly climate and from companies making money trading with Mexico: Dallas has been the great beneficiary of NAFTA. In the late 1990s the Metroplex was thriving; in 2000 it created 103,000 new jobs, the largest increase of any metro area in the nation.

Dallas's growth has now extended far into the countryside. The home of the city's elite may still be in the mansion-lined streets of Highland Park, only a few miles north of downtown. But the center of Dallas's entrepreneurial economy has moved north to the LBJ Freeway and edge cities beyond, and the residential center of Dallas's business and professional classes has moved ever farther north in Dallas county, to the rolling, scrub-covered hills, as they recently were, of Collin County to the north. Over the last 20 years Collin County has moved from a countrified area of 144,000 to an affluent urban area of half a million. North Dallas was once one of the most Republican parts of the nation; now the most Republican areas in the Metroplex are in Collin County and Plano, corporate headquarters and edge city, site of megamansion subdivisions, the new face of successful Texas.

The 3d Congressional District of Texas is centered in north Dallas and in Collin County; it includes middle-income Mesquite east of Dallas, higher-income Garland and Richardson to the northeast, and Plano in the north. This is a very Republican district, 70%–30% for George W. Bush in 2000.

The congressman from the 3d District is Republican Sam Johnson, first elected in 1991, a former Air Force fighter pilot and prisoner of war in Vietnam, including nearly three years in solitary confinement. Johnson grew up in Dallas, graduated from SMU and got a master's from George Washington University. After his F-4 was shot down over North Vietnam during his 25th mission, he was imprisoned from 1966–73 in the "Hanoi Hilton" and was left with a slight stoop in his walk and a disfigured hand. On his return, Johnson—who still flies his own plane "as a great way to get away"—started a home-building company and was elected to the Texas House in 1984. He won his congressional seat in a 1991 special election after incumbent Steve Bartlett was elected mayor of Dallas. Johnson ran second in the primary to former Peace Corps head Tom Pauken. In the runoff, he emphasized his war record and, although he showed limited knowledge of issues in debate, won 53%–47% over Pauken, later a sharp critic of Governor George W. Bush as Texas Republican chairman.

In the House, Johnson has a strong conservative record, opposing pork barrel projects of all kinds, voting for more IRAs and against extending unemployment benefits. He was a founder and chair of the Conservative Action Team, which pressed Republican leaders to stick with goals from budget targets to shutting down the National Endowment for the Arts. He criticized Newt Gin-grich's handling of the 1997 disaster-relief bill, and his support for Majority Leader Dick Armey to take over as speaker led to the July 1997 abortive coup. Every Congress he offers a constitutional amendment to repeal the 16th Amendment, which authorized the federal income tax. He was an early advocate of the successful repeal in 2000 of the earnings limit for Social Security recipients. He proposed the Good Samaritan Tax Act to permit corporations to take a tax deduction for charitable giving of food. He is now chairman of the Subcommittee on Employer-Employee Relations, which, now that George W. Bush is president, may revive worker-management cooperation measures it advanced in the mid-1990s. Unsurprisingly, Johnson has been a defender of the F-22 fighter jet, partly produced at the Lockheed Martin plant in Fort Worth. In early 2001, he passed an amendment to help domestic workers save for retirement.

Unlike some other former POWs in Congress, Johnson strongly opposed Bill Clinton's decision to extend diplomatic and trade recognition to Vietnam. On the 25th anniversary of his release as a POW, House colleagues paid tribute to him as "an American hero." Even though he was a POW with John McCain for a year and a half, Johnson strongly backed Bush in the 2000 primaries. McCain "cannot hold a candle to George Bush," he said. After the election, he and Representative Mac Thornberry introduced legislation to make the voting process easier for military personnel. Johnson has served on the Smithsonian Institution's Board of Regents, and for months he led criticism of the *Enola Gay* exhibit, which sentimentalized the plight of Japanese in World War II and totally ignored the Japanese attack on Pearl Harbor and Japanese mistreatment and torture of Americans captured in battle. Johnson was successful in getting a distinguished board to approve the withdrawal of the exhibit and the resignation of the museum director.

Collin County nearly doubled its population in the 1990s, and the 3rd was the second-fastest growing district in Texas, after the next-door 26th. This raises the possibility that another heavily Republican congressional district will be created in the Metroplex, as one of Texas's two new seats resulting from the 2000 Census. Johnson surely will find a congenial district to run in.

Cook's Call *Safe.* This is one of the safest Republican seats in the state—if not the country—and one of the fastest growing in the Texas during the 1990s. The 3rd District will need to shed more than 180,000 residents.

THE PEOPLE: Pop. 2000: 835,040; Pop. 1990: 567,383, up 47.2% 1990–2000. 72.9% White, 9.6% Black, 8% Asian, 0.5% Amer. Indian, 0.1% Hawaiian, 2.5% Two+ races, 6.4% Other; 15.4% Hispanic Origin.

2000 Presidential Vote			1996 Presidential Vote		
Bush (R)	185,390	(70%)	Dole (R)	103,465	(61%)
Gore (D)	80,293	(30%)	Clinton (D)	53,832	(32%)
			Perot (I)	13,402	(8%)

Rep. Sam Johnson (R)

Elected May 1991, 5th term; b. Oct. 11, 1930, San Antonio; home, Dallas; S. Methodist U., B.B.A. 1951, George Washington U., M.S. 1974; Methodist; married (Shirley).

Military Career: Air Force, 1950–79 (Korea & Vietnam).

Elected Office: TX House of Reps., 1984–91.

Professional Career: Home builder.

DC Office: 1030 LHOB 20515, 202-225-4201; Fax: 202-225-1485; Web site: www.house.gov/samjohnson.

District Office: Richardson, 972-470-0892.

Committees: *Education & the Workforce* (8th of 27 R): 21st Century Competitiveness; Employer-Employee Relations (Chmn.). *Ways & Means* (11th of 24 R): Health; Oversight; Social Security.

Group Ratings

	ADA	ACLU	AFS	LCV	CON	ITIC	NTU	COC	ACU	NTLC	CHC
2000	0	23	0	0	94	100	76	85	100	88	100
1999	0	—	0	6	85	—	73	88	96	—	—

National Journal Ratings

	1999 LIB —	1999 CONS	2000 LIB —	2000 CONS
Economic	0% —	84%	0% —	94%
Social	10% —	90%	0% —	79%
Foreign	3% —	92%	0% —	88%

Key Votes of the 106th Congress

1. Patient Bill of Rights	N	5. Bar RU-486 $ for FDA	Y	9. NATO War in Serbia	N
2. Accelerate Min. Wage	N	6. Display 10 Commandments	Y	10. Perm. Trade with China	Y
3. Strike Ban on Ergo. Stnd.	N	7. Gun Show Bkgrnd. Checks	N	11. Debt Relief for 3rd World	N
4. Ovrd. Estate Tax Veto	Y	8. Ban Part.-Birth Abortion	Y	12. Drop Cuba Econ. Embargo	N

Election Results

2000 general	Sam Johnson (R)	187,486	(72%)	($892,324)
	Billy Wayne Zachary (D)	67,233	(26%)	($6,702)
	Others	7,178	(3%)	
2000 primary	Sam Johnson (R)	40,802	(93%)	
	J.A. Gonnell (R)	2,843	(7%)	
1998 general	Sam Johnson (R)	106,690	(91%)	($601,473)
	Ken Ashby (Lib)	10,288	(9%)	

FOURTH DISTRICT

The Red River Valley is just one of the hearts of Texas. It is hardscrabble farm country along an unnavigable river. First settled in the 1830s, in the days of the Texas Republic, many counties here reached their population peak around 1900, when a large extended farm family worked every 160 acres. This was the part of Texas that first sent Sam Rayburn to Congress in 1913; he served as speaker from 1940 until his death in 1961 except for two terms in which Republicans had the majority; majestically, he declined to serve as minority leader then. The Red River then was one of the strongest Democratic parts of the country, with a sentimental regard for Confederate veterans and a seething hatred of Wall Street bankers. This was Rayburn's politics: He helped write the securities laws that, still today, so successfully regulate Wall Street, and other regulatory measures that have fared less well. Today Rayburn's politics has almost completely vanished from the area. The cause of the Confederacy has been left behind, populist suspicion of Wall Street has been replaced by active brokerage accounts, and allegiance to the Democratic Party is a thing of the distant past.

The 4th Congressional District is the lineal descendant of the seat that Rayburn held, and still includes his home town of Bonham in Fannin County, which houses a Rayburn museum. But almost one-third of the district's voters now live in the Dallas-Fort Worth Metroplex, with another third in the small oil (and now high-tech) cities of Tyler (famous for its annual Texas Rose Festival and the East Texas State Fair) and Longview. These are the homes of upwardly mobile families, far more trusting of free markets than of government regulation. Politics here has changed as well. In 1940, when Rayburn first became speaker, his district voted 90% for Franklin Roosevelt. In 1992, Bill Clinton finished third here, with 29%, behind George Bush and Ross Perot; in 2000 George W. Bush carried the district 72%–28%.

The congressman from the 4th is Ralph Hall, a conservative Democrat who votes almost always with Republicans, one of the few left in the House. He was first elected in 1980 after a 30-year career in local politics and business; he was a county judge as long ago as 1950 and from 1962–72 was in the Texas Senate. He usually has the most conservative voting record of any House Democrat and rarely backs his leadership except on purely party or procedural matters, and not always on those: He once declined to vote for Tip O'Neill for speaker. He opposed the Clinton budget and tax package in 1993 and supported just about everything in the Contract with America in 1995. He continues as a prime sponsor of the constitutional amendment to require two-thirds House and Senate votes to raise taxes. He was one of five House Democrats who voted to impeach Bill Clinton. Clinton's lying under oath "was perjury and perjury is a felony and it's impeachable," Hall said. "I'm not a big fan of his." But Hall is not a pure free marketeer: He voted against NAFTA. On the Commerce Committee he backed limits on the FCC's authority to regulate religious broadcasters but was skeptical about allowing the regional Bells into long distance and favored cable reregulation.

Those views are perhaps one reason why Hall did not join five other Democrats—some with less conservative voting records—who switched parties after Republicans won the House majority. If he had switched, he probably would have become a committee chairman by now. "I think it's my duty to stay [a Democrat] and try to pull them back toward the middle," he said. Hall is a hunting pal of Energy and Commerce's ranking Democrat John Dingell, and he was the ranking Democrat on the Energy and Power Subcommittee, a convenient slot for a booster of the oil and gas industry. He gave up that post in January 2001, when he became ranking Democrat on the Science Committee, where he has emphasized the use of space for biomedical research: "I fully and firmly believe that we're going to find some cures for the dreaded diseases, cancer and diabetes there, because we can't find them on Earth." He authored a 1997 law banning federal funding for physician-assisted suicide.

In recent years there has been speculation that Hall would retire or would face serious competition because of the district's growing Republican base in the north Dallas suburbs. But Hall has continued to win handily. He endorsed Republican Senator Phil Gramm for re-election in 1996 and he spoke favorably about George W. Bush in 2000; his affection for the Bushes was solidified in 1992 when then-President George Bush telephoned Hall to extend best wishes while he was at the Texas bedside of his grandson, who was suffering from a brain tumor. After the 2000 election, Hall worked with House centrists from both parties to promote bipartisanship; on key votes in early 2001, he was usually with Bush. It is not clear what will happen in redistricting. The current boundaries of the 4th District are irregular in the extreme, for reasons that were politically relevant 20 years ago but have now been forgotten. Demographically, the 4th should probably be replaced by a district even deeper within the Dallas-Fort Worth Metroplex, suburban and Republican—seemingly a misfit for the rural, small town Democrat Hall. But he may have his own way of adapting; in 2000 his son was elected a district judge back home, as a Republican.

Cook's Call *Probably Safe.* The fact that Hall continues to win big in the 4th District, even as Republicans rack up huge victories at the national level (Bush won here with 72%), is a testament to Hall's unique appeal. Republicans hope to give him some trouble in the redistricting process. Once the popular and conservative Hall retires, this seat will fall into Republican hands. But until then, he remains a tough target.

THE PEOPLE: Pop. 2000: 707,329; Pop. 1990: 567,231, up 24.7% 1990–2000. 85.1% White, 7.7% Black, 0.6% Asian, 0.7% Amer. Indian, 1.7% Two+ races, 4.2% Other; 8.8% Hispanic Origin.

2000 Presidential Vote		
Bush (R)	169,447	(72%)
Gore (D)	65,406	(28%)

1996 Presidential Vote		
Dole (R)	114,787	(56%)
Clinton (D)	71,784	(35%)
Perot (I)	18,021	(9%)

Rep. Ralph M. Hall (D)

Elected 1980, 11th term; b. May 3, 1923, Fate; home, Rockwall; U. of TX, TX Christian U., S. Methodist U., LL.B. 1951; United Methodist; married (Mary Ellen).

Military Career: Navy, 1942–45 (WWII).

Elected Office: Rockwall Cnty. Judge, 1950–62; TX Senate, 1962–72.

Professional Career: Practicing atty., 1951–80; Pres. & CEO, TX Aluminum Corp., 1967–68; Spec. Cnsl., Howmet Corp., 1970–74.

DC Office: 2221 RHOB 20515, 202-225-6673; Fax: 202-225-3332; Web site: www.house.gov/ralphhall.

District Offices: Gainesville, 940-668-6370; Rockwall, 972-771-9118; Sherman, 903-892-1112; Tyler, 903-597-3729.

Committees: *Energy & Commerce* (4th of 26 D): Energy & Air Quality; Health. *Science* (RMM of 22 D).

Group Ratings

	ADA	ACLU	AFS	LCV	CON	ITIC	NTU	COC	ACU	NTLC	CHC
2000	20	29	0	21	75	94	52	80	88	82	100
1999	20	—	16	0	92	—	54	71	84	—	—

National Journal Ratings

	1999 LIB —	1999 CONS		2000 LIB —	2000 CONS
Economic	46% —	53%		29% —	67%
Social	19% —	79%		0% —	79%
Foreign	15% —	81%		12% —	78%

Key Votes of the 106th Congress

1. Patient Bill of Rights	Y	5. Bar RU-486 $ for FDA	Y	9. NATO War in Serbia	N
2. Accelerate Min. Wage	N	6. Display 10 Commandments	Y	10. Perm. Trade with China	Y
3. Strike Ban on Ergo. Stnd.	N	7. Gun Show Bkgrnd. Checks	N	11. Debt Relief for 3rd World	N
4. Ovrd. Estate Tax Veto	Y	8. Ban Part.-Birth Abortion	Y	12. Drop Cuba Econ. Embargo	N

Election Results

2000 general	Ralph M. Hall (D)	145,887	(60%)	($739,496)
	Jon Newton (R)	91,574	(38%)	($132,984)
	Others	4,417	(2%)	
2000 primary	Ralph M. Hall (D)	unopposed		
1998 general	Ralph M. Hall (D)	82,989	(58%)	($597,793)
	Jim Lohmeyer (R)	58,954	(41%)	($246,101)
	Others	2,137	(1%)	

FIFTH DISTRICT

Not all of Dallas is glitz and postmodern marble. From each side of downtown, on one of the three street grids that skew to each other, is an older Dallas, with neighborhoods of high-ceilinged old mansions, modest bungalows and shotgun houses running out toward the old airport at Love Field or the State Fair Grounds and the Cotton Bowl in east Dallas, or south to the desolate treeless parks along the cement-lined Trinity River. Some of this older Dallas is being renovated and rebuilt, with chic cafes and trendy stores serving those who make their livings catering to the rich farther north. Other once middle-class neighborhoods are filling up with immigrants from Mexico and other parts of Latin America, once again noisy with children as they were in the 1950s when people moved here not from Mexico or Central America but from the almost all-Anglo counties of north and central Texas. The 2000 Census showed that 30% of the population in Dallas County is Hispanic.

Texas's 5th Congressional District, as redrawn in 1996, includes such neighborhoods just south and east of downtown Dallas. Added in the redistricting were the affluent Lakewood and Lake Highlands areas around and beyond White Rock Lake, out to the LBJ Freeway. Then, following the same lines used in the Democrats' creative 1991 redistricting, the 5th proceeds in a narrow corridor through the suburbs to combine this part of Dallas County with seven rural and small town counties about halfway between Dallas and Houston, plus black neighborhoods in Tyler and Bryan. The aim was to avoid including much Republican suburban territory and connecting hip inner-city neighborhoods with yellow-dog Democratic rural counties. The strategy has not quite worked. In 2000 the 5th District definitely had an ethnically varied makeup—17% black and 23% Hispanic, but it was not very Democratic. As rural areas swung away from Bill Clinton's Democrats, the affluent Dallasites within the district stuck with Republicans and George W. Bush attracted support from Latinos. This is a district that voted 48%–44% against Bill Clinton in 1996 and 60%–40% for George W. Bush in 2000.

The congressman from the 5th District is Pete Sessions, a Republican elected in 1996. Sessions grew up in Waco, graduated from Southwestern University, then worked at Southwestern Bell in Dallas for 16 years; his father William Sessions, a federal judge, served as FBI director from 1987–93. Pete Sessions ran in the 1991 special election in the 3d District and finished sixth. In 1993 he resigned from the phone company to run against 5th District Democrat John Bryant. A liberal and an active legislator, Bryant was a prime beneficiary of the Democratic districting plan, and he won easily in 1992. But in 1994, Sessions ran a vigorous campaign, making a two-day, 12-city tour of the district's rural portions with a livestock trailer full of horse manure and a sign saying "the Clinton health care plan stinks worse than this trailer." "A vulgar thing," Bryant sniffed. Although he outspent Sessions 2–1, Bryant won by just 50%–47%. In 1996, Bryant decided to run for the Senate against Phil Gramm; Bryant was the surprise loser, 51%–49%, in the low-turnout Democratic runoff to high school teacher Victor Morales, who lost 55%–44% to Gramm.

Sessions ran again in 1996 and won the March primary. That result was thrown out in the redistricting case in the summer, but only Sessions and the winner of the Democratic primary, John Pouland, a former regional GSA administrator, ran in November. Sessions was pleased that his home area in east Dallas was now included in the district. He charged that Pouland was a big government liberal and would abandon U.S. military bases overseas; Pouland criticized subsidizing the foreign bases while pursuing Medicare "cuts." Pouland charged that Sessions had changed to an anti-abortion stance after his 1991 race; Sessions sent out brochures graphically describing partial-birth abortions. This was a seriously contested race: Sessions won 53%–47%. He spent $1 million, Pouland $600,000. Redistricting made a big difference. Sessions won 56%–44% in Dallas County, 10% ahead of his 1994 showing there.

In the House Sessions has a solidly conservative voting record. He has chaired the Results Caucus, which oversees progress toward targets for government reform. In 1999 he was tapped for the Rules Committee, a sure sign that he is a leadership loyalist. He sponsored the constitutional amendment to require a two-thirds vote to raise taxes, and has been a leading advocate of the Republicans' proposal to put Social Security and Medicare surpluses in a lockbox. In a sign that he knows how to play across the aisle, he joined with Chuck Grassley, Ted Kennedy and Henry Waxman on a bill to permit families with disabled children to keep their Medicaid coverage even if their income rises; Sessions and his wife have a son with Down's syndrome. In 2000, he joined the fruitless effort to seek common ground on a managed-care reform bill. He was an early House organizer of the bandwagon for then-Governor Bush's presidential candidacy.

Sessions has faced competitive re-elections. His opponent in 1998 was Victor Morales, the nominee against Phil Gramm two years before, who again ran a shoestring campaign, criticizing Sessions for taking special-interest contributions. Sessions won 56%–43%; most of his margin came from the half of the electorate who voted in Dallas County, but he also carried seven of the 10 other counties. In 2000, Democrats spoke well of his challenger Regina Montoya Coggins, who was a Clinton White House liaison to local elected officials and whose husband was Clinton's U.S. attorney in the Dallas area; she was well known for her on-air work at KERA-TV in Dallas. She attacked the "politics of selfishness" and said that the incumbent was "in the pocket of the big drug companies." Sessions termed her "at the outer edges of the liberal agenda" and said that she was a "liar" in describing how he would benefit from tax cuts. With her Clinton and feminist contacts, Coggins was competitive financially. In a strong Republican year in Texas, Sessions had a slightly smaller victory margin, 54%–44%; Coggins won three rural counties. One big question in redistricting is whether the Democrats, arguing for incumbent protection, will seek to preserve an east-Dallas-and-rural-counties district, or redraw the lines to attach east Dallas and the rural counties both to similar territories nearby. Certainly the Democrats' desire to help incumbents does not extend to Sessions. But to draw a district like this, which is more Democratic but does not significantly reduce the Democratic percentage in the adjacent 24th and 30th Districts, may be beyond the capacities even of the 24th District's Martin Frost.

Cook's Call *Potentially Competitive.* Against both weak and strong Democratic opponents, Sessions has never won big in this Republican-leaning district. Republicans hope that redistricting will help him in 2002.

THE PEOPLE: Pop. 2000: 657,495; Pop. 1990: 566,887, up 16% 1990–2000. 67% White, 17.4% Black, 1.5% Asian, 0.6% Amer. Indian, 2.2% Two+ races, 11.3% Other; 23% Hispanic Origin.

2000 Presidential Vote			1996 Presidential Vote		
Bush (R)	125,064	(60%)	Dole (R)	97,057	(48%)
Gore (D)	84,518	(40%)	Clinton (D)	87,987	(44%)
			Perot (I)	16,045	(8%)

Rep. Pete Sessions (R)

Elected 1996, 3d term; b. Mar. 22, 1955, Waco; home, Dallas; SW U., B.A. 1978; Methodist; married (Juanita).

Professional Career: District Mgr., SW Bell Telephone Co., 1978–93; V.P., Public Policy, Natl. Center for Policy Analysis, 1994–95.

DC Office: 1318 LHOB 20515, 202-225-2231; Fax: 202-225-5878; Web site: www.house.gov/sessions.

District Offices: Athens, 903-675-8288; Dallas, 214-349-9996.

Committees: *Rules* (8th of 9 R): Rules & Organization of the House.

Group Ratings

	ADA	ACLU	AFS	LCV	CON	ITIC	NTU	COC	ACU	NTLC	CHC
2000	0	21	0	14	90	100	68	76	96	97	100
1999	5	—	0	6	82	—	70	84	96		

National Journal Ratings

	1999 LIB — 1999 CONS		2000 LIB — 2000 CONS	
Economic	24%	72%	6%	85%
Social	0%	96%	21%	78%
Foreign	3%	92%	33%	62%

Key Votes of the 106th Congress

1. Patient Bill of Rights	Y	5. Bar RU-486 $ for FDA	Y	9. NATO War in Serbia	N
2. Accelerate Min. Wage	N	6. Display 10 Commandments	Y	10. Perm. Trade with China	Y
3. Strike Ban on Ergo. Stnd.	N	7. Gun Show Bkgrnd. Checks	N	11. Debt Relief for 3rd World	N
4. Ovrd. Estate Tax Veto	Y	8. Ban Part.-Birth Abortion	Y	12. Drop Cuba Econ. Embargo	Y

Election Results

2000 general	Pete Sessions (R)	100,487	(54%)	($1,826,456)
	Regina Montoya Coggins (D)	82,629	(44%)	($1,636,875)
	Others	2,842	(2%)	
2000 primary	Pete Sessions (R)	unopposed		
1998 general	Pete Sessions (R)	61,714	(56%)	($747,685)
	Victor M. Morales (D)	48,073	(43%)	($107,870)

SIXTH DISTRICT

The Dallas-Fort Worth Metroplex—yes, the name is part of everyday speech there—has spread outward from its historic nodes in downtown Dallas and Fort Worth. Although Dallas is the larger population center, much of the development has moved west, across the dusty plains where one crosses the barely perceptible Balcones Escarpment, the geologist's boundary between green and grassy East Texas and the brown and barren West. This was empty territory a few decades ago; now it has mostly been filled in, with subdivisions and shopping centers that leave some feeling of the shape of this land under the enormous Texas sky.

The 6th Congressional District takes in much of this territory. It is the descendant of a more-rural district that stretched from Dallas-Fort Worth to Houston and was represented from 1979–85 by Phil Gramm. Now the 6th is entirely within the Metroplex, more than 80% of it in Tarrant County. It includes much of Dallas/Fort Worth International Airport and cargo-servicing Alliance Airport, developed by Ross Perot Jr. In between are rapidly growing and increasingly affluent suburbs—Colleyville, Grapevine, Euless, Bedford—and to the south is Arlington, home of the Texas Rangers' Ballpark and of Six Flags Over Texas. The local economy has diversified: away from once-heavy reliance on Pentagon contracts and toward high-tech firms like Texas Instruments and Electronic Data Systems, plus airport-related wholesale trade and transportation services. Essentially the 6th is a ring of suburban territory around Fort Worth, wrapping around the 12th District and part of the 24th. The boundaries were slightly smoothed out by a federal court in 1996. The original Democratic redistricters tried to concentrate Republicans in this district. Asked the court's motivation, 6th District Congressman Joe Barton responded, "I'd like to be able to talk to the federal judges and ask what the heck they were trying to accomplish."

Barton grew up in rural Ennis, in then-rural Ellis County just south of Dallas. He graduated from Texas A&M and Purdue, worked in business and was a White House Fellow. When Gramm ran for the Senate in 1984, Barton ran for the House, and won the Republican runoff by only 10 votes and the general with 57%. At first, Barton had two great causes, one defunct, the other successful—in a way. The first was the superconductor Supercollider, an enormous scientific laboratory that was to have been built in Waxahachie, south of Dallas, part of which is in the district. In retrospect this was a Texas project, alive only so long as George Bush was president; despite Barton's efforts, the House voted 282–143 to zero it out in 1993. His other cause has been sponsorship of the balanced budget amendment, requiring a two-thirds vote to raise taxes. When the House took up the issue in early 1995, many freshmen complained that party leaders were not doing enough to support Barton's version, while leaders whispered there was no way the tax-limitation measure could win the needed 290 votes. In fact it got 253. Newt Gingrich promised to schedule the two-thirds amendment for a vote on subsequent April 15ths until it passed, but the number of votes has never exceeded the 1995 bill. But Barton claimed progress across the country, where many states have approved tax-limitation plans. But the budget surpluses starting in 1998 changed the conversation, and the amendment has been mostly forgotten.

In the majority, Barton chaired the Energy and Commerce Oversight and Investigation Subcommittee and conducted extensive hearings on food and drug laws. These resulted in enactment, with bipartisan support, of major FDA modernization, encouraging the agency to more quickly review innovative drugs and medical devices. He was an official observer to the 1997 global warming talks in Kyoto, and said the treaty was overly stringent and would have adverse economic consequences. But he supported legislation to encourage companies to reduce greenhouse emissions on their own. In 1999 Barton became chairman of the Energy and Power Subcommittee. His goals were electricity deregulation—which Barton urged because of inconsistent state plans—and nuclear-waste disposal. Although the subcommittee was sympathetic to the oil and gas industry, he was unable to circumvent Bill Clinton's opposition, including a veto of the nuclear waste bill. The electricity bill also ran into clashes with outgoing committee chairman Thomas Bliley. In 2001, Barton maneuvered around the committee chairmanship clash between Billy Tauzin and Mike Oxley and expanded his subcommittee's jurisdiction to energy and air quality. He also hoped for close cooperation with the Bush Administration. "In the modern era, you can't do energy policy unless you do a fair amount of environmental policy," he said. "We're going to have a lot to do." Foes charged that Barton would place the Clean Air Act in jeopardy.

Barton can be stubborn and original. He has voted against compromise budgets backed by Republican leaders, opposed Permanent Normal Trade Relations with China because of its human rights record, sought unsuccessfully to require a three-fifths vote to break spending caps and pressed for mandatory random drug testing for the House. He has worked with Ed Markey on improving privacy of financial records. Back home, he assisted DFW Airport—which he predicted would become the world's busiest—with new radar consoles and computer software for its air-traffic system. He passed a relaxation of the Wright Amendment, named for former House Speaker Jim Wright, restricting flights to Dallas's Love Field. Barton has had some political disappointments. He ran for the Senate in 1993 after Lloyd Bentsen resigned to be Treasury secretary. Despite the support of former Governor Bill Clements, he finished third with just 14% of the vote in the May all-party primary. In 1994 he was outgoing Republican state Chairman Fred Meyer's choice to succeed him. But Clements opposed his candidacy, and Barton lost at the convention to Tom Pauken. In 1995 he became the House chairman of Gramm's hapless presidential campaign.

Barton has been re-elected easily and he almost surely will come out of redistricting with a solidly Republican district, though the boundaries surely will be far less irregular.

Cook's Call *Safe*. Barton is in solid standing for 2002 in this conservative Republican district. It was one of the fastest growing in Texas during the 1990s and will need to shed more than 100,000 residents.

THE PEOPLE: Pop. 2000: 759,418; Pop. 1990: 565,504, up 34.3% 1990–2000. 81.8% White, 8% Black, 3.7% Asian, 0.5% Amer. Indian, 0.1% Hawaiian, 2.1% Two+ races, 3.7% Other; 9.6% Hispanic Origin.

2000 Presidential Vote

Bush (R)	206,470	(71%)
Gore (D)	84,493	(29%)

1996 Presidential Vote

Dole (R)	143,067	(60%)
Clinton (D)	77,542	(33%)
Perot (I)	17,234	(7%)

Rep. Joe Barton (R)

Elected 1984, 9th term; b. Sept. 15, 1949, Waco; home, Ennis; Texas A&M U., B.S. 1972, Purdue U., M.S. 1973; United Methodist; married (Janet).

Professional Career: Asst. to V.P., Ennis Business Forms, 1973–81; White House Fellow, U.S. Dept. of Energy, 1981–82; Consultant, Atlantic Richfield Co., 1982–84.

DC Office: 2264 RHOB 20515, 202-225-2002; Fax: 202-225-3052; Web site: www.house.gov/barton.

District Offices: Arlington, 817-543-1000; Ennis, 817-875-8488; Fort Worth, 817-543-1000.

Committees: *Energy & Commerce* (3d of 31 R): Energy & Air Quality (Chmn.); Health; Telecommunications & The Internet. *Science* (7th of 25 R): Space & Aeronautics.

Group Ratings

	ADA	ACLU	AFS	LCV	CON	ITIC	NTU	COC	ACU	NTLC	CHC
2000	10	21	16	7	87	73	71	83	100	87	100
1999	5	—	0	0	75	—	65	86	91	—	—

National Journal Ratings

	1999 LIB —	1999 CONS		2000 LIB —	2000 CONS
Economic	0% —	84%		25% —	75%
Social	0% —	96%		0% —	79%
Foreign	3% —	92%		0% —	88%

Key Votes of the 106th Congress

1. Patient Bill of Rights	N	5. Bar RU-486 $ for FDA	Y	9. NATO War in Serbia	N
2. Accelerate Min. Wage	N	6. Display 10 Commandments	Y	10. Perm. Trade with China	N
3. Strike Ban on Ergo. Stnd.	N	7. Gun Show Bkgrnd. Checks	N	11. Debt Relief for 3rd World	N
4. Ovrd. Estate Tax Veto	Y	8. Ban Part.-Birth Abortion	Y	12. Drop Cuba Econ. Embargo	*

Election Results

2000 general	Joe Barton (R)	222,685	(88%)	($936,534)
	Frank Brady (Lib)	30,056	(12%)	
2000 primary	Joe Barton (R)	unopposed		
1998 general	Joe Barton (R)	112,957	(73%)	($1,117,657)
	Ben B. Boothe (D)	40,112	(26%)	($61,462)

SEVENTH DISTRICT

When the senior George Bush moved from Midland in West Texas to Houston in 1960, he bought a house in Briarwood, in what was then the western edge of the fast-growing city, beyond Memorial Park and Loop 610, long before the Galleria and high-rises went up around the intersection of Post Oak and Westheimer. Bush returned to Houston in 1993 and built a new house a mile from his old one, just west of Memorial Park, then the largest in Houston. Bush's favorite shopping mall is nearby on Sage and San Felipe and his favorite barbecue joint a mile east on Memorial; his office is atop the Park Laureate building at 10000 Memorial. But now all these landmarks are not at the edge of the vastly bigger—and economically vibrant—Houston metropolitan area, but near its epicenter, certainly its retail center and not far from its commercial center, though the industrial center of gravity remains far to the east, near the Ship Channel. Near the lavish Galleria, business leaders have made this area more than a shopping center. With extensive landscaping and art, they have sought to give it a unique and inviting image, and they have planned improvements on the 610 to increase mobility for commuters and shoppers.

The 7th Congressional District is the lineal descendant of the district that elected George Bush its first member of the House in 1966. It occupied far more territory then, but its boundaries have been pared back as the population of the west side of Houston has skyrocketed. There are more than 1.5 million people today in the area that had 350,000 when Bush was first elected. The district was pared back in 1992 so that it now starts just outside Memorial Park and extends west on Westheimer and the Katy Freeway and occupies most of Harris County west of Hillcroft and Bingle. It remains hyper-Republican, one of the most Republican districts in the nation.

The congressman from the 7th District is John Culberson, a Republican elected in 2000. He grew up in Houston and graduated from Southern Methodist University, then worked for his father's advertising agency. He graduated from South Texas College of Law and worked as a civil defense attorney. In 1986, at 29, Culberson won a seat in the Texas House, where he served for 14 years. Although he had few notable legislative accomplishments, he succeeded in challenging one federal judge's oversight of the state's prison system. George Bush's successor as congressman from the 7th District, Bill Archer, chairman of the House Ways and Means Committee since 1995, had long made it known that he would retire in 2000, after 30 years of service and when House Republicans' six-year term limit on committee chairmen kicked in. Archer never accomplished his goal of replacing the income tax with a broad-based consumption tax, but he did preside over significant cuts in tax rates and welfare reform; his purist approach to policy and his punctilious attention to duty (he insisted on preparing his own income tax return every year) meant that he did not easily accede to compromise, but he did move policy more in his direction than anyone would have predicted.

It was obvious that Archer's successor would be chosen in the March 2000 Republican primary, and it was seriously contested, with eight candidates. The clear front-runners were Culberson and Peter Wareing, a Houston merchant banker and son-in-law of Texas oilman Jack Blanton. Culberson led with 38% to Wareing's 27%; finishing third with 13% was Republican National Committeewoman Cathy McConn, who knocked on more than 10,000 doors and found that many residents were unaware that Archer was retiring. The runoff four weeks later turned into a contest about which candidate was more associated with Democrats—definitely a taboo in this district. Culberson charged that his opponent had contributed $5,000 to a Democrat, state comptroller candidate Paul Hobby, in the same year that Wareing chaired the Texas Republicans' Victory '98 drive and that he had voted for Democrats several times; Wareing countered that Culberson voted in a Democratic primary when he was 19 years old. The self-financing Wareing had a financial advantage: a budget of nearly $4 million, compared with Culberson's $650,000. But with an extensive grassroots campaign, Culberson won 60%–40%. "I wouldn't change one Culberson volunteer for all the $4 million," the winner said. The general election was no contest.

In the Archer tradition, Culberson says his goal is to junk the current tax system and replace it with a tax on consumption. He calls himself a "Jeffersonian Republican" who is passionate about transferring power from the federal to local governments. He opposes racial quotas and preferences, gun control, and abortion (except in cases of rape, incest, or to save the life of the mother). Whether, as with Archer, it will take two decades for him to rise to influence remains to be seen. He was the freshman representative on the Republican steering committee making House committee assignments.

Cook's Call   *Safe.* Culberson will have no trouble holding onto this heavily Republican district for as long as he likes.

THE PEOPLE: Pop. 2000: 772,147; Pop. 1990: 565,007, up 36.7% 1990–2000. 72.3% White, 7.5% Black, 7.2% Asian, 0.4% Amer. Indian, 0.1% Hawaiian, 3% Two+ races, 9.5% Other; 23.6% Hispanic Origin.

2000 Presidential Vote		
Bush (R)	185,186	(73%)
Gore (D)	69,151	(27%)

1996 Presidential Vote		
Dole (R)	146,923	(66%)
Clinton (D)	63,853	(29%)
Perot (I)	10,569	(5%)

Rep. John Culberson (R)

Elected 2000, 1st term; b. Aug. 24, 1956, Houston; home, Houston; Southern Methodist U., B.A. 1981; S. TX Col. of Law, J.D. 1988; Methodist; married (Belinda).

Elected Office: TX House of Reps., 1986–2000, Maj. Whip, 1999–2000.

Professional Career: Jim Culberson Advertising, 1981–85; Practicing atty., 1988–2000.

DC Office: 1728 LHOB 20515, 202-225-2571; Fax: 202-225-4381; Web site: www.house.gov/culberson.

District Office: Houston, 713-682-8828.

Committees: *Budget* (20th of 24 R). *Education & the Workforce* (27th of 27 R): Education Reform; Workforce Protections. *Transportation & Infrastructure* (40th of 42 R).

Group Ratings and Key Votes: Newly Elected

Election Results

2000 general	John Culberson (R)	183,712	(74%)	($1,085,071)
	Jeff Sell (D)	60,694	(24%)	($13,122)
	Others	4,187	(2%)	
2000 runoff	John Culberson (R)	29,968	(60%)	
	Peter Wareing (R)	20,017	(40%)	
2000 primary	John Culberson (R)	23,894	(38%)	
	Peter Wareing (R)	16,837	(27%)	
	Cathy McConn (R)	8,488	(13%)	
	Mark Brewer (R)	4,865	(8%)	
	Wallace Henley (R)	4,649	(7%)	
	Ron Kapche (R)	3,107	(5%)	
	Others	1,474	(2%)	
1998 general	Bill Archer (R)	111,010	(93%)	($346,064)
	Drew Parks (Lib)	7,889	(7%)	

EIGHTH DISTRICT

When Houston Intercontinental Airport opened in 1969, it was located far north of the city, in vacant ground near the small town of Humble (named for the oil company that was the predecessor of Exxon)—25 miles away from downtown Houston or from just about any other concentration of population. Today, the airport, known now as George Bush Intercontinental is still a jaunt from downtown Houston, but it is no longer in the middle of nowhere. It's in the middle of a zone of rapid metropolitan expansion and growth, of commercial office space and upscale residential subdivisions rising on land that once held roadside stands and barbecues and unpainted farmhouses with water pooling on low swampy fields. Greater Houston has spread far out into the countryside, past Loop 610 in the inner city, past the Sam Houston Tollway, past the now mislabeled Farm-Market 1960, out past Conroe and Woodbranch Village in once rural Montgomery County.

The 8th Congressional District of Texas occupies most of this territory. A district that once covered the docks along the Houston Ship Channel has moved out with the people, so that its southern boundary runs roughly along FM 1960, sometimes dipping south to the Sam Houston Tollway. Within its current boundaries, the 8th includes almost all of Montgomery County and two still mostly rural counties to the west and takes in College Station, home of Texas A&M University. This institution deserves more notice than it usually gets: It is one of Texas's two major state universities, with quite a different atmosphere from the University of Texas at Austin. A&M has an agricultural and military tradition and is the site of the George Bush Presidential Library; its students' test scores are similar to those at UT, but their political attitudes are far more conservative. Following the tragic death of 11 students and one former student in the November 1999 collapse of the tower built with logs for the traditional bonfire for the UT football game, a state investigating commission criticized the university administration for lack of control, and the bonfire tradition has been suspended till at least 2002. College Station is one college town that is staunchly Republican, like the rest of the 8th District: defiantly free market on economics (like former A&M economics professor Phil Gramm), respectful of tradition on cultural issues, firmly hawkish on military policy.

The congressman from the 8th District is Kevin Brady, a Republican first elected in 1996. Brady grew up and went to college in South Dakota, moved to Montgomery County in 1978 and headed the Woodlands Chamber of Commerce for 18 years. In 1990 he was elected to the Texas House. When Congressman Jack Fields announced in 1995 he was retiring, Brady decided to run. His main opponent in the obviously decisive Republican primary was Eugene Fontenot, a physician who wanted "to restore America to its Christian heritage." Two years before Fontenot had run in the open 25th District and had spent $4.7 million, most of it his own money; he lost the general election to Democrat Ken Bentsen 52%–45%. In 1996, Brady was the choice of party regulars—Fields, Governor George W. Bush, Senators Phil Gramm and Kay Bailey Hutchison; Fontenot was endorsed by Patrick Buchanan, Pat Robertson and Phyllis Schlafly. Fontenot attacked Brady for being one of two Republicans to vote against the carrying-concealed-weapons law. Brady had opposed most gun control bills, but not this one; when he was 12 his father was shot and killed while trying a case in a South Dakota courtroom. Brady and Fontenot ran against each other four separate times in that one year. In the March primary, Fontenot led Brady 36%–22% in a six-candidate field. In the April runoff Brady won 53%–47%. But the U.S. Supreme Court ruled in June 1996 that three of Texas's districts were invalid, and their boundaries and those of 10 adjoining districts were redrawn. One of them was the 8th. As a result there was an all-party primary on election day November 1996, in which Brady led Fontenot 41%–39%. In the December runoff, turnout was sharply down. This evidently helped party-regular Brady, who won 59%–41%, carrying every county. Fontenot did not spend as heavily on this contest as he had two years before; in the 8th District races he spent $1.3 million, not much more than Brady's $1.1 million.

In the House, Brady has compiled a conservative voting record. He called for renegotiating extradition treaties to deny safe harbors overseas to fugitives accused of heinous crimes in the U.S. With the murder of his father always a fresh memory, Brady has been an advocate of victims' rights and the death penalty. As he had in Austin, he called for sunsetting government agencies every 10 years, to require them to justify, if they can, their continued existence. He worked with Asa Hutchinson to require full disclosure of campaign contributions and to relax restrictions on soft money and issue ads. In a man-bites-dog tale, he refused to support a company's application for a $9.5 million grant for a riverwalk at The Woodlands: "I think projects that aren't essential can't be supported, even if they're in a congressman's district or hometown," he said. He criticized the Clinton EPA's clean-air standards for the Houston area as "unreasonable and unrealistic." In January 2001, he took Bill Archer's Houston-area seat on Ways and Means. "I can't hope to fill Bill Archer's shoes," he said, "but I can follow his path toward tax reform, thrift, individual responsibility and real fundamental change in the way Washington works." An advocate of abolishing the IRS and moving toward a consumption tax, he called for a national dialogue on a better tax system. He strongly backed the Bush tax cuts.

Since his four contests in 1996, Brady has had no problem winning re-election. Redistricting could change his district boundaries substantially, since this part of metro Houston has grown rapidly. Republicans would like to put some of the current 8th's heavily Republican precincts into more marginal districts, but there is sure to be a heavily Republican district on the north side of the metro area.

Cook's Call *Safe*. In a district where the Democratic nominee for president has routinely failed to break 30%, it's not hard to see why Brady is a sure bet for re-election.

THE PEOPLE: Pop. 2000: 776,623; Pop. 1990: 565,315, up 37.4% 1990–2000. 85.7% White, 5.3% Black, 2.5% Asian, 0.4% Amer. Indian, 0.1% Hawaiian, 1.8% Two+ races, 4.3% Other; 11.3% Hispanic Origin.

2000 Presidential Vote
Bush (R)	208,205	(78%)
Gore (D)	59,846	(22%)

1996 Presidential Vote
Dole (R)	149,402	(67%)
Clinton (D)	59,045	(26%)
Perot (I)	14,589	(7%)

Rep. Kevin Brady (R)

Elected 1996, 3d term; b. Apr. 11, 1955, Vermillion, SD; home, The Woodlands, TX; U. of SD, B.S. 1990; Catholic; married (Cathy).

Elected Office: TX House of Reps., 1990–96.

Professional Career: Exec., Woodlands Chamber of Commerce, 1978–96.

DC Office: 428 CHOB 20515, 202-225-4901; Fax: 202-225-5524; Web site: www.house.gov/brady.

District Offices: College Station, 979-846-6068; Conroe, 936-441-5700; Houston, 281-895-8892.

Committees: *Ways & Means* (23d of 24 R): Select Revenue Measures; Social Security.

Group Ratings
	ADA	ACLU	AFS	LCV	CON	ITIC	NTU	COC	ACU	NTLC	CHC
2000	0	21	0	7	83	94	66	80	100	84	100
1999	15	—	0	0	48	—	60	95	88	—	—

National Journal Ratings
	1999 LIB —	1999 CONS		2000 LIB —	2000 CONS
Economic	30%	70%		6%	85%
Social	25%	72%		0%	79%
Foreign	20%	78%		0%	88%

Key Votes of the 106th Congress
1. Patient Bill of Rights	Y	5. Bar RU-486 $ for FDA	Y	9. NATO War in Serbia	N
2. Accelerate Min. Wage	N	6. Display 10 Commandments	Y	10. Perm. Trade with China	Y
3. Strike Ban on Ergo. Stnd.	N	7. Gun Show Bkgrnd. Checks	N	11. Debt Relief for 3rd World	N
4. Ovrd. Estate Tax Veto	Y	8. Ban Part.-Birth Abortion	Y	12. Drop Cuba Econ. Embargo	N

Election Results
2000 general	Kevin Brady (R)	233,848	(92%)	($370,246)
	Gil Guillory (Lib)	21,368	(8%)	
2000 primary	Kevin Brady (R)	unopposed		
1998 general	Kevin Brady (R)	123,372	(93%)	($496,717)
	Don L. Richards (Lib)	9,576	(7%)	

NINTH DISTRICT

The spongy land of the Texas Gulf Coast, where the French explorer LaSalle and the Spanish colonizer Galvez dreamed of thriving settlements, remained mostly unsettled until well into the 20th Century. The elements here are not gentle, as Galveston learned when a hurricane in 1900 destroyed this city-on-a-sandspit. The summer heat is ferocious and the rains torrential; few crops grow well here. But this is a land of oil. Ever since the Spindletop strike in Beaumont in 1901, the coastal area has grown. First oil exploration, then petroleum refining, then petrochemicals: The straight-edged metal of oil rigs and the intricate curving metalwork of refineries shine through the swampy landscape of southeast Texas. And the rig workers and mechanical engineers they brought here have given a kind of permanent roughneck air to the region. To celebrate the centennial of Spindletop, thousands gathered to observe a solid stream—of water—gush out of the wellhead; former President George Bush was honorary chairman of the commemoration. In the early days, the town was so overrun by boomers who drained the local water supply that some doctors advised people to drink whiskey instead of water. That made the Women's Christian Temperance Union a prominent local force, for a while.

The 9th Congressional District of Texas occupies much of this territory. About half its people live in and around Beaumont and Port Arthur, still very much oil country and among the few places in Texas where labor unions have had any strength. The other half live south of Houston— in Galveston, now restoring its grand historic buildings (and the unlikely site of a Dickensian Christmas celebration every year); the refinery town of Texas City, where more than 500 died after two freighters containing ammonium nitrate fertilizer exploded in 1947; and the Lyndon B. Johnson Space Center, where America's space missions are planned, brought here originally by then-Vice President Johnson and longtime Houston Congressman Albert Thomas.

The congressman from the 9th District is Nick Lampson, a Democrat elected in 1996. Lampson grew up in Beaumont; he got his first job at age 12 when his father died. After graduating from Lamar University, he taught science in Beaumont schools, leading the first local Earth Day celebration in 1970, and then a real estate management course at Lamar; he also headed a home health care company. In 1977, at 32, he was elected Jefferson County tax assessor; he claimed to cut the cost of tax collections during 18 years on the job.

In 1996 Lampson ran against Congressmen Steve Stockman: one of the most controversial Republican freshmen elected in 1994, who won the seat by upsetting 42-year incumbent and Judiciary Committee Chairman Jack Brooks. Stockman stirred controversy by writing a letter to Attorney General Janet Reno expressing concern about raids allegedly planned on militias and for a garbled report about a threatening fax from a militia group his office received the day of the 1995 Oklahoma City bombing. Even so, he was in trouble in the 9th, if only because of the district's Democratic leanings. Lampson had solid backing for the Democratic nomination. But when the Supreme Court ruled three Texas districts unconstitutional, and the redistricting plan adopted by a three-judge federal court marginally shifted the 9th's boundaries and required a new election, the going got nasty. Stockman said Lampson's home health care company had been accused of defrauding Medicare, while Lampson accused Stockman of failing to repay his college loans on time. Democrats cried foul when one of their losing primary candidates, Geraldine Sam, ran in the open November 5 election; the Democratic vote was split, and Stockman led Lampson 46%–44%. Then Sam endorsed Stockman: more screams from Democrats. Labor unions worked Beaumont hard to get Lampson votes in the December runoff, and its county turnout fell only 29% compared to 50% in the rest of the district. Lampson won 53%–47%, winning more than his entire margin in the Beaumont area.

In the House, Lampson has a moderate voting record typical of Anglo Texas Democrats and is a member of the New Democrat Coalition. He promoted the Johnson Space Center from his Science Committee assignment and worked on the Transportation and Infrastructure Committee to improve the hurricane evacuation route on U.S. 69, deepen the Sabine-Neches Ship Channel, and restore estuary habitats. Following the abduction and murder of a 12-year-old girl, he became a national advocate for missing and exploited children and formed a Congressional Missing and Exploited Children's Caucus; in March 2001, he joined a State Department delegation in the Netherlands to discuss international abduction. On impeachment, Lampson was one of 31 Democrats to vote for the Republican impeachment inquiry, but he voted against all four counts of impeachment. Faithful to his labor allies, he voted against Permanent Normal Trade Relations with China; but he voted to override Bill Clinton's veto of the estate and gift tax repeal. He wants to lift the trade embargo on Cuba so that his local rice farmers can have a new market.

Back home, following new allegations of Medicare irregularities and declining business, his wife sold their home health care business. Lampson twice has been re-elected easily. In 2000 he was opposed by Republican Paul Williams, who was a fill-in quarterback during the 1987 National Football League strike, but Steve Stockman sent out fundraising letters attacking Lampson that suggested to many recipients that he was running. "I think he has a screw loose," Williams said. Lampson lost the Harris County portion of the district around the space center, but carried Galveston and Jefferson County handily. With neither party in total control, this district is not likely to be greatly changed in redistricting.

Cook's Call *Safe.* Although this district is very marginal (Clinton won here by 3% in 1996, Bush by 10% in 2000), Lampson has not had to put up much of a fight since defeating a Republican incumbent in 1996. The 9th will need to pick up about 20,000 new residents during redistricting.

THE PEOPLE: Pop. 2000: 636,960; Pop. 1990: 564,287, up 12.9% 1990–2000. 67.3% White, 21.7% Black, 2.7% Asian, 0.4% Amer. Indian, 1.9% Two+ races, 5.9% Other; 14.4% Hispanic Origin.

2000 Presidential Vote			**1996 Presidential Vote**		
Bush (R)	120,871	(55%)	Clinton (D)	97,268	(48%)
Gore (D)	99,116	(45%)	Dole (R)	89,942	(45%)
			Perot (I)	14,144	(7%)

Rep. Nick Lampson (D)

Elected 1996, 3d term; b. Feb. 14, 1945, Beaumont; home, Beaumont; Lamar U., B.S. 1968, M.Ed. 1971; Catholic; married (Susan).

Elected Office: Jefferson Cnty. Assessor, 1977–95.

Professional Career: Public schl. teacher, 1968–71; Instructor, Lamar U., 1971–76; Pres., Jefferson Cnty. Home Health Care, 1993–95.

DC Office: 417 CHOB 20515, 202-225-6565; Fax: 202-225-5547; Web site: www.house.gov/lampson.

District Offices: Beaumont, 409-838-0061; Galveston, 409-762-5877; Houston, 281-333-4884.

Committees: *Science* (11th of 22 D): Energy; Space & Aeronautics. *Transportation & Infrastructure* (26th of 34 D): Aviation; Water Resources & Environment.

Group Ratings

	ADA	ACLU	AFS	LCV	CON	ITIC	NTU	COC	ACU	NTLC	CHC
2000	75	64	85	57	11	72	24	57	24	18	13
1999	90	—	100	75	75	—	14	32	16	—	—

National Journal Ratings

	1999 LIB —	1999 CONS		2000 LIB —	2000 CONS
Economic	78% —	21%		61% —	38%
Social	61% —	39%		58% —	42%
Foreign	85% —	12%		69% —	28%

Key Votes of the 106th Congress

1. Patient Bill of Rights	Y	5. Bar RU-486 $ for FDA	N	9. NATO War in Serbia	Y
2. Accelerate Min. Wage	Y	6. Display 10 Commandments	N	10. Perm. Trade with China	N
3. Strike Ban on Ergo. Stnd.	Y	7. Gun Show Bkgrnd. Checks	N	11. Debt Relief for 3rd World	Y
4. Ovrd. Estate Tax Veto	Y	8. Ban Part.-Birth Abortion	Y	12. Drop Cuba Econ. Embargo	Y

Election Results

2000 general	Nick Lampson (D)	130,143	(59%)	($1,343,927)
	Paul Williams (R)	87,165	(40%)	($104,570)
	Others	2,508	(1%)	
2000 primary	Nick Lampson (D)	unopposed		
1998 general	Nick Lampson (D)	86,055	(64%)	($945,497)
	Tom Cottar (R)	49,107	(36%)	($57,990)

TENTH DISTRICT

Austin, the capital of the second-largest state in the United States and site of its largest Capitol building, is also the southernmost capital in the continental 48 states. It is one of many capitals with a first-rate university, the University of Texas, but one of the few (Nashville is the obvious other) with its own musical tradition, symbolized by Willie Nelson. Not long ago Austin seemed as laid-back and countrified as Nelson himself. There has never been much commerce here, and for much of the year the Capitol basked in a sun that seemed to ban gainful employment. Its skies were untainted with the smoke of industry, its ground unpocked with pumping oil rigs, its downtown streets lined not with business offices but with buildings holding a few lobbyists and the antique Driskill Hotel. Its biggest industry was the University of Texas, the nation's largest, endowed with thousands of west Texas acres that turned out to sit on top of oil, the university has long had a distinguished faculty and some of the world's great scholarly collections; it houses the LBJ Presidential Library with its 35 million documents, has spawned a community of liberal intellectuals since the 1940s and helped spark Austin's high-tech boom in the 1980s and 1990s.

Half a century ago, in Lyndon Johnson's time, Austin had a metropolitan population of 132,000. The compact Austin that was the home of J. Frank Dobie and Walter Prescott Webb in the 1940s, and which was Johnson's headquarters in 1948 when the Duval County returns came in and gave him the 87-vote victory that made his national career, is a very different Austin from the town that waited up in the rain, alternatively enthused and downcast, hoping to celebrate the election of George W. Bush in 2000. Today's high-tech Austin has grown out miles from the comfortable precincts of the old downtown and university, up and down the vast sloping hills to the west and north and south, bringing together subdivisions on dozens of square miles which were empty land in 1980, not to speak of 1948. Today's Austin is no longer a creation of the public sector, of state government and the University, though they are still prominent; it is also the home of Dell Computer, of the Sematech tech incubator of the 1980s, of the fourth largest number of high-tech employees in the nation. In the 1990s, the Austin metro area had some of the nation's fastest population growth, up 48% to 1,250,000, and its job growth skyrocketed 60% between 1989–98. Travis County alone had a 41% per cent increase to 812,000. "The rate of change in activity in venture capital has been larger in Austin than probably anywhere else in the country," local venture capitalist John Thornton told *The New York Times*. Austin has a new airport, the converted Bergstrom Air Force Base, handsome and conveniently located—one of the few closed military bases put to this obvious use. Even the music has changed; Austin now brags that it is the "Live Music Capital of the World" and hosts rising stars annually at its South-by-Southwest arts festival. One of America's most charming and idiosyncratic small cities has become one of America's fastest-growing and creative metropolitan areas.

Growth has also brought political change. For many years Austin was the central focus of Texas's hardy but almost always outnumbered liberals, thanks to the university, state government and the *Texas Observer*. Confident that the future was theirs, that Texas would follow America into the New Deal and the welfare state, they mocked the conservative business lobbyists who called the shots when the "lege" was in session and celebrated Texas zaniness with the verve of a Sixth Street band. But history—or at least Austin—has not moved in the direction Texas liberals expected. As Austin has grown, it has grown more conservative; as its private sector has led the local economy, the techies who settled in the south and west and the north hills going from Austin's Travis County to once-rural Williamson County have tended to vote Republican. The city core and the University area are still Democratic, and Texas liberals still are potent in the media. But this is a state capital in which George W. Bush could feel more at home than he would have 30 years before (when his application for admission was rejected by the UT Law School). Bush lost Austin and Travis County 59%–41% when he first ran for governor in 1994, but he carried Travis 60%–38% in 1998 for re-election and 47%–42% in 2000 for president (with 10% for Ralph Nader), a considerable achievement for a Republican.

The 10th Congressional District of Texas, which once spread over the Hill Country to the west and south, is now entirely within Travis County, including most of the now-sprawling city of Austin and its inner suburban fringe. It is the descendant of the 10th District that in April 1937 elected a gangly-looking 29-year-old New Dealer named Lyndon Johnson, who established a kind of dynasty here. When Johnson gave up the seat to make his second, and successful, run for the Senate in 1948, his friend Homer Thornberry won the seat and held it until he became a federal judge in December 1963; another LBJ backer, Jake Pickle, was elected that month and served until he retired in 1994—57 years of representation by three political allies, all born between 1908 and 1913.

The congressman today from the 10th District is Lloyd Doggett, first elected in 1994. He is a liberal Democrat with a dream resume and an up-and-down political career. Doggett grew up in Austin, finished first in his class and was president of UT's student body in 1967. In 1972, he was elected to the state Senate at 26, and as part of a surprisingly large liberal bloc in the 1970s, he pushed laws against job discrimination and cop-killer bullets and for generic drugs; he has always been a close ally of trial lawyers, the one strong institutional force supporting liberal Democrats in Texas. He had a certain flair. He was one of the "killer bees" who hid out to prevent a quorum on changing the rules in the Democratic primary and filibustered—wearing sneakers—against what he called anti-consumer bills. In 1984 he ran for the U.S. Senate, narrowly edging two congressmen, future Senator Bob Krueger in the primary and future Republican Kent Hance in the runoff. Then, despite the campaign help of James Carville, Doggett lost the general 59%–41% to party-switching Congressman Phil Gramm, who sharply attacked him for holding a fund raiser at a San Antonio gay strip bar. Doggett came back and, with strong support from trial lawyers, was elected to the Texas Supreme Court in 1988. When Pickle retired, Doggett left his judgeship and ran for Congress. He won the Democratic primary with token opposition and in the general outpolled black Republican Jo Baylor by the solid, but not quite overwhelming, margin of 56%–40%.

In the House, Doggett's voting record has been mostly but not totally liberal. He voted for the final version of welfare reform and voted to bring the Blue Dog budget to the floor (but not for it). With Tom Davis of Virginia, he formed an Information Technology Working Group. He was a vocal critic of Newt Gingrich and a close ally of Minority Whip David Bonior. "He's like a first-round draft choice," Bonior said. Doggett showed his legislative dexterity when he worked with Senator Paul Wellstone to limit nuclear waste dumping at Sierra Blanca, a poor Latino community near the Rio Grande. In 1999, he outmaneuvered other aspirants to become the first Texas Democrat assigned to the Ways and Means Committee since Jake Pickle retired. Although Republican control gave him few legislative opportunities at the committee, he succeeded with Amo Houghton in 2000 in requiring more disclosure by tax-exempt "Section 527" campaign groups. He complained when the Clinton administration backed a continuation of $100 million in annual tax breaks for tobacco products sold overseas; he also criticized Clinton's plan for a new gasoline pipeline in southern Travis County. But he voted with Clinton on Permanent Normal Trade Relations with China, and on key tax votes. In early 2001 he called George W. Bush's tax cuts "pretty wimpy help" for most taxpayers.

Doggett was re-elected 56%–41% in 1996 over Teresa Doggett (no relation) and has won easily since. Redistricting is likely to be kind to him. The 10th District has had phenomenal growth in the 1990s, and very much territory must be pared away. Republicans would like to remove Republican-leaning precincts, to create the nucleus of an entirely new (and Republican-leaning) district. That would leave Doggett with a district dominated by his core constituency, the heart of Austin, solidly Democratic and, despite George W. Bush's election as president, still hopeful liberals.

Cook's Call *Safe.* The fact that Doggett has consistently won this district by significant margins, even as state and national trends were going against Democrats, shows that it has a good Democratic base. The Austin region has grown heavily during the 1990s and the 10th needs to shed 140,000 people. But Doggett should not have any problems winning re-election in 2002.

THE PEOPLE: Pop. 2000: 791,117; Pop. 1990: 566,357, up 39.7% 1990–2000. 67.5% White, 9.5% Black, 4.6% Asian, 0.6% Amer. Indian, 0.1% Hawaiian, 2.9% Two+ races, 14.9% Other; 28.8% Hispanic Origin.

2000 Presidential Vote

Bush (R)	132,691	(52%)
Gore (D)	122,921	(48%)

1996 Presidential Vote

Clinton (D)	126,855	(54%)
Dole (R)	93,219	(40%)
Perot (I)	13,453	(6%)

Rep. Lloyd Doggett (D)

Elected 1994, 4th term; b. Oct. 6, 1946, Austin; home, Austin; U. of TX, B.B.A. 1967, J.D. 1970; Methodist; married (Libby).

Elected Office: TX Senate, 1973–85; TX Supreme Ct. Justice, 1989–94.

Professional Career: Practicing atty., 1970–89; Adjunct Prof., U. of TX Law Schl., 1989–94.

DC Office: 328 CHOB 20515, 202-225-4865; Fax: 202-225-3073; Web site: www.house.gov/doggett.

District Office: Austin, 512-916-5921.

Committees: *Ways & Means* (16th of 17 D): Human Resources; Social Security.

Group Ratings

	ADA	ACLU	AFS	LCV	CON	ITIC	NTU	COC	ACU	NTLC	CHC
2000	85	86	85	100	100	79	36	33	12	30	0
1999	100	—	83	94	100	—	36	24	4	—	—

National Journal Ratings

	1999 LIB —	1999 CONS		2000 LIB —	2000 CONS
Economic	70% —	30%		92% —	5%
Social	87% —	0%		91% —	6%
Foreign	71% —	27%		80% —	16%

Key Votes of the 106th Congress

1. Patient Bill of Rights	Y	5. Bar RU-486 $ for FDA	N	9. NATO War in Serbia	Y
2. Accelerate Min. Wage	Y	6. Display 10 Commandments	N	10. Perm. Trade with China	Y
3. Strike Ban on Ergo. Stnd.	Y	7. Gun Show Bkgrnd. Checks	Y	11. Debt Relief for 3rd World	Y
4. Ovrd. Estate Tax Veto	N	8. Ban Part.-Birth Abortion	N	12. Drop Cuba Econ. Embargo	Y

Election Results

2000 general	Lloyd Doggett (D)	203,628	(85%)	($232,268)
	Michael Davis (Lib)	37,203	(15%)	
2000 primary	Lloyd Doggett (D)	unopposed		
1998 general	Lloyd Doggett (D)	116,127	(85%)	($111,248)
	Vincent J. May (Lib)	20,155	(15%)	

ELEVENTH DISTRICT

Waco, at the intersection of lines from Dallas to Austin and Houston to Amarillo, is arguably the geographic and cultural heart of Texas. The city was named after Indians the Mexicans called Huecos; by the late 19th Century it was one of the largest cotton markets in the world, a rip-roaring town with legalized prostitution and with a graceful ox-cart-wide suspension bridge across the Brazos which, when it opened in 1870, was the longest single-span suspension bridge in the United States and the second longest in the world. Waco was the home of atheist William Cowper Brann, author and publisher of *The Iconoclast* magazine, who was shot down in the streets but managed to kill his attacker. Waco is famous now as the site of the tragedy of February 1993, when, in a dreadful misuse of government power, agents of the Bureau of Alcohol, Tobacco and Firearms moved in on David Koresh's Branch Davidian compound, Ranch Apocalypse, near Waco, and Koresh and his followers were burned to death. But Waco should be famous for other things as well. It is the home of Baylor University, the oldest college in Texas and the largest Baptist university in the world; its Armstrong Browning Library houses the papers of Robert and Elizabeth Barrett Browning. It is the largest city near Fort Hood, the Army's second largest installation, which occupies much of next-door Bell and Coryell counties and employs almost 50,000 military personnel and civilians. Even closer, in Waco's McLennan County, are the tiny town of Crawford, with its Rainey Creek, which traverses the ranch of George W. Bush: the White House press corps is going to see Waco a lot over the next four years. Waco is only a little more than an hour away from the gallerias of the Dallas-Fort Worth Metroplex, but it is still in touch with Texas's rural roots, with the days when cotton was Texas's major product.

The 11th Congressional District of Texas is centered on Waco and the Fort Hood area. It includes all or most of 12 counties, most of them still quite rural, all of them ancestrally Democratic. But that loyalty has slowly waned. This area voted for Democrat Hubert Humphrey in 1968, when most of the rural South went for George Wallace and Richard Nixon; it voted 53% Democratic when Texas first elected a Republican governor in 1978 and voted 51% for Democrat Ann Richards, a Waco native, in 1990. But in 1994 it voted 52% for George W. Bush, and in 2000 Bush carried the 11th District by a 66%–34% margin. No wonder Bush feels at home in Crawford.

The congressman from the 11th is Chet Edwards, a Democrat elected in 1990, and only the third congressman from this district since 1936. Edwards is one of those highly skilled and motivated Democrats who has made politics his life—and who kept the House Democratic until 1994. He graduated from Texas A&M, where he studied economics under Phil Gramm, then a conservative Democrat; from there, Edwards went to work as district director for 6th District Congressman Olin Teague. In 1978, at 27, Edwards ran for the 6th District seat when Teague retired. In the Democratic primary, Edwards wound up in third place, just 115 votes behind Gramm, who went on to win the seat; if Edwards had won just 116 more votes, a lot of Texas and national political history would be different. Edwards went off to Harvard to get an M.B.A., returned and moved to Duncanville in southwest Dallas County, and at age 31 ran for the state Senate in 1982 and won. There he had a moderate-to-liberal record, working to attract the Supercollider, bucking the unions and trial lawyers on workmen's compensation reform.

In 1990 when Democrat Marvin Leath retired, Edwards moved his residence to Waco, and ran for the 11th District seat unopposed in the Democratic primary. With a promise of an Armed Services Committee slot from Speaker Thomas Foley and strong support from Leath, Edwards got 56% in Waco's McLennan County for a 53%–47% victory. In the House, Edwards worked for Fort Hood and eventually won a seat on Appropriations, where he claims credit for nearly a quarter-billion dollars in construction there. He noted proudly that the $122 million appropriated for Fort Hood in 1999 was more than half the military construction funding in all of Texas. He bucked the Democratic leadership on the Gulf war resolution and he voted against the Clinton tax increase. He worked successfully to stop the designation of 33 Texas counties as a critical habitat for the allegedly endangered golden-cheeked warbler and supported the Private Property Owners Bill of Rights. He voted against the Brady bill but for the assault weapons ban and the 1994 crime bill. He tried to avoid publicity in the wake of the Waco tragedy, refusing invitations to appear on television, although at the request of Al Gore he visited ATF agents injured in the raid and attended every day of congressional hearings. "People in Waco would like to get this behind them. I'm saddened it's become part of political football already."

After Democrats lost their majority in 1994, Minority Leader Dick Gephardt asked Edwards to serve as one of four chief deputy whips. Edwards accepted, adding, "I did not ask for this job and I will not change my political independence to keep it." He promptly voted for the Contract with America's balanced budget amendment and line-item veto. In 1998 and 1999 he led opposition to the school-prayer constitutional amendment, citing the freedom that the Bill of Rights has "protected extraordinarily well for over two centuries." He opposed a resolution for a national day of prayer and fasting after the Columbine shootings in 1999, and later that year sponsored an amendment to ban government funds for "pervasively sectarian" groups; Baptist churches, it should be noted, have long favored a strict separation of church and state. But he supported the Fort Hood commander's granting of a request to have a Wiccan religious service on the base, and he opposed the partial-birth abortion ban. On several measures, he has worked with the Democratic leadership, supporting a waiting period for sales at gun shows and opposing repeal of the estate tax; he opposed the leadership and backed the Clinton administration in voting for Permanent Normal Trade Relations with China.

Edwards has won re-election by decisive but not overwhelming margins. In 1998, the expected Republican candidate decided at the last minute not to run, and Edwards had a free ride. In 2000, against a Republican who raised over $500,000 and attacked him on education, taxes and abortion, he won 55%–44%. If Republicans controlled redistricting, they would surely try to weaken Edwards, perhaps by including heavily Republican areas at the fringe of the Dallas-Fort Worth Metroplex. But the current 11th comes close to the population average for new districts, and could be left pretty much alone. In any case, this adept politician will have to work hard to hold onto the Republican president's home congressional district.

Cook's Call *Potentially Competitive.* Once home to yellow dog Democrats, this district has continued to trend toward Republicans at the national level. But Edwards is well established here and Republicans have yet to find the right candidate or formula to beat him. Republicans are hoping that redistricting may help them in 2002, but they may have to wait until Edwards leaves office before they can pick this seat up.

THE PEOPLE: Pop. 2000: 663,275; Pop. 1990: 566,280, up 17.1% 1990–2000. 70.3% White, 16.4% Black, 1.5% Asian, 0.6% Amer. Indian, 0.2% Hawaiian, 2.7% Two+ races, 8.2% Other; 16.4% Hispanic Origin.

2000 Presidential Vote		
Bush (R)	127,312	(66%)
Gore (D)	64,561	(34%)

1996 Presidential Vote		
Dole (R)	88,429	(50%)
Clinton (D)	74,063	(42%)
Perot (I)	14,671	(8%)

Rep. Chet Edwards (D)

Elected 1990, 6th term; b. Nov. 24, 1951, Corpus Christi; home, Waco; TX A&M U., B.A. 1974, Harvard U., M.B.A. 1981; Methodist; married (Lea Ann).

Elected Office: TX Senate, 1982–90.

Professional Career: Legis. & Dist. Dir., U.S. Rep. Olin Teague, 1975–77; Marketing Rep., Trammell Crow Co., 1981–85; Pres., Edwards Communications, 1985–90.

DC Office: 2459 RHOB 20515, 202-225-6105; Fax: 202-225-0350; Web site: www.house.gov/edwards.

District Offices: Belton, 254-933-2904; Waco, 254-752-9600.

Committees: *Chief Deputy Minority Whip. Appropriations* (18th of 29 D): Energy & Water Development; Military Construction.

Group Ratings

	ADA	ACLU	AFS	LCV	CON	ITIC	NTU	COC	ACU	NTLC	CHC
2000	80	64	71	57	69	75	22	52	8	15	13
1999	85	—	100	44	92	—	21	42	8	—	—

National Journal Ratings

	1999 LIB	—	1999 CONS		2000 LIB	—	2000 CONS
Economic	66%	—	34%		68%	—	31%
Social	62%	—	37%		66%	—	33%
Foreign	68%	—	30%		69%	—	28%

Key Votes of the 106th Congress

1. Patient Bill of Rights	Y	5. Bar RU-486 $ for FDA	N	9. NATO War in Serbia	Y
2. Accelerate Min. Wage	Y	6. Display 10 Commandments	N	10. Perm. Trade with China	Y
3. Strike Ban on Ergo. Stnd.	Y	7. Gun Show Bkgrnd. Checks	Y	11. Debt Relief for 3rd World	Y
4. Ovrd. Estate Tax Veto	N	8. Ban Part.-Birth Abortion	N	12. Drop Cuba Econ. Embargo	Y

Election Results

2000 general	Chet Edwards (D)	105,782	(55%)	($1,281,637)
	Ramsey Farley (R)	85,546	(44%)	($558,727)
	Others	1,590	(1%)	
2000 primary	Chet Edwards (D)	unopposed		
1998 general	Chet Edwards (D)	71,142	(82%)	($255,608)
	Vince Hanke (Lib)	15,161	(18%)	($8,215)

TWELFTH DISTRICT

Fort Worth, Texas, has a fair claim to being the quintessential mid-American city: halfway across the continent, just west of the Balcones Escarpment that divides the dry treeless grazing lands of West Texas from the humid green croplands of East Texas. It is Southern in heritage and Northern in its advanced post-industrial economy. It has the nation's longest row of Western wear shops and one of the nation's richest families, the Basses, whose steel-sheen skyscrapers, outlined at night by lights, dominate the skyline. This is where the West begins, Fort Worth boosters say, adding, as Will Rogers said, that Dallas is "where the East peters out."

But this is not a primitive West. Fort Worth has a high-tech economy, though one hard hit by defense cuts. The big General Dynamics plant that produced so many U.S. bombers was sold to Lockheed Martin, which produces the fuselage of the F-22 fighter there; next-door Carswell Air Force Base, the home of B-52s for years, was slated for closure in 1993 but was turned into a Joint Reserve Base. The assembly lines at Bell Helicopter Textron's nearby plant were kept going only when the Texas delegation and others overruled the cancellation of the accident-prone V-22 Osprey. Fort Worth also has some of the nation's premier small museums, the Amon Carter Museum of Western Art, Louis Kahn's gem, the Kimbell Museum, and the Will Rogers Coliseum with exhibits of Texas history. The downtown Bass Performance Hall has been acclaimed for its superb architectural design. Other cities have their claims, but the visitor from abroad who wants to see what is quintessentially American would be well advised to fly to Dallas/Forth Worth International Airport and head west.

The 12th Congressional District of Texas is centered on Fort Worth. Its highly convoluted boundaries drawn in 1991 include much of the city, though not the poor black southeast or rich white southwest areas, which are in the 24th and 6th Districts. It also extends south and west in a whirl around Fort Worth, taking in much of rural Johnson and Parker Counties, including Weatherford, where former House Speaker Jim Wright got his start in politics. Fort Worth's political heritage is Democratic, but lately it has been trending Republican and has become more diverse, with extensive rich as well as poor neighborhoods. Tarrant County, with a population boom in Arlington between Fort Worth and Dallas and in the north around DFW airport and Ross Perot Jr.'s Alliance cargo airport, has become more Republican than Dallas County. In 2000 George W. Bush carried Dallas County by only a 53%–45% margin, while he carried Tarrant County 61%–37%.

The congresswoman from the 12th District is Kay Granger, a Republican elected in 1996. Granger grew up in Fort Worth, graduated from Texas Wesleyan College, was a school teacher, raised three children and started her own insurance agency. In 1989 she was elected to the Fort Worth Council, and two years later was elected as the non-partisan mayor. She became very popular for her "Code: Blue" anti-crime initiatives and encouragement of citizen patrols, as violent crime dropped 49%. She also formed the Vision Coalition, a community-wide consensus-building organization, and attracted new business facilities from Motorola, Intel, FedEx and the Texas Motor Speedway. In 1995 Congressman Pete Geren, a conservative Democrat elected to replace Wright in 1989, announced his retirement; both Republican and Democratic leaders tried to recruit Granger. She said she was a Republican, and ran in the Republican primary. Attacked as a liberal, partly for her pro-choice stand on abortion, she won 69% in a three-candidate race. Granger's Democratic opponent was Hugh Parmer, also a former Fort Worth mayor, and the Democratic nominee against Senator Phil Gramm in 1990. That turned out to be a liability: it was revealed that he had large unpaid debts left over from that campaign. Parmer attacked Republican Medicare plans and Newt Gingrich. Granger called for a balanced budget and tax cuts for business and ran on her record as mayor. Granger won 58%–41%, a stunning victory in a district carried twice by Bill Clinton and represented a decade before by a Democratic Speaker of the House.

In the House, Granger's voting record has tended to be moderate on cultural issues and more conservative on economics. She became a favorite of Republican leaders, winning enactment of tax-free savings accounts for higher education expenses and serving as the only freshman on Dennis Hastert's health care task force. With other Republican women lawmakers, she filed a proposal to set new HMO regulations on obstetric and gynecological specialists. She split with most Republicans in applauding the FDA's approval of the RU-486 abortion pill. One setback was the Republican leadership's support of legislation that diluted the Wright Amendment's protection of Dallas/Fort Worth International Airport from competition by Dallas's Love Field; after that, Granger worked to create a local regional airport authority to encourage cooperation between the DFW and Love. In 1999 she became the third Texas Republican on the Appropriations Committee, where her seat on the Military Construction Subcommittee allows her to keep a close eye on local Pentagon spending. After the 2000 election, she considered running for Republican Conference secretary, but dropped out of the race, which was won by Wyoming's Barbara Cubin. Some members undoubtedly felt that Texas already has more than its share of House Republican leaders.

Granger has been reelected twice by wide margins; a greater threat was the March 2000 tornado that ripped apart her office and blew papers five miles away. Democratic Caucus Chairman Martin Frost, who represents the adjacent 24th District, said that if Granger was not defeated in 2000, she'll be there "as long as she wants to be." From Frost's view that may well be desirable. He would like to see redistricting maximize the number of Tarrant County black and Latino voters in his 24th District, which means reducing the number in Granger's 12th and keeping it solidly Republican.

Cook's Call *Safe.* By no means the most Republican district in the state, the 12th does have solid Republican underpinnings that help insulate Granger from serious challenges. She looks well positioned for 2002.

THE PEOPLE: Pop. 2000: 661,753; Pop. 1990: 565,988, up 16.9% 1990–2000. 74.4% White, 8.6% Black, 2.1% Asian, 0.7% Amer. Indian, 0.2% Hawaiian, 2.5% Two+ races, 11.6% Other; 25% Hispanic Origin.

2000 Presidential Vote			1996 Presidential Vote		
Bush (R)	110,472	(59%)	Clinton (D)	80,709	(46%)
Gore (D)	75,361	(41%)	Dole (R)	79,299	(46%)
			Perot (I)	14,187	(8%)

Rep. Kay Granger (R)

Elected 1996, 3d term; b. Jan. 18, 1943, Greenville; home, Ft. Worth; TX Wesleyan U., B.S. 1965; Methodist; divorced.

Elected Office: Ft. Worth City Cncl., 1989–91; Ft. Worth Mayor, 1991–96.

Professional Career: Teacher, 1965–78; Life Insurance Agent, 1978–85; Chmn., Ft. Worth Zoning Comm., 1981–88; Founder & Pres., Kay Granger Insurance Co., Inc., 1985–present.

DC Office: 435 CHOB 20515, 202-225-5071; Fax: 202-225-5683; Web site: www.house.gov/granger.

District Office: Ft. Worth, 817-338-0909.

Committees: *Appropriations* (29th of 35 R): Labor, HHS & Education; Military Construction; Transportation. *Budget* (18th of 24 R).

Group Ratings

	ADA	ACLU	AFS	LCV	CON	ITIC	NTU	COC	ACU	NTLC	CHC
2000	5	15	0	0	67	100	62	84	84	72	100
1999	5	—	0	6	28	—	53	95	78	—	—

National Journal Ratings

	1999 LIB	—	1999 CONS		2000 LIB	—	2000 CONS
Economic	0%	—	84%		15%	—	83%
Social	37%	—	61%		40%	—	60%
Foreign	31%	—	66%		0%	—	88%

Key Votes of the 106th Congress

1. Patient Bill of Rights	*	5. Bar RU-486 $ for FDA	N	9. NATO War in Serbia	N
2. Accelerate Min. Wage	*	6. Display 10 Commandments	Y	10. Perm. Trade with China	Y
3. Strike Ban on Ergo. Stnd.	N	7. Gun Show Bkgrnd. Checks	N	11. Debt Relief for 3rd World	N
4. Ovrd. Estate Tax Veto	Y	8. Ban Part.-Birth Abortion	*	12. Drop Cuba Econ. Embargo	N

Election Results

2000 general	Kay Granger (R)	117,739	(63%)	($671,838)
	Mark Greene (D)	67,612	(36%)	($83,280)
	Others	2,565	(1%)	
2000 primary	Kay Granger (R)	unopposed		
1998 general	Kay Granger (R)	66,740	(62%)	($883,397)
	Tom Hall (D)	39,084	(36%)	($622,443)
	Others	1,917	(2%)	

THIRTEENTH DISTRICT

Heading west in Texas, the population thins out, the land becomes browner until you can travel through whole counties containing only a few hundred people each—plus quite a few more head of cattle. And then the land rises nearly 1,000 feet in elevation, up steep hillsides from the gullies that surround the rivers that for most of the year are just tiny trickles, to the tilted tableland that is the High Plains of West Texas. The winds here sweep down from the Rockies, the land is barren except where irrigated, often with the now dangerously depleted waters of the Ogallala Aquifer. But here and there in this demanding environment—sticky-hot in the summer, swept by north winds from Canada in winter, always threatened in "Tornado Alley"—comfortable cities have been built to house the people and businesses that bring forth some of the nation's most abundant oil, natural gas, helium and other elements from the earth.

The 13th Congressional District of Texas spans more than 30,000 square miles and 38 counties of this territory. Population declined here in the 1980s, in some rural counties by as much as 30%, with only small gains in and around two of the three biggest cities, Wichita Falls and Amarillo. In the 1990s, the district's population increased 5%, but that was the smallest of any district in Texas, with population increasing in the larger cities but declining in most rural counties. Around Wichita Falls, in the eastern part of the district, is the agricultural land of the Red River Valley—dusty land with empty skylines, like Archer City, the boyhood home of novelist Larry McMurtry, chronicled in *The Last Picture Show* and *Texasville* and where he lives now and maintains an enormous used-book store. The area claims to produce more cotton than any other congressional district and is home to one of the nation's oldest and largest cattle auctions. It is also home to the county with the highest percentage of married couples in the U.S., King County. This is white Anglo Texas: Few blacks got this far west and relatively few Mexican-Americans go this far north. Up on the High Plains, the economy is different: it is based on natural resources. The largest city here is Amarillo, once the helium capital of North America (before Congress shut down production) and still—not Chicago—the windiest city in the United States. Just outside town is the Pantex Plant that secretly assembled the nation's thousands of nuclear warheads and was the epicenter of American defense in the Cold War; its 16,000 acres have been used to dismantle some disarmed weapons and now maintain the remainder of the arsenal.

Political traditions here differ. The Red River Valley, settled by Confederate veterans, was heavily Democratic up through the 1970s. The High Plains, settled overland from Kansas wheatlands, was for years more Republican. By 2000 things had changed: both the Red River Valley and the High Plains were overwhelmingly for George W. Bush, giving him county percentages as high as he won anywhere in the United States. Democrats drew the 13th's current boundaries in 1991 to protect a threatened Democratic incumbent; they split Amarillo and Lubbock, putting heavily black precincts into the 13th District. But the district has become so heavily Republican that there is no longer any point to such shenanigans, and most likely the boundaries will be smoothed out and the cities kept together in the lines that will be in effect in 2002.

The congressman from the 13th District is Mac Thornberry, a Republican elected in 1994. His great-great-grandfather Amos Thornberry, a Union Army veteran and staunch Republican, moved to Clay County, just east of Wichita Falls, in the 1880s; a year after Amos died in 1925, his son bought the cattle ranch that Mac Thornberry, his brothers and father now run. From the window of his ranch house, writes *The Texas Techsan*, "as far as the eye can see is the Golden Spread of Texas for which this part of the state is named. There are no buildings, no roadways, no signs of life. Gaze out long enough and you begin to think you can actually see the curvature of the earth." And, as the writer goes on, you can get a sense of why Thornberry is so unhappy with federal government intrusion into people's lives. But Thornberry is not just a local farmer: After college and law school in Texas he worked for Congressmen Tom Loeffler and Larry Combest and at the State Department in Washington. Then he returned to practice law in West Texas.

In 1994 the well-connected Thornberry took on three-term Democratic Congressman Bill Sarpalius. He attacked Sarpalius for voting for the Clinton budget and tax package. He profited from news stories about how Sarpalius did not pay a moving company that shipped his furniture to Washington, then accepted a fee for speaking at the company's convention in Las Vegas. The FBI investigated in October 1994: not helpful for Sarpalius's campaign. Thornberry won a solid 55%–45% victory, carrying the northern panhandle by wide margins and carrying Wichita Falls as well, trailing only in sparsely populated ranching counties.

In the House Thornberry has compiled a conservative voting record, though hardly the most ideological in the Texas delegation. He pressed hard for estate tax repeal and tax credits to encourage production in marginal wells. Responding to the punishing dip in oil prices in 1997 and 1998, he pushed to fill the Strategic Petroleum Reserve to its 750 million barrel capacity and urged a cutoff of the oil-for-food program that permitted Saddam Hussein's Iraq to flood the oil market. He worked with others along the Texas border with Oklahoma to precisely mark the boundaries of the Red River; their agreement in 2000 settled a 200-year dispute resulting from the river's shifts. He wants to reform the Endangered Species Act and to allow state-inspected meat to be sold in other states the same as foreign-inspected meat, which does not need USDA approval. On Armed Services, he won passage of his proposal barring transfer of Pantex Plant explosives work elsewhere. He has used his committee work to weigh in on military policy: Following reports that nuclear secrets from Los Alamos were missing, he put together a plan to tighten security at the nation's eight nuclear labs and weapons plants; Armed Services Chairman Bob Stump named him to head a special oversight panel on nuclear security. He urged the Bush administration to conduct a wide-ranging Pentagon review and tackle the difficult trade-offs. "If no one is complaining, you can bet that we're not making real changes," Thornberry said.

Thornberry has been re-elected easily. The 13th District needs to add 54,000 people in redistricting. Most likely the district will be moved east, to include territory that is, or is becoming, a heavily Republican part of the Dallas-Fort Worth Metroplex.

Cook's Call *Safe*. Though the 13th District elected a Democrat to Congress as recently as 1992, it will be very difficult for wrest it back from Thornberry. It was the slowest-growing district in Texas during the 1990s.

THE PEOPLE: Pop. 2000: 597,401; Pop. 1990: 566,682, up 5.4% 1990–2000. 74.3% White, 8.5% Black, 1.4% Asian, 0.8% Amer. Indian, 2.3% Two+ races, 12.6% Other; 24.6% Hispanic Origin.

2000 Presidential Vote			1996 Presidential Vote		
Bush (R)	120,544	(69%)	Dole (R)	92,815	(53%)
Gore (D)	54,492	(31%)	Clinton (D)	69,149	(39%)
			Perot (I)	14,030	(8%)

Rep. Mac Thornberry (R)

Elected 1994, 4th term; b. July 15, 1958, Clarendon; home, Clarendon; TX Tech. U., B.A. 1980, U. of TX Law Schl., J.D. 1983; Presbyterian; married (Sally).

Professional Career: Legis. Cnsl., U.S. Rep. Tom Loeffler, 1983–85; Chief of Staff, U.S. Rep. Larry Combest, 1985–88; Dpty. Asst. Secy. of State for Legis. Affairs, 1988–89; Practicing atty., 1989–94.

DC Office: 131 CHOB 20515, 202-225-3706; Fax: 202-225-3486; Web site: www.house.gov/thornberry.

District Offices: Amarillo, 806-371-8844; Wichita Falls, 940-692-1700.

Committees: *Armed Services* (13th of 32 R): Military Personnel; Military Procurement. *Budget* (7th of 24 R). *Resources* (15th of 28 R): Energy & Mineral Resources; National Parks, Recreation & Public Lands.

Group Ratings

	ADA	ACLU	AFS	LCV	CON	ITIC	NTU	COC	ACU	NTLC	CHC
2000	0	36	0	0	46	100	64	76	88	73	100
1999	5	—	0	0	56	—	60	76	88	—	—

National Journal Ratings

	1999 LIB —	1999 CONS		2000 LIB —	2000 CONS
Economic	24%	72%		6%	85%
Social	29%	69%		0%	79%
Foreign	39%	60%		12%	78%

Key Votes of the 106th Congress

1. Patient Bill of Rights	Y	5. Bar RU-486 $ for FDA	Y	9. NATO War in Serbia	N
2. Accelerate Min. Wage	N	6. Display 10 Commandments	Y	10. Perm. Trade with China	Y
3. Strike Ban on Ergo. Stnd.	N	7. Gun Show Bkgrnd. Checks	N	11. Debt Relief for 3rd World	N
4. Ovrd. Estate Tax Veto	Y	8. Ban Part.-Birth Abortion	Y	12. Drop Cuba Econ. Embargo	N

Election Results

2000 general	Mac Thornberry (R)	117,995	(68%)	($741,039)
	Curtis Clinesmith (D)	54,343	(31%)	($208,541)
	Others	2,137	(1%)	
2000 primary	Mac Thornberry (R)	30,867	(92%)	
	David G. Morris (R)	2,863	(8%)	
1998 general	Mac Thornberry (R)	81,141	(68%)	($448,727)
	Mark Harmon (D)	37,027	(31%)	($16,243)

FOURTEENTH DISTRICT

Retreating east from the Alamo, the ragtag army led by Sam Houston passed over what would become, after their bloody and conclusive victory at San Jacinto, some of the prime cropland in the new Republic and later the state of Texas. The hilly and river-crossed land between Houston and Austin, both named after Texas' first leaders, was settled early. The flat coastal plains, steamy and humid so much of the year, were settled later when the railroads came in. The Gulf of Mexico coastline, though it has plenty of inlets, never had any important ports in the stretch between Houston and Corpus Christi until the discovery of oil here made it worthwhile to build channels to ship the oil out.

This is the land of the 14th Congressional District of Texas. Made up of rural countrysides, small towns and a couple of small cities, it runs along the Gulf Coast and inland toward the old Texas German country. Its eastern and northern edges bring it within metropolitan range of Houston, Austin and San Antonio; more than one-third of its people live in these areas. Blanco County in the Hill Country west of Austin is the birthplace and first political base of Lyndon B. Johnson, and now site of the annual Christmas-season Hill Country Regional Lighting Trail. This country is ancestrally Democratic except for a couple of counties settled by Texas Germans, who were pro-Union in the Civil War and have remained Republican ever since. But it has trended Republican since the 1980s, twice rejecting Bill Clinton and casting a very large margin for George W. Bush.

The congressman from the 14th District is Ron Paul, a Republican elected in 1996, but also once a Libertarian candidate for president. Paul grew up in Pennsylvania, went to Duke medical school, served as a Air Force flight surgeon, then moved to Texas to practice obstetrics and gynecology in Brazoria County, just southwest of Houston. Paul was dismayed when Richard Nixon cut the connection between the dollar and gold in 1971 and became interested in politics. After winning election to the House in 1976 and serving four terms, he ran for the Senate in 1984 and lost the primary to Phil Gramm 73%–16%. His House seat was won by a young legislator and exterminating firm owner, Tom DeLay. In 1988, as the Libertarian candidate for president, Paul ran third with 432,000 votes, 0.47% of the total (more than Patrick Buchanan's 0.43% in 2000, achieved with the help of $12 million in federal funding). In his first congressional tenure, Paul advanced some ideas that in the mid-1990s became mainstream—term limits, which a majority of House members voted for, and abolition of the income tax. Other Paul ideas remain outside the political pale—endorsing a group that wants to end all government funding of education, cutting $150 billion from the defense budget and returning to the gold standard. Paul practices what he preaches. He will not accept payment by Medicare or Medicaid, he wouldn't let his children accept federal student loans and he refuses his congressional pension.

Paul re-entered congressional politics after Congressman Greg Laughlin switched parties in June 1995. Laughlin had a moderate voting record, but by no means the most conservative of Texas Democrats. Republicans offered him a seat on Ways and Means if he switched, and he did. Paul decided to run again as—well, as Ron Paul, raising money from his nationwide network of Libertarians, gold bugs and subscribers to the *Ron Paul Political Report*. "The [federal] government perpetually takes our money, lies to us and makes our lives worse," he said. After Laughlin led the primary with 43%, Paul won the runoff 54%–46%.

This set up an excruciating situation for Republican leaders. They did not want to lose the seat to Democrat Charles "Lefty" Morris, who ran as a "conservative Democrat," but omitted from his resume the fact that he had been president of the state trial lawyers' association. But they didn't want to get associated with Paul's wackier-seeming views either. Morris ("Lefty is right") hit Paul for favoring abolition of the minimum wage, repealing federal anti-drug laws and anti-prostitution laws. Researchers reported that Paul's newsletter in 1992 said that 95% of black men in Washington, D.C. are "semi-criminal or entirely criminal" and that black teenagers are "unbelievably fleet of foot." Paul ran 1% ahead of Bob Dole and won 51%–48% in a close race.

With his libertarian views, Paul's voting record is anything but rock-solid Republican and perversely places him toward the middle of the House. Frequently, his insistence on limited government made Paul the House's lonely dissenter—against bills to require states to report on their progress in improving student achievement, to urge Haiti to conduct fair and peaceful elections, and to award Rosa Parks and Pope John Paul II with Congressional Gold Medals. He says that he wants to "get rid of the special interests" and he worries about "the little guy." He was one of three House Republicans who opposed the high-tech industry on more than half his votes. He called U.S. membership in the World Trade Organization unconstitutional and filed a lawsuit challenging Bill Clinton's decision to bomb Yugoslavia. Paul gained a brief mention as the presidential candidate of the Reform Party in 2000, but he rejected the overture.

Paul has appeared on House Democrats' target lists, but easily survived in 1998 and 2000 the charges of Loy Sneary, a local rice farmer, that he votes "against Texas family farmers and ranchers" and attacks on his defense of medical marijuana. Paul's greater problem is redistricting. His district is larger than the state average, but its boundaries could be changed; Republicans would like to put one of Texas's two new seats in the high-tech area on the north side of metro Austin, and to do so would have to take away some of Paul's territory. He is not likely to have any protectors in Austin, and some politically adept legislators may be maneuvering to win his seat. But it may not be wise to underestimate someone who, however offbeat, has managed to be elected to the House seven times, at least once in each of the last four decades.

Cook's Call *Safe*. What keeps Paul in Congress is his tremendous fundraising abilities, and the conservative and Republican nature of this rural district. He is tough to beat.

THE PEOPLE: Pop. 2000: 688,604; Pop. 1990: 566,008, up 21.7% 1990–2000. 75.7% White, 9.1% Black, 0.7% Asian, 0.5% Amer. Indian, 2.1% Two+ races, 11.8% Other; 27.9% Hispanic Origin.

2000 Presidential Vote			1996 Presidential Vote		
Bush (R)	147,306	(65%)	Dole (R)	100,319	(50%)
Gore (D)	80,084	(35%)	Clinton (D)	84,317	(42%)
			Perot (I)	15,696	(8%)

Rep. Ron Paul (R)

Elected 1996, 3d term; b. Aug. 20, 1935, Pittsburgh, PA; home, Surfside; Gettysburg Col., B.A. 1957, Duke U., M.D. 1961; Protestant; married (Carol).

Military Career: Flight Surgeon, Air Force, 1963–68.

Elected Office: U.S. House of Reps., 1976, 1978–84.

Professional Career: Practicing physician, 1968–96.

DC Office: 203 CHOB 20515, 202-225-2831; Fax: 202-226-4871; Web site: www.house.gov/paul.

District Offices: Freeport, 979-230-0000; Victoria, 361-576-1231.

Committees: *Financial Services* (14th of 37 R): Capital Markets, Insurance & Government Sponsored Enterprises; Domestic Monetary Policy, Technology & Economic Growth; Oversight & Investigations (Vice Chmn.). *International Relations* (19th of 26 R): International Operations and Human Rights; Western Hemisphere.

Group Ratings

	ADA	ACLU	AFS	LCV	CON	ITIC	NTU	COC	ACU	NTLC	CHC
2000	30	64	57	29	95	41	91	45	76	91	73
1999	10	—	60	25	89	—	89	60	92	—	—

National Journal Ratings

	1999 LIB —	1999 CONS		2000 LIB —	2000 CONS
Economic	47% —	52%		49% —	51%
Social	46% —	53%		40% —	59%
Foreign	28% —	70%		56% —	42%

Key Votes of the 106th Congress

1. Patient Bill of Rights	N	5. Bar RU-486 $ for FDA	Y	9. NATO War in Serbia	N
2. Accelerate Min. Wage	N	6. Display 10 Commandments	Y	10. Perm. Trade with China	N
3. Strike Ban on Ergo. Stnd.	N	7. Gun Show Bkgrnd. Checks	N	11. Debt Relief for 3rd World	N
4. Ovrd. Estate Tax Veto	Y	8. Ban Part.-Birth Abortion	Y	12. Drop Cuba Econ. Embargo	Y

Election Results

2000 general	Ron Paul (R)	137,370	(60%)	($2,353,816)
	Loy Sneary (D)	92,689	(40%)	($1,033,842)
2000 primary	Ron Paul (R)	unopposed		
1998 general	Ron Paul (R)	84,459	(55%)	($1,987,457)
	Loy Sneary (D)	68,014	(44%)	($1,119,087)

FIFTEENTH DISTRICT

The Lower Rio Grande Valley of south Texas is one of America's 20th Century frontiers. A century ago, there was little here but desert wilderness. Only a handful of people lived anywhere near the shallow, sluggish Rio Grande; there was no Border Patrol because in this desert land no one bothered to cross it. Then came pioneers like Lloyd Bentsen Sr., father of the former senator and Treasury secretary, who arrived after World War I with $5 in his pocket and became one of the biggest Valley landowners. Bentsen and others cleared the land and dug canals, hired Mexican and Mexican-American workers, planted citrus groves, cornfields and palm windbreaks, ran cattle and drilled for oil and gas. Along U.S. 83 north of the Rio Grande these pioneers built a string of towns with Anglo names and storefronts. But most of the people here were Latino in culture and language. Wage levels higher than in Mexico (though low by U.S. standards) brought more Mexicans over the border. But if wages are low, so is the cost of living—which makes this a haven for low-income "winter Texan" retirees coming from the North in their RVs. The days are past when ranchers and oil men wielded absolute political power here. There is instead a robust, mostly Hispanic politics.

The 15th Congressional District of Texas is one of three districts dividing up the Lower Rio Grande Valley. Most of its residents live in Hidalgo County, in or near the string of towns from Mercedes through McAllen to Los Ebanos, just north of the river. The 15th then moves north through a narrow corridor of land between Corpus Christi and San Antonio to include Goliad, where 352 captured Texans were massacred by Santa Ana's troops in 1836, and Bee County, where former President George Bush goes to hunt quail at each year's end. The 15th's population is 79% Hispanic and mostly Democratic. This is the descendant of a district that elected Lloyd Bentsen Jr. to the House, before he went to Houston in 1955 to make his fortune and then on to national office.

The congressman from the 15th District is Ruben Hinojosa, a Democrat elected in 1996. His background is not in politics but in business and civic affairs. He grew up in Mercedes, between McAllen and Harlingen, where his family owns H&H Foods, which produces Mexican foods and beef patties and is one of the largest employers in the Valley. Hinojosa graduated from the University of Texas, then went into the family business and was active in civic affairs, primarily in education and regional development. He served on the state Board of Education and led an effort to create three regional magnet schools, including the South Texas School for Health Professions, a high school.

After former House Agriculture Committee Chairman Kika de la Garza announced he would not seek reelection in 1996, Hinojosa ran in the Democratic primary; his main political assets were his civic activities and cash; he spent $431,000 of his own money. In the primary he led Anglo lawyer Jim Selman 34%–33%. Selman promised to fight corruption; he questioned Hinojosa's Democratic credentials and profiting from government contracts. Hinojosa emphasized his interest in improving educational opportunities in the Lower Rio Grande Valley and extending I-69 to the Valley; he called for reducing the capital gains tax and giving investment tax credits to those making capital improvements. Hinojosa won the runoff 52%–48%. In effect, the more conservative of the two candidates won; only one of the three Lower Valley districts is represented by the sort of liberals who lead most national and Texas Hispanic organizations. Hinojosa won the general election over Mennonite minister Tom Haughey 62%–37%.

Hinojosa says his top priority in the House is increasing educational opportunity. He chairs the Hispanic Caucus's education task force, and has pushed to add $500 million to decrease dropout rates and boost educational attainment. He has sought to protect benefits for legal immigrants and to promote NAFTA. He claimed credit for progress on I-69 in the 1998 highway bill. He has enthusiastically supported the House's bipartisan "civility" retreats. He got $12 million in 2000 to help farmers in Cameron and Hidalgo Counties conserve and manage irrigation water. With Democrat Gregory Meeks, he was one of only two undecided Congressmen who took up the Clinton administration's offer of a visit to China to assess whether to approve permanent normal trade relations; Hinojosa got assurances of funding for the Cross-Border Institute for Regional Development before committing to vote for PNTR. In 2001 he was among the Democrats on the Education and the Workforce Committee who opposed subcommittee jurisdictional lines proposed by new committee chairman John Boehner because of the placement of oversight of historically Black and Hispanic-serving colleges; after they boycotted initial meetings, Boehner worked out a compromise with Democratic committee leaders.

The 1998 election saw a downtick in Hinojosa's support despite the pro-incumbent tenor of the year and his opponent's weak finances. Against the same opponent Hinojosa won 59%–41%, but he ran behind 52%–48% in the northern six counties. In 2000, he had no Republican opposition. Contrary to earlier expectations, the Lower Valley is not expected to gain a seat in redistricting. But the 15th District grew by 38%—by far, the largest of any Hispanic district in the state—mostly in Hidalgo County along the border. That means that some or most of the northern counties could be eliminated from the district, which would help Hinojosa.

Cook's Call *Safe.* Hinojosa will have no reelection problems in this solidly Democratic district. It is the most Hispanic in the state (79%) and was the fastest growing in southern Texas during the 1990s.

THE PEOPLE: Pop. 2000: 780,310; Pop. 1990: 566,805, up 37.7% 1990–2000. 76.8% White, 1.8% Black, 0.6% Asian, 0.5% Amer. Indian, 2.2% Two+ races, 18.1% Other; 78.9% Hispanic Origin.

2000 Presidential Vote		
Gore (D)	89,409	(55%)
Bush (R)	72,962	(45%)

1996 Presidential Vote		
Clinton (D)	86,707	(60%)
Dole (R)	49,595	(35%)
Perot (I)	7,093	(5%)

Rep. Ruben Hinojosa (D)

Elected 1996, 3d term; b. Aug. 20, 1940, Mercedes; home, Mercedes; U. of TX, B.B.A. 1962, M.B.A. 1980; Catholic; married (Marty).

Elected Office: TX Bd. of Educ., 1974–84.

Professional Career: Pres. & CEO, H&H Foods Inc., 1962–present.

DC Office: 1535 LHOB 20515, 202-225-2531; Fax: 202-225-5688; Web site: www.house.gov/hinojosa.

District Offices: Beeville, 512-358-8400; McAllen, 210-682-5545.

Committees: *Education & the Workforce* (11th of 22 D): 21st Century Competitiveness; Education Reform. *Financial Services* (26th of 32 D): Capital Markets, Insurance & Government Sponsored Enterprises; Domestic Monetary Policy, Technology & Economic Growth; Financial Institutions & Consumer Credit.

Group Ratings

	ADA	ACLU	AFS	LCV	CON	ITIC	NTU	COC	ACU	NTLC	CHC
2000	80	71	85	57	48	83	20	50	8	14	13
1999	100	—	100	63	12	—	10	40	4	—	—

National Journal Ratings

	1999 LIB —	1999 CONS		2000 LIB —	2000 CONS
Economic	66% —	33%		84% —	16%
Social	72% —	27%		69% —	30%
Foreign	89% —	8%		68% —	31%

Key Votes of the 106th Congress

1. Patient Bill of Rights	Y	5. Bar RU-486 $ for FDA	N	9. NATO War in Serbia	Y
2. Accelerate Min. Wage	Y	6. Display 10 Commandments	N	10. Perm. Trade with China	Y
3. Strike Ban on Ergo. Stnd.	Y	7. Gun Show Bkgrnd. Checks	Y	11. Debt Relief for 3rd World	Y
4. Ovrd. Estate Tax Veto	N	8. Ban Part.-Birth Abortion	Y	12. Drop Cuba Econ. Embargo	Y

Election Results

2000 general	Ruben Hinojosa (D)	106,570	(88%)	($470,513)
	Frank Jones (Lib)	13,167	(11%)	
	Others	711	(1%)	
2000 primary	Ruben Hinojosa (D)	46,247	(74%)	
	Diana Rivera-Martinez (D)	12,710	(20%)	
	Mel Buentello Hawkins (D)	3,928	(6%)	
1998 general	Ruben Hinojosa (D)	47,957	(58%)	($795,235)
	Tom Haughey (R)	34,221	(42%)	($15,009)

SIXTEENTH DISTRICT

El Paso, Texas, and Juarez, Mexico, face each other across the narrow Rio Grande, their tree-shaded streets spread out below the rough brown face of Comanche Peak, two border cities surrounded by hundreds of miles of some of North America's most rugged and desolate landscape—400 miles from Phoenix and 600 from Dallas-Fort Worth. There is much history here: Texas claims the first Thanksgiving took place in San Elizario near El Paso in 1598, and there were Spanish conquistadors coming through the pass of the north, El Paso del Norte, years before that. In the 1950s, El Paso and Juarez each had a population of 140,000; now the U.S. Census counted 679,000 in El Paso and estimates are that some 1.4 million live in and around Juarez. This is a bilingual, bicultural pair of cities, where most people have a Mexican heritage; the thrust of growth comes from the fertile union of a Spanish speaking people and an English-speaking economy. El Paso is one of the lowest-wage cities in the U.S., Juarez one of the highest-wage in Mexico; *maquiladora* plants pioneered a cross-border economy and the NAFTA strengthened it, and it is not all low-skill either; there is a big General Motors technical center, south of the border.

But free trade doesn't necessarily mean porous borders. In September 1993, El Paso Immigration and Naturalization Service leader Silvestre Reyes started Operation Hold the Line, positioning 400 officers on the border instead of trying to intercept illegals after they had already crossed into El Paso (amazingly enough, that had been firmly-rooted INS policy). Mexico complained about threats to its sovereignty, merchants worried about loss of sales, a few homeowners fretted about finding domestic help. But in El Paso auto thefts were down 30%, burglaries and robberies were down, beggars were absent from the streets, fewer Mexicans were having babies in El Paso hospitals; the move was almost universally popular north of the border and has been accepted to the south. The law finally was being enforced by an agency that had long said it was impossible; Californians began asking why the INS couldn't hold the line in their state.

The 16th Congressional District of Texas is made up of most of the city of El Paso, small communities along the Rio Grande, and giant Fort Bliss to the north. A full 78% of the people here are Latino. For many years politics divided people on ethnic lines, with most Anglos Republican and Latinos Democratic. El Paso feels distant from the rest of Texas; it is even in a different time zone. During his first four years as governor, George W. Bush paid close attention to El Paso, and in 1998 he carried El Paso County 50%–49%—a considerable achievement given the overwhelmingly Latino electorate. In 2000, when he ran for president, Bush lost the county to Al Gore, but still won a respectable 40%.

The congressman from the 16th District is Silvestre Reyes, who was elected as a Democrat in 1996. He grew up on a farm in Canutillo, five miles north of El Paso, the oldest of 10 children; he went to college in El Paso and Austin. He served in the Army in Vietnam, then "took as many civil service tests as I could, and the Border Patrol called" in 1969. He worked for the INS in four cities in Texas and Glynco, Georgia, and returned to El Paso in 1993 as chief patrol agent. When he got there he found that "people could basically cross the border at any time, wherever they wanted to." More than 40 boatmen ran "what were essentially international ferries" with 8,000 illegals crossing the border every day. By instituting his Operation Hold the Line against the wishes of many border agents eager to get credit for apprehending aliens, he reduced the flow by more than half. By November 1995 Reyes's name recognition was 65%, higher than most elected officials; he resigned from the INS and started running for Congress as a Democrat.

Reyes talked of the need for integrity and common sense. His target was Ron Coleman, a Democrat first elected in 1982, around whom scandals lurked: he had 673 overdrafts at the House bank, he was accused by Texas Attorney General Dan Morales on *60 Minutes* of trying to block prosecution of a local developer. In December 1995 Coleman announced he was retiring, but his legislative assistant for 13 years, Jose Luis Sanchez, ran with backing from Coleman and labor unions. Sanchez harshly attacked Reyes as a crypto-Republican, pointing out that his campaign treasurer had worked for Republicans in the past and that he had the support of Republican former Mayor Jonathan Rogers, and criticizing Reyes for backing a capital gains tax cut. One Sanchez mailing read, "Two of a kind: Gingrich and Reyes." Reyes hewed to his moderate platform, calling for water conservation research, a capital gains tax cut, promoting high-tech jobs, developing more highways and border crossings. After Reyes led the primary 42%–28%, Sanchez and the unions pressed hard in the runoff, but Reyes won 51%–49%. He won the general election 71%–28%. In surmounting political stereotypes, Reyes said, "The one thing I find curious is that people are amazed that Hispanics react like other groups. We're concerned about crime, taxes, education."

In the House, Reyes' voting record fell among moderates in the Democratic Caucus. He said that the permanent solution for the border is economic stabilization for Mexico. He said a border fence is unnecessary, and he opposed a national identification card. He objected when Bill Clinton failed to respond to a congressional mandate for 1,000 additional Border Patrol agents. He spoke out against decertification of Mexico for its drug enforcement record, saying it would upset the Mexican economy. He backs retraining for workers displaced by NAFTA, though he says that overall it is a great success. He was a late-deciding opponent of fast track in 1997, but backed permanent normal trade relations with China. Reyes has also worked on border environmental problems and water conservation, and to promote high-tech jobs and Fort Bliss, which he works to protect as an Armed Services Committee member. He actively backed the controversial pumping of gasoline through the Longhorn Pipeline from Houston to El Paso, and pressured to get a commitment from Clinton in exchange for supporting PNTR; Clinton granted approval despite objections from Environmental Protection Agency officials.

Reyes has easily won reelection. In 2001 he got a seat on the Intelligence Committee. He also became chairman of the Hispanic Caucus, and set as a major priority the expansion of its membership by recruiting and providing financial help to prospective candidates. With Census figures documenting the huge increase in Hispanic population nationwide, he set a formidable goal of electing an additional six to 10 Hispanics to Congress in the 2002 election; that could cause conflicts with Anglo and black Democrats in Texas, California and elsewhere. Another priority has been to increase economic growth along the Texas-Mexico boundary. Redistricting should be no problem. The 16th District is out in one corner of the state, connected to the rest of Texas by miles of desert; it needs only to add some more territory in El Paso County to meet the population standard.

Cook's Call *Safe*. This heavily Democratic district, one of only 10 in Texas carried by Gore in 2000, is a safe haven for Reyes. It will need to pick up about 30,000 people in redistricting.

THE PEOPLE: Pop. 2000: 620,847; Pop. 1990: 566,238, up 9.6% 1990–2000. 74.3% White, 3% Black, 1% Asian, 0.8% Amer. Indian, 0.1% Hawaiian, 3.2% Two+ races, 17.5% Other; 78% Hispanic Origin.

2000 Presidential Vote			1996 Presidential Vote		
Gore (D)	79,562	(60%)	Clinton (D)	80,475	(63%)
Bush (R)	54,070	(40%)	Dole (R)	40,983	(32%)
			Perot (I)	5,902	(5%)

Rep. Silvestre Reyes (D)

Elected 1996, 3d term; b. Nov. 10, 1944, Canutillo; home, El Paso; El Paso Commun. Col., A.A. 1977; Catholic; married (Carolina).

Military Career: Army, 1966–68 (Vietnam).

Elected Office: Canutillo Schl. Board, 1968–70.

Professional Career: Border Patrol Agent, 1969–95.

DC Office: 1527 LHOB 20515, 202-225-4831; Fax: 202-225-2016; Web site: www.house.gov/reyes.

District Office: El Paso, 915-534-4400.

Committees: *Armed Services* (10th of 28 D): Military Installations & Facilities; Military Research & Development. *Permanent Select Committee on Intelligence* (7th of 9 D): Human Intelligence, Analysis & Counterintelligence; Technical & Tactical Intelligence. *Veterans' Affairs* (6th of 14 D): Benefits (RMM).

Group Ratings

	ADA	ACLU	AFS	LCV	CON	ITIC	NTU	COC	ACU	NTLC	CHC
2000	80	50	85	79	57	88	18	42	16	12	29
1999	85	—	100	63	46	—	11	33	26	—	—

National Journal Ratings

	1999 LIB —	1999 CONS		2000 LIB —	2000 CONS
Economic	74% —	25%		85% —	11%
Social	61% —	39%		63% —	36%
Foreign	70% —	30%		56% —	42%

Key Votes of the 106th Congress

1. Patient Bill of Rights	Y	5. Bar RU-486 $ for FDA	N	9. NATO War in Serbia	*
2. Accelerate Min. Wage	Y	6. Display 10 Commandments	N	10. Perm. Trade with China	Y
3. Strike Ban on Ergo. Stnd.	Y	7. Gun Show Bkgrnd. Checks	Y	11. Debt Relief for 3rd World	Y
4. Ovrd. Estate Tax Veto	N	8. Ban Part.-Birth Abortion	Y	12. Drop Cuba Econ. Embargo	N

Election Results

2000 general	Silvestre Reyes (D)	92,649	(68%)	($406,530)
	Daniel S. Power (R)	40,921	(30%)	($30,621)
	Others	2,080	(2%)	
2000 primary	Silvestre Reyes (D)	unopposed		
1998 general	Silvestre Reyes (D)	67,486	(88%)	($340,427)
	Stu Nance (Lib)	5,329	(7%)	
	Lorenzo Morales (I)	3,952	(5%)	

SEVENTEENTH DISTRICT

West from Fort Worth, the West Texas plains stretch miles beyond the horizon, thousands and thousands of acres of rolling grazing land punctuated occasionally by oases of irrigated farmland (often in circles that show the reach of the sprinklers). This is primarily cattle country, with ranches specializing in Angora goats, ostriches and emus; there are cotton fields and pecan trees and mesquite, and many oil wells. On the interstate going west from Fort Worth, settlements start thinning out quickly. Before long, you are on open plains, with enormous skies and no people in sight: parched country in the drought of 2000. Then in the distance is a good-sized town, an oasis of activity. The largest towns here are Abilene and San Angelo. Settled by Confederate veterans suspicious of Eastern bankers and Yankee businessmen, this was one of the Democratic heartlands of America up through the 1970s; now it is voting Republican in top-of-the-ticket races.

Texas' 17th Congressional District takes up much of this "God's country," starting a few miles from Fort Worth and including most of three tiers of counties westward almost to New Mexico. This ancestrally Democratic region voted 70%–28% for George W. Bush in 2000.

The congressman from the 17th District is Charles Stenholm, one of several conservative Texas Democrats elected in 1978, and the only one remaining in the House. Stenholm is a farmer from a small town settled by Swedes near Abilene, a natural politician who went to Congress after leading the Rolling Plains Cotton Growers Association and the Stamford Electric Cooperative. Stenholm became a Democrat because in the 1970 Senate race Lloyd Bentsen was interested in his issues and the senior George Bush wasn't. In 1978, when 32-year incumbent Omar Burleson retired, Stenholm ran for the seat and easily won.

In the House, Stenholm and Phil Gramm were leaders of the "Boll Weevils," backing the 1981 Reagan budget and tax cuts. He threatened momentarily to run against Speaker Tip O'Neill in 1985, but desisted when conservatives were promised more attention. His voting record is conservative, the seventh- and eighth-most conservative of House Democrats in 1999 and 2000. In the 1980s and early 1990s Stenholm was the lead conservative Democrat on budget issues, as head of the Conservative Democratic Forum and on the Budget Committee. But that role faded as Republican leaders started viewing Stenholm as a conservative talker but a partisan Democratic doer, and the spotlight passed to other members of the Democratic Blue Dogs. "I think maybe people felt I was getting too much attention," he told *National Journal*. "I needed to step back and let others take some credit." More recently he has worked closely with other Democrats. In

2000 he co-sponsored with Charles Rangel a bill cutting the estate tax just 20% and raising the exemption for small businesses and farms to $2 million. He has co-sponsored a plan to include individual investment accounts as part of Social Security. He was one of five Democrats who voted to impeach Bill Clinton. In early 2001 he was one of the Blue Dogs who wanted to postpone tax cuts until the budget was passed. "Our primary focus is ensuring that our national budget meets a responsible and fiscally conservative model that prioritizes retiring the national debt," he and other Blue Dogs wrote to Bush in January 2001. House Democratic leaders let Stenholm and other Blue Dogs take the lead in arguing against the Bush income tax cut in March 2001.

Stenholm is now the ranking Democrat on the Agriculture Committee, working closely with Chairman Larry Combest of the next-door 19th District. Their prime charge is to reauthorize the Freedom to Farm Act of 1996. Stenholm argues that that bill was the product of Speaker Newt Gingrich, not the Agriculture Committee, and that it was based on the assumption, a faulty one he says, that American farmers would be able to sell surplus production on the world market. He points out that the European Union pays $55 billion yearly in subsidies to farmers and that, after farm prices collapsed in 1998, Congress has been voting roughly half that yearly in "disaster relief" to farmers, and that government payments amount to one-third to one-half of net farm income. In early 2001 he was supporting Combest's invitation to farm groups to suggest specific changes. He has worked to increase farm exports to China and to open up Cuba to U.S. farm exports. He has worked to reinsert the mohair and wool subsidies that were cut in the Gingrich era. He opposed and, with Combest, worked to delay the Clinton EPA non-point source pollution rules which would have required landowners to get pollution discharge permits from EPA—a prime reason why Al Gore did so poorly in farm areas, even at a time of low prices.

Stenholm has tried unsuccessfully to get into the leadership; in December 1994 he ran for minority whip, predictably losing to David Bonior 145–60. Now, with his seniority and ranking position on Agriculture, he seems more solidly committed to his party than ever. There was speculation that George W. Bush would nominate him for secretary of Agriculture, but that would have led to a special election in which Republicans would have had a good chance of picking up the seat, and the job went to a Californian instead. In the meantime, Stenholm's party label carries heavy costs in a district that has shed its long-held aversion to voting Republican. In 1996, Republican Rudy Izzard, a dentist and former San Angelo councilman, carried Abilene and eight other counties and Stenholm won by only 52%–47%. In 1998 Izzard ran again, and attacked Stenholm for supporting campaign finance legislation that would limit political speech by Christian conservative organizations. Stenholm argued that Newt Gingrich and Dick Armey wanted to defeat him because they opposed the needs of agriculture. Stenholm won 54%–45%. In 2000, running against a former judge who moved into the district from North Dallas, Stenholm won with a solid 59%–35%, carrying 31 of 32 counties. Now he must face redistricting. Three west Texas districts—the 13th, 19th and 17th—have all gained population sluggishly and must be expanded. Southward expansion would pose few problems for Stenholm, but going east would bring in heavily Republican counties at the edge of the Dallas-Fort Worth Metroplex.

Cook's Call *Potentially Competitive.* Republicans are hoping that redistricting (this seat needs to pick up about 30,000 residents) will give them the break they have needed to finally put this seat in their column. But they may just have to wait until Stenholm steps down to win here.

THE PEOPLE: Pop. 2000: 618,958; Pop. 1990: 566,255, up 9.3% 1990–2000. 84.1% White, 4% Black, 0.5% Asian, 0.6% Amer. Indian, 1.9% Two + races, 8.8% Other; 20.7% Hispanic Origin.

2000 Presidential Vote			**1996 Presidential Vote**		
Bush (R)	147,367	(71%)	Dole (R)	98,804	(51%)
Gore (D)	58,830	(29%)	Clinton (D)	76,057	(39%)
			Perot (I)	19,182	(10%)

Rep. Charles W. Stenholm (D)

Elected 1978, 12th term; b. Oct. 26, 1938, Stamford; home, Avoca; TX Tech. U., B.S. 1961, M.S. 1962; Lutheran; married (Cynthia).

Professional Career: Farmer; Vocational educ. teacher, 1962–65; Exec. V.P., Rolling Plains Cotton Growers, 1965–68; Mgr., Stamford Electric Co-op., 1968–76.

DC Office: 1211 LHOB 20515, 202-225-6605; Fax: 202-225-2234; Web site: www.house.gov/stenholm.

District Offices: Abilene, 915-673-7221; San Angelo, 915-655-7994; Stamford, 915-773-3623.

Committees: *Agriculture* (RMM of 24 D).

Group Ratings

	ADA	ACLU	AFS	LCV	CON	ITIC	NTU	COC	ACU	NTLC	CHC
2000	45	21	42	14	99	89	35	70	52	25	60
1999	55	—	66	0	87	—	24	68	54	—	—

National Journal Ratings

	1999 LIB	—	1999 CONS		2000 LIB	—	2000 CONS
Economic	52%	—	48%		56%	—	43%
Social	24%	—	75%		30%	—	68%
Foreign	58%	—	42%		51%	—	47%

Key Votes of the 106th Congress

1. Patient Bill of Rights	Y	5. Bar RU-486 $ for FDA	Y	9. NATO War in Serbia	Y
2. Accelerate Min. Wage	N	6. Display 10 Commandments	Y	10. Perm. Trade with China	Y
3. Strike Ban on Ergo. Stnd.	N	7. Gun Show Bkgrnd. Checks	N	11. Debt Relief for 3rd World	Y
4. Ovrd. Estate Tax Veto	N	8. Ban Part.-Birth Abortion	Y	12. Drop Cuba Econ. Embargo	Y

Election Results

2000 general	Charles W. Stenholm (D)	120,670	(59%)	($871,201)
	Darrell Clements (R)	72,535	(35%)	($68,388)
	Debra M. Monde (Lib)	11,180	(5%)	($50,824)
2000 primary	Charles W. Stenholm (D)	unopposed		
1998 general	Charles W. Stenholm (D)	75,367	(54%)	($1,529,708)
	Rudy Izzard (R)	63,700	(45%)	($572,253)

EIGHTEENTH DISTRICT

Houston contains, within its vast bounds, disparities of income and wealth as striking as any city in the United States. This is what one must expect in an expanding city with dynamic economic growth, vast immigration, absence of centralized planning and openness to cultural diversity. The contrast is most glaringly apparent at the edge of Houston's gleaming downtown with its keynote Pennzoil, Heritage Plaza and Bank of America buildings, plus Enron Field for baseball's Astros and the new basketball and hockey arena, and newly renovated housing in what was once the city's warehouse district. Only a few blocks away are the slums where blacks and Mexican-Americans live in unpainted frame houses full of cracks wide enough to let in Houston's humid, smoggy air. But the contrasts are less obvious as one moves out from Houston's historic center. Half a century ago, when Houston pioneers like Jesse Jones, millionaire cotton broker and newspaper publisher, started building downtown skyscrapers, they were operating in a town with a Third World economy, a low-skill producer of basic commodities, where a few got rich and many lived near subsistence level. Today, Houston has a high-tech advanced economy offering a myriad of opportunities and wide range of economic outcomes. One result is that as Houston's blacks and Hispanics have moved outward from the city, increasingly they are living in comfortable middle-class neighborhoods.

The 18th Congressional District of Texas contains central Houston and many of these out-lying neighborhoods, to the northeast, the south and especially the northwest. Its boundaries were redrawn by a three-judge federal court in 1996, after the Supreme Court ruled the previous boundaries unconstitutional because they were racially motivated. In its current form, the district has three spokes running out from Loop 610: northeast along the Eastex Freeway, to the south between the South Freeway and Telegraph Road, and a northwest spoke between the Northwest Freeway and Route 249. The previous boundaries were convoluted, so as to make the district's 1990 population 50% black and 15% Hispanic; within the 1996 boundaries the 1990 population was 45% black and 23% Hispanic. The 2000 Census showed that the balance had changed, to 40% black and 33% Hispanic.

The congresswoman from the 18th District is Sheila Jackson Lee, a Democrat first elected in 1994. A native of Queens, New York, she was educated at Yale and Virginia Law School, worked on Capitol Hill and practiced law in Houston, served as a local judge and won two terms in an at-large seat on the Houston Council. After a local term limits law took effect in 1994, she ran for Congress. The incumbent was Craig Washington, a talented but storm-tossed legislator, an iconoclast who voted against the space station and NAFTA, both of which are big pluses for the Houston-area economy. Jackson Lee supported NAFTA and raised lots of money from business interests who favored it. She won the Democratic primary unambiguously, 63%–37%, and has been re-elected easily since.

In the House Jackson Lee has a liberal voting record and has been prolific in offering amend-ments on the floor. More often than not, her proposals—for example, in favor of NASA funding and abortion—have been defeated, though she has won funds for science research at minority colleges. She voted "present" on the Defense of Marriage Act, the only Texan not to vote for it. As chair of the Children's Caucus, Jackson Lee has focused on improving child-care centers. During bankruptcy reform, she unsuccessfully sought to give child-support payments priority over everything except taxes. She wants a postage stamp issued to commemorate Mickey Leland, congressman from the district until his death in a plane crash in Africa in 1989.

Jackson Lee emerged into national prominence as an outspoken—and sometimes conten-tious—defender of President Clinton during impeachment. She called for censure as "right, pu-nitive and just" and called impeachment a "preposterous" trampling of the Constitution. She perhaps modeled herself on Barbara Jordan, the first black representative elected by the 18th District and an eloquent advocate of the impeachment of Richard Nixon in the Judiciary Com-mittee. Jackson Lee interposed comments often during the Judiciary hearings, spoke frequently in the debate on the floor, and during the trial was the only House member to sit on the Senate floor, silently at the back making copious notes. She "has become Congress's resident noodge, an endlessly loquacious presence here, there and everywhere," wrote *The New York Times*, perhaps unfairly, for her comments were often to the point and as defensible as those of many other members.

Jackson Lee is ranking Democrat on the Immigration and Claims Subcommittee, where she faces conflicting desires among her constituents: Latinos tend to favor greater immigration and more generous treatment of immigrants, but some African-Americans and union leaders see immigrants as dangerous competition for jobs. Frequently, but not always, she takes the pro-immigrant side: "We can't accept the goodness of immigration and what the immigrants have been able to do and at the same time characterize immigrants for all of the ailments and problems of America," she said, and she called for Guatemalans and Salvadorans to receive the same treatment as Nicaraguans and Cubans who are admitted as political refugees. But after Jackson Lee lectured high-tech firms about their failure to reach out to Black Caucus members, she opposed the bill to expand temporary H-1B visas for foreign workers because the proposal "does nothing" to recruit, hire or train domestic workers. She voted for permanent normal trade rela-tions with China, but only after presenting the White House "a list that dwarfs" the demands of other members, a Clinton aide said. She got Clinton to issue an executive order creating a Small Business Exports Task Force.

Cook's Call *Safe*. This district is probably the most Democratic in the state: Gore won here by 46% in 2000 and Clinton by 49% in 1996. It will also need to pick up more than 40,000 new residents in redistricting.

THE PEOPLE: Pop. 2000: 606,441; Pop. 1990: 568,146, up 6.7% 1990–2000. 38.8% White, 40.4% Black, 3.1% Asian, 0.4% Amer. Indian, 2.6% Two+ races, 14.7% Other; 33.4% Hispanic Origin.

2000 Presidential Vote			1996 Presidential Vote		
Gore (D)	123,707	(73%)	Clinton (D)	116,661	(73%)
Bush (R)	45,818	(27%)	Dole (R)	38,192	(24%)
			Perot (I)	5,699	(4%)

Rep. Sheila Jackson Lee (D)

Elected 1994, 4th term; b. Jan. 12, 1950, Queens, NY; home, Houston; Yale U., B.A. 1972, U. of VA Law Schl., J.D. 1975; Seventh Day Adventist; married (Elwyn).

Elected Office: Houston City Cncl., 1990–94.

Professional Career: Practicing atty., 1975–77, 1978–87; Staff Cnsl., U.S. House Select Assassinations Cmte., 1977–78; Houston Assoc. Municipal Judge, 1987–90.

DC Office: 403 CHOB 20515, 202-225-3816; Fax: 202-225-3317; Web site: www.house.gov/jacksonlee.

District Offices: Houston, 713-691-4882; Houston, 713-861-4070; Houston, 713-655-0050.

Committees: *Judiciary* (9th of 17 D): Crime; Immigration & Claims (RMM). *Science* (9th of 22 D): Energy; Space & Aeronautics.

Group Ratings

	ADA	ACLU	AFS	LCV	CON	ITIC	NTU	COC	ACU	NTLC	CHC
2000	80	86	85	79	32	65	19	50	4	12	14
1999	100	—	100	75	75	—	16	29	0	—	—

National Journal Ratings

	1999 LIB —	1999 CONS	2000 LIB —	2000 CONS
Economic	79% —	20%	95% —	0%
Social	87% —	0%	68% —	31%
Foreign	71% —	27%	85% —	15%

Key Votes of the 106th Congress

1. Patient Bill of Rights	Y	5. Bar RU-486 $ for FDA	N	9. NATO War in Serbia	Y
2. Accelerate Min. Wage	Y	6. Display 10 Commandments	N	10. Perm. Trade with China	Y
3. Strike Ban on Ergo. Stnd.	Y	7. Gun Show Bkgrnd. Checks	Y	11. Debt Relief for 3rd World	Y
4. Ovrd. Estate Tax Veto	N	8. Ban Part.-Birth Abortion	N	12. Drop Cuba Econ. Embargo	Y

Election Results

2000 general	Sheila Jackson Lee (D)	131,857	(76%)	($516,613)
	Bob Levy (R)	38,191	(22%)	($18,244)
	Others	2,330	(1%)	
2000 primary	Sheila Jackson Lee (D)	unopposed		
1998 general	Sheila Jackson Lee (D)	82,091	(90%)	($254,445)
	James Galvan (Lib)	9,176	(10%)	

NINETEENTH DISTRICT

On the High Plains of Texas, separated from the dusty cattlelands further east by rising gullies astride wide river courses, is some of the most productive cotton and wheat land in the United States, centered around the city of Lubbock. This is irrigated land, which gets its water from the giant Ogallala Aquifer that undergirds so much of the western Great Plains, making this part of

Texas a sort of green island in a vast brown sea of arid grazing land. It is also an area that has produced more than its share of popular musicians: Roy Orbison, Buddy Holly, Jimmy Dean, Tanya Tucker, Waylon Jennings, Larry Gatlin. The High Plains were settled relatively late, with most growth after World War II. Lubbock grew from 31,000 in 1940 to 128,000 in 1960 and 200,000 in 2000, with an economy that includes Texas Tech University as well as agribusiness. But the 1980s and 1990s were tough on the High Plains. The aquifer seemed to be going dry, populations declined in most rural counties, hospitals were closed in small towns.

The 19th Congressional District of Texas runs roughly 400 miles along the western edge of the High Plains, from the northern edge of the Panhandle south to the Permian Basin. Tantalizingly, it includes only part of each of its four major cities, Lubbock, Amarillo, Midland and Odessa. This was because Democrats, in control of redistricting, wanted to put the Democratic portions of each into the neighboring 13th and 23rd Districts, to shore up Democratic incumbents; both, however, lost in the early 1990s, and in early 2001 the chairman of the Texas House redistricting committee, Delwin Jones of Lubbock, said he wanted to put each of the cities entirely within one district.

The 19th District has an interesting political pedigree. When Mahon retired, the 19th was seriously contested by a young Midland oil man named George W. Bush, but he lost 53%–47% to Lubbock-based conservative Democrat Kent Hance. Co-sponsor of the Reagan tax cuts in 1981, Hance later became a Republican and lost in the 1990 primary for governor, the office Bush won four years later. Today of course Bush is the local celebrity; he made an emotional appearance in Midland just before his inauguration as president, saying, "This place has shaped the values that will shape my service to the nation," and the Midland Chamber of Commerce distributes a "George W. Bush lived here" fact sheet, with the location of schools, baseball fields and 10 home addresses, plus phone numbers of local residents who knew him back when. Bush carried Lubbock County 63%–37% for governor in 1994, 82%–18% for reelection in 1998, and 74%–24% for president in 2000. Overall, the 19th District was the most heavily Republican Texas district in 2000: Bush carried it 79%–19%, with percentages as high as 91% in some rural counties.

The congressman from the 19th District is Larry Combest, a Republican first elected in 1984. He graduated from West Texas State University, worked as a teacher, farmer and for the Soil Conservation Service; from 1971–78 he specialized on farm issues on Senator John Tower's staff. He then returned to Lubbock, where he owned an electronics company. In 1984, when Congressman Kent Hance ran for the Senate, Combest ran for the House. After a tough primary, runoff and general election that year, he has since won easily.

Combest has compiled a solidly conservative voting record and has been chairman of the House Agriculture Committee since 1999. Agriculture is a committee traditionally split not by party but by commodity; Combest and ranking Democrat Charles Stenholm from the next-door 17th District have worked closely and amicably together, and Combest invited all members of the committee to a weekend retreat. Combest opposed the 2000 EPA Total Maximum Daily Load regulations, which would have forced farmers to seek EPA pollution discharge permits for use of fertilizer; he and Stenholm sought to delay them, pending a National Academy of Sciences study. He has sought to open foreign markets to U.S. farm exports. And he has defended, against a slighting comment in one of Bill Clinton's State of the Union messages, the work of the Plant Stress Laboratory at Texas Tech, designed to foster plant growth on long-term space missions.

Combest was not an enthusiast for the 1996 Freedom to Farm Act; in 1995 he and three other Southern Republicans killed an earlier version in committee, and forced Senate Agriculture Committee Chairman Pat Roberts and Speaker Newt Gingrich to accept continuation of the cotton marketing program. Immediately after passage of the bill, Combest softened its farm credit terms when farmers in the 19th District were unable to get crop loans. Farm prices plummeted in 1998, and in the years since the committee has fashioned "disaster relief" packages each year— $18 billion in 1999, $15 billion in 2000—that dwarfed earlier subsidies. Combest started off not eager for changes in Freedom to Farm, which comes up for reauthorization in 2002. But in January 2001 he said, "The ag economy is much more fragile than most folks realize," and launched a series of committee hearings in which he demanded specific proposals for changes from farm groups; one hearing was canceled because the testimony was judged not specific enough. Combest and Stenholm seem determined to produce a bipartisan consensus bill which may revive subsidies in some form.

Combest was chairman of the Intelligence Committee in 1995 and 1996. He criticized CIA handling of the Aldrich Ames case and "the compartmented culture of the intelligence community," and proposed combining the CIA's Directorate of Operations with the Defense Department's Clandestine Services, a proposal that didn't make it out of committee. He was vice chairman of the Commission on Protecting and Reducing Government Secrecy, which produced a unanimous report in 1997 calling for both more and less secrecy. "The government must be made to discharge its superfluous secrets and behave in a more open manner," he said. "But in our rush to widen access, we must not compromise vital secrets, nor betray those who have risked their lives and fortunes to confide in us."

Redistricting will have to expand the 19th District, which is currently 54,000 people short of the state population average. Most likely Amarillo will be removed, while all of Lubbock and Midland will be included. Such a district should present Combest with no difficulty in winning reelection.

Cook's Call   *Safe.* This district gave Bush his largest winning percentage (79%) of any in the country.

THE PEOPLE: Pop. 2000: 607,535; Pop. 1990: 565,925, up 7.4% 1990–2000. 81% White, 3% Black, 1% Asian, 0.7% Amer. Indian, 2% Two+ races, 12.3% Other; 26.1% Hispanic Origin.

2000 Presidential Vote
Bush (R) 162,646 (80%)
Gore (D) 39,870 (20%)

1996 Presidential Vote
Dole (R) 133,397 (67%)
Clinton (D) 51,996 (26%)
Perot (I) 12,323 (6%)

Rep. Larry Combest (R)

Elected 1984, 9th term; b. Mar. 20, 1945, Memphis; home, Lubbock; W. TX St. U., B.B.A. 1969; United Methodist; married (Sharon).

Professional Career: Farmer; Teacher, 1970–71; Dir., U.S. Agric. Stabilization & Conservation Svc., Graham TX, 1971; Aide, U.S. Sen. John Tower, 1971–78; Founder & Pres., Combest Distrib. Co., 1978–85.

DC Office: 1026 LHOB 20515, 202-225-4005; Web site: www.house.gov/combest.

District Offices: Amarillo, 806-353-3945; Lubbock, 806-763-1611; Odessa, 915-550-0743.

Committees: *Agriculture* (Chmn. of 27 R). *Small Business* (2d of 19 R): Regulatory Reform Oversight.

Group Ratings

	ADA	ACLU	AFS	LCV	CON	ITIC	NTU	COC	ACU	NTLC	CHC
2000	0	21	0	14	43	100	63	100	88	84	100
1999	5	—	0	0	6	—	59	92	96	—	—

National Journal Ratings

	1999 LIB —	1999 CONS	2000 LIB —	2000 CONS
Economic	0%	84%	18%	76%
Social	0%	96%	0%	79%
Foreign	10%	86%	33%	62%

Key Votes of the 106th Congress

1. Patient Bill of Rights	N	5. Bar RU-486 $ for FDA	Y	9. NATO War in Serbia	N
2. Accelerate Min. Wage	N	6. Display 10 Commandments	Y	10. Perm. Trade with China	Y
3. Strike Ban on Ergo. Stnd.	N	7. Gun Show Bkgrnd. Checks	N	11. Debt Relief for 3rd World	N
4. Ovrd. Estate Tax Veto	Y	8. Ban Part.-Birth Abortion	Y	12. Drop Cuba Econ. Embargo	Y

Election Results

2000 general	Larry Combest (R)	170,319	(92%)	($556,470)
	John Turnbow (Lib)	15,579	(8%)	
2000 primary	Larry Combest (R)	unopposed		
1998 general	Larry Combest (R)	108,266	(84%)	($459,193)
	Sidney Blankenship (D)	21,162	(16%)	($8,937)

TWENTIETH DISTRICT

San Antonio, with its antique past and theme-park future, its Hispanic heritage, its military superstructure and its high-tech hopes, is unlike any other city in the United States. Here on a plaza is the Alamo, preserved by the Daughters of the Republic of Texas, where Davy Crockett, Jim Bowie and 184 others were wiped out in 1836 (Crockett was a Tennessee congressman for three terms; if he had not lost his reelection in 1834, he presumably would not have left Tennessee for Texas). The Spanish architecture recalls San Antonio's days as the most important town in Texas, when the state was part of Mexico, and contrasts with the 31-story Tower Life Building, which contrasts with the armadillo-like Alamodome; the stark terrain contrasts with the lushness of the Paseo, the 1970s-redeveloped Riverwalk along the tiny San Antonio River. The city includes old neighborhoods redolent of the Texas Germans who were its chief Anglo citizens for many years.

For most of the 20th Century, San Antonio's economy was built on the military: This has been the home of three Air Force bases and the Brooks Army Medical Center at Fort Sam Houston, contributing some $3 billion to the local economy. In 1995 Bill Clinton bent the rules of the base closing process to keep in San Antonio the thousands of depot jobs at Kelly Air Force Base, a move so resented that Congress blocked new rounds of base closings. Behind the bases as a local employer is the medical complex centered on the Health Science Center. San Antonio also has many military retirees and it has become a tourist center. For generations Texas schoolchildren made pilgrimages to the Alamo; in recent decades, they stop at the nearby HemisFair, preserved from the 1968 World's Fair, and the Riverwalk.

San Antonio is Texas's third-largest city, with 1,144,000 people in 2000, a 22% increase in the 1990s, though its metro area of 1.6 million is only about one-third the size of metro Houston or the Dallas-Fort Worth Metroplex. Notable as the only Hispanic-majority major city in the country, San Antonio has the low education and income levels one might expect from a city whose economy is affected by the proximity of the Mexican border. Yet it has mostly avoided the polarized politics and ethnic anger that were manifested in the urban black-white tensions of the 1960s, and it has made progress as a low-wage, high-tech center, making some linkage with nearby Austin.

The 20th Congressional District of Texas includes most of central San Antonio and its west side. Its boundaries on the north are irregular, since affluent Anglo neighborhoods are set off and placed in the 21st District. On the west it extends beyond I-410 to Loop 1604 and in some places past that highway. This is one of Texas' six Hispanic-majority districts, and the first to elect a Hispanic congressman. It is solidly Democratic.

The congressman from the 20th District is Charles Gonzalez, a Democrat elected in 1998. He is one of eight children of Henry B. Gonzalez, who held the seat since a 1961 special election and was for six years chairman of the Banking Committee. Charles Gonzalez grew up in San Antonio and was 16 when his father was elected to the House. He graduated from the University of Texas and St. Mary's University School of Law and served in the Texas Air National Guard. He was an elementary school teacher, practiced law and served as a judge from 1982–97. As a judge, he considered himself a reformer who created a statewide model for mediation to accelerate the justice system and protect children from broken families. He obviously benefited from his father's renown as the patron saint of Texas liberalism for many years; throughout his career, the elder Gonzalez brought a determination to do right and an indifference to what others may think. In September 1997, at 81 and in poor health, Gonzalez announced he would resign from the House at the end of the year. Later, he changed his mind but was absent from the House for most of 1998, returning only to vote against impeachment in December.

Charles Gonzalez was the frontrunner for the seat but the contest was more competitive than many had expected. With six other Democrats in the March primary, he campaigned as a consensus-builder, emphasizing his background in negotiation and compromise. Symbolizing the economic transformation of San Antonio, he said he would work for the entire district, not simply the low-income groups, and would promote San Antonio's future by stressing education. Taking a more feisty tone was Maria Berriozabal, a former city council member and the daughter of Mexican immigrants, who called for more outspoken leadership and had a picture of farmworkers-leader Cesar Chavez on her campaign walls. In a brash move, she used a picture of Henry in her campaign literature and claimed that she was more his model than was Charles. Just before the primary, his father issued a brief statement endorsing his son. Gonzalez led the first balloting with 44% to 22% for Berriozabal. In the April runoff, Gonzalez benefited from a fundraising advantage of more than 2–1 that reinforced his connection to his father—"Gonzalez Congress" read his campaign posters—and mostly ignored his opponent. He won 62%–38%. He won the general election with 63%.

In the House, Gonzalez has a generally liberal voting record and took his father's seat on the now-renamed Financial Services Committee. He filed a proposal to reform home-buying contracts and eliminate mandatory arbitration clauses, which have prevented consumers from going to court to seek compensation for damages for poor construction. He demanded the resignation of Reyn Archer, the Texas health commissioner, after Archer said that Hispanics had a high teen pregnancy rate because their community is more tolerant of such births. He became a leading proponent of census sampling for both the Democratic Caucus and the Hispanic Caucus—which his father had refused to join. "I consider this the civil rights issue of the decade," he said; but both the Census Bureau professionals and Commerce Secretary Donald Evans ruled that there was no justification. Following the Florida presidential recount, Gonzalez was named by Dick Gephardt as co-chair of the Democratic Caucus Special Committee on Election Reform. On local issues, he called for increased school funding, and he urged the Air Force to study why 66 former and current workers at the Kelly base had been diagnosed with amyotrophic lateral sclerosis, Lou Gehrig's disease.

In 2000 he had no major-party opposition. Although redistricting may produce big changes in San Antonio's outlying areas and the 20th needs to add 27,000, it probably won't have a significant impact.

Cook's Call *Safe.* Gonzalez can probably hold onto this seat for as long as he would like.

THE PEOPLE: Pop. 2000: 624,384; Pop. 1990: 564,865, up 10.5% 1990–2000. 66.3% White, 5.9% Black, 1.4% Asian, 1% Amer. Indian, 0.1% Hawaiian, 4.2% Two + races, 21.2% Other; 67% Hispanic Origin.

2000 Presidential Vote			1996 Presidential Vote		
Gore (D)	81,742	(56%)	Clinton (D)	82,892	(60%)
Bush (R)	63,675	(44%)	Dole (R)	48,488	(35%)
			Perot (I)	7,285	(5%)

Rep. Charles Gonzalez (D)

Elected 1998, 2d term; b. May 5, 1945, San Antonio; home, San Antonio; U. of TX, B. A. 1969; St. Mary's Law Schl., J. D. 1972.; Catholic; married (Becky Whetstone).

Military Career: TX Air Natl. Guard, 1969–75.

Elected Office: Judge, San Antonio Municipal Court; Judge, Bexar Cnty. Court at Law, 1983–87; Judge, 57th State Judicial Dist. Court, 1988–97.

Professional Career: Elem. schl. teacher, 1969–71; Practicing atty., 1972–82.

DC Office: 327 CHOB 20515, 202-225-3236; Fax: 202-225-1915; Web site: www.house.gov/gonzalez.

District Office: San Antonio, 210-472-6195.

Committees: *Financial Services* (22d of 32 D): Capital Markets, Insurance & Government Sponsored Enterprises; Domestic Monetary Policy, Technology & Economic Growth; Financial Institutions & Consumer Credit. *Small Business* (9th of 17 D): Regulatory Reform Oversight; Workforce, Empowerment & Government Programs.

Group Ratings

	ADA	ACLU	AFS	LCV	CON	ITIC	NTU	COC	ACU	NTLC	CHC
2000	80	86	85	93	57	83	19	50	8	15	13
1999	100	—	100	94	40	—	11	36	0	—	—

National Journal Ratings

	1999 LIB	—	1999 CONS		2000 LIB	—	2000 CONS
Economic	78%	—	21%		85%	—	11%
Social	80%	—	19%		77%	—	22%
Foreign	85%	—	12%		80%	—	16%

Key Votes of the 106th Congress

1. Patient Bill of Rights	Y	5. Bar RU-486 $ for FDA	N	9. NATO War in Serbia	Y
2. Accelerate Min. Wage	Y	6. Display 10 Commandments	N	10. Perm. Trade with China	Y
3. Strike Ban on Ergo. Stnd.	Y	7. Gun Show Bkgrnd. Checks	Y	11. Debt Relief for 3rd World	Y
4. Ovrd. Estate Tax Veto	N	8. Ban Part.-Birth Abortion	N	12. Drop Cuba Econ. Embargo	Y

Election Results

2000 general	Charles Gonzalez (D)	107,487	(88%)	($619,173)
	Alejandro (Alex) De Pena (Lib)	15,087	(12%)	
2000 primary	Charles Gonzalez (D)	unopposed		
1998 general	Charles Gonzalez (D)	50,356	(63%)	($657,280)
	James Walker (R)	28,347	(36%)	($89,200)

TWENTY-FIRST DISTRICT

The Texas German country, on the gently rolling plains between San Antonio and Austin and west into the Hill Country, is one of America's lesser known ethnic enclaves. Settled by refugees from the failed democratic revolutions of 1848, the German country has always been a set of orderly communities in rip-roaring Texas, economically prosperous in a state that considered itself poor until it struck oil. It was anti-slavery and politically Republican in a state whose enthusiasm for the Democratic Party had roots in Confederate loyalties and populist rebellions. The Texas Germans are entwined with the career of Lyndon Johnson: The death of Republican Congressman Harry Wurzbach of Guadalupe County gave Democrats a majority in the House in 1931 and enabled them to elect John Nance Garner of Uvalde as speaker, while Wurzbach's replacement in the House, Democrat Richard Kleberg (of the King Ranch family) gave the then 23-year-old Johnson to his first Washington job. And, though Johnson never emphasized this, his LBJ Ranch was neither in Blanco County nor poor Johnson City, where he grew up, but west in Gillespie County near the prosperous town of Fredericksburg, historically Texas German, heavily Republican (82% for George W. Bush in 2000), and now something of a tourist attraction with restored buildings, museums and quaint shops.

The 21st Congressional District has its demographic center in the old Texas German country, where the San Antonio and Austin metropolitan areas are now growing together. As with so many Texas districts under the 1991 redistricting, its boundaries are quite complex. About 40% is on the north side of San Antonio and Bexar County (pronounced like a drawn-out *bear*), mostly Anglo neighborhoods around Alamo Heights and out I-35, and in Guadalupe and Comal Counties just beyond—Texas German country now classified as part of metro San Antonio. Another 27% is in Williamson County, just north of Austin—one of the state's fastest-growing counties, with suburban overspill subdivisions full of high-tech and white-collar workers who are much more Republican than the liberals who live in older neighborhoods near downtown Austin and UT. These two areas are connected by sparsely populated Hill Country and Texas German counties, including Fredericksburg and the LBJ Ranch, the almost mountainous country around Kerrville, sheep and goat ranching country reaching northwest to San Angelo—America's wool and mohair capital—and all the way to Midland, headquarters of the high-income, oil-rich Permian Basin, where George Bush and George W. Bush lived from 1949–60. It is a big district geographically (it's 350 miles from Round Rock in Williamson County to Midland) and in population (801,000 in 2000, the third largest in Texas, up 42% in the 1990s) and heavily Republican (73%–24% for George W. Bush in 2000).

The congressman from the 21st District is Lamar Smith, a Republican first elected in 1986. Smith is from an old San Antonio and south Texas ranching family; he went to Yale and SMU Law School, worked as a reporter and a lawyer, was elected to the Texas House in 1980 and the Bexar County Commission in 1982. In 1986, when Congressman Tom Loeffler ran for governor, Smith ran for the House; at that time the 21st ranged even wider and had more acreage than Ohio. Smith won by beating two other San Antonio-based candidates in the primary and then winning the runoff, with help from Senator Phil Gramm, against a religious conservative. He has been re-elected easily since; 76%–22% in 2000, when the district cast 330,000 votes, the most of any Texas district and nearly three times as many as San Antonio's 20th District.

Smith compiled a conservative voting record and pursued original initiatives when Democrats held the majority. One bill added 100,000 acres to Big Bend National Park along the Rio Grande; another sponsored the first Bush administration's government-wide ethics act. By 1991, Smith was proposing cuts in every appropriations bill, with emphasis on cutting government overhead costs, especially travel; often Democrats prevented them from coming to a vote. In April 1993 he was appointed head of the Republicans' "theme team," organizing more than 800 one-minute speeches by members.

In the majority, Smith chaired the Immigration Subcommittee of Judiciary from 1995 to 2001. He had long believed in stronger action to stop illegal immigration and to reduce legal immigration, and in 1995 he steered his version of immigration reform through subcommittee. But on the House floor, a bipartisan group including liberal Democrats and freshmen Republicans successfully moved to strip almost all provisions on legal immigration—the effective end of Smith's move to reduce legal immigration. The bill passed by a wide margin, but House-Senate conferees removed almost all aid for illegals, even as the welfare bill barred states from aiding legal immigrants. The final version had harsher deportation and asylum proceedings, doubled the number of Border Patrol agents and mandated a 14-mile fence on the California-Mexico border. In the midst of his reelection campaign, Bill Clinton signed it.

Smith has supported some liberalizing provisions—a 1999 law giving citizenship to 3,000 immigrant children who turned 21 while the INS failed to act (sometimes for years) on their applications for citizenship, and a 2000 law providing for automatic citizenship for foreign children adopted by American parents, under which 150,000 children became U.S. citizens on February 27, 2001, the highest number on any day in history. He disagreed with his Senate counterpart Spencer Abraham's opposition to Section 110, requiring lengthy documentation at border crossings; they agreed in 2000 on a national computer database of information collected on INS spot checks. He opposed Bill Clinton's October 2000 demand for legalization of illegal immigrants living in the United States since 1985. His bill to split the INS into two agencies, one concentrating on law enforcement, the other on aid to immigrants, was passed by his subcommittee in March 2000, but went nowhere in the Senate; however, George W. Bush supported the idea in June 2000. Smith was initially skeptical about increasing the number of H-1B visas for high-skill immigrants. But in 2000 data convinced him that foreigners were needed to fill high-tech jobs, and he sponsored the House bill that removed the cap on the visas through 2002; a different version became law in October 2000. Smith rotated off the Immigration chairmanship as a result of the Republicans' six-year term limits on chairmen; he is now Chairman of the Crime Subcommittee.

From January 1999 to January 2001, Smith chaired the ethics committee (official name: Standards of Official Conduct Committee). He said he wanted to emphasize the panel's "advice and education" rather than its investigative duties. The practice of bringing ethics complaints for partisan reasons has been discontinued, and Smith had few cases to contend with. In September 2000 the committee said that it did not have sufficient evidence to agree with charges that Corinne Brown of Florida violated rules when her daughter accepted gifts from a foreigner whose side she took in a legal case. In October 2000 the committee issued a letter of reproval against Transportation Committee Chairman Bud Shuster for "official misconduct" in his relationship with lobbyist and former staffer Ann Eppard.

Cook's Call *Safe.* Smith is safely entrenched in this heavily Republican district. It was one of the faster-growing districts in Texas during the 1990s and will need to drop more than 150,000 people.

THE PEOPLE: Pop. 2000: 801,078; Pop. 1990: 566,105, up 41.5% 1990–2000. 86.4% White, 3.2% Black, 1.6% Asian, 0.5% Amer. Indian, 0.1% Hawaiian, 2.1% Two+ races, 6.1% Other; 18.3% Hispanic Origin.

2000 Presidential Vote		
Bush (R)	247,894	(75%)
Gore (D)	82,063	(25%)

1996 Presidential Vote		
Dole (R)	174,072	(63%)
Clinton (D)	81,940	(30%)
Perot (I)	18,474	(7%)

Rep. Lamar S. Smith (R)

Elected 1986, 8th term; b. Nov. 19, 1947, San Antonio; home, San Antonio; Yale U., B.A. 1969, S. Methodist U., J.D. 1975; Christian Scientist; married (Beth).

Elected Office: TX House of Reps., 1981–82; Bexar Cnty. Comm., 1982–85.

Professional Career: U.S. Small Business Admin., 1969–70; Business writer, *Christian Science Monitor*, 1970–72; Practicing atty., 1975–76.

DC Office: 2231 RHOB 20515, 202-225-4236; Fax: 202-225-8628; Web site: www.house.gov/lamarsmith.

District Offices: Georgetown, 512-931-3500; Kerrville, 830-895-1414; Midland, 915-687-5232; San Angelo, 915-653-3971; San Antonio, 210-821-5024.

Committees: *Judiciary* (5th of 21 R): Crime (Chmn.); Immigration & Claims; The Constitution. *Science* (2d of 25 R): Research; Space & Aeronautics. *Joint Economic Committee* (3d of 10 Reps.).

Group Ratings

	ADA	ACLU	AFS	LCV	CON	ITIC	NTU	COC	ACU	NTLC	CHC
2000	5	14	0	7	24	89	63	85	96	84	93
1999	0	—	0	0	19	—	52	88	84	—	—

National Journal Ratings

	1999 LIB —	1999 CONS		2000 LIB —	2000 CONS
Economic	0% —	84%		0% —	94%
Social	25% —	72%		30% —	68%
Foreign	15% —	81%		12% —	78%

Key Votes of the 106th Congress

1. Patient Bill of Rights	N	5. Bar RU-486 $ for FDA	Y	9. NATO War in Serbia	N
2. Accelerate Min. Wage	N	6. Display 10 Commandments	Y	10. Perm. Trade with China	Y
3. Strike Ban on Ergo. Stnd.	N	7. Gun Show Bkgrnd. Checks	N	11. Debt Relief for 3rd World	N
4. Ovrd. Estate Tax Veto	Y	8. Ban Part.-Birth Abortion	Y	12. Drop Cuba Econ. Embargo	N

Election Results

2000 general	Lamar S. Smith (R)	251,049	(76%)	($543,754)
	Jim Green (D)	73,326	(22%)	
	Others	6,503	(2%)	
2000 primary	Lamar S. Smith (R)	unopposed		
1998 general	Lamar S. Smith (R)	165,047	(91%)	($531,538)
	Jeffrey Charles Blunt (Lib)	15,561	(9%)	

TWENTY-SECOND DISTRICT

Spreading out in all directions from its historic center at Allen's Landing on Buffalo Bayou, Houston has become one of the great metropolises of North America. A half-century ago, the steaming flatlands south of Houston running down to the Gulf of Mexico did not seem a likely site for one of the world's most advanced civilizations. But they are today. It was Houston where most of the scientific work was done that put the first man on the moon—the first word spoken on the moon was "Houston." Houston is the undisputed center of expertise in the oil business, where the greatest concentration of experts in the world is within a few miles of each other. Houston has also become one of the great medical centers of the world, with the giant Texas Medical Center looming as impressively massive as any great office skyscraper complex. And Houston became one of the great surprise growth cities of the 1990s, creating thousands of small businesses, with special growth among immigrants. All this success and sophistication are testimony to human—and Texan—creativity, and to the triumph of air conditioning. For who supposed that all these people would move here if they had to sweat through Houston's steamy five-month summer?

The 22d Congressional District of Texas is made up of the southwest quadrant of metropolitan Houston, starting near Loop 610 and heading out into Fort Bend and Brazoria Counties. It also has a spur heading westward to a point near the Johnson Space Center and Galveston Bay. Much of the district's shape derives from the 1991 redistricting, but its lines in Houston and Harris County were smoothed out by the court-ordered redistricting plan of August 1996, adopted after the Supreme Court ruled the 18th and 29th Districts unconstitutional because they were racially motivated. The current 22d District, though mostly suburban, is by no means lily-white: in 2000 its population was 15% black, 22% Hispanic and 10% Asian—the last the highest in Texas. Politically, this is a heavily Republican district, 62%–36% for George W. Bush in 2000.

The congressman from the 22d District is Tom DeLay, the House majority whip and number three member of the House Republican leadership—an aggressive political operator, strong ideological conservative and one of the most powerful members of the House. DeLay was born in the border town of Laredo and spent much of his childhood in Venezuela, where his father drilled oil wells and where he says he witnessed three revolutions. After graduating from the University of Houston, he settled in Sugar Land, in Fort Bend County southwest of Houston, where he built a pest control business. He was elected to the state legislature in 1978, the first Republican legislator from Fort Bend County in the 20th Century. When 22d District Congressman Ron Paul (now congressman from the 14th District) ran for the Senate in 1984, DeLay ran for the House.

DeLay's voting record in the House has been very conservative; he has combined a strong ideological motivation and a knack for practical politics. In his first term, he was the freshman representative on the Republican Committee on Committees. In his second term he got a seat on the Appropriations Committee, where he has been known to seek money for his district, like grants for a bus system to ease traffic on the choked Southwest Freeway. But he opposed a $1.2 billion monorail, a sure clunker in this auto town. More recently he has pushed the designation of a new I-69 heading southwest from Houston and backed the May 1998 transportation bill, with its formula giving millions more to Texas. DeLay is an ardent booster of the space program and has worked mightily to save the space station from demise.

DeLay has been interested in leadership positions since the 1980s—and in the process became a master vote-counter. In March 1989, in only his third term, he managed the campaign of moderate Edward Madigan to replace Dick Cheney as minority whip; but Madigan lost 87–85 to Newt Gingrich—a result that made a revolutionary change in the House. Madigan's loss didn't stop DeLay from running in December 1992 against incumbent Bill Gradison for the post of Republican Conference secretary; DeLay won 95–71. It was clear that Robert Michel would retire as Minority Leader in 1994, and Gingrich would run to succeed him. DeLay started running for whip, presumed to be the second-highest leadership post at a time when almost no one thought Republicans would win a majority in the 1994 elections; that meant that DeLay was trying to leapfrog Dick Armey on the leadership ladder. Then Republicans won their majority in 1994, after which Gingrich was easily elected speaker and Armey majority leader. DeLay had serious opposition from Robert Walker, Gingrich's best friend in the House, and Bill McCollum. But he had done much more to prepare, campaigning in 25 states and contributing $2 million to Republican candidates. DeLay showed his vote-counting acumen by proclaiming that he was not interested in the second-ballot votes he would need if no one had a majority: "We are locked into winning this outright." He won with 119 votes to 80 for Walker and 28 for McCollum.

"I'm very aggressive. I'm a hard-working, aggressive, persistent whip. That's why I'm whip," says DeLay, who is often called "The Hammer." Not many would disagree. But his perspective goes beyond the House. Through increased use of risk assessment and cost-benefit analyses and a moratorium on new regulations, DeLay's goal has been to change the culture of federal regulatory agencies. Legislatively, this was not a success at first: Bill Clinton singled out DeLay's riders for vetoes, and moderate Republicans led by Sherwood Boehlert started opposing them. But DeLay has also had his successes and with George W. Bush as president will likely have more: as when the House voted down Clinton's proposed ergonomics rules in March 2001.

DeLay has also sought to change the culture of Washington lobbyists, a heavily Democratic group since the days of the New Deal. He has worked closely with sympathetic lobbyists, bringing them in on the drafting of legislation, and has also raised money from them in very large amounts. He argues that K Street (the generic Washington term for business lobbyists) should work with their natural allies among Republicans and abandon their alliances of convenience with Democrats when they seemed sure to be the majority party forever. Sometimes this has caused embarrassment. Many squawked in October 1998 when DeLay attacked the Electronics Industries Alliance for hiring former Democratic Congressman Dave McCurdy as president; the ethics committee privately rebuked him. As DeLay said in July 2000, "I haven't been able to change the culture of this town yet. And that's one of my goals—to change the culture of Washington, D.C."

But he has made headway, and nowhere more so than in fundraising. After the 1998 election, DeLay worked to replace National Republican Campaign Committee Chairman John Linder, a Georgian and ally of Newt Gingrich, with Tom Davis of Virginia, a moderate with a detailed knowledge of the politics of every district. In 1999 DeLay raised more than $15 million for Republican candidates, and was the chief fundraiser for the committee, while his own PACs raised more than $1 million. He also promoted a group called the US Family Network, a 501(c)4 group that raised $1.3 million in 1998 from five donors and to which the NRCC gave $500,000 in October 1999. And he started the Republican Majorities Issues Campaign, a Section 527 organization also not required to disclose contributors. These initiatives did not necessarily pay off. In May 2000 Patrick Kennedy, then head of Democratic Congressional Campaign Committee, brought a RICO suit charging that DeLay "extorted" funds from donors and laundered them through groups like US Family Network and RMIC, and the House in June 2000 passed a law requiring disclosure by Section 527 organizations. Many Democrats admitted that Kennedy's suit was an abuse of the RICO law, and DeLay threatened to take depositions of every House Democrat; the suit was eventually settled in April 2001. Regardless, DeLay had created an awesome fundraising apparatus, one responsible in considerable part for maintaining the Republican majority in 1998 and 2000.

DeLay's whip operation is awesome as well, generally conceded to be the best vote-counting operation in Congress. And DeLay has had great influence in selecting other Republican leaders. He supported Gingrich when his reelection as speaker was uncertain in January 1997, but in July 1997 he met with leaders of the coup against Gingrich, telling them the leadership would support a floor vote to oust him. But the coup failed, and at a Republican Conference meeting a few days later, DeLay came dramatically forward and admitted his participation in the coup attempt, while Dick Armey seemed to deny his. From that point forward, it was clear DeLay had much more support in the conference than Armey. In November 1998, when Gingrich quit after the disappointing results of the election, DeLay supported Bob Livingston for speaker. But on the morning of the impeachment vote in December 1998, Livingston shocked everyone by announcing that he would resign. Members began hovering around DeLay at the back of the chamber. Armey clearly did not have the support to win the speakership; DeLay, presumably aware of his polarizing reputation, made no move to run. Instead he threw his support to his chief deputy whip, Dennis Hastert, little known outside the House but respected by Republican members as a hard worker, consensus builder and party loyalist. Within hours it would be clear that Hastert would be the next speaker.

Many assumed that Hastert would be DeLay's puppet, but Hastert and DeLay often disagreed on basic strategy, and Hastert usually prevailed. In October 1999 DeLay wanted to pass stripped-down appropriations, even if they would be vetoed by Clinton, so that Republicans could argue that they preserved the Social Security surplus. But Hastert preferred to cut compromises with the Clinton White House. In October 2000 they agreed on not reaching an agreement with Clinton before the election, by refusing to drop language delaying the ergonomics rule. In the delayed session after the election, DeLay wanted to pass a one-year continuing resolution, daring Clinton to veto it; Hastert and Trent Lott preferred to negotiate with Clinton and avoid a government shutdown. Also in December 2000 DeLay backed Saxby Chambliss for Budget Committee chairman; Hastert backed Jim Nussle, who won. DeLay's relations with George W. Bush's campaign were not always smooth, even though DeLay's new chief deputy whip, Roy Blunt, was named the Bush campaign's liaison to House Republicans. But in October 1999 Bush attacked the leadership's—and DeLay's—proposal to save $8 billion in the next budget by sending out EITC payments every month instead of in one check in the spring. Bush said that was balancing the budget on the backs of the working poor; DeLay said, "It's obvious the governor's got a lot to learn about Congress." But in early 2001 DeLay worked hard to carry out Bush's legislative strategy.

DeLay is not all political maneuvering and fundraising. He operates from a hard core of conviction. He pushed the impeachment of Bill Clinton regardless of the political consequences. In the days after the November 1998 election, it was widely assumed that impeachment would fail; it passed, largely because of DeLay. He had no regrets; a year later he said Clinton "debased" the presidency and "poisoned" the national political dialogue. He strongly supported keeping Elian Gonzalez in the United States and said, "I consider the government's treatment of Elian to be the lowest point of the Clinton administration's tenure, a statement I make with full knowledge of its considerable excesses and transgressions." And he surprised many of his detractors by taking a personal interest in the deaths of children who were wards of the District of Columbia childcare services. DeLay and his wife have raised foster children in their home in Sugar Land, and he sought to reform the D.C. foster care system. "Lives are being destroyed every day because this agency does not do its job," he said.

DeLay attacked the Clinton foreign policy for ignoring "core American values" and called it "an inedible . . . stew of appeasement and social work." In June 2000 he sponsored a bill to bar the U.S. from cooperating with the international war crimes court established in the 1998 Rome treaty unless and until it was ratified by the Senate. On other foreign policy issues, Delay in February 2000 sponsored the Taiwan Security Act; despite the opposition of the Clinton administration it passed the House 341–70. He called for scrapping the "diplomatic fiction" of the one-China policy and to proclaim that threats against Taiwan will be met with the force required to deter aggression. But he supported permanent normal trade relations with China.

"I have a basic political philosophy: hard work wins every time. I have always won by out-working my opponents," DeLay has said. In November 2000, when the outcome of the presidential election was being disputed, DeLay sent out a memo to House Republicans pointing out that the House and the Senate could reject a state's electoral votes. A week before the Supreme Court settled the issue, he called 2000 "the most important election since the Civil War." When Bush was declared the winner, he exulted, "We have the House, we have the Senate, we have the White House, which means we have the agenda. Every Democrat who wants to work with us, we are open to working with them." With a Republican administration setting the priorities, DeLay is likely to be a less pivotal figure than he was in the late 1990s, but he is also more likely to see the changes in the culture of Washington that he has been seeking.

DeLay has been routinely re-elected in this heavily Republican district. Redistricting holds no terrors for him: the 22d District is far over the population average for districts, and there is plenty of Republican territory around in almost every direction.

Cook's Call *Safe.* Though DeLay's district is not as Republican as some other districts in the state, there is little chance that a Democrat could ever win here. It will need to shed about 130,000 residents during redistricting.

THE PEOPLE: Pop. 2000: 784,759; Pop. 1990: 569,350, up 37.8% 1990–2000. 62.8% White, 14.7% Black, 10% Asian, 0.4% Amer. Indian, 2.8% Two+ races, 9.3% Other; 22.3% Hispanic Origin.

2000 Presidential Vote
Bush (R) 163,375 (64%)
Gore (D) 93,648 (36%)

1996 Presidential Vote
Dole (R) 119,770 (56%)
Clinton (D) 80,280 (38%)
Perot (I) 12,278 (6%)

Rep. Tom DeLay (R)

Elected 1984, 9th term; b. Apr. 8, 1947, Laredo; home, Sugar Land; U. of Houston, B.S. 1970; Baptist; married (Christine).

Elected Office: TX House of Reps., 1978–84.

Professional Career: Owner, Albo Pest Control, 1973–84.

DC Office: 2370 RHOB 20515, 202-225-5951; Fax: 202-225-5241; Web site: tomdelay.house.gov.

District Office: Stafford, 281-240-3700.

Committees: *Majority Whip. Appropriations* (7th of 35 R): Transportation; VA, HUD & Independent Agencies.

Group Ratings

	ADA	ACLU	AFS	LCV	CON	ITIC	NTU	COC	ACU	NTLC	CHC
2000	0	14	0	0	88	94	68	84	88	85	100
1999	0	—	0	6	51	—	60	92	92	—	—

National Journal Ratings

	1999 LIB —	1999 CONS		2000 LIB —	2000 CONS
Economic	0%	84%		15%	85%
Social	4%	91%		0%	79%
Foreign	15%	81%		0%	88%

Key Votes of the 106th Congress

1. Patient Bill of Rights	N	5. Bar RU-486 $ for FDA	Y	9. NATO War in Serbia	N
2. Accelerate Min. Wage	N	6. Display 10 Commandments	Y	10. Perm. Trade with China	Y
3. Strike Ban on Ergo. Stnd.	N	7. Gun Show Bkgrnd. Checks	N	11. Debt Relief for 3rd World	N
4. Ovrd. Estate Tax Veto	Y	8. Ban Part.-Birth Abortion	Y	12. Drop Cuba Econ. Embargo	N

Election Results

2000 general	Tom DeLay (R)	154,662	(60%)	($1,298,995)
	Jo Ann Matranga (D)	92,645	(36%)	($6,597)
	Others	8,960	(3%)	
2000 primary	Tom DeLay (R)	41,901	(83%)	
	Michael (Fjet) Fjetland (R)	8,385	(17%)	
1998 general	Tom DeLay (R)	87,840	(65%)	($1,170,867)
	Hill Kemp (D)	45,386	(34%)	($75,849)

TWENTY-THIRD DISTRICT

The border country of Texas is a zone all its own. It is part of the United States but its culture and economy are not entirely Yanqui or Latino—a fluid mixture captured with great subtlety by John Sayles's 1996 movie *Lone Star*, which was filmed in and around the border town of Eagle Pass. The local economy fluctuates depending on, among other things, the strength of the peso and the aggressiveness of INS patrols. Years ago, movements like La Raza Unida—which got its beginnings here in 1969 when Hispanic youngsters wanted to elect high school cheerleaders in Crystal City—wanted the border country to become more like Mexico, with its union and party apparatchiks. More recently, Mexico, with its economic reforms and NAFTA, and with the election of President Vicente Fox in July 2000, has been trying to become more like the United States, and particularly like Texas, with open markets and privatized companies, less controlled by political or labor bosses. The border city of Laredo has been a boom town, with 40% of truck traffic between the United States and Mexico, some $80 billion worth; trucks lined up for three miles to get across the border before the opening of the Columbia Solidarity Bridge 17 miles upriver in 1997 and the World Trade Bridge in April 2000 (the latter witnessed by then-President Ernest Zedillo and then-Governor George W. Bush). Bustling also, but on a more even keel, is greater San Antonio, 150 miles from the border. In between is quiet ranching and oil country; and much quieter spots on the border, like Big Bend National Park, where on clear days you can see 180 miles.

The 23d Congressional District of Texas—geographically the largest by far in Texas, with more land area than 31 states—includes the longest portion of the 2,500-mile U.S.-Mexico border, following the Rio Grande from El Paso south past Laredo. The district includes Anglo neighborhoods on the north side of San Antonio and goes all the way to the Big Bend territory, where 7,000-foot peaks tower over stony desert. It covers miles of arid hills and rugged desert, of cattle grazing, sheep ranching and oil wells. Loving County, located halfway between El Paso and San Angelo, is the least-populated U.S. county, with only 67 residents in April 2000 but 155 voters in November. Most of the 23d's people live in a few widely scattered metropolitan areas—about one-third in or near San Antonio, with others in Laredo, parts of Midland and Odessa, and on the fringes of El Paso. Overall the population was 66% Hispanic in 2000, but only an estimated 40% of the voters are Hispanic. Politically, the border counties around Laredo and Eagle Pass are heavily Democratic, while many of the grazing counties inland are Republican. But the San Antonio suburbs are solidly Republican. The 23d has voted for Democrats in close statewide down-ballot races. But it voted 57%–41% for George W. Bush in 2000.

The congressman from the 23d is Henry Bonilla, a Republican first elected in 1992, when he beat a scandal-tarred incumbent. He was raised in a Latino neighborhood in San Antonio. His grandmother worked as a maid, and his father held down two jobs. Bonilla went to the University of Texas and then worked as a TV reporter, producer and executive in San Antonio, New York, Philadelphia and, starting in 1986, San Antonio again; his wife is an anchor for a San Antonio station. In 1991, Bexar County Republican leaders recruited Bonilla to run for Congress against incumbent Democrat Albert Bustamante, who reportedly was being investigated by the FBI for racketeering, who had 30 overdrafts on the House bank and who, after the election, was convicted of two counts of misuse of office for racketeering and bribery. Bonilla backed standard conservative planks but he crafted his own issues as well. He opposed two new hazardous waste dumps near Del Rio, backed tax and environmental policies more favorable to the oil industry, and sided with water-users over the endangered fountain darter fish in a dispute over Comal Springs. Bustamante called Bonilla "a eunuch for the plantation owners" for opposing a minimum wage bill, but Bonilla won by a large 59%–38%, with most of his margin in San Antonio's Bexar County, which he won 81%–16%.

Republicans gave Bonilla a seat on Appropriations, where he has displayed a talent for placing deregulatory riders on appropriations bills—to eliminate funding for enforcing a rule on cardboard balers and to block the Labor Department from developing ergonomic standards. Bonilla voted enthusiastically for NAFTA and against gun control; he bragged of getting $800 million for health centers and attacked the Clinton administration for diverting funds from bilingual education to school administration. The House approved his 1999 resolution urging the Supreme Court to allow student prayers before football games in a case involving the Santa Fe Independent School District. He worked to get $10 million to the Texas Workforce Commission for garment and farm workers who lost jobs due to NAFTA and to have Brooks Air Force Base declared a "city base," allowing businesses and universities to locate facilities there. He and Solomon Ortiz sponsored a bill in 2001 to create 18 new federal judgeships in the five districts on the Mexican border, which have 26% of all federal criminal court filings. In February 2001 he suggested that used U.S. trucks be sold in Mexico. Bonilla refuses to join the Hispanic Caucus, lamenting that it lacks a bipartisan agenda, but he is cautious about banning racial quotas and preferences. In January 2001 he became chairman of the Agriculture Appropriations Subcommittee.

Bonilla was an early and enthusiastic supporter of George W. Bush for president, and has held high-visibility positions—as one of three deputy permanent co-chairs of the Republican National Convention in Philadelphia, as head of the Republican National Committee's Victory 2000 outreach to minorities. Bonilla was re-elected three times with more than 60% of the vote and in 2000 won by 59%–39%. Republicans will surely seek to protect him in redistricting; the district must shed more than 100,000 people, and some of them will undoubtedly be in Democratic areas.

Cook's Call   *Safe*. This district is more marginal than Bonilla's solid victories would suggest. But he should have no real trouble in 2002.

THE PEOPLE: Pop. 2000: 762,627; Pop. 1990: 566,736, up 34.6% 1990–2000. 77% White, 2.7% Black, 1% Asian, 0.6% Amer. Indian, 0.1% Hawaiian, 2.7% Two + races, 15.9% Other; 66.3% Hispanic Origin.

2000 Presidential Vote		
Bush (R)	116,445	(58%)
Gore (D)	85,081	(42%)

1996 Presidential Vote		
Clinton (D)	83,965	(50%)
Dole (R)	73,282	(44%)
Perot (I)	9,372	(6%)

Rep. Henry Bonilla (R)

Elected 1992, 5th term; b. Jan. 2, 1954, San Antonio; home, San Antonio; U. of TX, B.A. 1976; Baptist; married (Deborah).

Professional Career: TV Reporter, 1976–80; Asst. Press Secy., PA Gov. Thornburgh, 1981; Writer/producer, WABC, New York, 1982–85; Asst. News Dir., WATF-TV, Philadelphia, 1985–86; KENS-TV, San Antonio, Exec. News Producer, 1986–89; Public Affairs, 1989–92.

DC Office: 2458 RHOB 20515, 202-225-4511; Fax: 202-225-2237; Web site: www.house.gov/bonilla.

District Offices: Del Rio, 830-774-6547; Laredo, 956-726-4682; Midland, 915-686-8833; San Antonio, 210-697-9055.

Committees: *Appropriations* (14th of 35 R): Agriculture, Rural Development, & FDA (Chmn.); Defense; Foreign Operations & Export Financing.

Group Ratings

	ADA	ACLU	AFS	LCV	CON	ITIC	NTU	COC	ACU	NTLC	CHC
2000	0	43	0	0	20	94	62	90	82	66	80
1999	0	—	16	0	37	—	54	84	91	—	—

National Journal Ratings

	1999 LIB —	1999 CONS		2000 LIB —	2000 CONS
Economic	0% —	84%		0% —	94%
Social	40% —	60%		40% —	59%
Foreign	10% —	86%		39% —	57%

Key Votes of the 106th Congress

1. Patient Bill of Rights	N	5. Bar RU-486 $ for FDA	Y	9. NATO War in Serbia	N
2. Accelerate Min. Wage	N	6. Display 10 Commandments	Y	10. Perm. Trade with China	Y
3. Strike Ban on Ergo. Stnd.	N	7. Gun Show Bkgrnd. Checks	N	11. Debt Relief for 3rd World	N
4. Ovrd. Estate Tax Veto	Y	8. Ban Part.-Birth Abortion	Y	12. Drop Cuba Econ. Embargo	N

Election Results

2000 general	Henry Bonilla (R)	119,679	(59%)	($1,050,250)
	Isidro Garza, Jr. (D)	78,274	(39%)	($364,440)
	Others	3,801	(2%)	
2000 primary	Henry Bonilla (R)	unopposed		
1998 general	Henry Bonilla (R)	73,177	(64%)	($820,842)
	Charlie Jones (D)	40,281	(35%)	($30,958)

TWENTY-FOURTH DISTRICT

The geographical heart of the Dallas-Fort Worth Metroplex was open country as late as the 1950s, when the Dallas-Fort Worth Turnpike was built over open land to link the two downtowns. Then, over the next three decades, the bottomlands of the West Fork of the Trinity River and the barren hills overlooking them filled up. Whole new Dallases and Fort Worths, with as many people as the central cities had in the 1940s—Grand Prairie and Arlington and Irving—grew up in these once impoverished lands and became central to one of America's richest and most productive metropolitan areas. Major landmarks have arisen here as well, from Six Flags Over Texas, celebrating its 40th anniversary in 2001 by opening the 255-feet Titan roller coaster, to The Ballpark in Arlington, the new old-style baseball stadium for the Texas Rangers built by then-managing partner George W. Bush. New subdivisions continue to grow here, but one can still see barren hills above the Metroplex. These new towns are taking on a graceful aging air, as trees grow, houses are renovated or expanded, and commercial buildings are adapted to new and unexpected uses. Not that all of the oldest areas are left behind: There are slums in the Metroplex, but large parts of neighborhoods like Oak Cliff, across the Trinity River south of Dallas, are being redeveloped by Texans appreciating their prairie architectural heritage.

When the Mid-Cities area, as some call it, started filling up in the 1950s, Dallas was Republican and Fort Worth Democratic. Now the most heavily Republican areas are counties that were rural in the 1950s. Dallas County, 20% black and 30% Hispanic, is trending toward Democrats, while Fort Worth's Tarrant County, 13% black and 20% Hispanic, is becoming more Republican, as Arlington starts outvoting Fort Worth.

The 24th Congressional District of Texas contains much of the Mid-Cities area. Since it was first established in 1972, the 24th's boundaries have changed several times, most recently in August 1996, following a Supreme Court decision declaring the adjacent 30th District unconstitutional. The 24th now includes Grand Prairie and the eastern half of Arlington, the older part of Oak Cliff and Duncanville and the south suburban fringe of Dallas County, the heavily black southeast side of Fort Worth and, to connect these areas, parts of rural Ellis and Navarro Counties south of Dallas. The 24th is 21% black and 35% Hispanic. It is the only district in the Dallas-Fort Worth Metroplex evenly divided between the parties: 51%–48% for Al Gore in 2000.

The congressman from the 24th District is Martin Frost, a Democrat first elected in 1978, now chairman of the House Democratic Caucus. He is the only member of Congress married to a general, Brigadier General Kathy Carlson Frost, whom he met on a courtesy visit to the Army and Air Force Exchange Service in Oak Cliff. Frost grew up in Fort Worth, went to the University of Missouri and Georgetown Law School. He clerked for Judge Sarah Hughes, who swore in Lyndon Johnson as president in November 1963, and worked for *Congressional Quarterly* in Washington and for Jim Lehrer at public TV in Dallas and appeared as a commentator himself on the channel. But politics has been most of his professional life. He first ran in the 24th in 1974, at 32, and lost the primary to incumbent Dale Milford; he ran again in 1978 and reversed the result. As a freshman he got a seat on the Rules Committee, thanks to then-Majority Leader Jim Wright of Fort Worth. Frost was a stalwart supporter of Wright to the end and has been a Democratic leadership man ever since. He lost two leadership bids in the 1980s, backing off a bid to chair the Budget Committee in 1984 and losing the race for caucus vice chairman to Vic Fazio in 1989 by 147–74. But he came back to chair the IMPAC 2000 redistricting panel from 1991–94, and was the chief architect of the Texas redistricting plan of 1991.

After the debacle of 1994, he was appointed chairman of the Democratic Congressional Campaign Committee. His efforts to restore optimism to his downtrodden party include coining the widely-cited depiction of Speaker Newt Gingrich as a "crybaby" following his complaints about his *Air Force One* treatment during the 1995 return trip from Yitzhak Rabin's funeral. He led Democrats to modest gains in 1996 and 1998, but they were left achingly short of a majority; he succeeded in holding down the number of Democratic retirees and, despite Republican Tom DeLay's efforts, has maintained the flow of PAC money to Democratic incumbents and even many open-seat candidates. He also kept money flowing into Texas: As much as 30% of DCCC soft money in 1996 was sent by Frost to Texas, much of it to Tarrant and Dallas counties, where it could help his campaign. In November 1998, despite many Democrats' desire to spotlight women in leadership positions, Frost defeated Rosa DeLauro 108–97 to replace Fazio as Democratic Caucus chairman. This was a rare case of the moderate defeating the more liberal Democrat; Frost assembled a coalition of moderates, Texans, black and Jewish members and new members he helped in the 1996 and 1998 campaigns. When some complained that the result left women without a leadership position in the party, Frost responded that he was the first Jew ever elected to the House leadership. Frost became the ranking Democrat on the Rules Committee after Joe Moakley died in May 2001.

Frost has worked on local causes, including funding the V-22 Osprey at Bell Helicopter Textron in Fort Worth, expanding Dallas/Fort Worth International Airport, building a Dallas-area light rail; he helped to keep open the GM plant in Arlington. He is proud of having sponsored the Amber Hagerman Child Protection Act, tacked onto an appropriation bill in October 1996 and named for an Arlington 9-year-old who was kidnapped and murdered; it mandates life in prison for anyone twice convicted of a sex offense against a child. He has obtained $12 million for flood control and parks on Johnson Creek, helped steer funding to Arlington's Handitran and, prompted by a 1998 murder in Arlington, sponsored a bill to require notification of a minor's or a disabled person's parents if they are working with an employee convicted of a violent crime. He was the highest-ranking member of the Democratic leadership to support permanent normal trade relations with China in May 2000.

Frost had some tough competition in the 1990s. In 1994 homebuilder Ed Harrison attacked him for voting with Bill Clinton 91% of the time; Frost switched to oppose the assault weapons ban, raised and spent more than $1.5 million and won 53%–47%—his lowest general election percentage ever. He lost the Dallas County portion of the district but was saved by large margins in southeast Fort Worth. Harrison ran again in 1996; Frost hit him as a clone of the now unpopular Gingrich and won 56%–39%, carrying both counties. He won by a robust 62%–37% in 2000, carrying Dallas County 60%–39% and Tarrant County 69%–29%.

Frost faces two challenges in 2002 and 2003. The first is redistricting. Republicans, remembering his role in the 1991 redistricting, have vowed to target him and would find it easy to give him an unfavorable district if they had control of the redistricting process. But Democrats have a 78–72 majority in the state House, and its redistricting committee chairman, Republican (and former Democrat) Delwin Jones, seems bent on keeping district lines pretty much as they are. Of Frost he said in early 2001, "I anticipate that he should not have any trouble getting elected." Frost himself was predicting a deadlock in the legislature and said in that case, "I'll take my chances in the federal courts. They've always been fair to me." His goal surely is to retain a district that includes both Oak Cliff and southeast Fort Worth, and he is fortunate that the adjacent 30th District, represented by Eddie Bernice Johnson, has to add only 17,000 people to meet the population standard. But linking Oak Cliff and southeast Fort Worth requires getting around heavily Republican territory, notably western Arlington, which is not in the present district. And some, including state Representative Domingo Garcia, want to create a Hispanic-majority or near-majority district in the Dallas-Fort Worth Metroplex, which would have to include much of Frost's territory and some of Johnson's. So there are perils.

Frost's other challenge is to establish a new place in the leadership, since the caucus chairmanship is term-limited. "If we're back in the majority, I would take a very long look at being majority leader," Frost has said. But Nancy Pelosi and Steny Hoyer have been running for the first vacant slot in anticipation of majority status since summer 2000. He might run for majority whip, but he may choose instead to become chairman of the Rules Committee. But all that assumes he gets safely through the 2002 election.

Cook's Call *Potentially Competitive.* Although Frost's victory margins have dipped in the last few elections, this district was one of only 10 in the state won by Al Gore in 2000 (albeit by just 3%). In redistricting, Republicans hope to pry minority voters away from the 24th District and replace them with Republicans overflowing from the Dallas suburbs, leaving Frost with a tougher seat to defend in 2002.

THE PEOPLE: Pop. 2000: 680,808; Pop. 1990: 567,791, up 19.9% 1990–2000. 55.1% White, 21.2% Black, 2.6% Asian, 0.7% Amer. Indian, 0.1% Hawaiian, 2.9% Two + races, 17.4% Other; 34.5% Hispanic Origin.

2000 Presidential Vote

Gore (D)	86,072	(52%)
Bush (R)	80,412	(48%)

1996 Presidential Vote

Clinton (D)	86,529	(53%)
Dole (R)	66,106	(40%)
Perot (I)	11,937	(7%)

Rep. Martin Frost (D)

Elected 1978, 12th term; b. Jan. 1, 1942, Glendale, CA; home, Dallas; U. of MO, B.A., B.J., 1964, Georgetown U., J.D. 1970; Jewish; married (Kathy).

Military Career: Army Reserves, 1966–72.

Professional Career: Legal commentator, KERA-TV, Dallas, 1971–72; Practicing atty., 1972–78.

DC Office: 2256 RHOB 20515, 202-225-3605; Fax: 202-225-4951; Web site: www.house.gov/frost.

District Offices: Corsicana, 903-874-0760; Dallas, 214-948-3401; Ft. Worth, 817-293-9231.

Committees: *Democratic Caucus Chairman. Rules* (RMM of 4 D): The Legislative & Budget Process (RMM).

Group Ratings

	ADA	ACLU	AFS	LCV	CON	ITIC	NTU	COC	ACU	NTLC	CHC
2000	80	69	85	57	50	82	19	47	12	15	7
1999	85	—	100	63	28	—	10	42	4	—	—

National Journal Ratings

	1999 LIB —	1999 CONS		2000 LIB —	2000 CONS
Economic	70% —	30%		73% —	26%
Social	70% —	30%		74% —	24%
Foreign	70% —	30%		66% —	33%

Key Votes of the 106th Congress

1. Patient Bill of Rights	Y	5. Bar RU-486 $ for FDA	N	9. NATO War in Serbia
2. Accelerate Min. Wage	Y	6. Display 10 Commandments	N	10. Perm. Trade with China	Y
3. Strike Ban on Ergo. Stnd.	Y	7. Gun Show Bkgrnd. Checks	Y	11. Debt Relief for 3rd World	Y
4. Ovrd. Estate Tax Veto	N	8. Ban Part.-Birth Abortion	N	12. Drop Cuba Econ. Embargo	N

Election Results

2000 general	Martin Frost (D)	103,152	(62%)	($1,983,181)
	James (Bryndan) Wright (R)	61,235	(37%)	($205,245)
	Others	2,561	(2%)	
2000 primary	Martin Frost (D)	unopposed		
1998 general	Martin Frost (D)	56,321	(57%)	($1,790,674)
	Shawn Terry (R)	40,105	(41%)	($789,196)
	Others	1,566	(2%)	

TWENTY-FIFTH DISTRICT

Houston is, among other things, a blue-collar city. The 54-mile long Ship Channel, which made it the nation's second-largest port, is lined with petrochemical plants and refineries and surrounded by factories, truck terminals and railroad-offloading platforms. Although some neighborhoods long have been close-knit places, others have sprouted up in and around Houston's wide city limits in the past three decades, with plain, contemporary houses and commercial strip highways. After all, physical mobility is easy in spread-out Houston and many people keep in touch through churches though they are miles apart.

The 25th Congressional District of Texas includes many such neighborhoods on the east and south sides of Houston. Its boundaries, once erose, were smoothed out by the 1996 federal court redistricting. On the east it includes Baytown and the industrial corridor to the north, Deer Park and Pasadena south of the Ship Channel, Highlands on the north. It includes the southern edge of Houston from Hobby Airport west to the Southwest Freeway. It includes Bellaire and the affluent neighborhoods just west of the Texas Medical Center and Rice University. The 1996 redistricting removed some black precincts and added some Hispanics; in 2000 the district was 24% black and 31% Hispanic. The redistricting change made the district more Republican, and in 2000 it was the most closely divided Houston-area district, voting 50%–48% for Al Gore.

The congressman from the 25th District is Ken Bentsen, a Democrat elected in 1994. He grew up in Houston, the son of an architect; his grandfather was the fabled Rio Grande Valley pioneer Lloyd Bentsen Sr., and his uncle is former Senator and Treasury Secretary Lloyd Bentsen Jr. After college in Houston, Ken Bentsen worked four years as a Capitol Hill staffer for Ron Coleman, spending much of his time at the Appropriations Committee; then he joined an investment banking firm in Houston and was elected Harris County Democratic chairman. In 1994, when incumbent Democrat Mike Andrews ran for the Senate, Bentsen ran for the House. In a light-turnout primary, Bentsen had only 26% to 37% for Beverley Clark, a black former Houston Council member, anti-abortion and supported by the Christian right, 23% for former legislator Paul Colbert and 13% for high-spending Carrin Patman, the daughter and granddaughter of Texas congressmen. In the runoff, Bentsen, pro-choice on abortion, concentrated on crime issues, supporting boot camps and more death penalties, and won 64%–36%. Republicans nominated Eugene Fontenot, a Christian conservative, who spent more than any other candidate in the country that year, $4.7 million. Bentsen, spending a comparatively modest $973,000, attacked Fontenot as "radical right" and called for a budget freeze with a pledge of universal health care coverage. Bentsen won 52%–45%, getting only 50% in Harris County but adding nearly 6,000 votes to his margin from the heavily black portion of Fort Bend County then in the district.

The 1996 court redistricting threw Bentsen for a loop, and reintroduced a cast of familiar characters. The November election was an all-party primary, and Bentsen's chances of avoiding a runoff became nil when Democrat Beverley Clark and 1992 Republican nominee Dolly Madison McKenna entered the race—two women at odds with most of their fellow party members on abortion. Bentsen led in November with just 34% of all votes; Clark and McKenna had 17% each, with McKenna ahead by 199 votes. Clark challenged the results, citing ballot irregularities; after a court dismissed her challenge, she endorsed McKenna two days before the runoff. Meanwhile, McKenna had been spending much time and energy trying to mollify abortion opponents. It failed to work. "The last thing Republicans need is a high-profile woman parading around Congress, being the darling of the pro-abortion forces," Al Clements of the Texas Right to Life Committee told the *Houston Chronicle*. Bentsen won the runoff 57%–43%.

Bentsen's voting record has been a bit to the left of the House's midpoint. He supported the moderate Blue Dog budget; he has sought more money for medical research, space exploration, education—Houston priorities. In March 2001 the Budget Committee voted down his amendment to prevent any budget raids on the Social Security and Medicare trust funds. In 2000 Bill Clinton signed his bill to make it easier for non-citizens to remain in the United States long enough to complete their medical treatment. He voted for permanent normal trade relations with China, after helping to get Clinton to create a commission to review worker training programs. On bankruptcy reform, he took credit for retaining the Texas homestead law, which allows bankrupt debtors to retain their homes no matter how expensive. On local issues, he called for ending the ethanol subsidy (not popular in oil-producing territory).

In 2000, Bentsen had another well-financed challenger: lawyer Phil Sudan, who contributed $3 million to his own campaign. But Sudan suffered some of the tribulations common to political newcomers, including embarrassing revelations about his two divorces and failure to pay alimony. He ran ads revealing a drunk-driving arrest of Bentsen and a photo of him dressed as Fidel Castro, and attempted to show that Bentsen has a voting record similar to that of Al Gore—even though they never served together. Some polls showed a close contest, but Bentsen won 60%–39%.

Bentsen's interest in redistricting also has been nationwide; he was chairman of IMPAC 2000, the House Democrats' redistricting project. As a Democrat who has had to deal with the consequences of redistricting—and who stands to be affected by it himself, since the Houston area can be divided up many ways—he was well prepared for the project. But he returned those duties to Martin Frost in 2001, and faced considerable uncertainty for 2002. The neighboring 18th District needs to add 45,000 people, and the easiest way to get them—indeed, the way the Voting Rights Act seems to require—would be to take heavily black precincts from the 25th.

Cook's Call *Potentially Competitive.* Bentsen has survived just about everything thrown at him over the last few cycles, including one very bad political climate (1994), one drastic re-mapping (1996), and one wealthy, self-funded Republican opponent (2000). Republicans hope that redistricting will make this seat more marginal. One potential threat to Bentsen is the dilution of the district's minority population.

THE PEOPLE: Pop. 2000: 662,264; Pop. 1990: 563,510, up 17.5% 1990–2000. 53.5% White, 23.8% Black, 5.4% Asian, 0.4% Amer. Indian, 0.1% Hawaiian, 2.9% Two+ races, 13.9% Other; 31.1% Hispanic Origin.

2000 Presidential Vote
Gore (D) 88,661 (51%)
Bush (R) 85,064 (49%)

1996 Presidential Vote
Clinton (D) 80,283 (51%)
Dole (R) 69,165 (44%)
Perot (I) 8,199 (5%)

Rep. Ken Bentsen (D)

Elected 1994, 4th term; b. June 3, 1959, Houston; home, Houston; U. of St. Thomas., B.A. 1982, American U., M.P.A., 1985; Presbyterian; married (Tamra).

Elected Office: Chair, Harris Cnty. Dem. Cmte., 1990–94.

Professional Career: Legis. Asst., U.S. Rep. Ronald Coleman, 1983–87; Staff Assoc., U.S. House Approprations Cmte., 1985–87; Investment Banker, 1987–94.

DC Office: 405 CHOB 20515, 202-225-7508; Fax: 202-225-2947; Web site: www.house.gov/bentsen.

District Offices: Baytown, 281-837-8225; Bellaire, 713-667-3554; Houston, 713-718-4100; Pasadena, 713-473-4334.

Committees: *Budget* (4th of 20 D). *Financial Services* (10th of 32 D): Capital Markets, Insurance & Government Sponsored Enterprises; Financial Institutions & Consumer Credit; International Monetary Policy & Trade; Oversight & Investigations.

Group Ratings

	ADA	ACLU	AFS	LCV	CON	ITIC	NTU	COC	ACU	NTLC	CHC
2000	90	79	85	71	50	78	22	47	8	15	13
1999	95	—	100	63	73	—	13	40	8	—	—

National Journal Ratings

	1999 LIB	—	1999 CONS		2000 LIB	—	2000 CONS
Economic	64%	—	36%		75%	—	24%
Social	71%	—	28%		72%	—	26%
Foreign	68%	—	32%		56%	—	42%

Key Votes of the 106th Congress

1. Patient Bill of Rights	Y	5. Bar RU-486 $ for FDA	N	9. NATO War in Serbia		*
2. Accelerate Min. Wage	Y	6. Display 10 Commandments	N	10. Perm. Trade with China		Y
3. Strike Ban on Ergo. Stnd.	Y	7. Gun Show Bkgrnd. Checks	Y	11. Debt Relief for 3rd World		Y
4. Ovrd. Estate Tax Veto	N	8. Ban Part.-Birth Abortion	N	12. Drop Cuba Econ. Embargo		N

Election Results

2000 general	Ken Bentsen (D)	106,112	(60%)	($1,354,444)
	Phil Sudan (R)	68,010	(39%)	($3,247,033)
	Others	2,400	(1%)	
2000 primary	Ken Bentsen (D)	unopposed		
1998 general	Ken Bentsen (D)	58,591	(58%)	($892,840)
	John M. Sanchez (R)	41,848	(41%)	($274,895)

TWENTY-SIXTH DISTRICT

On the northern edge of the Dallas-Fort Worth Metroplex, America's fastest-growing metropolitan area in the 1990s heads out into hardscrabble countryside. Here is a clash of cultures, the advance of one set of values and beliefs with another. On one side are the values of North Dallas, of the entrepreneurs who have created fortunes, starting from scratch with a good idea, a willingness to work, a determination to find good luck. They work in the dozens of high-rises that line the freeways of north Dallas or in smaller offices in industrial areas, they live in the affluent areas, starting with the super-wealthy Park Cities area not far north of downtown Dallas or in any one of dozens of comfortable neighborhoods running dozens of miles north. They believe in free markets, in personal responsibility, in traditional values, in the Republican Party: This is one of the most heavily Republican areas in the nation. And it is advancing into what used to be one of the most Democratic.

The tiers of Texas counties south of the Red River were the home of Sam Rayburn, speaker of the House and author of New Deal regulations, always suspicious of bankers and big corporations and eager to have government weigh in on the side of the little guy. They believed in economic redistribution, regulations and usury ceilings, and the Democratic Party. It is fairly clear which of these views is winning in North Texas. Forty years ago the Republican vote here was limited to affluent neighborhoods within a few miles of the Park Cities. Now it has spread out far into the countryside, into counties that once voted near-unanimously for Mr. Sam's Democrats.

The 26th Congressional District of Texas covers much of the northern part of the Dallas-Fort Worth Metroplex. Its boundaries were substantially changed by the August 1996 court-ordered redistricting. It now includes the Park Cities, Highland Park and University Park, the home of much of Dallas's elite, and the affluent quadrant of North Dallas between the Central Expressway and the Stemmons Freeway; this was the home not so long ago of George W. Bush and Richard Cheney. It includes Carrollton and Farmers Branch to the northwest and the wonderfully named Grapevine just north of the Dallas/Fort Worth International Airport. It also includes half of Denton County, once rural and Democratic, now with 433,000 people suburban and affluent (real property rose 23% in value between 1999 and 2000) and very heavily Republican. Overall, this is a very Republican district. A little more than half its voters are in Dallas County and about one-third in Denton County.

The congressman from the 26th District is Dick Armey, first elected in 1984, now the House majority leader. He is a free market economist who once was such a political nonentity that he did not even attend the 1984 Republican National Convention in nearby Dallas where Ronald Reagan was renominated. His political career could never have happened before the 1980s. He grew up on a farm in Cando, North Dakota—pronounced affirmatively as *can do*. At 18, working atop an electric pole at night when it was 30 below zero, he decided to become the first in his family to go to college. By 1984 Armey was an economics professor at the University of North Texas in Denton, a Northern-accented academic in the Red River Valley of Texas: not a likely candidate for anything. But as he was viewing House sessions on C-SPAN, it occurred to him that he could do as well as or better than a lot the people he was watching on the screen. He got the 1984 Republican nomination in the 26th District (then very differently shaped) unopposed, because no one thought incumbent Tom Vandergriff, the long-time mayor of Arlington, then the largest city in the district, could be unseated. But Armey won 51%–49%.

Armey arrived in Washington in modest circumstances—"When I came to Washington, the only congressman I'd known or spent much time with was the man I beat"—and he saved money by sleeping first in the House gym and, when forced to stop, on his office couch—a practice that he has since abandoned. Armey brought to the House a sometimes impolitic bluntness, but also fine political instincts and an appreciation of how to sell his principles to his colleagues. In 1987 Armey proposed a base closing commission operating outside of politics, but neither Congress nor then-Defense Secretary Caspar Weinberger were ready to delegate such power. After a long debate, Armey worked with the Pentagon, the Joint Chiefs of Staff and then-Armed Services Chairman Les Aspin to create an independent commission that would draw up a list of base closings that Congress would have to approve or reject in its entirety. The result: In 1988 Congress approved the first base closings in 12 years. The 1990 round of closings was rejected, but in 1993 the second round of base closings was approved. In 1995 a more modest third round was proposed by the Clinton administration and subsequently was approved. Congress refused to authorize another round of closings while Clinton was president. But for seven years Armey's bill had changed political incentives so that they ratcheted government spending down, not up. Armey had less immediate success with his next target, farm subsidies. He argued persuasively that subsidies are no more needed to maintain supplies of the six large subsidized crops than they are for the hundreds of crops that manage to be produced without subsidies and that farmers no more deserve subsidies than any other small businessmen. He forged an alliance on the issue with Brooklyn Democrat Charles Schumer, but was never able to prevail on the floor. The 1996 Freedom to Farm Act purported to phase out most subsidies over seven years, but when crop prices fell in 1998 Congress started legislating "disaster relief" every year.

Armey strongly opposed George Bush's 1990 budget summit tax increase and was determined to get "a seat at the table." After the 1992 election, Armey ran against Republican Conference Chairman Jerry Lewis, who had supported the budget summit. Armey won the number-three leadership position 88–84. This put Armey into leadership meetings at the White House, at one of the first of which he told Bill Clinton that passage of his budget and tax plan would make him a "one-term president"—not the first or last Armey breach of Washington's collegial etiquette. He is capable of bitter riposte: During the 1994 crime bill debate, when Democrats talked of the need to support Clinton, Armey said, "Your president is just not that important for us"—he soon apologized. When Newt Gingrich came up with the idea of having all Republican incumbents and candidates sign a pledge on the steps of the Capitol in September 1994, Armey spearheaded the effort to draw up and then sell—including to some doubters within his own party, let alone other parts of Washington's political class—many of the specifics of the Contract with America. After Republicans won control in November, Armey gained his just reward of being elected majority leader without opposition. And he then surprised many with his legislative skill in commanding the 100-day schedule that delivered on the Republicans' campaign promise to debate each item of the Contract, with the House passing everything except term limits. Later things got more ragged. Armey was frustrated when Southern Republicans preserved cotton subsidies in 1996 and when Gingrich yielded and let a minimum wage increase come to the floor.

Then in July 1997 came the attempted coup against Gingrich. Armey met with the aggrieved conservative junior members who wanted to get rid of Gingrich and listened to their case. He also met with fellow leadership members Tom DeLay, John Boehner and Bill Paxon; all said they had the impression he supported the coup, and said he had said he would run for speaker if Gingrich was ousted. But when DeLay met with the coup leaders, Tom Coburn said they wanted Paxon to replace Gingrich. The leaders had agreed to inform Gingrich of the coup, but Armey arrived first and told him. The coup collapsed and recriminations began. At a mid-July meeting of the Republican Conference, Armey insisted that he had never supported the coup, at which point Lindsey Graham knocked down a chair and tried to rush to the microphone. The belief was widespread that Armey supported the coup until he learned its leaders supported Paxon over him for speaker. But it was Paxon, not Armey, who resigned his leadership position. This episode killed Armey's chances of becoming speaker. When Gingrich announced his retirement three days after the November 1998 election, Armey did not run for speaker. Instead he was challenged for majority leader by Steve Largent—who had the support of many coup leaders and strong conservatives—and Jennifer Dunn. Chief Deputy Whip Denny Hastert was urged to run by Mike Castle and Thomas Ewing, and Hastert asked Armey to be relieved of his commitment to vote for him; Armey refused, and Hastert declined to run, though his name was put in nomination. On the first round of voting, Armey led with 100 votes to 58 for Largent, 45 for Dunn and 18 for Hastert. On the second round, Armey led with 99 to 73 for Largent and 49 for Dunn. Finally Armey beat Largent on the third round, 127–95, a decisive margin but scarcely an inspiring one for an incumbent. Then in December 1998 Bob Livingston announced his retirement on the morning of the impeachment vote, and votes were quickly rounded up for Hastert for speaker. As Armey said in 1999, "When I get in touch with my inner child, I regret that [I'm not speaker]. But I was not the right guy at the time."

Armey has had less turbulent times since Hastert became speaker, though they have not been without controversy. Hastert and Armey were accused of anti-Catholic prejudice when they passed over a Catholic priest who was the plurality choice of a committee recommending a new House chaplain in December 1999; eventually a different priest was appointed. On the legislative front, he sponsored the voucher amendment to provide as much as $3,200 for tuition for poor children at private schools in the District of Columbia in 1998, and offered a bill providing $3,500 to parents of children in failing schools in 1999; it was defeated 257–166. He has strongly criticized the IMF for imposing austerity on countries it is supposed to benefit. In 1999 he tried to block the IMF from selling gold to implement its policies; this became an issue in negotiations with Clinton that resulted in compromise. In 1998, while discussing the IMF, he noted that he had not been out of the United States since 1986 and said, "I've been to Europe once. I don't have to go again." But he did travel to the Balkans to visit troops in May 1999 and has taken more interest in international issues. In September 1999 he charged that Clinton's Russia policies had produced corruption and waste: "It's time for Congress to ask the question: Who lost Russia?"

Armey has had a package of high-tech legislation that earned him ratings as a "tech-savvy legislator." He strongly supported the Y2K bill that reduced the ability of trial lawyers to bring lawsuits. He blocked a measure to strip spectrum licenses from successful bidders at 1995 and 1996 auctions that had since gone bankrupt. He has supported a five-year extension of the ban on Internet taxation. Armey was a lead sponsor of the Republican version of HMO regulation in 1999, and in 2000 worked to exempt small businesses from a minimum wage increase. In January 2001 Armey called for a fast, front-loaded tax cut; in March he was calling for a bigger cut than George W. Bush's $1.6 trillion version. Also in March 2001 he wrote NAACP President (and former Congressman Kweisi Mfume) complaining of "racial McCarthyism" and "reverse race-baiting" and requested a meeting; they met and agreed on opposing racial profiling.

Armey still has a rough and ready style. He drives a pickup, wears cowboy boots, quotes country music lyrics and loves to go fishing, often with Justice Clarence Thomas (whose wife Virginia was an Armey staffer from 1993–98). He said that he has never tried to bring home pork, and in fact his base-closing law closed Carswell Air Force Base in Fort Worth. He has been re-elected by overwhelming margins, 72%–26% in 2000. The 26th was the fastest-growing district in Texas in the 1990s, up 50%. It is likely that there will be another heavily Republican district on the north side of the Metroplex; certainly there will be a heavily Republican district for Armey.

Cook's Call   *Safe.* Armey has consistently been re-elected by huge margins in this very Republican district. It was also the fastest growing in Texas during the 1990s and will need to shed almost 200,000 people.

THE PEOPLE: Pop. 2000: 845,541; Pop. 1990: 564,764, up 49.7% 1990–2000. 79.7% White, 6% Black, 4.7% Asian, 0.5% Amer. Indian, 2.2% Two+ races, 6.9% Other; 17.1% Hispanic Origin.

2000 Presidential Vote			1996 Presidential Vote		
Bush (R)	213,589	(72%)	Dole (R)	160,684	(62%)
Gore (D)	81,294	(28%)	Clinton (D)	79,441	(31%)
			Perot (I)	19,194	(7%)

Rep. Dick Armey (R)

Elected 1984, 9th term; b. July 7, 1940, Cando, ND; home, Cooper Canyon; Jamestown Col., B.A. 1963, U. of ND, M.A. 1964, U. of OK, Ph.D. 1969; Presbyterian; married (Susan).

Professional Career: Prof., West TX St. U., 1967–68, Austin Col., 1968–72, U. of N. TX, 1972–77, Chmn., Dept. of Economics, 1977–83.

DC Office: 301 CHOB 20515, 202-225-7772; Fax: 202-226-2028; Web site: armey.house.gov.

District Office: Irving, 972-556-2500.

Committees: *Majority Leader.*

Group Ratings

	ADA	ACLU	AFS	LCV	CON	ITIC	NTU	COC	ACU	NTLC	CHC
2000	0	21	0	0	34	100	62	90	92	88	100
1999	0	—	0	6	35	—	60	92	96	—	—

National Journal Ratings

	1999 LIB —	1999 CONS	2000 LIB —	2000 CONS
Economic	0%	84%	6%	85%
Social	4%	91%	0%	79%
Foreign	35%	64%	0%	88%

Key Votes of the 106th Congress

1. Patient Bill of Rights	N	5. Bar RU-486 $ for FDA	Y	9. NATO War in Serbia	N
2. Accelerate Min. Wage	N	6. Display 10 Commandments	Y	10. Perm. Trade with China	Y
3. Strike Ban on Ergo. Stnd.	N	7. Gun Show Bkgrnd. Checks	N	11. Debt Relief for 3rd World	N
4. Ovrd. Estate Tax Veto	Y	8. Ban Part.-Birth Abortion	Y	12. Drop Cuba Econ. Embargo	N

Election Results

2000 general	Dick Armey (R)	214,025	(72%)	($1,325,516)
	Steve Love (D)	75,601	(26%)	($8,040)
	Others	5,646	(2%)	
2000 primary	Dick Armey (R)	48,179	(88%)	
	Larry K. Thompson (R)	6,806	(12%)	
1998 general	Dick Armey (R)	120,332	(88%)	($2,125,437)
	Joe Turner (Lib)	16,182	(12%)	($257)

TWENTY-SEVENTH DISTRICT

South from Corpus Christi—the southernmost natural port on Texas' Gulf Coast and the nation's fifth-largest in trading volume with big petrochemical plants—to the Rio Grande and the Mexican border are two Texan versions of dreamland. One, fronting the Gulf of Mexico, is the sandspit of Padre Island, for most of its length a national seashore, at the southern tip of which is a high-rise resort to which college students throng for spring break. Remains of a 1554 Spanish shipwreck have been found offshore, and Portuguese settlers began cattle ranching here; today, developers want to dredge the local Packery Channel to encourage expanded tourism. The other, inland from the Laguna Madre, is the vast grazing and oil lands of the 825,000-acre (that's 1,289 square miles, partner) King Ranch. This still seemingly vacant land between the Nueces and the Rio Grande was the territory in contention in the Mexican-American War. The United States won that war and established its sovereignty. But today most people here are of Mexican ancestry: If their culture and economy, ultimately, are thoroughly *Norteamericano*, they also have a pronounced Mexican accent.

The 27th Congressional District of Texas includes this land from Corpus Christi south to the Rio Grande. More than half of the 27th's voters live in and around Corpus (as it is called locally). Most of the remainder live some 150 miles south in the Lower Rio Grande Valley around Brownsville and Harlingen. With a 71% Hispanic majority, the 27th is a Democratic district, though not quite as Democratic as some may suspect. In 1998 it cast a comfortable 60%–40% majority for Republican Governor George W. Bush; in 2000 it was 49%–49% in the presidential race.

The congressman from the 27th, since its creation following the 1982 redistricting, has been Solomon Ortiz. He grew up inland from Corpus in the Canta Ranas (singing frogs) neighborhood of Robstown, which is known for its political activism. His father died when he was 14, leaving him the eldest of four children who scratched out a living as migrant farm workers, sometimes working as far away as Colorado and Michigan. "I know what it is being poor, going home and nothing to eat," he says. When his father died, his employer at the local newspaper raised his wage, and then urged him to join the Army. Ortiz worked as an Army investigator and translator, using his Spanish to learn French, took a correspondence course in police work and returned home to run for constable. "If it wasn't for the military, I wouldn't be here today," he said. In 1976 he was the first Hispanic elected Nueces County sheriff. When he ran for Congress in 1982, he got only 26% in the primary, but he made a propitious alliance with party leaders in the Brownsville area and won the runoff with 52% and the general with 64%.

Ortiz's voting record has been moderate, especially on cultural issues. As the third-ranking Democrat on the Armed Services Committee, he watches out for the four military installations in the Coastal Bend, as he calls the area; they emerged from the 1995 base-closing review with more jobs than before. Looking after the Corpus Christi Army Depot, he authored the provision requiring 60% of military maintenance to be performed at military depots rather than by private contractors; noting that privatization has been sought by the Clinton White House, the Pentagon, major defense contractors and important senators (especially from California), he said, after the 60–40 formula survived, "I often felt like David going up against Goliath. In both cases, the Philistines went down." Not surprisingly, he remained an advocate of depot maintenance and adamantly opposed additional rounds of base closings. In September 2000, the Port of Corpus Christi dedicated its new conference center in his name. But five months later, the *San Antonio Express-News* reported that Ortiz received favored treatment when the Port awarded a contract to provide security to a firm that he owned even though it was not the low bidder. The newspaper claimed he was bringing home "political pork and eating it too." Ortiz defended the contract as awarded in open competition.

Ortiz is a sturdy internationalist: an enthusiastic supporter of NAFTA and permanent normal trade relations with China, and one of the few Democrats to back Bill Clinton's request for fast-track trade negotiating authority. He spoke against decertification of Mexico as a partner in good standing in the drug war. As co-chairman with Henry Bonilla of the Border Caucus, Ortiz convinced Mexican authorities to drop regulations requiring refundable deposits for U.S. automobiles traveling into Mexico; he has urged Mexico to repay its water debt, which comes from runoff of the Rio Grande. He fought successfully to get the proposed I-69 corridor ("the free trade highway") dedicated from Houston to the Lower Rio Grande Valley, and he is proud of the Birth Defects Prevention Act of 1998, which he initiated after a outbreak in Brownsville of infants born lacking most of their brains.

Ortiz has generally won reelection without difficulty. His most recent serious challenge was primary opposition in 1996 from Mary Helen Berlanga, whose husband represented part of the district in the Texas Senate, his first primary opposition since 1982. He won 70%–30%. Some local Hispanic leaders had hoped that the Census would show enough population increase to warrant a new southern district centered around Brownsville and McAllen, but the increase was less than expected and that is not likely. Cameron County on the border grew by 29% to 335,000, but Nueces County around Corpus grew by only 8% to 314,000. The district is now only 13,000 people over the population standard, and will probably be little changed by redistricting.

Cook's Call *Safe*. Though not as reliably Democratic as Texas' other minority-majority districts, Ortiz has never had much trouble winning here.

THE PEOPLE: Pop. 2000: 664,428; Pop. 1990: 565,992, up 17.4% 1990–2000. 76.3% White, 2.3% Black, 0.8% Asian, 0.5% Amer. Indian, 0.1% Hawaiian, 2.7% Two + races, 17.3% Other; 70.5% Hispanic Origin.

2000 Presidential Vote

Gore (D)	81,030	(50%)
Bush (R)	80,066	(50%)

1996 Presidential Vote

Clinton (D)	87,511	(57%)
Dole (R)	57,533	(38%)
Perot (I)	8,094	(5%)

Rep. Solomon P. Ortiz (D)

Elected 1982, 10th term; b. June 3, 1937, Robstown; home, Corpus Christi; Del Mar Col., Natl. Sheriffs Training Inst., 1977; Methodist; divorced.

Military Career: Army, 1960–62.

Elected Office: Nueces Cnty. Constable, 1965–68, Commissioner, 1969–76, Sheriff, 1976–82.

DC Office: 2304 RHOB 20515, 202-225-7742; Fax: 202-226-1134; Web site: www.house.gov/ortiz.

District Offices: Brownsville, 956-541-1242; Corpus Christi, 361-883-5868.

Committees: *Armed Services* (3d of 28 D): Military Installations & Facilities; Military Readiness (RMM). *Resources* (8th of 25 D): Energy & Mineral Resources; Fisheries Conservation, Wildlife & Oceans.

Group Ratings

	ADA	ACLU	AFS	LCV	CON	ITIC	NTU	COC	ACU	NTLC	CHC
2000	65	21	85	43	64	83	19	45	24	12	57
1999	60	—	100	44	28	—	7	33	32	—	—

National Journal Ratings

	1999 LIB —	1999 CONS	2000 LIB —	2000 CONS
Economic	71%	28%	73%	26%
Social	45%	54%	39%	60%
Foreign	66%	33%	49%	49%

Key Votes of the 106th Congress

1. Patient Bill of Rights	Y	5. Bar RU-486 $ for FDA	Y	9. NATO War in Serbia	Y
2. Accelerate Min. Wage	Y	6. Display 10 Commandments	Y	10. Perm. Trade with China	Y
3. Strike Ban on Ergo. Stnd.	Y	7. Gun Show Bkgrnd. Checks	N	11. Debt Relief for 3rd World	Y
4. Ovrd. Estate Tax Veto	N	8. Ban Part.-Birth Abortion	Y	12. Drop Cuba Econ. Embargo	N

Election Results

2000 general	Solomon P. Ortiz (D)	102,088	(63%)	($443,821)
	Pat Ahumada (R)	54,660	(34%)	($34,318)
	Others	4,324	(3%)	
2000 primary	Solomon P. Ortiz (D)	unopposed		
1998 general	Solomon P. Ortiz (D)	61,638	(63%)	($316,095)
	Erol A. Stone (R)	34,284	(35%)	($21,115)
	Others	1,476	(2%)	

TWENTY-EIGHTH DISTRICT

The Mexican-American tradition in the part of South Texas radiating from San Antonio is anchored in two culturally conservative but adaptive institutions, the Catholic Church and the United States military. Both are a major presence in San Antonio, just 150 miles north of the border, which for many years had the largest Mexican-American population of any American city, where Spanish has long been widely spoken and political refugees from Mexico's revolution could be sure of freedom. The church in San Antonio was led for years by liberal bishops who also ran St. Mary's University, which educated many Hispanic politicians and leaders, including two long-time House committee chairmen, Henry B. Gonzalez and Kika de la Garza. Just as visible a presence in San Antonio are the Army and Air Force, with huge Fort Sam Houston, Lackland Air Force Base, Randolph Air Force Base, and the Brooks Army Medical Center, all in or near the city limits. Mexican-Americans have long volunteered for military service in numbers higher than most ethnic groups, and for many years Mexican-Americans in San Antonio worked in civilian jobs for the military service: Uncle Sam has long been an equal opportunity employer. San Antonio's Mexican-American community has produced many politicians who are liberal on economic issues, civil rights and civil liberties. But it has not produced many who are hostile to the military or to traditional religious and cultural values.

The 28th Congressional District of Texas stretches from the southern half of San Antonio to the Mexican border. Some 61% of its people are in Bexar County, on the south and east sides of San Antonio. It has a salient north to Hispanic precincts in Guadalupe County and also heads south, through thinly settled ranch and oil well country, to the Lower Rio Grande. There it includes Starr County, home of many blatant and wealthy drug smugglers, and, to the north, Duval County, often the most Democratic county in the United States, whose then-boss George Parr provided the key votes Lyndon Johnson needed for his disputed 87-vote victory in the 1948 Democratic Senate runoff; in 2000 it voted 79%–20% for Al Gore over George W. Bush. This was a new district for 1992, when it was 60% Hispanic and solidly Democratic; in 2000 it was 65% Hispanic.

The congressman from the 28th District is Ciro Rodriguez, a Democrat chosen in the special election in April 1997 to replace Frank Tejeda, who died of a brain tumor. Rodriguez grew up in San Antonio, worked as a social worker, teacher and educational consultant, and spent 12 years on the Harlandale school board. In 1986 he was elected to the Texas House, where he had a liberal record, working on equalizing education funding and private development of Kelly Air Force Base. He started running for the U.S. House soon after Tejeda's death. Critical in the campaign was his endorsement by the San Antonio Central Labor Council; he raised $280,000 from PACs, mostly union PACs, more than half of his $505,000 total. His only serious competition for the House seat came from San Antonio Councilman Juan Solis. Like Tejeda, Solis was pro-life on abortion and against gun control, and he backed term limits and school vouchers; he called Rodriguez "more of a wild-eyed liberal, and that's not what we need in Congress." Rodriguez was backed by more prominent politicians and several Congress members and was promised Tejeda's seat on the Armed Services Committee by House Democratic leaders. Even more important, Rodriguez had the money to go on television and Solis didn't. In the March primary, Rodriguez led Solis 46%–27%; Rodriguez won the low-turnout runoff 67%–33%.

Rodriguez got Tejeda's seat on Armed Services and successfully fought to preserve the loan rate for the federal peanut program as set in the 1996 Freedom to Farm Act (the district produced $46 million worth of peanuts in 1996 and was the seventh-largest producing district in the nation). He was disappointed when the House voted against allowing public and private competition for depot maintenance at Kelly Air Force Base, which prepared for closure. He strongly opposes the closing of more military bases. He wants to designate the 2,580-mile El Camino Real de los Tejas, the Spanish "Royal Road," from Laredo to Natchitoches, Louisiana, as a National Historic Trail, which he said would symbolize the immigration and trade route's critical link between Mexico and the new American frontier. Unlike others from South Texas, he opposed permanent normal trade relations with China because he feared that local farmers would be hurt by "price-busting Chinese imports." In the 2000 defense bill, he got $4.8 million for a child development center at Lackland. During the presidential campaign, he called for a moratorium on the death penalty to permit more use of DNA testing; although he was a vocal critic of George W. Bush as governor, Rodriguez said that his action had nothing to do with election-year politics. He is first vice-chairman of the Hispanic Caucus, and chairs its health task force, which investigated Hispanic health disparities.

Despite speculation that Bexar County commissioner Robert Tejeda would seek to regain the seat his brother held, Rodriguez had no major-party opposition in 2000. Redistricting changes around rapidly growing San Antonio could affect his boundaries but appeared unlikely to cause him problems.

Cook's Call *Safe*. This is about as safe as it gets for a Democrat in Texas. Since winning a special election in 1997, Rodriguez has never dipped below 89%.

THE PEOPLE: Pop. 2000: 646,161; Pop. 1990: 566,447, up 14.1% 1990–2000. 66.6% White, 8.2% Black, 0.7% Asian, 0.8% Amer. Indian, 0.1% Hawaiian, 3.2% Two+ races, 20.4% Other; 65% Hispanic Origin.

2000 Presidential Vote

Gore (D)	90,864	(57%)
Bush (R)	68,656	(43%)

1996 Presidential Vote

Clinton (D)	93,147	(63%)
Dole (R)	47,338	(32%)
Perot (I)	8,211	(6%)

Rep. Ciro Rodriguez (D)

Elected April 1997, 2d term; b. Dec. 9, 1946, Piedras Negras, Coah., Mexico; home, San Antonio; St. Mary's U., B.A. 1973, Our Lady of the Lake U., M.S.W., 1978; Catholic; married (Carolina).

Elected Office: Harlandale Schl. Bd., 1975–87; TX House of Reps., 1986–97.

Professional Career: Substance Abuse Counselor, 1971–74, 1978–80; Educ. Consultant, 1980–87; Faculty, Our Lady of the Lake U., 1987–97.

DC Office: 323 CHOB 20515, 202-225-1640; Fax: 202-225-1641; Web site: www.house.gov/rodriguez.

District Offices: Roma, 956-847-1111; San Antonio, 210-924-7383; San Diego, 512-279-3907.

Committees: *Armed Services* (18th of 28 D): Military Installations & Facilities; Military Readiness. *Veterans' Affairs* (8th of 14 D): Health.

Group Ratings

	ADA	ACLU	AFS	LCV	CON	ITIC	NTU	COC	ACU	NTLC	CHC
2000	85	79	100	71	57	72	19	50	12	15	20
1999	100	—	100	81	65	—	11	21	8	—	—

National Journal Ratings

	1999 LIB —	1999 CONS		2000 LIB —	2000 CONS
Economic	84%	12%		78%	20%
Social	71%	28%		71%	28%
Foreign	74%	23%		66%	34%

Key Votes of the 106th Congress

1. Patient Bill of Rights	Y	5. Bar RU-486 $ for FDA	N	9. NATO War in Serbia		Y
2. Accelerate Min. Wage	Y	6. Display 10 Commandments	N	10. Perm. Trade with China		N
3. Strike Ban on Ergo. Stnd.	Y	7. Gun Show Bkgrnd. Checks	Y	11. Debt Relief for 3rd World		Y
4. Ovrd. Estate Tax Veto	N	8. Ban Part.-Birth Abortion	N	12. Drop Cuba Econ. Embargo		Y

Election Results

2000 general	Ciro Rodriguez (D)	123,104	(89%)	($294,228)
	William A. Stallknecht (Lib)	15,156	(11%)	
2000 primary	Ciro Rodriguez (D)	unopposed		
1998 general	Ciro Rodriguez (D)	71,849	(91%)	($762,187)
	Edward Elmer (Lib)	7,504	(9%)	

TWENTY-NINTH DISTRICT

"What built Houston," wrote John Gunther in *Inside U.S.A.*, "was a combination of cotton, oil, and the ship canal." The cotton and oil were gifts of nature, though they required much human effort and ingenuity to produce in commercial quantities; the Houston Ship Channel, by contrast, was almost totally man's creation. After the sand-spit port of Galveston was destroyed by a hurricane and tidal wave in 1900, Houston's elders decided to dredge out Buffalo Bayou and make their inland city a seaport. And so a sluggish, 6-foot-deep creek became a 40-foot-deep channel (45 feet by 2003, following a $570 million expansion) and Houston turned into the nation's busiest port for foreign trade, with more than 400 vessels daily generating 205,000 jobs and $7.7 billion a year for the local economy. On the west side of town, Houston—a world-class metropolis of 4.7 million people—seems entirely a white-collar, office-bound city. But on the east and north, around the turning basin in the port and through the maze of refinery towers and tubing, Houston is plainly blue collar, with blacks, Mexican-Americans and large numbers of whites from the rural South and even Michigan and California, who came here to move up in the world. The city's continuing growth has raised concerns that congestion and pollution could hamper long-term growth, and in 2001 stricter air pollution standards were imposed.

The 29th Congressional District of Texas covers much of the Ship Channel area and working-class Houston. It is one of three Texas districts declared unconstitutional by the Supreme Court in 1996 as racially gerrymandered (the others were the 18th and 30th). The current district lines, drawn by a three-judge federal court in 1996, are much more regular. Removed from the 29th were Baytown, Spring Branch and the Heights neighborhood in Houston. Added was much area on Houston's Northside, between the Eastex and North Freeways all the way out to Houston Intercontinental Airport and FM 1960, and blue-collar neighborhoods in northeast Houston. This district was 45% Hispanic and 15% black in 1990, 61% Hispanic and 16% black in 2000.

The congressman from the 29th District is Gene Green, a Democrat elected in 1992. Green grew up in Houston, worked as a printer's apprentice and was admitted to the bar at age 30; he was elected to the state House in 1972, at 25, and to the state Senate in a special election in 1985. He has been a faithful union and trial-lawyer man in Austin and Washington, and also an opponent of gun control—a politician whose natural base is Texas' small union, blue-collar class. He is a compulsive campaigner who goes door to door, with lawn signs and a hammer in his trunk; and a good thing, for him anyway, since otherwise he never would have won in the 29th. In the 1992 primary he faced Ben Reyes, a tempestuous Houston councilman who once protested official inaction by demolishing a crack house. In the primary, Reyes led 34%–28% over Green. For the runoff, Green came out ahead by 180 votes out of 31,508 cast. Then Reyes went to court and charged that Republican voters had illegally crossed over and voted in the runoff. That got him a July re-runoff, but to no avail. This time Green won with 52%, by 1,132 votes out of 36,722 cast. Green won the general election with 65%.

In his first term, Green voted against NAFTA and against the Brady bill. Reyes ran again in 1994, pro-NAFTA and pro-gun control, supported by downtown business money and most Latino politicians. Green won the primary 55%–45%, winning 80% of Anglos and 30% of Latinos. His voting record has been relatively moderate for a member in a heavily minority district. Since the lines were redrawn in 1996, no other Democrat has challenged him and he has been re-elected easily. After a spirited fight with other Texas Democrats, he won a seat in 1997 on the Commerce Committee. In 2000 the House passed a bill he co-sponsored to permit computer users to stop the distribution of "spam" to anyone who doesn't want e-mail ads. He wants to require Web site operators to post notice on their information collection practices and stop them from placing software cookies on computers of Internet users. He also added amendments to prohibit resale of tires in a recall following Firestone's problems. Following the 2000 election, he called for abolition of the Electoral College.

Green's most satisfying victory may have been to wrest the bulk of Harris County's grant money from the county's longstanding Head Start contractor. Always sensitive to his Hispanic constituents, Green complained to the Health and Human Services Department that Latinos in his district were being shut out of Head Start by the contractor's dysfunctional bureaucracy. This was "awkward," Green explained to *National Journal*, because the bureaucracy in question was run by African-Americans and supported, at least tacitly, by virtually all of the city's black leadership. After careful negotiations, a deal was struck to open three-quarters of the contract to bidding—a constructive agreement for a city that prides itself on easing racial discord rather than letting hostility into the open.

National and state Hispanic leaders are pressing for more seats in Congress, but the 29th already has a large Hispanic majority; it is slightly above the population standards, and its boundaries could be pretty much left as is. Latinos are probably not yet a majority of the electorate, but it is possible that Green could face serious primary opposition some time in the next decade.

Cook's Call   *Safe*. About the only threat to Green's political future would be a primary. Although he is an Anglo representing a district that is more than 60% Hispanic, Green has yet to face a significant primary challenge since his win here in 1992.

THE PEOPLE: Pop. 2000: 672,591; Pop. 1990: 568,250, up 18.4% 1990–2000. 50.7% White, 15.7% Black, 2.2% Asian, 0.6% Amer. Indian, 0.1% Hawaiian, 3.5% Two+ races, 27.1% Other; 60.9% Hispanic Origin.

2000 Presidential Vote			1996 Presidential Vote		
Gore (D)	70,412	(61%)	Clinton (D)	63,624	(61%)
Bush (R)	45,190	(39%)	Dole (R)	34,497	(33%)
			Perot (I)	5,994	(6%)

Rep. Gene Green (D)

Elected 1992, 5th term; b. Oct. 17, 1947, Houston; home, Houston; U. of Houston, B.A., 1971, Bates Col. of Law at U. of Houston, 1973–77; Methodist; married (Helen).

Elected Office: TX House of Reps., 1972–84; TX Senate, 1985–92.

Professional Career: Practicing atty., 1977–92.

DC Office: 2335 RHOB 20515, 202-225-1688; Fax: 202-225-9903; Web site: www.house.gov/green.

District Offices: Houston, 713-330-0807; Houston, 281-999-5716.

Committees: *Energy & Commerce* (17th of 26 D): Environment & Hazardous Materials; Health; Telecommunications & The Internet.

Group Ratings

	ADA	ACLU	AFS	LCV	CON	ITIC	NTU	COC	ACU	NTLC	CHC
2000	90	62	100	64	65	53	24	33	20	33	33
1999	70	—	100	75	47	—	22	24	26	—	—

National Journal Ratings

	1999 LIB —	1999 CONS		2000 LIB —	2000 CONS
Economic	70%	30%		68%	31%
Social	54%	46%		60%	39%
Foreign	65%	35%		56%	42%

Key Votes of the 106th Congress

1. Patient Bill of Rights	Y	5. Bar RU-486 $ for FDA	N	9. NATO War in Serbia	Y
2. Accelerate Min. Wage	Y	6. Display 10 Commandments	Y	10. Perm. Trade with China	N
3. Strike Ban on Ergo. Stnd.	Y	7. Gun Show Bkgrnd. Checks	N	11. Debt Relief for 3rd World	Y
4. Ovrd. Estate Tax Veto	N	8. Ban Part.-Birth Abortion	N	12. Drop Cuba Econ. Embargo	N

Election Results

2000 general	Gene Green (D)	84,665	(73%)	($626,951)
	Joe Vu (R)	29,606	(26%)	($50,896)
	Others	1,204	(1%)	
2000 primary	Gene Green (D)	unopposed		
1998 general	Gene Green (D)	44,179	(93%)	($392,122)
	Lea Sherman (I)	2,013	(4%)	
	Others	1,439	(3%)	

THIRTIETH DISTRICT

Dallas is, among other things, the westernmost city of the Deep South. Cotton was originally the major crop in this part of Texas, and many of Dallas's first enterprising businessmen, when the railroad reached the Trinity River here in the 1870s, were cotton brokers. Geographically, Dallas is directly west of the Black Belt of Alabama and the Mississippi Delta, both heavy cotton-producing areas in the days before the boll weevil. Many blacks and whites came west on U.S. 80—and now Interstate 20—to this metropolis, which is now the largest metro area in the South. The south side of Dallas, not much visited by tourists, is predominately black.

Texas' 30th Congressional District, designed to be the Dallas-Fort Worth Metroplex's black-majority district, includes most of Dallas' predominantly black neighborhoods. Its creation in 1991 was insisted on by Eddie Bernice Johnson, then chairwoman of the Texas Senate's committee on redistricting, and the precise lines were drawn by Bob Mansker, aide to 24th District Congressman Martin Frost, who made them exceedingly complex in order to create safe districts for Frost and then-5th District Democrat John Bryant. The result was one of the most grotesquely shaped districts in the country: Attached to the central body in south and east Dallas, were tentacles that appeared as complex and attenuated as a series of DNA molecules. A lawsuit was filed, claiming racial gerrymandering, and the Supreme Court ruled the 30th and two Houston districts unconstitutional. In August 1996 a three-judge federal court drew new lines for that year's election. The new 30th includes two compact geographic units connected by downtown Dallas. One consists of most of the south side of Dallas; the other runs northwest out Stemmons Freeway and includes most of Irving. This district was 45% black and 18% Hispanic in 1990, 39% black and 35% Hispanic in 2000.

The congresswoman from the 30th District is its creator, Eddie Bernice Johnson. She grew up in Texas and graduated from college as a registered nurse. She worked at St. Paul Hospital and was chief psychiatric nurse at the VA Hospital in Dallas. In 1972 she was elected to the Texas House—the first black woman elected to anything in Dallas. She became a regional HEW director in the Carter administration and was elected to the state Senate in 1986. She has never had effective opposition in the 30th District; she won the 1992 Democratic primary with 92% of the vote, and became the first African American to represent Dallas in the House. After the 1996 redistricting, she won comfortably with 55% against seven opponents in the November special election, thus avoiding a runoff. In 2000 she had no major-party opposition.

In the House, Johnson has a mostly liberal voting record, but she has been attentive to business interests in Dallas. Though she once pledged to unions to oppose NAFTA, she changed her mind and voted for it; Dallas probably exports more to Mexico than any other American city, and many jobs depend on those exports. She has worked to get NAFTA Superhighway status for I-35. Johnson also sided with business on permanent normal trade relations with China. She is concerned that "in too many high school classrooms, the world of work is distant and removed," and praises school-to-work programs for involving industry in education. She helped to enact in 1998 the Next Generation Internet Research Act, to support research on networking technologies, and promised additional initiatives to help improve the students' science and math skills while encouraging them to pursue technical careers; she has focused on reducing the Digital Divide in the minority community. As a health care professional, she has taken an interest in minorities' health care problems; she points out that some leading problems—sexually transmitted diseases, injuries to drivers and passengers not wearing seat belts, obesity—result from voluntary behavior. Serving on the Transportation and Infrastructure Committee, she got a seat on the Aviation Subcommittee, of great importance here: The 30th District includes half of Dallas/Fort Worth International Airport and three others, Love Field, Red Bird Airport and Lancaster Airport. On the Science Committee, she shared credit in 2000 for passing the Networking and Information Research and Development Act to double federal information research spending in five years.

In 2001, Johnson became chairwoman of the Congressional Black Caucus. Her priorities included support for black colleges to produce more black teachers, bridging the technology gap and reinvigorating the caucus PAC. During the Clinton impeachment trial, Johnson strongly rallied the black community on his behalf, saying, "He's been the best president on our issues." Redistricting will require the district to add 18,000 people, who will presumably come from the current 5th and 24th Districts; it is unlikely that redistricters will mess with the Texas district with the second-highest percentage of African Americans.

Cook's Call *Safe.* A court-ordered remapping of this once black-majority district in 1996 has had little impact on Johnson's ability to rack up large victories. She will need to pick up some population in redistricting, but this seat will remain a Democratic stronghold.

THE PEOPLE: Pop. 2000: 633,860; Pop. 1990: 564,902, up 12.2% 1990–2000. 37.8% White, 39.3% Black, 2.5% Asian, 0.5% Amer. Indian, 0.1% Hawaiian, 2.6% Two+ races, 17.3% Other; 34.7% Hispanic Origin.

2000 Presidential Vote

Gore (D)	101,911	(71%)
Bush (R)	41,673	(29%)

1996 Presidential Vote

Clinton (D)	95,841	(70%)
Dole (R)	35,205	(26%)
Perot (I)	6,466	(5%)

Rep. Eddie Bernice Johnson (D)

Elected 1992, 5th term; b. Dec. 3, 1935, Waco; home, Dallas; St. Mary's at Notre Dame, B.A. 1955, TX Christian U., B.S. 1967, S. Methodist U., M.B.A. 1976; Baptist; divorced.

Elected Office: TX House of Reps., 1972–1977; TX Senate, 1986–92.

Professional Career: Registered nurse; Regional Dir., U.S. Dept. of HEW, 1977–80; Mgmt. consultant, Sammons Corp., 1979–81; Owner, Eddie Bernice Johnson & Assoc., 1981–present.

DC Office: 1511 LHOB 20515, 202-225-8885; Fax: 202-226-1477; Web site: www.house.gov/ebjohnson.

District Offices: Dallas, 214-922-8885; Irving, 972-253-8885.

Committees: *Science* (5th of 22 D): Research (RMM). *Transportation & Infrastructure* (14th of 34 D): Aviation; Highways & Transit; Water Resources & Environment.

Group Ratings

	ADA	ACLU	AFS	LCV	CON	ITIC	NTU	COC	ACU	NTLC	CHC
2000	75	86	85	79	24	83	21	57	9	12	7
1999	90	—	100	81	28	—	12	36	0	—	—

National Journal Ratings

	1999 LIB	—	1999 CONS		2000 LIB	—	2000 CONS
Economic	83%	—	16%		80%	—	19%
Social	80%	—	19%		91%	—	9%
Foreign	95%	—	0%		80%	—	16%

Key Votes of the 106th Congress

1. Patient Bill of Rights	Y	5. Bar RU-486 $ for FDA	N	9. NATO War in Serbia	Y
2. Accelerate Min. Wage	*	6. Display 10 Commandments	N	10. Perm. Trade with China	Y
3. Strike Ban on Ergo. Stnd.	Y	7. Gun Show Bkgrnd. Checks	Y	11. Debt Relief for 3rd World	Y
4. Ovrd. Estate Tax Veto	N	8. Ban Part.-Birth Abortion	N	12. Drop Cuba Econ. Embargo	Y

Election Results

2000 general	Eddie Bernice Johnson (D)	109,163	(92%)	($243,072)
	Kelly Rush (Lib)	9,798	(8%)	
2000 primary	Eddie Bernice Johnson (D)	unopposed		
1998 general	Eddie Bernice Johnson (D)	57,603	(72%)	($241,756)
	Carrie Kelleher (R)	21,338	(27%)	($57,988)

★ UTAH ★

U tah is a triumph of man over nature, the creation of a productive and orderly civilization in a remote expanse of desert and mountain, arrayed around a desolate salt sea. Today's Utah and Mormonism have their roots in a very different landscape of more than 150 years ago, when a wave of religious enthusiasm, prophecy and utopianism swept across the "burnt-over district" of Upstate New York in the 1820s and 1830s. There Joseph Smith, a 14-year-old farmer, experienced a vision in which the angel Moroni appeared and told him where to unearth several golden tablets inscribed with hieroglyphic writings. With the aid of special spectacles, Smith translated the tablets and published them as the Book of Mormon in 1831. He later declared himself a prophet and founded the Church of Jesus Christ of Latter-day Saints.

The Mormons, as they were called, attracted thousands of converts and created their own communities; persecuted for their beliefs, they moved west to Ohio, Missouri and then Illinois. In 1844, the Mormon colony at Nauvoo, Illinois, had some 15,000 members living under the theocratic rule of Smith. It was here that Smith received a revelation sanctioning the practice of polygamy, which led to his death at the hands of a mob in 1844. After the murder, the new church president, Brigham Young, decided to move the faithful, "the saints," farther west into territory that was still part of Mexico and far beyond white settlement. In 1847 Young led a well-organized march across the Great Plains and into the Rocky Mountains on a path where Mormons re-enacted the march 150 years later in 1997. In 1847, they stopped on the western slope of the Wasatch Range and, as Young gazed over the valley of the Great Salt Lake spread out below, he uttered the now famous words, "This is the place."

The place was Utah. Young was governor of the territory for many years, and it is the only state that largely continues to live by the teachings of a church. The early pioneers laid out towns foursquare to the points of the compass with huge city blocks, built sturdy houses and planted dozens of trees. Young's home still stands a block away from Temple Square, where the Temple, closed to non-Mormons, stands in gleaming marble, topped by the golden angel Moroni, across from the oval Mormon Tabernacle where its great choir sings. For 150 years this "Zion" has attracted thousands of converts from the Midwest, the north of England and Scandinavia. The object of religious fear and prejudice, Utah was not granted statehood until 1896, after the church renounced polygamy. Utah has grown steadily since then, and remains heavily Mormon, its basic character is stamped on the desert, mountain-shadowed, often surrealistic landscape that without the Mormons would probably have remained as unpopulated as Nevada without gambling.

The LDS church remains distinctive in many ways. It cares deeply about its past: In caves in the mountains of Utah, the Church preserves America's most complete genealogical records in its Family History Library, which is also on the Internet. It tries to spread the faith: Young Mormons, 60,000 every year, spend missionary years in the United States and abroad, and their experiences in turn give Utah the biggest inventory of people with knowledge of obscure foreign languages of any state in the union, a nice commercial advantage. The church prohibits the consumption of tobacco, alcohol and caffeine; it encourages hard work and large families. Mormons are healthier than the average American; better educated, they work longer hours and earn more money. In an individualist country, the church fosters communitarian attitudes: The LDS Church has no clergy, but members serve in positions for which they are chosen, conducting religious services but also keeping in touch with members and counseling them when they need help. The church also maintains its own social service organizations. It evidently works: While American mainline denominations are losing members, the Mormon Church is growing. There were 2.9 million Mormons in 1970 and nearly 11 million in 2000, with more than half outside the United States and just 15% in Utah.

The church's influence in Utah is great—it owns one of the two leading Salt Lake City newspapers and a TV station, it has holdings in an insurance company, several banks, real estate—and it is sometimes resented. The conservative hold that the church has over the state can appear in political issues. In 1991 Utah passed the strictest abortion law of any state, banning abortion except in cases of rape and incest, or if the mother's life is endangered. Also in 1990, it became

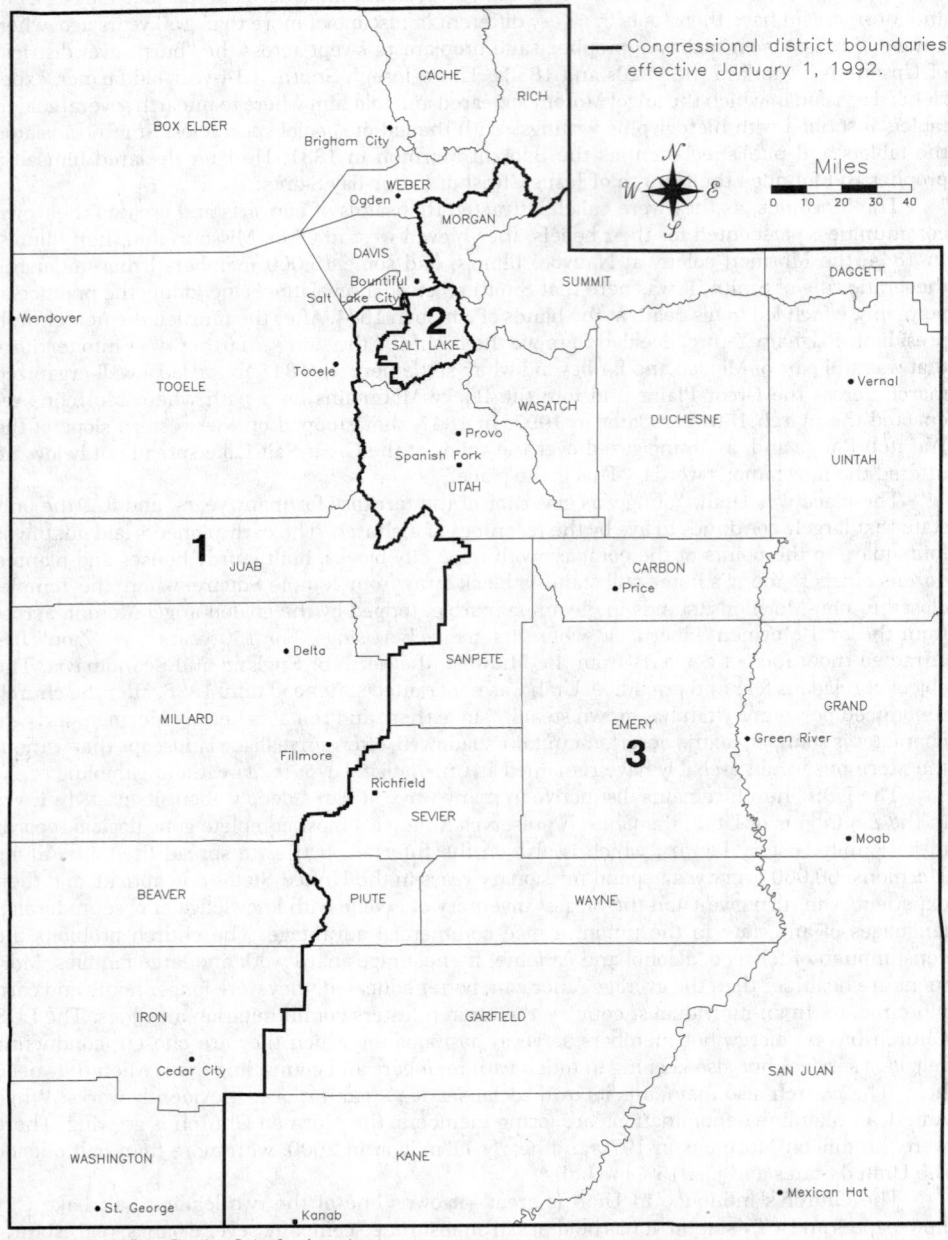

Congressional district boundaries effective January 1, 1992.

Miles
0 10 20 30 40

CACHE
RICH
BOX ELDER
Brigham City
WEBER
Ogden
MORGAN
DAVIS
Bountiful
Salt Lake City
SUMMIT
DAGGETT
Wendover
SALT LAKE
2
TOOELE
Tooele
WASATCH
DUCHESNE
Vernal
Provo
Spanish Fork
UTAH
UINTAH
1
JUAB
CARBON
Price
Delta
SANPETE
GRAND
MILLARD
EMERY
Green River
Fillmore
3
Richfield
SEVIER
BEAVER
PIUTE
WAYNE
Moab
IRON
GARFIELD
Cedar City
SAN JUAN
WASHINGTON
KANE
St. George
Kanab
Mexican Hat

the first state to ban the sale of vending machine cigarettes, although earlier in the year it became the last state to abolish the provision that stated hard liquor could not be served in public. And the church itself, financed by the tradition of tithing, runs its own high-quality welfare programs. This is a society that favors market economics and free enterprise, but also has a lively tradition of communal effort and responsibility.

If the moral underpinnings of life in Utah have not changed in 50 years, Utah's view of its place in the nation has. Before World War II, Utah saw itself as a colonial victim of East Coast bankers and financiers and Mormons saw themselves as suffering religious discrimination and bigotry—all with some cause. Utah's income levels were well below the national average, its cost of living higher, the prices paid for the things it produced seemed to be controlled elsewhere. Politically, this perspective translated into a Democratic allegiance: In 1940 Utah was represented by staunch New Dealers in Congress and cast 62% of its votes for Franklin Roosevelt. Today, Utah is more likely to see itself as a busy generator of wealth, with a raft of successful businesses and a knack for high-tech innovation. It has the youngest and most productive workforce of any state in the nation, sixth in job growth. Its population grew 30% in the 1990s, the fourth highest rate in the nation (after Nevada, Arizona and Colorado). Work weeks average 48 hours here, more than Japan and far more than anywhere else in America. It has fast-rising incomes, with wages outpacing inflation for six straight years, and in the mid-1990s America's fastest-rising house prices as thousands of people migrated from California. Utah has the largest families and the largest proportion of children of any state, by far, and low rates of divorce. In many ways, Utah looks like the America of the 1950s, but with a 21st Century high-tech look: in 2000 it was the number one state in households with computers. As Bill Cosby told the legislature, in a celebration of Utah's regaining the title of number one consumer of Jell-O back from Iowa, "You are the number one family state. You take your children with you when you go places. You cook for them. Feed them. Put them to sleep. Wake them up. And talk to them. You also get married here . . . before you have children." Utah is also a place with community spirit: It rejoiced when it won the 2002 Winter Olympics, and started a $1.6 billion reconstruction of I-15, an airport expansion, a downtown light rail system and building a winter sports park, new stadium space and an athlete's village.

Politically, Utah's special charactertistcs have made it a heavily Republican state since the middle 1960s. In the last 20 years, as traditional values thriving in Utah have come under attack elsewhere, it has become arguably the most Republican of states—standing out in national statistics politically just as it does demographically. In 1960, Richard Nixon carried Utah with 55% of the vote; by 1972, he won with 72%. Ronald Reagan won 73% here in 1980 and 75% in 1984; George Bush won 66% here in 1988 and George W. Bush won here with 67% in 2000. In five of the last seven presidential elections, Utah has been the nation's most Republican state, and in one of the others, 1992, it was the least Democratic: Ross Perot finished ahead of Bill Clinton, 27% to 25%. Utah is so Republican now that church leaders have been at pains to affirm that there is nothing contradictory about being a Mormon and voting Democratic. Interestingly, the Salt Lake City neighborhoods close to the church headquarters, with gracious old houses and a smaller street grid that attract academic and professional newcomers, have become the most heavily "gentile" and politically liberal parts of the state. As the Yankee hub of Boston filled up with Irish Catholic Democrats in the 1890s, so Salt Lake City is getting more than its share of secular liberal Democrats in the 1990s, people who cheer on the non-Church-owned *Salt Lake Tribune* when it runs stories attacking the Church for converting a block of Main Street into a plaza with restrictions on speech, dress, and conduct. But for the most part, Democrats are competitive only if they seem consistent with Utah values and attitudes, and even then are in jeopardy.

Not quite everything is rosy in Utah. Scandal appeared in late 1998 when it was revealed that members of the International Olympics Committee had received gifts—$400,000 for college scholarships, $28,000 in medical care, airline tickets, guns and skis—from Salt Lake Olympics organizers. Six members of the IOC resigned in January 1999, and two organizers were indicted in July 2000. As Governor Mike Leavitt said, "It didn't start here, but it must end here." The Olympics were not canceled, and Utah stands to gain $2.8 billion in spending and 20,000 man-years of employment; in early 2001 planning and construction seemed to be going ahead on schedule.

There are disputes as well about environmental protection, over the vast expanses of mostly empty land beyond the Wasatch Front from Ogden to Provo where 76% of Utahns live. There are still "downwinders," including Governor Mike Leavitt, who remember living downwind from the 1950s nuclear tests in Nevada, and some are uneasy about the new chemical weapons incinerator southwest of Tooele. Leavitt objected strongly to the Goshute Indians' contract to store nuclear waste in Skull Valley, between the Dugway Proving Grounds and the Tooele Army Depot. Utahns were furious in September 1996 when Bill Clinton, campaigning for re-election in Arizona with the Grand Canyon as a backdrop, announced that he was creating a 1.7 million acre new Grand Staircase-Escalante National Monument in southern Utah, which would bar coal mining and mineral exploration—without notification to Utah officials, although a planned coal mine would bring over $1 billion in royalties to Utah schools. But in 1998 the state and the Interior Department agreed on a land swap: The federal government would take 377,000 acres of state school trust land parcels, about half in the national monument, and would pay the state $50 million in cash and $13 million in future coal revenues, plus turn over 153,000 acres of exploitable lands elsewhere. And, out in the rural reaches of Utah, survives another vestige of the state's tradition, polygamy, though condemned by the LDS Church since 1890. In 2000 the state Senate authorized $500,000 for polygamy prosecutions, though none had been brought for 50 years, and one legislator estimated that there were 50,000 polygamists in the state—3% of the adult population! In May 2000 prosecutor David Leavitt, brother of the governor, instituted a polygamy prosecution of Tom Green, a telemarketer who has boasted openly of his multiple wives, claiming to have fathered 30 children by 10 women over the years. He had avoided marriage licenses, but he was convicted in May 2001. Utah, like other states, seldom if ever prosecutes men for fathering children outside legal marriages; Green maintained that he was being punished for his openness about a subject most Utahns would prefer not to have spotlighted as the world's eyes turn toward Salt Lake City in the Olympic month of February 2002.

Governor Mike Leavitt, a Republican, has been elected governor of Utah three times. He grew up in Cedar City, in the southwest corner of the state, graduated from Southern Utah University, worked for and in the 1980s ran the family businesses, including an insurance company that has spread all over the West and has land holdings in southern Utah and Nevada. In between, he managed the campaigns of Governor Norman Bangerter and Senator Jake Garn. In 1992, when Bangerter retired after two terms, Leavitt ran himself. He won the Republican primary 56%–44% over Richard Eyre, who backed a $1,200 school choice voucher; Leavitt had his own Strategic Plan for Education and opposed vouchers. In the general, liberal Democrat Stewart Hanson ran third, with only 23%; second was anti-tax crusader and later 2nd District Congressman Merrill Cook, with 34%; Leavitt won with 42%.

In office, Leavitt cut taxes in 1994, 1995 and 1996, as the state's economy surged, and pushed activist programs with catchy labels. One was the 1994 Healthprint insurance reforms; he boasted that Utah had lower health care costs than all but one other state. Another was a $120 million, seven-year Technology 2000 initiative. In 1995 he convened a Growth Summit, which came up with a 10-year, $2.6 billion highway-building program, with half the money to make I-15 in Salt Lake County a 10-lane (now a 12-lane) highway by 2001, in time for the 2002 Winter Olympics; for that he raised gas taxes while cutting the sales tax. In 1996 he proposed a Legacy Highway, to be built parallel to and west of I-15; that will come after the Olympics. He sponsored a Centennial Charter schools program and Highly Impacted Schools program for disadvantaged children; in 1998 he called for reading testing in early grades with summer school for those who fall short, and for competency testing in high school, with diplomas denied those who fail. He has worked to start, with other Western states, a Western Virtual University, and is completing UtahLINK, giving Internet access to all Utah schools.

On environmental issues, he backed a quality growth initiative, with incentives to local communities to preserve valuable open space, but no mandates. After discussions with Oregon's Democratic Governor John Kitzhaber, he advanced what he called Enlibra, "a symbol of balance and stewardship," based on collaboration, local decision-making and free market incentives rather than government command and control, "not to eliminate conflict but to shorten the conflict so as to increase the velocity of environmental problem-solving." Leavitt engineered land swaps with Clinton Interior Secretary Bruce Babbitt, but his consultative approach was unavailing against Clinton's election-year creation of the Grand Staircase-Escalante National Monument.

In 1996 Democrats had to scrounge to find a candidate to run against Leavitt; he was reelected 75%–23%. But as the 2000 election approached he was embroiled in controversy, often with members of his own party. His efforts to stop construction of a nuclear waste site at the Skull Valley Band of the Goshute Tribe in Tooele County seemed to be futile and his support of taxes on the Internet was frustrated by a federal ban. He signed a carrying concealed weapon bill in 1995, but ordered state employees to leave their guns home in 1996 and in 1999 called for a ban on guns in churches and schools; that, and a threat to call a special session on guns, infuriated conservatives. In March 2000 he vetoed a bill substituting abstinence advocacy for sex education, but said he would work to see that schools stressed abstinence.

In December 1999 Leavitt seemed to avoid primary opposition when he got House Speaker Marty Stephens to endorse him. But four little-known candidates ran anyway, and at the May 2000 state Republican convention, amid boos and catcalls, he failed to get the 60% required to win the nomination outright; on the final ballot he prevailed over the little-known Glen Davis by only 54%–46%. "I am in the mainstream of Republican thought," Leavitt insisted. "I'll take my message to the people." That message was a very conservative one in the primary; he stressed tax cuts, abstinence education, opposition to federal confiscation of private lands and opposition to trigger locks, without mentioning his abstinence veto, gun control measures and Enlibra. Davis promised to stress tax cuts, to give more control to local school districts, to fight harder against the federal government. Leavitt spent more than $1 million, Davis only $70,000; but Leavitt won by the uninspiring (for a two-term incumbent) 62%–38% margin.

His Democratic opponent was Bill Orton, three-term congressman from the heavily Republican 3rd District until he was defeated in 1996, who after a businessman withdrew in March (he found the state had a five-year residency requirement he didn't meet) decided to enter the race. Orton said the well-financed Leavitt was beholden to special interests and criticized him for not taking a stand on guns; he frequently cited LDS Church President Gordon Hinckley's admonition that there was no reason a good Mormon could not be a Democrat. Leavitt spent $1.9 million altogether, Orton just $140,000; Leavitt won again by an unimpressive margin, 56%–42%, as Orton carried Salt Lake County, Summit County (which contains Park City and voted 10% for Ralph Nader) and three small traditionally Democratic rural counties. At the same time, Utahns voted to make English the state's official language, a measure opposed by both Leavitt and Orton.

In his third term Leavitt advanced an initiative to spend $10 million on engineering and technology education and got the legislature to pass a bill banning nuclear waste in Utah; whether this could prevent federal law from applying to the proposed Goshute nuclear waste repository was not clear. There was little if any talk of Leavitt receiving a post in the Bush administration; his leadership in the fight for Internet taxation may have prevented that. He stands ready to welcome the world to Salt Lake City's Winter Olympics in February 2002.

Senior Senator Orrin Hatch is now serving his fifth term in the Senate—even though he had never planned a political career until he first ran in 1976. Hatch grew up in Pittsburgh, where his father was a metal lather; he worked his way through Brigham Young University, then Pittsburgh Law School, practiced law there and then moved to Salt Lake City. For a time he was an amateur boxer and at one point he and his wife lived in a refurbished chicken coop. He got into the 1976 Senate race late, filing the last day; an endorsement from Ronald Reagan helped him win the Republican nomination, and in the general he upset three-term Democrat Frank Moss 54%–45%. His toughest re-election fight came in 1982, when he was opposed by Salt Lake City Mayor Ted Wilson; Hatch won 58%–41%.

Hatch's Senate career has been shaped by two impulses which are sometimes in tension with each other: a strong conservative philosophy and a sense of responsibility for the superintendency of legislation. He first attracted attention in a Senate dominated by Democrats when he successfully filibustered the AFL-CIO's labor law reform, which had been expected to pass. Then, after just four years, he became chairman of the Labor Committee after Republicans won a Senate majority in 1980. He worked to convert federal programs to block grants to states, but became a fan of some programs, like the Job Corps. He worked for bipartisan compromise on child care, family and medical leave, immunizations, the WIC program and AIDS babies. He backed the Americans With Disabilities Act. But he remained a strong opponent of the striker replacement law sought by unions and eventually passed a subminimum wage for teens. On the Judiciary Committee, he fought abortion and a civil rights bill that produced racial quotas and preferences, and staunchly defended Supreme Court nominees Robert Bork and Clarence Thomas. He has also worked on less politically divisive issues—railway labor disputes, bankruptcy reform, sovereign immunity of states for patents and trademarks, patent protection for pharmaceuticals under GATT. He was the author of the 1994 law limiting the FDA's authority to test and regulate food supplements, working with Tom Harkin whom he had bonded with over the Americans With Disabilities Act; Hatch, like many Mormons, is a consumer of food supplements, and Utah has a $3 billion food supplement industry. He sponsored the 1990 legislation providing compensation for people exposed to radiation during nuclear tests or while working with uranium; that was followed with additional compensation in 2000, and in early 2001 Hatch was still working to fund the program.

In 1993 Hatch switched from ranking Republican on Labor to the same post on Judiciary, when it was vacated by Strom Thurmond; in 1995 he became chairman of Judiciary and left Labor altogether. On Judiciary he worked on tort reform and regulatory reform and managed the balanced budget amendment to one-vote defeats in 1995 and 1997. He worked also on the flag amendment, which fell four votes short of passage in March 2000, the anti-terrorism law and the Religious Freedom Restoration Act. On judicial appointments, Hatch promised in 1995 to cooperate with the Clinton administration; by early 1997 some Democrats were charging that he was stalling approval of nominees, while some Republicans were complaining that he was allowing too many liberal, activist judges on the bench. In 1999 he held up several nominations until his own choice in Utah was confirmed, and in early 2000 he allowed some nominations through—not enough to suit Democrats. In early 2001 Democrats seemed determined to retaliate by holding up George W. Bush's appointees.

In 1997 and 1998 Hatch passionately defended Independent Counsel Kenneth Starr against attacks by Clinton advisors. In March 1997 he revealed that the FBI had warned some members of Congress that China was planning to make illegal campaign contributions, and over the next two years criticized Attorney General Janet Reno for not seeking an independent counsel to investigate these and other allegations of misconduct. In 1999 he charged that Reno was unduly influenced by a palace guard of political advisers, and in January 2000 he said, "Faced with an astonishing range of allegations about illegal activities, from perjury by administration officials before Congress to damaging missile technology transfers and even theft of nuclear secrets, the Justice Department did not pursue corruption but thwarted its own lead attorney in the investigation as well as FBI Director Louis Freeh."

In 1997 Hatch again surprised some on both sides of the aisle when he joined Ted Kennedy in sponsoring a $24 billion program to get states to provide health insurance for children of low-income working parents who don't qualify for Medicaid; for Hatch, a tobacco opponent, one attraction must have been that the money would come from increasing the cigarette tax from 24 to 67 cents a pack. Hatch praised the Microsoft antitrust suit in May 1998; one of Microsoft's major competitors was Utah-based Novell. Hatch has worked to prevent specious suits on Y2K problems, to allow homeowners to claim capital losses on sales of homes, to bar the federal government from using racial or gender quotas, to stop operation of Oregon's assisted suicide law, and to ban stalking of celebrities by paparazzi. He tried to ban lawsuits against gun manufacturers, which he called "extortion." In 2000 he sponsored a bill to extend Schering-Plough's patent on Claritin, for which he was widely criticized. Presiding over hearings on Napster, he opined that the recording industry was going to have to sit down with Napster and owners of other copying software, which is what happened. In 2000 he sponsored a number of bills which were signed into law—a law giving religious groups a federal remedy when their religious rights are violated by land use policies, an increase in the number of H1-B visas, funding for agents and training aimed at methamphetamines. He proposed a ban on Internet sales of alcohol. In the March 2001 debate on campaign finance, he offered a payroll protection amendment aimed at both unions and corporations; sparring with his friend Edward Kennedy in debate, he said, "I admire the way he supports his special interest. We don't have anybody on our side who does it that well"—at which point Kennedy came over and hugged him.

In the midst of this productive legislative work, Hatch surprised just about everyone by announcing in June 1999 that he was running for president. He admitted that it would take a "miracle" to win, but argued that he had more experience in federal office than the other candidates and could work with Democrats, and that he was not "beholden to the Republican establishment." At the August 1999 Iowa straw poll he came in last, with 2% of the votes. He managed to raise $2 million, much of it in $36 "skinny cat" contributions. But in the Iowa caucuses in January 2000 he won only 1% of the votes, fewer than John McCain, who did not campaign in the state. Two days later he withdrew from the race and endorsed George W. Bush. He had one complaint. "I did find that there was a certain amount of prejudice against Mormons. The Gallup Poll said that 17% would not vote for a Mormon for president. . . . These people think that Mormons are not Christians, when the name of the church is 'Church of Jesus Christ of Latter-Day Saints.' We're very Christian."

Hatch immediately announced for re-election to the Senate. He attracted competition for the Republican nomination, and was greeted with jeers as well as applause at the very conservative May 2000 state party convention. But he got 61% of the votes, just above the 60% required to win the nomination outright, without a primary. For the fall campaign he was able to raise much more than he had for his presidential candidacy, and spent $3.1 million; his opponent, for eight years the Democratic leader in the Utah Senate, spent $296,000. Hatch won 66%–31%, and became the first Utahn popularly elected five times to the Senate; the only other five-term senator in Utah history, Reed Smoot, who served from 1903 to 1933, was elected to his first term by the legislature. Hatch's talents, by the way, extend beyond the political. He has long written poetry and in 1995 began writing songs. They have been recorded by a Utah firm, first in a 13-song album of Christmas music; some have been recorded by Gladys Knight, a convert to the LDS Church, and after Christian music publishers seemed uninterested in what Hatch has called his Latter-Day Sound, he began distributing his songs over the Internet (www.hatchmusic.com). He also appeared in the movie *Traffic,* but criticized the movie for its frequent obscenities.

Junior Senator Bob Bennett was first elected in 1992, but was no stranger to the Senate. He grew up in Salt Lake City, and was 17 when his father Wallace Bennett was elected in 1950 to the first of four terms in the Senate. Bob Bennett worked as a congressional staffer and was the Transportation Department's chief lobbyist during the Nixon administration. He also headed the public relations firm (and CIA front) that employed Watergate burglar Howard Hunt, but was involved in no wrongdoing himself; some Watergate buffs believe that Bennett was Bob Woodward's "Deep Throat," but both Bennett and Woodward have denied it, and Leonard Garment's *In Search of Deep Throat* makes a persuasive case that Deep Throat was not Bennett but John Sears. After that, Bennett headed Microsonics Corporation, which makes audio discs for talking toys, for three years, then became head of Franklin Quest, which produces the Franklin day planners and organizers; he increased it from four to 700 employees and brought in sales of $80 million; he sold his interest in 1991 for a reported $25 million. He headed a commission that produced Utah's Strategic Plan for Education and wrote *Gaining Control*, a book on how to control your daily life.

In 1992, when Jake Garn retired from the Senate, Bennett decided to run for the seat his father once held. He was not the only millionaire in the race. The initial favorite was Republican Joseph Cannon, who had taken over the old Geneva Steel plant and made it profitable, and who spent $5 million of his own money. But Bennett spent $1.4 million of his own and effectively attacked Geneva's environmental record and won 51%–49%. The Democratic nominee, Congressman Wayne Owens, was a familiar face, but his record in Washington was moderate—perhaps too liberal for Utah. Bennett won 55%–40%, with exit polls showing Owens carrying only the elderly—not a good omen for Utah Democrats.

Bennett has a moderate to conservative voting record. Bob Dole appointed Bennett head of a task force on health care in August 1994; he worked on the health insurance portability law that passed in 1996. He has worked for several years on bills to protect the confidentiality of medical records, with uniform rules for access by researchers and law enforcement personnel. He sponsored a bill to limit liability on debit cards as it is on credit cards, and one to establish a uniform "minimalist" framework for digital signatures and electronic verification over the Internet. In 1997, before most other senators were thinking about the problem, Bennett sponsored a bill to require businesses to disclose what they were doing to fix Y2K errors. In April 1998 Trent Lott made him chairman of a Select Committee on the Year 2000 Technology Problem. His first priorities were public utilities, telecommunications and transportation; later he spotlighted the unpreparedness of health care providers, and got the SEC to require disclosure of business spending on the problem. As businesses and government agencies retooled their computers, he grew more confident that problems could be avoided. "I was beginning to feel a lot better around April [1999], when the reports started coming in," he said, "The sky could have fallen, I do believe that." On December 31, 1999, he was at the Utah Capitol's emergency command center; the fact that so few problems arose may have been because Bennett and others worked to see they wouldn't. In April 2000 Bennett began working on collecting information about cybercrime. In July 2000 he moved successfully to reduce the time to review computer export controls from 180 days to 60 days; in March 2001 he moved to change the MTOPS (millions of theoretical operations per second) standards for exports, with new ones to be set by the Bush administration. He has embraced some new technology himself: He drives a gasoline-electric hybrid 2000 Honda Insight that gets 61 miles per gallon. He has come out in favor of sales taxes on Internet transactions; in his mail order business, he says, he charged customers sales tax in every state and no one protested.

Bennett has been a critic of new campaign finance regulation proposals, which he says would prescribe "ways in which the government itself will inject federal power into the process of determining who can speak, when they can speak, how they will speak." In October 1999 he reacted angrily when John McCain's website listed a Bennett amendment for $2.2 million for sewer infrastructure for the 2002 Winter Olympics as pork barrel spending won by political contributions. "Who gave the soft money? How much was it? Where did it go? And where's the quid pro quo?" he asked. In May 2000 he co-sponsored a bill to prohibit the FEC from regulating political speech over the Internet by individuals. In the campaign finance debate of March 2001 he offered an amendment to bar PACs from using soft money—supposedly the source of evil influence—for fundraising and operating expenses; opposed by unions, it was defeated by advocates of the McCain-Feingold bill. In 2001 he was co-sponsor of a bill to set up an election commission, and called for making Election Day a holiday.

Bennett has pressed for land exchanges between Utah and the federal government, to eliminate the checkerboard pattern of land ownership which prevents Utah from producing revenue for education from mining on state lands; he notes that the idea was pushed by his father 40 years ago and by Democratic Governor Scott Matheson 20 years ago. He and Congressman Chris Cannon sponsored a 2000 law to get the Energy Department to clean up uranium tailings at the Atlas uranium mill on the Colorado River at Moab; the law also returned traditional homelands to the Ute tribe which were taken by the federal government for oil shale. In September 2000 he came out against the proposed nuclear waste depository on the lands of the Skull Valley Band of the Goshute Indians, on the grounds that it would be located beneath the Utah Test and Training Range and because it might not prove temporary.

Bennett was re-elected 64%–33% in 1998 against a Democrat who was a surgeon with an interest in the microloan programs in Bangladesh. In 1992 he said he would run for only two terms, but in 1998 Bennett said he would not rule out running again in 2004. Longevity runs in the family: his father lived to be 95, and his grandfather Heber Grant was president of the LDS Church, a job that goes to the longest serving member of the Quorum of the Twelve Disciples.

Presidential politics Utah has been the most Republican state in five of the last seven presidential elections. Arguably it was in 2000 as well. The percentage of votes for George W. Bush, 67%, was slightly behind that in Wyoming and Idaho. But the Bush margin of 40.5% over Al Gore was larger than in either of those two other states.

Governor Mike Leavitt spent much time and effort promoting a Western regional primary for the Friday following Southern Super Tuesday, March 10, 2000. But only Colorado and Wyoming (with a caucus, not a primary) adopted the date, and candidates paid little attention to western issues as Leavitt had hoped. Bill Bradley and John McCain pulled out of their races before March 10, and only 10% of Utah's registered voters bothered to vote.

Congressional districting Utahns expected that the 2000 Census would give Utah a fourth seat in the House of Representatives. But, under the formula used for reapportionment, Utah fell 857 residents short of getting a new district; instead, North Carolina got an unexpected 13th seat. North Carolina had an edge because military personnel stationed abroad are counted in their states of residence. Utah sued, arguing that Mormon missionaries should be counted as well, since they, like military personnel, can be accurately tracked and matched with their home states. But in April 2001 a federal court threw out Utah's case, and one judge called Utah's theory "wildly unfair."

Redistricting is controlled by Republicans, and it is expected that they will try to weaken Democrat Jim Matheson, who won the Salt Lake City-based 2nd District in 2000. Republicans had removed the Democratic-leaning West Valley area from the district 10 years before, and now could excise other Democratic areas and add Republican precincts. If that is done, Democrats are likely to argue that such a plan, splitting Salt Lake County and other counties, violates the Voting Rights Act, since Salt Lake County was 12% Hispanic in 2000. This seems like a weak argument, but Matheson won by a healthy 56%–41% and could well be re-elected whatever the redistricters do.

THE PEOPLE: Pop. 2000: 2,233,169; Pop. 1990: 1,722,850, up 29.6% 1990–2000. 0.8% of U.S. total, 34th largest; 89.2% White, 0.8% Black, 1.7% Asian, 1.3% Amer. Indian, 0.7% Hawaiian, 2.1% Two+ races, 4.2% Other; 9% Hispanic Origin. 3.2% Unemployment. 2000 Voting age pop.: 1,514,471. 2000 Turnout: 784,582; 52% of VAP. Registered voters (2000): 1,123,238; no party registration.

POLITICAL LINEUP: Governor, Michael O. Leavitt (R); Lt. Gov., Olene S. Walker (R); Atty. Gen., Mark Shurtleff (R); Treasurer, Edward T. Alter (R); Auditor, Auston Johnson (R); State Senate, 29 (9 D, 20 R); Senate President, L. Alma Mansell (R); Majority Leader, L. Steven Poulton (R); State House, 75 (24 D, 51 R); House Speaker, Martin Stephens (R). Senators, Orrin G. Hatch (R) and Robert Bennett (R). Representatives, 3 (1 D, 2 R).

ELECTIONS DIVISION: 801-538-1041; **FILING DEADLINE FOR U.S. CONGRESS:** March 17, 2002.

2000 Presidential Vote

Bush (R)	515,096	(67%)
Gore (D)	203,053	(26%)
Nader (Green)	35,850	(5%)
Others	16,755	(2%)

2000 Republican Presidential Primary

Bush (R)	57,617	(63%)
Keyes (R)	19,367	(21%)
McCain (R)	12,784	(14%)
Other	1,285	(1%)

1996 Presidential Vote

Dole (R)	361,911	(54%)
Clinton (D)	221,633	(33%)
Perot (I)	66,461	(10%)
Others	15,623	(2%)

2000 Democratic Presidential Primary

Gore (D)	12,527	(80%)
Bradley (D)	3,160	(20%)

Gov. Michael O. Leavitt (R)

Elected 1992, term expires Jan. 2005, 3d term; b. Feb. 11, 1951, Cedar City; home, Salt Lake City; S. UT U., B.A. 1976; Mormon; married (Jacalyn).

Military Career: Army Natl. Guard, 1969–78.

Professional Career: Pres. & CEO, Leavitt Group Insurance Co., 1984–92; Chmn., S. UT U. Bd. of Trustees, 1985–89; UT Board of Regents, 1989–92.

Office: 210 State Capitol, Salt Lake City, 84114, 801-538-1000; Web site: www.state.ut.us.

Election Results

2000 general	Michael O. Leavitt (R)	424,837	(56%)
	Bill Orton (D)	321,979	(42%)
	Other	14,990	(2%)
2000 primary	Michael O. Leavitt (R)	122,289	(62%)
	Glen P. Davis (R)	75,719	(38%)
1996 general	Michael O. Leavitt (R)	503,693	(75%)
	Jim Bradley (D)	156,616	(23%)
	Others	11,570	(2%)

Sen. Orrin G. Hatch (R)

Elected 1976, seat up 2006, 5th term; b. Mar. 22, 1934, Pittsburgh, PA; home, Salt Lake City; Brigham Young U., B.S. 1959; U. of Pittsburgh, J.D. 1962; Ch. of Jesus Christ of LDS; married (Elaine).

Professional Career: Practicing atty., 1962–76.

DC Office: 104 HSOB, 20510, 202-224-5251; Fax: 202-224-6331; Web site: www.senate.gov/~hatch.

State Offices: Cedar City, 435-586-8435; Ogden, 801-625-5672; Provo, 801-375-7881; Salt Lake City, 801-524-4380; St. George, 435-634-1795.

Committees: *Finance*: Health Care; International Trade (RMM); Taxation & IRS Oversight. *Indian Affairs. Intelligence (Select). Judiciary* (RMM): Antitrust, Business Rights & Competition; Constitution, Federalism & Property Rights; Youth Violence. *Joint Committee on Taxation* (4th of 5 Sens.).

Group Ratings

	ADA	ACLU	AFS	LCV	CON	ITIC	NTU	COC	ACU	NTLC	CHC
2000	0	14	0	0	11	100	74	100	95	97	92
1999	0	—	0	0	8	—	69	88	84	—	—

National Journal Ratings

	1999 LIB	—	1999 CONS		2000 LIB	—	2000 CONS
Economic	46%	—	52%		0%	—	86%
Social	32%	—	67%		43%	—	56%
Foreign	40%	—	56%		36%	—	58%

Key Votes of the 106th Congress

1. Educ. Savings Accts.	Y	5. Review Movie Violence	Y	9. NATO War in Serbia	Y
2. Prescrip. Drug Benefit	N	6. Gun Show Bckgrnd. Checks	N	10. Table Cuba Travel Ban	Y
3. Delay Ergonomic Standards	Y	7. Ban Part.-Birth Abortion	Y	11. Nuclear Test-Ban Treaty	N
4. Phase Out Estate Tax	Y	8. Broaden Hate Crimes List	N	12. Perm. Trade with China	Y

Election Results

2000 general	Orrin G. Hatch (R)	504,803	(66%)	($3,130,550)
	Scott N. Howell (D)	242,569	(31%)	($296,839)
	Other	22,332	(3%)	
2000 primary	Orrin G. Hatch (R)	unopposed		
1994 general	Orrin G. Hatch (R)	357,297	(69%)	($4,209,993)
	Pat Shea (D)	146,938	(28%)	($311,491)
	Others	15,088	(3%)	

Sen. Robert Bennett (R)

Elected 1992, seat up 2004, 2d term; b. Sept. 18, 1933, Salt Lake City; home, Salt Lake City; U. of UT, B.S. 1957; Mormon; married (Joyce).

Military Career: Chaplain, Army Natl. Guard, 1957–60.

Professional Career: Staff Aide, U.S. Rep. Sherm Lloyd, 1962; Staff Aide, U.S. Sen. Wallace F. Bennett, 1963; Cong. Liaison, U.S. Dept. of Transp., 1969–70; Pres., Robert Mullen P.R., 1970–74; P.R. Dir., Summa Corp., 1974–78; Pres., Osmond Communications, 1978–79; Chmn., American Computers Corp., 1979–81; Pres., Microsonics Corp., 1981–84; CEO, Franklin Quest Co., 1984–91; Chmn., UT Educ. Strategic Plng. Comm., 1988.

DC Office: 431 DSOB, 20510, 202-224-5444; Fax: 202-228-1168; Web site: www.senate.gov/~bennett.

State Offices: Cedar City, 435-865-1335; Ogden, 801-625-5676; Provo, 801-379-2525; Salt Lake City, 801-524-5933; St. George, 435-628-5514.

Committees: *Appropriations*: Energy & Water Development; Foreign Operations; Interior; Legislative Branch (RMM); Transportation. *Banking, Housing & Urban Affairs*: Economic Policy; Financial Institutions (RMM); Securities & Investment. *Governmental Affairs*: International Security, Proliferation & Federal Services; Investigations (Permanent). *Small Business. Joint Economic Committee* (6th of 10 Sens.).

Group Ratings

	ADA	ACLU	AFS	LCV	CON	ITIC	NTU	COC	ACU	NTLC	CHC
2000	5	29	0	0	11	100	72	100	95	97	92
1999	0	—	0	0	8	—	71	94	84	—	—

National Journal Ratings

	1999 LIB —	1999 CONS		2000 LIB —	2000 CONS
Economic	40%	57%		0%	86%
Social	36%	59%		44%	55%
Foreign	23%	67%		17%	75%

Key Votes of the 106th Congress

1. Educ. Savings Accts.	Y	5. Review Movie Violence	Y	9. NATO War in Serbia	N
2. Prescrip. Drug Benefit	N	6. Gun Show Bckgrnd. Checks	N	10. Table Cuba Travel Ban	Y
3. Delay Ergonomic Standards	Y	7. Ban Part.-Birth Abortion	Y	11. Nuclear Test-Ban Treaty	N
4. Phase Out Estate Tax	Y	8. Broaden Hate Crimes List	N	12. Perm. Trade with China	Y

Election Results

1998 general	Robert Bennett (R)	316,652	(64%)	($1,546,219)
	Scott Leckman (D)	163,172	(33%)	($265,494)
	Others	15,085	(3%)	
1998 primary	Robert Bennett (R)	unopposed		
1992 general	Robert Bennett (R)	420,069	(55%)	($3,339,325)
	Wayne Owens (D)	301,228	(40%)	($1,904,750)
	Others	37,182	(5%)	

FIRST DISTRICT

In May 1869, a motley crowd of Irish and Chinese laborers, teamsters, engineers, train crews, officials and guests from California and Salt Lake City gathered in Promontory Point, Utah, to watch the opening of the transcontinental railroad. The Union Pacific train was late and Leland Stanford raised his hammer and totally missed the golden spike, but an alert telegrapher mimicked the sound over the wire and a photographer recorded the scene for posterity: United at last were the civilized East and the mostly untamed West. Here, beyond sight of the snow-capped mountains crossed by the Mormon pioneers, the salt flats still stretch out endlessly; the rail lines now pass north of here, and Promontory Point lies on uninhabited flat land beside the Great Salt Lake. Back in the middle 1980s the lake was rising and threatened to cover the historic site; the state legislature passed a law forbidding it to rise above a certain level and the local county commissioners called for a day of prayer for drought in May 1986; finally, for whatever reason, the lake level fell and the state didn't have to pump water through canals that would have formed a vast new lake in the salt flats to the west.

The 1st Congressional District includes the western half of Utah, from Promontory Point down to the small boom towns of Cedar City and St. George and to the Arizona and Nevada borders near Las Vegas, where the Colorado River flows south through Glen Canyon into Arizona; Zion National Park is in the south, there is mining country in the center and the desert lies west of the lake. Sixty percent of the people in this district live along the Wasatch Front, a thin strip of land on the east side of the Lake between the salt flats and the Wasatch Mountains. It takes in Brigham City and Logan near the Idaho border, goes south through Ogden, an old railroad town on the Union Pacific line and the nearest station stop to Promontory Point, and then proceeds through a strip of suburbs to the salt flats northwest of downtown Salt Lake City near the airport. The rest of the 1st's voters live in small communities, many entirely Mormon, in central and southern Utah.

The congressman from the 1st District is James Hansen, a Republican first elected in 1980. Hansen grew up in Farmington, Utah, served in the Navy, worked as an insurance agent and head of a land development company. He was elected to the City Council in Farmington, just north of Salt Lake City, and then to the Utah House in 1972, at 40; he was speaker in 1979 and 1980. In 1980 he ran against incumbent Democratic Congressman Gunn McKay and won 52%–48%; except in 1986 and 1990, he has won by wide margins ever since. Hansen, who describes himself as a "common kid from Utah," is now the chairman of the House Resources Committee, and also holds a senior seat on Armed Services. He was chairman of the ethics committee in 1997 and 1998, where he and ranking Democrat Howard Berman, for months the committee's only members, turned it around from the partisan circus it had been in 1996 and put through a set of reforms. In 1999 Hansen got his wish and left the committee.

Hansen has often decried what he considers extremist environmental groups; he called a Sierra Club plan to drain Lake Powell "ridiculous." He worked to complete the Central Utah Project to bring Colorado River water to the Wasatch Front in 1992, and helped crack down on cheap water rates in the Central Valley of California. He favors "multiple uses" of public land, including mining, timber, ranching and grazing. He was outraged when Bill Clinton created the Grand Staircase-Escalante National Monument in September 1996: "Without any public input, without any consideration under the National Environmental Policy Act and any consultation with Utah's elected officials, President Clinton with one stroke of the pen made a decision that will steal over $1 billion from Utah's school children and end up costing the state of Utah over $6.5 billion." In response, he sponsored bills to limit the president's power to create national monuments and to allow the Bureau of Land Management to turn over lands to state governments to manage. The end result was the Utah Land Exchange Act of 1998, which turned over federal lands and cash to Utah in compensation for about half of the national monument lands. In 1999 Hansen moved to halt implementation of an agreement between Governor Mike Leavitt and Interior Secretary Bruce Babbitt on Utah wilderness legislation, calling for a study of the effect on the Utah Test and Training Range first; that same year he nabbed the number H.R. 1500, used by former Democratic Congressman Wayne Owens to introduce Utah wilderness bills, to produce his own version requiring that wilderness designations be made within 10 years. In 2000 he introduced a bill to vastly increase the insurance costs for shipping nuclear waste to the proposed repository on the Skull Valley Band of the Goshute Indians' land west of Salt Lake City, and he also introduced Senator Bob Bennett's bill for an exchange of lands between Utah and the federal government.

Hansen worked to produce the national parks law of 1998. His first version was beaten badly, as Clinton threatened a veto and many Republicans opposed it at the behest of environmental groups. Hansen dropped some pet provisions, including the set-aside of the San Rafael Swell canyonlands, and a week later it passed with bipartisan support. The law set up a competitive bidding process for park concessions and kept 80% of concessionaire fees in the local site; it also required a study of whether proposed national parks are worthy of the designation.

In January 2001 Hansen called Bill Clinton's last-minute declaration of nearly one-third of federal forest lands off limits to logging "reckless" and "one of the most egregious abuses of the Clinton administration." It was delayed two months by the Bush administration. In February 2001 Hansen launched a formal review of all of Clinton's national monument designations, but said that he would not support changes unless they had broad support. Hansen also tackled the Endangered Species Act, which has been up for reauthorization since 1991. He argues that the Fish and Wildlife Service "has skewed it until you can't recognize it" by listing more than 2,000, mostly minor species; "the intent of Congress was to protect the big stuff," he says, like the bald eagle and the grizzly bear. In April he set up a bipartisan working group on the ESA. He applauded the Bush administration move in April to make it more difficult for outside groups to get the Fish and Wildlife Service to act on petitions to list species as endangered; this was a move largely supported by Babbitt as well. Hansen has called for more natural gas production on federal lands

On the Armed Services Committee, Hansen fought successfully to save Hill Air Force Base, Utah's largest employer, from the base closing commission in 1995. He has opposed the Clinton "privatization in place" plan designed to keep politically sensitive depot bases open in California and Texas, and has attacked the Pentagon for setting criteria that undercut Hill. "Hill Air Force Base wouldn't be there if it weren't for me and my staff," he said on election night 1998. Hansen is co-chairman of the Congressional Task Force on Tobacco and Health. In May 1998 he proposed a tobacco bill with a $1.50 per pack cigarette tax, the provisions sought by former Surgeon General Everett Koop, and with 55% of revenues devoted to lowering the deficit; it did not pass. In July 1998 he came within seven votes of getting the House to eliminate tobacco subsidies. In 2000 he sought to put graphic warnings on cigarette packages. Another Hansen cause: disclosure of the terms of private mortgage insurance, which is required on low-down-payment mortgages but which, as Hansen found out with his Crystal City, Virginia, condominium, is very hard to cancel when the borrower has built up the required equity. Hansen's bill to require disclosure of how to cancel passed the House 421–7 in April 1997; he persuaded Alfonse D'Amato to pilot a similar measure through the Senate, and it became law. "They picked on the wrong guy," Hansen said about his insurers. He sponsored a bill to allow beneficiaries of deceased persons to receive $10,000 for organ donations.

Hansen was re-elected by 68%–30% in 1996 and 1998 and 69%–27% in 2000. Redistricting should pose no problem for him.

Cook's Call *Safe*. Hansen is safely settled in this heavily Republican district.

THE PEOPLE: Pop. 2000: 765,156; Pop. 1990: 574,205, up 33.3% 1990–2000. 91.2% White, 0.9% Black, 1.2% Asian, 0.9% Amer. Indian, 0.3% Hawaiian, 1.9% Two+ races, 3.7% Other; 7.7% Hispanic Origin.

2000 Presidential Vote

Bush (R)	193,635	(72%)
Gore (D)	59,858	(22%)
Nader (Green)	8,742	(3%)
Others	5,540	(2%)

1996 Presidential Vote

Dole (R)	129,273	(59%)
Clinton (D)	64,104	(29%)
Perot (I)	22,893	(10%)
Others	4,548	(2%)

Rep. James V. Hansen (R)

Elected 1980, 11th term; b. Aug. 14, 1932, Salt Lake City; home, Farmington; U. of UT, B.A. 1960; Mormon; married (Ann).

Military Career: Navy, 1951–55.

Elected Office: Farmington City Cncl., 1962–72; UT House of Reps., 1972–80, Speaker, 1978–80.

Professional Career: Insurance agent, 1961–80; Land developer, 1970–80.

DC Office: 242 CHOB 20515, 202-225-0453; Fax: 202-225-5857; Web site: www.house.gov/hansen.

District Offices: Ogden, 801-393-8362; St. George, 435-628-1071.

Committees: *Armed Services* (4th of 32 R): Military Procurement; Military Readiness. *Resources* (Chmn. of 28 R).

Group Ratings

	ADA	ACLU	AFS	LCV	CON	ITIC	NTU	COC	ACU	NTLC	CHC
2000	0	14	0	7	22	94	66	85	95	76	100
1999	10	—	0	13	2	—	54	96	84	—	—

National Journal Ratings

	1999 LIB	—	1999 CONS		2000 LIB	—	2000 CONS
Economic	16%	—	78%		18%	—	76%
Social	4%	—	91%		36%	—	63%
Foreign	31%	—	69%		12%	—	78%

Key Votes of the 106th Congress

1. Patient Bill of Rights	N	5. Bar RU-486 $ for FDA	Y	9. NATO War in Serbia	N
2. Accelerate Min. Wage	N	6. Display 10 Commandments	Y	10. Perm. Trade with China	Y
3. Strike Ban on Ergo. Stnd.	N	7. Gun Show Bkgrnd. Checks	N	11. Debt Relief for 3rd World	N
4. Ovrd. Estate Tax Veto	Y	8. Ban Part.-Birth Abortion	Y	12. Drop Cuba Econ. Embargo	N

Election Results

2000 general	James V. Hansen (R)	180,591	(69%)	($338,572)
	Kathleen Collinwood (D)	71,229	(27%)	($74,137)
	Other	2,380	(4%)	
2000 primary	James V. Hansen (R)	unopposed		
1998 general	James V. Hansen (R)	109,708	(68%)	($291,891)
	Steve Beierlein (D)	49,307	(30%)	($284,627)
	Others	3,070	(2%)	

SECOND DISTRICT

The center of Utah and of the Mormon Church is Temple Square, illuminated by 300,000 lights during Christmas week, and nestled beneath the towering, snow-capped mountains that flank Salt Lake City. Here you can find the Mormon Tabernacle, home of the famous choir, and the Temple itself, crowned with the golden angel Moroni. Two long blocks north is the state Capitol, four blocks south is City Hall, and all around are Salt Lake City's impressive skyscrapers. Ironically, Salt Lake City is the least Mormon and most cosmopolitan part of Utah, with the state university and businesses bringing in outsiders. Some think it now has a non-Mormon majority, but most likely it doesn't; it grew by 14% in the 1990s, and the metro area has 1.3 million people now, but much of that growth is internally generated by Utah's large Mormon families.

Utah's 2d Congressional District, which includes most of Salt Lake County, has somewhat fewer families and children than the other two Utah districts. Its current boundaries exclude the western suburbs on the flats out toward the Great Salt Lake, which lean toward the Democrats—an attempt by the Republican legislature to help Republican chances. The 2d has most of Utah's affluent people, living in Salt Lake City and suburbs like East Millcreek, Holladay and Cottonwood, right next to the Wasatch Mountains, which rise at that point to 11,000 feet. It's just a 20-minute drive—well, 30—from offices to ski slopes, as Utah boosters like to tell prospective new residents. The district also includes a string of suburbs south of Salt Lake City: West Jordan, South Jordan, Murray, Sandy, Draper, Riverton, Bluffdale. By national standards, this is a Republican district, but it is the most Democratic of Utah's three House seats, and has been seriously contested in most elections since 1970. Since 1992, control of its congressional seat has gone through a revolving door and has been held by two Democrats and two Republicans—including two women and two men, and some peculiar personalities for a supposedly straight-laced area; none won more than 56% of the vote.

The latest congressman from the 2d District is Jim Matheson, a Democrat elected in 2000. He is an heir to one of Utah's most respected political families: His father Scott Matheson was elected governor in 1976 and 1980. Matheson grew up in Salt Lake City, graduated from Harvard and interned on Capitol Hill for Speaker Tip O'Neill. He worked for the Environmental Policy Institute, and then earned an M.B.A. from UCLA. Matheson returned to Salt Lake City to join Bonneville Pacific, an energy development company, where he was a project development manager. In 1992 he moved to Energy Strategies, a consulting firm, where he was a senior associate. In 1998 Matheson started his own business, the Matheson Group, to help businesses adapt to electricity deregulation, but he closed his office a year later to start campaigning. He served four years on the Salt Lake Public Utilities Board.

Matheson benefited enormously from fratricide among Republicans, which was prompted by the volatile behavior of two-term Congressman Merrill Cook. Cook was elected in 1996 when Republican Congressman Enid Greene Waldholtz turned out to have problems—to say the least. She had run (as Enid Greene) and lost a bid for an open seat in 1992; in August 1993 she married Joe Waldholtz, reportedly a rich political operative from Pennsylvania, and in 1994 she ran again and won against Democratic Representative Karen Shepherd and spent nearly $2 million, some $1.6 million of it supposedly her own money. Questions about Enid Waldholtz's personal finances and how she had paid for the campaign soon arose, and in November 1995 Joe Waldholtz disappeared for several days before turning himself over to the police. It became clear that he had embezzled the money from her father; she said he had passed it off as his own. In March 1996, she bowed to pressure from Utah and Washington and announced she would not seek re-election.

In stepped Cook, who got barely enough votes at the May 1996 party convention to make it onto the primary ballot. His primary opponent, Todd Neilson, charged that Cook would cut Social Security; Cook had written his Harvard Business School thesis on how to make Social Security fiscally sound and favored restructuring and portable private pensions. Cook, spending liberally of his own money, just barely beat Neilson in June, 52%–48%. In the general election Cook again peppered the district with TV ads and mailings, spending $1 million altogether, $866,000 of it his own. Against Democratic nominee Ross Anderson, Cook won 55%–42%.

Cook soon became known for his temper tantrums, staff turnover and ongoing feud with fellow Utah colleague Chris Cannon, and many Republicans in early 2000 saw him as vulnerable. Former Cannon chief of staff Mark Emerson talked about taking on Cook, but instead Emerson became the top consultant for millionaire businessman and political novice Derek Smith, who won enough support at the party nominating convention to force a primary. Cook attacked Smith for failing to pay Social Security and payroll taxes at his former company and for refusing to identify the purchaser of $500,000 in stock in another company which Smith used to finance his campaign. Smith responded that his business problems were typical of start-up firms, and he attacked Cook for allegedly using obscenities to refer to female staff members and for converting to personal use frequent flier miles that he earned on government trips. Six days before the primary, they faced off in a 45-minute confrontation outside the federal building in Salt Lake City—while reporters looked on—that was a continuation of their personal assaults and ended only when aides pulled the two away from each other. "The confrontation looked and sounded more like a schoolyard dust-up than a political debate," reported *The Salt Lake Tribune*. Smith won the primary 59%–41%; Cook was the only House Republican to lose his primary in 2000. Cook responded by blaming former employees and denouncing House Republican leaders for withholding full support.

In the general election, Matheson began with better name recognition. He played down his party affiliation and emphasized that he differed from most Democrats on gun licensing and registration and criticized Al Gore's prescription drug plan for Medicare. Smith campaigned on local antipathy toward Democrats—emphasizing Bill Clinton's creation of the Grand Staircase-Escalante National Monument by executive order in 1996—and contended Matheson was trying to run as a Republican. Smith sold $830,000 in stock to finance his campaign and benefited from about $1 million worth of advertisements paid for by national Republicans, more than four times what Democrats spent on Matheson. But Matheson's name—he even used his father's old campaign slogan, "Matheson Makes Sense"—plus voter malaise with Republicans proved mightier than Smith's money. Matheson won 56%–41%. In the House, he joined the New Democratic Coalition and got seats on the Budget, Science, and Transportation and Infrastructure Committees. He voted against George W. Bush's income-tax rate cut, but supported repeal of the marriage penalty and the estate tax.

Salt Lake City, which has had its share of problems in preparing to host the 2002 Winter Olympics, likely will become a battleground again in its House election. Republicans control redistricting, and will probably change the boundaries to make the district more Republican. The district needs to add 42,000 people, who will presumably come from fast-growing Republican suburbs, and some of its Democratic precincts may be put in other districts. But Matheson's 2000 margin was impressive, and even with redistricting he will likely be hard to beat in 2002.

Cook's Call *Competitive.* Matheson's solid 56%–41% win in 2000 belies the very marginal nature of this district, and Matheson could have problems in 2002. But his late father was a very popular governor and his moderate voting record could insulate him from Republican attacks. Matheson also intends to challenge in court any redistricting plan he feels is unfair.

THE PEOPLE: Pop. 2000: 702,102; Pop. 1990: 574,412, up 22.2% 1990–2000. 89.4% White, 0.9% Black, 2.2% Asian, 0.7% Amer. Indian, 0.7% Hawaiian, 2.2% Two+ races, 3.8% Other; 8.7% Hispanic Origin.

2000 Presidential Vote			1996 Presidential Vote		
Bush (R)	148,244	(57%)	Dole (R)	111,166	(47%)
Gore (D)	88,077	(34%)	Clinton (D)	96,037	(41%)
Nader (Green)	19,100	(7%)	Perot (I)	22,143	(9%)
Others	5,477	(2%)	Others	6,619	(3%)

Rep. Jim Matheson (D)

Elected 2000, 1st term; b. Mar. 21, 1960, Salt Lake City; home, Salt Lake City; Harvard, B.A. 1982; U.C.L.A., M.B.A. 1987; Mormon; married (Amy).

Professional Career: Staff, Environmental Policy Inst., 1982–85; Project Dev. Mgr., Bonneville Pacific, 1987–91; Sr. Assoc., Energy Strategies Inc., 1992–98; Founder & Pres., The Matheson Group, 1998–99.

DC Office: 410 CHOB 20515, 202-225-3011; Fax: 202-225-5638; Web site: matheson.house.gov.

District Office: Salt Lake City, 801-524-4394.

Committees: *Budget* (19th of 20 D). *Science* (19th of 22 D): Energy. *Transportation & Infrastructure* (32d of 34 D): Aviation; Highways & Transit.

Group Ratings and Key Votes: Newly Elected

Election Results

2000 general	Jim Matheson (D)	145,021	(56%)	($1,305,202)
	Derek W. Smith (R)	107,114	(41%)	($1,681,135)
	Other	7,466	(3%)	
2000 primary	Jim Matheson (D)	unopposed		
1998 general	Merrill Cook (R)	93,718	(53%)	($647,249)
	Lily Eskelsen (D)	77,198	(43%)	($677,327)
	Others	6,725	(4%)	

THIRD DISTRICT

The heartland of the Mormon Church in America is in a geographically isolated valley between 11,000-foot peaks of the Wasatch Range and the shores of Utah Lake. Here is Provo, the home of Brigham Young University, an institution long known for the rigorously conservative views of its faculty, the old-fashioned moral standards it encourages, and its welcoming of technological innovation. The Mormon commonwealth, after all, started off with a terrific shortage of both labor and water and was eager to use technology to make up for this and prosper in this fearsome terrain. In the 1990s this was one of America's high-tech centers, the home of WordPerfect and Novell and hundreds of other firms, some fleeing California's high taxes and cultural liberalism.

The 3d Congressional District includes Provo and Utah County and most of the west side of Salt Lake City and its suburb of West Valley. These two urban areas cast more than two-thirds of the district's votes; the rest are cast in towns scattered amid huge mountains, florid rock formations and deep canyons from Wyoming down to the Arizona border. Its northernmost point is in the Wasatch Range, and it includes the depressed uranium country in eastern Utah around Moab and the surreal rock formations of Canyonlands and Capitol Reef National Parks, described by John Wesley Powell in the 19th Century: "Wherever we look there is but a wilderness of rock. Deep gorges, where the rivers are lost below the cliffs and towers and pinnacles; and ten thousand strangely carved forms in every direction; and beyond them, mountains blending with the clouds." Today the area around Moab has one of the nation's premier stretches of whitewater, the famed Slickrock Trail for mountain bikes, dozens of unclimbed cliff faces, tree-lined back-country ski runs and a spidery maze of treacherous Jeep tracks; the Moab Citizens Alliance opposed development of additional luxury condominiums. Politically, the 3d District is one of the most Republican in presidential elections, and Utah County is one of the most heavily Republican areas in the United States. Bill Clinton finished a poor third here in 1992 with 22% of the vote and lost 58%–29% to Bob Dole in 1996; in 2000, Al Gore lost Utah County—the state's second largest—to George W. Bush 82%–14% and lost the district overall 72%–23% to Bush. Those figures are all the more striking because Republican redistricters for 1992 added the Democratic west side of Salt Lake County to make the 2nd District more Republican, which strengthened Democrats marginally in the 3rd.

The congressman from the 3d District is Chris Cannon, a Republican elected in 1996. Cannon is a great-grandson of Utah's first territorial delegate and counselor to Church President Brigham Young, George Q. Cannon, who had five wives and a lot of progeny. Chris Cannon grew up in Salt Lake City, practiced law, and from 1983–86 worked, sometimes controversially, in the Reagan Interior and Commerce departments, on coal surface mining and other issues. In 1987, with his brother Joe, he purchased and reopened the Geneva Steel plant near Provo, restoring 2,500 jobs. In 1988 they had a dispute about modernizing the plant. In 1990 Chris Cannon was bought out and set up his own venture capital investment firm. He was active in Republican politics, as was Joe, who ran for the Senate in 1992 and lost the primary 51%–49% to Bob Bennett.

In 1996 Chris Cannon ran for the 3d District seat held by Democrat Bill Orton, a conservative Democrat who first won it in 1990 after a fractious Republican primary. In the 1996 Republican primary, Cannon faced Tom Draschil, who called Cannon (a backer of Lamar Alexander for president) too moderate; Cannon said that Draschil was an extremist and had a lawn sign backing militia favorite Bo Gritz for president in 1992. Cannon won by only 56%–44%—a sign of how conservative the Republican core vote is here. In the general election, Cannon spent $1.8 million, $1.5 million of it his own money, against Orton's $709,000. He was helped when in September 1996, speaking in Arizona without consultation with Utah officials (including Orton), Bill Clinton announced that he was establishing a 1.7 million-acre Grand Staircase-Escalante National Monument in southern Utah. This was heartily opposed in the area: Much of the land was owned by a state school fund, which wanted to lease it for coal mining, and now would not get the revenue. Cannon ran an ad showing himself denim-clad, leading a horse, attacking Clinton, "I feel like I'm back in the 1850s again with the federal government encamped all around us." Orton said the designation was "a monumental blunder—pun intended." Orton carried the Salt Lake County portion, but Cannon won solidly in the Provo area and carried most of the rural counties, winning 51%–47%.

In the House, Cannon has a conservative voting record and has continued to attack the national monument. He supported what became the Utah Land Exchange Act of 1998. Even though he had support from Interior Secretary Bruce Babbitt, his proposal to set aside the San Rafael Swell was stripped from the year-end spending bill in 2000, reportedly because of opposition from Clinton's White House environmental adviser. Cannon got Clinton's signature in 2000 on his proposal directing a clean-up of uranium mill tailings on the Colorado River flood plain near Moab; but no money was provided, pending a study of options by the National Academy of Sciences. Clinton signed another Cannon bill to help state and local governments fight the spread of methamphetamines. On Judiciary, Cannon filed bills to ban both willful distribution of copyrighted material on the Internet and online gambling. With Democrat Anna Eshoo, he proposed to give consumers the opportunity to limit the use and disclosure of personal information on the Internet. Citing the close connections between Mormons and Jews, he has been a prominent booster of the Holocaust Museum, where he serves on the governing body.

Cannon's moment in the spotlight came during Clinton impeachment. He was one of the 13 House managers in the Senate trial prosecuting the case against the president. As it became clear that the Senate would not vote for removal, Cannon reflected that it was a mistake to release the salacious material in the Starr report. But he argued that it was Clinton who inserted such matters into public discussion, not only in his personal misconduct but in his official acts. In 1999, he set up the House Managers political action committee in response to impeachment, but it failed to generate much enthusiasm or money and he shut it down a year later.

In 2000 Cannon was opposed by a former Clinton White House intern who actually outspent him, but Cannon won 59%–37%. Cannon lost the district's slice of Salt Lake County, Summit County (the Park City ski resort) and the mining area of Carbon County. But he won Utah County, which cast nearly half the vote, by 66%–30%. Perhaps the biggest jolt in the campaign came the day before the election when Cannon was driving alone in his pickup truck in Provo, hit a patch of ice, slid off the road and tumbled down an embankment. A police officer said he was driving too fast, but did not charge him; Cannon, who had some bruises, said he was uninjured because he was wearing his seat belt, but his truck was destroyed. In redistricting, he may sacrifice some of his Republican base near Salt Lake City to aid the party's prospects in the 2nd District.

Cook's Call   *Safe.* Cannon's 59%–37% win in 2000 looks rather weak when compared with Bush's 72% here (his fifth-best showing in the nation), and this seat was held by conservative Democrat Bill Orton for six years. But it is highly unlikely that it will again fall into Democratic hands.

THE PEOPLE: Pop. 2000: 765,911; Pop. 1990: 574,233, up 33.4% 1990–2000. 87.2% White, 0.6% Black, 1.6% Asian, 2.3% Amer. Indian, 1.1% Hawaiian, 2.2% Two+ races, 5% Other; 10.7% Hispanic Origin.

2000 Presidential Vote		
Bush (R)	173,217	(72%)
Gore (D)	55,118	(23%)
Nader (Green)	8,008	(3%)
Others	5,738	(2%)

1996 Presidential Vote		
Dole (R)	121,472	(58%)
Clinton (D)	61,492	(29%)
Perot (I)	21,425	(10%)
Others	4,456	(2%)

Rep. Chris Cannon (R)

Elected 1996, 3d term; b. Oct. 20, 1950, Salt Lake City; home, Mapleton; Brigham Young U., B.S. 1974, J.D. 1980; Mormon; married (Claudia).

Professional Career: Practicing atty., 1980–83; Dpty. Assoc. Solicitor, Dept. of Interior, 1983–84, Assoc. Solicitor, 1984–86; Co-owner, Geneva Steel, 1987–90; Founder, Cannon Industries Inc., 1990–96.

DC Office: 118 CHOB 20515, 202-225-7751; Fax: 202-225-5629; Web site: www.house.gov/cannon.

District Office: Provo, 801-379-2500.

Committees: *Government Reform* (20th of 24 R): Census (Vice Chmn.); Energy Policy, Natural Resources and Regulatory Affairs. *Judiciary* (12th of 21 R): Courts, the Internet & Intellectual Property; Immigration & Claims. *Resources* (16th of 28 R): Energy & Mineral Resources; National Parks, Recreation & Public Lands. *Science* (14th of 25 R): Environment, Technology and Standards; Space & Aeronautics.

Group Ratings

	ADA	ACLU	AFS	LCV	CON	ITIC	NTU	COC	ACU	NTLC	CHC
2000	0	29	0	0	92	94	71	95	100	100	100
1999	10	—	0	6	6	—	59	92	92	—	—

National Journal Ratings

	1999 LIB	—	1999 CONS		2000 LIB	—	2000 CONS
Economic	30%	—	64%		6%	—	85%
Social	25%	—	72%		0%	—	79%
Foreign	0%	—	97%		0%	—	88%

Key Votes of the 106th Congress

1. Patient Bill of Rights	Y	5. Bar RU-486 $ for FDA	Y	9. NATO War in Serbia	N
2. Accelerate Min. Wage	N	6. Display 10 Commandments	Y	10. Perm. Trade with China	Y
3. Strike Ban on Ergo. Stnd.	N	7. Gun Show Bkgrnd. Checks	N	11. Debt Relief for 3rd World	N
4. Ovrd. Estate Tax Veto	Y	8. Ban Part.-Birth Abortion	Y	12. Drop Cuba Econ. Embargo	*

Election Results

2000 general	Chris Cannon (R)	138,943	(59%)	($340,723)
	Donald Dunn (D)	88,547	(37%)	($378,565)
	Other	9,858	(4%)	
2000 primary	Chris Cannon (R)	unopposed		
1998 general	Chris Cannon (R)	100,830	(77%)	($571,999)
	Will Christensen (AI)	20,720	(16%)	($6,197)
	Kitty K. Burton (Lib)	9,553	(7%)	

★ VERMONT ★

M aple syrup and Ben and Jerry's Ice Cream, tiny clapboard villages and carefully zoned towns complete with outlet malls, covered bridges and civil unions: Vermont is a mixture of the 19th and the 21st Centuries, with much of the 20th—its factories and suburbs, skyscrapers and shopping malls—left out. Not so long ago Vermont seemed an entirely antique state, almost as carefully preserved as its Shelburne Museum, with a barn and jail, railroad station and blacksmith shop, covered bridge, and 37 buildings of folk art. But it has been transformed by newcomers, who came here attracted to its antique look but have transformed its culture in their own image.

Vermont was first settled by flinty Yankees from Connecticut, and showed an independent streak from the beginning. After Ethan Allen's Green Mountain Boys repulsed the British in 1777, this was an independent republic for 14 years, claimed by New York and New Hampshire without avail, their argument settled when Vermont was admitted as the 14th state in 1791. The economy was almost entirely agricultural, as second sons and daughters from small New England farms struggled to scratch out livings from the rocky soil. In time they quit struggling and raised dairy cows instead, producing milk for the masses of New York City. Vermont developed commerce as well. With its legendary thriftiness, it accumulated capital that, invested wisely, was used to build the solid stone office buildings and courthouses, the thick-timbered houses and gold-topped state Capitol that have remained long after ramshackle wooden buildings of the 19th Century have crumbled into dust. But Vermont never developed labor-intensive industry, and so over the years it exported people, and aged. Today, millions of Americans have Vermont blood—far more than the 608,000 who live here now, many of whom have no Vermont roots at all. Two presidents were born here, but both made their careers elsewhere—Chester Arthur in New York, Calvin Coolidge in Massachusetts—while Vermont made no visible impression on two great writers who lived here for years—Rudyard Kipling and Aleksander Solzhenitsyn. From 1850 to the 1960s, as a result of continuous outmigration, Vermont's population hovered between 300,000 and 400,000.

Since then—perhaps the key date was 1963, when people started to outnumber cows—Vermont has changed rapidly. Its economy has boomed, led by leisure-time industries—ski resorts, summer homes—and IBM, with several big high-tech facilities around the Burlington area on the mostly undeveloped shores of glorious Lake Champlain. Vermont's tradition of cottage industries continues, with knitters seeking to overturn union-inspired federal bans on home production. Home-grown firms started by erstwhile Baby Boom rebels—Ben & Jerry's Ice Cream is the archetype, though some said its founders sold out when they sold the firm to Unilever in 2000—have flourished. The population rose from 390,000 in 1960 to 511,000 in 1980 and 608,000 in 2000. It hasn't been random settlement: While next-door New Hampshire, trumpeting its low taxes and aversion to government, attracted right-leaning migrants from Massachusetts happy to live in spanking-new developments and ravenous for low taxes, Vermont, proclaiming its desire to preserve the environment and the past, attracted left-leaning migrants from New York and elsewhere, willing to pay higher taxes and higher prices for the privilege of living in a seemingly pristine setting where the governor tries to confine Wal-Marts to the existing tiny downtowns. The result has been growth, not as lusty as New Hampshire's but also without as big a recession in the early 1990s. There is high-tech growth around Burlington but also a high dependence on tourism; as Vermont Preservation Trust Director Paul Bruhn says, "At least 30% of our economy is based upon Vermont being Vermont." People throng not only to ski resorts but to the Haskell Free Library and Opera House in Derby Line which spans the Canadian border; they protested when the skies over Breezy Hill, site of the annual Stellafane star watch, were threatened with bright lights from a proposed prison in Springfield.

Public policy played a part in the evolution of Vermont. Back in 1970, Republican Governor Deane Davis (the last Vermont native to hold the job), facing a primary challenge, pushed through a sweeping land use law (Act 250) that helped give Vermont its environmental reputation. Housing developments and new ski resorts were required to meet 10 environmental criteria and get the approval of a state commission. Davis also raised more money for education, authorized higher fines for water polluters and liberalized divorce laws. Since then, Vermont has passed its own

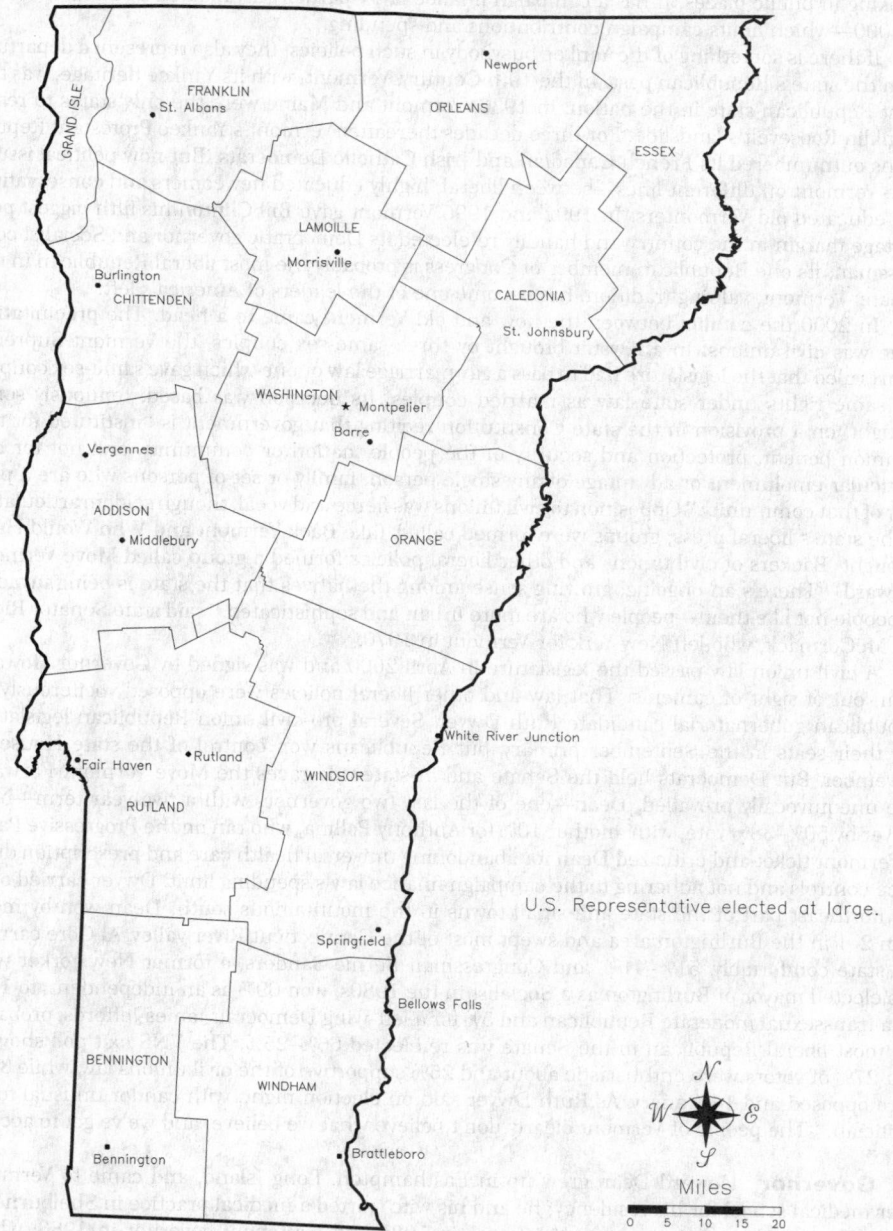

GRAND ISLE

FRANKLIN
• St. Albans

Newport

ORLEANS

ESSEX

LAMOILLE

• Morrisville

CALEDONIA

• Burlington

CHITTENDEN

• St. Johnsbury

WASHINGTON
★ Montpelier
• Barre

• Vergennes

ADDISON

ORANGE

• Middlebury

• White River Junction

• Rutland

WINDSOR

• Fair Haven

RUTLAND

U.S. Representative elected at large.

• Springfield

• Bellows Falls

BENNINGTON

WINDHAM

N
W   E
S

• Bennington

• Brattleboro

Miles
0 5 10 15 20

Clean Air Act that levies a tax on new cars that get less than 20 miles per gallon. It passed Act 60, which attempted to equalize property taxes throughout the state, and Act 200, which provided state support for regional planning boards. Although it has few gun control laws, Vermont has been busy regulating other things, banning clear-cutting of forests, requiring seat belt use, banning smoking in public places. It has a campaign finance law—partially invalidated by a federal court in 2000—which limits campaign contributions and spending.

If there is something of the Yankee busybody in such policies, they also represent a departure from the state's Republican past. In the 19th Century, Vermont, with its Yankee heritage, was the most Republican state in the nation; in 1936, Vermont and Maine were the only states to resist Franklin Roosevelt's landslide. For three decades thereafter Vermont's Yankee Protestant Republicans outnumbered its French Canadian and Irish Catholic Democrats. But now political issues slice Vermont on different lines—between liberal, highly educated newcomers and conservative, less educated old Vermonters. In 1992 and 1996 Vermont gave Bill Clinton his fifth biggest percentage margin in the country and handily re-elected its Democratic governor and Socialist congressman; its one Republican member of Congress is probably the most liberal Republican in the Senate. Vermont, valuing tradition, has become one of the leaders of America's left.

In 2000 the conflict between the new and old Vermont came to a head. The precipitating issue was civil unions. In a lawsuit brought by three same-sex couples, the Vermont Supreme Court ruled that the legislature had to pass a gay marriage law or one which gave same-sex couples the same rights under state law as married couples. Its decision was based, tenuously some thought, on a provision in the state Constitution reciting that government is "instituted for the common benefit, protection and security of the people, nation or community, and not for the particular emolument or advantage of any single person, family or set of persons who are a part only of that community." Opposition to civil unions was fierce and vocal, though seldom articulated in the state's liberal press; groups were formed called Take Back Vermont and Who Would Have Thought. Backers of civil unions and other liberal policies formed a group called Move Vermont Forward. "There's an ongoing, growing sense among the natives that the state is being invaded by people not like them—people who are more urban and sophisticated," said state Senator Richard McCormack, who left New York for Vermont in 1970.

A civil union law passed the legislature in April 2000 and was signed by Governor Howard Dean out of sight of cameras. That law and other liberal policies were opposed vociferously by Republican gubernatorial candidate Ruth Dwyer. Several pro-civil union Republican legislators lost their seats in the September primary, but Republicans won control of the state House in November. But Democrats held the Senate and in statewide races the Move Vermont Forward side unequivocally prevailed. Dean—one of the last two governors with a two-year term—beat Dwyer by 50%–38% vote, with another 10% for Anthony Pollina, who ran on the Progressive Party of Vermont ticket and criticized Dean for abandoning universal health care and prescription drug price controls and not adhering to the campaign finance law's spending limit. Dwyer carried only the northeast part of the state and small towns in the mountainous south; Dean won by more than 2–1 in the Burlington area and swept most of the Connecticut River valley. Al Gore carried the state comfortably, 51%–41%, and Congressman Bernie Sanders, a former New Yorker who was elected mayor of Burlington as a Socialist in the 1980s, won 69% as an independent, to 18% for a transsexual moderate Republican and 5% for a left-wing Democrat. James Jeffords, probably the most liberal Republican in the Senate was re-elected 66%–25%. The VNS exit poll showed that 27% of voters were enthusiastic about and 25% supportive of the civil unions law, while 32% were opposed and 14% angry. As Ruth Dwyer said on election night, with candor unusual for a politician, "The people of Vermont clearly don't believe what we believe, and we've got to accept that."

Governor Howard Dean grew up in Easthampton, Long Island, and came to Vermont after medical school for his residency; he and his wife started a medical practice in Shelburne in 1981. He was elected to the state legislature in 1982 and lieutenant governor in 1986; when Republican Governor Richard Snelling died suddenly in August 1991, Dean was given the news (while he was treating a patient) that he had become governor. Pleasant and articulate, he is probably one of the four or five most liberal governors on cultural issues, though he likes to say that he is the most fiscally conservative Vermont governor in 40 years.

Much of Dean's work has been on health care. In 1992 he tried to create a universal health insurance system, but it was rejected by the legislature in 1993, foreshadowing the fate of the Clinton health care plan. But he still says that "it is my view that health insurance ought to be universal, the right of every citizen in Vermont," and has tried to make that a reality step by step. He promoted an early childhood development program, offering home visits to babies, and his Dr. Dynasaur program guarantees free medical and dental care for children in families who make under $50,000. Adults with incomes below 150% of the poverty line get medical coverage for a nominal fee; health insurance companies must offer policies at the same cost to all, regardless of age or medical history. In 2000 he got Clinton Administration approval for making more elderly and middle-income people eligible for Medicaid so they could get prescription drug coverage at a 30% discount. As Dean admits, such reforms are easier in Vermont, with its small population and low poverty rates.

On education, Dean was prompted by a 1997 state Supreme Court ruling to get the legislature to pass Act 60, which levied a statewide property tax to provide each school district with $5,010 per student; taxes would be limited to 2% of income for those earning under $75,000. Half the districts would pay more property tax, half less. Districts wishing to raise money beyond that are required to donate a percentage of revenues to the state sharing pool—the shark pool, to Act 60 opponents—which ladles it out to other districts. But many strongly opposed the measure, some because it raised taxes, some because of fear of loss of local control. Dean has supported a limited school choice bill and, after a hazing incident forced cancellation of the University of Vermont's hockey season, an anti-hazing bill.

On welfare Dean has supported a 20-hour work requirement and the caseload has dropped about 40%. He wants to use state tax credits to encourage Vermonters to buy electric cars and has sought to get other states to join the Northeast Dairy Compact. When the state developed a large surplus in 2000—likely to balloon with capital gains from the sale of Ben and Jerry's to Unilever—he wanted to use the money to pay for projects usually funded by bonds, and not for a tax cut. Dean was a strong supporter of Vermont's 1997 campaign finance law, with its tight spending and contribution limits. But the day before the law took effect, he contributed $150,000 from his campaign treasury to the Democratic Party and, when a federal court overturned some of the provisions in 2000, he took his campaign out from under the law and raised and spent far more than its limits.

Dean was re-elected easily three times, with 75% in 1992, 69% in 1994 and 71% in 1996; Vermont and New Hampshire are the last states with two-year gubernatorial terms. But in 1998 and 2000 he got more vigorous opposition from Republican legislator Ruth Dwyer. She said she was on the side of the "forgotten Vermonter," opposed Act 60, and attacked Act 250 for squelching development where economically ailing local communities wanted it. She opposed Dean's proposal to expand childcare subsidies to higher-income families: It was against flinty self-reliance. This was a frontal attack on Vermont's governance over the past 30 years, and it struck something of a chord. Little known, poorly financed, Dwyer held Dean to a 56%–41% margin—by no means a defeat but far below his previous showings—and Democrats lost 12 seats in the state House.

In 2000 Dwyer came back again, this time better financed—she spent almost as much as Dean—and with an additional issue, the civil unions bill passed forced by the Supreme Court on the legislature and signed by Dean. She had opposition from a moderate Republican and prevailed 58%–41% in the September primary. Also running, as the nominee of the new Progressive Party of Vermont, was Anthony Pollina, who attacked Dean for abandoning universal health care in 1993 and prescription drug price controls in 2000, and stayed within Vermont's public campaign financing when Dean and Dwyer opted out. He said health care was a right and that school taxes should be based on income, not property.

Dwyer was an abrasive opponent. She charged that Dean offered bribes to push the civil unions bill in the legislature, but retreated later and said she was speaking from her own earlier experience in the state House. She attacked Dean's wife for not accepting Medicaid patients; evidently her medical group dropped one HMO in 1998 which had some Medicaid enrollees. She called for rolling back environmental regulations, reducing the government role in health care and school vouchers. She charged that Vermont was getting low grades on education scorecards. In a debate, Dean pointedly asked, "Where does tolerance fit into a Dwyer view?" She replied, "Governor, I wish you cared enough about the people of Vermont to stick to the issues and not bring up irrelevant things."

Dean's greatest problem turned out to be that Vermont requires its governors to win 50% of the vote; otherwise they are elected by the legislature, in which Republicans made significant gains. Dean won 50.4%–38%, with 10% for Pollina. So he was only narrowly elected, yet overall it was a clear rejection of Dwyer and the Take Back Vermont movement. Dwyer carried Catholics, who used to be the Democratic base, 48%–41%; the local bishop strongly opposed the civil unions law. She lost Protestants 49%–42% and those with no religion 61%–21%. She carried high school graduates 49%–41%, but lost college graduates 54%–32% and those with postgraduate degrees 69%–23%—the new Vermont speaking. She ran even among the elderly but far behind among those under 60. Most Vermonters clearly accepted, though they might not have initially voted for, civil unions. Dean said, "The number one task of the next governor is to establish a dialogue" on civil unions, because "we can't continue as a state where the feelings are so strong on either side."

Cook's Call   *Probably Safe.* The conventional wisdom has been that if Republicans were going to knock off Dean, it would have occurred last cycle when he was under fire for signing civil unions legislation, but he survived a spirited three-way race with 50%. There has been some recent polling that suggests that Vermont voters may be ready for a change and Republican interest in the race has increased. State Treasurer Jim Douglas and former state Human Services Secretary Cornelius Hogan are seeking the party's nomination.

Senior Senator   Patrick Leahy has held public office for most of his adult life. He grew up in Burlington, went to Georgetown Law School, then returned home to Burlington to practice law. He was elected Chittenden County state's attorney in 1966, at 26, and, after eight years in that post—and few public officials are scrutinized as closely as a local prosecutor—he was elected to the U.S. Senate at 34, the only Democratic senator elected in Vermont history. In October 1999 he became the 21st senator to cast 10,000 votes; he is closing in on the record of his predecessor, George Aiken, who served 33 years.

Leahy is ranking Democrat on the Judiciary Committee and was formerly chairman of Agriculture. A gadgeteer and fine amateur photographer, he was one of the first senators to go online; he begins his day by turning on his home computer, then heats up his coffee; his bookmarks include the Irish Times and the Grateful Dead. He has co-sponsored bills to remove export controls on encryption and opposed the Clinton Administration proposal to provide law enforcement agencies with encryption codes. He was the Senate's lead opponent of the 1996 Communications Decency Act, which was declared unconstitutional in 1997. He co-sponsored with Orrin Hatch the Digital Millennium Copyright law, passed to comply with the WIPO treaty, and with Jon Kyl the law making the theft of personal identification information a crime. He and Hatch also sponsored a satellite TV bill which would allow satellite services to transmit local stations' broadcasts. After considerable negotiation, he worked out an e-signature bill which passed the Senate unanimously, setting a national framework for giving on-line signatures legal status; it allowed consumers to agree to electronically signed contracts and consent to receiving records, while businesses had to verify electronic addresses. With Orrin Hatch and Charles Schumer he proposed a $125 million national cybercrimes support center. On the Napster controversy, on which he received 17,000 emails, he said, "You can't stop it. What we need to do, I think, is make sure copyrights and patent laws actually reflect the new reality."

Leahy has taken the initiative on other Judiciary issues. He has been concerned about medical privacy for some time, and led the fight to repeal portions of the 1996 health care law assigning medical identification numbers, and has sponsored a bill to allow individual access to and control of medical records. With Bob Torricelli he has sought to protect the privacy of personal information held by firms filing for bankruptcy. He has worked to expand funding to buy bulletproof vests for police officers. Appearing with former Death Row inmates who were exonerated, he sought to provide DNA testing for death row inmates who challenge their convictions. He blocked one bill inspired by the Firestone tire failures as too weak and promised to work with John McCain for a stronger measure. Inspired by the presence in Vermont of an accused Bosnian war criminal, he and Orrin Hatch moved to authorize the Justice Department Nazi-hunter unit to pursue contemporary war criminals. He has sought to legalize the presence in the U.S. of Haitian and Central American refugees living here for many years.

Another Leahy cause has been the elimination of land mines. Since 1989, he has been crusading against the export and use of landmines, which are easy and cheap to implant yet difficult and expensive to remove, and which injure thousands of civilians long after hostilities have ended. In 1994 he got the United Nations to approve unanimously their eventual elimination. In 1997 he and Chuck Hagel moved to support the treaty ban worked out in Ottawa; but the Clinton Administration, worried especially about U.S. forces in Korea, refused to support a total ban. Leahy continues to work to aid land mine victims and to deactivate the thousands of land mines still active in many parts of the world and to find alternatives for them. On foreign issues he tends to stand to the left of the Senate: He was one of three senators to vote against authorization of missile defense in March 1999 and has called for an end to the ban on travel ban to Cuba.

Leahy also serves on Appropriations and has procured funding for Vermont projects—$119,000 for the maple sugar industry, $400,000 to get rid of invasive species in Lake Champlain, $400,000 to repair brick walkways and add bicycle racks at the Church Street Marketplace, $2.4 million to compensate Vermont sheep owners for animals destroyed because of mad cow disease, $9.3 million for the Vermont Guard Aircraft Maintenance Complex (Leahy is head of the National Guard Caucus). He has sought to close old coal-fired plants grandfathered under the Clean Air Act and to impose an emissions control plan for mercury. He stopped his colleague James Jeffords's attempt to void Vermont utilities' contracts with Hydro-Quebec.

On the Agriculture Committee he worked with Chairman Richard Lugar on the Freedom to Farm Act of 1996. He worked hard to shape bill's conservation provisions to establish the Northeast Dairy Compact, to set milk prices in the six New England states. Separately, the Senate passed Leahy's Northern Forests bill, to protect privately owned New England and Upstate New York forests. In February 1998 he slipped into the Sea Grant College program a provision declaring Champlain one of the Great Lakes; the Michigan delegation squawked, and a bill passed in March revoked the designation but continued the Champlain research funds. With Lugar he has sought to expand the tax deduction for donations of food to the needy.

Leahy's overall voting record is quite liberal, except on some cultural issues. He has worked to confirm Clinton judicial appointments and stoutly defended Bill Clinton on impeachment. He criticized the Supreme Court decision stopping the hand counts of ballots in Florida: "Their credibility is so diminished, and their moral posture is so diminished, it will take years to repair."

To all this Leahy brings a quiet, thoughtful temperament and a puckish sense of humor, part of the Yankee heritage of Vermont, though his Irish and Italian ethnic origin is not standard Yankee. He is a Batman buff who had a bit part in the movie *Batman and Robin*. His standing in Vermont has been strong over the years: He narrowly survived the Republican sweep in 1980 and beat popular Governor Richard Snelling 63%–35% in 1986. In anti-incumbent 1992, against Republican state Treasurer Jim Douglas, who attacked him for voting for the congressional pay raise and for the loss of dairy jobs, he won 54%–43%—a decisive margin, but no landslide. In 1998 he had an easier time. The favorite for the Republican nomination, a Massachusetts businessman who had moved to Bennington to run, was upset 55%–45% by 77-year-old dairy farmer Fred Tuttle, the star of a 1996 documentary *A Man with a Plan* in which he is shown running for Congress. "I spend all my time in the barn. I'd just like to spend a little time in the House," Tuttle was shown as saying in his barely comprehensible accent. Of Leahy, Tuttle said in 1998, "I like Pat. He's a smart man, and he's done a good job." In October 1998, when *A Man With a Plan* was aired on PBS, Leahy had dinner at the Tuttles' home and contrasted this contest with the negative campaigns being waged elsewhere. "I had expected an opponent with deep pockets, not someone with holes in their pockets," Leahy said. Leahy won 72%–22%.

In 2000, though not up for re-election himself, Leahy actively campaigned for Governor Howard Dean and for Democratic legislative candidates. He was prompted by the outspoken opposition to the civil unions law, and arranged a joint appearance with his former Republican colleague Robert Stafford to denounce the tone of the campaign. Leahy's seat does not come up until 2004, and he looks in strong political shape; if re-elected he will pass Aiken's tenure in 2008.

Junior Senator Jim Jeffords, the senator whose departure in May 2001 from the Republican Party gave the Democrats a majority in the Senate, was elected to the House in 1974 and to the Senate in 1988, and over those years compiled one of the most liberal voting records of any Republican. He grew up in Rutland, son of a Vermont chief justice, went to Yale, served in the Navy, went to Harvard Law School and then returned to Shrewsbury in the Green Mountains to practice law. He was elected state senator in 1966, at 32, and then state attorney general in 1968 and 1970. In 1974, he was elected to the House and in 1988, when Senator Robert Stafford retired, to the Senate. There he has a record ever so slightly to the left of midpoint of the Senate, and has voted as often with Democrats as any Republican senator. In the Clinton years he voted for family and medical leave, motor voter, national service, the Brady bill and the 1994 crime package, despite Vermont's anti-gun control sentiment; in July 1993 he announced he was supporting the not-yet-written Clinton health care plan—the only Republican member of Congress who ever did. He was one of four Republican senators to vote for the Comprehensive Test Ban Treaty in October 1999, one of four to vote for the Democratic version of the minimum wage in November 1999; he voted for the Democratic version of the estate tax cut in July 2000 and in July 1999 cast the decisive vote for the Republicans' $792 billion tax cut only after inserting an increase in the Earned Income Tax Credit. In 1999 he backed a bill to increase funding of the National Endowments of the Art and the Humanities.

From 1997 to May 2001 Jeffords was chairman of the Health, Education, Labor and Pensions Committee. He was initially opposed by some conservatives, but backed by Majority Leader Trent Lott (they were part of the Singing Senators quartet); he promised, "I won't hold up legislation that all Republicans except me want." Sometimes he has opposed committee Democrats, led by Edward Kennedy. He took the lead on the Republican bill to allow worker-management consultation, vehemently opposed by labor unions. With Bill Frist he sponsored his own medical errors bill in June 2000, with voluntary reporting. He opposed the House version of the patients' rights HMO regulation. He opposed the Clinton proposal for 100,000 new teachers. On other issues he has worked with Democrats. His bill to allow import of prescription drugs from other countries passed 74–21 in July 2000 and was ultimately signed. He sponsored with Kennedy an Internet pharmacy bill, requiring disclosure of business locations and contact information. In July 2000 the Senate voted 58–40 for his bill to prevent insurance companies from using or requiring genetic information for determining coverage or rates. He proposed a "DrugGap" program to provide private health insurance with prescription drug coverage for low-income Medicare recipients. With Bill Frist and John Breaux, he proposed to create a $2,000 family health insurance tax credit, for those without employer-provided insurance and ineligible for Medicaid. He worked to overhaul the FDA and to double funding of the Ryan White CARE Act. He has backed funding for state services for the developmentally disabled and retaining federal benefits for the disabled who work. He has opposed school vouchers, even the limited number proposed by Republicans in Washington, D.C.

On other issues, he was the principal Republican co-sponsor of hate crimes legislation and of the bill to ban discrimination because of sexual orientation; he supported the Vermont civil unions law. Prompted by Chinese imprisonment of a Tibetan who had once studied at Middlebury College, he voted against permanent normal trade relations with China in order to retain the annual human rights review. He obtained funding for Vermont projects—$9.3 million for the Vermont Guard Aircraft Maintenance Complex, $2.4 million to compensate sheep owners for animals destroyed because of mad cow disease, $6 million for the Bennington Bypass, $1.25 million for technology upgrades for police departments. A history buff, he had a bill to catalogue and study unprotected Civil War sites, has sponsored a Revolutionary War and War of 1812 historic preservation act, and backs an historic corridor along the New York-Vermont border.

As the new chairman of the Environment and Public Works Committee, Jeffords is likely to follow the lead of environmental advocacy groups. It is unclear what the effect will be on the proposed Superfund changes sought by Republican Chairman Bob Smith and some Democrats.

In the runup to the 2000 election, Jeffords was able to strengthen his standing by using his seniority and clout. A February 1999 poll showed him leading Congressman Bernie Sanders, the Burlington Socialist, by only 42%–37%, and Sanders was giving serious thought to the race. Then in 1999 IBM, Vermont's biggest employer, announced it was shifting from defined-benefit to cash-balance pensions, a move that would sharply reduce the pensions of many workers over 45. Protest was loud, and Sanders leaked an IRS memo on the IBM plan and called for a 50% tax on a company's pension surplus if it didn't allow employees to opt out of cash-balance plans. Jeffords did not go as far, proposing instead that companies must notify workers of changes that would significantly reduce pensions, but after conferring with IBM executives was able to announce that the company would limit the scope of its pension conversion; it decided that workers over 40 with 10 years service could remain in the old plan. In addition, Jeffords supported a portability act that would allow workers to take retirement savings with them when they switched between private sector, public sector, and nonprofit jobs.

Then in November 1999 Jeffords obtained a major concession when he got Majority Leader Trent Lott and Speaker Dennis Hastert to agree to a two-year extension of the Northeast Dairy Compact and to reject the market-oriented reforms promised by the 1996 Freedom to Farm Act and supported by the Clinton administration. The compact allows much higher prices for milk in the Northeast, and is strongly opposed by Upper Midwest dairy farmers; overturning them was a major achievement. Meanwhile, House Democratic leaders, unwilling to give up a sure seat in Vermont, promised Sanders a seat on the Appropriations Committee if Democrats won a majority in the House. In November 1999 Sanders announced for reelection; Jeffords said, "I believe Congressman Sanders has made the decision that is right for Vermont."

That left Jeffords in strong shape for re-election. In 1994, against underfunded state Senator Jan Backus, he had won by only 50%–41%, a sharp decline from his 70%–30% win in 1988, when his real contest was in the Republican primary in which he beat a conservative 61%–39%. By early 2000 Jeffords's position was much stronger. He could demonstrate that his seniority had produced results from Vermont, and he had established a bipartisan reputation: he voted against both counts of impeachment, and Bill Clinton once referrred to him as "my favorite Republican." He was endorsed by NARAL and Planned Parenthood for his support of abortion rights, endorsed by the NEA and AFT for his opposition to vouchers and because he chaired their key committee, and co-endorsed by the Human Rights Campaign because of his support for gay rights.

Democrats had a contest in the September primary in which state Auditor Ed Flanagan beat Jan Backus by only 49%–46%. As state Auditor since 1992, Flanagan is a self-described "bulldog" street fighter, and had used his office to constantly criticize Governor Howard Dean's administration for wasting taxpayers' money on health care, child care, transportation, the environment, and the awarding of bids and tax breaks. He accused Jeffords of working in "lockstep" with Trent Lott and said he hadn't delivered sweeping change on universal health care, prescription drug benefits, and campaign finance reform. Playing little role in the campaign was the fact, announced by Flanagan in 1995, that he is gay, even despite the swirl of criticism of Vermont's civil unions law. Flanagan, who had not entered a civil union with his longtime partner, said this was "a great testament to Vermonters' commitment to human rights and to their insistence on judging an individual based on character and ability and performance and not on their private lives. It's a statement about what is possible, and where the rest of the country can go."

Jeffords ran far ahead in polls and declined to participate in debate unless two minor party candidates were included; he left a large part of his campaign treasury unspent. As he said in October, "After all these years, I don't think Vermonters have any misconceptions about me. They know who I am and what I stand for. Things look very good, to be honest with you." Jeffords won 66%–25%, and among demographic groups ran less well only with those under 30 (52%–43%). He won 70% and 71% among Protestants and Catholics and led 50%–41% among those with no religion. After the election, he said he might run for governor in 2002 if he lost his chairmanship, but that seems unlikely now. In a Senate equally divided, his penchant for bipartisan and his position at ideological midpoint makes him a potential major player. As he said in November, "There's no question that moderates on both sides—Republicans and Democrats—are aware that we have a great responsibility to try to make sure we can move forward to get things done. We don't want gridlock." The defeat of Rod Grams in Minnesota removed from Republican ranks its one Upper Midwest opponent of the Northeast Dairy Compact, which in early 2001 seemed likely to be renewed again. Since popular election of senators became law, no Vermont senator has been defeated for reelection; it doesn't seem likely to happen soon.

What prompted Jeffords's party switch in 2001? He had opposed the policies of Republican presidents, but had never before served in the Senate majority with a Republican president. His refusal to support the $1.6 trillion Bush tax cut left it one vote short in the Senate; the result was a $1.3 trillion cut, which Jeffords voted for even as he announced he was leaving the Republican Party. On education, he may have been dismayed that most of the negotiations on the Bush education program were conducted between Kennedy and Bush aide Sandy Kress. He sought $1.5 billion for special education in a meeting with Bush on April 3; after Bush aides agreed, he evidently decided that wasn't enough and demanded more. Much was made of the Bush White House's non-invitation of Jeffords to a ceremony honoring a Vermont teacher as teacher of the year. But no member of Congress was invited to the ceremony, and it is hard to believe that Jeffords switched parties because of such a small snub. He may have been more disturbed by conservative columnists' reports of further White House retaliation, including possible opposition to the Northeast Dairy Compact, but Democrats are unlikely to save that because it is fiercely opposed by the Democratic senators from Wisconsin and Minnesota. Jeffords attributed his switch to discomfort with a mostly conservative party, but such discomfort had not prompted him to switch during the previous 27 years. More likely he saw an opportunity to extract a chairmanship in return for switching, an opportunity unlikely to exist once Democrats got a majority by the replacement, which to many senators seemed increasingly likely, of Strom Thurmond by a Democrat.

Representative-At-Large Vermont's single House member is Bernie Sanders, a Socialist elected as an independent since 1990 but treated as a Democrat in the House. Sanders grew up in Flatbush, Brooklyn, the son of a paint salesman who had immigrated from Poland. "I know what it's like to live in a family without any money. Lack of money was a constant stress on my parents' relationship and in our household." He became involved in radical politics at the University of Chicago, then came to Vermont as part of the hippie invasion of 1968. His rumpled, tieless, sincere persona helped him win election as mayor of Burlington in 1981 by 10 votes, after losing four statewide races. There he governed ably for eight years, using the city's prosperity to start a municipal day-care center, expand low- and moderate-income housing, put a pollution control facility on Lake Champlain and switch the tax base from property to hotel and restaurant fees and a utility tax. In 1988, when Congressman Jim Jeffords ran for the Senate, Sanders ran for the House and lost to Republican Peter Smith. Two years later he ran again and reversed the result by capitalizing on Smith's support of the 1990 budget summit agreement and his vote for the ban on semiautomatic weapons. The National Rifle Association came out against Smith, and Sanders' opposition to gun control helped this urban-based Socialist carry 227 of Vermont's 251 cities and towns, and three gores and one grant. Sanders became only the third Socialist elected to the House, after Victor Berger of Milwaukee (1911–13, 1923–29) and Meyer London of Manhattan's Lower East Side (1915–23). "The reason why I am a democratic socialist is that I have a real problem with a society, the society in which we live today, in which the richest 1 percent of the population owns more wealth than the bottom 90 percent."

At first Democrats balked at accepting him in their caucus, but they have granted him seniority as a Democrat since 1991; he became ranking minority member on a subcommittee in 1997 over the objections of Elijah Cummings and, when a Banking subcommittee ranking position opened up in November 1997, he got that over the claims of Carolyn Maloney. Sanders adds to a heavily liberal voting record his own particular stamp. He formed a Progressive Caucus, with 53 members in the 106th Congress, with what is for the moment a quixotic agenda: progressive tax reform, a Canadian-style single-payer health care system, a 50% cut in military spending over five years, a national energy policy and—here Vermont speaks—support for family farms. He decries the tumbling of the barriers to international capital movement, and says the world economy is growing more slowly than at any time in the last 30 years; he joined conservative Republicans in voting against IMF funding.

But Sanders has also been a practical and sometimes successful legislator, gaining Republican allies in targeting what they consider corporate welfare. With Chris Smith of New Jersey, for example, he passed an amendment barring spending for defense contractor mergers ("payoffs for layoffs"). With Budget Chairman John Kasich, he got the House to pass a three-year phaseout of OPIC, which provides risk insurance for foreign investments. As a Banking subcommittee ranking member, he has criticized the IMF for subsidizing Russian mafias, undermining foreign economies and hurting the poor and middle class. He has been the House's leading backer of the Northeast Dairy Compact, which props up Northeast dairy prices. He got Majority Leader Dick Armey to agree to a vote in the 105th Congress banning "gag rules," HMO directives to doctors not to mention procedures not covered by insurance. He co-sponsored the 1998 law criminalizing identity fraud. His overall voting record is not entirely liberal and he has voted for relatively small amounts of additional spending.

Sanders backs a Canadian-style single-payer national health insurance system. Since the 1980s he has called for government programs to pay for prescription drugs, and led bus trips to Canada to buy drugs there. His bill passed the House, but not the Senate, mandating that drugs developed at taxpayer expense be offered at reasonable prices. He strongly backed Senator James Jeffords's bill to allow the import of prescription drugs and squawked loudly when he thought Jeffords and Republican leaders were watering it down. He seeks to restore funding to home health agencies lost in the Medicare reforms of 1997. He has called Social Security privatization "an umitigated disaster" and opposed the Medicare commission's recommended co-payments for home health care. He opposed the 1999 disaster reinsurance bill as "an unnecessary bailout of the insurance industry." When the Clinton Administration released oil from the Strategic Petroleum Reserve, he questioned the rationale and called for a temporary ban on exports of U.S.-refined heating oil. On local projects he worked for $1.5 million for a Burlington bus-train-bike path terminal, $1.2 million for low-income families to buy houses in Burlington, and $6 million to provide $50 a month free groceries to 10,000 Vermont seniors.

Sanders was re-elected 58%–31% in 1992, and considered running against Republican Senator Jim Jeffords in 1994, but decided not to. In 1994, after voting for the assault weapons ban and the crime bill with its gun control provisions, Sanders was opposed by the National Rifle Association-backed Vermont Sportsmen's Coalition. Sanders outspent state Senator John Carroll, but won by only 50%–47%. In 1996 Republican state Senator Susan Sweetser was expected to be a strong challenger. But a moderate Democrat may have hurt her more than Sanders; Sanders spent $942,000 and beat Sweetser 55%–33%. In pro-incumbent 1998, against a low-spending Republican and with no Democratic nominee, Sanders did better than ever, 63%–33%.

Sanders gave serious consideration to running against Jeffords in 2000. Polls showed him trailing only narrowly (42%–37% in February and 42%–39% in October). While he was pondering the race, IBM, the biggest employer in Vermont, announced it was shifting from defined-benefit to cash-balance pensions, a move that would reduce by as much as 40% the pensions of many workers over 45. Protest was loud and Sanders leaked an IRS memo on the IBM plan and called for a 50% tax on a company's pension surplus if it didn't allow employees to opt out of cash-balance plans and IRS disapproval of tax-exempt status for pension plans that discriminate by age. Jeffords did not go as far, proposing instead that companies must notify workers of changes that would significantly reduce pensions, but, after conferring with IBM executives, was able to announce that the company would limit the scope of its pension conversion and give greater protection to mid-career workers. Senators Tom Daschle and Bob Torricelli had been pressuring Sanders to run for the Senate, but House Democratic Leader Dick Gephardt promised him a seat on Appropriations if he remained in the House and Democrats won a majority. Auditor Ed Flanagan, one of two Democratic candidates for the Senate, said he'd run for the House if Sanders ran against Jeffords.

Against that background Sanders announced in November that he would run for re-election to the House. His re-election was not in doubt. The Republican nominee, Karen Kerin, is a woman who was formerly a man. The Human Rights Campaign endorsed Sanders. Also running was Peter Diamondstone of the leftist Liberty Union Party, which once supported Sanders. The only awkwardness for Sanders was the question of whom he would support for president and governor. Initially, he decided not to support Anthony Pollina, of the Progressive Party of Vermont, who took almost enough votes from Democrat Howard Dean to put him below 50% and send the election to the legislature. And after both party conventions, he declined to support either Al Gore or Ralph Nader, though he ultimately supported Gore.

Sanders won with 69% to 18% for Kerin and 5% for Diamondstone. But he ended up in a less strong position than he must have wished. If Sanders had run against Jeffords and won, he—not Jeffords—would have given Senate Democrats a 51–49 majority. Instead, he is still functionally part of the minority party in the House.

Cook's Call   *Safe.* Although Vermont is not as heavily Democratic as neighboring Massachusetts or New York, it has a Democratic core that helps insulate Sanders. He is unlikely to face a serious challenge in 2002.

Presidential politics   James A. Farley had a good laugh on Vermont in 1936 when he updated an adage to say "As goes Maine, so goes Vermont." Today's Vermont, liberal on cultural and foreign issues, not very conservative on economics, has become pretty solidly Democratic in presidential campaigns. Back in 1980, Ronald Reagan got his seventh lowest percentage here and John Anderson his best, 15%; in 1984 and 1988 Vermont was more Democratic than the nation; in 1992 and 1996 it gave Bill Clinton his fifth largest percentage margins. In 2000 Al Gore won 51%–41%, with 7% for Ralph Nader. The conflict between the old and new Vermonts is apparent in the VNS exit poll. Those without college degrees voted 48%–46% for Bush, but Gore carried college graduates 51%–36% and those with postgraduate degrees 62%–29%. The old divide between Protestants and Catholics has vanished; Bush carried them both by narrow margins. But Gore won those with no religion 64%–21%, with 12% for Nader.

The Vermont presidential primary, abolished for 1992, reappeared in 1996, but has achieved little notice; all the action is next door in New Hampshire.

THE PEOPLE: Pop. 2000: 608,827; Pop. 1990: 562,758, up 8.2% 1990–2000. 0.2% of U.S. total, 49th largest; 96.8% White, 0.5% Black, 0.9% Asian, 0.4% Amer. Indian, 1.2% Two+ races, 0.2% Other; 0.9% Hispanic Origin. 2.9% Unemployment. 2000 Voting age pop.: 461,304. 2000 Turnout: 297,146; 64% of VAP. Registered voters (2000): 427,354; no party registration.

POLITICAL LINEUP: Governor, Howard Dean (D); Lt. Gov., Douglas A. Racine (D); Secy. of State, Deborah Markowitz (D); Atty. Gen., William H. Sorrell (D); Treasurer, James H. Douglas (R); State Senate, 30 (16 D, 14 R); Majority Leader, Dick McCormack (D); State House, 150 (61 D, 83 R, 1 I, 4 Progressive, 1 vacancy); House Speaker, Michael Obuchowski (D). Senators, Patrick Leahy (D) and James M. Jeffords (I). Representative, 1 I at large.

ELECTIONS DIVISION: 802-828-2464; **FILING DEADLINE FOR U.S. CONGRESS:** July 15, 2002.

2000 Presidential Vote

Gore (D)	149,022	(51%)
Bush (R)	119,775	(41%)
Nader (Green)	20,374	(7%)
Others	5,137	(2%)

1996 Presidential Vote

Clinton (D)	137,894	(53%)
Dole (R)	80,352	(31%)
Perot (I)	31,024	(12%)
Others	9,179	(4%)

2000 Republican Presidential Primary

McCain (R)	49,045	(60%)
Bush (R)	28,741	(35%)
Other	3,569	(4%)

2000 Democratic Presidential Primary

Gore (D)	26,774	(54%)
Bradley (D)	21,629	(44%)
Other	880	(2%)

Gov. Howard Dean (D)

Assumed office, Aug. 1991, term expires Jan. 2003, 5th term; b. Nov. 17, 1948, New York, NY; home, Burlington; Yale U., B.A. 1977, Albert Einstein Col. of Medicine, M.D. 1978; Congregationalist; married (Judith).

Elected Office: VT House of Reps, 1982–86; VT Lt. Gov., 1986–91.

Professional Career: Practicing physician, 1981–91; Chmn., Natl. Govs. Assn., 1994–95; Chmn., Dem. Govs. Assn., 1997.

Office: Pavilion State Office Bldg., 109 State St., Montpelier, 05609, 802-828-3333; Web site: www.gov.state.vt.us.

Election Results

2000 general	Howard Dean (D)	148,059	(50%)
	Ruth Dwyer (R)	111,359	(38%)
	Anthony Pollina (PRG)	28,116	(10%)
	Other	5,939	(2%)
2000 primary	Howard Dean (D)	31,366	(84%)
	Brian Pearl (D)	4,357	(12%)
	Other	1,446	(4%)
1998 general	Howard Dean (D)	121,425	(56%)
	Ruth Dwyer (R)	89,726	(41%)
	Others	6,969	(3%)

Sen. Patrick Leahy (D)

Elected 1974, seat up 2004, 5th term; b. Mar. 31, 1940, Montpelier; home, Burlington; St. Michael's Col., B.A. 1961, Georgetown U., J.D. 1964; Catholic; married (Marcelle).

Elected Office: VT St. Atty., Chittenden Cnty., 1966–74.

Professional Career: Practicing atty., 1964–74.

DC Office: 433 RSOB, 20510, 202-224-4242; Web site: www.senate.gov/~leahy.

State Offices: Burlington, 802-863-2525; Montpelier, 802-229-0569.

Committees: *Agriculture, Nutrition & Forestry*: Forestry, Conservation & Rural Revitalization; Marketing, Inspection & Product Promotion; Research, Nutrition & General Legislation (Chmn.). *Appropriations*: Commerce, Justice, State & Judiciary; Defense; Foreign Operations (Chmn.); Interior; VA, HUD & Independent Agencies. *Judiciary* (Chmn.): Antitrust, Business Rights & Competition; Constitution, Federalism & Property Rights.

Group Ratings

	ADA	ACLU	AFS	LCV	CON	ITIC	NTU	COC	ACU	NTLC	CHC
2000	85	57	85	86	73	83	9	58	8	6	15
1999	95	—	100	100	51	—	5	41	4	—	—

National Journal Ratings

	1999 LIB	—	1999 CONS		2000 LIB	—	2000 CONS
Economic	75%	—	20%		82%	—	17%
Social	64%	—	31%		65%	—	34%
Foreign	78%	—	13%		95%	—	0%

Key Votes of the 106th Congress

1. Educ. Savings Accts.	N	5. Review Movie Violence	N	9. NATO War in Serbia	Y
2. Prescrip. Drug Benefit	Y	6. Gun Show Bckgrnd. Checks	Y	10. Table Cuba Travel Ban	N
3. Delay Ergonomic Standards	N	7. Ban Part.-Birth Abortion	Y	11. Nuclear Test-Ban Treaty	Y
4. Phase Out Estate Tax	N	8. Broaden Hate Crimes List	Y	12. Perm. Trade with China	Y

Election Results

1998 general	Patrick Leahy (D)	154,567	(72%)	($1,014,751)
	Fred H. Tuttle (R)	48,051	(22%)	
	Others	11,418	(5%)	
1998 primary	Patrick Leahy (D)	18,643	(97%)	
	Others	647	(3%)	
1992 general	Patrick Leahy (D)	154,762	(54%)	($1,202,445)
	James H. Douglas (R)	123,854	(43%)	($195,737)
	Others	7,123	(2%)	

Sen. James M. Jeffords (I)

Elected 1988, seat up 2006, 3d term; b. May 11, 1934, Rutland; home, Shrewsbury; Yale U., B.S. 1956, Harvard U., LL.B. 1962; Congregationalist; married (Elizabeth).

Military Career: Navy, 1956–59, Naval Reserves, 1959–90.

Elected Office: VT Senate, 1966–68; VT Atty. Gen., 1968–72; U.S. House of Reps. 1974–88.

Professional Career: Law clerk, 1962–63; Practicing atty., 1963–69, 1973–75; Shrewsbury Repub. Party Chmn., 1963–74; Town Agent, Grand Juror, 1964.

DC Office: 728 HSOB, 20515, 202-224-5141; Fax: 202-228-0776; Web site: www.senate.gov/~jeffords.

State Offices: Burlington, 802-658-6001; Montpelier, 802-223-5273; Rutland, 802-773-3875.

Committees: *Aging (Special). Environment & Public Works (Chmn.). Finance. Veterans' Affairs.*

Group Ratings

	ADA	ACLU	AFS	LCV	CON	ITIC	NTU	COC	ACU	NTLC	CHC
2000	55	71	57	71	20	80	44	73	36	60	31
1999	45	—	33	89	58	—	56	76	40	—	—

National Journal Ratings

	1999 LIB —	1999 CONS		2000 LIB —	2000 CONS
Economic	51% —	48%		52% —	47%
Social	54% —	45%		54% —	44%
Foreign	51% —	47%		89% —	5%

Key Votes of the 106th Congress

1. Educ. Savings Accts.	N	5. Review Movie Violence	Y	9. NATO War in Serbia	Y
2. Prescrip. Drug Benefit	N	6. Gun Show Bckgrnd. Checks	N	10. Table Cuba Travel Ban	N
3. Delay Ergonomic Standards	Y	7. Ban Part.-Birth Abortion	N	11. Nuclear Test-Ban Treaty	Y
4. Phase Out Estate Tax	N	8. Broaden Hate Crimes List	Y	12. Perm. Trade with China	N

Election Results

2000 general	James M. Jeffords (R)	189,133	(66%)	($1,889,243)
	Ed Flanagan (D)	73,352	(25%)	($1,054,977)
	Other	26,015	(9%)	
2000 primary	James M. Jeffords (R)	60,234	(78%)	
	Rick Hubbard (R)	15,991	(21%)	
	Other	1,204	(2%)	
1994 general	James M. Jeffords (R)	106,505	(50%)	($1,174,973)
	Jan Backus (D)	85,868	(41%)	($308,069)
	Gavin T. Mills (I)	12,465	(6%)	
	Others	6,834	(3%)	

Rep. Bernard Sanders (I)

Elected 1990, 6th term; b. Sept. 8, 1941, New York, NY; home, Burlington; U. of Chicago, B.A. 1964; Jewish; married (Jane).

Elected Office: Burlington Mayor, 1981–89.

Professional Career: Writer; Dir., Amer. People's History Soc.; Lecturer, Harvard U., 1989; Prof., Hamilton Col., 1989–90.

DC Office: 2135 RHOB, 20515, 202-225-4115; Fax: 202-225-6790; Web site: bernie.house.gov.

District Office: Burlington, 802-862-0697.

Committees: *Financial Services* (1st of 1 I): Domestic Monetary Policy, Technology & Economic Growth; International Monetary Policy & Trade (RMM). *Government Reform* (1st of 1 I): Criminal Justice, Drug Policy & Human Resources; National Security, Veterans' Affairs & Intl. Relations.

Group Ratings

	ADA	ACLU	AFS	LCV	CON ·	ITIC	NTU	COC	ACU	NTLC	CHC
2000	95	86	100	100	54	28	26	23	4	16	0
1999	100	—	100	100	58	—	30	8	12	—	—

National Journal Ratings

	1999 LIB —	1999 CONS		2000 LIB —	2000 CONS
Economic	75% —	23%		81% —	16%
Social	87% —	0%		94% —	0%
Foreign	61% —	37%		80% —	16%

Key Votes of the 106th Congress

1. Patient Bill of Rights	Y	5. Bar RU-486 $ for FDA	N	9. NATO War in Serbia	Y
2. Accelerate Min. Wage	Y	6. Display 10 Commandments	N	10. Perm. Trade with China	N
3. Strike Ban on Ergo. Stnd.	Y	7. Gun Show Bkgrnd. Checks	Y	11. Debt Relief for 3rd World	Y
4. Ovrd. Estate Tax Veto	N	8. Ban Part.-Birth Abortion	N	12. Drop Cuba Econ. Embargo	Y

Election Results

2000 general	Bernard Sanders (I)	196,118	(69%)	($323,561)
	Karen Ann Kerin (R)	51,977	(18%)	
	Pete Diamondstone (LU)	14,918	(5%)	
	Stewart Skrill (I)	11,816	(4%)	($21,501)
	Other	8,537	(3%)	
2000 primary	Bernard Sanders (I)	unopposed		
1998 general	Bernard Sanders (I)	136,403	(63%)	($529,499)
	Mark Candon (R)	70,740	(33%)	($103,631)
	Others	7,990	(4%)	

★ VIRGINIA ★

In Virginia, even as it helps lead the high-tech economy, traditions endure. Through nearly 400 years of history, Virginians have honored, and sometimes been fixated by, traditions going back to the Revolution and before. For half a century Virginia has been growing lustily, but the first state in the nation to elect a black governor still hews to a course close to its roots. In the first years after World War II, Virginia's growth came mainly from an expanding government, but in recent decades it has come more from a vibrant private sector. The first Virginia was a commonwealth ruled by a landed gentry which was, in the words of historian David Hackett Fischer, "elitist and libertarian." From the tobacco-growing counties emerged in the 1770s a group of leaders—George Washington, Patrick Henry, Thomas Jefferson, Richard Henry Lee, James Madison—who in learning, wisdom and strength of character, equal any such group from any similarly sized polity since Periclean Athens or republican Rome. They were slaveholders who insisted on liberty, armed men living on the marches of civilization who insisted on the rule of law, believers in racial inequality who set forth principles of equality that would in time form the basis of a non-racist society. The Virginia they led into the American Revolution was not only the most populous and the richest of the 13 colonies, it also was the indispensable creator of the Republic and the Constitution that has held together the world's greatest democracy.

After the Revolutionary War, gentry control continued even as Virginia was eclipsed in population and wealth by Pennsylvania and New York and, its tobacco fields all but exhausted, became a breeding ground for slaves. But Virginia had two more great heroes, Robert E. Lee and Stonewall Jackson, both of whom reluctantly and brilliantly fought for their state rather than their country. The state's leadership class was impoverished and embittered by the Civil War, so much of which was fought on Virginia soil. Industrialization was haphazard: Railroads were constructed to ship cotton up from the South and coal east to the seaports; textile mills were built in Southside towns and tobacco factories in Richmond; the giant Newport News Shipbuilding & Drydock Company was built by railroad magnate Collis Huntington. Politically, Virginia was ruled by a local gentry who worshipped their Revolutionary past and mourned their Lost Cause. They were pessimists, looking not for economic growth but for stability, bent on maintaining Virginia's segregation and content with its second-class economy. County courthouse organizations became the political machine of Harry Byrd, who ran Virginia politics from 1925, when he was elected governor, until 1965, when he retired from the Senate. In national politics, this machine lost battles more often than Lee lost on the battlefield, and less gallantly. But the machine succeeded in keeping most vestiges of the welfare state and racial equality out of Virginia, to the point of closing public schools in the 1950s rather than obeying federal court desegregation orders.

This "massive resistance" collapsed in the late 1950s, even as Virginia's demographics changed and it went through a quarter-century of political flux. The government-employee filled northern Virginia suburbs of Washington D.C. and the industrial Tidewater region around Norfolk and Newport News, plus the enfranchisement of blacks, provided a political base for liberal Democrats. But they were never quite a majority. In the 1970s they were held at bay by conservatives who left the Democratic Party and ran as independents or Republicans. In the 1980s three moderate Democrats were elected governor—Charles Robb in 1981, Gerald Baliles in 1985, Douglas Wilder in 1989—because they no longer represented an attempt to impose a labor-liberal agenda on an unwilling Virginia, and because they argued they could use government effectively to improve education and build Virginia's economy. Wilder's election was a national breakthrough, a successful attempt by a black politician to campaign and govern on equal terms; he won largely because of his margins in the Tidewater and Northern Virginia, where his pro-choice stand on abortion clearly helped, but he also ran solidly across the state. His fiscal conservatism, which resulted in sharp spending cuts in the early 1990s, like his elegant manners and thick Richmond accent, echoed Virginia's elitist and libertarian tradition.

Now Virginia seems to have developed ideological politics along party lines, where Republicans have made historic strides by winning majorities with traditional party platforms. George Allen was elected governor by a wide margin in 1993 as a Republican who believed in lower taxes,

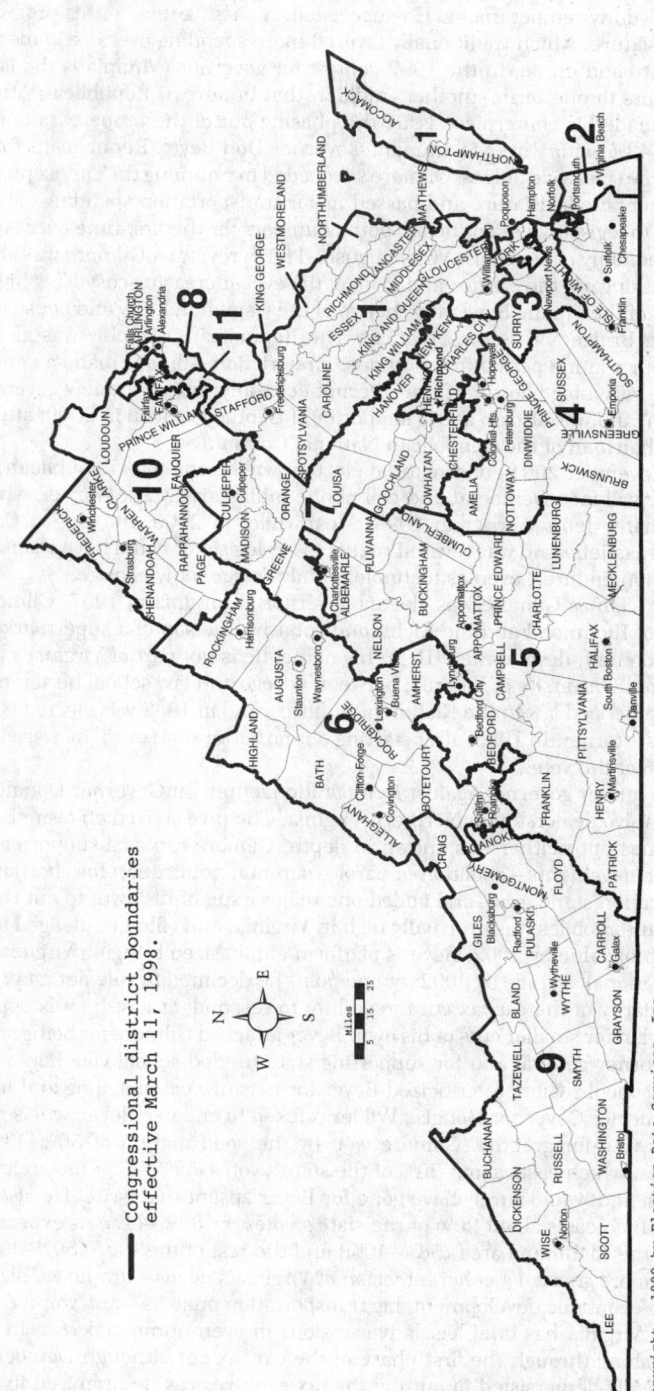

— Congressional district boundaries
effective March 11, 1998.

traditional cultural values, longer prison terms, and teaching basic skills, combining crunchy issue positions with a sunny temperament. He succeeded in passing most of his programs through a Democratic legislature, which traditionally favored more spending over discipline in the areas of education, welfare and crime. In the 1997 contest for governor (Virginia is the last state which limits its governors to one term, another tradition that endures), Republican Attorney General James Gilmore made his centerpiece issue the phasing out of the property tax on automobiles, and won a 56%–43% victory over Lieutenant Governor Don Beyer. Republicans for the first time swept the top three statewide offices. Gilmore succeeded in ramming the car tax phaseout through a reluctant Democratic legislature and passed major transportation spending. Then in 1999 he led Republicans to legislative majorities in both chambers for the first time ever. As the Internet- and high-tech economy of Northern Virginia gushed forth revenue, Gilmore was able to continue spending and phasing out the car tax, and to meet the ever-increasing cost of big highway projects, like the redesign of the Mixing Bowl interchange of the Capital Beltway and construction of a new Woodrow Wilson Bridge across the Potomac. The Republican assembly was also able to push through a 24-hour waiting period for abortions, a restriction Gilmore made a centerpiece of his agenda. Gilmore was a big booster of the Internet economy, one of the few governors to oppose Internet taxation, and was also an active supporter of George W. Bush in 2000; after the election, he was named chairman of the Republican National Committee.

Virginia's November 2001 gubernatorial election will be one test. Republican Attorney General Mark Earley will face Democrat and cell phone millionaire Mark Warner, who ran a strong race against Senator John Warner in 1996. Meanwhile, in 2000, the classic Capitol building designed by Thomas Jefferson was rewired so that every legislator could have a laptop on his desk: in Virginia tradition endures, even as technology and the economy change.

Governor James Gilmore was elected governor of Virginia in 1997. Gilmore grew up in the Fan district of Richmond and the Richmond suburbs, the son of a supermarket meat-cutter and a church secretary; despite the "III" in his name, he is not part of Virginia's ancestral elite. He graduated from University of Virginia; between college and law school he served in the Army. For 10 years he practiced law in the Richmond suburbs, and in 1987 was elected Henrico County commonwealth's attorney. In 1993, after starting out no better than even, he was elected attorney general with 56% of the vote.

In 1997, he ran for governor against Democratic Lieutenant Governor Donald Beyer, owner of a well-known Volvo dealership in Northern Virginia. The race started off even: both candidates had familiar names but neither was known in depth. Gilmore ran as a supporter of incumbent George Allen's achievements—abolition of parole, parental notification for abortions, welfare reform, strict education standards—and added one major issue of his own: to cut the car tax. The property tax on automobiles was unusually high in Virginia, and Gilmore pledged to cut it to zero on up to $20,000 of value by 2002. Beyer's platform emphasized bringing Virginia teachers' salaries up to the national average by 2002; at one point he declined to rule out a tax increase to do so. But the popularity of the car tax cut forced him to respond; at first he was opposed, then he came up with a plan for smaller cuts of his own. Beyer attacked Gilmore for being soft on polluters while he was attorney general and for supporting state funded school vouchers which could be used for private schools. Gilmore criticized Beyer for negative campaigning and for flip-flopping on the car tax. Former Governor Douglas Wilder refused to endorse Beyer, who some accused of taking the black vote for granted. Gilmore won by the solid margin of 56%–43%. He carried Northern Virginia, which casts about 30% of the state's votes, 52%–46%; the area has the state's highest car taxes, and would surely have gone for Beyer absent that issue. He also carried Tidewater Virginia, which casts about 20% of the state's votes, by 53%–44%. As expected, he won by wide margins in the Richmond area (58%–40%) and the rest of the state (59%–39%).

In office Gilmore showed a coherent vision of Virginia's needs—low taxes, high-quality education, high-tech economic development, big transportation projects—and worked aggressively to realize his goals. Virginia has brief legislative sessions in even-numbered year. In 1998 Gilmore succeeded in pushing through the first phase of the car tax cut although Democrats controlled the House. Doggedly he persisted in cutting the tax each year as he promised in his campaign, riling some by proposing to use tobacco settlement money; in early 2001 state Senate Republicans were complaining about his plan to finance the tax cut through selling bonds. He stoutly resisted pleas by Northern Virginia business leaders to allow the region to raise taxes for transportation projects. When Democrats called for eliminating the food tax, Gilmore agreed to cut it from 4.5% to 2.5%. On education, Gilmore implemented the Standards of Learning tests and created Best Practice Centers for schools and teachers. School systems were required to pay for the cost of remedial education for their graduates in the first two years of college—a form of accountability about which administrators and unions loudly squawked. He resisted efforts to water the standards down; in 2000 students showed gains on 21 of 27 tests. By 2004 students will have to pass six SOL tests to graduate; by 2007 schools will lose accreditation if less than 70% pass. Gilmore has pushed for more money for, and more accountability from, state universities.

The high-tech boom in Northern Virginia is one reason Gilmore has had plenty of money to spread around. He pleased high-tech leaders by appointing a secretary of Technology and provided tax breaks for AOL and other high-tech firms. As chairman of the Advisory Commission on Electronic Commerce, Gilmore cobbled together a majority out of tax opponents and businessmen and prevailed in getting endorsement of a five-year extension of the ban on Internet taxes over pro-tax forces led by Utah Governor Mike Leavitt. Bills to regulate software licensing agreements, filter out pornography in schools, and shield Internet providers for liability for pornography were passed. The high-tech boom has created terrible traffic problems in Northern Virginia. Gilmore's often-criticized VDOT moved forward on rebuilding the Mixing Bowl interchanges in Springfield, though cost estimates have risen alarmingly, and he negotiated with Congress and Maryland Governor Parris Glendening a federal payment of $1.58 billion toward rebuilding the Woodrow Wilson Bridge across the Potomac, with both states sharing cost overruns and upkeep. Gilmore objected to Glendening's insistence on hiring only union labor on the Maryland side. Gilmore has promoted SmarTrip pass cards for Metro, express buses on the Dulles Access Road, the Virginia Railway Express from Fredericksburg to Washington and extension of Metro to Tysons Corner and Dulles Airport.

On other issues, Gilmore took a hard stand against the dumping of New York garbage in landfills in Virginia. "We are very much on the rise and we don't want anyone to get the impression that Virginia is good only as a garbage depository." But the law passed to stop this was thrown out by a federal court in February 2000. He backed a museum in Richmond's Tredegar Ironworks on the role of blacks in the Civil War. In response to complaints, he worked for more blacks in the National Guard and state police. He backed a bill for an automatic five-year sentence for felons in illegal possession of a gun and another for preserving DNA evidence after trials. As chairman of a federal panel on domestic terrorism, he called in December 2000 for consolidation of anti-terrorist efforts in one office. He rebuked the Virginia Museum of Fine Arts for an exhibit of photos of naked children; the museum set up a review committee in response. He switched and accepted a Chesapeake Bay accord with Maryland, to cut sprawl, restore wetlands and maintain oyster population.

Through all this Gilmore has been a strong and effective partisan. He appointed popular Democratic legislators to administrative positions and then helped Republicans win their seats, so that by 1998 the Republicans had a 21–19 majority in the state Senate and got a power sharing arrangement in the House when the Democratic edge was cut to 50–49–1. In the 1999 elections Republicans held their majority in the Senate and gained a 52–47–1 majority in the House. He hailed this "Victory for conservatism. Liberalism is a washed-up relic of the past." This means that Republicans will control redistricting for the first time in Virginia's history. In the 2000 election Gilmore strongly backed George W. Bush, and after Virginia's primary said that John McCain's Straight Talk Express "ran out of gas in Virginia." In December 2000 Bush named Gilmore chairman of the Republican National Committee.

In the race to succeed Gilmore, Lieutenant Governor John Hager and Attorney General Mark Earley headed to the June Republican convention (Virginia Republican conventions have had as many as 13,000 delegates, the largest political assemblies in history, and nearly 9,000 turned out in 2001). Hager, a former tobacco executive who is wheelchair-bound by polio, traveled around the state extensively seeking support, but was outmaneuvered by Earley's organization, directed by former Gilmore and Allen strategists. A staunch social conservative, Earley supplemented his strong ties with Christian conservatives by reaching out to blacks and union leaders and won the nomination by about 3–1. In November he will face Mark Warner, a cell phone millionaire who was unopposed for the Democratic nomination; he won 47% of the vote in the 1996 race against (no relation) Senator John Warner. Earley says he has "experience that money cannot buy"; Warner has called for aiding non-Internet economic advance beyond the state's metropolitan areas. He had already raised $5.4 million by June, when he launched a $2 million ad campaign. He ran well for a Democrat in the rural areas in 1996, although one reason may have been resentment by some conservatives at John Warner's opposition two years before to Republican Senator Oliver North; that cause may not be burning so brightly five years later.

Cook's Call   *Highly Competitive.* Democrats are enthusiastic about wealthy businessman Mark Warner. Although Virginia trends Republican—Bush won by seven points here—the state's fiscal crunch, traffic problems in Northern Virginia and Gilmore's take-no-prisoners approach to the car tax may create a receptive environment for Warner. Republicans chose state Attorney General Mark Earley to be their nominee at a June 2001 convention. Expect a very competitive race.

Senior Senator   John Warner, first elected in 1978, is the senior Republican on the Senate Armed Services Committee. He grew up in Washington, D.C., with Virginia roots; his grandparents lived in Amherst County, Virginia. His father was a field surgeon in World War I; a great-uncle served in the Confederate Army and lost his arm in the Battle of the Wilderness. Warner volunteered for both the Army and Navy in 1944, at 17; the Navy snapped him up first. (There are only seven World War II veterans left in the Senate: Ted Stevens, Daniel Inouye, Daniel Akaka, Jesse Helms, Strom Thurmond, Ernest Hollings, John Warner; in contrast 34 senators were not born until after World War II.) He went to college at Washington & Lee and then interrupted his years at the University of Virginia Law School to serve in the Marine Corps in Korea. He worked as an assistant U.S. attorney and then practiced law in Washington and had a house in the horse country in Middleburg, Virginia. During the Nixon administration he was secretary of the Navy. He ran for the Senate in 1978 with few political assets other than his then-wife, Elizabeth Taylor. Finishing second at the huge Republican state convention, he graciously supported winner Richard Obenshain; then, when Obenshain died in a plane crash, Republican leaders reluctantly named Warner to fill his place. Warner won the general over Democrat Andrew Miller by a 4,721-vote margin. He was easily re-elected over a liberal Democrat in 1984 and had no serious opposition in 1990.

Warner can be grandiloquent and showy, yet he works hard on important issues and has shown steadfastness in his beliefs. His voting record is moderately conservative. He has voted for government funding of abortions in some cases, but favors parental consent laws and the partial-birth abortion ban. He cast a critical vote against the Supreme Court nomination of Judge Robert Bork in 1987. He voted for the Brady gun control bill and in May 1999 to control gun sales by non-licensed dealers at gun shows. He opposes term limits but would back sending a constitutional amendment to the states for a "national referendum." Representing a state which still has a large number of public employees (though the proportion is dropping), he favors higher federal pay and supported repeal of the Hatch Act.

Warner was the ranking Republican on the Armed Services committee from 1987–93, and he was looking forward to becoming chairman when he was bumped by the more senior Strom Thurmond. When both were re-elected in 1996 Warner expressed the hope he might be chairman some time within six years. In December 1997, on the day before his 95th birthday, Thurmond announced he would step down in January 1999 to give the younger generation a chance; he kept his word and Warner became chairman at 71. For years on the committee he had worked closely with Democratic Chairman Sam Nunn; but he opposed Nunn and led the fight in 1991 for the Gulf war resolution, which passed by only 52–47. Warner made harsh criticisms of Clinton administration defense policy. He had already opposed NATO expansion in March 1998. He was wary of U.S. troop commitments in the Balkans, though when Clinton sent in troops in May 1999 he said, "Once the president made the decision to join NATO in the Balkans, we have to support the troops." Warner was troubled when a British commander played "the red card," refusing to obey the order of American NATO commander to prevent Russians from occupying the Pristina airfield. In January 2000 he said the U.S. should solve its problems in Kosovo and Bosnia before taking on new commitments in Africa. In May 2000 he and Robert Byrd sponsored an amendment to end U.S. deployment in Kosovo by July 2001; it was beaten by only 53–47. In the first major bill of the 106th Congress, he hammered through the biggest military pay and pension increases in nearly 20 years. He created a new Emerging Threats Subcommittee to focus on terrorism, chemical and biological warfare and cyberwarfare; he is concerned about what might happen if the military's high-tech computers fail or are somehow jammed by low-tech countermeasures. He had supported previous rounds of base closings, but after Bill Clinton's politically-motivated tampering with the 1995 round of closings, he voted against another round in May 1999, saying, "Politics have destroyed the credibility of the process for closing bases." In 1999 he opposed the resolution clearing Admiral Husband Kimmel and General Walter Short of responsibility for Pearl Harbor and called for lifting the ban on official Navy contact with the Tailhook Association. When 24 Americans were detained by China in April 2001 after their spy plane crash-landed, Warner said he considered them "prisoners," much to the dismay of Defense secretary Donald Rumsfeld. Warner demanded accountability from the Navy in May 2001 after the terrorist attack on the USS Cole and the collision of the USS Greenville with a Japanese trawler.

Warner voted against the Comprehensive Test Ban Treaty in October 1999, arguing that it was impossible to monitor Russian compliance. In December 1999 he said that if the Vieques target range in Puerto Rico is closed down, the Navy should close the Roosevelt Roads naval base there too. He warned in early 2000 of the threat of China to Taiwan and in April secured increases in the defense budget. In important ways he worked to reshape defense policy. He strongly backs missile defense: "Russia and other nations must understand that the United States policy now calls for an eventual deployment of a system to protect ourselves," and he sternly pressed an Air Force general to "Look straight into the cameras and say, 'We are as a nation defenseless.'" Noting the unwillingness of the military and its civilian leaders to accept casualties, he called for a new set of unmanned weapons, and wants one-third of military aircraft to be unmanned by 2010 and one-third of ground vehicles to be unmanned by 2015. In a secret markup session in May 2000, he got approval of five new nuclear submarines of the Virginia class—a major increase in the submarine fleet. In October 2000 he secured coverage under the military Triad medical care plan of all military retirees, a change with a pricetag of $60 billion over 10 years. He has been willing, even eager to drop extraneous amendments from the defense authorization, even those he supports, including creation of a commission on Cuba, regulation of Section 527 campaign committees and hate crimes legislation. He gave strong support to Richard Holbrooke when he his nomination to be Ambassador to the UN was slowed up in 1999.

On some issues he has joined Democrats and opposed most Republicans, on gun control in May 1999 and on amendments to HMO regulation in July 1999. But he weighed in with solid support for his fellow Republican George Allen's $1,000 per-child tax credit when it was under attack from his Democratic colleague Charles Robb in October 2000. In commemoration of Virginia's most famous citizen, he sponsored a bill to require federal agencies to refer to Presidents' Day as George Washington's Birthday. As a subcommittee chairman, Warner worked on the giant 1998 transportation bill and conducted extensive negotiations to get a funding formula that would satisfy just about everyone, and in the process increased Virginia's annual transportation funding by $150 million. He led the bipartisan Virginia-Maryland delegation and in October 2000 raised the federal funding of the Woodrow Wilson Bridge across the Potomac to $1.5 billion. He fought against John McCain's 1999 efforts to open up slots at Washington Reagan National Airport, and got new slots reduced from 48 to 24. He supported the nomination of Roger Gregory to the 4th Circuit Court of Appeals, where he would be the first black judge; Warner previously appointed the first black and female federal trial judges in Virginia.

For a time in the 1990s Warner seemed to be in a war with many Virginia Republicans. In 1993, he refused to endorse lieutenant governor candidate Michael Farris, the leader of the national home schooling movement, and in 1994 he announced he could not support Senate nominee Oliver North, whose conviction on Iran-Contra charges was overturned on the grounds of inadmissibility of some critical evidence. Instead Warner backed independent (and twice Republican gubernatorial candidate) Marshall Coleman, and many blamed Warner for North's narrow loss to Charles Robb. Farris and North backers hoped to deny Warner renomination in 1996 at the gigantic Virginia Republican state convention. But Warner invoked a Virginia law that entitled him to insist on a primary. There he defeated James Miller, budget director under President Ronald Reagan and North's opponent at the 1994 convention, by 66%–34%. The Democratic nominee was Mark Warner, former state party chairman, a native of Connecticut who was criticized by John Warner for using his Democratic connections to win cellular phone licenses, amassing a personal fortune of over $100 million. Mark Warner spent liberally—$11.6 million in all, $10.3 million of it his own money. John Warner called himself a "common sense conservative" and, citing seniority, said, "Virginia's got an investment in me." But the incumbent hovered around only 50% in the polls and was placed on the defensive in October 1996 when his media consultant ran an ad superimposing Mark Warner's face on a picture of Charles Robb shaking hands with Douglas Wilder, as President Clinton looked on. John Warner fired the consultant and apologized for the deception, but did not repudiate the ad's quotation of a *Richmond Times-Dispatch* editorial calling Mark Warner "dirty, stupid, reckless, dangerous." John Warner won, but only narrowly, 52%–47%. He carried by narrow 51%–49% margins the usually Republican Richmond areas and non-metropolitan Virginia: evidence that some Farris and North enthusiasts cut him. He carried the Norfolk area by only 52%–47%: he was not yet Armed Services chairman. He ran best, 55%–45%, in Northern Virginia, where his highly visible opposition to Farris and North was an asset.

Warner's seat comes up in 2002, and he has announced that he plans to run. In early 2001 he faced no Republican opposition; memory of his apostasy on Farris and North has apparently dimmed.

Cook's Call *Safe.* Unlike the struggles Warner has faced against both Democratic and Republican opponents in recent years, 2002 should prove to be a much easier contest. There are no strong Democrats waiting in the wings and the party is not likely to focus on this race until after the 2001 gubernatorial election.

Junior Senator George Allen, a Republican elected in 2000, is one of only five Virginians to serve as governor and senator (the others were James Monroe, Claude Swanson, Harry Byrd Sr. and the man he beat, Charles Robb). Allen grew up in Illinois and California, graduating from high school in Palos Verdes. At that point his father had moved to Virginia to become the highly successful coach of the Washington Redskins ("Hit hard and good things will happen"), and he advised his son to go to college in the area. The younger George Allen graduated from college and law school at the University of Virginia. In 1977 he moved to a country home near Charlottesville and practiced law—wearing boots and chewing tobacco. In 1982 he was elected to the Virginia House of Delegates, where he was a conservative backbencher while Robb was governor. In a 1991 special election he won a seat in the U.S. House, which the Democratic legislature promptly redistricted out from under him.

Out of office, he started running for governor in 1993. He maneuvered smartly to get the support of religious conservatives at the 13,000-delegate June 1993 state convention, perhaps the largest legislative body in the history of democracy (and whose real enthusiasm was reserved for its lieutenant governor nominee, home schooling advocate Michael Farris). The Democratic nominee, Attorney General Mary Sue Terry, was better known and had a moderate record on many issues, though she backed some forms of gun control and was pro-abortion rights. Democrats thought gun control and the religious right would hurt Republicans. But Allen won by a whopping 58%–41% margin, Republican James Gilmore was elected attorney general and Farris lost to Democrat Lieutenant Governor Donald Beyer, who outspent him 10–1, by only 54%–45%.

Allen's term as governor (Virginia is the last state to limit governors to one term) was more successful than many had expected. His achievements included a more permissive concealed weapons law, abolition of parole (a big issue in the 1993 campaign), parental notification for abortions and welfare reform that required recipients to work after 90 days and cut off benefits after two years—which resulted in a big decline in welfare rolls. Allen was regarded by his foes as an intellectual lightweight, but his education reforms included Standards of Learning that were probably the toughest in the nation. The SOLs have been continued under his successor as governor, James Gilmore, and test scores have risen. But in 1995 the legislature rejected Allen's tax cut, and in elections that fall, despite a major effort by Allen, Republicans fell short of winning majorities in the legislature (they finally did so in 1999). Democrats disliked him for his partisanship and activist conservatism; he has a cheerful, sunny temperament but also a penchant for harsh conservative rhetoric. To the 1994 Republican state convention, he said, "My friends—and I say this figuratively—let's enjoy knocking their soft teeth down their whining throats." He calls for "capital punishment for death taxes" and depicts the federal government as a "grimy boot" trampling people's rights. But he had 68% job approval when he left the governorship.

Out of office in 1998, Allen joined a Richmond law firm, but it was widely expected that he would run against Charles Robb in 2000. Robb had been a public figure for one-third of a century, since he married Lynda Byrd Johnson in the White House in 1967, and then went off to command an infantry company in Vietnam. He was elected lieutenant governor of Virginia in 1977 and governor, by a 54%–46% margin over Republican Marshall Coleman, in 1981. As governor, he was widely popular and was given credit for much of Virginia's dynamic growth. His record in the Senate was among the more conservative of Democrats, but he found himself in political trouble in 1994 because of scandal. Robb had opposition in the Democratic primary from Delegate Virgil Goode (now an independent congressman who votes with Republicans) and won by the unimpressive margin of 58%–34%. But he was blessed by a general election opponent who also had high negatives, Oliver North, the epicenter of the Iran-contra scandal, whose conviction was overturned on the grounds of inadmissibility of some critical evidence. North had a national following, and raised and spent over $20 million. But many Republicans refused to support him. Robb won by only 46%–43%.

Many assumed that was Robb's last race, but he continued to compile a moderate voting record and worked hard on military issues and on programs with appeal in rural areas. A January 1999 poll showed Allen leading Robb 47%–38%, but he was undaunted. Senate Democrats' campaign committee made holding Robb's seat their number one priority, and he argued that his record of conservatism on defense and foreign policy and his support of abortion rights, gun control and environmental protections was in line with Virginians' values. Allen talked about bringing Virginia experience to Washington and, in reference to Robb's low public profile, said "A Senate seat is a terrible thing to waste." The centerpiece of Allen's campaign was a $1,000 per child tax credit for educational expenses for both public and private schools. He also called for cutting the cost of public college and for smaller elementary school class sizes. Robb argued that the money would be better invested in federal spending for education. Allen, a bit on the defensive on gun control, said he would vote to renew the assault weapons ban. Robb gained, at last, a lukewarm endorsement from his longtime adversary, former Governor Douglas Wilder; Allen gained a strong endorsement, and backing for his tax credits for education, from that sometime adversary of conservative Republicans, Senator John Warner. In the last weeks of the campaign, Robb accused Allen of an "intolerable" and "appalling" record on racial issues; Democratic flyers attacked him for opposing a federal Martin Luther King Holiday, for displaying a Confederate flag in his house and for displaying a noose in his law office.

Allen emerged the winner by a narrow 52%–48% margin. His votes tracked very closely with George W. Bush's. Robb, targeting the suburbs, carried Northern Virginia, but by only a 51%–49% margin. With his military credentials, he won in Tidewater Virginia, but by only 52%–48%. Allen carried the Richmond area 55%–45%, and won an even bigger margin, 57%–43%, in the one-third of the state outside these metropolitan areas. According to the VNS exit poll, Allen won among those married with children by 57%–42%, while the race was even among everyone else. A bad sign for Democrats in the future: Robb, elected governor in 1981, carried voters 60 and older; Allen, elected governor in 1993, carried voters under 60, and by wider margins. Allen serves on the Commerce committee, where he can promote the interests of the Dulles technology corridor.

Presidential politics Virginia remains one of the more Republican states in presidential races, but not as solidly as in the 1980s. In 1996 Bill Clinton lost here by only 48%–46%, and in 2000 George W. Bush won by 52%–44%, running only even in Northern Virginia and the Tidewater area around Norfolk, but winning 55% in the Richmond area and 56% in the rest of the state. In Virginia, as elsewhere, big metro areas have trended Democratic in the 1990s. Until 2000 Virginia's national convention delegates were chosen at state conventions, but an open primary was used this time by the Republican Party, and Bush took 53% to McCain's 44%. Virginia, within sight of the White House and the Capitol, sees relatively little presidential politicking.

Congressional districting Virginia's district lines for the 1990s were drawn by Democrats, and were redrawn twice. As often happens, they backfired on their makers. The Democrats wanted to end the brief House career of George Allen, and did; but he ran successfully for governor in 1993 and senator in 2000. The delegation, which was 7–4 Democratic after the 1992 election, has become 8–3 Republican if one counts Independent Virgil Goode with the Republicans. Now, thanks to their capture of both houses of the legislature in 1999, Republicans have control over redistricting for the first time in Virginia's history. Curiously, the result is likely to be not much different from the current districts. They will probably create another black-majority district running along the James River from Newport News to Richmond. They could marginally weaken Democrat Rick Boucher in the 9th District, but he has run well ahead of his party for years. They might try to weaken Democrat Jim Moran in the 8th District in Northern Virginia. But Arlington and Alexandria are now Democratic enough that no Republican incumbent will want them in his district. The likely result is a one-seat Republican gain.

THE PEOPLE: Pop. 2000: 7,078,515; Pop. 1990: 6,187,358, up 14.4% 1990–2000. 2.5% of U.S. total, 12th largest; 72.3% White, 19.6% Black, 3.7% Asian, 0.3% Amer. Indian, 0.1% Hawaiian, 2% Two + races, 2% Other; 4.7% Hispanic Origin. 2.2% Unemployment. 2000 Voting age pop.: 5,340,253. 2000 Turnout: 2,789,808; 52% of VAP. Registered voters (2000): 4,073,644; no party registration.

POLITICAL LINEUP: Governor, James S. Gilmore III (R); Lt. Gov., John H. Hager (R); Secy. of Commonwealth, Anne P. Petera (R); Atty. Gen., Randolph A. Beales (R); State Senate, 40 (18 D, 21 R, 1 Vacancy); Senate Pres. Pro Tempore, John H. Chichester (R); Majority Leader, Walter A. Stosch (R); House of Delegates, 100 (47 D, 52 R, 1 I); House Speaker, Vance Wilkins Jr. (R). Senators, John W. Warner (R) and George Allen (R). Representatives, 11 (3 D, 7 R, 1 I).

ELECTIONS DIVISION: 804-786-6551; **FILING DEADLINE FOR U.S. CONGRESS:** April 12, 2002.

2000 Presidential Vote

Bush (R)	1,437,490	(52%)
Gore (D)	1,217,290	(44%)
Nader (Green)	59,398	(2%)
Others	25,269	(1%)

1996 Presidential Vote

Dole (R)	1,137,171	(48%)
Clinton (D)	1,090,219	(46%)
Perot (I)	159,795	(7%)

2000 Republican Presidential Primary

Bush (R)	350,588	(53%)
McCain (R)	291,488	(44%)
Other	22,017	(3%)

Gov. James S. Gilmore, III (R)

Elected 1997, term expires Jan. 2002, 1st term; b. Oct. 6, 1949, Richmond; home, Richmond; U. of VA, B.A. 1971, J.D. 1977; Methodist; married (Roxane Gatling).

Military Career: Army, 1971–74.

Elected Office: Henrico Cnty. Commonwealth's Atty., 1988–93; VA Atty. Gen., 1994–97..

Professional Career: Practicing atty., 1977–87, 1997.

Office: State Capitol, Richmond, 23219, 804-786-2211; Fax: 804-371-6351; Web site: www.state.va.us.

Election Results

1997 general	James S. Gilmore III (R)	969,062	(56%)
	Don Beyer (D)	738,971	(43%)
	Sue Harris DeBauche (I)	25,777	(2%)
1997 primary	James S. Gilmore III (R)	nominated	
1993 general	George F. Allen (R)	1,045,319	(58%)
	Mary Sue Terry (D)	733,527	(41%)

Sen. John W. Warner (R)

Elected 1978, seat up 2002, 4th term; b. Feb. 18, 1927, Washington, D.C.; home, Middleburg; Washington & Lee U., B.S., 1949, U. of VA, LL.B. 1953; Episcopalian; divorced.

Military Career: Navy, 1944–46 (WWII), Marine Corps, 1950–52 (Korea).

Professional Career: Law Clerk, U.S. Court of Appeals, Chief Judge Barrett Prettyman, 1953–54; Practicing atty., 1954–56, 1960–69; Asst. U.S. Atty., 1956–60; U.S. Navy, Undersecy., 1969–72, U.S. Navy, Secy., 1972–74; Dir., Amer. Rev. Bicentennial Comm., 1974–76.

DC Office: 225 RSOB, 20510, 202-224-2023; Fax: 202-224-6295; Web site: www.senate.gov/~warner.

State Offices: Abingdon, 540-628-8158; Norfolk, 757-441-3079; Richmond, 804-771-2579; Roanoke, 540-857-2676.

Committees: *Armed Services* (RMM). *Environment & Public Works:* Fisheries, Wildlife & Water; Superfund, Waste Control & Risk Assessment; Transportation & Infrastructure. *Health, Education, Labor & Pensions:* Aging; Children & Families. *Rules & Administration.*

Group Ratings

	ADA	ACLU	AFS	LCV	CON	ITIC	NTU	COC	ACU	NTLC	CHC
2000	0	29	0	0	36	100	71	100	92	94	77
1999	10	—	0	33	8	—	72	100	84	—	—

National Journal Ratings

	1999 LIB	—	1999 CONS		2000 LIB	—	2000 CONS
Economic	32%	—	65%		27%	—	68%
Social	45%	—	54%		40%	—	57%
Foreign	48%	—	49%		36%	—	58%

Key Votes of the 106th Congress

1. Educ. Savings Accts.	Y	5. Review Movie Violence	Y	9. NATO War in Serbia	Y
2. Prescrip. Drug Benefit	N	6. Gun Show Bckgrnd. Checks	Y	10. Table Cuba Travel Ban	N
3. Delay Ergonomic Standards	Y	7. Ban Part.-Birth Abortion	Y	11. Nuclear Test-Ban Treaty	N
4. Phase Out Estate Tax	Y	8. Broaden Hate Crimes List	N	12. Perm. Trade with China	Y

Election Results

1996 general	John W. Warner (R)	1,235,744	(52%)	($5,819,157)
	Mark R. Warner (D)	1,115,982	(47%)	($11,600,424)
1996 primary	John W. Warner (R)	323,520	(66%)	
	James C. (Jim) Miller (R)	170,015	(34%)	
1990 general	John W. Warner (R)	876,782	(81%)	($1,219,726)

Sen. George Allen (R)

Elected 2000, seat up 2006, 1st term; b. Mar. 8, 1952, Whittier, CA; home, Earlysville; U. of VA, B.A. 1974, J.D. 1977; Presbyterian; married (Susan).

Elected Office: VA House of Delegates, 1982–91; U.S. House of Reps., 1991–92; VA Gov., 1993–97.

Professional Career: Practicing atty., 1977–91, 1998–99.

DC Office: 200 RSOB, 20510, 202-224-4024; Fax: 202-224-5432; Web site: allen.senate.gov.

State Office: Richmond, 804-771-2221.

Committees: *Commerce, Science & Transportation:* Communications; Consumer Affairs, Foreign Commerce & Tourism; Science, Technology & Space. *Foreign Relations:* International Economic Policy, Export & Trade Promotion; International Operations & Terrorism (RMM); Western Hemisphere, Peace Corps, Narcotics Affairs. *Small Business.*

Group Ratings and Key Votes: Newly Elected

Election Results

2000 general	George Allen (R)	1,420,460	(52%)	($9,995,980)
	Charles S. Robb (D)	1,296,093	(48%)	($6,610,252)
2000 primary	George Allen (R)	unopposed		
1994 general	Charles S. Robb (D)	938,376	(46%)	($5,501,697)
	Oliver L. (Ollie) North (R)	882,213	(43%)	($20,607,367)
	J. Marshall Coleman (I)	235,324	(11%)	($813,409)

FIRST DISTRICT

When British settlers first sailed up the estuaries that flow into the Chesapeake Bay, they were searching for gold, hoping to sail back soon with fortunes. But they couldn't help noticing that the spot where the James River feeds into the bay, now Hampton Roads, was a fine natural harbor, with calm, deep water and good anchorages. There they established a civilization whose elegance is recalled in the craftsmanship of restored Williamsburg and whose coarseness and brutality is brought to life by the story of Jamestown and the other beleaguered settlements. Tidewater Virginia brought slavery to America and tobacco to the world, and slave-raised tobacco was the center of its economy in the colonial era and in the years afterward, when its most talented sons left its depleted soil for better opportunities elsewhere.

Now the economy and tone of life in Tidewater Virginia are set by the American military. Sixty years ago, as America faced world war, the Navy base at Norfolk and the shipbuilding centers in Newport News across Hampton Roads became the center of American naval might in the Atlantic. There were fewer than 370,000 people living then on both sides of Hampton Roads. Today there are 1.5 million—a population collected from all over the country, making this a metropolitan area that is not so much Southern in atmosphere as it is, in the manner of military bases abroad, national. But you can still see this area's origins in the Newport News Shipbuilding and Drydock Company that lies over the flat neighborhoods lining the baysides, with ships looming larger than life, their turrets and superstructures bristling with armored might. This is the biggest private employer in Virginia. At the height of 1980s naval expansion, 30,000 people worked here and defense spending here topped $1 billion a year.

Virginia's 1st Congressional District contains much of this territory. Its boundaries are convoluted in order to accommodate the black-majority 3d District, although they were smoothed out in 1998 in response to a February 1997 federal court decision. Nearly half the district's residents live on the Peninsula, in and around Newport News, Williamsburg and other Hampton Roads area towns. It also includes the southern tip of the Delmarva Peninsula—Virginia's Eastern Shore, site of the annual roundup of wild Chincoteague ponies—and much of the Northern Neck between the Rappahannock and Potomac Rivers, where Robert "King" Carter, one of the great landowners of colonial Virginia, reigned, and where George Washington and Robert E. Lee were born; the Northern Neck is now growing robustly again for the first time in two centuries. Ancestrally, most of this area is Democratic, but with black precincts shorn away, the 1st now is reliably Republican in most elections.

The congresswoman from the 1st District is Jo Ann Davis, a Republican first elected in 2000. She was born in North Carolina; her father worked at a gas station and drove city buses in Hampton. She graduated from Hampton Roads Business College in 1971 and went to work as an executive secretary for a real estate firm for several years before becoming a stay-at-home mom, getting her real estate license and opening Davis Management Company in 1988 and Jo Ann Davis Realty in 1990. Davis was elected to the House of Delegates in 1997, defeating a 15-year incumbent who outspent her 3-to-1. When Bateman, who suffered from cancer and had heart surgery the previous year, announced his retirement in January 2000—he died in his sleep the following September at a local resort where he was scheduled to play in a golf tournament—Davis jumped into the race three days later. She faced four other candidates for the Republican nomination, including real estate entrepreneur Paul Jost, who spent almost $1 million of his own money and won the endorsement of Governor James Gilmore. Several better-known contenders failed to run, and Gilmore's initial favorite—his Commerce and Trade Secretary Barry DuVal—withdrew a month into his campaign. The low-profile Davis, who spent less than one-tenth of Jost's funds, appealed to conservative activists, especially in the district's rural counties. She favored a Social Security lockbox, more flexibility to the states on education funding, elimination of the marriage penalty and estate taxes, and protection of Second Amendment rights. Not surprisingly, she voiced strong support for military preparedness. Her religious faith and modest background are a stark contrast to the Richmond aristocrats who once ruled the local Republican Party—and the state. She led Jost 35%–30%, with just 14,274 votes, carrying nine of 23 counties. Political consultant Michael Rothfeld finished third with 22%.

In the general, she faced Democrat Lawrence Davies, a Baptist minister and former mayor of Fredericksburg for 20 years. Davies, who is black, in the 1960s served on a biracial commission that pushed for desegregation of the city's businesses. The two biggest issues of the campaign were abortion rights—Davis against, Davies for—and the proposed King William reservoir, which many local officials said is required to meet the peninsula's future water demand: Davis considered it too expensive to justify and Davies defended it as necessary for growth. Democrat Davies ran a quiet campaign, noting that Virginians are "genteel—they prefer a civil approach." Republican Davis won 58%–37%, with Davies winning Williamsburg, his home city of Fredericksburg plus two small counties.

Cook's Call *Safe.* This district is strongly Republican and it unlikely that Democrats will put much effort into this race in 2002. The 1st was one of the fastest-growing districts in Virginia during the 1990s and will have to drop about 66,000 people during redistricting.

THE PEOPLE: Pop. 2000: 709,060; Pop. 1990: 563,486, up 25.8% 1990–2000. 75.4% White, 19.7% Black, 1.5% Asian, 0.4% Amer. Indian, 0.1% Hawaiian, 1.8% Two+ races, 1.1% Other; 2.8% Hispanic Origin.

2000 Presidential Vote		
Bush (R)	161,116	(58%)
Gore (D)	109,084	(39%)
Nader (Green)	5,181	(2%)
Others	2,406	(1%)

1996 Presidential Vote		
Dole (R)	120,429	(51%)
Clinton (D)	96,475	(41%)
Perot (I)	17,195	(7%)

Rep. Jo Ann Davis (R)

Elected 2000, 1st term; b. June 29, 1950, Rowan Cnty., NC; home, Yorktown; Hampton Roads Bus. Col.; Assembly of God; married (Chuck).

Elected Office: VA House of Del., 1997–2000.

Professional Career: Real estate broker, 1984-present; Founder, Davis Mngmt. Co., 1988; Founder, Jo Ann Davis Realty, 1990.

DC Office: 1123 LHOB 20515, 202-225-4261; Fax: 202-225-4382; Web site: www.house.gov/joanndavis.

District Offices: Accomac, 757-787-7836; Fredericksburg, 540-373-3687; Warsaw, 804-333-1412; Yorktown, 757-874-6687.

Committees: *Armed Services* (29th of 32 R): Military Personnel; Military Procurement. *Government Reform* (17th of 24 R): Criminal Justice, Drug Policy & Human Resources. *International Relations* (26th of 26 R): Middle East & South Asia; Western Hemisphere.

Group Ratings and Key Votes: Newly Elected

Election Results

2000 general	Jo Ann Davis (R)	151,344	(58%)	($393,119)
	Lawrence A. Davies (D)	97,399	(37%)	($152,592)
	Sharon A. Wood (I)	9,652	(4%)	
	Others	4,619	(2%)	
2000 primary	Jo Ann Davis (R)	14,274	(35%)	
	Paul C. Jost (R)	12,171	(30%)	
	Michael I. Rothfeld (R)	8,932	(22%)	
	Robert L. Cunningham (R)	2,686	(7%)	
	Philip G. Short (R)	2,535	(6%)	
1998 general	Herbert H. Bateman (R)	76,474	(76%)	($304,245)
	Bradford L. Phillips (I)	13,235	(13%)	($53,862)
	Josh Billings (I)	9,492	(9%)	

SECOND DISTRICT

The United States Navy Atlantic fleet berthed in its home port of Norfolk is one of the great awe-inspiring sights in America, or anywhere. The aggregation of destructive power in the line of towering gray ships is probably greater than in any other single port in history—over 100 ships are based here, with some 100,000 sailors and Marines, some $2 billion in annual spending. Norfolk has been a Navy port since 1801, and has long been recognized as one of the best natural harbors on the East Coast, one that never freezes, has a channel 50 feet deep and is within 750 miles of three-quarters of U.S. manufacturing capacity.

Norfolk, once a small city, is now the center of a metropolitan area on both sides of Hampton Roads with over 1.5 million people. Nearly one-third of the total workforce here is employed by the military, but with its skilled labor force and lack of unions the Hampton Roads area has also attracted a lot of private employment; the port has taken a great deal of business away from the labor-torn piers of Baltimore. To the Hampton Roads area, this growth over the last half-century has brought a wider cross-section of people than usually found in the South. There is no heavy accent here: the brothy Tidewater accent is heard more often farther up the rivers toward Richmond. And Norfolk preserves its antique past more carefully now, developing cultural institutions and commercial amenities appropriate to a major metro area. Older parts of Norfolk have the look and feel of a working-class town, with shipyard workers and many blacks (39% in the city of Norfolk), but most of it is white middle-class suburbia, plus Virginia Beach's string of oceanfront motels.

The 2d Congressional District is made up of most of Norfolk and Virginia Beach, with boundaries that put most of Norfolk's heavily black neighborhoods in the black-majority 3d District. The politics here has changed as the area has become more heavily suburban, and the Democrats more associated with defense policy critics. In 1968, the 2d voted for Hubert Humphrey, as Norfolk cast 65,000 votes and Virginia Beach 37,000. In 2000 the two cities voted for George W. Bush, as Norfolk cast 62,000 votes and Virginia Beach 150,000.

The congressman from the 2d District is Edward Schrock, one of three freshman Republicans elected to the House from Virginia in 2000 and the one likely to make the biggest initial impact on Capitol Hill. He grew up in Ohio and joined the Navy in 1964 before graduating from college and served until 1988, retiring as a captain. He worked on public affairs throughout his Navy career, which included two tours in Vietnam and stints at the Pentagon and White House, and on the West Coast, where his assignment was to ensure that Hollywood accurately portrayed the Navy. From 1989 until 1995, he was an investment adviser in Norfolk with the Kidder Peabody firm. In 1995, he was elected to the Virginia Senate, defeating veteran Democratic incumbent Clarence Holland. Late in the 2000 campaign, he revealed that he suffered non-Hodgkin's lymphoma in 1975, possibly as the result of exposure in Vietnam to the chemical defoliant Agent Orange. At the time, his doctors gave him six months to live and he spent months drifting in and out of a coma, while dropping to 98 pounds.

Schrock was exploring a House race even before seven-term Democrat Owen Pickett announced his retirement in December 1999. Pickett was frustrated by congressional partisanship as he worked mostly on military issues. With no primary opposition, Schrock became the early front-runner in the Republican trending district. He emphasized his military experience, legislative record and many campaign donors. He endorsed a national missile defense system, increased defense spending and improved health care for military retirees. Although he's an anti-abortion conservative who wants lower taxes, he has sounded bipartisan notes on paying down the national debt, improving the environment and saving Social Security and Medicare. But Schrock faced an unexpectedly strong challenge from Democratic nominee Jody Wagner, a securities attorney who has worked with growing local companies, who made the race after better-known Democrats declined to run. Though a political novice, she was a successful fund-raiser, more than matching Schrock's $1 million-plus. Schrock won 52%–48%, winning 55% in Virginia Beach and 42% in Norfolk.

Schrock was elected head of his 28-member Republican freshman class. He won a seat on the Armed Services Committee, as well as Budget.

Cook's Call *Probably Safe.* The fact that Schrock won here with just 52% and Bush with 53% illustrates that the 2d is really a marginal district. Republicans, who control the redistricting process, are likely to boost its Republican registration: As one of the slowest-growing districts in the state, the 2d will need to pick up approximately 69,000 new residents.

THE PEOPLE: Pop. 2000: 574,058; Pop. 1990: 562,789, up 2% 1990–2000. 67.5% White, 23.1% Black, 4.5% Asian, 0.4% Amer. Indian, 0.1% Hawaiian, 2.7% Two+ races, 1.6% Other; 4.3% Hispanic Origin.

2000 Presidential Vote

Bush (R)	99,979	(53%)
Gore (D)	84,344	(45%)
Nader (Green)	3,139	(2%)
Others	1,855	(1%)

1996 Presidential Vote

Dole (R)	77,936	(48%)
Clinton (D)	73,367	(45%)
Perot (I)	11,637	(7%)

Rep. Edward Schrock (R)

Elected 2000, 1st term; b. Apr. 6, 1941, Middletown, OH; home, Virginia Beach; Alderson Broaddus Col., B.S. 1964; American U., M.A. 1974; Baptist; married (Judy).

Military Career: U.S. Navy, 1964–88 (Vietnam).

Elected Office: VA Senate, 1995–2000.

Professional Career: Stockbroker, Kidder Peabody, 1988–94.

DC Office: 128 CHOB 20515, 202-225-4215; Fax: 202-225-4218.

District Office: Virginia Beach/Norfolk, 757-497-6859.

Committees: *Armed Services* (30th of 32 R): Military Installations & Facilities; Military Personnel; Military Research & Development. *Budget* (19th of 24 R). *Government Reform* (23d of 24 R): National Security, Veterans' Affairs & Intl. Relations. *Small Business* (15th of 19 R): Tax, Finance & Exports; Workforce, Empowerment & Government Programs.

Group Ratings and Key Votes: Newly Elected

Election Results

2000 general	Edward Schrock (R)	97,856	(52%)	($1,067,074)
	Jody M. Wagner (D)	90,328	(48%)	($1,117,345)
	Others	145	(1%)	
2000 primary	Edward Schrock (R) .... nominated by convention			
1998 general	Owen Pickett (D) .... unopposed			($129,837)

THIRD DISTRICT

The history of African-American slavery literally began along the tidal expanse of the James River. In 1607, the first English colonists chose one of the marshiest, least healthy spots along the broad river as the site of their settlement at Jamestown. Only a dozen years later, the first slave ship sailed up the James and offloaded its human cargo, giving birth to the biracial society of the American South. In the 21st Century, the great plantation houses of the Tidewater, entire communities once adorned by the most impressive architecture of the day and attended by hundreds of slaves, still dot the banks of the James. Charles City County—the site of William Byrd II's Westover, Benjamin Harrison III's Berkeley, and John Carter's Shirley—also was the birthplace of two successive presidents, William Henry Harrison and John Tyler. The county's population continues to be heavily black: The demography of the plantation remains.

The 3d Congressional District is the descendant of a black-majority district formed in 1992, slightly redrawn in 1993 and then redrawn again in 1998 after a federal court ruled it unconstitutional. The current plan, agreed to by the five congressmen affected, smoothed out the boundaries and consolidated eight localities formerly split between districts; but the basic character of the district remains the same. It strings together black precincts and communities along the James River from Norfolk and Newport News upriver on the Peninsula past Jamestown and Charles City County all the way to Richmond and suburban Henrico County. Politically, with its majority-black population, the 3d is by far the most Democratic district in Virginia. But it also is sensitive to the needs of the businesses that supply its economic base—notably Newport News Shipbuilding and Drydock Company, the state's largest private employer.

The congressman from the 3d District is Bobby Scott, a Democrat elected when the district was created in 1992. He grew up in Newport News, the son of a doctor, went to Harvard, where he was a classmate of Al Gore, and then to Boston College Law School. He served in the National Guard and Army Reserves and returned home to practice law in 1973. In 1977, he was elected to the Virginia House of Delegates and in 1983 to the state Senate, representing a multi-racial district in a community where, because of the military tradition of integration, biracial politics came more naturally than in other places. In 1986 he ran a creditable race for Congress in the

1st District and lost to Republican Herb Bateman, 56%–44%. In 1992 he ran in the new 3d. With his base in the Peninsula, and against two Richmond-based candidates, Scott won the crucial Democratic primary with 67% of the vote. The general election made him the first black member of Congress elected from Virginia since Reconstruction.

Scott has had a solidly liberal voting record, except on some foreign and defense issues. On the Education and the Workforce Committee, he quickly jumped into the Clinton health care debate. Remembering how his father had been denied staff privileges in a Newport News hospital, he vowed that any health care bill would prohibit racial discrimination against patients and health care providers. On a range of issues, he has become one of the House's most outspoken civil libertarians. He opposes the death penalty and supports a requirement that it not be applied disproportionately by race. He opposed expelling problematic special-needs students in the IDEA debate: "the child still needs an education," he said. When bipartisan coalitions passed legislation to permit states to display the Ten Commandments in schools or government buildings, he raised First Amendment objections that the plans interfered with freedom of religion, as he did with President Bush's plan to fund faith-based social programs.

On the Judiciary Committee he was an outspoken defender of Bill Clinton against impeachment. He spoke out often against what he considered an unfair and partisan proceeding. Scott was the only Democrat to vote against Rick Boucher's motion to censure Clinton. But he also has shown skill as a consensus-builder. At the same time that he was engaging in partisan warfare in the highly publicized impeachment hearings, Scott was taking an active role in the highly technical and carefully bipartisan proceedings in the special committee on China chaired by Christopher Cox, to which he was appointed in June 1998. Amazingly, there were no leaks from this committee (until its draft report went to the Clinton White House in January 1999) and by all accounts Scott participated actively and helped build consensus for a unanimous report on an intellectually difficult and politically sensitive issue. On the ethics committee, reconstituted after the Newt Gingrich case was settled in 1997, Scott also contributed to a nonpartisan approach. With Judiciary Committee Republican Asa Hutchinson, he worked to enact a little-noted bill to require states to report the deaths of prisoners held in state or local custody; according to the sponsors, approximately 1,000 inmates annually die "questionable deaths."

Scott was unopposed in 2000. He has had aspirations to run for governor, but yielded to party leader's choices. After a disagreement with 2001 Democratic gubernatorial candidate Mark Warner, Scott in April 2001 quit his post on Warner's campaign. Republicans control redistricting, and they may remove some of the Richmond area from the 3d and add heavily black portions of the current 4th District in order to make the 4th more Republican. That would give Scott a more compact and still heavily Democratic constituency.

Cook's Call   *Safe.* Although this district was altered slightly due to court-ordered remapping in 1998, Scott has shown no signs of vulnerability. It was the slowest growing district in Virginia during the 1990s and will need to pick up about 76,000 new people, but will not be dramatically changed for 2002.

THE PEOPLE: Pop. 2000: 567,683; Pop. 1990: 560,280, up 1.3% 1990–2000. 38.3% White, 56.6% Black, 1.4% Asian, 0.5% Amer. Indian, 0.1% Hawaiian, 1.9% Two+ races, 1.3% Other; 2.7% Hispanic Origin.

2000 Presidential Vote
Gore (D)	117,113	(65%)
Bush (R)	57,002	(32%)
Nader (Green)	3,487	(2%)
Others	1,383	(1%)

1996 Presidential Vote
Clinton (D)	111,918	(66%)
Dole (R)	48,955	(29%)
Perot (I)	9,389	(6%)

Rep. Bobby Scott (D)

Elected 1992, 5th term; b. Apr. 30, 1947, Washington, D.C.; home, Newport News; Harvard U., B.A. 1969, Boston Col. Law Schl., J.D. 1973; Episcopalian; single.

Military Career: Army Natl. Guard, 1970–73; Army Reserves, 1973–76.

Elected Office: VA House of Delegates, 1977–82; VA Senate, 1983–92.

Professional Career: Practicing atty., 1973–91.

DC Office: 2464 RHOB 20515, 202-225-8351; Fax: 202-225-8354; Web site: www.house.gov/scott.

District Offices: Newport News, 757-380-1000; Richmond, 804-644-4845.

Committees: *Education & the Workforce* (8th of 22 D): Education Reform; Select Education. *Judiciary* (6th of 17 D): Crime (RMM); The Constitution.

Group Ratings

	ADA	ACLU	AFS	LCV	CON	ITIC	NTU	COC	ACU	NTLC	CHC
2000	95	93	100	86	50	40	19	42	4	12	20
1999	90	—	100	81	40	—	13	28	4	—	—

National Journal Ratings

	1999 LIB	—	1999 CONS		2000 LIB	—	2000 CONS
Economic	80%	—	18%		81%	—	16%
Social	87%	—	0%		79%	—	17%
Foreign	78%	—	17%		66%	—	33%

Key Votes of the 106th Congress

1. Patient Bill of Rights	Y	5. Bar RU-486 $ for FDA	N	9. NATO War in Serbia	Y
2. Accelerate Min. Wage	Y	6. Display 10 Commandments	N	10. Perm. Trade with China	N
3. Strike Ban on Ergo. Stnd.	Y	7. Gun Show Bkgrnd. Checks	Y	11. Debt Relief for 3rd World	Y
4. Ovrd. Estate Tax Veto	N	8. Ban Part.-Birth Abortion	N	12. Drop Cuba Econ. Embargo	Y

Election Results

2000 general	Bobby Scott (D) .... unopposed			($250,417)
2000 primary	Bobby Scott (D) .... nominated by convention			
1998 general	Bobby Scott (D) 48,129	(76%)		($182,679)
	Robert S. (Bob) Barnett (I) 14,453	(23%)		

FOURTH DISTRICT

The clash of arms resounds through much of the history of Tidewater Virginia. This was the scene of the first permanent English settlement in North America, at Jamestown, and of its first revolution, Bacon's Rebellion, in 1676. In 1781, George Washington's tattered and exhausted army finally pushed General Cornwallis to the sea, while the French Navy waited at Yorktown: the final victory of the Revolutionary War. The Tidewater also was the scene of bitter fighting more than 80 years later in the Civil War, as Union troops invested the battlements of the small industrial city of Petersburg, 25 miles south of Richmond. Today, the Tidewater region boasts one of the densest concentrations of military power in the world: the Hampton Roads area has the United States' largest accumulation of Navy bases, while Fort Lee, the big Army base near Petersburg, provides an estimated 17,000 local jobs.

The 4th Congressional District includes much of the Tidewater. More than half its people are in the Hampton Roads area, in Portsmouth—a Navy port and industrial town with a charming old section—and in the suburban expanse of Chesapeake and Suffolk. The district also takes in the flat lands of Southside Virginia fanning south from the James River. These were tobacco lands when the English first settled them in the 17th Century; today they also produce Virginia's peanut crop and its Smithfield hams. The district includes Petersburg and Hopewell, with its Allied Chemical plant facing 18th Century plantations. Historically, this was a Democratic area, and the 4th's

Democratic percentages are buoyed up by the fact that nearly 40% of its residents are black. Although race relations have improved mightily in the past half-century, nagging problems remain: At the Greensville County court house in Emporia, federal and state officials have been squabbling for years over which employees are permitted to eat in its lunch room; although both sides contend that race is not at issue, the conflict between white officials and black custodians continued. Increasingly in state elections, this area has been trending Republican. It voted for Governors George Allen and James Gilmore in the 1990s. But presidential elections have been virtual toss-ups: Bill Clinton in 1992 and George W. Bush in 2000 each won by less than 1,000 votes.

The congressman from the 4th District is Randy Forbes, a Republican who won a special election in June 2001 to fill the seat of Democrat Norm Sisisky, who died on March 29. Forbes grew up in Chesapeake, majored in government at Randolph-Macon and received his law degree from the University of Virginia. His first job in politics was as a legislative aide to the Democratic state delegate from Chesapeake. When that incumbent retired in 1989, Forbes ran for and won the seat as a Republican. Four years later, he became the floor leader—still in the minority in the House of Delegates. He held that position until 1997, when he was elected to the state Senate, where he replaced Mark Earley, who was elected that year as attorney general and became the Republican nominee for governor in June 2001. Forbes also was floor leader of Senate Republicans and he sponsored legislation that abolished parole for state prisoners and passed a bill that permitted teachers to purchase insurance that protects them from lawsuits if they enforce discipline in classrooms. Forbes became a close friend of both Allen and Gilmore when they attended law school together; all three graduated from UVA in 1977. Allen tapped him to chair the state party in 1996, and Forbes helped to engineer the Republicans' historic sweep in 1997 of the three statewide offices, including Gilmore's victory as governor.

After considering but deciding against a challenge to Sisisky in 2000, Forbes was a leading candidate for lieutenant governor in 2001. When Sisisky died eight days after cancer surgery, national and state party leaders tapped Forbes as their choice to run for the competitive seat. Delegate Kirkland Cox challenged Forbes at the Republican nominating convention on April 28, but Forbes succeeded by enforcing unity in the delegations from Chesapeake and Portsmouth, the two largest cities in the district. "Free the hostages," the Cox delegates shouted as they sought to seat their supporters.

Forbes won the convention with 468 votes to 333 for Cox. He dodged a bullet when the strongest potential Democrat—Norm Sisisky's son Mark—declined to run. Instead, Democrats chose state Senator Louise Lucas from Portsmouth, who is African-American and since 1992 has held a majority-black seat. Lucas worked for 18 years at the Norfolk Naval Shipyard, where she became its first woman shipfitter. She had three children by age 21, and then returned to college and graduate school before becoming executive director of the Southeastern Tidewater Opportunity Project, an anti-poverty agency.

Both national parties and their interest-group allies spent heavily, with estimates of more than $3 million by each side. Republicans attacked Lucas for opposing repeal of the sales tax on non-prescription drugs and for supporting a gasoline tax increase. Democrats criticized Forbes for backing privatization of Social Security. Forbes said that he favored President Bush's campaign proposal to permit young persons to invest some of their payroll taxes in private accounts, but his ads emphasized that he would preserve current benefits—"every penny of it." When Democrats distributed a flier that "six million minority families" would be "left behind" by the Bush budget, Republicans accused Lucas of playing the race card. With the prospect of switching party control of a seat in the narrowly divided House, both parties publicly downplayed their expectations; Democratic insiders predicted they would suffer a double-digit loss. But the Lucas campaign did an effective job of turning out her base vote. In a half-dozen heavily black precincts in Portsmouth, where the turnout was as high as 62%, Lucas got more than 98%; she won 63% in Portsmouth. Lucas also ran strongly in Petersburg, but Forbes took 61% in more populous Chesapeake and won a majority in 7 of the 10 rural counties, for an overall win of 52%–48%. Gilmore said that the significant victory validated Bush's tax cut and that voters rejected Democratic scare tactics on Social Security. Democrats said that the close call showed their strong grass-root efforts and that Lucas was the victim of negative ads. The result marked only the fourth time since 1977 that the president's party has won a special election for a House seat that the other party has held. In 14 other special elections, the president's party lost a House seat that it had controlled.

In the House, Forbes was promised a seat on the Armed Services Committee. Republicans control redistricting, and they will likely make the 4th District safer for Forbes, partly by moving some of its black precincts to Bobby Scott's redrawn 3rd District.

Cook's Call *Potentially Competitive.* Forbes' narrow win in the special election illustrates this district's marginal nature. But, with Republicans controlling redistricting, it is likely that this seat will become safer for Forbes in 2002.

THE PEOPLE: Pop. 2000: 645,733; Pop. 1990: 563,206, up 14.7% 1990–2000. 57.4% White, 39.1% Black, 1.2% Asian, 0.3% Amer. Indian, 1.3% Two+ races, 0.7% Other; 1.8% Hispanic Origin.

2000 Presidential Vote			1996 Presidential Vote		
Bush (R)	116,861	(49%)	Clinton (D)	107,109	(50%)
Gore (D)	116,388	(49%)	Dole (R)	91,241	(43%)
Nader (Green)	2,248	(1%)	Perot (I)	14,581	(7%)
Others	1,808	(1%)			

Rep. J. Randy Forbes (R)

Elected June 2001, 1st term; b. Feb. 17, 1952, Chesapeake; home, Chesapeake; Randolph-Macon Col., B.A. 1974; U. of VA, J.D. 1977; Baptist; married (Shirley).

Elected Office: VA House of Del., 1989–97; VA Senate, 1997–2001.

Professional Career: Practicing atty., 1977-present.

DC Office: 2371 Rayburn 20515, 202-225-6365; Fax: 202-226-1170.

Committees: *Armed Services* (32d of 32 R). *Science* (25th of 25 R).

Group Ratings and Key Votes: Newly Elected

Election Results

2001 special	J. Randy Forbes (R)	70,926	(52%)	($305,662)
	Louise Lucas (D)	65,189	(48%)	($375,018)
2000 general	Norman Sisisky (D)	unopposed		($56,828)
2000 primary	Norman Sisisky (D)	nominated by convention		
1998 general	Norman Sisisky (D)	unopposed		($75,130)

FIFTH DISTRICT

Southside Virginia is a geographic name which for years was shorthand for a state of mind. Here is Appomattox Court House, in the serene little hamlet where Robert E. Lee surrendered to his onetime subordinate Ulysses S. Grant; here is Danville, where the tobacco auction originated in 1858; here also is Prince Edward County, where Harry Byrd's massive resistance shut down public schools in 1957 rather than obey a federal court desegregation order. This land north of the dividing line Colonel William Byrd surveyed in 1728 has some variety. Its eastern counties are flat and humid—frontier in the late colonial period, plantation country by 1800, now peanut fields and pine forests. To the west, into the Piedmont, the land gradually gets hillier. Here are textile mill towns and furniture manufacturing centers—Danville, Martinsville—and hills where moonshine is still a significant part of the local economy. Nearby is Bedford, site of the new D-Day Memorial, which lost more men per capita, 23 of its 35 soldiers, in the Normandy invasion than any other in the nation. Westward, nearer to the mountains, is more livestock and less tobacco, and the thick syrupy tones of the Southside Virginia accent turn to mountain twangs.

The 5th Congressional District consists of much of Southside Virginia, west of metropolitan Richmond and at some points up to the Blue Ridge. It includes Charlottesville and much of surrounding Albemarle County, but skirts around Lynchburg. Historically, politics here were Democratic, segregationist and conservative, run by chain-smoking local bankers and courthouse lawyers. Such Democrats are a rare breed these days, on the way to becoming extinct, and Southside is increasingly one of the Republican heartlands of Virginia.

The congressman from the 5th District is Virgil Goode (rhymes with mood), elected as a Democrat in 1996 and officially an independent since January 2000. Goode grew up in Franklin County, where his father was a prominent enough figure that part of U.S. 220 was named after him. He attended the University of Richmond and the University of Virginia law school. In 1973, the same year he graduated from law school, he was elected to the Virginia Senate, at 27. In 1994, Goode ran against scandal-beleaguered Senator Charles Robb in the Democratic primary; he lost 58%–34%, but showed local strength. In 1995, his re-election in a Republican-leaning state Senate district enabled Democrats to hold control of the Senate with a 20–20 tie that could be broken by Democratic Lieutenant Governor Donald Beyer.

In 1996, when conservative Democratic Congressman L.F. Payne retired, Goode seemed the only Democrat with a strong chance to win the district. He ran emphasizing bipartisan cooperation with the slogan on the pencils and emery boards he handed out to voters: "Work together in Congress." Republicans had a convention in which Delegate Frank Ruff, recruited by 7th District Congressman Tom Bliley, lost to George Landrith, a former Albemarle County school board member who had lost 53%–47% to Payne in 1994. This time it was no contest. Goode carried Franklin County 87%–10%; Landrith carried only two counties, one by a single vote. Overall, Goode won by the impressive margin of 61%–36%.

In the House, Goode compiled an increasingly conservative voting record. He joined the Blue Dogs and supported the Shays-Meehan campaign finance bill. By 1999 he had the most conservative voting records of any House Democrat, far closer to that of Republican neighbor Bob Goodlatte than Democratic neighbor Rick Boucher. He passionately opposed one of the Clinton White House's favorite projects, the tobacco bill: "I'm not going to support legislation that bankrupts the companies, destroys the family farm and relegates land to a place where hope is a stranger and mercy will never reach!" In Washington, he runs a low-budget operation that defies the sometimes opulent culture of Capitol Hill; lobbyists who visit must sit on a oak stump he has had since his days as a state senator, and during off-hours, he answers his own phone and takes messages for his aides.

Goode was one of 31 Democrats to vote for the Republicans' impeachment inquiry in October 1998, and in December 1998 he voted for impeachment, evidently not a close issue for him. "The party line says that lying under oath in a court proceeding is not an impeachable offense. I disagree with that." Even in Southside Virginia local Democrats reacted angrily to Goode. In January 1999 the district Democratic Party decided not to invite him to a February fundraising dinner. His chief of staff, who had told friends he would leave if Goode switched parties, quit that month. More senior Democrats, understanding that no other Democrat had a chance of carrying this district, were more conciliatory. But in 1999 he kept voting with Republicans on key issues—on gun control in June, on the $792 billion tax cut in July, on the budget which passed 218–211 in October. His own bill to repeal the District of Columbia's gun control laws was beaten 250–175 in June. "I believe in the Second Amendment. The Constitution stands above home government."

The Republican leadership had been keeping in touch with Goode through Bob Goodlatte, who frequently urged him to switch parties, especially after November 1999 when Republicans won majorities in both houses of the legislature, and thus control of redistricting. In December 1999 Goode attended a fundraiser for Republican Senate candidate George Allen. On January 24, 2000, Goode announced that he would no longer attend the Democratic Caucus and would run for re-election as an independent. He said that he opposed Democrats' positions on spending and tobacco. Now "you don't have some Democrats telling you that you didn't vote the national party line enough. I will be voting as I have in the past." On January 27 he announced that he would be attending the Republican Conference and would contribute to House Republicans' campaign committee, though he would still remain an independent. Republicans promptly gave him a seat on the Appropriations Committee. In February, in Danville at the Piedmont Big Sale tobacco warehouse, he endorsed George W. Bush for president.

In May 2000 Goode wrote all his contributors offering refunds; in the first few days he got one letter requesting $50. In his well-financed 2000 campaign he attacked the Clinton administration for neglecting the woes of the Southside textile and apparel industries—Goode has voted against free trade agreements, including PNTR for China—and campaigned with George Allen. Opposed by a Democrat who headed a black farmers' advocacy group, he won 67%–31%, carrying every city and county except the university town of Charlottesville.

Was redistricting a factor in Goode's switch? Perhaps. He said no one promised him anything, but he had witnessed redistricting in the legislature in 1981 and 1991, and in 2000 said: "Anyone who focuses on that will stay awake at night and will have many sleepless nights over something they can't control." If he had remained a Democrat, Republicans might have put his base of Franklin County into the 9th District, where he would have had a tough time winning coal mining counties in a primary with the somewhat more liberal incumbent Rick Boucher. As it is, redistricters are more likely to extend his district north and perhaps east to include more Republican territory, while the 9th might extend into Roanoke and the 6th extended north in the Shenandoah Valley.

Cook's Call *Safe.* Goode's biggest threat in this conservative, Republican-leaning district comes not from Republicans, but from disgruntled members of his former party, angry at his decision to switch from Democrat to independent. But Goode's conservative record and down-home style make him tough to beat.

THE PEOPLE: Pop. 2000: 620,104; Pop. 1990: 562,273, up 10.3% 1990–2000. 73.4% White, 24% Black, 0.9% Asian, 0.2% Amer. Indian, 0.9% Two+ races, 0.6% Other; 1.6% Hispanic Origin.

2000 Presidential Vote			1996 Presidential Vote		
Bush (R)	134,391	(56%)	Dole (R)	103,796	(49%)
Gore (D)	96,097	(40%)	Clinton (D)	92,656	(43%)
Nader (Green)	4,819	(2%)	Perot (I)	16,867	(8%)
Others	3,648	(2%)			

Rep. Virgil H. Goode (I)

Elected 1996, 3d term; b. Oct. 17, 1946, Richmond; home, Rocky Mount; U. of Richmond, B.A. 1969, U. of VA, J.D. 1973; Baptist; married (Lucy).

Military Career: VA Natl. Guard, 1969–75.

Elected Office: VA Senate, 1973–96.

Professional Career: Practicing atty., 1973–96.

DC Office: 1520 LHOB 20515, 202-225-4711; Fax: 202-225-5681; Web site: www.house.gov/goode.

District Offices: Charlottesville, 804-295-6372; Danville, 804-792-1280; Farmville, 804-392-8331; Rocky Mount, 540-484-1254.

Committees: *Appropriations* (1st of 1 I): Agriculture, Rural Development, & FDA; Military Construction; VA, HUD & Independent Agencies.

Group Ratings

	ADA	ACLU	AFS	LCV	CON	ITIC	NTU	COC	ACU	NTLC	CHC
2000	10	36	14	7	66	67	68	66	100	15	93
1999	25	—	16	19	87	—	69	84	92	—	—

National Journal Ratings

	1999 LIB —	1999 CONS		2000 LIB —	2000 CONS
Economic	30%	64%		0%	94%
Social	10%	85%		0%	79%
Foreign	0%	97%		39%	57%

Key Votes of the 106th Congress

1. Patient Bill of Rights	N	5. Bar RU-486 $ for FDA	Y	9. NATO War in Serbia	N
2. Accelerate Min. Wage	N	6. Display 10 Commandments	Y	10. Perm. Trade with China	N
3. Strike Ban on Ergo. Stnd.	N	7. Gun Show Bkgrnd. Checks	N	11. Debt Relief for 3rd World	N
4. Ovrd. Estate Tax Veto	Y	8. Ban Part.-Birth Abortion	Y	12. Drop Cuba Econ. Embargo	N

Election Results

2000 general	Virgil H. Goode (I)	143,312	(67%)	($581,016)
	John W. Boyd, Jr. (D)	65,387	(31%)	($38,455)
	Others	4,006	(2%)	
2000 primary	Virgil H. Goode (I)	unopposed		
1998 general	Virgil H. Goode (D)	unopposed		($129,066)

SIXTH DISTRICT

The sturdy men and women who settled the Valley of Virginia west of the Blue Ridge were quite different from the "second sons" of the European aristocracy who cleared the marshy forests of the Tidewater and built grand plantations there. Even before the Revolutionary War, Englishmen and Scots, German Protestants and Mennonites and Moravians—members of religious communities and fiercely independent farmers—poured down the great Wagon Road from Pennsylvania to the Valley. They were looking not for the flat, mahogany-brown land that eastern tobacco growers sought, but for fields which could support wheat, corn and hay, crops which could be rotated and which an individual farmer and his family could handle. That same independent spirit nurtured the growth of higher education here. In Lexington alone are Washington and Lee University, which Robert E. Lee headed, and the Virginia Military Institute, where Stonewall Jackson taught philosophy and artillery tactics, and which began admitting women in 1996 under order from the U.S. Supreme Court. A quartet of the South's most distinguished women's private colleges are only a short drive away: Mary Baldwin College at Staunton, Randolph-Macon Woman's College at Lynchburg, Sweet Briar College at Sweet Briar, and Hollins College at Roanoke, farther south in the Valley. Industry flourished here more than in most of Virginia east of the Blue Ridge. In the 19th Century the Norfolk and Southern Railroad established its chief junction at Roanoke; as the years passed the city became the railroad's headquarters, and many major companies have plants here. In 1999, more than 16,000 people were working in technology companies in the Roanoke and New River valleys.

The 6th Congressional District covers the heart of the Valley of Virginia, from Harrisonburg south to Roanoke, and crosses over the Blue Ridge to take in Lynchburg. Politically, this area has a Republican tradition hospitable to economic assistance for the little guy, and fiercely opposed to Harry Byrd Democrats. But in more recent years, the ancestral conservatism of Byrd Democrats and the feisty politics of the mountain rebels have melded into a single conservative Republicanism, more populist than elite in tone, as concerned with moral values as economic freedom, prickly about interference from Washington or even Richmond.

The congressman from the 6th District is Bob Goodlatte, a Republican first elected in 1992. Goodlatte grew up in Massachusetts, attended college in Maine and then law school at Washington & Lee, and went to work in Congressman Caldwell Butler's office in Roanoke. Goodlatte then practiced law and stayed active in politics; in 1992, when Democratic Congressman Jim Olin retired, Goodlatte was nominated by convention and won the general 60%–40%.

Goodlatte has compiled a mostly conservative voting record. When Republicans took control in the 104th Congress, he rushed to confront OMB Director Alice Rivlin on the administration's unbalanced budget and was floor leader for the "loser pays" provision in Contract with America litigation reform legislation. Later, he sponsored the House-passed bill to limit class-action lawsuits against tobacco companies, gun makers and others companies. He favors scrapping the current tax code and replacing it with a much simpler tax. He has proposed limited campaign finance measures including requiring candidates' supporters to identify themselves on polls of more than 1,200 respondents, repealing voter registration by mail, banning fundraising in the White House and requiring disclosure of contributions and expenditures by computer.

With 9th District neighbor Rick Boucher, Goodlatte has become a leader among House members working on technology issues. He has been an enthusiast for the Internet, and chairman of Speaker Dennis Hastert's High-Tech Working Group. The Internet has provided rural Americans with economic opportunities once available only in urban hubs such as Wall Street, he contends. "Really, this technology is the future of my district," he told *National Journal*. With Boucher—the two have co-chaired the Congressional Internet Caucus—he has encouraged open access to broadband technology. Those two also cosponsored a loan-guarantee program to improve rural satellite owners' access to local broadcast stations. He has been chief sponsor, with Silicon Valley Democrat Zoe Lofgren, of bills to liberalize export controls on encryption technology. Although these were opposed by the NSA and FBI, which wanted law enforcement and intelligence agencies to possess keys to encryption, the Clinton White House agreed to the legislation under congressional pressure. He and Lofgren also have complained about federal on-line services, such as those operated by the Postal Service, that have unfair competitive advantages over private-sector services. Goodlatte sponsored the Communications Decency Act, allowing censorship of obscene material on the Internet, which was overturned by the Supreme Court. He sponsored a law imposing tougher penalties on commercial counterfeiters, especially important in the software industry; he sought tougher penalties for telemarketing fraud. The House defeated his bill to ban most forms of online gambling. He amended the Telecommunications Act to give local governments more say over the location of cellular phone towers.

In 1998 Goodlatte was opposed by David Bowers, mayor of Roanoke since 1992. Goodlatte was confident enough to leave $460,000 cash on hand after the campaign, which he won 69%–31%, carrying every city and county and winning in Roanoke 58%–42%. He was unopposed in 2000. Republicans redistricters are likely to move the district north in the Shenandoah Valley, leaving it still heavily Republican.

Cook's Call *Safe*. Since winning this formerly Democratic seat in 1992, Goodlatte has had no trouble racking up big re-election margins here.

THE PEOPLE: Pop. 2000: 609,802; Pop. 1990: 562,426, up 8.4% 1990–2000. 85.2% White, 11.7% Black, 1% Asian, 0.2% Amer. Indian, 1.2% Two+ races, 0.7% Other; 1.9% Hispanic Origin.

2000 Presidential Vote		
Bush (R)	135,417	(58%)
Gore (D)	89,524	(39%)
Nader (Green)	4,934	(2%)
Others	2,056	(1%)

1996 Presidential Vote		
Dole (R)	108,757	(51%)
Clinton (D)	87,883	(41%)
Perot (I)	16,116	(8%)

Rep. Bob Goodlatte (R)

Elected 1992, 5th term; b. Sept. 22, 1952, Holyoke, MA; home, Roanoke; Bates Col., B.A. 1974, Washington & Lee Law Schl., J.D. 1977; Christian Scientist; married (Maryellen).

Professional Career: Dist. Dir., U.S. Rep. Caldwell Butler, 1977–79; Practicing atty., 1979–92.

DC Office: 2240 RHOB 20515, 202-225-5431; Fax: 202-225-9681; Web site: www.house.gov/goodlatte.

District Offices: Harrisonburg, 540-432-2391; Lynchburg, 804-845-8306; Roanoke, 540-857-2672; Staunton, 540-885-3861.

Committees: *Agriculture* (3d of 27 R): Department Operations, Oversight, Nutrition & Forestry (Chmn.); Livestock & Horticulture. *Education & the Workforce* (21st of 27 R): 21st Century Competitiveness; Workforce Protections. *Judiciary* (7th of 21 R): Courts, the Internet & Intellectual Property; Crime.

Group Ratings

	ADA	ACLU	AFS	LCV	CON	ITIC	NTU	COC	ACU	NTLC	CHC
2000	0	29	0	7	74	100	68	85	100	91	100
1999	5	—	16	6	68	—	62	88	96	—	—

National Journal Ratings

	1999 LIB	—	1999 CONS		2000 LIB	—	2000 CONS
Economic	24%	—	72%		0%	—	94%
Social	4%	—	91%		0%	—	79%
Foreign	3%	—	92%		39%	—	57%

Key Votes of the 106th Congress

1. Patient Bill of Rights	N	5. Bar RU-486 $ for FDA	Y	9. NATO War in Serbia	N
2. Accelerate Min. Wage	N	6. Display 10 Commandments	Y	10. Perm. Trade with China	Y
3. Strike Ban on Ergo. Stnd.	N	7. Gun Show Bkgrnd. Checks	N	11. Debt Relief for 3rd World	N
4. Ovrd. Estate Tax Veto	Y	8. Ban Part.-Birth Abortion	Y	12. Drop Cuba Econ. Embargo	N

Election Results

2000 general	Bob Goodlatte (R)	....	unopposed		($395,342)
2000 primary	Bob Goodlatte (R)	....	nominated by convention		
1998 general	Bob Goodlatte (R)	....	89,177	(69%)	($824,510)
	David A. Bowers (D)	....	39,487	(31%)	($83,760)

SEVENTH DISTRICT

In the center of Virginia, on a hill in downtown Richmond above the James River, is Thomas Jefferson's Capitol, one of the first classical-style buildings in North America, chaste and simple in the Jefferson style. A mile or so west is Monument Avenue, Richmond's grand 140-foot-wide boulevard, punctuated by circles, each with a statue of a Confederate hero—Robert E. Lee (62 feet tall, dedicated Memorial Day 1890), Jeb Stuart, Jefferson Davis, Stonewall Jackson, Matthew Fountain Maury, "the Pathfinder of the Sea." Richmond is a monument to Jefferson and to the Confederacy; its metro area is only the third largest in the state, but it still sets the tone for Virginia, and is the home of many of the state's great institutions—Dominion Resources, Main Street banks, big law firms, and the Richmond *Times-Dispatch*. Richmond has long since grown out past its city borders, covering almost all of suburban Henrico and Chesterfield Counties and spreading out into what was until recently countryside. For many years Richmond was riven by sharp racial differences. It was from here that Virginia's leaders called for massive resistance to desegregation in the 1950s, and when Richmond elected its first black-majority council in the 1970s, the outgoing council deeded the statue of Lee to the state for fear it would be torn down. Now Richmond has come to a better place. Blacks have been a majority in the city for two decades now, and in 1989 Virginia elected a black governor, Douglas Wilder, who grew up on Church Hill, in a segregated neighborhood overlooking the Capitol. The state's Martin Luther King Jr. Holiday pays homage to Confederate heroes and to the civil rights leader, and a statue of Richmond-born African-American tennis champion Arthur Ashe has been added to Monument Avenue. Politically there remain differences. Black-majority Richmond is solidly Democratic; Henrico and Chesterfield and the counties beyond are heavily Republican.

The 7th Congressional District includes most of the Richmond area, but many black precincts in the city and Henrico County are in the black-majority 3d District, which extends downriver along the James to Newport News and Norfolk. The 1992 and 1993 districting plans were overturned by federal court decisions, and replaced with a 1998 plan which straightens the lines and adds three counties upriver from Richmond; the district also has an extension that runs north past James Madison's home at Montpelier to Culpeper County and the Blue Ridge Mountains. But nearly 80% of the 7th's population is in metro Richmond. This is the most heavily Republican district in Virginia.

The congressman from the 7th District is Eric Cantor, a Republican elected in 2000. He grew up in Henrico County and graduated from George Washington University and William and Mary Law School and got a master's degree in real estate from Columbia University. He then began practicing law in his family's firm in Richmond. In 1991 he was elected to the first of five terms in Virginia's House of Delegates. In the legislature, he was a leading ally of business, sponsoring a bill to limit the liability of Philip Morris in a Florida court decree and opposing restrictions on telemarketers. When 7th District Congressman Tom Bliley, after 20 years in the House and six years—the limit imposed by Republican rules—as chairman of the Commerce Committee, announced his retirement, Cantor entered the race. He had a big advantage: He had served as Bliley's campaign chairman for six years and had the backing of Bliley's political organization. He endorsed a $1,000 per child education tax credit, elimination of the marriage tax penalty, and an increase in the maximum IRA contribution. Cantor, who is Jewish, has strongly supported Israel, and helped create the Virginia-Israel Advisory and secured funding for a new building for the Virginia Holocaust Museum.

Still, Cantor faced a serious contest in the Republican primary, which was tantamount to victory here. His opponent was state Senator Stephen Martin, who quit school after the death of his father, a country preacher, and helped raise his five sisters; Martin emphasized his low-income background and he had a solid base of social and religious conservatives. Their contest turned negative: Cantor attacked Martin for supporting a back-door pay raise for legislators; Martin questioned Cantor's business dealings. Both supported gun rights and abolition of the National Endowment for the Arts, and opposed racial quotas and most abortions. Cantor supported permanent normal trade relations with China; Martin was opposed. Cantor, who was well-known in his Henrico County base, had a big fundraising advantage and put on a substantial advertising campaign. Martin raised less than $200,000—a quarter of what Cantor spent in the primary. Cantor got the endorsement of Governor Jim Gilmore, but won the primary by only 263 votes. Cantor won 74% in Henrico, while Martin won 77% in his Chesterfield County base; each county cast about one-third of the total vote. Cantor won 64% of the Richmond vote and won 53% in the remaining mostly rural nine counties, which cast 26% of the total vote. After the contest, Martin left the door open to another run for Congress.

The general election was something of an after-thought. Cantor beat former Goochland County school superintendent Warren A. Stewart by 67%–33%. Republicans control redistricting, and they may add some black precincts in Richmond as part of a maneuver to make the neighboring 4th District more Republican, and remove some of the rural counties. But that should leave the 3rd District still safely Republican.

Cook's Call *Safe.* Cantor will never have much trouble holding on to the 7th District, the most Republican in Virginia (Bush won by 27% here in 2000). This was one of the faster-growing districts in the state during the 1990s and will have to shed almost 50,000 residents in redistricting.

THE PEOPLE: Pop. 2000: 699,196; Pop. 1990: 562,729, up 24.3% 1990–2000. 81.6% White, 13.5% Black, 2.4% Asian, 0.3% Amer. Indian, 1.3% Two+ races, 1% Other; 2.3% Hispanic Origin.

2000 Presidential Vote			1996 Presidential Vote		
Bush (R)	194,807	(62%)	Dole (R)	158,918	(60%)
Gore (D)	109,312	(35%)	Clinton (D)	90,351	(34%)
Nader (Green)	6,618	(2%)	Perot (I)	16,647	(6%)
Others	2,392	(1%)			

Rep. Eric Cantor (R)

Elected 2000, 1st term; b. June 6, 1963, Richmond; home, Richmond; George Washington U., B.A. 1985; Col. of William & Mary, J.D. 1988; Columbia U., M.S., 1989; Jewish; married (Diana).

Elected Office: VA House of Del., 1991–2000.

Professional Career: Practicing atty., 1990-present.

DC Office: 329 CHOB 20515, 202-225-2815; Fax: 202-225-0011; Web site: cantor.house.gov.

District Offices: Culpeper, 540-825-8960; Glen Allen, 804-771-2809.

Committees: *Financial Services* (31st of 37 R): Financial Institutions & Consumer Credit; Housing & Community Opportunity; Oversight & Investigations. *International Relations* (23d of 26 R): Europe; Middle East & South Asia.

Group Ratings and Key Votes: Newly Elected

Election Results

2000 general	Eric Cantor (R)	192,652	(67%)	($1,336,548)
	Warren A. Stewart (D)	94,935	(33%)	($70,430)
2000 primary	Eric Cantor (R)	20,902	(50%)	
	Steven H. Martin (R)	20,639	(50%)	
1998 general	Tom Bliley (R)	77,044	(79%)	($817,037)
	Bradley E. Evans (I)	20,293	(21%)	($564)

EIGHTH DISTRICT

More than two hundred years ago, when George Washington trod the brick sidewalks of Alexandria, Virginia, on his way to market or court or church, this was the largest city in northern Virginia, and dwarfed Georgetown, Maryland, just up the Potomac River; what is now Capitol Hill and downtown Washington were hills above the river's mud flats. As Washington grew, Northern Virginia seemed left behind. In 1846 the District of Columbia retroceded its land south of the Potomac—now Alexandria and Arlington—to Virginia because it seemed obvious that the federal government would never need it, and it was 97 years before the first federal building was built on the Virginia side—the Pentagon; Franklin Roosevelt wondered out loud what they would do with all that space after the war. When the Pentagon was built, Alexandria and the rural countryside of Northern Virginia were represented in Congress by Judge Howard W. Smith, a Harry Byrd Democrat, who saw as his mission the maintenance of the standards of George Washington, Thomas Jefferson and Robert E. Lee. Yet by the 1960s, even as Judge Smith kept his law offices in Old Town, Alexandria, the area was changing around him. New subdivision dwellers with white-collar jobs and lots of children wanted schools with good academic programs—not the segregated schoolhouses Judge Smith's friends were willing to finance. The new generation wanted freeways and traffic lights, parks and recreation facilities. Smith's district was moved farther out into the countryside, two-party politics came to the suburbs, and local governments got to work. The congressional seat here, though often bitterly contested, was held from 1952–74 by Republican Joel Broyhill, a real estate developer who ran a fine constituency service operation in a district more than one-third of whose residents were federal employees.

Now the onetime suburbs of Arlington and Alexandria have become central cities of a sort—"edge cities," using Joel Garreau's term—themselves. Giant office developments sprang up from rail yards in Crystal City and from used car lots in Rosslyn. Vietnamese and Salvadorans, immigrants from Asia and Latin America have moved into these neighborhoods, and one of America's biggest Vietnamese commercial districts is in Clarendon, about a mile from Arlington National Cemetery and Fort Myer. Politically, Alexandria and Arlington, once hotly contested, are now solidly Democratic.

The 8th Congressional District consists of Arlington County and the cities of Alexandria and Falls Church. It also takes in two separate parts of Fairfax County: the portion of high-income McLean inside the Capital Beltway and several areas south of Alexandria's Old Town—the gentle landscapes of Mount Vernon, lower-income Groveton along the old U.S. 1, suburban Springfield and the more rural areas around Lorton and Fort Belvoir. This district was designed for the 1990s by a Democratic legislature and governor to be solidly Democratic. Where formerly there had been two marginal Northern Virginia districts, now there is the safely Democratic 8th, the safely Republican 10th and the closely divided 11th (Democratic in 1992, Republican since then.)

The congressman from the 8th District is Jim Moran, an oft-embattled Alexandria politician with traces in his accent of his Massachusetts roots. He graduated from Holy Cross and got a master's degree, worked in Washington for HEW, the Library of Congress and the Senate Appropriations Committee. He was elected to the Alexandria City Council in 1979 and vice mayor in 1982; in 1984 he pleaded no contest to a conflict of interest charge and resigned from the Council. The charges were eventually dropped (the law he supposedly violated was even changed), and in 1985 Moran was elected mayor. In 1990, he ran for Congress in what had become one of the most populous districts in the country, stretching from Alexandria south almost to Fredericksburg, against Republican incumbent Stanford Parris. It was a nasty race: Parris said Moran was a supporter of Saddam Hussein; Moran said he wanted to "break [Parris's] nose," and called him "a deceitful, fatuous jerk." The major substantive issue was abortion, on which Moran ran a pro-choice ad portraying Lady Liberty behind bars. With a big margin in Alexandria, Moran won 52%–45%.

In the House, Moran flip-flopped on his first big vote, the Gulf war resolution, which he ultimately voted against. He jousted—literally—with other Republicans, shoving Californian Duke Cunningham off the floor and out the House chamber doors in November 1995 after Cunningham said that Moran had "turned his back on Desert Storm." Moran later apologized and said, "I would prefer to be known as a statesman rather than a fighter in the literal way." He has engaged in a long and mostly unsuccessful fight to stop 11,000 Navy employees from being relocated out of Crystal City but he successfully fought the late Redskins owner Jack Kent Cooke's plan to build a football stadium at Potomac Yards in Alexandria. In 1993 he voted for the Clinton budget and tax package, despite its one-year pay freeze on federal employees—a tough vote in a district where 21% of workers are federal employees, the second highest in the country. He balked at Clinton's health care reform because it threatened federal employees' plan, and he blasted as "politically expedient" and based on "sound bites" Al Gore's reinventing government plan as threatening the most talented federal employees.

Moran, with Cal Dooley and Tim Roemer, founded in March 1997 the New Democrat Coalition, made up of moderate Democrats mostly from suburban districts to work for alternatives to "traditional Democratic policies." Working with other New Democrats and with Virginians, he became a strong ally of the local high-tech industry. He was an early supporter of fast track, which he struggled in vain to pass, and of permanent normal trade relations with China, which was successful. He actively backed Clinton's Kosovo initiative. He was the only Democrat to vote for a Republican program to allow local governments to consolidate federal grants into more flexible spending plans: his Alexandria experience counted. He criticized John Dingell for "doing the NRA's bidding" and harming Democrats in weakening gun-control legislation. On the Appropriations Committee, from his seat on the District of Columbia Subcommittee he has put in much bipartisan labor to straighten out the District's finances—and in the process helped force the District to close Lorton prison in Virginia; he also worked to reverse the federal ban on adoptions by gay couples in the District. He strongly opposed the Republican initiative to rename Washington National Airport after Ronald Reagan. He worked with others to approve financing for the new $2.1 billion Woodrow Wilson Bridge across the Potomac. He was strongly critical of Bill Clinton's conduct in the Lewinsky scandal and in September 1998 suggested the president should resign. He was one of 31 Democrats who voted for the Republicans' impeachment inquiry, but he voted against impeachment in December. He criticized the Pentagon for being intimidated by its employee, and ex-Lewinsky pal, Linda Tripp when Tripp was seeking job protection.

The 1992 redistricting gave Moran a solidly Democratic district, but he has had serious competition anyway; perhaps combativeness invites combativeness. He won 56% in 1992 and 59% in 1994 against Kyle McSlarrow, later a top aide to Bob Dole and Trent Lott and manager of Dan Quayle's presidential campaign. In 1998 and 2000 he was opposed by psychologist Demaris Miller, wife of Reagan OMB Director James Miller. But neither race got very close; Moran won 67% and 63%. He received negative headlines just before the 2000 election when *The Washington Post* reported that Maryland 8th District Democratic challenger—and pharmaceutical-company lobbyist—Terry Lierman gave his financially-troubled friend Moran a $25,000 loan on generous terms; but Moran quickly agreed to repay the loan and he suffered no apparent political damage. The Justice department ended its investigation in June 2001, but the Ethics Committee has launched its own inquiry.

Republicans control redistricting, and it is theoretically possible for them to reshape the three Northern Virginia as three pie-shaped wedges heading out from Arlington and Alexandria to the distant suburbs, each leaning mildly Republican. But that would risk losing all three in a heavily Democratic year and would not necessarily defeat Moran. The 11th District's Tom Davis, the chairman of House Republicans' campaign committee, fearing that his own district might go Democratic if he runs for statewide office, prefers to keep a safely Democratic 8th and leave the 11th and 10th solidly Republican. That is advice that the legislature seems likely to take. Joe

McCain, who is a freelance writer in Fairfax and Senator John McCain's younger brother, is said to be considering a run here in 2002.

Cook's Call   *Safe*. This district has seen some competitive races in the past, but is now one of the most reliably Democratic in the state. If Republicans opt to shore up Republican Tom Davis' Fairfax County district during redistricting, they will make the 8th even more Democratic.

THE PEOPLE: Pop. 2000: 627,849; Pop. 1990: 562,808, up 11.6% 1990–2000. 66.8% White, 14% Black, 8.7% Asian, 0.3% Amer. Indian, 0.1% Hawaiian, 4% Two+ races, 6.2% Other; 13.8% Hispanic Origin.

2000 Presidential Vote

Gore (D)	149,591	(55%)
Bush (R)	109,034	(40%)
Nader (Green)	9,866	(4%)
Others	2,138	(1%)

1996 Presidential Vote

Clinton (D)	130,177	(55%)
Dole (R)	95,839	(41%)
Perot (I)	9,439	(4%)

Rep. James P. Moran (D)

Elected 1990, 6th term; b. May 16, 1945, Buffalo, NY; home, Alexandria; Col. of Holy Cross, B.A. 1967, City U. of NY, 1968, U. of Pittsburgh, M.P.A. 1970; Catholic; divorced.

Elected Office: Alexandria City Cncl., 1979–82; Alexandria Vice Mayor, 1982–84, Alexandria Mayor, 1985–90.

Professional Career: Budget analyst & auditor, U.S. Dept. of H.E.W., 1968–74; Fiscal policy spec., Library of Congress, 1974–76; Staff, U.S. Senate Approp. Cmte., 1976–80; Investment broker, 1980–88.

DC Office: 2239 RHOB 20515, 202-225-4376; Fax: 202-225-0017; Web site: www.house.gov/moran.

District Office: Alexandria, 703-971-4700.

Committees: *Appropriations* (13th of 29 D): Defense; Interior; The Legislative Branch (RMM). *Budget* (10th of 20 D).

Group Ratings

	ADA	ACLU	AFS	LCV	CON	ITIC	NTU	COC	ACU	NTLC	CHC
2000	70	79	42	86	61	100	26	66	12	12	13
1999	90	—	100	75	83	—	19	64	12	—	—

National Journal Ratings

	1999 LIB —	1999 CONS		2000 LIB —	2000 CONS
Economic	56% —	44%		60% —	39%
Social	79% —	20%		70% —	29%
Foreign	61% —	37%		74% —	24%

Key Votes of the 106th Congress

1. Patient Bill of Rights	Y	5. Bar RU-486 $ for FDA	N	9. NATO War in Serbia	Y
2. Accelerate Min. Wage	Y	6. Display 10 Commandments	N	10. Perm. Trade with China	Y
3. Strike Ban on Ergo. Stnd.	Y	7. Gun Show Bkgrnd. Checks	Y	11. Debt Relief for 3rd World	Y
4. Ovrd. Estate Tax Veto	N	8. Ban Part.-Birth Abortion	Y	12. Drop Cuba Econ. Embargo	Y

Election Results

2000 general	James P. Moran (D)	164,178	(63%)	($1,203,058)
	Demaris H. Miller (R)	88,262	(34%)	($204,046)
	Others	6,759	(3%)	
2000 primary	James P. Moran (D)	nominated by convention		
1998 general	James P. Moran (D)	97,545	(67%)	($559,357)
	Demaris H. Miller (R)	48,352	(33%)	($643,434)

NINTH DISTRICT

One of the first areas to be settled from the seacoast to the great American interior was what is now southwest Virginia. As early as 1765, settlements were carved out of the great Valley of

Virginia, which bends westward and south toward Tennessee and the Cumberland Gap. Most settlers were of Scots-Irish lineage, and the mountainous area where they moved developed almost apart from the rest of Virginia. The fiercely independent settlers were first farmers, later often coal miners, as in West Virginia, which wasn't a separate state until 1863. Politically, this virtually all-white area opposed slavery and was skeptical if not hostile to the Confederacy. Out of the crucible of struggle between secessionists and unionists, southwest Virginia developed a robust two-party politics after the Civil War, with both parties resembling their national counterparts more closely than in the rest of Virginia.

The 9th Congressional District covers all of southwest Virginia west of Roanoke. Over the years, the district became known as the "Fighting Ninth," because of its taste for raucous politics, culturally conservative and economically populist. It has become somewhat more like the rest of Virginia, as development has moved down Interstate 81 to, and even past, Blacksburg, home of Virginia Tech. But mountain counties farther west continue to depend on coal and to lose population. The Fighting Ninth voted for Republican Governors George Allen and James Gilmore and for 1994 Republican Senate candidate Oliver North. It voted narrowly for Bill Clinton in 1992 and 1996 and for 1996 Democratic Senate candidate Mark Warner and by a much wider margin for George W. Bush in 2000. No other Virginia district voted for that combination.

The congressman from the 9th is Rick Boucher, a Democrat first elected in 1982. Boucher grew up in the antique town of Abingdon, went to Roanoke College and then the University of Virginia law school; he practiced law in Abingdon and was elected to the Virginia Senate in 1975, at 29. Politics runs in the family: his father was the Republican commonwealth's attorney in Washington County, while his mother was county Democratic chairwoman; his grandfather and great-grandfather were Democratic members of the House of Delegates. In 1982 Boucher ran for the U.S. House against veteran incumbent William Wampler and won with big margins in coal counties on the Kentucky border. Boucher tends to vote with House Democrats most but not all the time.

Boucher says that he has devoted 80% of his legislative time to technology issues, including his work on the Commerce Committee's Telecommunications Subcommittee. Back in 1988 he co-sponsored with Al Gore a bill to allow phone companies to offer cable TV and sponsored the Satellite Home Viewers Act, so viewers without over-the-air network reception could subscribe to satellite services carrying network channels: the beginning of the now booming satellite TV business. Cable TV had its start in mountainous areas where network TV signals were weak, and Boucher sees new technologies, from satellite TV to the Internet, as a means for out-of-the-way places like the 9th to compete on an equal commercial basis with urban areas. On the 1996 Telecommunications Act he helped write provisions intended to open up competition in the local telephone and cable TV markets. He has gotten Appalachian Regional Commission grant money to create an electronic classroom in Floyd County which will allow communication and instruction in all the schools in southwest Virginia. He has set up "electronic villages" in Blacksburg and Abingdon, with entire communities online. He convinced Colorado-based EchoStar Communications Corp. to establish a presence in southwest Virginia. "I think the arrival of the Internet as a revolutionary communications medium provides a breakthrough opportunity for economic improvements in rural areas because it spells the death of distance," he said in 2000. *Network Computing* magazine called him one of the 10 most important people of the 1990s.

Boucher was a co-founder of the House Internet Caucus in April 1996 with Rick White of Washington; he is now co-chair with Bob Goodlatte of the next-door 6th District. He worked on the Judiciary Subcommittee on Courts and Intellectual Property with Goodlatte to update copyright laws for the digital age and for a consensus on a National Information Infrastructure. He sponsored the law which permitted messages with commercial content to traverse the Internet backbone. With Goodlatte, he established a loan-guarantee program for private businesses to deliver television signals to satellite TV viewers in rural areas.

Boucher also has worked for binding arbitration to settle Superfund suits, for allowing state and local governments to engage in interstate shipment of municipal waste and for electricity deregulation, which he hopes will benefit the coal industry and stimulate investment in mine facilities. He opposed permanent normal trade relations with China, voicing concern about the impact on jobs in his district. In 1993 he set up a Commission on the Future of Southwest Virginia, which has called for a venture capital fund, a joint state legislative agenda and winterizing state parks. In 1998 he announced a $500,000 TVA grant to set up a Nature Conservancy Timber Bank, to which landholders can sell their timber rights. He conducts an active constituency service operation in an area where many people have problems with Social Security, veterans' benefits and black lung payments. He won approval for a $177 million Army Corps of Engineers project to move part of the often-flooded town of Grundy to higher ground from the Levisa River.

Boucher came into the national spotlight in the hearings on Clinton's impeachment. Far less strident than most other Judiciary Committee Democrats, speaking with old-fashioned formality in a businesslike manner, he pressed Kenneth Starr on whether a president can be prosecuted after leaving office. He was the author of the Democratic resolution to conduct a limited impeachment inquiry in October 1998. In December he was the author of the Democrats' censure resolution.

In this usually partisan district Boucher has become highly popular. His Commerce Committee seat helps him to raise large sums of money and he usually wins comfortably. In 2000 he spent $676,000 and had $585,000 cash on hand afterwards, following his 70%–30% victory over a Christian bookstore owner. Republicans control redistricting, and this corner-of-the-state district must add territory. To protect Virgil Goode in the next-door 5th District, redistricters will probably add territory in Roanoke County. That would make the district more Republican should Boucher not run but will not be much of a threat to his tenure.

Cook's Call   *Safe.* Though this conservative district has been quite competitive in presidential races, Boucher has continued to post impressive margins of victory since 1984. Republicans may make some changes in redistricting but acknowledge that they might not win this seat until Boucher decides to step down.

THE PEOPLE: Pop. 2000: 582,943; Pop. 1990: 562,508, up 3.6% 1990–2000. 95.1% White, 2.8% Black, 0.8% Asian, 0.2% Amer. Indian, 0.8% Two+ races, 0.4% Other; 1% Hispanic Origin.

2000 Presidential Vote

Bush (R)	116,851	(55%)
Gore (D)	90,916	(42%)
Nader (Green)	3,866	(2%)
Others	2,746	(1%)

1996 Presidential Vote

Clinton (D)	91,469	(46%)
Dole (R)	85,531	(43%)
Perot (I)	20,603	(10%)

Rep. Rick Boucher (D)

Elected 1982, 10th term; b. Aug. 1, 1946, Abingdon; home, Abingdon; Roanoke Col., B.A. 1968, U. of VA, J.D. 1971; United Methodist; single.

Elected Office: VA Senate, 1975–1983.

Professional Career: Practicing atty., 1971–83.

DC Office: 2187 RHOB 20515, 202-225-3861; Fax: 202-225-0442; Web site: www.house.gov/boucher.

District Offices: Abingdon, 540-628-1145; Big Stone Gap, 540-523-5450; Pulaski, 540-980-4310.

Committees: *Energy & Commerce* (5th of 26 D): Energy & Air Quality (RMM); Telecommunications & The Internet. *Judiciary* (4th of 17 D): Courts, the Internet & Intellectual Property.

Group Ratings

	ADA	ACLU	AFS	LCV	CON	ITIC	NTU	COC	ACU	NTLC	CHC
2000	75	71	85	71	8	70	29	55	29	22	14
1999	70	—	100	69	24	—	10	48	21	—	—

National Journal Ratings

	1999 LIB	—	1999 CONS		2000 LIB	—	2000 CONS
Economic	62%	—	37%		60%	—	39%
Social	67%	—	33%		62%	—	38%
Foreign	68%	—	30%		69%	—	28%

Key Votes of the 106th Congress

1. Patient Bill of Rights	Y	5. Bar RU-486 $ for FDA	N	9. NATO War in Serbia	Y
2. Accelerate Min. Wage	Y	6. Display 10 Commandments	N	10. Perm. Trade with China	N
3. Strike Ban on Ergo. Stnd.	Y	7. Gun Show Bkgrnd. Checks	N	11. Debt Relief for 3rd World	Y
4. Ovrd. Estate Tax Veto	Y	8. Ban Part.-Birth Abortion	N	12. Drop Cuba Econ. Embargo	Y

Election Results

2000 general	Rick Boucher (D)	137,488	(70%)	($676,127)
	Michael D. "OZ" Osborne (R)	59,335	(30%)	($33,501)
2000 primary	Rick Boucher (D)	nominated by convention		
1998 general	Rick Boucher (D)	87,163	(61%)	($795,457)
	J. A. (Joe) Barta (R)	55,918	(39%)	($443,938)

TENTH DISTRICT

Even as the Constitution was being hammered out in Philadelphia, the rolling green Piedmont of northern Virginia and the fertile mountain-bound lands of the Shenandoah Valley were buzzing with new settlers. They came up the rivers that flow into the Chesapeake, into the Valley from the great Wagon Road south from Pennsylvania, moving onto lands speculated on by George Washington and his peers. During the Civil War, this was some of the most heavily contested land on the continent; afterwards, the surge of movement having propelled new settlers much farther west, this part of Virginia was well-settled and became prime fox hunting country. Now metropolitan Washington has spread out into what was, 50 years ago, almost entirely rural land, punctuated by small villages and courthouse towns. There are still some horse farms in the Piedmont, long the first or second homes of some of the richest people in America, but they are increasingly flanked by subdivisions which sprout up in the fields overnight. Fairfax County, by many measures the most affluent county in the nation, had 98,000 people in 1950; it has ten times as many people today. Loudoun County, just past Dulles Airport, was the third-fastest growing county in the United States in the 1990s, doubling its population to 170,000 in just one decade; the growth triggered a movement called Voters to Stop Sprawl which won every seat on the county Board of Supervisors in 1999. The Washington metropolitan area, as defined by the government, now extends past Fairfax and Loudoun and over the Blue Ridge into the Shenandoah Valley.

Several decades ago the Virginia suburbs of Washington were just that: bedroom communities where most workers headed into the District of Columbia and where one-third of them were employed by the federal government. Today Northern Virginia is an employment center and focus of innovation on its own. Tysons Corner—the inspiration for Joel Garreau's *Edge City*—has not just shopping centers, but more office space than all but a few American downtowns, and it is only one of several edge cities in Northern Virginia. The Dulles Access Road, which ran through rural-looking territory 20 years ago, is now lined with office buildings holding high-tech firms and entrepreneurial startups—while the parallel toll road is jammed with traffic in morning and afternoon rush hour. And the federal government is no longer the dominant employer here. Some of Northern Virginia's private sector is the spawn of government—"Beltway Bandits" and defense contractors—but this area has also become one of the nation's major centers of high-tech and telecommunications firms: AOL has replaced Uncle Sam.

The 10th Congressional District covers much of Northern Virginia. It is all, literally, outside the Beltway. About one-third of its voters live in Fairfax County, in affluent and woodsy McLean and Great Falls, around the old crossroads of Centreville and the upscale Fair Oaks shopping mall area. This is a very upscale area, high-income, highly-educated, high-tech-oriented. Beyond Fairfax is Loudoun County, with one-fifth of the voters, its eastern portion with more modest but still affluent suburbs, the western portion much less developed, with farms bought up by developers trying to get permission to build. The 10th also includes part of Prince William County around

Manassas, including the Civil War battlefield, and the less-developed Fauquier and Rappahannock Counties. And it includes the northern Shenandoah Valley, with about one-fifth of the voters. Politically, Fairfax is about evenly split between the parties, with voters who are rather liberal on cultural issues and somewhat conservative on economics. As one gets farther into the country, or into what used to be the country, cultural attitudes become more conservative and voters more Republican. Overall this is a heavily Republican district, solidly for George W. Bush in 2000, even as he was losing suburban Montgomery County, Maryland, just across the Potomac, by 2–1.

The congressman from the 10th District is Frank Wolf, first elected in 1980 in a district most of whose residents were inside the Beltway. Wolf grew up in Philadelphia, went to law school at Georgetown, worked as a staffer on Capitol Hill and as an Interior Department appointee in the Nixon and Ford administrations and practiced law. In 1978 he ran for Congress against Joseph Fisher, a liberal who had won the district in 1974, and lost 53%–47%; in 1980 he ran again and won 51%–49%. He started off, in the suburban Washington manner, maintaining a crackerjack constituency service operation and concentrating on issues affecting federal employees. He has promoted on-site child care centers at federal workplaces, flextime and flexplace arrangements, leave-sharing and telecommuting (the first center was in Winchester). He opposed the Clinton health care reform in 1994 because it would have gutted the federal employee health plan, and he opposed the Contract with America tax cut in 1995 because it would have required higher pension payments by federal employees.

But over 20 years Wolf has come to specialize in three other areas—transportation, human rights and gambling. He used his seat on the Transportation Appropriations Subcommittee to work on projects in traffic-choked Northern Virginia—full funding for the 103-mile Metro subway system, widening I-66 from the Beltway to Gainesville, the Route 234 interchange in Manassas, express buses in the Dulles Airport corridor, improvements in the Virginia commuter rail system. He led the move to put Reagan National and Dulles airports under a regional authority, which built a new terminal for Reagan National and has vastly expanded Dulles, and pushed to get the National Air and Space Museum annex located at Dulles. As subcommittee chairman, he tangled with Transportation Committee Chairman Bud Shuster, who systematically offered members $15 million for earmarked projects in return for their votes for the giant transportation bill passed in May 1998. Wolf, in contrast, has consistently opposed earmarking funds for members' pet transportation projects in appropriations bills as "immoral." Wolf and Shuster also got into an epic war over the Office of Motor Carriers; Wolf cares deeply about truck safety and believes the agency has been lax in enforcement and fought to have it transferred out of the Federal Highway Administration. But in December 2000 Shuster failed to get an exemption from the six-year term limit House Republicans impose on committee chairmen, and as Congress assembled announced he was resigning from the House. In the meantime Wolf has used the subcommittee chairmanship to put through a national .08% blood alcohol limit for drunk driving. He opposed the OSHA letter that held employers responsible for health and safety conditions in employees' home offices as a barrier to telecommuting, and he proposed giving employers pollution credits for telecommuters. For the 107th Congress, Wolf chairs the Commerce Subcommittee of Appropriations which will give a voice on trade issues vital to the Dulles Tech corridor.

Wolf has been one of the House's leading crusaders for human rights and is co-chairman of the Congressional Human Rights Caucus. He traveled to El Salvador in 1982, Sudan in 1989, Romania in 1990, Tibet in 1997 (only the second time a congressman has been there since the Chinese takeover in 1959), East Timor in 1997 and Sierra Leone in 1999. He met with Li Peng in China and went to Beijing Prison No. 1 where Tiananmen Square protesters have been held, and where prisoners make jelly shoes for export to the West. With California's Nancy Pelosi, he led the annual moves to withdraw permanent normal trade relations for China because of human right violations; he strongly opposed PNTR in 2000, citing China's acts of jailing dissidents, killing Catholic priests, jailing evangelical pastors, persecuting Tibetan Buddhists and aiming missile at the United States. "Did trade change Nazi Germany?" he asked. "I don't think appeasement ever works." In 2000 he sought sanctions against oil companies doing business in Sudan, called for labeling the country of origin of diamonds (to identify those from Sierra Leone) and called for Intelligence Committee hearings on defectors' rights.

Wolf is probably Congress's leading opponent of gambling. "It leaves in its path the wreckage of human misery. Addiction, crime, corruption, loss of revenue to local business, bankruptcy and even suicide—these are the fruits of this industry which is sweeping America." He first proposed the National Gambling Impact Study Commission, passed in 1997, but was not pleased by the appointees; he hailed its call in June 1999 for a pause in granting licenses for new casinos and for federal oversight of Indian and Internet gambling. He sponsored a bill in 1999 to ban cruises to nowhere. He called on George W. Bush to reform the Bureau of Indian Affairs, citing a *Boston Globe* series on the creation of phony Indian tribes, and pointed out that just 2% of Indians earn 50% of the $10 billion in Indian gambling revenues, and two-thirds of Indians get nothing. He opposed the 8th District's Jim Moran's proposal to recognize eight tiny and perhaps dubious Indian tribes.

Wolf was re-elected by the identical margin, 72%–25%, in 1996 and 1998; he won 84% against two independents in 2000. Because of the population growth in Fairfax and Loudoun, redistricting may remove some of the outer counties of the 10th District, but it will likely remain safe Republican.

Cook's Call *Safe.* Wolf does a good job of balancing the needs of a district that has a conservative lean but is heavily populated by federal workers. Robust growth in once-rural Loudoun County helped make the 10th the most- populated district in Virginia: it will need to shed almost 150,000 people in redistricting. Still, Wolf remains a strong favorite for 2002.

THE PEOPLE: Pop. 2000: 792,534; Pop. 1990: 562,257, up 41% 1990–2000. 83.2% White, 6.7% Black, 5.3% Asian, 0.2% Amer. Indian, 0.1% Hawaiian, 2.2% Two+ races, 2.3% Other; 5.6% Hispanic Origin.

2000 Presidential Vote

Bush (R)	191,443	(58%)
Gore (D)	128,515	(39%)
Nader (Green)	7,665	(2%)
Others	2,657	(1%)

1996 Presidential Vote

Dole (R)	140,684	(55%)
Clinton (D)	99,510	(39%)
Perot (I)	16,476	(6%)

Rep. Frank R. Wolf (R)

Elected 1980, 11th term; b. Jan. 30, 1939, Philadelphia, PA; home, Vienna; PA St. U., B.A. 1961, Georgetown U., LL.B. 1965; Presbyterian; married (Carolyn).

Military Career: Army, 1962–63, Army Reserves 1963–67.

Professional Career: Legis. Asst., U.S. Rep. Edward Biester, 1968–71; Asst., U.S. Interior Secy. Rogers Morton, 1971–74; Dep. Asst. Secy., U.S. Dept. of Interior, 1974–75; Practicing atty., 1975–80.

DC Office: 241 CHOB 20515, 202-225-5136; Fax: 202-225-0437; Web site: www.house.gov/wolf.

District Offices: Herndon, 703-709-5800; Winchester, 540-667-0990.

Committees: *Appropriations* (6th of 35 R): Commerce, Justice & State (Chmn.); Transportation; Treasury, Postal Service & General Government.

Group Ratings

	ADA	ACLU	AFS	LCV	CON	ITIC	NTU	COC	ACU	NTLC	CHC
2000	10	7	14	14	21	78	58	71	72	58	93
1999	20	—	0	19	37	—	53	68	68	—	—

National Journal Ratings

	1999 LIB	—	1999 CONS		2000 LIB	—	2000 CONS
Economic	24%	—	72%		34%	—	64%
Social	28%	—	72%		37%	—	62%
Foreign	50%	—	48%		45%	—	53%

Key Votes of the 106th Congress

1. Patient Bill of Rights	Y	5. Bar RU-486 $ for FDA	Y	9. NATO War in Serbia	Y
2. Accelerate Min. Wage	N	6. Display 10 Commandments	Y	10. Perm. Trade with China	N
3. Strike Ban on Ergo. Stnd.	N	7. Gun Show Bkgrnd. Checks	N	11. Debt Relief for 3rd World	Y
4. Ovrd. Estate Tax Veto	Y	8. Ban Part.-Birth Abortion	Y	12. Drop Cuba Econ. Embargo	N

Election Results

2000 general	Frank R. Wolf (R)	238,817	(84%)	($465,729)
	Brian M. Brown (I)	28,107	(10%)	($6,826)
	Marc A. Rossi (I)	16,031	(6%)	
2000 primary	Frank R. Wolf (R)	nominated by convention		
1998 general	Frank R. Wolf (R)	103,648	(72%)	($465,350)
	Cornell W. Brooks (D)	36,476	(25%)	($116,526)
	Others	4,631	(3%)	

ELEVENTH DISTRICT

When author and *Washington Post* reporter Joel Garreau coined the term "edge city" to describe the autonomous urban centers developing on the rims of some of the nation's oldest municipalities, his prime example was Tysons Corner, Virginia. Rising on a hill west of Washington, Tysons Corner was a back-country intersection 50 years ago and a junction of several suburban roads 25 years ago; today it is home to the largest concentration of office space to be found anywhere between Washington and Atlanta, with a modern skyline and busy multi-lane avenues that serve as arteries to the nearby Capital Beltway. Fairfax County, which includes all of Tysons Corner, has changed just as dramatically since the end of World War II. At first only a few District of Columbia residents seeking breathing room in the suburbs trickled into Northern Virginia; initially they went to Arlington and Alexandria. But that trickle became a rush as young marrieds with large families and whites avoiding the increasingly high-crime District pushed farther out into Fairfax. Now Fairfax County is no longer Washington's country cousin. By 2000 it had 969,000 residents, nearly twice D.C.'s. 572,000. It had in 1990 the nation's highest median household income ($59,284), almost half its residents have a bachelor's degree or more and nearly 70% of its households have two or more vehicles. Fairfax has been transformed from a suburban county where people commute to government jobs in Washington, to a 21st Century urban county where people work somewhere around the Beltway and mostly for private sector employers.

The 11th Congressional District, the seat Virginia gained in the 1990 Census, went to fast-growing Fairfax County and its neighbor just to the south, Prince William County. The 11th straddles the Beltway; its inner portion includes older comfortable areas like Annandale, which has increasing Korean and Vietnamese populations, while the outer portion spans Tysons Corner and the office corridor out the Dulles Toll Road, to the airport. The 11th runs south through comfortable subdivision areas like Burke and covers the somewhat lower-income Woodbridge and Dale City areas of Prince William. This is a cosmopolitan district: 11% black, 13% Hispanic, 12% Asian; some 20% of residents speak a language other than English at home. The district is made up largely of two-income families, many with at least one spouse employed in one of the many divisions of high-tech companies that dot Fairfax County. Politically, the 11th's educated, mobile electorate produces a robust two-party politics. In the 1990s it voted 43%–42% for George Bush in 1992 and 49%–47% for Bill Clinton in 1996; in 2000 it voted for Gore, again by 49%–47%.

The congressman from the 11th District is Tom Davis, a Republican elected in 1994. Davis grew up in Northern Virginia, and was always interested in politics; by seventh grade he could name every member of the House. He got a job as a Senate page and was president of his class at the Capitol Page School; he was a friend of David Eisenhower at Amherst College, where almost everyone else was a Democrat or something further left; he served on active duty in the Army before earning a law degree. He practiced law in Northern Virginia and in 1979 was elected to the Fairfax County Board of Supervisors, a high visibility position. Over the years, he gained a reputation for financial savvy in municipal matters and for seeking compromise over confrontation. In 1991 he was elected board chairman, something in the nature of a mayor.

In 1994 Davis ran for the 11th District seat against Democrat Leslie Byrne, who had won

50%–45% in 1992. Byrne had voted solidly for Clinton administration positions and called for discipline against members of the Democratic Caucus who did not; she had strong support from labor and feminist groups, and spent $1.1 million. But Davis was able to raise and spend even more, $1.4 million. He won 53%–45%, even as Republican Oliver North fell to Democratic Senator Charles Robb in the 11th by 51%–36%.

As soon as he arrived on Capitol Hill, Davis was handed by Speaker Newt Gingrich one of the hottest potatoes of the new Congress: dealing with the affairs of the troubled District of Columbia government and its just re-elected mayor, Marion Barry. As chairman of the House Government Reform and Oversight Committee's D. C. Subcommittee, Davis first rejected Barry's request for massive federal aid, working closely with Gingrich and District Delegate Eleanor Holmes Norton to cut District spending. Together they passed in April 1995 a law establishing a five-member control board to oversee the D.C. government. He tended to oppose the appropriators' detailed policy prescription as micromanagement, but went along with the 1997 law taking power over nine agencies from Barry and giving it to the control board. In the process Congress ordered the closing of D.C.'s Lorton Prison in Fairfax County, long a goal of Northern Virginia politicians. In February 1999 Davis and Norton sponsored a bill restoring full management powers to the District and its new mayor, Anthony Williams; it was speedily passed. Davis and Norton also passed a bill suggested by *Washington Post* publisher Donald Graham to enable District students to attend Virginia and Maryland public colleges and universities at in-state tuition rates. When this was criticized as undercutting the University of the District of Columbia, they added funds for it.

Davis has a moderate voting record, near the midpoint of the House. He opposed the Contract with America tax cut in 1995 because it would have required higher pension payments by federal employees; he and suburban Washington's Frank Wolf and Connie Morella were three of only 11 Republicans who voted against the tax cut. He supported the Democratic Blue Dogs' budget as well as the Republicans'. He has worked for legislation to protect high-tech firms from the depredations of trial lawyers, including the securities litigation reform which was passed over Bill Clinton's veto in 1996 and the Y2K litigation which gave sued firms a 90-day window to solve problems, limited punitive damages and took cases out of state courts and into federal courts. He also worked on the law setting a national standard for digital signatures and for the increase in H1B1 visas. He has promoted telecommuting and he worked to overturn the OSHA advisory that held employers liable for conditions in telecommuting employees' home offices. He has kept in touch with the many immigrant groups in the 11th District, and favored amnesty to former refugees who have lived in the United States for many years. His bill to allow flexibility in education and experience requirements for federal information technology contractors passed the House. He worked to allow federal retirees to pay for federal employees' health care plans with before-tax money. Over several years Davis worked on getting federal financing for the new Woodrow Wilson Bridge, which totaled $1.58 billion in federal aid.

Davis is a political buff with a detailed knowledge of political statistics across the country. In Virginia's 1997 elections, he criss-crossed the state and created a PAC which gave some $150,000 to state legislative candidates. In September 1997, National Republican Congressional Committee Chairman John Linder named Davis to be his chief recruiter. He specialized in raising money from high-tech sources and argued that despite their cultural liberalism they were better protected by Republican principles of free trade, small government and laissez faire economic policies: "If you have a downturn, the New Economy will find out who its friends are. You get a cataclysmic event when the lines get drawn and the Democrats will go with their labor base and their underclass." After the November 1998 election, Newt Gingrich changed the rules and made the NRCC chairmanship elective rather than appointive, and Davis ran against Linder for the post. Many members blamed Linder for the disappointing 1998 results, which were far out of line with his predictions, and Tom DeLay put his whip organization to work for Davis. Davis won 130–77.

Davis had a delicate balancing act as a moderate in a mostly conservative party; he insisted that he was just trying to maximize the number of Republicans elected. "When you look at the extremes in American politics, I'm not part of either of those. In this election cycle, though, controlling the middle means controlling the game." He was criticized by the Family Research

Council for meeting with the Log Cabin Republicans of Northern Virginia in February 1999 (his response: "These are constituents of mine. As you know, I have a longstanding policy of meeting with everybody") and he risked further wrath by meeting with AFL-CIO leaders in March 1999. He was criticized by moderates for giving $750,000 to the U.S. Family Network and the National Right to Life Committee ("The fact of the matter is I'm not a lap dog for the right or for anyone"). In the New Jersey 12th District primary, he supported moderate Dick Zimmer while Tom DeLay and Dick Armey supported conservative Mike Pappas; the seat ended up staying Democratic. In 1999 he spent $2 million on a California ballot initiative to create a bipartisan redistricting commission, but a judge yanked it off the ballot. He spent $1 million on 1999 state legislative races in Virginia, in which Republicans captured both houses and won control of redistricting; within two months conservative incumbent Virgil Goode left the Democratic Party and announced he would caucus with Republicans, and later conservative Democrat Owen Pickett retired—a two-seat gain a year before an election in which Democrats needed only a five- or six-seat gain to win control.

Through most of the cycle Democrats were supremely confident they would win the House in 2000, and they matched and at some points exceeded Republicans' fundraising—a considerable achievement that owed much to the fame of their campaign committee chairman Patrick Kennedy. But Kennedy and the Gephardt staffers who advised him did not quite match Davis's political knowledge and instincts. He early on spotted open seats which had long voted Democratic but where conservative non-economic issues helped Republicans—Pennsylvania's 4th, West Virginia's 2d, Missouri's 6th, Michigan's 8th, Virginia's 2d—and won all of them. Against party-switcher Michael Forbes in New York's 1st he spent money on billboards thanking him for his solid support of Newt Gingrich and the Contract With America; Forbes was upset in the September Democratic primary, and the seat went Republican in November. He spotted early on the weakness of 20-year incumbent Democrat Sam Gejdenson in Connecticut's 2d. The Republican nomination in the open seat in Florida's 8th was not determined until the October runoff; but for two months before the NRCC spent heavily on ads attacking the Democratic nominee, who lost 51%–49%. Only four Republican incumbents lost, three in California and one in Arkansas 4th (the one district where a vote for impeachment hurt).

Davis was re-elected campaign committee chairman. With his knowledge of political demography, he will probably get involved in redistricting in many states; overall, redistricting looks likely to give Republicans a 10-seat advantage—a giant edge in such an evenly divided House. He will probably try to encourage incumbent Democrats in Republican-leaning districts to retire. And he will try to reestablish the Republican fundraising advantage that existed up to the 2000 cycle.

Through all this, Davis continues to work his district hard. In 1998 Democrats ran no candidate against him; in 2000 he won 62%–34%. He is known to be interested in running for the Senate some day—all that involvement in Virginia legislative races was not just aimed at picking up U.S. House seats—but he will not challenge Senators John Warner and George Allen, and so in all likelihood will have to wait till at least 2008.

Cook's Call *Safe.* Though this district has been a battleground for presidential contests in recent years, Davis has won re-election rather easily. His moderate image and high visibility in the D.C. media market make him a very tough target, and the 11th is sure to get at least a bit better for Davis after redistricting.

THE PEOPLE: Pop. 2000: 649,553; Pop. 1990: 562,596, up 15.5% 1990–2000. 66.6% White, 11.3% Black, 12.2% Asian, 0.3% Amer. Indian, 0.1% Hawaiian, 4.1% Two+ races, 5.5% Other; 12.9% Hispanic Origin.

2000 Presidential Vote

Gore (D)	126,406	(49%)
Bush (R)	120,589	(47%)
Nader (Green)	7,575	(3%)
Others	2,180	(1%)

1996 Presidential Vote

Clinton (D)	109,304	(49%)
Dole (R)	105,085	(47%)
Perot (I)	10,845	(5%)

Rep. Tom Davis (R)

Elected 1994, 4th term; b. Jan. 5, 1949, Minot, ND; home, Falls Church; Amherst Col. B.A. 1971, U. of VA, J.D. 1975; Christian Scientist; married (Peggy).

Military Career: Army, 1971–72; Army Reserves, 1972–79.

Elected Office: Fairfax Cnty. Bd. of Supervisors, 1979–94, Chmn., 1991–94.

Professional Career: Vice Pres. & Gen. Cnsl., PRC Inc., 1977–94.

DC Office: 306 CHOB 20515, 202-225-1492; Fax: 202-225-3071; Web site: www.house.gov/tomdavis.

District Offices: Annandale, 703-916-9610; Herndon, 703-437-1726; Woodbridge, 703-590-4599.

Committees: *NRCC Chairman. Energy & Commerce* (22d of 31 R): Telecommunications & The Internet. *Government Reform* (9th of 24 R): District of Columbia; Technology & Procurement Policy (Chmn.); Technology & Procurement Policy (Vice Chmn.).

Group Ratings

	ADA	ACLU	AFS	LCV	CON	ITIC	NTU	COC	ACU	NTLC	CHC
2000	5	29	0	50	36	100	60	80	70	64	87
1999	35	—	16	25	18	—	51	88	56	—	—

National Journal Ratings

	1999 LIB —	1999 CONS		2000 LIB —	2000 CONS
Economic	39%	61%		39%	60%
Social	51%	49%		48%	51%
Foreign	49%	50%		33%	62%

Key Votes of the 106th Congress

1. Patient Bill of Rights	Y	5. Bar RU-486 $ for FDA	N	9. NATO War in Serbia	Y
2. Accelerate Min. Wage	N	6. Display 10 Commandments	Y	10. Perm. Trade with China	Y
3. Strike Ban on Ergo. Stnd.	N	7. Gun Show Bkgrnd. Checks	Y	11. Debt Relief for 3rd World	N
4. Ovrd. Estate Tax Veto	Y	8. Ban Part.-Birth Abortion	Y	12. Drop Cuba Econ. Embargo	N

Election Results

2000 general	Tom Davis (R)	150,395	(62%)	($1,515,583)
	M.L. (Mike) Corrigan (D)	83,455	(34%)	($72,833)
	Others	9,118	(4%)	
2000 primary	Tom Davis (R)	nominated by convention		
1998 general	Tom Davis (R)	91,603	(82%)	($917,158)
	C. W. (Levi) Levy (I)	18,807	(17%)	
	Others	1,701	(2%)	

★ WASHINGTON ★

As never before, the eyes of the nation—and the world—were on Washington in 1999 and 2000—Washington state, that is, not Washington, D.C. From Starbucks coffee to grunge music, from America's leading exporter, Boeing, to America's leading software maker, Microsoft, to America's most visible dot-com, Amazon.com, Washington was a national trend-setter in the 1990s. An unusual environment and human creativity have combined to produce these achievements: Seattle's cold misty air and 225 overcast days a year stimulate the appetite for strong aromatic coffee, and the shapeless blue jeans and sweatshirts worn year-round in this moist climate by professionals and teenagers alike created a trend made famous by Nirvana and Soundgarden and other grunge artists. Boeing's airframe business took off during World War II because the Pacific Northwest's abundant hydroelectric power made cheap aluminum possible, and through booms and despite busts Boeing has mostly kept growing. Microsoft, founded by the usually tie-less and tousle-haired Bill Gates and based in Redmond, east of Lake Washington, became one of America's great success stories as its computer software business boomed as the computer hardware business elsewhere faced increasing problems. With flannel shirts and umbrellas, blue-collar types working off hangovers as if in a Raymond Carver story, and professionals relaxing on woodsy acreage, Washington set a tone for the 1990s, a style plainly Middle American but with attitude, an ordinariness so apt it is no longer ordinary.

All this comes to a state barely a century old, which in the two decades after statehood in 1889 built a new civilization, as transcontinental railroads reached the great ports of Puget Sound, the wheat-processing city of Spokane inland, orchard towns and fishing ports and lumber settlements. Shielded from the heavy rains and storms of the Pacific by the Olympic Mountains and the Sound, Seattle quickly became a serious American city, a lusty town full of lumbermen and railroad workers. When gold was struck in the Klondike and Alaska, Seattle became a metropolis of miners, prospectors and get-rich-quick operators, the site of the original "Skid Road" (skid row is a corruption propagated by a 1937 magazine article), where logs were rolled downhill to the port; today it's the focus of the restored Pioneer Square area. Booming, young Seattle had a turbulent class-warfare politics in the years before World War I, pitting the Industrial Workers of the World (the IWW, or Wobblies) against city business and civic leaders; the businessmen, after some violence, prevailed. Adding to the area's distinctiveness was its large numbers of Scandinavian immigrants, with their favorable views of cooperative enterprises and government ownership.

Over time, Washington was transformed by a series of national decisions which set its course for decades. One was government development of hydroelectric power. The Columbia River and its tributary, the Snake, falling thousands of feet in a relatively short distance, had far greater hydroelectric potential than any other American river system, and Franklin Roosevelt was always interested in these river valley projects. In 1937 Bonneville Dam was completed on the lower Columbia; in 1940 Grand Coulee Dam, the largest man-made structure in the world at the time, was opened where the Columbia cuts through the arid, surrealistically contoured plains of eastern Washington. Washington proved hospitable to the industrial union movement of the 1930s and became one of the nation's most heavily unionized states. When war came, Washington's hydroelectric power—the cheapest electricity in the country—made it the natural site for huge aluminum production plants, which require vast amounts of electricity, and the Seattle area became the home not only of shipbuilders, but of what became the biggest aircraft manufacturer in the country, Boeing, founded in 1916 by William Boeing after he bought a shipyard on the Duwamish River and turned it into an airplane factory. After the war, the Hanford plant on the Columbia was one of the government's main nuclear weapons manufacturing sites. Cheap power, aluminum, aircraft, nuclear weapons and high unionized wages: these became Washington's economic foundations in the post-World War II years.

Today, Washington is a commonwealth of nearly 6 million people, economically booming, pleased to the point of smugness with its physical environment and lifestyle. It lives less off the brawn of hydroelectric power and rail and ship tonnage and more off the brains that made Boeing

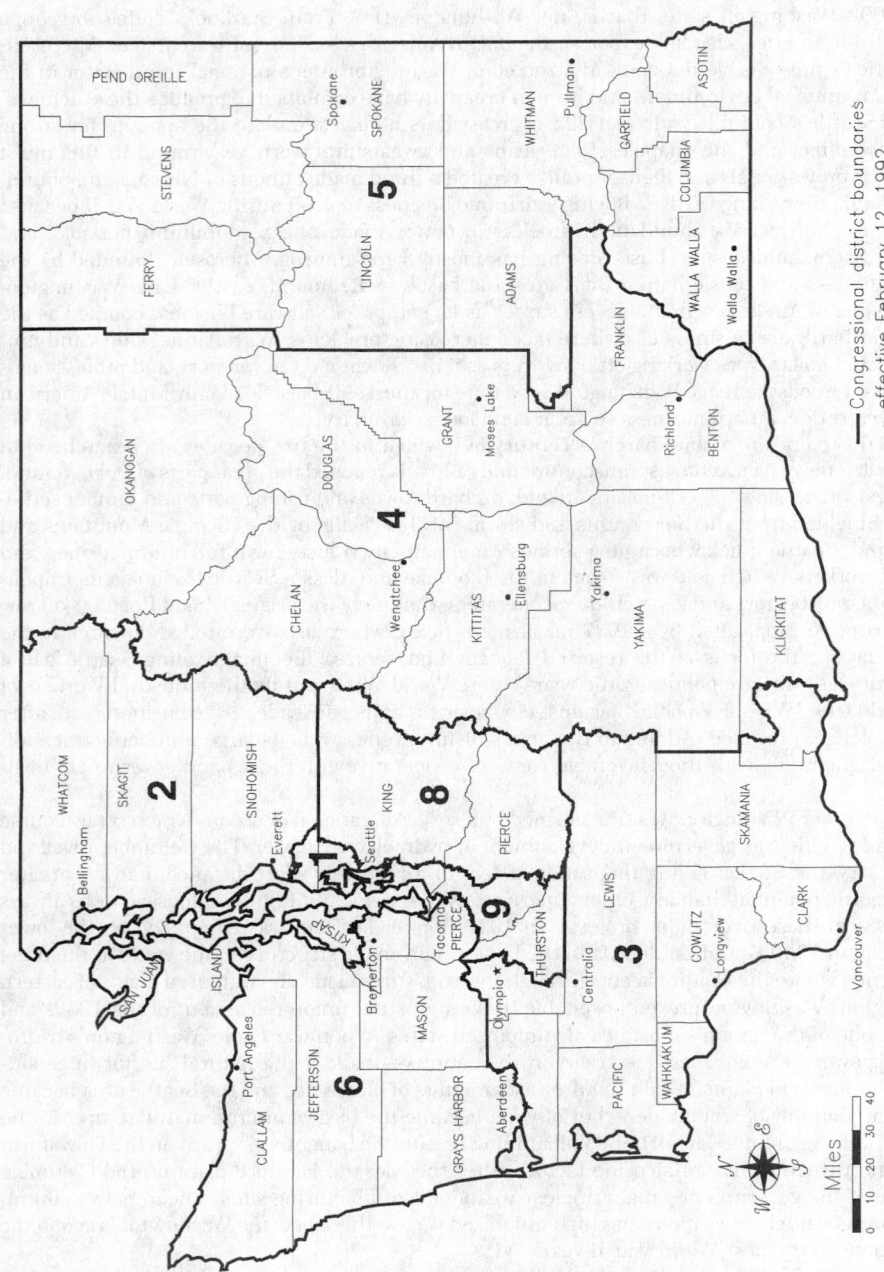

WASHINGTON

— Congressional district boundaries
effective February 12, 1992.

Copyright © 1993 by Election Data Services, Inc.

the world leader in aircraft and Microsoft the world leader in software. Yet there are problems in this moist paradise. They were perhaps most visible in December 1999, when Seattle hosted a meeting of the World Trade Organization. This was supposed to be an occasion for the city to shine in the international spotlighted. But demonstrators took control of the streets, smashing Starbucks' windows and preventing leaders from Bill Clinton on down from attending meetings; Seattle's liberal police chief and mayor did little to stop the violence, and even came out with statements, echoed by Clinton, expressing sympathy for the lawbreakers. Seattle became a symbol of mindless protest and lawless violence. Boeing has had its problems as well. In 1998 it cut payrolls as east Asian countries canceled orders, in 2000 white-collar engineers went on strike, and in March 2001 Boeing's chairman announced that the firm's headquarters would be moved out of Seattle. Politicians were aghast—Seattle Mayor Paul Schell complained that he was totally blind-sided and Governor Gary Locke said that the decision "leaves a void in our economic and cultural life." Only 500 employees will be moved to Chicago, but Boeing executives, removed from Seattle, can cast a cold eye on its expensive and strike-prone Washington operations, and some oldtimers remembered how Boeing cut its payroll from 100,000 in 1967 to 38,000 in 1971—although in 2001 it had 79,000 workers in Washington and 198,000 worldwide.

Microsoft was also under siege, sued in 1998 by the Justice Department's antitrust division and a number of states; Bill Gates, fresh from his huge high-tech mansion on the shore of Lake Washington, squirmed while giving Senate testimony in March 1998 and in videotaped testimony in November 1998. In November 1999 Judge Thomas Penfield Jackson ruled that Microsoft was a monopoly, and in June 2000 ordered the firm broken up. That decision seemed unlikely to stand up on appeal, but it was not clear whether the company's aggressive and innovative culture had been damaged. Even in energy production Washington seemed threatened. Washington still has the nation's lowest electricity prices, thanks to hydroelectric power; in late 2000 three aluminum companies shut down production lines but kept paying workers because they could sell the electricity they had coming from long-term contracts at much higher rates on the spot market—in one plant's case, selling electricity that cost them $22.50 per megawatt hour for $555 per megawatt hour. But in the winter of 2000–01 the snowpack was only about half the normal level, which would mean less water for producing electricity in summer 2001, while demand from energy-starved California seemed likely to draw down supply. Locke ordered emergency generators fired up, even at the cost of increased air pollution, and there were predictions that agricultural customers for the first time since the 1930s would not be able to buy electricity.

Electric supply was also threatened by proposals to breach four dams on the Snake River. Columbia and Snake River dams have reduced the number of salmon from 16 million to 1 million, despite government programs costing $3 billion, and Clinton environmental agencies recommended breaching the dams. That was highly unpopular in eastern Washington; Clinton decided in summer 2000 to delay a decision for five years, Al Gore refused to take a stand on the issue and George W. Bush came out point-blank against breaching the dams. But there is the possibility of action by a court—like the court decision that largely shut down Washington's logging industry a decade before to protect the supposedly endangered spotted owl. The Hanford Nuclear Reservation, which produced plutonium for the military, for years leaked radioactive waste and now must be cleaned up at the cost of billions, while new underground storage procedures have been criticized as unsafe. Washington's apples, half the nation's production, have long been barred from obvious markets in East Asia, and face stiff competition from China, while wheat sales can be cut off (as they nearly were for Pakistan in 1998) by U.S. foreign policy sanctions. And then there are earthquakes. Washington is the state second-most vulnerable to earthquakes, and in March 2001 the Seattle area was hit by a quake that measured 6.8 on the Richter scale. The state Capitol was cracked, the Sea-Tac Airport control tower was out of commission and there was $2 billion in damage. But thanks to skillful retrofitting by the state and private businesses, no one was killed and damage was far less than it would have been a decade before.

All these problems may turn out to be no more than footnotes to what is mainly a story of success. Look at a map that shows elevation of mountains and density of population. On both sides of the Pacific, vast numbers of people are squeezed into small margins of level land between steeply rising volcanic mountains and the sea, or tucked into valleys. These islands of settlement are surrounded by vast wildernesses—desert and mountains, open sea and Arctic lands. Yet the inhabitants of these pockets of the Pacific Rim in the last three decades have produced more economic growth than anywhere else in the world and, if there are occasional slumps, the Pacific Rim has always come surging back, as East Asia did in 1999. The question is whether Washington's laid-back tolerance can be so excessive as to undermine its impressive achievements.

Politically, Washington, with its Scandinavian and labor union heritage, was once one of the most Democratic states: Franklin Roosevelt's campaign manager James Farley used to refer to "the 47 states and the Soviet of Washington." Its mainstream Democrats—notably Warren Magnuson and Henry Jackson, who represented the state in Congress for a total of 87 years—believed in an active and compassionate federal government that built dams, aluminum plants and the Hanford Works at home, and pursued an internationalist, anti-Communist foreign policy abroad. Their political strength was built on a blue-collar base, augmented by the respect big businesses had for their political clout. Today, the fulcrum of the electorate has moved from blue collar to white collar, from economic class warfare to cultural wars. The balance is fairly close. In presidential races, Washington leans Democratic: big Seattle-area margins delivered the state for Michael Dukakis in 1988, Bill Clinton in 1992 and 1996 and Al Gore in 2000. Democrats have also won most downballot races in presidential years. Three different Democrats have held the governorship since 1984, and Democrats hold both Senate seats and six of its nine U.S. House seats. But there is also some Republican strength. In 1994 Republicans won seven of the nine House seats, and in 1998 and 2000 the state House of Representatives was split 49–49.

The political lines are fairly clear. The central city of Seattle is increasingly the liberal bastion, while old blue-collar lumber country strongholds have soured on many Democrats: Seattle's King County, by a wide margin the most affluent county in the state, is also its liberal stronghold. Republicans run best in the arid country east of the Cascades, with far lower income levels, this is a marchland between the culturally liberal Pacific Rim and the culturally conservative Rocky Mountains. Culture wars also are fought out in referenda. Washington rejected a "death with dignity" physician-assisted suicide measure in 1991 by 54%–46%. It voted for term limits, opposed by most liberals, 52%–48% in 1992. (One unanticipated result of term limits: with the churning of membership, 40% of Washington state legislators are women, the highest percentage in the country.) In 1993 voters adopted a measure restricting state spending increases to the combined rates of inflation and population increase. In 1997 voters rejected easing penalties for marijuana use and a ban on discrimination against (or for) gays; a gun control measure, requiring trigger locks for guns and safety tests for handgun owners, was rejected 71%–29%. In 1998, despite opposition from nearly every newspaper, all Democratic and some Republican politicians, Boeing, Starbucks, Microsoft and Eddie Bauer, voters approved by 58%–42% a ban on racial and gender quotas and preferences in state government. In 1999, against business and union opposition, voters passed 56%–44% Initiative 695, which eliminated the 2.2% car tax and replaced it with a $30 annual fee; this reduced state revenue $750 million, or 7.5% of the state budget—the state courts later ruled the initiative was unconstitutional so the legislature passed a law to do it instead. Washington likes its politicians liberal, but operating under conservative restraints.

Footnote: One of Washington's political innovations, the all-party primary, was ruled unconstitutional by the U.S. Supreme Court in June 2000. The all-party primary, copied in Alaska since statehood and adopted in modified form by California in the 1990s, provided that all candidates run in a primary in which voters can pick and choose any candidate for any office: no party registration. In practice, Washington's September all-party primary proved a pretty good forecast of the results in November, especially for incumbents. It had one last go 2000. Interestingly, Republicans ran a little better in September than they did in November, evidence of a possible shift of opinion during the campaign. After the legislature failed to come up with a new system, a temporary fix was agreed to for the 2001 primary that would require voters to choose from a single party's slate of candidates.

Governor Gary Locke, a Democrat elected in 1996 and 2000, is the first governor of Chinese descent elected in American history. Locke grew up in Seattle, the son of immigrants from Guandong and Hong Kong; he lived six years in a housing project and worked in his father's restaurant and grocery store; his grandfather worked as a houseboy less than a mile from the

Washington state Capitol. Locke graduated from Yale (a beneficiary of affirmative action, he says) and Boston University Law School, returned to Seattle and worked as a deputy prosecutor and community relations manager for US West. In 1982, at 32, he was elected to the state House from a liberal district in Seattle and rose to chair the Appropriations Committee; he supported an income tax (Washington still doesn't have one) and the 1993 tax increases that helped to make Democratic Governor Mike Lowry unpopular. That same year, Locke was elected King County executive where he cut the budget, established a savings incentive program and produced a growth management plan. His father was once shot at the family's grocery store, and Locke has been a supporter of tough penalties for crime and victim's rights legislation.

In February 1996 Lowry, a liberal and former congressman who was staggering under charges of sexual harassment, announced his retirement, and Locke decided to run for governor. It was a crowded field in Washington's all-party primary. Locke's main opponent, Seattle Mayor Norm Rice, shared the same base; they also faced former Congressman Jay Inslee from east of the mountains (he has since moved to the Seattle area and is now congressman from the 1st District). Locke won with 24% to 18% for Rice and 10% for Inslee. The Republican field was more fragmented, and the nomination was won by former state Senator Ellen Craswell, who emphasized her religious faith. Altogether Democrats won 52% of votes, Republicans 48%, indicating a close race in November. Republican legislators had cost the party some good campaign issues by repealing much of Lowry's tax increases, employer health care mandates and insurance premium caps. Craswell, however, emphasized what she called "God's plan" to cut state taxes 30% (later modified to 15%) and to privatize state universities, which evidently struck many voters as bizarre. Republican ads accusing Locke of supporting prostitution (a county prostitute-counseling service may have added to that impression). Locke, despite his liberal record in the legislature, took a moderate tack, abjuring tax increases and calling for more spending on education, with higher standards and accountability. Although some polls showed a close race, Locke won 58%–42%, fortified by a 62%–38% lead in the Seattle area; Craswell just barely carried the east.

Locke cultivated an image of moderation and compromise even as he vetoed more bills than any previous governor in his first months. But he and the legislature operate under the constraints of Initiative 601, passed in 1993, which limits spending increases to a formula based on population and inflation; that has forced the state into smart decisions, according to Syracuse University's Government Performance Project, which in February 2001 rated Washington one of the three best-managed state governments. Locke vetoed some changes in welfare reform but approved a business tax cut. He vetoed a bill banning gay marriage in February 1998; that was overridden in five hours as Democrats scampered to keep the issue off the November 1998 ballot. Left on was Referendum 49, a proposal to cut the auto tax at the expense of education funding and place the revenue, plus money from a huge bond issue, into a fund devoted to transportation; that passed 57%–43%. Locke campaigned hard against Initiative 200, to ban state racial and gender quotas and preferences, which passed; university administrators attempted to evade it by selecting the bottom third of their incoming classes by individual factors rather than test scores.

In 1998 Democrats won a 27–22 margin in the Senate and a 49–49 tie in the House, which left Locke to, in the words of David Postman of the *Seattle Times*, "stick to the middle ground, think bite-sized reform, press hard for results and focus on the direct delivery of state services." The evenly divided House, with co-speakers and co-chairmen of committees, in time worked out compromises on major state issues. It passed, by unanimous or near-unanimous margins, bills regulating HMOs and changing unemployment insurance. In November 1999 voters passed Initiative 695, eliminating the 2.2% car tab tax, which had provided 7.5% of state revenue and was replaced by a $30 annual fee; it also provided that voters would have to approve any new state or local tax increase or fee. It was opposed by business groups and unions and by Locke and many state and local government leaders; but a volunteer campaign led by Mukilteo wristwatch salesman Tim Eyman prevailed and voters approved it by a 56%–44% margin. A court struck down the latter portion in March 2000, but in the meantime the legislature worked out an emergency spending measure, and the $30 fee was left in place. Locke offered health benefits for the same-sex partners of state employees and offered senior citizens a chance to buy prescription drugs through the state employees' health plan. He and the legislature increased school spending, required testing of new teachers and passed a charter school initiative.

Approaching the 2000 election, Republicans attacked Locke for not asserting leadership, but had a hard time finding a candidate. Eventually they settled on radio talk show host John Carlson, a strong supporter of both a 1993 initiative to tie spending increases to the combined rates of inflation and population increases and a 1998 initiative to end racial and gender quotas and preferences in state government, both of which passed. Carlson called for lower taxes, more lanes on the Evergreen Point Floating Bridge and a new bridge to Portland to clear up traffic and more teachers. "No politician has talked more and done less than the incumbent governor," he said. In August Republicans ran ads criticizing Locke for vetoing a bill to bring methamphetamine crimes under the three-strikes law, and for the death of three-year-old Zy'Nyia Nobles, who was killed by her mother after Department of Social and Health Services workers took her out of a foster home and put her in the mother's custody. But for all the barrage of criticism, voters were in a consensus-minded, pro-incumbent mood, and Locke won by an impressive 58%–40% margin. He carried King County 66%–32%, a similar margin to 1996, and the rest of western Washington by 56%–42%; he even carried eastern Washington 51%–47%, thanks to a large margin in Spokane County.

In January 2001 Locke called for a complete overhaul of state education laws and sought control of the Department of Transportation; he had appointed a blue ribbon commission on transportation, which recommended $100 billion worth of improvements. With an eye on California's electricity shortage, and California's attempts to get electricity from Washington, he called for tax breaks on renewable resources and sought to require utilities to use solar and wind power. In February 2001 he called for "temporary" price caps on electricity.

Senior Senator Patty Murray is one of the Democrats whose election made 1992 "the year of the woman." Murray grew up in Bothell, the daughter of a disabled veteran, graduated from Washington State University in 1972, married and stayed home to raise her children. "Our culture needs to value parents who stay at home much more than they do," she said in 1996. In 1980, when she was in Olympia trying to save a parent education class she was teaching at Shoreline Community College from being cut from the budget, a state legislator told her gruffly, "You're just a mom in tennis shoes; you can't make a difference." As she had said later, "Almost every woman I've ever met in politics got into it because she was mad about something." But like many committed public employees, she won her fight; then she ran for the Shoreline School District board, lost, was appointed and then elected, and served as president. In 1988 she challenged a Republican state senator, knocked on 17,000 doors, and won the seat. Her first great cause there was extending a family leave bill to include leave for a parent whose child is sick or dying; she threatened to put the proposal on the ballot, and won the issue; she worked on school bus safety, "negative option" mail orders, accidental pesticide exposure—the warp and woof of everyday life. Then in late 1991 she decided to run against U.S. Senator Brock Adams, who was under a cloud from charges of sexual harassment and later decided not to seek reelection.

Amid a crowd of better-known conventional male politicians, Murray, with her flat accent and "mom in tennis shoes" line, attracted most of the attention and most of the votes. In the all-party primary, her main Democratic opponent was former Congressman Don Bonker, who had narrowly lost a Senate nomination in 1988. But Murray won 28% to Bonker's 19%. Meanwhile, three well-known Republicans vied: Congressman Rod Chandler won 20% to 16% for state Senator (and former opponent of George McGovern in South Dakota) Leo Thorsness and 11% for King County Executive Tim Hill. Murray sprinted to a big lead in polls, and in November won 54%–46%, carrying 60% in King County and winning Puget Sound and the west. Her margins over Chandler were similar to Bill Clinton's over George Bush, except in eastern Washington, which Clinton nearly carried but where Murray ran 10% behind.

In the Senate Murray has a largely liberal voting record and an unconventional approach. In her first years, she refused to see Washington industry lobbyists; in a scathing *Seattle Times* profile in 1996, Robert Nelson wrote of Murray, "Colleagues, lobbyists and former staff members view her as indifferent to issues that can't be explained through anecdotes about her family and neighbors." When Democrats were in control, she did not stake out areas of expertise, though she did get a seat on Appropriations. She attracted attention instead by demanding that the Senate Ethics Committee subpoena Oregon Senator Bob Packwood's diaries (he later resigned under threat of expulsion). In time she worked on Washington issues: seeking funding for cleanup of the Hanford Nuclear Reservation, trying to preserve the undammed Hanford Reach of the Columbia as a wild and scenic river, delaying with Slade Gorton the Alaska fisheries bill until a provision hurting Washington fishermen was removed. She opposed Gorton and Oregon's Mark Hatfield on timber cutting issues; their measure to allow some clear-cutting of old-growth forests passed in March 1995, and her plan to allow environmentalists to challenge timber sales in court failed.

Several years into her first term, Murray developed more legislative expertise and established a focus on certain issues; she also worked closely with Washington's economic interests and, on some issues, with Gorton. She pledges a "Commitment to Children," with money for children's health care, child care, and technology in the classroom. She formed the Senate Advisory Youth Involvement Team (SAY IT!) to meet with kids via her computer. She backed Clinton's commitment to 100,000 new teachers and tried to push it into an education bill without providing financing; that was beaten 50–49 in April 1998, with Gorton leading the opposition, instead arguing for unrestricted block grants for school districts. In May 1999 and June 2000 Murray's amendments to allow abortions in military hospitals were narrowly defeated. The Senate also rejected her 1999 amendment to maintain the five-acre limit on waste dumps in mines on federal lands. After a pipeline explosion in Bellingham killed three in June 1999, Murray sponsored a bill to let the states impose stricter safety requirements on pipelines; it passed the Senate in April 2000 and, the House having not acted, again in February 2001.

In June 2000 she had the satisfaction of seeing Clinton designate 200,000 acres of sagebrush country around the Hanford Reach as a national monument. Murray defended Microsoft against the antitrust case brought by the Clinton Justice Department; she criticized Judge Thomas Penfield Jackson's decision in November 1999. "Where is the consumer harm in constantly improving your products without raising prices?" she asked. "I join many commentators who question whether this case is even relevant, given the dynamic changes in the technology industry." She has sponsored bills to help apple farmers diversify their varieties and to help sell apples overseas. She and Congressman Jim McDermott sponsored a bill to name the Seattle federal courthouse after William Nakamura, a Washington G.I. who was killed in World War II and posthumously awarded the Medal of Honor. Murray is one of the Senate's strongest proponents of permanent normal trade relations with China—a position strongly backed by Boeing; "The best way we can affect human rights in China is to have a good conversation going with them," she said in 1996. She also favors relaxing export restrictions on encryption technology. In January 2001 she mediated a 45-day strike by the Pacific Northwest Newspaper Guild against the *Seattle Times.*

Murray was at first thought vulnerable in the 1998 election, but won handily. Her Republican opponent, Congresswoman Linda Smith, was another mom in tennis shoes—a strong opponent of abortion, backer of campaign finance regulation and opponent of free trade, a favorite of Ross Perot who was mistrusted by the Republican leadership. In the all-party primary, Smith won the Republican nomination, with 32% of all votes, to 15% for former King County prosecutor Christopher Bayley; Murray won 46% of all votes, with 2% for nuisance Democrats. But the primary was September 15, during the period when Bill Clinton's numbers were lowest in 1998; with the release of the Starr Report his numbers went up again, and Washington is one state where there was a perceptible move of opinion toward Democrats between September and October. Murray campaigned as a public official who had addressed issues of importance to Washington voters— "apples to aerospace, high-tech to Hanford, saving salmon to educating kids." She raised far more money than Smith, who spent much of her money on direct mail solicitations rather than TV ads. National Republican Senatorial Committee Chairman Mitch McConnell, the party's leading opponent of campaign finance reform, sent only about $100,000 to Smith; he argued that polls showed the race to be unpromising, which the results suggest may have been true. On election day and before (about one-third of Washington's votes are cast by absentee ballot) Murray won 58%–42%, winning 63% in the Seattle area and 55% in west Washington; Smith carried the east by only 51%–49%.

In December 1998 Murray was named vice chairwoman of the Democratic Senatorial Campaign Committee. In December 2000, just as the critical victory of Washington's Maria Cantwell was being clinched by absentee ballots, Murray was named chairwoman of the committee. Her responsibility is to match the $85 million raised by her and her predecessor Bob Torricelli.

Junior Senator   Maria Cantwell is a Democrat elected in the closest Senate race of 2000. Cantwell grew up in Indianapolis, where her father, a construction worker, served as county commissioner, city councilman and state legislator. She graduated from Miami University (Ohio) in 1980—the first in her family to graduate from college—and worked in Ohio for Jerry Springer's 1982 campaign for governor. Then she worked for Senator Alan Cranston's presidential campaign and went to Seattle to set up a regional campaign office. The Cranston campaign went nowhere, and so did Cantwell: she loved the Pacific Northwest and decided to stay. She moved to Mountlake Terrace, a suburb in Snohomish County just north of Seattle, where she organized a coalition to build a new library. In 1986, at 28, she was elected to the Washington House, where she managed the 1990 Growth Management Act during a 65-day session.

In 1992 Cantwell ran for the House, for the just redrawn 1st District seat being vacated by Republican John Miller. It included suburbs north and east of Seattle, including Redmond, the home of Microsoft, and it went across Puget Sound to include the semi-rural northern half of Kitsap County, just north of the Navy base town of Bremerton. She won a solid 55%–42% victory. In the House she supported the family and medical leave bill and the Clinton economic plan; she did not support the Clinton health care plan and only supported NAFTA at the last minute. She was a strong supporter of abortion rights and of stands backed by environmental advocacy groups. She worked to convince the Clinton administration to abandon its support of the "clipper chip": which would have enabled government to monitor personal electronic communications. But by fall 1994 some of those positions had become unpopular. In the September 1994 all-party primary she got just 44% of the vote, compared to 52% for three Republican candidates. In November she lost 52%–48% to Republican nominee Rick White.

Back in the Seattle area, she joined a startup firm called Progressive Networks in 1995; five years later it had become RealNetworks, a leader in Internet-based audio and visual software. In late 1999 her stock was worth about $40 million, and she decided to run against Republican Senator Slade Gorton. A brainy and hard-working veteran of Washington politics, Gorton served as attorney general from 1968 to 1980 and was elected Senator in 1980, 1988 and 1994 (he lost a race in 1986). Gorton had an increasingly conservative record on environmental and economic issues; he was also Microsoft's leading advocate on Capitol Hill. Cantwell was an answer to Democrats' prayers; their well-known House members had declined to run, and Insurance Commissioner Deborah Senn, who was running, was widely considered too liberal to win. Senn delivered revival-like speeches on the campaign trail, bringing out patients she had assisted against insurance companies. They had similar positions on many issues—both opposed breaching the Snake River dams—but Cantwell was for and Senn against permanent normal trade relations with China. They had different role models: Cantwell called herself a New Democrat in the Clinton mode, while Senn said her role model was Senator Barbara Mikulski. But the real difference was money. Cantwell, who liquidated more than $5 million of her RealNetworks stock, spent freely, while Senn was on TV only during the last two weeks before the September all-party primary. Cantwell won 37% of the total vote, to only 13% for Senn; Gorton, with 44% of the vote, was ahead but short of a majority.

For the general Cantwell said she would spend "whatever it takes" to win. At the same time, she made her support of McCain-Feingold-type campaign finance regulation a major issue, and refused to take contributions from PACs or soft money from the Democratic Party (though it put $640,000 into the state before Cantwell won the primary). She charged that Gorton was beholden to special interest contributors, singling out his last-night amendment to open a cyanide-leach gold mine in Okanogan County. Gorton called Cantwell an old-style liberal Democrat who would have government meddling in health care, education and local environmental issues. He emphasized his support of block grants to school districts and his bill to prohibit pharmaceutical companies from selling prescription drugs for lower prices in foreign countries than they do in the United States. Cantwell highlighted her experience in the high-tech private sector. "I've just spent the past five years in the private sector learning how to do things on the outside," she said. "Senator Gorton's been in office for 41 years. He seems to like government a lot." She called Gorton divisive, saying he pit eastern Washington against Seattle on environmental and other issues. Overall, Cantwell spent $11.5 million, $10.3 million of which she contributed; Gorton spent $6.4 million. Gorton was also hurt by more than $500,000 spent by Indian tribes, many flush with casino cash, who resented his efforts to have Indians bound by the laws which bind other people. And he was undoubtedly hurt by the fact that the Washington Republican Party after the election had $1.5 million cash left over; the state chairman, later deposed, had even spent $360,000 in cash for an office building.

Gorton led on election night, but not by much. Washington allows absentee voting, and 54% of the votes were cast absentee; two days after the election, one-quarter of the votes had yet to be counted. During the three weeks of counting, Gorton seemed to have the advantage. But the last two day's absentee ballots from King County put Cantwell over the top by 1,953. A mandated recount left the margin at 2,229 for Cantwell, out of 2.4 million cast. Cantwell carried only five counties—King, Snohomish, Thurston (which includes the state capital of Olympia) and two small counties in the west. She won King County 59%–39%; six years earlier Gorton had lost it by only 52%–48%. She also carried the rest of western Washington 50%–47%. Gorton carried eastern Washington 61%–36%—not quite enough to win. Cantwell's victory created a tie in the Senate, until James Jeffords became an independent in May 2001 and gave Democrats a razor-thin majority. This race was a very big loss for the Republican Party.

In the Senate Cantwell seems likely to be an advocate of high-tech industries; although Microsoft strongly backed Gorton, its president Steve Ballmer called her shortly after it was clear she had won. As she promised, she worked hard on campaign finance in the March 2001 two-week session on the issue. But she also had her own campaign finance problem. RealNetworks, like so many high-tech firms, saw its stock price plummet from $80 in spring 2000 to $6 in spring 2001. Cantwell had sold $5.6 million of her stock to finance her campaign, and borrowed another $3.8 million from a bank with RealNetworks stock as collateral. Suddenly she owed far more than the collateral was worth. She negotiated another loan due December 2001, guaranteed by the Democratic Senate Campaign Committee, which of course could use soft money to pay it off. And she began raising money, from committed Democrats and from some of those she might have called special interests during the campaign. But Cantwell had never shown much interest in an affluent lifestyle, and she proved the old rule that the smart thing to do with bubble money is to use it to buy something you want.

Presidential politics   For three decades Washington was one of the most contrarian states in presidential politics, voting for losers Richard Nixon in 1960, Hubert Humphrey in 1968, Gerald Ford in 1976 and Michael Dukakis in 1988. In the 1990s it was in sync with the nation, voting for Bill Clinton twice, but there has been an increasing divergence between coastal and interior voting patterns. In 1996 Clinton carried the state 50%–37%, winning by solid margins in Seattle's King County (57%–32%), which includes about one-third of the voters, and the rest of the west (49%–38%), which includes about half. He lost eastern Washington (45%–42%), which includes about one-fifth of the voters. In 2000 Al Gore carried the state 50%–45%, winning the same overall percentage as Clinton. But the vote was more polarized. Gore carried King County overwhelmingly (60%–34%) but only won narrowly in the rest of the west (49%–46%). He lost by a wide margin in eastern Washington (58%–37%). Clinton would have carried the state without King County; Gore would not. Gore carried union voters by a solid 62%–32% margin, while running marginally ahead among high income voters, who are heavily concentrated in culturally liberal King County.

Washington switched from a caucus system to primaries in 1992, when Pat Robertson won among Republicans and Jesse Jackson finished a solid second among Democrats: not much precedent for November there. In April 1999 Washington, which has never seen much of presidential primary candidates, set its primary for leap-year day, February 29, 2000. For the Democrats, this was a "beauty contest," since under party rules delegates chosen within five weeks of New Hampshire were not entitled to seating at the convention. In 2000 Bill Bradley, without any other contests in which to pick up momentum, campaigned here for six days, to no avail; Al Gore won by about 2–1. George W. Bush beat John McCain by a razor-thin margin.

Congressional districting In Washington congressional district lines are drawn by a bipartisan commission, which for the 1990s created at least four districts that were pretty evenly divided between the parties: only three of the nine districts were won by the same party in the five elections during which the lines were in effect. Because of slow population growth in the early 1990s, Washington did not gain a district in the Census in 2000, as it had in both 1990 and 1980, and the likelihood is that the commission will not make major changes. But given the close partisan division in some districts—especially the 1st, 2d , 3d and 9th, even minor changes could make a significant difference at some point in the next decade. Three of the commission's four voting members (the commission chairman does not vote) must agree on boundaries, which then can be changed only by two-thirds vote of the legislature; the governor has no say.

THE PEOPLE: Pop. 2000: 5,894,121; Pop. 1990: 4,866,692, up 21.1% 1990–2000. 2.1% of U.S. total, 15th largest; 81.8% White, 3.2% Black, 5.5% Asian, 1.6% Amer. Indian, 0.4% Hawaiian, 3.6% Two+ races, 3.9% Other; 7.5% Hispanic Origin. 5.2% Unemployment. 2000 Voting age pop.: 4,380,278. 2000 Turnout: 2,517,028; 57% of VAP. Registered voters (2000): 3,335,714; no party registration.

POLITICAL LINEUP: Governor, Gary Locke (D); Lt. Gov., Brad Owen (D); Secy. of State, Sam Reed (R); Atty. Gen., Christine Gregoire (D); Treasurer, Michael J. Murphy (D); Commissioner of Insurance, Mike Kreidler (D); Auditor, Brian Sonntag (D); Super. of Public Instruction, Teresa Bergeson; Commissioner of Public Lands, Doug Sutherland (R); State Senate, 49 (25 D, 24 R); Senate Pres. Pro Tempore, Rosa Franklin (D); Majority Leader, Sid Snyder (D); State House, 98 (49 D, 49 R); House Co-Speaker, Clyde Ballard (R); House Co-Speaker, Frank Chopp (D). Senators, Patty Murray (D) and Maria Cantwell (D). Representatives, 9 (6 D, 3 R).

ELECTIONS DIVISION: 360-902-4151; **FILING DEADLINE FOR U.S. CONGRESS:** August 2, 2002.

2000 Presidential Vote

Gore (D)	1,247,652	(50%)
Bush (R)	1,108,864	(45%)
Nader (Green)	103,002	(4%)
Others	27,915	(1%)

1996 Presidential Vote

Clinton (D)	1,123,323	(50%)
Dole (R)	840,712	(37%)
Perot (I)	201,003	(9%)
Others	90,465	(4%)

2000 Republican Presidential Primary

Bush (R)	402,287	(48%)
McCain (R)	399,980	(48%)
Other	31,391	(4%)

2000 Democratic Presidential Primary

Gore (D)	310,406	(65%)
Bradley (D)	162,727	(34%)

Gov. Gary Locke (D)

Elected 1996, term expires Jan. 2005, 2d term; b. Jan. 21, 1950, Seattle; home, Olympia; Yale U., B.A. 1972, Boston U., J.D. 1975; Protestant; married (Mona).

Elected Office: WA House of Reps., 1982–93; King Cnty. Chief Exec., 1994–97.

Professional Career: Dpty. King Cnty. Prosecuting atty., 1976–80; Staff atty., WA Senate, 1981; Legal Advisor, Seattle Human Rights Dept., 1981–82; Community Relations Mgr., U.S. West, 1988–92.

Office: Office of the Governor, P.O. Box 40002, Olympia, 98504, 360-753-6780; Fax: 360-753-4110; Web site: www.wa.gov.us.

Election Results

2000 general	Gary Locke (D)	1,441,973	(58%)
	John Eric Carlson (R)	980,060	(40%)
	Others	47,819	(2%)
2000 primary	Gary Locke (D)	701,929	(54%)
	John Eric Carlson (R)	446,142	(35%)
	Harold Hochstatter (R)	93,467	(7%)
	Others	50,764	(4%)
1996 general	Gary Locke (D)	1,296,492	(58%)
	Ellen Craswell (R)	940,538	(42%)

Sen. Patty Murray (D)

Elected 1992, seat up 2004, 2d term; b. Oct. 11, 1950, Seattle; home, Seattle; WA St. U., B.A. 1972; catholic; married (Rob).

Elected Office: Shoreline Schl. Bd., 1985–89, Pres., 1985–86; WA Senate, 1988–92.

DC Office: 173 RSOB, , 202-224-2621; Fax: 202-224-0238; Web site: www.murray.senate.gov.

Committees: *DSCC Chairman. Appropriations*: Commerce, Justice, State & Judiciary; Energy & Water Development; Interior; Labor, HHS & Education; Transportation (Chmn.). *Budget. Health, Education, Labor & Pensions*: Aging; Children & Families. *Veterans' Affairs.*

Group Ratings

	ADA	ACLU	AFS	LCV	CON	ITIC	NTU	COC	ACU	NTLC	CHC
2000	90	71	71	57	46	96	14	64	8	9	8
1999	100	—	100	100	64	—	1	59	4	—	—

National Journal Ratings

	1999 LIB —	1999 CONS		2000 LIB —	2000 CONS
Economic	83% —	16%		76% —	22%
Social	88% —	0%		66% —	21%
Foreign	78% —	13%		95% —	0%

Key Votes of the 106th Congress

1. Educ. Savings Accts.	N	5. Review Movie Violence	N	9. NATO War in Serbia	Y
2. Prescrip. Drug Benefit	Y	6. Gun Show Bckgrnd. Checks	Y	10. Table Cuba Travel Ban	N
3. Delay Ergonomic Standards	N	7. Ban Part.-Birth Abortion	N	11. Nuclear Test-Ban Treaty	Y
4. Phase Out Estate Tax	Y	8. Broaden Hate Crimes List	Y	12. Perm. Trade with China	Y

Election Results

1998 general	Patty Murray (D)	1,103,184	(58%)	($5,600,592)
	Linda Smith (R)	785,377	(42%)	($5,159,527)
1998 primary	Patty Murray (D)	479,009	(46%)	
	Linda Smith (R)	337,407	(32%)	
	Chris Bayley (R)	155,864	(15%)	
	Others	72,109	(7%)	
1992 general	Patty Murray (D)	1,197,973	(54%)	($1,342,038)
	Rod Chandler (R)	1,020,829	(46%)	($2,504,777)

Sen. Maria Cantwell (D)

Elected 2000, seat up 2006, 1st term; b. Oct., 13, 1958, Indianapolis, IN; home, Edmonds; Miami U. (OH), B.A. 1981; Catholic; single.

Elected Office: WA House of Reps., 1987–92; U.S. House of Reps., 1992–94.

Professional Career: Real Networks, 1995–2000.

DC Office: 717 HSOB, 20510, 202-224-3441; Fax: 202-228-0514; Web site: cantwell.senate.gov.

State Offices: Seattle, 206-220-6400; Spokane, 509-353-2507.

Committees: *Energy & Natural Resources*: Energy Research, Development, Production & Regulation; Forests & Public Land Management; Water & Power. *Judiciary*: Antitrust, Business Rights & Competition; Immigration; Technology, Terrorism & Government Information; Youth Violence. *Small Business*.

Group Ratings and Key Votes: Newly Elected

Election Results

2000 general	Maria Cantwell (D)	1,199,437	(49%)	($11,533,295)
	Slade Gorton (R)	1,197,208	(49%)	($6,402,488)
	Others	64,734	(3%)	
2000 primary	Slade Gorton (R)	560,787	(44%)	
	Maria Cantwell (D)	472,609	(37%)	
	Deborah Senn (D)	168,110	(13%)	
	Others	85,732	(7%)	
1994 general	Slade Gorton (R)	947,821	(56%)	($4,792,764)
	Ron Sims (D)	752,352	(44%)	($1,228,098)

FIRST DISTRICT

In the past 20 years, metropolitan Seattle spread out to the north and the east, as a growing wave of newcomers arrived seeking this area's distinctive blend of natural environmental beauty, free-wheeling culture and briskly expanding economy. In the process some of the distinctiveness of the old Seattle is left behind. The fishy odor of its docks does not permeate the new subdivisions built on what were once vegetable fields or vineyards; the Scandinavian heritage of old neighborhoods like Ballard has been mixed into a Pacific Northwest blend; the hoboes who used to hang around Yesler Way, the original "Skid Road," with its cast iron buildings and its street clocks, aren't allowed in the shopping malls off I-5 or I-405.

The heart of this new Seattle is east of Lake Washington, in the edge city of Redmond. Here the turquoise, pine-shaded low-rise buildings of the Microsoft campus—a tranquil environment for what has been the most booming and most controversial American company in the past decade. Microsoft set the standard for computer software and made billions for its founder Bill Gates by taking advantage of others' oversights, cobbling together innovative software that is sometimes barely "good enough" to put on the marketplace, and keeping fierce watch to see if its market niches are threatened by the new developments of others—so fierce, ruled Judge Thomas Penfield Jackson, that Microsoft violated antitrust laws. The company disagrees, and in early 2001 seemed to have a good chance of success on appeal; the question is whether its fierce corporate culture will continue to thrive under the Redmond pines. Not far away is the eastern shore of Lake Washington, home to many of the newly super-rich, where motorists on the causeway can make out from miles away the $60 million mansion that Bill and Melinda Gates took six years to complete—a 37,000-square-foot complex with a trampoline room with vaulted ceilings, video walls that can be electronically programmed with art from the world's great museums, and a garage large enough to hold 30 cars: Seattle's Xanadu.

The 1st Congressional District of Washington includes Redmond, Medina and a small part of Seattle, then stretches north to take in much of the northern and eastern suburbs of Seattle in Snohomish and King counties. It also runs west across Puget Sound, to Kitsap County, and gathers in Bainbridge Island, where you can commute by ferry to downtown Seattle each day and return home to what looks like the perfect American small town in the evening. Politically, this is an area torn by forces of roughly equal strength between the two parties. Most Seattle-area residents appreciate, and want to preserve, the region's unique natural aura: the evergreen smell of a well-watered land; the subtle regional style that is plainly American yet distinct from most of the nation. But it is impossible not to recognize the spectacular success of market economics in the 1st District—and to predict which way the district will lean if that success goes sour.

The congressman from the 1st District is Jay Inslee, a Democrat elected in 1998. Inslee grew up in north Seattle, the son of a high school biology teacher and football coach, and graduated from the University of Washington and Willamette School of Law. He moved to Selah, in Yakima County east of the Cascades, to practice law and served on the State Trial Lawyers board of directors. In 1988, at 37, he was elected to the state House over a former Yakima mayor; in 1990 he beat a well-known businessman who outspent him, with 62% of the vote. In 1992, when 4th District Congressman Sid Morrison ran for governor, Inslee entered the race and won the general 51%–49% over Doc Hastings, a conservative supported by the Christian Coalition. In the House Inslee voted for the Clinton budget and tax increase and for the crime bill with the assault weapons ban, despite promising to vote against gun control bills. In 1994 Hastings ran again and beat Inslee, 53%–47%.

After his defeat, Inslee moved to Bainbridge Island and practiced law in Seattle. In 1996 he ran for governor, attacking the Seattle Seahawks football stadium deal. He finished fifth, with 10%, in the primary. Briefly he was a regional director of HHS. Then he decided to run for Congress in the 1st District against Republican Congressman Rick White; another Democrat already running left the race. White was an economic conservative with liberal votes on some cultural issues, but he also had problems. In April 1998 he was divorced, though he had portrayed himself as a family man in his first campaign. And Bruce Craswell, whose wife Ellen Craswell lost to Governor Gary Locke in 1996, decided to run against him on the line of the conservative American Heritage Party. Inslee attacked White for voting to reduce spending on education and the environment and for supporting electricity deregulation, claiming that White was "willing to sell our reasonably priced electricity to California." White tried to paint Inslee as an opportunist. To the carpetbagger issue, Inslee replied that he had grown up in the 1st District and had lived there more years than White. In the September all-party primary White led 50%–44%; Craswell got 7%. The all-party primary, since abolished by the U.S. Supreme Court, was ordinarily a good forecast of the November vote. But two issues changed the balance. One was White's divorce: Although Inslee never mentioned it, his ad claimed that White intended to spend 10 years in the House and then be a lobbyist—a reference to a statement by his wife in the divorce papers. The second issue was impeachment: After White voted for the impeachment inquiry, and despite the fact that all but five members of the House voted for some form of impeachment inquiry, Inslee ran an ad for five days saying, "Rick White and Newt Gingrich shouldn't be dragging us through this. Enough is enough." The campaign became acrimonious; a debate went 45 minutes over the time limit. The primary numbers reversed: Inslee won with 50%, to 44% for White, while Craswell won 6%.

In the House, Inslee failed to win a seat on the Commerce Committee. But he voted as a centrist Democrat and found ways to work on high-tech issues, serving on Dick Gephardt's Democratic advisory group on high-tech issues. He joined in protecting the privacy of consumer financial records—a cause that is important to Microsoft. Congress approved his amendment, sponsored also by Senator Fred Thompson, to require that government inspectors general report how agencies collect and uses personal information on their web sites. He said that the World Trade Organization should take a "do no harm" approach to e-commerce and should extend duty-free cyberspace. When Congress passed the electronic signature bill, Inslee included an amendment to require that terms of consumer consent to receive electronic records be obvious and separate from other terms. On other issues, he helped to defeat a pipeline safety bill because he said that it failed to require stronger enforcement. He voted for permanent normal trade relations with China. He voted to override Bill Clinton's veto of the estate-tax and marriage-penalty repeal. He became ranking Democrat on the Forest and Forest Health Subcommittee in 2001 and attacked the Bush administration for cutting $500 million from a forest fire-fighting program. He complained that the Bush administration's failure to support short-term price caps in response to California's electricity crisis had caused prices to increase in the Pacific Northwest.

Inslee had another competitive re-election contest in 2000. Former Washington Senate Republican leader Dan McDonald, a state legislator for 22 years, called for tax cuts and local control of education. Inslee, who had fundraising help from Bill Clinton, attacked McDonald for voting for a bill that would let government agencies sell information without an individual's permission. Initially this seemed likely to be a close contest, but Inslee won by a decisive margin, 55%–43%. Redistricting could quite possibly change the lines of this sprawling and fast-growing district that straddles Puget Sound. It could lead to a fight between Inslee and freshman Democrat Rick Larsen in the 2d District, but it could also produce a district pretty much like this one.

Cook's Call *Competitive*. This swing district around Seattle has ousted two incumbents in 10 years and has never given any candidate more than 55%. It needs to pick up about 20,000 new residents in redistricting. If they come from Democratic-leaning Snohomish County, Inslee will be in much more comfortable position in 2002.

THE PEOPLE: Pop. 2000: 632,484; Pop. 1990: 540,315, up 17.1% 1990–2000. 83.6% White, 1.7% Black, 8.4% Asian, 0.9% Amer. Indian, 0.3% Hawaiian, 3.5% Two+ races, 1.6% Other; 4.2% Hispanic Origin.

2000 Presidential Vote			1996 Presidential Vote		
Gore (D)	159,462	(54%)	Clinton (D)	140,182	(51%)
Bush (R)	123,804	(42%)	Dole (R)	103,002	(37%)
Nader (Green)	11,656	(4%)	Perot (I)	21,352	(8%)
Others	2,795	(1%)	Others	10,527	(4%)

Rep. Jay Inslee (D)

Elected 1998, 2d term; b. Feb. 9, 1951, Seattle; home, Bainbridge Island; Stanford U., 1969–70, U. of WA, B.A. 1973, Willamette U., J.D. 1976.; Christian; married (Trudi).

Elected Office: WA House of Reps., 1988–92; U.S. House of Reps., 1992–94.

Professional Career: Practicing atty., 1976–92, 1995–96; Regional Dir., U.S. Dept. of H.H.S., 1997–98.

DC Office: 308 CHOB 20515, 202-225-6311; Fax: 202-226-1606; Web site: www.house.gov/inslee.

District Offices: Mountlake Terrace, 425-640-0233; Poulsbo, 360-598-2342.

Committees: *Financial Services* (19th of 32 D): Capital Markets, Insurance & Government Sponsored Enterprises; Oversight & Investigations. *Resources* (15th of 25 D): Energy & Mineral Resources; Forests & Forest Health (RMM).

Group Ratings

	ADA	ACLU	AFS	LCV	CON	ITIC	NTU	COC	ACU	NTLC	CHC
2000	70	86	57	100	95	94	42	71	28	45	13
1999	100	—	100	100	93	—	24	32	8	—	—

National Journal Ratings

	1999 LIB —	1999 CONS		2000 LIB —	2000 CONS
Economic	71%	28%		62%	37%
Social	69%	31%		77%	22%
Foreign	58%	41%		74%	24%

Key Votes of the 106th Congress

1. Patient Bill of Rights	Y	5. Bar RU-486 $ for FDA	N	9. NATO War in Serbia	Y
2. Accelerate Min. Wage	Y	6. Display 10 Commandments	N	10. Perm. Trade with China	Y
3. Strike Ban on Ergo. Stnd.	Y	7. Gun Show Bkgrnd. Checks	Y	11. Debt Relief for 3rd World	Y
4. Ovrd. Estate Tax Veto	Y	8. Ban Part.-Birth Abortion	N	12. Drop Cuba Econ. Embargo	Y

Election Results

2000 general	Jay Inslee (D)	155,820	(55%)	($2,009,131)
	Daniel McDonald (R)	121,823	(43%)	($1,462,965)
	Others	7,993	(3%)	
2000 primary	Jay Inslee (D)	80,362	(56%)	
	Daniel McDonald (R)	60,303	(42%)	
	Others	3,950	(3%)	
1998 general	Jay Inslee (D)	112,726	(50%)	($1,254,460)
	Rick White (R)	99,910	(44%)	($1,655,274)
	Bruce Craswell (AHP)	13,837	(6%)	($35,063)

SECOND DISTRICT

The 172 San Juan Islands, in the waters of Puget Sound at the far northwest corner of Washington, were the last part of the continental United States to be turned over to this country; these waters were great whaling ground, and not until 1860 did the British relinquish them. Today, ferry boats ply the waters of the Sound, connecting the islands to mainland Washington, and to British Columbia directly to the west. Whale-watching is popular not only with tourists, but also for scientists on both sides of the border. This is some of the most beautiful land and water of North America, the steely blue Sound with green forested hills rising behind; it is wet country, shielded from the full force of Pacific rains by the Olympic Mountains, but still seldom dry. The little towns, on bits of level land between the water and mountains, have the look of pristine New England villages or Midwestern historic towns, but are better preserved than the originals; the stores are full of fresh produce and local seafood. Here the Seattle metropolitan area has marched north along the shore of Puget Sound, to and beyond the old lumber port and railroad terminus of Everett, with the huge Boeing plant—the largest building in the world—where 747s, 767s and 777s are built. Far to the north are the small city of Bellingham and the town of Blaine on the 49th parallel, with America's most attractively landscaped border crossing and International Peace Arch, just south of British Columbia.

The 2d Congressional District of Washington includes the San Juan Islands, Whidbey Island and most of Puget Sound from Everett north, plus the margin of mainland along the Sound and the huge mountains, topped by snow-capped Mount Baker. The political tradition in most of the lumbering and fishing areas here is Democratic, while the rich agricultural areas, like the flower-bulb-growing Skagit Valley, are more Republican. Everett tends to be Democratic, some of the nearby new suburban towns Republican. Overall, this is a pretty evenly balanced district that tends to vote as the state does.

The congressman from the 2d District is Rick Larsen, a Democrat elected in 2000. He grew up in Arlington, in Snohomish County, graduated from Pacific Lutheran University and got a masters degree at the University of Minnesota. He spent a year as a research analyst for the Port of Everett, where he focused on economic development. For six years, he was director of public affairs for the Washington State Dental Association. In 1998 he won a seat on the Snohomish County Council and he later became its president. On the council, he claimed credit for preserving open space and cutting new spending initiatives.

In 2000 Republican Congressman Jack Metcalf kept his promise to retire after serving three terms, he had won the formerly Democratic seat three times by relatively narrow margins, and the 2d District became one of the premier open seat battles of the year. Each party settled on its choice early. The Democratic field was cleared for Larsen when state representative Jeff Morris, unpopular with labor union leaders, withdrew in September 1999. The Republican field was cleared for conservative state Representative John Koster when moderate state Representative Barry Sehlin, unable to raise much money, dropped out in April 2000. In the September all-party primary, Koster unexpectedly led 49%–46%, winning 49%–46% in Whatcom and 53%–42% in Skagit, the second- and third-largest counties, and trailing Larsen by only 757 votes in Snohomish, which cast 47% of the total vote. The contest became a major battleground for political action committees: anti-abortion groups and the National Rifle Association backed Koster, and unions and abortion rights groups fought for Larsen. Koster emphasized his anti-abortion views, including opposition to funds for family planning and fetal-tissue research, plus opposition to gay rights. Larsen turned up the heat on abortion, saying that the contest offered "a clear choice," and criticizing Koster for referring to "our American holocaust." Both parties' campaign committees focused on this district, with Speaker Dennis Hastert campaigning for Koster and Minority Leader Dick Gephardt for Larsen. In the general, Larsen benefited from the higher turnout generated by statewide contests, in which Democrats performed well. He won 50%–46%, improving his performance in each major county from the primary: winning 51%–46% in Snohomish and 50%–45% in Whatcom, and losing Skagit by only 76 votes.

In the House, Larsen won seats on the Agriculture and Transportation and Infrastructure Committees, and he joined the New Democrat Coalition. Spurred by a fatal pipeline explosion in Bellingham in 1999, he filed legislation to require more aggressive inspection and testing plus improved training for pipeline operators. Redistricting poses risks for Larsen. This corner-of-the-state district must lose some population, and the logical area to be chopped off is its southeast extremity, around Everett in Snohomish County. This is also the most Democratic part of the district. However, this will still be a swing district, in which an active incumbent can hope to have an advantage.

Cook's Call *Highly Competitive.* This swing district (which gave Gore just a 2% margin of victory) has been a battleground for years. Solid growth here means the 2nd needs to shed about 65,000 people. Republicans are hoping that Democratic-leaning Everett will be sloughed off. As of spring 2001, Republican state Representative Kelly Barlean had no opposition for his party's nomination.

THE PEOPLE: Pop. 2000: 719,487; Pop. 1990: 540,861, up 33% 1990–2000. 87.5% White, 1.3% Black, 3.2% Asian, 1.9% Amer. Indian, 0.2% Hawaiian, 3% Two+ races, 2.8% Other; 5.8% Hispanic Origin.

2000 Presidential Vote			1996 Presidential Vote		
Gore (D)	146,456	(48%)	Clinton (D)	123,729	(47%)
Bush (R)	140,437	(46%)	Dole (R)	103,901	(39%)
Nader (Green)	14,151	(5%)	Perot (I)	27,177	(10%)
Others	3,981	(1%)	Others	11,055	(4%)

Rep. Rick Larsen (D)

Elected 2000, 1st term; b. June 15, 1965, Arlington; home, Arlington; Pacific Lutheran U., B.A. 1987; U. of MN, M.P.A. 1990; Methodist; married (Tiia).

Elected Office: Snohomish City Cncl., 1998–2000, Pres., 1999–2000.

Professional Career: Econ. Dev. Ofcl., Port of Everett, 1990–91; Dir., Pub. Affairs, WA St. Dental Assn., 1991–98.

DC Office: 1529 LHOB 20515, 202-225-2605; Fax: 202-225-4420; Web site: www.house.gov/larsen.

District Offices: Bellingham, 360-733-4500; Everett, 425-252-3188.

Committees: *Agriculture* (20th of 24 D): General Farm Commodities & Risk Management; Livestock & Horticulture. *Transportation & Infrastructure* (34th of 34 D): Highways & Transit; Railroads.

Group Ratings and Key Votes: Newly Elected

Election Results

2000 general	Rick Larsen (D)	146,617	(50%)	($1,529,101)
	John Koster (R)	134,660	(46%)	($1,092,585)
	Others	11,903	(4%)	
2000 primary	John Koster (R)	72,244	(49%)	
	Rick Larsen (D)	68,315	(46%)	
	Others	6,686	(5%)	
1998 general	Jack Metcalf (R)	124,125	(55%)	($1,063,851)
	Margarethe Cammermeyer (D)	100,776	(45%)	($1,050,926)

THIRD DISTRICT

From the Pacific Ocean to the majestic row of active and inactive volcanoes from Mount Rainier to Mount St. Helens to Oregon's Mount Hood, southwest Washington is one of America's most productive lumber areas. The moist air and almost constant rains blown in from the Pacific keep the trees on the coast growing rapidly; in the valleys just past the Coast Range there is still plenty of precipitation and fast-growing forest. Then come the high mountains: The Cascades are a genuine divide, wrenching almost all precipitation out of the air so the climate eastward for a thousand miles is arid. Americans were reminded of the force of the volcanoes when Mount St. Helens, dormant for 123 years, erupted in 1980, killing 65 people, destroying its own peak and paving the land around with flows of lava. Americans used to be taught that there were no active volcanoes in the lower 48 states; but Mount St. Helens proved that wrong, and one of her sisters may prove it again soon.

Lewis and Clark came here in 1805, down the Columbia River to a rainy and foggy winter by the ocean, and for many years this part of Washington was sparsely settled, with lumber-mill and fishing-boat towns interspersed between mountains and water. It was flannel shirt country, Democratic since the New Deal days. In the early 1990s its resource-based economy was threatened by the environmental movement, which restricted fishing practices and got a court decision shutting down old-growth forest logging to save spotted owl habitat. This roiled local politics and gave Republicans an opening. More important recently has been the spread of the Pacific Northwest's great metropolitan areas into these valleys. Clark County across the Columbia from Portland, Oregon, has filled up with new residents, eager to avoid Oregon's income tax and still able to make big purchases in Oregon free of sales tax; its population grew by 45% in the 1990s, the largest increase in the state. The Seattle-Tacoma metro area has been moving down from the north past the small state capital of Olympia. This is one of America's great international trading areas, with big exports of logs and timber and vast imports on the docks of Portland and the Puget Sound.

The 3d Congressional District of Washington covers the land between the ocean and the Cascades, from Olympia on an inlet of Puget Sound, south to Vancouver in Clark County, site of the Hudson Bay Company headquarters in the 19th Century. Politically, this was long a solidly Democratic district. But economic growth and diversification and the coming of many new residents with no roots in the old industries have made the 3d now a politically marginal district.

The congressman from the 3d District is Brian Baird, a Democrat elected in 1998. Baird grew up in northern New Mexico and western Colorado. He got a Ph.D. in clinical psychology from the University of Wyoming, and worked with veterans and families dealing with cancer, with juvenile delinquents in prison, and families of murder victims. He also wrote a book called *Are We Having Fun Yet?* for couples on vacation. He moved to Washington in 1980 and was a professor at Pacific Lutheran University in Tacoma and living in Olympia when he ran for the House in 1996 against Republican incumbent Linda Smith. Smith was one of the most revolutionary of the 1994 Republican freshmen, an opponent of free trade and a backer of campaign finance reform, strongly supported by Christian conservatives. On election night Baird was ahead by 2,400 votes and was pronounced the winner by an overeager media; Baird spent five days in Washington, D.C., at freshman orientation. But when the more than 40,000 absentee votes outstanding were counted, Smith won by 887 votes, 50.2%–49.8%.

Baird returned to southwest Washington and, taking a leave from his job, never stopped running, while Smith decided to challenge Senator Patty Murray; she won the Republican nomination but lost the general election 58%–42%, running behind in the 3d District as well. Campaigning constantly, Baird picked up the consensus-minded inclination of voters and emphasized how confrontation-minded the Republicans were. "People really want to focus on a positive agenda," he said. "People are tired of candidates who just want to tear down government and tear down their opposition." He called for applying 100% of the budget surplus to Social Security, opposed school vouchers, favored campaign finance reform, opposed breaching the Columbia River dams and said Washington taxpayers should be able to deduct their sales tax payments—it is close to 8% in many counties—as they could before the Tax Reform Act of 1986.

Republicans nominated state Senator Don Benton, who called for a flat tax and respect for gun rights and property rights. He started far behind Baird in fundraising and took confrontational, crunchy stands on issues. Independent expenditure ads were run by Americans for Limited Terms (against Baird), the Sierra Club (against Benton) and the Republican Party. The last seized on the fact that on a Project Vote Smart questionnaire, Baird left blank the question whether he would prosecute as adults youths accused of murder and violent crimes. "Brian Baird wouldn't support trying even the most violent juveniles as adults," the ad said. Baird replied that "to make it a black-or-white blanket judgment and eliminate any judicial discretion is, I think, a big mistake. Voters are fed up with this kind of deception." It was unclear why, if Baird felt that way on the issue, he had not checked the yes box. But he framed the issue as one of positive versus negative campaigning and the media, very unsympathetic to conservatives here (*The Olympian* called Benton "an arrogant divisive blowhard"), accepted his argument that the ad was inaccurate. One Portland station pulled the ad and the issue probably worked for Baird. He spent twice as much money and won 55%–45%, exceeding 60% in the Olympia area and the coast and running barely ahead around Vancouver, Benton's home base.

Soon afterwards Baird got a quick dose of bad publicity. During his two campaigns, he had featured pictures of him and his wife embracing and holding hands by a river bank; he talked of how, with her two children in college, they avoided the "peace of an empty nest" by becoming hosts to an injured Bosnian teenager. But two days after the election the Bairds were divorced. Mary Baird said that her husband told her in April that he wanted a divorce but did not want to announce it until after the election for fear it would hurt his campaign. She stopped attending his rallies and asked that her pictures be dropped from his brochures and Website; most but not all were. Reporters recalled how Baird said during the campaign things like, "Voters demand and deserve honesty and integrity from their public officials." *The Seattle Times*, which endorsed Baird, wrote, "Baird squanders his potential when he puts short-term personal gain over long-term public trust." Baird replied, "It has never been my intention to deceive the public, only to protect my family's privacy in this painful time." In April 2000, Baird married Rachel Nugent, an economics professor at Pacific Lutheran; the event received little attention.

In the House, Baird was elected president of the Democratic freshman class and got a seat on the Transportation and Infrastructure Committee. He kept a campaign promise by filing a bill to restore income-tax deductibility for state sales tax payments, but of course no such law was enacted. He secured funds to dredge the Columbia River near Vancouver. And he passed legislation to authorize transfer to Vancouver of the former Army barracks in that city, which had been maintained as a military post since 1879. He proposed a new financial aid program for part-time students who also hold jobs. Although his voting record was rather liberal, he voted to override Bill Clinton's vetoes of the estate-tax and marriage-penalty repeal. He was among a handful of white Democrats who joined Black Caucus members in walking out of the Electoral College vote to protest the Florida result. When George W. Bush canceled U.S. assistance to international family-planning agencies, Baird said that he was "saddened" by the failure to recognize the problem of overpopulation: "This is not compassionate conservatism," he said.

Although Baird expected serious competition in 2000, he was re-elected easily. His challenger Trent Matson, a lobbyist for the Building Industry Association in Olympia, raised nearly $500,000, but was only 29 and had no campaign experience, and was not on Republicans' priority list. Baird won 56%–41%, winning more than 60% again in the Olympia area, and 55% in Clark County, even though George W. Bush defeated Al Gore there 50%–46%; Matson took rural Lewis County with 53%. Matson said he was thinking of running again in 2002. The district's large population gains will force some trimming in redistricting.

Cook's Call *Competitive.* Baird's convincing wins in 1998 and 2000 belie the underlying competitiveness of this district. But Republicans need to find stronger candidates than the ones they have put forth over the last two cycles. The 3d needs to lose about 44,000 residents and the new lines may determine how seriously this seat is contested in 2002.

THE PEOPLE: Pop. 2000: 698,038; Pop. 1990: 540,658, up 29.1% 1990–2000. 89.5% White, 1.3% Black, 2.7% Asian, 1.2% Amer. Indian, 0.3% Hawaiian, 3% Two+ races, 2% Other; 4.7% Hispanic Origin.

2000 Presidential Vote

Bush (R)	139,179	(48%)
Gore (D)	136,691	(47%)
Nader (Green)	13,345	(5%)
Others	3,520	(1%)

1996 Presidential Vote

Clinton (D)	124,864	(49%)
Dole (R)	97,985	(38%)
Perot (I)	24,407	(9%)
Others	9,895	(4%)

Rep. Brian Baird (D)

Elected 1998, 2d term; b. Mar. 7, 1956, Chama, NM; home, Olympia; U. of UT, B.A. 1977, U. of WY, M.S. 1980, Ph.D. 1984; Protestant; married (Rachael).

Elected Office: Dem. nominee for U.S. House of Reps., 1996.

Professional Career: Prof., Pacific Lutheran U., 1986–98.

DC Office: 1721 LHOB 20515, 202-225-3536; Fax: 202-225-3478; Web site: www.house.gov/baird.

District Offices: Olympia, 360-352-9768; Vancouver, 360-695-6292.

Committees: *Science* (16th of 22 D): Environment, Technology and Standards; Research. *Small Business* (12th of 17 D). *Transportation & Infrastructure* (29th of 34 D): Highways & Transit; Water Resources & Environment.

Group Ratings

	ADA	ACLU	AFS	LCV	CON	ITIC	NTU	COC	ACU	NTLC	CHC
2000	70	71	71	86	43	78	33	75	12	21	0
1999	95	—	100	88	88	—	23	33	4	—	—

National Journal Ratings

	1999 LIB	—	1999 CONS		2000 LIB	—	2000 CONS
Economic	78%	—	21%		64%	—	35%
Social	68%	—	32%		86%	—	12%
Foreign	71%	—	27%		85%	—	10%

Key Votes of the 106th Congress

1. Patient Bill of Rights	Y	5. Bar RU-486 $ for FDA	N	9. NATO War in Serbia	Y
2. Accelerate Min. Wage	Y	6. Display 10 Commandments	N	10. Perm. Trade with China	Y
3. Strike Ban on Ergo. Stnd.	Y	7. Gun Show Bkgrnd. Checks	N	11. Debt Relief for 3rd World	Y
4. Ovrd. Estate Tax Veto	Y	8. Ban Part.-Birth Abortion	N	12. Drop Cuba Econ. Embargo	Y

Election Results

2000 general	Brian Baird (D)	159,428	(56%)	($1,368,592)
	Trent Ross Matson (R)	114,861	(41%)	($487,812)
	Others	8,375	(3%)	
2000 primary	Brian Baird (D)	81,240	(56%)	
	Trent Ross Matson (R)	58,077	(40%)	
	Others	5,332	(4%)	
1998 general	Brian Baird (D)	120,364	(55%)	($1,602,437)
	Don Benton (R)	99,855	(45%)	($755,022)

FOURTH DISTRICT

The rugged peaks of the Cascade Mountains divide Washington State into two starkly different climate zones and two almost as starkly different political cultures. West of the Cascades, Washington is moist, green, full of watery inlets; to the east it is barren and brown, except where irrigation ditches feed the waters of the Columbia River into thirsty valleys, or where mountaintop waters fall east, as they do to water the apple orchards in the Yakima Valley. The federal government has been a presence in the East-of-the-Cascades since the 1930s, when it began to build dams that provided cheap power and boosted economic development in this forbidding, often surreal, landscape: A giant bust of Franklin Roosevelt gazes from a bluff on the Columbia out over 550-foot-high Grand Coulee Dam, which Roosevelt initiated and which was one of his favorite projects. Other dams are strung along downriver, like beads on the necklace of the Columbia, most of the way to Bonneville Dam near Portland, where the river breaks through the Cascades.

The one exception is the Hanford Reach, the last undammed, undeveloped stretch of the upper Columbia River, near the 560-square mile Hanford Nuclear Reservation, north of the Tri-Cities of Richland, Kennewick and Pasco. Hanford was built by the Army to manufacture pluto-nium for the Manhattan Project and was where the Nagasaki bomb was constructed. After the war the Hanford Works became the primary producer of materials for America's nuclear weapons and eastern Washington's largest employer. Then in 1988 Hanford's plutonium plant was shut down because of hazardous leaks and contaminated waste. There is a proposal to restart the Fast Flux Test Facility reactor, closed in 1992, to produce plutonium for space batteries and medical isotopes; it costs $40 million a year to keep on standby and would cost $371 million to restart and $120 million a year to operate—or $1.5 billion to dismantle. Construction is slated to begin in 2001 of a plant to convert million of gallons of nuclear waste to glass starting in 2006, which would cost about $4 billion.

The 4th Congressional District covers the western half of Washington east of the Cascades, running from the Canadian border past Grand Coulee and through the Hanford Works down to the Dalles Dam. Sentiment toward the federal government has soured in other parts of the district almost as much as around the Tri-Cities. The Yakima Valley, which produces more than half of the nation's apples, was angry that the groundless Alar scare in 1989 hurt sales, and farmers of other crops are furious at environmental groups' proposals to breach the Snake River dams upriver to save salmon. Lumber towns in the Cascades were furious when those who want to preserve the spotted owl tried to shut down logging businesses. In an area once pretty evenly divided between the parties, opinion has shifted toward Republicans; the cultural liberalism of Seattle seems very far away here. Said one Democrat when he looked at a party poll in 1998, "I don't know what Democrats did to these people, but it sure must have been bad."

The congressman from the 4th District is Doc Hastings, a Republican elected in 1994. Has-tings grew up in the Tri-Cities, went to college in Ellensburg, served in the Army Reserves and for 27 years ran the Columbia Basin Paper and Supply Company in Pasco. In 1979 he was elected to the state House, served as a Republican leader, then retired in 1987. In 1992 he ran for Congress, won the Republican nomination, but was beaten 51%–49% by moderate Democrat Jay Inslee. But Inslee voted for the Clinton budget and tax package in 1993 and the crime bill with its gun control provisions in 1994—big liabilities when Hastings ran again. Hastings led with 50% in the September all-party primary, to only 41% for Inslee. In November he won 53%–47%, despite losing Yakima.

In the House, Hastings has a solidly conservative voting record and, with a seat on the Rules Committee, has usually been a leadership loyalist. Much of his time has been spent on Hanford. With former Senator Slade Gorton, he sponsored a bill to make the state of Washington respon-sible for the cleanup, allowing privatization of cleanup work and avoiding the plethora of often impractical and duplicative federal regulations; this was supported also by Democratic Congress-man Norman Dicks and Senator Patty Murray. More recently, as chairman of the Nuclear Cleanup Caucus, he has worked to educate colleagues about the need for creative solutions. He worked closely with Dicks to stop a proposal by Lloyd Doggett of Texas to zero out the $230 million Environmental and Molecular Sciences Laboratory at Hanford; they even enlisted support from scientists in Austin, Doggett's hometown. The Fast Flux Test Facility reactor was ordered shut by Bill Clinton in his final days in office, but new Energy Secretary Spencer Abraham delayed this, at Hastings' urging, to explore the reactor's potential as a breeder for isotope production. When George W. Bush proposed cuts in the Energy Department budget, Hastings warned that cuts in the cleanup program were not acceptable.

Hastings opposed Murray's proposal, supported by Dicks, to designate the 51-mile Hanford Reach of the Columbia a wild and scenic river; it has been kept free from development by the Hanford Reservation and as a result is the closest thing to a free-flowing part of the river, producing most of its wild salmon run. Hastings argued for a county-state-federal management panel, with a quarter-mile on each side of the river kept free from development. "Nobody would argue that Hanford Reach is something that ought to be preserved and protected, but it ought to be accessible," he said. "There needs to be local decision making." In June 2000 Clinton unilaterally acted to create the Hanford Reach National Monument to be managed by the Fish and Wildlife Service, with the assistance of a local advisory board; Hastings opposed the action as an abuse of presidential authority. Clinton signed Hastings' bill to promote salmon recovery in the Yakima River and Hastings got $11 million for the Yakima River Basin Water Enhancement Project. When Clinton's Interior Secretary Bruce Babbitt said that he would like to tear down a major hydroelectric dam in Washington. Hastings opposed that, along with all of the Washington delegation; they and Governor Gary Locke also oppose the breaching of dams proposed by some environmentalists and Indian leaders.

Hastings has been re-elected three times. He had a serious opponent in 1996 in Rick Locke, who ran an ad in which a menacing voice said Hastings' votes were controlled by "someone back East named Newtie." Hastings retaliated with an ad with a Robin Leach-like voice saying: "Today we'll meet political candidate Rick Locke, the Seattle millionaire who just moved to central Washington to buy a seat in Congress. Of course, buying things comes naturally to Rick Locke. He still maintains several luxurious homes in Seattle and a 38-foot sailing yacht on nearby Puget Sound." Hastings won 53% in the general; Locke carried Yakima and Kittitas counties narrowly and Hastings carried everything else. Since then, Hastings has had easier going. With the slower growth of the 5th District to the east compared to the rest of the state, this district probably will move a bit to the west but that should not have much political impact on Hastings.

Cook's Call *Safe*. Hastings has found a foothold in this conservative, Republican-leaning district. It was Bush's best district in the state—he won it by 28%.

THE PEOPLE: Pop. 2000: 672,059; Pop. 1990: 540,701, up 24.3% 1990–2000. 75.8% White, 0.9% Black, 1.2% Asian, 2.8% Amer. Indian, 0.1% Hawaiian, 3% Two+ races, 16.1% Other; 25.4% Hispanic Origin.

2000 Presidential Vote			1996 Presidential Vote		
Bush (R)	147,675	(62%)	Dole (R)	101,963	(48%)
Gore (D)	80,316	(34%)	Clinton (D)	84,157	(40%)
Nader (Green)	6,033	(3%)	Perot (I)	20,516	(10%)
Others	3,231	(1%)	Others	4,868	(2%)

Rep. Doc Hastings (R)

Elected 1994, 4th term; b. Feb. 7, 1941, Spokane; home, Pasco; Columbia Basin Col., 1959–61, Central Washington U., 1963–64; Protestant; married (Claire).

Military Career: Army Reserves, 1964–69.

Elected Office: WA House of Reps., 1979–87; Repub. nominee for U.S. House of Reps., 1992.

Professional Career: Pres., Columbia Basin Paper & Supply, 1967–94.

DC Office: 1323 LHOB 20515, 202-225-5816; Fax: 202-225-3251; Web site: www.house.gov/hastings.

District Offices: Tri-Cities, 509-543-9396; Yakima, 509-452-3243.

Committees: *Budget* (14th of 24 R). *Rules* (6th of 9 R): The Legislative & Budget Process. *Standards of Official Conduct* (3d of 5 R).

Group Ratings

	ADA	ACLU	AFS	LCV	CON	ITIC	NTU	COC	ACU	NTLC	CHC
2000	0	29	0	0	24	94	61	94	92	82	100
1999	0	—	0	0	7	—	58	100	92	—	—

National Journal Ratings

	1999 LIB	—	1999 CONS		2000 LIB	—	2000 CONS
Economic	79%	—	20%		6%	—	85%
Social	16%	—	82%		0%	—	79%
Foreign	31%	—	66%		0%	—	88%

Key Votes of the 106th Congress

1. Patient Bill of Rights	N	5. Bar RU-486 $ for FDA	Y	9. NATO War in Serbia	N
2. Accelerate Min. Wage	N	6. Display 10 Commandments	Y	10. Perm. Trade with China	Y
3. Strike Ban on Ergo. Stnd.	N	7. Gun Show Bkgrnd. Checks	N	11. Debt Relief for 3rd World	N
4. Ovrd. Estate Tax Veto	Y	8. Ban Part.-Birth Abortion	Y	12. Drop Cuba Econ. Embargo	N

Election Results

2000 general	Doc Hastings (R)	143,259	(61%)	($761,774)
	Thomas James Davis (D)	87,585	(37%)	($433,054)
	Others	4,260	(2%)	
2000 primary	Doc Hastings (R)	79,683	(61%)	
	Thomas James Davis (D)	42,337	(32%)	
	Gordon Pross (R)	5,420	(4%)	
	Others	3,684	(3%)	
1998 general	Doc Hastings (R)	121,684	(69%)	($468,365)
	Gordon Pross (D)	43,043	(24%)	
	Peggy McKerlie (Ref)	11,363	(6%)	($11,538)

FIFTH DISTRICT

Eastern Washington is a land of great rivers and bare parched land, where the Columbia, Spokane and Snake Rivers wind among vast plateaus, bringing water from the Rockies to the desert. Spokane grew up at the falls of the Spokane River when the railroads first came through, and became a major wheat, mining, electrical and railroad center early in the 20th Century, the center of the so-called "Inland Empire"; it celebrated with the 1974 World's Exposition on the downtown riverfront. Nearby are some of the most fascinating landscapes in the United States: surreally undulating yellow wheatfields, the ridges of the Palouse where the topsoil is 200 feet deep, the bare-rock coulees rising above dammed-up lakes and barren desert. This is remote and inhospitable land: the summers can be blazing hot and winters bitter cold; many rivers run wildly. But it has been tamed by man, and the water from the Grand Coulee and other dams irrigates some of the richest farmland in the country. The economy has been strong, with Spokane recently among the top 25 per cent of metropolitan areas in job growth.

The 5th Congressional District covers the easternmost part of Washington. Two-thirds of the people here live in greater Spokane, a city whose voting habits are a fairly good proxy of the nation's. Its heritage leans Republican, but it is not as Republican as most of the nearby Rocky Mountain states. It is open to Democrats: Spokane County voted for Bill Clinton in 1992 and 1996, but George W. Bush won the county 52%–43% in 2000.

The congressman from the 5th District is George Nethercutt, a Republican elected in 1994 when he defeated House Speaker Thomas Foley—the first time a House speaker had been defeated in his home district since Galusha Grow lost in Pennsylvania in 1862. (Contrary to some local expectations, this did not make Nethercutt the new speaker.) He grew up in Spokane, graduated from Washington State University in Pullman and Gonzaga Law School in Spokane, served four years on the staff of Alaska Senator Ted Stevens, then returned home and practiced law. He was involved in civic work, representing clients in adoptions, heading the local Diabetes Foundation (his daughter was diagnosed with the disease), and starting a crisis nursery for abused children. Foley had served the district for 30 years and had wide personal popularity. But in 1992 his margin was not much larger than that of Bill Clinton's, whose popularity had plummeted, and many in the state were angry at Foley for filing a lawsuit against congressional term limits imposed by the voters in 1992. Nethercutt announced his candidacy in April 1994. In May two former Foley opponents also announced: Duane Alton, owner of a chain of tire stores who ran in 1976 and 1978; and John Sonneland, a physician who ran in 1980, 1982 and 1992. For a time the contest among Republicans seemed more intense than the race against Foley; Nethercutt won the all-party primary with 29% of the total vote, to 20% for Alton and 15% for Sonneland.

But the big news was that in the all-party primary, which often forecasts the November results, Foley won only 35%. Immediately Foley began spending heavily, emphasizing the work he had done for the district and what he could do in the future. However, he had to buck not only Nethercutt's ads but also campaigns by the National Rifle Association (furious that Foley, a long-time gun control opponent, backed the 1994 crime bill) and the National Taxpayers Union. Nethercutt in an ad promised never to sue the people of Washington—a swipe at Foley's lawsuit against the term-limits initiative—and pledged to serve only three terms himself. When attacked for his conservatism and support for budget cuts, Nethercutt responded with ads showing him walking out of a crisis nursery holding a baby and with his family walking in a park; he was helped also by a November 4th campaign appearance by Ross Perot. This was one of the most expensive House races in the nation: Foley spent $2.1 million; Nethercutt, $1.1 million. Foley carried Spokane County, but not by much, and lost all but one of the smaller counties; that gave Nethercutt a 51%–49% win.

In the House Nethercutt got a seat on Appropriations and supported most of the Contract with America. Initially noncommittal, he supported the Freedom to Farm Act, including the fixed payments to formerly subsidized farmers in its seven-year phaseout. He has a moderate voting record but has cast some surprising votes, notably in 1997 voting to take the United States out of the United Nations. In 1998 he helped put together the repeal of sanctions against Pakistan, the single largest buyer of winter wheat, in time for Washington grain sellers to qualify for a $35 million purchase; he pushed a bill to lift sanctions on farm products except in cases where the president exercises a national security waiver. He grilled Clinton Interior Secretary Bruce Babbitt about whether he would dismantle or breach the Columbia River dams; Babbitt said he had authority to do so, but could not act unless Congress provided money. Nethercutt strongly opposes getting rid of the dams and attacked Babbitt's "green sledge hammer." He has pushed hard for increased diabetes research, and made the Congressional Diabetes Caucus the largest such group on Capitol Hill. Locally, he won approval of a bill to rename the Spokane federal courthouse after Foley, and the plaza outside after Foley's predecessor, Walt Horan; together they represented the district for 52 years. He worked to build a $16 million dorm at Fairchild Air Force Base and backed a HUD loan to Spokane for downtown redevelopment opposed by the owner of NorthTown Mall. In 2000 the House narrowly approved his attempt to stifle the Clinton administration's new management rules for the Columbia River Basin.

In 2000 Nethercutt was the leader of the successful move to end the food and drug embargo on Communist Cuba. He assembled a coalition of free traders, left-wingers sympathetic to Castro and farm state members eager to export local products, which clearly had a majority. He was strongly opposed by Miami's two Republican Cuban-American members and by many conservatives and liberals opposed to Castro's totalitarian regime. The Republican leadership stepped in and helped negotiate an agreement. After weeks of negotiations, Nethercutt in September 2000 agreed to a limited victory that permits exports to Cuba, but on a cash-only basis and with no U.S. government financing; nor could Cuba export anything to the United States. The deal also expanded travel rights to Cuba by American grain and food exporters. Nethercutt called it "a fundamental shift in American foreign policy, and a new day for American agriculture." Miami's Lincoln Diaz-Balart responded, "I prefer this deal to current law." Those views suggested it had been a true compromise. Nethercutt won wide praise from the agricultural community.

Nethercutt generated national controversy by seeking reelection in 2000. His self-imposed term limit looming, he said in February 1999, "I meant it when I said six years is enough." But, he went on to say, he had found the issues so complicated that six years "is probably not enough," and he talked about the still-distant possibility of becoming a member of the college of cardinals—the 13 Appropriations subcommittee chairmen. That month, U.S. Term Limits put up a billboard thanking Nethercutt for keeping his pledge; in March, after he made no move to retire, they launched a $100,000 ad campaign that started with an ad showing Richard Nixon, George Bush and Bill Clinton making promises they were not to keep, then posing the question "Will George Nethercutt be next?" In June, he said: "I've changed my mind. . . . I made a mistake when I chose to set a limit on my service." U.S. Term Limits pledged to spend up to $1 million to defeat him, although the final amount spent was much less. Doonesbury lampooned him as "the Weasel King." Polls and political forecasters listed him in deep trouble for reelection. But Nethercutt had one big factor going his way: weak opposition. In the all-party primary, he easily won the Republican nomination 45%–20% against Spokane talk-radio host—and strong term-limits advocate— Richard Clear. Clear supported Democratic nominee Tom Keefe, who had received 21% of the total vote. But Keefe was a former congressional staffer and Washington lobbyist and a Seattle native who moved to Spokane a month before he declared his candidacy—a flawed messenger for a grass-roots citizenry. Nethercutt won 57%–39%, with a commanding lead in all 11 counties, including 55%–41% in Spokane.

The 5th District will need to be expand slightly in redistricting, into more Republican areas. Nethercutt has voiced interest in challenging Senator Patty Murray in 2004. It's been 60 years since Washington elected a Senator from east of the Cascades. But Nethercutt has a way of beating the odds.

Cook's Call   *Safe.* This conservative, Republican-leaning district is a tough sell for a Democrat, especially after Nethercutt withstood thousands of dollars of negative advertising by the national term-limits movement and reams of negative press nationally in 2000.

THE PEOPLE: Pop. 2000: 625,971; Pop. 1990: 540,865, up 15.7% 1990–2000. 90% White, 1.4% Black, 1.8% Asian, 1.8% Amer. Indian, 0.2% Hawaiian, 2.7% Two+ races, 2.3% Other; 4.9% Hispanic Origin.

2000 Presidential Vote			1996 Presidential Vote		
Bush (R)	142,185	(55%)	Clinton (D)	104,052	(44%)
Gore (D)	103,116	(40%)	Dole (R)	102,384	(43%)
Nader (Green)	8,992	(3%)	Perot (I)	25,250	(11%)
Others	3,367	(1%)	Others	6,826	(3%)

Rep. George Nethercutt (R)

Elected 1994, 4th term; b. Oct. 7, 1944, Spokane; home, Spokane; WA St. U., B.A. 1967, Gonzaga U. Law Schl., J.D. 1971; Presbyterian; married (Mary Beth).

Professional Career: Law Clerk, Fed. Judge Ralph Plumer, 1971–72; Chief of Staff & Cnsl., U.S. Sen. Ted Stevens, 1972–76; Practicing atty., 1976–94.

DC Office: 223 CHOB 20515, 202-225-2006; Fax: 202-225-3392; Web site: www.house.gov/nethercutt.

District Offices: Colville, 509-684-3481; Spokane, 509-353-2374; Spokane Valley, 509-924-7775; Walla Walla, 509-529-9358.

Committees: *Appropriations* (20th of 35 R): Agriculture, Rural Development, & FDA; Defense; Interior. *Science* (15th of 25 R): Energy; Space & Aeronautics.

Group Ratings

	ADA	ACLU	AFS	LCV	CON	ITIC	NTU	COC	ACU	NTLC	CHC
2000	5	29	0	0	61	100	62	80	88	72	93
1999	10	—	0	13	44	—	57	88	84	—	—

National Journal Ratings

	1999 LIB —	1999 CONS		2000 LIB —	2000 CONS
Economic	30%	64%		29%	67%
Social	37%	61%		37%	62%
Foreign	23%	73%		12%	78%

Key Votes of the 106th Congress

1. Patient Bill of Rights	N	5. Bar RU-486 $ for FDA	Y	9. NATO War in Serbia	N
2. Accelerate Min. Wage	N	6. Display 10 Commandments	Y	10. Perm. Trade with China	Y
3. Strike Ban on Ergo. Stnd.	N	7. Gun Show Bkgrnd. Checks	N	11. Debt Relief for 3rd World	N
4. Ovrd. Estate Tax Veto	Y	8. Ban Part.-Birth Abortion	Y	12. Drop Cuba Econ. Embargo	N

Election Results

2000 general	George Nethercutt (R)	144,038	(57%)	($1,749,203)
	Thomas P. Keefe, Jr. (D)	97,703	(39%)	($651,225)
	Greg Holmes (LIB)	9,473	(4%)	($5,688)
2000 primary	George Nethercutt (R)	64,341	(45%)	
	Thomas P. Keefe, Jr. (D)	30,263	(21%)	
	Richard Clear (R)	28,373	(20%)	
	Tom Flynn (D)	15,609	(11%)	
	Others	3,129	(2%)	
1998 general	George Nethercutt (R)	110,040	(57%)	($762,004)
	Brad Lyons (D)	73,545	(38%)	($187,781)
	John Beal (AHP)	9,673	(5%)	($37,866)

SIXTH DISTRICT

The rainiest part of the continental United States is at its far northwest corner, where the Olympic Mountains of Washington thrust into the Pacific Ocean. The waters of the Pacific evaporate, condense and then mist or rain down on the hills and mountains that jut up from the ocean and Puget Sound. The mountains here are always green, the trees that line the inlets towering, and during heavy rainfalls the rivers can rise six feet a day. This has long been lumbering and fishing country, where men go out to work at 6 a.m. in air cold enough to see your breath year round, and where dependence on the vagaries of nature and harsh environmental laws—like the ban on old-growth logging to protect the habitat of the spotted owl—have strengthened a traditional surly independence and suspicion of authority.

The inlets of Puget Sound, winding sinuously through the mountains, are among America's most picturesque waterways and strategically among its most important. Here during World War II shipyards built and sheltered much of the U.S. Navy's Pacific fleet, and here during the Cold War much of the nuclear submarine fleet anchored at the giant Bremerton Navy base. To the south is the Tacoma Straits Bridge, the replacement of the narrow span that, in a scene preserved on newsreel (and still viewed by civil engineering students), started vibrating on the wrong harmonic in high winds and collapsed in 1940. On the other side is Tacoma, long the second-ranking city on Puget Sound, with its massive docks, former pulp mills and pleasant hilly residential neighborhoods.

The 6th Congressional District of Washington contains the Olympic Peninsula, Bremerton and most of surrounding Kitsap County amid various inlets of Puget Sound and most of Tacoma. Politically, the Olympic Peninsula and Bremerton are working-class Democratic. Tacoma also is traditionally Democratic, though the 6th's portion of it is the more white-collar side of town. On balance the 6th is, after the central Seattle 7th, Washington's most Democratic district.

The congressman from the 6th District is Norman Dicks, a onetime University of Washington football player who was on Senator Warren Magnuson's staff when it was one of the best on Capitol Hill. Dicks returned home to Bremerton to run for Congress in 1976, when the 6th District incumbent got the judgeship for which he had been hankering for 12 years. Dicks was elected easily that year, and in every year since except 1980, when Magnuson lost. He has passed up several chances to run for the Senate, and seems firmly committed to the House, where he is a senior Democrat.

Dicks has brought to the House the aggressiveness and political shrewdness that were the hallmarks of the Magnuson staff in its golden days—"the word 'can't' leaves your vocabulary when you go to work for Norm," one former aide said—plus an interest in defense and intelligence reminiscent of Magnuson's colleague for 40 years, Henry Jackson. These talents would be deployed, he long assumed, from a place in the majority; in 1995 he said: "In 27 years I never once thought about being in the minority. It never, ever occurred to me until about noon on Election Day" in November 1994. But he has adapted smoothly to being part of the minority party, helped by the fact that on some issues, though not all, his goals are more congenial to Republicans than Democrats. "I still feel it's worth doing," he said. "And with Speaker Foley gone now, we've got to have a couple of people who know how to operate. I've got to be the person who takes the lessons of 27 years and puts them to use."

Dicks has a seat on the Appropriations Committee and on the Defense Subcommittee—a vital post for Kitsap County, where most workers depend on Pentagon payrolls, and for Washington generally. In these posts Dicks, even in the minority, has exerted pivotal influence on important policies, usually operating quietly and behind the scenes. In the early 1980s Dicks took the lead on restoring Export-Import Bank loan authority—Boeing is America's biggest exporter and user of the loans—when the Reagan administration wanted to cut it, and led a campaign that switched 80 House votes overnight. Later, he helped keep the MX missile alive in return for arms control commitments from the Reagan administration. During the post-Cold War downsizing of the Pentagon, he has looked out for the F-117 Stealth aircraft and especially for the B-2 Stealth bomber, for which he has been an enthusiast since Defense Secretary Harold Brown proposed the plane in 1980. In the mid-1990s he led the fight for more B-2s than the Clinton administration requested, arguing that their stealth capability might have deterred Saddam Hussein from invading Kuwait and prevented Scott O'Grady from being shot down over Bosnia. Dicks lobbied colleagues persistently at Camden Yards Stadium in September 1995, on the day Cal Ripken was setting his consecutive-games-played record, pausing only for the long fifth-inning ovation. The next day the B-2s were authorized, over the opposition of many Democrats and Budget Committee Chairman John Kasich, by a 213–210 vote; Dicks told Kasich he had six or seven votes in reserve. In 1996 and 1997 he won four straight votes on the B-2: "We are undefeated, untied, unscored on. That's the way I like it." Dicks complained when B-2s weren't used in 1998 air attacks on Iraq; he was vindicated when the B-2 was used in the bombing of Serbia and Kosovo in 1999, flying nonstop from Whiteman Air Force Base in Missouri and being refueled in-air, delivering weapons with pinpoint accuracy, with the pilots returning to sleep in their own beds.

Dicks has also used his Appropriations seat to help Washington communities, funneling money to lumber mill towns when logging in old-growth forests was banned, passing timber salvage riders to keep mills going, dealing with the cost of maintaining salmon runs in dammed rivers. He worked to maintain Washington's military bases during two rounds of base closings. In 1997 he called for reintroducing grey wolves into Olympic National Park after traveling to Canada's Algonquin Province Park and hearing them howl in response to his simulated howls; he pushed to tear down the Elwha River Dam to help salmon runs; he obtained a full-time tug boat for Neah Bay to help oil tankers through the Straits of Juan De Fuca. Naturally he looks after the interests of the Bremerton waterfront and has pushed for funding of a Tacoma waterfront development from which visitors can gaze upon Mount Rainier and see I-705, the last of the original interstate routes to be built. He was not able to keep the U.S.S. Missouri in Bremerton, but the largest construction project in the 1999 defense budget was dredging the Bremerton shipyard and building a new pier for the carrier U.S.S. Carl Vinson. Over several years, $100 million was earmarked for improvements at Tacoma's McChord Air Force Base, and the Todd Pacific Shipyards in Seattle got contracts for another $100 million to repair three carriers. Dicks worked for five years to settle the Puyallup Indian land claims and advanced the claim that Lewis and Clark ended their journey on the Washington, not the Oregon, side of the Columbia River. In 1999 he became ranking Democrat on the Interior Subcommittee, where he was vital in defending Bill Clinton's "lands legacy" from attacks by Western Republicans, and he was instrumental in the bipartisan approval of billions of dollars for new conservation projects.

Dicks served as ranking Democrat on the Intelligence Committee in the mid-1990s, operating quietly, knowledgeably and in a bipartisan manner—quite an accomplishment during the Gingrich years. In time that came to mix with his role on China. He has been a strong supporter of permanent normal trade relations with China; Washington accounts for one-quarter of U.S. exports to China and Boeing foresees a great market there. But Dicks knows there are problems: "We're trying to have a constructive engagement with China, and they just get worse and worse," he said in 1996. How much worse began to be apparent in 1998, when Gingrich set up a special committee to study technology transfers and, it turned out, espionage losses to China. Democratic Leader Dick Gephardt wanted to give the ranking minority post on the panel to Bob Menendez, a strong partisan, but was prevailed on to appoint Dicks instead. Dicks found panel Chairman

Christopher Cox and Republican leaders willing to take his suggestions seriously and determined to proceed in a factual, bipartisan manner. He took the same approach. Over the fall, during the impeachment controversy and campaign period, until the committee's report was delivered to the White House, there were no leaks of any kind, no hint of partisan wrangling. The committee held 22 hearings, took 200 hours of testimony from 75 witnesses, conducted another 700 hours of interviews with 150 more people and issued 21 subpoenas. Dicks went over the draft report with Cox until they reached agreement. "We were surprised at how ineffective our counterespionage has been," Dicks said later. The White House delayed in declassifying the report until May 1999, obviously seeking political advantage. But Dicks and Cox were ready with 38 specific recommendations for improving security and regulating technology transfers. And Dicks effectively warned Republicans that it would be unwise for them to seek partisan advantage from the revelations.

Dicks has had one other long-time cause, which he has fostered for many years: an enduring friendship with Al Gore, which began when both entered the House in January 1977. They worked together on the MX missile, and on the basketball court in the House gym. With Dicks' help, Vice President Gore worked on several Northwest issues, such as logging and salmon conservation. Gore tapped him in 1999 to rally support in Congress, and there was talk that a Gore win would have given Dicks a prime national-security job. After the bitter election setback, Dicks quickly found himself meeting with George W. Bush and, of course, making a pitch to build additional B-2s.

Cook's Call   *Safe*. Dicks has established a solid hold on this Democratic-leaning, though not solidly partisan district. He is unlikely to face stiff competition in 2002. The 6th was one of the slowest growing districts in Washington during the 1990s and will need to pick up 43,000 new residents in redistricting.

THE PEOPLE: Pop. 2000: 611,292; Pop. 1990: 540,836, up 13% 1990–2000. 80.9% White, 5.5% Black, 4.1% Asian, 2.3% Amer. Indian, 0.7% Hawaiian, 4.6% Two+ races, 1.9% Other; 5% Hispanic Origin.

2000 Presidential Vote		
Gore (D)	133,489	(51%)
Bush (R)	113,750	(43%)
Nader (Green)	11,113	(4%)
Others	3,759	(1%)

1996 Presidential Vote		
Clinton (D)	122,342	(50%)
Dole (R)	87,961	(36%)
Perot (I)	23,830	(10%)
Others	8,968	(4%)

Rep. Norman Dicks (D)

Elected 1976, 13th term; b. Dec. 16, 1940, Bremerton; home, Bremerton; U. of WA, B.A. 1963, J.D. 1968; Lutheran; married (Suzanne).

Professional Career: Legis. Asst., U.S. Sen. Warren Magnuson, 1968–73, A.A., 1973–76.

DC Office: 2467 RHOB 20515, 202-225-5916; Fax: 202-226-1176; Web site: www.house.gov/dicks.

District Offices: Bremerton, 360-479-4011; Tacoma, 253-593-6536.

Committees: *Appropriations* (3d of 29 D): Defense; Interior (RMM); Military Construction.

Group Ratings

	ADA	ACLU	AFS	LCV	CON	ITIC	NTU	COC	ACU	NTLC	CHC
2000	80	85	85	79	72	88	17	45	8	10	14
1999	90	—	100	81	31	—	14	28	0	—	—

National Journal Ratings

	1999 LIB —	1999 CONS		2000 LIB —	2000 CONS
Economic	69%	—	31%	85%	—	11%
Social	78%	—	22%	77%	—	22%
Foreign	70%	—	30%	69%	—	28%

Key Votes of the 106th Congress

1. Patient Bill of Rights	Y	5. Bar RU-486 $ for FDA	N	9. NATO War in Serbia	Y
2. Accelerate Min. Wage	Y	6. Display 10 Commandments	N	10. Perm. Trade with China	Y
3. Strike Ban on Ergo. Stnd.	Y	7. Gun Show Bkgrnd. Checks	Y	11. Debt Relief for 3rd World	N
4. Ovrd. Estate Tax Veto	N	8. Ban Part.-Birth Abortion	N	12. Drop Cuba Econ. Embargo	Y

Election Results

2000 general	Norman Dicks (D)	164,853	(65%)	($596,375)
	Bob Lawrence (R)	79,215	(31%)	($95,540)
	John A. Bennett (LIB)	10,645	(4%)	
2000 primary	Norman Dicks (D)	103,131	(66%)	
	Bob Lawrence (R)	38,817	(25%)	
	William Chovil (R)	7,882	(5%)	
	John A. Bennett (LIB)	6,311	(4%)	
1998 general	Norman Dicks (D)	143,308	(68%)	($495,257)
	Bob Lawrence (R)	66,291	(32%)	($30,031)

SEVENTH DISTRICT

Seattle was America's hot city of the 1990s. It first zoomed into the national consciousness with the 1897 Klondike gold strike, has been a major American city since around 1910, and hosted its own World's Fair in 1962. But only in the last decade has its combination of economic growth and creativity and its physical beauty and distinctive style made it a national leader. Seattle rises from the Puget Sound harbor of Elliott Bay on steep hills, once covered with 300-foot-high Douglas firs; behind the hills and buildings you can see on a clear day, from almost anywhere, the nimbus of Mount Rainier. On the waterfront, below gleaming high-rises, is the Pike Place market, where you can get fresh salmon and Dungeness crabs; nearby is Pioneer Square, where stores and warehouses from the turn of the century have been restored and renovated; and Yesler Way, America's original "Skid Road," now has upscale shops but still some homeless people. Seattle's upper class, like San Francisco's, continues to be anchored downtown, with its upscale stores and busy sidewalks; but the most remarkable growth has come east of Lake Washington, where Microsoft has dominated the computer software business from its turquoise-building campus.

Seattle still has its old ethnic neighborhoods, like Scandinavian Ballard, and comfortable working-class frame houses on steep hillsides. But it also has a new ethnic mix, with thousands of Asian immigrants, and the Capitol Hill neighborhood with shoppers jamming busy stores and clubs. Yet the dominant tone is set by highly educated, affluent, single professionals—the kind of people who have made the Victorian houses of Queen Anne overlooking the harbor or the 1940s houses lining the streets of Capitol Hill among the nation's highest priced residential real estate. But there are also still some blue-collar workers on the south side of the city and in valleys, or midway between Puget Sound and Lake Washington; factories, warehouses and railroad yards are still concentrated in a flat plain near Puget Sound and south of downtown. The big Boeing factories are located farther south, and younger blue-collar workers have followed them into the suburban areas directly south of the city: Burien, Tukwila, Kent and Renton, which lie at the southern end of Lake Washington.

For all its hipness, Seattle in many ways is an antique town, readily familiar to a time traveler from the 1940s. Its different neighborhoods are knit together by infrastructure that was high-tech for its time: the pontoon bridge across Lake Washington, the Lake Washington Ship Canal, connecting the Sound and the Lake, whose Chittenden Locks are the second-largest locks in this hemisphere, behind only the Panama Canal. Seattle has been booming, and exporting its own institutions: Boeing airplanes have been the world's best sellers for many years; Nordstrom department stores with their famously polite service (even in the New York area); Seattle espresso bars—especially Starbucks, named after the coffee-crazed first mate in Herman Melville's *Moby Dick*—have brought caffe latte across America.

But as the new century dawned, all was not well in the nation's new industrial center. In December 1999 rioters protesting globalism made a shambles of an international trade meeting at which Bill Clinton had hoped to chart new reductions in trade barriers—instead Clinton gave the rioters verbal concessions. At the end of the month, the city cancelled its New Year's Eve gala at the Space Needle because of terrorist threats. Then a federal judge back in the other Washington ruled that Microsoft was a monopoly. And, in perhaps the most stunning and unkindest cut, Boeing chairman Phil Condit announced in March 2001 that the company would relocate its corporate headquarters to Chicago, Dallas or Denver (he chose Chicago in May). That decision followed a series of bitter labor disputes plus less than hospitable treatment by Seattle-area officials. The headquarters accounts for relatively few jobs, and the company promised to maintain its big facilities in the Seattle area. But top executives will no longer feel the neighborly pressures to accommodate querulous workers and maintain economically marginal operations—such pressures are inevitable in a city where their company is such a big employer.

The 7th Congressional District of Washington includes almost all the city of Seattle, a little industrial suburban fringe to the south, plus rural-looking Vashon Island in Puget Sound. This is the Seattle area's minority district: 13% Asian, 9% black and 6% Hispanic. Central Seattle shares more with central San Francisco than hills and scenery: it is heavily populated by singles and gays, young professionals and elderly pensioners. A generation ago, the city of Seattle was roughly split between the parties; today, it is heavily Democratic and liberal, ready to support minority candidates like former King County Executive and now Governor Gary Locke and women like Senators Patty Murray and Maria Cantwell.

The congressman from the 7th District is Jim McDermott, one of the most liberal members of the House and its only (credentialed) psychiatrist. A Chicago native, McDermott was the first in his family to attend college, and went to conservative religious Wheaton College. After service in the Navy and stints in New York and Illinois hospitals, he came to the University of Washington Hospital in Seattle. Almost immediately, he was elected to the state House in 1970, ran for governor in 1972 and finished third in the primary, and was elected to the state Senate in 1974, where he worked on issues from clean water to health care. He ran for governor again in 1980, beat incumbent Dixy Lee Ray in the primary, then lost to Republican John Spellman; in 1984 he ran for governor a third time and lost the primary to Booth Gardner. In 1987 he retired from the legislature and went to Zaire (now Congo) as a medical officer in the Foreign Service. But when Congressman Mike Lowry ran for the Senate in 1988 (he lost, but in 1992 was elected governor), McDermott returned home and ran for the 7th District seat and easily won, beating Norm Rice 38%–29% in the primary and winning 76% in the general.

In the House, McDermott's great cause has been health care and his greatest publicity has come from ethics investigations; he has had some frustrations on both. He passed an AIDS Housing Opportunity Act in 1990, in his first term, and remains head of the Congressional Task Force on AIDS. He has long backed a single-payer, Canadian-style national health insurance program and had a bill, with some 90 co-sponsors in 1993, financed by a $2 cigarette tax and 50-cent handgun and ammunition excise. But he deferred to the Clinton health care plan, even while making the point that his was simpler to administer and more comprehensible to voters. Then in August 1994, as the Clinton plan was failing and Democratic leaders were scrambling to come up with an alternative, McDermott urged Congress to abandon all health care bills for the year. He evidently expected a more favorable political environment after the elections, and, like many, was surprised by the result. After Republicans took control, he said: "A lot of people around here have never been in the minority. I have. I know what to do: attack." He criticized Republicans for abandoning the refundability of their $500 per child tax credit, so that those with low income tax liabilities or receiving the Earned Income Tax Credit didn't get a payment. He served on the Medicare commission co-chaired by John Breaux, and opposed Breaux's plan for premium support or, as McDermott termed it, vouchers. Later McDermott argued that cost-control mechanisms were excluding people from Medigap insurance. In February 2001 he joined with Republican Jim McCrery on an innovative plan to replace the employer-based health insurance system with one that relied on tax credits to provide universal coverage.

Another measure, which seemed quixotic when McDermott first pushed it, was enacted in 2000. This was the African Growth and Opportunity Act, which reduces import quotas and tariffs on African goods and includes investment funds. McDermott was a co-sponsor with free-market Republican Philip Crane and Democrat Charles Rangel; as large parts of Africa moved toward free markets and political democracy, it became an idea whose time had come. He was among the handful of Democrats who actively supported permanent normal trade relations with China.

McDermott joined the ethics committee in 1991 and was made chairman in 1993 by Speaker Thomas Foley. For some time McDermott called for nonpartisan investigations and got along with his successor in the chair, Nancy Johnson. But that changed during the long hearings on charges against Speaker Newt Gingrich. McDermott was frustrated with what he considered Republican dilatoriness and successfully pressed for the appointment of special counsel James Cole, a former prosecutor, rather than a tax lawyer who might conduct a more limited review. McDermott was angry that Johnson would not make public Cole's report before the House voted for speaker on January 7, 1997, and he attacked Johnson for canceling a series of committee hearings after a meeting with Majority Leader Dick Armey. During the public hearing on January 17, the full committee approved the proposed sanctions of a House reprimand and a $300,000 penalty, which the House approved a few days later.

Amidst all this, on January 10, *The New York Times* printed an excerpt of a tape made by Florida Democratic activists John and Alice Martin of a December 1996 phone conversation between Gingrich and Republican leaders and advisers. It was presented as evidence that Gingrich was violating an agreement not to orchestrate a response to the committee's action, but much of it was taken up by discussions as to how to comply with the agreement. In any case it quickly became apparent that taping the call was a felony. The Martins said they ultimately gave the tape to McDermott, and it was widely assumed he was the *Times'* source; McDermott denied he ever possessed or knew anything about the tape. On January 14 the FBI announced it was investigating, and McDermott said he was conditionally excusing himself from the case against Gingrich, blasting the Republicans in the process. In ensuing days McDermott, long known as intellectually honest and candid, said he wouldn't give an explanation of the incident and said of the investigation, "Nobody has come out pure." The Martins eventually pleaded guilty to intercepting the call and were given a small fine; no action was taken against McDermott. In March 1998, John Boehner, one of the Republican leaders who had been taped, sued McDermott for infringing his privacy and property rights by disseminating the tape. McDermott refused to deny or admit that he passed the tape on, and argued that he was protected by the First Amendment. In July 1998 a federal judge dismissed the case, but the appeals court reversed that decision in September 1999, ruling that the First Amendment did not excuse the illegal obtaining of a tape. McDermott appealed to the Supreme Court, which heard the case in December 2000. In May 2001 the Supreme Court struck down the appeals court ruling, effectively ending the suit.

McDermott has been re-elected easily; he has had no major-party opponent since 1996. He thought about running against Senator Slade Gorton in 2000, but backed away soon after he underwent open-heart surgery; he said that he didn't want to raise the $8 million that would be required.

Cook's Call *Safe.* This Seattle-based district is the most solidly Democratic seat in Washington and one of the most Democratic in the country. It also has the distinction of being the least populated in the state and it will need to pick up more than 60,000 new residents in redistricting. But McDermott is still a safe bet for 2002.

THE PEOPLE: Pop. 2000: 590,062; Pop. 1990: 541,202, up 9% 1990–2000. 69.5% White, 8.6% Black, 13.2% Asian, 1% Amer. Indian, 0.5% Hawaiian, 4.5% Two+ races, 2.6% Other; 5.6% Hispanic Origin.

2000 Presidential Vote			1996 Presidential Vote		
Gore (D)	210,797	(72%)	Clinton (D)	182,671	(67%)
Bush (R)	58,480	(20%)	Dole (R)	53,437	(20%)
Nader (Green)	20,066	(7%)	Perot (I)	13,671	(5%)
Others	2,347	(1%)	Others	23,267	(9%)

Rep. Jim McDermott (D)

Elected 1988, 7th term; b. Dec. 28, 1936, Chicago, IL; home, Seattle; Wheaton Col., B.S. 1958, U. of IL, M.D. 1963; Episcopalian; married (Therese Hansen).

Military Career: U.S. Navy Medical Corps., 1968–70.

Elected Office: WA House of Reps., 1970–72; WA Senate, 1974–87; Dem. gubernatorial nominee, 1980.

Professional Career: Asst. Prof., U. of WA, Practicing psychiatrist, 1970–83; Medical Officer, U.S. Foreign Svc., Zaire, 1987–88.

DC Office: 1035 LHOB 20515, 202-225-3106; Web site: www.house.gov/mcdermott.

District Office: Seattle, 206-553-7170.

Committees: *Budget* (2d of 20 D). *Ways & Means* (7th of 17 D): Health; Human Resources.

Group Ratings

	ADA	ACLU	AFS	LCV	CON	ITIC	NTU	COC	ACU	NTLC	CHC
2000	80	83	83	93	92	75	31	42	0	10	0
1999	55	—	100	56	84	—	30	12	5	—	—

National Journal Ratings

	1999 LIB	—	1999 CONS		2000 LIB	—	2000 CONS
Economic	88%	—	12%		89%	—	11%
Social	87%	—	0%		91%	—	6%
Foreign	73%	—	27%		97%	—	0%

Key Votes of the 106th Congress

1. Patient Bill of Rights	Y	5. Bar RU-486 $ for FDA	N	9. NATO War in Serbia	Y
2. Accelerate Min. Wage	Y	6. Display 10 Commandments	N	10. Perm. Trade with China	Y
3. Strike Ban on Ergo. Stnd.	Y	7. Gun Show Bkgrnd. Checks	Y	11. Debt Relief for 3rd World	Y
4. Ovrd. Estate Tax Veto	N	8. Ban Part.-Birth Abortion	N	12. Drop Cuba Econ. Embargo	Y

Election Results

2000 general	Jim McDermott (D)	193,470	(73%)	($322,022)
	Joseph Brian Szwaja (Green)	52,142	(20%)	($33,331)
	Joel Grus (LIB)	20,197	(8%)	
2000 primary	Jim McDermott (D)	94,450	(78%)	
	Joseph Brian Szwaja (Green)	16,214	(13%)	
	Joel Grus (LIB)	10,546	(9%)	
1998 general	Jim McDermott (D)	183,076	(88%)	($332,241)
	Stan Lippmann (Ref)	19,545	(9%)	
	Others	4,921	(2%)	

EIGHTH DISTRICT

The land east of Seattle's Lake Washington half a century ago was quiet countryside. Orchards and vineyards flourished in the rich, moist soil just below the rise of the Cascades Mountains, while farms and broad pasturelands spread toward 14,410-foot Mount Rainier like a living green quilt. But as Seattle has grown over the years, people have crossed the pontoon bridge across Mercer Island to Bellevue and have made this Overlake area, sometimes called the Eastside, one of the most vibrant parts of metropolitan Seattle. Bellevue now has more than 109,000 people and enough office space to make it an edge city. While downtown Seattle specialized in banks and law firms and trading companies, Bellevue and other communities in Overlake specialized in high-tech startups. Redmond, just to the north, is the headquarters of Microsoft, and there are dozens of other firms here that make this one of America's leading high-tech centers.

The 8th Congressional District of Washington includes most of the eastern edge of metro Seattle, plus the scarcely inhabited territory of the Cascades. It includes most of Bellevue and all of Mercer Island, Issaquah at the edge of the Cascades and Renton at the south edge of Lake

Washington. It spreads south along Kent, Auburn and Puyallup to include the countryside and suburban fringe east of Tacoma, and includes Mount Rainier itself. This is the most affluent district in Washington, rivaled only by the 1st; politically it is market-oriented on economics, more liberal on the environment, mixed on cultural issues. In partisan terms, it is also one of the two most Republican districts in the state.

The congresswoman from the 8th District is Jennifer Dunn, a Republican elected in 1992. Dunn grew up in Bellevue, went to Stanford, worked as a systems engineer for IBM in the 1960s, then stayed home to raise her children (her younger son is named Reagan, after the then-California governor, whom she supported over Gerald Ford in 1976). She is a distant cousin of former Senator Slade Gorton. In 1981 she became Washington Republican Party chairwoman and served for 12 years. She is a peppery partisan, vigorous and knowledgeable about issues, persevering through bad times for her party and working to make them better. In 1992, when Congressman Rod Chandler ran for the Senate, she ran for the House and won in a walkover. In the House she was a vocal deficit hawk. With Georgia's Nathan Deal, she passed a Dunn-Deal bill to allow local communities to track convicted sex offenders. She served as the only freshman on the Joint Committee on the Organization of Congress. Her voting record has been conservative on economic and foreign policy, moderate on cultural issues.

When Republicans won the majority in 1994, Dunn was put on the transition team and Speaker Newt Gingrich's task force on committee review, and given a seat on Ways and Means. She worked on the child support provisions of the welfare reform bill and pushed for medical savings accounts in the 1996 health care bill. She sponsored an IRAs for homemakers amendment, which was vetoed, a small business tax relief package, a rise in the earning limits for seniors, and estate tax reductions. She backed a pension plan for employees of small companies with no plans of their own. She worked on the Medicaid formula for Washington state and on the preventive medicine provisions of Medicare reform. She worked to allow software firms to lower their taxes by setting up foreign sales corporations as other businesses can. On local issues, she worked against privatization of the Bonneville Power Administration and sought lower power rates.

Dunn, as one might expect of a longtime state party chairman, took political initiatives as well. She was a loyal supporter of Gingrich through his travails. Dunn spent much of her third term climbing—or trying to climb—up the leadership ladder. In November 1996 she was elected secretary of the Republican Conference. In May 1997, when Susan Molinari announced her resignation from the House, Dunn ran for her post of Conference vice chair. Just as the coup against Gingrich was disintegrating, Dunn had leadership support and defeated Jim Nussle of Iowa, by 129–85. Having won that position, she spurned running against Senator Patty Murray in 1998. Her real fight for a leadership position came two weeks after the 1998 election. Dunn had already moved to challenge Majority Leader Dick Armey, who was in low regard after the collapse of the anti-Gingrich coup. But the Tuesday Group and liberal Republicans did not endorse her, her longtime supporter Gingrich had announced his retirement, and Steve Largent, one of the most principle-bound of the 1994 freshmen, was running as well. Dunn stressed the importance of having a woman in the Republican leadership, but other women were running for other leadership positions. In the first round of voting, Armey led with 100 votes to 58 for Largent, 45 for Dunn and 18 for Denny Hastert, whose name was advanced by others as he stuck by a commitment to support Armey. At that point Largent asked Dunn to withdraw, in return for appointment to a new position as assistant majority leader should he win; Dunn refused and stayed in the race. On the second ballot, Armey got 99 votes, Largent 73 and Dunn 49—which meant that Dunn was eliminated; Armey won on the third ballot, 127–95. Shortly afterward, Tillie Fowler was elected Republican Conference vice chair. "I have no regrets," said Dunn.

Following that setback, Dunn returned to her strong support of tax cuts: in income tax rates, in the estate tax, in capital gains and through Education Savings Accounts. She has worked on addressing the gender gap for Republicans, urging candidates to relate their policies to women's lives—she talks often about how she coped as a divorced working mom, and of how two-thirds of new small businesses are being formed by women. As she explains, "We are developing speech-modules that are women-friendly." To help businesses, she called for a three-point (instead of the IRS's current 20-point) test of who is a subcontractor and who an employee; she has a bill to make it easier for start-up companies to offer stock options. She has been a strong backer of free trade and permanent normal trade relations with China. She strongly opposed the Shays-Meehan campaign finance bill. Despite all this—or perhaps because she campaigned all over the country and identified herself with partisan rather than consensus policies—she saw her share of the vote drop from 76% in 1994 to 65% in 1996 to a still safe but lower 60% in 1998.

In December 1998 she had dinner in Austin with George W. and Laura Bush and a few aides. Among other things, she was impressed with how Bush related to his wife. At the end of the dinner, she voiced her commitment of support to Bush and she soon became one of his staunchest backers in Congress, plus a leading fundraiser and adviser, especially on women's issues. She was one of three co-chairs of the 2000 national convention in Philadelphia, and then became a co-chair of the "Victory 2000" drive during the fall campaign. "She understands politics and she understands issues, and it's rare that you get someone who understands both," Bush political adviser Karl Rove told *The Seattle Times*. But the election victory did not give Dunn what she wanted: a job in his Cabinet. In part, she was a victim of Bush's decision not to take anyone from Congress, where the Republican margin was so narrow, especially since Al Gore carried the 8th District in November. Instead she focused on being one of Bush's leading allies in Congress. And she took a lead role in pushing for the estate-tax repeal.

Dunn was re-elected 62%–36% in 2000, an uptick from 1998. Redistricting will force her to give up some of her Republican constituency, but she will likely have a safe district to run in.

Cook's Call *Probably Safe*. The fact that Dunn has won this seat by 60% or more for four elections, despite strong performances by national Democrats here, shows how well positioned she is in this district. But Democrats are hoping that redistricting may make this already marginal seat more enticing for a serious Democratic challenger in 2002. Still, Dunn will be tough to beat.

THE PEOPLE: Pop. 2000: 695,277; Pop. 1990: 540,735, up 28.6% 1990–2000. 83.6% White, 2.4% Black, 7.7% Asian, 0.9% Amer. Indian, 0.3% Hawaiian, 3.4% Two+ races, 1.8% Other; 4.1% Hispanic Origin.

2000 Presidential Vote			1996 Presidential Vote		
Gore (D)	152,597	(49%)	Clinton (D)	130,472	(47%)
Bush (R)	145,410	(47%)	Dole (R)	112,463	(41%)
Nader (Green)	9,787	(3%)	Perot (I)	23,994	(9%)
Others	3,121	(1%)	Others	8,593	(3%)

Rep. Jennifer Dunn (R)

Elected 1992, 5th term; b. July 29, 1941, Seattle; home, Bellevue; U. of WA, 1960–62, Stanford U., B.A. 1963; Episcopalian; divorced.

Professional Career: Systems Engineer, IBM, 1964–69; P.R., King Cnty. Assessors Office, 1978–80; Chmn., WA Repub. Party, 1981–92; Delegate, U.N. Comm. on Status of Women, 1984 & 1990.

DC Office: 1501 LHOB 20515, 202-225-7761; Fax: 202-225-8673; Web site: www.house.gov/dunn.

District Office: Mercer Island, 206-275-3438.

Committees: *Ways & Means* (12th of 24 R): Health; Oversight; Trade. *Joint Economic Committee* (4th of 10 Reps.).

Group Ratings

	ADA	ACLU	AFS	LCV	CON	ITIC	NTU	COC	ACU	NTLC	CHC
2000	0	21	0	7	54	100	59	95	88	79	100
1999	10	—	0	6	50	—	62	96	80	—	—

National Journal Ratings

	1999 LIB	—	1999 CONS		2000 LIB	—	2000 CONS
Economic	0%	—	84%		18%	—	76%
Social	42%	—	56%		47%	—	52%
Foreign	43%	—	55%		12%	—	78%

Key Votes of the 106th Congress

1. Patient Bill of Rights	N	5. Bar RU-486 $ for FDA	Y	9. NATO War in Serbia	Y
2. Accelerate Min. Wage	N	6. Display 10 Commandments	Y	10. Perm. Trade with China	Y
3. Strike Ban on Ergo. Stnd.	N	7. Gun Show Bkgrnd. Checks	N	11. Debt Relief for 3rd World	N
4. Ovrd. Estate Tax Veto	Y	8. Ban Part.-Birth Abortion	Y	12. Drop Cuba Econ. Embargo	N

Election Results

2000 general	Jennifer Dunn (R)	183,255	(62%)	($1,731,507)
	Heidi Behrens-Benedict (D)	104,944	(36%)	($377,825)
	Others	6,269	(2%)	
2000 primary	Jennifer Dunn (R)	89,133	(61%)	
	Heidi Behrens-Benedict (D)	54,449	(37%)	
	Others	3,059	(2%)	
1998 general	Jennifer Dunn (R)	135,539	(60%)	($1,490,563)
	Heidi Behrens-Benedict (D)	91,371	(40%)	($172,349)

NINTH DISTRICT

The misty shores of Puget Sound have seen some of America's most vibrant economic growth over the last two decades. It has spread south from Seattle, over the mixed suburban territory, south and west to the once industrial city of Tacoma. The subdivisions along the Sound, which have some of the loveliest views in America, tend to be high-income. But much of greater Seattle's prime industrial territory lies between the ridges that run north and south inland. Weyerhaeuser, the world's largest private owner of softwood timber, has its headquarters here in Federal Way. Boeing is also a major presence in Renton, on the south end of Lake Washington; its aircraft and electronic components plants and its business services division, employing more than 20,000 people, have helped make the company America's number one exporter. A host of smaller factories cluster near the rail lines that run from Minneapolis-St. Paul across the Great Plains to Puget Sound. The military has influenced this area too. Fort Lewis is just west of Tacoma and active-duty and retired military personnel and their families make up perhaps one-fifth of the population.

The 9th Congressional District of Washington covers much of this area. It is a new seat created after the 1990 Census and confirmed by a 1992 Supreme Court decision that upheld the counting of servicemen abroad in their state of residence (otherwise, this seat would have gone to Massachusetts). The 9th District's northern end wraps around Sea-Tac International Airport and Renton, then winds south past Kent, Auburn and Federal Way, and reaches the shipyards and docks of Tacoma. It covers a piece of Tacoma, including McChord Air Force Base, and proceeds west, taking in the Army's vast Fort Lewis in Pierce County and stopping just shy of the boundaries of the state capital of Olympia. It is not heavily Democratic or Republican; as the district director for its first congressman said, "Everybody was happy to unload this district. It's sort of a mutt in a way." For three elections the 9th District was balanced at equipoise: it went Democratic in 1992, Republican in 1994, Democratic in 1996. Then, it settled down.

The congressman from the 9th District is Adam Smith, a Democrat first elected in 1996. He grew up in the Sea-Tac area; his father, a baggage handler for United Airlines and active in the Machinists' Union, died when Smith was 17. The family went on welfare; Smith worked his way through Fordham driving trucks for UPS, then went to the University of Washington Law School. He worked as a lawyer, then as a Seattle prosecutor, handling drunk driving and domestic abuse cases. In 1990, at 25, he was elected to the state Senate, beating an incumbent Republican by doorbelling the district twice. In July 1995 decided to run against Congressman Randy Tate. In many ways, the two were similar: born the same year to families of modest backgrounds, first elected to office at young ages, firm believers in doorbelling. A religious conservative and strong supporter of Speaker Newt Gingrich, Tate was an immediate target of the AFL-CIO in 1996, which spent somewhere between $500,000 and $1 million on ads against him. Smith campaigned as a moderate Democrat, a supporter of the death penalty and three-strikes legislation, and a believer in a more efficient and responsive government. Smith's campaign steadily attacked Tate for supporting Gingrich on 96% of House votes and for backing Medicare "cuts." Tate attacked Smith for opposing channeling youthful offenders to adult courts and prisons, and for voting for Governor Mike Lowry's $1.2 billion tax increase in 1993. This was one of the closest races in the country. In the September all-party primary, usually a good indicator of the final result in Washington, Smith led 49%–48%. The result in November was not quite as close: 50%–47% for Smith. Tate went on to become head of the Christian Coalition for two years.

In the House, Smith showed political acumen, winning good committee assignments—Resources and Armed Services. He announced he would not accept contributions from PACs or individuals outside Washington state in his first year, and kept doorbelling constituents. His voting record was moderate for a Democrat and he is communications chairman of the New Democrat Coalition. He voted for the balanced budget and for charter schools (but against school vouchers); he supported term limits and voted to allow concealed weapons permits to be transferred from state to state. In 1999 he was one of four House Democrats to vote for the Republicans' budget; a year later, he voted to override Bill Clinton's vetoes of the estate-tax and marriage-penalty repeals. Despite the pleas of Norm Dicks from the next-door 6th District, he voted against additional B-2 stealth bombers and against fast track—going against Boeing both times, though the fast track vote pleased his union backers. Later, though, he voted for permanent normal trade relations with China. He passed an amendment to the defense authorization bill in 1998 to cap overhead spending on cleanup at the Hanford Nuclear Reservation to 33% of the total cleanup budget, saying, "Too much money is going to management, and not enough is going to cleanup." After gaining unfavorable publicity for not introducing a single bill in his first term, Smith introduced seven bills in 1999–2000—from the handling of budget surpluses to enhancing military personnel benefits.

Smith's independence has worked well for him back home. He twice won reelection against credible opponents with more than 60% of the vote, an impressive performance in a district that had never before re-elected an incumbent. Redistricting will adjust, perhaps significantly shift, the partisan balance in this closely balanced district.

Cook's Call *Probably Safe.* The fact that Smith was able to win his last two races with more than 60% belies the inherent competitiveness of this district. It was drawn in 1991 to be competitive, but Smith's moderate image and easygoing style insulate him from charges that he is too liberal.

THE PEOPLE: Pop. 2000: 649,451; Pop. 1990: 540,519, up 20.2% 1990–2000. 73.9% White, 7% Black, 7.9% Asian, 1.4% Amer. Indian, 1.1% Hawaiian, 5.2% Two+ races, 3.4% Other; 7.2% Hispanic Origin.

2000 Presidential Vote

Gore (D)	124,726	(53%)
Bush (R)	97,941	(42%)
Nader (Green)	7,858	(3%)
Others	2,925	(1%)

1996 Presidential Vote

Clinton (D)	110,854	(51%)
Dole (R)	77,616	(36%)
Perot (I)	20,806	(10%)
Others	6,466	(3%)

Rep. Adam Smith (D)

Elected 1996, 3d term; b. June 15, 1965, Washington, DC; home, Kent; Fordham U. B.A. 1987, U. of WA, J.D. 1990; Christian; married (Sara).

Elected Office: WA Senate, 1990–96.

Professional Career: Practicing atty., 1991–92; Seattle Prosecutor, 1992–95.

DC Office: 116 CHOB 20515, 202-225-8901; Fax: 202-225-5893; Web site: www.house.gov/adamsmith.

District Office: Tacoma, 253-926-6683.

Committees: *Armed Services* (14th of 28 D): Military Procurement; Military Research & Development. *Resources* (12th of 25 D): Water & Power (RMM).

Group Ratings

	ADA	ACLU	AFS	LCV	CON	ITIC	NTU	COC	ACU	NTLC	CHC
2000	45	71	75	86	73	100	35	80	21	41	7
1999	85	—	83	88	98	—	24	56	20	—	—

National Journal Ratings

	1999 LIB	—	1999 CONS		2000 LIB	—	2000 CONS
Economic	55%	—	45%		66%	—	34%
Social	67%	—	33%		65%	—	34%
Foreign	58%	—	42%		73%	—	27%

Key Votes of the 106th Congress

1. Patient Bill of Rights	Y	5. Bar RU-486 $ for FDA	N	9. NATO War in Serbia	Y
2. Accelerate Min. Wage	*	6. Display 10 Commandments	N	10. Perm. Trade with China	Y
3. Strike Ban on Ergo. Stnd.	*	7. Gun Show Bkgrnd. Checks	N	11. Debt Relief for 3rd World	*
4. Ovrd. Estate Tax Veto	Y	8. Ban Part.-Birth Abortion	N	12. Drop Cuba Econ. Embargo	*

Election Results

2000 general	Adam Smith (D)	135,452	(62%)	($1,046,195)
	Christopher M. Vance (R)	76,766	(35%)	($634,816)
	Others	7,405	(3%)	
2000 primary	Adam Smith (D)	70,901	(60%)	
	Christopher M. Vance (R)	34,861	(29%)	
	Gary Snell (R)	9,322	(8%)	
	Others	3,569	(3%)	
1998 general	Adam Smith (D)	111,948	(65%)	($814,303)
	Ron Taber (R)	61,108	(35%)	($84,964)

★ WEST VIRGINIA ★

Almost heaven—that's what the song says about West Virginia. And indeed some things are looking up for this state, whose people have never lost their sense of hope or their affection for the hills and mountains that make this the most unhorizontal state in the nation. But West Virginia has had more than its share of tragedy and heartbreak. It was born out of the tragedy of the Civil War, when 55 mountain counties with few slaves seceded from Virginia, and it has made its living most of the years since on that cruelest of commodities, coal. Coal kept the sons of large mountaineer families here for much of the 20th Century, men who would otherwise have left for big cities; coal brought immigrants in, a few from odd corners of Europe, but more from adjacent areas of the South where the local farming economies were stagnant when West Virginia's coal economy was booming. Coal and local rock salt and brines brought the large concentration of chemical plants 50 years ago to the Kanawha Valley around Charleston; it built steel mills and glass factories in the panhandle and the Monongahela River valley, not far south of Pittsburgh.

But coal did not build a self-sustaining economy. When America was beleaguered abroad, demand for coal increased and energy prices rose, and West Virginia boomed, during World War II (the state reached its all-time population peak of 2 million in 1950) and the oil shocks of the 1970s. Coal changed West Virginia's politics too. West Virginia's heritage from the Civil War days was Republican, though some counties tilted toward the Confederacy and the Democrats. But after John L. Lewis's United Mine Workers organized most of the West Virginia mines, the coal country shifted toward the New Deal Democrats, and West Virginia for more than half a century was one of the most Democratic states, deserting the ticket only in Republican landslide years (1956, 1972, 1984) until George W. Bush carried it in 2000; its legislature has been controlled by Democrats since 1930. But neither Democratic administrations nor the pensions and medical benefits the UMW negotiated for retired miners were able to provide the economic growth to keep thousands of West Virginians from leaving their mountains to find work elsewhere—now more often south on I-77 to the booming Carolinas than north to the Great Lakes' industrial cities. As underground miners were replaced by strip-mining machines, coal tonnage went way up but coal mine employment dropped from 22% of the state's work force in 1950 to 10% in 1980 and only 4% in the late 1990s. The state's population, 1.95 million in 1980, fell to 1.8 million in 2000—the largest decrease, absolutely and in percentage terms, of any state. But West Virginians have a strong attachment to this unique state, where the accent sounds Southern and the early 20th Century factories and houses look Northern, where the landscape is rural and the economy industrial.

In the 1990s West Virginia was on the rebound, only to be threatened at the end of the decade with economic disaster. Population increased during the decade, though at the second-lowest rate of any state, and the number of jobs rose by 8%. Unemployment was down to 5.5% in 2000, the lowest since 1975. Government has played a role. Senator Robert Byrd, as both chairman and ranking Democrat on the Appropriations Committee, achieved his career goal of channeling $1 billion of federal projects into West Virginia, and more. They include offices for the FBI, Fish and Wildlife Service, NASA and the National Institute of Occupational Safety; federal jobs in West Virginia have grown 20% since 1988. Old mining towns like Nellis and Matewan have been given new firewalls and preservation funds to keep up their historic buildings; a memorial to the 130,000 men killed in underground coal mining is being planned for Nellis. State tax breaks promoted by Governor Gaston Caperton (1988–96) attracted investments from Georgia Pacific, Swearingen Aircraft, NGK Sparkplugs and Toyota; Lexus engines are produced in Buffalo, West Virginia. West Virginia's plastics and chemicals industries have been expanding, forest products are replacing coal in rural counties, health care is growing as everywhere and telemarketing is growing as well. Even the number of farms is increasing. West Virginia has finally completed its interstate highway network and in a computer age it is no longer isolated; with low wages, good work habits, low land costs, West Virginia has even developed a software industry in the corridor between Morgantown and Clarksburg. Governor Cecil Underwood, elected in 1956 and then again in 1996, notes that he started building the interstate highway system 40 years ago and worked to

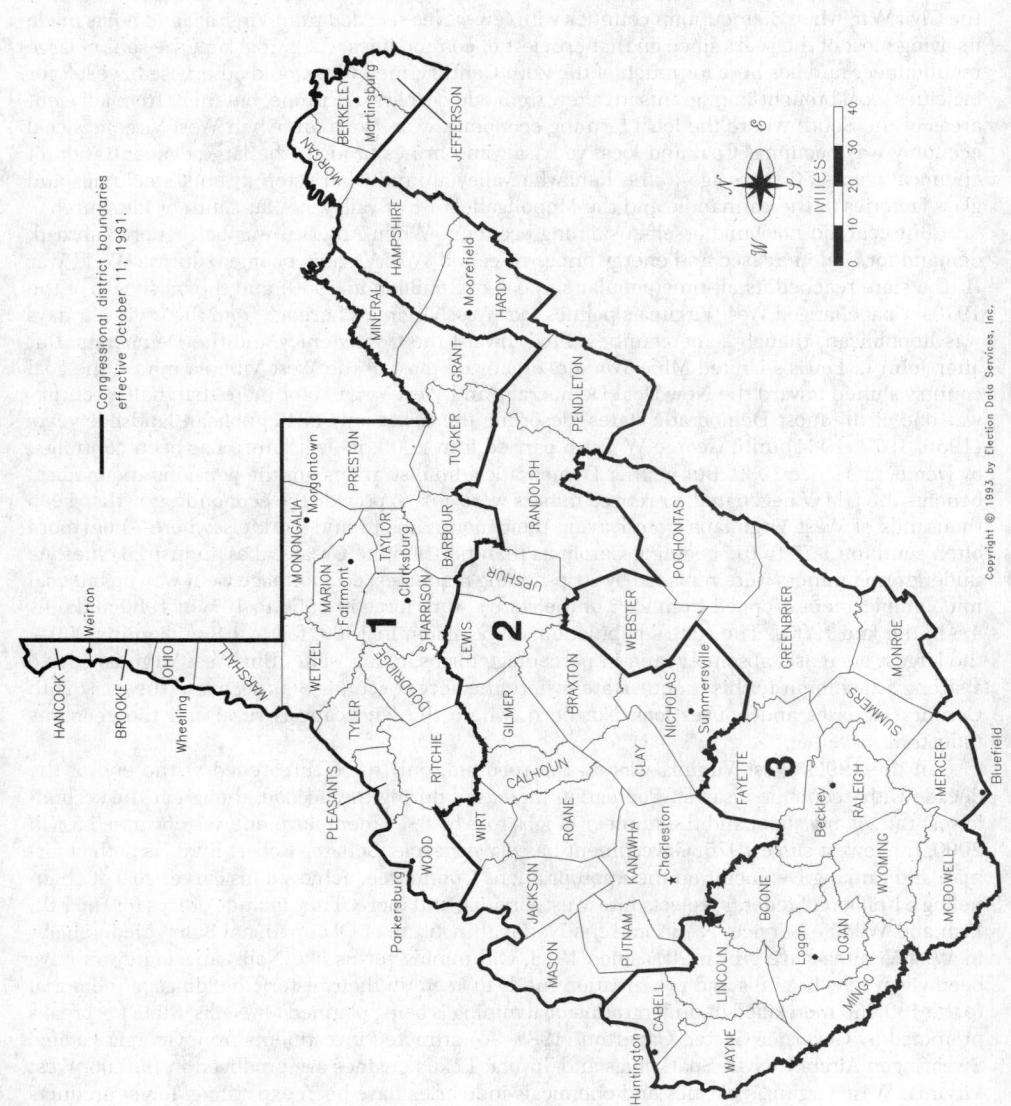

Congressional district boundaries
effective October 11, 1991.

build a "technology superhighway system"—the West Virginia State Unified Network, capable of carrying data, voice and video. And using the Internet, West Virginia's Appalachian by Design Inc. has created a mini-industry of home knitting, pairing West Virginia women who knit sweaters and pillows in their homes with national firms like Ethan Allen and Esprit.

The threat to West Virginia's economy came in October 1999, when federal judge Charles Haden in a case brought by environmental groups ruled that mountaintop mining violates federal environmental laws. Most underground mines in West Virginia have been closed; they were uneconomic and the most unsafe workplaces in the country except possibly for Alaskan fishing ships. Since the 1970s, mining companies have been leveling mountaintops with 20-story removal machines, exploding the loose dirt and rock and extracting low-sulfur coal from the resulting surface, and filling in local rivers and streams with piles of slag; when a mountain is mined, the companies are supposed to reclaim the land, and even some critics concede that some reclamation projects have been well done. Far fewer miners are needed for this work than in underground mining, but the pay is good and the jobs highly valued in counties which in some cases have half as many people as they did 50 years ago. Mining companies said that Judge Haden's decision would end coal mining in West Virginia. Senator Robert Byrd threatened to overturn the decision in an appropriations bill; Bill Clinton said he would veto any such bill, and the provision was dropped. But the issue became important—arguably crucial—in the 2000 presidential race. The Clinton administration came out in April 2000 opposing a ban on mountaintop mining but calling for stricter regulation; Al Gore was caught in the middle between environmentalists who supported it and West Virginia's all-Democratic congressional delegation which opposed it. George W. Bush, spotting an opening quickly, came out in favor of mountaintop mining and called for increased federal support of clean coal technology; he said that the Clinton administration "fears coal" and managed to bring up coal in one of the presidential debates. Bush's support of coal and his opposition to gun control enabled him to carry West Virginia 52%–46%—a stunning upset in a state that hadn't voted for a Republican in an open presidential race since 1928—and its five electoral votes were crucial: without them it would not have mattered who won Florida. The environmental stands which helped Gore in large East and West Coast states proved fatal to his candidacy in West Virginia. Bush ran well ahead of local Republicans: Democratic Congressman Bob Wise beat incumbent Republican Governor Cecil Underwood 50%–47%, and Republican Shelley Moore Capito, who won Wise's 2nd District House seat 48%–46%—the first Republican victory in a House race here since 1980—ran 6% behind Bush. After Bush was inaugurated, *Washington Post* reporter Eric Pianin wrote from West Virginia, "Slowed by Clinton administration environmental restrictions and shunted to the sideline in favor of cleaner-burning natural gas, coal for much of the past decade has been the stepchild of America's energy policy. A month into the Bush administration, however, there's a growing feeling here that coal is back." In April 2001 the Fourth Circuit Court of Appeals reversed Judge Haden and ruled that under the 1977 Surface Mining Control and Reclamation Act, West Virginia's mining standards superseded federal standards; unless that decision is reversed, mountaintop mining will continue.

Governor   Bob Wise, a Democrat, was elected governor of West Virginia in 2000. He grew up in Charleston in an affluent family and graduated from Duke and Tulane Law School. He returned home to start a law practice geared to low- and middle-income clients, and led a movement to force coal companies to pay higher taxes. A strong advocate of West Virginia culture—he is renowned for his clog dancing—he urges West Virginia students to make their careers, as he did, in their home state. In 1980 he was elected to the state Senate, at 32. In 1982 he ran for the 3rd District House seat (it was renumbered the 2nd in 1992), occupied by a Republican who had won in the Reagan year of 1980. It was widely assumed that the Democratic nominee would win the seat and hold it for a long time, and there was serious competition. But Wise, after just two years in office, beat the state House majority leader and a former Kanawha County sheriff with 45% of the vote and then beat the Republican incumbent 58%–42%.

In the House Wise had a generally liberal and often interesting voting record; he supported some conservative policies—repeal of the assault weapons ban, the flag amendment, welfare reform. He was a booster of alternative fuels and championed compressed natural gas an auto fuel. His biggest legislative success was the 1990 amendment, adopted 274–146, to provide benefits for workers displaced by compliance with the Clean Air Act, with a $250 million cap. He sponsored the 1986 Community Right to Know Act, requiring disclosure by chemical companies of discharges of hazardous chemicals. He moved to delay EPA's 1998 Clean Air guidelines which would require reductions of nitrous oxide in West Virginia to 44% below 1990 levels, the biggest drop in the nation.

In May 1999 he announced that he would run for governor in 2000. Incumbent Republican Cecil Underwood had a number of distinctions. When he was elected governor in 1956, he was at 34 the youngest governor in the nation; when, after a number of unsuccessful races he was elected governor again in 1996, he was at 74 the oldest. In 1996 he won largely because Democratic nominee Charlotte Pritt, backed by labor unions, was seen as too unfriendly to business and too far to the left; outgoing two-term Democratic Governor Gaston Caperton made little effort to hide the fact that he preferred Underwood. He gamely set about running for re-election and in 2000 proceeded to disperse $16 million from the governor's discretionary funds to presumably worthy projects throughout the state.

Wise ran with the support of West Virginia's teachers unions and the United Mine Workers, but sought to avoid the split between labor and business so prominent in the gubernatorial primary of 1996. "I want to stop this division between business and labor. It's a false division. I believe I'm the one to bring business and labor together." But he had spirited opposition from Jim Lees, who had run third, with 19% of the vote, in the 1996 primary but was now spending large sums of his own money on his campaign. He profited from the split among Democrats on mountaintop mining. Articulate liberals and environmentalist groups wanted to abolish the practice, and brought a lawsuit in federal court to do so; most elected officials, including Wise, were against, though in August 1998 Wise called for a moratorium on new permits for mountaintop mining pending the outcome of the court case. In October 1999 a federal judge ruled that mountaintop mining violated federal environmental laws; Wise backed Senator Robert Byrd's attempt to overturn the ruling through legislation. Lees outspent Wise 2–1 in the final two months before the May primary and was endorsed by the Charleston newspapers, the state Sierra Club and the social workers association. Wise won, by 63%–37%, but the fact that Lees doubled his vote from four years before showed the tension among Democrats.

Wise directed most of his fire all along at Underwood. He charged that the economy was not growing fast enough and issued a 28-page job growth plan. He charged that Underwood had failed to implement the CHIP child health care program and had taken the side of big insurance companies on HMO regulation. He promised to fully fund the 1999 Promise scholarships, providing funds to students with 3.0 averages in high school who maintained them in West Virginia colleges and universities. Key funding would come from taxing and regulating video poker machines—called gray machines in West Virginia—which were currently unlicensed and untaxed. In September Underwood unleashed a series of ads stressing his support for the partial-birth abortion ban and prayer in schools; he hailed his record of support for mountaintop mining and criticized Wise for seeking a moratorium in 1998. Wise got key endorsements from leading state Democrats. Gaston Caperton, now head of the College Board, returned home to say that the state's economic momentum had "dissipated" under Underwood. Senator Jay Rockefeller, who had backed Pritt ardently in 1996, backed Wise ardently in 2000. Senator Robert Byrd, who seldom had endorsed other candidates, cut a TV spot for Wise and traveled across the state urging West Virginians to vote for him.

This support from Byrd may have made the difference. While George W. Bush was carrying the state 52%–46%, Wise won 50%–47%; 21% of Bush voters voted for him. He did especially well in Charleston's Kanawha County, his home base, and in the northern panhandle; his support in the southern coal counties was below historic Democratic levels, and he carried only one county in the Republican-leaning eastern panhandle, though he had represented much of the area for eight years. Once in office, Wise ordered a 3% spending cut and ended Underwood's tax reform program by not requiring 11,000 businessmen to submit informational returns. Despite some setbacks, he steered his proposal for taxing gray machines and limiting them to 9,000 through the legislature, and appeared to be getting the necessary funding for Promise scholarships. Interestingly, such programs tend to redistribute money from the less affluent (who are more likely to play video poker) to the more affluent (who are more likely to have children who get good grades in college), but similar programs advocated by Democratic governors have been highly popular in Georgia and other states. In April 2001 a federal appeals court reversed the district court and ruled that mountaintop mining is regulated entirely by West Virginia's laws; presumably this means it will continue.

Senior Senator   Robert Byrd, longtime chairman and ranking minority member of the Senate Appropriations Committee, may come closer to the kind of senator the Founding Fathers had in mind than any other. He comes from the humblest of beginnings, and when first elected to the Senate, as part of the large and talented Democratic class of 1958, he was scarcely noticed. Now he is the last member of that class still in the Senate, and an authentic power whether in majority or minority. From a background as grindingly poor as that of any American politician, he has continually moved up with awesome persistence. Son of a coal miner, he was a welder in wartime shipyards and a meat cutter in a coal company town when he won his seat in the House of Delegates in 1946; he campaigned in every hollow in the county, playing his fiddle and even going to the length of joining the Ku Klux Klan (which he quickly quit and has ever since regretted joining). He worked hard in the legislature, and won a U.S. House seat when the incumbent retired in 1952; he made such a name for himself in West Virginia that by 1958, when he was 40, he was elected to the Senate even though the United Mine Workers initially opposed him and the coal companies never supported him.

In the Senate, he became a supporter of Majority Leader Lyndon Johnson and in return got a seat on Appropriations his first year. He backed Hubert Humphrey against John Kennedy in the 1960 West Virginia presidential primary not because he shared Humphrey's liberal politics—his voting record then was as conservative as any Southerner's and he opposed civil rights—but because Johnson wanted to stop Kennedy. Then, in the 1960s, Byrd's career took what in retrospect was a helpful detour. He became assistant majority whip, an unimportant position in 1965; in 1971, when Edward Kennedy neglected his duties as whip after Chappaquiddick, Byrd quietly lined up support and, with Richard Russell's deathbed vote, ousted Kennedy. There Byrd performed ably, managing Senate business and accommodating colleagues' needs, and when Majority Leader Mike Mansfield retired in 1976, Byrd easily won the job. All the while Byrd was working hard to keep in touch with West Virginians, to the point that he won 78% of the vote in 1970, becoming the first West Virginian in history to carry all 55 counties.

Byrd did not like being majority leader. Contrary to most people's assumptions, the post carries little power, because Senate rules requiring unanimous consent or supermajorities allow individual senators to block action; the office gained its reputation in the six years Lyndon Johnson held it, when his extraordinary abilities and compulsive personality, applied in a closely divided Senate, enabled him temporarily to become a national leader. No majority leader has since, and Byrd was aware that his power came from meeting other senators' needs and did not have a national issues agenda of his own, though his voting record became notably less conservative. In 1987, with Democrats back in the majority after six years out of power, Byrd established some legislative priorities and then announced he would leave the post after the 1988 election.

In 1989 Byrd got the position he had been aiming for all along, chairman of the Appropriations Committee. "I want to be West Virginia's billion dollar industry," he announced in 1990, and in the next dozen years succeeded handsomely. An FBI office went to Clarksburg, Treasury and IRS offices to Parkersburg, the Fish and Wildlife Training Center in Harper's Ferry, a Bureau of Alcohol, Tobacco and Firearms in Martinsburg, a NASA Research center in Wheeling. "All roads, they say, lead to Rome," he said in 1994 in Logan, West Virginia. "They haven't seen anything yet. All roads lead to Logan." The December 2000 final appropriations included more than $1 billion of spending in West Virginia. Some of it represents the ordinary operations of government, but much of it is Byrd's work: $322 million for expanding the FBI Fingerprinting Identification Center in Clarksburg; $15 million for drought relief and watershed projects; $6 million for forensic programs at Marshall University and West Virginia University; $9.2 million for the National White Collar Crime Center in Fairmont and Morgantown; $4 million for the Canaan Valley Institute, $25 million for a biometrics research facility in north central West Virginia; $8.2 million for renovations to the Allegheny Ballistics Laboratory in Mineral County; $53.7

million for the National Energy Technology Laboratory in Morgantown and Pittsburgh; $95 million for Clean Coal technology; $237 million for highways. He has worked hard to find funds for the depleted United Mine Workers health care program for retired miners and their widows. He has supported the state's coal mining industry, seeking funds for miners displaced by the Clean Air Act in 1990, co-sponsoring the 1997 resolution opposing the Kyoto Protocol so long as it excluded developing countries like China, which passed 95–0 and opposing EPA's 1999 proposed air quality standards. When a federal judge ruled in October 1999 that mountaintop mining violated federal environmental laws, he tried to pass an appropriations rider reversing the decision; he was angry when the Clinton administration, at first agreeable, decided to oppose such a rider with a veto. The issue helped George W. Bush carry West Virginia in 2000; in April 2001 a federal appeals court reversed the decision and ruled that state laws governed mountaintop mining.

It should be added that Byrd's positions are not just parochial but are the product of serious study of the Constitution and of history. He always carries a copy of the Constitution in his left breast pocket. With the assistance of Senate historian Richard Baker, he wrote *The Senate 1789–1989*, a two-volume history, plus two volumes of classic speeches and statistics; based on impressive research, gracefully written, full of arresting anecdotes and sound insights, it surpasses any previous work on the subject. Byrd earned his law degree while in the Senate and had his diploma presented to him by President Kennedy at the 1963 American University commencement where Kennedy delivered his most important foreign policy speech; in 1994 he was awarded his B.A. summa cum laude by Marshall University, which he had attended for one semester 43 years before and could not afford to continue, and where he earned As in all eight courses he took. Byrd has been educating himself as well, systematically reading the classics, and takes to quoting Shakespeare, Thucydides or Cato the Younger in debates on the balanced budget amendment and the line-item veto. He said the balanced budget amendment "would rudely disrupt the carefully balanced powers of the three branches so assiduously planned by the Framers." He said passage of the line-item veto in 1996 was "one of the darkest moments in the history of the republic," and with five other members of Congress brought suit against it; the Supreme Court rejected their challenge in July 1997; but it was ruled unconstitutional in June 1998. He objected as well to the October 1998 omnibus budget: "Only God knows what's in this monstrosity." In 1998 he objected to the Clinton administration's recess appointments as an undermining of the prerogatives of the Senate. "After 200 years," he wrote in his history, the Senate "is still the anchor of the Republic, the morning and evening star in the American constitutional constellation."

As might be expected, Byrd played a leading role on impeachment. In October 1998, when the White House sought to forestall a House vote by getting 34 Democratic senators to sign a letter saying they would never vote to remove Clinton, Byrd responded, "Don't tamper with this jury." The tampering stopped. After Clinton and most Democratic House members held a campaign-style rally at the White House after the House voted for impeachment, Byrd called it, "an egregious display of shameless arrogance the likes of which I don't think I have seen." To the senators-only meeting in the old Senate Chamber in January 1999 he delivered a 20-minute speech, saying, "The House has fallen into the black pit of partisan self-indulgence. The Senate is teetering on the brink of that same black pit." Later in January, he introduced a resolution to dismiss the charges, but that was defeated 56–44. In February 1999, he sounded ambivalent: "It would be very difficult to stand and say not guilty, very difficult. . . . Who's kidding whom here? I have to live with myself. I have to live with my conscience." But, though he evidently continued to believe that Clinton committed high crimes, he decided that a vote to remove would abet partisanship.

Byrd has upheld the Senate's prerogatives consistently and has responded fiercely when he believes the Senate has been slighted. He pushed in May 2000 for a requirement that U.S. troops be withdrawn from Kosovo by July 2001, which was beaten by only 53–47; he argued that deployment should not continue indefinitely unless authorized by the Senate. He brutally dressed down Energy Secretary Bill Richardson in June 2000 for skipping an Intelligence Committee hearing and warned ominously that he would "never again receive the support of the Senate of the United States for an appointive position." He opposed permanent normal trade relations with China in June 2000 and complained particularly about the administration's insistence that the

Senate approve the House legislation: "What weak dishwater is the excuse that we cannot add anything to the House-passed bill? What a sorry spectacle is a Senate completely cowed by the possibility that we might upset the Chinese." He attacked the procedure of keeping appropriations off the floor, to be settled by negotiations between the Republican leadership and the Clinton administration, saying in October 2000 that "senators will be reduced to nothing more than legislative automatons."

If Byrd is determined to uphold the prerogatives of the Senate, he is determined also to uphold the prerogatives of the Appropriations Committee. He sought a seat, as a junior member, on the Budget Committee in January 2001: "In recent years, unrealistically low funding levels have been included in the budget resolution, making it difficult for the Appropriations Committee to adequately fund many vital national priorities." George W. Bush went out of his way to shake Byrd's hand at his first speech to a joint session of Congress; Byrd had not attended State of the Union addresses since 1994 out of distaste for Bill Clinton: "His lifestyle and mine were so different I didn't care about coming to hear him." But Byrd opposed Bush's tax cut as "sheer madness," arguing that it was based on inevitably untrustworthy economic forecasts and complaining that it would cut off funds for appropriators. At Democratic caucuses he made impassioned pleas that Democrats not support tax cuts, and in February 2001 he clashed with Senate Parliamentarian Robert Dove over his interpretation that budget resolution procedures, which allow debate to be shut off by 50 senators, could be used on the tax cut. "The president's proposals are not an edict, and the Senate is not a quivering body of humble subjects who must obey. We must not shackle the intellects of 100 members of the Senate in this way." In this Byrd was consistent with his long-held beliefs. He had fired Dove in January 1987, when he became majority leader again (and Trent Lott fired him again in May 2001), and he opposed the use of budget resolution procedures to pass the Clinton economic plan in 1993. When Majority Leader George Mitchell suggested using budget resolution procedures to pass the Clinton health care plan, Byrd objected so strenuously that Mitchell and the Clintons dropped the idea.

In November 2000 Byrd was re-elected by a 78%–20% margin, his largest percentage margin ever, carrying all 55 counties for the third time. At a spirited rally at the end of the campaign he said, "West Virginia has always had four friends. God Almighty, Sears Roebuck, Carter's Liver Pills and Robert C. Byrd." He is the second senator to have been elected to eight six-year terms (the other is Strom Thurmond of South Carolina); he has served longer than any other senator but Thurmond and, assuming Thurmond retires as promised in January 2003, Byrd stands to beat his record in February 2007.

Junior Senator   Jay Rockefeller's full name, John D. Rockefeller IV, has a familiar ring to those who remember his great-grandfather as the oil billionaire who was America's richest man, and his grandfather as the heir who had more than enough money to build New York's Rockefeller Center, restore Colonial Williamsburg, and found the Museum of Modern Art during the Depression. Jay Rockefeller's father and uncles were men of impressive achievement in different fields. His uncle Winthrop Rockefeller moved to an impoverished state in the southern hills—in his case Arkansas—and won two terms as governor, running an honest and reforming administration. His other uncle, Nelson Rockefeller, became governor of the nation's then-biggest state and spent money expansively on generous welfare and gigantic monuments; Jay Rockefeller became governor of what turned out to be America's number one population-losing state of the 1980s, leaving behind a network of roads and highways and a progressive tax structure. Both Rockefellers were mentioned early on as presidential candidates: Nelson, never very shy about running, finally did so in 1964 at 56, and again in 1968 (he ultimately served briefly as vice president under Gerald Ford); Jay for years avoided projecting his name forward, then almost decided to run in the summer of 1991 at 54, but in 2001 said, "No, I'm not interested. If I'd wanted to do it, I would have in 1991."

The parallels stop here, for Jay Rockefeller lacks the aloof, imperial bearing of his Uncle Nelson; he is affable, full of self-deprecating humor, tall enough so that he stoops to get through doorways and uses hearing aids because of noise damage from frequent helicopter travel. He was careful to work his way up the political ladder. He grew up in New York, graduated from Harvard, and lived and studied in Japan for three years. He first came to West Virginia as a VISTA volunteer in 1969, was elected to the House of Delegates in Kanawha County in 1966 and as secretary of State in 1968, and then had the chastening experience of losing a race for governor to Republican Arch Moore in 1972. He served three years as president of West Virginia Wesleyan College in Buckhannon, and became more practical, dropping his opposition to strip mining. He was not shy about spending his own millions and was elected governor in 1976 and, against Moore, in 1980, after which the state was plunged into deep recession. In 1984, he ran for the U.S. Senate and beat Republican businessman John Raese by just 52%–48% after spending $12 million. Every penny helped, especially the huge sums needed to air ads on Washington and Pittsburgh TV. In most counties in the state, Rockefeller ran between 1% and 7% ahead of Walter Mondale's 45% showing; in all but one of the dozen or so panhandle counties in these hugely expensive media markets, he ran 12% to 18% ahead of Mondale.

Initially in the Senate Rockefeller deferred to Robert Byrd, compiled a conventional liberal voting record, somewhat more inclined to free trade because of his experience in East Asia. Then he began his concentration on health care. With a seat on the Finance Committee, he got a place on the Pepper Commission on long-term health care. As chairman he got majorities on the commission to back long-term care for all Americans regardless of age and, by 8–7, universal medical insurance coverage. But getting others to agree was harder. Rockefeller talked mostly about health care financing when he was mulling a presidential race; but he warmly endorsed Bill Clinton and applauded his emphasis on health care. He was motivated in part by anger at his mother's treatment during a long terminal illness—an experience that would be much worse for people of ordinary incomes, he thought—and he worked to increase the number of general practitioners, especially in states like West Virginia and Arkansas, at the risk of harming the major teaching hospitals. Efforts at compromise came far too late, after voters had turned against a government takeover of health care, and the health care bill crashed and burned in September 1994.

Rockefeller has worked on other health care issues since. Perhaps his biggest legislative achievement was his 1992 law, passed over furious opposition from Western coal states, which forced union and non-union coal companies and "reachback" companies that had gone out of the coal business to pay for the exploding cost of the United Mine Workers' health care trust funds; he has worked ever since to continue funding of this program for retired miners and their widows. He pushed through the children's health insurance bill passed in 1997, which requires state matching funds. With Bill Frist, he passed a law with incentives for primary care physicians in rural and inner city areas. Again with Frist, he sponsored a law to all physicians and hospitals to establish health provider organizations to contract directly with Medicare. Rockefeller was a member of the Medicare commission set up under a 1997 law. He opposed the recommendations of John Breaux of a premium-support system, under which seniors would be given a certain amount of money and could choose between offerings from different insurance companies, much as federal employees choose from among a series of approved plans today. Breaux won a 10–7 margin for his plan, but it was below the 11-vote supermajority required to make it an official recommendation; Rockefeller vigorously opposed the proposal and said it "threatens to void the Medicare contract." George W. Bush has made the similar proposals advanced by Breaux and Republican Bill Frist as the basis for his Medicare reform. Rockefeller, with a seat on the Finance Committee, seems likely to be one of their most vocal opponents.

Rockefeller supported the 1996 Welfare Reform Act, working to maintain programs for abused and neglected children. For a dozen frustrating years one of his major causes has been a uniform federal product liability law, to reduce the burden of expensive lawsuit settlements on manufacturers. One version was vetoed by Bill Clinton in May 1996; another was sidelines by the production of the Starr report in September 1998. Rockefeller was a key supporter of the adoption tax credit, raising it to $6,000 for special needs children. He was also chief sponsor for the 1998 law making the interest of the child, rather than the theory of family preservation, the chief criterion for decisions on adoption.

Steel has been a preoccupation of Rockefeller for a long time; he was one of those who helped Weirton Steel, now West Virginia's second largest employer, become empoloyee-owned in 1984. In the late 1990s he called for aid to steel makers in the face of what he regarded as a flood of subsidized steel imports, arguing that workers and companies that have "played by the book" should get government help to allow them to continue in their jobs and their homes. He sparred with Alan Greenspan on aid to the steel industry in April 2000 and in January 2001 called on George W. Bush to convene a national summit on steel. But he is not reflexively hostile to America's competitors in East Asia, where he once lived. He voted for permanent normal trade relations with China in September 2000 and in April 2001 traveled to Taiwan to confer with officials of Sino-Swearingen Aircraft, which has a factory in Martinsburg. That is one of the plants he has helped attract to the state; another is the Toyota factory in Buffalo, west of Charleston, which he is proud to say is the only plant outside of Japan that produces engines for the Lexus. He supported United Airlines' merger with USAirways, which serves West Virginia airports, and traveled to Midland, Michigan, to persuade executives of Dow Chemical, which absorbed Union Carbide, to continue Carbide's technical center in South Charleston and its factories in South Charleston and Institute.

Rockefeller is in strong shape politically, strong enough that he no longer spends any of his own money and wins handsomely. In 1990 he won 68%–32%; in 1996, against a nurse's aide who didn't like to see the ballot space empty, he won 77%–23%, duplicating Byrd's feat of winning all 55 counties.

Cook's Call *Safe*. Since his first Senate bid in 1984, Rockefeller has cruised to re-election. He is not expected to get a competitive race in 2002.

Presidential politics West Virginia was on few political reporters' radar screens in the 2000 presidential elections; after all, over the past 70 years the only Republican nominees it voted for were incumbents headed for landslide victories—Dwight Eisenhower in 1956, Richard Nixon in 1972, Ronald Reagan in 1984. But George W. Bush targeted the state early, and Al Gore paid it little heed until the very end of the campaign, when it was too late. Bush shrewdly took advantage of West Virginia's conservative cultural attitudes and of the threat to the coal industry. He carried two of the three congressional districts, and held Gore's margin to far below usual Democratic levels in the southern coal counties. This was the only state Bush carried which his father did not, though he came close in four others (Iowa, Minnesota, Oregon and Wisconsin); he ran ahead of his father's showing in almost every county except in the eastern panhandle which is part of the Washington metropolitan area. Gore had only a 51%–47% margin among union members, and Bush ran well ahead, 57%–37%, among voters under 30.

West Virginia's presidential primary, held in May, has not attracted much attention in years. But in 1960 it was the focus of the nation's attention when John Kennedy, reportedly fortified with large injections of cash from his father, took on Hubert Humphrey and beat him, proving that a Catholic could carry a virtually all-Protestant state.

Congressional districting West Virginia did not lose a House seat in the 2000 Census, as it did in 1990. The 2nd District is the only one of the three existing districts which gained population; it will have to be trimmed back by 33,000 people. But more drastic redrawing may be in store. The 2nd elected Republican, Shelley Moore Capito, in 2000, and the legislature and governorship are held by Democrats. They could remove five counties in the eastern panhandle from the 2nd and place them in the 1st; Capito carried these counties by 7,438 votes—more than her total margin of 5,766. But such a plan would also have to give Capito the Parkersburg area, which George W. Bush won with more than 60% of the vote, and if she, like most incumbents, can raise her percentage toward Bush's she will probably win again. And it is not clear whether 1st District Democrat Alan Mollohan will welcome the addition of the panhandle counties.

THE PEOPLE: Pop. 2000: 1,808,344; Pop. 1990: 1,793,477, up 0.8% 1990–2000. 0.6% of U.S. total, 37th largest; 95% White, 3.2% Black, 0.5% Asian, 0.2% Amer. Indian, 0.9% Two + races, 0.2% Other; 0.7% Hispanic Origin. 5.5% Unemployment. 2000 Voting age pop.: 1,405,951. 2000 Turnout: 638,523; 45% of VAP. Registered voters (2000): 1,067,822; 659,838 D (62%), 309,970 R (29%), 98,014 unaffiliated and minor parties (9%).

POLITICAL LINEUP: Governor, Robert E. Wise Jr. (D); Secy. of State, Joe Manchin III (D); Atty. Gen., Darrell V. McGraw Jr. (D); Treasurer, John Perdue (D); Auditor, Glen B. Gainer III (D); Commissioner of Agriculture, Gus R. Douglass (D); State Senate, 34 (28 D, 6 R); Senate President, Earl Ray Tomblin (D); State House, 100 (75 D, 25 R); House Speaker, Robert Kiss (D). Senators, Robert C. Byrd (D) and John D. Rockefeller IV (D). Representatives, (2 D, 1 R).

ELECTIONS DIVISION: 304-558-6000; **FILING DEADLINE FOR U.S. CONGRESS:** January 26, 2002.

2000 Presidential Vote		
Bush (R)	336,475	(52%)
Gore (D)	295,497	(46%)
Nader (Green)	10,680	(2%)
Others	5,472	(1%)

1996 Presidential Vote		
Clinton (D)	327,812	(52%)
Dole (R)	233,946	(37%)
Perot (I)	71,639	(11%)

2000 Republican Presidential Primary		
Bush (R)	87,050	(80%)
McCain (R)	14,121	(13%)
Keyes (R)	5,210	(5%)
Other	3,023	(3%)

2000 Democratic Presidential Primary		
Gore (D)	182,403	(72%)
Bradley (D)	46,710	(18%)
McDonald (D)	19,374	(8%)
LaRouche (D)	4,823	(2%)

Gov. Robert E. Wise, Jr. (D)

Elected 2000, term expires Jan. 2005, 1st term; b. Jan. 6, 1948, Washington, D.C.; home, Clendenin; Duke U., B.A. 1970, Tulane U., J.D. 1975; Episcopalian; married (Sandy).

Elected Office: WV Senate, 1980–82; U.S. House of Reps. 1982–2000.

Professional Career: Practicing atty., 1975–80; Dir., WV for Fair & Equitable Assessment of Taxes, 1977–80.

Office: State Capitol, Charleston, 25305, 304-558-2000; Fax: 304-558-2722; Web site: www.state.wv.us.

Election Results

2000 general	Robert E. Wise Jr. (D)	324,822	(50%)
	Cecil H. Underwood (R)	305,926	(47%)
	Other	17,299	(3%)
2000 primary	Robert E. Wise Jr. (D)	174,202	(63%)
	Jim Lees (D)	101,774	(37%)
1996 general	Cecil H. Underwood (R)	324,518	(52%)
	Charlotte Pritt (D)	287,870	(46%)
	Others	16,171	(3%)

Sen. Robert C. Byrd (D)

Elected 1958, seat up 2006, 8th term; b. Nov. 20, 1917, North Wilkesboro, NC; home, Sophia; American U., J.D. 1963; Baptist; married (Erma).

Elected Office: WV House of Delegates, 1946–50; WV Senate, 1950–52; U.S. House of Reps., 1952–58; U.S. Senate Majority Whip, 1971–76, Majority Ldr., 1977–80, 1987–88, Minority Ldr., 1981–86.

DC Office: 311 HSOB, 20510, 202-224-3954; Fax: 202-228-0002; Web site: byrd.senate.gov.

State Office: Charleston, 304-342-5855.

Committees: *President Pro-Tempore. Appropriations* (Chmn.): Defense; Energy & Water Development; Interior (Chmn.); Transportation; VA, HUD & Independent Agencies. *Armed Services*: Emerging Threats & Capabilities; Readiness & Management Support; Strategic Forces. *Budget. Rules & Administration.*

Group Ratings

	ADA	ACLU	AFS	LCV	CON	ITIC	NTU	COC	ACU	NTLC	CHC
2000	75	43	85	43	46	67	23	40	28	14	25
1999	80	—	100	22	75	—	10	47	20	—	—

National Journal Ratings

	1999 LIB —	1999 CONS		2000 LIB —	2000 CONS
Economic	72%	25%		59%	40%
Social	60%	38%		57%	39%
Foreign	53%	46%		62%	34%

Key Votes of the 106th Congress

1. Educ. Savings Accts.	Y	5. Review Movie Violence	Y
2. Prescrip. Drug Benefit	Y	6. Gun Show Bckgrnd. Checks	Y
3. Delay Ergonomic Standards	N	7. Ban Part.-Birth Abortion	Y
4. Phase Out Estate Tax	N	8. Broaden Hate Crimes List	N

9. NATO War in Serbia	Y
10. Table Cuba Travel Ban	Y
11. Nuclear Test-Ban Treaty	*
12. Perm. Trade with China	N

Election Results

2000 general	Robert C. Byrd (D)	469,215	(78%)	($1,045,993)
	David T. Gallaher (R)	121,635	(20%)	
	Other	12,627	(2%)	
2000 primary	Robert C. Byrd (D)	unopposed		
1994 general	Robert C. Byrd (D)	290,495	(69%)	($1,550,354)
	Stan Klos (R)	130,441	(31%)	($267,165)

Sen. John D. Rockefeller, IV (D)

Elected 1984, seat up 2002, 3d term; b. June 18, 1937, New York, NY; home, Charleston; Harvard U., B.A. 1961, Intl. Christian U., Tokyo, Japan, 1957–60; Presbyterian; married (Sharon).

Elected Office: WV House of Delegates, 1966–68; WV Secy. of State, 1968–72; Dem. gubernatorial nominee, 1972; WV Gov., 1976–84.

Professional Career: Natl. Advisory Cncl., Peace Corps, 1961; Asst., Peace Corps Dir. Sargent Shriver, 1962–63; VISTA worker, 1964–66; Pres., WV Wesleyan Col., 1973–75.

DC Office: 531 HSOB, 20510, 202-224-6472; Fax: 202-224-7665; Web site: www.senate.gov/~rockefeller.

State Offices: Beckley, 304-253-9704; Charleston, 304-347-5372; Fairmont, 304-367-0122; Martinsburg, 304-262-9285.

Committees: *Commerce, Science & Transportation*: Aviation (Chmn.); Communications; Consumer Affairs, Foreign Commerce & Tourism; Manufacturing & Competitiveness; Science, Technology & Space; Surface Transportation & Merchant Marine. *Finance*: Health Care (Chmn.); International Trade; Social Security & Family Policy. *Intelligence (Select)*. *Veterans' Affairs* (Chmn.). *Joint Committee on Taxation* (2d of 5 Sens.).

Group Ratings

	ADA	ACLU	AFS	LCV	CON	ITIC	NTU	COC	ACU	NTLC	CHC
2000	85	57	85	100	57	80	10	60	4	0	17
1999	100	—	100	89	51	—	3	41	4	—	—

National Journal Ratings

	1999 LIB —	1999 CONS		2000 LIB —	2000 CONS
Economic	87%	10%		78%	20%
Social	88%	0%		66%	21%
Foreign	87%	0%		88%	11%

Key Votes of the 106th Congress

1. Educ. Savings Accts.	N	5. Review Movie Violence	N	9. NATO War in Serbia	Y
2. Prescrip. Drug Benefit	Y	6. Gun Show Bckgrnd. Checks	Y	10. Table Cuba Travel Ban	N
3. Delay Ergonomic Standards	N	7. Ban Part.-Birth Abortion	N	11. Nuclear Test-Ban Treaty	Y
4. Phase Out Estate Tax	N	8. Broaden Hate Crimes List	Y	12. Perm. Trade with China	Y

Election Results

1996 general	John D. Rockefeller IV (D)	456,526	(77%)	($5,819,157)
	Betty A. Burks (R)	139,088	(23%)	
1996 primary	John D. Rockefeller IV (D)	280,303	(88%)	
	Bruce Barilla (D)	36,637	(12%)	
1990 general	John D. Rockefeller IV (D)	276,234	(68%)	($2,709,665)
	John Yoder (R)	128,071	(32%)	($22,904)

FIRST DISTRICT

The northern part of West Virginia is in many ways an extension of the Pittsburgh metropolitan area. People here are Steelers and Pirates fans, they drink Iron City and Rolling Rock beer, they watch Pittsburgh TV, they live in the crevasses between hills cut by the Monongahela and Ohio rivers, on terrain that seems forbidding to industrial and urban development. Yet this has been one of America's prime industrial areas; northern West Virginia is part of the same coal-and-steel economy that made Pittsburgh one of the nation's largest cities and filled the narrow bottomlands along the rivers with steel and glass factories, foundries and coal yards. In the 1980s and 1990s these were declining industries, or rather industries becoming far less labor-intensive. Replacing them are Japanese factories and high-tech startups, as well as federal office complexes obtained by Senator Robert Byrd.

The 1st Congressional District includes the northern third of West Virginia. On the panhandle along the Ohio River are Victorian Wheeling, once one of the richest cities in the country with its steel and glass company investors and executives, and where the radio show "Jamboree U.S.A." has been broadcast every Saturday night for more than 50 years, and Weirton, a steel company town and site of one of the most visible experiments in employee ownership, where steelworkers decided to cut their own pay in order to produce profits, but were still threatened with the loss of jobs. South of Pittsburgh on the Monongahela are Morgantown, site of West Virginia University, and Clarksburg and Fairmont. Far to the west, the district includes Parkersburg and the surrounding hills on the Ohio River. To the east, it extends to the upper Potomac River opposite Cumberland, Maryland. Politically, most of this territory is solidly Democratic, except for some mountain counties never heavily industrialized which have remained Republican since the Civil War.

The congressman from the 1st District is Alan Mollohan, a Democrat elected in 1982. His father Robert Mollohan was elected congressman in 1952 and 1954, ran for governor and lost in 1956, and then won the House seat again when his Republican successor, Arch Moore, was elected governor in 1968 and kept it until he retired in 1982. Alan Mollohan, a Washington lawyer for Consolidated Coal, among other clients, returned home in 1982 and won the seat. His one major challenge came in the 1992 primary, after he was redistricted in with another congressman who was also the son of a congressman, Harley Staggers Jr., and an ally of the National Rifle Association. Mollohan made his name as a member of the Appropriations Committee who hustled to bring jobs to northern West Virginia. Only 20% of the Democratic primary vote here was cast in Staggers's old district. He carried that part with 73%, but Mollohan won 70% in his old district and won overall, 62%–38%.

Mollohan has compiled a moderately liberal voting record—though more to the center on cultural issues—and concentrated on bringing projects to the district, working often with Senator Robert Byrd. He claims credit for a First District Federal Procurement Team and a West Virginia High-Technology Consortium, headquartered in the Alan B. Mollohan Innovation Center, and spurring a computer software testing center in Fairmont. He has worked to fund waterways, education projects, a flight simulator for Fairmont State College, a defense procurement center in Parkersburg, historic sites, and a law enforcement training system at the closed Moundsville prison. In April 1994 Mollohan joined the "college of cardinals" when he became chairman of the Commerce, Justice, State, and Judiciary Appropriations Subcommittee; but the Democrats' majority was short-lived and he is now the ranking member on the VA-HUD and Independent Agencies Subcommittee. Even in the minority, Mollohan got an SBA Business Information Center in Fairmont, favorable language on the use of high-sulfur coal for the Kammer power plant in Marshall County, an expansion of Morgantown's federal prison and renovation of the city's historic theater, plus community-based outpatient clinics in Wood and Tucker counties. He helped form the Canaan Valley Institute, to work with local watershed groups in West Virginia and adjoining states. To critics of pork, he was unapologetic: "I'm very proud of every one of my projects. If I was not very convinced of their merit, then I wouldn't fund the projects in the first place."

On national issues, Mollohan has worked to prevent what he considers unfair competition from foreign steelmakers, including Export-Import Bank financing to upgrade a steel mill in China. He was one of three members in September 2000 to vote against a Republican plan to set aside 90% of the next year's surplus to pay down the federal debt. He said that appropriations bills had been held hostage by "budget extremists"—who, among other things, were trying to reduce spending earmarks for influential local areas; but he opposed a plan to avoid year-end showdowns by moving to a biennial budget.

Mollohan has been re-elected without Republican opposition since 1994. Some redistricting plans have proposed giving Mollohan's district the eastern Panhandle, to remove Republican counties from Shelley Moore Capito's 2nd District; the rationale is that those areas have more in common with the northern Panhandle than with the Charleston area. Such a plan is sure to be opposed by Capito and probably by Mollohan; whether West Virginia's Democratic redistricters will pay attention is unclear. But Mollohan is a clear favorite for reelection in any case.

Cook's Call   *Safe.* Mollohan has not had major-party opposition in three elections, which shows just how safely entrenched he is in this Democratic-leaning district. Democrats, who control redistricting, may move part of the more-Republican eastern panhandle (now in the 2nd District) into the 1st to improve their prospects in the 2nd.

THE PEOPLE: Pop. 2000: 595,385; Pop. 1990: 598,056, down 0.4% 1990–2000. 96.3% White, 1.8% Black, 0.7% Asian, 0.2% Amer. Indian, 0.8% Two+ races, 0.2% Other; 0.7% Hispanic Origin.

2000 Presidential Vote		
Bush (R)	121,267	(54%)
Gore (D)	96,340	(43%)
Nader (Green)	4,612	(2%)
Others	2,710	(1%)

1996 Presidential Vote		
Clinton (D)	107,835	(49%)
Dole (R)	83,306	(38%)
Perot (I)	28,900	(13%)

Rep. Alan Mollohan (D)

Elected 1982, 10th term; b. May 14, 1943, Fairmont; home, Fairmont; Col. of William & Mary, A.B. 1966, WV U., J.D. 1970; Baptist; married (Barbara).

Military Career: Army, 1970, Army Reserves, 1970–83.

Professional Career: Practicing atty., 1970–82.

DC Office: 2346 RHOB 20515, 202-225-4172; Fax: 202-225-7564; Web site: www.house.gov/mollohan.

District Offices: Clarksburg, 304-623-4422; Morgantown, 304-292-3019; Parkersburg, 304-428-0493; Wheeling, 304-232-5390.

Committees: *Appropriations* (6th of 29 D): Commerce, Justice & State; District of Columbia; VA, HUD & Independent Agencies (RMM).

Group Ratings

	ADA	ACLU	AFS	LCV	CON	ITIC	NTU	COC	ACU	NTLC	CHC
2000	60	38	85	64	15	53	26	52	28	17	57
1999	60	—	80	25	50	—	18	36	31	—	—

National Journal Ratings

	1999 LIB —	1999 CONS	2000 LIB —	2000 CONS
Economic	58% —	41%	63% —	37%
Social	47% —	52%	45% —	54%
Foreign	60% —	39%	64% —	34%

Key Votes of the 106th Congress

1. Patient Bill of Rights	Y	5. Bar RU-486 $ for FDA	Y	9. NATO War in Serbia	Y
2. Accelerate Min. Wage	Y	6. Display 10 Commandments	Y	10. Perm. Trade with China	N
3. Strike Ban on Ergo. Stnd.	Y	7. Gun Show Bkgrnd. Checks	N	11. Debt Relief for 3rd World	Y
4. Ovrd. Estate Tax Veto	Y	8. Ban Part.-Birth Abortion	Y	12. Drop Cuba Econ. Embargo	N

Election Results

2000 general	Alan Mollohan (D)	170,974	(88%)	($335,864)
	Richard Kerr (LIB)	23,797	(12%)	($16,469)
2000 primary	Alan Mollohan (D)	unopposed		
1998 general	Alan Mollohan (D)	105,101	(85%)	($284,832)
	Richard Kerr (LIB)	19,013	(15%)	($21,232)

SECOND DISTRICT

Not all of West Virginia is coal country, not all of its valleys are industrial hollows choked with workingmen's homes and small factories, not all of its hills are scarred with strip mining wounds or piled with tailings. For miles you can see gentle hills and rugged mountains, stands of green trees and vistas stretching to far horizons. Yet over another hill you may find, amid scenery primeval and rural, sudden evidence of industrialization: a pulp mill or charcoal factory in a clearing scraped out of the forest; a small factory town, built close to a river in a cleft bordered with hills, its houses built in the same 1910s style as in the factory suburbs of Pittsburgh; the entrance to an underground coal mine or a mountaintop blasted open to allow surface mining. Large parts of this naturally beautiful state look as verdant and unchanged as they must have when George Washington was speculating in land here or taking the waters in Berkeley Springs, or when John Brown launched his assault at the federal arsenal at Harper's Ferry, or when the Civil War pitted brother against brother.

The 2d Congressional District is the central part of West Virginia, a belt of land from Berkeley Springs and Harper's Ferry in the Washington exurbs all the way west to the Ohio River town of Point Pleasant, where the Kanawha River (pronounced *kaNAW*) flows into the Ohio. It could easily take a full day to drive through this district that, if ironed out, would probably spread across the country. The 2d District includes the few fast-growing parts of West Virginia—the eastern panhandle counties, some of which are technically within the Washington, D.C., metro area, and Putnam County just west of Charleston, where Toyota opened its $400 million engine plant in 1998. The major urban center here is nearby Charleston, where on the banks of the Kanawha rises West Virginia's Capitol, built in 1932 and designed by Cass Gilbert with a dome higher than the U.S. Capitol and a chandelier with 10,000 pieces of cut glass. Charleston, with its two partisan newspapers, the Democratic *Gazette* and the Republican *Daily Mail*, is the state capital and the center of the state's political culture. Charleston is a major industrial center, with coal in the hills all around and, downriver from the Capitol, huge petrochemical plants that convert coal tar into everyday products. This was a center of American high tech in the 1940s, when it produced all the nation's lucite, polyethylenes and nylon, as well as much of its artificial rubber and antifreeze. More recently, these factories are seen as heavy polluters in a valley that has well above average rates of cancer. Charleston is also West Virginia's white-collar and professional center, with a few downtown skyscrapers and some pleasant affluent residential districts. Politically, the 2d has some mountain Republican counties, and Charleston's Kanawha County sometimes goes Republican too. In national terms this has been a solidly Democratic seat. But George W. Bush carried the 2nd 54%–44% in 2000—which helped him win West Virginia's five electoral votes, without which the 25 electoral votes of Florida would have been irrelevant.

The congresswoman from the 2d District is Shelley Moore Capito, a Republican elected in one of the key House races of 2000. She grew up in northern West Virginia and in the Washington area, when her father Arch Moore served in the House from 1957–69. He was elected governor in 1968 and (against Jay Rockefeller) in 1972, and then again in 1984; later he was convicted and served three years in jail for fraud and extortion. Shelley Moore Capito graduated from Duke University and earned a masters degree from the University of Virginia. She worked for two years as a career counselor at West Virginia State College, and then was director of the state's Educational Information Center from 1978–81, when Rockefeller was governor. She served two terms in the West Virginia state House, where she won praise for her work on children's health, domestic violence, and a new tax on smokeless tobacco. Her opportunity to follow in her father's footsteps came when Bob Wise, a Democratic congressman since 1982, ran for governor in 2000. She benefited from a divisive Democratic primary that was won by Jim Humphreys, a trial lawyer and former state senator and ally of labor unions, who made a fortune in asbestos litigation and spent $3 million of his own money to win the Democratic nomination with 43% against state senator and businesswoman Martha Walker, who took 26%, and 85-year-old Ken Hechler with 25%, a political maverick who was a speechwriter for Adlai Stevenson in 1956 and served in the House from 1959–77 and was later elected secretary of State.

In the general, Humphreys spent another $3 million of his own money and focused on health care issues. Capito, who supported abortion rights, started as the underdog but attacked Humphreys for voting to raise taxes as a state legislator, while she campaigned on job creation and economic revitalization in a state that has been left behind during the national prosperity. Humphreys' high-profile primary gave him an initial lead in the polls but he proved to be a poor candidate. Among the most effective Republican ads were attacks on the three liens that were placed on his home for unpaid state income taxes and on his vote as a state legislator against a bill to make it a criminal offense to sell drug paraphernalia to children. Capito had good name recognition and popularity, and she was able to tap into her father's political network. West Virginia's last Republican congressmen had been elected in 1980; with a Republican Congress, Capito argued that the state needed "a seat at the table." Capito received more than $500,000 in contributions from Republican members and PACs. She may have been one of the few congressional candidates in 2000 who benefited from George W. Bush's coattails, especially in the eastern Panhandle. She won 48%–46%, with big margins in the eastern panhandle counties, as Bush was carrying the district 54%–45%.

In the House, Capito got seats on the Financial Services and Transportation and Infrastructure Committees, and became one of two vice-chairwomen of the Congressional Women's Caucus. She proposed repeal of the New Deal-era ban on interest-bearing checking accounts for businesses. Capito surely will be a Democratic target in 2002. Redistricting will be controlled by the Democratic legislature and governor, and they might slice off the eastern panhandle counties, which she carried by more than her district-wide majority. But to do that, they would probably have to put the heavily Republican Parkersburg area into the district, and 1st district Democrat Alan Mollohan might resist taking the eastern panhandle. In early 2001 Humphreys sent signals that he planned to run again—probably a break for Capito. If she can use the benefits of incumbency to increase her vote in rural coal counties up to the levels achieved by Bush, she is likely to be re-elected.

Cook's Call *Highly Competitive*. Democrats will target Capito, only the third Republican in almost 80 years to hold this district, in 2002. Capito's 2000 Democratic opponent, lawyer Jim Humphreys, may return for a rematch but has heavy political and personal baggage. This will be a race to watch in 2002.

THE PEOPLE: Pop. 2000: 635,965; Pop. 1990: 597,921, up 6.4% 1990–2000. 94.6% White, 3.4% Black, 0.5% Asian, 0.2% Amer. Indian, 1% Two+ races, 0.2% Other; 0.8% Hispanic Origin.

2000 Presidential Vote		
Bush (R)	124,758	(54%)
Gore (D)	101,675	(44%)
Nader (Green)	3,555	(2%)
Others	1,645	(1%)

1996 Presidential Vote		
Clinton (D)	108,503	(49%)
Dole (R)	88,930	(40%)
Perot (I)	23,238	(10%)

Rep. Shelley Moore Capito (R)

Elected 2000, 1st term; b. Nov. 26, 1953, Glen Dale; home, Charleston; Duke U., B.S. 1975; U. of VA, M.Ed. 1976; Presbyterian; married (Charles).

Elected Office: WV House of Del., 1996–2000.

Professional Career: Career counselor, WV State Col., 1976–78; Dir., Educ. Info. Center, WV Board of Regents, 1978–81.

DC Office: 1431 LHOB 20515, 202-225-2711; Fax: 202-225-7856; Web site: www.house.gov/capito.

District Offices: Charleston, 304-925-5964; Martinsburg, 304-264-8810.

Committees: *Financial Services* (34th of 37 R): Domestic Monetary Policy, Technology & Economic Growth; Financial Institutions & Consumer Credit; International Monetary Policy & Trade. *Small Business* (18th of 19 R): Workforce, Empowerment & Government Programs. *Transportation & Infrastructure* (29th of 42 R): Economic Development, Public Buildings & Emergency Management; Highways & Transit; Railroads.

Group Ratings and Key Votes: Newly Elected

Election Results

2000 general	Shelley Moore Capito (R)	108,769	(48%)	($1,288,226)
	Jim Humphreys (D)	103,003	(46%)	($6,964,933)
	John Brown (LIB)	12,543	(6%)	
2000 primary	Shelley Moore Capito (R)	unopposed		
1998 general	Robert E. Wise Jr. (D)	99,357	(73%)	($433,816)
	Sally Anne Kay (R)	29,136	(21%)	
	John Brown (Lib)	7,660	(6%)	($5,105)

THIRD DISTRICT

Early in this century, the coalfields of southern West Virginia were one of America's boom areas. Into rural farmland and hollows, inhabited by the same families since they first arrived at these mountains 100 years before, came coal company lawyers with mineral rights' leases to sign, coal company engineers to design and sink the mineshafts, and men from other mountain counties, as well as Europe, to work the mines. Company houses were built, company stores were stocked with goods as the company dictated and company paymasters kept close tabs on the finances of every employee. These conditions bred dull discontent, ignited into the fire of industrial unionism by the tongue of John L. Lewis, president of the United Mine Workers, who organized most of the mines in the 1930s. Lewis was not only a militant unionist, but also an isolationist, and during and after World War II he called out his coal miners on strikes, to the fury of Franklin Roosevelt and Harry Truman. The entire national war effort and postwar economic recovery seemed gravely threatened by these labor stoppages involving perhaps 300,000 workers, centered in back corners of the country like southern West Virginia.

All that is history now. Coal is no longer central to the U.S. economy and there are only a few thousand coal miners left in southern West Virginia—and many are not UMW members anymore. In 1950, when coal area population peaked, there were 560,000 people in the eight counties that made up the heart of southern West Virginia's coal country; in 2000 those same counties had a population of 334,000: there are few parts of the United States, apart from some central city neighborhoods and some Great Plains farm counties, which have suffered such depopulation over the last half-century. Most of the old underground mines have been abandoned, leaving behind mineshafts and piles of tailings—and lives that were snuffed out by cave-ins or simple carelessness in America's deadliest industry.

The 3d Congressional District of West Virginia includes most of the coal country in the southern part of the state, the mountainous counties directly south of Charleston that are among America's most heavily Democratic—and in some cases most politically corrupt—jurisdictions:

Mingo County, where in the 1980s a sheriff bought his job for $100,000 and other politicos bought votes for $2 or a half-pint of bourbon. But the coal mining counties are now populous enough to make up only little more than half of the 3d District. About one-quarter is in and around the industrial city of Huntington on the Ohio River, and another quarter is to the east, in the farming uplands around the resort of White Sulphur Springs, where President John Tyler honeymooned in 1844, and the interstate junction at Beckley, which has become a popular whitewater rafting area. These two areas are much less Democratic than the coal counties.

The congressman here is Nick Rahall, a Democrat first elected in 1976, at 27; he was the youngest member of the 95th Congress. He comes from the thin economic upper crust of the coal country; his family owned radio and TV stations in Beckley and in St. Petersburg, Florida. Rahall has concentrated on bringing public works projects and jobs to his district. He got seats on Transportation and Infrastructure, and Resources early on, and is now senior on both; at the start of the 107th Congress, he replaced George Miller as ranking Democrat on Resources. He was the chief sponsor in the House of the law requiring union and non-union coal operators to bail out the United Mine Workers health care funds. He has worked for flood control in the Greenbrier River basin, for $25 million for southern West Virginia water and wastewater systems, a Lower Mud River flood control project in Milton, and the Hatfield-McCoy Trail System. He was a lead House sponsor of a bill establishing a new National Highway System comprised of interstate highways, leading arterial roads and other corridors designated by Congress. In 1998, Rahall criticized West Virginia regulators for improperly permitting mountaintop mining operations. This is a contentious local issue: 61 of 81 active mountaintop removal mines approved by state regulators since 1978 did not receive variances for flattening the land after mining is complete, according to an investigation by the Charleston *Gazette*. Rahall helped obtain $21 million in abandoned mine reclamation funds for 1999 and later sought to assure that the abandoned mine land reclamation program was used only to clean up high-priority projects. He passed laws creating a National Coal Heritage Area and expanding the boundaries of the New River Gorge National River. He has sought to improve airport service in West Virginia.

On national issues, Rahall has had a liberal voting record on economic and foreign issues but is more moderate on cultural issues. He was successful in opposing Cass Ballenger's revisions of the Coal Mine Health and Safety Act and Barbara Cubin's move to make enforcement of the Surface Mining Control and Reclamation Act a state rather than federal and state responsibility. When Congress closed the Interstate Commerce Commission, he succeeded in retaining rail pricing protections (or captive coal provisions) for coal shippers. In 1999, he voted to loosen gun control regulations. When members of both parties in early 2001 raised alarms about an energy crisis because of the supply shortage in California, Rahall was more cautious, terming it a problem "created and nurtured by California." Too often in the past, he added, energy policies have been abandoned when the outlook improved. He warned against opening more public lands—including the Arctic National Wildlife Refuge in Alaska—to energy production; instead he called for exploring use of the National Petroleum Reserve in Alaska, which was approved by the Clinton administration in 1998.

Rahall has mostly won re-election easily. In 1990, after negative publicity for gambling debts and a drunk driving arrest, he had close calls. In 1996 his Republican opponent withdrew for medical reasons and no Republican has run since then. Redistricting will force the 3rd District to gain 26,000 persons, which might make it marginally more Republican. But it was the only one of West Virginia's three districts to vote for Al Gore in 2000.

Cook's Call   *Safe*. Rahall has had no major-party opposition since 1994. He is about as safe as an incumbent can be.

THE PEOPLE: Pop. 2000: 576,994; Pop. 1990: 597,500, down 3.4% 1990–2000. 94.2% White, 4.3% Black, 0.4% Asian, 0.2% Amer. Indian, 0.8% Two+ races, 0.1% Other; 0.6% Hispanic Origin.

2000 Presidential Vote
Gore (D) 97,482 (51%)
Bush (R) 90,450 (47%)
Nader (Green) 2,513 (1%)
Others 1,270 (1%)

1996 Presidential Vote
Clinton (D) 111,474 (58%)
Dole (R) 61,710 (32%)
Perot (I) 19,501 (10%)

Rep. Nick J. Rahall, II (D)

Elected 1976, 13th term; b. May 20, 1949, Beckley; home, Beckley; Duke U., B.A. 1971; Presbyterian; divorced.

Professional Career: Civil Air Patrol, 1977–88; Staff Asst., U.S. Sen. Robert Byrd, 1971–74; Bd. of Dir., Rahall Communications Corp. 1974–76; Pres., Mountaineer Tour & Travel Agency, 1974–76; Pres., WV Broadcasting Corp. 1980–present.

DC Office: 2307 RHOB 20515, 202-225-3452; Fax: 202-225-9061; Web site: www.house.gov/rahall.

District Offices: Beckley, 304-252-5000; Bluefield, 304-325-6222; Huntington, 304-522-6425; Lewisburg, 304-647-3228; Logan, 304-752-4934.

Committees: *Resources* (RMM of 25 D): Energy & Mineral Resources. *Transportation & Infrastructure* (2d of 34 D): Aviation; Highways & Transit; Railroads.

Group Ratings

	ADA	ACLU	AFS	LCV	CON	ITIC	NTU	COC	ACU	NTLC	CHC
2000	70	50	85	64	11	39	23	42	28	9	43
1999	65	—	100	75	54	—	24	24	20	—	—

National Journal Ratings

	1999 LIB —	1999 CONS		2000 LIB —	2000 CONS
Economic	75%	23%		68%	31%
Social	51%	48%		50%	49%
Foreign	85%	12%		58%	40%

Key Votes of the 106th Congress

1. Patient Bill of Rights	Y	5. Bar RU-486 $ for FDA	Y	9. NATO War in Serbia	Y
2. Accelerate Min. Wage	Y	6. Display 10 Commandments	Y	10. Perm. Trade with China	N
3. Strike Ban on Ergo. Stnd.	Y	7. Gun Show Bkgrnd. Checks	N	11. Debt Relief for 3rd World	Y
4. Ovrd. Estate Tax Veto	Y	8. Ban Part.-Birth Abortion	Y	12. Drop Cuba Econ. Embargo	N

Election Results

2000 general	Nick J. Rahall II (D) 146,807	(91%)	($354,164)
	Jeff Robinson (LIB) 13,979	(9%)	
2000 primary	Nick J. Rahall II (D) .... unopposed		
1998 general	Nick J. Rahall II (D) 78,814	(87%)	($377,311)
	Joe Whelan (LIB) 12,196	(13%)	($22,647)

★ WISCONSIN ★

W isconsin, tucked off north of the main east-west routes across the country and squeezed between Lake Michigan and the Mississippi River, was a century ago one of America's premier "laboratories of reform," in Justice Louis Brandeis's phrase—and is still today: a state originating new public policies, seeing how they work, serving as an example for others. Wisconsin's first fame as a laboratory came during the Progressive era that began around 1900, and its primacy was due to an extraordinary governor, Robert LaFollette Sr., and to the state's unique history and German heritage. Wisconsin is the first state of the Old Northwest, that vast stretch of the United States reaching all the way to the Pacific, settled first by New England Yankees but even more by immigrants from Germany and Scandinavia. The German language is seldom heard now, the once plainly German beer brands now seem quintessentially American and few ties remain with the old country after two world wars. But in the late 19th and early 20th Centuries, Germans were among America's most numerous immigrants and until the 1890s probably the most distinct. They established, on the rolling dairyland of Wisconsin and the orderly streets of Milwaukee, their separate religions, often retaining their language and maintaining old customs, from country weddings to drinking beer—a source of friction in temperance-minded America—to eating bratwurst.

Politically, the Germans were not monolithic. Their origins were diverse and they were spread too widely across the nation. But where they were concentrated, there was a distinctive politics, basically American, but with echoes of progressive ideas current in German-speaking countries in Europe. Nowhere was the politics of German-Americans more apparent than in Wisconsin. This is one of the two states that gave birth to the Republican Party in 1854 (the other is Michigan), and Germans, then arriving in America in vast numbers, heavily favored it. They abhorred slavery and welcomed the free lands Republicans advocated in the Homestead Act, the free education promised by setting up land grant colleges, and the transportation routes constructed by subsidizing railroad builders. Then came the Progressive movement of Robert LaFollette, elected governor of Wisconsin in 1900. Up to that time a conventional Republican politician, LaFollette completely revamped the state government before going to the Senate in 1906. At a time when Germany was the world's leader in graduate education and the application of science to government, LaFollette had professors from the University of Wisconsin, just across town in Madison, help develop the state workmen's compensation system and income tax. The Progressive movement favored rational use of government to improve the lot of the ordinary citizen—an idea borrowed partly from German liberals and adopted by the New Dealers a generation later. All these programs were an attempt to bring bureaucratic rationality—Germanic systematization—to the seemingly disordered America of free markets and multiple cultures, gigantic fortunes and vast open spaces.

LaFollette became a national figure. He tried to run for president in 1912 as a Progressive, but was shoved aside by Theodore Roosevelt. He did run in 1924 on his Progressive ticket and won 18% of the vote, the best third-candidate showing between 1912 and 1992. He was strongest in the northern tier of states from Wisconsin west and along the West Coast—the same area of strength of later liberals George McGovern, Walter Mondale and Michael Dukakis. After LaFollette died in 1925, his sons carried on his tradition, progressive at home and isolationist abroad: Robert LaFollette Jr., for 22 years in the Senate; Philip, elected governor in 1930, 1934 and 1936. Philip created his own Progressive Party in 1934, with ominous overtones: a "Cross in Circle" symbol his critics called a circumcised swastika, huge rally-like parades reminiscent of some in Europe at the time and a call for the governor to propose all legislation. But Philip lost in 1938 and did not run again, and Robert Jr. decided to run for re-election in 1946 as a Republican but lost the primary to Joseph McCarthy. McCarthy's charges that Communists were influencing American foreign policy fed on the inarticulate convictions of many in Wisconsin and elsewhere that the U.S. should have been fighting Russia as well as Germany in World War II.

McCarthy's national prominence made Wisconsin seem like a Republican state. But he won by narrow margins and the LaFollette Progressive tradition was taken up by liberal Democrats

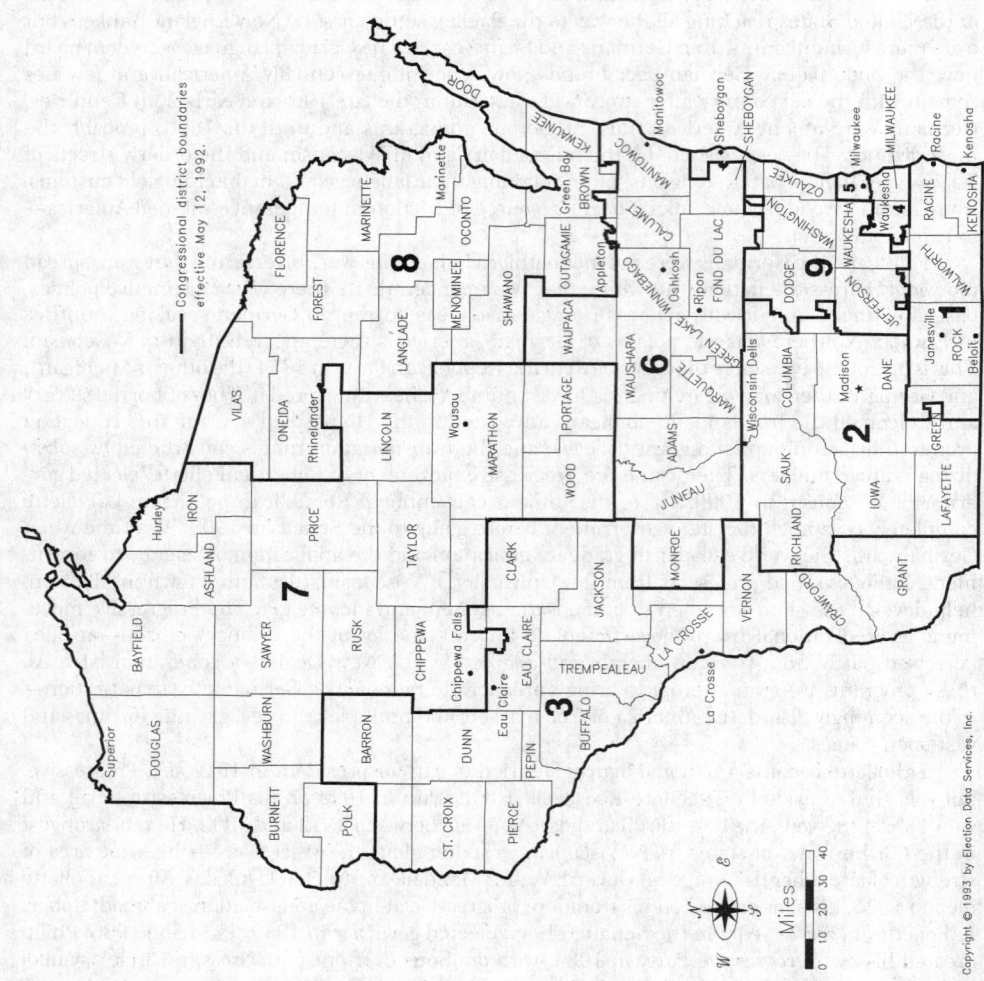

like Senators William Proxmire and Gaylord Nelson, and Governor Patrick Lucey. Like most liberals of their era, these progressives saw Washington rather than Madison as the main site of their laboratory of reform. Wisconsin, a mostly Republican state in the mostly Democratic years from 1944–64, became a mostly Democratic state in the mostly Republican years from 1968–88. It was one of the most dovish states, as if many Wisconsin voters were hit by the same impulse that led so many West German voters in the early 1980s to fear the presence of nuclear weapons and to favor disarmament.

In the 1990s Wisconsin moved in another direction, and was a laboratory for different reforms, for which the state's economy provided a favorable environment. Wisconsin's high-skill, precision manufacturing economy—its biggest companies include Allen Bradley, Johnson Controls, Harnischfeger, Briggs & Stratton, Harley-Davidson—jumped into gear in the late 1980s, and led the nation's export boom of the 1990s. The labor force is highly skilled and famously productive, with fewer hours lost to health, weather or strikes than average; unemployment fell to 3.5% in 2000, entry level-wages were $2 over the legal minimum wage, and Wisconsin's major economic problem was a shortage of workers. Population has been rising robustly, particularly in the ring of counties around Milwaukee, around Madison and in the Fox River Valley from Oshkosh to Green Bay, and in the once rural counties within commuting range of greater Minneapolis-St. Paul. Yet much of the political focus remains on the dwindling number of dairy farmers. Wisconsin ranks number two in milk production, number one in cheese, but thanks to improved productivity the number of dairy farms has declined from 105,000 in 1960 to 45,000 in 1980 and 21,000 in 2000. Waukesha County outside Milwaukee, once Cow County, U.S.A., now has only 67 dairy farms. The federal milk price fixing system is biased against Wisconsin, with prices higher the farther the farming operation is from Eau Claire; Wisconsin's members of Congress spend much time and psychic energy trying to change this. In the meantime, Wisconsin dairymen are adapting, producing specialty cheeses rather than bulk products, or turning land to more productive use.

The motivating force for reform in the 1990s has been, as in the early 1900s, a Republican governor, in this case Tommy Thompson, who beat a liberal Democrat in 1986 and went on to win some of the nation's highest job approval ratings. He cut taxes, sponsored a school choice program championed by Milwaukee black activist Polly Williams, and passed a series of welfare reforms—the nation's most thoroughgoing—which since 1987 cut caseloads by 93%. Thompson also provided yeoman support for Milwaukee's experiment with school vouchers, stifled by state bureaucrats and teachers' unions for several years, but backed by Milwaukee's Democratic Mayor John Norquist. The movement triumphed in 1998 when the Wisconsin Supreme Court ruled that vouchers could go to parochial schools and in 1999 when Milwaukee voters swept anti-voucher members off the school board despite heavy spending by the teachers' unions.

Thompson did not carry all before him. Wisconsin has two Democratic U.S. senators. It voted for Bill Clinton in 1992 and 1996 and, by 47.8%–47.6%, for Al Gore in 2000. Its U.S. House delegation is 5–4 Democratic. Republicans control the state House but Democrats have a narrow edge in the state Senate. Thompson himself went, somewhat reluctantly, to Washington to become Secretary of Health and Human Services in February 2001; his successor, Scott McCallum is not nearly so well-known and is not a cinch for a full term in 2002. Milwaukee Mayor Norquist, a Democrat, echoes some though not all of Thompson's themes. Norquist prides himself on lowering taxes while providing better services, and argues that central cities should see themselves not as hovels full of victims but as shining examples of excellence. Across the nation other governors and leaders of the Republican Congress have looked to learn from Wisconsin's experiments: it's a fair question whether the 1996 federal Welfare Reform Act would have passed without Wisconsin's example to give its backers confidence. Thompson and Wisconsin seem to have decided that the bureaucratic, supposedly rational state that the LaFollettes championed is now dysfunctional, and that individuals making their own choices, in the framework of a fair and orderly society, can achieve more than planners can ever conceive. The last of Milwaukee three Socialist mayors, Frank Zeidler, who served from 1948–60, in 1999 said mournfully, "What you're seeing in Wisconsin is a deconstruction of the progress we made in the first decades of the 20th Century." But most Wisconsin—and perhaps most American—voters apparently see the state's reforms as the construction of progress heading into the 21st.

Governor Scott McCallum, Republican lieutenant governor for 14 years, became governor of Wisconsin on February 1, 2001, when Tommy Thompson resigned to become a member of George W. Bush's cabinet. McCallum grew up in Fond du Lac, where his father worked on the assembly line at Giddings & Lewis and delivered mail and became president of the local Letter Carrier's Union. McCallum worked his way through Macalester College in St. Paul, Minnesota, and was captain of the football team. He got a masters degree from Johns Hopkins in 1974, and then went to work as a staffer for Congressman William Steiger, sponsor of the capital gains tax cut of 1978 that helped unleash the economic boom of the 1980s. He returned to Fond du Lac and worked as a real estate developer and in 1976, at 26, was elected to the state Senate; he beat an incumbent Republican in the primary by 32 votes. In the state Senate McCallum pressed for increased penalties for drunk driving (a controversial subject in beer-loving Wisconsin), creating a health insurance risk pool for the uninsured and indexing income tax rates to inflation. In 1982 he ran against Senator William Proxmire, who was highly popular after 25 years in the Senate and who spent virtually no money on his campaigns; Proxmire won 64%–34%, his lowest percentage since 1964. In 1986 McCallum was nominated to run for lieutenant governor on a ticket with Tommy Thompson; they were elected by 53%–46% over incumbent Democrats.

As lieutenant governor under the ebullient and hyperactive Thompson, McCallum made relatively little impression on voters. He worked for greater parental choice in schools, tried to retain more college graduates, promoted international trade, and set up the Lieutenant Governor's Excellence Awards to acknowledge accomplishments of "everyday Wisconsin citizens." After Thompson resigned, McCallum kept 14 of Thompson's 20 cabinet secretaries, but stirred controversy when he replaced Department of Natural Resources head George Meyer with former deputy Darrell Bazzell; the position had been appointed by the Natural Resources Board until 1995, when the governor was given power of appointment, and environmentalists were upset with McCallum's choice. He nominated state Senator Margaret Farrow to be lieutenant governor. His major problem was the budget: projections showed revenues would not be enough to cover spending. "My first priority as governor will be to do as much as I can to change the perception, and the reality, of Wisconsin being a high-tax state," McCallum said, even as taxpayers were about to receive refunds averaging $578 from a tax cut voted in 2000. He called for extending the sales tax to custom-made software and for increasing some state fees. In his budget he expanded school choice in Milwaukee. He offered a plan to pay for prescription drugs for seniors; it would cost less than either the Assembly Republicans' or Senate Democrats' plans. His first executive order was a ban on racial profiling. Reversing a previous stand, he said he saw no immediate need to ban the use of fetal tissue in medical research, since federal law bans buying fetal tissue. He barred three Chippewa tribes from building an off-reservation casino in Hudson on the Minnesota border even though it was approved by the Bush administration, noting that Wisconsin already had 17 casinos and 16,000 electronic games of chance. The proposed casino had been a source of embarrassment for the Clinton administration after the tribes charged that then-Interior Secretary Bruce Babbitt had ruled in favor of competing casinos planned by tribes that had contributed $350,000 to Bill Clinton and the Democratic National Committee.

In his first few months as governor, McCallum traveled incessantly across the state. His name recognition went way up: it was less than 50% in 2000, but by April 2001, 43% had a favorable impression and 82% knew his name. He seemed unlikely to have primary opposition in 2002, but several Democrats were lining up to run against him; it will have been 20 years since Wisconsin elected a Democratic governor, and one Democrat said it was time to "rotate crops."

Cook's Call *Highly Competitive.* Even though McCallum enjoys the perks of pseudo-incumbency he is untested and Democrats believe they will be very competitive, noting Gore's surprising victory here. Attorney General Jim Doyle, Congressman Tom Barrett and state Senator Gary George are definitely seeking the Democratic nod, while Congressman Ron Kind is exploring a candidacy.

Senior Senator Herb Kohl, a Democrat first elected in 1988, is one of the richest members of Congress, and one of the least flamboyant, a mild-mannered but persistent and successful politician. His parents immigrated to Milwaukee from Russia and Poland in the 1920s and opened a food store. Kohl's ultimately became a Wisconsin supermarket and retail chain and was sold in

1979, for great profit; Kohl's fortune has been estimated at $250 million. In 1985 he became a local celebrity, in a city smarting from sports franchises with lousy records and eager to move elsewhere, when he bought the Milwaukee Bucks basketball team to keep it from moving out of the city. When Senator William Proxmire retired in 1988, Kohl decided to run. He spent his own money liberally, running an extensive ad campaign with the theme, "Nobody's senator but yours." He won 47% in the primary to 38% for former Governor Tony Earl. In the general, against moderate Republican Susan Engeleiter, Kohl stressed his support of defense cuts—popular in dovish Wisconsin—and for requiring businesses to provide medical insurance; Engeleiter stressed her environmental stands, her legislative experience and her status as a wife and mother—in contrast to Kohl, a bachelor. This turned out to be one of the closest Senate races in the country, with Kohl winning 52%–48% after spending $7 million of his own money.

Kohl is a pleasant, shy, almost painfully earnest man, of transparent good will and seemingly little guile. He personally funds the Herb Kohl Educational Foundation, which has given more than $3.6 million in scholarships and grants to Wisconsin students, teachers and schools, and he donated $25 million to the University of Wisconsin for the Kohl Center arena which opened in 1998. His voting record has been mixed and at times one of the least liberal of Senate Democrats; he dislikes the clash of partisan fighting. He exerted great leverage when Democrats had a narrow majority in 1993 by insisting on paying for the Clinton stimulus package with spending cuts and by refusing to support a gas tax increase over 4.3 cents—otherwise Americans might have been paying a dime more a gallon for years. He opposed the Supercollider, the space station, and Trident II missiles, and has tried to keep defense spending increases down to Clinton budget levels. In 1994, prompted by Governor Tommy Thompson's welfare reforms, he sponsored a welfare-to-work bill, one of the predecessors of 1996's welfare reform. He has favored the balanced budget amendment and voted for the Chafee-Breaux bipartisan budget in May 1996. He was one of 12 Democratic senators who voted for a budget with a $1.3 trillion tax cut in May 2001.

Kohl was a sponsor of the Brady bill, and wrote the 1990 law banning guns in schools; when that was overturned by the Supreme Court in 1995 (on the ground it had nothing to do with interstate commerce). His amendment to require child safety locks on guns was rejected 61–39 in July 1998. But after the Littleton, Colorado, murders a version requiring that safety locks be sold with, but separate from, guns passed 78–20 in May 1999. In December 2000 he and Mike DeWine sponsored a bill to spend $45 million over three years to enter DNA samples of convicted violent criminals into a national law enforcement database and put it online. On bankruptcy reform, Kohl was the lead sponsor of amendments limiting the states' homestead exemption; states with high or no exemptions, like Florida and Texas, allow bankrupts to retain million-dollar homes exempt from creditors' claims. Kohl's amendment setting a $100,000 cap passed 76–22 in November 1999; his amendment to set a $125,000 cap passed by voice vote in March 2001. He and Judd Gregg sponsored a bill to make permanent the ban on Internet sales taxes; Kohl cited the plight of small Wisconsin cheese sellers. After Wisconsin suffered from highest-in-the-nation gas prices in June 2000, Kohl sponsored a bill authorizing price-fixing suits against OPEC. He has stood up for other Wisconsin interests. In 1990, as a subcommittee chairman, he stood stoutly against adjustment by sampling of the 1990 Census figures—a measure that, as it happens, would have cost Wisconsin a congressional seat, and contrary to the stand most Democrats took on the 2000 Census. He has supported Milwaukee Mayor John Norquist's light-rail projects and teardowns of freeways against Republican Governor Tommy Thompson and House Transportation Committee member Thomas Petri. In October 2000 he got a new federal judge for Green Bay and an increase in DEA officers in Wisconsin from 15 to 23.

Kohl has fought with uncharacteristic fierceness to change what he considers the unfair treatment of Wisconsin dairy farmers. Since 1937, the Agriculture Department has fixed milk prices by a formula that allows higher prices the farther a farmer is from Eau Claire, Wisconsin. This increases prices to consumers, creates an oversupply of milk and reduces dairy prices in the Upper Midwest. Further aggravating the problem is the Northeast Dairy Compact set up in the 1980s, which allows the New England states to set even higher prices; other Northeastern states have sought to join. In debate on the 1996 Freedom to Farm Act, Kohl got the Senate to vote 50–46 to end the Northeast Dairy Compact, but in conference it was extended to 1999 and the

Agriculture Secretary was ordered to set new milk marketing rules by then. In October 1999 New England senators inserted into an appropriations bill a two-year extension of the Northeast Dairy Compact and a rejection of Agriculture Secretary Dan Glickman's new rules; this was in part an effort to help then-Republican Jim Jeffords of Vermont, who was up for reelection in 2000. Kohl was outraged, and threatened to filibuster the bill and obstruct all business of the Senate. "This is very much unlike me," he told a reporter. "I hate it. I don't like to be a pain. I've never been an obstructionist before. But if this is what it takes, this is what I'll do." On November 18 and 19 he held the floor and filibustered. He was forced to desist, but got verbal support on the issue from party leaders Trent Lott and Tom Daschle and Agriculture Chairman Richard Lugar who promised the issue would be revisited. In the meantime, he and ranking House Appropriations Democrat David Obey worked for emergency assistance to dairy farmers. In October 2000 they got $473 million in emergency aid, targeted toward small family farmers. Farmers with 150 cows would get the maximum of $12,922. In February 2001 Kohl and Republican Rick Santorum proposed $500 million more in assistance for dairy farmers if milk prices fell below a threshold. In March 2001 Kohl announced that Lott and Daschle had agreed to co-sponsor a measure ending the Northeast Dairy Compact, due to expire in September 2001.

Kohl has been re-elected easily. His sincere, unprepossessing demeanor has helped—so has his money. He spent $6.5 million of his own money in 1994 (far more per voter, incidentally, than the much-ridiculed Michael Huffington was spending in California) and $4.8 million of his own money in 2000. The very fact that he is able to spend such sums has deterred many well-known Republicans from running against him. In 1994, against Republican legislator Robert Welch, he won 58%–41%. In 2000 he beat John Gillespie, founder of the Rawhide Boys Ranch for troubled teens, by 62%–37%. Kohl ran TV ads for five months; Gillespie ran radio ads for a few days before the election. Kohl lost eight counties, three in the Milwaukee suburbs, five around Gillespie's home base. From time to time there has been speculation that Kohl would run for governor, and he would obviously be a formidable candidate. In January 1998 he announced he would not run that fall; in spring 2001 he said he liked being a senator and was getting better at the job.

Junior Senator   Russ Feingold is a Democrat first elected to the Senate in 1992. He grew up in Janesville and said he wanted to be a senator someday; his father ran for district attorney as a Progressive and once lost an election to the country board by one vote. Feingold nurtured his ambition at the University of Wisconsin, as a Rhodes Scholar, and at Harvard Law School; he moved to Middleton, a not-so-academic suburb of Madison, and beat an incumbent state senator in 1982, at 29, by 31 votes. Feingold has a flair for publicity, and for political reform issues and novel arguments. His great goal in the legislature was to ban the use of bovine growth hormones, a Luddite measure aimed at keeping in business Wisconsin's numerous and long-subsidized dairy farmers, whose chief problem is that Americans drink less milk today than in the 1950s while cows are much more productive. Feingold also opposed Governor Tommy Thompson's welfare reforms and tax cuts and opposed capital punishment. Feingold's goal for 1992 was the Senate seat held by Bob Kasten, a free-market conservative who pushed tort reform and capital gains tax cuts, and had won by narrow margins in 1980 and 1986. In the Democratic primary, while Milwaukee businessman Joseph Checota and Congressman Jim Moody battered each other with negative ads, Feingold ran clever, humorous spots: one showing Elvis, alive and endorsing Feingold; another showing Feingold at home, opening up a closet and saying, "No skeletons." He also had detailed position papers, including an 82-point plan for reducing the deficit. Near primary day, Checota apologized for his ads and asked voters to vote for Feingold if they didn't vote for him. Feingold, already ahead in polls, zoomed to an astonishing 70% win in this three-way race. Feingold also bounced way ahead of Kasten, who ran his own Elvis ads attacking Feingold on issues; Feingold attacked Kasten's negativity and avoided engaging on specifics. The race narrowed, but Feingold won 53%–46%.

In the Senate, Feingold built a liberal record on cultural and foreign issues, somewhat more moderate on economics. He attacked spending virtually wherever he could find it: the Pentagon's medical school, helium subsidies and the Supercollider; he moved to eliminate the Extremely Low Frequency radio system—"a Cold War relic" in his words—embedded in northern Wisconsin. He voted against the 1997 budget agreement because it included tax cuts. He has opposed the

F/A-18E/F Super Hornet fighter-bomber, arguing that the F/A-18C/D Hornet is superior in some respects and that any improvements are not worth the doubled cost; his amendments to require the Pentagon to eliminate either the Super Hornet, the F-22 Raptor stealth figher or the Joint Strike Fighter were beaten by 4–1 margins. In 1999 he sought to end offsets, by which U.S. defense contractors agree to steer business to companies in foreign countries where they are working, and to cut off aid to Indonesia because of its brutality in East Timor. In February 2001 he moved to delay the Osprey program by a year.

Feingold has long said that the campaign finance system is "legalized bribery and influence-peddling"; democracy, he once said, "has been almost entirely corrupted in the last few years by soft money." In December 1995 he was surprised when John McCain called and asked if he would work with him against pork barrel spending—which McCain seems to regard as intended to please contributors, rather than voters. Out of this collaboration came the various versions of McCain-Feingold campaign finance bills. Most of those versions have banned soft money, contributions to parties that meet state but not federal limits, and to regulate or ban issue advertising by non-candidate groups in the weeks before elections. McCain-Feingold was filibustered to death in July 1996 and again in February 1998; House Republican leaders agreed under pressure to bring up the House version (Shays-Meehan), and it passed 252–179 in August 1998. But Feingold's efforts to end a filibuster failed again in September 1998. In 1999, while attacking oil companies for trying to limit federal royalty payments, he started citing oil PAC contributions to lawmakers, which evoked loud protests. In October 1999 McCain-Feingold was again beaten, far short of the 60 votes needed to end a filibuster. But they had other successes. They pushed through the bill requiring disclosure by Section 527 committees in June 2000.

McCain's presidential campaign and his threats to bring up the issue at every turn forced Trent Lott to schedule two weeks of debate on campaign finance in March 2001. This time McCain and Feingold prevailed. They beat an amendment for lesser changes by Chuck Hagel by 60–40 and beat non-severability (a provision that said if one provision was struck down the whole law would be invalid) by 57–43. This was important because of an amendment by Paul Wellstone, approved 51–46, that would bar non-profits running ads in the days before an election: it is hard to see how this can be squared with the First Amendment. McCain and Feingold did have to concede an increase in the individual contribution limit, unchanged since 1974, from $1,000 to $2,000. But were overjoyed when the bill passed 59–41 in early April. In the ensuing weeks, however, support in the House seemed to be waning: Democrats noted that they had equaled Republicans in soft money, but were behind them in hard money in the 2000 cycle, and were suddenly less eager to vote for a measure that seemed—unlike Shays-Meehan in 1998—likely to become law.

Feingold has pursued other ethics issues. He was one of the crusaders against lobbyists' gifts to lawmakers. He tried to extend the limit on retired members' lobbying from one year to two. He sought to prohibit members of Congress from using for personal travel frequent flier miles earned on business trips. He tried to ban the parties corporations financed for lawmakers at the two party conventions. He tried to ban cost-of-living adjustments to congressional pay—a provision likely to be noticed by him much more than most other senators, since he has one of the lowest net worths in the Senate. Feingold sponsored an amendment to the bankruptcy reform bill, which he strongly opposed, to make FEC penalties and fines undischargeable in bankruptcy.

Feingold did not respond in lockstep with other Democrats on the Clinton scandals. In February 1997 he called for an independent counsel on the Clinton-Gore fundraising operations. In January 1999 he was the only Democrat to vote against Robert Byrd's motion to dismiss the charges against Clinton. "I simply cannot say that the House managers cannot prevail," he said. He voted against removal in February.

On justice issues, Feingold is a strong opponent of the death penalty; he voted against the 1996 anti-terrorism bill because of its capital punishment provisions and in 1999 sponsored a bill to end the federal death penalty and urged states to end it too. With Orrin Hatch he sponsored a measure that passed in June 1997 that punishes crimes of sexual abuse and exploitation of children over the Internet. He is willing to cast lonely votes. He was the only Democrat on the Judiciary Committee to vote to confirm John Ashcroft. In March 1999 he was one of three Democratic senators to vote against air strikes in Serbia and Kosovo. He was one of two senators to vote against extending military health care benefits to retirees past age 65 in October 2000, and that same month he voted against an appropriation that included $100 million in emergency aid to dairy farms; he favored the aid, but objected to having it considered under emergency procedures.

Feingold has made it a practice to hold listening sessions in all 72 Wisconsin counties every year, speaking for five minutes and then taking all questions. And he has submitted voluntarily to some of the campaign restrictions he seeks to place on all candidates. In 1998 he faced a strong opponent in Congressman Mark Neumann, a conservative elected in 1994 who proposed to reserve all the budget surplus for paying down the national debt and retain money for Social Security—similar though not identical to Feingold's views—and touted his independence by saying he had been thrown off an Appropriations subcommittee for voting against the leadership. After some negotiation, they agreed to limit their campaign spending, Feingold to $3.8 million, Neumann to $4.7 million (he actually spent $4.4 million), and to limit PAC money to 10% of donations and out-of-state contributions to 25% and to impose a $2,000 limit on candidate contributions (more of a handicap for Neumann, a self-made home-builder millionaire, who spent $700,000 of his own money on a losing race in 1992). To Democrats who complained that Feingold was risking his seat in a race that was close in the polls, he said, "The issue is my issue now. We're on my playing field. Is Wisconsin going to become another state where money rules?"

The National Republican Senatorial Committee, then headed by Mitch McConnell, who led the fight against Feingold's campaign finance bill, spent heavily on this race, running anti-Feingold ads. But when the Democratic Senate Campaign Committee starting running anti-Neumann ads, Feingold responded: "Get the hell out of my state with those things"; the ads continued until the buy was finished. Neumann argued that Feingold's stand was hypocritical, since the Sierra Club, League of Conservation Voters and AFL-CIO all spent heavily on ads against Neumann. Republican attacks dominated the TV screens in August and into September; Feingold's leads of 10% or so melted away and the race became pretty much even in the polls. Feingold started out with positive ads: "Promises made, promises kept," they proclaimed, showing his van on his journeys to the state's 72 counties. But he also ran negative spots on Neumann's stands on HMOs and Social Security. Neumann ran humorous ads attacking Feingold for sending dollars to Russia to study monkeys in space and for voting for a study of cow flatulence (the ad showed smock-clad scientists out in a field trying to isolate samples of cow gas). He was one of the few Republicans in 1998 to run an ad on partial-birth abortion. Although the media scoffed at these, the VNS exit poll showed that of the 20% of voters who voted on abortion, 82% voted for Neumann—an even larger percentage than on taxes. In one of the nation's closest Senate races, Feingold won 50%–48%. This was not a big-city victory: metro Milwaukee voted for Feingold by only 50%–49%. His biggest margin came in Madison's Dane County, and he carried and ran ahead of Democratic norms in most counties in the Madison media market and along the Mississippi River—where Al Gore would run well in 2000—as well as in the Democratic Lake Superior counties. Neumann ran only about even in his own 1st District, but ran well ahead in the prosperous Fox River Valley and the Lake Michigan counties. Although the 2004 race was a long way off in early 2001, Neumann was saying he might run again.

Presidential politics Wisconsin has been seriously contested in six of the last seven presidential elections, and probably will be again in 2004. It was one of 10 states which voted for Michael Dukakis over the older George Bush in 1988, and came within 5,709 votes of voting for George W. Bush over Al Gore in 2000. In the process, some historic patterns were reversed. The younger Bush carried metro Milwaukee, which casts about one-third of the state's votes, by 49%–47%, thanks to big margins in the suburban counties, where he ran well ahead of his father's showing—the opposite of the pattern in most very large metro areas across the nation. But Gore carried many historically Republican or marginal counties in western Wisconsin, just as he carried many rural counties across the Mississippi River in eastern Iowa. Indeed, this was the only rural part of the country where Gore carried large numbers of counties and ran ahead of Democratic norms. Gore's biggest percentage margins were in Madison's Dane County and in Menominee County, which is an Indian reservation. Bush carried the Fox River Valley, though not by as big a margin as his father had, and ran well ahead of Republican norms in the far north, as he did in the Upper Peninsula of Michigan and northern Minnesota. Gore carried the elderly, but union members voted only 53%–43% for him, far less than in other industrial states; Gore did just as well among voters with postgraduate degrees. White Protestants voted 57%–40% for Bush, white Catholics were split 49%–49%.

Wisconsin once had one of the nation's most influential presidential primaries. It knocked Wendell Willkie out of the race in 1944, helped John Kennedy establish his lead over Hubert Humphrey in 1960, and prompted Lyndon Johnson to withdraw as Eugene McCarthy was about to beat him here in 1968. But now Wisconsin's primary, even after it was moved from April to March, tends to get lost. The national Democrats, incidentally, have allowed Wisconsin to continue its open primary (that is, there is no party registration), one of Bob LaFollette's reforms.

Congressional districting Wisconsin lost a congressional district in the 2000 Census, and every current district has a population well below the new state average. The only district to lose population was the 5th, which consists of the northern half of Milwaukee County. Control of redistricting is split between a Republican governor and House and a Democratic Senate. But Milwaukee County's loss of population makes one of the Milwaukee area districts the prime target for elimination. Two other factors push in this direction. In May 2001 5th District Democrat Tom Barrett announced he was running for governor, while the 4th District represented by Democrat Gerald Kleczka, with an increasing percentage of its votes cast in the Waukesha County suburbs, voted for George W. Bush. Kleczka would obviously benefit from getting the heavily Democratic portion of the city of Milwaukee now in the 5th District. So the likelihood is that most of Milwaukee County will be one heavily Democratic district, with realignments of other districts which will benefit other incumbents.

THE PEOPLE: Pop. 2000: 5,363,675; Pop. 1990: 4,891,769, up 9.6% 1990–2000. 1.9% of U.S. total, 18th largest; 88.9% White, 5.7% Black, 1.7% Asian, 0.9% Amer. Indian, 1.2% Two+ races, 1.6% Other; 3.6% Hispanic Origin. 3.5% Unemployment. 2000 Voting age pop.: 3,994,919. 2000 Turnout: 2,598,607; 65% of VAP. No state voter registration.

POLITICAL LINEUP: Governor, Scott McCallum (R); Lt. Gov., Margaret Farrow (R); Secy. of State, Douglas LaFollette (D); Atty. Gen., James E. Doyle (D); Treasurer, Jack C. Voight (R); Super. of Public Instruction, John Benson; State Senate, 33 (18 D, 15 R); Senate Pres. Pro Tempore, Gary George (D); Majority Leader, Chuck Chvala (D); Senate President, Fred Risser (D); State Assembly, 99 (43 D, 56 R); Assembly Speaker, Scott Jensen (R). Senators, Herb Kohl (D) and Russell Feingold (D). Representatives, 9 (5 D, 4 R).

ELECTIONS DIVISION: 608-266-8005; **FILING DEADLINE FOR U.S. CONGRESS:** July 9, 2002.

2000 Presidential Vote

Gore (D)	1,242,987	(48%)
Bush (R)	1,237,279	(48%)
Nader (Green)	94,070	(4%)
Others	22,375	(1%)

1996 Presidential Vote

Clinton (D)	1,071,970	(49%)
Dole (R)	845,028	(38%)
Perot (I)	227,310	(10%)
Others	51,881	(2%)

2000 Republican Presidential Primary

Bush (R)	343,292	(69%)
McCain (R)	89,684	(18%)
Keyes (R)	48,919	(10%)
Other	13,874	(3%)

2000 Democratic Presidential Primary

Gore (D)	328,682	(89%)
Bradley (D)	32,560	(9%)
Other	9,954	(3%)

Gov. Scott McCallum (R)

Assumed office, Feb. 2001, term expires Jan. 2003, 1st term; b. May 2, 1950, Fond du Lac; home, Fond du Lac; Macalester College, B.A. 1972; Johns Hopkins U., M.A. 1974; Christian Scientist; married (Laurie).

Elected Office: WI Senate, 1976–86; WI Lt. Gov., 1986–2001.

Professional Career: Aide, U.S. Rep. William Steiger, 1972–74; Mgr., M & P Development, 1977–87.

Office: State Capitol, 115 E. State Capitol, Madison, 53707, 608-266-1212; Web site: www.wisconsin.gov.

Election Results

1998 general	Tommy G.Thompson (R)	1,047,716	(60%)
	Ed Garvey (D)	679,553	(39%)
	Others	28,745	(2%)
1998 primary	Tommy G. Thompson (R)	229,916	(83%)
	Jeffrey A. Hyslop (R)	45,252	(16%)
1994 general	Tommy G. Thompson (R)	1,051,326	(67%)
	Chuck Chvala (D)	482,850	(31%)
	Others	29,659	(2%)

Sen. Herb Kohl (D)

Elected 1988, seat up 2006, 3d term; b. Feb. 7, 1935, Milwaukee; home, Milwaukee; U. of WI, B.A. 1956, Harvard U., M.B.A. 1958; Jewish; single.

Military Career: Army Reserves, 1958–64.

Professional Career: Businessman; Pres., Kohl Corp., 1970–79; Chmn., WI Dem. Party, 1975–77; Pres., Herbert Kohl Investments, 1979–88; Owner, Milwaukee Bucks pro basketball team, 1985–present.

DC Office: 330 HSOB, 20510, 202-224-5653; Fax: 202-224-9787; Web site: www.senate.gov/~kohl.

State Offices: Appleton, 920-738-1640; Eau Claire, 715-832-8424; La Crosse, 608-796-0045; Madison, 608-264-5338; Milwaukee, 414-297-4451.

Committees: *Aging (Special). Appropriations*: Agriculture & Rural Development (Chmn.); Commerce, Justice, State & Judiciary; Labor, HHS & Education; Transportation; VA, HUD & Independent Agencies. *Judiciary*: Antitrust, Business Rights & Competition (Chmn.); Technology, Terrorism & Government Information; Youth Violence.

Group Ratings

	ADA	ACLU	AFS	LCV	CON	ITIC	NTU	COC	ACU	NTLC	CHC
2000	85	71	71	86	63	79	17	60	20	12	15
1999	100	—	100	67	87	—	18	41	4	—	—

National Journal Ratings

	1999 LIB	—	1999 CONS		2000 LIB	—	2000 CONS
Economic	90%	—	0%		61%	—	38%
Social	75%	—	20%		64%	—	35%
Foreign	71%	—	24%		55%	—	44%

Key Votes of the 106th Congress

1. Educ. Savings Accts.	Y	5. Review Movie Violence	N	9. NATO War in Serbia	Y
2. Prescrip. Drug Benefit	Y	6. Gun Show Bckgrnd. Checks	Y	10. Table Cuba Travel Ban	Y
3. Delay Ergonomic Standards	N	7. Ban Part.-Birth Abortion	N	11. Nuclear Test-Ban Treaty	Y
4. Phase Out Estate Tax	N	8. Broaden Hate Crimes List	Y	12. Perm. Trade with China	Y

Election Results

2000 general	Herb Kohl (D)	1,563,238	(62%)	($4,991,364)
	John Gillespie (R)	940,744	(37%)	($582,221)
	Others	35,199	(1%)	
2000 primary	Herb Kohl (D)	184,920	(90%)	
	Jim Sigl (D)	20,858	(10%)	
1994 general	Herb Kohl (D)	912,662	(58%)	($8,249,531)
	Robert T. Welch (R)	636,989	(41%)	($1,180,382)

Sen. Russell Feingold (D)

Elected 1992, seat up 2004, 2d term; b. Mar. 2, 1953, Janesville; home, Middleton; U. of WI, B.A. 1975, Rhodes Scholar, Oxford U., 1977, Harvard Law Schl., J.D. 1979; Jewish; married (Mary).

Elected Office: WI Senate, 1982–92.

Professional Career: Practicing atty., 1979–83; Prof., Beloit Col., 1985–93.

DC Office: 506 HSOB, 20510, 202-224-5323; Fax: 202-224-2725; Web site: www.senate.gov/~feingold.

State Offices: Green Bay, 920-465-7508; LaCrosse, 608-782-5585; Middleton, 608-828-1200; Milwaukee, 414-276-7282; Wausau, 715-848-5660.

Committees: *Aging (Special). Budget. Foreign Relations*: African Affairs (Chmn.); East Asian & Pacific Affairs; Western Hemisphere, Peace Corps, Narcotics Affairs. *Judiciary*: Administrative Oversight & the Courts; Antitrust, Business Rights & Competition; Constitution, Federalism & Property Rights (Chmn.).

Group Ratings

	ADA	ACLU	AFS	LCV	CON	ITIC	NTU	COC	ACU	NTLC	CHC
2000	100	86	100	100	99	46	31	20	8	3	23
1999	100	—	100	100	100	—	25	24	8	—	—

National Journal Ratings

	1999 LIB —	1999 CONS		2000 LIB —	2000 CONS
Economic	75%	—	20%	94% —	4%
Social	69%	—	28%	66% —	21%
Foreign	54%	—	45%	66% —	31%

Key Votes of the 106th Congress

1. Educ. Savings Accts.	N	5. Review Movie Violence	N	9. NATO War in Serbia	N
2. Prescrip. Drug Benefit	Y	6. Gun Show Bckgrnd. Checks	Y	10. Table Cuba Travel Ban	N
3. Delay Ergonomic Standards	N	7. Ban Part.-Birth Abortion	N	11. Nuclear Test-Ban Treaty	Y
4. Phase Out Estate Tax	N	8. Broaden Hate Crimes List	Y	12. Perm. Trade with China	N

Election Results

1998 general	Russell Feingold (D)	890,059	(51%)	($3,846,089)
	Mark W. Neumann (R)	852,272	(48%)	($4,373,953)
1998 primary	Russell Feingold (D)	unopposed		
1992 general	Russell Feingold (D)	1,290,662	(53%)	($2,056,079)
	Robert W. Kasten Jr. (R)	1,129,599	(46%)	($5,427,163)

FIRST DISTRICT

Rolling dairy country, blanketed by snow during most of the winter, gloriously green under sunny blue skies in summer, the southern tier of Wisconsin from Lake Michigan inland to the Rock River Valley, is some of America's prime industrial country. Settled by Yankee and German farmers 170 years ago, it was once primarily dairyland. By the early 20th Century, the steady habits and high skills of the local dairy farmers provided a good labor pool for factories. Today there are still major plants here: the operations center for Johnson Wax (and its Frank Lloyd Wright-designed tower and Wingspread Center) in blue-collar Racine, and a General Motors Chevrolet plant in Janesville. Overriding local protests, Kenosha helped to revive its downtown by resurrecting a 1.2-mile trolley car line. In between are lake resorts, most notably Lake Geneva, a favorite of wealthy Chicagoans. To the untrained eye, this part of southern Wisconsin looks much the same as nearby northern Illinois; but politically there is a vast difference. The dotted line on the map is the boundary between the corruption-prone machine politics of Illinois and squeaky-clean progressive politics of Wisconsin.

This is the land of the 1st District of Wisconsin, from Lake Michigan west to the Rock River and beyond. It is a politically marginal area in Wisconsin politics and was a marginal district in congressional politics from 1958–70 and then again after 1993. In between, it was the district represented by the late Les Aspin, chairman of the House Armed Services Committee from 1985–93 and secretary of Defense from 1993–94.

The congressman from the 1st District is Paul Ryan, a Republican elected in 1998. He grew up in Janesville, in Rock County, where in 1884 his great-grandfather started a family construction firm now run by his cousins. Ryan got started in politics early, as a staffer for Senator Bob Kasten during college; then he worked as a speechwriter for Jack Kemp and William Bennett at Empower America and was legislative director to Kansas Senator Sam Brownback. Ryan returned to the 1st District in anticipation of the Senate candidacy of Congressman Mark Neumann who lost to Russell Feingold in 1998. Ryan's first test was to dispose of Republican primary opponents. One was state Senator George Petak, the only Wisconsin legislator to be recalled by voters, in June 1995, for voting for a tax increase for a new Milwaukee stadium; aware of his vulnerability on the issue, Petak withdrew in March 1998. A month later, beer distributor Brian Morello also withdrew. Ryan won 81% against an unknown in the September primary.

The Democratic primary was more closely contested. Kenosha County President Lydia Spottswood, who had lost to Neumann in 1996, was running again, and was expected to win easily. Her overall margin of 66%–34% was impressive, but in her home county, Kenosha, usually the most Democratic part of the district, she won by only 53%–47% over an unknown. One controversy revolved around her vote to put on the ballot in 1994 a ban on handguns. Her statements on the issue at the time were ambiguous, but she did say that as a nurse she had seen the devastating results of handgun violence, and many regarded her as an advocate of handgun bans; this didn't fly in a city where the Daimler Chrysler factory closes on the opening day of deer-hunting season. Ryan campaigned on the kind of overall theme that House Republican leaders in 1998 failed to provide. He called it his "Paycheck Protection Plan": he was for local control, against tax increases, in favor of gun ownership rights. He finessed the Social Security issue: "From day one, my Paycheck Protection Plan has advocated using Social Security surpluses to save Social Security and preserve the trust fund. I will not support any tax cuts unless they are paid for with cuts in government spending or non-Social Security surpluses, should they ever materialize." Spottswood dared him to sign a pledge to use the budget surplus to guarantee the solvency of Social Security; he said her pledge was too vague, and that he was going farther, even if it meant opposing House Republican leaders. He seized on her statement that she would consider removing the cap on the Social Security payroll tax, and accused her in ads, recalling her support of tax increases in Kenosha, of wanting to increase taxes by "a trillion dollars."

The candidates' personal backgrounds came into play. Spottswood campaigned on her "life experiences" as a nurse, a mother and a local official; at one appearance she said she was old enough to be Ryan's mother (she was 18 when he was born). Ryan, at age 28, proclaimed that he was old enough. "My five o'clock shadow shows up every day at four," he said, even while running ads about the five generations of Ryans in southern Wisconsin. This was a strenuously and expensively contested election, one of the Democrats' top 10 priorities in the nation. Spottswood spent $1.33 million, Ryan $1.24 million. But the final result was not that close. Ryan won 57%–43%, carrying Kenosha County by that margin and Racine County by just one point less. Curiously, his weakest area was his home county of Rock, which he carried 52%–48%; he carried heavily Republican Walworth County 67%–33%.

In the House, Ryan became a mainstream Republican who was not afraid to occasionally challenge his party. Following on his campaign pledge, he worked with Budget Committee chairman John Kasich to stop the "raid" on Social Security and put the trust funds in a lockbox. But he lost on the House floor when he pressed for language to require that any funds cut from appropriations bills be set aside to reduce total spending; appropriators in both parties objected that the provision would tie their hands. During the Midwest's gasoline crisis in the summer of 2000, he sought a waiver of the requirement to use reformulated gasoline, and he blamed the Environmental Protection Agency for causing higher prices. He criticized congressional leaders for reaching a dairy-pricing deal that violated "free-market principles" and tilted toward the Northeast. During the post-Columbine gun-control debate, Ryan was targeted by handgun-control groups for being a prime ally of gun control opponents. But in November 2000 he was reelected 67%–33% in this once-Democratic district.

In January 2001, he won a hard-fought campaign for a seat on the Ways and Means Committee. He immediately became an ally of the Wall Street-based Club for Growth in criticizing George W. Bush's proposed tax cut as too small. The success of this strong conservative in a swing district gives Republicans important lessons about establishing a personal bond with voters and working on constituent relations. His success at defining issues and setting an overall conceptual framework suggest he might be a strong statewide candidate some day—perhaps against Senator Russ Feingold in 2004. But first he must get by redistricting. If Milwaukee is given just one district, which seemed likely after Milwaukee Congressman Tom Barrett announced he was running for governor, he will probably be strengthened: adding any territory from suburban Waukesha County would make the district more Republican. But adding suburbs from southern Milwaukee County would be less helpful.

Cook's Call _Potentially Competitive._ Though he sits in a marginal district, Ryan should be considered pretty safe after big victories here in 1998 and 2000. But Wisconsin will lose one seat in redistricting and every incumbent will feel the impact. One scenario would merge Ryan's 1st District with Democrat Tammy Baldwin's 2nd District.

THE PEOPLE: Pop. 2000: 612,814; Pop. 1990: 543,380, up 12.8% 1990–2000. 88.7% White, 5.8% Black, 0.8% Asian, 0.3% Amer. Indian, 1.6% Two+ races, 2.8% Other; 6.3% Hispanic Origin.

2000 Presidential Vote		
Gore (D)	136,146	(49%)
Bush (R)	131,456	(47%)
Nader (Green)	8,296	(3%)
Others	2,419	(1%)

1996 Presidential Vote		
Clinton (D)	117,308	(50%)
Dole (R)	88,599	(38%)
Perot (I)	25,957	(11%)
Others	4,353	(2%)

Rep. Paul Ryan (R)

Elected 1998, 2d term; b. Jan. 29, 1970, Janesville; home, Janesville; Miami U. of OH, B.A., 1992; Catholic; married (Janna).

Professional Career: Aide, U.S. Sen. Bob Kasten, 1992; Advisor & speechwriter, Empower America, 1993–95; Legis. Dir., U.S. Sen. Sam Brownback, 1995–97; Mktg. consultant., Ryan Inc. Central, 1997–98.

DC Office: 1217 LHOB 20515, 202-225-3031; Fax: 202-225-3393; Web site: www.house.gov/ryan.

District Offices: Janesville, 608-752-4050; Kenosha, 262-654-1901; Racine, 262-637-0510.

Committees: _Ways & Means_ (24th of 24 R): Select Revenue Measures; Social Security. _Joint Economic Committee_ (2d of 10 Reps.).

Group Ratings

	ADA	ACLU	AFS	LCV	CON	ITIC	NTU	COC	ACU	NTLC	CHC
2000	5	29	0	21	85	94	66	90	88	88	100
1999	10	—	16	31	87	—	72	92	92	—	—

National Journal Ratings

	1999 LIB	—	1999 CONS		2000 LIB	—	2000 CONS
Economic	37%	—	61%		18%	—	76%
Social	29%	—	69%		0%	—	79%
Foreign	23%	—	73%		33%	—	62%

Key Votes of the 106th Congress

1. Patient Bill of Rights	N	5. Bar RU-486 $ for FDA	Y	9. NATO War in Serbia	N
2. Accelerate Min. Wage	N	6. Display 10 Commandments	Y	10. Perm. Trade with China	Y
3. Strike Ban on Ergo. Stnd.	N	7. Gun Show Bkgrnd. Checks	N	11. Debt Relief for 3rd World	N
4. Ovrd. Estate Tax Veto	Y	8. Ban Part.-Birth Abortion	Y	12. Drop Cuba Econ. Embargo	Y

Election Results

2000 general	Paul Ryan (R)	177,612	(67%)	($1,055,707)
	Jeffrey C. Thomas (D)	88,885	(33%)	($11,374)
2000 primary	Paul Ryan (R)	unopposed		
1998 general	Paul Ryan (R)	108,475	(57%)	($1,245,568)
	Lydia Spottswood (D)	81,164	(43%)	($1,339,361)

SECOND DISTRICT

On a narrow isthmus between Lakes Mendota and Monona is the center of Madison and, in many ways, the center of Wisconsin. Here the state Capitol rises at the one end of State Street; at the other end of several commercial blocks is the main campus of the University of Wisconsin, on a beautiful, parklike, sometimes windswept setting above Lake Mendota. For most of the 20th century, Wisconsin politics was dominated by the Madison-based LaFollettes and their liberal Democratic successors. And the traffic on State Street was two-way, with university faculty devoted to Bob LaFollette's "Wisconsin idea" of an apolitical bureaucracy, his Wisconsin Tax Commission and workmen's compensation law—both firsts in the nation. Now there is more division, with the liberal campus at odds with the welfare and school choice reforms enacted by Governor Tommy Thompson. But there is a steady debate carried on here between the liberal Madison *Capital-Times* and its conservative rival, the *Wisconsin State Journal*, with a much larger circulation; the two newspapers practice the kind of partisan journalism still seen in only a few major cities and state capitals (Detroit, Boston). Meanwhile, Madison's varied economy is thriving, with unemployment as low as 1.2% in recent years; this was the fastest-growing part of Wisconsin in the 1990s.

Madison is the center of Wisconsin's 2d Congressional District, which encompasses surrounding Dane County and several rural dairy counties that have traditionally been Republican; they include such picturesque Wisconsin scenes as Frank Lloyd Wright's home, Taliesin, the Swiss-settled town of New Glarus, and the headquarters of Lands' End in Dodgeville. Madison was LaFollette country for the first half of the century, and very liberal and Democratic for most of the second, enough so that, despite the Republican leanings of the rural counties, the 2d District voted for George McGovern in 1972 and Walter Mondale in 1984. Madison spawned an activist and sometimes violent student movement (during the Vietnam war, a grad student was killed in a laboratory by a bomb set off by a protester) and a permanent postgraduate proletariat. But there has been some mellowing out. In the 1990s, public sector employment rose 12%, while private sector jobs grew by 21%. *Money* magazine rated it among the best places to live in America. Madison has even been known to vote Republican, for Tommy Thompson and in congressional races in the 1990s. But in presidential politics the 2d district is solidly Democratic; it voted 55%–33% for Bill Clinton in 1996 and 58%–36% for Al Gore in 2000, as the rural counties here, unlike most rural counties in the nation, trended toward the Democrat.

The congresswoman from the 2d District is Tammy Baldwin, a Democrat elected in 1998. She grew up in Madison, where she was raised by her mother (a University of Wisconsin student when she was born) and her maternal grandparents, a UW biochemist and the theater department's head costume designer. She graduated first in her class at Madison West High School and went on to Smith College and UW Law School. In 1986, at 24, while still in law school, she was elected to the Dane County Board of Supervisors. In 1992 she was elected to the Wisconsin

Assembly from a heavily Democratic Madison seat; in her first term she chaired the Elections Committee. She was proud of a law requiring campaigns to file disclosure reports electronically; her greatest disappointment was passage of a 24-hour waiting period for abortions.

In 1998 the 2d District seat opened up when moderate Republican Scott Klug honored his promise to serve only four terms. This seemed a good chance for a Democratic open-seat pickup. The contest attracted four Democrats and six Republicans. But Baldwin had special advantages. As a woman with great political skills, she was supported by EMILY's List, which helped raised about one-quarter of her $1.5 million. And as a self-proclaimed lesbian, she had support from national gay and lesbian organizations, and raised money from a large and affluent national constituency. With almost all (86%) of Democratic primary votes cast in Dane County, this was mostly a Madison contest. Baldwin won with 37% of the vote.

Baldwin in some ways was the focus of the Republican primary as much as the Democratic. Most of the Republicans ran as pro-choice fiscal conservatives, including former state Insurance Commissioner Jo Musser, UW history professor John Sharpless, and beer distributor Don Carrig. But most prominent in the spotlight was Ron Greer, a black minister and Madison firefighter who was suspended from the force for distributing what many considered anti-gay literature. Greer relished the prospect of running against Baldwin, saying that she had a right to live as she wished, but that he opposed her allegedly radical gay rights agenda. He got vocal support from Green Bay Packer and preacher Reggie White, presidential candidates Alan Keyes and Gary Bauer, plus Christian conservative James Dobson. This was a race almost anybody could have won; the counties beyond Dane County cast 41% of the votes and made the difference. Musser ran first there; she ran third in Dane County, behind Sharpless and Greer. Overall, Musser had 21% of the vote, Greer 20%, Sharpless 18%, and Carrig 17%. Musser led Greer by only 394 votes.

The primary results guaranteed that Wisconsin would elect its first woman member to Congress (the other states that have not are an odd bunch: Alaska, Delaware, Iowa, Mississippi, New Hampshire and Vermont). But Baldwin's candidacy seemed to rouse the enthusiasm of Madison liberals in a way not seen in years. She called for a single-payer health insurance system, and suggested that Musser was dominated by cash from insurance companies; Musser, a nurse who founded the Madison Employers Health Care Alliance, argued that single-payer would reduce choices and create long waiting periods for elective surgery. Musser did not attack Baldwin for her support of same-sex marriage or public financing of campaigns—unpopular positions in most districts—but ran as a friend of small business and burdened taxpayers. Both sides were well-financed: Baldwin, fortified by national liberals, spent almost $1.5 million; Musser, with nearly $300,000 of her own money, spent $872,000. The difference may have been due to high turnout in Madison. Some precincts ran out of ballots and had to photocopy more. Dane County, which cast 73% of the district's votes, went 57%–42% for Baldwin; Musser's 59%–40% margin in the smaller counties was not enough to offset Dane's, and Baldwin won 53%–47%.

Baldwin thus became the first openly homosexual non-incumbent to win a seat in the House; the two other openly gay members of the House, Barney Frank and Jim Kolbe, divulged their sexual orientation after they had served several terms. Baldwin said that she did not want to be seen primarily as a lesbian congresswoman: "I have frequently said I will do more to advance gay and lesbian civil rights in this country if I become the congressperson associated with health care for everyone—who just happens to be lesbian." In an early appearance before the Washington Press Club Foundation, she deftly mocked herself: "You invited me because I'm one of the first elected officials who represents a group historically discriminated against. . . . A group that has been kept out of jobs, harassed at the workplace. A group that's been unfairly stereotyped and made the object of rude and base humor. Of course, I'm talking about . . . blonds. Especially, blonds named Tammy." Befitting Madison, she has a liberal voting record, though she prefers to be called a progressive. She sponsored the Health Security for All Americans Act to guarantee universal coverage. She sought to broaden federal hate crimes to include people targeted because of gender, sexual orientation or disability. Baldwin joined an odd alliance with Republican Bob Barr to outlaw the distribution over the Internet of recipes for methamphetamine, but a bipartisan coalition on the Judiciary Committee defeated them. During the fighting in Kosovo, she visited Macedonia and urged better care for refugees.

In the 2000 campaign Baldwin had a hard-fought contest against John Sharpless, who finished third in the 1998 Republican primary. In contrast to Musser, he was more moderate and better-known in Madison. His ads in campus newspapers called him "our professor, our Congressman, our voice," and he had students in senior campaign positions. He said that Baldwin had sparse accomplishments, had ignored farmers and raised most of her campaign money out of state. Baldwin responded that she helped to extend the Violence Against Women Act and led efforts to extend bankruptcy protection to farmers. Baldwin won by only 51%–49%, a smaller margin than in 1998, and a reversal of the usual pattern in which an incumbent, once elected, increases their vote. Baldwin ran far behind Al Gore: he carried Dane County 61%–33% in a high turnout, while she won there by 55%–45%. The rest of the district Gore won by 50%–46%, but Baldwin trailed there by 59%–41%.

Then-Governor Tommy Thompson urged Sharpless to run again in 2002. But Baldwin faces another problem: redistricting. The 2d district, despite its growth, must add 45,000 people, and the only adjacent area which is reliably Democratic is Rock County, which is the home of 1st District Republican Paul Ryan.

Cook's Call   *Competitive.* Baldwin's narrow 51%–49% win over an underfunded Republican in 2000 highlighted the competitiveness of this Madison-based district. But it could be merged with Republican Paul Ryan's 1st in redistricting. In any event, Baldwin will be impacted by redistricting in some way and could face an ambitious Republican in 2002.

THE PEOPLE: Pop. 2000: 624,959; Pop. 1990: 543,625, up 15% 1990–2000. 91.7% White, 3% Black, 2.4% Asian, 0.4% Amer. Indian, 1.4% Two+ races, 1.1% Other; 2.7% Hispanic Origin.

2000 Presidential Vote		
Gore (D)	188,419	(58%)
Bush (R)	118,311	(36%)
Nader (Green)	16,162	(5%)
Others	2,207	(1%)

1996 Presidential Vote		
Clinton (D)	146,819	(55%)
Dole (R)	88,072	(33%)
Perot (I)	21,682	(8%)
Others	12,743	(5%)

Rep. Tammy Baldwin (D)

Elected 1998, 2d term; b. Feb. 11, 1962, Madison; home, Madison; Smith Col., A.B. 1984; U. of WI Law Schl., J.D. 1989; No religious affiliation; companion (Lauren Azar).

Elected Office: Dane Cnty. Bd. of Supervisors, 1986–94; WI Assembly, 1992–98.

Professional Career: Practicing atty, 1989–92.

DC Office: 1022 LHOB 20515, 202-225-2906; Fax: 202-225-6942; Web site: www.house.gov/baldwin.

District Office: Madison, 608-258-9800.

Committees: *Budget* (12th of 20 D). *Judiciary* (14th of 17 D): Commercial & Administrative Law; Courts, the Internet & Intellectual Property.

Group Ratings

	ADA	ACLU	AFS	LCV	CON	ITIC	NTU	COC	ACU	NTLC	CHC
2000	90	85	100	100	83	37	29	23	4	16	0
1999	90	—	100	75	98	—	33	4	4	—	—

National Journal Ratings

	1999 LIB —	1999 CONS		2000 LIB —	2000 CONS
Economic	84% —	12%		92% —	5%
Social	87% —	0%		86% —	12%
Foreign	61% —	37%		92% —	6%

Key Votes of the 106th Congress

1. Patient Bill of Rights	Y	5. Bar RU-486 $ for FDA	N	9. NATO War in Serbia	Y
2. Accelerate Min. Wage	Y	6. Display 10 Commandments	N	10. Perm. Trade with China	N
3. Strike Ban on Ergo. Stnd.	Y	7. Gun Show Bkgrnd. Checks	Y	11. Debt Relief for 3rd World	Y
4. Ovrd. Estate Tax Veto	N	8. Ban Part.-Birth Abortion	N	12. Drop Cuba Econ. Embargo	Y

Election Results

2000 general	Tammy Baldwin (D)	163,534	(51%)	($1,680,093)
	John Sharpless (R)	154,632	(49%)	($637,530)
2000 primary	Tammy Baldwin (D)	unopposed		
1998 general	Tammy Baldwin (D)	116,377	(52%)	($1,469,905)
	Josephine W. Musser (R)	103,528	(47%)	($872,778)

THIRD DISTRICT

On the rolling land of western Wisconsin, in the knobby hills just east of the Mississippi River, is some of the most beautiful river landscape in the country. This is where Laura Ingalls Wilder's family built the "little house in the big woods" in the 1870s, before the first railroad came steaming up the narrow floodplain alongside the Mississippi River. Today, it is hard to imagine the big woods: The trees have long since been cut and the hillsides are covered with grass grazed by placid dairy cattle. Where pioneers tried to scratch out diversified crops, farmers soon created America's premier dairy region, producing milk, butter and especially cheese. Today the dairy industry is in trouble: more than half of family dairy farmers have gone out of business since 1980. Cows are more productive, while demand for milk has decreased because there are fewer children in America now than in the 1950s, and fewer Americans are descended exclusively from the northern European stock that carries the genes for the enzymes adults need to effectively digest milk. And Wisconsin has trouble competing against the European Common Market's hugely subsidized cheese and butter. In the 1980s many communities here lost population, but in the 1990s there was a steady 10% growth, especially rapid in the northern counties within commuting distance of Minneapolis-St. Paul.

The 3d Congressional District of Wisconsin follows the Mississippi and St. Croix River counties from the southern border of the state almost to Lake Superior, and here and there reaches east a county or two. This is probably the nation's number-one dairy district, with more cows than people. It was settled largely by German and Scandinavian immigrants (Laura's Yankee family moved away as Swedes were moving into the area), and it once voted for LaFollette Progressives. More recently, it has been fairly closely divided between Democrats and Republicans. In 2000 it voted 49%–46% for Al Gore, as he carried most of the rural counties and narrowly lost the counties nearest the Twin Cities; western Wisconsin and eastern Iowa, on either side of the Mississippi, were the one segment of rural America where Gore ran even with or ahead of historic Democratic percentages in 2000—which was vital to his narrow margins of victory in both states.

The congressman from the 3d District is Ron Kind, a Democrat elected in 1996. He grew up in a large family in La Crosse, the son of a telephone repairman and a secretary. He went to Harvard on scholarship and played quarterback, and worked as a summer intern for Senator William Proxmire, doing research for his Golden Fleece awards. He attended the London School of Economics and University of Minnesota Law School, practiced law in a big firm in Milwaukee, then returned home to La Crosse to work as an assistant prosecutor on rape and sexual abuse cases.

Kind started running for Congress soon after Steve Gunderson announced during the 1994 campaign that he would not run again in 1996. Early in the race to succeed him was Republican former state Senator Jim Harsdorf, from the northern part of the district near Minneapolis-St. Paul. Kind set a tone for the primary election by renting the Hollywood Theater in La Crosse for a special showing of *Mr. Smith Goes to Washington*. Kind's leading primary opponent, Lee Rasch, president of a La Crosse technical college, had run before and called for farmers to wean themselves from federal price supports. Kind talked of cutting corporate welfare and aiding the poor, and won the September primary 46%–29%.

Harsdorf won the Republican primary after Gunderson rejected pleas to run for re-election even though he might have become Agriculture Committee chairman. Harsdorf took hard-edged, well-defined stands, for the balanced budget and Governor Tommy Thompson's "Wisconsin Works" welfare reform (known as W-2). Kind complained the ads were misleading and called for an end to such campaigning, though the ads accurately set out the candidates' differences on two important issues: Kind said he was concerned whether W-2 provided enough job training and child care and wanted to see how Congress tackled the budget in 1997 before considering an amendment. He talked instead of campaign finance reform and presented his own balanced budget proposal. On November 1 Gunderson announced he was neutral on the candidates because he didn't agree with Harsdorf's views on civil and human rights and thought him too close to the Christian Coalition. In a district that Bill Clinton carried 50%–34%, Kind won 52%–48%.

In the House, Kind joined the New Democrat Coalition and compiled a moderate record on economics and cultural issues, and a more liberal one on foreign and defense issues. Like other Wisconsin members, he worked to reform the Federal Milk Marketing Order System, instituted in 1937, which pays higher prices the farther the farmer is from Eau Claire, Wisconsin. He opposed the Northeast Dairy Compact, which was temporarily preserved by the 1996 farm bill to allow New England states to set higher-than-federal milk prices and said that the federal milk pricing formula should include "weighted averages" to better reflect market forces; he argued that the basic price formula for cheese is not accurately determined by the market. He opposed delays in the end date of the Northeast Dairy Compact and predicted there might be new compacts in the Southeast and California.

Kind is a founder and co-chair of the Upper Mississippi River Congressional Task Force, where he sought an investigation of whether the Army Corps of Engineers was biased in favor of new lock and dam construction on the river and later filed a bill with Senator Russell Feingold to require independent review of the agency. He focused attention on runoff of nitrogen fertilizer from farm fields. He worked on the bipartisan task force on campaign finance, and made speeches for the Shays-Meehan bill on 98 consecutive days in 1997, in imitation of Proxmire's daily speeches urging ratification of the genocide treaty (it finally was ratified in 1986, his 30th year in the Senate). After strong lobbying by union leaders and dairy interests, he opposed fast track in 1997, even declining an invitation to play golf with Bill Clinton for fear he'd be lobbied. But he sided with Clinton—and local farmers—by voting yes on permanent normal trade relations with China, one of few Midwest Democrats taking that position. He joined a bill to prohibit Nevada sports books from taking bets on college games. In 2001 he got a temporary seat on the Agriculture Committee, charged with reauthorizing the 1996 farm bill.

After a tumultuous and heavily contested campaign in 1996, Kind twice won easy reelection in 1998 and 2000. In early 2001 he started traveling around Wisconsin and was frequently mentioned as a candidate for governor in 2002. Should he run, this would probably be a fiercely contested district, as it was in 1996.

Cook's Call *Potentially Competitive.* Although this district is very marginal, Kind has established himself in just four years. He was exploring a bid for governor in spring 2001, but will probably not run. Wisconsin will lose a seat in redistricting, however, and every district will have to be altered. This race is worth keeping an eye on.

THE PEOPLE: Pop. 2000: 600,914; Pop. 1990: 543,447, up 10.6% 1990–2000. 96.5% White, 0.5% Black, 1.3% Asian, 0.6% Amer. Indian, 0.8% Two+ races, 0.3% Other; 0.9% Hispanic Origin.

2000 Presidential Vote			**1996 Presidential Vote**		
Gore (D)	140,113	(49%)	Clinton (D)	120,717	(50%)
Bush (R)	131,692	(46%)	Dole (R)	82,678	(34%)
Nader (Green)	13,251	(5%)	Perot (I)	33,325	(14%)
Others	2,421	(1%)	Others	5,274	(2%)

Rep. Ron Kind (D)

Elected 1996, 3d term; b. Mar. 16, 1963, La Crosse; home, La Crosse; Harvard U., B.A. 1985, London Schl. of Econ., 1986, U. of MN, J.D. 1990; Lutheran; married (Tawni).

Professional Career: Practicing atty., 1990–92; Asst. St. Prosecutor, La Crosse Cnty., 1992–96.

DC Office: 1713 LHOB 20515, 202-225-5506; Fax: 202-225-5739; Web site: www.house.gov/kind.

District Offices: Eau Claire, 715-831-9214; La Crosse, 608-782-2558.

Committees: *Agriculture* (23d of 24 D): General Farm Commodities & Risk Management. *Education & the Workforce* (14th of 22 D): 21st Century Competitiveness; Education Reform. *Resources* (14th of 25 D): Energy & Mineral Resources (RMM).

Group Ratings

	ADA	ACLU	AFS	LCV	CON	ITIC	NTU	COC	ACU	NTLC	CHC
2000	80	64	83	86	94	83	32	50	8	12	13
1999	90	—	83	81	99	—	29	44	4	—	—

National Journal Ratings

	1999 LIB —	1999 CONS	2000 LIB —	2000 CONS
Economic	58%	42%	77%	22%
Social	73%	26%	74%	24%
Foreign	67%	33%	85%	10%

Key Votes of the 106th Congress

1. Patient Bill of Rights	Y	5. Bar RU-486 $ for FDA	N	9. NATO War in Serbia	Y
2. Accelerate Min. Wage	Y	6. Display 10 Commandments	N	10. Perm. Trade with China	Y
3. Strike Ban on Ergo. Stnd.	Y	7. Gun Show Bkgrnd. Checks	N	11. Debt Relief for 3rd World	Y
4. Ovrd. Estate Tax Veto	N	8. Ban Part.-Birth Abortion	Y	12. Drop Cuba Econ. Embargo	Y

Election Results

2000 general	Ron Kind (D)	173,505	(64%)	($564,246)
	Susan Tully (R)	97,741	(36%)	($124,818)
2000 primary	Ron Kind (D)	unopposed		
1998 general	Ron Kind (D)	128,256	(71%)	($457,273)
	Troy A. Brechler (R)	51,001	(28%)	($7,507)

FOURTH DISTRICT

The world's largest four-sided clock faces outward from all sides of the tower on the Allen-Bradley factory, looking out over the manufacturing city of Milwaukee. It is an apt symbol, a piece of precision engineering, in this high-skill manufacturing town, with its skyline of smokestacks and church steeples, the closest thing in America to the factory cities of the Germany whence so many Milwaukeeans' ancestors came. Chicago, just 90 miles away, provides much of the banking, advertising, insurance, accounting and legal services Milwaukee businesses need, and the retail and entertainment base as well, and Madison has the big research university. But Milwaukee leads the nation in industrial control equipment, mining gear, cranes and independent foundries. The work force, with German, Polish, Mitteleuropean work habits, is highly skilled and hard-working. German-Americans made Milwaukee the nation's major beer brewer for years, though brewing employs fewer than 4,000 here today. Milwaukee lost 60,000 manufacturing jobs in the 1979–82 recession years, but it stuck to its high-skill manufacturing strength and eventually prospered. Since then, Allen-Bradley has spent millions on improvements and new facilities, Rockwell International had a big increase in its sales, and Harnischfeger has recovered nicely to regain its status as a leader in mining equipment and papermaking machinery, after nearly going bankrupt.

Prospering quietly from this growth, for this is still a union, high-wage town, are the residents of Milwaukee's traditionally blue-collar south side. Here, in neighborhoods with sturdy houses that withstand northern winters and streets lined with bars emblazoned with beer signs, are Milwaukee's prototypical Polish neighborhoods and its even larger number of German-Americans; here also in old immigrant neighborhoods are the largest numbers of Wisconsin's Hispanics— 12% in 2000.

The 4th Congressional District, which has been the south-side Milwaukee district since 1892, has spread out with the population into the suburbs into Milwaukee County and farther west in Waukesha County. Historically this was the only securely Democratic part of Wisconsin. But Waukesha County is solidly Republican, and the 4th District is now far less Democratic than the north side 5th. In 1996 it went for Bill Clinton by only 49%–40%, less than some rural Wisconsin districts; in 2000 it voted for George W. Bush by a 50%–46% margin.

The congressman from the 4th District is Jerry Kleczka, a Democrat elected in 1984. Kleczka is a product of the south side, the sort of man who has remodeled his house from top to bottom and maintains the best lawn in the neighborhood. He was elected to the Wisconsin Assembly in 1968, at 24, to the state Senate in 1974, where he chaired several committees, and to the U.S. House after the death of Clement Zablocki, who represented the district for 35 years and chaired the Foreign Affairs Committee.

In the House Kleczka has a moderate-to-liberal voting record. He supported welfare reform in 1996, and opposed the 1998 omnibus budget because it cut $20 billion from the surplus. He has criticized Supplemental Security Income for providing benefits for children who are not disabled in any serious way and for drug addicts and alcoholics. He favors tax-free withdrawals from IRAs for first-time home-buying, college education, medical expenses, and during long-term unemployment. Inspired by the Pabst Brewery Company closure, he has sponsored a CARE Act to require employers to give six months' notice before changing health benefits; inspired by the Louis Allis Company bankruptcy, he wants to protect employee contributions to pension funds from being seized by banks and other creditors in bankruptcy proceedings. On the Ways and Means Committee, he has stood strongly against allowing private contracts between Medicare beneficiaries and doctors; that would create a two-tier system, he argues. He has sponsored a Personal Information and Privacy Act, to halt the sale and dissemination of Social Security numbers and other personal information, and wants to take other steps to stop identity fraud. He worked with Republican Amo Houghton to clarify tax rules on independent contractors. On other matters, he has sponsored bills to require school buses to be equipped with seat belts and—joined at his office by his dog Colby—to extend the ban on dog and cat fur in domestic clothing to imported clothing. He was the only Wisconsin Democrat to vote for the partial-birth abortion ban. On behalf of Waukesha, which has had drinking-water problems, he called for further studies of the health effects of radium in the water supply and then sought federal grants to help the city meet regulatory standards. Citing his district's sizable Serb constituency, he voted against support for Bill Clinton's air war against Yugoslavia, but did vote in favor of NATO peacekeeping operations.

Kleczka found himself in the middle of an unusual and bitter House conflict in 2000 over the selection of a new House chaplain. He recommended Father Tim O'Brien, a Marquette University professor, who was initially favored by a bipartisan selection committee and would have been the first Roman Catholic chaplain. But Kleczka said that Republican leaders "rigged" the process to select a Presbyterian minister. O'Brien said that he was the victim of anti-Catholic discrimination. Later, Speaker Dennis Hastert selected Father Daniel Coughlin, a Catholic priest from Chicago. Kleczka remained angry, contending that Republicans had "gone over the line" in politicizing the position.

As this district has become more suburban and Republican, Kleczka has had more serious challenges. In 1994, Tom Reynolds, a Christian conservative printer whose backyard print shop churned out anti-abortion as well as campaign literature, held him to a 54%–45% margin. In May 1995, after a second drunk driving arrest, Kleczka gave up drinking. He won the next two elections against Reynolds, 58%–42% in 1996 and 57%–43% in 1998. In 2000, against a little-known challenger Kleczka won 61%–38%. This district will change in 2002. Milwaukee County has had two congressional districts for 110 years, but its population dipped slightly in the 1990s. In May 2001 Tom Barrett, the Democratic congressman from the north side 5th District, announced he was running for governor. This increased the likelihood that the legislature, split between the parties, will create one Milwaukee district, with all or most of the city plus a few adjacent suburbs. This would give Kleczka much new territory, and perhaps primary opposition, but it would be a safe Democratic seat in November.

Cook's Call *Potentially Competitive.* Although this blue-collar Milwaukee district is pretty marginal (Bush won here by 5% in 2000), Kleczka is safely entrenched. His biggest threat is redistricting: Wisconsin must lose one seat, and Milwaukee, the slowest growing part of the state, could lose one of its two districts. Congressman Tom Barrett's decision to run for governor, means that it is likely that Barrett's 5th District will be partitioned or merged with the 4th.

THE PEOPLE: Pop. 2000: 578,409; Pop. 1990: 543,482, up 6.4% 1990–2000. 86.7% White, 2.2% Black, 2.1% Asian, 0.9% Amer. Indian, 2% Two+ races, 6.2% Other; 12.5% Hispanic Origin.

2000 Presidential Vote		
Bush (R)	140,422	(50%)
Gore (D)	126,687	(46%)
Nader (Green)	8,367	(3%)
Others	2,653	(1%)

1996 Presidential Vote		
Clinton (D)	115,466	(49%)
Dole (R)	94,003	(40%)
Perot (I)	21,373	(9%)
Others	5,032	(2%)

Rep. Gerald D. Kleczka (D)

Elected Apr. 1984, 9th term; b. Nov. 26, 1943, Milwaukee; home, Milwaukee; Catholic; married (Bonnie).

Military Career: Air Natl. Guard, 1963–69.

Elected Office: Milwaukee Cnty. Cncl., 1965–68; WI Assembly, 1968–74; WI Senate, 1974–84, Asst. Majority Ldr., 1977–82.

Professional Career: Accountant, 1982–84.

DC Office: 2301 RHOB 20515, 202-225-4572; Fax: 202-225-8135; Web site: www.house.gov/kleczka.

District Office: Milwaukee, 414-297-1140.

Committees: *Budget* (8th of 20 D). *Ways & Means* (8th of 17 D): Health.

Group Ratings

	ADA	ACLU	AFS	LCV	CON	ITIC	NTU	COC	ACU	NTLC	CHC
2000	85	64	100	93	87	67	25	30	20	27	27
1999	95	—	100	100	79	—	25	24	16	—	—

National Journal Ratings

	1999 LIB	—	1999 CONS		2000 LIB	—	2000 CONS
Economic	75%	—	23%		85%	—	11%
Social	68%	—	32%		65%	—	35%
Foreign	61%	—	39%		69%	—	28%

Key Votes of the 106th Congress

1. Patient Bill of Rights	Y	5. Bar RU-486 $ for FDA	N	9. NATO War in Serbia	Y
2. Accelerate Min. Wage	Y	6. Display 10 Commandments	N	10. Perm. Trade with China	N
3. Strike Ban on Ergo. Stnd.	Y	7. Gun Show Bkgrnd. Checks	Y	11. Debt Relief for 3rd World	Y
4. Ovrd. Estate Tax Veto	N	8. Ban Part.-Birth Abortion	Y	12. Drop Cuba Econ. Embargo	Y

Election Results

2000 general	Gerald D. Kleczka (D)	163,622	(61%)	($632,355)
	Tim Riener (R)	101,811	(38%)	($46,119)
	Other	3,705	(1%)	
2000 primary	Gerald D. Kleczka (D)	unopposed		
1998 general	Gerald D. Kleczka (D)	105,841	(58%)	($631,856)
	Tom Reynolds (R)	76,666	(42%)	($195,318)

FIFTH DISTRICT

Milwaukee is America's most German city, with an ethnic heritage noticeable not just in the names of its beers and its old German restaurants but in the solidness of its houses and the orderliness of its streets. Until World War I made this German character seem un-American, German was spoken on the streets and read in newspapers, German beer was produced in dozens of breweries and German cultural traditions breathed in churches, union halls and parlors. There was a German-type politics, with a Socialist mayor and an efficient, honest city government. Wisconsin's 5th Congressional District, which since 1892 has included the north side of Milwaukee, elected Socialist Victor Berger to Congress in 1910 and again from 1918–20 and 1922–26, even though he was denied his House seat after the 1918 election because of his opposition to World War I; in 1919 he was sentenced to 20 years in prison for writing anti-war articles, but his conviction was later reversed by the Supreme Court.

Though some ghetto neighborhoods here are beset by crime and drug use, most of Milwaukee is solid and upstanding, and some of it—Brewers Hill near the old Schlitz brewery—is gentrifying. There is an Oktoberfest (as well as an Irish Fest, summerfest, etc.); and there are large and efficiently run factories that pay high wages to highly-skilled and well-disciplined workers. This is also the place where state legislator Polly Williams, a Jesse Jackson backer in 1988, joined forces with Republican Governor Tommy Thompson and Democratic Mayor John Norquist to oppose the Democratic education bureaucracy and enact a school choice program, bitterly attacked by teachers' unions but upheld by the Wisconsin Supreme Court and perceptibly raising the testing scores of disadvantaged students. When Thompson became Secretary of Health and Human Services in 2001, Milwaukee had more students participating in voucher programs than anywhere else in the nation; one-third were in programs run by the Catholic Archdiocese. In April 2001 George W. Bush opened for the baseball Brewers the city's $400 million Miller Park, which has spurred downtown redevelopment.

The 5th Congressional District of Wisconsin includes the northern half of Milwaukee and Milwaukee County, including its black neighborhoods and the high-income suburbs on Lake Michigan. Overall, its tone is sturdily blue and white collar. Once German, Socialist and LaFollette Progressive, the 5th is now 43% black and the most heavily Democratic district in Wisconsin.

The congressman from the 5th District is Tom Barrett, a Democrat elected in 1992. He grew up in Milwaukee, went to college and law school in Madison, practiced law, and has spent most of his adult life in politics. He was elected to the state Assembly in 1984, at 30; in 1988 he was overwhelmingly elected to the state Senate in a district that conveniently was one of only two entirely within the 5th District. His legislation included bringing 911 emergency call service to Milwaukee and passing a state version of the Brady bill. Running for the House when the 5th District's Jim Moody ran for the Senate, Barrett presented detailed position papers on the economy and health care reform. He called for large defense cutbacks, a national police corps and federal encouragement of direct investment in "microenterprises" in depressed city neighborhoods. He won his primary with 41% over a black county supervisor, a former circuit judge who spent $200,000 of his own money, and a former Marquette basketball star; the general election was easy.

Barrett has a moderate-to-liberal voting record; he calls himself a "deficit hawk and military dove." He was a strong supporter of lobbying reform and the gift ban; he had a bill to prohibit congressmen from using frequent flier miles from official travel for personal vacations. In response to local concerns, he worked to require HUD to give owner-occupants preference in resales of HUD-owned houses and to allow public housing residents to ban firearms. He sponsored a bill to require companies that wish to terminate retiree benefits to notify employees and face a court hearing within 14 days if someone objects. He has supported the adoption tax credit, health insurance deductibility for the self-employed, trigger locks on guns, and a ban on the manufacture of cop-killer bullets. In 1996 he was one of two Wisconsin votes against welfare reform (David Obey was the other), arguing that there isn't enough child care capacity in Milwaukee County.

In September 1998 he was assigned to Judiciary to fill a vacancy, just in time for Independent Counsel Kenneth Starr's referral of the Clinton case. "If you are going to go to a prize fight, you might as well sit in the front row," Barrett said, but with his transparently good-hearted attempt to find common ground, he was soon frustrated at the impeachment hearings. "It was like watching concrete dry, watching both sides get farther and farther apart," he said. From early on, Barrett thought censure was the appropriate response, and he co-sponsored with Rick Boucher and William Delahunt a censure resolution that did not pass. Barrett then voted against impeachment. In 1999 he finally got the seat he had been seeking on the Commerce Committee. Republicans defeated his attempt there to add an amendment to the financial-services bill that would expand protections against insurance redlining in specific geographic areas to include all banking affiliates; Barrett vowed to continue the fight. In one of the Clinton administration's final actions, he got a waiver to permit BadgerCare to provide health insurance for the working poor with the same reimbursement as for children's coverage. But he criticized Donna Shalala, the former UW chancellor and Clinton's secretary of Health and Human Services, for her handling of new organ-donor rules. "We should be talking about how to help states procure more organs, not arguing about shuffling a limited supply or organs from state to state," he said.

Barrett has won reelection easily. But in early 2001 his future prospects were clouded by redistricting. Wisconsin lost a House seat in the 2000 Census, and the 5th was the only district in the state to lose population. The Republican chairman of the state House redistricting committee said that Milwaukee should have only one district, which would consist of all or some of the city plus a few adjacent suburbs. This would set up a primary between Barrett and the 4th District's Gerald Kleczka. Democrats, who controlled the state Senate by a narrow margin, said they wanted to keep two Milwaukee districts, but it was not clear they would prevail. In May 2001 Barrett announced he would run for governor. That probably, although not certainly, means that there will be only one Milwaukee district in 2002.

Cook's Call *Potentially Competitive.* Wisconsin needs to lose one seat in redistricting and Barrett's decision to run for governor in 2002 means that it is likely that his Milwaukee based district is portioned off among the surrounding districts or is merged with Jerry Kleczka's 4th District.

THE PEOPLE: Pop. 2000: 507,636; Pop. 1990: 543,607, down 6.6% 1990–2000. 50% White, 43.3% Black, 2.9% Asian, 0.4% Amer. Indian, 0.1% Hawaiian, 2.1% Two+ races, 1.3% Other; 3.3% Hispanic Origin.

2000 Presidential Vote				**1996 Presidential Vote**			
Gore (D)	153,447	(65%)		Clinton (D)	126,179	(63%)	
Bush (R)	72,230	(31%)		Dole (R)	58,560	(29%)	
Nader (Green)	7,563	(3%)		Perot (I)	10,182	(5%)	
Others	1,695	(1%)		Others	5,603	(3%)	

Rep. Tom Barrett (D)

Elected 1992, 5th term; b. Dec. 8, 1953, Milwaukee; home, Milwaukee; U. of WI, B.A. 1976, J.D., 1980; Catholic; married (Kristine).

Elected Office: WI Assembly, 1984–88; WI Senate, 1988–92.

Professional Career: FDIC bank examiner, 1977; Law Clerk, Fed. Dist. Judge Robert Warren 1980–82; Practicing atty., 1982–84.

DC Office: 1214 LHOB 20515, 202-225-3571; Fax: 202-225-2185; Web site: www.house.gov/barrett.

District Office: Milwaukee, 414-297-1331.

Committees: *Energy & Commerce* (21st of 26 D): Energy & Air Quality; Environment & Hazardous Materials; Health.

Group Ratings

	ADA	ACLU	AFS	LCV	CON	ITIC	NTU	COC	ACU	NTLC	CHC
2000	100	71	100	93	69	56	30	38	8	15	7
1999	100	—	100	100	99	—	36	12	4	—	—

National Journal Ratings

	1999 LIB	—	1999 CONS		2000 LIB	—	2000 CONS
Economic	80%	—	18%		95%	—	0%
Social	87%	—	0%		74%	—	24%
Foreign	77%	—	22%		85%	—	10%

Key Votes of the 106th Congress

1. Patient Bill of Rights	Y	5. Bar RU-486 $ for FDA	N	9. NATO War in Serbia	Y
2. Accelerate Min. Wage	Y	6. Display 10 Commandments	N	10. Perm. Trade with China	N
3. Strike Ban on Ergo. Stnd.	Y	7. Gun Show Bkgrnd. Checks	Y	11. Debt Relief for 3rd World	Y
4. Ovrd. Estate Tax Veto	N	8. Ban Part.-Birth Abortion	Y	12. Drop Cuba Econ. Embargo	Y

Election Results

2000 general	Tom Barrett (D)	173,893	(78%)	($221,766)
	Jonathan Smith (R)	49,296	(22%)	($16,339)
2000 primary	Tom Barrett (D)	unopposed		
1998 general	Tom Barrett (D)	121,129	(78%)	($139,501)
	Jack Melvin (R)	33,506	(22%)	

SIXTH DISTRICT

Central Wisconsin is solid country, a producer of basic commodities—milk, butter and cheese, paper products, Mirro pots and pans, Mercury outboard motors and Kleenex. Settled first by Yankee Protestants, it was one of the birthplaces of the Republican Party in February 1854, when a group of Whigs, Free Soilers and Democrats met in a small white schoolhouse in Ripon, Wisconsin, and proclaimed themselves Republicans; Jackson, Michigan, also claims to be the birthplace of the party. Whichever, the party grew rapidly, winning a near-majority in the House in the 1854 elections. But Republican roots here are not just Yankee. The 1850s brought the first surge of German migration into the United States, and central Wisconsin was a favorite destination. Here they built the dairy farms and factory towns that seemed steadfastly prosperous 50 years ago, and are now part of a manufacturing boom. Here also was the testing ground, in Fond du Lac County, of Governor Tommy Thompson's W-2 welfare reform; the welfare rolls there, never high, fell to zero after the program began in 1997.

The 6th Congressional District, which cuts a swath across Wisconsin from Manitowoc on Lake Michigan through Oshkosh and Ripon west almost to the Mississippi River, includes country that has voted Republican almost without interruption since that first meeting in Ripon. It has also elected Republican congressmen who have come up with thoughtful and original solutions to problems. One was William Steiger, first elected in 1966, whose chief monuments are the all-volunteer military and the 1978 Steiger amendment cutting capital gains tax rates—considerable accomplishments for a member of the minority party, and for one who died at age 40 in 1978.

The congressman from the 6th District is Tom Petri, a Republican first elected in the 1979 contest to succeed Steiger. Petri grew up in Fond du Lac, went to Harvard, was a Peace Corps volunteer in Somalia and was elected to the state Senate in 1972, at 32. In 1974 he was the Republican nominee against Senator Gaylord Nelson; he walked across the state campaigning but in that Democratic year lost 62%–36%. When he ran for the House, Petri beat Tommy Thompson in the primary 35%–19% and then won the special with 50.4%.

Some of Petri's ideas have been adopted. He long boosted the Earned Income Tax Credit, which results in payments to low-income people who work, targeting aid to families much better than the minimum wage; the Clinton administration agreed and increased the EITC when Democrats were in control, then dragged out the tattered arguments for the minimum wage when they wanted an issue to bash Republicans in 1996. Petri called for expanding the EITC concept with a $1,000 tax credit per child, in place of the current deduction; Congress and Bill Clinton agreed on a $500 per child credit, leaving the deduction in place. In 2000, he called for expanding the EITC to coordinate it with other programs for the poor, including housing subsidies and Medicaid. Petri favors making college loans repayable in amounts regulated by post-college earnings; Clinton adopted this in his direct student loan program. Other Petri successes have been stopping the Auburn Dam near Sacramento and slowing down the Animas-Las Palata water project in southwest Colorado—"dinosaurs," he calls them.

Some Petri reforms have been pretty much ignored. He would withdraw health care deductibility and substitute "Multicare," a fixed subsidy for catastrophic coverage, allowing people or employers to buy more insurance if they like. His campaign finance reform bill would include a 50% tax credit for up to $200 in contributions. He would privatize deposit insurance, on the theory that private insurers are better at spotting risks than government regulators. To supplement Social Security, he would provide every newborn with $1,000 in a tax-free retirement savings account; the miracle of compound interest over 67 years would pay for most of today's promised Social Security benefits, he says. Petri disdains "the outdated relic of Soviet-style central planning that is our federal dairy program." He is dismayed by the Northeast Dairy Compact's cartel and the exclusion of Wisconsin milk from other markets by the Eau Claire pricing system.

As chairman of the Surface Transportation Subcommittee, Petri played a major role in shaping the 1998 transportation bill. He strongly supported Chairman Bud Shuster's move to require all gas tax revenues to be taken off-budget and used for transportation; he passed an amendment raising Wisconsin's return on its gas tax dollars, which meant a 54% increase for the state. He brokered a compromise in the dispute between the city of Milwaukee—whose Mayor John Norquist has long opposed freeways and wanted to spend money on a light-rail system—and the state of Wisconsin, whose Governor Tommy Thompson wanted to rebuild the Marquette Interchange. He took credit for $4 million to widen Highway 10 to improve the link between Appleton and Stevens Point. On his subcommittee he also worked on natural gas and oil pipeline safety and safer transportation of hazardous materials. On education, his bid in 1999 to create vouchers for low-income students to go to private schools was defeated by Democrats and Republicans fearful of a Clinton veto.

Petri has usually been re-elected easily. In 2000 he faced his best-financed challenger in many years when Democrat Dan Flaherty, a former federal and state prosecutor, raised more than $200,000 and criticized Petri's support for "massive tax cuts." Petri won 65%–35%, carrying all 14 counties comfortably. But his career suffered a stinging setback in January 2001 when Republican leaders bypassed him for John Boehner in filling the vacancy for chairman on Education and the Workforce. Petri, who had seemed confident that he would prevail, argued that he was the most experienced member of the committee and deserved the chairmanship. But Republican leaders worried that he would be too quick to cooperate with Democrats on George W. Bush's education program. As consolation, he remained chairman of the renamed Highways and Transit Subcommittee. Perhaps in a display of his unhappiness with Republican and business leaders, Petri was one of 13 House Republicans in March 2001 to vote against repeal of Clinton's ergonomic regulations; the others were chiefly from heavily-labor districts. Like most other Wisconsin members, redistricting poses risks—in Petri's case because his district is the center of the state and could be sacrificed in pieces to neighboring districts.

Cook's Call   *Safe.* This district is pretty marginal at the national level (Bush won here with 53% in 2000, Clinton by 4% in 1996) and Democrats argue that the right candidate could give Petri a real race. It needs to pick up residents in redistricting, but it is not yet clear if that will make this seat more competitive.

THE PEOPLE: Pop. 2000: 606,416; Pop. 1990: 543,531, up 11.6% 1990–2000. 96.1% White, 0.8% Black, 1.1% Asian, 0.5% Amer. Indian, 0.8% Two+ races, 0.7% Other; 1.8% Hispanic Origin.

2000 Presidential Vote			**1996 Presidential Vote**		
Bush (R)	150,127	(53%)	Clinton (D)	108,004	(45%)
Gore (D)	122,374	(43%)	Dole (R)	99,650	(41%)
Nader (Green)	9,483	(3%)	Perot (I)	28,459	(12%)
Others	3,226	(1%)	Others	4,280	(2%)

Rep. Thomas E. Petri (R)

Elected Apr. 1979, 11th term; b. May 28, 1940, Marinette; home, Fond du Lac; Harvard U., B.A. 1962, J.D. 1965; Lutheran; married (Anne).

Elected Office: WI Senate, 1972–79.

Professional Career: Peace Corps, Somalia, 1966–67; Law Clerk, Fed. Judge James Doyle, 1965–66; White House aide, 1969; Practicing atty., 1970–79.

DC Office: 2462 RHOB 20515, 202-225-2476; Fax: 202-225-2356; Web site: www.house.gov/petri.

District Offices: Fond du Lac, 920-922-1180; Oshkosh, 920-231-6333.

Committees: *Education & the Workforce* (2d of 27 R): Education Reform; Select Education. *Transportation & Infrastructure* (2d of 42 R): Aviation; Highways & Transit (Chmn.); Railroads.

Group Ratings

	ADA	ACLU	AFS	LCV	CON	ITIC	NTU	COC	ACU	NTLC	CHC
2000	10	21	14	36	69	94	65	76	84	85	87
1999	20	—	16	19	65	—	71	88	80	—	—

National Journal Ratings

	1999 LIB —	1999 CONS		2000 LIB —	2000 CONS
Economic	37%	— 61%		41%	— 58%
Social	40%	— 59%		0%	— 79%
Foreign	23%	— 73%		49%	— 49%

Key Votes of the 106th Congress

1. Patient Bill of Rights	N	5. Bar RU-486 $ for FDA	Y	9. NATO War in Serbia	N
2. Accelerate Min. Wage	N	6. Display 10 Commandments	Y	10. Perm. Trade with China	Y
3. Strike Ban on Ergo. Stnd.	Y	7. Gun Show Bkgrnd. Checks	N	11. Debt Relief for 3rd World	N
4. Ovrd. Estate Tax Veto	Y	8. Ban Part.-Birth Abortion	Y	12. Drop Cuba Econ. Embargo	N

Election Results

2000 general	Thomas E. Petri (R)	179,205	(65%)	($703,496)
	Dan Flaherty (D)	96,125	(35%)	($213,059)
2000 primary	Thomas E. Petri (R)	31,113	(87%)	
	John L. Moder (R)	4,713	(13%)	
1998 general	Thomas E. Petri (R)	144,144	(93%)	($279,748)
	Timothy J. Farness (TXP)	11,267	(7%)	

SEVENTH DISTRICT

In the late 19th Century, on the rail lines radiating northwest from Chicago and Milwaukee, came thousands of migrants whose descendants have made the northern reaches of Wisconsin the most thickly settled land this far north in the United States east of the Mississippi. What brought people up so far was not cropland—there are no industrial-sized wheat farms as in the Red River Valley of North Dakota—but trees, iron and cows. This was one of America's largest virgin timberlands, and the river towns are still dotted with paper mills. Farther north, iron brought Finns and Italians to the port of Superior, Wisconsin, right next to Duluth, Minnesota, and to smaller towns on the chilly lake. Then on the cleared forestlands came dairy farms. Dairy cattle, properly cared for, thrive in these northern uplands, and the sons of Wisconsin dairymen, many of them immigrants from Germany and Norway, moved their dairy herds even farther north. On this base small cities grew, some with big enterprises. Wausau has paper mills and Wausau Insurance, Wisconsin Rapids has Georgia-Pacific, and Stevens Point has Sentry Insurance.

All these places are in Wisconsin's 7th Congressional District, which stretches from Stevens Point in the south to Lake Superior in the north. The politics of northern Wisconsin and the 7th District has a rough-hewn quality, a certain lumberjack populist flavor. Ancestrally Republican, this area favored the progressivism of the LaFollettes. Today, Superior and Stevens Point are heavily Democratic, while much of the country in between leans Republican. This district twice gave pluralities to Bill Clinton and in 2000 it voted 48%–46% for Al Gore.

The congressman from the 7th District is David Obey, a Democrat first elected in April 1969. Chairman of the Appropriations Committee from March 1994 to January 1995, and since then ranking minority member, he is one of the most capable and strongly motivated legislators on either side of the aisle. He grew up in Wausau, where his father worked in a roofing factory; he started off as a Republican, but was influenced by history teacher Arthur Henderson—who assigned papers on the politics of the 1920s and was attacked by McCarthyites—and between 1952 and 1956 Obey switched from supporting Dwight Eisenhower and Joe McCarthy to Adlai Stevenson and William Proxmire. By 1962, when he was 24, Obey was elected to the Wisconsin Assembly even before he got his master's degree. When Melvin Laird resigned his House seat to become Richard Nixon's Defense secretary, Obey won an upset in the April 1969 special election.

In the state legislature, Obey was inspired by older New Deal Democrats who fought hard for the little guy; when he entered the House, the driving energy came from liberal Democrats opposed to the Vietnam war. Obey preserves something of the force of each group. He is not a sentimental liberal: He has a prickly personality and a vigorous temper and does not suffer gladly those he considers fools or knaves. But he can leaven that with humor: he likes to quote Archy the Cockroach, the supposed writer of Don Marquis's *Archy and Mehitabel*, and he is part of a band called The Capitol Offenses, which plays rock music and hymns. Even as he has moved to the top of the seniority ladder, Obey has retained his sense of outrage and his eagerness to fight for what he believes in—a quality that even some Democrats complain has been too intense. But he continues to display abundant energy and leadership on a host of fronts. In the mid-1970s he chaired a special committee on ethics, pushing through a code requiring detailed disclosure of personal finances and limiting outside income: this was not forgiven by some of the oldtimers. From 1979 well into the 1980s he was the chief sponsor of campaign finance bills to limit PAC contributions, reduce individual donations and provide public financing. But he has come to believe that current campaign finance bills will make little difference so long as the "senile old men" of the Supreme Court continue to rule that political spending is speech protected by the First Amendment. In 1991 the office of House administrator was created—something Obey proposed 16 years before, and a recommendation that might have saved a lot of House Democrats and some House Republicans much trouble if it had been followed earlier. He had his disappointments. He lost the Budget Committee chairmanship to Oklahoma's Jim Jones in 1980 by 121–116. In 1984 he wanted to become Democratic Caucus chairman, but demurred when it became clear that Dick Gephardt had the votes. Even so, informally Obey became a key leader of liberal Democrats, in 1989 pushing Gephardt for majority leader when Jim Wright and Tony Coelho were resigning, and in 1990 pushing a rules change requiring Ways and Means subcommittee chairmen to be elected by the whole caucus.

Obey remains a true believer in traditional liberalism, in Keynesian economics and economic redistribution. He thinks that government should provide economic security, create jobs and build infrastructure through public investment, that it should control health care costs and guarantee coverage and a choice of providers. In 1994 he wanted to give the president power to lower taxes to counterbalance Federal Reserve interest rate increases, and stood ready to back middle-class tax cuts even as the economy by some measures was growing smartly. In two stints as chairman of the Joint Economic Committee, he prepared studies arguing that Reagan-Bush policies enriched the rich and hurt the middle class. He has bucked the Democratic leadership on behalf of principle, leading the opposition to the 1990 budget summit package. He also bucked the Clinton administration, vocally opposing NAFTA and, when Clinton seemed to be backing away from universal health care coverage in July 1994, said "then I will walk away from the Clinton health care plan" and supported his real preference, a single-payer system. In June 1995, when Clinton accepted the Republicans' goal of a budget balanced in seven years, Obey immediately issued a written statement reading, "I think most of us learned some time ago that if you don't like the president's position on a particular issue you simply need to wait a few weeks." Or months—Obey was pleased when Clinton started vetoing Republican appropriations bills in the fall. Obey also opposes some administration positions from the right. He has long opposed abortion, and backs the partial-birth abortion ban; he opposes gun control, and once pointed out that one of the guns singled out in the assault weapons ban was owned by 23,000 residents of the 7th District, including two sheriffs.

Obey is above all an appropriator, and takes some justifiable pride in his skill at this work. He first got his seat on Appropriations in August 1969, when he was just 30; when he became chairman, in March 1994, he was the youngest person to hold the post since James Good of Iowa in 1919. Obey has shown great skill, plus a determination to get things done on time—which is not always how appropriating works. For years much of his work was on the Foreign Operations Subcommittee, which he chaired from 1985–95. This panel handles rather small sums of money but deals with some very sensitive issues, and it was often rocked in disputes about aid to the Nicaraguan Contras, the pace of negotiations in the Middle East, the treatment of the liberated nations of Eastern Europe. Obey was inclined to think the Camp David agreements committed too much aid to Egypt and Israel and wanted to see more spent on humanitarian assistance. Obey has not always gotten his way, but in each case he worked to move appropriations bills forward in an orderly manner. He passed separate foreign operations appropriation bills nine out of 10 years, something that had only been accomplished twice in 10 years by his predecessors. Similarly, when Obey became chairman of the full committee, all 13 appropriations bills were signed into law prior to the beginning of the new fiscal year for the first time in 47 years; it hasn't happened since.

Obey's climb to the chairmanship was sudden. In January 1993 Jamie Whitten, whose health was impaired, was voted out after 14 years as chairman. William Natcher, holder of the record for consecutive roll call votes, performed ably for a year, but then his health visibly failed in January 1994. When he died in March 1994, Obey challenged the next Democrat in line, 74-year-old Neal Smith of Iowa. Smith had the support of other "cardinals," but Obey had more from non-committee liberals and less senior members, and won in the Democratic Caucus 152–106. But Obey was not as partisan as some may have hoped. "Our mission has been fairly well defined by circumstances," he said. "We've been trying to dig out of the Reagan-era deficits and manage the downsizing of programs while freeing up a tiny bit for the president's programs, and I want to do that in the most collegial and bipartisan way." Despite some loud arguments—both men are known for their tempers—Obey and Chairman Bob Livingston managed to work together on numerous occasions, sometimes to reach agreement, often to frame disagreement in orderly choices for other members; and he has worked amicably with Livingston's successor Bill Young. Along the way Obey has succeeded on some favorite causes—funding assistance for dairy farmers, promoting the National Endowment for the Arts, opposing nine new B-2 stealth bombers. He fought the May 1998 transportation bill, even though it increased funds for Wisconsin, because it took transportation spending off-budget, and beyond the reach of appropriators. He has opposed holding up appropriations on what he considers extraneous issues. In June 1999 he chastised the Republican leadership for "not facing up to budget reality" by sticking to the "fictional" budget caps; of course these make life difficult for appropriators. He and other committee members voted against a June 2000 amendment by Wisconsin Republican Paul Ryan to create a "spending accountability" lockbox of funds cut by appropriations subcommittees; appropriators argued that this would make it impossible to negotiate compromises with the Senate.

Obey is not one of those appropriators who load up their districts with earmarked projects, though he has supported some. But he has paid close attention to district interests. He and Senator Tom Daschle effectively killed the Clinton administration's ban on snowmobiles on federal lands; snowmobiling is popular in the long winters of northern Wisconsin, and many locals complained about the legislature's 50 mile per hour nighttime speed limit on snowmobiles. More important is the plight of Wisconsin dairy farmers; since 1937 the Agriculture Department has fixed milk prices by a formula that allows higher prices the farther a farm is from Eau Claire, Wisconsin. This increases prices to consumers, creates an oversupply of milk and reduces dairy prices in the Upper Midwest. Further aggravating the problem is the Northeast Daily Compact, which allows the new England states to set even higher prices. Obey and Senator Herb Kohl on their respective Appropriations Committees have worked for emergency aid for Wisconsin dairy farmers. In 1998 they got $200 million, in 1999, $125 million, and in October 2000 they got $473 million, targeted toward small family farmers. Farmers with 150 cows would get the maximum of $12,922. "This much-needed help isn't going to solve anyone's problems, but it will at least help those family farmers across Wisconsin who are fighting to keep their farms and put food on their tables," Obey said. His long-term proposal is for national pooling of high-priced fluid milk receipts, elimination of the federal milk marketing system and an end to milk marketing orders— a return to a free market in milk. But Obey has also sought to require labeling of cheese made of imported ultra-filtered milk and reporting of inspections to see that imported milk protein concentrates are not being used in cheese.

Obey has been re-elected fairly routinely, though in 1994 Republican Scott West held him to a 54%–46% margin. West ran twice more, and Obey's percentage rose each time. In 2000, against a candidate known as "Wrong Sean" from his previous work as a weathercaster, Obey won 63%–37%, carrying every county.

Cook's Call *Safe*. Despite the marginal nature of this district at the national level, Obey is well entrenched here.

THE PEOPLE: Pop. 2000: 582,884; Pop. 1990: 543,569, up 7.2% 1990–2000. 95.2% White, 0.3% Black, 1.7% Asian, 1.7% Amer. Indian, 0.9% Two + races, 0.3% Other; 0.9% Hispanic Origin.

2000 Presidential Vote			1996 Presidential Vote		
Gore (D)	134,085	(48%)	Clinton (D)	119,984	(49%)
Bush (R)	130,173	(46%)	Dole (R)	86,374	(35%)
Nader (Green)	12,444	(4%)	Perot (I)	34,328	(14%)
Others	3,728	(1%)	Others	5,257	(2%)

Rep. David R. Obey (D)

Elected Apr. 1969, 16th term; b. Oct. 3, 1938, Okmulgee, OK; home, Wausau; U. of WI, B.S. 1960, M.A., 1962; Catholic; married (Joan).

Elected Office: WI Assembly, 1962–69.

Professional Career: Asst., family-run supper club & motel, 1962–68.

DC Office: 2314 RHOB 20515, 202-225-3365; Web site: www.house.gov/obey.

District Offices: Superior, 715-398-4426; Wausau, 715-842-5606.

Committees: *Appropriations* (RMM of 29 D): Labor, HHS & Education (RMM).

Group Ratings

	ADA	ACLU	AFS	LCV	CON	ITIC	NTU	COC	ACU	NTLC	CHC
2000	95	57	100	79	81	41	32	15	4	12	27
1999	90	—	100	94	97	—	33	4	4	—	—

National Journal Ratings

	1999 LIB —	1999 CONS		2000 LIB —	2000 CONS
Economic	88% —	0%		85% —	11%
Social	66% —	34%		74% —	26%
Foreign	92% —	8%		97% —	0%

Key Votes of the 106th Congress

1. Patient Bill of Rights	Y	5. Bar RU-486 $ for FDA	N	9. NATO War in Serbia	*
2. Accelerate Min. Wage	Y	6. Display 10 Commandments	Y	10. Perm. Trade with China	N
3. Strike Ban on Ergo. Stnd.	Y	7. Gun Show Bkgrnd. Checks	N	11. Debt Relief for 3rd World	Y
4. Ovrd. Estate Tax Veto	N	8. Ban Part.-Birth Abortion	Y	12. Drop Cuba Econ. Embargo	Y

Election Results

2000 general	David R. Obey (D)	173,007	(63%)	($1,085,618)
	Sean Cronin (R)	100,264	(37%)	($192,479)
2000 primary	David R. Obey (D)	unopposed		
1998 general	David R. Obey (D)	115,613	(61%)	($848,023)
	Scott West (R)	75,049	(39%)	($71,534)

EIGHTH DISTRICT

In 1673, the French explorer and priest Father Marquette sailed from the open waters of Lake Michigan into what is now Green Bay. He had hoped to find the Northwest Passage to the Pacific. He actually found the Fox River, which leads to Lake Winnebago and, after a not-too-difficult portage, the Wisconsin River, which flows into the Mississippi. Green Bay and the Fox River Valley remained mostly wilderness and Indian country for more than 150 years. But once settled by Europeans, they became, as Father Marquette would have liked, one of the most heavily Catholic parts of the United States, though Indians still remain a presence; there was a long dispute over Chippewa Indian spearfishing rights and Green Bay's best hotel is now next to the Oneida Indian casino. This is a thriving area economically, with traditional paper mills joined by high-skill manufacturing in Green Bay and the Fox River Valley. And it thrived even more psychically, after the 1997 Super Bowl victory of the Green Bay Packers, the only community-owned franchise in the National Football League.

The 8th Congressional District of Wisconsin includes Green Bay and the Fox River Valley south to Appleton. It also includes several north woods and dairy counties inland, plus the Door County peninsula that juts out into Lake Michigan, a favorite summer vacation spot for Chicago and Milwaukee families. Politically, this has often been malleable country. Democrats, especially Catholics, can win here: John Kennedy carried the Fox River Valley in the primary and general election in 1960, and Bill Clinton carried it in 1996. But the 8th District more often votes Repulican; it voted for George W. Bush by 52%–44% in 2000.

The congressman from the 8th District is Mark Green, a Republican elected in 1998, the only Republican to beat a Democratic incumbent that year. Green grew up in the Green Bay area; his father was from South Africa and his mother from Britain. In high school and college he was a champion swimmer; after graduating from the University of Wisconsin at Eau Claire and UW Law School in Madison, he and his wife spent a year in Kenya, working in a WorldTeach program. He practiced law and in 1992, at 32, was elected to the Wisconsin Assembly, where he became Republican Caucus chairman. In 1998 he challenged freshman Democratic Congressman Jay Johnson, a former TV news anchor. Green brought a conceptual framework to his campaign. He listed 55 issues on which he would vote differently from Johnson, one for each day between the primary and general election; they ranged from taxes and spending to education to abortion and defense. It was a solidly conservative platform, in opposition to Johnson's moderate-to-liberal voting record. Green called for "restoration of American values," an end to partial-birth abortions, scrapping the tax code, increasing local control of education, and tougher crime laws. He carefully avoided any reference to the Clinton-Lewinsky scandal or to impeachment, saying that he had called for Clinton's resignation only to get the issue out of the way. He called for limits on out-of-state political contributions, and bringing troops home from Bosnia. He ran an ad showing himself with a halo (he checked with a minister on the propriety of this) saying that he was willing to scrap "the temple of big government's" holy book, the Internal Revenue Code.

Johnson made patients' rights a major issue and responded to the halo ad with an ad attacking Green for backing a $350,000 cap on jury awards in medical malpractice cases: "Green's a politician who took thousands in campaign cash from insurance companies, and voted to protect doctors who commit malpractice—even if they were drunk or on drugs. . . . Mark Green has a tarnished halo and can't be trusted." To that Green responded with an ad showing people watching TV in a diner, with a waitress disgustedly turning off the TV as Johnson's anti-halo ad was playing, saying he wasn't the "nice guy" she had thought. Johnson tried to stress the accomplishments of the 105th Congress—the first balanced budget in 30 years, tax cuts, IRS reform. But other Democrats called his campaign unfocused. Nor did he have the incumbent's usual financial advantage. Johnson spent $830,000, Green $823,000. Some 70% of Johnson's money was from PACs, mostly from unions—indeed no other House candidate in the country relied so heavily on PACs—which undercut his claim to be for campaign finance reform. But Johnson's greatest problem was that the 8th is not a very Democratic district: It had previously elected only three Democratic congressmen in the 20th Century, two of whom were defeated for re-election and another who lost a race for a third term. In November 1998 the 8th District went heavily for Governor Tommy Thompson and voted 55%–44% for Republican Mark Neumann over Senator Russ Feingold. Green won 54%–46%.

In the House, Green's voting record leans conservative, though he is more moderate on foreign policy issues. Majority Leader Dick Armey called him one of the Republicans' most "entrepreneurial" legislators. "My focus is on getting things done," Green said. His achievements included enactment of his "disabled housing initiative," a HUD pilot program that seeks to raise the fewer than 5% of individuals with disabilities who own homes. "It will genuinely improve the lives of disabled citizens in America," Green said. He also won approval of his bill to make it easier for tribal colleges to apply for federal aid and requires fairer distribution of funds to tribal colleges. He favors a "two strikes, you're out" law with imprisonment for repeat sex offenders who target children, similar to a requirement he passed in Wisconsin. He criticized House leaders for their decision in 1999 to continue the "anti-market" dairy system. In January 2001 he made a week-long visit to U.S.-backed education programs in Mali and Ghana and returned convinced that such programs are a "win-win" for both sides.

Green cemented the return of his district to Republican control when he won re-election by a 75%–25% margin over a Democrat who was a vocal opponent of the sales-tax increase to renovate Lambeau Field for the Packers. Redistricting is not likely to cause major change. Green didn't deny reports that he was interested in running statewide, though not necessarily in 2002.

Cook's Call   *Safe.* Green has not done anything to put himself in political jeopardy. But his statewide political ambitions (Green has been suggested as a candidate for both governor and attorney general) mean that this seat may be open in the near future.

THE PEOPLE: Pop. 2000: 617,575; Pop. 1990: 543,526, up 13.6% 1990–2000. 92.8% White, 0.7% Black, 1.5% Asian, 2.9% Amer. Indian, 1.1% Two+ races, 1% Other; 2.2% Hispanic Origin.

2000 Presidential Vote		
Bush (R)	152,703	(52%)
Gore (D)	129,155	(44%)
Nader (Green)	9,682	(3%)
Others	3,241	(1%)

1996 Presidential Vote		
Clinton (D)	116,073	(46%)
Dole (R)	105,131	(41%)
Perot (I)	28,567	(11%)
Others	3,862	(2%)

Rep. Mark Green (R)

Elected 1998, 2d term; b. June 1, 1960, Boston, MA; home, Green Bay; U. of WI, B.A. 1983, J.D. 1987; Catholic; married (Sue).

Elected Office: WI Assembly, 1992–98.

Professional Career: Teacher, Africa, 1988–89; Practicing atty., 1988–92.

DC Office: 1218 LHOB 20515, 202-225-5665; Fax: 202-225-5729; Web site: www.house.gov/markgreen.

District Offices: Antigo, 715-627-1511; Appleton, 920-380-0061; Green Bay, 920-437-1954.

Committees: *Financial Services* (25th of 37 R): Domestic Monetary Policy, Technology & Economic Growth; Housing & Community Opportunity (Vice Chmn.); International Monetary Policy & Trade. *Judiciary* (17th of 21 R): Commercial & Administrative Law; Crime.

Group Ratings

	ADA	ACLU	AFS	LCV	CON	ITIC	NTU	COC	ACU	NTLC	CHC
2000	5	29	14	14	75	89	64	85	84	82	100
1999	5	—	0	13	87	—	72	92	87	—	—

National Journal Ratings

	1999 LIB —	1999 CONS	2000 LIB —	2000 CONS
Economic	0%	84%	18%	76%
Social	29%	69%	0%	79%
Foreign	37%	62%	45%	53%

Key Votes of the 106th Congress

1. Patient Bill of Rights	N	5. Bar RU-486 $ for FDA	Y	9. NATO War in Serbia	N
2. Accelerate Min. Wage	N	6. Display 10 Commandments	Y	10. Perm. Trade with China	Y
3. Strike Ban on Ergo. Stnd.	N	7. Gun Show Bkgrnd. Checks	N	11. Debt Relief for 3rd World	N
4. Ovrd. Estate Tax Veto	Y	8. Ban Part.-Birth Abortion	Y	12. Drop Cuba Econ. Embargo	N

Election Results

2000 general	Mark Green (R)	211,388	(75%)	($553,153)
	Dean Reich (D)	71,575	(25%)	($13,904)
2000 primary	Mark Green (R)	unopposed		
1998 general	Mark Green (R)	112,418	(55%)	($847,692)
	Jay Johnson (D)	93,441	(45%)	($850,577)

NINTH DISTRICT

For decades, the orderly, heavily German-American factory city of Milwaukee has been spreading slowly, mostly west and north, into Wisconsin dairy country. There are high-income enclaves here, like close-in Elm Grove and Oconomowoc spread out around its lakes. There is office development in Brookfield; subdivisions spread out in Mequon and Menomonee Falls and farther, to reach small towns with roots deep in the 19th Century. This is comfortable but not fancy territory, and the economy here is still based heavily on skilled manufacturing. Not far from Milwaukee are Sheboygan, home of Kohler plumbing fixtures; Port Washington, with Allen-Edmonds shoes; West Bend, with West Bend kitchen appliances; Pewaukee, with Quad/Graphics printing.

The 9th Congressional District of Wisconsin includes most of the western, northwestern and northern suburbs of Milwaukee and spreads out into dairy farm country and to these factory towns. The large majority of precincts here vote Republican, and this is usually the most Republican district in the state; it voted 63%–34% for George W. Bush in 2000.

The congressman from the 9th District, James Sensenbrenner, first elected in 1978, is one of the most senior Republicans in the House. His Wisconsin roots are strong—his great-grandfather was a founder of Kimberly-Clark—and Sensenbrenner is among the richest members of Congress, and one of the few who lists his net worth ($10.2 million in 1999) and investments with meticulous detail every year. In December 1997 he won $250,000 in the District of Columbia lottery after buying two tickets at a Capitol Hill liquor store. "It was an impulse purchase. I was purchasing Wisconsin beer for my office's Christmas party, and I paid $2 for two Quick Cash tickets," Sensenbrenner explained. When he turned in the ticket and found he had won considerably more than the $10 he expected, he splurged and bought an $85 bottle of champagne. But the National Taxpayers Union Foundation labels him, approvingly, the second cheapest member of the House for his votes against spending.

Sensenbrenner grew up in the Milwaukee area, graduated from Stanford and the University of Wisconsin Law School and has spent most of his adult life in politics, briefly as a U.S. House staffer, and then serving 10 years in the Wisconsin legislature from 1968–78. For almost all that time, Sensenbrenner has been in the minority, gamely undertaking the Sisyphean task of moving amendments certain to lose. But he has persevered out of a dogged sense of principle. His voting record is mostly conservative, but not entirely. He supported the Brady bill, but led the fight against the assault weapons ban and voted for the Dingell amendment in June 1999. He was an original co-sponsor and floor manager of the Defense of Marriage Act, to let states refuse to recognize same-sex marriage if courts rule them legal in other states.

Sensenbrenner is chairman of the House Judiciary Committee, taking that position in January 2001 after the Republican Steering Committee declined to give Henry Hyde an exemption from the Republicans' six-year term limit on chairmanships. He immediately moved to reduce the number of hearings, which members had complained about, and to rein in subcommittee chairmen; they must give reasons in writing before holding subcommittee hearings. He helped to manage the bankruptcy reform measure to passage by 306–108 in March 2001, noting that "Every dollar that is written off in a bankruptcy is a dollar that's added to the cost of goods and services that are paid for by people who pay their bills." Prompted by the Microsoft case, he called for a commission to examine the antitrust laws, particularly the role of intellectual property, the global economy and the role of state attorneys general; it would report in three years. He signaled his skepticism about the intellectual property rights claims of the recording industry. Several years before, he moved to exempt from royalty fees small restaurants and bars that play recorded music; this issue aroused him when ASCAP auditors converged on Pewaukee Lake bars and demanded payments. Persevering, he negotiated in October 1998 an exemption for small businesses under 2,000 square feet and restaurants and bars under 3,750 square feet. "It was Main Street versus Hollywood and Nashville. And Main Street won," he said. He has promised hearings on the issues raised by the Napster case after it had ended, but of the operations of ASCAP and BMI he has said, "Sounds like an antitrust violation to me."

Sensenbrenner played a major role on Bill Clinton's impeachment. He has long been a stickler for ethics, and was one of the first to urge that Congress apply to itself the laws it imposes on the rest of the country. He served on the ethics committee in the early 1980s, when in the Abscam case the committee recommended and secured the first expulsions from the House since the Civil War era. In 1989 he helped to prosecute Judge Walter Nixon for perjury; in 1995 he sought to expel Congressman Walter Tucker for tax evasion and extortion, who resigned before the House could act. In 1994 he prepared motions to censure or expel Dan Rostenkowski if he pleaded guilty to any crimes—one reason, perhaps, why he did not. "I have a rather low tolerance for official misconduct. I've been extremely consistent on that," he noted dryly in 1998. Sensenbrenner seemed clearly inclined to vote for impeachment beginning in September 1998. He was one of the 13 House managers and was chosen by Hyde to lead off the managers' presentation to the Senate in January 1999. "We are here today because President William Jefferson Clinton decided to put himself above the law not once, not twice, but repeatedly," he said. Clinton "has not owned up to the false testimony, the stonewalling and legal hairsplitting and obstructing the courts from finding the truth. In doing so, he has turned his affair into a public wrong."

From 1997 to 2001 Sensenbrenner was chairman of the House Science Committee, after serving a term as chairman of its Space Subcommittee. On those bodies he has worked in a bipartisan manner with ranking Democrat George Brown. He supports the space station, which survived by a one-vote margin in 1993 and by larger margins since. He has generally supported manned space flight, but was persistently critical of the U.S.-Russia space agreement, particularly of the condition of the Russian Mir spacecraft. He was dismayed by the 1999 losses of Mars spacecraft, but generally backed NASA administrator Daniel Goldin's policy of "faster, better, cheaper" small missions. He has called for more privatization of the U.S. space program, and hailed the Pathfinder mission to Mars: "Our ecology is very fragile, and the earth is a unique place. If there ever was life on Mars, and Mars became a dead planet, finding out why that happened will be very useful in preventing something like that from happening on earth some time in the future." He was a leading critic of the December 1997 Kyoto Protocol on Climate Change. He supported without controversy federal research and development programs and in 1999 sought civil penalties for the operators of national laboratories for breaches of security.

On other issues, Sensenbrenner has spoken out strongly for Milwaukee's school choice experiment; he favors educational savings accounts and wants to replace federal K-12 regulations with block grants. He has long opposed racial quotas and preferences. He seeks repeal of the Northeast Dairy Compact, which he argues suffuses the national market with unfairly priced milk, butter and cheese. In 1999 he and Milwaukee Democrat Gerald Kleczka sought an EPA scientific study of the effects of small amounts of radium in water and criticized EPA on reformulated gas. Prompted by an airport meeting with the mayor of West Bend, Sensenbrenner got

$10 million in 1999 for the expansion of the West Bend's Wisconsin National Guard facility. He was one of the members of Congress who brought a lawsuit in May 1999 to force Bill Clinton to seek congressional approval of U.S. military action in Kosovo.

Sensenbrenner has not had a serious electoral challenge since the 1978 primary. In 2000 he was re-elected 74%–26%.

Cook's Call *Safe*. With Wisconsin losing one seat in redistricting (and with that seat possibly coming from the nearby Milwaukee area), Sensenbrenner may find his district changed in 2002. Regardless, he remains a serious favorite in 2002.

THE PEOPLE: Pop. 2000: 632,068; Pop. 1990: 543,602, up 16.3% 1990–2000. 96% White, 0.8% Black, 1.4% Asian, 0.3% Amer. Indian, 0.8% Two+ races, 0.7% Other; 2.1% Hispanic Origin.

2000 Presidential Vote			1996 Presidential Vote		
Bush (R)	210,165	(63%)	Dole (R)	141,961	(52%)
Gore (D)	112,561	(34%)	Clinton (D)	101,420	(37%)
Nader (Green)	8,822	(3%)	Perot (I)	23,437	(9%)
Others	2,681	(1%)	Others	5,477	(2%)

Rep. F. James Sensenbrenner, Jr. (R)

Elected 1978, 12th term; b. June 14, 1943, Chicago, IL; home, Menomonee Falls; Stanford U., A.B. 1965, U. of WI, J.D. 1968; Episcopalian; married (Cheryl).

Elected Office: WI Assembly, 1968–74; WI Senate, 1974–78.

Professional Career: Practicing atty., 1968–69; Staff asst., U.S. Rep. Arthur Younger, 1965.

DC Office: 2332 RHOB 20515, 202-225-5101; Fax: 202-225-3190; Web site: www.house.gov/sensenbrenner.

District Office: Brookfield, 262-784-1111.

Committees: *Judiciary* (Chmn. of 21 R).

Group Ratings

	ADA	ACLU	AFS	LCV	CON	ITIC	NTU	COC	ACU	NTLC	CHC
2000	20	29	14	21	99	78	90	70	88	88	100
1999	10	—	0	19	93	—	87	80	96	—	—

National Journal Ratings

	1999 LIB —	1999 CONS		2000 LIB —	2000 CONS
Economic	0%	— 84%		6%	— 85%
Social	16%	— 82%		0%	— 79%
Foreign	10%	— 86%		53%	— 45%

Key Votes of the 106th Congress

1. Patient Bill of Rights	N	5. Bar RU-486 $ for FDA	Y	9. NATO War in Serbia	N
2. Accelerate Min. Wage	N	6. Display 10 Commandments	Y	10. Perm. Trade with China	N
3. Strike Ban on Ergo. Stnd.	N	7. Gun Show Bkgrnd. Checks	N	11. Debt Relief for 3rd World	Y
4. Ovrd. Estate Tax Veto	Y	8. Ban Part.-Birth Abortion	Y	12. Drop Cuba Econ. Embargo	N

Election Results

2000 general	F. James Sensenbrenner Jr. (R)	239,498	(74%)	($464,515)
	Mike Clawson (D)	83,720	(26%)	($7,355)
2000 primary	F. James Sensenbrenner Jr. (R)	unopposed		
1998 general	F. James Sensenbrenner Jr. (R)	175,533	(91%)	($290,913)
	Jeffrey M. Gonyo (Ind)	16,419	(9%)	

★ WYOMING ★

Wyoming is "the land of the cowboy," as the *WPA Guide* called it 60 years ago. "Its mountains, plains, and valleys are essentially livestock country. A cowboy astride a bucking bronco greets the visitor from enameled license plates, from newspapers, magazines and painted signs." The cowboy is still on the license plates, and Wyoming remains the most western of states in spirit—largely unsettled, the least populous state, a thin veneer of civilization stretched over a forbidding and beautiful land. Wyoming "has a 'lean-to' look," writes Gretel Ehrlich. "Instead of big, roomy barns and Victorian houses, there are dugouts, low sheds, log cabins, sheep camps and fence lines that look like driftwood blown haphazardly into place. People here still feel pride because they live in such a harsh place, part of the glamorous cowboy past." "What you see now in Wyoming is the promotion of things we used to apologize for," says the state Commerce Department director. "Wide open spaces, a huge expansive sky with no pollution, uncluttered clean rivers with maybe a lone fly fisherman, a cowboy and his dog and a herd of cattle."

But Wyoming's economy now depends not on cowboys and cattle but, precariously, on mining and minerals. Wyoming boomed with oil prospectors during the energy price surge of the 1970s, but was hit hard by drops in oil prices in the early 1980s and again in the late 1990s. As the exploration for oil slumped, the production of other minerals has surged. The Clean Air Act put a premium on Wyoming's low-sulfur coal, and this is now the number one coal state, producing as much as West Virginia and Kentucky combined. The strip mines of the Powder River Basin produce 28% of the nation's coal, and a private company is building a new $1.4 billion rail line from there to the Mississippi River—the biggest U.S. rail construction project in a century. Wyoming is also the number seven oil and number five natural gas producer, and the nation's top producer of the mineral bentonite (used in oil drilling and cosmetics) and has the world's largest reserve of trona (used in glass and baking soda). But these are all capital-intensive industries, with few jobs for young people: About one-quarter of people 25 to 34 left the state in the 1990s, and about two-thirds of the graduates of the University of Wyoming leave, which means that the state's population is getting older and less educated. Wage levels, above the national average during the oil boom, are now well below. But Governor Jim Geringer, whose $21 million Wyoming Business Council has attracted eight new companies with 800 jobs, insists that, "Wyoming is going to grow."

Wyoming's second industry is now tourism. Yellowstone National Park continues to draw millions, and Jackson Hole just to the south has become one of America's elite resort areas year-round; its airport is Wyoming's busiest and the only one that accommodates jets, and Teton County is now trying to restore the Upper Snake River to its pre-levee condition with new islands and braiding. There has been growth as well in the scenic and pastoral country on the eastern slope of the Big Horn Mountains around Buffalo and Sheridan. The third industry is agriculture: Wyoming is second in the nation in wool production, third in sheep inventory and also produces sugar beets, barley, pinto beans and beef cattle.

Reliance on high-tech mineral extraction and high-end tourism may seem a contradiction of Wyoming's Old West heritage. But Wyoming has always depended on new technology to tame age-old nature. Cattle ranches after the open-range era were made possible only by the barbed wire that could fence in roaming herds, and the steam locomotives that could carry cattle to markets back east. This 19th Century high tech was brought to Wyoming by large capitalist operators, some of them onetime Texas cowhands or second sons of English landed gentry, who started the first big operations after the Civil War. And of course mining depends on high-tech machinery and responsiveness to markets that reward innovation and penalize stasis.

At the same time the old Wyoming is coming back. In the 1990s grey wolves were returned to the Yellowstone area, despite local ranchers' objections—nature edging man back just a little bit. Grizzly bears have done well enough in Yellowstone, despite hunters luring them outside the park with artificial salt licks, that they are likely to lose endangered status. The International Rocky Mountain Stage Stop Sled Race, run in daily stages over a 400-mile course, keeps Wyoming in touch with the past while promoting it for visitors. Coyote hunting contests are held to rid the

U.S. Representative elected at large.

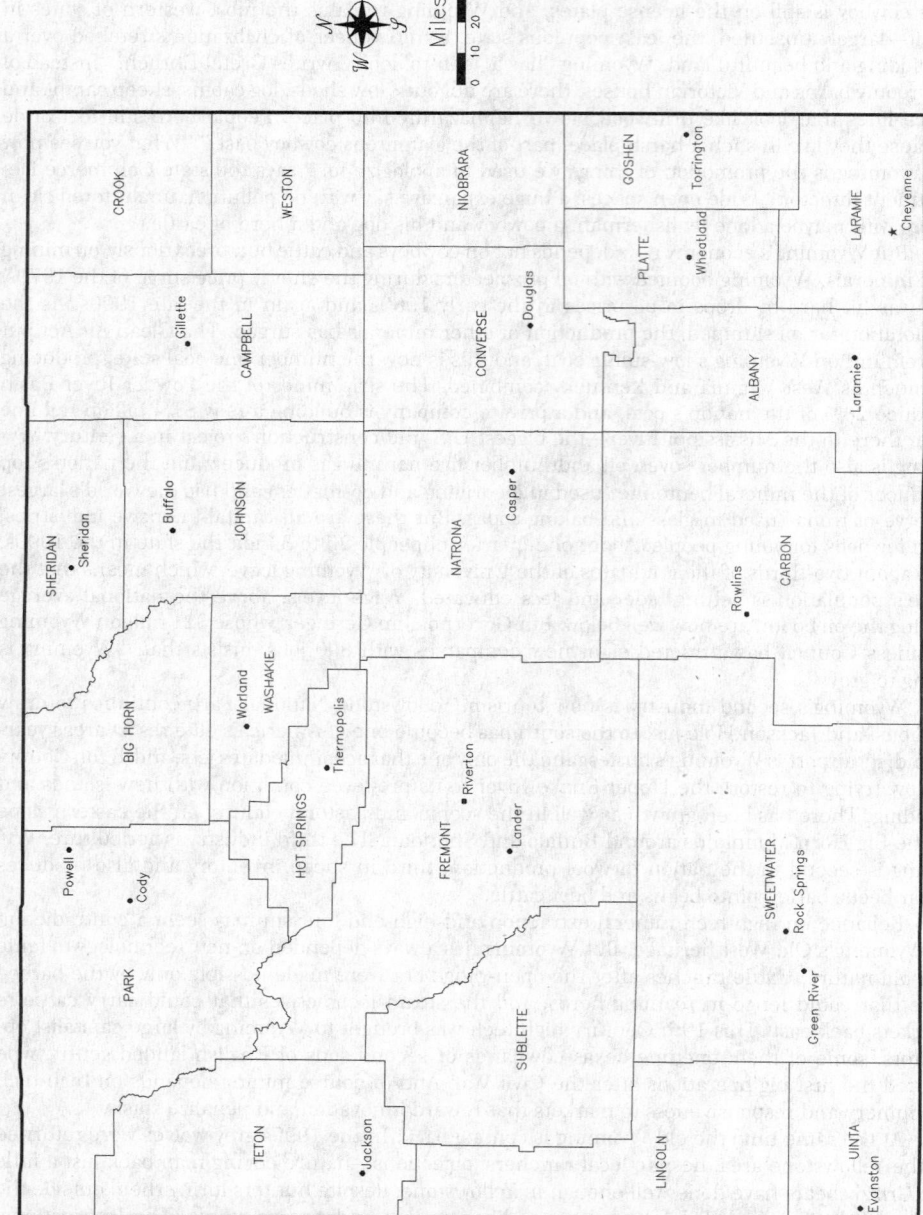

range of predators, while vandal-environmentalists cut barbed wire fences. Wyoming still is a kind of frontier: It was until recently one of the few states with more men than women—one reason it was the first part of the United States, when it was a territory in 1869, to give women the vote.

There is a settled part of Wyoming as well, in the medium-sized towns that are the state's largest cities, and among sheep and cattle ranches, sugar beet and malting barley farms and denizens of tiny settlements. This is a small state, a single community really, where people remember who played what position, when and how well, for what high-school football team; where because all locals know who your father's cousins married, you mostly live on the straight and narrow. The locals set the tone of life in Wyoming, and they were shocked and outraged in October, 1998, when Matthew Shepard, a gay student at the University of Wyoming, was gruesomely murdered; his killers were convicted and sentenced to life in prison in 1999.

There was once a sharp economic and regional split traditionally reflected in partisan politics. The big economic interests—cattle ranchers, organized in the Wyoming Stock Growers' Association, and the Union Pacific Railroad management always favored the Republicans, as did the wildcatters, independent producers and oil company geologists. The main Democratic constituency had been the Union Pacific Railroad workers who built the first transcontinental line across southern Wyoming in the 1860s; the southern tier of counties, from Cheyenne through Laramie to Evanston, once voted Democratic, but Laramie's Albany County is about the closest thing to a Democratic area left. Wyoming has been one of the most Republican states since the 1970s; it hasn't elected a Democrat to the Senate since 1970 or the House since 1976, though it has had mostly Democratic governors over that time. In presidential elections it is solidly Republican—the most Republican state in the nation in 2000, when it voted for George W. Bush and native son Dick Cheney by a 69%–28% margin.

Wyoming's Republican strength was tested in the 1990s, and has prevailed. The Clinton administration's environmental policies—proposing grazing fee increases, the reintroduction of grey wolves into Yellowstone, proposing threatened species status on the black-tailed prairie dog, banning snowmobiles in national parks, the moratorium on road building in the national parks—have not been popular here. That has hobbled even Democrats who have won state office and do well in the personal campaigning which has always remained important here: There aren't many people—not even half a million, less than the size of an average congressional district—and Wyoming voters expect to talk person-to-person with their governors, senators and congressmen every few years. Democrat Mike Sullivan was elected governor twice and had high job ratings. But nonetheless in 1994 he lost the Senate race 59%–39% to Congressman-at-Large Craig Thomas. Democrat Kathy Karpan became popular as secretary of State. But she lost the governorship to Jim Geringer in 1994 59%–40% and a Senate race to Mike Enzi in 1996, 54%–42%. Since then Republicans have continued to win: Geringer was re-elected 56%–40% in 1998, and in 2000 Thomas by 74%–22%, and Congresswoman-at-Large Barbara Cubin by 67%–29%. And Wyoming seems to be getting more Republican; Bush-Cheney won by only 56%–42% among voters over 65 but by 81%–17% by those under 30.

Governor   Jim Geringer, the governor of Wyoming, grew up in Wheatland, where his father, a Volga German, had immigrated early in the century. That was his Old West background; his high-tech experience came from service in the Air Force, where he worked on Air Force and NASA space boosters for 10 years. In 1977, Geringer returned to Wyoming, started from scratch and bought his own farm. He was elected to the state legislature in 1982. In 1994, when incumbent Mike Sullivan ran for the Senate, Geringer ran for governor. He won the four-way Republican primary with 43%, then beat Secretary of State Kathy Karpan in the general by 59%–40%, carrying all but one county.

Geringer says his goal is to use Wyoming's mineral resources and low taxes to build a more diversified, high-tech economy. But state government is highly dependent on volatile mineral revenues. In 1998 Geringer merged the state Commerce Department and other agencies into a Wyoming Business Council, to be run by a business with a 15-member board of directors and an economic development specialist as chief executive. He emphasizes that Wyoming is the cheapest state to do business in, with low taxes, low wages, low energy costs and little state government regulation. To critics who say that Wyoming is "the hole in the donut" of mountain state prosperity,

Geringer replies, "Are we growing as fast as our neighbors? No. Do we want to? I'm not sure that we do."

On other issues, Wyoming cut its welfare rolls by 74% in the 1990s. Geringer signed a contract with USWest to connect all the state's schools by Internet. He pushed for a Wyoming Comprehensive Assessment System of tests of 4th, 8th and 11th graders in reading, writing and math; these WyCAS tests were criticized when first administered in 1999, and in 2000 Geringer said that conclusions should not be drawn for another year. He supported a gas tax increase and expanded the scope of the line-item veto; when the state legislature forwarded to the secretary of State a proposed constitutional amendment limiting that veto to budget bills, Geringer sued. In 2000 the legislature approved an extension of the 4% sales tax beyond its expiration date of 2002. Geringer has argued that modest-income people should pay more for services. "The highest consumers of [government] services ought to have some skin in the game. They have very little right now. Why not have some sense of personal responsibility?"

Geringer has often opposed federal policies which he feels impinge unfairly on Wyoming. In June 1999 he asked the Fish and Wildlife Service to slim down the designated range of the Preble's meadow jumping mouse. In January 2000 he threatened to sue the Forest Service unless it gave states greater involvment in managing the Northern Plains grasslands; he feared federal regulators would impede mining and oil drilling. He applauded a 1999 U.S. Supreme Court ruling that coal bed methane rights belong to natural gas leaseholders and not to coal leaseholders, as argued by the Clinton Administration. He called for more incentives and fewer prohibitions in the Endangered Species Act.With the governors of Idaho and Montana he sought state management of grizzly bears in the Yellowstone area, but with federal funding. A strong opponent of gambling, he was sued by the Northern Arapaho tribe in November 2000 for refusing to negotiate in good faith to allow tribes to establish high-stakes gambling.

In 1998 Geringer had articulate opposition in both the primary and general election. In the primary sheep rancher Bill Taliaferro charged that Geringer had been ineffective in stimulating the Wyoming economy. He got 33% of the vote—more than challengers of sitting governors usually do. In the general veteran Democrat John Vinich attacked Geringer for hiring a Colorado expert to head the Wyoming Business Council and proposed to revive the state's link program—using state funds to generate low-interest business loans from banks. Geringer said that link lost money. He won 56%–40%, a decisive but not overwhelming margin. The legislature continues to be heavily Republican, dominated by farmers and ranchers not eager for economic development. Craig Thomas is now considering a run for governor, leaving other gubernatorial hopefuls anxiously waiting. A run by Thomas would leave Geringer with a Senate seat to himself pursue.

Cook's Call *Safe.* Bush won Wyoming by a whopping 41 points and Democrats do not hold out much hope that they can win here, even when the seat will be open. Potential Republican candidates are Senator Craig Thomas, Secretary of State Joe Meyer, state Treasurer Cynthia Lummis and former state House Speaker Eli Bebout. Don't expect much action from the Democratic side.

Senior Senator Craig Thomas grew up in Cody, where he knew his later Senate colleague Alan Simpson, graduated from the University of Wyoming and served in the Marines. He worked for the Wyoming Farm Bureau and the Wyoming Rural Electric Association, organizations with conservative political leanings that kept him in touch with hundreds of people active in their communities. In 1984 he was elected to the Wyoming House. In March 1989, when Congressman-at-Large Dick Cheney was appointed secretary of Defense, Thomas had serious competition from veteran Democrat John Vinich, who had just run a close race against Senator Malcolm Wallop. Vinich noted that national Republicans were backing Thomas and said voters shouldn't let outsiders make decisions for Wyoming. Thomas rallied and won with 53%.

In the House Thomas concentrated on Wyoming issues and was re-elected with 55% in 1990 and 58% in 1992. When Wallop retired in 1994, Thomas was the obvious Republican candidate and had no primary opposition. In the general, he faced Governor Mike Sullivan, personally popular and with a conservative record, but handicapped by his association with Bill Clinton at governors' conferences; Clinton personally asked him to run for the Senate. Thomas relentlessly attacked Sullivan as a "Friend of Bill" and ally of locally unpopular Interior Secretary Bruce Babbitt. Thomas won 59%–39%, losing only one southern tier county by 6 votes.

Thomas is the top Republican on the National Parks Subcommittee. In 1998, despite his disagreements with Babbitt, he steered to passage a national parks reauthorization bill which reformed the granting of park concessions, mandated that peer-reviewed scientific research should take primacy in park management, and set up a new process for studying potential park areas. For that he was given an award by the National Parks and Conservation Association. He opposed Babbitt's higher grazing fees on federal lands and opposed the ban on snowmobiles in national parks, calling instead for stricter pollution and noise limitations. He proposed a bill to provide for no net gain in federal lands in states where 25% of the land is federally owned. In 1999 he proposed changes in the Endangered Species Act, to require use of peer-reviewed scientific data open to the public, attacking the Fish and Wildlife Service's decision on the Preble's meadow jumping mouse. "The critical listing decisions ought to be made with quality, peer-reviewed science and not by federal bureaucrats reacting only to the threat of environmental lawsuits." In 2000 he pushed to passage a law increasing the amount of federal land coal companies could lease, and proposed to ban commercial air tours over Yellowstone and Grand Teton National Parks.

From his seat on the East Asian and Pacific Affairs Subcommittee of Foreign Relations, Thomas strongly backed Permanent Normal Trade Relations with China. Noting that nearly half of Wyoming's products are sold abroad, he said "Chinese trade barriers have stood like the Great Wall against Wyoming exports." Other Thomas causes include rural health: He wants higher Medicare reimbursement for rural areas, incentives to attract health care professionals and increased use of telemedicine. With Charles Grassley and two Democrats he moved to bar meatpackers from owning livestock. He favors a biennial budget, Social Security individual investment accounts and tax cuts. He takes an interest in special education; his wife teaches special needs children in Northern Virginia. Complaining about air service to Wyoming, he has complained about United Airlines's near-monopoly in Denver. With colleague Mike Enzi, he got a statue of Chief Washakie (1804–1900) in the Capitol's Statuary Hall.

Thomas did not have much trouble winning re-election in 2000. A backer of Lyndon LaRouche won the low-turnout and Democratic primary, and Thomas, campaigning on rural health care, highway spending and expanding agricultural trade, won the general 74%–22%. Signs for the future are good: His lead among voters under 30 was 84%–15%. Thomas is considering a run for governor in 2002, leaving the possibility that Governor Jim Geringer may pursue the open Senate seat.

Junior Senator Wyoming's junior senator is Michael Enzi, elected in 1996. Enzi grew up in Thermopolis and Sheridan, the son of a shoe salesman, got degrees in accounting and marketing, moved to Gillette and became an oil company accountant and founded NZ Shoes. He served eight years as mayor of Gillette, the center of Wyoming's coal belt and its fastest-growing town. In 1986 he was elected to the legislature, where he served for 10 years.

After Senator Alan Simpson announced his retirement in December 1995, Enzi was one of nine Republicans and two Democrats to run for the seat. With support from a grass roots network of conservatives, Enzi finished first in a straw poll at the May 1996 Republican state convention; in second place was John Barrasso, an orthopedic surgeon from Casper who had appeared on statewide TV discussing health issues for 12 years; his chief difference on issues was his support of abortion rights. Barrasso had more money, but Enzi won 32%–30%, with a big majority in his home area in northeast Wyoming and narrow margins in the Casper and Cheyenne areas.

In the Democratic primary Kathy Karpan, secretary of State from 1986–94 and gubernatorial candidate in 1994, beat a man who called for construction of a 22,000-mile-high tower into space to promote world peace. Karpan had an appealing story—she helped raise her siblings when her mother died, she worked her way through school and then was a prosecutor—and moderate stances on many issues. Her opposition to gun control led the National Rifle Association to stay neutral; her opposition to federally funded abortions kept her off EMILY's List. But she had the liabilities of having supported the presidential candidacies of Bill Clinton in 1992 and Bruce Babbitt in 1988. She opposed the balanced budget amendment and Senator Craig Thomas's bill to turn over BLM lands to state governments; Enzi favored both. It was a game effort by Karpan, but Enzi led in polls all the way and won 54%–42%.

Enzi started off in the Senate by presiding for 100 hours in the chair by July and seeking permission to bring his laptop on the floor (the Rules Committee said no). He voted against the budget agreement in October 1998 and opposed the Kyoto treaty at the Buenos Aires conference in November 1998. In 2000 he denounced U.S. acquiescence to a United Nations agreement allowing countries to ban imports of genetically modified food. In 1999 he managed to get unanimous support in the Banking Committee for reauthorizing the lapsed Export Administration Act, adding higher fines and dropping useless restrictions. But in October 2000 he agreed to reauthorize the 1979 law, to gain time "to put the finishing touches on a modernized EAA." As chairman of the Employment, Safety and Training Subcommittee he held hearings in 2000 in which he criticized OSHA's proposed ergonomics standard and sought to prevent it from taking effect. With Don Nickles, Enzi successfully sponsored the effort to have the rules rescinded in March 2001.

Enzi made up his mind to support Permanent Normal Trade Relations with China just a few days before the September 2000 vote. He criticized the Forest Service for holding a behind-closed-door meeting with environmental groups on its moratorium on road building in national forests. After the August 2000 forest fires, he charged that "most of this threat could have been prevented had our federal land management policies not been stymied by the Washington, D.C., one-size-fits-all-based policies that sacrificed forest health for political gain." He attacked the Park Service ban on snowmobiles in national parks as "a politically-biased, pre-determined conclusion that excludes the community and places the national parks out of reach for most Americans during the winter months." With colleague Craig Thomas, he got an amendment to help livestock producers to benefit from anti-dumping laws and a resolution to place a statue of Chief Washakie (1804–1900) in the Capitol's Statuary Hall.

Enzi comes up for reelection in 2002. In this most Republican of states in the 2000 presidential election, he seems to be a strong favorite.

Cook's Call *Safe.* Democrats have not won a Senate election here since 1958 and their prospects are unlikely to improve in 2002. Enzi should be fine as he seeks a second term.

Representative-At-Large Wyoming, the nation's least populous state, has elected one congressman-at-large since it was admitted to the Union in 1890. The current incumbent is Barbara Cubin, a Republican elected in 1994. The great-great-granddaughter of one of Wyoming's original homesteaders, she grew up in Casper, where she worked as a teacher, social worker, chemist and realtor; for 19 years she managed her husband's medical practice. She was divorced after an early first marriage, worked as a single mother, was subjected to sexual harassment, but insists: "I am not a feminist. I am not gender sensitive." She was elected to the legislature in 1986, where she was prime sponsor of a 1994 ballot measure authorizing life without parole sentences.

In 1994, when Congressman Craig Thomas ran for the Senate, Cubin was one of five Republicans and two Democrats to run for the House. She sharply attacked "the Clinton-Babbitt war on the West." In the Republican primary, she won 39% to 25% for House staffer Rob Wallace, 18% for sheep rancher Jim Magagna and 17% for state House Speaker Doug Chamberlain. The Democratic nominee was Bob Schuster, a law partner of high-profile Wyoming trial lawyer Gerry Spence, who spent $2.4 million, most of it his own money, on what was the third-highest spending campaign in the country. Schuster's big issue was abortion; she called him a "a slick trial-lawyer Clinton Democrat." Them was fightin' words in Wyoming in 1994: Schuster carried only four counties, three in the southern tier and the other in Jackson Hole, and Cubin won 53%–41%.

In the House Cubin has had a solidly conservative voting record and quickly became chairman of the Energy and Mineral Resources Subcommittee. She sought to overturn the Forest Service's ban on fixed climbing anchors for mountain and rock climbers and got $10 million for a National Historic Trails Interpretive Center (the Oregon Trail goes right through Wyoming). She has opposed bills to fund federal purchases of private lands and wants to limit the federal government to no-net-gain. She has backed laws to compensate landowners for expenses caused by endangered species listings and to require peer-reviewed science for them. In 2000 a Cubin bills passed the House to stop the federal government from charging states for the administrative expenses on mineral leases; Wyoming's $7.5 million savings, she said, would go for education. She sponsored the successful bill to allow coal companies larger leases of federal lands. She decried the October 2000 decision to ban snowmobiling in national parks. She worked to allow satellite TV to carry local stations and supported loans to satellite companies. She spearheaded the effort to obtain Medicare coverage for the breast cancer treatment Xeloda.

Cubin had a good year in elections in 2000. In May she was elected to the National Rifle Association board of directors. In November she was re-elected over a lightly-funded Democrat by 67%–29%. A week later she was elected Republican Conference secretary after calling for regional diversity in the party leadership.

Cook's Call   *Safe.* Democrats have little hope of ousting Cubin in a state that gave Bush his largest winning percentage (69%) in the country in 2000.

Presidential politics   Wyoming is one of the least likely states in the nation to be seriously contested in presidential general elections: it is too Republican, too remote and has only three electoral votes. Candidates have seldom visited, except when Dick Cheney went to his home in Jackson.

Wyoming holds presidential caucuses in early March. In 2000 they were held on March 10, the same day as the Colorado and Idaho primaries—a sort of western primary, which attracted little attention.

THE PEOPLE: Pop. 2000: 493,782; Pop. 1990: 453,588, up 8.9% 1990–2000. 0.2% of U.S. total, 51st largest; 92.1% White, 0.8% Black, 0.6% Asian, 2.3% Amer. Indian, 0.1% Hawaiian, 1.8% Two+ races, 2.5% Other; 6.4% Hispanic Origin. 3.9% Unemployment. 2000 Voting age pop.: 364,909. 2000 Turnout: 221,685; 61% of VAP. Registered voters (2000): 220,012; 63,994 D (29%), 133,927 R (61%), 22,091 unaffiliated and minor parties (10%).

POLITICAL LINEUP: Governor, Jim Geringer (R); Secy. of State, Joseph B. Meyer (R); Atty. Gen., Gay Woodhouse (R); Treasurer, Cynthia M. Lummis (R); Auditor, Max Maxfield (R); Super. of Public Instruction, Judith S. Catchpole (R); State Senate, 30 (10 D, 20 R); Senate President, Henry H. R. Coe (R); Majority Leader, April Brimmer Kunz (R); State House, 60 (14 D, 46 R); House Speaker, Rick Tempest (R). Senators, Craig Thomas (R) and Michael Enzi (R). Representative, 1 R at large.

ELECTIONS DIVISION: 307-777-7186; **FILING DEADLINE FOR U.S. CONGRESS:** May 31, 2002.

2000 Presidential Vote		
Bush (R)	147,947	(69%)
Gore (D)	60,481	(28%)
Others	5,298	(2%)

1996 Presidential Vote		
Dole (R)	105,388	(50%)
Clinton (D)	77,934	(37%)
Perot (I)	25,928	(12%)

Gov. Jim Geringer (R)

Elected 1994, term expires Jan. 2003, 2d term; b. Apr. 24, 1944, Wheatland; home, Wheatland; KS St. U., B.S. 1967; Lutheran; married (Sherri).

Military Career: Air Force, 1967–77, Air Force Reserves, 1977–91.

Elected Office: WY House of Reps., 1982–88; WY Senate, 1988–94.

Professional Career: Farmer, Rancher; Contract Admin., Missouri Basin Power Project, 1977–79.

Office: State Capitol Bldg., No. 124, Cheyenne, 82002, 307-777-7434; Fax: 307-632-3909; Web site: www.state.wy.us.

Election Results

1998 general	Jim Geringer (R)	97,235	(56%)
	John P. Vinich (D)	70,754	(40%)
	Others	6,899	(4%)
1998 primary	Jim Geringer (R)	56,015	(67%)
	Bill Taliaferro (R)	28,164	(33%)
1994 general	Jim Geringer (R)	118,016	(59%)
	Kathy Karpan (D)	80,747	(40%)

Sen. Craig Thomas (R)

Elected 1994, seat up 2006, 2d term; b. Feb. 17, 1933, Cody; home, Casper; U. of WY, B.S. 1954, LaSalle U., LL.B. 1968; Methodist; married (Susan).

Military Career: Marine Corps, 1955–59.

Elected Office: WY House of Reps., 1984–89; U.S. House of Reps., 1989–94.

Professional Career: V.P., WY Farm Bureau, 1960–66; Legis. staff, Amer. Farm Bureau, 1966–75; Gen. Mgr., WY Rural Electric Assn., 1975–89.

DC Office: 109 HSOB, 20515, 202-224-6441; Fax: 202-224-1724; Web site: www.senate.gov/~thomas.

State Offices: Casper, 307-261-6413; Cheyenne, 307-772-2451; Riverton, 307-856-6642; Rock Springs, 307-362-5012; Sheridan, 307-672-6456.

Committees: *Agriculture, Nutrition & Forestry*: Forestry, Conservation & Rural Revitalization; Marketing, Inspection & Product Promotion. *Energy & Natural Resources*: Energy Research, Development, Production & Regulation; Forests & Public Land Management; National Parks, Historic Preservation & Recreation (RMM). *Ethics (Select)*. *Foreign Relations*: East Asian & Pacific Affairs (RMM); International Economic Policy, Export & Trade Promotion; Near Eastern & South Asian Affairs. *Indian Affairs*.

Group Ratings

	ADA	ACLU	AFS	LCV	CON	ITIC	NTU	COC	ACU	NTLC	CHC
2000	0	29	0	0	85	100	73	92	92	94	92
1999	0	—	0	0	87	—	82	100	87	—	—

National Journal Ratings

	1999 LIB —	1999 CONS		2000 LIB —	2000 CONS
Economic	0%	83%		14%	75%
Social	3%	94%		10%	81%
Foreign	23%	67%		17%	75%

Key Votes of the 106th Congress

1. Educ. Savings Accts.	Y	5. Review Movie Violence	Y	9. NATO War in Serbia	N
2. Prescrip. Drug Benefit	N	6. Gun Show Bckgrnd. Checks	N	10. Table Cuba Travel Ban	Y
3. Delay Ergonomic Standards	Y	7. Ban Part.-Birth Abortion	Y	11. Nuclear Test-Ban Treaty	N
4. Phase Out Estate Tax	Y	8. Broaden Hate Crimes List	N	12. Perm. Trade with China	Y

Election Results

2000 general	Craig Thomas (R)	157,622	(74%)	($762,833)
	Mel Logan (D)	47,087	(22%)	($4,187)
	Margaret Dawson (LIB)	8,950	(4%)	
2000 primary	Craig Thomas (R)	unopposed		
1994 general	Craig Thomas (R)	118,754	(59%)	($1,068,335)
	Mike Sullivan (D)	79,287	(39%)	($712,991)
	Others	3,669	(2%)	

Sen. Michael Enzi (R)

Elected 1996, seat up 2002, 1st term; b. Feb. 1, 1944, Bremerton, WA; home, Gillette; George Washington U., B.S. 1966, Denver U., M.B.A. 1968; Presbyterian; married (Diana).

Military Career: WY Natl. Guard, 1967–73.

Elected Office: Gillette Mayor, 1975–82; WY House of Reps., 1986–90; WY Senate, 1990–96.

Professional Career: Owner, NZ Shoes, 1969–95; Dir. & Chmn., First WY Bank of Gillette, 1978–88; Accounting Mgr. & Computer Programmer, Dunbar Well Service, 1985–97; Educ. Comm. of States, 1989–93; Dir., Black Hills Corp., 1992–96; Western Interstate Comm. for Higher Educ., 1995–96.

DC Office: 290 RSOB, 20510, 202-224-3424; Fax: 202-228-0359; Web site: www.senate.gov/~enzi.

State Offices: Casper, 307-261-6572; Cheyenne, 307-772-2477; Cody, 307-527-9444; Gillette, 307-682-6268; Jackson, 307-739-9507.

Committees: *Aging (Special)*. *Banking, Housing & Urban Affairs*: Housing & Transportation; International Trade & Finance; Securities & Investment (RMM). *Health, Education, Labor & Pensions*: Employment, Safety & Training (RMM); Public Health. *Small Business*.

Group Ratings

	ADA	ACLU	AFS	LCV	CON	ITIC	NTU	COC	ACU	NTLC	CHC
2000	0	29	0	0	36	100	77	100	92	94	92
1999	0	—	0	0	87	—	83	94	92	—	—

National Journal Ratings

	1999 LIB — 1999 CONS		2000 LIB — 2000 CONS	
Economic	0%	— 83%	0%	— 86%
Social	3%	— 94%	0%	— 90%
Foreign	10%	— 84%	5%	— 86%

Key Votes of the 106th Congress

1. Educ. Savings Accts.	Y	5. Review Movie Violence	Y	9. NATO War in Serbia	N
2. Prescrip. Drug Benefit	N	6. Gun Show Bckgrnd. Checks	N	10. Table Cuba Travel Ban	N
3. Delay Ergonomic Standards	Y	7. Ban Part.-Birth Abortion	Y	11. Nuclear Test-Ban Treaty	N
4. Phase Out Estate Tax	Y	8. Broaden Hate Crimes List	N	12. Perm. Trade with China	Y

Election Results

1996 general	Michael Enzi (R)	114,116	(54%)	($953,572)
	Kathy Karpan (D)	89,103	(42%)	($814,258)
	Others	7,858	(4%)	
1996 primary	Michael Enzi (R)	27,056	(32%)	
	John Barrasso (R)	24,918	(30%)	
	Curt Meier (R)	14,739	(18%)	
	Nimi McConigley (R)	6,005	(7%)	
	Kevin P. Meenan (R)	6,000	(7%)	
	Others	4,610	(6%)	
1990 general	Alan K. Simpson (R)	100,784	(64%)	($1,435,814)
	Kathy Helling (D)	56,848	(36%)	($6,243)

Rep. Barbara Cubin (R)

Elected 1994, 4th term; b. Nov. 30, 1946, Salinas, CA; home, Casper; Creighton U., B.S. 1969; Episcopalian; married (Frederick).

Elected Office: WY House of Reps., 1986–92; WY Senate, 1992–94.

Professional Career: Office Mgr., Dr. Frederick Cubin, 1975–94.

DC Office: 1114 LHOB, 20515, 202-225-2311; Fax: 202-225-3057; Web site: www.house.gov/cubin.

District Offices: Casper, 307-261-6595; Cheyenne, 307-772-2595; Rock Springs, 307-362-4095.

Committees: *Republican Conference Secretary.* *Energy & Commerce* (15th of 31 R): Commerce, Trade & Consumer Protection; Health; Telecommunications & The Internet. *Resources* (12th of 28 R): Energy & Mineral Resources (Chmn.).

Group Ratings

	ADA	ACLU	AFS	LCV	CON	ITIC	NTU	COC	ACU	NTLC	CHC
2000	5	14	0	0	33	89	66	80	100	85	93
1999	5	—	0	6	17	—	60	91	88	—	—

National Journal Ratings

	1999 LIB —	1999 CONS	2000 LIB —	2000 CONS
Economic	0% —	84%	0% —	94%
Social	21% —	78%	0% —	79%
Foreign	15% —	81%	39% —	57%

Key Votes of the 106th Congress

1. Patient Bill of Rights	N	5. Bar RU-486 $ for FDA	Y	9. NATO War in Serbia	N
2. Accelerate Min. Wage	N	6. Display 10 Commandments	Y	10. Perm. Trade with China	Y
3. Strike Ban on Ergo. Stnd.	N	7. Gun Show Bkgrnd. Checks	N	11. Debt Relief for 3rd World	Y
4. Ovrd. Estate Tax Veto	Y	8. Ban Part.-Birth Abortion	Y	12. Drop Cuba Econ. Embargo	N

Election Results

2000 general	Barbara Cubin (R)	141,848	(67%)	($640,700)
	Michael Allen Green (D)	60,638	(29%)	
	Lewis Stock (LIB)	6,411	(3%)	
	Other	3,415	(1%)	
2000 primary	Barbara Cubin (R)	54,946	(78%)	
	Larry Herdt (R)	10,148	(14%)	
	Dino Wenino (R)	5,515	(8%)	
1998 general	Barbara Cubin (R)	100,687	(58%)	($569,704)
	Scott Farris (D)	67,399	(39%)	($134,427)
	Others	6,133	(4%)	

PUERTO RICO, VIRGIN ISLANDS,
★ GUAM, AMERICAN SAMOA ★

Four American insular territories—Puerto Rico, Virgin Islands, Guam, American Samoa—are represented in Congress by elected delegates who, like the District of Columbia's delegate, have floor privileges and votes on committees but not votes on the floor (though House Democrats let them vote in committee of the whole proceedings in the 103d Congress). Each territory's status—its relationship to the United States—is different, governed by a separate law, and status is often the pivot around which territorial politics turn.

PUERTO RICO

Puerto Rico has a unique history. For four centuries, from Columbus's landing here in 1493 until the Spanish-American War of 1898, Puerto Rico was a Spanish colony, and the port of San Juan was the gathering place for its annual convoy of gold and silver from the Americas to Spain. Today, with 3.8 million people, it is the largest American territory—about the same population as South Carolina; also, perhaps 3 million people of Puerto Rican descent live on the mainland. Fifty years ago, it was "the poorhouse of the Caribbean," heavily populated, devoted almost entirely to sugar and coffee cultivation. Now it has a recognizably First World economy, with per capita incomes about half of those of the least affluent American states and among the highest in Latin America.

Puerto Rico has elected a resident commissioner to Congress since 1900 (the only member of Congress with a four-year term) and its residents have been American citizens since 1917, but it didn't elect its own governor until 1948. In the 1940s, 1950s and early 1960s, Puerto Rico was transformed by Governor Luis Munoz Marin and his Popular Democratic Party. Munoz initiated "Operation Bootstrap" (called "Operation Hands to Work" by Puerto Ricans) to lure businesses to Puerto Rico with promises of low-wage labor and government-built factories and tax exemptions. Munoz also developed Puerto Rico's commonwealth form of government—better understood in Spanish, Estado Libre Asociado (ELA): Free Associated State—approved by plebiscite in 1952. Under ELA, Puerto Rico is part of the United States for purposes of international trade, foreign policy and war, but has its own separate laws, taxes and representative government; it is not subject to federal income taxes and is not eligible for federal benefits (though some have been approved). Puerto Rico has also developed its own political parties: Munoz's Popular Democrats, the New Progressives who favor statehood, and two Independence parties.

But the commonwealth solution, by its own terms, was open to amendment; ever since Munoz's voluntary retirement in 1964, the central issue in Puerto Rico's politics has been status: Should this island continue or modify ELA, should it seek statehood, or should it seek independence? Over time there was gradual movement toward statehood. In the July 1967 referendum, conducted when the Popular Democrats were in power, Puerto Ricans voted for ELA over statehood by 60%–39%; in the November 1993 referendum, conducted with New Progressive Governor Pedro Rossello in office, the vote was 48% for ELA, 46% for statehood. In March 1998 the U.S. House voted 209–208 for a referendum setting terms for statehood; this was a project of Speaker Newt Gingrich, who hoped to attract Hispanic votes, and of Resources Committee Chairman Don Young, who saw in statehood backers' demands echoes of Alaska's fight for statehood. But the bill went nowhere in the Senate. Rossello ordered a referendum on his terms (which are unlikely ever to be accepted in Congress) in December 1998; 46.5% voted for statehood and 50.3% for "none of the above," the option favored by the Popular Democrats. Independence has negligible support—4% in 1993, 2.5% in 1998—primarily from university students; nor are there many pro-independence abstentions, for voter turnout in the enthusiastic politics of Puerto Rico is the highest under the American flag, higher than in even the most affluent, long-settled suburbs of the mainland. Now, with the election of Popular Democrat Governor Sila Calderon in 2000, the move toward statehood has been at least temporarily solved; and in the campaign other issues surged forward—the Navy's bombing range in Vieques, corruption in Rossello's administration.

But status is likely to remain the chief determinant of political preference here, and the driving force behind electoral politics.

Even while Puerto Ricans were debating status in the 1990s, the island's economy was changing. In 1996 Congress voted to phase out through 2005 Section 936, the provision that shelters earnings of some Puerto Rico manufacturers from federal taxes and allows their products into the U.S. duty-free. Pharmaceutical companies in particular have set up highly visible plants in Puerto Rico—half of U.S. prescription drugs are manufactured in Puerto Rico—and ELA supporters have claimed that the island's economy depends on the tax exemptions. But if the number of manufacturing jobs has declined, Puerto Rico's overall economy has kept pace with the mainland's pace, growing about 4% a year; unemployment in 1999 was 12.5%, but that is far less than in the 1980s. Puerto Rico has long since lost low-wage garment jobs to lower-wage countries in the Caribbean and Latin America, and is developing new jobs in services, tourism, trading and exports.

Rossello supported the phaseout of 936, confident that Puerto Rico would grow without it, and made other changes to Puerto Rico's economy. In line with the trend toward privatization of state-owned firms in Latin America, Puerto Rico sold the longtime money-losing Navieras shipping company and, after protests and a two-day general strike, the Puerto Rico telephone company. The Aqueduct and Sewer Authority's facilities were privatized, as were seven hospitals and 78 health clinics. He reduced the corporate tax from 14.5% to 7%, with credits for job creation and investment reducing it to as low as 2%. Taxes on distributed dividends were eliminated and a 200% deduction allowed for research and development and job training. He started massive public works—a $300 million Superaqueduct, a $1.5 billion *Tren Urbano* (mass transit) in San Juan, and other major road projects. Puerto Rico provides health insurance to the poor via la tarjetita (the little card) and Rossello instituted school vouchers and five minutes of daily reflection in schools. This record proved popular enough that Rossello was re-elected 51%–44% in 1996.

His second term was stormier. Hurricane Georges in September 1998 wreaked $3 billion worth of damage—but also sparked the construction industry. More damaging to Rossello were corruption charges against many New Progressive officials. Federal prosecutors charged that $800,000 of public funds made their way to the party's treasury, mayors were indicted for bribes in the Georges cleanup, San Juan AIDS Institute officials were put on trial for diverting public monies, charges were made of mishandling of the bidding and contract provisions of the telephone company privatization. The Housing Department, which houses 250,000 people in 57,000 units in 328 projects—the second largest public housing department in the U.S., after New York's—had, in the words of HUD's inspector general, "flagrant fraud, waste and abuse." Rossello said that the media was "fabricating" the corruption issue, but had to testify in the AIDS Institute trial. Rossello was also embarrassed by a lawsuit brought by *El Nuevo Dia* after he yanked public advertising from it in 1997—the case was settled in 1999—and by revelations of the police spying on 100,000 people in the 1970s and 1980s, for which he apologized in 1999.

Past controversies also echoed in August 1999 when Bill Clinton announced he was granting conditional clemency to 14 members of the terrorist group FALN, some of whom had been imprisoned since 1981. In the 1970s and 1980s, the independence-supporting FALN had committed 130 bombings in which six people were killed and many more severely injured; the subjects of Clinton's grant had not been convicted of violent crimes, but had never expressed remorse for the activities of FALN of which they had been a willing part. The clemency grant was a foreshadowing of Clinton's January 2001 pardons, and political motives were suspected: Would this help Hillary Rodham Clinton's Senate candidacy in New York? The pardons were opposed by the FBI and the U.S. attorneys' offices which had prosecuted the criminals; they were harshly criticized by New York Mayor Rudolph Giuliani and Senator Daniel Patrick Moynihan; in a month Hillary Rodham Clinton herself felt obliged to oppose them. But in September 12 of the 14 convicts accepted Clinton's conditions (renunciation of violence, promises not to associate with other FALN members) and they were released. Most returned to Puerto Rico, where they were met by cheers from some and denunciations by others.

In April 1999 a Marine Corps jet dropped two 500-pound bombs in the wrong place in the Navy's bombing range on the island of Vieques, and a civilian guard was killed. The Vieques bombing range was established in 1941, and had long sparked protests from those who claimed the bombing jeopardized islanders' safety and polluted the environment; the Navy claimed that it was their most important training ground, the best place in the world for combined sea-land-air training exercises. For a year protesters streamed onto the range and prevented exercises; many were arrested, including Independence Party leader Ruben Berrios Martinez. Rossello and politicians of all parties demand that the range be shut down. But the Navy got support in Senate Armed Services Committee hearings in December 1999, in which Chairman John Warner said that if the bombing range was closed, the Navy should abandon its Roosevelt Roads base in San Juan harbor. The American military is an important part of Puerto Rico's economy, and personnel were relocated there in the 1990s as American forces left the Panama Canal Zone; Roosevelt Roads employs 2,500 Puerto Rican civilians and contributes $300 million to the island economy. In January 2000 Rossello—who stunned his supporters by announcing in June 1999 that he would not run for re-election—reached an agreement with the Clinton White House. The Navy would set a date for a referendum in which voters in Vieques (population 9,300) would decide whether to end the bombing in May 2003 or allow it to continue, with $40 million of federal aid for the town; in the meantime, exercises would continue 90 days a year. Protests continued. In February 2000 some 85,000 (or 150,000, depending on which group made the estimate) Puerto Ricans marched in San Juan for " *paz para Vieques.*" A month late some 90,000 New Progressive supporters marched in San Juan brandishing U.S. and Puerto Rican flags. Only in May was Vieques cleared of protesters. In December 2000 the Navy announced the Vieques referendum would be held in November 2001.

Bombing exercises using inert ordnance began again in April 2001 and were met with continued demonstrations. Among those detained this time were Illinois Congressman Luis Gutierrez, who complained of ill treatment by the Navy, and the Reverend Al Sharpton, who staged a hunger strike from his New York City jail; in total about 1,500 people had been arrested since April 1999. Then in June, George W. Bush announced that the Navy would halt all military exercises on Vieques by May 2003 and sought to cancel the pending referendum. Many Republican members of Congress objected to the decision, which was made by Navy Secretary Gordon England and Bush advisor Karl Rove; some interpreted it as an attempt to win Hispanic votes at the expense of military readiness.

In the meantime, a new governor was elected, Sila Maria Calderon of the Popular Democratic Party. Well known from her four years as mayor of San Juan, Calderon had been leading Rossello in polls when he announced his retirement and seemed well ahead of the lesser-known New Progressive candidate, former Transportation Secretary Carlos Pesquera. Status for once was not the headline issue, though Pesquera promised to lobby for statehood and Calderon backed ELA. Instead, Calderon emphasized Vieques and corruption, which 65% of voters thought was worse than in the past. She called for immediate eviction of the Navy from Vieques and opposed the sale of the telephone company and the hospitals and clinics. Despite her poll leads, these strong issues moved only a small percentage of voters from their ordinary party identification. Calderon won 49%–46%, with 5% for Berrios Martinez. The Popular Democrats won majorities in the legislature and won most mayoralties on the island, though the New Progressives won in San Juan, Bayamon and Guaynabo, the first, second and seventh largest *municipios*.

Calderon's election changes the calculus of Puerto Rican politics. Statehood is off the table, for at least four years; there will surely be no referendum in Puerto Rico and no push for one in Congress. She seems unlikely to reverse Rossello's privatizations and tax cuts, but she has every incentive to avoid the corruption that was so evident in his administration. The larger question is whether the events of 1999 and 2000—Vieques, the FALN clemency—will fray or rupture the ties between Puerto Rico and the United States. The poor showing of the Independence Party in 2000—Martinez won only 84,000 votes, less than his party's peak of 125,000 in 1952—suggests that support for independence has not grown and is still limited to a fringe of the electorate. But both major parties' platforms carry a risk of rupture with the mainland. If the New Progressives should manage to win a narrow majority for statehood, as they nearly did in 1998, Puerto Rico surely would not be granted statehood, as most Puerto Ricans expect. Congress, whichever party is in control, is unlikely to accept the New Progressives' terms and would likely require a consensus, not a narrow majority, for statehood; Alaska and Hawaii were admitted as states only after more than 80% of their voters supported statehood. Puerto Rico's ELA status is a compromise, an uneasy one. Munoz Marin's achievement of enthusiasm for a policy of compromise was an astonishing political achievement, unusual in any polity. But support for statehood and aggravation with the mainland have weakened that enthusiasm over the years, as the results of the compromise—economic growth and political freedom still unusual in Latin America—have come to be taken for granted. Puerto Rico is not much in the mind of most Americans, but officials in the federal government as well as in Puerto Rico have a responsibility to pay heed to Puerto Rico and take it seriously.

Presidential politics   One of the complaints of Puerto Rico's New Progressives is that it cannot vote for president, and in 2000 Governor Pedro Rossello tried to remedy that. On August 29, 2000, a federal judge in Puerto Rico ruled that Puerto Rican voters have a right to vote for president emanating from their U.S. citizenship and ordered that a vote be held and that Congress count eight electoral votes for Puerto Ricans' choice (eight was the number of electoral votes Puerto Rico would have had under the 1990 Census if it were a state). This ruling went against precedent and the language of the Constitution, which gives votes only to states which have been admitted to the Union and, in an amendment, to the District of Columbia. But Rossello and the New Progressive legislature were happy to pass a law putting the presidential election on the November 7 ballot. On October 13, the First Circuit Court of Appeals predictably reversed the rules and ordered the presidential contest off the ballot (although Guam has had a presidential straw vote on its November ballot). So no one knows for sure which candidate Puerto Rico would have preferred, George W. Bush (who nominally favors statehood, as Republican platforms long have) or Al Gore (who favors "self-determination" for Puerto Rico), although almost everyone assumes Gore would have won.

Puerto Rico does send delegates to the two mainland parties' national conventions. The Republicans, long identified with the New Progressives, though its two leading figures in 2000 identify with Democrats, held a primary in February in which the Spanish-speaking George W. Bush beat John McCain 93%–6%, even though Bush told the *San Juan Star*, "I was hoping to carry it without going down." That gave him 14 convention delegates, more than were elected by Vermont or Delaware and the same as Maine, Rhode Island and Hawaii. Al Gore won the March Democratic caucus, giving him 59 delegates, more than 24 states. Since Puerto Rico's Democratic delegates in the past have voted as a bloc, while Democratic rules require other states' delegates to be split proportionately, in a divided Democratic convention (if there ever is one again) Puerto Rico actually has more leverage than all but a half dozen or so states, as it did in the bitterly split convention in 1980.

Governor   Sila Maria Calderon, the first woman governor of Puerto Rico, was elected in 2000. She grew up in San Juan, graduated from Manhattanville College in New York and became a vice president of Citibank in Puerto Rico. She served as secretary of State under Popular Democratic Governor Rafael Hernandez Colon in the late 1980s. In 1996 she was elected mayor of San Juan—a notable upset victory, since San Juan ordinarily votes New Progressive. As mayor she was one of the most visible public figures in Puerto Rico and, as the most prominent Popular Democrat officeholder, the party's logical candidate for governor in 2000. When incumbent Pedro Rossello announced his retirement in June 1999, Calderon led him in a public poll by a solid 47%–30% margin.

Calderon, a supporter of ELA over statehood, did not campaign much on status. Instead, she emphasized her support of " *paz para Vieques*" and criticism of corruption in the Rossello administration. This was enough to change the 1990s balance of opinion in Puerto Rico and give her a 49%–46% victory over former Transportation Secretary Carlos Pesquera, whose trademark *Tren Urbano* did not carry the punch of Vieques. "Today the deep pride in our 'Puerto Ricanness' has triumphed," she said on election night. After George W. Bush announced plans to end the Navy's bombing exercises on Vieques by May 2003 and cancel the referendum that had been set for July 2001, Calderon had mixed emotions. "It satisfies us because of the certainty that there will be a definite end to the Navy in Vieques," she said. "But to continue the military exercises for two years, that cannot go on." Calderon said her administration would continue with a federal lawsuit alleging the bombing has harmed the health of Vieques residents—the preliminary findings of a 2001 HHS study found a high incidence of cardiac problems among Viequenses—and promised to press ahead with the referendum. On other issues, Calderon instituted audits of agencies which were the subject of corruption charges and indictments, and of course replaced New Progressive appointees with Popular Democrats.

Resident Commissioner   Anibal Acevedo Vila, former president of the Popular Democratic Party, was elected to a four-year term as Puerto Rico's resident commissioner—actually, non-voting delegate in Congress—in 2000. Acevedo was born in San Juan and lives in Guaynabo, graduated from the University of Puerto Rico and Harvard Law School and was a law clerk in the First Circuit Court of Appeals in Boston, which has jurisdiction over Puerto Rico. He returned to Puerto Rico to work on the staff of Governor Rafael Hernandez Colon from 1989 to 1992. In 1992 he was elected to the Puerto Rico House. Like all Puerto Rican politicians, he opposed the continuation of the Navy bombing range in Vieques and said he was "not satisfied" by the January 2000 agreement between Governor Pedro Rossello and Bill Clinton. He said Vieques would be his first priority, and said that he would try to create tax breaks for American companies in Puerto Rico—although the main tax break, Section 936, is being phased out.

His opponent in the 2000 election was incumbent Carlos Romero Barcelo, who was elected mayor of San Juan in 1968 and 1972, governor in 1976 and 1980 and resident commissioner in 1992 and 1996. Romero was known for his pugnacious temperament and strong advocacy of statehood, and unlike many other New Progressives always identified with the mainland Democratic Party. In 2000 Bill Clinton cut a spot for him: "For Carlos, Puerto Rico is always first." But Puerto Ricans tend to vote on straight party lines, and as the Popular Democrats' Sila Calderon was winning the governorship 49%–46%, Acevedo was elected by a 50%–45% margin, with 5% for the Independence Party candidate.

Del. Anibal Acevedo-Vila (D)

Elected 2000, 1st term; b. Feb. 13, 1962, San Juan; home, Guaynabo; U. of PR, B.A. 1982, J.D. 1985; Harvard U., J.D. 1987; Catholic; married (Luisa Gandara).

Elected Office: PR House of Reps., 1991–2000.

Professional Career: Clerk, PR Supreme Court, 1985–86; clerk, 1st Circuit Court of Appeals, Boston, 1987–88; staffer, Gov. Rafael Hernandez Colon, 1989–92; Pres., Popular Democratic Party, 1997–2000.

DC Office: 126 CHOB, 20515, 202-225-2615; Fax: 202-225-2154; Web site: www.house.gov/acevedo-vila.

District Offices: Ponce, 787-841-3209; San Juan, 787-723-6333.

Committees: *Agriculture* (22d of 24 D): Department Operations, Oversight, Nutrition & Forestry; General Farm Commodities & Risk Management. *Resources* (21st of 25 D): Forests & Forest Health; National Parks, Recreation & Public Lands. *Small Business* (17th of 17 D): Regulatory Reform Oversight; Tax, Finance & Exports.

VIRGIN ISLANDS

The United States' other insular territory in the Caribbean is the Virgin Islands, a very different sort of place from Puerto Rico. It is much smaller, with a resident population of only 110,000, mainly on the three islands of St. Thomas, St. John and St. Croix. They were settled not by Spaniards but by Dutch and Danes, and had a polyglot colonial society with one of the oldest Jewish communities in the Western Hemisphere; their most famous son is Alexander Hamilton, who grew up in St. Croix. The most famous contemporary son is Tim Duncan, the all-star basketball player for the San Antonion Spurs, who cuts promotional TV spots for the Virgin Islands. Puerto Rico is multiracial and not self-conscious about it, but most Virgin Islanders are black, and resent the clear divide between the races. While Puerto Rico has attracted all kinds of light industry, the Virgin Islands live off tourism and refineries (the Hovensa refinery on St. Croix is the largest refinery in the Western Hemisphere; it was built by Amerada Hess in the 1960s and is now half-owned by the Venezuela government oil company). These are industries that have produced higher income levels for its few citizens but have not provided the basis for a steady economy. One-third of the work force is on government payrolls, and the Virgin Islands government in late 2000 had a crushing debt of more than $1 billion and was in arrears on its payments to the U.S. Bureau of Prisons, had gas and armored car service cut off because of unpaid debts to Exxon and Brink's and saw teachers abandon classrooms to demand repairs.

One reason for these problems is that the Virgin Islands, blessed with beauty, have been cursed by bad weather for a decade. Hurricane Hugo in September 1989 destroyed 90% of the buildings on St. Croix, and tourism has never recovered; Hurricanes Luis and Marilyn in September 1995 caused terrible damage on St. Thomas; Hurricane Georges in September 1998 was not as bad, but still slowed down recovery; Hurricane Lenny in November 1999 caused $31.5 million of damage to St. Croix. St. Thomas has one-half the islands' population and four-fifths of its hotel rooms, but some 75% of tourists arrive on cruise ships and spend only about one-quarter as much time on shore as those who arrive by plane. St. John, lightly inhabited, remains mostly a natural paradise, with a few very high-end hotels. St. Croix is trying to stimulate tourism by building gambling casinos, the first of which opened in December 2000. But the islands' interests diverge: St. Thomas is against gambling, while Cruzans (the residents of St. Croix) resent the amount the V.I. government spends on promoting tourism. In the meantime, AIDS rates are high, and the Virgin Islands is a center for smuggling illegal Chinese immigrants into the United States.

Politics in the Virgin Islands is a personal thing, with big rivalries between St. Thomas and St. Croix; candidates for the highest offices tend to be physicians. There was a sort of political revolution here in 1994, with the replacement by independents of two longtime Democratic officeholders—Governor Alexander Farrelly, first elected in 1986, and Congressional Delegate Ron de Lugo, first elected in 1968 and in office since, except for one two-year interval. The next governor, oncologist Roy Schneider, was in turn defeated 59%–41% by Education Commissioner Charles Turnbull in 1998.

Governor Charles Turnbull was born in St. Thomas, the son of immigrants from the British Virgin Islands. He earned undergraduate and graduate degrees from Hampton University and a doctorate in education from the University of Minnesota, then returned home to teach. As Virgin Island's Education commissioner, Turnbull upgraded the curriculum, established a cultural education division to promote greater understanding and appreciation of the history and culture of the Caribbean region, and built enough new schools to eliminate double school-day sessions. Promising a "grander vision" than offered by independent Governor Roy Schneider—who focused on downsizing government, reducing spending and fighting drugs—Turnbull in 1998 defeated the one-term incumbent 59%–41%.

In April 1999, Turnbull said the government would be unable to pay its 10,000 workers because of $1 billion in debt from the previous administration. Turnbull tried to tackle this huge debt by cutting the government payroll through attrition and negotiated a memorandum of understanding with Interior Secretary Bruce Babbitt, promising to cut the budget, change the labor relations law and scrap five government holidays. Now he must deal with a new Interior secretary of another party, with uncertain results.

Delegate The delegate from the Virgin Islands is Donna Christian-Christensen, elected in 1996, when she beat Victor Frazer, a Republican who ran as an independent and the upset winner in 1994. Christensen (as her name is given in her press releases) is from an old St. Croix family; her father was Virgin Islands Chief District Court Judge Almeric Christian. She graduated from St. Mary's College and George Washington Medical School; she practiced medicine for more than 20 years in the Virgin Islands, in a family practice and in several public positions. She was elected a Democratic National committeewoman in 1984 and ran one losing race for delegate in 1994. In 1996 she attacked Frazer, who after some hesitation caucused with the Democrats, for foreign travel (11 trips to four continents), and for inaction in opposing the welfare reform bill. Frazer, who spent far less money, said, "What they don't realize is, these things are not possible," in reference to Christensen's promise that she would get the floor vote back for delegates. Christensen led Frazer 38%–34% on November 5; in the runoff two weeks later she won 52%–48%. It was a regional race: Christensen won 69% on St. Croix, Frazer 64% on St. Thomas and St. John.

In the House, Christensen has forged alliances with the Congressional Black Caucus and, when it was in office, the Clinton administration to achieve her goals; she works on health issues for the Black Caucus. She objected to government health guidelines recommending milk, since many blacks, Asians and Hispanics are lactose intolerant. She fought for the Virgin Islands to get the total rum tax of $13.50 per gallon, instead of the current $10.50; but the clout behind this proposal comes from Puerto Rico's friends in the New York delegation. She got the support of Resources Chairman Don Young, who can remember when his Alaska was a territory and subject to the whims of Congress, to a proposal to allow the Virgin Islands to write a constitution and to reduce the V.I. Senate from 15 to nine members. She boasted of getting $10 million for restoring damaged coral reefs. She backed the New Markets venture capital bill and with Bob Underwood of Guam sought reauthorization of Foreign Sales Corporations; the Virgin Islands is a center for franchising FSCs. She helped pass a 1999 law allowing the Virgin Islands to issue general obligation bonds to refinance tax and revenue anticipation notes, and tried to restore the law allowing import into the U.S. of Virgin Islands duty-free cigarettes.

Del. Donna M. Christian-Christensen (D)

Elected 1996, 3d term; b. Sept. 19, 1945, Teaneck, NJ; home, St. Croix; St. Mary's Col., B.S. 1966, George Washington U., M.D. 1970; Moravian; married (Christian).

Professional Career: Practicing physician, 1975–97; Territorial Asst., Commissioner of Health, 1988–94; Acting Commissioner of Health, 1994–95.

DC Office: 1510 LHOB, 20515, 202-225-1790; Fax: 202-225-5517; Web site: www.house.gov/christian-christensen.

District Offices: St. Croix, 340-778-5900; St. Thomas, 340-774-4408.

Committees: *Resources* (13th of 25 D): National Parks, Recreation & Public Lands (RMM). *Small Business* (5th of 17 D): Rural Enterprises, Agricultural and Technology; Workforce, Empowerment & Government Programs.

GUAM

Some 3,500 miles west of Hawaii, 19 hours of flying time from Washington, D.C., is Guam, the place where America's day begins. Guam lies just west of the International Date Line, and it is in the early hours of Tuesday there when the rest of us are just trying to get through Monday afternoon; the Interior Department came to Guam to see whether there were Y2K problems, as the clock struck midnight, January 1, 2000, while it was 9 a.m., December 31, in Washington. Geographically in the center of the Mariana Islands, Guam is legally separate: The Northern Marianas were administered by the U.S. as a United Nations trust territory until they became a commonwealth in 1978. Guam was ruled by Navy captains from 1898 to 1950, except for 32 months of Japanese occupation during World War II; in 1950 the Guam Organic Act made Guamanians U.S. citizens and allowed them to elect a local government, but Congress still retained final power over the territory; it started electing a non-voting delegate to Congress in 1972.

Guam is 36 miles long by four to nine miles wide, with 154,000 people; nearly half are Chamorro (descendants of the original islanders), 25% Filipino, 13% other Asian and 10% Caucasian; more than 75% of Guamanians are Catholic. (In 1990 Guam passed a law barring almost all abortions; it was overturned by a federal court in 1992, as clearly contrary to *Roe v. Wade*, and the Supreme Court dodged a direct challenge to that decision by refusing to hear the case.) There are about 4,000 U.S. military personnel here, on bases which occupy one-third of the island; they have room for refugees, and in recent years have been housing illegal immigrants from China and other parts of East Asia. Guam is tropical, but not an easy environment: in August 1993 it lived through an earthquake rated at 8.2 on the Richter scale, comparable to San Francisco in 1906; in December 1997 Typhoon Paka raged through with winds of 236 miles per hour. Guam has feral water buffalo, descendants of those imported from Asia hundreds of years ago; it has the brown tree snake, an import from somewhere in the Pacific, which has rid the island of native birds and many bats and has been known to try to eat sleeping babies; the island's coral reefs are being destroyed by erosion. There are other problems, including a rash of 22 teenage suicides in 1999–2001; teens were entering suicide pacts by email, and seemed to be emulating former Governor Ricky Bordallo, who in 1990 wrapped himself in the Guam flag, chained himself to the statue of Chief Quipuha and shot himself to avoid a prison term for bribery.

Economically, Guam depended for years on American military bases; now it is diversifying, with 1.5 million tourists a year, mostly from Japan. Military deployments declined with the closing of Agana Naval Air Station in 1995, but in October 2000 the Navy was considering transferring three nuclear submarines here from Hawaii, with 750 personnel. Tourism slumped in the late 1990s, when Japan's economy stagnated; unemployment in 2000 hovered around 15%. Guamanian entrepreneurs want to build garment and other low-wage factories here, to be staffed by guest workers from the Philippines and China, like those in the Commonwealth of the Northern Marianas (CNMI), where as Henry Hurt reported in *Reader's Digest* in 1997, many have been abused by employers. But Guam, unlike the CNMI, is covered by U.S. immigration laws. In the late 1990s guest workers from the CNMI entered Guam and claimed political asylum; in 1998 "snakehead" Chinese smugglers started bringing in Chinese from the Fujian province for a reputed $20,000 to $30,000 a head. In Guam they could claim asylum and seek an INS hearing in Seattle; the Clinton administration in April 1999 started shipping them to the CNMI instead. Guam is indeed "America in Asia," as its leaders like to proclaim, but that causes problems as much as it brings opportunity.

For much of the 1990s Guam sought a change in status, to give the Guam government control over immigration. Chamorros said they want to block others from coming in, establishing citizenship and making them minority; but another motive was to bring in guest workers as the CNMI has done, with local enforcement of labor laws. Guam's proposal also included "mutual consent," which would bar Congress from changing laws and treaties that affect Guam without Guam's consent; Guamanians remembered that its just-created watch and garment industries were destroyed by congressional action in the 1970s and 1980s. Guam's proposal for such commonwealth status was backed by Republican Governor Joe Ada, elected in 1986 and 1990, and Democratic Governor Carl Gutierrez, elected in 1994 and 1998, and was pushed in Congress by Guam's Delegate Robert Underwood, a Democrat first elected in 1992. The first Bush administration rejected the bill as inconsistent with the constitutional provision giving Congress full powers over territories. For a time the Clinton administration seemed sympathetic and inclined to agree to "mutual consent." But the election of the Republican Congress abruptly changed the provision's prospects. The Resources' Native American and Insular Affairs chairman at that time, Elton Gallegly of California, announced in January 1995 that he would block any mutual consent bill that seeks to bind future congresses. Guamanians, eager to get in Clinton's good graces, responded to a 1996 Democratic National Committee request for $250,000 by hosting Hillary Rodham Clinton on a stopover on her way to China and with generous contributions, ultimately $892,000, the largest amount per capita under the American flag. Gutierrez said, "Only when we showed Washington that there were people who could write a $1,000 check, a $5,000 check, a $25,000 check, did people begin to sit up and take notice."

In December 1996 Interior negotiator John Garamendi circulated a report backing commonwealth. But when the contributions attracted attention, the administration stepped back. In October 1997 Garamendi said, "We have been unable to find constitutional and otherwise appropriate ways of bridging the gap between the full extent of what Guam has originally proposed and what the executive branch is able to support under the American flag." He said the administration could not support mutual consent and could not support a referendum in which "only the indigenous Chamorro people" could vote and would not transfer control over labor and immigration policy nor a joint commission which could bind future congresses. Guam leaders responded in the tones of those who thought they had made an under-the-table deal only to find the table removed and nothing there. "We have been betrayed. We must continue to fight," said Ada. Underwood said the U.S.-Guam relationship was supposed to be a marriage but was more like a "kept woman." Negotiations sputtered out, and now with George W. Bush as president the chances for a change in status seem nil.

Guam of course does not cast any electoral votes for president, but has a part in presidential politics. It elects delegates to party national conventions—4 for Bush and 6 for Gore in 2000. Local politicians are happy to be at the conventions, but Underwood was irritated that Guam and other territories came up only at the end of the otherwise alphabetical roll call at the Democratic convention. "Even with the parties, the hurt doesn't stop. You're not even included in the alphabet." In November Guam has conducted a straw poll for president, and has voted for the winner every time since 1984; in 2000 Bush won 52%–47%. If only other Americans had paid heed to this indicator, a lot of trouble could have been avoided in Florida.

Governor   Carl Gutierrez is a Democrat elected in 1994. He went to high school in California, served in the Air Force, then set up the first data processing center in Guam and started a construction business; he was elected to the Guam Senate for all but four years from 1972–1994. He campaigned for commonwealth status, for return of federal lands to Guam, and for exemption from the Jones Act requirement that goods from the U.S. be shipped in U.S.-registered ships; only two lines serve Guam, and Gutierrez wants foreign competition. After the 1994 election Gutierrez attacked, Republican-style, the high-handedness of federal bureaucrats: "Guam has to survive with minor federal luminaries who operate with no apparent adult supervision," he said, and complained that the Fish and Wildlife Service seized 20% of Guam's land for a wildlife refuge. And when California Republican Dana Rohrabacher called Guam and other territories "economic basket cases" that are "backward and economically depressed," Gutierrez attacked "this ignorance and lack of sensitivity which run counter to our country's democratic traditions and which ensures the continuation of our status as second-class citizens in the American family." He is a vigorous presence in Guam and rushed to the scene when KAL 801 crashed on the island in August 1997 and even rescued an 11-year-old girl from the wreckage.

The 1998 election was a close contest between two familiar figures, Gutierrez and former Governor Joe Ada. Gutierrez raised the astonishing sum of $2.8 million, Ada $358,000—sums one thinks might have been enough to communicate with some 48,000 voters spread over an area three times the size of Washington, D.C. Initially the result was reported as a 51%–44% victory for Gutierrez, with 7% write-ins or defective ballots. But Republicans, who won most of the seats in the 15-member legislature, argued that 1,313 blank ballots should be counted as well, which would make the results 49.8%–43.58%, giving neither candidate the "majority of votes cast" required by the Guam Organic Act. The election commission certified Gutierrez's victory anyway by a quick 4–2 vote. It was reported that the FBI was conducting a criminal investigation. In December 1998 a federal judge ordered a runoff election; the order was suspended pending appeal. A week before that decision, Ada filed suit in Guam Superior Court, arguing that non-citizens and non-Guam residents and dead or underage people had voted; this was dismissed although earlier the Superior Court had found 571 non-citizens registered and that 151 voters shared the same Social Security number. The fraud case was dismissed in February 1999, after 45 witnesses testified at trial. In January 2000 Ada's efforts to get a runoff came to an end when the U.S. Supreme Court ruled unanimously that a runoff wasn't required.

Not surprisingly, relations between Gutierrez and the legislature have not been good. In August 1999, after the legislature refused to increase the budget $40 million as Gutierrez requested, Gutierrez signed a $20 million emergency spending bill to prevent a shutdown of the territorial government, which was four months behind on $15 million in bills. For 2000 Gutierrez sought a $469 million budget, though only $450 million was expected in revenues; the legislature voted $439 million but Gutierrez said it "isn't going to work." In September 2000 a court held that Gutierrez had improperly appointed members of the electoral commission. Republicans sought to put a referendum on recalling Gutierrez on the November ballot, on the grounds that he failed to provide a budget and financial information. Lieutenant Governor Madeleine Bordallo announced that if Gutierrez were removed and she succeeded him, she would appoint him lieutenant governor. In October, some Republicans demurred, recall got only an 8–7 vote (it required 10 votes to get on the ballot) and recall was abandoned in favor of a nine-point proposal for "peace and reconciliation of our people." One may wonder whether that will soon occur.

Delegate Robert Underwood, Guam's delegate in Congress since 1992, grew up in Guam and was educated in California. He started teaching at the University of Guam in 1976 and was known for his efforts promoting and preserving Chamorro language and culture; he was appointed to the Chamorro Language Commission in 1977 and served as its chairman for 12 years, until 1991. By 1990 he had become the university's academic vice president, and in 1992 he ran against Republican Delegate Ben Blaz, a former Marine general. Personal connections are often more important than party in Guam, and Underwood explained his victory thus: "I have a lot of relatives. His grandfather and my great-grandfather are first cousins. So I cut into his action when I ran—more of the relatives are closer to me." He was re-elected in 1994 and 1996 without opposition; he was re-elected 70%–22% in 1998 and 78%–22% in 2000. Evidently no one has more relatives.

Underwood on Armed Services (non-voting delegates can vote in committees) and is ranking member on the fisheries panel of the Resources Committee. He strongly backed the Guam Commonwealth Act but made little effort to push it forward in the House, where its chances were obviously dimmer than in the Clinton Interior Department. Instead he has produced a flurry of legislation, much of which has been passed, addressing Guam's practical problems and getting Guam and other territories treated on the same basis as the 50 states. In January 1994 he pushed through the House a bill transferring 3,200 acres from federal to GovGuam (as the government here is called) control. He has passed amendments providing for car rental reimbursement when Defense Department personnel's vehicles are shipped late, commissary and PX privileges for National Guard troops called up for disaster relief, and a $65 million reserve for Guam businesses on A-76 outsourcing contracts. He seeks help in eradicating, not just containing, the brown tree snake. He got Guam included in the State Commemorative Coin Act and the World War II memorial and got Pacific Islanders included in a resolution honoring minority veterans of World War II. In October 1998 he got the House to pass an amendment to the Guam Organic Act, allowing the legislature to create an elective office of attorney general, to redefine a quorum as a majority of those present (it has been 11 of 15), and to make laws over "rightful" subjects, not just local subjects. He persuaded the U.S. Board of Geographic Names to rename Agana Hagatna and got the Geological Survey to revise its topographic maps of Guam using Chamorro place names.

In the 106th Congress Underwood called for the elimination of political asylum in Guam and sought $4.4 million to reimburse Guam for maintaining hundreds of illegal Chinese aliens at its Department of Corrections. He helped get a $3 million increase in Compact aid for coastal improvements (up from $4.58 million) in 1999. After a shipload of PCB wastes from military bases was rejected in Canada, the military sent it to Japan; Underwood got it barred from Guam as well. In 2000 he got the Labor Department to issue an updated wage scale for federal contractors, giving Guamanians $2 an hour more. He persuaded the FDA to lift the 1992 ban on import of betel nuts. He got the House to pass a bill creating a commission to review the claims of Guamanians for compensation during the 32-month Japanese occupation in World War II and got the Defense Department to search records to identify World War II era dump sites in Guam; there is concern about unexploded mustard gas bombs buried in Agana Swamp. He got the time zone Guam is in renamed Chamorro Standard Time. He got a higher reimbursement rate for Guam's home health care providers. Underwood seems particularly assiduous about getting Guam treated as part of the United States. In 1999 he asked the Senate Foreign Relations Committee to include Guam in the definition of the U.S. in future tax treaties, and in 2000 secured the inclusion of Guam and the CNMI in mandated reports to assess the threat to the U.S. of ballistic missile development—an issue of great practical importance, since Guam is less than 2,000 miles from North Korea. And he introduced a bill to require OMB to provide an explanation when territories are excluded from presidential initiatives and executive orders.

Del. Robert Underwood (D)

Elected 1992, 5th term; b. July 13, 1948, Tamuning; home, Yona; CA St. U., B.A. 1969, M.A. 1971, U. of S. CA, Ph.D. 1988; Catholic; married (Lorraine).

Professional Career: Teacher, Admin., Guam Public Schls., 1972–76; Prof., U. of Guam, 1976–88, Dean, 1988–90, Academic Vice Pres., 1990–92.

DC Office: 2428 RHOB, 20515, 202-225-1188; Fax: 202-226-0341; Web site: www.house.gov/underwood.

District Office: Hagatna, 671-477-4272.

Committees: *Armed Services* (8th of 28 D): Military Installations & Facilities; Military Readiness. *Resources* (11th of 25 D): Fisheries Conservation, Wildlife & Oceans (RMM).

AMERICAN SAMOA

American Samoa, the only American territory south of the Equator, has been little influenced by Western settlers and remains almost as Polynesian today as it was when the United States took possession in 1900. These seven islands are 2,300 miles southwest of Hawaii, 1,600 miles northeast of New Zealand. American Samoa has 64,000 people, 89% of them Polynesian, mostly Christian (50% Congregationalist, 20% Catholic); they are U.S. nationals but not U.S. citizens. Its population has doubled in the last 20 years, and fear that outsiders will change the culture has prompted some demands for stricter immigration standards. American Samoa is an unincorporated territory administered by the Interior Department since 1951; minimum wages are set for industries by the U.S. Department of Labor. American Samoa elects a governor and a two house legislature known as the Fono. It is a bilingual society and government: Government is mostly conducted in English, Fono proceedings are in Samoan, and court sessions are conducted in English with each sentence then translated into Samoan. The islands of Ofu, Tau and Tutuila are the site of the National Park of American Samoa, opened in April 1997, preserving fruit bat habitat, tropical forests and coral reefs.

The market economy has not made much progress here: American Samoa lives off the federal government, which spends some $33 million annually, plus varying amounts for construction, and two big tuna canneries, which employ 5,200 workers, earn $451 million and provide one-third of all U.S. canned tuna. Residents are eligible for U.S. food stamps and welfare; local agriculture is minimal and sheltered (the territorial government in 2000 wanted to quadruple tariffs on bananas and taro) and efforts to attract investment brought in just one garment factory, which was closed in January 2001 after a Justice Department investigation found an extraordinary variety of abuses against workers committed there. Tourism for many years was minimal, but it increased in 2000 because of a coup in Fiji and political unrest in the Solomon Islands; 2000 also saw the opening of the first McDonalds here. The bedrock of the local economy is the territorial government, which under Governor Tauese Sunia has maintained payroll levels even though it has been stiffing creditors from the local utility to the IRS and has not been able to send out tax refunds on time.

One cause celebre is the renaming of nearby Samoa, formerly British Samoa and Western Samoa; the single name suggests to many in American Samoa that they are regarded as not full Samoans, and the legislature threatened not to recognize Samoan passports—a problem, since 85% of the cannery work force is from Samoa. But the governor, a nephew of the Samoan prime minister, promised to veto any such bill. Nationals of Samoa also made up 90% of the 107 prisoners who burned all three prison buildings in October 1999 after wardens refused to allow children to visit on White Sunday. But if American Samoans are proud Samoans, they are also proud Americans: On April 17, 2000, they celebrated the 100th anniversary of the American takeover, with a 60-foot American flag raised on Sogelau Hill, where the American flag was first raised; there was traditional singing and dancing at Veterans Stadium and a long boat race in Pago Pago Harbor, and a commemorative stamp was unveiled showing a Samoan alia (two-hull canoe) sailing in easterly winds near Suniatu Mountain in the Manu'a island group. Unfortunately, the celebration, which was budgeted at $100,000, ended up costing $625,000.

American Samoa does not cast electoral votes for president, but does send delegates to the parties' national conventions. In February 2000, George W. Bush won four delegates in a caucus. In March 2000, Al Gore beat Bill Bradley by 21–4—those are not percentages, but the actual number of votes; Bradley got one convention vote split between four delegates.

Governor Tauese Sunia, the son of Congregationalist ministers, taught high school in Nebraska and in American Samoa, and was the first Samoan television teacher. Tauese (it is Samoan tradition to refer to chieftans by their first names) headed the local department of education and the bar association and is the father of 10 children. He was elected lieutenant governor in 1992, serving under then-Governor A. P. Lutali, then was elected governor in 1996 as a Democrat; Lutali finished third in the first election, and in the runoff Tauese won by a 51%–49% margin over Lealaifuaneva Peter Reid.

In office Tauese had to struggle with American Samoa's $35.6 million debt, its difficulty in paying bills and in collecting taxes and fees. In 2000, the territorial government negotiated an $18.6 million, 26-year loan from the federal government to pay off debts contracted since 1992: It owed $6 million to the IRS for unpaid payroll deductions, $7 million to the authority providing trash collection, electricity and drinking water, which in turn owed $2.5 million to three oil companies. One of which, Tesoro South Pacific, announced it would no longer run the government-owned Gataivai oil tank farm and left the islands; American Samoa had to get permission from EPA to import unleaded gasoline from Australia and Singapore. It is hard to see why any company would want to start doing business with American Samoa. None of this seems to bother Tauese. Running for re-election, he said he could balance the budget in an hour, but would rather preserve government jobs than pay off the government debt. "Can anyone not respond to his child when he asks for something or is hungry? What's the use of the emphasis on balancing the budget if it deprives families of their keep?"

On other issues Tauese opposed video poker—it was declared illegal by the High Court of American Samoa—and wants to restrict immigration to men, on the grounds that they have more skills and do not produce babies. He wants to prevent non-"full-blooded Samoans" from owning land. He signed a bill outlawing roadside solicitations of money and told people to stop excavating coral. He called on the Fono to repeal the death penalty, but the Senate disagreed; he pointed out that the method of execution is not specified; the last execution, in 1951, was by hanging. He successfully sought "observer status" for American Samoa at the United Nations, but the territory decided it could afford to send an observer only during General Assembly meetings. In September 1998 Tauese's opponents tried to impeach him. They charged him with using $18,000 in school repair funds to build a sauna in the governor's mansion, using $10,000 in public funds to pay off a personal credit card, and selling government vehicles and spare parts without notice or competitive bidding. But nothing came of it. In 2000 he campaigned on his record, and the result was close; Tauese won 51%–48% over Senator Leala Reid out of 12,049 votes cast. Reid challenged the result, charging that absentee ballots were mishandled; his case was rejected by the High Court.

Delegate American Samoa has elected a delegate to Congress since 1980. Delegate Eni F. H. Faleomavaega is a Democrat first elected in 1988. He went to high school in Hawaii, to Brigham Young University, then to law school in Houston and Berkeley; he served in Vietnam in the Army. In the 1970s he worked on the Natural Resources Insular subcommittee staff and for former Utah Democrat Gunn McKay. In 1981 he became deputy attorney general of American Samoa, and in 1985 lieutenant governor.

Faleomavaega (he uses his last name in his press releases, rather than the first name used to refer to Samoan chiefs) serves on the Resources Committee, where he has been ranking Democrat on three subcommittees—Native Americans and Insular Affairs in January 1995; National Parks and Public Lands in January 1998; Fisheries, Conservation, Wildlife and Oceans in January 1999. He is also a member of International Affairs and ranking member on its East Asian and the

Pacific Subcommittee. Faleomavaega worked to improve conditions at the StarKist tuna plant and to get the British Ceramic Tile Company to make the largest investment in American Samoa since the canneries were built decades ago. He led the congressional protest against the French nuclear tests in the Pacific, and was stopped by the French for approaching the French nuclear testing site at Mururoa Atoll and imprisoned in Tahiti in 1996. In June 1998 he said it was difficult to believe the International Atomic Energy Agency study found little or no effect on plants or animals by French nuclear tests from 1966 to 1996. Faleomaveaga has also kept an eye on Indonesia, criticizing the Suharto government for the murder or "disappearance" of perhaps 300,000 Malanesians in western New Guinea; in March 1999 he and four other members called on Indonesia President B.J. Habibie to engage in dialogue with Irian Jaya. In September 2000 he met in Washington with Indian Prime Minister Atal Bihari Vajpayee and discussed the political strife in Fiji between island natives and the descendants of Indian laborers; he said it was not solely a racial conflict, but was rooted in colonialism.

Faleomavaega has expressed fears that American Samoa will be threatened by an "invasion" of Asian small businessmen, comparing it to Fiji. With help from Senator Daniel Inouye and Pennsylvania Democrat John Murtha, Faleomavaega got into the October 1998 omnibus budget free transportation on military aircraft for veterans approved for VA health care in Hawaii; in July 2000 he complained that the VA was not cooperating and only one veteran had flown to Hawaii. In late 2000 he urged American Samoa veterans to enroll as a first step in establishing a VA medical clinic in American Samoa. In January 1998 he had the pleasure of congratulating two Samoans who played in the Super Bowl, Maa Tanuvasa of the Denver Broncos and Esera Tuaolo of the Atlanta Falcons; he hailed other Samoan athletes, professional wrestler Dwayne Johnson, known as "The Rock" and heavyweight fighter David Tua, and helped arrange for the November 2000 championship fight between Tua and Lennox Lewis to be seen on free TV in American Samoa. Faleomavaega has been active in announcing federal grants and projects—$8.9 million to extend runways in Pago Pago International Airport in Tafuna and Fitiuta Airport on Ta'u, Manu'a, the U.S. Postal Service agreement with Evergreen International Airlines to deliver U.S. mail to American Samoa, and the FAA's ceding of 6.5 acres at Tafuna for a $20 million Army Reserve training facility. In 2000 his Fisheries Subcommittee passed bills to increase funding for coral reef preservation, to transfer a NOAA research vessel to the American Samoa government for future transport of cargo and passengers to the Manu'a islands and to prohibit the practice of shark finning in American waters. He strongly supported Native Hawaiian sovereignty in fall 2000 and decried the February 2000 Supreme Court decision that overturned Hawaii's native-Hawaiians-only elections to the state Office of Hawaiian Affairs.

In 1996 Faleomavaega fell just short of winning re-election on November 5, with 49.6%, to 26% for independent Gus Hanneman and 24% for Republican Aumua Amata Coleman; he won the runoff two weeks later 56%–44%. In 1998 he won 86%–14% over Seigafolava Pene; Coleman got perhaps 400 votes as a write-in, but they were voided since local law doesn't authorize write-ins. In 2000 he faced Hannemann again, and there was some bitterness; Faleomavaega had endorsed Honolulu Mayor Jeremy Harris in his September 2000 primary against Hannemann's brother, Honolulu Councilman Mufi Hannemann. On election day Faleomavaega won 46% of the vote, Hannemann 30% and Aumua Amata Coleman 22%. In the runoff two weeks later Faleomavaega won 61%–39%. American Samoa has the lowest number of votes cast in any congressional race, 12,021 in 2000.

Del. Eni F. H. Faleomavaega (D)

Elected 1988, 7th term; b. Aug. 15, 1943, Vailoatai; home, Pago Pago; Brigham Young U., B.A. 1972, U. of CA, LL.M. 1973; Mormon; married (Hinanui).

Military Career: Army, 1966–69 (Vietnam).

Elected Office: AS Lt. Gov., 1984–89.

Professional Career: A.A., U.S. Del. from AS, 1973–75; Cnsl., U.S. House Interior Cmte., 1975–81; AS Dpty. Atty. Gen., 1981–84.

DC Office: 2422 RHOB, 20515, 202-225-8577; Fax: 202-225-8757; Web site: www.house.gov/faleomavaega.

District Office: Pago Pago, 684-633-1372.

Committees: *International Relations* (4th of 23 D): East Asia & the Pacific (RMM); Western Hemisphere. *Resources* (6th of 25 D): Fisheries Conservation, Wildlife & Oceans; National Parks, Recreation & Public Lands.

HOUSE REDISTRICTING

State	107th House Composition	Gain/ Loss of Seats	Control of State House/Senate	Governor	Redistricting Responsibility
Alabama	2D/5R	0	D/D	D	Legislature, made up of a 22 rep. committee. Gov. has veto power.
Arizona	1D/5R	+2	R/tied	R	Redistricting commission. Gov. does not have veto power.
Arkansas	3D/1R	0	D/D	R	Legislature. Gov. has veto power but can be overridden by a majority vote in the legislature.
California	31D/20R	+1	D/D	D	Legislature. Gov. has veto power.
Colorado	2D/4R	+1	R/D	R	Legislature. Gov. has veto power.
Connecticut	3D/3R	−1	D/D	R	Bi-partisan reapportionment committee of 8 legislators. 2/3 majority vote in each chamber is required. Gov. does not have veto power.
Florida	8D/15R	+2	R/R	R	Legislature. Gov. has veto power.
Georgia	3D/8R	+2	D/D	D	Legislature. Gov. has veto power.
Hawaii	2D	0	D/D	D	9-member reapportionment commission made up of 2 members appointed by the president of the Senate, 2 appointed by the speaker, 2 by the minority party in each house. Those 8 members choose the 9th. Gov. does not have veto power.
Idaho	2R	0	R/R	R	6-member reapportionment commission. Gov. does not have veto power.
Illinois	10D/10R	−1	D/R	R	Legislature. Gov. has veto power.

Indiana	4D/6R	−1	D/R	D	Legislature. Gov. has veto power. If the legislature and the gov. can't agree on lines, the plan goes to a 5-member committee where Dems have the controlling vote.
Iowa	1D/4R	0	R/R	D	Non-partisan Legislative Services Bureau draws lines which the legislature has to approve. Gov. can veto.
Kansas	1D/3R	0	R/R	R	Legislature. Gov. has veto power.
Kentucky	1D/5R	0	D/R	D	Legislature. Gov. has veto power.
Louisiana	2D/5R	0	D/D	R	Legislature. Gov. has veto power, takes 2/3 vote to overturn veto.
Maine	2D	0	D/tied	I	Apportionment commission submits plan to legislature. Gov. has veto power.
Maryland	4D/4R	0	D/D	D	Legislature. Gov. has veto power.
Massachusetts	10D	0	D/D	R	Legislature. Gov. has veto power, takes 2/3 vote to overturn veto.
Michigan	9D/7R	−1	R/R	R	Legislature. Gov. has veto power.
Minnesota	5D/3R	0	R/D	I	Legislature. Gov. has veto power.
Mississippi	3D/2R	−1	D/D	D	Legislature. Gov. has veto power.
Missouri	4D/5R	0	D/R	D	Legislature. Gov. has veto power.
Nebraska	3R	0	unicameral	R	Legislature. Gov. has veto power.
Nevada	1D/1R	+1	D/R	R	Legislature. Gov. has veto power.
New Hampshire	2R	0	R/R	D	Legislature. Gov. has veto power.
New Jersey	7D/6R	0	R/R	R	Appointed 13-member redistricting com- mission. Gov. does not have veto power.

New Mexico	1D/2R	0	D/D	R	Legislature. Gov. has veto power, takes 2/3 vote to overturn veto.
New York	19D/12R	−2	D/R	R	Legislature. Gov. has veto power.
North Carolina	5D/7R	+1	D/D	D	Legislature. Gov. does not have veto power.
Ohio	8D/11R	−1	R/R	R	Legislature. Gov. has veto power.
Oklahoma	1D/5R	−1	D/D	R	Legislature. Gov. has veto power, takes 2/3 vote to overturn veto.
Oregon	4D/1R	0	R/R	D	Legislature. Gov. has veto power.
Pennsylvania	10D/10R	−2	R/R	R	Legislature. Gov. has veto power.
Rhode Island	2D	0	D/D	R	islature. Gov. has veto power.
South Carolina	2D/4R	0	R/R	D	Legislature. Gov. has veto power, takes 2/3 vote to overturn veto.
Tennessee	4D/5R	0	D/D	R	Legislature. Gov. has veto power which can be overridden by a majority vote in the legislature.
Texas	17D/13R	+2	D/R	R	Legislature. Gov. has veto power.
Utah	1D/2R	0	R/R	R	Legislature. Gov. has veto power.
Virginia	3D/7R/1I	0	R/R	R	Legislature. Gov. has veto power.
Washington	6D/3R	0	tied/D	D	4-member redistricting commission. Gov. does not have veto power.
West Virginia	2D/1R	0	D/D	D	Legislature. Gov. has veto power.
Wisconsin	5D/4R	−1	R/D	R	Legislature. Gov. has veto power.

Source: The Cook Political Report, April, 2001

GUBERNATORIAL ELECTION CYCLE

2001, 2 STATES

New Jersey (R)   **Virginia (R)**

2002, 36 STATES

Alabama (D)   Minnesota (Ind)
Alaska (D)   Nebraska (R)
Arizona (R)   Nevada (R)
Arkansas (R)   New Hampshire (D)
California (D)   **New Mexico (R)**
Colorado (R)   New York (R)
Connecticut (R)   Ohio (R)
Florida (R)   **Oklahoma (R)**
Georgia (D)   **Oregon (D)**
Hawaii (D)   **Pennsylvania (R)**
Idaho (R)   **Rhode Island (R)**
Illinois (R)   South Carolina (D)
Iowa (D)   **South Dakota (R)**
Kansas (R)   **Tennessee (R)**
Maine (I)   Texas (R)
Maryland (D)   Vermont (D)
Massachusetts (R)   Wisconsin (R)
Michigan (R)   **Wyoming (R)**

2003, 3 STATES

Kentucky (D)   Mississippi (D)
Louisiana (R)

2004, 11 STATES

Delaware (D)   North Dakota (R)
Indiana (D)   Utah (R)
Missouri (D)   Vermont (D)
Montana (R)   Washington (D)
New Hampshire (D)   West Virginia (D)
North Carolina (D)

29 Republicans, 19 Democrats, 1 Independent, 1 Independence

New Hampshire and Vermont have two year terms. All others are four year.
**Boldface indicates governors who may not succeed themselves in the election that
year.**

SENATE SEATS

2002 ELECTION CYCLE

REPUBLICANS (20)	PREVIOUS %	DEMOCRATS (13)	PREVIOUS %
Wayne Allard (CO)	51%	Max Baucus (MT)	50%
Thad Cochran (MS)	71%	Joseph R. Biden Jr. (DE)	60%
Susan Collins (ME)	49%	Jean Carnahan (MO)	appointed
Larry Craig (ID)	57%	Max Cleland (GA)	49%
Pete V. Dominici (NM)	65%	Richard J. Durbin (IL)	56%
Michael Enzi (WY)	54%	Tom Harkin (IA)	52%
Phil Gramm (TX)	55%	Timothy P. Johnson (SD)	51%
Chuck Hagel (NE)	56%	John F. Kerry (MA)	52%
Jesse Helms (NC)	53%	Mary L. Landrieu (LA)	50%
Tim Hutchinson (AR)	53%	Carl Levin (MI)	58%
James M. Inhofe (OK)	57%	Jack Reed (RI)	63%
Mitch McConnell (KY)	55%	John D. Rockefeller IV (WV)	77%
Pat Roberts (KS)	62%	Robert G. Torricelli (NJ)	53%
Jeff Sessions (AL)	52%	Paul Wellstone (MN)	50%
Bob Smith (NH)	49%		
Gordon H. Smith (OR)	50%		
Ted Stevens (AK)	77%		
Fred D. Thompson (TN)	61%		
Strom Thurmond (SC)*	53%		
John W. Warner (VA)	52%		

will not seek reelection in 2002

2004 ELECTION CYCLE

REPUBLICANS (15)	PREVIOUS %	DEMOCRATS (19)	PREVIOUS %
Robert Bennett (UT)	64%	Evan Bayh (IN)	64%
Christopher Bond (MO)	53%	Barbara Boxer (CA)	53%
Sam Brownback (KS)	65%	John Breaux (LA)	64%
Jim Bunning (KY)	50%	Thomas Daschle (SD)	62%
Ben Nighthorse Campbell (CO)	62%	Christopher Dodd (CT)	65%
Mike Crapo (ID)	70%	Byron Dorgan (ND)	63%
Peter Fitzgerald (IL)	50%	John Edwards (NC)	51%
Charles Grassley (IA)	68%	Russell Feingold (WI)	51%
Judd Gregg (NH)	68%	Bob Graham (FL)	62%
John McCain (AZ)	69%	Ernest Hollings (SC)	53%
Frank Murkowski (AK)	74%	Daniel Inouye (HI)	79%
Don Nickles (OK)	66%	Patrick Leahy (VT)	72%
Richard Shelby (AL)	63%	Blanche Lincoln (AR)	55%
Arlen Specter (PA)	61%	Barbara Mikulski (MD)	71%
George Voinovich (OH)	56%	Zell Miller (GA)	58%
		Patty Murray (WA)	58%
		Harry Reid (NV)	48%
		Charles Schumer (NY)	55%
		Ron Wyden (OR)	61%

CONGRESSIONAL LEADERSHIP

U.S. SENATE

DEMOCRATS

Majority Leader	Thomas A. Daschle (SD)
Majority Whip	Harry Reid (NV)
President Pro-Tempore	Robert Byrd (WV)
Democratic Policy Co-Chairman	Byron Dorgan (ND)
DSCC Chairman	Patty Murray (WA)
DSCC Vice Chairman	Bill Nelson (FL)
Democratic Conference Secretary	Barbara Mikulski (MD)
Democratic Steering Committee Chairman	John Kerry (MA)

REPUBLICANS

Minority Leader	Trent Lott (MS)
Minority Whip	Don Nickles (OK)
Republican Conference Chairman	Rick Santorum (PA)
Republican Conference Vice Chairman	Kay Bailey Hutchison (TX)
Republican Policy Committee Chairman	Larry Craig (ID)
NRSC Chairman	Bill Frist (TN)

U.S. HOUSE OF REPRESENTATIVES

REPUBLICANS

Speaker of the House	J. Dennis Hastert (IL-14)
Majority Leader	Dick Armey (TX-26)
Majority Whip	Tom DeLay (TX-22)
Republican Conference Chairman	J.C. Watts (OK-4)
Chief Deputy Majority Whip	Roy Blunt (MO-7)
Republican Leadership Chairman	Rob Portman (OH-2)
Republican Conference Vice Chairman	Deborah Pryce (OH-15)
Republican Conference Secretary	Barbara Cubin (WY-AL)
Republican Policy Committee Chairman	Christopher Cox (CA-47)
NRCC Chairman	Tom Davis (VA-11)
Chairman, Committee on Rules	David Dreier (CA-28)

DEMOCRATS

Minority Leader	Richard A. Gephardt (MO-3)
Minority Whip	David E. Bonior (MI-10)
Chief Deputy Minority Whip	Chet Edwards (TX-11)
Chief Deputy Minority Whip	John Lewis (GA-5)
Chief Deputy Minority Whip	Ed Pastor (AZ-2)
Chief Deputy Minority Whip	Maxine Waters (CA-35)
Democratic Caucus Chairman	Martin Frost (TX-24)
Democratic Caucus Vice Chairman	Robert Menendez (NJ-13)
Democratic Steering Committee Co-Chair	Steny Hoyer (MD-5)
DCCC Chairman	Nita Lowey (NY-18)

COMMITTEE CHAIRMEN

SENATE COMMITTEES	CHAIRMAN	RANKING MEMBER
Aging (Special)	John Breaux (LA)	Larry Craig (ID)
Agriculture, Nutrition & Forestry	Tom Harkin (IA)	Richard G. Lugar (IN)
Appropriations	Robert C. Byrd (WV)	Ted Stevens (AK)
Armed Services	Carl Levin (MI)	John Warner (VA)
Banking, Housing & Urban Affairs	Paul Sarbanes (MD)	Phil Gramm (TX)
Budget	Kent Conrad (ND)	Pete V. Domenici (NM)
Commerce, Science & Transportation	Ernest F. Hollings (SC)	John McCain (AZ)
Energy & Natural Resources	Jeff Bingaman (NM)	Frank Murkowski (AK)
Environment & Public Works	James Jeffords (VT)	Bob Smith (NH)
Ethics (Select)	Harry Reid (NV)	Pat Roberts (KS)
Finance	Max Baucus (MT)	Charles Grassley (IA)
Foreign Relations	Joseph R. Biden Jr. (DE)	Jesse Helms (NC)
Governmental Affairs	Joseph I. Lieberman (CT)	Fred D. Thompson (TN)
Health, Education, Labor & Pensions	Edward Kennedy (MA)	Judd Gregg (NH)
Indian Affairs	Daniel K. Inouye (HI)	Ben Nighthorse Campbell (CO)
Intelligence (Select)	Bob Graham (FL)	Richard C. Shelby (AL)
Judiciary	Patrick Leahy (VT)	Orrin G. Hatch (UT)
Rules & Administration	Christopher J. Dodd (CT)	Mitch McConnell (KY)
Small Business	John F. Kerry (MA)	Christopher S. Bond (MO)
Veterans' Affairs	John D. Rockefeller IV (WV)	Arlen Specter (PA)

HOUSE COMMITTEES	CHAIRMAN	RANKING MEMBER
Agriculture	Larry Combest (TX-19)	Charles W. Stenholm (TX-17)
Appropriations	C.W. (Bill) Young (FL-10)	David R. Obey (WI-7)
Armed Services	Bob Stump (AZ-3)	Ike Skelton (MO-4)
Budget	Jim Nussle (IA-2)	John M. Spratt Jr. (SC-5)
Education & The Workforce	John A. Boehner (OH-8)	George Miller (CA-7)
Energy & Commerce	W.J. (Billy) Tauzin (LA-3)	John D. Dingell (MI-16)
Financial Services	Michael G. Oxley (OH-4)	John J. LaFalce (NY-29)
Government Reform	Dan Burton (IN-6)	Henry A. Waxman (CA-29)
House Administration	Bob Ney (OH-18)	Steny H. Hoyer (MD-5)
Intelligence (Select)	Porter J. Goss (FL-14)	Nancy Pelosi (CA-8)
International Relations	Henry J. Hyde (IL-6)	Tom Lantos (CA-12)
Judiciary	F. James Sensenbrenner Jr. (WI-9)	John Conyers Jr. (MI-14)
Resources	James V. Hansen (UT-1)	Nick J. Rahall II (WV-3)
Rules	David Dreier (CA-28)	Joe Moakley (MA-9)
Science	Sherwood L. Boehlert (NY-23)	Ralph M. Hall (TX-4)
Small Business	Donald Manzullo (IL-16)	Nydia M. Velaquez (NY-12)
Standards of Official Conduct	Joel Hefley (CO-5)	Howard L. Berman (CA-26)
Transportation & Infrastructure	Don Young (AK-AL)	James L. Oberstar (MN-14)
Veterans’ Affairs	Christopher H. Smith (NJ-4)	Lane Evans (IL-17)
Ways & Means	Bill Thomas (CA-21)	Charles B. Rangel (NY-15)

SENATE COMMITTEES

As of early July 2001, Senate committees were still in the process of organizing. Full committee assignments were made, but subcommittee assignments were still subject to change, which would give Democrats a one-seat majority in most cases.

AGING (Special)
www.senate.gov/~aging

G-31 Dirksen
202-224-5364

Majority (D 11): Breaux (LA), Chmn.; Reid (NV), Kohl (WI), Jeffords (VT), Feingold (WI), Wyden (OR), Lincoln (AR), Bayh (IN), Carper (DE), Stabenow (MI), Carnahan (MO)
Minority (R 10): Craig (ID), RMM; Burns (MT), Shelby (AL), Santorum (PA), Collins (ME), Enzi (WY), Hutchinson (AR), Fitzgerald (IL), Ensign (NV), 1 vacancy

NO SUBCOMMITTEES

AGRICULTURE, NUTRITION & FORESTRY
www.senate.gov/~agriculture

SR-328-A Russell
202-224-2035

Majority (D 11): Harkin (IA), Chmn.; Leahy (VT), Conrad (ND), Daschle (SD), Baucus (MT), Lincoln (AR), Miller (GA), Stabenow (MI), Nelson (NE), Dayton (MN), Wellstone (MN)
Minority (R 10): Lugar (IN), RMM; Helms (NC), Cochran (MS), McConnell (KY), Roberts (KS), Fitzgerald (IL), Thomas (WY), Allard (CO), Hutchinson (AR), Crapo (ID)

SUBCOMMITTEES

Forestry, Conservation & Rural Revitalization
Majority (D 5): Lincoln, Chmn.; Leahy, Stabenow, Dayton, 1 vacancy
Minority (R 5): Crapo, RMM; McConnell, Thomas, Allard, Hutchinson

Marketing, Inspection & Product Promotion
Majority (D 5): Baucus, Chmn.; Leahy, Conrad, Nelson, Dayton
Minority (R 5): Fitzgerald, RMM; Helms, Cochran, Roberts, Thomas

Production & Price Competitiveness
Majority (D 5): Conrad, Chmn.; Baucus, Lincoln, Miller, 1 vacancy
Minority (R 5): Roberts, RMM; Helms, Cochran, Fitzgerald, McConnell

Research, Nutrition & General Legislation
Majority (D 5): Leahy, Chmn.; Conrad, Miller, Stabenow, Nelson
Minority (R 5): McConnell, RMM; Allard, Hutchinson, Crapo, Helms

APPROPRIATIONS
www.senate.gov/~appropriations

S-128 The Capitol
202-224-3471

Majority (D 15): Byrd (WV), Chmn.; Inouye (HI), Hollings (SC), Leahy (VT), Harkin (IA), Mikulski (MD), Reid (NV), Kohl (WI), Murray (WA), Dorgan (ND), Feinstein (CA), Durbin (IL), Johnson (SD), Landrieu (LA), Reed (RI)
Minority (R 14): Stevens (AK), RMM; Cochran (MS), Specter (PA), Domenici (NM), Bond (MO), McConnell (KY), Burns (MT), Shelby (AL), Gregg (NH), Bennett (UT), Campbell (CO), Craig (ID), Hutchison (TX), DeWine (OH)

SUBCOMMITTEES

Agriculture & Rural Development
Majority (D 6): Kohl, Chmn.; Harkin, Dorgan, Feinstein, Durbin, Johnson
Minority (R 6): Cochran, RMM; Specter, Bond, McConnell, Burns, Craig

Commerce, Justice, State & Judiciary
Majority (D 6): Hollings, Chmn.; Inouye, Mikulski, Leahy, Kohl, Murray
Minority (R 6): Gregg, RMM; Stevens, Domenici, McConnell, Hutchison, Campbell

Defense
Majority (D 9): Inouye, Chmn.; Hollings, Byrd, Leahy, Harkin, Dorgan, Durbin, Reid, Feinstein
Minority (R 9): Stevens, RMM; Cochran, Specter, Domenici, Bond, McConnell, Shelby, Gregg, Hutchison

District of Columbia
Majority (D 2): Landrieu, Chmn.; Durbin
Minority (R 2): DeWine, RMM; Hutchison

Energy & Water Development
Majority (D 6): Reid, Chmn.; Byrd, Hollings, Murray, Dorgan, Feinstein
Minority (R 6): Domenici, RMM; Cochran, McConnell, Bennett, Burns, Craig

Foreign Operations
Majority (D 7): Leahy, Chmn.; Inouye, Harkin, Mikulski, Durbin, Johnson, Landrieu
Minority (R 7): McConnell, RMM; Specter, Gregg, Shelby, Bennett, Campbell, Bond

Interior
Majority (D 7): Byrd, Chmn.; Leahy, Hollings, Reid, Dorgan, Feinstein, Murray
Minority (R 7): Burns, RMM; Stevens, Cochran, Domenici, Bennett, Gregg, Campbell

Labor, HHS & Education
Majority (D 7): Harkin, Chmn.; Hollings, Inouye, Reid, Kohl, Murray, Landrieu
Minority (R 7): Specter, RMM; Cochran, Gregg, Craig, Hutchison, Stevens, DeWine

Legislative Branch
Majority (D 2): Durbin, Chmn.; Johnson
Minority (R 2): Bennett, RMM; Stevens

Military Construction
Majority (D 4): Feinstein, Chmn.; Inouye, Johnson, Landrieu
Minority (R 4): Hutchison, RMM; Burns, Craig, DeWine

Transportation
Majority (D 6): Murray, Chmn.; Byrd, Mikulski, Reid, Kohl, Durbin
Minority (R 6): Shelby, RMM; Specter, Bond, Bennett, Campbell, Hutchison

Treasury & General Government
Majority (D 3): Dorgan, Chmn.; Mikulski, Landrieu
Minority (R 3): Campbell, RMM; Shelby, DeWine

VA, HUD & Independent Agencies
Majority (D 6): Mikulski, Chmn.; Leahy, Harkin, Byrd, Kohl, Johnson
Minority (R 6): Bond, RMM; Burns, Shelby, Craig, Hutchison, 1 vacancy

ARMED SERVICES
228 Russell
www.senate.gov/~armed_services
202-224-3871
Majority (D 13): Levin (MI), Chmn.; Kennedy (MA), Byrd (WV), Lieberman (CT), Cleland (GA), Landrieu (LA), Reed (RI), Akaka (HI), Nelson (FL), Nelson (NE), Carnahan (MO), Dayton (MN), Bingaman (NM)
Minority (R 12): Warner (VA), RMM; Thurmond (SC), McCain (AZ), Smith (NH), Inhofe (OK), Santorum (PA), Roberts (KS), Allard (CO), Hutchinson (AR), Sessions (AL), Collins (ME), Bunning (KY)

SUBCOMMITTEES

Airland Forces
Majority (D 6): Lieberman, Chmn.; Cleland, Nelson (FL), Nelson (NE), Carnahan, Dayton
Minority (R 6): Santorum, RMM; Inhofe, Roberts, Hutchinson, Sessions, Bunning

Emerging Threats & Capabilities
Majority (D 6): Landrieu, Chmn.; Kennedy, Byrd, Lieberman, Nelson (FL), Dayton
Minority (R 6): Roberts, RMM; Smith, Santorum, Allard, Hutchinson, Collins

Personnel
Majority (D 5): Cleland, Chmn.; Kennedy, Reed, Akaka, Carnahan
Minority (R 5): Hutchinson, RMM; Thurmond, McCain, Allard, Collins

Readiness & Management Support
Majority (D 6): Akaka, Chmn.; Byrd, Cleland, Landrieu, Nelson (NE), Dayton
Minority (R 6): Inhofe, RMM; Thurmond, McCain, Santorum, Roberts, Bunning

Seapower
Majority (D 5): Kennedy, Chmn.; Lieberman, Landrieu, Reed, Carnahan
Minority (R 5): Sessions, RMM; McCain, Smith, Collins, Bunning

Strategic Forces
Majority (D 5): Reed, Chmn.; Byrd, Akaka, Nelson (FL), Nelson (NE)
Minority (R 5): Allard, RMM; Thurmond, Smith, Inhofe, Sessions

BANKING, HOUSING & URBAN AFFAIRS

534 Dirksen
banking.senate.gov
202-224-7391
Majority (D 11): Sarbanes (MD), Chmn.; Dodd (CT), Johnson (SD), Reed (RI), Schumer (NY), Bayh (IN), Miller (GA), Carper (DE), Stabenow (MI), Corzine (NJ), Akaka (HI)
Minority (R 10): Gramm (TX), RMM; Shelby (AL), Bennett (UT), Allard (CO), Enzi (WY), Hagel (NE), Santorum (PA), Bunning (KY), Crapo (ID), Ensign (NV)

SUBCOMMITTEES

Economic Policy
Majority (D 3): Schumer, Chmn.; Miller, Corzine
Minority (R 3): Bunning, RMM; Bennett, Ensign

Financial Institutions
Majority (D 7): Johnson, Chmn.; Miller, Carper, Stabenow, Dodd, Reed, Bayh
Minority (R 7): Bennett, RMM; Ensign, Shelby, Allard, Santorum, Bunning, Crapo

Housing & Transportation
Majority (D 6): Reed, Chmn.; Carper, Stabenow, Corzine, Dodd, Schumer
Minority (R 6): Allard, RMM; Santorum, Ensign, Shelby, Enzi, Hagel

International Trade & Finance
Majority (D 3): Bayh, Chmn.; Miller, Johnson
Minority (R 3): Hagel, RMM; Enzi, Crapo

Securities & Investment
Majority (D 8): Dodd, Chmn.; Johnson, Reed, Schumer, Bayh, Corzine, Carper, Stabenow
Minority (R 8): Enzi, RMM; Shelby, Crapo, Bennett, Allard, Hagel, Santorum, Bunning

BUDGET

621 Dirksen
www.senate.gov/~budget
202-224-0642
Majority (D 12): Conrad (ND), Chmn.; Hollings (SC), Sarbanes (MD), Murray (WA), Wyden (OR), Feingold (WI), Johnson (SD), Byrd (WV), Nelson (FL), Stabenow (MI), Clinton (NY), Corzine (NJ)
Minority (R 11): Domenici (NM), RMM; Grassley (IA), Nickles (OK), Gramm (TX), Bond (MO), Gregg (NH), Snowe (ME), Frist (TN), Smith (OR), Allard (CO), Hagel (NE)

NO SUBCOMMITTEES

COMMERCE, SCIENCE & TRANSPORTATION

508 Dirksen
www.senate.gov/~commerce
202-224-5115
Majority (D 12): Hollings (SC), Chmn.; Inouye (HI), Rockefeller (WV), Kerry (MA), Breaux (LA), Dorgan (ND), Wyden (OR), Cleland (GA), Boxer (CA), Edwards (NC), Carnahan (MO), Nelson (FL)
Minority (R 11): McCain (AZ), RMM; Stevens (AK), Burns (MT), Lott (MS), Hutchison (TX), Snowe (ME), Brownback (KS), Smith (OR), Fitzgerald (IL), Ensign (NV), Allen (VA)

SUBCOMMITTEES

Aviation
Majority (D 9): Rockefeller, Chmn.; Hollings, Inouye, Breaux, Dorgan, Wyden, Cleland, Edwards, Carnahan
Minority (R 9): Hutchison, RMM; Stevens, Burns, Lott, Snowe, Brownback, Smith, Fitzgerald, Ensign

Communications
Majority (D 10): Hollings, Chmn.; Inouye, Kerry, Breaux, Rockefeller, Dorgan, Wyden, Cleland, Boxer, Edwards
Minority (R 10): Burns, RMM; Stevens, Lott, Hutchison, Snowe, Brownback, Smith, Fitzgerald, Ensign, Allen

Consumer Affairs, Foreign Commerce & Tourism
Majority (D 6): Dorgan, Chmn.; Rockefeller, Wyden, Boxer, Edwards, Carnahan
Minority (R 6): Fitzgerald, RMM; Burns, Brownback, Smith, Ensign, Allen

Manufacturing & Competitiveness
Majority (D 3): Wyden, Chmn.; Hollings, Rockefeller
Minority (R 3): Ensign, RMM; Brownback, Fitzgerald

Oceans & Fisheries
Majority (D 5): Kerry, Chmn.; Hollings, Inouye, Breaux, Boxer
Minority (R 5): Snowe, RMM; Stevens, Hutchison, Smith, Fitzgerald

Science, Technology & Space
Majority (D 7): Breaux, Chmn.; Rockefeller, Kerry, Dorgan, Cleland, Edwards, Carnahan
Minority (R 7): Brownback, RMM; Stevens, Burns, Lott, Hutchison, Fitzgerald, Allen

Surface Transportation & Merchant Marine
Majority (D 9): Inouye, Chmn.; Rockefeller, Kerry, Breaux, Dorgan, Wyden, Cleland, Boxer, Carnahan
Minority (R 9): Smith, RMM; Stevens, Burns, Lott, Hutchison, Snowe, Brownback, Fitzgerald, Ensign

ENERGY & NATURAL RESOURCES
364 Dirksen
energy.senate.gov
202-224-4971
Majority (D 12): Bingaman (NM), Chmn.; Akaka (HI), Dorgan (ND), Graham (FL), Wyden (OR), Johnson (SD), Landrieu (LA), Bayh (IN), Feinstein (CA), Schumer (NY), Cantwell (WA), Carper (DE)
Minority (R 11): Murkowski (AK), RMM; Domenici (NM), Nickles (OK), Craig (ID), Campbell (CO), Thomas (WY), Shelby (AL), Burns (MT), Kyl (AZ), Smith (OR), Hagel (NE)

SUBCOMMITTEES

Energy Research, Development, Production & Regulation
Majority (D 9): Graham, Chmn.; Akaka, Wyden, Johnson, Landrieu, Bayh, Feinstein, Schumer, Cantwell
Minority (R 9): Nickles, RMM; Domenici, Shelby, Hagel, Thomas, Kyl, Craig, Campbell, Burns

Forests & Public Land Management
Majority (D 8): Wyden, Chmn.; Akaka, Johnson, Landrieu, Bayh, Feinstein, Schumer, Cantwell
Minority (R 8): Craig, RMM; Burns, Domenici, Nickles, Smith, Thomas, Kyl, Shelby

National Parks, Historic Preservation & Recreation
Majority (D 6): Akaka, Chmn.; Dorgan, Graham, Landrieu, Bayh, Schumer
Minority (R 6): Thomas, RMM; Campbell, Burns, Smith, Hagel, Domenici

Water & Power
Majority (D 6): Dorgan, Chmn.; Graham, Wyden, Johnson, Feinstein, Cantwell
Minority (R 6): Smith, RMM; Kyl, Craig, Campbell, Shelby, Hagel

ENVIRONMENT & PUBLIC WORKS
410 Dirksen
www.senate.gov/~epw
202-224-6176
Majority (D 10): Jeffords (VT), Chmn.; Reid (NV), Baucus (MT), Graham (FL), Lieberman (CT), Boxer (CA), Wyden (OR), Carper (DE), Clinton (NY), Corzine (NJ)
Minority (R 9): Smith (NH), RMM; Warner (VA), Inhofe (OK), Bond (MO), Voinovich (OH), Crapo (ID), Chafee (RI), Specter (PA), Campbell (CO)

SUBCOMMITTEES

Clean Air, Wetlands, Private Property & Nuclear Safety
Majority (D 4): Lieberman, Chmn.; Carper, Clinton, Corzine
Minority (R 4): Voinovich, RMM; Inhofe, Crapo, Campbell

Fisheries, Wildlife & Water
Majority (D 5): Graham, Chmn.; Baucus, Wyden, Clinton, Corzine
Minority (R 5): Crapo, RMM; Bond, Warner, Chafee, Campbell

Superfund, Waste Control & Risk Assessment
Majority (D 5): Boxer, Chmn.; Wyden, Carper, Clinton, Corzine
Minority (R 5): Chafee, RMM; Warner, Inhofe, Crapo, Specter

Transportation & Infrastructure
Majority (D 5): Baucus, Chmn.; Graham, Lieberman, Boxer, Wyden
Minority (R 5): Inhofe, RMM; Warner, Bond, Voinovich, Chafee

ETHICS (Select)
ethics.senate.gov
220 Hart
202-224-2981
Majority (D 3): Reid (NV), Chmn.; Akaka (HI), Lincoln (AR)
Minority (R 3): Roberts (KS), RMM; Voinovich (OH), Thomas (WY)

NO SUBCOMMITTEES

FINANCE
www.senate.gov/~finance
219 Dirksen
202-224-4515
Majority (D 11): Baucus (MT), Chmn.; Rockefeller (WV), Daschle (SD), Conrad (ND), Graham (FL), Breaux (LA), Bingaman (NM), Kerry (MA), Torricelli (NJ), Lincoln (AR), Jeffords (VT)
Minority (R 10): Grassley (IA), RMM; Hatch (UT), Murkowski (AK), Nickles (OK), Gramm (TX), Lott (MS), Thompson (TN), Snowe (ME), Kyl (AZ), Thomas (WY)

SUBCOMMITTEES

Health Care
Majority (D 8): Rockefeller, Chmn.; Daschle, Bingaman, Kerry, Torricelli, Lincoln, Breaux, Graham
Minority (R 8): Snowe, RMM; Gramm, Grassley, Kyl, Hatch, Nickles, Thompson, 1 vacancy

International Trade
Majority (D 8): Baucus, Chmn.; Rockefeller, Daschle, Conrad, Kerry, Lincoln, Graham, Torricelli
Minority (R 8): Hatch, RMM; Grassley, Thompson, Murkowski, Gramm, Lott, Snowe, 1 vacancy

Long-Term Growth & Debt Reduction
Majority (D 3): Graham, Chmn.; Baucus, Conrad
Minority (R 3): Murkowski, RMM; Grassley, Kyl

Social Security & Family Policy
Majority (D 5): Breaux, Chmn.; Rockefeller, Bingaman, Daschle, Kerry
Minority (R 5): Kyl, RMM; Nickles, Lott, Gramm, 1 vacancy

Taxation & IRS Oversight
Majority (D 6): Conrad, Chmn.; Torricelli, Breaux, Bingaman, Lincoln, Baucus
Minority (R 6): Nickles, RMM; Lott, Hatch, Thompson, Snowe, Murkowski

FOREIGN RELATIONS
www.senate.gov/~foreign
450 Dirksen
202-224-4651
Majority (D 10): Biden (DE), Chmn.; Sarbanes (MD), Dodd (CT), Kerry (MA), Feingold (WI), Wellstone (MN), Boxer (CA), Torricelli (NJ), Nelson (FL), Rockefeller (WV)
Minority (R 9): Helms (NC), RMM; Lugar (IN), Hagel (NE), Smith (OR), Frist (TN), Chafee (RI), Allen (VA), Brownback (KS), Enzi (WY)

SUBCOMMITTEES

African Affairs
Majority (D 3): Feingold, Chmn.; Dodd, Boxer
Minority (R 3): Frist, RMM; Brownback, Smith

East Asian & Pacific Affairs
Majority (D 4): Kerry, Chmn.; Torricelli, Feingold, Biden
Minority (R 4): Helms, Lugar, Hagel, 1 vacancy

European Affairs
Majority (D 4): Biden, Chmn.; Sarbanes, Dodd, Wellstone
Minority (R 4): Smith, RMM; Lugar, Chafee, Hagel

International Economic Policy, Export & Trade Promotion
Majority (D 4): Sarbanes, Chmn.; Nelson, Wellstone, Torricelli
Minority (R 4): Hagel, RMM; Chafee, Allen, 1 vacancy

International Operations & Terrorism
Majority (D 4): Boxer, Chmn.; Kerry, Nelson, Biden
Minority (R 4): Allen, RMM; Helms, Frist, Brownback

Near Eastern & South Asian Affairs
Majority (D 4): Wellstone, Chmn.; Torricelli, Boxer, Sarbanes
Minority (R 4): Brownback, RMM; Smith, Frist, 1 vacancy

Western Hemisphere, Peace Corps, Narcotics Affairs
Majority (D 4): Dodd, Chmn.; Nelson, Kerry, Feingold
Minority (R 4): Chafee, RMM; Allen, Helms, Lugar

GOVERNMENTAL AFFAIRS

340 Dirksen
www.senate.gov/~gov_affairs
202-224-4751

Majority (D 9): Lieberman (CT), Chmn.; Levin (MI), Akaka (HI), Durbin (IL), Torricelli (NJ), Cleland (GA), Carper (DE), Carnahan (MO), Dayton (MN)
Minority (R 8): Thompson (TN), RMM; Stevens (AK), Collins (ME), Voinovich (OH), Domenici (NM), Cochran (MS), Bennett (UT), Bunning (KY)

SUBCOMMITTEES

Government Management, Restructuring and the District of Columbia
Majority (D 5): Durbin, Chmn.; Akaka, Torricelli, Carper, Carnahan
Minority (R 5): Voinovich, RMM; Stevens, Collins, Domenici, Cochran

International Security, Proliferation & Federal Services
Majority (D 6): Akaka, Chmn.; Levin, Torricelli, Cleland, Carper, Carnahan
Minority (R 6): Cochran, RMM; Stevens, Collins, Domenici, Bennett, 1 vacancy

Investigations (Permanent)
Majority (D 7): Levin, Chmn.; Akaka, Durbin, Torricelli, Cleland, Carper, Carnahan
Minority (R 7): Collins, RMM; Stevens, Voinovich, Domenici, Cochran, Bennett, 1 vacancy

HEALTH, EDUCATION, LABOR & PENSIONS

428 Dirksen
www.senate.gov/~labor
202-224-5375

Majority (D 11): Kennedy (MA), Chmn.; Dodd (CT), Harkin (IA), Mikulski (MD), Jeffords (VT), Bingaman (NM), Wellstone (MN), Murray (WA), Reed (RI), Edwards (NC), Clinton (NY), 1 vacancy
Minority (R 10): Gregg (NH), RMM; Frist (TN), Enzi (WY), Hutchinson (AR), Warner (VA), Bond (MO), Roberts (KS), Collins (ME), Sessions (AL), DeWine (OH)

SUBCOMMITTEES

Aging
Majority (D 5): Mikulski, Chmn.; Dodd, Murray, Edwards, Clinton
Minority (R 5): Hutchinson, RMM; Warner, Bond, Roberts, 1 vacancy

Children & Families
Majority (D 5): Dodd, Chmn.; Bingaman, Wellstone, Murray, Reed
Minority (R 5): Gregg, RMM; Frist, Warner, Bond, Collins

Employment, Safety & Training
Majority (D 4): Wellstone, Chmn.; Kennedy, Dodd, Harkin
Minority (R 4): Enzi, RMM; Gregg, Sessions, 1 vacancy

Public Health
Majority (D 7): Kennedy, Chmn.; Harkin, Mikulski, Bingaman, Reed, Edwards, Clinton
Minority (R 7): Frist, RMM; Gregg, Enzi, Hutchinson, Roberts, Collins, Sessions

INDIAN AFFAIRS

indian.senate.gov

838 Hart
202-224-2251

Majority (D 8): Inouye (HI), Chmn.; Conrad (ND), Reid (NV), Akaka (HI), Wellstone (MN), Dorgan (ND), Johnson (SD), Cantwell (WA)

Minority (R 7): Campbell (CO), Vice Chmn.; Murkowski (AK), McCain (AZ), Domenici (NM), Thomas (WY), Hatch (UT), Inhofe (OK)

NO SUBCOMMITTEES

INTELLIGENCE (Select)

intelligence.senate.gov

211 Hart
202-224-1700

Majority (D 9): Graham (FL), Chmn.; Levin (MI), Rockefeller (WV), Feinstein (CA), Wyden (OR), Durbin (IL), Bayh (IN), Edwards (NC), Mikulski (MD)

Minority (R 8): Shelby (AL), Vice Chmn.; Kyl (AZ), Inhofe (OK), Hatch (UT), Roberts (KS), DeWine (OH), Thompson (TN), Lugar (IN)

NO SUBCOMMITTEES

JUDICIARY

www.senate.gov/~judiciary

224 Dirksen
202-224-5225

Majority (D 10): Leahy (VT), Chmn.; Kennedy (MA), Biden (DE), Kohl (WI), Feinstein (CA), Feingold (WI), Schumer (NY), Durbin (IL), Cantwell (WA), Edwards (NC)

Minority (R 9): Hatch (UT), RMM; Thurmond (SC), Grassley (IA), Specter (PA), Kyl (AZ), DeWine (OH), Sessions (AL), Brownback (KS), McConnell (KY)

SUBCOMMITTEES

Administrative Oversight & the Courts
Majority (D 4): Schumer, Chmn.; Kennedy, Feingold, Durbin
Minority (R 4): Sessions, RMM; Grassley, Thurmond, Specter

Antitrust, Business Rights & Competition
Majority (D 5): Kohl, Chmn.; Leahy, Feingold, Schumer, Cantwell
Minority (R 5): DeWine, RMM; Hatch, Specter, Thurmond, Brownback

Constitution, Federalism & Property Rights
Majority (D 4): Feingold, Chmn.; Leahy, Kennedy, Durbin
Minority (R 4): Thurmond, RMM; Hatch, Kyl, McConnell

Immigration
Majority (D 5): Kennedy, Chmn.; Feinstein, Schumer, Durbin, Cantwell
Minority (R 5): Brownback, RMM; Specter, Grassley, Kyl, DeWine

Technology, Terrorism & Government Information
Majority (D 4): Feinstein, Chmn.; Biden, Kohl, Cantwell
Minority (R 4): Kyl, RMM; DeWine, Sessions, McConnell

Youth Violence
Majority (D 5): Biden, Chmn.; Kohl, Feinstein, Durbin, Cantwell
Minority (R 5): Grassley, RMM; Hatch, Sessions, Brownback, McConnell

RULES & ADMINISTRATION

www.senate.gov/~rules

305 Russell
202-224-6352

Majority (D 10): Dodd (CT), Chmn.; Byrd (WV), Inouye (HI), Feinstein (CA), Torricelli (NJ), Schumer (NY), Breaux (LA), Daschle (SD), Dayton (MN), Durbin (IL)

Minority (R 9): McConnell (KY), RMM; Warner (VA), Stevens (AK), Helms (NC), Cochran (MS), Santorum (PA), Nickles (OK), Lott (MS), Hutchison (TX)

NO SUBCOMMITTEES

SMALL BUSINESS
sbc.senate.gov
Majority (D 10): Kerry (MA), Chmn.; Levin (MI), Harkin (IA), Lieberman (CT), Wellstone (MN), Cleland (GA), Landrieu (LA), Edwards (NC), Cantwell (WA), Carnahan (MO)
Minority (R 9): Bond (MO), RMM; Burns (MT), Bennett (UT), Snowe (ME), Enzi (WY), Fitzgerald (IL), Crapo (ID), Allen (VA), Ensign (NV)

NO SUBCOMMITTEES

VETERANS' AFFAIRS
www.senate.gov/~veterans
Majority (D 8): Rockefeller (WV), Chmn.; Graham (FL), Jeffords (VT), Akaka (HI), Wellstone (MN), Murray (WA), Miller (GA), Nelson (NE)
Minority (R 7): Specter (PA), RMM; Thurmond (SC), Murkowski (AK), Campbell (CO), Craig (ID), Hutchinson (AR), 1 vacancy

NO SUBCOMMITTEES

HOUSE COMMITTEES

AGRICULTURE
www.house.gov/agriculture
Majority (R 27): Combest (TX), Chmn.; Boehner (OH), Goodlatte (VA), Pombo (CA), Smith (MI), Everett (AL), Lucas (OK), Chambliss (GA), Moran (KS), Schaffer (CO), Thune (SD), Jenkins (TN), Cooksey (LA), Gutknecht (MN), Riley (AL), Simpson (ID), Ose (CA), Hayes (NC), Fletcher (KY), Pickering (MS), Johnson (IL), Osborne (NE), Pence (IN), Rehberg (MT), Graves (MO), Putnam (FL), Kennedy (MN)
Minority (D 24): Stenholm (TX), RMM; Condit (CA), Peterson (MN), Dooley (CA), Clayton (NC), Hilliard (AL), Holden (PA), Bishop (GA), Thompson (MS), Baldacci (ME), Berry (AR), McIntyre (NC), Etheridge (NC), Boswell (IA), Phelps (IL), Lucas (KY), Thompson (CA), Hill (IN), Baca (CA), Larsen (WA), Ross (AR), Acevedo-Vila (PR), Kind (WI), Shows (MS)

SUBCOMMITTEES

Conservation, Credit, Rural Development & Research
Majority (R 8): Lucas, Chmn.; Moran, Thune, Ose, Osborne, Graves, Putnam, Kennedy
Minority (D 7): Baldacci, Phelps, Thompson (CA), Baca, Peterson, Clayton, 1 vacancy

Department Operations, Oversight, Nutrition & Forestry
Majority (R 7): Goodlatte, Chmn.; Pombo, Moran, Cooksey, Simpson, Rehberg, Putnam
Minority (D 6): Clayton, RMM; Berry, Acevedo-Vila, Hilliard, Holden, Baldacci

General Farm Commodities & Risk Management
Majority (R 18): Chambliss, Chmn.; Boehner, Smith, Everett, Lucas, Moran, Thune, Jenkins, Gutknecht, Riley, Ose, Hayes, Pickering, Johnson, Pence, Rehberg, Graves, Kennedy
Minority (D 17): Dooley, RMM; Thompson (MS), Bishop, Berry, McIntyre, Boswell, Phelps, Lucas, Hill, Baca, Ross, Acevedo-Vila, Larsen, Kind, Shows, Thompson (CA), Peterson

Livestock & Horticulture
Majority (R 9): Pombo, Chmn.; Boehner, Goodlatte, Gutknecht, Riley, Pickering, Osborne, Pence, Putnam
Minority (D 8): Peterson, RMM; Holden, Boswell, Larsen, Ross, Condit, Dooley, Etheridge

Specialty Crops & Foreign Agriculture Programs
Majority (R 9): Everett, Chmn.; Chambliss, Schaffer, Jenkins, Simpson, Hayes, Fletcher, Rehberg, Putnam
Minority (D 8): Condit, RMM; Bishop, McIntyre, Etheridge, Lucas, Hill, Thompson (MS), Thompson (CA)

APPROPRIATIONS

www.house.gov/appropriations

H-218 The Capitol
202-225-2771

Majority (R 35): Young (FL), Chmn.; Regula (OH), Lewis (CA), Rogers (KY), Skeen (NM), Wolf (VA), DeLay (TX), Kolbe (AZ), Callahan (AL), Walsh (NY), Taylor (NC), Hobson (OH), Istook (OK), Bonilla (TX), Knollenberg (MI), Miller (FL), Kingston (GA), Frelinghuysen (NJ), Wicker (MS), Nethercutt (WA), Cunningham (CA), Tiahrt (KS), Wamp (TN), Latham (IA), Northup (KY), Aderholt (AL), Emerson (MO), Sununu (NH), Granger (TX), Peterson (PA), Doolittle (CA), LaHood (IL), Sweeney (NY), Vitter (LA), Sherwood (PA)

Minority (D 29): Obey (WI), RMM; Murtha (PA), Dicks (WA), Sabo (MN), Hoyer (MD), Mollohan (WV), Kaptur (OH), Pelosi (CA), Visclosky (IN), Lowey (NY), Serrano (NY), DeLauro (CT), Moran (VA), Olver (MA), Pastor (AZ), Meek (FL), Price (NC), Edwards (TX), Cramer (AL), Kennedy (RI), Clyburn (SC), Hinchey (NY), Roybal-Allard (CA), Farr (CA), Jackson (IL), Kilpatrick (MI), Boyd (FL), Fattah (PA), Rothman (NJ)

Independent (1): Goode (I-VA)

SUBCOMMITTEES

Agriculture, Rural Development, & FDA
Majority (R 8): Bonilla, Chmn.; Walsh, Kingston, Nethercutt, Latham, Emerson, Goode, LaHood
Minority (D 5): Kaptur, RMM; DeLauro, Hinchey, Farr, Boyd

Commerce, Justice & State
Majority (R 8): Wolf, Chmn.; Rogers, Kolbe, Taylor, Regula, Latham, Miller, Vitter
Minority (D 5): Serrano, RMM; Mollohan, Roybal-Allard, Cramer, Kennedy

Defense
Majority (R 9): Lewis, Chmn.; Young, Skeen, Hobson, Bonilla, Nethercutt, Cunningham, Frelinghuysen, Tiahrt
Minority (D 6): Murtha, RMM; Dicks, Sabo, Visclosky, Moran, 1 vacancy

District of Columbia
Majority (R 6): Knollenberg, Chmn.; Istook, Cunningham, Doolittle, Sweeney, Vitter
Minority (D 3): Fattah, RMM; Mollohan, Olver

Energy & Water Development
Majority (R 8): Callahan, Chmn.; Rogers, Frelinghuysen, Latham, Wicker, Wamp, Emerson, Doolittle
Minority (D 5): Visclosky, RMM; Edwards, Pastor, Clyburn, Roybal-Allard

Foreign Operations & Export Financing
Majority (R 8): Kolbe, Chmn.; Callahan, Knollenberg, Kingston, Lewis, Wicker, Bonilla, Sununu
Minority (D 5): Lowey, RMM; Pelosi, Jackson, Kilpatrick, Rothman

Interior
Majority (R 8): Skeen, Chmn.; Regula, Kolbe, Taylor, Nethercutt, Wamp, Kingston, Peterson
Minority (D 5): Dicks, RMM; Murtha, Moran, Hinchey, Sabo

Labor, HHS & Education
Majority (R 10): Regula, Chmn.; Young, Istook, Miller, Wicker, Northup, Cunningham, Granger, Peterson, Sherwood
Minority (D 7): Obey, RMM; Hoyer, Pelosi, Lowey, DeLauro, Jackson, Kennedy

Military Construction
Majority (R 8): Hobson, Chmn.; Walsh, Miller, Aderholt, Granger, Goode, Skeen, Vitter
Minority (D 5): Olver, RMM; Edwards, Farr, Boyd, Dicks

The Legislative Branch
Majority (R 5): Taylor, Chmn.; Wamp, Lewis, LaHood, Sherwood
Minority (D 3): Moran, RMM; Hoyer, Kaptur

Transportation
Majority (R 9): Rogers, Chmn.; Wolf, DeLay, Callahan, Tiahrt, Aderholt, Granger, Emerson, Sweeney
Minority (D 6): Sabo, RMM; Olver, Pastor, Kilpatrick, Serrano, Clyburn

Treasury, Postal Service & General Government
Majority (R 8): Istook, Chmn.; Wolf, Northup, Sununu, Peterson, Tiahrt, Sweeney, Sherwood
Minority (D 5): Hoyer, RMM; Meek, Price, Rothman, Visclosky

VA, HUD & Independent Agencies
Majority (R 9): Walsh, Chmn.; DeLay, Hobson, Knollenberg, Frelinghuysen, Northup, Sununu, Goode, Aderholt, 1 vacancy
Minority (D 6): Mollohan, RMM; Kaptur, Meek, Price, Cramer, Fattah

ARMED SERVICES
www.house.gov/hasc

2120 Rayburn
202-225-4151

Majority (R 32): Stump (AZ), Chmn.; Spence (SC), Vice Chmn.; Hunter (CA), Hansen (UT), Weldon (PA), Hefley (CO), Saxton (NJ), McHugh (NY), Everett (AL), Bartlett (MD), McKeon (CA), Watts (OK), Thornberry (TX), Hostettler (IN), Chambliss (GA), Hilleary (TN), Scarborough (FL), Jones (NC), Graham (SC), Ryun (KS), Riley (AL), Gibbons (NV), Hayes (NC), Wilson (NM), Calvert (CA), Simmons (CT), Crenshaw (FL), Kirk (IL), Davis (VA), Schrock (VA), Akin (MO), Forbes (VA)
Minority (D 28): Skelton (MO), RMM; Spratt (SC), Ortiz (TX), Evans (IL), Taylor (MS), Abercrombie (HI), Meehan (MA), Underwood (GU), Blagojevich (IL), Reyes (TX), Allen (ME), Snyder (AR), Turner (TX), Smith (WA), Sanchez (CA), Maloney (CT), McIntyre (NC), Rodriguez (TX), McKinney (GA), Tauscher (CA), Brady (PA), Andrews (NJ), Hill (IN), Thompson (CA), Larson (CT), Davis (CA), Langevin (RI), 1 vacancy

SUBCOMMITTEES

Military Installations & Facilities
Majority (R 10): Saxton, Chmn.; Hostettler, Scarborough, Hayes, Vice Chmn.; Calvert, Crenshaw, Schrock, Hefley, McHugh, Everett
Minority (D 8): Abercrombie, RMM; Ortiz, Taylor, Underwood, Reyes, Snyder, Rodriguez, Thompson

Military Personnel
Majority (R 10): McHugh, Chmn.; Thornberry, Graham, Ryun, Vice Chmn.; Wilson, Simmons, Kirk, Davis, Schrock, Akin
Minority (D 8): Snyder, RMM; Sanchez, McKinney, Tauscher, Andrews, Hill, Davis, Langevin

Military Procurement
Majority (R 15): Spence, Chmn.; Hansen, Hefley, Everett, McKeon, Watts, Thornberry, Graham, Vice Chmn.; Ryun, Gibbons, Wilson, Simmons, Kirk, Davis, 1 vacancy
Minority (D 13): Taylor, RMM; Skelton, Spratt, Evans, Blagojevich, Allen, Turner, Smith, Maloney, McIntyre, McKinney, Tauscher, Brady

Military Readiness
Majority (R 12): Weldon, Chmn.; Bartlett, Chambliss, Jones, Riley, Vice Chmn.; Hunter, Hansen, McKeon, Watts, Hilleary, Gibbons, 1 vacancy
Minority (D 10): Ortiz, RMM; Evans, Underwood, Maloney, McIntyre, Rodriguez, Brady, Hill, Davis, 1 vacancy

Military Research & Development
Majority (R 15): Hunter, Chmn.; Hilleary, Vice Chmn.; Akin, Weldon, Saxton, Bartlett, Hostettler, Chambliss, Scarborough, Jones, Riley, Hayes, Calvert, Crenshaw, Schrock
Minority (D 13): Meehan, RMM; Spratt, Abercrombie, Blagojevich, Reyes, Allen, Turner, Smith, Sanchez, Andrews, Thompson, Larson, Langevin

BUDGET
www.house.gov/budget

309 Cannon
202-226-7270

Majority (R 24): Nussle (IA), Chmn.; Sununu (NH), Vice Chmn.; Hoekstra (MI), Bass (NH), Gutknecht (MN), Hilleary (TN), Thornberry (TX), Ryun (KS), Collins (GA), Fletcher (KY), Miller (CA), Toomey (PA), Watkins (OK), Hastings (WA), Doolittle (CA), Portman (OH), LaHood (IL), Granger (TX), Schrock (VA), Culberson (TX), Brown (SC), Crenshaw (FL), Putnam (FL), Kirk (IL)
Minority (D 20): Spratt (SC), RMM; McDermott (WA), Thompson (MS), Bentsen (TX), Davis (FL), Clayton (NC), Price (NC), Kleczka (WI), Clement (TN), Moran (VA), Hooley (OR), Baldwin (WI), McCarthy (MO), Moore (KS), Capuano (MA), Honda (CA), Hoeffel (PA), Holt (NJ), Matheson (UT), 1 vacancy

NO SUBCOMMITTEES

EDUCATION & THE WORKFORCE
www.house.gov/ed_workforce

2181 Rayburn
202-225-4527

Majority (R 27): Boehner (OH), Chmn.; Petri (WI), Roukema (NJ), Ballenger (NC), Hoekstra (MI), McKeon (CA), Castle (DE), Johnson (TX), Greenwood (PA), Graham (SC), Souder (IN), Norwood (GA), Schaffer (CO), Upton (MI), Hilleary (TN), Ehlers (MI), Tancredo (CO), Fletcher (KY), DeMint (SC), Isakson (GA), Goodlatte (VA), Biggert (IL), Platts (PA), Tiberi (OH), Keller (FL), Osborne (NE), Culberson (TX)

Minority (D 22): Miller (CA), RMM; Kildee (MI), Owens (NY), Payne (NJ), Mink (HI), Andrews (NJ), Roemer (IN), Scott (VA), Woolsey (CA), Rivers (MI), Hinojosa (TX), McCarthy (NY), Tierney (MA), Kind (WI), Sanchez (CA), Ford (TN), Kucinich (OH), Wu (OR), Holt (NJ), Solis (CA), Davis (CA), McCollum (MN)

SUBCOMMITTEES

21st Century Competitiveness

Majority (R 11): McKeon, Chmn.; Isakson, Vice Chmn.; Boehner, Castle, Johnson, Graham, Souder, Upton, Ehlers, Goodlatte, Osborne

Minority (D 9): Mink, RMM; Tierney, Kind, Holt, Wu, Rivers, McCollum, Andrews, Hinojosa

Education Reform

Majority (R 17): Castle, Chmn.; Schaffer, Vice Chmn.; Petri, Roukema, Greenwood, Souder, Upton, Hilleary, Ehlers, Tancredo, Fletcher, DeMint, Biggert, Platts, Keller, Osborne, Culberson

Minority (D 14): Kildee, RMM; Scott, Woolsey, Hinojosa, McCarthy, Sanchez, Ford, Solis, Davis, Owens, Payne, Roemer, Kind, Kucinich

Employer-Employee Relations

Majority (R 10): Johnson, Chmn.; Fletcher, Vice Chmn.; Boehner, Roukema, Ballenger, Hoekstra, McKeon, Tancredo, DeMint, Tiberi

Minority (D 7): Andrews, RMM; Payne, Kildee, Rivers, McCarthy, Tierney, Ford

Select Education

Majority (R 8): Hoekstra, Chmn.; Tiberi, Vice Chmn.; Petri, Greenwood, Norwood, Schaffer, Hilleary, Platts

Minority (D 6): Roemer, RMM; Scott, Holt, Davis, McCollum, Sanchez

Workforce Protections

Majority (R 8): Norwood, Chmn.; Biggert, Vice Chmn.; Ballenger, Graham, Isakson, Goodlatte, Keller, Culberson

Minority (D 6): Owens, RMM; Kucinich, Mink, Woolsey, Sanchez, Solis

ENERGY & COMMERCE
www.house.gov/commerce

2125 Rayburn
202-225-2927

Majority (R 31): Tauzin (LA), Chmn.; Bilirakis (FL), Barton (TX), Upton (MI), Stearns (FL), Gillmor (OH), Greenwood (PA), Cox (CA), Deal (GA), Largent (OK), Burr (NC), Vice Chmn.; Whitfield (KY), Ganske (IA), Norwood (GA), Cubin (WY), Shimkus (IL), Wilson (NM), Shadegg (AZ), Pickering (MS), Fossella (NY), Blunt (MO), Davis (VA), Bryant (TN), Ehrlich (MD), Buyer (IN), Radanovich (CA), Bass (NH), Pitts (PA), Bono (CA), Walden (OR), Terry (NE)

Minority (D 26): Dingell (MI), RMM; Waxman (CA), Markey (MA), Hall (TX), Boucher (VA), Towns (NY), Pallone (NJ), Brown (OH), Gordon (TN), Deutsch (FL), Rush (IL), Eshoo (CA), Stupak (MI), Engel (NY), Sawyer (OH), Wynn (MD), Green (TX), McCarthy (MO), Strickland (OH), DeGette (CO), Barrett (WI), Luther (MN), Capps (CA), Doyle (PA), John (LA), Harman (CA)

SUBCOMMITTEES

Commerce, Trade & Consumer Protection

Majority (R 15): Stearns, Chmn.; Upton, Deal, Vice Chmn.; Whitfield, Cubin, Shimkus, Shadegg, Bryant, Buyer, Radanovich, Bass, Pitts, Bono, Walden, Terry

Minority (D 12): Towns, RMM; DeGette, Capps, Doyle, John, Harman, Waxman, Markey, Gordon, Deutsch, Rush, Eshoo

Energy & Air Quality

Majority (R 17): Barton, Chmn.; Cox, Largent, Vice Chmn.; Burr, Whitfield, Ganske, Norwood, Shimkus, Wilson, Shadegg, Pickering, Fossella, Blunt, Bryant, Radanovich, Bono, Walden

Minority (D 14): Boucher, RMM; Hall, Sawyer, Wynn, Doyle, John, Waxman, Markey, Gordon, Rush, McCarthy, Strickland, Barrett, Luther

Environment & Hazardous Materials
Majority (R 15): Gillmor, Chmn.; Greenwood, Largent, Ganske, Shimkus, Vice Chmn.; Wilson, Fossella, Ehrlich, Buyer, Radanovich, Bass, Pitts, Bono, Walden, Terry
Minority (D 12): Pallone, RMM; Towns, Brown, Green, McCarthy, Barrett, Luther, Capps, Doyle, Harman, Waxman, Deutsch

Health
Majority (R 17): Bilirakis, Chmn.; Barton, Upton, Greenwood, Deal, Burr, Whitfield, Ganske, Norwood, Vice Chmn.; Cubin, Wilson, Shadegg, Pickering, Bryant, Ehrlich, Buyer, Pitts
Minority (D 14): Brown, RMM; Waxman, Strickland, Barrett, Capps, Hall, Towns, Pallone, Deutsch, Eshoo, Stupak, Engel, Wynn, Green

Oversight & Investigations
Majority (R 8): Greenwood, Chmn.; Bilirakis, Stearns, Gillmor, Largent, Burr, Whitfield, Vice Chmn.; Bass
Minority (D 6): Deutsch, RMM; Stupak, Strickland, DeGette, John, Rush

Telecommunications & The Internet
Majority (R 17): Upton, Chmn.; Bilirakis, Barton, Stearns, Vice Chmn.; Gillmor, Cox, Deal, Largent, Cubin, Shimkus, Wilson, Pickering, Fossella, Blunt, Davis, Ehrlich, Terry
Minority (D 14): Markey, RMM; Gordon, Rush, Eshoo, Engel, Green, McCarthy, Luther, Stupak, DeGette, Harman, Boucher, Brown, Sawyer

FINANCIAL SERVICES
www.house.gov/banking

2129 Rayburn
202-225-7502

Majority (R 37): Oxley (OH), Chmn.; Leach (IA), Roukema (NJ), Bereuter (NE), Baker (LA), Bachus (AL), Castle (DE), King (NY), Royce (CA), Lucas (OK), Ney (OH), Barr (GA), Kelly (NY), Paul (TX), Gillmor (OH), Cox (CA), Weldon (FL), Ryun (KS), Riley (AL), LaTourette (OH), Manzullo (IL), Jones (NC), Ose (CA), Biggert (IL), Green (WI), Toomey (PA), Shays (CT), Shadegg (AZ), Fossella (NY), Miller (CA), Cantor (VA), Grucci (NY), Hart (PA), Capito (WV), Ferguson (NJ), Rogers (MI), Tiberi (OH)
Minority (D 32): LaFalce (NY), RMM; Frank (MA), Kanjorski (PA), Waters (CA), Maloney (NY), Gutierrez (IL), Velazquez (NY), Watt (NC), Ackerman (NY), Bentsen (TX), Maloney (CT), Hooley (OR), Carson (IN), Sherman (CA), Sandlin (TX), Meeks (NY), Lee (CA), Mascara (PA), Inslee (WA), Schakowsky (IL), Moore (KS), Gonzalez (TX), Tubbs Jones (OH), Capuano (MA), Ford (TN), Hinojosa (TX), Lucas (KY), Shows (MS), Crowley (NY), Clay (MO), Israel (NY), Ross (AR)
Independent (1): Sanders (I-VT)

SUBCOMMITTEES

Capital Markets, Insurance & Government Sponsored Enterprises
Majority (R 25): Baker, Chmn.; Ney, Vice Chmn.; Shays, Cox, Gillmor, Paul, Bachus, Castle, Royce, Lucas, Barr, Jones, LaTourette, Shadegg, Weldon, Ryun, Riley, Fossella, Biggert, Miller, Ose, Toomey, Ferguson, Hart, Rogers
Minority (D 22): Kanjorski, RMM; Ackerman, Velazquez, Bentsen, Sandlin, Maloney (CT), Hooley, Mascara, Tubbs Jones, Capuano, Sherman, Meeks, Vice Chmn.; Inslee, Moore, Gonzalez, Ford, Hinojosa, Lucas, Shows, Crowley, Israel, Ross

Domestic Monetary Policy, Technology & Economic Growth
Majority (R 14): King, Chmn.; Leach, Vice Chmn.; Royce, Lucas, Paul, LaTourette, Ose, Green, Shays, Shadegg, Fossella, Grucci, Hart, Capito
Minority (D 12): Maloney (NY), RMM; Frank, Meeks, Sanders, Maloney, Hooley, Sandlin, Gonzalez, Capuano, Hinojosa, Clay, Ross, Lee

Financial Institutions & Consumer Credit
Majority (R 25): Bachus, Chmn.; Weldon, Vice Chmn.; Roukema, Bereuter, Baker, Castle, Royce, Lucas, Barr, Kelly, Gillmor, Ryun, Riley, LaTourette, Manzullo, Jones, Biggert, Toomey, Cantor, Grucci, Hart, Capito, Ferguson, Rogers, Tiberi
Minority (D 23): Waters, RMM; Maloney (NY), Watt, Ackerman, Bentsen, Sherman, Sandlin, Meeks, Gutierrez, Mascara, Moore, Gonzalez, Kanjorski, Velazquez, Maloney (CT), Hooley, Carson, Lee, Ford, Hinojosa, Lucas, Shows, Crowley

Housing & Community Opportunity

Majority (R 14): Roukema, Chmn.; Green, Vice Chmn.; Bereuter, Bachus, King, Ney, Barr, Kelly, Riley, Miller, Cantor, Grucci, Rogers, Tiberi

Minority (D 12): Frank, RMM; Velazquez, Carson, Lee, Schakowsky, Tubbs Jones, Capuano, Waters, Watt, Clay, Israel, 1 vacancy

International Monetary Policy & Trade

Majority (R 14): Bereuter, Chmn.; Ose, Vice Chmn.; Roukema, Baker, Castle, Ryun, Manzullo, Biggert, Green, Toomey, Shays, Miller, Capito, Ferguson

Minority (D 13): Sanders, RMM; Waters, Frank, Watt, Carson, Lee, Kanjorski, Sherman, Schakowsky, Maloney (NY), Gutierrez, Velazquez, Bentsen

Oversight & Investigations

Majority (R 11): Kelly, Chmn.; Paul, Vice Chmn.; King, Ney, Cox, Weldon, Jones, Shadegg, Fossella, Cantor, Tiberi

Minority (D 10): Gutierrez, Chmn.; Bentsen, Inslee, Schakowsky, Moore, Tubbs Jones, Capuano, Shows, Crowley, Clay

GOVERNMENT REFORM

2157 Rayburn

www.house.gov/reform

202-225-5074

Majority (R 24): Burton (IN), Chmn.; Gilman (NY), Morella (MD), Shays (CT), Ros-Lehtinen (FL), McHugh (NY), Horn (CA), Mica (FL), Davis (VA), Souder (IN), Scarborough (FL), LaTourette (OH), Barr (GA), Miller (FL), Ose (CA), Lewis (KY), Davis (VA), Platts (PA), Weldon (FL), Cannon (UT), Putnam (FL), Otter (ID), Schrock (VA), Duncan (TN)

Minority (D 19): Waxman (CA), RMM; Lantos (CA), Owens (NY), Towns (NY), Kanjorski (PA), Mink (HI), Maloney (NY), Norton (DC), Cummings (MD), Kucinich (OH), Blagojevich (IL), Davis (IL), Tierney (MA), Turner (TX), Allen (ME), Schakowsky (IL), Clay (MO), 2 vacancies

Independent (1): Sanders (I-VT)

SUBCOMMITTEES

Census

Majority (R 5): Miller, Chmn.; Cannon, Vice Chmn.; Souder, Barr, 1 vacancy
Minority (D 3): Clay, RMM; Maloney, Davis

Civil Service & Agency Organization

Majority (R 6): Scarborough, Chmn.; Weldon, Vice Chmn.; Morella, Mica, Souder, Otter
Minority (D 4): Davis, RMM; Owens, Norton, Cummings

Criminal Justice, Drug Policy & Human Resources

Majority (R 9): Souder, Chmn.; Gilman, Vice Chmn.; Ros-Lehtinen, Mica, Barr, Miller, Ose, Davis, Weldon
Minority (D 6): Cummings, RMM; Blagojevich, Sanders, Davis, Turner, Allen, 1 vacancy

District of Columbia

Majority (R 4): Morella, Chmn.; Platts, Vice Chmn.; Davis, Scarborough
Minority (D 3): Norton, RMM; 2 vacancies

Energy Policy, Natural Resources and Regulatory Affairs

Majority (R 8): Ose, RMM; Otter, Vice Chmn.; Shays, McHugh, LaTourette, Cannon, 2 vacancies
Minority (D 6): Tierney, RMM; Lantos, Towns, Mink, Kucinich, Blagojevich

Government Efficiency, Financial Management & Intergovernmental Relations

Majority (R 5): Horn, Chmn.; Lewis, Vice Chmn.; Miller, Ose, Putnam
Minority (D 4): Schakowsky, RMM; Owens, Kanjorski, Maloney

National Security, Veterans' Affairs & Intl. Relations

Majority (R 11): Shays, Chmn.; Putnam, Gilman, Ros-Lehtinen, McHugh, LaTourette, Lewis, Platts, Weldon, Otter, Schrock
Minority (D 9): Kucinich, RMM; Sanders, Allen, Lantos, Tierney, Schakowsky, Clay, 2 vacancies

Technology & Procurement Policy

Majority (R 4): Davis (VA), Chmn.; Davis (VA), Vice Chmn.; Horn, Ose
Minority (D 3): Turner, RMM; Kanjorski, Mink

HOUSE ADMINISTRATION
www.house.gov/cha

1309 Longworth
202-225-8281

Majority (R 6): Ney (OH), Chmn.; Ehlers (MI), Mica (FL), Linder (GA), Doolittle (CA), Reynolds (NY)
Minority (D 3): Hoyer (MD), RMM; Fattah (PA), Davis (FL)

NO SUBCOMMITTEES

INTERNATIONAL RELATIONS
www.house.gov/international_relations

2170 Rayburn
202-225-5021

Majority (R 26): Hyde (IL), Chmn.; Gilman (NY), Leach (IA), Bereuter (NE), Smith (NJ), Burton (IN), Gallegly (CA), Ros-Lehtinen (FL), Ballenger (NC), Rohrabacher (CA), Royce (CA), King (NY), Chabot (OH), Houghton (NY), McHugh (NY), Burr (NC), Cooksey (LA), Tancredo (CO), Paul (TX), Smith (MI), Pitts (PA), Issa (CA), Cantor (VA), Flake (AZ), Kerns (IN), Davis (VA)
Minority (D 23): Lantos (CA), RMM; Berman (CA), Ackerman (NY), Faleomavaega (AS), Payne (NJ), Menendez (NJ), Brown (OH), McKinney (GA), Hilliard (AL), Sherman (CA), Wexler (FL), Davis (FL), Engel (NY), Delahunt (MA), Meeks (NY), Lee (CA), Crowley (NY), Hoeffel (PA), Blumenauer (OR), Berkley (NV), Napolitano (CA), Schiff (CA), Watson (CA)

SUBCOMMITTEES

Africa
Majority (R 5): Royce, Chmn.; Houghton, Tancredo, Flake, Kerns
Minority (D 4): Payne, RMM; Meeks, Lee, Hilliard

East Asia & the Pacific
Majority (R 8): Leach, Chmn.; Rohrabacher, Smith (NJ), Royce, Chabot, Burr, Issa, Flake
Minority (D 7): Faleomavaega, RMM; Brown, Davis, Blumenauer, Ackerman, Meeks, 1 vacancy

Europe
Majority (R 10): Gallegly, Chmn.; Bereuter, King, Burr, Cooksey, Smith (MI), Gilman, Leach, Burton, Cantor
Minority (D 8): Hilliard, RMM; Sherman, Wexler, Davis, Engel, Delahunt, Lee, Crowley

International Operations and Human Rights
Majority (R 6): Ros-Lehtinen, Chmn.; Smith (NJ), Paul, Ballenger, Tancredo, Pitts
Minority (D 4): McKinney, RMM; Menendez, Napolitano, Schiff

Middle East & South Asia
Majority (R 11): Gilman, Chmn.; Burton, Chabot, McHugh, Pitts, Issa, Cantor, Davis, Rohrabacher, King, Cooksey
Minority (D 9): Ackerman, RMM; Berman, Sherman, Wexler, Engel, Crowley, Hoeffel, Berkley, Schiff

Western Hemisphere
Majority (R 6): Ballenger, Chmn.; Gallegly, Ros-Lehtinen, Paul, Smith (MI), Davis
Minority (D 5): Menendez, RMM; Delahunt, Napolitano, Faleomavaega, Payne

JUDICIARY
www.house.gov/judiciary

2138 Rayburn
202-225-3951

Majority (R 21): Sensenbrenner (WI), Chmn.; Hyde (IL), Gekas (PA), Coble (NC), Smith (TX), Gallegly (CA), Goodlatte (VA), Chabot (OH), Barr (GA), Jenkins (TN), Hutchinson (AR), Cannon (UT), Graham (SC), Bachus (AL), Scarborough (FL), Hostettler (IN), Green (WI), Keller (FL), Issa (CA), Hart (PA), Flake (AZ)
Minority (D 17): Conyers (MI), RMM; Frank (MA), Berman (CA), Boucher (VA), Nadler (NY), Scott (VA), Watt (NC), Lofgren (CA), Jackson Lee (TX), Waters (CA), Meehan (MA), Delahunt (MA), Wexler (FL), Baldwin (WI), Weiner (NY), Schiff (CA), 1 vacancy

SUBCOMMITTEES

Commercial & Administrative Law
Majority (R 7): Barr, Chmn.; Flake, Gekas, Green, Issa, Chabot, Hart
Minority (D 5): Watt, RMM; Nadler, Baldwin, Weiner, Waters

Courts, the Internet & Intellectual Property
Majority (R 12): Coble, Chmn.; Hyde, Gallegly, Goodlatte, Jenkins, Hutchinson, Cannon, Graham, Bachus, Scarborough, Hostettler, Keller
Minority (D 10): Berman, RMM; Conyers, Boucher, Lofgren, Delahunt, Wexler, Waters, Meehan, Baldwin, Weiner

Crime
Majority (R 8): Smith, Chmn.; Green, Coble, Goodlatte, Chabot, Barr, Hutchinson, Keller
Minority (D 5): Scott, RMM; Weiner, Jackson Lee, Meehan, Delahunt

Immigration & Claims
Majority (R 7): Gekas, Chmn.; Issa, Hart, Smith, Gallegly, Cannon, Flake
Minority (D 5): Jackson Lee, RMM; Frank, Berman, Lofgren, Meehan

The Constitution
Majority (R 8): Chabot, Chmn.; Jenkins, Graham, Bachus, Hostettler, Hart, Smith, Hutchinson
Minority (D 5): Nadler, RMM; Frank, Conyers, Scott, Watt

PERMANENT SELECT COMMITTEE ON INTELLIGENCE

H-405 The Capitol
202-225-4121

Majority (R 11): Goss (FL), Chmn.; Bereuter (NE), Vice Chmn.; Castle (DE), Boehlert (NY), Gibbons (NV), LaHood (IL), Cunningham (CA), Hoekstra (MI), Burr (NC), Hutchinson (AR), Chambliss (GA)
Minority (D 9): Pelosi (CA), RMM; Bishop (GA), Harman (CA), Condit (CA), Roemer (IN), Hastings (FL), Reyes (TX), Boswell (IA), Peterson (MN)

SUBCOMMITTEES

Human Intelligence, Analysis & Counterintelligence
Majority (R 7): Gibbons, Chmn.; Boehlert, Vice Chmn.; LaHood, Cunningham, Hoekstra, Burr, Hutchinson
Minority (D 4): Boswell, RMM; Hastings, Reyes, Condit

Intelligence Policy & National Security
Majority (R 6): Bereuter, Chmn.; LaHood, Vice Chmn.; Castle, Chambliss, Gibbons, Hutchinson
Minority (D 4): Condit, RMM; Bishop, RMM; Roemer, Peterson

Technical & Tactical Intelligence
Majority (R 7): Castle, Chmn.; Gibbons, Vice Chmn.; Boehlert, Cunningham, Hoekstra, Burr, Chambliss
Minority (D 5): Bishop, RMM; Harman, Hastings, Reyes, Boswell

RESOURCES

1324 Longworth
www.house.gov/resources
202-225-2761

Majority (R 28): Hansen (UT), Chmn.; Young (AK), Vice Chmn.; Tauzin (LA), Saxton (NJ), Gallegly (CA), Duncan (TN), Hefley (CO), Gilchrest (MD), Calvert (CA), McInnis (CO), Pombo (CA), Cubin (WY), Radanovich (CA), Jones (NC), Thornberry (TX), Cannon (UT), Peterson (PA), Schaffer (CO), Gibbons (NV), Souder (IN), Walden (OR), Simpson (ID), Tancredo (CO), Hayworth (AZ), Otter (ID), Osborne (NE), Flake (AZ), Rehberg (MT)
Minority (D 25): Rahall (WV), RMM; Miller (CA), Markey (MA), Kildee (MI), DeFazio (OR), Faleomavaega (AS), Abercrombie (HI), Ortiz (TX), Pallone (NJ), Dooley (CA), Underwood (GU), Smith (WA), Christian-Christensen (VI), Kind (WI), Inslee (WA), Napolitano (CA), Udall (NM), Udall (CO), Holt (NJ), McGovern (MA), Acevedo-Vila (PR), Solis (CA), Carson (OK), McCollum (MN), 1 vacancy

SUBCOMMITTEES

Energy & Mineral Resources
Majority (R 9): Cubin, Chmn.; Tauzin, Thornberry, Cannon, Gibbons, Tancredo, Otter, Flake, Rehberg
Minority (D 8): Kind, RMM; Rahall, Markey, Ortiz, Dooley, Inslee, Napolitano, Carson

Fisheries Conservation, Wildlife & Oceans
Majority (R 6): Gilchrest, Chmn.; Young, Tauzin, Saxton, Vice Chmn.; Pombo, Jones
Minority (D 5): Underwood, RMM; Faleomavaega, Abercrombie, Ortiz, Pallone

Forests & Forest Health
Majority (R 8): McInnis, Chmn.; Duncan, Peterson, Vice Chmn.; Souder, Simpson, Tancredo, Hayworth, Otter
Minority (D 7): Inslee, RMM; Kildee, Udall (NM), Udall (CO), Holt, Acevedo-Vila, McCollum

National Parks, Recreation & Public Lands
Majority (R 13): Hefley, Chmn.; Gallegly, Duncan, Gilchrest, Radanovich, Jones, Vice Chmn.; Thornberry, Cannon, Schaffer, Gibbons, Souder, Simpson, 1 vacancy
Minority (D 11): Christian-Christensen, RMM; Kildee, Faleomavaega, Pallone, Udall (NM), Udall (CO), Holt, McGovern, Acevedo-Vila, Solis, McCollum

Water & Power
Majority (R 9): Calvert, Chmn.; Pombo, Radanovich, Vice Chmn.; Walden, Simpson, Hayworth, Otter, Osborne, Flake
Minority (D 7): Smith, RMM; Miller, DeFazio, Dooley, Napolitano, Solis, Carson

RULES
H-312 The Capitol
www.house.gov/rules
202-225-9191
Majority (R 9): Dreier (CA), Chmn.; Goss (FL), Linder (GA), Pryce (OH), Diaz-Balart (FL), Hastings (WA), Myrick (NC), Sessions (TX), Reynolds (NY)
Minority (D 4): Frost (TX), RMM; Hall (OH), Slaughter (NY), Hastings (FL)

SUBCOMMITTEES

Rules & Organization of the House
Majority (R 5): Linder, Chmn.; Diaz-Balart, Vice Chmn.; Sessions, Reynolds, Dreier
Minority (D 2): Hall, RMM; Slaughter

The Legislative & Budget Process
Majority (R 5): Pryce, Chmn.; Goss, Vice Chmn.; Hastings, Myrick, Dreier
Minority (D 2): Frost, RMM; 1 vacancy

SCIENCE
2320 Rayburn
www.house.gov/science
202-225-6371
Majority (R 25): Boehlert (NY), Chmn.; Smith (TX), Morella (MD), Shays (CT), Weldon (PA), Rohrabacher (CA), Barton (TX), Calvert (CA), Smith (MI), Bartlett (MD), Ehlers (MI), Weldon (FL), Gutknecht (MN), Vice Chmn.; Cannon (UT), Nethercutt (WA), Lucas (OK), Miller (CA), Biggert (IL), Gilchrest (MD), Akin (MO), Johnson (IL), Pence (IN), Grucci (NY), Hart (PA), Forbes (VA)
Minority (D 22): Hall (TX), RMM; Gordon (TN), Costello (IL), Barcia (MI), Johnson (TX), Woolsey (CA), Rivers (MI), Lofgren (CA), Jackson Lee (TX), Etheridge (NC), Lampson (TX), Larson (CT), Udall (CO), Wu (OR), Weiner (NY), Baird (WA), Hoeffel (PA), Baca (CA), Matheson (UT), Israel (NY), Moore (KS), Honda (CA)

SUBCOMMITTEES

Energy
Majority (R 8): Bartlett, Chmn.; Rohrabacher, Calvert, Ehlers, Nethercutt, Biggert, Akin, Hart, Vice Chmn.
Minority (D 6): Woolsey, RMM; Costello, Jackson Lee, Wu, Matheson, Lampson

Environment, Technology and Standards
Majority (R 10): Ehlers, Chmn.; Morella, Shays, Weldon (PA), Smith (MI), Gutknecht, Cannon, Grucci, Vice Chmn.; Hart, Gilchrest
Minority (D 9): Barcia, RMM; Rivers, Lofgren, Udall, Weiner, Baird, Hoeffel, Baca, 1 vacancy

Research
Majority (R 11): Smith (MI), Chmn.; Smith (TX), Weldon (PA), Gutknecht, Lucas, Miller, Biggert, Akin, Johnson, Vice Chmn.; Grucci, Hart
Minority (D 9): Johnson, RMM; Etheridge, Israel, Rivers, Larson, Baird, Baca, Moore, Honda

Space & Aeronautics
Majority (R 12): Rohrabacher, Chmn.; Smith (TX), Barton, Calvert, Bartlett, Weldon (FL), Vice Chmn.;
Cannon, Nethercutt, Lucas, Miller, Pence, 1 vacancy
Minority (D 10): Gordon, RMM; Lampson, Larson, Moore, Lofgren, Jackson Lee, Etheridge, Udall, Wu,
Weiner

SMALL BUSINESS
www.house.gov/smbiz

2361 Rayburn
202-225-5821

Majority (R 19): Manzullo (IL), Chmn.; Combest (TX), Hefley (CO), Bartlett (MD), LoBiondo (NJ), Kelly
(NY), Chabot (OH), Toomey (PA), DeMint (SC), Thune (SD), Pence (IN), Ferguson (NJ), Issa (CA),
Graves (MO), Schrock (VA), Grucci (NY), Akin (MO), Capito (WV), Shuster (PA)
Minority (D 17): Velazquez (NY), RMM; Millender-McDonald (CA), Davis (IL), Pascrell (NJ), Christian-
Christensen (VI), Brady (PA), Udall (NM), Tubbs Jones (OH), Gonzalez (TX), Phelps (IL), Napolitano
(CA), Baird (WA), Udall (CO), Langevin (RI), Ross (AR), Carson (OK), Acevedo-Vila (PR)

SUBCOMMITTEES

Regulatory Reform Oversight
Majority (R 7): Pence, Chmn.; Combest, Kelly, Graves, Bartlett, Akin, Toomey
Minority (D 6): Brady, RMM; Pascrell, Gonzalez, Phelps, Langevin, Acevedo-Vila

Rural Enterprises, Agricultural and Technology
Majority (R 5): Thune, Chmn.; Bartlett, Grucci, Pence, Shuster
Minority (D 4): Udall (NM), RMM; Christian-Christensen, Phelps, Carson

Tax, Finance & Exports
Majority (R 8): Toomey, Chmn.; Chabot, Issa, Schrock, Akin, LoBiondo, DeMint, Thune
Minority (D 7): Pascrell, RMM; Langevin, Napolitano, Acevedo-Vila, Davis, Brady, Ross

Workforce, Empowerment & Government Programs
Majority (R 7): DeMint, Chmn.; LoBiondo, Ferguson, Grucci, Issa, Schrock, Capito
Minority (D 6): Millender-McDonald, RMM; Davis, Tubbs Jones, Gonzalez, Ross, Christian-Christensen

STANDARDS OF OFFICIAL CONDUCT
www.house.gov/ethics

HT-2 The Capitol
202-225-7103

Majority (R 5): Hefley (CO), Chmn.; Portman (OH), Hastings (WA), Hutchinson (AR), Biggert (IL)
Minority (D 5): Berman (CA), RMM; Sabo (MN), Pastor (AZ), Lofgren (CA), Tubbs Jones (OH)

NO SUBCOMMITTEES

TRANSPORTATION & INFRASTRUCTURE
www.house.gov/transportation

2165 Rayburn
202-225-9446

Majority (R 42): Young (AK), Chmn.; Petri (WI), Boehlert (NY), Coble (NC), Duncan (TN), Gilchrest
(MD), Horn (CA), Mica (FL), Quinn (NY), Ehlers (MI), Bachus (AL), LaTourette (OH), Kelly (NY);
Baker (LA), Ney (OH), Hutchinson (AR), Cooksey (LA), Thune (SD), LoBiondo (NJ), Moran (KS),
Pombo (CA), DeMint (SC), Bereuter (NE), Simpson (ID), Isakson (GA), Hayes (NC), Simmons (CT),
Rogers (MI), Capito (WV), Kirk (IL), Brown (SC), Johnson (IL), Kerns (IN), Rehberg (MT), Platts
(PA), Ferguson (NJ), Graves (MO), Otter (ID), Kennedy (MN), Culberson (TX), Shuster (PA), 1
vacancy
Minority (D 34): Oberstar (MN), RMM; Rahall (WV), Borski (PA), Lipinski (IL), DeFazio (OR), Clement
(TN), Costello (IL), Norton (DC), Nadler (NY), Menendez (NJ), Brown (FL), Barcia (MI), Filner
(CA), Johnson (TX), Mascara (PA), Taylor (MS), Millender-McDonald (CA), Cummings (MD), Blu-
menauer (OR), Sandlin (TX), Tauscher (CA), Pascrell (NJ), Boswell (IA), McGovern (MA), Holden
(PA), Lampson (TX), Baldacci (ME), Berry (AR), Baird (WA), Berkley (NV), Carson (OK), Matheson
(UT), Honda (CA), Larsen (WA)

SUBCOMMITTEES

Aviation
Majority (R 24): Mica, Chmn.; Petri, Duncan, Horn, Quinn, Ehlers, Bachus, Kelly, Baker, Hutchinson, Cooksey, Thune, LoBiondo, Moran, Simpson, Isakson, Hayes, Kirk, Johnson, Rehberg, Graves, Kennedy, 3 vacancies
Minority (D 20): Lipinski, RMM; Norton, Johnson, Boswell, Baldacci, DeFazio, Costello, Menendez, Brown, Millender-McDonald, Sandlin, Tauscher, Pascrell, Holden, Lampson, Berkley, Carson, Matheson, Honda, Rahall

Coast Guard & Maritime Transportation
Majority (R 5): LoBiondo, Chmn.; Coble, Gilchrest, DeMint, Simmons
Minority (D 4): Brown, RMM; Barcia, Taylor, DeFazio

Economic Development, Public Buildings & Emergency Management
Majority (R 5): LaTourette, Chmn.; Cooksey, Rogers, Capito, 1 vacancy
Minority (D 4): Costello, RMM; Berry, Norton, Barcia

Highways & Transit
Majority (R 30): Petri, Chmn.; Boehlert, Coble, Duncan, Mica, Quinn, LaTourette, Kelly, Baker, Thune, Moran, Pombo, DeMint, Isakson, Hayes, Simmons, Rogers, Capito, Kirk, Brown, Johnson, Kerns, Rehberg, Platts, Ferguson, Graves, Otter, Kennedy, 1 vacancy
Minority (D 25): Borski, RMM; Rahall, Barcia, Filner, Mascara, Millender-McDonald, Cummings, Sandlin, Pascrell, Holden, Berkley, Tauscher, Carson, Matheson, Honda, Larsen, Lipinski, Clement, Nadler, Johnson, Boswell, McGovern, Baird, Costello, Brown

Railroads
Majority (R 12): Quinn, Chmn.; Petri, Boehlert, Coble, Mica, Bachus, Moran, DeMint, Simmons, Capito, Platts, Ferguson
Minority (D 10): Clement, RMM; Nadler, Rahall, Borski, Filner, Cummings, Blumenauer, Baldacci, Larsen, Lipinski

Water Resources & Environment
Majority (R 19): Duncan, Chmn.; Boehlert, Gilchrest, Horn, Ehlers, LaTourette, Kelly, Baker, Hutchinson, Pombo, Bereuter, Simpson, Brown, Kerns, Rehberg, Otter, 3 vacancies
Minority (D 15): DeFazio, RMM; Menendez, Taylor, Blumenauer, McGovern, Lampson, Baird, Mascara, Berry, Borski, Filner, Johnson, Millender-McDonald, Pascrell, Honda

VETERANS' AFFAIRS
veterans.house.gov
335 Cannon
202-225-3527
Majority (R 17): Smith (NJ), Chmn.; Bilirakis (FL), Vice Chmn.; Stump (AZ), Spence (SC), Everett (AL), Buyer (IN), Quinn (NY), Stearns (FL), Moran (KS), McKeon (CA), Gibbons (NV), Simpson (ID), Baker (LA), Simmons (CT), Crenshaw (FL), Brown (SC), 1 vacancy
Minority (D 14): Evans (IL), RMM; Filner (CA), Gutierrez (IL), Brown (FL), Carson (IN), Reyes (TX), Snyder (AR), Rodriguez (TX), Shows (MS), Berkley (NV), Hill (IN), Udall (NM), 2 vacancies

SUBCOMMITTEES

Benefits
Majority (R 5): Simpson, Chmn.; Spence, Quinn, Crenshaw, Smith
Minority (D 4): Reyes, RMM; Brown, Evans, 1 vacancy

Health
Majority (R 9): Moran, Chmn.; Stearns, Vice Chmn.; McKeon, Gibbons, Simpson, Baker, Simmons, Crenshaw, Brown
Minority (D 7): Filner, RMM; Shows, Berkley, Rodriguez, Gutierrez, RMM; Carson, 1 vacancy

Oversight & Investigations
Majority (R 4): Buyer, Chmn.; Stump, Vice Chmn.; Bilirakis, Everett
Minority (D 3): Snyder, RMM; Hill, Udall

WAYS & MEANS
www.house.gov/ways_means

1102 Longworth
202-225-3625

Majority (R 24): Thomas (CA), Chmn.; Crane (IL), Shaw (FL), Johnson (CT), Houghton (NY), Herger (CA), McCrery (LA), Camp (MI), Ramstad (MN), Nussle (IA), Johnson (TX), Dunn (WA), Collins (GA), Portman (OH), English (PA), Watkins (OK), Hayworth (AZ), Weller (IL), Hulshof (MO), McInnis (CO), Lewis (KY), Foley (FL), Brady (TX), Ryan (WI)

Minority (D 17): Rangel (NY), RMM; Stark (CA), Matsui (CA), Coyne (PA), Levin (MI), Cardin (MD), McDermott (WA), Kleczka (WI), Lewis (GA), Neal (MA), McNulty (NY), Jefferson (LA), Tanner (TN), Becerra (CA), Thurman (FL), Doggett (TX), Pomeroy (ND)

SUBCOMMITTEES

Health
Majority (R 8): Johnson (CT), Chmn.; McCrery, Crane, Johnson (TX), Camp, Ramstad, English, Dunn
Minority (D 5): Stark, RMM; Kleczka, Lewis, McDermott, Thurman

Human Resources
Majority (R 8): Herger (CT), Chmn.; Johnson (CT), Watkins, McInnis, McCrery, Camp, English, Lewis
Minority (D 5): Cardin, RMM; Stark, Levin, McDermott, Doggett

Oversight
Majority (R 8): Houghton, Chmn.; Portman, Weller, Hulshof, McInnis, Foley, Johnson (TX), Dunn
Minority (D 5): Coyne, RMM; McNulty, Lewis, Thurman, Pomeroy

Select Revenue Measures
Majority (R 7): McCrery, Chmn.; Hayworth, Weller, Lewis, Foley, Brady, Ryan
Minority (D 4): McNulty, RMM; Neal, Jefferson, Tanner

Social Security
Majority (R 8): Shaw, Chmn.; Johnson (TX), Collins, Hayworth, Hulshof, Lewis, Brady, Ryan
Minority (D 5): Matsui, RMM; Doggett, Cardin, Pomeroy, Becerra

Trade
Majority (R 9): Crane, Chmn.; Shaw, Houghton, Camp, Ramstad, Dunn, Herger, English, Nussle
Minority (D 6): Levin, RMM; Rangel, Neal, Jefferson, Becerra, Tanner

JOINT COMMITTEES

JOINT COMMITTEE ON TAXATION
www.house.gov/jct

1015 Longworth
202-225-3621

House (5): Thomas (CA), Chmn.; Crane (IL), Shaw (FL), Rangel (NY), Stark (CA)
Senate (5): Baucus (MT), Vice Chmn.; Rockefeller (WV), Grassley (IA), Hatch (UT), Murkowski (AK)

Joint Economic Committee
www.house.gov/jec

1537 LHOB
202-226-3234

House (10): Saxton (NJ), Chmn.; Ryan (WI), Smith (TX), Dunn (WA), English (PA), Putnam (FL), Stark (CA), Maloney (NY), Watt (NC), 1 vacancy
Senate (11): Reed (RI), Vice Chmn.; Kennedy (MA), Sarbanes (MD), Bingaman (NM), Corzine (NJ), Torricelli (NJ), Bennett (UT), RMM; Brownback (KS), Sessions (AL), Crapo (ID), Chafee (RI)

CAMPAIGN FINANCE

All data are derived from candidate and party reports as well as other official studies available from the Federal Election Commission (FEC) located at 999 E Street, N.W., Washington, DC 20463. Telephone (202) 694-1100 (or toll-free 800-424-9530). Individuals listed in italics were losing candidates in that election.

U.S. SENATE

The following charts show the 15 top 2000 Senate candidates in terms of the highest total net receipts, net expenditures, political action committee (PAC) contributions, individual contributions, cash on hand and debts owed during the 1999–2000 election cycle.

2000 SENATE: TOP RAISERS

1. Hillary Rodham Clinton (D-NY) $41,752,247
2. *Rick Lazio (R-NY)* 39,020,511
3. *Rudolph W. Giuliani (R-NY)*† 23,532,604
4. *Spencer Abraham (R-MI)* 11,838,542
5. Dianne Feinstein (D-CA) 10,464,194
6. George Allen (R-VA) 10,073,255
7. Rick Santorum (R-PA) 9,126,046
8. *John Ashcroft (R-MO)* 8,925,706
9. Mel Carnahan (D-MO)* 8,530,447
10. Deborah Ann Stabenow (D-MI) 8,297,375
11. *Bill McCollum (R-FL)* 7,936,639
12. Maria Cantwell (D-WA) 7,774,040
13. Edward Kennedy (D-MA) 6,623,179
14. Bill Nelson (D-FL) 6,539,259
15. *Bob Franks (R-NJ)* 6,423,214

2000 SENATE: TOP SPENDERS

1. Jon Corzine (D-NJ) $63,209,506
2. Hillary Rodham Clinton (D-NY) 41,469,898
3. *Rick Lazio (R-NY)* 40,576,273
4. *Rudolph Giuliani (R-NY)†* 20,766,961
5. *Spencer Abraham (R-MI)* 13,028,636
6. Mark Dayton (DFL-MN) 11,957,114
7. Maria Cantwell (D-WA) 11,533,295
8. Rick Santorum (R-PA) 10,616,262
9. Dianne Feinstein (D-CA) 10,346,170
10. George Allen (R-VA) 9,995,980
11. *John Ashcroft (R-MO)* 9,378,581
12. Mel Carnahan (D-MO)* 8,800,864
13. *Bill McCollum (R-FL)* 8,664,112
14. Deborah Ann Stabenow (D-MI) 7,892,518
15. *Charles S. Robb (D-VA)* 6,610,252

2000 SENATE: TOP PAC RECIPIENTS

1. *Spencer Abraham (R-MI)* $2,485,419
2. *Rick Lazio (R-NY)* 2,380,043
3. *John Ashcroft (R-MO)* 2,040,748
4. Rick Santorum (R-PA) 1,878,625
5. *Slade Gorton (R-WA)* 1,770,339
6. *William Roth (R-DE)* 1,727,178
7. John Ensign (R-NV) 1,715,992
8. Conrad Burns (R-MT) 1,683,501
9. *Rod Grams (R-MN)* 1,623,289
10. *Charles S. Robb (D-VA)* 1,622,753
11. George Allen (R-VA) 1,581,172
12. Kent Conrad (D-ND) 1,443,306
13. *Bill McCollum (R-FL)* 1,391,571
14. Benjamin Nelson (D-NE) 1,298,059
15. Dianne Feinstein (D-CA) 1,245,727

2000 SENATE: TOP INDIVIDUAL CONTRIBUTIONS

1. *Rick Lazio (R-NY)* $35,885,552
2. Hillary Rodham Clinton (D-NY) 24,191,963
3. *Rudolph Giuliani (R-NY)†* 22,567,091
4. *Spencer Abraham (R-MI)* 8,759,626
5. Dianne Feinstein (D-CA) 8,192,183
6. George Allen (R-VA) 7,981,748
7. *Bill McCollum (R-FL)* 6,562,401
8. Deborah Ann Stabenow (D-MI) 6,560,892
9. Mel Carnahan (D-MO)* 6,035,654
10. Rick Santorum (R-PA) 5,794,892
11. *John Ashcroft (R-MO)* 5,584,825
12. Edward Kennedy (D-MA) 5,478,801
13. Bill Nelson (D-FL) 4,888,080
14. *Bob Franks (R-NJ)* 4,829,307
15. *Charles S. Robb (D-VA)* 4,353,994

2000 SENATE: TOP CASH-ON-HAND

1.	Kay Bailey Hutchison (R-TX)	$4,622,229
2.	Edward Kennedy (D-MA)	4,008,748
3.	Rudolph Giuliani (R-NY)†	3,014,241
4.	Bill Frist (R-TN)	2,139,518
5.	Trent Lott (R-MS)	1,330,389
6.	Joseph I. Lieberman (D-CT)	1,098,721
7.	Jon Kyl (R-AZ)	991,980
8.	Mike DeWine (R-OH)	688,577
9.	Orrin G. Hatch (R-UT)	621,340
10.	*Brendan Thomas Byrne Jr. (D-NJ)*	492,424
11.	James M. Jeffords (R-VT)	482,884
12.	Olympia Snowe (R-ME)	447,789
13.	Craig Thomas (R-WY)	446,479
14.	Robert C. Byrd (D-WV)	424,114
15.	Dianne Feinstein (D-CA)	422,585

2000 SENATE: TOP DEBTS OWED

1.	Jon Corzine (D-NJ)	$60,048,968
2.	Mark Dayton (DFL-MN)	8,360,000
3.	Maria Cantwell (D-WA)	4,286,936
4.	*Rick Lazio (R-NY)*	3,087,910
5.	*Michael Ciresi (DFL-MN)*	1,500,000
6.	Bill Frist (R-TN)	1,440,000
7.	*Elliott Rustad (R-NE)*	1,078,010
8.	*Ed Bernstein (D-NV)*	988,000
9.	Rick Santorum (R-PA)	505,180
10.	*Rebecca Yanisch (DFL-MN)*	442,255
11.	*Charles S. Robb (D-VA)*	409,000
12.	*James Florio (D-NJ)*	400,000
13.	*Richard Licht (D-RI)*	341,745
14.	*Philip Giordano (R-CT)*	327,536
15.	Lincoln Chafee (R-RI)	300,000

* *died October 16, 2000*
† *withdrew from race*

U.S. HOUSE OF REPRESENTATIVES

The following charts show the 25 top 2000 House candidates in terms of the highest total net receipts, net expenditures, political action committee (PAC) contributions, individual contributions, cash on hand and debts owed during the 1999–2000 election cycle.

2000 HOUSE: TOP RAISERS

1.	*James E. Rogan (R-CA)*	$6,871,077
2.	Adam Schiff (D-CA)	4,352,754
3.	Richard A. Gephardt (D-MO)	3,816,891
4.	Bob Barr (R-GA)	3,442,211
5.	Anne Northup (R-KY)	2,896,393
6.	E. Clay Shaw Jr. (R-FL)	2,755,056
7.	Henry J. Hyde (R-IL)	2,744,677
8.	Rush Holt (D-NJ)	2,659,446
9.	Ernie Fletcher (R-KY)	2,493,053
10.	Ron Paul (R-TX)	2,413,684
11.	J. Dennis Hastert (R-IL)	2,385,649
12.	*Bill Federer (R-MO)*	2,377,050
13.	Patrick J. Tiberi (R-OH)	2,374,205
14.	David E. Bonior (D-MI)	2,336,205
15.	Don Sherwood (R-PA)	2,330,100
16.	Heather Wilson (R-NM)	2,241,534
17.	Mike Rogers (R-MI)	2,224,233
18.	*Dick Zimmer (R-NJ)*	2,223,722
19.	Robert Menendez (D-NJ)	2,188,542
20.	Mike Honda (D-CA)	2,153,003
21.	Dennis Rehberg (R-MT)	2,146,239
22.	*Elaine Bloom (D-FL)*	2,111,353
23.	James H. Maloney (D-CT)	2,086,534
24.	Mark Kirk (R-IL)	2,068,719
25.	Shelley Berkley (D-NV)	2,067,764

2000 HOUSE: TOP SPENDERS

1.	*Jim Humphreys (D-WV)*	$6,964,933
2.	*James E. Rogan (R-CA)*	6,889,947
3.	Richard A. Gephardt (D-MO)	5,580,964
4.	Adam Schiff (D-CA)	4,351,025
5.	*Peter Wareing (R-TX)*	3,896,840
6.	*Roger F. Kahn (D-GA)*	3,859,860
7.	Bob Barr (R-GA)	3,495,641
8.	*Phil Sudan (R-TX)*	3,247,033
9.	E. Clay Shaw Jr. (R-FL)	3,086,708
10.	Anne Northup (R-KY)	2,916,818
11.	William P. (Bill) Luther (D-MN)	2,597,244
12.	Rush Holt (D-NJ)	2,566,080
13.	*Shawn Margaret Donnelley (R-IL)*	2,444,398
14.	Henry J. Hyde (R-IL)	2,436,839
15.	*Elaine Bloom (D-FL)*	2,378,327
16.	Ron Paul (R-TX)	2,353,816
17.	Patrick J. Tiberi (R-OH)	2,349,872
18.	*Bill Federer (R-MO)*	2,319,819
19.	David E. Bonior (D-MI)	2,312,101
20.	Ernie Fletcher (R-KY)	2,300,940
21.	Darrell Issa (R-CA)	2,300,907
22.	J. Dennis Hastert (R-IL)	2,299,072
23.	Mike Ferguson (R-NJ)	2,294,820
24.	*Terry Lierman (D-MD)*	2,217,488
25.	Heather Wilson (R-NM)	2,203,322

2000 HOUSE: TOP PAC RECIPIENTS

1.	E. Clay Shaw Jr. (R-FL)	$1,316,733
2.	J. Dennis Hastert (R-IL)	1,307,648
3.	Ernie Fletcher (R-KY)	1,139,810
4.	James H. Maloney (D-CT)	1,130,622
5.	*Steven T. Kuykendall (R-CA)*	1,119,862
6.	Anne Northup (R-KY)	1,102,290
7.	Martin Frost (D-TX)	1,101,824
8.	Calvin Dooley (D-CA)	1,099,483
9.	Charles B. Rangel (D-NY)	1,081,195
10.	James E. Rogan (R-CA)	1,012,593
11.	David E. Bonior (D-MI)	997,301
12.	*Brian Bilbray (R-CA)*	990,366
13.	Don Sherwood (R-PA)	962,656
14.	Patrick J. Tiberi (R-OH)	954,423
15.	Roy Blunt (R-MO)	940,446
16.	Mike Rogers (R-MI)	937,385
17.	Nancy L. Johnson (R-CT)	902,306
18.	Joe Baca (D-CA)	897,077
19.	Heather Wilson (R-NM)	884,156
20.	Shelley Berkley (D-NV)	879,780
21.	Melissa Hart (R-PA)	871,124
22.	Tom Delay (R-TX)	863,586
23.	Bill Thomas (R-CA)	857,933
24.	John D. Dingell (D-MI)	847,208
25.	Richard A. Gephardt (D-MO)	838,109

2000 HOUSE: TOP INDIVIDUAL CONTRIBUTIONS

1.	*James E. Rogan (R-CA)*	$5,640,866
2.	Adam Schiff (D-CA)	3,563,953
3.	Bob Barr (R-GA)	2,911,436
4.	*Bill Federer (R-MO)*	2,298,240
5.	Henry J. Hyde (R-IL)	2,286,801
6.	Ron Paul (R-TX)	2,254,193
7.	Rush Holt (D-NJ)	1,744,913
8.	Elaine Bloom (D-FL)	1,662,593
9.	Anne Northup (R-KY)	1,657,801
10.	*Dick Zimmer (R-NJ)*	1,579,203
11.	*Jay W. Dickey (R-AR)*	1,543,412
12.	*Peter Wareing (R-TX)*	1,500,740
13.	*Noach Dear (D-NY)*	1,484,178
14.	Mike Honda (D-CA)	1,479,030
15.	Carolyn McCarthy (D-NY)	1,448,655
16.	*Lauren Beth Gash (D-IL)*	1,447,419
17.	Jane Harman (D-CA)	1,431,974
18.	Robert Menendez (D-NJ)	1,423,132
19.	*Susan Levin (D-NJ)*	1,414,659
20.	Mark Kirk (R-IL)	1,404,401
21.	Susan Davis (D-CA)	1,399,396
22.	Loretta Sanchez (D-CA)	1,389,089
23.	Patrick J. Tiberi (R-OH)	1,378,322
24.	David Vitter (R-LA)	1,346,949
25.	*Dianne Byrum (D-MI)*	1,336,246

2000 HOUSE: TOP CASH-ON-HAND

1.	Peter R. Deutsch (D-FL)	$2,360,082
2.	David Dreier (R-CA)	2,318,497
3.	Martin T. Meehan (D-MA)	1,965,917
4.	Lloyd Doggett (D-TX)	1,770,900
5.	Robert Menendez (D-NJ)	1,682,851
6.	Nita M. Lowey (D-NY)	1,545,122
7.	Nick J. Rahall II (D-WV)	1,426,833
8.	Loretta Sanchez (D-CA)	1,263,638
9.	Ileana Ros-Lehtinen (R-FL)	1,242,393
10.	Scott McInnis (R-CO)	1,233,841
11.	Cliff Stearns (R-FL)	1,158,724
12.	Sherrod Brown (D-OH)	1,105,021
13.	Dan Burton (R-IN)	1,046,381
14.	William D. Delahunt (D-MA)	1,040,886
15.	Robert Andrews (D-NJ)	1,018,385
16.	Mark Foley (R-FL)	1,001,480
17.	Jerry Lewis (R-CA)	978,187
18.	Richard E. Neal (D-MA)	928,231
19.	Rod R. Blagojevich (D-IL)	915,328
20.	Michael N. Castle (R-DE)	909,781
21.	Richard Burr (R-NC)	904,365
22.	John J. Duncan Jr. (R-TN)	880,331
23.	Patrick J. Kennedy (D-RI)	855,625
24.	Joe Barton (R-TX)	827,194
25.	Bud Cramer Jr. (D-AL)	802,903

2000 HOUSE: TOP DEBTS OWED

1.	*James F. Humphreys (D-WV)*	$6,105,000
2.	*Philip P. Sudan Jr. (R-TX)*	3,275,000
3.	*Roger F. Kahn (D-GA)*	2,932,500
4.	Darrell Issa (R-CA)	1,820,000
5.	Chris Cannon (R-UT)	1,664,044
6.	*Derek W. Smith (R-UT)*	1,455,938
7.	Doug Ose (R-CA)	1,433,125
8.	*Terry Lierman (D-MD)*	1,315,000
9.	*William E. Peacock (D-CA)*	1,268,344
10.	*Ronald A. Kapche (R-TX)*	1,218,105
11.	*Paul C. Jost (R-VA)*	1,216,500
12.	*Carl J. Mayer (Green-NJ)*	997,055
13.	*Jose A. Hernandez-Mayoral (D-PR)*	966,028
14.	*Monica L. Monica (R-LA)*	955,000
15.	Mike Ferguson (R-NJ)	814,541
16.	*Martha Fuller Clark (D-NH)*	718,302
17.	*Leigh Harvey McNairy (D-NC)*	641,000
18.	*Jeffrey E. Wright (R-UT)*	640,000
19.	Norman Sisisky (D-VA)*	639,183
20.	*Melissa Brown (R-PA)*	570,800
21.	*John Brewer (R-TX)*	559,846
22.	*John H. Cox, (R-IL)*	558,000
23.	*David Treen (R-LA)*	553,000
24.	Anibal Acevedo-Vila (D-PR)	545,263
25.	*John J. Kelly (D-NM)*	495,801

*died March 29, 2001

DEMOGRAPHICS

POPULATION. All population figures are from the Bureau of the Census, U.S. Department of Commerce, Washington, D.C. 20233, 301-457-3030. Figures for 1970, 1980, 1990, and 2000 are final Census Bureau population counts as of April 1 of those years. (The District of Columbia is included as a state in all the following charts.)

VOTING AGE POPULATION. This figure indicates all persons at least 18 years of age who are eligible to vote, including the Armed Forces, aliens and institutional members.

Chart I shows the total U.S. population and total U.S. voting age population for 2000, 1990, 1980 and 1970.

CHART I

Total U.S. Population		Total U.S. Voting Age Population	
April 1, 2000	281,421,906	April 1, 2000	209,128,094
April 1, 1990	248,709,873	April 1, 1990	185,105,441
April 1, 1980	226,545,805	April 1, 1980	163,997,000
April 1, 1970	203,302,031	April 1, 1970	135,290,000

Chart II indicates the range of highest and lowest state population changes in percentage growth and absolute change for 1990–2000.

CHART II
1990–2000 Population Change
(National Avg.: up 13.2%)

State	Highest		State	Lowest	
Nevada	66.3	796,424	District of Columbia	−5.7	−34,841
Arizona	40.0	1,465,404	North Dakota	0.5	3,400
Colorado	30.6	1,006,867	West Virginia	0.8	14,867
Utah	29.6	510,319	Pennsylvania	3.4	399,411
Idaho	28.5	287,204	Connecticut	3.6	118,449
Georgia	26.4	1,708,237	Maine	3.8	46,995
Florida	23.5	3,044,452	Rhode Island	4.5	44,855
Texas	22.8	3,865,310	Ohio	4.7	506,025
North Carolina	21.4	1,420,676	Iowa	5.4	149,569
Washington	21.1	1,027,429	New York	5.5	986,002
			Massachusetts	5.5	332,672

Chart III shows the ten highest and the ten lowest state populations.

CHART III
2000 U.S. Population: Ten Highest and Lowest States

State	Highest	State	Lowest
California	33,871,648	Wyoming	493,782
Texas	20,851,820	District of Columbia	572,059
New York	18,976,457	Vermont	608,827
Florida	15,982,378	Alaska	626,932
Illinois	12,419,293	North Dakota	642,200
Pennsylvania	12,281,054	South Dakota	754,844
Ohio	11,353,140	Delaware	783,600
Michigan	9,938,444	Montana	902,195
New Jersey	8,414,350	Rhode Island	1,048,319
Georgia	8,186,453	Hawaii	1,211,537

Chart IV shows the states with the highest and lowest average unemployment rates for 2000. These figures are from the U.S. Department of Labor, Bureau of Labor Statistics, and were compiled independently of the Census Bureau figures.

CHART IV
2000 Average Unemployment Rate
(National Avg.: 4.0%)

Highest		Lowest	
Alaska	6.6	Virginia	2.2
District of Columbia	5.8	Connecticut	2.3
Mississippi	5.7	South Dakota	2.3
Louisiana	5.5	Iowa	2.6
West Virginia	5.5	Massachusetts	2.6
Washington	5.2	Colorado	2.7
California	4.9	New Hampshire	2.8
Idaho	4.9	Vermont	2.9
Montana	4.9	Nebraska	3.0
New Mexico	4.9	North Dakota	3.0
Oregon	4.9	Oklahoma	3.0

ETHNIC BREAKDOWN. The racial and ethnic breakdowns illustrate the potential ethnic vote as opposed to the overall population. The concepts of race and ethnicity as defined by the Census Bureau reflect self-identification and not clear-cut biological definitions. The following statistics are drawn from respondents reporting only one race category.

Chart V lists voting age and total state population figures for the seventeen states with black populations above the national average of 12.3% in 2000. Black ethnic classification refers to those persons who indicated their race as Black on the Census questionnaire.

CHART V
2000 Black Population: Total State Population

State	% of voting age pop.	% of total state pop.	State	% of voting age pop.	of total state pop.
District of Columbia	56.2	60.0	Delaware	17.6	19.2
Mississippi	33.1	36.3	Tennessee	14.8	16.4
Louisiana	29.7	32.5	New York	14.8	15.9
South Carolina	27.2	29.5	Arkansas	13.9	15.7
Georgia	26.6	28.7	Illinois	13.8	15.1
Maryland	26.4	27.9	Florida	12.7	14.6
Alabama	24.0	26.0	Michigan	13.1	14.2
North Carolina	20.0	21.6	New Jersey	12.6	13.6
Virginia	18.4	19.6			

Chart VI illustrates voting age and total state population figures for the nine states with Hispanic origin concentrations above the national average of 12.5% in 2000. The Hispanic origin classification includes three specific categories—Mexican, Puerto Rican and Cuban—as well as those who indicated that they were of other Spanish or Hispanic origin (origin can be viewed as ancestry, nationality group, lineage or country of birth of the person or the person's parents or ancestors prior to their arrival in the United States). Persons of Hispanic origin may be of any race.

CHART VI
2000 Hispanic Origin: Total State and Voting Age Population

State	% of voting age pop.	% of total state pop.	State	% of voting age pop.	% of total state pop.
New Mexico	38.7	42.1	Colorado	14.9	17.1
California	28.1	32.4	Florida	16.1	16.8
Texas	28.6	32.0	New York	13.8	15.1
Arizona	21.3	25.3	New Jersey	12.3	13.3
Nevada	16.7	19.7			

Chart VII illustrates the voting age and total population figures for the seventeen states with American Indian concentrations above the national average of 0.9% in 2000. The American Indian classification includes persons who classified themselves as American Indian, Eskimo, or Aleut.

CHART VII
2000 American Indian: Total State and Voting Age Population

State	% of voting age pop.	% of total state pop.	State	% of voting age pop.	% of total state pop.
Alaska	13.8	15.6	Idaho	1.3	1.4
New Mexico	8.3	9.5	Nevada	1.2	1.3
South Dakota	6.2	8.3	Oregon	1.2	1.3
Oklahoma	6.8	7.9	Utah	1.2	1.3
Montana	5.1	6.2	North Carolina	1.1	1.2
Arizona	4.1	5.0	Minnesota	0.9	1.1
North Dakota	3.8	4.9	California	0.9	1.0
Wyoming	1.9	2.3	Colorado	1.0	1.0
Washington	1.4	1.6			

Chart VIII illustrates the voting age and total state population figures for the ten states with Asian concentrations above the national average of 3.6% in 2000. The Asian classification includes persons who classified themselves as Asian.

CHART VIII
2000 Asian Origin: Total State and Voting Age Population

State	% of voting age pop.	% of total state pop.	State	% of voting age pop.	% of total state pop.
Hawaii	45.4	41.6	Nevada	4.8	4.5
California	11.5	10.9	Alaska	4.2	4.0
New Jersey	5.6	5.7	Maryland	4.1	4.0
Washington	5.6	5.5	Massachusetts	3.7	3.8
New York	5.7	5.5	Virginia	3.7	3.7

Chart IX illustrates the voting age and total state population figures for the seven states with Native Hawaiian and other Pacific Islander concentrations above the national average of 0.1% in 2000. The Native Hawaiian and other Pacific Islander classification includes persons who classified themselves as Native Hawaiian and other Pacific Islander.

CHART IX
2000 Native Hawaiian and other Pacific Islander Origin:
Total State and Voting Age Population

State	% of voting age pop.	% of total state pop.	State	% of voting age pop.	% of total state pop.
Hawaii	8.3	9.4	Nevada	0.4	0.4
Utah	0.6	0.7	California	0.3	0.3
Alaska	0.4	0.5	Oregon	0.2	0.2
Washington	0.4	0.4			

Chart X illustrates the Congressional Districts with the highest Black population percentage.

CHART X
2000 Black Population: By Congressional District

District	% of total state pop.	District	% of total state pop.
Mich.-14	79%	N.Y.-11	69%
Ill.-2	76%	La.-2	67%
Md.-7	75%	Tenn.-9	66%
Ill.-1	70%	Miss.-2	65%
Ala.-7	70%	Md.-4	65%
Mich.-15	70%	Ohio-11	65%

Chart XI illustrates the Congressional Districts with the highest Hispanic population percentage. The Hispanic origin classification includes three specific categories—Mexican, Puerto Rican and Cuban—as well as those who indicated that they were of other Spanish or Hispanic origin (origin can be viewed as ancestry, nationality group, lineage or country of birth of the person or the person's parents or ancestors prior to their arrival in the United States). Persons of Hispanic origin may be of any race.

CHART XI
2000 Hispanic Population: By Congressional District

District	% of total state pop.	District	% of total state pop.
Calif.-33	86%	Fla.-18	71%
Texas-15	79%	Texas-27	70%
Texas-16	78%	Ill.-4	70%
Fla.-21	78%	Texas-20	67%
Calif.-34	72%	Texas-23	66%

Chart XII illustrates the Congressional Districts with the highest American Indian population percentage. The American Indian classification includes persons who classified themselves as American Indian, Eskimo, or Aleut.

CHART XII
2000 American Indian Origin: By Congressional District

District	% of total state pop.	District	% of total state pop.
N.M-3	20%	N.C.-7	7%
Okla.-2	17%	Mont.-1	6%
Alaska-1	16%	N.D.-1	5%
Ariz.-6	16%	Okla.-1	
Okla.-3	11%	Okla.-4	5%
S.D.-1	8%	Okla.-6	5%

Chart XIII illustrates the Congressional Districts with the highest Asian population percentage.

CHART XIII
2000 Asian Origin: By Congressional District

District	% of total state pop.	District	% of total state pop.
Hawaii-1	53%	Calif.-16	27%
Hawaii-2	31%	Calif.-30	20%
Calif.-12	31%	Calif.-28	19%
Calif.-13	30%	Calif.-14	19%
Calif.-8	28%	N.Y.-5	19%
Calif.-31	28%		

INDEX

The 50 States and the names of all the Governors, Senators and Representatives appear in boldface type. The number of the page that includes Members' corresponding biographical, voting and campaign finance information also appears in bold.

THE AUTHORS

MICHAEL BARONE, a senior writer at *U.S. News and World Report*, is a regular panelist on *The McLaughlin Group* and a Fox News Channel contributor. *The Chicago Tribune* says, "Michael Barone is to politics what statistician-writer Bill James is to baseball, a mix of historian, social observer, and numbers cruncher who illuminates his subject with perspective and a touch of irreverence." He is the author of *The New Americans: How the Melting Pot Can Work Again,* published by Regnery in May 2001.

RICHARD E. COHEN brings to the *Almanac* 24 years of experience covering Capitol Hill. He is the 1990 winner of the Everett McKinley Dirksen Award for distinguished reporting on Congress and *National Journal*'s congressional correspondent since 1977. Cohen is an active author of books about Congress, including a 1999 biography of former Rep. Dan Rostenkowski.

THE PUBLISHER

❝ The nation's most respected nonpartisan source of information about how Washington policymaking machinery really works. ❞

That's how *Newsweek* described *National Journal*. For more than 30 years, *National Journal* has reached subscribers with an award-winning weekly magazine noted for its dedication to "facts only" reporting. *National Journal* speaks to people who make it their business to know what's going on in the world's largest business—the United States Government.

Only *National Journal* is exclusively devoted to the coverage of what the government is doing today, what it's going to do tomorrow, and how its actions affect our lives.

This 2002 edition of *The Almanac of American Politics* marks the tenth volume to be published by National Journal Group Inc. In addition to the *Almanac* and *National Journal*, National Journal Group publishes *Government Executive*, a monthly magazine for senior federal managers; *CongressDaily*, a twice-daily news service covering Congress; *The Hotline*, a daily briefing on American politics; National Journal's *Technology Daily*, a twice-daily news service on information technology politics and policy; NationalJournal.com, the online source for political and policy professionals; *UN Wire*, a daily briefing on the United Nations; the *The Capital Source*, a semi-annual Washington directory; and the *National Journal Convention Daily*, a daily newspaper published at the Democratic and Republican Conventions.

1501 M Street, NW, Washington, DC 20005 Telephone (202) 739-8400